The Reader's Adviser

The Reader's Adviser
14th EDITION

Marion Sader, Series Editor

Volume 1
The Best in Reference Works, British Literature, and American Literature
David Scott Kastan and Emory Elliott, Volume Editors

Books About Books • Bibliography • Reference Books: General • Reference Books: Literature • Medieval Literature • Renaissance Literature • Shakespeare • Restoration and Eighteenth-Century Literature • The Romantic Period • The Victorian Period • Modern British and Irish Literature • British Literature: Popular Modes • Early American Literature: Beginnings to the Nineteenth Century • Early Nineteenth-Century American Literature • Middle to Late Nineteenth-Century American Literature • Early Twentieth-Century American Literature • Middle to Late Twentieth-Century American Literature • Modern American Drama • American Literature: Some New Directions • American Literature: Popular Modes

Volume 2
The Best in World Literature
Robert DiYanni, Volume Editor

Introduction to World Literature • Hebrew Literature • Yiddish Literature • Middle Eastern Literatures • African Literatures • Literature of the Indian Subcontinent • Chinese Literature • Japanese Literature • Korean Literature • Southeast Asian Literatures • Greek Literature • Latin Literature • Italian Literature • French Literature • Spanish Literature • Portuguese Literature • German Literature • Netherlandic Literature • Scandinavian Literatures • Russian Literature • East European Literatures • Latin American Literatures • Canadian Literature • Literature of the Caribbean • Australian Literature • New Zealand Literature • Comparative Literature

Volume 3
The Best in Social Sciences, History, and the Arts
John G. Sproat, Volume Editor

Social Sciences and History: General Reference • Anthropology • Economics • Geography • Political Science • Psychology • Sociology • Education • World History • Ancient History • European History • African History • Middle Eastern History • History of Asia and the Pacific • United States History • Canadian History • Latin American History • Music and Dance • Art and Architecture • Mass Media • Folklore, Humor, and Popular Culture • Travel and Exploration

Volume 4
The Best in Philosophy and Religion
Robert S. Ellwood, Volume Editor

Philosophy and Religion: General Reference • General Philosophy • Greek and Roman
Philosophy • Medieval Philosophy • Renaissance Philosophy • Modern Western
Philosophy, 1600–1900 • Twentieth-Century Western Philosophy • Asian and African
Philosophy, 1850 to the Present • Contemporary Issues in Philosophy • Ancient
Religions and Philosophies • Eastern Religions • Islam • Judaism • Early and Medieval
Christianity • Late Christianity, 1500 to the Present • The Bible and Related Literature •
Minority Religions and Contemporary Religious Movements • Contemporary Issues in
Religious Thought

Volume 5
The Best in Science, Technology, and Medicine
Carl Mitcham and William F. Williams, Volume Editors

Science, Technology, and Medicine: General Reference • A General View: Science,
Technology, and Medicine • History of Science, Technology, and Medicine • Philosophy
of Science, Technology, and Medicine • Ethics in Science, Technology, and Medicine •
Science, Technology, and Society • Special Issues in Science, Technology, and Society •
Engineering and Technology • Agriculture and Food Technology • Energy •
Communications Technology • Medicine and Health • Illness and Disease • Clinical
Psychology and Psychiatry • Mathematics • Statistics and Probability • Information
Science and Computer Science • Astronomy and Space Science • Earth Sciences •
Physics • Chemistry • Biological Sciences • Ecology and Environmental Science

THE
Reader's Adviser®

14th EDITION

Volume 1

The Best in Reference Works, British Literature, and American Literature

David Scott Kastan and Emory Elliott, Volume Editors

Marion Sader, Series Editor

R. R. Bowker®

A Reed Reference Publishing Company
New Providence, New Jersey

Published by R. R. Bowker
A Reed Reference Publishing Company
Copyright © 1994 by Reed Publishing (USA) Inc.

International Standard Book Numbers
0-8352-3320-0 (SET)
0-8352-3321-9 (Volume 1)
0-8352-3322-7 (Volume 2)
0-8352-3323-5 (Volume 3)
0-8352-3324-3 (Volume 4)
0-8352-3325-1 (Volume 5)
0-8352-3326-X (Volume 6)
International Standard Serial Number 0094-5943
Library of Congress Catalog Card Number 57-13277

R. R. Bowker has used its best efforts in collecting and preparing
material for inclusion in *The Reader's Adviser*, but does not warrant
that the information herein is complete or accurate, and does not
assume, and hereby disclaims, any liability to any person for any
loss or damage caused by errors or omissions in *The Reader's Adviser*
whether such errors or omissions result from negligence, accident
or any other cause.

The paper used in this publication meets the minimum requirements
of American National Standard for Information Sciences—Permanence
of Papers for Printed Library Materials, ANSI Z39.48-1984.

ISBN 0 - 8352 - 3320 - 0

9 780835 233200

Contents

Preface

Libraries are busy places and rarely is there time for the reader and the
librarian to sit down, discuss and analyze the reader's book problem, direct
his interest or locate the book he wants. . . . In answer to this demand
readers' advisers are appearing on many library staffs.
—JENNIE M. FLEXNER

When Jennie M. Flexner, founder of the New York Public Library's famous
Reader's Advisory service, wrote those words in *Library Journal* in 1938,
R. R. Bowker's own *Reader's Adviser* had already been a Baedeker for
overwhelmed library patrons for nearly a generation. Known then as *The
Bookman's Manual*, it had, as its name suggests, actually been conceived, not by
a librarian, but by a bookseller, Bessie Graham. Graham's first edition,
published in 1921, was based on an enormously popular bookselling course she
had recently taught at the William Penn Evening High School in Philadelphia.
Just over 400 pages, that first *Bookman's Manual* was intended to give novice
book retailers a basic inventory of essential in-print titles, both to stock and to
recommend to customers. (It did, admittedly, fail to mention Shakespeare—a
shortcoming that so appalled Mildred C. Smith, the young Bowker employee
who had been asked to organize Graham's material, that more than four
decades later, as editor of *Publishers Weekly*, Smith still vividly recalled the
omission.) Not surprisingly, however, *The Bookman's Manual* was quickly
adopted by librarians facing much the same task with their own patrons—and
through 13 editions the work, in its various guises, has been successfully
matching good books with grateful readers for more than 70 years.

Because of its roots in bookselling, *The Reader's Adviser* has always been far
more than a guide to "the classics"—those time-honored treasures that, as Mark
Twain once insisted, "everybody talks about but nobody reads." From the very
first edition, its chapters reflected current literary, social, and political trends,
embracing not only such mainstream categories as "Great Names in English
Poetry" and "Essays and Letters" but also, as befitted the new era of universal
suffrage, "American Fiction—Contemporary *Men* Writers" and "American
Fiction—Contemporary *Women* Writers." Modern British authors experienced
the same sexual differentiation in the second edition, published three years
later, by which time Shakespeare had returned from exile and books on such
extraliterary subjects as "Nature," "Music," and "Travel" had also been added.

Throughout the 1920s and 1930s, *The Bookman's Manual* continued to grow
explosively—so much so that, by the time Bessie Graham bid farewell to her
"lifework" (as she called it in her preface to the fifth edition of 1941), it had
nearly doubled in size. "I commend its future editions to my unknown
successor," she wrote, "and take leave of a task that holds only pleasant

associations for me now that I pass 'Out of the stress of the doing, Into the peace of the done.'" Sadly, the United States's entry into World War II would soon interrupt that peace as well as the arrival of "future editions."

With the war near an end in June 1945, Bowker's Mildred Smith recommended Hester R. Hoffman, a bookseller with nearly 30 years' experience at the Hampshire Bookshop in Northampton, Massachusetts, to compile the next peacetime edition of Graham's *The Bookman's Manual*. Unfortunately, Hoffman's start was frustrated by more than a wartime paper shortage; Bowker's proposal reached her (as she later put it) while she was "lying flat in a room in a South Boston Hospital recovering from, of all things, a broken neck." Undaunted by her predicament, by the dearth of current titles on publishers' lists, and even by her typesetter's utter lack of foreign accents for the chapter on French literature, she succeeded in pulling together the sixth edition of *The Bookman's Manual* by 1948. The war, though, had taken its toll: despite a seven-year hiatus between editions, Hoffman's first effort was 62 pages *shorter* than Graham's last.

As the 1950s unfolded and the nuclear age cast a lengthening shadow, Hester Hoffman strove to keep *The Bookman's Manual* at the forefront of breaking literary and nonliterary events worldwide. A new chapter on science in the seventh edition of 1954 helped readers make sense of the profound legacy of such diverse theorists as Einstein and Freud. Thanks to Russian literature editors Helen Muchnic and Nicolai Vorobiov, anyone searching for contemporary Soviet novelists could have discovered the great Boris Pasternak (then known in the West only as a poet) fully three years before *Doctor Zhivago* made him an international sensation. In the eighth edition of 1958, the chapter on bibles updated readers who were eager to learn more about one of the seminal discoveries in Judeo-Christian history: a tattered collection of Hebrew and Aramaic parchments, concealed in pottery jars in caves near Qumran, that soon became known as the Dead Sea Scrolls.

Renamed *The Reader's Adviser and Bookman's Manual*, in 1960, the work continued to grow precipitously—struggling to reward the newfound postwar affluence, leisure, and cosmopolitan curiosity of American readers. With the baby boom at that time came a publishing boom, and, as Americans opened the New Frontier, they hungered for books about everything from rockets and space travel to parapsychology to segregation and the South. Indeed, just a glimpse of the new reading lists added during this heady and tumultuous era recaptures a time when readers were discovering ideas, arts, peoples, and places as perhaps they never had discovered before. There were books on the North American Indian and the opening of the West, Soviet history and policy, and the Civil War (as it reached its centenary); there were books by authors from Africa, Japan, China, India, Latin America, and, at long last, black America, as well as books about the lively arts of jazz, cinema, children's theater, and, yes, McLuhan's "cool medium," television.

By 1968, when Winifred F. Courtney guided the eleventh edition to press, one volume could no longer hold it all: It took two. The twelfth edition, published from 1974 to 1977, then blossomed to three volumes. As Bowker's own *Books in Print* continued to document a book market that was all but doubling in size every 10 years (from 245,000 titles in 1967 to 750,000 in 1987), the thirteenth edition, published in two installments, in 1986 and 1988, swelled to five volumes (plus a separately bound index). *The Reader's Adviser*, which always had been a reference tool built on the contributions of subject specialists, now had become virtually an encyclopedia—requiring separate editors for the set, for the individual volumes, for the sections . . . and even for the chapters!

As little as today's *Reader's Adviser* may resemble Bessie Graham's once modest *Bookman's Manual*, the work still adheres to tradition. More than ever the essential starting point for anyone who is setting out to read about the world of literary, artistic, philosophical, or scientific endeavor, the work's individual volumes are designed to carry users from the general to the specific—from overarching reference guides, critical histories, and anthologies about a genre or a field to the lives and works of its leading exemplars. As always, booksellers, reference and acquisitions librarians, lay readers, teachers, academics, and students alike can readily use it to identify the best of nearly everything available in English in the United States today, from the poetry of the ancients to Renaissance philosophy to meditations on the ethics of modern medicine.

Choosing what to include and what to leave out is never easy. As specialists, the volume and chapter editors know their field's most noted and popular figures, current and historic, and the body of literature on which the reputations of those individuals stand. Although I have asked each editor, when possible, to revise an "out of vogue" author's profile and bibliography rather than simply to eliminate it, paring is inevitable with any new edition. Then, too, the mere availability of an author's work can play its own editorial role. Although it is customary to list only titles published as books and (according to the latest monthly release of *Books in Print* on CD-ROM) currently for sale in the United States, exceptions are made for invaluable out-of-print works deemed likely to appear in the stacks of an established, modest-sized municipal library.

Revisions to the fourteenth edition have been judicious. Most noticeably, the set itself is longer and has a larger trim size—up from 6" x 9" to 7" x 10"—to give the pages a more open look. As the heart of *The Reader's Adviser*, the bibliographies have been more extensively annotated than ever before, and the lists of "books by" that accompany each profiled author in Volumes 1 and 2 are now helpfully subcategorized into genres (fiction, nonfiction, poetry, plays, etc.). Furthermore, ISBNs have been added to the usual bibliographic data (again, drawn from the latest monthly release of *Books in Print* on CD-ROM) of publisher, price, and year of publication. In addition, on the sensible assumption that the author profiles preceding bibliographies should be a tantalizing appetizer for the entrée to come, the editors have done their best to season them all with rich, lively biographical detail. Finally, the reader should be aware that not all in-print editions of a work are necessarily listed but, rather, only those editions selected because of their quality or special features.

Another change in this edition is the addition of a "Chronology of Authors" section before the alphabetical arrangement of profiled authors in each chapter—a complement to the chronology that appears at the outset of each volume and a quick and easy means of placing each chapter's profiled entrants in historical perspective. Finally, to boost *The Reader's Adviser's* reference utility, the subject index of each volume has been greatly expanded, and the chapters on "Books about Books," "General Bibliography," and "General Reference" (which were previously split between Volumes 1 and 2) have been brought together and now appear at the beginning of Volume 1.

Of course, much about this new edition of *The Reader's Adviser* remains uniquely similar to the previous edition. The six-volume organization begun with the thirteenth edition continues: Volume 1 encompasses general reference works and American and British literature; Volume 2, world literature in translation; Volume 3, the social sciences, history, and the arts; Volume 4, the literature of philosophy and world religions; and Volume 5, the literature of science, technology, and medicine. Similarly, Volume 6 incorporates the name, title, and subject indexes of each of the previous volumes. Also retained are convenient cross-references throughout, which guide inquiring readers to related authors, chapters, sections, or volumes. A "see" reference leads the reader to the appropriate volume and chapter for information on a specific author. "See also" refers the reader to additional information in another chapter or volume. Within any sections of narrative, the name of an author who appears as a main listing in another chapter or volume is printed in large and small capital letters. If the chapter cross-referenced is to be found in a different volume from the one being consulted, the volume number is also given. Furthermore, to make basic research easier, the annotated bibliographies accompanying profiled individuals separately list works "by" and "about" those authors.

To assure that all volumes of the fourteenth edition are compiled concurrently and arrive together, I have relied on the contributions of countless authorities. Special thanks are due to both *The Reader's Adviser's* team of volume editors and the chapter contributors, whose names are listed in each volume. The book production experts at Book Builders Incorporated directed the almost Herculean task of coordinating the 110 chapters by 120 authors through numerous editing and production stages; to everyone's satisfaction, the system succeeded, as the reader can affirm from a glance at these six volumes. In particular, I must recognize Book Builders' Lauren Fedorko, president and guiding spirit, for her unfailing good spirits and intelligent decisions; Diane Schadoff, editorial coordinator; and Paula Wiech, production manager. Many thanks to them and their staffs for the extra hours and care that they lavished on our "magnum opus." Very special appreciation is due to Charles Roebuck, managing editor *extraordinaire*, whose concerns for accuracy, detail, and style made perfection almost attainable. Charles's contributions are countless, and much of the success of this edition is due to his tact and diplomacy in managing many people, many deadlines, and many pages of manuscript. Here at Bowker, I am especially grateful to my assistant, Angela Szablewski, who has had the monumental responsibility of coordinating all stages of the books' production.

In her 1938 article, Ms. Flexner wrote that "libraries are made up of good, old books as well as good, new books." In agreement with her view, I have continued in the *Reader's Adviser* tradition by including in this new fourteenth edition titles that are timeless, as well as those that are timely; the aim is to provide the user with both a broad and a specific view of the great writings and great writers of the past and present. I wish you all satisfaction in your research, delight in your browsing, and pleasure in your reading.

Marion Sader
Publisher
Professional & Reference Books
R.R. Bowker
September 1993

Contributing Editors

Susan Allen, REFERENCE BOOKS: LITERATURE
Director of Libraries and Media Services, Upjohn Library, Kalamazoo College, Kalamazoo, Michigan

Vareen Bell, EARLY TWENTIETH-CENTURY AMERICAN LITERATURE
Professor of English, Vanderbilt University

Sidney Berger, BOOKS ABOUT BOOKS
Head of Special Collections, Rivera Library, University of California at Riverside

Joseph Childers, THE VICTORIAN PERIOD
Assistant Professor of English, University of California at Riverside

Harry Eiss, AMERICAN LITERATURE: POPULAR MODES (CHILDREN'S LITERATURE) AND BRITISH LITERATURE: POPULAR MODES (CHILDREN'S LITERATURE)
Associate Professor of English, Eastern Michigan University

Emory Elliott, VOLUME EDITOR, EARLY AMERICAN LITERATURE: BEGINNINGS TO THE NINETEENTH CENTURY
Professor of English, University of California at Riverside

Richard K. Emmerson, MEDIEVAL LITERATURE
Professor and Chair, Department of English, Western Washington University, Bellingham, Washington

Clarissa Cullerton Erwin, RESTORATION AND EIGHTEENTH-CENTURY LITERATURE
Librarian, Community College of Southern Nevada, Las Vegas, Nevada

Timothy Erwin, RESTORATION AND EIGHTEENTH-CENTURY LITERATURE
Associate Professor of English, University of Nevada at Las Vegas

Jennifer Fleischner, MIDDLE TO LATE TWENTIETH-CENTURY AMERICAN LITERATURE
Assistant Professor of English, State University of New York at Albany

Marilyn Gaull, THE ROMANTIC PERIOD
Professor of English, New York University

Gary Hoppenstand, BRITISH LITERATURE: POPULAR MODES (Popular Genres)
Assistant Professor, Department of American Thought and Languages, Michigan State University

David Scott Kastan, VOLUME EDITOR, SHAKESPEARE
Professor of English and Comparative Studies, Columbia University

Candace Klaschus, AMERICAN LITERATURE: POPULAR MODES (Popular Genres)
Assistant Professor of English, University of Hartford, Hartford, Connecticut

Randy Malamud, MODERN BRITISH AND IRISH LITERATURE
Assistant Professor of English, Georgia State University, Atlanta, Georgia

Claire McEachern, RENAISSANCE LITERATURE
Assistant Professor of English, University of California at Los Angeles

Kathy A. Mitchell, BIBLIOGRAPHY
Doctoral student, Graduate School of Library and Information Science, University of California at Los Angeles

John V. Richardson, Jr. BIBLIOGRAPHY AND REFERENCE BOOKS: GENERAL
Associate Professor, Graduate School of Library and Information Science, University of California at Los Angeles

Warren Robertson, MODERN AMERICAN DRAMA
Professor of Theatre, College of Arts and Sciences, East Tennessee State University, Johnson, City, Tennessee

Carol Sapora, MIDDLE TO LATE NINETEENTH-CENTURY AMERICAN LITERATURE
Assistant Professor of English, Villa Julie College, Westminster, Maryland

Carol-Anne Tyler, AMERICAN LITERATURE: SOME NEW DIRECTIONS
Assistant Professor of English, University of California at Riverside

Thomas Wortham, EARLY NINETEENTH-CENTURY AMERICAN LITERATURE
Professor of English, University of California at Los Angeles

Margaret R. Zarnosky, REFERENCE BOOKS: GENERAL
User Education Librarian, Newman Library, Virginia Polytechnic Institute and State University

Abbreviations

abr.	abridged
A.D.	in the year of the Lord
annot(s).	annotated, annotator(s)
B.C.	before Christ
B.C.E.	before the common era
B.P.	before the present
Bk(s)	Book(s)
c.	circa
C.E.	of the common era
Class.	Classic(s)
coll.	collected
comp(s).	compiled, compiler(s)
ed(s).	edited, editor(s), edition(s)
fl.	flourished
fwd.	foreword
gen. ed(s).	general editor(s)
ill(s).	illustrated, illustrator(s)
intro.	introduction
Lit.	Literature
o.p.	out-of-print
Pr.	Press
pref.	preface
pt(s).	part(s)
repr.	reprint
rev. ed.	revised edition
Ser.	Series
Supp.	Supplement
trans.	translated, translator(s), translation
U. or Univ.	University
Vol(s).	Volume(s)

Throughout this series, publisher names are abbreviated within bibliographic entries. The full names of these publishers can be found listed in Volume 6, the Index to the series.

Chronology of Authors

Main author entries appear here chronologically by year of birth. Within each chapter, main author entries are arranged alphabetically by surname.

1. **Books About Books**

2. **Bibliography**

3. **Reference Books: General**

4. **Reference Books: Literature**

5. **Medieval Literature**
Ballads and Lyrics. 1250–1700
Gower, John. c.1330–1408
Chaucer, Geoffrey. c.1342–1400
Langland, William. fl. 1370–1390
Pearl-Poet. fl. 1390
Kempe, Margery. c.1373–c.1440
Malory, Sir Thomas. fl. 1470

6. **Renaissance Literature**
Skelton, John. c.1460–1529
More, Sir Thomas, St. 1478–1535
Bale, John. 1495–1563
Wyatt, Sir Thomas the Elder. 1503–1542
Baldwin, William. 1518–1563
Deloney, Thomas. 1543–1600
Spenser, Edmund. 1552–1599
Lyly, John. c.1554–1606
Sidney, Sir Philip. 1554–1586
Peele, George. c.1556–1596?
Greene, Robert. 1558–1592
Kyd, Thomas. 1558–1594
Lodge, Thomas. 1558–1606
Chapman, George. c.1559–1634
Drayton, Michael. 1563–1631
Marlowe, Christopher. 1564–1593

Campion, Thomas. 1567–1620
Nashe, Thomas. 1567–1601
Dekker, Thomas. c.1572–c.1632
Jonson, Ben. 1572?–1637
Donne, John. 1573–1631
Heywood, Thomas. c.1573–1641
Marston, John. c.1575–1634
Tourneur, Cyril. c.1575–1626
Fletcher, John. 1579–1625
Middleton, Thomas. c.1580–1627
Webster, John. c.1580–c.1634
Massinger, Philip. 1583–1640
Beaumont, Francis. c.1584–1616
Ford, John. 1586–c.1639
Herrick, Robert. 1591–1674
Herbert, George. 1593–1633
Milton, John. 1608–1674
Crashaw, Richard. 1613–1649
Marvell, Andrew. 1621–1678
Vaughan, Henry. 1622–1695
Bunyan, John. 1628–1688

7. **Shakespeare**

8. **Restoration and Eighteenth-Century Literature**
Dryden, John. 1631–1700
Etherege, Sir George. c.1635–c.1691
Behn, Aphra. 1640–1689
Wycherley, William. 1640–1716
Otway, Thomas. 1652–1685
Defoe, Daniel. 1660–1731
Vanbrugh, Sir John. 1664–1726

Swift, Jonathan. 1667–1745

Congreve, William. 1670–1729

Addison, Joseph. 1672–1719

Steele, Sir Richard. 1672–1729

Farquhar, George. 1678–1707

Gay, John. 1685–1732

Pope, Alexander. 1688–1744

Montagu, Lady Mary Wortley. 1689–1762

Richardson, Samuel. 1689–1761

Chesterfield, 4th Earl of. 1694–1773

Thomson, James. 1700–1748

Fielding, Henry. 1707–1754

Johnson, Samuel. 1709–1784

Sterne, Laurence. 1713–1768

Gray, Thomas. 1716–1771

Walpole, Horace. 4th Earl of Orford. 1717–1797

Collins, William. 1721–1759

Smollett, Tobias George. 1721–1771

Smart, Christopher. 1722–1771

Goldsmith, Oliver. 1728–1774

Cowper, William. 1731–1800

Boswell, James. 1740–1795

Sheridan, Richard Brinsley. 1751–1816

Burney, Frances. 1752–1840

9. The Romantic Period

Chatterton, Thomas. 1752–1770

Crabbe, George. 1754–1832

Blake, William. 1757–1827

Burns, Robert. 1759–1796

Baillie, Joanna. 1762–1851

Hogg, James. 1770–1835

Wordsworth, William. 1770–1850

Scott, Sir Walter. 1771–1832

Coleridge, Samuel Taylor. 1772–1834

Southey, Robert. 1774–1843

Austen, Jane. 1775–1817

Lamb, Charles. 1775–1834

Landor, Walter Savage. 1775–1864

Hazlitt, William. 1778–1830

Hunt, Leigh. 1784–1859

De Quincey, Thomas. 1785–1859

Peacock, Thomas Love. 1785–1866

Lord Byron, George Gordon. 1788–1824

Shelley, Percy Bysshe. 1792–1822

Clare, John. 1793–1864

Keats, John. 1795–1821

Shelley, Mary Wollstonecraft. 1797–1851

10. The Victorian Period

Trollope, Frances Milton. 1779–1863

Marryat, Captain Frederick. 1792–1848

Carlyle, Thomas. 1795–1881

Chadwick, Sir Edwin. 1800–1890

Macaulay, Thomas Babington, 1st Baron. 1800–1859

Martineau, Harriet. 1802–1876

Bulwer-Lytton. 1803–1873

Coyne, Joseph Stirling. 1803–1868

Jerrold, Douglas William. 1803–1857

Disraeli, Benjamin. 1804–1881

Kay-Shuttleworth, Sir James Phillips. 1804–1877

Browning, Elizabeth Barrett. 1806–1861

Mill, Harriet Taylor. 1807–1858

Norton, Caroline Sheridan. 1808–1877

Tennyson, Alfred, 1st Baron. 1809–1892

Gaskell, Elizabeth. 1810–1865

Thackeray, William Makepeace. 1811–1863

Browning, Robert. 1812–1889

Dickens, Charles. 1812–1870

Mayhew, Henry. 1812–1887

Reade, Charles. 1814–1884

Trollope, Anthony. 1815–1882

Brontë, Charlotte. 1816–1855

Lewes, George Henry. 1817–1878

Taylor, Tom. 1817–1880

Brontë, Emily Jane. 1818–1848

Clough, Arthur Hugh. 1819–1861

Eliot, George. 1819–1880

Kingsley, Charles. 1819–1875

Ruskin, John. 1819–1900

Boucicault, Dionysius Lardner.
  1820–1890

Brontë, Anne. 1820–1849

Arnold, Matthew. 1822–1888

Collins, Wilkie. 1824–1889

Bodichon, Barbara. 1827–1891

Butler, Josephine Grey. 1828–1906

Meredith, George. 1828–1909

Oliphant, Margaret. 1828–1897

Rossetti, Dante Gabriel. 1828–1882

Robertson, T(homas) W(illiam).
  1829–1871

Rossetti, Christina. 1830–1894

Du Maurier, George. 1834–1896

Morris, William. 1834–1896

Butler, Samuel. 1835–1902

Gilbert, Sir William Schwenck.
  1836–1911

Braddon, Mary Elizabeth.
  1837–1915

Swinburne, Algernon Charles.
  1837–1909

Pater, Walter Horatio. 1839–1894

Hardy, Thomas. 1840–1928

Hudson, William Henry. 1841–1922

Hopkins, Gerard Manley.
  1844–1889

Stevenson, Robert Louis.
  1850–1894

Jones, Henry Arthur. 1851–1929

Moore, George. 1852–1933

Wilde, Oscar. 1854–1900

Pinero, Sir Arthur Wing.
  1855–1934

Gissing, George. 1857–1903

Barrie, Sir J(ames) M(atthew).
  1860–1937

Kipling, Rudyard. 1865–1936

11. Modern British and Irish Literature

Gregory, Lady Isabella Augusta.
  1852–1932

Shaw, George Bernard. 1856–1950

Conrad, Joseph. 1857–1924

Housman, A(lfred) E(dward).
  1859–1936

Barrie, Sir James Matthew, Bart.
  1860–1937

Yeats, William Butler. 1865–1939

Wells, H. G. 1866–1946

Bennett, Arnold. 1867–1931

Galsworthy, John. 1867–1933

Belloc, Hilaire. 1870–1953

Munro, H(ector) H(ugh).
  1870–1916

Synge, John Millington. 1871–1909

Beerbohm, Sir H(enry)
  M(aximilian) 1872–1956

de la Mare, Walter. 1873–1956

Ford, Ford Madox. 1873–1939

Richardson, Dorothy. 1873?–1957

Chesterton, G(ilbert) K(eith).
  1874–1936

Maugham, W(illiam) Somerset.
  1874–1965

Masefield, John. 1878–1967

Thomas, Edward. 1878–1917

Forster, E(dward) M(organ).
  1879–1970

O'Casey, Sean. 1880–1964

Colum, Padraic. 1881–1972

Joyce, James. 1881–1941

Woolf, Virginia. 1882–1941

Lewis, Wyndham. 1884–1957

O'Casey, Sean. 1884–1964

Lawrence, D(avid) H(erbert).
  1885–1930

Firbank, Ronald. 1886–1926

Hall, Radclyffe. 1886–1943

Sassoon, Siegfried. 1886–1967

Brooke, Rupert. 1887–1915

Muir, Edwin. 1887–1959

Sitwell, Edith. 1887–1964

Cary, Joyce. 1888–1957

Eliot, T(homas) S(tearns).
  1888–1965

Rosenberg, Isaac. 1890–1918

Compton-Burnett, Dame Ivy.
  1892–1969

MacDiarmid, Hugh. 1892–1978

Sackville-West, Vita. 1892–1962

Tolkien, J.R.R. 1892–1973
West, Dame Rebecca. 1892–1983
Owen, Wilfred. 1893–1918
Huxley, Aldous. 1894–1963
Priestley, J(ohn) B(oynton). 1894–1984
Graves, Robert. 1895–1985
Hartley, L(eslie) P(oles). 1895–1972
Jones, David. 1895–1974
Clarke, Austin. 1896–1974
Lewis, C(live) S(taples). 1898–1963
Bowen, Elizabeth. 1899–1973
Coward, Sir Noel. 1899–1973
Bunting, Basil. 1900–1985
Hughes, Richard. 1900–1976
O'Faolain, Sean. 1900–1991
Pritchett, Sir V(ictor) S(awden). 1900–
Smith, Stevie. 1902–1971
O'Connor, Frank. 1903–1966
Orwell, George. 1903–1950
Waugh, Evelyn. 1903–1966
Greene, Graham. 1904–1991
Isherwood, Christopher. 1904–1986
Lewis, C(ecil) Day. 1904–1972
Green, Henry. 1905–1974
Kavanagh, Patrick. 1905–1967
Powell, Anthony. 1905–
Snow, Lord C. P. 1905–1980
Beckett, Samuel. 1906–1989
Betjeman, Sir John. 1906–1984
Watkins, Vernon. 1906–1967
Auden, W(ystan) H(ugh). 1907–1973
Fry, Christopher. 1907–
MacNeice, (Frederick) Louis. 1907–1963
Spender, Sir Stephen. 1909–
Golding, William. 1911–1993
O'Brien, Flann. 1911–1966
Rattigan, Sir Terence. 1911–1977
Durrell, Lawrence. 1912–1990
Fuller, Roy. 1912–1991
Pym, Barbara. 1913–1980
Wilson, Angus. 1913–1991
Thomas, Dylan. 1914–1953

Burgess, Anthony. 1917–
Spark, Muriel. 1918–
Murdoch, Iris. 1919–
Amis, Kingsley. 1922–
Braine, John. 1922–1986
Davie, Donald. 1922–
Larkin, Philip. 1922–1985
Behan, Brendan. 1923–1964
Bolt, Robert. 1924–
Fowles, John. 1926–
Jennings, Elizabeth. 1926–
Shaffer, Peter. 1926–
Tomlinson, Charles. 1927–
Brookner, Anita. 1928–
Nichols, Peter. 1928–
Sillitoe, Alan. 1928–
Friel, Brian. 1929–
Gunn, Thom(son). 1929–
Osborne, John. 1929–
Arden, John. 1930–
Hughes, Ted. 1930–
Pinter, Harold. 1930–
Wilson, Colin. 1931–
Bradbury, Malcolm. 1932–
MacBeth, George. 1932–
Wesker, Arnold. 1932–
Orton, Joe. 1933–1967
Bond, Edward. 1934–
Lodge, David (John). 1935–
Potter, Dennis. 1935–
Byatt, A(notonia) S(usan). 1936–
Gray, Simon. 1936–
Stoppard, Tom. 1937–
Churchill, Caryl. 1938–
Ayckbourn, Alan. 1939–
Drabble, Margaret. 1939–
Heaney, Seamus. 1939–
Carter, Angela. 1940–1992
Brenton, Howard. 1942–
Hare, David. 1947–

12. British Literature: Popular Modes

Walpole, Horace. 1717–1797
Radcliffe, Ann. 1764–1823
Lewis, Matthew Gregory. 1775–1818

Lear, Edward. 1812–1888
Le Fanu, J. Sheridan. 1814–1873
MacDonald, George. 1824–1905
Carroll, Lewis. 1832–1898
Morris, William. 1834–1896
Crane, Walter. 1845–1915
Caldecott, Randolph. 1846–1886
Greenaway, Kate. 1846–1901
Stoker, Bram. 1847–1912
Haggard, H. Rider. 1856–1925
Doyle, Arthur Conan. 1859–1930
Grahame, Kenneth. 1859–1932
James, M. R. 1862–1936
Potter, Beatrix. 1866–1943
Wallace, Edgar. 1875–1932
Dunsany, Lord. 1878–1957
Milne, A(lan) A(lexander).
   1882–1956
Rohmer, Sax. 1883–1959
Christie, Dame Agatha. 1890–1976
Sayers, Dorothy. 1893–1957
Cartland, Barbara. 1901–
Du Maurier, Daphne. 1907–1989
Fleming, Ian. 1908–1964
Travers, P(amela) L(yndon). 1906–
Peters, Ellis. 1913–
Clarke, Arthur C. 1917–
Pilcher, Rosamunde (Scott). 1924–
Aldiss, Brian W. 1925–
Rendell, Ruth. 1930–
Le Carré, John. 1931–
Moorcock, Michael. 1939–
Barker, Clive. 1952–

13. Early American Literature: Beginnings to the Nineteenth Century

Bradford, William. 1590–1657
Bradstreet, Anne. c. 1612–1672
Taylor, Edward. c. 1642–1729
Edwards, Jonathan. 1703–1758
Franklin, Benjamin. 1706–1790
Paine, Thomas. 1737–1809
Jefferson, Thomas. 1743–1826
Freneau, Phillip. 1752–1832
Barlow, Joel. 1754–1812
Wheatley, Phillis. c. 1754–1784

Tyler, Royall. 1757–1826
Rowson, Susanna Haswell.
   1762–1824
Brown, Charles Brockden.
   1771–1810

14. Early Nineteenth-Century American Literature

Irving, Washington. 1783–1859
Cooper, James Fenimore.
   1789–1851
Sedgwick, Catharine Maria.
   1789–1867
Longstreet, Augustus Baldwin.
   1790–1870
Bryant, William Cullen. 1794–1878
Prescott, William Hickling.
   1796–1859
Emerson, Ralph Waldo. 1803–1882
Hawthorne, Nathaniel. 1804–1864
Simms, William Gilmore.
   1806–1870
Longfellow, Henry Wadsworth.
   1807–1882
Whittier, John Greenleaf.
   1807–1892
Holmes, Oliver Wendell.
   1809–1894
Poe, Edgar Allan. 1809–1849
Fuller, Margaret. 1810–1850
Fern, Fanny. 1811–1872
Stowe, Harriet Beecher. 1811–1896
Jacobs, Harriet Ann. 1813–1897
Very, Jones. 1813–1880
Harris, George Washington.
   1814–1869
Dana, Richard Henry, Jr.
   1815–1882
Thorpe, Thomas Bangs. 1815–1878
Thoreau, Henry David. 1817–1862
Douglass, Frederick. 1818–1895
Lowell, James Russell. 1819–1891
Melville, Herman. 1819–1891
Whitman, Walt. 1819–1892
Tuckerman, Frederick Goddard.
   1821–1873
Parkman, Francis. 1823–1893
Timrod, Henry. 1828–1867

15. Middle to Late Nineteenth-Century American Literature

Tuckerman, Frederick Goddard.
1821–1873

Chesnut, Mary Boykin Miller.
1823–1886

Harper, Frances E(llen) W(atkins).
1825–1911

De Forest, John Willima.
1826–1903

Timrod, Henry. 1828–1867

Dickinson, Emily (Elizabeth).
1830–1886

Davis, Rebecca Harding.
1831–1910

Jackson, Helen Maria (Fiske) Hunt.
1831–1885

Twain, Mark. 1835–1910

Aldrich, Thomas Bailey. 1836–1907

Harte, (Francis) Bret(t).
1836?–1902

Howells, William Dean. 1837–1920

Adams, Henry. 1838–1918

Woolson, Constance Fenimore.
1840–1894

Bierce, Ambrose (Gwinnet).
1842–1914?

James, William. 1842–1910

Lanier, Sidney. 1842–1881

James, Henry. 1843–1916

Cable, George Washington.
1844–1925

Harris, Joel Chandler. 1848–1908

James, Alice. 1848–1892

Jewett, Sarah Orne. 1949–1909

Lazarus, Emma. 1849–1887

Riley, James Whitcomb. 1849–1916

Bellamy, Edward. 1850–1898

Chopin, Kate. 1851–1904

Freeman, Mary Eleanor (Wilkins).
1852–1930

Washington, Booker T(aliaferro).
1856–1915

Chesnutt, Charles Wadell.
1858–1932

Eastman, Charles A. 1858–1939

Addams, (Laura) Jane. 1860–1935

Cahan, Abraham. 1860–1951

Garland, (Hannibal) Hamlin.
1860–1940

Gilman, Charlotte Perkins.
1860–1935

Wister, Owen. 1860–1938

Henry, O. 1862–1910

Wharton, Edith (Jones). 1862–1937

Austin, Mary (Hunter). 1868–1934

Moody, William Vaughn.
1869–1910

Norris, (Benjamin) Frank(lin).
1870–1902

Crane, Stephen. 1871–1900

Johnson, James Weldon.
1871–1938

London, Jack. 1876–1916

16. Early Twentieth-Century American Literature

Masters, Edgar Lee. 1869–1950

Du Bois, W(illiam) E(dward)
B(urghardt). 1868–1963

Robinson, Edwin Arlington.
1869–1935

Dreiser, Theodore. 1871–1945

Frost, Robert. 1874–1963

Glasgow, Ellen. 1874–1945

Lowell, Amy. 1874–1925

Stein, Gertrude. 1874–1946

Anderson, Sherwood. 1876–1941

Cather, Willa. 1876–1947

Sandburg, Carl. 1878–1967

Sinclair, Upton. 1878–1968

Lindsay, Vachel. 1879–1931

Stevens, Wallace. 1879–1955

Mencken, H(enry) L(ouis).
1880–1956

Roberts, Elizabeth Madox.
1881–1941

Williams, William Carlos.
1883–1963

Lardner, Ring(gold Wilmer).
1885–1933

Lewis, Sinclair. 1885–1951

Pound, Ezra. 1885–1972

H. D. (Hilda Doolittle) 1886–1961

Jeffers, Robinson. 1887–1962

Moore, Marianne. 1887–1972

Ransom, John Crowe. 1888–1974
Aiken, Conrad. 1889–1973
Benchley, Robert. 1889–1945
McKay, Claude. 1889–1948
Porter, Katherine Anne. 1890–1980
Larsen, Nella. 1891–1964
Miller, Henry. 1891–1980
Barnes, Djuna. 1892–1982
MacLeish, Archibald. 1892–1982
Millay, Edna St. Vincent.
    1892–1950
Parker, Dorothy. 1893–1967
Cummings, E(dward) E(stlin).
    1894–1962
Thurber, James. 1894–1961
Toomer, Jean. 1894–1967
Schuyler, George. 1895–1977
Wilson, Edmund. 1895–1972
Dos Passos, John. 1896–1970
Fitzgerald, F(rancis) Scott.
    1896–1940
Burke, Kenneth. 1897–
Faulkner, William. 1897–1962
Wilder, Thornton. 1897–1975
Benét, Stephen Vincent. 1898–1943
Cowley, Malcolm. 1898–1989
Crane, Hart. 1899–1932
Hemingway, Ernest. 1899–1961
Tate, Allen. 1899–1979
White, E(lwyn) B(rooks).
    1899–1985
Wolfe, Thomas. 1900–1938
Hurston, Zora Neale. 1901–1960
Riding, Laura. 1901–1991
Bontemps, Arna. 1902–1973
Hughes, Langston. 1902–1967
Steinbeck, John. 1902–1968
Caldwell, Erskine. 1903–1987
Cullen, Countee. 1903–1946
Nin, Anaïs. 1903–1977
Blackmur, R(ichard) P(almer).
    1904–1965
Farrell, James T(homas).
    1904–1979
Perelman, S(idney) J(oseph).
    1904–1979
West, Nathanael. 1904–1940

O'Hara, John. 1905–1970
Warren, Robert Penn. 1905–1989
Barzun, Jacques. 1907–
Wright, Richard. 1908–1960
Welty, Eudora. 1909–

17. Middle to Late Twentieth-Century American Literature

Gordon, Caroline. 1895–1981.
Bogan, Louise. 1897–1970.
Burke, Kenneth. 1897–
Nabokov, Vladimir. 1899–1977.
Brown, Sterling Allen. 1901–1989
Johnson, Edgar. 1901–
Cozzens, James Gould. 1903–1978
Eberhart, Richard. 1904–
Singer, Isaac Bashevis. 1904–1991
Zukofsky, Louis. 1904–1978
Kunitz, Stanley. 1905–
Rexroth, Kenneth. 1905–1983
Trilling, Lionel. 1905–1975
Brooks, Cleanth. 1906–
Roth, Henry. 1906–
Edel, Leon. 1907–
Petry, Ann. 1908–
Roethke, Theodore. 1908–1963
Agee, James. 1909–1955
Stegner, Wallace. 1909–1993
Morris, Wright. 1910–
Olson, Charles. 1910–1970
Bishop, Elizabeth. 1911–1979
Patchen, Kenneth. 1911–1972
Abrams, M. H. 1912–
Cheever, John. 1912–1982
Frye, Northrop. 1912–1991
McCarthy, Mary. 1912–1989
Hayden, Robert E(arl). 1913–1980
Olsen, Tillie. 1913–
Rukeyser, Muriel. 1913–1980
Schwartz, Delmore. 1913–1966
Shapiro, Karl. 1913–
Berryman, John. 1914–1972
Burroughs, William S. 1914–
Ellison, Ralph. 1914–
Ignatow, David. 1914–
Jarrell, Randall. 1914–1965

Malamud, Bernard. 1914–1986
Stafford, William. 1914–
Bellow, Saul. 1915–
Kazin, Alfred. 1915–
Percy, Walker. 1916–
Auchincloss, Louis. 1917–
Brooks, Gwendolyn. 1917–
Fiedler, Leslie A(aron). 1917–
Lewis, R(ichard) W(arrington)
    B(aldwin). 1917–
Lowell, Robert. 1917–1977
McCullers, Carson. 1917–1967
Powers, J(ames) F(arl). 1917–
Ellmann, Richard. 1918–
De Man, Paul. 1919–1983
Duncan, Robert. 1919–
Jackson, Shirley. 1919–1965
Salinger, J(erome) D(avid). 1919–
Swenson, May. 1919–1989
Clampitt, Amy. 1920–
Howe, Irving. 1920–1993
Nemerov, Howard. 1920–1991
Jones, James. 1921–1977
Van Duyn, Mona. 1921–
Wilbur, Richard. 1921–
Gaddis, William. 1922–
Kerouac, Jack. 1922–1969
Vonnegut, Kurt, Jr. 1922–
Dickey, James. 1923–
Dugan, Alan. 1923–
Hecht, Anthony. 1923–
Hugo, Richard. 1923–1982
Levertov, Denise. 1923–
Logan, John. 1923–
Mailer, Norman. 1923–
Purdy, James. 1923–
Simpson, Louis. 1923–
Baldwin, James. 1924–1987
Berger, Thomas. 1924–
Capote, Truman. 1924–1984
Gass, William. 1924–
Hawkes, John. 1925–
Justice, Donald. 1925–
Kizer, Carolyn. 1925–
Koch, Kenneth. 1925–
Merrill, James. 1925–

O'Connor, Flannery. 1925–1965
Styron, William. 1925–
Vidal, Gore. 1925–
Ammons, A(rchie) R(andolph).
    1926–
Bly, Robert. 1926–
Creeley, Robert. 1926–
Ginsberg, Allen. 1926–
Lurie, Alison. 1926–
O'Hara, Frank. 1926–1966
Snodgrass, W(illiam) D(ewitt).
    1926–
Ashbery, John. 1927–
Kinnell, Galway. 1927–
Merwin, W(illiam) S(tanley). 1927–
Wright, James. 1927–1980.
Angelou, Maya. 1928–
Hall, Donald. 1928–
Kennedy, William. 1928–
Levine, Philip. 1928–
Ozick, Cynthia. 1928–
Sexton, Anne. 1928–1977
Wiesel, Elie. 1928–
Dorn, Edward. 1929–
Howard, Richard. 1929–
Kennedy, X. J. 1929–
Marshall, Paule. 1929–
Potok, Chaim. 1929–
Rich, Adrienne. 1929–
Steiner, George. 1929–
Barth, John. 1930–
Corso, Gregory. 1930–
Elkin, Stanley. 1930–
Snyder, Gary. 1930–
Barthelme, Donald. 1931–
Doctorow, E(dgar) L(aurence).
    1931–
McPhee, John. 1931–
Morrison, Toni. 1931–
Coover, Robert. 1932–
Heller, Joseph. 1932–
McClure, Michael. 1932–
Plath, Sylvia. 1932–1963
Updike, John. 1932–
Bercovitch, Sacvan. 1933–
Gardner, John. 1933–1982

Kosinski, Jerzy. 1933–1991
Roth, Philip. 1933–
Sontag, Susan. 1933–
Baraka, Imamu Amiri. 1934–
Didion, Joan. 1934–
Momaday, N. Scott. 1934–
Sanchez, Sonia. 1934–
Strand, Mark. 1934–
Allen, Woody. 1935–
Kesey, Ken. 1935–
Said, Edward W. 1935–
Wright, Charles. 1935–
Baym, Nina. 1936–
McMurtry, Larry. 1936–
Silverman, Kenneth. 1936–
Pynchon, Thomas. 1937–
Stone, Robert. 1937–
Carver, Raymond. 1938–1988.
Fish, Stanley. 1938–
Harper, Michael. 1938–
Oates, Joyce Carol. 1938–
Reed, Ishmael. 1938–
Simic, Charles. 1938–
Bambara, Toni Cade. 1939–
Banks, Russell. 1940–
Kingston, Maxine Hong. 1940–
Pinsky, Robert. 1940–
Apple, Max. 1941–
Hass, Robert. 1941–
Showalter, Elaine. 1941–
Tyler, Anne. 1941–
Irving, John. 1942–
Rose, Phyllis. 1942–
Baker, Houston A., Jr. 1943–
Glück, Louise. 1943–
Tate, James. 1943–
Walker, Alice. 1944–
Strouse, Jean. 1945–
Beattie, Ann. 1947–
Ackerman, Diane. 1948–
Boyle, T. Coraghessan. 1948–
Goldbarth, Albert. 1948–
Silko, Leslie Marmon. 1948–
Smiley, Jane. 1949–
Naylor, Gloria. 1950–
Hijuelos, Oscar. 1951–

Dove, Rita. 1952–

18. Twentieth-Century American Drama

Kelly, George Edward. 1887–1974
Anderson, Maxwell. 1888–1959
O'Neill, Eugene. 1888–1953
Kaufman, George S. 1889–1961
Rice, Elmer. 1892–1967
Green, Paul. 1894–1981
Barry, Philip. 1896–1949
Wilder, Thornton. 1897–1975
Hellman, Lillian. 1905–1984
Odets, Clifford. 1906–1963
Saroyan, William. 1908–1981
Williams, Tennessee. 1911–1983
Inge, William. 1913–1973
Miller, Arthur. 1915–
Anderson, Robert. 1917–
McCullers, Carson. 1917–1967
Baldwin, James. 1924–1987
Simon, Neil. 1927–
Albee, Edward. 1928–
Gurney, A. R., Jr. 1930–
Hansberry, Lorraine. 1930–1965
Linney, Romulus. 1930–
Terry, Megan. 1932–
Baraka, Imamu Amiri (LeRoi
    Jones). 1934–
Bullins, Ed. 1935–
Van Itallie, Jean-Claude. 1935–
Jones, Preston. 1936–1979
Zindel, Paul. 1936–
Kopit, Arthur. 1937–
Wilson, Lanford. 1937–
Guare, John. 1938–
Horovitz, Israel. 1939–
McNally, Terrence. 1939–
Rabe, David. 1940–
Shepard, Sam. 1943–
Wilson, August. 1945–
Mamet, David. 1947–
Norman, Marsha. 1947–
Durang, Christopher. 1949–
Wasserstein, Wendy. 1950–
Henley, Beth. 1952–
Hwang, David Henry. 1957–

L'Amour, Louis Dearborn.
  1908–1988
Short, Luke. 1908–1975
Fisher, Clay/Henry, Will.
  1912–1991
Manfred, Frederick. 1912–
Fast, Howard. 1914–
Macdonald, Ross. 1915–1983
MacDonald, John D. 1916–1986
Robbins, Harold. 1916–
Wallace, Irving. 1916–1990
Yerby, Frank. 1916–1992
Sheldon, Sidney. 1917–
Farmer, Philip Jose. 1918–
Spillane, Mickey. 1918–
Pohl, Frederick. 1919–
Asimov, Isaac. 1920–1992
Bradbury, Ray. 1920–
Sanders, Lawrence. 1920–
Herbert, Frank. 1920–1986
Highsmith, Patricia. 1921–
Miller, Walter M., Jr. 1923–
Hillerman, Tony. 1925–
Leonard, Elmore. 1925–
McBain, Ed. 1926–
Dick, Philip K. 1928–1982
Sendak, Maurice. 1928–

Le Guin, Ursula. 1929–
Jakes, John. 1932–
Paterson, Katherine. 1932–
Silverstein, Shel(by). 1932–
Anthony, Piers. 1934–
Russ, Joanna. 1937–
Zelazny, Roger. 1937–
Niven, Larry. 1938–
Woodiwiss, Kathleen. 1939–
Andrews, V(irginia) C(leo). ?–1986
Michaels, Fern (pseud. of
  Roberta Anderson, 1942–
  and Mary Kuczkir, 1939–)
Grafton, Sue. 1940–
Rice, Anne. 1941–
Delaney, Samuel R. 1942–
Saul, John. 1942–
Holland, Cecelia. 1943–
Straub, Peter. 1943–
Koontz, Dean. 1945–
Dailey, Janet. 1947–
Deveraux, Jude. 1947–
King, Stephen. 1947–
Paretsky, Sara. 1947–
Steel, Danielle. 1947–
Van Allsburg, Chris. 1949–
McCammon, Robert R. 1952–

Introduction: British Literature

Reference books serve as atlases or maps of intellectual territories, allowing readers to see both where they want to go and how they might get there. The fourteenth edition of *The Reader's Adviser* is among the most valuable of these reference books. It is, in fact, a collection of treasure maps pointing the way to a wealth of books, many of which lie hidden in the almost impenetrable jungle of publishers' lists.

This new edition of Volume 1 of *The Reader's Adviser* is completely revised; yet it proudly continues the distinguished tradition of its predecessors. Once again, a team of renowned scholars has gathered together to reconsider their fields of expertise and to identify the most important literary landmarks in them. These scholars have worked diligently to translate their considerable knowledge and judgment into new, comprehensive listings of what is most important to know—the central primary texts in a field of the most useful secondary readings. The contributors have, for the most part, reconceptualized their fields of expertise, taking stock of recent scholarship and their own individual experiences of teaching and writing to see these fields as they appear today, both in their own integrity and as they touch us in our present moment. The contributors of the individual chapters reveal a remarkable command of their field, and the chapters are marked by comprehensive and incisive listings of books, generously and judiciously introduced and usefully annotated.

In many significant ways, this volume is truly new. It does not merely add materials that have appeared since the thirteenth edition, but it has reconsidered and revised everything that previously appeared and has significantly reconfigured the chapter organization to allow its achievement to be more useful to users. The most obvious difference between the thirteenth and fourteenth editions is that Volume 1 now includes, within a single volume, the whole of British Literature and American Literature, as well as important reference chapters. With regard to British literature, the new arrangement is based on accepted periodizations rather than on the broader historical divisions and generic categories of the thirteenth edition. This arrangement brings greater clarity and coherence, and will certainly enable readers to use this volume more easily. However, perhaps more significantly, the new chapters and their organization now correspond more closely to the fields in which scholars in British literature actually work, thus insuring that the chapters are truly informed and informative, and accurately reflect the present state of knowledge in the field.

In addition to this major reorganization of chapters, the current edition includes a greatly expanded list of profiled authors and thousands of new, as well as revised, bibliographic entries. More than 300 authors are now included in the section on British literature. The British literature section also includes a new chapter, "British Literature: Popular Modes," which contains sections on children's literature and popular fiction in such genres as adventures and thrillers, Gothic and horror, mystery and detective, science fiction and fantasy, and romances.

This new edition of Volume 1 of *The Reader's Adviser*, then, is not only an outstanding bibliography but also a map of current literary concerns and understandings. The contributors have struggled with remarkable integrity and intelligence to organize the great quantity of material available. The result is that chapters not only provide valuable guides to the most important materials of various authors and literary periods but also serve to trace the compelling interests and concerns of literary study today.

David Scott Kastan

Introduction: American Literature

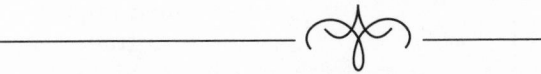

Since the publication of the thirteenth edition of *The Reader's Adviser*, there have been several important developments in the research and study of American literature. Shifts in theoretical perspectives stemming from new directions in philosophy have encouraged some critics to redefine the very meaning of "literature." As a result, new serious study is now being devoted in literature and English departments to a number of genres such as film and television, which previously were not included within literary criticism. Similarly, the questioning of the familiar distinction between high culture and popular culture has led some scholars to explore the previously overlooked artistic, cultural, and historical significance and substance of such popular modes as westerns, detective stories, and children's literature. A deeper and more thoughtful assessment of the roles of gender and race in literature, and the contributions to American literary heritage by women, gays and lesbians, and ethnic minority group writers has, furthermore, expanded the accepted canon of the literature and broadened and deepened our understanding of the rich complexity of American literature.

As a result of these and other trends within American literature, this Volume 1 of the fourteenth edition reflects a number of significant changes from the thirteenth edition. Most noticeable is the chronological breakdown of American literature into several major periods, combining all genres within each period, rather than the breakdown, by both genre and overly-broad historical periods, that characterized the previous edition. This organization presents a more coherent approach to the subject, one that follows a more traditional division among chapters and, importantly, avoids a break between genres that does not reflect the fact that many writers produce works in a variety of genres. Along with this new organization, the fourteenth edition provides many exciting additions to the materials within each chapter and adds several new chapters as well. Throughout, the authors of each chapter have added many authors previously excluded and have updated and expanded the lists of primary and secondary works. After taking into account recent trends, it further was decided to add two completely new chapters: "American Literature: Some New Directions," which focuses on new literary theory, gay and lesbian literature, and film studies, and "American Literature: Popular Modes," which examines both children's literature and popular fiction genres such as westerns, romances, mystery and detective, horror, historical fiction, and science fiction. In each chapter on American literature, not only are current critical perspectives and the most recent bibliographic information present, but the sections build thoughtfully upon the foundations established in previous editions.

Emory Elliott

The Reader's Adviser

Part One

Reference Works

CHAPTER 1

Books About Books

Sidney E. Berger

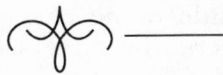

> . . . the newcomer to research, whatever his discipline, can be forgiven
> dismay at the sheer bulk of the sources at his disposal, sources which seem to
> multiply with undisciplined rapidity. The threat to enlightenment lies less in
> the insufficiency of information than in its overwhelming flood.
> —R. C. ALSTON, "The Grammar of Research"

There is a wonderful irony that, in spite of the growth of electronic publishing
and optical storage, "the book"—in traditional codex form as well as new
electronic form—continues to fascinate. The literature about the development
of writing, printing, and publishing provides both entertainment and education
for those who care about communication. Such literature demonstrates the
classical, historical, and futuristic bases from which to explore the world of the
book as it has been, as it is now, and as it is becoming.

One of the catchword phrases of library schools and of information scientists
during the last 10 years has been "the paperless society." The phrase designates
a new era of communication technologies that use electricity rather than more
tangible media (papyrus, vellum, paper). In the "ideal world" of the paperless
society, all publications would appear in electronic form, available instantly at
the touch of a few buttons, completely indexed and searchable, and ready for
instant updates so that no text would become obsolete.

In fact, with electronic mail, scanners, and a host of other marvels of the
modern electronic era, some of this has already come to pass. Not remarkably,
more books—tangible, physical objects made of paper, ink, glue, and boards—
are being produced each year than ever before in history. And the interest in
books as physical objects has burgeoned as well.

In the thirteenth edition of *The Reader's Adviser*, the opening chapter on
"Books About Books" was a comprehensive guide indicating the interests of the
author's audience. Since that edition, however, there has been a shift in the
focus of interest of scholars looking at books about books. This shift manifests
itself in a reduction of concentration on the book industry and a concomitant
increase in concentration on the book arts, or, more specifically, an interest in
the arts and crafts of book production. This shift comes partly from the effects of
the return to the hand crafts of the 1960s through the present and partly from
continuing efforts of descriptive and historical bibliographers to learn about the
book as an artifact.

Because of these new concentrations, the present chapter takes the material
from the previous edition and reorganizes much of it, while creating entirely
new sections of bibliographical references, first presenting books about the
production of books (broken down into appropriate categories such as writing
surfaces, printing, calligraphy and letterforms, printing types, ink, bookbinding,

book illustration, and so forth) and then moving on to categories pertaining to book industry history.

Many older titles have been included in lists for this chapter, since they have taken on importance because of new trends in scholarship, along with titles included in the thirteenth edition and also many titles that have appeared since the publication of the previous edition.

Additionally, little has been added to the previous author's excellent sections on book industry history. Those listings were both retrospective and forward looking, and they need little or no change. Readers wanting to do further research in the areas covered by these sections will be amply rewarded by following the leads included here.

WRITING SURFACES

There is a vast body of literature about paper, papyrus, parchment, vellum, and other writing surfaces. This section gives just a brief overview, mentioning some of the key texts in a variety of areas, for example, dictionaries of terms, histories of the crafts, and practical handbooks. Naturally, one must be selective since there are so many volumes on scores of aspects of the topics.

It should be noted that the W. J. Barrow Research Laboratory was one of the first to recognize the importance of alkaline papers in the production of books and other documents. As early as 1960 the laboratory was doing research on the durability and longevity of papers. Before closing down, the laboratory produced a series of influential pamphlets, pointing up many issues that were the foundation of modern studies on acidity and alkalinity in papers. Among the pamphlets produced were *The Manufacture and Testing of Durable Book Papers* (1960); *Permanence/Durability of the Book: A Two-Year Research Program* (1963); *Permanence/Durability of the Book—II: Test Data of Naturally Aged Pages* (1964); *Permanence/Durability of The* [sic] *Book—III: Spray Deacidification* (1964); *Permanence/Durability of the Book—IV: Polyvinyl Acetate (PVA) Adhesives for use in Library Binding* (1965); *Permanence/Durability of the Book—V: Strength and Other Characteristics of Book Papers 1800–1899* (1967); *Permanence/Durability of the Book—VI: Spot Testing for Unstable Modern Book and Record Papers* (1969); and *Permanence/Durability of the Book—VII: Physical and Chemical Properties of Book Papers, 1507–1949* (1974). The work of W. J. Barrow and his laboratory was at the forefront of a whole new field of study: scientific book conservation.

Balston, Thomas. *James Whatman, Father and Son.* Garland 1978 o.p. On one of the
greatest and most important papermakers in English history.
_____. *William Balston, Paper Maker, 1759–1849.* Garland 1978 o.p. A biography and a
company history of the firm that took over the prestigious Whatman watermark and
produced quality papers for nearly a century.
Barrett, Timothy. *Japanese Papermaking: Traditions, Tools, and Techniques.* Weatherhill
1983 $29.95. ISBN 0-8348-0255-4. A thorough study, well illustrated, of materials and
methods.
Clapperton, Robert H. *Paper: An Historical Account of Its Making by Hand From the
Earliest Times Down to the Present Day.* OUP 1934 o.p. An excellent and often-quoted
study.
*The Dictionary of Paper: Including Pulp, Paperboard, Paper Properties, and Related
Papermaking Terms.* American Paper and Pulp Assoc. 1980 $20.00. ISBN 0-685-
45519-X. Five hundred pages of terms and definitions.

Easton, Phoebe Jane. *Marbling: A History and a Bibliography*. Dawsons 1983 o.p. Looks at marbling in the Near East, Europe, and America, with discussions of its uses, collectors, patterns, mechanization, and so on.

Gaur, Albertine. *Writing Materials of the East*. ALA 1979 o.p. Looks at such surfaces as palm leaves, tortoise shells and bone, stones, ivory, wood, bamboo, bark, copper, clay, papyrus, and others.

Gravell, Thomas L., and George Miller. *A Catalogue of American Watermarks 1690–1835*. Garland 1979 o.p. Lists and illustrates 734 watermarks used by American papermakers.

_____. *A Catalogue of Foreign Watermarks Found on Paper Used in America 1700–1835*. Garland 1983 o.p. Illustrates 788 watermarks.

Hills, Richard L. *Papermaking in Britain 1488–1988: A Short History*. Humanities 1988 $35.00. ISBN 0-485-11346-5. An overview of British papermaking, looking at people and techniques, machines and fibers, and other issues.

Hughes, Sukey. *Washi: The World of Japanese Paper*. Kodansha 1981 $300.00. ISBN 0-87011-350-X. Excellently illustrated study, showing methods, materials, and techniques.

Hunter, Dard. *My Life with Paper: An Autobiography*. Knopf 1958 o.p. The life of one of the world's most learned and influential paper historians.

_____. *Papermaking: The History and Technique of an Ancient Craft*. Dover 1978 repr. of 1943 ed. $11.95. ISBN 0-486-23619-6. Contains more than 600 pages of valuable information about the subject, from its beginnings in the Orient to its mechanization and its modern manufacture.

_____. *Papermaking in Pioneer America*. Garland 1978 o.p. A history of the earliest mills in the first 18 states. An important study that gives a directory of American papermakers from 1680 to 1817, along with chapters on the mills and their equipment and on paper-mould manufacture.

Labarre, E. J. *Dictionary and Encyclopaedia of Paper and Paper-making*. Swets North Am. 1952 o.p. Perhaps the most famous of the dictionaries of paper and papermaking terms. The first edition offers equivalent terminology in French, German, Dutch, Italian, and it has a section of 45 paper samples bound in. The second edition lacks the paper samples, but adds Spanish and Swedish to the equivalent terminology.

Leif, Irving P. *An International Sourcebook of Paper History*. Archon Bks. 1978 o.p. A bibliographical guide to histories of paper and watermarks, and papermaking in Asia and Australia, Europe and the former Soviet Union, and North and South America.

Loeber, E. G. *Paper Mould and Mouldmaker*. Paper Pubns. Soc. 1982 o.p. Well-illustrated, extensive study of the prime piece of equipment in the making of handmade paper: the mould.

_____. *Supplement to E. J. Labarre, Dictionary and Encyclopaedia of Paper and Paper-making*. Swets North Am. 1967 o.p. Contains over 100 pages of additions and corrections.

Loring, Rosamond B. *Decorated Book Papers: Being an Account of their Designs and Fashions*. Harvard Coll. Lib. Department of Printing and Graphic Arts 1973 repr. of 1942 ed. o.p. Reprint of the scarce limited first edition. Gives a history and description of many kinds of decorated papers.

Mason, John. *Paper Making as an Artistic Craft: With a Note on Nylon Paper*. Faber & Faber 1959 o.p. This book came out in a number of editions. A minor classic on hand papermaking, with illustrations of materials, equipment, and techniques.

Munsell, Joel. *Chronology of the Origin and Progress of Paper and Paper-Making*. Garland 1978 repr. of 1876 ed. o.p. An important nineteenth-century account, drawn from Munsell's experience and firsthand observation.

Papermaking: Art and Craft. Lib. Congress 1968 o.p. Brief but well-illustrated guide to the history of hand and machine papermaking.

Sandstrom, Alan R., and Pamela Effrein Sandstrom. *Traditional Papermaking and Paper Cult Figures of Mexico*. U. of Okla. Pr. 1986 $26.95. ISBN 0-8061-1972-1. Offers a history of the making of bark papers, along with a discussion of materials, processes, and uses.

Sutermeister, Edwin. *Chemistry of Pulp and Paper Making.* Routledge Chapman & Hall 1941 o.p. Extensive scientific study about raw materials, rags, processes, bleaching, sizing, coloring, and many other topics. There are chapters on printing and paper testing.

————. *The Story of Papermaking.* S. D. Warren Company 1954 o.p. Informative history and technical guide to the subject. Looks at materials, processes, machinery, and paper grades.

Von Hagen, Victor Wolfgang. *The Aztec and Maya Papermakers.* J. J. Augustin 1944 o.p. An important study, considering the makers, their materials and techniques, and the uses to which these papers were put.

Weeks, Lyman Horace. *A History of Paper-Manufacturing in the United States, 1690–1916.* Lockwood Trade Journal Co. 1916 o.p. An in-depth examination of papermaking.

Wolfe, Richard J. *Marbled Paper: Its History, Techniques, and Patterns, With Special Relationship of Marbling to Bookbinding in Europe and the Western World.* U. of Pa. Pr. 1990 $125.00. ISBN 0-8122-8188-8. Wide-ranging and beautifully illustrated study.

PRINTING

Many bibliographies exist on all of the contributory crafts that go into the making of books. A bibliography on printing, perhaps the central craft in the history of bookmaking, could fill many volumes. In fact, the Theodore Besterman bibliography on this subject lists over 600 pages in the field, and this listing is only of bibliographies. The following listing, therefore, can give only the most superficial coverage to a gargantuan field. Included under the rubric "printing" are books on typography, printing presses, design in printing, and printers' manuals. For this last topic alone, one could compile a list of over 200 volumes. The selections here are of only the most influential or prominent manuals.

Adams, Thomas F. *Typographia; or, The Printer's Instructor. A Brief Sketch of the Origin, Rise, and Progress of the Typographic Art.* . . . o.p. The standard printer's manual from about 1836 until 1866, with the publication of MacKellar's famous manual. (See MacKellar.)

Allen, Lewis. *Printing With the Handpress.* Krieger 1976 o.p. A generally reliable manual that discusses equipment, presses, paper, ink, bearers, and so forth.

American Dictionary of Printing and Bookmaking. 1894. B. Franklin 1970 o.p. Nearly 600 pages, in small type, of information on all aspects of printing.

Arner, Robert D. *Dobson's Encyclopaedia: The Publisher, Text, and Publication of America's First Britannica, 1789–1803.* U. of Pa. Pr. 1991 $35.95. ISBN 0-8122-3092-2. A thorough study of the massive efforts and expenses Dobson went through to publish the encyclopedia. A valuable study in printing, book illustration, subscription selling, and early American scholarship and the reading public.

Bailyn, Bernard, and John B. Hench, eds. *The Press and the American Revolution.* NE U. Pr. 1981 $37.50. ISBN 0-930350-32-4. Eight essays.

Barber, G. G. *Book Making in Diderot's Encyclopédie.* Gregg Intl. 1973 o.p. Illustrations and text from Diderot, with an introduction by Barber.

Barker, Nicolas. *Stanley Morison.* HUP 1972 $38.00. ISBN 0-674-83425-9. Morison, who died in 1967, was without question the greatest influence in the mid-twentieth century on type and typography. A massive biography.

Bennett, Paul A., ed. *Books and Printing: A Treasury for Typophiles.* Beil repr. of 1951 ed. $29.95. ISBN 0-913720-72-0. Forty-two essays by distinguished scholars, covering many areas of printing and book history (e.g., the alphabet, printers' marks, types, design, ornaments, the book trade, and private presses). A wonderful selection of important essays.

Berger, Sidney E. *The Design of Bibliographies: Observations, References and Examples.* Greenwood 1991 $85.00. ISBN 0-313-28425-3. The first study on the subject; offers basic guidance on book design, with particular reference to bibliographies. With an annotated bibliography and many examples.

Bernard, Auguste. *Geofroy Tory: Painter and Engraver, First Royal Printer, Reformer of Orthography and Typography under François I.* Trans. by George B. Ives. Kraus 1969 o.p. Extensive and thorough biography.

Berry, W. Turner, and H. Edmund Poole. *Annals of Printing: A Chronological Encyclopaedia from the Earliest Times to 1950.* Blandford Pr. 1966 o.p. Traces bookish events from the reputed invention of paper in A.D. 105 (a date now discredited) to 1950. A useful compendium.

Besterman, Theodore. *Printing, Book Collecting and Illustrated Books: A Bibliography of Bibliographies.* 2 vols. Rowman 1971 o.p. Lists thousands of items under many topics, including printing, book collecting, illustrated books, broadsides and pamphlets, book production, paper, publishing and bookselling, and special subjects.

Biggs, John R. *Basic Typography.* Watson-Guptill 1968 o.p. A good, basic introduction to the principles, mechanics, and practice of typography.

Bigmore, F. C., and C. W. H. Wyman, comps. *A Bibliography of Printing.* 1880. Saifer 1982 $75.00. ISBN 0-87556-157-8. The first great such bibliography, listing thousands of items in nearly a thousand pages, and often with extensive commentary.

Blades, William. *The Life and Typography of William Caxton, England's First Printer.* 2 vols. B. Franklin 1861–1863 o.p. A standard biography.

Blumenthal, Joseph. *The Art of the Printed Book, 1455–1955: Masterpieces of Typography through Five Centuries.* Godine 1974 $50.00. ISBN 0-87923-082-7. Contains 125 facsimiles of beautifully printed pages throughout the centuries, representing some of the best printing to be found in the Pierpont Morgan Library collection.

_____. *Bruce Rogers: A Life in Letters, 1870–1957.* W. T. Taylor 1989 $95.00. ISBN 0-935072-16-0. Excellent, well-illustrated biography, with a foreword by John Dreyfus. Many of the 57 plates are in two colors.

_____. *The Printed Book in America.* Godine 1989 $50.00. ISBN 0-87451-485-1. Beautifully designed and printed, well-illustrated book with a good historical text.

_____. *Typographic Years: A Printer's Journey through a Half Century, 1925–1975.* Beil 1982 $26.50. ISBN 0-913720-38-0. Blumenthal's reminiscences of his work at the Spiral Press, one of the finest publishing establishments in the country.

Carter, John, and Percy Muir, comps. and eds. *Printing and the Mind of Man: A Descriptive Catalogue Illustrating the Impact of Print on the Evolution of Western Civilization During Five Centuries.* HR&W Schl. Div. 1967 o.p. A massive landmark catalog, emanating from a smaller paperback volume of the same title that accompanied the original exhibit. Describes fully 424 volumes "which, for the ideas that they brought to the world for the first time, are of prime importance to the mind of man" (dust-jacket blurb). A second edition under the same title, revised and enlarged (Karl Pressler 1983), contains a new bibliographical section with 550 references, along with a corrected and augmented index and a new introduction by Percy Muir.

Chapell, Warren. *A Short History of the Printed Word.* Godine 1980 $10.95. ISBN 0-87923-312-5. A concise history by this well-known artist, designer, and teacher.

Clair, Colin. *A Chronology of Printing.* Greenwood 1969 o.p. Begins in A.D. 105, the (now discredited) date of the invention of paper, and ends in 1967 with the death of Stanley Morison. A comprehensive history.

_____. *A History of European Printing.* Acad. Pr. 1977 o.p. The origins of printing in all countries and its spread from the early beginnings constitute Clair's broad field of interest.

Cobden-Sanderson, Thomas James. *The Journals of Thomas James Cobden-Sanderson 1879–1922.* Together with *The Ideal Book or Book Beautiful—A Tract on Calligraphy, Printing, and Illustration and on the Book Beautiful as a Whole.* 1926. 2 vols. B. Franklin 1969 o.p. Cobden-Sanderson was a friend of William Morris and was one of the turn-of-the-century printers returning to the hand crafts and trying to reach perfection in book design and typography. His Doves Press and Doves Bindery were famous for the beauty of their products. His journals are a treasure trove of information about printing, binding, and contemporary practitioners of these arts. His *Ideal Book or Book Beautiful* is a classic statement about the role of typography in printing.

Cohen, Arthur A. *Herbert Bayer: The Complete Work.* MIT Pr. 1984 $75.00. ISBN 0-262-02206-0. The famous émigré from the Bauhaus, a towering influence on graphic and industry design. With many illustrations.

Comparato, Frank F. *Books for the Millions.* Labyrinthos 1971 $12.50. ISBN 0-8117-0263-4. The inventions that made possible the modern industry of printing and binding books.

Dair, Carl. *Design With Type.* U. of Toronto Pr. rev. ed. 1982 $19.95. ISBN 0-8020-6519-8. A comprehensive and succinct treatment of design principles from this famous typographer.

Eisenstein, Elizabeth. *The Printing Press as an Agent of Change.* 2 vols. in 1. Cambridge U. Pr. 1980 $39.95. ISBN 0-521-29955-1. This scholar points out that all agree that printing led to a change in every aspect of life, but the process by which this came about and what the cause-and-effect connections were need much deeper examination. A controversial book, criticized by some.

———. *The Printing Revolution in Early Modern Europe.* Cambridge U. Pr. 1984 o.p. A one-volume, heavily illustrated abridgment of *The Printing Press as an Agent of Change.* For college courses and the general reader.

Emery, Edwin, and Michael Emery. *The Press and America: An Interpretative History of the Mass Media.* P-H 1991. ISBN 0-13-739277-X. Looks at how mass media handle important events in American history, from the English heritage of the American press to the 1970s.

Febvre, Lucien, and Henri-Jean Martin. *The Coming of the Book: The Impact of Printing 1450–1800.* Trans. by David Gerard. Routledge Chapman & Hall 1976 $17.95. ISBN 0-86091-797-5. Looks at the technical preconditions and the social pressures that shaped the transition from the manuscript to the printed page in Europe. Shows that printing changed the way people could think. Tremendously influential study.

Gill, Eric. *An Essay on Typography.* Godine 1988 $15.95. ISBN 0-87923-762-7. A reprint of this 1936 classic volume on composition, lettering, typography, the production of printing types, paper and ink, and so forth.

Glick, William J. *William Edwin Rudge.* Typophiles 1984 o.p. Short but carefully researched account of the company and its founder that did some of the finest book printing in the first third of the twentieth century and produced many of the best designers and printers.

Grabhorn, Jane. *The Compleat Jane Grabhorn.* Grabhorn 1968 o.p. Writings and many reproduced or tipped-in actual specimens of the work of a great printer who died in 1973. Foreword by her husband, Robert Grabhorn, who, along with Jane and his brother Edwin, was a partner in the historic Grabhorn Press.

Grannis, Chandler B., ed. *Heritage of the Graphic Arts.* Bowker 1972 o.p. A selection of 22 of the lectures arranged in New York City by Dr. Robert L. Leslie on leaders in the graphic arts and bookmaking.

Harris, Elizabeth, and Clint Sisson. *The Common Press: Being a Record, Description and Delineation of the Early Eighteenth-Century Handpress in the Smithsonian Institution.* 2 vols. Godine 1978 o.p. Harris wrote the history and documentation; Sisson made the drawings and advises readers how to construct such a press.

Hart, James D. *Fine Printing: The San Francisco Tradition.* Lib. Congress 1985 $20.00. ISBN 0-8444-0472-1. Accounts of the Grabhorns and others, produced by Andrew Hoyem of the Arion Press, a major inheritor of the tradition.

Hindman, Sandra L., ed. *Printing the Written Word: The Social History of Books, circa 1450–1520.* Cornell Univ. Pr. 1992 $45.00. ISBN 0-8014-2578-6. Thirteen essays from a 1987 conference in Chicago, considering how printing developed out of the standards and practices of the manuscript book. Looks at printers, authors, artists, and readers.

Ing, Janet. *Johann Gutenberg and His Bible: A Historical Study*. Typophiles 1988 $27.50. ISBN 0-945074-00-X. A summary of the Gutenberg scholarship from the fifteenth century to the twentieth. Tells us what we know and how we came to know it.

Joyce, William L., and others, eds. *Printing and Society in Early America*. Am. Antiquarian 1983 $37.50. ISBN 0-912296-55-0. Ten essays on various aspects of the American book trade.

Labuz, Ronald. *Typography and Typesetting: Type Design and Manipulation Using Today's Technology*. Van Nos. Reinhold 1988 $39.95. ISBN 0-442-25966-2. A broad, well-illustrated study, considering modern typography, the anatomy and history of type, legibility, book design, layout, copyfitting, and many other subjects.

Lehmann-Haupt, Hellmut. *The Göttingen Model Book*. U. of Mo. Pr. 1972 o.p. An edition with translation and commentary of a fifteenth-century manuscript book giving patterns and models of decorations for use by illuminators. All reproduced in full color.

_____. *Gutenberg and the Master of the Playing Cards*. Yale U. Pr. 1967 o.p. A most interesting speculation, with illustrative evidence, about a decorative printing experiment that Gutenberg may have pursued.

_____. *One Hundred Books about Bookmaking*. Greenwood 1976 repr. of 1949 ed. $45.00. ISBN 0-8371-8546-7. Reprint of a small classic.

Levarie, Norma. *The Art and History of Books*. Da Capo 1982 $24.50. ISBN 0-306-80181-7. Heavily illustrated folio volume, its subject matter ranging throughout Europe from the origins of the book through the twentieth century.

Lewis, John. *Anatomy of Printing: The Influences of Art and History on Its Design*. Watson-Guptill 1970 o.p. Contains 228 pages, lavishly illustrated, surveying the influences on printing design over the centuries.

_____. *The Twentieth-Century Book: Its Illustration and Design*. Van Nos. Reinhold 1984 o.p. Contains over 400 illustrations, primarily from the Arts and Crafts Movement of the 1890s to the Swiss influences of the twentieth century.

_____. *Typography: Design and Practice*. Taplinger 1978 o.p. A broad overview dealing with the influences that have shaped typographic design since the nineteenth century.

McLean, Ruari. *Modern Book Design*. OUP 1958 o.p. The range is from William Morris and his work in the nineteenth century to design in the late 1950s.

_____. *Victorian Book Design and Colour Printing*. U. CA Pr. 1972 o.p. Lavishly illustrated with color and black-and-white plates.

McMurtrie, Douglas C. *The Book: The Story of Printing and Bookmaking*. OUP 1943 o.p. The romantic story of printing and bookmaking from primitive human records to modern methods.

MacKellar, Thomas. *The American Printer: A Manual of Typography*. MacKellar, Smiths & Jordan o.p. Many editions, from 1866 on. This became the standard printer's manual, going into eighteen editions (the eighteenth being published in 1893). Contains a vast amount of detailed information.

Mardersteig, Giovanni. *The Officina Bodoni: An Account of the Work of a Hand Press, 1923–1977*. Ed. and trans. by Hans Schmoller. Chiswick Book Shop 1980 o.p. Extensive account of one of the greatest handpress printers of the twentieth century.

Meynell, Sir Francis, and Herbert Simon, eds. *The Fleuron Anthology*. Godine 1980 o.p. Twenty-three colorful and scholarly articles reproduced from the famous journal, 1923–1930, devoted to the modern typographic revival and the history of printing.

Moran, James. *Printing Presses: History and Development from the Fifteenth Century to Modern Times*. U. CA Pr. 1973 $52.50. ISBN 0-520-02245-9. A well-illustrated and scholarly treatment.

Morison, Stanley. *First Principles of Typography*. Cambridge U. Pr. 1951 o.p. An essential essay on clear, unobtrusive typography.

Morison, Stanley, and Kenneth Day. *The Typographic Book, 1450–1935: A Study of Fine Typography through Five Centuries Exhibited in Upwards of Three Hundred and Fifty Title and Text Pages Drawn from Presses Working in the European Tradition*. U. Ch. Pr. 1963 o.p. Sixty-six pages of text precede the wonderful selection of plates.

Morris, William. *The Ideal Book: Essays and Lectures on the Arts of the Book.* Ed. by William S. Peterson. U. CA Pr. 1982 $47.50. ISBN 0-520-04563-7. The most important of the essays and lectures, some not reprinted since the 1890s, on the book arts by the proprietor of the Kelmscott Press.

Moxon, Joseph. *Mechanick Exercises on the Whole Art of Printing.* 1683. Ed. by Herbert Davis and Harry Carter. Astragal Pr. 1989 repr. of 1683 ed. $22.50. ISBN 0-9618088-1-0. The first and perhaps the most thorough manual of typography ever written. This modern edition contains all the original illustrations and text, and has an excellent 55-page introduction, scholarly notes, and an extensive index.

Needham, Paul. *The Printer & the Pardoner: An Unrecorded Indulgence Printed by William Caxton for the Hospital of St. Mary Rounceval, Charing Cross.* Lib. Congress 1986 $35.00. ISBN 0-8444-0508-6. An important study of a newly discovered broadside from England's first printer. Well illustrated.

Nineteenth-Century Book Arts and Printing History. Ed. by John Bidwell. Garland o.p. This is a series of reprints in 23 volumes of 26 texts, mostly printer's manuals and other books on papermaking, typography, type design, typefounding, and illustration processes. Some of the more important titles are listed separately in this bibliography.

Oswald, John Clyde. *Printing in the Americas.* Gregg Intl. 1937 o.p. The dust-jacket blurb says, "A Complete History of Printing in the Western Hemisphere." Over 600 pages of information.

Pederson, Johannes. *The Arabic Book.* Ed. by Robert Hillenbrand. Trans. by Geoffrey French. Princeton U. Pr. 1984 $32.50. ISBN 0-691-06564-0. The production of books in medieval Islam.

Polk, Ralph. *The Practice of Printing.* The Manual Arts Pr. 1945 o.p. A practically ubiquitous book on all aspects of printing (the industry, type, type cases, spacing materials, setting type, proofing and correcting) and much more.

Rice, Stanley. *Book Design: Systematic Aspects.* Bowker 1978 $34.95. ISBN 0-8352-1044-8. Manual on the essential, permanent features in a book.

———. *Book Design: Text Format Models.* Bowker 1978 $34.95. ISBN 0-8352-1045-6. Alternate specifications, with visual samples, for all special items in a book: front matter, back matter, captions, and so on. Companion volume to *Book Design: Systematic Aspects.*

Ringwalt, J. Luther, ed. *American Encyclopaedia of Printing.* Garland 1978 repr. of 1871 ed. o.p. A good source of information on printing equipment, bookbinding, lithography, paper, type, and many other subjects, as well as biographical sketches of famous printers.

Rogers, Bruce. *A Hodge-Podge of the Letters, Papers and Addresses Written during the Last Sixty Years.* Ayer 1973 $18.00. ISBN 0-8369-2669-2. Formal and informal statements by the graphic artist who led the modern movement for excellence in book design.

———. *Paragraphs on Printing.* Dover 1980 $6.95. ISBN 0-486-23817-2. Commentary on quality in the handling of type and presswork by one of the most respected twentieth-century U.S. designers.

Rollins, Carl Purington. *Theodore Low De Vinne.* 2 vols. Typophiles 1968 o.p. Biographical essay by Rollins and an annotated bibliography and several major articles by the highly influential turn-of-the-century printer, typographer, and teacher.

Ryder, John. *The Case for Legibility.* Moretus Pr. 1979 $8.50. ISBN 0-89679-002-9. Claims that legibility should be the guiding principle of typography, even in the computer age. Looks at book design in general with legibility as the key issue. A small but important book.

———. *Printing for Pleasure.* Trafalgar rev. ed. 1976 o.p. Covers many topics, including printing on a small press for pleasure and profit, choosing a typeface, how to handle and arrange movable types, inking and proofing, the aesthetics of printing, getting equipment. With a glossary of printing terms.

Sanders, Norman, and William Bevington. *Graphic Designer's Production Handbook.* Hastings 1982 $10.95. ISBN 0-8038-5896-5. Offers information about 191 topics concerned with printing. Fine illustrations by Bevington.

Saxe, Stephen O. *American Iron Hand Presses*. Oak Knoll 1992 $35.00. ISBN 0-938768-35-2. Stories of the presses, their inventors and users. With fine wood engravings by John DePol.

Schreiber, Fred. *The Estiennes: An Annotated Catalogue of 500 Highlights of Their Various Presses*. Schreiber 1982 o.p. Major aspects of printing and publishing by the Estienne family in Paris and elsewhere in the tumultuous times, 1502–1664. Introduction by Nicholas Barker.

Simon, Herbert. *Introduction to Printing: The Craft of Letterpress*. Faber & Faber 1968 o.p. Another popular book on the subject, covering typesetting, ancillary equipment of the printing shop, makeup and imposition, machine printing, distribution of type and proofreading, book design, and so on.

Simon, Oliver. *Introduction to Typography*. Ed. by David Bland. Faber & Faber 1969 o.p. One of the enduring classic studies on many aspects of typography, such as rules of composition, setting type, page layout, use of illustration, paper, presswork, binding, dust jackets, and more.

Spencer, Herbert. *The Liberated Page: A Typographica* [sic] *Anthology*. Humanities 1987 o.p. A superb collection of avant-garde typography from the pages of the journal *Typographica*. With Spencer's illuminating commentary.

Steinberg, S. H. *Five Hundred Years of Printing*. Viking Penguin rev. ed. 1974 o.p. A one-volume, concise, handy reference to the people, places, machines, and events from the winepress to electronics. Though sometimes dry reading, it is filled with valuable information.

Stower, Caleb. *The Printer's Manual, an Abridgment of Stower's Grammar, Comprising all the Plans in that Work for Imposing Forms, Several Tables and other Useful Articles*. 1817. Garland 1978 o.p. With an introduction by John Bidwell. The first printer's manual to be published in America.

Taylor, John B. *The Art Nouveau Book in Britain*. Taplinger 1980 o.p. The William Morris era and later.

Thames & Hudson Manual of Typography. Thames Hudson 1980 $14.95. ISBN 0-500-68022-1. A thorough manual to all aspects of printing, with especial reference to contemporary practices, but with an eye on the tradition.

Thomas, Isaiah. *Diary of, 1805–1828*. 2 vols. Johnson Repr. repr. of 1909 ed. $35.00 ea. ISBN 0-384-60174-X. Source material on the pioneer U.S. bookman, founder of the American Antiquarian Society, and one of the influential early U.S. printers.

_____. *The History of Printing in America: With a Biography of Printers and an Account of Newspapers*. 2 vols. Ed. by Marcus McCorison. Gordon Pr. $400.00. ISBN 0-8490-0345-8. Despite its errors, this is still the starting point for any investigation into the history of the American press.

Thompson, Susan Otis. *American Book Design and William Morris*. Bowker 1977 o.p. Turn-of-the-century designs and typography. The impact of the Arts and Crafts Movement on publishing up to the 1930s.

Tschichold, Jan. *Asymmetric Typography*. Van Nos. Reinhold 1968 o.p. One of the most influential statements about "modern" typography in the twentieth century. Tschichold, a Swiss (formerly German) typographer, in the 1920s advocated the use of many nontraditional design elements, and while he later recanted some of his pronouncements, this nonetheless remains one of the most cogent and imaginative statements about typography in this century. Covers a rich array of subjects, including decorative typography, functional typography, types, hand-versus-machine composition, words, lines, leading, line length and grouping, indentation, justification, type size, headings, type mixtures, the use of space, tables, and so on.

_____. *The Form of the Book: Essays on the Morality of Good Design*. Trans. by Hajo Hadeler. Hartley & Marks 1992 $24.95. ISBN 0-88179-034-6. A collection of 23 important essays, meticulously anatomizing book design.

Tufte, Edward R. *The Visual Display of Quantitative Information*. Graphics Pr. 1983 $40.00. ISBN 0-9613921-0-X. Important and respected text, looking at charts, tables, graphs of various kinds, data maps, time-series, space-time narrative designs, and relational graphics. A practical and useful guide.

Victor Hammer: Artist and Printer. The Anvil Pr. 1981 o.p. Chapters written by several scholars on Hammer, one of the most revered typographers and type designers of the twentieth century.

Walker, Gay, ed. *The Works of Carl P. Rollins.* Yale U. Pr. 1982 o.p. Based on the collection left to Yale by Rollins, who was a major force for classical excellence in typography and printing in the first half of the twentieth century.

Warde, Beatrice. *The Crystal Goblet: Sixteen Essays on Typography.* Ed. by Henry Jacob. World Publishing Co. 1956 o.p. Writings by the promotion director of the Monotype Corporation, authority on typography and book design, who preached: "Printing should be invisible and should above all serve the text."

William Morris and the Art of the Book: With Essays on William Morris as Book Collector by Paul Needham, as Calligrapher by Joseph Dunlap, and as Typographer by John Dreyfus. Pierpont Morgan 1976 o.p. Scholarly treatments of Morris, with a catalog of William Morris's library. Lavishly illustrated with 114 plates.

Williamson, Hugh. *Methods of Book Design: The Practice of an Industrial Craft.* Yale U. Pr. 1983 $18.00. ISBN 0-300-03035-5. Covers many aspects of book design, from typescript to final bound product. Attractive, detailed volume, valuable for anyone in the book production field.

Wilson, Adrian. *The Design of Books.* Gibbs Smith Pub. 1974 o.p. Treats layout, typography, printing methods, paper, the constituent parts of books, design theories, binding, dust jackets and paperback covers, trade book design, textbooks, reference books, manuals, and limited editions. Well illustrated.

Winckler, Paul A., ed. *Reader in the History of Books and Printing.* Greenwood 1983 $35.00. ISBN 0-313-24038-8. A lengthy study.

Winship, George Parker. *The Cambridge Press 1638–1692: A Reexamination of the Evidence Concerning The Bay Psalm Book and the Eliot Indian Bible, as Well as Other Contemporary Books and People.* Ayer repr. of 1945 ed. $22.50. ISBN 0-8369-1004-4. Covers a wide range of topics, including the complications of ownership of the Cambridge Press, its relation to Harvard College, the printers who were in charge of it, and a description of the printing done there.

————. *Gutenberg to Plantin: An Outline of the Early History of Printing.* 1926. B. Franklin 1968 o.p. This overview by a distinguished scholar relates to the period 1450–1600 in Europe.

————. *Printing in the Fifteenth Century.* U. of Pa. Pr. 1940 o.p. Posits that 110 presses were established in the incunabula period, employing 350 people. Looks at the amazingly quick spread of the craft of printing in its infancy.

Winterich, John T. *Early American Books and Printing.* 1935. Omnigraphics Inc. 1992 $37.00. ISBN 1-55888-965-5. An excellent recapitulation of the subject. Anecdotal and easy to read, about pre- and postcolonial printers in America. Discusses, *inter alia*, The Bay Psalm Book, presses, newspapers and periodicals, and print shops and their tools.

Wroth, Lawrence C. *The Colonial Printer.* U. Pr. of Va. 1964 o.p. On the beginnings of printing and publishing in the United States, including accounts of presses, typefounding, ink, paper, binding, employment and economic conditions, content and physical nature of products.

Zapf, Hermann. *Manuale Typographicum.* MIT Pr. 1970 o.p. Contains 100 pages of quotations in 16 languages (with English translations) in elegant typographic layouts by Zapf. Mostly printed in two colors throughout. Notable as much for its own typography as for the information and observations in the quotations.

PRINTING TYPES: CALLIGRAPHY AND LETTERFORMS

This section, as is the case with most of the others in this chapter, could contain thousands of entries. The attempt here has been to suggest a wide range of sources, covering all aspects of the history of Western alphabets, the development of letterforms and printing types, and the relationship between handwriting and the printed word. Cited here are only a few type-specimen manuals. For a more thorough (but by no means definitive) listing of American catalogs, see Maurice Annenberg, *Type Foundries of America and their Catalogs* (Baltimore and Washington: Moran Printing Services, 1975). A great deal of scholarship has been expended on these subjects in recent years. The attempt here has been to direct readers to good starting places from which they can then launch more in-depth research. Where appropriate, volumes with especially good bibliographies on these subjects are noted. Included also are a few recent items on typesetting machines.

Adkins, Jan. *Letterbox: The Art and History of Letters.* Walker & Co. 1981 o.p. Brief text on the history of lettering, with small section on preparing one's tools.

American Type Founders Company. *American Specimen Book of Type Styles.* Amer. Type Founders Co. 1912 o.p. One of the great type specimen and printing equipment catalogs of all time. Over 1,300 pages of specimen pages, showing all printing types and equipment available from the company. Printed in several colors.

_____. *Specimen Book and Catalogue.* Amer. Type Founders Co. 1923 o.p. Another huge catalog (with 1,148 pages), produced in thousands of copies. A treasure trove of information.

Anderson, Donald M. *The Art of Written Forms: The Theory and Practice of Calligraphy.* Dover 1992 repr. of 1968 ed. $17.95. ISBN 0-486-27212-5. Covers topics from "The Origins of Writing" to "The Grand Age of Manuscripts" to "The Origin of Modern Letter Forms." Looks at types, calligraphy, graphic design and the alphabet, and much more. Considers Western and Oriental writing.

Avis, F. C. *Edward Philip Prince: Type Punchcutter.* F. C. Avis 1967 o.p. A biographical sketch of one of the great modern punchcutters, with much information on the process of designing and casting types. Contains smoke proofs of punches in the process of being cut.

Baker, Arthur. *Calligraphic Alphabets.* Dover 1974 $6.95. ISBN 0-486-21045-6. No prose text. A series of full-page plates showing full alphabets in calligraphy.

_____. *Calligraphy.* Dover 1973 $7.95. ISBN 0-486-22895-9. No prose text; similar to the previous volume, showing full alphabets in calligraphy.

_____. *Mastering Italic Calligraphy.* Scribner 1985 o.p. Contains a brief text and many plates showing the strokes and equipment for writing in italic script.

Ball, Johnson. *William Caslon, 1693–1766: The Ancestry, Life and Connections of England's Foremost Letter-Engraver and Type-Founder.* Roundwood Pr. 1973 o.p. An exhaustive biography, with illustrations and an excellent bibliography.

Barker, Nicolas. *Aldus Manutius and the Development of Greek Script and Type in the Fifteenth Century.* Fordham 1992 $150.00. ISBN 0-8232-1247-5. An interesting historical study; includes bibliographical references and an index.

Barnhart Brothers & Spindler. *Catalog 25: Type Faces, Border Designs, Typecast Ornaments, Brass Rule . . .* Barnhart Bros. o.p. Typical of the blockbuster catalogs of this century. This contains over 700 pages printed in several colors, showing types, ornaments, rule, furniture, equipment, and sample settings.

Bickham, George. *The Universal Penman: Engraved by George Bickham, London 1743.* Dover repr. of 1941 ed. $15.95. ISBN 0-486-20616-5. Bickham was one of the greatest of British calligraphers. Contains 212 plates showing Bickham's brilliant calligraphic and engraving skills. Foreword by Philip Hofer.

Bigelow, Charles, Paul Hayden Duensing, and Linnea Gentry, eds. *Fine Print on Type: The Best of Fine Print Magazine on Type and Typography.* Pro Arte Libri. 1989. ISBN 0-9607290-1-1. A collection of 35 essays on many aspects of type design and printing.

Brewer, Roy. *Eric Gill: The Man Who Loved Letters.* Frederick Muller Ltd. 1973 o.p. A brief biography of one of this century's most influential type theorists, focusing on Gill's work as a type designer and typographer, with a careful look at the types he created.

Brightly, Charles. *The Method of Founding Stereotype.* 1809. Garland 1982 o.p. Bound
with Thomas Hodgson's *An Essay on the Origin and Progress of Stereotype Printing.*
With a new introduction by Michael L. Turner. Two important early treatises on this
method of printing, which used printing types to create printing plates.

Brown, Frank Chouteau. *Letters and Lettering: A Treatise with 200 Examples.* Bates &
Guild 1921 o.p. Over 200 pages of text with commentary. Looks at roman capitals,
modern roman letters, gothic letters, and italic and script writing.

Carr, Melbert B., Jr. *Modern Alphabets.* Bridgman Pubs. 1930 o.p. A two-page introduction, followed by showings of full alphabets of nearly three dozen faces.

Carter, Harry, and H. D. L. Vervliet. *Civilité Types.* OUP 1966 o.p. Scholarly treatment on
these French types, relating them to handwritings, giving their history, showing full
fonts, and listing works printed in them. With a short bibliography.

Catich, Edward M. *The Origin of the Serif: Brush Writing & Roman Letters.* St. Ambrose U.
1968. ISBN 0-9629740-0-5. Well-illustrated text that covers, among other things, the
history, lineage, and development of the roman alphabet, letter cutting in stone, the
brush versus other writing tools, and much more.

———. *Reed, Pen, and Brush Alphabets for Writing and Lettering.* Hastings 1972 $8.95.
ISBN 0-8038-5891-4. Contains a text volume with a brief introduction and descriptions of all of the plates. Also with a portfolio containing the plates showing the
design and construction of each of the letters of the alphabet.

Child, Heather. *Calligraphy Today.* Pentalic Corp. 1971 o.p. The text covers definitions of
key terms, historical background, italic and other handwritings, elements of the
craft, and many examples drawn from Europe and the United States.

———, and others. *More than Fine Writing: Irene Wellington, Calligrapher (1904–84).*
Viking Penguin 1986 o.p. A collection of essays and appreciations, beautifully
illustrated with many color examples.

Cirker, Hayward, and Blanche Cirker. *Monograms and Alphabetic Devices.* Dover 1970
$8.95. ISBN 0-486-22330-2. ". . . contains the entire contents of four fine volumes of
monograms and allied devices published between 1830 and 1881. Over 2,500
monogrammatic and alphabetic designs are displayed" (from cover blurb). An
attractive volume.

Contemporary Calligraphy: Modern Scribes and Lettering Artists. Trefoil 1986 o.p. A
catalog showing examples of the work of many modern artists, mostly in black and
white. Shows work in various media (e.g., on paper or vellum, in stone).

David, Stuart. *How to Become a Professional Calligrapher.* Taplinger 1985 $9.95. ISBN 0-
8008-3959-5. Showing many examples of writing, but concentrating on the business
end of the profession. Looks at business practices, employment possibilities,
copyfitting, and so on.

Davis, Jinnie Y., and John V. Richardson. *Calligraphy: A Sourcebook.* Libs. Unl. 1982
$27.50. ISBN 0-8728-727-7-7

Dawson, Giles E., and Laetitia Kennedy-Skipton. *Elizabethan Handwriting, 1500–1650: A
Manual.* Norton 1966 o.p. A scholarly introduction, followed by 50 plates with facing
commentaries and transcriptions. With a bibliography.

Diringer, David. *The Alphabet: A Key to the History of Mankind.* 2 vols. Funk & Wagnalls
rev. ed. 1968 o.p. Completely revised edition with the assistance of Reinhold
Regensburger. Vol. I contains an extensive text covering nonalphabetic systems of
writing and alphabetic scripts throughout the world. Vol. II contains hundreds of
plates. With a bibliography.

———. *A History of the Alphabet.* Gresham Pub. 1977 o.p. A short text, based on the
scholarship in his earlier work, with much information on the alphabet, memory-aid
devices, stages of writing, analytic systems of writing, phonetic and alphabetic
writing, and so on.

Douglass, Ralph. *Calligraphic Lettering with Wide Pen and Brush.* Watson-Guptill 1967
$14.95. ISBN 0-8230-0551-8. A practical manual with a bibliography. Spiral bound.

Drogin, Marc. *Medieval Calligraphy: Its History and Technique.* Dover 1989 $10.95. ISBN
0-486-26142-5. Excellent text with original medieval examples and much instruction
to reproduce the medieval hands.

Dürer, Albrecht. *Of the Just Shaping of Letters: From the Applied Geometry of Albrecht Dürer, Book III*. Peter Smith $13.25. ISBN 0-8446-2016-5. Dürer's treatise offering precise rules for the geometric construction of roman majuscules. Well illustrated.

Eason, Ron, and Sarah Rookledge. *Rookledge's International Handbook of Type Designers*. Ed. by Phil Bains and Gordon Rookledge. Seven Hills Bk. Dists. 1991 o.p. Concise biographical sketches of more than 175 type designers, discussing their personalities and the faces they originated. With an essay on trends in type design and indexes of subject and typeface.

Evetts, L. C. *Roman Lettering: A Study of the Letters of the Inscription at the Base of the Trajan Column, with an Outline of the History of Lettering in Britain*. 1938. Taplinger 1979 o.p. Well illustrated by the author.

Fairbank, Alfred. *A Book of Scripts*. 1949. Faber & Faber 1977 o.p. Showing of the great scripts, classic and modern, with commentary by the distinguished British calligrapher. Much used by teachers.

———. *The Story of Handwriting*. Watson-Guptill 1976 repr. of 1970 ed. o.p. Script and the origins of letterforms and type.

Finlay, Michael. *Western Writing Implements in the Age of the Quill Pen*. Plain Bks. 1990 o.p. A carefully documented study covering all aspects of the quill pen and its various ancillary materials—how to prepare a quill, the history of the penknife, inks, paper and parchment, pounce-pots, pencils, seals, and early fountain pens. Well illustrated.

Fisher, Leonard Everett. *Alphabet Art: Thirteen ABCs from Around the World*. Macmillan Child. Grp. 1984 $14.95. ISBN 0-02-735230-7. Brief historical notes, followed by full-page printings of many alphabets (Arabic, Cherokee, Chinese, Cyrillic, Eskimo, Gaelic, German, Greek, Hebrew, Japanese, Sanskrit, Thai, and Tibetan).

Furber, Alan. *Layout and Design for Calligraphers*. Taplinger 1984 $6.95. ISBN 0-8008-4573-0. Along with the title focus, shows balance, contrast, dominance, headings, linespacing, initials, and much more.

Goins, David Lance. *A Constructed Roman Alphabet: A Geometric Analysis of the Greek and Roman Capitals and of the Arabic Numerals*. Godine 1982 o.p. A leading calligrapher demonstrates how the majuscule letters are and have been made. A prize-winning work of book art. Beautifully printed letterpress, in two colors.

Goudy, Frederic W. *The Alphabet, and Elements of Lettering: Revised and Enlarged with Many Full-Page Plates and Other Illustrations Drawn & Arranged by the Author*. Dorset Pr. 1989 $29.95. ISBN 0-88029-330-6. Offset printed version of Goudy's two classic works.

———. *The Alphabet: Fifteen Interpretative Designs Drawn and Arranged with Explanatory Text and Illustrations*. Mitchell Kennerley 1918 o.p. A wonderful folio volume on "What Letters Are," a history of letters, the various hands of different nations, the development of gothic forms, the beginnings of printing types, and much more. Printed letterpress, with full-page illustrations of each letter of the alphabet in various manifestations.

———. *Elements of Lettering*. 1922. Mitchell Kennerley 1926 o.p. A matching volume to *The Alphabet*, discussing and depicting many letterforms.

———. *Goudy's Type Designs: His Story and Specimens*. Myriade 1978 $19.95. ISBN 0-918142-05-9. A facsimile of The Typophiles Chap Books 13 and 14 (*A Half Century of Type Design* and *Typography*). Contains a great deal of information about type design and letterforms; with a bibliography of Goudy's writings and a list of his types.

———. *Typologia: Studies in Type Design & Type Making—With Comments on the Invention of Typography, The First Types, Legibility and Fine Printing*. 1940. U. CA Pr. 1978 $10.95. ISBN 0-520-03278-0. This classic book is by the most prolific of U.S. type designers, who was an expert in all the areas mentioned in the title. This is an illustrated, detailed study of type manufacture and design, looking at tradition and the history of types, design problems, "What Type Is," details of the construction of an alphabet, pattern and matrix making, and so on.

Gray, Nicolete. *A History of Lettering: Creative Experiment and Letter Identity*. Godine 1987 $30.00. ISBN 0-87923-612-4. An excellent, well-illustrated study, from the origins of the roman alphabet to the present, "from medieval manuscripts to neon signs, and from shop fronts to Ceefax" (from the dust-jacket blurb). Over 300 illustrations. With a bibliography.

———. *Nineteenth Century Ornamented Typefaces.* U. CA Pr. 1976 $75.00. ISBN 0-520-03074-5. Originally published as *XIXth Century Ornamented Types & Title Pages.* 1938. This edition has an additional chapter by Ray Nash on ornamented types in America. Well-illustrated chronological survey.

A Handbook of Printing Types with Notes on the Style of Composition and Graphic Processes Used by Cowells. Faber & Faber 1947 o.p. An attractive volume on text and display faces, the preparation of copy, and other subjects; illustrated throughout.

Hewitt, Graily. *Lettering.* Seely, Service & Co. 1954 o.p. Contains 336 pages of text with 403 illustrations covering a wide array of topics in 30 chapters.

Hlasta, Stanley C. *Printing Types and How to Use Them.* Carnegie Pr. 1950 o.p. A work displaying book and magazine faces and advertising and display faces, with discussions about each face and sample settings.

Hodgson, Thomas. *An Essay on the Origin and Progress of Stereotype Printing; Including a Description of the Various Processes.* Garland 1982 o.p. With an introduction by Michael L. Turner.

Holub, Rand. *Applied Lettering and Design.* Watson-Guptill 1953 o.p. A well-illustrated guide to the materials and methods of lettering. Considers type, scripts, cartoon lettering, advertisements, book jackets, logotypes, letterheads, and so on.

Horicke, Baldri van. *Master Album of Pictorial Calligraphy and Scrollwork: An Antique Copybook Rediscovered.* Dover 1985 $4.95. ISBN 0-486-24974-3. Reproduces the complete text of a calligraphy copybook from about 1633. The first printing of a wonderful book.

Humez, Alexander, and Nicholas Humez. *A B C et Cetera: The Life and Times of the Roman Alphabet.* Godine 1985 $14.95. ISBN 0-87923-664-7. A historical guide to each of the letters of the roman alphabet. A popular treatment, but with a good bibliography. Each chapter (on a different letter) talks about the cultures that shaped the letters.

———. *Alpha to Omega: The Life & Times of the Greek Alphabet.* Godine 1981 o.p. A brief historical guide to each of the Greek letters. A popular treatment, but with a good bibliography.

Huss, Richard E. *The Development of Printers' Mechanical Typesetting Methods 1822–1925.* U. Pr. of Va. 1973 o.p. More than 300 pages of text and illustrations, offering a thorough chronological look at various machinery. With a bibliography.

———. *The Printer's Composition Matrix: A History of Its Origin and Development.* Oak Knoll 1985 o.p. Illustrated study covering punches, typesetting methods, hot- and cold-metal machines, and so on.

Hutchinson, James. *Letters.* Van Nos. Reinhold 1983 o.p. An illustrated, scholarly text on nonalphabetic writing, alphabetic writing, manuscripts in the Latin alphabet, and printing types. With a bibliography.

Hutt, Allen. *Fournier: The Compleat Typographer.* Rowman 1972 o.p. One of the great type designers, known for his ability to modernize traditional letterforms, thus creating the transitional types between old face and modern styles. Also known for his italics, flowers, ornaments, and decorated types.

Isaac, Frank, coll. and annot. *English and Scottish Printing Types 1501–35, 1508–41.* OUP 1930 o.p. Folio volume with facsimiles and illustrations and discussions of each typeface depicted.

———. *English and Scottish Printing Types 1535–58, 1552–58.* OUP 1932 o.p. A companion volume to the previous book.

Jaspert, W. Pincus, W. Turner Berry, and A. F. Johnson. *The Encyclopaedia of Type Faces.* 1953. Blandford 1990 $50.00. ISBN 0-7137-2186-3. Depicts full fonts for nearly 2,000 faces, with information on designers, dates of design, and foundries.

Jenkinson, Hilary. *The Later Court Hands in England: From the Fifteenth to the Seventeenth Century.* 1927. 2 vols. OUP 1967 o.p. Excellent volume, with explanatory text and a portfolio volume with plates, depicting the writing of scriveners, English writing masters, and public records.

Johnson, Charles, and Hilary Jenkinson. *English Court Hand, A.D. 1066 to 1500: Illustrated Chiefly from the Public Records*. 1915. 2 vols. OUP 1967 o.p. A classic in scholarship. Vol. I discusses the evolution of the court hand and has an extensive discussion of abbreviations, ligatures, transcription, histories of individual letters, runes, and special signs, punctuation, and so on, with transcriptions of the 44 plates found in Vol. II.

Johnston, Edward: Lessons in Formal Writing. Ed. by Heather Child and Justin Howes. Humanities 1986 $55.00. ISBN 0-85331-502-7. Johnston was one of the twentieth century's greatest practitioners. A collection of essays and appreciations with 243 large pages of text with 71 illustrations.

Johnston, Edward. *Writing and Illuminating and Lettering*. Taplinger 1977 o.p. Johnston was the father of the modern movement in writing and lettering whose ideas and type designs influenced Stanley Morison. A classic work.

Jones, Herbert. *Stanley Morison Displayed: An Examination of His Early Typographic Work*. Frederick Muller 1976 o.p. Well-illustrated text on Morison's work.

Kapr, Albert. *The Art of Lettering: The History, Anatomy and Aesthetics of the Roman Letter Forms*. K. G. Saur 1983 $75.00. ISBN 3-598-10464-2. Detailed history of letterforms from the earliest times to the era of modern typography. Well illustrated.

Kelly, Rob Roy. *American Wood Type: 1828–1900: Notes on the Evolution of Decorated and Large Types and Comments on Related Trades of the Period*. Da Capo 1977 $8.95. ISBN 0-306-80059-4. Splendidly illustrated historical and analytical study with an excellent bibliography.

Kubler, George A. *Historical Treatises, Abstracts and Papers on Stereotyping*. 1936 o.p. Contains seven essays on stereotype printing.

Lancaster, John. *Calligraphy Techniques*. B. T. Batsford 1992 $22.95. ISBN 0-7134-4370-7. Well illustrated with many samples of writing and with a good text on materials and equipment, a brief history, instructions on various hands, design and layout, and so on.

Lawson, Alexander. *Anatomy of a Typeface*. Godine 1990 $40.00. ISBN 0-87923-332-X. Anatomizes many specific typefaces, the development and use of type over the ages, their antecedents and offsprings, newspaper types, scripts and cursives, decorative types, and so on. Looks also at the making of letters from punchcutting to computers. With a fine bibliography.

———. *Printing Types: An Introduction*. Beacon Pr. 1974 $11.95. ISBN 0-8070-6661-3. An excellent text, well illustrated, discussing many topics: historical development, mechanization of typesetting, phototypesetting, computerized setting, photolettering devices, protection of type designs, nomenclature, type classification, and so on.

Lesiak, Michaeline, Sister. *The Art of Fine Lettering: Basic Skills and Techniques*. U. of Notre Dame Pr. 1965 o.p. Nearly 300 pages of information on paper, pens, ink, composition, books, freehand lettering, the use of a brush and a reed, and sample illustrations showing many alphabets, layouts, and applications. With a bibliography.

Lindegren, Erik. *ABC of Lettering and Printing Typefaces: A Complete Guide to the Letters and Typefaces Used for Typesetting and Printing*. Greenwich House 1982 o.p. Very short text (on a classification of printing types) and a whole volume full of illustrations of alphabets and texts set in several typefaces.

Lucas, Elizabeth. *Calligraphy: The Art of Beautiful Writing*. P-H 1984 $18.50. ISBN 0-13-112269-X. A spiral-bound book covering history, basic materials, suppliers, and a good deal of how-to information.

Mahoney, Dorothy. *The Craft of Calligraphy*. Taplinger 1981 o.p. Historical information along with sections on tools and materials, various hands, and applications.

Martin, Judy. *The Complete Guide to Calligraphy: Techniques and Materials*. Phaidon UK 1984 o.p. An excellent, well-illustrated text, discussing history and development of writing, materials, tools, basic letterforms, layout and design, and more.

McGew, Mac. *American Metal Typefaces of the Twentieth Century*. Myriade 1986 o.p. Called a 'preliminary edition' in order to be distributed to scholars and practitioners who could help fill in the volume's gaps. The aim was to publish an augmented edition when further information had been gathered. An informative text showing hundreds of faces.

McLean, Ruari. *Reynolds Stone.* Faber & Faber 1984 o.p. Stone was one of the greatest modern calligraphers, letterers, and engravers, in wood or stone or on paper.

Middleton, Robert Hunter. *Robert Hunter Middleton: The Man and His Letters, Eight Essays on His Life and Career.* Caxton 1985 o.p. Essays on this type designer, with illustrations of his work.

Modern Scribes and Lettering Artists. Godine 1991 $19.95. ISBN 0-87923-874-7. A fully illustrated source book on calligraphers, showing many samples of their work on paper, glass, slate, and stone.

Morante, Pedro Díaz, Giuliano Sellari, and Leopardo Antonozzi. *Pictorial Calligraphy and Ornamentation.* Dover 1972 o.p. Eighty-six marvelous plates selected from the works of Morante, Sellari, and Antonozzi.

Morison, Stanley. *John Fell, 1745–1831: Bookseller, Printer, Publisher, Typefounder, Journalist.* Garland 1978 repr. of 1940 ed. o.p. Thorough account of this famous British printer and type designer.

———. *John Fell: The University Press and the 'Fell' Types.* Garland 1980 o.p. A monumental study of one of Oxford's great eighteenth-century printers and the typefaces he introduced. Fell was the chief founder of the first corporately owned university press. With much historical background, information on the types (roman, italic, Greek, exotic, etc.), a bibliography of Fell's published writings, and much more. The first edition of 1967 was printed from hand-set type cast in the matrices left to the press by Fell.

———. *Politics and Script: Aspects of Authority and Freedom in the Development of Graeco-Latin Script from the Sixth Century B.C. to the Twentieth Century A.D.* Ed. by Nicolas Barker. U. Pr. of Va. 1972 o.p. Morison's classical scholarship comes into play here, along with his political concerns.

———. *Selected Essays in the History of Letter Forms in Manuscript and Print.* 2 vols. Ed. by David McKitterick. Cambridge U. Pr. 1981 $335.00. ISBN 0-521-22338-5. Heavily illustrated volumes on one of Morison's main interests.

———. *A Tally of Types: With Additions by Several Hands.* Cambridge U. Pr. 1973 $55.00. ISBN 0-521-20043-1. A historical, critical, and functional account of the types cut by the Monotype Corporation under Morison's direction of its typographic revival program in the early 1920s and 1930s. Discusses 20 typefaces.

Nesbitt, Alexander, ed. *Decorative Alphabets and Initials.* Dover 1959 $6.95. ISBN 0-486-20544-4. Contains 123 full-page plates with 91 complete alphabets in many different styles; compiled by a prominent practitioner and teacher.

———. *The History and Technique of Lettering.* Dover 1957 $6.95. ISBN 0-486-20427-8. Originally published under the title *Lettering: The History and Technique of Lettering and Design.* Thorough history of letterforms from the perspective of a typographer and artist. From early pictographs and hieroglyphs to the work of twentieth-century designers. With a practical handbook on the techniques of lettering and a bibliography.

———. *Two Hundred Decorative Title Pages.* Dover 1964 $8.95. ISBN 0-486-21264-5. A good source book for designers.

Ogg, Oscar. *The 26 Letters.* 1948. Thomas Y. Crowell 1971 o.p. Classic study, tracing the history of the alphabet. Well illustrated with line drawings and letterforms. Relates the origins of calligraphy and lettering, development of the roman alphabet, and the progress of printing.

Pardoe, F. E. *John Baskerville of Birmingham: Letter-Founder & Printer.* Frederick Muller Ltd. 1975 o.p. Pardoe's aim is to depict Baskerville as the greatest printer in British history. A biography and an assessment of Baskerville's achievements. With a bibliography.

Pearce, Charles. *The Anatomy of Letters: A Guide to the Art of Calligraphy.* Taplinger 1987 $10.95. ISBN 0-685-17522-7. Offers much information on history, tools, materials, layout, design, use of color, and more. Pleasant illustrations.

_____. *The Little Manual of Calligraphy.* Taplinger 1981 $3.95 ISBN 0-8008-4923-X. Contains "A Brief History of Writing" with many illustrations and a guide on how to be a calligrapher.

Reed, Talbot Baines. *A History of the Old English Letter Foundries: With Notes Historical and Bibliographical on the Rise and Progress of English Typography.* Faber & Faber rev. ed. 1952 o.p. An authoritative text on many topics. Looks at English type-bodies and faces, printer letter-foundries, the letter-founding trade, particular foundries and practitioners, mechanical inventions of the trade, and a great deal more. With a fine bibliography. A new edition revised and enlarged by A. F. Johnson.

Romano, Frank J. *The TypEncyclopedia: A User's Guide to Better Typography.* Bowker 1984 $34.95. ISBN 0-8352-1925-9. Key terms and definitions needed in copy-specifying and judging the quality of typesetting.

Rondthaler, Edward, and others, eds. *Alphabet Thesaurus.* Vol. 2. Van Nos. Reinhold 1965 o.p. The dust jacket says, "probably contains the largest showing of letter designs ever put between book covers." Contains over 4,500 type designs in nearly 950 pages by more than 200 designers, letterers, and calligraphers. Vols. 3 and 4 are shorter versions of this massive compendium.

Rookledge, Gordon, and Christopher Perfect. *Rookledge's International Typefinder: The Essential Handbook of Typeface Recognition and Selection.* Moyer Bell Limited 1991 $34.95. ISBN 1-55921-052-4. An exceptional book for the identification of typefaces, depicting hundreds of full fonts both for texts and for decorative printing.

Sassoon, Rosemary. *The Practical Guide to Lettering & Applied Calligraphy.* Thames Hudson 1985 $10.95. ISBN 0-500-27366-9. Contains 225 illustrations with examples and advice.

Shaw, Paul. *Black Letter Primer: An Introduction to Gothic Alphabets.* Taplinger rev. ed. 1982 $4.95. ISBN 0-8008-0810-X. With many examples of black-letter writing and instructions on doing it yourself.

Shepherd, Margaret. *Calligraphy Now: New Light on Traditional Letters.* Putnam Pub. Group 1984 $17.95. ISBN 0-3991-2975-8. Well-illustrated book covering new pens and pen strokes, visual possibilities, historical examples, and much more.

Silver, Rollo G. *Typefounding in America, 1787–1825.* Bks. Demand 1965 $50.00. ISBN 0-317-10827-1. The best source on the subject, looking at the typefounding industry, typefounders and punchcutters, inventions and patents, the spread of the craft, and the importation of type. Though lacking a bibliography, the footnotes are wide-ranging and provocative.

Society of Scribes and Illuminators (London). *Modern Scribes and Lettering Artists.* Godine 1991 $19.95. ISBN 0-87923-874-7. Presents a wide variety of contemporary scribal styles, mostly British and European. Omits several outstanding U.S. calligraphers.

Standard, Paul. *Calligraphy's Flowering, Decay and Restoration.* Taplinger 1977 $3.95. ISBN 0-8008-1183-6. A contemporary master calligrapher, historian, and teacher who produced, largely in his own hand, this study of the years before the revival of calligraphy in the United States. Standard was a dedicated promoter of the revival.

_____, trans. *Arrighi's Running Hand.* Taplinger 1979 o.p. A presentation of the writing of the Renaissance master who was the chief inspirer of modern calligraphy.

Stanley Morison: A Portrait. Smithsonian 1971 o.p. A catalog for an exhibit, with a biographical sketch and many illustrations. Morison was one of this century's most important type designers.

Stribley, Miriam, comp. *The Calligraphy Source Book.* Macdonald 1986 $19.95. ISBN 0-89471-468-6. Beautifully illustrated book showing many alphabets and with a section on illumination and ornamentation. Discusses many writing styles.

Studley, Vance. *Left-Handed Calligraphy.* Dover 1979 $3.95. ISBN 0-486-26782-4. With a brief history of letters and then a good manual for left-handers.

Sutton, James, and Alan Bartram. *Typefaces for Books.* New Amsterdam Bks. 1990 $65.00. ISBN 1-56131-016-6. A showing of specimen settings of a text in more than a hundred typefaces, depicting various type sizes in bold, roman, italic, sloped roman, and small caps. With a brief bibliography.

Tannenbaum, Samuel A. *The Handwriting of the Renaissance: Being the Development and Characteristics of the Script of Shakespere's* [sic] *Time.* 1930. Continuum 1967 o.p. "A comprehensive array of practical and historical information, including thousands of handwriting facsimiles" (from the dust-jacket blurb of the reprint). With a good bibliography.

Thompson, Tommy. *The Script Letter: Its Form, Construction and Application.* Studio Pubns. 1949 o.p. Heavily illustrated showing equipment and materials, slope, principal strokes, letter formation in capitals and lower case, spacing, joining letters, and so on.

Tracy, Walter. *Letters of Credit: A View of Type Design.* Godine 1986 $27.50. ISBN 0-87923-636-1. In two broad sections ("Aspects of Type Design" and "Some Designers and Their Types"), covers a tremendous range of information: the vocabulary of type, type measure, legibility and readability, type production, proportion in letters, letterforms, italic and boldface types, numerals, character spacing, slab- and sans-serif types, and much more. With a good bibliography.

Tschichold, Jan. *Treasury of Alphabets and Lettering.* Omega LA 1985 o.p. With a brief but illuminating introductory text, this volume covers what is good and what is bad in letterforms, old and new forms, the use of capitals, word and line spacing of capitals, lowercase letters, proportions, layout, and other things. Followed by nearly 175 plates demonstrating many faces and typographical layouts.

Type for Books: A Designer's Manual. Trafalgar rev. ed. 1976 o.p. A type-specimen book showing 61 alphabets and many specimen pages set in these faces. With character-count and word-count tables.

Type Metals: Their Characteristics and Their Performance. Imperial Type Metal Co. 1950 o.p. Contains a general discussion of metals and looks at many kinds used for printing.

Updike, Daniel Berkeley. *Printing Types: Their History, Forms, and Use.* 2 vols. Dover 1951 o.p. The classic study, still unrivalled. A comprehensive study of printing types from their earliest use to the twentieth century. With 367 illustrations.

Wallis, L. W. *A Concise Chronology of Typesetting Developments 1886–1986.* Humanities 1988 o.p. An illustrated chronology showing the mechanization and computerization of the craft.

Weiss, Egon. *The Design of Lettering: With an Original Method for Spacing Inscriptions.* The Pencil Point Pr. Inc. 1932 o.p. A well-produced, 174-page folio volume with historical information and many chapters on fundamentals of lettering, equipment, spacing, roman and other alphabets, uncials, italics and scripts, commercial lettering, numerals, and a great deal more.

Whitehill, Clayton. *The Moods of Type.* B & N Imports 1947 o.p. ". . . analyzes and interprets the great creative periods of civilization from classical Greece through the Renaissance until the present day in terms of the alphabets and types which were at the same time their expression and a part of their basic structure" (from the dust-jacket blurb).

Wilson, Victor T. *Free-Hand Lettering: Being a Treatise on Plain Lettering from the Practical Standpoint for Use in Engineering Schools and Colleges.* Routledge Chapman & Hall 1905 o.p. A well-illustrated text with much theoretical and practical advice on letter design, spacing, writing instruments, particular design problems (lines and titles, technical lettering), and so on.

Zapf, Hermann. *About Alphabets: Some Marginal Notes on Type Design.* MIT Pr. 1970 o.p. Contains many observations on type design, printing types, printing. Though focusing primarily on letterforms, many examples of his calligraphy are included.

_____. *Hermann Zapf and His Design Philosophy: Selected Articles and Lectures on Calligraphy and Contemporary Developments in Type Design.* Society of Typographic Arts 1987 o.p. Splendidly illustrated folio volume by one of the great calligraphers and type designers of the twentieth century. Nearly two dozen of Zapf's articles, along with much ancillary bibliographical information.

INK AND ROLLERS

Bloy, Colin H. *A History of Printing Ink, Balls and Rollers 1440–1850*. Beil 1980 o.p. One of the more authoritative texts on the subject. Looks at various kinds of inks, both black and in colors, methods of manufacture, implements, inkballs and rollers, inking tables, and much more. Excellent bibliography, though only a handful of items in it are specifically on ink.

Earhart, John F. *The Harmonizer*. Earhart & Richardson 1897 o.p. A printer's sample book showing how various colored printer's inks will look on various kinds and colors of papers. Over 240 pages of samples.

Leach, R. H., and others, eds. *The Printing Ink Manual*. Von Nos. Reinhold 1988 $119.95. ISBN 0-7476-0000-7. Nearly 900 pages of information in 15 chapters, written by various experts. Covers such topics as the nature of printing inks, printing processes, color and color matching, raw materials, various kinds of inks (letterpress, lithographic, gravure, flexographic, screen), and a tremendous amount of other information.

Lehner, Sigmund. *The Manufacture of Ink: Comprising the Raw Materials, and the Preparation of Writing, Copying, and Hektograph Inks, Safety Inks, Ink Extracts and Powders, Colored Inks, Solid Inks, Lithographic Inks and Crayons, Printing Ink, Ink or Aniline Pencils, . . .* Henry Carey Baird & Co. 1892 o.p. An extensive and authoritative treatise, the contents of which are indicated in the title.

Van Son Holland Ink Corporation. *Handbook of Helpful Press Hints*. Van Son Holland 1975 o.p. A 48-page booklet on the proper use of many kinds of inks, ink additives, and printing rollers.

Vanderwalker, F. N. *The Mixing of Colors and Paints: Description, Properties, Theory, Harmony, and Management of Colors*. F. J. Drake 1950 o.p. A general treatise on color selection, the properties of color and light, various kinds of pigments, thinners and driers, color theory, and so on. Contains a chapter on printing inks (history, pigments and dyes, oils and varnishes, waxes, and so on).

The Vibrator: A Handbook on Printers' Rollers. Bingham Bros. Co. 1925 o.p. Contains 106 pages of text about rollers.

Williams, Roger L. *Paper & Ink Relationships*. Roger L. Williams. Practical Print Management 1988 $29.95. ISBN 0-961828-0-2. Considers the relationships between these two media in the offset printing process. Looks at the components of papers and inks, paper testing, paper grades, ink manufacturing and properties, the designs of presses and their influence on printing, color inks, and so on.

BOOKBINDING AND BOOK CONSERVATION

There is an enormous body of literature on bookbinding and conservation. As with other sections of this volume, the following list just scratches the surface. The attempt here is to suggest a few important or classical studies. Books on conservation have been included because this field is closely related to binding, and, perhaps since the Florence flood, conservation has been one of the most active fields in the world of books.

Ball, Douglas. *Victorian Publishers' Bindings*. Bookpress Ltd. 1985 $38.50. ISBN 0-916271-01-3. Thirteen scholarly chapters (with only twelve plates and seven figures) covering this broad topic. Includes discussions of the introduction of cloth, binding technology, decoration and cover design, designers, publishers, and so on.

Barrow, W. J. *Manuscripts and Documents: Their Deterioration and Restoration*. U. Pr. of Va. 1972 o.p. An important study by the man responsible for extensive studies on the longevity and durability of papers. Discusses inks, papers, storage conditions, deacidification, effects of air pollution, light rays, high temperatures and humidity, vermin, and lamination of documents. Written at the dawn of modern, scientific conservation studies.

Baynes-Cope, A. D. *Caring for Books and Documents*. ALA 1989 $12.95. ISBN 0-941553-68-9. A useful and brief guide to the handling, care, storage, and treatment of books.

Bearman, Frederick A., Nati H. Krivatsy, and J. Franklin Mowery. *Fine and Historic Bindings from the Folger Shakespeare Library*. Abrams 1992 $49.50. ISBN 0-8109-3312-8. Folio volume, with many illustrations and scholarly descriptions.

Blades, William. *The Enemies of Books*. Trubner 1881 o.p. The classic study of the means by which books are destroyed (e.g., fire, water, rodents, heat and gas, insects, dust and neglect; bookbinders, collectors).

Bookbinding in America 1680–1910: From the Collection of Frederick E. Maser. Bryn Mawr Coll. Lib. 1983 o.p. Fine, hardbound exhibition catalog, illustrated with black-and-white (and a few color) plates.

Bosch, Gulnar, John Carswell, and Guy Petherbridge. *Islamic Bindings and Bookmaking*. U. Ch. Pr. 1981 o.p. A well-illustrated (in black and white) catalog of an exhibit, with a scholarly introduction.

Broomhead, Frank. *The Zaehnsdorfs (1842–1947): Craft Bookbinders*. Oak Knoll 1986 $40.00. ISBN 0-900002-74-3. A biographical and historical sketch of the family of binders, with a discussion of their bindings and their work as conservators and restorers.

Burdett, Eric. *The Craft of Bookbinding: A Practical Handbook*. David & Charles 1975 o.p. A 400-page illustrated manual on tools and equipment, binding styles, preparatory work, forwarding, covering, finishing, cover design, and repairs to books.

Callery, Bernadette G., and Elizabeth A. Mosimann, comps. *The Traditions of Fine Bookbinding in the Twentieth Century*. David & Warde 1979 $25.00. ISBN 0-686-65642-3. An attractive exhibition catalog, with 124 illustrations, some in color.

Carter, John. *Binding Variants with More Binding Variants*. Oak Knoll 1989 $55.00. ISBN 0-938768-16-6. A single-volume reprint of Carter's two books: *Binding Variants in English Publishing 1820–1900*. (Constable & Co. 1932); and *More Binding Variants*. (Constable & Co. 1938). The two volumes treat the period from the introduction of cloth into binding from about 1820 to the end of the nineteenth century. Carter looks extensively at particular examples.

Clarkson, Christopher. *Limp Vellum Binding and Its Potential as a Conservation Type Structure for the Rebinding of Early Printed Books: A Break with Nineteenth and Twentieth Century Rebinding Attitudes and Practices*. Red Gull Pr. 1982 o.p. An important essay, with fine illustrations, discussing the current trend in conservation to use limp bindings for conservation purposes.

Cloonan, Michèle Valerie. *Early Bindings in Paper: A Brief History of European Hand-Made Paper-Covered Books with a Multilingual Glossary*. Mansell 1991 $38.50. ISBN 0-8161-1971-6. An illustrated history, with binding and paper terms in English, French, German, and Italian, and an extensive bibliography.

Cockerell, Douglas. *Bookbinding, and the Care of Books*. John Hogg 1901 o.p. A classic on the binding and care of books. Contains 336 pages of minutely detailed information and illustrations.

———. *Some Notes on Bookbinding*. OUP 1929 o.p. A small volume that covers paper, mending and sewing, forwarding, edge gilding and covering, covering material, lettering and decoration, binding valuable books, judging a binding, and binding as a career.

Cockerell, Sydney M. *The Repairing of Books*. Sheppard Pr. 1958 o.p. Summarizes the ways books can be repaired, from simple, quick measures to more complicated ones.

Craig, Maurice. *Irish Bookbindings*. Eason & Son 1976 o.p. Well-illustrated pamphlet.

Crane, W. J. E. *Bookbinding for Amateurs: Being Descriptions of the Various Tools and Appliances Required and Minute Instructions for their Effective Use*. L. Upcott Gill o.p. A text sophisticated beyond most amateurs' abilities; with over 150 illustrations. Looks at tools, appliances, materials, folding, sawing and sewing, endpapers, boards, and many other topics.

Cunha, George M., and Dorothy G. Cunha. *Conservation of Library Materials: A Manual & Bibliography on the Care, Repair, and Restoration of Library Materials*. 2 vols.

Scarecrow 1972 $59.50. ISBN 0-8108-2015-3. A comprehensive and useful guide, written by long-time practitioners-pioneers in the field.

Darling, Pamela W., and others. *Preservation Planning Program: An Assisted Self-Study Manual for Libraries.* OMS 1987 $30.00. ISBN 0-318-03507-3. A guide for libraries showing how to do a self-study of their preservation needs.

Davenport, Cyril. *Royal English Bookbindings.* Seeley and Co. 1896 o.p. To its day, the only authoritative text on the subject, primarily from the eighteenth to the nineteenth centuries. With eight colored plates and many illustrations in the text.

Diehl, Edith. *Bookbinding: Its Background and Technique.* Dover 1980 $14.95. ISBN 0-486-24020-7. One of the enduring classics on the subject.

Dirda, Michael. *Caring for Your Books.* Book-of-the-Month Club 1990 o.p. A small book of basic advice for the care and handling of books. Covers such things as temperature and humidity, shelving, checking for mildew and infestation, opening a book, use of bookmarks, marking in books, lending books, and so on.

Duncan, Alastair, and Georges De Bartha. *Art Nouveau and Art Deco Bookbinding: French Masterpieces 1880–1940.* Abrams 1989 $67.50. ISBN 0-685-25301-5. Contains 230 color photographs of elegant bindings; with a brief introductory text.

Early American Bookbinding from the Collection of Michael Papantonio. Am. Antiquarian 1985 $22.50. ISBN 0-912296-75-5. A catalog of the collection, with 61 plates.

Fletcher, W. Y. *Bookbinding in England and France.* Seeley and Co. 1897 o.p. Discusses binders, their styles, and the collectors who commissioned them, from the Middle Ages to the end of the nineteenth century. Only a brief text, primarily on leather bindings.

Foot, Mirjam M. *The Henry Davis Gift: A Collection of Bookbindings.* ALA Vol. 1 *Studies in the History of Bookbinding.* 1978 o.p. Vol. 2 *A Catalogue of North-European Bindings.* 1983 o.p. A major study, with scholarly text and many illustrations of bindings from Great Britain, France, Switzerland, the Netherlands, Spain, Germany, Italy (in Vol. 1), and from England, Ireland, Scotland, the Netherlands, Germany, Austria, and Denmark (Vol. 2).

———. *Pictorial Bookbindings.* ALA 1986 o.p. A small but well-illustrated volume showing the various kinds of decorations on bindings: leather and vellum, onlays and inlays, cut leather, ink and paint, wood and straw, paper, and so on.

French, Hannah Dustin. *Bookbinding in Early America: Seven Essays on Masters and Methods.* U. Pr. of Va. 1986 $49.95. ISBN 0-912296-76-3. A compilation of fine essays on many subjects (e.g., Scottish-American bindings and particular binders).

———. "Early American Bookbinding by Hand 1636–1820." In *Bookbinding in America: Three Essays.* Ed. by Hellmut Lehmann-Haupt. Bowker 1941 o.p. A 127-page essay covering materials, technique, decoration and binding styles, plain bindings, centers of activity, names of binders, and much more.

Goldschmidt, E. Ph. *Gothic and Renaissance Bookbindings: Exemplified and Illustrated from the Author's Collection.* 2 vols. N. Israel 1967 o.p. Volume 1 contains extensive text with descriptions; Volume 2 contains over 100 plates.

Grimm, Francis W. *A Primer to Bookbinding.* HM 1939 o.p. A well-illustrated and succinct manual, discussing paper and various kinds of bindings (simple, signature, pamphlet, full, half, and so on).

Haldane, Duncan. *Islamic Bookbindings in the Victoria and Albert Museum.* Interlink Pub. 1987 $69.95. ISBN 0-317-59305-6. Splendid color and black-and-white illustrations and a scholarly text.

Harthan, John P. *Bookbindings.* Trafalgar 1985 o.p. An essay on the development of bookbinding design, with notes and bibliography and many plates.

Hewitt-Bates, J. S. *Bookbinding.* Branford 8th rev. ed. 1967 o.p. A historical and practical text, covering equipment, materials, various kinds of bindings, tooling, and marbling.

The History of Bookbinding 525–1950 A.D. Rowman 1965 $34.50. ISBN 0-87471-091-X. An oft-cited and splendid catalog of an exhibit, filled with valuable information in 275 pages of text and 106 plates. Foreword by Dorothy Miner.

The History of Bookbinding and Design. 19 vols. Garland 1990 o.p. A series of reprints, original monographs, and translations on the art of bookbinding, under the general editorship of Sidney F. Huttner. The series includes many important titles long out of print, some volumes containing more than one text. They are listed in this bibliography only by author and title.

Hobson, Anthony. *Humanists and Bookbinders: The Origins and Diffusion of the Humanistic Bookbinding, 1459–1559, with a Census of Historiated Plaquette and Medallion Bindings of the Renaissance*. Cambridge U. Pr. 1989 $145.00. ISBN 0-521-35536-2. A monumental study, illustrated in black and white.

Horton, Carolyn. *Cleaning and Preserving Bindings and Related Materials*. ALA 1967 o.p. Covers many topics, offering information on the work area, moving books, vacuuming and dusting, sorting books, labels, book jackets, larger books, and so on. A circumspect text with many fine illustrations by Aldren A. Watson.

Howe, Ellic. *The London Bookbinders 1780–1806*. Merrion Pr. 1988 o.p. A history, citing many binders by name and discussing their business practices and affairs.

Ikegami, Kojiro. *Japanese Bookbinding: Instructions from a Master Craftsman*. Weatherhill 1986 $32.50. ISBN 0-8348-0196-5. Adapted by Barbara B. Stephan. A well-illustrated manual showing many kinds of Oriental binding techniques, equipment, and materials, along with techniques of mending.

James, David. *Qur'ans and Bindings from the Chester Beatty Library*. Interlink Pub. 1988 o.p. Large, paperbound exhibit catalog, showing 115 pieces, with descriptions.

Johnson, Arthur W. *The Practical Guide to Book Repair and Conservation*. Thames Hudson 1992 $14.95. ISBN 0-500-27518-1. Contains 100 of Johnson's usual fine illustrations, covering a great breadth of topics: principles of restoration, equipment, materials, adhesives, chemicals, insects, book construction, book furniture, paper and vellum cleaning and repair, and many other subjects.

———. *The Practical Guide to Craft Bookbinding*. Thames Hudson 1985 $14.95. ISBN 0-500-27360-X. A 96-page, well-illustrated manual covering forwarding, working procedures, and finishing.

———. *The Thames and Hudson Manual of Bookbinding*. Norton 1981 $14.95. ISBN 0-500-68011-6. Offers detailed information and instruction for hand binding, with excellent illustrations throughout.

Johnson, Pauline. *Creative Bookbinding*. Dover 1990 $10.95. ISBN 0-486-26307-X. Looks mostly at new styles of artistic bindings.

Kuhn, Hilde, comp. *Wörterbuch . . . Dictionary of Bookbinding and Restauration of Papyri, Manuscripts . . . Bindings, and Globes in German, English, French and Italian*. Schlütersche 1979 o.p. A valuable multilingual glossary.

Langwell, W. H. *The Conservation of Books and Documents*. Greenwood 1974 $35.00. ISBN 0-8371-6810-4. Covers many topics, including paper history, causes and prevention of paper damage, animal skins, inks, sewing materials, adhesives, techniques, and so forth.

Lehmann-Haupt, Hellmut, ed. *Bookbinding in America*. Bowker 1967 o.p. Contains three essays: "Early American Bookbinding" by Hannah Dustin French; "The Rise of American Edition Binding" by Joseph W. Rogers; and "On the Rebinding of Old Books" by Hellmut Lehmann-Haupt. The Lehmann-Haupt essay discusses what is wrong with current methods, remedies, historical perspective, practical approaches, pamphlet bindings, library bindings, lettering, materials, the care of old volumes, and so on.

Leighton, Douglas. *Modern Bookbinding: A Survey and a Prospect*. J. M. Dent and Sons 1935 o.p. With a brief historical section, followed by discussions of styles, processes, equipment, materials (e.g., leather, boards, cloth), prices, gold blocking, the trade, and much more.

Lepeltier, Robert. *The Restorer's Handbook of Drawings and Prints*. Van Nos. Reinhold 1977 o.p. A discussion of conservation and restoration, followed by practical advice on how to analyze works of art for deterioration of various kinds, and additional information on restoration.

Lewis, A. W. *Basic Bookbinding*. Dover 1957 o.p. Another manual, this one particularly focusing on "binding in the simpler styles." Deals with equipment, materials, basic operations, pamphlets, case binding, endpapers, and much more.

Lewis, Roy Harley. *Fine Bookbinding in the 20th Century*. Arco 1984 o.p. Backgrounds, development of new attitudes, styles, and techniques. Attention to Philip Smith, Ivor Robinson, and other leading contemporary binding artists of Europe and the United States.

Lydenberg, Harry Miller, and John Archer. *The Care and Repair of Books*. Bks. Demand 4th rev. ed. 1960 $32.00. ISBN 0-317-10303-2. Contains many informative chapters covering such topics as repair and mending, treatment of paper, vellum, leather, and cloth. Revised by John Alden.

McLean, Ruari. *Victorian Publishers' Book-bindings in Paper*. U. CA Pr. 1983 $65.00. ISBN 0-520-05102-5. Extensively illustrated study (mostly in color).

Matthews, William F. *Bookbinding: A Manual for Those Interested in the Craft of Bookbinding*. NAL-Dutton o.p. A manual with information on many aspects of forwarding and finishing.

Mehtha, S. P. *Art and Science of Book Preservation*. Swaraj Pubn. (India). 1976 o.p. A scientific study that considers the parts of a book, its materials and their treatment (cloth, papers, leathers, threads, inks, etc.), deterioration and treatments, gases, fungi, insects, and so on.

Middleton, Bernard C. *A History of English Craft Bookbinding Technique*. Holland Pr. 1988 $130.00. ISBN 0-946323-13-5. One of the standard texts on the subject of the history of the craft from the beginnings to the present day. Looks at both decorative and commercial aspects of the trade.

———. *Restoration of Leather Bindings*. ALA 1984 $40.00. ISBN 0-8389-0391-6. The definitive text on the subject, written from many years of experience.

Miura, Kerstin Tini. *A Master's Bibliophile Bindings: Tini Miura 1980–1990*. Kyoiku Shoseki 1990 o.p. A splendid volume showing Miura's magnificent bindings, all illustrations in color. One of the most innovative and artistic of today's binders.

———. *My World of Bibliophile Binding*. U. CA Pr. 1984 o.p. Another spectacularly produced folio volume showing Miura's bindings, and with a 52-page prose section containing about 200 black-and-white illustrations demonstrating her tools and technique.

Needham, Paul. *Twelve Centuries of Bookbindings 400–1600*. OUP 1979 o.p. Emanating from an exhibition, this heavily illustrated volume is a great storehouse of information.

Nixon, Howard M. *Five Centuries of English Bookbinding*. Scholarly 1979 o.p. A catalog of 100 important bindings from c. 1483 to 1928. Each is illustrated and accompanied by a discussion. An often-quoted text.

Nixon, Howard M., and Mirjam M. Foot. *The History of Decorated Bookbinding in England*. OUP 1992 $72.00. ISBN 0-19-818182-5. Covers the subject from 1520 to the modern movement, with greatest emphasis on the period up through 1800. With 128 black-and-white and 12 colored illustrations. Looks at binders, binding styles, tooling, the business of binding, and much more.

Oliphant, Dave, ed. *Conservation and Preservation of Humanities Research Collections: Essays on Treatment and Care of Rare Books, Manuscripts, Photography, and Art on Paper and Canvas*. U. of Tex. Pr. 1989 $17.95. ISBN 0-87959-109-9. Ten informative essays on various restoration and conservation treatments, offering not only practical details of the conservation projects, but also much theoretical underpinnings.

Percival, George, and Rigby Graham. *Unsewn Binding*. Branford 1979 o.p. A useful work covering equipment, materials, adhesives, and various kinds of rebindings.

Philip, Alex. J. *The Business of Bookbinding*. Trafalgar 1912 o.p. "Bookbinding from the point of view of the binder, the publisher, the librarian and the general reader" (title-page blurb). Contains many samples of leathers and cloths, and sections on paper and its deterioration, library and reinforced bindings, materials, machine binding,

binding specifications, fine bindings, etc. See also *The History of Bookbinding and Design*.

Plenderleith, H. J. *The Preservation of Leather Bookbindings*. Parkwest Pubns. 1947 o.p. On the decay and revitalization of leather on books.

Plumbe, W. J. *The Preservation of Books in Tropical and Subtropical Countries*. OUP 1964 o.p. A general discussion of conservation practices along with the narrower topic of the title.

Pollard, Graham, and Esther Potter. *Early Bookbinding Manuals: An Annotated List of Technical Accounts of Bookbinding to 1840.* Oxford Bibliographical Soc., Bodleian Lib. 1984 o.p. Occasional Publication No. 18. Lists 141 manuals in Latin, Arabic, German, French, Swedish, Dutch, English, Italian, and other sources.

Prideaux, S. T. *Bookbinders and Their Craft*. Scribner 1903 o.p. A collection of eight essays on English and Scottish nineteenth-century bindings, the binder Roger Payne, bookbinding design, French binders, stamped and Italian bindings, and other subjects.

Ramsden, Charles. *London Bookbinders 1780–1840*. Trafalgar 1988 $125.00. ISBN 0-7134-5078-9. An alphabetical listing of binders, giving addresses and other information, with a useful historical introduction and 40 plates.

Reed, Ronald. *Ancient Skins, Parchments and Leathers*. Seminar Pr. 1972 o.p. A scientific study of the materials that go into bookbindings, with chapters on skins, their method of processing, parchment, conservation, and so on.

———. *The Nature and Making of Parchment*. Elmete Press 1977 o.p. A thorough examination of parchment, its preparation and uses.

Roberts, Matt T., and Don Etherington. *Bookbinding and the Conservation of Books: A Dictionary of Descriptive Terminology*. Lib. Congress 1982 $27.00. ISBN 0-8444-0366-0. Nearly 300 folio pages with many illustrations (by Margaret R. Brown), aimed primarily at conservators and binders.

Rogers, Joseph W. "The Rise of American Edition Binding." In *Bookbinding in America: Three Essays*. Ed. by Hellmut Lehmann-Haupt. Bowker 1941 o.p. Looks at the introduction of cloth and cased bindings, mechanization of the process, manufacture and decoration of cloth, and the growth of the industry.

Smith, Keith A. *Non-Adhesive Binding*. The Sigma Fairport 1990 $30.00. ISBN 0-927159-04-X. With 318 well-illustrated pages covering a wide array of topics, such as books with one or two folds, triads, dovetails, supplies, pamphlet stitching with various numbers of holes, Oriental styles, stab covers, albums, different kinds of lacing and stitches, covers of various kinds, and so on.

Smith, Philip. *The Book: Art & Object*. Merstham 1982 o.p. Illustrated with drawings and many color photographs, showing the new directions in the decorative designs of bookbindings.

———. *New Directions in Bookbinding*. Van Nos. Reinhold 1974 o.p. Depicts bookbinding as a modern art, with many of Smith's and others' creative modern bindings as examples.

Sterne, Harold E. *Catalogue of Nineteenth Century Bindery Equipment*. Ye Olde Printery 1978 $14.95. ISBN 0-932606-01-6. With 270 pages of illustrations of folding machines, paper cutters, blank-book equipment, edition-binding equipment, and miscellaneous machinery.

Tidcombe, Marianne. *The Bookbindings of T. J. Cobden-Sanderson: A Study of His Work 1884–1893, based on his Time Book (British Library Add. MS. 49061), with a Biographical Introduction*. ALA 1984 o.p. A scholarly and well-written study containing over 400 pages of information and illustrations.

———. *The Doves Bindery*. Oak Knoll 1991 $185.00. ISBN 0-938768-17-4. A companion volume to the previous book, showing the work of the Doves Bindery from 1893–1922, when Cobden-Sanderson designed the bindings but had a skilled group of craftsmen do the bindings. With hundreds of illustrations, and an authoritative text on the founding and history of the bindery, its pupils and books, patterns and sources. A rich resource.

Titcombe, Marianne Fletcher. *The Bookbinding Career of Rachel McMasters Miller Hunt.* Hunt Botanical Lib. 1974 o.p. A biographical and historical sketch, with a list of the books bound by Hunt.

Walden, Sarah. *The Ravished Image: Or How to Ruin Masterpieces by Restoration.* St. Martin 1985 o.p. Challenges conservators' practices of repairing and restoring items. This is "an elegant philosophical and practical presentation of the case against overzealous 'cleaning up' of old masterpieces" (from blurb on dust jacket).

Waters, Peter. *Procedures for Salvage of Water-Damaged Library Materials.* Lib. Congress 1979 o.p. A useful pamphlet, covering assessment of damage, the effect of water on books and unbound materials, freezing, procedures for salvage, cleaning and drying, and many other topics.

Watson, Aldren A. *Hand Bookbinding: A Manual of Instruction.* Macmillan 1986 $19.95. ISBN 0-02-624430-6. One of the more ubiquitous manuals, with many fine illustrations showing procedures, materials, tools, and equipment.

Wolf, Edwin, 2nd. *From Gothic Windows to Peacocks: American Embossed Leather Bindings 1825–1855.* Lib. Co. Phila. 1990 $85.00. ISBN 0-914076-82-5. A major study, with 226 illustrations. Discusses background, methods, materials, styles, binders and die-engravers, costs. Illustrations depict many different styles.

Zaehnsdorf, Joseph W. *The Art of Bookbinding: A Practical Treatise.* 1890. Gregg Intl. 1969 o.p. One of the classic treatises by one of England's premiere binders. The Zaehnsdorf bindery was in the family for generations, producing for the most part decorative bindings of high quality for nearly one-and-a-half centuries.

Zigrosser, Carl, and Christa M. Gaehde. *A Guide to the Collecting and Care of Original Prints.* Crown Pub. Group 1965 o.p. Discusses fine prints, collecting, techniques of printmaking, and the handling, care, and conservation of prints.

BOOK ILLUSTRATION

Listed below are books on the history and practice of book illustration. Included are books that not only discuss the history of the art but also teach one how to produce illustrations, as well as books that will help one determine the mechanical process that produced a given illustration. Only the smallest sampling of books on this topic is possible. There is a vast sea of information beyond the items listed, including books on graphic processes of various kinds and the artists who practice them.

Bader, Barbara. *American Picturebooks from Noah's Ark to The Beast Within.* Macmillan 1976 o.p. Lavishly illustrated historical and analytical study, with nearly 700 illustrations, 130 in color. Looks at artists, authors, social trends, artistic currents, the effects of changes in printing technology, market conditions, and so on. With an excellent bibliography.

Banister, Manley. *Lithographic Prints from Stone and Plate.* Littlefield 1974 o.p. Well-illustrated manual covering stones, drawing onto the stone, crayons, papers and presses, printing methods, printing in color, and so on.

Beedham, R. John. *Wood Engraving.* Faber & Faber 1938 o.p. Historical sketch followed by a manual discussing tools, equipment, wood, drawing, techniques, taking proofs, and so on. With an introduction and appendix by Eric Gill.

Biegeleisen, J. I. *The Complete Book of Silk Screen Printing Production.* Dover 1963 o.p. A brief historical account followed by sections on equipment, tools, stencil-making techniques, photo-stencil methods, multicolor work, and much more. With a bibliography.

Biegeleisen, J. I., and E. J. Busenbark. *The Silk Screen Printing Process.* McGraw 1941 o.p. A thorough, well-illustrated practical manual.

Biegeleisen, J. I., and Max Arthur Cohn. *Silk Screen Techniques.* Dover 1952 o.p. A corrected and enlarged edition of the earlier McGraw-Hill edition of 1942. Thorough volume looking at origin and development, basic principles, equipment, various stencil methods, the use of colors, and printing.

Bland, David. *A History of Book Illustration: The Illuminated Manuscript and the Printed Book.* U. CA Pr. 2nd rev. ed. 1974 o.p. Perhaps one of the most comprehensive studies on the subject. Looks at illustration in books from throughout the world in all media. With more than 400 illustrations and a bibliography.

Brewer, Frances J. *Book Illustration.* Gebrüder Mann Verlag 1963 o.p. Six essays from a conference held in Florida in 1962. All essays, well illustrated, by experts in such fields as Baroque book illustration, illustration in Colonial Spanish America, early America, magazine illustration, and so on.

Cirker, Blanche, and others, eds. *1800 Woodcuts by Thomas Bewick and His School.* Dover 1962 $11.95. ISBN 0-486-20766-8. Excellent reproductions of the work of Bewick (1752–1828), one of the more prolific artists of the woodcut. Organized into convenient categories such as animals (subdivided by animal), birds, fish, insects, trees, flowers and plants, rocks and cliffs, people (subdivided into such categories as fashions, military costumes, eating), business and trades, and scores of other categories.

Curwen, Harold. *Processes of Graphic Reproduction in Printing.* Faber & Faber 1963 o.p. Covers many methods of printing illustrations: relief methods, intaglio methods, stencilling, lithography; also photographic reproduction of many kinds. An excellent, well illustrated text with a good bibliography. Revised by Charles Mayo.

Daniels, M. *Victorian Book Illustration.* St. Mut. 1990 $60.00. ISBN-0-685-36747-9. How the development of new printing processes continuously changed book illustration throughout the nineteenth century.

de Maré, Eric. *The Victorian Woodblock Illustrators.* Beil 1982 o.p. The development of illustration by engraving the end-grain of boxwood, from Thomas Bewick to William Morris. The craft and its role as a social force. With about 200 illustrations.

Elliott, Brian. *Silk-Screen Printing.* OUP 1971 o.p. With a historical note and information on screens and other equipment, ink and paper, stencils, transfer printing, vacuum forming, mould blowing, and so on.

Garrett, Albert. *British Wood Engraving of the 20th Century: A Personal View.* Scholarly 1980 $25.00. ISBN 0-85967-608-0. A good selection of work by top artist-illustrators. Brief biographies of over 100 artists with more than 300 prints.

Harthan, John. *The History of the Illustrated Book: The Western Tradition.* Thames Hudson 1981 $60.00. ISBN 0-500-23316-0. A well-illustrated volume, with 465 plates, 33 in color. Looks at manuscripts, early printed books, the Renaissance, and so on to the twentieth century.

Hindman, Sandra, ed. *The Early Illustrated Book: Essays in Honor of Lessing J. Rosenwald.* Lib. Congress 1982 $50.00. ISBN 0-8444-0398-9. A handsome work, based on some of the lavish Rosenwald gifts to the library. Special attention to the major Dutch and Belgian presses.

Hunnisett, Basil. *Steel-Engraved Book Illustration in England.* Godine 1980 o.p. A detailed survey of the illustrators, firms, styles, and methods of a previously little-researched period in the eighteenth and nineteenth centuries.

Ivins, William M., Jr. *How Prints Look: Photographs with a Commentary.* Beacon Pr. 1987 $12.95. ISBN 0-8070-6647-8. A close examination of many prints to show how one can determine their printing process. Revised by Marjorie B. Cohn.

———. *Notes on Prints: Being the Texts of Labels Prepared for A Special Exhibit of Prints from the Museum Collection.* 1930. Da Capo 1967 $37.50. ISBN 0-306-70957-0. The notes include information on changing artistic styles, methods of making the prints, and so on.

Johnson, Fridolf, ed. *Treasury of American Pen-and-Ink Illustrators, 1881 to 1938.* Dover 1982 $7.95. ISBN 0-486-24280-3. Portrayal of an intensely creative period in U.S. book and periodical art; introductory essay, 236 drawings by 103 artists.

Jones, Stanley. *Lithography for Artists.* OUP 1967 o.p. A historic note, followed by principles, methods, equipment, tools, color, and so on.

Kingman, Lee, and others, eds. *Illustrators of Children's Books, 1967–1976*. Horn Bk. 1978 $35.95. ISBN 0-87675-018-8. Latest in an ongoing series that highlights prominent children's illustrators.

Klemin, Diana. *The Art of Art for Children's Books*. Murton Pr. 1982 $16.95. ISBN 0-9608042-0-X. Relation of art to text demonstrated, with comment, in reproduced pages of approximately 60 books.

———. *The Illustrated Book: Its Art and Craft*. 1965. Murton Pr. 1983 $19.95. ISBN 0-9608042-1-8. Examples and explanations of works and techniques of 74 book illustrators.

Larson, Judy L. *Enchanted Images: American Children's Illustration 1850–1925*. Santa Barb. Mus. Art 1980 o.p.

Lewis, John. *The Twentieth-Century Book:s from the arts and crafts movement Its Illustration and Design*. Reinhold 1984 o.p. Highlights from the arts-and-crafts movement of the 1890s to the Swiss influences of the twentieth century; more than 400 illustrations.

Lindley, Kenneth. *The Woodblock Engravers*. David & Charles 1970 o.p. A history of wood engraving, especially in the commercial world, with a section on how it was done.

Linton, William J. *American Wood Engraving: A Victorian History*. Am. Life Foun. 1976 repr. of 1882 ed. $25.00. ISBN 0-89257-010-5. Formerly entitled *American Victorian Wood Engraving*. Extensive new bibliography by Nancy Carlson Shrock.

Lumsden, E. S. *The Art of Etching: A Complete & Fully Illustrated Description of Etching, Drypoint, Soft-Ground Etching, Aquatint and Their Allied Arts*. Peter Smith repr. of 1929 ed. $19.00. ISBN 0-8446-2497-7. With 208 illustrations and a very thorough practical and historical text.

McClean, Ruari. *Victorian Book Design and Colour Printing*. U. CA Pr. 1972 o.p. The flowering of book illustration in Britain, 1830–80. Lavishly illustrated (mostly in black and white).

Mahony, Bertha, and Elinor Whitney. *Contemporary Illustrators of Children's Books*. Omnigraphics Inc. 1992 repr. of 1930 ed. $65.00. ISBN 0-55888-944-02. By early editors of the *Horn Book*.

Meyer, Susan E. *A Treasury of the Great Children's Book Illustrators*. Abrams 1987 $24.95. ISBN 0-8109-8081-9. Examples and accounts of the work of 13 major illustrators from about 1840 to about 1920.

Osborne, Carol Margot. *Pierre Didot the Elder and French Book Illustration 1789–1822*. Garland 1985 $34.00. ISBN 0-8240-6862-9. An in-depth study of the illustrations in Didot's works, with 334 illustrations and a good bibliography. Originally done as a dissertation at Stanford University, 1979.

Peterdi, Gabor. *Printmaking Methods Old and New*. Macmillan 1961 o.p. Well-illustrated manual on line engraving, dry point, stipple engraving and etching, dotted print, mezzotint, etching, equipment and tools, color printing, woodcut and wood engraving, and so on.

Pippin, Brigid, and Lucy Mickle Thwaite. *Book Illustration of the 20th Century*. Arco 1984 o.p. Short encyclopedia-style accounts of illustrators and portrayals of them and their work.

Plowman, George T. *Etching and Other Graphic Arts: An Illustrated Treatise*. John Lane 1914 o.p. Gives information on pencil drawing and composition, pen drawing, wood-engraving lithography, line engraving, dry-point, soft ground, materials, preparing and working on the plate, and so on.

The Process Engraver's Compendium for Users of Photo-Process Engraving. The Federation of Master Process Engravers 1932 o.p. Considers many forms of engraving processes: the photo-process engraving, the line process, half-tones, three-color process, the use of tints or stipples, color line blocks, and many other topics.

Ray, Gordon N. *The Art of the French Illustrated Book, 1700–1914*. Dover 1986 $24.95. ISBN 0-486-25086-5. Careful scholarship, full documentation, well illustrated. A major reference work on an exciting field.

————. *The Illustrator and the Book in England from 1790–1914*. Dover 1992 $24.95. ISBN 0-486-26955-8. Catalog, heavily annotated, with sectional and general essays. A landmark exhibition.

Reed, Walt, and Roger Reed. *The Illustrator in America, 1880–1980*. Madison Square 1990 $48.50. ISBN 0-8230-5849-2. Hundreds of brief biographies with samples of the artists' works.

Reilly, Elizabeth Carroll. *A Dictionary of Colonial American Printers' Ornaments and Illustrations*. Am. Antiquarian 1975 $60.00. ISBN 0-912296-06-2. Reproduces more than 2,000 relief-cut ornaments used by American printers from 1640 to 1776. Well-indexed by printers and dates.

Sampler of Book Illustration Processes Issued in Connection with an Exhibition of Techniques in Book Illustration. Am. Instit. of Graphic Arts 1939 o.p. Pamphlet with examples of letterpress printing on four kinds of paper, sheetfed gravure, collotype, and offset printing.

Smith, Charles W. *Linoleum Block Printing*. Charles W. Smith 1925 o.p. A brief handbook on how to make linoleum blocks, with good illustrations.

Taft, Robert. *Artists and Illustrators of the Old West: 1850–1900*. Princeton U. Pr. 1982 $55.00. ISBN 0-691-03995-X. Looks at many media of illustration. Not specifically about book illustration, but presents information about many artists whose works wound up in books.

Tooley, R. V. *English Books with Coloured Plates, 1790 to 1860: A Bibliographical Account of the Most Important Books Illustrated by English Artists in Colour Aquatint and Colour Lithography*. Batsford 1987 o.p. Offers hundreds of bibliographical descriptions for works with colored plates, listing all the plates in each volume. Not illustrated but nonetheless, a valuable reference tool.

Twyman, Michael. *Lithography, 1800–1850: The Technique of Drawing on Stone in England and France and Their Application to Works of Typography*. OUP 1970 o.p. Written by a leading English historian of printing.

Tymms, W. R., and M. Digby Wyatt. *The Art of Illuminating as Practised in Europe from the Earliest Times, Illustrated by Borders, Initial Letters, and Alphabets*. 1860. Chartwell Bks. 1987 o.p. Beautifully illustrated reprint, with more than 100 color plates showing different styles of ornament and decoration. Wyatt's contribution is an informative essay on the history of illuminating and a practical manual of how the art should be practiced.

BIBLIOPHILIA, BOOK COLLECTING, AND READING

As with other subtopics in this chapter, there is no paucity of literature on the love and collecting of books. In fact, there are thousands of books on the subject. There is practically nothing that is not collected. The following list tries to cover the field in its breadth, from simple how-to-collect and what-to-collect manuals to accounts of such passionate collectors as Sir Thomas Phillipps, who said, "I wish to have one copy of every book in the world" and then went out to achieve that goal, bankrupting his family in the attempt. The listing here also includes titles on the love of reading as an adventure, and the encouragement of reading in others.

Ahearn, Allen. *Book Collecting: A Comprehensive Guide*. Putnam. Pub. Group 1989 $24.95. ISBN 0-3991-3456-5. Single-volume guide to values with six introductory chapters; values of 3,520 books by frequently requested authors.

Altick, Richard D. *The Scholar Adventurers*. Ohio St. U. Pr. 1987 $13.95. ISBN 0-8142-0435-X. Great episodes in literary detection: the exposure of the Wise forgeries, the discovery of the lost Boswell papers at Malahide Castle, and the use of codes and ciphers in literature are among the stories told.

Arnold, William Harris. *Ventures in Book Collecting*. Scribner 1923 o.p. On the makings of a collector, with chapters on various collecting areas.

Booth, Richard, ed. *Book Collecting*. Ballantine 1976 o.p. Covers how and what to collect, the book before 1800, illustrated books, fields of collecting (e.g., natural history, philosophy and religion, children's books), first editions, and so on. Some of the chapters are written by others.

Brook, G. L. *Books and Book-Collecting*. Westview 1980 o.p. A learned text on many aspects of the field, including what to collect, bibliographical issues, trends, care, booksellers, forgeries, selling a collection, and so on.

Cannon, Carl L. *American Book Collectors and Collecting from Colonial Times to the Present*. Wilson 1941 o.p. Twenty-nine chapters on dozens of collectors, including Thomas Jefferson, Isaiah Thomas, George Ticknor, John Carter Brown, Rover Hoe III, Henry E. Huntington, Henry Clay Folger, J. P. Morgan, and many others

Carter, John. *ABC for Book Collectors*. Oak Knoll 1992 $25.00. ISBN 0-938768- 30-1. Perhaps the most important book on the subject of book collecting, if only for the humor and learning the author brings to the topic. This book is a glossary of terms that all collectors and booksellers must know. With corrections and additions by Nicolas Barker.

_____. *Taste and Technique in Book-Collecting: A Study of Recent Developments in Great Britain and the United States*. Bowker 1948 o.p. A classic study covering the evolution and method of collecting and discussing many aspects of the field, including the education of the collector, tools and terminology, bookshop and auction room, rarity, and condition.

Chapman, R. W., John Hayward, John Carter, and Michael Sadleir. *Book Collecting: Four Broadcast Talks*. Bowes & Bowes 1950 o.p. Four lectures for radio broadcast on various aspects of the subject. A slender but informative little book.

Chidley, John. *Discovering Book Collecting*. Lubrecht & Cramer 1982 o.p. A compact, succinct, but very informative little book on what a collector needs to know. Chapters on printing (historical and practical), various collecting areas, and terminology. Good for the beginning collector.

Collison, Robert L. *Book Collecting: An Introduction to Modern Methods of Literary and Bibliographical Detection*. Essential Bks. Inc. 1957 o.p. Covers a wide range of topics, including bibliography, bookbindings, manuscripts and proofreading, paper and watermarks, printers and printing, title pages, and many more topics. The aim is to educate the collector on terminology, techniques, history, care of books, and so on, in order to make the collector more informed and thus more responsible.

Currie, Barton. *Fishers of Books*. Little 1931 o.p. Amusingly written on how one begins to collect, first editions, dealers and dealer psychology, and a great deal more.

de Bury, Richard (Bishop of Durham). *Love of Books: Philobiblon of Richard de Bury*. 1599. Ed. by I. Gollancz. Trans. by E. C. Thomas. Cooper Sq. repr. of 1926 ed. o.p. First translated in 1834. The oldest book about books.

Donaldson, Gerald. *Books: Their History, Art, Power, Glory, Infamy, and Suffering According to Their Creators, Friends and Enemies*. Van Nos. Reinhold 1981 o.p. A collection of vignettes, tidbits, and miscellanies pertaining to books. Well illustrated.

Downs, Robert B. *Books and History*. U. of Ill. Pr. 1974 o.p. On the role of books in affecting historical development.

_____. *Books That Changed America*. Macmillan 1970 o.p. Selection and comment.

_____. *Books That Changed the World*. NAL-Dutton 1956 $5.99. ISBN 0-451-62698-2. Durable reference work.

Dunbar, Maurice. *Books and Collectors*. Book Nest 1980 $11.95. ISBN 0-686-27441-5. A wide-ranging text, with much information on collecting, first editions, limited editions, bestsellers, book club editions, care and handling, books as investments, and a great deal more.

Elton, Charles Isaac, and Mary Augusta Elton. *The Great Book-Collectors*. 1893. Ayer 1977 $15.00. ISBN 0-8369-6972-3. A series of biographical sketches about great collectors from classical times to the end of the last century throughout the world.

Ettinghausen, Maurice L. *Rare Books and Royal Collectors: Memoirs of an Antiquarian Bookseller*. S&S Trade 1966 o.p. Reminiscences of this dealer about the books and clients he dealt with.

Fasick, Adele M., Margaret Johnson, and Ruth Osler, eds. *Lands of Pleasure: Essays on Lillian H. Smith and the Development of Children's Libraries*. Scarecrow 1990 $22.50. ISBN 0-8108-2266-0. Seeks to celebrate the accomplishments of a noted children's librarian and her work to encourage reading in children.

Fitzgerald, Percy. *The Book Fancier, or The Romance of Book Collecting*. 2nd rev. ed. 1887 o.p. Discusses collectors and dealers and then looks at the many areas of collecting popular in his day.

Glaister, Geoffrey Ashall. *Glaister's Glossary of the Book: Terms Used in Papermaking, Printing, Bookbinding and Publishing, with Notes on Illuminated Manuscripts and Private Presses*. Paul & Co. Pubs. 2nd rev. ed. 1979 o.p. A usually reliable glossary of 3,200 entries indispensable to collectors.

Hanff, Helene. *Eighty-four Charing Cross Road*. Avon 1982 $5.95. ISBN 0-380-00122-5. A novel told in the form of trans-Atlantic correspondence between the staff of a London bookstore and a breezy New York City customer. It became a Broadway play and a movie.

Hazlitt, W. Carew. *The Book-Collector: A General Survey of the Pursuit and of Those Who Have Engaged in It at Home and Abroad from the Earliest Period to the Present Time, With an Account of Public and Private Libraries and Anecdotes of their Founders or Owners and Remarks on Bookbinding and on Special Copies of Books*. John Grant 1904 o.p. The title says it all.

Howell, R. Patton. *Beyond Literacy: The Second Gutenberg Revolution*. Saybrook 1989 $7.95. ISBN 0-933071-32-9. Nobel laureates, writers, educators, and scientists affirm reading as humanity's most important tool.

Iacone, Salvatore J. *The Pleasures of Book Collecting*. HarpC 1976 o.p. Looks at the nature and the mechanics of collecting. Covers a wide range of topics.

Jackson, Holbrook. *The Anatomy of Bibliomania*. AMS Pr. 1981 $30.00. ISBN 0-404-15337-2. A classic on the maniacal obsessions of all true bibliophiles, covering all the pleasures that books afford under 23 headings, with voluminous quotations.

———. *A Bookman's Holiday*. Folcroft 1973 o.p. One of this literary historian's many books about books, authors, and bibliophilia.

Lanes, Selma. *Down the Rabbit Hole: Adventures and Misadventures in the Realm of Children's Literature*. Atheneum 1976. Assessments and observations.

Lang, Andrew. *Books and Bookmen*. AMS Pr. repr. of 1886 ed. $10.00. ISBN 0-404-03818-2. A standard work by a literary classicist and teacher.

Lewis, John. *Printed Ephemera*. Antique Collect. 1990 $69.50. ISBN 1-85149-116-3. Discusses many areas of collecting ephemera, such as indulgences and proclamations, licenses and certificates, almanacs, all kinds of broadsides, and many others. Beautifully illustrated.

Lewis, Roy Harley. *Antiquarian Books: An Insider's Account*. David & Charles 1978 o.p. An anecdotal tour around the world of books, touching on buying and selling, forgeries, auctions, binding, and trends.

McCullough, David W. *People, Books and Book People*. Crown Pub. Group 1981 o.p. Essays and interviews by a contemporary book-trade observer and literary critic.

Magee, David. *Infinite Riches: The Adventures of a Rare Book Dealer*. Eriksson 1973 o.p. An entertaining account of the life of this bookseller and the collectors he dealt with.

Makepeace, Chris E. *Ephemera: A Book on Its Collection, Conservation and Use*. Sheridan 1985 $59.95. ISBN 0-566-03439-5. A comprehensive guide defining the field, discussing how to build a collection, and treating conservation and preservation issues; cataloging and classifying and indexing ephemera, and appraising pieces. With a bibliography.

Merryweather, F. Somner. *Bibliomania in the Middle Ages*. 1933. Gordon Pr. 1977 $59.95. ISBN 0-8490-1503-0. A perfectly descriptive title.

Mitchell, Edwin Valentine. *Morocco Bound: Adrift Among Books*. Farrar & Rinehart 1929 o.p. On book collecting and bookselling. Readable and informative, with such chapter titles as "The Human Procession," "Book Thieves and Author Snatching," and "The Sense and Nonsense of Collecting."

Morley, Christopher. *The Haunted Bookshop*. Amereon Ltd. 1983 repr. of 1919 ed. $17.95. ISBN 0-88411-887-8. Along with *Parnassus on Wheels*, a famous novel about bookselling.

―――――. *Parnassus on Wheels*. Booksellers Pub. 1983 repr. of 1917 ed. $12.95. ISBN 1-879923-01-7. Both *The Haunted Bookshop* and *Parnassus on Wheels* are famous novels about bookselling—a detective tale and a clever romance—that have become part of the lore of book lovers.

Muir, P. H., ed. *Talks on Book-Collecting: Delivered under the Authority of The Antiquarian Booksellers' Association*. Cassell and Co. 1952 o.p. Seven lectures by P. H. Muir, E. P. Goldschmidt, John Carter, and others. Topics discussed: the nature and scope of book collecting, manuscripts, terminology, fashions in collecting, binding and binders, and so on.

Munby, A. N. L. *Portrait of an Obsession: The Life of Sir Thomas Phillipps, the World's Greatest Book Collector*. Putnam Pub. Group 1967 o.p. An engaging account of Phillipps's maniacal collecting. Adapted by Nicolas Barker from the five volumes of *Phillipps Studies* by A. N. L. Munby.

Nell, Victor. *Lost in a Book: The Psychology of Reading for Pleasure*. Yale U. Pr. 1988 $40.00. ISBN 0-300–4115-2. Examines the feelings people have when reading books.

Newton, A. Edward. *The Amenities of Book-Collecting and Kindred Affections*. Little 1918 o.p. Another book of Newton's reminiscences as a collector, among other collectors and a world of books. Looks at collecting at home and abroad, book prices, collectors, and much more.

―――――. *This Book-Collecting Game*. Little 1928 o.p. The reminiscences of this indefatigable collector and author. Discusses bindings, points of editions, the rewards and perils of collecting, and much more. With 133 illustrations.

Orcutt, William Dana. *In Quest of the Perfect Book*. Ayer 1969 repr. of 1926 ed. $26.00. ISBN 0-8369-1769-3. A booklover's classic.

―――――. *The Kingdom of Books*. Little 1927 o.p. Well illustrated and wide ranging, a book about collectable books, great printers, book decoration, and many other topics.

Pearson, Edmund L. *Books in Black or Red*. Ayer 1975 repr. of 1923 ed. $21.50. ISBN 0-8369-1267-5. Pearson was an entertaining essayist and literary historian.

Peters, Jean, ed. *Book Collecting: A Modern Guide*. Bowker 1977 $39.95. ISBN 0-8352-0985-7. A dozen fine essays on many aspects of collecting, written by experts. An important collection.

Powell, Lawrence Clark. *Bookman's Progress*. Ed. by William Targ. Holmes Pub. 1968 $15.00. ISBN 0-910740-25-9. Writings, selected by a publisher-bibliographer, of essays by a famous librarian-bibliophile.

―――――. *Books in My Baggage: Adventures in Reading and Collecting*. Greenwood 1973 repr. of 1960 ed. $52.50. ISBN 0-8371-6784-1. Librarian, book collector, and lecturer, Powell was a popular interpreter of the pleasures of books.

―――――. *A Passion for Books*. Greenwood repr. of 1958 ed. $39.75. ISBN 0-8371-6783-3

Quayle, Eric. *The Collector's Book of Books*. Crown Pub. Group 1971 o.p. Attractive folio volume, well illustrated, looking at many specific collecting areas. With glossary and bibliography.

Raabe, Tom. *Biblioholism: The Literary Addiction*. Fulcrum Pub. 1991 $8.95. ISBN 1-5559-080-7. An amusing discussion of the fanatic, maniacal addiction of book buying.

Rees-Mogg, William. *How to Buy Rare Books: A Practical Guide to the Antiquarian Book Market*. Phaidon UK 1985 o.p. Discusses the book trade, buying at auction, the construction and composition of books, and so on. Well-illustrated.

Richkards, Maurice. *Collecting Printed Ephemera*. BDD Promo. Bk. Co. 1988 $9.98. ISBN 0-7924-8276-X

Rosenbach, A. S. W. *Book Hunter's Holiday: Adventures with Books and Manuscripts*. Ayer 1968 repr. of 1936 ed. $21.50. ISBN 0-8369-0834-1

―――――. *Books and Bidders: The Adventures of a Bibliophile*. Little 1927 o.p. The reminiscences of this famous and controversial dealer. Looks at many collectors and books.

Rostenberg, Leona, and Madeleine B. Stern. *Between Boards: New Thoughts on Old Books*. Modoc Pr. 1989 $11.95. ISBN 0-929246-02-0. Collectible books from the perspective of these well-known booksellers. Much information on catalogs and collecting, with chapters on innovative collecting areas and what traits a dealer needs to be a dealer.

Sabine, Gordon, and Patricia Gordon. *Books That Made a Difference: What People Told Us*. Shoe String 1983 $21.50. ISBN 0-208-02022-5. A Center for the Book project. Two professional journalists interviewed people all over the country who told about books that "made the greatest difference in their lives."

Spiegel, Dixie L. *Reading for Pleasure: Guidelines*. Bks. Demand repr. of 1981 ed. $25.00. ISBN 0-8357-2633-9. Looks at ways of maximizing the pleasure gained from reading.

Starrett, Vincent. *Bookman's Holiday: The Private Satisfactions of an Incurable Collector*. Ayer repr. of 1942 ed. $18.00. ISBN 0-8369-2475-4

Stewart, Seumas. *Book Collecting: A Beginner's Guide*. David & Charles 1972 o.p. Offers advice on many subjects, such as the anatomy of a book, first editions, collecting literature, collecting fine books, illustrated volumes, and much more on various other fields of collecting. With a glossary and bibliography.

Storm, Colton, and Howard Peckham. *An Invitation to Book Collecting: Its Pleasures and Practices, with Kindred Discussions of Manuscripts, Maps, and Prints*. Bowker 1947 o.p. Defines "rare books" and offers information on collectors and collecting, specific fields, bibliography, buying and selling rare books, book prices, fakes and forgeries, thefts, and planning and building a collection.

Thomas, Alan G. *Fine Books*. Putnam Pub. Group 1967 o.p. Looks at four popular areas of collecting: manuscripts, early printing, English books with color plates, and private presses. Well illustrated.

_____. *Great Books and Book Collectors*. Weidenfeld and Nicolson 1975 o.p. A splendid well-illustrated folio volume on manuscripts, early printing, bookbinding, collecting areas, first editions, fakes and forgeries, great collectors, and much more.

Thwaite, Mary F. *From Primer to Pleasure in Reading*. Horn Bk. 1972 repr. of 1963 ed. o.p. On children's books printed in England from the 1400s to 1914, including authors, illustrators, publishers, representative books, and notes on other countries.

Uden, Grant. *Understanding Book-Collecting*. Antique Collect. 1986 $29.50. ISBN 0-907462-13-8. Covers many aspects of the subject, including terminology, various collecting areas, bookbinding, and so forth. A great deal of good information; with illustrations.

Waldhorn, Arthur, Olga S. Weber, and Arthur Zeiger, eds. *Good Reading: A Guide for Serious Readers*. Bowker 1990 $44.00. ISBN 0-8352-2707-3. Notes on 2,500 outstanding books, in five broad areas, many subgroups, and special lists.

Webber, Winslow L. *Books about Books, A Bio-bibliography for Collectors*. Hale, Cushman & Flint 1937 o.p. A bibliography of books about books by famous book people.

Williams, Iolo A. *The Elements of Book-Collecting*. Stokes 1927 o.p. Contains chapters on the pleasures and logic of collecting books, book sizes, the parts of a book, condition, issue and editions, book description, first editions, and so on.

Wilson, Robert A. *Modern Book Collecting*. Lyons & Burford 1992 $14.95. ISBN 1-55821-179-9. A book with varying value from chapter to chapter. Looks at what to collect, how to build an author collection, dealers and collectors, condition, first editions, and bibliographies.

Winterich, John T. *Collector's Choice*. Greenberg Pub. Co. 1928 o.p. A rambling text covering collecting, selling, book prices, condition of books, buying and selling, the rise and fall of collections, the "completeness" of any collection, first editions, and so on.

Winterich, John T., and David A. Randall. *A Primer of Book Collecting*. Crown Pub. Group 3rd rev. ed. 1966 o.p. A famous but not always carefully written book on many aspects of collecting. Has chapters on first editions, association books, condition, rarity, collecting, value, and so on.

Wolf, Edwin, 2nd, with John F. Fleming. *Rosenbach: A Biography*. World Pub. Co. 1960 o.p. A biography of A. S. W. Rosenbach, the bookseller.

FORGERY

Listed here are but a few of the books on the subject of forgery.

Barker, Nicolas, and John Collins. *A Sequel to An Enquiry into the Nature of Certain Nineteenth Century Pamphlets by John Carter and Graham Pollard: The Forgeries of H. Buxton Forman & T. J. Wise Re-Examined.* Oak Knoll 1992 $55.00. ISBN 0-938768-32-8. A continuation of Carter and Pollard's studies on the Wise forgeries, based on their papers. With a good bibliography.

Bozeman, Pat, ed. *Forged Documents: Proceedings of the 1989 Houston Conference.* Oak Knoll 1990 $25.00. ISBN 0-938768-22-0. A wide-ranging conference, discussing forgery from many perspectives (legal, library, book dealer, among others). A most informative volume.

Carter, John, and Graham Pollard. *An Enquiry into the Nature of Certain Nineteenth Century Pamphlets.* 1934. Oak Knoll 1992 $55.00. ISBN 0-938768-31-X. By now a classic of detection. The first exposure of Thomas James Wise, the respected bibliographer and collector, as the forger of a great number of pamphlets. A sensation when it came out, ruining the otherwise glorious career of Wise, who died in ignominy.

―――. *The Firm of Charles Ottley, Landon and Co.: Footnote to an Enquiry.* Scribner 1948 o.p. A continuation of these authors' *Enquiry*, with additional damning evidence of Wise's forgeries.

Collins, John. *The Two Forgers: A Biography of Harry Buxton Forman and Thomas James Wise.* Oak Knoll 1992 $55.00. ISBN 0-938768-29-8. Collins's excellent biographies, which naturally focus on the forgeries of the two, Forman having been implicated with Wise in the latter's scandalous fabrications.

Grafton, Anthony. *Forgers and Critics: Creativity and Duplicity in Western Scholarship.* Princeton U. Pr. 1990 $14.95. ISBN 0-691-05544-0. Looks at forgery and scholarship (his word for sophisticated methods of detection) over the centuries. Concludes that as the means of detection get more and more sophisticated, so does the work of the forgers—and vice versa.

Grebanier, Bernard. *The Great Shakespeare Forgery.* Norton 1965 o.p. About the William Henry Ireland forgeries of Shakespeare texts.

Hamilton, Charles. *Great Forgers and Famous Fakes: The Manuscript Forgers of America and How They Duped the Experts.* Crown Pub. Group 1980 o.p. An amusing and informative text by one of the country's premiere manuscript sellers and an authority on autographs.

―――. *Scribblers and Scoundrels.* Eriksson 1968 o.p. Another of Hamilton's chatty books about his dealings with forgers. Amusing and instructive.

Lindsey, Robert. *A Gathering of Saints: A True Story of Money, Murder and Deceit.* Dell 1990 $4.95. ISBN 0-440-20558-1. One of the accounts of Mark Hofmann's crimes and forgeries of Mormon documents. This and two other volumes (see the Naifeh and Sillitoe volumes) reveal, among other things, Hofmann's methods of forgery.

Myers, Robin, and Michael Harris. *Fakes and Frauds: Varieties of Deception in Print and Manuscript.* Omnigraphics Inc. 1989 $55.00. ISBN 0-906795-77-X. Seven essays on various forms of forgery, e.g., false statements in colophons, false and misleading imprints, piracies, forgery among scriveners, forged handwriting, and so on.

Naifeh, Steven, and Gregory White Smith. *The Mormon Murders: A True Story of Greed, Forgery, Deceit, and Death.* NAL-Dutton 1989 $5.95. ISBN 0-451-40152-2. One of the accounts of the forgeries and other crimes of Mark Hofmann, who fabricated many Mormon and other documents.

Partington, Wilfred. *Forging Ahead: The True Story of the Upward Progress of Thomas James Wise, Prince of Book Collectors, Bibliographer Extraordinary, and Otherwise.* Putnam Pub. Group 1939 o.p. An engaging biography of Wise, perhaps the most famous literary forger in history.

Sillitoe, Linda, and Allen D. Roberts. *Salamander: The Story of the Mormon Forgery Murders.* Signature Bks. 1990 $5.95. ISBN 0-941214-87-7. The third account of the Mormon forgeries of Mark Hofmann.

Taylor, W. Thomas. *Texfake: An Account of the Theft and Forgery of Early Texas Printed Documents*. W. T. Taylor 1991 $45.00. ISBN 0-935072-20-9. An authoritative and thorough account of this bookseller's discovery of the forgeries, his investigations into their provenance, and his testimony on their perpetrators. With a bibliography.

Todd, William B. *Suppressed Commentaries on The Wisean Forgeries: Addendum to an Enquiry*. U. of Tex. Pr. 1969 $15.00. ISBN 0-87959-052-1. Correspondence between Wise and others that shed light on his forgeries and his attempts to suppress the evidence against him.

————, ed. *Thomas J. Wise: Centenary Studies*. U. of Tex. Pr. 1959 o.p. Essays by John Carter, Graham Pollard, and William B. Todd, assessing new evidence on Wise's operations, identifying another forgery, discussing Wise's method of distribution of his forgeries and his association with H. Buxton Forman, and so on.

Whitehead, John. *This Solemn Mockery: The Art of Literary Forgery*. British Am. Books 1973 $22.50. ISBN 0-89979-044-5. Describes the careers of more than 20 literary forgers from ancient Assyria to the twentieth century. Very readable.

Wiegand, Wayne A. *The History of a Hoax: Edmund Lester Pearson, John Cotton Dana, and The Old Librarian's Almanack*. Beta Phi Mu 1979 o.p. An account of a literary hoax that involved well-known librarians.

BOOK INDUSTRY HISTORY

General and British

Bennett, Henry S. *English Books and Readers*. 3 vols. Cambridge U. Pr. 1969. Vol. 1 $75.00. ISBN 0-521-07609-9. Vol. 2 $89.95. ISBN 0-521-04153-8. Vol. 3 $49.50 ISBN 0-521-07701-X. History of books from Caxton to the eve of the Civil War.

Bonham-Carter, Victor. *Authors by Profession*. 2 vols. Kaufmann 1978–84 o.p. Called "the most readable and current economic history of authorship."

Bookselling in Britain: A Comprehensive Assessment of Bookselling in the U.K. Jordan & Sons 1989 $495.00. ISBN 0-85938-324-5

Briggs, Asa, ed. *Essays in the History of Publishing: In Celebration of the 250th Anniversary of the House of Longman*. Longman 1974 o.p. A handsome work; valuable historical articles, plus assessments of the future.

Carpenter, Kenneth E., ed. *Books and Society in History*. Bowker 1983 o.p. Eleven papers on different periods in history, European and American, exploring the role of the book. Given at the Association of College and Research Libraries pre-conference in June 1980.

Curwin, Henry. *A History of Booksellers: The Old and the New*. 1873. Gordon Pr. $59.95. ISBN 0-8490-0318-0. A seminal study of British bookselling.

Darnton, Robert. *The Business of the Enlightenment: A Publishing History of the "Encyclopédie," 1775–1800*. HUP 1979 $14.95. ISBN 0-674-08786-0. Archives found by the author made possible a massive study of the renowned French encyclopedia.

————. *The Literary Underground of the Old Regime*. HUP 1982 $20.00. ISBN 0-674-53656-8. A leading scholar of French publishing and printing history presents studies of prerevolutionary antiestablishment publishing, underground and in exile.

Darton, F. J. Harvey. *Children's Books in England: Five Centuries of Social Life*. Ed. by Brian Anderson. 1932. Cambridge U. Pr. 1982 $37.50. ISBN 0-521-24020-4. Illustrated scholarly material on John Newbery, Thomas Day, Peter Parley, and others.

Davenport, Cyril. *The Book: Its History and Development*. 1930. Gale 1977 $59.95. ISBN 0-8490-1528-6. The story prior to film composition and electronic data processing.

Diringer, David. *The Book before Printing: Ancient, Medieval, and Oriental*. Dover 1983 repr. of 1953 ed. $10.95. ISBN 0-486-24243-9. Long a standard work.

Fitch, Noel R. *Sylvia Beach and the Lost Generation: A History of Literary Paris in the Twenties and Thirties*. Norton 1983 $25.00. ISBN 0-393-01713-3. A comprehensive account of the personalities of the era and of Beach's shop, Shakespeare and Company.

Ford, Hugh D. *Published in Paris: American and British Writers, Printers and Publishers in Paris, 1920–1939*. Peter Smith 1992 $23.75. ISBN 0-8446-6488-X. The many aspects of a legendary era.

Greg, W. W. *Some Aspects and Problems of London Publishing between 1550 and 1650*. OUP 1956 o.p. Six lectures looking at how the Stationers' Company did business in its first century of operation. On the many regulations in the trade, copyright, the reliability of books' imprints, and other topics.

Kenney, E. J. *The Classical Text: Aspects of Editing in the Age of the Printed Book*. U. CA Pr. 1974 $40.00. ISBN 0-520-02711-6. Converting scribal editions of classical texts into printed form raised new editorial questions.

Kenyon, Frederic G. *Books and Readers in Ancient Greece and Rome*. Ares 1980 $15.00. ISBN 0-89005-340-5. Bookmaking and early publishing methods from the time of Homer, c.850 B.C., to A.D. 400.

Lehmann-Haupt, Hellmut. *The Life of the Book*. Greenwood 1975 repr. of 1957 ed. $38.50. ISBN 0-8371-8293-X. Addressed to young readers, but of general value.

Levarie, Norma. *The Art and History of Books*. Da Capo 1982 $24.50. ISBN 0-306-80181-7. Some emphasis on the book arts.

Norrie, Ian, ed. *Mumby's Publishing and Bookselling in the 20th Century*. Bowker 1982 o.p. Revised and enlarged from Edward A. Mumby's classic work, updating the story of the book trade (primarily British) from Roman times to 1980.

Pollard, M. *Dublin's Trade in Books, 1550–1800*. OUP 1989 $72.00. ISBN 0-19-818409-3. The first book to examine the Irish book trade apart from the English trade. Looks at the expansion of the trade, especially in the eighteenth century, and at Ireland's imports and exports of books.

Rostenberg, Leona. *English Publishers in the Graphic Arts, 1599–1700*. B. Franklin 1963 $23.50. ISBN 0-8337-3060-6

———. *Literary, Political, Scientific, Religious and Legal Publishing, Printing and Bookselling in England, 1551–1700*. 2 vols. B. Franklin 1963 o.p.

Taubert, Sigfred, ed. *The Book Trade of the World*. 4 vols. Bowker 1972–84 $70.00 ea. ISBN 0-317-11847-1. Country-by-country survey of bookselling and publishing today, reported by leading figures in the book industry.

Taylor, Isaac. *History of the Transmission of Ancient Books to Modern Times*. 1875. Haskell 1971 $75.00. ISBN 0-8383-1317-5. A century-old piece of scholarship, still valued.

Thompson, James Westfall, ed. and trans. *The Frankfort Book Fair (1574)*. B. Franklin 1968 $29.00. ISBN 0-8337-3519-5. Reprint of the Caxton Club's (Chicago) edition of 1911; fully and heavily illustrated account of the fair and its meaning in book-trade history.

Thwaite, Mary F. *From Primer to Pleasure in Reading*. Horn Bk. 1972 o.p. History of children's books in England from the invention of printing to 1914, with an outline of developments in Australia, North America, and Western Europe.

Winship, George Parker. *The Cambridge Press, 1638–1692*. *Essay Index Repr. Ser*. Ayer repr. of 1945 ed. o.p. A scholarly account of the beginnings of printing and bookmaking in Massachusetts.

Winterich, John T. *Early American Books and Printing*. Dover 1992 $37.00. ISBN 1-55888-965-5. Winterich was always painstaking in his scholarship—and irrepressible in his humor and his love of the illuminating fact.

Woodfield, Denis B. *Surreptitious Printing in England, 1550–1640*. Biblio. Soc. Amer. 1973 $17.50. ISBN 0-914930-04-4. Unauthorized, though not necessarily "underground," publishing of works in English, French, Italian, Spanish, and Dutch.

North American

Bader, Barbara. *American Picture Books: From Noah's Ark to the Beast Within*. Macmillan 1976 o.p. Beautifully color-reproduced pages of hundreds of children's books, with accounts of the significant writers, illustrators, and publishers of these books during a decisive 80-year period.

Belok, Michael V. *Forming the American Minds: Early School Books and Their Compilers, 1783–1837*. Heinemann Ed. 1973 o.p. Aims, contents, and editor-authors of school textbooks in the early U.S. Republic.

Bonn, Thomas L. *Under Cover: An Illustrated History of American Mass Market Paperbacks*. Viking Penguin 1982 o.p. Almost 200 illustrations, more than 100 in full color; relation of packaging to editorial and marketing decisions; roles of artist, art director; notes on top firms.

Charvat, William. *Literary Publishing in America, 1790–1850*. U. of Pa. Pr. 1959 o.p. Includes relation of publishing to early U.S. geography and transport.

Cole, John Y., ed. *Books in Action: The Armed Services Editions*. Lib. Congress 1984 $6.95. ISBN 0-8444-0466-9. Historical review of the World War II project in which publishers cooperated in issuing soft-cover editions of hundreds of current and standard titles, distributed free to service people.

Davis, Kenneth C. *Two-Bit Culture: The Paperbacking of America*. HM 1984 $18.95. ISBN 0-395-34398-4. Broad study of the mass-market paperback revolution, its origins, personalities, methods, and relation to authorship and reading.

Dennison, Sally. *Alternative Publishing: Five Modern Histories*. U. of Iowa Pr. 1984 o.p. How "small press" publishing established Eliot, Woolf, Joyce, Nin, and Nabokov.

Ford, Worthington. *The Boston Book Market, 1679–1700*. B. Franklin 1973 repr. of 1917 ed. $21.00. ISBN 0-8339-1181-4. A significant part of the story of early bookselling in the United States.

Hudak, Leona M. *Early American Women Printers and Publishers: 1639–1820*. Scarecrow 1978 o.p. Examines the role of women in the early development of the U.S. book industry.

Lehmann-Haupt, Hellmut, Lawrence C. Wroth, and Rollo G. Silver. *The Book in America: A History of the Making and Selling of Books in the United States*. 1939. Bowker rev. ed. 1951 o.p. The most detailed, comprehensive single volume on the subject.

Madison, Charles A. *Book Publishing in America*. McGraw 1966 o.p. Leading companies and personalities from 1630 to 1965.

———. *Irving to Irving: Author-Publisher Relations 1800–1974*. Bowker 1974 o.p. The love-hate relations between some U.S. writers and their publishers.

———. *Jewish Publishing in America*. Hebrew Pub. 1976 $15.00. ISBN 0-88482-902-2. History of leading companies, personalities, trends.

Meckler, Alan Marshall. *Micropublishing: A History of Scholarly Micropublishing in America, 1938–1980*. Greenwood 1982 $38.50. ISBN 0-313-23096-X. One aspect of publishing in the new age; an answer to the "knowledge explosion" and its deluge of paper.

Schick, Frank L. *The Paperbound Book in America*. Bks. Demand $70.00. ISBN 0-317-10717-8. A history up to the late 1950s; highly detailed; includes European backgrounds.

Sheehan, Donald. *This Was Publishing*. Ind. U. Pr. 1952 o.p. How U.S. publishing was conducted in "old line" houses, 1865–1915.

Stern, Madeleine B. *Books and Book People in 19th-Century America*. Bowker 1978 o.p. Includes a 75-year history of *Publishers Weekly*, 1872–1947; also many episodes and personalities in the book world.

———. *Imprints on History: Book Publishing and American Frontiers*. AMS Pr. 1976 repr. of 1956 ed. $31.50. ISBN 0-404-06261-X. Accounts of 16 publishing houses of different kinds, with notes on approximately 200 others.

———, ed. *Publishers for Mass Entertainment in Nineteenth-Century America*. G. K. Hall 1980 o.p. Accounts of almost 50 firms, their chief publications, personnel, changes in location, ownership, and programs.

Tebbel, John. *Between Covers: The Rise and Transformations of Book Publishing in America*. OUP 1987 $35.00. ISBN 0-19-504189-5. A single-volume edition of Tebbel's classic four-volume *History of Book Publishing in the United States*.

———. *A History of Book Publishing in the United States*. 4 vols. Bowker 1972–81 o.p. Era-by-era (1630–1980), highly detailed, readable; the publishers, the unfolding

developments, the economic and social environments, and the other parts of the
book industry.

Winterich, John T. *Early American Books and Printing*. Dover 1992 repr. of 1935 ed.
$37.00. ISBN 0-55888-965-5. Author was a bibliophile, historian, journalist, and a
coeditor of the *Colophon*.

BOOK INDUSTRY

Biographies of Persons, Companies, and Organizations

A great many of the biographies of people or units in the book industry are
printed in short-run scholarly editions, in editions for special circulation, or in
small trade editions that sell out and are not reprinted. Hence, many valuable
titles are soon out of print. However, since a number of these are in library
collections, we include some of these out-of-print titles in this section for the
benefit of those who would like to read these fascinating accounts.

ABINGDON PRESS

Pilkington, James Penn. *The Methodist Publishing House: A History*. Vol. 1 Abingdon 1968
o.p. This volume covers the first 100 years (to 1870) of the Methodist publishing
enterprises in the United States.

AMERICAN BOOKSELLERS ASSOCIATION

Anderson, Charles B., ed. *Bookselling in America and the World*. Random 1975 o.p.
History of the ABA, 1900–1975; lists and chronologies; articles on world bookselling;
American bookselling history to 1900.

D. APPLETON CO.

Wolfe, Gerard R. *The House of Appleton*. Scarecrow 1981 o.p. History of a once
prominent publisher, now a merged imprint.

ASSOCIATION OF BOOK TRAVELERS

Chaney, Beverley D., ed. *The First Hundred Years: Association of Book Travelers,
1884–1984*. Chaney 1984 o.p. History and memoirs of the publishers' traveling
representatives to the book trade in the United States.

BALLANTINE BOOKS, INC.

Aronovitz, David. *Ballantine Books: The First Decade*. Bailiwick Bks. 1987 $16.95. ISBN
0-317-67995-3

BANTAM BOOKS

Petersen, Clarence. *The Bantam Story: Twenty-Five Years of Paperback Publishing*.
Bantam 1970 o.p. A narrative that emphasizes Bantam but places the firm in context;
title list.

BEACH, SYLVIA

Beach, Sylvia. *Shakespeare and Company*. HarBraceJ 1959 o.p. The author's American
bookshop in Paris was the first publisher of *Ulysses* and a literary center of the 1920s.

BLACKWELLS

Norrington, A. L. P. *Blackwell's, 1879–1979: The History of a Family Firm*. Blackwell
Pubs. 1984 $20.00. ISBN 0-946344-00-0. The English companies—retailers, export-
ers, publishers—that evolved from the famous antiquarian bookshop in Oxford,
England.

R. R. BOWKER CO.

Fleming, E. McClung. *R. R. Bowker: Militant Liberal.* Bowker 1952 o.p. Life of the versatile journalist, New York political reformer, entrepreneur, and publisher, cofounder of *Publishers Weekly* (1872) and associated publications, who guided the firm until 1933.

CAMBRIDGE UNIVERSITY PRESS

Black, Michael H. *Cambridge University Press, 1584–1984.* Cambridge U. Pr. 1984 $49.95. ISBN 0-521-26473-1. Concise account of the evolution, through stresses and successes, of the first formally chartered university press (charter 1534, continuous publishing since 1584).

CANFIELD, CASS

Canfield, Cass. *Up and Down and Around: A Publisher Recollects the Time of His Life.* Harper's Mag. Pr. 1971 o.p. The author's career in book publishing; the statesmen, other public figures, and writers he knew; leadership at Harper.

CAPE, JONATHAN

Howard, Michael S. *Jonathan Cape: Publisher.* Merrimack 1980 o.p. A leading twentieth-century British publisher with close ties to the United States.

CAREY, MATTHEW

Bradsher, Earl L. *Matthew Carey, Editor, Author and Publisher.* AMS Pr. repr. of 1912 ed. $12.00. ISBN 0-404-00969-7. Basic study of the U.S. book-trade pioneer in the early years of the Republic.

CERF, BENNETT A.

Cerf, Bennett A. *At Random: The Reminiscences of Bennett Cerf.* Random 1977 $16.95. ISBN 0-394-47877-0. Edited by the late publisher's wife and associates; colorful memoirs from written and oral records.

COCKERELL, SIR SYDNEY CARLYLE

Blunt, Wilfrid. *Cockerell.* Knopf 1965 o.p. Cockerell (1867–1962) was associated with famous literary and artistic figures, worked with William Morris, Emery Walker, and others in the important private presses—Kelmscott, Doves, and Ashendene.

COLUMBIA UNIVERSITY PRESS

Wiggins, Henry H. *Columbia University Press, 1893–1983.* Col. U. Pr. 1983 o.p. History and analysis of one of the two or three largest university presses in the United States.

COMMINS, SAXE

Commins, Dorothy. *What Is an Editor? Saxe Commins at Work.* U. Ch. Pr. 1978 $5.95. ISBN 0-226-11428-7. How the great Random House editor worked with O'Neill, Faulkner, Irwin Shaw, and others.

CURLL, EDMUND

Straus, Ralph. *The Unspeakable Curll: Being Some Account of Edmund Curll, Bookseller, To Which Is Added a Full List of His Books.* Kelley 1970 o.p. An engaging text about the piracies and other publishing tricks of the eighteenth-century printer/publisher. One of Alexander Pope's enemies.

CURWEN PRESS

A Spirit of Joy: Notes From an Exhibition of Books, Periodicals and Ephemera Printed at the Curwen Press During Its Heyday, 1916–1956. Alta Pr. 1990 $15.00. ISBN 0-88864-

760-3. Striking catalog with a brief history of the press, good descriptions of the items exhibited, and many illustrations.

DAIGH, RALPH

Daigh, Ralph. *Maybe You Should Write a Book*. P-H 1979 $7.95. ISBN 0-13-566372-5. Cheerfully scrappy memoirs of mass-market publishing and advice on authorship.

DELL PUBLISHING COMPANY

Lyles, William H. *Putting Dell on the Map: A History of Dell Paperbacks*. Greenwood 1983 $47.95. ISBN 0-313-23666-4. One of the most successful mass-market publishers.
_____, comp. *Dell Paperbacks, 1942 to Mid–1962: A Catalog-Index*. Greenwood 1983 $55.00. ISBN 0-313-23668-2. A comprehensive catalogue-index of Dell paperbacks published during the years indicated; useful for collectors, readers, and researchers.

DORAN, GEORGE H.

Doran, George H. *Chronicles of Barabbas, 1884–1934*. H. Holt & Co. 1952 o.p. The well-told story of the pains and pleasures of publishing, full of interesting anecdotes of a brilliant period.

GOLLANCZ, VICTOR

Hodge, Sheila, *Gollancz: The Story of a Publishing House, 1928–1978*. Random 1978 o.p. The brilliant, innovative, left-liberal Victor Gollancz and his successful career in British publishing.

GOODSPEED, CHARLES E.

Goodspeed, Charles E. *Yankee Bookseller*. Greenwood 1974 repr. of 1937 ed. o.p. A legend in modern times: Goodspeed's Bookshop, Boston, and its proprietor.

HALDEMAN, E. JULIUS

Haldeman, E. Julius. *The First Hundred Million*. Ayer 1975 $24.00. ISBN 0-405-06377-6. The maverick publishing effort that produced hundreds of titles in vest-pocket-sized, center-stapled "Little Blue Books."
Hamady, Walter S. *Two Decades of Hamady and the Perishable Press Limited . . .* Perishable Pr. 1984 $15.00. ISBN 0-318-03765-3. A splendid, lavishly illustrated retrospective catalog.

HARLEQUIN BOOKS

Harlequin's 30th Anniversary, 1949–1979. Harlequin Bks. 1979 o.p. House history; a mass-market paperback publisher's shift from general books to an all-out romance publishing program.

HARPER & ROW

Exman, Eugene. *The Brothers Harper, 1817–1853*. Harper 1965 o.p. How the Harpers established their famous house; methods of promotion and sale; relations with U.S. and British writers; printing practices; business ventures and profits.
_____. *The House of Harper: One Hundred and Fifty Years of Publishing*. HarpC 1967 $15.95. ISBN 0-06-011201-8. A broad portrait of the firm and its people, candid about failures and foibles, entertainingly written. (See also Cass Canfield.)

HAYDN, HIRAM

Haydn, Hiram. *Words and Faces*. Harcourt 1974 o.p. Outspoken memoirs of the author and editor at Bobbs-Merrill, Harcourt, and Atheneum.

THE HOGARTH PRESS

Woolf, Leonard. *Beginning Again*. Peter Smith 1992 $19.75. ISBN 0-8446-6515-0

————. *Downhill All the Way: An Autobiography, 1919–1939*. Peter Smith 1972 $19.75. ISBN 0-8446-6516-9. The writer describes the private press operated by himself and his wife, the essayist and novelist Virginia Woolf; their life together; his work as publisher, editor, writer, and political worker; and the Woolfs' literary and artistic circle.

HOLT, RINEHART & WINSTON

Madison, Charles A. *The Owl among Colophons: Henry Holt as Publisher and Editor*. H. Holt & Co. 1966 o.p. A short account by a former head of Holt's college department.

HOUGHTON MIFFLIN COMPANY

Ballou, Ellen B. *The Building of the House: Houghton Mifflin's First Half Century*. HM 1970 $12.95. ISBN 0-395-07383-9. Achievements and failures of a major publishing firm up to 1921; includes printing-plant and design development, mergers, trade publishing, and the *Atlantic Monthly*.

HUBBARD, ELBERT

Champney, Freeman. *Art and Glory: The Story of Elbert Hubbard*. Crown Pub. Group 1968 o.p. Life of the turn-of-the-century publisher, populist, and arts-and-crafts proponent.

JOHNSTON, EDWARD

Johnston, Priscilla. *Edward Johnston*. Pentalic 1976 $7.95. ISBN 0-8008-2367-2. A full-scale personal and artistic biography of the great English calligrapher, type designer, and teacher, by one of his daughters.

KNOPF, ALFRED A.

Portrait of a Publisher, 1915–1965. Ed. by Paul A. Bennett. 2 vols. Knopf 1965 o.p. Essays by dozens of well-known book people; many fine photos. Worth seeking out.

KRAUS, HANS PETER

Kraus, Hans Peter. *A Rare Book Saga: The Autobiography of H. P. Kraus*. Putnam Pub. Group 1978 o.p. Kraus, a refugee from Nazi Vienna, founded in New York an outstanding book and manuscript business that is also involved in related services and publishing.

LANE, ALLEN

Morpurgo, J. E. *Allen Lane, King Penguin: A Biography*. Methuen 1980 o.p. More than any other individual, Lane showed what could be done with pocket-sized paperback reprints of quality; scholarly and witty career of a modern pioneer.

LIVERIGHT, HORACE

Gilmer, Walker. *Horace Liveright: Publisher of the Twenties*. David Lewis 1970 o.p. The short, brilliant career of a publisher who brought out important new writers.

LUSTY, ROBERT

Lusty, Robert. *Bound to Be Read*. Doubleday 1976 o.p. Memoirs of a leading contemporary English publisher, executive with Hutchinson and Michael Joseph, with close ties to the United States.

MARION PRESS

Larremore, Thomas A., and Amy Hopkins. *The Marion Press: A Survey and a Checklist*. Oak Knoll 1981 repr. of 1943 ed. $35.00. ISBN 0-938768-04-2

MASSEE, MAY

Hodowanec, George V., ed. *The May Massee Collection: Creative Publishing for Children, 1923–1963*. Emporia State 1979 $25.00. ISBN 0-686-25585-2. The famous Viking

Press editor's complete files are on view and form the center of a research collection at Emporia.

McGraw-Hill

Burlingame, Roger. *Endless Frontiers: The Story of McGraw-Hill*. McGraw 1959 o.p. A detailed record of the firm's role in the expansion of U.S. scientific and technical book publishing.

Meynell, Sir Francis: The Nonesuch Press

Dreyfus, John. *A History of the Nonesuch Press: With an Introduction by Geoffrey Keynes and a Descriptive Catalogue by David McKittrick, Susan Randall, and John Dreyfuss*. Nonesuch 1981 o.p. Meynell's distinguished, commercial, fine press.

Meynell, Francis. *My Lives*. Random 1971 o.p. A twentieth-century Renaissance man—poet, journalist, publisher, industrialist, radical, book designer, founder of the Nonesuch Press in London.

Oxford University Press

Barker, Nicolas. *The Oxford University Press and the Spread of Learning: An Illustrated History*. OUP 1978 $35.00. ISBN 0-19-951086-5. Oversize; 64-page historical review, 236 pages of plates. Issued in connection with the five-hundredth anniversary of printing in Oxford.

Sutcliffe, Peter. *The Oxford University Press: An Informal History*. OUP 1978 $24.95. ISBN 0-19-951084-9. Pleasant reading, but detailed; reviews struggles from the first press in the city of Oxford in 1478, but concentrates on the university press itself since 1860.

Perkins, Maxwell E.

Berg, A. Scott. *Maxwell Perkins: Editor of Genius*. NAL-Dutton 1978 o.p. The famed Scribner editor of Wolfe, Fitzgerald, Hemingway, and others.

Princeton University Press

Darrow, Whitney, and Herbert S. Bailey, Jr. *Princeton University Press, 1905–1980*. Princeton U. Pr. 1980 o.p. Founding and growth of one of the leading scholarly presses.

Regnery, Henry

Regnery, Henry. *Memoirs of a Dissident Publisher*. Regnery Gateway 1979 $12.95. ISBN 0-89526-752-7. Experiences and views of a general publisher and political conservative.

Reynolds, Paul R.

Reynolds, Paul R. *Middle Man: The Adventures of a Literary Agent*. Morrow 1972 o.p. The author represented many of the recent era's outstanding authors.

Rosenbach, A. S. W.

Wolf, Edwin, II, and John F. Fleming. *Rosenbach: A Biography*. World Publishing 1960 o.p. Founded in 1903, the firm gave new status to the entire rare book and manuscript business as an aid to important collections and literary scholarship.

Scholastic

Lippert, Jack E. *Scholastic: A Publishing Adventure*. Scholastic Inc. o.p. Maurice ("Robbie") Robinson and the innovative educational program of schoolroom periodicals, books, and other materials that he built; by his partner.

CHARLES SCRIBNER'S SONS

Burlingame, Roger. *Of Making Many Books: A Hundred Years of Writing and Publishing.* Scribner 1971 repr. of 1948 ed. o.p. A great publisher and his role in U.S. literature; correspondence with authors. (See also Maxwell E. Perkins.)

SIMON & SCHUSTER

Schwed, Peter. *Turning the Pages: An Insider's Story of Simon & Schuster, 1924–1984.* Macmillan 1984 o.p. Cheerful, candid account of perhaps the most colorful and successful of the publishing houses that grew out of the turbulent 1920s into the corporate 1980s.

STELOFF, FRANCES

Rogers, W. G. *Wise Men Fish Here: The Story of Frances Steloff and the Gotham Book Mart.* HarBraceJ 1965 o.p. Still regarded by many as the prototype of "a real bookshop," Frances Steloff's enterprise has been identified with the forward trends in U.S. writing since 1920.

THE STINEHOUR PRESS

Farrell, David, comp. *The Stinehour Press: A Bibliographical Checklist of the First Thirty Years.* Meriden-Stinehour Pr. 1988 $60.00. ISBN 0-87792-009-5. With an introduction by Roderick Stinehour. Offers information on the founding and output of this press, whose printed work, primarily done letterpress, has won many awards. The checklist contains 1,006 entries plus a list of serials printed at the press.

TARG, WILLIAM

Targ, William. *Indecent Pleasures.* Macmillan 1975 o.p. A leading trade-book editor, publisher, and bibliophile offers short, incisive pieces on books.

THOMAS, ISAIAH

Nichols, Charles Lemuel. *Isaiah Thomas: Printer, Writer and Collector.* B. Franklin 1971 repr. of 1912 ed. o.p. Work of the leading U.S. bookman of the revolutionary period and after; includes a bibliography of books he produced. First issued by Boston's Club of Odd Volumes.

TICKNOR & FIELDS

Tryon, Warren S. *Parnassus Corner: A Life of James T. Fields, Publisher to the Victorians.* HM 1963 o.p. Account of one of the most outstanding New England publishers in the decades after 1854.

TONSON, JACOB

Geduld, Harry M. *Prince of Publishers: A Study of the Work and Career of Jacob Tonson.* Bks. Demand repr. of 1969 ed. $65.00. ISBN 0-317-10301-6. London publishers (all three with the same name—1655–1736; 1682–1735; 1713–1753); literary publishers, owning rights to all the major contemporary authors.

UNIVERSITY OF CALIFORNIA PRESS

Frugé, August. *A. F.: Reflections from a Publishing Career—Prepared by His Staff and Friends. . . .* U. CA Pr. 1977 o.p. Made up mostly of 89 pages of writings on scholarly publishing by the director of the press on the occasion of his retirement.

UNIVERSITY OF NORTH CAROLINA PRESS

A Statesman of the Republic of Books. U. of NC Pr. 1970 o.p. Prepared by the staff of the press; includes statements by and in honor of Lambert Davis upon his retirement as director.

The Unwins

Unwin, Philip. *The Publishing Unwins*. Heinemann Ed. 1972 o.p. Saga of the English publishing family and its leading members since early in the nineteenth century.

Unwin, Sir Stanley. *The Truth about a Publisher*. Bowker 1960 o.p. The sprightly English bookman was active until he died at 83. His autobiography gives a lively picture of his youth and his long professional career, the writers and other publishers he encountered, and his battles for copyright and the book trade.

The Ward Ritchie Press

Ritchie, Ward. *The Ward Ritchie Press and Anderson, Ritchie & Simon*. Ward Ritchie 1961 o.p. Outstanding among the fine commercial printers and publishers for which California is known.

Jazzar, Bernard N., and Wendy M. Mayfield. *Ward Ritchie: The Lagune Verde Imprenta Years, 1975–1990*. CSU 1991. ISBN 0-936270-31-4

Warne, Frederick K.

King, Arthur, and A. R. Stuart. *The House of Warne: One Hundred Years of Publishing*. Warne 1965 o.p. Publisher of Kate Greenaway, Randolph Caldecott, Beatrix Potter, and many more makers of children's books.

Weems, Mason Locke

Leary, Lewis. *The Book-eddling Person: An Account of the Life of Mason Locke Weems. . . .* Algonquin Bks. 1984 $15.95. ISBN 0-912697-09-1. Readable biography of the publisher, bookseller, author who invented the story of George Washington's cherry tree.

Weybright, Victor

Weybright, Victor. *The Making of a Publisher: A Life in the 20th-Century Book Revolution*. Morrow 1967 o.p. The beginning of the New American Library, growth and conflict; founding of Weybright & Talley.

John Wiley & Sons

The First One Hundred and Fifty Years: A History of John Wiley and Sons, Incorporated, 1807–1957. Wiley 1957 o.p. A collection of 28 essays by different authors on various aspects of the company's history.

Moore, John Hammond. *Wiley: 175 Years of Publishing*. Wiley o.p. The growth of a leading publisher of science, technology, business, and college books; authors, company leaders, world connections.

H. W. Wilson Co.

Lawler, John Lawrence. *H. W. Wilson Company: Half a Century of Bibliographic Publishing*. Ed. by Lee Ash. 1950. Gregg Intl. 1972 o.p. Ingenious and persistent, Wilson systematically built a complex of major services for libraries, schools, and the book industry.

Education and Operations

Alexander, E. Curtis, ed. *How to Publish and Market Your Own Book as an Independent Black Publisher*. E.C.A. Associates 1988 $14.95. ISBN 0-938818-09-0.

American Booksellers Association, ed. *A Manual on Bookselling: How to Open and Run Your Own Bookstore*. Crown Pub. Group 1987 $16.95. ISBN 0-517-56648-6. The definitive how-to-book.

Andersen, Arthur, and Company. *Book Distribution in the United States: Issues and Perspectives*. Bk. Indus. Study 1982 $60.00. ISBN 0-940016-12-5. Tables, analysis.

Appelbaum, Judith, and Nancy Evans. *How to Get Happily Published: A Complete and Candid Guide*. NAL-Dutton 1982 $8.95. ISBN 0-452-26125-2. Practical guide for the author, about publishers and about successful relations with them.

Association of American Publishers. *AAP Industry Statistics*. AAP annual. For members of the AAP.

———. *Professional and Reference Books: A Guide for Booksellers*. AAP 1983. Prepared by the Marketing Committee of the AAP's Professional and Scholarly Publishing Division. Includes advice on stocking and selling books in these areas.

———. *Survey of Compensation and Personnel Practices in the Publishing Industry*. AAP 1984 $195.00. Available only to AAP members.

Association of American University Presses, ed. *One Book, Five Ways: Procedures of Five University Presses*. Kaufmann 1978 o.p. The memos, forms, and specifications that each one of five publishers would use in the process of publishing the same book, from manuscript to sales plan.

An Author's Primer to Word Processing. AAP 1984 o.p. New technology and the writer.

Bailey, Herbert S., Jr. *The Art and Science of Book Publishing*. U. of Tex. Pr. 1990 $14.95. ISBN 0-8214-0970-0. By the director of Princeton University Press. Financial management for a creative industry; addressed to students and actual or aspiring managers.

Belkin, Gary S. *Getting Published: A Guide for Business People and Other Professionals*. Wiley 1983 o.p. Includes special problems of special fields.

Bermont, Hubert. *The Handbook of Association Publishing*. Bermont 1978 o.p. Publishing for institutional purposes, more than for general commercial reasons.

Bernstein, Leonard S. *Getting Published: The Writer in the Combat Zone*. Morrow 1986 $7.95. ISBN 0-688-06423-X. Discusses the challenges of getting published in a competitive market.

Blissett, William, ed. *Editing Illustrated Books*. AMS Pr. 1987 $29.50. ISBN 0-404-63665-9. Scholarly papers on historical and current practice, given at a conference at the University of Toronto in 1979.

Bliven, Bruce, Jr. *Book Traveler*. Dodd 1975 o.p. The daily work of George Scheer, well-known publishers' sales representative to booksellers. A *New Yorker* profile.

Bodian, Nat G. *Bodian's Publishing Desk Reference: A Comprehensive Dictionary of Practices & Techniques for Book & Journal Marketing & Bookselling*. Oryx Pr. 1988 $49.50. ISBN 0-89774-454-3. A dictionary of 4,000 definitions and 18 appendixes with tips for book marketers.

———. *The Book Marketing Handbook*. 2 vols. Bowker 1980–83 $64.95 ea. ISBNs 0-8352-1286-6, 0-8352-1685-3. Hundreds of short segments on techniques of promoting and selling scientific, technical, and other professional books and journals by many channels.

———. *Copywriter's Handbook*. ISI Pr. 1984 $29.95. ISBN 0-89495-040-1. Writing the advertising and sales promotion material for scholarly and other specialized books and journals.

———. *How to Choose a Winning Title: A Guide for Writers, Editors & Publishers*. Oryx Pr. 1989 $25.00. ISBN 0-89774-540-X. Informative guide to chosing an appropriate title for a book.

Cain, Michael Scott. *An Intelligence Guide to Book Distribution*. Dustbooks 1981 o.p. Especially pertinent to small operations.

Carter, Robert A., ed. *Trade Book Marketing*. Bowker 1983 $29.95. ISBN 0-8352-1693-4. Comprehensive, including the marketing environment, relations with editors, retailing of hardcover and paperback books, rights, advertisements, publicity, and more.

Children's Book Council Staff. *Illustrating Children's Books*. Child. Bk. Coun. o.p. Including a selection of related titles.

———. *Writing Books for Children and Young People*. Child. Bk. Coun. o.p. Including selective lists of other sources.

Clifton, Merritt. *Help! For Small Press People*. Samisdat 1985 $5.00. ISBN 0-317-16911-4

Congrat-Butlar, Stefan, comp. *Translation and Translators.* Bowker 1979 o.p. Background and growth of translated books, the structure of the field, and lists of translators and their markets.

Curtis, Richard. *How to Be Your Own Literary Agent.* HM 1984 $10.70. ISBN 0-395-36142-7. A subject not often covered at length.

Dessauer, John P. *Book Industry Trends.* Bowker 1985 o.p. Analysis and voluminous tabulations of book-publishing data; includes charts, graphs, and tables that publishers, librarians, and so on, can use to forecast their future growth.

_____. *Book Publishing: A Basic Introduction.* Continuum 1989 $24.95. ISBN 0-8264-0446-4. Revised, expanded edition of Dessauer's *Book Publishing: What It Is, What It Does;* an excellent book documenting the general history of the book-publishing industry and the various book-publishing processes.

_____. *Book Publishing: What It Is, What It Does.* Bowker 1981 o.p. Concise but full instruction on every step in book publishing and each of its major divisions.

DuBoff, Leonard D. *Book Publishers' Legal Guide.* Rothman 2nd rev. ed. 1992 $65.00. ISBN 0-8377-0559-2. Important basic information.

Duke, Judith S. *Religious Publishing and Communication.* Knowledge Indus. 1980 o.p. One of several area surveys; books are included.

_____. *The Technical, Scientific and Medical Publishing Market.* Knowledge Indus. 1984 o.p. Survey of a vast field that is actually not one field, but many.

Geiser, Elizabeth, and Arnold Dolin, eds. *The Business of Book Publishing.* Westview 1985 $76.00. ISBN 0-89158-998-8. Chapters by 31 contributors describe the successive functions and the different areas of the industry.

Glenn, Peggy. *Publicity for Books and Authors: A Do-It-Yourself Manual for Small Publishing Firms and Enterprising Authors.* Aames-Allen 1984 $16.95. ISBN 0-9369-30-92-6. A comprehensive review.

Grannis, Chandler B., ed. *What Happens in Book Publishing.* Bks. Demand 1967 $128.00. ISBN 0-7837-0435-6. Twenty chapters, by specialists, on the functions and principal branches of publishing.

Greenfeld, Howard. *Books: From Writer to Reader.* Crown Pub. Group 1976 o.p. The successive steps in general book publishing, with useful illustrations; for young and adult readers.

Guidelines for Bias-Free Publishing. McGraw 1983. ISBN 0-07-045033-1. For editors, writers, and others.

Harman, Eleanor, and Ian Montagnes, eds. *The Thesis and the Book.* U. of Toronto Pr. 1976 $12.95. ISBN 0-8020-6293-8. Describes the work required to make a publishable book out of a thesis.

Henderson, Bill, ed. *The Publish-It-Yourself Handbook: Literary Tradition and How To.* Pushcart Pr. 1987 $11.95. ISBN 0-916366-44-8. Accounts by writers who have produced and sold their own books without resorting to vanity publishers. Some literary history.

Hill, Mary, and Wendell Cochran. *Into Print: A Practical Guide to Writing, Illustrating, and Publishing.* W. Kaufmann 1977 o.p. Relations among author, publisher, and illustrator.

Holt, Robert Lawrence. *Publishing: A Complete Guide for Schools, Small Presses and Entrepreneurs.* CA Health Pubns. 1982 o.p. Writing, editing, design, producing, selling, with an antivanity emphasis.

_____. *How to Publish, Promote, and Sell Your Own Book.* St. Martin 1986 $8.95. ISBN 0-312-39619-8

Horn, David. *Boards and Buckram.* U. Pr. of New Eng. 1980 o.p. Entertaining but seriously intended essays on the operations, author relations, and markets of the scholarly press.

Huenefeld, John. *The Huenefeld Guide to Book Publishing.* Mills Sanderson 1990 $29.95. ISBN 0-938179-17-9. The author and his firm are leading advisers and producers of business information for new and small publishers.

Huenefeld, John, and Virginia Wiley. *Planning and Control Guides and Forms: For Small Book Publishers.* Huenefeld o.p. Management tools.

Hyde, Sidney T., ed. *Selling the Book: A Bookshop Promotion Manual*. Shoe String 1977 o.p. A variety of materials.

Marsh, Carole. *Self Publishing By the Seat of Your Pants!* Gallopade Pub. Group 1989 $19.95. ISBN 1-55609-962-2

Meyer, Carol. *Writer's Survival Manual: The Complete Guide to Getting Your Book Published Right*. Bantam 1984 $4.50. ISBN 0-553-26376-5. Comprehensive.

Poets and Writers Newsletter (CODA), eds. *The Writing Business: A Poets and Writers Handbook*. Poets and Writers 1985 $11.95. ISBN 0-913734-19-5. Details about book contracts, small-press publishing, and earning by writing.

Poynter, Dan. *The Self-Publishing Manual: How to Write, Print and Sell Your Own Book*. Para 1991 $19.95. ISBN 0-915516-74-8. Covers a lot of ground.

Reynolds, Paul R. *The Writing and Selling of Fiction*. Morrow 1980 rev. ed. o.p. A famous literary agent's experience regarding relations among agent, author, and publisher.

Seuling, Barbara. *How to Write a Children's Book and Get It Published*. Macmillan rev. ed. 1991 $12.95. ISBN 0-684-19343-4. A successful author and editor describes the writing, illustrating, placing, and publishing of children's books.

Smith, Datus C., Jr. *Economics of Book Publishing in Developing Countries*. UNIPUB 1977 $5.00. ISBN 92-3-101422-6. Problems and prospects, incisively summed up by the former head of Franklin Book Programs, a technical assistance agency.

Smith, Roger H. *Paperback Parnassus*. Westview 1976 o.p. Details of the mass-market paperback industry and its intricate distribution system.

Stainton, Elsie Myers. *Author and Editor at Work: Making a Better Book*. U. of Toronto Pr. 1981 $7.95. ISBN 0-8020-6449-3. Advice to authors and editors about their own crafts and their relations with each other.

———. *The Fine Art of Copyediting*. Col. U. Pr. 1992 $25.00. ISBN 0-231-06960-X. Guide to editing procedures for trade, scholarly, text, professional, and reference books and for journals.

To Be a Publisher: A Handbook on Some Principles and Programs of Book Publishing Education. AAP 1979 o.p. Organizing education for, in, and about book publishing. Prepared by the AAP's former Education for Publishing Committee.

Ward, Audrey, and Philip Ward. *The Small Publisher: A Manual and Case Histories*. Oleander Pr. 1979 $35.00. ISBN 0-900-891-59-9. One of the service guides for the small-press movement.

White, Ken. *Bookstore Planning and Design*. McGraw 1982 o.p. White, architect and designer for business, has specialized in bookstores.

The World of Translations. Pen Amer. Ctr. 1971 o.p. Thirty-nine conference papers on world problems of translating literary manuscripts and materials.

Trends, Issues, Commentary

Altbach, Philip G., and Sheila McVey, eds. *Perspectives on Publishing*. Lexington Bks. 1976 o.p. A full issue of the *Annals of the American Academy of Political and Social Sciences*. U.S. and world trends in book publishing.

Altbach, Philip G., and Eva Marie Rathgeber. *Publishing in the Third World: Trend Report and Bibliography*. Greenwood 1980 o.p. The varied status of publishing in the different countries of Africa, Asia, and Latin America.

Altbach, Philip G., and others, eds. *Publishing in the Third World: Knowledge and Development*. Heinemann Ed. 1985 $35.00. ISBN 0-435-08006-7

Benjamin, Curtis G. *A Candid Critique of Book Publishing*. Bowker 1977 o.p. Provocative views and recommendations on book industry practice by the late head of McGraw-Hill.

———. *U.S. Books Abroad: Neglected Ambassadors*. Lib. Congress 1982. U.S. book export trends, previous aid programs, proposals for improvement, and growth. Has influenced policy.

Bernstein, Robert, and others. *Book Publishing in the U.S.S.R.: Reports of the Delegations of U.S. Book Publishers Visiting the U.S.S.R., 1962 and 1970*. HUP 1972 $6.95. ISBN

0-674-07874-8. After these discussions, the U.S.S.R. acceded to international copyright and began paying royalties directly to foreigners.

Book Industry Study Group Special Reports:

Lambert, Douglas M. *Physical Distribution: A Profit Opportunity for Printers, Publishers, and Their Customers.* Bowker 1982 o.p.

Noble, J. Kendrick, Jr. *Trends in Textbook Markets 1984.* Bowker 1984 o.p. Examines various textbook markets.

Boorstin, Daniel. *Books in Our Future: A Report from the Librarian of Congress to the Congress.* USGPO 1984 o.p. Analysis of the present condition of reading and books, and recommendations to combat illiteracy and aliteracy.

Bowker Lectures on Book Publishing. Bowker 1957 o.p. Memorial series of 17 lectures from 1934–57.

Bowker (R. R.) Memorial Lectures. Bowker 2nd series 1973–82 o.p. Contains the following individual titles: Harriet F. Pilpel, *Obscenity and the Constitution*; Barbara A. Ringer, *The Demonology of Copyright*; Frances E. Henne, *The Library World and the Publishing of Children's Books*; Samuel S. Vaughan, *Medium Rare: A Look at the Book and Its People*; Herbert S. Bailey, Jr., *The Traditional Book in the Electronic Age*; Peter Mayer, *The Spirit of the Enterprise*; Richard De Gennaro, *Research Libraries Enter the Information Age*; Oscar Dystel, *Mass-Market Publishing*; Robert Giroux, *The Education of an Editor*; Lowell A. Martin, *The Public Library: Middle-Age Crisis or Old Age.*

Cheney, O. H. *Economic Survey of the Book Industry 1930–1931.* 1931. Bowker 1960 o.p. Still cited. Introduction by Robert W. Frase.

Cole, John Y., ed. *The Audience for Children's Books.* Viewpoint Ser. Lib. Congress 1980 o.p. Symposium on ways and means of bringing books to children.

———. *Books in Our Future: Perspectives and Proposals.* Lib. Congress 1987 $16.00. ISBN 0-8444-0554-X. Presents various views by members of the Library of Congress project on the forecasts for future books, reading, and electronic publishing.

———. *The International Flow of Information: A Trans-Pacific Perspective.* Viewpoint Ser. Lib. Congress 1981 o.p. Record of a useful symposium.

———. *Responsibilities of the American Book Community.* Lib. Congress 1981 o.p. Papers from two seminars on financial concentration and related issues in publishing and bookselling.

———. *Television, the Book, and the Classroom.* Lib. Congress 1978 $4.95. ISBN 0-8444-0303-2. Papers by Mortimer J. Adler, Frank Stanton, and other experts.

Cole, John Y., and Thomas G. Sticht, eds. *The Textbook in American Society.* Lib. Congress 1982 $5.95. ISBN 0-8444-0355-5. Papers by 18 educators, writers, critics, and publishers.

Coser, Lewis A., Charles Kadushin, and Walter Powell. *Books: The Culture and Commerce of Publishing.* U. Ch. Pr. 1985 $16.95. ISBN 0-226-11593-3. Three sociologists deeply probe social and business forces affecting trade, college, and scholarly publishing. Lively and provocative.

Davison, Peter, and others, eds. *Bookselling, Reviewing and Reading.* Chadwyck-Healey 1978 $90.00. ISBN 0-85964-047-7. Selections on the book trade and its customers.

Fitzgerald, Frances. *America Revised: History Schoolbooks in the Twentieth Century.* Random 1980 $3.95. ISBN 0-394-74439-X. Analysis and strong criticism of bland, inadequate contemporary texts and the policies that produce them.

Graubard, Stephen, ed. *Reading in the 1980s.* Bowker o.p. The state of reading, the book industry, technology, criticism, and prospects for change: 18 essays, all but one from the winter 1983 issue of *Daedalus* (American Academy of Arts and Sciences). (See also Roger H. Smith.)

Gross, Gerald, ed. *Editors on Editing.* Putnam Pub. Group. 1962 o.p. Still valuable; 25 pieces by editors in different fields.

———. *Publishers on Publishing.* Putnam Pub. Group. 1961 o.p. In all, 36 selections from publishers' writings.

Henderson, Bill, ed. *The Art of Literary Publishing: Editors on Their Craft.* Pushcart Pr. 1980 $15.00. ISBN 0-916-366-05-7. Articles and statements by distinguished contemporary book editors.

Jovanovich, William. *Now Barabbas.* HarpC 1964 o.p. Essays on publishers' and editors' relations with authors and others.

Kazin, Alfred, Dan M. Lacy, and Ernest L. Boyer. *The State of the Book World. Viewpoint Ser.* Lib. Congress 1981 o.p. Papers on criticism, books in the future, books and schools.

Kefauver, Weldon A., ed. *Scholars and Their Publishers.* Modern Lang. 1977 $10.00. ISBN 0-87352-005-X. A report by a university press director.

Kerr, Chester. *A Report on American University Presses.* 1949. Assn. Am. Univ. o.p. A landmark study, still consulted. Worth seeking out.

Kobrak, Fred and Beth Luey, eds. *The Structure of International Publishing in the 1990s.* Transaction 1991 $22.95. ISBN 0-65000-568-8

Kujoth, Jean S., ed. *Publishing: Inside Views.* Scarecrow 1981 o.p. Fifty articles by expert observers on issues and trends of the 1960s.

L'Engle, Madeleine. *Dare to Be Creative.* Lib. Congress 1984 o.p. Lecture cosponsored by the library's Center for the Book and Children's Literature Center. Eloquent plea for integrity and freedom in the writing and publishing of children's books.

Machlup, Fritz, and Kenneth W. Leeson. *Information through the Printed Word: The Dissemination of Scholarly, Scientific and Intellectual Knowledge.* 4 vols. Greenwood. Vol. 1 *Book Publishing.* 1978 $49.95. ISBN 0-275-90301-X. Vol. 2 *Journals.* 1928 $49.95. ISBN 0-275-90302-8. Vol. 3 *Libraries.* 1978 $45.00. ISBN 0-275-90303-6. Vol. 4 *Books, Journals, and Bibliographic Services.* 1980 $55.00. ISBN 0-275-90516-0. Massive research, facts, and figures.

National Enquiry into Scholarly Communication. *Scholarly Communication: The Report of the National Enquiry.* Johns Hopkins 1979 $25.00. ISBN 0-8018-2267-X. Result of a major collaboration among leading scholarly, library, and publishing groups concerning the dissemination of the great masses of scholarly work now being produced. Includes recommendations.

Nemeyer, Carol A. *Scholarly Reprint Publishing in the United States.* Bowker 1972 o.p. Description and analysis of a major publishing phenomenon, now past its peak but still important.

Peattie, Noel. *A Passage for Dissent: The Best of SIPAPU, 1970–1988.* McFarland 1989 $35.00. ISBN 0-89950-399-3. Reprints from the magazine *SIPAPU*, the courageous review and interview journal for librarians. Covers small-press journals, monographs, the publishing process, and intellectual freedom from the standpoint of social responsibility.

Shatzkin, Leonard. *In Cold Type: Overcoming the Book Crisis.* HM 1983 o.p. Analyses and exhortations on the marketing and other functions of book publishers.

Smith, Roger H., ed. *The American Reading Public: What It Reads, Why It Reads.* Bowker 1963 o.p. The publishers' markets, how they are reached, how readers respond. The winter 1961 issue of *Daedalus*, with additional essays.

Sutherland, Zena. *The Best in Children's Books: The University of Chicago Guide to Children's Literature, 1966–1972.* U. Ch. Pr. 1976 $25.00. ISBN 0-226-78057-0

————. ————, *1973–1978.* U. Ch. Pr. 1980 $25.00. ISBN 0-226-78059-7

————. ————, *1979–1984.* U. Ch. Pr. 1986 $35.00. ISBN 0-226-78060-0

————. ————, *1985–1990.* U. Ch. Pr. 1991 $37.50. ISBN 0-226-78064-3

Sutherland, Zena, and May Hill Arbuthnot. *Children and Books.* HarpC 1990 $45.00. ISBN 0-673-46357-5. Wide-ranging work on children's reading, books, and authors.

Turow, Joseph G. *Getting Books to Children: An Exploration of Publisher-Market Relations.* ALA 1979 o.p. Insightful. Heavy sociological language at times.

Unwin, Stanley, and Philip Unwin. *The Truth about Publishing.* Unwin Hyman 1976 $24.95. ISBN 0-04-655014-3. An outspoken, lively classic on the fundamentals of book publishing by a great English publisher. Updated by his son.

Van Nostrand, Albert. *The Denatured Novel.* Greenwood 1973 repr. of 1960 ed. o.p. Critique of presumed effect of market policies on writing.

Walker, Gregory. *Soviet Book Publishing Policy*. Bks. Demand repr. of 1978 ed. $46.80. ISBN 0-685-20577-0. An extensive updating of information, which, however, continues to change.

Whiteside, Thomas. *The Blockbuster Complex: Conglomerates, Show Business and Book Publishing*. Bks. Demand repr. of 1981 ed.$56.50. ISBN 0-8357-6878-3. A *New Yorker* series on the state of popular publishing. It aroused furious controversy.

Bestsellers

Bestseller lists are provided weekly and annually by trade, specialized, and general media. *Publishers Weekly* reports fiction, nonfiction, and paperback bestsellers weekly, with major cumulations, statistical reviews, and analysis in the annual summary number, usually an early March issue of the magazine. Current and annual lists are provided by leading news media and special-interest periodicals. Annual bestseller listings and analyses published in Bowker periodicals are reprinted each year in the *Bowker Annual Library and Book Trade Almanac: Facts, Figures, and Reports*. For additional information, see the section "Book Industry: Trends, Issues, Commentary," found earlier in this chapter.

Hackett, Alice Payne, and James Henry Burke. *80 Years of Best Sellers, 1895–1975*. Bowker 1977 o.p. Bestsellers, year by year, all-time lists, lists by major subjects, historical notes.

Hart, James D. *The Popular Book: A History of America's Literary Taste*. Greenwood 1976 repr. of 1950 ed. $35.00. ISBN 0-8371-8694-3. Books for "popular" reading: their authors, publishers, history, and place in U.S. culture.

Hinckley, Karen, and Barbara Hinckley. *American Best Sellers: A Reader's Guide to Popular Fiction*. Ind. U. Pr. 1989 $29.95. ISBN 0-253-32728-8. Discusses the role of bestsellers in U.S. publishing history.

Kujoth, Jean S. *Best-Selling Children's Books*. Scarecrow 1973 o.p. Overall review.

Mott, Frank Luther. *Golden Multitudes: The Story of Best Sellers in the United States*. 1947. Bowker 1960 o.p. Important and readable literary, economic, and cultural history; still cited.

Book Industry References

This section includes some of the most widely used reference materials needed by people who work in the book industry. Several statistical sources are included in the section "Book Industry: Education and Operations," found earlier in this chapter. Bibliographies are listed in Chapter 2, and books needed in editing manuscripts, in Chapter 3.

AB Bookman's Yearbook. Antiquarian Bookman annual $15.00. Free with a subscription to *AB Bookman's Weekly*. Review and forecast for the out-of-print and specialized book trade, with principal *AB* articles of the past year reprinted.

An Advertiser's Guide to Scholarly Publishing. Am. Univ. Pr. Services 1985. Hundreds of journals with full data desired by advertisers. Cross-references.

American Book Trade Directory. Bowker 39th ed. 1993 $215.00. ISBN 0-8352-3156-9. State and local listing of more than 27,000 U.S. and Canadian book outlets showing principal stock, specialties, contacts. Also includes appraisers, auctioneers, private book clubs, foreign-language and other specialties. Available in book form and on CD-ROM.

American Library Directory. 2 vols. Bowker 46th ed. 1993 $225.00. ISBN 0-8352-3282-4. Detailed listing of approximately 38,000 U.S. and Canadian libraries above high school level, including geographical arrangement, with top personnel, departments, and statistics for each library. Available in book form and on CD-ROM.

American National Standard for Compiling Book Publishing Statistics. ANSI 1977 $6.00.
ISBN 0-686-01885-0. Compiled by Committee Z-39, a cooperative group dealing with
book-industry standards of all kinds.

Basic Book List. ABA o.p. Basic lists for bookstore stock, both hardcover and paperback.

Book Buyer's Handbook. ABA 1984. Comprehensive directory, continuously updated, of
publishers' terms and policies, wholesalers and other suppliers, and data useful to
booksellers. Essential for store operation, valuable as data source.

Books in Print, 1993–94. 10 vols. Bowker 1993 $425.00. ISBN 0-8352-3354-5. Contains
more than 1.2 million titles and publisher entries. Available in book form and on CD-
ROM.

Books in Series, 1985–88. 2 vols. Bowker 1989 $199.95. ISBN 0-8352-2679-4

Bowker Annual Library and Book Trade Almanac: Facts, Figures, and Reports. Bowker
38th ed. 1993 $149.95. ISBN 0-8352-3345-6. Compendium of yearly information and
trend analysis on publishing and the library world. Many statistical tables. Reviews of
legislation, funding, education, salaries, research, reference sources. Directories of
library and book trade organizations. Available in book form and on CD-ROM.

Brownstone, David M., and Irene M. Franck. *The Dictionary of Publishing.* Van Nos.
Reinhold 1982 o.p. Legal, financial, business, and technical terms related to the
special language of book, newspaper, or magazine publishing.

Cassell and the Publishers Association Directory of Publishing, 1992. Vol. 1 *U.K.—
Commonwealth—Overseas.* $40.00. ISBN 0-304-32403-5. Vol. 2 *Continental Europe.*
$55.00. ISBN 0-304-32321-7

Children's Books: Awards and Prizes. Child. Bk. Coun. rev. ed. 1985 $50.00. ISBN 0-
933633-00-9. Approximately 120 U.S., British Commonwealth, and other international awards, including the history of each award and the names of winners up to
1984–85.

*Children's Book Awards International: A Directory of Awards and Winners, from Inception
through 1990.* Ed. by Laura Smith. McFarland & Co. 1992 $75.00. ISBN 0-89950-
686-0

Directory of Literary Magazines, 1992–93. Coord. Coun. Lit. Mag. annual 1992 $9.95.
ISBN 1-55921-065-6. Describes more than 350 member magazines.

Glaister, Geoffrey. *Glaister's Glossary of the Book: Terms Used in Paper-Making, Printing,
Bookbinding, and Publishing.* U. CA Pr. 1979 o.p. Far more than a glossary; virtually
an encyclopedic dictionary.

Gottlieb, Robin. *Publishing Children's Books in America, 1919–1976.* Child. Bk. Coun.
1978 $10.00. ISBN 0-685-11568-2. Fully annotated listings of books, articles, and
other materials covering children's book publishing houses, leaders and editors, and
specialized bookstores, starting with the first *Children's Book Week.*

Graphic Designer's Production Handbook. Hastings 1983 o.p. Concise, practical.

IMS/Ayer Directory of Publications. IMS Pr. 1984 o.p. A famous old standby. Details
publications in the United States and other markets; includes demographic data and
maps.

Index Translationum. UNIPUB annual, various prices. International bibliography of
translations from and into the principal languages. Breakdowns are by nation, world
area, language, topic, and so on.

International Directory of Little Magazines and Small Presses. Dustbooks annual 1992
$42.95. ISBN 0-916685-32-2. Serves a growing area of publishing.

International Literary Market Place. Bowker 1993 $164.00. ISBN 0-8352-3232-8. Similar
pattern to *Literary Market Place,* below, but covering more than 160 countries and
more than 13,000 book trade organizations, publishers, import-export services, and
related units. Annual. Available in book form and on CD-ROM.

Katz, William A. and Linda Sternberg Katz. *Magazines for Libraries.* 7th ed. Bowker 1992
$139.95. ISBN 0-8352-3166-6. Evaluates and describes 6,500 periodicals suitable for
all libraries; since 1969, a major source of information.

Kingman, Lee, ed. *Newbery and Caldecott Medal Books, 1976–1985.* Horn Bk. 1986
$24.95. ISBN 0-87675-004-8. Accounts of and excerpts from each of the annual prize
winners for children's literature and illustration, with each acceptance speech.

Earlier volumes include: *Newbery Medal Books, 1922–1955,* edited by Bertha Mahony Miller and Elinor Whitney Field (1955) $22.00; *Caldecott Medal Books, 1938–1957,* edited by Bertha Mahony Miller and Elinor Whitney Field (1957) $22.00; *Newbery and Caldecott Medal Books, 1956–1965,* edited by Lee Kingman (1965) $22.00; *Newbery and Caldecott Medal Books, 1966–1975,* ed. by Lee Kingman (1975) $22.00.

Knowledge Industry Publications. *U.S. Book Publishing Yearbook and Directory.* Facts on File 1982 o.p. Chronology, operating-expense ratios, financial reports, statistical tables, associations.

Literary Agents of North America. Ed. by Arthur Ormont and Leonie Rosensteil. 3rd ed. Author Aid 1988 $19.95. ISBN 0-911085-04-1. A vast guide for writers listing information on over 1,000 agents in the U.S. and Canada.

Literary Agents of North America Marketplace, 1984–1985. Aid-Research Associates 1984 $16.95. ISBN 0-911085-00-9. A new source.

Literary Market Place (LMP): The Directory of American Book Publishing. Bowker 1994 ed. $158.00. ISBN 0-8352-3346-4. Names, addresses, departments, personnel, and types of products or services, of the active U.S. and Canadian publishers. Also includes book-related and national associations, production services, review media, reference sources, and suppliers. Approximately 1,800 pages: includes a yellow-page section of Names and Numbers with quick contact information for 25,000 key people in book publishing. Available in book form and on CD-ROM.

Mayer, Debby. *Literary Agents: A Writers' Guide.* Pushcart Pr. 1983 $6.95. ISBN 0-913734-17-9. Where authors can get help in finding publishers.

Peters, Jean, ed. *The Bookman's Glossary.* Bowker 1983 $39.95. ISBN 0-8352-1686-1. Extensive revision. More than 1,800 terms plus 150 biographical notes. Publishing, bookselling, graphic arts, bibliography; includes current technology.

Plotnik, Arthur. *The Elements of Editing: A Modern Guide for Editors and Journalists.* Macmillan 1982 $5.95. ISBN 0-02-047430-X. A distinguished editor provides practical advice on copyright, permissions, relations among author, publisher, and printer.

Publishers Directory, A Guide to New and Established, Commercial and Nonprofit, Private and Alternative, Corporate and Association, Government and Institution Publishing Programs and Their Distributors. 14th ed. Gale 1993 $235.00. ISBN 0-8103-8156-7. Notes on more than 18,000 private, special, avant-garde, organizational, governmental, and institutional presses.

Sanders, Norman, and William Bevington. *Graphic Designer's Production Handbook.* Hastings 1982 $10.95. ISBN 0-8038-5896-5

Smith, Peggy. *Proofreading Manual and Reference Guide.* Edit. Experts 1981 o.p. Comprehensive reference and self-study text. Examples, workbook.

_____. *Simplified Proofreading.* Edit. Experts 1987 o.p. Instructional text covering over 100 subjects.

Sutherland, Zena, and others. *Children and Books.* Scott F. 7th ed. 1986 o.p. Children's books and their audience. A comprehensive, standard reference.

Ulrich's International Periodicals Directory. 5 vols. Bowker 1993–94 ed. $395.00. ISBN 0-8352-3368-5. Subject-arranged, detailed data about more than 140,000 publications; worldwide, including buying and bibliographic information. Available in book form and on CD-ROM. Now includes over 7,000 newspapers.

UNESCO Statistical Yearbook. UNIPUB 1986 $85.00. ISBN 92-3-002445-7. Massive collection of worldwide tabulations, by nation and region, on education, book output, libraries, newspapers and periodicals, museums, film, broadcasting, and cultural expenditures.

COPYRIGHT

Listed here are a few useful books on a complicated subject—copyright. The U.S. Copyright Act, which became effective January 1, 1978, has been followed by many regulatory changes and some court actions, and has required the revision or replacement of many books on the subject. Thorny issues continue to include the application of international copyright agreements and questions arising from contemporary technology, notably electronic data storage and delivery systems and quick, cheap copying. The literature of copyright will continue to change accordingly. The few items listed here are suggestive of the kinds of possible problems that one may encounter in learning about copyright. The best thing one can do is to follow the many publications of the U.S. Copyright Office, a few of which are listed here.

The ABC of Copyright. UNESCO 1981 o.p. A 73-page book on copyright, historically and currently. Discusses the moral and economic right of authors, protected works, copyright ownership, transfer and duration of copyright, infringement and remedies, international copyright, and so on.

Barnes, James J. *Authors, Publishers, and Politicians: The Quest for an Anglo-American Copyright Agreement, 1815–1854.* Ohio St. U. Pr. 1974 o.p. More than 300 pages of wide-ranging information. Historical study covering the depression of 1837–43, British periodicals in America, the Canadian market, British and American laws, and much more.

Berenbeim, Ronald E. *Safeguarding Intellectual Property.* Conference Bd. 1989 o.p. Reports on the protection of intellectual property, including discussions on patents and trademarks, copyright, trade secrets, litigation and arbitration, noncompetition and nondisclosure contracts with key employees, U.S. protective mechanisms, international legal protection for software, and more.

Chickering, Robert B., and Susan Hartman. *How to Register a Copyright and Protect Your Creative Work: A Basic Guide to the Copyright Law and How It Affects Anyone Who Wants to Protect Creative Work.* Macmillan 1987 $11.95. ISBN 0-684-18878-3. A thorough guide with 216 pages of advice on registering a claim to copyright, the length of time the rights are in effect, proper copyright notices, special copyright situations, copyright exemptions for nonprofit governmental and religious use, and other forms of protection.

Gorman, Robert A. *Copyright Law.* Fed. Judicial Ctr 1991. Offers historical view, discussion of copyright acts of 1909 and 1976, the 1989 and 1990 amendments to the 1976 act, patents, trademarks, subject matter of copyright, copyright and property law, duration and renewal, ownership, rights and limitations, and so on.

Johnston, Donald F. *Copyright Handbook.* Bowker 1982 $39.95. ISBN 0-8352-1488-5. Based on the new copyright law, with continuing interpretations and regulations.

Kozak, Ellen M. *Every Writer's Guide to Copyright and Publishing Law.* H. Holt & Co. 1990 $7.95. ISBN 0-8050-1222-2. Contains 22 chapters covering the things writers need to know about copyright; e.g., definition of copyright, getting works copyrighted, duration of protection, the copyright notice, contracts, work-for-hire, libel and privacy, aliases, infringement and suits, and many other topics.

Lawrence, John Shelton, and Bernard Timberg, eds. *Fair Use and Free Inquiry: Copyright Law and the New Media.* Ablex Pub. 1989 $65.00. ISBN 0-89391-484-3. Deals with copyright law, fair use, piracies, the impact of copyright law on scholars and publishers, archives and libraries, and more. Considers television, radio, videobooks, private archives, duplication, and more.

Library of Congress. *Copyright Registration for Derivative Works.* Lib. Congress 1991. A five-page brochure explaining what a derivative work is and how to register it for copyright.

————. *Extension of Copyright Terms.* Lib. Congress 1991. A four-page pamphlet explaining when to renew copyright and how works copyrighted in the past will have automatic extensions of protection under the 1976 copyright law.

————. *Reproduction of Copyrighted Works by Educators and Librarians.* Lib. Congress 1991. A 26-page brochure discussing exclusive rights, fair use, reproduction by librarians and archives, liability for infringement, and other issues.

———. *Sorry . . . But you didn't send us everything we need to register your claim to copyright, and we're going to have to start all over.* Lib. Congress 1991. A single-page explanation of how to get something copyrighted. Tells what a person must submit and to whom.

———. *Supplementary Copyright Registration.* Lib. Congress 1991. A four-page brochure defining supplemental registration, which is designed to correct errors in, or to amplify the information in, an already existing filed copyright registration.

———. *Works-Made-for-Hire Under the 1976 Copyright Act.* Lib. Congress 1992. A two-page circular, briefly explaining what works-made-for-hire are, both for an employee and for a party specially commissioned to contribute to a larger work.

Nimmer, David, and Melville B. Nimmer. *Nimmer on Copyright: A Treatise on the Law of Literary, Musical and Artistic Property, and the Protection of Ideas.* Bender 1992. ISBN 0-8205-1465-9. Five large ring-bound volumes covering all aspects of the subject. Perhaps the definitive and most up-to-date treatment in published volumes. The ring binder allows for constant updates, and, in fact, there is a special supplement on computer law, software protection, and so forth.

Nissley, Meta, and Nancy Melin Nelson. eds. *CD-ROM Licensing and Copyright Issues for Libraries.* Meckler Corp. 1990 $29.95. ISBN 0-88736-701-1. Five essays that deal with protecting CD-ROM texts. With a sample licensing agreement.

Patry, William F. *The Fair Use Privilege in Copyright Law.* Bernan Pr. 1985 $88.00. ISBN 0-87179-451-9. A 544-page volume on the origin and development of fair use, its legislative history, First Amendment issues, and procedural issues.

Patterson, Lyman Ray. *The Nature of Copyright: A Law of Users' Rights.* U. of Ga. Pr. 1991 $30.00. ISBN 0-8203-1347-5. Contains 275 pages including a historical sketch, the evolution of copyright laws, copyright and free speech, the scope of the right to copy, authors', publishers', and users' rights.

Saunders, David. *Authorship and Copyright.* Routledge 1992 $49.95. ISBN 0-415-04158-9. Offers a history of copyright laws in England, France, Germany, and the United States. Has a chapter on "The Internationalisation of Copyright and authorship." Considers cultural as well as legal issues.

United States. Congress. Senate. Committee on the Judiciary. *Fair Use of Unpublished Works.* USGPO 1991. Aims to clarify the application of the fair-use doctrine to unpublished works. Discusses common-law protection versus protection by federal statute. Shows the impact on the publication world of the barring of the use of unpublished materials, which are protected under copyright. Attempts to define Fair Use.

———. Subcommittee on Patents, Copyrights, and Trademarks. *The Copyright Clarification Act.* USGPO 1990. Congressional Sales Office. Transcript of a hearing of the one-hundred-and-first Congress containing extensive discussion on what constitutes copyright, who has rights, what to do about their infringement, liability for damages, and related issues.

Weil, Ben H., and Barbara Friedman Polansky. *Modern Copyright Fundamentals: Key Writings on Technological and Other Issues.* Amer. Soc. for Info. Science 1989 $39.50. ISBN 0-938734-33-4. Emphasis on the effect of changing technologies on copyright.

Weinstein, David A. *How to Protect Your Creative Work: All You Need to Know about Copyright.* Wiley 1987 $49.95. ISBN 0-471-85270-8. Contains 343 pages of information on copyright, trademarks, patents, what can be protected, what cannot, how to determine copyright ownership, fair use, limitations on rights, duration of protection, copyright notices, transferring copyright ownership, recovering ownership of transferred rights, licenses, copyright infringement and remedies, and income tax considerations.

A Writer's Guide to Copyright. Poets and Writers 1990 $6.95. ISBN 0-913734-21-7. Summarizes existing laws, gives a glossary of key terms, talks about writers' rights, publishing, how to deal with the Copyright Office, infringement, and so on.

CENSORSHIP AND THE FREEDOM TO READ

Throughout the world, "intellectual freedom" denotes a struggle for freedom of access to information. In the United States, this freedom is the foundation of democracy. Censorship—the banning, prohibition, suppression, or restriction of access to information—denies that freedom. The last word is never said about censorship, nor is the necessity of the freedom to read ever sufficiently emphasized. The books named here cover the subject in fairly comprehensive, though often detailed, terms. More specialized studies may be found in the *Subject Guide to Books in Print.*

From the 1960s to the present, different majorities on the U.S. Supreme Court have issued sharply differing—often confusing—rules concerning "community standards," "redeeming social value," privacy, civil rights, and the secrecy of information held by units of government. Certain government personnel face lifetime restrictions on speech and publication because of the sensitive nature of their jobs and national security issues. Military censorship may be on the rise; during the Persian Gulf War, for example, journalists were restricted access to types of information that had been available in similar previous situations. "Whistle blowers" are often persecuted. Publishers face the continual threat and expense of litigation for alleged libel and other reasons. Self-censorship becomes increasingly tempting for publishers, editors, and authors to adopt as an option. If untrammeled historical research and a robust press are to be maintained, the classic rule applies: "Eternal vigilance is the price of liberty."

Adams, Michael. *Censorship: The Irish Experience.* U. of Ala. Pr. 1968 o.p. Until Irish censorship was greatly mitigated in the middle 1960s, it sadly inhibited Irish literary publishing.

American Library Association, Office for Intellectual Freedom. *Censorship Litigation and the Schools.* ALA 1983 o.p. Deals with the increasing attacks against school-library operations and textbooks.

――――. *Intellectual Freedom Manual.* ALA 1983 $25.00. ISBN 0-8389-3412-9. Guidance for defense of reading and libraries. Includes background history, documents, policies, and procedures.

Bennett, James R. *Control of Information in the United States: An Annotated Bibliography.* Greenwood 1987 $69.50. ISBN 0-313-28097-5. A 900-page bibliography on all aspects of censorship worldwide. Lists items with annotations.

Berninghausen, David K. *The Flight from Reason: Essays on Intellectual Freedom in the Academy, the Press and the Library.* ALA 1975 o.p. Statements by a leading association figure in this field.

Bosmajian, Haig A., comp. *Censorship, Libraries, and the Law.* Neal-Schuman 1983 $45.00. ISBN 0-918212-54-5. Compilation of 33 court cases on school-library censorship and U.S. Supreme Court decisions relied on by the lower courts in library-censorship cases.

Calvocoressi, Peter, assisted by Ann Bristow. *Freedom to Publish: A Report on Obstacles to Freedom in Publishing Prepared for the Congress of International Publishers Association.* Humanities 1980 o.p. Has chapters on the censor; The Defense of the State; The Defense of Morals; Civil Law; State Competition, Patronage, and Taxation; Social Constraints and Pressure Groups; and The Public Trade. With an international focus.

Censorship: 500 Years of Conflict. OUP 1984 $34.50. ISBN 0-19-503529-1. A pictorial history containing eleven essays on the subject. An exhibition catalog.

de Grazia, Edward. *Censorship Landmarks.* Bowker 1969 o.p. Monumental compilation, with history and interpretation, by an attorney deeply involved in many such cases.

Demac, Donna A. *Liberty Denied: The Current Rise of Censorship in America.* 2nd rev. ed. Rutgers U. Pr. 1990 $30.00. ISBN 0-8135-1544-0. Preface by Arthur Miller; introduction by Larry McMurtry.

Downs, Robert, and Ralph E. McCoy. *The First Freedom Today: Critical Issues Related to Censorship and to Intellectual Freedom.* ALA 1984 $20.00. ISBN 0-8389-0412-2. Specific kinds of attacks on free expression emerging in the 1980s.

D'Souza, Frances, ed. *Information, Freedom, and Censorship, World Report, 1991, Article 19.* ALA 1991 $45.00. ISBN 0-8389-2156-6. Censorship examined in the context of the Universal Declaration of Human Rights.

Green, Jonathan. *The Encyclopedia of Censorship.* Facts on File 1990 $45.00. ISBN 0-8160-1594-5. Comprehensive, international focus from early times to the present, with emphasis on the West.

Gregorian, Vartan. *Censorship: Five Hundred Years of Conflict.* OUP 1984 $34.50. ISBN 0-19-503529-1. Lavishly illustrated catalog of a spectacular exhibit at the New York Public Library, by its former director. Includes essays and references.

Haight, Anne Lyon. *Banned Books: 387 B.C. to 1978 A.D.* Bowker 1978 o.p. Updated and enlarged by Chandler B. Grannis, with opening essay on censorship in the United States by Charles Rembar. Chronology of censored books and authors.

Intellectual Freedom Manual. ALA 1992 $25.00. ISBN 0-8389-3412-9. With a wide scope. Presents a Library Bill of Rights. Looks at expurgation of library materials, diversity in collection development, evaluating library collections, challenged materials, exhibitions and meeting rooms in libraries, freedom to read, and a great deal more.

Jenkinson, Edward B. *Censors in the Classroom.* S. Ill. U. Pr. 1979 o.p. Effects of censorship activities on schools and libraries: why it happens, court rulings, the case for free access, free inquiry, and an open society.

Levy, Leonard W. *Treason against God: A History of the Offense of Blasphemy.* Schocken 1981 o.p. Book banning and burning has been only one aspect of this story.

Lewis, Felice Flannery. *Literature, Obscenity and the Law.* S. Ill. U. Pr. 1978 $12.95. ISBN 0-8093-0870-3. Thorough, brightly written account of all aspects of the issue.

Long, Robert Emmet, ed. *Censorship.* Wilson 1990 o.p. Twenty essays on many aspects of censorship, e.g., censorship in Great Britain, censorship of books in libraries and schools, censorship of the fine arts.

Milton, John. *Areopagitica.* Saifer 1972 repr. of 1644 ed. $15.00. ISBN 0-87556-219-1. Milton's famous statement against licensing of books.

Moon, Eric, ed. *Book Selection and Censorship in the Sixties.* Bowker 1969 o.p. A selection of essays in 55 chapters, covering many areas of censorship: theory, surveys, magazines and news publications, audiovisual materials, children's books, selection tools and reviewing, book censorship, libraries, and more.

Noble, William. *Bookbanning in America: Who Bans Books?—And Why?* Eriksson 1990 $14.95. ISBN 0-8397-1081-X. Shows how and why censorship takes place, and how it affects politics, religion, social status, education, and publishing. With a bibliography.

Oboler, Eli M., ed. *Censorship and Education.* Wilson 1982 o.p. Strong, representative, differing points of view. Discusses the impact of censorship on schools and libraries and major legal decisions.

————. *To Free the Mind: Libraries, Technology and Intellectual Freedom.* Libs. Unl. 1983 o.p. Essays on interrelated issues by the late university librarian, a leader in the defense of freedom of inquiry, writing, and reading.

Perrin, Noel. *Dr. Bowdler's Legacy: History of Expurgated Books in England and America.* Godine 1992 $14.95. ISBN 0-87923-861-5. Not "banned" books, but "bowdlerized" ones. Amusing, factual.

Reisner, Robert George. *Show Me the Good Parts: The Reader's Guide to Sex in Literature.* Carol Pub. Group. 1964 $2.45. ISBN 0-8065-0049-2. Examples of what may be censored.

Rembar, Charles. *The End of Obscenity.* Random 1968 o.p. Accounts of the trials of *Lady Chatterley's Lover, Tropic of Cancer,* and *Fanny Hill* by the attorney for their defense.

CHAPTER 2

Bibliography

Kathleen A. Mitchell

> The business of bibliography is to take heed of all publications, old or new,
> great or small, cheap or dear, and to describe, and catalogue, and index them
> in such a clear and sufficient manner that the whole literature of the world
> on any given subject, or by any given author, shall be placed at the service of
> the humblest inquirer. . . . If once it is recognized that bibliography is really
> the index and guide to all past and existing knowledge, enabling any class of
> inquirer to find quickly the book which can answer his question, then there
> will be some hope of the science being set in its proper place as a key to the
> knowledge stored, and too often hidden, in books.
> —JAMES DUFF BROWN, *A Manual of Practical Bibliography*

Derived from two Greek word stems, *biblios* and *graphia*, the word *bibliography*
literally means "the writing or copying of books." For the first three centuries of
the Christian era, *bibliographia* was used by the Greeks to describe the copying
of books by hand; from the twelfth century, it was used to refer to the activity of
composing books. Occasionally, the word *bibliographia* was used during the
fifteenth and sixteenth centuries; however, it could refer to a writer, a copier, or
a printer of books. It was not until the seventeenth century that the word was
used by scholars to refer to the writing *about* books. More precisely, *bibliographia* was used to refer to the activity of and end product of book description.
This product frequently took the form of both essays about books and lists of
books. During the eighteenth century, *bibliographia* came to refer to those
activities related to the description of books and the knowledge of books rather
than to lists of books. "Thus the term *Bibliographia* (which originally designated
the process of book description, then usually denoted its product, a descriptive
list of books) came to be understood in a general and collective sense and to
stand for the description of books in general and for the totality of book
descriptions—if knowledge of books was meant." (Blum, *Bibliographia*)

As bibliography became a field of knowledge in its own right, three major
forms emerged: *enumerative, analytical,* and *historical*. Moreover, various
scholars divided the field differently as well, adding such categories as textual,
descriptive, and systematic. Over time, a wealth of other terms have been used
to describe the subcategories of bibliography, such as author, annotated,
comparative, national, personal, retrospective, and selective. Nevertheless,
North American usage and practice validate the formulation of three major
categories: enumerative, analytical, and historical. British scholars tend to
combine analytic and historical bibliography, frequently referring to these as
critical or textual bibliography.

One area closely related to bibliography, both in character and historical
development, is the book trade, particularly that which deals in rare and unique
books. During the sixteenth and seventeenth centuries, printed books were

added to manuscript collections. Collectors then, as now, added to their libraries in those areas that were of special interest to them. This practice of collecting books in particular subject areas led to the development of extensive collections in particular subject areas. Collectors made lists of their holdings, organizing them into subject categories. It was not long before scholars began to expand their lists to include materials that they did not have in their personal collections. Up to the eighteenth century, these lists contained only materials published as individual items. With the rise of journal literature in the eighteenth century, materials published collectively began to appear in subject bibliographies.

During the nineteenth century, book collectors began to amass the works of a single author. This was also a period when the development of extensive descriptive lists of books that had been printed during fifteenth, sixteenth, and seventeenth centuries began to occur. With these developments, the basic forms and formats of modern bibliography were set.

In the twentieth century, all bibliographic activity, whether analytic, historical or enumerative, can be characterized as refinements of the techniques and methods developed by bookpersons during the first four centuries after the invention of printing.

Enumerative Bibliography

Sometimes known as systematic bibliography, enumerative bibliography most closely conforms to the sixteenth- and seventeenth-century view of a bibliography as a list of books. The guiding principle of enumerative bibliography is that materials are brought together by some coordinating feature; that is, the books have a recognized relationship to each other. While some bibliographies may be annotated as to content or quality, such descriptions are not necessary to the definition of enumerative bibliography. Enumerative bibliographies have been known from antiquity. Some were created to record the materials available on a particular subject, whereas others defined what was and was not part of the canonical works of a particular author.

As books and other forms of recorded materials have proliferated, the need for more inclusive and exclusive bibliographies has increased. More inclusive bibliographies are needed so that all materials on a particular subject are represented. Yet, at the same time, the sheer mass of materials available have made it necessary for ever more restricted definitions of the subject to be covered by the bibliography.

Included in the listing of types of enumerative bibliographies are subject, author, and national (country specific) bibliographies. Union lists, booksellers' catalogs, periodical indexes and subject specific on-line information services are also part of the family of enumerative bibliography.

Perhaps the most important thing to remember about enumerative bibliographies is that they are tools—tools for the study of all disciplines. Under ideal circumstances they have been compiled by specialists in the field. The oldest of the enumerative bibliographies give insight into the life and scholarship of their time. Thus, they are tools, not only for the study of a particular subject, but also for the study of the time and circumstances of their compilation.

Analytical Bibliography

Analytical bibliography is sometimes known as critical bibliography and deals with the book as a physical object. In this, study is directed to the materials of which books are and have been made. This includes type, paper, ink, bindings, and binding materials. In addition, those who are involved in this type of study also look at editions, issues, states, printings, and recensions of a particular work. There is a concerted effort on the part of the analytic bibliographer to describe the copies in hand as compared with an ideal copy, that is, a copy that may not exist but that is as it was intended to have been produced; a copy composed not only of real words, correctly spelled but also of the correct words correctly spelled.

The product of such intensive study of the physical book and its textual idiosyncrasies is what is known as a descriptive bibliography. Custom dictates the format for these descriptions, although they can vary, depending on the demands of the materials and the purposes for which they were designed. They are as detailed as has been shown to be necessary in order to distinguish one seemingly identical item from another. It is the level of description that distinguishes these bibliographies from library catalogs.

To summarize, analytical bibliography is the examination of books as material objects, with the purposes of discovering the details of their production process and analyzing the effects of this process on the physical characteristics of any given copy of a book.

Historical Bibliography

Whereas analytical bibliography looks at the book as a physical object, historical bibliography views the book as a historical object. This includes the history of the book, in general, as well as the history of a book, in particular. Also included in this field of study is the history of printing and publishing.

The skills of analytical bibliography—that is, knowledge of type, paper, ink, and bindings—when applied to the study of the book as a historical object, enable the historical bibliographer to make determinations concerning the history of the transmission of literary texts. Such study has resulted in discernment concerning the chronological and textual relationship of various editions of Shakespeare to one another. In this sort of study, historical bibliography overlaps with textual criticism, with both striving to illuminate an author's original intent concerning his or her work.

The study of the transmission of texts also investigates how a work came to exist in its own time, as well as how it came to be in its modern form. In the broadest sense, the social, political, economic, and historical forces that helped to form and shape the work and the transmitted text are also a part of the study of historical bibliography.

GENERAL READINGS

Overviews and Anthologies

The Bibliographical Society of America, 1904–79: A Retrospective Collection. U. Pr. of Va. 1980 $20.00. ISBN 0-914930-80-7. A collection of nine articles taken from the society's *Papers* to commemorate its seventy-fifth anniversary in 1979. The selections represent, in the society's words, "the highest degree of excellence—articles of critical importance that have moved forward the art of bibliography."

Blum, Rudolf. *Bibliographia: An Inquiry into Its Definition and Designations.* Trans. by Mathilde V. Rovelstad. ALA 1980 o.p. A dense but elegant text that traces the origins and history of bibliography.

Bowers, Fredson T. *Essays in Bibliography, Text and Editing*. Bks. Demand 1975 $145.10. ISBN 0-8357-7900-9. Published for the Bibliographic Society of the University of Virginia.

Harmon, Robert B. *Elements of Bibliography: A Simplified Approach*. Scarecrow 1989 $32.50. ISBN 0-8108-2218-0. New edition of a guide to the literature of bibliography.

Schneider, Georg. *Theory and History of Bibliography*. 1934. Trans. by Ralph R. Shaw. Gordon Pr. 1977 $69.95. ISBN 0-8490-2741-1

Stokes, Roy. *The Function of Bibliography*. 1971. Lexington Bks. 2nd ed. 1983 o.p. An excellent introduction to the various forms of bibliography; concise without being terse.

Tanselle, G. Thomas. *Selected Studies in Bibliography*. Bks. Demand 1979 $160.70. ISBN 0-7837-1234-X. A collection of 11 articles, selected by the author and reprinted from the annual *Studies in Bibliography*. They are the most significant of the articles by G. Thomas Tanselle that appeared in the *Studies in Bibliography*. The council of the Bibliographical Society of the University of Virginia points out in the Foreword to the collection that "the *SB* articles as a group have had a major influence on the theory and practice of bibliography and textual criticism."

———. *Introduction to Bibliography—Seminar Syllabus*. Col. U. Pr. 1990 o.p. Described by the author as a brief list of readings on various topics in bibliography, it provides an overview of the richness of material available in the field; a working document that is frequently updated.

Enumerative Bibliography

Berger, Sidney E. *The Design of Bibliographies: Observations, References and Examples*. Greenwood 1992 $85.00. ISBN 0-313-28425-3. Discusses the various elements of book design.

Besterman, Theodore. *The Beginnings of Systematic Bibliography*. Rprt. Serv. 1988 repr. of 1935 ed. $75.00. ISBN 0-7812-0258-2

Harner, James L. *On Compiling an Annotated Bibliography*. Modern Lang. 1985 $10.00. ISBN 0-87352-138-2

Hauer, Mary G. *Books, Libraries, and Research*. Kendall-Hunt 2nd ed. 1983 o.p. Provides guidelines for both researching and compiling a bibliography.

Krummel, D. W. *Bibliographies: Their Aims and Methods*. Mansell 1984 o.p. A practical book for compilers of enumerative bibliographies and for those interested in bibliographic theory and practice. It examines the features that characterize the most respected bibliographies and suggests what makes other lists flawed. It concludes with a bibliography of major writings on the compiling of bibliographies (1883–1983) and a list of bibliographies that have received awards for graphic excellence.

Malcles, Louise N. *Bibliography (La Bibliographie)*. 1956. Trans. by Theodore C. Hines. Scarecrow 1973 repr. of 1961 ed. o.p.

Van Hoesen, Henry B., and Frank K. Walter. *Bibliography, Practical, Enumerative, Historical: An Introductory Manual*. 1928. B. Franklin 1971 o.p.

Because the work of enumerative bibliography requires extensive research, the following books are included as beginning guides to working in a research library.

Beasley, David R. *How to Use a Research Library*. OUP 1988 $29.95. ISBN 0-19-50425-X. Covers the catalog, research tools, and ILL, and gives details about several national libraries.

The New York Public Library Book of How and Where to Look it Up. Ed. by Sherwood Harris. P-H 1991 $30.00. ISBN 0-13-61428-3. Compiled by freelance writers as a good source for lay researchers.

Other good sources of both bibliographies and information that is useful in the construction of bibliographies are the following:

Walford's Guide to Reference Material. Ed. by A. J. Walford. UNIPUB 6th ed. 1993 Vol. 1 $210.00. ISBN 1-85604-015-1. 5th ed. 1991 Vol. 2 $180.00. ISBN 0-85365-539-1. Vol. 3 $240.00. ISBN 0-85365-549-9. A guide to reference books published by the British Library Association. Although British items are given prominence, much U.S., Russian, French, German, and other material is included. Volume 1 is on science and technology; Volume 2 on history, social science, philosophy, and religion; Volume 3 on generalia, language and literature, and the arts.

Wynar, Bohdan S., Anna G. Patterson, and D. A. Rothschild, eds. *American Reference Books Annual.* Libs. Unl. 1970–present. Vol. 24 $87.50. ISBN 1-56308-076-1. Reviews current reference works on all subjects, many of them not reviewed by the standard reviewing sources, and includes increasing numbers of books from Canada.

Analytical Bibliography

The books listed below complement one another and are basic guides.

Bowers, Fredson T. *Principles of Bibliographical Description.* Omnigraphics Inc. 2nd ed. 1987 $80.00. ISBN 0-906795-86-9. A detailed treatment of analytical bibliography as applied to the description of books.

Gaskell, Philip. *A New Introduction to Bibliography.* OUP 1972 $29.95. ISBN 0-19-818150-7. Updates and extends the period of coverage in McKerrow, listed below.

McKerrow, Ronald B. *An Introduction to Bibliography for Literary Students.* OUP 1928 o.p. Covers all aspects of the making of the printed book up to about 1800 and provides the background of knowledge requisite for bibliographic description.

Tanselle, G. Thomas. *Textual Criticism Since Gregg: A Chronicle, 1950–1985.* U. of Va. Pr. 1988 $12.95. ISBN 0-8139-1166-4

The following books provide or direct the reader to more specific information on some of the topics discussed in the basic guides to analytic bibliography.

Apicella, Vincent F. *The Concise Guide to Type Identification.* TAB Bks. 1990 $24.95. ISBN 0-8306-3449-5. Some 1,700 laser typefaces from the linotype library are displayed.

The Art and History of Book Printing: A Topical Bibliography. Comp. by Vito J. Brenni. Greenwood 1984 $42.95. ISBN 0-313-24306-9. A bibliography arranged by subject that should be of use to anyone seeking to learn more about the book as a physical object.

Bauermeister, Benjamin. *A Manual of Comparative Typography: The Panrose System.* Van Nos. Reinhold 1988 o.p.

Bookbinding: A Guide to the Literature. Comp. by Vito J. Brenni. Greenwood 1982 $42.95. ISBN 0-313-23718-2. Inconsistent but useful introduction to the literature on this topic.

Carvalho, David Numes. *Forty Centuries of Ink.* Banks-Baldwin 1904 o.p.

Edmunds, Desmond. *The International Type Book.* Van Nos. Reinhold 1990 $17.95. ISBN 0-442-30503-6

Grant, Julius. *Books and Documents: Dating, Permanence and Preservation.* Gordon Pr. 1980 $59.95. ISBN 0-8490-3157-5

Haley, Allan. *ABCs of Type.* Watson-Guptill Pubs. 1990 $29.95. ISBN 0-8230-0053-2. Compilation of articles that originally appeared in *Step-by-Step* graphics magazine. Describes the characteristics, suggests the best use, and surveys the historical background of 20 of the most popular families of modern typefaces.

Jaspert, W. Pincus. *The Encyclopedia of Type Faces.* Sterling 1990 $50.00. ISBN 0-7137-2186-3

Historical Bibliography

The basic sources listed for analytical bibliography will also provide an introduction to the study of historical bibliography; the following will help to expand that knowledge.

A *Dictionary of Book History.* Ed. by John Feather. Routledge 1991 o.p.

McMurtie, Douglas C. *The Book: The Story of Printing and Bookmaking.* OUP 1950 o.p. A classic work on the printed book.

Morison, Stanley. *Four Centuries of Fine Printing.* E. Benn 1960 o.p.

Schreyer, Alice D. *The History of Books: A Guide to Selected Resources in the Library of Congress.* USGPO 1987 $15.00. ISBN 0-16-004024-8. A guide to the Library of Congress's collections for those who are studying the history of the book. Part One describes each of the relevant collections in the Manuscript Division, the Rare Books Room, and the Special Collections Division. Part Two discusses the value to the researcher of the Copyrights Records and Deposits Office, the Law Library, the Geography and Map Division, the Music Division, and the Prints and Photographs Division.

Williams, William Proctor, and Craig S. Abbott. *An Introduction to Bibliographical and Textual Studies.* Modern Lang. 1989 $37.00. ISBN 0-87352-176-5. Its chapters summarize the general kinds of bibliography.

Bibliographies of Bibliographies

Bibliographies of bibliographies provide lists of lists created on various subjects. These lists can be used as guidelines and sources of information for new bibliographies.

Beaudiquez, Marcelle. *Bibliographical Services throughout the World.* 2 vols. Unipub Vol. 1 *1975–1979.* 1985 $25.00. ISBN 92-3-101982-1. Vol. 2 *1970–74.* 1977 $14.00. ISBN 92-3-101394-7. The volumes covering the periods 1950–1959, edited by Robert L. Collison, and 1960–1964 and 1965–1969, compiled by Paul Avicenne, are out of print.

Besterman, Theodore. *A World Bibliography of Bibliographies and of Bibliographical Catalogues, Calendars, Abstracts, Digests, Indexes, and the Like.* 5 vols. Rowman 4th ed. 1963 $383.00. ISBN 0-87471-294-7. The classic of its type, recording approximately 117,000 volumes of bibliography under 16,000 headings. Worth the time of anyone interested in compiling a bibliography.

The Bibliographic Index: A Cumulative Bibliography of Bibliographies. 26 vols. Wilson 1937–92. Vols. 1–4 $120.00 ea. ISBN 0-685-22234-9. Vols. 5–8 $225.00 ea. ISBN 0-685-22233-0. Vols. 9–19 $180.00 ea. Vols. 20–26 $180.00 ea. Write publisher for information. Published twice a year, with a cumulative annual edition.

LeFontaine, Joseph R. *The Collector's Bookshelf: A Comprehensive Listing of Authors, Their Pseudonyms, & Their Books.* Prometheus Bks. 1990 $69.95. ISBN 0-87975-605-5. Lists 33,614 works of fiction by 731 British and American authors.

Sheehy, Eugene P. *Guide to Reference Books.* ALA 10th ed. 1986 $80.00. ISBN 0-8389-0390-8. A superior work, this is a guide to reference books published primarily in the United States, although much foreign material is also included. Based on an earlier edition by Constance M. Winchell. Supplement edited by Robert Balay (1992).

Toomey, Alice F. *A World Bibliography of Bibliographies, 1964–1974: a List of Works Represented by the Library of Congress Printed Catalog Cards.* 2 vols. Rowman 1977 o.p.

TYPES OF ENUMERATIVE BIBLIOGRAPHIES

Although there is considerable overlap among the various types of enumerative bibliographies, they can be categorized as follows.

General bibliographies (also called *universal*) attempt to be all-inclusive and list books without limitations as to place of publication, time, subject, or author.

National bibliographies list books published *in* or *about* a country or a region.

Trade bibliographies list books that are in print or for sale, and when, where, and by whom they were published. They usually also include the price of each item listed.

Author bibliographies list the complete works of an author, or works both by and about an author. They can run the gamut from the most simple, which provide only minimum identifying information (title and publication date), called *checklists*, to those that provide descriptions extensive enough to approach the characteristics of a full-dressed descriptive bibliography.

Subject bibliographies list books about a specific subject. They may be comprehensive or selective, or merely a reading list appended to an article or book. Unlike the other types of bibliographies just described, the items listed are connected by *content*.

Bibliographies by *form* or *genre* include lists based either on the physical form in which the items were published, such as newspapers or periodicals (bibliographies of bibliographies fall into this category), or on genre, such as poetry or science fiction.

This chapter includes general bibliographies, national bibliographies, and trade bibliographies. For other types of enumerative bibliographies (author, subject, and form or genre), consult the appropriate chapters in this volume and the other volumes of the series.

General Bibliographies

It is generally accepted that there will probably never be a truly universal bibliography complete and unlimited by language, period, or subject: The material is too vast. Attempts have been made to achieve this ideal, and some results are of great value. However, these materials tend to be available only in major research libraries or through on-line services. Union catalogs, which are the collective catalogues of two or more libraries, are the vehicles used to identify the holdings of other libraries. These catalogs are found in two forms: printed and CD-ROM. In most cases today, CD-ROM is the form usually used to issue regional unions lists, because it provides the opportunity for both rapid and cumulative updating. In addition, since the early 1970s, very large union catalogs have also become available online. The following items are presented as representative, and the reader is advised to consult his or her local library for further information regarding access to these materials.

National Bibliographies

Bell, Barbara L. *An Annotated Guide to Current National Bibliographies.* Chadwyck/Healey 1986 $100.00. ISBN 0-85964-123-6. A source of further information regarding the available national bibliographies.

UNITED STATES

National Union Catalog. Lib. of Congress o.p. The *National Union Catalog* ceased publication as a book catalog at the end of 1982. Since January 1983, it has been published in computer-output microfiche and is available from the Cataloging Distribution Service, Library of Congress.

National Union Catalog: A Cumulative Author List, 1953–57. 28 vols. Rowman o.p.

National Union Catalog: A Cumulative Author List, 1958–67. 125 vols. Rowman o.p.

National Union Catalog: A Cumulative Author List, 1968–72. 119 vols. J. W. Edwards 1973 $1,950.00. ISBN 0-910546-06-1

National Union Catalog: Audiovisual Materials. Prepared under the editorial coordination of the Catalog Management and Publication Division, Lib. of Congress. Issued quarterly in 48x microfiche, with separate cumulative name, title, subject, and series indexes. 1983 register, $7.00; 1984 register, $12.00; 1985 subscription, $65.00. Includes bibliographic records for motion pictures, filmstrips, transparency and slide sets, video recordings, and kits currently cataloged by the Library of Congress.

National Union Catalog: Author List, 1973–77. 135 vols. Rowman $1,518.30. ISBN 0-8476-6142-3. Cumulation includes *Films and Other Materials for Projection* and *Music, Books on Music, and Sound Recordings.*

National Union Catalog: Books. Prepared under the editorial coordination of the Catalog Management and Publication Division, Lib. of Congress. Issued monthly on 48x microfiche, with separate cumulative name, title, subject, and series indexes. 1983 December index plus 12 monthly registers, $100.00; 1984 December index plus 12 monthly registers, $110.00; 1985 subscription, $350.00. Contains bibliographic or catalog entries prepared by the Library of Congress or by one of the libraries that contribute reports to the *National Union Catalog* for books, pamphlets, and manuscripts, such as typescripts of theses, map atlases, monographic microform publications, and monographic government publications, both foreign and domestic. Entries encompass publications from all countries and in virtually every language.

National Union Catalog: U.S. Books. Prepared under the editorial coordination of the Catalog Management and Publication Division, Lib. of Congress. Issued monthly on 48x microfiche, with separate name, title, subject, and series indexes. 1983 December index plus 12 monthly registers, $150.00; 1984 December index plus 12 monthly registers, $145.00; 1985 subscription, $245.00. Consists of records for monographs published in the United States in any language. This is a subset of the *National Union Catalog: Books.*

National Union Catalog: Cartographic Materials. Prepared under the editorial coordination of the Catalog Management and Publication Division, Lib. of Congress. Issued quarterly on 48x microfiche, with five separate indexes (name, title, subject, series, geographical classification code). 1983 registers, $33.00; 1984 registers, $6.50; 1985 subscriptions, $130.00. Includes catalog records of single-sheet maps, map sets, atlases, and maps treated as serials catalogued by the Library of Congress and records for atlases that have been cataloged by 1,500 contributing libraries. In 1983 the entire retrospective Library of Congress's maps database was added to this publication.

The National Union Catalog Pre-1956 Imprints. National Union Catalog Pre-1956 Imprints (Vienna, Virginia) 754 vols. 1968–81, price available on request from the distributor. A cumulative author list representing Library of Congress printed cards and titles reported by other U.S. libraries. Also available on microfiche. A comprehensive retrospective catalog containing some 12 million entries for books, pamphlets, maps, atlases, music, and periodicals, and indicating locations in some 1,100 libraries. A monumental work that supersedes the basic Library of Congress *Catalog of Books . . . and its Supplement (1942–47),* the *Library of Congress Author Catalog, 1948–52,* the *National Union Catalog . . . 1952–55 Imprints,* and the *National Union Catalog . . . 1953–57.* It also incorporates entries from the Union Catalog card file at the Library of Congress.

National Union Catalog, 1972: A Cumulative Author List Representing Library of Congress Printed Cards and Titles Reported by Other American Libraries. Lib. of Congress (Card Division) nine monthly issues, three quarterly cumulations, and annual cumulation, $375.00. This price also covers the *Catalog on Motion Pictures and Film Strips* (three quarterly issues and annual cumulation, $20.00) and *Catalog on Music and Phonorecords* (semiannual issue and annual cumulation).

The National Union Catalog ceased publication as a book catalog at the end of 1982, and, since January 1983, has been available on computer-generated microfiche.

GREAT BRITAIN

British Museum General Catalogue of Printed Books and the Catalogues of The Bodleian Library and of the University Library Cambridge, an Author Union Catalogue Extracted from the: "Eighteenth-Century British Books." 5 vols. Ed. by F.J.G. Robinson and others. Wm. Dawson. o.p.

British Museum General Catalogue of Printed Books, Subject Catalogue Extracted from the: "Eighteenth-Century British Books." 4 vols. Wm. Dawson o.p.

British Museum-Library. *General Catalogue of Printed Books: Compact Edition.* Readex Bks. *First Supplement, 1956–65.* 5 vols. 1974 $180.00. ISBN 0-918414-05-9. *Second Supplement, 1966-70.* 3 vols. 1974 $150.00. ISBN 0-918414-06-7. *Third Supplement, 1971–75.* 2 vols. 1980 $180.00. ISBN 0-918414-07-5

Retrospective National Bibliographies

EARLY AND RARE BOOKS

British Museum. Department of Printed Books. *Catalogue of Books Printed in the XVth Century Now in the British Museum.* British Lib. UK 1908–62 o.p. A major source of information on British incunabula, or early printed books.

The Eighteenth Century Short Title Catalogue. Ed. by R. C. Alston and M. J. Crump. British Lib. UK 1990 220 fiches $1,500.00. Now available in CD-ROM in North America by Research Publications. The machine-readable catalog is accessible in the United States through the Research Libraries Information Network (RLIN). The publication of this microfiche catalog of eighteenth-century imprints printed in Britain and in the English language anywhere in the world completes phase one of the *Eighteenth Century Short Title Catalog.* Phase Two, the expansion of the database with records of the holdings of other libraries, is in progress. In the United States, the recording of North American copies of British eighteenth-century imprints is under way at the University of California, Riverside.

Goff, Frederick Richmond. *Incunabula in American Libraries: A Third Census of Fifteenth Century Books Recorded in North American Collections.* 1964. Kraus 1973 $125.00. ISBN 0-527-34200-9. Originally published by the Bibliographical Society of America. The Kraus reprint includes substantial marginal annotations by the author to update the entries. The first census was compiled by the Bibliographical Society in 1919, and the second was compiled by Margaret Bingham Stillwell in 1940.

Incunable Short-Title Catalogue. Ed. by Lotte Hellinga. British Lib. UK Records compiled are accessible in machine-readable form through the British Library Automated Information Services (BLAISE). This is the only bibliography to record all surviving editions of books and other items printed from movable type in Europe from the beginning of printing in the mid-fifteenth century to 1500, and to list all known copies of each edition. Restricting its description of each edition to only what is required for identification, it will not supersede already existing bibliographies of incunabula, but rather is intended to offer far broader coverage of the period than has ever before been provided.

The Nineteenth Century Short Title Catalogue. Chadwyck-Healey Ser. 1 1801–15. 5 vols. 1984 $2,230.00. Series 2 1816–70. 25 vols. Vols. 1–5 1986 $2,140.00. ISBN 0-685-48783-0. Vols. 6–10 1987 $2,140.00. ISBN 0-685-48784-9. Vols. 11–15 1988 $2,140.00. ISBN 0-685-48785-7. Vols. 16–20 1990 $2,140.00. ISBN 0-685-48786-5. Vols. 21–25 1991 $2,250.00. ISBN 0-685-48787-3. A union catalog of all nineteenth-century imprints in English, wherever published, held by the Bodleian Library; the British Library; the University Library, Cambridge; Trinity College Library, Dublin; the National Library of Scotland; and the University Library, Newcastle.

Stillwell, Margaret Bingham. *The Beginning of the World of Books, 1450–1470: A Chronological Survey of the Texts Chosen for Printing during the First Twenty Years of the Printing Art.* Biblio. Soc. Am. 1972 $10.00. ISBN 0-914930-03-6

———. *Incunabula and Americana, 1450–1800: A Key to Bibliographical Study.* 1930. Cooper Sq. 1968 o.p.

UNITED STATES

Evans, Charles. *The American Bibliography: A Chronological Dictionary of All Books, Pamphlets and Periodical Publications Printed in the United States of America from the Genesis of Printing in 1639 Down to and Including the Year 1800; with Bibliographical and Biographical Notes.* 1903–34. Peter Smith repr. of 1942 ed. Vols. 1, 6–9, 11, 12 $15.00. ea. ISBN 0-8446-1173-5. Vol. 13 $30.00. ISBN 0-8446-1174-3. Vol. 14 *Index.* $30.00. ISBN 0-8446-1175-1. Vols. 2–5 10 o.p. This is the most important general list of early American publications. For each book the author's name, along with birth and death dates, full title, date and place of publication, publisher or printer, number of pages, size, and, where possible, the name of a library owning a copy are supplied. In each volume, there is an index by author, subject, and publisher or printer. The first volume of this work was published in 1903; the twelfth, covering the years 1798–1799, was published in 1934, just one year before the bibliographer's death.

Kelly, James. *The American Catalogue of Books (Original and Reprints). Published in the United States 1861 [to Jan. 1871].* 2 Vols. Peter Smith 1938 $19.00 ea. ISBNs 0-8446-1257-X, 0-8446-1258-8. A continuation of Roorbach's *Bibliotheca Americana.*

Leypoldt, Frederick. *American Catalogue of Books (Original and Reprints), Published in the United States . . . 1876–1910.* 13 vols. Peter Smith 1941 o.p. A monumental bibliographic work, recording books in print and for sale, arranged by author, title, and subject.

The New Sabin: Books Described by Joseph Sabin and His Successors, Now Described Again on the Basis of Examination of Originals, and Fully Indexed by Title, Subject, Joint Authors, and Institutions and Agencies. Ed. by Lawrence S. Thompson. 10 vols. Whitston Pub. Vol. 1 1973 $25.00. ISBN 0-87875-049-5. Vol. 2 1975 $25.00. ISBN 0-87875-060-6. Vol. 3 1976 $25.00. ISBN 0-87875-103-3. Vol. 4 1977 $25.00. ISBN 0-87875-134-3. Vol. 5 1979 $25.00. ISBN 0-87875-153-X. Vol. 6 1979 $25.00. ISBN 0-87875-159-9. Vol. 7 1980 $25.00. ISBN 0-87875-183-1. Vol. 9 1983 $30.00. ISBN 0-87875-262-5. Vol. 10 1984 $25.00. ISBN 0-87875-287-0

Roorbach, Orville Augustus. *Bibliotheca Americana: A Catalogue of American Publications, Including Reprints and Original Works, from 1820 [to Jan. 1861].* 1852–61. Peter Smith 1939 Vol. 1 o.p. Vols. 2–4 $30.00. ISBN 0-8446-1389-4. This is the direct ancestor of *The United States Catalog* and *The Cumulative Book Index;* see under "Trade Bibliographies, United States."

Sabin, Joseph, Wilberforce Eames, and R.W.G. Vail. *A Dictionary of Books Relating to America, from Its Discovery to the Present Time. 1868–1936.* 29 vols. Scarecrow 1966 $325.00. ISBN 0-8108-0033-0. Sabin's *Dictionary* is one of the great bibliographic reference works on the world in that it gives the bibliographic facts (including collations, locations, and notes on contents) of more than 100,000 books relating to U.S. history and social life. The *Dictionary* was begun in the middle of the nineteenth century by Joseph Sabin, distinguished American antiquarian. After approximately 15 years of research, Sabin published the first part of Volume 1 in 1868. He continued the work until his death in 1881, by which time he had gone as far as Volume 14, Part 82. After his death, the great task was continued by one of America's greatest bibliographers, Wilberforce Eames, who carried out the work from Volume 14, Part 83, through Volume 20, Part 1126, p. 196 (to the entry "Smith, Henry Hollingsworth"). The continuation by R.W.G. Vail completed the set. The Scarecrow edition in miniprint is said to be readable without aids, but a free bar magnifier is included with each set. It is "the most handy Sabin for bookmen to use" (*Antiquarian Bookman*).

Shaw, Ralph R., and Richard H. Shoemaker. *American Bibliography: A Preliminary Checklist*. 1801–19. Scarecrow 1983 $45.00. ISBN 0-8108-1607-5. A preliminary checklist gathered from secondary sources, designed to partially fill the gap in U.S. national bibliography between 1800, when Evans stops, and 1820, when Roorbach begins. Each volume covers one year.

Shipton, Clifford K., and James E. Mooney, eds. *National Index of American Imprints through 1800: The Short-Title Evans*. U. Pr. of Va. 1969 $75.00. ISBN 0-8271-6908-6. Provides an index to the Readex Microprint edition of Evans and also incorporates into the single alphabetical listing 10,035 additional items that have been identified since the publication of Evans's *The American Bibliography*.

Shoemaker, Richard H., and others. *Checklist of American Imprints*. Scarecrow 1972–92. *1820–29*. $20.00. ISBN 0-8108-0567-7. *1830*. $45.00. ISBN 0-8108-0520-0. *1831*. $45.00. ISBN 0-8108-0828-5. *1832*. $45.00. ISBN 0-8108-1019-0. *1833*. $45.00. ISBN 0-8108-1191-X. *1834*. $45.00. ISBN 0-8108-1487-0. *1835*. $47.50. ISBN 0-8108-1828-0. *1836*. $55.00. ISBN 0-8108-1839-6. *1837*. $45.00. ISBN 0-8108-1841-8. *1838*. $39.50. ISBN 0-8108-2123-0. *1839*. $42.50. ISBN 0-8108-2124-9. *1840*. $65.00. ISBN 0-8108-2376-4. *1841*. $55.00. ISBN 0-8108-2377-2. *1842*. $52.50. ISBN 0-8108-2533-3. *1844*. $52.50. ISBN 0-8108-2654-2. Designed as a continuation of Shaw's *American Bibliography*, giving more complete listings than those in Roorbach. The purpose of this series (see preceding entry) is to make an initial identification of materials published in America during each year from 1820 to 1875. The bibliography is based upon the work of the American Imprints Inventory of the Depression-era WPA but draws heavily upon more recently published national and state bibliographies. Arrangement is by author. The essential elements of description are given, and, in most cases, locations of several extant copies are provided.

GREAT BRITAIN

British National Bibliography. British Lib. UK 1989 o.p. An annual reference catalog of the new books published in Great Britain. Based on new books and new editions deposited with the Agent for the Copyright Libraries, with full bibliographic descriptions of every book. Dewey Decimal Classification (with modifications); author, title, and subject index. First issued in 1950.

Lowndes, William Thomas. *The Bibliographer's Manual of English Literature: Containing an Account of Rare, Curious, and Useful Books, Published in or Relating to Great Britain and Ireland, from the Invention of Printing; with Bibliographical and Critical Notices, Collations of the Rarer Articles, and the Prices at Which They Have Been Sold*. 1834. 8 vols. Ed. by Henry G. Bohn. 1967 repr. of 1964 ed. o.p. Corrected and enlarged edition.

Pollard, A. W., and G. R. Redgrave. *A Short-Title Catalogue of Books Printed in England, Scotland and Ireland, and of English Books Printed Abroad, 1475–1640*. 2 vols. Ed. by N. A. Jackson, F. S. Ferguson, and K. F. Pantzer. OUP 2nd rev. ed. Vol. 1 *A–H*. $275.00. ISBN 0-19-721789-3. Vol. 2 *I–Z*. 1976 $195.00. ISBN 0-19-721790-7

Wing, Donald Godard, and Timothy J. Crist. *A Short-Title Catalogue of Books Printed in England, Scotland, Ireland, Wales and British America and of English Books Printed in Other Countries, 1641–1700*. 3 vols. Modern Lang. 2nd ed. Vol. 1 *A–E*. 1972 $225.00. ISBN 0-87352-044-0. Vol. 2 *E–O*. 1982 $400.00. ISBN 0-87352-045-9. Vol. 3 *P–Z*. 1988 $400.00. ISBN 0-87352-046-7. A continuation of Pollard and Redgrave's *Short-Title Catalogue*.

BOOK TRADE

The book trade encompasses a wide range of activities with respect to books. From publishing and distribution to new and used sales, virtually all books pass through several aspects of the book trade during their existence.

Book Trade and Library Terminology

Included here are glossaries dealing with the language of the book trade. For glossaries dealing specifically with the terminology of book collecting and the rare book, see under "Book Collecting, Glossaries of Terminology" in this chapter.

Genre Terms: A Thesaurus for Use in Rare Books and Special Collections Cataloging. ACRL/ALA 1991 $19.95. ISBN 0-8389-7516-X

Glaister, Geoffrey A. *Glaister's Glossary of the Book.* U. CA Pr. 1979 o.p. Contains terms used in papermaking, printing, bookbinding, and publishing.

Orne, Jerrold. *The Language of the Foreign Book Trade: Abbreviations, Terms and Phrases.* 1949. ALA 3rd ed. 1976 o.p. Designed as a working tool for librarians and personnel in book trade who may not have sufficient familiarity with any of the major languages of Western Europe, Central Europe, Latin America, or the former Soviet Union.

Peters, Jean, ed. *The Bookman's Glossary.* Bowker 6th ed. 1983 $39.95. ISBN 0-8352-1686-1. Classic desktop dictionary of the book trade. Provides precise definitions of more than 1,800 terms.

Prytherch, Ray. *Harrod's Librarian's Glossary and Reference Book.* Ashgate Pub. Co. 7th ed. 1990 $89.95. ISBN 0-566-03620-7

Directories

American Book Trade Directory. Bowker 38th ed. 1992–93 $189.95. ISBN 0-8352-3156-9. Annual that includes lists of booksellers, book clubs, rental library chains, wholesalers, and so on in the United States and Canada.

Cassell and the Publishers Association Directory of Publishing. 2 vols. Oryx Pr. Vol. 1 *UK— Commonwealth Overseas.* 1992 $40.00. ISBN 0-304-32403-5. Vol. 2 *Continental Europe.* 1991 $55.00. ISBN 0-304-32321-7. Covers book publishing and its ancillary services.

International Literary Market Place. Bowker 1993 $164.00. ISBN 0-8352-3232-8. An annual directory to approximately 10,000 active publishers throughout the world.

Literary Market Place. Bowker 1993 $148.00. ISBN 0-8352-3237-9. Lists publishers with addresses, specializations, and some editors. Useful to writers who want their work published and to others in the book trade. Also includes listings on other publishing-related specialists, such as designers, translators, printers, and so on. Published annually, this tracks all aspects of the publishing industry.

Publishers Directory, 1984–85: A Guide to New and Established, Commercial and Nonprofit, Private and Alternative, Corporate and Association, Government and Institution Publishing Programs and Their Distributors. Gale 14th ed. 1993 $235.00. ISBN 0-8103-8156-7; *Supplement.* 1994 $175.00. ISBN 0-8103-8157-5. Includes information on approximately 20,000 publishers in the United States and Canada, excluding only vanity presses and publishers listed in Bowker's *Literary Market Place.*

Publishers, Distributors, and Wholesalers of the United States, 1993–1994: A Directory of 57,000 Publishers, Distributors, Associations, Wholesalers and Software Producers and Manufacturers Listing Editorial and Ordering Addresses, and an ISBN Publisher Prefix Index. 2 vols. Bowker 1993 $165.00. ISBN 0-8352-3382-0. An annual.

Publishers' International ISBN Directory. 3 vols. K. G. Saur 1992 $315.00. ISBN 3-598-21601-7. Provides names and addresses of publishers around the world—arranged geographically. Includes an index listing publishers by subject interests; a guide to publishers' and booksellers' associations, and lists of national and international book trade associations around the globe.

Taubert, Sigfred, and Peter Wiedhaus, eds. *The Book Trade of the World.* 4 vols. K. G. Saur 1972–84 $280.00. ISBN 0-317-11847-1. A country-by-country survey of publishing and bookselling around the world, describing in detail the structure of each country's book trade, providing such information as history, statistics, and industry organizations and publications.

Library Directories

The search for bibliographic information almost inevitably leads one to use the library for either materials or assistance. The following will assist the student or compiler of a bibliography in finding those libraries that may be useful to them.

American Library Directory 1993–94. Bowker 46th ed. 1993 $225.00. ISBN 0-8352-3282-4. Includes public libraries, county and regional extension systems, college and university libraries, junior college libraries, major research libraries overseas, and so on. Arranged geographically by state and city, with information as to key personnel, volumes, budget, special departments, branches, salaries, and so on.

The Bowker Annual Library and Book Trade Almanac 1993. Bowker 1993 $149.95. ISBN 0-8352-3345-6. Sources of listings, charts, associations, and articles of interest to the library and book world.

Directory of Special Libraries and Information Centers. Gale 15th ed. 1991 $399.00. ISBN 0-8103-7138-3

Subject Collections: A Guide to Special Book Collections and Subject Emphases as Reported by University, College, Public, and Special Libraries and Museums in the United States and Canada. Ed. by Lee Ash and William G. Miller. 2 vols. Bowker 7th ed. 1993 $275.00. ISBN 0-8352-3141-0. A companion to the "American Library Directory," this volume indexes the book resources of college, special, and public libraries under subjects based upon Library of Congress subject headings, plus innumerable author, place, and name collections. Within the subject categories, entries are arranged alphabetically in geographic order. Typical entries include name and location of library holding the collection, name of curator, whether indexed, book budget, and so on.

Subject Collections in European Libraries. Ed. by Richard C. Lewanski. Bowker 2nd ed. 1978. o.p. Provides such information as name and location of collection, its size and type of material, name of curator, interlibrary loan and photoreproduction facilities, copyright privileges, number of volumes held, and a bibliographic citation of printed catalogs, guides, and other descriptive and historical monographs on the library.

World Guide to Libraries. Ed. by Bettina Bartz. K. G. Saur 11th ed. 1993 $350.00. ISBN 3-598-20720-4. Lists special, university, and public libraries from countries in Europe, Africa, America, Asia, and Oceania. For each library, the guide provides the name and address, subject specialities, year of establishment, and number of books. The subject index, subdivided by country, pinpoints all of the libraries of any country with particular subject collections.

World Guide to Special Libraries. Ed. by Helga Lengenfelder. K. G. Saur 2nd ed. 1990 $325.00. ISBN 3-598-22230-0. Lists more than 32,000 libraries in 160 countries.

Trade Bibliographies

Trade bibliographies are the basic reference tools for librarians, bibliographers, and booksellers who are seeking information as to which books are in print and when, where, by whom, and at what price they were published and made available for sale. The following list includes both current and retrospective sources. Many of these titles are available also in nonprint formats.

UNITED STATES

The American Book Publishing Record Annual Cumulative Bowker 1970–present. 1992 vol. $211.00. ISBN 0-8352-3365-0. Provides quick access to over 500,000 titles, arranged in Dewey sequence with sections for Fiction and Juvenile Fiction. In addition to annual volumes, cumulative volumes covering five-year periods are also available under the title *The American Book Publishing Record Cumulatives*.

Books in Print. 10 vols. Bowker 46th ed. 1993–94 $425.00 set. ISBN 0-8352-3354-5. An annual publication listing all the in-print books of some 17,000 U.S. publishers by title and by author—more than 692,000 titles in all. Information provided includes author, title, edition, Library of Congress number, series information, language (if other than English), whether illustrated or not, grade range, year of publication, type of binding, price, International Standard Book Number, publisher's order number, imprint, and publisher. Also available in CD-ROM.

Books in Print Supplement. 3 vols. Bowker 1993–94 $229.95. ISBN 0-8352-3387-1. An annual publication issued six months after the publication of *Books in Print* to update the information that appears there. Includes titles that have had price or other major changes, titles that have gone out of print, and titles that have been published or announced since the last edition of *Books in Print*. Also contains listings of new titles by subject.

The Cumulative Book Index, 1969–1985. Wilson $180.00. ea. ISBN 0-685-22244-6. The *CBI* began publication in 1898. Since 1928, the last single-volume cumulation, it has been an author, title, and subject index to current books in the English language published worldwide. Monthly supplements are published cumulatively quarterly and then annually in bound volumes. Permanent volumes now in print are 1938–42, 1943–48, 1953–56, 1957–58, 1959–60, 1961–62, 1963–64, 1965–66, 1967–68, and annual volumes for each year from 1969 to 1982; continually updated.

The Cumulative Paperback Index, 1939–59: A Comprehensive Bibliographic Guide to 14,000 Mass-Market Paperback Books Issued under 69 Imprints. Ed. by Robert Reginald and M. R. Burgess. Borgo Pr. 1990 $50.00. ISBN 0-89370-022-3

Guide to Reprints: An International Bibliography of Scholarly Reprints. Guide to Reprints 1991 $160.00. ISBN 0-918086-17-5. An annual guide to books, journals, and other materials that are available in reprint form.

Paperbound Books in Print. 6 vols. Bowker 1993 $375.00. ISBN 0-8352-3314-6. A spring and fall semiannual. Contains more than 413,000 titles. Arranged by author, title, and subject. Fiction titles in the author index are identified as General Fiction, Mysteries, Westerns, or Science Fiction. Subject index includes a Literature heading, with subheadings for Novels, Poetry, and Short Stories.

Publishers' Trade List Annual. 4 vols. Bowker 1993 $250.00. ISBN 0-8352-3375-8. A collection of the booklists and catalogs of some 1,800 U.S. publishers bound together alphabetically.

Subject Guide to Books in Print. 5 vols. Bowker 1993–94 $299.00. ISBN 0-8352-3348-0. A subject guide to the nonfiction titles listed in *Books in Print*; titles arranged under some 66,000 headings, with numerous cross-references. Also available on-line and on CD-ROM.

The United States Catalog: Books in Print. Wilson 1929 o.p. Continued by *The Cumulative Book Index*.

GREAT BRITAIN

British Paperback Books in Print. J. Whitaker UK semiannual £25.00. A complete record of all paperbacks in print in the United Kingdom.

Whitaker's Books in Print. 4 vols. Bowker 1993 $426.00. ISBN 0-85021-230-8. All British books in print at the end of April of each year. This is the continuation of *British Books in Print*, which continued *The Reference Catalogue of Current Literature* first published in 1874 and subsequently in four- or five-year intervals; provides access to 400,000 titles.

Whitaker's Cumulative Books List. J. Whitaker UK annual $25.00. A complete record of British publishing each year, with details as to title, subtitle, author, size, number of pages, price, month of publication, publisher, and classification.

CANADA

Canadian Books in Print 1992: Author and Title Index. U. of Toronto Pr. 1992 $135.00. ISBN 0-8020-4661-4

Canadian Books in Print 1992: Subject Index. U. of Toronto Pr. 1992 $115.00. ISBN 0-8020-4662-2

Tools for Periodical and Newspaper Identification

Periodicals, magazines, and newspapers are difficult to identify and to locate because of frequent changing patterns of publication. The standard tools listed below will assist in identification of these items worldwide.

To access information in these materials, the reader is referred to the appropriate subject chapter in this work and the periodical indexes listed therein.

Ayer Directory of Publications. Ayer o.p. Indexes newspapers and magazines published in the United States and its territories; also includes Canada, Bermuda, Panama, and the Philippines. Arranged geographically, with classified lists. Now incorporated in *Gale Directory of Publications and Broadcast Media.*

Gale Directory of Publications and Broadcast Media 94 and Update. Ed. by Julie Winklepleck. Gale 1993 $280.00. ISBN 0-8103-8059-5

Katz, William, and Linda Sternberg Katz. *Magazines for Libraries.* Bowker 7th ed. 1992 $139.95. ISBN 0-8352-3166-6. Completely rewritten to reflect current serials trends and offers recommendations on over 6,500 periodicals.

————. *Magazines for Young People.* Bowker 1991 $38.00. ISBN 0-8352-3009-0. Lists and annotates more than 1,100 magazines in 74 subjects. Covers materials for children ages 3 to 18.

New Serial Titles, 1950–70, Subject Guide. 2 vols. Bowker 1975 $138.50. ISBN 0-8352-0820-6. It includes approximately 260,000 titles, arranged alphabetically. Information includes issuing body, place of publication, date of first issue, and date of last issue if publication has ceased. Dewey Decimal Classification number, country code, and International Standard Serial Number are included.

Spahn, Theodore J., Janet M. Spahn, and Robert H. Muller. *From Radical Left to Extreme Right: A Bibliography of Current Periodicals of Protest, Controversy, Advocacy or Dissent, with Dispassionate Content-Summaries to Guide Librarians and Other Educators.* Scarecrow 1987 $59.50. ISBN 0-8108-1967-8. Includes a geographical index; an index of titles, editors, and publishers; and a subject index.

The Standard Periodical Directory. Oxbridge Comm. 15th ed. 1992 $445.00. ISBN 0-917460-37-5. A guide to more than 75,000 U.S. and Canadian periodicals. Alphabetical subject arrangement with author index and subject guide. Gives names and address of publisher, editorial content and scope, year founded, subscription rate and so on.

Ulrich's International Periodicals Directory. 5 vols. Bowker 32nd ed. 1993–94 $395.00. ISBN 0-8352-3368-5. Provides in-depth information for some 126,000 regularly and irregularly issued serials from all over the world, arranged by subject. Special sections list periodicals that have been launched or ceased publication since 1983, and indexing and abstracting services are also included. Includes addresses for 65,000 publishers in 200 countries. Includes irregular serials and annuals.

Working Press of the Nation. 5 vols. Bowker 1992 $330.00. ISBN 0-912670-91-3. Includes Volume 1, *Newspaper Directory*; Volume 2, *Magazine Directory*; Volume 3, *TV and Radio Directory*; Volume 4, *Feature Writer and Photographer Directory*; Volume 5, *Internal Publications Directory.* With cross-references and indexes.

Tools for Book Selection

Many book lists are compiled annually by libraries, wholesalers, and various organizations. The American Library Association catalogs are the highest type of evaluative bibliography. Entries are arranged according to the Dewey Decimal Classification. Each entry gives the author, birth and death dates, title, publisher, date of publication, price, number of pages, and a description and evaluation of the contents.

GENERAL BOOK SELECTION TOOLS

Best Books for Public Libraries. Ed. by Steve Arozena. Bowker 1992 $75.00. ISBN 0-8352-3073-2. Based on positive reviews from respected sources (*New York Times,* etc.), this one-volume annotated bibliography lists more than 1,000 fiction and nonfiction titles best for public libraries. Nonfiction is arranged according to Dewey classification; fiction according to genre. Review citations are given for each entry. Author, title, and subject indexes are included.

Book Review Digest. 1905–present. Wilson Annual, 1905–1924. $110.00. ea. Annual, 1925–1959 $135.00. ISBN 0-686-66570-8. Annual, 1960–1985 $150.00. ISBN 0-686-66571-6. Annual, 1980–1990. o.p. Approximately 6,000 books a year are listed by author with price, publisher, and descriptive notes. Published monthly (except February and July) with permanent bound annual accumulations. Annual volumes from 1905 to present are available at prices ranging from $90.00 to $125.00.

Books for College Libraries: A Core Collection of 50,000 Titles. 6 vols. ALA 3rd ed. 1988 $600.00. ISBN 0-8389-3353-X. The titles included are considered the minimum essential for the four-year undergraduate college. Subject specialists evaluated the titles in the earlier editions as well as titles published between 1972 and 1985. Titles are arranged by Library of Congress classification and are entered in the main catalog only once. Volume 6 contains author, title, and subject indexes.

Books for Public Libraries. ALA 1981 o.p. Professional book-selection tool developed by the Public Library Association.

The Fiction Catalog. Wilson 12th ed. 1991 $98.00. ISBN 0-8242-0804-8. Lists over 5,000 works of fiction that have been found most useful by experienced and outstanding librarians in U.S. and Canadian libraries. The four annual supplements cover approximately 1,600 additional titles.

Public Library Catalog (Standard Catalog for Public Libraries). Wilson 9th ed. 1989 $180.00. ISBN 0-8242-0778-5. A classified and annotated list of some 8,000 nonfiction titles recommended for small and medium-sized libraries. Part 1 is a classified catalog arranged by Dewey Decimal Classification, with subject headings based on the *Sears List of Subject Headings.* Part 2 is an author, title, and subject index to Part 1, with analytical entries for parts of books. Part 3 is a directory of publishers and distributors.

REFERENCE BOOKS

Bopp, Richard E., and Linda C. Smith. *Reference and Information Services: An Introduction.* Libs. Unl. 1991 $47.50. ISBN 9-87287-788-4. Offers chapter-length discussions of principles and goals with equal coverage of sources. Solid introductory work.

General Reference Books for Adults. Bowker 1988 $75.00. ISBN 0-8352-2393-0. Compiled in cooperation with experienced librarians and subject experts. Evaluates over 200 basic adult reference works—atlases, dictionaries, encyclopedias, word books, and large-print reference works. Features facsimile pages and entries, comparison charts, at-a-glance fact boxes, review excerpts, and results of a librarian reference-rating survey.

Katz, William A. *Introduction to Reference Work.* 2 vols. McGraw 1987 $29.82. ea. Vol. 1 ISBN 0-07-033638-5. Vol. 2 ISBN 0-07-033639-3. Acquaints students, librarians, and library users with reference works in order to help them use the library more effectively. An essential tool.

Kister, Kenneth F. *Best Encyclopedias: A Guide to General and Specialized Encyclopedias.* Oryx Pr. 1993 $44.95. ISBN 0-89774-744-5

_____. *Kister's Atlas Buying Guide: General English-Language World Atlases Available in North America.* Oryx Pr. 1984 $10.95. ISBN 0-912700-62-9

Reference Books for Young Readers. Bowker 1988 $52.95. ISBN 0-8352-2366-3. Rates and evaluates reference books aimed at young readers. Compiled by a board of children's/young adult librarians and subject experts.

Reference Sources for Small and Medium-Sized Libraries. Ed. by Jovian P. Lang. ALA 5th ed. 1992 $37.00. ISBN 0-8389-3406-4

Sheehey, Eugene P. *Guide to Reference Books.* ALA 10th ed. 1986 $35.00. ISBN 0-8389-0390-8. *Supplement* covers books published 1985–1990.

Taylor, Margaret, and Ronald R. Powell. *Basic Reference Sources: A Self-Study Manual.* Scarecrow Pr. 4th ed. 1990 $27.50. ISBN 0-8108-2244-X

Topical Reference Books. Bowker 1991 $109.00. ISBN 0-8352-3087-2. Selects and recommends today's best specialized reference books. Provides titles, authors, publishers, and ordering information. Includes expert evaluations of over 2,000 titles in 40 categories; with indexes.

Walford, A. J. *Walford's Guide to Reference Material.* UNIPUB Vol. 1 1993 ISBN 1-85604-015-1. Volume 1 deals with science and technology; Volume 2 with philosophy and religion; and Volume 3 with generalities, languages, and arts and literature.

Wynar, Bohdan S. *American Reference Books Annual.* Libs. Unl. 1993 $87.50. ISBN 1-56308-076-1

CHILDREN'S BOOKS

The field of children's books has a literature of its own that goes beyond the scope of this chapter. Listed below are some of the basic tools for selecting books for children.

Children's Books in Print. 2 vols. Bowker 1993 $139.00 ISBN 0-8352-3229-8. Author, title, and illustrator index to over 80,000 books. Includes children's book awards.

Children's Catalog. Wilson 16th ed. 1991 $90.00. ISBN 8242-0805-6. A catalog of children's books found useful in public and elementary school libraries. The catalog is arranged in three parts: Part 1 is a classified catalog giving full cataloging information for each book; Part 2 is an author, title, and subject index with analytical entries; Part 3 is a directory of publishers and distributors. Annual supplements.

The Elementary School Library Collection: A Guide to Books and Other Media. Ed. by Lauren K. Lee and Gary D. Hoyle. Brodart 18th ed. 1992 $99.95. ISBN 0-87272-095-0. Covers books, periodicals, sound filmstrips, sound recordings, videocassettes, microcomputer programs, and CD-ROM products. Not an annual tool and very selective.

Gillespie, John T. *Best Books for Junior High Readers.* Bowker 1991 $43.00. ISBN 0-8352-3020-1. Recommends over 6,000 books as selected by leading journals. An appendix lists over 750 challenging titles for advanced young teenagers.

_____. *Best Books for Senior High Readers.* Bowker 1991 $48.00. ISBN 0-8352-3021-X. Offers annotaed selections of over 10,000 recommended books for older teens. Titles where chosen based on sources such as *School Library Journal, Booklist,* and *Voice of Youth Advocates.* Main section entries are arranged by subject.

Gillespie, John T., and Corinne J. Naden. *Best Books for Children.* Bowker 4th ed. 1990 $48.00. ISBN 0-8352-2668-9. Evaluative listing of over 11,000 titles, each with two or three recommendations from leading journals. Provides review citations; separate author, title, and illustrator indexes.

Junior High School Library Catalog. Wilson 6th ed. 1990 $105.00. ISBN 0-8242-0799-8. An annotated list of approximately 4,000 in-print fiction and nonfiction titles essential to the junior high school library collection (grades 7–9).

Lima, Carolyn W., and John A. Lima. *A to Zoo: Subject Access to Children's Picture Books.* Bowker 4th ed. 1993 $49.95. ISBN 0-8352-3201-8. Lists more than 15,000 fiction and nonfiction titles for preschool through the second grade. Complete bibliographic information is included. Additional indexes list all entries by author, title, and illustrator. Caldecott Award winners are noted.

Nichols, Margaret Irby. *Guide to Reference Books for School Library Media Centers*. Libs. Unl. 1992 $38.50. ISBN 0-87287-833-3. Addresses reference needs of students from kindergarten to high school.

Senior High School Library Catalog (Standard Catalog for High School Libraries). Wilson 14th ed. 1992 $115.00. ISBN 0-8242-0831-5

Subject Guide to Children's Books in Print. Bowker 1993 $139.00. ISBN 0-8352-3262-X. A subject listing of over 45,000 juvenile titles under more than 7,100 subject headings. Provides complete ordering information: author, title, publisher, date of publication, price, and, when available, grade level, binding, and edition.

The Young Adult Reader's Adviser. 2 vols. Bowker 1992 $79.95. ISBN 0-8352-3068-6. Patterned after *The Reader's Adviser*, this set features 17,000 bibliographic entries, more than 850 biographical profiles, and author, title, and subject indexes.

LISTS OF "BEST" BOOKS

The making of lists of "best books" is a form of book selection that is ever popular, both with the makers of books and with the readers. One of the earliest lists is Sir John Lubbock's famous Hundred Best Books in *The Pleasures of Life*, first published in 1887 and now out of print.

Dickinson, Asa Don. *The World's Best Books: Homer to Hemingway; 3000 Books of 3000 Years, 1050 B.C. to 1950 A.D. Selected on the Basis of a Consensus of Expert Opinion*. Wilson 1953 o.p. This brief volume unifies and revises its four predecessors. Brief descriptions of each title; useful for individual reading programs.

Downs, Robert B. *Books That Changed the World*. NAL-Dutton 1956 $5.99. ISBN 0-451-62698-2

_____. *Famous American Books*. McGraw 1971 o.p.

Fadiman, Clifton. *The Lifetime Reading Plan*. HarpC 1988. $10.00. ISBN 0-06-096174-0. A guide to his famous "100 books."

The Reader's Adviser. 6 vols. Bowker 14th ed. 1993 $500.00. Provides a useful survey of the world's writers and writings. Five volumes on the best books in reference, British and American literature, world literature, social science, history, the arts, philosophy and religion, science, technology, and medicine. Each volume includes comprehensive name, title, and subject indexes. Sixth volume is an index volume to the complete set.

The Reader's Catalog: An Annotated Selection of More Than 40,000 of the Best Books in Print in 205 Categories. Ed. by Geoffrey O'Brien. Reader's Catalog 1989 $24.95. ISBN 0-924322-00-4. The book's aim, according to the introduction, is to provide access for book buyers to a wide range of titles.

Waldhorn, Arthur, and others, eds. *Good Reading: A Guide for Serious Readers*. Bowker 23rd ed. 1990 $44.00. ISBN 0-8352-2707-3. An annotated guide to more than 3,000 enduring nonfiction titles. Entries are indexed under five major subject headings: historical periods, regional and American minority cultures, literary types, humanities and social sciences, and sciences.

BOOK COLLECTING

The books included here relate to the individual collector, the institutional collector, and the book dealer. They are a representative selection from the vast literature of book collecting. Also listed are directories for the rare and antiquarian book trade.

Glossaries of Terminology

Included here are glossaries of terms used specifically in book collecting and the rare book trade. Glossaries that include the terminology of book collecting as one aspect of the language of the book trade can be found in this chapter under "Book Trade and Library Terminology."

ABC for Book Collectors. Ed. by John Carter. Oak Knoll 6th rev. ed. 1992 $25.00. ISBN 0-938768-30-1. Revised by Nicolas Barker.

Malkin, Sol M. *ABC of the Book Trade.* AB Bookman's Weekly o.p.

General Introductions and Manuals

Ahearn, Allen. *Book Collecting: A Comprehensive Guide.* Putnam Pub. Group 1989 $24.95. ISBN 0-3991-3456-5. Single-volume guide to the values of books, with six introductory chapters. Gives the values of 3,500 books by frequently requested authors.

Berkeley, Edmund, Jr., and others. *Autographs and Manuscripts: A Collector's Manual.* Scribner 1978 o.p. A collection of articles sponsored by the Manuscript Society, offering the collector of autographs a comprehensive manual covering the history and fundamentals of autograph collecting.

Book Collecting: A Modern Guide. Ed. by Jean Peters. Bowker 1977 $39.95. ISBN 0-8352-0985-7. A collection of 12 original essays by a group of prominent book professionals on the techniques of book collecting, offering advice on practical ways of building, organizing, and caring for a personal or special collection of books and manuscripts. Concludes with an excellent bibliographic essay on "The Literature of Book Collecting" by G. Thomas Tanselle.

Carter, John. *Taste and Technique in Book Collecting.* Private Libs. Assoc. 1970 o.p. A gracefully written and intelligent work on the nature of book collecting; one of the great classics in the field.

———, ed. *New Paths in Book Collecting: Essays by Various Hands.* 1934. Ayer repr. of 1967 ed. $16.00. ISBN 0-8369-0279-3. A collection of essays by a group of English collectors and dealers, offering excellent examples of imaginative approaches to book collecting. Areas covered include detective fiction, "yellow backs," serial fiction, and musical first editions.

Collectible Books: Some New Paths. Ed. by Jean Peters. Bowker 1979 $39.95. ISBN 0-8352-1154-1. A collection of essays by a group of librarians, scholars, and book collectors on nontraditional areas of collecting. Among the collecting areas covered are nonfirsts, anthologies, mass market paperbacks, American trade bindings, photography as book illustration, publishers' imprints, and American fiction since 1960.

Connolly, Joseph. *Modern First Editions: Their Value to Collectors.* Trans. Atl. Phila. 3rd ed. 1987 $42.50. ISBN 0-356-14212-4

Jackson, Holbrook. *The Anatomy of Bibliomania.* Beil 1989 $35.00. ISBN 0-913720-70-4

Raabe, Tom. *Biblioholism: The Literary Addiction.* Fulcrum Pub. 1991 $8.95. ISBN 1-55591-080-7. A lighter look at the subject of book collecting.

Uden, Grant. *Understanding Book-Collecting.* Antique Collect. 1986 $29.50. ISBN 0-907462-13-8

Wilson, Robert A. *Modern Book Collecting.* Knopf 1980 o.p. A guide for the beginning collector of modern first editions. Included is a key to identifying first editions of nearly 200 American and British publishers and a list of bibliographies of collected modern authors.

Zempel, Edward N., and Linda A. Verkler. *First Editions: A Guide to Identification.* Spoon River 1989 $28.00. ISBN 0-930358-08-2. Statements of selected North American, British Commonwealth, and Irish publishers on their methods of designating first editions.

RARE BOOK TRADE

Keys to Anonymous Books

The anonymous book begs for identification. The books listed below, which are either reprints of earlier books or are books currently out of print, form the basis for identifying books without an author. From 1950 on, authorship of anonymous and pseudonymous works in English and U.S. literature can usually be found in the British National Bibliography and in the National Union Catalog.

Cushing, William. *Anonyms: A Dictionary of Revealed Authorship.* 1889. Adlers Foreign Bks. 1968 $148.00. ISBN 3-487-02714-3

Halkett, Samuel, and John Liang. *Dictionary of Anonymous Literature.* Haskell repr. of 1971 ed. $490.00. ISBN 0-8383-1245-4. Covers 1475 to 1640.

Initials and Pseudonyms: A Dictionary of Literary Disguises. 1885. Gale 1982 o.p. Covers English and American literary territory from the eighteenth century to the time of the book's publication.

Ossman, Jennifer, ed. *Pseudonyms and Nicknames Dictionary.* 2 vols. Gale 3rd ed. 1986 $235.00. ISBN 0-8103-0541-0

Room, Adrian. *A Dictionary of Pseudonyms and Their Origins, with Stories of Name Changes.* McFarland & Co. 1989 $35.00. ISBN 0-89950-450-7. Four thousand entries document the pseudonym together with real name, vital dates, nationality, profession or sphere of activity, and country of settlement (where different from native land).

Stonehill, Charles A. Andrew Block, and H. Winthrop Stonehill. *Anonyma and Pseudonyma.* 1927. 4 vols. Longwood 1977 o.p.

Taylor, Archer, and Frederic J. Mosher. *The Bibliographical History of Anonyma and Pseudonyma.* U. of Ch. Pr. 1951 o.p.

Rare Book Collectors and Dealers

AB Bookman's Yearbook. 12 pts. Ed. by Jacob L. Chernofsky. AB Bookman's Weekly 1993 ed. $15.00. Free with AB subscription. The *Yearbook* includes such book trade features as a "Directory of Specialist and Antiquarian Booksellers."

Bookdealers in North America: A Directory of Dealers in Secondhand and Antiquarian Books in Canada and the United States, 1983–85. Seven Hills Bk. 9th ed. 1983 o.p.

The Collector's Guide to Antiquarian Bookstores. Macmillan 1984 o.p. With an introduction by Leona Rostenberg and Madeleine B. Stern.

Dealers in Books: A Directory of Dealers in Secondhand and Antiquarian Books in the British Isles, 1984–86. Seven Hills Bk. 1982 o.p. Dated but potentially useful until more current listings are available.

Directory of Specialized American Bookdealers, 1984–1985. Moretus Pr. 1984 $35.00. ISBN 0-89679-012-6. Prepared by the staff of *American Book Collector.*

European Bookdealers: A Directory of Dealers in Secondhand and Antiquarian Books on the Continent of Europe, 1982–84. Seven Hills Bk. 1982 $39.95. ISBN 0-904929-24-8. This material is dated but remains one of the few sources for this information that is currently available.

Rare Books 1983–84: Trends, Collections, Sources. Ed. by Alice D. Schreyer. Bowker 1984 o.p. A combination directory and year-in-review that covers the antiquarian and rare book trade. The directory section contains full contact and descriptive listings for rare book libraries, antiquarian book dealers, and appraisers.

Robinson, Ruth E., and Daryush Farudi. *Buy Books Where—Sell Books Where: A Directory of Out of Print Booksellers and their Author-Subject Specialities.* Robinson Bks. 8th rev. ed. 1992 $29.75. ISBN 0-9603556-9-3. Current directory that lists more than 2,000 active out-of-print booksellers and more than 6,000 subject and author listings.

Rostenberg, Leona, and Madeleine B. Stern. *Old and Rare: Forty Years in the Book Business*. Modoc Pr. 1988 repr. of 1974 ed. $11.95. ISBN 0-929246-00-4

Sheppard, Roger, and Judith Sheppard, eds. *The International Directory of Book Collectors, 1985–1987*. Bowker 4th ed. 1985 $39.95. ISBN 0-904929-26-8

Rare Book Prices

American Book Prices Current Annual. 1895–present. Ed. by Daniel Leab and Katherine Leab. Bancroft Parkman Vol. 97. 1991 $135.00. ISBN 0-914022-25-3. Earlier volumes are all out of print. This distinguished series, issued continuously for more than 75 years, covers all principal book auction sales in the United States and London and, with the newest volumes, covers also some major Continental sales. It was issued originally by Dodd, later by Dutton, then by Bowker, and from 1953 through 1965 by Edward Lazare, a leading rare book expert, as editor and Ramona J. Lazare as publisher. It was subsequently issued by Columbia University Press for five years before it was acquired by its present owner.

American Book Prices Current Index. American Book Prices Current 1916–1983 12 vols. o.p. Useful for identifying trends in prices and demand in the rare book trade.

Author Price Guides. Quill and Brush 1984–to date. o.p. Separate guides issued for each author, printed on three-ring binder paper. A series of bibliographic checklists of the first editions of collectible authors, with estimated retail price ranges noted.

Book Auction Records 1988–1989, Vol. 86. Intl. Pubns. Serv. 1990 $175.00. ISBN 0-7129-1049-2. A priced and annotated annual record of book auctions throughout the world.

Bradley, Van Allen. *The Book Collector's Handbook of Values 1982–83*. Putnam Pub. Group 1982 o.p. The Chicago book critic, journalist, and one-time bookseller lists (by author) some 15,000 old and contemporary editions desired by collectors, along with approximate prices. Bradley's popular column about rare books, "Gold in Your Attic," led to a book by that title and a sequel, *New Gold in Your Attic*.

Howes, Wright. *U.S. Iana*. Bowker 2nd ed. 1978 $49.95. ISBN 0-8352-0103-1. A selective bibliography of Americana identifying significant and collectible works. Titles are keyed to relative grades of value, importance, and scarcity.

International Rare Book Prices: Early Printed Books, 1988. Ed. by Michael Cole. Spoon River 1988 $38.00. ISBN 1-870773-02-0

International Rare Book Prices: Modern First Editions, 1988. Ed. by Michael Cole. Spoon River 1988 $38.00. ISBN 1-870773-03-9

McGrath, Daniel, ed. *The Bookman's Price Index, Vol. 48*. Gale 1994 $208.00. ISBN 0-8103-5602-3. Each volume contains entries selected from the catalogs of leading antiquarian and specialist book dealers of the United States and Great Britain.

Mandeville's Used Book Price Guide. Ed. by Richard L. Collins. Price Guide 1989 $89.95. ISBN 0-911182-88. Since used book prices are constantly in a state of flux, this will serve as a guideline only.

Shiflett, Lee. *Bookman's Guide to Americana*. 10th ed. Scarecrow 1991 $49.50. ISBN 0-8108-2464-7. An alphabetical cumulation from antiquarian booksellers' catalogs in Americana.

Bibliographies and Checklists

Whether one collects an author, subject, or a printing or publishing imprint, bibliographies are essential in helping to identify and to describe the material to be collected. In the nineteenth century, it was still possible to prepare comprehensive bibliographies that attempted to list *all* rare and collectible books. Today, works such as this have been superseded by hundreds of specialized bibliographies, so that it is necessary now to consult such works as Theodore Besterman's *A World Bibliography of Bibliographies*, the Wilson Company's *Bibliographic Index*, and others grouped together under the section on "Bibliographies of Bibliographies" to learn what individual bibliographies are available on a particular collecting interest.

In the field of literature, where author collecting is probably the most predominant form, the collecting rules are set down in descriptive author bibliographies. These may be collective, providing the descriptions of the works of a number of authors, such as the monumental *Bibliography of American Literature* compiled by Jacob Blanck, or they may be of individual authors, such as John C. Sherwood's *Stephen Crane: An Annotated Bibliography*. A full range of descriptive author bibliographies in English and American literature can be located in the works listed below.

Ghodes, Clarence, and Sanford E. Marovitz. *Bibliographical Guide to the Study of the Literature of the U.S.A.* Duke 1984 $35.00. ISBN 0-8223-0592-5

Howard-Hill, T. H. *Bibliography of British Literary Bibliographies*. OUP 1987 $160.00. ISBN 0-19-818184-1. Supplemented by the last half of his *Shakespearean Bibliography and Textual Criticism: A Bibliography* (Oxford 1971 $39.95).

LeFontaine, Joseph Raymond. *A Handbook for Booklovers: A Survey of Collectible Authors, Books and Values*. Prometheus Bks. 1988 $69.95. ISBN 0-87975-491-5. For the bibliophile.

Cambridge New Bibliography of English Literature, 4 vols. Ed. by G. Watson. Cambridge U. Pr. 1987 $470.00. ISBN 0-521-34378-X

Tanselle, G. Thomas. *Guide to the Study of United States Imprints*. 2 vols. HUP 1971 $100.00. ISBN 0-674-36761-8. Published research concerning the history of U.S. printing and publishing, divided into nine different categories.

CHAPTER 3

Reference Books: General

John V. Richardson, Jr. and Margaret R. Zarnosky

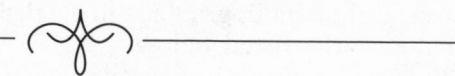

"Knowledge is of two kinds. We know a subject ourselves, or we know where
we can find information upon it."

—SAMUEL JOHNSON, *Boswell's Life*

When the reader wants to find the answer to his own questions, a good place to
start is with general reference books. Reference books can be defined in several
ways. Administratively, libraries consider certain publications noncirculating;
that is one kind of reference work. More theoretically, the format of reference
books is structured in such a way that it makes them less likely to be read from
cover to cover, for instance, like a novel. Hence, librarians refer to those books
as "reference," and probably this definition makes the most sense. The point is
that there are numerous publications that probably qualify as reference books
that may not be found in the reference collection of your local library. Be sure
to ask for assistance at the "Reference" or "Information Service" department.

For the last fiscal year in which data were available, the American Library
Association estimated that 129 million questions were asked in American
libraries. To answer these questions reliably, reference librarians drew upon
traditional print-based publications, but increasingly used on-line bibliographic
databases as well as CD-ROM resources. When they did not actually know a
specific source that contained the answer, they employed a trick of the trade,
sometimes called the Mudge Method or the Hutchins Heuristic, which is to
classify the question by type of reference source; in other words, what reference
format would be likely to contain the answer to a question. Either implicitly or
explicitly, the reference works cited draw upon this technique to teach novices
how to answer reference questions.

The importance of format cannot be overemphasized in the process of
answering questions. Hence, the following sections are organized according to
format. It should be noted that bibliography as a format is not included here; the
reader should see Chapter 2, entitled "Bibliography," for lists of books and
specific library holdings.

GENERAL REFERENCE WORKS

Cheney, Frances N., and Wiley J. Williams. *Fundamental Reference Sources*. ALA 2nd ed.
1980 $15.00. ISBN 0-8389-0308-8. Although now somewhat dated, this source covers
more than 500 landmark reference sources.

Hutchins, Margaret. *Introduction to Reference Works*. ALA 1944 o.p. Emphasizing know-
how rather than know-what, this text is most valuable for its procedural approach to
answering reference questions.

Katz, William. *Introduction to Reference Work.* 2 vols. McGraw 1982 $33.40 ea. Vol 1 *Basic Information Sources.* ISBN 0-07-033638-5. Vol. 2 *Reference Services.* ISBN 0-07-033639-3. The most current textbook for this field. Strong on recent reference materials.

Sader, Marion, ed. *General Reference Books for Adults.* Bowker 1988 $69.95. ISBN 0-8352-2393-0. Contains more than 200 basic adult reference works. Compiled in cooperation with librarians and subject experts. Features facsimile pages and entries, comparison charts, fact boxes, review excerpts, and librarian reference-rating survey results.

————. *Reference Books for Young Readers.* Bowker 1988 $49.95. ISBN 0-8352-2366-3. Rates and evaluates encyclopedias, atlases, and dictionaries for young readers. Compiled by a board of children's/young adult librarians and subject experts.

————. *Topical Reference Works.* Bowker 1991 $104.95. ISBN 0-8352-3087-2. Selects and recommends specialized reference books on a variety of subjects. Contains more than 2,000 titles in 50 different categories. Features headnotes with background information and suggestions, core title suggestions for building a reference collection, and reviewer quotes.

Sheehy, Eugene P. *Guide to Reference Books.* 10th ed. ALA 1986 $80.00. ISBN 0-8389-0390-8. The most comprehensive American guide, listing more than 14,000 useful reference books for academic libraries. *Supplement* to 10th edition (covering 1985–90) is edited by Robert Balay.

Shores, Louis. *Basic Reference Books.* ALA 1954 o.p. Probably the most extensive coverage of the different formats of reference materials.

Thomas, Diana, Ann Hinckley, and Elizabeth Eisenbach. *The Effective Reference Librarian.* Academic Pr. 1980 $33.00. ISBN 0-12-688720-9. No specific reference books are discussed; however, the psychological aspects of asking questions in the reference interview, called "question negotiation," is thoroughly covered here.

Wyer, James. *Reference Work.* ALA 1930 o.p. The first textbook for teaching reference work to novices.

Almanacs and Yearbooks

Almanacs and yearbooks offer quick, direct access to recent, factual data, usually in a single volume. Factual information may be organized by time period, subject, or geography (either nationally or on a worldwide basis). Typically, these kinds of sources are issued annually. Readers needing more current information should consult the section on "Indexes and Abstracting Services" or the statistical sources listed in the section "Government Publications." Up-to-the-minute information can be found in newspapers and their respective indexes.

The Almanac of American Politics. Ed. by Michael Barone and Grant Ujifus. 1970–present. Nat'l. Journal 1990 $44.95. ISBN 0-89234-043-6. Information about senators and representatives and their districts, including major votes and ratings by interest groups.

Almanacs of the United States. Comp. by Milton Drake. 2 vols. Scarecrow 1962 o.p. This checklist of 14,300 entries includes almanacs and calendars published from 1639 on, arranged geographically by state, then chronologically by year of publication.

The American Jewish Yearbook. Ed. by David Singer. 1899–present. JPS Phila. 1991 $30.00. ISBN 0-8276-0402-5. Published since 1899 and issued by the office of the American Jewish Committee since 1909, it contains an almanac, statistical and directory material, and special articles on contemporary issues.

The Annual Register 1989: A Record of World Events (Annual Register: A Review of Public Events at Home and Abroad). Ed. by H. V. Hodson. 1758–present. Longman 1991 $147.00. ISBN 0-582-07926-8. "Articles written by distinguished contributors chronicle the leading events of the year concerning every country, the UN and other international organizations, social and economic trends, and major developments in all fields. Statistics, text of important documents, a chronology of events, charts and photographs add to the work's reference value".

Britain: An Official Handbook. 1948–present. UNIPUB 1991 $40.00. ISBN 0-11-701550-4. Prepared by the Great Britain Central Office of Information, London, British Information Services. "An excellent handbook . . . it is a factual account of the administration and national economy of the United Kingdom." (*LJ*).

Britannica Book of the Year. 1983–present. Ency. Brit. Inc. o.p. An excellent review of the past year issued annually by Encyclopaedia Britannica, Inc. Information is provided on important events and people of the year, as well as relevant articles on timely subjects. Arranged by subject.

Canadian Almanac and Directory 1985. Ed. by Susan Bracken. 1847–present. 1993 $102.00. ISBN 0-8103-9656-4. Contains legal, commercial, statistical, governmental, ecclesiastical, educational, financial, and general information. Directory sections provide names and addresses of many organizations and companies.

Catholic Almanac: An Annual. Ed. by Felician Foy and Rose M. Avato. Our Sunday Visitor 1992 $19.95. ISBN 0-87973-268-7. An excellent and detailed one-volume source of facts and information concerning the Catholic Church.

CQ Almanac. 1945–present. Cong. Quarterly Annual 1991 $205.00. ISBN 0-685-57411-3. Topical presentation of the activities of the U.S. Congress for the year. Reorganizes and indexes the material that appears in the *CQ Weekly Report.*

Europa Yearbook. 1926–present. 2 vols. Gale 34th ed. 1993 $450.00. Vol. 1 *International Organizations and Europe including the U.S.S.R. and Turkey.* ISBN 0-8103-9654-8. Vol. 2 *Africa, the Americas, Asia and Australasia.* ISBN 0-8103-9655-6. Annual two-volume edition, containing detailed information on the political, economic, and commercial institutions of the world. Volume one contains international organizations and the first part of the alphabetically arranged survey of the world's nations; Volume two continues this survey. This survey and directory provides economic and statistical data as well as details on the constitution, government, political parties, legal system, and education in each country. A directory section for each country lists major newspapers and periodicals, publishers, radio and television stations, banks, insurance companies, chambers of commerce, trade associations and unions, transport companies, learned societies, research institutes, libraries, museums, and universities. Major international organizations, their organization and purpose, are described in detail.

Facts on File Yearbooks. 1941–present. Facts on File 1992 $95.00. ISBN 0-8160-2757-9. All previous annual volumes in print at various prices. Republication in a single bound volume, with a cumulative index, of the 52 weekly issues of *Facts on File Weekly New Reference Service,* an indexed weekly news summary of 20–30 pages.

Hattendorf, Lynn C. *Educational Rankings: Annual.* Gale 1992. ISBN 0-8103-8230-X. Provides over 1,500 rankings on colleges and universities from many vantage points. The very best tool for assistance in educational rankings.

Information Please Almanac. Ed. by Dan Golenpaul Associates. 1947–present. HM 1993 $21.45. ISBN 0-395-62886-9. The popular single-volume yearbook and atlas containing information on a wide variety of subjects. Excellent as a quick and easy reference guide.

Middle East and North Africa: Survey and Directory of Lands of Middle East and North Africa. 1948–present. Gale 39th ed. 1993 $280.00. ISBN 0-8103-9935-8. Similar to *Europa Yearbook;* includes a who's who section.

The Negro Almanac: A Reference Work on the Afro-American. Ed. by Harry Ploski and James Williams. Gale 7th ed. 1992 $110.00. ISBN 0-8103-7867-1. Offers both retrospective data, as well as statistics and current information, on subjects concerning the needs of African Americans. Published every six or seven years, it is the best single source of timely information on African Americans.

The New York Public Library Desk Reference. P-H 1989 $34.95. ISBN 0-13-620444-9. Assembles into one volume basic information on popular subjects from a library system that answers five million reference questions a year.

The Old Farmer's Almanac: Ed. by Rob Trowbridge and Judson Hale. 1792–present. Yankee Pub. 1993 $3.95. ISBN 0-89909-246-2. This little publication, "established in 1792 by Robert B. Thomas," has delighted New Englanders for its 202 years of continuous publication, in the same format.

Political Handbook of the World. CSA 1991 $89.95. ISBN 0-933199-07-4. Annual review of governments and intergovernmental organizations.

Reader's Digest Almanac and Yearbook, 1985. Ed. by David C. Whitney. 1966–present. Random 1987 o.p. An appealing compendium of data and statistics arranged by subject. Concentrates more on summaries and standard yearbook materials than on statistics.

Statesman's Yearbook: Statistical and Historical Annual of the States of the World. Ed. by Brian Hunter. 1864–present. St. Martin 128th ed. 1991 $75.00. ISBN 0-318-0667-7. Includes information on individual countries and international organizations.

United Nations, Statistical Office. *Statistical Yearbook*. 1946–present. UN 1991 $150.00. ISBN 92-1-061141-1. Summary volume of the international series of statistical reports published by the United Nations and its specialized agencies, which include *Demographic Yearbook*, *UNESCO*, *Statistical Yearbook*, and others.

U.S. Bureau of the Census. *Statistical Abstract of the United States*. 1878–present. Ref. Press 1992 $19.95. ISBN 1-878753-08-8. Office annual. Standard summary of statistics on the social, political, and economic condition of the United States. Introductory texts to each major division (such as population, education, income, energy, etc.), and the source notes appearing below each statistical table serve as guides to additional sources. Detailed subject index.

Weather Almanac. Ed. by James A. Ruffner and Frank E. Bair. Gale 7th ed. 1994 $120.00. ISBN 0-8103-6980-X. Climatic data for the United States for the period 1951–80.

Whitaker's Almanac. Gale 125th ed. 1993 $70.00. ISBN 0-8103-9743-9. "Noted for its accuracy and detachment in covering the events and personalities that affect the entire world, *Whitaker's* is especially useful for its detailed reporting of current events and social, political, and economic developments in Great Britain."

World Almanac and Book of Facts. Ed. by Mark S. Hoffman. 1868–present. Pharos Bks. NY 1992 $16.95. ISBN 0-88687-659-1. Published without interruption since 1868. Strongest in its record of the United States.

World Fact File. Facts on File 1990 $60.00. ISBN 0-8160-2522-3. Based on research by the Cambridge International Reference on World Affairs. Includes data on each nation's economy, political systems, history, mortality, and commerce.

World of Learning. 1950–present. Gale 43rd ed. 1993 $330.00. ISBN 0-8103-9747-1. A comprehensive, up-to-date directory of educational, cultural, and scientific resources all over the globe.

The Yearbook of the United Nations. 1946–present. Intl. Pubs. Co. Vol. 60 1991 $95.00. ISBN 0-7923-1076-4. Earlier volumes available from various publishers. Annual summary of U.N. activities throughout the world. Publication delay averages three years.

Atlases and Gazetteers

To answer spatial or "where is"-type questions, atlases can be consulted most profitably. Atlases vary in their coverage of physical features (such as climate, geology, forestry, minerals, and hydrology), political subdivisions, and thematic or cultural concerns (such as historical developments, agriculture, commerce, economic matters, transportation, and demography). On the other hand, gazetteers are most useful in providing the origins of place names, and readers seeking extensive narrative information will find guidebooks even more useful. Readers must keep in mind that world events change the political boundaries of some countries. Whereas atlases normally go out of date at the rate of 5 percent per year, recent world events such as the dissolution of the Soviet Union mean that even the newer atlases are dated in their coverage of these areas. In other

words, readers should carefully examine the copyright date of their geographical tools for currency. Electronic sources, such as CD-ROMs or on-line
geographical information systems, which are updated in a timely fashion, may
be more useful than some of the reference books listed below. Again, one must
check the copyright dates for currency.

Although the index to an atlas can serve as a kind of gazetteer, some readers
will be better served by a separately published index (i.e., gazetteer) if they are
seeking the location of more esoteric places. Interested readers also may want
to consult the section on government publications, because the U.S. government plays an important role by establishing place names in the United States;
furthermore, the Defense Mapping Agency produces and distributes foreign
gazetteers as part of its overall mission of supporting area studies.

Ambassador World Atlas. Hammond Inc. 1992 $54.95. ISBN 0-8437-1292-9. A large,
   general atlas with color maps and a substantive index.
Columbia-Lippincott Gazetteer of the World. With 1961 Supplement. Ed. by Leon E.
   Seltzer. Col. U. Pr. 1952 $200.00. ISBN 0-231-01559-3. Although increasingly dated,
   this source provides extensive worldwide coverage along with a brief narrative on
   each place named.
Cosmopolitan World Atlas. Rand McNally 1992 $60.00. ISBN 0-528-83553-X. A medium-
   sized general atlas with color maps and 82,000 index entries. North America receives
   coverage in about half of the volume.
Economist Atlas. H. Holt & Co. 1992 $48.00. ISBN 0-8050-1987-1. Updated edition
   incorporates recent political changes. Includes over 200 country and regional
   profiles and extensive tables and graphs.
Geo-Data: The World Geographical Encyclopedia. Ed. by George T. Kurian. Gale 1983
   $120.00. ISBN 0-914746-31-6. Profiles 204 nations' physical environment.
Gold Medallion World Atlas. Hammond Inc. 1992 $85.00. ISBN 0-8437-1291-0. Despite its
   North American bias, this large volume with color plates is strong on political
   boundaries; an excellent world atlas for adults.
Maps on File Annual Update. Facts on File 1991 $35.00. ISBN 0-8160-2639-4. An 8½ by 11-
   inch looseleaf collection covering the world's countries and regions, as well as
   special topics. Handy outline maps for classroom use.
National Atlas of the United States of America. USGPO 1970 o.p. Now dated, this source is
   the official national atlas; thematic (especially agriculture, climate, population, and
   vegetation) as well as political coverage of the United States. The index is oft-
   reprinted as a free-standing gazetteer. Result of Geologic Survey division of U.S.
   Department of the Interior.
National Gazetteer of the United States of America. USGPO 1991-in progress. A joint
   venture of the U.S. Geological Survey and the U.S. Board on Geographic Names,
   each state's gazetteer alphabetically lists geographical names.
National Geographic Atlas of the World. Ed. by Alice J. Hall. Natl. Geog. 6th ed. 1990
   $59.95. ISBN 0-87044-398-4. Similar in coverage to Hammond's *Ambassador*, this
   world atlas contains an extensive index with more than 155,000 entries.
New International Atlas. Anniversary Edition. Rand McNally 1991 $125.00. ISBN 0-528-
   83459-2. A large, general atlas with 309 pages of color maps and 160,000 index
   entries. All world regions are evenly represented, and place names are given in local
   languages.
New York Times Atlas of the World. Random 1992 $75.00. ISBN 0-8129-2075-9. Up-to-date
   resource including information about states and territories and lists of geographic
   comparisons. Highly recommended for family use.
Rand McNally Goode's World Atlas. Rand McNally 18th ed. 1989 $28.95. ISBN 0-528-
   83128. Best children's atlas because of its extensive introductory material; this atlas
   is strong on physical features.
Rand McNally Road Atlas, 1993. Rand McNally 1993 $11.95. ISBN 0-528-81072-3. The
   standard road atlas; provides the necessary information for automobile touring
   throughout the U.S.

Times Atlas of the World. Random 9th ed. 1992 $174.58. ISBN 0-8129-2077-5. Based on the five-volume *London Times Atlas* published in the 1950s, this is the best single-volume world atlas available. Its large format, superb maps, and comprehensive index make it an indispensible geographic reference tool.

Webster's New Geographical Dictionary. Merriam-Webster Inc. 1984 $19.95. ISBN 0-87779-446-4. Contains more than 47,000 entries. Strong on orthography and pronunciation.

BIOGRAPHICAL SOURCES

Readers with innate curiosity will be attracted to biographical sources because these sources contain information about other people. In addition to biographical sources, local as well as national telephone directories should also be consulted for addresses and telephone numbers (see the section, "Directories," found later in this chapter). Biographical data on obscure individuals can be exceedingly difficult to find, and even the best sources are selective in their coverage of people. The more background knowledge of the subject and the respective information needed (i.e., whether the person is living or deceased, male or female, or of a particular ethnic group; whether one wants factual or evaluative entry, a photograph or portrait), the easier the search will be. In any event, readers interested in answering "who"-type questions may find the following sources the most useful in getting started.

General Biographical Sources

Black Biography: 1790–1950. 3 vols. Chadwyck-Healey 1991 $900.00. ISBN 0-89887-085-2. Compiled under the auspices of the W. E. B. Dubois Institute for Afro-American Research at Harvard University.

Biography and Genealogy Master Index. 1980–present. Gale 1994 $275.00. ISBN 0-8103-8002-1. A comprehensive index to more than six million entries in other current and retrospective biographical sources. Quite useful when the readers have exhausted other possibilities or are unsure about the status of a person (e.g., living or deceased). An annual publication.

Biography Index. Wilson 1946–present. $180.00. Quarterly with bound annual and permanent multiple-year cumulations. Indexes biographical information found in books and magazines. Each issue includes a useful index to occupations and professions.

Contemporary Authors: Permanent Series. 2 vols. Gale Vol. 1 1975 $109.00. ISBN 0-8103-0036-2. Vol. 2 1978 $109.00. ISBN 0-8103-0037-0. An up-to-date source that includes many lesser-known authors. Brief biographical sketches accompany a list of the author's published works.

Current Biography Yearbook. 1940–present. Wilson 1990 $52.00. ISBN 0-685-45837-7. Well-written, medium-length biographical articles on newsworthy, living men and women. Appendixes list subjects by professions and occupations. Includes photographs. This is an annual cumulation of a reference source issued monthly.

Dictionary of American Biography. 17 vols. Macmillan 1981 $1,399.00. ISBN 0-684-17323-9. Known as the DAB, it provides excellent coverage of deceased Americans. Signed evaluative entries noted for their balance and objectivity. Bibliographies. Eight supplements available. Supplement 8, released in 1988, includes such notables as Spencer Tracy, Herbert Hoover, and Thomas Merton.

Dictionary of National Biography. 22 vols. OUP 1882–1953 $1,600.00. Supplements 2–9 $89.00. ISBN 0-19-865101-5. This set, on which the DAB was modeled, covers British figures. Signed articles in the DNB vary in length according to the importance of the person discussed. Bibliographies.

Dockstader, Frederick. *Great North American Indians.* Van Nos. Reinhold 1977 o.p. Lengthy narratives on deceased American Indians. Portraits.

International Who's Who. 1935–present. Taylor & Francis 1993 $250.00. ISBN 0-946653-58-5. Includes reigning royal families followed by an alphabetic listing of 12,000 to 15,000 brief biographies. An annual publication.

Notable American Women, 1607–1950: A Biographical Dictionary. Ed. by Edward T. James and Janet W. James. 3 vols. HUP 1971 $45.00. ISBN 0-674-62734-2. Three-volume biographical dictionary of noteworthy American women from 1607–1950. A useful complement to the *Dictionary of American Biography.*

Notable American Women: The Modern Period. HUP 1980 $19.95. ISBN 0-674-62733-4. One of the few reference works worth reading for its literary quality.

Stetler, Susan. *Almanac of Famous People.* 3 vols. Gale 5th ed. 1993 $95.00. ISBN 0-8103-6988-5. Update of the *Biography Almanac.* Lists over 25,000 names in more than 300 biographical works.

Webster's New Biographical Dictionary. Merriam-Webster Inc. 1988 $21.95. ISBN 0-87779-543-6. Handy, single-volume source of more than 40,000 individuals. Updates but does not replace *Webster's Biographical Dictionary* (1980). Over 30,000 persons described in short biographies.

Who's Who. St. Martin 1993 $195.00. ISBN 0-312-09426-4. Current biographical sketches of prominent, living Britons.

Who's Who Among Black Americans. Gale 7th ed. 1993 $115.00. ISBN 0-8103-5461-6. Brief biographical sketches of living black Americans.

Who's Who in America. 1898–date. Marquis 48th ed. 1993 $429.95. ISBN 0-8379-0151-0. Brief, biographical sketches of 80,000 prominent living American men and women. Current addresses.

Who's Who in American Art. Bowker 20th ed. 1993 $176.00. ISBN 0-8352-3274-3. Profiles over 11,000 artists from all segments of the art world in the U.S., Canada, and Mexico.

Who's Who in American Law. Marquis 8th ed. 1993 $249.95. ISBN 0-8379-3509-1

Who's Who in American Politics. 2 vols. Bowker 14th ed. 1993 $225.00. ISBN 0-8352-3285-9. Includes over 26,000 biographical sketches.

Who's Who of American Women. Marquis 18th ed. 1993 $225.00. ISBN 0-8379-0418-8. Includes more than 28,000 prominent achievers from all fields.

On The Writing of Biography and Autobiography

Altick, Richard D. *Lives and Letters: A History of Literary Biographies in England and America.* Greenwood 1979 repr. of 1965 ed. $38.50. ISBN 0-313-21116-7. A chronological examination of the historical background of literary biography in America and England. Examines the role of the biographer.

Andrews, William L. *To Tell a Free Story: The First Century of Afro-American Autobiography, 1760–1865.* U. of Ill. Pr. 1986 $29.95. ISBN 0-252-01222-4. A study of autobiographies of African Americans written between 1760 and 1865. The author surmises that these autobiographies "tell a free story" and reflect freedom as a theme and goal of life.

Benstock, Shari, ed. *The Private Self: Theory and Practice of Women's Autobiographical Writings.* U. of NC Pr. 1988 $37.50. ISBN 0-8078-1791-0

Bowen, Catherine D. *The Adventures of a Biographer.* Little 1959 o.p.

_____. *Biography: The Craft and the Calling.* Greenwood 1978 repr. of 1969 ed. o.p. An enjoyable description of the way of life of a biographer. First-person account by the author about the people and places she met while on research travels.

Briscoe, Mary L. *A Bibliography of American Autobiography, 1945–1980.* U. of Wis. Pr. 1982 $35.00. ISBN 0-299-09090-6. Provides access to over 5,000 American autobiographies published in book format by commercial and private presses from 1945 to 1980. A companion volume to *A Bibliography of American Autobiographies* by Louis Kaplan.

Brumble, H. David, III. *American Indian Autobiography*. U. CA Pr. 1988 $42.50. ISBN 0-520-06245-0. Examines Native American autobiographies and suggests relationships between published autobiographies and oral autobiographical traditions.

Cockshut, A. O. *The Art of Autobiography in Nineteenth and Twentieth Century England*. Yale U. Pr. 1984 o.p. Selective study of autobiographical works in English. Emphasis is on nineteenth and twentieth century works.

————. *Truth to Life: The Art of Biography in the Nineteenth Century*. HarBraceJ 1974 o.p. An examination of the role of the biographer and biography in the nineteenth century.

Daghlian, Philip B., ed. *Essays in Eighteenth-Century Biography*. Bks. Demand 1968 $35.30. ISBN 0-317-27814-2. A volume of papers originally delivered at Indiana University in 1967. Emphasis is on biographical topics in the eighteenth century. Includes selective bibliographies and suggested reading lists for further study.

Edel, Leon. *Writing Lives: Principia Biographica*. Norton 1987 $15.95. ISBN 0-393-01882-2. A collection of essays by a master of the biographical art—its principles, problems, and noted practitioners.

Kaplan, Louis, and others, eds. *A Bibliography of American Autobiographers*. U. of Wis. Pr. 1961 o.p. Selective list of 6,377 American autobiographies published before 1945.

Kendall, Paul M., and Stephen B. Oates. *The Art of Biography*. Norton 1985 $4.95. ISBN 0-393-06411-2. A study of biography from its beginnings to contemporary times.

Mandell, Gail. *Life Into Art: Conversations with Seven Biographers*. U. of Ark. Pr. 1991 $27.50. ISBN 1-55728-180-7. Insightful interviews with seven distinguished biographers on a variety of writing techniques.

Matthews, William, comp. *British Autobiographies: An Annotated Bibliography of British Autobiographies Published or Written Before 1951*. U. CA Pr. 1984 repr. of 1951 ed. $45.00. ISBN 0-520-05357-5. Intended for use by scholars, this work contains an alphabetically arranged annotated bibliography.

Pachter, Marc, ed. *Telling Lives: The Biographer's Art*. New Republic Bks. 1981 $16.95. ISBN 0-8122-1118-9. Essays by current biographers or historians practicing the art, including Leon Edel and Barbara Tuchman.

Rosenwald, George C., and Richard L. Ochberg. *Storied Lives: The Cultural Politics of Self Understanding*. Yale U. Pr. 1992 $35.00. ISBN 0-300-05455-6. A series of varied investigations into the stories people relate about their own lives.

DATES AND FACTS

For quick access to facts and dates, the reader might consult a variety of sources, such as almanacs, encyclopedias, biographical dictionaries, statistical yearbooks, and similar reference tools. The value of these works in supplying this kind of information depends on their organization and indexing. The titles listed below are a selection from the many works in all fields that are devoted to particular kinds of factual information.

American Book of Days. Ed. by Jane M. Hatch. Wilson 3rd ed. 1978 $80.00. ISBN 0-8242-0593-6. Presents more than 700 articles that explore, day by day, our nation's history through the lives of distinguished citizens, anniversaries of great events, religious and secular holidays, and various celebrations connected with sports, commerce, and local customs. The book describes each occasion in detail, from its origin to the present day.

The Book of Calendars. Ed. by Frank Parise. Facts on File 1982 $35.00. ISBN 0-87196-467-8. Explanation and conversion tables for 40 calendars used in ancient and modern times.

The Book of Lists #3. Ed. by Amy Wallace. Bantam 1985 $5.95. ISBN 0-553-2786-8. Lists of everything, such as fungi that changed history, notable marriage proposals, winners of the Golden Fleece Award, and strange deaths.

Chase's Annual Events. 1957–to date. Contemp. Bks. 1992 $38.95. ISBN 0-8092-3897-7. Traces previous year and notes upcoming events, arranged in calendar format.

Cottrell, Philip L. *Events in the Twentieth Century.* OUP 1992 $40.00. ISBN 0-19-520923-0. Year-by-year list of events in four categories: politics, society, culture, science. Covers 1900–91.

de Ford, Miriam Allen, and Joan S. Jackson. *Who Was When? A Dictionary of Contemporaries.* Wilson 3rd ed. 1976 $47.00. ISBN 0-8242-0532-4. A chronologically arranged list of the birth and death dates of 10,000 important figures in history. Index of names, with birth and death dates.

Diggs, Ellen Irene. *Black Chronology: From 4,000 B.C. to the Abolition of the Slave Trade.* G. K. Hall 1983 $50.00. ISBN 0-8161-8543-3. "Every source is cited in the text and referenced in an extensive bibliography" (Publisher's catalog). Proper name index.

Facts on File. 1940–to date. 1991 Yearbook. 1992 $95.00. ISBN 0-8160-2757-9. Facts on File annual subscription to weekly loose-leaf news service $400.00. Individual yearbooks from 1941 through 1991 are available at $85.00 per vol. Summarizes current events around the world. Indexes cumulate throughout the year. Five-year indexes from 1946 to 1990 are available for $85.00 each. No sources of information are given.

The Guinness Book of World Records. Ed. by Donald Mc Farlan. 1955–present. Bantam rev. ed. 1991 $6.95. ISBN 0-553-28954-3. A subjective selection of world records, arranged by categories. The top-selling copyright book in publishing history.

Holidays and Anniversaries of the World. Ed. by Jennifer Mossman. Gale 2nd ed. 1989 $85.00. ISBN 0-8103-4870-5. Holidays, anniversaries, holy days, birthdays of famous persons, significant dates in history, and special events are listed for each month and day of the year. Detailed index.

Kane, Joseph Nathan. *Facts about the Presidents.* Wilson 5th ed. 1989 $45.00. ISBN 0-8242-0774-2. A chapter for each president includes data about their lives, families, careers, and administration. Much comparative data.

_____. *Famous First Facts.* Wilson 4th ed. 1981 $78.00. ISBN 0-8242-0661-4. Lists more than 9,000 inventions, discoveries, and first happenings that took place on the American continent from 1007 to the present. Alphabetical subject arrangement with cross-references and indexes by year, month, and day, personal names, and state and municipality.

Kurian, George Thomas. *The New Book of World Rankings.* Facts on File $40.00. ISBN 0-8160-1931-2. Ranks more than 150 countries in more than 300 categories, including climate, defense, crime, and politics.

Leonard, Thomas M. *Day by Day: The 40's.* Facts on File 1977 $125.00. ISBN 0-87196-375-2. Major events day by day for the ten-year period. Detailed index.

_____. *Day by Day: The 70's.* 2 vols. Facts on File 1988 $195.00. ISBN 0-8160-1020-X. Major events day by day for the ten-year period.

Merritt, Jeffrey. *Day by Day: The 50's.* Facts on File 1979 $125.00. ISBN 0-87196-383-3. Major events day by day for the ten-year period. Detailed index.

Parker, Thomas, and Douglas Nelson. *Day by Day: The 60's.* 2 vols. Facts on File 1983 $195.00. ISBN 0-87196-648-4. Major events day by day for the 10-year period. Detailed index.

Twentieth Century American Nicknames. Ed. by Laurence Urdang. Wilson 1979 $35.00. ISBN 0-8242-0642-8. Lists 4,000 nicknames for persons, places, events, and things. Nicknames and proper names are listed in one alphabet with see references. Gives full identification and birth and death dates.

Wallenchinsky, David. *The Complete Book of the Olympics.* Little 1992 $14.95. ISBN 0-316-92053-3. All the records from 1896 to 1980.

Walter, Claire. *Winners: The Blue Ribbon Encyclopedia of Awards.* Facts on File rev. ed. 1982 o.p. Winners in all fields of endeavor, emphasizing major U.S. awards with some important foreign awards. Excludes hall-of-fame lists.

What They Said. Ed. by Alan Pater and Jason R. Pater. 1969–present. Monitor 1992 $41.00. ISBN 0-917734-24-6. A yearbook of spoken opinion by individuals prominent during each year.

DICTIONARIES

When one thinks of a dictionary, many images may come to mind. Some variations include the desktop dictionary found in schools, the unabridged volume frequently found in the library reference room, and the venerable *Oxford English Dictionary* (or *OED*), frequently seen in colleges and universities. No longer bound to print format, dictionaries such as the *OED* are now found on-line and in CD-ROM versions.

Frequently, dictionaries may be grouped into functional types. Aside from the basic English-language dictionaries, there are also foreign-language and etymological dictionaries, as well as volumes focusing upon such aspects of language as spelling, abbreviations, pronunciation, and the like. In addition, such specialized fields as medicine and law have developed their own dictionaries for terms that are relevant to their areas. With these variations of dictionaries available, selecting a dictionary that will be appropriate for the need at hand can be a challenging task, since many factors must be considered. Aspects such as vocabulary, word treatment, illustrations, use of abbreviations, and special features are some such considerations. To help choose the appropriate dictionary, there are several guidebooks available: *General Reference Books for Adults: Authoritative Evaluations of Encyclopedias, Atlases, and Dictionaries.* (Bowker); *Reference Books for Young Readers: Authoritative Evaluations of Recommended Resources in Specialized Subject Areas* (Bowker); and *Dictionary Buying Guide* (Oryx).

Whether the need is to say *thank you* in a foreign language, to trace the history of the usage of a term, or to learn the spelling of a pluralized version of a word, chances are that there is a dictionary available to fill that need.

English-Language Dictionaries

The American Heritage Desk Dictionary. HM 1981 $12.70. ISBN 0-395-31256-6. A condensed version of the *American Heritage Dictionary*, with shorter etymologies and definitions.

The American Heritage Dictionary of the English Language. HM 3rd ed. 1992 $38.95. ISBN 0-395-44895-6. A refreshingly readable, attractive, and candid source of lexical information, newly updated with the addition of more than 16,000 words. "Continuously," although not greatly revised, this edition updates a standard and respected dictionary.

The Concise Oxford Dictionary of Current English. Ed. by R. E. Allen. OUP 8th ed. 1990 $24.95. ISBN 0-19-861200-1. Based upon the well-known *Oxford English Dictionary* and its supplements, this work also contains new words and technical terms. A distinction is made between British and American terms. The dictionary utilizes a compact format and small type, but serves as a handy alternative to its parent.

Dictionary of American English on Historical Principles. Ed. by William A. Craigie and James R. Hulbert. 4 vols. U. Ch. Pr. 1960. $300.00. ISBNs 0-226-11737-5, 0-226-11738-3, 0-226-11739-1, 0-226-11740-5. A monumental work begun in 1936 and completed in 1943. Directed by Sir William A. Craigie, one of the editors of the *Oxford English Dictionary*, this work is similar in format in that its purpose is to trace each word to its entrance into the language and to its earliest users. It aims to present "those features by which the English of the American colonies and United States is distinguished from that of England and the rest of the English-speaking world . . . including not only words or phrases which are clearly or apparently of American origin, or have greater currency here than elsewhere, but also every word denoting something which has a real connection with the development of the country and the history of its people. . . ." Neither slang nor dialect is included.

A Dictionary of Americanisms on Historical Principles. Ed. by Mitford McLeod Mathews. 3 vols. U. Ch. Pr. 1951 o.p. Narrower in scope than the *Dictionary of American English on Historical Principles.* This work covers words and phrases that first made their appearance in English in this country, words formerly in the language but having acquired new meanings in the United States, terms first used in this country but made up of older words, and American nicknames and slang expressions well entrenched in the language or having some historical significance.

Longman Dictionary of Contemporary English. Ed. by Paul Proctor. Longman 1987 $21.95. ISBN 0-582-84223-9. Intended for use by those unfamiliar with the English language, this work is a compilation of approximately 2,000 words with concise definitions.

The Merriam-Webster Dictionary. Merriam-Webster Inc. 1989 $4.95. ISBN 0-87779-900-8. Based upon *Webster's Third*, this work contains approximately 57,000 entries.

Merriam-Webster's Collegiate Dictionary Tenth Edition. Merriam-Webster Inc. 10th ed. 1993 $21.95. ISBN 0-87779-709-9. Considered one of the best abridged dictionaries around, this work has been extensively revised and updated, including the special sections. Sometimes faulted for a slowness to reflect change, it still includes many thousands of new terms and senses of definitions, and gives dates of first use of senses. Included is a section on foreign words. Formerly *Webster's Ninth New Collegiate Dictionary*; title has been changed with the 10th edition.

Oxford American Dictionary. Ed. by Eugene Ehrlich and others. OUP 1980 $18.95. ISBN 0-19-502795-7. An American counterpart to the *Oxford English Dictionary*, this work sets the standard for American-English usage. An abridged version that does not contain etymologies or additional informational material.

The Oxford-Duden Pictorial English Dictionary. Ed. by John Pheby. OUP 1984 $14.95. ISBN 0-19-864155-9. Useful for non-English speakers attempting to identify common objects.

Oxford English Dictionary: Being a Corrected Re-Issue, with an Introduction, Supplement and Bibliography of a New English Dictionary on Historical Principles. Ed. by James A. H. Murray, Henry Bradley, William A. Craigie, and Charles T. Onions. 20 vols. OUP 1989 $2,750.00. ISBN 0-19-861186-2. The original *Oxford English Dictionary: A New English Dictionary on Historical Principles* (10 vols., published in 1898–1928) was begun in 1879 and was founded mainly on materials collected by the Philological Society as far back as 1857. The *Oxford* was planned to meet the need for a dictionary that would trace the history of a word in the English language, as well as indicate which of the senses of a word were original, and when an obsolete word became obsolete. The set was designed to supplement all other dictionaries and contains quotations illustrating the first and last appearance of every word. A reprint of the original ten-volume work has been made from the same plates and printed on thinner paper. Typographic errors have been corrected and a supplementary volume includes a bibliography of books quoted in the original work. The entire *OED* is now available on CD-ROM. A four-volume supplement, *A Supplement to the Oxford English Dictionary*, is also available.

Random House Dictionary of the English Language. Ed. by Stuart Berg Flexner. Random 2nd ed. 1987 $89.95. ISBN 0-394-50050-4. This unabridged work contains over 315,000 entries, which are formatted to include sample sentences, synonyms and antonyms, and usage notes. Also included within the volume are concise French, Spanish, Italian, and German dictionaries, copies of the Declaration of Independence and the Constitution, and a manual of style.

The Scribner-Bantam English Dictionary. Ed. by Edwin B. Williams and others. Bantam 1984 $4.50. ISBN 0-553-26496-6. Entries include proper names of people and places, current vocabulary and idioms, and straightforward, concise entries. Contains extensive added information, including weights and measures and lists of colleges.

The Shorter Oxford English Dictionary on Historical Principles. Ed. by William Little and others. Rev. and ed. by Charles T. Onions. 2 vols. OUP 3rd ed. rev. and enl. 1973 $185.00. ISBN 0-19-861127-7. A condensed 2,500-page version of the original work of 15,500 pages, omitting quotations showing word usage and utilizing abbreviations.

The vocabulary of the *Shorter Oxford Dictionary* includes all words in regular literary and colloquial use, with a selection of technical, archaic, and obsolete words. Designed as a dictionary for written rather than spoken English.

Third Barnhart Dictionary Of New English. Ed. by Robert K. Barnhart and others. Wilson 1990 $49.00. ISBN 0-8242-0796-3. Defines over 12,000 new terms adopted in the last thirty years.

Twelve Thousand Words: A Supplement to Webster's Third New International Dictionary. Merriam-Webster Inc. 1986 $10.95. ISBN 0-87779-207-0. The most recent supplement to *Webster's Third*, includes new words and those words omitted from the two previous editions.

Webster's New World Dictionary of the American Language, College Edition. P-H 3rd ed. 1988 $18.95. ISBN 0-13-947169-3. Updated edition of a standard favorite, comparable in many ways to the *American Heritage Dictionary*. Includes sections on etymology, editorial style, and signs and symbols.

Webster's Third New International Dictionary of the English Language Unabridged. Ed. by Philip Babcock Gove and others. Merriam-Webster Inc. 3rd ed. 1992 $100.00. ISBN 0-87799-202-X. A work that has been the subject of much controversy due to numerous revisions and deletions from the second edition, the *New International*, published in 1934. These revisions include the omission of 150,000 words from the second edition. However, the work is noted for its clear, concise, and authoritative definitions, as well as its descriptive approach to the language, whereby its focus is to relate what terms are currently in use. Includes more than 10,000,000 citations and was produced with more than 200 special consultants as well as a large staff.

British-English Dictionaries

The American-British, British-American Dictionary with Helpful Hints to Travelers. Ed. by William Q. de Funiak. Oak Tree Pubns. 1978 o.p. Compiled to help interpret the differences between American and British English. Also contains various suggestions to the traveler concerning language usage and idiomatic usage.

Dictionary of Contemporary American English: Contrasted with British English. Ed. by Givi Zviadadze. Humanities 1983 o.p. An interesting volume in that it was compiled in Soviet Georgia from written sources and contains quotations for every entry from newspapers, periodicals, and books. Indicates whether a use is primarily British or American. Thesauri and index.

Fowler, Henry W., and F. G. Fowler. *The King's English*. OUP 3rd ed. 1985 $9.95. ISBN 0-19-881330-9. This is essentially a reprint of a 1931 edition of a classic work, which emphasizes graceful and correct writing with its sections on vocabulary, syntax, punctuation, and others.

Moss, Norman. *British-English Language Dictionary: For More Effective Communication Between Americans and Britons*. NTC Pub. Grp. 1991 $14.95. ISBN 0-8442-9115-3

Schur, Norman W. *English English*. Gale. 3rd ed. in press. $46.00. ISBN 0-8103-9885-0. A revision of the author's 1973 *British Self-Taught: With Comments in American*, this book includes many words and phrases used in the living speech of the majority of the British, as well as a number of literary and regional uses no longer commonly encountered. In two-column dictionary format, with some cross-references, it also defines a number of the entries for meanings in both American and British English.

Current English-Usage Dictionaries

Bell, James K., and Adrian Cohn. *Bell and Cohn's Handbook of Grammar, Style and Usage*. Macmillan 2nd ed. 1976 o.p.

Evans, Bergen, and Cornelia Evans. *A Dictionary of Contemporary American Usage*. Random 1957 o.p. The authors' premise is that no one use of language is "correct." An interesting and authoritative volume.

Follett, Wilson. *Modern American Usage: A Guide*. Ed. by Jacques Barzun. *Amer. Century Ser*. Hill & Wang 1966 $14.95. ISBN 0-8090-139-X. "This is an unusual and a

valuable . . . intensely personal book, based firmly on and edited consistently in
accord with certain of Follett's basic beliefs about language" (*LJ*). In his introduction
the author said of linguists such as those who prepared *Webster's Third New
International Dictionary*: "[They] deny that there is any such thing as correctness,"
but Follet argued "there is a right way to use words and construct sentences, and
many wrong ways."

Fowler, Henry W. *A Dictionary of Modern English Usage*. Ed. by Ernest Gowers. OUP 1983
repr. of 1965 ed. $10.95. ISBN 0-19-869115-7. Although Fowler died in 1933, this
work remains the classic on English style, with a British focus. This is a volume not
merely to be consulted, but to be browsed in and read by those who love the
language.

Kenyon, John S. *Pronouncing Dictionary of American English*. Merriam-Webster Inc. 2nd
ed. 1953 $14.95. ISBN 0-87779-047-7. Colloquial English pronunciation, using the
international phonetic alphabet.

Martin, Phyllis. *Word Watcher's Handbook: A Deletionary of the Most Abused and Misused
Words*. St. Martin 3rd ed. 1991 $14.95. ISBN 0-312-05540-4. Includes bibliography
and index.

Morris, William, and Mary Morris. *Harper Dictionary of Contemporary Usage*. HarpC
1992 2nd ed. repr. of 1977 ed. $13.00. ISBN 0-06-181608-X. An excellent handbook
of correct usage of the English language. Reflects collaborative efforts of over 165
experts in the field of language and answers many questions fielded by readers.

Neaman, Judith, and Carole Silver. *Kind Words: A Thesaurus of Euphemisms*. Facts on
File 1989 $22.95. ISBN 0-8160-1896-0. A collection of euphemisms concerning
familiar and popular subjects. Etymologies of many words and phrases are included.
Entries are arranged alphabetically by subject.

Nicholson, Margaret. *A Dictionary of American-English Usage*. NAL-Dutton 1957 o.p.
Continues Fowler's *Modern English Usage* and includes new words and idioms, as
well as American variations in spelling, pronunciation, and usage.

Shaw, Henry. *Dictionary of Problem Words and Expressions*. McGraw 1987 $18.95. ISBN
0-07-056517-1. Selects, defines, explains, and illustrates more than 1,500 of the most
common mistakes in word usage in the English language.

Urdang, Laurence, ed. *Suffixes: and Other Word-Final Elements of English*. Gale 1982
$92.00. ISBN 0-8103-1123-2. Forms are listed from right to left, with an alphabetical
index for each form quoted going from left to right. Short etymologies and general
meanings are given for each form.

Slang and Colloquial Dictionaries

Berrey, Lester V., and Melvin Van den Bark. *The American Thesaurus of Slang: A
Complete Reference Book of Colloquial Speech*. Crowell rev. ed. 1953 o.p. Over
100,000 expressions arranged in several ways, including according to dominant idea
and occupation. Includes an alphabetical word index.

Byrne, Josefa H. *Mrs. Byrne's Dictionary of Unusual, Obscure, and Preposterous Words,
Gathered from Numerous and Diverse Authoritative Sources*. Ed. by Robert Byrne.
Citadel Pr. 1976 $7.95. ISBN 0-8065-0498-6. A personal selection of unusual terms.
Although the definitions do not provide all senses of a word, the volume can be
useful in conjunction with an abridged dictionary.

Chapman, Robert L. *New Dictionary of American Slang*. HarpC 1986 $30.00. ISBN 0-06-
181157-2. A full-scale dictionary of slang, examining both past and current usage.

Farmer, John S., and W. E. Henley. *Slang and Its Analogues, Past and Present*. 7 vols. in 3.
Kraus repr. of 1890–1904 ed. $25.00. ISBN 0-527-28300-2. Three centuries of slang
with synonyms in English, French, German, and Italian. Entries are labeled
colloquial, provincial, vulgar, and so on.

Grose, Francis. *Classical Dictionary of the Vulgar Tongue*. Ed. by Eric Partridge. *Select
Bibliographies Repr. Ser.* Ayer repr. of 1963 ed. $23.50. ISBN 0-8369-6652-X. The
earliest-known dictionary of English slang, updated by Eric Partridge. Partridge,
perhaps the leading authority on slang in English, has said that it "has contributed

illuminating notes" and a biographical sketch of that "antiquarian Falstaff." The early compiler "would be astonished to learn that a few terms he considered vanishing vogue words—'bore' and 'twaddle,' for example—are still very much alive, just as some of us may be astonished to find that certain other terms—such as 'douse the glim' and 'elbow grease'—date to his time. An incidental asset of the book is the way it brings to sparkling life the mores, the humor and the foibles of the 18th century" (*N.Y. Times*).

Partridge, Eric. *A Dictionary of Catch Phrases: American and British, From the Sixteenth Century to the Present Day*. Madison Bks UPA rev. ed. 1992 $24.95. ISBN 0-8128-3101-2. A detailed work of colloquialisms, catch phrases, solecisms, catachreses, slang, nicknames, and vulgarisms. Designed to be a companion to the *Oxford English Dictionary*.

————. *A Dictionary of Slang and Unconventional English*. Macmillan 8th ed. 1985 $75.00. ISBN 0-02-594980-2. An immense body of work compressed into one volume by means of abbreviations. It deals not only with slang, but also with scabrous language.

Thorne, Tony. *Dictionary of Contemporary Slang*. Pantheon. 1991 $15.00. ISBN 0-679-73706-5. Intended to describe the core of English slang between 1950 and 1990, this collection includes over 15,000 definitions from a variety of English-speaking countries.

Urdang, Laurence, ed. *Idioms and Phrases Index*. 3 vols. Gale 1983 $97.00. ISBN 0-8103-1196-8. Entries by significant words, alphabetically arranged.

Urdang, Laurence, and Charles Hoequist, Jr., eds. *-Ologies and -Isms: A Thematic Dictionary*. Gale 3rd ed. 1986 $92.00. ISBN 0-8103-5513-2. Includes *-ist*, *-ic*, and *-phobia* endings as well as *-ology (-ies)* and *-isms*, with definitions and historical notes.

Acronym and Abbreviation Dictionaries

Douglas, Auriel, and Michael Strumpf. *Webster's New World Dictionary of Acronyms and Abbreviations*. P-H 1988 $7.95. ISBN 0-13-947136-7. Includes more than 15,000 of the most important acronyms and abbreviations from varied fields; all entries are defined. Presented in a handy pocket-sized volume.

International Acronyms, Initialisms and Abbreviations. Gale 3rd ed. 1993 $165.00. ISBN 0-8103-7431-5. A guide to over 110,000 foreign and international acronyms, initialisms, abbreviations, alphabetic symbols, contractions, and condensed appellations in all fields. Alphabetically arranged by abbreviations.

Miller, Stuart W. *Concise Dictionary of Acronyms & Initialisms*. Facts on File 1988 $24.95. ISBN 0-8160-1577-5

Reverse Acronym, Initialisms & Abbreviations Dictionary. Gale 18th ed. 1993 $250.00. ISBN 0-685-48515-3. Terms arranged alphabetically by meaning of the acronym, initialism, or abbreviation. A companion volume to the *New Acronyms, Initialisms, and Abbreviations Dictionary*.

Synonym, Antonym, and Homonym Dictionaries

Chapman, Robert L. *Roget's International Thesaurus*. HarpC 5th ed. 1992 $18.95. ISBN 0-06-270014-6. In the original format by topical arrangement, updated to include recent vocabulary in its more than 325,000 entries, with an extensive alphabetical index.

Kloe, Donald R. *A Dictionary of Collective Onomatopoeic Sounds, Tones and Noises in English and Spanish: Including Those of Animals, Man, Nature, Machinery and Musical Instruments, Together with Some that are not Imitative or Echoic*. Ethridge Blaine Bks. 1977 o.p. A convenient reference work for translations of onomatopoeic works. Includes a bidirectional bilingual dictionary with two different monolingual dictionaries; one with Spanish definitions, the other with English definitions.

Laird, Charlton. *Webster's New World Thesaurus*. Warner Bks. rev. ed. 1990 $3.99. ISBN 0-446-36027-9. Lists main entries, followed by synonyms and antonyms. A concise work, with no definition of the word given.

Landau, Sidney, and Ronald Bogus, eds. *The Doubleday Roget's Thesaurus in Dictionary Form*. Doubleday 1991 $11.95. ISBN 0-385-23996-3. Each entry refers one back to a main category, within which the terms are listed by noun form, with synonyms following. There are no illustrations of use or distinctions for shades of meaning.

The Merriam-Webster Thesaurus. PB 1989 $4.95. ISBN 0-87779-902-9. Easy-to-use volume based upon *Webster's Third New International Dictionary of the English Language Unabridged*. In addition to referring the user to a more appropriate or alternative word, it provides synonyms, antonyms, related words, definitions, and illustrations of the main term. Includes good cross-references that refer one back to a dictionary when necessary.

Morehead, Philip D. *The New American Roget's College Thesaurus in Dictionary Form*. NAL-Dutton rev. ed. 1985 $7.95. ISBN 0-452-00732-1. Second edition, which includes a number of added slang and colloquial expressions.

Newhouse, Dora. *Homonyms, "Sound Alikes": A Bilingual Reference Guide to Most Mispronounced, Misspelled, and Confusing Words in the English Language: English-Spanish*. Newhouse Pr. 1978 o.p. Useful mostly for those whose second language is English, this volume's 3,500 words are some of the most problematic for all English speakers. Has brief definitions and cross-references under all spellings.

Powell, David. *Look-Alike, Sound-Alike, Not-Alike Words: An Index of Confusables*. U. Pr. of Amer. 1982 o.p. The words here are in sets, arranged alphabetically, with cross-references. There are no definitions, but finding the right spelling would allow access back to any good dictionary.

Random House Thesaurus. Ed. by Jess Stein and Stuart Berg Flexner. Random 1984 $14.95. ISBN 0-394-52949-9. Compiled to help readers find the most effective words to express themselves. Main entries are boldfaced and used in context, with synonyms listed under each meaning. Lists of antonyms are included.

Reid, Stuart. *Verb Synonyms and Related Words*. Exposition Press 1974 o.p. A popular book of synonyms. Definitions of the words are given, followed by the synonym for maximum comprehension. Antonyms are included when applicable.

Rodale, J. I. *The Synonym Finder*. Rodale Pr. Inc. rev. ed. 1978 $21.95. ISBN 0-857-236-8. A comprehensive collection of synonyms, this revision includes more senses of meanings than the 1961 edition and is updated with slang terms. Alphabetically arranged and indicates the kind of use, i.e., technical or informal, but does not give examples of use.

Roget's II: The New Thesaurus. By the editors of the *American Heritage Dictionary*. HM 1988 $12.95. ISBN 0-395-48317-4. A revision of the original *Roget's Thesaurus*, presented in dictionary form with definitions included for each listing.

Roget's University Thesaurus. Ed. by Sylvester Mawson. HarpC 1981 $10.95. ISBN 0-06-463537-6. A reprint of the "classic" and well-known *Roget's Thesaurus*, and one of several revisions by Mawson; expanded subject categories and updated vocabulary.

Room, Adrian. *Room's Dictionary of Confusibles*. Routledge 1979 o.p. A handbook of usage for easily confused terms. Includes many cross-references for ease of use. Fun to browse through.

————. *Room's Dictionary of Distinguishables and Confusibles*. 2 vols. Routledge 1981 o.p. Covers words that are related, such as *hare* and *rabbit*, but whose differences are not easy to distinguish. Illustrations are particularly helpful.

Sparkes, Ivan G., ed. *Dictionary of Collective Nouns and Group Terms*. Gale 2nd ed. 1985 $80.00. ISBN 0-8103-2188-2. A dictionary of terms for groups of things, dating from the medieval to modern times, and including a number of punning terms listed alphabetically and by subject.

Webster's Collegiate Thesaurus. Merriam-Webster Inc. 1976 $14.95. ISBN 0-87779-069-8. A thesaurus in dictionary format, with excellent introductory material. May be easier for some to use than *Roget's*.

Webster's New Dictionary of Synonyms. Merriam-Webster Inc. 1984 $14.95. ISBN 0-87779241-0. Useful for its lists of related words that are carefully defined for their shades of meaning. Includes quotations illustrating correct usage.

Rhyming Dictionaries

Cahn, Sammy. *Sammy Cahn's Rhyming Dictionary.* Astor Bks. 1991 $16.95. ISBN 0-943351-51-0. Organized by vowel sounds and arranged phonetically. Designed for the songwriter.

Daughterty, Sue. *American Rhyming Dictionary of Words and Phrases.* Morrow 1991 $24.95. ISBN 0-688-10360-X. More comprehensive work including slang, colloquialisms, phrases, and near rhymes. Designed to be easier to use than previous rhyming dictionaries.

Walker, J. *Walker's Rhyming Dictionary of the English Language: In Which the Whole Language is Arranged According to Its Terminations.* Routledge rev. ed. 1983 $19.95. ISBN 0-7100-9306-3. Standard rhyming dictionary, arranged by last syllable and with British pronunciation.

Whitfield, Jane S. *Whitfield's University Rhyming Dictionary.* Ed. by Frances Stillman. B & N Imports 1981 $8.95. ISBN 0-06-463538-4

Wood, Clement. *The Complete Rhyming Dictionary.* Ed. by Ronald J. Bogus and others. Doubleday 1990 $25.00. ISBN 0-385-41350-5. An excellent guide for the poet or reader. Contains a full rhyming dictionary and chapters on technique, patterns, and form.

Spelling Dictionaries

The works cited in this section are used to determine the correct spelling of words, terms, names, and so on, rather than to provide definitions. Some also provide help in hyphenation, proper syllable division, and pronunciation.

Bolander, D. *New Webster's Spelling Dictionary.* Grolier Inc. 1987 $2.95. ISBN 0-7172-4538-1

Downing, David. *Dictionary of American Spelling.* NTC Pub. Grp. 1991 $9.95. ISBN 0-8442-5476-2

Dougherty, Margaret M. *Instant Spelling Dictionary.* Warner Bks. 3rd ed. 1990 $4.99. ISBN 0-446-36082-1

The Random House Speller/Divider. Ballantine 1981 o.p. Very comprehensive work that includes geographical and biographical names and how to hyphenate, divide, spell, and pronounce them. Distinguishes between homonyms.

Zoubek, Charles E. and G. A. Condon. *Twenty Thousand Words.* McGraw 8th ed. 1985 $7.88. ISBN 0-07-037462-7. Basic-level speller/divider, with a number of referrals to homonyms. Although not complete in coverage, does include sections on usage and rules.

Etymological Dictionaries

Etymological dictionaries trace the origins and development of words and phrases, showing how meaning and usage change over time.

Barnhart Dictionary of Etymology. Ed. by Robert K. Barnhart. Wilson 1988 $59.00. ISBN 0-8242-0745-9. Contains over 30,000 entries emphasizing the development of American English. "It makes the complicated processes of language development accessible to users at all levels."

Claiborne, Robert. *The Roots of English: A Reader's Handbook of Word Origins.* Times Bks. 1989 $18.95. ISBN 0-8129-1716-2. Comprehensive dictionary of selected Indo-European roots in English. Gives basic form of each root.

Funk, Charles E. *Heavens to Betsy and Other Curious Sayings.* HarpC 1986 $6.95. ISBN 0-06-091353-3. A personalized collection of sayings designed for browsing.

———. *Hog on Ice and Other Curious Expressions.* HarpC 1985 $6.95. ISBN 0-06-091259-6. A short history of selected common and curious sayings in the English language. An entertaining work, arranged in no particular order.

———. *Thereby Hangs the Tale: Stories of Curious Word Origins.* HarpC 1985 repr. of 1950 ed. $6.95. ISBN 0-06-0911260-X. This lexicographer wrote a wonderful series of books on origins and meanings of odd words and phrases.

Funk, Charles E., and Charles E. Funk, Jr. *Horsefeathers and Other Curious Words.* HarpC 1986 $6.95. ISBN 0-06-09352-5. This book was completed by Funk's son after his father's death.

Klein, Ernest. *A Comprehensive Etymological Dictionary of the English Language.* Elsevier 1986 repr. of 1971 ed. $131.00. ISBN 0-444-40930-0. Recommended for libraries. Designed for scholarly research.

Morris, William, and Mary Morris. *Morris Dictionary of Word and Phrase Origins.* HarpC 2nd ed. 1988 $28.00. ISBN 0-06-015862-X. A less formal dictionary of etymology, including coverage of slang terms and cliches. Alphabetical order by first word, with an index supplying access via other parts of the phrases.

Onions, Charles T., ed. *The Oxford Dictionary of English Etymology.* OUP 1966 $60.00. ISBN 0-19-861112-9. The most complete and reliable etymological dictionary of the English language. Also useful for etymology is the *Oxford English Dictionary.*

Partridge, Eric. *Origins: A Short Etymological Dictionary of Modern English.* Macmillan 1977 o.p. Intimately cognate groups of words are arranged into single unified treatments. Thus, "can," "could," "con," "cough," "uncouth," "kith," "cunning," "keen," "ken," "kenning," "know," and "knowledge" are all treated in six numbered paragraphs under "can," to which the others are cross-referenced.

Pinkerton, Edward C. *Word for Word: A Dictionary of Etymological Cognates.* Gale 1982 o.p. An etymological dictionary that groups words in families and that is interesting and easy to understand. The index of more than 15,000 terms refers back to each numbered line, making it easy to use as well.

The Shorter Oxford English Dictionary on Historical Principles. Prepared by William Little, Henry W. Fowler, and Jessie Coulson. Revised and edited by Charles T. Onion. 2 vols. OUP 1973 o.p. Includes updated etymologies and addenda list with new words, making it the best historical dictionary of its size. It is also a good supplement to use with the compact edition of the *Oxford English Dictionary.*

Skeat, Walter W., ed. *Concise Etymological Dictionary of the English Language.* Putnam Pub. Group 1963 $11.95. ISBN 0-399-50049-9. History of selected words of curious or disputed derivation. Skeat alone explains many "lost" meanings of words in the Bible, Shakespeare, and so on. For example, Cinderella's slipper was originally fur, not glass; Skeat explains how the word became *glass.*

Smith, Logan P. *The English Language.* Century Bookbindery 1982 repr. of 1912 ed. o.p. The author was an American who lived in England and preferred English fashions of speech. His work on English idioms explains the origin of expressions like "hoist with his own petard," "to the manor born," "sour grapes," "curry favor," and so on.

Foreign-English Dictionaries

MULTILANGUAGE DICTIONARIES

De Lafayette, Jean M. *The Nine Language Universal Dictionary: How to Write it and Say it in Arabic, English, French, German, Italian, Japanese, Portuguese, Russian and Spanish.* Ed. by the American Council for University Planning and Academic Excellence. ACUPAE 1991 $30.00. ISBN 0-939877-28-7. Access to multiple languages. Arranged alphabetically in English, with foreign terms translated phonetically. Includes key to pronunciation, geographical terms, and weights and measures.

ANGLO-SAXON

Bosworth, Joseph, and Alistair Campbell, eds. *An Anglo-Saxon Dictionary.* OUP 1972 repr. of 1898 ed. $225.00. ISBN 0-19-863101-4. 1921 supplement $135.00. ISBN 0-19-863112-X. Contains the classical references for Anglo-Saxon.

Hall, John R. *A Concise Anglo-Saxon Dictionary.* Supplement by Herbert D. Meritt. U. of Toronto Pr. 1984 repr. of 1960 ed. $17.95. ISBN 0-8020-6548-1. Useful particularly due to the addenda and revisions made by Meritt in his 20-page supplement, containing 1,700 new entries not in the Bosworth-Campbell volume (above).

ARABIC

Doniach, N. S. *The Concise Oxford English-Arabic Dictionary of Current Usage.* OUP 1982 $29.95. ISBN 0-19-864321-7. An abridged edition of the *Oxford English-Arabic Dictionary of Current Usage,* also edited by Doniach. Includes American usage, with common phrases.

English-Arabic Vocabulary: Students' Pronouncing Dictionary. Comp. by Merrill Y. Van Wagoner. Spoken Lang. Serv. 1980 $10.00. ISBN 0-87950-028-X. Both the English and Arabic lists used to compile this work are dated to the mid-1940s.

Hinds, Martin. *A Dictionary of Egyptian Arabic: Arabic-English.* Fr. & Eur. 1986 $125.00. ISBN 0-8288-0434-6. Focuses upon spoken language.

The Oxford English-Arabic Dictionary of Current Usage. Ed. by N. S. Doniach. OUP 1972 $75.00. ISBN 0-19-869312-8. Designed to meet the needs of English and Arabic speakers who are learning each other's language. A useful reference tool as well.

Shaikh, Shafi. *Handbook of English-Arabic for Professionals.* OUP 1983 $28.00. ISBN 0-19-561385-6. Emphasizes technical terms in many fields.

Wehr, Hans. *A Dictionary of Modern Written Arabic.* Ed. by J. M. Cowan. Spoken Lang. Serv. 5th ed. 1985 $195.00. ISBN 0-8288-0995-X. Enlarged and improved version of Wehr's German language lexicon, including 13,000 additional entries.

CHINESE

The Basic English-Chinese, Chinese-English Dictionary. Ed. by Peter Bergman and others. Humanities 1980 $5.75. ISBN 0-451-16826-7. Uses the Pinyin system of transliteration. Chinese characters are arranged by number of strokes, English entries are arranged alphabetically.

Beginner's Dictionary of Chinese-Japanese Characters: With Common Abbreviations, Variants, and Numerous Compounds. Comp. by Arthur Rose-Innes. Dover 1977 $11.95. ISBN 0-486-23467-3. A revision of a 1959 work, including new terms and modifications of characters.

Beijing Language Institute Staff. *Everyday Chinese-English Dictionary.* Hippocrene Bks. rev. ed. 1990 $12.95. ISBN 0-87052-862-9. Contains over 3,800 single-character entries and 19,000 compound-character entries, all frequently used in everyday life. A handy quick-reference book.

Chi, Wen Shun, and others, comps. *Chinese-English Dictionary of Contemporary Usage.* U. CA Pr. 1977 $50.00. ISBN 0-520-02655-1. More than 20,000 terms included emphasize modern vocabulary and usage, utilizing the Wade-Giles system of romanization with a conversion table from Pinyin.

Chinese-English Dictionary of Idioms: Compiled by Specialists of English From Sichuan Province. Hippocrene Bks. 2nd ed. 1988 $12.95. ISBN 0-87052-454-2. Entries of over 4,000 Chinese idioms, with English translations of 150,000. Precise Chinese entries, transcribed in Hanyu Pinyin. An excellent reference tool for all levels of language ability.

Dobson, W. A. *A Dictionary of the Chinese Particles, with a Prolegomenon in Which the Problems of the Particles Are Considered and They Are Classified by Their Grammatical Functions.* U. of Toronto Pr. 1974 $160.00. ISBN 0-317-55768-9. Includes 684 particles used from the eleventh century B.C. to the sixth century A.D., with many still presently in use. Arrangement is by the National Romanization system, with a Wade-Giles conversion table included.

Lin Yutang. *Chinese-English Dictionary of Modern Usage.* St. Mut. 1986 $195.00. ISBN 0-317-59312-9. An excellent dictionary that reflects the scholarly reputation of its author. Based upon contextual semantics, the way in which a word changes in context. Characters are listed in the regular-to-simplified form and vice versa.

The Oxford-Duden Pictorial English & Chinese Dictionary: Simplified Character Edition.
   OUP 1989 $45.00. ISBN 0-19-584203-8. Uses numbered illustrations to identify
   objects and terms, which are given in English and Chinese. An excellent, comprehensive tool for students of both languages.
The Pinyin Chinese-English Dictionary. Ed. by Wu Jingrong and others. Wiley 1982
   $35.00. ISBN 0-471-86796-9. Entries are given in the Pinyin romanization and many
   Chinese characters, which one must know to use. Includes many modern terms and
   expressions.

DANISH

Danish-English, English-Danish Dictionary. Hippocrene Bks. 1989 $9.95. ISBN 0-87052-
   823-8
Vinterberg, H., and others. *Danish-English Dictionary: Dansk-Engelsk Urdbog.* Fr. & Eur.
   1981 $250.00. ISBN 0-8288-4429-1. A current Danish-English dictionary, containing
   many modern and important words. Meanings of words are defined by means of
   examples for greater reader comprehension.

DUTCH

Berlitz Editors. *Dutch-English Dictionary.* Berlitz 1988 $6.95. ISBN 2-8315-0942-4
Bruggencate, K. Ten. *Dutch-English, English-Dutch Dictionary.* 2 vols. IBD Ltd. 19th ed.
   1981 Dutch-English $34.50. ISBN 90-01-96819-8. English-Dutch $34.50. ISBN 90-01-
   96818-X. A good, standard two-volume desktop set.
Cassel's Editors.*Cassel's New Dutch Dictionary: English-Dutch, Dutch-English.* Macmillan
   1982 $50.00. ISBN 0-02-522940-0. A standard desk dictionary, with clear pronuncia-
   tion given.

FRENCH

Atkins, Beryl T., and others. *Collins-Robert French Dictionary.* Collins 2nd ed 1987
   $35.00. ISBN 0-8288-0059-6. Also, *French-English/English-French* $29.95. ISBN 0-
   313-45617-2. Offers superior coverage, with timely new technical entries. An
   authoritative reference work for the serious student.
Berlitz editors. *French-English Dictionary.* Berlitz 1989 $6.95. ISBN 2-8315-0940-8
Cassell Staff. *Cassell's French & English Dictionary.* Macmillan 1986 $5.00. ISBN 0-02-
   013680-3. An excellent standard bilingual work, with easy pronunciation instructions. Includes slang words, idioms, and common lay terms.
Collins Staff. *Harper Collins French Dictionary.* HarpC 1990 $14.95. ISBN 0-06-055250-6.
   Up-to-date revision with current terms; emphasis is on American usage.
Corbeil, Jean-Claude. *The Facts on File English-French Visual Dictionary.* Facts on File
   1987 $35.00. ISBN 0-8160-1545-6. An excellent pictorial resource reflecting modern
   terminology. Intended for all users.
Dubois, M. M. *Larousse Saturne French-English/English-French Dictionary.* Fr. & Eur. In
   progress. $49.95. ISBN 0-685-19997-5. Designed for the widest variety of interests
   and professions. Includes over 35,000 definitions, pronunciation keys, idioms, and
   conjugations in both languages.
Harrap's Concise French Dictionary. P-H 1990 $16.95. ISBN 0-13-383035-7. Provides the
   user of any level with up-to-date practical terms.
Oxford-Duden Pictorial French & English Dictionary. OUP 1989 $17.95. ISBN 0-19-
   864153-2. Provides the meanings of French/English vocabulary words through a
   pictorial approach.
Steiner, Roger. *The Bantam New College French & English Dictionary.* Bantam 1989
   $4.95. ISBN 0-553-27411-2

GERMAN

Berlitz Editors. *German-English Dictionary.* Berlitz 1989 $6.95. ISBN 2-8315-0941-6. A
   handy and compact dictionary with more than 12,000 terms in each language.
   Designed for the traveler.

Betteridge, Harold. *Cassell's German-English, English-German Dictionary: Deutsch-Englisches, Englisch-Deutsches Wörterbuch*. Macmillan rev. ed. 1978 $24.95. ISBN 0-02-522930-3. This revised edition includes a key to German pronunciation and phonetic transcriptions of German keywords.

Buck, Timothy. *German-English Dictionary*. Viking Penguin 1992 $14.00. ISBN 0-14-051073-7

Cassell's New German Dictionary (German-English and English-German). Funk & Wagnalls rev. ed. 1958. o.p. The 1940 edition was called the "bible" of the Allied Control Commission in Germany. Thoroughly revised by Betteridge, this expanded version includes literary language, as well as colloquial terms. Set in roman, instead of Gothic type.

Harper Collins German Dictionary. HarpC 1990 $24.95. ISBN 0-06-017801-9. Standard desktop edition, with an emphasis on current spoken language.

Keller, Howard H. *German Root Lexicon*. U. of Miami Pr. 1973 $11.95. ISBN 0-87024-244-X. Alphabetical arrangement by English word. Useful in selecting equivalent terms in German.

———. *A German World Family Dictionary: Together with English Equivalents*. U. CA Pr. 1978 $25.00. ISBN 0-520-03291-8. Groups German words in families in columns.

Langenscheidt New College German Dictionary: German-English, English-German. Langenscheidt 1973 $25.95. ISBN 0-88729-018-3. Designed for the English-speaking user, this is an excellent standard work. Strong in contemporary, colloquial, and idiomatic usage.

The Oxford-Duden Pictorial German-English Dictionary. Ed. by John Pheby. OUP 1980 $49.95. ISBN 0-345-34600-9. Illustrations and word lists allow users in both languages to name familiar objects. There are 28,000 items here.

Webster's New World German Dictionary: A Collins Concise Dictionary. P-H 1987 $16.95. ISBN 0-671-63815-7

GREEK

Liddell, H. G., and R. Scott. *Greek-English Lexicon*. Rev. by H. S. Jones and others. 2 vols. OUP rev. ed. 1968 $98.00. ISBN 0-19-84214-8. The authoritative Greek-English dictionary, carefully prepared and edited by leading scholars in the field.

———. *Intermediate Greek-English Lexicon*. OUP 1959 $35.00. ISBN 0-19-912206-6. Based on the *Greek-English Lexicon*, with expanded listings and further explanations of the words.

Pring, J. T., ed. *The Oxford Dictionary of Modern Greek: Greek-English, English-Greek*. OUP 1986 $29.95. ISBN 0-19-864137-0. This work has been critically praised.

Swanson, Donald C. *Vocabulary of Modern Spoken Greek (English-Greek and Greek-English)*. Ed. by Theofanis G. Stavrou. Nostos Bks. 1982 $15.00. ISBN 0-935476-11-3. Information on derivation, structure, and pronunciation. Includes sections on names, food and drink, and greetings. Very good for student-residents or tourists.

Wharton, E. R. *Etymological Lexicon of Classical Greek*. Ares 1975 $15.00. ISBN 0-89005-033-3

HEBREW

Balstan, Hayim. *Webster's New World Hebrew-English Dictionary*. P-H 1992 $35.00. ISBN 0-13-944547-1

Ben-Yehuda, Eliezer, ed. *Dictionary and Thesaurus of the Hebrew Language*. Oak Tree Pubns. 8 vols. $150.00. ISBN 0-498-07038-7. Complete international centennial edition.

Berlitz Editors. *Hebrew Phrase Books*. Berlitz 1989 $5.95. ISBN 2-8315-0757-X. Designed for the visitor to Israel, this handy little book contains phrases and vocabulary for use in many typical situations.

Gross, David C. *Concise Phonetic English-Hebrew/Hebrew-English Conversational Dictionary*. Hippocrene Bks. 1991 $7.95. ISBN 0-87052-625-1

HUNGARIAN

Berlitz Editors. *Hungarian-English Dictionary*. Berlitz 1992 $6.95. ISBN 2-8315-0982-3. Newly revised edition in an easy-to-carry volume. Good for the traveler.

Maqay, Tamas. *English-Hungarian, Hungarian-English Dictionary*. Hippocrene Bks. 1990 $9.95. ISBN 0-88254-986-3

Maqay, Tamas, and others. *A Concise English-Hungarian Dictionary*. OUP 1990 $39.95. ISBN 0-19-864170-2. Standard and concise work including more than 65,000 terms.

ITALIAN

Andrews, Joyce, ed. *The Oxford Paperback Italian Dictionary: Italian-English/English-Italian*. OUP 1989 $5.95. ISBN 0-19-282184-9

Berberi, Dilaver, and Edel A. Berberi. *Italian Dictionary*. Putnam Pub. Group 1975 $3.95. ISBN 0448-14030-6

Berlitz Editors. *Italian-English Dictionary*. Berlitz 1989 $6.95. ISBN 2-8315-0945-9. Condensed volume of standard Italian-English terms. Intended for use by the traveler.

Cassell's Italian Dictionary: Italian-English, English-Italian. Macmillan 1977 $19.95. ISBN 0-02-522530-8. Thumb indexed $23.95. ISBN 0-02-552540-5. A standard bilingual dictionary. Includes contemporary word usage, as well as obsolete phrases for the student of classic Italian literature.

Collins staff. *Harper Collins Italian Dictionary*. HarpC 1991 $4.95. ISBN 0-06-100246-1. A portable, compact, and authoritative dictionary. Provides excellent coverage of contemporary Italian language usage.

The Concise Cambridge Italian Dictionary. Comp. by Barbara Reynolds. Viking Penguin 1975 $10.95. ISBN 0-19-051064-8. Emphasizes current Italian usage.

Concise Italian Dictionary. P-H 1990 $16.95. ISBN 0-13-383381-X

Hall, Robert A., Jr., ed. *The Random House Basic Dictionary: Italian*. Ballantine 1986 $10.95. ISBN 0-345-34603-3

Lipton, Gladys C., and John Colaneri. *Beginning Italian Bilingual Dictionary*. Barron 2nd rev. ed. 1989 $4.95. ISBN 0-8120-4272-7

Melzi, Robert C. *Bantam New College Italian and English Dictionary*. Bantam 1989 $4.50. ISBN 0-553-26306-4

JAPANESE

All-Romanized English-Japanese Dictionary. Fr. & Eur. 9th ed. 1980 $12.95. ISBN 0-8288-1611-5. In addition to terms, includes a section on Japanese grammar.

Corwin, Charles, and others. *A Dictionary of Japanese and English Idiomatic Equivalents*. Kodansha 1980 $24.95. ISBN 0-87011-111-6

Hadamitzky, Wolfgang, and Mark Spahn. *Kanji and Kana: A Handbook Dictionary of the Japanese Writing System*. C. E. Tuttle 1981 $19.95. ISBN 0-8048-1373-6. A systematic and comprehensive introduction to the Japanese writing system. Intended primarily for use as a textbook, it is also useful as a concise dictionary of Japanese writing.

Halpern, Jack. *Webster's New World Kenkyusha Japanese-English Character Reading Dictionary*. P-H 1992 $60.00. ISBN 0-13-945858-1

Martin, Samuel. *Basic Japanese Conversation Dictionary: English-Japanese and Japanese-English*. C. E. Tuttle 1957 $6.95. ISBN 0-8048-0057-X. Contains 6,000 of the most common English and Japanese words in Japanese characters and in standard romanization.

Miura, Akira. *English Loanwords in Japanese: A Selection*. C. E. Tuttle 1979 $19.95. ISBN 0-8048-1248-9

———. *Japanese Words and Their Uses*. C. E. Tuttle 1983 $12.95. ISBN 0-8048-1639-5. Includes 300 expressions that cause difficulty for English speakers of Japanese.

The Oxford-Duden Pictorial Japanese and English Dictionary. OUP 1989 repr. of 1983 ed. $19.95. ISBN 0-19-86427-6. Identifies 28,000 objects by using numbered illustrations, accompanied by their Japanese and English names. Arranged by subject category.

KOREAN

English-Korean/Korean-English Dictionary. Hippocrene Bks. 1991 $9.95. ISBN 0-87052-092-X

Grant, Bruce K. *A Guide to Korean Characters: Reading and Writing Hangul and Hanja.* Hollym Intl. 1989 $27.50. ISBN 0-930878-13-2

Rhie, Gene S., and B. J. Jones, eds. *Standard English-Korean and Korean-English Dictionary for Foreigners.* Hollym Intl. 1992 $15.95. ISBN 0-930878-06-X

LATIN

Glare, P. G., ed. *Oxford Latin Dictionary.* OUP 1982 $215.00. ISBN 0-19-864224-5. A one-volume edition of a nine-volume set started in 1967. The most comprehensive of available Latin dictionaries.

Latham, R. E. *Dictionary of Medieval Latin from British Sources.* OUP 2 fascicules 1984 $125.00. ISBN 0-19-706023-3. In-depth dictionary of medieval Latin terms compiled from British sources. Includes a useful bibliography.

Simpson, D. P., and others. *Cassell's Latin & English Dictionary.* Macmillan 1987 $4.95. ISBN 0-02-013340-5. For quick, easy reference. Contains thousands of words, phrases, and idioms used in scholarly and academic sources. Includes tables of verbs and a section on Roman culture.

NORWEGIAN

Berlitz Editors. *Norwegian-English Dictionary.* Berlitz 1989 $6.95. ISBN 2-8315-0948-3. A compact volume designed primarily for the traveler. Also contains basic phrases and a menu reader.

Kirkeby, Willy A. *English-Norwegian Dictionary.* OUP 1989 $49.95. ISBN 82-00-18293-2. A standard, comprehensive Norwegian-English work, with Americanisms included.

Norwegian-English, English-Norwegian Pocket Dictionary. IBD Ltd. 19th ed. 1987 $24.75. ISBN 82-517-8012-8. A small, concise, dictionary for users of all levels. Especially handy for travelers.

PHILIPPINE

Bickford, Sam. *Philipino Concise Dictionary.* Hippocrene Bks. 1989 $6.95. ISBN 0-87052-491-7. Contains over 5,000 entries for students and travelers. Employs a concise format.

Enriquez. *English-Tagalog, Tagalog-English Pocket Dictionary.* Colton Bk. 1989 repr. of 1949 ed. $5.00. ISBN 0-686-00861-8

POLISH

Borkowski, P. *An English-Polish Dictionary of Idioms and Phrases.* Fr. & Eur. 1982 $9.95. ISBN 0-8288-1630-1. A dictionary of English idioms and phrases for Poles, particularly those who settled in English-speaking countries after World War II.

Bulas, Kazimierz, Francis J. Whitfield, and Lawrence L. Thomas. *The Kosciuszko Foundation English-Polish, Polish-English Dictionary.* 2 vols. Kosciuszko 1986 $27.50. ea. English-Polish ISBN 0-917004-00-0, Polish-English ISBN 0-917004-16-7. A comprehensive Polish dictionary, with American spelling favored over British form. Includes cross-references and colloquialisms.

Pogonowski, Iwo. *Dictionary: Polish-English, English-Polish.* Hippocrene Bks. 3rd rev. ed. $22.50. ISBN 0-87052-908-0. A practical guide to the language that includes phonetic descriptions.

PORTUGUESE

Berlitz Editors. *Portuguese-English Dictionary.* Berlitz 1989 $6.95. ISBN 2-8315-0949-1. Designed as a companion volume for visitors to Brazil and Portugal; contains common terms and phrases for various situations.

Houaiss, Antonio, and I. Cardin. *Portuguese-English, English-Portuguese Dictionary*. Hippocrene Bks. rev. ed. 1991 $14.95. ISBN 0-87052-980-3. A small, practical bilingual dictionary; includes contemporary usage and idiomatic phrases.

Oxford-Duden Pictorial Portuguese & English Dictionary. OUP 1992 $19.95. ISBN 0-19-864172-9. A current pictorial dictionary prepared by specialists in the field. Includes specialized words and technical terms.

ROMANIAN

Romanian-English/English-Romanian Dictionary. IBD Ltd. 1991 $35.00. ISBN 0-88431-075-2

Schonkron, Marcel. *Romanian-English/English-Romanian Dictionary*. Hippocrene Bks. 1991 $19.95. ISBN 0-87052-986-2. Comprehensive and practical, with over 40,000 entries. Also includes contemporary and colloquial terms.

RUSSIAN

Coulson, Jessie, and others. *The Pocket Oxford Russian Dictionary: Russian-English/English-Russian*. OUP 1981 $12.95. ISBN 0-12-864122-2. Based upon the *Oxford Russian-English Dictionary* and designed primarily for the English-speaking user. Offers translations rather than definitions or explanations.

Macura, P. *Elsevier's Russian-English Dictionary*. Elsevier 1990 $307.75. ISBN 0-444-88467-X. A four-volume set divided into the Sciences, Humanities, Social Sciences, and the Russian language.

Smirnitsky, A. I. *Russian English Dictionary*. St. Mut. 13th ed. 1990 $90.00. ISBN 0-569-00006-8. Source of standard Russian vocabulary and terms.

Wilson, E. A. *The Modern Russian Dictionary for English Speakers: English-Russian*. Pergamon 1983 $46.00. ISBN 0-08-020554-2. Emphasis on colloquial Russian and actual equivalents to the English language.

SERBO-CROATIAN

An English-Serbocroatian Dictionary. Comp. by Zivajin Simic. Fr. & Eur. 1979 $14.95. ISBN 0-686-97375-5. Compiled to satisfy a timely need for an up-to-date English-Serbocroatian lexicon, this dictionary seeks to utilize standard American English.

Oxford-Duden Pictorial Serbo-Croat & English Dictionary. OUP 1988 $59.00. ISBN 0-19-869165-3. Conveys information through pictures, as well as by definitions and explanations.

SPANISH

American Heritage Larousse Spanish Dictionary. Ed. by the Houghton Mifflin Company staff. HM 1986 $21.45. ISBN 0-317-65694-5. An excellent bilingual dictionary jointly produced by Houghton Mifflin and Larousse. Emphasis is on Spanish usage in the United States and Latin America.

Berlitz editors. *Spanish-English Dictionary*. Berlitz 1989 $6.95. ISBN 2-8315-0944-0

Boggs, R. S., and J. I. Dixon. *Everyday Spanish Idioms*. P-H 1978 $5.95. ISBN 0-88345-326-6

Cassell's Spanish-English, English-Spanish Dictionary: Diccionario Espanol-Ingles, Ingles-Espanol. Comp. by Anthony Gooch and Angel Garcia de Paredes. Macmillan 1978 $21.95. ISBN 0-02-522910-9. Includes tables of verbs and colloquial expressions.

Castillo, Carlos, and Otto F. Bond. *The University of Chicago Spanish Dictionary*. PB 4th ed. 1991 $4.99. ISBN 0-317-56745-4. A staple in many reference collections.

Corbeil, Jean-Claude. *Facts on File English-Spanish Visual Dictionary*. Facts on File 1992 $39.95. ISBN 0-8160-1546-5. Divided into three sections: table of contents, illustrations, and alphabetical indexes. Illustrations arranged by subject.

Cuyas, Arturo. *New Appleton's Cuyas English-Spanish and Spanish-English Dictionary*. P-H 5th ed. 1974 $26.95. ISBN 0-13-611749-X. A comprehensive and standard English-Spanish dictionary for all users.

El Diccionario del Espanol Chicano: The Dictionary of Chicano Spanish. Comp. by Roberto A. Galvan and Richard V. Teschner. NTC Pub. Grp. 1991 $9.95. ISBN 0-8325-9634-5. A revised edition of *El Diccionario del Espanol de Tejas/The Dictionary of the Spanish of Texas* that contains regionalized expressions.

Jump, James R. *Penguin Spanish Dictionary.* Viking Penguin 1990 $12.00. ISBN 0-14-051068-0

Oxford-Duden Pictorial Spanish & English Dictionary. OUP 1989 $17.95. ISBN 0-19-869155-6. A pictorial dictionary, with each double page containing a plate illustrating the vocabulary of an entire subject, along with exact Spanish names and the English equivalent. Includes many specialized and technical terms.

Parnwell, E. C. *Oxford Picture Dictionary of American English.* OUP 1980 English-Spanish ed. $6.95. ISBN 0-19-502333-1

Williams, Edwin B. *Diccionario Espanol-Ingles/English-Spanish Dictionary.* McGraw 2nd ed. 1989 $19.95. ISBN 0-07-070421-X

SWAHILI

Gilmore, T. *Swahili Phrasebook: For Travelers in Eastern and Southern Africa.* Hippocrene Bks. 1991 $6.95. ISBN 0-87052-970-6. A slim volume for the student or traveler providing a practical guide to simple communication. Arranged by topic.

Jahadhmy, Ali A. *Learner's Swahili-English/English-Swahili Dictionary.* Trafalgar 1992 $3.95. ISBN 0-237-50467-7

SWEDISH

Berlitz Editors. *Swedish-English Dictionary.* Berlitz 1989 $6.95. ISBN 2-8315-0943-2

Tornberg, Astrid. *Swedish-English, English-Swedish Dictionary: Svensk-Engelsk-Svensk Ordbok.* Fr. & Eur. 1986 $29.95. ISBN 0-8288-0525-3

TURKISH

Berlitz Editors. *Turkish-English Dictionary.* Berlitz 1991 $6.95. ISBN 2-8315-0981-5. Pocket volume with over 12,500 concepts; includes 350 pages of key words for the traveler.

Concise Oxford Turkish Dictionary. Ed. by Anthony D. Alderson and others. OUP 1959 $55.00. ISBN 0-19-864109-5

VIETNAMESE

Nguyen, Dihn-Hoa. *Vietnamese-English Dictionary.* C. E. Tuttle 1991 $19.95. ISBN 0-8048-1712-X. A compact and concise dictionary designed as a study aid to students of Vietnamese. Includes morphemes and words most frequently used in the language.

YIDDISH

Gross, David C. *English-Yiddish/Yiddish-English Concise Conversational Dictionary: In the Roman Alphabet.* Hippocrene Bks. 1991 $7.95. ISBN 0-87052-969-2

Harkavy, Alexander, ed. *Yiddish-English-Hebrew Dictionary.* Schocken 1988 $35.00. ISBN 0-8052-4027-6. A standard desktop Yiddish-Hebrew dictionary.

Kogos, Fred. *Dictionary of Yiddish Slang.* Citadel Pr. 1983 $5.95. ISBN 0-8065-0347-5

DIRECTORIES

Directories can provide brief, but current, facts about individuals, groups, organizations (such as business and trade groups), government, and other institutions. They often contain such facts about organizations as names of its officers, membership, budget, functions, and publications.

Guides to Directories

City and State Directories in Print. Gale 2nd ed. 1993 $145.00. ISBN 0-8103-6901-X. An annotated guide to more than 45,000 state, city, and local directories, rosters, guides, and lists covering a wide variety of subjects.

Directories in Print. 2 vols. Gale 1992 10th ed. $270.00. ISBN 0-8103-7627-X. Formerly *Directory of Directories.* Lists commercial directories, trade and professional directories, biographical directories, professional societies. Annual publication.

International Directories in Print. Gale 1988 o.p. Lists 5,000 directories published outside the United States, or with an international scope. Includes business, industrial, scientific, and professional directories.

Organizations Master Index. Gale 1986 $125.00. ISBN 0-8103-2079-7. A consolidated index to approximately 50 directories, yearbooks, and guides providing information on 150,000 organizations in the United States and Canada.

General Directories

American Library Directory. Bowker Annual 1908–present. 46th ed. 1993 $225.00. ISBN 0-8352-3282-4. An annual comprehensive listing of 50,000 U.S. and Canadian public, academic, special, and government libraries. Addresses, telephone numbers, staff members, budgets, collection size, and special collections. Arranged by state and city, with indexes for other access points.

Annual Register of Grant Support: A Directory of Funding Sources. Bowker 26th ed. 1993 $165.00. ISBN 0-8352-3293-X. Describes over 3,000 programs of governmental agencies, foundations, unions, and professional associations.

Awards, Honors & Prizes. Gale 10th ed. 1992 $390.00. ISBN 0-8103-7641-5. Single most comprehensive source of information on awards offered by U.S. and Canadian organizations.

Directory of Online Databases. Elsevier $95.00. ISBN 0-685-17450-6. An alphabetical listing of more than 3,000 electronically accessible resources.

Directory of Special Libraries and Information Centers. 3 vols. Gale 17th ed. 1993 $345.00–$415.00 ea. ISBNs 0-8103-8017-X, 0-8103-8020-X, 0-8103-8016-X. Describes collections found in businesses, government agencies, foundations. Subject access.

Encyclopedia of Associations: International Organizations. Gale 1992 $455.00. ISBN 0-8103-7673-3. A guide to over 12,000 international nonprofit membership organizations including multinational and binational groups. Strong U.S. emphasis. Available on-line and in CD-ROM.

Encyclopedia of Associations: National Organizations of the U.S. Gale Annual 1993 $340.00. ISBN 0-8103-8314-4. Comprehensive detailed source of information concerning more than 30,000 nonprofit organizations; 270,000-line alphabetical "Name and Keyword Index." Available on-line and in CD-ROM.

Encyclopedia of Associations: Regional, State, Local. 5 vols. Gale 3rd ed. 1992 $469.00. ISBN 0-8103-7696-2. Great Lakes, Northeastern, South Middle Atlantic, South Central Great Plains, Western volumes. Encompasses nonprofit organizations. Available on-line and in CD-ROM.

Europa Yearbook. 2 vols. Gale 1993 ISBNs 0-8103-9654-8, 0-8103-9655-6. Similar to the *Encyclopedia of Associations,* except that it provides better coverage of international organizations.

Foundation Directory. Col. U. Pr. 14th ed. 1992 $165.00. ISBN 0-87954-438-4. Provides information on the finance, governance, and giving interests of the largest grant-making foundations with annual giving of at least $100,000.

Foundation Grants Index. Col. U. Pr. 20th ed. 1991 $110.00. ISBN 0-87954-401-5. The 1992 *Index* covers 57,443 grants totaling $4.47 billion.

Government Research Directory. Gale 7th ed. 1992 $405.00. ISBN 0-8103-7526-5. Provides information for over 3,500 research centers of the U.S. Government. Companion volume to *The Research Center Directory.* Available on-line through the database, Research Center and Service Directory.

Information Industry Directory. 2 vols. Gale Annual 1992 $475.00. ISBN 0-8103-7625-3. Formerly the *Encyclopedia of Information Systems and Services.* A comprehensive, international, descriptive guide to more than 4,500 organizations, systems, and services involved in the production and distribution of information in electronic form.

International Research Centers Directory. Gale 7th ed. 1993 $395.00. ISBN 0-8103-7909-0. Covers all categories of research including government, university, commercial, and laboratory. Companion to *The Research Center Directory.* Available on-line with companion volumes through the database, Research Center and Service Directory.

National Fax Directory. Gale 1992 $85.00. ISBN 0-8103-7638-5. Lists over 80,000 FAX users with voice phone number and mailing address.

The Official Museum Directory. Bowker 24th ed. 1994 nonmembers $185.00, members $134.00. ISBN 0-8352-3372-3. Published for the American Association of Museums. Features profiles and statistics on more than 7,000 institutions in the United States. Lists national and international museum organizations. Includes zoos, aquariums, nature centers, all types of museums.

The Research Center Directory. Gale 1992 $420.00. ISBN 0-8103-8006-5. Guide to nearly 13,000 university-related and other nonprofit organizations. Companion to *International Research Centers Directory, State Government Research Directory* and *Government Research Directory.* Available on-line through the database, Research Center and Services Directory.

State Government Research Directory. Gale 1986. $175.00. ISBN 0-8103-1591-2. Covers over 800 state-level research agencies. Companion to *Government Research Directory.* Available through the on-line database, Research Center and Service Directory.

Subject Collections. 2 vols. Comp. by Lee Ash and William G. Miller. Bowker 7th ed. 1993 $275.00. ISBN 0-8352-3141-0. Subject index to 65,000 special books and manuscript collections housed in academic, public, and special libraries and museums in the United States and Canada. Listings are organized under 18,000 subject headings.

Washington Information Directory 1992–93. Congr. Quarterly 1992 $89.95. ISBN 0-87187-692-2. Lists information for agencies of the U.S. Government and nonprofit organizations in Washington.

World of Learning. Gale 43rd ed. 1993 $330.00. ISBN 0-8103-9747-1. Information on learned societies, universities, museums, and libraries throughout the world.

Worldwide Government Directory. Belmont Pubns. 1992 $325.00. ISBN 0-9629283-2-1. Lists every independent country in the world—covers 50,000 officials for 170 nations.

ENCYCLOPEDIAS

Since PLINY THE ELDER's (see Vol. 5) *Historia Naturalis* (A.D. 77), attempts have been made to produce encyclopedic summaries of human knowledge. One of the most renowned and influential encyclopedias, the French *Encyclopédie*, was completed in 1772 by DENIS DIDEROT (see Vols. 2 and 4). The famous *Encyclopaedia Britannica*, first published in 1771, has grown dramatically in size and reputation over the years. Today, encyclopedias continue to have a useful place in homes, schools, and libraries. As a result of advances in technology, encyclopedias are no longer restricted to print format, as these sources may also be found online and on CD-ROM.

Regardless of the format in which encyclopedias may be found, they are useful for answering questions and providing basic background or introductory matter on a wide range of topics. Articles in general encyclopedias are generally written with the beginner in mind. Those who are interested in more specific information may use a subject encyclopedia in virtually any field of their choice. Information contained in encyclopedia articles frequently progress from a broad, simple orientation to more advanced concepts. When entries are accompanied by a bibliography, the user is afforded a brief introduction to other sources of information on that topic available at the time that the article was prepared. Further, a well-prepared index can assist the reader in using the work. Those interested in learning more about encyclopedias may consult Bowker's *General Reference Books for Adults* (1988) and *Reference Books for Young Readers* (1988), Kenneth Kister's *Best Encyclopedias: A Guide to General and Specialized Encyclopedias* (Phoenix, AZ: Oryx, 1986), or *Kister's Concise Guide to Best Encyclopedias* (Phoenix, AZ: Oryx, 1988), which provide critical evaluations of many multivolume or single-volume encyclopedias that are presently available. An additional source for reviews of encyclopedias is the *American Reference Books Annual*. The prices and edition dates listed below should be taken only as an indication.

Multivolume Encyclopedias

Academic American Encyclopedia. 21 vols. Grolier Inc. rev. ed. 1993 ISBN 0-7172-2047-8. Designed for adults and older students, the *AAE* is noted for its illustrations and index. Articles are generally 500 words or fewer and are frequently accompanied by a bibliography. In the current edition, there are 32,000 articles, 16,000 illustrations, and 1,100 maps. The work is also available on-line through systems such as BRS, Dow Jones News/Retrieval, and PRODIGY.

Children's Britannica. 20 vols. Ency. Brit. Inc. 1992 $299.00. ISBN 0-85229-229-5. A revision of the *Britannica Junior Encyclopedia* focusing on children ages 7 through 12. Includes approximately 4,000 articles and 6,000 illustrations.

Collier's Encyclopedia. 24 vols. Macmillan 1992 $959.00. ISBN 0-02-942157-4. Intended for use by high school students and adults, this work falls between the *World Book* and *Encyclopaedia Britannica* in scope and depth of articles. The most recent edition contains an 11,500-title bibliography for advanced research on topics. One of the limitations of the work is that users must rely on the index volume to locate all aspects of a topic. However, currency of the work is made possible through the accompanying *Collier's Yearbook*.

The Encyclopedia Americana. 30 vols. Grolier Inc. 1993. ISBN 0-7172-0124-4. "The Encyclopedia Americana is a well-balanced and clearly written authoritative work prepared by an experienced editorial staff, with an excellent index and well-designed illustrations. New editions appear every year with varied degrees of revision" (Bohdan S. Wynar, *American Reference Books Annual*). The set includes a comprehensive index to entries and is updated through a separate one-volume *Americana Annual*.

Funk and Wagnalls New Encyclopedia. Ed. by Leon L. Bram and Robert S. Phillips. 29 vols. Funk & Wagnalls 1983 o.p. *"Funk and Wagnalls New Encyclopedia (FWNE)* is intended for home use as well as for junior high school students. It is designed for the reader with little or no background in the material being researched. The majority of articles are concise, a page or less in length. For long articles containing complicated subject matter, the material is presented from the simple to the complex and from the general to the specific. . . . The *FWNE* has prepared well for its audience. . . . It is not intended to compete with encyclopedias like *Collier's* or *World Book*" (Marilyn Strong-Noronha, *American Reference Books Annual*). The *FWNE* includes more than 9,000 illustrations and more than 300 maps and is accompanied by a 250-page bibliography.

The New Book of Knowledge. 21 vols. Grolier Inc. 1992 ISBN 0-7172-0520-7. Designed for third- through sixth-graders, the *New Book* is considered "a relatively current, well-written encyclopedia that is responsive to the school and home needs of the elementary school-aged student" (Janet H. Littlefield, *American Reference Books*

Annual). The 1992 edition includes 13,000 illustrations, a majority of which are in color.

The New Encyclopaedia Britannica. 32 vols. Ency. Brit. Inc. 15th ed. 1992 $1,199.00. ISBN 0-85229-553-7. The *Britannica*, by far the most complex of those encyclopedias listed here, is published in three parts. The *Propaedia* is a one-volume topical outline of knowledge, intended to serve the user as a guide to the information found in the longer *Macropaedia* articles. The *Macropaedia* contains within its 17 volumes in-depth examinations and annotated bibliographies. The 12-volume *Micropaedia* consists of alphabetically arranged brief articles. In general, information located within the *Britannica* can be more challenging to locate, due to its three-part arrangement. However, most reviewers agree that the *Britannica* is an authoritative encyclopedia that provides more information on almost all subject areas than any other English-language encyclopedia. The work is updated through the annual *Britannica Book of the Year.*

The World Book Encyclopedia. 22 vols. World Bk. 1992 ISBN 0-7166-0092-7. One of the most popular and easily recognizable encyclopedias, the *World Book* is known for its clear, readable articles and simple design. Intended for use by elementary, junior high, and high school students, as well as adults, its content is based in part on school curriculum analysis and classroom testing. Longer articles include outlines and a list of related articles and suggested readings. Cross-references may be found throughout the set, and the index is easy to use. Includes thousands of articles and over 30,000 illustrations and maps, of which a majority are in color; the Research Guide/Index includes over 150,000 index entries. The work is updated through the annual *World Book Yearbook.*

One-Volume Encyclopedias

Columbia Encyclopedia. Col. U. Pr. 5th rev. ed. 1993 $99.00. ISBN 0-231-08098-0

The Concise Columbia Encyclopedia. Col. U. Pr. 2nd ed 1989 $39.95. ISBN 0-394-58450-3. A compact one-volume desk encyclopedia intended to provide concise up-to-date factual information.

The Random House Encyclopedia. Random rev. ed. 1990 $129.95. ISBN 0-394-58450-3. A one-volume encyclopedia designed for general readership, the *Random House* contains a wide range of information and numerous illustrations. Arranged in two sections, the *Colorpedia* contains information and illustrations relating to the following groupings: The Universe, The Earth, Life on Earth, Man, History and Culture, Man and Science, and Man and Machines. The *Alphapedia* includes over 25,000 entries and cross-references to the *Colorpedia*. The volume also contains a Rand-McNally atlas.

GOVERNMENT PUBLICATIONS

The reader who is searching for authoritative sources of information on a wide range of material, but especially statistics, must consider using official government sources. Sometimes the government, whether at the federal, state, local, or international level, is the sole source of information. Government publications often can be an inexpensive source as well.

Libraries in the United States often create separate divisions staffed with well-educated specialists who deal with this type of material, so interested readers would do well to seek out the Government Publications Department (or whatever it may be called) in order to receive the best assistance in their search for relevant information. It is also worth keeping in mind that historically much of this material has not been fully catalogued using the Dewey Decimal or Library of Congress Classification schemes, so readers cannot depend upon the local library's catalog, whether card or on-line, to reveal the entire holdings of governmental publications. The reader should also be prepared to deal with physical formats other than hard-copy printed sources. For instance, the U.S. government has been issuing material primarily in microformats since the late 1970s. Furthermore, statistical information is increasingly being issued on CD-ROM, so that readers may also have to be familiar with microcomputer hardware and software if they want to work with this kind of material without the informed assistance of document librarians.

To aid the reader in locating relevant information, the following sections are organized according to level of government: U.S. federal, state, local, and international after general sources of information about U.S. government publications.

Guides to the Use of U.S. Government Publications

Boyd, Anne M., and Elizabeth Rips. *U.S. Government Publications*. Wilson 3rd ed. 1949 o.p. Although outdated, this textbook is occasionally still useful on historical agencies such as the Works Progress Administration.

Hernon, Peter, and Charles R. McClure. *Public Access to Governmental Information*. Ablex Pub. 2nd ed. 1988 $69.50. ISBN 0-89391-522-X. Strong on policies that influence the reader's ability to obtain federal government information as well as strategies to deal with restrictive access. Modest coverage of the publications of the 50 states and the UN.

Morehead, Joe, and Mary Fetzer. *Introduction to U.S. Government Information Sources*. 4th ed. Libs. Unl. 1992 $38.50. ISBN 0-87287-909-7. The current textbook on U.S. federal government publications. Supersedes the Schmeckebier volume.

Robinson, Judith S. *Tapping the Government Grapevine: The User-Friendly Guide to U.S. Government Information Sources*. Oryx Pr. 1993 $34.50. ISBN 0-89774-712-7. Extensive, annotated bibliography of federal government publications.

Schmeckebier, Laurence F., and Roy B. Eastin. *Government Publications and Their Use*. Bks. Demand 2nd ed. 1969 $128.50. ISBN 0-317-26160-6. Though dated, this volume still covers landmark government publications at the federal level.

Sears, Jean L., and Marily Moody. *Using Government Publications*. 2 vols. Oryx Pr. 1986 $41.50. ISBN 0-89774-124-2. Valuable bibliography of federal government publications as well as federal information services.

U.S. Government Publications

The U.S. government is one of the world's largest publishers and the U.S. Government Printing Office (GPO) issues 20–30 thousand government publication titles annually. The GPO makes much of their material available for selection to libraries. Many academic and public libraries throughout the United States have been designated as Depository Libraries, and these maintain a collection of federal publications for the general public's use. Besides these depository titles, many libraries select so-called "non-depository" titles as well.

American Statistics Index. CIS 1974–present. ISBN 0-0091-1658. Congressional Information Service subscription to annual cumulation and monthly supplements sold on a service basis. All annual volumes are in print at various prices. Detailed subject, name, title, and report-number indexing of nearly all statistical publications of the U.S. government. The *Index* correlates to a separate Abstract section, giving content, organization, currency, and source of the publications. A complete set of the full text of the publications indexed is available on microfiche from CIS. An excellent source for federal statistical data because of the strong indexing.

CCH Congressional Index. Commerce 1993 ISBN 0162-1203. A loose-leaf service that provides the current status of Congressional bills in the U.S. House of Representatives and Senate.

Census Bureau Catalog. U.S. Department of Commerce. USGPO 1992 $17.00. SuDoc Number C3.163/3:992. A complete listing of authoritative Census publications covering agriculture, business, commerce, government, housing, industry, population, and transportation data.

CIS Congressional Committee Hearings Index. CIS 1833–1969. Index by title, subject, organization, personal name, and bill, report, or document number to more than 30,000 congressional hearings from 1833 to 1969, when it was superseded by the *CIS Index.* The hearings are available on microfiche from CIS and are also held in many large research libraries.

CIS Index. CIS 1992. Since 1970, the major catalog and index of congressional publications. Attempts to catalog, abstract, and exhaustively index all publications of Congress (except the *Congressional Record* and bills). Reports, documents, hearings and testimony, and committee prints are thoroughly covered. Indexes by subject, name (author, witness, etc.), bill, report, and document number. All congressional publications covered in the *CIS/Index* are available on microfiche from CIS. Most are also available in depository and large research libraries. An excellent source of congressional information because of the strong indexing and abstracting of publications.

CIS U.S. Serial Set Index. CIS. Subject and keyword index to the *American State Papers* and the U.S. serial set of congressional reports and documents. The serial set (available from CIS on microfiche and also held in many large libraries) contains more than 11 million pages of information published between 1789 and 1969 and includes most significant federal publications through the early part of the twentieth century. After 1969 this work was superseded by the *CIS Index.*

Document Catalog. USGPO 1894–1940. Issued biennially, and discontinued with the volume covering 1939–40. This catalog is arranged by subjects, personal authors, and government authors. Replaced for the years since 1940 by the expanded *Monthly Catalog of U.S. Government Publications.*

Historical Statistics of U.S. Bureau of the Census. USGPO 1989 $68.00. SuDoc Number C3.134:H62/970/pt.1–2. Based on the decennial censuses, this source provides retrospective statistical information from 1790 to the present.

List of Depository Libraries. Superintendent of Documents. USGPO 1992 $3.50. Organized alphabetically by state and city, this publication lists the depository library number that must be used in conjunction with the *Sales Publication Reference File.*

Monthly Catalog of U.S. Government Publications. Superintendent of Documents. USGPO 1895–present $185.00. ISBN 0362-6830. The most comprehensive current listing of government publications since 1940 (replaces the *Document Catalog*). Provides the item number of a publication, so that a reader can consult the *Union List* (see below) for the actual location of a publication. Monthly and annual cumulations are available as well as special quenquennial and decennial indexes. Available on-line and in CD-ROM by various vendors; machine-readable tapes are available via the bibliographic utilities OCLC and RLIN.

Official Congressional Directory. USGPO 1989 $20.00. ISBN 0-16-006312-4. Complete listing of representatives and senators, their party affiliations, and committee assignments.

Poore, Benjamin Perley. *Poore's Descriptive Catalogue of the Government Publications of the United States, Sept. 4, 1774–March 4, 1881.* 2 vols. Johnson repr of 1885 ed. o.p. The first and only attempt to list completely all government publications. Entries are arranged chronologically and are annotated.

Sales Publication Reference File. USGPO 1992 $850.00. GP3.22/3-2:992. Organized by stock number (i.e., S/N), this work is the "Books In Print" of federal government publications. If the reader wants to purchase a government publication, this microformat publication is the definitive source on availability after verifying a publication's existence in the *Monthly Catalog* (see above).

Statistical Abstract. Bureau of the Census. USGPO 1992 $29.00. ISBN 0081-4741. The best current source of statistical information in tabular form. If the answer is not

digesting the article's contents. Depending upon the amount of literature being written, many subject areas and most academic disciplines will have indexing as well as abstracting services. Book-reviewing sources offer the reader a critique of the publication under review. Quotation books can give the exact location of who said what.

General Indexing and Abstracting Services

Abstracting and Indexing Services Directory. Ed. by John Schmittroth, Jr. Gale 1982 $200.00. ISBN 0-8103-1649-8. Describes more than 2,000 current and continuing abstracts, indexes, digests, bibliographies, and catalogs in all fields, including indexes that appear as a regular feature in journals and on-line bibliographic databases.

Arts and Humanities Citation Index. Institute for Scientific Information, quarterly, with annual cumulation 1977–present $4,375.00. ISBN 0-162-8445. A massive computer-produced index to international journals in the arts and humanities that provides author and title word-pair indexing. Its special feature is citation indexing, which indexes current articles by the items cited in their bibliographies and thus makes it possible to follow a chain of research forward from key books and articles in a field. Available on-line and on CD-ROM.

Bibliographic Index. 1937–present. Wilson. ISSN 0006-1255. Vols. 1–4 1937–55 $140.00 ea. Vols. 5–8 1956–58 $230.00 ea. Vols. 9–25 1969–85 $180.00 ea. Vols. 26–32 1986–92 sold on service basis. Published in April and August, with a permanent bound cumulation in December sold on a service basis. A subject index to bibliographies published separately as books or articles and those appearing as parts of books or articles with 50 or more bibliographic references. More than 2,800 periodicals are regularly scanned for bibliographic material. Available on Wilson-line.

Book Review Digest. 1905–present. Wilson. ISSN 0006-7326. Published monthly, except for February and July, with annual cumulations sold on a service basis. Reprints of annual volumes for 1905–92 are available at prices ranging from $110.00 to $150.00. Includes full publishing information and price, a descriptive note, and excerpts from generally three to five reviews selected to reflect the full range of critical opinion, for more than 6,000 books a year. Limited to English-language books, published or distributed in the United States, which are reviewed in at least 2 (4 for fiction) of the 95 journals scanned for reviews. Arrangement is by author of the books reviewed, with a title and subject index. Every fifth year, the annual volume contains a combined index for the past five years.

Book Review Digest Author/Title Index, 1905–1984 Wilson 1986 $65.00. ISBN 0-8242-0729-7. A useful cumulation that also includes references to a few publications not indexed by *Book Review Digest*. Available on Wilsonline and CD-ROM.

Book Review Index. 1965–present. Gale. Cumulation 1994 $195.00. ISBN 0-8103-5596-5. Bimonthly with quarterly and annual cumulations for an annual subscription of $195.00. All annual cumulations are permanently in print for $195.00 each. There is a master cumulation (1965–84) in 10 volumes for $1,250.00. Indexes all reviews in more than 400 English-language journals. No summaries or excerpts are included. Title index. Available on-line.

Books in Print. 1948–present. 10 vols. Bowker annual. 1993 $425.00. ISBN 0-8352-3354-5. Annual listings by author and title of books currently available from publishers in the United States. Each entry includes full publishing information, price, grade level, whether illustrated or not, LC card number, and ISBN. A directory of publishers' addresses is also included. The spring *Supplement* and bimonthly *Forthcoming Books* update *Books in Print*. *Paperbound Books in Print* is a similar Bowker publication. Available in many formats—microfiche, CD-ROM, and on-line.

Books in Series 1985–1989. 2 vols. Bowker 1989 $199.95. ISBN 0-8352-2679-4. Access to 240,000 titles published in 25,000 popular, scholarly, and professional series.

Author/title and subject indexes. Directory of publishers' addresses. Also available are earlier volumes covering 1876 through 1984.

British Books in Print (Whitaker's) 1993. 4 vols. Bowker 1993 $426.00. ISBN 0-85021-230-8. Titles currently available from British publishers, with full bibliographic and publishing information. Directory of publishers' addresses.

Canadian Books in Print. 2 vols. U. of Toronto Pr. 1992 $115.00–$135.00. ISBNs 0-8020-4661-4, 0-8020-4661-2. Titles currently available from Canadian publishers. Arranged by author, with title and publisher indexes.

Consumer Index to Product Evaluation and Information Sources. 1973–present. Annual. Pierian Pr. ISBN 0094-0534. Quarterly updated annually. Indexes more than 110 periodicals and services. Aimed at the general consumer and the library/education community.

Cumulative Book Index. 1898–present. Wilson. ISSN 0011-300X. 1898–1927 o.p. 1928–1956, 5-yr. vols. $200.00 ea. 1957–1968, 2-yr. vols. $265.00 ea. 1969–1985, 2-yr. vols. $180.00 ea. 1986–1992 sold on service basis. Monthly, with quarterly and annual cumulations sold on a service basis. The *CBI* is a combined author, title, and subject listing of books published in English in all countries during the time period covered by the issue or volume. Publishing information and price are given. A directory of publishers' addresses is included. Available on-line via Wilsonline or on CD-ROM via Wilsondisc.

Directory of Online Databases. Semi-annual. Elsevier 1991 $95.00. ISBN 0-685-17450-6. Provides up-to-date information on over 5,000 databases and distinctly named files within database families.

Essay and General Literature Index. 1900–present. Wilson. ISSN 0014-083X. Subscription to January to June issue and annual cumulation at $115.00. Subscriber receives five-year cumulations at no extra cost. Five-year cumulations are permanently in print from 1900–89 at $230.00 each. Author and subject index to essays in published collections, emphasizing the social sciences and humanities.

Forthcoming Books. Bowker bimonthly annual subscription $227.00, with *Subject Guide to Forthcoming Books* $199.00. Includes books to be published within the next five months and a cumulative index of books published since the latest annual edition of *Books in Print.* Author and title indexes. Available on-line.

Gale Directory of Publications and Broadcast Media. 1869–present. Gale. Originally *Ayer Directory of Publications.* Basic data about 1,800 newspapers.

Humanities Index. 1974–present. Wilson ISSN 0095-5981. Quarterly with annual cumulation sold on a service basis. Vols. 1–11 1974–85 $190.00 ea. Vols. 12–18 1985–92 sold on service basis. With *Social Sciences Index*, a successor to *Social Sciences and Humanities Index* (1964–74) and *International Index* (1900–64). Both are author and subject indexes to English-language periodicals of a scholarly nature. Includes a separate book-review index. Also available on Wilsonline and CD-ROM.

InfoTrac (Magazine Index). Information Access Grp. "InfoTrac" is really an umbrella term for IAG's CD-ROM products including the *National Newspaper Index*, but the term "InfoTrac" is used so widely to denote the *Magazine Index* it is listed here. InfoTrac's *Magazine Index* indexes more than 400 titles (compared to about 200 for the *Readers' Guide*.) Provides annotations. Available on-line and in printed form.

Magazines for Libraries, 7th ed. Ed. by Bill Katz and Linda Sternberg Katz. Bowker 7th ed. 1992 $139.95. ISBN 0-8352-3166-6. Some 6,500 magazines selected and annotated by more than 137 subject experts to represent the most useful titles for school, public, and academic libraries. Broad subject arrangement with detailed subject index.

National Newspaper Index. 1979–present. Information Access Grp. Part of the "InfoTrac" services. Subject indexing of the *New York Times*, *Wall Street Journal*, *Christian Science Monitor*, *Washington Post*, and *Los Angeles Times*. Available on-line and on CD-ROM.

New Serial Titles 1950–1970. Bowker 1975 $138.50. ISBN 0-8352-0820-6. Microfilm format. Supplements the *Union List of Serials* by listing serials and periodicals that began publication since 1949. Provides bibliographic data for 220,000 serials held by 800 libraries in the United States and Canada reporting to the Library of Congress.

Entries include issuing body, Dewey decimal number, and place and first date of publication. Cessations and changes are listed in separate sections.

New York Times Book Review 1896–1981. 141 vols. including 5-vol. index. Random $9,781.00. ISBN 0-6853-2624-1. Republication of the full text of the *N.Y. Times* reviews. The five-volume index is available from Ayer (1973 $600.00. ISBN 0-405-12494-5).

The New York Times Index. 1851–present. NY Times. Semimonthly with annual cumulations. Available on-line.

Nineteenth-Century Readers' Guide to Periodical Literature: 1890–1899. 2 vols. Wilson 1944 $180.00. ISBN 0-8242-0584-7. Author and subject index to 51 American and English periodicals; includes indexing for some periodicals up to the time they were included in a later Wilson index. Includes many references to book reviews. Superseded by *Reader's Guide to Periodical Literature*.

Periodical Title Abbreviations. Ed. by Leland G. Alkire, Jr. 2 vols. Gale 9th ed. $175.00 ea. Vol. 1 *By Abbreviation* 1989. ISBN 0-8108-4935-3. Vol. 2 *By Title* 1989. ISBN 0-8108-4936-1. Some 80,000 abbreviations and full titles.

Poole's Index to Periodical Literature. 16 vols. Peter Smith $252.00. Vol. 1 (1802–81) Vol. 2 (1882–87) Vol. 3 (1887–92) Vol. 4 (1892–96) Vol. 5 (1897–1902) Vol. 6 (1902–06). Subject index to nineteenth-century British and U.S. periodicals.

Popular Periodical Index. 1973–present. Popular Periodical Index biannual $30.00. ISBN 0092-9727. Subject index to popular periodicals such as *Discover, Rolling Stone, Yankee*.

Publishers Directory. Ed. by Linda S. Hubbard. 2 vols. Gale 14th ed. 1993 $235.00. ISBN 0-8103-8156-7. Supplement. Directory of U.S. and Canadian publishers of books, classroom materials, databases, software, and other print and nonprint publications. Subject and geographical indexes.

Publishers' Trade List Annual. 4 vols. Bowker 1993 $250.00. ISBN 0-8352-3375-8. *PTLA* is a collection of the catalogs and booklists of 1,800 U.S. publishers bound together alphabetically. Subject and series indexes to publishers.

Readers' Guide to Periodical Literature. 1900–present. Wilson $180.00 ea. Semimonthly in March, April, September, October, and December; monthly in January, February, May, June, July, August, and November, with quarterly and annual cumulations. Annual subscriptions. Vols. 1–52 available at $180.00 each. Author and subject index to articles in 240 U.S. general-interest periodicals. The *Abridged Readers' Guide* indexes 68 of the most popular periodicals covered by *Readers' Guide*. Also available as *Readers' Guide Abstracts* through Wilsonline (on-line) and Wilsondisc (CD-ROM).

Short Story Index. 1900–present. Wilson. ISSN 0360-9774. Identifies stories in periodicals and book collections. Available as an annual subscription; multi-year retrospective volumes available at from $50.00 to $130.00.

Social Sciences Citation Index. 1969–present. Institute for Scientific Information quarterly with annual cumulation. $4,300.00. ISSN 0091-3707. A massive computer-produced index to more than 25 international journals in the social and behavior sciences, it provides author and title word-pair indexing. Its special feature is citation indexing, which indexes current articles by the items cited in the bibliographies and thus makes it possible to follow a chain of research forward from key books and articles in a field. Also available on-line.

Social Sciences Index. 1974–present. Wilson. ISSN 0094-4920. 1974–85 $190.00 ea. 1985–92 sold on service basis. Quarterly with annual cumulations. With *Humanities Index*, a successor to *Social Sciences and Humanities Index* (1964–74) and *International Index* (1900–64). Both are author and subject indexes to more than 342 English-language periodicals of a scholarly nature. Includes a separate book-review index. Also available on Wilsonline and CD-ROM.

The Standard Periodical Directory. Ed. by Patricia Hagood. Oxbridge. Comm. 15th ed. 1992 $445.00. ISBN 0-917460-37-5. Listing of more than 66,000 U.S. and Canadian periodicals. Broad subject arrangement, with title and subject indexes. Gives publisher and address, editorial content and scope, first year of publication, and subscription rate.

Ulrich's International Periodicals Directory. 5 vols. Bowker 1993 $395.00. ISBN 0-8352-3368-5. Lists more than 140,000 periodicals from 200 countries. Arrangement is by broad subject, with a title index. Entries include full publishing and subscription information, ISBN, indication of titles that carry advertising and book or movie reviews, and selected periodical indexes that index the title. Now includes irregular serials and annuals and newspapers.

Union List of Serials in Libraries of the United States and Canada. 5 vols. Wilson 3rd ed. 1965 $175.00. Lists holdings of 156,499 serial titles in 956 libraries in the United States and Canada. Continued by *New Serial Titles.*

U.S. Library of Congress, Catalog Division. *Newspapers in Microfilm: United States, 1948–1972.* Supplements 1973–77 and 1978–present. Lib. Congress. The basic volume lists 34,289 newspapers published from colonial times to the present, with holdings in major libraries.

Whitaker's Books in Print 1993 (British). See *British Books in Print* in this section.

PROVERBS AND MAXIMS

Many books of proverbs are available in print; many others that are no longer in print are held in library collections. A large number of these works are devoted to the proverbs of a particular people or civilization or are in a particular language. Only a representative few of the more general English-language collections are listed below.

The Concise Oxford Dictionary of Proverbs. Ed. by J. A. Simpson. OUP 1992 $23.00. ISBN 0-19-866177-0. Based on the *Oxford Dictionary of English Proverbs*, this work includes only proverbs in common use in Great Britain today.

Fergusson, Rosalind, comp. *The Facts on File Dictionary of Proverbs.* Facts on File 1983 $27.95. ISBN 0-87196-298-5. Topical arrangement of 7,000 proverbs from all periods and nationals. Comprehensive keyword index.

Glazer, Mark. *A Dictionary of Mexican American Proverbs*, Greenwood 1987 $49.95. ISBN 0-313-25385-4. A multi-faceted and systematic dictionary of Mexican American proverbs. Based on currently utilized proverbs and previously published materials.

Hazlitt, William C. *English Proverbs & Proverbial Phrases.* Gordon Pr. 1972 $59.95. ISBN 0-3490-0117-X. Alphabetically arranged and annotated, this work contains an in-depth collection of proverbs and proverbial phrases.

Houghton, Patricia, ed. *The Cassell Book of Proverbs.* Sterling $14.95. ISBN 0-304-34165-7. A standard, comprehensive collection of proverbs.

Mieder, Wolfgang. *Dictionary of American Proverbs.* OUP $49.95. ISBN 0-19-505399-0. Alphabetical listing of U.S. and Canadian proverbs cross-referenced for related proverbs.

———. *The Prentice Hall Encyclopedia of World Proverbs: A Treasury of Wit and Wisdom.* S&S Trade 1986 $34.95. ISBN 0-13-695586-X. An entertaining encyclopedia collection of proverbs; contains the largest collection of proverbs available in one volume.

The Oxford Book of Aphorisms. Ed. by John Gross. OUP 1987 $29.95. ISBN 0-19-214111-2. Entries are divided into 58 topical sections, such as nature, good and evil, and knowledge and ignorance. Author index, but no keyword index.

Stevenson, Burton. *The Macmillan Book of Proverbs, Maxims and Famous Sayings.* Macmillan 1987 $75.00. ISBN 0-02-614500-6

Whiting, Bartlett J. *Early American Proverbs and Proverbial Sayings.* HUP 1977 $39.95. ISBN 0-674-21981-3. Collection of proverbs used by writers in North America from the beginnings of the seventeenth century to about 1820.

———. *Modern Proverbs and Proverbial Sayings.* HUP 1989 $39.95. ISBN 0-674-58053-2. A collection of twentieth-century proverbs and proverbial phrases. Entries are alphabetized by key words. Includes cross-references.

Wilson, Frank P. *The Oxford Dictionary of English Proverbs.* OUP 3rd ed. 1970 $49.95. ISBN 0-19-869118-1

QUOTATIONS

Books of quotations are to be judged by their content and indexes. The four kinds of indexes are author, straight quotation, concordance, and topical. The author index is common to all. The straight quotation index gives the first word of the quotation just as it occurs in the text. A concordance indexes the principal words in the quotation. For instance, "All that glitters is not gold," in a straight quotation index, will be found under "All"; in a concordance index, it will be found under "gold" and "glitter." A topical index lists under general headings all quotations that bear on that particular subject. The quotation "All that glitters is not gold" might be found under the topic "Appearance." The purpose of a topical index is to suggest quotations on various topics. The collections listed below are among the larger and better known, although there are many others. Most overlap to some degree; none is complete, and the one quote you need will be in the last place you look.

Adler, Mortimer J., and Charles Van Doren. *The Great Treasury of Western Thought: A Compendium of Important Statements on Man and His Institutions by the Great Thinkers in Western History*. Bowker 1977 $49.50. ISBN 0-8352-0833-8. Contains more than 8,000 quotations from Homer to Freud. Author and keyword indexes.

Allusions—Cultural, Literary, Biblical, and Historical: A Thematic Dictionary. Ed. by Laurence Urdang. Gale 2nd ed. $85.00. ISBN 0-8103-1828-8. Identifies more than 7,000 literary, biblical, and cultural allusions and metaphors. Entries are arranged alphabetically under 628 thematic headings. More than 1,000 biblical, literary, folklore, and other sources of allusions were consulted, with most of them being listed in the dictionary's extensive bibliography. Index."

Andrews, Robert. *The Concise Columbia Dictionary of Quotations*. Col. U. Pr. 1990 $19.95. ISBN 0-231-06990-1. A compilation of quotations on a broad range of subjects. Brief descriptions are given of people not well known. Entries arranged alphabetical by subject.

Augarde, A. J. *The Oxford Dictionary of Modern Quotations*. OUP 1991 $29.95. ISBN 0-19-866141-X. Contains over 5,000 quotations, including common quotes from books, magazines, and newspapers by various people from British and American culture.

Bartlett, John. *Bartlett's Familiar Quotations: Fifteenth & 125th Anniversary Edition*. Little 1992 $40.00. ISBN 0-316-08277-5. John Bartlett (1820–1905), a bookseller in Cambridge, Massachusetts, and partner of Little, Brown, compiled two famous books of reference: *A Complete Concordance to Shakespeare* (1894) and *Familiar Quotations* (1855). Bartlett lived to be 85 and brought out nine editions of his earlier book, enlarging it from 295 pages to 1,158. The present edition has 936 pages of quotations. Some quotations have been dropped, and sayings from non-Western cultures have been added as well as quotations from persons previously overlooked: Chekhov, Brandeis, Flaubert, Freud, Jung, and others. The subject-matter index, prepared with the aid of a computer, now runs to almost 600 pages.

Cohen, J. M., *The Penguin Dictionary of Modern Quotations*. Viking Penguin rev. ed. 1971 $10.95. ISBN 0-14-051038-9. Arranged by author, with keyword index.

The Concise Oxford Dictionary of Quotations. OUP rev ed. 1981 $9.95. ISBN 0-19-281324-2

Evans, Bergen. *Dictionary of Quotations*. Dell 1968 o.p. [A] reference book which keeps the best from the past while utilizing choice items from the present. Thousands of familiar quotations, with the addition of many other new, contemporary, bright sayings chosen for wit as well as wisdom, and about 2,000 illuminating and amusing comments (set in italics) by the humorist and word specialist Bergen Evans. His remarks make this book a gem and a delight for the browser. A very broad and thorough subject index [locates] and cross-indexes each quotation under each of its key words and under [general subjects].

Magill, Frank N., ed. *Magill's Quotations in Context: Second Series*. 2 vols. Salem Pr. 1969 $75.00. ISBN 0-89356-136-3. Familiar sayings, important passages from esteemed works, and proverbs are given in a few paragraphs of their original context with commentary. The first series has 2,020 entries, the second, 1,500.

Mencken, H. L., ed. *A New Dictionary of Quotations on Historical Principles from Ancient and Modern Sources.* Knopf 1942 $74.50 ISBN 0-394-40079-8. Arranged by subject in a single alphabet, this collection includes some quotations from the 1930s and a few from the 1940s, but they are mainly from the eighteenth and early nineteenth centuries. Of interest as a browsing volume, reflecting the compiler's vigorous individuality. No index.

Mottoes. Ed. by Laurence Urdang and others. Gale 1986 $85.00. ISBN 0-8103-2076-2. Some 9,000 mottoes of individuals, families, and institutions. Arranged by theme, with indexes by motto and person or organization.

The New York Public Library Book of 20th Century American Quotations. Warner Bks. 1992 $24.95. ISBN 0-446-51639-2. Valuable collection of quotations covering over 40 different topics.

The Oxford Dictionary of Quotations. OUP 3rd ed. 1979 $49.95. ISBN 0-19-211560-X. Arranged alphabetically by author and indexed by keyword. Exact reference to source is given. More than 7,000 index entries.

Palmer, Alan, comp. *Quotations in History: A Dictionary of Historical Quotations—c.800 A.D. to the Present.* B & N Imports. 1976 o.p.

Pater, Alan F., and Jason R. Pater, eds. *What They Said in 1991: The Yearbook of Spoken Opinion.* Monitor annual 1992 $41.00. ISBN 0-917734-24-6. Quotations are documented with date, place, and circumstance information.

Picturesque Expressions: A Thematic Dictionary. Ed. by Walter W. Hunsinger and Laurence Urdang. Gale 2nd ed. $84.00. ISBN 0-8103-1606-4. More than 7,000 picturesque expressions like "hands down" are topically arranged, with explanation, date of origin, and illustrative quotations.

Seldes, George. *The Great Quotations.* Citadel Pr. 1983 $12.95. ISBN 0-8065-0817-5

Slogans. Ed. by Laurence Urdang and Celia Dame Robbins. Gale 1984 $82.00. ISBN 0-8103-1549-1. Some 6,000 slogans from a variety of fields, including advertising and politics, topically arranged and giving origin and use. Index.

Stevenson, Burton Egbert. *Home Book of Quotations: Classical and Modern.* 1967. Dodd 10th ed. 1984 $34.95. ISBN 0-396-083-4. Includes more than 73,000 quotations from 4,700 authors. The concordance index has more than 100,000 entries. Quotations are grouped under such subjects as love, government, religion, and law, making the index indispensable. The work is particularly strong in U.S. political quotations, campaign slogans, new coinages, and catchlines from popular songs.

Tripp, Rhoda Thomas, ed. *The International Thesaurus of Quotations.* HarpC 1987 $14.95. ISBN 0-06-59382-7. Topical arrangement. Author and keyword indexes.

Tuttle Dictionary of Quotations for Speeches. C. E. Tuttle 1992 $9.95. ISBN 0-8048-1779-0

WRITING GUIDES

For dictionaries, thesauri, and other "word" books, see earlier sections of this chapter. Many books currently in print offer guidance in writing for publication.

Barzun, Jacques. *Simple and Direct: A Rhetoric for Writers.* HarpC rev. ed. 1985 $7.95. ISBN 0-06-091122-0

Chicago Guide to Preparing Electronic Manuscripts. U. Ch. Pr. 1986 ISBN 0-226-10392-7. Detailed reference guide providing information on all aspects of electronic publishing. Useful to both writers and publishers.

The Chicago Manual of Style. U. Ch. Pr. rev. ed. 1982 $37.50. ISBN 0-226-10390-0. The standard style manual at many publishing houses and universities. Includes sections on new technology in the publishing and editing process, copyright law, manuscript preparation and script editing, and many examples of documentation (footnotes, bibliography, notes, etc.).

Conrad, Barnaby. *The Complete Guide to Writing Fiction.* Writers Digest 1990 $18.95. ISBN 0-89879-395-5. Compiled in collaboration with the Santa Barbara Writers Conference.

Coyle, William. *The Macmillan Guide to Writing Research Papers.* Macmillan 1990 ISBN 0-02-325291-X. Aimed at college students.

Crews, Frederick B. *The Random House Handbook.* Random 5th ed. 1988 $15.80. ISBN 0-07-505429-1. Covers grammar, usage, punctuation, documentation, and the process of composition.

Fishman, Stephen. *Copyright Handbook: How To Protect and Use Written Works.* Nolo Pr. 1991 $24.95. ISBN 0-87337-130-5. A good basic source on copyright protection for writers, publishers, researchers, and the general public.

Flesch, Rudolf, and A. H. Lass. *A New Guide to Better Writing.* Warner Bks. 1990 $3.95. ISBN 0-446-31504-4

French, Christopher W. *The Associated Press Stylebook and Libel Manual.* Addison-Wesley 1992 $11.49. ISBN 0-201-56760-1. The "journalist's bible"; a helpful work stating rules of grammar, style, spelling, and usage for 156,000 terms. Includes a libel manual. Organized in an A–Z listing.

Gibaldi, Joseph, and Walter S. Achtert. *MLA Handbook for Writers of Research Papers.* Modern Lang. 3rd ed. 1988 $9.95. ISBN 0-87352-379. The recommended style for the preparation of scholarly manuscripts and research papers. Intended as a supporting text in writing courses or as a reference book to be used alone.

Harbrace College Handbook. Ed. by John C. Hodges and others. HarBraceJ 1990 $15.00. ISBN 0-15-531862-4. Standard college handbook for composition.

Heller, James, and Sarah Wiant. *Copyright Handbook.* Rothman 1984 $15.00. ISBN 0-8377-0121-X. A useful reference manual, offering guidance with respect to the application of copyright law to new technologies. Published by the American Association of Law Libraries.

Johnston, Donald. *Copyright Handbook.* Bowker 2d ed. 1982 $39.95. ISBN 0-8352-1988-5. A guide to the Copyright Law of 1976 and its revisions.

Leggett, Glenn, and others. *Prentice-Hall Handbook for Writers.* P-H 11th ed. 1990 ISBN 0-13-716093-3

Literary Market Place. 1994. Bowker 1993 $158.00. ISBN 0-8352-3346-4. Editorial addresses, phone numbers, key personnel, publications specialities, number of titles published annually, imprints, and other pertinent information; for publishers, librarians, etc.

Longyear, Marie. *The McGraw-Hill Style Manual: Concise Guide for Writers and Editors.* McGraw 1983 $36.50. ISBN 0-07-038676-5. Designed for anyone who desires to prepare manuscript for publication. Examines style standards.

Luey, Beth. *Handbook for Academic Authors.* Cambridge U. Pr. rev. ed. 1990 $12.95. ISBN 0-521-39646-8. A complete guide for academic authors who desire to be published. Includes a bibliography.

Sears, Donald A. *Harbrace Guide to the Library and the Research Paper.* HarBraceJ 4th ed. 1984 $12.00. ISBN 0-15-5350-65-X. Designed to acquaint individuals with the resources available in libraries; leads step-by-step through the process of preparing a research paper.

Skillin, Marjorie E., and Robert M. Gay. *Words into Type.* P-H 3rd ed. 1986 $39.95. ISBN 0-13-964262-5. One of the references most favored by book editors.

Strunk, William, Jr., and E. B. White. *Elements of Style: With Index.* 1918. Macmillan 3rd ed. 1979 ISBN 0-02-418200-1. Concise guide for those who wish to use English style with simplicity and grace. "Distinguished by brevity, clarity, and prickly good sense, it is, unlike most such manuals, a book as well as a tool" (*New Yorker*).

Turabian, Kate L. *A Manual for Writers of Term Papers, Theses, and Dissertations.* U. Ch. Pr. 6th ed. 1980 $8.95. ISBN 0-685-50252-X. Widely used by college students.

Writer's Market. Writers Digest 1992 $26.95. ISBN 0-89879-579-6

CHAPTER 4

Reference Books: Literature

Susan M. Allen

I think of the world's literature as a kind of forest, I mean it's tangled and it
entangles us but it's growing.
—JORGE LUIS BORGES, *Conversations with Jorge Luis Borges*

In recent years scholarship in literature has been at the same time exciting and
controversial. Wars have been waged over the standard literary canon, and the
consequence has been a wide and growing acceptance of the teaching of
multiculturalism in place of what heretofore have been called the classics of
Western civilization.

Since reference materials generally follow trends in scholarship, it is not
surprising that special reference tools have been developed that provide
bibliographic control and access to these new areas of multicultural interest, for
example, the African American, Native American, Hispanic American, and
Asian American literatures. Unfortunately, some of the reference tools developed in the last decade to support this new scholarship have come and gone
rapidly, disappearing from print just as quickly as they have appeared. Yet, such
comprehensive, scholarly reference books as the Oxford and Cambridge
histories of British and American literature, which have been used for decades,
are only now slowly going out of print, to be replaced eventually, one would
assume, with ones rewritten from the perspective of the late twentieth century.

In spite of the seeming comprehensive list of reference books provided, one
must remember that some writers are no longer in print and that there are no
biographies of them or bibliographies of their work. However, as new studies in
literature are undertaken and new authors are discovered and rediscovered,
new reference materials and tools will no doubt be developed or old ones
will be rewritten to provide greater access for scholars and other interested
persons. For specialized reference books on specific topics, see the appropriate
chapters in this volume. It should also be noted that, although the focus of this
volume is on British and American literature, this chapter also contains some
general reference works on world literature. However, for works related to
specific world literatures—French, German, Russian, and so on—please refer
to Volume 2.

BIBLIOGRAPHIES

General

Abstracts of English Studies. U. of Alberta 1958–present. ISSN 0001-3560. Abstracts
articles from 500 journals on U.S., English, Commonwealth, and related literatures.
Longer annotations than MLA entries, but coverage is not as comprehensive.

Allibone, Samuel Austin. *A Critical Dictionary of English Literature and British and American Authors, Living and Deceased: From the Earliest Accounts to the Latter Half of the Nineteenth Century, Containing over 46,000 Articles (Authors) with 40 Indexes of Subjects.* 3 vols. Gordon Pr. 1972 repr. of 1872 ed. $300.00. ISBN 0-87968-965-X. A valuable standard work.

Annual Bibliography of English Language and Literature. 1921–present. Modern Humanities Res. ISSN 0066-3786. Includes a section on U.S. literature but is heavily weighted toward English scholarship.

Annals of English Literature, 1475–1950: The Principal Publications of Each Year Together with an Alphabetical Index of Authors and Their Works. Ed. by R. W. Chapman and others. OUP 1961 o.p. Chronological tables of each year's publication. Useful and reliable.

Besterman, Theodore. *World Bibliography of Bibliographies.* 5 vols. Rowman 4th ed. 1963 $383.00. ISBN 0-87471-294-7

The Bibliographic Index: A Cumulative Bibliography of Bibliographies. Wilson 1937–present. ISSN 0006-1255 1987–92. Vols. 1–4 1937–55 $140.00 ea. ISBN 0-685-22234-9. Vols. 5–8 1956–68 $230.00. ISBN 0-685-22233-0. Vols. 9–25 1969–85 $180.00 ea. Vols. 26–32 1986–92 sold on service basis. A subject list of English and foreign-language bibliographies, which contain 40 or more bibliographic citations. Includes bibliographies published separately or as parts of books and pamphlets. In addition, the editors search 1,900 periodicals for material. Published in April and August, with a bound cumulative edition each December.

Biggs, Frederick M., and others, eds. *Sources of Anglo-Saxon Literary Culture: A Trial Version.* MRTS 1990 $20.00. ISBN 0-86698-084-9

Howard-Hill, Trevor H. *Bibliography of British Literary Bibliographies.* OUP 2nd ed. 1987 $160.00. ISBN 0-19-818184-1. "Revision of the *Bibliography of British Literary Bibliographies* and its resetting by computer has afforded an opportunity to bring its conventions into line with those adopted in later volumes of the Index" (Preface). More than 1,800 entries have been added; coverage is 1890–1969. Includes comprehensive index.

———. *British Literary Bibliography, 1970–79: A Bibliography.* OUP 1992 $185.00. ISBN 0-19-818183-3

Modern Language Association (MLA) International Bibliography of Books and Articles on the Modern Languages and Literatures. 1921–present. Modern Lang. 1991 ed. $500.00. ISBN 0-87352-640-6. Most comprehensive annual listing of books and articles on modern languages and literature in the United States and Great Britain. Includes sections on U.S., English, and other national literatures, as well as Medieval, neo-Latin, and Celtic literatures and folklore, and linguistics. Divided first by century, then by authors writing in that century. Also available on-line with DIALOG, Wilsonline; also available on CD-ROM from

New Cambridge Bibliography of English Literature. 5 vols. Cambridge U. Pr. 1972. Vol. 1 $130.00. ISBN 0-521-04499-5. Vol. 2 $130.00. ISBN 0-521-04500-2. Vol. 3 o.p. Vol. 4 $160.00. ISBN 0-521-08535-7. Vol. 5 $89.95 ISBN 0-521-04503-7. Covers British authors from 600 A.D. to 1950.

Pownall, David E., comp. *Articles on Twentieth Century Literature: An Annotated Bibliography, 1954–1970.* 7 vols. Kraus $630.00. ISBN 0-527-72150-6. Based on the annotated bibliographies appearing in the journal *Twentieth Century Literature.* Includes scholarly and critical articles.

Schwartz, Narda L., ed. *Articles on Women Writers, 1976–1984: A Bibliography,* Vol. 2 ABC-CLIO 1986 $65.00. ISBN 0-87436-438-8. English-language articles published between 1974 and 1984 on about 1,000 mostly American and British women authors; Volume 1 covers 1960–1975 but is out of print.

The Year's Work in English Studies. Humanities Pr. 1921–present. Humanties ISSN 0084-4144. Evaluative, narrative bibliography of scholarly writing (in English) of Great Britain, America, Africa, Australia, Canada, the Caribbean, and India.

British Literature

Boos, Florence Saunders. *Bibliography of Women and Literature*. Holmes & Meier 1989 $22.00. ISBN 0-8419-0693-9 (set; 2 vols.) Lists books, articles, and dissertations on literature in English. Includes author indexes.

Tucker, Lena L. *Bibliography of Fifteenth Century Literature, with Special Reference to the History of English Culture*. Gordon Pr. 1974 $49.95. ISBN 0-87968-738-X

Watson, George, ed. *Cambridge New Bibliography of English Literature*. 4 vols. Cambridge U. Pr. 1987 $470.00. ISBN 0-521-34378-X. Based on the *CBEL* published in 1940 and the supplement published in 1957. Expanded and brought up to date, it retains the systematic arrangement of the earlier work, but does omit some materials. Focuses on literature of the British Isles, both primary and secondary works. Owners of *CBEL* were urged to retain their volumes while adding *CNBEL*.

———, ed. *The Cambridge Shorter Bibliography of English Literature*. Cambridge U. Pr. 1981 $130.00. ISBN 0-521-22600-7. Intended for smaller libraries, for which the cost of the CNBEL is prohibitive. A greatly abridged edition of the *CNBEL*, offering a select list of the best editions by, and secondary works about, the major British writers.

American Literature

American Literary Scholarship: An Annual. Ed. by James L. Woodress and others. 1963–present. Duke. ISSN 0065–9142. Authoritative survey of essays that assess the state of literary research each year. A counterpart to *The Year's Work in English Studies*.

Bibliography of American Literature. 9 vols. Comp. by Jacob Blanck. Yale U. Pr. 1955–91. Vols. 1–7 o.p. Vol. 8 1989 $80.00. ISBN 0-300-03839-9. Vol. 9 1991 $80.00. ISBN 0-300-05141-7. A selective bibliography that includes approximately 300 U.S. literary figures from the beginnings of the federal period through 1930.

Cheung, King-Kok, and Stan Yogi, eds. *Asian American Literature: An Annotated Bibliography*. Modern Lang. 1988 $37.00. ISBN 0-87352-960-X. "Reference guide to literature written by Asian American writers in the United States and Canada" (Preface).

Eger, Ernestina N. *Bibliography of Criticism of Contemporary Chicano Literature*. UC Chicano Lib. 1982 $16.50. ISBN 0-685-05653-8. More than 2,000 articles, books, reviews, and dissertations, most of which have been published after 1960.

Gohdes, Clarence, and Stanford E. Marovitz, eds. *Bibliographical Guide to the Study of the Literature of the U.S.A.* Duke 5th rev. ed. 1984 $35.00. ISBN 0-8223-0592-5. More than 400 new items have been added to the latest revision.

Leary, Lewis, and John Auchard, comps. *Articles in American Literature, 1968–1975*. Duke 1979 o.p. A supplement to Leary's earlier out-of-print works, which covered the periods 1900–1950 and 1950–1967. An important reference tool.

Mainiero, Lina, and Langdon L. Faust, eds. *American Women Writers: A Critical Reference Guide from Colonial Times to the Present*. 4 vols. Continuum 1982 $600.00. ISBN 0-8044-3150-7. Contains bio-bibliographic essays on well-known and neglected U.S. women authors from such fields as anthropology, history, and religion; each entry includes data on birth, ancestry, marriage, a summary of the writer's life, and a description and evaluation of major works.

World Literature

There are many bibliographic tools for researching the literature of nations other than Great Britain or the United States. For information on specific national literatures, see Volume 2. A comprehensive listing can be found in Eugene P. Sheehy's *Guide to Reference Books* and *Supplement*, both published by the American Library Association.

Hornstein, Lillian H., and others. *The Reader's Companion to World Literature*. NAL-Dutton 1956 $5.95. ISBN 0-451-62441-6

Magill, Frank N., ed. *Masterpieces of World Literature*. HarpC 1989 $40.00. ISBN 0-06-016144-2. Works listed by title, then summarized.

Thompson, George A., Jr. *Key Sources in Comparative and World Literature: An Annotated Guide to Reference Materials*. Continuum 1983 $40.00. ISBN 0-8044-3281-3. Scholarly coverage of all literatures; includes annotations.

Fiction

Coan, Otis W., and Richard G. Lillard. *America in Fiction: An Annotated List of Novels That Interpret Aspects of Life in the United States, Canada, and Mexico*. Pacific Bks. 6th ed. o.p. Provides lists of novels, a volume of short stories, and collections of folklore organized under such headings as "Pioneering" and "Industrial America." Designed to help readers interested in the civilizations of Canada, the United States, and Mexico.

Davis, Barbara K. *Read All Your Life: A Subject Guide to Fiction*. McFarland & Co. 1989 $24.95. ISBN 0-89950-370-5

Dickinson, A. T., Jr. *American Historical Fiction*. Scarecrow 3rd ed. 1971 o.p. Classifies more than 3,000 novels, all related to American history, into chronological periods from Colonial times to the 1970s.

Dyson, A. E., ed. *The English Novel: Select Bibliographical Guides*. OUP 1974 o.p. Contains 20 helpful guides to major English novelists, with a discussion of their texts and critical commentaries.

Fiction 1876–1983: A Bibliography of United States Editions. 2 vols. Bowker 1983 $99.50. ISBN 0-8352-1726-4. About 170,000 titles listed; from Bowker's *Books in Print* and *American Book Publishing Record*.

Grimes, Janet, and Diva Daims. *Novels in English by Women, 1891–1920: A Preliminary Checklist*. Ed. by Doris Robinson. Garland 1981 $29.00. ISBN 0-8240-9522-7. Lists 15,000 novels by 5,000 writers, most of which are annotated.

Husband, Janet, and Jonathan K. Husband. *Sequels: An Annotated Guide to Novels in Series*. ALA 2nd ed. 1990 $45.00. ISBN 0-8389-0533-1. Now includes detective fiction and titles published from 1982–1989.

McCaffery, Lawrence F., ed. *Postmodern Fiction: A Bio-bibliographical Guide*. Greenwood 1986 $79.95. ISBN 0-313-24170-8. Examines texts from the early 1960s. "Biographical and bibliographical information, as well as critical assessments, about many of the important figures in the field of postmodern literature." (Introduction.)

McGarry, Daniel D., and Sarah H. White. *World Historical Fiction Guide: Annotated, Chronological, Geographical and Topical List of Selected Historical Novels (Historical Fiction Guide)*. o.p. Works are arranged by geography and chronology. Contains author-title index. All works are in English, although some are translations into English.

Nagel, James, and Gwen L. Nagel, eds. *Facts on File Bibliography of American Fiction: 1866–1918*. Facts on File 1992 $95.00. ISBN 0-8160-2116-3. Consists of entries with brief headnotes, which place writers in the context of American literary history; also includes a vade mecum of 100 basic reference tools for U.S. literature.

Nield, J. A. *Guide to the Best Historical Novels and Tales*. Gordon Pr. 1972 $59.95. ISBN 0-8490-0270-2. More than 2,000 titles listed chronologically and annotated; some in translation.

Radcliffe, Elsa J. *Gothic Novels of the Twentieth Century: An Annotated Bibliography*. Scarecrow 1979 $25.00. ISBN 0-8108-1190-1. Mostly English and American novelists; almost 2,000 titles listed by author.

Rosenberg, Betty, and Diana T. Herald. *Genreflecting: A Guide to Reading Interests in Genre Fiction*. Libs. Unl. 3rd ed. 1991 $35.00. ISBN 0-87287-930-5. Identifies genres of authors; invaluable for bookstore clerks and librarians. Also serves as a textbook for library school students.

Drama

Arata, Esther S. *More Black American Playwrights: A Bibliography.* Scarecrow 1978 $30.00. ISBN 0-8108-1158-8. Supplement to *Black American Playwrights.*

Arata, Esther S., and Nicholas J. Rotoli. *Black American Playwrights, 1800 to the Present: A Bibliography.* Scarecrow 1976 o.p. Listed by playwright's name; includes published and unpublished works.

Baker, Blanch M. *Dramatic Bibliography.* Ayer 1968 repr. of 1933 ed. $22.00. ISBN 0-405-08229-0. Lists almost 6,000 titles published between 1885 and 1948, almost all in English.

———. *Theatre and Allied Arts.* Ayer repr. of 1953 ed. $43.50. ISBN 0-405-08230-4. Based on *Dramatic Bibliography* but focuses more specifically on theater and theater arts.

Critical Survey of Drama: English Language. Ed. by Frank N. Magill. 6 vols. Salem Pr. 1986 $350.00. ISBN 0-89356-382-X

Boyer, Robert D., comp. *Realism in European Theater and Drama, 1870–1920: A Bibliography.* Greenwood 1979 $45.00. ISBN 0-313-20607-4. Covers material by and about 62 European dramatists.

Burton, Ernest J. *The British Theatre: Its Repertory and Practice, 1100–1900 A.D.* Greenwood 1977 repr. of 1960 ed. $45.00. ISBN 0-8371-9739-2. Emphasizes the problems in presenting period plays today. Includes an extensive bibliography.

Drury, Francis K. W. *Drury's Guide to Best Plays.* Scarecrow 4th ed. 1987 $39.50. ISBN 0-8108-1980-5. Information on 1,500 plays in English from 400 B.C. to 1985.

Fletcher, Steve, and Norman Jopling, eds. *The Book of a Thousand Plays.* Facts on File 1989 $24.95. ISBN 0-8160-2122-8. A guide to the most popular plays in Britain and the United States during this century.

Harris, Richard H. *Modern Drama in America and England, 1950–1970: A Guide to Information Sources.* Gale 1982 o.p. Covers the United States, England, and other world literatures in English.

Litto, Fredric M. *American Dissertations on the Drama and the Theatre: A Bibliography.* Bks. Demand repr. of 1969 ed. $132.30. ISBN 0-8357-5362-X

Palmer, Helen H. *European Drama Criticism, 1900–1975.* Shoe String 2nd ed. 1977 o.p. Cumulative from earlier editions and adds new material through 1975; stresses English-language material.

Steadman, Susan M. *Dramatic Re-Visions: An Annotated Bibliography of Feminism and Theatre, 1972–1988.* ALA 1991 $50.00. ISBN 0-8389-0577-3. A useful bibliography that draws together a wide range of material from many sources.

Poetry

Congdon, Kirby. *Contemporary Poets in American Anthologies, 1960–1977.* Scarecrow 1978 $20.00. ISBN 0-8108-1168-5. Covers poets published in almost 400 anthologies, 1960–1977.

Literary Recordings: A Checklist of the Archive of Recorded Poetry and Literature in the Library of Congress. Gordon Pr. 1986 $79.95. ISBN 0-8490-3540-6. Lists recordings for almost 1,000 poets.

Reardon, Joan. *Poetry by American Women, 1975–1989: A Bibliography.* Scarecrow 1990. ISBN 0-8108-2366-7. Updates *Poetry by American Women, 1900–1975.*

Reardon, Joan, and Kristine A. Thorsen. *Poetry by American Women, 1900–1975: A Bibliography.* Scarecrow 1979 $37.50. ISBN 0-8108-1173-1. Includes 9,500 volumes of poetry. written by more than 5,500 women.

Sefami, Jacobo, comp. *Contemporary Spanish American Poets: A Bibliography of Primary and Secondary Sources.* Greenwood 1992 $45.00. ISBN 0-313-27880-6

INDEXES

General

Comprehensive Index to English-Language Little Magazines, 1890–1970: Series One. Ed. by Marion Sader. 8 vols. Kraus 1976 $695.00. ISBN 0-527-00370-0. Author and title index to 100 magazines; both text and illustrations are indexed. Includes poetry, drama, and fiction.

Drama

Chicorel, Marietta, ed. *Chicorel Theater Index to Plays in Anthologies and Collections: 1970–1976.* Am Lib. Pub. Co. 1976 $125.00. ISBN 0-934598-68-1

Connor, Billie M., and Helene Machedlover. *Ottemiller's Index to Plays in Collections: An Author and Title Index to Plays Appearing in Collections Published Between 1900 and 1985.* Scarecrow 7th ed. 1988 $42.50. ISBN 0-8108-208-1. The first edition (1943) covered 1900–1942; this edition extends that edition by 10 years. Indexes plays by 2,555 different authors; 1,350 collections are analyzed. Limited to books published in England and the United States. Only complete texts are indexed. Foreign plays translated into English are entered under English titles with cross-references.

Firkins, Ina. *Index of Plays Eighteen Hundred to Nineteen Twenty-Six.* AMS Pr. repr. of 1927 ed. $24.50. ISBN 0-404-02386-X. Indexes more than 7,500 plays by more than 2,000 playwrights.

Index to Full-Length Plays, 1895–1925. Faxon 1956 $11.00. ISBN 0-87305-085-1. Title, author, and subject indexes. Subject approach makes this very useful. The volumes *1926–1944* and *1944–1964* are out of print.

Index to One-Act Plays, 1900–1924. Comp. by Hannah Logasa and Winifred VerNooy. Faxon 1924 o.p. *Supplement, 1924–31.* 1932 $11.00. ISBN 0-87305-046-0. *Second Supplement, 1932–40.* 1941 o.p. *Third Supplement, 1941–48.* 1950 o.p. *Fourth Supplement, 1948–57.* 1958 o.p. *Fifth Supplement, 1958–64.* 1966 o.p. The index covers thousands of one-act plays. Indexed by title, author, and subject; states the number of characters in each play.

Keller, Dean H. *Index to Plays in Periodicals, 1977–1987.* Scarecrow 1990 $42.50. ISBN 0-8108-2288-1. Supplements earlier editions now out of print; arranged by playwright, with title index.

Patterson, Charlotte A. *Plays in Periodicals: An Index to English Language Scripts in Twentieth-Century Journals.* G. K. Hall 1972 o.p. More than 4,000 plays printed in 97 English-language journals published from 1900 through 1968.

Play Index. 7 vols. Wilson 1953–88. Vol. 1 *1949–52.* 1953 $17.00. ISBN 0-686-66657-7. Vol. 2 *1953–60.* 1963 $22.00. ISBN 0-686-66658-5. Vol. 3 *1961–67.* 1968 $25.00. ISBN 0-686-66659-3. Vol. 4 *1968–72.* 1973 $30.00. ISBN 0-686-66660-7. Vol. 5 *1973–77.* 1978 $38.00. ISBN 0-686-66661-5. Vol. 6 *1978–82.* 1983 $45.00. ISBN 0-685-05422-5. Vol. 7 *1983–1987.* 1988 $55.00. ISBN 0-685-45835-0. Indexed by author, title, and subject, with cast analysis and publisher.

Fiction

Fiction Catalog. Wilson 12th ed. 1991 $98.00. ISBN 0-8242-0804-8. Standard index that annotates the best fiction in English. Lists more than 5,000 works that have been found most useful by experienced librarians in U.S. and Canadian libraries.

Gerhardstein, Virginia B. *Dickinson's English Historical Fiction.* Scarecrow 5th ed. 1986 $35.00. ISBN 0-8108-1867-1. "A total of 3,048 novels casting light on some aspect of American history are classified into natural chronological periods from Colonial days to the 1970's." (Preface)

Hartman, Donald K. *Themes and Settings in Fiction: A Bibliography of Bibliographies.* Greenwood 1988 $45.00. ISBN 0-313-25866-X. Lists bibliographies, bibliographic essays, review articles, and literary surveys of novels and short stories in English from 1900 to 1985.

Husband, Janet. *Sequels: An Annotated Guide to Novels in Series.* ALA 2nd ed. 1990 $50.00. ISBN 0-8389-0533-1. Covers 1982–89 and detective fiction. Continuation of a 1982 publication by the same author.

McGarry, Daniel D., and Sarah H. White. *World Historical Fiction Guide: Annotated Chronological, Geographical and Topical List of Selected Historical Novels (Historical Fiction Guide).* Scarecrow 2nd ed. 1973 o.p. Contains 6,455 works arranged by geography and chronology to 1900. All works are in English, although some are translations into English. Includes an author-title index.

McPherow, William. *The Bibligraphy of American Fiction, 1945–1988.* Meckler 1989 o.p.

Magill, Frank N. *Critical Survey of Long Fiction.* 8 vols. Salem Pr. rev. ed. 1991 $475.00. ISBN 0-89356-825-2. Provides, among other things, principal works within the genre and a biography of each author profiled.

Menendez, Albert J. *The Catholic Novel: An Annotated Bibliography.* Garland 1988 $48.00. ISBN 0-8240-8534-5. Lists nearly 500 works with an author list of 1,700 novels.

Short Story Index: Basic Volume, 1900–1949. Wilson 1953 $50.00. ISBN 0-8242-0384-4. About 60,000 short stories indexed.

Short Story Index: Collections Indexed 1900–1978. Wilson 1979 $40.00. ISBN 0-8242-0643-6. A single, alphabetical author-editor and title index to the 8,400 story collections published from 1900 to 1978.

Poetry

Brogan, T.V.F. *Verseform: A Comparative Bibligraphy.* Johns Hopkins 1989 $26.00. ISBN 0-8108-3362-0

The Columbia Granger's Index to Poetry. Ed. by Edith Hazen and Deborah Fryer. Col. U. Pr. 9th ed. 1990 $175.00. ISBN 0-231-07104-3. Also available on CD-ROM. A useful index to standard and popular collections of poetry.

Critical Survey of Poetry: English Language Series. 8 vols. Salem Pr. 1992 $475.00. ISBN 0-89356-834-1. Includes 300 writers from all literary periods. Additional writers included in the *Supplement.*

Hoffman, Herbert H. *Hoffman's Index to Poetry: European and Latin American Poetry in Anthologies.* Scarecrow 1985 $49.50. ISBN 0-8108-1831-0. Serves as non-English-language supplement to *Granger's Index.*

Index of American Periodical Verse, 1990. Ed. by Rafael Catala and others. Scarecrow 1992 $59.50. ISBN 0-8108-2587-2. This twentieth annual volume indexes poems published by 289 participating periodicals from Canada, the United States, and Puerto Rico. The 1983 volume indexed 170 U.S. periodicals.

Index to Poetry by Black American Women. Comp. by Dorothy H. Chapman. Greenwood 1986 $55.00. ISBN 0-313-25152-5. Over 4,000 poems indexed by title, first line, poet, and subject.

Poetry Index Annual, 1988. Roth Pub. Inc. 1989 $54.99. ISBN 0-89609-283-6. Serves as a supplement to *Granger's Index.*

Poetry Index Annual, 1989. Roth Pub. Inc. 1990 $54.99. ISBN 0-89609-296-8

Reardon, Joan. *Poetry by American Women* 2 vols. Scarecrow Vol. 1 1900–1975. (1979) $37.50. ISBN 0-8108-1173-1. Vol. 2 1975–1989. (1990) $29.50. ISBN 0-8109-2366-7. Lists separately published volumes by U.S. women poets.

Sears, Minnie E., and Phyllis Crawford, eds. *Song Index: An Index to More than 12,000 Songs.* Rprt. Serv. 1990 repr. of 1926 ed. $109.00. ISBN 0-7812-9019-8. Contains poems set to music. Many of the titles are not included in *Granger's Index.* Includes more than 7,000 songs.

BIOGRAPHICAL REFERENCE WORKS

General

Allibone, Samuel Austin. *Critical Dictionary of English Literature and British and American Authors.* 3 vols. Gale 1972 $300.00. ISBN 0-87968-965-X. Contains over 46,000 articles (authors), with 40 indexes of subjects. A two-volume *Supplement* contains 37,000 articles (authors).

Author Biographies Master Index. Gale 4th ed. 1993 $250.00. ISBN 0-8103-7582-6. Indexes biographies of major literary figures plus those of minor authors.

Biography Index. 15 vols. Wilson 1946–present. $170.00 ea. A quarterly index with annual and 3-year cumulations. Covers biographical material appearing in approximately 2,600 periodicals indexed in other Wilson indexes; current books of individual and collective biography in the English language; obituaries, and incidental biographical material in otherwise nonbiographical books. Bibliographies and portraits and other illustrations are noted when they appear in connection with indexed material. Consists of a main or name alphabet and an index by professions and occupations.

Contemporary Authors. 136 vols. Gale 1962–present. $109.00 ea. Includes more than 100,000 writers in a wide range of media—fiction, nonfiction, journalism and other media, literary greats.

Contemporary Dramatists. Ed. by D. L. Kirkpatrick. St. James Pr. 4th ed. 1991 $149.50. ISBN 0-912289-62-7. Biography and criticism on about 600 playwrights alive at the time that the edition was updated.

Contemporary Novelists. Ed. by Leslie Henderson. St. James Pr. 5th ed. 1991 $115.00. ISBN 1-55862-036-2. Bio-bibliographical information; earlier edition updated. Contains information on novelists, both living and dead, since the 1950s.

Contemporary Poets. Ed. by Tracy Chevalier. St. James Pr. 5th ed. 1991 $115.00. ISBN 1-55862-035-4. Covers more than 1,000 poets, both living and dead, since 1950.

Dictionary of Literary Biography. 134 vols. Gale 1978–1993. $120.00. ea. A bio-bibliographical guide to topics in literature. Each volume focuses on a specific genre and literary movement. Related works are the *Dictionary of Literary Biography Yearbook*, which includes literary highlights of the year in review, and *Literary Biography: Documentary Series*, which concentrates on the major figures of particular literary periods, movements, or genres using selections from authors' letters, diaries, or interviews.

European Authors, 1000–1900: A Biographical Dictionary. Ed. by Stanley J. Kunitz and Vineta Colby. Wilson 1967 $70.00. ISBN 0-8242-0013-6. Contains biographies of authors born after 1000 A.D. and dead by 1925.

Havlice, Patricia P. *Index to Literary Biography.* 2 vols. Scarecrow 1975 $85.00. *Supplement.* 2 vols. 1983 $85.00. ISBNs 0-8108-0745-9, 0-8108-1613-X. Contains biographical information on 68,000 authors appearing in collective biographies and dictionaries of literature.

Magill, Frank N., ed. *Cyclopedia of World Authors, No. II.* Salem Pr. 1989 $300.00. ISBN 0-89356-512-1. A fine collection of 753 biographies and appraisals by authorities; signed articles.

Twentieth-Century Authors. Ed. by Stanley J. Kunitz and Howard Haycraft. Wilson 1942 $87.00. ISBN 0-8242-0049-7. *Supplement.* 1955 $77.00. ISBN 0-8242-0050-0. A revision of Kunitz's *Living Authors* (o.p.) and *Authors Today and Yesterday* (o.p.), with additional material. Contains 1,850 biographies. The supplement brings the original biographies and bibliographies up to 1955, adding some 700 biographies.

The Writer's Directory: 1980-1982. St. Martin 1979 $40.00. ISBN 0-312-89426-0. Includes 17,000 living authors, each of whom has published at least one full-length book. Useful since it lists many minor writers not found in other biographical sources. Published irregularly.

Great Britain

Blain, Virginia. *The Feminist Companion to Literature in English: Women Writers from the Middle Ages to the Present*. Yale U. Pr. 1990 $49.95. ISBN 0-300-04854-8. Includes women from all national traditions writing in English.

British Authors before Eighteen Hundred. Ed. by Stanley J. Kunitz and Howard Haycraft. Wilson 1952 $48.00. ISBN 0-8242-0006-3. Biographies of 650 writers from the beginning of English literature to Cowper and Burns.

British Authors of the Nineteenth Century. Ed. by Stanley J. Kunitz and Howard Haycraft. Wilson 1936 $50.00. ISBN 0-8242-0007-1. Complete in one volume, with 1,000 biographies and 350 portraits.

British Women Writers: A Critical Reference Guide. Ed. by Janet Todd. Continuum 1989 $59.50. ISBN 0-8044-3334-8. Signed essays arranged alphabetically by writer (440 are included). Emphasis on twentieth-century subjects. Includes indexes.

Great Writers of the English Language. 3 vols. Ed. by James Vinson and Daniel L. Kirkpatrick. St. Martin 1979 Vol. 1 *Poets*. $55.00. ISBN 0-312-34640-9. Vol. 2 *Novelists and Prose Writers*. $55.00. ISBN 0-312-34624-7. Vol. 3 *Dramatists*. $50.00. ISBN 0-312-34570-4. Essays, biography, bibliography, and criticism on a select group of writers.

Scott-Kilvert, Ian, ed. *British Writers*. 8 vols. Scribner 1979–84 $60.00–$85.00 ea. ISBNs 0-684-15798-5, 0-684-16407-8, 0-684-16408-6, 0-684-16635-6, 0-684-16636-4, 0-684-16637-2, 0-684-16638-0, 0-684-17417-0. *Supplement 1*. ISBN 0-684-18612-8. Contains signed articles on major figures and traditions of British literature from the fourteenth century to the late twentieth century; includes bibliographies and an index. *Supplement 1* (1987) continues, beginning with Graham Greene.

Twayne's English Authors Series. G. K. Hall. More than 500 volumes; for some authors, the Twayne studies are the sole source of biographical information. Approximately 20 new volumes are printed annually.

Vrana, Stan A. *Interviews and Conversations with 20th Century Authors Writing in English: An Index*. Scarecrow 1990 $42.50. ISBN 0-8108-2352-7. At least 5,600 entries index almost 2,500 contemporary writers.

Writers and Their Work Series. Ed. by Bonamy Dobree and Geoffrey Bullough. British Bk. Ctr. 1950–present o.p. Almost 300 monographs on English-language authors. Begun in 1950, each monograph has a biocritical essay and bibliography. These are brief introductions to the writers, and the biographical information is not intended to be complete.

United States

American Authors, 1600–1900: A Biographical Dictionary of American Literature. Ed. by Stanley J. Kunitz and Howard Haycraft. Wilson 8th ed. 1977 $68.00. ISBN 0-8242-0001-2. Biographies of nearly 1,300 authors who contributed to the development of American literature from the first English settlement at Jamestown to the close of the nineteenth century.

Beachler, Lea, and A. Walton Litz, eds. *American Writers: A Collection of Literary Biographies*. Macmillan 1991 $169.00. ISBN 0-684-19196-2. Contains information about the lives, careers, and works of such American authors as Henry Adams and T. S. Eliot. Twenty-nine essays supplement earlier volumes.

Faust, Langdon L., ed. *American Women Writers*. Continuum 1988 $59.50. ISBN 0-8044-3157-4. A more affordable alternative to the four-volume edition by Mainiero and Faust but abridged, with only about 40 percent of the original 1,000 entries.

Mainiero, Linda, and Langdon L. Faust, eds. *American Women Writers: A Critical Reference Guide*. 4 vols. Continuum 1982 $300.00. ISBN 0-8044-3150-7. Contains bio-bibliographic essays on U.S. women writers of all periods.

Newby, James Edward. *Black Authors: A Selected Annotated Bibliography*. Garland 1990 $80.00. ISBN 0-8240-3329-9. Lists 3,200 works authored by black Americans, covering mostly the time period from 1973 to 1990.

Rush, Theressa G., and others. *Black American Writers Past and Present: A Biographical and Bibliographical Dictionary.* 2 vols. Scarecrow 1975 $72.50. ISBN 0-8108-0785-8. Contains bio-bibliographic information on 2,000 African American writers.

Twayne's United States Authors Series. Macmillan 1962–present. More than 575 volumes, all of which contain a concise critical introduction to the author and his or her complete oeuvre, including biographical and historical background and readings of major works. For some authors, the Twayne studies are the sole source of biographical information.

Unger, Leonard, ed. *American Writers: A Collection of Literary Biographies.* 8 vols. Macmillan 1981 $625.00. ISBN 0-684-17322-0. Includes the supplement edited by A. Walton Litz.

Who's Who in America: A Biographical Dictionary of Notable Living Men and Women. 1899–present. 3 vols. Marquis 1993 $429.95. ISBN 0-8379-0151-0. Now an annual publication listing 80,000 leaders from every field. Along with *Who Was Who,* the standard and essential reference.

Who's Who in Writers, Editors and Poets: United States and Canada, 1989/90. Ed. by Curt Johnson. December Pr. 3rd ed. 1989 $76.80. ISBN 0-913204-21-8. ISSN 1049-8621. Profiles 9,500 people, presenting personal and professional data.

World

European Authors, 1000–1900. Ed. by Stanley J. Kunitz and Vineta Colby. Wilson 1967 $63.00. ISBN 0-8242-0013-6. Contains 967 biographies of authors from more than 30 countries born after 1000 A.D. and dead by 1925. *Supplement* in 1955 added 700 biographies.

European Writers Ed. by William T. H. Jackson. 14 vols. Scribner 1983–1990 o.p. Contains signed essays on authors and subjects with selective bibliographies. Last volume is an index volume.

Magill, Frank N. *Cyclopedia of World Authors.* 3 vols. Salem Pr. 1989 $300.00. ISBN 0-8935-6512-1. A fine collection of 1,000 biographies and appraisals by authorities; signed articles.

World Authors, 1980–1985: Authoritative Biographies of 320 Contemporary Writers. Ed. by Vineta Colby. Wilson 1991 $80.00. ISBN 0-8242-0797-1. A companion to earlier editions.

World Authors, 1950–1970: A Companion Volume to Twentieth Century Authors. Ed. by John Wakeman. Wilson 1975 $95.00. ISBN 0-8242-0419-0. Biographical or autobiographical articles on 950 authors whose work has been published in English and who gained attention between 1950 and 1970.

World Authors, 1970–1975: A Biographical Dictionary. Ed. by John Wakeman and Stanley J. Kunitz. Wilson 1980 $78.00. ISBN 0-8242-0641-X. A companion to *World Authors, 1950–1970.* Articles on 348 of the most influential and popular authors who came into prominence between 1970 and 1975.

ANTHOLOGIES

General

Brooks, Cleanth, and Robert Penn Warren. *An Approach to Literature.* P-H 5th ed. 1975 $26.95. ISBN 0-13-043802-2. A fine general anthology, one of the best introductions to literature. Includes a glossary of literary terms.

Ellman, Richard, and Charles Feidelson, Jr. *The Modern Tradition: Backgrounds of Modern Literature.* OUP 1965 o.p. Attempts to assemble the texts from 101 poets, novelists, scientists, artists, and speculative thinkers whose writings constitute the main documents of "the modern tradition." A provocative collection, constituting the intellectual baggage of the modern literary scholar up to the mid-1960s.

Elements of Literature. OUP 1986 o.p. Excellent general anthology of essays, fiction, poetry, and drama, with critical introductions.

Trilling, Lionel. *The Experience of Literature.* P-H o.p.

_____ . *Prefaces to the Experience of Literature.* HarBraceJ 1979 $12.95. ISBN 0-15-173915-3. Contains 1,316 pages of drama, fiction, and poetry, beginning with Sophocles up to the present. "Occasionally . . . there comes along a text so remarkably good and interesting that it can no longer be merely studied; it demands to be read" *(N.Y. Times).*

British Literature

Abrams, M. H., and others. *Norton Anthology of English Literature.* 2 vols. Norton 5th ed. 1988 $37.95 ea. ISBNs 0-393-95469-2, 0-393-95472-2. One of the best of the blockbuster anthologies. Includes explanatory notes, bibliographies, biographical and critical commentaries, and generous excerpts from writers of each period.

Allison, Alexander W. *The Norton Anthology of Poetry.* Ed. by Herbert Barrows and others. Norton 3rd ed. 1986 $33.95. ISBN 0-393-95242-8. Provides readers with a sampling of the best poetry of the English language from early medieval times to relatively recent times; includes 11 more women authors and twice the number of Canadian authors as represented in the last edition.

Baugh, Albert C. and G. W. McClelland. *English Literature: A Period Anthology.* 2 vols. Appleton 1954 o.p. Still a standard and very useful anthology.

Bloom, Harold, ed. *Twentieth-Century British Literature.* 6 vols. Chelsea Hse. 1985–87 $395.00. ISBN 0-87754-808-0. Biographical information and criticism for authors from the United Kingdom and its former colonies.

Kermode, Frank, and John Hollander, eds. *The Oxford Anthology of English Literature.* 2 vols. OUP 1973. Vol. 1 *Middle Ages through the Eighteenth Century.* $28.00. ISBN 0-19-501657-2. Vol. 2 *1800 to the Present.* $28.00. ISBN 0-19-501658-0. "The 4600-page work features a general introduction to each of the six periods; brief biographical and critical essays on major authors; glossaries of literary and historical terms; modernized texts . . . explanatory notes; lists of suggested further readings; indexes; and 192 pages of illustrations." *(Library Journal)*

McEwan, Neil, ed. *The Twentieth Century.* St. Martin 1990 $29.95. ISBN 0-312-04475-5. One of St. Martin's *Anthologies of English Literature Series.*

American Literature

Barkan, Stanley H., and Dorothea Neale, eds. *Americana Anthology: Bicentennial Edition 1776–1976, Vol. 1.* Cross Cult. 1976 $20.00. ISBN 0-89304-011-8. First volume of a projected multivolume set. Includes 97 poems about America from its discovery to the time of its bicentennial.

Baym, Nina, and others, eds. *The Norton Anthology of American Literature.* 2 vols. Norton 3rd ed. 1989 $33.95 ea. ISBNs 0-393-95736-5, 0-393-95738-1. A very comprehensive anthology that divides the twentieth century into three sections: American literature between the wars (1914–1945), American prose since 1945, and American poetry since 1945. The latest edition emphasizes the work of four authors: William Bradford, Anne Bradstreet, Jonathan Edwards, and Benjamin Franklin.

Benet, William Rose, and Norman Holmes Pearson, eds. *The Oxford Anthology of American Literature.* 2 vols. OUP 1938 o.p. Although dated, this is still a valuable collection.

Blanche, Jerry. *Native American Reader: Speeches, Poems and Stories of the American Indian.* Denali Pr. 1990 $25.00. ISBN 0-938737-20-1. Interesting anthology of Native American works, including many by contemporary writers.

Chan, Jeffrey P. *The Big Aiiieeeee! An Anthology of Chinese-American and Japanese-American Literature.* NAL-Dutton 1991 $15.00. ISBN 0-452-01076-4. A useful anthology; many works are not anthologized in any other sources.

Chapman, Abraham, ed. *Jewish American Literature: An Anthology.* NAL-Dutton 1974 o.p.

Elliott, Emory, and others. *American Literature: A Prentice Hall Anthology*. P-H 1991. Vol. 1 ISBN 0-13-025750-8. Vol. 2 $20.00. ISBN 0-13-027269-8

Gates, Henry Louis, ed. *Norton Anthology of Afro-American Literature*. Norton 1990

Keller, Gary D. *Hispanics in the United States: An Anthology of Creative Literature*. Bilingual Rev-Pr. 1980 $13.00. ISBN 0-916950-19-0

Lauter, Paul, and others. *The Heath Anthology of American Literature*. 2 vols. Heath 1990 $19.50 ea. ISBNs 0-669-12064-2, 0-669-12065-0. An anthology of unprecedented richness spanning more than 200 years, with time-honored authors placed alongside women and minority writers.

Long, Richard A., and Eugenia W. Collier. *Afro-American Writing*. Pa. St. U. Pr. 1990 $14.95. ISBN 0-271-00376-6.

McMichael, George, and Frederick Crews, eds. *Anthology of American Literature*. 2 vols. Macmillan 1992 ISBN 0-02-379606-5

Rubin, Louis D., Jr., ed. *The Literary South*. La. State U. Pr. 1986 $16.95. ISBN 0-8071-1359-X

Russell, Sandi. *Render Me My Song: African-American Women Writers from Slavery to the Present*. St. Martin 1992 $9.95. ISBN 0-312-07074-8. Interesting anthology on an often neglected subject.

World Literature

Arkin, Marian, and Barbara Schollar *The Longman Anthology of World Literature by Women*. Longman 1989 $27.16. ISBN 0-582-28559-3

Gilbert, Sandra M., and Susan Gubar. *Norton Anthology of Literature by Women: The Tradition in English*. Norton 1985 $47.50. ISBN 0-393-01940-3. Brings together works by 150 women authors from many different English-speaking countries; serves as an overview of the ambition and imaginative vision of the female literary tradition.

Hunt, Douglas G. *The Riverside Anthology of Literature*. HM 1988 $34.76. ISBN 0-395-43264-2

Mack, Maynard, ed. *Norton Anthology of World Masterpieces*. 2 vols. Norton 6th ed. 1992 $38.95 ea. ISBNs 0-393-96140-0, 0-393-96142-7. Highly respected anthology of some of the best-known works in world literature.

Specialized Subjects

Lewis, Arthur O. *Of Men and Machines*. NAL-Dutton 1963 o.p. A fascinating collection of writings on the relationship of men and machines: the problem, machine as friend, machine as thing of beauty, machine as enemy, futures.

MacDonald, Dwight, and Veronica Geng, eds. *Parodies: An Anthology from Chaucer to Beerbohm and After*. Quality Pap. Ser. Da Capo 1985 repr. of 1960 ed. $12.95. ISBN 0-306-80239-2. A malicious gathering of parodies from many languages and cultures, with emphasis on the English language. Contains an interesting discussion of the distinctions among satire, burlesque, parody. For those who lived through the Eisenhower years, the Gettysburg Address as Eisenhower might have delivered it is not to be missed.

Moffat, Mary J. *In the Midst of Winter: Selections from the Literature of Mourning*. Random 1992 $12.00. ISBN 0-679-73827-4

Rabin, Jonathan. *Oxford Book of the Sea*. OUP 1993 $12.95 ISBN 0-19-283148-8. Collection of stories about sailing and the seas.

Seaver, Richard, and others. *Writers in Revolt: An Anthology*. Fell 1963 o.p. Rebels from the Marquis de Sade to writers of the present, such as Henry Miller, Iris Murdoch, Genet, Ionesco, Beckett.

Swados, Harvey, ed. *American Writers and the Great Depression*. Bobbs 1966 o.p. "Part of the 'American Heritage Series,' this brilliantly edited anthology offers selections from novels, poems and other writings, with photographs, from the Depression years" (*LJ*).

Wells, Carolyn. *A Parody Anthology*. Gordon Pr. 1972 $59.95. ISBN 0-8490-0803-4. Provides diverse parodies of many authors, including Chaucer, Tennyson, Browning, and Wordsworth.

White, E. B., and Katherine S. White, eds. *A Subtreasury of American Humor*. Telegraph Bks. repr. of 1941 ed. o.p. Divides entries into different genres, including stories, parodies, folklore, satire, and verse.

ENCYCLOPEDIAS

Bede, Jean-Albert, and William Edgerton, eds. *Columbia Dictionary of Modern European Literature*. Col. U. Pr. 2nd ed. 1980 $163.00. ISBN 0-231-03717-1. Includes 1,853 writers selected on the basis of their relevance to twentieth-century literature, as well as survey articles on various national literatures.

Benét, William R., ed. *Benét's Reader's Encyclopedia*. 3rd ed. HarpC 1987 $45.00. ISBN 0-06-181088-6. Contains more than 9,000 entries covering author biographies, plot summaries of important works, fictional characters, and literary styles and periods. International in scope, the work covers both classic and contemporary literature.

Buchanan-Brown, John. *Cassell's Encyclopedia of World Literature*. 3 vols. Morrow 1973 o.p. Includes histories, general articles, and biographies of literary figures.

Gassner, John, and Edward Quinn. *The Reader's Encyclopedia of World Drama*. Crowell 1969 o.p. Signed essays on the history and development of theater, as well as entries for playwrights, titles, and so on.

Holman, C. Hugh. *A Handbook to Literature*. Macmillan 5th ed. 1986 $27.50. ISBN 0-02-553430-0. Encyclopedic listing of more than 1,560 entries, including literary terms and movements, British and U.S. literary history, winners of major literary prizes, structuralism, semiotics, and phenomenology.

Klein, Leonard S., ed. *Encyclopedia of World Literature in the 20th Century*. 5 vols. Ungar 1981–1993. Vol. 1 *A–D*. $100.00. ISBN 0-8044-3135-3. Vol. 2 *E–K*. $100.00. ISBN 0-8044-3136-1. Vol. 3 *L–Q*. $100.00. ISBN 0-8044-3137-X. Vol. 4 *R–Z*. $130.00. ISBN 0-8044-3138-8. Vol. 5 *Supplement*. 1993 $150.00. ISBN 0-8264-0571-1. *Index*. $40.00. ISBN 0-8044-3131-0. A reliable reference work that upholds the standards established by the first edition. Articles on living authors and bibliographies have been updated. Especially strong in covering European authors.

McGraw-Hill Encyclopedia of World Drama. 5 vols. Ed. by Stanley Hochman. McGraw 2nd ed. 1984 $395.00. ISBN 0-07-079169-4. Concerned with dramatists, the literature of the theater, and aspects of production and stagecraft around the world.

Preminger, Alex, ed. *The Princeton Encyclopedia of Poetry and Poetics*. Princeton U. Pr. 1974 $29.50. ISBN 0-691-01317-9. An authoritative and scholarly encyclopedia with 1,000 articles written by authorities on the subject. International in scope.

LITERARY GUIDES, HANDBOOKS, DICTIONARIES

General

Abrams, M. H. *A Glossary of Literary Terms*. HarBraceJ 5th ed. 1988 $14.50. ISBN 0-03-011953-7. Defines and discusses terms, concepts, and points of views commonly used in analyzing works of literature. Ranked among the outstanding literary handbooks.

Barnet, Sylvan, and others. *A Dictionary of Literary, Dramatic and Cinematic Terms*. Scott F. 2nd ed. 1987 $11.50. ISBN 0-673-39194-9. Offers some of the fullest and most allusive definitions; bibliographies.

Brewer, E. Cobham. *Brewer's Dictionary of Phrase and Fable*. Ed. by Ivor H. Evans. HarpC 14th ed. 1992 $20.00. ISBN 0-06-272022-8. References colloquial and proverbial phrases, mythological and biographical figures, and so forth.

Cuddon, J. A. *Dictionary of Literary Terms*. Viking Penguin 1982 $9.95. ISBN 0-14-051112-1. Contains more than 2,000 literary terms in use today, representing a dozen languages, explained by means of quotes and illustrations from world literature.

Deutsch, Babette. *Poetry Handbook: A Dictionary of Terms*. B & N Imports 4th ed. 1982 $10.00. ISBN 0-06-463548-1. Dictionary format; appropriate for students.

Fowler, Roger, ed. *A Dictionary of Modern Critical Terms*. Routledge 1987 $12.95. ISBN 0-7102-1022-1. Three hundred essays on theoretical concepts; includes terminology of contemporary literary criticism.

Scott, A. F., ed. *Current Literary Terms*. St. Martin repr. of 1980 ed. $18.95. ISBN 0-312-17956-1. Alphabetical arrangement of literary and critical terms used in poetry and drama.

Seigneuret, Jean-Charles, ed. *Dictionary of Literary Themes and Motifs*. Greenwood 1988 $225.00. ISBN 0-313-22943-0. Discusses 143 themes, ranging from "utopia" to "grotesque." Includes cross-references and a detailed index.

Seymour-Smith, Martin. *Dictionary of Fictional Characters*. Writer 1992 $17.75. ISBN 0-87116-166-4. Indexes fictional characters from literature, plays, and operas written in English during the last six centuries. Based on Freeman's *Dictionary of Fictional Characters*.

British Literature

Drabble, Margaret, ed. *The Oxford Companion to English Literature*. OUP 5th ed. 1985 $49.95. ISBN 0-19-866130-4. Authors, characters, plots, mythological references, general topics, and so on; ". . . pigheaded and fussy, but still admirable volume." (*New York Times*)

Drabble, Margaret, and Jenny Stringer, eds. *The Concise Oxford Companion to English Literature*. OUP 1987 $24.95. ISBN 0-19-866140-1. An abridged version of the 5th edition of *The Oxford Companion to English Literature*.

Eagle, Dorothy, and others, eds. *The Oxford Illustrated Literary Guide to Great Britain and Ireland*. OUP 2nd ed. 1992 $45.00. ISBN 0-19-212988-0. Provides information on such things as homes and universities and includes quotations and exquisite illustrations.

Gray, Martin. *A Chronology of English Literature* Longman 1989 $20.00. ISBN 0-582-05141-X. Tabulates historical and literary events from the beginnings of English literature to 1980. Contains winners of prizes and bestseller lists.

Ousby, Ian, ed. *Cambridge Guide to Literature in English*. Cambridge U. Pr. 1992 $24.95. ISBN 0-521-42904-8. Provides detailed biographies and critical entries on major poets, playwrights, novelists, authors of literature for children, and critics originally published in English.

Wynne-Davies, Marion, ed. *Prentice-Hall Guide to English Literature*. P-H 1990 $35.00. ISBN 0-13-083619-2. Alphabetical list of authors, works, names, historical and literary figures, plus essays.

American Literature

Duyckinck, Evert A., and George L. Duyckinck. *Cyclopedia of American Literature*. 2 vols. Omnigraphics Inc. 1992 repr. of 1875 ed. $250.00. ISBN 1-55888-949-3. This older work, cited in bibliographies, is arranged chronologically. Still a very useful book.

Ehrlich, Eugene, and Gorton Carruth. *The Oxford Illustrated Literary Guide to the United States*. OUP 1982 $45.00. ISBN 0-19-503186-5. Locates places associated with 1,527 U.S. authors in 1,586 cities and towns in the United States, covering U.S. literature from the beginning to publication date.

Hart, James D. *The Oxford Companion to American Literature*. OUP 5th ed. 1983 $49.95. ISBN 0-19-503074-5. Standard reference tool.

Magill, Frank N., ed. *Masterpieces of African-American Literature*. HarpC 1992 $40.00. ISBN 0-06-270066-9. Guide to important works of African American literature, including Baldwin, DuBois, Hughes, Malcom X, and Morrison.

Perkins, George, and others, eds. *Benet's Reader's Encyclopedia of American Literature*. HarpC 1991 $45.00. ISBN 0-06-270027-8. Includes biographies of writers and historical figures, plot summaries of important literary works, and sketches of principal characters from these works. Revises two earlier editions and adds 1,500 entries, for a total of more than 9,000 information-packed entries.

Salzman, Jack. *The Cambridge Handbook of American Literature*. Cambridge U. Pr. 1986 $24.95. ISBN 0-521-30703-1. Useful work containing 750 entries covering authors, works, and themes.

Wiget, Andrew O. *Native American Literature*. Macmillan 1985 $20.95. ISBN 0-8057-7408-4. Evaluates Native American literature, using the term most diversely to include works from the Arctic, Canada, and meso-America; also includes recent contributions in fiction and poetry.

Classical and Mythological Works

Cotterell, Arthur. *A Dictionary of World Mythology*. OUP 1990 $9.95. ISBN 0-19-217747-8. Breaks down major myths of the world by the following regions: West Asia, South Asia, Central Asia, East Asia, Europe, Africa, America, and Oceania; stresses balance between assessment and analysis.

Gayley, Charles M. *The Classic Myths in English Literature and Art*. Buccaneer Bks. 1991 $42.95. ISBN 0-89966-769-4. Includes sketches of *The Fall of Troy*, the *Odyssey*, and the *Aeneid*; useful for students who are unfamiliar with mythology.

Grant, Michael. *Greek and Latin Authors, 800 B.C.–A.D. 1000*. Wilson 1980 $55.00. ISBN 0-8242-0640-1. Brief biographies of 370 classical authors; some bibliography.

Harsh, Philip W. *A Handbook of Classical Drama*. Stanford U. Pr. 1944 $60.00. ISBN 0-8047-0380-9. "Convenient brief guide to further critical material." (Preface)

Howatson, M. C., ed. *Oxford Companion to Classical Literature*. OUP 2nd ed. 1989 $45.00. ISBN 0-19-866121-5. Revision of earlier edition "pays more attention to the philosophy and political institutions." (Preface)

Oxford Classical Dictionary. Ed. by N. G. Hammond and H. H. Scullard. OUP 2nd ed. 1970 $55.00. ISBN 0-19-869117-3. A compendium of modern scholarship designed to meet the needs of the general reader and of the specialist in all fields of ancient Greek and Roman civilization.

LITERARY HISTORY

Great Britain

Cambridge History of English Literature. Ed. by A. W. Ward and A. R. Waller. 15 vols. Bks. Demand repr. of 1927 ed. ISBN 0-8357-7981-5. Every chapter of this monumental work is written by a specialist. In the original edition, each volume was indexed separately, but now Volume 15 is the general index to the entire work. The unique feature is the discussion according to type: "Political Literature," "Ballad Literature," "Memoir Writers," etc.

Garnett, Richard, and Edmund Gosse. *English Literature: An Illustrated Record*. 4 vols. Somerset Pub. repr. of 1935 ed. $33.00. ISBN 0-686-02073-1. Provides literary history and biographical and critical sketches of authors.

The Oxford History of English Literature Series. OUP o.p. A standard multivolume reference history that is now out of print.

Rogal, Samuel J. *A Chronological Outline of British Literature*. Greenwood 1980 $39.95. ISBN 0-313-21477-8. Listing by year of authors, works, political and literary events in England, Scotland, Ireland, and Wales.

United States

Cambridge History of American Literature. Ed. by Sacvan Bercovitch and Cyrus Patell. Cambridge U. Pr. 1993. ISBN 0-521-30105-X. This work, now out of print, was modeled on the *Cambridge History of English Literature*.

Elliott, Emory, ed. *The Columbia Literary History of the United States*. Col. U. Pr. 1988 $67.50. ISBN 0-231-05812-8. "Mostly post-modern; it acknowledges diversity, complexity, and contradiction." (Preface)

Rogal, Samuel J. *A Chronological Outline of American Literature*. Greenwood 1987 $49.95. ISBN 0-313-25471-0. Covers the sixteenth century through the 1980s. Lists, for each year, names of authors and editors, political and literary events, and literary publications. Indexes included.

Ruoff, A. LaVonne, Jr., and Jerry W. Ward, eds. *Redefining American Literary History*. Modern Lang. 1990 $45.00. ISBN 0-87352-187-0. Most comprehensive introduction currently available to the genres and major authors of Native American oral and written literature.

Spiller, Robert E., and others. *Literary History of the United States: Bibliography*. 2 vols. Macmillan 1974 o.p. Volume 1, the literary history, contains articles by distinguished contributors, divided according to historical periods; Volume 2 is the bibliographic supplement.

LITERARY CRITICISM

Bloom, Harold, ed. *Twentieth-Century American Literature*. 8 vols. Chelsea Hse. 1985 $535.00. ISBN 0-87754-800-5. Excerpts from criticism; arranged alphabetically by author.

———. *Twentieth-Century British Criticism*. 6 vols. Chelsea Hse. 1985–87 $395.00. ISBN 0-87754-809-9. Excerpts from published criticism: memoirs, book reviews, articles, book-length studies.

Bullock, Chris, and David Peck. *Guide to Marxist Literary Criticism*. Ind. U. Pr. 1980 $29.95. ISBN 0-253-13144-8. Useful to access this school of literary criticism.

Contemporary Literary Criticism Series. 73 vols. 1973–present. Gale $108.00 ea. Excerpts from criticism of the works of living writers; some photographs.

Curley, Dorothy N., ed. *Modern American Literature*. *Library of Literary Criticism Series*. 5 vols. Continuum 4th ed. 1969–85. Vols. 1–3 $225.00. ISBN 0-8044-3046-2. Vol. 4 *Supplement*. 1976 $75.00. ISBN 0-8044-3050-0. Vol. 5 *Supplement*. $75.00. ISBN 0-8044-3265-1. Expands the original Moulton edition by providing samples of criticism of modern American writers.

Dunn, Richard, ed. *The English Novel: Twentieth-Century Criticism, Defoe through Hardy*. Ohio U. Pr. 1976 $20.00. ISBN 0-8040-0742-X. Checklist of twentieth-century criticisms on the English novel, divided into two parts: alphabetical listing of novelists and novels, and general studies of the novel.

Eddleman, Floyd E., ed. *American Drama Criticism: Interpretations, 1890–1977*. Shoe String 2nd ed. 1979 $45.00. ISBN 0-208-01713-5. *Supplement I*. 1984 $39.50. ISBN 0-208-01978-2. *Supplement II*. 1989 $47.50. ISBN 0-208-02138-8. *Supplement III*. 1992 $55.00. ISBN 0-208-02270-8. "Interpretations of American plays." (Preface)

Humm, Maggie. *Annotated Critical Bibliography of Feminist Criticism*. Macmillan 1987 $40.00. ISBN 0-8161-8937-4. Chapters on broad subject areas; indexes.

Moulton, Charles A.. *Moulton's Library of Literary Criticism of English and American Authors through the Beginning of the 20th Century*. 4 vols. Ed. by Martin Tucker. Continuum 1966 $260.00. ISBN 0-8044-3190-6. Biographical data and excerpts from criticism.

Nineteenth-Century Literary Criticism Series. 44 vols. Ed. by Paula Kepos. Gale 1981–present. $108.00 ea. Furnishes extensive excerpts from published criticism on the great novelists, poets, and playwrights of the nineteenth century. All genres and nationalities are represented, including important political, social, and economic writers.

Poetry Criticism Series. 8 vols. Gale 1990–94 $75.00 ea. ISBNs 0-8103-5450-0, 0-8103-5539-6, 0-8103-5540-X, 0-8103-5541-8, 0-8103-8333-0, 0-8103-8334-9, 0-8103-8335-7, 0-8103-8460-4. A new, illustrated publication that covers the poets most frequently discussed and studied in high school and undergraduate literature courses; follows the format of Gale's other literature criticism series, providing substantial critical excerpts and biographical information on 12–15 major poets from all eras in each biannual volume.

Rice, Philip, and Patricia Waugh, eds. *Modern Literary Theory: A Reader*. Routledge Chapman & Hall 2nd ed. 1992 $17.95. ISBN 0-340-57599-9

Schlueter, Paul, and June Schlueter. *English Novel Twentieth-Century Criticism*. Swallow 1982 $35.00. ISBN 0-8040-0424-2. A thorough bibliography of criticism of "mainstream" twentieth-century British novels; contains 7,500 entries.

Tucker, Martin, ed. *The Critical Temper: A Survey of Modern Criticism on English and American Literature from the Beginnings to the Twentieth Century*. Lib. of Literary Criticism Ser. 3 vols. Continuum 1969 $225.00. ISBN 0-8044-3303-8. *Supplement.* 1979 $75.00. ISBN 0-8044-3307-0. Excerpts of criticism on about 220 authors.

Twentieth-Century Literary Criticism Series. 41 vols. Ed. by Paula Kepos. Gale 1978–present. $104.00 ea. Excerpts from criticism of the works of major novelists, poets, and playwrights who died between 1900 and 1960.

Wellek, René. *History of Modern Criticism Series, 1700–1950*. Vol. 2 *The Romantic Age*. Bks. Demand $120.90. ISBN 0-8357-8167-4. Vol. 5 *The First Half of the Twentieth Century: English*. Yale U. Pr. 1986 $37.00. ISBN 0-300-03378-8. Vol. 6 *The First Half of the Twentieth Century: American*. Yale U. Pr. 1986 $37.00. ISBN 0-300-03486-5. Vol. 7 *German, Russian, and East European Criticism, 1900–1950*. Yale U. Pr. 1981 $42.50. ISBN 0-300-05039-9. Vol. 8 *French, Italian, and Spanish Criticism, 1900–1950*. Yale U. Pr. 1993 $42.50. ISBN 0-300-05451-3. A monumental, comprehensive work; valuable to scholars, students, and interested laypersons.

LITERARY AWARDS

Clapp, Jane. *International Dictionary of Literary Awards*. Scarecrow 1963 o.p. "A selected list of major literary honors granted internationally and in countries other than the United States, Canada, and the United Kingdom." (Preface)

Hohenberg, John. *The Pulitzer Prize Story: News Stories, Editorials, Cartoons, and Pictures from the Pulitzer Prize Collection at Col. University*. Col. U. Pr. 1971 $17.00. ISBN 0-231-08663-6

————. *The Pulitzer Prize Story II: 1959–1980*. Col. U. Pr. 1980 $47.50. ISBN 0-231-04978-2. Builds on the author's *The Pulitzer Prize Story*.

The National Book Foundation. *The National Book Awards: Forty One Years of Literary Excellence*. National Book Foundation 1992

Pribic, Rado. *Nobel Laureates in Literature: A Biographical Dictionary*. Garland 1990 $95.00. ISBN 0-8240-5741-4. Includes biographical information on the laureates and a limited amount of critical analysis on the laureates' works.

Roginski, Jim. *Newbery and Caldecott Medalists and Honor Book Winners: Bibliographies and Resource Material through 1991*. Ed. by Muriel Brown and Rita S. Foundray. Neal-Schuman 2nd ed. 1992 $59.95. ISBN 1-55570-118-3. Collectors of children's literature will find this tool of great value.

Siegman, Gita, ed. *Awards, Honors and Prizes*. 2 vols. Gale 11th ed. 1994 $375.00. ISBN 0-8103-7906-6. Includes awards and prizes in different areas, one being literature.

Stuart, Sandra Lee. *Who Won What When*. Carol Pub. Group 1980 $12.00. ISBN 0-8184-0295-4. Lists winners of U.S. and major foreign prizes since 1900.

Weber, Olga S., ed. *Literary and Library Prizes*. Bowker 10th ed. 1980 o.p. Provides information on the history, condition, and rules of international, U.S., Canadian, and British prizes. Hundreds of winning authors and their works are listed.

Wills, Kendall J. *Pulitzer Prizes, 1990*. S&S Trade 1990 $9.95. ISBN 0-671-72583-1

World Dictionary of Awards and Prizes. Europa 1979 o.p. Includes international and national awards.

Part Two

British Literature

CHAPTER 5

Medieval Literature

Richard K. Emmerson

Ye knowe ek that in forme of speche is chaunge Withinne a thousand year.
–Chaucer, *Troilus and Criseyde*

The literature of medieval England is remarkably rich and varied. Covering some eight hundred years, from Caedmon (c.675) to Malory (fl. 1470), it includes genres and themes that are uniquely medieval and that may strike modern readers as quite foreign. The literature represents, as well, the beginnings of poetic forms and concerns that have come to characterize English literature in subsequent periods. The period encompasses several crucial historical events, starting with the conquest of Britain in the fifth century by the Anglo-Saxons, a Germanic semibarbaric people whose culture was inferior to the Romanized Celtic peoples then occupying the British Isles. Politically in that time span, King Alfred of Wessex made the first attempts to shape a centralized monarchy from the several petty kingdoms of Britain; the organization of feudalism was introduced by William the Conqueror; and parliamentary government after the Magna Carta emerged. Near its conclusion, in the fourteenth and fifteenth centuries, there occurred significant social and political disruptions, including the catastrophic Black Death, the Peasants' Revolt, and the Wars of the Roses which brought the nation to the brink of destruction and yet led ultimately into the Tudor monarchy and the expansion of the English peoples beyond the British Isles.

At first, the Anglo-Saxons remained involved primarily with their Germanic cousins to the east and the north. During the ninth and tenth centuries, for example, Viking invaders settled a substantial portion of eastern and northern England in an area known as the Danelaw, and Canute of Denmark became king of England in 1016. After the Norman Conquest fifty years later, however, England's history was increasingly linked with the south, especially France, where English kings' claims to territory later led to the Hundred Years' War. Similarly, English religion shifted from the Germanic north to the Latinate south. The period was dominated initially by a pagan religion based on northern mythology like that described much earlier in *Germania* (A.D. 98), written by the Roman historian Tacitus. Following the arrival of Saint Augustine in Canterbury in 597, however, England was quickly Christianized; after the Synod of Whitby, at which England rejected Irish Christianity, the English Church was tied to Rome. Roman Catholicism thus had a great impact on English thought and everyday life, as is evident even today in the numerous remains of monasteries and friaries. Toward the end of the period, though, influenced by the writings of John Wycliffe (c.1328–1384) and the spread of heretical Lollardy, England became more independent of Rome.

Culturally, the period begins with art that is particularly appropriate to a migratory people: fine metalwork decorated with interlace designs and representing mythological concerns, and an oral literature that interweaves various traditional myths and historical events. The two supreme artistic achievements of Anglo-Saxon culture, the metalwork discovered by archaeologists at Sutton Hoo (c.625) and the poem BEOWULF (c.750), reflect this style which the Anglo-Saxons shared with other Germanic peoples. With the introduction of Benedictine monasticism and the Christianization of society, the Anglo-Saxon kingdoms became centers of culture and learning, as is evident in the work of Alcuin of York, who in 782 became the imperial schoolmaster for Emperor Charlemagne. By the high Middle Ages, English culture, under the influence of Christianity and continental Latinate culture, had been institutionalized and was closely connected to the church and the court. It boasted fine architectural monuments, including impressive Romanesque and Gothic cathedrals and imposing castles; a fine tradition of craftwork, including sculpture, stained glass, ivory carving, and manuscript illuminations; leadership in theology and natural philosophy, culminating in the establishment of two respected universities; and a highly bookish literature which combined native and continental influences into a new English poetic. The growth of the reading public and the new patronage of a powerful middle class, furthermore, became an important factor during the fourteenth and fifteenth centuries, as the popularity of the poetry of GEOFFREY CHAUCER and the introduction of the printing press by William Caxton in 1476 indicate.

Medieval literature is traditionally divided into two major periods based upon the form of English spoken during each: Old English and Middle English. Old English (c.650–1100), a language that evolved from the Germanic dialects of the Angles, Saxons, and Jutes, is available today primarily in the late West Saxon form in which most Old English literature is preserved in manuscript. Although the latest example of Old English—the prose of the East Midland *Peterborough Chronicle* (1154)—differs significantly from the much earlier Northumbrian dialect of Caedmon's "Hymn," linguistic as well as stylistic continuity is evident in Old English literature. This continuity, however, was shattered when Norman French was established as the language of the aristocracy because of the Norman Conquest. It wasn't until 1362 that Parliament was opened in English, and not much earlier that a vigorous literature developed in Middle English, the stage of the language—from 1100 to 1500—between Old and Modern English. During the early part of this period, English was spoken primarily by peoples who were disenfranchised by the French-speaking aristocracy and the Latin-speaking clergy and educational elite. England was, in other words, trilingual through most of this period. Thus, although English was clearly in the ascendancy by the fourteenth century, Chaucer's friend JOHN GOWER wrote long poems in French and Latin as well as in English. Contributing to the problem of establishing English as a literary language were the many dialects of Middle English, which included Kentish, Southern, East and West Midland, and Northern forms. Literary awareness of these forms is evident in Chaucer's use of a northern dialect to portray the two students in *The Reeve's Tale* as country bumpkins or in the use of southern forms in *The Second Shepherds' Play* (late fifteenth century) to portray the villainous Mak as a pompous hypocrite. The three masterpieces of the late fourteenth century, Chaucer's *Canterbury Tales* (1387–1400), WILLIAM LANGLAND's *Piers Plowman* (1370–1390), and the anonymous *Sir Gawain and the Green Knight* (c.1395), reflect the variety of Middle English dialects as well as the range of interests of its literature. Even by the end of the period, Caxton would still despair of the numerous dialectical differences apparent in the English language.

HISTORY AND CRITICISM

Blake, N. F. *The English Language in Medieval Literature*. Routledge Chapman & Hall 1979 $10.95. ISBN 0-416-72470-1. Excellent treatment of both Old and Middle English and their literary forms.

Bolton, W. F. *The Middle Ages*. P. Bedrick Bks. 1987 $39.50. ISBN 0-87226-125-5. Helpful historical survey of the entire period.

Emmerson, Richard K. *Antichrist in the Middle Ages: A Study of Medieval Apocalypticism, Art, and Literature*. U. of Wash. Pr. 1981 $35.00. ISBN 0-7190-0829-8. Examination of Old and Middle English prose, poetry, and drama, including *Piers Plowman* and the Chester cycle.

Swanton, Michael. *English Literature before Chaucer*. Longman 1987 $29.95. ISBN 0-582-49241-6. Best recent history.

Zesmer, David M. *Guide to English Literature from Beowulf through Chaucer and Medieval Drama*. Greenwood 1982 $42.50. ISBN 0-313-23619-4. Handy for quick background information.

COLLECTIONS

Robertson, D. W., ed. *Literature of Medieval England*. McGraw 1970 $40.43. ISBN 0-07-053158-7

Trapp, J. B., ed. *Medieval English Literature*. OUP 1973 $21.00. ISBN 0-19-501624-6. Excellent anthology, with helpful background materials.

OLD ENGLISH PROSE AND POETRY

Old English poetry, as is clear even in its earliest recorded forms—for example, Caedmon's "Hymn" in Bede's *Ecclesiastical History of the English People* (731)—is essentially oral and formulaic. Composed to be sung by a *scop*, or bard, perhaps with the accompaniment of a harp, the works are built on conventional devices such as inherited epithets, phrases for describing repeated gestures and actions, and traditional topics and themes related to heroic ideology and deeds. These formulas were arranged to fit the four-stressed rhythm and alliterative patterns of Old English poetry. Rather than rhyme, or aural echoes—a device not established in English poetry until the Middle English period—this poetic stressed a kind of thought echo or variation in which formulas that retained stress and alliteration could be repeated to underscore particular actors and actions. Thus Caedmon in just nine lines represents God's creative activity in seven distinct ways, varying "heaven-kingdom's Guardian" with "Glory-Father," "eternal Lord," and "Master almighty," among others. To this device, Old English poets added an intense form of metaphor known as the *kenning*, which depicts a place or person by encapsulating an activity, such as "dispenser of rings" for lord or "riding place of the whale" for sea. These stylistic forms are best exemplified in *Beowulf* (c.750), which includes kennings and a series of standard actions such as boasting, distributing gifts, and shaking one's spear before speaking. Traditional heroic *topoi*, or themes, such as the appearance of the "Birds of Battle" to feast on the dead after a particularly violent encounter, or the notion that the best heroes represent *sapientia et fortitudo*—both wisdom and strength—are also exemplified in *Beowulf*. That they and the alliterative, formulaic style continue to be the basis for much later poems suggests the power and flexibility of the traditional Old English poetic. For example, *The Battle of Maldon*, which describes a skirmish in 991 when a Viking band defeated an English army, although based on a historical rather than a mythological subject, includes many of these devices.

While it is unified by its style and many of its shared themes, Old English poetry may be classified, for convenience, into three groups. In addition to such heroic poems as *Beowulf* and *Maldon*, a group of elegiac and more contemplative poems is extant. Influenced by Christian morality, they nevertheless reflect the Germanic ethos of the *comitatus*, described by Tacitus as the band of warriors in which the thane, or warrior, is tied to his leader. Elegiac poems such as "The Seafarer" and "The Wanderer" concentrate on the nostalgic thoughts of a warrior who has been exiled from his leader, the "gift giver," and who must therefore wander alone in search of a new band. Because, in one sense, this is the situation of all Christians—who, according to medieval theology, are pilgrims in a foreign land—these elegiac poems have allegorical elements as well. The third group of Old English poetry, then, is related to the second for it is composed of explicitly religious poetry. The finest example is the dramatic vision of the cross, *The Dream of the Rood*, which describes a heroic Christ climbing onto the cross as a warrior king conquering death. The poetry of Cynewulf, along with Caedmon the only Old English poet known by name, similarly develops this oral-formulaic style for his renditions of biblical, hagiographic, and eschatological subjects. Although, at one time, scholars assumed that the vast bulk of religious poetry was composed by Cynewulf, only the poems that include his signature inscribed in runic characters are now attributed to him. These include the particularly powerful *Elena*, which describes the discovery of the True Cross by Saint Helena, the mother of Constantine.

Prose written in Old English can similarly be divided into three types. The first includes a series of translations from Latin, particularly those associated with King Alfred, in the ninth century. The second type, the historical, includes the remarkable *Anglo-Saxon Chronicle*, which, while tracing history back to its origins, concentrates on English events. Its record of the Norman Conquest and the subsequent domination of England by the French under William the Conqueror is especially moving. The third type of prose, cycles of homilies or sermons, evolved from the Benedictine monastic revival of the late tenth century. Aelfric of Eysham (c.955–1012) and Wulfstan of York (d. 1023) are the two most prominent homiletic writers. Especially in Wulfstan's *Sermo Lupi ad Anglos* (Sermon of the Wolf to the English) (c.1010), written after renewed Viking attacks, one senses the apocalyptic concerns of the English near the turn of the millennium and the end of the Old English period.

History and Criticism

Fowler, David C. *The Bible in Early English Literature*. U. of Wash. Pr. 1976 $18.95. ISBN 0-295-95438-8. An excellent survey of biblical influence on all aspects of Old English literature.

Fulk, R. D. *A History of Old English Meter*. U. of Pa. Pr. 1992 $48.95. ISBN 0-8122-3157-0. Excellent on both history of Old English poetry and history of the English language.

Godden, Malcolm, and Michael Lapidge. *The Cambridge Companion to Old English Literature*. Cambridge U. Pr. 1991 $49.50. ISBN 0-521-37438-3. Best introduction for students; excellent series of essays.

Greenfield, Stanley B., and Daniel G. Calder. *A New Critical History of Old English Literature*. NYU Pr. 1986 $30.00. ISBN 0-8147-3002-7. Best historical survey.

Greenfield, Stanley B., and Fred C. Robinson, eds. *Bibliography of Publications on Old English Literature*. U. of Toronto Pr. 1980 $35.00. ISBN 0-8020-6505-8. The place to begin research; covers publications to 1972.

Hermann, John Patrick. *Allegories of War: Language and Violence in Old English Poetry*. U. of Mich. Pr. 1989 $32.50. ISBN 0-472-10147-1. Critical reading that focuses on a pervasive feature of Old English poetry.

Queen, Karen J., and Kenneth P. Quinn. *A Manual of Old English Prose*. Garland 1990 $51.00. ISBN 0-8240-9032-2. Good overview and bibliography.

Collections

Alexander, Michael, tr. *The Earliest English Poems*. Viking Penguin 1992 $7.95. ISBN 0-14-044594-3. Best collection for general readers and students.

Bradley, S. A. J. *Anglo-Saxon Poetry*. C. E. Tuttle 1982 $12.95. ISBN 0-460-87086-6

Crossley-Holland, Kevin, ed. *The Anglo-Saxon World: An Anthology*. OUP 1984 $8.95. ISBN 0-19-281632-2. Includes chronicles, letters, and poetry.

Farmer, D. H., ed. *The Age of Bede*. Viking Penguin 1981 $6.95. ISBN 0-14-04437-8. Includes translations of saints' lives.

Garmonsway, G. N. *The Anglo-Saxon Chronicle*. C. E. Tuttle 1972 $7.95. ISBN 0-460-87038-6

Sweet, Henry, and Dorothy Whitelock, eds. *Anglo-Saxon Reader in Prose and Verse*. OUP 1969 $14.95. ISBN 0-19-811169-X. Best Old English reader.

BEOWULF. c.750

The earliest epic and one of the first poems in any European vernacular, *Beowulf*, in 3,182 lines of unrhymed accentual and alliterative Old English verse, describes the numerous valiant deeds of Beowulf the Geat. Employing formulaic incidents, descriptions, and themes, the poem narrates three major events that trace the hero's growth from young and audacious leader of a band of warriors to elderly and wise king. In the first incident Beowulf sails to Denmark to battle without weapons against the humanoid monster Grendel, who is described as the kin of Cain. In the second, using a marvelous sword he discovers in an underwater cave, Beowulf kills Grendel's mother, a water monster who, in good Germanic tradition, avenges her son's death by attacking the Danish court. In the third, the hero slays a fire-breathing dragon who guards an ancient treasure that is disturbed by one of the hero's subjects. Beowulf dies from his wounds and is consumed with the treasure on a huge funeral pyre. As generous in gift-giving as he is impulsive in his violence, as quick with his tongue as he is with his sword, Beowulf exemplifies the ideal heroic virtues of fortitude and wisdom.

Beowulf reflects three distinct historical cultures: the period of the Germanic migrations of fifth- and sixth-century northern Europe, during which the action of the poem is set; the culture of the eighth-century kingdom of Mercia, in the English Midlands, when the Anglo-Saxon scop composed an oral version of the poem; and the early eleventh-century cultural revival of southwest England, when the unique West Saxon manuscript containing the only extant copy of the poem was written. The poem interweaves Germanic legend with accounts of historical battles, portraying in some detail the transitory joys of the mead hall and the incessant violence of these feuding tribes, but from the perspective of a later settled and peaceful Christian culture. In its fatalistic depiction of ancestral blood feuds and the necessity to avoid shame and to gain fame at all costs, *Beowulf* resembles the culture described by Tacitus in *Germania*. Combining pagan codes and Christian moralizing, folkloric patterns and biblical allusions, it is similar in spirit to the archaeological discoveries unearthed at Sutton Hoo in 1939, which include beautifully adorned metalwork objects whose interlace designs are visual analogues to the poem's intricate narrative structure.

The one extant copy of the *Beowulf* manuscript, which is in the British Museum, at one time was owned by the sixteenth-century British collector, Sir Robert Bruce Cotton. In 1700, Cotton's descendants turned his library over to the government, but much of the collection was destroyed in a fire in 1731. An Icelandic scholar, Grimur Jonsson Thorkelin, while in London searching for historical data, copied *Beowulf* without realizing its literary significance. His transcripts, in The Great Royal Museum of Denmark, survived the British bombardment of Copenhagen in 1807 and were part of an ambitious plan to preserve valuable Anglo-Saxon manuscripts.

EDITIONS OF *BEOWULF*

Beowulf. Trans. by Michael Alexander. Viking Penguin 1973 $2.95. ISBN 0-14-044268-5
Beowulf. Trans. by E. Talbot Donaldson. Ed. by Joseph F. Tuso. Norton 1975 $7.95. ISBN 0-393-09225-9
Beowulf. Trans. by Ruth P. M. Lehman. U. of Tex. Pr. 1988 $5.95. ISBN 0-292-70771-1
Beowulf. Trans. by Burton Raffel. NAL-Dutton 1987 $2.50. ISBN 0-451-62627-3
Beowulf and Other Old English Poems. Trans. by Constance B. Hieatt. Bantam 1988 $2.25. ISBN 0-553-21347-4
Beowulf and the Fight at Finnsburg. Ed. by F. Klaeber. Heath 3rd ed. 1936 o.p. With bibliography, notes, and glossary. Considered the best edition.

BOOKS ABOUT *BEOWULF*

Bessinger, Jess B., Jr., and Robert F. Yeager, eds. *Approaches to Teaching Beowulf.* Modern Lang. 1984 $34.00. ISBN 0-87352-481-0. An accessible collection with a series of helpful short essays and a good bibliography.
Chambers, Raymond W., ed. *Beowulf: An Introduction.* 3rd ed. Cambridge U. Pr. 1963 o.p. The authoritative, indispensable critical work.
Fry, Donald K. *Beowulf and the Fight at Finnsburg: A Bibliography.* U. Pr. of Va. 1969 $25.00. ISBN 0-8139-0268-1
Irving, Edward B., Jr. *Rereading Beowulf.* U. of Pa. Pr. 1989 $25.95. ISBN 0-8122-8155-1. A rare example of a scholar thoughtfully revising earlier positions; now emphasizes the poem's oral-formulaic features.
Kiernan, Kevin S. *Beowulf and the Beowulf Manuscript.* Rutgers U. Pr. 1981 $50.00. ISBN 0-8135-0925-4. An important, controversial study concentrating on manuscript and dating problems.
Nicholson, Lewis E., ed. *An Anthology of Beowulf Criticism.* U. of Notre Dame Pr. 1963 $11.95. ISBN 0-268-00006-9. Major articles from British and American scholarly journals.
Short, Douglas D. *Beowulf Scholarship: An Annotated Bibliography.* Garland 1980 $53.00. ISBN 0-8340-9530-8. Most comprehensive bibliography.

MIDDLE ENGLISH PROSE AND POETRY

No early forms of Middle English literature have survived because, after the Norman Conquest, English was replaced as a literary language by French and

Latin. The earliest extant examples of poetry thus show significant changes from Old English literary style and themes. For example, Middle English lyrics, although they include alliteration, do not follow the four-stressed line of Old English poetry. Some stress remains, but it is now combined with the syllabic tradition of French poetry to make the syllabic foot. Along with the tendency of English to accent the first syllable of a word and to use prepositions, articles, and other function words, the syllabic foot led, during this period, to the development of iambic meter. Also under the influence of French and Latin verse, Middle English began to use rhyme, often in couplets. The combination of the rhymed couplet and the iambic-pentameter line, a form established by Chaucer in *The Canterbury Tales* (c.1387–1400), led to the heroic couplet, one of the most enduring poetic forms in English literature. The fourteenth century, especially outside London, witnessed a revival of heavily alliterative poetry, although scholars debate the extent to which the alliterative revival can be traced to Old English models. Some of this poetry, such as *Sir Gawain and the Green Knight* (c.1390), combines paragraphs of the new alliterative long line with shorter, rhyming stanzas, a mixture of native and continental forms. But in general, as Chaucer makes clear when his Parson states that as a southern man he is unable to "rum, ram, ruf," alliterative poetry was associated with the north and the west and rhymed metric poetry with the south and especially London.

In addition to the long poems by the great authors of the late fourteenth-century Middle English literature renaissance—Chaucer, Gower, Langland, and the *Pearl*-Poet—Middle English poetry includes several anonymous works of varying type. Secular lyrics and ballads are particularly fresh and enduring in their themes; they often praise a lover or complain of unrequited love, linking these emotions to the beauty or harshness of nature. Many lyrics are set during spring, which provides the objective correlative not only for love but also for the religious poems on the Passion of Christ and the suffering of the Virgin Mary. The longer poem *The Owl and the Nightingale* (c.1195), a witty debate between two birds that symbolize opposing human outlooks, is a secular version of a popular genre, the debate, which often features the opposition between body and soul. The spring setting is also typical of dream visions, which are often allegorical poems that describe the dream experience of a confused or wandering narrator. Although they may develop love themes, as is evident in Chaucer's early poetry, dream visions may be satirical, as is *Piers Plowman* (1370–1390), or elegiac and visionary, as is *Pearl* (c.1390).

Romances are the largest category of Middle English poetry. Unlike the Old English epic, they are as much about chivalry, courtly love, and the motivating power of women as about heroic activity. They are often classified by their subject matter into four types: those representing the deeds of ancient heroes (e.g., the twelfth-century *Kyng Alisaunder*); of the great French heroes, especially Roland, Charlemagne, and the leaders of the Crusades; and of English heroes, especially ancestral stories (e.g., *Guy of Warwick*, c.1260); and those relating to folk heroes (e.g., the late thirteenth-century *Havelok the Dane*) or more recent history (e.g., *Richard the Lion-Hearted*, c.1300). The most important group of romances—the matter of Britain—are those that narrate the adventures of King Arthur and his Knights of the Round Table. The Arthurian legend, elements of which can be traced back to Gildas's *On the Destruction and Conquest of Britain* (548), combines Celtic mythology with English landscape and traditions as well as with the historical nostalgia that connects Britain to Rome and to the heroes of classical epics; this is evident in Geoffrey of Monmouth's *History of the Kings of Britain* (1137). The legend first flourished in

France in the romances of Chrétien de Troyes (fl. 1160–1190), who added its characteristic interest in courtly love. A poetic tradition soon developed in England, though, as evidenced by the Anglo-Norman *lais* of Marie de France (fl. 1180–1195) and the earliest Middle English version, Layamon's *Brut* (1205). By the fourteenth century, the Arthurian tradition was more likely to focus on individual knights, such as Lancelot, Gawain, and Yvain, than on Arthur. The finest Middle English example, *Sir Gawain and the Green Knight* (c. 1190), exemplifies this tendency. Exceptions to this rule, however, are alliterative and stanzaic Middle English versions of the *Morte Arthure*, two mid-fourteenth-century examples of this complex tradition.

The fifteenth century is usually seen as a period of decline after the flowering of Middle English literature in the second half of the fourteenth century. Two poets, however, are worth attention. The amazingly prolific John Lydgate (c.1370–c.1450) composed some 145,000 lines of verse, including *The Siege of Thebes* (1421), which relates the story of the sons of Oedipus. The Scottish schoolmaster Robert Henryson (c.1429–1508), who wrote fables and ballads, is best known for his *Testament of Cresseid* (c.1460), a sequel to Chaucer's great romance in which Criseida becomes a leper. In addition, the fifteenth century saw two remarkable works of English prose, the *Book of Margery Kempe*, an autobiographical account of the spiritual and personal life of a fascinating middle-class woman, and THOMAS MALORY's *Morte d'Arthur*, the culmination of the Arthurian tradition. Middle English prose also includes homiletic and didactic works such as sermons, creeds, and chronicles. *The Ancrene Wisse* (c.1200), a manual written for the spiritual guidance of three sisters, is the earliest important prose work in Middle English and a key element in tracing the continuity between the Old English works of Aelfric and the later prose of Malory. Mystical and contemplative works by Richard Rolle and Julian of Norwich, as well as the anonymous *Cloud of Unknowing* (mid to late fourteenth century) are also important examples of Middle English prose and moving works of religious thought.

History and Criticism

Baron, W. R. *English Medieval Romance.* Longman 1987 $32.50. ISBN 0-582-49221-1. Excellent study of development of romance in Europe and England.

Bennett, H. S. *Chaucer and the Fifteenth Century.* Vol. 2 *Oxford History of Eng. Lit.* OUP 1990 $59.00. ISBN 0-19-812230-6. More helpful on the fifteenth century than on Chaucer.

Bennett, J. A. W., and Douglas Gray. *Middle English Literature.* OUP 1990 $59.00. ISBN 0-19-812228-4. Standard literary history of the period.

Boitani, Piero. *English Medieval Narrative in the Thirteenth and Fourteenth Centuries.* Cambridge U. Pr. 1986 $18.95. ISBN 0-521-31149-7. Excellent study of romance and other narrative forms.

Burrow, John A. *Medieval Writers and Their Work: Middle English Literature and Its Background, 1100–1500.* OUP 1982 $12.95. ISBN 0-19-289122-7. A superb introduction for students.

――――. *Ricardian Poetry: Chaucer, Gower, Langland, and the Gawain Poet.* Bks. Demand o.p. Helpful in establishing notion of late fourteenth-century court poetry.

Cable, Thomas. *The English Alliterative Tradition.* U. of Pa. Pr. 1991 $25.95. ISBN 0-8122-3063-9. An important book focusing on Middle English alliterative poetry and its relation to Renaissance poetry.

Chambers, E. K. *Malory and Fifteenth-Century Drama, Lyrics, and Ballads.* Vol. 3 *Oxford History of Eng. Lit.* OUP 1990 $45.00. ISBN 0-19-812230-6. A reprint, still useful, of standard study.

Emmerson, Richard K., and Ronald B. Herzman. *The Apocalyptic Imagination in Medieval Literature.* U. of Pa. Pr. 1992 $27.95. ISBN 0-8122-3122-8. Wide-ranging study of the influence of the Book of Revelation on medieval literature, including Chaucer's *Canterbury Tales.*

Fowler, David C. *The Bible in Middle English Literature.* U. of Wash. Pr. 1984 $25.00. ISBN 0-295-96130-9. Good survey, particularly helpful on lyrics and *Piers Plowman.*

Ganin, John. *Style and Consciousness in Middle English Narrative.* Princeton U. Pr. 1983 $27.50. ISBN 0-691-06779-1. One of few studies that concentrate on stylistic matters.

Hopkins, Andrea. *The Sinful Knights: A Study of Middle English Penitential Romance.* OUP 1990 $69.00. ISBN 0-19-811762-0. Concentrates on popular Middle English romances, such as *Guy of Warwick.*

Lewis, Clive S. *Allegory of Love: A Study of Medieval Tradition.* OUP 1936 $11.95. ISBN 0-19-281220-3. Although dated, a good introduction to medieval romances.

———. *Studies in Medieval and Renaissance Literature.* Cambridge U. Pr. 1980 $12.95. ISBN 0-521-29701-X. A collection of often witty essays.

Medcalf, Stephen. *The Later Middle Ages.* Holmes & Meier 1981 $39.50. ISBN 0-8419-0725-0. Excellent essays on historical, social, and artistic contexts.

Pearsall, Derek, ed. *Manuscripts and Texts: Editorial Problems in Later Middle English Literature.* Boydell & Brewer 1987 $48.00. ISBN 0-85991-231-0. Good collection of essays focused on problems of editing Middle English.

Salter, Elizabeth. *Fourteenth-Century English Poetry: Contexts and Readings.* OUP 1983 $12.95. ISBN 0-19-871102-6. Insightful readings by a fine critic of Middle English poetry.

Spearing, A. C. *Medieval Dream-Poetry.* Cambridge U. Pr. 1976 o.p. Best overview of this medieval genre.

———. *Medieval to Renaissance in English Poetry.* Cambridge U. Pr. 1985 $54.50. ISBN 0-521-24769-1. A collection of essays stressing the continuity of the English poetic tradition.

———. *Readings in Medieval Poetry.* Cambridge U. Pr. 1989 $16.95. ISBN 0-521-31133-0. Thoughtful, close reevaluations of several Middle English poems.

Vasta, Edward, ed. *Middle English Survey: Critical Essays.* U. of Notre Dame Pr. 1965 $9.95. ISBN 0-268-00175-8. Good collection of earlier criticism.

Collections

Bennett, J. A. W., and G. V. Smithers, eds. *Early Middle English Verse and Prose.* OUP 2nd ed. 1982 $26.00. ISBN 0-19-871101-8

Dunn, Charles W., and Edward T. Byrnes, eds. *Middle English Literature.* Garland 1991 $55.00. ISBN 0-8240-5298-6. Excellent and wide-ranging anthology of texts, with good glossing.

Gray, Douglas, ed. *The Oxford Book of Late Medieval Verse and Prose.* OUP 1989 $12.95. ISBN 0-19-282245-4. Anthologizes writings in English from 1400 to 1520.

Millett, Bella, and Jocelyn Wogan-Browne. *Medieval English Prose for Women.* OUP 1990 $64.00. ISBN 0-19-811205-X. Includes the important *Ancrene Wisse.*

Mills, Maldwyn, ed. *Three Middle English Arthurian Romances.* C. E. Tuttle 1992 $10.95. ISBN 0-460-87077-7. Includes *Yvain* and *Gawain.*

Ross, James Bruce, and Mary Martin McLaughlin, eds. *The Portable Medieval Reader.* Viking Penguin 1977 $9.95. ISBN 0-14-015046-3. Includes Middle English and continental poetry, philosophy, and mystical works.

Stone, Brian, trans. *King Arthur's Death.* Viking Penguin 1989 $7.95. ISBN 0-14-044445-9. Translations of the alliterative and stanzaic versions of the Middle English *Morte Arthure.*

Weiss, Judy, ed. *The Birth of Romance: An Anthology.* C. E. Tuttle 1992 $12.95. ISBN 0-460-87048-3. Includes *Haveloc.*
Wolters, Clifton, trans. *The Cloud of Unknowing and Other Works.* Viking Penguin 1978 $5.95. ISBN 0-14-044385-1. Accessible translations of major works of mysticism.

CHRONOLOGY OF AUTHORS AND WORKS

Ballads and Lyrics. 1250–1700
Gower, John. c.1330–1408
Chaucer, Geoffrey. c.1342–1400
Langland, William. fl. 1370–1390

Pearl-Poet. fl. 1390
Kempe, Margery. c.1373–c.1440
Malory, Sir Thomas. fl. 1470

BALLADS AND LYRICS, c.1250–1700

The English ballads (anonymous narrative songs preserved by oral transmission) were probably composed over a period of some 450 years, from about 1250 to 1700; but very few were printed before the eighteenth century, when Bishop Thomas Percy discovered a seventeenth-century manuscript containing a number of ballads and other poems. He published these under the title *Reliques of Ancient English Poetry* in 1765; this volume stimulated an interest in the subject on the part of other writers. Ballads are typically simple in form (normally combining tetrameter quatrains with a repeated refrain), spare, and dramatically tragic in content. The ballads crossed the Atlantic with Scottish and Irish immigrants to America and thrived in various regions of the United States. Middle English lyrics, many composed as songs, date from the thirteenth century and flourished in the fifteenth century, when several manuscript anthologies were written. They are usually divided into two types. Religious lyrics, including Christmas carols, concentrate on the lives of the Virgin Mary and Christ and on preparing the soul to meet death. Secular lyrics are mostly focused on varieties of love, ranging from idealized to erotic, but include debates such as *The Owl and the Nightingale* and historical and political poems.

EDITIONS AND ANTHOLOGIES OF BALLADS AND LYRICS

Early English Lyrics. Ed. by E. K. Chambers and F. Sidgwick. October Hse. 1967 $8.95. ISBN 0-8079-0039-7
English and Scottish Popular Ballads. Ed. by Francis J. Child. Dorset Pr. 1990 o.p.
English and Scottish Popular Ballads. 2 vols. Ed. by George L. Kittredge and C. H. Sargent. Gordon Pr. $250.00 ISBN 0-87968-295-7. Good headnotes.
Faber Book of Ballads. Ed. by Matthew Hodgart. Faber & Faber 1971 o.p.
Lyrics of the Middle Ages: An Anthology. Ed. by James J. Wilhelm. Garland 1990 $50.00. ISBN 0-8240-3345-0. Contains English renderings of nearly 300 lyrics from an impressive range of languages.
Medieval English Lyrics: A Critical Anthology. Ed. by R. T. Davies. Faber & Faber 1987 $11.95. ISBN 0-571-06571-6. Excellent commentary.
Medieval English Verse. Trans. by Brian Stone. Viking Penguin 1964 $5.95. ISBN 0-14-044144-1. Most accessible edition.
Middle English Lyrics. Ed. by Maxwell Luria and Richard Hoffman. Norton 1974 $10.95. ISBN 0-393-09338-7. Wide-ranging selection accompanied by helpful critical essays.
The Oxford Book of Ballads. 1911. Ed. by Arthur Quiller-Couch. OUP 1955 o.p. Only the older ballads. No introduction; some music.
Religious Lyrics of the Thirteenth, Fourteenth, and Fifteenth Centuries. 3 vols. Ed. by Carleton Brown. Gordon Pr. 1932-57 $300.00. ISBN 0-8490-0942-1

A Selection of Religious Lyrics. Ed. by Douglas Gray. OUP 1975 $19.95. ISBN 0-19-871085-2

The Traditional Tunes of the Child Ballads. 4 vols. Ed. by Bertrand H. Bronson. Princeton U. Pr. 1962 $210.00. ISBN 0-685-23096-1. Covers more than the tunes; a valuable supplement to the Francis J. Child edition.

BOOKS ABOUT BALLADS AND LYRICS

Brown, Carleton, and Rossell H. Robbins, eds. *Index of Middle English Verse.* Modern Lang. 1943 $60.00. ISBN 0-87352-017-3. Essential for research on Middle English lyrics.

Dronke, Peter. *The Medieval Lyric.* HarpC 1968 o.p. Best overview of English lyrics within the European tradition.

Fowler, David C. *A Literary History of the Popular Ballad.* Bks. Demand repr. of 1968 ed. $90.00. ISBN 0-317-28961-6. Insightful literary analysis of ballads.

Gummere, Francis B. *The Popular Ballad.* Gordon Pr. $69.95. ISBN 0-87968-285-X. Still valuable overview.

Hodgart, Matthew J. *The Ballads.* Norton 1966 o.p.

CHAUCER, GEOFFREY. c.1342–1400

Chaucer has been called the "Prince of Story-tellers" because of his great narrative skill, his acute penetration, his mixture of humor and somber realism, and his remarkable accuracy in describing the real world. The technical perfection and extraordinary grace of Chaucer's verse are a discovery of recent centuries. Although he borrowed widely from a range of sources throughout his career, for convenience scholars often divide his work into three major periods: French, Italian, and English. In the first he was influenced by the major French poets of the time; the second results from his trip to Italy, and especially the influence of Boccaccio; the final period includes his greatest works, especially *The Canterbury Tales* (1387–1400) and *Troilus and Criseyde* (c.1385). The sources and dates of many Chaucer works remain disputed, nor are all questions of authorship settled.

The Canterbury Tales is one of the world's chief collections of stories. Its sources include contemporary poetry, traditional saints' lives and folktales, and classical narratives; few, if any, are Chaucer's own invention. (Originality was not, at this time, regarded as a literary virtue.) The 24 stories are told by pilgrims journeying on horseback from the Tabard Inn, Southwark, to the shrine of the martyred Saint Thomas of Becket in Canterbury Cathedral. Chaucer never completed his vast scheme, which might have summarized the whole of medieval society. What he did achieve fully justifies Dryden's immortal statement: "Here is God's plenty."

His poems are usually printed today with a glossary, as a key to his Middle English; but his language does not vary from our own nearly so much in vocabulary as in spelling, and reading them in the original is well worth the effort.

Of the *Canterbury Tales,* any list of the best and most popular would include *The Pardoner's Tale, The Wife of Bath's Prologue and Tale, The Merchant's Tale, The Miller's Tale,* and *The Nun's Priest's Tale* (of Chanticleer and the Fox). *Troilus and Criseyde,* a moving romance set during the Trojan War and reflecting the nostalgic codes of chivalry and courtly love, is Chaucer's masterpiece. His other major poems include *The Book of the Duchess,* an elegy in the form of a dream about the death of Blanche, the duchess of Lancaster; *The Parliament of Fowls,* an allegorical dream focusing on the mating rituals of birds; *The House of Fame,* an incomplete vision in which the narrator is carried into the heavens by an eagle; and *The Legend of Good Women*, written, the poet tells us, at the command of the God of Love in recompense for the poet's more jaundiced view of romance in *Troilus and Criseyde* and *The Romance of the Rose*, parts of which Chaucer translated from Old French.

Chaucer is the greatest poet of his age and one of the three or four major figures in the history of English poetry. Modern English derives from the Middle English London dialect in which he wrote. Chaucer created and used two metrical forms: the seven-line stanza, which was later called "rhyme royal" because James I of Scotland used it in *The King's Quair*, and the rhyming, or "heroic," couplet. Chaucer's later and best work was done in such couplets, the form of *The Knight's Tale*, *The Nun's Priest's Tale*, and *The Legend of Good Women*.

Son of a London wine merchant, Chaucer served as a page to Elizabeth, countess of Ulster; as a soldier in Edward's army in France; as a diplomat; and as a government official in various capacities. He is buried in Westminster Abbey, the first to be interred in what has become known as "Poet's Corner."

POEMS BY CHAUCER

The Canterbury Tales. Ed. by A. Kent Hieatt and Constance Hieatt. Bantam 1982 $3.50. ISBN 0-553-21082-3

The Canterbury Tales. Ed. by Donald R. Howard and James M. Dean. NAL-Dutton 1988 $3.50. ISBN 0-451-52400-4

The Canterbury Tales. Trans. by David Wright. *World's Class. Ser.* OUP 1986 $2.95. ISBN 0-19-281597-0

The Canterbury Tales. Trans. by Nevill Coghill. Viking Penguin 1951 $2.95. ISBN 0-14-044022-4

Canterbury Tales: Nine Tales and the General Prologue. Ed. by V. A. Kolve and Glending Olson. Norton 1989 $9.95. ISBN 0-393-95245-2

The Complete Poetry and Prose of Geoffrey Chaucer. Ed. by John H. Fisher. H. Holt & Co. 2nd ed. 1988 $39.00. ISBN 0-03-028612-3. Best student text.

Complete Works. 7 vols. Ed. by Walter W. Skeat. OUP 2nd ed. 1894-1900 $245.00. ISBN 0-19-811314-5. Still the basic text.

The Legend of Good Women. Ed. by Ann McMillan. Rice Univ. 1987 $10.95. ISBN 0-89263-264-X

Love Visions. Trans. by Brian Stone. Viking Penguin 1983 $8.95. ISBN 0-14-044408-4

The Riverside Chaucer. Ed. by Larry D. Benson. HM 1987 $60.00. ISBN 0-395-29031-7. Most complete and annotated one-volume edition.

Troilus and Criseyde. Ed. by Maldwyn Mills. C. E. Tuttle 1974 $8.95. ISBN 0-460-87098-X

Troilus and Criseyde. Trans. by Nevill Coghill. Viking Penguin 1971 $5.95. ISBN 0-14-044239-1

BOOKS ABOUT CHAUCER

Boitani, Piero, and Jill Mann, eds. *The Cambridge Chaucer Companion.* Cambridge U. Pr. 1986 $13.95. ISBN 0-521-31689-8. Valuable essays on all the major poems.

Brewer, Derek, ed. *Chaucer: The Critical Heritage.* 2 vols. *Critical Heritage Ser.* Routledge Chapman & Hall 1978. Vol. 1 $42.50. ISBN 0-7100-0223-8. Vol. 2 $42.50. ISBN 0-7100-0224-6. Most thorough collection of commentary on Chaucer, beginning with the writer's contemporaries.

Cooper, Helen. *Oxford Guides to Chaucer: The Canterbury Tales.* OUP 1991 $19.95. ISBN 0-19-811978-X. The best introduction to Chaucer's most popular work.

――――. *The Structure of the Canterbury Tales.* U. of Ga. Pr. 1983 o.p. Insights into the influences on and thematic reasons for the ordering of the tales and their links.

Dinshaw, Carolyn. *Chaucer's Sexual Poetics.* U. of Wis. Pr. 1990 $15.00. ISBN 0-299-12274-3. First systematic feminist reading of Chaucer; especially good on *Pardoner's Tale*.

Donaldson, E. Talbot. *Speaking of Chaucer*. Labyrinth Pr. 1983 repr. of 1970 ed. $8.95. ISBN 0-939464-15-2. The best example of old-style New Criticism, with compelling readings of characters and narrator.

Fisher, John H., and Mark Allen. *The Essential Chaucer: An Annotated Bibliography of Major Modern Studies*. G. K. Hall 1987 $35.00. ISBN 0-8161-8739-8. The best place to begin a research project.

Hansen, Elaine Tuttle. *Chaucer and the Fictions of Gender*. U. CA Pr. 1992 $42.50. ISBN 0-520-97133-6. A feminist critique of Chaucer and critics who see him as a protofeminist poet countering medieval misogyny.

Howard, Donald R. *Chaucer: His Life, His Works, His World*. Fawcett 1989 $12.95. ISBN 0-449-90341-9. Scans the public and private events of Chaucer's life for their significance to his humanistic art.

_____. *The Idea of the Canterbury Tales*. U. CA Pr. 1976 $10.95. ISBN 0-520-03492-9. One of the best studies of Chaucer, with implications for reading the tales and poem as a unified whole.

Kiser, Lisa J. *Telling Classical Tales: Chaucer and the "Legend of Good Women."* Cornell Univ. Pr. 1983 $22.50. ISBN 0-8014-1601-9. Excellent on Chaucer's use of sources.

Kittredge, George L. *Chaucer and His Poetry*. Intro. by B. J. Whiting. HUP 1970 o.p. A classic study.

Knapp, Peggy. *Chaucer and the Social Context*. Routledge Chapman & Hall 1990 $35.00. ISBN 0-415-90150-2. Excellent study placing the tales within the context of their time; good introduction for students.

Kolve, V. A. *Chaucer and the Imagery of Narrative: The First Five Canterbury Tales*. Stanford U. Pr. 1984 $49.50. ISBN 0-8047-1161-5. A groundbreaking, heavily illustrated iconographic study.

Lumiansky, R. M. *Of Sondry Folke: The Dramatic Principle in the "Canterbury Tales."* U. of Tex. Pr. 1980 $8.95. ISBN 0-292-76019-5. Argues for a reading of the tales as dramatic representations of the storytellers.

Mann, Jill. *Chaucer and Medieval Estates Satire: The Literature of Social Classes and the General Prologue of the Canterbury Tales*. Cambridge U. Pr. 1973 o.p. Best for understanding the pilgrim portraits in *The General Prologue*.

Miller, Robert P., ed. *Chaucer: Sources and Backgrounds*. OUP 1977 $14.95. ISBN 0-19-502167-3. Wide-ranging collection of sources; valuable for backgrounds.

Muscatine, Charles. *Chaucer and the French Tradition*. U. CA Pr. 1957 $11.95. ISBN 0-520-00908-8. Highly influential critical study of Chaucer, still worth reading for its insights on style.

Patterson, Lee. *Chaucer and the Subject of History*. U. of Wis. Pr. 1991 $45.00. ISBN 0-299-12830-X. A new historicist study of Chaucer's career and poetry within late medieval society.

Robertson, D. W. *Preface to Chaucer: Studies in Medieval Perspectives*. Princeton U. Pr. 1962 $24.95. ISBN 0-691-01294-6. The most important historicist study of Chaucer; controversial and insightful, especially on medieval art and religion.

Rowland, Beryl, ed. *Companion to Chaucer Studies*. OUP 1979 $15.95. ISBN 0-19-502489-3. A highly useful introduction, with scholarship by major authorities.

Wagenknecht, Edward, ed. *Chaucer: Modern Essays in Criticism*. OUP 1959 o.p. A useful collection of early critical studies.

Wetherbee, Winthrop. *Chaucer and the Poets: An Essay on Troilus and Criseyde*. Cornell Univ. Pr. 1984 $26.95. ISBN 0-8014-1684-1. The best recent study of Chaucer's masterpiece.

_____. *Chaucer: The Canterbury Tales*. Cambridge U. Pr. 1989 $19.95. ISBN 0-521-32331-2. A handy introductory guide.

Windeatt, Barry A. *Chaucer's Dream Poetry: Sources and Analogues*. Boydell & Brewer 1981 $62.00. ISBN 0-85991-072-5. A useful collection of backgrounds for Chaucer's early poetry.

GOWER, JOHN. c.1330-1408

Best known as "moral Gower," as he is called by his friend Chaucer in the dedication of *Troilus and Criseyde*, Gower composed "balades" in the French fashion as well as three long poems, representing the trilingual status of the cultural and political elite of late fourteenth-century England. *Mirour de l'Homme* (Mirror of Man) (c.1376–78), a mammoth French poem of some 30,000 lines, deals with the seven deadly sins. *Vox Clamantis* (Voice of One Crying) (c.1379–81), in Latin, is a prophetic attack on contemporary political and social abuses in response to the Peasants' Revolt of 1381. Gower's lengthy and occasionally dreary Middle English poem *Confessio Amantis* (Lover's Confession) (1390), portions of which influenced Chaucer, is set as an allegorical confession of the poet-lover to Genius, the priest of Venus. In 34,000 lines, he retells several classical love stories and examples illustrating cupidity and the other deadly sins.

POETRY BY GOWER

Confessio Amantis. Ed. by Russell A. Peck. U. of Toronto Pr. 1981 $14.95. ISBN 0-8020-6438-8. Most accessible edition.

English Works of John Gower. Ed. by G. C. Macauley. 2 vols. *Early Eng. Text Soc.* OUP 1900–01 $27.00 ea. ISBNs 0-19-722530-6, 0-19-722531-4. Standard edition.

The Major Latin Works of John Gower. Trans. by Eric W. Stockton. U. of Wash. Pr. 1962 o.p.

BOOKS ABOUT GOWER

Fisher, John H. *John Gower: Moral Philosopher and Friend of Chaucer.* NYU Pr. 1964 o.p. Still the best study of Gower.

Minnis, A. J., ed. *Gower's Confessio Amantis: Responses and Reassessments.* Boydell & Brewer 1983 $56.00. ISBN 0-85991-142-X. Excellent collection of essays.

Minnis, A. J., and Robert F. Yeager. *John Gower's Poetic: The Search for a New Arion.* Boydell & Brewer 1990 $66.00. ISBN 0-85991-280-9. Good set of essays on Gower's poetic art in its own right.

Yeager, Robert F., ed. *John Gower: Recent Readings.* Medieval Inst. 1989 $35.95. ISBN 0-918720-99-0. Essays that seek to remove Gower from Chaucer's shadow.

KEMPE, MARGERY. c.1373–c.1440

One of the most interesting and eccentric works of "autobiography" in English literature, *The Book of Margery Kempe* is extant in a fifteenth-century manuscript discovered in 1934. Dictated to at least two scribes and written in the third person, it details the personal, social, and spiritual life of Kempe, a woman of great strength and strong will. Often compared with Chaucer's Wife of Bath because of her outspokenness, Kempe, despite bearing fourteen children, became involved in preaching, meditation, and pilgrimages, challenged church authority, and was accused of heresy. Her several visions—especially of the passion of Christ and of his semierotic relationship to her as his "bride"—exemplify one mystical strand of the spirituality of laypersons in the late Middle Ages. The prose, sometimes rambling, is strong and worth comparison with THOMAS MALORY.

PROSE BY KEMPE

The Book of Margery Kempe. Ed. by Sanford B. Meech and Hope Emily Allen. *Early Eng. Text Soc.* OUP 1940 $38.00. ISBN 0-19-722112-9. Standard edition.

The Book of Margery Kempe. Trans. by B. A. Windeatt. Viking Penguin 1986 $8.95. ISBN 0-14-043251-5. Most accessible edition.

The Cell of Self Knowledge: Seven Early English Mystical Treatises. Ed. by John Griffiths. Crossroad NY 1981 $8.95. ISBN 0-8245-0082-2

BOOKS ABOUT KEMPE

Atkinson, Clarissa W. *Mystic and Pilgrim: The "Book" and the World of Margery Kempe.* Cornell Univ. Pr. 1983 $31.95. ISBN 0-8014-1521-7. Best introductory study.

Lochrie, Karma. *Margery Kempe and Translations of the Flesh.* U. of Pa. Pr. 1992 $24.95. ISBN 0-8122-3107-4. Strongly argued feminist study of Kempe.

LANGLAND, WILLIAM. fl. 1370–1390

Little is known of the life of this early English poet, who was a contemporary of Chaucer. Langland represents the height of Middle English alliterative verse. His *Vision of Piers Plowman*, an allegorical and satirical poem in the form of several dreams, survives in many manuscripts, representing three separate versions known as the A, B, and C texts. The A text is about 2,500 lines long (c.1367); the B text (c.1381) continues A, adding about 4,000 lines; the C text (c.1385) is a sometimes extensive revision of B. The poem contains vivid pictures of contemporary life, religious practice, personified moral states, and events from Christian history. It is in two parts: the *Visio*, set in fourteenth-century England, examines the proper use of material possessions and introduces the idealized Christian worker Piers Plowman. The second part, the *Vita*, is traditionally divided into three further sections, examining the inner life of the dreamer, Will; portraying the crucial events of Christian history, including the Crucifixion of Christ and the establishment of the church; and prophesying the apocalyptic end of history and the coming of Antichrist. In the second part, Piers Plowman assumes greater allegorical significance, becoming associated with Jesus and the papacy. *Piers Plowman* is one of the supreme, if also one of the most difficult, medieval poems.

It is not certain who Langland was, whether he was the author of *Piers Plowman*, and if so, whether he was responsible for all three versions. Most scholars, however, now connect him to the poem based upon a brief "autobiographical" passage in the C text. Some 52 manuscripts exist, testifying to the poem's great popularity in the fourteenth and fifteenth centuries; it was also printed in the sixteenth century and interpreted as a proto-Protestant attack on church corruption.

POEMS BY LANGLAND

Piers Plowman: The A Version. Ed. by George Kane. U. CA Pr. 1988 $135.00. ISBN 0-520-06229-9. The standard edition of A text.

Piers Plowman: The B Version. Ed. by George Kane and E. Talbot Donaldson. U. CA Pr. 1988 $145.00. ISBN 0-520-06230-2. The standard edition of B text.

Piers Plowman by William Langland: An Edition of the C-Text. Ed. by Derek Pearsall. U. CA Pr. 1979 $65.00. ISBN 0-520-03793-6. The standard critical edition of C text.

The Vision of Piers Plowman. Trans. by J. F. Goodridge. Viking Penguin 1959 $5.95. ISBN 0-14-044087-9. Prose translation.

The Vision of Piers Plowman: A Complete Edition of the B-Text. Ed. by A. V. C. Schmidt. C. E. Tuttle 1978 $16.95. ISBN 0-460-10571-X. Good classroom edition.

Vision of William Concerning Piers the Plowman, in Three Parallel Texts. 2 vols. Ed. by Walter W. Skeat. OUP 1886 $125.00. ISBN 0-19-811366-8. Still useful for comparing all three versions.

William Langland: Piers Plowman: An Alliterative Verse Translation. Trans. by E. Talbot Donaldson. Norton 1990 $25.00. ISBN 0-393-02772-4. The best translation.

BOOKS ABOUT LANGLAND

Alford, John A. *A Companion to Piers Plowman*. U. CA Pr. 1988 $11.95. ISBN 0-520-06007-5. The essential book on the poem. Superb essays on text, language, and interpretation.

Blanch, Robert J., ed. *Style and Symbolism in Piers Plowman: A Modern Critical Anthology*. Bks. Demand repr. of 1969 ed. $72.50. ISBN 0-317-557-85-8. Good collection of critical essays.

Bloomfield, Morton W. *Piers Plowman as a Fourteenth Century Apocalypse*. Rutgers U. Pr. 1962 o.p. Influential study of the poem's monastic and apocalyptic elements.

Colaianne, A. J. *Piers Plowman: An Annotated Bibliography of Editions and Criticism, 1550–1977*. Garland 1978 o.p.

Donaldson, E. Talbot. *Piers Plowman: The C-Text and Its Poet*. Yale U. Pr. 1959 o.p. Ranges well beyond its title; one of the best studies of Langland.

Fowler, David C. *Piers the Plowman: Literary Relations of the A & B Texts*. U. of Wash. Pr. 1961 $20.00. ISBN 0-295-73879-0. Best study of this complex issue.

Kane, George. *Piers Plowman: The Evidence for Authorship*. Athlone Pr. o.p. Strongest argument for Langland as single author of three versions.

Kerby-Fulton, Kathryn. *Reformist Apocalypticism and Piers Plowman*. Cambridge U. Pr. 1990 $54.95. ISBN 0-521-34298-8. Compelling argument for reading the poem as both apocalyptic and reformist.

Pearsall, Derek. *An Annotated Critical Bibliography of Langland*. U. of Mich Pr. 1990 $42.50. ISBN 0-472-10185-4. Offers solid critical guidance to authoritative editions of *Piers Plowman* and to about 600 significant twentieth-century general and topical studies associated with Langland and the poem.

MALORY, SIR THOMAS. fl. 1470

Sir Thomas Malory's works (consisting of the legends of Sir Lancelot, Sir Gareth, Sir Tristram, and the Holy Grail, as well as the stories of Arthur's coming to the throne, his wars with the Emperor Lucius, and his death) are the most influential expression of Arthurian material in English. The author's sources are principally French romances; his own contributions are substantial, however, and the result is a vigorous and resonant prose. *Le Morte d'Arthur*, finished between March 1469 and March 1470, was first printed in 1485 by William Caxton, the earliest English printer.

Malory is presumed to have been a knight from an old Warwickshire family, who inherited his father's estates about 1433 and spent 20 years of his later life in jail accused of various crimes. The discovery of a manuscript version of *Le Morte d'Arthur* in 1934 in the library of Winchester College supported the identification of Malory the author with Malory the traitor, burglar, and rapist and showed that many of the inconsistencies in the printed text were traceable to the printing house rather than to the author. The most reliable modern version, therefore, is one like Eugène Vinaver's that is based on the Winchester manuscript.

PROSE BY MALORY

King Arthur and His Knights. Ed. by Eugène Vinaver. OUP 1975 $8.95 ISBN 0-19-501905-9

Le Morte d'Arthur. Ed. by D. S. Brewer. Northwestern U. Pr. 1968 $8.95. ISBN 0-8101-0031-2

Le Morte d'Arthur. 2 vols. Ed. by Janet Cowen. Viking Penguin 1970 $4.95 ea. ISBNs 0-14-043043-1, 0-14-043044-X

Le Morte d'Arthur. Ed. by Robert M. Lumiansky. Macmillan 1986 $19.95. ISBN 0-02-022560-1

Le Morte d'Arthur. Trans. by Keith Baines. NAL-Dutton 1962 $5.99. ISBN 0-451-62567-6

The Winchester Malory: A Facsimile. Intro. by N.R. Ker. *Early English Text Soc.* OUP 1976
  o.p.
Works. Ed. by Eugène Vinaver. OUP 2nd ed. 1971 $24.95. ISBN 0-19-281217-3
The Works of Sir Thomas Malory. 3 vols. Ed. by Eugène Vinaver. OUP 3rd rev. ed. 1990.
  Vol. 1 $125.00. ISBN 0-19-812344-2. Vol. 2 $135.00. ISBN 0-19-812345-0. Vol. 3
  $145.00. ISBN 0-19-812346-9

BOOKS ABOUT MALORY

Hicks, Edward. *Sir Thomas Malory: His Turbulent Career—A Biography.* Rprt. Serv. 1992
  repr. of 1928 ed. $69.00. ISBN 0-7812-7186-X. Interesting study of a fascinating life.
Ihle, Sandra N. *Malory's Grail Quest: Invention and Adaptation in Medieval Prose
  Romance* U. of Wis. Pr. 1983 $30.00. ISBN 0-299-09240-2. Excellent on use of French
  sources.
Life, Page W. *Sir Thomas Malory and the Morte d'Arthur: A Survey of Scholarship and
  Annotated Bibliography.* U. Pr. of Va. 1980 $28.50. ISBN 0-8139-0868-X
Lumiansky, Robert M., ed. *Malory's Originality: A Critical Study of Le Morte d'Arthur.* Ayer
  $25.50. ISBN 0-405-10612-2. A standard, still useful study.
Vinaver, Eugène. *The Rise of Romance.* Boydell & Brewer 1984 $50.00. ISBN 0-85991-
  158-6. Best study of *Morte d'Arthur* within its generic context.

THE *PEARL*-POET. fl. 1390

The Pearl is a poet's exquisite lament, depicting a mystical, allegorical vision
set in a garden near the grave of a baby girl, possibly the narrator's daughter
Margaret (from the French *Marguerite,* meaning "pearl" or "daisy," both
symbols of virginity). It is one of four anonymous alliterative poems all in the
same handwriting and in the same difficult West Midland dialect, extant in a
British Museum manuscript. The resemblances among the four poems have
persuaded scholars that they are the work of a single poet, who is sometimes
also called the *Gawain*-Poet.

The four poems differ significantly in genre and subject. *Pearl* is a dream
vision in which the bereft narrator—standing on the lush banks of a river—
converses with the soul of a young maiden, one of the brides of the Lamb in
heaven. It merges theological doctrine with rich descriptions of the visionary
landscape and the New Jerusalem. *Cleanness* and *Patience* are based on Old
Testament stories, including the destruction of Sodom and the story of Jonah.
Sir Gawain and the Green Knight, the gem of medieval English metrical
romances and one of the finest poetic narratives in English, is unrivaled for its
artistic unity, stylistic color, and ability to merge religious sensibility with the
demands of the chivalric code. It tells of the adventures resulting from Gawain's
meeting the challenge of a mysterious Green Knight, who engages the Arthurian
court in a "game" of decapitation.

POEMS BY THE *PEARL*-POET

Pearl: A New Verse Translation. Trans. by Marie Borroff. Norton 1977 $5.95. ISBN 0-393-
  09144-9
Pearl Poems: An Omnibus Edition. 2 vols. Ed. by William Vantuono. Garland 1984. o.p.
The Poems of the Pearl Manuscript. Ed. by Malcolm Andrew and Ronald Waldron. U. CA
  Pr. 1979 $16.95. ISBN 0-520-04631-5
Sir Gawain and the Green Knight. Trans. by Marie Borroff. Norton 1967 $3.95. ISBN 0-
  393-09754-4. The best translation.
Sir Gawain and the Green Knight. Trans. by Burton Raffel. NAL-Dutton 1970 $2.50. ISBN
  0-451-62456-4
Sir Gawain and the Green Knight, Pearl, Cleanness, Patience. Ed. by A. C. Cawley and J. J.
  Anderson. C. E. Tuttle 1991 $6.95. ISBN 0-460-87101-3

Books about the *Pearl*-Poet

Benson, Larry. *Art and Tradition in Sir Gawain and the Green Knight*. Rutgers U. Pr. 1965
o.p. Perhaps the best book on the subject.

Blanch, Robert J. *Sir Gawain and Pearl: Critical Essays*. Ind. U. Pr. 1966 o.p. Excellent
collection of essays.

Burrow, J. A. *A Reading of Sir Gawain and the Green Knight*. Routledge 1965 o.p.
Analyzes the poem section by section, using many allusions to other literature, and
many quotations.

Howard, Donald R., and Christian K. Zacher, eds. *Critical Studies of Sir Gawain and the
Green Knight*. U. of Notre Dame Pr. 1968 o.p. A collection of critical essays written
since 1960.

Miller, Miriam Youngerman, and Jane Chance, eds. *Approaches to Teaching Sir Gawain
and the Green Knight*. Modern Lang. 1986 $34.00. ISBN 0-87352-491-8. Good
introduction and essays on contexts and language.

Spearing, A. C. *The Gawain-Poet*. Cambridge U. Pr. 1976 $14.95. ISBN 0-521-29119-4. A
discussion of *Pearl, Cleanness, Patience,* and *Sir Gawain*, beginning with a general
study of the whole group, followed by an analysis of each one individually.

Stanbury, Sarah. *Seeing the Gawain-Poet: Description and the Act of Perception*. U. of Pa.
Pr. 1992 $22.95. ISBN 0-8122-3109-0. Draws on aesthetics, narrative theory, and
iconographics to elucidate these highly visual poems.

MEDIEVAL DRAMA

Beginning in late tenth-century Winchester as a local development of an
Easter ritual, medieval drama in England was at first Latin and liturgical and
limited to monasteries. It commemorated the Nativity, the Crucifixion, and the
Resurrection of Christ and, starting in the twelfth century, other scenes
celebrated by the liturgy of the medieval Christian church. The relationship
between this early Latin drama and later vernacular drama is uncertain.
Scholars have rejected arguments that the liturgical plays developed into large
cycles and that they were simply translated into the vernacular because there is
no evidence of such evolution. Nevertheless, the various forms of drama are
clearly related by their subject matter and occasionally by their dialogue; this is
so because the emphasis upon events central to Christian theology remained a
feature of medieval drama throughout its history, and the Bible and brief
selections from church liturgy continued to influence the plots and dialogues of
later plays. In any case, by the late fourteenth century, a popular vernacular
drama, now distinct from church ceremony and produced for the general
populace, had emerged, as is known from Chaucer's allusion in *The Miller's Tale*
to Absalom playing Herod on stage: "Somtyme, to shewe his lightnesse and
maistrye, / He pleyeth Herodes upon a scaffold hye."

The cycle plays, usually staged by amateurs outdoors, sometimes on pageant
wagons or on stationary scaffolds, were extremely popular in the fifteenth
century. They represented a series of plays linked in a full-day cycle by their
biblically based plots. Although the cycles concentrated on the life of Christ,
they traced all human history from Creation to the Last Judgment and usually
included scenes drawn from each of the seven ages of world history, a common
means of structuring the past evident in medieval historiography. Receiving
strong civic support, they flourished into the mid-sixteenth century. The biblical
plays were joined, in the fifteenth century, by miracle and morality drama.
These were not staged as cycles but were distinct plays teaching moral and
doctrinal truths and celebrating the lives of Christian saints. All these forms of

medieval drama, although religious, included much comic action and occasional blasphemy and obscenity, usually associated with devils and other evil characters such as Cain and Herod. In addition to these major genres of medieval drama, a tradition of theater evolved in Cornwall. The extant texts, in Cornish—a Celtic language now extinct—are also cyclical, once again concentrating on the Passion of Christ. Finally, other dramatic entertainments during the Middle Ages were secular. These included mummings, disguisings, masques, and interludes, folk festivals, and various forms of civic pageantry such as processions and other spectacles. While texts for these dramatic forms do not survive, some contemporary descriptions are extant.

The growing professionalism of medieval drama is evident in fifteenth-century records. These records reveal that payments were made to actors who played important roles, such as those of Christ and Mary. The collection of fees by the actors in *Mankind* provides similar evidence. The actors extract payment from the audience before Titivillus comes on stage: "We shall gather mony onto—Ellys ther shall no man him se." The form of the morality plays particularly influenced later Tudor drama, as is evident in the plays of JOHN BALE, who manipulated the morality form to further his Protestant polemic. Their concern with moral dilemmas could also be transformed into an emphasis on ethical and civic virtues, thus moving drama toward the more secular theater of the Elizabethan age. The influence of their personified characters remains in the presentation of the Seven Deadly Sins in CHRISTOPHER MARLOWE's *Dr. Faustus* (c.1588), and scholars have noted the similarity between the demonic evil of Iago in Shakespeare's *Othello* and the vice figures of late medieval moralities. All forms of medieval drama have been successfully revived in the twentieth century.

History and Criticism

Bevington, David, ed. *Homo, Memento Finis: The Iconography of Just Judgment in Medieval Art and Drama*. Medieval Inst. 1985 $22.95. ISBN 0-918720-60-5. Essays dealing with liturgical, cycle, and moral plays in relation to the visual arts.

Briscoe, Marianne G., and John C. Coldewey, eds. *Contexts for Early English Drama*. Ind. U. Pr. 1989 $29.95. ISBN 0-253-31413-5. Excellent collection of essays on urban, artistic, religious, and social contexts.

Davidson, Clifford, ed. *Drama in the Middle Ages: Comparative and Critical Essays*. AMS Pr. 1982 $39.50. ISBN 0-404-61434-5. Includes important critical essays.

Emmerson, Richard. *Approaches to Teaching Medieval English Drama*. Modern Lang. 1990 $34.00. ISBN 0-87352-531-0. Seventeen essays on medieval drama, including theatrical and literary aspects.

Hardison, O. B., Jr. *Christian Rite and Christian Drama in the Middle Ages*. Johns Hopkins 1983 repr. of 1965 ed. $65.00. ISBN 0-313-24121-X. A major study of medieval drama, arguing against the evolutionary development of drama from Latin to vernacular.

Simon, Eckehard, ed. *The Theatre of Medieval Europe: New Research in Early Drama*. Cambridge U. Pr. 1991 $54.95. ISBN 0-521-38514-8. Essays surveying scholarship on medieval drama.

Stratman, Carl J., ed. *Bibliography of Medieval Drama*. Continuum 1972 o.p. Still helpful, although dated.

Tydeman, William. *The Theatre in the Middle Ages*. Cambridge U. Pr. 1979 $52.50. ISBN 0-521-21891-8. Emphasizes theatrical traditions rather than literary; good on continental as well as English drama.

Wickham, Glynne. *The Medieval Theatre*. Cambridge U. Pr. 1987 $54.95. ISBN 0-521-32069-0. Particularly valuable on forms of secular drama.
_____. *Early English Stages*. 3 vols. Col. U. Pr. Vol. 1 1959 $20.00. ISBN 0-231-08935-X. Vol. 2 1963 $77.00. ISBN 0-231-08936-8. Vol. 3 1981 $77.00. ISBN 0-231-08938-4. Best on staging.

Collections

Bevington, David, ed. *Medieval Drama*. HM 1975 $48.76. ISBN 0-395-13915-5. Best student edition, with translations of liturgical and continental plays.
Cawley, A. C., ed. *Everyman and Medieval Miracle Plays*. C. E. Tuttle 1991 $5.95. ISBN 0-460-87032-7. Most accessible anthology.
Gassner, John, ed. *Medieval and Tudor Drama*. Applause Theatre Bk. Pubs. 1987 $10.95. ISBN 0-936839-84-8. Twenty-four plays, including the Cornish Passion play.

CHRONOLOGY

Cycle Plays. c.1370–c.1570
Morality Plays. c.1415–c.1550
Miracle Plays. fl. fifteenth century

CYCLE PLAYS. c.1370–c.1570.

Emerging in the fourteenth century and flourishing in the fifteenth and sixteenth centuries until the political rise of puritanical Protestantism led to their suppression, the cycle plays were a series of biblical, apocryphal, and other religious pageants arranged historically and ranging from the Fall of Lucifer and the creation of Adam and Eve to the arrival of Antichrist and the Last Judgment. They are also called "mystery plays" (after the French *mystère*), "craft plays" (they were often produced by the craft or trade guilds), and Corpus Christi plays (they were sometimes staged on the annual feast of Corpus Christi in late May or early June). The feast of Corpus Christi—which celebrates not only the "body of Christ" but also all members of the body of Christ, or the church throughout history—may have provided the impetus for these plays through its ritual processions and pageants. In most cases, however, the plays were staged by civic, guild, or other secular organizations; their records, especially in Chester and York, reveal that the cycles were of great financial and political importance and were considered a way not only to praise God but also to bring renown to their cities.

Cycle plays were particularly popular in the Midlands and East Anglia. Although fragments are known from Coventry, Norwich, and Newcastle, only four major cycles are extant in nearly complete form. The largest is from York, one of the most important late medieval cities; it has revived the plays regularly since 1952. The *York Cycle* comprises 48 pageants, some of which, including the Crucifixion, were revised by an anonymous late medieval playwright. He is known as the "York Realist," and his plays emphasize realistic settings and colloquial speech. The *Chester Cycle*, which includes twenty-four pageants staged on three days over Whitsuntide (Feast of Pentecost), is the smallest cycle and the only one extant in more than one manuscript, some dating into the early seventeenth century and reflecting the influence of religious reform. The *Towneley Plays*, named for a former owner of the manuscript, are sometimes called the Wakefield cycle because of their possible connection with the town of Wakefield in Yorkshire, but this provenance is strongly disputed. Some of the 32 pageants were borrowed from York. Several were later revised by the so-called Wakefield Master, who is best known for bawdy and blasphemous dialogue, use of anachronisms and localisms, and expressions of complaints from the rural poor. *The Second Shepherd's Play* is his masterpiece and probably the most famous medieval cycle play. It introduces a traditional Nativity scene by parodying Mary, Joseph, and the Christ child in the characters of a sheep stealer, his duplicitous wife, and a real lamb. The fourth cycle, the *N-Town Play*, is associated with the East Midlands and East Anglia. The manuscript includes a "Banns," the announcement of a forthcoming performance, which states that it will be performed in "N Town." This suggests that the cycle was produced by a touring company that would announce the "Name" of the town where it would next be staged. Its 43 pageants focus on the life of the Virgin Mary.

Editions of Cycle Plays

The Chester Mystery Cycle. Ed. by R. M. Lumiansky and David Mills. *Early Eng. Text Soc. Ser.* OUP Vol. 1 1975 $36.00. ISBN 0-19-722403-2. Vol. 2 1985 $39.95. ISBN 0-19-722408-3. Standard critical edition.

The Chester Mystery Cycle: A New Edition with Modernized Spelling. Ed. by David Mills. Colleagues Pr. Inc. 1992 $38.00. ISBN 0-937191-29-9. Excellent student edition in modernized English.

English Mystery Plays. Ed. by Peter Happé. Viking Penguin 1976 $9.95. ISBN 0-14-043093-8. Thirty-eight plays selected from all four cycles.

The N-Town Play. 2 vols. Ed. by Stephen Spector. *Early Eng. Text Soc.* OUP 1992. Vol. 1 $59.00. ISBN 0-19-0722411-3. Vol. 2 $45.00. ISBN 0-19-722412-1. Standard critical edition.

The Wakefield Mystery Plays. Ed. by Martial Rose. Norton 1969 $12.95. ISBN 0-393-00483-X. Acting edition, modernized, with some editorial changes.

The Wakefield Pageants in the Towneley Cycle. Ed. by A. C. Cawley. Manchester Univ. Pr. 1958 o.p. Helpful notes and introduction.

York Mystery Plays: A Selection in Modern Spelling. Ed. by Richard Beadle and Pamela King. OUP 1984 $16.95. ISBN 0-19-811197-5. Good student edition.

Books about Cycle Plays

Davidson, Clifford. *From Creation to Doom: The York Cycle of Mystery Plays.* AMS Pr. 1984 $39.50. ISBN 0-404-61435-3. Good on visual elements in plays.

Diller, Hans-Jurgen. *The Middle English Mystery Play: A Study in Dramatic Speech and Form.* Cambridge U. Pr. 1992 $69.95. ISBN 0-521-32062-3. Emphasizes dramatic features of the plays, especially speeches, prayers, and dialogues.

Elliott, John R., Jr. *Playing God: Medieval Mysteries on the Modern Stage.* U. of Toronto Pr. 1989 $45.00. ISBN 0-8020-5606-7. Best study of the history of postmedieval productions.

Gibson, Gail McMurray. *The Theater of Devotion: East Anglian Drama and Society in the Late Middle Ages.* U. Ch. Pr. 1989 $34.95. ISBN 0-226-29101-4. Best study of social and religious contexts.

Kolve, V. A. *The Play Called Corpus Christi.* Stanford U. Pr. 1966 $39.95. ISBN 0-8047-0277-2. Most influential study of cycle plays; highly recommended.

Lumiansky, R. M., and David Mills, eds. *The Chester Mystery Cycle: Essays and Documents.* U. of NC Pr. 1983 o.p. Excellent collection of primary documents.

Stevens, Martin. *Four Middle English Mystery Cycles: Textual, Contextual, and Critical Interpretations.* Princeton U. Pr. 1987 $50.00. ISBN 0-691-06714-7. Best recent study of all four cycles; emphasizes their literary and dramatic unity.

Travis, Peter W. *Dramatic Design in the Chester Cycle.* U. Ch. Pr. 1982 $20.00. ISBN 0-226-81164-6. Best study of Chester.

Woolf, Rosemary. *The English Mystery Plays*. U. CA Pr. 1980 $13.95. ISBN 0-520-04081-3.
Excellent readings of individual plays drawn from all cycles.

MIRACLE PLAYS fl. fifteenth century

Also known as conversion plays or saints plays, because of their emphasis upon the conversions and lives of saints, these dramas were particularly popular in the late Middle Ages when they were often lengthy and elaborately staged. Developing romantic and sensational plots, they often depicted the confrontation between Christians and unbelievers. Many are continental, but three Middle English miracle plays are well known. *The Conversion of Saint Paul*, extant in a later fifteenth-century manuscript from the East Midlands that includes *Mary Magdalene* and other plays, enacts Saul's opposition to early Christianity and his spectacular conversion, when he was renamed Paul. *Mary Magdalene*, the most complex, in 2,144 lines mixes biblical and legendary sources to trace Mary's life from her aristocratic origins and her temptation by Satan, the World, and the Flesh, to her conversion and ultimate sainthood, including her voyage across the Mediterranean to convert to Christianity the king of Marseilles and ultimately all France. *The Play of the Sacrament* (c.1465) stages a miracle that was supposed to have occurred in 1461. It is intended to convince unbelievers that the bread of the Mass really represents the Body of Christ.

EDITIONS OF MIRACLE PLAYS

The Digby Plays. Ed. by F. J. Furnivall. *Early Eng. Text Soc*. Kraus 1967 $15.00. ISBN 0-685-09932-6
The Late Medieval Plays of Bodleian MSS Digby 133 and e Museo 160. Ed. by Donald C. Baker and others. *Early Eng. Text Soc*. OUP 1982 o.p.
Non-Cycle Plays and Fragments. Ed. by Norman Davis. *Early Eng. Text Soc*. OUP 1970 o.p.

BOOK ABOUT MIRACLE PLAYS

Davidson, Clifford, ed. *The Saint Play in Medieval Europe*. Medieval Inst. 1987 $25.95. ISBN 0-918720-77-X. Includes lengthy essay on Middle English plays.

MORALITY PLAYS c.1415–c.1550

From the early fifteenth century to the mid-sixteenth century, morality plays were the most direct medieval dramatic predecessors of the masterpieces of the Elizabethan theater. Also known as moral plays, these elaborately staged and often lengthy dramas probably were produced in the round, using colorful costumes, several stages, and much movement, mime, and vigorous action. The plays present the dialogue and combat of several allegorical and supernatural characters. The protagonist usually represents all Christians in a personified form, such as Anima, Everyman, Human Nature, or Mankind. Numerous antagonists include the Seven Deadly Sins, the Flesh, World, and Satan, and demons, whose comic antics provide great entertainment. Fewer good characters support the protagonist, but they are always victorious; they include the Seven Virtues, angels, Good Deeds, and God and variations such as Wisdom. Three moralities are extant in the East Anglian Macro manuscript now in the Folger Library. They include the most complex and earliest full-fledged morality, *The Castle of Perseverance*, which has 35 speaking parts and in 3,650 lines traces the entire life of Mankind. It is accompanied by an enigmatic stage diagram that suggests that the play was staged in the round. The most humorous morality, *Mankind* (c.1465–70), stages the frustrations of a farmer tempted by a particularly witty vice named Titivillus. Apparently very popular and requiring only six actors, it is one of the first plays known to have been produced by an itinerant troup of professional performers. The third of the Macro moralities, recently revived successfully, is *Wisdom*, which stresses much pomp and circumstance. The best known, but least typical, moral play is *Everyman*, which dates from around 1495. One of the first plays published in England, it may be based on a Dutch original. Its highly formal and somber mood reflects the late medieval "arts of dying," which underscored the need to prepare to meet death.

EDITIONS OF MORALITY PLAYS

Early English Drama: An Anthology. Ed. by John C. Coldewey. Garland 1992 o.p. Morality and noncycle plays.

Everyman. Ed. by Geoffrey Cooper and Christopher Wortham. Intl. Spec. Bk. 1980 $8.95. ISBN 0-85564-167-3. Excellent introduction and commentary.

Four Morality Plays. Ed. by Peter Happé. Viking Penguin 1987 o.p. Includes *Castle of Perseverance*.

Macro Plays. Ed. by David Bevington. Folger Bks. 1972 $42.00. ISBN 0-686-16149-1. Facsimile of the important Macro manuscript.

The Macro Plays: The Castle of Perseverance, Wisdom, Mankind. Ed. by Mark Eccles. *Early Eng. Text Soc.* OUP 1969 o.p. Standard critical edition.

BOOKS ABOUT MORALITY PLAYS

Bevington, David M. *From Mankind to Marlowe: Growth of Structure in the Popular Drama of Tudor England*. HUP 1962 o.p. Remains the best study of the relation between moralities and later Tudor drama.

Kelley, Michael R. *Flamboyant Drama: A Study of "The Castle of Perseverance," "Mankind," and "Wisdom"*. S. Ill. U. Pr. 1979 $12.95. ISBN 0-8083-0915-7. Argues a relation between morality plays and the late Gothic flamboyant style.

Potter, Robert. *The English Morality Play*. Routledge 1975 o.p. Still the best study of the genre.

Riggio, Milla Cozart. *The Play of Wisdom: Its Texts and Contexts*. AMS Pr. 1986 $32.50. ISBN 0-404-61444-2. First full study of the play.

_____, ed. *The Wisdom Symposium*. AMS Pr. 1986 $32.50. ISBN 0-404-61441-8. Essays on contexts, staging, and themes.

Schell, Edgar. *Strangers and Pilgrims: From the Castle of Perseverance to King Lear*. U. Ch. Pr. 1983 $22.50. ISBN 0-226-73673-3. Good thematic readings of the major moralities.

Southern, Richard. *Medieval Theatre in the Round*. Theatre Arts Bks. 1975 $25.00. ISBN 0-87830-085-6. Controversial, but still one of the best studies of medieval staging.

CHAPTER 6

Renaissance Literature

Claire McEachern

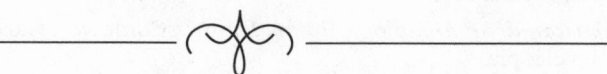

> They are never alone that are accompanied, with noble thoughts.
> —SIR PHILIP SIDNEY, *Arcadia, Book I*

Generously defined, "the Renaissance" of English literature spans a period of 175 years, from 1485 to 1660: From the accession of Henry VII to that of Charles II; from authors JOHN SKELTON to JOHN MILTON. In between these points lies what has been considered England's most striking cultural revolution. In concurring with such a definition of this nearly two-century span, we collaborate with the self-description of writers of the age to describe it as unique. For as C. S. LEWIS (see also Vol. 4) remarks, "our legend of the Renaissance is itself a Renaissance legend." Such an impulse had its roots in a complex web of cultural, material, and ideological circumstances.

With the end of the Wars of the Roses, the island we now call Great Britain had been made safe for new forms of literary production. The victory of Henry VII brought not only an end to a century of civil war but also the beginnings of a centralized state apparatus focused in and by the royal court. The relatively peaceful successions within this monarchic family allowed such centralization to be elaborated and bureaucratically implemented. The coincidental invention of the printing press in the late fifteenth century provided the mechanism by which a market for literature was both created and satisfied. This literal machinery of reading and writing collaborated with the Reformation's emphasis on the crucial role of the vernacular text—and "the Word"—in the development of an individual's moral and political identity. Finally, the urban center of London helped provide a pool of both writers and readers of the new textual production, while the diversification of the economy made possible, for members of increasingly varied social statuses, the leisure time to consume the results of proliferating textual practices.

Perhaps even more important, for the development of a lively and vigorous national literary culture, than a certain political stability was the existence of political contest. Political anxieties permeate Tudor and Stuart rules, whether about internal rebellion or external invasion. With reliance of the aristocracy on the wool trade came the dislocation of husbandry and farmers in favor of sheep, and thus enclosure riots. Inflation spirals, famine, and frequent plague also contributed to the contradiction of an official propaganda that held a hierarchical social order to be a natural and beneficent divinely ordained patriarchy. The split of the English church from the papacy created a powerful site of ideological turbulence whose effects were to be felt through the next set of civil wars and beyond. Monarchs throughout the sixteenth and seventeenth centuries viewed the national church as a potential organ for the consolidation of official goals. *The Book of Common Prayer* (1547), for instance, prescribed a uniform order of ritual reading to be implemented throughout the polity, "so that," in the words of one royal proclamation, "every one of his Majesty's loving subjects . . . learn thereby to observe God's commandments, and to obey their sovereign lord and high powers, without murmur or grudgings." However, at the same time, and with increasing vociferousness throughout the next century, individual reformers viewed the proliferation of the Word as providing a vocabulary for the individual regulation and investigation of selfhood. In conjunction with the official dissolution of the Roman Catholic institutional apparatuses for the regulation of personal identity (such as confession and pardons), such individuality produced both an exhilarating and frightening departure from traditional vocabularies of personhood and salvation. The effects of such a departure collaborated, in turn, to produce the social schisms of the English Revolution.

Renaissance means "rebirth." Appropriately enough for a description of a cultural movement largely reliant on the importation of foreign models, it is a French-derived term. Coincidental to England's developing internal cultural coherence was, of course, its articulation of relationship to other cultures, both contemporary (those of the Continent and the "new" world of the Americas) and ancient. While the Renaissance—the importation, through translation and imitation, of the texts and conventions of classical civilization—came relatively late to provincial England, it came with a vengeance. As early as 1548, JOHN BALE compiled his catalog *Illustrium Maioris Britanniae Scriptorum . . . Summarium* to publicize his country's literary riches to the world in the language of international community. *Tottel's Miscellany* (1559) marked the first poetry anthology of the age, in which the "courtly makers" WYATT and Surrey could be read to signal, in their translations of PETRARCH (see Vol. 2), England's recognition of the fourteenth-century Italian appropriation of classical tropes. By 1579, EDMUND SPENSER prefaced his Vergilian-inspired pastoral *The Shepheardes Calendar* with an assertion that "our Mother tongue . . . truly of itself is both full enough for prose and stately enough for verse." And by 1589, George Puttenham, in his *Arte of English Poesie*, announced one of the first canons of English literature "so that their names should not be defrauded of such honour as seemeth due to them for having by their thankefull studies so much beautified our English tongue, as at this day it will be found our nation is nothing inferior to the French or the Italian."

Hand in hand with such self-consciousness about the competitive status of English language went an increasing consciousness, and curiosity, about the relationship of language and the self. The proliferation of imaginative literature, in combination with the Protestant emphasis on the importance of the individual's attention to the state of his or her own soul, helped to invent new vocabularies of interiority in which the role of the text was central. When SIR PHILIP SIDNEY wrote, in his *Apology for Poesy* (1589), that literature "nothing affirmeth, and therefore never lieth", he displayed a defensiveness about literature's function as a moral tool; when he claimed that poetry excelled both history and philosophy as a teacher of virtue, he demonstrated conviction of the essential role of literature in the development of moral identity. With such reliance on textuality comes a double-edged freedom: The "Renaissance man" denoted an ideal of discovery and the power of self-invention, coupled with a disturbing consciousness of the fragile, artificial, and isolating limits of such autonomy. "Renaissance woman" tended to be almost exclusively an invention of a male imagination; in recent years, there has been a renaissance of the work of the period's female authors, such as Katherine Parr, Aemilia Lanyer, Mary

Sidney, and Mary Wroth, although, unfortunately, most of their work remains unavailable in modern editions.

Sidney's attempt to describe and defend the function of imaginative literature reveals a notion of it as something different from other kinds of writing. Yet Renaissance literature takes many forms, and a modern understanding of the term can deny the extent to which many kinds of texts in this period engaged the efforts of writers. In addition to the diversity of literary genres, such as lyric, pastoral, or epic, were extrafictional ones: Sermons, polemical tracts, histories, and official propaganda are among the many other forms in which Renaissance authors worked. If assiduous in search of patrons, few made their living by their fictional pens alone. Many were civil servants; others were preachers; and an anomalous few, usually dramatists, survived (often just barely) as professional writers. Complementing this range of genres is the array of social stations from which writers emerged. While many were aristocrats, and poetry writing the marker of a specific class location, what is perhaps truly remarkable about the English Renaissance is the degree to which nonaristocratic authors were capable of aspiring to an audience.

POETRY

Perhaps most important to an understanding of Renaissance poetry is the notion of genre: the literary convention, or pattern, or gesture, that imports an authorial posture, an ideological location, and a set of affective expectations. For Tudor-Stuart authors, genres functioned as codes to signal both their acknowledgment and self-inscriptions within literary tradition, and simultaneously their departure from it. For instance, a sonnet (little song) typically signaled the poetry of love in a compact 14-line structure, its speaker often a disaffected or disappointed suitor of, in the tradition inherited from the Italian PETRARCH (see Vol. 2), a remote and ideal mistress. The pastoral, a fashionable form among aristocrats (and would-be aristocrats) at the turn of the century, usually celebrated rural life and condemned a courtly one in the songs of rather eloquent shepherds. In a more serious vein, there was the epic, with its glorification of military and chivalric values, its length, and its civilization-founding narrative. Much of English writers' approaches to the classical norms of genre involved a subtle tension between imitation and originality. The earliest writers, as well as the late ones, often engage in translations, such as WYATT's of PETRARCH (see Vol. 2), or JOHNSON's of CATULLUS (see Vol. 2); yet, at the other extreme, authors could aggressively signal their transformation of ancient models, and MILTON's *Paradise Lost* (1667, 1674) redefines the epic as a rejection of the military valor of the fallen angels in favor of the moral fortitude of humankind.

Poetry tended to be a gentleman's activity: Some poetry, like that of SIDNEY, was written for circulation among a coterie of friends and acquaintances who would have been more able than ourselves to read between its lines. Indeed, a crucial presence in a great deal of the poetry of this age is that of the court and its inhabitants, whether as patrons or audience. Echoes of court power and ambition can be read in the disappointed but ambitious verses of the sonneteers; and particularly during Elizabeth's reign, the monarch herself appeared both as audience and subject of poetry. SPENSER, for instance, dedicated his unfinished epic *The Faerie Queene* (1590) to the ruler and refers to her allegorically throughout. Poets were fond of proclaiming the relevance of poetry to the social order; and in keeping with their self-conscious articulation of a national literary culture, they made much of the medieval inheritance of literary styles and forms such as allegory, personification, and a self-consciously native dialect and orthography.

By the seventeenth century, England had accumulated its own body of recent literary tradition to act as both spur and guide to further invention. With the death of Elizabeth and the accession of the Stuart monarchs, and ultimately the civil wars, came both an idealized nostalgia for the first flower of Tudor literary production and a darker sensibility of the poetic self.

Sixteenth Century—History and Criticism

Bush, Douglas. *Mythology and the Renaissance Tradition in English Poetry*. HUP rev. ed. o.p. Masterful studies of a crucial subject.

Colie, Rosalie B. *The Resources of Kind: Genre-Theory in the Renaissance*. U. CA Pr. 1974 $47.50. ISBN 0-520-02397-8. A study of the roles of literary convention in the period.

Ferguson, Margaret, and others, eds. *Rewriting the Renaissance: The Discourses of Sexual Difference in Early Modern Europe*. U. Ch. Pr. 1986 $50.00. ISBN 0-226-24313-3. A seminal collection of essays about literature's exploration of conventions of gender.

Ferry, Anne. *The "Inward" Language: Sonnets of Wyatt, Sidney, Shakespeare and Donne*. U. Ch. Pr. 1983 $25.00. ISBN 0-226-24466-0. A study of the sonnet and the elaboration of vocabularies of interiority.

Greenblatt, Stephen J. *Renaissance Self-Fashioning: From More to Shakespeare*. U. Ch. Pr. 1983 $12.95. ISBN 0-226-30654-2. An important study of six authors (More, Tyndale, Wyatt, Spenser, Marlowe, and Shakespeare) in the context of systems of cultural power.

Helgerson, Richard. *The Elizabethan Prodigals*. U. CA Pr. 1977 $37.50. ISBN 0-520-03264-0. A study of England's inaugural generation of Renaissance authors.

———. *Self-Crowned Laureates: Spenser, Jonson, and the Literary System*. U. CA Pr. 1983 $37.50. ISBN 0-520-04808-3. A study of the literary invention of categories of authorship.

Lewis, Clive S. *English Literature in the Sixteenth Century (Excluding Drama)*. Oxford History of Eng. Lit. Ser. OUP 1954 o.p. The standard literary history of the period.

Smith, Hallett D. *Elizabethan Poetry: A Study in Conventions, Meaning, and Expression*. Bks. Demand repr. of 1952 ed. $98.10. ISBN 0-7837-1725-3. Probably the best general survey.

Tuve, Rosemond. *Elizabethan and Metaphysical Imagery*. U. Ch. Pr. 1961 o.p. A study of common habits of symbolism.

Sixteenth Century—Collections

Auden, W. H. *An Elizabethan Song Book*. Ed. by Noah Greenberg. Faber & Faber 1968 o.p. Unique for the poet's later views of Elizabethan work.

Jones, Emrys, ed. *The New Oxford Book of Sixteenth-Century Verse*. OUP 1992 $16.95. ISBN 0-19-282971-8. A useful anthology.

Rollins, H. E., ed. *Tottel's Miscellany, 1557–1587*. 2 vols. HUP 1965 $50.00. ISBN 0-674-89610-6. The inaugural anthology of Renaissance poetry, including the work of Wyatt and Surrey, among others.

Sylvester, Richard S., ed. *Anchor Anthology of Sixteenth-Century Verse*. Peter Smith $18.25. ISBN 0-8446-5087-0. A collection of verse by lesser, as well as well-known, authors.

Seventeenth Century—History and Criticism

Bennett, Joan. *Five Metaphysical Poets: Donne, Herbert, Vaughan, Crashaw, Marvell*. Cambridge U. Pr. 1934 $32.50. ISBN 0-521-04156-2. An influential study of common themes.

Bradbury, Malcolm, and David Palmer, eds. *Metaphysical Poetry*. Crane Russak & Co. 1970 o.p.

Bush, Douglas. *The Earlier Seventeenth Century, 1600–1660*. Oxford History of Engl. Lit. Ser. OUP 1990 $59.00. ISBN 0-19-812233-0. A masterful analysis.

Cruttwell, Patrick. *The Shakespearian Moment and Its Place in the Poetry of the Seventeenth Century*. Col. U. Pr. 1954 o.p. A discussion of the common style and mood of Shakespeare and Donne.

Keast, William R., ed. *Seventeenth-Century English Poetry*. OUP 1971 o.p. Twenty-nine essays discussing seventeenth-century poetry generally, and the major poets of the era, exclusive of Milton.

Lewalski, Barbara. *Protestant Poetics and the Seventeenth-Century Religious Lyric*. Bks. Demand repr. of 1979 ed. $146.40. ISBN 0-8357-4284-9. A study of the influence of a common context of religious belief upon genre, language, and symbolism.

Martz, Louis. *The Poetry of Meditation: A Study of English Religious Literature of the Seventeenth Century*. Bks. Demand repr. of 1962 ed. $105.30. ISBN 0-8357-8272-7. A study of the meditative sensibility of Donne and his school.

Seventeenth Century—Collections

Fowler, Alistair, ed. *The New Oxford Book of Seventeenth-Century Verse*. OUP 1992 $39.95. ISBN 0-19-214164-3. A convenient collection of verse by a range of writers.

Gardner, Helen. *The Metaphysical Poets*. Penguin Poets Ser. Viking Penguin 1960 $6.95. ISBN 0-14-042038-X. More than 200 poems by some 40 poets, among them Donne, Herbert, Crashaw, Vaughan; provides explanatory and biographical notes.

Lewalski, Barbara K., and A. J. Sabol, eds. *Major Poets of the Earlier Seventeenth Century*. Bobbs 1973 o.p. Copious selections from Donne, Herbert, Vaughan, Crashaw, Jonson, Herrick, and Marvell.

Sylvester, R. S., ed. 2 vols. *The Anchor Anthology of Sixteenth Century Verse*. Peter Smith. $18.95 ISBN 0-8446-5087-0. A collection of verse by lesser, as well as well-known, authors.

PROSE FICTION

As the compound term betrays, *prose fiction* is an unwieldy accommodation of a modern taxonomy to an earlier period. The novel as we acknowledge it, with its conventions of character, plot, and structure, did not develop until the eighteenth century, and much of the prose of the Renaissance was not what we would consider fictional: The sermon, the history, the rhetorical oration, and the essay were among its governing forms; JOHN DONNE, John Foxe, JOHN MILTON, and FRANCIS BACON (see Vol. 4) were among their most accomplished practitioners. Translations of the Bible were no doubt the chief forge of an English prose style. Yet fictional narratives freed from the structures and strictures of verse did indeed exist during this period; one of the earliest literary masterpieces of the period, *Utopia* (1516) by THOMAS MORE (see also Vol. 4), was what we would recognize as an antecedent of later forms of narrative.

Unlike the sources of either poetry or drama, the chief models for English prose narrative were more immediately continental than classical. The Italian novella, often drawn from Ovidian sources, made its way to England in story collections such as that of William Painter's *Palace of Pleasure* (1566) or George Pettie's *Petite Palace of Pettie His Pleasures* (1576). As their titles perhaps suggest, such collections provided stories of erotic, dangerous, and fantastic adventures—"the lives, gests, and conquests of corageous personages." They found an eager audience among the newly literate aristocratic and middle classes. The market composed of the latter, particularly, would be reflected in the work of such authors as THOMAS DELONEY, who depicted the adventures of heroes of the middling sort. The picaresque structures of medieval romance were readily adapted to the expression of a nonchivalric culture.

In addition to narratives chiefly informed by the vagaries of plot and the fantasies of class transcendence, prose fiction served as a vehicle for social and moral commentary. *Utopia* is, of course, the chief example, but the work of WILLIAM BALDWIN also functioned to comment on polemical issues of the Reformation. PHILIP SIDNEY's *Arcadia* (1590) took pastoral romance, with its veiled commentary on aristocratic power structures, to new lengths, and THOMAS NASHE's *The Unfortunate Traveller* (1594) turned a rollicking travel picaresque into the most scathing of social criticism of contemporary Europe. JOHN LYLY's *Euphues* (1580), on the other hand, used the form to explore the stylistic intricacies of prose itself and was widely imitated and parodied in other forms such as the drama.

History and Criticism

Ashley, Robert, and E. M. Moseley, eds. *Elizabethan Fiction.* Peter Smith 1953 o.p. A substantial collection.

Davis, Walter R. *Idea and Art in Elizabethan Fiction.* Bks. Demand repr. of 1969 ed. $80.90. ISBN 0-8357-8915-2.

Harner, James L. *English Renaissance Prose Fiction, 1500–1660: An Annotated Bibliography of Criticism 1976–1983.* G. K. Hall 1983 o.p. Includes the most significant criticism written during the period covered.

———. *English Renaissance Prose Fiction: An Annotated Bibliography of Criticism, 1984–1990.* G. K. Hall 1992 $35.00. ISBN 0-8161-9088-7. A guide to the most recent criticism of Renaissance fiction.

Lewis, C. S. *English Literature in the Sixteenth Century (Excluding Drama).* Oxford History of Eng. Lit. Ser. OUP 1954 o.p. On the medieval literature of Scotland and the works of Sidney, Spenser, and Hooker.

Miller, Edwin Haviland. *The Professional Writer in Elizabethan England: A Study of Nondramatic Literature.* HUP 1959 o.p. A scholarly examination analyzing the social, political, and aesthetic tensions in the development of the professional writer.

Mueller, Janet M. *The Native Tongue and the Word: Developments in English Prose Style, 1380–1580.* U. Ch. Pr. 1984 $27.50. ISBN 0-226-54562-8. A study of habits of prose location (chiefly in nonliterary works).

Schlauch, Margaret. *Antecedents of the English Novel, 1400–1600: From Chaucer to Deloney.* Greenwood 1979 repr. of 1963 ed. $45.00. ISBN 0-313-21219-8. A study of medieval precedents.

DRAMA

To consider "Renaissance Drama" as a single entity is to simplify a practice diverse in geographic site, social function, literary form, and chronological location. In the early sixteenth century, theatrical activity occurred primarily either in the royal or the aristocratic banqueting hall, or in the public streets. Tudor interludes, stylistically reliant on both medieval morality plays and the resources of humanist debate forms, staged political and theological conflicts of contemporary concern to their elite patrons. At the other extreme, the liturgical calendar was punctuated, and the public spaces of inn yards and markets populated, by the religious cycle plays, a practice that continued well into the early seventeenth century, despite official Reformation efforts to suppress the practice. Mobile troupes of actors traveled between these two locations; for instance, the Lord Protector Cromwell commissioned playwright and polemicist JOHN BALE to write plays of Protestant propaganda to disseminate the messages of the Reformation throughout the realm. While theater was often prohibited in times of social unrest, early official attitudes toward playgoing and playacting were relatively tolerant: Henry VIII proclaimed in 1543 that "it is lawfull to all and every person and persons, to set forth songes, plays and interludes, to be used and exercise in this realme, and other the kinges dominions, for the rebuking and reproducing of vices, and the setting forth of vertue." Similarly, Sir Thomas Elyot answered the charge that dramatic representation of vice encouraged its practice with the claim that "by the same argument not only entreludes in Englishe, but also sermones, wherein some vice is declared, should be to the beholders and hearers like occasion to encrease sinners."

With the construction of the first permanent public theater in the 1570s, the conditions of theatrical production and reception changed dramatically. Officially classified as vagabonds by royal statute, actors and theater companies were permitted to play only by means of aristocratic license and patrons, a system that evolved a select number of monopolies by the end of the sixteenth century (Shakespeare's company, the Lord Chamberlain's Men, later the King's Men, was among them). Condemned by the municipal officials of London, and vilified by an increasingly vocal religious radicalism, the newly professional and economically independent theater enjoyed the complex geographical location of the London suburbs (the "liberties," site of leper houses, brothels, and other forms of paid entertainment) and the ideological sanction of the royal license. Objections to the theater ranged from reprehension of its representational content ("lewd comedies") to its transgressive practices, including the cross-dressing of boy actors; actors' violation of sumptuary laws; and the congregation of an audience diverse by gender and class. Despite (or perhaps because of) the campaign against it, the professional theaters, sustained by a combination of economic success and royal permission, thrived until their closure by Parliament in 1642; the ostensible (if inadequate) excuse for the Elizabethan theater was that the queen liked to see plays: "her majesty being pleased at some time to take delight and recreation in the sight and hearing of them."

This richness of ideological location was seconded in the formal constituents of Renaissance drama. Classical influences such as revenge tragedy (from SENECA) (see Vol. 2) and farce (from PLAUTUS (see Vol. 2) and TERENCE (see Vol. 2)) combined with the resources of humanist rhetorical practice and the parallel practices of medieval theater. New forms were invented to match and create public taste; the history play represented and interrogated the Tudor myth of kingship; domestic tragedy explored the sensational temper of the relationship between the family and the state. By the seventeenth century, a diverse body of indigenous work had evolved and was available for imitation and self-conscious parody. Playwrights acted, collaborated, and appropriated both the plots and the styles of other literary forms—as well as of other playwrights. Theater companies imitated the structure of the more conventional guilds and competed with each other for the large and diverse London audiences. Stages such as Blackfriars provided an indoor venue, where plays were presented by exclusively boy companies. Theaters such as the Rose or the Globe gave a spare, open-air backdrop for the verbal virtuosity of the drama, where ARISTOTLE's (see Vols. 3, 4, and 5) laws of unity of time, place, and action were shamelessly and successfully violated. At the court, the masque tradition developed and thrived to compliment and criticize its aristocratic subjects and audience and to produce a new illusionist theater. Such diversity, if discontinuous, was inarguably productive; the drama produced in the period has yet to be rivaled.

History and Criticism

Barish, Jonas. *The Anti-theatrical Prejudice.* U. CA Pr. 1981 o.p. A useful guide to the cultural resistance to the Elizabethan and Jacobean theater.

Belsey, Catherine. *The Subject of Tragedy: Identity and Difference in Renaissance Drama.* Routledge Chapman & Hall 1985 $29.95. ISBN 0-416-32700-1. A study of the drama's elaboration of a liberal subject, from medieval through Jacobean plays.

Bentley, Gerald E. *The Jacobean and Caroline Stage.* 7 vols. AMS Pr. 1982 repr. of 1968 ed. o.p. A magisterial account of the period that continues Edmund K. Chambers, *The Elizabethan Stage,* and improves on it.

Bevington, David M. *From Mankind to Marlowe.* HUP 1962 o.p. A study of the structural and thematic development of Elizabethan drama in light of medieval precedent.

_____. *Tudor Drama and Politics: A Critical Approach to Topical Meaning.* Bks. Demand repr. of 1968 ed. $97.20. ISBN 0-7837-1672-9. Focuses on drama's relationship to contemporary political issues.

Boas, Frederick S. *An Introduction to Tudor Drama.* AMS Pr. repr. of 1933 ed. $14.00. ISBN 0-404-14509-4. A useful overview of themes and conventions.

Bowers, Fredson. *Elizabethan Revenge Tragedy, 1587-1642.* Peter Smith 1958 $11.75. ISBN 0-8446-1085-2. A standard account of the subject.

Bradbrook, Muriel C. *Artist and Society in Shakespeare's England.* B & N Imports 1982 o.p. A general introduction to the literary context.

_____. *The Growth and Structure of Elizabethan Comedy.* Cambridge U. Pr. 1979 $12.95. ISBN 0-521-29526-2. A study of comic forms and forebears.

_____. *The Rise of the Common Player.* History of Elizabethan Drama Ser. Cambridge U. Pr. 1979 $12.95. ISBN 0-521-29527-0. A theater history.

_____. *Themes and Conventions of Elizabethan Tragedy.* History of Elizabethan Drama Ser. Cambridge U. Pr. 1980 $59.95. ISBN 0-521-29695-1. An excellent brief account of a large subject.

Braunmuller, A. R., and others. *The Cambridge Companion to English Renaissance Drama.* Cambridge U. Pr. 1990 $49.95. ISBN 0-521-34657-6. A thorough guide to the stylistic, dramaturgic, and social conventions governing theatrical production in the period.

Butler, Martin. *Theatre and Crisis, 1632–1642.* Cambridge U. Pr. 1987 $24.95. ISBN 0-521-31049-0. An indispensable guide to the years and political contexts preceding the closing of the theaters.

Chambers, Edmund K. *The Elizabethan Stage.* 4 vols. OUP 1923 o.p. Special index volume by Beatrice White (includes Chambers, *William Shakespeare*). An indispensable guide to the history and social conditions of the drama.

Craik, T. W., and others. *The Revels History of Drama in English, 1500–1576.* Vol. 2. Routledge Chapman & Hall 1980 $59.95. ISBN 0-416-1303-5. Contributions by Norman Sanders, Richard Southern, T. W. Craik, and Lois Potter; good bibliography.

Doran, Madeleine. *Endeavors of Art: A Study of Form in Elizabethan Drama.* U. of Wis. Pr. 1963 $12.50. ISBN 0-299-01084-8. Studies dramaturgic assumptions of Elizabethan playwrights.

Eliot, T. S. *Elizabethan Essays.* Gordon Pr. 1973 $250.00. ISBN 0-87968-043-1. Essays, most originally written as reviews, that are still trenchant and have a knack for quoting apt passages.

Gurr, Andrew. *Playgoing in Shakespeare's London.* Cambridge U. Pr. 1989 $59.95. ISBN 0-521-36824-3. An exploration of the issues surrounding the audience composition of Renaissance theater.

———. *The Shakespearean Stage, 1574–1642*. Cambridge U. Pr. 1992 $59.95. ISBN 0-521-42240-X. An essential account of the conditions of theatrical production in the period.

Harbage, Alfred. *Annals of English Drama, 975–1700*. Ed. by S. Schoenbaum. Univ. of Penn. Pr. rev. ed. 1964 o.p. A crucial book that attempts to date plays year by year.

Hattaway, Michael. *Elizabethan Popular Theatre: Plays in Performance. Theatre Production Studies* Routledge 1982 o.p. A guide to performance considerations and issues.

Henslowe, Philip. *Henslowe's Diary*. Ed. by R. A. Foakes and others. Cambridge U. Pr. 1961 o.p. The account book of the Elizabethan impresario.

Kastan, David Scott, and Peter Stallybrass, eds. *Staging the Renaissance: Reinterpretations of Elizabethan and Jacobean Drama*. Routledge 1991 $45.00. ISBN 0-415-90166-9. An informative collection of essays on the cultural conditions of early modern theatrical productions, as well as on individual authors.

Leech, Clifford, and T. W. Craik. *The Revels History of Drama in English, 1576–1613*. Vol. 3. Routledge Chapman & Hall 1975 o.p. Contributions by J. Leeds Barroll, Alexander Leggatt, Richard Hosley, and Alvin Kernan.

Levin, Richard. *Multiple Plot in English Renaissance Drama*. U. Ch. Pr. 1971 $22.00. ISBN 0-226-47526-3. A detailed and practical study.

———. *New Readings vs. Old Plays: Recent Trends in the Reinterpretation of English Renaissance Drama*. U. Ch. Pr. 1979 $24.00. ISBN 0-226-47520-4. Many cogent objections to the ahistorical, thematic trends in modern scholarship and criticism.

Logan, Terence P., and Denzell S. Smith, eds. *The Later Jacobean and Caroline Dramatists. Survey and Bibliography of Recent Studies in Eng. Renaissance Drama Ser*. Bks. Demand repr. of 1978 ed. $79.70. ISBN 0-8357-2912-5. A guide to criticism.

———. *The New Intellectuals. Survey and Bibliography of Recent Studies in Eng. Renaissance Drama Ser*. U. of Nebr. Pr. 1977 $31.00. ISBN 0-8032-0859-6. A guide to criticism.

———. *The Popular School. Survey and Bibliography of Recent Studies in Eng. Renaissance Drama Ser*. Bks. Demand repr. of 1975 ed. $84.60. ISBN 0-7837-1467-X. A guide to criticism.

———. *The Predecessors of Shakespeare. Survey and Bibliography of Recent Studies in Eng. Renaissance Drama Ser*. U. of Nebr. Pr. 1973 o.p. Four volumes, indispensable for anyone working in this area.

Potter, Lois. *The Revels History of Drama in English, 1613–1660*. Vol. 4. Routledge Chapman & Hall 1983 o.p. Studies a period generally neglected in literary history; good bibliography.

Rose, Mary Beth, ed. *Renaissance Drama as Cultural History: Essays from Renaissance Drama, 1977–1987*. Northwestern U. Pr. 1990 $39.95. ISBN 0-801-0683-3. A collection that considers the drama in its historical and cultural moment.

Shapiro, Michael. *Children of the Revels: The Boy Companies of Shakespeare's Time and Their Plays*. Col. U. Pr. 1977 $48.00. ISBN 0-231-04112-8. An authoritative statement on this special topic.

Shepherd, Simon. *Amazons and Warrior Women: Varieties of Feminism in 17th-Century Drama*. St. Martin 1982 $35.00. ISBN 0-312-02155-0. A study of gender types.

Wickham, Glynne. *Early English Stages 1300–1660*. 3 vols. Routledge 1959–81 o.p. A history of the evolution of the drama from its earliest liturgical forms to the professional theater.

Collections

The Revels Plays, modeled on the Arden edition of Shakespeare, is the most important edition of Elizabethan and pre-Shakespearean drama. *The Regents Renaissance Drama Series*, under the general editorship of Cyrus Hoy, is also of high quality. The old Mermaid editions of Elizabethan dramatists, published from the 1880s to the early 1900s, make available some hard-to-find texts. The series has been reedited since 1956 in single volumes called *New Mermaid*

Series, under the general editorship of Philip Brockbank and Brian Morris. Many of the better-known plays appear in *Crofts Classics Series*. Facsimile reprints of Tudor and Elizabethan plays are available from the Malone Society and *The Tudor Facsimile Texts Series*. The Scolar Press has published photographic facsimiles of many English Renaissance plays. Under the editorship of Stephen Orgel, Garland Publishers has undertaken an extensive *Renaissance Drama* series, especially of lesser-known plays.

Brooke, Charles F., and Nathaniel B. Paradise. *English Drama, 1580–1642*. Heath 1983 $32.00. ISBN 0-669-06144-1. A general overview.

Fraser, Russell A., and Norman Rabkin. *Drama of the English Renaissance*. 2 vols. Macmillan 1976. ISBNs 0-02-339570-2, 0-02-339580-X. The best of the big student anthologies.

Gomme, A. H., ed. *Jacobean Tragedies*. Oxford Pap. Ser. OUP 1969 $14.95. ISBN 0-19-281059-6. Useful introduction; contains *The Malcontent, The Revenger's Tragedy, The Atheist's Tragedy, The Changeling,* and *Women Beware Women*.

Harrier, Richard C., ed. *An Anthology of Jacobean Drama*. 2 vols. Stuart Eds. Ser. NYU Pr. 1963 o.p. A collection of often-read works.

McIlwraith, Archibald K., ed. *Five Elizabethan Comedies*. World's Class Ser. OUP 1934 o.p.

_____. *Five Elizabethan Tragedies*. Oxford Pap. Ser. Greenwood 1981 repr. of 1938 ed. $59.50. ISBN 0-313-22528-1. Contains *Gordudac, The Spanish Tragedy, Arden of Fevershahn, A Woman Killed with Kindness, Thyestes*.

Salgado, Gamini, ed. *Three Jacobean Tragedies*. Viking Penguin 1965 $7.95. ISBN 0-14-043006-7. Contains *The Revenger's Tragedy, The White Devil, The Changeling*.

Wine, Martin. *Drama of the English Renaissance*. Viking Penguin 1969 $7.95. ISBN 0-14-043006-7

CHRONOLOGY OF AUTHORS

Skelton, John. c.1460–1529
More, Sir Thomas, St. 1478–1535
Bale, John. 1495–1563
Wyatt, Sir Thomas the Elder. 1503–1542
Baldwin, William. 1518–1563
Deloney, Thomas. 1543–1600
Spenser, Edmund. 1552–1599
Lyly, John. c.1554–1606
Sidney, Sir Philip. 1554–1586
Peele, George. c.1556–1596?
Greene, Robert. 1558–1592
Kyd, Thomas. 1558–1594
Lodge, Thomas. 1558–1606
Chapman, George. c.1559–1634
Drayton, Michael. 1563–1631
Marlowe, Christopher. 1564–1593
Campion, Thomas. 1567–1620
Nashe, Thomas. 1567–1601

Dekker, Thomas. c.1572–c.1632
Jonson, Ben. 1572?–1637
Donne, John. 1573–1631
Heywood, Thomas. c.1573–1641
Marston, John. c.1575–1634
Tourneur, Cyril. c.1575–1626
Fletcher, John. 1579–1625
Middleton, Thomas. c.1580–1627
Webster, John. c.1580–c.1634
Massinger, Philip. 1583–1640
Beaumont, Francis. c.1584–1616
Ford, John. 1586–c.1639
Herrick, Robert. 1591–1674
Herbert, George. 1593–1633
Milton, John. 1608–1674
Crashaw, Richard. 1613–1649
Marvell, Andrew. 1621–1678
Vaughan, Henry. 1622–1695
Bunyan, John. 1628–1688

BALDWIN, WILLIAM. 1518–1563

After studying at Oxford, William Baldwin became a corrector to the press for the Edwardine printer Edward Whitchurch. Perhaps not surprisingly, Baldwin's prose narrative, *Beware the Cat*, engages issues of the relative merits of the printed versus the spoken word. Baldwin also published verse translations of Scripture and superintended (and contributed to) the publication of the historical poem *The Mirror of Magistrates* (1559). *Beware the Cat* is an inventive and lively anti-Catholic satire that combines verse and prose ostensibly to address the question of animal speech; in the process it delivers a critique of Catholic forms of the production and transmission of knowledge.

PROSE FICTION BY BALDWIN

Beware the Cat: The First English Novel. Ed. by William A. Ringler, Jr., and Michael Flachmann. Huntington Lib. 1988 $25.00. ISBN 0-87328-087-3

BALE, JOHN. 1495–1563

John Bale's life embodied the turbulent contradictions of the early Reformation. Reared from age 12 as a Carmelite friar, he converted to Protestantism as an adult and soon became one of its most ardent polemicists. Much of Bale's work consists of vituperative prose attacks on the institutional corruption of the Roman church, a style for which he received the nickname "Billious Bale." However, Bale was also an energetic dramatist, whose zeal in staging Protestant propaganda earned him the sponsorship of Cromwell. While his drama bears evidence of the medieval morality plays, he is remarkable for authoring the first Tudor history play, *King Johan* (1539), which displays the English monarch as a proto-Protestant enemy of the papacy. In his choice of topic and invention of genre, Bale anticipated SHAKESPEARE's history plays. Bale's martyrology *A Brief Chronicle Concerning the Examination and Death of Sir John Oldcastle* (1544) may have provided the Bard with a source for his portrait of Falstaff.

PLAYS BY BALE

Complete Plays. 3 vols. Ed. by D. S. Brewer. Boydell & Brewer 1985 o.p. The standard edition.

King Johan. 1539. Ed. by Barry B. Adams. Huntington Lib. 1969 $12.50. ISBN 0-87328-039-3

WORKS BY BALE

Three Laws. AMS Pr. repr. of 1908 ed. $49.50. ISBN 0-404-53323-X. A useful edition of Bale's morality play.

The Vocacyon of Johan Bale. Ed. by Peter Happe and John N. King. MRTS 1990 $20.00. ISBN 0-86698-079-2. Bale's moving autobiography of his own conversion and persecution.

BOOKS ABOUT BALE

Fairfield, Leslie. *John Bale: Mythmaker for the English Reformation.* Purdue U. Pr. 1976 o.p. A biographical analysis of the writer's work.

BEAUMONT, FRANCIS. c.1584–1616, and JOHN FLETCHER. 1579–1625

Beaumont and Fletcher are the best-known collaborators of Elizabethan literature. John Aubrey reports that, when they lived together, they shared one wench and one cloak between them, and everything encourages the myth of literary twins. The collaboration, however, could not have lasted for more than five years, beginning in 1608 and ending in 1613, when Beaumont married the heiress Ursula Isley. After that time, Fletcher collaborated with other dramatists, such as MASSINGER, MIDDLETON, Shirley, and perhaps SHAKESPEARE. We do not yet understand how to untangle the various shares in Elizabethan dramatic collaborations. A Beaumont and Fletcher play was generally understood to be a tragicomedy with a complex and swiftly moving plot, a good deal of spectacle, upper-class and genteel characters contrasted with low characters (as love is with lust), sentimental effusions, and a smoothly articulated, elegant, and fluent style. *A King and No King* (1611), which is and is not about royal incest, is typical. Beaumont and Fletcher were extremely inventive in setting up actions based on some improbable assumption. The play then became an exercise in disproving the original proposition.

PLAYS BY BEAUMONT AND FLETCHER

The Dramatic Works in the Beaumont and Fletcher Canon. 4 vols. Ed. by Fredson Bowers. Cambridge U. Pr. 1983 o.p. A splendid modern edition, with separate editors for the individual plays.

A King and No King. 1611. *Eng. Experience Ser.* Walter J. Johnson repr. of 1619 ed. $15.00. ISBN 90-221-0290-4

The Knight of the Burning Pestle. 1613. Ed. by Sheldon P. Zitner. St. Martin 1988 $59.95. ISBN 0-7190-1532-4. A satiric view of social and literary pretensions.

The Maid's Tragedy. 1619. Ed. by T. W. Craik. St. Martin 1988 $59.95. ISBN 0-7190-1548-0. An exploration of court roles and themes.

Philaster, or, Love Lies a-Bleeding. 1620. Walter J. Johnson 1968 repr. of 1620 ed. $20.00. ISBN 90-221-0018-9. A tragicomic romance of identity and betrayal.

BOOKS ABOUT BEAUMONT AND FLETCHER

Finklepearl, Philip J. *Court and Country Politics in the Plays of Beaumont and Fletcher*. Princeton U. Pr. 1990 $35.00. ISBN 0-691-06825-9. Drama's relationship to a commonly conceived social context of the revolution.

Pearse, Nancy C. *John Fletcher's Chastity Plays: Mirrors of Modesty*. Bucknell U. Pr. 1973 $22.50. ISBN 0-8387-1151-0. A study of an important theme.

Thorndike, Ashley H. *Influence of Beaumont and Fletcher on Shakespeare*. Rprt. Serv. 1992 repr. of 1901 ed. $69.00. ISBN 0-7812-7295-5. A source study.

Waith, Eugene. *The Pattern of Tragicomedy in Beaumont and Fletcher*. Yale Studies in *Eng. Ser.* Shoe String 1969 repr. of 1952 ed. $32.50. ISBN 0-208-00777-6. Generic history and concerns.

Wallis, Lawrence B. *Fletcher, Beaumont and Company*. Hippocrene Bks. 1968 repr. of 1947 ed. $20.00. ISBN 0-374-98208-2. A study of theatrical practice.

BUNYAN, JOHN. 1628–1688

John Bunyan was a "braseuer," or tinker, who created the most intense prose allegories in English. A deeply religious man, he was imprisoned for most of 1660–72 for preaching Puritan doctrine in an England barely recovering from a religious civil war. In his first, autobiographical work, *Grace Abounding* (1666), he found his main theme—spiritual conversion. He treated this subject most magnificently in his *Pilgrim's Progress* (1678). He wrote this most famous allegory while imprisoned again in 1675 for six months. In this work, the character Christian, the ordinary man, makes the painful journey from the City of Destruction to the Heavenly Gates through dangers set up by others and by his own mind. Bunyan's theme is universal; he brought to it intense conviction, brilliant economy and vigor of statement, and the ability to evoke living characters in the guise of allegorical figures. Although *Mr. Badman* (1680), *The Holy War* (1682), and *Pilgrim's Progress, Part II* (1684) are not quite up to the masterpiece, they constitute an impressive expansion of Bunyan's range of prose fiction. *Pilgrim's Progress* was one of the few books that the American pioneer carried along with the Bible; with the return to favor of allegory and symbolism, a resurgence of interest in Bunyan is evident.

PROSE FICTION BY BUNYAN

Works: With an Introduction to Each Treatise, Notes and a Sketch of His Life, Times and Contemporaries. 3 vols. Ed. by George Offor. AMS Pr. repr. of 1856 ed. $225.00. ISBN 0-404-09250-0. The standard edition.

Grace Abounding to the Chief of Sinners. 1666. Baker Bks. 1986 $6.95. ISBN 0-8010-0925-1

The Pilgrim's Progress from This World to That Which Is to Come. 1678. Ed. by James B. Wharey. Rprt. Serv. 1992 repr. of 1928 ed. $89.00. ISBN 0-7812-7326-9. A collation of the 11 editions published during Bunyan's lifetime and the first really authentic text, with bibliographical analysis.

The Holy War. 1682. Ed. by Roger Sharrock and James F. Forrest. *Oxford Eng. Texts Ser.* Baker Bks. 1986 $6.95. ISBN 0-8010-0924-3

BOOKS ABOUT BUNYAN

Brown, John. *John Bunyan, 1628–1688: His Life, Times, and Work.* Rprt. Serv. 1988 repr. of 1928 ed. $75.00. ISBN 0-7812-0346-5. The standard biography.

Harrison, George B. *John Bunyan: A Study in Personality.* Rprt. Serv. 1992 repr. of 1928 ed. $69.00. ISBN 0-7812-7327-7. A biographical sketch.

Hill, Christopher. *A Tinker and a Poor Man: John Bunyan and His Church, 1628–1688.* Knopf 1988 $22.95. ISBN 0-394-57242-4. A contextual account by the excellent materialist historian.

Tindall, William York. *John Bunyan, Mechanick Preacher.* Russell 1964 repr. of 1934 ed. o.p. Bunyan in his times.

CAMPION, THOMAS. 1567–1620

A practicing physician and musician throughout his life, Campion wrote poetry, songs, masques, and a treatise on music and poetry. His lyrics possess rare charm and freshness, as well as a melodiousness and metrical variety that reflect their musical origin. In his introduction to Campion's collected works, Walter R. Davis says, "Campion's pursuit of the movements of sound is recorded in that strange but subtle treatise, *Observations in the Art of English Poesie* (1602), and its fruits are preserved in his songbooks. He is a poet— perhaps *the* poet—of the auditory rather than the visual imagination. . . . He offers us experiences that strike the ear."

POETRY BY CAMPION

Observations in the Art of English Poesie. 1602. Walter J. Johnson 1972 repr. of 1602 ed. $7.00. ISBN 0-90-221-0441-9

The Selected Songs of Thomas Campion. Godine 1972 o.p. A collection of Campion's lyrics, with an introduction by John Hollander.

WORK BY CAMPION

Works of Thomas Campion. Ed. by Walter R. Davis. Norton 1970 $2.95. ISBN 0-393-00439-2. The most convenient edition.

BOOKS ABOUT CAMPION

Davis, Walter R. *Thomas Campion.* Twayne 1987 $26.95. ISBN 0-8057-6949-8. Proceeds from a discussion of Campion's life through chapters on song, poetry, and music, to a final consideration of his reputation.

Lindley, David. *Thomas Campion.* E. J. Brill 1986 $48.50. ISBN 90-04-07601-8. Scholarly study of the author and his work.

CHAPMAN, GEORGE. c.1559–1634

Chapman had a reputation in his own time for being a learned writer. On the payroll of the Elizabethan impresario, Philip Henslowe, he wrote for the Admiral's Men and was imprisoned with BEN JONSON for supposedly seditious theater. He translated HOMER's (see Vol. 2) *Iliad* and *Odyssey* and completed MARLOWE's *Hero and Leander*. His works are full of humanist scholarship from classical sources, while his tragedies are mostly based on contemporary French history. In *Bussy d'Ambois* (1607), the best known of this series, the hero is the aspiring, stoic man who is doomed to extinction in a crass world. Chapman's comedies, which are much more lighthearted, experiment in the comedy of "humours" that Jonson was to perfect. The plays are mostly written for the boy companies.

PLAYS BY CHAPMAN

All Fools. 1605. Ed. by Frank Manley. *Regents Renaissance Drama Ser.* U. of Nebr. Pr. 1968 $2.75. ISBN 0-8032-5256-0

Bussy d'Ambois. 1607. Ed. by Nicholas Brooke. *Revels Plays Ser.* St. Martin 1988 repr. of 1964 ed. $40.00. ISBN 0-7190-1505-7

The Comedies. 2 vols. Ed. by Thomas Marc Parrott. Russell 1961 repr. of 1914 ed. o.p. The standard edition.

The Gentleman Usher. 1606. Ed. by John H. Smith. *Regents Renaissance Drama Ser.* U. of Nebr. Pr. 1970 $16.95. ISBN 0-8032-0285-7

The Plays of George Chapman: The Comedies. Ed. by Allan Holaday and Michael Kiernan. U. of Ill. Pr. 1970 o.p. Contains a useful introduction.

The Tragedies. 2 vols. Ed. by Thomas Marc Parrott. Russell 1961 repr. of 1910 ed. o.p. The standard collection.

The Widow's Tears. 1605. Ed. by Akihiro Yamada. *Revels Plays Ser.* St. Martin 1988. $59.95. ISBN 0-7190-1510-3. A satire on the inconstancy of women.

BOOKS ABOUT CHAPMAN

Braunmuller, A. R. *Natural Fictions: George Chapman's Major Tragedies.* U. Delaware Pr. 1991 $32.50. ISBN 0-87413-404-8. An insightful study of Chapman's major concerns.

Ide, Richard S. *Possessed with Greatness: The Heroic Tragedies of Chapman and Shakespeare.* U. of NC Pr. 1980 $27.50. ISBN 0-8078-1429-6. A study of character and the heroic personality.

Rees, Ennis. *The Tragedies of George Chapman.* Hippocrene Bks. 1979 repr. of 1954 ed. $18.00. ISBN 0-374-96767-9. A study of thematic patterns.

Waddington, Raymond B. *The Mind's Empire: Myth and Form in George Chapman's Narrative Poems.* Bks. Demand repr. of 1974 ed. $58.00. ISBN 0-317-42063-1. A study of Chapman's treatment of literary conventions.

CRASHAW, RICHARD. 1613–1649

Crashaw differs from other English Metaphysical poets chiefly by virtue of his intense attachment to Roman Catholicism and to the spirit of the Counter Reformation. The son of a Puritan clergyman, he took Anglican orders in 1638; but during the Civil Wars he was converted to the Church of Rome and (in 1646) went to Italy, where he was made a canon shortly before his death there. His poetry is strongly influenced by Spanish and Italian models, notably the work of GIAMBATTISTA MARINO (see Vol. 2), whose poetry is marked by extravagantly sensuous conceits. Crashaw obsessively employs the imagery of wounds, kisses, nests, breasts, milk, and blood. After many years of neglect, and even contemptuous dismissal, Crashaw's poetry has experienced an extraordinary revival and is now much admired for its originality and dazzling imagery.

POETRY BY CRASHAW

The Complete Poetry of Richard Crashaw. Ed. by George W. Williams. NYU Pr. 1972 o.p. The standard edition.

Poems, English, Latin and Greek, of Richard Crashaw. Ed. by Leonard C. Martin. *Oxford Eng. Texts Ser.* OUP 1957 o.p. A useful collection.

BOOKS ABOUT CRASHAW

Bennett, Joan. *Five Metaphysical Poets: Donne, Herbert, Vaughan, Crashaw, Marvell.* Cambridge U. Pr. 1934 $13.95. ISBN 0-521-09238-8. One of the best introductions to a remarkable group of poets.

Cooper, Robert M. *A Concordance to the English Poetry of Richard Crashaw*. Whitston Pub. 1980 $35.00. ISBN 0-87875-188-2. A guide to Crashaw's frequency and site of language use.

Healy, Thomas F. *Richard Crashaw*. E. J. Brill 1986 $40.00. ISBN 90-04-07864-9

Roberts, John R., ed. *New Perspectives on the Life and Art of Richard Crashaw*. U. of Mo. Pr. 1990 $32.50. ISBN 0-8262-0739-1. Collection of 10 original critical and historical essays on the life and art of Crashaw; introduction surveys the history of Crashavian criticism and signals new directions for future scholarship.

Willey, Basil. *Richard Crashaw*. Folcroft repr. of 1949 ed. o.p.

Williams, George W. *Image and Symbol in the Sacred Poetry of Richard Crashaw*. U. of SC Pr. 1967 $24.95. ISBN 0-87249-087-4. A study of Crashaw's religious hopes.

DEKKER, THOMAS. c.1572–c.1632

Dekker was a popular, prolific writer who had a hand in at least 40 plays, which he wrote for Philip Henslowe, the theatrical entrepreneur. In the plays that seem to be completely by Dekker, he shows himself as a realist of London life, but even his most realistic plays have a strong undertone of romantic themes and aspirations. *The Shoemaker's Holiday* (1600), for example, glorifies the gentle craft of the shoemaker, and the character Simon Eyre speaks in an extravagant, hyperbolic style that is far from realistic. The two parts of *The Honest Whore* (1604) are both vivid and realistic. Dekker also wrote such prose pamphlets as the *Bellman of London* (1608) and *The Gull's Hornbook* (1609), the latter an entertaining account of the behavior of a country yokel and dupe in London. He died in debt.

PLAYS BY DEKKER

The Dramatic Works of Thomas Dekker. 4 vols. Ed. by Fredson Bowkers. Cambridge U. Pr. 1961. Vol. 1 $75.00. ISBN 0-521-04808-7. Vol. 2 $77.50. ISBN 0-521-04809-5. Vol. 3 $75.00. ISBN 0-521-04810-9. Vol. 4 $75.00. ISBN 0-521-04811-7. The standard edition in old spelling.

The Shoemaker's Holiday. 1600. Ed. by Stanley Wells. *Revels Plays Ser.* Johns Hopkins 1979 $32.00. ISBN 0-8018-2293-9

The Witch of Edmonton. 1621. Methuen 1988 $9.95. ISBN 0-404-53423-6. Written in collaboration with William Rowley.

NONFICTION BY DEKKER

The Gull's Hornbook. 1609. Ed. by R. M. McKerrow. AMS Pr. repr. of 1904 ed. $14.00. ISBN 0-404-02069-0

The Wonderful Year and Other Pamphlets. Ed. by Eric D. Pendry. *Stratford-upon-Avon Libr.* HUP 1968 o.p. Dekker's lesser-known writings.

BOOKS ABOUT DEKKER

Adler, Doris R. *Thomas Dekker: A Reference Guide*. G. K. Hall o.p. A guide to the critical tradition.

Shirley, Peggy F. *Serious and Tragic Elements in the Comedy of Thomas Dekker. Salzburg Studies in Eng. Lit., Jacobean Drama Studies*. Humanities 1975 o.p. A consideration of Dekker's eclecticism.

DELONEY, THOMAS. 1543–1600

Little is known about the life of Thomas Deloney; fellow writer THOMAS NASHE referred to him as a "balleting Silke weaver"; and Will Kemp, the comic actor, reported that he "died poorly" but was "honestly buried." Most of Deloney's literary production seems to have taken the form of ballads; however, his four prose narratives are admired for their depiction of character and popular bourgeois culture, and their handling of dialogue. *The Gentle Craft* (1 and 2) (1597–98) (like the dramatist THOMAS DEKKER's *Shoemaker's Holiday*) portrays the world of cobblers, while *Thomas of Reading* (1599?) resembles—in its mingling of the world of weavers with the story of Robert, duke of Normandy and his love Margaret—later historical novels. *Jack of Newbery* (1597–98), published in eight editions by 1619, presents the adventures of an upwardly mobile apprentice who marries his master's widow and goes on to become a power in the realm.

PROSE FICTION BY DELONEY

The Novels of Thomas Deloney. Ed. by Merrit Lawlis. Greenwood 1978 repr. of 1961 ed. $55.00. ISBN 0-313-20105-6. Useful introduction and notes.
The Works of Thomas Deloney. Ed. by Francis Oscar Mann. Repr. Serv. 1992 repr. of 1912 ed. $99.00. ISBN 0-7812-7202-5. The standard edition.

BOOK ABOUT DELONEY

Simons, John. *Realistic Romance: The Prose Fiction of Thomas Deloney*. Winchester Pr. 1983 o.p. Styles and themes of Deloney's work.

DONNE, JOHN. 1573–1631

The dean of St. Paul's, the foremost preacher of his day, Donne has had an influence of English literature that is singularly wide and deep. In his own time he was far more famous as a preacher than as a poet, and for generations after his death his poetry was regarded as eccentric and rhythmically ungainly. Yet it is no exaggeration to say that he was the greatest single influence on English poetry between the two world wars. The great revival of Donne in the twentieth century is reflected in the poetry of many poets, notably T. S. ELIOT.

Donne was educated at Oxford and Cambridge. He became a member of Parliament in 1600, but his early career was ruined by his secret marriage to the niece of his employer, the Lord Keeper Sir Thomas Egerton. His early poetry—sensual love lyrics and satires on society—was cynical and realistic. After 1601, when he began his satirical *Progresse of the Soule*, it became more serious in tone. The greatest of the Metaphysical poets, he was an exquisite shaper of ideas in compact form and characteristically made use of conceits and inversions to produce verse of great subtlety and power. He became dean of St. Paul's in 1619, and his prose *Sermons* and satires are his most important contribution to literature after some of the lyrics and elegies. His earnest and vigorous mind, expressed in flashing wit and startling beauty, his daring phrases—coupled with a certain roughness of form—have made him attractive to modern readers. Izaak Walton, his intimate and adoring friend, wrote the famous contemporary biography in his *Lives*, first published in 1640.

POETRY BY DONNE

The Complete English Poems: John Donne. Ed. by A. J. Smith. *Penguin Poets Ser.* Viking
    Penguin 1977 $9.95. ISBN 0-14-042209-9. A convenient collection.
The Divine Poems. Ed. by Helen Gardner. *Oxford Eng. Texts Ser.* OUP 1979 $17.95. ISBN
    0-19-871100-X. Supersedes all previous editions.
The Elegies, and the Songs and Sonnets. Ed. by Helen Gardner. *Oxford Eng. Texts Ser.*
    OUP 1965 o.p. Contains useful introduction and notes.
Poems. Ed. by Herbert J. Grierson. 2 vols. OUP 1933 $14.95. ISBN 0-19-281113-4. The
    standard edition for decades, but containing many disputed readings.

PROSE WORKS BY DONNE

*John Donne's Sermons on the Psalms and Gospels: With a Selection of Prayers and
    Meditations.* Ed. by Evelyn M. Simpson. U. CA Pr. 1963 $10.95. ISBN 0-520-00340-3.
    Contains 10 sermons and a few prayers and meditations with explanatory footnotes:
    a good introduction to Donne's prose.
Paradoxes and Problems. Ed. by Helen Peters. OUP 1980 $75.00. ISBN 0-19-812753-7. The
    standard edition.
Satires, Epigrams, and Verse Letters. Ed. by Wesley Milgate. *Oxford Eng. Texts Ser.* OUP
    1967 $79.00. ISBN 0-19-811842-2. Supersedes all previous editions.
The Sermons of John Donne. 10 vols. Ed. by Evelyn M. Simpson. U. CA Pr. 1984 $495.00.
    ISBN 0-520-05255-2. The standard edition, with essays on the bibliography of the
    printed sermons; a study of manuscripts, textual problems, and literary value; and an
    introduction on background and context.

BOOKS ABOUT DONNE

Bald, R. C. *John Donne: A Life.* Ed. by Wesley Milgate. OUP 1986 $32.50. ISBN 0-19-
    812870-3. A biographical treatment of Donne, with critical analysis of his work.
Carey, John. *John Donne: Life, Mind and Art.* Faber & Faber critical analysis of his work.
    1991 $9.95. ISBN 0-571-14337-7. A brilliant book by a remarkably gifted critic and
    scholar.
Grant, Patrick. *The Transformation of Sin: Studies in Donne, Herbert, Vaughan, and
    Traherne.* U. of Mass. Pr. 1974 $30.00. ISBN 0-87023-158-8. A comparative consider-
    ation of religious sensibility and psychology.
Lewalski, Barbara K. *Donne's Anniversaries and the Poetry of Praise: The Creation of a
    Symbolic Mode.* Bks. Demand repr. of 1973 ed. $103.80. ISBN 0-8357-3689-X. One of
    the most influential studies of the past generation.
Marotti, Arthur F. *John Donne, Coterie Poet.* U. of Wis. Pr. 1986 $35.00. ISBN 0-299-
    10490-7. A study of Donne's poetry in the context of his culture's social roles.
Roberts, John R. *John Donne: An Annotated Biography of Modern Criticism, 1968–1978.*
    U. of Mo. Pr. 1982 $44.00. ISBN 0-8262-0364-7. A guide to studies of Donne.
––––––, ed. *Essential Articles for the Study of John Donne's Poetry. Essential Articles Ser.*
    Shoe String 1975 o.p. A useful selection of key readings.
Sanders, Wilbur. *John Donne's Poetry.* Cambridge U. Pr. 1975 $34.50. ISBN 0-521-09909-
    9. A consideration of themes and styles.
Smith, A. J., ed. *John Donne: The Critical Heritage. Critical Heritage Ser.* Routledge 1975
    o.p. A superb survey of Donne criticism from the beginnings to the present.
Spencer, Theodore, ed. *A Garland for John Donne, 1631–1931.* Peter Smith $11.25. ISBN
    0-8446-1418-1. Valuable essays by T. S. Eliot and others.
Stein, Arnold S. *John Donne's Lyrics.* Hippocrene Bks. 1980 repr. of 1962 ed. o.p. A
    location of Donne in his stylistic context.
Tayler, Edward. *Donne's Idea of a Woman.* Col. U. Pr. 1991 $42.50. ISBN 0-231-07594-4.
    Battles the current interpretations of John Donne's ideas of women in his two poems
    of 1611 and 1612.
Winny, James. *A Preface to Donne.* Longman 1983 o.p.

DRAYTON, MICHAEL. 1563–1631

Born to a family of Warwickshire gentry and reared as a page, Drayton was a poet whose career spanned both Elizabethan and Jacobean eras. Like SPENSER (whom he admired greatly), he wrote in a variety of genres, according to the Vergilian pastoral-to-epic trajectory of the civic poet (he also wrote for the stage). Some of his most interesting poetry takes up historical subjects, often of a notorious exemplarity: His *Heroicall Epistles* (1597) are versified imaginary love letters of the *amours* of English monarchs, and his *Barons Warres* (1603) (first published as *Mortimeradios* in 1596) views the history of Edward II from the usurper's vantage point. Drayton's longest poem is the chorographical epic *Poly-Olbion* (1613, 1622, with annotations by the lawyer John Selden), in which Drayton attempts to provide a vocabulary of national identity in his description of the geographical features of Britain.

WORK BY DRAYTON

Works. Ed. by J. W. Hebel. OUP 1931–41 o.p. The standard edition.

BOOKS ABOUT DRAYTON

Hardin, Richard F. *Michael Drayton and the Passing of Elizabethan England*. U. Pr. of KS 1973 $19.95. ISBN 0-7006-0103-1. A study of Drayton's literary generation.
Newdigate, B. H. *Michael Drayton and His Circle*. OUP 1941 o.p. A biographical account of the poet and dramatist.

FLETCHER, JOHN. 1579–1625

[SEE Francis Beaumont.]

FORD, JOHN. 1586–c.1639

Ford, the second son of a landed gentleman, did not begin his career as a playwright until 1621, with his collaboration with Dekker on *The Witch of Edmonton*. As a dramatist, Ford was extremely interested in psychology, especially abnormal psychology, and his best-known plays are studies in frustration and quiet suffering. His plots tend to be static and deterministic, with the characters unable to act against a crushing destiny. In *The Broken Heart* (1629), because all the crucial events are fixed before the play begins, there is a heavy emphasis on pathos. *'Tis Pity She's a Whore* (1632) rewrites *Romeo and Juliet* with brother-sister incest and a violent revenge action. *Perkin Warbeck* (1633) is the last of the history plays. In it, the pretender to the throne of Henry VII hardly makes much pretense to establish his legitimate claims. Ford writes in an unusually plain, lyric style that resembles that of passionate and melancholy speech.

PLAYS BY FORD

The Broken Heart: A Tragedy. 1629. Ed. by T. J. B. Spencer, *Revels Plays Ser*. Johns Hopkins 1981 $32.00. ISBN 0-8018-2479-6
The Chronicle Historie of Perkin Warbeck. 1633. *Eng. Experience Ser*. Walter J. Johnson repr. of 1634 ed. 1972 $20.00. ISBN 90-221-0447-8
The Lovers Melancholy. Eng. Experience Ser. Walter J. Johnson 1970 repr. of 1629 ed. $35.00. ISBN 90-221-0271-8. A story of love's frustrations.
The Selected Plays: The Broken Heart, 'Tis Pity She's a Whore, Perkin Warbeck. Ed. by C. Gibson. Cambridge U. Pr. 1986 $69.95. ISBN 0-521-22543-4
'Tis Pity She's a Whore. 1932. Ed. by Derek Roper. *Revels Plays Ser*. St. Martin 1988 $59.95. ISBN 0-7190-1511-1

BOOKS ABOUT FORD

Anderson, Donald K., Jr. *John Ford. Twayne's Eng. Authors Ser.* G. K. Hall o.p. A general
    introduction.
Farr, Dorothy M. *John Ford and the Caroline Theatre.* B & N Imports 1979 o.p. Ford and
    the later Stuart theatrical conventions and conditions.
Huebert, Ronald. *John Ford: Baroque English Dramatists.* U. of Toronto Pr. 1978 $34.95.
    ISBN 0-7735-0286-6. Ford's work in light of the Baroque tradition in art and
    literature.
Senasbaugh, George F. *The Tragic Muse of John Ford.* Ayer repr. of 1944 ed. $17.00. ISBN
    0-405-08949-X. Ford's work and the intellectual climate of his time.
Stavig, Mark. *John Ford and the Traditional Moral Order.* U. of Wis. Pr. 1968 $25.00. ISBN
    0-299-04680-X. A general overview of attitudes and treatments.

GREENE, ROBERT. 1558–1592

Greene was a notorious figure in his own time, leading a life of excess and
debauchery (or at least so he represents himself in his many journalistic
pamphlets). His exposés of the Elizabethan underworld may or may not be
based on real experience. He died, according to his friend THOMAS NASHE, from
a "banquet of Rhenish wine and pickled herring." In addition to his plays,
Greene wrote many charming prose romances, with interpolated lyric poems.
His works helped lay the foundations of the English drama, and even his worst
plays have historical value.

PLAYS BY GREENE

Friar Bacon and Friar Bungay, c.1594. AMS Pr. repr. of 1914 ed. $49.50. ISBN 0-404-
    53370-1
James the Fourth. 1598. Ed. by Norman Sanders. *Revels Plays Ser.* St. Martin 1990 $59.95.
    ISBN 0-7190-1606-1. A historical romance of the Scottish king.
The Tragical Reign of Selimus. Ed. by Alexander Grosart. Richard West repr. of 1898 ed.
    o.p.

WORK BY GREENE

The Life and Complete Works in Prose and Verse of Robert Greene. 15 vols. Ed. by
    Alexander Grosart. Rprt. Serv. 1992 repr. of 1886 ed. $1,125.00. ISBN 0-7812-7242-4.
    The standard edition.

BOOK ABOUT GREENE

Hayashi, Tetsumaro. *Robert Greene Criticism: A Comprehensive Bibliography. Author
    Bibliographies Ser.* Scarecrow 1971 $20.00. ISBN 0-8108-0340-2

HERBERT, GEORGE. 1593–1633

A member of a distinguished Anglo-Welsh family, George Herbert was one of
the most important of the English Metaphysical poets. Herbert was educated at
Trinity College, Cambridge, and began following a path that seemed destined to
a worldly career. Soon, however, a growing sense of religious vocation led him
to the Church. The remainder of his life, though brief, was singularly pure,
pious, and intensely devoted to his office as an Anglican priest. The 129 sacred
poems in the collection known as *The Temple* (1633) are a spiritual autobiography of extraordinary intensity. Herbert was fond of traditional poetic forms, but
he infused them with a meditative pathos that results in original effects. He was
fond of simple diction and the rhythms of speech, at the same time that he freely
used arcane symbols and arranged the poems in strange shapes on the page.

POETRY BY HERBERT

The English Poems of George Herbert. Ed. by C. A. Patrides. C. E. Tuttle 1991 $6.95. ISBN 0-460-87039-4. An inexpensive selection.

George Herbert and the Seventeenth Century Religious Poets. Ed. by Mario Di Cesare. *Norton Critical Eds.* Norton 1978 o.p. Excellent selection of poems, valuable critical articles, and a useful selected bibliography.

The Williams Manuscript of George Herbert's Poems. Ed. by Amy Charles. Schol. Facsimiles 1977 $55.00. ISBN 0-8201-1286-0. A reprint of the original.

Works. Ed. by F. E. Hutchinson. *Oxford Eng. Ser.* OUP 1941 o.p. The standard edition.

BOOKS ABOUT HERBERT

Benet, Diana. *Secretary of Praise: The Poetic Vocation of George Herbert.* U. of Mo. Pr. 1984 $23.00. ISBN 0-8262-0408-2

Bennett, Joan. *Five Metaphysical Poets: Donne, Herbert, Vaughan, Crashaw, Marvell.* Cambridge U. Pr. 1934 $13.95. ISBN 0-521-09238-8. One of the best introductions to a remarkable group of poets; a comparative study of theme, tone, and imagery.

Block, Chana. *Spelling the Word: George Herbert and the Bible.* U. CA Pr. 1985 $45.00. ISBN 0-521-09238-8. A study of Herbert's scriptural inflections.

Charles, Amy. *A Life of George Herbert.* Cornell Univ. Pr. 1977 o.p. a biographical treatment.

Di Cesare, Marion, and Rigo Mignani, eds. *A Concordance to the Complete Writings of George Herbert.* Cornell Univ. Pr. 1977 $88.50. ISBN 0-8014-1106-8. A guide to Herbert's frequency and location of word usage.

Fish, Stanley E. *The Living Temple: George Herbert and the Catechizing.* U. CA Pr. 1978 $37.50. ISBN 0-520-02657-8. A fine, original study by an outstanding critic and scholar.

Harmon, Barbara L. *Costly Monuments: Representations of the Self in George Herbert's Poetry.* HUP 1982 $22.95. ISBN 0-674-17465-8. A study of Herbert's poetic persona.

Patrides, C. A., ed. *George Herbert: The Critical Heritage. Critical Heritage Ser.* Routledge 1983 $69.50. ISBN 0-7100-9240-7

Roberts, John R., ed. *Essential Articles for the Study of George Herbert.* Shoe String 1979 $47.50. ISBN 0-208-01770-4. A handy collection.

_____. *George Herbert: An Annotated Bibliography of Modern Criticism, 1905–1974.* U. of Mo. Pr. 1988 $42.00. ISBN 0-8262-0487-2. A guide to the criticism.

Schoenfeldt, Michael C. *Prayer and Power: George Herbert and Renaissance Courtship.* U. Ch. Pr. 1991 $49.95. ISBN 0-226-74001-3. A study of Herbert in relation to conventions of court power.

Stein, Arnold. *George Herbert's Lyrics.* Bks. Demand repr. of 1968 ed. $69.50. ISBN 0-8357-6626-8. A work of permanent value.

Strier, Richard. *Love Known: Theology and Experience in George Herbert's Poetry.* U. Ch. Pr. 1986 $25.00. ISBN 0-226-77716-2. An essential study.

Tuve, Rosemond. *A Reading of George Herbert. Midway Repr. Ser.* Bks. Demand repr. of 1982 ed. $56.70. ISBN 0-685-23855-5

Westerweel, Bart. *Patterns and Patterning: A Study of Four Poems by George Herbert.* Humanities Pr. 1984 o.p.

HERRICK, ROBERT. 1591–1674

Herrick is one of the Cavalier lyricists, and the most gifted of "The Tribe of Ben," the small band of poets much under the influence of Ben Jonson. Herrick has been called one of the very greatest of English songwriters, and certainly the conflict within him between the pagan and the priest infuses his best poetry with a peculiar power and complexity. Herrick published only one volume of verse, the astonishing collection of 1,200 poems known as the *Hesperides and Noble Numbers* (1648). Many of the poems deal with wine, women, and song— the need to *carpe diem* (seize the day), for youth and joy are fleeting. Intensely musical, his verse is by no means trivial, reflecting as it does classical and Anglican ceremony, English folklore, and timeless myth. Herrick lived a long life in holy orders, but with the Puritan victory he was pushed out of favor. Herrick almost disappeared from English literature until well into the nineteenth century. Since then his fame has steadily grown, and some of his poems are among the most popular in the language.

POETRY BY HERRICK

The Complete Poetry of Robert Herrick. Ed. by J. Max Patrick. *Norton Lib.* Norton 1968 o.p.

Poetical Works. Ed. by Leonard C. Martin. *Oxford Eng. Texts Ser.* OUP 1956 o.p. The poetry only.

Works. Ed. by F. E. Hutchinson. *Oxford Eng. Texts Ser.* OUP 1941 o.p. The standard edition.

BOOKS ABOUT HERRICK

Coiro, Ann B. *Robert Herrick's Hesperides and the Epigram Book Tradition.* John Hopkins 1988 $35.00. ISBN 0-8018-3571-2. An insightful study of Herrick's work in the context of a lesser-known literary tradition.

MacLeod, Malcolm L. *A Concordance to the Poems of Robert Herrick.* Haskell 1970 repr. of 1936 ed. $75.00. ISBN 0-8383-0991-7. A guide to the frequency and location of Herrick's word usage.

Moorman, Frederick. *Robert Herrick: A Biographical and Critical Study.* Russell 1962 o.p. A general introduction.

Rollin, Robert B., and J. Max Patrick, eds. *Trust to Good Verses: Herrick Tercentenary Essays.* U. of Pittsburgh Pr. 1977 o.p. A useful collection of readings.

HEYWOOD, THOMAS. c.1573–1641

Heywood is a good example of the professional dramatist who worked for Philip Henslowe, the theatrical manager, both as a playwright and an actor. By his own admission, Heywood claimed to have "either an entire hand or at least the main finger" in 220 plays, of which less than 30 survive. His best-known play, *A Woman Killed with Kindness* (1603), exemplifies domestic tragedy, in which sentiment and homely details are equally mingled. Heywood wrote an eloquent defense of the theater against Puritan attack called *An Apology for Actors* (1607–08).

PLAYS BY HEYWOOD

Dramatic Works of Thomas Heywood. 6 vols. Ed. by R. H. Shepherd. Russell 1964 repr. of 1874 ed. o.p. The standard edition.

The Fair Maid of the West. c.1631. Ed. by Robert K. Turner, Jr. Bks. Demand repr. of 1967 ed. $60.60. ISBN 0-8357-3823-X. A swashbuckling adventure story of romance and death.

A Woman Killed with Kindness. 1603. Ed. by Brian Scobie. Norton 1986 $6.95. ISBN 0-393-90052-5

WORK BY HEYWOOD

An Apology for Actors. 1612. *Eng. Stage Ser.* Johnson Repr. repr. of 1612 ed. $32.00. ISBN 0-384-22855-0

BOOKS ABOUT HEYWOOD

Bergeron, David M. *Thomas Heywood's Pageants: A Critical Edition.* Garland 1986 $20.00. ISBN 0-8240-5464-4. An informative guide to Heywood's civic commissions.

Boas, Frederick S. *Thomas Heywood.* Phaeton 1974 repr. of 1950 ed. $40.00. ISBN 0-87753-056-4. A useful, general guide.

JONSON, BEN. 1572?–1637

Next to SHAKESPEARE, Jonson was the most creative and energetic playwright and poet of the Elizabethan-Jacobean period. Son of a clergyman, and stepson of a master bricklayer, Jonson was learned in the classics, especially Latin literature, and throughout his career he attempted to apply neoclassical principles to his writing. In *The Alchemist* (1620), for example, he strictly adheres to unity of time and place. In his critical opinions expressed in *Timber* and in his conversations with William Drummond of Hawthornden, he is constantly attacking romantic assumptions and a failure to observe classical precedent. His great comedies—Volpone (1606), *Epicoene* (1609), *The Alchemist* (1610), and *Bartholomew Fair* (1614)—are satirical and display an enormous energy in language and characterization. A moralist, he sought to teach improvement by exaggerating the foibles and passions (or humours) of his characters. Jonson developed the "humours" theory of comedy in *Every Man in His Humour* (1598), and *Every Man Out of His Humour* (1600): The purpose of comedy is to purge eccentricity and whimsical monomania. Jonson wrote two tragedies, *Sejanus* (1603), and *Catiline* (1611), strongly founded on classical sources. His comedies after *The Devil Is an Ass* in 1616 represent a decline and are sometimes unfairly referred to as his "dotages."

Jonson's poetry, noted for its balance, control, and unadorned simplicity, prefigured the later lyrics of the seventeenth-century Cavalier poets, the "sons of Ben." Among his most well-known poems are two mourning the death of his first daughter and his seven-year-old son. For generations after his death, Jonson was considered as almost the equal of Shakespeare as a playwright, as well as a poet of outstanding achievement. During the twentieth century, however, his reputation began to suffer an undeserved decline. The excellent Yale edition of Jonson, published in individual volumes, is the most fully annotated collection of his works now available.

PLAYS BY JONSON

The Alchemist. 1610. Ed. by F. H. Mares. *Revels Plays Ser.* St. Martin 1988 repr. of 1967 ed. $12.95. ISBN 0-7190-1617-7

Ben Jonson's Plays and Masques. Ed. by Robert M. Adams. *Norton Critical Eds.* Norton 1979 $12.95. ISBN 0-393-09035-3. A convenient collection, with a good introduction.

Bartholomew Fair. 1614. Ed. by E. A. Horsman. *Revels Plays Ser.* St. Martin 1988 $59.95. ISBN 0-7190-1520-0

The Complete Masques. Ed. by Stephen Orgel. Yale U. Pr. 1969 $60.00. ISBN 0-300-01181-4. The definitive edition of Jonson's court productions.

The Complete Plays of Ben Jonson. Ed. by G. A. Wilkes. Vol. 2 OUP 1981 $149.00. ISBN 0-19-812601-8. The standard edition.

Sejanus. 1603. Ed. by Philip Ayres and others. *Revels Plays Ser.* 1990 $59.95. ISBN 0-7190-1542-1

Three Comedies. Ed. by Michael Jamieson. *Penguin Eng. Lib. Ser.* Viking Penguin 1966 $5.95. ISBN 0-14-043013-X

Volpone. 1606. Ed. by Philip Brockbank. *New Mermaid Ser.* Norton 1976 $5.95. ISBN 0-393-90010-X

POETRY BY JONSON

Ben Jonson and the Cavalier Poets. Ed. by Hugh MacLean. *Norton Critical Eds.* Norton 1975 $12.95. ISBN 0-393-09308-5.

Ben Jonson: The Complete Poems. Ed. by George Parfitt. *Eng. Poets Ser.* Bks. Demand 1989 $160.00. ISBN 0-8357-8076-7. The standard edition.

Works by Jonson

Works of Ben Jonson. 11 vols. Ed. by C. H. Herford and others. OUP 1925–52 $79.00 ea.
ISBNs 0-19-811352-8, 0-19-811353-6, 0-19-811356-0, 0-19-811358-7, 0-19-811359-5, 0-
19-811361-7, 0-19-811362-5. The standard edition.

Books about Jonson

Barish, Jonas A. *Ben Jonson and the Language of Prose Comedy. Norton Lib.* Norton 1970
repr. of 1967 ed. o.p. An important and influential study.

Barton, Anne. *Ben Jonson, Dramatist.* Cambridge U. Pr. 1984 $65.00. ISBN 0-521-27748-
5. An indispensable introduction to themes, form, and social context.

Bentley, Gerald E. *Shakespeare and Jonson, Their Reputations in the Seventeeth Century
Compared.* 2 vols. U. Ch. Pr. 1965 o.p.

Chan, Mary. *Music in the Theatre of Ben Jonson.* OUP 1980 o.p. Jonson's relations to
contemporary performance conventions.

Di Cesare, Mario A., and Ephim Fogel, eds. *A Concordance to the Poems of Ben Jonson.*
Cornell Univ. Pr. 1978 $82.50. ISBN 0-8014-1217-X. A guide to Jonson's frequency
and location of word use in the poetry.

Dutton, Richard. *Ben Jonson: To the First Folio. British and Irish Authors Ser.* Cambridge
U. Pr. 1984 $44.95. ISBN 0-521-24313-0. A study of the significance of Jonson's
unprecedented publication of his works.

Evans, Robert C. *Ben Jonson and the Poetics of Patronage.* Bucknell U. Pr. 1989 $45.00.
ISBN 0-8387-5136-9. Jonson's relations to the shaping constraints of literary
production.

Hyland, Peter. *Disguise and Role-Playing in Ben Jonson's Drama. Salzburg Studies in Eng.
Lit., Jacobean Drama Studies.* Humanities 1977 o.p. A study of a prevalent conceit.

Knoll, Robert E. *Ben Jonson's Plays: An Introduction.* Bks. Demand repr. of 1964 ed.
$58.80. ISBN 0-8357-7126-1

Loewenstein, Joseph. *Responsive Readings: Versions of Echo in Pastoral, Epic, and the
Jonsonian Masque. Yale Studies in Eng. Ser.* 1984 o.p. A study of imitation and
allusion.

Meagher, John C. *Method and Meaning in Jonson's Masques.* U. of Notre Dame Pr. 1969
o.p. A detailed analysis of the masque's form, themes, and virtues.

Orgel, Stephen. *The Jonsonian Masque.* Col. U. Pr. 1981 repr. of 1967 ed. $43.50. ISBN 0-
231-05370-3. The main authority on Jonson's masques.

Parfitt, George. *Ben Jonson: Public Poet and Private Man.* B & N Imports 1976 o.p. A
biographical treatment of the work.

Partridge, Edward B. *The Broken Compass: A Study of the Major Comedies of Ben Jonson.*
Greenwood 1976 repr. of 1958 ed. $47.50. ISBN 0-8371-8662-5. A study of imagery
and theme.

Peterson, Richard S. *Imitation and Praise in the Poems of Ben Jonson.* Yale U. Pr. 1981
$30.00. ISBN 0-300-02586-6. Jonson and the epideictic tradition.

Riggs, David. *Ben Jonson: A Life.* HUP 1989 $14.95. ISBN 0-674-06626-X. A sensitive
psychoanalytic account of the writer.

Summers, Claude J., and Ted Larry Pebworth. *Ben Jonson. Twayne's Eng. Authors Ser.* G.
K. Hall 1979 o.p.

Trimpi, Wesley. *Ben Jonson's Poems: A Study of the Plain Style.* Stanford U. Pr. 1962
$35.00. ISBN 0-8047-0097-4. Jonson's stylistic concerns.

Watson, Robert N. *Ben Jonson's Parodic Strategy: Literary Imperialism in the Comedies.*
HUP 1987 $25.00. ISBN 0-674-00601-4. An incisive account of Jonson's competitive
literary relations to contemporary playwrights.

KYD, THOMAS. 1558–1594

Son of a scrivener, Kyd is best known as the author of *The Spanish Tragedy*
(c.1586) an extremely popular revenge tragedy of the late 1580s and one of the
most parodied of Elizabethan plays. Kyd's only other acknowledged authorship

is the translation of Robert Garnier's Senecan tragedy, *Cornélie*, in 1594. He may also have written the lost *Hamlet* play that precedes SHAKESPEARE'S. Although Kyd's balanced rhetoric seems old fashioned, *The Spanish Tragedy* is notable for its searing passions and intensely dramatic rendering of revenge-tragedy themes.

PLAY BY KYD

The Spanish Tragedy. c.1586. Ed. by Philip Edwards. *Revels Plays Ser.* St. Martin 1988 repr. of 1969 ed. $12.95. ISBN 0-7190-1609-6. Concerns the killing of a Spanish nobleman by a Portuguese prince and the revenge that follows.

BOOKS ABOUT KYD

Barber, C. L. *Creating Elizabethan Tragedy: The Theater of Marlowe and Kyd.* Ed. by Richard P. Wheeler. U. Ch. Pr. 1988 $11.95. ISBN 0-226-03704-5. A sensitive and subtle account of the cultural place and work of these two dramatists.

Murray, Peter B. *Thomas Kyd. Twayne's English Authors Ser.* o.p. A general introduction.

LODGE, THOMAS. 1558–1606

While primarily remembered for composing the story that would provide the source for SHAKESPEARE's *As You Like It*, Thomas Lodge was a prolific author in his own right, who made prose fiction his chief concern. Son of a one-time London mayor, Lodge began his career as a lawyer but quickly found literature more attractive, perhaps because of the encouragement of his friend ROBERT GREENE. Lodge was also a playwright—his first published work appears to be *A Defense of Stage Plays* (1580), an answer to the attack by Stephen Gosson—but the majority of his efforts were devoted to prose romances, such as *The Delectable History of Forbonius and Prisceria* (1584), *Scilla's Metamorphosis* (1589), and *Robert, Duke of Normandy* (1591). *Rosalynde* (1590) is, like SIDNEY's *Arcadia*, a pastoral romance, a form popular with urban Elizabethans for its idealized depiction of rural *otium*.

PROSE FICTION BY LODGE

Rosalynde. Ed. by W. W. Greg. Ayer repr. of 1907 ed. $15.00. ISBN 0-8369-5510-2

WORK BY LODGE

Works. Printed for the Hunterian Club 1883 o.p. The standard edition.

BOOKS ABOUT LODGE

Rae, Welsey D. *Thomas Lodge. Twayne's English Authors Ser.* G. K. Hall 1967 $17.95. ISBN 0-89197-964-6. A general introduction.

Sisson, Charles Jasper, ed. *Thomas Lodge and Other Elizabethans.* Hippocrene Bks. 1966 $37.00. ISBN 0-374-97467-5. Lodge in his contemporary context.

LYLY, JOHN. c.1554–1606

Lyly wrote eight elegant and refined comedies for the boy companies and for court performance. His witty and elaborate prose style, drawing many allusions from classical mythology, was honed in his prose romance, *Euphues: The Anatomy of Wit* (1578), and its sequel, *Euphues and His England* (1580). These works are the basis for the "euphuistic" style, characterized by an intensity of antithesis, alliteration, and simile. Lyly's comedies are notable for their graceful and incisive portraits of women.

PLAYS BY LYLY

Campaspe and *Sappho and Phao*. Ed. by G. K. Hunter and others. *Revels Plays Ser.* St. Martin 1992 $59.95. ISBN 0-7190-1550-2. A good introduction and notes.

Endymion: The Man in the Moon. Ed. by George P. Baker. Folcroft 1977 o.p. A good introduction to the courtly play.

Gallathea (and *Midas*). Ed. by Anne B. Lancashire. *Regents Renaissance Drama Ser.* U. of Nebr. Pr. 1970 $20.00. ISBN 0-8032-0268-7. A useful edition to the play about the consequences of cross-dressing.

Mother Bombie. 1594. *Malone Society Repr. Ser.* AMS Pr. repr. of 1939 ed. o.p.

WORKS BY LYLY

Complete Works. 3 vols. Ed. by R. Warwick Bond. Rprt. Serv. 1992 repr. of 1902 ed. $225.00. ISBN 0-7812-7212-2. The standard edition.

Euphues, the Anatomy of Wit. Ed. by Edward Arber. Saifer repr. of 1868 ed. $25.00. ISBN 0-87556-213-2

BOOKS ABOUT LYLY

Saccio, Peter. *The Court Comedies of John Lyly: A Study in Allegorical Dramaturgy.* Princeton U. Pr. 1969 o.p. A seminal study of Lyly's method.

Scragg, Leah. *The Metamorphosis of Galathea: A Study in Creative Adaptation.* U. Pr. of Amer. 1982 o.p.

Wilson, John D. *John Lyly.* Haskell 1969 repr. of 1905 ed. $49.95. ISBN 0-8383-0261-0. A useful overview.

MARLOWE, CHRISTOPHER. 1564–1593

Marlowe was born in the same year as SHAKESPEARE and, by the time of his early death in 1593, his achievement towered over that of his longer-lived contemporary. Son of a shoemaker, and a graduate of Cambridge, Marlowe burst into the theatrical scene around 1588 with the two parts of *Tamburlaine*, and grand conqueror play whose mighty hero threatens the world "with high astounding terms." Marlowe's blank verse—his "mighty line"—was strong and passionate and offered a model for later dramatists. He was also a poet, and his unfinished poem in the style of OVID (see Vol. 2)—*Hero and Leander* (continued by GEORGE CHAPMAN)—is remarkable for its wry handling of both erotic conventions and gender roles. All of Marlowe's seven plays test limits or show a protagonist striving against a humdrum and uncomprehending world. Doctor Faustus is a typically Marlovian hero who dares damnation to achieve a more than human scope. Marlowe himself during his lifetime was accused of atheism and homosexuality. He seems to have been a secret agent in the government service and was killed in a tavern brawl at Deptford under mysterious circumstances. The Marlowe Society in the United States publishes a regular periodical with reviews.

PLAYS BY MARLOWE

Complete Plays. Ed. by J. B. Steanie. Viking Penguin 1969 $9.95. ISBN 0-14-043037-7

Doctor Faustus. 1604. AMS Pr. repr. of 1914 ed. $49.50. ISBN 0-404-53402-3

Edward the Second. 1594. Ed. by W. Moelwyn Merchant. *New Mermaid Ser.* Norton 1976 $4.95. ISBN 0-393-90018-5. Marlowe's history play.

The Jew of Malta. 1633. Ed. by H. S. Bennett. Gordian 1966 repr. of 1931 ed. $35.00. ISBN 0-87752-189-1

Tamburlaine the Great. 1590. 2 vols. Ed. by U.M. Ellis-Fermor. Gordian 1966 repr. of 1930 ed. $35.00. ISBN 0-87752-192-1

WORKS BY MARLOWE

Complete Plays and Poems. Ed. by E. D. Pendry. C. E. Tuttle 1991 $9.95. ISBN 0-460-87043-2. A convenient edition.

The Complete Works of Christopher Marlowe. 2 vols. Ed. by Fredson Bowers. Cambridge U. Pr. 1981 $170.00. ISBN 0-521-22759-3

BOOKS ABOUT MARLOWE

Bakeless, John E. *The Tragicall History of Christopher Marlowe.* 2 vols. Greenwood repr. of 1942 ed. o.p. A biographical account.

Cartelli, Thomas. *Marlowe, Shakespeare, and the Economy of Theatrical Experience.* U. of Pa. Pr. 1991 $36.95. ISBN 0-8122-3102-3. Argues that the playgoer sought pleasure rather than moral enrichment.

Cole, Douglas. *Suffering and Evil in the Plays of Christopher Marlowe.* Gordian 1971 repr. of 1962 ed. text ed. o.p.

Eccles, Mark. *Christopher Marlowe in London.* Hippocrene Bks. 1967 o.p.

Friedenreich, Kenneth. *Christopher Marlowe: An Annotated Bibliography of Criticism Since 1950.* Scarecrow 1979 $20.00. ISBN 0-8108-1239-8. A useful guide to critical discussion.

Hotson, J. Leslie. *The Death of Christopher Marlowe.* Rprt. Serv. 1992 repr. of 1925 ed. $59.00. ISBN 0-7812-7250-5. Discovery of the sensational circumstances of Marlowe's death.

Ingram, John H. *Christopher Marlowe and His Associates.* Cooper Sq. 1970 repr. of 1904 ed. $35.00. ISBN 0-8154-0326-7. Marlowe's life and contemporaries.

Kocher, Paul H. *Christopher Marlowe: A Study of His Thought, Learning and Character.* Russell 1962 repr. of 1946 ed. o.p.

Leech, Clifford. *Christopher Marlowe: Poet for the Stage.* AMS Pr. 1986 $39.50. ISBN 0-404-62281-X. Insightful analysis of language and themes.

Levin, Harry. *The Overreacher: A Study of Christopher Marlowe.* Peter Smith o.p. Insightful criticism, especially on style.

MacLure, Millar. *Marlowe: The Critical Heritage. 1588–1896.* Routledge 1979 $69.50. ISBN 0-7100-0245-9. The indispensable guide to Marlowe's reception.

Sanders, Wilbur. *The Dramatist and the Received Idea.* Cambridge U. Pr. 1980 $19.95. ISBN 0-521-29800-8

Shepherd, Simon. *Marlowe and the Politics of Elizabethan Theatre.* St. Martin 1986 $35.00. ISBN 0-312-51546-4

Sims, James H. *Dramatic uses of Biblical Allusions in Marlowe and Shakespeare.* U. Press Fla. 1966 $9.00. ISBN 0-8130-0206-0. A reference guide.

Steane, J. B. *Marlowe: A Critical Study.* Cambridge U. Pr. 1970 $54.00. ISBN 0-521-06545-3. A good introduction.

Weil, Judith. *Christopher Marlowe.* Cambridge U. Pr. 1977 $54.95. ISBN 0-521-21554-4. A good overview.

MARSTON, JOHN. c.1575–1634

Marston studied law in the Middle Temple but abandoned the law to write biting verse satires in the Roman style of JUVENAL (see Vol. 2). His best-known satires are *The Scourge of Villainie* (1598) and *The Metamorphosis of Pygmalion's Image* (1598). When verse satires were forbidden in 1599, Marston turned his satiric talent to the theater. *The Malcontent* (1604) is his best-known play. There is a sharp distinction between the banished Altofronto, who speaks in verse, and his disguise as Malevole, who expresses himself in a scurrilous and misanthropic prose. *The Dutch Courtesan* (1604) is preoccupied with sexuality and is at once moralistic, satirical, cynical, and grotesque. These mixtures of tone are part of the passionate attitudinizing of Marston. All of his plays were written for performance by children's companies in the private theaters.

PLAYS BY MARSTON

Antonio and Mellida. 1599. Ed. by Reavley Gair and others. *Revels Plays Ser.* St. Martin 1992 $49.95. ISBN 0-7190-1547-2

Antonio's Revenge. 1599. Ed. by George K. Hunter. *Regents Renaissance Drama Ser.* U. of Nebr. Pr. 1965 o.p. With *Antonio and Mellida*, two parts of a double play.

The Dutch Courtesan. 1604. Ed. by M. L. Wine. *Regents Renaissance Drama Ser.* Bks. Demand repr. of 1965 ed. $40.60. ISBN 0-8357-7933-5

The Fawn. c.1605. Ed. by Gerald A. Smith. *Regents Renaissance Drama Ser.* U. of Nebr. Pr. 1965 $12.95. ISBN 0-8032-5275-7

The Malcontent. 1604. Ed. by M. L. Wine. *Regents Renaissance Drama Ser.* Bks. Demand repr. of 1964 ed. $37.80. ISBN 0-685-15565-X

Select Plays. Ed. by M. Jackson and others. Cambridge U. Pr. 1986 $69.95. ISBN 0-521-21746-6

The Scourge of Villanie. Haskell 1974 $57.95. ISBN 0-8383-1828-2

WORK BY MARSTON

Works. 3 vols. Ed. by A. H. Bullen. Adlers Foreign Bks. 1970 repr. of 1887 ed. o.p. The standard edition.

BOOKS ABOUT MARSTON

Geckle, George L. *John Marston's Drama: Themes, Images, Sources*. Fairleigh Dickinson 1978 $29.50. ISBN 0-8386-2157-0. A useful introduction.

Jensen, Ejner. *John Marston, Dramatist. Salzburg Studies in Eng. Lit., Jacobean Drama Studies*. Humanities 1980 o.p.

Scott, Michael. *John Marston Plays: Themes, Structure and Performance*. B & N Imports 1978 o.p.

MARVELL, ANDREW. 1621–1678

This enchanting poet was at once a Puritan and sympathetic to the Cavaliers. A partisan of Charles I, he became tutor to Cromwell's ward, a friend of JOHN MILTON, and assistant Latin Secretary in the Cromwell government; he was later a member of the Restoration Parliament, surviving very well in the shifting political climate of his age. Close to the Metaphysical poets in method and diction, Marvell is usually secular in approach; he is fascinated by the charm and also the rude power of nature, with which his poetry is centrally concerned. His best-known poem, *To His Coy Mistress*, rings witty changes of the theme on *carpe diem* (seize the day).

Marvell's reputation has never stood higher than it does today. His verse combines wit, satire, intellectual depth, playfulness, complexity, and deep seriousness in a way perfectly suited to modern taste.

POETRY BY MARVELL

The Complete Poems. Ed. by Elizabeth S. Donno. *Poets Ser.* Viking Penguin 1977 $7.95. ISBN 0-14-042213-7

The Poems of Andrew Marvell. Ed. by Hugh MacDonald. Routledge 1969 o.p.

WORK BY MARVELL

Poems and Letters. 2 vols. Ed. by H. M. Margoliouth. *Oxford Eng. Texts Ser.* OUP 1971 o.p. Contains the complete poems and letters.

BOOKS ABOUT MARVELL

Bennett, Joan. *Five Metaphysical Poets: Donne, Herbert, Vaughan, Crashaw, Marvell*. Cambridge U. Pr. 1934 $13.95. ISBN 0-521-09238-8. One of the best introductions to a remarkable group of poets. A comparative study of styles and images.

Cullen, Patrick. *Spenser, Marvell, and Renaissance Pastoral.* Bks. Demand repr. of 1970 ed. $42.60. ISBN 0-685-15242-1. A study of Marvell's work in relation to Renaissance models of pastoral poetry.

Donno, Elizabeth S., ed. *Andrew Marvell: The Critical Heritage. Critical Heritage Ser.* Routledge 1978 $69.50. ISBN 0-7100-8791-8

Guffey, George R., ed. *A Concordance to the English Poems of Andrew Marvell.* U. of NC Pr. 1974 o.p. A guide to the frequency and location of Marvell's word use.

Kermode, Frank, and others, eds. *Andrew Marvell.* OUP 1991 $45.00. ISBN 0-19-54183-8. Includes a brief introduction to the life and writings of Marvell, a chronology, explanatory notes, and a selected bibliography.

King, Bruce. *Marvell's Allegorical Poetry.* Oleander Pr. 1977 $25.00. ISBN 0-902675-60-5. A guide to Marvell's allegory.

Legouis, Pierre. *Andrew Marvell: Poète, Puritain, Patriote, 1621–1678.* Russell 1965 repr. of 1929 ed. o.p. A biographical treatment.

Patterson, Annabel M. *Marvell and the Civic Crown.* Bks. Demand repr. of 1978 ed. $71.50. ISBN 0-8357-6202-5. A consideration of Marvell's public identity.

Wallace, John M. *Destiny His Choice: The Loyalism of Andrew Marvell.* Cambridge U. Pr. 1981 $47.50. ISBN 0-521-06725-1. A seminal political reading.

MASSINGER, PHILIP. 1583–1640

Massinger is a prolific dramatist who wrote, or had a hand in, more than 50 plays. His specialty was tragicomedy, in which he imitated John Fletcher. His best-known play is *A New Way to Pay Old Debts* (1621), based on MIDDLETON's *A Trick to Catch the Old One.* Sir Giles Overreach reflects the historical Sir Giles Mompesson, a notorious capitalist and extortionist, who was tried in 1621. There is a good deal of snobbery in Massinger's play, and the class hatred of Sir Giles is frenzied and passionate. *A New Way to Pay Old Debts* has had an active theatrical history from its own day to the present, especially as a vehicle for the grandly histrionic role of Overreach.

PLAYS BY MASSINGER

City Madam. 1632. *New Mermaid Ser.* Norton 1984 o.p.

A New Way to Pay Old Debts. 1621. Ed. by M. St. Clare Byrne. *New Mermaid Ser.* Norton 1984 $6.95. ISBN 0-393-90009-6

The Plays and Poems of Philip Massinger. 5 vols. Ed. by Philip Edwards and Colin Gibson. *Oxford Eng. Texts Ser.* OUP 1976 o.p. An admirable modern edition of Massinger's extensive works.

Plays of Philip Massinger. 4 vols. Ed. by William Gifford. AMS Pr. repr. of 1813 ed. $160.00. ISBN 0-404-04280-5. The standard edition.

BOOKS ABOUT MASSINGER

Howard, Douglas, ed. *Philip Massinger: A Critical Reassessment.* Cambridge U. Pr. 1985 $49.95. ISBN 0-521-25895-2. A collection of essays on Massinger's themes, language, and use of form.

McManaway, James G. *Philip Massinger and the Restoration Drama.* Folcroft repr. of 1934 ed. o.p.

Maxwell, Baldwin. *Studies in Beaumont, Fletcher and Massinger.* Hippocrene Bks. 1966 o.p. A collection of critical approaches.

MIDDLETON, THOMAS. c.1580–1627

Middleton, who wrote in a wide variety of genres and styles, was a thoroughly professional dramatist. His comedies are generally based on London life but are seen through the perspective of Roman comedy, especially those of PLAUTUS (see Vol. 2). Middleton is a masterful constructor of plots. *A Chaste Maid in Cheapside* (1630) is typical of Middleton's interests. It is biting and satirical in tone: the crassness of the willing cuckold Allwit is almost frightening. Middleton was very preoccupied with sexual themes, especially in his tragedies, *The Changeling* (1622), written with William Rowley, and *Women Beware Women* (1621). The portraits of women in these plays are remarkable. Both Beatrice-Joanna in *The Changeling* and Bianca in *Women Beware Women* move swiftly from innocence to corruption, and Livia in *Women Beware Women* is noteworthy as a feminine Machiavelli and manipulator. In his psychological realism and his powerful vision of evil, Middleton is close to SHAKESPEARE.

PLAYS BY MIDDLETON

The Changeling (coauthored with William Rowley). 1622. Ed. by N. W. Bawcatt. *Revels Plays Ser.* St. Martin 1988 $12.95. ISBN 0-7190-1610-X

A Chaste Maid in Cheapside. 1630. Ed. by Alan Brissenden. *New Mermaid Ser.* Norton 1976 $4.95. ISBN 0-393-90023-1

A Game at Chess. 1625. Ed. by J. W. Harper. *New Mermaid Ser.* Norton 1976 $4.95. ISBN 0-393-90026-6. A striking political commentary.

A Mad World, My Masters. 1608. Ed. by Standish Henning. *Regents Renaissance Drama Ser.* Bks. Demand repr. of 1965 ed. $34.10. ISBN 0-8357-7877-0. A satiric, farcical portrait of a rapacious opportunist.

Michaelmas Term. 1607. Ed. by Richard Levin. *Regents Renaissance Drama Ser.* Bks. Demand repr. of 1966 ed. $44.60. ISBN 0-7837-0147-0. A city comedy of an entrepreneurial woolen draper.

No Wit, No Help Like a Woman's. Ed. by Lowell E. Johnson. *Regents Renaissance Drama Ser.* U. of Nebr. Pr. 1976 $15.95. ISBN 0-8032-0300-4. A city comedy of disguise, marriage, and intrigue.

The Roaring Girl (coauthored with Thomas Dekker). 1611. Ed. by A. H. Gomme. AMS Pr. repr. of 1914 ed. $49.50. ISBN 0-404-53430-0. The adventures of a cross-dressed heroine.

A Trick to Catch the Old One. 1608. Ed. by C. J. Watson. *New Mermaid Ser.* Norton 1976 $4.95. ISBN 0-393-90025-8

Women Beware Women. 1621. Ed. by J. R. Mulryne. *Revels Plays Ser.* St. Martin $55.00. ISBN 0-7190-1509-X

WORK BY MIDDLETON

The Works of Thomas Middleton. 8 vols. Ed. by A. H. Bullen. AMS Pr. repr. of 1886 ed. $360.00. ISBN 0-404-04330-5. The standard edition.

BOOKS ABOUT MIDDLETON

Covatta, Anthony. *Thomas Middleton's City Comedies.* Bucknell U. Pr. 1974 $18.00. ISBN 0-8387-1196-0. An overview of themes and satiric techniques.

Heinemann, Margot. *Puritanism and Theatre: Thomas Middleton and Opposition Drama under the Early Stuarts.* Cambridge U. Pr. 1982 $17.95. ISBN 0-521-27052-9. An essential reaction of Middleton's political valence.

Kistner, A. L., and M. K. Kistner. *Middleton's Tragic Themes.* P. Lang Pubs. 1984 $23.00. ISBN 0-8204-0120-X. A reading of concerns common to the plays.

Rowe, George E., Jr. *Thomas Middleton and the New Comedy Tradition.* U. of Nebr. Pr. 1979 $25.00. ISBN 0-8032-3853-3. A discussion of Middleton's relation to his literary inheritance.

Schoenbaum, Samuel. *Middleton's Tragedies.* Gordian 1970 repr. of 1955 ed. $50.00. ISBN 0-87752-132-8

Steene, Sara J. *Thomas Middleton: A Reference Guide.* G. K. Hall 1984 o.p.

MILTON, JOHN. 1608–1674

John Milton was born in London, the son of a notary. Recognizing talent in his son at an early age, his father made sure that Milton had the best of educations. After private tutoring, Milton entered St. Paul's School and then Cambridge University, where he began to prepare for the ministry. While at Cambridge, however, he decided to become a poet instead.

Milton's tremendous poetic gift showed itself early: in the two companion pieces written in 1633, *L'Allegro* (the mirthful man) and *Il Penseroso* (the contemplative man); in *Comus, A Masque*, which was acted in 1634; and *Lycidas* (1637), a pastoral elegy mourning the death of the poet's college friend Edward King, who was drowned crossing the Irish Channel.

Milton's prose belongs to his middle life, when he turned away from poetry for a time, to help bring about "the establishment of real liberty" (as he wrote in 1654); from 1640 to 1660, he actively supported the Puritan cause, serving Cromwell as Latin Secretary from 1649 to 1655. His greatest prose work, the *Areopagitica* (1644) or *Speech for the Liberty of Unlicensed Printing*, took its name from the hill of Ares, on the site of the Acropolis in Athens, where a judicial court met.

Paradise Lost, one of the world's supreme epics, was published in 1667, in 10 books; the second edition (1674) contains 12 books, of which Books 1, 2, 4, and 9 are the most admired. Its mighty theme is the fall of humankind from the Garden of Eden, and its purpose is "to justify the ways of God to man." Milton had been destined for the church, but while in Cambridge gave up his intention of taking orders. Theology continued throughout his life to occupy his thoughts, particularly in the great epic poem *Paradise Lost*. *Paradise Regained* (1671) is its sequel.

For the last 22 years of his life, Milton was blind. His three daughters, children of his first wife, Mary Powell, read aloud to him in Greek, Latin, and Hebrew, and the youngest took down all of *Paradise Lost* in dictation. Mary Powell died in 1652; Milton married Katherine Woodcock in 1656, and, after her death in 1658, married Elizabeth Minshull in 1663. These later marriages seemed to have alienated his children. Something of Milton's unhappy experience in marriage certainly echoes in his last great poem, *Samson Agonistes* (Samson the Athlete or Wrestler) (1671). Written in the style of a Greek tragedy, the story is founded on the biblical account of Samson's blindness and his deception at the hands of Delilah.

Milton's sonnets are few in number but are unsurpassed; *On His Blindness* (1652–58) is perhaps the most famous. He was a great Latin scholar who wrote poetry in Latin that has been widely admired by classicists. Milton is one of the two or three greatest poets ever to write in English, and the peculiar power of his blank verse has earned him the title "the organ voice of England."

POETRY BY MILTON

John Milton: Complete Shorter Poems. Ed. by John Carey. Longman 1971 o.p. A useful introduction to the minor poems.

Paradise Lost. Ed. by Scott Elledge. *Norton Critical Eds.* Norton 1975 $19.95. ISBN 0-393-04406-8. Excellent text, good section on backgrounds and sources, major critical essays, and useful biography.

The Poetical Works. Ed. by Helen Darbishire. 2 vols. *Oxford Eng. Texts Ser.* OUP Vol. 1 1952 $55.00. ISBN 0-19-811819-8. Vol. 2 1955 $55.00. ISBN 0-19-811820-1. Volume One contains *Paradise Lost;* Volume Two contains *Paradise Regained, Samson Agonistes,* and *Poems upon Several Occasions.*

Works. 2 vols. Ed. by Frank Allen Patterson and others. Col. U. Pr. 1931 o.p. The first complete and definitive edition containing all the poetry considered to be genuine and all the variant readings of other editors, together with translations of works not originally written in English.

PROSE WORKS BY MILTON

The Complete Prose Works. 8 vols. Ed. by Don M. Wolfe and others. Yale U. Pr. 1953–1982 $70.00–$95.00 ea. ISBNs 0-300-00956-9, 0-300-01288-8, 0-300-02015-5, 0-300-02561-0, 0-300-00581-4. Good notes and introduction.

WORKS BY MILTON

John Milton: Complete Poems and Major Prose. Ed. by Merritt Y. Hughes. Odyssey Pr. 1957 $26.56. ISBN 0-672-63178-4. In many respects the best one-volume edition; contains fine commentary and copious notes.

The Portable Milton. Ed. by Douglas Bush. *Viking Portable Lib.* Viking Penguin 1976 $9.95. ISBN 0-14-015044-7. Includes *Paradise Lost, Paradise Regained, Samson Agonistes,* complete early poems and sonnets; selections from prose works, including *Areopagitica* complete.

BOOKS ABOUT MILTON

Barker, Arthur E., *Milton: Modern Essays in Criticism.* OUP 1965 o.p. A collection of standard readings.

Broadbent, John. *Introduction to Paradise Lost.* Cambridge U. Pr. 1972 $34.50. ISBN 0-521-08068-1. An insightful guide.

Empson, William. *Milton's God.* Cambridge U. Pr. 1981 $19.95. ISBN 0-521-29910-1. A controversial discussion of the religion of *Paradise Lost* by the eminent British critic.

Fish, Stanley E. *Surprised by Sin: The Reader in Paradise Lost.* U. CA Pr. 1971 $12.95. ISBN 0-520-01897-4. One of the most influential recent readings of the epic.

Frye, Northrop. *The Return of Eden: Five Essays on Milton's Epics.* Bks. Demand repr. of 1975 ed. $39.80. ISBN 0-8357-41389. Absorbing essays by one of the century's most respected critical theorists.

Gardner, Helen. *A Reading of Paradise Lost.* OUP 1965 o.p. A defense of Milton's style.

Hanford, James H. *John Milton: Poet and Humanist.* Case Western Reserve U. Pr. 1966 o.p. A series of essays on Milton's poetic development.

Hanford, James, H., and James G. Taaffe. *A Milton Handbook.* 1939. Appleton & Lange 1970 o.p. Invaluable. A collection of bibliographic, biographic, and historical contexts.

Hill, Christopher. *Milton and the English Revolution.* Viking Penguin 1979 o.p. Milton in his turbulent political context.

Hughes, Merritt Y., ed. *A Variorum Commentary on the Poems of John Milton.* 2 vols. Col. U. Pr. o.p. The indispensable history of response.

Hunter, William B., Jr. *A Milton Encyclopedia.* 9 vols. Bucknell U. Pr. $220.00. ISBN 0-686-85742-9. An all-purpose guide to Milton's sources and references.

Ingram, William, and Kathleen M. Swain, eds. *A Concordance to Milton's English Poetry.* OUP 1972 o.p. A guide to Milton's frequency and location of word use.

Leonard, John. *Naming in Paradise Lost: Milton and the Language of Adam and Eve.* OUP 1990 $59.00. ISBN 0-19-812958-0. A study of the poem's philosophy of language.

Lewalski, Barbara K. *Milton's Brief Epic: The Genre, Meaning, and Art of "Paradise Regained."* U. Pr. of New England 1966 $55.00. ISBN 0-87057-095-1. An insightful overview.

Lewis, Clive S. A Preface to Paradise Lost. OUP 1942 $9.95. ISBN 0-19-500345-4. An interpretation of Milton's purpose in writing the epic.

McColley, Diane K. *Milton's Eve.* U. of Ill. Pr. 1983 $24.95. ISBN 0-252-00980-0. Milton's notion of woman.

Nicolson, Marjorie H. *John Milton: A Reader's Guide to His Poetry.* FS&G 1971 $27.50. ISBN 0-88254-967-7

Parker, William R. *Milton: A Biography.* 2 vols. OUP 1968 o.p. Authoritative, scholarly biography.

Patrides, C. A., ed. *Milton's "Lycidas": The Tradition and the Poem.* U. of Mo. Pr. rev. ed. 1983 o.p. A study of the elegiac pastoral tradition.

Patterson, Annabel, ed. *John Milton*. Longman 1992 $44.95. ISBN 0-582-04550-9. A collection of a recent range of critical approaches.

Radzinowicz, Mary Ann. *Toward Samson Agonistes: The Growth of Milton's Mind*. Princeton U. Pr. 1978 $65.00. ISBN 0-691-06357-5. A thorough study of the tragedy in the context of Milton's corpus.

Ricks, Christopher. *Milton's Grand Style*. OUP 1963 $16.95. ISBN 0-19-812090-7. The classic justification of Milton's style.

Rumrich, John O. *Matter of Glory: A New Preface to Paradise Lost*. U. of Pittsburgh Pr. 1987 $24.95. ISBN 0-8229-3564-3. A study of the relation of chaos and glory in the epic.

Schwartz, Regina M. *Remembering and Repeating: Biblical Creation in Paradise Lost*. Cambridge U. Pr. 1989 $39.95. ISBN 0-521-34357-7

Turner, James Grantham. *One Flesh: Paradisial Marriage and Sexual Relations in the Age of Milton*. OUP 1987. $69.00. ISBN 0-19-821866-5. A study of Milton's culture with regard to affective and sexual attitudes.

Warner, Rex. *John Milton*. Haskell 1975 $75.00. ISBN 0-8383-2097-X. A general overview.

Wilson, A. N. *The Life of John Milton*. OUP 1983 $22.95. ISBN 0-19-211776-9. An informative, sentimental life.

Woodhouse, A. S. *The Heavenly Muse: A Preface to Milton*. Ed. by Hugh R. MacCallum. Bks. Demand repr. of 1972 ed. $101.20. ISBN 0-8357-8165-8. A historically inflected consideration of several works.

MORE, SIR THOMAS, ST. 1478–1535

Born in London, the son of a judge, More became an important statesman and scholar. He was also one of the most eminent humanists of the Renaissance. Educated at Oxford, More became an under-sheriff of London and, later, a member of Parliament. Under King Henry VIII he served as Treasurer of the Exchequer, speaker of the House of Commons, and, finally, Lord Chancellor.

More is probably best known for his *Utopia*, which was written in Latin (then the language of literary and intellectual Europe). It was translated into English in 1551. As the first part of this small masterpiece indicates, when More was weighing the offer to be an adviser to Henry VIII he was well aware of the compromises, bitterness, and frustration that such an office involved. In the second part, More develops his famous utopia—a Greek word punning on the meanings "a good place" and "no place"—a religious, communistic society where the common ownership of goods, obligatory work for everyone, and the regular life of all before the eyes of all ensure that one's baser nature will remain under control. Inspired by PLATO's (see Vols. 3 and 4) *Republic*, More's *Utopia* became in turn the urbane legacy of the humanistic movement (in which More's friends were most notably ERASMUS (see Vol. 4), John Colet, and William Grocyn) to succeeding ages. More also wrote a history, *Richard III*, which, if arguably the first instance of modern historiography in its attention to character and its departure from chronicle, is also, in its responsiveness to the Tudor polemic of divine rights, largely responsible for the notorious reputation of Richard as an evil ruler. More's refusal to recognize Henry VIII as Head of the Church led to a sentence of high treason. Imprisoned for more than a year, he was finally beheaded. Eventually, More was granted sainthood.

PROSE FICTION BY MORE

Utopia. 1516. Trans. by Robert M. Adams. *Norton Critical Eds*. Norton 1991 $6.95. ISBN 0-393-96145-1

WORKS BY MORE

The Complete Works of St. Thomas More. Complete Works of St. Thomas More Ser. 16
   vols. Yale U. Pr. 1963–1988 Vols. 1-9 o.p. Vol. 10 1988 $65.00. ISBN 0-300-03376-1.
Correspondence. Ed. by Elizabeth Frances Rogers. *Select Bibliographies Repr. Ser.* Ayer
   repr. of 1947 ed. $30.00. ISBN 0-8369-5404-1. The letters.
The History of King Richard III and Selections from the English and Latin Poems. Yale U.
   Pr. 1976 $30.00. ISBN 0-300-01925-4
Thomas More's Prayer Book: A Facsimile Reproduction of the Annotated Pages. Trans. by
   Louis L. Martz and Richard S. Sylvester. *Elizabethan Club Ser.* Yale U. Pr. 1969
   $35.00. ISBN 0-300-00179-7. A facsimile reproduction of the annotated pages, with
   the English translation; intended as a companion volume to *The Complete Works of
   St. Thomas More.*

BOOKS ABOUT MORE

Bolt, Robert. *A Man for All Seasons.* Random 1990 $7.95. ISBN 0-679-72822-8. The
   thoughtful and immensely successful play and movie.
Guy, J. A. *The Public Career of Sir Thomas More.* Yale U. Pr. 1980 o.p. More as a public
   servant.
Harpsfield, Nicholas. *The Life and Death of St. Thomas More.* Ed. by E. V. Hitchcock.
   Rprt. Serv. 1988 repr. of 1932 ed. $99.00. ISBN 0-7812-0274-4
Kenyon, Timothy. *Utopian Communism and Political Thought in Early Modern England.*
   Col. U. Pr. 1990 $39.00. ISBN 0-86187-772-1. A study of More's work in relation to
   contemporary political discourse.
Logan, George M. *The Meaning of More's Utopia.* Princeton U. Pr. 1983 $42.50. ISBN 0-
   691-06557-8
Marius, Richard. *Thomas More: A Biography.* Knopf 1984 o.p. Standard biography of the
   author.
Martz, Louis L. *Thomas More: The Search for the Inner Man.* Yale U. Pr. 1990 $16.95.
   ISBN 0-300-04784-3. Cuts down the revived charge of More as a bloodthirsty hunter
   of heretics, a furious, sexually repressed, and frustrated man.
Roper, William. *The Mirror of Vertue, or The Life of Thomas More.* 1625. Ed. by Richard S.
   Sylvester and Davis P. Harding. Yale U. Pr. o.p. A biography by More's son-in-law.
Surtz, Edward Louis. *The Praise of Pleasure: Philosophy, Education, and Communism in
   More's Utopia.* HUP 1957 o.p. An intense and scholarly study that endeavors to
   reconcile *Utopia's* communist and Epicurean principles with More's Catholicism.
Sylvester, Richard S., and Germaine Marc'hadour, eds. *Essential Articles for the Study of
   Thomas More. Essential Articles Ser.* Shoe String 1977 o.p. A useful collection of
   critical approaches.

NASHE, THOMAS. 1567–1601

Thomas Nashe arrived in London from Cambridge in 1588, the year of the
Armada. Known as a member of the group of "University Wits," he went on to
turn his lively and prolific energy to a number of literary endeavors. He began
his career with an attack on recent efforts (including those by THOMAS KYD) and
soon joined in the controversial Marprelate polemic, writing against the
Puritans. Other satires followed, but Nashe's most engaging work is the
picaresque relation of the adventures of Jack Wilton in *The Unfortunate
Traveller* (1594). The hero's journey through Reformation Europe provides
Nashe with many an opportunity for his dark and irreverent sarcasm; themes of
violence, disease, and erotic corruption combine to deliver what is perhaps the
period's finest parody of both literary and religious institutions. Nashe also
wrote for the stage and was among the people sent to the Fleet prison for his
role in the Isle of Dogs controversy (in this play, which is lost, he attacked
abuses in society). Nashe died in poverty at the age of 33.

PROSE FICTION BY NASHE

The Unfortunate Traveller and Other Stories. Ed. by J. B. Steane. Viking Penguin 1972 $7.95. ISBN 0-14-043067-9

WORKS BY NASHE

Works. Ed. by Ronald B. McKerrow. Sidgewick and Jackson 1910 o.p. The standard edition.

BOOKS ABOUT NASHE

Crewe, Jonathan V. *Unredeemed Rhetoric: Thomas Nashe and the Scandal of Authorship.* Bks. Demand repr. of 1982 ed $35.10. ISBN 0-8357-6608-X
Hutson, Lorna. *Thomas Nashe in Context.* OUP 1989 $69.00. ISBN 0-19-812876-2. Considers Nashe's work in its literary, historical, and political context.

PEELE, GEORGE. c.1556–1596?

Peele wrote a variety of plays: *Edward I,* an English Chronicle history; *The Battle of Alcazar,* a foreign history; *The Old Wives' Tale* (1595), a folkloric narration; *The Arraignment of Paris* (1584), a mythological pastoral; and *David and Bethsabe* (1599), a biblical tragedy. Peele is predominantly a courtly dramatist best known for his fluent lyrical gifts.

PLAYS BY PEELE

The Chronicle of King Edward the First, Surnamed Longshanks: With the Life of Luellen, Rebel in Wales. Ed. by G. K. Dreber. Longshanks Bk. 1974 $5.95. ISBN 0-9601000-1-6
The Dramatic Works of George Peele. 3 vols. Ed. by Mark R. Benbow. Yale U. Pr. 1970 o.p. An excellent scholarly edition.
The Old Wives' Tale. Ed. by Patricia Binnie. *Revels Plays Ser.* Johns Hopkins 1980 $20.00. ISBN 0-8018-2410-9

BOOKS ABOUT PEELE

Ashley, L.R. *George Peele.* Irvington 1970 $34.00. ISBN 0-8290-0175-1
Braunmuller, A. R. *George Peele.* Twayne English Authors Ser. 1983 o.p. A historically informed overview of themes and technique.
Horne, David H. *The Life and Minor Works of George Peele.* Greenwood 1978 repr. of 1952 ed. o.p. A useful biographical treatment.

SIDNEY, SIR PHILIP. 1554–1586

Sidney is perhaps the supreme example of the ideal Elizabethan gentleman, embodying those traits as soldier, scholar, and courtier that Elizabethans most admired. As the nephew of Robert Dudley, earl of Leicester (the favorite of Queen Elizabeth), and the son of a lord deputy of Ireland, his social and court connections were impeccable. He traveled widely in France, Germany, and Italy, and served the queen as courtier and ambassador before his death in battle in the Low Countries, a death that only added to his glamour. His writings in prose and poetry were not intended for publication but for private circulation among aristocratic friends. His pastoral prose romance *Arcadia* (1590) is sprinkled with poetry and was much admired in his day, as it is in ours. His *A Defence of Poesie* (1595) is one of the great critical treatises in English and brilliantly summarizes the Renaissance ideal in literature: to instruct as well as to delight. His sonnet sequence *Astrophil and Stella* (1591) is one of the first and perhaps the finest of the great Elizabethan sonnet cycles. Its influence on subsequent love poetry has been enormous. What gives the sequence its special appeal is Sidney's ability to bring fresh vigor to poetical conventions and to dramatize the entire sequence of 108 sonnets.

POETRY BY SIDNEY

The Poems of Sir Philip Sidney. Ed. by William A. Ringler, Jr. *Oxford Eng. Texts Ser.* OUP 1962 $98.00. ISBN 0-19-811834-1. The definitive edition.

PROSE WORKS BY SIDNEY

Arcadia. 1590. Ed. by Maurice Evans. *Penguin Eng. Lib. Ser.* Viking Penguin 1977 $9.95. ISBN 0-14-04311-X
The Countesse of Pembroke's Arcadia. Ed. by Katherine Duncan-Jones. OUP 1985 $9.95. ISBN 0-19-281690-X. A guide to a complicated textual history.
A Defence of Poetry. Ed. by Jan A. Van Dorsten. OUP 1966 $8.95. ISBN 0-19-911022-0. An inexpensive edition with notes.

BOOKS ABOUT SIDNEY

Duncan-Jones, Katherine. *Sir Philip Sidney: Courtier Poet.* Yale U. Pr. 1991 $29.95. ISBN 0-300-05099-2. A biographical treatment of Sidney's work.
Hamilton, A. C. *Sir Philip Sidney.* Cambridge 1980 o.p. A biographically informed reading of the works.
Kalstone, David. *Sidney's Poetry.* Norton Lib. 1970 repr. of 1965 ed. $1.85. ISBN 0-393-00516-X. The best general study of Sidney's art.
McCoy, Richard C. *Sir Philip Sidney: Rebellion in Arcadia.* Rutgers U. Pr. 1979 $45.00. ISBN 0-8135-0869-X. A consideration of Sidney's joint political and literary ambitions.
Myrick, Kenneth. *Sir Philip Sidney as a Literary Craftsman.* U. of Nebr. Pr. 1966 o.p. A study of Sidney's uses of form.
Nichols. *The Poetry of Sir Philip Sidney.* State Mutual Bk. 1982 o.p.
Osborn, James M. *Young Philip Sidney: 1572–1577.* Bks. Demand repr. of 1972 ed. $147.80. ISBN 0-317-29286-2. The best of the fairly recent books on Sidney.
Waller, Gary F., and Michael Moore, eds. *Sir Philip Sidney and the Interpretation of Renaissance Culture.* B & N Imports 1984 $37.25. ISBN 0-389-20514-1. A collection exploring Sidney's origins and reception in Renaissance contexts.

SKELTON, JOHN. c.1460–1529

As a royal tutor, parson, orator, poet-satirist, and courtier, Skelton has been called one of the most remarkable poets between CHAUCER and SPENSER, an imaginative, unpredictable precursor of the Renaissance. *A Ballade of the Scottysshe Kynge* (1513) celebrates the victory of the English forces of Henry VIII under the Earl of Surrey over the army of James IV at the battle of Flodden. *Magnificence* (1516) is an allegory in which the generous prince Magnificence is first destroyed by his own ill-advised generosity, then restored by Goodhope, Perseverance, and related virtues.

He was awarded the degree of laureate by the universities of Oxford and Cambridge and was chosen as tutor to the young Prince Henry, who became Henry VIII. When ERASMUS (see Vol. 4) visited England, he called Skelton "the one light and glory of British letters," mainly because of his translations of the classics and his Latin verses.

Skelton directed his satire against the clergy, particularly Cardinal Wolsey, the target of *Colin Clout* (1522). After a lifelong hatred of Henry's chancellor, Skelton was finally forced to the sanctuary of Westminster in 1523 for writing *Why Came Ye Not To Court* (1522). While in confinement, he purified and simplified his style. He died before Wolsey met his downfall.

POETRY BY SKELTON

The Complete English Poems. Ed. by John Scattergood. Viking Penguin 1992 $12.95.
ISBN 0-14-042233-1. Supersedes all previous editions.
John Skelton: A Selection from His Poems. Ed. by Vivian De Sola. AMS Pr. repr. of 1950
ed. $22.00. ISBN 0-404-20235-7. Some of the more popular works.
Magnificence. Ed. by Paula Neuss. *Revels Plays Ser.* Bks. Demand repr. of 1980 ed.
$63.70. ISBN 0-8357-4032-3

BOOKS ABOUT SKELTON

Fish, Stanley E. *John Skelton's Poetry. Yale Studies in Eng. Ser.* Shoe String 1976 repr. of
1965 ed. $29.50. ISBN 0-208-01613-9. A major reevaluation and explication of the
Skelton canon.
Heiserman, Arthur Ray. *Skelton and Satire.* U. Ch. Pr. 1961 o.p. A study of Skelton's
parodic method.
Kinney, Arthur F. *John Skelton, Priest as Poet: Seasons of Discovery.* U. of NC Pr. 1987
$27.50. ISBN 0-8078-1730-9. A study of Skelton's religious identity.
Nelson, William. *John Skelton, Laureate.* Russell 1964 repr. of 1939 ed. o.p. A general
overview.
Walker, Greg. *John Skelton and the Politics of the 1520s.* Cambridge U. Pr. 1988 $54.95.
ISBN 0-521-35124-3. Discusses Skelton in the political context of his times.

SPENSER, EDMUND. 1552–1599

"The poet's poet"—as CHARLES LAMB was to call Spenser two centuries
later—was born in London, where he attended school before going to
Cambridge in 1569. About 1579 he came to know Sir PHILIP SIDNEY; his first
significant work, *The Shepheardes Calendar*, published under a pseudonym in
1579 and consisting of 12 "ecologues" (one for each month of the year), was
dedicated to Sidney. Spenser hoped for advancement at the court of Queen
Elizabeth, but in August 1580 he took a minor position in Ireland, where he
spent the rest of his life, save for two visits to England. In 1594 he married
Elizabeth Boyle, in Cork; the sonnet sequence *Amoretti* (1595) bears on his
courtship, and the great marriage hymn, *Epithalamion* (1595), celebrates the
wedding.

The first three books of Spenser's allegorical epic romance, *The Faerie
Queene*, appeared in 1590; three more appeared in 1596. A fragment, the *Cantos
of Mutabilitie*, which may or may not have been intended to form part of the
great poem, appeared in 1609, after Spenser's death. Spenser appended a letter
to his friend Sir Walter Raleigh to the edition of 1590, explaining that the
"general end . . . of all the book is to fashion a gentleman or noble person in
vertuous and gentle discipline." Although Spenser planned to write 12 books in
all, only 6, and the two *Cantos of Mutabilitie*, survive. The rest may possibly have
been destroyed by Irish rebels when, in 1598, they sacked Spenser's Irish
residence at Kilcolman, but it is equally possible that the poet never managed to
bring his massively planned work to completion.

Spenser's *Amoretti* (1595) is one of the more idealized sonnet sequences, and
Colin Clout's Come Home Again (1595) is an allegorical attack on the taste of the
court. Like many Renaissance authors, his writings extend beyond the narrowly
literary; his tract "A View of the Present State of Ireland" (1596) provides a
series of brutal recommendations for the colonial suppression of England's
Irish territories. Spenser's complex range of styles and genres served as both a
model and a challenge for his contemporaries and for later authors.

POETRY BY SPENSER

Edmund Spenser's Poetry. Ed. by Hugh MacLean. *Norton Critical Eds.* Norton 1982 o.p. Probably the most useful edition, with much valuable criticism and a helpful bibliography.

The Faerie Queene. Ed. by Thomas P. Roche. *Eng. Poets Ser.* Yale U. Pr. 1981 o.p. One of the best editions, with very full notes.

Minor Poems. Ed. by Ernest de Selincourt. *Oxford Eng. Texts Ser.* OUP 1910 o.p. The less considered works.

The Poetical Works. Ed. by J. C. Smith and Ernest de Selincourt. *Oxford Eng. Texts Ser.* OUP 1961 $17.95. ISBN 0-19-281070-7. Inexpensive access to the complete works.

Spenser: The Faerie Queene. Ed. by A. G. Hamilton. Longman 1977 $32.95. ISBN 0-685-42243-7. Copiously annotated; very helpful.

A View of the Present State of Ireland. Scholarly repr. of 1934 ed. $29.00. ISBN 0-403-01224-4

The Works of Edmund Spenser: A Variorum Edition. 11 vols. Ed. by Edwin Greenlaw and others. Johns Hopkins 1932–57 $425.00. ISBN 0-8018-2131-2. Follows in the main the edition of 1596, all other important editions and variants being noted, and summarizes all the older scholarship.

BOOKS ABOUT SPENSER

Alpers, Paul J. *Edmund Spenser.* Viking Penguin 1970 o.p. A standard introduction.

Berger, Harry, Jr. *Revisionary Play: Studies in the Spenserian Dynamics.* U. CA Pr. 1988 $15.95. ISBN 0-520-07180-8. A provocative series of readings.

Cain, Thomas H. *Praise in* The Faerie Queene. Bks. Demand repr. of 1978 ed. $66.20. ISBN 0-7837-0227-2. Spenser and the epideictic tradition.

Goldberg, Jonathan. *Endlesse Worke: Spenser and the Structure of Discourse.* Johns Hopkins 1981 o.p. A study of Spenser's narrative habits and strategies.

Gross, Kenneth. *Spenserian Poetics: Idolatry, Iconclasm and Magic.* Cornell Univ. Pr. 1985 $29.95. ISBN 0-8014-1805-4. Spenser and the Reformation discourse of iconography.

Hamilton, Albert Charles, ed. *Essential Articles for the Study of Edmund Spenser.* Shoe String 1972 o.p. A useful collection of approaches.

––––––. *The Spenser Encyclopedia.* U. of Toronto Pr. 1990 $250.00. ISBN 0-8020-2676-1. An exhaustive guide to Spenser's themes, sources, and analogues.

Hoffman, Nancy J. *Spenser's Pastorals: The Shepheardes Calendar and "Colin Clout."* Bks. Demand repr. of 1978 ed. $42.90. ISBN 0-8357-6614-4. Spenser and the pastoral mode.

Hume, Anthea. *Edmund Spenser: Protestant Poet.* Cambridge U. Pr. 1984 $49.95. ISBN 0-521-25807-3. A considered attempt to place Spenser in the religious controversy of his era.

Judson, A. C. *Notes on the Life of Edmund Spenser.* Kraus 1978 repr. of 1949 ed. $15.00. ISBN 0-527-46940-8. Definitive consideration of the biographical elements.

King, John N. *Spenser's Poetry and the Reformation Tradition.* Princeton U. Pr. 1990 $39.50. ISBN 0-691-06800-3. Studies Spenser in the context of Reformation discourse, including iconographic issues.

Krier, Theresa M. *Gazing on Secret Sights: Spenser, Classical Imitation, and the Decorums of Vision.* Cornell Univ. Pr. 1990 $32.95. ISBN 0-8014-2345-7. An insightful study of Spenser's visual tropes.

MacCaffrey, Isabel G. *Spenser's Allegory: The Anatomy of Imagination.* Bks. Demand repr. of 1976 ed. $118.90. ISBN 0-8357-3548-6

McNeir, Waldo F., and Foster Provost. *An Annotated Bibliography of Edmund Spenser.* AMS Pr. repr. of 1962 ed. o.p. A guide to the criticism.

Miller, David Lee. *The Poem's Two Bodies: The Poetics of the 1590* Faerie Queene. Princeton U. Pr. 1991 $39.50. ISBN 0-691-06744-9. A provocative historical account.

Nohrnberg, James. *The Analogy of* The Faerie Queene. Princeton U. Pr. 1976 $105.00. ISBN 0-691-06307-9. An exhaustive guide to Spenser's allegorical resonance.

O'Connell, Michael. *Mirror and Veil: The Historical Dimension of Spenser's* Faerie Queene. U. of NC Pr. 1977 $24.95. ISBN 0-8078-1307-9. A study of the epic in the context of Elizabethan historiographical tradition.

Osgood, Charles G. *A Concordance to the Poems of Edmund Spenser.* Peter Smith repr. of 1915 ed. $42.00. ISBN 0-8446-1332-0. A guide to the frequency and location of Spenser's word use.

Wells, Robin Headlam. *Spenser's* Faerie Queene *and the Cult of Elizabeth.* B & N Imports 1983 o.p. A discussion of the poem's relation to the discourses of sovereignty surrounding the female monarch.

TOURNEUR, CYRIL. c.1575–1626

Little is known about the life of Cyril Tourneur. In 1600 he published a verse satire, *The Transformed Metamorphosis,* and the two plays associated with his name—*The Revenger's Tragedy* (1607) and *The Atheist's Tragedy* (1611)—are both strongly satirical. *The Revenger's Tragedy* is a masterpiece of tragic farce and black comedy, with an impassioned contempt-of-the-world rhetoric. Its authorship has been questioned, with THOMAS MIDDLETON the leading candidate. *The Atheist's Tragedy* directly engages the theological theme of atheism; it is both grotesque and homiletic in its proof of the existence of God.

PLAYS BY TOURNEUR

The Atheist's Tragedy. 1611. Ed. by Brian Morris and Roma Gill. *New Mermaid Ser.* Norton 1976 $4.95. ISBN 0-393-90030-4

The Plays and Poems of Cyril Tourneur. Select Bibliographies Repr. Ser. 2 vols. Ayer repr. of 1878 ed. $34.50. ISBN 0-8369-6787-9. Introduction and notes by John C. Collins.

The Revenger's Tragedy. 1607. Ed. by R. A. Foakes. *Revels Plays Ser.* St. Martin 1988 $12.95. ISBN 0-7190-1612-6

BOOK ABOUT TOURNEUR

Jacobson, Daniel. *The Language of the Revenger's Tragedy. Salzburg Studies in Eng. Lit., Jacobean Drama Studies.* Humanities 1974 o.p. Critical analysis of Tourneur's masterpiece, focusing on the author's literary style.

VAUGHAN, HENRY. 1622–1695

Henry Vaughan was born in South Wales. He studied at Oxford with his twin brother, Thomas; Thomas became an alchemist and a dealer in magic, and studied the hermetic philosophy that is also reflected in Henry's poems. Henry left Oxford for London, and, after serving as a Royalist soldier during the Civil War, retired to Wales, where he served as a physician for the last 20 years of his life. His early work was secular, but he is best remembered for his religious verse in *Silex Scintillans* (1650; second part, 1655). The best of his work shines with a childlike innocence and clarity of vision. He wrote about nature as a reflection of God: "All things that be, praise him . . . Stones are deep in admiration." Vaughan's views on nature and childhood may have influenced WORDSWORTH.

POETRY BY VAUGHAN

The Complete Poems. Ed. by Alan Rudrum. *Eng. Poets Ser.* Yale U. Pr. 1981 repr. of 1976 ed. $55.00. ISBN 0-300-02680-3. The most recent comprehensive edition, incorporating the results of modern scholarship.

The Complete Poetry of Henry Vaughan. Ed. by French Fogie. *Norton Lib.* Norton 1969 repr. of 1964 ed. o.p. A convenient edition.

BOOKS ABOUT VAUGHAN

Grant, Patrick. *The Transformation of Sin: Studies in Donne, Herbert, Vaughan and Traherne*. U. of Mass. Pr. 1974 $30.00. ISBN 0-87023-158-8. A comparative consideration of religious sensibility and psychology.

Martz, Louis. *The Paradise Within: Studies in Vaughan, Traherne, and Milton*. Yale U. Pr. 1966 $12.00. ISBN 0-300-00164-9. An approach from the standpoint of the Augustinian concept of interior "illumination."

Post, Jonathan F. *Henry Vaughan: The Unfolding Vision*. Princeton U. Pr. 1983 $32.50. ISBN 0-691-06527-6. An essential reading of literary and social contexts.

Simmonds, James D. *Masques of God: Form and Theme in the Poetry of Henry Vaughan*. U. of Pittsburgh Pr. 1972 $29.95. ISBN 0-8229-3236-9. Close readings of the poetic concerns and influences.

Wall, John W., Jr. *Transformations of the Word: Spenser, Herbert, Vaughan*. U. of Ga. Pr. 1988 $40.00. ISBN 0-8203-0930-3. An important book that explores the ties between liturgy and poetry.

WEBSTER, JOHN. c.1580–c.1634

Webster seems to have participated in many dramatic collaborations, but his undisputed work consists of only three plays: *The White Devil* (1612), *The Duchess of Malfi* (1614), and *The Devil's Law Case* (1623). His two great tragedies, *The White Devil* and *The Duchess of Malfi*, are darkly poetic and brooding, especially in their sardonic villain-spokesmen, Flamineo and Bosola. As critic Robert Dent has shown, Webster plundered other authors for his laborious, jewel-like, sententious, and epigrammatic style, but the overall effect is one of a soaring and passionate poetry. Webster employs the full gamut of violent and sensational effects, especially in *The Duchess of Malfi*, to render a physical sense of horror. His plots are drawn from the political and amorous intrigues of Renaissance Italy.

PLAYS BY WEBSTER

The Devil's Law-Case. 1623. Ed. by Elizabeth M. Brennan. *New Mermaid Ser.* Norton 1976 $4.95. ISBN 0-393-90033-9

The Duchess of Malfi. 1614. Ed. by Elizabeth M. Brennan. *New Mermaid Ser.* Norton 1984 $6.95. ISBN 0-393-90049-5

The Selected Plays: The White Devil, The Duchess of Malfi, The Devil's Law Case. Ed. by Jonathan Dollimore and Alan Sinfield. *Plays by Renaissance and Restoration Dramatists Ser.* Cambridge U. Pr. 1983 $42.50. ISBN 0-521-24927-9

Webster: Three Plays. Ed. by D. C. Gunby. *Penguin Eng. Lib. Ser.* Viking Penguin 1973 $6.95. ISBN 0-14-043081-4

The White Devil. 1612. Ed. by Elizabeth M. Brennan. *New Mermaid Ser.* Norton 1976 $6.95. ISBN 0-393-90037-1

WORKS BY WEBSTER

Complete Works of John Webster. 4 vols. Ed. by F. L. Lucas. Rprt. Serv. 1966 repr. of 1927 ed. $300.00. ISBN 0-7812-7314-5

BOOKS ABOUT WEBSTER

Bliss, Lee. *The World's Perspective: John Webster and the Jacobean Drama*. Rutgers U. Pr. 1983 $40.00. ISBN 0-8135-0967-X. A contextual reading of Webster's forms and themes.

Bogard, Travis. *Tragic Satire of John Webster*. Russell 1965 repr. of 1955 ed. o.p. An important study.

Boklund, Gunnar. *The Sources of the White Devil*. Kraus repr. of 1957 ed. $24.00. ISBN 0-8115-0215-5. Webster's literary background.

Bradbrook, Muriel C. *John Webster*. Col. U. Pr. 1980 $39.50. ISBN 0-231-05162-X

Corballis, Richard. *A Concordance to the Works of John Webster.* 4 vols. Ed. by J. M. Harding. *Salzburg Studies in Eng. Lit., Jacobean Drama Studies.* Humanities 1979 o.p. A guide to Webster's frequency and location of word use.

Forker, Charles R. *Skull Beneath the Skin: The Achievement of John Webster.* S. Ill. U. Pr. 1986 $50.00. ISBN 0-8093-1279-4

Leech, Clifford. *John Webster.* Haskell 1969 repr. of 1951 ed. $75.00. ISBN 0-8383-0690-X. Principally a study of Webster's stylistic achievement.

Moore, Don. *Webster: The Critical Heritage. Critical Heritage Ser.* Routledge $69.50. ISBN 0-7100-0773-6. A good account of the enormous volume of Webster criticism.

Morris, Brian, ed. *John Webster. Mermaid Critical Ser.* Verry 1970 o.p.

Waage, Frederick O. *The White Devil Discover'd: Backgrounds and Foregrounds to Webster's Tragedy.* P. Lang Pubs. 1984 $19.70. ISBN 0-8204-0055-6. A study of sources.

Wang, Tso-Liang. *The Literary Reputation of John Webster to 1830 Salzburg Studies in Eng. Lit., Jacobean Drama Studies.* Humanities 1976 o.p. Webster's reception.

WYATT (OR WIAT), SIR THOMAS THE ELDER. 1503–1542

Wyatt served King Henry VIII as a diplomat and as ambassador to Spain. He was imprisoned twice (once for brawling, in 1534, and once on suspicion of treason, in 1536) and was the reputed lover of Henry VIII's second wife, Anne Boleyn. His poetry reflects the influence of French and Italian literature (notably the Italian sonneteer PETRARCH) (see Vol. 2), and also the troubled course of his career as a courtier. Wyatt introduced the Italian sonnet into English verse, for the most part translating and paraphrasing Petrarchan originals, and employing rhyme schemes derived from other Italian poets. The sonnet, of course, was to become one of the chief English poetic forms; in Wyatt's handling, it displays a peculiarly biting edge. As C. S. LEWIS writes, "Poor Wyatt seems to be always in love with women he dislikes." Wyatt's poetry also includes epigrams, satires, and devotional works, as well as many lyrics that look to Chaucerian precedent in form and outlook.

He and Henry Howard, earl of Surrey, who established the "English" sonnet form (three quatrains and a couplet, rhyming *abab, cdcd, efef, gg*), have justly been called the first reformers of English meter and style. The work of both was first published in *Tottel's Miscellany* (1557).

POETRY BY WYATT

Collected Poems of Sir Thomas Wyatt. Ed. by Kenneth Muir. HUP 1950 o.p.

Poetry of Sir Thomas Wyatt: A Selection and Study by E. M. W. Tillyard. Somerset Pub. repr. of 1929 ed. $29.00. ISBN 0-403-08614-0

Wyatt: Complete Poems. Ed. by R. A. Rebholz. Viking Penguin 1989 $7.95. ISBN 0-14-042227-7

BOOKS ABOUT WYATT

Hangen, Eva C. *A Concordance to the Complete Poetical Works of Sir Thomas Wyatt. English Literary Reference Ser.* Johnson Repr. 1969 repr. of 1941 ed. $45.00. ISBN 0-384-21300-6. A guide to the frequency and location of Wyatt's word use.

Muir, Kenneth, ed. *The Life and Letters of Sir Thomas Wyatt.* State Mutual Bk. 1963 o.p. The standard biography.

Thomson, Patricia. *Sir Thomas Wyatt and His Background.* Stanford U. Pr. 1964 o.p. Wyatt in his cultural and literary moment.

———. *Wyatt: The Critical Heritage. Critical Heritage Ser.* Routledge 1974 o.p. A collection of Wyatt's receptions.

CHAPTER 7

Shakespeare

David Scott Kastan

> Soule of the Age!
> The applause! delight! the wonder of our stage!
> My *Shakespeare* rise!
>
> Ben Jonson, 1623

William Shakespeare (1564–1616) was a successful man of the emerging entertainment industry of Elizabethan England. He was an actor, a "sharer" in his acting company (that is, no mere "hireling" but a partner entitled to share in its profits), and, of course, a playwright. Beginning in the middle of the nineteenth century, however, he became much more—the very standard of literary value, his genius the virtual mark of the greatness of England and Englishness. His dominating presence in the world of letters stood as an aesthetic parallel and prop to the progress of the British Empire. The greatness of both spread over the globe.

He began, of course, more humbly. We know a remarkable amount about Shakespeare and his family. He was born in late April of 1564 in Stratford-upon-Avon. The parish church records his baptism on April 26 (and his unrecorded birthday has been plausibly set on April 23, St. George's Day, and also, apparently, the day of his death). His father was John Shakespeare, a glover and later a wool merchant, and his mother was Mary Arden, daughter of a farmer in the nearby village of Wilmcote. We can safely assume that he attended the King's New School, the Stratford grammar school with its strenuous classically based curriculum, but we know for certain that at age 18 he married Anne Hathaway, also of Stratford, and that a daughter, Susanna, was born to them, as the parish records note, on May 26, 1583. On February 2, 1585, the register records the birth of twins, Hamnet and Judith.

Shakespeare was well established in London by the early 1590s as an actor and a playwright. When a severe outbreak of plague beginning in the summer of 1592 closed the theaters until the spring of 1594, he wrote two narrative poems, *Venus and Adonis* and *The Rape of Lucrece*, both dedicated to Henry Wriothesley, the third earl of Southampton, and printed by a former fellow-resident of Stratford, Richard Field. But Shakespeare's primary work was in the theater, writing, acting, and managing. Tax and legal records allow us to plot his various residences in London, and the money he made as a sharer in the Lord Chamberlain's company permitted him in 1597 to purchase New Place, a fine, three-floor house in Stratford, indeed its second largest dwelling. His profits from the acting company enabled him to continue his real estate investments both in Stratford and in London.

His family's lives and deaths can be traced in the parish register of Holy Trinity Church in Stratford. His son, Hamnet, died at age 11 and was buried on

August 11, 1596. Shakespeare's father died in September of 1601; his mother, in 1608. Shakespeare's elder daughter, Susanna, married John Hall, a well-respected Stratford physician, in Holy Trinity on June 5, 1607. His younger daughter, Judith, married Thomas Quiney on February 10, 1616. Shakespeare's wife died on August 6, 1623; she had lived to see a monument of her husband installed in Holy Trinity but passed away just before the publication of the first folio of his plays, the more lasting monument to his memory.

Shakespeare himself had died in late April of 1616, having left a will written that January. He left 10 pounds to the poor of Stratford, remembered Stratford friends, and donated money for memorial rings for his theatrical colleagues Richard Burbage, John Heminges, and Henry Condell. He left a sizable sum to Judith, but the bulk of the assigned estate went to Susanna. His wife is mentioned only once, in an apparent afterthought to the document: "Item, I give unto my wife my second best bed with the furniture." The bequest of bed and bedding has led many to speculate that this was a deliberate slight, but English customary law provided the wife with a third of the estate, and the "second best bed" was almost certainly their own, the best being saved for visitors.

Yet in spite of the detailed records that remain, allowing us to trace major and minor events in the life of Shakespeare and his family, some critics have passionately held that the author of the plays was someone other than the glover's son from Stratford. It wasn't until the eighteenth century that anyone challenged Shakespeare's authorship, but since then many, including MARK TWAIN, HENRY JAMES, and SIGMUND FREUD (see Vols. 3 and 5) have been tempted by the anti-Stratfordian heresy. Various candidates have been put forth. CHRISTOPHER MARLOWE, FRANCIS BACON (see Vol. 4), the seventeenth Earl of Oxford, Queen Elizabeth, even DANIEL DEFOE (who wasn't even born until 1661) have all been proposed as the "real" author of "Shakespeare's" plays and poems. The controversy has, however, little to recommend it except for its unintended humor; anti-Stratfordian champions have sometimes had unfortunate names like Looney, Battey, and Silliman. Although usually energetically asserted, the belief that someone other than Shakespeare wrote the plays seemingly derives only from simple social snobbery: a certainty that only someone educated at university or at court would be capable of such artistry. But the desire to give the plays a more socially distinguished patrimony than they in fact had at least attests to the elevated position they have come to assume in our culture.

In Shakespeare's own lifetime, drama was considered a subliterary form. The plays first appeared in print only in individual quarto editions of various degrees of authority, which at least initially were published because of the theater company's need to generate revenue while the theaters were closed during outbreaks of plague. Nineteen of Shakespeare's plays appeared in these small, relatively inexpensive volumes between 1594 and 1622, the first few without any indication of authorship. *Venus and Adonis* and *The Rape of Lucrece*, on the other hand, appeared about the time of the earliest quartos in finely edited and printed editions to which Shakespeare contributed elaborate dedications. Shakespeare's growing reputation, however, soon established even his plays as worthy of careful editing. An unauthorized attempt by Thomas Pavier to produce a collected edition in 1619 was stopped by the Stationers' Company, but in 1623, seven years after Shakespeare's death, two of Shakespeare's fellow sharers, John Heminges and Henry Condell, working with Pavier's printer, William Jaggard, succeeded in producing the first folio. The handsome book, which sold for one pound, contained 36 plays, 17 of which had never before appeared in print.

The plays of the first folio, along with *Pericles,* which was added only in the second issue of the third edition (1664), have generally been taken to comprise the total of Shakespeare's individual dramatic work (though *Henry VIII* has been thought to be by Shakespeare and John Fletcher, and *Pericles* is itself possibly the product of collaboration). *The Two Noble Kinsman* seems clearly to be partly Shakespeare's. First published in 1634, its title page declares it to be "by the memorable worthies of their time, Mr. John Fletcher, and Mr. William Shakespeare." It also seems likely that Shakespeare wrote some of *Sir Thomas More,* a play existing only in manuscript and written in several hands, one of which, the so-called hand D, is often thought to be Shakespeare's and, as such, provides the only substantive text in his own writing. Other plays were attributed to Shakespeare in his lifetime. Some, like *Love's Labor's Won* and *Cardenio,* have not survived; others, like *The London Prodigal* (1605) and *The Yorkshire Tragedy* (1608), opportunistically exploit his name in the interest of sales. But that such cynical appropriation was possible in the first decade of the seventeenth century attests to the fact that the myth of Shakespeare had already begun to grow at that early date.

BIOGRAPHIES

Shakespeare's life has occasioned almost as much interest as his plays. It has been documented, invented, sometimes even denied. An imaginary history was literally forged, first, in the eighteenth century, by William Henry Ireland and then in the nineteenth by John Payne Collier. Shakespeare's life has been more overtly fictionalized by many, including novelists SIR WALTER SCOTT and ANTHONY BURGESS and the playwright EDWARD BOND. And, of course, there is the Shakespeare who exists only as a cover for the "real" author, be it the Earl of Oxford, FRANCIS BACON (see Vol. 4), or Queen Elizabeth, in the various anti-Stratfordian conspiracy theories that seem continually to circulate. Nonetheless, Shakespeare lived and much is known about him, and the steady appearance of thoughtful biographies attests to the fascination the man himself, as well as his art, continues to hold for us.

Bentley, G. E. *Shakespeare: A Biographical Handbook.* Greenwood 1986 $52.50. ISBN 0-313-25042-1. Readable account of the known facts.

Chambers, E. K. *William Shakespeare: A Study of Facts and Problems.* 2 vols. OUP 1989 repr. of 1930 ed. Vol. 1 $95.00. ISBN 0-19-811773-6. Vol. 2 $82.00. ISBN 0-19-811774-4. Essential collection of information relating to Shakespeare's life and his poems and plays.

Dutton, Richard. *William Shakespeare: A Literary Life.* St. Martin 1989 $35.00. ISBN 0-312-03091-6. Informative biography focusing on Shakespeare's literary and theatrical life.

Eccles, Mark. *Shakespeare in Warwickshire.* U. of Wis. Pr. 1961 $15.00. ISBN 0-299-02330-3. Focuses on Shakespeare's family and its social relations in Stratford and its environs.

Fraser, Russell. *Shakespeare, the Later Years.* Col. U. Pr. 1992 $27.95. ISBN 0-231-06766-6. Lively biography attempting to connect the life and the art.

———. *Young Shakespeare.* Col. U. Pr. 1988 o.p. Critical biography focusing on early years.

Honigmann, E. A. J. *Shakespeare, the Lost Years.* Manchester Univ. Pr. 1985 $34.50. ISBN 0-389-20765-9. A speculative but thoughtful attempt to account for Shakespeare's activities between 1585 and 1592.

Lee, Sidney. *A Life of William Shakespeare*. Scholarly 1971 repr. of 1903 ed. $59.00. ISBN 0-403-01069-1. Remained the standard biography until the middle of the twentieth century.

Levi, Peter. *The Life and Times of William Shakespeare*. H. Holt & Co. 1989 $29.95. ISBN 0-8050-1199-4. Examines the critical evidence of Shakespeare's life and career from a historical and literary perspective.

Rowse, A. L. *William Shakespeare the Man*. Macmillan 1973 o.p. Rowse's claim, among other assertions, that he discovered the identity of the "dark lady."

Schoenbaum, S. *Shakespeare's Lives*. OUP 1991 $35.00. ISBN 0-19-818618-5. Analyzes the many biographies that have been written and provides a concise account of Shakespeare's life.

_____. *William Shakespeare: A Compact Documentary Life*. OUP rev. ed. 1987 $14.95. ISBN 0-19-505161-0. An inexpensive and convenient abridgment of the *Documentary Life*, lacking most of the illustrations.

_____. *William Shakespeare: A Documentary Life*. OUP 1975 o.p. Includes facsimiles and transcriptions of about 200 documents essential to our knowledge of Shakespeare's life.

_____. *William Shakespeare: Records and Images*. OUP 1981 o.p. A handsome sequel to the *Documentary Life*, containing 165 of the facsimiles.

TEXTS AND TEXTUAL STUDIES

The plays and poems of Shakespeare are available to us only because they have been preserved in print. We read not the unmediated genius of Shakespeare—or any author, for that matter—but black marks on white pages that have been produced by the labor of many people other than the writer. The inevitable interference of the material process of book publication with the intention of the author is intensified in the case of Shakespeare, as his plays were written not to be read but to be performed. Play texts even belonged to the acting company, not to the playwright, and few, if any, were scrutinized by the author before they were printed. Textual scholars have carefully examined the early quarto and folio editions and studied the processes by which they were printed, all with the aim of discovering what Shakespeare actually wrote. Modern editors, exactly as did John Heminges and Henry Condell, who put together the first folio in 1623, attempt to present readers with texts that are, as they wrote, "as he conceived them." Yet it is an impossible task perfectly to reconstruct Shakespeare's intentions. Modern scholarship has taught us that there will never be an "authentic" text; the texts that we read will always be at least in part as their editors have "conceived them."

Editions

COLLECTED EDITIONS

Allen, Michael J. B., and Kenneth Muir. *Shakespeare's Plays in Quarto: A Facsimile Edition of Copies Primarily in the Henry E. Huntington Library*. U. CA Pr. 1981 $185.00. ISBN 0-520-04077-5. Facsimiles of 22 quartos of Shakespeare's plays published between 1594 and 1634.

Barnet, Sylvan, gen. ed. *The Complete Signet Classic Shakespeare*. HarBraceJ 1972 $37.00. ISBN 0-15-512610-5. Collection of individually edited plays arranged chronologically.

Bevington, David, ed. *Complete Works of Shakespeare*. HarpCollege 1991 $51.50. ISBN 0-637-38873-5. Carefully edited texts and sound introductions.

Clark, William George, and William Aldis Wright, eds. *The Complete Works: Globe Edition*. AMS Pr. repr. of 1864 ed. $95.00. ISBN 0-404-05950-3. Out-of-date but interesting as the most influential edition until the mid-twentieth century.

Evans, G. Blakemore, and others, eds. *The Riverside Shakespeare*. HM 1974 $99.00. ISBN 0-395-17226-8. Somewhat fussy text but excellent introductory materials in a handsome volume.

Harbage, Alfred, gen. ed. *The Complete Pelican Shakespeare*. Viking Penguin 1974 $35.00. ISBN 0-14-071449-9. Collection of individually edited plays, arranged generically.

Hinman, Charlton, ed. *Norton Facsimile: The First Folio of Shakespeare*. Norton 1987 repr. of 1968 ed. $100.00. ISBN 0-393-09843-5. Facsimile of the first folio compiled from the best examples of individual pages in the folios owned by the Folger Library.

Wells, Stanley, and Gary Taylor, eds. *William Shakespeare: The Complete Works*. OUP 1987 $49.95. ISBN 0-19-812926-2. The most thorough revision of the textual tradition, but without notes and with only brief introductory comments.

———. *William Shakespeare: The Complete Works. Compact Edition*. OUP 1988 $29.95. ISBN 0-19-811747-7. A brilliant rethinking of the text, but limited in usefulness for students by the absence of notes and significant introductions.

EDITIONS OF INDIVIDUAL PLAYS

Barnet, Sylvan, and others, eds. *The Signet Classic Shakespeare*. 38 vols. New Amer. Lib. 1963–68. Rev. and reissued 1988–. Good editions with critical material excerpted and fine introductory essays.

Bevington, David, and others, eds. *Bantam Shakespeare*. 29 vols. Bantam 1988. Well-edited texts with good introductions, stage histories, excerpts from source material, and annotated bibliographies of criticism.

Brockbank, Philip, Brian Gibbons, and others, eds. *New Cambridge Shakespeare*. Cambridge U. Pr. 1984–. Carefully prepared editions with substantial introductions attentive to the play on the stage.

Brooks, Harold F., and Harold Jenkins, gen. eds. *The Arden Shakespeare*. 39 vols. Methuen 1951–82.

Furness, Horace Howard, and others, eds. *A New Variorum Edition of Shakespeare*. Lippincott 1871–1912. Old-spelling texts with valuable collection of notes.

Harbage, Alfred, gen. ed. *The Pelican Shakespeare*. 29 vols. Viking Penguin 1956–67. Individually edited volumes with critical introductions.

La Mar, Virginia A., and Louis B. Wright. *The Folger Library Shakespeare*. 39 vols. WSP 1957–68. o.p. Low-priced volumes popular because of the page of facing notes; being reedited by Barbara Mowat and Paul Werstine.

Quiller-Couch, Sir Arthur, John Dover Wilson, and J. C. Maxwell, gen. eds. *The New Shakespeare*. 39 vols. Cambridge U. Pr. 1921–66 o.p Original and sometimes controversial interpretations, under the guiding spirit of Wilson.

Spencer, Terence J. B., gen. ed. *The New Penguin Shakespeare*. 36 vols. Viking Penguin 1967–. $4.50–$5.50 ea. Handy paperback editions with introductions and useful notes at the back.

Wells, Stanley, gen. ed. *The Oxford Shakespeare*. OUP 1984–. $35.00–$69.00 ea. Rigorously edited texts with comprehensive introductions and useful index.

EDITIONS OF POEMS

Bevington, David, and others, eds. *William Shakespeare: The Poems*. Bantam 1988 $4.95. ISBN 0-553-21309-1. Edition of *Venus and Adonis, The Rape of Lucrece, The Phoenix and the Turtle, A Lover's Complaint*, and the sonnets, with notes, introductory essays, and annotated bibliographies.

Booth, Stephen, ed. *Shakespeare's Sonnets, Edited with Analytic Commentary*. Yale U. Pr. 1977 $19.00. ISBN 0-300-02495-9. Old-spelling and modern text on facing pages, with wonderfully sensitive and nuanced commentary.

Kerrigan, John, ed. *The New Penguin Shakespeare: The Sonnets and A Lover's Complaint.* Viking Penguin 1986 $20.00. ISBN 0-670-81466-0

Lever, J. W. *The New Penguin Shakespeare: The Rape of Lucrece.* Viking Penguin 1971 o.p.

Prince, F. T. *The Arden Shakespeare: The Poems.* Methuen 1960 $49.95. ISBN 0-416-47610-4. Text of *Venus and Adonis, Rape of Lucrece, The Passionate Pilgrim,* and *The Phoenix and the Turtle,* with introductory essay and commentary.

Roe, John, ed. *The New Cambridge Shakespeare: The Poems.* Cambridge U. Pr. 1992 $39.95. ISBN 0-521-22231-1. ISBN 0-521-29411-8

Rollins, H. E., ed. *The New Variorum "Poems."* Lippincott 1938 o.p. Text of the poems with extensive commentary.

_____. *The New Variorum "Sonnets."* 2 vols. Lippincott 1944 o.p. Text of the sonnets with extensive commentary; in Vol. 2, essays on the date, the sonnet order, and questions of autobiography.

Textual Studies

Blayney, Peter W. M. *The First Folio of Shakespeare.* Folger 1991 $6.95. ISBN 0-9629254-3-8. Exhibition catalog that is a remarkably readable and informative account of textual and social history of the first folio.

Bowers, Fredson. *On Editing Shakespeare.* U. Pr. of VA 1966 o.p. Invaluable collection of essays on the function of textual scholarship for Shakespeare studies.

Greg, W. W. *The Editorial Problem in Shakespeare.* OUP 1954 o.p. Analysis of the nature and foundation of the text of each of Shakespeare's plays.

_____. *The Shakespeare First Folio: Its Bibliographical and Textual History.* OUP 1955 o.p. Though superseded in part by Hinman (below), a still indispensable account of the printing and the text of the first folio.

Hinman, Charlton. *The Printing and Proof-reading of the First Folio Shakespeare.* 2 vols. OUP 1963 o.p. Detailed study of the printing and proofreading of the folio.

Honigmann, E. A. J. *The Stability of Shakespeare's Text.* U. of Neb. Pr. 1965 o.p. Influential analysis of variants in the texts of Shakespeare's plays.

Ioppolo, Grace. *Revising Shakespeare.* HUP 1991 $35.00. ISBN 0-674-76696-2. A study of Shakespeare as reviser, focusing on the variant texts of his plays.

Pollard, Alfred W. *Shakespeare Folios and Quartos: A Study in the Bibliography of Shakespeare's Plays, 1594–1685.* Methuen 1909 o.p. Descriptive bibliography of the early texts of Shakespeare's plays.

Walker, Alice. *Textual Problems of the First Folio.* Cambridge U. Pr. 1953 o.p. Important study of the relationship between the quarto and folio versions of six plays.

Wells, Stanley, and Gary Taylor, eds. *Modernizing Shakespeare's Spelling: With Three Studies in the Text of* Henry V. OUP 1979 o.p. Essay on the problems and process of modernization, plus study of *Henry V* that argues for the quarto text as a substantive version.

_____. *Re-editing Shakespeare for the Modern Reader.* OUP 1984 $13.95. ISBN 0-19-812934-3. Interesting collection of essays on the problems of editing Shakespeare today.

_____. *William Shakespeare: A Textual Companion.* Clarendon Pr. 1987 $125.00. ISBN 0-19-812914-9. Indispensable compilation of information and analysis about the texts of Shakespeare's plays.

Wilson, F. P. *Shakespeare and the New Bibliography.* Ed. by Helen Gardner. Clarendon Pr. 1970 o.p. Edition of Wilson's essay, left incompletely revised at his death, that usefully surveys the practice of textual scholarship.

CRITICAL STUDIES

Shakespeare's works have provoked an astounding quantity of criticism (fifty percent of which, said one critic, is very good; "the problem is knowing which fifty percent"). If the amount is daunting, not possibly assimilable by any one reader, the abundance of the scholarship testifies to the vitality of Shakespeare's work, which continues to demand new readings and new approaches, allowing every generation not to reinvent Shakespeare in its own image but to find fresh terms in which the study of Shakespeare illuminates its own needs and interests.

General Studies

ANTHOLOGIES OF CRITICISM

Calderwood, James L., and Harold E. Toliver, eds. *Essays in Shakespearean Criticism.* Prentice-Hall 1970 o.p. A wide-ranging selection of essays on the complexities of Shakespeare's artistry.

Crane, Milton, ed. *Shakespeare's Art: Seven Essays.* U. Ch. Pr. 1973 $11.00. ISBN 0-226-11835-5. A collection of essays originally presented in George Washington University's series of Tupper Lectures.

Dollimore, Jonathan, and Alan Sinfield, eds. *Political Shakespeare: New Essays in Cultural Materialism.* Cornell Univ. Pr. 1985 $11.95. ISBN 0-8014-9325-0. An influential collection of essays challenging traditional readings of Shakespeare's plays.

Drakikis, John, ed. *Alternative Shakespeare.* Methuen 1985 $12.95. ISBN 0-415-02528-1. A provocative collection self-consciously devoted to "the demystification of the 'myth' of Shakespeare."

Howard, Jean E., and Marion O'Connor, eds. *Shakespeare Reproduced: The Text in History and Ideology.* Methuen 1987 $15.95. ISBN 0-416-00932-8. An important collection of essays originally presented at the International Shakespeare Congress in Berlin in 1986.

Kernan, Alvin, ed. *Modern Shakespearean Criticism: Essays on Style, Dramaturgy, and Major Plays.* HarBraceJ 1970 $13.00. ISBN 0-15-563375-9. A collection of sensible essays on the style and structure of the major plays.

Kettle, Arnold, ed. *Shakespeare in a Changing World.* Lawrence and Wishart 1964 o.p. A collection of essays on the social conditions in which Shakespeare's plays were written and continue to be produced.

Lenz, Carolyn, Ruth Swift, Gayle Greene, and Carol Thomas Neely, eds. *The Woman's Part: Feminist Criticism of Shakespeare.* U. of Ill. Pr. 1980 $13.95. ISBN 0-252-01016-7. An extremely influential collection of feminist studies of Shakespeare's plays.

Parker, Patricia, and Geoffrey Hartman, eds. *Shakespeare and the Question of Theory.* Methuen 1985 $27.00. ISBN 0-4143-36920-0. A fine collection of essays displaying the provocative use of contemporary literary theories to explore the textual density of Shakespeare's work.

Schwartz, Murray M., and Coppélia Kahn, eds. *Representing Shakespeare: New Psychoanalytic Essays.* Johns Hopkins 1980 $12.95. ISBN 0-8018-2825-2. Thirteen essays using psychoanalytic approaches to articulate the defining features of Shakespeare's plays.

INDIVIDUAL CRITICAL WORKS

Adelman, Janet. *Suffocating Mothers: Fantasies of Maternal Origin in Shakespeare's Plays, "Hamlet" to "The Tempest."* Routledge 1992 $15.95. ISBN 0-415-90039-5. Rich, suggestive essays on the plays' profound concern with maternal power.

Burckhardt, Sigurd. *Shakespearean Meanings.* Princeton U. Pr. 1968 o.p. Brilliantly attentive and original readings of a number of Shakespeare's plays.

Coleridge, Samuel Taylor. *Coleridge's Writings on Shakespeare: A Selection of the Essays, Notes, and Lectures.* Ed. by Terence Hawkes. Viking Penguin 1969 o.p. A fine selection of Coleridge's thoughtful meditation on Shakespeare's works.

Cox, John. *Shakespeare and the Dramaturgy of Power.* Princeton U. Pr. 1989 $35.00. ISBN 0-691-06765-1. Discusses Shakespeare's drama in terms of its medieval dramatic and theological heritage.

Dusinberre, Janet. *Shakespeare and the Nature of Women.* 1975 o.p An early feminist approach that finds in the variety of Shakespeare's women a challenge to the patriarchal values of his culture.

Eagleton, Terry. *William Shakespeare.* Blackwell Pubs. 1986 $24.95. ISBN 0-631-14553-2. A short, suggestive account of the complexity of Shakespeare's understanding of language and society.

Fiedler, Leslie. *The Stranger in Shakespeare.* Stein and Day 1973 o.p. A collection of provocative essays about the alien figures in Shakespeare's universe.

Frye, Northrop. *Northrop Frye on Shakespeare.* Yale U. Pr. 1988 $10.00. ISBN 0-300-04208-6. Collection of essays on individual plays from one of the greatest modern critics.

Garber, Marjorie. *Shakespeare's Ghost-Writers: Literature as Uncanny Causality.* Routledge 1988 $45.00. ISBN 0-416-07342-5. Dazzling psychoanalytic account of Shakespeare's uncanny ability to "haunt our culture."

Goldman, Michael. *Shakespeare and the Energies of Drama.* Princeton U. Pr. 1972 o.p. A study of the meaning of the dramatic experience of Shakespeare's plays.

Greenblatt, Stephen. *Shakespearean Negotiations: The Circulation of Social Energy in Renaissance England.* U. CA Pr. 1988 $29.95. ISBN 0-520-06159-4. Influential "new historicist" essays exploring the social dimension of Shakespeare's vitality.

Hapgood, Robert. *Shakespeare: The Theatre-Poet.* OUP 1989 $59.00. ISBN 0-19-812990-4. Essays on how the texts of Shakespeare's plays function as "guides to enactment."

Hawkes, Terence. *That Shakespeherian Rag: Essays on a Critical Process.* Methuen 1986 $10.95. ISBN 0-416-38540-1. Essays on how and for what purposes Shakespeare has been interpreted.

Holland, Norman N. *The Shakespearean Imagination.* Macmillan 1964 o.p. A psychoanalytic account of Shakespeare's imaginative language.

Jardine, Lisa. *Still Harping on Daughters: Women and Drama in the Age of Shakespeare.* Col. U. Pr. 1989 $14.95. ISBN 0-231-07063-2. A feminist approach measuring Shakespeare's representations of gender against Renaissance social conditions.

Johnson, Samuel. *Samuel Johnson on Shakespeare.* Ed. by H. R. Wouhuysen. Viking Penguin 1989 $8.95. ISBN 0-14-053020-7. A collection of Johnson's witty and perceptive writings on Shakespeare.

Kahn, Coppélia. *Man's Estate: Masculine Identity in Shakespeare.* U. CA Pr. 1981 $35.00. ISBN 0-520-03899-1. A study of the psychological dimensions of masculinity in Shakespeare's plays.

Kastan, David Scott. *Shakespeare and the Shapes of Time.* U. Pr. of New Eng. 1982 $30.00. ISBN 0-87451-237-9. A study of Shakespeare's literary response to the human understanding and experience of time.

Kernan, Alvin B. *The Playwright as Magician: Shakespeare's Image of the Poet in the English Public Theater.* Yale U. Pr. 1979 $22.50. ISBN 0-393-00736-7. Essays on Shakespeare's understanding of the changing social and literary world of the professional playwright.

Kott, Jan. *Shakespeare Our Contemporary.* Trans. by Boleslaw Taborski. Norton 1980 $10.95. ISBN 0-393-00736-7. Brilliant rereadings of Shakespeare's plays through the filter of Kott's experiences of Soviet-dominated Eastern Europe.

Marcus, Leah. *Puzzling Shakespeare: Local Reading and Its Discontents.* U. CA Pr. 1988 $37.50. ISBN 0-520-06417-8. New interpretations of plays focusing on their relation to the society in which they were produced.

Mullaney, Stephen. *The Place of the Stage: License, Play, and Power in Renaissance England.* U. Ch. Pr. 1988 $12.95. ISBN 0-520-07191-3. An important study of the cultural position of popular drama in Shakespeare's England.

Neely, Carol Thomas. *Broken Nuptials in Shakespeare's Plays.* Yale U. Pr. 1985 $27.50. ISBN 0-300-03341-9. A sensitive exploration of the meaning of women's public and private action in the plays, focusing on the motif of the interrupted wedding.

Patterson, Annabel. *Shakespeare and the Popular Voice.* Blackwell Pubs. 1989 $39.95. ISBN 0-631-16872-9. Challenging readings of seven plays, assessing Shakespeare's developing social vision.

Rabkin, Norman. *Shakespeare and the Problem of Meaning*. U. Ch. Pr. 1981 $4.95. ISBN 0-226-70178-6. Argues for the multivalence of Shakespeare's plays as the essence of their intellectual and artistic achievement.

Righter (Barton), Anne. *Shakespeare and the Idea of the Play*. 1977 Greenwood repr. of 1962 ed. $35.00. ISBN 0-8371-9446-6. Essays on Shakespeare's changing attitude toward the theater and theatricality.

Rossiter, A. P. *Angel with Horns: Fifteen Lectures on Shakespeare*. Longman 1989 repr. of 1961 ed. $15.95. ISBN 0-582-01499-9. An edition of Rossiter's lectures demonstrating the complexity of Shakespeare's thought and art.

Shaw, George Bernard. *Shaw on Shakespeare*. Ed. by Edwin Wilson. NAL–Dutton 1961 $26.50. ISBN 0-8369-2175-5. A selection of Shaw's incisive, iconoclastic commentary on Shakespeare.

Tennenhouse, Leonard. *Power on Display: The Politics of Shakespeare's Genres*. Methuen 1986 $13.50. ISBN 0-416-01281-7. An effort to understand in Shakespeare's theatrical art the interrelationship of political and aesthetic concerns.

Traversi, Derek. *An Approach to Shakespeare*. 2 vols. 1968 o.p. Sensitive essays on each of the plays.

Weimann, Robert. *Shakespeare and the Popular Tradition in the Theater: Studies in the Social Dimension of Dramatic Form and Function*. Trans. by Robert Schwartz. Johns Hopkins 1978 $14.95. ISBN 0-8018-3506-2. An important account of the social meaning of the conventions of Shakespeare's theater.

Criticism of the Comedies

Comedy is always a challenge for critics. Unlike tragedy, comedy is *As You Like It;* its apparent willingness to pander to our desire for happy endings seems trivial and mocks scholarly efforts to account for its richness. Shakespeare's comedies, however, in their variety and complexity clearly repay serious study, and critics have worked hard to find appropriate terms to expose and explore their sophisticated aesthetic and psychological, social, and moral concerns. Some indication of our growing sense of the variety of Shakespeare's comic art may be found in the usual critical insistence today upon subdividing the group of plays that the editors of the folio of 1623 grouped together as "comedies" into "romantic comedies" (like *As You Like It*), "problem" or "dark" comedies (like *Measure for Measure*), and "romances" or tragicomedies (like *The Tempest*), each subgenre marking a stage in Shakespeare's developing understanding of the deepest logic of comedy itself.

Barber, C. L. *Shakespeare's Festive Comedy*. Princeton U. Pr. 1957 $11.95. ISBN 0-691-01304-7. An influential study of dramatic form and its relation to social custom.

Berry, Edward. *Shakespeare's Comic Rites*. Cambridge U. Pr. 1984 $39.50. ISBN 0-521-26303-4. Uses anthropological notions of rites of passage to explore the distinctive shape and appeal of the comedies.

Bradbrook, M. C. *The Growth and Structure of Elizabethan Comedy*. Rev ed. Chatto & Windus UK 1973 o.p. Traces the development of the characteristic forms of Elizabethan comedy.

Carroll, William. *the Metamorphoses of Shakespeare's Comedy*. Princeton U. Pr. 1985 $34.50. ISBN 0-691-06633-7. A study of the reiterated action of transformation that marks the comedies.

Evans, Bertrand. *Shakespeare's Comedies*. OUP 1960 o.p. Studies of the individual plays' characteristic exploitation of different levels of awareness and control.

Felperin, Howard. *Shakespearean Romance*. Princeton U. Pr. 1972 o.p. Discovers the power of Shakespeare's romances within the conventions and traditions of romance.

Frye, Northrop. *The Myth of Deliverance: Reflections on Shakespeare's Problem Comedies*. U. of Toronto Pr. 1983 $10.95. ISBN 0-8020-6503-1. Studies of *All's Well, Measure for Measure,* and *Troilus and Cressida* as comic mixtures of the festive and the ironic.

————. *A Natural Perspective: The Development of Shakespearean Comedy and Romance*. HarBraceJ 1969 repr. of 1965 ed. $6.95. ISBN 0-15-665414-8. Focuses on the structures of the plays as they enact patterns of rebirth and renewal.

Hunter, Robert Grams. *Shakespeare and the Comedy of Forgiveness*. Col. U. Pr. 1965 o.p. Finds a shared thematic and structural interest in forgiveness, derived from their medieval forebears, in six of the comedies.

Leggatt, Alexander. *Shakespeare's Comedy of Love*. 1974 o.p. Thoughtful essays on the individuality of each of the comedies.

Mowat, Barbara A. *The Dramaturgy of Shakespeare's Romances*. U. of Ga. Pr. 1976 $18.00. ISBN 0-8203-0389-5. Finds the meaning of these last plays in their radical dramatic strategies.

Nevo, Ruth. *Comic Transformations in Shakespeare*. Methuen 1980 $18.95. ISBN 0-416-73890-7. Sees the comedies as a developing experiment in formal complexity and psychological significance.

Newman, Karen. *Shakespeare's Rhetoric of Comic Character*. Methuen 1985 $18.95. ISBN 0-416-37990-7. Sensitive examination of the rhetorical devices that Shakespeare used in achieving psychological complexity.

Salinger, Leo. *Shakespeare and the Traditions of Comedy*. Cambridge U. Pr. 1974 o.p. An important study of the diverse literary traditions that underlie the variety of Shakespeare's comic achievement.

Wheeler, Richard P. *Shakespeare's Development and the Problem Comedies: Turn and Counter-Turn*. U. CA Pr. 1981 $32.50. ISBN 0-520-03902-5. The problem comedies as crucial in the development of Shakespeare's artistry, especially in the tension between trust and autonomy.

Williamson, Marilyn. *The Patriarchy of Shakespeare's Comedies*. Wayne St. U. Pr. 1986 $29.95. ISBN 0-8143-1807-X. Feminist reconsideration of the representation of gender identities and roles in the comedies.

Criticism of the History Plays

Criticism of the histories, while subtle and various, has tended to focus on problems of definition. What is a history play? The form, existing virtually without classical precedent or precept, flowered briefly in the late sixteenth century, and unquestionably Shakespeare is its finest practitioner. Critical responses to the history plays have usually attempted to account for the vitality of the form by differentiating the plays from the chronicles on which they were based or by tracing the political meanings they carried for Elizabethan or modern audiences.

Berry, Edward I. *Patterns of Decay: Shakespeare's Early Histories*. Cambridge U. Pr. 1975 o.p. A study of the first tetralogy, the three parts of *Henry VI* and *Richard III*, focusing on the theme of social disintegration.

Blanpied, John W. *Time and the Artist in Shakespeare's English Histories*. U. Delaware Pr. 1983 $35.00. ISBN 0-87413-230-4. Finds coherence in the plays' focus on the relation of history and drama.

Calderwood, James L. *Metadrama in Shakespeare's Henriad: "Richard II" to "Henry V."* U. CA Pr. 1979 $30.00. ISBN 0-520-03652-2. Examines the plays' self-conscious engagement with language and art.

Campbell, Lily B. *Shakespeare's Histories: Mirrors of Elizabethan Policy*. Huntington Lib. 1978 repr. of 1947 ed. $12.95. ISBN 0-87328-004-0. Probes the plays not as medieval history but as a mirror of Elizabethan political values.

Hodgdon, Barbara. *The End Crowns All: Closure and Contradiction in Shakespeare's History*. Princeton U. Pr. 1991 $35.00. ISBN 0-691-06833-X. Sensitive account of how theatrical aspects of the histories collaborate with and contest the claims of power.

Holderness, Graham. *Shakespeare's History*. St. Martin 1985 $27.50 ISBN 0-312-71581-1. Considers the plays both in the historical moment of their writing and in the history of their performance and reception.

Jones, Robert C. *These Valiant Dead: Renewing the Past in Shakespeare's Histories*. U. of Iowa Pr. 1991 $24.00. ISBN 0-87745-308-X. Essays focusing on the history plays' own engagement with history.

Ornstein, Robert. *A Kingdom for a Stage*. Arden Pr. OH 1988 repr. of 1972 ed. $19.75. ISBN 0-9620257-0-4. A fine account of the complexity of the histories, denying their dependence on the Tudor historical myth.

Rackin, Phyllis. *Stages of History: Shakespeare's English Chronicles*. Cornell Univ. Pr. 1990 $10.95. ISBN 0-8014-9698-5. Sensitive readings of the plays in terms of their relationship to Tudor historiography.

Ribner, Irving. *The English History Play in the Age of Shakespeare*. B & N Imports rev. ed. 1965 o.p. Extensive study of the genre of the history play.

Saccio, Peter. *Shakespeare's English Kings*. OUP 1977 $9.95. ISBN 0-19-502156-8. Useful summary of the historical material on which Shakespeare based his plays.

Sprague, Arthur Colby. *Shakespeare's Histories: Plays for the Stage*. Soc. for Theatre Research 1964 o.p. Readable essays on the stage histories of the plays.

Tillyard, E. M. W. *Shakespeare's History Plays*. B & N Imports 1964 repr. of 1944 ed. o.p. Influential argument that the plays are an orthodox demonstration of the unfolding of the Tudor myth of history.

Wilder, John. *The Lost Garden: A View of Shakespeare's English and Roman History Plays*. Macmillan 1978 o.p. Finds in the plays a consistent view of human nature shaped by and shaping history.

Criticism of the Tragedies

Shakespeare's tragedies have generally been seen as the finest expression of his artistry, but the preeminence of the genre in modern criticism reflects an anachronistic bias, perhaps determined by the grimness of modern life that tells us that the tragedies are somehow more "true" than the comedies and more profound than the histories. Nevertheless, Shakespeare's tragedies are great artistic achievements, and one measure of their greatness is the quality of the criticism they have provoked. While Shakespeare's contemporaries seemed not to recognize what we usually see as the four "major" tragedies (*Hamlet*, *Othello*, *King Lear*, and *Macbeth*) as different in kind from the other tragedies, in recent years these have generated so much influential criticism that bibliographies of full-length studies of each follow the general listings.

GENERAL STUDIES

Booth, Stephen. *"King Lear, "Macbeth," Indefinition, and Tragedy*. Yale U. Pr. 1983 $22.50. ISBN 0-300-02850-4. Finds the essence of Shakespearean tragedy in the plays' resistance to categorization and closure.

Bradley, A. C. *Shakespearean Tragedy*. Viking Penguin 1991 repr of 1904 ed. $10.95. ISBN 0-14-053019-3. The most influential single work on the plays, focusing on tragic characterization.

Brooke, Nicholas. *Shakespeare's Early Tragedies*. Methuen 1968 o.p. Essays on the style of the early tragedies, from *Titus Andronicus* to *Hamlet*.

Charney, Maurice. *Shakespeare's Roman Plays: The Function of Imagery in the Drama*. HUP 1961 o.p. A study of the style and imagery of the Roman plays.

Danson, Lawrence. *Tragic Alphabet: Shakespeare's Drama of Language*. Bks. Demand repr. of 1974 ed. $55.00. ISBN 0-8357-8768-0. Focuses on a persistent concern of the tragedies with the difficulty of finding adequate expression for the tragic experience.

Dollimore, Jonathan. *Radical Tragedy: Religion, Ideology, and Power in the Drama of Shakespeare and His Contemporaries*. U. Ch. Pr. 1984 $12.50. ISBN 0-226-15539-0. Finds skeptical and subversive power in these plays.

Everett, Barbara. *Young Hamlet: Essays on Shakespeare's Tragedies.* OUP 1990 $18.95. ISBN 0-19-812993-9. Subtle readings of Shakespeare's tragedies to show how they are rooted in "ordinary human experience."

Felperin, Howard. *Shakespearean Representation: Mimesis and Modernity in Elizabethan Tragedy.* Princeton U. Pr. 1977 $27.50. ISBN 0-691-06341-9. Discovers the meaning of the tragedies in their relation to the literary models on which they are based.

Frye, Northrop. *Fools of Time: Studies in Shakespearean Tragedy.* U. of Toronto Pr. 1967 $12.95. ISBN 0-8020-6215-6. Identifies the essence of the tragic vision as "being in time."

Goldman, Michael. *Acting and Action in Shakespearean Tragedy.* Princeton U. Pr. 1985 $24.50. ISBN 0-691-06630-2. Essays on five plays, focusing on the challenges faced by characters, by actors in constructing those characters, and by audiences.

Knight, G. Wilson. *The Wheel of Fire: Interpretation of Shakespeare's Tragedies.* Routledge Chapman & Hall rev. ed. 1949 $13.95. ISBN 0-416-67620-0. Sensitive essays on the meaning of the plays' imagery.

McElroy, Bernard. *Shakespeare's Mature Tragedies.* Princeton U. Pr. 1986 repr. of 1973 ed. $14.50. ISBN 0-691-10201-5. Suggestive essays on the major tragedies, focusing on the experience of the tragic hero.

Miola, Robert. *Shakespeare's Rome.* Cambridge U. Pr. 1983 $34.50. ISBN 0-521-25307-1. Thoughtful account of Shakespeare's sustained interest in Rome and Roman values.

Muir, Kenneth. *Shakespeare's Tragic Sequence.* B & N Imports 1979 repr. of 1972 ed. $13.95. ISBN 0-06-495022-0. Useful introductory treatment of Shakespeare's tragedies, arguing for their individuality.

Nevo, Ruth. *Tragic Form in Shakespeare.* Princeton U. Pr. 1972 o.p. Detailed essays on the developing structure of the tragedies as a five-phased process of discovery.

Snyder, Susan. *The Comic Matrix of Shakespeare's Tragedies.* Princeton U. Pr. 1979 o.p. Explores the complex interrelationship of comedy and tragedy.

THE MAJOR TRAGEDIES

HAMLET CRITICISM

Alexander, Nigel. *Poison, Play, and Duel: A Study in "Hamlet."* U. of Nebr. Pr. 1971 o.p. Focuses on the play's presentation of the difficulty of moral choice and action.

Calderwood, James L. *To Be and Not to Be: Negation and Metadrama in "Hamlet."* Col. U. Pr. 1983 $12.00. ISBN 0-231-05629-X. Exploration of the play's proliferation of tensions and uncertainties.

Clayton, Thomas, ed. *The "Hamlet" First Published (Q1, 1603): Origins, Form, Intertextuality.* U. Delaware Pr. 1992 $42.50. ISBN 0-87413-4277. Interesting collection of essays assessing the textual and literary status of the first quarto of *Hamlet*.

Charney, Maurice. *Style in "Hamlet."* Princeton U. Pr. 1969 o.p. Sustained analysis of the verbal and visual patterns in the play.

Frye, Roland Mushat. *The Renaissance "Hamlet": Issues and Responses in 1600.* Princeton U. Pr. 1984 $39.50. ISBN 0-691-06579-9. Exhaustive study of the historical and intellectual background of the play.

Jones, Ernest. *Hamlet and Oedipus.* Norton repr. of 1949 ed. $6.95. ISBN 0-393-00799-5. Psychoanalytic account of Hamlet's character.

Levin, Harry. *The Question of Hamlet.* OUP 1970 repr. of 1959 ed. $5.95. ISBN 0-19-500808-1. Influential essay focusing on the play's relentless questioning and often unexpected answers.

Prosser, Eleanor. *Hamlet and Revenge.* Stanford U. Pr. 1971 $10.95. ISBN 0-8047-0317-5. Examination of the play's moral universe in light of Elizabethan attitudes toward revenge and ghosts.

Rosenberg, Marvin. *The Masks of "Hamlet."* U. Delaware Pr. 1992 $69.50. ISBN 0-88277-930-3. Uses critical and performance history to explore the richness of the play in a scene-by-scene analysis.

OTHELLO CRITICISM

Adamson, Jane. *"Othello" as Tragedy: Some Problems of Judgment and Feeling.* Cambridge U. Pr. 1980 $39.50. ISBN 0-521-22368-7. Finds the unity of the play in the relationship between the characters' effort to judge morals and motive and the audience's own.

Calderwood, James L. *The Properties of "Othello."* U. of Mass. Pr. 1989 $22.50. ISBN 0-87023-666-0. Subtle tracing of the concept of property as it informs the play's theme and structure.

Heilman, Robert B. *Magic in the Web: Action and Language in "Othello."* Greenwood 1977 repr. of 1956 ed. $35.00. ISBN 0-871-9784-8. Sensitive focus on the play's imagery and action.

Jones, Eldred. *Othello's Countrymen: The African in English Renaissance Drama.* OUP 1965 o.p. Survey of Elizabethan knowledge of Africans and of dramatic representations of African characters.

Rosenberg, Marvin. *The Masks of "Othello": The Search for the Identity of Othello, Iago, and Desdemona by Three Centuries of Actors and Critics.* U. Delaware Pr. 1992 repr. of 1961 ed. o.p. Examines theatrical and critical approaches to the play from the eighteenth to the twentieth century.

KING LEAR CRITICISM

Colie, Rosalie L., and F. T. Flahiff, eds. *Some Facets of "King Lear": Essays in Prismatic Criticism.* Bks. Demand 1974 $64.00. ISBN 0-317-27054-0. Twelve essays on various aspects of the play.

Elton, William R. *"King Lear" and the Gods.* U. Pr. of KY 1988 $12.00. ISBN 0-8131-0178-6. A powerful challenge to redemptive readings of the play.

Heilman, Robert B. *This Great Stage: Image and Structure in "King Lear."* Greenwood 1976 repr. of 1948 ed. $37.50. ISBN 0-8371-8523-8. Detailed exploration of the play's language and imagery.

Lusardi, James P., and June Schlueter. *Reading Shakespeare in Performance: "King Lear."* Fairleigh Dickinson 1991 $37.50. ISBN 0-8386-3394-3. Explores the text as a guide to performance and performance as an interpretation of the text.

Mack, Maynard. *"King Lear" in Our Time.* U. CA Pr. 1965 o.p. Influential study of the play's stage history, its sources, and its appeal to modern readers.

Rosenberg, Marvin. *The Masks of "King Lear."* U. Delaware Pr. 1992 repr. of 1972 ed. $30.00. ISBN 0-520-01718-8. Scene-by-scene analysis, using the play's stage and critical history.

Taylor, Gary, and Michael Warren, eds. *Division of the Kingdoms: Shakespeare's Two Versions of* King Lear. OUP 1983 $24.00. ISBN 0-19-812950-5. Important studies arguing that the 1608 quarto and the 1623 folio are independent and substantive versions of the play.

MACBETH CRITICISM

Bartholomeusz, Dennis. *"Macbeth" and the Players.* Cambridge U. Pr. 1984. $49.50. ISBN 0-521-06925-4. Survey of the history of the play on stage.

Brown, John Russell, ed. *Focus on "Macbeth."* Routledge Chapman & Hall 1982 $25.00. ISBN 0-7100-9015-3. Interesting essays on various aspects of the play.

Calderwood, James L. *If It Were Done: "Macbeth" and Tragic Action.* U. of Mass. Pr. 1986 o.p. Subtle account of the play's resistances to closure and completeness.

Jorgensen, Paul. *Our Naked Frailties: Sensational Art and Meaning in "Macbeth."* U. CA Pr. 1971 $27.50. ISBN 0-520-01915-6. Sensitive essay on the play's poetic texture.

Paul, Henry P. *The Royal Play of "Macbeth."* Hippocrene 1971 repr. of 1950 ed. $26.00. ISBN 0-374-96319-3. Argues that the play was written for a performance at the court of King James.

Rosenberg, Marvin. *The Masks of "Macbeth."* U. Delaware Pr. 1992 repr. of 1978 ed. $30.00. Scene-by-scene analysis, using the play's stage and critical history.

Criticism of the Nondramatic Poetry

Shakespeare was a poet of distinction as well as a great dramatist, though the nondramatic poetry was added to collected editions of his work only in 1778. *Venus and Adonis* was published in 1593 and was followed the next year by the *The Rape of Lucrece*. Both were published in fine, carefully printed editions, and both were widely admired. *The Phoenix and the Turtle* first appeared in 1601 in a volume called *Love's Martyr*. The sonnets, which of course are the best known and most often read of Shakespeare's nondramatic poetry, were published first in 1609 by Thomas Thorpe. It is not known exactly when they were written or even if Thorpe's order is authoritative.

Baldwin, T. W. *On the Literary Genetics of Shakespeare's Poems and Sonnets.* U. of Ill. Pr. 1950 o.p. Exhaustive account of Shakespeare's models and sources.

Booth, Stephen. *An Essay on Shakespeare's Sonnets.* Yale U. Pr. 1969 o.p. Ingenious tracing of formal patterns that structure the reader's experience of the sonnets.

Bush, Douglas. *Mythology and the Renaissance Tradition in English Literature.* Norton rev. ed 1963 o.p. Fine account of subject, with a chapter *"Venus and Adonis* and *Lucrece."*

Dubrow, Heather. *Captive Victors: Shakespeare's Narrative Poems and Sonnets.* Cornell Univ. Pr. 1987 $31.50. ISBN 0-8014-1975-1. Focuses on the moral and psychological issues expressed by the poetry's elaborate rhetorical surface.

Fineman, Joel. *Shakespeare's Perjured Eye: The Invention of Poetic Subjectivity in the Sonnets.* U. CA Pr. 1986 $12.95. ISBN 0-520-06331-7. Dense, original study of the poems' development of a persona as the model of literary subjectivity.

Hulse, Clarke. *Metamorphic Verse: The Elizabethan Minor Epic.* Princeton U. Pr. 1981 $35.00. ISBN 0-691-06483-0. Locates *Venus and Adonis* and *The Rape of Lucrece* within the Ovidian tradition of verse narrative.

Knight, G. Wilson. *The Mutual Flame: On Shakespeare's Sonnets and "The Phoenix and the Turtle."* Macmillan 1955 o.p. Considers the central images in the poetry and their role in structuring the poet's meditation on time and eternity.

Kreiger, Murray. *A Window to Criticism: Shakespeare's Sonnets and Modern Poetics.* Bks. Demand repr. of 1964 ed. $59.00. ISBN 0-317-27580-1. Examines the relationship of the aesthetic object and its historical existence.

Leishman, J. B. *Themes and Variations in Shakespeare's Sonnets.* Hillary Hs. 1961 o.p. Exploration of the sonnets' themes and their sources in classical and Renaissance literature.

Muir, Kenneth. *Shakespeare's Sonnets.* Paul & Co. Pubs. 1979 o.p. A sensible introduction to bibliographic, stylistic, and thematic issues.

LANGUAGE AND STYLE

Shakespeare's art is, of course, an art of language that has been studied from a variety of illuminating perspectives. Scholars have explored the linguistic and rhetorical resources available to Shakespeare and his remarkable use of what existed. English itself was still in flux in Shakespeare's time. Grammar, orthography, pronunciation, vocabulary—all were changing and all were hotly debated, in a climate of linguistic and stylistic self-consciousness that Shakespeare's art engages.

Dictionaries and Concordances

Dent, R. W. *Shakespeare's Proverbial Language: An Index.* U. CA Pr. 1981 $49.95. ISBN 0-520-03894-0. A list of all proverbs in the works, citing origins and analogues.

Onions, Charles T. *Shakespeare Glossary.* Ed. by Robert D. Eagleson. OUP 1986 $13.95. ISBN 0-19-812521-6. An indispensable small lexicon based on the *Oxford English Dictionary.*

Partridge, Eric. *Shakespeare's Bawdy.* Routledge 1990 $15.95. ISBN 0-415-05076-6. In addition to its glossary, includes an essay on sexual language.

Rubinstein, Frankie. *A Dictionary of Shakespeare's Sexual Puns and Their Significance.* Scholars Bookshelf 2nd ed. n.d. $18.95. ISBN 0-945726-35-X

Schmidt, Alexander. *Shakespeare Lexicon: A Complete Dictionary of All the English Words, Phrases and Constructions in the Work of the Poet.* 2 vols. 1901. Ed. by Gregor Sarrazin. Ayer 1968 $95.00. ISBN 0-405-08935-X; De Gruyter 1971 $164.30. ISBN 3-11-002203-6. A large Shakespeare dictionary with illustrations.

Spevack, Martin, ed. *A Complete and Systematic Concordance to the Works of Shakespeare.* 9 vols. Adlers Foreign Bks. 1967–80 $1,782.00. ISBN 3-487-01817. Computer-generated concordance, based on *The Riverside Shakespeare.*

———. *The Harvard Concordance to Shakespeare.* Belknap Pr. 1974 $80.00. ISBN 0-674-37475-4. A valuable single-volume abridgment of Spevack's nine-volume work.

Studies

Abbott, E. A. *A Shakespearean Grammar.* Haskell 1972 $75.00. ISBN 0-8383-1571-2. Survey of grammatical constructions, with copious examples.

Blake, N. F. *Shakespeare's Language: An Introduction.* St Martin 1984 $11.95. ISBN 0-312-71430-0. Excellent introductory account of the state of English in Shakespeare's time.

Cercignani, Fausto. *Shakespeare's Works and Elizabethan Pronunciation.* OUP 1981 o.p. An extensive and authoritative work, emphasizing the difference between Elizabethan and modern pronunciation.

Clemen, Wolfgang H. *The Development of Shakespeare's Imagery.* Repr. and trans. by HUP 1951 o.p.

Dobson, E. J. *English Pronunciation, 1500–1700.* 2 vols. OUP 1968 o.p. The essential phonological study of early modern pronunciation.

Doran, Madeleine. *Shakespeare's Dramatic Language.* U. of Wis. Pr. 1976 $32.50. ISBN 0-299-07010-7. Concentrating on the tragedies, a study of the thematic implications of style.

Donawerth, Jane. *Shakespeare and the Sixteenth-Century Study of Language.* U. of Ill. Pr. 1984 $29.95. ISBN 0-252-01038-8. Examines the ideas about language available to Shakespeare and their use in the plays.

Edwards, Philip, Inga-Stina Ewbank, and G. K. Hunter. *Shakespeare's Styles: Essays in Honour of Kenneth Muir.* Cambridge U. Pr. 1980 o.p. A collection of essays on the diverse rhetorical styles of Shakespeare's art.

Evans, B. Ifor. *The Language of Shakespeare's Plays.* Greenwood 1985 $43.75. ISBN 0-313-24987-3. Individual essays analyzing the use of language in the plays.

Houston, John P. *Shakespeare's Sentences: A Study in Style and Syntax.* La. State U. Pr. 1988 $32.50. ISBN 0-8071-1399-9. An analysis of the effects of Shakespeare's characteristic syntactical forms.

Hulme, Hilda M. *Explorations in Shakespeare's Language.* Bks. Demand 1962 $90.80. ISBN 0-317-28358-8. Examines the various linguistic contexts that provide Shakespeare's verbal resources.

Hussey, S. S. *The Literary Language of Shakespeare.* 1982 o.p.

Kökeritz, Helge. *Shakespeare's Names: A Pronouncing Dictionary.* Bks. Demand repr. of 1959 ed. $22.50. ISBN 0-8357-9507-1. A pronunciation guide to the names in Shakespeare's plays.

———. *Shakespeare's Pronunciation.* Yale U. Pr. 1959 o.p. A conservative but comprehensive account of the pronunciation of Shakespeare's English.

Mahood, M. M. *Shakespeare's Wordplay.* Methuen 1957 o.p. Subtle and sensitive tracing of the wordplay, largely punning, in the plays and poems.

Miriam Joseph, Sister. *Shakespeare's Use of the Arts of Language.* Col. U. Pr. 1947 o.p. Scholarly account of rhetorical theory in Elizabethan England and Shakespeare's use of it.

Ness, Frederic W. *The Use of Rhyme in Shakespeare's Plays.* Yale U. Pr. 1941 o.p.

Spurgeon, Caroline. *Shakespeare's Imagery and What It Tells Us.* Cambridge U. Pr. 1935 $24.95. ISBN 0-521-09258-2. Pioneering census and study of patterns of imagery.

Thompson, Ann, and John O. Thompson. *Shakespeare: Meaning and Metaphor.* U. of Iowa Pr. 1987 $27.00. ISBN 0-87745-166-4. A sophisticated account of Shakespeare's use of metaphor.

Trousdale, Marion. *Shakespeare and the Rhetoricians.* U. of NC Pr. 1982 $27.50. ISBN 0-8078-1482-2. Uses Elizabethan attitudes toward language to develop a notion of Shakespeare's literary practice.

Vickers, Brian. *The Artistry of Shakespeare's Prose.* B & N Imports 1968 o.p. Examination of Shakespeare's prose style as it develops in the plays.

Wright, George T. *Shakespeare's Metrical Art.* U. CA Pr. 1988 $47.50. ISBN 0-520-06057-1. A subtle study of Shakespeare's metrical practice.

THEATERS, ACTING, STAGE HISTORY, AND DRAMATURGY

An enormous amount has been discovered about Shakespeare's stage and stagecraft. Studies of the theaters' structure, size, and location, of actors and acting companies, of the audiences, of theatrical conventions, and of government regulation have given us insight into the theatrical environment that shaped Shakespeare's art.

Beckerman, Bernard. *Shakespeare at the Globe, 1599–1609.* Macmillan 1962 o.p. Account of staging demands and possibilities.

Bentley, Gerald E. *Shakespeare and His Theater.* Bks. Demand 1964 $35.40. ISBN 0-685-23968-3. Readable essays on the theatrical environment, physical and professional, in which Shakespeare functioned.

Berry, Herbert. *Shakespeare's Playhouses.* AMS Pr. 1987 $34.50. ISBN 0-404-62289-5. A collection of essays on the four playhouses used by Shakespeare's acting company.

Berry, Ralph, ed. *On Directing Shakespeare: Interviews with Contemporary Directors.* Viking Penguin 1990 $21.95. ISBN 0-241-12689-4. Interesting discussions with important directors about contemporary productions.

Bethell, S. L. *Shakespeare and the Popular Dramatic Tradition.* Duke 1944 o.p. Examines Shakespeare's relation to his immediate dramatic forebears on the English stage.

Bevington, David. *Action Is Eloquence: Shakespeare's Language of Gesture.* Bks. Demand 1984 $65.10. ISBN 0-7837-1510-2. A study of how action, blocking, and gesture produce meanings that clarify or contest the verbal meanings of the plays.

Bulman, J. C., and H. R. Coursen, eds. *Shakespeare on Television.* U. Pr. of New Eng. 1988 $35.00. ISBN 0-87451-435-5. A collection of essays on television productions of Shakespeare's plays.

Cook, Ann Jennalie. *The Privileged Playgoers of Shakespeare's London, 1576–1642.* Princeton U. Pr. 1981 $40.00. ISBN 0-691-06454-7. A study of the audiences of Shakespeare's theater, stressing upper-class participation.

Gurr, Andrew. *The Shakespearean Stage, 1574–1642.* Cambridge U. Pr. 1992 $59.95. ISBN 0-521-41005-3. Readable summary of the most recent scholarship on Shakespeare's theatrical environment.

———. *Playgoing in Shakespeare's London.* Cambridge U. Pr. 1989 $59.95. ISBN 0-521-25336-5. Interesting study of Shakespeare's theater, based on an examination of every known playgoer in Shakespeare's day.

Gurr, Andrew, and John Orrell. *Rebuilding Shakespeare's Globe.* Routledge Chapman & Hall 1989 $25.00. ISBN 0-685-26528-5. Account of Sam Wanamaker's effort to rebuild the Globe theater today on the south bank of the Thames.

Hogan, Charles B. *Shakespeare in the Theater, 1701–1800*. 2 vols OUP 1952–57 o.p. Index to English performances in the eighteenth century.

Howard, Jean E. *Shakespeare's Art of Orchestration: Stage Technique and Audience Response*. U. of Ill. Pr. 1984 $24.95. ISBN 0-252-01116-3. Sensitive account of relation of stage technique and literary meaning.

Jorgens, Jack J. *Shakespeare on Film*. U. Pr. of Amer. 1991 $24.75. ISBN 0-8191-8157-9. Examination of major film versions of Shakespeare.

Joseph, Bertram. *Acting Shakespeare*. Routledge Chapman & Hall 1969 $11.95. ISBN 0-87830-522-X. An account both of what is known about Elizabethan acting styles and what can be inferred from the texts.

King, T. J. *Shakespearean Staging, 1599–1642*. HUP 1971 o.p. A scrupulous account of the theatrical requirements for staging the plays of the period.

_____. *Casting Shakespeare's Plays: London Actors and Their Roles, 1590-1642*. Cambridge U. Pr. 1992 $59.95. ISBN 0-521-32785-7. Study of Elizabethan playhouse procedures through analysis of casting requirements.

Knutson, Roslyn L. *The Repertory of Shakespeare's Company, 1594-1613*. U. of Ark. Pr. 1991 $32.00. ISBN 1-55728-191-2. Valuable analysis of the dramatic repertory of Shakespeare's acting company.

McGuire, Philip C., and David A. Samuelson, eds. *Shakespeare: The Theatrical Dimension*. AMS Pr. 1979 $34.50. ISBN 0-404-16002-6. Collection of essays that consider Shakespeare's plays as scripts for the stage.

Muir, Kenneth, and others, eds. *Shakespeare: Man of the Theater*. U. Delaware Pr. 1983 $35.00. ISBN 0-87413-217-7. Collection of stage-centered essays.

Nungezer, J. M. *A Dictionary of Actors and Other Persons Associated with the Public Representation of Plays in England before 1642*. Greenwood 1969 $45.00. ISBN 0-8371-0593-5. A biographical dictionary of the playwrights, actors, and theatrical personnel.

Odell, George C. *Shakespeare—From Betterton to Irving*. 2 vols Ayer repr. of 1920 ed. $55.00. ISBN 0-405-08824-8. The standard history of Shakespeare on the English stage from 1660 through the nineteenth century.

Orrell, John. *The Quest for Shakespeare's Globe*. Cambridge U. Pr. 1983 $59.95. ISBN 0-521-24751-9. Scholarly effort to recover the physical dimensions of the Globe theater.

Rutter, Carol, and others. *Clamorous Voices: Shakespeare's Women Today*. Routledge Chapman & Hall 1989 $39.95. ISBN 0-87830-036-8. Focuses on recent actresses' approach to major roles.

Shattuck, Charles H. *The Shakespearean Promptbooks: A Descriptive Catalogue*. Bks. Demand 1965 $140.80. ISBN 0-685-23650-1. A list and description of existing prompt books.

_____. *Shakespeare on the American Stage: From the Hallams to Edwin Booth*. Folger Bks. 1978 $25.00. ISBN 0-918016-50-9. A fine stage history of Shakespeare in America through the nineteenth century.

Speaight, Robert. *Shakespeare on the Stage: An Illustrated History of Shakespearean Performance*. Little 1973 o.p. Attractive, informal history of Shakespeare on the stage.

Sprague, Arthur C. *Shakespeare and the Actors: The Stage Business in His Plays, 1660–1905*. HUP 1944 o.p. Stage history focusing on memorable moments in important productions.

Styan, J. L. *Shakespeare's Stagecraft*. Cambridge U. Pr. 1967 o.p. A useful guide to the stage practice demanded by Shakespeare's theater.

Thomson, Peter. *Shakespeare's Theatre*. Routledge 1992 $14.95. ISBN 0-415-05148-7. Surveys information on the physical and commercial aspects of Shakespeare's theater.

Trewin, J. C. *Shakespeare on the English Stage, 1900–1964*. Barrie and Rockliff 1964 o.p. Selective but thoughtful survey of Shakespeare in the British theater, with appendixes listing all West End, Old Vic, and Stratford productions.

Wiles, David. *Shakespeare's Clown: Actor and Text in the Elizabethan Playhouse.* Cambridge U. Pr. 1987 o.p. A comprehensive history of the role of the clown on the Elizabethan stage.

SOURCE STUDIES

Shakespeare was not an impressively learned man. He was not a scholar, but he read widely and obviously read well. Since Langbaine in 1691, scholars have explored his indebtedness to earlier writers, and they have sought to understand his artistic intentions by comparing his work with what it was based upon. What he read was easily available: the classics that were the basis of the school curriculum, the historical chronicles that celebrated the English nation, popular prose fiction translated from French and Italian, and, of course, the Bible, which he read most probably in the 1560 Geneva translation. But perhaps Shakespeare's most important source is Shakespeare himself; he returns again and again to plots, characters, and images in his own plays and poetry, continually reimagining his own artistic and thematic concerns.

Bluestone, Max. *From Story to Stage: The Dramatic Adaptation of Prose Fiction in the Period of Shakespeare and His Contemporaries.* De Gruyter 1974 $45.50. ISBN 90-2792-697-2. Important study of Shakespeare's use of contemporary prose fiction.

Boswell-Stone, W. G. *Shakespeare's Holinshed.* Ayer 1967 repr. of 1909 ed. $30.00. ISBN 0-405-08291-6. An edition of Holinshed's *Chronicles,* essential for any study of Shakespeare's histories.

Bullough, Geoffrey, ed. *Narrative and Dramatic Sources of Shakespeare.* 8 vols. Col. U. Pr. 1957–75. Indispensable collection of sources and analogues for all Shakespeare's plays.

Donaldson, E. Talbot. *The Swan at the Well: Shakespeare Reading Chaucer.* Yale U. Pr. 1985 $25.00. ISBN 0-300-03349-4. A major scholar assessing Shakespeare's use of Chaucer.

Gesner, Carol. *Shakespeare and the Greek Romance: A Study of Origins.* U. Pr. of Ky. 1970 $59.80. ISBN 0-8357-8594-7. Assessment of Shakespeare's knowledge and use of ancient Greek romance.

Griffin, Alice, ed. *The Sources of Ten Shakespearean Plays.* Crowell 1966 o.p. Modernized text of the major source of *Romeo and Juliet, Taming of the Shrew, Twelfth Night, Henry IV, Henry V, Julius Caesar, Othello, Macbeth,* and *Antony and Cleopatra.*

Hart, Alfred. *Shakespeare and the Homilies.* Octagon 1970 repr. of 1934 ed. $16.00. ISBN 0-374-93699-4. Study of Shakespeare's use of the homilies read in church and other religious influences.

Hosley, Richard, ed. *Shakespeare's Holinshed.* Putnam 1968 o.p. Useful selection from Holinshed, but includes only what Shakespeare actually used.

Martindale, Charles, and Michelle Martindale. *Shakespeare and the Uses of Antiquity: An Introductory Essay on Shakespeare and English Renaissance Classicism.* Routledge 1990 $45.00. ISBN 0-415-02388-2. A valuable study of the critical implications of Shakespeare's handling of his classical sources.

Milward, Peter. *Shakespeare's Religious Background.* Loyola 1985 repr. of 1973 ed. $10.95. ISBN 0-8294-0508-9. A study of religious thought in Shakespeare's England and its reflection in the plays.

Miola, Robert S. *Shakespeare and Classical Tragedy: The Influence of Seneca.* OUP 1992 $49.95. ISBN 0-19-811264-5. Traces Shakespeare's stylistic and intellectual debt to Senecan tragedy.

Muir, Kenneth. *The Sources of Shakespeare's Plays.* Yale U. Pr. 1978 o.p. Considers Shakespeare's sources, in individual essays on each of the plays.

Noble, Richmond S. *Shakespeare's Biblical Knowledge and Use of the Book of Common Prayer: As Exemplified in the Plays of the First Folio.* Gordon Pr. 1972 repr. of 1935 ed. $59.95. ISBN 0-8490-1039-X. Essential study of major religious sources.

Pinciss, Gerald M., and Roger Lockyer, eds. *Shakespeare's World: Background Readings in the English Renaissance.* Continuum 1989 $24.50. ISBN 0-8264-0421-9. Excerpts from a range of influential texts, showing the ideas shaping Elizabethan culture.

Root, Robert K. *Classical Mythology in Shakespeare.* Rprt. Serv. 1992 repr. of 1903 ed. $69.00. ISBN 0-7812-7306-4. Useful if underanalyzed account of Shakespeare's mythological reference, mainly drawn from Ovid.

Satin, Joseph Henry. *Shakespeare and His Sources.* HM 1966 o.p. Modernized texts of major source of *Richard III, Richard II, Henry V, Twelfth Night, Merchant of Venice, Julius Caesar, Hamlet, Othello, King Lear, Macbeth,* and *Antony and Cleopatra.*

Shaheen, Naseeb. *Biblical References in Shakespeare's History Plays.* U. Delaware Pr. 1989 $36.50. ISBN 0-87413-341-6. Census of biblical and liturgical references.

———. *Biblical References in Shakespeare's Tragedies.* U. Delaware Pr. 1987 $35.00. ISBN 0-87413-293-2. Census of biblical and liturgical references.

Sims, James H. *Dramatic Uses of Biblical Allusions in Marlowe and Shakespeare.* U. Press Fla. 1966 $9.95. ISBN 0-8130-0206-0. Discussion of the playwrights' thematic and structural use of biblical references.

Spencer, T. J., ed. *Shakespeare's Plutarch.* Viking Penguin 1991 repr. of 1964 ed. $9.95. ISBN 0-14-053004-5. Selections from the 1595 edition of Thomas North's translation of Plutarch's *Lives.*

Thompson, Ann. *Shakespeare's Chaucer: A Study in Literary Origins.* Liverpool U. Pr. 1978 o.p. Argues for Shakespeare's extensive knowledge of Chaucer's poetry.

Thomson, J. A. K. *Shakespeare and the Classics.* Greenwood 1978 $32.50. ISBN 0-313-20388-1. Casual play-by-play account of Shakespeare's use of Ovid and Plutarch.

Whitaker, Virgil K. *Shakespeare's Use of Learning.* Huntington Lib. 1964 o.p. Learned study of Shakespeare's changing relation to his sources.

GENERAL REFERENCE

Bibliographies

Bergeron, David M., and Geraldo U. De Sousa. *Shakespeare: A Study and Research Guide.* U. Pr. of KS 1987 $27.50. ISBN 0-7006-0339-5. Annotated guide to reference and critical materials for college students.

Berman, Ronald. *A Reader's Guide to Shakespeare's Plays: A Discursive Bibliography.* Scott, Foresman 1973 o.p. Useful, if opinionated, guide to criticism.

Bevington, David, ed. *Shakespeare. Goldentree Bibliographies in Language and Lit. Ser.* Harlan Davidson 1978 $14.95. ISBN 0-88295-555-1. Carefully organized listings of scholarly publications from 1930 to 1977.

Champion, Larry S. *The Essential Shakespeare: An Annotated Bibliography of Major Modern Studies.* Macmillan 1986 $65.00. ISBN 0-8161-8731-2. A selective bibliography of criticism with descriptive annotations, containing about 1,500 entries.

Ebisch, Walther, and Levin L. Schucking, comps. *Shakespeare Bibliography.* Ayer 1968 repr. of 1931 ed. $24.50. ISBN 0-405-08482-X. Thorough listing of criticism from the first part of the twentieth century.

———. *A Supplement for the Years 1930–1935.* Ayer 1972 repr. of 1937 ed. $24.50. ISBN 0-405-08483-8

Godshalk, William, gen. ed. *Garland Shakespeare Bibliographies.* Garland 1980–. A series of volumes, each on an individual play, issued as they are completed.

Howard-Hill, T. H. *Shakespearean Bibliography.* Clarendon Pr. 1971 o.p. A bibliography of bibliographies, plus a chronological bibliography of textual studies.

Jacobs, Henry E., and Claudia D. Johnson, comps. *An Annotated Bibliography of Shakespearean Burlesques, Parodies and Travesties.* Garland 1975 o.p

Jaggard, William. *Shakespeare Bibliography*. A Wofsy Fine Arts 1971 repr. of 1911 ed. o.p. The first scholarly bibliography of Shakespeare, containing over 36,000 entries.

McLean, Andrew M. *Shakespeare: Annotated Bibliographies and Media Guide for Teachers*. NCTE 1980 o.p. Useful bibliography on teaching as well as a guide to visual resources.

McManaway, James G., and Jeanne A. Roberts, comps. *Selective Bibliography of Shakespeare: Editions, Textual Studies, Commentary*. Folger Bks. 1978 $20.00. ISBN 0-918016-02-9. A valuable bibliography of materials relating to Shakespeare's plays.

Parker, Barry. *The Shakespeare Folger Filmography: A Directory of Feature Films Based on the Works of Shakespeare*. Folger Bks. 1979 $7.95. ISBN 0-918016-19-3

Quinn, Edward, and others. *The Major Shakespearean Tragedies: A Critical Bibliography*. Macmillan 1973 o.p. Valuable, if dated, annotated bibliography of criticism of *Hamlet, King Lear, Othello*, and *Macbeth*.

Sajdak, Bruce T., ed. *Shakespeare Index: An Annotated Bibliography of Critical Articles on the Plays 1959–1983*. Kraus Intl. 1991. $295.00. ISBN 0-527-78932-1

Shakespeare Quarterly. Vol. 1. Folger 1950–. Indispensable annual bibliography of Shakespeare studies.

Smith, Gordon Ross, ed. *Classified Shakespeare Bibliography 1936-1958*. Pa. St. U. Pr. 1963 $60.00. ISBN 0-271-73053-6. Exhaustive bibliography of criticism of the period.

Velz, John W. *Shakespeare and the Classical Tradition: A Critical Guide to Commentary, 1660–1960*. Bks. Demand 1968 $119.80. ISBN 0-317-27789-8. An extensive bibliography of work assessing Shakespeare's relation to Greek and Latin literature.

Wells, Stanley, ed. *Shakespeare: Select Bibliographical Guides*. OUP 1973 o.p. Sensitive essays outlining the criticism of the plays and poems.

Reference Works

Andrews, John F. *William Shakespeare: His World, His Work, His Influence*. 3 vols. Macmillan 1985. $199.00. ISBN 0-684-17851-6. A fine collection of essays on a variety of key topics.

Chambers, E. K. *The Elizabethan Stage*. 4 vols. Clarendon Pr. 1923 o.p. Essential collection of information about the social, material, and literary conditions of Elizabethan playmaking.

Greg, W. W. *A Bibliography of the English Printed Drama to the Restoration*. 4 vols. OUP 1939–59 o.p. Comprehensive account of the early textual histories of the drama of Shakespeare's age.

_____. *Dramatic Documents from the Elizabethan Playhouses*. 2 vols. OUP 1931 o.p.

Harbage, Alfred. *Annals of English Drama, 975–1700*. 3rd ed. rev. by Sylvia S. Wagonheim. Methuen 1989 $79.95. ISBN 0-415-01099-3. A chronological listing of all the plays produced in England before 1700.

Ingleby, C. M., and others, eds. *The Shakespeare Allusion-Book: A Collection of Allusions to Shakespeare from 1591–1700*. 2 vols. 1932. Ayer $55.00. ISBN 0-8369-5512-9

Lewis, Benjamin R. *Shakespeare Documents: Facsimiles, Transliterations, Translations and Commentary*. 2 vols. Stanford U. Pr. 1940 o.p.

Long, John. *Shakespeare's Use of Music: Comedies*. Da Capo 1977 $32.50. ISBN 0-306-77423-2. Essential information about the practice and effects of music in the plays.

_____. *Shakespeare's Use of Music: Final Comedies*. Da Capo 1977 $29.50. ISBN 0-306-77424-0

_____. *Shakespeare's Use of Music: Histories and Tragedies*. U. Press Fla. 1971 $17.95. ISBN 0-8130-0311-3

Seng, Peter J. *The Vocal Songs in the Plays of Shakespeare*. HUP 1967 o.p. Brings together all locations, texts, sources, and functions of songs in the plays.

Stevenson, Burton, ed. *The Standard Book of Shakespeare Quotations*. Funk & Wagnalls 1953 o.p.

Vickers, Brian. *Shakespeare: The Critical Heritage*. 6 vols. Routledge Chapman & Hall 1974–81. Comprehensive collection of critical response to Shakespeare, including parodies, adaptations, and commentary, beginning in the 1590s.

Handbooks

Brown, John R. *Discovering Shakespeare: A New Guide to the Plays.* Col. U. Pr. 1986 $15.50. ISBN 1550-05359-2. Emphasizes performance and theatrical history.

Campbell, Oscar J., and Edward G. Quinn, eds. *The Reader's Encyclopedia of Shakespeare.* Crowell 1966 o.p. An informative source; illustrated, with extensive bibliography.

Fox, Levi, ed. *The Shakespeare Handbook: The Essential Companion to Shakespeare's Works, Life and Times.* G. K. Hall 1987 $29.95. ISBN 0-8161-8905-6. Incorporates historical and biographical information.

Granville-Barker, Harley, and George B. Harrison. *A Companion to Shakespeare Studies.* Cambridge U. Pr. 1934 $75.00. ISBN 0-521-05132-0. A standard handbook.

Harbage, Alfred. *William Shakespeare: A Reader's Guide.* Hippocrene Bks. 1985 $30.00. ISBN 0-88254-8379. A standard handbook; good source for general information.

Harrison, George B. *Introducing Shakespeare.* Somerset repr. of 1939 ed. $39.00. ISBN 0-403-08926-3; Rprt. Serv. 1939 ed. $49.00. ISBN 0-7812-0132-2; Viking Penguin 1950 repr. of rev. ed. $6.95. ISBN 0-14-020043-6. A general work for secondary school students first encountering Shakespeare.

Lee, Sidney, and Charles T. Onions, eds. *Shakespeare's England: An Account of the Life and Manners of His Age.* OUP 1917 o.p. Numerous illustrations and references to the plays.

Muir, Kenneth, and S. Schoenbaum, eds. *A New Companion to Shakespeare Studies.* Cambridge U. Pr. 1971 $15.95. ISBN 0-521-09645-6. Addresses many topics not covered in the first *Companion.*

Schoenbaum, S. *Shakespeare: The Globe and the World.* OUP 1979 o.p. Catalog for the Folger Library exhibition; many illustrations.

Wells, Stanley, ed. *The Cambridge Companion to Shakespeare Studies.* Cambridge U. Pr. 1986 $54.95. ISBN 0-521-26737-4. Excellent illustrated handbook.

Zesmer, David M. *Guide to Shakespeare.* B & N Imports 1991 $35.00. ISBN 0-8095-9106-5. Convenient source for briefly stated general information.

CHAPTER 8

Restoration and Eighteenth-Century Literature

Timothy Erwin and Clarissa Cullerton Erwin

> Words are the daughters of the earth, and things the sons of heaven.
> —SAMUEL JOHNSON , *Preface to the Dictionary*

The forms and modes adopted by British writers during the Restoration and the eighteenth century vary perhaps more widely than at any other time in literary history. The works of the writers of that period looked back to those of classical Greece and Rome as a model and also anticipated the reading tastes and habits of contemporary and later readers. JOHN DRYDEN and ALEXANDER POPE ensured the future popularity of the epics of VIRGIL (see Vol. 2) and HOMER (see Vol. 2) by creating new translations of the *Aeneid*, the *Iliad*, and the *Odyssey*; they also diverted readers with that sprightly, satiric cousin to the epic, the mock-epic. The return of the Stuart monarchy with Charles II restored the theater to life after a long Cromwellian slumber and sponsored the creation of a sophisticated dramatic mode mixed in equal parts of wit, charm, poignancy, and cynicism— Restoration comedy. One among many kinds of lyric poetry, the great ode was lifted on the pinions of a new critical idea, the sublime, to heights that would carry it well into the second generation of romantic poetry. Meanwhile, the novelist, a new breed of writer, began to entertain masses of middle-class readers, many, if not most, of whom were women, by creating narratives about people much like themselves. So, in 1740, SAMUEL RICHARDSON took the reading public by storm with *Pamela*, a story told in the form of letters about the courtship and marriage of an innocent young maidservant and her predatory master.

Although it once was fashionable to speak of the Restoration and the eighteenth century as a peaceful era in British history, the exuberant, formal experimentation of its writers in actuality took place against a backdrop of rapid social change and met the contradictory needs of many different types of readers. Between the Restoration in 1660 and the fall of the Bastille in 1789, eight monarchs from three royal lines ruled England. Although a Whig ministry held sway for most of the period, there were Jacobite rebellions in 1715 and 1745, several wars—from 1720 to 1729 (with Spain), from 1756 to 1763 (the Seven Years' War, with France), and from 1775 to 1783 (War of Independence, with America)—as well as several major urban riots (most notably the Gordon Riots of 1780). So, just as the complex, architectonic plot of HENRY FIELDING's *Tom Jones* takes place against the background of the uprising of 1745, the unusual order and symmetry of much of the literature of the period can be understood as a complicated response to the flux and disorder of contemporary life.

As might be expected, the eighteenth century has a nomenclature problem. The rational skepticism inherent in the label "the Age of Reason" was, in reality, not so pervasive. The intellectual awakening that we call the Enlightenment might have suited the native development of an empirical philosophy, but it also spoke to progressive European ideals that had been rejected by many Englishmen. A term such as the Augustan Age, which likens the cultural aspirations of eighteenth-century writers and artists to the reign of the Roman emperor Augustus (63 B.C. – A.D. 14), with its outpouring of verse by HORACE (see Vol. 2), Virgil and OVID (see Vol. 2), accurately reflects some of the imitative aims of Pope, Fielding, and OLIVER GOLDSMITH but not those of many other writers. Goldsmith, in his works, limited the range of the Augustan Age to the reign of Queen Anne (1702–14). The problem may be best solved by treating all labels as only partially applicable.

The major political division throughout the century was between the Whig party of commercial and moneyed interests and its opposition, the Tory party. To one degree or another, the major writers of the period belonged to the opposition party. Most, in other words, were spokespersons for communitarian values. The philosophical mode of the day was the skeptical empiricism of JOHN LOCKE (see Vols. 3 and 4) and his followers, which sought to set reliable limits to what the human mind could know with certainty. A key metaphor of Locke likens the mind to a tabula rasa, or blank slate, which receives sense impressions and then reflects on them in order to create ideas. In another of Locke's metaphors, which was important to JOSEPH ADDISON's theory of the imagination, the mind is compared to a camera obscura, which receives pictures from the external world. Locke's influence on the eighteenth century was as considerable as that of FREUD (see Vols. 3 and 5) on the twentieth century, and his understanding of moral choice in the second book of the *Essay Concerning Human Understanding* shaped a major theme in the work of SAMUEL JOHNSON, the most important author of the eighteenth century.

Because the era was intensely religious, its philosophy and literature were often allied to theology. As Leslie Stephen, a student of eighteenth-century thought, pointed out: "The doctrine accepted alike by reason and the imagination was that the world was created, governed, and sustained by a Supreme Being of infinite perfection. . . . Strike away this central truth, and chaos would come again; truth be unattainable, and the world a blind congeries of shifting and changing forces." Sermons and other religious works were immensely popular, and many novels of the period, like Fielding's *Joseph Andrews*, retrace an unstated but understood biblical narrative. The literary criticism of the era began with a rhetorical rethinking of the classical tenets of ARISTOTLE, Horace, and LONGINUS (see Vol. 2), as passed down by Renaissance humanism, and ended with the invention of a new, romantic theory of the imagination. In the meantime, criticism addressed some important questions: "How can we understand *wit* and *judgment* as complementary yet contrary principles of literary enjoyment?" "When we talk about *nature*, do we mean what we usually call *human nature* or the *nature* comprising the natural world outside our window?" "How can we formulate a theory of genre that will include the novel (not yet thought to be a serious literary form) on its own terms?" "Is the relationship of poetry to the other arts a necessary imaginative connection or merely an accident of taste?" In answer to these and other questions, the canon of English literature became more expansive and self-conscious than before, especially in such a late collection as Johnson's *Lives of the Poets*. On the whole, readers approached literature with an increasingly democratic taste and gradually came to prefer the contemporary novel to the neoclassical epic.

If we understand the history of criticism as a contest between ancient rule and modern freedom, then modernism during the eighteenth century enjoyed a decided victory—one celebrated in LAURENCE STERNE's *Tristram Shandy*. Historical shift is more complex than that, of course. "Thought moves in a spiral curve, not in a straight line," as Leslie Stephen stated. Among many neoclassical concepts that were never abandoned by either the later Augustan novel or romantic poetry was the notion that an informed criticism should guide the creation of poetry; in fact, an extended neoclassical variety persists even in the novelized shaping of the last great British epic, LORD BYRON's *Don Juan*.

HISTORY AND CRITICISM

Barrell, John. *The Birth of Pandora and the Division of Knowledge*. U. of Pa. Pr. 1992 $38.95. ISBN 0-8122-3153-8. Seven excellent essays on British literature and painting and the cultural values they represent.

Brown, Marshall. *Preromanticism*. Stanford U. Pr. 1991 $45.00. ISBN 0-8047-1561-0. Cosmopolitan and often fascinating critical readings of several more forward-looking writers from the period; especially insightful on Goldsmith and Wordsworth.

Canfield, J. Douglas, and J. Paul Hunter, eds. *Rhetorics of Order: Ordering Rhetorics in English Neoclassical Literature*. U. of Delaware Pr. 1989 $32.50. ISBN 0-87413-374-2. Nine essays by various authors, analyzing some of the several rhetorics of order in neoclassical literature.

Damrosch, Leo, ed. *The Profession of Eighteenth-Century Literature: Reflections on an Institution*. U. of Wis. Pr. 1992 $62.00. ISBN 0-299-13300-1. Twelve informal and somewhat personal essays by as many distinguished practitioners.

Davie, Donald. *Purity of Diction in English Verse*. Schocken 1967 o.p. Superb discussions of eighteenth-century poetry.

Engell, James, ed. *Forming the Critical Mind: Dryden to Coleridge*. HUP 1989 $32.50. ISBN 0-674-30943-X. Examines some ideas and concepts of eighteenth-century critical approaches, concentrating specifically on English critical thought from Dryden to Coleridge.

———. *Johnson and His Age*. HUP 1984 $25.00. ISBN 0-674-48075-9. Essays examining Johnson and the literary culture of the late eighteenth century.

Ezell, Margaret J. M. *The Patriarch's Wife: Literary Evidence and the History of the Family*. U. of NC Pr. 1987 $27.50. ISBN 0-8078-1741-4. A detailed, carefully researched study of the norms and expectations established for women by ordinary seventeenth-century domestic life.

Folkenflik, Robert, ed. *The English Hero 1660–1800*. U. of Delaware Pr. 1982 $32.50. ISBN 0-87413-174-X. Ten considerations of various aspects of exemplary heroic ideals.

Grundy, Isobel, and Susan Wiseman, eds. *Women, Writing, History 1640–1740*. U. of Ga. Pr. 1992 $40.00. ISBN 0-8203-1440-4. A collection of essays examining the interrelationships of writing, gender, and historical circumstances in the writings of women authors from 1640 to 1740.

Hagstrum, Jean H. *Eros and Vision: The Restoration to Romanticism*. Northwestern U. Pr. 1989 $34.95. ISBN 0-8101-0828-3. A spirited collection of 12 essays on literature and the visual arts from a distinguished pioneer scholar in the field.

Levine, Joseph M. *The Battle of the Books: History and Literature in the Augustan Age*. Cornell Univ. Pr. 1991 $29.95. ISBN 0-8014-2537-9. A prize-winning study of the intellectual and cultural formation of an association of Jonathan Swift, Alexander Pope, and others, known as the Scriblerus club.

McIntosh, Carey. *Common and Courtly Language: The Stylistics of Social Class in 18th-Century English Literature*. U. of Pa. Pr. 1986 $27.95. ISBN 0-8122-7998-0. A detailed and groundbreaking study of social differences in the uses of eighteenth-century literary language.

Messenger, Ann, ed. *Gender at Work: Four Women Writers of the Eighteenth Century.* Wayne St. U. Pr. 1990 $29.95. ISBN 0-8143-2147-X. Interesting essays on gender differences in writing; examines works of Anne Finch, Mary Whateley, Laetitia Pilkington, and Mary Pix.

Myers, Sylvia Harcstark. *The Bluestocking Circle: Women, Friendship, and the Life of the Mind in Eighteenth-Century England.* OUP 1990 $69.00. ISBN 0-19-811767-1. An informative and readable account of the shared intellectual life of Elizabeth Montagu, Elizabeth Carter, and Elizabeth Vesey (who coined the term "bluestocking"), among others.

Nussbaum, Felicity, and Laura Brown, eds. *The New Eighteenth Century: Theory, Politics, English Literature.* Routledge Chapman & Hall 1987 $35.00. ISBN 0-416-01631-6. An interesting collection of 12 essays arguing for the application of more theoretical approaches to period authors.

Rawson, Claude Julien. *Order From Confusion Sprung: Studies in Eighteenth-Century Literature from Swift to Cowper.* Allen & Unwin 1985 $19.95. ISBN 0-04-800019-1. A wide-ranging, masterful collection of essays and reviews bringing the present to bear on the past in interesting ways.

Rivers, Isabel. *Books and Their Readers in Eighteenth-Century England.* Leicester U. Pr. 1982 $30.00. ISBN 0-312-09248-2

———. *Reason, Grace, and Sentiment: A Study of the Language of Religion and Ethics in England, 1600–1780.* Vol. 1, *Whichcote to Wesley.* Cambridge U. Pr. 1991 $49.95. ISBN 0-521-38340-4

Rogers, Pat. *Eighteenth-Century Encounters: Studies in Literature and Society in the Age of Walpole.* B & N Imports 1985 $35.75. ISBN 0-389-20090-5. Ten learned historical essays about Swift, Pope, Gay, Defoe, and others, loosely assembled around the reign of George I (1714–27).

Roston, Murray. *Changing Perspectives in Literature and the Visual Arts, 1650–1820.* Princeton U. Pr. 1990 $59.50. ISBN 0-691-06795-3. An impressive synchronic overview of relationships between the arts, from Milton to Wordsworth, or from the late baroque to the picturesque.

Salvaggio, Ruth. *Enlightened Absence: Neoclassical Configurations of the Feminine.* U. of Ill. Pr. 1988 $24.95. ISBN 0-252-01541-X. A feminist critique of the classical systems epitomized in English Enlightenment literature and science.

Sambrook, James. *The Eighteenth Century: The Intellectual and Cultural Context of English Literature*, 1700–1789. Longman 1986 $29.95. ISBN 0-582-49306-4. Concise chapters on religion, philosophy, aesthetics, and politics, making this text an indispensable resource for all students of the period.

Sitter, John E.. *Arguments of Augustan Wit.* Cambridge U. Pr. 1991 $44.95. ISBN 0-521-41120-3. Argues convincingly that the sometimes slighted Augustan emphasis on wit offers an analytic opportunity for critics interested in alternative imaginative models.

Weinbrot, Howard D. *Eighteenth-Century Satire: Essays on Text and Context from Dryden to Peter Pindar.* Cambridge U. Pr. 1988 $44.50. ISBN 0-521-32513-7. Thirteen ways of looking at the muse of satire in essays published by a distinguished ironist between 1965 and 1988.

Welsh, Alexander. *Strong Representations: Narrative and Circumstantial Evidence in England.* Johns Hopkins 1992 $29.95. ISBN 0-8018-4271-9. An intriguing critical investigation of the quasi-legal uses of circumstantial evidence in eighteenth- and nineteenth-century fiction.

Willey, Basil. *Eighteenth-Century Background: Studies in the Idea of Nature in the Thought of the Period.* Col. U. Pr. 1941 o.p. Classic study of nature as a theme in eighteenth-century literature.

COLLECTIONS

Brady, Frank, and Martin Price, eds. *English Prose and Poetry, 1660–1800: A Selection*. HR&W Schl. Div. 1961 o.p.

Lonsdale, Roger, ed. *The New Oxford Book of Eighteenth-Century Verse*. OUP 1989 $15.95. ISBN 0-19-282054-0. A huge original selection.

Tillotson, Geoffrey, Paul Fussell, Jr., and Marshall Waingrow, eds. *Eighteenth-Century English Literature*. HarBraceJ 1969 $34.00. ISBN 0-15-520957-4. A very useful anthology, although it should be supplemented with more selections by women writers.

Uphaus, Robert W., and Gretchen M. Foster, eds. *The "Other" Eighteenth Century: English Women of Letters, 1660–1800*. Colleagues Press Inc. 1991 $15.95. ISBN 0-937191- 40-X. A good representative selection of verse, drama, and nonfiction prose by authors from Aphra Behn to Mary Wollstonecraft.

POETRY

Eighteenth-century poets produced their polished rhymes in satire and panegyric, in the ode greater and lesser, georgic and pastoral, in elegy, mock-epic, and in countless songs and ballads. Their primary mode of versification was the heroic couplet, and, whereas the metaphysical and romantic poets composed relatively private lyrics, Augustan poets generally addressed public themes. Theirs was a cultural poetics of biblical creation, of the faults of their fellow poets, of the anatomy of the emotions, and of the English landscape allegorized as a historical or emotional progress. Following the lead of a Christian benevolence, several longer poems from the period compared the decadence of the city of their time to the mythic natural goodness of the countryside of the past. Several midcentury odes of THOMAS GRAY and WILLIAM COLLINS exemplify the difference. Other cases in point are SAMUEL JOHNSON's *London*, an imitation of the third satire of JUVENAL (see Vol. 2) that attacks the corrupt administration of Sir Robert Walpole, and *The Deserted Village* by OLIVER GOLDSMITH, which laments the encroachments of new wealth on rural labor and the consequent disappearance of rural happiness.

History and Criticism

Colomb, Gregory G. *Designs on Truth: The Poetics of the Augustan Mock-Epic*. Pa. St. U. Pr. 1991 $32.50. ISBN 0-271-00805-9. A detailed study of the poetics of the Augustan mock-epic.

Doody, Margaret Anne. *The Daring Muse: Augustan Poetry Reconsidered*. Cambridge U. Pr. 1985 $59.95. ISBN 0-521-25825-1. A description and analysis of the complexity and richness of Augustan poetry in England.

Dowling, William C. *The Epistolary Moment: The Poetics of the Eighteenth-Century Verse Epistle*. Princeton U. Pr. 1991 $35.00. ISBN 0-691-06891-7. A critical study of the verse epistle as the dominant form in eighteenth-century English poetry.

Landry, Donna. *The Muses of Resistance: Laboring-Class Women's Poetry in Britain, 1739–1796*. Cambridge U. Pr. 1990 $44.95. ISBN 0-521-37412-X. An in-depth examination of poetry by and about British working-class women from 1739 to 1796.

Williams, Anne. *Prophetic Strain: The Greater Lyric in the Eighteenth Century*. U. Ch. Pr. 1984. $22.00. ISBN 0-226-89916-0. Examines the relationship between the use of the lyric in English poetry and its function in eighteenth-century poetry.

Collections

Lonsdale, Roger, ed. *Eighteenth-Century Women Poets: An Oxford Anthology*. OUP 1990 $12.95. ISBN 0-19-282775-8. An inclusive and well-organized collection.

Nokes, David. *An Annotated Critical Bibliography of Augustan Poetry*. St. Martin 1989
$35.00. ISBN 0-312-01961-0. An annotated list of major books and articles dealing
with Augustan poetry, with a selective bibliography of leading eighteenth-century
English poets.
Spacks, Patricia Meyer. *Late Augustan Poetry*. P-H 1973 o.p.

DRAMA

Restoration drama begins immediately after the return of Charles II (1660)
with the granting of patents to theater managers Thomas Killigrew and William
Davenant, who quickly introduced revivals of works by BEN JONSON and
WILLIAM SHAKESPEARE. Comedy once again became popular, heroic drama
appeared, and women for the first time began to play women's roles. JOHN
DRYDEN became the leading playwright by introducing both the epic scope of
The Conquest of Granada and the mixed tragicomedy of *Secret Love*. Then, like
the magician's dove, a form appeared—Restoration comedy—which flourished
in the hands of WILLIAM CONGREVE, SIR GEORGE ETHEREGE, and WILLIAM
WYCHERLEY and which was later given a saucy, somewhat farcical turn by APHRA
BEHN. Its appearance was not for long, however, for, with the Glorious
Revolution of William of Orange and his wife Mary (1688), the theater
discovered a sober, even stoic sensibility that would eventually produce JOSEPH
ADDISON's severe tragedy, *Cato*. Perhaps the most popular comedy of the entire
century is *The Beggar's Opera*, the "Newgate pastoral" that JONATHAN SWIFT
asked his friend JOHN GAY to write. With Walpole's Licensing Act of 1737, the
theater was subject to government censorship, and it was not until after 1760,
with the works of OLIVER GOLDSMITH and RICHARD BRINSLEY SHERIDAN, that
writers of comedy were again free to decide whether they wanted to portray, in
Goldsmith's distinction, a laughing or a sentimental muse.

History and Criticism

Bevis, Richard W. *English Drama: Restoration and Eighteenth Century, 1660–1789*.
Longman 1988 $32.76. ISBN 0-582-49393-5.
Ellis, Frank H. *Sentimental Comedy: Theory & Practice*. Cambridge U. Pr. 1991 $49.95.
ISBN 0-521-39431-7. A detailed study of eighteenth-century printed plays, with
analyses of several sentimental comedies.
Hume, Robert D. *The Rakish Stage: Studies in English Drama, 1660–1800*. S. Ill. U. Pr.
1983 $35.00. ISBN 0-8093-1100-3. A collection of essays on English dramatic plays
written between 1660 and 1800; focuses on the values found in the plays and their
impact upon an audience.
Zimbardo, Rose A. *A Mirror to Nature: Transformations in Drama and Aesthetics,
1660–1732*. U. Pr. of Ky. 1986 $25.00. ISBN 0-8131-1590-6

Collections

Cox, Jeffrey N., ed. *Seven Gothic Dramas, 1789–1825*. Ohio U. Pr. 1992 $45.00. ISBN 0-
685-54526-1. A collection of seven plays with a short, informative framework on the
history of Gothic dramas.
Kenny, Shirley Strum, ed. *The Performers and Their Plays*. Garland 1982 o.p. A
comprehensive collection of over 200 representative plays reproduced in facsimile,
with critical introductions by leading scholars.
McMillin, Scott. *Restoration and Eighteenth-Century Comedy: Authoritative Texts of The
Country Wife, The Man of Mode, The Way of the World, The Conscious Lovers, The*

School for Scandal. Norton 1973 $12.95. ISBN 0-393-09997-0. Includes background information and criticism of each play.

Steeves, Edna, ed. *The Plays of Mary Pix and Catherine Trotter*. Garland 1982 o.p. Provides a brief life history of each playwright, followed by their collected plays.

Sutcliffe, Barry, ed. *Plays by George Colman the Younger and Thomas Morton*. Cambridge U. Pr. 1983. $49.50. ISBN 0-521-24019-0. Includes a short biographical sketch and critical introduction of each playwright, in addition to the selected plays themselves.

Taylor, George, ed. *Plays by Samuel Foote and Arthur Murphy*. Cambridge U. Pr. 1984 o.p. Selected plays, with short critical introductions and biographical sketches of the two men.

Wood, E. R., ed. *Plays by David Garrick and George Colman the Elder*. Cambridge U. Pr. 1982 $44.50. ISBN 0-521-23590-1. Includes a brief introduction, biographical sketches of each playwright, and representative plays.

FICTION

For a long time the fiction of the Restoration and the eighteenth century, especially the work of DANIEL DEFOE, SAMUEL RICHARDSON, and TOBIAS GEORGE SMOLLETT, was seen as an outgrowth of emerging realistic, individualist, and somewhat privatized middle-class values. The view is entirely to the credit of its formulators. These are indeed the values of many early novelists, and they could have only been arrived at as a result of certain types of social change. More recent critics have revised the standard view by reading the novel in terms of other large shifts of cultural consciousness. Some of these involve the role of a skeptical empiricism in reformulating ideas of truth and virtue; the new religious attitudes toward penitence; and other new ideas made available through the practice of journalism. Whatever its origins, the eighteenth-century novel captured the attention of readers as no previous genre had done. In part, it succeeded by denying its own imaginative status and pretending to the unusual factual status of, say, autobiography or biography. Partly for this reason, many eighteenth-century novels took for their titles the names of individuals. Yet, in another way, by alluding to other examples of the form, the novel subtly acknowledged its imaginative status. In *Shamela* and *Joseph Andrews*, for example, HENRY FIELDING responded directly to Richardson's *Pamela* by parodying its form and manner, confirming what many of his readers already knew, that, despite his claim that he was creating a comic epic poem in prose, what he was really doing was writing a novel. Later novelists agreed, drawing upon both the contingent form of Richardson and the traditional plots of Fielding.

History and Criticism

Bender, John B. *Imagining the Penitentiary: Fiction and the Architecture of Mind in Eighteenth-Century England*. U. Ch. Pr. 1987 $34.95. ISBN 0-226-04228-6. A prize-winning, "new-historical" consideration of prison architecture and the structures of novelistic consciousness.

Brophy, Elizabeth Bergen. *Women's Lives and the 18th-Century English Novel*. U. Press Fla. 1991 $29.95. ISBN 0-8130-1036-5. An excellent assessment of the accuracy in the portrayal of women in novels and the influence this may have had on women readers.

Damrosch, Leopold. *God's Plot and Man's Stories: Studies in the Fictional Imagination from Milton to Fielding*. U. Ch. Pr. 1985 $25.00. ISBN 0-226-13579-9. Considers how specific eighteenth-century narratives both embraced and questioned the religious ideas held by their authors and readers; examines specific works.

Davis, Lennard J. *Factual Fictions: The Origins of the English Novel*. Bks. Demand 1983
    $66.30. ISBN 0-8357-6368-6
Frank, Frederick S. *The First Gothics: A Critical Guide to the English Gothic Novel*.
    Garland 1987 $60.00. ISBN 0-8240-8501-9. A well-written selective survey of the
    English Gothic novel during its major phase—from 1764 to the late 1820s.
Green, Katherine Sobba. *The Courtship Novel, 1740–1820: A Feminized Genre*. U. Pr. of
    Ky. 1991 $23.00. ISBN 0-8131-1736-4. Examines the historical parameters of the
    courtship novel, with detailed attention to specific authors.
Hunter, J. Paul. *Before Novels: The Cultural Contexts of Eighteenth-Century English
    Fiction*. Norton 1992 $12.95. ISBN 0-393-30861-8
Kahn, Madeleine. *Narrative Transvestism: Rhetoric and Gender in the Eighteenth-Century
    English Novel*. Cornell Univ. Pr. 1991 $29.95. ISBN 0-8014-2536-0. Explores the
    concept of "narrative transvestism," in which a male author employs the use of a
    first-person female narrator, and its impact on the eighteenth-century English novel.
Kraft, Elizabeth. *Character and Consciousness in Eighteenth-Century Comic Fiction*. U.
    of Ga. Pr. 1992 $35.00. ISBN 0-8203-1365-3. Critical examination of the central
    consciousness of eighteenth-century comic fiction and the development of the
    comic character.
McKeon, Michael. *The Origins of the English Novel, 1600–1740*. Johns Hopkins 1987
    $17.50. ISBN 0-8018-3746-4
Raven, James. *British Fiction, 1750–1770: A Chronological Check-List of Prose Fiction
    Printed in Britain and Ireland*. U. of Delaware Pr. 1987 $45.00. ISBN 0-87413-324-6. A
    chronological listing of prose fiction; provides a context for the work of the period.
Spacks, Patricia Ann Meyer. *Desire and Truth: Functions of Plot in Eighteenth-Century
    English Novels*. U. Ch. Pr. 1990 $32.00. ISBN 0-226-76845-7. Analyzes the various
    uses of plot in eighteenth-century novels as a means of placing them in a historical
    context.
Todd, Janet M. *The Sign of Angellica: Women, Writing, and Fiction, 1660–1800*. Col. U. Pr.
    1989 $45.00. ISBN 0-231-07134-5. A scholarly study of eighteenth-century fiction,
    focusing particularly on the role and achievements of women.
Varey, Simon. *Space and the Eighteenth-Century English Novel*. Cambridge U. Pr. 1990
    $47.95. ISBN 0-521-37483-9. Considers the idea of space in the major novels of
    Defoe, Fielding, and Richardson, and its relationship to the theory and practice of
    eighteenth-century architecture.
Yeazell, Ruth Bernard. *Fictions of Modesty: Women and Courtship in the English Novel*. U.
    Ch. Pr. 1991 $24.95. ISBN 0-226-95096-4. Surveys the popularity of the modest
    woman as a subject in eighteenth-century narrative, and considers the ways in which
    English novelists adopted the conventions of modesty, especially in their heroines.

Collections

Brady, Frank, and Martin Price, eds. *English Prose and Poetry, 1660–1800: A Selection*.
    HR&W 1961 o.p.

NONFICTION

If we except philosophy and theology from the category of nonfiction prose,
most of the nonfiction prose of the eighteenth century would qualify in one way
or another as higher journalism. Although there was the occasional odd
presentiment, notably the *Apology for His Life* of Colley Cibber, the celebrity
autobiography of our present day was as yet unheard of, and biography was still
categorized as a subgenre of history. Only after midcentury was a subgenre of
biography, literary biography, much in evidence. A surprising number of
eighteenth-century authors, on the other hand, either themselves wrote, or else
contributed to, the periodical essay. Not only JOSEPH ADDISON and SIR RICHARD

STEELE in the *Guardian* and *Spectator* papers, but also JAMES BOSWELL in the *Hypochondriac*, OLIVER GOLDSMITH in the *Bee*, and SAMUEL JOHNSON in the *Rambler* and *Idler* all used the forum of the periodical essay to improve the language and to comment on politics and society.

History and Criticism

Batten, Charles. *Pleasurable Instruction: Form and Convention in Eighteenth-Century Travel Literature.* U. CA Pr. 1978 $35.00. ISBN 0-520-03260-8. A generic description of a popular literary form of the eighteenth century, the nonfiction travelogue.

Cafarelli, Annette. *Prose in the Age of Poets: Romanticism and Biographical Narrative from Johnson to De Quincey.* U. of Pa. Pr. 1990 $29.95. ISBN 0-8122-8198-5. A series of textual studies demonstrating methods of reading nonfiction narrative as a literary form.

Corns, Thomas N., ed. *The Literature of Controversy: Polemical Strategy from Milton to Junius.* Intl. Spec. Bk. 1987 $25.00. ISBN 0-7146-3292-9

Damrosch, Leopold. *Fictions of Reality in the Age of Hume and Johnson.* U. of Wis. Pr. 1989 $15.50. ISBN 0-299-12384-7. Examines the differences between realistic writing and imaginative modes during the era of Hume and Johnson.

McKenzie, Alan T. *Certain, Lively Episodes: The Articulation of Passion in Eighteenth-Century Prose.* U. of Ga. Pr. 1990 $35.00. ISBN 0-8203-1167-7. Argues that, during the eighteenth century, passion was regarded as having a clearer and more elaborate meaning than today.

Nussbaum, Felicity. *The Autobiographical Subject: Gender and Ideology in Eighteenth-Century England.* Johns Hopkins 1989 $32.50. ISBN 0-8018-3825-8. Focuses on the ideologies of autobiography and questions how an autobiographical subject can be held in place by class and gender relations.

Shevelow, Kathryn. *Women and Print Culture: The Construction of Femininity in the Early Periodical.* Routledge 1989 $29.95. ISBN 0-415-01222-8

Collections

Spacks, Patricia Ann Meyer. *Late Augustan Prose.* P-H 1971 o.p. A representative selection of prose works by various authors of the late Augustan era.

CHRONOLOGY OF AUTHORS

Dryden, John. 1631–1700
Etherege, Sir George. c.1635–c.1691
Behn, Aphra. 1640–1689
Wycherley, William. 1640–1716
Otway, Thomas. 1652–1685
Defoe, Daniel. 1660–1731
Vanbrugh, Sir John. 1664–1726
Swift, Jonathan. 1667–1745
Congreve, William. 1670–1729
Addison, Joseph. 1672–1719
Steele, Sir Richard. 1672–1729
Farquhar, George. 1678–1707
Gay, John. 1685–1732
Pope, Alexander. 1688–1744
Montagu, Lady Mary Wortley. 1689–1762
Richardson, Samuel. 1689–1761

Chesterfield, 4th Earl of. 1694–1773
Thomson, James. 1700–1748
Fielding, Henry. 1707–1754
Johnson, Samuel. 1709–1784
Sterne, Laurence. 1713–1768
Gray, Thomas. 1716–1771
Walpole, Horace. 4th Earl of Orford. 1717–1797
Collins, William. 1721–1759
Smollett, Tobias George. 1721–1771
Smart, Christopher. 1722–1771
Goldsmith, Oliver. 1728–1774
Cowper, William. 1731–1800
Boswell, James. 1740–1795
Sheridan, Richard Brinsley. 1751–1816
Burney, Frances. 1752–1840

ADDISON, JOSEPH. 1672–1719

Addison, son of the Dean of Litchfield, took high honors at Oxford University and joined the army. He first came to literary fame by writing a poem, "The Campaign" (1704), to celebrate the Battle of Blenheim. When RICHARD STEELE, whom he had known in his public school Charterhouse, started *The Tatler* in 1709, Addison became a regular contributor. But his contributions to a later venture, *The Spectator* (generally considered the zenith of the periodical essay), were fundamental: Steele can be credited with the editorial direction of the journal; but Addison's essays, ranging from gently satiric to genuinely funny, secured the journal's success. In *The Spectator*, No. 10, Addison declared that the journal aimed "to enliven morality with wit, and to temper wit with morality." His brilliant character of Sir Roger de Coverley (followed from rake to reformation) distinguishes the most popular essays.. He is buried in Westminster Abbey.

NONFICTION BY ADDISON

The Coverley Papers from The Spectator. Scholarly 1980 $39.00. ISBN 0-686-71913-1. Contains all issues of the *Spectator* that concern the history and character of Sir Roger de Coverly.

Critical Essays from The Spectator. Ed. by Donald F. Bond. OUP 1970 o.p. Offers selections from the standard five-volume scholarly edition prepared by Professor Bond, among them the highly influential essays on the pleasures of the imagination.

Criticism of Milton's Paradise Lost, from The Spectator, 1711–1712. 1868. Ed. by Edward Arber. Saifer 1983 $15.00. ISBN 0-87556-550-6

Essays in Criticism and Literary Theory. Ed. by John Loftis. *Crofts Class. Ser.* Harlan Davidson 1975. ISBN 0-88295-106-8. A two-volume collection of Joseph Addison's works, including poems, plays, and prose works.

The Freeholder, or Political Essays. Scholarly 1976 repr. of 1761 ed. $39.00. ISBN 0-403-05788-4

The Miscellaneous Works of Joseph Addison. 2 vols. Ed. by A. C. Guthkelch. Scholarly 1971 repr. of 1914 ed. o.p.

The Spectator. 5 vols. Ed. by Donald F. Bond. OUP 1987 $120.00 ea. ISBNs 0-19-818610-X, 0-19-818611-8, 0-19-818612-6, 0-19-818613-4, 0-19-818614-2

BOOKS ABOUT ADDISON

Ketcham, Michael G. *Transparent Designs: Reading, Performance, and Form in the "Spectator" Papers.* U. of Ga. Pr. 1985 $25.00. ISBN 0-8203-0771-8. A fine study of Whig ideology and the role of the reader in the *Spectator* papers.

Smithers, Peter. *The Life of Joseph Addison.* OUP 1968. o.p. An excellent and detailed full-length biography of Addison.

BEHN, APHRA. 1640–1689

Unquestionably the leading woman playwright of the Restoration period, Aphra Behn is also notable for her poetry and fiction. While still in her twenties, she traveled with her family to Surinam, where she witnessed a slave insurrection, much like the rebellion that figures prominently in her novel *Oroonoko* (1688), a work that introduced the character of the noble savage. She was well connected at court and for a brief time was sent to Antwerp as a spy. Around 1670, with the help of JOHN DRYDEN, she established a career in the theater, and, during the following two decades, rarely was her work absent from the London stage. Among the comedies that bear the special stamp of her libertine, feminist, and Tory political views are *The Dutch Lover* (1673), *The*

Feign'd Curtezans (1679), and her best-known works, *The Rover* (1677) and *The Rover, Part II* (1681). Behn is often called the first Englishwoman to support herself by being a writer.

Readers seeking a good introduction to the skill and sensibility of Aphra Behn will do well to look into her lyric poetry, which is often represented in recent anthologies of women writers.

NOVELS BY BEHN

Love Letters Between a Nobleman and His Sister. Viking Penguin 1987 $7.95. ISBN 0-14-016160-0. A novel of love and politics, written partly as a reaction to censure and for political revenge.

Novels of Mrs. Aphra Behn. Greenwood 1970 repr. of 1913 ed. $45.00. ISBN 0-8731-2824-2. Contains 10 collected novels of Behn, the first Englishwoman to become a novelist and a playwright.

Oroonoko: Or, the Royal Slave. 1688. Norton 1973 $5.95. ISBN 0-393-00702-2

PLAYS BY BEHN

Five Plays. Routledge Chapman & Hall 1990 $14.95. ISBN 0-416-17090-X. With an introduction by Maureen Duffy.

The Rover: A Comedy. 1677. Ed. by Frederick Link. U. of Nebr. Pr. 1967 $5.95. ISBN 0-8032-5350-8

WORKS BY BEHN

Works of Aphra Behn. 6 vols. Ed. by Montague Summers. Ayer 1967 repr. of 1915 ed. $27.50 ea. ISBNs 0-405-08254-1, 0-405-08255-X, 0-405-08256-8, 0-405-08257-6, 0-405-08258-4, 0-405-08259-2

BOOK ABOUT BEHN

Link, Frederick M. *Aphra Behn*. Twayne 1968 o.p. A dependable, brief biography in a standard series.

BOSWELL, JAMES. 1740–1795

As a young man, Boswell was ambitious to have a literary career but reluctantly obeyed the wishes of his father, a Scottish Judge, and instead followed a career in the law. He was admitted to the Scottish bar in 1766 and was married to Margaret Montgomerie in 1769. His legal practice did not prevent him from writing a series of periodical essays, *The Hypochondriac* (1777–83), and his *Journal of a Tour of the Hebrides* (1785), an account of the journey to the outer islands of Scotland undertaken with SAMUEL JOHNSON in 1773, as well as the impulsively frank *Journals*, private papers lost to history until they were discovered by modern scholars and issued in a multivolume set. Known during much of his life as "Corsican" Boswell for his authorship of *An Account of Corsica* in 1768, his first considerable work, Boswell now bears a name that is synonymous with biographer; the reason for this rests in the achievement of his *Life of Samuel Johnson*, published in 1791, seven years after the death of Johnson. Boswell recorded in his diary the anxiety of the long-awaited encounter with Johnson, on May 16, 1763, in the back parlor of a London bookstore, and upon their first meeting he began collecting Johnson's conversations and opinions. Johnson was a daunting subject for a biographer, in part because of his extraordinary, outsized presence and, in part because Johnson himself was a pioneer in the art of literary biography. Boswell met the challenge by taking an anecdotal, year-by-year approach to the wealth of biographical material he gathered. If the *Life of Johnson* lacks the magisterial critical judgment of Johnson's own *Lives of the Poets* (1779–81), it remains nonetheless a painstaking tribute to a true giant of letters and a monument of lively, telling detail.

NONFICTION BY BOSWELL

Boswell: The Applause of the Jury: 1782–1785: The Yale Editions of the Private Papers of James Boswell. McGraw 1981 o.p.

Boswell, The English Experiment, 1785–1789. The Yale Editions of the Private Papers of James Boswell. Ed. by Irma S. Lustig and Frederick A. Pottle. McGraw 1986 o.p.

Boswell, Laird of Auchinleck: 1778–1782: The Yale Editions of the Private Papers of James Boswell. McGraw 1977 o.p.

Boswell for the Defence, 1769–1774: The Yale Editions of the Private Papers of James Boswell. McGraw 1962 o.p. This volume "records his marital ups and downs, his drinking bouts and occasional wenching, and his unsuccessful defense of John Reid, a sheep-stealer, who, unfortunately for James's peace of mind, was executed" (*Library Journal*).

Boswell in Extremes, 1776–1778: The Yale Editions of the Private Papers of James Boswell. McGraw 1970 o.p.

Boswell in Holland, 1762–1764: The Yale Editions of the Private Papers of James Boswell. McGraw 1952 o.p. Includes his correspondence with Belle de Zuylen (Zélide).

Boswell in Search of a Wife, 1766–1769: The Yale Editions of the Private Papers of James Boswell. McGraw 1956 o.p. "Most entertaining since the first sensational 'London Journal.' It has every ingredient to make it popular—a succession of amorous adventures, scenes of high comedy in Boswell's most artful manner, long conversations with Samuel Johnson, and even a conventional happy ending" (*N.Y. Times*).

Boswell on the Grand Tour: Germany and Switzerland, 1764: The Yale Editions of the Private Papers of James Boswell. McGraw 1953 o.p.

Boswell on the Grand Tour: Italy, Corsica, and France, 1765–1766: The Yale Editions of the Private Papers of James Boswell. McGraw 1955 o.p.

Boswell's London Journal, 1762–1763. Ed. by Frederick A. Pottle. Yale U. Pr. 1992 $15.00. ISBN 0-300-05735-0. Published from the original manuscript.

Correspondence of James Boswell and John Johnston of Grange. Ed. by Ralph S. Walker. McGraw 1966 o.p. This work, which covers the years 1759–86, is Volume 1 of the planned 40-volume series of the *Private Papers of James Boswell*, research edition, "designed chiefly for scholars and libraries." John Johnston was "Boswell's alter ego, his 'constant resort in moments of distress'" (*Library Journal*).

Journals of James Boswell, 1761–1795. Ed. by John Wain. Yale U. Pr. 1992 $28.50. ISBN 0-300-05652-4

A Journey to the Western Islands of Scotland. Ed. by Allan Wendt. HM 1965 $9.16. ISBN 0-395-05181-9. Includes Boswell's *The Journal of a Tour to the Hebrides*.

Life of Johnson. Ed. by R. W. Chapman and J. D. Fleeman. OUP 1982 $14.95. ISBN 0-19-281537-7

Ominous Years, 1774–1776. Ed. by C. A. Ryskamp and Frederick A. Pottle. McGraw 1963 o.p. The eighth volume in the series covers 20 months of indecisiveness, hypochondria, self-delusions, and downright despair, with ample Johnsoniana and other records of a busy, frenetic London.

The Private Papers of James Boswell. Ed. by Frederick A. Pottle and others. McGraw 1950–to date o.p.

BOOKS ABOUT BOSWELL

Clingham, Greg, ed. *New Light on Boswell: Critical and Historical Essays on the Occasion of the Bicentenary of the Life of Johnson.* Cambridge U. Pr. 1991 $44.95. ISBN 0-521-38047-2. Excellent collection of articles on Boswell's life and placement in eighteenth-century Scottish culture.

Cochrane, Hamilton E. *Boswell's Literary Art: An Annotated Bibliography of Critical Studies, 1900–1985.* Garland 1991 $29.00. ISBN 0-8240-1516-9. Excellent introduction to Boswell; highly recommended for researchers.

BURNEY, FRANCES (OR FANNY) (MME D'ARBLAY). 1752–1840

Although lovers of JANE AUSTEN may think of Frances Burney as merely an essential precursor, her own novels, and especially *Evelina* (1778), deserve their loyal devotees. Consisting largely of the letters of the heroine, a young marriageable girl visiting London and registering freshly the responses to the metropolis and its people, the novel shows sharp observations, a precise sense of the shifting feelings of the girl and the men who are interested in her, and a delight in and fear of the grotesque middle class and the foreign relatives she meets. After Frances Burney was revealed as the author of the widely admired novel, she left the intellectually exciting household of her father, Charles Burney, the leading musicologist of his time and a friend of SAMUEL JOHNSON, for the onerous boredom of being a lady-in-waiting to Queen Charlotte. She married late, wrote *Cecilia* (1782), *Camilla* (1796), and *The Wanderer* (1814), and lived with apparent contentment to a very old age.

NOVELS BY BURNEY

Camilla. 1796. Ed. by Edward A. Bloom and Lillian D. Bloom. OUP 1983 $9.95. ISBN 0-19-281662-4

Evelina, or A Young Lady's Entrance in the World. 1778. Norton 1965 $11.95. ISBN 0-393-00294-2

The Wanderer. 1814. Ed. by Margaret A. Doody and others. OUP 1991 $11.95. ISBN 0-19-282133-4

NONFICTION BY BURNEY

Fanny Burney: Selected Letters and Journals. Ed. by Joyce Hemlow. OUP 1986 $45.00. ISBN 0-19-818528-6. A wonderfully readable abbreviated version of the magisterial 12-volume scholarly edition by the same editor and publisher (1972–84).

BOOKS ABOUT BURNEY

Hemlow, Joyce. *The History of Fanny Burney.* OUP 1958 o.p. Based largely on her journal-letters, notebooks, unpublished works, voluminous correspondence, and on other previously unpublished sections of Burney papers. A standard reference book.

Simons, Judy. *Fanny Burney.* B & N Imports 1987 $33.00. ISBN 0-389-20693-8. The story of Frances Burney's life, with an examination of her literary heroines and excerpts from her journals and plays.

CHESTERFIELD (PHILIP DORMER STANHOPE), 4th Earl of. 1694–1773

An English statesman, and celebrated wit and conversationalist, Lord Chesterfield achieved lasting fame through his letters to his natural son and to his adopted godson. The brilliant *Letters to His Son*, first published by his widow in 1774, was written to acquaint the boy with, and encourage him to acquire, the manners and standards of a man of the world. The letters are "shrewd and exquisitely phrased observations, witty, elegant, cynical." The similar *Letters to His Godson*, of which 236 are extant, was not published until 1890. Chesterfield was an intimate of POPE and SWIFT and corresponded with VOLTAIRE (see Vol. 2). As the patron of SAMUEL JOHNSON, he provoked Johnson's famous February 1755 letter of rebuke after Lord Chesterfield's belated praise of Johnson's *Dictionary*, which he had ignored in prospectus since 1747. In this letter, Johnson said: ". . . the notice which you have been pleased to take of my labors, had it been early, had been kind; but it has been delayed till I am indifferent, and cannot enjoy it; till I am solitary, and cannot impart it; till I am known, and do not want it.''

NONFICTION BY CHESTERFIELD

Letters. 6 vols. Ed. by Bonamy Dobrée. AMS Pr. repr. of 1932 ed. o.p.
Letters to His Son. 1774. NAL-Dutton o.p.
Lord Chesterfield's Letters. OUP 1993 $11.95. ISBN 0-19-282864-9. With an introduction by David Roberts.

BOOK ABOUT CHESTERFIELD

Shellabarger, Samuel. *Lord Chesterfield and His World.* Biblo 1971 repr. of 1951 ed. $26.00. ISBN 0-8196-0271-X. Analyzes the life of Lord Chesterfield by examining the man, his age, and his philosophy.

COLLINS, WILLIAM. 1721–1759

Collins published only a handful of poems before insanity clouded the remainder of his brief life. In 1754 he was confined to an asylum, having suffered from mental illness since 1751. Neglected in his own time, Collins is one of the few eighteenth-century poets whose reputation has continued to grow. His odes and lyrics, often difficult for the casual reader to grasp, have come to be regarded by some eminent critics as masterworks and touchstones of political taste. The young COLERIDGE wrote that Collins's *Ode on the Poetical Character* (1747) had moved him as much as anything in SHAKESPEARE. Two of his other best-known works are *Ode to Evening* and *Ode Written in the Beginning of the Year 1746.*

POETRY BY COLLINS

Gray and Collins: Poetical Works. Ed. by Roger Lonsdale. OUP 1986 $16.95. ISBN 0-19-281169-X. The poetry of Gray, Collins, and Goldsmith, with extensive translations and critical examinations of the works.
Poems of Gray, Collins, Goldsmith. Ed. by Roger Lonsdale. *Annotated Eng. Poets Ser.* Longman 1976 o.p.

WORK BY COLLINS

Works of William Collins. Ed. by Richard Wendorf and Charles Ryskamp. *Oxford Eng. Texts. Ser.* OUP 1979 o.p. A critical edition of Collins's works, with full references to manuscripts and early printings to aid the modern reader.

BOOKS ABOUT COLLINS

Garrod, H. W. *Collins.* Hippocrene Bks. 1973 repr. of 1928 ed. $16.50. ISBN 0-374-93011-2. An acutely perceptive brief study of the life and works of William Collins.
Sigworth, Oliver F. *William Collins. Twayne's Eng. Authors Ser.* Irvington 1965 $15.95. ISBN 0-8290-1729-1. Serves as a useful guide to understanding and appreciating Collins's poetry.
Wendorf, Richard. *William Collins and 18th-Century Poetry.* U. of Minn. Pr. 1981 o.p.
Williams, W. T., and G. H. Vallins. *Gray, Collins, and Their Circle.* Richard West repr. of 1937 ed. o.p.

CONGREVE, WILLIAM. 1670–1729

Congreve was born in England but grew up and was educated in Ireland. While attending Trinity College in Dublin, he became a friend of JONATHAN SWIFT. Although he studied law, he never practiced it, turning his attention instead to writing for the theater. When he was just 30, however, Congreve turned his back upon the theater after publishing his most polished and brilliant comedy, *The Way of the World* (1700). Whether he was stung by Jeremy Collier's attack on the Restoration comedy of manners in *A Short View of the Immorality and Profaneness of the English Stage* (1698) or was simply disappointed by the lukewarm reception of his play, Congreve doubtless also recognized a change in the cultural temper. Public interest in the artificial world of the haute-monde that he described was on the wane. There is already a nostalgic element in the teasing courtship of Millamant and Mirabell; the scintillating proviso scene for their marriage echoes with the diffidence of their milieu; and yet, an essential compatibility is to be understood by the way each completes the other's couplets. Congreve's earlier comedies, *The Old Bachelor* (1693), *The Double Dealer* (1693), and *Love for Love* (1695), all sparkle with graceful and witty dialogue, and all were successful. Congreve also wrote one blank-verse tragedy, *The Mourning Bride* (1697), and a novel of intrigue, *Incognita* (1691).

PLAYS BY CONGREVE

The Comedies of William Congreve: The Old Bachelor, The Double Dealer, Love for Love, The Way of the World. Ed. by Anthony Henderson. Cambridge U. Pr. 1982 $59.95. ISBN 0-521-24747-0

The Complete Plays of William Congreve. Ed. by Herbert Davis. U. Ch. Pr. 1967 $35.00. ISBN 0-226-11485-6

Love for Love. Ed. by Malcolm Kelsall. Norton 1976 $4.95. ISBN 0-393-90003-7

The Way of the World. Ed. by Brian Gibbons. Norton 1976 $6.95. ISBN 0-393-90004-5

BOOKS ABOUT CONGREVE

Mann, David D. *A Concordance to the Plays of William Congreve.* Cornell Univ. Pr. 1973 $82.50. ISBN 0-8014-0767-2. A concordance based on *The Complete Plays of William Congreve*, edited by Herbert Davis; the first concordance devoted to Restoration drama and dramatic prose.

Williams, Aubrey L. *An Approach to Congreve.* Yale U. Pr. 1979 $30.00. ISBN 0-300-02304-9. An excellent, brief introduction by a distinguished scholar.

COWPER, WILLIAM. 1731–1800

WORDSWORTH and COLERIDGE regarded Cowper as the greatest of living poets, the master of the most natural blank verse written in the late eighteenth century. For generations Cowper's profound influence on the English romantic revolution was taken for granted. His easy, intimate, and completely unaffected personal correspondence marked a new departure in the art of letter writing, and recent reexaminations of his poetic and epistolary art suggest that a revival of interest is well under way. Cowper suffered from intermittent attacks of mental illness throughout his life. His powerful poem *The Castaway* (1796) carries a terrifying sense of despair and isolation. He was deeply religious and convinced that he was destined to eternal damnation. Devoted friends like the Unwins sheltered him against the constant threat of overwhelming dread. After their deaths, he sank into a frightful apathy. Although he and Mary Unwin had planned to marry after her husband's death, his deep depression prevented it; they did, however, live together until Cowper's death. His *Olney Hymns* (1779) have long been popular devotional works. It is ironic that his most beloved poem should be the comic narrative of John Gilpin.

POETRY BY COWPER

The Poems of William Cowper. Vol. 1. Ed. by John D. Baird and Charles Ryskamp. *Oxford Eng. Texts Ser*. OUP 1980 $110.00. ISBN 0-19-811875-9. As with the edition of prose by King and Ryskamp (cited below), when complete this will be standard for generations to come.

Verse and Letters. Ed. by Brian Spiller. *Reynard Lib*. HUP 1968 o.p. A wide selection of Cowper's poems and a representation of his letters, all left as unedited as possible.

WORK BY COWPER

The Letters and Prose Writings of William Cowper. 5 vols. Ed. by James King and Charles Ryskamp. OUP 1979–86. Vol. 1 $115.00. ISBN 0-19-811863-5. Vol. 2 $149.00. ISBN 0-19-812607-7. Vol. 3 $110.00. ISBN 0-19-812608-5. Vol. 4 $150.00. ISBN 0-19-812681-6. Vol. 5 $72.00. ISBN 0-19-812690-5. A multivolume edition of Cowper's personal letters to friends and acquaintances; one volume contains prose work and a cumulative index.

BOOKS ABOUT COWPER

Cecil, David. *The Stricken Deer or the Life of Cowper*. Richard West repr. of 1929 ed. o.p. A candid, beautifully written story of William Cowper and his life, including an analysis of his character and those of his friends.

Fausset, Hugh I. *William Cowper*. Rprt. Serv. 1991 repr. of 1928 ed. $89.00. ISBN 0-7812-7339-0. A well-received biography of Cowper, with special emphasis on his religious impulses.

Hutchings, Bill. *The Poetry of William Cowper*. Longwood MA 1983 o.p. An excellent introduction.

King, James. *William Cowper: A Biography*. Duke 1986 $37.50. ISBN 0-8223-0513-0. An excellent and now standard scholarly biography.

Neve, J. *Concordance to the Poetical Works of William Cowper*. *Studies in Poetry*. Haskell 1969 repr. of 1887 ed. $69.95. ISBN 0-8383-0287-0. A concordance of Cowper's poetry compiled from the Aldine edition of the British poets.

Newey, Vincent. *Cowper's Poetry: A Critical Study and Reassessment*. *Eng. Texts and Studies*. B & N Imports 1982 $41.25. ISBN 0-387-20079-4. Especially good on *The Task*. This and Hutchings's volume (cited above) are the most comprehensive modern studies.

Nicholson, Norman. *William Cowper*. Folcroft 1973 o.p. Examines the extent to which the evangelical revival influenced William Cowper's thoughts, life, and poetry.

Priestman, Martin. *Cowper's Task: Structure and Influence*. Cambridge U. Pr. 1983 $44.95. ISBN 0-521-23643-6. An in-depth examination of the structure and influence of Cowper's poem *The Task*.

Quinlan, Maurice J. *William Cowper: A Critical Life*. Greenwood 1970 repr. of 1953 ed. $45.00. ISBN 0-8371-3725-0. A critical biography of Cowper, focusing on the man in relation to his works, and his works in relation to his life.

Ryskamp, Charles. *William Cowper of the Inner Temple*. Cambridge U. Pr. 1959 o.p. Concentrates on the poet's early life. A fine biography by one of the leading Cowper scholars.

DEFOE, DANIEL. 1660–1731

Defoe was born Daniel Foe, the son of a London chandler. He changed his surname in 1703, adding the more genteel "De" before his own name to suggest a higher social standing. Long considered the father of the novel, Defoe should in all fairness share parentage with APHRA BEHN and other lesser-known writers, and yet it is undeniable that, with the appearance of the immediately successful *Robinson Crusoe* (1719) and *Moll Flanders* (1722), the interior consciousness of the individual was explored in ways entirely new and the landscape of British literature was peopled as never before with a striking diversity of character and incident. Although *Robinson Crusoe*, with its realistic narrative of isolation and independence, is probably better known to young readers, many students prefer *Moll Flanders* for its dazzling yet troubling recollection of a lifetime in the London underworld, told from the point of view of a reformed criminal. Since Defoe wrote an enormous amount on all sorts of topics (and was sometimes in such a hurry to write more that he declined to revise what he had already written), and since he could become a notable ironist on occasion (see, for instance, *The Shortest Way with Dissenters*, 1702), it is difficult to know how seriously he meant readers to take the artfulness of his seeming nuances and the sincerity of Moll's late religious conversion. Nonetheless, Defoe's uniquely realistic detail, fostered by a career in journalism, and his compassionate sense of the individual courage needed to prosper in a society that was much harsher than our own, remain a legacy to later eighteenth-century novelists, and to generations of readers ever since. Notable among his other works (much of it irretrievably anonymous, to the frustration of those who prefer the work of a writer neatly organized into a canon) are the novels *Roxana* (1724), praised by Virginia Woolf; *Captain Singleton* (1720); and *Colonel Jack* (1722).

Defoe's reputation is on the rise. The listings below reflect a strong upsurge of readerly interest, deriving partly from the unusual role that social history plays in Defoe's narratives, many of which seem to have written themselves from the materials of daily life, and partly from more local problems and pleasures.

NOVELS BY DEFOE

Captain Singleton (The Life, Adventures and Piracies of the Famous Captain Singleton). 1720. AMS Pr. repr. of 1895 ed. $32.50. ISBN 0-404-07916-4
Colonel Jack. 1722. Ed. by S. H. Monk. OUP 1989 $8.95. ISBN 0-19-282224-1
A Journal of the Plague Year. 1722. AMS Pr. repr. of 1895 ed. $32.50. ISBN 0-404-07919-9. Defoe's observations of the great plague in Marseilles from 1720 to 1721; written as an eyewitness account.
Moll Flanders (The Fortunes and Misfortunes of the Famous Moll Flanders). 1722. 2 vols. AMS Pr. repr. of 1895 ed. $32.50 ea. ISBNs 0-404-07917-2, 0-404-07918-0
Robinson Crusoe (The Life and Strange Surprizing Adventures of Robinson Crusoe, of York, Mariner). 1719–20. AMS Pr. repr. of 1895 ed. $32.50. ISBN 0-404-07911-3
Roxana; or the Fortunate Mistress. 1724. Ed. by Jane Jack. OUP 1981 $5.95. ISBN 0-19-281563-6

NONFICTION BY DEFOE

Defoe's Review. 9 vols. AMS Pr. repr. of 1938 ed. o.p. A representative selection of Defoe's *Review* essays, which reveal the man Defoe, as well as eighteenth-century England; with an introduction and bibliography by Arthur Wellesley Secord.
A General History of the Robberies and Murders of the Most Notorious Pyrates. 1724. Ed. by Manuel Schonhorn. U. of SC Pr. 1972 o.p. Defoe's account of the activities of pirates around the island of Providence in the West Indies; uses factual circumstances enlivened by fiction.
Letters. Ed. by George Harris Healey. Century Bookbindery 1984 repr. of 1955 ed. o.p. A collection of 251 letters that provide authentic information about Defoe; penned from 1703 to 1730.
A Tour through the Whole Island of Great Britain. 1724–27. Ed. by P. N. Furbank and others. Yale U. Pr. 1991 $45.00. ISBN 0-685-40169-3. Gives the entire account of Defoe's travels through England, Scotland, and Wales; also provides a full and well-informed account of life and conditions in the early eighteenth century.

WORKS BY DEFOE

Novels and Miscellaneous Works. 20 vols. AMS Pr. repr. of 1841 ed. $630.00. ISBN 0-404-09300-0. With biographical memoir, notes, and literary prefaces attributed to Sir Walter Scott.

Novels and Selected Writings. Shakespeare Head Ed. 14 vols. Rowman 1974 repr. of 1923 ed. $383.00. ISBN 0-87471-521-0. Fourteen volumes of the novels and selected writings of Defoe.

Romances and Narratives. 16 vols. Ed. by George A. Aitken. AMS Pr. repr. of 1895 ed. $520.00. ISBN 0-404-07910-5. With an etched portrait and 48 rotogravure illustrations.

Books about Defoe

Alkon, Paul. *Defoe and Fictional Time.* U. of Ga. Pr. 1979 o.p. Explores how extensively and successfully Defoe's narratives dealt with time in his works and how his work marked the beginning of new traditions in narrative writing.

Backscheider, Paula R. *Daniel Defoe: Ambition and Innovation.* U. Pr. of Ky. 1986 $25.00. ISBN 0-8131-1596-5. Traces Defoe's development as a writer by demonstrating that everything he wrote was the result of his extensive knowledge of English culture and politics.

_____. *Daniel Defoe: His Life.* Johns Hopkins 1989 $40.00. ISBN 0-8018-3785-5. A lengthy and comprehensive biography.

_____. *Moll Flanders: The Making of a Criminal Mind.* Twayne 1990 $20.95. ISBN 0-8057-9429-8. An excellent, detailed study of one of Defoe's most vivid novels.

Blewett, David. *Defoe's Art of Fiction: Robinson Crusoe, Moll Flanders, Colonel Jack, and Roxana.* U. of Toronto Pr. 1979 o.p. A critical analysis of four major novels by Defoe and of his vision of the human experience.

Boardman, Michael M. *Defoe and the Uses of Narrative.* Rutgers U. Pr. 1983 o.p. A critical study of Defoe and his use of the narrative; provides insight into Defoe's complexity as a man.

Dijkstra, Bram. *Defoe and Economics: The Fortunes of Roxana in the History of Interpretation.* St. Martin 1987 $35.00. ISBN 0-312-00535-0

Furbank, P. N., and W. R. Owens. *The Canonization of Daniel Defoe.* Yale U. Pr. 1988 $25.00. ISBN 0-300-04119-5. An intriguing proposal that the broad assortment of texts attributed to Defoe in actuality may not have been written by him.

Novak, Maximillian E. *Realism, History, and Myth in Defoe's Fiction.* U. of Nebr. Pr. 1983 o.p. A short study, depicting Defoe as one of the great writers of his time and attempting to pinpoint his excellence in his ability to create a complexity of style and language in his fiction.

Richetti, John J. *Daniel Defoe.* Twayne 1987 $19.95. ISBN 0-8057-6955-2. A thorough and comprehensive general study of Defoe's life and works.

_____. *Defoe's Narratives: Situations and Structures.* OUP 1975 o.p. A commentary on the author's reading of Defoe; critically examines specific characters from his novels.

Schonhorn, Manuel. *Defoe's Politics: Parliament, Power, Kingship, and Robinson Crusoe.* Cambridge U. Pr. 1991 $42.95. ISBN 0-521-38452-4. A comprehensive study of the politics of Defoe, which challenges the view that we must see Defoe as modern; his political writings are restored to the context in which they were written.

Sill, Geoffrey. *Defoe and the Idea of Fiction, 1713–1719.* U. of Delaware Pr. 1983 $29.50. ISBN 0-87413-227-4. An in-depth study of the formative period of Defoe (1713–19), with specific attention paid to the process by which he came to regard fiction as a valid means for regarding the human experience.

DRYDEN, JOHN. 1631–1700

As one of the first English writers to make a living by his pen alone, Dryden had to cater to popular public taste. His long career was astonishingly varied, and he turned his exceptional gifts to almost all of the major literary forms. He dominated the entire Restoration period as a poet, playwright, and all-around man of letters. He was the third poet laureate of England, but he was dismissed when he refused to take the oath of allegiance to William and Mary (Protestants) after the Revolution of 1688. In his old age, he was the acknowledged literary dictator of England, and his influence on eighteenth-century poetry was immense, especially on ALEXANDER POPE. His development of the couplet form and his brilliant satires became models for other poets to imitate but rarely equal. His many plays were popular in his own time, but it is his *MacFlecknoe* (1682), a devastating assault on his literary rival Thomas Shadwell, and *Absalom and Achitophel* (1681, 1682), a masterful satire on the political scene, that are especially admired today.

Dryden defended the Church of England in his *Religio Laici* (1682), and when he became a Roman Catholic wrote *The Hind and the Panther* (1697), a religious allegory in which the Roman Catholic Church is hounded by various wild beasts. Dryden was also a master of lyrical forms and of translation. His *Essay of Dramatic Poesy* (1668) is a classic critical statement. Dryden's last work, the *Fables* of 1699, is regarded by some as his greatest achievement. In part because Dryden wrote before the advent of the novel and in part because his satire is somewhat topical, Dryden may not be as familiar to general readers as, say, DANIEL DEFOE or JONATHAN SWIFT, yet SAMUEL JOHNSON called him the father of English criticism and placed his odes at the very pinnacle of lyric poetry.

POEMS BY DRYDEN

Complete Poetical Works. Ed. by George R. Noyes. HM o.p. Excellent notes.
Dryden. Ed. by Keith Walker. *Oxford Authors Ser*. OUP 1987 $55.00. ISBN 0-19-254192-7
Dryden: Poems. Penguin Poetry Lib. Ser. Viking Penguin 1985 $5.95. ISBN 0-14-058503-6
Poems and Fables of John Dryden. Ed. by James Kinsley. *Oxford Stand. Authors Ser*. OUP 1962 o.p. A complete text of Dryden's original poems and verse translations, based upon a critical review of all of the early printings.
Poems of John Dryden. 4 vols. Ed. by James Kinsley. *Oxford Eng. Texts Ser*. OUP 1958 o.p. Superior texts.

NONFICTION BY DRYDEN

An Essay of Dramatic Poesy and Other Critical Writings. Ed. by John L. Mahoney. Irvington 1982 $7.95. ISBN 0-8290-1006-8
Literary Criticism of John Dryden. Ed. by Arthur C. Kirsch. Bks. Demand repr. of 1966 ed. $36.50. ISBN 0-8357-9709-0. An examination of critical essays by Dryden, published from 1664 to 1700.
Selected Criticism. Ed. by James Kinsley and G. A. Parfitt. OUP 1970 o.p.

WORKS BY DRYDEN

Selected Poetry and Prose. Modern Lib. College Ed. Ser. Random 1969 $5.24. ISBN 0-07-553553-X. A modernized edition of selected pieces of Dryden's poetry and prose.
Works. 21 vols. U. CA Pr. 1973–87 o.p. In progress since 1956, this will be the standard edition for generations.

BOOKS ABOUT DRYDEN

Bredvold, Louis I. *The Intellectual Milieu of John Dryden: Studies in Some Aspects of Seventeenth-Century Thought*. U. of Mich. Pr. 1956 o.p. One of the most influential books ever written about Dryden, later superseded by Phillip Harth.
Bywaters, David A. *Dryden in Revolutionary England*. U. CA Pr. 1991 $25.00. ISBN 0-520-07061-5
Corse, Taylor. *Dryden's Aeneid: The English Virgil*. U. of Delaware Pr. 1991 $27.50. ISBN 0-87413-385-8. A comparison of Dryden's translations with those of other poets of the period, identifying Dryden as a narrative poet.
Eliot, T. S. *Homage to John Dryden*. Haskell 1970 $39.95. ISBN 0-8383-0024-3. Three brief essays examining the poetry of Dryden, metaphysical poetry and poets, and Andrew Marvell.

Frost, William. *John Dryden: Dramatist, Satirist, Translator.* AMS Pr. 1988 $39.50. ISBN 0-404-61723-9. A chronological examination of Dryden in three roles—man of the theater, creator of English satire, and translator.

Hall, James M. *John Dryden: A Reference Guide.* G. K. Hall 1984 o.p. An excellent bibliography of and research guide to the works of Dryden.

Harth, Philip. *Contexts of Dryden's Thought.* U. Ch. Pr. 1968 o.p. A study of Dryden's religious thought and of his use of religious ideas in his writings.

———. *New Homage to John Dryden: Papers Read at a Clark Library Conference.* Clark Library 1983 o.p. With an introduction by Alan Roper.

Hopkins, David. *John Dryden. British and Irish Authors Ser.* Cambridge U. Pr. 1986 $39.50. ISBN 0-521-30914-X. An introduction to Dryden's work; valuable for those who are reading his works for the first time.

Kinsley, James, and Helen Kinsley. *Dryden: The Critical Heritage.* Routledge 1978 $69.50. ISBN 0-7100-6977-4. Representative collection of critical comments on Dryden, ranging from 1663 to 1810.

Miner, Earl. *Dryden's Poetry.* Ind. U. Pr. 1967 o.p. Indispensable.

Montgomery, Guy, ed. *Concordance to the Poetical Works of John Dryden.* Russell 1967 repr. of 1957 ed. o.p. An alphabetically organized concordance, based on the *Cambridge Edition of the Poetical Works of John Dryden.*

Nicoll, Allardyce. *Dryden and His Poetry.* Folcroft repr. of 1923 ed. o.p. A brief volume on the life and personality of Dryden, as expressed through his poetry; representative poems included.

Saintsbury, George E. *Dryden.* Ed. by John Morley. *Eng. Men of Letters.* AMS Pr. repr. of 1888 ed. $7.80. ISBN 0-404-51726-9. A short account of the life and works of Dryden, in a chronological survey.

Scott, Walter. *The Life of John Dryden.* Ed. by Bernard Kreissman. U. of Nebr. Pr. 1963 $9.95. ISBN 0-8032-5177-7. A masterful history of the Restoration period, with Dryden as the central figure of interest.

Smith, David N. *John Dryden.* Folcroft repr. of 1950 ed. o.p. Four lectures on "John Dryden of Trinity College," delivered in Oxford, England, in 1948.

Swedenborg, H. T., Jr. *Essential Articles for the Study of John Dryden.* Shoe String 1966 o.p. A collection of informative articles by various authors on the life and work of Dryden.

Van Doren, Mark. *The Poetry of John Dryden.* Haskell 1969 repr. of 1920 ed. $75.00. ISBN 0-8383-1207-1. A lengthy and scintillating essay on the life and work of Dryden.

Ward, Charles E. *The Life of John Dryden.* U. of NC Pr. 1961 o.p.

Winn, James A. *John Dryden and His World.* Yale U. Pr. 1987 $40.00. ISBN 0-300-02994-2. An excellent, highly readable scholarly biography.

Zwicker, Steven N. *Politics and Language in Dryden's Poetry.* Princeton U. Pr. 1984 $37.50. ISBN 0-691-06618-3. A critical examination of the political culture influencing Dryden's work and the role of disguise in his poetry.

ETHEREGE, SIR GEORGE. c.1635–c.1691

Etherege helped to develop the comedy of manners, or society comedy, in which the brilliant world of wits and fops is both portrayed and satirized. In his best-known comedy, *The Man of Mode* (1676), Dorimant is hardly a model for how the young man about town should behave. Etherege is a cool observer of manners. Sir Fopling Flutter is clearly a Frenchified fop and dandy, yet he is also lovable. Harriet is a prototype of the witty, liberated woman, coquettish, teasing, and intelligent. Etherege's other comedies are *The Comical Revenge*, or *Love in a Tub* (1664) and *She Would If She Could* (1668).

PLAYS BY ETHEREGE

The Dramatic Works of Sir George Etherege. Ed. by H. F. Brett-Smith. Scholarly 1971 repr. of 1927 ed. $39.00. ISBN 0-403-00956-1. A two-volume collection of the plays of Etherege.

The Man of Mode. 1676. Ed. by John Barnard. *New Mermaid Ser.* Norton 1979 $7.95.
  ISBN 0-393-90041-X
The Plays of Sir George Etherege. Ed. by Michael Cordner. *Plays by Renaissance and
  Restoration Dramatists Ser.* Cambridge U. Pr. 1982 o.p.
She Would If She Could. 1668. Ed. by Charlene M. Taylor. *Regents Restoration Drama
  Ser.* Bks. Demand repr. of 1971 ed. $42.20. ISBN 0-8357-7770-7
The Works of Sir George Etherege. Ed. by A. W. Verity. Folcroft 1974 o.p. Selected plays
  and poems by Etherege, with an introduction and critical notes by A. Wilson Verity.

WORK BY ETHEREGE

The Letters of Sir George Etherege. Ed. by Frederick Bracher. U. CA Pr. 1974 $52.00. ISBN
  0-520-02218-1. A compilation of Etherege's surviving letters.

BOOKS ABOUT ETHEREGE

Huseboe, Arthur R. *Sir George Etherege.* Twayne 1987 $29.95. ISBN 0-8057-6946-3
Jantz, Ursula. *Targets of Satire in the Comedies of Etherege, Wycherley and Congreve.*
  Salzburg Studies in Eng. Lit., Poetic Drama and Poetic Theory. Humanities 1978 o.p.
McCamic, Frances S. *Sir George Etherege.* Folcroft repr. of 1931 ed. o.p.
Mann, David D. *A Concordance to the Plays and Poems of Sir George Etherege.*
  Greenwood 1985 $115.00. ISBN 0-313-20976-6
_____. *Sir George Etherege: A Reference Guide.* G. K. Hall 1981 o.p. An in-depth
  bibliography of the works of Etherege, noting trends in the criticism of his work.
Markley, Robert. *Two-Edg'd Weapons: Style and Ideology in the Comedies of Etherege,
  Wycherley, and Congreve.* OUP 1988 $64.00. ISBN 0-19-812960-2. A study of the
  relationship of style and ideology in selected plays.

FARQUHAR, GEORGE. 1678–1707

Farquhar was Irish by birth and education (he left Trinity College in Dublin to
become an actor). He is most notable for bringing to English comedy a fresh
good humor and an emphasis on country settings. One of his plays, *The
Recruiting Officer* (1706), which BERTOLT BRECHT rewrote, is a lively takeoff on
the author's own military experiences. His best-known play, *The Beaux'
Stratagem* (1707), engages the marriage debate and the difficulty of divorce,
drawing on JOHN MILTON's divorce tracts. It is a lively, very natural comedy of
sensibility. Farquhar wrote *Discourse upon Comedy in a Letter to a Friend*, in
which he defended the genre as "a well-framed tale, handsomely told, as an
agreeable vehicle for counsel or reproof." Farquhar married a woman he
thought to be wealthy. He was mistaken, however; he died penniless in London
at the age of 29.

PLAYS BY FARQUHAR

The Beaux' Stratagem. 1707. Ed. by Michael Cordner. *New Mermaid Ser.* Norton 1976
  $4.95. ISBN 0-393-90007-X
Complete Works. 2 vols. Ed. by Charles Stonehill. Bks. Demand 1967 repr. of 1930 ed.
  $47.10. ISBN 0-8357-4104-4
The Recruiting Officer. 1706. Ed. by John Ross. *New Mermaid Ser.* Norton 1977 $5.95.
  ISBN 0-393-90039-8
The Works of George Farquhar. 2 vols. Ed. by Shirley S. Kenney. OUP 1988. Vol. 1
  $145.00. ISBN 0-19-811858-9. Vol. 2 $140.00. ISBN 0-19-812342-6. A two-volume set
  of Farquhar's plays and nondramatic works; excellent and informative introduction
  to each work.

BOOKS ABOUT FARQUHAR

Connely, Willard. *Young George Farquhar.* Arden Lib. 1980 repr. of 1949 ed. o.p. A
  biography of Farquhar; provides excellent insight into English Restoration drama.

James, Eugene M. *George Farquhar: A Reference Guide*. G. K. Hall 1986 $40.00. ISBN 0-8161-8182-9. The first full-length bibliography by a leading scholar, on works by and about Farquhar.

Rothstein, Eric. *George Farquhar*. Twayne 1967 $17.95. ISBN 0-8290-1725-9

FIELDING, HENRY. 1707–1754

A successful playwright in his twenties, Fielding turned to the study of law and then to journalism, fiction, and a judgeship after his *Historical Register*, a political satire on the Walpole government, contributed to the censorship of plays that put him out of business. As an impoverished member of the upper classes, he knew the country squires and the town nobility; as a successful young playwright, the London "jet set"; as a judge at the center of London, the city's thieves, swindlers, petty officials, shopkeepers, and vagabonds; and as a political journalist (editor-author of *The Champion, 1739–41*; *The True Patriot, 1745–46*; *The Jacobite's Journal, 1747–48*; *The Covent-Garden Journal, 1752*), he participated in argument and intrigue over everything from London elections to national policy, knowledgeably attacking and defending a range of politicians, from ward heelers to the Prince of Wales.

When Fielding undertook writing prose fiction to ridicule the simple morality of SAMUEL RICHARDSON's *Pamela*, he first wrote the hilarious burlesque *Shamela* (1741). Shortly, however, he found himself considering all the forces working on man, and in *Joseph Andrews* (1742) (centering on his invented brother of Pamela), he played with the patterns of HOMER (see Vol. 2), the Bible, and CERVANTES (see Vol. 2) to create what he called "a comic epic poem in prose." His preface describing this new art form is one of the major documents in literary criticism of the novel. *Jonathan Wild*, a fictional rogue biography of a year later, plays heavily with ironic techniques that leave unsettled Fielding's great and recurring theme: the difficulty of uniting goodness (an outflowing love of others) with prudence in a world where corrupted institutions support divisive pride rather than harmony and self-fulfillment.

In his masterpiece *Tom Jones* (1749), Fielding not only faces this issue persuasively but also shows for the first time the possibility of bringing a whole world into an artistic unity, as his model Homer had done in verse. Fielding not only develops a coherent and centered sequence of events—something CONGREVE had done casually on a small scale in *Incognita* 60 years before—but relates the plot organically to character and theme, giving us all of eighteenth-century England (if not indeed, as he wished, all humanity) in a vision of the archetypal good man (Tom) on a journey toward understanding, with every act by every character both reflecting the special and typical psychology of that character and incurring the proper moral response.

If in *Tom Jones* Fielding affirms the existence of an order under the surface of chaos, in his last novel, *Amelia* (1751), which realistically examines the misery of London, he can find nothing reliable except the prudent good heart, and that only if its possessor escapes into the country. Fielding based the title character on his second wife, with whom he was deeply in love. However himself ill, still saddened by the deaths of his intensely loved first wife and daughter, and depressed by a London magistrate's endless toil against corruption, he saw little hope for goodness in that novel or in his informal *Journal of a Voyage to Lisbon* (1755). Shortly after traveling to that city for his health, he died at the age of 47, having proved to his contemporaries and successors that the lowly novel was capable of the richest achievements of art.

NOVELS BY FIELDING

Amelia. Ed. by Martin C. Battestin. *Works of Henry Fielding*. Wesleyan U. Pr. 1988 $50.00. ISBN 0-8195-5084-1

The History of Tom Jones, a Foundling. 2 vols. Ed. by Fredson Bowers. *Works of Henry Fielding*. Wesleyan U. Pr. 1974 $60.00. ISBN 0-8195-4068-4

Jonathan Wild. Ed. by David Nokes. *Penguin English Lib. Ser.* Viking Penguin 1982 $5.95. ISBN 0-14-043151-9

Joseph Andrews. Ed. by Martin Battestin. Wesleyan U. Pr. 1967 $50.00. ISBN 0-8195-3070-0

NONFICTION BY FIELDING

Covent Garden Journal and A Plan of the Universal Register-Office. Ed. by Bertrand A. Goldgar. Wesleyan U. Pr. $75.00. ISBN 0-8195-5167-8

An Enquiry into the Causes of the Late Increase of Robbers, and Related Writings. Ed. by Malvin R. Zirker. Wesleyan U. Pr. 1988 $75.00. ISBN 0-8195-5166-X. A critical, unmodernized text of Fielding's work, offering Fielding's own elaborate solution to problems that Parliament was currently debating; other similar types of writings included.

The Jacobite's Journal and Related Writings. Ed. by W. B. Coley. Wesleyan U. Pr. 1975 $60.00. ISBN 0-8195-4072-2

The True Patriot. Ed. by W. B. Coley. Wesleyan U. Pr. 1987 $65.00. ISBN 0-8195-5127-9

WORKS BY FIELDING

The Complete Works of Henry Fielding. 16 vols. Ed. by William E. Henley. B & N Imports 1967 repr. of 1902-1903 ed. o.p. A 16-volume collection of Fielding's complete works.

Works of Henry Fielding. Wesleyan U. Pr. 1972 repr. of 1743 ed. $50.00. ISBN 0-8195-4046-3. The first of a three-volume set of Fielding's works, including short poems, formal essays, satirical sketches, and Lucianic dialogues.

BOOKS ABOUT FIELDING

Battestin, Martin C. *The Moral Basis of Fielding's Art: A Study of Joseph Andrews*. Wesleyan U. Pr. 1959 $10.95. ISBN 0-8195-6038-3. A textual, critical, and annotated edition of Fielding's novel, *Joseph Andrews*.

————. *New Essays by Henry Fielding: His Contributions to the Craftsman (1734–1739) and Other Journalism*. U. Pr. of Va. 1989 $50.00. ISBN 0-8139-1221-0. An attempt to prove that 41 essays published anonymously or pseudonymously in *The Craftsman* from 1734 to 1739 were actually written by Fielding.

Battestin, Martin C., and Ruthe K. Battestin. *Henry Fielding: A Life*. Routledge 1990 $45.00. ISBN 0-415-01438-7. A lengthy and interesting account of the life and works of Fielding.

Cleary, Thomas R. *Henry Fielding: Political Writer*. Wilfrid Laurier U. Pr. 1984 $35.00. ISBN 0-88920-131-5. A thorough, comprehensive study of the political aspects of Fielding's work.

Dircks, Richard J. *Henry Fielding*. Twayne 1983 $17.95. ISBN 0-8057-6768-1. A critical study of Fielding's life, his comedies, his fiction, and his mature novels, especially *Tom Jones* and *Amelia*.

Golden, Morris. *Fielding's Moral Psychology*. U. of Mass. Pr. 1966 $22.50. ISBN 0-87023-022-0. Describes Fielding's theory of psychology and examines its connection to his view of morality.

Hume, Robert D. *Henry Fielding and the London Theatre, 1728–1737*. OUP 1988 $65.00. ISBN 0-19-812864-9. A contextual history of Fielding as a dramatist and a theater manager.

Hunter, J. Paul. *Occasional Form: Henry Fielding and the Chains of Circumstance*. Johns Hopkins 1976 $32.50. ISBN 0-8018-1672-6. Places Fielding's career and major works in the context of the historical forces that influenced his mind and art.

Reilly, Patrick. *Tom Jones: Adventure and Providence*. Twayne 1991 $21.95. ISBN 0-8057-9422-0. A critical study that looks at the novel *Tom Jones* as Fielding's master work.
Rivero, Albert J. *The Plays of Henry Fielding: A Critical Study of His Dramatic Career*. U. Pr. of Va. 1989 $24.50. ISBN 0-8139-1228-8
Rogers, Pat. *Henry Fielding*. Scribner 1979 o.p. A short presentation of the major occurrences and concerns in Fielding's career.
Varey, Simon. *Henry Fielding*. Cambridge U. Pr. 1986 $42.50. ISBN 0-521-26244-5. A concise study, introducing the major work of Fielding; includes a discussion of both Fielding the dramatist and the great comic novelist.
Wright, Andrew H. *Henry Fielding, Mask and Feast*. Bks. Demand repr. of 1965 ed. $55.70. ISBN 0-685-44039-7. An examination and comparison of three of Fielding's novels: *Joseph Andrews*, *Tom Jones*, and *Amelia*.

GAY, JOHN. 1685–1732

Gay is a highly original poet and dramatist who experimented in various forms and genres. His *The What D'Ye Call It: A Tragi-Comical Pastoral Farce* (1715) is a burlesque of high seriousness, as is also *Three Hours after Marriage*, which he wrote with his fellow members of the Scriblerus Club ALEXANDER POPE and Dr. John Arbuthnot. *The Beggar's Opera* (1728) is his best-known work. It started the vogue for ballad operas, with tunes drawn from popular airs (Gay's are mostly from Thomas D'Urfey's *Pills to Purge Melancholy*, a popular sourcebook for ribald songs). *The Beggar's Opera* satirizes gentility and vulgarity alike, and its topical political allusions are so direct that the government forbade its sequel, *Polly*. BERTOLT BRECHT (see Vol. 2) caught the spirit of the work in his *Threepenny Opera*.

PLAYS BY GAY

The Beggar's Opera. Ed. by Bryan Loughrey and T. O. Treadwell. Viking Penguin 1987 $4.95. ISBN 0-14-043220-5
John Gay: Dramatic Works. 2 vols. Ed. by John Fuller. *Oxford English Texts Ser*. Vol. 1 $95.00. ISBN 0-19-812701-4. Vol. 2 $135.00. ISBN 0-19-812320-5. A two-volume collection of Gay's dramatic works.

WORK BY GAY

Poetical, Dramatic, and Miscellaneous Works. 6 vols. AMS Pr. repr. of 1795 ed. $180.00. ISBN 0-404-02790-3

BOOKS ABOUT GAY

Armens, Sven. *John Gay, Social Critic*. Hippocrene Bks. 1966 $21.50. ISBN 0-374-90285-2. An analysis of Gay's poetry, with particular attention paid to the use of the pastoral lyric in his work.
Hebert, Alan P. *Mr. Gay's London*. Greenwood repr. of 1948 ed. $38.50. ISBN 0-8371-4805-7
Klein, Juliet. *John Gay: An Annotated Checklist of Criticism*. Whitston Pub. 1973 $7.50. ISBN 0-87875-041-X
Lewis, Peter, and Nigel Wood. *John Gay and the Scriblerians*. St. Martin 1989 $35.00. ISBN 0-312-02422-3. A collection of critical essays by various authors, on the life and works of Gay and his relationship with other members of the Scriblerus Club.

GOLDSMITH, OLIVER. 1728–1774

As SAMUEL JOHNSON said in his famous epitaph on his Irish-born and educated friend, Goldsmith ornamented whatever he touched with his pen. A professional writer who died in his prime, Goldsmith wrote the best comedy of his day, *She Stoops to Conquer* (1773); one of its finest poems, "The Deserted Village"

(1770); its most engaging essays, particularly in his newspaper column of *Chinese Letters*, which were reprinted as *The Citizen of the World* (1762); histories of Rome, Greece, and England that remained in use in schools for a century; a *History of the Earth and Animated Nature* that at times, as Johnson predicted, is as amusing as a Persian tale; biographies and even book reviews that still give pleasure in their wit and sympathy; and *The Vicar of Wakefield* (1766), which, despite major plot inconsistencies and the intrusion of poems, essays, tales, and lectures apparently foreign to its central concerns, remains one of the most engaging fictional works in English. One reason for its appeal is the character of the narrator, Dr. Primrose, who is at once a slightly absurd pedant, an impatient traditional father of teenagers, a Job-like figure heroically facing life's blows, and an alertly curious, helpful, loving person. Another reason is Goldsmith's own mixture of delight and amused condescension (analogous to, though not identical with, LAURENCE STERNE's in *Tristram Shandy* and Johnson's in *Rasselas*, both contemporaneous) as he looks at the vicar and his domestic group, fit representatives of a ludicrous but workable world. Never married and always facing financial problems, he died in London and was buried in Temple Churchyard.

PLAY BY GOLDSMITH

She Stoops to Conquer. Ed. by J. A. Lavin. Norton 1980 $6.95. ISBN 0-393-90046-0

NOVEL BY GOLDSMITH

The Vicar of Wakefield. Ed. by Arthur Friedman. OUP 1981 $3.50. ISBN 0-19-281560-1

NONFICTION BY GOLDSMITH

New Essays by Goldsmith. Ed. by Ronald S. Crane. Greenwood 1969 repr. of 1927 ed. $35.00. ISBN 0-8371-0447-5. Eighteen essays originally appearing anonymously between 1760 and 1762, attributed by Crane to Goldsmith.

WORKS BY GOLDSMITH

Collected Letters. Ed. by Katharine C. Balderston. Richard West 1980 repr. of 1928 ed. o.p. A collection of Goldsmith's letters, arranged around a variety of topics.

Collected Works. 5 vols. Ed. by Arthur Friedman. OUP 1966 o.p. Includes Goldsmith's reviews, essays, biographies, novel, poems, plays, and miscellaneous pieces; the standard scholarly edition.

Oliver Goldsmith: Poems and Plays. C. E. Tuttle 1991 $8.95. ISBN 0-460-87019-X. With an introduction by Tom Davis.

BOOKS ABOUT GOLDSMITH

Dixon, Peter. *Oliver Goldsmith Revisited.* Twayne 1991 $24.95. ISBN 0-8057-7008-9. A timely retrospective of Goldsmith's life and works.

Jackson, Robert. *Oliver Goldsmith: Essays Towards an Interpretation.* Ayer repr. of 1951 ed. $9.25. ISBN 0-8369-8199-5

Quintana, Ricardo. *Oliver Goldsmith: A Georgian Study.* Macmillan 1967 o.p. An interesting study of the life and works of Goldsmith.

Swarbrick, Andrew. *The Art of Oliver Goldsmith.* B & N Imports 1984 $30.25. ISBN 0-389-20462-5. A collection of critical essays by various authors on the literature of Goldsmith, offering a broad survey of his works.

Woods, Samuel H., Jr. *Oliver Goldsmith, A Reference Guide.* G. K. Hall 1982 $35.00. ISBN 0-8161-8339-2. An annotated list of writings about Goldsmith and his works, from the beginning of his literary career through 1978.

GRAY, THOMAS. 1716–1771

Gray was an extremely shy, almost reclusive person. His nature was scholarly, and he sought perfection in everything he did. He did not write much poetry, but what he did finish is of such high quality that he is sometimes considered the most important figure in English poetry between POPE and BLAKE. His *Elegy Written in a Country Churchyard* (1751) has long been one of the supremely popular poems in the English language, rivaling any poem ever written for quotable lines. Gray's language is extremely formal, often archaic. Much influenced by the Greek and Roman poets, and by DRYDEN, Gray later turned to Norse mythology for thematic material. *The Progress of Poesy* (1757) and *The Bard* (1757) contributed to the revival of the ode form, especially among the romantics. His letters have long been admired as among the best in the English language. WORDSWORTH regarded his *Hymn to Adversity* (1742) as a masterpiece.

POETRY BY GRAY

Gray and Collins: Poetical Works. Ed. by Roger Lonsdale. OUP 1986 $16.95. ISBN 0-19-281169-X

WORKS BY GRAY

Gray: Poetry and Prose. AMS Pr. repr. of 1926 ed. $18.50. ISBN 0-404-15304-6. A selection of poetry and prose works by Gray, with essays by Johnson, Goldsmith, and others.
Works of Thomas Gray in Verse and Prose. Ed. by Edmund Gosse. AMS Pr. repr. of 1884 ed. $70.00. ISBN 0-404-02900-0

BOOKS ABOUT GRAY

Brooks, Cleanth. *The Well-Wrought Urn: Studies in the Structure of Poetry.* HarBraceJ 1956 $9.95. ISBN 0-15-695705-1
Cook, Albert S. *A Concordance to the English Poems of Thomas Gray.* Peter Smith repr. of 1908 ed. $16.50. ISBN 0-8446-1124-7
Golden, Morris. *Thomas Gray.* Twayne 1988 $22.95. ISBN 0-8057-6961-7. Provides information about Gray, his poetry, and his age, and examines all of the included poems as works of literature.
Ketten-Cremer, R. W. *Thomas Gray: A Biography.* Cambridge U. Pr. 1955 o.p. Still the standard scholarly biography.
McKenzie, Alan T. *Thomas Gray: A Reference Guide.* G. K. Hall 1982 o.p.
Weinfield, Henry. *The Poet Without a Name: Gray's "Elegy" and the Problem of History.* S. Ill. U. Pr. 1990 $34.95. ISBN 0-8093-1652-8. A study of Gray's *Elegy* from the dual standpoint of both literary history and literary theory. The author states that this poem was an important turning point in the history of English poetry.

JOHNSON, SAMUEL. 1709–1784

As literary critic, essayist, biographer, and lexicographer, Johnson so dominates the eighteenth century that it is easy to neglect his accomplishments as a poet. Yet T. S. ELIOT believed that Johnson's imitations of JUVENAL (see Vol. 2), *London* (1738), and *The Vanity of Human Wishes* (1749), were achievements almost unique in English verse. Son of a bookseller, Johnson left Oxford without attaining a degree because of a lack of funds. Failing as a schoolteacher, he arrived in London in the company of his student, David Garrick, who later became the most brilliant actor of the century. There Johnson apprenticed himself as a jack-of-all-literary-trades to a monthly publication called the *Gentleman's Magazine.* Within a few years, he had become its managing editor. From the beginning, Johnson valued the creative imagination in large part for its potential for moral instruction. Among the works drawn from his early career, besides *London*, is the groundbreaking *Life of Mr. Richard Savage* (1744), a youthful biography that urges writers to adopt a guild mentality and that would later be included in the crowning achievement of his career, the *Lives of the Poets* (1779–81). Often called "The Age of Johnson," the second half of the eighteenth century brought to a close the traditional dependence of the writer on patronage; the classic declaration of the writer's independence is the letter in which Johnson refuses LORD CHESTERFIELD the belated sponsorship of his *Dictionary of the English Language* (1755). Two decades later Johnson was awarded an Oxford doctorate, primarily for his contributions to learning during the nine years he spent compiling the *Dictionary*.

During the 1750s, Johnson began to write his thoughtful and popular periodical essays *The Rambler* and *The Idler* and to contribute papers to another series called *The Adventurer*. Before long he also published *Rasselas* (1759), a compelling "oriental" tale treating LOCKE's (see Vols. 3 and 4) theme of the choice of life. Johnson was already famous when in 1763 the young JAMES BOSWELL made his acquaintance and decided to write his biography. It is somewhat ironic that Johnson, who wrote so often about the developmental stages of human life and who in the *Preface to Shakespeare* (1765) honored the slow maturing of a writer's reputation, should come down through the pages of Boswell as such a finished personality and full-fledged literary celebrity. As rich and wonderful as Boswell's *Life of Johnson* is, readers will come to know the compassion, integrity, and intellectual power of Johnson much better by reading Johnson's own works.

POETRY BY JOHNSON

The Poems of Samuel Johnson. Ed. by David N. Smith and Edward L. McAdam. 2nd ed. 1974 $59.00. ISBN 0-19-812702-2 A collection of Johnson's poems, placing original texts in chronological order.

NONFICTION BY JOHNSON

Journey to the Western Islands of Scotland and the Journal of a Tour to the Hebrides. Viking Penguin 1984 $7.95. ISBN 0-14-043221-3. The account of Johnson's visit to the western islands of Scotland in 1773; includes an introduction by Peter Levi.

FICTION BY JOHNSON

History of Rasselas, Prince of Abissinia. OUP 1989 $4.95. ISBN 0-19-281778-7. A fictional account of the life of Prince Rasselas of Abissinia, first published in 1759; includes an introduction by J. P. Hardy.

WORKS BY JOHNSON

Johnson: Selected Writings. Ed. by Patrick Cruttwell. Viking Penguin 1982 $9.95. ISBN 0-14-04033-4

The Letters of Samuel Johnson, with Mrs. Thrale's Genuine Letters to Him. 3 vols. Ed. by R. W. Chapman. OUP 1984 $36.00 ea. ISBNs 0-19-818536-7, 0-19-818537-5, ISBN 0-19-818538-3

Samuel Johnson. Ed. by Donald Greene. OUP 1984 $15.95. ISBN 0-19-281340-4

Works of Samuel Johnson. 11 vols. Ed. by Francis P. Walesby. AMS Pr. repr. of 1825 ed. $357.50. ISBN 0-404-03610-4. Supersedes all previous editions.

BOOKS ABOUT JOHNSON

Bate, Walter J. *Samuel Johnson*. HarBraceJ 1979 $10.95. ISBN 0-15-679259-1. A distinguished literary biography.

Boswell, James. *Life of Johnson.* Ed. by R. W. Chapman and J. D. Fleeman. OUP 1982 $14.95. ISBN 0-19-281537-7. The classic biography of Samuel Johnson.

Boulton, James T., ed. *Johnson: The Critical Heritage.* Routledge 1978 $69.50. ISBN 0-7100-7030-6. Documents the development of Johnson's reputation by providing extracts from criticism written during his lifetime and up to 1832.

Brownell, Morris. *Samuel Johnson's Attitudes to the Arts.* OUP 1989 $55.00. ISBN 0-19-812956-4. Presents the thesis that past tradition has misrepresented Johnson's attitude toward the arts and points out his contributions to the eighteenth-century nonliterary arts.

Folkenflik, Robert. *Samuel Johnson, Biographer.* Cornell Univ. Pr. 1978 $26.95. ISBN 0-8014-0968-3. An analysis of Johnson as biographer and a recognition of his achievement in this role.

Fussell, Paul. *Samuel Johnson and the Life of Writing.* Norton 1986 $6.95. ISBN 0-393-30258-X. A study of Johnson's life as a writer; presents some conceptions about writing that governed Johnson's achievements.

Greene, Donald. *The Politics of Samuel Johnson.* U. of Ga. Pr. 2nd ed. 1990 $20.00. ISBN 0-8203-1206-1. Examines the political life and beliefs of Johnson.

Grundy, Isobel. *Samuel Johnson and the Scale of Greatness.* U. of Ga. Pr. 1986 $30.00. ISBN 0-8203-0867-6. A study of Johnson's fascination with the concept of greatness and of his belief that goodness is a necessary step toward it.

Hinnant, Charles H. *Samuel Johnson: An Analysis.* St. Martin 1988 $32.50. ISBN 0-312-01346-9. Explores the Newtonian dimension of Johnson's philosophy.

Naugle, Helen H., ed. *A Concordance to the Poems of Samuel Johnson.* Cornell Univ. Pr. 1973 $60.00. ISBN 0-8014-0769-9. An authoritative concordance to Johnson's poems, divided into three sections: poems in English, poems in Latin, and poems of doubtful attribution.

Parke, Catherine N. *Samuel Johnson and Biographical Thinking.* U. of Mo. Pr. 1991 $34.95. ISBN 0-8262-0789-8

Tomarken, Edward. *Samuel Johnson on Shakespeare: The Discipline of Criticism.* U. of Ga. Pr. 1991 $35.00. ISBN 0-8203-1358-0

MONTAGU, LADY MARY WORTLEY. 1689–1762

Lady Mary, as Montagu is known, was among the truly independent women of eighteenth-century England. During her lifetime she was much admired as a poet of stylish wit; afterward she was highly regarded as a correspondent of keen observation. While still a young woman, she eloped with Edward Wortley Montagu and, when he was appointed ambassador, accompanied him to Constantinople. On her return to England, she brought with her the vaccine for smallpox (she had meanwhile contracted the disease). She was the leading woman of letters of her day, and, while she quarreled in print with her friends ALEXANDER POPE and JONATHAN SWIFT, she returned their attacks with at least equal force. From 1739 until just before her death in 1762, she left England and her husband for Italy; from Brescia she wrote to her daughter letters so brimming with learning that Voltaire compared them favorably to those of MME DE SÉVIGNÉ (see Vol. 2).

WORKS BY MONTAGU

The Complete Letters. 3 vols. Ed. by Robert Halsband. OUP 1965-67 o.p. A three-volume set of all of the letters penned by Montagu.

Essays and Poems and Simplicity, a Comedy. Ed. by Robert Halsband and Isobel Grundy. OUP 1977 o.p. Selected essays and poems by Montagu on a wide range of topics and in a variety of styles.

Letters. Knopf 1992 $20.00. ISBN 0-679-41747-8

Letters and Works of Lady Mary Wortley Montagu. 2 vols. Ed. by Lord Wharncliffe. AMS Pr. repr. of 1861 ed. $55.00. ISBN 0-404-04378-X

Letters from the Levant: During the Embassy to Constantinople, 1716–18. Eastern European Collection Ser. Ayer 1970 repr. of 1838 ed. $22.00. ISBN 0-405-02767-2

BOOK ABOUT MONTAGU

Halsband, Robert. *Life of Lady Mary Wortley Montgu.* OUP 1956 o.p. This has been the standard biography.

OTWAY, THOMAS. 1652–1685

Otway was probably the best writer of tragedies during the Restoration period. His *Venice Preserved* (1682) is rivaled only by DRYDEN's *All for Love*. As the Royal Shakespeare Company's production so well demonstrated, *Venice Preserved* is still a dark and passionate play. The love versus honor conflict echoes the heroic drama, but Jaffier's vacillation between the demands of a friend and a wife reflects the somberness of a world in chaos—a Jacobean tragic theme. Otway's *The Orphan* (1680) set the fashion for a serious play based on pathos, if not actual tears. Otway had an unrequited passion for Mrs. Elizabeth Barry, the actress who appeared in most of his dramas. Penniless at the end of his life, he died while in a London tavern.

PLAYS BY OTWAY

The Orphan. 1680. Ed. by Aline M. Taylor. *Regents Restoration Drama Ser.* U. of Nebr. Pr. 1976 $15.00. ISBN 0-8032-0383-7
Venice Preserved. 1682. Ed. by Malcolm Kelsall. Bks. Demand repr. of 1969 ed. $39.50. ISBN 0-8357-4080-3

WORK BY OTWAY

Complete Works. 3 vols. Ed. by Montague Summers. AMS Pr. repr. of 1926 ed. $180.00. ISBN 0-404-04860-9. The edited, collated, and annotated plays and poems of Otway, in a three-volume set.

BOOKS ABOUT OTWAY

Armistead, J. M. *Four Restoration Playwrights: A Reference Guide to Thomas Shadwell, Aphra Behn, Nathaniel Lee, and Thomas Otway.* G. K. Hall 1984 o.p.
Pollard, Hazel M. *From Heroics to Sentimentalism: A Study of Thomas Otway's Tragedies. Salzburg Studies in Eng. Lit., Poetic Drama and Poetic Theory.* Humanities 1974 o.p. A detailed study of the principles behind critically analyzing both tragic and comedic works.
Schumacher, Edgar. *Thomas Otway.* Franklin 1970 repr. of 1924 ed. $18.50. ISBN 0-8337-3176-9
Taylor, Aline M. *Next to Shakespeare.* AMS Pr. repr. of 1950 ed. $17.50. ISBN 0-404-06351-9
Warner, Kerstin P. *Thomas Otway. Twayne's Eng. Authors Ser.* G. K. Hall 1982 o.p.

POPE, ALEXANDER. 1688–1744

Pope claimed to have "lisped in numbers" (i.e., to be born a poet), and he was unusually precocious: His *An Essay on Criticism* (1711), *The Rape of the Lock* (1712), and *Windsor Forest* (1713) all were published before he was 25 years old. Deprived of a university education because of ill health and his Catholic religion, Pope devoted himself entirely to classical and humanistic learning, and his verse sparkles with a dense, allusive texture while commenting upon the foibles of the modern world. The *Rape of the Lock*, his best-known poem, is especially dazzling for its description of the magical sylphs, creatures who mimic the fallen angels in JOHN MILTON's work, as well as for the closing lines, in which the stolen lock of hair is transformed into a celestial comet. Yet, an alternating current of loss and even dismay runs beneath the preposterous humor of this youthful mock-epic. Pope patterned his career after those of his heroes, VIRGIL (see Vol. 2) and JOHN DRYDEN. Like Dryden, he undertook the translation of epic poetry, and his versions of the *Iliad* (1715–20) and *Odyssey* (1725–26) of HOMER (see Vol. 2) brought him financial security as well as fame. Meanwhile, he collaborated with his fellow members of the Scriblerus Club, JONATHAN SWIFT and JOHN GAY, on such joint projects as the comedy *Three Hours After Marriage* (1717). The spirit of ridicule inherited from Dryden's MACFLECKNOE and honed against the keen wit of his fellow members of the Scriblerus Club finds its sharpest expression in the two versions of the *Dunciad* published in 1728 and 1742. However, there are many other sides to Pope's verse, from his early efforts to recreate the effects of painting in poetry, to the sentimentalism of *Eloisa to Abelard* (1717), to the philosophical spirit of the *Essay on Man* (1733–34). After an eclipse of some decades, his reputation as poet par excellence now enjoys new interest, in part for his extraordinary tonal mastery of a variety of verse forms.

POETRY BY POPE

Alexander Pope: Collected Poems. C. E. Tuttle 1991 $7.95. ISBN 0-460-87062-9

Poems of Alexander Pope: A One-Volume Edition of the Twickenham Text with Select Annotations. Ed. by John Butt. Yale U. Pr. 1963 $17.95. ISBN 0-300-00030-8

Poetical Works. Ed. by Herbert Davis. OUP 1966 $16.95. ISBN 0-19-281246-7

The Rape of the Lock. Ed. by J. S. Cunningham. OUP 1966 $6.95. ISBN 0-19-911012-3

Twickenham Edition of the Poems of Alexander Pope. 11 vols. Yale U. Pr. 1967 o.p. The standard scholarly edition.

NONFICTION BY POPE

Selected Prose. Ed. by Paul Hammond. Cambridge U. Pr. 1987 $49.50. ISBN 0-521-25011-0

BOOKS ABOUT POPE

Brower, Reuben A. *Alexander Pope: The Poetry of Allusion*. OUP 1986 $19.95. ISBN 0-19-881149-7

Damrosch, Leopold, Jr. *The Imaginative World of Alexander Pope*. U. CA Pr. 1987 $42.50. ISBN 0-520-05975-1. A study of how Pope's imaginative world attempted to embrace an increasingly practical external world.

Kowalk, Wolfgang. *Alexander Pope: An Annotated Bibliography of Twentieth-Century Criticism, 1900–1979*. P. Lang Pubs. 1981 $63.95. ISBN 3-8204-5881-6. An annotated bibliography of criticism of Pope's work from the years 1900 to 1979; entries listed chronologically by subject matter.

Mack, Maynard. *Alexander Pope: A Life*. Yale U. Pr. 1985 $40.00. ISBN 0-300-03391-5

Morris, David B. *Alexander Pope: The Genius of Sense*. HUP 1984 $28.95. ISBN 0-674-01522-3. A critical analysis of Pope's writings, with appropriate historical background.

Rousseau, G. S., and Pat Rogers, eds. *The Enduring Legacy: Alexander Pope Tercentenary Essays*. Cambridge U. Pr. 1988 $49.50. ISBN 0-521-30581-0. Essays on Pope by a variety of contributing authors.

Rumbold, Valerie. *Woman's Place in Pope's World*. Cambridge U. Pr. 1989 $49.50. ISBN 0-521-36308-X. Sets Pope's writing to and about women in its cultural and personal contexts.

RICHARDSON, SAMUEL. 1689–1761

A printer and bookseller who wrote love letters for servant girls as an apprentice, studied nights to improve himself, and married the boss's daughter,

Samuel Richardson undertook at age 50 to write a book of sample courtesy notes, marriage proposals, job applications, and business letters for young people. While imagining situations for this book, he recalled an old scandal and developed it into *Pamela, or Virtue Rewarded* (1740–44), a novel about a servant girl whose firmness, vitality, literacy, and superior intelligence turn her master's lust into a decorous love that leads to their marriage. All of *Pamela's* virtues of fresh characterization, immediacy (what Richardson called "writing to the moment" of the character's consciousness), and the involvement of the reader in the character's intense and fluctuating fantasies, together with a much more focused seriousness, a more varied and differentiated cast of letter writers, and a more fundamental examination of moral and social issues, make his second novel, *Clarissa Hawlowe* (1747–48), a masterpiece. Although anyone who reads this huge novel for its plot may hang himself (as Richardson's friend SAMUEL JOHNSON said), readers have been fascinated by the complex conflict between Clarissa Harlowe and Robert Lovelace, two of the most fully realized characters, psychologically and socially, in all of literature. Like such great successors as ROUSSEAU (see Vol. 3), an acknowledged follower of Richardson, DOSTOEVSKY (see Vol. 2), and D. H. LAWRENCE, Richardson understands and shows us, in DIDEROT's (see Vols. 2 and 4) appreciative image, the black recesses of the cave of the mind.

Although Richardson's last novel, *Sir Charles Grandison* (1753–54), like *Pamela Part II*, mainly undertakes comic delineation of manners, it also examines the serious issues of love between a Protestant and a Catholic, and experiments technically with flashbacks, with stenographic reports, and most assertively with a pure hero, a male Clarissa of irresistible charm and power. At its best, Richardson's work fuses the epistolary technique, the use of dramatic scenes, the traditions of religious biography, and the elements of current romantic fiction to achieve precise analysis, an air of total verisimilitude, and a vision of a world of primal psychological forces in conflict.

NOVELS BY RICHARDSON

Clarissa Harlowe, or The History of a Young Lady—Comprehending the Most Important Concerns of Private Life. 8 vols. AMS repr. of 1751 ed. $765.00. ISBN 0-404-64100-8. With a new introduction by Florian Stuber and a bibliographic note by O. M. Brack.

The History of Sir Charles Grandison. 1753–54. 3 vols. Ed. by Jocelyn Harris. OUP 1972 o.p.

Novels of Samuel Richardson. 19 vols. AMS Pr. 1970 repr. of 1902 ed. $855.00. ISBN 0-404-05310-6

Pamela, or Virtue Rewarded. Ed. by Peter Sabor. Viking Penguin 1981 $5.95. ISBN 0-14-043140-3

WORKS BY RICHARDSON

Correspondence of Samuel Richardson. Ed. by Anna L. Barbauld. AMS Pr. repr. of 1804 ed. $210.00. ISBN 0-404-05300-9. Includes Richardson's written correspondence, a biographical account of the author, and observations on his various writings.

Selected Letters of Samuel Richardson. Ed. by John Carroll. OUP 1964 o.p.

BOOKS ABOUT RICHARDSON

Brophy, Elizabeth. *Samuel Richardson.* Twayne 1987 $20.95. ISBN 0-8047-6951-X

Castle, Terry. *Clarissa's Ciphers: Meaning and Disruption in Richardson's Clarissa.* Cornell Univ. Pr. 1982 $26.95. ISBN 0-8014-1495-4

Doody, Margaret, and Peter Sabor, eds. *Samuel Richardson: Tercentenary Essays.* Cambridge U. Pr. 1989 $54.50. ISBN 0-521-35383-1. Essays by various authors, commemorating the tercentenary of Richardson's birth in 1689.

Flynn, Carol Houlihan. *Samuel Richardson: A Man of Letters*. Princeton U. Pr. 1982
    $45.00. ISBN 0-691-06506-3. Examination of the tension between Richardson's
    moral and aesthetic principles in his letters and novels.
Harris, Jocelyn. *Samuel Richardson*. Cambridge U. Pr. 1987 $44.50. ISBN 0-521-30501-2
Myer, Valerie G. *Samuel Richardson: Passion and Prudence*. B & N Imports 1986 $35.75.
    ISBN 0-389-20650-4. A collection of critical essays by contributing authors on varied
    works by Richardson and on characters in his works.
Sale, William M. *Samuel Richardson: Master Printer*. Greenwood 1978 repr. of 1950 ed.
    $38.50. ISBN 0-8371-9732-5
Smith, Sarah W. *Samuel Richardson: A Reference Guide*. G. K. Hall 1984 $55.00. ISBN 0-
    8161-8170-5

SHERIDAN, RICHARD BRINSLEY. 1751–1816

The son of Thomas Sheridan, the Irish actor and theater manager, Richard
Brinsley Sheridan began writing plays as a youngster in Bath. He went on to
become one of the most successful playwrights of the later eighteenth century,
manager of the Drury Lane Theater, and also a politician and orator of some
note in the House of Commons. Along with his friends DAVID GARRICK (see
Vol. 3) and OLIVER GOLDSMITH, Sheridan was a member of the Literary Club of
SAMUEL JOHNSON, having been proposed for membership by Johnson himself.
Like Goldsmith, Sheridan also attacks "The Sentimental Muse" of weeping
comedy. In his best-known play, *The School for Scandal* (1777), Sheridan
revives the Restoration comedy of manners with its portrait of the beau monde
and its deflation of hypocrisy. The play is indebted to WILLIAM CONGREVE as well
as to MOLIÈRE (see Vol. 2), and the picture of society is based on Bath and
London. In *The Rivals* (1775), Sheridan amuses himself with the language
games of Mrs. Malaprop and her "nice derangement of epitaphs." The allusions
are consistently literary, as in her simile "as headstrong as an allegory on the
banks of the Nile." Sheridan's acute ear for banalities and truisms is best seen in
The Critic (1779), a burlesque of sentimental and inflated plays as well as self-
important criticism. The play ridicules "false Taste and brilliant Follies of
modern dramatic Composition." Sheridan's sparking dialogue, lively scenes,
and masterful dramatic construction have proved to be enduringly popular.

PLAYS BY SHERIDAN

Dramatic Works of Richard Brinsley Sheridan. 2 vols. Ed. by Cecil Price. OUP 1973 o.p.
    Authoritative two-volume collection of the dramatic works of Sheridan; also examines
    his life and achievements.
The Rivals. 1775. Ed. by Cecil Price. OUP 1971 $7.95. ISBN 0-19-831908-8
The School for Scandal. 1777. Ed. by Cecil Price. OUP 1971 $7.95. ISBN 0-19-911008-5
Sheridan's Plays. Ed. by Cecil Price. OUP 1975 $14.95. ISBN 0-19-281158-4

WORK BY SHERIDAN

Letters of Richard Brinsley Sheridan. 3 vols. Ed. by Cecil Price. OUP 1966 o.p. A
    collection of the letters of Sheridan, revealing his character and his career.

BOOKS ABOUT SHERIDAN

Auburn, Mark S. *Sheridan's Comedies: Their Contexts and Achievements*. U. of Nebr. Pr.
    1977 $19.50. ISBN 0-8032-0914-2
Darlington, William A. *Sheridan*. Haskell 1974 $75.00. ISBN 0-8383-1926-2
Durant, Jack D. *Richard Brinsley Sheridan*. Twayne's Eng. Authors Ser. G. K. Hall 1975
    o.p.

————. *Richard Brinsley Sheridan: A Reference Guide.* G. K. Hall 1981 $40.00. ISBN 0-8161-8146-2. A reference guide, listing essays and books written about Sheridan since 1816.

Foss, Kenelm. *Here Lies Richard Brinsley Sheridan.* Folcroft repr. of 1940 ed. o.p. A vivid biography of Sheridan.

Gibbs, Lewis. *Sheridan.* Richard West 1973 repr. of 1947 ed. o.p. A compact biographical account of Sheridan's life.

Loftis, John. *Sheridan and the Drama of Georgian England.* HUP 1977 $17.95. ISBN 0-674-80632-8. Probably the best book on the subject.

Rae, W. Fraser. *Sheridan.* 2 vols. Richard West 1973 repr. of 1896 ed. o.p. A thorough biography, in two volumes, of Sheridan.

Sadler, Michael T. *The Political Career of Richard Brinsley Sheridan: The Stanhope Essay for 1912.* Folcroft 1974 repr. of 1912 ed. o.p. Examines Sheridan's political career and includes some hitherto unpublished letters of Mrs. Sheridan.

SMART, CHRISTOPHER. 1722–1771

Son of a viscount, Smart was educated at Cambridge, where he was a lecturer in philosophy and rhetoric until 1752. Smart also spent his early years as a journalist and a writer of occasional verse. Subject to religious mania and an overexcited mind, Smart suffered a breakdown and spent several years in mental asylums. It is said that during his confinement, deprived of paper and pen, he scratched with a key on the wainscot of his room his masterpiece, *A Song to David* (1763). In 1771, in debt and sunk in drunkenness, Smart was confined to King's Bench Prison, where he died.

In his greatest poetry, Smart wrote rationally but ecstatically, shedding the narrow poetic shackles of his time. His verse anticipates the poetry of BLAKE, especially in *Jubilate Agno* (*Rejoice in the Lamb*), also from Smart's "mad" period, in which the poet glorifies all the creatures of God; there is a charming section on his cat Jeoffry. BENJAMIN BRITTEN (see Vol. 3) has set *Rejoice in the Lamb* to music.

POETRY BY SMART

Jubilate Agno. Ed. by W. H. Bond. Greenwood repr. of 1954 ed. $38.50. ISBN 0-8371-2331-3

My Cat Jeoffry: A Poem by Christopher Smart. Viking Penguin 1992 $8.95. ISBN 0-7207-2018-4

The Poetical Works of Christopher Smart. 4 vols. Ed. by Karina Williamson. OUP. Vol. 1 1980 $65.00. ISBN 0-19-811869-4. Vol. 2 $95.00. ISBN 0-19-812767-7. Vol. 3 $120.00. ISBN 0-19-812771-5. Vol. 4 $115.00. ISBN 0-19-812768-5. The standard scholarly edition.

WORK BY SMART

The Annotated Letters of Christopher Smart. Ed. by Betty Rizzo and Robert Mahoney. S. Ill. U. Pr. 1991 $24.50. ISBN 0-8093-1609-9. The first collected edition of Smart's letters, with annotations preceding each letter.

BOOKS ABOUT SMART

Rizzo, Betty, and Robert Mahoney. *Christopher Smart: An Annotated Bibliography.* Garland 1983 o.p. An annotated record of the appearance of Smart's works and of published references to him; arranged chronologically within four major sections.

Sherbo, Arthur. *Christopher Smart: Scholar of the University.* Mich. St. U. Pr. 1967 $8.50. ISBN 0-87013-110-9. A compelling biography of Smart.

SMOLLETT, TOBIAS GEORGE. 1721–1771

Smollett, the only major eighteenth-century English novelist whose work can seriously be called picaresque, came to the writing of novels with a strong sense of Scottish national pride (an alienating element in the London of the 1750s and 1760s), a Tory feeling for a lost order, horrifying experiences as a physician, and a fierce determination to make his way in the literary world. Prolific in a variety of literary forms, he was particularly successful as a popular historian, magazine editor, translator of CERVANTES (see Vol. 2), and author of novels about adventurous, unscrupulous, poor young men. His work is marked by vigorous journalistic descriptions of contemporary horrors, such as shipboard amputations or the filthy curative waters of Bath; by a flair for racy narrative often built on violence and sentiment, and for comedy that often relies on practical jokes and puns; and by a great gift for creating comic caricatures. His peppery *Travels through France and Italy* (1766) was something of a spur to LAURENCE STERNE's *Sentimental Journey*, in which Smollett is referred to as Dr. Smelfungus, who "set out with the spleen and jaundice, and every object he passed by was discolored or distorted—He wrote an account of them, but 'twas nothing but the account of his miserable feelings."

Smollett's most notable novels are *Roderick Random* (1748), *Peregrine Pickle* (1751), *Ferdinand Count Fathom* (1753), *Sir Launcelot Greaves* (1762), which set a precedent by first being serialized in his *British Magazine* (January 1760–December 1761), and especially *The Expedition of Humphrey Clinker* (1771), a relatively mellow work that follows the travels of Matthew Bramble, an excitable Welshman, from his home through chaotic England to idyllic Loch Lomond and back. Bramble himself finds what Smollett had irrecoverably lost—his health—as well as a son from his youth. Smollett died in 1771, the year of the novel's appearance, in Leghorn, Italy, and is buried in the English cemetery there.

NOVELS BY SMOLLETT

The Adventures of Ferdinand Count Fathom. U. of Ga. Pr. 1988 $40.00. ISBN 0-8203-1010-7

The Adventures of Peregrine Pickle. Ed. by James L. Clifford. OUP 1983 $8.95. ISBN 0-19-281663-2

The Adventures of Roderick Random. Ed. by Paul-Gabriel Bouce. OUP 1981 $6.95. ISBN 0-19-281261-0

The Expedition of Humphrey Clinker. Ed. by Thomas Preston. U. of Ga. Pr. 1991 $45.00. ISBN 0-8203-1203-7

The History and Adventures of an Atom. Ed. by Robert A. Day. U. of Ga. Pr. 1990 $45.00. ISBN 0-8203-1073-5. Smollett's narrative work about the principal events of the Seven Years' War, with extensive notes and background information provided.

The Life and Adventures of Sir Launcelot Greaves. Ed. by Peter Wagner. Viking Penguin 1988 $6.95. ISBN 0-14-043306-6

NONFICTION BY SMOLLETT

Travels through France and Italy. 1766. Ed. by Frank Feldstein. *World's Classics Ser.* OUP 1981 $7.95. ISBN 0-19-281569-5

WORKS BY SMOLLETT

Letters. Ed. by Edward S. Noyes. *Select Bibliographies Repr. Ser.* Ayer repr. of 1926 ed. $23.50. ISBN 0-8369-5100-X. The collected and edited letters of Smollett, arranged chronologically.

Poems, Plays, and the Briton. Ed. by Bryon Gassman. U. of Ga. Pr. 1993 $50.00. ISBN 0-8203-1428-5

BOOKS ABOUT SMOLLETT

Basker, James G. *Tobias Smollett, Critic and Journalist.* U. of Delaware Pr. 1988 $39.50. ISBN 0-87413-311-4. A study of the journalistic career of Smollett and his innovations in that field; includes a discussion of his writings.

Spector, Robert. *Tobias George Smollett.* Twayne 1968 $17.95. ISBN 0-89197-968-9

STEELE, SIR RICHARD. 1672–1729

Steele was born in the same year as JOSEPH ADDISON, whom he knew at Charterhouse School and at Oxford, which Steele left before receiving his degree. In 1709 he began the first of a series of periodicals that established the characteristics of the "periodical essay." This essay form, which was short and usually addressed personal topics, evolved primarily from journalistic sources and for journalistic purposes. Nevertheless, the essays appearing in *The Tatler* (from 1709) and *The Spectator* (from 1711) exerted a tremendous influence. Addison, who was a frequent contributor to both periodicals, displayed insight and elegance in his 42 numbers of *The Tatler*; Steele, with less elegance and wit, produced 188 and showed a warmth and sympathy that many readers preferred to Addison's cool intelligence. Steele's best-known play, *The Conscious Lovers* (1722), retreats from the artifice and aristocratic notions of Restoration drama, promoting instead a sound middle-class gentility. Married twice, Steele died in Wales, where he lived because of his debts.

NONFICTION BY STEELE

The Tatler. 3 vols. Ed. by Donald F. Bond. OUP 1987. Vol. 1 $135.00. ISBN 0-19-812484-8. Vol. 2 $120.00. ISBN 0-19-818533-2. Vol. 3 $120.00. ISBN 0-19-818534-0

Tracts and Pamphlets. Ed. by Rae Blanchard. Hippocrene Bks. 1966 $46.00. ISBN 0-374-90646-7. A collected edition of the tracts and pamphlets of Steele brought together for rereading.

PLAY BY STEELE

The Conscious Lovers. Ed. by Shirley S. Kenney. U. of Nebr. Pr. 1968 $11.95. ISBN 0-8032-0369-1

NONFICTION BY STEELE AND ADDISON

Critical Essays from The Spectator. Ed. by Donald F. Bond. OUP 1970 o.p.

Coverley Papers from the Spectator. Rprt. Ser. 1988 repr. of 1897 ed. $49.00. ISBN 0-685-21430-3. A collection of 33 letters of the Coverly Papers from *The Spectator.*

Selected Essays from the Tatler, The Spectator, and The Guardian. Ed. by Daniel McDonald. Macmillan 1973 $5.95. ISBN 0-672-60990-8

The Spectator. 5 vols. Ed. by Donald F. Bond. OUP 1987. Vol. 1 $120.00. ISBN 0-19-818610-X. Vol. 2 $120.00. ISBN 0-19-818611-8. Vol. 3 $120.00. ISBN 0-19-818612-6. Vol. 4 $120.00. ISBN 0-19-818613-4. Vol. 5 $120.00. ISBN 0-19-818614-2

BOOKS ABOUT STEELE

Ketcham, Michael G. *Transparent Designs: Reading, Performance, and Form in the "Spectator" Papers.* U. of Ga. Pr. 1985 $25.00. ISBN 0-8203-0771-8. An extended commentary on the eighteenth-century periodical *The Spectator.*

Winton, Calhoun. *Sir Richard Steele, M. P.: The Later Career.* Bks. Demand repr. of 1970 ed. $70.80. ISBN 0-317-42062-3. A biography presenting the major events in the later career of Steele, from 1714 to 1729.

STERNE, LAURENCE. 1713–1768

If Fielding showed that the novel (like the traditional epic or drama) could make the chaos of life coherent in art, Sterne only a few years later in *The Life and Opinions of Tristram Shandy, Gentleman* (1760–67) laughed away the notion of order. In Sterne's world, people are sealed off in their own minds so that only in unpredictable moments of spontaneous feeling are they aware of another human being. Reviewers attacked the obscenity of Tristram's imagined autobiography as it was published (two volumes each in 1759, early 1761, late 1761, 1765, and one in 1767), particularly when the author revealed himself as a clergyman, but the presses teemed with imitations of this great literary hit of the 1760s.

Through the mind of the eccentric hero, Sterne subverted accepted ideas on conception, birth, childhood, education, and the contemplation of maturity and death, so that Tristram's concerns touched his contemporaries and are still important. Since *Tristram Shandy* is patently a great and lasting comic work that yet seems, as E. M. FORSTER said, "ruled by the Great God Muddle," much recent criticism has centered on the question of its unity or lack of it; and its manipulation of time and of mental processes has been considered particularly relevant to the problems of fiction in our day.

Sterne's *Sentimental Journey* (1768) has been immensely admired by some critics for its superb tonal balance of irony and sentiment. His *Sermons of Mr. Yorick* (1760) catches the spirit of its time by dramatically preaching benevolence and sympathy as superior to doctrine. Whether as Tristram or as Yorick, Sterne is probably the most memorably personal voice in eighteenth-century fiction.

NOVELS BY STERNE

The Life and Opinions of Tristram Shandy, Gentleman. Ed. by Ian Ross. OUP 1983 $5.95. ISBN 0-19-281566-0

The Life and Opinions of Tristram Shandy, Gentleman: The Notes. Ed. by Melvyn New. U. Press Fla. 1984 $42.95. ISBN 0-8130-0738-0

The Life and Opinions of Tristram Shandy, Gentleman: The Text. 2 vols. Ed. by Melvyn New. U. Press Fla. 1978 Vol. 1 $42.95. ISBN 0-8130-0580-9. Vol. 2 $40.95. ISBN 0-8130-0599-X

NONFICTION BY STERNE

A Sentimental Journey through France and Italy with *Journal to Eliza* and *A Political Romance.* Ed. by Ian Jack. OUP 1984 $3.95. ISBN 0-19-281685-3

WORKS BY STERNE

Complete Works and Life of Laurence Sterne. 12 vols. Ed. by Wilbur Cross. AMS Pr. repr. of 1904 ed. $405.00. ISBN 0-404-52356-0. Depicts the life, travels, letters, and complete works of Sterne.

Memoirs of Mr. Laurence Sterne, The Life and Opinions of Tristram Shandy, A Sentimental Journey, Selected Sermons and Letters. Ed. by Douglas Grant. HUP 1950 $20.00. ISBN 0-685-42164-3

Works of Laurence Sterne. 6 vols. Ed. by George Saintsbury. AMS Pr. repr. of 1894 ed. $60.00. ISBN 0-404-08080-4

BOOKS ABOUT STERNE

Cash, Arthur H. *Laurence Sterne: The Early and Middle Years.* Routledge Chapman & Hall 1975 $85.00. ISBN 0-416-82210-X. A detailed history of Sterne's life and career, from 1713 to 1760.

————. *Laurence Sterne: The Later Years*. Routledge Chapman & Hall 1986 $60.00. ISBN 0-416-32930-6. A continuation of Sterne's life and illustrious career, from 1760 to his death in 1768.

DePorte, Michael V. *Nightmares and Hobbyhorses: Swift, Sterne, and Augustan Ideas of Madness*. Huntington Lib. 1974 $24.95. ISBN 0-87328-061-X. Examines theories of mental disorder formulated by English post-Restoration philosophers and doctors, and determines their criteria for establishing sanity.

Hammond, Lansing. *Laurence Sterne's Sermons of Mister Yorick*. Shoe String repr. of 1948 ed. $29.50. ISBN 0-208-00922-1. A critical examination of the passages in *The Sermons of Mr. Yorick* that signify an indebtedness to other authors, with an analysis of each sermon.

Holtz, William. *Image and Immortality: A Study of Tristram Shandy*. U. Pr. of New Eng. 1970 $25.00. ISBN 0-87057-121-4. A study of Sterne's *Tristram Shandy*, exploring the pictorial relationships noted in the work.

Howes, Alan B. *Yorick and the Critics: Sterne's Reputation in England, 1760–1868*. Shoe String repr. of 1958 ed. $30.00. ISBN 0-208-01129-3. A critical examination of the literary works of Sterne.

Lamb, Jonathan. *Sterne's Fiction and the Double Principle*. Cambridge U. Pr. 1989 $37.50. ISBN 0-521-37273-9. Analyzes the set of skeptical commonplaces exemplified in Sterne's fiction, which fosters experiments in characterization, narrative, and aesthetics.

Loveridge, Mark. *Laurence Sterne and the Argument about Design*. B & N Imports 1982 $31.50. ISBN 0-389-20106-5. A detailed examination of Sterne's use of the concepts of pattern, design, and form, with literary illustrations of these concepts.

Moglen, Helen. *The Philosophical Irony of Laurence Sterne*. U. Press Fla. 1975 $16.00. ISBN 0-8130-0363-6. An in-depth study of the philosophical irony of Sterne through consideration of sources of Sterne's vision and its expression in the novel *Tristram Shandy*.

Myer, Valerie G. *Laurence Sterne: Riddles and Mysteries*. B & N Imports 1984 $35.75. ISBN 0-389-20473-0

Traugott, John. *Tristram Shandy's World: Sterne's Philosophical Rhetoric*. Russell repr. of 1954 ed. o.p. A study of the comedic work *Tristram Shandy* and Sterne's use of philosophical rhetoric.

SWIFT, JONATHAN. 1667–1745

Apparently doomed to an obscure Anglican parsonage in Laracor, Ireland, even after he had written his anonymous masterpiece, *A Tale of a Tub* (c.1696), Swift turned a political mission to England from the Irish Protestant clergy into an avenue to prominence as the chief propagandist for the Tory government. His exhilaration at achieving importance in his forties appears engagingly in his *Journal to Stella* (1710–13), addressed to Esther Johnson, a young protégée for whom Swift felt more warmth than for anyone else in his long life. At the death of Queen Anne and the fall of the Tories in 1714, Swift became dean of St. Patrick's Cathedral, Dublin. In Ireland, which he considered exile from a life of power and intellectual activity in London, Swift found time to defend his oppressed compatriots, sometimes in such contraband essays as his *Drapier's Letters* (1724), and sometimes in such short mordant pieces as the famous *A Modest Proposal* (1729); and there he wrote perhaps the greatest work of his time, *Gulliver's Travels* (1726).

Using his characteristic device of the persona (a developed and sometimes satirized narrator, such as the anonymous hack writer of *A Tale of a Tub* or Isaac Bickerstaff in *Predictions for the Ensuing Year*, who exposes an astrologer), Swift created the hero Gulliver, who in the first instance stands for the bluff, decent, average Englishman and in the second, humanity in general. Gulliver is a full and powerful vision of a human being in a world in which violent passions, intellectual pride, and external chaos can degrade him or her—to animalism, in Swift's most horrifying images—but in which humans do have scope to act, guided by the Classical-Christian tradition. *Gulliver's Travels* has been an immensely successful children's book (although Swift did not care much for children), so widely popular through the world for its imagination, wit, fun, freshness, vigor, and narrative skill that its hero is in many languages a common proper noun. Perhaps as a consequence, its meaning has been the subject of continuing dispute, and its author has been called everything from sentimental to mad. Swift died in Dublin and was buried next to his beloved "Stella."

POETRY BY SWIFT

The Complete Poems. Ed. by Pat Rogers. Viking Penguin 1989 $14.95. ISBN 0-14-042261-7
Poetical Works. Ed. by Herbert Davis. OUP 1967 o.p.

FICTION BY SWIFT

Gulliver's Travels. Ed. by L. A. Landa. HM 1960 $7.16. ISBN 0-395-05146-0
Gulliver's Travels and Other Writings. Ed. by Richard Quintana. Random 1950 $4.00. ISBN 0-685-03396-1
The Prose Works of Jonathan Swift. 12 vols. Ed. by Temple Scott. AMS Pr. $495.00. ISBN 0-404-10050-3. A 12-volume collection of Swift's prose works.
A Tale of a Tub. Ed. by Edward Hodnett. AMS Pr. repr. of 1930 ed. $15.00. ISBN 0-404-06308-X
A Tale of a Tub with Other Earlier Works, 1696–1707. Ed. by Herbert Davis. Blackwell Pubs. 1986 $60.00. ISBN 0-631-00180-8
The Writings of Jonathan Swift. Ed. by Robert A. Greenberg and William Piper. Norton 1973 $14.95. ISBN 0-393-09415-4

NONFICTION BY SWIFT

The Correspondence of Jonathan Swift. Vols. 4–5. Ed. by Harold Williams. OUP 1965 $82.00. ISBN 0-19-811443-5. Includes letters from 1732 to 1745, with appendixes and indexes.
Miscellaneous and Autobiographical Pieces, Fragments and Marginalia. Ed. by Herbert Davis and L. A. Landa. Blackwell Pubs. 1986 $60.00. ISBN 0-631-00220-0
A Proposal for Correcting the English, Polite Conversations, etc. Ed. by Herbert Davis and L. A. Landa. Blackwell Pubs. 1986 $60.00. ISBN 0-631-00210-3

WORK BY SWIFT

The Portable Swift. Ed. by Carl Van Doren. Viking Penguin 1977 $8.95. ISBN 0-14-015037-4. Representative works of Swift; includes essays, poems, letters, journals, and *Gulliver's Travels.*

BOOKS ABOUT SWIFT

Ehrenpreis, Irvin. *Swift: The Man, His Works, and the Age.* 3 vols. HUP. Vol. 1 *Mr. Swift and His Contemporaries.* 1983 $35.00. ISBN 0-674-85830-1. Vol. 2 *Dr. Swift.* 1983 $40.00. ISBN 0-317-54487-X. Vol. 3 *Dean Swift.* 1983 $45.00. ISBN 0-674-85835-2. A masterful scholarly biography.
Eilon, Daniel. *Factions' Fictions: Ideological Closure in Swift's Satire.* U. of Delaware Pr. 1991 $33.50. ISBN 0-87413-391-2. Presents the theory that Swift's work is continuously concerned with the holding powers of the group ethic.
Fabricant, Carole. *Swift's Landscape.* Johns Hopkins 1982 $40.00. ISBN 0-8018-2721-3. Explores the meaning and significance of the physical features of Swift's surroundings, and the ways in which he perceived them.

Golden, Morris. *The Self-Observed: Swift, Johnson, Wordsworth.* Johns Hopkins 1972 $23.00. ISBN 0-8018-1289-5. An exploration of the works of Swift, Johnson, and Wordsworth in an attempt to understand their unique visions of the place of humankind in the world.

Paulson, Ronald. *Theme and Structure in Swift's Tale of a Tub.* Elliots Bks. 1960 o.p. An analysis of Swift's *Tale of a Tub.*

Rawson, Claude, ed. *The Character of Swift's Satire: A Revised Focus.* U. of Delaware Pr. 1983 $39.50. ISBN 0-87413-209-6

Schakel, Peter. *Critical Approaches to Teaching Swift.* AMS Pr. 1991 $42.50. ISBN 0-404-63521-0

THOMSON, JAMES. 1700–1748

Thomson, the son of a Scottish clergyman, was educated for the ministry at Edinburgh University but went instead to London, where he joined ALEXANDER POPE's literary circle. His boyhood in the country greatly influenced his mature poetry. *The Seasons* (1730), a series of nature poems, grew to more than 5,000 lines in its final version; it became the most popular poem of the eighteenth century and inspired JOSEPH HAYDN's (see Vol. 3) great musical setting. Thomson can justly be credited with undermining the supremacy of the couplet and with changing poetic taste. With Thomson, the center of poetic interest moved from the city to the country. Thomson was a deeply committed humanitarian poet, convinced that human nature was basically benevolent and that physical nature was a manifestation of the divine spirit. For this reason, he is often regarded as a "preromantic." He is also the author of the supremely famous song *Rule, Britannia* (1740).

POETRY BY THOMSON

Liberty, the Castle of Indolence and Other Poems. Ed. by James Sambrook. OUP 1986 $135.00. ISBN 0-19-812759-6

Poems and Some Letters of James Thomson. Ed. by Anne Ridler. Bks. Demand $85.30. ISBN 0-8357-6670-5. Presents annotated critical texts of all of Thomson's poetical works, excluding dramas and *The Seasons.*

The Seasons and the Castle of Indolence. Ed. by James Sambrook. OUP 1972 $14.95. ISBN 0-19-871070-4

BOOKS ABOUT THOMSON

Cohen, Ralph. *The Art of Discrimination: Thomson's "Seasons" and the Language of Criticism.* U. CA Pr. 1963 o.p.

Sambrook, James. *James Thomson (1700–1748), A Life.* OUP 1991 $59.00. ISBN 0-19-811788-4. An in-depth biography of Thomson's life from 1700 to 1748.

Scott, Mary Jane W. *James Thomson, Anglo-Scot.* U. of Ga. Pr. 1988 $40.00. ISBN 0-8203-0973-7. A biographical and literary-critical study, with particular emphasis on the influences of Thomson's Scottish background on his work.

Walker, Imogene. *James Thomson (B.V.), a Critical Study.* Greenwood repr. of 1950 ed. $38.50. ISBN 0-8371-3738-1

VANBRUGH, SIR JOHN. 1664–1726

Vanbrugh was an architect as well as a playwright, and his massive style of building provoked the following mock-epitaph: "Lie heavy on him, Earth! for he/ Laid many heavy loads on thee!" Vanbrugh is best known for two comedies. In *The Relapse* (1696), which is a sequel to the sentimental play of Colley Cibber, *Love's Last Shift,* Vanbrugh questions the essential goodness of human beings, especially when presented in the form of an inveterate rake. The foppish Lord Foppington in this play is a memorable character. In *The Provoked Wife*

(1697), Vanbrugh has fun with the serious issue of marital incompatibility. Sir John Brute, played with great success by DAVID GARRICK (see Vol. 3), is a caricature of a drunken, dim-witted, loutish aristocrat. Brute's attitudinizing is admirably rendered on stage.

PLAYS BY VANBRUGH

Complete Works. Ed. by Bonamy Dobree and Geoffrey Webb. AMS Pr. repr. of 1928 ed. $225.00. ISBN 0-404-06760-3. Four-volume set of the complete works of Vanbrugh, arranged by type of work.
The Provoked Wife. Ed. by Antony Coleman. St. Martin 1988 $59.95. ISBN 0-7190-1526-X
The Relapse. Ed. by Bernard Harris. Norton 1976 $4.95. ISBN 0-393-90032-0

BOOK ABOUT VANBRUGH

Whistler, L. *Sir John Vanbrugh, Architect and Dramatist, 1664–1726.* Kraus repr. of 1938 ed. $23.00. ISBN 0-527-95850-6. An interesting biography of Vanbrugh.

WALPOLE, HORACE, 4th Earl of Orford. 1717–1797

Born in London, Walpole was educated at Eton and Cambridge. Like his father before him, he entered politics, although his role was more as a chronicling spectator than as a serious participant. After his father died, Walpole inherited a substantial estate. In 1747 he purchased the former coachman's cottage at Twickenham and converted it to a Gothic-style castle, which he named Strawberry Hill. In the process, he began an architectural revival in England.

Walpole's first novel, *The Castle of Otranto* (1764), was Gothic in style, and it became a model for many later Gothic novels in England as well as abroad. Another Gothic work is *The Mysterious Mother* (1768), a strong but gruesome thriller.

Walpole's charming, vivacious, and often brilliant letters (7,000 extant letters written and received) are "a monument to his writing skill as well as an invaluable picture of Georgian England." He always professed to be an amateur in literary affairs, as he amused himself with his private printing press at his Strawberry Hill estate, where he printed many of the first editions of his own works and THOMAS GRAY's *Odes.* An extraordinarily wealthy bachelor, Walpole lived a life of collecting and leisure.

NOVEL BY WALPOLE

The Castle of Otranto. Ed. by W. S. Lewis and Joseph W. Reed. OUP 1982 $3.93. ISBN 0-19-281606-3. A Gothic romance novel about chivalry and knighthood.

NONFICTION BY WALPOLE

Anecdotes of Painting in England. 4 vols. Ayer repr. of 1937 ed. $48.00. ISBN 0-405-02229-8. Short commentaries on the history of painting and artists in England from early times to the accession of George III.
Anecdotes of Painting in England, 1700–1795. Vol. 5. Ed. by F. W. Hilles and P. B. Daghlian. Elliots Bks. 1937 $100.00. ISBN 0-685-45657-9
Honest Diplomat at the Hague: Private Letters, 1715–1716. Ed. by John J. Murray. Ayer repr. of 1955 ed. $22.00. ISBN 0-8369-8112-X. A collection of the private letters of Walpole from 1715 to 1716, providing insight into the domestic situation in Holland and Anglo-Dutch diplomacy of the time.
Memoirs of the Reign of King George II. 3 vols. AMS Pr. repr. of 1846 ed. $115.00. ISBN 0-404-06830-8

Memoirs of the Reign of King George III. Ed. by G. Russell Barker. AMS Pr. repr. of 1894 ed. $105.00. ISBN 0-404-06840-5. The four-volume chronological compilation of the life of King George III.

WORKS BY WALPOLE

Selected Letters of Horace Walpole. Ed. by W. S. Lewis. Bks. Demand $86.00. ISBN 0-317-29273-0. A collection of selected letters of Horace Walpole, aimed at first-time readers.

Yale Edition of Horace Walpole's Correspondence. 48 vols. Ed. by Edwine M. Martz and others. Yale U. Pr. Vols. 1–42 1937–1982 o.p. Vol. 43 1983 $70.00. ISBN 0-300-02711-7. Vols. 44–48 1983 $360.00. ISBN 0-300-02718-4

BOOKS ABOUT WALPOLE

Judd, Gerrit. *Horace Walpole's Memoirs.* NCUP 1959 $8.95. ISBN 0-8084-0161-0

Lewis, Wilmarth. *Horace Walpole.* Natl. Gallery Art o.p. Lectures delivered in 1960 on the life of Walpole.

Sabor, Peter. *Horace Walpole: The Critical Heritage Series.* Routledge 1988 $69.50. ISBN 0-7100-9956-8

Smith, Warren Hunting. *Horace Walpole, Writer, Politician, and Connoisseur.* Yale U. Pr. 1967 o.p. A collection of 19 essays by selected authors, discussing various facets of Walpole's life and works.

WYCHERLEY, WILLIAM. 1640–1716

Wycherley is best known for his dark comedy, which is strong, ironic, and complex. The character of Manly in *The Plain Dealer* (1677) was taken to be a portrait of the author, although Manly is clearly based on Alceste in MOLIÈRE's (see Vol. 2) *Misanthrope. The Country Wife* (1675), Wycherley's most popular play, has a cynical vitality. Taking a hint from a comedy by TERENCE (see Vol. 2), Horner pretends that he is impotent in order to have his way with the ladies, but his success does little to please him. The play demonstrates curious contrasts between truth-speakers and feigners, neither of which can be classified as entirely good or bad. Wycherley's other comedies are *Love in a Wood* (1671) and *The Gentleman Dancing Master* (1673).

PLAYS BY WYCHERLEY

Complete Plays of William Wycherley. Ed. by Gerald Weakes. Norton 1972 o.p.

The Country Wife. Ed. by David Cook and John Swannel. St. Martin 1988 $59.95. ISBN 0-7190-1513-8

The Plain Dealer. Ed. by James L. Smith. Norton 1980 $7.95. ISBN 0-393-90042-8

The Plays of William Wycherley. Ed. by Arthur Friedman. OUP 1979 o.p. The plays of Wycherley, with explanatory notes by renowned editor Arthur Friedman.

BOOKS ABOUT WYCHERLEY

Connely, Willard. *Brawny Wycherley.* Assoc. Faculty Pr. repr. of 1930 ed. o.p. An excellent and enjoyable biography of Wycherley.

McCarthy, B. Eugene. *William Wycherley: A Reference Guide.* G. K. Hall 1985 $55.00. ISBN 0-8161-8184-5. A reference guide listing all editions of the works of Wycherley from 1669 to the present; lists and annotates all works concerning him.

Thompson, James. *Language in Wycherley's Plays: Seventeenth-Century Language Theory and Drama.* U. of Ala. Pr. 1984 $17.75. ISBN 0-8173-0176-3. An examination of Wycherley's plays in the context of Restoration concepts of language, or semantic theory.

CHAPTER 9

The Romantic Period

Marilyn Gaull

> . . . What we have loved
> Others will love, and we will teach them how,
> Instruct them how the mind of Man becomes
> A thousand times more beautiful than the earth
> On which he dwells. . . .
> —WILLIAM WORDSWORTH, *The Prelude*

Chronologically, the romantic period is defined by two kings, George III (1760–1821) and George IV (1821–30); two wars, the American War of Independence (1775–83) and the Napoleonic Wars (1793–1815); a political revolution in France and an industrial revolution in England; the emergence of a popular press and with it the development of a reading public; and a politically engaged middle class. It is this new, unknown, and growing reading public that defined new possibilities of authorship, creating from among themselves and through their tastes and needs the writers we call romantic: WILLIAM BLAKE, SAMUEL TAYLOR COLERIDGE, WILLIAM WORDSWORTH, SIR WALTER SCOTT, ROBERT SOUTHEY, WILLIAM HAZLITT, THOMAS DE QUINCEY, CHARLES LAMB, LORD BYRON, PERCY BYSSHE SHELLEY, MARY WOLLSTONECRAFT SHELLEY, JOHN KEATS, JANE AUSTEN, and such lesser-known figures as William Godwin and JOHN CLARE.

Mostly poets, they formed no school, shared no dogma, and more often than not rejected one another's work, interests, values, and style. Contemporary reviewers and critics identified them by geography, personality, or mannerisms into such groups as the Lake school, the Satanic school, and the Cockney or Regency poets. Yet they did form a kind of community, for, however diverse, they were all reflecting or reacting to the same cultural phenomena: the empowerment of the middle and lower classes, the development of large urban centers, the loss of a traditional agrarian society, the secularization of nature and of art, the development of competitive forces that drove the economy and of aggressive ones that would make England a world power and the English language a universal measure of literacy and culture before the century was over.

In painting as well as writing, some artists turned to traditional subjects, nature and rural lives, while others cultivated a nostalgia for an illusory medieval world, with its ornamental spiritualism and sense of order; still others found in a pastoral Hellenic past, with its myths and formalized eroticism, models for the art they wished to produce. A few, like Byron, Austen, and THOMAS LOVE PEACOCK, cultivated a curious form of parody to point out the hypocrisy and excess that made literature and its readers look ridiculous.

Whatever they used for models or sources of inspiration, however—either nature or earlier art forms—these were modified by the single most powerful faculty cultivated during that period: the creative imagination. In fact, if anything were to characterize this period in literature, architecture, painting, and music—even in philosophy, political life, and science—it was the importance of the imagination.

HISTORY AND CRITICISM

Abrams, Meyer H. *The Mirror and the Lamp: Romantic Critical Tradition.* OUP 1971 $12.95. ISBN 0-19-501471-5. A history of the idea of imagination focusing on the romantic period.

_____. *Natural Supernaturalism: Tradition and Revolution in Romantic Literature.* Norton 1973 repr. of 1971 ed. $14.95. ISBN 0-393-00609-3. Traces the secularization of nature and literature in European romanticism.

Altick, Richard. *The English Common Reader: A Social History of the Mass Reading Public, 1800–1900.* U. Ch. Pr. 1983 repr. of 1957 ed. $22.00. ISBN 0-226-01540-8. Looks at the best-sellers, periodicals, and newspapers that were read by the British public between 1800 and 1900.

Bate, Jonathan. *Shakespeare and the English Romantic Tradition.* OUP 1986 o.p. A study of Shakespeare's influence on the minds and works of the major English romantic poets.

Bush, Douglas. *Mythology and the Romantic Tradition in English Poetry.* HUP 1969 o.p. An exhaustive study of the relationship of classical mythology to the work of the romantic poets.

Dabundo, Laura, ed. *Encyclopedia of Romanticism: Culture in Britain, 1780–1830.* Garland 1992 $95.00. ISBN 0-8240-6997-8. Well-rounded guide to the consciousness of Britain during the late 1700s and 1800s.

Engell, James. *The Creative Imagination: Enlightenment to Romanticism.* HUP 1981 $23.95. ISBN 0-674-17572-7. Examines the creative impulses of English writers from the period of the Enlightenment to the romantic period.

Frye, Northrop. *A Study of English Romanticism.* U. Ch. Pr. 1968 o.p. Includes essays on Beddoes's *Death Jest Book,* Shelley's *Prometheus Unbound,* and Keats's *Endymion;* examines the changes in the language of romantic writers.

Gaull, Marilyn. *English Romanticism: The Human Context.* Norton 1988 $15.95. ISBN 0-393-95547-8. A comprehensive cultural history of the English romantic period.

Halévy, Elie. *England in 1815.* Trans. by E. I. Watkins and D. A. Barker. B & N Imports 1968 o.p.

Hungerford, Edward B. *Shores of Darkness.* Col. U. Pr. 1941 $10.75. A study of the mythic revival in Europe.

Jack, Ian. *English Literature, 1815–1832. Oxford History of English Literature.* Vol. 12. OUP 1963 o.p. A comprehensive analysis of the romantic period; part of a series that examines the major writers of the period.

Jordan, Frank, Jr., ed. *The English Romantic Poets: A Review of Research and Criticism.* Modern Lang. 1985 $50.00. ISBN 0-87352-262-1. The most comprehensive introduction to the criticism and scholarship of English romanticism; periodically updated.

Klancher, Jon. *The Making of English Reading Audiences, 1790–1832.* U. of Wis. Pr. 1986 $27.50. ISBN 0-299-10780-9. A careful and impressively researched essay on cultural history, examining a wide range of writings for diverse audiences—periodicals, political works, travel diaries, and romantic theoretical texts.

Lockridge, Laurence. *The Ethics of Romanticism.* Cambridge U. Pr. 1989 $59.95. ISBN 0-521-35256-8. A monumental study of the idea of ethics in romantic art.

Low, Donald A. *That Sunny Dome: A Portrait of Regency England.* Rowman 1977 o.p.

McGann, Jerome. *The Romantic Ideology: A Critical Investigation.* U. Ch. Pr. 1985 $9.95. ISBN 0-226-55850-9. A controversial study in the critical school called neo-historicism, which attempts to find the suppressed political biases in literary works.

Mellor, Anne K. *English Romantic Irony*. HUP 1980 $20.00. ISBN 0-674-25690-5.
Examines the range of literary structures, styles, and tonalities in romantic irony,
especially in the works of Byron, Keats, and Carlyle.

———. *Romanticism and Feminism*. Ind. U. Pr. 1988 $39.95. ISBN 0-253-35083-2. A
series of compelling new perspectives on the significance of gender in romanticism.

Peckham, Morse. *Beyond the Tragic Vision: The Quest for Identity in the Nineteenth
Century*. Braziller 1962 o.p. A wide-ranging meditation on the personal significance
of public art, literature, and architecture.

Reiman, Donald. *English Romantic Poetry, 1800–1835: A Guide to Information Sources*.
Gale 1979 o.p. Provides information on sources dealing with romantic poetry;
includes an index and bibliography.

———. *Romantics Reviewed: Contemporary Reviews of British Romantic Writers*. 9 vols.
1972 o.p. Original reviews of romantic poetry; indexed.

Renwick, W. L. *English Literature, 1789–1815*. Oxford History of English Literature. 1963
o.p. A historical overview of English literature during the romantic period.

Stillinger, Jack. *Multiple Authorship and the Myth of Solitary Genius*. OUP 1991 $32.50.
ISBN 0-19-506861-0. A series of texts, based in the romantic period, showing that
creativity is collaborative, not isolated.

Wellek, René. *The Romantic Age. A History of Modern Criticism*. Yale U. Pr. 1955 o.p.

White, R. J. *From Waterloo to Peterloo*. Macmillian 1957 o.p.

———. *Life in Regency England*. Putnam Pub. Group 1965 o.p. Excellent social histories.

Williams, Raymond. *Culture and Society, 1780–1950*. Col. U. Pr. 1983 repr. of 1958 ed.
$82.00. ISBN 0-231-02287-5. Examines present-day responses to English society of
the eighteenth century.

Wittreich, J. A. *The Romantics on Milton: Formal Essays and Critical Asides*. Case Western
1970 o.p.

Wordsworth, Jonathan. *Ancestral Voices: Fifty Books from the Romantic Period*. Woodstock 1992 o.p. Chronological survey of the romantic period through a discussion of
50 outstanding books of the period.

———. *William Wordsworth and the Age of English Romanticism*. Rutgers U. Pr. 1987
$65.00. ISBN 0-8135-1273-5

COLLECTIONS

Abrams, M. H., ed. *The Norton Anthology of English Literature*. Vol. 2. Norton 1993
$39.95. ISBN 0-393-96287-3

McGann, Jerome J. *The New Oxford Book of Romantic Verse*. OUP 1993 $30.00. ISBN 0-
19-214158-9

Noyes, Russell, ed. *English Romantic Poetry and Prose*. OUP 1956 $34.50. ISBN 0-19-
501007-8. Biographies, bibliographies, chronologies, personal letters, and background materials that influenced the romantic writers.

Perkins, David, ed. *English Romantic Writers*. HarBraceJ 1967 $45.25. ISBN 0-15-
522660-6. An anthology of poetry and prose, concentrating on 20 major authors;
includes biographies and bibliographies.

POETRY

Romantic poetry is on every level about the poets themselves and how they
conceived their tasks. In their letters, prefaces, and poems, they explored the
nature and function of poetry, the poet, and the experience of the creative
imagination, trying to find a place for the aesthetic in an increasingly technical,
practical, and political world. Their self-conception ranged from the divinely
inspired BLAKE in his prophecies, the demonic COLERIDGE in "Kubla Khan," the
prophetic WORDSWORTH in *The Excursion*, the alienated BYRON in *Childe Harold*,

the politically martyred SHELLEY in *Prometheus Unbound*, and the sensualist KEATS in *The Fall of Hyperion*. All of them attempted in some way to reconcile the claims of the imagination, however conceived, with the demands of reality, society, and specifically their reading public. But the imagination itself is a wayward faculty, not easily controlled or directed, or even stimulated. Consequently, at some point in most of their careers, they all wrote an ode lamenting the loss of the imagination and their poetic powers: Coleridge's "Dejection: An Ode," Wordsworth's *Ode on the Intimations of Immortality*, Shelley's "Ode to the West Wind," and Keats's "Ode to a Nightingale."

The importance of the imagination arose in part from the belief that it accounts for the way reality is perceived, that art originates in the individual perception rather than in the object perceived, a concept illustrated in Blake's aphorism "As a man is, so he sees." Indeed, it is from imaginative perception that the lifeless, meaningless, alien universe and human life itself acquire meaning. This "capacity to imagine what we know," as Shelley explained it, constitutes the "poetry of life." Poetry, dramas, or novels that concentrate on the nature of perception, as opposed to a re-creation of the object perceived, is common to all romantic literature, exemplified in the title of Wordsworth's poem beginning, "My heart leaps up when I behold / A rainbow in the sky." The poem traces the history of his feeling toward the rainbow from childhood to anticipated old age, but nowhere is the rainbow itself described.

This intensely personal and imaginative apprehension of experience or of nature extends to human beings, history, and art. For such unique visions, traditional forms of poetry were also reinvented. Coleridge, for example, adapted the ballad form for the highly artful and mysterious *Rime of the Ancient Mariner*. Wordsworth, Blake, and JOHN CLARE abandoned poetic diction completely in favor of the colloquial. Wordsworth chose the epic of MILTON for his autobiographical *Prelude*, as did Blake for his giant myths and Keats for his pagan ones. Spenserian romance influenced both Byron's *Childe Harold* and Keats's *Eve of St. Agnes*. Elegies, sonnets, odes, and the meditative-descriptive poem all reflected the priority that the poets placed on the subjective, the personal, or the imaginative experience. Their major struggle was to communicate this private life to a new reading public, to justify themselves by relating their art to the demands of contemporary life.

History and Criticism

Bate, Walter Jackson. *The Burden of the Past and the English Poet*. HUP 1970 $13.95. ISBN 0-674-08586-8. Traces the sense of creative paralysis some poets felt from the great achievements of the past.

Beers, Henry A. *A History of English Romanticism in the Eighteenth Century*. Gordian 1966 $75.00. ISBN 0-87752-006-2. A fruitful survey and reevaluation of substreams found in the romantic literary movement; an unabridged and unaltered edition of the 1899 original work.

Bloom, Harold. *Poetry and Repression: Revisionism from Blake to Stevens*. Yale U. Pr. 1976 o.p. Continues a series of studies on the creative ways that poets react to the influence of the past and the anxiety it produces.

_____. *The Visionary Company: A Reading of English Romantic Poetry*. Cornell Univ. Pr. 1971 $15.95. ISBN 0-8014-9117-7. Relates major poets to the prophetic tradition of Spenser and Milton.

Bostetter, Edward E. *The Romantic Ventriloquists: Wordsworth, Coleridge, Keats, Shelley, Byron*. U. of Wash. Pr. 1975 $10.00. ISBN 0-295-95318-7. Depicts the way these major poets projected their voices and values on the world around them.

Butler, Marilyn. *Romantics, Rebels, and Reactionaries: English Literature and Its Background, 1760–1830.* OUP 1982 $27.00. ISBN 0-19-520384-4. A detailed discussion of the ideas comprising the romantic movement; examines individual voices from the eighteenth and nineteenth centuries.

Curran, Stuart. *Poetic Form and British Romanticism.* OUP 1986 $42.50. ISBN 0-19-504019-8. Shows the creative and adaptive ways the major poets used traditional poetic forms.

Fogle, Richard H., comp. *Romantic Poets and Prose Writers.* Harlan Davidson 1967. ISBN 0-88295-513-6. A bibliography intended for use by graduate or advanced undergraduate students; a convenient guide to scholarship of the romantic poets and prose writers.

Hayden, John O. *Romantic Bards and British Reviewers: A Selected Edition of Contemporary Reviews of the Works of Wordsworth, Coleridge, Byron, Keats, and Shelley.* U. of Nebr. Pr. 1976 $35.00. ISBN 0-8032-0773-5

Jackson, J. R. de J. *Poetry of the Romantic Period. Routledge History of English Poetry.* Vol. 4. Routledge 1984 o.p. A comprehensive history and criticism of English poetry during the eighteenth and nineteenth centuries.

Jackson, Wallace. *The Probable and the Marvelous: Blake, Wordsworth, and the Eighteenth Century Critical Tradition.* U. of Ga. Pr. 1978 $25.00. ISBN 0-8203-0439-5. Examines the roles of Blake and Wordsworth within the tradition of romantic thought.

Langbaum, Robert. *The Poetry of Experience: The Dramatic Monologue in Modern Literary Tradition.* U. Ch. Pr. 1986 $9.95. ISBN 0-226-46872-0. Examines the influence of the romantic tradition on later poetry.

Martin, Philip, and Robin Jervis, eds. *Reviewing Romanticism.* St. Martin 1992 $49.95. ISBN 0-312-06801-8. A selection of papers given at King Alfreds College, April 1989, including such topics as editing the Waverly novels, and the politics of the Gothic heroines during the late eighteenth century, among others.

Noyes, Russell, ed. *English Romantic Poetry and Prose.* OUP 1956 $31.00. ISBN 0-19-501007-8

Perkins, David. *The Quest for Permanence: The Symbolism of Wordsworth, Shelley, and Keats.* Bks. Demand repr. of 1969 ed. $84.60. ISBN 0-7837-4175-8

Phelps, William L. *Beginnings of the English Romantic Movement: A Study in Eighteenth Century Literature.* Gordian 1968 $50.00. ISBN 0-87752-084-4

Riasanovsky, Nicholas V. *The Emergence of Romanticism.* OUP 1992 $21.95. ISBN 0-19-507341-X

Shapiro, Barbara. *The Romantic Mother: Narcissistic Patterns in Romantic Poetry.* Johns Hopkins 1983 $22.00. ISBN 0-8018-2896-1. Examines the image of woman as a central figure in romantic poetry.

Watson, J. R. *English Poetry of the Romantic Period, 1789–1830.* Longman 1985 $15.16. ISBN 0-582-49258-0. Discusses English poetry of the romantic period in general terms.

Wilkie, Brian. *Romantic Poets and the Epic Tradition.* U. of Wis. Pr. 1965 o.p. A pioneering work analyzing the principle works of several important English romantic poets—Rossetti, Swinburne, Wilde, Lionel Johnson, Arthur Symons—within the epic tradition.

Woodring, Carl. *Politics in English Romantic Poetry.* HUP 1970 $30.50. ISBN 0-674-68882-1. Examines the politics contained within the works of Romantic poets.

Collections

Ashfield, Andrew, ed. *Women Romantic Poets, 1770–1838: An Anthology.* St. Martin 1993. ISBN 0-7190-3789-1. An anthology of aristocratic and working-class women poets; contains a critical introduction and detailed bibliography.

Heath, William, ed. *Major British Poets of the Romantic Period.* Macmillan 1973. ISBN 0-02-352900-8

Lonsdale, Roger. *The New Oxford Book of Eighteenth Century Verse*. OUP 1989 $15.95. ISBN 0-19-282054-0

Scrivener, Michael. *Poetry and Reform: Periodical Verse from the English Democratic Press, 1792–1824*. Wayne St. U. Pr. 1992 $34.95. ISBN 0-8143-2378-2

Wright, David, ed. *The Penguin Book of English Romantic Verse*. Viking Penguin 1985 o.p.

FICTION

Like the drama of the romantic period, the novel was also extremely popular. It had a wide audience of newly literate, mostly female, middle-class readers who were often censored for reading fiction. But, as JANE AUSTEN explains in *Northanger Abbey*, a novel about the pleasures and perils of novel reading, novels were never held in high esteem by reviewers, and they made few lasting contributions to the literary tradition. The most popular novels were the Gothic tales produced in the closing decades of the eighteenth century: novels set in exotic places, mostly castles in the mountains of Italy, about ill-fated love, disputed property, sinister villains, unspeakable crimes, restless ghosts, victimized heroines, and the virtuous heroes who overcame real or imagined danger to rescue them. ANN RADCLIFFE's *The Mysteries of Udolpho* (1794) was the best of these. The characters in such novels displayed the refinements of sentiment and excess of emotion portrayed in Henry Mackenzie's *Man of Feeling* (1771) from which they all seemed to be descended. Another popular form, the horror novel, depicted unrelieved and often gratuitous torture, violence, and, usually, anticlerical feeling inspired by the French Revolution. The early horror novel, such as William Beckford's *The History of Caliph Vathek* (1786) and MATTHEW GREGORY LEWIS's *Ambrosio, or, the Monk* (1796), was primarily visual in effect, but it took a psychological turn with MARY SHELLEY's *Frankenstein, or, The Modern Prometheus* (1818), John Polidori's *The Vampyre* (1819), Charles Maturin's *Melmouth the Wanderer* (1820), and JAMES HOGG's *Private Memoirs and Confessions of a Justified Sinner* (1824).

The major novelists of the period were Jane Austen, whose subdued and subtle representation of ordinary human behavior in colloquial language set a standard for what came to be known as the well-crafted novel, and Sir WALTER SCOTT, who single-handedly invented the historical romance.

History and Criticism

Allen, Walter. *The English Novel: A Short Critical History*. Phoenix 1954 o.p. Finest critical histories of the English novel, from Bunyan to Lawrence.

Auerbach, Nina. *Communities of Women: An Idea in Fiction*. HUP 1978 $19.95. ISBN 0-674-15168-2. Studies the idea of community among women in novels of the romantic period.

Baker, Ernest Albert. *A History of the English Novel*. 11 vols. B & N Imports 1966–77. Vol. 6. *Edgeworth, Austen, Scott*. 1979 $22.50. ISBN 0-06-480051-2. This volume focuses on the romantic novel.

Beer, Patricia. *Reader, I Married Him: A Study of the Women Characters of Jane Austen, Charlotte Brontë, Elizabeth Gaskell and George Eliot*. B & N Imports 1977 repr. of 1974 ed. o.p. A compilation of essays evaluating the depictions of women in English novels.

Block, Andrew. *The English Novel, 1740–1850: A Catalogue Including Prose Romances, Short Stories, and Translations of Foreign Fiction*. Greenwood rev. ed. 1982 repr. of 1961 ed. $59.50. ISBN 0-313-23224-5. A valuable reference source.

Cotton, Daniel. *The Civilized Imagination: A Study of Ann Radcliffe, Jane Austen, and Sir Walter Scott.* Cambridge U. Pr. 1985 $10.95. ISBN 0-521-30172-6. An in-depth intertextual study examining the works of Radcliffe, Austen, and Scott in the social context of their time.

Fleishman, Avrom. *The English Historical Novel: Walter Scott to Virginia Woolf.* Johns Hopkins 1971 $13.95. ISBN 0-8018-1433-2. A history of historical fiction.

Gilbert, Sandra M., and Susan Gubar. *The Madwoman in the Attic: A Study of Women and the Literary Imagination in the Nineteenth Century.* Yale U. Pr. 1979 $19.95. ISBN 0-300-02596-3. Examines the fall of humankind in English literature; discusses the influence of Milton on Emily Dickinson's work.

Kelly, Gary. *English Fiction of the Romantic Period, 1789–1830.* Longman 1989 $44.95. ISBN 0-582-49261-0

Kiely, Robert. *The Romantic Novel in England.* Bks. Demand repr. of 1972 ed. $76.20. ISBN 0-7837-4160-X. Defines the intellectual context—premises of taste, the philosophical and psychological preoccupations—in which the romantic novel flourished; examines particular works.

Kroeber, Karl. *Romantic Narrative Art.* U. of Wis. Pr. 1966 $10.95. ISBN 0-299-02244-7. The first comprehensive survey of narrative poetry in the romantic era; examines the ballad, imaginative story, realistic tale.

Levine, George. *The Realistic Imagination: English Fiction from Frankenstein to Lady Chatterley.* U. Ch. Pr. 1983 $10.95. ISBN 0-226-47551-4. Literary theory and criticism on the "realistic" in nineteenth-century literature; contains a bibliography and indexes.

Lucas, John. *The Literature of Change: Studies in the Nineteenth-Century Provincial Novel.* B & N Imports 1980 o.p. Examines the nature of social change in provincial novels; excludes George Eliot.

Ousby, Ian. *Bloodhounds of Heaven: The Detective in English Fiction from Godwin to Doyle.* HUP 1976 $17.95. ISBN 0-674-07657-5

Railo, Eilo. *The Haunted Castle: A Study of the Elements of English Fiction.* Gordon Pr. 1973 $300.00. ISBN 0-87968-072-6. An extensive study of romanticism in English literature.

Tracy, Ann. *The Gothic Novel (1790–1830).* U. Pr. of Ky. 1981 $24.00. ISBN 0-8131-1397-0. Includes plot summaries and index to motifs.

Twitchell, James B. *The Living Dead: A Study of the Vampire in Romantic Literature.* Duke 1981 $12.95. ISBN 0-8223-0789-8

Van Ghent, Dorothy. *The English Novel: Form and Function.* HarpC 1961 o.p.

Varma, Devendra P. *The Gothic Flame: Being a History of the Gothic Novel in England— Its Origin, Efflorescence, Disintegration, and Residuary Influences.* Scarecrow 1987 repr. of 1957 ed. $25.00. ISBN 0-8108-2077-3. A study of the nature and importance of the Gothic impulse in Gothic novels; traces the growth of the Gothic novel in literature. Thorough, entertaining, and scholarly.

DRAMA

Although the theater flourished during the romantic period, little of the drama has survived, for several curious reasons. The theaters themselves still operated under the severe licensing restrictions imposed in 1737 (which were not suspended until 1843). A potent social force, the licensing acts were designed to discourage political unrest and religious deviation by restricting the spoken drama to a few carefully censored "patent" theaters, primarily Drury Lane and Covent Garden. Since most of the great dramas from the time of the Greeks were about kings or gods, eliminating these figures as subjects for the stage effectively ended the great dramatic tradition. Cavernous theaters and raucous audiences overwhelmed whatever dialogue escaped the censors. In place of the dramas, such unlicensed theaters as Sadler's Wells or Astley's

Circus presented spectacles, melodramas (a form of drama with musical accompaniment imported from France), pantomime (a seasonal comic improvisation with a standard plot and technically creative stagecraft), or animal shows resembling the contemporary circus.

SHAKESPEARE and MARLOWE and other major playwrights from the past were adapted to the contemporary stage by eliminating allusions to mad kings (because George III was considered insane) and religion. Contemporary writers used the dramatic form and attempted to have their plays staged: WORDSWORTH's *The Borderers* (1796–97); BYRON's *Manfred* (1817), *Cain* (1821), and *Werner* (1821–22); SHELLEY's *Prometheus Unbound* (1821), *The Cenci* (1819), and *Hellas* (1821); KEATS's *Otho the Great* (1819); and COLERIDGE's *Remorse* (1813), which actually was produced on stage. It was not nearly so successful, however, as Charles Maturin's *Bertram, or, The Castle of St. Aldobrand* (1816), which Coleridge attacked as a symptom of the depraved state of public taste. Ironically, the more the government censored the political and religious content of plays, the more playwrights drew on other forbidden areas of experience, depicting necrophilia, incest, and all forms of evil associated with the abuse of power.

Two dramatists are remembered for their literary influence: JOANNA BAILLIE (1762–1851), whose 1798 collection *Plays on the Passions* showed a series of characters struggling with some master passion, and T. L. Beddoes (1803–1849), whose *Death's Jest-Book* (1829; published 1850), a verse-drama, recalls the Renaissance in style, reflects the romantic period in substance, and, in its antic humor, anticipates the modern theater of the absurd.

History and Criticism

Altick, Richard. *The Shows of London.* HUP 1978 $40.00. ISBN 0-674-80731-6. An encyclopedic illustrated collection of popular entertainments in London during the eighteenth and nineteenth centuries.

Arundell, Dennis. *The Story of Sadler's Wells, 1683–1977.* Rowman 1978 o.p.

Barranger, Milly S. *Theatre Past and Present: An Introduction.* Wadsworth Pub. 1984 o.p. An unusually complete and well-designed introductory textbook.

Beaumont, Cyril W. *History of Harlequin.* Ayer 1967 repr. of 1926 ed. $18.00. ISBN 0-405-08248-7. Discusses the Harlequin; lists principal works consulted for sources on the Harlequin.

Booth, Michael R. *English Melodrama.* Jenkins 1965 o.p. Defines the golden age of melodrama in the nineteenth century; traces drama's background.

Booth, Michael R., and others, eds. *The Revels History of Drama in English.* Vol. 6. Routledge Chapman & Hall o.p. A history of the theater neglected by earlier sources; includes illustrations and an index of plays.

Conolly, Leonard W. *The Censorship of English Drama: 1737–1824.* Huntington Lib. 1976 $17.97. ISBN 0-87328-068-7. Examines the progression of censorship in English drama through the eighteenth and nineteenth centuries; includes a bibliography and index.

Cox, Jeffrey. *In the Shadows of Romance: Romantic Tragic Drama in Germany, England, and France.* Ohio St. U. Pr. 1987 o.p. About melodrama, the key dramatic form during the period.

Disher, Maurice W. *Clowns and Pantomimes.* 1925. Ayer 1968 repr. of 1925 ed. $36.95. ISBN 0-405-08446-3

Donohue, Joseph W., Jr. *Dramatic Character in the English Romantic Movement.* Princeton U. Pr. 1970 o.p. A study of drama, theater, and criticism in the English romantic age and the period leading up to it; discusses the romantic concept of dramatic character.

————. *Theater in the Age of Kean*. Rowman 1975 o.p. Examines the state of the theater in the 1790s; follows the growth of, and focuses on, the "patent" theater.

Evans, Bertrand. *Gothic Drama from Walpole to Shelley*. U. CA Pr. 1947 o.p. An intense yet accessible study of the Gothic novel's relationship to drama in the romantic movement.

Fletcher, Richard. *English Romantic Drama, 1795–1843: A Critical History*. Exposition Pr. 1966 o.p.

Genest, John. *Some Account of the English Stage from the Restoration in 1660 to 1830*. B. Franklin 1965 o.p. A remarkable contemporary account of the English stage, originally published in 1832.

Gillespie, Patti P., and Kenneth M. Cameron. *Western Theatre: Revolution and Revival*. Macmillan 1984 o.p. Considers the changing relation between stage, actor, and audience through Western history.

Hartnoll, Phyllis, ed. *Concise Oxford Companion to the Theatre*. OUP 1993 $14.95. ISBN 0-19-282574-7

————. *Oxford Companion to the Theatre*. OUP 1983 $55.00. ISBN 0-19-211564-4. A valuable reference tool, with full bibliography and many illustrations.

Heller, Janet Ruth. *Coleridge, Lamb, Hazlitt, and the Reader of Drama*. U. of Mo. Pr. 1990 $32.50. ISBN 0-8262-0718-9. Focuses on romantic dramatic theory and the belief that stage spectacle is inappropriate for Shakespeare.

Leacroft, Richard, and Helen Leacroft. *Theatre and Playhouse*. Heinemann Ed. 1988 $17.95. ISBN 0-413-52940-1. Isometric cutaways of theater buildings from all periods; uniquely valuable for the student.

Nicoll, Allardyce. *British Drama*. Ed. by J. C. Trewin. B & N Imports 6th rev. ed. 1978 o.p.

————. *A History of English Drama, 1660–1900*. 6 vols. Cambridge U. Pr. 1959 o.p.

Richardson, Alan. *A Mental Theater: Poetic Drama and Consciousness in the Romantic Age*. Pa. St. U. Pr. 1988 $22.50. ISBN 0-271-00612-9. Romantic theater as a drama of the internal world.

Saxon, A. H. *Enter Foot and Horse: A History of the Hippodrama in England and France*. Yale U. Pr. 1968 o.p.

Strathan, Carl. *Britain's Theatrical Periodicals, 1720–1967*. NY Pub. Lib. 1972 $20.00. ISBN 0-87104-034-4. Evidence, from magazines and journals, of the popularity of the theater during the romantic period.

Collections

Booth, Michael R., ed. *English Plays of the Nineteenth Century*. 5 vols. OUP 1969–76. Vol. 1 o.p. Vol. 2 o.p. Vol. 3 $82.00. ISBN 0-19-812465-1. Vol. 4 $79.00. ISBN 0-19-812466-X. Vol. 5 o.p. Looks at dramas during the eighteenth century, including comedies, farces, pantomimes, extravaganzas, and burlesques.

Cox, Jeffrey N., ed. *Seven Gothic Dramas: 1789–1825*. Ohio U. Pr. 1992 $45.00. ISBN 0-8214-1015-6. A must-have for students of British drama and of literary gothicism; includes *The Kentish Barons*, *Julia of Louvain*, *The Castle Spectre*, *The Capture*, *De Monfort*, *Bertram*, and *Presumption*.

Rogers, Katherine, ed. *The Signet Classic Book of Eighteenth and Nineteenth Century British Drama*. NAL-Dutton 1979 o.p. Contains Boucicault, *The Octaroon*; Gilbert, *Ruddigore*; Wilde, *Importance of Being Earnest*.

Rowell, George, ed. *Nineteenth-Century Plays*. Oxford Pap. Ser. OUP 1972 o.p. Contains Jerrold, *Black Ey'd Susan*; Bulwer-Lytton, *Money*; Reade and Taylor, *Masks and Faces*; Boucicault, *The Colleen Bawn*; Bradon and Hazlewood, *Lady Audley's Secret*; Taylor, *The Ticket-of-Leave Man*; Robertson, *Caste*; Albery, *Two Roses*; Lewis, *The Bells*; and Grundy, *A Pair of Spectacles*.

NONFICTION

The proliferation of essays and new forms of nonfiction prose during the romantic period may be attributed to the new popularity of two kinds of periodicals: the magazine (a monthly collection of miscellaneous writing) and reviews (quarterly collections of book reviews and literary commentaries). New machinery for producing inexpensive paper and efficient printing lowered the cost of such periodicals and made them more available to a wider audience than novels and volumes of poetry. Extended literacy, increased political awareness, an enlarged urban population engaged in manufacturing or trade, and the productive use of leisure time created an audience for the practical, informative, inspiring, opinionated, didactic, or merely diverting informal or familiar essay. Presented in nontechnical language, in a relaxed and nonargumentative tone, intimate manner, and colloquial diction, the subjects were an index to the culture of the period: history, architecture, public figures, holidays, education, the theater, religion, morals, fashions, social customs, poetry, novels, contemporary events, travel, or practical matters relating to domestic life, economy, topography, and science.

The most famous essayists, WILLIAM HAZLITT, THOMAS DE QUINCEY, and CHARLES LAMB, all cultivated unique styles and narrative voices, authoritative, engaging, and personal, capturing the subjectivity that characterized the poetry being written by their friends—WORDSWORTH, COLERIDGE, and KEATS. And they all contributed to the *London Magazine*, a free-wheeling and urbane publication founded in 1820 that reflected the tastes and interests of the London literary community. More profitable than other forms of writing, the essay provided an alternative means of income to poets such as Coleridge and SOUTHEY, while it sustained a whole occupation practiced by writers who came to be called "men of letters."

The literary commentary that appeared in *The Edinburgh Review*, founded in 1802, set a standard for derision, scathing invective, and ill-mannered contempt that other periodicals, such as *The Quarterly*, founded in 1808, imitated. Claiming to protect public taste, these commentaries sent authors into such despair that BYRON and SHELLEY thought that Keats, who died of tuberculosis, had been killed by a review of *Endymion* in *The Quarterly*. THOMAS LOVE PEACOCK's cynical attack on contemporary verse in *The Literary Miscellany* (1820) evoked Shelley's *Defense of Poetry* (1821). Indeed, the antagonism between the reviews and the experimental and politically liberal poets produced a whole series of literary essays defining, defending, promoting poetry—teaching, as Wordsworth said, the art by which poems were to be seen, creating the taste by which they were to be enjoyed.

History and Criticism

Bauer, Josephine. *The London Magazine, 1820–29.* Rosenkilde & Boyger 1953 o.p.

Cafarelli, Annette Wheeler. *Prose in the Age of Poets: Romanticism and the Biographical Narrative from Johnson to De Quincey.* U. of Pa. Pr. 1990 $31.95. ISBN 0-8122-8198-5. Examines experimentation in style in the biographical narrative, starting with Johnson.

Clive, John. *Scotch Reviewers: "The Edinburgh Review," 1802–1815.* HUP 1957 o.p.

Collins, Arthur S. *The Profession of Letters, 1780–1832.* Routledge 1928 o.p.

Gross, John. *The Rise and Fall of the Man of Letters: English Literary Life Since 1800.* I. R. Dee 1992 $14.95. ISBN 1-56663-000-2

McFarland, Thomas. *Romantic Cruxes: The English Essayists and the Spirit of the Age.* OUP 1988 $36.00. ISBN 0-19-812895-9. Explores the reasons for the decline of Lamb, Hazlitt, and De Quincey's influence in the twentieth century.

Nabholtz, John R. *"My Reader, My Fellow-Labourer": A Study of English Romantic Prose.* U. of Mo. Pr. 1986 $22.00. ISBN 0-8262-0491-0. Distills decades of thought into a valuable, concentrated study.

Roper, Derek. *Reviewing before "The Edinburgh," 1788–1802.* U. of Delaware Pr. 1978 $35.00. ISBN 0-87413-128-6. A collection of review articles and an appraisal of them; sets the articles in context.

Shine, Hill, and Helen Chadwick Shine. *"The Quarterly Review" under Gifford.* U. of NC Pr. 1949 o.p.

Sullivan, Alvin, ed. *British Literary Magazines: The Romantic Age, 1789–1836.* Greenwood 1983 $69.50. ISBN 0-313-22872-8. Introduction by John O. Hayden; a research tool providing profiles of 84 journals.

Thomas, Donald. *A Long Time Burning: The History of Literary Censorship in England.* 1969 o.p.

Williams, Raymond. *The Long Revolution.* Greenwood 1975 repr. of 1961 ed. $35.00. ISBN 0-8371-8244-1. Traces the role of the periodical press in the extension of literacy in England.

Collections

Hayden, John O. *Romantic Bards and British Reviewers: A Selected Edition of the Contemporary Reviews of the Works of William Wordsworth, Samuel Taylor Coleridge, Byron, Keats, and Shelley.* U. of Nebr. Pr. 1976 $35.00. ISBN 0-8032-0773-5. Explains why reviewing was popular during the romantic period; reviewers of Wordsworth, Coleridge, Byron, Keats, and Shelley represented.

Nabholtz, John, R. *Prose of the British Romantic Movement.* Macmillan 1974 o.p. Mostly critical pieces by poets; with biographies and bibliographies.

Reiman, Donald. *The Romantics Reviewed: Contemporary Reviews of British Romantic Writers.* 9 vols. Gale 1972 o.p. Facsimile reprints of reviews published in various British periodicals, from 1793 to 1824: includes the Lake poets, Byron and Regency society poets, Shelley, Keats, and London radical writers.

Ward, William S. *Literary Reviews in British Periodicals, 1798–1820: A Bibliography.* 2 vols. Garland 1972 o.p. Contains 15,000 reviews.

CHRONOLOGY OF AUTHORS

Chatterton, Thomas. 1752–1770	Landor, Walter Savage. 1775–1864
Crabbe, George. 1754–1832	Hazlitt, William. 1778–1830
Blake, William. 1757–1827	Hunt, Leigh. 1784–1859
Burns, Robert. 1759–1796	De Quincey, Thomas. 1785–1859
Baillie, Joanna. 1762–1851	Peacock, Thomas Love. 1785–1866
Hogg, James. 1770–1835	Lord Byron, George Gordon.
Wordsworth, William. 1770–1850	1788–1824
Scott, Sir Walter. 1771–1832	Shelley, Percy Bysshe. 1792–1822
Coleridge, Samuel Taylor. 1772–1834	Clare, John. 1793–1864
Southey, Robert. 1774–1843	Keats, John. 1795–1821
Austen, Jane. 1775–1817	Shelley, Mary Wollstonecraft.
Lamb, Charles. 1775–1834	1797–1851

AUSTEN, JANE. 1775–1817

The seventh of eight children (six of whom were brothers), Jane Austen grew up in the sheltered atmosphere of a country parsonage and was educated at home by her father. She supplemented his vast library with contemporary novels borrowed from a lending library and with periodic visits to the London theater. Except for these visits to London and a brief stay at fashionable Bath during her father's final illness, she spent most of her life in the country—a maiden aunt involved in raising children, caring for aging parents and for her sister, Cassandra, who also remained unmarried. Her most fruitful years, between 1809 and 1817, were spent in a cottage in Chawton, inherited by one of her brothers upon the death of a childless cousin who had adopted him. She wrote to amuse herself and her family, focusing on the topics that interested them: social relations, courtship, marriage, property, and propriety.

Before she died at age 42, Jane Austen wrote six novels that altered the course of literary history. She sold *Northanger Abbey*, a parody of Gothic romance readers and reviewers, to a publisher in 1798, but, when he did not publish it, she repurchased the copyright and the book appeared posthumously in 1818. *Sense and Sensibility*, published anonymously in 1811, explores the dangers of fashionably excessive feeling; *Pride and Prejudice*, her most popular novel, published in 1813, focuses on marriage and property; *Mansfield Park* (1814) concerns a young girl who wins a wealthy husband through her virtue; *Emma* (1815), about a wealthy, witty, but intrusive heroine, interested both the Prince Regent and SIR WALTER SCOTT; and *Persuasion* (1818) explores loss through the long separation that a heroine endures between a rejected marriage proposal and a second chance. The incomplete *Sanditon* reflects the satirical direction Austen was moving in, but all of the novels share that rare comic spirit, the wry perspective, the sense of fun that Austen brought to the serious problems of her age and class.

About Austen's work Somerset Maugham wrote, "Nothing very much happens in her books, and yet, when you come to the bottom of a page, you eagerly turn it to learn what will happen next. . . . The novelist who has the power to achieve this has the most precious gift a novelist can possess."

NOVELS BY AUSTEN

The Complete Novels of Jane Austen. Viking Penguin 1989 $15.00. ISBN 0-14-010649-9. Includes *Sense and Sensibility, Pride and Prejudice, Mansfield Park, Emma, Northanger Abby*, and *Persuasion*.

Emma. 1816. Ed. by Stephen U. Parrish. Norton 1993 $9.95. ISBN 0-393-96014-5. The story of beautiful, clever, and rich Emma Wodehouse and her hunt for a husband.

Mansfield Park. 1814. Knopf 1992 $20.00. ISBN 0-679-41269-7. Young Fanny Price, one of nine children of a very poor family, is sent to live with her wealthy aunt at Mansfield Park where she is received with little welcome from everyone except her cousin Edmund, with whom she falls in love.

Northanger Abbey. 1818. Knopf 1992 $14.50. ISBN 0-679-41715-X. The romantic folly of young Catherine Morland and her visit to ancient Northanger Abbey, the ancestral home of the novel's handsome hero, where her hopes of romance are sparked amid Gothic horrors.

Persuasion. 1818. McKay 1992 $14.50. ISBN 0-679-40986-6. After years apart, unmarried Anne Elliot encounters the dashing naval officer others persuaded her to reject, as he now courts the rash and younger Luisa Musgrove.

Pride and Prejudice. 1813. Dearborn Trade 1993 $5.95. ISBN 0-582-07720-6. Delicate but telling satire of the English country gentlefolk of Austen's day, featuring Elizabeth Bennet, one of the most delightful heroines of all time.

Sense and Sensibility. 1811. McKay 1992 $16.50. ISBN 0-679-40987-4. Story of two sisters—Marianne and Elinor—who have to overcome many difficulties in order to achieve happiness and success.

The Watsons. 1805. Humanities 1985 repr. of 1927 ed. $18.95. ISBN 0-485-10503-9. Tantalizing and highly delightful story whose vitality and optimism center on the marital prospects of the Watson sisters in a small provincial town. Unfinished fragment, first published posthumously in 1871.

WORKS BY AUSTEN

Catharine and Other Writings. Ed. by Margaret Anne Doody and Douglas Murray. OUP 1993 $9.95. ISBN 0-19-282823-1. Collection of Austen's poetry and "youthful prose" (*Publishers Weekly*).

The History of England. 1791. Algonquin 1993. Witty and satiric journal by Austen, illustrated by her sister Cassandra and with an introduction by A. S. Byatt.

Letters, 1796–1817. Ed. by R. W. Chapman. *World's Class. Ser.* OUP 1952 o.p.

Letters to Her Sister Cassandra and Others. Ed. by R. W. Chapman. OUP repr. of 1952 ed. o.p. Letters covering rare periods when the two sisters were apart.

Oxford Illustrated Jane Austen. 6 vols. Ed. by R. W. Chapman. OUP 1987 $85.00. ISBN 0-19-254707-0. Includes juvenilia.

BOOKS ABOUT AUSTEN

Apperson, George. *Jane Austen Dictionary. Studies in Fiction Ser.* Haskell 1969 repr. of 1932 ed. $75.00. ISBN 0-8383-0909-7. A citation of every person, place, book, and author mentioned in Austen's works.

Austen-Leigh, J. E. *Memoir of Jane Austen, by Her Nephew.* Rprt. Serv. 1992 repr. of 1926 ed. $79.00. ISBN 0-7812-7428-1. First-hand account by Austen's nephew; contains vivid, personal recollections.

Brown, Julia Polwitt. *Jane Austen: Social Change and Literary Form.* HUP 1979 o.p.

Butler, Marilyn,. *Jane Austen and the War of Ideas.* OUP 1988 $19.95. ISBN 0-19-812968-8. Examines the different schools of writings with which Austen is associated.

Chapman, R. W. *Jane Austen: Facts and Problems.* OUP 1948 o.p. Biographical and critical problems with bibliography, chronology, iconography.

Halperin, John. *The Life of Jane Austen.* Johns Hopkins 1984 $25.00. ISBN 0-8018-3410-4. In-depth biography of Austen, focusing on her family and including a discussion of each of her completed novels.

Hardwick, Michael. *A Guide to Jane Austen.* Scribner 1982 o.p.

Johnson, Claudia L. *Jane Austen: Women, Politics, and the Novel.* U. Ch. Pr. 1990 $27.50. ISBN 0-226-40138-3. Places Austen in a tradition of eighteenth-century women novelists who are skeptical of conservative ideology.

Lascelles, Mary. *Jane Austen and Her Art.* 1977 Arden Lib. repr. of 1939 ed. o.p. A masterly study of the writer and of the craft of fiction.

Litz, A. Walton. *Jane Austen: A Study of Her Artistic Development.* Chatto 1965 o.p. An excellent critical study of Austen and her writings.

Mansell, Darrel. *The Novels of Jane Austen: An Interpretation.* Humanities 1978 repr. of 1973 ed. o.p. Study of how Austen's heroines prepare themselves for their positions in the world.

Moler, Kenneth L. *Jane Austen's Art of Allusion. Landmark Ed.* U. of Nebr. Pr. 1968 o.p. Discusses Austen's frequent use of borrowed literary material.

Monaghan, David, ed. *Jane Austen in a Social Context.* B & N Imports 1981 o.p. Collection of essays on the social life of Austen's characters.

Mudrick, Marvin. *Jane Austen: Irony as Defense and Discovery.* U. CA Pr. 1968 o.p.

Paris, Bernard J. *Character and Conflict in Jane Austen's Novels: A Psychological Approach.* Wayne St. U. Pr. 1979 o.p. Examines Austen's novels as models of organic unity.

Tave, Stuart M. *Some Words of Jane Austen.* U. Ch. Pr. 1973 o.p. A classic study of a novelist's linguistic habits, showing what repetitive use of key words reveals about her value system.

BAILLIE, JOANNA. 1762–1851

Although only five of them were produced during her lifetime, Joanna Baillie's 22 plays on the passions, published between 1798 and 1812, supposedly initiated a revival of the drama during the romantic period. Born into a dour and religious family in Glasgow, Scotland, educated at a girls' boarding school, Baillie moved to London in 1783, when her brother inherited the school of anatomy and museum founded earlier by their uncle, William Hunter. Although Baillie remained unmarried, her home in Hampstead, which she shared with her mother and unmarried sister, attracted the most famous writers in England, including COLERIDGE, BYRON, SOUTHEY, LANDOR, and her most forceful advocate, SIR WALTER SCOTT.

According to the introduction that she wrote to the plays, each one was supposed to demonstrate the inner struggle of an individual with a dominating passion. However appealing actors may have found the opportunity to present boundless anger, hate, jealousy, pride, and revenge, plays about single passions were too monotonous, subtle, introspective, and philosophical for contemporary taste—and they were written in unfashionable blank verse as well. But the psychology was interesting—to see how people with dominant passions respond to crises, the way in which they reveal or fail to reveal intense feelings in intimate situations. Baillie contributed to the development of a secular morality suited to a stage from which religion and religious texts had been banished. And she translated contemporary theories of human behavior into drama. The mystery of Joanna Baillie was how anyone from such a sheltered environment and with such limited experience could conceive of the vast range of material from which she created her dramas.

PLAYS BY BAILLIE

A Series of Plays. 1798. Woodstock 1990 o.p. With an introduction by Jonathan Wordsworth.

BOOK ABOUT BAILLIE

Carhart, Margaret. *The Life and Work of Joanna Baillie.* Shoe String 1970 repr. of 1923 ed. $29.50. ISBN 0-208-00917-5

BLAKE, WILLIAM. 1757–1827

Blake, an engraver by training, is unique in English literature as a man who was a great pictorial artist as well as a great poet. He printed and published all of his own works. Every page was hand-lettered and had to be cut in reverse, mirror-image fashion, in copper, before being printed. It was then ornamented and illustrated and painted over in watercolors by the poet-engraver and his wife. Every copy was in a sense a first edition, because every copy differed from every other copy. Blake's illustrations of the Book of Job, reproduced in *Blake's Job*, and for Robert Blair's *Grave* (published as *Blake's Grave*), are his masterpieces. He also illustrated the *Divine Comedy* by DANTE (see Vol. 2), the poems of THOMAS GRAY, *The Canterbury Pilgrims*, and *Paradise Lost* by MILTON.

Blake was a visionary whose social criticism was much ahead of his day. He worked as an illustrator and engraver against financial odds and in poor health—for clients whom his independence often displeased—assisted by his acquiescent wife and encouraged by a few believing friends. He was quite isolated from other poets of his time and was usually considered slightly mad when noticed at all in the literary world. But the short poems of the *Innocence* (1789) and *Experience* (1794) volumes—such as "The Tyger"—have come to be recognized as among the finest and most enduring of the English language. The long and difficult "Prophetic Books" develop an elaborate religious mythology, which Blake said he derived from his "visions." He was a Christian with a difference, despising the hypocrisy he found in religious institutions and preaching a sort of natural Christianity in which human beings were free to develop—and to love each other—without artificial restraints. His genius has been fully appreciated only in the twentieth century, and an enormous body of commentary has developed around all of his works. Even his most complex "prophetic" poems are now held to be fully intelligible, and the simplest of his lyrics may contain the essence of a profound philosophy. Critical disputes abound, and sharply divergent interpretations are commonplace.

POETRY BY BLAKE

The Book of Thel: A Facsimile and a Critical Text. 1789. Ed. by Nancy Bogen. Bks. Demand repr. of 1971 ed. $24.50. ISBN 0-8357-7343-4. A reproduction in full color of the copy in the Berg Collection of the New York Public Library.

The Book of Urizen. 1794. U. of Miami Pr. 1966 $7.95. ISBN 0-87024-065-X. A poetic work that tells of the fall of humankind through the alienation of reason.

Poems and Prophecies. Ed. by Max Plowman. Biblio Dist. 1978 repr. of 1927 ed. o.p.

Songs of Innocence and of Experience. 1794. OUP 1977 $11.95. ISBN 0-19-281089-8. With an introduction by Geoffrey Keynes.

WORKS BY BLAKE

Blake's America, a Prophecy, and Europe, a Prophecy. Fine Arts Ser. Dover 1984 $7.95. ISBN 0-486-24548-9. Blake's criticism of Christianity.

The Complete Poetry and Prose of William Blake. Ed. by David V. Erdman. U. CA Pr. rev. ed. 1981 $47.50. ISBN 0-520-04473-8. A standard edition, but with sparse punctuation and often eccentric commentary.

Complete Writings of William Blake, with Variant Readings. Ed. by Geoffrey Keynes. *Oxford Stand. Authors Ser.* OUP 1966 $39.95. ISBN 0-19-254157-9. An accessible standard edition.

The Marriage of Heaven and Hell. 1790. OUP 1975 $12.95. ISBN 0-19-281167-3. Blake's principal prose work; sets forth his doctrine of Contranes and emphasizes the negative side of his dualistic thinking.

Portable Blake. Ed. by Alfred Kazin. *Viking Portable Lib.* Viking Penguin 1977 $11.00. ISBN 0-14-015026-9. Good introduction.

Selected Prose and Poetry. Ed. by Northrop Frye. *Modern College Lib. Ser.* Random 1966 o.p. Judicious selection, introduction, and notes by a preeminent Blake scholar.

William Blake's Illustrations of the Book of Job. Ed. by S. Foster Damon. U. Pr. of New Eng. 1966 o.p. Contains some of Blake's most famous engravings.

William Blake's Poetry and Designs. Ed. by John E. Grant and Mary L. Johnson. *Norton Critical Eds.* Norton 1979 o.p. An especially useful volume; valuable criticism and good bibliography.

William Blake's Writings. 2 vols. Ed. by Gerald E. Bentley, Jr. *Oxford Eng. Texts Ser.* OUP 1979 o.p. Reliable standard edition.

BOOKS ABOUT BLAKE

Behrendt, Stephen C. *Reading William Blake.* St. Martin 1992 $45.00. ISBN 0-312-06835-2

Bentley, Gerald E., Jr., ed. *William Blake: The Critical Heritage. Critical Heritage Ser.* Routledge 1975 $69.50. ISBN 0-7100-8234-7. Especially valuable in demonstrating the extraordinary shifts in the critical attitudes toward Blake.

Blackstone, Bernard. *English Blake.* Shoe String 1966 repr. of 1949 ed. o.p. Useful as a guide for beginners.

Bloom, Harold. *Blake's Apocalypse.* Cornell Univ. Pr. 1970 o.p. Poem-by-poem commentary.

Bronowski, Jacob. *William Blake: A Man without a Mask.* Gordon Pr. 1976 $59.95. ISBN 0-8490-1300-3

Butlin, Martin, and others. *William Blake and His Circle*. Huntington Lib. 1989 $12.95. ISBN 0-685-25595-6. Biography that traces the development of Blake's writing and his close relationships with other writers.

Damon, S. Foster. *A Blake Dictionary: The Ideas and Symbols of William Blake*. U. Pr. of New Eng. 1988 $22.00. ISBN 0-87451-436-3. An extremely useful guide to the meanings of Blake's language and symbols, but should be supplemented by opposing views.

_____. *William Blake: His Philosophy and Symbols*. Peter Smith o.p. One of the pioneering books in the modern study of Blake.

DeLuca, Vincent. *Words of Eternity: Blake and the Poetics of the Sublime*. Princeton U. Pr. 1991 $32.50. ISBN 0-691-06874-7

Erdman, David V. *Blake: Prophet against Empire*. Dover 1991 $14.95. ISBN 0-486-26719-9. Demonstrates Blake's unexpectedly deep involvement in the political controversies of his day.

_____. *Concordance to the Writings of William Blake*. 2 vols. *Concordance Ser.* Cornell Univ. Pr. 1968 o.p.

Fisher, Peter. *The Valley of Vision: Blake as Prophet and Revolutionary*. Ed. by Northrop Frye. U. of Toronto Pr. 1961 o.p. A basic guide to Blake's thought.

Frye, Northrop. *Fearful Symmetry: A Study of William Blake*. Princeton U. Pr. 1947 $15.95. ISBN 0-691-01291-1. Perhaps the most influential study of Blake ever written.

Gilchrist, Alexander. *The Life of William Blake*. 2 vols. Phaeton 1969 $100.00. ISBN 0-87753-017-3. Flawed, but still a necessary source.

Gleckner, Robert. *The Piper and the Bard: A Study of William Blake*. Wayne St. U. Pr. 1959 o.p. Discusses "Songs of Innocence" and "Songs of Experience," "Tiriel," "The Book of Thel," "The Marriage of Heaven and Hell," and "Visions of the Daughters of Albion."

Gleckner, Robert, and Mark L. Greenberg, eds. *Approaches to Teaching Blake's Songs of Innocence and of Experience*. Modern Lang. 1989 $19.50. ISBN 0-87352-518-3

Hilton, Nelson, ed. *Essential Articles for the Study of William Blake, 1970–1984*. Archon 1986 o.p. Contains 13 essays and informative articles about Blake.

Murry, John M. *William Blake*. Haskell 1971 repr. of 1933 ed. $75.00. ISBN 0-8383-1344-2. A fascinating study of the "doctrine" of William Blake, with reference to his works.

Percival, Milton O. *William Blake's Circle of Destiny*. Kessinger Pub. 1993 $21.00. ISBN 1-56459-315-0. A controversial guide to Blake's thought.

Schorer, Mark. *William Blake: The Politics of Vision*. Peter Smith o.p. An interpretation of the moral and intellectual structure of Blake's "visionary" art.

Swinburne, Algernon C. *William Blake: A Critical Essay*. U. of Nebr. Pr. 1970 o.p. Excellent study of Blake's life and work.

Wilkie, Brian, and Mary Lynn Johnson. *Blake's Four Zoas: The Design of a Dream*. HUP 1978 $20.50. ISBN 0-674-07645-1. A guide, along with text, of the Four Zoas; explains the references and Blake's philosophy.

Wilson, Mona. *The Life of William Blake*. Ed. by Geoffrey Keynes. OUP 1971 o.p. Not altogether reliable, but highly readable.

BURNS, ROBERT. 1759–1796

Born to a stern but affectionate tenant farmer, Burns spent most of his life trying to earn a living from the unyielding soil of southern Scotland on one unprofitable farm after another. Self-educated and well read, he briefly experimented with conventional poetic forms before he began collecting native songs and composing original poems to earn a living. His first publication, *Poems, Chiefly in the Scottish Dialect* (1786), attracted the attention of the socially prominent, although his major topics and themes would seem to have been distasteful to them: drinking, local customs, sentiment, sex, repressive religion, superstition among the ignorant, and social hypocrisy. His poetry reflected his life—lusty, convivial, quarrelsome, a man bedeviled by his own nature. He fathered many children by at least four women, one of whom he married and all of whom he provided for, although his conscientiousness required his taking a position as a tax collector.

Burns found inspiration in the Scottish dialogue, captured, purified, dignified, and disseminated through his verse. He unearthed the commonplace and universal passions that lay beneath provincial or dialectical idiosyncrasies. In poetry, he reconciled the genteel, the antiquarian, and the vernacular tradition. He was an iconoclast who challenged the fashionable, sentimental, and artificial symbols of rustic bards, and the artful folk and pastoral traditions. Ironically, after his death he was venerated by such poets as WORDSWORTH and KEATS as a lonely minstrel who lived in impoverished solitude and died in neglect. Burns died at age 37—the poet of love, physical pleasure, friendship, drinking, Scotland, and author of the most sociable song in the English-speaking world: "Auld Lang Syne."

POETRY BY BURNS

The Jolly Beggars. Ed. by John C. Weston. U. of Mass. Pr. 1967 o.p.

The Merry Muses of Caledonia. c.1800. Ed. by James Barke and Sidney G. Smith. St. Mut. 1983 o.p.

Poems, Chiefly in the Scottish Dialect. AMS Pr. repr. of 1786 ed. $12.50. ISBN 0-404-08977-1

Poems and Songs of Robert Burns. 3 vols. Ed. by James Kinsley. *Oxford Eng. Texts Ser.* OUP 1969 $13.95. ISBN 0-19-281114-2. Includes all extant poems and songs, with their eighteenth-century musical settings.

Songs of Robert Burns. Ed. by James C. Dick. AMS Pr. repr. of 1903 ed. $67.50. ISBN 0-404-08511-3. Contains words and music of all 361 songs, with James Dick's notes; includes bibliography and indexes of first lines and tunes.

WORK BY BURNS

The Letters of Robert Burns. 2 vols. Ed. by J. De Lancey Ferguson and G. Ross Roy. OUP 1985. Vol. 1 $105.00. ISBN 0-19-812478-3. Vol. 2 $110.00. ISBN 0-19-812321-3. Collection of letters from 1759 to 1796.

BOOKS ABOUT BURNS

Bentman, Raymond. *Robert Burns.* Twayne 1987 $22.95. ISBN 0-8037-6952-8. Discusses Burns's main themes in the context of his intellectual, historical, and literary background.

Bold, Alan. *A Burns Companion.* St. Martin 1991 $35.00. ISBN 0-312-04500-X. Exemplary biographical and critical guide to Robert Burns.

Crawford, Thomas. *Burns: A Study of the Poems and Songs.* Stanford U. Pr. 1960 $49.50. ISBN 0-8047-0055-9. One of the best critical studies and particularly good on Burns's sources.

Daiches, David. *Robert Burns and His World.* Thames & Hudson 1978 o.p. A delightful, frank, and erudite study, more critical than biographical.

Ferguson, J. De Lancey. *Pride and Passion: Robert Burns, 1759–1796.* Russell 1964 repr. of 1939 ed. o.p.

Hecht, Hans. *Robert Burns: The Man and His Work.* St. Martin 1988 $70.00. ISBN 0-907526-04-7. Examines the universality of Burns's work by presenting him against the broad background of British civilization.

Lindsay, Maurice. *The Burns Encyclopedia.* St. Martin 1980 o.p. Invaluable guide to readers of Burns's poems and letters.

———. *Robert Burns: The Man, His Works, the Legend.* St. Mut. 1988 $35.00. ISBN 0-7091-7598-1. Popular study of Burns and his work, with bibliographic footnotes.

Lockhart, John G. *Life of Robert Burns*. Ed. by William S. Douglas. AMS Pr. repr. of 1892 ed. $20.00. ISBN 0-404-08517-2. The best of the older biographies.

Low, Donald A., ed. *Robert Burns: The Critical Heritage*. *Critical Heritage Ser*. Routledge 1974 o.p. A selection of the most important early critical views by reviewers of Burns's work.

Reid, J. B. *A Complete Word and Phrase Concordance to the Poems and Songs of Robert Burns*. Rprt. Serv. 1992 repr. of 1889 ed. $99.00. ISBN 0-7812-7468-0. Includes a glossary of Scots words, with notes, index, and appendix of readings.

Snyder, Franklin B. *The Life of Robert Burns*. Shoe String 1968 repr. of 1932 ed. o.p.

LORD BYRON, GEORGE GORDON (sixth Baron Byron of Rochdale). 1788–1824

Born into an aristocratic Scottish family, Byron was afflicted from birth with a club foot and a conviction that he was doomed as a sinner, a belief derived from his Calvinist upbringing and his notorious ancestors. After succeeding to the title as the sixth Baron Byron in 1798, he attended Harrow and then Cambridge, where he began to acquire his reputation as a reprobate and to write poetry. His first volume, *Hours of Idleness* (1807) was blasted in the *Edinburgh Review*, prompting his *English Bards and Scotch Reviewers* (1809), which attacked not only the reviews but also such contemporary poets as COLERIDGE, SOUTHEY, WORDSWORTH, and SCOTT and established his allegiance to eighteenth-century writers such as POPE.

From 1809 to 1811, he traveled in the Middle East, Malta, Albania, Greece, and Turkey, swam the Hellespont, engaged in a number of sexual adventures, and began writing a romance called *Childe Harold* (1812), in which he introduced a "hero," a brooding figure of great mystery who projected an aura of guilt, evil, nameless sins, social alienation, and immense courage in defying authority. The first two books were published in 1812, and, in part because the public was hungry for such adventure, the work was an unprecedented success. Byron claimed he awoke to find himself famous. Because most people believed he himself was his "hero," he was pursued by the decadent, fashionable society of the Regency period and became entangled in scandal. However, he was so productive a poet that it is difficult to believe that he was as active a lover as he claimed. In 1813 he published *The Giaour* and *The Bride of Abydos*; soon after, *The Corsair* and *Lara* (1814), *Hebrew Melodies* (1815), and *The Siege of Corinth* and *Parisina* (1816), all long, exotic, and fascinating poems. Seeking respectability, in 1814 he married the intellectual but unsuitable Annabelle Millbanke, who left him shortly after the birth of their daughter, Augusta Ada (who grew up to be a famous mathematician), on the grounds that he was committing incest with his half sister.

Ostracized from society because of this scandal, Byron wandered around Europe accompanied by a few companions and his own bad reputation. SHELLEY, having abandoned his wife, Harriet, to wander in Europe with Mary Godwin and her sister Clare, found him at the Villa Diodati, and there it was that MARY SHELLEY wrote *Frankenstein* as part of a ghost story competition. In *Manfred* (1817), a verse drama, Byron allowed his "hero" to expire; when he moved to Italy, he began writing satire: *Beppo* (1818), *Mazeppa* (1819), and *Don Juan* (1819–24), a long poem ridiculing excess, hypocrisy, and social conventions of all sorts. During the four years he was composing *Don Juan*, Byron also wrote a series of poetic dramas: *Marino Faliero, The Two Foscari, Sardanapalus*, and *Cain*, all of which were published in 1821.

In 1823 Byron left Italy to help Greece in its war of independence against Turkey, but he died of an obscure fever before he could fight the first battle—an apt symbol of the irony he found in human experience. Nearly all of his poetry and dramas illustrate the contradiction between divine or heroic aspirations and human limitations—the flaws, distractions, and inadequacies that keep people from reaching their goals or realizing their ideals. Even during his short lifetime he was unquestionably the most popular writer in Europe.

POETRY BY BYRON

Byron's Hebrew Melodies. Ed. by Thomas L. Ashton. U. of Tex. Pr. 1971 $16.95. ISBN 0-292-70141-1

Byron's Poetry. Ed. by Frank D. McConnell. *Norton Critical Eds.* Norton 1978 $12.95. ISBN 0-393-09152-X. Judicious selection, important critical articles, and excellent bibliography to 1978.

Childe Harold's Pilgrimage (1812–1818). Ed. by Samuel C. Chew. Odyssey Pr. 1936 o.p. Superb notes.

The Complete Poetical Works of Byron. 5 vols. Ed. by Jerome J. McGann. *Oxford Eng. Texts Ser.* OUP. Vol. 1 1980 $119.00. ISBN 0-19-811890-2. Vol. 2 1980 $135.00. ISBN 0-19-812754-5. Vol. 3 1981 $155.00. ISBN 0-19-812755-3. Vol. 4 1986 $135.00. ISBN 0-19-812756-1. Vol. 5 1986 $145.00. ISBN 0-19-812757-X. An analysis of the connections between texts of the known works; more than 80 new poems, as well as poetic fragments have been added to the collected works.

Don Juan. 1819–24. Ed. by Leslie A. Marchand. HM 1972 $9.16. ISBN 0-395-05138-X

WORKS BY BYRON

Byron's Letters and Journals. 12 vols. Ed. by Leslie A. Marchand. HUP. Vol. 1 *In My Hot Youth: Seventeen Ninety-Eight to Eighteen Ten.* 1973 $19.95. ISBN 0-674-08940-5. Vol. 2 *Famous in My Time: Eighteen Ten to Eighteen Twelve.* 1974 $18.50. ISBN 0-674-08941-3. Vol. 3 *Alas! The Love of Women: Eighteen Thirteen to Eighteen Fourteen.* 1974 $18.50. ISBN 0-374-08942-1. Vol. 4 *Wedlock's the Devil: Eighteen Fourteen to Eighteen Fifteen.* 1975 $22.50. ISBN 0-674-08944-8. Vol. 5 *So Late into the Night.* 1976 $18.50. ISBN 0-674-08945-6. Vol. 6 *The Flesh Is Frail: Eighteen Eighteen to Eighteen Nineteen.* 1976 $18.50. ISBN 0-674-08946-4. Vol. 7 *Between Two Worlds: Eighteen Twenty.* 1977 $18.50. ISBN 0-674-08947-2. Vol. 8 *Born for Opposition: Eighteen Twenty-One.* 1978 $22.50. ISBN 0-674-08948-0. Vol. 9 *In the Wind's Eye: Eighteen Twenty-One to Eighteen Twenty-Two.* 1979 $19.95. ISBN 0-674-08949-9. Vol. 10 *A Heart for Every Fate: Eighteen Twenty-Two to Eighteen Twenty-Three.* 1980 $18.50. ISBN 0-674-08952-9. Vol. 11 *For Freedom's Battle.* 1981 $18.50. ISBN 0-674-08953-7. Vol. 12 *The Trouble of an Index.* 1982 $19.95. ISBN 0-674-08954-5. The only unexpurgated edition of Byron's incomparably vivid correspondence.

Byron: A Self-Portrait: Letters and Diaries. OUP 1990 $17.95. ISBN 0-19-282754-5. Byron's letters and diaries, from 1798 to 1824; includes unpublished letters.

Works. Ed. by E. H. Coleridge and R. E. Prothero. 13 vols. Rprt. Serv. 1992 repr. of 1905 ed. $975.00. ISBN 0-7812-7472-9. Prose and poetry, with notes and supporting materials much worth consulting.

BOOKS ABOUT BYRON

Asimov, Isaac. *Asimov's Annotated Don Juan.* Doubleday 1972 o.p.

Boyd, Elizabeth F. *Byron's Don Juan: A Critical Study.* Humanities 1975 repr. of 1945 ed. o.p.

Cooke, Michael G. *The Blind Man Traces the Circle: On the Patterns and Philosophy of Byron's Poetry.* Princeton U. Pr. 1969 o.p. A serious scrutiny of Byron's poetry, devoted to the lyrics and intertextual synthesis.

Dubois, Charles. *Byron and the Need of Fatality.* Haskell 1970 repr. of 1932 ed. $49.95. ISBN 0-8383-0971-2. An old but still influential study by an eminent French scholar.

Faulkner, Claude W. *Byron's Political Verse Satire*. Folcroft repr. of 1947 ed. o.p. Study of Byron's political satire.

Fuess, Claude M. *Lord Byron as a Satirist in Verse*. Haskell 1974 $75.00. ISBN 0-8383-0554-7

Gleckner, Robert. *Critical Essays on Lord Byron*. Macmillan 1991 $42.00. ISBN 0-8161-8859-9. A collection of articles and essays on Byron ranging from Jerome J. McGann's "On Reading *Childe Harold's Pilgrimage*" to Donald H. Reiman's "The Poetry of Byron's Italian Years."

_____. *Byron and the Ruins of Paradise*. Greenwood 1980 repr. of 1967 ed. $55.00. ISBN 0-313-22421-8. A study of the evolution of Byron's poetic ideas.

Graham, Peter. *"Don Juan" and Regency England*. U. Pr. of Va. 1990 $30.00. ISBN 0-8139-1254-7. Series of essays written to help readers understand the relationship between time, place, and culture in Byron's poems.

Guiccoli, Countess. *My Recollections of Lord Byron*. Gordon Pr. 1972 $59.95. ISBN 0-8490-0690-2

Hagelman, Charles W., Jr., and Robert J. Barnes, eds. *Concordance to Byron's "Don Juan."* Concordance Ser. Cornell Univ. Pr. 1967 $79.50. ISBN 0-8014-0169-0. Indexes the complete poem, in addition to the "16" rejected stanzas and 634 complete-line variant readings.

Hunt, Leigh. *Lord Byron and Some of His Contemporaries*. AMS Pr. repr. of 1828 ed. $25.00. ISBN 0-404-03419-5. Examines the work of Byron in relation to that of his contemporaries.

Lansdown, Richard. *Byron's Historical Dramas*. OUP 1992 $59.00. ISBN 0-19-811252-1. Excellent chapter on the Drury Lane Theater.

Looper, Travis. *Byron and the Bible: A Compendium of Biblical Usage*. Scarecrow 1978 $27.50. ISBN 0-8108-1123-5. A chronological examination of the literature with regard to the relationship of the Bible and Byron's work.

Lovell, Ernest J., Jr., ed. *His Very Self and Voice: Collected Conversations of Lord Byron*. Hippocrene Bks. 1980 repr. of 1954 ed. o.p. Printed books and articles from which accounts of Byron's conversations have been extracted.

_____. *Lady Blessington's Conversations of Lord Byron*. Princeton U. Pr. 1969 o.p. Intended as a companion to *His Very Self and Voice*.

McGann, Jerome J. *Don Juan in Context*. U. Ch. Pr. 1976 o.p. A study of high romantic experience in *Don Juan*; examines the nature of imagination.

_____. *Fiery Dust: Byron's Poetic Development*. U. Ch. Pr. 1980 $22.00. ISBN 0-226-55844-4. A brilliant work by a preeminent Byron scholar.

Manning, Peter J. *Byron and His Fictions*. Bks. Demand repr. of 1978 ed. $80.20. ISBN 0-7837-3667-3. An intertextual evaluation of Byron's more famous texts, with a view of his personality.

Marchand, Leslie A. *Byron: A Portrait*. U. Ch. Pr. 1979 $7.95. A one-volume condensation of the standard biography.

_____. *Byron's Poetry: A Critical Introduction*. HUP 1965 $18.50. ISBN 0-674-08950-2. A masterful distillation of learning and critical acumen.

Marshall, William H. *The Structure of Byron's Major Poems*. U. of Pa. Pr. 1974 o.p.

Martin, Philip W. *Byron: A Poet before His Public*. Cambridge U. Pr. 1982 o.p. Provocative, dissenting estimate of Byron's poetry.

Maurois, André. *Byron*. Arden Lib. 1979 repr. of 1930 ed. o.p. A biography concerned with papers that shed light on Byron's religious perplexities.

Nicolson, Harold G. *The Poetry of Byron*. Folcroft repr. of 1943 ed. o.p.

Page, Norman. *A Byron Chronology*. Macmillan 1988 $38.50. ISBN 0-8161-8952-8. Outlines important events in the writer's personal and professional life.

Quennel, Peter. *Byron in Italy*. Ayer repr. of 1941 ed. $16.25. ISBN 0-8369-7147-7. Well written.

_____. *Byron: The Years of Fame*. Haskell 1974 o.p.

Raphael, Frederic. *Byron*. Thames & Hudson 1982 $18.95. ISBN 0-500-01278-4. A study of Byron that highlights Byron's personality and travails.

Ridenour, George M. *The Style of "Don Juan."* Yale U. Pr. 1960 o.p. Examines the intertextual similarities in *Don Juan* in order to discuss its theme and evaluate its style.

Robinson, Charles E. *Shelley and Byron: The Snake and the Eagle Wreathed in Flight.* Johns Hopkins 1976 $38.00. ISBN 0-8018-1707-2. An analysis of the relationship between Shelley and Byron, and the negative influence each had on the other's "spirit."

Robson, W. W. *Byron as Poet.* Folcroft repr. of 1957 ed. o.p.

Rutherford, Andrew. *Byron: A Critical Study.* Stanford U. Pr. 1961 $37.50. ISBN 0-8047-0072-9. Excellent study of Byron and his work.

Shilstone, Frederick, ed. *Approaches to Teaching Byron's Poetry.* Modern Lang. 1991 $34.00. ISBN 0-87352-545-0. Editions, materials, and aids provided by master teachers.

_____. *Byron and the Myth of Tradition.* U. of Nebr. Pr. 1988 $27.50. ISBN 0-8032-4197-6. Treats the conflict between self and tradition in Byron's consciousness.

Steffan, Truman Guy, and Willis Pratt, eds. *Byron's "Don Juan": A Variorum Edition.* 4 vols. U. of Tex. Pr. 1957 o.p.

Thomas, Gordon K. *Lord Byron's Iberian Pilgrimage.* Brigham 1983 $7.95. ISBN 0-8425-2139-9. A description of Byron's travels through Spain and Portugal and how they are reflected in his literature.

Thorslev, Peter. *The Byronic Hero: Types and Prototypes.* U. of Minn. Pr. 1962 o.p. The classic and comprehensive study of the sources and inspirations for the Byronic hero.

Trelawney, Edward J. *Recollections of the Last Days of Shelley and Byron. Select Bibliographies Reprint Ser.* Corner Hse. 1975 repr. of 1858 ed. $22.50. ISBN 0-87928-060-3. Reviews the significant aspects of the latter part of their lives.

Trueblood, Paul Graham. *The Flowering of Byron's Genius: Studies in "Don Juan."* Stanford U. Pr. 1945 o.p. The first modern study of Byron's style, and still the most original.

Young, Ione D., ed. *A Concordance to the Poetry of Byron.* 4 vols. I. Young 1985 repr. of 1975 ed. $32.00. ISBN 0-9605660-0-7. An indispensable work for scholars and readers of Byron's works.

CHATTERTON, THOMAS. 1752–1770

To a whole generation of artists and writers, including WORDSWORTH, COLERIDGE, KEATS, and HAZLITT, Chatterton was a symbol of neglected genius, of talent wasted on a materialistic world. That he was a forger did not seem to interfere with the magic of this myth.

Born in an age of antiquarian discovery and blessed with a talent for fabrication, Chatterton was capable, by the age of 12, of inventing convincing poems by the fictional fifteenth-century Bristol monk Thomas Rowley, whose work he claimed to have found among the illuminated parchment manuscripts in the church of St. Mary's Redcliffe. The poems circulated for some time among the citizens of Bristol. The obvious contrivances and anachronisms, and the disordered syntax and spelling, made them difficult to read, and no one would publish them. In 1770, at age 17, he moved to London and, unable to survive on the money he earned writing for magazines, committed suicide. Seven years after his death, in 1777, the poems were finally published, initiating an age of artful imitations of medieval ballads, such as Coleridge's *Rime of the Ancient Mariner* and Keats's "La Belle Dame Sans Merci."

POETRY BY CHATTERTON

Poems Supposed to Have Been Written at Bristol in the 15th Century by Thomas Rowley, 1794. Woodstock 1990 o.p. A series of facsimile reprints chosen and introduced by Jonathan Wordsworth.

The Rowley Poems. Ed. by S. E. Hare. Rprt. Serv. 1992 repr. of 1911 ed. $89.00. ISBN 0-7812-7331-5. Good introduction.

WORK BY CHATTERTON

The Complete Works of Thomas Chatterton. 2 vols. Ed. by Donald S. Taylor and B. B. Hoover. *Oxford Eng. Texts Ser.* OUP o.p. The standard edition.

BOOK ABOUT CHATTERTON

Meyerstein, Edward H. *A Life of Thomas Chatterton.* Richard West repr. of 1930 ed. o.p. The standard life.

CLARE, JOHN. 1793–1864

Born in rural Northamptonshire, the son of an agricultural laborer, Clare worked as ploughman, reaper, and thresher while educating himself by means of whatever books were available. At age 13, he began to write verse and by 1820 published his first book: *Poems Descriptive of Rural Life.* Its success is partly attributable to Clare's fitting the sentimental ideal, fashionable at the time, of the born poet, the natural, unspoiled, untutored genius, such as primitives Robert Bloomfield and Stephen Duck (with ROBERT BURNS as the prototype). Clare's publisher, John Taylor, who also published KEATS, brought him to London, where he met LAMB, HAZLITT, and WORDSWORTH, returning then to find his little farm threatened by the Enclosure acts.

His poetry then acquired a new purpose: to memorialize and record a way of rural life, of independent farming, that was soon to be lost. In 1821, Clare published *The Village Minstrel* and, six years later, *The Shepherd's Calendar.* But his mental health began to deteriorate, and in 1837 he was committed to a private asylum from which he escaped. Later he was admitted to the Northampton General Lunatic Asylum, where he died in 1864. But even in his madness and subsequent neglect, he fulfilled another fashionable pattern of the poet, the tragic poet exemplified by CHATTERTON. As Wordsworth wrote of him in "Resolution and Independence," "We Poets in our youth begin in gladness" but end up in "despondency and madness."

POETRY BY CLARE

The Early Poems of John Clare, 1804–1822. Ed. by Eric Robinson. OUP 1989 $145.00. ISBN 0-19-812314-0

Later Poems of John Clare: 1837–1861. Ed. by Eric Robinson and Geoffrey Summerfield. OUP 1984 $225.00. ISBN 0-19-811874-0. A collection of poetry from 1837 to 1869; includes notes to individual poems and author's footnotes.

The Shepherd's Calendar: With Village Stories and Other Poems, 1827. OUP 1973 repr. of 1964 ed. $29.95. ISBN 0-19-211249-X

NONFICTION BY CLARE

John Clare's Autobiographical Writings. Ed. by Eric Robinson. OUP 1983 $19.95. ISBN 0-19-211774-2. Traces Clare's life from infancy to adulthood; includes woodcarvings by John Lawrence.

The Natural History Prose Writings of John Clare. Ed. by Margaret Grainger. OUP 1983 $89.00. ISBN 0-19-818517-0. Looks at Clare's knowledge of natural history in his manuscripts about Northamptonshire, England.

WORKS BY CLARE

John Clare: Selected Letters. Ed. by Mark Storey. OUP 1988 $55.00. ISBN 0-19-818585-5. Letters covering all of Clare's life, providing a portrait of him; a comprehensive, scholarly edition.

John Clare: Selected Poetry and Prose. Ed. by Merryn Williams and Raymond Williams.
    Routledge Chapman & Hall 1987 $9.95. ISBN 0-416-41120-7. A selection of Clare's
    works, covering the period before the Industrial Revolution to his "modern" poems.
The Letters of John Clare. Ed. by Mark Storey. OUP 1986 $79.00. ISBN 0-19-812669-7.
    Provides absorbing information about the poet's life.

BOOKS ABOUT CLARE

Brownlow, Timothy. *John Clare and the Picturesque Landscape.* OUP 1983 $55.00. ISBN
    0-19-812808-8. An outline of Clare's verse and prose, from first signs of maturity
    (1821) to the beginning of the "asylum" period (1841).
Dendurent, H. O. *John Clare: A Reference Guide.* G. K. Hall 1978 o.p. Annotated guide to
    all writings about John Clare.
Storey, Edward. *A Right to Song: The Life of John Clare.* Routledge Chapman & Hall 1982
    o.p. An exhaustive biography describing the origins of Clare's creative impulse.
_____. *Clare: The Critical Heritage.* Routledge o.p. Includes most of the reviews and
    notices of Clare's work that appeared during his lifetime, with the exception of
    biographies.

COLERIDGE, SAMUEL TAYLOR. 1772–1834

Coleridge wrote almost all of his great poems in just 14 months, soon after he
and WORDSWORTH became neighbors. *The Ancient Mariner, Kubla Khan*, the first
part of *Christabel*—the so-called "mystery poems"—were part of this miraculous year (1798), as were the best of the "conversation poems," such as *"Frost at
Midnight."* Four years later, he wrote his heartbreaking *"Ode to Dejection"*
(1802), a kind of farewell to poetry. Opium addiction, a desperately unhappy
private life, and severe personality disorders combined to destroy his confidence and his capacity to work effectively.

In middle age he became a permanent guest-patient of a young doctor and his
wife, with whom he spent the rest of his life. Although the great poetic gift never
returned, Coleridge made a spectacular recovery as a critic, aesthetician, and
philosopher. His lectures on SHAKESPEARE and *Biographia Literaria* (1817) are
among the masterworks of world criticism. Today he is regarded as one of the
supreme figures in English literature, and his influence extends everywhere.

Coleridge's reputation has been embroiled in constant controversy because of
the repeated disclosures of unacknowledged borrowings in his major prose
works, mainly from German philosophers and critics. But the major poetry
remains untouched by such charges. The comprehensive edition of Coleridge's
writings has considerably extended the range of his intellectual activities, and
his reputation is higher than ever. Coleridge is an extremely complex figure,
who has aroused sharply divergent responses, but it is universally agreed that
his greatest poetry is inimitable, an unforgettable amalgam of mystery, beauty,
and intellectual depth.

POETRY BY COLERIDGE

Coleridge: Selected Poems. Ed. by R. C. Bald. *Crofts Class. Ser.* Harlan Davidson 1956.
    ISBN 0-88295-023-1
Complete Poetical Works. 2 vols. Ed. by E. H. Coleridge. *Oxford Eng. Texts Ser.* OUP 1912
    o.p. A standard edition.
Poems. Ed. by John Beer. Knopf 1991 $17.00. ISBN 0-679-40669-7
Poems of Samuel Taylor Coleridge. Ed. by E. H. Coleridge. *Oxford Stand. Authors Ser.*
    OUP 1912 $13.95. ISBN 0-14-015048-X

NONFICTION BY COLERIDGE

Biographia Literaria. Ed. by James Engell and W. J. Bate. Princeton U. Pr. 1984 o.p. Highly tendentious, with partisan notes and introduction; includes annotation of German sources.

Biographia Literaria. 2 vols. Ed. by John Shawcross. OUP 1907 o.p. Highly influential introduction, with notes not easy to consult.

Biographia Literaria. Ed. by George Watson. C. E. Tuttle 1906 $8.95. ISBN 0-460-87108-0. Lightly annotated, omits the two chapters added by Coleridge that were not part of his original plan.

Coleridge on Shakespeare: The Texts of the Lectures of 1811–12. Ed. by R. A. Foakes. Folger Bks. 1978 $12.95. ISBN 0-918016-54-1. Based on previously unpublished transcripts of J. P. Collier's notes, now in the Folger Shakespeare Library.

Inquiring Spirit: A New Presentation of Coleridge from His Published and Unpublished Writings. Ed. by Kathleen Coburn. Hyperion Conn. 1990 repr. of 1951 ed. $39.00. ISBN 0-88355-837-8

Notebooks. 3 vols. Ed. by Kathleen Coburn. Princeton U. Pr. 1957–73 o.p. Among the most amazing notebooks ever written.

Shakespearean Criticism. 2 vols. Ed. by T. M. Rayser. Biblio Dist. repr. of 1960 ed. 1974–80 o.p. Excerpts from Coleridge's criticism of Shakespeare's plays and poetry, from the first published appraisals to later evaluations.

Table Talk of Samuel Taylor Coleridge. Richard West repr. of 1884 ed. o.p.

WORKS BY COLERIDGE

Collected Letters of Samuel Taylor Coleridge. 6 vols. Ed. by Earl L. Griggs. OUP. Vols. 1–2 1956 $98.00. ISBN 0-19-811318-8. Vols. 3–4 1959 o.p. Vols. 5–6 1971 $110.00. ISBN 0-19-811458-3. Full representation of Coleridge's philosophy, metaphysics, and daily life.

The Collected Works. Ed. by Kathleen Coburn and others. 14 vols. Princeton U. Pr. 1970–84. Vols. 1–4 o.p. Vol. 5 $125.00. ISBN 0-691-09872-7. Vols. 6–11 o.p. Vol. 12 $125.00. ISBN 0-691-09889-1. Vols. 13–14 o.p. Authoritative, but represents a single perspective about Coleridge.

The Portable Coleridge. Ed. by Ivor A. Richards. *Viking Portable Lib.* Viking Penguin 1977 $11.00. ISBN 0-14-015048-X. Authoritative one-volume edition that includes "The Rime of the Ancient Mariner," "Christabel," "Kubla Khan," and most of the shorter poems.

Selected Poetry and Prose. Ed. by Donald Stauffer. McGraw 1951 $8.36. ISBN 0-07-553638-2. An ample introduction for the beginning student or general reader.

BOOKS ABOUT COLERIDGE

Barth, J. Robert. *Coleridge and the Power of Love.* U. of Mo. Pr. 1988 o.p. Explores human and religious aspects of love in Coleridge's thought.

Bate, Walter Jackson. *Coleridge.* HUP 1987 $12.95. ISBN 0-674-13680-2. The best one-volume biography.

Beer, John, ed. *Coleridge's Variety: Bicentenary Studies.* U. of Pittsburgh Pr. 1974 o.p. Contains a group of lectures on Coleridge given by Cambridge scholars.

Brandl, Alois. *Samuel Taylor Coleridge and the English Romantic School.* Haskell 1969 repr. of 1887 ed. $75.00. ISBN 0-838-05122-1

Chambers, Edmund K. *Samuel Taylor Coleridge: A Biographical Study.* Greenwood 1978 repr. of 1967 ed. o.p. Dull, but thoroughly reliable as to facts.

Coburn, Kathleen, ed. *Coleridge: A Collection of Critical Essays.* P-H 1967 o.p. Essays on Coleridge by a group of distinguished international critics, including I. A. Richards, Herbert Read, L. C. Knights, and Elisabeth Schneider.

Crawford, Walter B., and others. *Samuel Taylor Coleridge: An Annotated Bibliography of Criticism and Scholarship, 1900–1939.* Vol. 2. G. K. Hall 1983 o.p.

Doughty, Oswald, *Perturbed Spirit: The Life and Personality of Samuel Taylor Coleridge*. Fairleigh Dickinson 1981 $45.00. ISBN 0-8386-2353-0. Studies Coleridge through his own words and through the writings of his friends and colleagues.

Everest, Kevin. *Coleridge's Secret Ministry: The Context of the Conversation Poems 1795–1798*. B & N Imports 1979 o.p. Attempts to analyze Coleridge's social consciousness through works written between 1795 and 1798.

Foakes, R. A. *Samuel Taylor Coleridge, Lectures 1808–1819: On Literature*. Princeton U. Pr. 1987 o.p.

Fruman, Norman. *Coleridge: The Damaged Archangel*. Braziller 1971 o.p. One of the most controversial books ever written about Coleridge.

Holmes, Richard. *Coleridge*. OUP 1982 $4.95. ISBN 0-19-2875915. Provides a unified portrait of Coleridge in which each work is given its place.

Jackson, J. R., ed. *Coleridge: The Critical Heritage*. Routledge 1970 o.p. Contains most of the critical reviews of Coleridge's work written during his lifetime.

Lefebure, Molly. *Samuel Taylor Coleridge: A Bondage of Opium*. Stein & Day 1974 o.p. Attributes Coleridge's many personal and creative problems to his opium addiction; well written but unreliable.

Levere, Trevor. *Poetry Realized in Nature: Samuel Taylor Coleridge and Early Nineteenth-Century Science*. Cambridge U. Pr. 1981 $49.95. ISBN 0-521-23920-6. Explores Coleridge's ideas of science and nature through a study of his notebooks.

Lockridge, Laurence. *Coleridge the Moralist*. Cornell Univ. Pr. 1977 o.p. A careful, illuminating study of Coleridge's ethics.

Logan, Eugenia. *A Concordance to the Poetry of Samuel Taylor Coleridge*. Telegraph Bks. 1983 repr. of 1940 ed. o.p.

Lowes, John L. *The Road to Xanadu: A Study in the Ways of the Imagination*. Princeton U. Pr. 1986 $68.00. ISBN 0-691-06645-0. Traces the sources of *The Ancient Mariner* and *Kubla Khan* in an attempt to unravel the mysteries of the imagination.

McKusick, James. *Coleridge's Philosophy of Language*. Bks. Demand repr. of 1986 ed. $49.20. ISBN 0-8357-3752-7. Presents a persuasive argument that Coleridge's linguistic theories form a coherent body of thought underlying his poetry, criticism, and aesthetics.

McNiece, Gerald. *The Knowledge That Endures: Coleridge, German Philosophy and the Logic of Romantic Thought*. St. Martin 1991 $55.00. ISBN 0-312-06799-2

Milton, Mary Lee. *The Poetry of Samuel Taylor Coleridge: An Annotated Bibliography of Criticism, 1935 to 1970*. Garland 1981 o.p.

Nethercot, Arthur H. *The Road to Tryermaine: A Study of the History, Background and Purposes of Coleridge's "Christabel."* Greenwood 1978 repr. of 1962 ed. $35.00. ISBN 0-313-20001-7

Potter, Stephen. *Coleridge and S. T. C.: A Study of Coleridge's Dual Nature*. Russell 1965 repr. of 1935 ed. o.p.

Prickett, Stephen. *Coleridge and Wordsworth*. Cambridge U. Pr. 1980 o.p. Comparison of the romanticism of Coleridge and Wordsworth; examines their creativity and their artistic development.

Schneider, Elisabeth. *Coleridge, Opium and Kubla Khan*. Hippocrene Bks. 1966 o.p. A brilliant scholarly and critical study that has undermined belief in the famous "dream" origin of *Kubla Khan*.

Wallace, C. M. *The Design of* Biographia Literaria. Allen & Unwin 1983 o.p. Examines the order and design of Coleridge's work as it relates to literary discourse.

Woodring, Carl R. *Politics in the Poetry of Coleridge*. U. of Wis. Pr. 1961 $25.00. ISBN 0-299-02440-7. The best book on the subject.

Wylie, Ian. *Young Coleridge and the Philosophers of Nature*. OUP 1989 $55.00. ISBN 0-19-812983-1. Imposes an admirable order on a confusion of texts and thinkers.

CRABBE, GEORGE. 1754–1832

Crabbe was a parson as well as a poet. He was as ordinary a parson as he was an extraordinary poet; the extraordinariness lay in his power to put mussels, eels, colds, weeds, teapots, and so on, and also whole villages of sympathetically observed characters, into couplets that are undeniably poetry. Benjamin Britten's highly popular opera *Peter Grimes* is based on a section of Crabbe's *The Borough* (1810). His deeply pessimistic view of human nature and his rejection of rural life as spiritually ennobling have made him seem a cynic to some, a sober realist to others. He was JANE AUSTEN's favorite poet.

POETRY BY CRABBE

George Crabbe: The Complete Poetical Works. 3 vols. Ed. by Norma Dalrymple-Chumpneys. OUP 1988. Vol. 1 $155.00. ISBN 0-19-811882-1. Vol. 2 $165.00. ISBN 0-19-812787-1. Vol. 3 $120.00. ISBN 0-19-812788-X

The Poetical Works of George Crabbe. 1914. Ed. by A. J. Caryle and R. M. Caryle. Scholarly 1971 repr. of 1932 ed. o.p. Reproduction of the text of the author's own edition, adding some posthumous works.

Selected Poems. Ed. by C. Day Lewis. Viking Penguin 1973 o.p. Modern poet C. Day Lewis's own edition of Crabbe's work. Includes critical reactions and intriguing insights.

Tales, 1812, and Other Selected Poems. Ed. by Howard W. Mills. Cambridge U. Pr. 1967 o.p. A large selection of poems, especially useful for the general reader.

NONFICTION BY CRABBE

Selected Letters and Journals. Ed. by Thomas C. Faul. OUP 1985 o.p. Selected for their relevance to the poet's work; includes bibliographical references and indexes.

BOOKS ABOUT CRABBE

Bareham, Terence, and S. Gatrell. *Bibliography of George Crabbe*. Shoe String 1978 o.p. A critical reassessment of Crabbe's work and life. Chronological approach to his political and religious thinking.

_____. *George Crabbe. Critical Studies Ser.* B & N Imports 1977 o.p. Examines the influence of Anglicanism and pastoral duties on Crabbe's life and work.

Burne, Neville B. *The Restless Ocean*. St. Mut. 1979 o.p. Comprehensive examination of Crabbe's life and works; includes illustrations and an index.

Chamberlain, Robert L. *George Crabbe. English Authors Ser.* Irvington 1965 o.p. Provides a detailed analysis of Crabbe's most important works.

Crabbe, George, Jr. *The Life of George Crabbe*. Arden Lib. repr. of 1980 ed. o.p. Written by his son; an enduring, minor classic.

Edgecombe, Rodney S. *Theme, Embodiment and Structure in the Poetry of George Crabbe*. Humanities 1983 o.p. An intertextual examination of Crabbe's thought; focuses on his romanticism.

Evans, John H. *The Poems of George Crabbe: A Literary and Historical Study*. Ayer o.p. Still much worth consulting.

Haddakin, Lilian. *The Poetry of Crabbe*. Humanities 1955 o.p. Excellent.

Nelson, Beth. *George Crabbe and the Progress of Eighteenth-Century Narrative Verse*. Bucknell U. Pr. 1976 $18.00. ISBN 0-8387-1736-5. An authoritative examination of Crabbe's novels and their use of Augustan verse satire.

Pollard, Arthur. *Crabbe: The Critical Heritage. Critical Heritage Ser.* Routledge 1975 $69.50. ISBN 0-7100-7258-9

Sigworth, Oliver. *Nature's Sternest Painter: Five Essays on the Poetry of George Crabbe*. Bks. Demand repr. of 1964 ed. $51.00. ISBN 0-317-26796-5. One of the best modern studies.

DE QUINCEY, THOMAS. 1785–1859

Born in Manchester, the son of a merchant, De Quincey is best know for his masterful *Confessions of an English Opium Eater*, written for *Blackwood's Magazine* in 1822 and much later enlarged by retrospection. He began taking opium at Oxford for relief from a toothache and fought the addiction, with occasional success, for more than 20 years. His life and works are marked by contrast: He was born to a patrimony but lost it; he had immense intellectual gifts (he could read Greek at 15 without study and could translate and interpret the German romanticists) but would not submit to disciplined study for an Oxford degree. His own experiences and reminiscences formed the major subject of his essays; even in literary criticism, he contrived to interweave biographical details obtained from personal knowledge. His *Reminiscences of the English Lake Poets* (1834–40) reveals a sharp and unique view of the great romantic poets of his day, including WORDSWORTH and COLERIDGE, with whom he was closely associated in the Lake District.

NONFICTION BY DE QUINCEY

Collected Writings. 14 vols. Ed. by David Masson. AMS Pr. repr. of 1889–90 ed. $315.00. ISBN 0-404-02100-X. The most comprehensive collection of De Quincey's writings.
Confessions of an English Opium Eater. 1822. Trans. by Aileen Ward. Carroll & Graf 1985 $4.95. ISBN 0-88184-130-7
English Mail-Coach and Other Essays. Biblio Dist. repr. of 1912 ed. o.p.

BOOKS ABOUT DE QUINCEY

Barrell, John. *The Infection of Thomas De Quincey: A Psychopathology of Imperialism.* Yale U. Pr. 1991 $30.00. ISBN 0-300-04932-3. A brilliant analysis of the psychological backgrounds to De Quincey's political ideas.
Baxter, Edmund. *De Quincey's Art of Autobiography.* B & N Imports 1990 $46.75. ISBN 0-685-50138-8. Takes note of the major studies of De Quincey published over the last three decades.
Jordan, John E. *Thomas De Quincey, Literary Critic.* Gordian 1973 repr. of 1952 ed. $50.00. ISBN 0-87752-160-3. Analyzes De Quincey's critical methods and discusses his literary theory.
Lindop, Grevel. *The Opium-Eater: A Life of Thomas De Quincey.* St. Mut. 1981 $45.00. ISBN 0-460-04358-7. Interesting biography that synthesizes other biographies of De Quincey; captures his personality and concentrates on his opium addiction.
Snyder, Robert Lance, ed. *Thomas De Quincey: Bicentenary Studies.* U. of Okla. Pr. 1986 $38.50. ISBN 0-8061-1849-0. Contains a group of essays, noted for their scholarship.

HAZLITT, WILLIAM. 1778–1830

Born in Maidstone, Kent, Hazlitt was the son of a Unitarian minister. At age 15 he went to Hackney College to study for the ministry, but he soon abandoned that pursuit in favor of painting. That too, however, never came to fruition, because Hazlitt was forced by economic circumstances to become a journalist. His early literary tastes were guided by COLERIDGE, WORDSWORTH, and LAMB. His political convictions gave him violent prejudices, made him quarrel with these three and other friends, and marred his essays with many digressions. He was a great admirer of Napoleon, and his longest work is a biography of that leader. Most of his essays combine a loose association of ideas with rapt comparison. He wanted to balance reason and feeling: "To feel what is good and give reasons for the faith that is in me." And, though his passionate commitment to liberal causes made his personal preferences occasionally unsound, his judgment of literature in general seems to have been excellent—formed by what KEATS described as "his depth of taste."

NONFICTION BY HAZLITT

Criticisms on Art. Folcroft repr. of 1856 ed. o.p. Essays on art written from the perspective of Hazlitt's own painting experience.

The Hazlitt Sampler: Selections from His Familiar, Literary and Critical Essays. Ed. by Hershel M. Sikes. Peter Smith o.p.

Hazlitt on Theater: Selections from the View of the English Stage and Criticisms and Dramatic Essays. Ed. by William Archer and Robert Lowe. Hyperion Conn. 1991 repr. of 1957 ed. $26.00. ISBN 0-88355-847-5. With an introduction by William Archer.

Lectures on the English Comic Writers. Russell 1969 repr. of 1819 ed. o.p. Lectures delivered at the Surry Institution.

Lectures on the English Poets. 1818. Ed. by William Hazlitt, Jr. Rprt. Serv. 1992 repr. of 1924 ed. $79.00. ISBN 0-7812-7065-0. Eight intensive lectures on major English poets from Chaucer to Keats.

The Round Table: A Collection of Essays and Characters of Shakespeare's Plays. 1817. Biblio Dist. 1957 o.p. Mostly by Hazlitt, but with ten contributions by Leigh Hunt.

Selected Essays. Ed. by John R. Nabholtz. *Crofts Class. Ser.* Harlan Davidson 1970. ISBN 0-88295-042-8. Four groups of essays dealing with life in general, writers on writing, painters on painting, and actors on acting.

Selected Writings. Ed. by William Blythe. Viking Penguin 1982 o.p.

Sketches and Essays. Darby Pub. 1983 repr. of 1903 ed. o.p.

The Spirit of the Age or Contemporary Portraits: Coleridge, Scott, Byron, Wordsworth. 1825. Darby Pub. 1983 repr. of 1904 ed. o.p. Biographical treatment of these four major Romantic poets.

Table Talk: 1821–22. Folcroft repr. of 1906 ed. o.p.

Works. 21 vols. Ed. by Percival P. Howe. AMS Pr. repr. of 1934 ed. $630.00. ISBN 0-404-03210-9. The standard centenary edition.

BOOKS ABOUT HAZLITT

Jones, Stanley. *Hazlitt: A Life: From Winterslow to Frith Street.* OUP 1991 repr. of 1990 ed. $15.95. ISBN 0-19-282897-5. Well-written, authoritative biography.

Kinnard, John. *William Hazlitt, Critic of Power.* Col. U. Pr. 1978 $52.50. ISBN 0-231-04600-6. Critical biography of Hazlitt as revealed through his works.

Wardle, Ralph Martin. *Hazlitt.* Bks. Demand repr. of 1971 ed. $149.10. ISBN 0-7837-1829-2. Includes bibliographic references.

HOGG, JAMES. 1770–1835

Son of a Scottish shepherd and descended from minstrels, Hogg led a life that has the fictional quality THOMAS HARDY was to capture later in the century in his novels of country life. After meeting SIR WALTER SCOTT in 1802, Hogg adopted the name "Ettrick Shepherd," a pseudonym under which he published original lyrics and ballads. In 1814 Hogg met WILLIAM WORDSWORTH and enjoyed literary friendships in the Lake District, although he parodied the other poets' styles and mannerisms in *The Poetic Mirror* (1816). He married at age 50 and fathered five children, whom he tried to support by the same kind of unproductive farming at which ROBERT BURNS had labored a generation before. Like Burns, his convivial nature and verbal talents won him a following in fashionable society, especially after the publication of his first novel, *The Private Memoirs and Confessions of a Justified Sinner* (1824), when he was 53 years old. The first novel to explore psychological aberrations, it traces the collapse of a personality under the pressure of social conformity, native superstition, and religious excess. Since the introduction by ANDRÉ GIDE (see Vol. 2) to the 1947 Cresset edition, it has acquired an academic following and a new popularity. There is a James Hogg Society, founded in 1982, which publishes a newsletter.

NONFICTION BY HOGG

Poetic Mirror and *New Poetic Mirror.* 1816, 1829–31. Ed. by David Groves. P. Lang Pubs. 1990 $59.80. ISBN 3-361-42959-2

POETRY BY HOGG

Songs by the Ettrick Shepherd. 1831. Woodstock 1989 o.p. With an introduction by
Jonathan Wordsworth.

NOVEL BY HOGG

The Private Memoirs and Confessions of a Justified Sinner. 1824. Ed. by David Groves.
Trafalgar 1992 $8.95. ISBN 0-86241-340-0. The only complete edition since the
novel's original appearance.

BOOKS ABOUT HOGG

Groves, David. *James Hogg: The Growth of a Writer.* Scot. Acad. Pr. UK 1988 o.p. Traces
the development of Hogg as a writer, based on published works and reviews.
Smith, Nelson. *James Hogg.* Twayne 1980 o.p. Comprehensive evaluation of Hogg's
diverse accomplishments; analyzes his strengths and weaknesses.

HUNT, (JAMES HENRY) LEIGH. 1784–1859

Leigh Hunt was so prolific that, if his writing were ever collected, it would
exceed 100 volumes of mostly unmemorable prose. He was so eccentric and
socially visible that even DICKENS's caricature of Hunt as the perennially
cheerful Harold Skimpole in *Bleak House* is immediately recognizable. But his
philosophy of cheer, however eccentric among such doleful writers of his
generation as COLERIDGE and BYRON, appealed to middle-class public taste,
which accounts for his immense following.

Educated, like Coleridge and LAMB, at Christ's Hospital, Hunt became a
journalist, helping his brother John edit the weekly *Examiner.* As a result of the
paper's liberal policy, they were both fined and imprisoned for two years for
writing a libelous description of the Prince Regent on his birthday. Hunt turned
his prison cell into a salon and enjoyed visits from Jeremy Bentham, Byron,
KEATS, Lamb, and HAZLITT. After his release, Hunt settled in Hampstead,
London, a political martyr and a model of domesticity.

His writing includes *The Feast of the Poets* (1814), a satire of contemporary
writers; *The Story of Rimini* (1816), a saccharine Italianate romance; and *Hero
and Leander* (1819). Young poets such as Keats found the sensual surfaces easy
to imitate. But mostly Hunt wrote essays and edited dozens of short-lived
magazines and journals, providing an insight into the literary life of London
during this period.

NONFICTION BY HUNT

The Autobiography. Ed. by J. E. Morpurgo. Cresset Pr. 1949 o.p. A charitable, good-
humored work; includes an appendix of material gathered by Hunt.
The Feast of the Poets, 1814. Woodstock 1989 o.p. With an introduction by Jonathan
Wordsworth.
Leigh Hunt's Dramatic Criticism, 1808–1831. Ed. by Laurence Houtchens. Hippocrene
Bks. 1977 $23.00. ISBN 0-374-93988-8. A complete collection of Hunt's literary
criticism from the years cited.
Leigh Hunt's Literary Criticism. Ed. by Laurence Houtchens. Col. U. Pr. 1956 o.p. A
companion volume to *Leigh Hunt's Dramatic Criticism.*

BOOKS ABOUT HUNT

Blainey, Ann. *Immortal Boy: A Portrait of Leigh Hunt.* St. Martin 1985 o.p.
Thompson, James R. *Leigh Hunt. Twayne's English Authors Ser.* Irvington 1977 $17.95.
ISBN 0-8057-6679-0. Basic assessment of Hunt's life and work utilizing his essays,
letters, prose, and poetry.

KEATS, JOHN. 1795–1821

Keats was born in London, the oldest of four children. His father, who was a livery-stable keeper, died when Keats was 8 years old, and his mother died six years later. At age 15, he was apprenticed to an apothecary-surgeon. In 1815 he began studying medicine but soon gave up that career in favor of writing poetry.

The critic Douglas Bush has said that, if one poet could be recalled to life to complete his career, the almost universal choice would be Keats, who now is regarded as one of the three or four supreme masters of the English language. His early work is badly flawed in both technique and critical judgment, but, from his casually written but brilliant letters, one can trace the development of a genius who, through fierce determination in the face of great odds, fashioned himself into an incomparable artist.

In his tragically brief career, cut short at age 25 by tuberculosis, Keats constantly experimented, often with dazzling success, and always with steady progress over previous efforts. The unfinished *Hyperion* is the only English poem after *Paradise Lost* that is worthy to be called an epic, and it is breathtakingly superior to his early *Endymion* (1818), written just a few years before. *Isabella* is a fine narrative poem, but *The Eve of St. Agnes* (1819), written soon after, is peerless. In *Lamia* (1819) Keats revived the couplet form, long thought to be dead, in a gorgeous, romantic story.

Above all it was in his development of the ode that Keats's supreme achievement lies. In just a few months, he wrote the odes *"On a Grecian Urn"* (1819), *"To a Nightingale"* (1819), *"To Melancholy"* (1819), and the marvelously serene *"To Autumn"* (1819). Keats is the only romantic poet whose reputation has steadily grown through all changes in critical fashion. Once patronized as a poet of beautiful images but no intellectual content, Keats is now appreciated for his powerful mind, profound grasp of poetic principles, and ceaseless quest for new forms and techniques. For many readers, old and young, Keats is a heroic figure.

POETRY BY KEATS

The Complete Poems. Ed. by Miriam Allott. *Annotated Eng. Poets Ser.* Longman 1972 o.p. Probably the most useful student edition.

The Complete Poems. Ed. by John Barnard. *Penguin Poets Ser.* Viking Penguin 1977 $7.95. ISBN 0-14-042210-2. Easy-to-use one-volume edition; good notes.

Endymion: A Poetic Romance 1818. Woodstock 1991 o.p. Facsimile reproduction of Keats's poem about the shepherd Endymion's love for the Moon. With an introduction by Jonathan Wordsworth.

John Keats: Complete Poems. Ed. by Jack Stillinger. HUP 1982 $14.95. ISBN 0-674-15431-2. The most reliable text, with detailed textual but no critical notes.

Lamia, Isabella, The Eve of St. Agnes . . . 1820. Woodstock 1990 o.p. With an introduction by Jonathan Wordsworth.

Poetical Works of John Keats. Ed. by H. W. Garrod. *Oxford Eng. Texts Ser.* OUP 1956 $27.50. ISBN 0-19-254132-3. Long the standard edition; still worth consulting.

WORKS BY KEATS

Complete Poems and Selected Letters. Ed. by Clarence D. Thorpe. Odyssey Pr. 1935 o.p. Copious notes; superb introduction.

The Keats Circle, 1816–1878. 1948. 2 vols. Ed. by Hyder E. Rollins. HUP 1965 o.p. Invaluable materials dealing with Keats and his family and friends.

Letters of John Keats. Ed. by Robert Giddings. *Oxford Pap. Ser.* OUP 1970 $15.95. ISBN 0-19-281081-2. The best one-volume edition; very good notes.

Letters of John Keats, 1814–1821. 2 vols. Ed. by Hyder E. Rollins. HUP 1958 $71.00. ISBN 0-674-52700-3. The standard edition.

Selected Poems and Letters. Ed. by Douglas Bush. HM 1959 $7.96. ISBN 0-395-05140-1. Authoritative notes that are masterpieces of compression and critical judgment.

BOOKS ABOUT KEATS

Aske, Martin. *Keats and Hellenism.* Cambridge U. Pr. 1985 o.p. Explores the influence of classical Greek and Hellenistic culture on Keats.

Baker, Jeffrey. *John Keats and Symbolism.* St. Martin 1986 o.p. Examines character as a symbolic persona and analyzes the importance of symbolism in Keats's work.

Bate, Walter J., ed. *John Keats.* HUP 1979 o.p. A superb life, particularly strong on critical analysis of poems.

Becker, Michael G., and Robert Dilligan. *A Concordance to the Poems of John Keats.* Garland 1979 o.p. An inclusive and accurate reference work reflecting recent progress in textual criticism.

Bush, Douglas. *John Keats: His Life and Writings.* Macmillan 1966 o.p. The best brief life and critical study; beautifully written.

Dickstein, Morris. *Keats and His Poetry: A Study in Development.* U. Ch. Pr. 1974 $4.25. ISBN 0-226-14796-7. An elegant and insightful study.

Evert, Walter H. *Aesthetic and Myth in the Poetry of Keats.* Princeton U. Pr. 1965 o.p. Original and illuminating.

Evert, Walter H., and Jack W. Rhodes, eds. *Approaches to Teaching Keats's Poetry.* Modern Lang. 1991 $34.00. ISBN 0-87352-543-4. Provides examples of the ways in which Keats's poetry can be taught in the classroom.

Finney, Claude L. *Evolution of Keats's Poetry.* 2 vols. Russell repr. of 1936 ed. o.p. A huge, immensely rewarding study.

Ford, George. *Keats and the Victorians.* Yale U. Pr. 1944 o.p. Examines the impact of Keats on Victorian writers.

Giddings, Robert. *John Keats.* Greenwood 1978 repr. of 1968 ed. o.p. A comprehensive, fact-laden, authoritative biography.

_____. *The Mask of Keats.* Darby Pub. repr. of 1979 ed. o.p.

Hagstrum, Jean H. *The Romantic Body: Love and Sexuality in Keats, Wordsworth, and Blake.* U. of Tenn. Pr. 1986 $19.95. ISBN 0-87049-482-1. Examines the Romantic idea of love and how love and sexuality are expressed in the works of Keats, Wordsworth, and Blake.

Little, Judy. *Keats as a Narrative Poet: A Test of Invention.* U. of Nebr. Pr. 1975 $20.00. ISBN 0-8032-0846-4. A detailed intertextual and historical study of Keats's narrative poetry.

Lowell, Amy. *John Keats.* 2 vols. Rprt. Serv. 1992 repr. of 1925 ed. $50.00. ISBN 0-7812-7573-3

Murry, John M. *Keats.* Hippocrene Bks. 1976 repr. of 1955 ed. o.p. A companion piece to *Keats and Shakespeare.*

_____. *Keats and Shakespeare: A Study of Keats' Poetic Life from 1816–1820.* Greenwood 1978 repr. of 1951 ed. $35.00. ISBN 0-313-20581-7. One of the most widely-read excursions into Keats and his influence on other poets.

Perkins, David. *The Quest for Permanence: Symbolism of Wordsworth, Shelley, and Keats.* HUP 1959 o.p.

Ricks, Christopher. *Keats and Embarrassment.* OUP 1984 $14.95. ISBN 0-19-812829-0. Discusses Keats and his work in the social context of his time.

Ridley, M. R. *Keats' Craftsmanship: A Study in Poetic Development.* Rprt. Serv. 1992 repr. of 1923 ed. $89.00. ISBN 0-7812-7574-1. A masterpiece that brings the reader close to the creative process.

Ryan, Robert M. *Keats: The Religious Sense.* Princeton U. Pr. 1976 $35.00. ISBN 0-691-06316-8. Comprehensive, intertextual study focusing on Keats's attitudes toward religion and the religious aspects in his work.

Sperry, Stuart M., Jr. *Keats the Poet.* Princeton U. Pr. 1973 o.p. Traces the intellectual and poetic development of Keats from the beginning to the end of his career.

Van Ghent, Dorothy. *Keats: The Myth of the Hero*. Ed. by Jeffrey C. Robinson. Princeton U. Pr. 1983 $39.50. ISBN 0-691-06569-1. Distills Van Ghent's career-long involvement in the works of Keats. Focuses on myth, story, plot, action, and recurring figures in Keats's work.

Vendler, Helen. *The Odes of John Keats*. HUP 1983 $22.50. ISBN 0-674-63075-0. An acclaimed work by one of the most respected of contemporary critics.

Walker, Carol Kyros. *Walking North with Keats*. Yale U. Pr. 1992 $35.00. ISBN 0-300-04824-6. A beautifully illustrated guide to the walking tour Keats took in the north of England with his friend Brown.

Ward, Aileen. *John Keats: The Making of a Poet*. FS&G 1986 $11.95. ISBN 0-374-52029-1. Not a detailed biographical account but good on Keats's artistic psychology.

LAMB, CHARLES. 1775–1834

Although COLERIDGE called him "gentle hearted" and he was generally considered one of the most beloved figures of his generation, Charles Lamb knew more about violence, disappointment, and insanity than any of his contemporaries who were depicting such emotions in their writings. Educated with Coleridge at Christ's Hospital, Lamb was unable to attend university because of a speech impediment. He spent his life as a clerk at the East India Company, 33 years, 6 days a week, 9 hours a day doing mindless tasks in which he had no interest. One day he came home to find that his sister Mary had murdered their mother in a fit of insanity; to keep her from a life of confinement, he took care of her for the rest of his life. Together they entertained his friends, took brief journeys to the country, and wrote books for children: *Tales from Shakespeare* (1807) and *Mrs. Leicester's School* (1809). But mostly he is remembered for his essays written under the pseudonym Elia, published in the *London Magazine* and collected in 1823. They are sociable, cheerful, simple essays written in a variety of styles on commonplace themes: childhood memories, vacations, playing cards, poor relations, theatrical performances, growing old, retirement, various holidays, and social customs. Lamb died an urban gentleman, resisting to the very end the charms of nature that had captivated his friends WORDSWORTH and Coleridge.

NONFICTION BY LAMB

Essays of Elia (and *Last Essays of Elia*). 1823, 1833. Biblio Dist. repr. of 1906 ed. o.p. Contains all the "Elia" essays that Lamb collected in book form; includes explanatory notes.

Lamb as Critic. Ed. by Roy Park. U. of Nebr. Pr. 1980 o.p. Carefully chosen selection from Lamb's criticism; includes an introduction discussing Lamb as a critic.

Lamb's Criticism: Selection from the Literary Criticism of Charles Lamb. Ed. by E. M. Tillyard. Rprt. Serv. 1992 repr. of 1923 ed. $69.00. ISBN 0-7812-7015-4. Contains some of the best examples of Lamb's criticism.

Selected Essays. Ed. by John R. Nabholtz. *Crofts Class. Ser.* Harlan Davidson 1967. ISBN 0-88295-052-5

WORKS BY LAMB

The Portable Charles Lamb. Ed. by John Mason Brown. *Viking Portable Lib*. Viking Penguin 1975 repr. of 1949 ed. $38.50. ISBN 0-8371-8202-6. Includes letters, poems, and essays, arranged to show various aspects of Lamb's character and interests.

The Works of Charles and Mary Lamb. 7 vols. Rprt. Serv. 1992 repr. of 1905 ed. $525.00. ISBN 0-7812-7584-9. Essays, poems, and letters by both Charles and Mary Lamb.

BOOKS ABOUT LAMB

Aaron, Jane. *A Double Singleness: Gender and the Writings of Charles and Mary Lamb*. OUP 1991 $55.00. ISBN 0-19-812890-8. A lively provocative book that explores the unique relationship between the Lambs and its effect on their writing.

Barnett, George L. *Charles Lamb*. Irvington 1976 $17.95. ISBN 0-8057-6668-5. Biography tracing Lamb's life and works, with special focus on his essays and criticism.

Blunden, Edmund. *Charles Lamb and His Contemporaries*. Shoe String 1967 $26.00. ISBN 0-208-00461-0. Brief biography noting early influences and the development of Lamb's essay persona, Elia; originally delivered as lectures at Trinity College, Cambridge.

Courtney, Winifred. *Young Charles Lamb, 1775–1802*. NYU Pr. 1982 o.p. A fine selection of informal essays that attempt to draw the modern general reader into Lamb's earlier life and writings.

Frank, Robert. *"Don't Call Me Gentle Charles": Discourses on Charles Lamb's* Essays of Elia. Oreg. St. U. Pr. 1976 $13.95. ISBN 0-87071-082-6. Includes seven detailed essays about Lamb's Elia essays.

Monsman, Gerald. *Confessions of a Prosaic Dreamer: Charles Lamb's Art of Autobiography*. Duke U. Pr. 1984 $29.95. ISBN 0-8223-0596-8. Examines Lamb's skill at capturing salient aspects of others in his work.

Randel, Fred. *The World of Elia: Charles Lamb's Essayistic Romanticism*. Kennikat Pr. 1975 o.p. A glowing tribute to Charles Lamb as a critic and prose writer.

LANDOR, WALTER SAVAGE. 1775–1864

Landor's long life was filled with endless quarrels, lawsuits, and controversy. His temper was violent; his convictions, absolute. But his poetic writings are astonishingly serene, disciplined, and elevated. His youthful *Gebir* (1798) is the best of his long narrative poems, but it is with the short lyric that he is an enduring master. His prose *Imaginary Conversations* (1824–53) remains widely read.

POETRY BY LANDOR

Poetical Works. 3 vols. Ed. by Stephen Wheeler. OUP 1937 o.p.

NONFICTION BY LANDOR

Imaginary Conversations. 10 vols. AMS Pr. 1983 repr. of 1893 ed. $445.00. ISBN 0-404-07680-7

Selected Imaginary Conversations of Literary Men and Statesmen. Ed. by Charles L. Proudfit. U. of Nebr. Pr. 1969 $24.95. ISBN 0-8032-0097-8. Thoroughly annotated and documented collection of eight "conversations" about leading authors and statesmen; based on an 1846 edition.

WORKS BY LANDOR

The Complete Works of Walter Savage Landor. Ed. by T. E. Welby and Stephen Wheeler. 16 vols. AMS Pr. repr. of 1936 ed. o.p.

Poetry and Prose. Ed. by E. K. Chambers. AMS Pr. repr. of 1946 ed. o.p. Excellent selection; important critical articles by major critics.

BOOKS ABOUT LANDOR

Bradley, William. *Early Poems of Walter Savage Landor*. Folcroft repr. of 1914 ed. o.p.

Davie, Donald. *Purity of Diction in English Verse*. Schocken 1967 o.p. An interesting dissent.

Elwin, Malcolm. *Savage Landor*. Arden Lib. 1983 repr. of 1941 ed. o.p. Good biography.

Pinsky, Robert. *Landor's Poetry*. U. Ch. Pr. 1968 o.p. An important modern study.

Super, Robert H. *Walter Savage Landor*. Greenwood 1977 repr. of 1954 ed. o.p. A standard resource.

PEACOCK, THOMAS LOVE. 1785–1866

The witty, erudite, quirky Peacock, renowned for his range of knowledge, was largely self-educated. While working at the East India Company as a clerk to support his invalid wife and children, he mastered Greek, Latin, Italian, French, and Welsh. In his youth he associated with a number of free-thinking intellectuals, including SHELLEY (who called him "Greeky Peaky" for his fondness of ancient Greek literature), Jeremy Bentham, and JOHN STUART MILL. Peacock's daughter married and later abandoned GEORGE MEREDITH, who expressed his anguish in the sonnet sequence *Modern Love* (1862) and his novels *The Ordeal of Richard Feverel* (1859) and *The Egoist* (1879). Peacock's own fiction parodied the fashionable excesses of taste for the supernatural, medieval, melancholy, and sensibility that appeared in the popular novels, poetry, and melodramas. He also parodied the writers themselves—COLERIDGE, BYRON, and Shelley among others—for their eccentricities and attitudinizing. In a series of novels written over a long creative life (he died at age 81), with titles caricaturing the fashion for castles and abbeys—*Headlong Hall* (1816), *Melincourt* (1817), *Nightmare Abbey* (1818), *Crotchet Castle* (1831), and *Gryll Grange* (1861)—Peacock tried to show that the proper function of literature, as he said in *Nightmare Abbey*, was "to reconcile man as he is to the world as it is."

NOVELS BY PEACOCK

Headlong Hall and *Nightmare Abbey*. 1816. Biblio Dist. 1965 o.p.
Nightmare Abbey and *Crotchet Castle* and *The Misfortunes of Elphin*. 1818. Viking Penguin 1982 $9.95. ISBN 0-14-043045-8

POETRY BY PEACOCK

Songs from the Novels of Thomas Love Peacock. Folcroft 1972 o.p.

NONFICTION BY PEACOCK

Peacock's Memoirs of Shelley, With Shelley's Letters to Peacock. Rprt. Serv. 1992 repr. of 1909 ed. $79.00. ISBN 0-7812-7655-1. Personal recollections of Shelley, with an introduction by Humbert Wolfe.

WORK BY PEACOCK

Works. 10 vols. Ed. by H. F. Brett-Smith and C. E. Jones. Rprt. Serv. 1992 repr. of 1934 ed. $750.00. ISBN 0-7812-7616-0. Contains novels, poems, fugitive pieces, and criticism. Includes a preface by Lord Houghton and a biographical notice by Peacock's granddaughter, Edith Nicolls.

BOOKS ABOUT PEACOCK

Able, Augustus H. *George Meredith and Thomas Love Peacock: A Study in Literary Influence*. Gordon Pr. 1973 $59.95. ISBN 0-8490-0224-9
Butler, Marilyn. *Peacock Displayed: A Satirist in His Context*. Routledge 1979 o.p. Competent introduction to Peacock's writings and his humor.
Burns, Bryan. *The Novels of Thomas Love Peacock*. B & N Imports 1985 $48.25. ISBN 0-389-20532-X
Campbell, Olwen W. *Thomas Love Peacock. Select Bibliographies Repr. Ser.* Ayer 1972 repr. of 1953 ed. $14.00. ISBN 0-8369-5787-3
Mills, Howard W. *Peacock: His Circle and His Age*. Cambridge U. Pr. 1969 o.p. A critical look at Peacock's relationships with Hazlitt, Byron, Crabbe, and others.
Prance, Claude A. *The Characters in the Novels of Thomas Love Peacock*. E. Mellen 1992 $79.95. ISBN 0-7734-9510-X
Van Doren, Carl. *The Life of Thomas Love Peacock*. Russell 1966 repr. of 1911 ed. o.p. A comprehensive chronological survey of Peacock's life; also deals with his most important works.

SCOTT, SIR WALTER. 1771–1832

Scott was born in Edinburgh, Scotland, the son of a writer. As a young boy, he contracted polio and was sent to his grandfather's farm to recuperate. While there, he came to know and love the Border country, which figures prominently in his work.

Scott began his literary career by writing metrical tales. "The Lay of the Last Minstrel," "Marmion," and "The Lady of the Lake" made him the most popular poet of his day. Sixty-five hundred copies of "The Lay of the Last Minstrel" were sold in the first three years, a record sale for poetry. His later romances in verse, "The Vision of Don Roderick," "Rokeby," and "The Lord of the Isles," met with waning interest owing to the rivalry of BYRON, whose more passionate poetic romances superseded Scott's in the public favor. Scott then abandoned poetry for prose. In 1814 he anonymously published a historical novel, *Waverly, or, Sixty Years Since*, the first of the series known as the Waverley novels. He wrote 23 novels anonymously during the next 13 years. The first master of historical fiction, Scott wrote novels that are historical in background rather than in character: A fictitious person always holds the foreground. In their historical sequence, the Waverley novels range in setting from the year 1090, the time of the First Crusade, to 1700, the period covered in *St. Roman's Well* (1824), set in a Scottish watering place. Scott wrote novels covering every period of European history from the eleventh to nineteenth centuries, except the thirteenth century. Scott's last years were plagued by illness, yet in 1831 and 1832 he toured the Mediterranean aboard a government frigate. He died at Abbotsford soon after his return and was buried in the ruins of Dryburgh Abbey.

NOVELS BY SCOTT

THE WAVERLEY NOVELS

The Abbot. Biblio Dist. 1969 repr. of 1906 ed. o.p. A romantic adventure about Queen Mary's escape from Bockleven Castle. ·

The Antiquary. 1816. Biblio Dist. 1969 o.p.

The Bride of Lammermoor. 1819. Biblio Dist. 1979 $6.95. ISBN 0-460-01129-4. Story of the lovers Ravenswood and Lucy who are torn apart by a family feud.

The Fair Maid of Perth. 1828. NAL-Dutton o.p.

The Fortunes of Nigel. 1822. 2 Vols. Rprt. Serv. 1992 repr. of 1893 ed. $150.00. ISBN 0-7812-7641-1

Guy Mannering. 1815. Biblio Dist. 1954 o.p. The tale of an unfortunate, melancholy man whose efforts at goodness result in ultimate victory.

The Heart of Midlothian. 1818. Biblio Dist. 1980 $5.95. ISBN 0-460-01134-0. Effie Dean is accused of murdering her own child, but her sister Jeanie sets out to prove her innocence.

Ivanhoe. 1820. Bantam 1988 $3.50. ISBN 0-553-21326-1. Story of the struggles between the Norman conquerors and the native Saxons in twelfth-century England, told through the love story of Ivanhoe and Rowena.

Kenilworth. 1821. *Airmont Class. Ser.* Airmont 1968 $2.25. ISBN 0-8049-0312-5. The events that led to the mysterious death of Amy Robsart in 1560.

The Monastery. 1826. Biblio Dist. 1969 repr. of 1906 ed. o.p. A tale of religious conflict during the Reformation; focuses on the lives of two characters in a monastery.

Old Mortality. 1817. Ed. by Angus Calder. Viking Penguin 1975 $6.95. ISBN 0-14-043098-9

Quentin Durward. 1823. Airmont 1969 $2.50. ISBN 0-8049-0312-5. Story of a young Scot of the 1400s caught up in the intrigues of King Louis XI of France.

Redgauntlet. 1824. Ed. by Kathryn Sutherland. OUP 1985 $7.95. ISBN 0-19-281668-3. A tale of intrigue based on the Jacobite rebellion of 1745.

Rob Roy. 1818. C. E. Tuttle 1991 $7.95. ISBN 0-460-87089-0. Chronicles the travails of a Scottish chieftain in the Highlands of Scotland.

The Talisman. 1825. C. E. Tuttle 1991 $7.95. ISBN 0-460-87088-2. Deals with the
  adventures of King Richard and the Persians during the period of the Crusades.
Waverley, or, Sixty Years Since. 1814. OUP 1986 $6.95. ISBN 0-19-281722-1. Waverly, a
  soldier, is torn between his loyalty to England and his love of Scotland.
Woodstock. 1826. Rprt. Serv. 1992 repr. of 1894 ed. $150.00. ISBN 0-7812-7643-0.
  Ghostly adventures at the village of Woodstock in 1649.

NONFICTION BY SCOTT

The Bannatyne Miscellany. 1827–1855. 3 vols. AMS Pr. repr. of 1927 ed. $70.00. ISBN 0-
  404-52720-5. Volume 1 edited by Scott. Contains Scottish documents of historical
  and literary interest.
The Journal of Sir Walter Scott. 1890. Greenwood 1978 repr. of 1950 ed. o.p. From the
  original manuscript at Abbotsford.
Letters on Demonology and Witchcraft. Gordon Pr. 1973 $250.00. ISBN 0-87968-180-2.
  Letters addressed to J. G. Lockhart, Esquire, dealing with the subject of demons and
  demonology; includes explanatory notes.
Life of Dryden. 1808. Ed. by Bernard Kreissman. U. of Nebr. Pr. 1963 o.p.
The Prefaces to the Waverley Novels. Ed. by Mark A. Weinstein. U. of Nebr. Pr. 1978
  $23.95. ISBN 0-8032-4700-1. Collection of Scott's prefaces to his Waverley novels;
  one of the most important series of revelations by a writer about his own work.

POETRY BY SCOTT

Complete Poetical Works. HM 1980 $8.95. ISBN 0-395-07493-2. Contains every known
  verse poem and fragment.
The Lady of the Lake and Other Poems. 1810. *Airmont Class. Ser.* Airmont 1967 $1.75.
  ISBN 0-8049-0137-6
The Lord of the Isles. 1815. Rprt. Serv. 1988 repr. of 1914 ed. $59.00. ISBN 0-7812-0077-6
Minstrelsy of the Scottish Border. 1802. Ed. by T. F. Henderson. 4 vols. Gale 1968 repr. of
  1902 ed. $150.00. ISBN 1-55888-189-1. Edited by Scott.
Selected Poems. Ed. by Thomas Crawford. OUP 1972 o.p. A good collection for the
  general reader; includes introductions to each poem.

WORK BY SCOTT

Letters. Ed. by Herbert J. Grierson and others. 12 vols. AMS Pr. repr. of 1932–37 ed. o.p.
  Includes many letters not published before, or printed in an abridged or garbled
  form.

BOOKS ABOUT SCOTT

Ball, Margaret. *Sir Walter Scott as a Critic of Literature.* Assoc. Faculty Pr. repr. of 1907
  ed. o.p. A standard work.
Beiderwell, Bruce. *Power and Punishment in Scott's Novels.* U. of Ga. Pr. 1992 $30.00.
  ISBN 0-8203-1351-3
Carswell, Donald. *Scott and His Circle.* Ayer 1972 repr. of 1930 ed. $19.00. ISBN 0-8369-
  6607-4. Also interesting for materials on such authors as James Hogg.
Corson, J. C. *Bibliography of Sir Walter Scott. Bibliography and Reference Ser.* B. Franklin
  repr. of 1943 ed. o.p. Notes and index to the *Letters of Sir Walter Scott*; epitomizes
  the whole of Scott's work.
Duncan, Jan. *Modern Romance and Transformations of the Novel: The Gothic, Scott, and
  Dickens.* Cambridge U. Pr. 1992 $49.95. ISBN 0-521-39535-6
Ferris, Ina. *The Achievement of Literary Authority: Gender, History, and the Waverly
  Novels.* Cornell Univ. Pr. 1991 $34.50. ISBN 0-8014-2630-8
Gell, William. *Reminiscences of Sir Walter Scott's Residence in Italy, 1832.* Richard West
  1973 repr. of 1937 ed. o.p. Gell's personal notes of Scott's last journey to Italy.
Grierson, Herbert. *Sir Walter Scott, Bart.* Folcroft repr. of 1938 ed. o.p. One of the earlier
  biographies.

Hillhouse, J. T. *The Waverley Novels and Their Critics.* Hippocrene Bks. 1968 o.p. Useful study.

Johnson, Edgar. *Sir Walter Scott: The Great Unknown.* 2 vols. Macmillan 1970 o.p. An exhaustive and definitive modern biography, awarded the American Heritage Biography Prize.

Kerr, James. *Fiction Against History: Scott as Storyteller.* Cambridge U. Pr. 1989 $44.95. ISBN 0-521-36425-6

Lauber, John. *Sir Walter Scott. Twayne's Eng. Authors Ser.* G. K. Hall 1966 o.p. Includes a brief biographical sketch and chapters on Scott's poetry, critical essays, and novels.

Lockhart, John Gibson. *The Life of Sir Walter Scott.* 10 vols. AMS Pr. 1983 repr. of 1902 ed. $345.00. ISBN 0-404-07700-5. An abridgment of the *Memoirs* below.

————. *Memoirs of Sir Walter Scott.* 10 vols. AMS Pr. repr. of 1902 ed. o.p. The standard authorized biography by Scott's son-in-law, regarded as one of the great literary biographies.

Mayhead, Robin. *Walter Scott. British Authors Ser.* Cambridge U. Pr. 1973 $35.50. ISBN 0-685-15593-5. Part of a series of short, introductory critical studies of significant British authors.

Millgate, Jane. *Sir Walter Scott: The Making of a Novelist.* U. of Toronto Pr. 1984 $14.95. ISBN 0-8020-6692-5. Criticism and interpretation with a bibliography.

Rogers, May. *The Waverley Dictionary.* Gordon Pr. 1972 $75.00. ISBN 0-8490-1279-7

Welsh, Alexander. *The Hero of the Waverley Novels.* Atheneum 1968 o.p. A thematic study examining Scott's heroes in terms of their morality.

Wilson, A. N. *The Laird of Abbotsford: A View of Sir Walter Scott.* OUP 1989 $12.95. ISBN 0-19-282588-7. An attempt to view Scott's life and work as complementary.

SHELLEY, MARY WOLLSTONECRAFT (GODWIN). 1797–1851

Mary Godwin (the daughter of William Godwin, the English philosopher and writer, and Mary Wollstonecraft, author of the *Vindication of the Rights of Women*, 1792) fell in love with the poet PERCY BYSSHE SHELLEY, traveled to the Continent with him in 1814, and married him after the suicide of his first wife, in 1816. She is best known for her novel of horror, *Frankenstein* (1818), which she wrote when BYRON proposed that he and each of his companions write a tale of the supernatural. It was as part of this competition that John Polidori wrote *The Vampyre* (1819). After Shelley's death, she edited his writings and wrote biographies, articles, and fiction in order to raise money to educate their surviving son. Because of her association with BYRON, Edward J. Trelawny, and LEIGH HUNT, her *Letters* and *Journal* are excellent sources of literary material on the period. *My Best Mary*, written by Percy Bysshe Shelley, reveals in detail his life and loves as well as his wife's feelings and flirtations. Mary Shelley's seminal use of a combination of a creation myth and science in *Frankenstein* and her notoriety as Shelley's mistress have made her especially interesting to modern audiences.

NOVELS BY MARY SHELLEY

Frankenstein; or, The Modern Prometheus. 1818. U. CA Pr. 1984 $40.00. ISBN 0-520-05281-1

The Last Man. 1826. Ed. by Hugh J. Luke, Jr. U. of Nebr. Pr. 1993 $10.95. ISBN 0-8032-9217-1

Falkner: A Novel. 3 vols. in 1 AMS Pr. repr. of 1837 ed. $44.50. ISBN 0-404-62110-4

POETRY BY MARY SHELLEY

The Choice: A Poem on Shelley's Death. Folcroft repr. of 1876 ed. o.p.

SHORT STORY COLLECTION BY MARY SHELLEY

Mary Shelley: Collected Tales and Stories, with Original Engravings. Ed. by Charles E. Robinson. Johns Hopkins 1976 o.p.

WORKS BY MARY SHELLEY

The Journals of Mary Shelley, Part I, 1814–July 1822. 2 vols. Ed. by Diana Scott-Kilvert and Paula R. Feldman. OUP 1987 $115.00. ISBN 0-19-812571-2

The Journals of Mary Shelley, Part II, July 1822–1844. Ed. by Diana Scott-Kilvert and Paula R. Feldman. OUP $98.00. ISBN 0-19-812674-3

The Letters of Mary Wollstonecraft Shelley. 2 vols. Ed. by Betty Bennett. Johns Hopkins Vol. 1 *A Part of the Elect.* 1980 $49.50. ISBN 0-8018-2275-0. Vol. 2 *Treading in Unknown Paths.* 1983 $42.50. ISBN 0-8018-2645-4. Vol. 3 *What Years I Have Spent.* 1988 $45.00. ISBN 0-8018-2646-2

The Letters of Mary Wollstonecraft Shelley. Ed. by Howard Harper. Folcroft 1974 repr. of 1918 ed. o.p.

BOOKS ABOUT MARY SHELLEY

Baldick, Chris. *In Frankenstein's Shadows: Myth, Monstrosity, and Nineteenth-Century Writing.* OUP 1990 repr. of 1988 ed. $16.95. ISBN 0-19-812249-7

Behrendt, Stephen C., ed. *Approaches to Teaching Shelley's* Frankenstein. Modern Lang. 1990 $34.00. ISBN 0-87352-539-6. Collected essays reflecting the diverse ways in which *Frankenstein* is dealt with in the classroom.

Farry, Stephen. *Hideous Progeny: Dramatizations of Frankenstein from Mary Shelley to the Present.* U. of Pa. Pr. 1990 $41.95. ISBN 0-8122-8131-4. A fascinating investigation of one of the most intriguing characters of the imagination.

Giddings, Robert, and Jo Manton. *Claire Clairmont and the Shelleys, 1798-1879.* OUP 1992 $39.95. ISBN 0-19-818594-4. A well-written and well-researched book.

Levine, George, and U. K. Knoepflmacher, eds. *The Endurance of Frankenstein: Essays on Mary Shelley's Novel.* U. CA Pr. 1979 $10.95. ISBN 0-520-04640-4. Twelve essays that examine the persistent hold that *Frankenstein* continues to have on the contemporary reader.

Lyles, W. H. *Mary Shelley: An Annotated Bibliography.* Garland 1975 o.p. A fairly comprehensive listing of works by and about Shelley; the majority are annotated.

Mellor, Anne K. *Mary Shelley: Her Life, Her Fiction, Her Monsters.* Routledge 1988 $14.95. ISBN 0-415-90147-2. Examines the entire range of Mary Shelley's life and writing, taking her out of the shadow of her famous husband and acknowledging the originality of Frankenstein.

St. Clair, William. *The Godwins and the Shelleys: A Biography of a Family.* Johns Hopkins 1991 $16.95. ISBN 0-8018-4233-6. Reprint of the Norton edition.

Spark, Muriel. *Mary Shelley.* NAL-Dutton 1988 $8.95. ISBN 0-452-00951-0. A welcome biography that covers the facts of Shelley's life.

———. *Child of Light: A Reassessment of Mary Shelley.* 1951 o.p. A sympathetic life by another woman novelist.

Sunstein, Emily. *Mary Shelley: Romance and Reality.* Little 1989 $24.95. ISBN 0-316-82246-9. Biography of the creator of *Frankenstein*; for advanced readers.

Walling, William. *Mary Shelley.* Twayne 1972 o.p. A brief but reliable treatment of her life and works.

SHELLEY, PERCY BYSSHE. 1792–1822

Born in Field Place, near Horsham in Sussex, Shelley was educated at Syon House Academy and Eton, where he acquired the sobriquet "Mad Shelley" for his independent spirit. While at Eton he published *Zastrozzi* (1810), a Gothic novel. Expelled from Oxford because he refused to retract his atheistic beliefs, Shelley quarreled with his wealthy father and was banished from home. Shelley married impulsively and then abandoned his young wife to run off to Italy with

the 16-year-old MARY WOLLSTONECRAFT GODWIN (the daughter of the radical
feminist and the anarchist philosopher, who was eventually to write *Frankenstein*). While in Italy, Shelley became close friends with BYRON, and the two
became objects of endless, notorious rumor.

Shelley's personal character was revered by almost everyone who knew him.
Extremely generous toward others, frugal with himself, he strove tirelessly for
the betterment of humanity. *Prometheus Unbound* (1820), a lyrical drama in
four acts, calls for the regeneration of society through love and for the
destruction of all repressive institutions. *The Cenci* (1819), a verse drama based
on real events, is one of the few plays from the romantic period still produced.
Shelley's lyrics are marvelously varied and rich in sound and rhythm.
WORDSWORTH regarded him as the best artist among living poets. *Adonais*
(1821), written to honor the memory of JOHN KEATS, is one of the supreme
elegies in English. *The Triumph of Life*, which was left incomplete at his death,
has been hailed by T. S. ELIOT as the nearest approach in English to DANTE (see
Vol. 2). The "Ode to the West Wind" and "To a Skylark" are anthologized
everywhere. Shelley's early death by drowning ended his career just as it was
coming into full flower. A revolutionary in his art and life, Shelley is considered
by many to be an inspired polemicist and poetic genius. As one of his
contemporaries wrote in *Etonian* (1821), "He is one of the many whom we
cannot read without wonder, or without pain. . . ."

POETRY BY PERCY SHELLEY

The Complete Poetical Works of Percy Bysshe Shelley: 1814–1817. 2 vols. Ed. by Neville
    Rogers. OUP 1972–74 o.p. Provides a textual history of Shelley's poems; includes
    discussions about each poem. Volume I includes poems written from 1802 to 1813;
    Volume II covers 1814–17.
The Triumph of Life. Ed. by Donald H. Reiman. Garland 1984 o.p.

PLAY BY PERCY SHELLEY

Prometheus Unbound. 1820. Ed. by Vida D. Scudder. Century Bookbindery 1980 repr. of
    1904 ed. o.p.

NONFICTION BY PERCY SHELLEY

Shelley's Literary and Philosophical Criticism. Ed. by John Shawcross. Folcroft 1973 o.p.

WORKS BY PERCY SHELLEY

Selected Poetry and Prose. Ed. by Kenneth N. Cameron. *Rinehart Ed*. H. Holt & Co. 1951
    o.p. Excellent selection and notes.
Shelley. Ed. by Kathleen Raine. *Penguin Poets Ser*. Viking Penguin 1978 o.p.
Shelley on Love: An Anthology. Ed. by Richard Holmes. U. CA Pr. 1981 $27.50. ISBN 0-
    520-04322-7. A particularly interesting anthology by one of Shelley's most original
    biographers.
Shelley's Poetry and Prose. Ed. by Donald H. Reiman. *Norton Critical Eds*. Norton
    1977 $13.95. ISBN 0-393-09164-3. Excellent selection, introduction, notes, and
    bibliography.

BOOKS ABOUT PERCY SHELLEY

Abbey, Lloyd. *Destroyer and Preserver: Shelley's Poetic Skepticism*. Bks. Demand repr. of
    1979 ed. $49.50. ISBN 0-7837-1815-2. Study showing that skepticism is both a central
    theme of Shelley's poetry and a primary cause of its artistic excellence.
Allott, Miriam, ed. *Essays on Shelley*. *Eng. Texts and Studies*. B & N Imports 1982 $28.50.
    ISBN 0-389-20127-8. Analysis of Shelley's thought, work, and reputation.

Barcus, James E., ed. *Shelley: The Critical Heritage. Critical Heritage Ser.* Routledge 1975 $69.50. ISBN 0-7100-8148-0. A worthy selection of critical essays; includes letters, journals, and conversations by Shelley's friends and enemies.

Behrendt, Stephen. *Shelley and His Audiences.* U. of Nebr. Pr. 1989 $35.00. ISBN 0-8032-1208-9

Blank, G. Kim. *The New Shelley: Later Twentieth-Century Views.* St. Martin 1991 $45.00. ISBN 0-312-05344-4

Bloom, Harold. *Shelley's Mythmaking.* Cornell Univ. Pr. 1969 repr. of 1959 ed. o.p. A key work in the reassessment of Shelley.

Cameron, Kenneth N. *Shelley: The Golden Years.* HUP 1974 $38.00. ISBN 0-674-80605-0. A continuation of Cameron's *The Young Shelley*; examines his period of greatest productivity and genius.

———. *The Young Shelley: Genesis of a Radical.* Century Bookbindery 1980 repr. of 1951 ed. o.p. Indispensable study tracing Shelley's literary development.

Cronin, Richard. *Shelley's Poetic Thoughts.* St. Martin 1981 o.p. Deals with Shelley's handling of language and poetic forms.

Curran, Stuart. *Shelley's Annus Mirabilis: The Maturing of an Epic Vision.* Huntington Lib. 1975 $17.95. ISBN 0-87328-064-4. An especially lucid study.

———. *Shelley's Cenci: Scorpions Ringed with Fire.* Princeton U. Pr. 1970 $45.00. ISBN 0-691-06196-3. Thorough investigation into Shelley's writings based on the sixteenth-century Italian beauty, Beatrice Cenci.

Ellis, Frederick S. *A Lexical Concordance to the Poetical Works of Percy Bysshe Shelley.* Rprt. Serv. 1992 repr. of 1892 ed. $109.00. ISBN 0-7812-7651-9. Attempt to classify every word found in Shelley's poetry according to its significance.

Fogle, Richard H. *The Imagery of Keats and Shelley: A Comparative Study.* U. of NC Pr. repr. of 1949 ed. o.p. Analyzes the poetry of both Shelley and Keats in order to compare and dispute stereotypes in their imagery.

Grabo, Carl A. *Prometheus Unbound: An Interpretation.* Gordian 1968 repr. of 1935 ed. $45.00. ISBN 0-87752-045-3

Hall, Spencer, ed. *Approaches to Teaching Shelley's Poetry.* Modern Lang. 1990 $34.00. ISBN 0-87352-528-0

Holmes, Richard. *Shelley: The Pursuit.* Viking Penguin 1987 $12.95. ISBN 0-14-058037-8. Provocative, controversial, and highly readable life.

Keach, William. *Shelley's Style.* Routledge Chapman & Hall 1985 $32.50. ISBN 0-416-30320-X. Technical but lucid analysis of special characteristics.

King-Hele, Desmont. *Shelley: His Thought and Work.* Fairleigh Dickinson 1984 $35.00. ISBN 0-8386-3199-1. Valuable because of its attention to Shelley's scientific interests.

Knerr, Anthony D. *Shelley's Adonais: A Critical Edition.* Col. U. Pr. 1984 $37.00. ISBN 0-231-05466-1. Synthesizes extensive scholarship since the eighteenth century; provides a transcription of the manuscript drafts of the poem.

O'Neill, Michael. *Percy Bysshe Shelley: A Literary Life.* St. Martin 1989 $35.00. ISBN 0-312-03248-X

Peacock, Thomas L. *Peacock's Memoir of Shelley, with Shelley's Letters to Peacock.* Rprt. Serv. 1992 repr. of 1909 ed. $79.00. ISBN 0-7812-7655-1. Includes an introduction by Humbert Wolfe; fully illustrated with eighteen pen and ink drawings and sixteen photogravure portraits.

Pulos, C. E. *Deep Truth: A Study of Shelley's Scepticism.* U. of Nebr. Pr. 1962 o.p. A very influential study.

Raine, Kathleen, ed. *Shelley. Penguin Poets Ser.* Viking Penguin 1978 o.p.

Reiman, Donald H. *Percy Bysshe Shelley. Twayne's Eng. Authors Ser.* G. K. Hall 1970 $14.50. ISBN 0-8057-1488-X. General introduction; overview integrating Shelley's life and work.

Rieger, James. *Mutiny Within.* Braziller o.p. Interesting biography of Shelley, focusing on the conflicts in his life.

Roe, Ivan. *Shelley: The Last Phase.* Cooper Sq. 1973 repr. of 1953 ed. $35.00. ISBN 0-8154-0464-6

Trelawney, Edward J. *Records of Shelley, Byron, and the Author.* 2 vols. Rprt. Serv. 1992 repr. of 1878 ed. $150.00. ISBN 0-7812-7253-7. Contemporary account of Shelley and Byron, by the English author and adventurer Edward Trelawney.

Wasserman, Earl R. *Shelley: A Critical Reading.* Johns Hopkins 1971 $15.95. ISBN 0-8018-2017-0. Extreme critical readings, highly influential.

Weaver, Bennett. *Toward the Understanding of Shelley.* 1966. Hippocrene Bks. 1967 $18.50. ISBN 0-374-98284-8

Webb, Timothy. *Shelley: A Voice Not Understood.* Humanities 1977 o.p. Probing study of Shelley's poetry and prose.

White, Newman Ivey. *Shelley.* 2 vols. Hippocrene Bks. 1972 o.p. The definitive biography of Shelley.

Wilson, Milton T. *Shelley's Later Poetry.* Greenwood 1974 repr. of 1959 ed. o.p. A sensible and useful guide through some difficult works.

SOUTHEY, ROBERT. 1774–1843

Southey was known to his contemporaries for his industrious habits, his methodical nature, his generosity, his hospitality, and his composition of "The Three Bears," as part of *The Doctor* (1834–47), an extended prose epic that he wrote to amuse himself and his large family. With his friend COLERIDGE, the youthful, revolutionary Southey planned an ideal community in America called Pantisocracy; the two writers married sisters whom they thought would be suitable for that project. Southey instead spent time in the civil service, then settled in Keswick in the Lake District. By 1813 he had sufficiently recanted his revolutionary ideals to be appointed poet laureate. To support his large family of seven children, and Coleridge's three children as well, Southey literally wrote himself to death in what he called "miscellaneous authorship": journalism, histories, biographies, translations, editions, reviews, and long exotic poems with titles such as *The Curse of Kehama* (1810) and *Thalaba the Destroyer* (1801). Because he wrote whatever would sell, Southey was treated with contempt by authors such as BYRON, who felt that a writer's pen should not be for sale. But he was so generous, helpful, and compassionate that to those who knew him his character was impeccable. His home, Greta Hall, with its massive library and view of the mountains, has now appropriately become a school for young children.

NONFICTION BY SOUTHEY

History of Brazil. 1819. 3 vols. B. Franklin 1971 o.p.

The Life of Nelson. 1813. Naval Inst. Pr. 1990 $29.95. ISBN 0-87021-301-6. Interesting account of the famous English naval commander.

The Life of Wesley; and the Rise and Progress of Methodism. 1820. OUP 1925 o.p. With Coleridge's copious notes.

Sir Thomas More, or, Colloquies on the Progress and Prospects of Society. 1829 o.p.

POETRY BY SOUTHEY

Joan of Arc: An Epic Poem. 1796. o.p. Based on the life of the French saint.

Omniana. 1812. Ed. by Robert Giddings. S. Ill. U. Pr. 1969 o.p.

The Poetical Works of Southey, Collected by Himself. 1837–38. 10 vols. o.p.

Thalaba the Destroyer. 1801. Woodstock 1991 o.p.

PLAY BY SOUTHEY

The Fall of Robespierre: An Historic Drama. 1794. Cambridge U. Pr. o.p. Acts 2 and 3, by Southey; Act 1, by Coleridge. Details the life of the French revolutionary.

WORKS BY SOUTHEY

The Doctor. 1834–47. Ed. by M. H. Fitzgerald. Bell 1930 o.p. Selections from the original seven-volume work.

Letters from England by Don Manuel Alvarez Espriella. Ed. by Jack Simmons. Cresset Pr. 1951 o.p. Helpful notes and introduction.

The Life and Correspondence of Robert Southey. 6 vols. Rprt. Serv. 1992 repr. of 1850 ed. $450.00. ISBN 0-7812-7661-6

New Letters. 2 vols. Ed. by Kenneth Curry. Col. U. Pr. 1965 o.p.

BOOKS ABOUT SOUTHEY

Bernhardt-Kabisch, Ernest. *Robert Southey*. Irvington 1977 $17.95. ISBN 0-8057-6692-8. Overview of Southey's work and its historical significance.

Carnall, Geoffrey. *Robert Southey and His Age: The Development of a Conservative*. OUP 1960 o.p. Examines Southey and his work in the political context of his time.

Curry, Kenneth. *Southey*. Routledge 1975 o.p. Interesting and informative biography.

_____. *Robert Southey: A Reference Guide*. G. K. Hall 1977 o.p. An annotated guide to all Southey scholarship.

WORDSWORTH, WILLIAM. 1770–1850

Born in the "Lake Country" of northern England, the great English poet William Wordsworth was orphaned at an early age. After an undistinguished career at Cambridge, he spent a year in revolutionary France, before returning to England a penniless radical. For five years he and his sister Dorothy lived very frugally in rural England, where they met COLERIDGE. *Lyrical Ballads*, published anonymously in 1798, led off with Coleridge's *Ancient Mariner* and ended with Wordsworth's *Tintern Abbey*. Between these two masterworks are at least a dozen other great poems. *Lyrical Ballads* is often said to mark the beginning of the English romantic revolution. A second, augmented edition in 1800 was prefaced by one of the great manifestos in world literature, an essay that called for natural language in poetry, subject matter dealing with ordinary men and women, a return to emotions and imagination, and a conception of poetry as pleasure and prophecy.

Before he was 30, Wordsworth had begun the supreme work of his life, *The Prelude*, an immensely long autobiographical work on "The Growth of the Poet's Mind," a theme unprecedented in poetry. Although first finished in 1805, *The Prelude* was never published in Wordsworth's lifetime. Between 1797 and 1807, he produced a steady stream of magnificent works, but little of his work over the last four decades of his life matters greatly. *The Excursion*, a poem of epic length, was considered by HAZLITT and KEATS to be among the wonders of the age.

After *Lyrical Ballads*, Wordsworth turned to his own life, his spiritual and poetical development, as his major theme. More than anyone else, he dealt with mysterious affinities between nature and humanity. Poems like the *Ode on the Intimations of Immortality* have a mystical power quite independent of any particular creed, and simple lyrics like "The Solitary Reaper" produce amazingly powerful effects with the simplest materials. Wordsworth also revived the sonnet and is one of the greatest masters of that form. Wordsworth is one of the giants of English poetry and criticism, his work ranging from the almost childishly simple to the philosophically profound.

POETRY BY WORDSWORTH

Benjamin the Waggoner. Ed. by Paul Betz. Cornell Univ. Pr. 1980 $62.50. ISBN 0-8014-1270-6. Includes complete texts of the two primary pre-publication stages of the poem (1806 and 1812) and reprints of the 1819 first edition.

The Borderers. Ed. by Robert Osborn. Cornell Univ. Pr. 1981 $99.50. ISBN 0-8014-1283-8. Includes the complete text of the 1796 edition.

Descriptive Sketches. Ed. by Eric Birdsall and Paul M. Zall. Cornell Univ. Pr. 1983 $55.00. ISBN 0-8014-1536-5. The 1793 version, with sustained critical discussion of the work by the editor.

An Evening Walk. Ed. by James Averill. Cornell Univ. Pr. 1983 $49.95. ISBN 0-8014-1474-1. Complete text of Wordsworth's first long poem (1794); includes a full textual history of the poem.

The Excursion. Woodstock 1991 o.p. Facsimile edition with introduction by Jonathan Wordsworth.

Home at Grasmere: Part First, Book First, of "The Recluse." Ed. by Beth Darlington. Cornell Univ. Pr. 1977 $77.50. ISBN 0-8014-1055-X. A "reading text" and photographs of many manuscript pages; valuable for detailed study of textual variants and stages of development in the poem.

Lyrical Ballads, 1798. (coauthored with Samuel Taylor Coleridge). Ed. by W. J. Owen. OUP 1969 $5.95. ISBN 0-19-911006-9

Peterbell. Ed. by John E. Jordan. Cornell Univ. Pr. 1985 $75.00. ISBN 0-8014-1620-5. Wordsworth's great imaginative work; includes copies of earlier manuscripts.

Poems, in Two Volumes, & Other Poems, 1800–1807. Ed. by Jared Curtis. Cornell Univ. Pr. 1982 $99.50. ISBN 0-8014-1445-8. Presents all textual evidence of Wordsworth's lyric and shorter narrative poems composed between 1800 and 1807.

Poetical Works. Ed. by Thomas Hutchinson and Ernest de Selincourt. *Oxford Stand. Authors Ser.* 1950 $35.00. Superb one-volume edition.

The Prelude: 1799, 1805, 1850. Ed. by Jonathan Wordsworth. *Norton Critical Eds.* 1979 $15.95. ISBN 0-393-09071-X. Contains the 1799, 1805, and 1850 versions of this much-revised poem.

William Wordsworth. Ed. by Stephen Gill. *Oxford Authors Ser.* 1984 $13.95. ISBN 0-19-281333-1. Original versions of the poems, not as later revised.

Wordsworth: Poetical Works. Ed. by Ernest de Selincourt. *Oxford Stand. Authors Ser.* OUP rev. ed. 1950 repr. of 1936 ed. o.p.

Wordsworth and Coleridge: Lyrical Ballads, 1805. (coauthored with Samuel Taylor Coleridge). Ed. by Derek Roper. International Ideas 1986 o.p.

WORKS BY WORDSWORTH

The Letters of William Wordsworth: A New Selection. Ed. by Alan G. Hill. OUP 1991 $45.00. ISBN 0-19-818529-4. Letters written during Wordsworth's later years, 1821–1850.

Letters of the Wordsworth Family from 1787 to 1855. 3 vols. Rprt. Serv. 1992 repr. of 1907 ed. $225.00. ISBN 0-7812-7647-0

The Love Letters of William and Mary Wordsworth. Ed. by Beth Darlington. Cornell Univ. Pr. 1981 $34.95. ISBN 0-8014-1261-7. Letters throwing invaluable light on the poet's marriage and middle years.

BOOKS ABOUT WORDSWORTH

Abrams, Meyer H, ed. *Wordsworth: A Collection of Critical Essays.* P-H (Spectrum Bks.) 1972 $12.95. ISBN 0-685-03922-6. Collection of critical essays representing the best in twentieth-century critical opinion.

Bate, Jonathan. *Romantic Ecology: Wordsworth and the Environmental Tradition.* Routledge 1991 $14.95. ISBN 0-415-06116-4

Bateson, Frederick W. *Wordsworth: A Re-interpretation.* AMS Pr. repr. of 1954 ed. $27.50. ISBN 0-404-20020-6. A controversial book about Wordsworth because of its claim that William and Dorothy felt more than family affection for each other.

Beatty, Arthur. *William Wordsworth: His Doctrine and Art in Their Historical Relations.* AMS Pr. repr. of 1927 ed. $32.50. ISBN 0-404-14003-3

Bewell, Alan. *Wordsworth and the Enlightenment: Nature, Man, and Society in the Experimental Poetry.* Yale U. Pr. 1989 $40.00. ISBN 0-300-04393-7. A remarkable study showing Wordsworth's eighteenth-century intellectual origins.

Chandler, James K. *Wordsworth's Second Nature: A Study of the Poetry and Politics.* U. Ch. Pr. 1984 $14.95. ISBN 0-226-10081-2. Examines the relationship of philosophy and power in Wordsworth's writings.

Coleridge, Samuel Taylor. *Biographia Literaria.* Ed. by George Watson. C. E. Tuttle 1906 $8.95. ISBN 0-460-87108-0. Still regarded as the classic analysis of Wordsworth's art.

Darbishire, Helen. *The Poet Wordsworth.* Greenwood 1980 repr. of 1965 ed. $35.00. ISBN 0-313-21483-2. A miracle of compression and judicious criticism.

Ferry, David. *The Limits of Mortality: An Essay on Wordsworth's Major Poems.* Greenwood 1978 repr. of 1959 ed. o.p.

Garrod, H. W. *Wordsworth: Lectures and Essays.* Arden Lib. 1978 repr. of 1923 ed. o.p. Compilation of noted lectures and essays about the poet's work and influence.

Gill, Stephen. *William Wordsworth: A Life.* OUP 1990 $13.95. ISBN 0-19-282747-2. Currently the standard life.

Grob, Alan. *The Philosophic Mind: A Study of Wordsworth's Poetry and Thought, 1797–1805.* Ohio State U. Pr. 1973 o.p. Includes the work of Wordsworth critics who share the same philosophical orientation.

Hall, Spencer, and Jonathan Ramsey, eds. *Approaches to Teaching Wordsworth's Poetry.* Modern Lang. 1986 $34.00. ISBN 0-87352-495-0. Evaluates the best approaches to use in teaching Wordsworth.

Harper, George M. *William Wordsworth: His Life, Works and Influence.* Russell 2 vols. in 1 repr. of 1929 ed. rev. ed. 1960 o.p. Superb for intellectual background and critical penetration.

Hartman, Geoffrey H. *Wordsworth's Poetry, 1785–1814.* Bks. Demand repr. of 1964 ed. $115.00. ISBN 0-8357-8382-0. Among the most influential studies of the century; absorbing, but lacks balance.

Havens, Raymond D. *The Mind of a Poet: A Study of Wordsworth's Thought with Reference to* The Prelude. 2 vols. AMS Pr. repr. of 1941 ed. $57.50. ISBN 0-404-14090-4. A masterful analysis of *The Prelude.*

Johnston, Kenneth. *Wordsworth and "The Recluse."* Yale U. Pr. 1984 o.p. Carefully reconstructs the manuscripts of Wordsworth major long poem.

Jones, Henry J. *The Egotistical Sublime: A History of Wordsworth's Imagination.* Greenwood 1979 repr. of 1954 ed. o.p. Well-written examination of Wordsworth's literalness, his masculinity, and his ego.

Legouis, Emile. *Early Life of William Wordsworth, 1770–1798.* Paul & Co. Pubs. 1992 repr. of 1991 ed. $60.00. ISBN 0-870352-30-0

Levinson, Marjorie. *Wordsworth's Great Period Poems: Four Essays.* Cambridge U. Pr. 1986 $49.95. ISBN 0-521-30829-1. A controversial interpretation of the poems mainly of 1807.

Lindenberger, Herbert S. *On Wordsworth's Prelude.* Greenwood 1976 repr. of 1963 ed. $60.50. ISBN 0-8371-8417-7. Series of closely related essays dealing with Wordsworth's language, style, and images.

Liu, Alan. *Wordsworth: The Sense of History.* Stanford U. Pr. 1989 $59.50. ISBN 0-8047-1373-1. A detailed reading of the historical background of Wordsworth's poetry.

McFarland, Thomas. *William Wordsworth: Intensity and Achievement.* OUP 1992 $45.00. ISBN 0-19-811253-X

Magnuson, Paul. *Coleridge and Wordsworth: A Lyrical Dialogue.* Princeton U. Pr. 1988 $42.00. ISBN 0-691-06732-5. A textually based reading of the relationship between Coleridge and Wordsworth.

Miles, Josephine. *Wordsworth and the Vocabulary of Emotion.* Hippocrene Bks. 1965 $18.00. ISBN 0-374-95681-2. Scholarly look at meaning and feeling in Wordsworth's poetry.

Moorman, Mary. *William Wordsworth.* 2 vols. OUP 1957–65 o.p. The standard life, but needs to be augmented by other perspectives.

Parrish, Stephen M. *The Art of the Lyrical Ballads.* HUP 1973 $19.95. ISBN 0-674-04810-5. Considers the ideas of Coleridge and Wordsworth in regard to the "language of conversation" in their poetry.

Perkins, David. *Quest for Permanence: Symbolism of Wordsworth, Shelley, and Keats.* HUP 1959 $18.50. Examines imagery and symbolism in Romantic poetry and its function as a means of reflecting nineteenth-century society.

Simpson, David. *Wordsworth's Historical Imagination.* Methuen 1987 o.p. The least controversial of the historical readings of Wordsworth.

Wordsworth, Dorothy. *The Grasmere Journals.* OUP 1993 $12.95. ISBN 0-19-283130-5. Complete journals of Wordsworth's sister Dorothy, with explanatory notes.

CHAPTER 10

The Victorian Period

Joseph W. Childers

> The first of the leading peculiarities of the present age is, that it is an age of transition. Mankind have outgrown old institutions and doctrines, and have not yet acquired new ones.
>
> —JOHN STUART MILL, "The Spirit of the Age"

The Victorian period—that time between the passage of the first Reform Bill in 1832 and the death in 1901 of the monarch who lent her name to the era—was an age of unparalleled change in Great Britain. Not only, as JOHN STUART MILL (see Vols. 3 and 4) says, were the institutions of the previous era outworn and useless, but also material change was happening so quickly that it was difficult to know what new institutions would allow the Victorians to make sense of their world. In many ways it was an age of contradictions, an age that produced countless self-made millionaires while the destitution experienced by so many of the working classes grew steadily worse. It was a period in which many of the greatest writers were women, yet women could neither vote nor possess private property in their marriages. It was a time of intense religiousness and also a time of decadence. The Victorian Age looked eagerly forward to a future when humanity would harness the raw power of nature and looked longingly back to the "simpler" middle ages and "jolly old England." It was a time in which revolutions—political, economic, and industrial—were both dreaded and longed for. It was a period that Mill could characterize as the offspring of the conservative SAMUEL TAYLOR COLERIDGE and the radical JEREMY BENTHAM (see Vol. 3). It was, as MATTHEW ARNOLD has said of himself in "Stanzas from the Grande Chartreuse," "caught between two worlds, one dead, the other powerless of being born."

This is not to say that the Victorian period was one of ambivalence. Convictions were firmly held. But increasingly, or so it seemed, the number of possible convictions that one could hold on any given issue was robbing the world of any sense of certainty. The Victorians were faced with making themselves over so that they could make sense of their world. The result in the literature of the period was incredible diversity and the singular *lack* of a dominant view of the world. While it is true that many writers of the period agreed on the importance of the issues of faith, industrialization, education, aesthetics, and politics, it would be both simple-minded and wrong to assume that these thinkers all thought the same way or to understand the age as a period of self-satisfaction and complacency. In the arena of politics, for instance, it is possible to find every stripe of political theory, from the paternalistic conservatism of someone like BENJAMIN DISRAELI to the cautious progressivism of THOMAS BABINGTON MACAULAY to the articulate liberalism of John Stuart Mill to the socialism of GEORGE GISSING and WILLIAM MORRIS.

Politics is an especially good place to begin a discussion of the Victorian period, because in many ways it was a quintessentially political age. The inwardness that had characterized so much of the great literature of the romantics who preceded the Victorians still found voice in novels, poems, and nonfiction (sometimes it seems as though every Victorian author wrote an autobiography), but usually this emphasis on the self was subordinated to a sense of the inchoate social self. From ALFRED LORD TENNYSON's "Locksley Hall" to THOMAS HARDY's *Jude the Obscure*, there is the insistence that, however isolated one may be and however much a pawn one may be of an indifferent universe or a compassionate God, there is no existence outside the demands of society. What one thinks and how one acts are largely the result of one's relationship with other people. Ironically, however, and despite this insistence on the social, many were disenfranchised in one way or another during the Victorian era—often denied their political and juridical rights. As a result, they and those who sympathized with them often turned to literature as a way of expressing their dissatisfaction. The "woman question" finds its issues articulated not only in the essays of BARBARA BODICHON and JOSEPHINE BUTLER but also in the poetry of ELIZABETH BARRETT BROWNING and the fiction of CHARLOTTE BRONTË. The difficulties of the working classes are written in the novels of ELIZABETH GASKELL, CHARLES KINGSLEY, and CHARLES DICKENS, as well as in the works of JAMES PHILIP KAY-SHUTTLEWORTH, EDWIN CHADWICK, and HENRY MAYHEW; and the complacency of the middle classes is commented upon by HENRY ARTHUR JONES, MATTHEW ARNOLD, ARTHUR HUGH CLOUGH, and WILLIAM MAKEPEACE THACKERAY alike.

The most remarkable aspect of the Victorian Age as a period of literary history was the prominence attained by the novel. So popular were some authors, like Dickens, that even the illiterate person had access to his works. Kathleen Tillotson, in *Novels of the 1840s*, recalls an instance of Dickens's in-laws' charwoman going to a gathering to *hear* the latest issue of *Dombey and Son*. Before 1850 Dickens and Thackeray were the literary giants, each seeming to mirror the prodigious output of the other; and each month would see the blue-covered number of the current Dickens novel vying for space at the bookseller's stall with Thackeray's yellow-jacketed installment. The novel became so influential in shaping the tastes of the reading public that historians like Macaulay admittedly imitated their form, hoping to displace the "current novel on the night table of young ladies" with their own work. Other novelists, such as the BRONTË SISTERS, Gaskell, Disraeli, and EDWARD BULWER-LYTTON, as well as scores of lesser talents, were immensely popular during the early years of the period. Later they would be replaced by such authors as GEORGE ELIOT, ANTHONY TROLLOPE, THOMAS HARDY, and the sensationalist novelists of the 1860s like MARY ELIZABETH BRADDON and WILKIE COLLINS.

Despite the popularity of the novel, poetry still had a tremendous audience. Two of the Victorian Age's best poets, Tennyson and ROBERT BROWNING, had long careers and attained considerable prominence during their own lifetimes, although their work is extremely different in style and tone. Matthew Arnold, who turned almost exclusively to essay writing after 1851, had a shorter but nonetheless distinguished career as a poet, whose works are marked by a carefully articulated doubt about himself and his age. The pre-Raphaelites, such as D. G. ROSSETTI, his sister CHRISTINA, and their later associates William Morris and ALGERNON CHARLES SWINBURNE introduced a new "fleshly school" of poetry that focused on the sensual and erotic, often shocking readers. Still others, like Charles Kingsley, George Eliot, and Thomas Hardy, who are remembered primarily for their novels, all turned their hand to poetry; and Hardy, from about 1892 until his death in 1928, wrote poetry exclusively, and very successfully.

Poetry and the novel tend to be regarded as the primary genres of the Victorian period, but two other genres flourished during the era—nonfiction prose and the drama. With the institution of the factory and Sunday schools across England during the nineteenth century, literacy rose at an astounding rate. The result was an explosion of the popular press, especially newspapers and periodicals. These became the forums of the day, where everything from Corn Laws to MILTON were debated and commented upon. It is in these periodicals that some of the most informative minds of the century—THOMAS CARLYLE, Macaulay, CARDINAL JOHN NEWMAN (see Vol. 4), HARRIET MARTINEAU, Bodichon—first came to prominence, and in these that political opinions were formed and battle lines drawn on the issues of the day. The theater was also extremely popular during Queen Victoria's reign. Early in the period, plays tended toward historical dramas, farces, and "spectaculars," and the most popular playwrights were people like DOUGLAS WILLIAM JERROLD and Bulwer-Lytton. By midcentury, however, THOMAS WILLIAM ROBERTSON, Jones, and ARTHUR WING PINERO began to articulate the social concerns of the period, even as they continued to produce comedy and melodrama. WILLIAM GILBERT and Arthur Sullivan took the British penchants for opera and melodrama and turned them into a new art form; and, by the end of the century, OSCAR WILDE, with his witty drawing-room comedies and spoof of middle-class pretensions, had set the stage, so to speak, for the strong resurgence of the theater during the early twentieth century.

In some ways it is easy to say the Victorian period ended with the death of the queen in 1901, but many of the issues—both literary and social—that confront our postmodern existence were first expressed in something like their present forms in the nineteenth century. It is no accident that some of the most important work being done currently in Victorian studies attends to issues of gender, class, and race, for between the "woman question," the debates surrounding the needs of the working classes, and the concern over the building of empire, one can see that, in many ways, the world we inhabit today was significantly shaped by the Victorians.

HISTORY AND CRITICISM

Altick, Richard Daniel. *Victorian People and Ideas.* Norton 1974 $10.95. ISBN 0-393-09376-X. Excellent introduction to the period.

Baldick, Chris. *The Social Mission of English Criticism, 1848–1932.* OUP 1983. $34.50. ISBN 0-19-812821-5. Useful for its investigation of the political ramifications of literary criticism in the Victorian era; especially good on Arnold.

Brantlinger, Patrick. *Rule of Darkness: British Literature and Imperialism, 1830–1914.* Cornell Univ. Pr. 1988 $34.95. ISBN 0-8014-2090-3. Seminal study of imperialism and its representations in England.

Briggs, Asa. *The Age of Improvement, 1783–1867.* Longman 1979 $10.00. ISBN 0-582-49100-2. Important discussion of the political history of the first portion of the Victorian era.

———. *The Collected Essays of Asa Briggs.* 3 vols. U. of Ill. Pr. Vol. 1 1985 $32.50. ISBN 0-252-011216-X. Includes a number of important essays, including "The Language of Class."

_____. *Victorian Cities.* HarpC 1970 o.p. Important study of the major urban centers of Victorian England; includes essay on Manchester as "shock city" of the nineteenth century.

_____. *Victorian People: A Reassessment of Persons' Themes, 1851–67.* U. Ch. Pr. 1975 $15.95. ISBN 0-226-07488-9. Collection of essays about important Victorian personalities.

_____. *Victorian Things.* U. Ch. Pr. 1989 $29.95. ISBN 0-226-07483-8. Companion volume to *Victorian Cities* and *Victorian People*; excellent survey of the materiality of Victorian culture.

Bulwer-Lytton, Edward. *England and the English.* 1833. Ed. by Standish Meacham. U. Ch. Pr. 1970 $22.50. ISBN 0-226-08014-5. Insightful and witty observations of the first years of the Victorian period.

Dawson, Carl. *Victorian Noon: English Literature in 1850.* Johns Hopkins 1979 $38.50. ISBN 0-8018-2110-X. Discussion of the state of English literature and culture just prior to the Crystal Palace exhibition; compares with Stein's *Victoria's Year.*

Dyos, H. J., and Michael Wolff, eds. *The Victorian City.* 2 vols. Routledge 1977 o.p. Excellent collection of essays by leading Victorianists on the social conditions in the cities.

Gallagher, Catherine, and Thomas W. Laqueur, eds. *The Making of the Modern Body: Sexuality and Society in the Nineteenth Century.* U. CA Pr. 1987 $45.00. ISBN 0-520-05960-3. Originally published as an issue of *Representations;* useful collection of essays on the breadth of the topic.

Hobsbawm, E. J. *The Age of Capital, 1848–1875.* Peter Smith 1992 $17.50. ISBN 0-8446-6606-8. Important materialist discussion of economic basis of Victorian politics and culture.

_____. *The Age of Empire, 1875–1914.* Pantheon 1987 $19.95. ISBN 0-394-56319-0. Landmark book on the politics of empire at the end of the last century.

Hoggart, Richard. *The Uses of Literacy.* Transaction Pubs. 1992 $21.95. ISBN 0-88738-892-2. Seminal work on cultural materialism; important examination of the political and social ramifications of literacy.

Houghton, Walter Edwards. *The Victorian Frame of Mind, 1830–1870.* Yale U. Pr. 1963 $15.00. ISBN 0-300-00122-3. Excellent encyclopedic information about the literary culture of the age.

Inkster, Ian, and Jack Morrell, eds. *Metropolis and Province: Science in British Culture, 1780–1850.* U. of Pa. Pr. 1983 $55.95. ISBN 0-8122-7855-0. Collection of essays concerning aspects of science such as geology and medicine and their relations to other facets of Victorian culture.

Jones, Gareth Stedman. *Outcast London: A Study in the Relationship between Classes in Victorian Society.* OUP 1971 o.p. Especially good on the conditions of the working classes in the city.

Kitson Clark, G. S. R. *The Making of Victorian England.* Atheneum 1966 o.p. Good introduction to the period; wide-ranging and useful.

Marcus, Steven. *The Other Victorians: A Study of Sexuality and Pornography in Mid-Nineteenth-Century England.* NAL-Dutton 1977 o.p. Important rethinking of the myth of sexual repression as a Victorian characteristic.

Michie, Helena. *The Flesh Made Word: Female Figures and Women's Bodies.* OUP 1987 $29.95. ISBN 0-195-04107-0. Important study of the representation of women's bodies in Victorian culture.

Mitchell, Sally, ed. *Victorian Britain: An Encyclopedia.* Garland 1988 $125.00. ISBN 0-8240-1513-4. Useful encyclopedia of all things Victorian.

Morris, Jan. *The Spectacle of Empire: Style, Effect and the Pax Britannica.* Doubleday 1982 o.p. Study of the ways in which empire was represented in Victorian England.

Poovey, Mary. *Uneven Developments: The Ideological Work of Gender in Mid-Victorian England.* U. Ch. Pr. 1988 $39.95. ISBN 0-226-67529-7. Important new-historicist study of the formation of gender in the Victorian era; includes discussions of Florence Nightingale, Josephine Butler, and Charles Dickens.

Reader, W. J. *Victorian England*. Putnam Pub. Group 1974 o.p. Excellent survey; especially good on the social aspects.

Richardson, Ruth. *Death, Dissection, and the Destitute*. Viking Penguin 1988 o.p. Fascinating study of the poor and of medicine in Victorian England.

Shires, Linda M., ed. *Rewriting the Victorians: Theory, History and the Politics of Gender*. Routledge 1992 $49.95. ISBN 0-415-05524-5. Good collection of theoretical approaches to gender issues in Victorian literature.

Stein, Richard L. *Victoria's Year: English Literature and Culture, 1837–1838*. OUP 1988 $38.00. ISBN 0-19-504922-5. Excellent "thick description" of English culture in the year Victoria ascended to the throne.

Thompson, E. P. *The Making of the English Working Class*. Random 1966 $25.00. ISBN 0-394-70322-7. Groundbreaking study of the culture of the working classes and its formation in the eighteenth and nineteenth centuries.

Thompson, F. M. L. *The Rise of Respectable Society: A Social History of Victorian Britain, 1830–1900*. HUP 1988 $35.00. ISBN 0-674-77285-7. Useful, though predictable, survey of the formation of respectability as a middle-class trait.

Viswanathan, Gauri. *Masks of Conquest: Literary Study and British Rule in India*. Col. U. Pr. 1989 $34.50. ISBN 0-231-07084-5. Analysis of English studies in India and the effect on colonial rule.

Walkowitz, Judith R. *Prostitution and Victorian Society: Women, Class, and the State*. Cambridge U. Pr. 1982 $15.95. ISBN 0-521-27064-2. First-rate study of the connections between prostitution and class.

Webb, R. K. *The British Working Class Reader, 1790–1848: Literacy and Social Tension*. Kelley 1971 repr. of 1955 ed. $29.50. ISBN 0-678-00578-8. Important collection of "literature" for the working classes.

_____. *Modern England: From the Eighteenth Century to the Present*. HarpC 1990 $28.00. ISBN 0-06-046974-9. Good on the Victorian's political history.

Williams, Raymond. *The Country and the City*. OUP 1975 repr. of 1973 ed. $10.95. ISBN 0-19-519810-7. Good on the dual experiences of English literary culture in the nineteenth century.

_____. *Culture and Society, 1780–1950*. Col. U. Pr. 1983 $82.00. ISBN 0-231-02287-5. Landmark study of the concept of culture in English studies.

Young, G. M. *Portrait of an Age*. 1952. OUP 1988 $9.95. ISBN 0-19-281005-7. Classic introduction to the period.

Zedner, Lucia. *Women, Crime, and Custody in Victorian England*. OUP 1992 $72.00. ISBN 0-19-820264-4. Study of women as criminals and their treatment.

POETRY

The poets of the Victorian period in many ways recognized that they were caught in a period of transition. In 1837 the important poets of the second generation of romantics (BYRON, KEATS, and SHELLEY) had all been dead for more than a decade. The longer-lived first generation (WORDSWORTH and COLERIDGE) had been subsumed by a conservatism that sprang from their philosophy of poetry and nature but that was strangely out of joint with Victorian poetic sensibilities. Thus ROBERT BROWNING writes of Wordsworth's acceptance of the post of laureate, "Just for a handful of silver he left us, just for a ribbon to put in his coat" ("The Lost Leader"). The Victorian poets, especially the early ones like ALFRED TENNYSON and Browning, struggled mightily with the legacy of the romanticism that overshadowed them not only poetically but also politically. Suddenly, or so it seemed, romanticism had become the status quo, had lost its radical edge, and no longer seemed to be about change. In striking contrast, the Victorian poets' work was in some ways *always* about change and new opportunities. For them, as for many Victorians, the sense of self-confident progress was uppermost in their minds. "The best is yet to be," writes Browning in "Rabbi Ben Ezra," while Tennyson's *In Memoriam* looks forward to a continual spiritual renewal and a beckoning transcendent reward. For someone like MATTHEW ARNOLD, whose poetry is much more riddled with doubt, self-consciousness, and mortality, and who sees himself as "between two worlds, one dead, the other powerless to be born," the practice of poetry proved too emotionally straining. As a result, Arnold abandoned his promising career as a poet, turning instead to the essay and the social instead of the highly personal self, which is the subject of poetry.

Despite their differences with those of Wordsworth and Coleridge's generation, however, the Victorian poets did find an affinity with the romantics who died young or relatively neglected. Keats, Shelley, and WILLIAM BLAKE could be embraced as models for the Victorians' developing ideas on poetry, for in many respects that first generation of Victorian poets—Tennyson, Robert Browning and ELIZABETH BARRETT BROWNING, and Arnold—shared in the romantic ferment that roused the world in the early nineteenth century: political reform, religious evangelism, literary and philosophical upheaval, and technological innovation. However, as that generation moved toward middle age and the middle of the century, it, too, was subsumed by its own success. Tennyson, upon the death of the venerable Wordsworth, became poet laureate, and by 1851 the poetic standards that were in place were adamantly Victorian. The hope for great change became increasingly fraught with doubt that such change was possible. The economic depressions of the 1840s, the European revolutions of 1848–49, Britain's fiasco of a war in Crimea, and the Indian Mutiny all seemed to reveal a system that was more capable of derailing positive change than accommodating it. Thus, the nostalgia for a simpler, more aesthetically pleasing era—a nostalgia that had always been present in Victorian thought—was expressed yet again in the works of such poets as WILLIAM MORRIS, ALGERNON CHARLES SWINBURNE, and the Pre-Raphaelites. As with so many of the activities of the Victorian period, theirs, too, were riddled with contradiction and inconsistency. For, even as Morris, saddled with doubt, can write, "Why should I strive to set the crooked straight?" ("The Earthly Paradise"), he and others of his generation never abandoned a hope for the possibility of progress. Thus, in their looking backward, they did, in fact, *strive* for beauty in the arts and political and juridical justice for English men and women.

Already by the 1860s, though, such doubts had begun to generate a sense of disillusionment in those who can be designated the third generation of Victorians. "Day and night I deplore / My . . . foundering own generation" laments GERARD MANLEY HOPKINS ("The Loss of the Eurydice"). His (and HARDY's) was a generation that would adopt neither revolution nor reform as its rallying cry, merely sensation. Trading the sense of a world reborn for the despairing conviction of a world in shreds and tatters, a world slowly winding down, these last of the Victorians abandoned the tradition that they had inherited from the romantics and the first two generations of Victorian poets. If any are truly "between two worlds," it is this generation, whose skepticism ultimately gave way to the aesthetic excesses of the *fin-de-siècle* and the codification of new poetic and aesthetic forms in the modernism of the following century.

History and Criticism

Ball, Patricia M. *The Heart's Events: The Victorian Poetry of Relationships*. Longwood MA 1976 o.p. Analysis of Victorian poems and of lyrics, tracing the course of close personal relationships.

Bloom, Harold, ed. *Pre-Raphaelite Poets*. Chelsea Hse. 1986 $34.95. ISBN 0-87754-667-3. Good collection of essays on the Pre-Raphaelite Brotherhood.

Buckley, Jerome H. *The Victorian Temper: A Study in Literary Culture*. HUP 1969 $22.50. ISBN 0-674-93680-9. A clear, well-structured overview of the period.

Christ, Carol T. *Victorian and Modern Poetics*. U. Ch. Pr. 1982 $16.00. ISBN 0-226-10458-3. An addition to the argument over just how Victorian turned into modern.

Colville, Derek. *Victorian Poetry and the Romantic Religion*. State U. NY Pr. 1970 $19.95. ISBN 0-87395-074-7. Reexamines Victorian poetry against a background of romantic thought.

Edmond, Rod. *Affairs of the Hearth: Victorian Poetry and Domestic Narrative*. Routledge 1988 $45.00. ISBN 0-415-00656-2. Examines connections between issues of domesticity and poetry of the period.

Faas, Ekbert. *Retreat into the Mind: Victorian Poetry and the Rise of Psychiatry*. Princeton U. Pr. 1991 $42.00. ISBN 0-691-06748-1. Interesting cultural study on the connections between poetic self-reflection and psychiatric practices.

Faverty, Frederic E., ed. *Victorian Poets: A Guide to Research*. HUP 1968 $78.90. ISBN 0-783-74144-8. The starting point for any serious study of Victorian poets.

Fletcher, Pauline. *Gardens and Grim Ravines: The Language of Landscape in Victorian Poetry*. Princeton U. Pr. 1983 $45.00. ISBN 0-691-06556-X. Excellent examination of the significance of landscape in Victorian poetry.

Gaunt, William. *The Pre-Raphaelite Dream (The Pre-Raphaelite Tragedy)*. Richard West repr. of 1943 ed. o.p. Explores the personalities and philosophies of the main writers of the Pre-Raphaelite movement.

Harrison, Antony H. *Victorian Poets and Romantic Poems: Intertextuality and Ideology*. U. Pr. of Va. 1990 $35.00. ISBN 0-8139-1253-9. Examines the romantic intertext of several poets, including Tennyson.

Houghton, Walter E. *The Victorian Frame of Mind, 1830–1870*. Yale U. Pr. 1963 $15.00. ISBN 0-300-00122-3. Analyzes more than a dozen themes and attitudes in the public and private writings of the early Victorians.

Hunt, John D. *The Pre-Raphaelite Imagination, 1848–1900*. U. of Nebr. Pr. 1977 $27.50. ISBN 0-8032-0083-8

Langbaum, Robert. *The Poetry of Experience: The Dramatic Monologue in Modern Literary Tradition*. U. Ch. Pr. 1986 $9.95. ISBN 0-226-46872-0. The book that defined how the dramatic monologue works.

———, ed. *The Victorian Age: Essays in History and in Social and Literary History*. Academy Chi. Pubs. 1983 repr. of 1967 ed. $8.00. ISBN 0-89733-055-2

Levine, Richard A., ed. *The Victorian Experience: The Poets*. Ohio U. Pr. 1982 $12.00. ISBN 0-8214-0748-1

Lucas, John. *England and Englishness: Ideas of Nationhood in English Poetry, 1688–1900*. U. of Iowa Pr. 1990 $24.95. ISBN 0-87745-275-X. Study of the discursive and poetic formation of Englishness.

Mermin, Dorothy. *The Audience in the Poem: Five Victorian Poets*. Rutgers U. Pr. $35.00. ISBN 0-8135-0988-2

Pearce, Lynn. *Woman—Image—Text: Readings in Pre-Raphaelite Art and Literature*. Harvester Wheatsheaf 1991 o.p. Brief but useful examination of Pre-Raphaelites' representations of women.

Sambrook, James. *Pre-Raphaelitism: A Collection of Critical Essays*. U. Ch. Pr. 1976 o.p. Reviews the most significant definitions of the term "Pre-Raphaelite" and draws distinctions between them.

Slinn, E. Warwick. *The Discourse of Self in Victorian Poetry*. U. Pr. of Va. 1991 $35.00. ISBN 0-8139-1309-8. Examination of the Victorian shift to "self" in a context much different from that of the romantics.

Stevenson, Lionel. *The Pre-Raphaelite Poets.* U. of NC Pr. 1972 o.p.

Tennyson, G. B. *Victorian Devotional Poetry: The Tractarian Mode.* HUP 1981 $22.50. ISBN 0-674-93586-1. Discusses verse associated with Oxford and the Tractarian movement.

Collections

Barnes, William. *A Selection from Poems of Rural Life in the Dorset Dialect.* Century Bookbindery 1977 repr. of 1909 ed. An important collection of dialect poetry, which was influential in the late Victorian era.

Buckler, William E., ed. *The Major Victorian Poets.* HM 1973 $9.16. ISBN 0-395-14024-2. A good, usable text edition.

Caldwell, Thomas, ed. *The Golden Book of Modern English Poetry: 1870–1920.* Arden Lib. 1978 repr. of 1922 ed. o.p. A fascinating index of Georgian taste.

Carr, Arthur S. *Victorian Poetry: Clough to Kipling.* Irvington 1982 repr. of 1972 ed. o.p.

Garrett, Edmund H., ed. *Victorian Songs. Granger Index Repr. Ser.* Ayer repr. of 1895 ed. $18.00. ISBN 0-8369-6145-5. A useful collection of a neglected genre. Introduction by E. Grosse.

Hayward, John, ed. *The Oxford Book of Nineteenth-Century English Verse.* OUP 1964 o.p.

Hickock, Kathleen. *Representations of Women: Nineteenth-Century British Women's Poetry.* Greenwood 1984 $42.95. ISBN 0-313-23837-5. Not a true anthology, since the poetry is available in short quotations only, but makes available far more women's poetry than has been accessible before.

Houghton, Walter E., and G. Robert Stange. *Victorian Poetry and Poetics.* HM 1972 $49.56. ISBN 0-395-04646-7. Perhaps the most comprehensive text.

Lang, Cecil Y., ed. *The Pre-Raphaelites and Their Circle.* U. Ch. Pr. 1975 $15.95. ISBN 0-226-46866-6. The best anthology of Pre-Raphaelite works.

Miles, Alfred H., and others. *The Poets and the Poetry of the Nineteenth Century.* 12 vols. AMS Pr. repr. of 1907 ed. $510.00. ISBN 0-404-015120-0. The official collection of romantic and Victorian poets, selected by the Victorians.

Richards, Bernard. *English Verse, 1830–1890.* Longman 1980 o.p. Includes 18 Victorian poets and over 13,000 lines of verse; completely annotated.

Ricks, Christopher B., ed. *The New Oxford Book of Victorian Verse.* OUP 1987 $30.00. ISBN 0-19-214154-6. Good anthology by a preeminent Tennysonian.

Scheckner, Peter, ed. *An Anthology of Chartist Poetry: Poetry of the British Working Class, 1830s–1850s.* Fairleigh Dickinson 1989 $47.50. ISBN 0-8386-3345-5. Poetry by working-class radicals or in association with them.

Stanford, Derek, ed. *Pre-Raphaelite Writing.* Biblio Dist. 1984 o.p.

Symons, Arthur, ed. *An Anthology of Nineties' Verse.* Rprt. Serv. 1988 repr. of 1928 ed. $49.00. ISBN 0-7812-0044-X

Thomas, Donald Serrell, ed. *The Everyman Book of Victorian Verse: The Post-Romantics.* C. E. Tuttle 1992 $8.95. ISBN 0-460-87102-1. Fairly good collection, though selective; contains a bibliography.

Wright, David, ed. *Seven Victorian Poets.* Heinemann Ed. 1964 o.p. Contains work by William Barnes, Arthur Clough, Matthew Arnold, and others.

THE NOVEL

British fiction exploded into sustained greatness in the Victorian Age. The popular phenomenon that was SIR WALTER SCOTT, the Waverly novelist, became the standard of aesthetic and, perhaps as important, commercial evaluation in the Victorian period. Early in the 1830s, writers like BULWER-LYTTON and FREDERICK MARRYAT attempted to imitate the romanticism of Scott's works, even as they turned their attention to the social and political events of their own day. The formation of new genres of fiction, like the Newgate novel, which dwelt on the underworld and the seamier, criminal side of everyday life, as well as attempts by authors such as Bulwer-Lytton to reproduce the greatness (and popularity) of Scott in historical fiction, became commonplaces of the market. But until 1836, despite the efforts of a number of writers, the Victorian novel was still finding its way, seeking to establish itself as *the* popular literary art form.

In 1836 *Sketches by Boz* was published, and a new luminary burst on the scene—CHARLES DICKENS. For the next 34 years, no other star would burn brighter. In some ways it is possible to argue that Dickens single-handedly reshaped the nineteenth-century publishing industry and the novel form. Between him and his rival THACKERAY, there seemed little room for any other lights in the literary sky of novel writing. Beside these two, the other authors of the 1830s and 1840s were relegated to the status of satellites, circling, perhaps even reflecting, the light of these two writers but never equaling their brilliance.

Such a glowing evaluation of Thackeray and Dickens should be taken with a grain of salt, however. For there were other writers of the period who were as popular and, arguably, as talented. Part of what makes such statements about Thackeray and Dickens possible is the way in which novel writing and publishing became a business, and novelists became public figures. Whatever one may think of Thackeray and Dickens as novelists, there were few writers who were better at self-promotion; their very recognizability contributed greatly to their sales.

Nevertheless, there were other novelists of the early part of the era who experienced tremendous commercial success. One of these was HARRIET MARTINEAU, whose nine-volume *Illustrations of Political Economy*, while perhaps more properly considered a series of tracts than a novel, was immensely popular. Also popular were the BRONTË SISTERS, who, in a span of about five years at midcentury, produced some of Victorian England's most memorable fiction; ELIZABETH GASKELL, whose compassionate representations of working-class life drew the approbation of Dickens and garnered her the mixed blessing of his acting as her editor; and BENJAMIN DISRAELI, the future prime minister, who began writing novels in the 1830s and in the 1840s published his *Young England* trilogy of political novels to much acclaim.

As the century progressed, a number of artists emerged. GEORGE ELIOT epitomized a new kind of novelist—one whose works were the product of a different type of intellect. Rather than the biting satire of a Thackeray or the bustling world of a Dickens, Eliot's novels were devoted to a realistic representation of the world and the minds of the people who inhabited it. Rather than hurtling from one adventure to another, Eliot's plots are contemplative and, in comparison with many other Victorian novelists', relatively uneventful. In direct contrast, and flourishing at about the same time, were the sensationalist novelists, like WILKIE COLLINS and MARY ELIZABETH BRADDON. The works of these writers were intended to shock; their plots were tangled and intricate; and they were immensely popular.

Still other novelists of the period deserve some mention, for the variety of fiction in the Victorian period was nearly as staggering as the number of novels that were written. Flourishing somewhat later than Dickens was the prolific ANTHONY TROLLOPE, who managed to write political novels, urban novels, Irish novels, novels of social norms, and novels of parish life. In recent years, Trollope's critical stock has risen considerably, and he is now often considered in the first rank of Victorian novelists. Later even than Trollope were THOMAS HARDY and RUDYARD KIPLING. Hardy, who preferred to think of himself as a poet, may be characterized as the novelist of late Victorian pessimism and doubt. However bleak one finds Dickens's *Little Dorrit* or Thackeray's *Vanity Fair*, they are positively cheery compared with Hardy's *Tess* or *Jude the Obscure*. Kipling at his best is Hardy's exact contrast, for he is the optimistic novelist of empire, and his *Kim* is a perfect jumping-off point for a literary study of the British raj.

No period in the history of the English novel reflects so dramatically the movement from the past to the present, from pastoral containment to urban chaos, from aristocratic forbearance to democratic emotionalism, from belief in firm opinions and a settled faith to uncertainty and relativism. At the same time, no literature since the Renaissance in England has communicated quite the fullness and variety of life, the sense of sustained explorations of the relationship between people and themselves and people and society, as the fiction of the Victorian period.

History and Criticism

Auerbach, Nina. *Communities of Women: An Idea in Fiction*. HUP 1978 $19.95. ISBN 0-674-15168-2. Explores changing visions of female independence, along with reactions to the idea of communities of women.

Baker, Ernest Albert. *A History of the English Novel*. Vol. 7 *Age of Dickens and Thackeray*. B & N Imports 1968 repr. of 1936 ed. o.p.

Block, Andrew. *The English Novel, 1740–1850: A Catalogue Including Prose Romances, Short Stories and Translations of Foreign Fiction*. Greenwood rev. ed. 1982 repr. of 1961 ed. $59.50. ISBN 0-313-23224-5. A valuable reference source.

Bloom, Harold, ed. *Victorian Fiction*. Chelsea Hse. 1989 $64.95. ISBN 0-87754-980-X. Good collection of recent essays on a variety of novels.

Bodenheimer, Rosemarie. *The Politics of Story in Victorian Social Fiction*. Cornell Univ. Pr. 1988 $27.95. ISBN 0-8014-2099-7. Successful use of Jamesonian paradigm on issues of gender as well as class in the social novels.

Buckley, J. H. *Season of Youth: The Bildungsroman from Dickens to Golding*. HUP $30.00. ISBN 0-674-79640-3. Explores novels about youth and growing up.

Caserio, Robert L. *Plot, Story, and the Novel: From Dickens and Poe to the Modern Period*. Princeton U. Pr. 1979 $47.00. ISBN 0-691-06382-6. Examines the growing antagonism to plot and storytelling in English and American fiction since the early nineteenth century.

Cohen, Paula Marantz. *The Daughter's Dilemma: Family Process and the Nineteenth-Century Domestic Novel*. U. of Mich. Pr. 1991 $32.50. ISBN 0-472-10234-6. Discussion of the role of the daughter in domestic plots.

Cunningham, Valentine. *Everywhere Spoken Against: Dissent in the Victorian Novel*. OUP 1975 o.p.

Deidre, David. *Fictions of Resolution in Three Victorian Novels*. Col. U. Pr. 1981 $49.00. ISBN 0-231-04980-3

Feltes, N. N. *Modes of Production of Victorian Novels*. U. Ch. Pr. 1986. $18.95. ISBN 0-226-24117-3. Useful Marxian analysis of publishing of Victorian fiction.

Ford, Boris, ed. *From Dickens to Hardy*. Viking Penguin 1983 $7.95. ISBN 0-14-022269-3

Ford, G. H., ed. *Victorian Fiction: A Second Guide to Research*. Modern Lang. 1978 $37.00. ISBN 0-87352-254-0

Gallagher, Catherine. *The Industrial Reformation of English Fiction: Social Discourse and Narrative Form*. U. Ch. Pr. 1985 $12.95. ISBN 0-226-27932-4. Excellent study of social-problem novels.

Garrett, Peter K. *The Victorian Multiplot Novel: Studies in Dialogical Form*. Yale U. Pr. 1980 o.p. Explores works by Dickens, Eliot, Thackeray, and Trollope.

Gilbert, Sandra M., and Susan Gubar. *The Madwoman in the Attic: A Study of Women and the Literary Imagination in the Nineteenth Century*. Yale U. Pr. 1979 $19.95. ISBN

0-300-02596-3. Argues for a distinctively female imagination in the work of great nineteenth-century women novelists.

Houghton, Walter E., and others, eds. *The Wellesley Index to Victorian Periodicals, 1824–1900.* 5 vols. U. of Toronto Pr. Vols. 1–3 o.p. Vol. 4 1987 $175.00. ISBN 0-8020-5271-7. Vol. 5 1989 $195.00. ISBN 0-8020-2688-5. An important, influential work.

James, Lewis. *Fiction for the Working Man, 1830–1850.* Viking Penguin 1974 o.p. Detailed and scholarly study of popular literature of Victorian England.

Keating, P. J. *The Haunted Study: A Social History of the English Novel, 1875–1914.* Secker & Warburg 1989 o.p. Worthwhile study of the late Victorian and Edwardian novel.

King, Jeannette. *Tragedy in the Victorian Novel: Theory and Practice in the Novels of George Eliot, Thomas Hardy, and Henry James.* Cambridge U. Pr. 1980 o.p. Explores the rise of the novel in the nineteenth century and how it came to embody a tragic vision of life.

Kucich, John. *Repression in Victorian Fiction: Charlotte Brontë, George Eliot, and Charles Dickens.* U. CA Pr. 1987 $37.50. ISBN 0-520-05980-8. Psychoanalytic study of three important authors; argues for the productiveness of repression in fiction.

Leavis, F. R. *The Great Tradition: George Eliot, Henry James, Joseph Conrad.* NYU Pr. 1963 o.p. Important study of the novel.

Levine, George Lewis. *Darwin and the Novelists: Patterns of Science in Victorian Fiction.* HUP 1988 $29.95. ISBN 0-674-19285-0. Examines the influence of science, especially evolution, on realist novels.

Lucas, John. *The Literature of Change: Studies in the Nineteenth-Century Provincial Novel.* B & N Imports 1980 $28.50. ISBN 0-389-20020-4. Examines the works of three "provincial novelists: Mrs. Gaskell, William Hale White, and Thomas Hardy.

Miller, D. A. *The Novel and the Police.* U. CA Pr. 1988 $22.50. ISBN 0-520-06281-7. Important study of the "carceral" in Victorian fiction.

Miller, J. Hillis. *The Form of Victorian Fiction.* Bellflower 1980 $17.50. ISBN 0-934958-00-9

Musselwhite, David E. *Partings Welded Together: Politics and Desire in the Nineteenth-Century Novel.* Routledge Chapman & Hall 1987 $57.50. ISBN 0-416-06162-1. Wide-ranging study; good discussion of the creation of Dickens's movement away from his Boz persona.

Newton, Judith Lowder. *Women, Power, and Subversion: Social Strategies in British Fiction, 1778-1860.* U. of Ga. Pr. 1981 $24.00. ISBN 0-8203-0564-2

Polhemus, Robert M. *Erotic Faith: Being in Love from Jane Austen to D. H. Lawrence.* U. Ch. Pr. 1990 $29.95. ISBN 0-226-67322-7. Surveys representations of love throughout the nineteenth-century novel.

Qualls, Barry. *The Secular Pilgrims of Victorian Fiction: The Novel as Book of Life.* Cambridge U. Pr. 1982 o.p. Uses Carlyle as the context to study the works of such writers as Dickens and Eliot.

Rothfield, Lawrence. *Vital Signs: Medical Realism in Nineteenth-Century Fiction.* Princeton U. Pr. 1992 $27.50. ISBN 0-691-06896-8. Foucauldian analysis of realist fiction; argues that realist paradigm has its basis in medical discourse.

Sanders, Andrew. *The Victorian Historical Novel, 1840–1880.* St. Martin 1979 $25.00. ISBN 0-312-04293-7. Examines how Victorian historical novels gave new dimension to contemporary moral and social questions.

Sedgwick, Eve Kosofsky. *Between Men: English Literature and Male Homosocial Desire.* Col. U. Pr. 1985 $38.00. ISBN 0-231-05860-8. Groundbreaking work on theorizing homosexuality in reading Victorian texts; excellent chapter on *Our Mutual Friend.*

Showalter, Elaine. *A Literature of Their Own: British Women Novelists from Brontë to Lessing.* Princeton U. Pr. 1976 $14.95. ISBN 0-691-01343-8. Analyzes the contributions of British female novelists in terms of three historical phases: feminine, female, and feminist.

Tillotson, Kathleen. *Novels of the Eighteen-Forties.* OUP 1983 o.p. Discusses these novels in the context of their relationship to each other, their time, and their first readers.

Tuchman, Gaye, and Nina Fortin. *Edging Women Out: Victorian Novelists, Publishers, and Social Change*. Yale U. Pr. 1989 $32.00. ISBN 0-300-04316-3. Useful examination of gender politics in Victorian publishing.

Wilt, Judith. *Ghosts of the Gothic: Austen, Eliot, and Lawrence*. Princeton U. Pr. 1980 $44.50. ISBN 0-691-06439-3

Yeazell, Ruth Bernard. *Fictions of Modesty: Women and Courtship in the English Novel*. U. Ch. Pr. 1991 $24.95. ISBN 0-226-95096-4. New-historicist examination of the discourse of courtship and marriage in the novel.

DRAMA

Drama in the Victorian period was a thriving enterprise, and Victorian audiences had specific tastes. Under the old patent system, only three theaters—Drury Lane, Covent Garden, and, in the summertime, the Haymarket—were licensed to operate within London. Until the beginning of the nineteenth century, their bill of fare was fairly predictable: tragedy, comedy, and the plays of WILLIAM SHAKESPEARE. Other "illegitimate" theaters had been set up outside central London to accommodate recitations, equestrian events, and performing animal acts. In 1802, however, Thomas Holcroft's melodrama, *A Tale of Mystery*, was produced at Covent Garden. Suddenly the old generic conventions had been exploded. Theater owners and managers had recognized that their audiences wanted more than the same old eighteenth-century "legitimate" theater. In 1843, partly in response to the great demand for theaters and partly as a wink at the number of theaters that were operating despite the patent law, the Theater Regulation Act abolished the old patenting system. Thus, while the enormous Drury Lane and Convent Garden theaters remained, other smaller venues had emerged that had become known by their management and the types of plays that they presented. The Adelphi, for instance, was the place to see sensationalist melodrama, while, for extravaganza, genteel burlesque, and light comedy, one visited the Olympic. The Princess Theater's specialties were Shakespearean revivals and literary melodrama; the Lyceum was known for spectacular melodrama and Shakespearean revivals, and the Prince of Wales was known for comedy.

Whereas the types of plays that were performed were various and are often categorized as melodrama, comedies, comedy dramas, burlesques, extravaganzas, burlettas, tragedies, comediettas, romantic comedies, and the like, far and away the most prolific form was the melodrama. Nearly all of the successful playwrights of the era wrote melodramas, and the form became so well wrought that it produced its own subgenres, such as the nautical melodrama, domestic melodrama, and sensation drama. Works like Seymour Hicks and Fred Latham's *Flying Colors* (1899) indicate the enduring popularity of the nautical melodrama, which, properly speaking, was at its peak of popularity between 1825 and 1835. Domestic melodramas were much more central to the Victorian theater, and some of the best plays of the period—TOM TAYLOR's *Ticket-of-Leave Man* (1863), DOUGLAS JERROLD's *Martha Willis* (1831), and HENRY ARTHUR JONES's *The Dancing Girl* (1891)—are of this genre. Typically, these plays contain a hero or heroine who is corrupted (often by the lures of the city) but who is redeemed at the play's end. Often it is avarice that leads the play's characters to gambling (then usually drinking) and eventually to a life of crime. Unlike nautical or Gothic melodrama, these plays focused on the recognizable, the everyday, rather than the exotic, and even as they became more sophisticated in plotting and thematics, they continued to attract large audiences who identified the world of the play with their own world.

On the opposite side of the coin from domestic melodrama and its insistence on the familiar were the very popular extravaganzas, burlesques, and pantomimes. These types of plays often indulged in great spectacle, and pantomime, especially, frequently implied the propriety of a short tenure of misrule, chaos, or carnival. The firmly entrenched moral codes of the melodrama were turned upside down, and it is quite easy to trace the influence of such plays to the moral and social invertedness of the works of W. S. GILBERT. By the end of the century, the pantomimes of Augustus Harris—*Aladdin* (1885) and *Dick Whittington* (1891)—had become massive spectacles, requiring huge numbers of extras and equally huge sums of money for costume and sets. Akin to pantomime and spectacular drama was the extravaganza in which, as one of the form's leading authors, J. R. Planché, explains, a poetical subject is treated whimsically. His works, like *The Sleeping Beauty in the Wood* (1840) and *The Golden Branch* (1847), were based on reducing the world of classical mythology to a spectacular absurdity. By the 1870s, burlesques and extravaganzas were increasingly moving off the primary stages of the large theaters and into the music halls.

The reach of drama in the Victorian Age should not be underestimated. While it is a commonplace of critical accounts of English drama to speak of the decline of the theater until about 1850, this may in part be accounted for by the vestiges of the romantic period among the critics and poets of the age. Despite writing dramas, none of the great romantic figures enjoyed much success in the theater; similarly ROBERT BROWNING, who desired a theatrical career, never particularly prospered as a playwright. On the other hand, TENNYSON's *Becket* and *Queen Mary* were relatively successful as vehicles for the popular actor Henry Irving. Another notable figure who was much influenced by the theater was CHARLES DICKENS, who was himself a rather good amateur actor and who was constantly volunteering his services for private productions. Together with his friend WILKIE COLLINS, he authored a (mercifully) rarely produced play, *The Frozen Deep*. Less successful as a novelist, but comparing quite favorably with Dickens as a playwright, was the historical novelist CHARLES READE, who collaborated successfully with Tom Taylor on a number of popular dramas, such as *Masks and Faces* (1852), which helped to establish Taylor with the Haymarket theater.

Other important playwrights of the era were THOMAS WILLIAM ROBERTSON, HENRY ARTHUR JONES, and ARTHUR WING PINERO. Robertson's work is often considered the turning point of Victorian theater. His ability to capture the temper of his audiences in his comic works sets him apart from his predecessors. His most famous and most often revived play is *Caste* (1867), but he was extremely popular during his short career, and, as Victor Emeljanow has pointed out, he was highly imitated; his work became "the yardstick for future writing as well as a landmark in its own right." Jones and Pinero were contemporaries and friends, and, before the arrival of GEORGE BERNARD SHAW on the scene, were the grand old men of the theater. Both men saw drama as a serious, literary calling. Jones wrote in 1883, "The truth is that audiences want literature, they want poetry, but they do not want unactable, intractable imitations of Shakespeare's form, without his vitality. They want life, they want reality." Early in his career, Jones sympathized with the plight of the working classes, an attitude that brought him to the attention of Shaw; later, however, Jones turned increasingly reactionary, and by the onset of World War I had completely abandoned the sentiments he had expressed in such works as *The Middleman* (1891). Pinero, like Jones, turned from farce and comedy to plays dealing with social problems during the 1890s, writing works such as *The Second Mrs. Tanqueray* (1893). Unlike Jones, however, Pinero was castigated by Shaw for his "timid morality" and conventional characterization; Shaw found Pinero's version of the "new" drama lacking in both intensity and commitment.

By the end of the century, Shaw had begun to write and produce his own plays and eventually eclipsed Jones and Pinero (both of whom lived well into this century). But it was their work, and their predecessors', that made so much of Shaw's writing possible. If Shaw is the epitome of the theater's rejuvenation, then it is at least partly the emerging vitality of Victorian drama that helps to grant him his place as the leading figure in early twentieth-century English drama. Very clearly the modernism of Shaw has its antecedents in the Victorian theater.

History and Criticism

Auerbach, Nina. *Private Theatricals: The Lives of the Victorians.* HUP 1990 $15.00. ISBN 0-674-70755-9. Interesting work linking theatricality to Victorian life.

Booth, Michael R. *English Melodrama.* H. Jenkins 1965 o.p. Important work on English melodrama of the nineteenth century.

_____. *Prefaces to English Nineteenth-Century Theatre.* Manchester Univ. Pr. 1980 o.p. The prefaces of Booth's *English Plays of the Nineteenth Century* collected in one volume.

_____. *Theatre in the Victorian Age.* Cambridge U. Pr. 1991 $49.50. ISBN 0-521-34351-8. Comprehensive survey of the social and cultural context of the theater as well as the works.

Booth, Michael, and others, eds. *The Revels History of Drama in English. Volume 6: 1750–1880.* Routledge Chapman & Hall 1975 o.p. Excellent history; covers theater as well as plays and playwrights.

Bratton, Jacqueline S., ed. *Acts of Supremacy: The British Empire and the Stage, 1790–1830.* Manchester Univ. Pr. 1991 $59.95. ISBN 0-7190-2583-4. Good collection of essays on the presentation, on the British stage, of the imperialized other.

Cross, Gilbert B. *Next Week East Lynne: Domestic Drama in Performance, 1820–1874.* Bucknell U. Pr. 1977 $37.50. ISBN 0-8387-1646-6. Superficial but useful examination of the reception of domestic melodrama: useful chapter on the semiology of melodrama.

Donohue, Joseph W. *Theatre in the Age of Kean.* Blackwell Pubs. 1975 o.p. Discussion of the historical context of the theater as well as plays from the 1790s through the early 1830s; only tangentially Victorian, but good for precursors.

Eigner, Edwin M. *The Dickens Pantomime.* U. CA Pr. 1989 $28.00. ISBN 0-520-06255-8. Excellent work on the connection between Dickens and the theater.

Emeljanow, Victor. *Victorian Popular Dramatists.* Twayne 1987 $25.95. ISBN 0-8057-6935-8. Good introduction; includes chapters on Jerrold, Robertson, Taylor, and Jones.

Fisher, Judith Law, and Stephen Watt, eds. *When They Weren't Doing Shakespeare: Essays on Nineteenth-Century British-American Theater.* U. of Ga. Pr. 1989 $40.00. ISBN 0-8203-1108-1. Essays on nineteenth-century American and British popular drama.

Foulkes, Richard, ed. *British Theatre in the 1890s: Essays on Drama and the Stage.* Cambridge U. Pr. 1992 $54.95. ISBN 0-521-41478-4. Useful discussion of all aspects of theater, including design, as well as a number of important playwrights.

Jackson, Russell, ed. *Victorian Theatre.* Blackwell Pubs. 1989 $29.95. ISBN 0-941533-69-7. Essays on the formation of Victorian theater.

Jenkins, Anthony. *The Making of Victorian Drama*. Cambridge U. Pr. 1991 $54.95. ISBN 0-521-40205-0. Up-to-date analysis of Victorian playwrights' concern with social issues: includes discussions of Bulwer-Lytton, Pinero, and Robertson.

Meisel, Martin. *Shaw and the Nineteenth Century Theater*. Princeton U. Pr. 1976 $75.00. ISBN 0-8371-8416-9. Important work on Shaw's connection to the Victorian theater.

Mullin, Donald C. *Victorian Plays: A Record of Significant Productions on the London Stage, 1837–1901*. Greenwood 1987 $65.00. ISBN 0-313-24211-9. Checklist of important productions; incomplete and somewhat idiosyncratic.

Nelson, Walter W. *Oscar Wilde and the Dramatic Critics: A Study in Victorian Theatre*. Bloms Boktryckerll 1989 o.p. Interesting study of Wilde's relations to the critical reception of his plays; good for context of the Victorian theater.

Nicoll, Allardyce. *A History of Early Nineteenth-Century Drama, 1800–1850*. University MT 1930 o.p. The standard history; includes handlists of the plays of the period.

_____. *A History of Late Nineteenth-Century Drama, 1850–1900*. University Pr. 1949 o.p. Second volume of the standard history; includes handlists of plays; indispensable.

Rowell, George. *The Victorian Theatre, 1792–1914*. 1956 Cambridge U. Pr. 1978 o.p. One of the best single-volume surveys

Stephens, John Russell. *The Profession of the Playwright: British Theatre, 1800–1900*. Cambridge U. Pr. 1992 $54.95. ISBN 0-521-25913-4. Account of the rise of professionalism for dramatists; includes discussion of copyright and publishing reform.

Taylor, George. *Players and Performances in the Victorian Theatre*. Manchester Univ. Pr. 1989 $59.95. ISBN 0-7190-3167-2. Discussion of notable actors and their roles.

Collections

Ashley, Leonard R. N., ed. *Nineteenth-Century British Drama: An Anthology of Representative Plays*. Scott F. 1967 o.p. Broad selection includes plays by Robertson, Jerrold, Wilde, Pinero, Boucicault, Jones, and Wilde.

Bailey, James Osler, ed. *British Plays of the Nineteenth Century: An Anthology to Illustrate the Evolution of the Drama*. Odyssey Pr. 1966 o.p. Useful edition; includes plays from the romantic era.

Booth, Michael R., ed. *English Plays of the Nineteenth Century*. 5 vols. OUP 1969–76. Vols. 1–2 o.p. Vol. 3 $82.00. ISBN 0-19-812465-1. Vol. 4 $79.00. ISBN 0-19-812466-X. Vol. 5 o.p. Excellent, quite extensive collection; volumes organized by subgenre.

_____. *Prefaces to English Nineteenth-Century Theatre*. Manchester Univ. Pr. 1980 o.p. The prefaces of Booth's *English Plays of the Nineteenth Century* collected in one volume.

Mackin, Dorothy, ed. *Melodrama Classics: Six Plays and How to Stage Them*. Sterling 1982 o.p. Includes *The Ticket-of-Leave Man*.

NONFICTION

Many of the most important issues of the Victorian period found their expression in the articles, essays, and books of what came to be a professional class of "men" of letters. The political press was divided among three important organs: *The Edinburgh Review*, which was the forum for Whigs and Whiggish interests; *The Quarterly Review*, which was *The Edinburgh Review*'s conservative (Tory) counterpart; and the less venerable (founded in 1823) but nonetheless important *Westminster Review*, which was affiliated with the Philosophic Radicals (Utilitarians) and which promulgated the views of JEREMY BENTHAM (see Vol. 3), HARRIET MILL, and JOHN STUART (see Vols. 3 and 4). It was in these journals that writers like THOMAS BABINGTON MACAULAY and THOMAS CARLYLE first found their large audiences. Other journals, like *Cornhill* and *Punch*, also played an important role in the formation of the careers of certain writers.

WILLIAM MAKEPEACE THACKERAY, for instance, was associated with both those journals, while HENRY MAYHEW, DOUGLAS JERROLD, and J. S. COYNE were all involved in the founding of *Punch*. Other miscellanies that catered to an audience less concerned with politics and more interested in lighter entertainment included *Blackwoods* and *The London Magazine*, both of which provided forums for the most important writers of the period.

It is necessary to remember that many of the most influential books of the period found their first audiences through the periodical press: JOHN HENRY NEWMAN, Carlyle, Macaulay, Mill, MATTHEW ARNOLD, JOHN RUSKIN, BARBARA BODICHON, JOSEPHINE BUTLER, HARRIET MARTINEAU, and others often took advantage of this venue, primarily because the issues that these authors wrote about were topics that concerned most of society. Almost all of these writers confronted current political and social issues concerning the extension of the franchise, the conditions of the lower classes, the subjection of women, or the status of religion (never an apolitical issue in Victorian England). But many also wrote autobiographies. Sometimes, as in the case of Mill or Martineau, the texts are relatively straightforward, if not always forthcoming about many of the most interesting aspects of the subjects' lives. Other times, as with Carlyle's *Sartor Resartus* or Newman's *Apologia pro Vita Sua*, the effort is more a record of a spiritual and intellectual journey (often a conversion) than a mere account of the subject's life.

Another great concern of the Victorian period was that of aesthetics. Here John Ruskin's work is perhaps the greatest example of the way in which the Victorian preoccupation with aesthetics is ultimately converted to a social issue; by the 1860s Ruskin had completed *Modern Painters* (five volumes), *The Seven Lamps of Architecture*, and *The Stones of Venice* and had turned his attention to the difficulties of "political economy" in collections of essays such as *Unto This Last* and *Munera Pulveris*. Quite the opposite of Ruskin is WALTER PATER, whose works on aesthetics are concerned much more with the impressions of the individual than with the social harmony of the work. It is Pater who, in the phrase "to burn with a hard, gem-like flame," succinctly characterizes the subjective aspect of impressionism and who, somewhat unwillingly, acts as instigator of the "art for art's sake" movement and the beginning of the *fin-de-siècle* decadence that is so often associated with OSCAR WILDE.

History became a recognized academic discipline in the Victorian period, and Carlyle, perhaps the most influential thinker of the age, always considered himself a historian, first and foremost. Though his masterpiece is often considered to be *Sartor Resartus*, he first came to public prominence with the publication of *The French Revolution* (1837). Similarly, despite Macaulay's essays on JOHN MILTON and ROBERT SOUTHEY's "Colloquies," it is his *History of England* that he considered his most important project. It is also important to remember that the Victorians were inveterate letter writers. And, although a number of their letters were published in newspapers and periodicals, some of the most revealing information about many of these personalities is found in their private correspondences. Fortunately, many of these figures have had their letters collected along with their works, and such collections offer an important source of material.

In recent years there has been a steady increase in the representation in prose of marginal groups, such as the working classes and women. A number of critical works have lately appeared that deal with travel writing by women, especially to the edges of the empire. Other works, such as those by JAMES KAY-

SHUTTLEWORTH, EDWIN CHADWICK, and Mayhew, give us an idea of the extent to which the middle classes claimed the problems of the poor as their own and the ways in which they confronted those problems and represented them to the uninformed public. Important materials, especially on immigration and colonialism, remain to be gathered, but many of the secondary works on Victorian prose have begun to comment upon these issues.

History and Criticism

Arac, Jonathan. *Commissioned Spirits: The Shaping of Social Motion in Dickens, Carlyle, Melville, and Hawthorne.* Rutgers U. Pr. 1979 $41.00. ISBN 0-231-07116-7. Important book on the historical context and intertext of these authors.

Corbett, Mary Jean. *Representing Femininity: Middle-Class Subjectivity in Victorian and Edwardian Women's Autobiographies.* OUP 1992 $38.00. ISBN 0-195-06858-0. Important theoretical study of female subjectivity and autobiography.

DeLaura, David J., ed. *Victorian Prose: A Guide to Research.* Modern Lang. 1973 $25.00. ISBN 0-87352-251-6. Still indispensable, though somewhat dated.

Gagnier, Regenia. *Subjectivities: A History of Self-Representation in Britain, 1832–1920.* OUP 1991 $38.00. ISBN 0-195-06096-2. Outstanding work on Victorian working-class autobiography.

Henderson, Heather. *The Victorian Self: Autobiography and Biblical Narrative.* Cornell Univ. Pr. 1989 $25.95. ISBN 0-8014-2294-9. Associates Victorian autobiography with the impulse to incorporate elements of biblical narrative.

Holloway, John. *The Victorian Sage: Studies in Argument.* Norton 1965 o.p. Important study of rhetorical aspects of Victorian prose.

Knights, Ben. *The Idea of the Clerisy in the Nineteenth Century.* Bks. Demand 1978 $73.90. ISBN 0-685-20555-X. Discussion of the promulgation of the idea of an intellectual "class" by nineteenth-century prose writers.

Landow, George P., ed. *Approaches to Victorian Autobiography.* Ohio U. Pr. 1979 $24.95. ISBN 0-8214-0400-8. Collection of essays on autobiography in the period.

Levine, George Lewis. *The Boundaries of Fiction: Carlyle, Macaulay, Newman.* Princeton U. Pr. 1968. o.p. Discussion of the connection of prose fiction to the nonfiction essays of the three writers.

Levine, George Lewis, and W. A. Madden, eds. *The Art of Victorian Prose.* OUP 1968 o.p. Essays on Victorian prose and prose writers.

Levy, Anita. *Other Women: The Writing of Class, Race, and Gender, 1832–1898.* Princeton U. Pr. 1991 $35.00. ISBN 0-691-06865-8. Good work on women's writing in Victorian era.

Loesberg, Jonathan. *Fictions of Consciousness: Mill, Newman, and the Reading of Victorian Prose.* Rutgers U. Pr. 1986 $20.00. ISBN 0-8135-1204-2. Examines psychological implications of the autobiographies of J. S. Mill and Newman.

McPherson, Bruce. *Between Two Worlds: Victorian Ambivalence about Progress.* U. Pr. of Amer. 1983 o.p. Discussion of "progress" as the informing discourse of the Victorian period.

Mills, Sara. *Discourses of Difference: An Analysis of Women's Travel Writing and Colonialism.* Routledge 1991 $55.00. ISBN 0-415-04629-7. Good work on women's writing about their experiences outside England.

Sanders, Valerie. *The Private Lives of Victorian Women: Autobiography in Nineteenth-Century England.* St. Martin 1989 $35.00. ISBN 0-312-00961-5. Women's autobiography and the formation of private subjectivities.

Stevenson, Catherine Barnes. *Victorian Women Travel Writers in Africa.* Twayne 1982 o.p. Early and useful introduction on the topic of women travel writers.

Swindells, Julia. *Victorian Writing and Working Women.* U. of Minn. Pr. 1985 $39.95. ISBN 0-8166-1476-8. Very useful study of the ways working women expressed themselves outside professionalized literature.

Collections

Bellringer, Alan W., and C. B. Jones, eds. *The Victorian Sages: An Anthology of Prose.* Rowman 1975 o.p. Somewhat limited selections.

Brownell, William Crary. *Victorian Prose Masters: Thackeray, Carlyle, George Eliot, Matthew Arnold, Ruskin, George Meredith.* Scribner 1931 $79.00. ISBN 0-7812-7112-6. Interesting older collection.

Buckler, William Earl, ed. *Prose of the Victorian Period.* HM 1958 $9.16. ISBN 0-395-05128-2. Affordable collection, but very limited and idiosyncratic.

Foster, Shirley. *Across New Worlds: Nineteenth-Century Women Travellers and Their Writings.* Harvester Wheatsheaf 1990 o.p. Useful volume on a topic currently receiving much attention.

Haight, Gordon Sherman, ed. *The Portable Victorian Reader.* Viking Penguin 1976 $4.95. ISBN 0-14-015068-4. Interesting collection; contains some often neglected material.

Harrold, Charles Frederick, and W. D. Templeman, eds. *English Prose of the Victorian Era.* OUP 1961 o.p. For years the standard teaching collection; has been superseded by Tennyson and Gray.

Jay, Elisabeth, and Richard Jay, eds. *Critics of Capitalism: Victorian Criticism of Political Economy.* Cambridge U. Pr. 1986 $54.95. ISBN 0-521-26588-6. Good collection on a specific topic.

Nadel, Ira Bruce, ed. *Victorian Biography: A Collection of Essays from the Period.* Garland 1986 o.p. Reprint of works originally published between 1832 and 1929.

Tennyson, G. B., and Donald J. Gray, eds. *Victorian Literature: Prose.* Macmillan 1976 o.p. Standard classroom volume.

Trilling, Lionel, and Harold Bloom, eds. *Victorian Prose and Poetry.* OUP 1973 $22.00. ISBN 0-19-501616-5. Good selection, if limited.

CHRONOLOGY OF AUTHORS

Trollope, Frances Milton. 1779–1863
Marryat, Captain Frederick. 1792–1848
Carlyle, Thomas. 1795–1881
Chadwick, Sir Edwin. 1800–1890
Macaulay, Thomas Babington, 1st Baron. 1800–1859
Martineau, Harriet. 1802–1876
Bulwer-Lytton. 1803–1873
Coyne, Joseph Stirling. 1803–1868
Jerrold, Douglas William. 1803–1857
Disraeli, Benjamin. 1804–1881
Kay-Shuttleworth, Sir James Phillips. 1804–1877
Browning, Elizabeth Barrett. 1806–1861
Mill, Harriet Taylor. 1807–1858
Norton, Caroline Sheridan. 1808–1877
Tennyson, Alfred, 1st Baron. 1809–1892
Gaskell, Elizabeth. 1810–1865
Thackeray, William Makepeace. 1811–1863
Browning, Robert. 1812–1889
Dickens, Charles. 1812–1870

Mayhew, Henry. 1812–1887
Reade, Charles. 1814–1884
Trollope, Anthony. 1815–1882
Brontë, Charlotte. 1816–1855
Lewes, George Henry. 1817–1878
Taylor, Tom. 1817–1880
Brontë, Emily Jane. 1818–1848
Clough, Arthur Hugh. 1819–1861
Eliot, George. 1819–1880
Kingsley, Charles. 1819–1875
Ruskin, John. 1819–1900
Boucicault, Dionysius Lardner. 1820–1890
Brontë, Anne. 1820–1849
Arnold, Matthew. 1822–1888
Collins, Wilkie. 1824–1889
Bodichon, Barbara. 1827–1891
Butler, Josephine Grey. 1828–1906
Meredith, George. 1828–1909
Oliphant, Margaret. 1828–1897
Rossetti, Dante Gabriel. 1828–1882
Robertson, T(homas) W(illiam). 1829–1871
Rossetti, Christina. 1830–1894
Du Maurier, George. 1834–1896
Morris, William. 1834–1896

Butler, Samuel. 1835–1902
Gilbert, Sir William Schwenck.
1836–1911
Braddon, Mary Elizabeth. 1837–1915
Swinburne, Algernon Charles.
1837–1909
Pater, Walter Horatio. 1839–1894
Hardy, Thomas. 1840–1928
Hudson, William Henry. 1841–1922
Hopkins, Gerard Manley. 1844–1889

Stevenson, Robert Louis. 1850–1894
Jones, Henry Arthur. 1851–1929
Moore, George. 1852–1933
Wilde, Oscar. 1854–1900
Pinero, Sir Arthur Wing. 1855–1934
Gissing, George. 1857–1903
Barrie, Sir J(ames) M(atthew).
1860–1937
Kipling, Rudyard. 1865–1936

ARNOLD, MATTHEW. 1822–1888

Son of the famous headmaster at Rugby, Arnold established himself in an Oxford professorship (of poetry in 1857) and pursued relentlessly the theme of social integration. A poet and literary critic influenced initially by GOETHE (see Vol. 2) and WILLIAM WORDSWORTH, Arnold gradually became a trenchant social critic. In his essay "Culture and Anarchy" (1869), he inveighed against the barbarian aristocracy for its materalism, against the philistine middle class for its vulgarity, and against the populace lower class for its ignorance. He sought wider respect for education and coined the phrase "disinterestedness" to suggest that culture should be disseminated equally among all social classes. His *Essays in Criticism* (1865) established a broader intellectual scope for the literary critic: Criticism was to be more comprehensive, with social and political considerations equal in importance to scholarship. In his efforts to integrate literature and life, and to bring higher cultural standards to all ranks of society, Arnold had an influence extending well beyond his own time.

Arnold's career as a poet was brief, however. As a young man, Arnold attempted to create poems through which contemporary readers could touch worlds of remoteness—the people and places of legend. But by 1855 he had realized that his poetry could never achieve the popularity of ALFRED TENNYSON's nor the influence among the great that might have compensated for his smaller audience. Declaring that "it is a pity that power should be wasted" (preface to *Poems*, 1855), he turned to prose. Then, after the death of his dear college friend and fellow poet, ARTHUR HUGH CLOUGH, in 1861, Arnold wrote a number of poems on the subject of doubt and willed conviction, including *Thyrsis* (1867), often called his greatest poem. Arnold's works are characterized by brilliant romantic images, set within earnestly Victorian discourse.

POETRY BY ARNOLD

Poems. Biblio Dist. 1965 o.p.
Poetical Works. Ed. by C. B. Tinker and Howard F. Lowry. *Oxford Stand. Authors Ser.* OUP 1950 o.p. An acceptable collection.
The Poetical Works of Matthew Arnold. Arden Lib. 1978 repr. of 1893 ed. o.p.

NONFICTION BY ARNOLD

On the Study of Celtic Literature and Other Essays. 1867. Biblio Dist. 1976 o.p.
On Translating Homer. 1862. AMS Pr. 1978 repr. of 1905 ed. $16.25. ISBN 0-404-00388-5

WORKS BY ARNOLD

The Complete Prose Works of Matthew Arnold. 11 vols. U. of Mich. Pr. 1960–76 $47.50 ea. ISBNs 0-472-11651-7, 0-472-11652-5, 0-472-11653-3, 0-472-11654-1, 0-472-11655-X,

0-472-11656-8, 0-472-11657-6, 0-472-11658-4, 0-472-11659-2, 0-472-11660-6, 0-472-11661-4

Essays and Poems of Arnold. Ed. by Frederick W. Roe. Richard West 1980 repr. of 1928 ed. o.p.

Letters of Matthew Arnold, 1848–1888. 2 vols. Rprt. Serv. 1992 repr. of 1895 ed. $150.00. ISBN 0-7812-7424-9

The Portable Matthew Arnold. Ed. by Lionel Trilling. *Viking Portable Lib.* Viking Penguin 1980 o.p.

Unpublished Letters of Matthew Arnold. Folcroft 1977 repr. of 1923 ed. o.p.

The Works of Matthew Arnold. 15 vols. AMS Pr. 1970 repr. of 1903–04 $395.00. ISBN 0-403-00201-X. Includes essays on criticism, as well as poetry, letters, etc.

The Yale Manuscript. Ed. by S. O. Ullman. U. of Mich. Pr. 1989 $49.50. ISBN 0-472-10105-6. Publication of a significant portion of the Yale collection of Arnold's works in manuscript. Includes commentary by Ullman.

BOOKS ABOUT ARNOLD

Bloom, Harold, ed. *Matthew Arnold.* Chelsea Hse. 1987 $19.95. ISBN 0-877-54686-X. Useful collection of perspectives on Arnold.

Buckler, William E. *On the Poetry of Matthew Arnold: Essays in Critical Reconstruction. Gotham Lib.* NYU Pr. 1982 $40.00. ISBN 0-8147-1039-5. Dismisses myths about Arnold's poetry and argues that it is actually more exciting than previously realized.

Collini, Stefan. *Arnold. Oxford Past Masters Ser.* OUP 1988 $20.00. ISBN 0-19-287660-0. Introductory, short, judicious essay on Arnold.

Eells, John S., Jr. *The Touchstones of Matthew Arnold.* AMS Pr. repr. of 1955 ed. $22.50. ISBN 0-404-02263-4. Explores the possibility of links between Arnold's criticism and his poetry.

Honan, Park. *Matthew Arnold: A Life.* HUP 1983 $14.95. ISBN 0-674-55465-5. Authoritative biography that presents Arnold's development as an influential social thinker, literary critic, and poet.

Johnson, W. Stacy. *The Voices of Matthew Arnold.* Greenwood 1973 repr. of 1961 ed. $39.75. ISBN 0-8371-6693-4. Critical study tracing Arnold's evolution as a successful poet.

MacDonald, Isobel. *The Buried Self: A Background to the Poems of Matthew Arnold.* Folcroft 1974 repr. of 1949 ed. o.p.

Machann, Clinton, and Forrest D. Burt. *Matthew Arnold in His Time and Ours: Centenary Essays.* U. Pr. of Va. 1988 $30.00. ISBN 0-813-91173-7. Good, diverse collection of essays.

Riede, David G. *Matthew Arnold and the Betrayal of Language.* U. Pr. of Va. 1987 $30.00. ISBN 0-8139-1149-4. Examines Arnold's poetry as caught in a tradition he could neither avoid nor control.

Smart, Thomas B. *Bibliography of Matthew Arnold.* B. Franklin repr. of 1892 ed. o.p. Contains over 300 critical reviews of Arnold's writings, with special reference to his poetical works.

Stange, G. Robert. *Matthew Arnold: The Poet as Humanist.* Gordian 1979 repr. of 1967 ed. $50.00. ISBN 0-87752-202-2. Differs from other studies in that it examines Arnold's work in terms of Goethe's lyrics and the traditions of classical humanism.

Trilling, Lionel. *Matthew Arnold.* HarBraceJ 1979 $6.95. ISBN 0-15-657734-8. Focuses on the development of Arnold's thought in relation to his times.

BARRIE, SIR J(AMES) M(ATTHEW). 1860–1937

Barrie was born in Kirriemuir, Fofarshire, Scotland, the ninth child, to David (a weaver by trade) and Margaret Barrie. As a child, he was an avid reader, especially of adventure stories. He married the actress Mary Ansell in 1894 and was divorced in 1909. After receiving an M.A. from Edinburgh University in 1882, he worked as a freelance journalist in London. He was the rector of St.

Andrews University, 1919–22, the chancellor of Edinburgh University, 1930–37, and a member of the Society of Authors.

When he was 6 years old, his 13-year-old brother David, his mother's favorite child, died in an accident, and, as a result, his mother suffered a nervous collapse. The trauma led Barrie to strive to replace his brother in his mother's affections, and all of his life he was consumed with winning her love. His mother often told him stories of her own childhood, and he later said that his writing stemmed from being able to see her as a child wandering confidently through the pages.

Although James Barrie wrote 45 plays (some, such as *Dear Brutus*, still get performed), 7 novels for adults, and many short stories, his fame rests on one play, *Peter Pan* (1904). The idea apparently began as entertainment for five little boys whom he befriended in London in 1897 and ultimately adopted. In 1901 he compiled a book of captioned photographs that he had taken of the boys acting out these adventures and titled it *The Boy Castaways of Black Lake Island*. The story first appeared in print as part of *The Little White Bird, or, Adventures in Kensington Gardens* (1902), one of his novels for adults. In it, the infant Peter flies away from home and finds another little boy sleeping in his bed when he attempts to return home. The work was rewritten as a play. It was first produced in London at Duke of York's Theatre in 1904 and has since been adapted in various forms many times, most notably as a Broadway musical starring Mary Martin and as a Disney film in 1952. The play was rewritten as a novel, *Peter Pan and Wendy* (1911). The popular play and subsequent narrative of Peter Pan has received both criticism and praise. The criticism centers on the fact that Peter Pan does not want to grow up, something Barrie said applied to his own life, as well as the complex relationships of mother and child, thus raising questions about arrested child development. The praise lauds the creative, imaginative, mythical quality of the work.

In regard to his other work, Barrie's novels of homely Scottish life, with their blended pathos and humor, made Scots dialect popular. The publication of *The Little Minister* (1891) established him as a successful novelist, and its dramatization was what started his career as a successful playwright. Other novels included *A Window in Thrums* (1889), which was largely autobiographical. In addition to the popular *Peter Pan*, his plays included *The Admirable Crichton* (1902), a social satire, *What Every Woman Knows* (1908), and his last play, *The Boy David* (1936), which was based on the biblical character David.

NOVEL BY BARRIE

The Little Minister. 1891. Buccaneer Bks. 1981 repr. of 1891 ed. $18.95. ISBN 0-89966-329-X

SHORT STORY COLLECTION BY BARRIE

Auld Licht Idylls and *Better Dead*. Ayer repr. of 1896 ed. $18.00. ISBN 0-8369-3182-X

PLAYS BY BARRIE

Pantaloon. Players Pr. 1993 $5.00. ISBN 0-88734-316-3
Peter Pan. Macmillan Child. Grp. 1980 $19.95. ISBN 0-684-16611-9
Rosalind. Players Pr. 1993 $6.00. ISBN 0-88734-331-7
The Twelve Pound Look. Players Pr. 1993 $6.00. ISBN 0-88734-330-9
The Will. Players Pr. 1993 $6.00. ISBN 0-88734-329-5

WORKS BY BARRIE

The Letters of James Matthew Barrie. Ed. by Viola Meynell. AMS Pr. 1976 repr. of 1947 ed.
   $18.50. ISBN 0-404-10640-1
The Little White Bird, or Adventures in Kensington Gardens. Longwood MA 1977 repr. of
   1902 ed. o.p.
Selections from the Prose Works. Richard West repr. of 1929 ed. o.p.
Works. 18 vols. AMS Pr. repr. of 1929–41 ed. o.p.

BOOKS ABOUT BARRIE

Asquith, Cynthia Mary Evelyn. *Portrait of Barrie.* NAL-Dutton 1967 o.p. An affectionate
   reminiscence by his private secretary.
Cutler, Bradley D. *Sir James M. Barrie: A Bibliography with Full Citations of the British
   Unauthorized Editions.* B. Franklin 1967 repr. of 1931 ed. o.p. Useful for locating
   other sources.
Dunbar, Janet. *J. M. Barrie: The Man behind the Image.* HM 1970 o.p.
Jack, Ronald D. S. *The Road to the Never Land: A Re-assessment of J. M. Barrie's Dramatic
   Art.* Aberdeen U. Pr. 1991 $50.00. ISBN 0-08-037742-4. Discusses Barrie's dramatic
   works as much more important than generally acknowledged.
Kennedy, John. *Thurms and The Barrie Country.* Cranton Heath 1930 o.p. A painstaking,
   honest biography by a devoted follower.
Mackail, Denis G. *Barrie: The Story of J. M. B.* Select Bibliographies Repr. Serv. Ayer repr.
   of 1941 ed. $ 34.00 ISBN 0-8369-6734-8. A complete, extremely detailed, and well-
   researched biography of Barrie.
Markgraf, Carl. *J. M. Barrie: An Annotated Secondary Bibliography.* ELT Pr. 1989 $35.00.
   ISBN 0-944-31803-7. A useful, up-to-date bibliography of works about Barrie and his
   writing.
Ormond, Leonee. *J. M. Barrie.* Scot. Acad. Pr. UK 1987 o.p. A worthwhile recent
   biography of Barrie.

BODICHON, BARBARA (LEIGHTON SMITH). 1827–1891

Suffragist, education reformer, essayist, and feminist, Barbara Bodichon was
one of the most influential women of Victorian England. The eldest of five
children, she was born in Sussex to William Smith and Anne Longdon.
Bodichon came from a long line of radical Unitarians. Her father, an MP and
himself interested in social reform, was the son of a wealthy merchant and
became rich in his own right as a successful distiller. Her mother was a
milliner's assistant. Her mother and father lived together for 11 years until the
former's death, in 1834, but never married. The resulting stigma of illegitimacy
was made easier to bear by her father's unconventional views and, according to
Bodichon, in later life by her wealth.

Early in her adult life, Bodichon made the acquaintance of GEORGE ELIOT. The
two formed a close friendship that lasted more than 30 years, until Eliot's death
in 1880. The novelist even used Bodichon as the model for her heroine Romola,
in her historical novel of the same name. Bodichon's own writing helped
galvinize the feminist movement in England in the mid-1850s. Her *Brief
Summary . . . of the Most Important Laws of England Concerning Women* (1854)
focused on the property rights of women, especially the inequitable laws
concerning married women's property. In *Women and Work* (1857), Bodichon
argues for the salutary effects of work, encouraging employment for married as
well as single women—an unheard-of consideration for middle- and upper-class
females. In the 1860s Bodichon turned her energies to the suffrage movement
and was influential in America as well as in England. In the following decade
she, along with Emily Davies, worked to institute higher education for women

in England; together they helped establish Girton College, Cambridge, where for the first time women could matriculate at the university.

Interest in Bodichon's work has increased in recent years, but the greatest amount of the scholarship has appeared as journal articles rather than as book-length studies.

NONFICTION BY BODICHON

An American Diary. Ed. by Joseph W. Reed. Routledge 1972 o.p. Diary of Bodichon's trip to America in 1857–58; first published from the manuscript in 1972.
Barbara Leighton Smith Bodichon and the Langham Place Group. Ed. by Candida Ann Lacey. Routledge 1986 o.p.
A Brief Summary in Plain Language of the Most Important Laws of England Concerning Women. Holyoake 1854 o.p. Important document discussing the rights and lack of them extended to women under British law.
Women and Work. 1857. Bosworth & Harrison o.p.

BOOKS ABOUT BODICHON

Bradbrook, M. C. *Barbara Bodichon, George Eliot, and the Limits of Feminism.* Somerville Coll. 1975 o.p. Focuses on the writers' interest in women's progress.
Burton, Hester. *Barbara Bodichon, 1827–1891.* Murray 1949 o.p. Adequate but dated.
Herstein, Sheila R. *A Mid-Victorian Feminist: Barbara Leigh Smith Bodichon.* Yale U. Pr. 1985 o.p. The most comprehensive coverage of Bodichon's work as a feminist.

BOUCICAULT, DIONYSIUS (DION) LARDNER. 1820–1890

Dublin-born playwright of Huguenot extraction, Boucicault (originally Boursiquot) attended University College in London and began his stage career as an actor in 1838. His first success as playwright came in 1841 with *London Assurance.* Thereafter, he wrote or adapted some 250 plays, including *The Corsican Brothers* (1852), *The Poor of New York* (1857), *The Colleen Bawn, or, The Brides of Garryowen* (1860), and *The Shaughraun* (1874), all extremely popular. Queen Victoria, for example, saw *The Corsican Brothers* four times. Boucicault was one of the premier playwrights of the period, although his career was tempestuous, distinguished by both great successes and devastating failures. Especially toward the end of his life, Boucicault's plays fell increasingly out of favor, as farce and romance became less fashionable and were replaced on the London stage by the realist dramas of such authors as GEORGE BERNARD SHAW and HENRIK IBSEN (see Vol. 2). Along with his contributions to Victorian drama, Boucicault helped transform the business of the theater and the writing of plays in the nineteenth century by introducing such important innovations as royalties for playwrights and copyright for dramatists in America.

PLAYS BY BOUCICAULT

Arrah-na-Pogue, or, The Wicklow Wedding. Dramatic Pr. 1912 o.p. Popular Irish drama, produced in 1865.
The Colleen Bawn, or, The Brides of Garryowen. Lacy 1860 o.p. One of Boucicault's most popular plays; typical of the Irish drama for which he became famous.
Forbidden Fruit & Other Plays. 1940. Ed. by Allardyce Nicoll and Theodore F. Clark. Ind. U. Pr. 1963 o.p. Selected collection of Boucicault's more prominent works.
Led Astray. French 1873 o.p. One of Boucicault's most popular comedies.
London Assurance. Ed. by James L. Smith. Norton 1984 $4.95. ISBN 0-393-90050-9. Boucicault's earliest play, often considered his best.
The Octaroon. Ayer repr. of 1861 ed. $8.75. ISBN 0-8369-8521-4. Adapted from Mayne Reid's novel *The Quadroon*; originally produced in 1859.
Plays. Ed. by Peter Thomson. Cambridge U. Pr. 1984 $59.95. ISBN 0-521-23997-4

Selected Plays of Dion Boucicault. Cath. U. Pr. 1987 $29.95. ISBN 0-813-20616-2. A recent collection of Boucicault's works.

The Shaughraun. 1874. French o.p. Late, popular Irish drama.

Rip Van Winkle. Dodd 1895 o.p. One of Boucicault's most popular adaptations. A vehicle for famous American actor Joseph Jefferson for many years.

WORK BY BOUCICAULT

Dion Boucicault, the Shaughraun. Ed. and comp. by Robin Goodefellowe and Sven Eric Molin. Proscenium Pt. 1 1979 o.p. Pt. 2 1982 $3.95. ISBN 0-912262-78-8. Pt. 3 1985 $4.95. ISBN 0-912262-85-0. Pt. 4 1989 $4.95. ISBN 0-912262-89-3. Pt. 5 1991 $4.95. ISBN 0-912262-90-7. Useful, firsthand biographical information.

BOOKS ABOUT BOUCICAULT

Fawkes, Richard. *Dion Boucicault*. Charles River Bks. 1979 $21.95. ISBN 0-685-42065-5. Accessible biography.

Steele, William Paul. *The Character of Melodrama: An Examination through Dion Boucicault's* The Poor of New York. U. of Maine Pr. 1968 $5.95. ISBN 0-89101-017-3. Includes text of play.

Walsh, Townsend. *The Career of Dion Boucicault*. 1915. Ayer repr. of 1915 ed. $22.00. ISBN 0-405-09052-8. Reprint of early literary-historical evaluation of Boucicault's work.

BRADDON, MARY ELIZABETH. 1837–1915

Braddon, the daughter of a solicitor, was educated privately. As a young woman, she acted under an assumed name for three years in order to support herself and her mother. In 1860 she met John Maxwell, a publisher of periodicals, whose wife was in an asylum for the insane. Braddon acted as stepmother to Maxwell's five children and bore him five illegitimate children before the couple married, in 1874, when Maxwell's wife died.

Braddon's most famous novel, *Lady Audley's Secret* (1862), was first published serially in *Robin Goodfellow* and *The Sixpenny Magazine*. One of the earliest sensationalist novels, it sold nearly 1 million copies during Braddon's lifetime. Its plot involves bigamy, the protagonist's desertion of her child, her murder of her first husband, and her thoughts of poisoning her second husband. The novel shocked and outraged her contemporary, MARGARET OLIPHANT, who said Braddon had invented "the fair-haired demon of modern fiction." Throughout her long literary career, during which she wrote more than 80 novels and edited several magazines, she was often excoriated for her penchant for sensationalizing violence, crime, and sexual indiscretion. Nevertheless, Braddon had many well-known devotees, among them WILLIAM MAKEPEACE THACKERAY, EDWARD BULWER-LYTTON, and ROBERT LOUIS STEVENSON.

NOVELS BY BRADDON

Aurora Floyd. 1863. Garland 1979 repr. of 1863 ed. $96.00. ISBN 0-824-04350-2. Work that helped establish Braddon as a popular sensation novelist. Introduction by Jennifer Uglow.

The Black Band, or, The Mysteries of Midnight. 1861. George Vickers 1877 o.p. Originally published pseudonymously; interesting for its illustrations by Gustave Doré, Janet Lange, and other artists.

The Doctor's Wife. Ward, Lock & Tyler 1864 o.p. One of several popular sensation novels written by Braddon during the 1860s.

Henry Dunbar. Ward, Lock, & Tyler 1864 o.p. Sensation novel typical of Braddon's early career.

The Infidel: A Story of the Great Revival. 1900 o.p. A historical novel.

Ishmael. John & Robert Maxwell 1884 o.p. One of Braddon's several historical novels.
Lady Audley's Secret. OUP 1987 $7.95. ISBN 0-19-281741-8. Useful scholarly edition of
the novel.
London Pride, or, When the World Was Younger. Simpkin 1896 o.p. Historical novel
characteristic of Braddon's work at the turn of the century.
The Rose of Life. Hutchinson 1905 o.p. Late novel of manners and character.

BOOK ABOUT BRADDON

Wolff, Robert Lee. *Sensational Victorian: The Life and Fiction of Mary Elizabeth Braddon.*
Garland 1979 $20.00. ISBN 0-824-01618-1. Thorough biography.

THE BRONTË SISTERS

The Brontë sisters—Anne (1820–49), Charlotte (1816–55), and Emily
(1818–48)—lived most of their lives at the parsonage in Haworth, in Yorkshire,
where their father, the Reverend Patrick Brontë, had been appointed perpetual
curate. Their mother had died soon after they moved there, leaving six small
children, who were cared for by Elizabeth Branwell, their mother's oldest sister.
The two older girls died of tuberculosis within the next five years. Left very
much to their own devices, the three remaining sisters and their brother,
Branwell, entertained themselves with creative writings recorded in tiny
volumes. When Charlotte went away to school, Emily and Anne started an
imaginative saga of their own called *Gondal.* When Charlotte returned, she
attempted to revive their earlier work and expand it into a realm named Angria,
but without success. From that time on, Charlotte and Branwell played and
wrote about Angria; Emily and Anne, about Gondal. These experiments in
writing led to a joint volume of verse printed at their own expense in 1846,
Poems by Currer, Ellis and Acton Bell, of which only two copies were sold.
Currer, Ellis, and Acton Bell were pseudonyms that the sisters adopted and
retained throughout their later work.

WORK BY THE BRONTË SISTERS

*The Life and Works of the Sisters Brontë (The Life and Works of Charlotte Brontë and Her
Sisters).* 7 vols. AMS Pr. repr. of 1903 ed. $45.00 ea. $315.00 set. Includes Elizabeth
Gaskell's biography of Charlotte, with annotations of Clement K. Shorter.

BOOKS ABOUT THE BRONTË SISTERS

Allott, Miriam, ed. *The Brontës: The Critical Heritage.* Routledge 1974 o.p. Includes a
wide selection of criticism; the author's argument is that *Wuthering Heights* is
actually more popular than *Jane Eyre.*
Bloom, Harold, ed. *The Brontës.* Chelsea Hse. 1987 $19.95. ISBN 0-877-54687-8.
Collection of essays on all of the Brontës.
Dimnet, Ernest. *The Brontë Sisters.* Richard West repr. of 1927 ed. o.p. Includes some
early letters.
Eagleton, Terry. *Myths of Power: A Marxist Study of the Brontës.* Macmillan 1988 o.p.
Important Marxist reading of the novels.
Pascal, Anne, ed. *Charlotte and Emily Brontë: An Annotated Bibliography. Reference Lib.
of the Humanities* Garland 1979 o.p. Covers a multitude of topics, including
mysticism in Emily Brontë's poetry and Charlotte Brontë's contributions to feminist
philosophy.
Ratchford, Fannie E. *The Brontë's Web of Childhood.* Russell 1964 repr. of 1941 ed. o.p.
Shorter, Clement K. *The Brontës: Life and Letters.* 2 vols. Haskell 1992 repr. of 1908 ed.
$150.00. ISBN 0-7812-7451-6. Told from the perspective of Ellen Nussey, who knew
the Brontë family.
_____. *The Brontës and Their Circle.* Kraus repr. of 1917 ed. o.p. Includes some early
letters.

Tayler, Irene. *Holy Ghosts: The Male Muses of Emily and Charlotte Brontë*. Col. U. Pr. 1990 $35.00. ISBN 0-231-07154-X. Interesting book on the male paradigm out of which the Brontës wrote.

Winnifrith, Tony. *The Brontës and Their Background: Romance and Reality*. Humanities 1973 o.p. Distinguishes the real-life tragedies in the Brontë family from the literature they created.

BRONTË, ANNE ("Acton Bell," pseud.). 1820–1849

Considered by most to be the least talented Brontë sister, Anne wrote two novels. *Agnes Grey* (1847) is the story of a governess, and *The Tenant of Wildfell Hall* (1848), a tale of the evils of drink and profligacy. Her acquaintance with sin and wickedness, as shown in her novels, was so astounding that Charlotte Brontë saw fit to explain in a preface that the source of her sister's knowledge of evil was her brother Branwell's dissolute ways. A habitué of drink and drugs, he finally became an addict. Anne Brontë's other notable work is her *Complete Poems*.

NOVELS BY ANNE BRONTË

Agnes Grey. 1847. OUP 1991 $5.95. ISBN 0-19-282711-1
The Tenant of Wildfell Hall. 1848. Viking Penguin 1980 $5.95. ISBN 0-14-043137-3

POETRY BY ANNE BRONTË

Complete Poems. Ed. by Clement K. Shorter. Scholarly 1971 repr. of 1924 ed. $49.00. ISBN 0-403-01758-0
The Poems of Anne Brontë: A New Text and Commentary. Ed. by Edward Chitham. Rowman 1979 o.p.

BOOKS ABOUT ANNE BRONTË

Gérin, Winifred. *Anne Brontë: A Biography*. Rowman 1976 o.p. Tribute to Anne Brontë and her often overlooked poetry.
Harrison, Ada, and Derek Stanford. *Anne Brontë: Her Life and Work*. Shoe String 1970 repr. of 1959 ed. o.p. An excellent study.

BRONTË, CHARLOTTE ("Currer Bell," pseud.). 1816–1855

A psychological novelist whose depictions of feminine heroines, particularly Jane Eyre, have risen to the level of cultural myth, Charlotte Brontë's books were based on her somber surroundings and the tragic events of her life. *The Professor* was a short early sketch that she enlarged in *Villette* (1853). In *Jane Eyre* (1847) she introduced the first "ugly" heroine in fiction and immediately achieved success. This novel, in essence, constituted a plea for female equality with men in the avowal of their passions. The heroine of *Shirley* (1849) is modeled on her sister Emily, and the story describes the misery that followed the introduction of machinery into Yorkshire. *Villette* is set in Brussels, where the author once taught school. While in Brussels, Charlotte formed an unreciprocated attachment to a married man, and he is scornfully satirized in this novel. The original ending, so painful to her readers that she changed it in later editions, enforced her bleak view of the position of the sensitive woman in a hostile society.

The first biography of Charlotte was the famous one by ELIZABETH GASKELL (known as Mrs. Gaskell), which appeared two years after Charlotte's death. The discovery of Charlotte's "Lost Letters to Constantin Heger" (the original of *The Professor*), juvenilia, and other later letters and data has led to several new interpretations. Of these, Margaret Lane's *The Brontë Story* is an excellent sequel to Gaskell's book. In the foreword, Lane says: "This book, in fact, is offered as a sort of footnote to Mrs. Gaskell, bringing the reader back to every point in her incomparable text, and at the same time putting him in possession of everything of importance that has come to light in the century since she wrote. Provided with this footnote as well as her 'Life,' he will, I hope, have in his hands the whole of the Brontë story."

Charlotte Brontë married her father's curate, Arthur Bell Nichols, in 1854, and died during pregnancy the following year. She left behind an unfinished novel, *Emma*.

NOVELS BY CHARLOTTE BRONTË

Jane Eyre. 1847. *Bantam Class. Ser.* Bantam 1983 $1.95. ISBN 0-553-21140-4. The story of a love relationship between a master and pupil, Rochester and Jane.

The Professor. OUP 1991 $5.95. ISBN 0-19-282741-3

The Secret and Lily Hart: Two Tales. Ed. by William Holtz. U. of Mo. Pr. 1979 o.p. Two stories from juvenilia and a high-quality facsimile of original manuscript.

Shirley. 1849. Ed. by Margaret Smith and Herbert Rosengarten. OUP 1987 $4.95. ISBN 0-19-281562-8

The Spell: An Extravaganza. Ed. by George MacLean. Arden Lib. 1979 repr. of 1931 ed. o.p. An examination of Charlotte's unfinished novel.

Villette. 1853. Ed. by Mark Lilly. *Penguin Eng. Lib. Ser.* Viking Penguin 1980 $5.95. ISBN 0-14-043118-7

POETRY BY CHARLOTTE BRONTË

Complete Poems of Charlotte Brontë. Rprt. Serv. 1988 repr. of 1924 ed. $59.00. ISBN 0-7812-0136-5. Broad collection that provides insight into author's style.

Legends of Angria. Ed. by Fannie E. Ratchford and William C. DeVane. Kennikat 1973 o.p. Five stories from juvenilia, including the undated "Farewell to Angria."

BOOKS ABOUT CHARLOTTE BRONTË

Fraser, Rebecca. *Charlotte Brontë and Her Family*. Fawcett 1990 $12.95. ISBN 0-449-90465-2. Psychoanalytic and historical evaluation.

Gaskell, Elizabeth Cleghorn. *The Life of Charlotte Brontë*. Biblio Dist. 1982 $4.95. ISBN 0-460-01318-1. A classic study, vivid, charming, and revealing of an age and an artist.

Gates, Barbara T., ed. *Critical Essays on Charlotte Brontë*. Macmillan 1989 $40.00. ISBN 0-8161-8772-X. Contains essays on juvenilia, *The Professor*, *Jane Eyre*, *Shirley*, and other works by Charlotte Brontë.

Gérin, Winifred. *Charlotte Brontë: The Evolution of Genius*. OUP 1967 o.p. An excellent definitive biography.

Lane, Margaret. *The Brontë Story*. Greenwood 1971 repr. of 1953 ed. $35.00. ISBN 0-8371-3817-5. Intended for the general reader rather than the specialist.

Martin, Robert B. *The Accents of Persuasion: Charlotte Brontë's Novels*. Arden Lib. 1983 repr. of 1966 ed. o.p. Examines Charlotte Brontë's four complete novels in terms of the nineteenth-century conflict between passion and moral intelligence.

Pinion, F. B. *A Brontë Companion: Literary Assessment, Background and Reference*. B & N Imports 1975 o.p. Brontë's novels are given close analysis, as are her views on subjects like marriage and religion.

BRONTË, EMILY JANE ("Ellis Bell," pseud.). 1818–1848

In her one novel, *Wuthering Heights* (1847), Emily Brontë draws on the Gothic horror tradition and the romantic obsession with Byronic intensity and wildness of feeling. *Wuthering Heights* depicts a series of tumultuous and passionate relationships that dramatize the power of love. Set in the wild Yorkshire moors, the novel emphasizes the connection between landscape and character, between the physical environment and the psychological contours of those who inhabit it. It is noteworthy, among other reasons, for its innovative handling of point of view and narrative structure, its resonant but flexible style, and its dramatic psychological realism. Widely read in its own day, *Wuthering Heights* is even more widely read and highly thought of today. MATTHEW ARNOLD said of her that "for passion, vehemence, and grief she had no equal since Byron."

NOVEL BY EMILY BRONTË

Wuthering Heights. 1847. Ed. by Richard Dunn. Norton 1989 $6.95. ISBN 0-393-95760-8

POETRY BY EMILY BRONTË

Complete Poems. Ed. by C. W. Hatfield. Col. U. Pr. 1941 $27.50. ISBN 0-231-01222-5. Edited from original manuscripts.

Gondal Poems. Ed. by H. Brown and J. Mott. Folcroft repr. of 1938 ed. o.p. Verses from a notebook presented to the British Museum in 1933; with an introduction on the history of the manuscript.

Gondal's Queen: A Novel in Verse. 1855. Ed. by Fannie E. Ratchford. U. of Tex. Pr. 1977 o.p. A novel in verse about Augusta Geraldine Almeda.

BOOKS ABOUT EMILY BRONTË

Benvenuto, Richard. *Emily Brontë*. *Twayne's Eng. Authors Ser*. G. K. Hall 1982 $12.50. ISBN 0-8057-7436-X. Focuses on Brontë's independent spirit and surveys the various readings of *Wuthering Heights*.

Crandall, N. *Emily Brontë: A Psychological Portrait*. Kraus repr. of 1957 ed. o.p. Recreates the psychological atmosphere at Haworth Parsonage, where Brontë lived and wrote.

Gérin, Winifred. *Emily Brontë*. OUP 1971 $9.95. ISBN 0-19-281251-3. Separates the facts about Brontë from the inferences and focuses on her development as a person.

Homans, Margaret. *Women Writers and Poetic Identity: Dorothy Wordsworth, Emily Brontë, and Emily Dickinson*. Princeton U. Pr. 1987 $14.95. ISBN 0-691-10218-X. Study of these three nineteenth-century women poets and their response to a literary tradition that defined "poet" as a male.

Visick, Mary. *The Genesis of Wuthering Heights*. Garland 1980 $41.50. ISBN 0-313-27687-0. A study of the apotheosis of the Gondal people of the poems into the immortals of *Wuthering Heights*.

BROWNING, ELIZABETH BARRETT. 1806–1861

Elizabeth Barrett was born in Coxhoe Hall, Durham. Most of her childhood was spent on her father's estate, reading the classics and writing poetry. A sickly invalid for a long time, Barrett met the poet ROBERT BROWNING in 1845, and the two eloped the following year.

The story of Elizabeth Barrett's elopement with Robert Browning has been told many times, most succinctly perhaps by Samuel C. Chew: "Browning's virile confidence triumphed over paternal despotism and ill-health" (*A Literary History of England*). When the lovers left England on September 12, 1846, Barrett was a famous poet and Browning was known more as a difficult and obscure thinker; her *Poems*, first published in 1844, had already made her a voice for women of her generation. That reputation was reinforced with the publication of her second edition of *Poems* in 1850, containing *Sonnets from the Portuguese*, and reached its peak with her publication in 1857 of *Aurora Leigh*.

Barrett Browning's enduring fame has rested on these last two works, one of which is a celebration of woman as man's other half and the second of which is a celebration of woman's potential to stand on her own. During the Edwardian and later periods, it was *Sonnets from the Portuguese* that embodied Barrett Browning; since the rise of feminism, it has been *Aurora Leigh*. More recently, a third side of Barrett Browning has been revealed: the incisive critical and political commentator, seen in her letters. As an invalid and a resident in Italy, she was of necessity a detached observer of events; but she was a passionately interested one.

POETRY BY ELIZABETH BARRETT BROWNING

Aurora Leigh. 1857. Academy Chi. Pubs. 1989 $12.00. ISBN 0-915864-85-1

The Complete Works of Elizabeth Barrett Browning. 6 vols. Ed. by Charlotte Porter and Helen A. Clarke. AMS Pr. repr. of 1900 ed. $240.00. ISBN 0-404-08840-6. The standard edition, extensively annotated.

The Earlier Poems of Elizabeth Barrett Browning, 1826–1833. Arden Lib. 1978 repr. of 1878 ed. o.p.

Poetical Works of Elizabeth Barrett Browning. Cambridge Eds. Ser. HM 1974 $39.00. ISBN 0-395-18012-0. Introduction by Ruth Adams.

Sonnets from the Portuguese. 1850. Doubleday 1990 $12.95. ISBN 0-385-41618-0

WORKS BY ELIZABETH BARRETT BROWNING

The Brownings' Correspondence. 4 vols. Ed. by Philip Kelley and Ronald Hudson. Wedgestone Pr. 1984–86 $60.00 ea. ISBNs 0-685-08297-0, 0-911459-10-3, 0-911459-11-1, 0-911459-12-X

The Letters of Elizabeth Barrett Browning. 2 vols. Ed. by Frederic G. Kenyon. Telegraph Bks. 1981 repr. of 1897 ed. o.p.

The Letters of Elizabeth Barrett Browning to Mary Russell Mitford, 1836–1854. 3 vols. Ed. by Mary R. Sullivan. Wedgestone Pr. 1983 $160.00. ISBN 0-911459-00-6. Traces the affection and differing tastes of Browning and Mitford through unpublished letters.

Robert Browning and Elizabeth Barrett: The Courtship Correspondence. Ed. by Daniel Karlin. OUP 1989 $37.50. ISBN 0-198-18547-2. Interesting insights into the relationship between Robert and Elizabeth Browning before their marriage.

Twenty-Two Unpublished Letters of Elizabeth Barrett Browning and Robert Browning. Haskell 1971 repr of 1935 ed. $75.00. ISBN 0-8383-1313-2

Women of Letters: Selected Letters of Elizabeth Barrett Browning and Mary Russell Mitford. Ed. by Meredith B. Raymond and Mary Rose Sullivan. Twayne 1987 $29.95. ISBN 0-805-79023-3. Useful, if limited, selection of letters.

BOOKS ABOUT ELIZABETH BARRETT BROWNING

Dally, Peter. *Elizabeth Barrett Browning: A Psychological Portrait.* Macmillan 1989 o.p. Good analysis of the effects of Barrett Browning's "invalid" life in her father's home.

Forster, Margaret. *Elizabeth Barrett Browning: A Biography.* Doubleday 1989 $19.95. ISBN 0-385-24959-4. Worthwhile biography aimed at broad audience.

Hudson, Gladys W., ed. *Elizabeth Barrett Browning Concordance.* 4 vols. Gale 1973 o.p. Lists roughly 20,000 entries drawn from Browning's poetic writing.

Leighton, Angela. *Elizabeth Barrett Browning.* Harvester Pr. UK 1986 o.p. Introduction to Browning and her work.

Loth, David. *The Brownings: A Victorian Idyll.* Richard West 1973 repr. of 1932 ed. o.p.

Lubbock, Percy. *Elizabeth Barrett Browning in Her Letters.* AMS Pr. repr. of 1906 ed. $21.45. ISBN 0-404-08879-1

Mermin, Dorothy. *Elizabeth Barrett Browning: The Origins of a New Poetry.* U. Ch. Pr. 1989 $49.95. ISBN 0-226-52038-2. Browning's poetics and their influence.

Radley, Virginia L. *Elizabeth Barrett Browning.* Macmillan 1972 $19.95. ISBN 0-8057-1064-7. Reassesses Browning's contributions to the genre of Belle Lettres.

Woolf, Virginia. *Flush: A Biography.* HarBraceJ 1986 $4.95. ISBN 0-15-631952-7. The life of Elizabeth Barrett Browning as seen through the eyes of Browning's dog, Flush.

BROWNING, ROBERT. 1812–1889

Browning's reputation has suffered, both during his lifetime and since, from the charge of obscurity. "Sordello," published in 1840, only his third published work, remains an enigma even to those who read it with the benefit of a recent annotated edition. Marriage to ELIZABETH BARRETT in 1846 brought a new lightness and openness of voice to Browning's verse during the next 21 years, resulting in the great dramatic monologues of *Men and Women* in 1855 and the epic *The Ring and the Book* in 1867. It is not that these are the most beautiful poems of the Victorian Age, but they are the most perceptive; they reveal more clearly the men and women who speak the monologues, and the poet who conceived them, than any comparable works of the century. During the last 20 years of his career, however, the clotted quality of his verse returned, aggravated by his efforts to transform such subjects as contested wills (in "Red-Cotton Night Cap Country") and the political career of George Bubb Dodding-ton (in "Parleyings with Certain People of Importance in Their Day") into poetry.

These notorious difficulties with Browning's poetry have led successive editors into apparently impassable morasses. Between the demands of textual exegesis, on the one side, and the long-time bias toward encyclopedic annotation of the Browning Society, on the other, any editor foolhardy enough to tackle Browning's works deserves thanks for even partial success.

POETRY BY ROBERT BROWNING

The Complete Works of Robert Browning, with Variant Readings and Annotations. 9 vols. Ed. by Roma A. King, Jr. Ohio U. Pr. 1967–90. Vols. 1–7 o.p. Vol. 8 $50.00. ISBN 0-8214-0380-X. Vol. 9 $55.00. ISBN 0-8214-0381-8. An ambitious effort to record all the poetry, in all its states.

A Critical Edition of Robert Browning's "Bishop Blougram's Apology". Ed. by Frank C. Allen. Humanities Pr. 1976 o.p.

Dramatic Idylls. Found. Class Reprints 1981 repr. of 1879 ed. o.p.

Pauline. Folcroft 1977 repr. of 1931 ed. o.p.

The Pied Piper of Hamelin. HarBraceJ 1988 $10.95. ISBN 0-15-200566-8

Poetical Works, 1833 to 1864. Ed. by Ian Jack. OUP 1987 $100.00. ISBN 0-19-194002-X

The Poetical Works of Robert Browning. Cambridge Eds. Ser. HM 1974 $39.00. ISBN 0-395-18485-1. Introduction by G. Robert Stange.

The Ring and the Book. Ed. by Richard O. Altick. Viking Penguin 1989 $8.95. ISBN 0-14-042294-3

Robert Browning: Men and Women and Other Poems. Ed. by J. W. Harper. Biblio Dist. 1985 o.p.

Robert Browning: The Poems. 2 vols. Ed. by John Pettigrew. Yale U. Pr. 1981 o.p.

Robert Browning's Poetry. Ed. by James M. Loucks. Norton 1980 $14.95. ISBN 0-393-09092-2

Sordello: A Marginally Annotated Edition. Ed. by Morse Peckham. Whitston Pub. 1977 $15.00. ISBN 0-87875-114-9

WORKS BY ROBERT BROWNING

The Brownings' Correspondence. 4 vols. Ed. by Ronald Hudson and Philip Kelley. Wedgestone Pr. 1984–86 $60.00 ea. ISBNs 0-685-08297-0, 0-911459-10-3, 0-911459-11-1, 0-911459-12-X. Scholarly collection of the letters.

Learned Lady: Letters from Robert Browning to Mrs. Thomas Fitzgerald, 1876–1889. Ed. by Edward C. McAleer. HUP 1966 $20.00. ISBN 0-674-51900-0. Reveals Robert Browning's poetry, social life, and friendships through his letters to Mrs. Thomas Fitzgerald.

The Letters of Robert Browning and Elizabeth Barrett Browning, 1845–1846. 2 vols. Arden Lib. 1899 o.p.

Robert Browning and Elizabeth Barrett: The Courtship Correspondence. Ed. by Daniel Karlin. OUP 1989 $45.00. ISBN 0-19-818547-2

BOOKS ABOUT ROBERT BROWNING

Berdoe, Edward. *The Browning Cyclopedia: A Guide to the Study of the Works of Robert Browning.* Longwood MA 1980 repr. of 1916 ed. o.p. Includes notes and references to the more difficult passages in Browning's work.

Brady, Ann P. *Pompilia: A Feminist Reading of Robert Browning's "The Ring and the Book".* Ohio U. Pr. 1988 $19.95. ISBN 0-821-40886-0. Feminist approach to Browning's most ambitious project.

Bristow, Joseph. *Robert Browning.* St. Martin 1991 $45.00. ISBN 0-312-06774-7. Introduction to Browning and his poetry.

Broughton, Leslie N. *Robert Browning: A Bibliography, 1830–1950.* B. Franklin 1970 repr. of 1953 ed. o.p. A comprehensive and useful work.

Broughton, Leslie N., and Benjamin F. Stelter. *Concordance to the Poems of Robert Browning, 1924–1925.* 4 vols. Haskell 1970 repr. of 1924 ed. $325.00. ISBN 0-8383-1101-6. Includes musical settings to the poems of Browning, whose work attracted more musical composers than any other author except Shakespeare.

Buckler, William E. *Poetry and Truth in Robert Browning's "The Ring and the Book".* NYU Pr. 1985 $45.00. ISBN 0-8147-1072-7

Davies, Hugh S. *Browning and the Modern Novel.* Folcroft 1976 repr. of 1962 ed. o.p.

Drew, Philip. *Annotated Critical Bibliography of Robert Browning.* St. Martin 1990 o.p. Useful for beginning scholars.

Erickson, Lee. *Robert Browning: His Poetry and His Audiences.* Cornell Univ. Pr. 1984 $34.95. ISBN 0-8014-1618-3

Gibson, Mary Ellis. *History and the Prism of Art: Browning's Poetic Experiments.* Ohio St. U. Pr. 1987 $25.00. ISBN 0-8142-0418-X. Argues that Browning's vision of history significantly affected his poetic form.

Gridley, Roy E. *The Brownings and France: A Chronicle with Commentary.* Longwood MA 1982 o.p. Especially helpful in illuminating Browning's French poems.

Hassett, Constance W. *The Elusive Self in the Poetry of Robert Browning.* Ohio U. Pr. 1982 $19.95. ISBN 0-8214-0629-9. Identifies, for the first time, Browning's development of confession *manqué.*

Honan, Park. *Browning's Characters: A Study in Poetic Technique.* Shoe String 1969 repr. of 1961 ed. o.p. Examines Browning's poetic technique in dramatic monologue.

Korg, Jacob. *Browning and Italy.* Ohio U. Pr. 1983 $24.95. ISBN 0-8214-0725-2

Litzinger, Boyd, and K. L. Knickerbocker, eds. *The Browning Critics.* Bks. Demand repr. of 1965 ed. $116.50. ISBN 0-8357-7448-1. Shows the development of Browning's criticism, and traces fluctuations of his reputation.

Maynard, John R. *Browning's Youth.* HUP 1977 $33.00. ISBN 0-674-08441-1. Reconstructs circumstances of Browning's youth, including his ancestry and his eccentric family.

Mayne, Ethel C. *Browning's Heroines.* Richard West 1973 o.p.

Pearsall, Robert B. *Robert Browning.* Twayne's Eng. Authors Ser. Macmillan 1974 $19.95. ISBN 0-8057-1065-5. Places Browning's work in the context of his life.

Ryals, Clyde De L. *Becoming Browning: The Poems and Plays of Robert Browning, 1833–1846.* Ohio St. U. Pr. 1983 $36.75. ISBN 0-8142-0352-3. Stresses the development of Browning's ironic stance.

———. *Browning's Later Poetry, 1881–1889.* Cornell Univ. Pr. 1975 $34.95. ISBN 0-8014-0964-0

Slinn, E. Warwick. *Browning and the Fictions of Identity.* B & N Imports 1982 $40.00. ISBN 0-389-20273-8. Develops a new analysis of what Browning meant by "action in character."

Southwell, Samuel B. *Quest for Eros: Browning and "Fifine".* U. Pr. of Ky. 1980 o.p. Fascinating life-into-art study.

Thomas, Donald. *Robert Browning: A Life within Life.* Viking Penguin 1983 o.p. Intelligently compares and contrasts Browning's public and private personae.

BULWER-LYTTON (Edward George Earle Lytton, after 1st Baron Lytton of Knebworth). 1803–1873

Immensely popular in his own lifetime, Bulwer-Lytton introduced the "silver spoon" novel with *Pelham* (1828) and initiated a series of historical romances with *Falkland* (1827), the most notable of which are *The Last Days of Pompeii* (1834), *Rienzi* (1835), and *Harold, the Last of the Saxons* (1848). Bulwer-Lytton's versatility was equaled only by his eccentricity. He wrote essays, travel volumes, drama, poetry, heroicized romance, fictionalized fact and factualized fiction, domestic fiction (*The Caxtons*, 1849), mystery tales; and, as a deeply committed adept of magic and the occult, novels of the supernatural, the most readable of which is *Zanoni: A Rosicrucian Tale* (1842). The standard life is *The Life, Letters, and Literary Remains* (1883), edited by his son, who wrote under the pseudonym "Owen Meredith." Robert L. Wolff's *Strange Stories: An Examination of Victorian Literature* contains a long section on Bulwer-Lytton's fascination with the occult.

NOVELS BY BULWER-LYTTON

The Caxtons, A Family Picture. 1849. 3 vols. Scholarly 1971 repr. of 1898 ed. $225.00. ISBN 0-7812-7590-3
Falkland. 1827. Ed. by Herbert Van Thal. *First Novel Lib.* Dufour 1967 o.p.
The Last Days of Pompeii. 1834. Buccaneer Bks. 1983 $29.95. ISBN 0-89966-309-5
Pelham, or, The Adventures of a Gentleman. 1828. Ed. by Jerome J. McGann. U. of Nebr. Pr. 1972 $29.50. ISBN 0-835-77934-3
Rienzi: The Last of the Roman Tribunes. 1835. Scholarly 1971 repr. of 1885 ed. $69.00. ISBN 0-403-01079-9
A Strange Story and the Haunted and the Haunters: Or the House and the Brain. Kessinger Pub. 1992 $35.00. ISBN 1-56459-000-3
Vril: The Power of the Coming Race (The Coming Race). 1871. *Spiritual Fiction Publications Ser.* Garber Comm. 1982 repr. of 1972 ed. $12.00. ISBN 0-8334-0016-9
Zanoni: A Rosicrucian Tale. *Spiritual Fiction Publications Ser.* Garber Comm. 1982 repr. of 1842 ed. $22.00. ISBN 0-89345-014-6

NONFICTION BY BULWER-LYTTON

England and the English. U. Ch. Press 1970 $22.50. ISBN 0-226-08014-5

WORK BY BULWER-LYTTON

Letters of the Late Edward Bulwer, Lord Lytton, to His Wife. AMS Pr. repr. of 1889 ed. $24.50. ISBN 0-404-08884-8. Includes extracts from his wife's manuscript "Autobiography" and other documents, published in vindication of her memory by Louisa Devey.

BOOKS ABOUT BULWER-LYTTON

Campbell, James L. *Edward Bulwer-Lytton.* Twayne 1986 o.p. Introduction to Bulwer-Lytton and his writing.
Escott, T. H. *Edward Bulwer, First Baron Lytton of Knebworth: A Social, Personal, and Political Monograph.* Arden Lib. 1977 repr. of 1910 ed. $30.00. o.p.
Sadleir, Michael. *Bulwer: A Panorama.* Folcroft 1977 repr. of 1931 ed. o.p.

BUTLER, JOSEPHINE GREY. 1828–1906

Josephine Butler was born in Northumberland, the seventh child of John Grey and Hannah Annent. Her father was a cousin of Lord Grey, the prime minister, and her cousin was Charles Grey, an equerry of Prince Albert. Butler's childhood was happy and privileged, and, in addition to the usual training that girls received, her father insisted that she, and all of his children, be politically educated. As a result, she was familiar with the work of her father's friend, EDWIN CHADWICK, on the Poor Laws and on the sanitary condition of the working classes. This, along with a strong religious upbringing, helped prepare her for her later role as a champion of women's and children's rights.

The work by which Butler is best remembered is her *Personal Reminiscences of a Great Crusade* (1898), in which she recalls successful efforts to repeal the Contagious Diseases Acts of 1864, 1866, and 1868. Although the intent of the acts was to control the spread of venereal diseases by instituting state brothels for the military and requiring prostitutes to undergo medical examination, the acts, in effect, did away with the civil rights of every woman in England. Because of these laws, the police could take into custody any woman suspected of prostitution; failure to comply with the demand that she be examined was punishable by imprisonment. Butler's prolific writing on the topic included *An Appeal to the People of England on the Recognition and Superintendence of Prostitution by Government* and *On the Moral Reclaimability of Prostitutes* (1870) and *The Constitutional Iniquity of the Contageous Diseases Acts* and *The Constitution Violated* (1871). She ultimately drew a large number of people to her cause, although oddly many who were sympathetic to the plight of the prostitutes, like Gladstone, were bitterly opposed to her efforts. In 1886 the acts were repealed. In later years Butler worked to enact temperance laws and to stop the child sex-slave trade of England.

As with other early feminists, such as BARBARA BODICHON, much scholarship remains to be done on Josephine Butler. A number of articles have appeared, but few book-length studies. *Portrait of Josephine Butler*, by her grandson A. S. G. Butler, is interesting for its reminiscences, but it is more panygeric than critical. Also useful is her own *Autobiographical Memoir* (1909). Glenn Petrie's *A Singular Iniquity* (1971) is a worthwhile account of Butler's activism.

NONFICTION BY JOSEPHINE GREY BUTLER

An Appeal to the People of England on the Recognition and Superintendence of Prostitution by Government. Banks 1870 o.p.

The Constitutional Iniquity of the Contageous Diseases Acts. 1871 o.p.

The Constitution Violated. Edmonston & Douglas 1871 o.p.

Josephine G. Butler: An Autobiographical Memoir. Ed. by George W. Johnson and Lucy A. Johnson. Arrowsmith 1909 o.p.

On the Moral Reclaimability of Prostitutes. National Assoc. 1870 o.p.

Personal Reminiscences of a Great Crusade. Hyperion Conn. 1989 $27.00. ISBN 0-88355-257-4

Some Thoughts on the Present Aspect of the Crusade. Brakell 1874 o.p. Discussion of the work against the Contageous Diseases Acts.

BOOKS ABOUT JOSEPHINE GREY BUTLER

Bell, E. Moberly. *Josephine Butler, Flame of Fire.* Constable 1963 o.p. A biography.

Butler, A. S. G. *Portrait of Josephine Butler.* Faber & Faber 1954 o.p.

Petrie, Glenn. *A Singular Iniquity: The Campaigns of Josephine Butler.* Viking Penguin 1971 o.p.

BUTLER, SAMUEL. 1835–1902

The son of a clergyman and grandson of an Anglican bishop, Butler also seemed destined for a life in the church. After graduating from Cambridge, however, religious doubts made him abandon such plans. Instead, he pursued a number of different interests. A versatile genius, Butler was an artist who exhibited in the Royal Academy, a musician who composed a cantata and an oratorio of distinction, a man of science who contributed several books to the study of evolution (not taken very seriously by scientists), a translator of HOMER (see Vol. 2), and the author of various books of travel and at least one enduring novel. *The Way of All Flesh* (1903) is a biographical novel depicting three generations of the same family. It satirizes the hypocrisy of the ecclesiastical and educational systems in a surprisingly modern tone. *Erewhon* (1872) (an anagram for "nowhere") and its sequel are utopias. *Erewhon*, his satiric masterpiece, attacked contemporary attitudes in science, religion, and social mores. *Erewhon Revisited* (1901) continues his attack on religion. Another work, *The Fair Haven* (1873), is another subtle attack on religion, presented in the guise of a defense of the Gospels, though it actually undermines them.

The Family Letters is a selection from the correspondence of Butler and his father, with several letters to and from his mother and sisters and one or two other relatives. Those between Butler and his father show how close the early part of *The Way of All Flesh* was to the events in the son's life. A brilliant, versatile writer, Butler was one of the most searching critics of his time.

NOVELS BY SAMUEL BUTLER

Erewhon. 1872. Viking Penguin 1970 $8.95. ISBN 0-14-043057-1
Erewhon Revisited (and *Erewhon*). 1901. Biblio. Dist. 1979 repr. of 1932 ed. o.p.
The Fair Haven: A Work in Defence of the Miraculous Element in Our Lord's Ministry upon Earth. Ed. by Robert L. Wolff. *Victorian Fiction Ser*. Garland 1975 repr. of 1873 ed. o.p.
The Way of All Flesh. 1903. Knopf 1992 $16.50. ISBN 0-679-41718-4

NONFICTION BY SAMUEL BUTLER

The Authoress of the Odyssey. 1897. U. Ch. Pr. 1967 o.p. Butler's discussion of why he believed *The Odyssey* to have been written two centuries after *The Iliad* by a Sicilian noblewoman. Introduction by David Grene.
Essays on Life, Art and Science. 1904. Ed. by Richard A. Streatfeild. Assoc. Faculty Pr. 1970 repr. of 1908 ed. o.p.
The Family Letters of Samuel Butler, 1841–1846. Ed. by Arnold Silver. Fernhill 1962 o.p.
The Notebooks of Samuel Butler. Ed. by Henry F. Jones. Richard West repr. of 1919 ed. o.p.
Prose Observations. Ed. by Hugh De Quehen. OUP 1979 $110.00 ISBN 0-19-812728-6

WORK BY SAMUEL BUTLER

Works. Ed. by Henry F. Jones and A. T. Bartholomew. 20 vols. AMS Pr. repr. of 1923–26 ed. $800.00. ISBN 0-404-01320-1

BOOKS ABOUT SAMUEL BUTLER

Cole, G. D. H. *Samuel Butler*. Folcroft 1973 o.p.
Harkness, Stanley. *The Career of Samuel Butler, 1835–1902. Bibliography and Reference Ser*. B. Franklin 1968 repr. of 1955 ed. o.p. Allows the reader to approach Butler from many angles, and to appreciate his versatility.
Holt, Lee E. *Samuel Butler*. Macmillan 1989 $20.95. ISBN 0-8057-6974-9. Cursory but useful survey of Butler and his work.
Jeffers, Thomas. *Samuel Butler Revalued*. Pa. St. U. Pr. 1981 $19.95. ISBN 0-271-00281-6. Presents Butler in many perspectives, including his roles as theologian, moralist, and teacher.
Muggeridge, Malcolm. *Earnest Atheist: A Study of Samuel Butler. Eng. Lit. Ser*. Haskell 1971 repr. of 1936 ed. $75.00. ISBN 0-8383-1242-X. Butler presented as the epitome of a Victorian writer, rather than as a rebel against his times.
Raby, Peter. *The Life of Samuel Butler: A Biography*. U. of Iowa Pr. 1991 $32.95. ISBN 0-877-45331-4. Thorough literary biography.

CARLYLE, THOMAS. 1795–1881

Scottish-born writer Thomas Carlyle, although an erratic student at Edinburgh University, read widely in the classics, mathematics, Newtonian physics, history, and philosophy. He acquired a thorough knowledge of German, and his earliest works were a life of Schiller for *The London Magazine* and a translation of *Wilhelm Meister*. His favorite style was vivid, majestic, and dramatic; his favorite devices were pathos, satire, and denunciation. He often coined a word when he needed one. His philosophical *Sartor Resartus* (1837) and his essays in *On Heroes and Hero-Worship* (1841) and *Past and Present* (1843) are perhaps better known to the general reader than are his histories. In his essays, deeply influenced by the German romantics, Carlyle revolted against the rationalism of the eighteenth century, gradually espousing the glories of enlightened despotism, in which the "heroes" ruled the less intelligent. His *French Revolution* (1837) history brought him great contemporary acclaim. Carlyle is probably best remembered for his attacks on sham, hypocrisy, and materialism; his distrust of democracy and mob rule; and his romantic belief in the power of the individual.

NONFICTION BY CARLYLE

Montaigne: And Other Essays, Chiefly Biographical. Essay Index Repr. Ser. Ayer repr. of 1897 ed. $23.00. ISBN 0-404-09800-2
On Heroes, Hero-Worship and the Heroic in History. 1841. Ed. by Carl Niemeyer. U. of Nebr. Pr. 1966 $8.95. ISBN 0-8032-5030-4
Past and Present. 1843. Ed. by Richard D. Altick. *Gotham Lib.* NYU Pr. 1977 $15.00. ISBN 0-8147-0562-6
Reminiscences. 2 vols. Ed. by James A. Froude. Scholarly 1972 repr. of 1881 ed. $29.00. ISBN 0-403-00898-0. Biographical work in which Carlyle drew portraits of his family and such contemporaries as William Wordsworth.
Sartor Resartus. 1837. OUP 1987 $7.95. ISBN 0-19-281757-4
Sartor Resartus and *On Heroes and Hero-Worship.* Biblio Dist. 1967 repr. of 1908 ed. o.p.

POETRY BY CARLYLE

The Collected Poems of Thomas and Jane Welsh Carlyle. Ed. by Fleming McClelland and Rodger L. Tarr. Penkevill 1986 $30.00. ISBN 0-913-28309-6. Interesting collection of seldom-read texts.

WORKS BY CARLYLE

A Carlyle Reader. Ed. by G. B. Tennyson. Cambridge U. Pr. 1984 $14.95. ISBN 0-521-27873-2
Letters of Thomas Carlyle, 1826–1836. Scholarly 1971 repr. of 1923 ed. $39.00. ISBN 0-403-00897-2
Works of Thomas Carlyle. 30 vols. Ed. by H. D. Traill. AMS Pr. repr. of 1899 ed. $1,200.00. ISBN 0-404-09800-2

BOOKS ABOUT CARLYLE

ApRoberts, Ruth. *The Ancient Dialect: Thomas Carlyle and Comparative Religion.* U. CA Pr. 1988 $25.00. ISBN 0-520-06116-0. Important study of Carlyle's religious ideas and religious influences on his writing.
Bloom, Harold, ed. *Thomas Carlyle.* Chelsea Hse. 1986 $19.95. ISBN 0-877-54688-6. Good collection of recent essays on Carlyle.
Kaplan, Fred. *Thomas Carlyle: A Biography.* Cornell Univ. Pr. 1983 $52.50. ISBN 0-8014-1508-X. A sensitive and frank portrait tracing Carlyle's intellectual and spiritual development through the use of unpublished documents.

Lehman, B. H. *Carlyle's Theory of the Hero*. AMS Pr. repr. of 1928 ed. $17.25. ISBN 0-7812-7491-5. A classic study of its sources, history, and appearance in Carlyle's writings.

Neff, Emery. *Carlyle and Mill*. Hippocrene Bks. 1964 $26.00. ISBN 0-374-96042-9. An examination of a famous friendship.

Timko, Michael. *Carlyle and Tennyson*. U. of Iowa Pr. 1988 $28.00. ISBN 0-87745-184-2. Biographical and literary-historical discussion of the relationship between these two "sages" of the Victorian era.

Vanden Bossche, Chris. *Carlyle and the Search for Authority*. Ohio St. U. Pr. 1991 $35.95. ISBN 0-814-20538-0. Discussion of Carlyle's attempts at establishing hermeneutic and political authority in his writing.

CARROLL, LEWIS (pseud. of Rev. Charles Lutwidge Dodgson). 1832–1898

[SEE Chapter 12 in this volume.]

CHADWICK, SIR EDWIN. 1800–1890

Chadwick, the son of a radical journalist and grandson of an important Wesleyan minister, was one of the most influential public men during the Victorian period. He began his career as an attorney, but, in order to support himself, he turned to journalism. An 1829 essay, "Preventative Police," caught the eye of JEREMY BENTHAM (see Vol. 3). The two men soon met, and, within a few weeks, Chadwick became Bentham's amanuensis, serving him until Bentham's death, in 1832. In 1834 Chadwick, along with the economist NASSAU WILLIAM SENIOR (see Vol. 3), published the *Report on the Poor Laws*, which advocated reform of the old Poor Laws along utilitarian lines, including the establishment of a central governing body to administer the laws. With the passage of the New Poor Law Act in 1834, based primarily on Chadwick and Senior's recommendations, a commission was established, with Chadwick as its secretary. In this capacity he oversaw an inquiry into the living conditions of the working classes; the findings were published as the *Report on the Sanitary Condition of the Labouring Population of Great Britain* (1842). Instantly popular (by some accounts as many as 100,000 copies were distributed), it became the basis for the sanitation laws passed in the 1850s.

Often considered the first modern professional bureaucrat, Chadwick was vilified for his role in the creation of the New Poor Laws. As his reputation grew, however, his associations with such writers as HARRIET MARTINEAU and JOHN STUART MILL (see Vols. 3 and 4) became the foundation for a large circle of literary acquaintances—including CHARLES DICKENS, who, despite his initial distrust of Chadwick, ultimately came to rely on his judgment on many public issues.

NONFICTION BY CHADWICK

The Health of Nations. A Review of the Works of Edwin Chadwick. With a Bibliographical Dissertation by Benjamin Ward Richardson. 1887. Dawsons 1965 o.p. Extracts from Chadwick's most important statements on the prevention of poverty, crime, and disease.

On the Progress of Sanitation, Civil and Military, to the year 1888. o.p. Read at the Congress of the Sanitary Inspectors of Great Britain, held at Brighton, August 25, 1888.

Report on the Sanitary Condition of the Labouring Population of Great Britain. 1842. Ed. by M. W. Flinn. Col. U. Pr. 1965 $28.00. ISBN 0-85224-145-3

BOOKS ABOUT CHADWICK

Brundage, Anthony. *England's "Prussian Minister": Edwin Chadwick and the Politics of Government Growth, 1832–1854*. Pa. St. U. Pr. 1988 $24.95. ISBN 0-271-00629-3. Good study of Chadwick's contribution to the growth of bureaucracy in England.

Finer, S. E. *The Life and Times of Sir Edwin Chadwick*. Routledge Chapman & Hall 1952 o.p. The standard biography; very good.

Hutchins, B. L. *The Public Health Agitation, 1833–48*. Fifield 1909 o.p. Places Chadwick in the context of health conditions in early Victorian England.

Watson, Roger. *Edwin Chadwick, Poor Laws and Public Health*. Longman 1969 o.p. Examines Chadwick's public career.

CLOUGH, ARTHUR HUGH. 1819–1861

The Victorians' insistence on facing doubts, and prevailing through them to achieve true conviction, made it inevitable that there would be failures: those who succumbed to their doubts. Some turned to Catholicism; some turned to a secularized "muscular Christianity"; some, like Arthur Hugh Clough, found no place to stand. But in the course of his search, while his loss of faith could still be thought of as healthy skepticism, Clough wrote three fine poems that keep his name and mind alive after a century and a half: *The Bothie* (1848), *Amours de Voyage* (1858), and *Dipsychus* (unfinished). During the same period, he was MATTHEW ARNOLD's closest friend and most earnest correspondent; most of Arnold's critical ideas were worked out in letters to Clough before they were published in essays or prefaces. Clough's works have all been well edited, making study of his poems and letters a pleasure, not just a requirement.

POETRY BY CLOUGH

Amours de Voyage. Ed. by Patrick G. Scott. U. of Queensland Pr. 1974 o.p.

The Bothie: The Text of 1848. Ed. by Patrick G. Scott. U. of Queensland Pr. 1977 o.p.

The Poems of Arthur Hugh Clough. Ed. by F. L. Mulhauser. *Oxford Eng. Texts Ser.* OUP 1974 o.p. An authoritative edition of the poems.

Selections from the Poems of Arthur Hugh Clough. Norwood 1977 repr. of 1894 ed. o.p.

WORKS BY CLOUGH

The Oxford Diaries of Arthur Hugh Clough. Ed. by Anthony John Patrick Kenny. OUP 1990 $52.00. ISBN 0-19-811739-6. Important record of Clough's student days.

Poems and Prose Remains of Arthur Hugh Clough. 2 vols. Scholarly 1992 repr. of 1869 ed. $150.00. ISBN 0-7812-7499-0

BOOKS ABOUT CLOUGH

Greenberger, Evelyn B. *Arthur Hugh Clough: Growth of a Poet's Mind*. HUP 1970 $20.50. ISBN 0-674-04849-0. Competent study contradicting the traditional view that Clough was an ineffectual and uncommitted literary failure within his own time.

Houghton, Walter E. *The Poetry of Clough*. Hippocrene Bks. 1979 repr. of 1963 ed. $18.50. ISBN 0-374-93982-9. A reassessment of Clough's work in which the author suggests that *Amours de Voyage* and *Dipsychus* are masterpieces in their right.

Scott, Patrick G. *The Early Editions of Arthur Hugh Clough*. *Reference Lib. of the Humanities* Garland 1977 o.p.

Thorpe, Michael, ed. *Clough: The Critical Heritage*. Routledge 1972 $69.50. ISBN 0-7100-7156-6. Essays, reviews, and extracts representing a cross-section of contemporary responses to Clough's work.

COLLINS, WILKIE. 1824–1889

Born in London, the son of artist William Collins, Wilkie Collins was educated at Highbury and spent four years in Italy with his parents. Upon his return to

England, he worked first in business and then law, but eventually turned to literature. Collins created the crime novel of intricate plot and baffling mystery. *The Woman in White* (1860) was his first success, followed in 1863 by his masterpiece *The Moonstone.* Both novels demonstrate Collins's fascination with psychological portraiture and sensationalistic complication. Other books include *The Haunted Hotel* (1875), *Antonia* (1850), and *Heart and Science* (1883). Collins was a close friend of CHARLES DICKENS and collaborated with him. His mastery of plot influenced Dickens, and he was influenced by Dickens's mastery of character. T. S. ELIOT remarked, "To anyone who knows the bare facts of Dickens's acquaintance with Collins, and who has studied the work of the two men, their relationship and their influence upon one another is an important subject of study."

NOVELS BY COLLINS

Armadale. 2 vols. Scholarly 1972 repr. of 1866 ed. $69.00. ISBN 0-403-00433-0. Praised by T. S. Eliot as among "the best of Collins's masterpieces."

The Dead Secret. 1857. Dover 1979 $7.95. ISBN 0-486-23775-3. Collins's first full-length puzzle romance novel.

The Haunted Hotel. 1875. Dover 1982 $3.95. ISBN 0-486-24333-8. A popular ghost story that transcended the conventions of its genre and was highly praised by T. S. Eliot.

Hide and Seek. 1854. Dover 1982 $7.95. ISBN 0-486-24211-0. Collins's first mystery novel; combines detective elements with domestic comedy and pathos.

The Moonstone. 1863. Biblio Dist. 1977 $4.95. ISBN 0-460-01979-1

Poor Miss Finch: A Novel. Lit. Ser. Scholarly 1972 repr. of 1872 ed. $69.00. ISBN 0-403-00559-0. One of Collins's more sensational novels; the bizarre story of a blind woman who falls in love with one brother of a set of twins.

The Woman in White. 1860. Ed. by Julian Symons. *Penguin Eng. Lib. Ser.* Viking Penguin 1975 $3.95. ISBN 0-14-043096-2

SHORT STORY COLLECTIONS BY COLLINS

Little Novels. Dover 1978 $6.95. ISBN 0-486-23506-8. Collection of stories published toward the end of Collins's life.

The Queen of Hearts. Ayer 1976 repr. of 1859 ed. $35.50. ISBN 0-405-07868-4. Features stories from Collins's periodical collection.

WORK BY COLLINS

Works. 30 vols. AMS Pr. repr. of 1900 ed. $1,200.00. ISBN 0-404-01750-9

BOOKS ABOUT COLLINS

Andrew, Ray Vernon. *Wilkie Collins: A Critical Survey of His Prose Fiction with a Bibliography.* Ed. by E. F. Bleiler. *Fiction of Popular Culture Ser.* Garland 1979 o.p.

Heller, Tamar. *Dead Secrets: Wilkie Collins and the Female Gothic.* Yale U. Pr. 1992 $25.00. ISBN 0-300-04574-3. Feminist readings of Collins; strong on *The Woman in White.*

Page, Norman, ed. *Wilkie Collins: The Critical Heritage. Critical Heritage Ser.* Routledge 1974 $69.50. ISBN 0-7100-7843-9. An extensive collection of whole and fragmentary reviews of Collins's books.

Robinson, Kenneth, *Wilkie Collins: A Biography.* Greenwood 1973 repr. of 1951 ed. o.p. The first full-length biography, and a good one.

Sayers, Dorothy L. *Wilkie Collins: A Critical and Bibliographical Study.* Ed. by E. R. Gregory. Friends Univ. Toledo 1977 $12.50. ISBN 0-918160-01-4. Study by noted mystery writer emphasizing Collins's influence on the mystery novel.

Taylor, Jenny. *In the Secret Theatre of Home: Wilkie Collins, Sensation Narrative, and Nineteenth-Century Psychology.* Routledge 1988 $47.50. ISBN 0-415-00707-0. Focuses on Collins as sensation novelist.

COYNE, JOSEPH STIRLING. 1803–1868

Although there is little scholarly criticism of the works of J. S. Coyne, he was a popular playwright, the sole author of more than 55 vehicles for the stage and the collaborator on nearly as many more. An Irishman, he originally intended law as his career but, encouraged by the publication of some of his literary articles in Dublin, he forsook the bar and undertook a literary career. In the early 1830s, he came to London, where he contributed to periodicals and joined the staff of *The Morning Gazette*, one of the first cheap dailies. Like HENRY MAYHEW, Coyne was also associated with *Punch* magazine as a staff writer in the early years of its existence. He eventually became drama critic for the *Sunday Times* and secretary of the Dramatic Authors Society.

The bulk of Coyne's dramatic output was farces, which were produced mainly at the Haymarket and Adelphi theaters. A number of his plays were adaptations of French drama. The most notable of his works include *The Hope of the Family*, *The Secret Agent*, and *The Black Sheep*. His writing is vigorous; often the plays are genuinely funny. Unlike THOMAS WILLIAM ROBERTSON, he rarely dealt with serious social issues, but the best farces of the later portion of his career increasingly incorporate lower-middle and working-class characters and, consequently, comic techniques peculiar to those social strata.

PLAYS BY COYNE

Plays. French o.p. Collected plays.

DARWIN, CHARLES. 1809–1882

[SEE Volume 5.]

DICKENS, CHARLES. 1812–1870

With a reputation that now places him among the half dozen most significant and formidable literary artists in English literature, Charles Dickens dominates modern critical opinion of the Victorian novel to the same extent that he dominated his contemporaries. Dickens was richly educated in the trials of a bankrupt household, in the difficulties of earning his own way from a young age, and in the pressures of modern urban life. London becomes in his fiction the symbol of the condition of modern man; the pressures of economic survival become the illuminator of character and environment; and the experiences of childhood are transformed into a threatening landscape of exploitation.

Born in Landport, a suburb of Portsmouth, England, Charles Dickens had a difficult and unhappy childhood. His father, a navy clerk, was constantly in debt. When he was thrown into a debtors prison, the young Dickens was sent to work in a factory at age 12. Dickens responded to his hardship by working very hard. In time, he became an office boy in a law firm, then a county reporter, and finally a reporter in Parliament. From there, Dickens secured a position on a London newspaper and was sent all around the country on assignments. At the same time, he also began working on writings of his own.

Dickens's first success, *Sketches by Boz* (1836), a series of vignettes on London life and character, was followed by the immensely popular *Pickwick Papers* (1836–37), which, like all of Dickens's novels, was published in serial form. His reputation was firmly established by a succession of novels between 1837 and 1848, in which the dominant tone of ironic satire, outraged liberalism, comic extravagance, and imaginative fancy dramatized his concern with the themes of power, ambition, exploitation, self-destruction, and dehumanization. He drew on traditions of fairy tale and fantasy, developed immense skill with narrative and characterization, and revealed a brilliant flair for metaphor, psychological realism, and symbolic action. After *David Copperfield* (1849–50), his "favorite" but flawed child, Dickens's novels became dark with a kind of visionary pessimism. His earlier liberalism and optimism were replaced in *Bleak House* (1852–53), *Little Dorrit* (1855–57), and *Our Mutual Friend* (1864–66) with an increasing sense of the corruption and imperfectibility of humankind and society in general, although he maintained his belief in the capability of special individuals to live productive and even happy lives. Dickens's fiction, in its richness and variety, its fascination with people and society, its embrace of humankind and acceptance of the withdrawal of God, its emphasis on urban life, economic pressures, and psychological realism both embodies and transcends Victorian culture.

NOVELS AND NOVELLAS BY DICKENS

Barnaby Rudge: A Tale of the Riots of Eighty. 1841. Ed. by G. W. Spence. *Penguin Eng. Lib. Ser.* Viking Penguin 1974 $5.95. ISBN 0-14-043090-3. A historical romance set in the late eighteenth century, showing the effect of the anti-Catholic Gordon riots on a humble family and a pair of young lovers.

Bleak House. 1852–53. *Bantam Class. Ser.* Bantam 1985 $4.95. ISBN 0-553-21223-0

The Chimes. 1844. o.p.

Christmas Books. OUP 1989 $7.95. ISBN 0-19-281790-6. Five of Dickens's long stories, all with a Christmas theme, first published in 1852.

A Christmas Carol. 1843. Bantam 1986 $1.95. ISBN 0-553-21244-3. The past, present, and future come together to help miser Ebenezer Scrooge discover the true meaning of Christmas.

Christmas Stories. OUP 1956 $10.95. ISBN 0-19-254517-5

The Cricket on the Hearth. 1845 Rprt. Serv. 1992 repr. of 1914 ed. $69.00. ISBN 0-7812-7510-5

David Copperfield (The Personal History of David Copperfield). 1849–50. *Bantam Class. Ser.* Bantam 1981 $3.50. ISBN 0-553-21189-7

Dombey and Son. Buccaneer Bks. 1990 $29.95. ISBN 0-89966-678-1

Great Expectations. 1861. Bantam 1982 $3.95. ISBN 0-553-21265-6. The story of Pip, a poor young boy whose whole life changes when he receives a fortune from a mysterious donor.

Hard Times (Hard Times for These Times). 1854. *Bantam Class. Ser.* Bantam 1981 $2.25. ISBN 0-553-21016-5. The shortest and perhaps driest of all Dickens's novels. The story of the Gradgrind family and their unhappy lives, brought about, in part, by their inability to see the human side of life.

Little Dorrit. 1855–57. *Penguin Eng. Lib. Ser.* Viking Penguin 1968 $5.95. ISBN 0-14-043025-3

Martin Chuzzlewit (The Life and Adventures of Martin Chuzzlewit). 1843–48. Viking Penguin 1968 $6.95. ISBN 0-14-043025-3. Story about a man's struggles with his wealthy, misanthropic grandfather.

Master Humphrey's Clock. 1841. OUP 1958 $10.95. ISBN 0-19-254520-5. Reintroduces the characters of Pickwick and Sam Weller.

The Mystery of Edwin Drood. 1870. Ed. by A. Cox. Viking Penguin 1986 $3.95. ISBN 0-14-009258-X. The story of a young engineer who is reported missing, apparently killed.

Nicholas Nickleby. 1838–39. Bantam 1981 $4.95. ISBN 0-553-21265-6. The story of Nicholas Nickleby, his fatherless youth, and his miserly uncle.

The Old Curiosity Shop. 1840–41. Viking Penguin 1972 $5.95. ISBN 0-14-043075-X. The trials of Little Nell and her grandfather, who are hounded by the evil Daniel Quilp.

Oliver Twist. 1839. Bantam 1982 $2.50. ISBN 0-553-21102-1. The young orphan Oliver falls in with criminals that keep him from his kindly benefactor.

Our Mutual Friend. Random 1992 $19.00. ISBN 0-679-60022-1. Like *Little Dorrit*, a novel of failures and a parable about the corrupting influence of money.

The Pickwick Papers. 1836–37. Bantam 1983 $4.95. ISBN 0-553-21123-4. The humorous
   adventures of Samuel Pickwick, his servant Sam Weller, and the other gentlemen of
   the Pickwick Club.
Sketches by Boz: Illustrative of Every-Day Life and Every-Day People. 1836. OUP 1957
   $10.95. ISBN 0-19-254518-3
A Tale of Two Cities. 1859. *Bantam Class. Ser*. Bantam 1989 $2.50. ISBN 0-553-21176-5

NONFICTION BY DICKENS

American Notes. 1842. Rprt. Serv. 1993 $69.00. ISBN 0-7812-5121-4
A Child's History of England. 1853. Biblio Dist. 1978 repr. of 1907 ed. o.p.
Uncollected Writings from Household Words, 1850–1859. Ed. by Harry Stone. Ind. U. Pr.
   1969 o.p.
The Uncommercial Traveler (and *Reprinted Pieces*). 1860. In *New Oxford Illustrated
   Dickens*. OUP 1958 o.p.

WORKS BY DICKENS

Dickens' Working Notes for His Novels. Ed. by Harry Stone. U. Ch. Pr. 1987 $74.95. ISBN
   0-226-14590-5. Very useful for studying Dickens's method of writing.
Letters. Ed. by Madeline House, Graham Storey, Kathleen Tillotson, and K. J. Fielding.
   OUP 1965–81 o.p.
Mr. and Mrs. Charles Dickens: His Letters to Her. Ed. by Walter Dexter. *Studies in Dickens*.
   Haskell 1972 repr. of 1935 ed. $75.00. ISBN 0-8383-1429-5. Foreword by Dickens's
   daughter, Kate Perugin.
Oxford Illustrated Dickens. 21 vols. OUP 1987 $200.00. ISBN 0-19-254522-1. The
   complete novels, short fiction, and assorted journalism.
The Unpublished Letters of Charles Dickens: to Mark Lemon. Ed. by Walter Dexter.
   Haskell 1971 repr. of 1927 ed. $59.95. ISBN 0-8383-1281-0. Letters to the first editor
   of *Punch*, who shared with Dickens an interest in the stage.

BOOKS ABOUT DICKENS

Bentley, Nicolas, Nina Burgis, and Michael Slater, eds. *The Dickens Index*. OUP 1988
   $45.00. ISBN 0-192-11665-7. Excellent index of the Dickens oeuvre.
Bolton, H. Philip. *Dickens Dramatized*. G. K. Hall 1987 $65.00. ISBN 0-816-18924-2.
   Interesting study of the appropriation of Dickens's work by the dramatic arts.
Chesterton, G. K., and F. G. Kitton. *Charles Dickens*. Folcroft 1973 o.p.
Chittick, Kathryn. *Dickens and the 1830's*. Cambridge U. Pr. 1990 $39.95. ISBN 0-521-
   38174-6. Well-done study of Dickens as journalist and aspiring novelist.
Cohen, Jane R. *Charles Dickens and His Original Illustrators*. Ohio St. U. Pr. 1980 $52.00.
   ISBN 0-685-03707-X
Collins, Philip, ed. *Dickens: Interviews and Recollections*. 2 vols. B & N Imports 1981 o.p.
   Presents a varied picture of Dickens through the hundreds who knew or met him.
_____, ed. *Dickens: The Critical Heritage. Critical Heritage Ser*. Routledge 1971 o.p. A
   collection of contemporary criticism, grouped for each work and arranged chrono-
   logically.
Collins, Philip Arthur William, and Joanne Shattock, eds. *Dickens and Other Victorians:
   Essays in Honor of Philip Collins*. St. Martin 1988 $35.00. ISBN 0-312-02101-1.
   Collection of essays, primarily on Dickens, by noted scholars.
Davies, Paul B. *The Lives and Times of Ebenezer Scrooge*. Yale U. Pr. 1990 $32.00. ISBN
   0-300-04664-2. Study of the historical reception and variations of *A Christmas Carol*.
Dickens Studies Annual 1970–1992: Essays on Victorian Fiction. 21 vols. AMS Pr. $45.00
   ea. ISBN 0-404-18520-7. First series, 1970–78, edited by Robert Partlow; second
   series, 1979–92, edited by Michael Timko, Fred Kaplan, and Edward Guiliano.
Fielding, K. J. *Charles Dickens: A Critical Introduction*. HM 1958 o.p. A study of his career
   as a novelist, arranged as a biography.

Ford, George H., and Lauriat Lane, Jr., eds. *The Dickens Critics*. Greenwood 1972 repr. of 1961 ed. $55.00. ISBN 0-8371-6029-4. A compilation of essays and articles from 1841 to 1961 examining Dickens's fiction.

Forster, John. *The Life of Charles Dickens*. NAL-Dutton o.p. Written by Dickens's most intimate friend, a professional biographer.

Gissing, George. *Critical Studies of the Works of Charles Dickens*. Haskell 1969 repr. of 1924 ed. $75.00. ISBN 0-8383-0557-1. A critical handbook plus nine papers that Gissing originally wrote as introductions to Dickens's novels.

Hardwick, Michael, and Mollie Hardwick. *The Charles Dickens Encyclopedia*. Carol Pub. Group 1993 $14.95. ISBN 0-8065-1403-5. Includes works, people, places, and quotes associated with Dickens.

Hayward, Arthur L. *Dickens Encyclopedia*. Rprt. Serv. 1992 $69.00. ISBN 0-7812-7513-X. Provides a wealth of information on the most commonly read Dickens works.

House, Humphrey. *The Dickens World*. Richard West 1950 o.p. Shows in a broad way the connection between what Dickens wrote and the times he wrote in.

Jaffe, Audrey. *Vanishing Points: Dickens, Narrative, and the Subject of Omniscience*. U. CA Pr. 1991 $32.50. ISBN 0-520-06918-8. Intelligent study of Dickens's narrative techniques, especially third-person narration.

Johnson, Edgar. *Charles Dickens: His Tragedy and Triumph*. Viking Penguin 1986 $12.95. ISBN 0-14-058027-1. A fine biography.

Kaplan, Fred. *Dickens: A Biography*. Morrow 1988 $24.95. ISBN 0-688-04341-0. Excellent biography.

Kent, William C. *London for Dickens Lovers*. Studies in Dickens. Haskell 1972 repr. of 1935 ed. $59.95. ISBN 0-8383-1480-5. London backgrounds of Dickens's life and work.

Kitton, Frederic G. *Dickens and His Illustrators*. AMS Pr. repr. of 1899 ed. $32.50. ISBN 0-404-08872-4. Contains 22 portraits and 70 facsimiles of original drawings.

Leavis, F. R., and Q. D. Leavis. *Dickens the Novelist*. Rutgers U. Pr. 1979 $15.00. ISBN 0-8135-0881-9. Argues that Dickens was one of the world's most creative thinkers.

Levit, Fred. *A Dickens Glossary*. Garland 1990 $53.00. ISBN 0-824-05542-X. Useful glossary of terms and names used in Dickens's novels.

Ley, J. W. T. *The Dickens Circle*. Studies in Dickens. Haskell 1972 repr. of 1919 ed. $75.00. ISBN 0-8383-1415-5. An intimate portrait of Dickens, his family, and his friends.

Lucas, John. *Melancholy Man: A Study of Dickens' Novels*. B & N Imports 1980 o.p. Disputes charges that Dickens's characters are either wooden or not realistically drawn.

Mackenzie, Norman, and Jeanne Mackenzie. *Dickens: A Life*. OUP 1979 o.p.

Marcus, Steven. *Dickens: From Pickwick to Dombey*. Norton 1987 $6.95. ISBN 0-393-30286-5. A guide to the seven novels written during Dickens's early period.

Meckier, Jerome. *Hidden Rivalries in Victorian Fiction: Dickens, Realism, and Revaluation*. U. Pr. of Ky. 1987 $35.00. ISBN 0-813-11622-8. Uneven study of the marketplace rivalries between George Eliot, Dickens, and others.

———. *Innocent Abroad: Charles Dickens' American Engagements*. U. Pr. of Ky. 1990 $34.00. ISBN 0-813-11707-0. Examines the critical and biographical implications of Dickens's two trips to America.

Miller, J. Hillis. *Charles Dickens: The World of His Novels*. HUP 1959 $22.50. ISBN 0-674-11000-5. Study of Dickens's novels from a social and cultural perspective.

Monod, Sylvère. *Dickens the Novelist*. U. of Okla. Pr. 1968 o.p. The author's own translation and revision of *Dickens Romancier*, originally published in 1953.

Patten, Robert L. *Charles Dickens and His Publishers*. OUP 1978 $104.00. ISBN 0-19-812076-1. Examines Dickens's relationships with his many publishers, both English and foreign, and how conditions of publishing shaped his success.

Pierce, Gilbert A. *The Dickens Dictionary*. Studies in Dickens. Haskell repr. of 1878 ed. $75.00. ISBN 0-8383-1526-7. Organized by the title of Dickens's work; includes a directory of characters.

Pope-Hennessy, Dame Una. *Charles Dickens, 1812–1870*. Telegraph Bks. 1983 repr. of 1945 ed. o.p. Based on the 8,000 collected letters published by Nonesuch Press in 1938.

Raina, Badri. *Dickens and the Dialectic of Growth*. U. of Wis. Pr. 1986 $27.50. ISBN 0-299-10610-1. Marxist reading of the novels; examines the development of the "martyred self" through the works.

Slater, Michael. *Dickens and Women*. Stanford U. Pr. 1983 $52.50. ISBN 0-8047-1180-1. Intelligently compares the women in Dickens's life with those in his writings.

Stewart, Garrett. *Dickens and the Trials of Imagination*. HUP 1974 $19.95. ISBN 0-674-20440-9. Analyses verbal wit, metaphor, syntax, and diction in language of Dickensian heroes and heroines.

Welsh, Alexander. *From Copyright to Copperfield: The Identity of Dickens*. HUP 1987 $27.50. ISBN 0-674-32342-4. Examines Dickens's advocation of international copyright laws and the effect of that advocacy on his works.

Wilson, Angus. *The World of Charles Dickens*. Academy Chi. Pubs. 1985 $15.00. ISBN 0-89733-172-9. Shows how Dickens's private and public life fed the creative imagination of the novelist; with 200 black-and-white illustrations and 40 color plates.

DISRAELI, BENJAMIN (1st Earl of Beaconsfield). 1804–1881

A great master of the political novel, Disraeli may be said to have originated the genre. ANTHONY TROLLOPE in his parliamentary novels is his closest rival. Disraeli's early books were all *romans à clef*, novels in which he introduced real personages who were easily recognizable beneath fictitious names. With *Coningsby* (1844), *Sybil* (1845), and *Tancred* (1847), Disraeli produced his best work. All of them are political novels and more or less comprise a trilogy, since the same characters appear and reappear. In these novels Disraeli dramatized ambition, romantic egoism, and the role of the outsider, particularly the Jew, and revealed a strong sense of the social and economic problems of mid-Victorian Britain. He then gave up writing temporarily, gradually rose to be chancellor of the exchequer, and finally, prime minister from 1867 to 1868 and again from 1874 to 1880. During his second term of office, when he was knighted, he took a name from his first novel and became the first Earl of Beaconsfield. In his later years, he resumed his writing and became an intimate friend of Queen Victoria, who referred to his death as "a national calamity."

NOVELS BY DISRAELI

Coningsby. 1844. Buccaneer Bks. 1989 $35.95. ISBN 0-89966-637-X

Lothair. 1870. Greenwood repr. of 1906 ed. o.p.

Sybil. Viking Penguin 1980 $6.95. ISBN 0-14-043134-9

Tancred, or The New Crusade. 1847. Greenwood repr. of 1877 ed. $35.00. ISBN 0-8371-3072-7

Vivian Grey. 1826. Dufour 1969 o.p.

The Voyage of Captain Popanilla. 1828. Bks. for Libraries o.p.

The Young Duke: A Moral Tale, though Gay. 1853. Folcroft repr. of 1853 ed. o.p.

WORKS BY DISRAELI

Benjamin Disraeli: Letters, 1815–1834. Ed. by J. A. Gunn and others. U. of Toronto Pr. 1982 $60.00. ISBN 0-8020-5523-0

Benjamin Disraeli: Letters, 1835–1837. Ed. by J. A. Gunn and others. U. of Toronto Pr. 1982 $60.00. ISBN 0-8020-5587-7

The Works of Benjamin Disraeli, Earl of Beaconsfield. 20 vols. AMS Pr. repr. of 1904 ed. $800.00. ISBN 0-404-08800-7

BOOKS ABOUT DISRAELI

Blake, Robert. *Disraeli*. OUP o.p. A penetrating study of a complex personality.

———. *Disraeli's Grand Tour: Disraeli in the Holy Land, 1830–31*. OUP 1982 o.p.
Bradford, Sarah. *Disraeli*. Madison Bks. UPA 1986 $12.95. ISBN 0-8128-6251-1. Modern
    biography that views Disraeli both as a young man and as prime minister.
Braun, Thomas. *Disraeli the Novelist*. Allen & Unwin 1981 o.p.
McGuirk, Carol. *Disraeli. World Leaders—Past and Present Ser*. Chelsea Hse. 1987
    $17.95. ISBN 0-87754-565-0. General biography of the nineteenth-century British
    prime minister.
Schwarz, Daniel R. *Disraeli's Fiction*. B & N Imports 1979 $40.00. ISBN 0-06-496124-9
Vincent, John. *Disraeli*. OUP 1990 $6.95. ISBN 0-19-287-681-3

DOYLE, SIR ARTHUR CONAN. 1859–1930

[SEE Chapter 12 in this volume for Main Entry.]

DU MAURIER, GEORGE. 1834–1896

Du Maurier was first famous as an artist, contributing incomparable satirical
drawings of society to *Punch* and illustrating novels by authors such as
ELIZABETH GASKELL, WILLIAM MAKEPEACE THACKERAY, and GEORGE MEREDITH.
Peter Ibbetson (1892), his own first novel, is a fanciful romance of dream life, a
work of rare imagination and charm of style. *Trilby* (1894) created a literary
sensation and brought the name of the character Svengali—an evil person who
bends others to his will—into the English language. The story is set in the Latin
Quarter in Paris and is thoroughly French in atmosphere. Du Maurier was born
in Paris, studied art there, and illustrated his own novels. *Trilby* contained a
portrait of Whistler in caricature, which du Maurier was forced by law to
change. Du Maurier is the grandfather of DAPHNE DU MAURIER, popular novelist
of the 1930s.

NOVELS BY DU MAURIER

The Martian: A Novel. Scholarly 1971 repr. of 1897 ed. $69.00. ISBN 0-403-00919-7
Peter Ibbetson. 1892. Scholarly 1971 repr. of 1932 ed. $69.00. ISBN 0-403-00920-0
Trilby. 1894. Biblio Dist. 1977 o.p.

WORK BY DU MAURIER

Young George du Maurier: A Selection of His Letters, 1860–67. Ed. by Daphne du Maurier.
    Darby Pub. 1982 repr. of 1951 ed. o.p. Includes illustrations from contemporary
    drawings by du Maurier.

BOOK ABOUT DU MAURIER

Ormond, Leonée. *George du Maurier*. U. of Pittsburgh Pr. 1969 o.p. A critical biography.

ELIOT, GEORGE (pseud. of Mary Ann, or Marian, Evans, afterward Cross). 1819–1880

Mary Ann Evans, known by the pen name George Eliot, was born in
Warwickshire, England. Eliot was the daughter of a land agent, a man of strong
religious convictions. When her mother died in 1836, Eliot took entire charge of
the family household and also studied music and foreign languages. She was
always an avid reader. In 1841 Eliot and her father moved to Coventry, where
she met Charles Bray and Charles Hennel, both writers on philosophy. Under
their influence, she rejected the fervent Christianity of her father in favor of
rationalistic thought. This separation from her father's religion became a source
of conflict for her and a great distress for him.

After her father's death in 1849, Eliot traveled on the Continent, returning to
England in 1850, at which time she began writing for the *Westminster Review*.

From 1851 to 1854, Eliot served as assistant editor for that journal and, while there, she met GEORGE HENRY LEWES. Lewes was separated from his wife but could not obtain a divorce. In 1854 Eliot and Lewes entered into a liaison that lasted until his death in 1878; they lived as husband and wife and were accepted as such by their friends, even though they never married.

Eliot asserted her intellect in her early translations and journalism, her imagination in a series of extraordinary novels, and her independence in her pseudonym and in her personal life. Her first four novels moved from social to psychological realism. English rural life became the carefully delineated background for serious dramatizations of human character tested by the interplay between environment and moral choice. Her concern for philosophical and moral issues was illumined by her wide learning and deep compassion for the human situation. Her versatility and learning propelled her into trying the historical novel (*Romola*, 1863), the political novel (*Felix Holt*, 1866), and a novel revealing Eliot's pro-Jewish sentiments (*Daniel Deronda*, 1876). Her style resembled that of other Victorian novelists, particularly CHARLES DICKENS, in the triumph of selective realism and psychological perceptiveness. Although HENRY JAMES thought *Silas Marner* (1861) "nearly a masterpiece," recent opinion holds that her supreme achievement is *Middlemarch* (1871).

Toward the end of her life, Eliot fell in love again with a banker, John Walter Cross, who was 20 years younger than she. Shortly after they were married in May 1880, Eliot died. She was buried in Highgate Cemetery in the grave next to her first love, George Lewes. As a novelist, Eliot stands among the greatest in the Victorian Age. Her portrayals of farmers, tradesmen, and the lower middle class are among the finest in English literature.

NOVELS BY ELIOT

Adam Bede. 1859. *Penguin Eng. Lib. Ser.* Viking Penguin 1980 $4.95. ISBN 0-14-016188-0. A tragic love story about the consequences of misplaced affections; Eliot's father served as the model for the title character.

Brother Jacob. Virago 1989 $4.95. ISBN 1-853-81040-1. Good edition of novella; with a new afterword by Beryl Gray.

Daniel Deronda. 1876. Ed. by Graham Handley. OUP 1988 $5.95. ISBN 0-19-281787-6. A story about the difficulties and romances of a group of people in English society; deals with anti-semitism in Victorian England.

Felix Holt, the Radical. 1866. Ed. by Fred C. Thompson. OUP 1988 $5.95. ISBN 0-19-281781-7

Middlemarch: A Study of Provincial Life. 1871. Ed. by David Carroll. OUP 1988 $4.95. ISBN 0-19-281760-4. Story of the lives of seven people in rural England and how they affect each other, focusing on the intelligent Dorothea's unhappy marriage to a pompous older man.

The Mill on the Floss. 1860. Bantam 1987 $3.95. ISBN 0-553-21319-9. Story of a brother and sister torn apart by society's different treatment of men and women.

Romola. 1863. Ed. by Andrew Sanders. Viking Penguin 1980 $5.95. ISBN 0-14-043139-X. A historical novel set in Renaissance Florence.

Scenes of Clerical Life. 1858. OUP 1989 $4.95. ISBN 0-19-281786-8

Silas Marner. 1861. Bantam 1981 $1.95. ISBN 0-553-21229-X. Story of the miser Silas Marner, whose life is changed forever when he finds a baby girl on his doorstep.

WORKS BY ELIOT

Essays. 1879. Ed. by Thomas Pinney. Col. U. Pr. 1963 o.p.

The George Eliot Letters: 1836-80. 9 vols. Ed. by Gordon S. Haight. Yale U Pr. Vol. 1 1954 $97.50. ISBN 0-300-00529-6. Vols. 2–3 o.p. Vol. 4 1955 $97.50. ISBN 0-300-01090-7. Vol. 5 1955 $97.50. ISBN 0-300-01091-5. Vol. 6 1955 $97.50. ISBN 0-300-01092-3.

Vol. 7 o.p. Vol. 8 1978 $97.50. ISBN 0-300-01968-8. Vol. 9 1978 $97.50. ISBN 0-300-02251-4

George Eliot's Life as Related in Her Letters and Journal. 3 vols. Rprt. Serv. 1992 repr. of 1885 ed. $225.00. ISBN 0-7812-7525-3

Selections from George Eliot's Letters. Ed. by Gordon S. Haight. Yale U. Pr. 1985 $19.95. ISBN 0-300-04050-4

Writings of George Eliot. 25 vols. AMS Pr. repr. of 1908 ed. $1,125.00. ISBN 0-404-02280-4. With the *Life* by J. W. Cross.

BOOKS ABOUT ELIOT

Auster, Henry. *Local Habitations: Regionalism in the Early Novels of George Eliot.* HUP 1970 $18.95. ISBN 0-674-53676-2. A fresh study of the early fiction of George Eliot.

Beer, Gillian. *George Eliot.* Ind. U. Pr. 1986 $29.95. ISBN 0-253-30100-9. Feminist reading of the life and works.

Bennett, Joan. *George Eliot: Her Mind and Her Art.* Cambridge U. Pr. 1948 o.p.

Bonaparte, Felicia. *The Triptych and the Cross: A Key to the Central Myths of George Eliot's Poetic Imagination.* NYU Pr. 1979 o.p. Critical analysis of what is generally considered Eliot's least popular novel, *Romola.*

Carroll, David. *George Eliot and the Conflict of Interpretations: A Reading of the Novels.* Cambridge U. Pr. 1992 $59.95. ISBN 0-521-40366-9. Examines Eliot within the crisis of belief acted out in the mid-nineteenth century.

——, ed. *George Eliot: The Critical Heritage.* B & N Imports 1971 o.p.

Cottom, Daniel. *Social Figures: George Eliot, Social History and Literary Representation.* U. of Minn. Pr. 1987 $35.00. ISBN 0-816-61547-0. Examination of Eliot's liberal humanist assumptions as informative of her fiction.

Dodd, Valerie. *George Eliot: An Intellectual Life.* St. Martin 1990 $39.95. ISBN 0-312-02694-3. Interesting biography; for broad audience.

Emery, Laura Comer. *George Eliot's Creative Conflict: The Other Side of Silence.* U. CA Pr. 1976 $37.50. ISBN 0-520-02979-8. Explores the conflicts in Eliot's novels.

Gray, Beryl. *George Eliot and Music.* Macmillan 1989 $35.00. ISBN 0-333-45899-0. Excellent study of Eliot's use of music in her work and its influence on her life.

Haight, Gordon S. *George Eliot: A Biography.* OUP 1976 o.p. A judicious, carefully written, and definitive biography, the first to draw fully on the author's edition of the letters.

Handley, Graham. *George Eliot: A Guide through the Critical Maze.* Bristol Pr. 1990 o.p. Good, though highly biased, guide to critical writing on Eliot.

Hardy, Barbara. *The Novels of George Eliot.* Humanities 1981 $10.95. ISBN 0-485-12005-4. Collection of essays (1964–1980) exploring such subjects as the "womanliness" of Eliot's imagination.

——. *Particularities: Readings in George Eliot.* Ohio U. Pr. 1983 $21.95. ISBN 0-8214-0741-4

Jones, R. T. *George Eliot. British Authors Ser.* Cambridge U. Pr. 1971 $24.95. ISBN 0-521-07832-6. Discusses the novels in chronological order.

Levine, George Lewis, and Patricia O'Hara. *An Annotated Critical Bibliography of George Eliot.* St. Martin 1988 $35.00. ISBN 0-312-01959-9. Useful bibliography.

Mintz, Alan. *George Eliot and the Novel of Vocation.* HUP 1978 $20.00. ISBN 0-674-34873-7. Discusses conceptions of self and work in Victorian times, with particular attention to *Middlemarch.*

Paxton, Nancy L. *George Eliot and Herbert Spencer: Feminism, Evolutionism, and the Reconstruction of Gender.* Princeton U. Pr. 1991 $32.95. ISBN 0-691-06841-0. Interesting look at Eliot's friendship with Spencer and the effect it had on her fictional and personal views on gender.

Pinion, F. B. *A George Eliot Companion: Literary Achievement and Modern Significance. Companion Ser.* B & N Imports 1981 $41.25. ISBN 0-389-20208-8

Pratt, John C., and Victor A. Neufeldt. *George Eliot's Middlemarch Notebooks.* U. CA Pr. 1979 $52.50. ISBN 0-520-02867-8

GASKELL, ELIZABETH (CLEGHORN STEVENSON). 1810–1865

Elizabeth Gaskell was the daughter of an important Unitarian minister, William Stevenson. In 1832 she married William Gaskell, minister of the Cross Street Unitarian Chapel in Manchester. As a way of occupying herself after the death of her infant son, she wrote her first novel, *Mary Barton*, which was published in 1848. Subtitled *A Tale of Manchester Life*, the novel focuses on the problems of the urban working classes and was partly drawn from Gaskell's experiences as a minister's wife working among Manchester's poor. The novel was a success and caught the attention of CHARLES DICKENS, who became her editor and published much of her subsequent work in his journals *Household Words* and *All the Year Round*. This was only the beginning of Gaskell's movement in literary circles, and she became good friends with a number of luminaries, including JOHN RUSKIN, THOMAS CARLYLE and Jane Carlyle, CHARLES KINGSLEY, and CHARLOTTE BRONTË.

Gaskell's critical legacy has been somewhat checkered. For many years her most important novels were considered to be *Mary Barton* and *North and South* (1855). These works, which detail the effects of the industrialization of northern England on the relations between the middle and working classes, are often discussed as significant but flawed contributions to the "social problem" novel of the Victorian period. The primary critical objections to these works fasten on Gaskell's sometimes awkward plot devices, which tend to resolve narrative crises in facile ways. As a result, Gaskell was often considered a notable but second-rate talent. Recent criticism, however, especially Marxist, post-Marxist, and feminist work, has helped raise Gaskell's stock considerably. There has been a keen, renewed attention given to her "industrial" novels by critics who are interested in the social and political issues associated with class struggle in Victorian England. And feminist critics have increasingly looked to Gaskell's other works, such as *Ruth* (1853) and *Cranford* (1853), as ways of examining the status of women in the nineteenth century. *Ruth*, in particular, has become an important text for feminists, for in it Gaskell rewrites the figure of the "fallen women" as a redeemable, sympathetic character rather than as an object of scorn and condemnation. Although her attempt has brought her critical notoriety among late-twentieth-century critics, many of Gaskell's contemporary readers were shocked.

Gaskell also enjoys a reputation as a biographer. She was a good friend of CHARLOTTE BRONTË, and two years after that novelist's death in 1855, Gaskell published *The Life of Charlotte Brontë*. The biography caused a considerable stir because of some supposedly defamatory statements, which had to be excised from the book. Throughout much of this century, this biography was seen as Gaskell's major contribution to literary history, and it remains an important work for Brontë scholars.

NOVELS BY GASKELL

Lizzie Leigh and Other Tales. 1854. *Short Story Index Repr. Ser.* Ayer repr. of 1865 ed. $16.00. ISBN 0-8369-4102-0

Mary Barton. 1848. Ed. by Stephen Gill. Viking Penguin 1970 $5.95. ISBN 0-140-43053-9

North and South. 1855. Scholarly 1971 repr. of 1914 ed. $69.00. ISBN 0-403-00985-5

Ruth. Ed. by Alan Shelston. OUP 1985 $5.95. ISBN 0-19-281669-1

Sylvia's Lovers. 1863. OUP 1982 $8.95. ISBN 0-19-281571-7. Romantic story set in a northeastern seaport during the Napoleonic wars.

Wives and Daughters. 1866. Viking Penguin 1986 $5.95. ISBN 0-14-043046-6. The story of Mr. Gibson's new marriage and its influence on the lives of those closest to him.

SHORT STORY COLLECTIONS BY GASKELL

Cousin Phillis and Other Tales. Ed. by Angus Easson. *World's Class. Ser.* OUP 1981 $3.95.
ISBN 0-19-281554-7
Cranford and Other Tales. 1851–53. Ayer repr. of 1886 ed. $24.50. ISBN 0-8369-3815-1.
Gaskell's most acclaimed work.
The Grey Woman and Other Tales. Short Story Index Repr. Ser. Ayer repr. of 1865 ed.
$16.00. ISBN 0-8369-3942-5
My Lady Ludlow and Other Stories. Ed. by Edgar Wright. OUP 1989 $8.95. ISBN 0-19-
28183-4. Collection of stories, most first appearing in *Household Words.*

NONFICTION BY GASKELL

Life of Charlotte Brontë. Ed. by Alan Shelston. Viking Penguin 1975 $8.95. ISBN 0-14-
043099-7. Written at the request of Mr. Brontë (Charlotte's father).

WORKS BY GASKELL

The Letters of Mrs. Gaskell. Ed. by J. A. V. Chapple and Arthur Pollard. HUP 1966 $80.00.
ISBN 0-674-52675-9. Letters dating from her marriage to her death, 1832–64.
Works. 8 vols. Ed. by A. W. Ward. AMS Pr. repr. of 1906 ed. $380.00. ISBN 0-404-07250-X

BOOKS ABOUT GASKELL

Chapple, J. A. V., and J. G. Sharps. *Elizabeth Gaskell: A Portrait in Letters.* St. Martin 1988
$17.95. ISBN 0-7190-0985-5. Examines Mrs. Gaskell, a vivacious letter writer,
through her letters to various people.
Easson, Angus. *Elizabeth Gaskell.* Routledge 1979 o.p. History of the critical reception of
Gaskell's works.
Gérin, Winifred. *Elizabeth Gaskell: A Biography.* OUP 1976 o.p. Treats its subject, Mrs.
Gaskell, very sympathetically as an admirable mother to four daughters, a gracious
hostess, and a dedicated social worker.
Haldane, Elizabeth. *Mrs. Gaskell and Her Friends. Select Bibliographies Repr. Ser.* Ayer
repr. of 1931 ed. $20.00. ISBN 0-8369-5599-4
Sanders, Gerald DeWitt. *Elizabeth Gaskell.* Rprt. Serv. 1992 repr. of 1929 ed. $79.00.
ISBN 0-7812-7531-8
Schor, Hilary M. *Scheherezade in the Marketplace: Elizabeth Gaskell and the Victorian
Novel.* OUP 1992 $29.95. ISBN 0-19-507388-6. Good for narrative and analysis of
Gaskell's work.
Stoneman, Patsy. *Elizabeth Gaskell.* Ind. U. Pr. 1987 $29.95. ISBN 0-253-30103-3. Another
in a good series on key women writers; up-to-date critical analysis of the novels.

GILBERT, SIR WILLIAM SCHWENCK. 1836–1911

Born in London, William S. Gilbert served a term as a government clerk and
was called to the bar as a barrister before being diverted into the bohemian
world of Victorian comic journalism. He first achieved popularity as the author
of several volumes of "Bab Ballads" (Max Beerbohm praised them as "silly").
Moving on to theater, Gilbert contributed to the current rage for travesties of
opera and for one-act musical "entertainments" until a blank-verse burlesque of
TENNYSON's *Princess* led to commissions and full-length comedies, both
mythological and "modern." Still highly regarded by critics, some of these—
perhaps *Sweethearts* (1874) and *Engaged* (1877)—should be investigated by
today's readers and producers. As it is, their best memorial is the early work of
GEORGE BERNARD SHAW, who, although he polemically rejected their cynicism,
was clearly influenced by Gilbert's comedies and their inversion of social
values.

By the time of *Engaged,* however, a second dramatic career had overtaken
Gilbert. Collaboration with the composer Arthur Sullivan, begun in 1871

(*Thespis*), achieved theatrical success with *Trial by Jury* in 1875. In the comic operas that followed, Sullivan's generally allusive music enriched the sometimes shrill pessimism of Gilbert's wit. An unlikely jostle of theatrical parody, contemporary satire, intricate meters, and logical fantasy, the librettos have often been compared with the comedies of ARISTOPHANES (see Vol. 2) and have influenced English playwrights from OSCAR WILDE to TOM STOPPARD. (Gilbert, too, wrote a *Rosencrantz and Guildenstern*.)

Uncomfortable, often acrimonious, the partnership nevertheless lasted through 25 years and 13 Savoy operas (so called because many were staged by Richard D'Oyly Carte at his Savoy Theatre). Gilbert, whose merely theatrical connections (as opposed to Sullivan's serious musical credentials) held him back from formal honors, was knighted in 1907, only a few years before his death.

PLAYS BY GILBERT

The Annotated Gilbert and Sullivan. Ed. by Ian Bradley. Viking Penguin 1983 $10.95. ISBN 0-14-070848-0

Asimov's Annoted Gilbert & Sullivan. Ed. by Isaac Asimov. Doubleday 1988 $50.00. ISBN 0-385-23915-7. Interesting, if idiosyncratic, annotations.

The Bab Ballads. 1869. Ed. by James Ellis. HUP 1970 o.p.

The Complete Gilbert and Sullivan. Ed. by Diana Bell. Bk. Sales Inc. 1989 $29.98. ISBN 1-55521-440-1

The Complete Plays of Gilbert and Sullivan. Norton Lib. Norton 1976 repr. of 1941 ed. $12.95. ISBN 0-393-00828-2

The Gilbert and Sullivan Lexicon: In Which Is Gilded the Philosophic Pill. Ed. by Harry Benford. Jennings Pr. 1991 $20.00. ISBN 0-931781-08-6. Featuring new illustrations and the complete libretto for *The Zoo.*

Gilbert before Sullivan: Six Comic Plays. Ed. by Jane W. Stedman. Bks. Demand repr. of 1967 ed. $99.00. ISBN 0-685-15528-5. One-act musical "entertainments": *No Cards* (1869); *Ages Ago: A Musical Legend* (1869); *Our Island Home* (1870); *A Sensational Novel in Three Volumes* (1871); *Eyes and No Eyes, or The Art of Seeing* (1875); and *Happy Arcadia* (1872).

Martyn Green's Treasury of Gilbert and Sullivan. Ed. by Martyn Green. S & S Trade 1985 o.p. The librettos of 11 works, more than 100 songs simply arranged for voice and piano, and a full commentary by Green, comic lead of the D'Oyly Carte Opera Company for more than two decades.

New and Original Extravagances. Ed. by Sir Isaac Goldberg. Branden Pub. Co. 1931 o.p.

Plays by W. S. Gilbert. Ed. by George Rowell. Cambridge U. Pr. 1982 o.p.

BOOKS ABOUT GILBERT

Allen, Reginald. *Gilbert and Sullivan in America.* Pierpont Morgan 1979 o.p.

Dark, Sidney, and Rowland Grey. *W. S. Gilbert: His Life and Letters.* Ayer repr. of 1923 ed. o.p. Entertaining biography that includes extracts from Gilbert's writings, reproductions of his sketches, and critical evaluation of his work.

Dillard, Philip H. *How Quaint the Ways of Paradox!: An Annotated Gilbert & Sullivan Bibliography.* Scarecrow 1991 $25.00. ISBN 0-810-82445-0. Useful bibliography.

Dixon, Geoffrey. *The Gilbert and Sullivan Concordance: A Word Index to W. S. Gilbert's Libretti for the Fourteen Savoy Operas.* Garland 1987 o.p. Worthwhile index of the libretti.

Dunn, George E. *A Gilbert and Sullivan Dictionary.* Da Capo 1971 repr. of 1936 ed. $25.00. ISBN 0-306-70007-7

Eden, David. *Gilbert & Sullivan: The Creative Conflict.* Fairleigh Dickinson 1986 $32.50. ISBN 0-838-63282-3. Examination of the relationship between the two men.

Fischler, Alan. *Modified Rapture: Comedy in W. S. Gilbert's Savoy Operas.* U. Pr. of Va.
1991 $25.00. ISBN 0-813-91334-9. Examination of the comic technique and its
attendance to Victorian stage and social convention.
Godwin, A. H. *Gilbert and Sullivan: A Critical Approach to the Savoy Operas.* Assoc.
Faculty Pr. 1969 repr. of 1926 ed. o.p. Analyzes Gilbert and Sullivan's operettas, with
an emphasis on their structure and significance.
Hayter, Charles. *Gilbert and Sullivan.* St. Martin 1987 $25.00. ISBN 0-312-00446-X.
Intended for a nonscholarly audience.
Hibbert, Christopher. *Gilbert and Sullivan and Their Victorian World.* Putnam Pub.
Group 1976 o.p.
Pearson, Hesketh. *Gilbert and Sullivan.* Amereon Ltd. repr. of 1935 ed. $17.95. ISBN 0-
89190-868-4. Anecdotal biography that deals with the personalities of Gilbert and
Sullivan rather than their works and explores the rift that broke up their partnership.
Searle, Townley. *A Bibliography of Sir William Schwenck Gilbert.* B. Franklin 1967 repr.
of 1931 ed. o.p.
Sutton, Max K. *W. S. Gilbert. Twayne's Eng. Authors Ser.* G. K. Hall 1975 o.p.

GISSING, GEORGE (ROBERT). 1857–1903

Recent years have seen a strong revival of interest in Gissing, many of whose
novels are now available in reprints. A bridge between late Victorianism and
early modernism, Gissing's novels combine two essential themes of the period,
the isolation and struggle of the artist and the economic bondage of the
proletariat. *New Grub Street* (1891) and his own indirect autobiography, *The
Private Papers of Henry Ryecroft* (1903), reveal the close connection in Gissing
between fiction and autobiography, and *Workers in the Dawn* (1880) and
Demos: A Story of English Socialism (1892) dramatizes Gissing's conviction that
economic and class divisions are central to human character and individual
destiny.

Novels by Gissing

The Crown of Life. AMS Pr. repr. of 1899 ed. $24.50. ISBN 0-404-02814-4. Story of
illegitimate Piers Otwar, a man of soulful erotic faith, and his encounter with the
"ideal" woman.
Demos: A Story of English Socialism. AMS Pr. repr. of 1892 ed. $15.00. ISBN 0-404-
02778-4
Eve's Ransom. Dover 1980 $4.95. ISBN 0-486-24016-9. Hilliard, who regards himself as a
"living machine" condemned forever to be a draftsman, inherits money, falls in love,
and becomes a successful architect.
In the Year of Jubilee. AMS Pr. repr. of 1894 ed. $21.50. ISBN 0-404-02797-0. Depicts the
boorish offspring of parents who have themselves climbed from an uneducated class
into middle-class comfort.
Life Morning. AMS Pr. repr. of 1888 ed. o.p. Affected idealism and snobbery make for a
sordid tale of two young people in love.
The Nether World. 1889. OUP 1992 $8.95. ISBN 0-19-281769-8. Story of a working-class
woman's travails, as her rich grandfather demands fidelity for philanthropic duties.
New Grub Street. 1891. Ed. by Bernard Bergonzi. Viking Penguin 1976 $6.95. ISBN 0-14-
043032-6
The Odd Women. AMS Pr. repr. of 1893 ed. $30.00. ISBN 0-404-02788-1. Deals
compassionately with the story of a single woman who is relegated to second-rate
jobs.
Paying Guest. AMS Pr. repr. of 1895 ed. $16.00. ISBN 0-404-02799-7. Centers around
Louise Derreck's spirited vulgarity and her tenant Mumford's fearful gentility.
The Private Papers of Henry Ryecroft. 1903 Rprt. Serv. 1992 repr. of 1927 ed. $79.00.
ISBN 0-7812-7535-0

Sleeping Fires. 1895. U. of Nebr. Pr. 1983 $4.95. ISBN 0-8032-7011-9. An aristocratic heroine admits that she should not have rejected the father of her illegitimate child.

The Unclassed. AMS Pr. repr. of 1896 ed. $15.00. ISBN 0-404-02811-X. The story of poor, but literate, men on the edges of squalor who become involved with three well–to–do women.

Veranilda: A Romance. AMS Pr. repr. of 1904 ed. $15.00. ISBN 0-404-02816-0. Classical romance about sixth–century Rome.

The Whirlpool. 1897. Fairleigh Dickinson 1978 $24.50. ISBN 0-8386-2172-4. The tale of Harvey Rolfe, who stands aloof amid lurid events including ruined reputations, unnatural deaths, and extramarital affairs.

Will Warburton: A Romance of Real Life. AMS Pr. repr. of 1905 ed. $10.00. ISBN 0-404-02817-9. Deals with a grocer's life and times.

Workers in the Dawn.. AMS Pr. repr. of 1880 ed. $55.00. ISBN 0-404-02777-6

SHORT STORY COLLECTIONS BY GISSING

The House of Cobwebs. Ayer repr. of 1906 ed. $20.00. ISBN 0-8369-3911-5. Includes "The Work of George Gissing: An Introduction" by Thomas Seccombe.

Thyrza: A Tale. 1887. AMS Pr. repr. of 1893 ed. $30.00. ISBN 0-404-02789-X. Thyrza, once lowly seamstress, rises from the working class through her "artistic soul".

A Victim of Circumstances and Other Stories. Short Story Index Repr. Ser. Ayer repr. of 1927 ed. $17.00. ISBN 0-8369-4013-X. Story of a talentless man who believes himself to be Michelangelo, and his truly artistically gifted wife who regards her own work as worthless.

NONFICTION BY GISSING

Charles Dickens: A Critical Study. Rprt. Serv. repr. of 1898 ed. $79.00. ISBN 0-7812-0309-0. Examination of social patterns that cut across individual works; organized thematically.

WORKS BY GISSING

The Collected Letters of George Gissing. 4 vols. Ed. by Paul F. Mattheisen, Arthur C. Young, and Pierre Coustillas. Ohio U. Pr. Vol. 1 1990 $49.95. ISBN 0-8214-0955-7. Vol. 2 1991 $55.00. ISBN 0-8214-0984-0. Vol. 3 1992 $55.00. ISBN 0-8214-1014-8. Vol. 4 1993 $55.00. ISBN 0-8214-1054-7. Important contribution to Gissing scholarship; good source for information on his life.

George Gissing and H. G. Wells: Their Friendship and Correspondence. Ed. by Royal A. Gettmann. Telegraph Bks. 1983 repr. of 1961 ed. o.p. The famous author's account of Gissing.

Letters of George Gissing to Members of His Family. Ed. by Algernon Gissing and Ellen Gissing. *Eng. Lit. Ser.* Haskell 1970 repr. of 1927 ed. $75.00. ISBN 0-8383-1158-X. Profound illustration of Gissing's turbulent life.

BOOKS ABOUT GISSING

Collie, Michael. *George Gissing: A Biography.* Shoe String 1977 o.p. Traces Gissing's life, from his bourgeois bohemian beginnings to his two collapsed marriages to his death.

Coustillas, Pierre, and Colin Partridge, eds. *Gissing: The Critical Heritage. Critical Heritage Ser.* Routledge 1972 $69.50. ISBN 0-7100-7367-4. Contemporary and near-contemporary criticisms and comments.

Goode, John. *George Gissing: Ideology and Fiction. Critical Studies Ser.* B & N Imports 1979 o.p. Analyzes the implications of Gissing's works within an economic and historical framework.

Halperin, John. *Gissing: A Life in Books.* OUP 1982 o.p. Develops an awareness of Gissing's work; proceeds chronologically through his life and work.

Selig, Robert L. *George Gissing. Twayne's Eng. Authors Ser.* G. K. Hall 1983 o.p. Places Gissing's creative achievement within an accompanying cultural and historical perspective.

Wolff, Joseph J. *George Gissing: An Annotated Bibliography of Writings about Him. Annotated Secondary Bibliography Ser. of Eng. Lit. in Transition, 1880–1920*. N. Ill. U. Pr. 1974 $30.00. ISBN 0-87580-038-6

HARDY, THOMAS. 1840–1928

Hardy achieved his initial fame as a novelist, winning acclaim with three early novels, *Under the Greenwood Tree* (1872), *A Pair of Blue Eyes* (1873), and *Far from the Madding Crowd* (1874). The last of these was especially successful commercially and allowed him to abandon architecture, the vocation for which he had been formally trained, and to marry. His start as a novelist, despite the ultimate fame that was to be his, was hardly auspicious. The publisher Chapman and Hall rejected his first novel, *The Poor Man and His Lady*, at the advice of their reader, GEORGE MEREDITH. Upset at the criticism that the novel "had not enough plot," Hardy destroyed the manuscript.

The setting of nearly all of Hardy's novels is the area of the ancient kingdom of Wessex (used as a fictitious county name by Hardy), the part of England that includes Dorsetshire, where Hardy grew up and where he settled after attaining literary success. As characteristic of Hardy's novels as their insistent Wessex setting is the underlying theme of his works, since nearly all of them deal with the struggle of their characters against an indifferent and deterministic world. The humor that is present in Hardy's works—and there is a good deal—is typically double-edged, simultaneously sardonic and sympathetic. Between 1874 and 1896, Hardy published a dozen novels, the most famous of which are *The Return of the Native* (1878), *The Mayor of Casterbridge* (1886), *Tess of the d'Urbervilles* (1891), and *Jude the Obscure* (1896). Both *Tess* and *Jude* were controversial and considered by many to be immoral and indecent. HENRY JAMES wrote of *Tess* that it was full of "faults and falsity," while *The Pall Mall Gazette* excoriated *Jude* as "dirt, drivel, and damnation." As Hardy writes in the 1912 preface to *Jude*, the book was burned by a bishop, "probably in despair at not being able to burn me." The furor the book aroused led Hardy to give up fiction for poetry.

Hardy's reputation as a poet was considerable during his lifetime and still attracts many casual readers as well as serious scholars. Between 1898 and 1928, he published eight volumes of poetry, which were collected in 1930 and are now available in *The Complete Poetical Works* edited by Samuel Hynes. Some of the most notable works of this period are *Poems of 1912–13*, which were composed in the year following the death of his first wife and look back over their often difficult life together. Hardy's most ambitious poem is *The Dynasts*, a long work in blank verse and prose published in three volumes (1904, 1906, 1908). Of his more than 900 poems, many like "The Blow," "The Convergence of the Twain," and "The Darkling Thrush" have demonstrated a remarkable endurance and have established themselves as important, if minor, works.

Although single-author scholarship has fallen somewhat out of fashion among Victorianists, a number of important works on Hardy emerge every year, and an edition of selected letters has recently been edited by Michael Millgate, whose *Thomas Hardy: A Biography* replaced Carl Weber's *Hardy of Wessex* as the standard critical biography. Another excellent recent addition to scholarly works on Hardy is Peter Widdowson's *Hardy in History*, which goes a good distance to explain the enduring interest in Hardy's works.

NOVELS BY HARDY

Desperate Remedies. 1871. St. Martin 1977 $3.95. ISBN 0-312-19494-3. First novel; published anonymously.

Far from the Madding Crowd: An Authoritative Text, Backgrounds, Criticism. 1874. Ed. by Robert C. Schweik. Norton 1988 $8.95. ISBN 0-393-95408-0. Story of impulsive Bathsheba Everdene and the three men in her life.

The Hand of Ethelberta: A Comedy in Chapters. St. Martin 1978 $3.95. ISBN 0-312-35736-2. Hardy associates Pugin's principles with the "true and eternal spirit of art."

Jude the Obscure. 1896. Ed. by Patricia Ingham. OUP 1985 $2.50. ISBN 0-19-281670-5. The talented and ambitious Jude Frawley hoped for much from life but received little.

A Laodicean. 1881. Ed. by Jane Gatewood. OUP 1991 $7.95. ISBN 0-19-282783-9. Represents the triumph of the creative architect and the return of high Victorian Gothic back into culture.

The Mayor of Casterbridge. 1886. Ed. by Dale Kramer. OUP 1987 $2.00. ISBN 0-19-281728-0. Tragic story of a man who sells his wife and child.

A Pair of Blue Eyes. 1873. Ed. by Roger Ebbatson. Viking Penguin 1986 $5.95. ISBN 0-14-043266-3. Successful novel.

The Return of the Native. 1878. Ed. by Simon Gatrell. OUP 1990 $4.95. ISBN 0-19-282717-0. Story of Clym Yeobright's return from Paris to his native town and his love for the ambitious and flighty Eustacia Vye.

Tess of the d'Urbervilles. 1891. Ed. by Juliet Grindle and Simon Gatrell. OUP 1988 $3.00. ISBN 0-19-281826-0. Tragic story of Tess, who is rejected by the man she loves and pursued by one she fears.

The Trumpet-Major. 1880. Ed. by Richard Nemesvari. OUP 1991 $3.00. ISBN 0-19-282718-9. A fictitious chronicle of historical fiction; an imaginative study of ordinary people and their faith. Includes a map of Wessex.

Two on a Tower: A Romance. St. Martin 1977 $3.95. ISBN 0-312-82742-3

Under the Greenwood Tree. 1872. Ed. by Simon Gatrell. OUP 1985 $1.65. ISBN 0-19-281706-X. His second novel; published anonymously. Life in rural Wessex through the story of Fanny Day and the three men who love her.

The Woodlanders. Ed. by Dale Kramer. OUP 1985 $4.95. ISBN 0-19-281600-4. Story of Grace Melbury who is trapped in a marriage arranged by her wealthy father.

SHORT STORY COLLECTION BY HARDY

Wessex Tales. 1888. Ed. by Kathryn R. King. OUP 1991 $3.00. ISBN 0-19-282720-0. A collection of short stories, including "The Three Strangers," "The Melancholy Hussor," and "The Son's Veto."

POETRY BY HARDY

The Complete Poems. Ed. by James Gibson. Macmillan 1982 $14.95. ISBN 0-02-069600-0. The student text.

The Complete Poems of Thomas Hardy. Macmillan 1989 $60.00. ISBN 0-02-632943-3. Superseded by Gibson's variorum edition and the Oxford, but still usable.

The Complete Poetical Works. 3 vols. Ed. by Samuel Hynes. OUP 1982–85 Vol. 1 1982 $79.00. ISBN 0-19-812708-1. Vol. 2 1984 $95.00. ISBN 0-19-812783-9. Vol. 3 1985 $69.00. ISBN 0-19-812784-7. The new standard edition.

The Variorum Edition of the Complete Poems of Thomas Hardy. Ed. by James Gibson. Macmillan 1980 o.p.

WORKS BY HARDY

The Collected Letters of Thomas Hardy. 7 vols. Ed. by Richard L. Purdy and Michael Millgate. OUP 1978–88 $59.00–$88.00 ea. ISBNs 0-19-812470-8, 0-19-812619-0, 0-19-812620-4, 0-19-812621-2, 0-19-812622-0, 0-19-812623-9, 0-19-812624-7

The Life and Work of Thomas Hardy. Ed. by Michael Millgate. U. of Ga. Pr. 1985 $40.00.
   ISBN 0-8203-0752-1. The reconstructed work of the manuscripts by Hardy originally
   published under his wife's name, Florence Hardy.
The Thomas Hardy Omnibus. St. Martin 1979 o.p.
Thomas Hardy: Selected Letters. OUP 1990 $41.00. ISBN 0-198-18546-4
The Works of Thomas Hardy in Prose and Verse. Johnson Repr. $3,000.00. ISBN 0-3842-
   1360-X. All the works, novels, and poetry.

Books about Hardy

Bailey, J. O. *An Essay on Hardy*. Cambridge U. Pr. 1978 $59.95. ISBN 0-521-28462-7
   _____. *Thomas Hardy and the Cosmic Mind: A New Reading of "The Dynasts."*
   Greenwood 1977 repr. of 1956 ed. $45.00. ISBN 0-8371-9743-0. A careful reading of
   The Dynasts, examining Hardy's philosophy and influences.
Bowra, C. M. *The Lyrical Poetry of Thomas Hardy*. Haskell 1975 $75.00. ISBN 0-8383-
   2098-8. Contains all of the lyrical poetry written by Hardy; includes a bibliography
   and index.
Carpenter, Richard C. *Thomas Hardy*. Macmillan 1964 $18.95. ISBN 0-8057-1244-5. An
   intelligent and perceptive analysis of Hardy's work.
Clements, Patricia, and Juliet Grindle, eds. *The Poetry of Thomas Hardy*. B & N Imports
   1980 o.p. Essays of a consistently high standard.
Das, Manas M. *Thomas Hardy—Poet of Tragic Vision: A Study of Hardy's Poetic
   Sensibility*. Humanities 1983 o.p. A doctoral dissertation springing from a disagree-
   ment on interpretation and evaluation of Hardy by other scholars; combines Indian
   ideals.
Davie, Donald. *Thomas Hardy and British Poetry*. OUP 1972 o.p. One of the best works of
   criticism of modern poetry generally.
Dean, Susan. *Hardy's Poetic Vision in The Dynasts: The Diorama of a Dream*. Princeton U.
   Pr. 1977 $47.00. ISBN 0-691-06324-9. Introduces a way of understanding *The Dynasts*
   by means of dissection and explanation.
Draper, Ronald P., and Martin Ray. *An Annotated Critical Bibliography of Thomas Hardy*.
   U. of Mich. Pr. 1989 $37.50. ISBN 0-472-10116-1. Recent critical bibliography.
Gatrell, Simon. *Hardy, the Creator: A Textual Biography*. OUP 1988 $45.00. ISBN 0-198-
   12810-X. Biography of Hardy through his writing.
Gerber, Helmut E., and W. Eugene Davis, eds. *Thomas Hardy: An Annotated Bibliography
   of Writings about Him*. 2 vols. N. Ill. U. Pr. Vol. 1 1973 $45.00. ISBN 0-87580-039-4.
   Vol. 2 1983 $50.00. ISBN 0-87580-091-2
Goode, John. *Thomas Hardy: The Offensive Truth*. Blackwell Pubs. 1988 $33.00. ISBN 0-
   631-13954-0. Discussion of Hardy's fiction and the reaction to it.
Hardy, Florence Emily Dugdale, comp. *The Life of Thomas Hardy*. Shoe String 1970 repr.
   of 1962 ed. o.p. Compiled by Hardy's second wife, largely from contemporary notes,
   letters, diaries, and biographical memoranda, as well as from oral information from
   conversations extending over many years.
Howe, Irving. *Thomas Hardy*. Masters of World Lit. Ser. Macmillan 1985 $6.95. ISBN 0-
   02-052010-7. Critical analysis of Hardy's major works, early and lesser novels, lyric
   poems, and verse trilogy; discussion of Hardy scholarship in preface.
Ingham, Patricia. *Thomas Hardy*. Humanities 1989 $29.95. ISBN 0-312-03734-1. Dis-
   cusses Hardy's uneasiness with the "new woman" of the late nineteenth century.
Johnson, Trevor. *A Critical Introduction to the Poems of Thomas Hardy*. St. Martin 1991
   $39.95. ISBN 0-312-05790-3. Helps to resituate Hardy as poet.
Lewis, C. Day. *Lyrical Poetry of Thomas Hardy*. Folcroft repr. of 1953 ed. o.p.
Meisel, Perry. *Thomas Hardy: The Return of the Repressed—A Study of the Major Fiction*.
   Yale U. Pr. 1972 $49.20. ISBN 0-835-78349-9. Essay discussing the intertextual
   tension in Hardy's writings.
Miller, J. Hillis. *Thomas Hardy: Distance and Desire*. HUP 1970 o.p. Discusses the
   characteristics of Hardy's writing; examines character development and plot.

Millgate, Michael. *Thomas Hardy: A Biography*. OUP 1985 $13.95. ISBN 0-19-281472-9.
Definitive biography that draws extensively on diaries, notebooks, letters, local
records, and contemporary newspapers to explore Hardy as man and artist.

Page, Norman. ed. *Thomas Hardy: The Writer and His Background*. St. Martin 1980
$27.50. ISBN 0-312-80132-7. Sets Hardy in both his contexts.

Paulin, Thomas. *Thomas Hardy: The Poetry of Perception*. Rowman 1975 o.p. Probably
the best single book on Hardy's poetry.

Pinion, F. B. *A Commentary on the Poems of Thomas Hardy*. B & N Imports 1976 o.p.
Mainly biographical and geographical notes.

_____. *A Thomas Hardy Dictionary*. NYU Pr. 1989 $50.00. ISBN 0-8147-6610-2. Useful
guide to Hardy's life and his Wessex novels.

Richardson, James. *Thomas Hardy: The Poetry of Necessity*. U. Ch. Pr. 1977 o.p. One of
the few books on Thomas Hardy's poetry by a poet.

Saxelby, F. Outwin. *A Thomas Hardy Dictionary: The Characters and Scenes of the Novels
and Poems Alphabetically Arranged and Described*. Greenwood 1980 repr. of 1911 ed.
$35.00. ISBN 0-313-22078-6. The characters and scenes of the novels and poems
alphabetically arranged and described.

Taylor, Dennis. *Hardy's Poetry, 1860–1928*. Col. U. Pr. 1981 o.p. Evaluates Hardy's "plot"
and its implications for his development and style of writing.

Vigar, Penelope. *The Novels of Thomas Hardy: Illusion and Reality*. Humanities 1974 o.p.

Weber, Carl J. *Hardy in America: A Study of Thomas Hardy and His American Readers*.
Russell 1966 repr. of 1946 ed. o.p.

_____. *Hardy of Wessex*. 1940. Col. U. Pr. 1965 o.p. An outstanding critical biography,
notable for its scholarly accuracy and balanced appraisal, but now replaced by
Millgate.

Widdowson, Peter. *Hardy in History*. Routledge 1989 $49.50. ISBN 0-415-01330-5.
Excellent analysis of Hardy's role in literary history.

Williams, Merryn. *A Preface to Hardy*. Longman 1976 $6.95. ISBN 0-582-09563-8. A
readable and unexpectedly positive study of Hardy's prose and verse; examines the
depth and power of tragic emotions.

Wright, T. R. *Hardy and the Erotic*. St. Martin 1989 $39.95. ISBN 0-312-8204-0939-1.
Demonstrates Hardy's "undercutting of liberal-humanist" myths about sexuality.

HOPKINS, GERARD MANLEY. 1844–1889

Hopkins and his near contemporary OSCAR WILDE represent the two extremes
of the late Victorian dichotomy. Starting in the aesthetic center shared by
RUSKIN and PATER, the heroes of the university, one moved toward flamboyance,
decadence, and ruin; the other moved toward asceticism, self-denial, and what
some might call an equivalent end.

Before Hopkins converted to Catholicism and became a Jesuit in 1868, he had
been considered the star of Balliol College at Oxford; however, when he entered
the novitiate, he burned all of his youthful poems. Seven years later, at the
instigation of his superiors, he resumed the practice of poetry in the composition of his finest long work, *The Wreck of the Deutschland*, a poem about the
1875 sinking of a German ship carrying five exiled German nuns. The Jesuit
magazine to which he submitted it declined to print it, and declined again with a
later poem, so none of his poems had more than manuscript existence until
1918, when his closest friend and fellow poet, Robert Bridges, collected them,
wrote a short prefatory study of Hopkins's innovations, and published the
Poems.

Hopkins's verse, with its fusion of romantic and Christian images and its
sophisticated metrical patterning, can appear difficult at first reading. However,
because Hopkins was a brilliant theorist and analyst of his own work, and left so
many letters explaining his otherwise obscure concepts, such as "inscape,"

"instress," and "sprung rhythm," his poetry has been well served by critics. With the *Poems*, a selection of the prose, and any one of the secondary works listed below, a reader will encounter few obstacles to Hopkins's grandeur.

POETRY BY HOPKINS

Gerard Manley Hopkins. Pocket Poets Ser. Dufour 1969 o.p. Examines Hopkins's major poems, ranging throughout his entire career.

Major Poems. Biblio Dist. 1979 o.p. Discusses the poems on which his reputation as a major poet was formed; goes through the years 1875–1889.

Poems. 1918. Ed. by W. H. Gardner and Norman H. Mackenzie. OUP 1967 $10.95. ISBN 0-19-281094-4. The definitive edition.

The Wreck of the Deutschland. Godine 1971 $6.00 o.p.

WORKS BY HOPKINS

The Early Poetic Manuscripts and Note-Books of Gerard Manley Hopkins in Facsimile. Ed. by Norman H. MacKenzie. Garland 1989 $100.00. ISBN 0-824-03898-3. Collection of Hopkins's early work, much never before published.

Gerard Manley Hopkins: Selected Letters. Ed. by Catherine Phillips. OUP 1990 $37.00. ISBN 0-19-818582-0. Useful, eclectic selection.

The Later Poetic Manuscripts of Gerard Manley Hopkins in Facsimile. Ed. by Norman H. MacKenzie. Garland 1991 $125.00. ISBN 0-8240-7444-0. Good facsimile edition of Hopkins's manuscripts; of interest to textual scholars.

Poems and Prose of Hopkins. Ed. by W. H. Gardner. Viking Penguin 1953 $8.95. ISBN 0-14-042015-0. The student text, combining poems and letters.

BOOKS ABOUT HOPKINS

Bender, Todd K. *Gerard Manley Hopkins: The Classical Background and Critical Reception of His Work.* Bks. Demand repr. of 1966 ed. $45.50. ISBN 0-317-55514-6. Incorporates reviews of the author's work and a sketch of his background.

Bump, Jerome. *Gerard Manley Hopkins.* Macmillan 1982 $20.95. ISBN 0-8057-6819-X. Rises far above the usual biographical treatment.

Downes, David A. *The Great Sacrifice: Studies in Hopkins.* U. Pr. of Amer. 1983 o.p.

Dunne, Tom. *Gerard Manley Hopkins: A Comprehensive Bibliography.* Omnigraphics Inc. 1978 repr. of 1976 ed. $70.00. ISBN 0-906795-21-4. A chronological overview of the author's published writings.

Ellsberg, Margaret R. *Created to Praise: The Language of Gerard Manley Hopkins.* OUP 1987 $15.95. ISBN 0-19-504098-8. Formalist-linguistic reading of the poetry.

Harris, Daniel A. *Inspirations Unbidden: The "Terrible Sonnets" of Gerard Manley Hopkins.* U. CA Pr. 1982 $37.50. ISBN 0-520-04539-4. An outstanding study.

Kenyon Critics. *Gerard Manley Hopkins.* New Dir. Pr. 1973 $2.45. ISBN 0-812-0479-0. Eight essays reprinted from *The Kenyon Review;* includes a biographical sketch and studies of the poet's verse, symbolism and imagery, religious nature, and Victorian heritage.

Lichtmann, Maria R. *The Contemplative Poetry of Gerard Manley Hopkins.* Princeton U. Pr. 1989 $29.50. ISBN 0-691-07345-7. Discussion of Hopkins's poetry as meditation and prayer.

MacKenzie, Norman H. *A Reader's Guide to Gerard Manley Hopkins.* Cornell Univ. Pr. 1981 $13.95. ISBN 0-8014-9221-1. Handy reference providing authoritative interpretations of Hopkins's poetry and background on his life; includes cross-references to other critical works and extended bibliography.

Roberts, Gerald. *Gerard Manley Hopkins.* Routledge 1987 $88.50. ISBN 0-7102-0414-0. Selective collection of the critical reception of Hopkins's work.

Robinson, John. *In Extremity.* Cambridge U. Pr. 1980 o.p. Evaluates Hopkins's religious commitment; examines his religious ideals in his writing.

Schneider, Elisabeth. *The Dragon in the Gate: Studies in the Poetry of Gerard Manley Hopkins.* U. CA Pr. 1968 o.p.

Sprinker, Michael. *A Counterpoint of Dissonance: The Aesthetics and Poetry of Gerard Manley Hopkins*. Johns Hopkins 1980 $20.00. ISBN 0-8018-2402-8. A poststructuralist account.

Storey, Graham. *A Preface to Hopkins*. Longman 1981 o.p. The best general introduction.

Walhout, Donald. *Send My Roots Rain: A Study of Religious Experience in the Poetry of Gerard Manley Hopkins*. Ohio U. Pr. 1981 $16.95. ISBN 0-8214-0565-9. A full-length study of how the structure of Hopkins's religious experience characteristically informs his poetry.

White, Norman. *Hopkins: A Literary Biography*. OUP 1992 $25.00. ISBN 0-19-812099-0. Good, up-to-date biography.

HUDSON, WILLIAM HENRY. 1841–1922

William Henry Hudson, born in South America of American parents, was both a naturalist and a novelist. He chose to serve each of two masters and reached distinction under both. His book *The Purple Land* (1885) is a story of Uruguay, "the land that England lost." *A Crystal Age* (1906) is a utopia, a picture of a paragon world. *Green Mansions* (1904), perhaps his best-known work, is an idyllic allegorical romance of South America. His autobiography, *Far Away and Long Ago* (1918), has a matchless charm. *W. H. Hudson's Diary, 1874: Voyages from Buenos Aires to Southampton* contains descriptions of great force and beauty. Hudson is a stylist whose books are rich in beautiful lyric prose. In all his works, he combined a gift for storytelling with a deep feeling for nature.

NOVELS BY HUDSON

A Crystal Age. 1906. AMS Pr. repr. of 1922 ed. $35.00. ISBN 0-404-03392-X

Fan: The Story of a Young Girl's Life. 1892. AMS Pr. repr. of 1923 ed. $35.00. ISBN 0-404-03394-6

Green Mansions: A Romance of the Tropical Forest. 1904. AMS Pr. repr. of 1923 ed. $35.00. ISBN 0-404-03402-0

A Little Boy Lost: Together with the Poems. 1905. AMS Pr. repr. of 1923 ed. $35.00. ISBN 0-404-03403-9

The Purple Land: Being the Narrative of One Richard Lamb's Adventures in the Banda Oriental in South America as Told by Himself. AMS Pr. repr. of 1922 ed. $35.00. ISBN 0-404-03391-1

SHORT STORY COLLECTION BY HUDSON

El Ombú and Other South American Stories. 1902. AMS Pr. repr. of 1923 ed. $35.00. ISBN 0-404-03400-4

NONFICTION BY HUDSON

Dead Man's Plack; An Old Thorn; and Miscellanea. 1920. AMS Pr. repr. of 1923 ed. $25.00. ISBN 0-404-03414-4

Hampshire Days. 1903. AMS Pr. repr. of 1923 ed. $35.00. ISBN 0-404-03401-2. Notes on the natural history of the area, its animals, plants, and sights.

A Hind in Richmond Park. 1922. AMS Pr. repr. of 1923 ed. $35.00. ISBN 0-404-03413-6. With a prefatory note by Morley Roberts.

Idle Days in Patagonia. 1893. AMS Pr. repr. of 1923 ed. $35.00. ISBN 0-404-03395-4

The Land's End: A Naturalist's Impression in West Cornwall. 1908. AMS Pr. repr. of 1923 ed. $35.00. ISBN 0-404-03404-7. Travel notes, a history of the area, the peoples of the area, its animals and vegetation, and so forth.

A Shepherd's Life: Impressions of the South Wiltshire Downs. 1910. AMS Pr. repr. of 1923 ed. $35.00. ISBN 0-404-03406-3. A fascinating study of Wiltshire animals, vegetation, and shepherds.'

A Traveller in Little Things. 1921. AMS Pr. repr. of 1923 ed. $35.00. ISBN 0-404-03412-8

WORKS BY HUDSON

Collected Works. 24 vols. AMS Pr. repr. of 1923 ed. $840.00. ISBN 0-404-03390-3.
  Contains volumes of fiction also listed here under NOVELS.
Far Away and Long Ago. 1918. AMS Pr. repr. of 1923 ed. $35.00. ISBN 0-404-03408-X

BOOKS ABOUT HUDSON

Payne, John R. *W. H. Hudson: A Bibliography.* U. Pr. of Va. 1977 o.p.
Roberts, Morley. *W. H. Hudson: A Portrait.* Richard West repr. of 1924 ed. o.p. A
  biography that delves into Hudson's life and writings.
Tomalin, Ruth. *W. H. Hudson: A Biography.* Greenwood repr. of 1954 ed. o.p.
Wilson, G. F. *A Bibliography of the Writings of W. H. Hudson. Eng. Lit. Ser.* Haskell 1972
  repr. of 1922 ed. $55.95. ISBN 0-8383-1510-0

HUXLEY, THOMAS HENRY. 1825–1895

[SEE Volume 5.]

JERROLD, DOUGLAS WILLIAM. 1803–1857

Jerrold became a well-known wit and playwright, and even turned his hand at novel writing, but his beginnings were humble at best. Born into a theatrical family, he was educated haphazardly as a child. He was enrolled for a short time in a school in Sheerness, but in 1813, at the age of 10, he enlisted in the navy, serving in the final phases of the Napoleonic wars. In the 1820s he returned to the theater and became the dramatic author for the Surrey Theatre. In 1829 his first big hit, *Black-Eyed Susan*, was produced, and his career as a dramatist began. Other dramatic successes included *Fifteen Years of a Drunken's Life* (1828), *Rent Day* (1832), and *The Prisoner of War* (1842), but none ever equaled the success of *Black-Eyed Susan* either in popularity or in quality.

By 1835 Jerrold had also established himself as a prominent journalist, writing for works like *Blackwood's Magazine* and, along with HENRY MAYHEW and J. S. COYNE, helping to found *Punch* magazine in 1841. His was the dominant satiric voice of the magazine until 1847, when he was replaced by WILLIAM MAKEPEACE THACKERAY. At about the same time, he undertook to establish *Douglas Jerrold's Shilling Magazine* and *Douglas Jerrold's Weekly Newspaper*. Both ultimately failed. In 1845 he published what John Sutherland has called "his one novel proper," *The History of St. Giles and St. James*. In it his politics are at their most liberal, and his intense loathing of tyranny, which he apparently developed in the navy, is articulated in an attempt to demonstrate "the ignorant disregard of the social claims of the poor upon the rich, of the governed millions on the governing few" (Preface, 1851 edition).

Most scholarship on Jerrold concentrates on his contributions to the theater or is included in works on the history of *Punch*. His biographies *The Life and Remains of Douglas Jerrold*, by W. Blanchard Jerrold, and *Douglas Jerrold, Dramatist and Wit*, by Walter Jerrold, by his son and grandson, respectively, are somewhat flawed by their sentimental and anecdotal character. Nevertheless, they remain fairly good sources for information about Jerrold's life.

NOVEL BY JERROLD

The History of St. Giles and St. James. Bradbury & Evans 1859 o.p. Issued in serial, 1845.

WORK BY JERROLD

Writing of Douglas Jerrold. Bradbury & Evans 1853–54 o.p.

BOOKS ABOUT JERROLD

Jerrold, Walter. *Douglas Jerrold and "Punch," by Walter Jerrold.* Macmillan 1910 o.p. Good on Douglas Jerrold's affiliation with *Punch.*

————. *Douglas Jerrold, Dramatist and Wit.* Hodder & Stroughton 1914 o.p. More even-handed than the W. Blanchard Jerrold biography. Good on the plays.

Jerrold, W. Blanchard. *The Life and Remains of Douglas Jerrold.* Bentley 1859 o.p.

Kelly, Richard Michael. *Douglas Jerrold.* Twayne 1972 o.p. Connects Jerrold's dramatic writing to his journalistic career.

JONES, HENRY ARTHUR. 1851–1929

Jones was the oldest son of a Buckinghamshire farmer. His formal education lasted only until he was 12, when he went to work for his uncle, who kept a drapery shop. Although he may have begun writing dramas as early as 1869, his first play was not produced until 1878 in a small theater in Exeter; four years later he achieved success in London with *The Silver King.* He was a contemporary and good friend of ARTHUR WING PINERO, who was also his strongest rival for audiences. Jones's plays were extremely popular, and he was encouraged early in his career by GEORGE BERNARD SHAW and MAX BEERBOHM. Although he wrote many comedies, including *The Liars* (1897), his most provocative works treat social themes, especially double standards for the sexes and sexual prudery. In *Michael and His Lost Angel* (1895), he outraged London audiences both by depicting a church scene and by having one of his characters, a clergyman, participate in an adulterous affair.

With Pinero, Jones is greatly responsible for reestablishing serious themes in late Victorian drama and in marking an important transition from the melodrama and spectacle that had characterized the early and middle years of nineteenth-century theater. The author of a number of periodical articles on drama, Jones was a leading advocate in the repeal of censorship laws. Although early in his career he was a socialist and a friend of Emery Walker and WILLIAM MORRIS, in later life he became an entrenched conservative and often argued in print with leftist men of letters, like H. G. WELLS and Shaw. His works are still admired for their dramatic construction and, at their best, their flexible and convincing dialogue. Although he was neither as clever a wit as OSCAR WILDE nor as shrewd a social commentator as Shaw, Jones was an important precursor to both. There are few full-length studies of Jones, though Penny Griffin has published a work on Jones and Pinero that is intended for a broad audience.

PLAYS BY JONES

Representative Plays. 4 vols. Scholarly 1925 $295.00. ISBN 0-403-01054-3. Collected plays of Jones.

WORKS ABOUT JONES

Cordell, Richard Albert. *Henry Arthur Jones and the Modern Drama.* 1932. Kennikat 1968 o.p. A bit old-fashioned but still useful.

Griffin, Penny. *Arthur Wing Pinero and Henry Arthur Jones.* St. Martin 1991 $19.95. ISBN 0-312-05572-2

Jones, Doris Arthur. *Taking the Curtain Call: The Life and Letters of Henry Arthur Jones.* Macmillan 1930 o.p. Best source of information on Jones's life.

KAY-SHUTTLEWORTH, SIR JAMES PHILLIPS. 1804–1877

James P. Kay-Shuttleworth was born into a prominent Lancashire family. As a youth he worked in the bank of a relative and seemed set on finance as a profession. However, in 1824 he enrolled in the University of Edinburgh as a medical student and soon proved to be one of the most promising of his class. While a student he assisted the famed Dr. Alison (of CARLYLE's *Past and Present* and CHADWICK's *Sanitary Report*). This experience, together with time spent studying in Dublin and the beginning of his practice in one of the poorer sections of Manchester, brought the plight of the urban working classes directly to his attention. The result is one of his most famous texts, *The Moral and Physical Condition of the Working Classes Employed in the Cotton Manufacture in Manchester* (1832), in which he describes the horrendous unsanitary conditions that the working classes faced daily. In 1835 he became an assistant Poor Law commissioner and began his investigations into the training of pauper children, the first report on which he published in 1841. His efforts in this area led him to become interested in the establishment of publicly funded education in England.

Along with E. Carleton Tufnell, Kay-Shuttleworth established the first training college for teachers at Battersea. He advocated the use of student teachers: older students who would teach elementary school children and in return receive secondary school education from the elementary school headmasters. He was also a strong advocate of a school inspection system and was instrumental in establishing British public education.

Although little work has been done on Kay-Shuttleworth, he was one of the most influential men of the period. His early work on the conditions of the working class in Lancashire is unparalleled for its investigative rigor and its unflinching gaze at the opprobrium that the manufacturing towns produced.

NONFICTION BY KAY-SHUTTLEWORTH

Memorandum on Popular Education. 1868. Kelley 1969 o.p. Important public document on the state of education in England in the mid-nineteenth century.

The Moral and Physical Condition of the Working Classes Employed in the Cotton Manufacture in Manchester. 1832. Kelley 1970 $25.00. ISBN 0-678-05107-0. With a new preface by W. H. Chaloner; Kay's most famous work, an early sociological investigation of the working classes in England.

Sir James Kay-Shuttleworth on Popular Education. Ed. by Trygve R. Tholfsen. Tchrs. Coll. 1974 o.p. Collection of Kay's writings on education for the lower classes.

Thoughts and Suggestions on Certain Social Problems, Contained Chiefly in Addresses to Meetings of Workmen in Lancashire. 1873. E. J. Morten 1973 o.p. Puts forward Kay's utilitarian views, especially on education.

The Training of Pauper Children: Report Published by the Poor Commissioners in Their Fourth Annual Report. 1841. E. J. Morten 1970 o.p.

WORKS ABOUT KAY-SHUTTLEWORTH

Smith, Frank, and Ughtred James Shuttleworth. *The Life and Work of Sir James Kay-Shuttleworth.* J. Murray UK 1923 o.p. Standard biography. With an introduction by Sir Michael Sadler and a chapter by Lord Ughtred James Shuttleworth.

KINGSLEY, CHARLES. 1819–1875

Charles Kingsley, a clergyman of the Church of England, who late in his life held the chair of history at Cambridge University, wrote mostly didactic historical romances. He put the historical novel to new use, not to teach history, but to illustrate some religious truth. *Westward Ho!* (1855), his best-known work, is a tale of the Spanish main in the days of Queen Elizabeth I. *Hypatia: New Foes with Old Faces* (1853) is the story of a pagan girl-philosopher who was torn to pieces by a Christian mob. The story is strongly anti-Roman Catholic, reflecting Kingsley's controversy with JOHN HENRY NEWMAN (see Vol. 4) at the time of the Oxford movement. *Hereward the Wake, or The Watchful* (1866) is a tale of a Saxon outlaw. *The Water-Babies* (1863), written for Kingsley's youngest child, "would be a tale for children were it not for the satire directed at the parents of the period," said Andrew Lang. *Alton Locke* (1850) and *Yeast* (1851) reflect Kingsley's leadership in "muscular Christianity" and his dramatization of social issues.

Kingsley used the pseudonym "Parson Lot" on papers he wrote for magazines. Of his poems, the most characteristic is the ballad-song "Sands of Dee."

NOVELS BY KINGSLEY

Alton Locke: Tailor and Poet. 1850. Scholarly 1971 repr. of 1928 ed. $39.00. ISBN 0-403-01056-X

At Last: A Christmas in the West Indies. 1871. Folcroft repr. of 1900 ed. o.p. Notes on places visited, places Kingsley's mother had described, with notes on the vegetation.

The Hermits. 1878. Folcroft repr. o.p.

Hereward the Wake, or The Watchful. 1866. AMS repr. of 1935 ed. $36.00. ISBN 0-404-20146-6

Hypatia: New Foes with Old Faces. 1853. Garber Comm. 1987 repr. of 1882 ed. $14.50. ISBN 0-8334-0020-7

Two Years Ago. 1857. Arden Lib. 1983 repr. of 1887 ed. o.p. Tells the story of a love-struck dilettante's pursuit across Europe of a beautiful quadroon, a former slave, who is pretending to be an Italian actress.

The Water-Babies. 1863. Crown Pub. Group 1986 $7.98. ISBN 0-517-61817-6. A "fable."

Westward Ho! 1855. Macmillan Child Grp. 1992 $26.95. ISBN 0-684-19444-9

Yeast: A Problem. 1851. Biblio Dist. 1976 o.p.

WORKS BY KINGSLEY

Charles Kingsley: His Letters and Memories of His Life. 2 vols. AMS Pr. repr. of 1877 ed. $37.50. ISBN 0-404-08869-4. A standard source of printed material on Kingsley; the official biography.

The Heroes of Greek Fairy Tales for My Children. 1856. Folcroft o.p. A retelling of the legends of Perseus, the Argonauts, and Theseus.

Life and Works of Charles Kingsley. 28 vols. Adlers Foreign Bks. 1969 repr. of 1880 ed. o.p. The most nearly complete edition of Kingsley's work.

BOOKS ABOUT KINGSLEY

Colloms, Brenda. *Charles Kingsley: The Lion of Eversley.* B & N Imports 1975 o.p. Emphasizes Kingsley's attitudes toward the working classes.

Stubbs, Charles W. *Charles Kingsley and the Christian Social Movement.* AMS Pr. repr. of 1899 ed. $17.50. ISBN 0-404-08914-3

Uffelman, Larry K. *Charles Kingsley.* Twayne's Eng. Authors Ser. G. K. Hall 1949 o.p.

KIPLING, RUDYARD. 1865–1936 (NOBEL PRIZE 1907)

Kipling, who as a novelist dramatized the ambivalence of the British colonial experience, was born of English parents in Bombay and as a child knew Hindustani better than English. He spent an unhappy period of exile from his parents (and the Indian heat) with a harsh aunt in England, followed by the public schooling that inspired his "Stalky" stories. He returned to India at 18 to work on the staff of the Lahore *Civil and Military Gazette* and rapidly became a prolific writer. His mildly satirical work won him a reputation in England, and he returned there in 1889. Shortly after, his first novel, *The Light That Failed* (1890) was published, but it was not altogether successful.

In the early 1890s, Kipling met and married Caroline Balestier and moved with her to her family's estate in Brattleboro, Vermont. While there he wrote

Many Inventions (1893), *The Jungle Book* (1894–95), and *Captains Courageous* (1897). He became dissatisfied with life in America, however, and moved back to England, returning to America only when his daughter died of pneumonia. Kipling never again returned to the United States, despite his great popularity there.

Short stories form the greater portion of Kipling's work and are of several distinct types. Some of his best are stories of the supernatural, the eerie and unearthly, such as "The Phantom Rickshaw," "The Brushwood Boy," and "They." His tales of gruesome horror include "The Mark of the Beast" and "The Return of Imray." "William the Conqueror" and "The Head of the District" are among his political tales of English rule in India. The "Soldiers Three" group deals with Kipling's three musketeers—an Irishman, a Cockney, and a Yorkshireman. The Anglo-Indian Tales, of social life in Simla, make up the larger part of his first four books.

Kipling wrote equally well for children and adults. His best-known children's books are *Just So Stories* (1902), *The Jungle Books* (1894-95), and *Kim* (1901). Some critics, like GEORGE ORWELL and LIONEL TRILLING, have dismissed him from serious consideration; others, such as T. S. ELIOT and Bonamy Dobrée, have affirmed his genius. EDMUND WILSON, in *The Wound and the Bow*, sees his great failing as an artist in the fact that, although he sometimes appeared to be torn between two cultures, he avoided significant dramatic conflict (which would have brought his work stature) by ending up, predictably, on the side of authority. His short stories—although their understanding of the Indian is often moving—became minor hymns to the glory of Queen Victoria's empire and the civil servants and soldiers who staffed her outposts. *Kim*, an Irish boy in India who becomes the companion of a Tibetan lama, at length joins the British Secret Service, without, says Wilson, any sense of the betrayal of his friend this actually meant. Nevertheless, Kipling has left us a vivid panorama of the India of his day.

Kipling is England's first Nobel Prize winner in literature and the only nineteenth-century English poet to win the Prize; he won not only on the basis of his short stories, which more closely mirror the ambiguities of the declining Edwardian world than has commonly been recognized, but also on the basis of his tremendous ability as a popular poet. His reputation was first made with *Barrack Room Ballads* (1892), and in "Recessional" he captured a side of Queen Victoria's final jubilee that no one else dared to address. Kipling's genius lies neither in his patriotic fervor nor in his music hall rhythms but rather in the underlying spirit that, as J. I. M. Stewart said in his study of Kipling, always manages to "pluck something affirmative from the abyss."

NOVELS BY KIPLING

Captains Courageous. 1897. Bantam 1985 $2.25. ISBN 0-553-21190-0. Story of a teenage boy's adventures on a New England fishing boat.
The Jungle Books. 1894–95. Ed. by Daniel Karbin. Viking Penguin 1987 $2.95. ISBN 0-14-043282-5. Story of Mowgli, a boy raised in the wild among animals.
Kim. 1901. Ed. by Edward W. Said. Viking Penguin 1987 $2.95. ISBN 0-14-043281-7. Good edition.
The Light That Failed. 1890. Viking Penguin 1988 $5.95. ISBN 0-14-43283-3. Introduction by John Lyon; inexpensive, well-edited edition. Story of a young artist and soldier who faces blindness and the loss of a woman's love.
The Second Jungle Book. 1895. Doubleday 1923 o.p.
The Seven Seas. Longwood Pr. 1978 repr. of 1897 ed. o.p. Verse collection tributes to "tommies" and "tars" everywhere—British fighting men.

SHORT STORY COLLECTIONS BY KIPLING

The Courting of Dinah Shadd and Other Stories. Short Story Index Repr. Ser. Ayer repr. of 1890 ed. $12.50. ISBN 0-8369-3773-2

The Day's Work. Short Story Index Repr. Ser. Ed. by Thomas Pinney. OUP 1987 $2.95. ISBN 0-19-281714-0

Just So Stories. 1902. Ed. by Peter Levi. Viking Penguin 1987 $2.95. ISBN 0-14-043302-3

Kipling: Short Stories. 2 vols. Ed. by Andrew Rutherford. Viking Penguin 1977 o.p. Twenty-eight tales by the master.

Kipling's India: Uncollected Sketches, 1884–88. Ed. by Thomas Pinney. Macmillan 1986 o.p. A selection of newspaper articles about Kipling's work in India from 1884 to 1888.

The Man Who Would Be King and Other Stories. Ed. by Louis L. Cornell. OUP 1987 $7.95. ISBN 0-19-281652-7. Two adventurers, released from the British Army in India, aspire to riches and meet with disaster.

Mulvaney Stories. Short Story Index Repr. Ser. Ayer repr. of 1897 ed. $15.00. ISBN 0-8369-4045-8

Plain Tales from the Hills. Ed. by Andrew Rutherford. OUP 1987 $5.95. ISBN 0-19-281652-7. Short stories focusing on the British Colonial experience in India.

Soldier Stories. Short Story Index Repr. Ser. Ayer. repr. of 1899 ed. $16.00. ISBN 0-8369-3356-7

Stalky and Company. Puffin Bks. 1988 $2.25. ISBN 0-317-69643-2. A collection of stories previously published in magazines.

POETRY BY KIPLING

A Choice of Kipling's Verse. Ed. by T. S. Eliot. Faber & Faber 1963 $8.95. ISBN 0-571-05444-7. Verse selected by T. S. Eliot; includes an essay by Eliot on the poet.

Complete Verse. Kyle Cathie 1990 o.p. Introduction by M. M. Kaye.

Early Verse by Rudyard Kipling, 1879–1889: Unpublished, Uncollected, and Rarely Collected Poems. Ed. by Andrew Rutherford. OUP 1986 $34.50. ISBN 0-19-812323-X. Verse that has not been published because it was thought to be his "younger" work or was found only recently.

Rudyard Kipling's Verse. Doubleday 1940 $19.95. ISBN 0-385-04407-0. The definitive edition; includes the verses he liked to append to his stories.

NONFICTION BY KIPLING

American Notes. Foreign Travelers in Amer. Ayer 1974 repr. of 1891 ed. $13.00. ISBN 0-405-05463-7. Description of travels in the United States from 1865 to 1918.

Book of Words. Essay Index Repr. Ser. Ayer repr. of 1928 ed. $17.00. ISBN 0-8369-1884-3. Contains 31 speeches.

Something of Myself and Other Autobiographical Writings. Ed. by Thomas Pinney. Cambridge U. Pr. 1990 $10.95. ISBN 0-521-35515-X. Personal accounts of others by Kipling; represents the author's thoughts on society and his circle.

WORKS BY KIPLING

Collected Works. 28 vols. AMS Pr. repr. of 1941 ed. o.p.

The Letters of Rudyard Kipling, 1: 1872–1889; 2: 1890–1899. 2 vols. Ed. by Thomas Pinney. U. of Iowa Pr. 1991 $42.95 ea. ISBNs 0-87745-305-5, 0-87745-306-3. An insightful representation of letters by the author revealing his thoughts, loves, and disappointments.

Letters of Travel, 1892–1913. 1920. Amereon Ltd. o.p.

O Beloved Kids: Rudyard Kipling's Letters to his Children. HarBraceJ 1984 o.p.

War Stories and Poems. Ed. by Andrew Rutherford. OUP 1990 $6.95. ISBN 0-19-282656-5

BOOKS ABOUT KIPLING

Bloom, Harold, ed. *Rudyard Kipling.* Chelsea Hse. 1987 $19.95. ISBN 0-88754646-0. Good collection of recent essays.

————, ed. *Rudyard Kipling's "Kim."* Chelsea Hse. 1987 $24.95. ISBN 1-55546-022-4. Good collection of essays on the novel.

Cornell, Luis L. *Kipling in India.* Telegraph Bks. 1982 repr. of 1966 ed. o.p. A study of Kipling's literary apprenticeship; contains 23 uncollected and unpublished early works.

Dobrée, Bonamy. *Rudyard Kipling: Realist and Fabulist.* OUP 1967 o.p. A study of Kipling's work by an eminent critic, who rallies to his defense as a writer "grotesquely misunderstood" and "misrepresented."

Durback, Renee. *Kipling's South Africa.* Chameleon Bks. 1988 o.p. A useful study of the role of South Africa in Kipling's works.

Green, Roger L., ed. *Kipling: The Critical Heritage.* Critical Heritage Ser. Routledge 1971 $33.75. ISBN 0-7100-6978-2. Contemporary and near-contemporary criticism, reviews, and comments.

Kemp, Sandra. *Kipling's Hidden Narratives.* Blackwell Pubs. 1988 $45.00. ISBN 0-631-15577-5. Examines Kipling's politics as seen in his works.

McClure, John. *Kipling and Conrad: The Colonial Fiction.* HUP 1981 $22.00. ISBN 0-674-50529-8. Conrad and Kipling each bear the stamp of their time; examines the effects of authoritarianism on both personalities.

Moore-Gilbert, B. J. *Kipling and "Orientalism."* St. Martin 1986 $27.50. ISBN 0-312-45644-1. Interesting study of Kipling and representations of the East.

Moss, Robert F. *Rudyard Kipling and the Fiction of Adolescence.* St. Martin 1982 $23.95. ISBN 0-312-69549-7. Examines Kipling's early works; shows the roots of his genius and its manifestation in later life.

Orel, Harold, ed. *Critical Essays on Rudyard Kipling.* G. K. Hall 1989 $40.00. ISBN 0-8161-8767-3. Uneven collection.

Rao, K. Bhaskara. *Rudyard Kipling's India.* U. of Okla. Pr. 1967 o.p. A critical view of Kipling's political and racial attitudes (as expressed in his work), which Rao, an Indian living in the United States, regards as having strengthened the reactionary forces of British imperialism.

Rutherford, Andrew, ed. *Kipling's Mind and Art: Selected Critical Essays.* Stanford U. Pr. 1964 $37.50. ISBN 0-8047-0212-8. A collection of 11 essays by English and American scholars who agree that Kipling has been too easily dismissed.

Wilson, Angus. *The Strange Ride of Rudyard Kipling: His Life and Works.* Viking Penguin 1978 o.p. High intellectual adventure and a moving narrative.

Younge, W. Arthur, and John H. McGivering. *A Kipling Dictionary.* Gordon Pr. 1972 $250.00. ISBN 0-8490-0473-X. Includes entries on about 1,000 titles by Kipling.

LEWES, GEORGE HENRY. 1817–1878

Today Lewes is remembered primarily as the consort of GEORGE ELIOT, with whom he lived—but never married—from 1854 until his death. Because he had condoned his wife Agnes's adulterous relationship with T. L. Hunt, Lewes was unable to obtain a divorce. In 1850 Agnes bore the first of four of Hunt's children, whom Lewes adopted as his own.

Lewes was well known and respected as an intellectual, traveling in the most progressive and free-thinking society that Victorian London could offer. Always a great encourager of the somewhat retiring Eliot, he was also a prolific author in his own right, making significant contributions in philosophy and literary criticism. He was the author of one of the first books in English on the philosophy of AUGUSTE COMTE (see Vols. 3 and 4), *Comte's Philosophy of Science* (1853), and wrote essays on a number of topics, including Hegelian aesthetics, political economy, and popular drama. Lewes's *Biographical History of Philosophy* (1845), notable for its adherence to THOMAS CARLYLE's dictum that history is made up of the "biographies of great men," is devoted to the Victorian (and Comtean) notion of progressive change. The best-known literary criticism by

Lewes is the excellent *Life and Works of Goethe* (1855), which he researched, with Eliot's assistance, in Germany in 1854–55.

Outside of criticism, philosophy, and science—his last work, unfinished at his death but completed by Eliot, was the multivolume *Problems of Life and Mind* (1874)—Lewes's writings were not overly popular. Under the pseudonym Slingsby Lawrence, he wrote a number of plays, none of which fared well. He also wrote two novels, *Ranthorpe* (1847) and *Rose, Blanche, and Violet* (1848), neither of which were well received, although the first is an interesting example of the *Bildungsroman* and is written in imitation of GOETHE (see Vol. 2). In the 1860s Lewes served briefly as editor for both *Cornhill Magazine* and *Fortnightly Review*.

Criticism of Lewes is based primarily on his relationship with George Eliot, whose literary star considerably outshines his. His ideas on philosophy, the social sciences, and physiology have long been superseded, but, as a contributor to the vibrant intellectual milieu of his age, it is difficult to find his equal.

NONFICTION BY LEWES

A Biographical History of Philosophy from Its Origin in Greece Down to the Present Day. Gregg Intl. 1968 repr. of 1857 ed. $210.00. ISBN 0-576-29116-1

Comte's Philosophy of Science. Bell 1853 o.p.

The Life and Works of Goethe: With Sketches of His Age and Contemporaries, from Published and Unpublished Sources. 2 vols. Nutt 1855 o.p.

Literary Criticism of George Henry Lewes. Ed. by Alice R. Kaminsky. U. of Nebr. Pr. 1964 $20.00. ISBN 0-8032-0456-6. Good collection of his essays.

Problems of Life and Mind. AMS Pr. repr. of 1874 ed. $180.00. ISBN 0-404-60870-1

NOVELS BY LEWES

Ranthorpe. 1847. Ed. by Barbara Smalley. Ohio U. Pr. 1974 $12.00. ISBN 0-82140167-X

Rose, Blanche, and Violet: Three Sisters and Three Fortunes. 3 vols. AMS Pr. repr. of 1848 ed. $84.50. ISBN 0-404-61975-4

BOOKS ABOUT LEWES

Ashton, Rosemary. *G. H. Lewes: A Life.* OUP 1991 $45.00. ISBN 0-19-812827-4. Excellent biography.

Hirshberg, Edgar U. *George Henry Lewes.* Twayne 1970 o.p. Useful introduction; contains a bibliography.

Kaminsky, Alice R. *George Henry Lewes as Literary Critic.* Syracuse U. Pr. 1968 $58.50. ISBN 0-317-52009-1

Tjoa, Hock Guan. *George Henry Lewes: A Victorian Mind.* HUP 1977 $15.00. ISBN 0-674-34874-5. An intellectual biography.

Williams, David. *Mr. George Eliot: A Biography of George Henry Lewes.* Watts 1983 $17.95. ISBN 0-531-09813-3. Primarily on his relationship with Eliot.

MACAULAY, THOMAS BABINGTON, 1ST BARON. 1800–1859

The grouping of Macaulay's essays according to the classification of Cotter Morison in his monograph on Macaulay—as English history, foreign history, literary criticism—has been followed strictly in some editions of his prose. It has been hard to live down the persistent influence of some of Macaulay's essays. His strongly biased remarks (and he was not beyond conscious misstatements)—on ADDISON, BACON (see Vol. 4), BYRON, DRYDEN, WALPOLE, and others—made and unmade reputations. Since even his basest opinions were uttered in the purest English prose, Macaulay's reputation as a scholar and a historian flourished. Trained in law, he became a member of Parliament and rose to the peerage in 1857. Although Macaulay held a number of important cabinet posts, the effects of his sweeping educational reform while in India are his most enduring contribution to the Whig government.

NONFICTION BY MACAULAY

Critical and Historical Essays. 2 vols. 1843. Biblio Dist. 1966 repr. of 1907 ed. o.p.
Selected Writings. Ed. by John Clive and Thomas Pinney. U. Ch. Pr. 1972 o.p. Biographies, literary essays, narrative, occasional verse, political speeches, official papers, and personal letters.

WORK BY MACAULAY

Lays of Ancient Rome and Miscellaneous Essays and Poems. 1954. Biblio Dist. 1976 o.p. A rich and varied selection of Macaulay's prose and verse; memorable portraits of Dante, Petrarch, Goldsmith, and Johnson.

BOOKS ABOUT MACAULAY

Clive, John. *Macaulay: The Shaping of the Historian.* HUP 1987 $15.95. ISBN 0-674-54005-0. First-rate biography, with an emphasis on Macaulay as writer of history.
Roberts, Sidney C. *Lord Macaulay: The Pre-eminent Victorian.* 1927. Folcroft 1973 o.p.

MARRYAT, CAPTAIN FREDERICK. 1792–1848

A master of the sea tale, Marryat wrote novels that deal with life in the English Navy, in which he himself served. His stories were written for children but were read by old and young alike. *Masterman Ready* (1841) at one time stood next to *Robinson Crusoe* in popularity with boy readers. *Peter Simple* (1834) is the most autobiographical of the novels, *Mr. Midshipman Easy* (1836), the most humorous. *Percival Keene* (1842), the least estimable of his heroes, is a melodramatic story. *The Little Savage* (1848) is a horror tale of remarkable power, strong in plot and character development. Marryat's novels are all didactic, but his moral lessons never intrude or offend. The details of his adventurous life, so far as they are known, are well described in Oliver Warner's *Captain Marryat: A Rediscovery.* *A Diary in America* appeared first in 1839. The recognition now given to Marryat as a source for social history is fully deserved, since his opinionated account of his journey gives us "an invaluable view of American life at the time when Jacksonian democracy was in full development in the new nation" (*Library Journal*).

NOVELS BY MARRYAT

The Children of the New Forest. 1847. Buccaneer Bks. 1990 $21.95. ISBN 0-89966-700-7
Jacob Faithful. 1834. House Fire Pr. 1989 $12.00. ISBN 0-929491-01-7. The story of a sailor who does his duty despite fearful obstacles.
Masterman Ready. 1841. Biblio Dist. 1970 repr. of 1907 ed. o.p.
The Mission, or Scenes in Africa. 1845. *Colonial Novel Ser.* Holmes & Meier 1970 repr. of 1845 ed. o.p. Introduction by Tony Harrison.
Mr. Midshipman Easy. 1836. Biblio Dist. 1970 $2.50. ISBN 0-460-01082-4. Tale of a young man who comes of age at sea, with sometimes hilarious results.
Narratives of the Travels and Adventures of Monsieur Violet. 1843. Gregg Intl. 1970 o.p.
The Novels of Captain Marryat. 24 vols. Ed. by Johnson R. Brimley. Arden Lib. 1978 repr. of 1895 ed. o.p.
Peter Simple. 1834. Biblio. Dist. 1970 $14.95. ISBN 0-460-00232-5. Adventures at sea with the British Navy.
The Phantom Ship. 1839. AMS Pr. repr. of 1839 ed. $44.50. ISBN 0-404-6206-4. An eerie tale of mystery and suspense at sea.

BOOK ABOUT MARRYAT

Warner, Oliver. *Captain Marryat: A Rediscovery*. Hyperion Conn. repr. of 1953 ed. o.p.

MARTINEAU, HARRIET. 1802–1876

Martineau, from a devout and strict Unitarian family in Norwich, was born without the sense either of taste or of smell and, by the age of 12, showed signs of severe deafness. Throughout the early years of her life, she battled poverty and illness. At her mother's insistence, Martineau was educated, at first at home by her brothers and then for a short time at school. Because her loss of hearing became worse, she was sent home. Within a space of about three years during the late 1820s, Martineau's favorite brother, Thomas, died; her father lost his fortune and died; and her fiancé became insane and died. By 1829 the last of the family money was gone, and she was reduced to helping support her mother and sisters with her needlework. At about this time, she began to review for the Unitarian periodical *The Monthly Repository* and in 1831 won all three prizes in the magazine's contest for the best essays on the conversion of Catholics, Jews, and Muslims. During 1832–33 she published the tales *Illustrations of Political Economy* and its sequel, *Poor Laws and Paupers*, in monthly parts. Despite their pointed didacticism, the works were a tremendous success. Other works of fiction followed. In 1839 she published her first novel, *Deerbrook*, and, three years later, her fictionalized biography of Toussaint L'Ouverture, *The Hour and the Man*, appeared.

Despite her forays into fiction, however, Martineau is better known today for her historical, political, and philosophical writings. Early in her career she was influenced by the classical economies of DAVID RICARDO (see Vol. 3) and THOMAS MALTHUS (see Vol. 3). She was friends with EDWIN CHADWICK and JAMES KAY-SHUTTLEWORTH, and acquainted with JOHN STUART MILL (see Vols. 3 and 4). A strong, often radical proponent of utilitarian reform, early in her career she wrote a number of instructive texts that advocated the same curriculum for men and women. By the mid-1840s, Martineau had completely thrown off her Unitarianism and in 1851 published her antitheological *Laws of Man's Social Nature*.

Some good work has been done on Martineau's life and writings, especially on the political aspects of her public life. Books on Martineau as a literary artist are scarcer; Deirdre David's *Intellectual Women and Victorian Patriarchy* (1987) contains an excellent discussion of Martineau, and Valerie Sanders's *Reason over Passion* (1986) discusses Martineau as a novelist. One of the most insightful books on Martineau, and one of the most readable, is her own *Autobiography* (1877).

NOVELS BY MARTINEAU

Deerbrook. 1839. 3 vols. AMS Pr. repr. of 1839 ed. $84.50. ISBN 0-404-62034-5. Reprint of the Smith, Elder 1892 edition.

The Hour and the Man: A Historical Romance. 1841. AMS Pr. 1974 $40.00. ISBN 0-404-08890-2. Reprint of the 1841 edition, published by E. Moxon, London.

Illustrations of Political Economy. 9 vols. Charles Fox 1834 o.p. Immense bestseller; contains salutary tales based on political and legal ideas.

Ireland. 1832. Garland 1979 o.p. Reprint of the edition published by Charles Fox, London, issued as Volume 9 of *Illustrations of Political Economy*.

Poor Laws and Paupers. 1833. 4 vols. Charles Fox o.p. Written as a sequel to *Illustrations of Political Economy* at the urging of Lord Brougham.

Principle and Practice, or The Orphan Family: A Tale. Houlston 1827 o.p.

NONFICTION BY MARTINEAU

British Rule in India: An Historical Sketch. Elder Smith 1857 o.p.

Eastern Life, Present and Past. 3 vols. Saunders and Otley 1838 o.p. Travel book of a trip to the Middle East.

Harriet Martineau on Women. Ed. by Gayle Graham Yates. Rutgers U. Pr. 1985 $29.00. ISBN 0-8135-1057-0. Collection of Martineau's work on the Woman Question.

Harriet Martineau's Autobiography. 2 vols. 1877. Virago 1983 o.p. Introduction by Gaby Weiner.

Miscellanies. AMS Pr. 1975 $49.50. ISBN 0-404-08887-2. Contributions to periodicals, 1829–32. Reprint of the 1836 edition published by Hilliard, Gray.

The Positive Philosophy of Auguste Comte. 2 vols. London 1853 o.p. Condensation and translation of Comte's work.

Society in America. 1837. Ed. by Seymour Martin Lipset. Transaction Pubs. 1981 $17.95. ISBN 0-87855-420-3. Unfavorable critiques of America.

Suggestions towards the Further Government of India. Elder Smith 1858 o.p. Written in response to the Indian Mutiny.

WORK BY MARTINEAU

Harriet Martineau: Selected Letters. Ed. by Valerie Sanders. OUP 1990 $69.00. ISBN 0-19-818604-5

BOOKS ABOUT MARTINEAU

David, Deirdre. *Intellectual Women and Victorian Patriarchy: Harriet Martineau, Elizabeth Barrett Browning, George Eliot.* Cornell Univ. Pr. 1987 $35.00. ISBN 0-333-32493-5. Excellent on Martineau; examines difficulty of intellectual life among the patriarchal conventions of Victorian England.

Hoecker-Drysdale, Susan. *Harriet Martineau: First Woman Sociologist.* St. Martin 1992 $29.75. ISBN 0-85496-645-5

Nevill, John C. *Harriet Martineau.* Fredrick Muller 1943 o.p. Early popular biography; accessible, with good introduction.

Pichanick, Valerie Kossew. *Harriet Martineau: The Woman and Her Work 1802–76.* U. of Mich. Pr. 1980 $32.50. ISBN 0-472-10002-5. Sound historical work, but with little critical discussion of Martineau's writing.

Sanders, Valerie. *Reason over Passion: Harriet Martineau and the Victorian Novel.* St. Martin 1986 $32.50. ISBN 0-312-66511-4

Smith, Sidonie. *A Poetics of Women's Autobiography: Marginality and the Fictions of Self-Representation.* Ind. U. Pr. 1987 $29.95. ISBN 0-253-34505-7. Employs Martineau's texts to support thesis that female autobiography is often a response to the marginalization and silencing of women in Western patriarchal society.

Thomas, Gillian. *Harriet Martineau.* Twayne 1985 o.p. Good introduction to her life and works.

Webb, R. K. *Harriet Martineau: A Radical Victorian.* Heinemann Ed. 1960 o.p. Political biography; little on her literary life.

MAYHEW, HENRY. 1812–1887

Henry Mayhew had a varied career as a London writer of the mid-Victorian period. He was the son of a London solicitor, Joshua Mayhew, who reputedly was a rather tyrannous father. Apparently, Henry was a bitter disappointment to his father; the younger Mayhew had been educated at the Westminster School but, in objection to a flogging he had received, ran away from school and went to sea for a year. On his return he was articled to his father, but after three years he abandoned the law to seek a career as a journalist and a dramatist. Mayhew achieved some early success as a dramatist, most notably with his 1834 farce, *The Wandering Minstrel.* In the late 1830s, he was the joint editor of a successful satirical weekly, *Figaro in London,* and later helped to found *Figaro's* most significant and long-lived successor, *Punch*. Evidently, a fairly serious rift developed between Mayhew and his magazine colleagues, although the details of this falling-out remain a mystery—one of the many unanswered questions about Mayhew's life.

Mayhew was never without financial worries, and, as a means of making quick money, he collaborated on a number of comic novels with his younger brother, Augustus (1826–75). Their most successful work is *The Greatest Plague of Life* (1847), which was issued in monthly numbers and proved very popular. They followed it with *Whom to Marry and How to Get Married* (1848); later Mayhew singly authored *1851, or, The Adventures of Mr. and Mrs. Sandbags* (1851). Mayhew's attempt, in 1851, to publish the 82 "letters" he had written for the *Morning Chronicle*, in which he investigates the plight of London's urban poor, was a financial failure. They were issued in 1861, however, in four volumes under the title *London Labour and the London Poor*. It is for this classic work that Mayhew is today best known. In it he unhesitatingly depicts the opprobrium under which most of the London working classes led their lives. In many ways *London Labour and the London Poor* epitomizes the Victorian tendency to be simultaneously repulsed and fascinated by the working classes, the "Great Unwashed" huddled together in the urban centers of England. Along with EDWIN CHADWICK and J. P. KAY-SHUTTLEWORTH, Mayhew stands as one of the earliest of urban sociologists.

Although recent years have witnessed an increase in interest in Henry Mayhew, a "definitive" biography remains to be written. The introductions to his work, notably John Rosenberg's preface to the Dover facsimile edition of *London Labour and the London Poor* and the essays framing the edition of *The Unknown Mayhew*, are good sources of information.

NONFICTION BY MAYHEW

The Criminal Prisons of London, and Scenes of Prison Life (coauthored with John Binny). 1862. Kelley 1968 $49.50. ISBN 0-678-05072-4. A study similar to *London Labour and the London Poor* in method.

German Life and Manners as Seen in Saxony at the Present Day. AMS Pr. repr. of 1964 ed. $82.50. ISBN 0-404-16520-6. An interesting travel book.

The Illustrated Mayhew's London: The Classic Account of London Street Life and Characters in the Time of Charles Dickens and Queen Victoria. Ed. by John Canning. Weidenfeld & Nicolson 1986 o.p. Good introduction by Asa Briggs.

London Characters: Illustrations of the Humor, Pathos, and Peculiarities of London Life by Henry Mayhew and Other Writers. Chatto & Windus UK 1874 o.p. Famous edition illustrated by Sir W. S. Gilbert of Gilbert and Sullivan fame.

London Labour and the London Poor. 1861. Viking Penguin 1985 $9.95. ISBN 0-14-043241-8. Abridgement of Mayhew's most famous work, with introduction by Victor Neuburg.

The Unknown Mayhew: Selections from the Morning Chronicle, *1849–50.* Ed. by E. P. Thompson and Eileen Yeo. Viking Penguin 1984 o.p. Excellent selection from the "Labour and the Poor" letters.

Voices of the Poor: Selections from the Morning Chronicle *"Labour and the Poor" (1849–1850).* Ed. by Anne Humpherys. Cass 1971 $37.50. ISBN 0-7146-2929-4

NOVELS BY MAYHEW

1851, or, The Adventures of Mr. and Mrs. Sandbags and Family, Who Came up to London to "Enjoy Themselves," and to See the Great Exhibition. 1851 o.p. The world's show, illustrated by George Cruikshank.

The Image of His Father, or, One Boy Is More Trouble than a Dozen Girls, Being a Tale of a "Young Monkey" (coauthored with Augustus Mayhew). H. Hurst 1848 o.p. Illustrated by Halbot Knight Browne.

The Magic of Kindness, or, The Wondrous Story of the Good Huan (coauthored with Augustus Mayhew). HarpC 1849 o.p. Illustrated by Walter Crane.

Whom to Marry and How to Get Married, or, The Adventures of a Lady in Search of a Good Husband (coauthored with Augustus Mayhew). David Bogue 1848 o.p. Illustrated by George Cruikshank.

PLAY BY MAYHEW

The Wandering Minstrel: A Farce, in One Act. 1834. French o.p.

BOOKS ABOUT MAYHEW

Humphreys, Anne. *Henry Mayhew.* Twayne 1984 o.p. A good introduction.
_____. *Travels into the Poor Man's Country: The Work of Henry Mayhew.* U. of Ga. Pr. 1977 $12.50. ISBN 0-8203-0416-6. The only book-length study of Mayhew's work as a social observer.

MEREDITH, GEORGE. 1828–1909

An intellectual novelist, George Meredith was leisurely, epigrammatic, and involved at a time when the public admired the swift narrative flow of DICKENS and THACKERAY. His novels were designed to penetrate the hidden motivations of character. He boasted that he never wrote a word to please the public and counted as the greatest compliment ever paid to him the statement that he had brought about a change in public taste. Meredith's reputation grew slowly. His first important novel, *The Ordeal of Richard Feverel* (1859), a fine study of the emotional growth of a young man, is his most epigrammatic work and had little popular success. *The Egoist* (1879), a comedy in narrative, regarded by most critics as his masterpiece, was the first to receive popular attention. *Diana of the Crossways* (1885), his most popular book, gave to fiction a new and particularly well-drawn heroine, the woman of fine brain and strong body.

His *The Essay on Comedy, and the Uses of the Comic Spirit* (1897) has been described as the key to his novels. But Meredith, like THOMAS HARDY, thought more of his poems than of his novels and preferred to be remembered as a poet. In notes for *The Selected Poetical Works of George Meredith* (1955), G. M. TREVELYAN (see Vol. 3) writes: "His poems are more especially concerned with his philosophy, and the novels with his application of it to ethical problems." Meredith's philosophy was one of optimism, but it was "the optimism of temperament and not of creed."

NOVELS BY MEREDITH

The Adventures of Harry Richmond. 1871. Ed. by L. T. Hergenhan. U. of Nebr. Pr. 1970 $35.00. ISBN 0-8032-0712-3

The Adventures of Harry Richmond: The Unpublished Parts. Ed. by Sven-Johan Spanberg. U. of Uppsala Pr. 1990 o.p. Useful scholarly completion of the novel.

Beauchamp's Career. Ed. by Margaret Harris. OUP 1989 $8.95. ISBN 0-19-281751-5. Looks at social class and political party in Victorian England through the life and adventures of a young naval officer.

Diana of the Crossways. 1885. Scholarly 1971 repr. of 1931 ed. $89.00. ISBN 0-403-01105-1

The Egoist. 1879. Ed. by Robert M. Adams. Norton 1979 $11.95. ISBN 0-393-09171-6. A comic novel about the refined selfishness of Sir Willoughby Patterne.

Evan Harrington. 1860. Boydell & Brewer 1983 o.p. A romance of social climbing.

The Ordeal of Richard Feverel: A Story of a Father and Son. 1859. Dover 1983 $8.95. ISBN
    0-486-24463-6
The Tragic Comedians: A Study in a Well-Known Story. 1880. Ayer rev. ed. 1975 repr. of
    1922 ed. $14.00. ISBN 0-405-06735-6

SHORT STORY COLLECTION BY MEREDITH

Short Stories. 1898. Ayer repr. of 1898 ed. $18.00. ISBN 0-8369-3777-5

POETRY BY MEREDITH

The Poems of George Meredith. Ed. by Phyllis B. Bartlett. Yale U. Pr. 1978 $155.00. ISBN
    0-300-01283-7

NONFICTION BY MEREDITH

The Essay on Comedy, and the Uses of the Comic Spirit. Norwood 1980 repr. of 1897 ed.
    o.p.

WORKS BY MEREDITH

Letters of George Meredith. 2 vols. Rprt. Serv. 1992 $150.00. ISBN 0-7812-7594-6
Letters of George Meredith to Alice Meynell: With Annotations There to 1896–1907. Ed. by
    E. Meynell. Folcroft repr. of 1923 ed. o.p.
Works. 29 vols. Ed. by William M. Meredith. Russell repr. of 1909–12 ed. $2,175.00. ISBN
    0-7812-7593-8

BOOKS ABOUT MEREDITH

Collie, Michael. *George Meredith: A Bibliography*. U. of Toronto Pr. 1976 o.p.
Muendel, Renate. *George Meredith*. Twayne 1986 $20.95. ISBN 0-8057-6932-3. Worth-
    while introduction to Meredith's life and career.
Olmstead, John Charles. *George Meredith: An Annotated Bibliography, 1925–1975*.
    Garland 1978 o.p.
Stevenson, Lionel. *The Ordeal of George Meredith*. Russell 1967 repr. of 1953 ed. o.p.
Williams, Ioan, ed. *Meredith: The Critical Heritage. Critical Heritage Ser*. Routledge 1978
    $69.50. ISBN 0-7100-6961-8. Contemporary criticisms of both novels and poetry,
    arranged chronologically.
Wright, Walter F. *Art and Substance in George Meredith: A Study in Narrative*. Greenwood
    1980 repr. of 1953 ed. $39.75. ISBN 0-313-22514-1

MILL, HARRIET TAYLOR. 1807–1858

Not much is known about Harriet Mill. There is no biography, and almost any
information about her is filtered through the scholarship on her husband, JOHN
STUART MILL (see Vols. 3 and 4). Mill himself was careful to guard his wife's
privacy, even after her death. When the American suffragist Pauline Wright
Davis asked Mill in 1870 about the possibility of composing a memoir about his
wife, he responded that it would be of great benefit to humanity to portray in
biography a mind like hers. "But such a psychological history is seldom
possible," he argued, "and in her case the materials for it do not exist. All that
could be furnished is her birth-place, parentage, and a few dates." Mill may have
destroyed the materials that could have shed light on his wife's life, but more
likely she led a relatively uneventful life and was most preoccupied with
intellectual matters. We do know that she was born Harriet Hardy and in 1826
married John Taylor, a merchant. When she met Mill (probably in 1830), she
was already the mother of two sons; her daughter, Helen, was born in 1831, by
which time Mill and Harriet had already forged a strong friendship. After a trial
separation in 1833, Taylor accepted his wife's friendship with Mill, but at least
one of Mill's friends seems to have broken with him over what was thought by

some to be an "improper" relationship. Taylor died in 1849, and, in 1851, when both Mill and Harriet were in failing health, they married. They took up residence in Avignon, where Harriet died seven years later.

There is much speculation as to the true nature of the relationship between Harriet and Mill during the years when Taylor still lived. Though in 1831 Harriet said that her relationship with both her husband and Mill was one of "Seelenfreundin," or "soul-kinship," her explanation does little to defuse conjecture. Her intellectual contribution seems much clearer, but even here there is little empirical evidence of how much or how little she actually had to do with the composition of some of Mill's most important writings. Some scholars have postulated that she is the unacknowledged coauthor of *On Liberty* (1859), *The Subjection of Women* (1869), and the *Autobiography* (1873), all of which were published after her death. Yet the only work for which she is indisputably credited is her essay "Enfranchisement of Women." Whatever her contribution, Mill, in the introduction of *On Liberty*, calls her "the inspirer, and in some part the author of all that is best in my writings." Certainly she was a tireless advocate of women's and workers' rights throughout her life.

NONFICTION BY MILL

Enfranchisement of Women and *The Subjection of Women* (coauthored with John Stuart Mill). Virago 1983 o.p. Inexpensive paper edition.

Essays on Equality, Law, and Education. Ed. by John M. Robson. U. of Toronto Pr. 1988 $70.00. ISBN 0-802-05629-6. Includes "The Subjection of Women" and "Enfranchisement of Women."

Essays on Sex Equality. Ed. by Alice S. Rossi. U. Ch. Pr. 1970 $8.95. ISBN 0-226-52545-7. Excellent introductory essay on Mill and Taylor's life together.

Woman's Rights Tracts (coauthored with Wendell Phillips, Theodore Parker, Thomas Wentworth Higginson, and Clarina Irene Howard Nichols). Robert F. Wallcut 1854 o.p.

WORKS BY MILL

John Stuart Mill and Harriet Taylor: Their Correspondence and Subsequent Marriage. Ed. by Friedrich August von Hayek. U. Ch. Pr. 1951 o.p. A standard source for biographies of both Harriet Taylor Mill and her husband.

BOOKS ABOUT MILL

Kamm, Josephine. *John Stuart Mill in Love.* Gordon & Cremonesi 1977 o.p. Focuses primarily on Mill, but has some material on Taylor.

Pappe, H. D. *John Stuart Mill and the Harriet Taylor Myth.* Melbourne U. Pr. 1960 o.p. Discussion of the questions of Taylor's contributions to Mill's work.

MILL, JOHN STUART. 1806–1873

[SEE Volumes 3 and 4.]

MOORE, GEORGE. 1852–1933

George Moore, "the master of the most subtle rhythm in modern prose" (Austin Clarke, *N.Y. Times*), was an exponent of the experimental novel of EMILE ZOLA (see Vol. 2), the naturalistic fiction written with a polished and careful artistry. Many regard *Sister Teresa* (1901) as his masterpiece, although *Esther Waters* (1894), his objective story of a servant girl's seduction and struggle, is more widely read.

As an autobiographer, Moore was prolific. His *Confessions of a Young Man* (1888), *Memoirs of My Dead Life* (1906), and the trilogy *Hail and Farewell!*

(1911–14) are books about himself and his friends. In the latter, says Austin Clarke, "He had mocked at his fellow writers, invented ludicrous conversations for them and succeeded in turning literary Dublin into delightful, irresistible legend. He . . . made many enemies by his candor." *Conversations in Ebury Street* (1924) is a volume of actual talks between Moore and his friends in his London home.

NOVELS BY MOORE

The Brook Kerith. 1916. Liveright 1969 o.p.
Esther Waters. 1894. OUP 1983 $7.95. ISBN 0-19-281578-4
Evelyn Innes (and *Sister Teresa*). Ed. by Robert L. Wolff. *Victorian Fiction Ser.* Garland 1975 repr. of 1898 ed. o.p.
The Lake. 1905. Dufour 1980 $30.00. ISBN 0-900675-75-6
A Story-Teller's Holiday. 1918. 2 vols. Rprt. Serv. 1992 repr. of 1928 ed. $150.00. ISBN 0-7812-7602-0

SHORT STORY COLLECTIONS BY MOORE

In Single Strictness. Short Story Index Repr. Ser. Ayer repr. of 1922 ed. $20.00. ISBN 0-8369-4116-0
The Untilled Field. Short Story Index Repr. Ser. Ayer repr. of 1903 ed. $19.95. ISBN 0-8369-3600-0. A group of excellent short stories.

NONFICTION BY MOORE

A Communication to My Friends. Haskell 1974 $49.95. ISBN 0-8383-1910-6. The essay used as the preface to the uniform and later editions of *A Mummer's Wife.*
Confessions of a Young Man. 1888. *Lit. Ser.* Scholarly 1972 repr. of 1925 ed. $29.00. ISBN 0-403-0113-2. Autobiography.
Hail and Farewell. 1911–14. Dufour 1976 $60.00. ISBN 0-900675-64-0. Autobiography.

WORKS BY MOORE

George Moore in Transition: Letters to T. Fisher Unwin and Lena Milman, 1894–1910. Bks. Demand repr. of 1968 ed. $85.80. ISBN 0-685-15627-3. About 300 items from Moore's correspondence with his publisher and the woman who introduced him to Russian literature.
George Moore on Parnassus: Letters (1900–1933) to Secretaries, Publishers, Printers, Agents, Literati, Friends, and Acquaintances. Ed. by Helmut E. Gerber and O. M. Brack, Jr. U. of Delaware Pr. 1986 $75.00. ISBN 0-87413-152-9. Collection of Moore's letters from late in life.
Letters of George Moore. Folcroft 1977 o.p.
Letters to Lady Cunard, 1895–1933. Greenwood 1979 repr. of 1957 ed. o.p.

BOOKS ABOUT MOORE

Cave, Richard Allen. *A Study of the Novels of George Moore. Irish Literary Studies.* B & N Imports 1978 o.p.
Freeman, John. *Portrait of George Moore in a Study of His Work.* Scholarly repr. of 1922 ed. $23.00. ISBN 0-403-00598-1
Gilcher, Edwin. *Bibliography of George Moore.* N. Ill. U. Pr. 1970 o.p.
Langenfeld, Robert. *George Moore: An Annotated Secondary Bibliography of Writings about Him.* AMS Pr. 1987 $76.50. ISBN 0-404-61583-X. Lengthy bibliography, with useful annotations.
Mitchell, Susan L. *George Moore. Irish Culture and History Ser.* Assoc. Faculty Pr. 1970 repr. of 1916 ed. o.p.
Sechler, Robert P. *George Moore: A Disciple of Walter Pater.* Folcroft repr. of 1931 ed. o.p.

MORRIS, WILLIAM. 1834–1896

Morris was the Victorian Age's model of the Renaissance man. Arrested in 1885 for preaching socialism on a London street corner (he was head of the Hammersmith Socialist League and editor of its paper, *The Commonweal*, at the time), he was called before a magistrate and asked for identification. He modestly described himself upon publication (1868–70) as "Author of 'The Earthly Paradise,' pretty well known, I think, throughout Europe." He might have added that he was also the head of Morris and Company, makers of fine furniture, carpets, wallpapers, stained glass, and other crafts; founder of the Society for the Protection of Ancient Buildings; and founder, as well as chief designer, for the Kelmscott Press, which set a standard for fine book design that has carried through to the present. His connection to design is significant. Morris and Company, for example, did much to revolutionize the art of house decoration and furniture in England.

Morris's literary productions spanned the spectrum of styles and subjects. He began under the influence of DANTE GABRIEL ROSSETTI with a Pre-Raphaelite volume called *The Defence of Guenevere and Other Poems* (1858); he turned to narrative verse, first in the pastoral mode ("The Earthly Paradise") and then under the influence of the Scandinavian sagas ("Sigurd the Volsung"). After "Sigurd," his masterpiece, Morris devoted himself for a time exclusively to social and political affairs, becoming known as a master of the public address; then, during the last decade of his life, he fused these two concerns in a series of socialist romances, the most famous of which is *News from Nowhere* (1891).

NOVELS BY MORRIS

News from Nowhere. Routledge 1970 $10.95. ISBN 0-7100-6756-9. Classic account of Morris's Socialist idealism.

The Story of the Glittering Plain or The Land of Living Men. Dover 1987 $7.95. ISBN 0-486-25467-4. Facsimile of the 1894 Kelmscott edition, with 23 woodcuts by Walter Crane.

WORKS BY MORRIS

Collected Letters. 2 vols. Ed. by Norman Kelvin. Princeton U. Pr. vol. 1 1984 $84.00. ISBN 0-691-06501-2. Vol. 2 1987. Pt. 1 $52.50. ISBN 0-691-06723-6. Pt. 2 $63.00. ISBN 0-691-06723-6

Collected Works. 24 vols. Ed. by May Morris. Gordon Pr. 1973 repr. of 1910–15 ed. $600.00. ISBN 0-8796-8895-5. The standard edition of Morris's works, with revealing biographical introductions.

The Letters of William Morris to His Family and Friends. Ed. by Philip Henderson. AMS Pr. repr. of 1950 ed. $28.25. ISBN 0-404-14711-9

News from Nowhere and *Selected Writings and Design.* Ed. by Asa Briggs. Viking Penguin 1984 $6.95. ISBN 0-14-043115-2. A student edition, weighted toward the late work.

Stories in Prose, Stories in Verse, Shorter Poems, Lectures and Essays. Ed. by G. D. H. Cole. AMS Pr. repr. of 1934 ed. $31.50. ISBN 0-404-14690-2

William Morris by Himself: Designs and Writings. Little 1988 $50.00. ISBN 0-8212-1710-0

The Work of William Morris. Ed. by Paul Thompson. OUP 1991 $35.00. ISBN 0-19-212279-7. Collection of Morris's most important work.

BOOKS ABOUT MORRIS

Faulkner, Peter. *Against the Age: An Introduction to William Morris.* Allen & Unwin 1980 o.p. The best general introduction to the man and his milieu.

———. *William Morris: The Critical Heritage.* Routledge 1973 $69.50. ISBN 0-7100-7520-0

Harvey, Charles, and John Press. *William Morris: Design and Enterprise in Victorian England*. Manchester Univ. Pr. 1991 $79.95. ISBN 0-7190-2418-8. Study of Morris as designer and businessman.

Hodgson, Amanda. *The Romances of William Morris*. Cambridge U. Pr. 1987 $39.50. ISBN 0-521-32075-5. Worthwhile study of Morris's historical romances, such as *The Story of the Glittering Plain*.

Kirchhoff, Frederick. *William Morris. Twayne's Eng. Authors Ser.* G. K. Hall 1979 o.p.

_____. *William Morris: The Construction of the Male Self, 1856–1872*. Ohio U. Pr. 1990 $29.95. ISBN 0-8214-0954-9. Study of Morris's early work and the developing representation of the masculine in it.

Latham, David, and Sheila Latham. *An Annotated Critical Bibliography of William Morris*. St. Martin 1991 $45.00. ISBN 0-312-05656-7. Useful bibliography.

Lindsay, Jack. *William Morris: His Life and Work*. Taplinger 1979 o.p.

Mackail, J. W. *The Life of William Morris*. 2 vols. Ayer 1968 repr. of 1899 ed. $33.00. ISBN 0-405-08767-5. One of the best Victorian official biographies.

Needham, Paul, ed. *William Morris and the Art of the Book: A Pierpont Morgan Library Volume*. OUP 1976 o.p.

Oberg, Charlotte. *A Pagan Prophet: William Morris*. U. Pr. of Va. 1978 o.p.

Silver, Carole. *The Romance of William Morris*. Ohio U. Pr. 1982 $12.95. ISBN 0-8214-0706-6. A good critical study.

Stansky, Peter. *Redesigning the World: William Morris, the 1880's, and the Arts and Crafts*. Princeton U. Pr. 1984 $45.00. ISBN 0-691-06616-7

Thompson, E. P. *William Morris: Romantic to Revolutionary*. Stanford U. Pr. 1988 $19.95. ISBN 0-8047-1509-2. Reprint of important biography of Morris, stressing his political development and influence.

Thompson, Paul Van K. *The Work of William Morris*. OUP 1992 $52.00. ISBN 0-19-212279-7

Vallance, Aymer. *William Morris: His Art, His Writings, and His Public Life: A Record*. Dover 1986 o.p. Interesting contemporaneous compilation of Morris's work; reprint of an 1897 edition.

_____. *William Morris Full Color Patterns and Designs*. Dover 1988 $7.95. ISBN 0-486-25615-6. Reproduces all the color plates from *The Art of William Morris*, by Aymer Vallance (1897).

NEWMAN, JOHN HENRY, CARDINAL. 1801–1890

[SEE Volume 4.]

NORTON, CAROLINE SHERIDAN (afterward, Lady Stirling-Maxwell). 1808–1877

Caroline Norton is primarily remembered today for her work in repealing the divorce and child custody laws of the Victorian period. The granddaughter of RICHARD BRINSLEY SHERIDAN, the famous Restoration playwright, Norton, herself a prolific and widely read poet and novelist, married George Chapple Norton in 1827. The marriage was a notoriously unhappy one that culminated in separation in 1836, when her husband brought suit of adultery against Lord Melbourne. The suit failed, but, in accordance with the matrimonial laws of the time, her husband retained custody of their children. Norton immediately began a long fight for custody. Because the laws of the time denied married women most rights of property and even juridical status, the popular press was the arena for her struggle; in 1839 she published *A Plain Letter to the Lord Chancellor on the Infant Custody Bill* under the pseudonym Pearce Stevenson. When her youngest son died in 1842, largely due to neglect on the part of her husband, he relented and granted her custody of their two surviving children.

Between 1827 and 1842, despite the difficulties of what was rapidly becoming a very public private life and the demands of her writing to reform child custody laws, Norton published a book of verse, *The Sorrows of Rosalie* (1829), a long poem, *The Undying One* (1830), her first novel, *The Wife and Woman's Reward* (1835), and her important factory reform poem, *A Voice from the Factories* (1836). In 1853, she was sued for debt by her husband, who upon the death of Norton's mother had been cut short of allowance and seized her copyright interests. In response to this lawsuit, Norton once again pamphleteered for her cause, this time in support of the Divorce Bill. Her open *Letter to the Queen* on this topic was published in 1855. Although she was still active as a writer, she was nearing the end of her literary career. She had published a novel, *Stuart of Dunleath*, in 1851, but her last long poem, *The Lady of La Garaye*, appeared in 1862 and her last novel, *Old Sir Douglas*, in 1867.

Norton's poetry and novels today remain relatively unread, although her work for women's rights has been thoroughly documented and remains an important record of English laws for women during the nineteenth century. Throughout her life, Norton was renowned for her wit, grace, and beauty. GEORGE MEREDITH's *Diana of the Crossways* is putatively based on Norton's affair with Melbourne.

POETRY BY NORTON

Aunt Carry's Ballads for Children. Cundall 1847 o.p. Popular collection of children's verse, containing "Adventures of a Wood Sprite" and "Story of Blance and Brutikin." Illustrated by John Absolon.

The Child of the Islands: A Poem. Routledge Chapman & Hall 1845 o.p.

The Dream, and Other Poems. Colburn 1840 o.p.

The Lady of La Garaye. Macmillan 1862 o.p.

The Sorrows of Rosalie: A Tale, with Other Poems. Ebers 1829 o.p.

The Undying One, and Other Poems. Colburn & Bentley 1830 o.p.

A Voice from the Factories: In Serious Verse. J. Murray UK 1836 o.p. Semi-autobiographical collection emphasizing themes of social protest.

NOVELS BY NORTON

Lost and Saved. 1863. Schol. Facsimiles 1988 $60.00. ISBN 0-8201-1434-0. Reprint of one of Norton's late novels, with an introduction by S. Bailey Shurbutt.

The Wife, and Woman's Reward. 3 vols. Saunders & Otley 1835 o.p. Semi-autobiographical.

Stuart of Dunleath: A Story of Modern Times. 3 vols. Colburn & Bentley 1851 o.p.

NONFICTION BY NORTON

English Laws for Women in the Nineteenth Century. 1854. Hyperion Conn. 1981 repr. of 1854 ed. $17.00. ISBN 0-8305-0111-8. Originally printed for private circulation; useful scholarly edition, with an introduction by Joan Huddleston.

A Letter to the Queen on Lord Chancellor Cranworth's Marriage and Divorce Bill. Longman 1855 o.p.

A Letter to the Right Reverend Lord Bishop of Exeter on the Custody of Infants. Churton 1839 o.p.

A Plain Letter to the Lord Chancellor on the Infant Custody Bill, by Pearce Stevenson. Ridgeway 1839 o.p.

WORKS BY NORTON

The Coquette, and Other Tales and Sketches, in Prose and Verse. 2 vols. Churton 1835 o.p.

Kate Bouverie, and Other Tales and Sketches, in Prose and Verse. 2 vols. Carey 1835 o.p.

Letters of Caroline Norton to Lord Melbourne. Ed. by James O. Hoge and Clarke Olney. Ohio St. U. Pr. 1974 $26.75. ISBN 0-8142-0208-X. Good source of firsthand information on the Norton-Melbourne affair.

Selected Writings of Caroline Norton: Facsimile Reproductions. Schol. Facsimiles 1978 $58.00. ISBN 0-8201-1312-3. A useful collection of Norton's most important writings. Introduction and notes by James O. Hoge and Jane Marcus.

BOOK ABOUT NORTON

Acland, Alice. *Caroline Norton.* Constable 1948 o.p. Interesting, though dated, biography.

OLIPHANT, MARGARET. 1828–1897

Margaret Oliphant was one of the most prolific writers of the Victorian period. During her nearly 50-year career, the Scotswoman published more than 100 books and countless articles. The untimely death of her husband, in 1859, left her nearly destitute, pregnant, and the sole support of their two small children. She had, however, already embarked upon a literary career and had won some reputation with her first novel, *Some Passages in the Life of Mrs. Margaret Maitland of Sunnyside* (1849), a tale of Scottish life. Never in very secure financial circumstances, even while her husband was alive, she had continued to write, publishing a well-received historical novel, *Caleb Field* in 1851, and, six years later, the most highly regarded of her many domestic romances, *The Athelings.* After her husband's death, both the speed of Oliphant's composition and her productivity increased dramatically.

Although she published a number of nonfiction works—a biography of her distant relative, the novelist, bureaucrat, and adventurer Laurence Oliphant (1891); *Cervantes* (1880); her *Autobiography* (1899); *The Literary History of England* (1882); and *The Annals of a Publishing House* (1897), which commemorated her long association with Blackwood's—she is best remembered for two series of novels. The first, the *Carlingsford Chronicles,* is sometimes likened to ANTHONY TROLLOPE's *Chronicles of Barsetshire* or GEORGE ELIOT's *Scenes of Clerical Life* in its subject matter of small-town intrigues and religious themes. The five novels in the Carlingsford series are *The Rector and the Doctor's Family* and *Salem Chapel* (both published in 1863), *The Perpetual Curate* (1864), *Miss Marjoriebanks* (1866)—probably the most widely read of her novels today—and *Phoebe Junior* (1876). The other notable group is *Stories of the Seen and Unseen,* a series whose central theme is death and the experiences of the soul; it begins with *A Beleaguered City* (1880) and continues with *A Little Pilgrim* (1882). Despite her incredible output, Oliphant never achieved first-rank status as a novelist, although her work has begun to generate a good deal of interest among critics and theorists.

NOVELS BY OLIPHANT

The Athelings, or, The Three Gifts. Harper's 1857 o.p.
The Curate in Charge. Harper's 1876 o.p.
Miss Marjoriebanks. 1866. Chatto & Windus UK 1969 o.p. Introduction by Q. D. Leavis.
The Perpetual Curate. 1864. Garland 1975 o.p.
Phoebe Junior, a Last Chronicle of Carlingsford. Garland 1976 o.p.
The Rector and the Doctor's Family. 1863. Viking Penguin 1986 $6.95. ISBN 0-14-016151-1
Salem Chapel. 1863. Garland 1976 o.p.
Stories of the Seen and the Unseen. 1885. Ayer repr. of 1889 ed. $33.00. ISBN 0-8369-3411-3

NONFICTION BY OLIPHANT

The Autobiography of Margaret Oliphant: The Complete Text. Ed. by Elisabeth Jay. OUP
    1990 $39.95. ISBN 0-19-818615-0
Cervantes. Blackwood 1880 o.p.
*The Literary History of England in the End of the Eighteenth and Beginning of the
    Nineteenth Century.* 1882. 3 vols. AMS Pr. 1970 $45.00. ISBN 0-404-04830-7
Memoir of the Life of Laurence Oliphant and of Alice Oliphant, His Wife. 1891. Arno Press
    1976 $32.00. ISBN 0-405-07970-2
The Victorian Age of English Literature. 2 vols. Dodd 1892 o.p.

BOOK ABOUT OLIPHANT

Williams, Marryn. *Margaret Oliphant: A Critical Biography.* St. Martin 1986 $25.00. ISBN
    0-312-51447-6. One of the few book-length works on Oliphant's career and writings.

PATER, WALTER HORATIO. 1839–1894

Pater's personal life was rather uneventful. His father, a surgeon, died when
the boy was 3, at which time his family moved to the London suburb of Chase
Side, Enfield. An unremarkable student, in 1858 he matriculated at Queen's
College, Oxford, where, as before, he did not especially distinguish himself.

Pater was early influenced by JOHN RUSKIN, but, after a trip to the Continent in
1865, he became less concerned with the social idealism that comprises much
of Ruskin's aesthetic writing and increasingly focused on expressing the
concrete and individual experience of the work of art. His earliest work, an
essay on SAMUEL TAYLOR COLERIDGE, appeared in 1866 in *The Westminster
Review*; Pater soon became a regular contributor to a number of serious
reviews, especially *The Fortnightly*, which published his essays on LEONARDO DA
VINCI (see Vol. 3), PICO DELLA MIRANDOLA (see Vol. 4), Botticelli, and the poetry
of MICHELANGELO (see Vol. 3). All were included in his first, and perhaps most
influential, book, *Studies in the History of the Renaissance* (1873; reissued as *The
Renaissance*, 1877). It is in the famous conclusion to this book that Pater asserts
that to "burn with a hard, gem-like flame, to maintain this ecstasy, is success in
life."

Although not universally well received by the literary establishment, many of
whom believed his aesthetics to be morbid, unscholarly, and solipsistic, Pater
became a somewhat reluctant intellectual role model for many of the
undergraduates, among them OSCAR WILDE. Pater never was comfortable with
the more outrageous expressions of the "art for art's sake" movement,
preferring instead the retiring life of the university don. Nonetheless, he
counted among his friends a number of London literati, including ALGERNON
CHARLES SWINBURNE and DANTE GABRIEL ROSSETTI.

In 1885 Pater's only novel, *Marius the Epicurean*, appeared. Ostensibly *Marius*
is a historical novel, set in the time of MARCUS AURELIUS (see Vol. 4) and tracing
the philosophical development of its young protagonist and his gradual
approach to Christianity. Practically, however, *Marius* is more a meditation of
the philosophical choices that confronted Pater, or any thinker, during the late
Victorian period. In light of the work's underrealized characterizations and the
lack of any but intellectual action, it is difficult to justify calling it a novel in the
usual sense of the term. Yet, as a highly polished prose piece, and as an
argument for an austere yet intensely experienced way of life, it holds a singular
place in Victorian literature.

Following *Marius*, Pater published *Imaginary Portraits* (1887), a series of
philosophical depictions of historical characters, and *Appreciations: With an*

Essay on Style (1889). This latter work established Pater as a master prose stylist. Toward the end of his life, in works like "Emerald Uthwart" (1892) and "Apollo in Picardy" (1893), as well as in his unfinished *Gaston de Latour*, Pater evinced a continuing affinity for the themes of morbid violence, early promise, and early death that had significantly informed *Imaginary Portraits*.

Pater's stock as a subject to critics has risen and fallen dramatically in the twentieth century. Except for *The Renaissance*, his major writings are difficult to characterize, and this may account for some of the ambivalence toward them.

NONFICTION BY PATER

Appreciations: With an Essay on Style. 1889. Northwestern U. Pr. 1987 o.p.
The Child in the House: An Imaginary Portrait. Thomas B. Mosher 1896 o.p. A revealing, semiautobiographical piece.
Gaston de Latour: An Unfinished Romance. AMS Pr. repr. of 1896 ed. $44.50. ISBN 0-404-62093-0
Imaginary Portraits. 1887. AMS Pr. 1978 repr. of 1924 ed. $16.50. ISBN 0-404-14038-6
Plato and Platonism. Greenwood repr. of 1910 ed. $62.50. ISBN 0-8371-1151-X
The Renaissance: Studies in Art and Poetry. 1877. Ed. by Donald L. Hill. U. CA Pr. 1980 $47.50. ISBN 0-520-03325-6
Three Major Texts: "The Renaissance," "Appreciations," and "Imaginary Portraits." Ed. by William E. Buckler. NYU Pr. 1986 $22.50. ISBN 0-8147-1089-1. A useful teaching text.

NOVEL BY PATER

Marius the Epicurean: His Sensations and Ideas. 1885. Ed. by Ian Small. OUP 1986 $6.95. ISBN 0-19-2817051. Generally considered to be Pater's finest work.

WORK BY PATER

The Letters of Walter Pater. Ed. by Lawrence Evans. OUP 1970 o.p.

BOOKS ABOUT PATER

Brake, Laurel, and Ian Small, eds. *Pater in the 1990s.* ELT Pr. 1991 $30.00. ISBN 0-944318-05-3. Collection of recent essays on Pater.
Buckler, William E. *Walter Pater: The Critic as Artist of Ideas.* NYU Pr. 1987 $45.00. ISBN 0-8147-1092-1. Argues that Pater's criticism is informed by imaginative intuition rather than abstract theory.
Inman, Billie Andrew. *Walter Pater and His Reading, 1874–1877: With a Bibliography of His Library Borrowings, 1878–1894.* Garland 1990 $103.00. ISBN 0-8240-8562-0
Iser, Wolfgang. *Walter Pater: The Aesthetic Moment.* 1960. Trans. by David Henry Wilson. Cambridge U. Pr. 1987 $42.50. ISBN 0-521-30962-X. Examination of Pater's philosophical and religious skepticism.
Keefe, Robert, and Janice A. Keefe. *Walter Pater and the Gods of Disorder.* Ohio U. Pr. 1988 $24.95. ISBN 0-8214-0892-5. Argues that Pater was caught between a desire for Dionysian chaos and the Victorian conventions of the Greek as serenely ordered.
Levey, Michael. *The Case of Walter Pater.* Thames Hudson 1978 o.p. Competent biography.
Loesberg, Jonathan. *Aestheticism and Deconstruction: Pater, Derrida, and de Man.* Princeton U. Pr. 1991 $35.00. ISBN 0-691-06884-4. Examines Pater's aesthetic theories in conjunction with the relativism of de Man and Derrida.
McGrath, F. C. *The Sensible Spirit: Walter Pater and the Modernist Paradigm.* U. Press Fla. 1986 $32.95. ISBN 0-8130-0829-8. Pater as protomodernist.
Monsman, Gerald. *Pater's Portraits: Mythic Pattern in the Fiction of Walter Pater.* Johns Hopkins 1967 o.p. Contains an excellent discussion of *Marius*.
———. *Walter Pater.* Twayne 1977 $17.95. ISBN 0-8057-6676-6. A good introduction to the writer's work and ideas.

_____. *Walter Pater's Art of Autobiography.* Yale U. Pr. 1980 $47.90. ISBN 0-8357-3753-5. Study of Pater's tendency toward autobiography in his prose.

Williams, Carolyn. *Transfigured World: Walter Pater's Aesthetic Historicism.* Cornell Univ. Pr. 1989 $35.00. ISBN 0-8014-2151-9

Wright, Samuel. *An Informative Index to the Writings of Walter H. Pater.* Locust Hill Pr. 1987 $40.00. ISBN 0-933951-11-6. Useful concordance.

PINERO, SIR ARTHUR WING. 1855–1934

Arthur Wing Pinero, a former actor, remained a shrewd judge of theatrical taste. After a period of writing comedies and farces (*Dandy Dick*, in 1887, among the best), in the 1890s Pinero fastened on London's newly aroused interest in social-problem plays. But, instead of following the difficult example of IBSEN (see Vol. 2), whose plays were just then beginning to be produced in English translations, Pinero turned to the French playwrights of an earlier generation. The *demimondaine* of Guillaume Augier and ALEXANDRE DUMAS (fils) (see Vol. 2) became, in plays like *The Second Mrs. Tanqueray* (1893), the "woman with a past." The inevitable (and inevitably effective) theatrical business of recognition and confession led to acts of renunciation—in Mrs. Tanqueray's case, suicide—which permitted characters and audiences to escape the moral problems that had been posed for them. Although OSCAR WILDE admired and imitated Pinero, GEORGE BERNARD SHAW (as a critic) denounced the timid morality and conventional characterization of this supposedly "new" drama.

Pinero's one lasting achievement is not a problem play at all, but the affectionate homage of a theater man to an earlier era of the London stage. *Trelawney of the "Wells"* (1898) has had successful modern productions at London's National Theatre and New York's Lincoln Center.

PLAYS BY PINERO

Dandy Dick. 1887. Heinemann Ed. 1959 o.p.

Plays. Ed. by George Rowell. Cambridge U. Pr. 1986 $59.95. ISBN 0-521-24103-0. New collected edition of the plays.

Social Plays. Ed. by Clayton Hamilton. 4 vols. AMS Pr. repr. of 1922 ed. $150.00. ISBN 0-404-05080-8. With a general introduction and critical preface to each play by Clayton Hamilton.

Three Plays. Routledge Chapman & Hall 1985 o.p. Contains *The Magistrate, The Second Mrs. Tanqueray,* and *Trelawney of the "Wells."* Introduction by Stephen Wyatt.

WORK BY PINERO

The Collected Letters of Sir Arthur Pinero. Ed. by J. P. Wearing. Bks. Demand repr. of 1974 ed. $81.70. ISBN 0-318-39674-2

BOOKS ABOUT PINERO

Dunkel, Wilbur D. *Sir Arthur Pinero: A Critical Biography with Letters.* Assoc. Faculty Pr. repr. of 1941 ed. o.p.

Griffin, Penny. *Arthur Wing Pinero and Henry Arthur Jones.* St. Martin 1991 $24.95. ISBN 0-312-05572-2. Recent study of two of the most prolific and important of the Victorian playwrights.

Lazenby, Walter. *Arthur Wing Pinero.* Twayne's Eng. Authors Ser. G. K. Hall o.p.

Smith, Leslie. *Modern British Farce: A Selective Study of British Farce from Pinero to the Present Day.* B & N Imports 1989 $46.00. ISBN 0-389-20820-5. Examines Pinero in the tradition of modern farce.

READE, CHARLES. 1814–1884

An energetic playwright and dramatizer of the novel for the stage, Reade wrote the didactic novel, the novel with a lesson. But he also wrote, probably influenced by CHARLES DICKENS, such interesting psychological romances as *Hard Cash* (1863), in which sexual tension and sensationalism dominate. His one historical romance, his masterpiece *The Cloister and the Hearth* (1861), is a picture of life in Germany and Italy at the close of the Middle Ages, the hero being the father of ERASMUS (see Vol. 4). Such novels were compiled rather than written. Reade did endless historical research and investigation for the facts they contain.

NOVELS BY READE

The Cloister and the Hearth. 1861. Biblio Dist. 1955 o.p. Reade's best-known work. Introduction by Algernon Charles Swinburne.
It Is Never Too Late to Mend: A Matter-of-Fact Romance. 3 vols. AMS Pr. repr. of 1857 ed. o.p.

WORK BY READE

Works. 17 vols. AMS Pr. repr. of 1896 ed. $637.50. ISBN 0-404-05260-6

BOOKS ABOUT READE

Elwin, Malcolm. *Charles Reade: A Biography.* Russell 1969 repr. of 1931 ed. o.p.
Reade, Charles L. *Charles Reade: Dramatist, Novelist, Journalist.* 2 vols. Folcroft 1977 repr. of 1887 ed. o.p.
Smith, Elton E. *Charles Reade.* Twayne's Eng. Authors Ser. Twayne o.p.

ROBERTSON, T(HOMAS) W(ILLIAM). 1829–1871

Robertson was born into an old theatrical family and as early as 1834 began playing children's roles. As a young boy, he was sent to Henry Young's School at Spalding and later to a school at Whitlesea. In 1843 he left school to work for his father, then manager of the Lincoln Company, as a prompter and roustabout. Robertson acted a number of roles there, including Hamlet, but, when the company disbanded in 1848, he went to London, finding work as an actor in a number of lesser-known theaters. Within a few years, his first play, *A Night's Adventure* (1851), was produced, followed by *Castles in the Air* (1855). Robertson's success was limited, however, and he continued to work at a number of odd acting and stage manager jobs. He even attempted to join the army but was rejected. The 1861 staging of *Cantab* brought him to the notice of bohemian London but did little to improve his financial situation. Finally, after the production of *David Garrick* (1864) and *Society* (1865), Robertson's career began in earnest; he went on to write a number of successful comedies, including *Ours* (1866), *Caste* (1867)—which many believe to be his best play— *Play* (1868), *School* (1869), and *M.P.* (1870).

Robertson's significance is in his introduction, to the mid-Victorian stage, of a new, more natural type of comedy, in which the characters evinced a combination of sentiment and shallow worldliness. He has fallen out of favor among critics, and his plays are today seldom produced. A fairly recent edition of the plays have been collected by William Tydeman; a good collection of his most important works is available in *Six Plays*. The older collection of his plays, from 1889, is notable primarily for the biographical memoir by his son.

PLAYS BY ROBERTSON

Plays by Tom Robertson. Ed. by William Tydeman. Cambridge U. Pr. 1982 $54.95. ISBN 0-521-23386-0

Six Plays. Amber Lane Pr. 1980 $7.95. ISBN 0-9063-9916-5. Excellent introduction by Michael R. Booth.

The Principal Dramatic Works of Thomas William Robertson, with Memoir by His Son. 2 vols. (coauthored with Thomas William Shaft Robertson). Low, Marston, Searle & Rivington 1889 o.p.

BOOKS ABOUT ROBERTSON

Pemberton, Thomas Edgar. *The Life and Writings of T. W. Robertson.* Bentley 1983 o.p.

Savin, Maynard. *Thomas William Robertson: His Plays and Stagecraft.* Bks. Demand repr. of 1950 ed. $40.00. ISBN 0-685-15773-3. Literary study of the plays.

ROSSETTI, CHRISTINA. 1830–1894

Christina Rossetti was for decades treated primarily as the sister of DANTE GABRIEL ROSSETTI. She rejected her brother's flamboyance, remained at home, and wrote a far greater volume of poetry than her brother. With the rise of feminism and the growing recognition of the aesthetic possibilities of religious poetry, Christina Rossetti's work has become the subject of an increasing volume of study. She is known primarily for her ballads and her mystical religious lyrics. Her work is also marked by its symbolism, vivid detail, and intensity of feeling.

Although *Goblin Market*, published in 1862, remains her best-known poem, the sonnet sequence *Monna Innominata* has attracted growing attention as a work that can bear comparison with ELIZABETH BARRETT BROWNING's *Sonnets from the Portuguese* on the one side, and GEORGE MEREDITH's *Modern Love* on the other.

POETRY BY CHRISTINA ROSSETTI

A Choice of Christina Rossetti's Verse. Ed. by Elizabeth Jennings. Faber & Faber 1970 $8.95. ISBN 0-571-09018-9

The Complete Poems of Christina Rossetti. 2 vols. Ed. by Rebecca W. Crump. La. State U. Pr. Vol. 1 1979 $37.50. ISBN 0-8071-0358-6. Vol. 2 1986 $40.00. ISBN 0-8071-1246-1.

Goblin Market. Dover 1983 repr. of 1893 ed. $2.95. ISBN 0-486-24516-0

Poetical Works. Rprt. Serv. 1992 repr. of 1906 ed. $99.00. ISBN 0-7812-7623-3. To date, the standard work.

Selected Poems. Ed. by C. H. Sisson. Humanities 1984 o.p.

Sing Song: A Nursery Rhyme Book. Dover 1969 repr. of 1872 ed. $4.50. ISBN 0-486-22107-5. Collection of children's verse.

WORKS BY CHRISTINA ROSSETTI

Family Letters of Christina Georgina Rossetti, with Some Supplementary Letters and Appendices. Ed. by William M. Rossetti. *Eng. Lit. Ser.* Haskell 1969 repr. of 1908 ed. $75.00. ISBN 0-8383-0237-8

Maude: Prose and Verse. Ed. by Rebecca W. Crump. Shoe String 1976 o.p.

BOOKS ABOUT CHRISTINA ROSSETTI

Battiscombe, Georgina. *Christina Rossetti.* St. Mut. 1981 o.p.

Bell, Mackenzie. *Christina Rossetti: A Biographical and Critical Study.* AMS Pr. repr. of 1898 ed. $12.50. ISBN 0-404-08724-8. For years the only work on Christina Rossetti.

Bellas, Ralph A. *Christina Rossetti.* Twayne's Eng. Authors Ser. G. K. Hall 1977 o.p.

Crump, Rebecca W. *Christina Rossetti: A Reference Guide.* G. K. Hall 1976 o.p.

Edmond, Rod. *Affairs of the Hearth: Victorian Narrative Poetry and the Ideology of the Domestic.* Routledge 1988 $45.00. ISBN 0-415-00656-2. Good on Christina Rossetti.

Harrison, Antony H. *Christina Rossetti in Context.* U. of NC Pr. 1988 $14.95. ISBN 0-8078-1755-4. Examines Rossetti as squarely within the Pre-Raphaelite tradition.

Kent, David A., ed. *The Achievement of Christina Rossetti.* Cornell Univ. Pr. 1987 $15.95. ISBN 0-8014-1937-9. Makes a strong case for inclusion of Christina Rossetti in first rank of Victorian poets.

Mayberry, Katherine J. *Christina Rossetti and the Poetry of Discovery.* La. State U. Pr. 1989 $25.00. ISBN 0-8071-1529-0. A somewhat new critical reading of Rossetti's work.

Rosenblum, Dolores. *Christina Rossetti: The Poetry of Endurance.* S. Ill. U. Pr. 1986 $26.95. ISBN 0-8093-1269-7. Feminist reading that situates Rossetti outside the female tradition and necessarily passive in the male poetic tradition.

ROSSETTI, DANTE GABRIEL. 1828–1882

Around Rossetti swirled the currents of high Victorian revolt. From his formative influence on the Pre-Raphaelite Brotherhood (1847–54) and his publication of the magazine *The Germ* in 1850, to his later infamy as the butt of Robert W. Buchanan's 1871 moralistic attacks in *The Fleshly School of Poetry*, Dante Gabriel Rossetti attracted the scorn of many and the wholehearted admiration of growing numbers. Rossetti's poetry ranged from the grand guignol of "A Last Confession," through the imagistic brilliance of "The Blessed Damozel" (1850), to his masterwork, the sonnet sequence *The House of Life*, upon which Rossetti's contemporary poetic fame rests.

Rossetti was also known as a translator, producing the first modern translation of the early Italian poets and publishing the best Victorian translation of DANTE's (see Vol. 2) *Vita Nuova* in 1861. A noted painter as well, his paintings stand out among the general academic ruck of Victorian England and have been the subject of exhibitions at the Delaware Art Museum, the Fogg Art Museum, and the Yale University Art Gallery. Finally, he was an important model for the generations that followed him, both in his willingness to indulge in sexual irregularities and, even more important, in his eagerness to *épater les bourgeoisie* (walking his pet wombat on the streets of London, for example), which became a religion for the decadents who grew up during the 1860s.

In 1860, after a prolonged courtship, Rossetti married his painting model Eizabeth Siddal. When she died in 1862 he was grief-stricken, and his work took on a morbid quality. Her death affected him for many years, contributing to deep depression and a suicide attempt in 1872. At one point he was even considered to be insane.

POETRY BY DANTE GABRIEL ROSSETTI

The Essential Rossetti. Ed. by John Hollander. Ecco Pr. 1989 $6.00. ISBN 0-88001-196-3. Nice selection of the most often read poems.

Poems. Ed. by Oswald Doughty. Biblio Dist. 1977 repr. of 1961 ed. o.p.

The Poetical Works of Dante Gabriel Rossetti. Folcroft repr. of 1903 ed. o.p.

WORKS BY DANTE GABRIEL ROSSETTI

Dante and His Circle with the Italian Poets Preceding Him. 2 vols. Norwood 1980 repr. of 1900 ed. o.p.

Dante Gabriel Rossetti: His Family Letters. 2 vols. AMS Pr. repr. of 1895 ed. $72.50. ISBN 0-404-05434-X

The Early Italian Poets. U. CA Pr. 1982 $27.50. ISBN 0-520-04468-1. Introduction by John Wain.

Letters. Ed. by Oswald Doughty and John R. Wahl. 4 vols. OUP 1965–67 o.p. Letters that are less revelatory than one would hope.

The Letters of Dante Gabriel Rossetti to His Publishers, F. S. Ellis. Folcroft 1977 repr. of 1928 ed. o.p.

Pre-Raphaelite Diaries and Letters. Ed. by William M. Rossetti. AMS Pr. repr. of 1900 ed. o.p. Essential source material for the Pre-Raphaelite Brotherhood and for much of the Rossetti family's activities.

Works. Ed. by William M. Rossetti. Adlers Foreign Bks. 1972 repr. of 1911 ed. o.p. In the absence of anything more definitive, the standard edition.

BOOKS ABOUT DANTE GABRIEL ROSSETTI

Angeli, Helen R. *Dante Gabriel Rossetti.* Ayer repr. of 1949 ed. $22.50. ISBN 0-405-08206-1. Study of Rossetti in relation to his family and the men and women who knew him.

Bass, Eben E. *Dante Gabriel Rossetti: Poet and Painter.* P. Lang Pubs. 1990 $55.00. ISBN 0-8204-1028-4. A well-researched and well-written biography.

Beerbohm, M. *Rossetti and His Circle.* Gordon Pr. 1972 $59.95. ISBN 0-8490-0974-X. An early study of the Pre-Raphaelites by the rapier-penned satirist.

Buchanan, Robert W. *The Fleshly School of Poetry and Other Phenomena of the Day.* AMS Pr. 1871 $14.00. ISBN 0-404-08821-X. Explains to the serious student of Rossetti, Swinburne, and their contemporaries just what the attacks on Rossetti were based on.

Dobbs, Brian, and Judy Dobbs. *Dante Gabriel Rossetti: An Alien Victorian.* Humanities 1977 o.p.

Doughty, Oswald. *A Victorian Romantic: Dante Gabriel Rossetti.* Telegraph Bks. 1981 repr. of 1949 ed. o.p. The standard biography, although much has come to light in the past few decades.

Faxon, Alicia Craig. *Dante Gabriel Rossetti.* Abbeville Pr. 1989 $85.00. ISBN 0-89659-928-0. Unexceptional story of the poet and artist's life.

Fennell, Francis L. *Dante Gabriel Rossetti: An Annotated Bibliography.* Ed. by Duane Devries. Garland 1981 o.p.

Howard, Ronnalie R. *The Dark Glass: Vision and Technique in the Poetry of Dante Gabriel Rossetti.* Ohio U. Pr. 1972 o.p.

Johnston, Robert D., ed. *Dante Gabriel Rossetti.* Twayne 1969 o.p. Analysis of Rossetti's poetry and art that traces the theme of love to show the effect of his early thought on his mature work; minor emphasis on biography; contains a chronology and selected bibliography.

Rees, Joan. *The Poetry of Dante Gabriel Rossetti: Modes of Self-Expression.* Cambridge U. Pr. 1981 $47.95. ISBN 0-521-23537-5. One of the better recent studies.

Riede, David G. *Dante Gabriel Rossetti and the Limits of Victorian Vision.* Cornell Univ. Pr. 1983 $33.95. ISBN 0-8014-1552-7. One of the best books on Rossetti and on Victorian poetry generally.

Rossetti, William M. *Bibliography of the Works of Dante Gabriel Rossetti.* AMS Pr. repr. of 1905 ed. $17.00. ISBN 0-404-05439-0

Scott, William B. *Autobiographical Notes and Notes on His Artistic and Poetic Circle of Friends, 1830–1882.* Ed. by M. Minto. 2 vols. AMS Pr. 1970 repr. of 1892 ed. $47.50. ISBN 0-404-05643-1. Fascinating memoirs by Rossetti's friend and fellow artist.

Surtees, Virginia. *Rossetti's Portrait Drawings of Elizabeth Siddall: A Catalogue of the Drawings and Watercolours.* Gower UK 1991 o.p.

RUSKIN, JOHN. 1819–1900

Ruskin was, after CARLYLE, probably the most influential man of letters of the nineteenth century. An only child, Ruskin was born in Surrey. He attended Christ Church, Oxford, from 1839 to 1842. His ties to his parents, especially his mother, were very strong, and she stayed with him at Oxford until 1840, when, showing ominous signs of consumption, he left for a long tour of Switzerland

and the Rhineland with both parents. His journeys to France, Germany, and, especially, Italy formed a great portion of his education. Not only did these trips give him firsthand exposure to the art and architecture that would be the focus of much of his long career; they also helped shape what he felt was his main interest, the study of nature. Around this time Ruskin met the landscape artist J. M. W. TURNER (see Vol. 3), for whose work he had developed a deep admiration and whom he lauded in his *Modern Painters* (1843).

In 1848 Ruskin married Euphemia (Effie) Gray, a distant cousin 10 years his junior. This relationship has been the focus of much scholarship, for six years later the marriage was annulled on the grounds of nonconsummation, and in 1855 Effie married John Everett Millais, the Pre-Raphaelite painter and an acquaintance of Ruskin. During the years 1849–50 and 1850–52, Ruskin lived in Venice, where he pursued a course of architectural studies, publishing *The Seven Lamps of Architecture* (1849) and where he began *The Stones of Venice* (1851–53). It was also during this period that Ruskin's evangelicalism weakened, leading finally to his "unconversion" at Turin in 1858. His subsequent interest in political economy was clearly stated when, echoing his "hero," Carlyle, Ruskin remarked in the last volume of *Modern Painters* that greed is the deadly principle that guides English life. In a series of essays in *Cornhill Magazine* attacking the "pseudo-science" of political economists like J. S. MILL (see Vols. 3 and 4), DAVID RICARDO (see Vol. 3), and THOMAS MALTHUS (see Vol. 3), Ruskin argues that England should base its "political economy" on a paternalistic, Christian-based doctrine instead of on competition. The essays were not well received, and the series was canceled short of completion, but Ruskin published the collected essays in 1862 as *Unto This Last*. At the same time, he renewed his attacks on the political economists in *Fraser's Magazine*, later publishing these essays as *Munera Pulveris* (1872).

From about 1862 until the end of his life, Ruskin unsuccessfully fought depression. He was in love with Rose La Touche, whom he met when she was 11 and he 41. When she turned 18, Ruskin proposed, but the marriage was opposed by Rose's parents, and religious differences (she was devout; Ruskin was at this time a freethinker) kept them from ever marrying. La Touche died in 1875, insane, and three years later Ruskin experienced the first of seven attacks of madness that would plague him over the next 10 years. By 1869 Ruskin had accepted the first Slade Professorship of Fine Art at Oxford, begun his serial *Fors Clavigera*, been sued and found guilty of libel for his attack on Whistler in *Fors Clavigera* (he was fined a farthing), and resigned his professorship.

Whatever the oddness of Ruskin's life, his work was instrumental in the formation of art history as a modern discipline. Himself a capable artist, he complemented his technical understanding of art with insightful analysis and passionately held social ideals. Much of his social writings are of interest today primarily as artifacts of the age, but his art criticism still holds an important place in the canon, especially in his appreciation of Turner. There is a vast number of works on Ruskin. From a literary standpoint, John Rosenberg's study, although dated because of many of its assumptions, is still an outstanding book. Jay Fellows's work is interesting and has caused much controversy among Ruskin scholars. Two good, recent biographies are Joan Abse's *John Ruskin: The Passionate Moralist* and John Dixon Hunt's *The Wider Sea*.

NONFICTION BY RUSKIN

Lectures on Art. 1870. Garland 1978 o.p. Reprint of the 1870 edition.

Modern Painters. 1834. 2 vols. Ed. by David Barrie. Knopf 1987 $45.00. ISBN 0-394-56846-X. Reprint of the books that made Ruskin famous as an art critic.

Munera Pulveris: Six Essays on the Elements of Political Economy. 1872. Greenwood 1969 repr. of 1891 ed. $35.00. ISBN 0-8371-0642-7

Praeterita: The Autobiography of John Ruskin. 1885–89. OUP 1978 $16.95. ISBN 0-19-281253-X

Ruskin on Turner. Ed. by Dinah Birch. Bulfinch Pr. 1990 $50.00. ISBN 0-8212-1808-5. Collection of Ruskin's appreciations of the landscape artist J. M. W. Turner.

Sesame and Lilies: The Two Paths and the King of the Golden River. Scholarly 1971 repr. of 1907 ed. $69.00. ISBN 0-403-01190-6

The Seven Lamps of Architecture. 1849. Peter Smith 1991 $19.75. ISBN 0-8446-6469-3. Helped establish Ruskin as a noted art critic.

The Stones of Venice. 1851–53. Ed. by Jan Morris. Moyer Bell Limited 1989 $34.95. ISBN 0-918825-13-X. Study of architecture in Venice and the city's artistic decay.

A Tour to the Lakes in Cumberland: John Ruskin's Diary for 1830. Ed. by James S. Dearden. Gower UK 1990 $39.95. ISBN 0-85967-812-1. Ruskin's travel diary from his youthful visit to the Lake District; introduction by Van Akin Burd.

Unto This Last, and Other Writings. Ed. by Clive Wilmer. Viking Penguin 1985 $5.95. ISBN 0-14-043211-6. Good selection on Ruskin's works on the need for social and economic reforms.

WORKS BY RUSKIN

The Correspondence of John Ruskin and Charles Eliot Norton. Ed. by John Lewis Bradley and Ian Ousby. Cambridge U. Pr. 1987 $89.95. ISBN 0-521-32091-7. Interesting collection of the letters between the two art critic-theorists.

The Diaries of John Ruskin. 3 vols. Ed. by Joan Evans and John Howard Whitehouse. OUP 1956–59 o.p. Covers the years 1835–89.

The Genius of John Ruskin. Ed. by John Rosenberg. Routledge 1979 o.p. Good, judicious, one-volume selection of Ruskin's most famous works.

The Order of Release: The Story of John Ruskin, Effie Gray, and John Everett Millais Told for the First Time in Their Unpublished Letters. Ed. by Sir William James. J. Murray UK 1947 o.p. Important for information about Ruskin's marriage.

The Ruskin Family Letters: The Correspondence of John James Ruskin, His Wife, and Their Son, John, 1801–1843. 2 vols. Ed. by Van Akin Burd. Cornell Univ. Pr. 1973 $88.50. ISBN 0-8014-0725-7. Good for understanding Ruskin's relation to his parents.

Ruskin's Letters from Venice, 1851–1852. Ed. by John Lewis Bradley. Greenwood repr. of 1955 ed. $38.50. ISBN 0-313-20456-X. Letters to his parents, indicating Ruskin's growing religious doubts.

The Works of John Ruskin. 39 vols. Ed. by E. T. Cook and Alexander Wedderburn. George Allen 1903–12 o.p. The standard edition.

BOOKS ABOUT RUSKIN

Abse, Joan. *John Ruskin: The Passionate Moralist*. Quartet UK 1980 o.p.

Austin, Linda Marilyn. *The Practical Ruskin: Economics and Audience in the Late Work*. Johns Hopkins 1991 o.p. Discussion of Ruskin as economic and social theorist.

Bloom, Harold, ed. *John Ruskin*. Chelsea Hse. 1986 $19.95. ISBN 0-8775-4692-4. Good collection of essays on Ruskin.

Bradley, John L. *An Introduction to Ruskin*. HM 1971 o.p. Short but good appraisal of the work.

Brooks, Michael W. *John Ruskin and Victorian Architecture*. Rutgers U. Pr. 1987 $29.95. ISBN 0-8135-1205-0. Ruskin as advocate of Gothic revival and his role as critic of architecture.

Burd, Van Akin, ed. *John Ruskin and Rose La Touche: Her Unpublished Diaries of 1861 and 1867*. OUP 1967 o.p. Excellent for firsthand information on Ruskin's relationship with the unfortunate young woman.

Cate, George Allan. *John Ruskin, a Reference Guide: A Selective Guide to Significant and Representative Works about Him*. G. K. Hall 1988 $45.00. ISBN 0-8161-8908-0. Useful for sifting through a large amount of material.

Fellows, Jay. *The Failing Distance: The Autobiographical Impulse in John Ruskin*. Johns Hopkins 1975 $26.50. ISBN 0-8018-1671-8

———. *Ruskin's Maze: Mastery and Madness in His Art*. Princeton U. Pr. 1981 $83.20. ISBN 0-8357-6931-3. Discussion of Ruskin's subjectivity in his writing.

Helsinger, Elizabeth K. *Ruskin and the Art of the Beholder*. HUP 1982 $33.00. ISBN 0-674-78082-5. Discussion of the influence on and context of Ruskin's thought.

Hewison, Robert. *John Ruskin: The Argument of the Eye*. Bks. Demand repr. of 1976 ed. $61.60. ISBN 0-7837-1939-6. Worthwhile introduction to Ruskin's work.

Hunt, John Dixon. *The Wider Sea: A Life of John Ruskin*. J. M. Dent 1982 o.p.

Kemp, Wolfgang. *The Desire of My Eyes: The Life and Work of John Ruskin*. Trans. by Jan van Heurck. FS&G 1990 $40.00. ISBN 0-374-17996-4. For a broad audience, though the work has some scholarly value.

Kirchhoff, Frederick. *John Ruskin*. Twayne 1984 o.p. Good overview with valuable, if biased, bibliography.

Penny, Nicholas. *Ruskin's Drawings in the Ashmolean Museum*. Phaidon UK 1988 o.p. Reproductions of Ruskin's own sketches.

Proust, Marcel. *On Reading Ruskin: Prefaces to "La Bible d'Amiens" and "Sesame et les Lys," with Selections from Notes to the Translated Texts*. Trans. and ed. by Jean Autret, William Burford, and Phillip J. Wolfe. Yale U. Pr. 1987 $25.00. ISBN 0-300-03513-6. Essays by one of the most famous of Ruskin's readers; introduction by Richard Macksey.

Rhodes, Robert, and Del Ivan Janik, eds. *Studies in Ruskin: Essays in Honor of Van Akin Burd*. Ohio U. Pr. 1982 o.p. Good collection by prominent Ruskin scholars.

Rosenberg, John D. *The Darkening Glass*. Col. U. Pr. 1986 $18.00. ISBN 0-231-06387-3

Wheeler, Michael, and Nigel Whiteley, eds. *The Lamp of Memory: Ruskin, Tradition, and Architecture*. St. Martin 1992 $79.95. ISBN 0-7190-3710-7. Collection of essays about Ruskin's influence on Victorian architecture and architecture criticism.

SPENCER, HERBERT. 1820–1903

[SEE Volume 4.]

STEVENSON, ROBERT LOUIS. 1850–1894

Novelist, poet, and essayist Robert Louis Stevenson was born in Edinburgh, Scotland. A sickly child, Stevenson was an invalid for part of his childhood and remained in ill health throughout his life. He began studying engineering at Edinburgh University but soon switched to law. His true inclination, however, was for writing. For several years after completing his studies, Stevenson traveled on the Continent, gathering ideas for his writing. His *Inland Voyage* (1878) and *Travels with a Donkey* (1878) describe some of his experiences there. A variety of essays and short stories followed, most of which were published in magazines. It was with the publication of *Treasure Island* in 1883, however, that Stevenson achieved wide recognition and fame. This was followed by his most successful adventure story, *Kidnapped*, which appeared in 1886.

With stories such as *Treasure Island* and *Kidnapped*, Stevenson revived DANIEL DEFOE's novel of romantic adventure, adding to it psychological analysis. While these stories and others, such as *David Balfour* and *The Master of Ballantrae* (1889), are stories of adventure, they are at the same time fine studies of character. *The Master of Ballantrae*, in particular, is a study of evil character, and this study is taken even further in *The Strange Case of Dr. Jekyll and Mr. Hyde* (1886).

In 1887 Stevenson and his wife, Fanny, went to the United States, first to the health spas of Saranac Lake, New York, and then on to the West Coast. From there they set out for the South Seas in 1889. Except for one trip to Sidney, Australia, Stevenson spent the remainder of his life on the island of Samoa with his devoted wife and stepson. While there he wrote *The Wrecker* (1892), *Island Nights Entertainments* (1893), and *Catriona* (1893), a sequel to *Kidnapped*. He also worked on *St. Ives* and *The Weir of Hermiston*, which many consider to be his masterpiece. He died suddenly of apoplexy, leaving both of these works unfinished. Both were published posthumously; *St. Ives* was completed by Sir ARTHUR QUILLER-COUCH, and *The Weir of Hermiston* was published unfinished. Stevenson was buried on Samoa, an island he had come to love very much.

Although Stevenson's novels are perhaps more accomplished, his short stories are also vivid and memorable. All show his power of invention, his command of the macabre and the eerie, and the psychological depth of his characterization.

NOVELS BY STEVENSON

The Black Arrow. Airmont 1964 $1.95. ISBN 0-8049-0020-5. In fifteenth-century England, a band of outlaws called The Brotherhood of the Black Arrow fights against tyranny.

Dr. Jekyll and Mr. Hyde. 1886. Signet 1987 $2.25. ISBN 0-451-52138-2. Through his experiments, a scientist releases his own evil nature.

Kidnapped. Bantam Class. Ser. Bantam 1982 $2.25. ISBN 0-553-21249-4. In the Scots uprising of 1775, young David Balfour is kidnapped and has to fight for his life and his honor.

Kidnapped and *Catriona*. Ed. by Emma Letley. OUP 1986 $4.50. ISBN 0-19-281726-4. Two of the Scottish romances.

The Master of Ballantrae. 1889. Airmont 1964 $1.95. ISBN 0-8049-0047-7. A lifelong feud between two brothers extends from Scotland to America.

St. Ives. 1894. Biblio Dist. 1958 o.p.

The Strange Case of Dr. Jekyll and Mr. Hyde and *Weir of Hermiston*. Ed. by Emma Letley. OUP 1987 $4.50. ISBN 0-19-281740-X. Reprint of the classic tale and Stevenson's unfinished last novel.

Treasure Island. 1883. Ed. by Emma Letley. OUP 1982 $2.25. ISBN 0-19-281681-0. Jim Hawkins discovers a treasure map, and the adventure begins.

The Wrecker. 1892. (coauthored with Lloyd Osbourne). Dover 1982 o.p. Written in collaboration with his stepson Lloyd Osbourne.

The Wrong Box. 1889. North Bks. 1992 $20.00. ISBN 0-939495-32-5

SHORT STORY COLLECTIONS BY STEVENSON

Robert Louis Stevenson: The Complete Shorter Fiction. Ed. by Peter Stoneley. Carroll & Graf 1991 $28.95. ISBN 0-88184-741-0

Island Nights Entertainments. Rprt. Serv. 1992 repr. of 1921 ed. $79.00. ISBN 0-7812-7666-7. Written during the last years of Stevenson's life while living on the island of Samoa.

POETRY BY STEVENSON

A Child's Garden of Verses. 1885. Crown Pub. Group 1986 $6.98. ISBN 0-517-39777-X. Poems about the joys of childhood that will delight readers of all ages.

Complete Poems. Gordon Pr. 1973 $250.00. ISBN 0-87968-101-2

Moral Emblems and Other Poems. Polygon Pr. UK 1986 o.p. Illustrated by Stevenson, with an introduction by Allan Massie.

New Poems and Variant Readings. Century Bookbindery 1981 repr. of 1918 ed. o.p.

Poems. Rprt. Serv. 1992 repr. of 1925 ed. $79.00. ISBN 0-7812-7665-9

NONFICTION BY STEVENSON

An Inland Voyage by Robert Louis Stevenson: With a Travel Guide to the Route by Andrew Sanger. Seven Hills Bk. Dists. 1992 $19.95. ISBN 1-873054-02-5. Based on Stevenson's experiences traveling in France.

In the South Seas. 1896. Routledge $14.95. ISBN 0-7103-0140-5

The Lantern-Bearers and Other Essays. FS&G 1988 $25.00. ISBN 0-374-25792-2. Selected and with an introduction by Jeremy Treglown.

WORKS BY STEVENSON

Letters. 4 vols. Ed. by Sidney Colvin. Rprt. Serv. 1992 repr. of 1911 ed. $300.00. ISBN 0-7812-7668-3

The Scottish Stories and Essays. Ed. by Kenneth Gelder. Edinburgh U. Pr. 1989 o.p. Includes "Thrawn Janet" and "The Beach of Falseá."

Selected Writings. Ed. by Saxe Commins. *Essay Index Repr. Ser.* Ayer repr. of 1947 ed. $42.50. ISBN 0-8369-2523-8. Three novels, ten short stories, three books of travel, and a selection of verse.

Vailima Letters. Rprt. Serv. 1992 repr. of 1895 ed. $150.00. ISBN 0-7812-7669-1

Works. Ed. by L. Osbourne and F. Van de G. Stevenson. 26 vols. AMS Pr. repr. of 1921–23 ed. $1,950.00. ISBN 0-7812-7664-0

Works. 10 vols. Richard West repr. o.p.

BOOKS ABOUT STEVENSON

Balfour, Sir Graham. *The Life of Robert Louis Stevenson.* Rprt. Serv. 1992 repr. of 1901 ed. $150.00. ISBN 0-7812-7670-5. Reveals a great family pride and maintains loyal silences on many passages in Stevenson's career; written by Stevenson's cousin.

Daiches, David. *Stevenson and the Art of Fiction.* Darby Pub. 1980 repr. of 1951 ed. o.p.

Eigner, E. M. *Robert Louis Stevenson and Romantic Tradition.* Princeton U. Pr. 1966 o.p.

Furnas, Joseph Chamberlain. *Voyage to Windward: The Life of Robert Louis Stevenson.* Richard West 1980 o.p.

Hillier, Robert Irwin. *The South Seas Fiction of Robert Louis Stevenson.* P. Lang Pubs. 1989 $30.00. ISBN 0-8204-0889-1. Discussion of Stevenson's late fiction.

Knight, Alanna, ed. *R. L. S. in the South Seas: An Intimate Photographic Record.* Paragon Hse. 1987 o.p. Photos of Stevenson's voyage to the Pacific.

Maixner, Paul, ed. *Robert Louis Stevenson: The Critical Heritage. Critical Heritage Ser.* Routledge 1981 $53.00. ISBN 0-7100-0505-9

Saposnik, Irving S. *Robert Louis Stevenson. Twayne's Eng. Authors Ser.* G. K. Hall 1974 $14.95. ISBN 0-8057-1517-7. Introduction to Stevenson's works; includes a biographical sketch and a discussion of literary forms, from essay to novel.

Veeder, William R., and Gordon Hirsch, eds. *Dr. Jekyll and Mr. Hyde: After One Hundred Years.* U. Ch. Pr. 1988 $45.00. ISBN 0-226-85228-8. Collection of essays on the famous horror story.

SWINBURNE, ALGERNON CHARLES. 1837–1909

Swinburne was just old enough to get caught up in the Pre-Raphaelite maelstrom. In 1857, when DANTE GABRIEL ROSSETTI, WILLIAM MORRIS, and their friends painted the ceiling of the new Oxford Union, Swinburne fell away from his politically minded friends at Balliol College and into the set of aesthetic young graduates. Within a year he had left Oxford, one step ahead of expulsion. In less than 10 years, he was the most notorious poet of Europe, accepted by WALTER SAVAGE LANDOR but savaged by the critic John Morley; these early poems are still his best known: *Atalanta in Calydon* (1865), *Poems and Ballads* (1866), and "A Song of Italy" (1867).

Stung by the critical attacks on *Poems and Ballads*, Swinburne turned for a time to prose, writing the manifesto "Art for Art's Sake" in his *Notes on Poems and Reviews*, as well as still readable essays on WILLIAM BLAKE, BYRON, and

SHAKESPEARE. He also composed two novels, *Lesbia Brandon* (c. 1864) and *Love's Cross-currents* (1877).

But Swinburne's reputation rests on his poems: the several above, *Songs before Sunrise* (1871), *Tristram of Lyonesse* (1882), and the many others that flowed, with increasing regularity but diminishing vitality, from the retreat at Putney where he was taken in 1879 to recover from the effects of his alcoholic and other debauches—and where he stayed for 30 years under the care of Theodore Watts. David G. Riede has written eloquently of these late poems, attributing to them a mythopoeic power equal to the rhythmic and melodic power of the early works; however, to most readers, although the late poems may be masterful, they reveal little of that erotic energy that led TENNYSON to call Swinburne's verses "poisonous honey."

POETRY BY SWINBURNE

Ballads of the English Border. Folcroft 1973 o.p.
Poems and Ballads and *Atalanta in Calydon.* Ed. by Morse Peckham. Macmillan 1970 $10.00. ISBN 0-672-51119-3
Poems of Algernon Charles Swinburne. 6 vols. AMS Pr. repr. of 1905 ed. $265.00. ISBN 0-404-08930-5. Originally prepared by Swinburne himself.
Selected Poems: Swinburne. Ed. by L. M. Findlay. Carcanet 1987 $8.50. ISBN 0-85635-728-6

NOVELS BY SWINBURNE

The Novels of Algernon Charles Swinburne: Love's Cross-currents, Lesbia Brandon. Greenwood 1978 repr. of 1962 ed. o.p.

WORKS BY SWINBURNE

The Swinburne Letters. 6 vols. Ed. by Cecil Y. Lang. Yale U. Pr. 1959–62 $85.80. ISBN 0-317-29712-0. The model for all later collections.
A Year's Letters. Ed. by Francis J. Sypher. NYU Pr. 1974 o.p.

BOOKS ABOUT SWINBURNE

Beetz, Kirk H. *Algernon Charles Swinburne: A Bibliography of Secondary Works, 1861–1980. Author Bibliographies Ser.* Scarecrow 1982 $25.00. ISBN 0-8108-1541-9
Chew, Samuel C. *Swinburne.* Shoe String repr. of 1929 ed. $29.00. ISBN 0-208-00557-9. An accessible general account of Swinburne, though silent about sexual matters.
Harrison, Antony. *Swinburne's Medievalism: A Study in Victorian Love Poetry.* La. State U. Pr. 1988 $27.50. ISBN 0-8071-1327-1. Argues that Swinburne's lifelong interest in medievalism was a major influence on his poetry.
Hyder, Clyde K., ed. *Swinburne: The Critical Heritage.* Routledge 1970 $69.50. ISBN 0-7100-6656-2. Useful for its tracing of Swinburne's violent reception.
Louis, Margot Kathleen. *Swinburne and His Gods: The Roots and Growth of an Agnostic Poetry.* McGill CN 1990 $34.95. ISBN 0-7735-0715-9. Study of Swinburne's development as an agnostic and hedonist.
McSweeney, Kerry. *Tennyson and Swinburne as Romantic Naturalists.* U. of Toronto Pr. 1981 $30.00. ISBN 0-8020-2381-9
Riede, David G. *Swinburne: A Study in Romantic Mythmaking.* U. Pr. of Va. 1978 o.p.
Thomas, Donald. *Swinburne: The Poet of His World.* OUP 1979 $22.95. ISBN 0-19-520136-1. Biography that provides a brief overview of the "darker sides" of Swinburne's life.

TAYLOR, TOM. 1817–1880

Taylor, a prolific dramatist, was the editor of *Punch* from 1874 to 1880. He was educated at Glasgow University, where he distinguished himself as a student; later he studied at Trinity College, Cambridge, and served for two years as a professor of English at University College, London. When Taylor settled in

London, he worked for both the *Morning Chronicle* and *The Daily News*. Despite his journalism, however, he is best remembered as the author of more than 100 plays over a 35-year span. While few survive as outstanding literary achievements, Taylor was immensely successful in his own day, and apparently only one of his plays was an outright failure. In 1871 the playwright was accused by the *Atheneum* of plagiarizing most of his works—a common practice in the early-nineteenth-century theater but less savory during the later Victorian years. Only one-tenth of his plays were adaptations, he replied; the rest were original. Indeed, some of the most popular plays were adaptations of works by VICTOR HUGO (see Vol. 2) and CHARLES DICKENS. The most successful plays were the domestic comedies *Our American Cousin* (1858) and *The Ticket-of-Leave Man* (1863). *Our American Cousin* is memorable as the play that was being performed at Ford's Theater in Washington the night that Abraham Lincoln was assassinated. Taylor is also notable for his collaboration with the novelist CHARLES READE on a number of historical dramas, the most famous of which is *Two Loves and a Life*.

PLAY BY TAYLOR

Plays. Ed. by Martin Banham. Cambridge U. Pr. 1985 $54.95. ISBN 0-521-24102-2. The principal plays; includes *Still Water Run Deep*, *The Ticket-of-Leave Man*, and *Our American Cousin*.

BOOK ABOUT TAYLOR

Tolles, Winton. *Tom Taylor and the Victorian Drama*. AMS Pr. 1966 repr. of 1940 ed. $20.00. ISBN 0-404-06474-4. The only full-length study of Taylor.

TENNYSON, ALFRED. 1ST BARON. 1809-1892

If there were a contest for the title "greatest Victorian poet," Tennyson would in death, as in life, obtain the prize. He had the finest ear of any English poet, admitting to know the metrical value of every word in the English language except "scissors." In addition, his ability to evoke a closely rendered scene was unsurpassed. Therefore, although those who sought to attack Tennyson called him "the stupidest of the English poets," he remains the only one ennobled for his poetry.

Tennyson was born at Somersby rectory in Lincolnshire, the son of the rector there, and was educated at Louth Grammar School and Trinity College, Cambridge. His earliest published verse, *Poems Chiefly Lyrical* (1830) and *Poems* (1833), were considered too sentimental by many critics. Signs of future greatness could be detected in some of the poems in these collections, however. In 1842, a new volume entitled *Poems* was published. This work, consisting of heavily revised poems from the two earlier collections as well as many new poems, helped to establish Tennyson's fame. His masterpiece, *In Memoriam* (1850), crowned his fame. The work is a tribute to his close friend Arthur Henry Hallam, whose sudden death in 1833 was a crucial event in the poet's life. The year it was published he succeeded WORDSWORTH as poet laureate of England. Thereafter, he became tremendously popular and held the respect and admiration of the nation, including Queen Victoria and Prince Albert. From that point, Tennyson also became the poet of the establishment, and for the next 40 years he was the Parnassian idol whom younger poets would vainly seek to topple.

In many of his poems, including "Ulysses," "The Princess," and *Idylls of the King* (1859–1885), Tennyson trumpeted the creed of the benevolent tyrant. It was this embrace of an authoritarian universe that, as much as his versecraft, had earned him the respect of the British monarchs. His lifelong fascination with King Arthur was the inspiration for *Idylls of the King*, a series of 12 narrative poems published over a period of 26 years. In 1888, Tennyson chronologically arranged these 12 poems, thus depicting the full story of Arthur and his vision of the perfect state. Tennyson's last poem, "Crossing the Bar," was a 16-line lyric written while crossing from Lymington to the Isle of Wight. It was included in a collection entitled *Demeter and Other Poems* published in 1889.

Tennyson's most characteristic form of poetry was the idyl, a poem of country life. These poems frequently take the form of dramatic reveries that tell a story. Mood is often created through the power of richly described settings. All of Tennyson's work reflects his talent for achieving fine shades of poetic expression, and his lyrics express the emotions and experiences shared by all people. His work is also notable for its heroic quality.

In 1883, Tennyson was awarded the title of Baron Tennyson by Queen Victoria; his full title was Baron of Aldworth and Farringford. When he died in 1892, he was buried in the Poet's Corner of Westminster Abbey.

Tennyson's letters show almost nothing of the vividness and brilliance of his poetry, but Cecil Y. Lang and Edgar F. Shannon have been publishing them for their sidelights. More important for an understanding of Tennyson's poetry, the century-long ban on publishing the contents of Tennyson's notebooks, held by Trinity College in Cambridge, was lifted not long ago; an edition of *In Memoriam*, incorporating these variants, was brought out by Susan Shatto and Marion Shaw in 1982.

POETRY BY TENNYSON

Alfred Tennyson: "In Memoriam," "Maud," and Other Poems. Ed. by John D. Jump. Rowman 1974 o.p.

Idylls of the King. Viking Penguin 1989 $6.95. ISBN 0-14-042253-6. The best working edition of the *Idylls*.

Idylls of the King and a Selection of Poems. NAL-Dutton $3.95. ISBN 0-451-52258-3

In Memoriam. Ed. by Susan Shatto and Marion Shaw. OUP 1982 $85.00. ISBN 0-19-012747-2. Essential for any serious study.

The Lover's Tale. Porter 1977 o.p.

Poems of 1842. Ed. by Christopher Ricks. International Ideas 1981 repr. of 1968 ed. o.p.

Poems of Tennyson. Ed. by Jerome H. Buckley. HM 1958 $9.16. ISBN 0-395-05124-X

Poetical Works of Tennyson. HM 1974 $25.00. ISBN 0-395-18014-7. Introduction by G. Robert Strange.

The Poems of Tennyson. 3 vols. Ed. by Christopher Ricks. U. CA Pr. 1987 $325.00. ISBN 0-520-06012-1. Definitive edition.

Unpublished Early Poems. Ed. by Charles Tennyson. Arden Lib. 1980 repr. of 1932 ed. o.p.

Selected Poems. Ed. by Michael Millgate. Viking Penguin 1992 $9.95. ISBN 0-14-044545-5

Tennyson's Poetry. Ed. by Robert W. Hill, Jr. Norton 1972 $14.95. ISBN 0-393-09953-9

Tennyson: A Selected Edition. Ed. by Christopher Ricks. U. CA Pr. 1989 $49.95. ISBN 0-520-06588-3. Excellent collection.

Tennyson: A Selected Edition Incorporating the Trinity College Manuscripts. Ed. by Christopher Ricks. U. CA Pr. 1989 o.p. Useful, scholarly collection.

Tennyson's Maud: *A Definitive Edition.* Ed. by Susan Shatto. U. of Okla. Pr. 1986 $45.00. ISBN 0-8061-19861. Scholarly edition of one of Queen Victoria's favorite poems.

WORKS BY TENNYSON

The Letters of Alfred Lord Tennyson. Ed. by Cecil Y. Lang and Edgar F. Shannon. Vol. 1 1821–1850. HUP 1981 $35.00. ISBN 0-674-52583-3. Vol. 2 1851–1870. HUP 1987

$39.95. ISBN 0-674-52584-1. Vol. 3 OUP 1990 $50.00. ISBN 0-19-812692-1. An excellent edition of material that illuminates little about Tennyson.

Tennyson: The Harvard Manuscripts, Loose Papers. 3 vols. Ed. by Christopher Ricks and Aidan Day. Garland 1987 $100.00 ea. ISBNs 0-8240-4207-7, 0-8240-4208-5, 0-8240-4209-3.

Tennyson: The Harvard Manuscripts, Notebooks 1–[70] (MS Eng 952). 7 vols. Ed. by Christopher Ricks and Aidan Day. Garland 1987 $100.00 ea. ISBN 0-8240-4200-X

Tennyson: The Manuscripts and Proofs at the Tennyson Research Centre. Ed. by Christopher Ricks and Aidan Day. Garland 1989 $163.00. ISBN 0-8240-4215-8

Tennyson: The Manuscripts at the Beinecke Library, Yale University. Ed. by Christopher Ricks and Aidan Day. Garland 1990 $100.00. ISBN 0-8240-4223-9

Tennyson: The Manuscripts at the Berg Collection of the New York Public Library and the Harry Ransom Humanities Research Center, the University of Texas at Austin. Ed. by Christopher Ricks and Aidan Day. Garland 1992 $100.00. ISBN 0-8240-4227-1

Tennyson: The Manuscripts at the British Library. Ed. by Christopher Ricks and Aidan Day. Garland 1990 $100.00. ISBN 0-8240-4224-7

Tennyson: The Manuscripts at the Fitzwilliam Museum, the Bodleian Library of Oxford University and the Sterling Library of the University of London. Ed. by Christopher Ricks and Aidan Day. Garland 1992 $100.00. ISBN 0-8240-4228-X

Tennyson: The Manuscripts at the Huntington Library and the Free Library of Philadelphia. Ed. by Christopher Ricks and Aidan Day. Garland 1991 $100.00. ISBN 0-8240-4226-3

Tennyson: The Manuscripts at Trinity College, Cambridge. 5 vols. Ed. by Christopher Ricks and Aidan Day. Garland 1988 $100.00. ISBN 0-8240-4210-7

Tennyson: The Manuscripts at the University Library, Cambridge. Ed. by Christopher Ricks and Aidan Day. Garland 1991 $100.00. ISBN 0-8240-4225-5

Works of Alfred Lord Tennyson, Annotated. 9 vols. Ed. by Hallam Tennyson. AMS Pr. repr. of 1907–08 ed. $202.50. ISBN 0-404-06370-5. The official text, incorporating all author's revisions.

BOOKS ABOUT TENNYSON

Baker, Arthur E. *A Concordance to the Poetical and Dramatic Works of Alfred, Lord Tennyson.* B & N Imports 1966 repr. of 1914 ed. o.p.

Buckler, William E. *Man and His Myths: Tennyson's "Idylls of the King" in Critical Context.* NYU Pr. 1984 o.p.

Buckley, Jerome H. *Tennyson: The Growth of a Poet.* HUP 1974 o.p. The ideal critical introduction to Tennyson's poetry and life.

Colley, Ann C. *Tennyson and Madness.* U. of Ga. Pr. 1983 $20.00. ISBN 0-8203-0648-7. Must be read with care, but thought provoking.

Culler, Arthur D. *The Poetry of Tennyson.* Yale U. Pr. 1977 o.p. An excellent overview of the poetry.

Goslee, David. *Tennyson's Characters: "Strange Faces, Other Minds."* U. of Iowa Pr. 1989 $39.95. ISBN 0-87745-246-6. Psychoanalytic examination of the characters in Tennyson's poems.

Gray, J. M. *Thro' the Vision of the Night: A Study of Source, Evolution and Structure in Tennyson's "Idylls of the King."* U. of Toronto Pr. 1980 $34.95. ISBN 0-7735-0519-9. Lacks a complete sense of recent critical work.

Hair, Donald S. *The Domestic and Heroic in Tennyson's Poetry.* U. of Toronto Pr. 1981 o.p.

——. *Tennyson's Language.* U. of Toronto Pr. 1991 $50.00. ISBN 0-8020-5905-8. Study of Tennyson's prosody and use of language.

Hughes, Linda K. *The Manyfacéd Glass: Tennyson's Dramatic Monologues.* Ohio U. Pr. 1987 $29.95. ISBN 0-8214-0853-4. Excellent study of Tennyson's use of the form most often associated with Browning.

Jordan, Elaine. *Alfred Tennyson.* Cambridge U. Pr. 1988 $42.95. ISBN 0-521-30822-4. Good introduction to Tennyson's work.

Joseph, Gerhard. *Tennyson and the Text: The Weaver's Shuttle*. Cambridge U. Pr. 1992 $54.95. ISBN 0-521-42390-7. Analyzes the gendering of Tennyson's characters in light of recent literary theories.

Killham, John, ed. *Critical Essays on the Poetry of Tennyson*. Darby Pub. 1981 repr. of 1960 ed. o.p. Mostly superseded now, but several of these essays were critical in the Tennyson revival.

Kissane, James D. *Alfred Tennyson. Twayne's Eng. Authors Ser.* Macmillan 1970 $20.95. ISBN 0-8057-1544-4

Kozicki, Henry. *Tennyson and Clio: History in the Major Poems*. Johns Hopkins 1979 $54.10. ISBN 0-8357-6619-5

Martin, Robert B. *Tennyson: The Unquiet Heart*. Faber & Faber 1983 o.p. A full recent biography marred only by its overemphasis on the strain of madness in the Tennyson family.

Pattison, Robert. *Tennyson and Tradition*. HUP 1980 $17.00. ISBN 0-674-87415-3. A study of the idyll tradition and its relation to the domestic and heroic poems.

Pinion, F. B. *A Tennyson Companion: Life and Works*. St. Martin 1984 $29.95. ISBN 0-312-79107-0. Broadly chronological survey of Tennyson's works, emphasizing later poetry; includes biographical introduction and selection of illustrations.

Pitt, Valerie. *Tennyson Laureate*. Telegraph Bks. 1981 repr. of 1962 ed. $79.10. ISBN 0-8357-4166-4

Rader, Ralph W. *Tennyson's Maud: The Biographical Genesis. Lib. Repr. Ser.* U. CA Pr. 1978 $45.00. ISBN 0-520-03617-4. A stimulating essay in the life-into-art tradition.

Ricks, Christopher B. *Tennyson*. U. CA Pr. 1989 $38.00. ISBN 0-520-06784-3. Updated and corrected edition of Ricks's earlier (1972) biography.

Rosenberg, John D. *The Fall of Camelot: A Study of Tennyson's Idylls of the King*. HUP 1973 $10.95. ISBN 0-674-29175-1

Shannon, Edgar F. *Tennyson and the Reviewers: A Study of His Literary Reputation and of the Influence of the Critics upon His Poetry, 1827–1951*. Shoe String 1967 repr. of 1952 ed. $32.50. ISBN 0-208-00566-8

Shaw, Marion. *Alfred Lord Tennyson*. Humanities 1988 o.p. Worthwhile introduction to Tennyson's life and work.

Shaw, Marion, and Clifton U. Snaith. *An Annotated Critical Bibliography of Alfred, Lord Tennyson*. St. Martin 1989 $35.00. ISBN 0-312-01962-9. Useful, though selective, bibliography.

Shaw, W. David. *Tennyson's Style*. Cornell Univ. Pr. 1976 o.p.

Staines, David. *Tennyson's Camelot: The Idylls of the King and Its Medieval Sources*. Humanities 1982 $22.95. ISBN 0-88920-115-3. Study of *Idylls* that follows the chronology of the poem's composition and analyzes Tennyson's approach to his sources.

Tennyson, Charles, *Alfred Tennyson*. 1949. Shoe String 1968 repr. of 1949 ed. $49.50. ISBN 0-208-00716-4. The fuller, nearly definitive biography by the poet's grandson.

Tennyson, Hallam, ed. *Studies in Tennyson*. B & N Imports 1981 o.p. Foreword by John Benjamin.

Tennyson, Hallam T. *Alfred Lord Tennyson: A Memoir by His Son*. 2 vols. Scholarly repr. of 1899 ed. $32.00. ISBN 0-403-00274-5. The "authorized," collaborative biography, containing all the material Tennyson, his wife, and his son wanted to see preserved.

Tucker, Herbert F. *Tennyson and the Doom of Romanticism*. HUP 1988 $39.95. ISBN 0-674-87430-7. One of the best recent studies of Tennyson.

THACKERAY, WILLIAM MAKEPEACE. 1811–1863

William Makepeace Thackeray was born in Calcutta, India, where his father was in service to the East India Company. After the death of his father in 1816, he was sent to England to attend school. Upon reaching college age, Thackeray attended Trinity College, Cambridge, but he left before completing his degree. Instead, he devoted his time to traveling and journalism.

Generally considered the most effective satirist and humorist of the mid-nineteenth century, Thackeray moved from humorous journalism to successful fiction with a facility that was partially the result of a genial fictional persona and a graceful, relaxed style. At his best, he held up a mirror to Victorian manners and morals, gently satirizing, with a tone of sophisticated acceptance, the inevitable failure of the individual and of society. He took up the popular fictional situation of the young person of talent who must make his way in the world and dramatized it with satiric directness in *The Luck of Barry Lyndon* (1844), with the highest fictional skill and appreciation of complexities inherent within the satiric vision in his masterpiece *Vanity Fair* (1847), and with a great subtlety of point of view and background in his one historical novel, *Henry Esmond* (1852). *Vanity Fair*, a complex interweaving in a vast historical panorama of a large number of characters, derives its title from JOHN BUNYAN's *Pilgrim's Progress* and attempts to invert for satirical purposes the traditional Christian image of the City of God. *Vanity Fair*, the corrupt City of Man, remains Thackeray's most appreciated and widely read novel. It contrasts the lives of two boarding-school friends, Becky Sharp and Amelia Smedley.

Constantly attuned to the demands of incidental journalism and his sense of professionalism in his relationship with his public, Thackeray wrote entertaining sketches and children's stories and published his humorous lectures on eighteenth-century life and literature. His own fiction shows the influence of his dedication to such eighteenth-century models as HENRY FIELDING, particularly in his satire, which accepts human nature rather than condemns it and takes quite seriously the applicability of the true English gentleman as a model for moral behavior.

Thackeray requested that no authorized biography of him should ever be written, but members of his family did write about him, and these accounts were subsequently published.

NOVELS BY THACKERAY

The Book of Snobs. 1848. Ed. by John Sutherland. St. Martin 1978 $25.00. ISBN 0-312-09011-0. Book of satire.

Henry Esmond (The History of Henry Esmond, Esquire). 1852. Biblio Dist. 1976 o.p. The life of Henry Esmond, from his youth through his adventures as a soldier to his move to America.

The Luck of Barry Lyndon. 1844. Buccaneer Bks. 1982 o.p.

The Newcomes. 1853. NAL-Dutton o.p. A story about young love at the mercy of scheming relatives and mean-spirited rival suitors.

Pendennis. 1850. NAL-Dutton o.p. Introduction by M. R. Ridley. A story of class snobbery in England and the efforts of its middle class protagonists to become gentlemen and aristocrats.

Thee Rose and the Ring, or The History of Prince Giglio and Prince Bulbo. 1854. NAL-Dutton o.p.

Vanity Fair. 1847. Knopf 1991 $20.00. ISBN 0-679-40566-6

The Virginians. 1859. NAL-Dutton o.p. Sequel to *Henry Esmond.*

NONFICTION BY THACKERAY

Contributions to the Morning Chronicle. Ed. by Gordon N. Ray. U. of Ill. Pr. 1955 o.p.

The English Humorists (and *The Four Georges*). 1851. Biblio Dist. repr. of 1912 ed. o.p.

The Hitherto Unpublished Contributions of W. M. Thackeray to "Punch." AMS Pr. repr. of 1899 ed. o.p. Includes a complete and authoritative bibliography, 1843–48, by M. H. Spielman, with numerous illustrations and explanatory notes.

WORKS BY THACKERAY

Centenary Biographical Edition of the Works of Thackeray. 26 vols. AMS Pr. repr. of
1910–11 ed. $1,128.50. ISBN 0-404-18310-7. Introduction by Anne T. Richie; memoir
by Leslie Stephens, Thackeray's son-in-law.
The Letters and Private Papers of William Makepeace Thackeray. 4 vols. Ed. by Gordon N.
Ray. Hippocrene Bks. 1980 repr. of 1945 ed. $287.50. ISBN 0-374-97855-7
Stray Papers: Reviews, Verses, Sketches. Ed. by Lewis Melville (pseud. of Lewis Saul
Benjamin). Kraus repr. of 1901 ed. o.p.

BOOKS ABOUT THACKERAY

Bloom, Harold. ed. *William Makepeace Thackeray.* Chelsea Hse. 1987 $27.50. ISBN 1-
555-46288-X. Useful collection of essays on Thackeray.
_____. *William Makepeace Thackeray's "Vanity Fair."* Chelsea Hse. 1987 $19.95. ISBN
0-87754-747-5. Essays on *Vanity Fair.*
Carey, John. *Thackeray: Prodigal Genius.* Faber & Faber 1980 o.p.
Colby, Robert A. *Thackeray's Canvass of Humanity: An Author and His Public.* Ohio St. U.
Pr. 1979 $42.00. ISBN 0-8142-0282-9
Collins, Philip, ed. *Thackeray: Interviews and Recollections.* 2 vols. St. Martin 1983
$22.50 ea. ISBNs 0-312-79488-6, 0-312-79489-4
Flamm, Dudley. *Thackeray's Critics: An Annotated Bibliography of British and American
Criticism, 1836–1901.* U. CA Pr. 1967 o.p. An interesting introduction describing
Thackeray's critical fortunes in his own century; more than 700 entries.
Goldfarb, Sheldon. *William Makepeace Thackeray: An Annotated Bibliography,
1976–1987.* Garland 1989 $29.00. ISBN 0-8240-1212-7. Useful, selective bibliogra-
phy.
Harden, Edgar F., ed. *Annotations for the Selected Works of William Makepeace
Thackeray: The Complete Novels, the Major Non-fictional Prose, and Selected Shorter
Pieces.* 2 vols. Garland 1990 $171.00. ISBN 0-8240-3140-7. Bibliography.
_____. *The Emergence of Thackeray's Serial Fiction.* U. of Ga. Pr. 1979 o.p.
Loofbourow, John. *Thackeray and Form of Fiction.* Gordian 1976 repr. of 1964 ed. $45.00.
ISBN 0-87752-177-8
Peters, Catherine. *Thackeray's Universe: Shifting Worlds of Imagination and Reality.* OUP
1987 $35.00. ISBN 0-19-504855-5. Discussion of Thackeray's realism in the major
works.
Prawer, Siegbert Salomon. *Israel at Vanity Fair: Jews and Judaism in the Writings of W. M.
Thackeray.* E. J. Brill 1992 $123.00. ISBN 90-04-09403-2. Discussion of Thackeray's
representations of Jews.
Rawlins, Jack. *Thackeray's Novels: A Fiction That Is True.* U. CA Pr. 1975 $45.00. ISBN 0-
520-02562-8
Ray, Gordon N. *The Buried Life.* Haskell 1974 $49.95. ISBN 0-8383-1984-X
Ritchie, Anne Thackeray. *Two Thackerays: Anne Thackeray Ritchie's Centenary Biograph-
ical Introductions to the Works of William Makepeace Thackeray.* 2 vols. AMS Pr.
1988 $165.00. ISBN 0-404-61483-3. Useful introductions to the works; with a critical
introduction by Carol Hanbery MacKay and a bibliographical introduction by Peter
L. Shillingsburg and Julia Maxey.
Stevenson, Lionel. *The Showman of Vanity Fair: The Life of William Makepeace
Thackeray.* Russell 1968 repr. of 1947 ed. o.p.
Sutherland, John. *Thackeray at Work.* Longwood 1979 o.p.
Taylor, Theodore. *Thackeray the Humorist and the Man of Letters. Eng. Lit. Ser.* Haskell
$59.95. ISBN 0-8383-1339-6. Based on information from source material and from
Thackeray's friends, while memories of him were still sharp.
Tillotson, Geoffrey, and Donald Hawes, eds. *Thackeray: The Critical Heritage. Critical
Heritage Ser.* Routledge 1968 o.p. First edition reviews from Thackeray's time.

TROLLOPE, ANTHONY. 1815–1882

Born in London, Trollope was the son of Thomas A. Trollope, an unsuccessful
lawyer and barrister. As a result of his father's failure, his school days at Harrow

and Winchester were miserable. When the family's finances were at their worst, they moved first to Cincinnati, Ohio, and then to Belgium, where Thomas Trollope died. The family survived after this due to the writing of Trollope's mother, FRANCES TROLLOPE, who became a well-known writer of novels and travel articles. In 1834 Anthony Trollope became a postal clerk, and he worked as a postal officer for many years. During that time, however, he also became a prolific writer, producing a large number of novels dealing with Victorian life.

In recent decades, Trollope's reputation has grown considerably, with particular emphasis on his effectiveness as a gentle satirist and as a shrewd observer of British manners and morals in provincial and urban settings, in politics, in the church, and in finance. Trollope's comic novels present the panorama of Victorian British pride and power while dramatizing traditional and conservative virtues in their conflict with changing values. His works number 100 or more volumes, including novels, tales, history, travel, and biography. Forty-odd novels are divided into three series: *The Chronicles of Barsetshire, or The Cathedral Stories*; *The Parliamentary Novels*; and *The Manor House Novels*. In each series, the same characters appear repeatedly, but each volume is complete in itself. The Barsetshire novels, the most popular of the group, are all set in the imaginary town of Barchester (based on Winchester, according to Trollope), and the characters are mainly clergy of various ranks and their families.

Trollope's autobiography, published posthumously in 1883, has been blamed for the eclipse of Trollope's fame right after his death. In it he confesses his custom of writing with his watch before him, requiring of himself 250 words every quarter hour. He began work at 5:30 every morning without fail and prided himself on living a full, varied life the rest of the day. But Trollope's mechanical work habits did not produce mechanical novels, and his modern reputation acknowledges his comic genius, his social insights, and his general seriousness. In recent years many of Trollope's novels, for years out of print or available only in costly editions, have been republished by Oxford University Press in affordable paperback versions.

NOVELS BY ANTHONY TROLLOPE

Barchester Towers. 1857. McKay 1992 $19.50. ISBN 0-679-40587-9
Dr. Thorne. 1858. Viking Penguin 1991 $7.95. ISBN 0-14-043326-0
Framley Parsonage. 1861. OUP 1980 $5.95. ISBN 0-19-281545-8
The Last Chronicle of Barset. 1867. OUP 1980 $7.95. ISBN 0-19-281544-X
The Small House at Allington. 1864. OUP 1980 $6.95. ISBN 0-19-281552-0
The Warden. 1855. Knopf 1991 $15.00. ISBN 0-679-40551-8

THE PARLIAMENTARY NOVELS

Can You Forgive Her? 1864. OUP 1991 $16.95. ISBN 0-19-520895-1
The Duke's Children. 1880. Ed. by Hermione Lee. OUP 1983 $16.95. ISBN 0-19-520900-1
The Eustace Diamonds. 1873. OUP 1983 $16.95. ISBN 0-19-520897-8
Phineas Finn. 1869. OUP 1982 $6.95. ISBN 0-19-281587-3
Phineas Redux. 1874. Ed. by John C. Whale. OUP 1983 $16.95. ISBN 0-19-520898-6
The Prime Minister. 1876. Ed. by Jennifer Uglow. OUP 1983 $16.95. ISBN 0-19-520899-4

THE MANOR HOUSE NOVELS

The Belton Estate. 1866. OUP o.p.
Is He Popenjoy? 1878. Ed. by John Sutherland. OUP 1986 $4.60. ISBN 0-19-281716-7.
    Introduction by John Sutherland.
Orley Farm. 1862. Dover 1981 $11.95. ISBN 0-486-24181-5
The Way We Live Now. 1875. Dover 1982 $8.95. ISBN 0-486-24360-5

OTHER NOVELS

The American Senator. 1877. Ed. by John Halperin. OUP 1986 $4.60. ISBN 0-19-281739-6. Introduction by John Halperin.

Ayela's Angel. 1881. Ed. by Julian Thompson-Furnival. OUP 1986 $4.55. ISBN 0-19-281747-7. One of the "Australian" novels; introduction by Julian Thompson-Furnival.

The Bertrams. 1859. Ed. by Geoffrey Harvey. OUP 1991 $6.00. ISBN 0-19-282645-X. Introduction by Geoffrey Harvey.

Castle Richmond. 1860. Ed. by Mary Hamer. OUP 1989 $10.95. ISBN 0-19-282173-3. Introduction by Mary Hamer.

The Claverings. 1867. OUP 1986 $6.95. ISBN 0-19-281727-2. Introduction and notes by David Skilton.

Cousin Henry. 1879. Ed. by Julian Thompson. OUP 1987 $6.95. ISBN 0-19-281784-1

The Fixed Period. 1882. OUP 1993 $4.99. ISBN 0-19-282842-8

He Knew He Was Right. 1869. OUP 1985 $8.95. ISBN 0-19-281692-6

Kept in the Dark. 1882. OUP 1992 $8.95. ISBN 0-19-282740-5

Lady Anna. 1874. Ed. by Stephen Orgel. OUP 1990 $7.95. ISBN 0-19-282134-2. Introduction by Stephen Orgel.

The Landleaguers. 1883. Ed. by R. H. Super. U. of Mich. Pr. 1992 $39.50. ISBN 0-472-09485-8. Unfinished; appeared posthumously.

The Macdermonts of Ballycloran. 1847. Ed. by Robert Tracy. OUP 1989 $10.00. ISBN 0-19-282181-4. One of the early "Irish" novels. Introduction by Tracy.

Miss Mackenzie. 1865. Ed. by A. O. J. Cockshut. OUP 1988 $7.50. ISBN 0-19-281846-5. Introduction by Cockshut.

Mr. Scarborough's Family. 1883. Ed. by Geoffrey Harvey. OUP 1989 $7.95. ISBN 0-19-287808-2. Published posthumously; introduction by Harvey.

Nina Balatka and *Linda Tressel.* 1867, 1868. Ed. by Robert Tracy. OUP 1991 $7.00. ISBN 0-19-282723-5. Introduction by Tracy.

An Old Man's Love. 1884. Ed. by John Sutherland. OUP 1991 $7.95. ISBN 0-19-282646-8. Published posthumously; introduction by Sutherland.

Rachel Ray. 1863. OUP 1988 $7.50. ISBN 0-19-281890-0. Introduction and notes by P. D. Edwards.

Ralph the Heir. 1871. Ed. by John Sutherland. OUP 1990 $8.95. ISBN 0-19-281805-8. Introduction by Sutherland.

The Three Clerks. 1858. Ed. by Graham Handley. OUP 1989 $8.95. ISBN 0-19-281829-5. Introduction by Handley.

The Vicar of Bullhampton. 1870. Ed. by David Skilton. OUP 1988 $9.50. ISBN 0-19-282163-9. Introduction by Skilton.

NONFICTION BY ANTHONY TROLLOPE

An Autobiography. 1883. Ed. by P. D. Edwards. OUP 1980 $6.95. ISBN 0-19-281509-1

South Africa. 1878. Humanities o.p.

The West Indies and the Spanish Main. 1859. Biblio Dist. 1968 o.p. Provides an intimate and comprehensive picture of Victorian England.

SHORT STORY COLLECTIONS BY ANTHONY TROLLOPE

Collected Short Stories. Dover 1987 $8.95. ISBN 0-486-25484-4

The Complete Short Stories. 5 vols. Tex. Christian 1979–83 o.p.

WORKS BY ANTHONY TROLLOPE

The Letters of Anthony Trollope. 2 vols. Ed. by N. John Hall. Stanford U. Pr. 1983 $115.00. ISBN 0-8047-1076-7

The Selected Works of Anthony Trollope. 62 vols. Ed. by N. John Hall. *Selected Works of Anthony Trollope Ser.* Ayer 1981 $1,994.00. ISBN 0-405-14114-9

BOOKS ABOUT ANTHONY TROLLOPE

Bloom, Harold, ed. *Anthony Trollope's "Barchester Towers" and "The Warden."* Chelsea Hse. 1988 $24.50. ISBN 0-877-54748-3. Good collection of essays on the two novels.

Hall, N. John. *Trollope: A Biography.* OUP 1991 $35.00. ISBN 0-19-812627-1. Important biography; complete and scholarly.

———, ed. *The Trollope Critics.* B & N Imports 1981 o.p.

Halperin, John, ed. *Trollope Centenary Essays.* St. Martin 1982 $22.50. ISBN 0-312-81894-7

Hamer, Mary. *Writing by Numbers: Trollope's Serial Fiction.* Cambridge U. Pr. 1987 $49.95. ISBN 0-521-32528-5. Discussion of Trollope's writing technique for serialization.

Herbert, Christopher. *Trollope and Comic Pleasure.* U. Ch. Pr. 1987 $24.00. ISBN 0-226-32741-8. Examination of satire and comedy in the novels.

Lansbury, Coral. *The Reasonable Man: Trollope's Legal Fictions.* Princeton U. Pr. 1981 $32.50. ISBN 0-691-06457-1

Letwin, Shirley R. *The Gentlemen in Trollope: Individuality and Moral Conduct.* HUP 1982 $27.50. ISBN 0-674-34755-2

MacDonald, Susan. *Anthony Trollope.* Twayne 1987 $20.95. ISBN 0-8057-6945-5. A useful introduction to his life and work.

Macmaster, Juliet. *Trollope's Palliser Novels: Theme and Pattern.* OUP 1978 o.p.

Pope-Hennessy, James. *Anthony Trollope.* Little 1972 o.p. A critical biography that includes 25 illustrations from the original editions of the novels.

Smalley, Donald, ed. *Trollope: The Critical Heritage. Critical Heritage Ser.* Routledge 1969 o.p. A collection of contemporary criticisms.

Stebbins, Lucy, and Richard Stebbins. *The Trollopes: The Chronicle of a Writing Family.* AMS Pr. repr. of 1945 ed. $26.50. ISBN 0-404-06228-8. Based on family journals and other writings; includes Frances and her two sons, the historian Thomas Adolphus and the novelist Anthony.

Super, R. H. *The Chronicler of Baretshire: A Life of Anthony Trollope.* U. of Mich. Pr. 1988 $35.00. ISBN 0-472-10102-1. Worthwhile biography.

Swingle, L. J. *Romanticism and Anthony Trollope: A Study in the Continuities of Nineteenth-Century Thought.* U. of Mich. Pr. 1990 $37.50. ISBN 0-472-10189-7. Examines Trollope in connection with his romantic antecedents.

Tingay, Lance. *The Trollope Student: An Annotated List of Full Length Studies (1833–1990) and a Check List of the Writings of Anthony Trollope and Other Members of the Trollope Family (1734–1909).* Silverbridge 1990 o.p. Useful bibliography for the serious Trollopian.

TROLLOPE, FRANCES MILTON. 1779–1863

Frances Trollope, the mother of the prolific mid-Victorian novelist ANTHONY TROLLOPE, was an accomplished novelist and travel writer in her own right. In all, she was the author of 35 novels, many of them quite popular. Born the second daughter of a vicar, she was raised in the town of Bristol. In 1809 she married Thomas Trollope, a promising young barrister. Although Thomas had a profitable legal practice, a number of pecuniary crises strained the Trollopes financially. In 1827, partly in an attempt to escape her husband's sullenness over their money matters and partly to help rebuild the family's fortune, she took three of her six children to the United States, where she remained until 1830. There (in Cincinnati) she set up a retail store that was to provide this region of provincial America with European culture. When the scheme failed, Trollope turned to writing as a means of self-preservation. The result was *Domestic Manners of the Americans*, which was immensely popular, and *The Refugee in America*, her first novel, both published in 1832. Soon after she established a professional relationship with the publisher Richard Bentley, who went far to publicize her work. The finances of the family did not improve, however, and in 1835, finally bankrupt, the Trollopes moved to Belgium, where Thomas died. Frances's agreement with Bentley, who paid her £600 per novel, and her remarkable output of two novels per year restored the family fortunes.

During her life Trollope's fiction was considered rough and inelegant, and she was not a favorite of the critics. In recent years her work has begun to attract considerable attention for its insightful political and social analysis and its strong stand on issues of the day.

NOVELS BY FRANCES TROLLOPE

The Abbess. 3 vols. Whittaker 1833 o.p. One of Trollope's earliest works.

The Barnabys in America, or Adventures of the Widow Wedded. 3 vols. Colburn 1843 o.p. Third in the famous *Widow Barnaby* trilogy. Illustrated by John Leech.

Charles Chesterfield, or, The Adventures of a Youth of Genius. 3 vols. Colburn 1841 o.p. Comedy of modern life and manners. Illustrated by Halbot Knight Browne.

Father Eustace: A Tale of the Jesuits. 2 vols. 1847. Garland 1975 o.p. Anti-Catholic propaganda novel.

Gertrude, or Family Pride. 3 vols. Hurst & Blackett 1855 o.p.

Jessie Phillips: A Tale of the Present Day. 3 vols. Colburn 1843 o.p.

The Life and Adventures of a Clever Woman. 3 vols. Hurst & Blackett 1854 o.p.

The Life and Adventures of Jonathan Jefferson Whitlaw, or Scenes on the Mississippi. 3 vols. Bentley 1836 o.p. Antislavery novel.

The Life and Adventures of Michael Armstrong, the Factory Boy. 1840. Cass 1968 o.p. Exposes factory abuse.

The Old World and the New. 3 vols. Colburn 1849 o.p.

One Fault. 3 vols. Bentley 1840 o.p. Autobiographical; reflections on Trollope's own marriage.

The Refugee in America. 3 vols. Whittaker 1832 o.p.

The Three Cousins. 3 vols. Colburn 1847 o.p.

Tremordyn Cliff. 2 vols. Wilmans 1835 o.p.

The Vicar of Wrexhill. 3 vols. Garland 1975 $27.50. ISBN 0-824-01563-0. Antievangelical novel.

The Ward of Thorpe-Combe. Baudry's European Lib. 1842 o.p.

The Widow Barnaby. 3 vols. AMS Pr. repr. of 1839 ed. $84.50. ISBN 0-404-62141-4. First in the *Widow Barnaby* trilogy.

The Widow Married: A Sequel to "The Widow Barnaby." 3 vols. Colburn 1840 o.p. Second in the *Widow Barnaby* series.

The Young Heiress. 3 vols. Hurst & Blackett 1853 o.p.

Young Love. 3 vols. Colburn 1844 o.p.

NONFICTION BY FRANCES TROLLOPE

Belgium and Western Germany in 1833. 2 vols. J. Murray UK 1834 o.p.

Domestic Manners of the Americans. 1832. 2 vols. Rprt. Serv. 1993 repr. of 1901 ed. $150.00. ISBN 0-7812-5137-0

Paris and the Parisians. 1835. Hippocrene Bks. 1985 o.p.

Vienna and the Austrians: With Some Account of a Journey through Swabia, Bavaria, the Tyrol, and the Salzbourg. 2 vols. Bentley 1838 o.p.

A Visit to Italy. 2 vols. Bentley 1842 o.p.

BOOKS ABOUT FRANCES TROLLOPE

Bigland, Eileen. *The Indomitable Mrs. Trollope.* Lippincott 1954 o.p. Dated biography.

Heineman, Helen. *Frances Trollope.* Twayne 1984 o.p. Good introduction to Trollope's life and works.

_____. *Mrs. Trollope: The Triumphant Feminine in the Nineteenth Century.* Ohio U. Pr. 1979 $22.00. ISBN 0-8214-0354-0. Best recent study of Trollope.

Johnston, Johanna. *The Life, Manners, and Travels of Fanny Trollope: A Biography*. Hawthorn Bks. 1978 o.p. Worthwhile biography.

Trollope, Frances Eleanor. *Frances Trollope, Her Life and Literary Work from George III to Victoria*. 2 vols. Bentley 1895. AMS Pr. repr. of 1975 ed. $65.00. ISBN 0-404-08917-8. The standard biography, written by her daughter.

WILDE, OSCAR. 1854–1900

Flamboyant man-about-town, Oscar Wilde had a reputation that preceded him, especially in his early career. He was born to a middle-class Irish family (his father was a surgeon) and was trained as a scholarship boy at Trinity College, Dublin. He subsequently won a scholarship to Magdalen College, Oxford, where he was heavily influenced by JOHN RUSKIN and WALTER PATER, whose aestheticism was taken to its radical extreme in Wilde's work. By 1879 he was already known as a wit and a dandy; soon after, in fact, he was satirized in GILBERT and Sullivan's *Patience*. Largely on the strength of his public persona, Wilde undertook a lecture tour to the United States in 1882, where he saw his play *Vera* open—unsuccessfully—in New York. His first published volume, *Poems*, which met with some degree of approbation, appeared at this time. In 1884 he married Constance Lloyd, the daughter of an Irish lawyer, and within two years they had two sons. During this period he wrote, among others, *The Picture of Dorian Gray* (1891), his only novel, which scandalized many readers and was widely denounced as immoral. Wilde simultaneously dismissed and encouraged such criticism with his statement in the preface, "There is no such thing as a moral or an immoral book. Books are well written or badly written. That is all."

In 1891 Wilde published *A House of Pomegranates*, a collection of fantasy tales, and in 1892 gained commercial and critical success with his play, *Lady Windermere's Fan*. He followed this comedy with *A Woman of No Importance* (1893), *An Ideal Husband* (1895), and his most famous play, *The Importance of Being Earnest* (1895). During this period he also wrote *Salomé*, in French, but was unable to obtain a license for it in England. Performed in Paris in 1896, the play was translated and published in England in 1894 by Lord Alfred Douglas and was illustrated by Aubrey Beardsley.

Lord Alfred was the son of the Marquess of Queensbury, who objected to his son's spending so much time with Wilde because of Wilde's flamboyant behavior and homosexual relationships. In 1895, after being publicly insulted by the marquess, Wilde brought an unsuccessful slander suit against the peer. The result of his inability to prove slander was his own trial on charges of sodomy, of which he was found guilty and sentenced to two years of hard labor. During his time in prison, he wrote a scathing rebuke to Lord Alfred, published in 1905 as *De Profundis*. In it he argues that his conduct was a result of his standing "in symbolic relations to the art and culture" of his time. After his release, Wilde left England for Paris, where he wrote what may be his most famous poem, *The Ballad of Reading Gaol* (1898), drawn from his prison experiences. Among his other notable writing is *The Soul of Man under Socialism* (1891), which argues for individualism and freedom of artistic expression.

There has been a revived interest in Wilde's work; among the best recent volumes are Richard Ellmann's *Oscar Wilde* and Regenia Gagnier's *Idylls of the Marketplace*, two works that vary widely in their critical assumptions and approach to Wilde but that offer rich insights into his complex character.

PLAYS BY WILDE

The Definitive Four Act Version of "The Importance of Being Earnest": A Trivial Comedy for Serious People. Ed. by Ruth Berggren. Vanguard 1987 o.p. Introduction by Berggren.

An Ideal Husband. 1895. Smithers 1899 o.p.

The Importance of Being Earnest. Ed. by Robert Wilson. Longman 1983 $5.72. ISBN 0-582-33134-X

Lady Windermere's Fan. 1892. Routledge Chapman & Hall 1985 $7.95. ISBN 0-413-57790-2. Wilde's first truly successful play.

The Plays of Oscar Wilde. Vin. 1988 $9.95. ISBN 0-394-75788-2

Salome. 1894. Trans. by Lord Alfred Douglas. Faber & Faber 1989 $9.95. ISBN 0-571-14350-4.

Vera; or, the Nihilist. 1880. E. Mellen 1989 $69.95. ISBN 0-88946-931-8

Wilde: Complete Plays. Routledge Chapman & Hall 1988 $11.95. ISBN 0-413-18760-8. Scholarly edition; introduction by H. Montgomery Hyde.

A Woman of No Importance. Lane 1894 o.p. Successful follow-up to *Lady Windermere's Fan.*

NOVEL BY WILDE

The Picture of Dorian Gray. 1891. Ed. by Donald L. Lawler. Norton 1988 $10.95. ISBN 0-393-95568-0. Concerns a beautiful youth, Dorian Gray, who, after having his portrait painted, ceases to age, while the portrait reflects his state of degeneracy.

POETRY BY WILDE

The Ballad of Reading Gaol. 1898. Intemprte. Stage 1991 $5.00. ISBN 0-881355-01-2. Study of a man condemned to die; drawn from Wilde's experiences in prison.

The Poems of Oscar Wilde. Buckles 1906 o.p. The collected poetry.

NONFICTION BY WILDE

De Profundis and Other Writings. 1905. Viking Penguin 1976 $5.95. ISBN 0-14-043089-X

The Soul of Man under Socialism, and Other Essays. 1891. HarpC 1970 $22.95. ISBN 0-8828-6057-7

CHILDREN'S FICTION BY WILDE

The Happy Prince and Other Stories. 1888. Morrow Jr. Bks. 1991 $16.95. ISBN 0-688-10390-1. Originally written for Wilde's sons.

A House of Pomegranates. Osgood 1891 o.p.

WORKS BY WILDE

Complete Works of Oscar Wilde. HarpC 1989 $27.50. ISBN 0-06-055170-4. Affordable edition; with introduction by Vyvyan Holland, one of Wilde's sons.

Letters. Ed. by Rupert Hart-Davis. HarBraceJ 1962 o.p.

More Letters of Oscar Wilde. Ed. by Rupert Hart-Davis. Vanguard 1985 o.p.

Oscar Wilde's Oxford Notebooks: A Portrait of a Mind in the Making. Ed. by Philip E. Smith II and Michael S. Helfand. OUP 1989 $38.00. ISBN 0-19-505133-5

Selected Letters of Oscar Wilde. Ed. by Rupert Hart-Davis. OUP 1989 o.p.

Writings of Oscar Wilde. 14 vols. Edinburgh Soc. 1911 o.p. The standard edition.

BOOKS ABOUT WILDE

Bloom, Harold, ed. *Oscar Wilde's "The Importance of Being Earnest."* Chelsea Hse. 1988 $24.50. ISBN 1-555-46022-4. Good collection of recent essays on *The Importance of Being Earnest.*

Ellmann, Richard. *Oscar Wilde.* Knopf 1987 $24.95. ISBN 0-394-55484-1. Has replaced Pearson's as the standard biography.

Gagnier, Regenia, ed. *Critical Essays on Oscar Wilde.* G. K. Hall 1991 o.p. Good collection of essays on Wilde, covering all aspects of his career.

————. *Idylls of the Marketplace: Oscar Wilde and the Victorian Public*. Stanford U. Pr. 1986 $35.00. ISBN 0-8047-1334-0. Study of Wilde's readership and his reception.

Nelson, Walter W. *Oscar Wilde and the Dramatic Critics: A Study in Victorian Theatre*. 1989 o.p. Study of Wilde as dramatist and his contributions to late Victorian theater.

Pearson, Hesketh. *The Life of Oscar Wilde*. Greenwood 1978 repr. of 1975 ed. $37.50. ISBN 0-313-20491-8

Powell, Kerry. *Oscar Wilde and the Theatre of the 1890's*. Cambridge U. Pr. 1990 $42.95. ISBN 0-521-18008-1. Wilde as dramatist.

Raby, Peter. *Oscar Wilde*. Cambridge U. Pr. 1988 $12.95. ISBN 0-521-26078-7. Introductory critical study of Wilde's works from his early poems to his plays, with emphasis on his contribution to modern drama.

CHAPTER 11

Modern British and Irish Literature

Randy Malamud

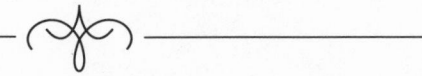

These fragments I have shored against my ruins.
—T. S. ELIOT, *The Waste Land*

Several movements and schools have contributed to the major developments in twentieth-century British and Irish literature, and some of these may provide coherent guidance in attempting to establish an overview of the period. Imagism was technically a movement that arose in poetry, although its demands for hardness and concision certainly influenced all genres of modern literature, as well as other modern arts. The times were felt to be overwhelming, and a profusion of stimuli threatened to bombard the artist into muteness; so, out of this, the imagist chose a symbol, a token, an ember of an aesthetic insight that could preserve its integrity and power. Vorticism, similarly, aspired to harness the power and furies of the modern age and rescue them from the tepidities of mass culture. Existentialism, though more continental in origin, certainly pervaded and shaped British and Irish literature, from T. S. ELIOT's protoexistentialist angst in *The Waste Land* (1922) to HAROLD PINTER's dramatic minimalism. In the darker recesses of a play by SAMUEL BECKETT or a novel by EVELYN WAUGH, this existentialism fizzles exhaustedly into nihilism. Traces of surrealism are more prominent in the visual arts and in European literature than in British and Irish literature, but they still certainly contribute to the fusion of sensibilities in, for example, JAMES JOYCE's novels and THOM GUNN's poetry. A dawning feminist consciousness made itself felt in a generation of women writers, mostly novelists, who drew upon the strengths of their Victorian antecedents but embodied a newly empowered vision of a world filled with sexism, hypocrisy, and the pathetic vestiges of a Victorian patriarchal pomposity.

Indeed, the contrast with the Victorian Age is one of the most poignantly defining features of twentieth-century British and Irish literature. In place of a Victorian consciousness of material splendor, the modern writers perceive themselves wallowing amid the jetsam of gawdy debris that the previous century bequeathed them. Victorian logical certainties are undercut by modern doubts, fears, and a sense of alienation from social or natural order. The spirit of Victorian adventures barely lingers in some of the century's early literature—in H. G. WELLS's fantasies or JOSEPH CONRAD's narratives of exploration and espionage—but in a parodied or perverted remove from its literary antecedent. Much of the richness of modern British and Irish literature, ironically, derives from a sense of devolution of institutions and sensibilities; this generates a literature replete with entrancing vicissitudes, if somewhat devoid of succor.

Modern British and Irish literature was once synonymous with "modernism," the general term under which it was categorized within the canon when it first entered the scholarly and academic arenas in the 1930s and 1940s. The defining works of modernism—such as Eliot's *The Waste Land*, EZRA POUND's *Cantos* (1925), Joyce's *Ulysses* (1922), VIRGINIA WOOLF's *To the Lighthouse* (1927)— among them established a stylistic and aesthetic plane, marked by path-blazing experimental narratives and unfettered explorations of the crucial crevices of human life, genteelly overlooked by previous generations but central to an understanding of the modern condition.

More recently, it has become fashionable to be skeptical of any coherent modernist movement; its originators, it is argued, exerted too subjective and manipulative an influence upon its early foundations, merely establishing a forum for their own literature (as Eliot did, for example, in "Tradition and the Individual Talent") that was exclusive of other movements that should have had a claim on the contemporary spotlight; and, too often, what masqueraded as a daring avant-garde was, in fact, a cover for a conservative or even reactionary agenda, both politically and stylistically.

But, despite caveats about the formation of the modernist canon, it remains true that, to a considerable extent, readers can recognize in the language of modern British and Irish literature a force of coherence and unity. At first the works may seem confusing, opaque, intentionally difficult. As the literature is read more intensely, though, one realizes that it is written according to certain recurring codes, dialects, variants. One's eyes focus, at first tentatively, on an anarchic style that is meant to challenge the orderliness of the British and Irish literary tradition up to the twentieth century. While the Victorians had in their literature a sense of confident self-completion, subsequent generations of writers looked back at it and found it somewhat devoid of the originality that was deemed necessary to speak of the modern age. Victorian poetry had been soft, Pound opined; modern poetry must be hard.

The newness of modernist style invests it with a sharpness, keenness, accuracy, and sense of truth that relates to a world newly perceived as stark, dangerous, urban, eclectic, technological, jarring. The language of modernism, given to extremism in the service of experiment, fits in with what FORD MADOX FORD called the incoherence, the tenuousness, and the odd vibrations of life. Writers have in common, to a considerable extent, a fixation on the challenge of language: the inadequacy of the poetic of the past and the multiple possibilities that might replace it. Their sensibility reflects their belief that literature, in the modern age, had to be stretched—had to say more than it had been able to previously; had to embody more, and paradoxically, at the same time, obscure more, because any text that was too easily accessible was implicitly of less value than a dense and rigorous work, such as *The Waste Land*, which demanded intense study and arcane exegesis.

Among the many cultural and historical events that could be taken as emblematic of the modern sensibility—the death of Queen Victoria after a 64-year reign, the sinking of the *Titanic*, the increasing empowerment of women in the workplace and in political and suffrage movements—certainly World War I stands as a consummate embodiment of the period. Besides generating a vast amount of writing explicitly about the effects of the Great War (such as WILFRED OWEN's and ISAAC ROSENBERG's poetry and novels by ARNOLD BENNETT, D. H. LAWRENCE, and Wells), a great deal of literature more subliminally dealt with the aftereffects of the war, the "shell-shock" effect of the cataclysm that wreaked havoc on a scale previously unimaginable. A sense of irony—linked to the lethality of the technology that had been heralded as the savior of the new age and to the perversely inhuman stasis of the soldiers in the trenches—pervades much of the literature that appeared for over a decade after the end of the war. That we now think of the 1920s and 1930s as the years between two wars reflects the fact that in many ways the war affected the literature throughout much of the first half of the century.

In contrast with the earlier uniformity seen in what has been called "high modernism," the century's literature is now regarded as flourishing in myriad directions. In the works of Woolf, Ford, DOROTHY RICHARDSON, and Joyce, modern writers created new models for narrative and authorial voices. Political exhortation and invective are effusively manifest in the writing of GEORGE ORWELL, W. B. YEATS, and at least subliminally in that of Conrad. Eliot's wry, cynical elitism was once considered to be the attitude toward the contemporary situation, *de rigueur,* of the modernist in good standing; now critics and readers perceive a wider range of sensibility that includes Waugh's dark humor, KINGSLEY AMIS's irreverent farce, DYLAN THOMAS's exuberant decadence, DAVID LODGE's drily intellectual parody, MURIEL SPARK's indignant rebukes, PHILIP LARKIN's weary resignation, and STEVIE SMITH's escapist insouciance.

Earlier in the twentieth century, most writers' work embodied some attempt, often desperate and unsuccessful, to relate the contemporary situation— positively or subversively—to the traditions and order of the Victorian past. By the midcentury, a more prominent trend in British literature was the accep- tance of a society somewhat adrift and an attempt to voice this situation new to a culture that had historically been so secure—economically, politically, and intellectually—in its certainty of endurance, dignity, and triumph. Plays such as JOHN OSBORNE's *Look Back in Anger* (1956) and Harold Pinter's *The Birthday Party* (1957), novels such as those of BARBARA PYM and MARGARET DRABBLE, and poetry such as that of Larkin all reflected a weariness and bleakness indicative of Britain's fall from a position of superiority and assurance. Literature of this period may tend to be less grandiose, less magnificent, than the works that emerged from the high modernist reign of energy, avant-garde enthusiasm, and self-assured establishment of literary styles, schools, fads, and movements. At the same time, however, it is perhaps more sincere in its humility and more courageous for its attempt to probe the unmomentous but eminently human pathos of an aesthetic of bittersweet decline.

HISTORY AND CRITICISM

Bergonzi, Bernard. *The Twentieth Century.* Sphere 1970 o.p. Survey.

Blamires, Harry. *Twentieth-Century English Literature.* Schocken 1982 $8.95. ISBN 0-8052-3827-1. Focuses on the upheaval of World War I and the birth of literary modernism.

Bradbury, Malcolm. *Modernism.* Viking Penguin 1978 $7.95. ISBN 0-14-021933-1. Comprehensive survey of the period.

———. *The Social Context of Modern English Literature.* Blackwell Pubs. 1971 o.p.

Edel, Leon. *Bloomsbury: A House of Lions.* Viking Penguin 1979 o.p. Biographically based study of the influential writers and thinkers known as the Bloomsbury Group.

Ford, Boris, ed. *The Present.* Vol. 8 *New Pelican Guide to English Lit.* Viking Penguin 1983 $5.95. ISBN 0-14-022271-5. Social and cultural settings; overview of literary scene; discussion of significant writers.

Gilbert, Sandra M., and Susan Gubar. *No Man's Land: The Place of the Woman Writer in the Twentieth Century.* Vol. 1 *The War of the Words.* Yale U. Pr. 1988 $29.95. ISBN

0-300-04005-9. Social, literary, and linguistic conflicts between men and women that mark modernism.

_____. *No Man's Land: The Place of the Woman Writer in the Twentieth Century.* Vol. 2 *Sexchanges.* Yale U. Pr. 1989 $29.95. ISBN 0-300-04735-9. Feminism and fantasy, reconceptions of gender roles as a motif of modernism.

Karl, Frederick R. *Modern and Modernism: The Sovereignty of the Artist 1885–1925.* Atheneum 1988 $14.95. ISBN 0-689-11564-4. Traces modernism through literature, art, music, science, and psychoanalysis.

Kenner, Hugh. *A Colder Eye: The Modern Irish Writers.* Knopf 1983 $16.95. ISBN 0-394-04225-2. A piquant, idiosyncratic survey of modern Irish literary and cultural history.

_____. *The Pound Era.* U. CA Pr. 1971 $37.50. ISBN 0-520-01860-5. Examines Pound's role as the central figure in modernism; analysis of modernist sensibilities.

_____. *A Sinking Island: The Modern English Writers.* Johns Hopkins 1987 $12.95. ISBN 0-8018-3837-1. Somewhat whimsical account of the decline of modern English literature.

Korg, Jacob. *Language in Modern Literature: Innovation & Experiment.* B & N Imports 1979 $40.00. ISBN 0-06-493892-1. Examines the upheaval in literary language and its role in modernism.

Levenson, Michael. *A Genealogy of Modernism: A Study of English Literary Doctrine, 1908–1922.* Cambridge U. Pr. 1984 $15.95. ISBN 0-521-33800-X. Theoretical and critical foundations of modernism.

Malamud, Randy. *The Language of Modernism.* Bks. Demand 1989 $56.20. ISBN 0-8357-2030-6. Considers linguistic and stylistic experimentation as a force in modernism.

Menand, Louis. *Discovering Modernism: T. S. Eliot and His Context.* OUP 1987 $14.95. ISBN 0-19-505717-1. Reexamination of Eliot's role in the canonization of modernism.

Morrison, Blake. *The Movement: English Poetry and Fiction of the 1950s.* OUP 1980 o.p. Critical overview of the literary group known as the Movement.

Sabin, Margery. *The Dialect of the Tribe: Speech and Community in Modern Fiction.* OUP 1987 $42.50. ISBN 0-19-504153-4. Comparative study of the language of Beckett, Joyce, Lawrence, and James.

Tindall, William York. *Forces in Modern British Literature, 1885–1956.* Ayer repr. of 1947 ed. $26.50. ISBN 0-8369-1730-8. Classic survey of modernist themes: Exile, disenchantment, symbolism, and myth.

COLLECTIONS

Faulkner, Peter. *The English Modernist Reader, 1910–1930.* U. of Iowa Pr. 1986 $23.00. ISBN 0-87745-158-3. Collection of contemporary critical essays on modernism.

Lodge, David. *Twentieth-Century Literary Criticism: A Reader.* Longman 1972. ISBN 0-582-48422-7

Scott, Bonnie Kime. *The Gender of Modernism: A Critical Anthology.* Ind. U. Pr. 1990 $45.00. ISBN 0-253-35122-7. Critical statements exploring the engendering of modernism.

POETRY

In the late 1920s, EZRA POUND declared that "The language is now in the keeping of the Irish (Yeats and Joyce); apart from Yeats, since the death of Hardy, poetry is being written by Americans. . . . All the developments in English verse since 1910 are due almost wholly to Americans." Pound's exaggeration contains an important kernel of truth. Until almost the end of the nineteenth century, the most important poetry in the English language was written in Great Britain. But the situation changed in the twentieth century, largely because of the immense contribution of American poetry and the independence from Britain of countries such as Ireland and other Commonwealth nations. As a result British poetry now ranks as only one strand, albeit an important one, of poetry being written in English. A glance at three of the major poets covered in this chapter—W. B. YEATS, T. S. ELIOT, and W. H. AUDEN—illustrates the point. Yeats considered himself an Irish poet and served in the senate of his country after its independence. Eliot was born and raised in the United States and only became a British subject in 1927, well after the composition of *"The Love Song of J. Alfred Prufrock"* (1915), *The Waste Land* (1922), and other important works. Only Auden was born in England, and he chose to become a U.S. citizen in 1946 after several years of residency.

During the first part of the century, British poetry bore a close relation to political and social events. The extensive slaughter, horrifying new weaponry, and political ineptitude of the war years destroyed the complacency, optimism, and sense of fixity of much prewar culture. The savage war poetry of WILFRED OWEN and others replaced the sentimental patriotism of RUPERT BROOKE. Postwar poetry combined social pessimism with technical experimentation, as exemplified in the early and influential poetry and criticism of T. S. Eliot, whose title *The Waste Land* caught much of the intellectuals' response to their era. With the economic problems of the 1930s, the generation of Auden, STEPHEN SPENDER, LOUIS MACNEICE, and C. DAY LEWIS turned temporarily leftward, toward a more socially engaged poetry. The economic crisis in turn yielded to World War II, from which England emerged victorious but diminished. Many of the best poets who came to prominence during the 1950s, such as PHILIP LARKIN, formed a loose group called the Movement and produced a polished, restrained, ironic verse eschewing the large claims of the high modernist mode. Meanwhile, contemporary British verse has opened up to a variety of influences and has taken a number of directions. During the twentieth century, of course, many poets took independent paths, such as the neoromantic Dylan Thomas, who produced his great poetry of vibrant rhetoric from the 1930s through the early 1950s. And Irish poetry, like Irish politics (Ireland remained neutral during World War II), took a separate course. After the great achievement of Yeats, the generation of PATRICK KAVANAGH and AUSTIN CLARKE dealt more with Irish themes and the shadow of Yeats than with the modernist main current. A different group of poets succeeded them, and of the newest generation SEAMUS HEANEY seems to many the strongest voice.

Although several decades ago critics tended to think of modern poetry as antiromantic, more recent voices have argued plausibly that it is more properly postromantic, whether overtly continuing or opposing romantic tradition. Certainly, the romantics began a poetry of mind (WILLIAM WORDSWORTH called the human mind "my haunt, and the main region of my song"), which poets have followed ever since. Recent critics have argued that the structure, imagery, and subjects of modern verse owe much to romantic forebears. Yeats avowed the connection frankly, calling himself and his coworkers "the last romantics," and even the antiromantic polemics of Eliot betray a continuing connection. But modernism has not merely repeated romanticism. It drew also on traditions as disparate as the folk, the French, the classical, and even the oriental. Adding to these disparate traditions are the regional and internationalist strains of recent years. From the regional focus of the 1960s and 1970s to the much broader cultural base of today, British writing is perhaps best defined now as only a space within which great differences are found. Within this space, the restless technical explorations and troubled modes of consciousness of contemporary poets have resulted in a varied, yet distinctive, poetry of high quality.

History and Criticism

Alvarez, A. *Stewards of Excellence: Studies in Modern English and American Poets.* Gordian 1971 repr. of 1958 ed. $40.00. ISBN 0-87752-152-2. Readable comments on Yeats, Auden, William Empson, and D. H. Lawrence, together with various American poets.

Bedient, Calvin. *Eight Contemporary Poets: Charles Tomlinson, Donald Davie, R. S. Thomas, Philip Larkin, Ted Hughes, Thomas Kinsella, Stevie Smith, W. S. Graham.* OUP 1974 $3.95. ISBN 0-19-519825-5. Perceptive essays and a bibliography.

Bornstein, George. *Transformations of Romanticism in Yeats, Eliot and Stevens.* U. Ch. Pr. 1976 o.p. Modern poetry as an "act of mind" for poets both continuing and opposing romantic tradition.

Brooks, Cleanth. *Modern Poetry and the Tradition.* 1939. U. of NC Pr. 1970 o.p. Historically important and still worth reading; heavily influenced by the views of T. S. Eliot.

Cook, Albert. *On Shakespeare, Modern Poetry, Plato & Other Subjects.* Wayne St. U. Pr. 1991 $34.95. ISBN 0-8143-2331-6. A collection of essays including Cook's retrospective on modern poetry.

Daiches, David. *The Present Age in British Literature.* Ind. U. Pr. 1958 o.p. Survey of trends since 1914; includes bibliography.

Davie, Donald. *Thomas Hardy and British Poetry.* OUP 1972 o.p. Important argument for the "native strain" in modern British verse.

Fallis, Richard. *Irish Renaissance.* Syracuse U. Pr. 1977 $29.95. ISBN 0-8156-2187-6. The best general history of its subject.

Feder, Lillian. *Ancient Myth in Modern Poetry.* Princeton U. Pr. 1972 $17.95. ISBN 0-691-01336-5. Emphasis on Yeats, Pound, Eliot, and Auden.

Gross, Harvey. *Sound and Form in Modern Poetry: A Study of Prosody from Thomas Hardy to Robert Lowell.* U. of Mich. Pr. 1964 $11.95. ISBN 0-472-06141-0

Harrison, John R. *The Reactionaries—Yeats, Wyndham, Lewis, Pound, Eliot, Lawrence: A Study of the Anti-Democratic Intelligentsia.* Schocken 1967 o.p. Explores the political stance of the great modernists.

Hollander, John, ed. *Modern Poetry: Essays in Criticism.* OUP 1968 o.p. A good collection of essays by both poets and critics.

Kermode, Frank. *The Romantic Image.* Chilmark Pr. 1963 o.p. Important study of the postromantic in modern poetry, with emphasis on Yeats, Eliot, and T. E. Hulme.

Langbaum, Robert. *The Poetry of Experience: The Dramatic Monologue in Modern Literary Tradition.* U. Ch. Pr. 1985 $9.95. ISBN 0-226-46872-0. An influential study aligning modern poetry with that of the nineteenth century.

Leavis, Frank R. *New Bearings in English Poetry: A Study of the Contemporary Situation.* AMS Pr. repr. of 1938 ed. $26.50. ISBN 0-404-14035-1. An influential interpretation, with particular emphasis on T. S. Eliot and Ezra Pound.

Loftus, Richard J. *Nationalism in Modern Anglo-Irish Poetry.* U. of Wis. Pr. 1964 o.p. The standard book in its field.

Miller, J. Hillis. *Poets of Reality: Six Twentieth-Century Writers.* Atheneum 1969 repr. of 1965 ed. o.p. Study of, among others, Yeats, Eliot, and Thomas, with an introductory chapter on Conrad.

Perkins, David. *History of Modern Poetry: From the Eighteen Nineties to the High Modernist Mode.* HUP 1976 $14.95. ISBN 0-674-39945-5. The most encyclopedic history of the period, including a very large number of poets.

Pinsky, Robert. *The Situation of Poetry: Contemporary Poetry and Its Traditions. Princeton Essays in Lit. Ser.* Princeton U. Pr. 1977 $12.95. ISBN 0-691-01352-7

Press, John. *Map of Modern English Verse.* OUP 1969 o.p. Useful survey.

Rosenthal, M. L. *Modern Poets: A Critical Introduction.* OUP 1960 o.p. Good survey of poetry from Yeats to World War II, with a final chapter on postwar poetry.

_____. *The New Poets: American and British Poetry since World War II*. OUP 1967 o.p. Good survey of the first 20 years of postwar poetry in America, Britain, and Ireland.

Scully, James, ed. *Modern Poetics*. McGraw 1965 o.p. Essays on poetry by 15 modern poets from Yeats to Robert Lowell.

Spears, Monroe K. *Dionysus and the City: Modernism in Twentieth-Century Poetry*. OUP 1970 o.p. Considers the major changes around World War I and again after World War II.

Spender, Stephen. *The Struggle of the Modern*. U. CA Pr. 1963 o.p. Fascinating study by an important poet, with emphasis on the poetic imagination.

Stead, Christian K. *The New Poetic: Yeats to Eliot*. U. of Pa. Pr. 1987 $17.95. ISBN 0-8122-1244-4. Covers a variety of figures besides the two mentioned in the title; particularly good on Eliot.

Welch, Robert. *Changing States: Transformation in Modern Irish Writing*. Routledge 1993 $59.95. ISBN 0-415-08666-3

Wilson, Edmund. *Axel's Castle: A Study in the Imaginative Literature of 1870–1930*. Norton 1984 repr. of 1931 ed. $9.95. ISBN 0-393-30194-X. A classic older study, still worth reading.

Collections

Bradley, Anthony, ed. *Contemporary Irish Poetry*. U. CA Pr. 1988 $45.00. ISBN 0-520-05927-1. Begins with poets who started their careers after World War I; useful introduction and biographical sketches.

Brown, H., and M. Berry, eds. *Speak to the Hills: An Anthology of Twentieth Century British and Irish Mountain Poetry*. Macmillan 1985 $29.00. ISBN 0-08-030406-0

Cameron, Moven, ed. *Voices of Our Kind: An Anthology of Contemporary Scottish Verse*. State Mutual Bk. 1975 $25.00. ISBN 0-85411-000-3

Ellmann, Richard, and Robert O'Clair, eds. *The Norton Anthology of Modern Poetry*. Norton 1988 $37.95. ISBN 0-393-95636-9. Excellent, capacious gathering (1,456 pages) with helpful, brief bibliographies.

Harmon, Maurice, ed. *Irish Poetry after Yeats: Seven Poets*. Dufour 1987 $14.95. ISBN 0-905473-22-1. Ample representations of the poets and useful introduction.

Heath-Stubbs, John F., and David H. Wright, eds. *The Faber Book of Twentieth Century Verse: An Anthology of Verse in Britain*. Rprt. Serv. 1988 $69.00. ISBN 0-7812-0287-6

Jones, Gwyn, ed. *The Oxford Book of Welsh Verse in English*. OUP 1977 $24.95. ISBN 0-19-211858-7

Larkin, Philip, ed. *The Oxford Book of Twentieth Century English Verse*. OUP 1973 $35.00. ISBN 0-19-812137-7. An important collection.

Lindsay, Maurice, ed. *Modern Scottish Poetry: An Anthology of the Scottish Renaissance 1925–1975*. Humanities 1976 o.p.

MacQueen, John, and Tom Scott, eds. *Oxford Book of Scottish Verse*. OUP 1989 $14.95. ISBN 0-19-282600-X

Montague, John, ed. *The Book of Irish Verse: An Anthology of Irish Poetry from the Sixth Century to the Present*. Macmillan 1983 o.p.

Philip, Neil, ed. *A New Treasury of Poetry*. Stewart, Tabori & Chang 1990 $25.00. ISBN 0-55670-145-4. A 256-page collection of English poetry that celebrates rich traditions in poetic forms.

Roth Publishing staff, eds. *Survey of British Poetry, Vol 5: Twentieth Century*. Roth Pub. 1993 $59.95. ISBN 0-89609-278-X

Sanders, G. D., and others, eds. *Chief Modern Poets of Britain and America*. 2 vols. Macmillan 1970 $13.95. ISBNs 0-02-405890-4, 0-02-405900-5

Thwaite, Anthony, and John Mole, eds. *Poetry, 1945–1980*. Longman 1983 o.p. Good short gathering of mostly British and Irish poets; contains notes and biographical sketches.

Untermeyer, Louis. *Modern British Poetry*. HarBraceJ 1969 o.p. Contains critical introductions to each poet.

Williams, Oscar, ed. *The Mentor Book of Major British Poets*. NAL-Dutton 1985 $5.99. ISBN 0-451-62637-0

Yeats, William Butler, ed. *Oxford Book of Modern Verse, 1892–1935*. OUP 1936 o.p. Historically important gathering of British, Irish, and American verse, with a brilliant if biased introduction by a great poet.

FICTION

In 1927, E. M. FORSTER wrote in *Aspects of the Novel* that "No English novelist is as great as Tolstoy—that is to say has given so complete a picture of man's life. . . . No English novelist has explored man's soul as deeply as Dostoevsky. . . . English poetry fears no one. . . . But English fiction is less triumphant." Certainly the writers Forster mentions have few equals; but his remarks indicate that he was only partially aware of the greatness of some of his contemporaries.

Forster's appraisal of the accomplishments of his compatriots illustrates the difficulty of attempting, even in the most sensible and well-informed manner, to judge the art of one's contemporaries accurately. In discussing contemporary writers, one finds it almost impossible to avoid praising mediocrity or ignoring greatness; the objects closest to us are the ones most difficult to see. And this perhaps is why Forster, five years after the publication of JAMES JOYCE's *Ulysses* (1922), assumed that no novelist could rival MARCEL PROUST (see Vol. 2) in analyzing the modern consciousness.

Forster's remarks came at the end of an unusually productive period in British and Irish fiction. In the 25 or 30 years prior to the publication of his comments, outstanding novels were published by realists such as ARNOLD BENNETT and JOHN GALSWORTHY; by masters of psychological symbolism such as JOSEPH CONRAD and D. H. LAWRENCE; by social observers such as HENRY JAMES and FORD MADOX FORD; and by experimental innovators such as James Joyce and VIRGINIA WOOLF. Forster himself contributed to the large number of masterpieces produced in this era: Though he lived until 1970, his last great work, *A Passage to India*, was completed in 1924.

The best British novelists of the next generation, of the 1930s and 1940s, were ALDOUS HUXLEY, GRAHAM GREENE, GEORGE ORWELL, EVELYN WAUGH, and ANTHONY POWELL. All are noted for their skill in writing social commentary and satire—and satire, of course, is a form of social commentary. Because they worked in turbulent times, it is natural enough to find these novelists preoccupied with social questions; and the turbulence may explain a decline both in the productivity and variety of English fiction in this period.

After World War II, enough similarities appeared among the new novelists to make generalizations about the state of fiction possible once again. At one point the phrase "Angry Young Men" was very much in vogue; and when the writers in question protested that they were not really very angry, their protest was taken as a sign that they were. What many of these newer novelists did seem to have in common—unlike some of their American and French counterparts— was a fictional style that ignored almost entirely the experimental writing of the early decades of the century.

Novelists such as ANGUS WILSON, C. P. SNOW, KINGSLEY AMIS, JOHN BRAINE, ALAN SILLITOE, IRIS MURDOCH, and DORIS LESSING have, for the most part, returned to the traditional naturalism of the Victorian or the Edwardian novel. Few of these writers use devices such as symbolism or stream of consciousness or try to develop new techniques of their own; their main interest is in storytelling. Those British and Irish writers most interested in experiment—

SAMUEL BECKETT, LAWRENCE DURRELL, and ANTHONY BURGESS—all (for a variety of reasons) went to live abroad, and the expatriate experience of alienation was central to their writings.

Some interesting novels have been produced in the modern period, many of them by religious writers such as GRAHAM GREENE, MURIEL SPARK, and WILLIAM GOLDING. Otherwise, the most compelling recent novels seem to be by current and former academics—MALCOLM BRADBURY, ANGELA CARTER, JOHN FOWLES, DAVID LODGE, Iris Murdoch—many of whom are both successful critics and self-conscious novelists aware of the full responsibilities of both their craft and their art. They seek, like Amis in *Lucky Jim* (1954), to make the ivory tower representative of larger social spheres, to explore the universal in the university. To some critics today, English fiction does not seem as exciting as it once did. But of course this is perhaps an illusion; we may, like Forster in 1927, be guilty of underestimating the quality of the newest writers. Indeed, the diversity of the contemporary English novel is a sign of the genre's vitality and its ability to engage the reader on many levels.

History and Criticism

Aldridge, John W. *Time to Murder and Create: The Contemporary Novel in Crisis. Essay Index Repr. Ser.* Ayer repr. of 1966 ed. $26.50. ISBN 0-8369-2682-X

———, ed. *Critiques and Essays on Modern Fiction, 1920–1951: Representing the Achievement of Modern American and British Critics.* Scott F. 1952 o.p.

Allen, Walter. *The Novel To-Day.* Folcroft repr. of 1955 ed. o.p.

Atkins, John. *Six Novelists Look at Society.* Riverrun NY 1980 $9.95. ISBN 0-7145-3863-9

Auerbach, Erich. *Mimesis: The Representation of Reality in Western Literature.* Trans. by W. R. Trask. Princeton U. Pr. 1953 $59.50. ISBN 0-691-06078-9. Rich, complex study; brilliant on the vast subject indicated by its title.

Baker, Ernest A. *A History of the English Novel.* 11 vols. B & N Imports Vol. 1 1977 $31.50. ISBN 0-06-480046-6. Vol. 2 1966 $24.75. ISBN 0-06-480047-4. Vol. 3 1969 $31.50. ISBN 0-06-480048-2. Vol. 4 o.p. Vol. 5 1975 $31.50. ISBN 0-06-480050-4. Vol. 6 1979 $31.50. ISBN 0-06-480051-2. Vol. 7 1968 $22.50. ISBN 0-06-480052-0. Vol. 8 1972 $31.50. ISBN 0-06-480053-9. Vol. 9 1975 $31.50. ISBN 0-480054-7. Vols. 10-11 o.p.

Bergonzi, Bernard. *Heroes' Twilight.* Humanities 1980 o.p. Excellent analysis of the writings resulting from World War I.

———. *Wartime and Aftermath: English Literature and Its Background, 1939-60.* OUP 1993 $13.95. ISBN 0-19-289222-3

Blamires, Harry, ed. *A Guide to Twentieth-Century Literature in English.* Routledge Chapman & Hall 1983 o.p.

Booth, Wayne C. *Rhetoric of Fiction.* U. Ch. Pr. 1983 $30.00. ISBN 0-226-06556-1

Bradbury, Malcolm, and David Palmer, eds. *The Contemporary English Novel.* Holmes & Meier 1980 $19.50. ISBN 0-8419-0571-1

Brown, E. K. *Rhythm in the Novel.* U. of Nebr. Pr. 1978 $17.50. ISBN 0-8032-1150-3

Cross, W. L. *Four Contemporary Novelists.* AMS Pr. repr. of 1930 ed. $12.50. ISBN 0-404-01867-X. Examines Conrad, Bennett, Galsworthy, and Wells.

Daiches, David. *The Novel and the Modern World.* U. Ch. Pr. 1984 repr. of 1939 ed. o.p. Looks at Galsworthy, Conrad, Mansfield, Joyce, Woolf, and Huxley.

DeKoven, Marianne. *Rich and Strange: Gender, History, Modernism.* Princeton U. Pr. 1992 $39.50. ISBN 0-691-06869-0. Feminist reading of British literature of the late nineteenth and early twentieth centuries; shows how modernist works both assert and subvert conventional masculine and feminine polarities and established hierarchies of class and race.

Edel, Leon. *Modern Psychological Novel (The Psychological Novel, 1900–1950).* 1955. Peter Smith $11.25. ISBN 0-8446-2020-3. A brilliant analysis of the stream of consciousness technique in the works of Joyce, Proust, Virginia Woolf, Dorothy Richardson, and Faulkner.

Forster, E. M. *Aspects of the Novel*. HarBraceJ 1956 $7.95. ISBN 0-15-609180-1. An important study of the aesthetics of fiction, in which Forster introduces his idea of "flat" and "round" characters.

Fraser, George S. *The Modern Writer and His World*. Greenwood 1976 repr. of 1965 ed. $70.00. ISBN 0-8371-8549-1

Friedman, Alan W. *Multivalence: The Moral Quality of Form in the Modern Novel*. La. State U. Pr. 1978 $35.00. ISBN 0-8071-0399-3. Relates narration and ethical concerns in Conrad, Ford, Cary, Waugh, and others.

Gilpin, George H. *The Art of Contemporary English Culture*. St. Martins 1993 $39.95. ISBN 0-312-04496-8. Analyzes contemporary English culture by examining shifting attitudes expressed in both art and literature.

Gindin, James. *Postwar British Fiction*. Greenwood 1976 repr. of 1962 ed. $38.50. ISBN 0-8371-8800-8

Hall, James. *The Tragic Comedians: Seven Modern British Novelists*. Greenwood 1978 $35.00. ISBN 0-313-20106-4. A thoughtful critique of the modern British comic novel as exemplified in Forster, Huxley, Evelyn Waugh, and others.

Hayman, David. *Re-forming the Narrative: Toward a Mechanics of Modernist Fiction*. Cornell Univ. Pr. 1987 $24.95. ISBN 0-8014-2005-9. Takes significant steps toward re-forming narrative theory to account for the practice of twentieth-century novels.

Howe, Irving. *Politics and the Novel*. *Essay Index Repr. Ser*. Ayer repr. of 1957 ed. $18.00. ISBN 0-8369-1710-3. An intelligent, penetrating examination of the novel in modern life.

Humphrey, Robert, *Stream of Consciousness in the Modern Novel*. U. CA Pr. 1962 o.p. A rewarding discussion of the methods used by Joyce, Faulkner, Woolf, and Dorothy Richardson.

Iser, Wolfgang. *The Implied Reader: Patterns of Communication in Prose Fiction from Bunyan to Beckett*. Johns Hopkins 1978 $13.95. ISBN 0-8018-2150-9. Pioneering study of reader-response criticism.

Johnstone, Richard. *The Will to Believe: Novelists of the 1930s*. OUP 1982 o.p.

Karl, Frederick R. *A Reader's Guide to the Contemporary English Novel*. Hippocrene Bks. 1972 $25.00. ISBN 0-374-94523-3. An evaluation of the main movements in the British and Irish novel since Joyce.

Karl, Frederick R., and Marvin Magalaner. *A Reader's Guide to Great Twentieth-Century English Novels*. Hippocrene Bks. 1972 $22.50. ISBN 0-87052-003-2. An examination of the works of Conrad, Forster, Woolf, Lawrence, Joyce, and Huxley.

Kazin, Alfred. *Contemporaries, from the Nineteenth Century to the Present*. Horizon Pr. rev. ed. 1981 o.p. Essays, some originally published as book reviews, covering modern novelists.

Kenner, Hugh. *A Colder Eye: The Modern Irish Writers*. Johns Hopkins 1989 repr. of 1983 ed. $12.95. ISBN 0-8018-3838-X

_____. *Gnomon: Essays in Contemporary Literature*. Astor-Honor 1958 o.p.

Kermode, Frank. *The Art of Telling: Essays on Fiction*. HUP 1983 $20.00. ISBN 0-674-04828-8

_____. *Sense of an Ending: Studies in the Theory of Fiction*. OUP 1967 $8.95. ISBN 0-19-500770-0

Kettle, Arnold. *Introduction to the English Novel*. 2 vols. Humanities 1974 repr. of 1963 ed. o.p. Studies of Butler, Hardy, Joyce, Forster, Huxley, Cary, and Greene.

Knowles, Sebastian D. *A Purgatorial Flame: Seven British Writers in the Second World War*. U. of Pa. Pr. 1990 $34.95. ISBN 0-8122-8213-2. Considers the modernist aspects of Woolf, MacNeice, Eliot, Tolkien, C. S. Lewis, Charles Williams, and Evelyn Waugh and their treatment of wartime themes.

Kostelanetz, Richard, ed. *On Contemporary Literature: An Anthology of Critical Essays on the Major Movements and Writings of Contemporary Literature*. *Essay Index Repr. Ser*. Ayer repr. of 1964 ed. $40.00. ISBN 0-8369-2406-1. Contains sections on British writing and on Burgess, Lawrence Durrell, Golding, Lessing, Murdoch, and Spark.

Krieger, Murray. *Classic Vision: The Retreat from Extremity in Modern Literature.* Johns Hopkins 1971 o.p.

Kumar, Shiv K. *Bergson and the Stream of Consciousness Novel.* Greenwood 1979 repr. of 1963 ed. $35.00. ISBN 0-313-20806-9. Uses Bergson's concepts to analyze the work of Richardson, Woolf, and Joyce.

Lodge, David. *The Language of Fiction: Essays in Criticism and Verbal Analysis of the English Novel.* Col. U. Pr. 1967 o.p.

———. *Working with Structuralism: Essays and Reviews on Nineteenth and Twentieth Century Literature.* Routledge 1981 o.p.

McCafferey, Lawrence F. *Postmodern Fiction: A Bio-biographical Guide.* Greenwood 1986 $75.00. ISBN 0-313-24170-8. Consists of 15 essays and some 100 short bio-bibliographical essays.

Mansfield, Katherine. *Novels and Novelists.* Somerset repr. of 1930 ed. $49.00. ISBN 0-403-02290-8

Miller, J. Hillis. *Fiction and Repetition: Seven English Novels.* HUP 1982 $18.95. ISBN 0-674-29925-6

Newby, Peter. *The Novel, 1945–1950.* Folcroft 1974 repr. of 1951 ed. o.p.

O'Connor, William V. *The New University Wits and the End of Modernism. Crosscurrents Modern Critiques Ser.* S. Ill. U. Pr. 1963 o.p. An early study of the writers who emerged after World War II, with a discussion of their literary antecedents.

O'Faolain, Sean. *Vanishing Hero. Essay Index Repr. Ser.* Ayer repr. of 1957 ed. $16.00. ISBN 0-8369-2065-1. On the novelists of the 1920s, including Bowen, Greene, Huxley, Joyce, Waugh, and Woolf.

Russell, John. *Style in Modern British Fiction: Studies in Joyce, Lawrence, Forster, Lewis, and Green.* Johns Hopkins 1978 $26.50. ISBN 0-8018-2029-4

Shapiro, Charles, ed. *Contemporary British Novelists. Crosscurrents Modern Critiques Ser.* S. Ill. U. Pr. 1969 $5.95. ISBN 0-8093-0353-1. Preface by Harry T. Moore. Essays by various hands on the most important post–World War II English writers.

Spender, Stephen. *The Creative Element: A Study of Vision, Despair, and Orthodoxy among Some Modern Writers. Select Bibliographies Repr. Ser.* Ayer repr. of 1953 ed. $20.00. ISBN 0-8369-5911-6

———. *Destructive Element.* Saifer 1970 $12.50. ISBN 0-87556-325-2

Tindall, William Y. *Forces in Modern British Literature, 1885–1946. Essay Index Repr. Ser.* Ayer repr. of 1947 ed. $26.50. ISBN 0-8369-1730-8. Literary criticism of all the major writers, as well as many minor figures, written with wit and understanding.

Vinson, James, ed. *Contemporary Novelists of the English Language.* St. Martin 1972 o.p. Preface by Walter Allen. An excellent reference work with a short essay and bibliography describing the works of every important contemporary novelist.

Watson, George. *British Literature since 1945.* St. Martins 1991 $39.95. ISBN 0-312-05339-8. Insular approach that distinguishes postwar British literature from European and other English-speaking endeavors of the same period.

Webster, Harvey C. *After the Trauma: Representative British Novelists since 1920.* U. Pr. of Ky. 1970 o.p. Includes discussions on Rose Macaulay, Huxley, Compton-Burnett, Waugh, Greene, Hartley, Snow, and others.

West, Rebecca. *Ending in Earnest, A Literary Log. Essay Index Repr. Ser.* Ayer 1967 repr. of 1931 ed. $15.50. ISBN 0-8369-0983-6

Williams, Raymond. *English Novel from Dickens to Lawrence.* Trafalgar 1990 $17.95. ISBN 0-7012-0558-X. Examines the links between the late nineteenth and early twentieth centuries and the social change that occurred during that period.

Collections

Bradbury, Malcolm, ed. *The Penguin Book of Modern British Short Stories.* Viking Penguin 1989 $12.00. ISBN 0-14-006306-4

Craig, Patricia, ed. *The Penguin Book of British Comic Stories.* Viking Penguin 1992 $12.95. ISBN 0-14-012292-3

Davis, Robert G. *Ten Modern Masters*. HarBraceJ 1972 $20.00. ISBN 0-15-590281-4.
   Several stories each by Anderson, Chekhov, Conrad, Faulkner, James, Joyce, Mann,
   Mansfield, and O'Connor.
Garrity, Devin A., ed. *Forty-four Irish Short Stories: An Anthology of Irish Short Fiction
   from Yeats to Frank O'Connor*. Devin 1980 $18.95. ISBN 0-685-45582-3
Hayman, David, and Eric S. Rabkin. *Form in Fiction*. St. Martin 1974 o.p.
Hudson, Derek, ed. *Modern English Short Stories*. Somerset repr. of 1956 ed. $27.00.
   ISBN 0-404-51801-X. A comprehensive anthology, with minor writers as well as
   familiar names represented.
Miller, Karl. *Writing in England Today: The Last Fifteen Years*. Peter Smith o.p. An
   anthology of recent British writing; includes poets and essayists as well as novelists.
Schorer, Mark, ed. *Story: A Critical Anthology*. P-H 1967 o.p.
Trevor, William, ed. *The Oxford Book of Irish Short Stories*. OUP 1989 $29.95. ISBN 0-19-
   214180-5. Includes classic as well as contemporary tales, magical folk tales and fairy
   stories.

DRAMA

At the end of the nineteenth century, HENRY JAMES lamented the enfeebled
state of English dramatic writing. Perhaps in response to this criticism, shortly
after the turn of the century, in 1904, Harley Granville-Barker and GEORGE
BERNARD SHAW took over the management of London's Court Theatre and began
making a deliberate effort to create a modern British literary drama. The critics
and actor-managers, who had been complaining for decades that there were no
original plays, had recently been tempted to accept the weak work of ARTHUR
WING PINERO and HENRY ARTHUR JONES as a substitute. But now, as a revelation,
the Court Theatre began staging JOHN GALSWORTHY, ARNOLD BENNETT, Granville-
Barker and, of course, Shaw (who brought 12 plays to the repertory). Writers of
the stature of RUDYARD KIPLING, JOSEPH CONRAD, and H. G. WELLS were also
invited to contribute. And, although it never became the national theater that
Shaw and Barker had hoped it would, the Court Theatre eventually played three
seasons and was surprisingly profitable and immensely influential.

In 1899, a short time before Barker and Shaw embarked on their Court
Theatre venture, W. B. YEATS founded an Irish national theater, the Abbey, in
Dublin in collaboration with Edward Martyn, and LADY ISABELLA AUGUSTA
GREGORY. The Abbey Theatre became one of the most experimental European
theaters of its time, offering grand mystical verse drama by Yeats and the more
earthy, poetic prose works of JOHN MILLINGTON SYNGE. It should be noted that it
is generally the custom to group under Irish drama not only the writers who
were born in Ireland (which would include Shaw and OSCAR WILDE, as well as
many of the important playwrights back to the Restoration), but also the writers
whose dramas are Irish in subject and setting. This being the case, it can be said
that the birth of modern Irish theater came about with Yeats's decision to turn
his back on HENRIK IBSEN (see Vol. 2) and prose and use the lives of gods and
heroes of ancient Irish legend as the material for a poetic national drama. Such
folklore, however, was largely discarded by SEAN O'CASEY and others, who tried
to introduce social and political realism to the Dublin stage.

These attempts to develop a serious intellectual drama on both sides of the
Irish Sea had little immediate impact on London's West End. The Court Theater
venture had played itself out by 1907, and, by the end of World War I, the
English theater had become as insular as ever, with the main emphasis on quick
profit through light musical entertainment. This situation did not change until

several decades later, when George Devine established his English Stage Company at the same old Sloane Square Playhouse that had housed the earlier Court Theater. Devine began soliciting plays from young dramatists, many of whom had no professional connections to the theater—teachers, architects, bakers. His aim was again to establish a repertory that could support new writing. From the stage of the new Royal Court, playwrights such as JOHN ARDEN, ARNOLD WESKER, and JOHN OSBORNE—the "new wave" of the late 1950s—as well as later figures such as EDWARD BOND, JOE ORTON, HOWARD BRENTON, and DAVID HARE made their way into the London theater.

Ironically, as the movement for a British national theater was again gaining force, the Irish national theater (the Abbey) was in decline. The life of the Abbey had frequently been turbulent. Rioting greeted the masterpieces of both Synge and O'Casey, and in time the theater became as well known for the plays it refused—Shaw's *John Bull's Other Island* (1904), O'Casey's *Silver Tassie* (1929), BRENDAN BEHAN's *The Quare Fellow* (1956)—as for those it produced. By 1951, when a fire destroyed the original building, the Abbey had lost most of the prestige that it had enjoyed in its first decades, although its acting graduates—Barry Fitzgerald, Cyril Cusack, Siobhan McKenna—were internationally famous.

When England finally attained its National Theatre in the wake of the Royal Court-led revitalization, it was natural that Devine's (and Shaw's) ideal should be perpetuated. From 1963 to 1972, the National Theatre engaged Kenneth Tynan, most articulate of critics, as its literary adviser, and, under his guidance, Arden, Osborne, PETER SHAFFER, and an unknown TOM STOPPARD brought their new plays to the National stages. The period of the 1960s and 1970s were years of great excitement and experimentation in the theater. The years since, while continuing to advance serious dramatic writing, have nevertheless also been more troubled. Economic recession and cutbacks have had some limiting effect on the endeavors of theaters and theater companies. Some critics fear that, without new challenges and provocations, the theater may be in danger of slipping back into complacency.

Not that every important dramatist is a writer in the theater. Sometimes he or she is a theater writer, a professional writer such as SOMERSET MAUGHAM, NOEL COWARD, TERENCE RATTIGAN, or ALAN AYCKBOURN, who is eager to work in the traditional commercial forms. The well-made plays or bedroom farces of other playwrights are often eventually acknowledged as classic by an originally contemptuous literary criticism. Sometimes the playwright refuses to think of himself or herself as literary at all, preferring the title of political agitator or performance artist. (It was the Royal Court Theatre that quite naturally became the target of resentment against the literary establishment during the 1970s. Boycotting a playwrighting conference in its auditorium, Hare, Brenton, Trevor Griffiths, and other radicals set about composing their seminal collective piece *Lay-By*.)

It is largely true that, in the plays of the modern period, the reader will find the special qualities of literary drama. In them is an unusual openness to foreign influence. For example, Edward Bond would be impossible without BERTOLT BRECHT (see Vol. 2), just as, in years past, JEAN ANOUILH (see Vol. 2), ANTON CHEKHOV (see Vol. 2), and HENRIK IBSEN have had as much to do with the making of British drama as any native writer. Then again, this literary drama has serious intentions. Beginning with "problem plays" in the 1890s, the British stage has since made room for philosophical and religious debate, outbursts of social anger and political hatred, poetic introspection, and even the meta-seriousness of nonsense. Literary plays, finally, make language their subject as much as their medium. And from *Pygmalion* (1913) to Wester's *Roots* (1959), from Jimmy Porter's rant to the resonant cliché of Pinter's characters, twentieth-century British drama displays the power of the voice to limit and to liberate.

History and Criticism

Acheson, James M., ed. *British and Irish Drama since 1960*. St. Martin 1993. ISBN 0-312-08046-8

Bennett, Benjamin. *Theatre as Problem: Modern Drama and Its Place in Literature*. Cornell Univ. Pr. 1990 $34.50. ISBN 0-8014-2443-7. A theoretical study of modern drama's contribution to literature.

Bull, John. *New British Political Dramatists*. Modern Dramatist Ser. Grove Pr. 1984 o.p. Concentrates on Howard Brenton, David Hare, Trevor Griffiths, and David Edgar.

Cave, Richard A. *New British Drama in Performance on the London Stage: 1970-1985*. St. Martin 1988 $29.95. ISBN 0-312-01912-2. A survey of modern British drama focusing on eight contemporary playwrights: Pinter, Aychbourn, Stoppard, Beckett, Storey, Hare, Griffiths, and Bond.

Cook, Judith. *Director's Theatre*. Harrap 1974 o.p. Interviews with John Barton, Peter Brook, John Dexter, Peter Hall, Joan Littlewood, Jonathan Miller, and Trevor Nunn (among others).

Davison, Peter. *Contemporary Drama and the Popular Dramatic Tradition in England*. B & N Imports 1983 $40.00. ISBN 0-389-20232-0. Explores the important relation of modern British drama and the music hall.

Donoghue, Dennis. *The Third Voice: Modern British and American Verse Drama*. Princeton U. Pr. 1959 o.p. Yeats and Eliot are treated as crucial figures. Includes shorter studies of Fry and Auden, among others.

Esslin, Martin. *The Theatre of the Absurd*. Overlook Pr. rev. ed. 1973 repr. of 1961 ed. $35.00. ISBN 0-87951-005-6. Attempts to assimilate Pinter and Simpson to a continental dramatic tradition.

Evans, Gareth, and Barbara Evans. *Plays in Review, 1956–1980*. Routledge Chapman & Hall 1985 o.p. First-night reviews by a variety of English critics.

Gooch, Steve. *All Together Now*. Heinemann Ed. 1984 $8.95. ISBN 0-413-53480-4. A manifesto for the community and touring groups who have rejected both the West End and the subsidized theater.

Griffiths, Trevor R., and Margaret Llewellyn-Jones. *British and Irish Women Dramatists Since 1958: A Critical Handbook*. Taylor & Francis 1993 $94.00. ISBN 0-335-09603-4

Hayman, Ronald. *British Theatre since 1955: A Reassessment*. OUP 1979 o.p.

———. *Playback*. Horizon 1974 o.p.

———. *The Set-Up: An Anatomy of the English Theatre Today*. Methuen 1973 o.p.

Hinchcliffe, Arnold P. *British Theatre, 1950–1970*. OUP 1974 o.p.

Itzin, Catherine. *Stages in the Revolution: Political Theatre in Britain since 1968*. Heinemann Ed. 1989 $14.95. ISBN 0-413-61505-7

Kennedy, A. *Six Dramatists in Search of a Language*. Cambridge U. Pr. 1975 o.p. Discusses Shaw, Pinter, Osborne, and others.

Kerensky, Oleg. *The New British Drama: Fourteen Playwrights since Osborne and Pinter*. Taplinger 1979 o.p. Valuable mainly for its interview material.

Marowitz, Charles, and others, eds. *New Theatre Voices of the Fifties and Sixties: Selections from "Encore" Magazine, 1956–1963*. Routledge Chapman & Hall 1981 o.p. Introduction by Michael Billington. Articles from *Encore* magazine (1956–63), forum of the anticommercial theater movement.

Marowitz, Charles, and Simon Trussler, eds. *Theatre at Work: Playwrights and Productions of the Modern British Theatre*. Hill & Wang 1968 o.p.

Page, Adrian, and Clive Bloom, eds. *The Death of the Playwright?: Modern British Drama and Literary Theory*. St. Martin 1992 $45.00. ISBN 0-312-06537-X. Examines drama through various theories, from psychoanalytic to structuralist.

Peacock, D. Keith. *Radical Stages: Alternative History in Modern British Drama*. Greenwood 1991 $45.00. ISBN 0-313-27888-1. Well-researched, intelligently presented account of historical/political drama in Britain since 1956.

Rabey, David I. *British and Irish Political Drama in the Twentieth Century: Implicating the Audience*. St. Martin 1986 $35.00. ISBN 0-312-10030-2. Examines the work of more than 30 playwrights.

Roy, Emil. *British Drama since Shaw. Crosscurrents Modern Critiques Ser*. S. Ill. U. Pr. 1972 $8.50. ISBN 0-8093-0579-8

Spanos, William V. *Christian Tradition in Modern British Verse Drama: The Poetics of Sacramental Time*. Rutgers U. Pr. 1967 o.p.

Taylor, John Russell. *Anger and After: A Guide to the New British Drama*. Routledge Chapman & Hall 1977 o.p. A thorough journalistic account of the new wave playwrights and their plays. Includes a good survey of London theatrical conditions in the 1950s.

———. *The Rise and Fall of the Well-Made Play*. Hill & Wang o.p.

———. *The Second Wave: British Drama for the Seventies*. Hill & Wang 1971 o.p. Nichols, Bond, Stoppard, Orton, Storey, and others; a successor to *Anger and After*.

Trussler, Simon, ed. *New Theatre Voices of the Seventies: Interviews from "Theatre Quarterly," 1970–1980*. Routledge Chapman & Hall 1981 o.p.

Tynan, Kenneth. *Curtains*. Atheneum 1961 o.p. Reprints Tynan's important views of the 1950s.

———. *Show People*. S & S Trade 1980 o.p. Contains profiles of Tom Stoppard and Ralph Richardson.

———. *The Sound of Two Hands Clapping*. Da Capo 1982 repr. of 1975 ed. $7.95. ISBN 0-306-80164-7

———. *Tynan Right and Left: Plays, Films, Places, People and Events*. Atheneum 1967 o.p. Includes reviews of new wave theater.

Wilmut, Roger. *From Fringe to Flying Circus: Celebrating a Unique Generation of Comedy, 1960–1980*. Heinemann Ed. 1985 $15.95. ISBN 0-413-50770-X

Worth, Katharine. *Revolutions in Modern English Drama*. Bell 1973 o.p. Locates new wave plays in the continuum of British drama.

Theaters and Companies

Arundell, Dennis. *The Story of Sadler's Wells, 1683–1977*. Rowman 1978 o.p.

Beauman, Sally. *The Royal Shakespeare Company: A History of Ten Decades*. OUP 1982 $29.95. ISBN 0-19-212209-6

Browne, Terry. *Playwright's Theatre: The English Stage Company at the Royal Court*. Wesleyan U. Pr. 1975 o.p.

Chambers, Colin. *Other Spaces: New Theatre and the Royal Shakespeare Company*. Routledge Chapman & Hall 1981 o.p.

The Complete Guide to Britain's National Theatre. Ed. by Richard Findlater and others. Heinemann Ed. 1977 o.p.

Doty, Gresdna A., and Billy J. Harbin. *Inside the Royal Court Theatre, 1956–1981: Artists Talk*. La. St. U. Pr. 1990 $35.00. ISBN 0-8071-1550-9. Consists of discussions held between various artists associated with the company and a panel chaired by U.S. theater professionals at Louisiana State University celebrating the company's 25th anniversary.

Findlater, Richard, ed. *At the Royal Court: Twenty-Five Years of the English Stage Company*. Grove Pr. 1981 o.p.

McCarthy, Desmond. *The Court Theatre, 1904–1907: A Commentary and Criticism*. Ed. by Stanley Weintraub. U. of Miami Pr. 1966 $10.95. ISBN 0-87024-068-4. Chronicle of a brilliantly successful early experiment in repertory theater.

Wearing, J. P. *The London Stage 1940–1949: A Calendar of Plays & Players.* 2 vols. Scarecrow 1991 $115.00. ISBN 0-8108-2500-7. Day by day calendar of plays produced at the major London theatres from January 1, 1940 to December 31, 1949.

Collections

Landmarks of Modern British Drama. 2 vols. Heinemann Ed. 1988 $12.95 ea. ISBNs 0-413-59080-1, 0-413-59090-9. Introductions by Roger Cornish and Violet Ketels. Vol. 1: *The Sixties*: Contains Wesker, *Roots*; Arden, *Serjeant Musgrave's Dance*; Pinter, *The Caretaker*; Osborne, *A Patriot for Me*; Bond, *Saved*; Orton, *Loot*; Barnes, *The Ruling Class*. Vol. 2: *The Seventies*: Contains Ayckbourn, *Just Between Ourselves*; Brenton, *Weapons of Happiness*; Stoppard, *Every Good Boy Deserves Favor*; Shaffer, *Amadeus*; Nichols, *Passion Play*; Gray, *Quartermaine's Terms*; Churchill, *Top Girls*.

Wandor, Michelene, ed. *Plays by Women.* 4 vols. Heinemann Ed. 1988 $11.95 ea. ISBNs 0-413-50020-9, 0-413-51030-1, 0-413-54300-5, 0-413-56740-0. Vol. 1: Churchill, *Vinegar Tom*; Gems, *Dusa, Fish, Stas and Vi*; Page, *Tissue*; Wandor, *Aurora Leigh*. Vol. 2: Luckman, *Trafford Tanzi*; Goldenberg, *Letters Home*; Duffy, *Rites*; Wymark, *Find Me*. Vol. 3: Gems, *Aunt Mary*; Horsfield, *Red Devils*; Pollock, *Blood Relations*; Wakefield and others, *Time Pieces*. Vol. 4: Churchill, *Objections to Sex and Violence*; Dayley, *Rose's Story*; Lochhead, *Blood and Ice*; Lyssa, *Pinball*.

Warnock, Robert. *Representative Modern Plays: British.* Scott F. 1953 o.p. Contains Barrie, *The Admirable Crichton*; Shaw, *The Doctor's Dilemma*; Galsworthy, *Loyalties*; Synge, *Riders to the Sea*; O'Casey, *Juno and the Paycock*; Maugham, *The Constant Wife*; Coward, *Blithe Spirit*; Eliot, *Murder in the Cathedral*; Fry, *A Phoenix Too Frequent*.

Bibliography and Reference

Adelman, Irving, and Rita Dworkin. *Modern Drama: A Checklist of Critical Literature on 20th-Century Plays.* Scarecrow 1967 o.p. A guide to critical articles and sections of books but not reviews.

Breed, Paul F., and Florence M. Sniderman. *Dramatic Criticism Index: Bibliography of Commentaries on Playwrights from Ibsen to the Avant Garde.* Gale 1972 o.p. More than 300 playwrights, most from the twentieth century.

Carpenter, Charles A. *Modern British Drama.* Harlan Davidson 1979. ISBN 0-88295-568-3. A select bibliography covering general works as well as individual English and Irish dramatists.

Coleman, Arthur, and Gary Tyler. *Drama Criticism.* 2 vols. Ohio U. Pr. o.p. Interpretive criticism from 1940.

Harris, Richard H. *Modern Drama in America and England, 1950-1970: A Guide to Information Sources.* Gale 1982 o.p. Lists relevant bibliographies and selected critical writings.

King, Kimball. *Twenty Modern British Playwrights: A Bibliography, 1956 to 1976.* Garland 1977 o.p. Includes both well-known and lesser-known figures. Lists the dramatists' works and bibliographies of critical writings and reviews

Mikhail, E. H. *Contemporary British Drama, 1950–1976.* Rowman 1976 $20.00. ISBN 0-87471-854-6. A checklist of books and articles.

Nightingale, Benedict. *A Reader's Guide to Fifty Modern British Plays.* B & N Imports 1982 o.p. General introduction to playwrights and comments on specific plays, from Barrie's *Admirable Crichton* to Trevor Griffiths's *Comedians*.

Salem, James M. *A Guide to Critical Reviews Part III: British and Continental Drama from Ibsen to Pinter.* Scarecrow 1979 $37.50. ISBN 0-8108-1226-6. Indexes reviews of productions, not scholarly or critical studies.

Theatre Year. Routledge Chapman & Hall 1984 o.p. Introduction by Michael Coveney, photographs by Donald Cooper. Photographic record of the London theater season, with brief credit lists and an essay.

Thompson, John C. *A Reader's Guide to Fifty British Plays: 1660–1900.* B & N Imports
    1980 o.p. Includes biographical information and plot summaries.
Vinson, James, ed. *Contemporary Dramatists. Contemporary Writers Ser.* St. Martin 1982
    $30.00. ISBN 0-312-16660-5. Preface by Ruby Cohn. Lists more than 300 playwrights.
    Includes biography, playlist, production date, bibliography, critical essays, and other
    relevant material.
_____, ed. *Great Dramatists.* St. Martin 1979 o.p. English dramatists of all historical
    periods.
Weintraub, Stanley, ed. *Modern British Dramatists, 1900 to 1945. Dictionary of Literary
    Biography Ser.* 2 vols. Gale 1982 $226.00. ISBN 0-8103-0937-8
_____, ed. *British Dramatists: Since World War II. Dictionary of Literary Biography Ser.* 2
    vols. Gale 1983 $226.00. ISBN 0-8103-0936-X. Long biographical-critical essays,
    including illustrations, selective bibliographies.

NONFICTION

In the modern period, the essay in British and Irish literature lacks the importance that it had in earlier periods, such as the Romantic era, when it was a vehicle for the unfettered and eloquent exposition of self and the world. Modern writers such as HILAIRE BELLOC and G. K. CHESTERTON, known primarily for their nonfiction prose, are not acclaimed as central voices of modernism. Even the appeal of a dedicated, industrious, and talented essayist like GEORGE ORWELL is, to an extent, legitimized by his works of fiction. The modern period is characterized by stylistic experimentation, avant-garde formal reconsiderations, and radical extensions of the realms of literary consciousness; nonfiction writing is poorly poised to draw upon these attributes of modernism, and so it tends to be relegated to a subordinate position in the canon of modern British and Irish literature.

Perhaps the most prominent essays of the period are those whose writers had alternate claims to literary reputation. T. S. ELIOT, for example, wrote hundreds of essays—book reviews, literary criticism, examinations of the Christian condition in the modern world—which exerted a considerable influence on the aesthetic sensibility of modernism and the constitution of contemporary and traditional literary canons. H. G. WELLS wrote copious essays of social and cultural observation, which complemented the agendas inherent in his novels. Yet, both writers are known primarily for their work in poetry and fiction, respectively.

"Little magazines" of the period—*Athenaeum, The Little Review, Criterion, Poetry,* and others—have offered a forum for writers who intended their nonfiction prose to serve, in a sense, as a manifesto for their literature. The modernist text itself is intricate, complex, often only marginally fathomable on its own terms; the genre of the literary essay has made possible a more prosaic and straightforward explanation of the aesthetic *zeitgeist.* When VIRGINIA WOOLF, for example, wrote in her famous essay "Mr. Bennet and Mrs. Brown" that human character simply changed sometime around December 1910, she encouraged her readers to examine, in her own fiction, what constituted this change—how the modern generation set itself against the sensibility of its Victorian antecedents, and what, precisely, was meant by the idea of human character in the modern period. During this period, nearly every literary figure of appreciable stature found it politic to supplement his or her creative writing with at least the occasional review or prose pronouncement, to be suitably collected, eventually, in a volume of essays that provided readers with the author's version of his or her platform.

While other traditional genres of nonfiction writing certainly existed during the modern period, again they tended to be co-opted by the more famous literary canon of a given writer and considered as an outgrowth of that (as with EVELYN WAUGH and his travel writing), or else—as with much of the most important biography and autobiography—set off from the literary and aesthetic mainstream and treated as a separate entity, closer to journalism and mass-market publishing than to the canon of high literary art.

History and Criticism

Altick, Richard. *Lives and Letters: A History of Literary Biographies in England and America*. Greenwood 1979 repr. of 1965 ed. $30.50. ISBN 0-313-21116-7. Discusses Gosse's writing and the impact of Strachey's biographical sensibility.

Beum, Robert Lawrence, ed. *Modern British Essayists*. Gale 1990 o.p. Biographies and bibliographies of 63 essayists.

Brown, Christopher C., and William B. Thesing, eds. *English Prose and Criticism, 1900–1950: A Guide to Information Sources*. Gale 1983 $68.00. ISBN 0-8103-1236-0. Bibliographies of individual writers and genres including literary history, biography and autobiography, essays, literary criticism, and travel writing.

Dawson, Carl. *Prophets of Past Time: Seven British Autobiographers, 1880–1914*. Johns Hopkins 1988 $38.00. ISBN 0-8018-3587-9. Memory and imagination in the autobiographies of writers including Yeats, Ford, and Gosse.

Dobrée, Bonamy. *Modern Prose Style*. Greenwood 1978 repr. of 1964 ed. $38.50. ISBN 0-313-20124-2. Descriptive, explanatory, and emotional prose.

Ellmann, Richard. *Literary Biography*. OUP 1971 o.p. The difficulties of literary biography, with reference to such authors as Joyce, Lawrence, Yeats, Forster, Gosse.

Finney, Brian. *The Inner I: British Literary Autobiography of the Twentieth Century*. OUP 1985 $35.00. ISBN 0-19-503738-3. Versions of truth and identity in the works of such writers as John Mortimer, V. S. Pritchett, Osbert Sitwell, Edwin Muir, and H. G. Wells.

Fussell, Paul. *Abroad: British Literary Traveling Between the Wars*. OUP 1980 $25.00. ISBN 0-19-502767-1. Includes discussion of travel writing.

Good, Graham. *The Observing Self: Rediscovering the Essay*. Routledge 1988 o.p. Chapters on Woolf, Eliot, Orwell.

Gross, John. *The Rise and Fall of the Man of Letters: English Literary Life since 1800*. I. R. Dee 1992 $14.95. ISBN 0-56663-000-2. Covers Eliot, Chesterton, Murry, Orwell, Leavis, and others.

Hynes, Samuel. *Edwardian Occasions: Essays on English Writing in the Twentieth Century*. Routledge 1972 o.p. Discusses such prose writers as Wells, Shaw, Conrad, Chesterton, Belloc, Forster, Hulme.

Keith, W. J. *The Rural Tradition: A Study of the Non-Fiction Prose Writers of the English Countryside*. U. of Toronto Pr. 1974 $81.00. ISBN 0-3173-9690-0. Edward Thomas, Henry Williamson, H. J. Massingham, and other writers on rural themes.

Miles, Josephine. *Style and Proportion: The Language of Prose and Poetry*. Little 1967 o.p. Historical development of British prose style.

Routh, Harold V. *English Literature and Ideas in the Twentieth Century*. Russell 1970 o.p. Prose styles and ideologies of Beerbohm, Gosse, Eliot, Richards, Strachey, and other non-fiction writers.

Shelston, Alan. *Biography*. HarpC 1977 o.p. Problems of balancing fact and fiction, author and subject.

Thomson, J. A. K. *Classical Influences on English Prose*. Rprt. Serv. 1988 repr. of 1956 ed. $49.00. ISBN 0-7812-0567-0. Classical models of genres such as biography, travel literature.

Collections

Cahill, Kevin M. *Irish Essays*. John Jay Pr. 1980 $9.00. ISBN 0-89444-028-4. A wide-ranging collection of essays on a variety of subjects.

Daiches, David J., ed. *A Century of the Essay, British and American*. HarBraceJ 1951 o.p. An extensive anthology covering significant British and American essays.

Edes, Mary Elisabeth. *The Age of Extravagance: An Edwardian Reader*. Rinehart 1954 o.p. A collection of early twentieth-century prose.

Eglinton, John. *Anglo-Irish Essays*. Gordon Pr. 1971 $59.95. ISBN 0-87968-635-9. Interesting anthology of modern essays.

Freeman, John. *English Portraits and Essays*. Rprt. Serv. 1992 repr. of 1924 ed. $79.00. ISBN 0-7812-7012-X. Includes some essays from the beginning of the modern period.

Glover, Jon, and Jon Silkin, eds. *The Penguin Book of First World War Prose*. Viking Penguin 1991 $11.95. ISBN 0-14-005802-8. War writers and other prominent figures offer a sense of the period's sensibility.

Gross, John J., ed. *The Oxford Book of Essays*. OUP 1991 $30.00. ISBN 0-19-214185-6. Older and recent essays by acclaimed nonfiction writers.

Hoy, Pat C. III and Rogert Diyanni. *Modern American and British Prose*. McGraw 1988 $17.56. ISBN 0-07-555113-6. A selective collection of modern prose.

Milford, Humphrey S., ed. *Selected Modern English Essays*. Greenwood 1981 repr. of 1932 ed. $47.50. ISBN 0-313-22763-2

Moulton, Charles W. *The Library of Literary Criticism of English and American Authors*. 8 vols. Rprt. Serv. 1992 $600.00. ISBN 0-7812-7004-9. Collections of criticism by modern British and American authors.

Scholes, Robert E., ed. *Some Modern Writers*. OUP 1971 o.p. Collection of essays by a number of modern authors, including Conrad, Lawrence, and Orwell.

Smallwood, Philip. *Modern Critics in Practice: Critical Portraits of British Literary Critics*. St. Martin 1990 $39.95. ISBN 0-312-04763-0

Wellek, René. *A History of Modern Criticism, 1750–1950*. Yale U. Pr. 1986 $37.00. ISBN 0-300-03378-8. A comprehensive collection of critical essays on the works of major British and American critics of the past 50 years.

CHRONOLOGY OF AUTHORS

Gregory, Lady Isabella Augusta. 1852–1932

Shaw, George Bernard. 1856–1950

Conrad, Joseph. 1857–1924

Housman, A(lfred) E(dward) 1859–1936

Barrie, Sir James Matthew, Bart. 1860–1937

Yeats, William Butler. 1865–1939

Wells, H. G. 1866–1946

Bennett, Arnold. 1867–1931

Galsworthy, John. 1867–1933

Belloc, Hilaire. 1870–1953

Munro, H(ector) H(ugh). 1870–1916

Synge, John Millington. 1871–1909

Beerbohm, Sir H(enry) M(aximilian) 1872–1956

de la Mare, Walter. 1873–1956

Ford, Ford Madox. 1873–1939

Richardson, Dorothy. 1873?–1957

Chesterton, G(ilbert) K(eith). 1874–1936

Maugham, W(illiam) Somerset. 1874–1965

Masefield, John. 1878–1967

Thomas, Edward. 1878–1917

Forster, E(dward) M(organ). 1879–1970

O'Casey, Sean. 1880–1964

Colum, Padraic. 1881–1972

Joyce, James. 1881–1941

Woolf, Virginia. 1882–1941

Lewis, Wyndham. 1884–1957

O'Casey, Sean. 1884–1964

Lawrence, D(avid) H(erbert). 1885–1930

Firbank, Ronald. 1886–1926

Hall, Radclyffe. 1886–1943

Sassoon, Siegfried. 1886–1967

Brooke, Rupert. 1887–1915

Muir, Edwin. 1887–1959
Sitwell, Edith. 1887–1964
Cary, Joyce. 1888–1957
Eliot, T(homas) S(tearns). 1888–1965
Rosenberg, Isaac. 1890–1918
Compton-Burnett, Dame Ivy. 1892–1969
MacDiarmid, Hugh. 1892–1978
Sackville-West, Vita. 1892–1962
Tolkien, J.R.R. 1892–1973
West, Dame Rebecca. 1892–1983
Owen, Wilfred. 1893–1918
Huxley, Aldous. 1894–1963
Priestley, J(ohn) B(oynton). 1894–1984
Graves, Robert. 1895–1985
Hartley, L(eslie) P(oles). 1895–1972
Jones, David. 1895–1974
Clarke, Austin. 1896–1974
Lewis, C(live) S(taples). 1898–1963
Bowen, Elizabeth. 1899–1973
Coward, Sir Noel. 1899–1973
Bunting, Basil. 1900–1985
Hughes, Richard. 1900–1976
O'Faolain, Sean. 1900–1991
Pritchett, Sir V(ictor) S(awden). 1900–
Smith, Stevie. 1902–1971
O'Connor, Frank. 1903–1966
Orwell, George. 1903–1950
Waugh, Evelyn. 1903–1966
Greene, Graham. 1904–1991
Isherwood, Christopher. 1904–1986
Lewis, C(ecil) Day. 1904–1972
Green, Henry. 1905–1974
Kavanagh, Patrick. 1905–1967
Powell, Anthony. 1905–
Snow, Lord C. P. 1905–1980
Beckett, Samuel. 1906–1989
Betjeman, Sir John. 1906–1984
Watkins, Vernon. 1906–1967
Auden, W(ystan) H(ugh). 1907–1973
Fry, Christopher. 1907–
MacNeice, (Frederick) Louis. 1907–1963
Spender, Sir Stephen. 1909–
Golding, William. 1911–1993

O'Brien, Flann. 1911–1966
Rattigan, Sir Terence. 1911–1977
Durrell, Lawrence. 1912–1990
Fuller, Roy. 1912–1991
Pym, Barbara. 1913–1980
Wilson, Angus. 1913–1991
Thomas, Dylan. 1914–1953
Burgess, Anthony. 1917–
Spark, Muriel. 1918–
Murdoch, Iris. 1919–
Amis, Kingsley. 1922–
Braine, John. 1922–1986
Davie, Donald. 1922–
Larkin, Philip. 1922–1985
Behan, Brendan. 1923–1964
Bolt, Robert. 1924–
Fowles, John. 1926–
Jennings, Elizabeth. 1926–
Shaffer, Peter. 1926–
Tomlinson, Charles. 1927–
Brookner, Anita. 1928–
Nichols, Peter. 1928–
Sillitoe, Alan. 1928–
Friel, Brian. 1929–
Gunn, Thom(son). 1929–
Osborne, John. 1929–
Arden, John. 1930–
Hughes, Ted. 1930–
Pinter, Harold. 1930–
Wilson, Colin. 1931–
Bradbury, Malcolm. 1932–
MacBeth, George. 1932–
Wesker, Arnold. 1932–
Orton, Joe. 1933–1967
Bond, Edward. 1934–
Lodge, David (John). 1935–
Potter, Dennis. 1935–
Byatt, A(notonia) S(usan). 1936–
Gray, Simon. 1936–
Stoppard, Tom. 1937–
Churchill, Caryl. 1938–
Ayckbourn, Alan. 1939–
Drabble, Margaret. 1939–
Heaney, Seamus. 1939–
Carter, Angela. 1940–1992
Brenton, Howard. 1942–
Hare, David. 1947–

AMIS, KINGSLEY. 1922–

Kingsley Amis, born "of Baptist stock originating in southeast London," received his degree in English language and literature from St. John's College, Oxford, in 1947. He has written poems, stories, and criticism for various periodicals. Until 1961 Amis lectured in English at University College, Swansea, and was a fellow of Peterhouse (Cambridge) until 1963, when he decided to devote all of his time to writing. It was W. SOMERSET MAUGHAM who first attacked that group of English writers called the "Angry Young Men," of whom Amis is one of the best known.

Lucky Jim (1954), an entertaining satire on the fortunes of a frivolous young scholar at an English university, won the Somerset Maugham Award in 1955 and made Amis's reputation. He followed with *That Uncertain Feeling* (1956), which the *Times Literary Supplement* praised: "His dialogue is brilliant, his timing of comic situations could hardly be bettered . . . yet by intention he is a serious comic writer, one who apparently means to say something about society." There was a great diversity of critical opinion about *Take a Girl Like You* (1960), but the *New Yorker* considered it his best work since *Lucky Jim*: "Mr. Amis treats his subject . . . with wit, shrewdness, and humanity, and he shows an uncommon understanding of a kind of girl who exists by the million and who has not been taken seriously in literature for quite some time." In *The Anti-Death League* (1966), at once a comedy and a spy thriller with serious undertones, "what Mr. Amis has done, with some of his best writing, is to expound his philosophies through a vivid, exciting story and a superior character analysis that challenges your imagination and absorbs your interest" (*Baltimore Sunday Sun*). With Robert Conquest, he has edited *Spectrum*, science fiction anthologies of short stories by masters who write with imagination and style. A longtime James Bond devotee—who had proved his interest with a study of the superhero, *The James Bond Dossier* (1965)—Amis was delegated to produce more Bond books in the manner of the late IAN FLEMING, Bond's creator. "The critics," said the *N.Y. Times*, "were outraged, but the public seems to be delighted." Amis's more recent works include *Jake's Thing* (1978); *Stanley and the Women* (1984); *The Old Devils* (1986), which won the Booker Prize; and *The Crime of the Century* (1989). His son Martin Amis is also a well-known novelist.

NOVELS BY AMIS

The Alteration. 1976. Carroll & Graf 1988 $3.95. ISBN 0-88184-432-2

The Crime of the Century. Mysterious Pr. 1989 $75.00. ISBN 0-89296-403-0. Story of a criminal inquiry to investigate a number of fatal stabbings in London parks.

The Folks That Live on the Hill. G. K. Hall 1991 $21.95. ISBN 0-7451-7255-5

The Green Man. Academy Chi. Pubs. 1986 $6.95. ISBN 0-89733-220-2

Jake's Thing. 1978. Viking Penguin 1980 $7.95. ISBN 0-14-005096-5

Lucky Jim. 1954. Viking Penguin 1976 $6.00. ISBN 0-14-001648-1. Lampoons academic pretensions.

One Fat Englishman. Transaction Pubs. 1989 repr. of 1963 ed. $18.95. ISBN 0-85089-223-7

Stanley and the Women. Summit Bks. 1985 o.p.

Take a Girl Like You. David & Charles 1960 o.p.

POETRY BY AMIS

Collected Poems, 1944–1979. Viking Penguin 1980 o.p.

NONFICTION BY AMIS

Harold's Years: Impressions of the Harold Wilson Era. Charles River Bks. $12.95. ISBN 0-7043-2143-2

New Maps of Hell. Ayer repr. of 1975 ed. $18.95. ISBN 0-405-06321-0

Rudyard Kipling. Thames Hudson 1986 $9.95. ISBN 0-500-26019-2. Admirable study of the noted author.

BOOKS ABOUT AMIS

Gardner, Philip. *Kingsley Amis.* Twayne 1981 o.p. Overview of his life.

McDermott, John. *Kingsley Amis: An English Moralist.* St. Martin 1989 $24.95. ISBN 0-312-02103-8. Discussion of moral conditions in Amis's writing.

Salwak, Dale, ed. *Kingsley Amis: In Life and Letters.* St. Martin 1991 $29.95. ISBN 0-312-05365-7. Essays by friends and readers offering anecdotes, criticism, and colorful background.

————. *Kingsley Amis: A Reference Guide.* G. K. Hall 1978 o.p. Bibliography.

————. *Kingsley Amis: Modern Novelist.* B & N Imports 1992 $58.75. ISBN 0-389-20992-9. Critical study examining Amis's comedy and disillusionment.

ARDEN, JOHN. 1930–

John Arden's is a striking case of the alienation that has overtaken a number of the original "angry" playwrights—ARNOLD WESKER and JOHN OSBORNE also come to mind—in an age of subsidized theater and broadly tolerant audiences. Trained as an architect, Arden was one of the Royal Court discoveries. His plays of the 1950s, *Live Like Pigs* (1958) and, particularly, *Serjeant Musgrave's Dance* (1958), while not initially successes, have become modern classics. (In 1972, John McGrath's theater company paid *Musgrave* homage by producing a version, updated to a Northern Irish situation, called *Serjeant Musgrave Dances On*.) But Arden today, still a prolific and committed playwright, claims he cannot get an English theater to produce his plays and, with his wife, Margaretta D'Arcy, has retreated to Ireland, where most of his recent work has been staged.

The problem apparently lies in the political dogmatism, absorption with Irish problems, and militancy that have entered Arden's drama since 1967, when he became a full-time collaborator in writing with his wife. D'Arcy's dramatic instincts, Arden has admitted, are the opposite of his own: She thinks of a subject needing illustration; he thinks of language and action and characters to suit them. His own plays—from *The Water of Babylon* (1957) through *Armstrong's Last Goodnight* (1964) and *Left-Handed Liberty* (1965)—are imaginative, often balladlike, and (politically) inconclusive. Poetic qualities are not altogether absent from later plays, such as the Arthurian *The Island of the Mighty* (1972). But typically Arden demands a sharper emphasis. Arden and D'Arcy bitterly criticized the Royal Shakespeare Company's 1970s production of *The Island* as imperialist and corrupted, and actually picketed the performances.

PLAYS BY ARDEN

Left-Handed Liberty: A Play about Magna Carta. 1965. Grove Pr. 1966 o.p.

Plays: One. Grove Pr. o.p. Contains *Serjeant Musgrave's Dance, The Workhouse Donkey,* and *Armstrong's Last Goodnight.* The first of these, *Serjeant Musgrave's Dance,* is Arden's best-known play and concerns deserters from a colonial war.

Three Plays. Grove Pr. 1966 o.p. Introduction by John Russell Taylor. Contains *Live Like Pigs, The Waters of Babylon,* and *The Happy Haven.*

Two Autobiographical Plays: The True History of Squire Jonathan and *The Unfortunate Treasure.* Methuen 1971 o.p.

NONFICTION BY ARDEN

To Present the Pretence: Essays on the Theatre and Its Public. Holmes & Meier 1979 o.p. Arden's selection of his own critical writings on the theater, complete with his own commentary.

PLAYS BY ARDEN AND MARGARETTA D'ARCY

The Business of Good Government. Heinemann Ed. 1984 $8.95. ISBN 0-413-53460-X. One act Christmas play; first collaboration between the duo.

The Hero Rises Up. Methuen 1969 o.p. Tales of an admiral's conquests at sea, told in nineteenth-century melodrama style.

The Island of the Mighty. Methuen 1975 o.p.

The Royal Pardon. Methuen 1967 $8.95. ISBN 0-413-33410-4. Children's plays set in a legendary past that relate the story of a soldier back from war who joins a theater troupe.

Vandaleur's Folly: An Anglo-Irish Melodrama. Methuen 1981 o.p. A play about Ireland.

BOOK ABOUT ARDEN

Page, Malcolm. *Arden on File*. Heinemann Ed. 1988 $10.95. ISBN 0-413-56280-8. Surveys Arden's stage plays, radio and television work, and nondramatic writing.

AUDEN, W(YSTAN) H(UGH). 1907–1973

The most important British poet of the generation after T. S. ELIOT, W. H. Auden was born in York, England. The son of a doctor and a nurse, he passed through a series of private schools on his way to Oxford University, where he intended to study science but then changed to English literature instead. Although Auden graduated from Oxford with only a mediocre degree, the force of his personality and the brilliance of his intellect established him as an important figure even during his student days. After graduation, he quickly gained recognition as the foremost poet in a brilliant literary circle that also included C. DAY LEWIS, STEPHEN SPENDER, LOUIS MACNEICE, and CHRISTOPHER ISHERWOOD. In 1938, Auden married Erika Mann, the daughter of German novelist THOMAS MANN (see Vol. 2) and an ardent anti-Nazi. Auden was a homosexual, but he married Mann so that she could obtain British citizenship and leave Germany.

Auden had a lifelong passion for travel, and in 1939 he immigrated to the United States, where he became a naturalized citizen in 1946. Two years later, in 1948, he won a Pulitzer Prize for his book of poetry, *The Age of Anxiety*. Between 1947 and 1962, he was editor of the Yale Younger Poets series. During that time, a series of academic opportunities also culminated in a position as professor of poetry back at Oxford from 1956 to 1961. While in America, Auden divided his time principally between Greenwich Village and California. In later life, he also maintained a residence in Kirchstetten, Austria, where he died in 1973.

Auden produced work in a bewildering variety of forms, including long poems, short poems, verse drama, light and occasional verse, songs, opera libretti, and verse epistles, along with numerous editions and translations. He also deserves high status as a critic; three important collections are *The Enchafed Flood* (1950), his study of romanticism; *The Dyer's Hand* (1962), which includes many pieces written while he held the chair of poetry at Oxford; and *Forewords and Afterwords* (1973). Auden's habit of continually revising his verse makes it particularly difficult to study his career and even the establishment of his basic canon.

Auden's prolific output in both verse and prose was matched by a number of stylistic and thematic changes. As a teenager, he composed copious verses in the tradition of WILLIAM WORDSWORTH but tore them up at Oxford because they were "based on Wordsworth. No good nowadays." Soon after, Auden found a new mentor in T. S. Eliot, whose urbanity, intellectual compression, and modernistic technique attracted him. During the 1930s, Auden's work entered its most political phase, with an amalgam of KARL MARX (see Vols. 3 and 4) and SIGMUND FREUD (see Vol. 5) driving his verse intellectually and a new-found affinity for GEORGE GORDON, LORD BYRON affecting it literarily. At this time, his leftist politics led him to both Spain and China, where he reported on the

Spanish Civil War and the Sino-Japanese war in collaboration with Christopher Isherwood. (He also collaborated with Isherwood on several plays, including *The Dog Beneath the Skin*, 1935; *The Ascent of F6*, 1936; and *On the Frontier*, 1938.) By the end of the 1930s, Auden moved toward a more religious phase, and his later poetry took on a decidedly Christian cast. Simultaneously, Auden came to doubt the social efficacy of verse, writing in his great elegy for WILLIAM BUTLER YEATS that "poetry makes nothing happen." Towards the end of his life, Auden became a rather isolated figure, quite different from his early career, when he had seemed to be the voice of a generation. Some of his later works and editions include *About the House* (1966), *City Without Walls* (1969), and *Epistle to a Godson* (1972). Among the many honors Auden received during his life were the Pulitzer Prize, the Bollingen Prize, and the National Book Award.

POETRY BY AUDEN

Collected Poems. Random 1991 $22.50. ISBN 0-679-73197-0

The Double Man. Greenwood repr. of 1941 ed. 1979 $35.00. ISBN 0-313-21073-X. Poems expressing the fullest exposition of Auden's philosophical problems; also known as *New Year Letter*.

Epistle of a Godson and Other Poems. Random 1972 o.p. Auden as a mentor to the poets of the future. The last volume published in his lifetime.

Homage to Clio. Random 1960 o.p. Expressions of striking tensions and divisions in uncertain relationships.

Look, Stranger! AMS Pr. repr. of 1936 ed. o.p. Poems of spiritual dilemma.

Nones. Random 1951 o.p. Lyrical poems and witty choral songs.

Selected Poems of W. H. Auden. Ed. by Edward Mendelson. Random 1979 $11.00. ISBN 0-679-72483-4. Contains 50 years' worth of poems.

NONFICTION BY AUDEN

The Dyer's Hand. 1962. Random 1990 $15.00. ISBN 0-679-72484-2

The Enchafed Flood. 1950. U. Pr. of Va. 1979 repr. of 1967 ed. $16.50. ISBN 0-8139-0828-0. A study of romanticism.

Forewords and Afterwords. Random 1973 $15.00. ISBN 0-679-72485-0.

The Orators: An English Study. Scholarly repr. of 1932 ed. $39.00. ISBN 0-403-00500-0. Acute and vigorous attack on the state of England.

WORKS BY AUDEN

Complete Works of W. H. Auden. 2 vols. Princeton U. Pr. Vol. 1 1989 $50.00. ISBN 0-691-06740-6. Vol. 2 1993 $49.50. ISBN 0-691-03301-3. These first few volumes of a planned eight-volume set include early stage, film, and radio scripts, as well as several of Auden's earlier dramatic writings.

The English Auden: Poems, Essays, and Dramatic Writings. Faber & Faber 1978 $15.00. ISBN 0-571-11502-0. Selection of suppressed and unpublished prose and verse from Auden's early period.

"The Map of All my Youth": Early Works, Friends, and Influences. OUP 1990 $59.00. ISBN 0-19-812964-5. Contains important new works and completions of earlier essays.

BOOKS ABOUT AUDEN

Beach, Joseph W. *Making of the Auden Canon*. Russell 1971 repr. of 1957 ed. o.p. Controversial, somewhat critical study of Auden's revisions.

Bloomfield, B. C., and Edward Mendelson. *W. H. Auden, A Bibliography, 1924–1969*. U. Pr. of Va. 1973 $35.00. ISBN 0-8139-0395-5. Lists pamphlets, edited works, and contributions to periodicals by Auden.

Callan, Edward. *Auden: A Carnival of Intellect*. OUP 1983 $30.00. ISBN 0-19-503168-7. Traces the development of Auden's poetry from the political romanticism of the 1930s to the influence of Kierkegaard and Tillich.

Carpenter, Humphrey. *W. H. Auden: A Biography*. HM 1982 $10.95. ISBN 0-395-32439-X. Definitive biography, using access to private and previously unpublished material.
Fuller, John. *A Reader's Guide to Auden*. FS&G 1970 o.p. Poem-by-poem commentary.
Haffenden, John, ed. *W. H. Auden: The Critical Heritage. Critical Heritage Ser.* Routledge 1983 $69.50. ISBN 0-7100-9350-0. Historical anthology of criticism about Auden.
Hynes, Samuel. *The Auden Generation: Literature and Politics in England in the 1930's.* Princeton U. Pr. 1982 repr. of 1977 ed. $58.00. ISBN 0-691-01395-0. Especially good on the literary and political context of the 1930s.
Johnson, Richard. *Man's Place: An Essay on Auden*. Cornell Univ. Pr. 1973 o.p. Essay exploring the effect on Auden's poetry of his attitudes towards human existence.
McDiarmid, Lucy. *Saving Civilization: Yeats, Eliot, and Auden Between the Wars.* Cambridge U. Pr. 1984 $37.95. ISBN 0-521-26930-X
Mendelson, Edward. *Early Auden*. HUP 1983 $12.95. ISBN 0-674-21986-4. The fullest study of this phase of Auden's career.
Replogle, Justin. *Auden's Poetry. Washington Pap. Ser.* U. of Wash. Pr. 1971 repr. of 1969 ed. o.p. Examines the influence of Kierkegaard, Marx, and Freud in Auden's poetry.
Spears, Monroe K. *The Poetry of Auden: The Disenchanted Island*. OUP 1963 o.p. Analyzes Auden's poetry in regard to its style, themes, and the influences upon it.
_____, ed. *Auden: A Collection of Critical Essays*. P-H 1964 o.p. Essays assessing and analyzing Auden's poetry.
Wright, George T. *W. H. Auden. Twayne's U.S. Authors Ser.* Macmillan 1981 $20.95. ISBN 0-8057-7346-0. An in-depth review of Auden's life and a study of his work.

AYCKBOURN, ALAN. 1939–

Many American tourists who flock to the annual Ayckbourn offering on the West End think of this playwright as Britain's NEIL SIMON. The analogy holds true to the extent that the relationship between Ayckbourn's and Simon's plays illustrates the corollary difference between British and American theater and audiences. Both writers capture the social machinations of middle-class characters (very much like the audience members) in quotidian situations that are made compelling simply by the addition of clever (albeit conventional) dramatic intrigues, twists, and discoveries.

But, whereas Simon's plays tend to evolve into a condition of broad pathos or comedy, luxuriating in bittersweet melodrama, Ayckbourn's offerings revel in ever-increasing intricacy, sharply incisive verbal dueling, and a dark social resonance that sounds much greater depths than in Simon's drama.

Ayckbourn's scripts embody boggling challenges for directors and actors as well as audiences; *Intimate Exchanges* (1985), for example, a sequence of plays for 10 characters played by only 2 actors, involves numerous moments when an actor chooses to send the script off on one of two alternative directions. *The Norman Conquests* (1975) typifies Ayckbourn's determination to squeeze as much as possible out of a dramatic construct. The trilogy's first play, *Table Manners*, offers a typical Ayckbourn scenario: interwoven family traumas played against each other in the constrained setting of a dining room. In the second and third plays, *Living Together* and *Round and Round the Garden*, the audience is exposed to simultaneous layers of action that occur in two other venues, the living room and garden, when characters are not onstage in the dining room. Each play makes sense on its own, but the trilogy taken as a whole embodies a vision of this family that is larger than the sum of the individual parts. Aychbourn has also been known for rather experimental staging. *The Way Upstream* (1982), for example, is set on and around a boat and requires flooding the stage.

Among his later plays, *Woman in Mind* (1985) and *Henceforward* (1987) reflect a bleak vision of society. In some of these later plays, Aychbourn's characters have become increasingly complex, and he reveals himself as an intense social commentator. Other recent plays include *It Could Be Any One of Us* (1983), *Man of the Moment* (1990), and *Body Language* (1991). Since the 1970s, Ayckbourn has written at least one play a season; the premieres are always at a small local theater that he runs in the resort town of Scarborough.

PLAYS BY AYCKBOURN

A Chorus of Disapproval. Faber & Faber 1986 $8.95. ISBN 0-571-13917-5
Intimate Exchanges. 1985. 2 vols. French 1985 o.p.
Invisible Friends. Faber & Faber 1991 $8.95. ISBN 0-571-14476-4
Joking Apart and Other Plays. Chatto & Windus UK o.p. Includes *Just between Ourselves, Sisterly Feelings*, and *Ten Times Table*.
Man of the Moment. 1990. Faber & Faber 1990 $7.95. ISBN 0-571-15475-1
The Norman Conquests: Table Manners, Living Together, Round and Round the Garden. 1975. Grove Pr. 1988 $8.95. ISBN 0-8021-3134-4
The Revenger's Comedies. 1990. Faber & Faber 1991 $10.95. ISBN 0-571-14358-X. Depicts two suicidal characters who plan to gain revenge on each other's enemies.
Sisterly Feelings and *Taking Steps*. Chatto & Windus UK 1981 o.p. Two plays about relationships.
A Small Family Business. Faber & Faber 1987 $8.95. ISBN 0-571-14970-7. Farce which explores modern consumerism's effect on human morality.
Three Plays: Absurd Person Singular; Absent Friends; Bedroom Farce. Grove Pr. 1989 $9.95. ISBN 0-8021-3157-3. Plays about couples and their relationships.
Woman in Mind. 1985. Faber & Faber 1986 $7.95. ISBN 0-571-14520-5. Woman fantasizes about an ideal family after being hit on the head.

BOOKS ABOUT AYCKBOURN

Billington, Michael. *Alan Ayckbourn*. St. Martin 1990 $24.95. ISBN 0-312-04242-6. Surveys his career.
Dukore, Bernard Frank. *Alan Ayckbourn: A Casebook*. Garland 1991 $30.00. ISBN 0-8240-5759-1. Collected essays on such topics as the tradition of farce, British comedy, gender, and directing Ayckbourn's plays.
Page, Malcolm. *File on Ayckbourn*. Heinemann Ed. 1989 $10.95. ISBN 0-413-42010-8. Production details, reviews, and bibliography.
Watson, Ian. *Conversations with Ayckbourn*. Macdonald 1981 o.p. Ayckbourn's self-analysis of his writings.
White, Sidney Howard. *Alan Ayckbourn*. Twayne 1984 o.p. Overview traces Ayckbourn's development from a writer of slick farces to a Chekhovian comic.

BARRIE, SIR J(AMES) M(ATTHEW). 1860–1937

Barrie was born in Kirriemuir, Fofarshire, Scotland, the ninth child of David (a weaver by Trade) and Margaret Barrie. As a child, he was an avid reader, especially of adventure stories. When he was 6 years old, his 13-year-old brother David, his mother's favorite child, died in an accident, which caused his mother to suffer a nervous breakdown. The trauma led Barrie to strive to replace his brother in his mother's affections, and all of his life he was consumed with winning her love. His mother often told him stories of her own childhood, and he later said that much of his writing stemmed from being able to see her as a child wandering confidently through the pages.

Although Barrie wrote seven novels for adults, theater criticism, and many stories, he is best known for his plays, especially *Peter Pan* (1904). Barrie began writing drama in 1890, toying with the problem play he found in vogue. He soon turned to the whimsical romanticism for which he is remembered (or, mostly, forgotten). But it would be a mistake to ignore the realistic substratum in his plays. *The Admirable Crichton* (1903), in which shipwrecked aristocrats are forced to acknowledge the natural superiority of their servant, is not very far from the comic fantasies of Barrie's friend GEORGE BERNARD SHAW. *What Every Woman Knows* (1908) has been called a Scottish *Candida*. And even *Peter Pan*, appears to be an oblique confrontation with the sexual and psychological pathologies of the playwright's life (the situation of a woman confronted with a man's inability to mature). The play was first produced in London at Duke of York's Theatre in 1904 and has since been adapted in various forms, including a Broadway musical and a Disney film.

Outdoing Shaw (who had introduced the readable play text to British and Irish publishing), Barrie spent long intervals before publication preparing novelistic stage directions and comments for his plays, and sometimes changing their endings. Consequently, the date of its appearance as a book is often no guide to when one of his plays was originally performed.

Barrie married the actress Mary Ansell in 1894 and was divorced in 1909. In addition to his writing, he served as rector of St. Andrews University from 1919 to 1922 and as chancellor of Edinburgh from 1930 until his death in 1937.

PLAYS BY BARRIE

Peter Pan. 1904. Knopf 1992 $12.95. ISBN 0-679-41792-3. A sentimental fantasy of youth.
Plays of J. M. Barrie. Scribner 1928 o.p. Twenty plays, including *Peter Pan.*
Sentimental Tommy. Rprt. Serv. 1992 repr. of 1924 ed. $99.00. ISBN 0-7812-7430-3
A Window in Thrums. Rprt. Serv. 1992 repr. of 1896 ed. $79.00. ISBN 0-7812-7431-1

WORKS BY BARRIE

The Letters of James Matthew Barrie. Ed. by Viola Meynell. AMS Pr. 1976 repr. of 1947 ed. $18.50. ISBN 0-404-10640-4. Letters written from 1884–1937, touching on Barrie's personal life and career.
The Works of J. M. Barrie. 18 vols. AMS Pr. repr. of 1929–41 ed. $585.00. ISBN 0-404-08780-9

BOOKS ABOUT BARRIE

Allen, David. *Peter Pan & Cricket.* Constable 1988 o.p. Biography.
Birkin, Andrew. *J. M. Barrie and the Lost Boys: The Love Story That Gave Birth to Peter Pan.* Crown Pub. Grp. 1979 o.p. Biographical background of Barrie's most famous play.
Braybrooke, Patrick. *J. M. Barrie: A Study in Fairies and Mortals.* Haskell 1972 repr. of 1924 ed. $49.95. ISBN 0-8383-1349-3
Dunbar, Janet. *J. M. Barrie: The Man Behind the Image.* HM 1970 o.p.
Markgraf, Carl. *J. M. Barrie: An Annotated Secondary Bibliography.* ELT Pr. 1989 $35.00. ISBN 0-944318-03-7
Rose, Jacqueline. *The Case of Peter Pan: or, The Impossibility of Children's Fiction.* U. of Pa. Pr. 1993 repr. of 1990 ed. $12.95. ISBN 0-8122-1435-8. Examines Barrie's place within the genre of children's literature.

BECKETT, SAMUEL. 1906–1989 (NOBEL PRIZE 1969)

Born into a Protestant middle-class family in suburban Dublin, Samuel Beckett was educated, like OSCAR WILDE, at Portora Royal School and Trinity College, Dublin. From 1928 to 1930, he was a reader in English at the École Normale Supérieure in Paris, where he became acquainted with JAMES JOYCE; the two remained close friends until Joyce's death in 1941. When Joyce's eyesight was failing, Beckett served for a time as his secretary, sometimes taking dictations of Joyce's final extravaganza, *Finnegans Wake* (1939). Some critics have conjectured that, after the direct experience of such literary vastness and incontinence, Beckett felt unable to compete and thus retreated into his trademark minimalism.

Beckett's first book, *Whoroscope*—an abstract dramatic monologue spoken by René Descartes—was awarded a prize by Nancy Cunard's Hours Press in Paris and published in 1930. A keen scout for experimentalism, Cunard recognized the strain of the stylistically and technically unusual that would characterize Beckett's writing throughout his career. Returning to Dublin, he took a post lecturing in Romance languages at Trinity College but soon decided that teaching was not his métier. Beckett traveled around Europe, settling in Paris in 1937 and publishing his first novel, *Murphy* (1938), a grotesque depiction of a man who severs his links to humanity and society; the themes from this novel were further explored in a trilogy that Beckett published after World War II. It was about this time that he met Suzanne Dechevaux-Dumesnil, whom he married in 1961.

Waiting for Godot (1953), written, like most of Beckett's later work, in French, brought Beckett's work to a wide audience and revolutionized the modern theater. Alternatingly comic, tragic, profound, inane, existential, and juvenile, the play simultaneously frustrates the audience's compulsion for dramatic engagement and forces the spectators to extrapolate, energetically, beyond the boundaries of the play space, in an attempt to impose coherence on the spectacle. *Watt* (1954) is the last novel he wrote in English; its title is a pun on the word "what." The play *Krapp's Last Tape* (1959), another avant-garde landmark, written in English, dramatizes the devastating monologue of a man who plays the autobiographical tape he had recorded on his thirty-ninth birthday, 30 years later. Other well-known plays include *End Game* (1957), *Happy Days* (1961), *Not I* (1973), and *Quad* (1982). Beckett is considered to be one of the most influential playwrights of the century.

PLAYS BY BECKETT

Ends and Odds. Grove Pr. 1976 $10.00. ISBN 0-8021-1190-4. Short dramatic pieces including *Footfalls, Theater I* and *Theater II,* and the television play *Ghost Trio.*

Happy Days. 1961. Grove Pr. 1987 $7.95. ISBN 0-8021-3076-3. Figurative paralysis and the quest for meaning.

Krapp's Last Tape and Other Dramatic Pieces. Grove Pr. 1960 $7.95. ISBN 0-8021-5134-5. Includes the radio plays *All That Fall* and *Embers.*

Waiting for Godot. 1953. Grove Pr. 1987 $6.95. ISBN 0-8021-3034-8. A minimalist search for meaning.

NOVELS BY BECKETT

Dream of Fair to Middling Women. Arcade Pub. Inc. 1993 $21.95. ISBN 0-55970-217-6. Written by Beckett at age twenty-six, this autobiographical first novel remained unpublished during his lifetime.

Murphy. 1938. Grove Pr. 1970 $12.50. ISBN 0-8021-1198-X

Three Novels. Grove Pr. 1965 $9.95. ISBN 0-8021-5091-8. Novels (originally written in French) sharing the theme of physical or mental isolation from the external reality in order to reach the truth of personality. The works are *Molloy* (1951), *Malone Dies* (1952), and *The Unnamable (1953).* He wrote this as a trilogy.

POETRY BY BECKETT

Collected Poems in English and French. Grove Pr. 1977 $10.00. ISBN 0-8021-1187-4

Collected Poems in English. Grove Pr. 1977 $10.00. ISBN 0-8021-3096-8. Collection of poems that Beckett wished to preserve.

WORK BY BECKETT

As the Story Was Told. Riverrun NY 1990 $20.95. ISBN 0-7145-4113-3. The first posthumous collection of his work containing writings from the forties, fifties, sixties.

BOOKS ABOUT BECKETT

Alvarez, A. *Samuel Beckett.* Viking Penguin 1973 o.p. General overview.

Andonian, Cathleen Culotta. *Samuel Beckett: A Reference Guide.* Macmillan 1988 $60.00. ISBN 0-8161-8570-0. Bibliography and sourcebook.

Bair, Deirdre. *Samuel Beckett: A Biography.* 1978 o.p.

Connor, Steven. *Samuel Beckett: Repetition, Theory, and Text.* Blackwell Pubs. 1988 $55.00. ISBN 0-63-116017-5. Explores Beckett's style and technique and the effects of repetition.

Doll, Mary Aswell. *Beckett and Myth: An Archetypal Approach.* Syracuse U. Pr. 1988 $23.95. ISBN 0-8156-2447-6. Investigates mythic and archetypal patterns in Beckett's writing.

Fitch, Brian T. *Beckett and Babel: An Investigation into the Bilingual Work.* U. of Toronto Pr. 1988 $35.00. ISBN 0-8020-5778-0. Examines the production and reception of Beckett's texts and the problematics of self-translation.

Harrington, John P. *The Irish Beckett.* Syracuse U. Pr. 1991 $29.95. ISBN 0-8156-2528-6. Explores the roots of Beckett's writing in Irish culture.

Miller, Lawrence. *Samuel Beckett: The Expressive Dilemma.* St. Martin 1992. ISBN 0-312-07960-5. Examines Beckett's criticism and critical phases: Disciple, expressivist, amateur.

Sabin, Margery. *The Dialect of the Tribe: Speech and Community in Modern Fiction.* OUP 1987 $42.50. ISBN 0-19-504153-4. Comparative study of the language of Beckett, Joyce, Lawrence, and James.

Smith, Joseph H. *The World of Samuel Beckett.* Johns Hopkins 1991 $42.50. ISBN 0-8018-4079-1. Psychoanalytic approaches to Beckett.

BEERBOHM, SIR (HENRY) MAX(IMILIAN). 1872–1956

When Beerbohm succeeded GEORGE BERNARD SHAW as drama critic of the *Saturday Review* in 1898, Shaw introduced his successor as "the incomparable Max." Beerbohm was decadent, witty, graceful, and urbane—fitting for a critic who carried on the high tradition of satire in British letters. His works of social and literary criticism, and of fiction, mask serious dissatisfaction with contemporary pretenses and poses behind a patina of highly polished prose. In *A Christmas Garland* (1912), Beerbohm uses parody to expose the artifice of literary manner in his contemporaries (including ARNOLD BENNET, JOSEPH CONRAD, H. G. WELLS, and G. K. CHESTERTON). His only novel, *Zuleika Dobson* (1911), is a delightful burlesque of his own college days at Oxford University. Like his essays and short stories, it is light, witty, and stimulating. Beerbohm was an accomplished caricaturist. Of his 46 portrait drawings in *Max's Nineties: Drawings 1892–1899* (1958), most were taken from periodicals of that period.

NONFICTION BY BEERBOHM

Around Theaters. 1898–1903. Greenwood 1969 repr. of 1954 ed. $35.00. ISBN 0-8371-0303-7. Essays originally published in the *Saturday Review.*

Last Theaters. 1904–10. Ed. by Rupert Hart-Davis. Taplinger 1970 o.p.

Mainly on the Air. 1946. *Essay Index Reprint Ser.* Ayer repr. of 1957 ed. o.p. Collection of his World War II broadcasts for the BBC in London.

More. 1899. *Essay Index Repr. Ser.* Ayer 1921 $17.00. ISBN 0-8369-0181-9. Twenty essays expressing Beerbohm's taste for the unpopular and distaste for the popular.

Observations. Haskell 1971 repr. of 1925 ed. $75.00. ISBN 0-8383-1249-7. A series of topical caricatures critical of the modern world.

Works and More. Scholarly repr. of 1896 ed. $49.00. ISBN 0-403-00144-7. Twenty-seven essays reflecting Beerbohm's rebellion against accepted norms.

NOVEL BY BEERBOHM

Zuleika Dobson: An Oxford Love Story. 1911. Heinemann Ed. 1991 $7.50.

WORKS BY BEERBOHM

Works of Max Beerbohm. Rprt. Serv. 1985 repr. of 1896 ed. $39.00. ISBN 0-932051-90-1

BOOKS ABOUT BEERBOHM

Denson, Lawrence. *Max Beerbohm and the Act of Writing.* OUP 1989 $33.75. ISBN 0-19-812683-0. Examines fluctuating boundaries between Beerbohm's fiction, parody, caricatures, and essays.

Riewald, Jacobus Gerhardus, ed. *The Surprise of Excellence: Modern Essays on Max Beerbohm.* Archon Bks. 1974 o.p. Discussions of irony and deception, Beerbohm and Wilde, manners, and the aesthete as realist.

Viscusi, Robert. *Max Beerbohm, Or The Dandy Dante: Rereading with Mirrors.* Johns Hopkins 1986 $38.50. ISBN 0-8018-2927-5. Explores the themes of pretense, allegory of beauty, and transmutability in Beerbohm's prose.

BEHAN, BRENDAN. 1923–1964

A Dublin slum boy, Behan at the age of 16 was arrested in Liverpool with a suitcase full of explosives. Sent to the Borstal (reform school) as an IRA terrorist, he was to be arrested and sentenced several more times, once to deportation, before he settled down, in the mid-1950s, to writing. Plays and books began to appear with regularity, but by 1964 Behan was dead, having escaped, through drink and diabetes, the "bent old legs and twisted buniony toes" of an old age he dreaded.

A "quare fellow" is a condemned man about to be hanged, the absent subject about whom the prison society uneasily stirs in Behan's first play (1954). After rejection by the Abbey, it was staged by a small Dublin theater, the Pike, and brought to England by Joan Littlewood in 1956. (The Abbey recanted after *The Quare Fellow*'s London success.) The British soldier in *The Hostage* (1958) is another condemned prisoner, held in a brothel in exchange for an Irish captive. But after his death—typical of Littlewood's fantastic music-hall staging of the play—the soldier stands up again to lead the cast in song.

Littlewood was criticized for expanding the play with music and improvisations, although Behan's thin text certainly profited from the brilliant theatricality of her Theatre Workshop, whose Brechtian productions were important influences on the next decade of London theater. *Richard's Cork Leg*, Behan's unfinished last script, was even more seriously in need of the revisions and additions made by Alan Simpson after the author's death. It was produced posthumously at the Abbey Theatre in 1972.

PLAYS BY BEHAN

After the Wake. Ed. by Peter Fallon. Devin 1983 $15.95. ISBN 0-905140-97-4

The Complete Plays. Grove Pr. 1988 $9.95. ISBN 0-8021-3070-4. Introduction by Alan Simpson. Includes *The Quare Fellow, The Hostage,* and *Richard's Cork Leg.*

WORKS BY BEHAN

Borstal Boy. Godine 1982 repr. of 1959 ed. $12.95. ISBN 0-87923-415-6. An autobiographical novel.

Brendan Behan's Island: An Irish Sketch Book. Little 1985 o.p. Anecdotes, two short
  stories, a one-act play, and several poems.
The Letters of Brendan Behan. U. of Toronto Pr. 1992 $49.95. ISBN 0-7735-0888-0. Also
  includes some unpublished poems and early writings.

BOOKS ABOUT BEHAN

Arthurs, Peter. *With Brendan Behan.* St. Martin 1981 o.p. A well-written and very
  informative biography.
Kearney, Colbert. *The Writings of Brendan Behan.* St. Martin 1977 $20.00. ISBN 0-312-
  89442-2. Focuses on Behan's drama as well as his extratheatrical writing.
Mikhail, E. H. *Brendan Behan: An Annotated Bibliography of Criticism.* B & N Imports
  1980 $23.50. ISBN 0-06-494826-9. A collection of more than 100 interviews and brief
  memoirs by Behan's family, friends, contemporaries, and critics.

BELLOC, HILAIRE. 1870–1953

Belloc was born in France, educated at Oxford, and naturalized as a British
subject in 1902. Although he began as a humorist—with children's verse—his
works include satire, poetry, history, biography, fiction, and many volumes of
essays. With his close friend and fellow Catholic, G. K. CHESTERTON, Belloc
founded the *New Witness,* a weekly newspaper opposing capitalism and free
thought and supporting a philosophy known as distributism. The pair were so
close in thought and association that GEORGE BERNARD SHAW nicknamed them
"Chesterbelloc." Belloc lived quietly in the country in England until his tragic
death in 1953 from burns caused when his dressing gown caught fire from the
hearth. During his life, Belloc published over 150 books. Today, however, he is
best remembered for only a few works, most notably his light verse such as
Cautionary Tales (1907) and *A Bad Child's Book of Beasts* (1896). In *Shandygaff*
(1918), Christopher Morley said: "In Belloc we find the perfect union of the
French and English minds. Rabelaisian in fecundity, wit, and irrepressible
sparkle, he is also of English blood and sinew."

NONFICTION BY BELLOC

At the Sign of the Lion, and Other Essays. Essay Index Repr. Ser. Ayer repr. of 1916 ed.
  $12.00. ISBN 0-8369-1318-3
Avril. Essay Index Repr. Ser. Ayer repr. of 1904 ed. $19.00. ISBN 0-8369-1339-6. Essays on
  the poetry of the French Renaissance.
Conversation with a Cat and Others. 1929. *Essay Index Repr. Ser.* Ayer repr. of 1931 ed.
  $17.00. ISBN 0-8369-0035-9. Historical essays on a variety of subjects.
Conversation with an Angel, and Other Essays. Essay Index Repr. Ser. Ayer 1968 repr. of
  1929 ed. $20.00. ISBN 0-8369-0187-8. A series of comical essays with no serious
  point.
Characters of the Reformation. Essay Index Repr. Ser. Ayer repr. of 1936 ed. $24.00. ISBN
  0-8369-1696-4
Essays of a Catholic. Essay Index Repr. Ser. Ayer repr. of 1931 ed. $18.00. ISBN 0-8369-
  0188-6. Essays on Christianity and other religious issues.
First and Last. Essay Index Repr. Ser. Ayer repr. of 1911 ed. $18.00. ISBN 0-8369-0059-6.
  Satirical essays on social issues.
Great Heresies. Essay Index Repr. Ser. Ayer repr. of 1938 ed. $21.95. ISBN 0-8369-0189-4
On. Essay Index Repr. Ser. Ayer repr. of 1923 ed. $17.00. ISBN 0-8369-0190-8. Essays on a
  variety of topics.
On Anything. Essay Index Repr. Ser. Ayer repr. of 1910 ed. $18.00. ISBN 0-8369-0003-0.
  Essays written while Belloc was working in the House of Lords.
On Everything. Essay Index Repr. Ser. Ayer repr. of 1910 ed. $19.00. ISBN 0-8369-1865-7.
  Collection of newspaper essays covering a variety of subjects.

On Nothing and Kindred Subjects. Essay Index Repr. Ser. Ayer repr. of 1908 ed. $19.00. ISBN 0-8369-1448-1. Satirical non-partisan political essays.

On Something. Essay Index Repr. Ser. Ayer 1968 repr. of 1910 ed. $15.00. ISBN 0-8369-0191-6. A series of elegiac essays.

Short Talks with the Dead, and Others. Essay Index Repr. Ser. Ayer repr. of 1926 ed. $18.00. ISBN 0-8369-0192-4. Essays on literary criticism, writers, and different literary genres.

This and That and the Other. Essay Index Repr. Ser. Ayer 1968 repr. of 1912 ed. $21.50. ISBN 0-8369-0193-2

BOOKS ABOUT BELLOC

McCarthy, John P. *Hilaire Belloc: Edwardian Radical.* Liberty Fund 1979 $8.00. ISBN 0-913966-43-6

Markel, Michael H. *Hilaire Belloc.* Twayne 1982 o.p. Overview and bibliography.

Morton, J. B. *Hilaire Belloc: A Memoir.* Gordon Pr. 1984 $90.00. ISBN 0-8490-3236-9

Wilson, A. N. *Hilaire Belloc.* Hamilton 1984 o.p. Biographical treatment of Belloc based on letters, papers, and personal recollection by Belloc's friends.

BENNETT, ARNOLD. 1867–1931

"In his time, Arnold Bennett was the shrewdest and most successful tradesman in English letters" (V. S. PRITCHETT, *New Yorker*). *The Old Wives' Tale* (1908) is the masterpiece of this novelist, who wrote about the lives of shopkeepers and potters in the north of England—his own boyhood background, although he became immensely successful. "A merchant of words, frankly writing for money," he was able nonetheless to make the dullest characters interesting. In 1968, reviewing *Darling of the Day*, a successful musical adaptation of *Buried Alive* (1923), Walter Kerr wrote: "I'd forgotten some of the nicer twists of . . . 'Buried Alive' . . . and so was charmed all over again." Bennett's other important novels are *The Clayhanger Trilogy* (1910), *Hilda Lessways* (1911), *These Twain* (1916), and *Riceyman Steps* (1923). Bennett's voluminous *Journal* (1932–33) is of special value for the light it throws on the novelist at work.

NOVELS BY BENNETT

Anna of the Five Towns. 1902. Viking Penguin 1978 $6.95. ISBN 0-14-000033-X

Clayhanger. Ayer 1976 repr. of 1910 ed. $43.25. ISBN 0-518-19093-5

Grand Babylon Hotel: A Fantasia on Modern Themes. 1904. Scholarly 1904 $27.00. ISBN 0-403-00004-1. A serial comic thriller with complicated plot turns, escapes, and romance.

The Old Wives' Tale. 1908. Ayer 1976 repr. of 1911 ed. $43.25. ISBN 0-518-19142-7. Classic realist story of two sisters from the potteries.

Pretty Lady. Scholarly 1971 repr. of 1918 ed. $18.00. ISBN 0-403-00863-8. Examines the relationships between men and women during the First World War.

NONFICTION BY BENNETT

Author's Craft and Other Critical Writings of Arnold Bennett. Ed. by Samuel Hynes. *Regents Critics Ser.* U. of Nebr. Pr. 1968 $6.50. ISBN 0-8032-5451-2. Short talks and discussion on the subject of the novel.

Journal of Arnold Bennett. 3 pts. Ayer 1976 repr. of 1932–33 ed. $29.00–$33.00. ISBNs 0-518-19118-4, 0-518-19120-6, 0-518-19121-4

Things That Have Interested Me. 3 vols. Ayer 1976. Vol. 1 $27.50. ISBN 0-518-19161-3. Vol. 2 $24.25. ISBN 0-518-19162-1. Vol. 3 $22.75. ISBN 0-518-19163-X

SHORT STORY COLLECTION BY BENNETT

The Matador of the Five Towns and Other Stories. Collected Works of Arnold Bennett Ser.
Ayer 1976 repr. of 1912 ed. $31.50. ISBN 0-518-19134-6. Short stories expressing
revulsion against organized religion.

WORKS BY BENNETT

The Collected Works of Arnold Bennett. 90 vols. Ayer repr. of 1976 ed. $1,897.50. ISBN 0-
8369-7057-8

BOOKS ABOUT BENNETT

Broomfield, Olga R. *Arnold Bennett.* Twayne 1984 o.p. Examines Bennett's relation to the
emerging conception of the novel as art; bibliography.
Drabble, Margaret *Arnold Bennett: A Biography.* G.K. Hall 1986 o.p.
Miller, Anita. *Arnold Bennett: An Annotated Bibliography, 1887–1932.* Garland 1977
$65.00. ISBN 0-82-409954-0. Comprehensive listing of books by and about the author
and his work.
Roby, Kinley E. *A Writer at War: Arnold Bennett, 1914–1918.* La. State U. Pr. 1972 o.p.
Explores the impact of the Great War on Bennett's writing and life.
Swinnerton, Frank. *Arnold Bennett: A Last Word.* Hamilton 1978 o.p. A biography of
Bennett told through letters; written by a close friend.
Wright, Walter Francis. *Arnold Bennett: Romantic Realist.* U. Nebr. Pr. 1971 $18.95. ISBN
0-803-20798-0. Examines tensions between romance and realism in Bennett's
novels.

BETJEMAN, SIR JOHN. 1906–1984

A leading modern champion of the values of an older England, John
Betjeman was born in Highgate, London, to a well-off merchant family. The
loneliness and suffering of his upbringing, first under nursemaids and then at a
series of schools culminating in Marlborough, often surface in his poetry. He
went to Magdalene College, Oxford, where he belonged to the same smart social
set as EVELYN WAUGH. Betjeman worked in a variety of media and achieved wide
public attention as host for a television series on the history of British
architecture, one of his prime enthusiasms (he was particularly fond of
Victorian Gothic). In fact, he wrote a great deal on architecture, especially for
the *Architectural Review*.

Deliberately free from the difficulties of much modern verse, Betjeman's
poetry harks back to a more accessible British tradition that includes ALFRED,
LORD TENNYSON and THOMAS HARDY. With quiet wit he resisted the debasements
of modern mass culture in favor of an older England—simpler, more rural, and
more religious than the current one. Both W. H. AUDEN and PHILIP LARKIN
especially admired his work, and Auden even edited a selection of it. His
harsher critics have found him unintellectual and sentimental. His poetry has
achieved a huge circulation in Britain, with the *Collected Poems* (1958)
reputedly selling more than 100,000 copies. Considered a national institution,
he succeeded CECIL DAY LEWIS as poet laureate in 1972.

POETRY BY BETJEMAN

Collected Poems. Greenwood 1982 repr. of 1959 ed. $45.00. ISBN 0-313-23319-5.
Introduction by Lord Birkenhead. Enormously popular collection, first published in
1958.
John Betjeman. Pocket Poets Ser. Dufour 1967 $3.50. ISBN 0-8023-9040-4
A Nip in the Air. Norton 1976 $2.50. ISBN 0-393-04423-8. Written over a nine-year period,
these poems reflect a variety of subjects and themes.

NONFICTION BY BETJEMAN

An American's Guide to English Parish Churches. Astor-Honor 1959 $20.00. ISBN 0-8392-1004-3. Celebrates the diverse character of parish churches; with illustrations.
Victorian and Edwardian London. David & Charles 1969 o.p. An examination of London during the Victorian and Edwardian age; includes an introduction and commentary.

BOOKS ABOUT BETJEMAN

Hillier, Bevis. *John Betjeman: A Life in Pictures.* Herbert Pr. 1984 o.p. A competently written biography.
Stapleton, Margaret L. *Sir John Betjeman: A Bibliography of Writings by and about Him.* Scarecrow 1974 $20.00. ISBN 0-8108-0758-0. A sourcebook of works by Betjeman and analytical writings about him and his work.

BOLT, ROBERT. 1924–

Born in Manchester, where he attended the university, Bolt was teaching school in 1957 when his play *Flowering Cherry*, with Ralph Richardson in the title role, was staged in London. Its success persuaded him to devote himself to the theater, and *The Tiger and the Horse* (1960), which, like its predecessor, concerns the paradoxes of idealism and detachment, appeared three years later. In the meanwhile, Bolt had written for BBC radio the short play about SIR THOMAS MORE (see also Vol. 4) he was to expand into his international triumph, *A Man for All Seasons* (1960). Stylistically, the earlier works had been (Bolt conceded) "uneasily straddled between naturalism and nonnaturalism." But *A Man for All Seasons* made a double move, projecting the familiar themes upon historical myth and presenting them in the trappings of a fashionable Brechtian theatricality. The resulting simplification, or clarification, of his ideas brought Bolt the New York Drama Critics Circle Award in 1962, and, for the screenplay, an Academy Award.

Aside from the schematic but interesting experiment *Gentle Jack* (1963), Bolt wrote a series of screenplays for David Lean (*Lawrence of Arabia*, 1962; *Doctor Zhivago*, 1965; and *Ryan's Daughter*, 1970) in which personal melodrama is again played out against romanticized history. The stage work *Vivat! Vivat Regina!* (1970) confronts Queen Elizabeth's rigidity with the femininity of Mary of Scotland. *State of Revolution* (1977), written for the National Theatre, is a portrait of LENIN (see Vol. 3) as a sensitive leader imprisoned in his ideals.

PLAYS BY BOLT

Gentle Jack. 1963. Heinemann Ed. 1965 o.p. Unusual exploration of high finance versus nature: discusses the human condition in the industrial world.
A Man for All Seasons. 1960. Random 1990 $7.95. ISBN 0-679-72822-8
State of Revolution. Heinemann Ed. 1977 o.p.
The Thwarting of Baron Bolligrew. Heinemann Ed. 1966 $5.95. ISBN 0-435-23103-0

BOND, EDWARD. 1934–

Because of its pivotal scene, which involves the stoning to death of a baby by a gang of young toughs in a London park, Edward Bond's first major production, *Saved* (1965), was banned in its entirety by the Lord Chamberlain. This last heroic effort of English stage censorship necessarily drew attention away from the play's dry rendering of an inarticulate and insensitive existence. Even without the censor, though, this difficulty remains. A distracting violence is still the center of Bond's work—the surrealist murders and cannibalism of *Early Morning* (1968), the mutilations of the Shakespearean travesty *Lear* (1970), the drowning man refused assistance in *The Sea*, or infanticide again in *The Bundle*

(1978), a Brechtian parable that intentionally inverts the humane *Caucasian Chalk Circle*.

Bond's violence is not simply an image of evil or crude dramatic shock. It is meant as something to come to terms with intellectually, or even—as in *The Bundle*—to be agreed to, as the price of effective action. In its obviousness, Bond's brutality challenges the audience to acknowledge its own hidden, structural ruthlessness. But, despite his presumption to a "rational theater," the playwright's ideas often seem inadequately worked out (and are certainly inadequately expressed in prefaces that share nothing of GEORGE BERNARD SHAW's vivacity and clarity). Bond has never lost touch, meanwhile, with an impressive stiff poetry of the stage, clearest in stylistically spare works like *Bingo* (about SHAKESPEARE's last days) and *The Fool* (1976) (about the madness of the poet JOHN CLARE). Among his more recent works are *The Worlds* (1979) and a trilogy, *The War Plays* (1985).

PLAYS BY BOND

Bingo and *The Sea: Two Plays*. Hill & Wang 1975 o.p.

The Bundle. 1978. Heinemann Ed. 1978 $9.95. ISBN 0-413-39360-7

Derek and Choruses from "After the Assassinations." Heinemann Ed. 1984 $9.95. ISBN 0-413-54700-0

Early Morning. 1968. Riverrun NY 1980 $9.95. ISBN 0-7145-0206-5

The Fool and *We Come to the River*. Heinemann Ed. 1988 $9.95. ISBN 0-413-34770-2

Narrow Road to the Deep North. 1968. Heinemann Ed. 1988 $9.95. ISBN 0-413-30840-5. A play based on the life of the Japanese poet Bashō; discusses freedom and people in cities.

Plays. Methuen 2 vols. 1977–78 o.p. Vol. 1: *Saved, Early Morning, The Pope's Wedding*. Vol. 2: *Lear, The Sea, Narrow Road to the Deep North, Black Mass, Passion*.

Restoration and the Cat. Methuen 1982 o.p. These two plays—*Restoration* and *The Cat*— are quirky moral dramas about society.

Saved. 1965. Heinemann Ed. 1965 $9.95. ISBN 0-413-31360-3

Summer. Methuen 1982 o.p. Based on war and its aftermath, this play deals with the morality of brotherhood and friendship in daily life.

War Plays. 1985. Heinemann Ed. 1991 $19.95. ISBN 0-413-64600-9. Contains *Red, Black and Ignorant, Tin Can People*.

The Woman. 1978. Dramatic Pub. 1981 $5.45. ISBN 0-87129-081-2. Based on the Greek myth of the Trojan War; introduces a variety of new characters and subplots.

BOOKS ABOUT BOND

Bond, Edward, Malcolm Hay, and Philip Roberts. *Edward Bond: A Companion to the Plays*. TQ 1978 o.p. A production sourcebook, useful for understanding the original productions.

Hay, Malcolm. *Bond: A Study of His Plays*. Heinemann Ed. 1981 $15.95. ISBN 0-413-47060-1. Attempts to clear up confusion about Bond's main preoccupations and theatrical methods; divides his works into three different historical phases.

Hirst, David L. *Edward Bond*. St. Martin 1990 $11.95. ISBN 0-333-32032-8. A detailed explanation of the sources for Bond's plays and a discussion of their performance; investigates Bond's place in British theater.

Lappin, Lou. *The Art and Politics of Edward Bond*. P. Lang Pubs. 1987 $34.00. ISBN 0-8204-0455-1. Explores the artist's avocation and commercial culture as well as sexual politics.

Roberts, Philip. *Bond on File*. Heinemann Ed. 1985 $9.95. ISBN 0-413-54040-5. Overview of Bond's plays, music theater, translations and adaptations, and nondramatic writing.

BOWEN, ELIZABETH. 1899–1973

Elizabeth Bowen, distinguished Anglo-Irish novelist, was born in Dublin, traveled extensively, lived in London, and inherited the family estate—Bowen's Court—in County Cork. Her account of the house, *Bowen's Court* (1942), with a detailed fictionalized history of the family in Ireland through three centuries, has "sober charm" and "a warmth and insight that suggest extraordinary imaginative virtuosity." *Seven Winters* is a fragment of autobiography published in England in 1942. The "Afterthoughts" of the original edition are critical essays, "indispensable documents," in which she discusses and analyzes, among others, such literary figures as VIRGINIA WOOLF, E. M. FORSTER, KATHERINE MANSFIELD (see Vol. 2), ANTHONY TROLLOPE, and EUDORA WELTY. Her stories, mostly about people of the British upper middle class, portray relationships that her analysis shows are never simple, except, perhaps, on the surface. Her concern with time and memory is a major theme. Beautifully and delicately written, her stories, with their oblique psychological revelations, are symbolic, subtle, and terrifying. *A Time in Rome* (1960) is her brilliant evocation of that city and its layered past. In 1948 she was made a Commander of the British Empire.

NOVELS BY BOWEN

Bowen's Court. 1942. Ecco Pr. 1979 $6.95. ISBN 0-912946-67-9

The Death of the Heart. 1938. Viking Penguin 1991 $8.95. ISBN 0-14-018300-0. Examines psychological resonances of love and marriage.

Friends and Relations. Viking Penguin 1987 $5.95. ISBN 0-14-000398-3. An oblique novel describing the shadow cast on the younger generation by the errors of their elders.

Good Tiger. Knopf 1965 o.p.

The Heat of the Day. 1949. Buccaneer Bks. 1981 $25.95. ISBN 0-89966-259-5. Set in wartime London; examines conditions that led up to World War II.

The Hotel. 1927. Viking Penguin 1986 $5.95. ISBN 0-14-000449-1. Tragi-comedic novel about an English family on the Italian Riviera.

The House in Paris. 1936. Avon 1979 o.p. Study of generational family antipathies.

The Little Girls. 1963. Viking Penguin 1992 $9.95. ISBN 0-14-018305-1. A story about the comedic reunion of three friends; deals with the theme of time and memory in relationships.

SHORT STORY COLLECTIONS BY BOWEN

Ann Lee's and Other Stories. Short Story Index Repr. Ser. Ayer repr. of 1926 ed. $16.00. ISBN 0-8369-3239-0. The second compilation of Bowen's short stories.

The Collected Stories of Elizabeth Bowen. Knopf 1981 $25.00. ISBN 0-394-51666-4. A complete edition of Bowen's short stories; with an introduction by Angus Wilson discussing the form and shape of the stories.

Joining Charles and Other Stories. Scholarly 1971 repr. of 1929 ed. o.p. The fourth compilation of Bowen's short stories; the stories deal primarily with social settings and interactions.

NONFICTION BY BOWEN

Collected Impressions. AMS Pr. repr. of 1950 ed. o.p. Expansive essays reflecting the author's feelings about writing and her work.

The Mulberry Tree: Writings of Elizabeth Bowen. Ed. by Hermione Lee. HarBraceJ 1987 $19.95. ISBN 0-15-163240-5. Comprehensive collection of essays, book reviews, radio broadcasts, book prefaces, and autobiographical writings showcasing Bowen's intelligent, highly dignified style.

Seven Winters. Biblio Dist. 1971 repr. of 1942 ed. o.p. Her only autobiographical work.

Why Do I Write? Haskell 1975 $75.00. ISBN 0-8383-2094-5. An exchange of views among
   Bowen, Graham Greene, and V. S. Pritchett.

BOOKS ABOUT BOWEN

Austin, Allan E. *Elizabeth Bowen.* Macmillan 1989 $21.95. ISBN 0-8057-6972-2. Survey of
   her life and overview of her work.
Craig, Patricia. *Elizabeth Bowen.* Viking Penguin 1986 o.p.
Glendinning, Victoria. *Elizabeth Bowen: Portrait of a Writer.* Grove Pr. 1977 o.p. Richly
   detailed, illustrative biography exploring Bowen's contradictions and complexities.
Jordan, Heather Bryant. *How Will the Heart Endure: Elizabeth Bowen and the Landscape
   of War.* U. of Mich. Pr. 1992 $32.50. ISBN 0-472-10218-4. The presence of war—
   specifically, World Wars I and II and the Irish civil war—in Bowen's novels.
Lassner, Phyllis. *Elizabeth Bowen.* B & N Imports 1986 $46.00. ISBN 0-389-20878-7.
   Biographical and critical overview.
_____. *Elizabeth Bowen: A Study of the Short Fiction.* Macmillan 1991 $22.95. ISBN 0-
   8057-8336-9. Examines the artistic achievement in Bowen's short stories, generally
   read as glosses on her longer fiction.
Lee, Hermione. *Elizabeth Bowen: An Estimation.* B & N Imports 1981 o.p. A comprehen-
   sive critical study.
Sellery, J. M., and William O. Harris. *Elizabeth Bowen: A Descriptive Bibliography.* U. of
   Tex. Pr. 1981 $25.00. ISBN 0-87959-080-7. Useful sourcebook of primary and
   secondary sources.

BRADBURY, MALCOLM (STANLEY). 1932–

   A professor of English literature and American studies who has published
numerous critical works (on WILLIAM SHAKESPEARE, EVELYN WAUGH, E. M.
FORSTER, SAUL BELLOW, and twentieth-century fiction, among others), Malcolm
Bradbury is also a novelist whose protagonists are academics who make
muddles of their personal and professional lives. He maintains, however, that
his "settings are relatively incidental . . . and my main concern has been,
within a more or less comic framework, to explore problems and dilemmas of
liberalism and issues of moral responsibility." The targets of Bradbury's satires
include intellectual pretension, cultural myopia, and official smugness. His
protagonists are largely sympathetic, if comic, failures at mastering their own
fates in a world of absurd rules and regulations. His best novels include *Eating
People Is Wrong* (1959), *Stepping Westward* (1965), and *The History Man* (1975).
This last, a novel of intellectual and political conflict at an English university in
the late 1960s, was made into a successful television minidrama. More recent
novels include *Rates of Exchange* (1983) and *Cuts* (1987).

NOVELS BY BRADBURY

Cuts. 1987. Viking Penguin 1988 $5.95. ISBN 0-14-010846-7
Doctor Criminale. Viking Penguin 1992 $22.00. ISBN 0-670-84677-5. Clever satire
   exploring the corruption and confusion of post-Communist Europe.
Rates of Exchange. Viking Penguin 1985 $10.00. ISBN 0-14-007631-X. A fictional look at
   barter on every level—spiritual, mental, and verbal.

NONFICTION BY BRADBURY

All Dressed Up and Nowhere to Go. Merrimack River 1983 o.p. Comedic essays about
   Bradbury's experiences in America; discusses the differences between British and
   American culture.

BOOK ABOUT BRADBURY

Morace, Robert A. *The Dialogic Novels of Malcolm Bradbury and David Lodge.* S. Ill. U.
   Pr. 1989 $29.95. ISBN 0-8093-1519-X. Comparison of the two contemporary writers.

BRAINE, JOHN. 1922–1986

John Braine, a Yorkshireman by birth and inclination, started to write *Room at the Top* (1957) while hospitalized and recovering from tuberculosis. It is the story of a man (Joe Lampton) obsessed by the need for success who believes he can become an "insider" by donning the proper mask but who finds that he must compromise everything he values. The film version of *Room at the Top* won top film honors in Great Britain and was widely acclaimed in the United States. *From the Hand of the Hunter* deals with the fight against failure by a tubercular. *Life at the Top* (1962) is concerned with the hero of *Room at the Top* after he marries the boss's daughter. In *The Jealous God* (1964), "an author whose earlier concerns have been mainly fiscal and physical now turns his attention to the soul" in what is "perhaps his best novel since 'Room at the Top'" (*Library Journal*). *Waiting for Sheila* (1976), Braine's most interesting formal experiment, occurs in a single evening during which the protagonist recounts the failures of his past and present. Braine's theme of aggressive ambition and determination to break through rigid social barriers, expressed in both *Room at the Top* and *Life at the Top*, identified him as one of the "angry young men" of the 1950s.

NOVELS BY BRAINE

Life at the Top. Routledge Chapman & Hall 1980 repr. of 1962 ed. $3.95. ISBN 0-4160-0591-8
Waiting for Sheila. 1976. Methuen 1977 o.p.

NONFICTION BY BRAINE

Writing a Novel. McGraw 1975 $8.95. ISBN 0-07-007112-8. Braine's analysis of the writing process.

BOOKS ABOUT BRAINE

Lee. James W. *John Braine*. Irvington 1968 $17.95. ISBN 0-8057-1056-6. Comprehensive overview of Braine's life and work.
Salwak, Dale. *John Braine and John Wain: A Reference Guide*. G.K. Hall 1979 o.p.

BRENTON, HOWARD. 1942–

Howard Brenton trained in the fringe theaters of the late 1960s, radical experiments in political consciousness-raising, which dispensed with theatrical scenery, stage venues, and formally constructed, full-length plays. After leaving Cambridge, he worked with a group in Brighton until the London production of *Revenge* in 1969 brought him a commission from Portable Theatre, an important touring agitprop company that had been founded by two other Cambridge graduates, DAVID HARE and Tony Bicat. For them, he wrote *Christie in Love*, a stylistically disorienting confrontation of the Rillington Place murderer and the police. Brenton also participated in a seminal collaboration of the early 1970s, *Lay-By*, and joined Hare in writing a chronicle of British profiteers, *Brassneck* 1973. In the same year, *Magnificence* (1973), with its famous nihilistic conclusion—an accidental detonation that kills both a radical terrorist and his innocent victim—found its way to the stage of the Royal Court.

The scandal of Brenton's work has since then been raised to a higher power by his insistence on leaving the fringe behind and finding new scope for his ideas on the stages of the establishment—if not in the commercial West End, then in the subsidized theaters. The National Theatre produced his study of an industrial strike, *Weapons of Happiness* (1974), and, most notoriously, *The*

Romans in Britain (1980). Violent scenes in this epic of colonialism, which parallels the Roman occupation of Britain to the English presence in Northern Ireland, drew the wrath of citizens' groups, and a lawsuit. More recent subjects include nuclear arms—in *The Genius* (1983), ironically challenging the optimism of BERTOLT BRECHT's (see Vol. 2) *Galileo* (which Brenton translated)—and the relationship of power and journalism—in *Pravda* (1985), a collaboration with Hare. One of his more recent works is *Diving for Pearls* (1989), a political thriller.

PLAYS BY BRENTON

The Churchill Play. Heinemann Ed. 1974 $9.95. ISBN 0-413-33390-6. A political play based on Churchill's hereditary syphilis as a symbol for Britain's crippled economy; develops a theory for activism in politics.
Dead Head. Heinemann Ed. 1988 $9.95. ISBN 0-413-15180-8
Epsom Downs. Heinemann Ed. 1988 $8.95. ISBN 0-413-38930-8. Exuberant play about a secular English festival, filled with subplots and colorful characters.
A Fleet Street Comedy. Heinemann Ed. 1988 $9.95. ISBN 0-413-58480-1
The Genius. 1983 Heinemann Ed. 1988 $7.95. ISBN 0-413-54650-0
Greenland. Heinemann Ed. 1989 $8.95. ISBN 0-413-19530-9
Hitler Dances. Heinemann Ed. 1988 $8.95. ISBN 0-413-50060-8. A play that examines attitudes towards popular myths of World War II.
Lay-By. Riverrun NY 1988 $9.95. ISBN 0-7145-0928-0
Magnificence: A Play. 1973. Heinemann Ed. 1988 $8.95. ISBN 0-413-46750-3
Plays for the Poor Theatre: Five Short Plays. Heinemann Ed. 1988 $9.95. ISBN 0-413-47080-1. Contains *The Saliva Milk Shake, Christie in Love, Gum and Goo, Heads, The Education of Skinny Spew.*
Pravda. (coauthored with David Hare). Heinemann Ed. 1988 $9.95. ISBN 0-413-58480-1.
Revenge. 1969. Heinemann Ed. 1988 $9.95. ISBN 0-413-50010-1
The Romans in Britain: A Play. 1980. Heinemann Ed. 1988 $9.95 ISBN 0-685-03354-6
Sore Throats and Sonnets of Love and Opposition. Methuen 1979 o.p. A dark and cynical play about love and the different forms it can take.
Thirteenth Night and A Short Sharp Rock. 1980. Methuen 1981 o.p. Serious drama about a mad socialist family countering Thatcher's government.
Weapons of Happiness. Heinemann Ed. 1988 $8.95 ISBN 0-413-36650-2

BROOKE, RUPERT. 1887–1915

The best known of the poets who took a patriotic, somewhat idealized, view of World War I, Brooke was born in Rugby, where his father was headmaster of a house at the elite Rugby School. Blond, athletic, and intelligent, Brooke embodied the English stereotype of the golden youth; even WILLIAM BUTLER YEATS called him "the handsomest man in England." Graduating from Rugby School to King's College, Cambridge, Brooke joined the Apostles, a venerable intellectual club, which counted ALFRED LORD TENNYSON among its earlier members. Brooke published his first collection of poetry, entitled simply *Poems*, in 1911. His verse moved from fashionably decadent to nearly Georgian, often with a quiet pastoralism that now seems conventional. Brooke joined the Royal Navy Volunteer Reserve in August 1914, served in Belgium, and was sent to Gallipoli with the Hood Battalion but died of blood poisoning en route in the Aegean. He is best remembered for his war sonnets, which idealize both combat and patriotic feelings in a way that other war poets would later react against sharply.

POETRY BY BROOKE

The Collected Poems of Rupert Brooke. 1915. Dodd 1980 o.p. Includes an introduction by George Edward Woodberry and a biographical note by Margaret Lavington.

The Complete Poems of Rupert Brooke. AMS Pr. repr. of 1942 ed. $17.50. ISBN 0-404-14647-3
The Poetical Works of Rupert Brooke. 1946. Faber & Faber 1970 $8.95. ISBN 0-571-04704-1. The standard edition; includes an introduction by Geoffrey Keynes.
Rupert Brooke. Dufour 1968 $3.50. ISBN 0-8023-9042-0

BOOKS ABOUT BROOKE

De La Mare, W. *Rupert Brooke and the Intellectual Imagination.* Haskell 1972 repr. of 1919 ed. $75.00. ISBN 0-8383-1515-1. Examines the intellectual basis of Brooke's artistic production.
Keynes, Geoffrey. *A Bibliography of Rupert Brooke.* Hart-Davis 1954 o.p. A detailed bibliography with a preface by Keynes; includes illustrated reproductions of title pages of manuscripts.
Lehmann, John. *The Strange Destiny of Rupert Brooke.* H. Holt & Co. 1980 o.p. An interesting and well-written biography.

BROOKNER, ANITA. 1928–

Anita Brookner's novels evoke a near-contemporary, BARBARA PYM: like Pym (and certainly, following Pym, in the tradition of JANE AUSTEN and CHARLOTTE BRONTË), Brookner's forte is the meticulous examination of the lives of unremarkable women. Portraying these women with a dignity and tolerance that authors rarely expend on them, Brookner generates novels of intellectual and emotional compulsion.

Pym's women, like Austen's, remain ultimately tame and calm, at least manifestly. Brookner's women reflect the realities of a generation later than Pym: For Brookner, a simple, pacific femininity no longer provides a respite from a danger that lurks throughout her world. Unhappiness, which Pym's characters bear with resignation, torments Brookner's sensibility. *Hôtel du Lac* (1984) won the Booker Prize and remains Brookner's most acclaimed work. Cunning and formal in tenor, it probes the repressed secrets and fragile psychological condition of a writer, Edith Hope, who is recovering from the external world's threats and bruises and trying to reconcile the life of human passions with the life of the artist. Critics have rated the novel as one of the most important works in the genre of *Künstlerroman* for the late modern period.

A professor of art history, Brookner has taught at Cambridge University and the Cortauld Institute. Specializing in eighteenth- and nineteenth-century painting, she has written, in addition to her fiction, scholarly works about Jacques Louis David, Jean Baptiste Greuze, and JEAN-ANTOINE WATTEAU (see Vol. 3).

NOVELS BY BROOKNER

Brief Lives. Random 1990 $20.00. ISBN 0-394-58548-8. A scrutinizing look at an odd friendship between two women.
A Closed Eye. Random 1991 $21.00. ISBN 0-679-40447-3. Depiction of the limits imposed by convention on a woman's quest for love.
The Debut. Random 1990 $8.95. ISBN 0-679-72712-4. A detached novel about a young woman's adventures outside of books.
Family and Friends. PB 1986 $6.95. ISBN 0-317-53641-9. Set in prewar London, this novel follows a family through their travels as far afield as Paris, Hollywood, and the Italian Riviera.
Fraud. Random 1993 $20.50. ISBN 0-679-41606-4. A poignant exploration of one woman's self-sacrifice.
A Friend from England. HarpC 1989 repr. of 1988 ed. $6.95. ISBN 0-06-097202-5
Hôtel du Lac. Pantheon 1984 $13.95. ISBN 0-394-54215-0

Latecomers. Random 1990 $8.95. ISBN 0-679-72668-3. Portrays the friendship between
two men and their quite different reflections on their shared past.

Lewis Percy. Random 1991 $10.00. ISBN 0-679-72944-5. A portrayal of a young man
coping with his mother's death and unsuccessful marriage that explores the different
life expectations and understandings between men and women.

The Misalliance. HarpC 1988 $9.00. ISBN 0-06-097134-7

BOOKS ABOUT BROOKNER

Sadler, Lynn Vetch. *Anita Brookner*. Macmillan 1990 $21.95. ISBN 0-8057-6991-9.
Overview focusing on the ironies and discomfitures of Brookner's heroines.

Skinner, John. *The Fictions of Anita Brookner: Illusions of Romance*. St. Martin 1992
$35.00. ISBN 0-312-06862-8. Interesting look at romantic themes in Brookner's
fiction.

BUNTING, BASIL. 1900–1985

Ever the maverick, Basil Bunting was one of the most English as well as the
most Americanized of modern British poets. Born in Northumbria, in northern
England, and educated largely at Quaker boarding schools, he declared himself
a conscientious objector in World War I and served a term in prison. After a
year and a half at the London School of Economics, he traveled extensively—
particularly to Paris and then Italy—and supported himself through journalism,
often doing music reviews. During World War II, he worked for the British
merchant navy and was then sent to Persia by the government, eventually
becoming Persian correspondent for the *London Times*. Work for an English
provincial newspaper followed, and in the mid-1960s he returned to poetry and
achieved his first public success with the autobiographical poem *Briggflatts*
(1965).

The unlikely duo of WILLIAM WORDSWORTH and EZRA POUND exerted major
influences on Bunting's work. From WORDSWORTH came the preoccupation with
rural life in his native Northumbria, which constitutes his best subject. From
Pound came the verse techniques of American modernism with which Bunting
presents his material. WILLIAM BUTLER YEATS described him as "one of Ezra's
more savage disciples," and Pound helped him get his first volume of verse
published. Almost ignored in Britain until the late 1960s, Bunting later became
an influential conduit of modernist techniques into native British poetry. His
own formal innovations consist principally in his detailed adaptations of
musical structures and forms for verbal art.

POETRY BY BUNTING

Collected Poems. Moyer Bell Limited 1985 $22.50. ISBN 0-918825-16-4. A compilation of
forty years of poetry; includes an introduction by Bunting.

Uncollected Poems. Ed. by Richard Caddel. OUP 1991 $11.95. ISBN 0-19-282870-3

BOOKS ABOUT BUNTING

Forde, Victoria. *Basil Bunting*. Dufour 1991 $55.00. ISBN 1-85224-047-4. Competent,
well-written biography.

Guedalla, Roger. *Basil Bunting: A Bibliography of Works and Criticism*. Folcroft 1976 o.p.
A chronologically arranged list of all of Bunting's work; includes descriptions of the
books by appearance and title.

Terrell, Carroll F., ed. *Basil Bunting: Man and Poet. Man and Poet Ser*. Nat. Poet. Foun.
1981 $35.00. ISBN 0-915032-51-1. Comprehensive collection of essays, with annotat-
ed bibliography.

BURGESS, ANTHONY (JOHN ANTHONY BURGESS WILSON). 1917–

Anthony Burgess wrote his first novel in 1949 while he was a teacher of linguistics and composer of music; *A Vision of Battlements* (1953) resulted from his being "empty of music but itching to create." Later he became a British colonial officer in Southeast Asia, and in that capacity produced the trilogy *The Long Day Wanes*. This so called "Malayan Trilogy," which includes *Time for a Tiger* (1956), *The Enemy in the Blanket* (1958), and *Beds in the East* (1959), aptly describes British colonial life. He has since scored an impressive record—some 15 works of fiction published within a decade. "Although there are suggestions of what has come to be called 'black humor' in both *A Vision of Battlements* and *The Long Day Wanes*, it was only when he turned to the English scene, as he did in 1960 with *The Doctor is Sick* and *The Right to an Answer*, that Burgess showed how wry and bitter he could be" (*Saturday Review*). These two successful satires on present-day England paved the way for two more on the England of the future: *The Wanting Seed* (1962) shows a society where people are governed by rigorous laws, and homosexuality is encouraged to control a mounting population; *A Clockwork Orange* (1962) paints the bleak picture of a nation overridden by teenage gangs. These two exhibit Burgess's fascination (like that of JAMES JOYCE and VLADIMIR NABOKOV [see Vol. 2]) with oddities of language.

Other works include *Honey for the Bears*, which describes the United States and the former Soviet Union as overconformist societies. In *Tremor of Intent*, "using the spy as missile-era folk-hero, he creates a gleaming novel of ideas— troubling ideas about the survival value of ideology, the disease of our appetites, our malevolent innocence as we perpetuate incredible atrocities and feel no guilt. Brazenly clever, Burgess is . . . guided by a foolproof intellectual homing device and possessed by a black sense of humor that barely hold his hostility in check. Outraged by blasphemies against life, he attacks unreason with satire so swift we hardly know we've been hit before we're pronounced morally dead" (*N.Y. Times*). *Enderby* (1963), about an antisocial poet confined to the bathroom of a small apartment and then pitched into the world again, inaugurated a marvelous series on a most unusual character. Burgess has also written several books of literary criticism.

NOVELS BY BURGESS

Any Old Iron. PB 1990 $5.95. ISBN 0-671-72708-7

Beard's Roman Women. McGraw 1976 o.p. A surrealistic story about a man haunted by his first wife; somewhat autobiographical.

A Clockwork Orange. 1962. Norton 1963 $14.95. ISBN 0-393-30553-8. Violent futurist vision of social devolution.

The Clockwork Testament, or Enderby's End. 1976. McGraw 1984 o.p. Follows Enderby on his last, violent rampage against art, original sin, and proper nourishment.

Devil's Mode. Random 1989 $18.95. ISBN 0-394-57670-5. Collection of short stories informed by Burgess's cynicism about civilization.

The Doctor Is Sick. Norton 1979 repr. of 1960 ed. $8.95. ISBN 0-393-00959-9

Earthly Powers. Avon 1981 o.p. An epic novel portraying a revolution in the church.

Enderby. 1963. Norton 1968 o.p.

Enderby Outside. 1968. McGraw 1984 o.p. A scintillating saga of Enderby in Morocco; continues Enderby's adventures.

Enderby's Dark Lady: Or, No End to Enderby. McGraw 1984 o.p. A resurrection of the character Enderby; places the middle-aged poet in Indiana.

The End of the World News: An Entertainment. McGraw 1983 o.p. Three novellas bound together as one; about the life of Freud, a Broadway musical about Trotsky's visit to America, and an Earth crushed by aliens.

The Eve of St. Venus. 1970. Norton 1979 o.p. A light parody of the British aristocracy.
Honey for the Bears. Norton 1978 $5.95. ISBN 0-393-00905-X
Inside Mr. Enderby. 1963. McGraw 1984 o.p. Portrait of a middle-aged poet.
The Long Day Wanes: A Malayan Trilogy. 1956–59. Norton 1993 $10.95. ISBN 0-393-
    30943-6. Contains *Time for a Tiger, The Enemy in the Blanket,* and *Beds in the East.*
Man of Nazareth. McGraw 1979 o.p. Burgess's personal interpretation of Jesus of
    Nazareth; developed as a screenplay for Franco Zeffirelli.
Napoleon Symphony. Norton 1980 o.p. An ambitious fictional account of Napoleon's life;
    includes four sequences—emerging, triumphant, descending, and finished.
Nineteen Eighty-Five. Pantheon 1984 $4.95. ISBN 0-394-72482-8. A fictional response to
    Orwell's *1984*; includes commentary about Orwell.
The Pianoplayers. PB 1987 $4.95. ISBN 0-685-19178-8
The Right to an Answer. 1960. Norton 1978 $3.95. ISBN 0-393-00887-8
Tremor of Intent. Norton 1966 $6.95. ISBN 0-393-00416-3
The Wanting Seed. 1962. Norton 1976 repr. of 1963 ed. $9.95. ISBN 0-393-00808-8

BOOKS ABOUT BURGESS

Aggeler, Geoffrey. *Anthony Burgess: The Artist as Novelist.* U. of Ala. Pr. 1979 o.p.
    Burgess's views of contemporary art and life.
———, ed. *Critical Essays on Anthony Burgess.* Hall 1986 $40.00. ISBN 0-8161-8757-6.
    Interview, and essays on the futility of history, sex and art, politics and modernity.
Boytinck, Paul W. *Anthony Burgess: An Annotated Bibliography and Reference Guide.*
    Garland 1985 o.p. A comprehensive bibliography including reviews from magazines.
Brewer, Jeutonne. *Anthony Burgess: A Bibliography.* Scarecrow 1980 $22.50. ISBN 0-
    8108-1286-X. An extensive listing of Burgess's work; includes a foreword by Burgess.
Matthews, Richard. *The Clockwork Universe of Anthony Burgess.* Borgo Pr. 1978 $10.00.
    ISBN 0-89370-127-0. Focuses on novels from the mid-1960s and earlier.
Stinson, John J. *Anthony Burgess Revisited.* Macmillan 1991 $22.95. ISBN 0-8057-7000-3.
    Overview of his life; bibliography.

BYATT, A(NTONIA) S(USAN). 1936–

Like her sister MARGARET DRABBLE, A. S. Byatt writes of the common aspects
in the lives of women but invests her writing with an energy and an eloquent
appreciation for the heroism of their lives that generates a charged narrative. A
contemporary feminist awareness combines in many of her novels with a
reverence for the beauties and potentials of the Victorian novel. This fusion
occurs most exuberantly in her Booker Prize-winning novel *Possession* (1990),
which finally brought Byatt to the attention of international audiences. The
vagaries of modern literary scholarship are intertwined with romance and
mystery in a narrative that, for its sheer compelling power, is considered by
many to be one of the most striking stories in contemporary fiction.

Educated at Cambridge University, Byatt has lectured in English and
American literature and regularly broadcasts on BBC radio. Her critical
reputation stands apart from her literary talents, based upon her scholarly
examinations of WILLIAM WORDSWORTH, SAMUEL TAYLOR COLERIDGE, and IRIS
MURDOCH. A volume of essays, *Passions of the Mind* (1991), solidifies her
reputation as a critical presence.

NOVELS BY BYATT

Angels and Insects: Two Novellas. Random 1993 $21.00. ISBN 0-679-40512-7. Two
    postmodern novellas dealing with the ideas of Darwinism and spiritualism in
    Victorian settings.
The Game. Random 1992 $10.00. ISBN 0-679-74256-5. Disturbing memories, shared by
    two sisters, of a strange childhood.

Possession: A Romance. Random 1991 $22.95. ISBN 0-685-48550-1. Postmodern parable of intersecting Victorian and modern lives.

Still Life: A Novel. 1985. Random 1991 $10.00. ISBN 0-02-017855-7. An in-depth saga portraying the art world and history.

The Virgin in the Garden. 1978. Random 1992 $12.00. ISBN 0-679-73829-0. Erudite novel about a family mired in sexuality.

NONFICTION BY BYATT

Degrees of Freedom: The Novels of Iris Murdoch. Chatto & Windus UK 1965 o.p. Examines the novels of Iris Murdoch and discusses her position historically within the symbolist movement.

Passions of the Mind: Selected Writings. Random 1993 $12.00. ISBN 0-679-73678-6. Essays and other writings on a variety of subjects.

Unruly Times: Wordsworth and Coleridge in Their Time. Trafalgar 1990 $17.95. ISBN 0-7012-0857-0. Examines the two great romantic poets and analyzes their work in the context of their age.

SHORT STORY COLLECTION BY BYATT

Sugar and Other Stories. 1987. Random 1992 $10.00. ISBN 0-679-74227-1. The first collection of Byatt's short stories.

CARTER, ANGELA. 1940–1992

A powerful and disturbing writer, Angela Carter created haunting fiction about travelers surviving their passage through a disintegrating universe. Often based on myth or fairy tale—borrowed or invented for the occasion—her work evokes the most powerful aspects of sexuality and selfhood, of life and death, of apocalypse. Carter's most successful novels include *The Magic Toyshop* (1967), which won the John Llewellyn Rhys Prize; *Several Perceptions* (1968), which won the Somerset Maugham Award; and *The Passion of New Eve* (1977), a story of the end of the world and its possible new beginning with failed mankind replaced by a self-generating womankind. She translated many fairy tales and wrote several collections of short stories, including *The Bloody Chamber* (1979) which won the Cheltenham Festival of Literature Award and was the basis for the powerful movie *A Company of Wolves.* She worked as a journalist and teacher (including appointments at Brown and the University of Texas), and published two nonfiction books of interest: *Nothing Sacred,* selected writings, and *The Sadeian Woman* (1979).

NOVELS BY CARTER

Come unto These Yellow Sands. Dufour 1985 $35.00. ISBN 0-906427-67-3

Heroes and Villains. Viking Penguin 1991 $9.00. ISBN 0-14-011930-2

Infernal Desire Machines of Doctor Hoffman. Viking Penguin 1986 $7.95. ISBN 0-14-005651-3

Love. Viking Penguin 1988 $5.95. ISBN 0-14-010851-3

Nights at the Circus. 1984. Viking Penguin 1986 $11.00. ISBN 0-14-007703-0

Saints and Strangers. 1986. Viking Penguin 1986 $13.95. ISBN 0-670-81139-4

The War of Dreams. Harcourt 1974 $6.95. Avon 1977 pap. $1.95. Fictional memories of a war; a picaresque tale of a great war hero.

Wise Children. FS&G 1991 $21.00. ISBN 0-374-29133-0. Comic saga of theatrical families.

SHORT STORY COLLECTION BY CARTER

The Bloody Chamber. Viking Penguin 1990 $10.00. ISBN 0-14-017821-X

Fireworks: Nine Stories in Various Disguises. 1974. HarpC 1981 $10.53. 1982 pap. $4.09

NONFICTION BY CARTER

The Sadeian Woman and the Ideology of Pornography. Pantheon 1988 repr. of 1979 ed. $8.95. ISBN 0-394-75893-5

BOOK ABOUT CARTER

Robinson, Sally. *Engendering the Subject: Gender and Self-Representation in Contemporary Woman's Fiction*. State U. NY Pr. 1991 $49.50. ISBN 0-7914-0727-6 Feminist consideration of Carter and Doris Lessing.

CARY, JOYCE. 1888–1957

Poet, amateur painter, political scientist, and novelist, Cary was born in Ireland of an old Devonshire family. His autobiographical novels, *Castle Corner* (1938) and *A House of Children* (1941), represent Cary's family life in County Clare up to the time of his own youth. He studied art for several years but gave it up to enter Oxford University. There, he first studied history but changed to law. Resolved to become a writer when he left Oxford, he was eager for adventure and went to the Balkan War of 1912–13. Later, in Africa, Cary served with the Nigerian colonial service, and during World War I with the West African Frontier Force in campaigns in the Cameroons. Having had some success at writing and selling short stories, he settled in Oxford and devoted himself full time to his writing. But it was more than 10 years before he published his first novel, and more than 20 before he attained financial security.

Aissa Saved (1932) was the first of many books that established his reputation as a novelist of great vigor and imagination. Some of the early ones about Nigeria show his knowledge of Africa and his perception, compassion, and imaginative power. *Mr. Johnson* (1939) is the most powerful of these. Among his later works is the marvelous *The Horse's Mouth* (1944), the portrait of a good artist who is also an outrageous one—perhaps his masterpiece, although the other books of that trilogy (1941–44) are also compelling. The Nimmo trilogy (1952–55) treats British parliamentary politics through intensely clashing perspectives and values. Cary's genius in the trilogies and his other successful novels lies in a kind of ventriloquism, the ability to create and sustain extraordinary vital characters, each of whom tells his or her own story with remarkable intensity and sympathy.

NOVELS BY CARY

The Captive and the Free. 1959. Amereon Ltd. repr. of 1959 ed. $19.95. ISBN 0-88411-309-4. An unfinished last novel; examines issues about religion through a freakish faith healer.

Except the Lord. New Dir. Pr. 1985 repr. of 1962 ed. $7.95. ISBN 0-8112-0965-2

A Fearful Joy: A Novel. Greenwood 1973 repr. of 1949 ed. $66.00. ISBN 0-8371-6777-9. The story of Tabitha Bassitt; subordinates *The Horse's Mouth*.

Herself Surprised. 1941. Amereon Ltd. 1976 repr. of 1948 ed. $18.95. ISBN 0-89244-070-8. The first novel of the first trilogy, followed by *To Be a Pilgrim* (1942, o.p.).

The Horse's Mouth. 1944. HarpC 1965 $5.95. ISBN 0-06-080046-1. The third novel of the first trilogy. Cary's masterpiece about an artist's Blakean attempts to capture and present his visions. Narrated by a scoundrel, Gully Jimson.

House of Children. 1941. New Dir. Pr. 1986 $8.95. ISBN 0-8112-1008-1

Mister Johnson. 1939. New Dir. Pr. 1989 $8.95. ISBN 0-8112-1174-6

Not Honour More. 1955. New Dir. Pr. 1985 $7.95. ISBN 0-8112-0966-0

Prisoner of Grace. 1952. New Dir. Pr. 1985 repr. of 1962 ed. $7.95. ISBN 0-8112-0964-4

NONFICTION BY CARY

Art and Reality: Ways of the Creative Process. Ayer repr. of 1958 ed. $19.00. ISBN 0-8369-1906-8

BOOKS ABOUT CAREY

Bloom, Robert. *The Indeterminate World: A Study of the Novels of Joyce Cary.* U. of Pa. Pr. 1962 o.p. Examines Cary's moral stances, which are often perplexed or exasperated.

Cook, Cornelia. *Joyce Cary: Liberal Principles.* B & N Imports 1981 $40.00. ISBN 0-389-20201-0. Themes of creativity, power, freedom, and their manifestations in the world.

Echeruo, Michael J. C. *Joyce Cary and the Dimensions of Order.* B & N Imports 1979 $16.50. ISBN 0-06-49187-0. Discusses Cary's late novels, which reflect a resolution of his philosophical doubts.

_____. *Joyce Cary and the Novel of Africa.* Africana Pub. 1973 o.p. Examines conflicts between paganism and Christianity, order and civilization, tragedy and absurdity in Cary's African novels.

Fisher, Barbara. *Joyce Cary Remembered: In Letters and Interviews by His Family and Others.* Smythe 1988 o.p. Biographical reminiscences.

Mahood, M. M. *Joyce Cary's Africa.* Methuen 1964 o.p. Explores the facts and fictions about the Africa of which Cary writes.

Makinen, Merja, and Kevin Harris. *Joyce Cary: A Descriptive Bibliography.* Mansell 1989 o.p. Lists Cary's major works; delineates each title by genre.

O'Connor, William V. *Joyce Cary.* Col. U. Pr. 1966 $7.50. ISBN 0-231-02680-3

Roby, Kinley E. *Joyce Cary.* Twayne 1984 o.p. Overview of his life; bibliography.

CHESTERTON, G(ILBERT) K(EITH). 1874–1936

Chesterton was HILAIRE BELLOC's devoted friend and ally in literary pursuits. He was a humorist, a historian, a literary critic, and an ardent Roman Catholic. His essays combine these qualifications most successfully. As a critic he wrote several noteworthy literary studies, among them *Robert Browning* (1903) and *George Bernard Shaw* (1909). His *Victorian Age in Literature* (1913) was once a standard work. In the Father Brown detective stories, Chesterton created a mild-mannered priest, Father Brown, a character who became popular with mystery fans. His own colorful dress and manner were later characterized in John Dickson Carr's Gideon Fell mysteries. *The Father Brown Omnibus* has been in print continuously for decades.

NONFICTION BY CHESTERTON

All I Survey. Essay Index Repr. Ser. Ayer repr. of 1933 ed. $20.00. ISBN 0-8369-0293-9. Broad selection of essays covering subjects from blonds to traffic.

All Things Considered. Essay Index Repr. Ser. Ayer repr. of 1908 ed. $19.00. ISBN 0-8369-2275-1. Essays discussing the sport of the upper class in the future.

As I Was Saying. Essay Index Repr. Ser. Ayer repr. of 1936 ed. $17.00. ISBN 0-8369-0295-5

Autobiography. Arden Lib. 1978 repr. of 1936 ed. o.p.

Come to Think of It. Essay Index Repr. Ser. Ayer repr. of 1931 ed. $18.00. ISBN 0-8369-2042-2

Do We Agree? A Debate. Haskell 1969 repr. of 1928 ed. $39.95. ISBN 0-8383-0525-3

Generally Speaking. Essay Index Repr. Ser. Ayer repr. of 1929 ed. $19.00. ISBN 0-8369-0296-3. Essays on a variety of subjects ranging from detective novels to the work of Thomas Hardy.

George Bernard Shaw. Arden Lib. 1978 repr. of 1909 ed. o.p.

Heretics. Essay Index Repr. Ser. Ayer repr. of 1905 ed. $19.00. ISBN 0-8369-1869-X

Lunacy and Letters. Ed. by Dorothy Collins. *Essay Index Repr. Ser.* Ayer repr. of 1958 ed. $15.00. ISBN 0-8369-2937-3. Contains 38 nonpolitical light essays, some rich in fantasy, from the *Daily News*, 1901–12. Edited by Chesterton's literary executor.

Miscellany of Men. Essay Index Repr. Ser. Ayer repr. of 1912 ed. $21.00. ISBN 0-8369-1281-1. Essays discussing various men and their eccentricities.

Robert Browning. Richard West 1973 repr. of 1903 ed. o.p.

Utopia of Usurers, and Other Essays. Essays Index Repr. Ser. Ayer repr. of 1917 ed. $15.00. ISBN 0-8369-0299-8. Essays on Great Britain's politics and government.

Wit and Wisdom of G. K. Chesterton. Folcroft 1980 repr. of 1911 ed. o.p. Discusses Chesterton's forms of satire and what lies underneath.

NOVEL BY CHESTERTON

The Father Brown Omnibus. Dodd 1983 o.p.

WORK BY CHESTERTON

The Man Who Was Chesterton. Ed. by Raymond T. Bond. *Essay Index Repr. Ser.* Ayer repr. of 1937 ed. $42.00. ISBN 0-8369-1908-4. Essays, stories, poems, and other writings.

BOOKS ABOUT CHESTERTON

Conlon, D. J., ed. *G. K. Chesterton: A Half Century of Views.* OUP 1987 $21.00. ISBN 0-19-212260-6. Essays on Chesterton and Dickens, Chesterton as practical mystic.

Finch, Michael. *G. K. Chesterton.* Grove Pr. 1986 o.p. Interesting biography illustrating Chesterton's inner turmoil and conversion to Roman Catholicism.

Hunter, Lynette. *G. K. Chesterton: Explorations in Allegory.* St. Martin 1979 $18.50. ISBN 0-313-31492-2. Examines Chesterton's artistic explorations, encampments, and inner landscape.

CHRISTIE, DAME AGATHA. 1890–1976

[SEE Chapter 12 in this volume.]

CHURCHILL, CARYL. 1938–

In the early 1980s, Churchill suddenly became one of the contemporary British dramatists best represented on New York stages, as three of her plays were produced in succession. *Cloud Nine* (1978), directed by Tommy Tune, held the stage for two years and won an Obie (as did *Top Girls*, 1982). In England Churchill's career has been less abrupt, a long migration among the characteristic outlets of the new drama. From 1961 to 1972, she wrote radio plays. *Owners* (1972) was her first stage work (aside from college productions), commissioned by the Royal Court, where she became resident dramatist in 1974, and which staged *Objections to Sex and Violence* in 1975. In the next year, Churchill began working with two of the important fringe theater companies—Joint Stock (for which she wrote *Light Shining in Buckinghamshire*, 1976; *Cloud Nine*, and *Fen* 1982) and a feminist group, Monstrous Regiment (*Vinegar Tom*, 1976: contributions to the revue *Floorshow*). The Lucille Lortel Theatre (New York) production of *Cloud Nine* in 1981 ushered in the most recent, transatlantic phase of Churchill's career. New York's Public Theater, as well as London's Royal Court, staged versions of *Top Girls* in 1982.

Churchill writes plays of many different sorts—Ortonesque (the grotesques of *Owners*), historical (versions of the seventeenth century in *Light Shining*, about the English Civil War, and *Vinegar Tom*, about witchcraft), expressionist (the cross-sexual casting and doubling in *Cloud Nine*), and formally experimental (the permutations of situation in her dramatic Möbius strip, *Traps*). She is increasingly feminist in outlook. But, if her demonstrations of sexual liberation are sometimes pat (as in the second half of *Cloud Nine*), her theatrical adventurousness is always invigorating.

PLAYS BY CHURCHILL

Churchill Plays: One. Routledge 1985 $7.95. ISBN 0-415-90196-0. Contains *Owners, Traps, Vinegar Tom, Light Shining in Buckinghamshire* and *Cloud Nine.*

Churchill Plays: Two. Heinemann Ed. 1990 $12.95. ISBN 0-413-62270-3

Cloud Nine. Routledge 1984 $6.95. ISBN 0-415-90135-9

Serious Money. Heinemann Ed. 1988 $9.95. ISBN 0-413-16660-0. A satirical study of the effects of the financial world.

Softcops and *Fen.* Heinemann Ed. 1988 $9.95. ISBN 0-413-41200-8. *Softcops* satirizes Michel Foucault as a music hall freak; *Fen* scrutinizes the life of low-paid female potato pickers.

Top Girls. Heinemann Ed. 1988 $9.95. ISBN 0-413-55480-5. About brilliant women of history struggling against oppression and poverty.

BOOKS ABOUT CHURCHILL

Cousin, Geraldine. *Churchill, the Playwright.* Methuen 1989 o.p.

Fitzsimmons, Linda. *File on Churchill.* Heinemann Ed. 1989 $9.95. ISBN 0-413-14730-4. Bibliography, sourcebook, and reviews.

Kritzer, Amelia Howe. *The Plays of Caryl Churchill: Theatre of Empowerment.* St. Martin 1991 $39.95. ISBN 0-312-06091-2. Explores Churchill's handling of the issues of power, freedom, choice, gender, and myth.

Randall, Phyllis R. *Caryl Churchill: A Casebook.* Garland 1988 o.p. Bibliography and scholarly essays on early radio and stage plays, gender.

CLARKE, AUSTIN. 1896–1974

One of the leading Irish poets of the generation after WILLIAM BUTLER YEATS, Clarke also wrote verse drama, novels, and criticism. From his parents he imbibed the Irish nationalism of his father and the stern religious conscience of his mother. As a boy he attended the same Belvedere College as JAMES JOYCE and later attended University College, Dublin. He was appointed to a teaching post for a three-year term, but a nervous breakdown, an abortive marriage (it lasted 10 days), and the nonrenewal of his teaching job led to Clarke's departure in 1922 for England, where he spent most of the next 15 years. Chosen as a charter member of the Irish Academy of Letters in 1932, Clarke returned to Dublin permanently in 1937 and devoted himself largely to writing verse drama. A lifelong Roman Catholic, he took a leading role in the battle against censorship, which had already banned some of his books from his native country. His final years saw a renewed outpouring of poetry, much of it on social issues.

Clarke's early poetry turned to Celtic themes and adaptations. Unlike Yeats and others, he knew enough Gaelic to read his sources in the original, and he tried to reproduce some of their complex patterns of assonance in his own verse. For the last 20 years of his career, he focused more on contemporary social issues. Throughout his poetry, Clarke displayed both technical skill (particularly in his complex assonance) and a thematic preoccupation with the struggle between conscience and repression. When asked by ROBERT FROST to describe his poetry, he remarked, "I load myself with chains and then try to get out of them."

POETRY BY CLARKE

The Collected Poems of Austin Clarke. AMS Pr. repr. of 1936 ed. $30.50. ISBN 0-404-14523-X. Collection of Clarke's romantic poetry; Gaelic prosody and metrical verse translated into English.

Echo at Coole and Other Poems. Dufour 1968 $13.95. ISBN 0-8023-1155-5. Classic Gaelic
    poems about the countryside of Ireland and love poems to women.
The Frenzy of Sweeney. Humanities 1980 o.p.
Poems. OUP 1964 o.p. The standard edition.
Poetry in Modern Ireland. Arden Lib. 1978 repr. of 1951 ed. o.p. Published as part of a
    series written for the Cultural Relations Committee of Ireland in 1951.
The Selected Poetry of Austin Clarke. Ed. by Thomas Kinsella. Wake Forest 1976 o.p.
    Poems written between 1925 and 1971; with an introduction by Thomas Kinsella.
The Singing Men at Cashel. Humanities 1980 o.p. Based on the legendary story of
    Gormalai, the wife of Cormac MacGuillenan.

PLAYS BY CLARKE

Liberty Lane: A Ballad Play of Dublin in Two Acts with a Prologue. Humanities 1978. o.p.
The Third Kiss. Humanities 1976 o.p.

NONFICTION BY CLARKE

Celtic Twilight and the Nineties. Dufour 1970 $13.95. ISBN 0-85105-010-7. Introduction
    by R. McHugh.
Twice around the Black Church. 1962 o.p. An autobiographical volume.

BOOKS ABOUT CLARKE

Halpern, Susan. *Austin Clarke: His Life and Works.* Dolmen 1974 o.p. Surveys Clarke's
    poetry, criticism, drama, and prose romances.
Harmon, Maurice. *Austin Clarke: 1886–1974: A Critical Introduction.* B & N Imports 1989
    $56.00. ISBN 0-389-20864-7. Traces parallels between Clarke's literature and the rise
    of modern Ireland.
Schirmer, Gregory A. *The Poetry of Austin Clarke.* Notre Dame 1983 o.p. Survey of the
    narrative, public, and erotic poems and Gaelic translations.
Tapping, G. Craig. *Austin Clarke: A Study of his Writings.* B & N Imports 1981 o.p.
    Examines Clarke's tradition: Modern classicism; myth and poetry.

COLUM, PADRAIC. 1881–1972

Born in a Longford workhouse where his father was first teacher and then
master, Padraic Colum grew into an important figure in the Irish literary
renaissance before immigrating to the United States. Invited by the Fay brothers
to join the National Theatre Society, Colum soon came into contact with
WILLIAM BUTLER YEATS, JOHN MILLINGTON SYNGE, LADY ISABELLA AUGUSTA
GREGORY, and other major figures of the day. In 1912 he married the teacher
and writer Mary Maguire, with whom he undertook several joint projects. The
Colums immigrated to the United States in 1914. They eventually settled in New
York, with intervening periods in Europe and in Connecticut. Colum kept up a
varied production of verse, plays, fiction, criticism, and children's literature,
together with active lecturing. His most extended teaching appointment was at
Columbia University, where he and his wife offered a joint course in comparative literature.

Colum felt that his Roman Catholic and peasant roots gave him a closer tie to
the Irish folk than did the Protestant, Anglo-Irish background of many writers of
the Irish renaissance. His poetry usually deals with common people and rural
landscapes in a forthright manner. Colum was resolutely Irish, and his work for
the most part avoids didacticism or sentimental nationalism in favor of
straightforward presentation. As his best critic Zack Bowen remarked, Colum
puts his trust in the "world of visible experience."

POETRY BY COLUM

Collected Poems. Devin 1953 $25.00. ISBN 0-8159-5203-1. Deluxe edition of his poems, revised and reedited.

Images of Departure: Poetry. Dufour o.p. Twenty poems in remembrance of his dead wife.

Irish Elegies. 1966. Humanities 1976 o.p. Eleven poems commemorating the dead heroes of Ireland; includes revisions of earlier Irish poems.

The Poet's Circuits. Dufour 1984 $14.95. ISBN 0-685-20030-2. Colum's last book of poems; memories of the Irish countryside.

NONFICTION BY COLUM

Our Friend James Joyce. 1958. Peter Smith o.p. Personal experiences with James Joyce and his family; written in conjunction with Colum's wife, Mary.

SHORT STORY COLLECTIONS BY COLUM

Selected Short Stories. Ed. by Sanford Sternlicht. Syracuse U. Pr. 1985 $22.50. ISBN 0-8156-2327-5. Stories set in the Ireland of Colum's youth; with an introduction by Sanford Sternlicht.

A Treasury of Irish Folklore. Outlet Bk. Co. 1992 $12.99. ISBN 0-517-42046-5

PLAYS BY COLUM

Selected Plays of Padraic Colum. Ed. by Sanford Sternlicht. Syracuse U. Pr. 1986 $18.00. ISBN 0-8156-2386-0. Contains *The Land*; *Betrayal*; *Glendalough*; and *Monasterboice.*

WORKS BY COLUM

The Children of Odin: The Book of Northern Myths. Macmillan Child Grp. 1984 $15.95. ISBN 0-02-722890-8. A retelling of Norse myths; includes "The Dwellers of Asgard," "Odin the Wanderer," "The Witches Heart," "The Sword of the Volsungs," and "The Twilight of the Gods."

Golden Fleece. Macmillan 1967 o.p. An account of Jason's search for the golden fleece; children's book.

Golden Fleece and the Heroes Who Lived before Achilles. Macmillan Child Grp. 1983 $15.95. ISBN 0-02-723620-X. An epic for children that recounts the tales of Greek heroes, including the travels of Jason and the Argonauts.

BOOKS ABOUT COLUM

Bowen, Zack R. *Padraic Colum: A Biographical-Critical Introduction.* S. Ill. U. Pr. 1970 o.p. Comprehensive look at the full scope of Colum's literary works.

Sternlicht, Sanford V. *Padraic Colum.* Twayne 1985. ISBN 0-8057-6901-3. An appreciation and critical study of Colum's life and work.

COMPTON-BURNETT, DAME IVY. 1892–1969

English novelist Dame Ivy Compton-Burnett was born in London and studied classics at Royal Holloway College, London University. After publishing her first novel, *Dolores*, in 1911 she went on to become a prolific writer. All Compton-Burnett's many novels, which have been called "morality plays for the tough-minded," are satires of the least admirable qualities of the nobility and landed gentry of the late Victorian world. She writes with subtle brilliance—her melodramatic plots are developed almost exclusively in "dense, sometimes cryptic" dialogue. *The Mighty and Their Fall* (1961), centering on a late Victorian family of three generations living in a country house attended by four servants, is a compelling analysis of character; its suspense leads to insightful revelation. Many of her works contain dark themes of murder, abuse, and fraud. Although her works can be initially difficult, the reader is rewarded by Compton-Burnett's intelligent and unsentimental style. In 1956 she won the

James Tait Black Memorial Award for Fiction for *Mother and Son* (1955). A decade later, she was made a Dame Commander of the Order of the British Empire.

NOVELS BY COMPTON-BURNETT

Brothers and Sisters. 1930. Schocken 1987 $5.95. ISBN 0-8052-8213-0. A frank story of incest.

Daughters and Sons. Schocken 1984 o.p.

Dolores. 1911 St. Mut. 1981 o.p. Story of a Victorian heroine who sacrifices for the ideal of duty.

Elders and Betters. Trafalgar 1944 $18.95. ISBN 0-575-02371-6. A vibrant comedic portrayal of a family and its difficulties.

A Family and a Fortune. David & Charles 1939 o.p. Domestic and economic tyrannies.

A God and His Gifts. David & Charles 1963 o.p. Story about a novelist father battling the erosion of his family unit.

A Heritage and Its History. Trafalgar 1992 $10.95. ISBN 1-85381-281-1. Revolving around the birth of a child, this novel explores the instinctive forces in its characters' lives.

Manservant and Maidservant. AMS Pr. repr. of 1948 ed. $29.50. ISBN 0-404-20067-2. Also published in the United States under the title *Bullivant and the Lambs.* Deals with social pressures within a household; explores social class differences among members of an extended family.

The Mighty and Their Fall. Trafalgar 1992 $10.95. ISBN 1-85381-177-7

More Women than Men. Schocken 1987 $5.95. ISBN 0-8052-8210-6. Set in a girl's school, this novel challenges the heterosexual model and its expression of sexuality.

Mother and Son. David & Charles 1955 o.p.

Pastors and Masters. 1925. Schocken 1987 $5.95. ISBN 0-8052-8212-2. Set in a boy's school; the characters discuss the pros and cons of religion.

The Present and Past. Viking Penguin 1986 $6.95. ISBN 0-14-003347-5. The tale of a pathetic patriarch named Cassius Clave.

Two Worlds and Their Ways. Trafalgar 1992 $10.95. ISBN 1-85381-176-9. Portrays two teachers at a boy's school engaged in a homosexual relationship.

BOOKS ABOUT COMPTON-BURNETT

Baldanza, Frank. *Ivy Compton-Burnett.* Irvington 1964 $17.95. ISBN 0-8290-1728-3. Overview and bibliography.

Burkhart, Charles, ed. *The Art of I. Compton-Burnett: A Collection of Critical Essays.* Gollancz 1972 o.p. Interviews, reviews, and scholarly essays.

———, ed. *I. Compton-Burnett.* Gollancz 1965 o.p. Overview of Compton-Burnett's career as "eccentric novelist"; her ethos and conventions.

Liddell, Robert. *Elizabeth and Ivy.* Dufour 1986 $26.00. ISBN 0-7206-0644-6. Compton-Burnett's association with the novelist Elizabeth Taylor.

Spurling, Hilary. *Ivy: The Life of I. Compton-Burnett.* Knopf 1984 o.p. A thorough examination of Compton-Burnett's home life and writings; fully illuminates her craft and her character.

CONRAD, JOSEPH. 1857–1924

From a young age, Józef Teodor Konrad Nałecz Korzeniowski experienced the uncertainty and oppression that were to become trademarks of his modernist fiction. He was born into a Polish nation and culture that was being scavenged, dissected, and divided by Austria, Russia, and Prussia. After an 1863 uprising, his father, Apollo, was arrested and exiled with his family to Vologda, hundreds of miles north of Moscow; the trip nearly killed the 6-year-old boy, and the brutal conditions in Vologda led to his parents' premature deaths.

Orphaned at the age of 12, Józef was cared for by an uncle, who sent him to school in Krakow and Geneva. (Polish was Conrad's first language, and French became his second.) Finding a schoolboy's regimen restrictive, the young man abandoned this for the French merchant navy. In four years filled with exotic adventures, Conrad indulged in fortune hunting, gambling, political insurrection, and amorous intrigues. Forbidden from continuing in the French merchant marine fleet in 1878, he switched to a British ship and worked on British vessels for 16 years; he became a subject of Great Britain in 1887, adopting English as his language. His voyages, especially those to Asia and Central America, generated the experiences and atmosphere that he would channel into his fiction. *Almayer's Folly* (1895), the first of these works, marked the end of his naval career and the beginning of his life as a writer. A year after its publication, Conrad married and settled at Ashford in Kent. He remained there for the rest of his life, living a rather quiet, secluded existence devoted to his writing.

In his fiction, Conrad helped renew the form of the novel. Building on the techniques begun by HENRY JAMES, GUSTAVE FLAUBERT (see Vol. 2), and IVAN TURGENEV (see Vol. 2), Conrad abolished the omnisciently logical authorial narration, substituting a more uncertain and murky impressionism that was rich in detail but oblique in plot and direction.

Conrad's subject matter is grounded in adventure, danger, and quests for personal achievement; his fiction is filled with challenges undertaken by heroes and antiheroes who metaphorically represent the nature of the European character and soul. Conrad's writing thus offers a subtext of geopolitical quandaries, issues of historical and economic imperialism, and ultimately moral conundrums about personal, social, and national ethics that are rarely resolved but, rather, left simmering and potent.

Conrad's deconstruction, in his macrocosmic fictive portraits, of the notion of a stable and majestic European sensibility likely reflects his experience of being tossed about in a rapidly changing and seemingly impenetrable culture. Glimpsing this society both from the inside (as he wandered through Europe, adopting different literatures and nationalities) and from the outside (as he traveled to Europe's colonial and imperial outposts, gauging the toll of this crumbling culture of far-flung innocent victims), Conrad generates a literature replete with the trademarks of modernism: alienation, anomie, ambiguity, and a pervasive atmosphere of physical and moral decadence.

His most famous works are *Nostromo* (1904), a subtle examination of how politics and capitalism corrupt personal relationships, and *Heart of Darkness* (1902), derived from Conrad's personal experience in the Congo in 1890—an exposé of the brutality and exploitation underlying the enterprise of trading and exploring. By the time of his death in 1924, Conrad was one of the most revered of English authors. Moreover, his work is considered an important link between nineteenth century realism and twentieth century modernism.

NOVELS BY CONRAD

Heart of Darkness and *The Secret Sharer*. Buccaneer Bks. 1978 repr. of 1910 ed. $17.95. ISBN 0-89966-054-1. Two of Conrad's best-known adventures of exploration by sea.

Lord Jim. 1900. Knopf 1992 $16.50. ISBN 0-679-40544-5

The Nigger of the Narcissus. 1897. Buccaneer Bks. 1991 $18.95. ISBN 0-89966-055-X

Nostromo. 1904. Knopf 1992 $19.50. ISBN 0-679-40990-4. Revolution, deception, and self-betrayal.

An Outcast of the Islands. 1896. Buccaneer Bks. 1983 $16.95. ISBN 0-89966-263-3. A South Seas trader betrays his friend for love.

The Secret Agent. 1907. Knopf 1992 $16.50. ISBN 0-679-41723-0. A chilling story of espionage based on a real attempt to blow up the Greenwich Observatory.

Under Western Eyes. 1911. Knopf 1991 $20.00. ISBN 0-679-40554-2. A story of European revolutionaries.

BOOKS ABOUT CONRAD

Berman, Jeffrey. *Joseph Conrad: Writing as Rescue.* Astra 1977 o.p. Examines the effect of Conrad's suicide attempt on his writing.

Bloom, Harold, ed. *Joseph Conrad.* Chelsea Hse. 1986 $24.50. ISBN 0-8775-4642-8. Investigates Conrad's handling of impressionism and symbolism, women as moral force, and repetition and organic form.

Daleski, H. M. *Joseph Conrad: The Way of Dispossession.* Faber & Faber 1977 o.p. Examines depictions of loss of self in Conrad's work.

Erdinast-Vulcan, Daphna. *Joseph Conrad and the Modern Temper.* OUP 1991 $52.00. ISBN 0-19-811785-X. The failures of myth, metaphysics, and textuality in Conrad's novels.

Gillon, Adam. *Joseph Conrad.* Macmillan 1982 $19.95. ISBN 0-8057-6820-3. Overview of his life; bibliography.

Hawthorn, Jeremy. *Joseph Conrad: Narrative Technique and Ideological Commitment.* Arnold 1990 o.p. Examines Conrad's technical craftsmanship and his artistic conception.

Karl, Frederick. *Joseph Conrad: The Three Lives.* FS&G 1979 o.p. Interesting biography exploring the many facets of Conrad's life and work.

Knowles, Owen. *A Conrad Chronology.* G. K. Hall 1990 $35.00. ISBN 0-8161-1839-6
———. *An Annotated Critical Bibliography of Joseph Conrad.* St. Martin 1992 $39.95. ISBN 0-312-07556-1. Comprehensive source book of primary and secondary sources.

Meyers, Jeffrey. *Joseph Conrad: A Biography.* Macmillan 1991 $27.50. ISBN 0-684-19230-6. Contains new information on Conrad's seafaring career, his marriage, his friendship with Ford, and his affair with Jane Anderson.

Nadelhaft, Ruth L. *Joseph Conrad.* Humanities 1991 $45.00. ISBN 0-391-03721-8. Feminist interpretations of Conrad.

Ressler, Steve. *Joseph Conrad: Consciousness and Integrity.* NYU Pr. 1988 $35.00. ISBN 0-8147-7405-9. Examines loss of self, failure, integrity, and affirmation of action.

Secor, Robert, and Debra Moddelmog. *Joseph Conrad and American Writers: A Bibliographical Study of Affinities, Influences, and Relations.* Greenwood 1985 $42.95. ISBN 0-313-24601-7. Annotated listing of materials reflecting the influence of American authors in Conrad's work.

Teets, Bruce E. *Joseph Conrad: An Annotated Secondary Bibliography.* Garland 1990 $103.00. ISBN 0-8240-7037-2. Comprehensive bibliography covering the critical reception of his works from his early years up until 50 years after his death.

Winner, Anthony. *Culture and Irony: Studies in Joseph Conrad's Major Novels.* U. Pr. of Va. 1988 $25.00. ISBN 0-8139-1170-2. A synthesis of Conrad's narrative and his ideas of cultural irony; discusses his portrayal of the collapse of Victorian culture.

COWARD, SIR NOEL (PIERCE). 1899–1973

In 1964, when *Hay Fever* (1925) was placed in the repertory of the newly organized National Theatre, Noel Coward professed to be grateful: "Bless you for admitting that I'm a classic." The admission has by now grown to a chorus of affirmation. A week-long series of Coward played on BBC television in 1969; there have been major revivals in London and New York; plays long out of print have been republished in popular collections. At the start of the 1960s, though, Coward's reputation had been at an ebb, as he skirmished with the angry new drama (he called it the "scratch and mumble school"), which in turn classified him with TERENCE RATTIGAN as a figurehead of the establishment. Coward had enjoyed no big success since *Blithe Spirit* of 1941—a considerable dry spell for a playwright who had once seen five of his plays staged in a single season.

There have been attempts to assimilate the rehabilitated Coward to contemporary drama. Kenneth Tynan, for instance, professed to see a connection between the playwright's famous bare, unepigrammatic dialogue, which depended entirely on the actors for its life, and the style of HAROLD PINTER. And Coward himself profited from the new freedom when, in 1965, his *Song at Twilight* forthrightly discussed homosexuality, a personal subject that he had carefully evaded throughout his career.

There is really no way to take Coward except on his own terms. A juvenile prodigy, he was by turns actor, director, composer, lyricist, autobiographer, and author of nearly 60 theater pieces. He even wrote screenplays, notably for *In Which We Serve* (1942) and *Brief Encounter* (1946). Although he specialized in light comedy, the so-called comedy of manners, he worked in many forms—patriotic spectacle, revue, musical, farce, even the problem play. (He associated *The Vortex*, 1923, a particularly overheated example, with PINERO.) *Hay Fever*, *Blithe Spirit*, and *Private Lives* (1930) have proved to be the most durable of his comedies, along with nine short plays presented as *Tonight at 8:30*. In each, characters demonstrate the combination of perpetual role playing, cool hedonism, and energizing self-absorption—the stance that may be Coward's most enduring creation.

PLAYS BY COWARD

The Lyrics of Noel Coward. Overlook Pr. 1983 repr. of 1965 ed. $25.00. ISBN 0-87951-197-4. Includes a narrative introduction by Coward.

Plays: One. Grove Pr. 1981 o.p. Contains *Hay Fever*, *Fallen Angels*, and *Easy Virtue*.

Plays: Two. Grove Pr. 1981 o.p. Contains *Private Lives*, *Bitter-Sweet (1929 operetta)*, *The Marquise*, and *Post Mortem*. The first of these, a honeymoon farce.

Plays: Three. Grove Pr. 1981 o.p. Contains *Design for Living (1933)*, *Cavalcade*, *Conversation Piece*, and three plays from *Tonight at 8:30 (Hands across the Sea, Still Life*, and *Fumed Oak)*.

Plays: Four. Grove Pr. 1981 o.p. Contains *Blithe Spirit*, *Present Laughter*, *This Happy Breed*, and three plays from *Tonight at 8:30 (Ways and Means, The Astonished Heart*, and *Red Peppers)*.

Plays: Five. Grove Pr. 1983 o.p. Contains *Relative Values*, *Looking after Lulu*, *Waiting in the Wings*, and *Suite in Three Keys*.

Spangled Unicorn. Frisch H. 1982 repr. of 1932 ed. $8.95. ISBN 0-910638-00-4

Three Plays. Grove Pr. 1979 $9.95. ISBN 0-8021-5108-6. Contains *Blithe Spirit*, *Hay Fever*, and *Private Lives*. Introduction by Edward Albee.

NONFICTION BY COWARD

Future Indefinite: An Autobiography. Da Capo 1980 repr. of 1954 ed. $9.95. ISBN 0-306-80126-4

Present Indicative: An Autobiography. Da Capo 1980 repr. of 1947 ed. $9.95. ISBN 0-306-80112-4

BOOKS ABOUT COWARD

Cole, Lesley, Graham Payn, and Sheridan Morley. *Noel Coward and His Friends*. Morrow 1979 o.p. A colorful biography of Coward and his personal life.

Fisher, Clive. *Noel Coward*. St. Martin 1992 $24.95. ISBN 0-312-07044-6. A well-researched and witty biography.

Kiernan, Robert F. *Noel Coward*. Continuum 1986 $15.95. ISBN 0-8044-2456-X. Examines the Coward legend; his comedies of manners, melodramas, and revues.

Levin, Milton. *Noel Coward*. Macmillan 1989 $20.95. ISBN 0-8057-6978-1. Overview of his life; includes a bibliography.

DAVIE, DONALD. 1922–

Along with KINGSLEY AMIS, THOM GUNN, and PHILIP LARKIN, Donald Davie was at the forefront of the poetic school of the 1950s known as the Movement. The group's aesthetic was characterized by simplicity, in contrast to the extravagant rhetoric and stylistic excesses that they felt marked neoromantic poetic trends typified by DYLAN THOMAS. Unlike other Movement poets, though, Davie generally eschews a casual tenor or informal voice, resorting instead to a more traditional prosody and affirming the influence of late Augustan poets.

Hugh Kenner, in *A Sinking Island*, calls Davie the one fine critical intelligence of the Movement. Davie's most durable contribution to poetic debates of the period was a work of literary criticism called *Purity of Diction in English Verse* (1952). The laws of poetic syntax, he argues there, are as momentous as the laws of human society and should be appreciated equally.

Davie was born in Barnsley, a place that figures gloomily in much of his work. He has taught at universities in both Great Britain and the United States.

POETRY BY DAVIE

Brides of Reason. 1955 o.p. A collection of Davie's early poetry.
Collected Poems. U. Ch. Pr. 1991 $40.00. ISBN 0-226-13760-0
Collected Poems, 1950–1970. 1972 o.p. Compilation of poems published in previous collections; includes Davie's descriptive notes for the poems.
Collected Poems, 1970–1983. 1983 o.p. Includes all poems not published in the 1950–1970 edition of collected poems.
To Scorch or Freeze: Poems About the Sacred. U. Ch. Pr. 1988 $24.00. ISBN 0-226-13754-6. Speculates on philosophical and religious themes, using the Psalms as a base.

NONFICTION BY DAVIE

Slavic Excursions: Essays on Russian and Polish Literature. U. Ch. Pr. 1990 $29.95. ISBN 0-226-13758-9
Under Briggflatts: A History of Poetry in Great Britain. U. Ch. Pr. 1989 $24.95. ISBN 0-226-13756-2. A historical survey which also serves as a valuable guide to Davie's own remarkable career as a poet.

BOOK ABOUT DAVIE

Wright, Stuart T. *Donald Davie: A Checklist of His Writings, 1946–1988.* Greenwood 1991 $45.00. ISBN 0-3132-7701-X. Includes Davie's known writings; reviews, notes, translations and recordings.

DE LA MARE, WALTER. 1873–1956

Born in a Kent village, Walter de la Mare grew up with late Victorian tastes, which he never wholly left behind. After he left St. Paul's Cathedral Choir School in London, he joined the London office of the Anglo-American Oil Company (a branch of Standard Oil) as a bookkeeper in 1890. He continued with that firm until 1908, when a Civil List pension enabled him to retire from business and concentrate entirely on writing. Devoted to children's literature and to prose tales as well as to poetry, de la Mare began his career with a volume of children's verse, followed it with a novel, and only in 1906 produced his first book of poetry for adults. *The Listeners and Other Poems* (1912) established his reputation. Other poetry collections include *The Veil* (1921), *Memory and Other Poems* (1938), and *Collected Poems* (1942). Along with adult verse, he continued his interest in prose and in children's literature throughout his career; *Memoirs of a Midget* (1921) is his finest novel. Another well-known novel is *Henry Brocken* (1904), and *On the Edge* (1930) is a notable collection of short stories.

De la Mare's early success was an early casualty of the modernist movement and of the academic criticism (chiefly by the Leavis group in England and the New Critics in the United States) that supported it. They saw him as a typical promulgator of a nineteenth-century dream world detached from modern life. Yet, at his best, de la Mare was more than that, with his pervasive sense of a lost visionary world of childhood or of a symbolic one behind nature coexisting with the frustrations of an unsuccessful quest to recover it. He was also a skilled craftsman and would count both W. H. AUDEN and T. S. ELIOT among the admirers of his technical ability. In some ways, his mixture of formal technique with somewhat conventional appearance recalls the poetry of the Georgians, who respected him and included his verse in their anthologies.

POETRY BY DE LA MARE

A Choice of de la Mare's Verse. Ed. by W. H. Auden. Faber & Faber 1963 o.p.
Collected Poems. Faber & Faber 1979 $19.95. ISBN 0-571-11382-6
Complete Poems. Faber & Faber 1969 o.p.
Peacock Pie: A Book of Rhymes. 1913. Faber & Faber 1988 $8.95. ISBN 0-571-14963-4. Children's verse.
Selected Poems. Ed. by R. N. Green-Armitage. Faber & Faber 1973 o.p.
Songs of Childhood. Dover repr. of 1902 ed. $4.50. ISBN 0-4862-1972-0. His first book of verse.

SHORT STORY COLLECTION BY DE LA MARE

Best Stories of Walter de la Mare. Faber & Faber 1983 o.p. A selection made by the author himself.

NOVELS BY DE LA MARE

Early One Morning. Hippocrene Bks. 1977 repr. of 1935 ed. $49.00. ISBN 0-374-92098-2
Memoirs of a Midget. 1921. AMS Pr. repr. of 1941 ed. $38.00. ISBN 0-404-20076-1. The finest of de la Mare's five novels.

NONFICTION BY DE LA MARE

Pleasures and Speculations. *Essay Index Repr. Ser.* Ayer repr. of 1940 ed. $21.50. ISBN 0-8369-1255-1. A collection of essays.
Private View: Essays on Literature. Hyperion Conn. 1986 repr. of 1953 ed. $25.00. ISBN 0-88355-786-X. Another collection of essays.

BOOKS ABOUT DE LA MARE

Atkins, John Alfred. *Walter de la Mare: An Exploration*. Haskell 1975 $46.95. ISBN 0-8383-2105-4. A short critical appreciation.
McCrosson, Doris Ross. *Walter de la Mare*. Twayne 1966 o.p. Well-written biography, with attention to the writer's short stories, poetry, and novels; includes an overview and bibliography.

DRABBLE, MARGARET. 1939–

Margaret Drabble graduated from Cambridge University, worked for a while as an actress, and then married Clive Swift (an actor). The plots of a number of her novels reflect situations in her own life. *A Summer Bird-Cage* (1963) tells of two sisters. One, very bright, has recently graduated from Oxford University; the other, very pretty, is about to marry. *The Garrick Year* (1964) is based on her experiences in the theatrical world. The heroine of *The Needle's Eye* (1972) is a divorced woman with three children; her involvement with a lawyer leads to

Jamesian subtleties as the moral and spiritual dilemmas of her characters are set forth.

Drabble herself has three children, and the central problem in a number of her books is one that has received a good deal of attention recently: the divided loyalties of a mother who seeks more than the simple joys of family life. Like those of a number of her contemporaries, Drabble's books are written in a traditional novelistic style, with an emphasis on the social and moral issues raised by the predicaments of her characters. She is a feminist and socialist. She has edited some of JANE AUSTEN (whose writings have greatly influenced her own), as well as the fifth edition of the *Oxford Companion to English Literature* (1985). Divorced from Clive Swift in 1972, Drabble was remarried in 1982 to the biographer Michael Holroyd. Her sister is the novelist A.S. BYATT. Among her more recent works are *The Radiant Way* (1987) and *A Natural Curiosity* (1990).

NOVELS BY DRABBLE

The Ice Age. 1977. NAL-Dutton 1985 $7.95. ISBN 0-452-26046-9. An imaginative account of what women think of men and each other.

Jerusalem the Golden. 1967. NAL-Dutton 1987 $8.95. ISBN 0-452-25935-5

The Middle Ground. 1980. Ivy Books 1989 $4.95. ISBN 0-8041-0362-3. Journalistic focus on social and moral dilemmas.

The Millstone. 1965. NAL-Dutton 1989 $7.95. ISBN 0-452-26126-0. Autobiographically resonant story of educated sisters.

A Natural Curiosity. Viking Penguin 1989. $10.00. ISBN 0-14-012228-1. Ironic depiction of post-imperial, post-industrial Britain. A sequel to *The Radiant Way*.

The Needle's Eye. 1972. Ivy Books 1989 $4.95. ISBN 0-8041-0364-X

The Radiant Way. Ivy Books 1987 $4.95. ISBN 0-8041-0365-8

Realms of Gold. 1975. Ivy Books 1989 $4.95. ISBN 0-8041-0363-1. About a divorced woman's journey to Africa; and the journey through the psychology of a family.

A Summer Bird-Cage. 1963. NAL-Dutton 1985 $8.95. ISBN 0-452-26050-7

The Waterfall. 1969. NAL-Dutton 1989 $8.95. ISBN 0-317-02811-1

BOOKS ABOUT DRABBLE

Moran, Mary Hurley. *Margaret Drabble: Existing within Structures.* S. Ill. U. Pr. 1983 $18.95. ISBN 0-8093-1080-5. Examines Drabble's characters' will to survive in a world devoid of freedom, nurturance, and imagination.

Myer, Valerie Grosvenor. *Margaret Drabble: A Reader's Guide.* St. Martin 1991 $24.95. ISBN 0-312-06104-8. Solid reference to Drabble's works.

———. *Margaret Drabble: Puritanism and Permissiveness.* Vision 1974 o.p. Explores influence of Drabble's Quaker background.

Packer, Joan Garrett. *Margaret Drabble: An Annotated Bibliography.* Garland 1988 o.p. Comprehensive list of Drabble's complete writings; includes significant critical and biographical information.

Rose, Ellen Cronan, ed. *Critical Essays on Margaret Drabble.* G. K. Hall 1985 o.p. Analysis of Drabble's cautious feminism, fantasy, and femaleness, and visions of power.

Sadler, Lynn Vetch. *Margaret Drabble.* Macmillan 1986 $19.95. ISBN 0-8057-6907-2. Overview of her life; bibliography.

DURRELL, LAWRENCE. 1912–1990

A prolific and protean writer since the early 1930s, Durrell led a life as rich and varied as his writings. Born of Anglo-Irish parents in Himalayan India, Durrell attended school in England but spent most of his life abroad. Along with numerous odd jobs, he taught at the English Institute in Athens and at the Greek gymnasium on Cyprus; edited (along with HENRY MILLER) a witty and avant-garde magazine in Paris; founded and edited several poetry magazines; worked as press attaché in Egypt and Yugoslavia; and lectured for the British Council in Argentina. The popular success of *The Alexandria Quartet* (1957–60) enabled him to live solely by writing.

Durrell's first important work, *The Black Book* (1938), was greeted by T. S. ELIOT as "the first piece of work by a new English writer to give me any hope for the future of prose fiction." In it, Durrell has said, "I first heard the sound of my own voice. . . . This is an experience no artist ever forgets." *A Chronicle of the English Death* (the book's original subtitle)—spiritual sterility embodied by smug, decadent, cold England—*The Black Book* heralded Durrell's emergence into Greece's warmth, color, and fecundity, the setting for much of his later work. Appropriately, *The Black Book* was unavailable until 1962 in the English-speaking world that it attacked as smug, decadent, and cold.

Durrell's fiction includes two apprentice novels, *Pied Piper of Lovers* (1935) and *Panic Spring* (1937); a psychological mystery set on Crete, *The Dark Labyrinth* (1947); *The Revolt of Aphrodite* (1974); and *The Avignon Quintet* (1974–85). *Aphrodite*, a not wholly successful satire of science fiction, Gothic romance, and business exposé novels, concerns a young inventor's misadventures with modern technology and love. He is constrained to create an exact "living" replica of a beautiful, deceased Greek actress, but the machine—the perfect illusion—commits suicide rather than inhabit the world's harsh reality.

The subject of much controversy, *The Alexandria Quartet* is Durrell's major achievement. It is a self-reflexive novel of great structural complexity; a rich evocation of a cultural crossroads in a time of rapid change (a city "the most various and colorful I could remember"); a political and diplomatic thriller; an analysis of art and love from a myriad of angles; an education and a romance; a fairy tale that *ends* with "Once upon a time . . . ," and many other things— perhaps, above all, a work self-delighted with the rhythms and nuances of language.

The Avignon Quintet shares the *Quartet*'s aesthetic and thematic concerns. One of its narrators tells us that a quincunx is a form bearing mystical meaning derived from the pattern of trees in "an ancient Greek temple grove"—one at each corner of a square and one at the center. The mysticism expresses ancient Gnostic beliefs and relates to the Knights Templar (about whom one of the characters is writing a history), who were destroyed in the early fourteenth century but supposedly left a vast treasure buried at the quincunx's center. All of the characters, who are less vividly conceived than their *Quartet* counterparts, seek some metaphysical treasure or another.

Durrell's other writings include three verse plays with ancient settings, a dozen books of poetry, including his *Collected Poems* (1956), five island books (the best of which, *Bitter Lemons*, 1959, won the Duff Cooper Prize), and several collections of "Sketches from Diplomatic Life." Durrell's brother is Gerald Durrell, a well known zoologist and writer.

NOVELS BY DURRELL

The Alexandria Quartet: Justine, Balthazar, Mountolive, Clea. 1957–60. Viking Penguin 1991 $36.00. ISBN 0-14-015317-9. Lush and erotic Egyptian adventures.

The Avignon Quintet: Monsieur, or, the Prince of Darkness; Livia, or, Buried Alive; Constance, or, Solitary Practices; Sebastian, or, Ruling Passions; Quinx, or, The Ripper's Tale. 1974–85. Viking Penguin o.p.

The Black Book. 1938. Carroll & Graf 1990 $7.95. ISBN 0-88184-600-7

The Dark Labyrinth. 1947. Viking Penguin 1978 o.p.

The Revolt of Aphrodite: Tunc. 1968. Viking Penguin 1979 o.p.

Sauve Qui Peut. 1966. Fr. & Eur. 1972 $10.95. ISBN 0-8288-3791-0. Further accounts of the manic adventures of the "Dips".

POETRY BY DURRELL

Collected Poems. Viking Penguin 1980 o.p.
The Ikons and Other Poems. Black Swan CT 1981 $15.00. ISBN 0-933806-01-9
Vega and Other Poems. Overlook Pr. 1974 $14.95. ISBN 0-87951-009-9

NONFICTION BY DURRELL

Bitter Lemons. 1957. Viking Penguin 1991 $9.00. ISBN 0-14-015318-7. The narrative of his life in a small village on Cypress as civil war erupts.
The Greek Islands. Viking Penguin 1980 $14.95. ISBN 0-14-005661-0. Durrell's personal memoirs and reflections on Greece; illustrated.
Prospero's Cell. 1945. Viking Penguin 1978 o.p. About Corfu.
Reflections on a Marine Venus: A Companion to the Landscape of Rhodes. 1953. Viking Penguin 1978 o.p.
Sicilian Carousel. Viking Penguin 1977 o.p. Chronicles Durrell's travels in Sicily; includes poems and illustrations.
The Spirit of Place: Letters and Essays on Travel. Ed. by Alan G. Thomas. Leefes Isl. 1984 $8.95. ISBN 0-918172-17-9. Eight reproductions of paintings by the author.
Stiff Upper Lip. 1958. NAL-Dutton 1959 o.p. Durrell's account of life among diplomats.
Art and Outrage: A Correspondence about Henry Miller. Porter 1982 o.p. Coauthored with Alfred Perlès.

BOOKS ABOUT DURRELL

Begnal, Michael H. *On Miracle Ground: Essays on the Fiction of Lawrence Durrell.* Bucknell U. Pr. 1990 $35.00. ISBN 0-8387-5158-X. Examines love, incest, and writing; authorial conscience; the writer as painter.
Friedman, Alan Warren. *Critical Essays on Lawrence Durrell.* G. K. Hall 1987 o.p. Analyses of the baroque novel, romantic anachronism, Gnostic heresy, and the quest for wholeness.
Kersnowski, Frank L. *Into the Labyrinth: Essays on the Art of Lawrence Durrell.* Univ. Rochester Pr. 1989 $50.00. ISBN 0-8357-2024-1. Durrell's plays; love, culture, and poetry; his paintings and poetry; Durrell and Henry Miller.
Perlès, Alfred. *My Friend Lawrence Durrell.* Scorpion 1961 o.p. Personal memoir.
Pine, Richard. *The Dandy and the Herald.* St. Martin 1988 $35.00. ISBN 0-312-00521-0
Vander Closter, Susan. *Joyce Cary and Lawrence Durrell: A Reference Guide.* Macmillan 1985 $55.00. ISBN 0-8161-8627-8. Bibliographical sourcebook.
Weigel, John A. *Lawrence Durrell.* Macmillan 1989 $21.95. ISBN 0-8057-6986-2. Overview of his life; bibliography.

ELIOT, T(HOMAS) S(TEARNS). 1888–1965 (NOBEL PRIZE 1948)

Poet, critic, and scholar, T. S. Eliot is considered by many to be a literary genius, a writer who became perhaps the most influential man of letters during the half-century after World War I. Born in St. Louis, Missouri, he traced his descent from Andrew Eliot, who emigrated to Massachusetts from East Coker, Somerset, in the mid-seventeenth century, through a distinguished line of New England forebears. Eliot received his early education at Smith Academy in St. Louis. He then went on to Harvard University, both as undergraduate and graduate student from 1906 to 1914, with time abroad pursuing graduate studies at the Sorbonne, Marburg, and finally Oxford University. The outbreak of World War I prevented him from returning to the United States, and, persuaded by EZRA POUND to remain in England, he decided to settle there permanently. In 1915 he married Vivien Haigh-Wood, but the marriage turned out to be an unhappy one. The two were separated in 1932 but were never divorced. Haigh-Wood died in 1947, however, and Eliot married Valerie Fletcher in 1957.

After marrying Haigh-Wood, Eliot worked first as a schoolteacher and then in the foreign department of Lloyds Bank. During this time he published his influential early criticism, much of it written as occasional pieces for literary periodicals. He developed such doctrines as the "dissociation of sensibility" and the "objective correlative" and elaborated his views on wit and on the relation of tradition to the individual talent. Conceived partly to defend the kind of poetry he was writing, his critical theories shaped the taste of a generation, particularly through their impact on such critics as F. R. Leavis and I. A. Richards in England and the New Critics in America. Under the encouragement of Ezra Pound, Eliot by this time had left his early, derivative verse far behind and had begun to publish avant-garde poetry (including "The Love Song of J. Alfred Prufrock." (1915), which exploited fresh rhythms, abrupt juxtapositions, contemporary subject matter, and witty allusion. This period of creativity also resulted in another collection of verse (which included "Gerontian") and culminated in The Waste Land, a masterpiece published in 1922 and produced partly during a period of psychological breakdown.

In 1922, Eliot became a director of the Faber & Faber publishing house, and in 1927 he became a British citizen and joined the Church of England. Thereafter, his career underwent a change. With the publication of Ash Wednesday in 1930, his poetry became more overtly Christian. As editor of the influential literary magazine The Criterion, he also turned his hand to social as well as literary criticism, with an increasingly conservative orientation. His religious poetry culminated in the great sequence Four Quartets, published individually from 1936 onward and collectively in 1943. This work is considered by most critics to be his greatest poetic achievement. During this period Eliot also wrote poetry in a much lighter vein, such as Old Possum's Book of Practical Cats (1939), a collection that was used during the early 1980s as the basis for the popular Andrew Lloyd Webber musical, Cats. The end of this creative period marked the end of Eliot's poetic career.

In addition to his contributions in poetry and criticism, Eliot is the pivotal verse dramatist of this century. He followed the lead of WILLIAM BUTLER YEATS in attempting to revive metrical language in the theater and left to CHRISTOPHER FRY, after the war, an alternative to realism in dialogue, which nevertheless did not revert to the Shakespeareanizing of the Victorians. But, unlike Yeats (and to some extent Fry), Eliot wanted a dramatic verse that would be self-effacing, an elastic medium capable of expressing the most prosaic passages in a play, and an insistent, undetected presence nevertheless capable of elevating itself at a moment's notice. His progression from the pageant The Rock (1934) and Murder in the Cathedral (1935), written for the Canterbury Festival, through The Family Reunion (1939) and The Cocktail Party (1949), a West End hit, was thus a matter of neutralizing obvious poetic effects and bringing prose passages into the flow of verse.

In contrast to his period of greatest influence, when Eliot's literary views were accepted as gospel, more recent critics have seen him as a more divided figure, often covertly attracted to the very elements (romanticism, personality, heresy) and he overtly condemned. His early attacks on romantic poets, for example, often reveal him as a romantic against the grain, and his work shows the strong impress of his personality. The same divisions carry over into his verse, where violence struggles against restraint, emotion against order, and imagination against ironic detachment. This Eliot is at once more human and

more attractive to contemporary taste. During his lifetime, Eliot received many
honors and awards, including the Nobel Prize for literature in 1948 as "a trail-
blazing pioneer of modern poetry."

POETRY BY ELIOT

Collected Poems, 1909–1962. HarBraceJ 1963 $16.95. ISBN 0-15-118978-1. Eliot's final
collection; fine selection of poems spanning his career.
Four Quartets. 1943. HarBraceJ 1968 $4.95. ISBN 0-15-633225-6. Eliot's last great
sequence.
Old Possum's Book of Practical Cats. HarBraceJ 1982 $11.95. ISBN 0-15-168656-4.
Delightful comic verse on a variety of feline types; the basis for the musical *Cats.*
Poems Written in Early Youth. FS&G 1967 o.p. Juvenilia not included in the collected
editions.
Selected Poems. HarBraceJ 1967 $6.95. ISBN 0-15-680647-9. The best short selection.
*The Waste Land: A Facsimile and Transcript of the Original Drafts, Including the
Annotations of Ezra Pound.* 1922. Ed. by Valerie Eliot. HarBraceJ 1971 $25.00. ISBN
0-15-194760-0

PLAYS BY ELIOT

The Confidential Clerk. HarBraceJ 1964 $6.95. ISBN 0-15-622015-6
The Cocktail Party. 1949. HarBraceJ 1964 $6.95. ISBN 0-15-618289-0
The Elder Statesman. FS&G 1959 o.p.
The Family Reunion. 1939. HarBraceJ 1964 $6.95. ISBN 0-15-630157-1
Murder in the Cathedral. 1935. HarBraceJ 1963 o.p. Based on the murder of Thomas à
Becket, the twelfth century archbishop of Canterbury.

NONFICTION BY ELIOT

Christianity and Culture. HarBraceJ 1960 $7.95. ISBN 0-15-617735-8. Social criticism.
Elizabethan Essays. Gordon Pr. 1973 $250.00. ISBN 0-87968-043-1. Series of critical
essays on Elizabethan playwrights.
On Poetry and Poets. Hippocrene Bks. 1975 repr. of 1957 ed. $21.50. ISBN 0-374-92530-5.
Important collection of critical essays on the state of modern poetry.
Sacred Wood. Routledge Chapman & Hall 1960 $13.95. ISBN 0-416-67610-3. Famous
early collection of prose.
Selected Essays. HarBraceJ 1950 $19.95. ISBN 0-15-180387-0. The most capacious
collection of his prose.
Selected Prose of T. S. Eliot. HarBraceJ 1975 $10.95. ISBN 0-15-180702-7. The best one-
volume selection, with notes by a leading scholar.
To Criticize the Critic and Other Writings. U. of Nebr. Pr. 1992 repr. of 1965 ed. $8.95.
ISBN 0-8032-6721-5. An influential work on literary criticism and critics.
The Use of Poetry and the Use of Criticism. HUP 1986 $6.95. ISBN 0-674-93150-5.
Originally given as the Charles Eliot Norton Lectures at Harvard University,
1932–33.

WORK BY ELIOT

The Complete Poems and Plays, 1909–1950. HarBraceJ 1952 $24.95. ISBN 0-15-
121185-X. Includes the first three of Eliot's five plays.

BOOKS ABOUT ELIOT

Ackroyd, Peter. *T. S. Eliot: A Life.* S & S Trade 1984 o.p. Extremely readable biography
that also explicates much of Eliot's poetry.
Bagchee, Shyamal. *T. S. Eliot: A Voice Descanting: Centenary Essays.* St. Martin 1990
$39.95. ISBN 0-312-03697-3. Investigates Eliot and Poe; Eliot's use of *vers libre*; the
mutations of objectivity; and the drama of images in *The Waste Land.*

Bush, Ronald. *T. S. Eliot: A Study in Character and Style.* OUP 1983 $25.00. ISBN 0-19-503376-0. Examines the tension between romantic yearning and compulsive intellectual detachment in Eliot's life and poetry.

Browne, E. Martin. *The Making of T. S. Eliot's Plays.* Cambridge U. Pr. 1969 $54.50. ISBN 0-521-07372-3. Invaluable textual and performance details about the plays by the man who directed them.

Gallup, Donald Clifford. *T. S. Eliot: A Bibliography.* HarBraceJ 1969 o.p. Primary sources and translations.

Gordon, Lyndall. *Eliot's Early Years.* 1977. FS&G 1988 $8.95. ISBN 0-374-52110-7. First of two volumes considered to be the definitive biographical study.

_____. *Eliot's New Life.* FS&G 1989 $19.95. ISBN 0-374-14741-8. Second of two-volume biography.

Kearns, Cleo McNelly. *T. S. Eliot and Indic Traditions: A Study in Poetry and Belief.* Cambridge U. Pr. 1987 $44.95. ISBN 0-521-32439-4. Examines Hindu and Buddhist traditions in Eliot's writing, metaphysics, and wisdom.

Malamud, Randy. *T. S. Eliot's Drama: A Research and Production Sourcebook.* Greenwood 1992 $49.95. ISBN 0-313-27813-X. Surveys production details and critical reception of Eliot's seven plays; traces other aspects of Eliot's dramatic career.

Martin, Mildred. *A Half-Century of Eliot Criticism: An Annotated Bibliography of Books and Articles in English, 1916–1965.* Bucknell U. Pr. 1975 $45.00. ISBN 0-8387-7808-9. An important reference of secondary sources dealing with Eliot and his work.

Olney, James, ed. *T. S. Eliot: Essays from the Southern Review.* OUP 1988 $45.00. ISBN 0-19-818575-8. Surveys the concept of literary influence and Eliot's language of theory and of poetry.

Pinkney, Tony. *Women in the Poetry of T. S. Eliot: A Psychoanalytic Approach.* Macmillan 1984 o.p. Interesting analysis of Eliot's female characters and his misogyny.

Reibetanz, Julia Maniates. *A Reading of Eliot's Four Quartets.* Bks. Demand 1983 o.p. Detailed and incisive exegesis of Eliot's final poetic sequence.

Ricks, Beatrice. *T. S. Eliot: A Bibliography of Secondary Works.* Scarecrow 1980 $35.00. ISBN 0-8108-1262-2. Contains references to many important critical studies of Eliot.

Ricks, Christopher. *T. S. Eliot and Prejudice.* U. CA Pr. 1989 $25.00. ISBN 0-520-06578-6. Exhaustively examines the roots of Eliot's prejudices.

Riquelme, John Paul. *Harmony of Dissonances: T. S. Eliot, Romanticism and Imagination.* Johns Hopkins 1990 $36.00. ISBN 0-8018-4058-9. Examines imagination, allegory, and wit; writing as Heraclitean process.

Roby, Kinley, ed. *Critical Essays on T. S. Eliot: The Sweeney Motif.* G. K. Hall 1985 o.p. Essays about the shadowy character of Sweeney in Eliot's early poems and his play, *Sweeney Agonistes.*

Scofield, Martin. *T. S. Eliot: The Poems.* Cambridge U. Pr. 1988 o.p. Survey, with attention to Eliot's patterns and beliefs.

Sigg, Eric Whitman. *The American T. S. Eliot: A Study of the Early Writings.* Cambridge U. Pr. 1989 $39.95. ISBN 0-521-36561-9. Studies Eliot's debt to American literary traditions.

Smith, Carol H. *T. S. Eliot's Dramatic Theory and Practice: From* Sweeney Agonistes *to* The Elder Statesman. Gordian 1977 repr. of 1963 ed. $50.00. ISBN 0-87752-201-4. The definitive study of Eliot's drama; examines parallel levels of meaning in each of the plays.

Williams, Geoffrey Bernard. *The Reason in a Storm: A Study of the Use of Ambiguity in the Writings of T. S. Eliot.* Univ. Pr. of Amer. 1991 $49.00. ISBN 0-8191-8270-2. Explores Eliot's language of transcendence; erasure of meaning; and the limits of language.

FIRBANK, (ARTHUR ANNESLEY) RONALD. 1886–1926

Born in London, the son of a wealthy businessman, Firbank was educated at Uppingham and Cambridge University. In 1909 he converted to Roman Catholicism and left the university without taking a degree. Instead, he embarked on extensive travels in Spain, Italy, the Middle East, and North Africa.

By nature he was a rather solitary individual, perhaps due to his rather delicate health and his homosexuality. Firbank's first novel, *Vainglory* (1915), was originally published privately, as were other early works. He wrote his novels on blue postcards; though slight, these works were innovative and prefigured the works of such writers as IVY COMPTON-BURNETT and EVELYN WAUGH.

EDMUND WILSON called Firbank "one of the finest English writers of his period." Firbank lived the life of a leisured aesthete and died, still a young man, in Rome. His original and subtle novels have appealed to a small but appreciative audience, and, during the 1950s and early 1960s, he "posthumously acquired a band of devoted disciples." Firbank had a fine disdain for plot and a taste for eccentric characters. "All in all, a felicity, undisturbed by fugues and hints of nonfulfillment, reigns over his novels. There can be no doubt that Firbank has earned his niche of fame. . . . As literature goes, it is a small and creditable world, a true one, looking back at the reader with laughter and sorrow" (*TLS*). From Firbank descend elements in the work of Waugh, Compton-Burnett, ALDOUS HUXLEY, ANGUS WILSON, and IRIS MURDOCH. *The Complete Ronald Firbank* (1961), with a preface by Anthony Powell, is a worthwhile edition of his works.

NOVELS BY FIRBANK

Five Novels. 1949. New Dir. Pr. 1981 $12.95. ISBN 0-8112-0799-4. Contains *Valmouth, The Artificial Princess, The Flower beneath the Foot, The Prancing Nigger*, and *Cardinal Pirelli*. Introduction by O. Sitwell.
The Prancing Nigger. 1924. Biblio Dist. 1977 o.p.
Valmouth. 1919. Biblio Dist. 1977 o.p. Wealthy wastrels at a health spa.

BOOKS ABOUT FIRBANK

Benkovitz, Miriam J. *A Bibliography of Ronald Firbank*. OUP 1982 o.p. A comprehensive annotated sourcebook of materials by and about Firbank.
———. *Ronald Firbank: A Biography*. Knopf 1969 o.p. An interesting, readable account of Firbank's life and work.
Brophy, Brigid. *Prancing Novelist: A Defence of Fiction in the Form of a Critical Biography in Praise of Ronald Firbank*. B & N Imports 1973 o.p. A stirring homage to Firbank.
Firbankiana: Being a Collection of Reminscences on the Life of Ronald Firbank. Hanuman Bks. 1989 $4.95. ISBN 0-937815-29-2
Kiernan, Robert F. *Frivolity Unbound: Six Masters of the Camp Novel*. Continuum 1990 $18.95. ISBN 0-8264-0465-0. A flamboyant and illuminating look at Firbank and five other writers (Wodehouse, Beerbohm, Compton-Burnett, Peacock, and E. F. Benson).
Merritt, James Douglas. *Ronald Firbank*. Twayne 1969 o.p. Overview of his life; bibliography.

FORD, FORD MADOX (originally Ford Madox Hueffer). 1873–1939

Ford, who changed his German name legally in 1919, was a grandson of the painter Ford Madox Brown, who, together with his cousins CHRISTINA and DANTE GABRIEL ROSSETTI, founded the Pre-Raphaelite Brotherhood. While helping JOSEPH CONRAD master English, Ford collaborated with him on *The Inheritors* (1901) and *The Nature of a Crime* (1924). Ford established the *English Review* in 1908. Among its distinguished contributors were Conrad, THOMAS HARDY, JOHN GALSWORTHY, JOHN MASEFIELD, and WILLIAM JAMES. In 1922 he founded in Paris one of the most influential "little magazines" of the twentieth century, *The Transatlantic Review*. In it, he "discovered" JAMES JOYCE and ERNEST HEMINGWAY. His reminiscences, *Return to Yesterday* (1931), are a valuable record of these editorial years; the volume was suppressed in England because it quotes King George V as threatening to abdicate the throne.

Ford's masterpiece is *The Good Soldier* (1915), a work that many critics number among the finest British novels of the century. This novel contains an outstanding example of what Ford and Conrad called *progression d'effet*, a technique for the chronological rearrangement of incidents in a story in order to provide the greatest emotional impact on the reader. Ford's *Parade's End* (1924–28), a tetralogy set primarily in England during World War I, is a major achievement on a grand scale. Even more than the war, Ford's concern in these novels is a study of the psychology and interrelationships of people going through violent change.

Ford's reputation grew slowly, perhaps because of his association with so many of the great literary figures of his time. His *Portraits from Life* (1960) contains memories and criticisms of HENRY JAMES, Conrad, Hardy, H. G. WELLS, D. H. LAWRENCE, Galsworthy, and others. But, as shown in some of the recent critical appraisals, Ford is now considered an innovator, a major twentieth-century novelist. He also wrote several volumes of literary criticism, including *The March of Literature* (1938), his last published work.

NOVELS BY FORD

The Fifth Queen. 1906. Ecco Pr. 1986 $12.95. ISBN 0-88001-101-7. Contains *The Fifth Queen, Privy Seal, The Fifth Queen Crowned*—a trilogy based on the life of Catherine Howard, wife of King Henry VIII.

The Good Soldier. 1915. Peter Smith 1992 $19.50. ISBN 0-8446-6637-8. A "Tale of Passion" with an interpretation by Mark Schorer. A story of tangled romances and marriages, probably his best novel.

Parade's End. 1924-28. Knopf 1992 $19.50. ISBN 0-679-41728-1. The four novels of "The Tietjans Saga": *Some Do Not, No More Parades, A Man Could Stand Up, The Last Post.*

The Rash Act. Century Bookbindery 1982 repr. of 1933 ed. o.p.

POETRY BY FORD

Collected Poems. AMS Pr. repr. of 1914 ed. $21.00. ISBN 0-404-17114-1. The definitive edition of Ford's poetry.

NONFICTION BY FORD

It Was the Nightingale. 1933. Ecco Pr. 1984 $9.50. ISBN 0-88001-034-7. A memoir.

No Enemy. Ecco Pr. 1984 repr. of 1929 ed. $8.50. ISBN 0-88001-062-2

Return to Yesterday. 1931. Liveright 1983 $7.95. ISBN 0-87140-271-8. Early memoirs.

Thus to Revisit: Some Reminiscences. Hippocrene Bks. 1966 o.p. Memoirs revealing many facets of Ford's life and work.

BOOKS ABOUT FORD

Cassell, Richard A. *Critical Essays on Ford Madox Ford*. Macmillan 1987 $35.00. ISBN 0-8161-8761-4. Examines historical novels and romances; images of collapse and reconstruction; Ford as impressionist.

Green, Robert. *Ford Madox Ford: Prose and Politics*. Cambridge U. Pr. 1981 o.p. Ford's novels as vehicles for his political agenda.

Hoffmann, Charles G. *Ford Madox Ford*. Macmillan 1989 $23.95. ISBN 0-8057-6987-0. Overview of his life; bibliography.

Huntley, H. Robert. *The Alien Protagonist of Ford Madox Ford*. U. of NC Pr. 1970 o.p. Examines the alien ethics and temperaments of Ford's protagonists.

Lindberg-Seyerstad, Brita, ed. *Pound-Ford: The Story of a Literary Friendship*. New Dir. Pr. 1982 $22.95. ISBN 0-8112-0833-8. The personal and professional relations of the two writers.

MacShane, Frank. *Ford Madox Ford: The Critical Heritage*. Routledge 1972 $69.50. ISBN 0-7100-6957-X. Contemporary reviews and responses.

Mizener, Arthur. *The Saddest Story: A Biography of Ford Madox Ford*. Carroll & Graf 1985 o.p.

Moser, Thomas. *The Life in the Fiction of Ford Madox Ford*. Princeton U. Pr. 1980 $96.50. ISBN 0-8357-4645-3. Psychobiographical interpretation of Ford's writing.

Snitow, Ann Barr. *Ford Madox Ford and the Voice of Uncertainty*. La. State U. Pr. 1984 $32.50. ISBN 0-8071-1113-9. Explores Ford's comedy, irony, and ambiguity.

Stang, Sondra J. *The Presence of Ford Madox Ford: A Memorial Volume of Essays*. U. of Pa. Pr. 1981 o.p. Topics include Ford as literary critic; the artist as propagandist; memoirs and impressions of Ford.

FORSTER, E(DWARD) M(ORGAN). 1879–1970

E. M. Forster is noted for "the easy grace and lucidity of his style; his humor, his good taste, the wise humanism of his outlook" (C. J. Rolo, *Atlantic*). His *Collected Tales* display wit and irony in the use of fantasy, of which "The Celestial Omnibus" (1914) is a most delightful example. His most popular book, *A Passage to India* (1924), won both the James Tait Black and the Femina-Vie Heureuse prizes. It is a brilliant, discerning study of the British-Indian dilemma well before the days of Indian independence. The play *A Passage to India* opened in London in 1960 and on Broadway in 1962.

Howard's End (1910), another very fine novel, deals with the problems of the changing English class structure. *Maurice*, about homosexual love, was suppressed during the author's lifetime and published posthumously in 1972. Forster's last three novels are serious and deal with important social problems. His earlier novels often have similar concerns but are less successful. The best of these is *A Room with a View* (1908), which contrasts English gravity and Italian lightheartedness; the book is warm, witty, and sensitive. Several of Forster's novels, including *A Passage to India*, *A Room With a View*, and *Howard's End*, have been made into movies.

His most important critical work is *Aspects of the Novel* (1927), long considered a classic on the art of fiction. *Two Cheers for Democracy* (1951) is divided into two parts, "The Second Darkness" (political reflections) and "What I Believe" (his faith in the arts and personal relationships). *Abinger Harvest* (1936) is "one of the most notable miscellanies of our time" (JOHN CROWE RANSOM, *Yale Review*)—a collection of articles, essays reviews, and poems. In 1953, Forster received high recognition for his work from the queen—the Order of Companion of Honor. Until his death in 1970, he lived quietly in a small apartment in King's College, Cambridge, where he was an honorary fellow.

NOVELS BY FORSTER

The Abinger Edition of E. M. Forster. 9 vols. Ed. by Oliver Stallybrass. HarBraceJ 1978–83 o.p. The best scholarly and textual edition of Forster's novels.

Howard's End. 1910. Buccaneer Bks. 1981 $23.95. ISBN 0-89966-301-X. Antiquated patrilineage versus modern moralities.

The Longest Journey. 1907. Buccaneer Bks. 1989 $27.95. ISBN 0-89966-632-9. A philosophical novel.

Maurice. Buccaneer Bks. 1990 $25.95. ISBN 0-89966-751-1. Posthumously published story of homosexual romance.

A Passage to India. 1924. Buccaneer Bks. 1981 $25.95. ISBN 0-89966-300-1. Personal exploration of colonial inequities and oppression.

A Room with a View. 1908. Buccaneer Bks. 1987 $23.95. ISBN 0-89966-607-8. Romance of the English in Italy.

Where Angels Fear to Tread. 1905. Random 1992 $9.00. ISBN 0-679-73634-4. A story of love and passion in Italy.

Short Story Collections by Forster

Collected Tales of E. M. Forster. Knopf 1947 $19.95. ISBN 0-394-41978-2
The Eternal Moment and Other Stories. HarBraceJ 1970 repr. of 1928 ed. $4.95. ISBN 0-15-629125-8
The Life to Come: And Other Stories. Norton 1987 $8.95. ISBN 0-393-30442-6. Introduction by Oliver Stallybrass.

Books about Forster

Das, G. K. *Forster's India*. Macmillan 1977 o.p. Cultural background of *Passage to India*.
Finkelstein, Bonnie Blumenthal. *Forster's Women: Eternal Differences*. Col. U. Pr. 1975 o.p. Forster's treatment of female characters.
Furbank, P. N. *E. M. Forster: A Life*. HarBraceJ 1981 $8.95. ISBN 0-15-628651-3. Considered the definitive biography.
Herz, Judith Scherer. *The Short Narratives of E. M. Forster*. St. Martin 1988 $29.95. ISBN 0-312-00912-7. Forster's "writing between genres": Mythic fictions and narrative modes.
King, Francis. *E. M. Forster and His World*. Scribner 1978 o.p. Biography and overview of Forster's contemporary sensibility.
Kirkpatrick, B. J. *A Bibliography of E. M. Forster*. OUP 1985 $84.00. ISBN 0-19-818191-4. A very useful annotated sourcebook of materials by and about Forster.
Shahane, Vasant Anant. *Approaches to E. M. Forster: A Centenary Volume*. Humanities 1981 o.p. Hellenic heroines; Forster on love and liberty; Indian themes.
Summers, Claude J. *E. M. Forster: A Guide to Research*. Garland 1991 $48.00. ISBN 0-8240-4624-2.
Wilde, Alan. *Critical Essays on E. M. Forster*. G. K. Hall 1985 $40.00. ISBN 0-8161-8754-1. Questions of morality and sexuality; fiction as history; treatments of the major novels.

FOWLES, JOHN. 1926–

John Fowles's first novel, *The Collector* (1963), is a "psychological thriller" about a lower-class young man who wins a lottery and thus is able to afford the expenses of acting out a fantasy: He abducts a pretty, talented girl whom he has admired from afar. Fowles is good at maintaining suspense and in providing realistic details of the kidnapping; however, his understandable distaste for the demented protagonist limits the psychological depth of his characterizations. In *The Magus* (1966), as in *The Collector*, Fowles is concerned with the issues of enslavement, moral responsibility and perspective, and psychological aberration.

The French Lieutenant's Woman (1969), perhaps Fowles's best-known book because of the excellent movie made from it, takes place in Lyme Regis, the small seacoast village where he makes his home. The time, setting, and plot of the novel are old-fashioned: a story about a betrayed woman who lived 100 years ago. But this is much more than the remake of a Victorian novel; Fowles's narrator often reminds the reader that he lives in the twentieth century—anachronisms, philosophical speculations, parodies, and literary allusions are all used to provide a very modern effect. The novel is that rare beast—a work that utilizes unconventional techniques and still manages to get onto the bestseller lists. *The Aristos* (1964) is an essay in which Fowles sets forth the ideas that concern him most; prominent among these is his elevation of an ideal of excellence, which, he says, should always be at the core of an artist's motivating instinct. Those who can achieve only mediocrity despise excellence: It intimidates them. The artist's struggle, therefore, is not only to achieve excellence in his or her own works but also to resist damaging or envious criticism from inferiors. Fowles, who published a collection of poems written over the course of 20 years, has said that he considers poetry a relief after the rigors of writing fiction.

NOVELS BY FOWLES

The Collector. Little 1963 $17.95. ISBN 0-316-29096-3. A novel of kidnapping, sexual oppression, and psychological deviance.
Daniel Martin. Little 1977 $19.95. ISBN 0-316-28959-0. A story about a writer's past.
The French Lieutenant's Woman. Little 1969 $24.95. ISBN 0-316-29099-8. A romance juxtaposing Victorian and modern sensibilities.
The Magus. 1966. Little 1978 $19.95. ISBN 0-316-29092-0. Occult quest.
Mantissa. Little 1982 $16.95. ISBN 0-316-28980-9
Shipwreck. Little 1983 $9.95. ISBN 0-316-29091-2. An exciting maritime adventure.

SHORT STORY COLLECTIONS BY FOWLES

The Ebony Tower. Little 1974 $19.95. ISBN 0-316-29093-9
Islands. Little 1979 $10.95. ISBN 0-316-28960-4
The Tree. Ecco Pr. 1983 $13.50. ISBN 0-88001-040-1

POETRY BY FOWLES

Poems. Ecco Pr. 1973 $7.50. ISBN 0-912946-03-2

NONFICTION BY FOWLES

The Aristos. 1964. Little 1970 $14.95. ISBN 0-316-29094-7

BOOKS ABOUT FOWLES

Aubrey, James R. *John Fowles: A Reference Companion.* Greenwood 1991 $49.95. ISBN 0-3132-6399-X. Sourcebook and overview.
Cooper, Pamela. *The Fictions of John Fowles: Power, Creativity, Femininity.* Univ. of Ottawa Pr. 1991 o.p. Feminist analysis of power and freedom in Fowles's writing.
Olshen, Barry N. *John Fowles.* Continuum 1978 o.p. One in a series of reference guides, with plot summaries of each of John Fowles's works.
_____. *John Fowles: A Reference Guide.* G. K. Hall 1980 o.p. Bibliographical sourcebook.
Onega Jaen, Susana. *Form and Meaning in the Novels of John Fowles.* Univ. Rochester Pr. 1989 $50.00. ISBN 0-8357-1949-9. Fowles's solution to the tension between realism and experimentalism; metafictional mechanisms and parody.
Pifer, Ellen. *Critical Essays on John Fowles.* G. K. Hall 1986 $40.00. ISBN 0-8161-8759-2. Existence as authorship; Fowles's tarot quest; unities in his fiction; a deconstructive interpretation.
Salami, Mahmoud. *John Fowles's Fiction and the Poetics of Postmodernism.* Fairleigh Dickinson 1992 $42.50. ISBN 0-8386-3446-X. Narrative and imprisonment; history, ideology, and politics of seduction; philosophy and history as narratives.
Tarbox, Katherine. *The Art of John Fowles.* U. of Ga. Pr. 1988 o.p. Analysis of Fowles's fiction in terms of his demand that the reader "see whole."
Woodcock, Bruce. *Male Mythologies: John Fowles and Masculinity.* B & N Imports 1984 $44.50. ISBN 0-389-20497-8. Investigates the notion of masculinity in Fowles's work and how he attempts to escape the script of gender.

FRIEL, BRIAN. 1929–

A schoolteacher until his stories achieved recognition in *The New Yorker*, Brian Friel has maintained a transatlantic reputation with his plays. His American debut piece was *Philadelphia, Here I Come!* (1964), the story of Gar, an Irish youth about to leave, reluctantly, for America. Gar's "public" and "private" faces, hopeful and hopeless, were played by two actors. In the year of *Philadelphia*'s long run, 1966, *The Loves of Cass McGuire* failed in New York, but it became a solid hit the next year in Dublin. Appropriately, it concerns a disillusioned old woman who returns to Ireland after a half-century's stay in America. Friel's 1967–68 triumph in Dublin was *Lovers*, which ended its run only to make room for the Dublin Drama Festival. Consisting of two one-acters, *Winners* (a sort of tragedy) and *Losers* (called "hilarious"), it opened at Lincoln Center in 1968. Also in that year, *Crystal and Fox*, concerning the private life of a traveling show company, was produced in Dublin and Los Angeles. The Abbey Theatre maintained a deplorable tradition by turning down Friel's next play, *The Munday Scheme*. But the political satire (in which it is proposed that the West of Ireland be converted for profit into an international cemetery) eventually took the stage, both in Dublin and New York, in 1969.

Inevitably, Friel came to the subject of Northern Ireland's troubles. *The Freedom of the City* (1973) confronts the problem directly, but in a more recent approach, the playwright utilized the form of a historical analogy. *Translations* (1980) represents the encounter of peasants and Royal Engineers on a survey in the Donegal of 150 years ago. A London success, it was transferred from a Hampstead stage to the National Theatre. Other recent works include *Dancing at Lughnasa*, which had a run on Broadway in New York, and *Aristocrats* (1988).

PLAYS BY FRIEL

The Communication Cord. Faber & Faber 1983 o.p.
Dancing at Lughnasa. Faber & Faber 1991 $8.95. ISBN 0-571-14479-9. About three Irish spinster sisters and the people who come and go from their lives.
The Faith Healer. Faber & Faber 1980 o.p. About people's desperate search for salvation.
Living Quarters. Faber & Faber 1978 o.p.
Philadelphia, Here I Come! 1964. FS&G 1966 o.p.
Selected Plays of Brian Friel. Cath. U. Pr. 1986 $33.50. ISBN 0-8132-0626-X. With an introduction by Seamus Deane.
Two Plays. FS&G 1970 o.p.
Translations. Faber & Faber 1980 o.p.
Volunteers. Faber & Faber 1980 o.p.

SHORT STORY COLLECTION BY FRIEL

The Diviner. Graywolf 1990 $7.95. ISBN 1-55597-141-5

BOOKS ABOUT FRIEL

Maxwell, D.E.S. *Brian Friel*. Bucknell U. Pr. 1973 $1.95. ISBN 0-8387-7666-3. Themes and variations; private conversation and public address.
O'Brien, George. *Brian Friel*. Macmillan 1989 $23.95. ISBN 0-7171-1737-5. Focuses on the uncompromising humanity of Friel's vision.
Pine, Richard. *Brian Friel and Ireland's Drama*. Routledge 1990 $69.95. ISBN 0-415-04753-6. Nationalist themes and characteristics of Friel's plays.

FRY, CHRISTOPHER (born Christopher Harris). 1907–

Success came to Christopher Fry after 38 years of living close to poverty. He was born in Bristol, where his father, a poor architect, turned to lay missionary work in the slums. In 1940, after alternating between teaching and acting, Fry became the director of the excellent Oxford Playhouse. As a Quaker conscientious objector, he refused to bear arms in World War II.

He was first discovered by critics and connoisseurs in 1946, when a small London theater staged *A Phoenix Too Frequent*, his version of the perennial story of the widow who accepts a new lover while mourning beside her husband's grave. Three years later, John Gielgud's production of *The Lady's Not for Burning* (1949) brought Fry popular success in London and the provinces. This clever medieval conceit was produced in New York, and received the Drama Critics Circle Award for 1950. Sir Laurence Olivier commissioned *Venus Observed* (1950), a play about middle age, the autumn section of what has come to be a cycle of seasonal plays. The winter play, *The Dark Is Light Enough* (1954), followed two years later. Set in 1848, during the Hungarian revolution against the Austrian empire, it takes a moral stand against any use of violence. (An antiwar morality play, *A Sleep of Prisoners*, had been produced in 1951.) It was more than a decade before Fry's summer comedy, *A Yard of Sun* (1970), was published.

Fry's relation to T. S. ELIOT is interesting. Like him, Fry is a Christian verse dramatist. He has set a play (like Eliot) in a church (*A Sleep of Prisoners*); he has written a historical study of Becket and Henry II (*Curtmantle*, 1962). And, like Eliot, Fry has achieved a loose, speakable verse. Yet their differences are equally instructive. Fry's verse, unlike Eliot's functional amble, strives to be poetic, with flamboyant energy and arresting wit. The same theatricality is evident in, say, his Becket play, in which he replaces the introspection of Eliot's martyr with the strong clash of personalities. *The Lady's Not for Burning*—which was performed alongside Eliot's *The Cocktail Party* (1949) in 1949—is a downright, if intellectual, comedy, unlike the dry drawing-room enigma of Eliot.

As a translator-adaptor, Fry seems almost single-handedly responsible for the postwar English vogue of modern French writers. His version of JEAN GIRAUDOUX's (see Vol. 2) *The Trojan War Will Not Take Place* (a transatlantic success in 1959, when it was retitled *Tiger at the Gates*) was revived at the National Theatre in 1984, directed by HAROLD PINTER. Fry is also a screenwriter (John Huston's *The Bible*, William Wyler's *Ben Hur*) and composer.

PLAYS BY FRY

The Dark is Light Enough. Dramatists Play 1990 $4.75. ISBN 0-8222-0272-7
The Firstborn. 1948. Dramatists Play 1990 $4.75. ISBN 0-8222-0403-7
The Lady's Not for Burning. Dramatists Play 1990 $4.75. ISBN 0-8222-0630-7
One Thing More, or Caedmon Construed. Dramatists Play 1987 $4.75. ISBN 0-8222-0854-7
A Phoenix Too Frequent. 1946. Dramatists Play 1990 $2.75. ISBN 0-8222-0891-1
Selected Plays. OUP 1985 $15.95. ISBN 0-19-281873-2
A Sleep of Prisoners. Dramatists Play 1990 $4.75. ISBN 0-8222-1040-1
Venus Observed. Dramatists Play 1990 $4.75. ISBN 0-8222-1206-4. An astronomer learns to accept impermanence.
A Yard of Sun. OUP 1970 o.p.

BOOKS ABOUT FRY

Buning, Sietze. *More Than the Ear Discovers: God in the Plays of Christopher Fry*. Loyola 1983 o.p. Explores Fry's religion, ethics, theology.
Leeming, Glenda. *Christopher Fry*. Macmillan 1990 $22.95. ISBN 0-8057-6998-6. Overview of his life; bibliography.

FULLER, ROY. 1912–1991

Like the American WALLACE STEVENS, Roy Fuller pursued simultaneous careers as writer and solicitor. Born of a middle-class family in Lancashire (his father managed a factory), he qualified as a solicitor in 1933 and spent most of his career with the Woolwich Equitable Building Society, of which he became a director in 1959. He married in 1936 and during the war served as a radar mechanic with the Royal Navy. From 1968 to 1973, he was a professor of poetry at Oxford University, and in 1972 became a governor of the BBC. Besides poetry, Fuller wrote numerous novels, including several for children, and some literary criticism. His only child is the poet and critic John Fuller.

Fuller first came to notice as a war poet during World War II. He named W. H. AUDEN as a major influence on his verse, which in its regular form and restrained tone ultimately harks back to the English tradition of THOMAS HARDY. Always conscious of the relationship between poetry and society, Fuller sought a steady accessibility rather than recondite arcana. He often wrote of domestic or natural subjects and resisted what he saw as the debasement of traditional English culture. Fuller's inclusion in Robert Conquest's 1961 anthology *New Poetry* resulted in his being viewed as part of the loose grouping of postwar poets known as the Movement.

POETRY BY FULLER

Buff: Poems. Dufour 1965 o.p.

Collected Poems. Dufour 1962 $18.95. ISBN 0-8023-1046-X. Collection of Fuller's early poetry.

From the Joke Shop. Dufour 1975 o.p. Observations of contemporary culture.

The Individual and His Times: A Selection of the Poetry of Roy Fuller. Ed. by V. J. Lee. Humanities 1982 $8.95. ISBN 0-485-61008-6. Wide-ranging selection of poetry.

New Poems. Dufour 1968 $14.95. ISBN 0-8023-1180-6. Series of poems about ordinary daily life.

Professors and Gods. St. Martin 1974 $20.00. ISBN 0-312-64785-9

The Second Curtain. Academy Chi. Pubs. 1986 repr. of 1962 ed. $5.95. ISBN 0-89733-197-4

Souvenirs. St. Mut. 1980 o.p. Poems about truth and hope.

NOVEL BY FULLER

Stares. Trafalgar 1991 $22.95. ISBN 1-85619-008-0. Story of an actor's stay at a psychiatric facility.

NONFICTION BY FULLER

Owls and Artificers: Oxford Lectures on Poetry. Open Court 1971 o.p. Important collection of criticism.

Spanner and Pen: An Autobiography. Trafalgar 1991 $29.95. ISBN 1-85619-040-4

BOOK ABOUT FULLER

Austin, Allan E. *Roy Fuller. Twayne's Eng. Authors Ser.* G. K. Hall 1979 o.p. Standard biography; with an annotated bibliography.

GALSWORTHY, JOHN. 1867–1933 (NOBEL PRIZE 1932)

At age 28, after a gentlemanly education at Harrow and Oxford, and a training at law (that links him with British playwrights from ARTHUR WING PINERO to JOHN MORTIMER), Galsworthy settled into simultaneous careers as a novelist and a playwright. He was encouraged in this endeavor by Ada Galsworthy, who was unhappily married to his cousin. The two also began a relationship that eventually, after her divorce, resulted in their marriage in 1905.

The Silver Box, Galsworthy's first successful drama, was staged in 1906, the year he published the first volume of what was to become *The Forsyte Saga*.

His one-word titles—*Justice* (1910), *Strife* (1909), *Loyalties* (1922)—suggest the nature of Galsworthy's artistic ambition: to generalize a social indictment, keeping faith with the objective methods of naturalism. Systematically, without any apparent imaginative will toward a particular subject, his drama turns a cold eye on a series of institutional problems: "One law for the rich and one for the poor" (*The Silver Box*); the futility of charity in relieving the "submerged tenth" (*The Pigeon*, 1912); the counterclaims of capital and labor (*Strife*); the intersections of class, race, family, and friendship (*Loyalties*); and nationalistic jingoism (*Mob*). In each Galsworthy favors an austere irony and unresolvable situations, and balanced moral positions are displayed in the cabinetwork of "well-made" playwrighting. Reputed to have led to reforms in its time, his realism today seems contrived to produce aesthetic distance and a sense of resignation that is precisely what contemporary political dramatists strain hardest to avoid. Not surprisingly, critics have come away from revivals with the sense that (especially in his spare language) Galsworthy anticipates HAROLD PINTER rather than more socially engaged playwrights.

Galsworthy wrote novels and plays alternately throughout his life. His masterwork, *The Forsyte Saga*, begun in 1906 and finished in 1928, and consisting of six separate novels and two linking interludes, is the most famous example of the sequence novel in English literature. It is a study of the property sense, the possessive spirit, in different individuals and generations of English middle-class society. He also completed a second trilogy dealing with the Forsyte family, called *A Modern Comedy* (1928). His last trilogy, a study of the Charwell family, is called *End of the Chapter* (1933).

Galsworthy's later years brought him many honors, including the presidency of P.E.N. and honorary degrees from Oxford, Cambridge, and several other universities. After World War I, he was offered a knighthood, which he refused. He did, however, accept the Order of Merit in 1929, and in 1932 he was awarded the Nobel Prize. He was, however, too ill to attend the Nobel ceremony and died within two months of receiving the award.

Although his posthumous reputation had waned, the centenary of his death, in 1967, brought a re-creation of *The Forsyte Saga* on British and American television in serial form. Interest in him skyrocketed, and the Forsyte novels again became bestsellers. With new popularity came fresh critical analysis. Pamela Hansford Johnson called *The Forsyte Saga* "a work of profound social insight and patchy psychological insight" (*N.Y. Times*). His critical writings include *The Inn of Tranquility: Studies and Essays* (1911) and *Author and Critic*.

NOVELS BY GALSWORTHY

Captures. Scholarly 1971 repr of 1923 ed. $29.00. ISBN 0-403-00973-1
Dark Flower. 1913. Scholarly 1971 repr. of 1923 ed. $39.00. ISBN 0-403-00974-X
Five Tales. 1915. Scholarly 1971 repr. of 1918 ed. $39.00. ISBN 0-403-00975-8
The Forsyte Saga. 1906–21. Buccaneer Bks. 1983 $32.95. ISBN 0-89966-443-1. Contains
     The Man of Property, In Chancery, and *To Let*. An Edwardian soap opera.
Fraternity. Scholarly 1971 repr. of 1923 ed. $59.00. ISBN 0-403-00976-6
Jocelyn. Greenwood 1970 repr. of 1898 ed. $45.00. ISBN 0-8371-3104-4
Motley. Scholarly 1971 repr. of 1910 ed. $59.00 ISBN 0-403-00978-2

PLAYS BY GALSWORTHY

Galsworthy: Five Plays. Heinemann Ed. 1988 $9.95. ISBN 0-413-54290-4. With an
     introduction by Benedict Nightingale; plays focusing on upper-middle class life.
The Plays of John Galsworthy. Richard West 1980 repr. of 1929 ed. o.p.
Representative Plays. Scribner 1924 o.p.
Strife. Heinemann Ed. 1988 $9.95. ISBN 0-413-54270-X. Bitter conflicts between an
     employer and striking employees.

NONFICTION BY GALSWORTHY

Letters from John Galsworthy, 1900–1932. Ed. by Edward Garnett. Scholarly 1971 $59.00. ISBN 0-403-00601-5

BOOKS ABOUT GALSWORTHY

Coustillas, Pierre, Earl E. Stevens, and H. Ray Stevens. *John Galsworthy: An Annotated Bibliography of Writings about Him.* N. Ill. U. Pr. 1980 $45.00. ISBN 0-87580-073-4. An important collection of secondary sources on Galsworthy.

Dupré, Catherine. *John Galsworthy: A Biography.* Collins 1976 o.p.

Sternlicht, Sanford V. *John Galsworthy.* Macmillan 1987 $20.95. ISBN 0-8057-6947-1. Overview, with attention to Galsworthy as gentleman writer and playwright of conscience.

GOLDING, WILLIAM (GERALD). 1911–1993 (NOBEL PRIZE 1983)

Born in Cornwall and brought up as a scientist, Golding changed to English literature after two years at Oxford University. Interested in classical Greek and archeology, he says his literary influences have been EURIPIDES (see Vol. 2) and the anonymous Anglo-Saxon author of *The Battle of Maldon.* E. M. FORSTER called Golding's *Lord of the Flies* (1954) "the outstanding novel of the year." In the United States, it got off to a slow start, however, until the paperback edition of 1959 led to its popularity among college students. Golding himself describes its theme as "an attempt to trace the defects of human nature. The moral is that the shape of a society must depend on the ethical nature of the individual and not on any political system however logical or respectable" (Introduction). It became a runaway bestseller and was made into a film in 1963.

Other novels include *The Inheritors* (1955), which tells the story of innocent Neanderthal man's defeat and supersession by Homo sapiens; *Free Fall* (1959), an artist's autobiographical search for the mechanism of transition from the relatively guiltless sins of his free childhood to those in his unfree adult life; *The Spire* (1964), in which Golding re-creates the story behind the building of a great English cathedral, which might have been Salisbury; and *The Pyramid* (1967), a lighthearted comedy of manners. *The Hot Gates and Other Occasional Pieces* (1965) consists of 20 brief essays (two are autobiographical). Among the most interesting is "Fable," in which he tells how the war transformed him into a moralist and how he came to write *Lord of the Flies.*

In 1940 Golding joined the Royal Navy and spent five years in command of a rocket ship. In 1961–62, he was a visiting professor at Hollins College in Virginia and lectured at American colleges and universities. He won the Nobel Prize for Literature in 1983. Golding lives with his family in Salisbury.

NOVELS BY GOLDING

Close Quarters. FS&G 1987 $16.95. ISBN 0-374-12510-4. The follow-up to *Rites of Passage.*

Darkness Visible. FS&G 1979 $14.95. ISBN 0-374-13502-9. Golding's modern vision of hell.

Fire Down Below. G. K. Hall 1990 $20.95. ISBN 0-7451-7238-5

Free Fall. 1959. HarBraceJ 1962 $8.95. ISBN 0-15-633468-2. A story of youthful love and its devastating consequences.

The Inheritors. 1955. HarBraceJ 1963 $7.95. ISBN 0-15-644379-1. Story about the destruction of the Neanderthals.

Lord of the Flies. 1954. Buccaneer Bks. 1992 $16.95. ISBN 0-89966-905-0. Study of the nature of human oppression.

The Paper Men. FS&G 1984 $13.95. ISBN 0-374-22980-5. Story of the struggle between a
    British writer and an American professor.
Pincher Martin (The Two Deaths of Christopher Martin). HarBraceJ 1968 repr. of 1957 ed.
    $7.95. ISBN 0-15-671833-2. Survival story of a shipwrecked naval officer.
The Pyramid. 1967. HarBraceJ 1968 $3.95. ISBN 0-15-674703-0
Rites of Passage. 1980. White Pine 1990 $10.00 ISBN 1-877727-12-1. Winner of the
    prestigious Booker Prize.
The Scorpion God: Three Short Novels. 1971. HarBraceJ 1984 $3.95. ISBN 0-15-679658-9.
    Includes *The Scorpion God, Clonk, Clonk,* and *Envoy Extraordinary.*
The Spire. 1964. HarBraceJ 1965 $6.95. ISBN 0-15-684741-8. Medieval theology and
    ecclesiastical architecture.

PLAY BY GOLDING

The Brass Butterfly. Faber & Faber 1969 $4.95. ISBN 0-571-09073-7

NONFICTION BY GOLDING

An Egyption Journal. Faber & Faber 1985 $12.95. ISBN 0-571-12547-6. An account of
    Golding's month-long cruise up the Nile.
The Hot Gates. Transaction Pubs. 1990 $22.95. ISBN 1-85290-016-4
A Moving Target. 1982. FS&G 1984 $7.95. ISBN 0-374-51850-5

BOOKS ABOUT GOLDING

Anderson, David, and Jack I. Biles. *William Golding: Some Critical Considerations.* U. of
    Ky. Pr. 1978 $73.80. ISBN 0-3172-6707-8. Explores Christian theology, Golding's
    existential vision, and the language of Caliban; includes bibliography.
Baker, James R., ed. *Critical Essays on William Golding.* G. K. Hall 1988 $40.00. ISBN 0-
    8161-8764-9. A selection of essays focusing on Golding's morality and its expression
    in his work.
Boyd, S. J. *The Novels of William Golding.* St. Martin 1988 $35.00. ISBN 0-312-01957-2.
    Examines Golding's handling of innocence and experience, divine tragicomedy, and
    eschatology.
Carey, John. *William Golding: The Man and His Books.* Faber & Faber 1986 o.p.
    Biographical tribute.
Crompton, Don. *A View from the Spire: William Golding's Later Novels.* Blackwell Pubs.
    1986 $14.95. ISBN 0-631-14911-2. Analyzes Golding's later novels.
Dick, Bernard F. *William Golding.* Macmillan 1987 $20.95. ISBN 0-0057-6925-0.
    Overview of his life; bibliography.
Redpath, Philip. *William Golding: A Structural Reading of His Fiction.* B & N Imports
    1986 $53.00. ISBN 0-389-20647-4. Scholarly study of Golding's fictional narratives.

GRAVES, ROBERT. 1895–1985

Born in Wimbledon, near London, to an Irish father and German mother,
Robert Graves led one of the most varied and productive careers in twentieth-
century literature. Although devoted primarily to his poetry, Graves produced a
vast array of other works, including historical novels such as *I, Claudius* (1934),
plays, criticism, translations, and his moving autobiography, *Goodbye to All That*
(1929). His interest in myth and mythology also prompted several works, most
notably *Greek Myths* (1955); *Greek Gods and Heroes* (1960), a retelling of
ancient Greek legends; and *Hebrew Myths* (1963).

Graves was educated at Charterhouse School, and after serving in France
during World War I, he completed his formal education at St. John's College,
Oxford University. His tangled private life has included, besides his two
marriages, a liaison with the poet LAURA RIDING from 1926 to 1939. During his
time with Riding, he settled in Majorca, where he spent most of his life. Both
accomplished and quirky, Graves's early poetic criticism was more influential

than his later attacks on the great modernists. From 1961 to 1966, he was professor of poetry at Oxford.

Graves's early, Georgian poetry soon yielded to a more psychological orientation. Treated after the war by the psychiatrist W.H.R. Rivers, Graves developed a theory of poetry as the writer's expression of internal psychological conflicts, which informed much of his work during the 1920s. Under Riding's tutelage he turned outward in the 1930s toward a more objective stance in which the poet discovers a reality beyond himself. From the 1940s onward, his work was dominated by the theories he explicated in *The White Goddess* (1947), which he subtitled *A Historical Grammar of Poetic Myth*. For Graves, the ancient Greeks and Hebrews perverted an originally matriarchal society, whose underlying mythology of a White Goddess with three aspects—mother, beloved, and crone—true poets must seek to recover. Scholars do not agree with all of Graves's conclusions, but the book does illuminate the most obscure area of a poetry otherwise clear, craftsmanlike, and accessible.

NOVELS BY GRAVES

Claudius the God. 1934. Random 1989 $14.00. ISBN 0-679-72573-3. Continues the story of Claudius.

I, Claudius. 1934. Random 1989 $11.00. ISBN 0-679-72477-X. Historical fiction about the life of the Roman emperor Claudius.

Wife to Mr. Milton. Academy Chi. Pub. 1979 repr. of 1944 ed. o.p.

POETRY BY GRAVES

Collected Poems. 1975. OUP 1988 $35.00. ISBN 0-19-505143-2

Over the Brazier. Folcroft repr. of 1916 ed. o.p. Reprint of Graves's first volume.

Poems, 1938–1945. FS&G 1946 o.p. A collection of poems, written during wartime, reflecting the concerns of the time.

Poems about War. Moyer Bell Limited 1992 $9.95. ISBN 1-55921-030-3. Includes several drafts and memorable works.

NONFICTION BY GRAVES

Goodbye to All That. Peter Smith 1992 $19.50. ISBN 0-8446-6491-X. Famous autobiography.

On English Poetry: Being an Irregular Approach to the Psychology of This Art, from Evidence Mainly Subjective. Haskell 1972 repr. of 1922 ed. $75.00. ISBN 0-8383-1386-8

A Survey of Modernist Poetry. (coauthored with Laura Riding). Doubleday 1928 o.p.

Whipperginny. Folcroft repr. of 1923 ed. o.p.

The White Goddess. 1947. Peter Smith 1983 $24.00. ISBN 0-8446-5983-5. Amended and enlarged edition.

WORKS BY GRAVES

Between Moon and Moon: Selected Letters of Robert Graves. Moyer Bell Limited 1990 $10.95. ISBN 1-55921-031-1. Letters depicting Graves's interests as a novelist, poet, and mythographer.

Greek Myths. Viking Penguin 1992 $16.00. ISBN 0-14-007602-6. Graves's classic renditions of the Greek myths.

BOOKS ABOUT GRAVES

Bryant, Hallman Bell. *Robert Graves: An Annotated Bibliography.* Garland 1986 o.p. Useful list of secondary sources on Graves and his work.

Canary, Robert H. *Robert Graves.* Twayne 1980 o.p. Overview and bibliography, with attention to Graves as lyric and Georgian poet.

Carter, D.N.G. *Robert Graves: The Lasting Poetic Achievement*. B & N Imports 1989 $40.00. ISBN 0-389-20818-3. Survey, with discussions on love poetry and the irrational.

Graves, Richard Perceval. *Robert Graves*. Grove Pr. 1986 o.p. Biography.

―――― . *Robert Graves: The Years with Laura, 1926–1940*. Viking 1990 $24.95. ISBN 0-670-81327-3

Keane, Patrick J. *A Wild Civility: Interactions in the Poetry and Thought of Robert Graves*. U. of Mo. Pr. 1980 $9.95. ISBN 0-8262-0296-9. Short general survey.

Seymour-Smith, Martin. *Robert Graves: His Life and Works*. Paragon Hse. 1987 $10.95. ISBN 0-913729-18-3

Snipes, Katherine. *Robert Graves*. Continuum 1979 o.p. Focuses on Graves's use of Greek and Hebrew myth, satire, and historical novels.

GRAY, SIMON. 1936–

Simon Gray's plays seem to have traced the recent history of British comedy, backward. He began in 1967 with the outrageous *Wise Child*, which kept Alec Guinness, playing a fugitive criminal in woman's clothing, an Ortonian *Charley's Aunt*. By 1971 Gray had arrived, in *Butley*, at the nonstop rant of a disaffected provincial university teacher, recalling the tone and temper of JOHN OSBORNE's Jimmy Porter and KINGSLEY AMIS's Lucky Jim. *Otherwise Engaged* (1975) was cooler in its wit, more elegantly situated in the world of publishing, but no less a monologue, as Simon Hench detaches himself, with disconcerting reasonableness, from wife, friends, and other claimants, including a suicide. In *Quartermaine's Terms* (1981) and *The Common Pursuit* (1984), Gray seems at last to have rediscovered the interplay of character without effacing his bitter vision of isolation and sterility.

Gray has edited a literary review (like the characters in *The Common Pursuit*) and taught English in universities, both major and provincial. He has written television plays and novels, and adapted FYODOR DOSTOEVSKY's (see Vol. 2) *The Idiot* for the National Theatre. Gray published *An Unnatural Pursuit* (1985), a diary of the London production of *The Common Pursuit*, describing his work with the director, his friend HAROLD PINTER, who has staged several of his plays.

PLAYS BY GRAY

Butley. 1971. Methuen 1971 o.p. Character study of an academic who faces personal and emotional turmoil.

Close of Play and *Pig in a Poke*. Heinemann Ed. 1988 $8.95. ISBN 0-413-46960-3

The Common Pursuit. 1984. Dramatists Play 1990 $4.75. ISBN 0-8222-0234-4

Dutch Uncle. Faber & Faber 1969 o.p.

Gray Plays: One. Heinemann Ed. 1988 $9.95. ISBN 0-413-40420-X

Hidden Laughter. Faber & Faber 1991 $10.95. ISBN 0-571-14433-0

Melon: A Play. Heinemann Ed. 1988 $9.95. ISBN 0-413-16550-7

Old Flames and *a Month in the Country*. Faber & Faber 1991 $8.95. ISBN 0-571-14229-X

Otherwise Engaged and Other Plays. Methuen 1984 o.p. Gray's first collection of dramatic works.

Quartermaine's Terms. 1981. Heinemann Ed. 1983 $8.95. ISBN 0-413-52830-8

The Rear Column and Other Plays. Heinemann Ed. 1988 $8.95. ISBN 0-413-39170-1. Presents a postmodern view of English culture.

Spoiled. Methuen 1971 o.p.

Wise Child. 1967. Faber & Faber 1968 o.p.

GREEN, HENRY (pseud. of Henry Vincent Yorke). 1905–1974

ELIZABETH BOWEN called Henry Green "one of the novelists most to be reckoned with today," and W. H. AUDEN referred to him as "the best English novelist alive." Green's "subtly designed" novels, with their one-word titles, are what Green called "an advanced attempt to break up the old-fashioned type of novel." He does not describe his characters but "has made pioneer explorations of all the ways in which they can describe themselves." He is especially cognizant of the way people converse with each other. "Anything which has a voice is invited to use it," he explains, "but the reader is left to supply the shapes and colors out of his own head." This oblique method and a fondness for symbols make his novels difficult for readers who expect straight plot and action but fascinating to others. He has described his background in the autobiographical *Pack My Bag* (1952), his only book of nonfiction. Among his best-known novels are *Living* (1929), *Back* (1946), and *Loving* (1945), a story about life in an English country house during World War II.

NOVELS BY GREEN

Back. New Dir. Pr. 1981 repr. of 1946 ed. o.p. Novel about the life of a disabled prisoner of war.

Blindness. 1926. Viking Penguin 1978 o.p.

Concluding. Kelley 1970 repr. of 1950 ed. $25.00. ISBN 0-678-05158-4. Green's first novel. A futuristic examination of humanistic oppression. Foreword by Eudora Welty.

Doting. Kelley 1970 repr. of 1952 ed. $25.00. ISBN 0-678-03159-2

Living. Scholarly 1971 repr. of 1929 ed. $49.00. ISBN 0-403-01001-2. A story of workers in a Midland's factory.

Loving-Living-Party Going. Viking Penguin 1993 $15.95. ISBN 0-14-018691-3. Introduction by John Updike. Contains the complete text of all three works.

Nothing. Kelley 1970 repr. of 1950 ed. $25.00. ISBN 0-678-03160-6

Nothing-Doting-Blindness. Viking Penguin 1993 $14.95. ISBN 0-14-018692-1

Party Going. Kelley 1970 repr. of 1951 ed. $25.00. ISBN 0-678-03161-4. An exposé of upper-class vapidity.

NONFICTION BY GREEN

Pack My Bag: A Memoir. 1940. New Dir. Pr. 1993 $19.95. ISBN 0-8112-1234-3

BOOKS ABOUT GREEN

Gorra, Michael Edward. *The English Novel at Mid-Century: From the Leaning Tower*. St. Martin 1990 $39.95. ISBN 0-312-04023-7. Consideration and comparison of Green and Evelyn Waugh.

Holmesland, Oddvar. *A Critical Introduction to Henry Green's Novels: The Living Vision*. St. Martin 1986 $29.95. ISBN 0-312-17471-3. Overview of his life; montage approach to Green's tone.

Mengham, Rod. *The Idiom of the Time: The Writings of Henry Green*. Cambridge U. Pr. 1983 $44.95. ISBN 0-521-24813-2. Survey of Green's best work.

North, Michael. *Henry Green and the Writing of His Generation*. U. Pr. of Va. 1984 $63.20. ISBN 0-8357-3132-4. Explores the literature of debility, the powers of memory, and the fictive life.

Odom, Keith C. *Henry Green*. Twayne 1978 o.p. Overview; examines the novel theorist and the role of World War II in Green's fiction.

GREENE, (HENRY) GRAHAM. 1904–1991

Novelist, short story writer, essayist, and playwright, Graham Greene was born in Berkhamsted and educated at the Berkhamsted School, where his father was headmaster. His father's position at the school made school life rather difficult for Greene, and he reacted in a rebellious manner, playing Russian roulette at age 13 and cutting open his leg with a penknife. While attending

Balliol College at Oxford, he published his first book, *Bubbling April* (1925), a collection of verse.

Converting to Roman Catholicism in 1926, Greene became "primarily and passionately concerned with good and evil," with God in a fallen world of frail mortals. Greene's characters always fall short of the standards by which they are being judged, but their anguish earns them great sympathy.

Greene spent periods on the staff of the London *Times* and the *Spectator.* In World War II, he served at the Foreign Office, with special duties in West Africa. *The Man Within* (1929), his first published novel, was not a complete success. He wrote several thrillers, which he called "entertainments," but *The Power and the Glory* (1940) and *The Heart of the Matter* (1948), considered his two finest novels, convinced critics of his serious intent, subtle characterization, and accomplished craftsmanship.

Greene named as two great influences on his writing John Buchan, a master of the spy thriller, and the Roman Catholic novelist FRANÇOIS MAURIAC (see Vol. 2). Greene's work follows this split character, from those sinister spy-chase tales to works of serious moral and religious reflection. A number of his novels and short stories have been made into successful films, and two of his plays, *The Living Room* (1954) and *The Potting Shed* (1957), were produced on Broadway. *Carving a Statue*, which played off-Broadway in 1968, had its premiere in London in 1964. His 1967 film adaptation of *The Comedians*, a best-selling novel set in contemporary Haiti under the terror-ridden dictatorship of President François Duvalier, drew protest from the Haitian government upon its release. In 1952 Greene received the Catholic Literary Award for *The End of the Affair* (1951), a powerful study of love and religion. His nonfictional writings include *The Lost Childhood and Other Essays* (1951), an excellent critical collection, mostly on contemporaries. Considered by many as the best English writer of the past fifty years, Greene was said to be a candidate for the Nobel Prize in literature on several occasions, but he never received the award.

NOVELS BY GREENE

The Bear Fell Free. Folcroft repr. of 1935 ed. o.p.
Brighton Rock. 1938. Viking Penguin 1977 $5.95. ISBN 0-14-000442-4. A tale of gang warfare and racketeering.
A Burnt-Out Case. 1961. Viking Penguin 1977 $4.95. ISBN 0-14-001894-8. About a philanderer's atonement at a leper colony.
The Comedians. 1965. Viking Penguin 1991 $8.95. ISBN 0-14-018494-5
The Confidential Agent. Viking Penguin 1981 $4.95. ISBN 0-14-001895-6
Dr. Fisher of Geneva or the Bomb Party. 1980. Viking Penguin 1981 $20.00. ISBN 0-670-27522-0
The End of the Affair. 1951. Viking Penguin 1991 $7.95. ISBN 0-14-018495-3
A Gun for Sale. Viking Penguin 1992 $7.95. ISBN 0-14-018540-2. A story of violence and morality.
The Heart of the Matter. 1948. Viking Penguin 1991 $8.95. ISBN 0-14-018496-1. Story of sin, martyrdom, and ethical chaos set in West Africa.
The Honorary Consul. 1973. Transaction Pubs. 1985 $15.95. ISBN 1-85089-004-8
The Human Factor. 1978. S & S Trade 1988 $5.99. ISBN 0-671-64850-0
It's a Battlefield. 1934. Viking Penguin 1991 $7.95. ISBN 0-14-018541-0. Contemporary satire.
The Man Within. 1929. Viking Penguin 1982 $4.95. ISBN 0-14-003283-5
Monsignor Quixote. 1982. S & S Trade 1982 $12.95. ISBN 0-671-45818-3
Orient Express. 1933. Viking Penguin 1982 o.p.
Our Man in Havana. 1958. Viking Penguin 1991 $8.95. ISBN 0-14-018493-7. An exciting adventure of espionage in Cuba.

The Power and the Glory (The Labyrinthine Ways). 1940. Viking Penguin 1991 $8.95. ISBN 0-14-018499-6. Story set in Mexico, reflecting its culture and people.

The Quiet American. 1955. Random 1992 $13.50. ISBN 0-679-60014-0

Travels With My Aunt. 1969. Viking Penguin 1991 $9.95. ISBN 0-14-018501-1

Short Story Collections by Greene

Collected Stories. Viking Penguin 1987 $8.95. ISBN 0-14-008070-8. Stories dealing with the darker, more arid side of religion, love, and life.

Twenty-one Stories. Viking Penguin 1981 $5.95. ISBN 0-14-003093-X. Three stories added and one withdrawn from *Nineteen Stories* form this collection.

Nonfiction by Greene

Collected Essays. Viking Penguin 1981 $7.95. ISBN 0-14-003159-6

Getting to Know the General: The Story of an Involvement. S & S Trade 1984 o.p.

In Search of a Character. 1961. Viking Penguin 1981 $4.95. ISBN 0-14-002822-6. Greene's collection of raw material for *A Burnt-Out Case.*

Journey Without Maps. 1961. Viking Penguin 1992 $9.95. ISBN 0-14-018579-8. Greene's account of a trip across Liberia.

A Sort of Life. 1971. S & S Trade 1978 o.p. An autobiographical look at Greene's life and work.

Ways of Escape. S & S Trade 1981 $13.95. ISBN 0-6707-5262-2. An autobiography.

Work by Greene

The Portable Graham Greene. Ed. by Philip Stratford. Viking Penguin 1977 o.p. A cross section, chosen with the collaboration of the author.

Books about Greene

Allain, Marie-Françoise. *The Other Man: Conversations with Graham Greene.* S & S Trade 1981 o.p. Interviews.

Cassis, A. F. *Graham Greene: An Annotated Bibliography of Criticism.* Scarecrow 1981 $37.50. ISBN 0-8108-1418-8. Secondary sources.

De Vitis, A. A. *Graham Greene.* Macmillan 1986 $21.95. ISBN 0-8057-6911-0. Overview of his life; bibliography.

Erdinast-Vulcan, Daphna. *Graham Greene's Childless Fathers.* St. Martin 1988 $29.95. ISBN 0-312-00742-6. Secular and Christian themes of paternity.

Gatson, George M. *The Pursuit of Salvation: A Critical Guide to the Novels of Graham Greene.* Whitston Pub. 1984 $18.50. ISBN 0-87875-289-7. Focuses on Greene's Christian vision.

Meyers, Jeffrey. *Graham Greene: A Revaluation.* St. Martin 1990 $35.00. ISBN 0-3120-3230-7. Essays on religious aspects of Greene's literary criticism, travel books, and spy fiction, and on Greene as a Roman Catholic novelist.

Miller, R. H. *Understanding Graham Greene.* U. of SC Pr. 1990 $29.95. ISBN 0-87249-704-6. Explores the use of religion, politics, and fables in Greene's writing.

Sherry, Norman. *The Life of Graham Greene, Vol. 1: 1904–1939.* Viking Penguin 1990 $15.95. ISBN 0-14-014450-1. A massive study, "going to the heart of Greene's darkly anguished world view and the anxieties, guilt, and demons that have driven him to create," according to *Publisher's Weekly.*

Thomas, Brian. *An Underground Fate: The Idiom of Romance in the Later Novels of Graham Greene.* U. of Ga. Pr. 1988 $32.00. ISBN 0-8203-0984-2. Argues that romantic themes tend to dominate Greene's later works.

Wobbe, R. A. *Graham Greene: A Bibliography and Guide to Research.* Garland 1979 o.p.

GREGORY, LADY ISABELLA AUGUSTA (née PERSSE). 1852–1932

Lady Gregory's literary life did not blossom until after the death of her husband, Sir William Gregory, in 1892. At that time, she became very interested in Irish literature and history. After meeting William Butler Yeats in 1898, she dedicated her talent, wealth, and position to nurturing Irish national consciousness, and the growing renaissance of Irish literature.

Lady Gregory was one of the founders of the Irish National Theatre Society, the author of books on Irish folklore, and an important playwright. Her story of the revival of native drama for the Irish stage is told in *Our Irish Theatre* (1913). Her journals reveal her as courageous and honest, with the gift of bringing out the best in the many people she befriended, among them W. B. Yeats, whose close friend and collaborator she remained from their meeting in the 1890s. She directed the Abbey Theatre with him until her death and with him wrote the play *Kathleen ni Houlihan* (1902). Her own, usually brief, plays were Irish legendary fantasies, patriotic historical dramas, and the comedies of peasant life for which she is best known. Simplicity, which Lady Gregory as a writer always sought, should not be confused with naiveté. Her balanced dialogue and "constant stripping away of easy sentiment" have been commented on by her editor, Ann Saddlemyer. Among the eclectic Abbey Theatre playwrights, Lady Gregory was a source of unity and consistency.

PLAYS BY GREGORY

Collected Plays. 4 vols. Ed. by Ann Saddlemyer. OUP 1970 o.p. Vol. 1: *The Comedies.* Vol. 2: *The Tragedies and Tragi-comedies.* Vol. 3: *The Wonder and Supernatural Plays.* Vol. 4: *Translations and Adaptations and Her Collaborations with Douglas Hyde and W. B. Yeats.*

Seven Short Plays. Scholarly 1970 repr. of 1909 ed. $29.00. ISBN 0-403-00614-7. Includes *Kathleen ni Houlihan.*

Three Last Plays. Scholarly 1971 repr. of 1928 ed. $59.00. ISBN 0-403-00615-5

NONFICTION BY GREGORY

Irish Folk History Plays. 2 vols. Scholarly 1971 repr. of 1912 ed. $39.50. ISBN 0-403-01006-3

Lady Gregory's Journals. 2 vols. Ed. by Daniel J. Murphy. NY Pub. Lib. Vol. 1 o.p. Vol. 2 1987 $79.00. ISBN 0-87104-308-4. Highlights Lady Gregory's role in Irish cultural movements.

Our Irish Theatre: A Chapter of Autobiography. Dufour 1972 $50.00. ISBN 0-900675-28-4

WORK BY GREGORY

A Book of Saints and Wonders: Put Down Here by Lady Gregory According to the Old Writings and Memory of the People of Ireland. OUP 1971 o.p. Contains a series of folk tales and legends collected by Lady Gregory.

BOOKS ABOUT GREGORY

Adams, Hazard. *Lady Gregory.* Bucknell U. Pr. 1973 $6.50. ISBN 0-8387-1207-X. Short overview of Lady Gregory's career and her use of myth.

Kohfeldt, Mary Lou. *Lady Gregory: A Biography.* Atheneum 1985 o.p. An interesting study of Lady Gregory's life and work.

Kopper, Edward A. *Lady Isabella Persse Gregory.* Twayne 1976 o.p. Overview, with attention to Lady Gregory's sources of inspiration, folklore and mythology, and her work with the Abbey Theatre.

Mikhail, E. H. *Lady Gregory: An Annotated Bibliography of Criticism.* Whitston Pub. 1981 $20.00. ISBN 0-87875-216-1. Useful listing of secondary sources on Lady Gregory and her work.

Saddlemyer, Ann, and Colin Smythe. *Lady Gregory: Fifty Years After.* Smythe 1987 o.p. A retrospective look at her life and work.

GUNN, THOM(SON). 1929–

Both literally and figuratively, Thom Gunn may have traveled the farthest of any of the original Movement poets of the 1950s in Britain. Born in Gravesend, he moved often as a child because his journalist father frequently worked for different newspapers. After two years in the British army and some months in Paris, he enrolled in Trinity College, Cambridge, from which he graduated in 1953. He then went to the United States for graduate study at Stanford University and an assistant professorship from 1958 to 1966 at the University of California, Berkeley. Important influences during that period were the older poets Yvor Winters and J. V. Cunningham and his contemporaries GARY SNYDER and TED HUGHES (who was at Cambridge with Gunn). Since then he has lived in San Francisco and supported himself as a freelance writer.

Gunn's literal journeys mirror psychological ones reflected in his poetry. Influenced by French existentialist thought, he first came to public attention as a skilled craftsman of anguished lyrics in traditional forms. Moving to California, he experimented with the drug LSD and a looser artistic structure, which he used to present often violent subjects (such as motorcycle gangs). Correspondingly, Gunn's erotic verse changed from the early heterosexual lyrics to a frank portrayal of homosexual love. Although he claims to be an atheist, Gunn often conveys a passionate, nearly mystical, identification with the world of nature. The title poem of his important volume *Moly* (1971) shows his understandable fascination with the theme of metamorphosis.

POETRY BY GUNN

Jack Straw's Castle. Small Pr. Dist. 1975 $3.50. ISBN 0-685-57066-5. Poems about identity and the search for meaning in life.

The Man with Night Sweats: Poems. FS&G 1992 $15.00. ISBN 0-374-20175-7

The Menace. Man-Root 1982 o.p.

Moly and My Sad Captains. FS&G 1973 o.p. LSD-influenced poetry.

The Passages of Joy. FS&G 1982 $6.95. ISBN 0-374-51796-7. Series of poems about sexuality and escape.

Positives: Verses by Thom Gunn. (coauthored with Ander Gunn). U. Ch. Pr. 1967 $10.00. ISBN 0-226-31067-1. Contains verse by Gunn and photographs by his brother, Ander Gunn.

Selected Poems. Faber & Faber 1962 o.p. Gunn's earliest collection of poetry.

Selected Poems, 1950–1975. FS&G 1979 o.p.

The Sense of Movement. Faber & Faber 1968 o.p. A selection of poems influenced by the Beat Generation.

Talbot Road. Helikon NY 1981 $25.00. ISBN 0-685-02252-8. Illustrated by Bill Schuessler.

To the Air. Ed. by Jan Schreiber. Godine 1974 o.p.

NONFICTION BY GUNN

The Occasions of Poetry: Essays in Criticism and Autobiography. Ed. by Wilmer Clive. FS&G 1982 o.p.

BOOKS ABOUT GUNN

Bold, Alan Norman.. *Gunn & Hughes: Thom Gunn and Ted Hughes*. B & N Imports 1976 o.p. Comparative study and survey of the two writers.

Hagstrom, Jack W. C., Thom Gunn, and George Bixby. *Thom Gunn: A Bibliography*. Bertram Rota 1979 o.p. A highly useful sourcebook.

HALL, RADCLYFFE. 1886–1943

Born Marguerite Radclyffe Hall, the writer called herself John as an adult. Educated at King's College, London, Hall began her career writing poetry set to music and performed prominently before World War I. Under the influence of the socialite Mabel Batten, Hall became devoutly Roman Catholic and met Una, Lady Troubridge, who was to become Hall's lifelong companion.

The Well of Loneliness (1928), a frank and touching portrayal of lesbian sensibilities, was banned in Britain and America (despite GEORGE BERNARD SHAW's comment that the novel told of things people should know about), nearly ruining her literary career. Copies of the book were widely confiscated; censors expressed moral outrage, especially because Hall's characters showed no contrition for their "vices" and were portrayed sympathetically. Despite aggressive attempts at censorship, though, audiences clamored for the novel, which attained a strong popularity.

Hall wrote of lesbianism as natural and pleaded for tolerance, yet her writing manifests a degree of guilt that in some way affirms her society's widespread prejudice that homosexuality was a deformity. Still, though Hall was less self-accepting than contemporary gay writers, *The Well of Loneliness* endures as a relatively rare and valuable documentation of lesbian lives and aesthetics in the early twentieth century.

Despite her fierce defense of *The Well of Loneliness*, none of Hall's later writing explicitly deals with homosexual themes.

NOVELS BY HALL

Adam's Breed. 1929. Virago 1985 o.p. Story about an Italian orphan seeking spirituality.
A Saturday Life. 1925. Virago 1987 o.p.
The Unlit Lamp. 1929. Rprt. Serv. 1988 $80.00. ISBN 0-7812-0150-0. A novel focusing on people's social aspirations and decadence.
The Well of Loneliness. 1928. Buccaneer Bks. 1992 $31.95. ISBN 0-89966-948-4

BOOKS ABOUT HALL

Baker, Michael. *Our Three Selves: The Life of Radclyffe Hall*. Hamilton 1985 o.p. Well written, interesting biography of Hall.
Franks, Claudia Stillman. *Beyond the Well of Loneliness: The Fiction of Radclyffe Hall*. Ashgate Pub. Co. 1982 o.p. Study of Hall's social isolation.
O'Rourke, Rebecca. *Reflecting on The Well of Loneliness: Stephen Gordon, A Lesbian's Heroine?* Routledge 1989 $9.95. ISBN 0-415-01841-2. Detailed examination of Hall's most famous protagonist, Stephen Gordon, focusing on heroes, gender, and sexuality.

HARE, DAVID. 1947–

David Hare was one of the founders of the Portable Theatre and, later, Joint Stock, important companies on the British theatrical left. He has collaborated in two of the seminal radical dramas of the seventies—*Lay-By* and *England's Ireland*. He favors writing with the provocateur HOWARD BRENTON. Yet, in notable ways, Hare's drama keeps itself apart from the agitprop, assaultive techniques of the contemporary political theater. His plays are constructions—allusions to, if not actually specimens of, the well-made play. Their dialogue is witty. Without epic ambitions, they seek out small societies (not often working-class) and confined situations—a girls' school (*Slag*, 1970), the home of a diplomat (*The Great Exhibition*, 1972), May Ball at a Cambridge college (*Teeth n' Smiles*, 1975), an international conference on the problems of developing nations (*A Map of the World*, 1983). And in the midst of a theater that largely derides the notion of character, Hare has focused constantly on personal drama.

Not that this is simply classicism, or regression. Hare has kept his political convictions onstage by situating his character studies in a historical perspective—in *Plenty* (1978), *Licking Hitler* (1978), and the film *Wetherby* (1985), testing actions against the moral touchstone of World War II. And, in *Fanshen* (1975), the reenactment of the collectivization of a Chinese village, he seems to have deliberately adopted the radical theater's simplicities of language and scene, as well as its subject matter. But even *Fanshen*, as critics have pointed out, takes a detached and ambivalent view of the radical process it describes. And a sense of the playwright's detachment hovers over many of Hare's works— from the early comedy of feminism, *Slag*, to the later *Map of the World*, which gives most of its best lines to a conservative novelist deriding the emptiness of utopian idealism. In *Pravda* (1985)—a return to collaboration with the committed Brenton—Hare seems to be as fascinated with the figure of the Machiavellian newspaper czar as he is interested in exposing the mechanics of capitalist exploitation.

PLAYS BY HARE

The Asian Plays: Fanshen, Saigon, and A Map of the World. Faber & Faber 1986 $14.95. ISBN 0-571-13990-6. Politically and emotionally compelling portrayals of Third World development.

The Bay at Nice and *Wrecked Eggs*. Faber & Faber 1987 $7.95. ISBN 0-571-14694-5. Plays revolving around the conflict between personal freedom and responsibility within married life.

Dreams of Leaving. Faber & Faber 1980 o.p.

The Early Plays: Slag, the Great Exhibition, Teeth 'n' Smiles. Faber & Faber 1992 $10.95. ISBN 0-571-16220-7

Fanshen. Faber & Faber 1976 o.p.

The Great Exhibition. Faber & Faber 1972 o.p.

Heading Home: With Weatherby and Dreams of Living. Faber & Faber 1992 $12.95. ISBN 0-571-16244-4

The History Plays: Plenty, Knuckle, and Licking Hitler. Faber & Faber 1986 $10.95. ISBN 0-571-13132-8. Focuses on the ways recent history has warped the lives of the formerly principled English middle class.

Plenty. NAL-Dutton 1985 $7.95. ISBN 0-452-25956-8

Pravda. (coauthored with Howard Brenton). Methuen 1985 o.p.

Saigon: Year of the Cat. Faber & Faber 1984 o.p. A contemporary morality play about the Vietnam experience.

The Secret Rapture. Grove Pr. 1989 $9.95. ISBN 0-8021-3175-1

Teeth n' Smiles. Faber & Faber 1976 o.p.

BOOKS ABOUT HARE

Dean, Joan Fitzpatrick. *David Hare*. Macmillan 1990 $22.95. ISBN 0-8057-6997-8. Discussion of Hare's collaborations and adaptations, television plays, and films.

Oliva, Judy Lee. *David Hare: Theatricalizing Politics*. Bks. Demand 1990 $58.40. ISBN 0-8357-2048-9. The individual, national, and international concerns of Hare's political drama.

Page, Malcolm. *File on Hare*. Heinemann Ed. 1990 $9.95. ISBN 0-413-15620-6. Survey of productions and reviews.

HARTLEY, L(ESLIE) P(OLES). 1895–1972

Novelist, short-story writer, and literary critic, L. P. Hartley won the James Tait Black Memorial Prize in 1947 for *Eustace and Hilda*. Part of a trilogy that offers a penetrating and disturbing psychological study of what Hartley called "sisteritis" in an upper-middle-class family, the three books were described by the London *Times* as "unique in modern writing . . . diverting and disturbing. Beneath a surface 'almost overcivilized' the reviewer found 'a hollow of horror.'" One of Hartley's special interests is HENRY JAMES, with whom he has been compared.

In *The Tragic Comedians*, James Hall devotes a chapter to Hartley, who is respected but not popular in Britain, read by few in America, but praised by discerning critics in both countries: "Along with Green and Powell, Hartley has changed the direction of the comic novel, raising even more seriously than they the question of whether it remains comic at all. . . . His freshness consists at first in simply changing the patterns of the naturalist novel from social insights to emotional ones; yet in doing so he departs from both the older solid way of conceiving character and the more recent fluid way of conceiving consciousness." David Cecil called *The Go-Between* (1953) "impressive," and wrote: "Hartley is for me the first of living novelists in certain important respects; beauty of style, lyrical quality of feeling and, above all, the power and originality of his imagination, which wonderfully mingles ironic comedy, whimsical fancy and a mysterious Hawthorne-like poetry." *The Novelist's Responsibility* is a collection of essays and letters.

NOVELS BY HARTLEY

Eustace and Hilda: A Trilogy. Madison Bks. UPA 1986 $24.95. ISBN 0-8128-3033-4. Trilogy detailing the lives of middle-class siblings.
The Go-Between. Madison Bks. UPA 1980 $9.95. ISBN 0-8128-6073-X
Hireling. Dufour 1973 repr. of 1957 ed. o.p. A story focusing on social ideas and personal awareness.

NONFICTION BY HARTLEY

The Novelist's Responsibility. o.p.

HEANEY, SEAMUS (JUSTIN). 1939–

Often viewed as the leading poet of his generation, Seamus Heaney was born into a Catholic farming family in Castledawson, County Derry, in Northern Ireland. Educated entirely in Irish schools, he graduated from Queen's University, Belfast, with a first-class honors degree in English. He has held a variety of teaching jobs, including a post at Queen's University from 1966 to 1972. In 1972 he left the turbulence of Belfast for a four-year stay in a cottage at Glanmore, County Wicklow, where he produced the *Glanmore Sonnets* and other works. He and his family now live in Dublin, and he spends part of each year teaching at Harvard University. A gifted critic as well as poet, Heaney has also written a book of literary essays.

Heaney's first book, *Death of a Naturalist* (1966), established his reputation, which has grown with each successive volume. He often writes of rural life in his native Ulster in an unsentimental and moving way. A poem such as "Digging" establishes analogies between rural hardship and the poet's own labor. When he turns to the past, he favors the Viking rather than the Celtic heroes of most Irish poets. Under the fascination of P. V. Glob's book *The Bog People*, he produced a powerful group of poems about the preservation of ancient tribal culture in Irish peat bogs, again finding analogies to the poet's own condition. Political themes connected to the troubles in Northern Ireland also appear in his work. Heaney published a superb version of the story of one

Irish hero who fascinates him, the medieval king Sweeney, in *Sweeney Astray* (1984). Among his more recent works are *Station Island* (1985), *The Haw Lantern* (1987), and *The Cure at Troy* (1991).

POETRY BY HEANEY

The Cure at Troy: A Version of Sophocles' Philoctetes. FS&G 1991 $20.00. ISBN 0-374-52289-8

Death of a Naturalist. 1966. Faber & Faber 1969 $9.95. ISBN 0-571-09024-9. Irish observations and anecdotal poetry.

Door into the Dark. 1969. Faber & Faber 1972 $8.95. ISBN 0-571-10126-7. Poems reflecting Heaney's cultural observations.

Field Work. 1979. FS&G 1981 $7.95. ISBN 0-374-51620-0

The Haw Lantern. FS&G 1987 $12.95. ISBN 0-374-16837-7. A melancholy, introspective collection inspired by myth and history.

North. 1975. Faber & Faber 1985 $5.95. ISBN 0-571-10813-X

Poems, 1965–1975. FS&G 1980 o.p. Combined printing of his first four volumes.

Seeing Things: Poems. FS&G 1991 $19.00. ISBN 0-374-25776-0

Selected Poems 1966–1987. FS&G 1991 $15.00. ISBN 0-374-52280-4

Station Island. FS&G 1986 $12.00. ISBN 0-374-51935-8. Collection focusing on the culture of Heaney's native Ireland.

WORK BY HEANEY

The Government of the Tongue: Selected Prose 1978–1987. FS&G 1990 $8.95. ISBN 0-374-52220-0

Sweeney Astray. FS&G 1984 $25.00. ISBN 0-374-27221-2. Translation of the medieval Irish work.

Sweeney's Flight. FS&G 1992 $35.00. ISBN 0-374-27219-0

BOOKS ABOUT HEANEY

Andrews, Elmer. *The Poetry of Seamus Heaney.* St. Martin 1988 $35.00. ISBN 0-312-01597-6. Survey of Heaney's poetry.

Burris, Sidney. *The Poetry of Resistance: Seamus Heaney and the Pastoral Tradition.* Ohio U. Pr. 1990 $24.95. ISBN 0-8214-0951-4. Examines Heaney's portrayal of Northern Irish rural communities for insights into the political tenor of his poetry.

Buttel, Robert. *Seamus Heaney.* Bucknell U. Pr. 1975 $6.50. ISBN 0-8387-1567-2. Overview of Heaney's life and work.

Corcoran, Neil. *Seamus Heaney.* Faber & Faber 1986 o.p. Biographical and critical background.

Curtis, Tony. *The Art of Seamus Heaney.* Dufour 1985 $21.00. ISBN 0-802-31279-9. Explores Heaney's craft and technique, his manuscript drafts, and his social voice.

Foster, Thomas C. *Seamus Heaney.* Macmillan 1989 $21.95. ISBN 0-8057-6984-6. Survey of his life; bibliography.

Hart, Henry. *Seamus Heaney, Poet of Contrary Progressions.* Syracuse U. Pr. 1991 $29.95. ISBN 0-8156-2536-7. Heaney's diagnosis of Irish ills balanced against self-deconstructive doubts about poetry.

Tamplin, Ronald. *Seamus Heaney.* Taylor & Francis 1990 $17.95. ISBN 0-335-15261-9. Overview focusing on nature, language, and history in Heaney's work.

HOUSMAN, A(LFRED) E(DWARD). 1859–1936

A professor of Latin at University College, London, and at Cambridge University, A. E. Housman was a meticulous and detached classical scholar. His personal life, similarly, was exceedingly reserved. During his lifetime, he published only two slender volumes of poetry, which bespeak a fervent but muted passion and a repressed homosexuality. Influenced by Greek and Latin poetry, his own verse is spare, delicate, and concentrated. Its importance in relation to modern poetry derives from Housman's tentative yet compelling attempt to reconcile this classical and Victorian composure with a more contemporary sense of energy and expression. The poetry of *A Shropshire Lad* (1896) fuses the conventional strains of the pastoral with an anticipation of a more modernist tension and uncertainty.

POETRY BY HOUSMAN

Collected Poems. Buccaneer Bks. 1983 $21.95. ISBN 0-89966-451-2. Well-rounded selection covering most of Housman's best works.

Last Poems. 1922. Rprt. Serv. 1992 $59.00. ISBN 0-7812-7566-0. Series of poems reflecting pastoral ideals.

A Shropshire Lad. 1896. Bucaneer Bks. 1981 $20.95. ISBN 0-89966-285-4

NONFICTION BY HOUSMAN

The Name and Nature of Poetry: And Other Selected Prose. New Amsterdam Bks. 1989 repr. of 1961 ed. $10.95. ISBN 0-941533-61-1

BOOKS ABOUT HOUSMAN

Bayley, John. *Housman's Poems.* OUP 1992 $49.95. ISBN 0-19-811763-9. Biographically based critical study focusing on love, the romantic personality, and the nature of poetry.

Carter, John. *A. E. Housman: A Bibliography.* Omnigraphics Inc. 1982 repr. of 1952 ed. $50.00. ISBN 0-906795-05-2. A comprehensive and highly useful collection of secondary sources.

Graves, Richard Perceval. *A. E. Housman, the Scholar-Poet.* Scribner 1980 o.p. Excellent biography of Housman.

Leggett, Bobby Joe. *The Poetic Art of A. E. Housman: Theory and Practice.* U. of Nebr. Pr. 1978 $20.00. ISBN 0-8032-0969-X. Critical overview, focusing on Housman's metaphors, the limits of the intellect, persona, and point of view.

HUGHES, RICHARD (ARTHUR WARREN). 1900–1976

Welsh by descent, Richard Hughes had a varied university life at Oxford—on vacations, he tramped, begged, acted as a pavement artist, and once led an expedition through Central Europe on some obscure mission that involved political intrigue. As an undergraduate, he wrote *The Sisters' Tragedy* (1922), which GEORGE BERNARD SHAW called "the finest one-act play ever written." Drama was his first effort—which he then abandoned for fiction.

A High Wind in Jamaica (1929), a modern classic, is an extraordinary tale about the casual cruelty in children—captured, in this case, by softhearted pirates. *In Hazard* (1938), the vivid description of sailors battling a crippling storm, is, in fact, an allegory of the collapse of the British Empire. The story of a young Englishman's visit to his cousin's home near Munich in 1923, the year of Hitler's aborted beer-hall putsch, *The Fox in the Attic* (1961) is a novel of extraordinary brilliance. It was the first volume of a projected series, *The Human Predicament*, which the author described as a long historical novel of his own times, culminating in World War II. The second volume of the series, *The Wooden Shepherdess* (1972), was less successful. Hughes worked as a civilian for the Admiralty during World War II and later collaborated on its official history. An unpredictable writer, he "preserves the devastating innocence of the child reflected through a highly sophisticated mature intellect. . . . Hughes is inspired as Tolstoy was by the compulsion to create. Everything that he touches comes to life in a gusty, laughing, tender, tragic interpretation of the weird contradictions that jostle each other so pitifully in the human heart" (*Saturday Review*). His nonfiction works include *Theology and the Cain Complex* and *Fiction as Truth: Selected Literary Writings by Richard Hughes.*

NOVELS BY HUGHES

The Fox in the Attic. HarpC 1962 o.p. The first volume of the series *The Human Predicament,* which explored the roots of the Second World War.
A High Wind in Jamaica: or, The Innocent Voyage. 1929. Amereon Ltd. repr. of 1929 ed. $15.95. ISBN 0-884-11128-8. An English family as prey to pirates. Became a play in 1943 and a film in 1965.
In Hazard: A Novel. Peter Smith 1938 $11.75. ISBN 0-844-60714-2. Adventures on the seas.

PLAY BY HUGHES

The Sisters' Tragedy. 1924. Branden Pub. Co. o.p.

SHORT STORY COLLECTION BY HUGHES

In the Lap of Atlas: Stories of Morocco. Merrimack River 1980 o.p. Collection of stories about Morocco and Arab-Islamic culture.

WORKS BY HUGHES

Fiction as Truth: Selected Literary Writings. Dufour 1984 $36.00. ISBN 0-907476-18-X. Interesting collection touching on the writing process and literary production.

HUGHES, TED (EDWARD JAMES). 1930–

Hughes attended a grammar school in his native Yorkshire before spending two years as a ground mechanic in the Royal Air Force. He went on to Pembroke College, Cambridge, where he studied first literature and then anthropology in amassing some of the primitive lore that underlies his work. There he also met the American poet SYLVIA PLATH, whom he married in 1956. Their troubled marriage produced two children and ended with Plath's suicide in 1963. Hughes remarried in 1970. He has worked as a rose gardener and night watchman as well as reader for the Rank Organisation, and in 1965 became coeditor of the magazine *Modern Poetry in Translation.* Besides his adult poetry, he has done children's verse, translations of East European poets, and several plays. Hughes's long list of honors and prizes culminated in his appointment as poet laureate in December 1984.

Violent in both subject matter and technique, Hughes stands as a major force against the more restrained and traditional verse of the Movement poets. His first book, *The Hawk in the Rain,* created a sensation on publication in 1957. Hughes finds a favorite subject in animals, particularly horses and birds of prey, and has developed a character called Crow in several volumes. His poetry aims to shock and disturb. Often it favors atavistic and instinctual forces beyond human involvement; the animal poems often stem from the point of view of the animal rather than of a human observer and have something in common with the work of the American poet ROBINSON JEFFERS. Hughes's predilection for raw energy, rarer in British than in American poetry, displays itself technically in daring diction, compression, and jarring rhythms.

POETRY BY HUGHES

Crow: From the Life and Songs of the Crow. HarpC 1971 o.p.
Gaudete. HarpC 1977 o.p.
The Hawk in the Rain. 1957. Faber & Faber 1968 $7.95. ISBN 0-571-08614-4

Lupercal. Faber & Faber 1970 $6.95. ISBN 0-571-09246-2
Moortown. HarpC 1980 o.p. A series of longer poetic sequences.
New Selected Poems. HarpC 1982 $15.00. ISBN 0-06-090925-0. Series of poems about the natural world. The best one-volume edition.
Remains of Elmer. HarpC 1979 o.p. For children.
River. HarpC 1984 o.p. Poems about the patterns of the natural world.
Season Songs. Ultramarine Pub. 1975 $20.00. ISBN 0-670-62725-9. Poems on the theme of time and nature.
Selected Poems, 1957–1967. HarpC 1974 o.p.
Under the North Star. Viking Penguin 1981 o.p.
Wolfwatching. FS&G 1991 $18.95. ISBN 0-374-29199-3

PLAYS BY HUGHES

Cave Birds: An Alchemical Cave Drama. Viking Penguin 1978 $15.00. ISBN 0-670-20927-9
The Tiger's Bones and Other Plays for Children. Viking Penguin 1974 o.p.

NONFICTION BY HUGHES

Shakespeare and the Goddess of Complete Being. FS&G 1992 $35.00. ISBN 0-374-26204-7. Ambitious critique of Shakespeare's use of religious myth.

WORK BY HUGHES

Wodwo. Faber & Faber 1971 $8.95. ISBN 0-571-09714-6

BOOKS ABOUT HUGHES

Bishop, Nicholas. *Re-making Poetry: Ted Hughes and a New Critical Psychology.* St. Martin 1991 $45.00. ISBN 0-312-07200-7. Formulates a psychologically based critical approach and applies this to Hughes's canon.
Faas, Ekbert. *Ted Hughes: The Unaccommodated Universe.* Black Sparrow Pr. 1980 $7.50. ISBN 0-87685-459-5. Studies Hughes's language, myths, and primitivism. Includes selected critical writings by Hughes along with two interviews.
Gifford, Terry, and Neil Roberts. *Ted Hughes: A Critical Study.* Faber & Faber 1981 o.p. Focuses on finding Hughes's voice, concerning nature and death.
Hirschberg, Stuart. *Myth in the Poetry of Ted Hughes: A Guide to the Poems.* B & N Imports 1981 o.p. Survey from a mythic perspective.
Sagar, Keith M., and Stephen Tabor. *Ted Hughes: A Bibliography, 1946–1980.* Mansell 1983 o.p. A detailed critical account of Hughes's work as well as a comprehensive bibliography of writings by and about him.
Scigaj, Leonard M. *Ted Hughes.* Macmillan 1991 $22.95. ISBN 0-8057-7006-2. Overview and bibliography; focuses on language and ecology, dissolution and rebirth, aggression and a new divinity.
Uroff, Margaret Dickie. *Sylvia Plath and Ted Hughes.* U. of Ill. Pr. 1979 o.p. Examines the work and lives of the married couple (1956–1963).

HUXLEY, ALDOUS. 1894–1963

Aldous Huxley was a grandson of the great Darwinian apostle THOMAS HENRY HUXLEY (see Vol. 5). A graduate of Eton and of Oxford, he had a reputation for the wit and the wide, curious learning that he packed into his books. Vincent Spalding thought him enormously cultured but not a great novelist because he was not a storyteller; indeed, he produced fewer novels than books of nonfiction. While he is always interesting and engages our intelligence, Huxley seldom touches our emotions. Differentiating his characters by their views and opinions, he wrote novels of ideas, abounding in passages of moralizing and of nonnarrative matter. Huxley was a very influential writer, at once the satirist and the fascinated chronicler of the hedonism of the 1920s. *Brave New World* (1932), his avid, but entertaining—and in some respects prophetic—vision of the mechanized near future, became the classic satire on technology carried to extremes.

In *Literature and Science* (1963), his forty-fifth and last book, he "is more concerned with the use that Literature can make of Science, and the proper attitude of a man of letters towards Science, than with what a scientist might derive from Literature or how Science might recognize, assimilate, and employ the realities proper to Literature." He believed that it was necessary to connect the worlds of science and art.

After immigrating to California in 1937, he became involved with the techniques of mysticism, and the possibilities of reaching "reality" through the drug mescaline were explored in some of his writings.

Huxley received the Award of Merit Medal (1959) from the American Academy of Arts and Letters. In 1962 he was elected a Companion of Literature of the British Royal Society of Literature, (restricted to 10 members), one of the highest literary awards in Britain.

NOVELS BY HUXLEY

After Many a Summer Dies the Swan. 1939. Amereon Ltd. 1977 $20.95. ISBN 0-89190-395-X

Antic Hay. 1923. Buccaneer Bks. 1991 $22.95. ISBN 0-89966-848-8

Brave New World. Buccaneer Bks. 1982 $21.95. ISBN 0-89966-423-7. Futuristic prophecy of intellectual and physical oppression.

Crome Yellow. Buccaneer Bks. 1991 $22.95. ISBN 0-89966-847-X

Eyeless in Gaza. Carroll & Graf 1989 $10.95. ISBN 0-88184-460-8

Island. Borgo Pr. 1991 $20.00. ISBN 0-8095-9048-4. A sequel and alternative to *Brave New World.*

NONFICTION BY HUXLEY

Beyond the Mexique Bay. Academy Chi. Pubs. 1985 o.p.

Brave New World Revisited. 1958. Borgo Pr. 1991 $20.00. ISBN 0-8095-9047-6

Huxley and God: Essays on Mysticism, Religion, and Spirituality. Harper SF 1992 $13.00. ISBN 0-06-250536-X. Essays on classical mysticism that present mystical practice as the noblest human endeavor.

WORKS BY HUXLEY

World of Aldous Huxley. Ed. by C. J. Rollo. Peter Smith o.p. An omnibus collection of fiction and nonfiction covering three decades.

Collected Short Stories. I. R. Dee 1992 repr. of 1957 ed. $14.95. ISBN 0-929587-81-2

BOOKS ABOUT HUXLEY

Baker, Robert S. *The Dark Historic Page: Social Satire and Historicism in the Novels of Aldous Huxley, 1921–1939.* U. of Wis. Pr. 1982 $29.50. ISBN 0-299-08940-1. Huxley's vision of social history and historical ideology.

Bass, Eben E. *Aldous Huxley: An Annotated Bibliography of Criticism.* Garland 1981 o.p. Wide-ranging and useful list of secondary sources.

Dunaway, David King. *Huxley in Hollywood.* Doubleday 1991 $14.95. ISBN 0-385-41591-5. Biographical focus on Huxley's American screenwriting career from 1937 until his death.

Eschelbach, Claire, and Joyce Lee Shober. *Aldous Huxley: A Bibliography, 1916–1959.* Hippocrene Bks. 1979 $16.00. ISBN 0-374-92626-3. Surveys the major critical works of Huxley and his writing.

Firchow, Peter Edgerly. *The End of Utopia: A Study of Aldous Huxley's* Brave New World. Bucknell U. Pr. 1984 o.p. Examines Huxley's vision of the future in terms of literature, history, politics, science, and sociology.

Kuehn, Robert E., ed. *Aldous Huxley: A Collection of Critical Essays*. P-H 1974 o.p. Huxley and the novel of ideas; Huxley's quest for values; Huxley as biographer; his early poetry.

Nance, Guinevera A. *Aldous Huxley*. Continuum 1989 $18.95. ISBN 0-8044-2639-2. Biographical and critical examination of Huxley, focusing on his novels and how they are affected by his philosophical explorations.

Watt, Donald. *Aldous Huxley: The Critical Heritage*. Routledge 1975 o.p.

Watts, Harold H. *Aldous Huxley*. Macmillan 1969 $18.95. ISBN 0-8057-1284-4. Survey of his life; bibliography.

ISHERWOOD, CHRISTOPHER. 1904–1986

Isherwood met W. H. AUDEN at an English boarding school. They collaborated on three fantasy verse plays. In 1938 the two went to China together, financed by their publishers. *Journey to a War* (1939) is their diary, kept alternately. In 1939 they came to the United States, intending to become permanent residents. In 1946 Isherwood became a U.S. citizen, and in 1949 he was elected a member of the National Institute of Arts and Letters.

His excellent brief novels, largely autobiographical, are written with precision. He is still best known for the brilliance of his Berlin stories, written before World War II. He spent about four years in Germany; the eccentrics of *The Berlin Stories* (1946) symbolize the decadence of pre-Nazi Berlin. John Van Druten adapted his successful play, *I Am a Camera* (1951), from these stories. Its 1966 musical version, *Cabaret*, won the N.Y. Drama Critics Circle Award and a Tony; it was later also made into a popular film.

"Hinduism and homosexuality have long been favorite themes of Christopher Isherwood. [*A Meeting by the River*, 1967] combines them in a short novel, composed entirely of letters and diaries, that is rather old-fashioned in form but distinctly up-to-date in its descriptions of post-British India and post-Genet California" (*N.Y. Times*). The book, says Stanley Kauffmann (*New Republic*), "is credible, moving, and ultimately ironic. [Its] considerable work is accomplished with beautifully spare means, seemingly easy but possible only to an artist who has always been good and who has lost no refinement." *A Single Man* (1964), on the theme of homosexual love, portrays a college professor distraught over the death of his male lover. Isherwood was one of the first prominent international figures to admit his homosexuality and was an early spokesperson for gay rights.

In California Isherwood wrote movie scripts and, with Huxley, became interested in the ancient Indian philosophy of the Vedas. With Swami Prabhavanda, he translated from the Sanskrit, in prose and poetry, the Mahabharata Bhagavadgita, *The Song of God*, with an introduction by ALDOUS HUXLEY. He edited a number of books on Vedanta and Yoga. *Exhumations* contains poems, articles, essays, and stories.

NOVELS BY ISHERWOOD

All the Conspirators. 1928. New Dir. Pr. 1979 $7.95. ISBN 0-8112-0725-0

The Berlin Stories. Bentley 1979 repr. of 1946 ed. $18.00. ISBN 0-8376-0449-4. Explores the cosmopolitan and intellectual decadence of Germany on the eve of World War II.

Down There on a Visit. FS&G 1987 $8.95. ISBN 0-374-52052-6

A Meeting by the River. 1967. FS&G 1988 $7.95. ISBN 0-374-52076-3

The Memorial. FS&G 1988 $8.95. ISBN 0-374-52067-4

Prater Violet. FS&G 1987 $5.95. ISBN 0-374-52053-4

A Single Man. FS&G 1987 $10.95. ISBN 0-374-52038-0

NONFICTION BY ISHERWOOD

Christopher and His Kind. FS&G 1987 $8.95. ISBN 0-374-52036-4. Autobiography.
People One Ought to Know. Doubleday 1982 o.p. Foreword by Andre Mangeot.

WORKS BY ISHERWOOD

Where Joy Resides: A Christopher Isherwood Reader. FS&G 1991 $12.95. ISBN 0-374-52255-3. With an introduction by Gore Vidal.

BOOKS ABOUT ISHERWOOD

Fryer, Jonathan. *Isherwood: A Biography of Christopher Isherwood.* Trafalgar 1977 o.p. Well-written account of Isherwood's life and work.

Funk, Robert W. *Christopher Isherwood: A Reference Guide.* G. K. Hall 1979 o.p. Bibliography of Isherwood's primary works and criticism.

Lehmann, John. *Christopher Isherwood: A Personal Memoir.* Grove Pr. 1987 o.p. A friend's colorful biographical reminiscences.

Piazza, Paul. *Christopher Isherwood: Myth and Anti-myth.* Col. U. Pr. 1978 $36.50. ISBN 0-231-04118-7. Biographical focus on Isherwood's personal and literary experiences of family, war, heroism, and homosexuality.

Schwerdt, Lisa M. *Isherwood's Fiction: The Self and Technique.* St. Martin 1989 $39.95. ISBN 0-312-02789-3. Examines the nature of Isherwood's autobiographically based fiction.

White, James. *Christopher Isherwood: A Bibliography of His Personal Papers.* Texas Ctr. Writers 1987 $10.95. ISBN 0-916092-11-9. Sourcebook for Isherwood's letters, diaries, and unpublished journals.

JENNINGS, ELIZABETH. 1926–

Elizabeth Jennings was born in Boston, England. Educated at Oxford High School and St. Anne's College, Oxford, she worked in the Oxford City Library from 1950 to 1958 and then as a reader for the publisher Chatto & Windus. Since 1961 she has been a freelance writer. She lives in Oxford but has often visited Italy, where many of her poems are set. After a difficult period, which included stays in a mental hospital, Jennings has written strongly religious verse. She has said that "my Roman Catholic religion and my poems are the most important things in my life."

Jennings is one of the major figures associated with the Movement, one of the most important "movements" in postwar British poetry. Movement poetry is meticulously crafted, controlled and common-sensical, sardonic, lucid, and self-consciously ironic. Jennings writes a restrained, sometimes lapidary, poetry of lucid diction and traditional meters. The Italian setting and profound religious conviction distinguish her work from that of the other Movement writers, as does her more personal and confessional stance. She has done numerous translations, including an interesting version of MICHELANGELO's (see Vol. 3) sonnets.

POETRY BY JENNINGS

The Animals Arrival. Dufour 1969 $13.95. ISBN 0-8023-1207-1
Celebrations and Elegies. Humanities 1982 o.p.
Consequently I Rejoice. Humanities 1980 o.p. Focuses on Jennings's personal morality.
In Praise of Our Lady. David & Charles 1982 o.p. A series of spiritual devotions.
Moments of Grace. Humanities 1980 o.p. Poems celebrating Christian beliefs and worship.
The Secret Brother and Other Poems. Dufour 1966 $13.95. ISBN 0-8023-1194-6. Verse for children.
Selected Poems. 1979. Carcanet o.p. A series of confessional poems.

BOOK ABOUT JENNINGS

Schmidt, Michael, and Grevel Lindop, eds. *British Poetry since 1960*. Carcanet 1972 o.p.
    Contains a study of Jennings by Margaret Byers.

JONES, DAVID (MICHAEL). 1895–1974

David Jones did not publish his first book of poetry until his forties. Although
he was born in Kent, his Welsh father instilled in him a love for the culture of
Wales that pervades his work. At first Jones intended to be an artist, and he left
grammar school for Camberwell School of Art. With the outbreak of war, he
enlisted in the Royal Welsh Fusiliers (ROBERT GRAVES served as an officer in the
same regiment) and served in Flanders and France. After the war, he completed
his education and began a successful artistic career, during which he became
perhaps best known as an engraver and watercolorist. Immersed in legend,
myth, and romance, he held that humans are fundamentally religious. His own
religious beliefs led him to convert to Roman Catholicism in 1921.

Although W. B. YEATS saluted his first book, Jones stood apart from the
literary mainstream of his day, despite obvious debts to the methods of EZRA
POUND, T. S. ELIOT, and JAMES JOYCE. His first volume, *In Parenthesis* (1937),
combines both poetry and prose in chronicling the wartime career of its major
figure, John Ball. His even more ambitious second book, *The Anathemata:
Fragments of an Attempted Writing* (1952), uses the structure of the Tridentine
Mass to chronicle the history of Britain from early geological times through
preindustrial London. Some of its techniques of presentation and counterpart-
ing of myths and factual materials resemble Pound's *Cantos*. W. H. AUDEN
judged it the best modern long poem in English. The later works *The Tribune's
Visitation* and *The Sleeping Lord* (1974) deal with the Roman Empire in the time
of Jesus. Readers will appreciate Jones's inclusion of his own notes to his
difficult, allusive verse.

POETRY BY JONES

The Anathèmata: Fragments of an Attempted Writing. 1952. Faber & Faber 1972 o.p. His
    major poem.
The Dying Gaul and Other Writings. Ed. by Harman Grisewood, Faber & Faber 1978 o.p.
In Parenthesis. 1937. Faber & Faber 1975 $10.95. ISBN 0-571-05661-X. His first book of
    poetry, mingled with prose.
Roman Quarry and Other Sequences. Sheep Meadow 1981 $14.95. ISBN 0-935296-24-7. A
    collection of minor works.
The Sleeping Lord and Other Fragments. Faber & Faber 1974 o.p.

WORKS BY JONES

Dai Greatcoat: A Self-Portrait of David Jones in His Letters. Ed. by René Hague. Faber &
    Faber 1980 o.p. Interesting autobiographical look at Jones as reflected in his letters.
Epoch and Artist. Faber & Faber 1973 o.p. Criticism of art and artists.
Introducing David Jones: A Selection of His Writings. Ed. by John Matthias. Faber & Faber
    1980 o.p. Wide-ranging collection.

BOOKS ABOUT JONES

Blamires, David Malcolm. *David Jones: Artist and Writer*. Manchester 1971 o.p. Compares
    Jones's art and literature.
Blissett, William. *The Long Conversation: A Memoir of David Jones*. OUP 1981 o.p.
    Biographical study.

Dilworth, Thomas. *The Shape of Meaning in the Poetry of David Jones*. U. of Toronto Pr. 1988 $47.50. ISBN 0-802-02613-3. Discusses genre and technique, form, typology, sequence, and secular and sacred mythos in Jones's poetry.

Hague, René. *A Commentary on* The Anathemata *of David Jones*. D.G.S. Skelton 1977 o.p. Meticulous elucidation of sources, allusions, and references.

Matthias, John, ed. *David Jones: Man and Poet*. Nat. Poet. Foun. 1989 $55.00. ISBN 0-943-37303-4. Collection includes critical and biographical excerpts.

Rees, Samuel. *David Jones*. Twayne 1978 o.p. Survey of his life; bibliography.

_____. *David Jones: An Annotated Bibliography and Guide to Research*. Garland 1977 o.p.

JOYCE, JAMES. 1881–1941

For many critics, James Joyce is the most important novelist of the twentieth century. He perfected the stream-of-consciousness monologue (which Edouard Dujardin and DOROTHY RICHARDSON had used before him); emerged as the most inventive of the experimental novelists; was a polyglot who could pun in a dozen languages; and antagonized his friends because of his egoism, yet could write about characters unlike himself with great compassion. Joyce's life was filled with contrasts: He abandoned his home to become an artist and spent his life in exile writing about the city he had abandoned. He was thought of as a great writer by people who had read little of his work, for his books were banned in English-speaking countries. Though *Ulysses* (1922) was suppressed for its supposed obscenity, few books stress the virtues of family life as strongly.

There is always more to Joyce's works than first meets the eye. The stories in *Dubliners* (1914) are, on the surface, naturalistic descriptions of city life; but Joyce's irony and symbolism show the true sterility of Dublin. One of the stories, "The Dead," seems to be about a festive occasion, the Morkans' annual dance; but the ghostly imagery reveals that the dance is a dance of the dead.

A Portrait of the Artist as a Young Man (1916) is similarly undercut by irony. The novel tells of Stephen Daedalus—a protagonist seemingly very much like the young Joyce, though ultimately quite different—and his struggle to become a writer. The novel vibrates between the alternatives of greatness and inexperience, triumph and failure, art and sham. It is filled with subtleties and hidden beauty: intricate imagery; compact, powerful prose; and musical, flowing language.

In Joyce's early works, the innovative techniques are always subtle, concealed beneath a plain, seemingly conventional story. In his later works, this is no longer true. The reader is immediately aware of the experimental techniques; the prose may seem strange or unusual; and very often the story is difficult or impossible to discern.

Ulysses is such a work—a novel with many strata of meaning. On one level, the book tells of the need Stephen Daedalus has for a father, of Leopold Bloom's yearning for a son, and of how the two meet during the one day on which the novel takes place: June 16, 1904. It was a day of great significance for Joyce, because on it he met Nora Barnacle, who later became his wife. On another level, Stephen is Telemachus, Bloom is Odysseus, and their story is a modern "odyssey." But here, again, irony is important, for it is in the way that Bloom is *not* Odysseus, in his compassionate and extraordinary humanity, that his greatness and universality are revealed.

Every chapter of *Ulysses* has its own technique, style, central symbols, colors—all ingeniously used to enhance the action. In a chapter in which the chief event is the birth of a child, the style delineates the birth and evolution of the English language. Joyce accomplishes this by parodying great English writers, moving forward chronologically from the earliest to the most recent. *Ulysses* is a very demanding book; but after the initial difficulties are surmounted, it yields many rewards.

Ulysses was so inventive that it seemed to exhaust the possibilities for innovation in the English novel. Joyce, therefore, moved beyond English and wrote *Finnegans Wake* (1939) in a language of puns, allusions, and neologisms. The prose demands a slow reading pace, for the words themselves are as important as the ideas they represent. It cannot be read like most novels, in a few sittings; it must be savored slowly, bit by bit, over months and years. A reader must come to it with a great store of patience, intelligence, and humor and perhaps also with a good supply of critical commentaries.

Seven decades ago, Joyce's frankness seemed obscene to some, and he encountered difficulty in finding publishers for his works. Typesetters refused to work on his books; *Ulysses* was published in Paris because it was banned in Britain and the United States; and Americans who were eager to read it had to smuggle the book past customs inspectors until 1933, when, in a historic decision, Judge Woolsey declared that it was not obscene.

Today, enthusiasm for Joyce continues to be strong. In 1967 the exciting film versions of *Ulysses* and of passages from *Finnegans Wake* played to eager audiences, as did the play *Stephen D*—an adaptation of *A Portrait of the Artist* and *Stephen Hero* (1944)—and the revival of *The Coach with the Six Insides*, Jean Erdman's award-winning dramatic dance interpretation of *Finnegans Wake*. The year 1967 was also notable for the discovery of "Giacomo Joyce," a poetic love story Joyce wrote for a young woman, his pupil in Trieste, with whom he became infatuated. Joyce himself did not publish it, but he worked passages from it into *Ulysses* and *Finnegans Wake*.

Joyce spent most of his life away from his native Ireland—mostly in Trieste, Rome, and Paris, it being his belief that exile was necessary for his art. He and his family were visiting in Vichy when France fell in 1940; they took refuge in Zurich, where Joyce soon died, thus ending a lifetime of struggle against poverty, obtuse and fearful publishers, and his daughter's madness.

NOVELS BY JOYCE

Dubliners. 1914. Random 1993 $13.50. ISBN 0-679-60049-3. Stories of paralysis and emotional tepidity.

Finnegans Wake. 1939. Viking Penguin 1982 $11.95. ISBN 0-14-006286-6. A linguistic dream-fantasy, written in stream-of-consciousness style.

A Portrait of the Artist as a Young Man. 1916. Buccaneer Bks. 1992 $26.95. ISBN 0-89966-899-2. Autobiographical novel, with text and criticism.

A Shorter Finnegans Wake. Ed. by Anthony Burgess. Viking Penguin 1968 o.p. An accessible shortening of a difficult work.

Stephen Hero. 1955. New Dir. Pr. 1969 $9.95. ISBN 0-8112-0074-4. Introduction by Theodore Spencer, with five subsequently discovered manuscript pages.

Ulysses. 1922. Random 1992 $20.00. ISBN 0-679-60011-6. The long-awaited corrected text in the Random House paperback.

PLAY BY JOYCE

Exiles: A Play. 1918. Ed. by Michael Groden. Garland 1978 repr. of 1951 ed. o.p. Includes hitherto unpublished notes by the author, discovered after his death. Introduction by Padraic Colum.

WORKS BY JOYCE

Letters of James Joyce. 3 vols. Viking Penguin 1957–66 o.p.

The Portable James Joyce. 1947. Viking Penguin 1976 $12.00. ISBN 0-14-015030-7.
Introduction by Harry Levin. Includes *A Portrait of the Artist as a Young Man,
Collected Poems, Exiles, Dubliners*, selections from *Ulysses* and *Finnegans Wake.*

BOOKS ABOUT JOYCE

Attridge, Derek, and Daniel Ferrer, eds. *Post-structuralist Joyce: Essays from the French.*
Cambridge U. Pr. 1984 o.p. Explores intertextuality in Joyce and the uses and ruses
of writing; includes a meditation by Derrida on two words of Joyce's.

Beja, Morris, and Shari Benstock. *Coping with Joyce: Essays from the Copenhagen
Symposium.* Ohio St. U. Pr. 1989 $37.50. ISBN 0-8142-0467-8. Examines the language
of *Exiles*; Joycean pedagogy; and Joyce and modernist ideology.

Benstock, Bernard, ed. *Critical Essays on James Joyce.* G. K. Hall 1985 $40.00. ISBN 0-
8161-8751-7. Discusses the cubism of *Portrait* as well as Joyce's Eucharistic imagery;
presents a deconstructive perspective on *Finnegans Wake.*

_____, ed. *James Joyce: The Augmented Ninth.* Syracuse U. Pr. 1988 $35.00. ISBN 0-
8156-2446-8. Discusses Joyce, Derrida, and the discourse of the other; Joyce and
clichés; women in Joyce's Dublin; and Joyce and the ideology of character.

Bowen, Zack, and James F. Carens, eds. *A Companion to Joyce Studies.* Greenwood 1984
$85.00. ISBN 0-313-22832-9. Includes chapters surveying all Joyce's works; a textual
and publishing history; and a history of Joyce criticism and schólarship.

Brown, Richard. *James Joyce and Sexuality.* Cambridge U. Pr. 1989. $17.95. ISBN 0-521-
36852-9. Examines sex, sex roles, love, and women in Joyce's writing.

Cheng, Vincent, and Timothy Peter Martin, eds. *Joyce in Context.* Cambridge U. Pr. 1992
$59.95. ISBN 0-521-41358-3. Discusses Joyce and cartoons as well as Joyce's relation
to Ford Madox Ford, Virginia Woolf, Sigmund Freud, and Homer.

DiBernard, Barbara. *Alchemy and* Finnegans Wake. State U. of NY Pr. 1980 $64.50. ISBN
0-87395-388-6. Explores occult and alchemical themes and influences in Joyce's
final novel.

Dunleavy, Janet Egleson. ed. *Reviewing Classics of Joyce Criticism.* U. of Ill. Pr. 1991 o.p.
Analysis of such seminal critics of Joyce as Kain, Tindall, Budgen, Glasheen, Gilbert,
and Levin.

Gluck, Barbara Reich. *Beckett and Joyce: Friendship and Fiction.* Bucknell U. Pr. 1979
$27.50. ISBN 0-8387-2060-9. Comparative study of the two writers' styles and
influences.

Halper, Nathan. *Studies in Joyce.* Bks. Demand 1983 $46.10. ISBN 0-6852-0451-0. Essays
on Joyce's relation to Rebecca West, T. S. Eliot, and Ezra Pound, as well as on design
in *Dubliners.*

Henke, Suzette A. *James Joyce and the Politics of Desire.* Routledge 1990 $45.00. ISBN 0-
415-01056-X. Feminist examination of Joyce's lust, desire, fantasy, vulnerability, and
fear.

Herr, Cheryl. *Joyce's Anatomy of Culture.* U. of Ill. Pr. 1986 $29.95. ISBN 0-252-01234-8.
Examines Irish social and popular culture in Joyce's fiction.

Kenner, Hugh, and Edmund L. Epstein. *A Starchamber Quiry: A James Joyce Centennial
Volume, 1882–1982.* Routledge Chapman & Hall 1982 $35.00. ISBN 0-416-31560-7.
Explores such topics as Joyce and the body, Joyce and the soul, and Joyce and his
civilization.

Lobner, Corinna del Greco. *James Joyce's Italian Connection: The Poetics of the Word.*
U. of Iowa Pr. 1989 $20.00. ISBN 0-87745-226-1. Examines Italian influences on
Joyce's writing.

Loss, Archie K. *Joyce's Visible Art: The Work of Joyce and the Visual Arts, 1904–1922.*
Bks. Demand 1984 $36.40. ISBN 0-8357-1576-0. Investigates artistic themes,
backgrounds, and influences in Joyce's writing.

Maddox, Brenda. *Nora: A Biography of Nora Joyce.* Fawcett 1989 $12.95. ISBN 0-449-
90410-5. Controversial biography of Joyce's wife, often critical of the writer.

Peterson, Richard F., Alan M. Cohn, and Edmund L. Epstein, eds. *Work in Progress: Joyce
Centenary Essays.* S. Ill. U. Pr. 1983 $22.50. ISBN 0-8093-1094-5. Essay topics include
epiphanies in *Dubliners*, Joycean psychology, and narrative movement and place.

Rabaté, Jean-Michel. *James Joyce: Authorized Reader*. Johns Hopkins 1991 o.p. Examines Circe's stagecraft, Molly's yarn, and Idiolects and idiolex.

————. *Joyce upon the Void: The Genesis of Doubt*. Macmillan 1991 o.p. Examines belief and doubt in Joyce's fiction.

Restuccia, Frances L. *Joyce and the Law of the Father*. Yale U. Pr. 1989 $24.00. ISBN 0-30-004444-5. Psychological criticism, focusing on Joyce's themes of fathers and patriarchy.

Rice, Thomas Jackson. *James Joyce: A Guide to Research*. Garland 1982 $36.00. ISBN 0-824-09383-6

Senn, Fritz, and John Paul Riquelme, eds. *Joyce's Dislocutions: Essays on Readings as Translation*. Bks. Demand repr. of 1984 ed. $69.40. ISBN 0-7837-3395-X. Investigates the illusion of translatability, foreign readings, and metastasis.

Staley, Thomas F. *An Annotated Bibliography of James Joyce*. Harvester Pr. 1989 o.p.

KAVANAGH, PATRICK. 1905–1967

"My life has in many ways been a tragedy and a failure," wrote Patrick Kavanagh toward his death. Yet posterity has increasingly viewed him as one of the major Irish poets after W. B. YEATS. Born in Innishkeen, County Monaghan, Kavanagh ended his formal education after grammar school. He lived on a farm in his native parish until moving to Dublin in 1939, which he later described as one of the great mistakes of his life. There he supported himself primarily through journalism until awarded a sinecure of £400 a year for extramural lectures at University College, Dublin. After an illness in the mid-1950s, he grew resigned to obscurity and mellowed in his long literary war with both Irish repression and the Irish literary establishment. Besides his journalism, he also wrote novels of an autobiographical cast. He married for the first time during the last years of his life.

Sprung from Roman Catholic peasant stock, Kavanagh saw himself as voicing his own heritage against more anglicized (and more famous) writers. His first volume, *Ploughman and Other Poems*, established the rural themes that mark much of his verse. His best-known, and perhaps his greatest poem, *The Great Hunger* (1942), follows a potato farmer named Patrick Maguire through the famine of the 1840s and presents a blistering attack on the sexual and spiritual deprivation of rural Irish peasantry. Kavanagh later criticized the poem as lacking humor, and his subsequent work shows a more temperate acceptance of the ironic comedy of life, as in "Canal Bank Walk." He never lost his acerbity.

POETRY BY KAVANAGH

Collected Poems of Kavanagh. Norton 1973 $8.95. ISBN 0-393-00694-8. Series of poems about rural culture.

Complete Poems. Kavanagh 1972 $30.00. ISBN 0-914612-04-2. A definitive collection of Kavanagh's poems.

The Great Hunger. Biblio Dist. 1971 repr. of 1942 ed. o.p. Reprint of his best-known poem.

NOVELS BY KAVANAGH

By Night Unstarred: An Autobiographical Novel. Kavanagh 1978 $30.00. ISBN 0-914612-07-7. Strongly reflects Kavanagh's Irish roots.

The Green Fool. Irish Bk. Ctr. 1975 o.p. Heavily autobiographical novel.

Tarry Flynn. Proscenium 1977 $2.50. ISBN 0-912262-40-0. Heavily autobiographical novel, later made into a play.

NONFICTION BY KAVANAGH

Lapped Furrows: Correspondence, 1933–1967. Kavanagh 1969 $30.00. ISBN 0-914612-02-6

WORK BY KAVANAGH

November Haggard: Uncollected Prose and Verse. Kavanagh 1971 $30.00. ISBN 0-914612-03-4

BOOKS ABOUT KAVANAGH

Kavanagh, Peter, and Patrick Kavanagh. *Patrick Kavanagh: Man and Poet.* Nat. Poet. Foun. 1986 $32.00. ISBN 0-915032-63-5. Biographical and critical essays.
———. *Sacred Keeper: A Biography of Patrick Kavanagh.* P. V. Goldsmith 1980. Comprehensive, well-written account of Kavanagh and his work.
Nemo, John. *Patrick Kavanagh.* Twayne 1979 o.p. Overview of his life; bibliography.
O'Brien, Darcy. *Patrick Kavanagh.* Bucknell U. Pr. 1975 $6.50 ISBN 0-8387-7884-4. Short survey of Kavanagh as poetic nationalist.
Quinn, Antoinette. *Patrick Kavanagh: Born-Again Romantic.* Gill 1991 o.p. Examines Kavanagh's sensibility as a present-day incarnation of romanticism.
———. *Patrick Kavanagh: A Critical Study.* Syracuse U. Pr. 1991 $39.95. ISBN 0-8156-2549-9. A complement to Nemo's critique.

LARKIN, PHILIP. 1922–1985

Born in Coventry, where his father served as city treasurer for 22 years, Larkin was educated at King Henry VIII School in his native city and at St. John's College, Oxford. Perhaps his most important friend at Oxford University was KINGSLEY AMIS, who dedicated the novel *Lucky Jim* (1954) to him; Larkin reciprocated by dedicating *XX Poems* (1950) to Amis. A librarian by profession, Larkin held various posts in British libraries after graduation from college, including librarian of Brynmor Jones Library, University of Hull. Besides his verse, Larkin wrote two novels in the 1940s, *Jill* (1940) and *A Girl in Winter* (1947). An enthusiastic jazz buff, he did feature stories on that subject for the newspaper *The Daily Telegraph* from 1961 to 1971, and reviews of jazz recordings. Larkin was a private man who discouraged publication of details of his life. Recently, however, his correspondence has been published and some aspects of his life, such as his anti-Semitic views, have surfaced.

Influenced at first by W. B. YEATS, Larkin soon became perhaps the finest of the Movement poets, who eschewed both rhetorical excess and cosmic themes in the service of a restrained, conversational idiom presenting more ordinary subjects. Never a prolific poet, Larkin earned his high public esteem through the quality rather than quantity of his verse. Poems such as "Church Going" or "The Whitsun Weddings" combine extraordinary skill with an ironic integrity to succeed in making major statements in spite of themselves. Like W. H. AUDEN, Larkin can also excel in wryly comic verse, as in his toad poems. In the introduction to his volume *The North Ship* (1946), he declared THOMAS HARDY his favorite poet.

POETRY BY LARKIN

Collected Poems. FS&G 1993 $14.95. ISBN 0-374-52275-8
High Windows. FS&G 1983 $8.95. ISBN 0-374-51212-4. Focuses on the decline of traditions.
The North Ship. Faber & Faber 1974 $8.95. ISBN 0-571-10503-3
The Whitsun Weddings. Faber & Faber 1971 $7.95. ISBN 0-571-09710-3

NOVELS BY LARKIN

Jill. 1940. Overlook Pr. 1984 $22.50. ISBN 0-87951-038-2
A Girl in Winter. 1947. Overlook Pr. 1985 $22.50. ISBN 0-87951-039-0. Tells the story of a
   fateful winter day in the life of a European woman who has fled to England during
   World War II.

WORKS BY LARKIN

All What Jazz: A Record Diary. FS&G 1985 $19.95. ISBN 0-374-10340-2. Collection of
   record reviews Larkin originally wrote for England's Daily Telegraph.
(ed.). *The Oxford Book of Twentieth Century English Verse.* OUP 1973 $35.00. ISBN 0-19-
   812137-7. Reflections of life in contemporary England.
Required Writing: Miscellaneous Pieces, 1955–1982. FS&G 1984 $9.95. ISBN 0-374-
   51840-8. A wide-ranging collection of essays.
Selected Letters: 1940–1985. Ed. by Anthony Thwaite. FS&G 1993 $40.00. ISBN 0-374-
   25829-5

BOOKS ABOUT LARKIN

Bloomfield, B. C. *Philip Larkin: A Bibliography, 1933–1976.* Faber & Faber 1979 o.p.
   Primary sources.
Booth, James. *Philip Larkin: Writer.* St. Martin 1992 $39.95. ISBN 0-312-08360-2.
   Overview of his life.
Hassan, Salem K. *Philip Larkin and His Contemporaries: An Air of Authenticity.* St. Martin
   1988 $35.00. ISBN 0-312-01184-9. Examines Larkin in relation to his contemporaries
   of the 1950s movement.
Martin, Bruce. *Philip Larkin.* Twayne 1978 o.p. Overview of his life; and bibliography.
Motion, Andrew. *Philip Larkin: A Writer's Life.* FS&G 1993 $30.00. ISBN 0-571-15174-4.
   Devoted to his writing and work as a librarian. Larkin's somewhat unhappy
   childhood and his later moodiness, prejudices, and shyness are depicted here by
   Motion, who was a colleague of Larkin at the University of Hull.
Rossen, Janice. *Philip Larkin: His Life's Work.* U. of Iowa Pr. 1990 $24.95. ISBN 0-87743-
   271-7. Explores Larkin's use of lyrical distancing and melancholy as well as his
   attempt to preserve and celebrate England in his work.
Thwaite, Anthony. *Larkin at Sixty.* Faber & Faber 1982 o.p.
Timms, David. *Philip Larkin.* B & N Imports 1973 o.p. A study of Larkin's role in the
   Movement and his parochialism.
Tolley, A. T. *My Proper Ground: A Study of the Work of Philip Larkin and Its Development.*
   Carleton Pr. 1991 $29.95. ISBN 0-8862-9139-9. Examines the formation of Larkin's
   style.
Whalen, Terry. *Philip Larkin and English Poetry.* Macmillan 1986 o.p. General consider-
   ation of Larkin's poetry.

LAWRENCE, D(AVID) H(ERBERT). 1885–1930

   One of Lawrence's finest novels, traditional in form and unlike his later work,
is *Sons and Lovers* (1913), an epic of family life in a colliery district and
"unabashed autobiography." Lawrence himself was the fourth child of a miner
who was a heavy drinker. Born in the coal region of Nottinghamshire, he earned
a scholarship to Nottingham University and briefly pursued a teaching career
before devoting his life to writing. *The Rainbow* (1915), with its forthright
treatment of sexual passion, was condemned as obscene in 1915 and the entire
edition destroyed. *Lady Chatterley's Lover* (1928), which Lawrence considered
his greatest work, was written in three versions. It was privately printed in
Florence, Italy, and banned both in Britain and the United States until 1959,
when Grove Press undertook publication of the third manuscript version and
issued the first U.S. unexpurgated version. It was immediately banned by the

U.S. Post Office, but in a now-famous opinion, Judge Frederick van Pelt Bryan ruled the ban "unconstitutional" and confirmed it as "illegal and void."

Always in search of warm climates for his tuberculosis, Lawrence spent some time in New Mexico in 1924 on a ranch presented to him by Mabel Dodge Luhan. Here "he found himself as much at harmony as he was ever to be with any place." After his death, the battle waged by Lawrence's (often jealous) disciples turned to civil warfare. Abuse, libel, and recriminations fill many of the early books about him. He left behind him "an extraordinarily large body of work for so short a career, nearly all of it strongly marked by his unmistakable literary and philosophical imprint."

Novels by Lawrence

Aaron's Rod. 1922. Viking Penguin 1990 $6.95. ISBN 0-14-018196-2

The Boy in the Bush. (coauthored with M. L. Skinner). 1924. Viking Penguin 1992 $9.95. ISBN 0-14-018446-5

Four Short Novels. Viking Penguin 1976 $5.00. ISBN 0-14-003726-8. Includes *Love among the Haystacks, The Ladybird, The Fox,* and *The Captain's Doll.*

Kangaroo. 1923. Viking Penguin 1992 $9.95. ISBN 0-14-018201-2. Autobiographical novel about fascism, set in Australia.

Lady Chatterley's Lover. 1928. Buccaneer Bks. 1981 $23.95. ISBN 0-89966-375-3. About an aristocratic woman's earthy passion for her gamekeeper.

The Lost Girl. 1920. Cambridge U. Pr. 1981 $74.95. ISBN 0-521-22263-X

Plumed Serpent. 1926. Random 1955 $10.00. ISBN 0-394-70023-6. Mexican religious cults. Introduction by W. Y. Tindall.

The Rainbow. 1915. Buccaneer Bks. 1989 $35.95. ISBN 0-89966-644-2. Generations of a Nottinghamshire family.

Sons and Lovers. 1913. Knopf 1991 $17.00. ISBN 0-679-40572-0

The White Peacock. 1911. Viking Penguin 1990 $7.95. ISBN 0-14-018219-5. Deals with the social mores of the time.

Women in Love. 1920. Buccaneer Bks. 1984 $27.95. ISBN 0-89966-496-2. A novel about different generations of a Nottingham family.

Short Story Collections by Lawrence

Complete Short Stories of D. H. Lawrence. 3 vols. Viking Penguin 1977 $5.95–$7.00 ea. ISBNs 0-14-004382-9, 0-14-004255-5, 0-14-004255-5. Includes the collections originally published as *A Modern Lover, The Lovely Lady, Love among the Haystacks,* and others.

The Prussian Officer, and Other Stories. 1914. *Short Story Index Repr. Ser.* Ayer repr. of 1914 ed. $21.00. ISBN 0-8369-3918-2

St. Mawr. 1925. Random 1959 $7.00. ISBN 0-394-70071-6. Bound with *The Man Who Died.*

Poetry by Lawrence

Complete Poems. Ed. by Vivian de Sola Pinto and F. Warren Roberts. Viking Penguin 1977 o.p.

Plays by Lawrence

The Complete Plays. Viking Penguin 1966 o.p. Contains all eight of Lawrence's finished plays and two fragments.

Nonfiction by Lawrence

Collected Letters. Ed. by Harry T. Moore. 2 vols. Viking Penguin 1962 o.p. Contains 1,200 letters with a useful "Who's Who in the Lawrence Letters" by the editor.

The Centaur Letters: Unpublished Letters by D. H. Lawrence. U. of Tex. Pr. 1970 $25.00. ISBN 0-87959-060-2. Foreword by Edward D. McDonald.

Etruscan Places. 1932. A travel classic.

Reflections on the Death of a Porcupine. 1925. Cambridge U. Pr. 1988 $89.95. ISBN 0-521-
    26622-X. Puts down, sometimes in a poetic and allegorical vein, sometimes
    satirically, Lawrence's views on life and love, on war and peace, and on the writer's
    craft.

WORK BY LAWRENCE

The Portable D. H. Lawrence. Ed. by Diana Trilling. Viking Penguin 1977 $12.00. ISBN 0-
    14-015028-5. A broad collection of Lawrence's works.

BOOKS ABOUT LAWRENCE

Bell, Michael. *D. H. Lawrence: Language and Being.* Cambridge U. Pr. 1992 $54.95. ISBN
    0-521-39200-4. Focuses on language as a way of understanding Lawrence's wisdom
    and sense of craft.

Daiches, David. *D. H. Lawrence.* Folcroft 1977 o.p. A good general overview of Lawrence
    and his work.

Draper, R. P., ed. *D. H. Lawrence: The Critical Heritage. Critical Heritage Ser.* Routledge
    1970 $69.50. ISBN 0-7100-6591-4. An important collection of reviews and criticism.

Goodheart, Eugene. *The Utopian Vision of D. H. Lawrence.* U. Ch. Pr. 1963 o.p. Focuses
    on Lawrence's social concerns and evidence of them in his work.

Gregory, Horace. *D. H. Lawrence: Pilgrim of the Apocalypse. Select Bibliographies Repr.
    Ser.* Ayer repr. of 1933 ed. $15.00. ISBN 0-8369-5598-6. Views Lawrence as a prophet
    of the modern age.

Hochman, Baruch. *Another Ego: The Changing View of Self and Society in the Work of
    D. H. Lawrence.* U. of SC Pr. 1970 $25.95. ISBN 0-87249-168-4. Discusses Lawrence's
    modernist visions of individuality.

Hough, Graham. *The Dark Sun: A Study of D. H. Lawrence.* Hippocrene Bks. 1972 $21.00.
    ISBN 0-88254-840-9. A critical survey of Lawrence's work and his literary themes.

Humma, John B. *Metaphor and Meaning in D. H. Lawrence's Later Novels.* U. of Mo. Pr.
    1990 $22.50. ISBN 0-8262-0742-1. Examines the use of metaphor and other language
    strategies in eight of Lawrence's later novels.

Hyde, G. M. *D. H. Lawrence.* St. Martin 1990 $24.95. ISBN 0-312-04038-5. A brief
    introductory guide to Lawrence's novels.

Jackson, Dennis. *Critical Essays on D. H. Lawrence.* G. K. Hall 1988 $40.00. ISBN 0-8161-
    8765-7. Excellent volume providing invaluable studies on and editions of Lawrence's
    work.

Lawrence, Ada, and George S. Gelder. *Young Lorenzo: The Early Life of D. H. Lawrence.*
    Russell 1966 repr. of 1931 ed. o.p. Coauthored by Lawrence's sister.

Leavis, F. R. *D. H. Lawrence: Novelist.* U. of Ch. Pr. 1979 $6.95. ISBN 0-226-46971-9. A
    study by one of Lawrence's leading advocates in England.

Luhan, Mabel G. *Lorenzo in Taos.* Scholarly repr. of 1932 ed. $59.00. ISBN 0-403-01077-2

Meyers, Jeffrey. *D. H. Lawrence: A Biography.* Random 1992 $14.00. ISBN 0-679-73065-6.
    A penetrating profile.

Miko, Stephen J. *Toward* Women in Love: *The Emergence of a Lawrentian Aesthetic.* Yale
    U. Pr. 1972 $80.40. ISBN 0-8357-8354-5. Analyzes the thematic development of
    Lawrence's novels.

Moore, Harry T. *The Life and Works of D. H. Lawrence.* Darby Pub. 1981 repr. of 1951 ed.
    o.p. A good general survey of Lawrence.

———. *The Priest of Love: A Life of D. H. Lawrence.* FS&G 1974 o.p.

Moynahan, Julian. *Deed of Life: The Novels and Tales of D. H. Lawrence.* Princeton U. Pr.
    1963 o.p. A chronological analysis of 10 novels and a group of shorter pieces.

Nehls, Edward H., ed. *D. H. Lawrence: A Composite Biography.* 3 vols. U. of Wis. Pr.
    1957–59 $35.00 ea. Vol. 1 ISBN 0-299-81501-3. Vol. 2 ISBN 0-299-81502-1. Vol. 3 o.p.
    A highly detailed, well-written work.

Pinkney, Tony. *D. H. Lawrence and Modernism.* U. of Iowa Pr. 1990 $25.00. ISBN 0-87745-294-6. Examines how Lawrence's novels can be seen as classical examples of modernism.

Ruderman, Judith. *D. H. Lawrence and the Devouring Mother: The Search for a Patriarchal Ideal of Leadership.* Duke 1984 $37.50. ISBN 0-8223-0598-4. Examines gender in Lawrence's work.

Sagar, Keith. *The Art of D. H. Lawrence.* Cambridge U. Pr. 1976 o.p. A comprehensive view of Lawrence's writings in many genres.

———. *D. H. Lawrence: A Calendar of His Works.* U. of Tex. Pr. 1979 o.p.

Smith, Anne, ed. *Lawrence and Women. Critical Studies Ser.* B & N Imports 1978 o.p. A feminist study of Lawrence and his portrayal of women.

Spender, Stephen, ed. *D. H. Lawrence: Novelist, Poet, Prophet.* HarpC 1973 o.p. Essays by Diana Trilling, Denis Donoghue, A. Alvarez, and others; edited by the well-known British poet and critic.

Spilka, Mark. *Love Ethic of D. H. Lawrence.* Ind. U. Pr. 1955 o.p. Foreword by F. L. Ravagli; examines the romance and passion in Lawrence's work.

———, ed. *D. H. Lawrence: A Collection of Critical Essays.* P-H 1963 $12.95. ISBN 0-13-526855-9. Provides important textual, biographical, and cultural background.

Stoll, John E. *Novels of D. H. Lawrence: A Search for Integration.* U. of Mo. Pr. 1971 o.p. A rather conventional overview of Lawrence's novels.

Vivas, Eliseo. *D. H. Lawrence: The Failure and the Triumph of Art.* Bks. Demand repr. of 1960 ed. $60.80. ISBN 0-8357-9452-0. An interesting study of Lawrence's aesthetics.

Weiss, Daniel. *Oedipus in Nottingham: D. H. Lawrence.* U. of Wash. Pr. 1962 o.p.

Worthen, John. *D. H. Lawrence: A Literary Life.* St. Martin 1989 $35.00. ISBN 0-312-03524-1. Chronicles Lawrence's literary and financial travails.

———. *D. H. Lawrence and the Idea of the Novel.* Rowman 1979 $33.00. ISBN 0-8476-6175-X

LEWIS, C(ECIL) DAY. 1904–1972

The grandfather of C. Day Lewis changed the family name of Day to Day-Lewis. In a fit of inverse snobbery, the poet dropped the hyphen, to the confusion of librarians and bibliographers ever since. His own father was a priest in the Church of Ireland, and the poet was born in Ballintubber, Northern Ireland but was educated in English boarding schools and at Oxford University. There he met the young W. H. AUDEN and eventually became part of the circle that Auden once facetiously dubbed "Daylewisaudenmacneicespender." After a stint as a schoolteacher, he married and supported himself partly through writing a series of highly successful detective novels under the pseudonym Nicholas Blake. Active in leftist political affairs during the 1930s, he left the Communist party, and political activity generally, in 1938.

His later honors include a year as Charles Eliot Norton professor of poetry at Harvard University and as Clark lecturer at Cambridge University, and a term as professor of poetry at Oxford University from 1951 to 1956. He served as director of the publishing house of Chatto & Windus from 1954 until his death in 1972, and was named poet laureate in 1968.

C. Day Lewis began as a nearly Georgian poet but changed direction radically at Oxford under the influence of Auden. His verse for the next decade and a half showed greater intellectual tightness, contemporary diction, and social relevance. In his influential literary manifesto *A Hope for Poetry* (1934), he named GERARD MANLEY HOPKINS, WILFRED OWEN, and T. S. ELIOT as literary ancestors. Moving to the Devon village of Musbury in 1938, Lewis entered a new phase of more private poetry marked by a strong interest in nature. An avid student of VIRGIL (see Vol. 2), he translated the *Georgics*, the *Aeneid*, and *Eclogues*. In his autobiography, Lewis confessed that he found it difficult "to decide between contrary opinions, or to form any coherent idea of my own identity." Perhaps because he wrote well in a variety of styles but lacked a distinctive speaking voice, the public reputation of his poetry has declined somewhat in recent years.

POETRY BY C. DAY LEWIS

The Complete Poems of C. Day Lewis. Stanford U. Pr. 1992 $49.50. ISBN 0-8047-2070-3. Comprehensive volume with an introduction by Lewis's widow, Jill Balcon.
Poems, 1925–1972. Hogarth Pr. 1977 o.p. Reflects Lewis's contemporary social observations.

NONFICTION BY C. DAY LEWIS

A Hope for Poetry. 1934. Porter 1978 o.p. Prose manifesto.

BOOKS ABOUT C. DAY LEWIS

Handley-Taylor, Geoffrey, and Timothy Smith. *C. Day Lewis, the Poet Laureate: A Bibliography.* St. James Pr. 1968 o.p. A comprehensive, useful sourcebook of works by and about Lewis.
Riddel, Joseph N. *C. Day Lewis.* Twayne 1971 o.p. Overview of his life; bibliography.

LEWIS, C(LIVE) S(TAPLES) (pseud. of Clive Hamilton). 1898–1963

C. S. Lewis, fellow at Oxford University and then professor of medieval and Renaissance English at Cambridge University, 1954–63, was a writer of varied and exceptional gifts. He wrote novels of fantasy, scholarly literary essays, and expositions of Christian doctrine. He became known in the United States for the demoniacal *The Screwtape Letters* (1942)—letters of instruction and encouragement from a shrewd old devil to an undergraduate imp on earth, a revelation of hell's best official secret, and for *The Chronicles of Narnia* (1950–56), a seven-volume Christian allegory in the form of a children's adventure fantasy. *Out of the Silent Planet* (1938), and *Perelandra* (1943), and *That Hideous Strength* (1946) form a trilogy of strange and exciting philosophical fantasies of life on other planets and, at last, in the earthly setting of a college community. Other novels include *The Great Divorce, Four Loves,* and *Studies in Words.* Among his scholarly works on literature, *The Allegory of Love: A Study of Medieval Tradition* (1936) has become a classic.

NOVELS BY C. S. LEWIS

Four Loves. 1960. HarBraceJ 1971 $6.95. ISBN 0-15-632930-1. Focuses on the themes of spirituality and love.
The Great Divorce. 1946. Macmillan 1978 $6.00. ISBN 0-02-086890-1
Out of the Silent Planet. 1938. Macmillan 1990 repr. $45.00. ISBN 0-02-570795-7. Space exploration and fallen humanity.
Perelandra. 1944. Macmillan 1968 $40.00. ISBN 0-02-570845-7
The Screwtape Letters. 1943. Macmillan 1967 $14.95. ISBN 0-02-571240-3. A plot by the devil to win a human soul.
Studies in Words. Cambridge U. Pr. 1990 $10.95. ISBN 0-521-39831-2
That Hideous Strength. 1946. Macmillan 1990 $60.00. ISBN 0-02-571255-1
Till We Have Faces: A Myth Retold. 1957. HarBraceJ 1980 $8.95. ISBN 0-15-690436-5

NONFICTION BY C. S. LEWIS

Surprised by Joy: The Shape of My Early Life. 1954. HarBraceJ 1956 $14.95. ISBN 0-15-187011-X. A fascinating autobiographical account of Lewis's early years.

Works by C. S. Lewis

Letters to an American Lady. Ed. by Clyde S. Kilby. Eerdmans 1967 $7.99. ISBN 0-8028-1428-X. More than 100 letters, Christian in theme, to an American (her identity is withheld) whom Lewis had never met.

Letters to Malcolm: Chiefly on Prayer. HarBraceJ 1973 repr. of 1963 ed. $6.95. ISBN 0-15-650880-X. Letters addressed to a probably fictitious person.

Books about C. S. Lewis

Beversluis, John. *C. S. Lewis and the Search for Rational Religion.* Eerdmans 1985 $10.99. ISBN 0-8028-0046-7. Attempts to disprove Lewis's arguments for the existence of God.

Christopher, Joe R. *C. S. Lewis.* Macmillan 1987 $19.95. ISBN 0-8057-6944-7. Overview of his life; bibliography.

Edwards, Bruce L., ed. *The Taste of the Pineapple: Essays on C. S. Lewis as Reader, Critic, and Imaginative Writer.* Bowling Green Univ. 1988 $36.95. ISBN 0-87972-407-2. Examines Lewis's theory of literature, critical and fictional pairing, the role of metaphor and symbol, and Lewis and Chesterton.

Glover, Donald E. *C. S. Lewis: The Art of Enchantment.* Ohio U. Pr. 1981 $24.95. ISBN 0-8214-0566-7. Applies Lewis's theory of fiction to his own work.

Hannay, Margaret P. *C. S. Lewis.* Continuum 1981 $19.95. ISBN 0-8044-2341-5. Survey of Lewis's fiction, Narnia chronicles, literary criticism, apologetics, poems, and stories.

Hart, Dabney Adams. *Through the Open Door: A New Look at C. S. Lewis.* U. of Ala. Pr. 1984 o.p. Investigates myth, the power of language, pedagogical style, and prophetic theme in Lewis's work.

Manlove, C. N. *C. S. Lewis: His Literary Achievement.* St. Martin 1987 $35.00. ISBN 0-312-00899-6. Survey.

Schakel, Peter J., and Charles A. Huttar. *Word and Story in C. S. Lewis.* U. of Mo. Pr. 1991 $37.50. ISBN 0-8262-0760-X. Essays on sanctifying the literal, the making of metaphor, and language and myth.

Wilson, A. N. *C. S. Lewis: A Biography.* Norton 1990 $22.50. ISBN 0-393-02813-5. Best book to date on Lewis.

LEWIS, (PERCY) WYNDHAM. 1884–1957

Distinguished and highly original, Wyndham Lewis is known for his sharp wit and sardonic insight. A modern master of satire, expert at deflating the pretensions of democracy, he was born off the coast of Maine in his English father's yacht and grew up in England. He was associated with Roger Fry and Ezra Pound on the vorticist magazine *Blast* (1914–15). Lewis served in France in World War I, and his dynamic paintings of war scenes soon gained him wide recognition for his art, now represented in the Tate Gallery and the Victoria and Albert Museum, London, and in the Museum of Modern Art, New York. After the publication of his naturalistic novel *Tarr* (1918), he became prominent as a writer. His major work of fiction is the tetralogy *The Human Age* (1955–56). Lewis "was one of those high-powered, controversial and prophetic figures to whom no one can react with indifference. He was a fellow-traveller with fascism who wrote enthusiastically about Hitler. . . . A toughy, you see: a would-be shocker: a braggart. But his eye for the comic surface of things is marvelous" (Philip Toynbee, *Observer*). T. S. Eliot called Wyndham Lewis "the most fascinating personality of our time" and he was described by W. B. Yeats as having that rare quality in writers, intellectual passion. Yet his reactionary views, especially his anti-Semitism, have more or less consigned him to oblivion today. His views are clearly expressed in such works as *Hitler, the Germans and the Jews* and *The Jews, Are They Human?*

NOVELS BY WYNDHAM LEWIS

The Apes of God. Black Sparrow 1984 repr. of 1930 ed. $25.00. ISBN 0-87685-513-3. Sarcastic overview of the art world of the 1920s.

The Caliph's Design. Black Sparrow 1986 repr. of 1919 ed. $20.00. ISBN 0-87685-665-2

The Childermass. Scholarly 1972 repr. of 1928 ed. $49.00. ISBN 0-403-01072-1

Doom of Youth. Haskell 1973 repr. of 1932 ed. $75.00. ISBN 0-8383-1475-9

Journey into Barbary. Ed. by C. J. Fox. Black Sparrow 1983 $20.00. ISBN 0-87685-518-4

Malign Fiesta. Riverrun NY 1981 $7.95. ISBN 0-7145-0355-X

Rotting Hill. Black Sparrow 1986 repr. of 1952 ed. $20.00. ISBN 0-87685-647-4

Self Condemned: A Novel of Exile. Black Sparrow 1983 repr. of 1954 ed. $20.00. ISBN 0-87685-575-3. With an afterword by Smith Rowland.

The Snooty Baronet. Black Sparrow 1984 $20.00. ISBN 0-87685-600-8. With an afterword by Bernard Lafourcade.

Tarr. 1918. Dufour 1970 repr. of 1918 ed. o.p. Bohemian prewar Paris scenes.

SHORT STORY COLLECTION BY WYNDHAM LEWIS

The Wild Body. Haskell 1971 repr. of 1927 ed. $59.95. ISBN 0-8383-1225-X. Includes short stories: "A Soldier of Humour," "Beau Jejour," "Bestre," "The Cornac and His Wife," "The death of the Ankou," "Franciscan Adventures," "Brotcotnaz," "Inferior Religions."

NONFICTION BY WYNDHAM LEWIS

Blasting and Bombardiering: An Autobiography, 1914–1926. 1937. Riverrun NY 1982 $9.95. ISBN 0-7145-0130-1. Lewis's interaction with the literary avant-garde.

Creatures of Habit and Creatures of Change: Essays on Art, Literature, and Society, 1914–1956. Ed. by Paul Edwards. Black Sparrow 1989 $15.00. ISBN 0-87685-769-1

Men Without Art. 1914. Black Sparrow 1987 $20.00. ISBN 0-87685-687-3

Time and Western Man. 1927. Black Sparrow 1993 $30.00. ISBN 0-87685-879-5

WORK BY WYNDHAM LEWIS

Letters of Wyndham Lewis. Ed. by W. K. Rose. New Dir. Pr. 1964 $10.00. ISBN 0-8112-0305-0. Letters to Pound, Eliot, Joyce, Augustus John, and others.

BOOKS ABOUT WYNDHAM LEWIS

Ayers, David. *Wyndham Lewis and Western Man*. St. Martin 1992 $35.00. ISBN 0-312-07166-3. Valuable examination of Lewis's anxieties about self.

Bridson, D. G. *The Filibuster: A Study of the Political Ideas of Wyndham Lewis*. Cassell 1972 o.p. Biography focusing on Lewis's attraction to Mussolini and Hitler.

Kush, Thomas. *Wyndham Lewis's Pictorial Integer*. Bks. Demand 1981 o.p. Discusses the modern painter as critic, the metaphysics of art, and vorticism.

Meyers, Jeffrey. *The Enemy: A Biography of Wyndham Lewis*. Routledge 1980 o.p. An account of Lewis focusing on his anti-Semitism and other damaging views.

Morrow, Bradford. *A Bibliography of the Writings of Wyndham Lewis*. Black Sparrow 1978 $40.00. ISBN 0-87685-419-6. A sourcebook of primary sources; indispensable for a comprehensive look at Lewis.

Schenker, Daniel. *Wyndham Lewis: Religion and Modernism*. U. of Ala. Pr. 1991 $29.95. ISBN 0-8173-0535-1. Examines the aesthetics of deadness, morality and metaphysics, and the modernist apocalypse as they pertain to Lewis.

LODGE, DAVID (JOHN) . 1935–

Novelist and critic David Lodge was born in London and educated at London University. In 1976, he became Professor of Modern English Literature at the University of Birmingham and remained there only until the 1980s, when he retired to write full time. Lodge writes criticism and fiction that self-consciously reflect each other. He is, for example, sympathetic toward narrative experimentation in both. Nonetheless, he writes in what he calls "a tradition of realistic fiction [about] what the writer has himself experienced and observed . . . lower-middle-class life in the inner suburbs of South East London; a war-time childhood and a post-war 'austerity' adolescence; Catholicism; education and the social and physical mobility it brings; military service, marriage, travel, etc." His earliest novels, especially *The Picturegoers* (1960) and *Out of the Shelter* (1970), reflect his own early years, whereas *Ginger, You're Barmy* (1962) is a seriocomic evocation of army life. *The British Museum is Falling Down* (1965), his first experimentally interesting novel, is both a parodic pastiche of earlier literature (JAMES JOYCE's *Ulysses*, for example) and a witty complaint against the Roman Catholic prohibition against contraception. In *How Far Can You Go?* (1980) he traces the lives of young adults in the 1960s as they turn away from outmoded Roman Catholicism only to discover their lives devoid of all spiritual values. His finest novels to date are hilarious academic satires—*Changing Places* (1975) and its sequel, *Small World* (1984)—on the petty quarrels, rigid structures, intellectual pretentiousness, erotic and professional jealousies, and jet-setting conferences of present-day university life.

NOVELS BY LODGE

Changing Places. 1975. Viking Penguin 1993 $10.00. ISBN 0-14-017098-7
Nice Work. 1988. Viking Penguin 1990 $10.00. ISBN 0-14-013396-8. Provocative take on modern British society.
Out of the Shelter. 1970. Viking Penguin 1989 $7.95. ISBN 0-14-012279-6. Semi-autobiographical novel depicting the maturation of a young Londoner during World War II.
Paradise News. Viking Penguin 1992 $21.00. ISBN 0-670-84228-1. Academic travel novel.
Small World: An Academic Romance. 1984. Warner Bks. 1991 $8.99. ISBN 0-446-39327-4. Lodge's most popular parody of academia.
The Writing Game. Trafalgar 1991 o.p. A witty social comedy.

NONFICTION BY LODGE

After Bakhtin: Essays on Fiction and Criticism. Routledge 1990 $49.95. ISBN 0-415-05037-5. Collection of essays incorporating the ideas of Mikhall Bakhtin which provide a valuable insight into the theory and practice of narrative fiction.
The Art of Fiction. Viking Penguin 1993 $22.00. ISBN 0-670-84848-4
Language of Fiction: Essays in Criticism and Verbal Analysis of the English Novel. Routledge 1966 o.p. An important study of critical theory and the use of language.
Working with Structuralism: Essays and Reviews on Nineteenth and Twentieth Century Literature. 1980. Routledge Chapman & Hall 1981 o.p.

BOOK ABOUT LODGE

Morace, Robert A. *The Dialogic Novels of Malcolm Bradbury and David Lodge*. S. Ill. U. Pr. 1989 $29.95. ISBN 0-8093-1519-X

MACBETH, GEORGE (MANN). 1932–

Born in the Scots mining village of Shotts but educated at King Edward VII School in Sheffield, Yorkshire, George MacBeth graduated with first-class honors from New College, Oxford. In the late 1950s, he belonged to The Group, an informal association of young writers, mostly poets, which in 1965 became the more structured Writers' Workshop. For 21 years, beginning in 1955, MacBeth produced programs on poetry and the arts for the BBC. Both the oral presentations of The Group and the BBC broadcasts whetted MacBeth's interest in the oral aspect of his own work. He has published numerous volumes of poetry, along with plays and (beginning in 1975) novels.

A prolific poet, MacBeth has worked in an almost chameleonlike variety of forms and styles. This eclecticism has made it difficult to establish a distinctive voice, yet his different styles have influenced numerous contemporaries in England. He has also tried to keep his poems accessible to the general public, and has achieved a reasonably wide popularity. Sometimes didactic, MacBeth often treats his subjects—death and life, war and love, tradition and the present day—with a linguistic playfulness that delights in the resources of language itself. His rephrasing of JOHN KEATS's "Ode on a Grecian Urn" and pseudotranslations of Chinese poetry are memorably comic.

POETRY BY MACBETH

Anna's Book. H. Holt & Co. 1984 o.p.
The Book of Cats. Dufour 1992 repr. of 1983 ed. $19.95. ISBN 0-185224-163-2. Edited with Martin Booth.
Buying a Heart. Atheneum 1978 o.p.
Collected Poems, 1958–1970. Atheneum 1972 o.p.
The Katana. S & S Trade 1982 o.p.
The Long Darkness. Atheneum 1984 o.p.
Poems from Oby. Macmillan 1983 $5.95. ISBN 0-689-11374-9
Poems of Love and Death. Atheneum 1980 o.p.
Shrapnel and the Poet's Year. Atheneum 1974 o.p. Two volumes in one.

NOVEL BY MACBETH

The Survivor. HarBraceJ 1978 o.p.

MACDIARMID, HUGH (pseud. of Christopher Murray Grieve). 1892–1978

The leading Scottish poet of the twentieth century, Hugh MacDiarmid was the son of a letter carrier in the Scottish border country. Educated at a local school, Langholm Academy, and at Edinburgh University, he served in World War I and then worked as a journalist and lecturer. His active political life involved membership in the Communist party, which expelled but later readmitted him, and in the Scottish Nationalist party, which he helped to found. These elements combined in his poetry, which often uses Scottish dialect and confronts political themes. His Scottish poetry reached perhaps its highest point in his major sequence *A Drunk Man Looks at the Thistle* (published in 1926, revised 1956) and his English poetry in the *Second Hymn to Lenin*, published in 1935. Tempestuous, irascible, surprising, and brilliant, MacDiarmid sought struggle rather than calm and suffered through periods of poverty and neglect as well as of public recognition. Throughout his long life, he strove to create a Scottish culture in opposition to the dominant English one; in *Who's Who*, he listed "Anglophobia" as his preferred recreation. A pioneer of the Scottish literary renaissance, MacDiarmid dedicated his life to reclaiming the Scottish literary language as well as celebrating its culture. For his achievements he was awarded the Foyle Poetry Prize, the Fletcher of Saltoun Medal, and an honorary doctoral degree from Edinburgh University.

POETRY BY MACDIARMID

Complete Poems of Hugh MacDiarmid. 2 vols. Ed. by Michael Grieve and William Aitken. Flatiron Bk. Distributors 1983 o.p. The definitive edition of MacDiarmid's poetry.
A Drunk Man Looks at the Thistle. 1926. Ed. by John C. Weston. U. of Mass. Pr. 1971 o.p.
The Hugh MacDiarmid Anthology: Poems in Scots and English. Ed. by Michael Grieve and Alexander Scott. Routledge 1972 o.p. Many of the poems in this collection are based on political themes.

More Collected Poems. Ohio U. Pr. 1970 $8.95. ISBN 0-8040-0213-4. Poetry that strongly reflects MacDiarmid's Scottish culture and heritage.

Seven Poets. St. Mut. 1989 $85.00. ISBN 0-906474-14-0. Includes the works of MacDiarmid and six other poets.

NONFICTION BY MACDIARMID

Aesthetics in Scotland. Ed. by Alan Bold. B & N Imports 1985 $28.00. ISBN 0-389-20558-3. Collection of excerpts on Scottish aesthetics.

Lucky Poet: A Self-Study in Literature and Political Ideas, Being the Autobiography of Hugh MacDiarmid. U. CA Pr. 1972 o.p. Interesting personal reflections on his life, politics, and literary career.

BOOKS ABOUT MACDIARMID

Baglow, John. *Hugh MacDiarmid: The Poetry of Self.* U. of Toronto Pr. 1987 $39.95. ISBN 0-7735-0571-7. Examines world and self, problems of modern poetry, and MacDiarmid and his age.

Bold, Alan Norman. *MacDiarmid: A Critical Biography.* U. of Mass. Pr. 1990 $35.00. ISBN 0-87023-714-4. Examines his life as both a poet and political activist.

———. *MacDiarmid: The Terrible Crystal.* Routledge 1983 o.p. Survey of MacDiarmid's poetry.

Boutelle, Ann Edwards. *Thistle and Rose: A Study of Hugh MacDiarmid's Poetry.* Bucknell U. Pr. 1981 $30.00. ISBN 0-8387-5023-0. Discusses MacDiarmid as a poet of paradox and disparities.

Gish, Nancy K. *Hugh MacDiarmid: The Man and His Work.* Macmillan 1984 o.p. A survey paying close attention to language and Scots dialect.

Glen, Duncan. *Hugh MacDiarmid: A Critical Survey.* B & N Imports 1972 o.p. Essays on Gaelic literature, poetry and knowledge, Scots traditions, and MacDiarmid as Marxist poet.

Riach, Alan. *Hugh MacDiarmid's Epic Poetry.* Col. U. Pr. 1991 $35.00. ISBN 0-7486-0257-7. Explores the themes of history and nationalism in MacDiarmid's work.

Wright, Gordon. *MacDiarmid: An Illustrated Biography of Christopher Murray Grieve (Hugh MacDiarmid).* Wright 1977 o.p. Well-written and interesting biography.

MACNEICE, (FREDERICK) LOUIS. 1907–1963

Born in Belfast and raised in Carrickfergus, MacNeice was the son of an Anglican clergyman who became a bishop. His education in English schools and Oxford University made him ill at ease with his Puritan upbringing, but it never caused him to lose his sense of northern Irish roots. At Oxford, MacNeice became friends with STEPHEN SPENDER and later, W. H. AUDEN, with whom he collaborated on *Letters from Iceland* (1937). After graduating with a double first, MacNeice accepted a lectureship in the classics at Birmingham University and, after the traumatic elopement of his first wife, at Bedford College of the University of London. He joined the BBC as scriptwriter and producer in 1941 and remained with it for the remainder of his career. He also did an admired translation of AESCHYLUS's (see Vol. 2) *Agamemnon* and the well-known book *The Poetry of W. B. Yeats* (1941).

MacNeice defended his own poetry and that of Auden, Spender, and C. DAY LEWIS in his book *Modern Poetry* (1938). There he called for an "impure poetry" that would react against the giants of the previous generation by embracing the partisanship that he missed in W. B. YEATS and involvement with life that he found lacking in T. S. ELIOT, both of whom had otherwise influenced him. While engaged with personal and political issues of the 1930s, MacNeice maintained a more skeptical stance than many of his contemporaries. His best verse—such as "Valediction" or "Bagpipe Music"—brings wit and strong rhythms to bear on contemporary life and often harks back to scenes of his youth. After joining the BBC, he also wrote more than 150 scripts, of which a dozen radio dramas have been published. An autobiography, *The Strings Are False*, was published posthumously in 1966. During his lifetime, MacNeice was overshadowed by Auden, but in recent years, reevaluation of his work has regarded him as a major literary figure.

POETRY BY MACNEICE

Collected Poems. 1967. Ed. by E. R. Dodds. Faber & Faber 1979 $16.95. ISBN 0-571-11353-2

Modern Poetry: A Personal Essay. Haskell 1969 repr. of 1938 ed. $75.00. ISBN 0-8383-0991-5

Selected Poems. Faber & Faber 1964 o.p. Many poems in this collection are about the decline of contemporary culture.

NONFICTION BY MACNEICE

The Poetry of W. B. Yeats. Greenwood 1979 repr. of 1941 ed. $38.50. ISBN 0-313-22102-2

Selected Prose of Louis MacNeice. Ed. by Alan Heuser. OUP 1990 $49.95. ISBN 0-19-81825-1

PLAY BY MACNEICE

Christopher Columbus, A Radio Play. AMS Pr. repr. of 1944 ed. $20.00. ISBN 0-404-20165-2. An interesting historical drama about the famous explorer.

BOOKS ABOUT MACNEICE

Armitage, Christopher M., and Neil Clark. *A Bibliography of the Works of Louis MacNeice*. Kaye & Ward 1973 o.p. A useful sourcebook for scholars and researchers.

Coulton, Barbara. *Louis MacNeice in the BBC*. Faber & Faber 1980 o.p. Bibliographical focus on MacNeice's work at the British Broadcasting Corporation.

Longley, Edna. *Louis MacNeice: A Study*. Faber & Faber 1988 o.p. Overview, focusing on MacNeice's Irish roots and transition to English culture, the impact of World War II on his work, and his handling of the themes of belief and myth.

Marsack, Robyn. *The Cave of Making: The Poetry of Louis MacNeice*. OUP 1982 $27.50. ISBN 0-19-811718-3. Examines MacNeice's relationship to the other 1930s poets, his use of nostalgia, and his lyricism.

McDonald, Peter. *Louis MacNeice: The Poet in His Contexts*. OUP 1991 $55.00. ISBN 0-19-811766-3. Survey of MacNeice's poetry.

MASEFIELD, JOHN. 1878–1967

Once one of the most popular English poets of the century, Masefield has fallen into undeserved neglect since his death. He was born in a Victorian house with rural vistas, which he later recalled as "living in Paradise." In childhood he had a series of intense, visionary experiences inspired by both nature and literature, which gave him a habitual sense of participation in a greater life. These had weakened by 1891, when he entered training for the merchant naval service. An officer on the White Star Line's *Adriatic*, he jumped ship in New York in 1895 and roamed across America, returning to England two years later when a recovery of his intense childhood visions convinced him he could succeed as a writer.

Masefield excelled more at narrative than at symbolism. His first book, *Salt Water Poems and Ballads* (1902), displayed the allegiance to outcasts and wanderers that marks his subject matter. The musicality of that volume derives partly from the strong early influence of W. B. YEATS. Increasingly, Masefield experimented with colloquial diction, particularly from the lower classes; his

The Everlasting Mercy (1911) recounted the conversion of a rural scoundrel in language that astonished many readers. Highly prolific, he produced more than 20 volumes of fiction, 17 plays, and other prose work besides his major volumes of poetry. Masefield still appeals particularly to the common reader. He was appointed poet laureate in 1930.

POETRY BY MASEFIELD

Poems. Macmillan 1935 o.p. The most comprehensive collected edition of Masefield's poetry.
Salt Water Poems and Ballads. 1902. Macmillan 1953 o.p.

NONFICTION BY MASEFIELD

Grace before Plowing: Fragments of an Autobiography. Macmillan 1966 o.p. Traces his development as a poet.
Some Memories of W. B. Yeats. Biblio Dist. 1971 repr. of 1940 ed. o.p.

SHORT STORY COLLECTION BY MASEFIELD

Tarpaulin Muster. Short Story Index Repr. Ser. Ayer repr. of 1907 ed. $14.00. ISBN 0-8369-3677-9

CHILDREN'S BOOKS BY MASEFIELD

Box of Delights: When the Wolves Were Running. Transaction Pubs. 1988 repr. of 1935 ed. $14.95. ISBN 1-85089-925-8
Midnight Folk. Transaction Pubs. 1988 repr. of 1927 ed. $14.95. ISBN 1-85089-927-4

BOOKS ABOUT MASEFIELD

Drew, Fraser Bragg. *John Masefield's England: A Study of the National Themes in His Work.* Fairleigh Dickinson 1973 $24.50. ISBN 0-8386-1020-X. Sociohistorical survey of Masefield's poetry.
Dwyer, June. *John Masefield.* Continuum 1987 $18.95. ISBN 0-8044-2164-1. Survey, with attention to Masefield's early lyrics, narratives, novels, sonnets, plays, and laureate poetry.
Handley-Taylor, Geoffrey. *John Masefield, or, the Queen's Poet Laureate: A Bibliography and Eighty-first Birthday Tribute.* Saifer 1960 $15.00. ISBN 0-87556-680-4. Biographical tribute to Masefield.
Spark, Muriel. *John Masefield.* Hutchinson 1992 o.p. New release of Spark's 1962 general survey.
Sternlicht, Sanford V. *John Masefield.* Twayne 1977 o.p. Survey focusing on narratives and Masefield's critical, historical, and autobiographical prose; bibliography.

MAUGHAM, W(ILLIAM) SOMERSET. 1874–1965

This master of the modern short story and noted novelist was born in Paris but was of Irish origin. Orphaned at age 10, Maugham was raised by an aunt and uncle. He received his early education at King's School, Canterbury, studied philosophy and literature at Heidelberg University in Germany, and qualified as a surgeon at St. Thomas's Hospital in London. During his student days, he decided to try his hand at writing. His first novel, *Liza of Lambeth*, a lurid tale about the London slums, was published in 1897.

Maugham's personal life was filled with travels and experiences. During World War I, he served in a Red Cross unit in France and then as a secret agent in Geneva and Petrograd (St. Petersburg), Russia. Between the wars, he traveled to the South Seas and the Far East. In World War II, he again served as a British agent, but only for a short time before going to the United States, where he lived until 1946. His adventures figure prominently in much of his writing.

In 1959, when Maugham was 85, the *N.Y. Times* reported that he had decided that it was time to stop writing except for himself. He had retired gracefully from writing drama in 1934. Of his formidable body of work, his autobiographical novel *Of Human Bondage* (1915) has become a modern classic. It reflects his early experiences as a physician in St. Thomas's Hospital. *The Moon and Sixpence* (1919), based on the life of the artist PAUL GAUGUIN (see Vol. 3), is still read. Many of his stories are set in far outposts of the British Empire, where he himself had observed the effect of tropical lands on the uprooted European. Two of his most famous stories, "Miss Thompson" (later known as *Rain*) and "The Letter" became films. Maugham said of himself, "I have never pretended to be anything but a storyteller. It has amused me to tell stories and I have told a great many." *The Summing Up* (1938), a review of his writing career, which might well be used as a handbook of authorship, largely explains his competent craftsmanship and his thoroughgoing professionalism as a writer.

A multimillionaire, Maugham sold 38 of his art treasures at auction in 1962 for more than $1,400,000; the funds, as well as much of the rest of his assets, he bequeathed to a society for authors in need. His last years were marred by a public dispute with his daughter over the disposition of some of his paintings. Before his death, he stipulated that none of his unpublished work should be printed posthumously.

NOVELS BY MAUGHAM

Ashenden, or The British Agent. 1928. Ayer 1977 repr. of 1941 ed. $25.00. ISBN 0-405-07805-6

Cakes and Ale. 1930. Viking Penguin 1977 $5.95. ISBN 0-14-000651-6. Satirical portrait of Hugh Walpole.

The Making of a Saint: A Romance of Mediaeval Italy. 1898. Ayer 1977 repr. of 1966 ed. $24.50. ISBN 0-405-07815-3. A historical romance.

The Moon and Sixpence. 1919. Viking Penguin 1977 $5.95. ISBN 0-14-000468-8. Fictionalized account of Gauguin's life.

The Narrow Corner. Ayer 1977 repr. of 1932 ed. $20.00. ISBN 0-405-07818-8

Of Human Bondage. 1915. Doubleday 1955 $22.50. ISBN 0-385-04899-8. Disabled hero confronting the bondage of Christianity.

The Razor's Edge. 1944. Viking Penguin 1992 $7.95. ISBN 0-14-018523-2

NONFICTION BY MAUGHAM

Points of View: Five Essays. Ayer 1977 repr. of 1959 ed. $20.00. ISBN 0-405-07827-7. Contains several essays on social criticism.

A Writer's Notebook. Viking Penguin 1984 $6.95. ISBN 0-14-002644-4. Discusses the craft of fiction writing.

The Writer's Point of View. Folcroft repr. of 1951 ed. o.p.

SHORT STORY COLLECTION BY MAUGHAM

Collected Short Stories. Viking Penguin 1993 $9.95. ISBN 0-14-018589-5

WORK BY MAUGHAM

The Works of W. Somerset Maugham. 47 vols. Ayer 1977 o.p.

BOOKS ABOUT MAUGHAM

Burt, Forrest D. *W. Somerset Maugham*. Macmillan 1985 $20.95. ISBN 0-8057-6885-8. Overview focusing on Maugham's period of apprenticeship and his autobiographical novels.

Curtis, Anthony, and John Whitehead. *W. Somerset Maugham: The Critical Heritage*. Routledge 1987 o.p. Collection of contemporary and current reviews and essays.

Loss, Archie K. *Of Human Bondage: Coming of Age in the Novel*. Macmillan 1989 $20.95. ISBN 0-8057-8067-X. Study of Maugham's best-known work.

———. *W. Somerset Maugham*. Continuum 1988 $19.95. ISBN 0-8044-2544-2. General overview of the life and work of Somerset Maugham.

Maugham, Robin. *Conversations with Willie*. S & S Trade 1978 o.p. Biography.

Morgan, Ted. *Maugham: A Biography*. S&S Trade 1980 o.p.

Sanders, Charles. *W. Somerset Maugham: An Annotated Bibliography of Writings about Him*. N. Ill. U. Pr. 1970 o.p. A thorough sourcebook, useful for both scholars and general readers.

Whitehead, John. *Maugham: A Reappraisal*. B & N Imports 1987 o.p. Study of Maugham in the context of the different periods in which he wrote.

MUIR, EDWIN. 1887–1959

One of the foremost practitioners of modern Scottish letters, Edwin Muir was born to a farming family in the remote Orkney Islands. Forced to move with his family to the industrial city of Glasgow when he was 13, Muir held a series of minor and often grubby jobs before supporting himself mainly through journalism and occasional teaching. In 1919, he married Willa Anderson, and in his *An Autobiography* (1940) would describe their marriage as "the most fortunate event in my life." Willa Muir not only encouraged her husband to write but collaborated with him on numerous translations and other works. They were the first to translate the works of FRANZ KAFKA (see Vol. 2) into English. Her own, moving autobiography, *Belonging*, is both an engrossing account and a minor masterpiece in its own right. In later life, Muir worked for the British Council, was warden of an adult educational college in Scotland, and served as visiting Charles Eliot Norton professor at Harvard University.

Muir's poetry stands somewhat aloof from more flamboyant varieties of modernism, yet won the respect of both T. S. ELIOT and W. B. YEATS. Often cast in seemingly traditional rhymes and meters, his verse depended on a vision, which Kathleen Raine described as "the perennial philosophy." Muir looked beneath surfaces of the world for archetypes of a primal and now-lost unity of the soul with the world. Sometimes he used the Scottish landscape and sometimes earlier mythology to convey his vision, as in *One Foot in Eden* (1956). Muir's criticism and translations are still worth reading as well. Among his critical works are *Scott and Scotland* (1936), Essays on Literature and Society (1949), and *Structure of the Novel* (1928). Though not known as a novelist, his most notable is *The Marionette* (1927).

POETRY BY MUIR

Collected Poems. 1960. Faber & Faber 1984 o.p. The standard edition, published posthumously.

Selected Poems. Faber & Faber 1965 o.p.

NONFICTION BY MUIR

An Autobiography. 1940. Graywolf 1990 repr. of 1954 ed. $10.95. ISBN 1-55597-128-8. Revised version of *The Story and the Fable: An Autobiography*.

The Estate of Poetry. 1962. Graywolf 1993 $11.00. ISBN 1-55597-182-2. Critical essays originally delivered as the Charles Eliot Norton lectures at Harvard. Foreword by Archibald MacLeish.

John Knox: Portrait of a Calvinist. Ayer repr. of 1929 ed. $21.00. ISBN 0-8369-5656-7

Selected Letters. Ed. by Peter H. Butter. Hogarth Pr. 1974 o.p. An interesting and revealing collection of letters.

Scott and Scotland: The Predicament of the Scottish Writer. 1936. Folcroft repr. of 1936 ed. o.p. Examines the sources of Scottish literary culture.

Scottish Journey. Norwood 1979 repr. of 1935 ed. o.p. An account of travels through Scotland.

Transition: Essays on Contemporary Literature. Rprt. Serv. 1992 repr. of 1926 ed. $79.00. ISBN 0-7812-7061-8

BOOKS ABOUT MUIR

Hoy, Peter C., and Elgin W. Mellown. *A Checklist of Writings about Edwin Muir.* Whitston Pub. 1971 $7.50. ISBN 0-87875-012-6. A useful and accessible bibliography.

Huberman, Elizabeth. *The Poetry of Edwin Muir: The Field of Good and Ill.* OUP 1971 o.p. Explores Muir's major themes and poetic traditions.

Knight, Roger. *Edwin Muir: An Introduction to His Work.* Longman 1980 o.p. Biographically linked critical survey.

Mellown, Elgin W. *Edwin Muir.* G. K. Hall 1979 o.p. Overview and bibliography, with attention to Muir's literary criticism and autobiographical writing.

Phillips, Michael Joseph. *Edwin Muir: A Master of Modern Poetry.* Hackett Pub. 1978 o.p. Examines Muir's handling of despair and affirmation, his use of persona, and his place poems.

MUNRO, H(ECTOR) H(UGH) ("Saki"). 1870–1916

H. H. Munro, better known as "Saki," was born in Burma, the son of an inspector-general for the Burmese police. Sent to England to be educated at the Bedford Grammar School, he returned to Burma in 1893 and joined the police force there. In 1896, he returned again to England and began writing first for *The Westminster Gazette* and then as a foreign correspondent for *The Morning Post.*

Best known for his wry and amusing stories, Saki depicts a world of drawing rooms, garden parties, and exclusive club rooms. His short stories at their best are extraordinarily compact and cameolike, wicked and witty, with a careless cruelty and a powerful vein of supernatural fantasy. They deal, in general, with the same group of upper-class Britishers, whose frivolous lives are sometimes complicated by animals—the talking cat who reveals their treacheries in love, the pet ferret who is evil incarnate. The nom de plume "Saki" was borrowed from the cupbearer in OMAR KHAYYAM's (see Vol. 2) *The Rubáiyát.* Munro used it for political sketches contributed to the *Westminster Gazette* as early as 1896, later collected as *Alice in Westminster.* The stories and novels were published between that time and the outbreak of World War I, when he enlisted as a private, scorning a commission. He died of wounds from a sniper's bullet while in a shell hole near Beaumont-Hamel. One of his characters summed up Saki's stories as those that "are true enough to be interesting and not true enough to be tiresome."

SHORT STORY COLLECTION BY MUNRO

The Short Stories of Saki (H. H. Munro). Ed. by Corbin Hoopes. Darby repr. o.p.

WORKS BY MUNRO

Best of Saki. Viking Penguin 1977 $6.95. ISBN 0-14-004484-1

The Complete Works of Saki. Dorset Pr. 1989 $19.95. ISBN 0-88029-259-8

The Novels and Plays of Saki. Scholarly 1971 repr. of 1945 ed. $39.00. ISBN 0-403-01123-X

BOOKS ABOUT MUNRO

Gillen, Charles H. *H. H. Munro (Saki).* Twayne 1969 o.p. Overview of his life; includes a bibliography.

Langguth, A. J., and H. H. Munro. *Saki, a Life of Hector Hugh Monroe: With Six Short Stories Never Before Collected.* S & S Trade 1981 o.p. Includes biographical material.

MURDOCH, IRIS. 1919–

Wit, variety, and unpredictability characterize the work of this Irish philosopher-novelist. Murdoch was born in Dublin and educated in England, where she attended Somerville College, Oxford. After several government jobs, she returned to academic life, studying philosophy at Newnham College, Cambridge. Since 1948, she has been a fellow and tutor at St. Anne's College, Oxford. In 1959 she lectured at Yale University. Her husband, John Bayley, is a novelist, poet, and critic.

ELIZABETH BOWEN has said: "Everything that she has written has been remarkable—stamped by the unmistakable authority of mind and vision." Her first novel, *Under the Net* (1954), already showed "a deft touch, a delight in strange, intricate and puzzling plots, a wild intelligence and a defiance of the pigeonhole" (*PW*). In the world of *A Severed Head* (1961), she depicted a London society devoid of passion or conviction, a modern world in which are contrasted the artificial and the real in her characters' emotions. Her subtle irony, her wit, and her sense of the comic combine in this astonishing novel. Murdoch also wrote *An Unofficial Rose* (1962), *The Unicorn* (1963), *The Red and the Green* (1965) and *The Time of the Angels* (1966). Of *The Nice and the Good* (1967), which treats the multiple facets of love, Elizabeth Janeway said in the *N.Y. Times*: "Sparkling, daring, great fun, the book sweeps up black magic, science fiction, thriller, and half-a-dozen kinds of novel into the wittiest sort of concoction. It is hard to imagine anyone not enjoying it."

Murdoch has also written a book on JEAN-PAUL SARTRE (see Vol. 2) and several nonfiction works, including *The Sovereignty of Good* (1971), in which she sets forth her ideas on ethics, and *The Fire and the Sun: Why Plato Banished the Artists* (1977).

NOVELS BY MURDOCH

The Black Prince. Viking Penguin 1983 $9.95. ISBN 0-14-003934-1. Betrayals of marriage and friendship.
Bruno's Dream. 1969. Viking Penguin 1976 $8.95. ISBN 0-14-003176-6. A man's meditations on death, love, and happiness.
A Fairly Honorable Defeat. 1970. Viking Penguin 1979 $8.95. ISBN 0-14-003332-7
Henry and Cato. Viking Penguin 1977 $10.00. ISBN 0-14-004569-4
The Italian Girl. 1964. Viking Penguin 1979 $5.95. ISBN 0-14-002559-6
The Nice and the Good. 1967. Viking Penguin 1978 $9.95. ISBN 0-14-003034-4. An exotic tale of black magic and eroticism.
Nuns and Soldiers. Viking Penguin 1982 $6.95. ISBN 0-14-006143-6. A tale about the tragic consequences of philosophy.
The Philosopher's Pupil. Viking Penguin 1984 $7.95. ISBN 0-14-007614-X
The Sacred and Profane Love Machine. Viking Penguin 1984 $10.00. ISBN 0-14-004111-7. A story of perversions of love and marriage.
The Sand Castle. 1957. Viking Penguin 1978 o.p. A novel about art and marital infidelity.
The Sea, the Sea. Viking Penguin 1980 $8.95. ISBN 0-14-005199-6
A Severed Head. 1961. Viking Penguin 1976 $9.95. ISBN 0-14-002003-9. Portrays three couples whose unfaithful sexual conduct illustrates their shallow, self-centered philosophies.
Under the Net. 1954. Viking Penguin 1977 $7.95. ISBN 0-14-001445-4. Exposes how abstract systems of behavior can cut people off from spontaneous, loving relationships.
A Word Child. 1976. Viking Penguin 1987 $6.95. ISBN 0-14-008153-4

BOOKS ABOUT MURDOCH

Baldanza, Frank. *Iris Murdoch*. Twayne 1974 o.p. Survey of her life; with a comprehensive bibliography.

Bove, Cheryl Browning. *A Character Index and Guide to the Fiction of Iris Murdoch*. Garland 1990 o.p. Useful reference guide to Murdoch's characters and other details in her novels.

Conradi, Peter J. *Iris Murdoch: The Saint and the Artist*. St. Martin 1986 $25.00. ISBN 0-312-43614-9. Examines Murdoch's moral psychology, novelistic structure, and use of romanticism.

Dipple, Elizabeth. *Iris Murdoch: Work for the Spirit*. U. Ch. Pr. 1982 $30.00. ISBN 0-2261-5363-0. Philosophical approach to Murdoch's literature.

Fletcher, John, and Cheryl Bove. *Iris Murdoch*. Garland 1990 $72.00. ISNB 0-8240-8910-3

Johnson, Deborah. *Iris Murdoch*. Ind. U. Pr. 1987 $25.00. ISBN 0-253-30104-1. Survey of Murdoch's writing.

Ramananathan, Suguna. *Iris Murdoch: Figures of Good*. St. Martin 1990 $39.95. ISBN 0-312-04504-2. Study of ethics in Murdoch's fiction.

Todd, Richard. *Iris Murdoch: The Shakespearian Interest*. B & N Imports 1979 $40.00. ISBN 0-06-496935-5. Investigates the Bard's sensibility as an informing conception behind Murdoch's oeuvre.

Tominaga, Thomas T., and Wilma Schneidermeyer. *Iris Murdoch and Muriel Spark: A Bibliography*. Scarecrow 1976 $20.00. ISBN 0-810-80907-9. Includes primary and secondary sources.

NICHOLS, PETER. 1928–

A Bristol-born former actor and schoolteacher, Peter Nichols got his start writing some 14 plays for television and has continued to write for that medium even since attaining success in the West End. *A Day in the Death of Joe Egg*, his first stage play, was produced in England in 1967 and on Broadway a year later. *Joe Egg* (as a squeamish American management insisted it be retitled) concerns a couple whose marriage is slowly being destroyed by their attempt to raise a hopelessly spastic daughter (Josephine, alias Joe Egg, their "living parsnip"). They survive in their situation as long as they do only by ceaselessly joking about it. However, this is not black humor, Nichols insists. The black humorist "sets himself at a distance from his characters and [laughs] at them. The characters [in my play] set themselves at a distance from their own situation. . . ."

This comic distancing, as much as its autobiographical revelation, was to be the common characteristic of Nichols's later plays. *Forget-Me-Not-Lane* (1971), distinctly personal in its middle-aged re-examination of a World War II childhood, has characters stepping back and forth through time and in and out of the dramatic situation. In *Passion Play* (1981), Nichols's characters even break away from themselves, each partner in a bickering couple splitting into mutually critical components. *The National Health* (1969), produced to general acclaim at the National Theatre, achieves its distancing through the alternation of realistic scenes of suffering and dying in a hospital ward with episodes of an outrageous medical soap opera, *Nurse Norton's Affair*, shown on a simulated television screen. And in the ironic musical episodes of *Privates on Parade* (1977), the story of an army entertainment troupe in the 1950s, Nichols entered the area of alienating theatricalism explored by JOHN OSBORNE's *The Entertainer* (1957) and Joan Littlewood's *Oh, What a Lovely War*. *Privates*, a Royal Shakespeare Company hit of 1977, has been made into a film, as have *Joe Egg* and *The National Health*. (Nichols also wrote the screenplay for the 1966 film satire *Georgy Girl*.)

PLAYS BY NICHOLS

Born in the Gardens. Faber & Faber 1980 o.p. Details the experiences of a family at a funeral.

Chez Nous: A Domestic Comedy in Two Acts. Faber & Faber 1974 o.p. Focuses on a pediatrician's dilemma.

Joe Egg. Grove Pr. 1968 $9.95. ISBN 0-8021-5115-9. The problems of a young couple with a spastic daughter.

Forget-Me-Not-Lane. 1971. Faber & Faber 1971 o.p

The Freeway. 1974. Faber 1975 o.p. A witty domestic comedy.

The National Health, or Nurse Norton's Affair. 1969. Grove Pr. 1975 o.p.

Passion Play. 1981. Heinemann Ed. 1981 $5.95. ISBN 0-413-47800-9

A Piece of My Mind. Heinemann Ed. 1988 $9.95. ISBN 0-413-17360-7

Poppy. Heinemann Ed. 1989 $9.95. ISBN 0-413-49490-X

Privates on Parade. 1977. Faber & Faber 1977 o.p.

O'BRIEN, FLANN (pseud. of Brian O'Nolan or O'Nuallain). 1911–1966

This gifted Irish writer had three identities: Brian O'Nolan, an Irish civil servant and administrator; Myles na gCopaleen, columnist for the *Irish Times*, poet and author of *An Beal Bocht (The Poor Mouth: A Bad Story about the Hard Life*, 1941), a satire in Gaelic on the Gaelic revival; and Flann O'Brien, playwright and avant-garde comic novelist praised by JAMES JOYCE, GRAHAM GREENE, DYLAN THOMAS, and WILLIAM SAROYAN. Although these writers, as well as a few intellectuals on both sides of the Atlantic, were quick to grasp O'Brien's genius, his masterpiece, *At Swim-Two-Birds* (1939), went almost unrecognized in its time. This novel, which plays havoc with the conventional novel form, is about a man writing a book about characters in turn writing about him. O'Brien starts off with three separate openings: "One beginning and one ending for a book was a thing I did not agree with." ANTHONY BURGESS has called it "one of the five outrageous fictional experiments of all time that come completely and triumphantly off. What a fuss the French antinovelists make about their tedious exercises in *chosisme*; how little fuss has been made about Flann O'Brien's humour, humanity, metaphysics, theology, bawdry, mythopoeia, word-play and six-part counterpoint." *The Third Policeman* (1967), funny but grim, plunges into the world of the dead, though one is not immediately aware that the protagonist is no longer living. This book, says the *Nation*, "secures his place, already indicated by 'At Swim-Two-Birds,' as the most original comic artist, after Joyce, to come out of Ireland in this century."

NOVELS BY O'BRIEN

At Swim-Two-Birds. 1939. NAL-Dutton 1976 $11.00. ISBN 0-452-25913-4. Experimental novel.

The Dalkey Archive. 1964. Dalkey Arch. 1993 repr. of 1965 ed. $9.95. ISBN 1-56478-019-8

The Hard Life: A Novel. 1962. Viking Penguin 1977 o.p.

The Poor Mouth: A Bad Story about the Hard Life. 1941. Seaver Bks. 1981 o.p. A story of the Irish working classes.

The Third Policeman. 1967. NAL-Dutton 1976 $9.00. ISBN 0-452-25912-6. Written in 1940, but published posthumously in 1967. Molecules from a policeman and a bicycle become intermixed.

WORKS BY O'BRIEN

A Flann O'Brien Reader. Ed. by Stephen Jones. Viking Penguin 1978 o.p.

Stories and Plays. Viking Penguin 1976 o.p.

BOOKS ABOUT O'BRIEN

Asbee, Sue. *Flann O'Brien*. Macmillan 1991 $22.95. ISBN 0-8057-7001-1. Overview of his
   life; bibliography.
Cronin, Anthony. *No Laughing Matter: The Life and Times of Flann O'Brien*. Grafton Bks.
   1989 o.p. Biography.
Gallagher, Monique. *Flann O'Brien*. Dufour 1991 $10.95. ISBN 0-86140-329-0. Interesting
   and authoritative study of O'Brien's life and work.
Shea, Thomas F. *Flann O'Brien's Exorbitant Novels*. Bucknell U. Pr. 1992 $32.50. ISBN 0-
   8387-5220-9. In-depth look at O'Brien's most important novels.

O'CASEY, SEAN. 1880–1964

Unlike the directors of the Abbey Theatre, Sean O'Casey was slum-born and
bred, self-educated, and deeply involved in the political and labor ferment that
preceded Irish independence. His famous group of realistic plays produced at
the Abbey form, in effect, a commentary on each stage of the independence
movement. The melodramatic *The Shadow of a Gunman* (1923), the first to be
staged, deals with the guerrilla war conducted by the IRA until the peace treaty
was signed in 1921. *Juno and the Paycock* (1925), cast in the mold of classic
comedy, describes the civil war and failure of hopes that followed the
settlement. The last to be produced, *The Plough and the Stars* (1926), set off
howls of resentment by returning to the Easter 1916 uprising itself, and
condemning the vanity of the nationalists and the dogmatism of labor, who
squabble while Dublin, in the person of its women, suffers martyrdom. (No less
offended was the prudery of the Abbey audience, which responded to the
presence of Rosie Redmond, the prostitute, much as it had to Christy Mahon's
reference to "shifts" in J. M. SYNGE's *The Playboy of the Western World*, 1907.)

It was expected that the Abbey audience would be unsympathetic. However,
when even the Abbey management, in the person of W. B. YEATS, turned against
the antiwar play, *The Silver Tassie* (1928), O'Casey (who had already taken up
residence in London and married) determined to remain in "exile." It was an
ill-chosen moment to throw himself upon the mercy of a commercial theater,
because O'Casey was just embarking on a series of dramatic experiments:
Within the Gates (1934), in which the stylized polyphony of urban activities
recalls the panorama of *The Plough and the Stars* and anticipates more modern
works such as ARNOLD WESKER's *Kitchen* (1959); *The Star Turns Red* (1940), a
vision of an anti-fascist revolution; and *Purple Dust* (1940), a fantasy cleansing of
the remnants of imperialism from Ireland. Without an assured theater, these
and his later plays were condemned to productions often amateurish and
unhelpful to the reviser, sometimes coming years after O'Casey had reluctantly
published the text. (An exception was the exemplary New York production of
Within the Gates in 1934. But Irish playwrights have often done better in New
York than London.)

After World War II, O'Casey turned to a third, still more idiosyncratic form of
drama, of which his own favorite example was *Cock-A-Doodle-Dandy* (1949).
Broadly satirical depictions of rural Ireland in the grip of church and
complacency, these were Aristophanic comedies with a great deal of folk
culture and music hall in their constitution. Their reception was appropriately
divided: *Cock-A-Doodle-Dandy* received its first production at the Royal Court in
1959; *The Drums of Father Ned* was forced out of the Dublin Festival of 1958
(and SAMUEL BECKETT withdrew his own play in protest).

In the 1930s, O'Casey served as a drama critic for London's *Time and Tide*,
producing a group of scathing comments on West End conventionality, which

have been published as *The Flying Wasp* (1937). Other essays on theater appear in *The Green Crow* (1956), *Under a Colored Cap* (1963), and *Blasts and Benedictions* (1967).

PLAYS BY O'CASEY

Collected Plays. 4 vols. St. Martin o.p. Vol. 1: *Juno and the Paycock; The Shadow of the Gunman; The Plough and the Stars; The End of the Beginning; A Pound on Demand.* Vol. 2: *The Silver Tassie; Within the Gates; The Star Turns Red.* Vol. 3: *Purple Dust; Red Roses for Me; Hall of Healing.* Vol. 4: *Oak Leaves and Lavender; Cock-A-Doodle-Dandy; Bedtime Story; Time to Go.*

Five One-Act Plays: The End of the Beginning, A Pound on Demand, Hall of Healing, Bedtime Story, and Time to Go. St. Martin 1966 o.p.

Selected Plays of Sean O'Casey. Braziller 1956 o.p. *The Shadow of a Gunman; Juno and the Paycock; The Plough and the Stars; The Silver Tassie; Within the Gates; Purple Dust; Red Roses for Me; Bedtime Story; Time to Go*; a foreword on playwrighting by the dramatist and a comprehensive introduction by John Gassner.

Seven Plays by Sean O'Casey. Ed. by Ronald Ayling. St. Martin 1985 $32.50. ISBN 0-312-71323-1

Three Plays: Juno and the Paycock, The Shadow of a Gunman, and *The Plough and the Stars.* St. Martin 1969 $6.95. ISBN 0-312-80290-0

Three More Plays: Silver Tassie, Purple Dust, and *Red Roses for Me.* St. Martin 1965 o.p.

WORKS BY O'CASEY

Blasts and Benedictions: Articles and Stories. Ed. by Ronald Ayling. Greenwood 1976 repr. of 1967 ed. $45.00. ISBN 0-8371-8158-5

The Letters of Sean O'Casey, 1942–1954. 4 vols. Ed. by David Krause. Cath. U. Pr. Vols. 1–3 o.p. Vol. 4 1992 $49.95. ISBN 0-8132-0678-2

BOOKS ABOUT O'CASEY

Hunt, Hugh. *Sean O'Casey.* Gill 1980 o.p. A well-written, thorough biography.

Kosok, Heinz. *O'Casey the Dramatist.* B & N Imports 1985 $51.50. ISBN 0-389-20552-4. Explores O'Casey's experiments, ideology, bitterness, and reconciliation, as well as forces of continuity and originality in his work.

Mikhail, E. H. *Sean O'Casey and His Critics: An Annotated Bibliography, 1916–1982.* Scarecrow 1985 $32.50. ISBN 0-8108-1747-0. Overview of criticism.

O'Connor, Garry. *Sean O'Casey: A Life.* Hodder & Stoughton 1988 o.p. An interesting and authoritative account of O'Casey's life and work.

Rollins, Ronald Gene. *Sean O'Casey's Drama: Verisimilitude and Vision.* U. of Ala. Pr. 1979 o.p. Contrasts poetic and pragmatic forces of O'Casey's Irish subjects; discusses his uses of ritual, ceremony, and myth.

Scrimgeour, James. *Sean O'Casey.* Twayne 1978 o.p. Overview of his life; includes a bibliography.

O'CONNOR, FRANK (pseud. of Michael O'Donovan). 1903–1966

An Irish master of the short story, Frank O'Connor was born Michael O'Donovan in Cork. It is not surprising to learn in the first part of his autobiography, *An Only Child* (1961), that he took his adored mother's name. O'Connor's absorbing interest was the literary treasury of Ireland. He labored tirelessly over masterful translations of ancient Gaelic works. O'Connor wrote the well-received *A Short History of Irish Literature: A Backward Look* and edited an anthology of prose and poetry, *A Book of Ireland* (1959), which contains some of his own translations from the Gaelic. His *Shakespeare's Progress* (1960) is an appraisal of the bard. In *The Lonely Voice: A Study of the Short Story* (1963), he examines the work of those he considers the great short story writers of the past. The subjects of his own stories are the middle and lower-middle classes of his beloved Ireland. In his last years, O'Connor lived mostly in the United States, where he taught at Harvard and Northwestern universities.

SHORT STORY COLLECTIONS BY O'CONNOR

The Big Fellow. 1937. Dufour 1979 repr. of 1937 ed. $9.95. ISBN 0-905169-84-0. Stories about Irish culture.
Collected Stories. 1952. Random 1982 $18.00. ISBN 0-394-71048-7. A definitive edition of O'Casey's short fiction.
Mirror in the Roadway. Select Bibliographies Repr. Ser. Ayer repr. of 1956 ed. $22.00. ISBN 0-8369-5339-8
A Picture Book. Biblio Dist. 1971 repr. of 1943 ed. o.p.
Three Tales. Biblio Dist. 1971 repr. of 1942 ed. o.p.

NONFICTION BY O'CONNOR

My Father's Son. 1969. G.K. Hall 1985 o.p. Another autobiography.
My Oedipus Complex. Creative Ed. 1986 $19.95. ISBN 0-88682-062-6
An Only Child. 1961. G. K. Hall 1985 o.p. Autobiographical depiction of Irish experiences.

BOOKS ABOUT O'CONNOR

Matthews, James. *Frank O'Connor.* Bucknell U. Pr. 1975 $6.50. ISBN 0-8387-7756-2. Competent look at O'Connor's life and work.
Steinman, Michael. *Frank O'Connor at Work.* Syracuse U. Pr. 1989 $32.50. ISBN 0-8156-2474-3. Survey of O'Connor's short stories, drawing on unpublished manuscripts and typescripts.
Tomory, William M. *Frank O'Connor.* Twayne 1980 o.p. Overview of his life; bibliography.

O'FAOLAIN, SEAN. 1900–1991

"There is an element in Irish fiction that someone has aptly described as malicious affection. O'Faolain has it to the greatest degree. All of the 11 stories in . . . [*I Remember! I Remember!,* 1962] bare the faults and failings of the characters without losing the reader's sympathy and understanding for those same characters. There is a melancholy strain along with the quiet chuckle, the nostalgic findings of a man who has lived and learned well. He is indeed a past master of the short story" (*Library Journal*), as evidenced in *The Heat of the Sun* (1966). In his autobiography, *Vive Moi!* (1965), which contains lovely passages descriptive of the Irish countryside, he tells about his six years in the rebel Irish Republican Army, about Irish Roman Catholicism, and about the position of the Irish writer who at one time or another usually finds himself in voluntary exile. The first literary work of "Ireland's leading prose writer" was in Gaelic, although this was acquired and not his native tongue. He first attracted wide attention with *A Nest of Simple Folk* (1933). After his IRA experiences, O'Faolain did graduate work at Harvard University. He returned to Ireland but frequently lectured, taught, and traveled in the United States.

SHORT STORY COLLECTIONS BY O'FAOLAIN

The Collected Stories of Sean O'Faolain. Little o.p. The definitive edition of O'Faolain's short stories.
The Man Who Invented Sin. Devin 1974 repr. of 1948 ed. $12.95. ISBN 0-8159-6212-6. Stories about struggle and insurrection.
Midsummer Night Madness and Other Stories. 1932. Irish Bk. Ctr. 1982 o.p. Short stories.

NOVELS BY O'FAOLAIN

And Again. 1979. Carol Pub. Group 1989 $16.95. ISBN 1-55972-003-4
Come Back to Erin. Greenwood 1972 repr. of 1940 ed. o.p. Rebellious Irish life.

NONFICTION BY O'FAOLAIN

King of the Beggars. Greenwood 1975 repr. of 1938 ed. o.p.

WORKS BY O'FAOLAIN

Silver Branch. Ayer repr. of 1938 ed. $12.00. ISBN 0-8369-6035-1. An edition of
translations from Gaelic.
Vanishing Hero. Ayer repr. of 1957 ed. $16.00. ISBN 0-8369-2065-1

BOOKS ABOUT O'FAOLAIN

Bonaccorso, Richard. *Sean O'Faolain's Irish Vision.* State U. NY Pr. 1987 $64.50. ISBN 0-
88706-536-8. Discusses O'Faolain's nationality, physical life, and extensions of
Irishness as they pertained to his work.
Doyle, Paul A. *Sean O'Faolain.* Twayne 1968 o.p. Overview of his life; bibliography.
Harmon, Maurice. *Sean O'Faolain: A Critical Introduction.* Notre Dame U. Pr. 1967
$60.50. ISBN 0-3172-9672-8. Explores O'Faolain's handling of the themes of the
national mind, imagination and faith, and revolution and dislocation.
Rippier, Joseph Storey. *The Short Stories of Sean O'Faolain.* Dufour 1976 $26.00. ISBN 0-
901072-30-3. Examines O'Faolain's literary influences as well as his use of character,
nature, metaphor, and meaning.

ORTON, JOE. 1933–1967

Born in Leicester, Orton trained as an actor but soon turned to writing plays
instead. Before his career had barely begun, however, he was murdered by his
homosexual lover, apparently in a fit of jealousy over his success.

Orton's shocking murder is too easily made the biographical focus for
discussion of his plays, devoted as they are to the grotesque, the perverse, and
the violent. A more relevant landmark in the playwright's life might be the jail
term he served for the bizarre crime of defacing library books, replacing
illustrations with uproarious collages, and rewriting jacket blurbs in "mildly
obscene" parodies of journalistic cliché. Assaulting the cultural consumer by
transposing familiar icons and vocabulary was the key to Orton's theatrical
method. But it was supplemented by a growing verbal power and stage imagery
with aspirations to myth.

As Orton's literary powers grew, so did the outrage of social response. The
Pinterian ambiance and language of his first works, *Entertaining Mr. Sloan*
(1964) and the radio play *The Ruffian on the Stair* (1966), were well received.
Sloane was chosen best new British play of 1964 and won the blessing of
TERENCE RATTIGAN himself. But *Loot*, joking with death, religion, sex, and family,
proved more disturbing (it involves a slapstick charade centered on a corpse
and a coffin). The first production, directed by Peter Wood, closed on tour
without reaching London. It was not until 1966 that the play was staged, to
acclaim, in Charles Marowitz's fringe theater. In 1969, *What the Butler Saw*
failed in the West End, despite a cast of many famous names, including Ralph
Richardson. Only the Royal Court revival of 1975 gave Orton's undoubted
masterpiece its due. But by then the playwright had been dead for eight years.

In the phallic epiphany with which *Butler* ends, as in his version of EURIPIDES'
(see Vol. 2) *Bacchae, The Erpingham Camp* (1965), Orton calls attention to his
Dionysian ambitions—his serious use of farce as a means of disruption and
liberation. His last plays, in which violent animal spirits subvert dialogue of

extreme—even Victorian—formality and outrageous authority figures, represent probably the greatest comic achievement of contemporary British drama.

PLAYS BY ORTON

The Complete Plays. Grove Pr. 1990 $11.95. ISBN 0-8021-3215-4. Introduction by John Lahr. Contains *Entertaining Mr. Sloane, Loot, What the Butler Saw,* and four shorter plays (*The Ruffian on the Stair, The Erpingham Camp, The Good and Faithful Servant, Funeral Games*).

BOOKS ABOUT ORTON

Bigsby, C.W.E. *Joe Orton.* Methuen 1982 o.p. Discusses the death of character, anarchic farce, and sexuality in Orton's plays.
Charney, Maurice. *Joe Orton.* Macmillan 1984 o.p. Overview focusing on sardonic intellectualizing, quotidian farce, and black comedy.
Gallix, Andrew. *Joe Orton's Comedy of the Last Laugh.* Garland 1992 $20.00. ISBN 0-8153-0146-4. Examines the comedic aspects of Orton's work.
Lahr, John, ed. *The Orton Diaries.* Methuen 1986 o.p. Personal journals reflecting many facets of Orton's colorful personal life.
———. *Prick Up Your Ears: The Biography of Joe Orton.* Limelight Edns. 1986 repr. of 1978 ed. $14.95. ISBN 0-87910-057-5. Well-written, highly readable account of Orton's life and work.

ORWELL, GEORGE (pseud. of Eric Blair). 1903–1950

A Bengal-born novelist, critic, and political satirist, a product of Eton, an anti-Communist wounded while fighting for the Republicans in Spain, Orwell was an independent radical who courageously battled all forms of dictatorship. He first gained recognition in the United States with *Animal Farm* (1945), his satiric fable on JOSEPH STALIN's (see Vol. 3) Russia. His best-selling *1984* (1949) depicts the future horrors of a well-established totalitarian regime; "Big Brother," the government spy, has become common American parlance for the official snooper and the term "Orwellian" is now used as an adjective to refer to the type of society described in his works. Several posthumous volumes of essays have appeared, including *Shooting an Elephant* (1950) and *Collection of Essays.*

NOVELS BY ORWELL

Animal Farm. 1946. Buccaneer Bks. 1982 $21.95. ISBN 0-89966-369-9. Parody of political totalitarianism.
Burmese Days. HarBraceJ 1974 repr. of 1934 ed. $8.95. ISBN 0-15-614850-1. Autobiographical novel that attacks British imperialism.
A Clergyman's Daughter. 1935. HarBraceJ 1969 repr. of 1960 ed. $12.95. ISBN 0-15-618065-0. A story of politics and morality.
Coming Up for Air. 1939. HarBraceJ 1969 repr. of 1950 ed. $7.95. ISBN 0-15-619625-5. A plea for the individual against big business.
Keep the Aspidistra Flying. 1936. HarBraceJ 1969 repr. of 1956 ed. $7.95. ISBN 0-15-646899-9
1984. 1949. NAL-Dutton 1950 $4.95. ISBN 0-451-52493-4. Authoritarian repression.
Orwell's 1984: Text, Sources, Criticism. Ed. by Irving Howe. HarBraceJ 1982 $18.75. ISBN 0-15-565811-5

WORKS BY ORWELL

Collected Essays, Journalism and Letters of George Orwell. 3 vols. HarBraceJ 1968 $15.95–$17.95 ea. ISBNs 0-15-118546-8, 0-15-118547-6, 0-15-118548-4
The Orwell Reader: Fiction, Essays, and Reportage. HarBraceJ 1961 $10.95. ISBN 0-15-670176-6. Introduction by R. H. Rovere.

BOOKS ABOUT ORWELL

Bolton, W. F. *The Language of 1984: Orwell's English and Ours.* U. of Tenn. Pr. 1984 $24.95. ISBN 0-870-49412-0. Discussion of language changes, varieties, and mixtures, with reference to Orwell.

Gardner, Averil. *George Orwell.* Macmillan 1987 $20.95. ISBN 0-805-76956-0. Overview of his life; bibliography.

Kubal, David L. *Outside the Whale: George Orwell's Art and Politics.* Notre Dame U. Pr. 1972 o.p. Study of Orwell's political odyssey and his rejection of old political myths.

Meyers, Jeffrey, ed. *George Orwell: The Critical Heritage.* Routledge 1975 $69.50. ISBN 0-7100-8255-X. Collection of reviews and general critical essays.

Meyers, Jeffrey, and Valerie Meyers. *George Orwell: An Annotated Bibliography of Criticism.* Garland 1977 $18.00. ISBN 0-824-09955-9. Useful list of secondary sources on Orwell and his work.

Meyers, Valerie. *George Orwell.* St. Martin 1991 $24.95. ISBN 0-312-05567-6. Perceptive introductory study.

Oldsey, Bernard Stanley, and Joseph Browne, eds. *Critical Essays on George Orwell.* G. K. Hall 1986 o.p. Discusses Orwell and the lower-middle-class novel, conflicts between art and life, and the antinomies of *1984.*

Shelden, Michael. *Orwell: The Authorized Biography.* HarpC 1991 $25.00. ISBN 0-06-016709-2. A comprehensive and authoritative look at Orwell and his writing.

Stansky, Peter, and William Miller Abrahams. 2 vols. Knopf. Vol. 1 *The Unknown Orwell.* 1972 o.p. Vol. 2 *Orwell, the Transformation.* 1980 o.p. Two-volume biography.

Wemyss, Courtney T., and Alexej Ugrinsky, eds. *George Orwell.* Greenwood 1987 $42.95. ISBN 0-3132-6079-6. Covers Orwell's rhetoric, the problematics of nonfiction, and comparisons with Jack London, Arthur Koestler, Thomas Pynchon, and G. K. Chesterton.

Williams, Raymond, ed. *George Orwell: A Collection of Critical Essays.* P-H 1974 o.p. Examines the politics of truth, Orwell as satirist, and Orwell's postwar prophecy and his world view.

OSBORNE, JOHN. 1929–

John Osborne, it is fairly well known, started the new wave rolling. He had worked intermittently as an actor and journalist, and had had two plays performed outside London, when, at 26, he sent a script to the English Stage Company, George Devine's new repertory group, which hoped to establish a writer's theater in London. With *Look Back in Anger* (1956) and its oratorial hero, Jimmy Porter, the company at the Royal Court inaugurated a revitalization of the British drama and gave a name to a generation of young writers and their protagonists—"angry young men." In reviews, Osborne found himself crowded together with ARNOLD WESKER, David Storey, Ann Jellicoe, Shelagh Delaney, and JOHN ARDEN, playwrights with whom he shared little beyond their working-class origins and antiestablishment attitudes.

Osborne went on, however, to write plays about figures definitely not young or even angry, exactly. Archie Rice, of *The Entertainer* (1957), is a faded music-hall comedian whose son has been killed in Cyprus. His squalid life alternates between scenes of aggressive and embittered performances before bored holiday audiences, a brilliantly distancing use of the theatrical that turns Archie's show into a metaphor for waning England. That Rice was played by Lawrence Olivier was also significant—a gesture of the establishment theater accepting the new drama, meeting it (symbolically) on the common ground of the music hall, a shared popular dramatic tradition.

Luther (1961) might be described as an inconclusive attempt to find a historical analogue for Jimmy Porter. But, with *Inadmissible Evidence* (1964), Osborne succeeded in creating the third of his archetypes for the modern stage, the decomposing solicitor Bill Maitland, hallucinating in the shadows of his office as business, daughter, mistress, and self slip through his fingers. *As Look Back* is a defiant inversion of TENNESSEE WILLIAMS's *Streetcar Named Desire*, *Inadmissible Evidence* is Osborne's *Death of a Salesman*. Stylistically, the play joined *Look Back* and *The Entertainer* in defining the three courses to be taken by new wave British theater: socially committed naturalism, theatricalism (influenced by the popular stage), and a shadowy interiority, to be fully realized only a decade later in the work of HAROLD PINTER. So Osborne did not just begin it all—in a sense, he went through it all as well.

Not that he has ever been anything but himself. Characteristic of all three plays are invective and pleading and aggressive vulnerability, in Osborne's peculiar modern version of GEORGE BERNARD SHAW's stage-dominating monologue. If there has been any marked development in the plays he has written since 1965, it has been in the direction of engaging the speaker with others, in finding an ensemble of voices, as he tried to do in *The Hotel in Amsterdam* (1968) and *West of Suez* (1972). Meanwhile, without real commitment, Osborne has been theatrically experimental (in *A Sense of Detachment*, 1972, actors planted in the audience interrupt the performance) and thematically daring. *A Patriot for Me*, the homosexual subject that provoked the Lord Chamberlain's censorship in 1966, was triumphantly revived in 1983 in the very heart of the establishment, moving from the Chichester Festival to the Theatre Royal, Haymarket. Osborne's increasingly reactionary social views have detached him in everyone's mind from the "angries" into whose ranks he was unfairly conscripted some four decades ago. His more recent works include *A Better Class of Person* (1985) and *God Rot Tunbridge Wells* (1985).

PLAYS BY OSBORNE

The Entertainer. 1957. Viking Penguin 1983 o.p.

The End of Me Old Cigar and *Jack and Jill.* 1974–75. Faber & Faber 1975 o.p.

Four Plays. Dodd 1973 o.p. Contains *West of Suez, A Patriot for Me, Time Present,* and *The Hotel in Amsterdam.*

Inadmissible Evidence. Faber & Faber 1964 o.p.

Look Back in Anger. 1956. Viking Penguin 1982 $6.00. ISBN 0-14-048175-3. Bleak portrait of working-class life, which gave rise to the movement known as "angry young men."

Luther. 1961. NAL-Dutton 1963 $3.95. ISBN 0-451-14474-0. A historical chronicle.

A Patriot for Me and *A Sense of Detachment.* Faber & Faber 1983 $8.95. ISBN 0-571-13041-5

Tom Jones: A Film Script. Faber & Faber 1964 o.p. Period drama about a likeable rogue and his amorous adventures.

Watch It Come Down. 1975. Faber & Faber 1975 o.p. A work that focuses on the theme of social dissolution.

You're Not Watching Me, Mommy (and *Try a Little Tenderness*). Faber & Faber 1983 o.p.

BOOKS ABOUT OSBORNE

Carter, Alan. *John Osborne.* Oliver & Boyd 1973 o.p. Biographical, critical approach examining Osborne's themes, language, and public and private voices.

Goldstone, Herbert. *Coping with Vulnerability: The Achievement of John Osborne.* University Pr. 1982 o.p. Survey of Osborne's plays.

Hinchliffe, Arnold P. *John Osborne.* Twayne 1984 o.p. Overview of his life; bibliography.

Northouse, Cameron, and Thomas P. Walsh. *John Osborne: A Reference Guide.* G. K. Hall 1974 o.p. A useful bibliography of sources.

Trussler, Simon. *The Plays of John Osborne: An Assessment.* Trafalgar 1969 o.p. General overview of the writer.

OWEN, WILFRED. 1893–1918

Born in the village of Oswestry in Shropshire, Owen began to compose poems at age 10 or 11 and continued steadily thereafter. He honed his technique during a checkered academic career, which included Shrewsbury Technical School, a brief stint at University College, Reading, matriculation and then withdrawal from the University of London, a short effort at studying for priestly orders, and language teaching at the Berlitz school in Bordeaux. Returning to England in 1915 to enlist in the army, he was commissioned in the Manchester Regiment and went to the front in January 1917. Sent back to England to recuperate from the rigors of a winter campaign, he met SIEGFRIED SASSOON at the Craiglockhart War Hospital in Edinburgh. During the year from August 1917 to September 1918, he produced much of his best work. Sent back to the front in 1918, he was awarded the Military Cross for gallantry in action and was killed by machine-gun fire on November 4 while in action at the Sambre Canal.

Although he produced other work, Owen's reputation depends on his war poetry. "My subject is War, and the pity of War," he wrote. Yet as his sometime mentor Sassoon observed, "He pitied others; he did not pity himself." Owen's realistic depiction of the carnage of war, and his savage indignation at it, inform his best work. His themes gain power through his skillful technique, particularly the play of sound. He pioneered the technique of pararhyme, the use of rhyming words with similar consonants but differing vowels (as in "flashes/fleshes"). "Strange Meeting" is one of his finest poems.

POETRY BY OWEN

Collected Poems. Ed. by C. Day Lewis. New Dir. Pr. 1964 $8.95. ISBN 0-8112-0132-5. The definitive collection.

The Complete Poems and Fragments. 2 vols. Ed. by Jon Stallworthy. Norton 1984 $65.00. ISBN 0-393-01830-X

Poetry of the First World War. Ed. by Edward Hudson. Lerner Pubns. 1990 $16.95. ISBN 0-685-45375-8

WORKS BY OWEN

Collected Letters. Ed. by Harold Owen and John Bell. OUP 1967 o.p. A revealing collection of letters.

Selected Letters of Wilfred Owen. Ed. by John Bell. OUP 1986 $13.95. ISBN 0-19-281914-3

Wilfred Owen. Ed. by Jennifer Breen. Routledge 1988 $12.95. ISBN 0-415-00733-X. Wide-ranging collection of Owen's work, including poetry and prose.

BOOKS ABOUT OWEN

Hibberd, Dominic. *Owen the Poet.* U. of Ga Pr. 1986 $30.00. ISBN 0-8203-0858-7. Biographical treatment of Owen's origins as a poet, his religious crisis, and his experiences and death in war.

Lane, Arthur E. *An Adequate Response: The War Poetry of Wilfred Owen and Siegfried Sasson.* Bks. Demand repr. of 1972 ed. $51.60. ISBN 0-7837-3795-5. Comparative and thematic study of the two war poets.

Stallworthy, Jon. *Wilfred Owen.* OUP 1978 $4.95. ISBN 0-19-281215-7. Includes tables, maps, and other graphics on Owen's life and places of residence.

White, Gertrude. *Wilfred Owen.* Twayne 1969 o.p. Overview of his life; bibliography.

PINTER, HAROLD. 1930–

Harold Pinter was born in London's poor East End, the son of a tailor of Portuguese-Jewish ancestry (da Pinta). After attending the Royal Academy of Dramatic Art, he worked as an actor and published poetry. In 1958 his third play, *The Birthday Party*, lasted for only 16 performances in London. Two years later, he had plays running successfully both at the Royal Court Theatre and in the West End.

Pinter is perhaps the most established of the contemporary dramatists, with almost every one of his plays in print, and one who has eluded final critical definition. This last is not entirely the fault of the critics. Although the earliest attempts at categorization, such as Irving Wardle's "comedy of Menace," soon proved inadequate, they did help readers cope with Pinter's plays of intentional ambiguity and mysterious violence, such as *The Dumbwaiter* (1957) and *The Birthday Party*. Then *The Caretaker* (1960), *The Collection* (1962), and the screenplay for *The Servant* (1963) seemed to move Pinter into a plainer and more familiar style of playwriting, one concerned with subtle reversals of power in Strindbergian contests to establish "the stronger."

But, by *The Homecoming* (1964), critics could no longer ignore the sense that something more was going on. In Peter Hall's Royal Shakespeare production, Vivien Merchant, then Pinter's wife, played the role of a young woman who crosses the Atlantic with her husband to meet his (entirely male) family and ends up staying on, by mutual agreement, as their private whore who will do public whoring to support herself. (The apparently unaffected husband amiably returns to their children in America.) Such tribal behavior suggested that a framework of mythic criticism might best contain *The Homecoming* (and related works like *A Slight Ache*, 1961).

But just as articles began to appear elaborating this new explanation, Pinter again shifted style, this time to a dramatic minimalism, announced in the experimental short works *Landscape* (1969) and *Silence* (1969). The full-length plays *Old Times* (1971) and *No Man's Land* (1975), which followed, are intentionally static dramas absorbed with events sometimes literal, sometimes remembered, sometimes imagined, among which the audience cannot definitely discriminate. These were difficult plays. *Betrayal* (1980), his next major work, was deceptively easy, its disorientation so slight, that playgoers might mistake it for an ordinary triangle of lovers. Criticism had been left behind again.

Pinter's marriage to Vivian Merchant ended in 1980, at which time he married the writer and biographer Lady Antonia Fraser. In 1981, Pinter wrote the brilliant screenplay for JOHN FOWLES's *The French Lieutenant's Woman*. Other recent works, such as *One for the Road* (1984), *Mountain Language* (1988), and *Party Time* (1991), also reaffirm the playwright's creative powers.

PLAYS BY PINTER

Betrayal. Grove Pr. 1988 $8.95. ISBN 0-8021-3080-1. Explores the anatomy of a marriage's decline.

The Homecoming. Grove Pr. 1989 $6.95. ISBN 0-8021-5105-1

One for the Road: A Play. Grove Pr. 1986 $7.95. ISBN 0-8021-5188-4

Three Plays. Grove Pr. 1962 o.p. Contains *A Slight Ache*, *The Collection*, and *The Dwarfs*.

WORK BY PINTER

Complete Works. 4 vols. Grove Pr. 1990 $10.95 ea. ISBNs 0-8021-5096-9, 0-8021-3237-5, 0-8021-5049-7, 0-8021-5050-0. Vol. 1: *The Birthday Party, The Room, The Dumbwaiter, A Slight Ache*, and *A Night Out*. Vol. 2: *The Caretaker, Night School, The Dwarfs, The Collection, The Lover*, five revue sketches, and an essay "Writing for Myself." Vol. 3: *The Homecoming, Landscape, Silence, The Basement*, revue sketches, and other writings. Vol. 4: *Old Times, No Man's Land, Betrayal*, and other writings.

BOOKS ABOUT PINTER

Diamond, Elin. *Pinter's Comic Play*. Bucknell U. Pr. 1985 $35.00. ISBN 0-838-75068-0. Discusses Pinter's poses, parody, and comic language.

Gale, Stephen H. *Critical Essays on Harold Pinter*. G. K. Hall 1990 $40.00. ISBN 0-8161-8853-X. Contains a bibliography, interviews, and essays discussing Pinter's scenic imagery as well as individual films and plays.

_____. *Harold Pinter: An Annotated Bibliography* G. K. Hall 1978 o.p.

_____. *Harold Pinter: Critical Approaches*. Fairleigh Dickinson 1986 $32.50. ISBN 0-8386-3215-7. Essays on Pinter and Proust, Pinter's radio plays, his disjunctive chronology, and his ironic modes of identification.

Ganz, Arthur F. *Pinter: A Collection of Critical Essays*. P-H 1972 o.p. Essays on such topics as family, naturalism, and language and silence.

Gordon, Lois G. *Harold Pinter: A Casebook*. Garland 1990 $37.00. ISBN 0-8240-2949-6. Essays on the relationship between Pinter's film scripts and his plays, Pinter's politics, Pinter in New York, and a structuralist reading of his work.

Hinchliffe, Arnold. *Harold Pinter*. Macmillan 1981 $20.95. ISBN 0-8057-6784-3. Overview of his life; bibliography.

Trussler, Simon. *The Plays of Harold Pinter: An Assessment*. Trafalgar 1973 o.p. Survey.

POTTER, DENNIS. 1935–

Educated at Oxford, Dennis Potter's aesthetic resonates with the strains of postmodernism proliferated by TOM STOPPARD and THOMAS PYNCHON: a combination of the bizarre and a compelling and somehow old-fashioned narrative. Operating simultaneously with this is a wryly cynical undertone that challenges the smug conventionality of the narrative. His novels, *Ticket to Ride* and *Blackeyes*, are vintage slick postmodern texts, evocative of ROBERT COOVER's or Don DeLillo's with their tricks, twists, dazzling opacity, and masterful stylized tone.

Potter's most notable distinction, though, is in bringing his work to the television screen—adapting his work to an industry that was (especially in the 1960s and 1970s, when he began writing) a highly unlikely forum for his avant-garde offerings. Yet Potter can be credited with creating a stunning canon of television plays that won acclaim despite the seemingly inauspicious mix of the medium and the drama; beyond this, he has energetically expanded the reach of popular culture (from within that culture), garnering admiration for the seriousness and incisiveness of such television plays as *Pennies from Heaven* (1978) and *The Singing Detective* (1986). The latter is an autobiographically based story about a hack writer's anxieties and the relationship between text and reality. Typical of Potter's rich filmic technique, it features a visual and musical panorama brimming with seamlessly intermixed stimuli ranging from 1930s song and dance numbers to psychoanalytic probing of childhood and sexuality.

NOVELS BY POTTER

Blackeyes. Random 1988 $6.95. ISBN 0-679-72047-2. A murder straddles the line between fact and fiction.

Ticket to Ride. Random 1986 $6.95. ISBN 0-679-72353-6. A man is divorced from his memory and sanity.

PLAYS BY POTTER

The Singing Detective. Random 1988 $6.95. ISBN 0-679-72046-4. Potter's most acclaimed television miniseries.

Waiting for the Boat. Faber & Faber 1984 $9.95. ISBN 0-571-13081-X. Television plays:
   Blue Remembered Hills, Joe's Ark, Cream in My Coffee; in preface, discussion by
   Potter of his career.

POWELL, ANTHONY (DYMOKE). 1905–

Powell was born in London and educated at Eton and Balliol College, Oxford,
where he met GRAHAM GREENE and EVELYN WAUGH. Before World War II, he had
worked in journalism and publishing and had several early works of his own
published. After the war, he began a series of novels he called *A Dance to the
Music of Time.* Waugh once said: "Each succeeding volume of Mr. Powell's
'Music of Time' series enhances its importance. The work is dry, cool,
humorous, elaborately and accurately constructed and quintessentially English.
It is more realistic than 'A la Recherche du Temps Perdu,' to which it is often
compared, and much funnier." It has been Powell's fate, according to some
critics, to be praised for writing like someone else, and in the 1930s, he was
praised for writing like Waugh. He was of Waugh's world, and the conflicts in
his work develop out of the rebellions of the first quarter of the century. With
The Kindly Ones, he reached the halfway mark in his chronicle, the end of the
uneasy decades between two world wars. The third trilogy is devoted to World
War II and the fourth, to the following decades. The whole is a complex 12-
volume fictional history of the first two-thirds of the twentieth century. Powell
thinks of his work as one long novel appearing a volume at a time, and not like,
say, C. P. SNOW's *Strangers and Brothers,* a series of connected novels. Since the
completion of the cycle with *Hearing Secret Harmonies* (1975), he has published
a number of other works, including two novels, *O, How the Wheel Becomes It!*
(1983) and *The Fisher King* (1986).

NOVELS BY POWELL

At Lady Molly's. Warner Bks. 1985 $3.95. ISBN 0-445-20055-3
A Dance to the Music of Time. 4 vols. Little 1963–76. Vol. 1: *A Question of Upbringing, A
   Buyer's Market,* and *The Acceptance World.* o.p. Vol. 2: *At Lady Molly's, Casanova's
   Chinese Restaurant,* and *The Kindly Ones.* o.p. Vol. 3. *The Valley of Bones, The
   Soldier's Art,* and *The Military Philosophers.* o.p. Vol. 4: *Books Do Furnish a Room,
   Temporary Kings,* and *Hearing Secret Harmonies.* $24.95. ISBN 0-316-71548-4
The Fisher King. 1986. Transaction Pubs. 1988 $18.95. ISBN 1-85089-188-5
Hearing Secret Harmonies. 1975. Warner Bks. 1986 $4.50. ISBN 0-445-20146-0
O, How the Wheel Becomes It! 1983. H. Holt & Co. 1983 o.p.

NONFICTION BY POWELL

Miscellaneous Verdicts. U. Ch. Pr. 1992 $34.95. ISBN 0-226-67710-9. Collection of
   Powell's commentaries on key writers of the nineteenth and twentieth centuries.
To Keep the Ball Rolling. Viking Penguin 1984 o.p. Powell's four volume set of
   autobiographical memoirs; includes *Infants of the Spring* (1977), *Messengers of the
   Day* (1978), *Faces in My Time* (1980), and *The Strangers All Are Gone* (1982).

BOOK ABOUT POWELL

Tucker, James. *The Novels of Anthony Powell.* Col. U. Pr. 1976 $42.00. ISBN 0-231-
   04150-0

PRIESTLEY, J(OHN) B(OYNTON). 1894–1984

English novelist, playwright, and critic J. B. Priestley was born in Bradford in
Yorkshire, the setting for many of his stories, and was educated at Cambridge
University. Although he first established a reputation with critical writings such
as *The English Comic Characters* (1925), *The English Novel* (1927), and *English*

Humor (1928), it is for his novels and plays that he is best known. Priestley was, like JOHN GALSWORTHY and SOMERSET MAUGHAM, a novelist only partially committed to his playwriting. Yet he became the dominant literary figure in the London West End during the 1930s, as he attempted to make realistically rendered domestic conversation the vehicle for a mature study of personality and emotion. Philosophical theories about time, Socialist dogmatism (often erupting into sermons), and a taste for dramatic expressionism may be said to have finally deflected him from his goal. Priestley's experimental bent nevertheless yielded, among his more than 25 plays, a number of striking theatrical situations—the soliloquies of *Ever since Paradise*, the reviewed life in *Johnson over Jordan* (1939), the replay of an ill-fated conversational turn in *Dangerous Corner* (his most successful play, 1934), and the supernatural visitation in *An Inspector Calls* (his acknowledged masterpiece, 1946).

A prolific essayist and reviewer (as well as screenwriter), Priestley often wrote on the drama. His introduction to his collected plays includes witty and candid comments on each. A lecture, *The Art of the Dramatist* (1957), has also been published. Priestley also wrote books on travel, such as *English Journey* (1934), and *Midnight on the Desert* (1937), about travels through the American Southwest.

PLAYS BY PRIESTLEY

The Plays of J. B. Priestley. 3 vols. HarpC 1950–52 o.p. Vol. 1: *Dangerous Corner, I Have Been Here Before, Johnson over Jordan, Music at Night, The Linden Tree, Eden End, Time and the Conways*. Vol. 2: *Laburnum Grove; Bees on the Boat Deck; When We Are Married; Good Night, Children; The Good Companions; How Are They at Home?; Ever since Paradise*. Vol. 3: *Cornelius, People at Sea, They Came to a City, Desert Highway, An Inspector Calls, Home is Tomorrow, Summer Day's Dream*.

NOVELS BY PRIESTLEY

Angel Pavement. 1930. U. Ch. Pr. 1983 o.p.
Bright Day. U. Ch. Pr. 1983 $7.95. ISBN 0-226-68211-0
The Good Companions. 1929. U. Ch. Pr. 1983 $9.95. ISBN 0-226-68223-4
The Magicians. 1954. Beil 1993 $17.95. ISBN 0-913720-73-9

NONFICTION BY PRIESTLEY

The English Comic Characters. 1925. Phaeton 1972 repr. of 1925 ed. $30.00. ISBN 0-87753-052-1
English Journey. 1934. U. of Ch. Pr. 1984 $24.95. ISBN 0-226-68212-9
The English Novel. 1927. Scholarly 1971 repr. of 1931 ed. $14.00. ISBN 0-403-01311-9

BOOKS ABOUT PRIESTLEY

Atkins, John. *J. B. Priestley: The Last of the Sages*. Riverrun NY 1983 $24.95. ISBN 0-7145-3804-3
Brome, Vincent. *J. B. Priestley*. B & N Imports 1979 o.p. Biography.
Day, Alan Edwin. *J. B. Priestley: An Annotated Bibliography*. Garland 1980 o.p. An extensive, useful sourcebook on Priestley and his work.
De Vitis, A. A., and Albert E. Kalson. *J. B. Priestley*. Twayne 1980 o.p. Overview of his life; includes a bibliography.
Klein, Holger Michael. *J. B. Priestley's Plays*. St. Martin 1988 $35.00. ISBN 0-312-01599-2. Examines place and unity; language, characters, and situations; and ideas of gender, society, and time in Priestley's plays.

PRITCHETT, SIR V(ICTOR) S(AWDEN). 1900–

Born in Ipswich and educated at Alleyn's School, Dulwich, and Dulwich College, novelist and critic V. S. Pritchett worked in the leather trade and later as a commercial traveler and shop assistant. After World War II, he was literary editor of the *New Statesman and Nation* and has frequently contributed to American periodicals and the *N.Y. Times Book Review*. He is a distinguished short story writer who has often appeared in the *New Yorker*. Pritchett has also collaborated with the photographer Evelyn Hofer on three charming and excellent portraits of London, New York, and Dublin. Pritchett, who has been lauded for his fine literary criticism, has also written about many other writers.

NOVELS BY PRITCHETT

Midnight Oil. Random 1973 o.p.
The Turn of the Years. Random 1982 o.p.

SHORT STORY COLLECTIONS BY PRITCHETT

Careless Widow and Other Stories. Random 1989 $16.95. ISBN 0-394-57612-8. Delightful collection.
Complete Collected Stories. Random 1992 $20.00. ISBN 0-679-73892-4. The definitive collection of Pritchett's short fiction.
On the Edge of the Cliff and Other Stories. Random 1979 $11.95. ISBN 0-394-50485-2

NONFICTION BY PRITCHETT

Complete Collected Essays. Random 1992 $34.50. ISBN 0-679-41112-7
Lasting Impressions: Essays 1961–1987. Random 1990 $19.95. ISBN 0-394-58720-0. Essays probing the personal, artistic, and sociopolitical sides of great writers.
The Myth Makers. 1979. Random 1979 $11.95. ISBN 0-394-50472-0

BOOKS ABOUT PRITCHETT

Baldwin, Dean R. *V. S. Pritchett.* Twayne 1987 o.p. Overview of his life; bibliography.
Stinson, J. *V. S. Pritchett: A Study of the Short Fiction.* Macmillan 1992 $22.95. ISBN 0-8057-8341-5

PYM, BARBARA. 1913–1980

Novelist Barbara Pym was born in Shropshire and educated at Oxford University. An editor of *Africa*, an anthropological review, for many years, she published her first novel, *Some Tame Gazelle*, in 1950. Since then, a number of popular works have been published. Often compared with the works of JANE AUSTEN in both manner and subject, Pym's novels are apparently guileless evocations of the foibles of aging and isolated characters. She has a sure, if understated, sense of her characters' psychology and of their unintentionally comic revelations about themselves and their futile lives. After the publication of *No Fond Return of Love* (1961), all her books were out of print until she was cited, coincidentally by both David Cecil and PHILIP LARKIN, as among the most underestimated novelists of the twentieth century. She subsequently completed two successful novels, *The Sweet Dove Died* (1978) and *Quartet in Autumn* (1978), the latter a comic-pathetic study of two men and two women in their sixties who work in the same office but lead separate, lonely lives outside. Many of her earlier books have since been reprinted, including *Excellent Women* (1952) and *A Glass of Blessings* (1958), both perceptive psychological studies of aging women taken advantage of by others. A posthumous novel, *A Few Green Leaves* (1980), is a superb comedy of provincial village life.

NOVELS BY PYM

An Academic Question. NAL-Dutton 1987 $9.00. ISBN 0-452-25996-7. A young woman's attempt to help her husband with eccentric neighbors throws their small college town into a muddle.

Crampton Hodnet. NAL-Dutton 1986 $8.95. ISBN 0-452-25816-2

Excellent Women. 1952. NAL-Dutton 1988 $9.00. ISBN 0-452-26730-7. Search by heroine for her place in a man's world.

A Few Green Leaves. 1980. NAL-Dutton 1989 $8.95. ISBN 0-525-48511-2. A mesmerizing portrait of a small English village.

A Glass of Blessings. 1958. NAL-Dutton 1989 $8.95. ISBN 0-525-48512-0. An understated psycho-drama about the conflict between religious faith and sexual desire.

Jane and Prudence. NAL-Dutton 1990 $8.95. ISBN 0-525-48570-0. A story of two women and their lonely lives.

Less Than Angels. 1955. NAL-Dutton 1990 $8.95. ISBN 0-525-48571-6. A novel about personal and spiritual quests.

No Fond Return of Love. 1961. NAL-Dutton 1992 $9.00. ISBN 0-452-26920-2. Dulcie Mainwaring likes to help others more than herself, especially in matters concerning love.

Quartet in Autumn. 1978. NAL-Dutton 1988 $7.95. ISBN 0-525-48379-9. Portrait of four elderly friends, all single and dreading a lonely retirement.

Some Tame Gazelle. 1950. NAL-Dutton 1992 $9.00. ISBN 0-452-26919-9. A novel of contemporary manners.

The Sweet Dove Died. 1978. NAL-Dutton 1988 $7.95. ISBN 0-525-48380-2

An Unsuitable Attachment. HarpC 1986 repr. of 1982 ed. $7.95. ISBN 0-06-097055-3

NONFICTION BY PYM

Very Private Eye: An Autobiography in Diaries and Letters. Ed. by Hazel Holt and Hilary Holt. NAL-Dutton 1984 o.p. Pym's life and work as revealed through personal documents.

BOOKS ABOUT PYM

Ackley, Katherine Anne. *The Novels of Barbara Pym.* Garland 1989 $29.00. ISBN 0-8240-5621-3. Study of family relationships and isolation in Pym's novels.

Benet, Diana. *Something to Love: Barbara Pym's Novels.* U. of Mo. Pr. 1986 $10.95. ISBN 0-8262-0493-7. Survey, focusing on the role of love in Pym's writing.

Cotsell, Michael. *Barbara Pym.* St. Martin 1989 $24.95. ISBN 0-312-02054-6. Survey and study of literary influences.

Holt, Hazel. *A Lot to Ask: A Life of Barbara Pym.* NAL-Dutton 1991 $19.95. ISBN 0-525-24937-0. An authoritative and interesting biography.

Salwak, Dale. *Barbara Pym: A Reference Guide.* Macmillan 1991 $34.95. ISBN 0-8161-9076-3. Bibliography and sourcebook.

———. *The Life and Work of Barbara Pym.* U. of Iowa Pr. 1986 $27.95. ISBN 0-87745-159-1. Essays on Pym and Austen, the novelist as anthropologist, and Pym's long-neglected stature.

Weld, Annette. *Barbara Pym and the Novel of Manners.* St. Martin 1992 $39.95. ISBN 0-312-06808-5. Survey, focusing on Pym's use of the genres of the mannerly and the comic novel.

RATTIGAN, SIR TERENCE (MERVYN). 1911–1977

Rattigan, who had been a playwright since leaving Oxford University at the age of 22, boasted of his workmanship—"I believe sloppy construction, untidy technique, and lack of craftsmanship to be great faults"—and of his ability to please the British playgoer, the archetypal "Aunt Edna," a "middle-class, middle-aged maiden lady with time on her hands." Not surprisingly, he fell out of favor in the Britain of the 1960s. (He had never been particularly popular in the United States, which looked on his work as inspirationally lacking.) At the time of his death, criticism, still taking him at his word, faintly praised Rattigan's expositions, his management of interleaving characters (as in *Separate Tables*, 1954), and his artful episodic development in *Ross* (1960). But Darlow and Hodson's revelations of Rattigan's tormented personal life have helped readers acknowledge that, despite imposed or sentimental endings, his plays are often full of genuine anguish—in the relations of parents and children (*Man and Boy*, 1963) and obsessed lovers (*The Deep Blue Sea*, 1952), and in recognition of weakness that vitiates heroism (*Ross*, 1960, which is based on the life of T. E. LAWRENCE [see Vol. 5]). And revivals of the 1948 play *The Browning Version* (at the National Theatre) and of *The Winslow Boy* (1946) moved the critic Harold Hobson to concede that "there are many things in Rattigan that have not yet been properly perceived."

PLAYS BY RATTIGAN

The Browning Version. 1948. French o.p. About a failed public school master.
The Deep Blue Sea. 1952. French o.p. Realistic play in the Chekhovian tradition.
Man and Boy. 1963. Boulevard 1964 $10.95. ISBN 0-910278-42-3
O Mistress Mine. Boulevard 1949 $10.95. ISBN 0-910278-43-1
Plays: One. Grove Pr. 1982 o.p. Contains *French without Tears*, *The Winslow Boy*, *Harlequinade*, and *The Browning Version*.
Separate Tables. 1954. French o.p. A study of loneliness set in an English seaside resort.
The Sleeping Prince. Boulevard 1954 $10.95. ISBN 0-910278-44-X
While the Sun Shines. 1945. French o.p. Examines several ethical dilemmas.
The Winslow Boy. 1946. Dramatists Play 1990 $4.75. ISBN 0-8222-1264-1. A father defends his son against an accusation of theft.

BOOKS ABOUT RATTIGAN

Darlow, Michael, and Gillian Hodson. *Terence Rattigan: The Man and His Work.* Interlink Pub. 1979 $25.00. ISBN 0-7043-2160-2. Critical biography stressing the similarity between Rattigan's plays and his personal life.
Rusinko, Susan. *Terence Rattigan.* Twayne 1983 o.p. Overview of his life; bibliography.
Young, B. A. *The Rattigan Version: Sir Terence Rattigan and the Theatre of Character.* Hamilton 1986 o.p. An interesting account of Rattigan's life and work.

RICHARDSON, DOROTHY (MILLER). 1873–1957

The work of Dorothy Richardson is significant in the development of the modern British and Irish novel. Like MARCEL PROUST (see Vol. 2), JAMES JOYCE, and VIRGINIA WOOLF—though her talent was less than theirs—she was one of the first to write in the stream-of-consciousness manner, although she hated this term. Her autobiographical novel, in 12 book-length "chapters," had enjoyed few recent readers until the posthumous discovery and publication of a thirteenth section, *March Moonlight*, in 1967, aroused new interest and brought fresh evaluations of her work. Although she displayed astonishing self-perceptions, most critics find her writing flawed by its egotistical tone and by her unpoetic, humorless style. The fact that she was treated like a son by her father perhaps explains the strong feminist orientation of her life (and of *Pilgrimage*, 1915–38) and her general distrust of men. She gloried in loneliness and independence in a day when these were difficult for women, but tempered these virtues with love affairs both lesbian and heterosexual. She was briefly a mistress of H. G. WELLS (who is portrayed as "Hypo" in *Pilgrimage*), an affair that ended in pregnancy and miscarriage, and eventually married an artist, Alan Odle, in 1917. Disdaining "plot," *Pilgrimage* runs to 2,210 pages, and some of it is heavy going, largely because it lacks selectivity and intensity. Richardson was "hopelessly vague" about her birth date, says Horace Gregory, but on her gravestone (which contains an error in her name), it is given as May 17, 1873.

NOVELS BY RICHARDSON

Backwater. Buccaneer Bks. 1977 repr. of 1916 ed. $13.85. ISBN 0-89966-154-8. A stream-of-consciousness novel.

Honeycomb. Buccaneer Bks. 1977 repr. of 1919 ed. $13.95. ISBN 0-89966-155-6. A highly experimental novel for its time.

BOOKS ABOUT RICHARDSON

Hanscombe, Gillian E. *The Art of Life: Dorothy Richardson and the Development of Feminist Consciousness*. Ohio U. Pr. 1983 o.p. Examines the nature of women's writing as manifested in Richardson's canon.

Radford, Jean. *Dorothy Richardson*. Ind. U. Pr. 1992 $29.95. ISBN 0-253-30108-4. Investigates Richardson's quests, her feminist enigmas, and her use of *l'écriture féminine*.

Staley, Thomas F. *Dorothy Richardson*. Twayne 1976 o.p. Overview of her life; includes a bibliography.

ROSENBERG, ISAAC. 1890–1918

The son of poor immigrants from Lithuania and Russia, Rosenberg spent his youth as an apprentice to an engraver. He attended the Slade School of Art, where he became competent as a portraitist. In 1915, he joined the army, to help support his family, and spent two years in the French trenches. He was killed while on dawn patrol in 1918. His poetry, which reached a mature style and resonance only at the end of his life, starkly and brutally reveals the sensibility of the soldier amid the miasma of the Great War. His best-known poems, such as "Louse Hunting," "Returning, We Hear the Larks," and "Break of Day in the Trenches," are keenly modern in their ironic displacement of the overwhelming realities of war; the focus of these poems is, respectively, lice, birds, and a "queer sardonic rat." Yet in these seemingly marginal aspects of the war, Rosenberg brilliantly embeds its banal horrors. His *Collected Poems* was published posthumously in 1922.

POETRY BY ROSENBERG

Collected Works. Ed. by Ian Parsons. 1979 o.p. Poems exploring the theme of war and its horrors.

BOOKS ABOUT ROSENBERG

Cohen, Joseph. *Journey to the Trenches: The Life of Isaac Rosenberg, 1890–1918*. Basic 1975 o.p. Interesting study of Rosenberg's work and brief life, focusing on the influences that shaped his work.

Liddiard, Jean. *Isaac Rosenberg: The Half Used Life*. Trafalgar 1975 o.p. Competent study of Rosenberg's life and work that examines his unfulfilled potential as a writer.

SACKVILLE-WEST, VITA (VICTORIA MARY). 1892–1962

Poet and novelist Vita Sackville-West began writing as a child. Born at elegant Knole Castle, scene of VIRGINIA WOOLF's novel *Orlando* (1928), Sackville-West was educated in that 365-room dwelling. In 1913 she married HAROLD NICOLSON (see Vol. 3), journalist, diplomat, and biographer. Despite Nicolson's homosexuality and her own lesbian affair with Violet Trefusis, this marriage survived. *Poems of East and West*, her first book, was published in 1917. She remained unknown except by a small group of literary connoisseurs until 1927, when she received the Hawthornden Prize for a second volume of poetry. At this time she lived in London and was part of the Bloomsbury group, which also included LYTTON STRACHEY (see Vol. 3), E. M. FORSTER, JOHN MAYNARD KEYNES (see Vol. 3), and Woolf.

Sackville-West published many novels and volumes of poetry, biography, and family history, and several books on gardening, as well as book reviews and criticism. All of her writings reflect the same unhurried approach, deep reflection, and brilliantly polished style. Her influence on other writers, especially Woolf, was perhaps greater than her own individual achievement. *The Edwardians* (1930) and *All Passion Spent* (1931) are her best-known novels.

Sackville-West's son, Nigel Nicholson, recounted the close, but unconventional relationship of his parents in the memoir *Portrait of a Marriage*, published in 1973.

NOVELS BY SACKVILLE-WEST

All Passion Spent. 1931. Buccaneer Bks. 1990 $29.95. ISBN 0-89966-745-7
The Easter Party. Greenwood 1972 repr. of 1953 ed. $38.50. ISBN 0-8371-5763-3
The Edwardians. 1930. Amereon Ltd. $16.95. ISBN 0-88411-140-7. Social portrait of the aristocracy.

SHORT STORY COLLECTION BY SACKVILLE-WEST

The Heir. Ayer repr. of 1922 ed. $10.00. ISBN 0-8369-3731-7. Stories of upper-class life and morality.

BOOKS ABOUT SACKVILLE-WEST

Glendinning, Victoria. *Vita: A Bibliography of Vita Sackville-West.* Morrow 1985 $12.00. ISBN 0-688-04111-6. A useful reference to works by and about Sackville-West.
Stevens, Michael. *V. Sackville-West: A Critical Biography.* Joseph 1973 o.p. An authoritative account of Sackville-West's life and work.
Watson, Sara Ruth. *V. Sackville-West.* Twayne 1972 o.p. Overview of her life; includes a bibliography.

SASSOON, SIEGFRIED. 1886–1967

Sassoon is unusual among the generation of World War I poets in that he survived the war and was able to write of it both immediately and retrospectively. Born into a wealthy family, Sassoon grew up steeped in the genteel pleasures of the Edwardian aristocracy. He enlisted as a second lieutenant in World War I, serving in France. Like many poets, Sassoon wrote of the war at first as a noble, chivalric undertaking. But, under the influence of ROBERT GRAVES, Sassoon soon developed a more cynical aesthetic. His poem "Repression of War Experience" helps explain the development of his war poetry: It describes the frustration of the soldier trying to communicate the nature of the war to those safe at home and vividly connotes the horror and madness that pervade the soldiers' sustained experience in the trenches. His eventual pacifism and distrust of the military are reflected in his short poem "The General," which blames an uncomprehending and facile wartime leadership for the needless deaths of masses of soldiers.

POETRY BY SASSOON

Collected Poems, 1908–1956. Faber & Faber 1986 $15.95. ISBN 0-571-13262-6
The War Poems of Siegfried Sassoon. Ed. by Rupert Hart-Davis. Faber & Faber 1983 $8.95. ISBN 0-685-06444-1

WORK BY SASSOON

Siegfried Sassoon Diaries. 3 vols. Ed. by Rupert Hart-Davis. Faber & Faber 1983. Vol. 1 *1915–1918.* $22.95. ISBN 0-571-11997-2. Vol. 2 *1920–1922.* $23.95. ISBN 0-571-11685-X. Vol. 3 *1923–1925.* $27.95. ISBN 0-571-13322-3

BOOKS ABOUT SASSOON

Keynes, Geoffrey. *A Bibliography of Siegfried Sassoon.* Hart-Davis 1962 o.p. A handy sourcebook for scholars and general readers.

MacDonald, Stephen. *Not about Heroes: The Friendship of Siegfried Sassoon and Wilfred Owen.* Faber & Faber 1983 o.p. Examines the companionship influences of the two war poets.

Thorpe, Michael. *Siegfried Sassoon: A Critical Study.* OUP 1967 o.p. Discusses Sassoon's lyrics and satire and his religious concerns.

SHAFFER, PETER (LEVIN). 1926–

The psychiatrist Dysart and the composer Salieri, the protagonists of Shaffer's most successful plays, are overcivilized men, each faced with a figure of tormented inspiration—the horse mutilator Strang and the simpering and sublime WOLFGANG AMADEUS MOZART (see Vol. 3). The envy felt by the cultivated and repressed for a mind capable of confronting its own demons (and angels) is a subject that runs back through Shaffer's earlier pairings of liberal and reactionary in *Shrivings* (1970), of conquistador and Inca in *The Royal Hunt of the Sun* (1964). It may even be traceable, in some way, to Shaffer's own equivocal position in the British drama.

Shaffer burst into public attention at the very moment the new drama found its voice—*Five Finger Exercise* won him a citation as the most promising British playwright in 1958, the same year that HAROLD PINTER and ARNOLD WESKER had their first London productions. Yet from the start, Shaffer was chided for the impersonality—the overconstructed and underinspired quality—of his playwrighting. (*Five Finger Exercise* was, as its title suggests, an essay in traditional domestic melodrama.) Director John Dexter made heroic efforts to enrich the texture of *The Royal Hunt of the Sun* with ritual, mime, and music in a grand National Theatre production. He was more successful in *Equus* (1973), in which he brought some of the audience onstage and placed horse-head masks on actors. But Dexter's near-collaborative efforts, and the extensive rewriting that marked Peter Hall's production of *Amadeus* (1980), suggest that Shaffer, despite his successes, is too reticent for the overheated contemporary stage, a Salieri clever enough to acknowledge his own exclusion.

Born in Liverpool, Shaffer spent three years working in coal mines before entering Cambridge University, and several more employed by a music publisher and the New York Public Library. The twin of playwright Anthony Shaffer (*Sleuth,* 1970), he has also written detective novels and music criticism.

PLAYS BY SHAFFER

Amadeus. 1979. HarpC 1981 $9.00. ISBN 0-06-090783-5. Extravagant biographical treatment of Mozart.

Equus. 1973. Viking Penguin 1984 $5.95. ISBN 0-14-048185-0

Five Finger Exercise. 1958. HarBraceJ 1959 o.p.

Lettice and Lovage: A Comedy. 1987. HarpC 1990 $16.95. ISBN 0-685-32430-3. Delightful play about the relationship between two eccentric middle-aged women.

The Private Ear and the Public Eye. 1962. Stein & Day 1964 o.p. An entertaining farce.

The Royal Hunt of the Sun. 1964. Stein & Day 1965 o.p.

BOOKS ABOUT SHAFFER

Cooke, Virginia, and Malcolm Page. *File on Shaffer*. Heinemann Ed. 1988 $9.95. ISBN 0-413-42000-0. Survey of Shaffer's productions and reviews.

Gianakaris, C. J. *Peter Shaffer*. St. Martin 1992 $24.95. ISBN 0-312-06052-1. Provides insightful analyses of each of Shaffer's plays, enhanced with biographical details and production histories.

———. *Peter Shaffer: A Casebook*. Garland 1991 $27.00. ISBN 0-8240-6889-0. Source-book and bibliography.

Klein, Dennis A. *Peter Shaffer*. Twayne 1979 o.p. Overview of his life; bibliography.

Plunka, Gene A. *Peter Shaffer: Roles, Rites, and Rituals in the Theater*. Fairleigh Dickinson 1988 $34.50. ISBN 0-8386-3329-3. Discusses Shaffer as dramatic sociologist as well as form and function in his plays.

Thomas, Eberle. *Peter Shaffer: An Annotated Bibliography*. Garland 1991 $38.00. ISBN 0-8240-7645-1. The most complete Shaffer reference guide to date.

SHAW, GEORGE BERNARD. 1856–1950   (NOBEL PRIZE 1925)

Irish dramatist, essayist, and critic George Bernard Shaw was born in Dublin of Irish-Protestant parents. After short and unhappy periods at several schools, he entered a firm of land agents in 1871. He disliked his work, however, and soon left Ireland for good, and went to London to pursue a literary life. His early years in London were a period of struggle and impoverishment; the novels he wrote during this time were all rejected by publishers. However, an interest in socialism resulted in the publication of many well-known Socialist tracts, and it was this type of journalism, as well as music criticism, that helped build his reputation.

The rest of Shaw's life, especially after his marriage to Charlotte Payne-Townshend in 1898, was devoted primarily to his plays. Ten of Shaw's most important plays—including *Arms and the Man* (1894), *Candida* (1894), and *Caesar and Cleopatra* (1900)—were written before the turn of the century. But only the epoch-making Court Theatre season of 1904–07 brought these plays before the British public.

Unmistakably the work of a drama reviewer who made his attacks on theatrical convention inseparable from his criticism of society, these early plays are (at the very least) a wonderful celebration of the theatricalities of the nineteenth-century British stage. Less overtly given to parody, the major works of the next decade and a half remain Shaw's most popular: *Man and Superman* (1903), *Major Barbara* (1905), *The Doctor's Dilemma* (1906), *Pygmalion* (1913). The experience of World War I, as Stanley Weintraub has shown in *Journey to Heartbreak*, had a profound effect on the playwright's work. His bitter memorial of the war, *Heartbreak House* (1919), which was apparently his favorite play, is in some ways his most difficult. It foreshadows the open-form fantasies and political extravaganzas that largely occupied Shaw for the next three decades. Except for *Saint Joan* (1924), the rich work of this period is unjustly neglected by anthologists and producers today. Shaw's later plays, such as *Too True to Be Good* (1932) and *The Simpleton of the Unexpected Isles* (1934) have also received very little attention. Nevertheless, they continue to reflect the stern Shavian concern for individual responsibility, self-discipline, utmost integrity, and heroic effort without thought of reward, that mark his earlier, more well-known works.

During his 60 years of literary activity, Shaw produced a tremendous body of work. Contrary to received opinion, his prefaces, polemics, and press releases are almost as uniformly thoughtful as they are uniformly, magnificently, readable. In recognition of his outstanding literary achievements, Shaw was awarded the Nobel Prize for literature in 1925.

Plays by Shaw

Androcles and the Lion. 1912. Viking Penguin 1988 $4.95. ISBN 0-14-045013-0

Arms and the Man. 1894. Garland 1981 $20.00. ISBN 0-8240-4578-5. The story of a cynical mercenary.

The Apple Cart. 1929. Viking Penguin 1956 $4.95. ISBN 0-14-048008-0

Caesar and Cleopatra. 1899. Macmillan 1974 $4.20. ISBN 0-672-61154-6

Candida. 1897. Viking Penguin 1950 $5.95. ISBN 0-14-048103-6

Captain Brassbound's Conversion. 1901. Ed. by Rodelle Weintraub. Garland 1981 $16.00. ISBN 0-8240-4586-6. A witty social satire.

The Devil's Disciple. 1901. Ed. by Robert F. Whitman. Garland 1981 $20.00. ISBN 0-8240-4581-5. An Ibsenian morality play.

The Doctor's Dilemma. 1911. Ed. by Margery M. Morgan. Garland 1981 $16.00. ISBN 0-8240-4584-X. Explores the ethical dilemma of which of two dying men should be saved.

Four Plays by Bernard Shaw. PB 1968 $.75. ISBN 0-671-46863-4

Heartbreak House. 1919. Viking Penguin 1965 $3.95. ISBN 0-14-048053-6

Major Barbara. 1905. Ed. by Bernard Dukore. Garland 1981 $20.00. ISBN 0-8240-4583-1

Man and Superman. 1903. Viking Penguin 1950 $2.95. ISBN 0-14-048006-4. Shaw's life force in action.

The Millionairess. Viking Penguin 1961 o.p.

Plays: Major Barbara, Heartbreak House, Saint Joan, Too True to Be Good. Ed. by Warren S. Smith. Norton 1970 o.p.

Plays Unpleasant. Viking Penguin 1950 $3.95. ISBN 0-14-048012-9. Contains *Widower's Houses, The Philanderer,* and *Mrs. Warren's Profession.*

Pygmalion. 1913. PB 1989 $4.50. ISBN 0-671-70496-6

Saint Joan. 1924. Viking Penguin 1950 $2.50. ISBN 0-5827-8286-4. The martyrdom of Joan of Arc.

Selected One-Act Plays. Viking Penguin 1976 o.p. Contains *The Shewing-Up of Blanco Posnet, He Lied to Her Husband, O'Flaherty V.C., The Inca of Perusalem, Annajanska, The Bolshevik Empress, A Village Wooing, The Six of Calais, Overruled, Dark Lady of the Sonnets, Great Catherine, Augustus Does His Bit.*

You Never Can Tell. 1898. Ed. by Daniel J. Leary. Garland 1981 $16.00. ISBN 0-8240-4580-7. A comic portrait of the New Woman.

Novel by Shaw

Cashel Byron's Profession. 1886. Viking Penguin 1979 $4.95. ISBN 0-14-004886-3

Nonfiction by Shaw

Bernard Shaw's Letters to Granville Barker. Ed. by C. B. Purdom. Theatre Arts Bks. o.p.

Collected Letters. Ed. by Dan H. Laurence. 3 vols. Viking Penguin 1985 o.p. Shaw's letters, estimated at 250,000.

The Collected Music Criticism of Bernard Shaw. 4 vols. Vienna Hse. 1973 $75.00. ISBN 0-8443-0063-2

Major Critical Essays. Scholarly 1971 repr. of 1932 ed. $49.00. ISBN 0-403-01205-8

Prefaces by Bernard Shaw. Scholarly 1971 repr. of 1934 ed. $89.00. ISBN 0-403-00785-2

The Quintessence of Ibsenism. Hill & Wang 1959 o.p. A revolt against the nineteenth-century "well-made play."

Selected Non-dramatic Writings of Bernard Shaw. Ed. by Dan H. Laurence. HM 1965 $9.16. ISBN 0-395-05166-5. Contains *An Unsocial Socialist, The Quintessence of Ibsenism,* and essays and reviews.

Shaw on Shakespeare. Ed. by Edwin Wilson. *Essay Index Repr. Ser.* Ayer repr. of 1961 ed. $26.50. ISBN 0-8369-2175-5

Shaw's Dramatic Criticism from the Saturday Review, 1895–1898. Ed. by John F. Matthews. Peter Smith o.p. Reviews from the London *Saturday Review.*

An Unsocial Socialist. 1887. Rprt. Serv. 1992 repr. of 1928 ed. $79.00. ISBN 0-7812-7646-2

WORK BY SHAW

The Portable Bernard Shaw. Ed. by Stanley Weintraub. Viking Penguin 1977 $10.00. ISBN 0-14-015090-0. Contains *Devil's Disciple, Pygmalion, In the Beginning, Heartbreak House,* and *Shakes vs. Shav,* with the "Don Juan in Hell" section of *Man and Superman, The Adventures of the Black Girl,* and other writings.

BOOKS ABOUT SHAW

Adams, Elise Bonita, ed. *Critical Essays on George Bernard Shaw.* G.K. Hall 1991 o.p. Series of essays exploring Shaw's dramatic forms and sources.

Gibbs, A. M. *The Art and Mind of Shaw.* St. Martin 1983 $29.95. ISBN 0-312-04992-7. Discusses Shavian themes—the failure of politics, romance and anti-romance, the economics of love—as well as Shaw's formative years.

Gordon, David J. *Bernard Shaw and the Comic Sublime.* Macmillan 1990 $35.00. ISBN 0-333-49632-9. Explores the development, compromise, and negation of Shaw's comic sublime.

Holroyd, Michael. *Bernard Shaw.* Random 1988 o.p. The definitive biography of Shaw.

Laurence, Dan H. *Bernard Shaw: A Bibliography.* 2 vols. OUP 1983 $215.00. ISBN 0-19-818179-5. An indispensable sourcebook on Shaw and his work.

May, Keith M. *Ibsen and Shaw.* St. Martin 1985 $25.00. ISBN 0-312-40371-2. Comparative study tracing similarities and influences of the two playwrights.

Peters, Margot. *Bernard Shaw and the Actresses.* Doubleday 1980 o.p. Examines Shaw's relations with the women who performed in his plays.

Silver, Arnold Jacques. *Bernard Shaw: The Darker Side.* Stanford U. Pr. 1982 $42.50. ISBN 0-8047-1091-0. Biographically based criticism.

Smith, Warren Sylvester. *Bishop of Everywhere: Bernard Shaw and the Life Force.* Pa. St. U. Pr. 1982 $25.00. ISBN 0-271-00306-5. Investigates the nature of religion and ethics in Shaw's drama.

Turco, Alfred. *Shaw's Moral Vision: The Self and Salvation.* Cornell Univ. Pr. 1976 $36.95. ISBN 0-8014-0965-9. Examines the role of the individual in Shaw's moralistic sensibility.

Wearing, J. P. *G. B. Shaw: An Annotated Bibliography of Writings about Him.* N. Ill. U. Pr. 1986 $45.00. ISBN 0-8758-0125-0. A critical sourcebook that details important works about Shaw.

Weintraub, Stanley. *Bernard Shaw: A Guide to Research.* Pa. St. U. Pr. 1992 $35.00. ISBN 0-27-100831-8. Bibliography.

―――――. *Bernard Shaw on the London Art Scene, 1885–1950.* Pa. St. U. Pr. 1989 $50.00. ISBN 0-271-00665-X. Explores Shaw's interaction with the contemporary art world.

Whitman, Robert F. *Shaw and the Play of Ideas.* Cornell Univ. Pr. 1977 $36.95. ISBN 0-8014-1072-X. Philosophically based study of Shaw's plays.

Wiesenthal, J. L. *Shaw's Sense of History.* OUP 1988 $55.00. ISBN 0-19-812892-4. Examines Shaw's background in history and discusses his plays as historical drama.

SILLITOE, ALAN. 1928–

Alan Sillitoe grew up in the slums of the industrial city of Nottingham. He began to write while in the Royal Air Force, stationed in Malaya. After the war he went to Majorca, where he became a friend of ROBERT GRAVES, who encouraged him to write *Saturday Night and Sunday Morning* (1958). The *N.Y. Herald Tribune* said: "Alan Sillitoe has given us one of the better pictures of English working-class life since Arnold Bennett dealt with the Five Towns or D. H. Lawrence with Nottingham collieries." His author's fee for the manuscript rescued him and his wife, the American poet Ruth Fainlight, from poverty and enabled him to afford the balanced diet to which he attributes his recovery from tuberculosis. *Saturday Night* won the Author's Club Prize for the best British novel of 1958 and was made into a superb movie in 1960. His second book, *The Loneliness of the Long-Distance Runner* (1959), was awarded Britain's Hawthornden Prize for 1960 and was made into an excellent film in 1962.

William Posters is Sillitoe's play on words of the British "Bill Posters Will Be Prosecuted" (U.S. version—"Post No Bills"), a sentence that has haunted him. *The Death of William Posters* (1965) is a novel about yet another young man who must escape from the philistinism of the social milieu to which he has been born. *Tree on Fire* (1967), a novel with autobiographical elements, was published in Britain in 1968. *Travels in Nihilon* (1971) is a satirical novel about a country controlled by nihilism. *Raw Material* (1972) is a fictionalized memoir of his childhood and an exploration of the making of a writer.

NOVELS BY SILLITOE

Her Victory. 1982. Academy Chi. o.p.
The Loneliness of the Long-Distance Runner. NAL-Dutton 1992 repr. $8.00. ISBN 0-452-26908-3. Short stories.
The Lost Flying Boat. Little 1984 o.p. A parable of the welfare state.
Out of a Whirlpool. 1987. Transaction Pubs. 1988 repr. of 1987 ed. $18.95. ISBN 1-85089-225-5
Saturday Night and Sunday Morning. Knopf 1959 $16.95. ISBN 0-394-44377-2. Working-class life in the Midlands.

BOOKS ABOUT SILLITOE

Atherton, Stanley S. *Alan Sillitoe: A Critical Assessment*. Allen 1979 o.p. Examines Sillitoe's views on writing, working-class attitudes, and meeting points of art and life.
Gerard, David. *Alan Sillitoe: An Annotated Bibliography*. Greenwood 1988 $49.95. ISBN 0-313-27672-2. A useful sourcebook of primary and secondary sources.
Hitchcock, Peter. *Working-Class Fiction in Theory and Practice: A Reading of Alan Sillitoe*. Univ. Rochester Pr. 1989 $39.00. ISBN 0-8357-1976-6. Surveys the working-class influences on Sillitoe's work.
Penner, Allen Richard. *Alan Sillitoe*. Twayne 1972 o.p. Overview of his life; bibliography.

SITWELL, (DAME) EDITH. 1887–1964

The first child of Sir George Sitwell and Lady Ida Sitwell, Edith Sitwell became famous both as poet and bohemian. Reacting against what she called the "dim bucolics" of the Georgians, she and her brothers Osbert and Sacheverell constituted a kind of aristocratic bohemian vanguard after World War I. SERGEI DIAGHILEV's (see Vol. 3) Russian Ballet joined T. S. ELIOT and, improbably, ALEXANDER POPE among the early influences on her work. A skilled publicist as well as poet, Sitwell exploited her upper-class nonconformity in numerous public controversies. Her collaboration with William Walton to produce musical settings of the *Façade* poems (1923) created an uproar when the work was performed. Sitwell also put her talents to work for young writers in whom she believed, chief among them DYLAN THOMAS, whose reputation she helped launch. Despite later public honors—Elizabeth II created her a Dame Grand Cross of the British Empire, and Oxford and Cambridge bestowed honorary degrees—she remained proudly eccentric throughout her celebrated career.

Sitwell's early poetry displayed a pyrotechnic surface of dazzling images and leaps. She saw Eliot's *Prufrock and Other Observations* (1917) as heralding "a new era in poetry," which would lead to poets seeing the world with new eyes. Breakthroughs in perception often became the themes as well as goals of her poetry. Interested particularly in French symbolist theories of sound, she developed an intricate tonal play of verbal patterns in her verse. Her work displayed an increasingly religious orientation, and during World War II, she engaged such public themes as politics more overtly in works like *Three Poems for an Atomic Age*. Besides her own verse, she wrote several books of prose and edited numerous anthologies of poetry.

POETRY BY SITWELL

Bath. Greenwood 1980 repr. of 1932 ed. $45.00. ISBN 0-313-20815-8
Collected Poems. Vanguard 1954 o.p. The definitive collection of Sitwell's poems.
Poetry and Criticism. Folcroft 1977 repr. of 1925 ed. o.p.
The Shadow of Cain. 1947. Folcroft 1977 repr. of 1947 ed. o.p.

NOVEL BY SITWELL

I Live Under a Black Sun: A Novel. Greenwood repr. of 1938 ed. o.p.

NONFICTION BY SITWELL

Aspects of Modern Drama. Scholarly repr. of 1934 ed. $15.00. ISBN 0-403-00720-8
Aspects of Modern Poetry. *Essay Index Repr. Ser*. Ayer repr. of 1934 ed. $17.00. ISBN 0-8369-1684-0
Edith Sitwell: Selected Letters, 1919–1964. Vanguard 1970 o.p.
The English Eccentrics. 1933. Vanguard o.p.
Music and Ceremonies. Vanguard 1963 o.p.
A Poet's Notebook. Greenwood 1972 repr. of 1950 ed. $35.00. ISBN 0-8371-6040-5
Taken Care Of: The Autobiography of Edith Sitwell. Atheneum 1965 o.p.

BOOKS ABOUT SITWELL

Brophy, James. *Edith Sitwell: The Symbolist Order*. S. Ill. U. Pr. 1968 o.p. Sitwell's relation to the tradition of symbolism.
Cevasco, G. A. *The Sitwells: Edith, Osbert, and Sacheverell*. Macmillan 1987 $21.95. ISBN 0-8057-6953-6. Overview of their lives; bibliography.
Fifoot, Richard. *A Bibliography of Edith, Osbert, and Sacheverell Sitwell*. Archon Bks. 1971 o.p. A useful sourcebook that includes materials by and about Sitwell.
Glendinning, Victoria. *Edith Sitwell: A Unicorn among Lions*. Knopf 1981 o.p. A well-written, interesting biography.
Pearson, John. *Façades: Edith, Osbert, and Sacheverell Sitwell*. Macmillan 1978 o.p. Biography.
Villa, Jose Garcia, ed. *A Celebration for Edith Sitwell*. New Dir. Pr. 1948 o.p. Tributes by such writers as W. B. Yeats, Stephen Spender, and Gertrude Stein.

SMITH, STEVIE (pseud. of Florence Margaret Smith). 1902–1971

Florence Margaret Smith adopted her nickname, Stevie, as a nom de plume after a friend's joking comparison of her petite stature to that of the jockey Steve Donoghue. She was born in Hull but after her parents' separation moved with her mother, aunt, and sister to a house in the London suburb of Palmers Green. There she lived for the rest of her outwardly uneventful life. After graduation from school, she worked as a private secretary with the London magazine publishing firm George Newnes until 1953, when partly due to ill health she retired to devote her full time to writing and to BBC broadcasts. Besides her verse, her other works include three novels published between 1936 and 1949.

Although she had a minor success with *Novel on Yellow Paper* (1936) and subsequent verse in the late 1930s, Smith came to wider public attention after the publication of her *Selected Poems* in Britain in 1962 and the United States in 1964. Praised by ROBERT LOWELL and others, her poetry does not fit easily into any school or influence. Rather, her mixture of nursery or children's rhythms with a mature irony leads to a voice at once individualized yet accessible. Smith's poems often deal with death, loneliness, absent parents, and what she described as a backsliding rejection of orthodox Christianity. After 1938 she illustrated her own books with line drawings that some critics find distracting but others judge as often ironic commentaries on the text. "Not Waving but Drowning," perhaps her best-known poem, illustrates her disconcerting blend of wit and seriousness at its best. Smith was awarded the Chomondeley Award in 1966 and the Queen's Gold Medal for Poetry in 1969. In 1981, a film based on her life entitled *Stevie* was released.

POETRY BY SMITH

Collected Poems. Ed. by James MacGibbon. New Dir. Pr. 1983 repr. of 1975 ed. $16.95. ISBN 0-8112-0882-6. The definitive collection of Smith's poetry.
New Selected Poems. New Dir. Pr. 1988 $18.95. ISBN 0-8112-1067-7. Wide-ranging selection of poems, including some previously unpublished.
Selected Poems. New Dir. Pr. 1964 o.p.

NOVELS BY SMITH

The Holiday. 1949. Trafalgar 1992 $10.95. ISBN 0-86068-067-3
Novel on Yellow Paper. 1936. Trafalgar 1992 $10.95. ISBN 0-86068-146-7
Over the Frontier. 1938. Trafalgar 1992 $10.95. ISBN 0-86068-130-0. Smith explores the use of experimental narrative in this novel.

WORKS BY SMITH

Me Again: The Uncollected Writings of Stevie Smith, Illustrated by Herself. Ed. by Jack Barbera and William McBrien. Random 1983 repr. of 1981 ed. o.p. Includes a number of personal artifacts and other writings.
Stevie Smith: A Selection. Ed. by Hermione Lee. Faber & Faber 1983 o.p.

BOOKS ABOUT SMITH

Barbera, Jack, and William McBrien. *Stevie: A Biography of Stevie Smith.* OUP 1988 $35.00. ISBN 0-19-520549-9. A comprehensive, interesting look at Smith's life and work.
Barbera, Jack, and Helen Bajan. *Stevie Smith: A Bibliography.* Greenwood 1987 $47.50. ISBN 0-313-27666-8. Thorough reference to Smith's work and books about her and her work.
Rankin, Arthur C. *The Poetry of Stevie Smith: "Little Girl Lost".* B & N Imports 1985 $39.25. ISBN 0-389-20508-7. Thematic study emphasizing Smith's religious and spiritual values.
Spalding, Frances. *Stevie Smith: A Biography.* Norton 1991 $14.95. ISBN 0-393-30718-2. Critical biography of Smith.
Sternlicht, Sanford. *In Search of Stevie Smith.* Syracuse U. Pr. 1991 $27.50. ISBN 0-8156-2503-0. Interviews, biographical reminiscences; essays on the melancholy and macabre, untrue myths.
———. *Stevie Smith.* Macmillan 1990 $21.95. ISBN 0-8057-6990-0. Overview of her life; includes a bibliography.

SNOW, LORD C(HARLES) P(ERCY) (Baron Snow of Leicester). 1905–1980

Trained as a physicist and at one time a fellow in physics at Cambridge University, C. P. Snow wrote a number of papers on the problems of molecular structure. He was knighted in 1957 for his important work in organizing scientific personnel for the Ministry of Labour during World War II and for his

NONFICTION BY SPARK

Curriculum Vitae. HM 1993 $14.95. ISBN 0-395-65372-X. An autobiography describing
the first 39 years of her life. Deals with her childhood, schooling, marriage, and early
success as a writer. "The whole thing is sheer pleasure." (*Booklist*)

BOOKS ABOUT SPARK

Bold, Alan Norman. *Muriel Spark.* Routledge Chapman & Hall 1986 $7.50. ISBN 0-416-
40360-3. Survey.

Edgecombe, Rodney Stenning. *Vocation and Identity in the Fiction of Muriel Spark.* U. of
Mo. Pr. 1990 $22.50. ISBN 0-8262-0750-2. Investigates secular and divine vocations
and travesties of vocation in Spark's fiction.

Hynes, Joseph. *The Art of the Real: Muriel Spark's Novels.* Fairleigh Dickinson 1988 o.p. A
study of deception versus reality and of Spark's comic texture.

Page, Norman. *Muriel Spark.* St. Martin 1990 $24.95. ISBN 0-312-04039-3. Survey of
Spark's life and work.

Randisi, Jennifer Lynn. *On Her Way Rejoicing: The Fiction of Muriel Spark.* Cath. U. Pr.
1991 $29.95. ISBN 0-8132-0730-4. Discusses demons and mysteries in Spark's fiction
as well as her work as spiritual autobiography.

Sproxton, Judy. *The Women of Muriel Spark.* St. Martin 1992 $35.00. ISBN 0-312-08116-2.
Examines Spark's women characters.

Tominaga, Thomas T., and Wilma Schneidermeyer. *Iris Murdoch and Muriel Spark: A
Bibliography.* Scarecrow 1976 $24.00. ISBN 0-8108-0907-9. A fairly comprehensive
bibliography of Spark's work and books about her.

Walker, Dorothea. *Muriel Spark.* Macmillan 1988 $19.95. ISBN 0-8057-6960-9. Complete
treatment of Spark and her work; contains a chronology, bibliography, and index.

SPENDER, SIR STEPHEN (HAROLD). 1909–

The youngest of the group that included W. H. AUDEN, C. DAY LEWIS, and LOUIS
MACNEICE, Stephen Spender was born in London and educated at Oxford
University. He produced his most memorable verse in the 1930s, when his leftist
orientation led him briefly to join the Communist party. Coeditor of *Horizon*
magazine before World War II, he served in the National Fire Service during the
war. He worked as an editor of *Encounter* magazine from 1953 to 1967,
resigning after the revelation that the magazine had relied on funding from the
American CIA. Since World War II, Spender has produced more prose than
poetry, including the fine autobiography *World within World* (1951) and the
valuable literary analysis *The Struggle of the Modern* (1963). After his first visit to
the United States in 1947 to see his old friend Auden, Spender began to spend
half the year in Britain and the other half abroad, often in the United States on
visiting appointments at universities. In 1970 he was appointed professor of
English literature at the University of London.

Spender's poetry lacks both the wit and quietly authoritative tone of Auden's.
Instead, he takes a more questioning, self-divided stance, in which his modern
diction and subjects often serve a romantic preoccupation with the self.
Spender's prose shows him the most proromantic of his circle. Even in the
socially engaged verse of the 1930s, Spender often dramatized individual
yearnings or projected them onto only apparently objective social circumstances. He has found his true themes in relationships, whether of individuals or
of groups. A gifted critic, his recent work has included studies of T. S. ELIOT, the
1930s poets, and the sculptor Henry Moore. In 1962, he was made a CBE
(Commander, Order of the British Empire).

POETRY BY SPENDER

Collected Poems: 1928–1985. Random 1986 $19.95. ISBN 0-394-54601-6. Collection of Spender's best works, many newly revised.
Selected Poems. Random 1964 $8.95. ISBN 0-394-40445-9. The definitive collection of Spender's poetry.

NOVELS BY SPENDER

Engaged in Writing: Two Novels. Saifer $15.00. ISBN 0-87556-519-0

PLAY BY SPENDER

Oedipus Trilogy: A Play in Three Acts Based on the Oedipus Plays of Sophocles. Random 1987 $19.95. ISBN 0-394-54483-8

NONFICTION BY SPENDER

The Creative Element: A Study of Vision, Despair, and Orthodoxy Among Some Modern Writers. Ayer repr. of 1953 ed. $20.00. ISBN 0-8369-5911-6
The Destructive Element: A Study of Modern Writers and Beliefs. Saifer 1970 $12.50. ISBN 0-87556-325-2. Interesting collection of essays about writers and their personal philosophies.
Forward from Liberalism. Arden Lib. 1977 repr. of 1937 ed. o.p.
Learning Laughter. Greenwood repr. of 1953 ed. o.p. On Israel.
The Thirties and After: Poetry, Politics, People, 1930s–1970s. Random 1979 o.p. Series of memoirs, essays, and other prose spanning 40 years of Spender's career.

WORKS BY SPENDER

Journals 1939–1983. OUP 1987 $12.95. ISBN 0-19-505209-9
Letters to Christopher: Stephen Spender's Letters to Christopher Isherwood, 1929–1939, with "The Line of the Branch"—Two Thirties Journals. Ed. by Lee Bartlett. Black Sparrow 1980 $20.00. ISBN 0-87685-470-6

BOOKS ABOUT SPENDER

Kulkarni, Hemant Balvantrao. *Stephen Spender, Works and Criticism: An Annotated Bibliography*. Garland 1976 o.p. Collection of primary and secondary sources.
Sternlicht, Sanford V. *Stephen Spender*. Twayne 1992 $24.95. ISBN 0-8057-7009-7. Overview of his life; includes a useful bibliography.
Weatherhead, Andrew Kingsley. *Stephen Spender and the Thirties*. Bucknell U. Pr. 1975 $22.50. ISBN 0-685-00935-1. Examines Spender's poetry and aesthetic against the background of the contemporary sensibility.

STOPPARD, TOM (born Tom Straussler). 1937–

When the National Theatre needed a last-minute substitute for a canceled production of *As You Like It*, Kenneth Tynan decided to stage *Rosencrantz and Guildenstern Are Dead*, a work by an unfamiliar author that had received discouraging notices from provincial critics at its Edinburgh Festival debut. Of course, the play, when it opened in April 1967, met with universal acclaim. In New York the next year, it was chosen best play by the Drama Critics Circle.

In such an unlikely way, Tom Stoppard came to light. Born in Czechoslovakia, a country he left (for Singapore) when he was an infant, he began his literary career as a journalist in Bristol, where play reviewing led to playwriting. After *Rosencrantz and Guildenstern*, Stoppard's reputation suffered through the production of a number of minor works, whose intellectual preoccupations were shrugged off by reviewers: *Enter a Free Man* (1968; "an adolescent twinge of a play," *N.Y. Times*), *The Real Inspector Hound* (1968; "lightweight," *N.Y. Times*), and *After Magritte*. But in the 1970s, the initial enthusiasms aroused by

Rosencrantz and Guildenstern were more than vindicated by the production of two full-length plays, *Jumpers* (1974) and the antiwar play *Travesties* (1975), whose immense verbal and theatrical inventiveness made them absolute successes on both sides of the Atlantic.

Stoppard's method from the start has been to contrive explanations for highly unlikely encounters—of objects (the ironing board, old lady, and bowler hat of *After Magritte*), characters (Joyce, Lenin, and Tzara in *Travesties*), and even plays (*Hamlet, Rosencrantz and Guildenstern, The Importance of Being Earnest, Travesties,* and *The Real Thing,* 1982). In the 1970s, Tynan called for Stoppard—as a Czech and as an artist—to engage himself politically. But although political subjects have since found their way into pieces from *Every Good Boy Deserves Favor* (1977) to *Squaring the Circle* (1985), politics and art seem to have become just two more of the playwright's irreconcilables, which meet, but never join, in the logical frames of his comedy. The presence of political material—such as the Lenin sections that nearly ruin the second part of *Travesties*—has occasionally strained the structure of the plays. But in *The Real Thing* Stoppard is comfortable enough with the satire on art and activism to bring a third subject, love, into the mix. Stoppard has acknowledged his Eastern European heritage nonpolitically, in a series of adaptations of plays by ARTHUR SCHNITZLER (see Vol. 2), Johann Nestroy, and Ferenc Molnár.

PLAYS BY STOPPARD

The Dog It Was That Died, and Other Plays. Faber & Faber 1983 o.p. Includes a number of dark comedies.
Enter a Free Man. Faber & Faber 1991 $8.95. ISBN 0-571-08794-9
Every Good Boy Deserves Favor and *Professional Foul.* 1977. Grove Pr. 1988 $7.95. ISBN 0-8021-5045-4
Hapgood. 1988. Faber & Faber 1989 $8.95. ISBN 0-571-15160-4
Jumpers. 1972. Grove Pr. 1989 $7.95. ISBN 0-8021-5100-0
Night and Day. Grove Pr. 1979 o.p.
The Real Inspector Hound and *After Magritte.* Grove Pr. 1970 $8.95. ISBN 0-8021-5205-8
The Real Thing. 1982. Faber & Faber 1983 $8.95. ISBN 0-685-26862-4
Rosencrantz and Guildenstern Are Dead. Grove Pr. 1988 $7.95. ISBN 0-8021-3275-8. Two minor Shakespearean characters taking center stage.
Rough Crossing and *On the Razzle.* Faber & Faber 1991 $10.95. ISBN 0-571-16401-3. Adaptations of Molnár and Johann Nestroy, respectively.
Travesties. 1975. Grove Pr. 1989 $5.95. ISBN 0-8021-5089-6

BOOKS ABOUT STOPPARD

Billington, Michael. *Stoppard The Playwright.* Heinemann Ed. 1988 $11.95. ISBN 0-413-45850-4. Overview, focusing on Stoppard's philosophy and his work in the context of contemporary drama.
Brassell, Tim. *Tom Stoppard: An Assessment.* St. Martin 1985 $29.95. ISBN 0-312-80888-7. Examines Stoppard's style, puzzles, and farces.
Delaney, Paul. *Tom Stoppard: The Moral Vision of the Major Plays.* St. Martin 1990 $39.95. ISBN 0-312-03556-X. Discusses art as a moral matrix and moral absolutes and action in Stoppard's plays.
Jenkins, Anthony. *Critical Essays on Tom Stoppard.* G. K. Hall 1990 $36.00. ISBN 0-8161-8854-8. Discusses Stoppard's philosophy and farce, his puns, his portrayal of women, and his treatment of the theme of ethics on the wane.
———. *The Theatre of Tom Stoppard.* Cambridge U. Pr. 1989 $34.95. ISBN 0-521-33266-4. Examines language, perspective, ethics, and manners in Stoppard's drama.
Kelly, Katherine E. *Tom Stoppard and the Craft of Comedy: Medium and Genre at Play.* U. of Mich. Pr. 1990 $29.95. ISBN 0-4721-0188-9. Covers Stoppard's plays, journalism, fiction, radio and television drama, as well as satire and silence.

Page, Malcolm. *File on Stoppard*. Heinemann Ed. 1986 $9.95. ISBN 0-413-57280-3. Surveys Stoppard's productions and reviews.

Sammells, Neil. *Tom Stoppard: The Artist as Critic*. St. Martin 1988 $35.00. ISBN 0-312-00534-2. Discusses formalism and Stoppard's aesthetics of engagement as well as dissent and dissidents.

SYNGE, JOHN MILLINGTON. 1871–1909

After graduating from Trinity College, Dublin, Synge left for Europe to write poetry. If W. B. YEATS had not discovered him in Paris and persuaded him to return to Ireland and absorb its native traditions, the Irish renaissance might have lost its best playwright. As it was, Synge's poetry of Celtic romanticism was rather more tempered with a European realism than Yeats and his renaissance had anticipated.

Yeats sent Synge to the West of Ireland to get to know the peasants there. The result was, in addition to the journal *The Aran Islands* (1907), two short plays for the Abbey: *The Shadow of the Glen* (1903), in which a comic resurrection interrupts a widow's marriage bargaining, and *Riders to the Sea* (1904), about a mother's loss of her last son, a perfect condensed tragedy and probably the finest one-act play. The poorly received *The Well of the Saints* (1905), whose characters vehemently reject reality for comfortable illusion, offered the Abbey audience a warning of what was to come. This was Synge's masterpiece, *The Playboy of the Western World* (1907), which touched off rioting at the theater. The playboy is Christy Mahon, a lout who becomes a hero among the Mayo peasantry when he boasts he has murdered his father. Satire on Irish romanticism conceals a parable of the poet's development and estrangement from his public. But Dublin nationalists heard only the people slandered, and Dublin prudery heard only the forbidden word "shifts" on Christy's lips.

Playboy was the last play Synge saw staged. He died of cancer at age 37, never having completed *Deirdre of the Sorrows* (1910), his only work in the Celtic legendary mode.

PLAYS BY SYNGE

The Complete Plays of John M. Synge. Random 1960 $10.00. ISBN 0-394-70178-X. The definitive collection of plays.

The Complete Plays of Synge. Heinemann Ed. 1988 $11.95. ISBN 0-413-48520-X

The Playboy of the Western World. 1907. Dufour 1990 $6.95. ISBN 0-85342-406-3. Cynical comedy about the adulation of a murderer.

The Plays. 2 vols. Ed. by Ann Saddlemyer. Cath. U. Pr. o.p.

Riders to the Sea. 1904. Biblio Dist. 1969 o.p. About the grief of a woman who has lost her sons to the sea.

The Well of the Saints. 1905. Ed. by Nicholas Grene. Cath. U. Pr. 1982 $12.95. ISBN 0-8132-0571-9. Recovery of their sight by a blind couple, and discovery of their ugliness.

WORKS BY SYNGE

The Collected Letters of John Millington Synge, 1871–1907. Ed. by Ann Saddlemyer. OUP 1983 $79.00. ISBN 0-19-812678-6

Plays, Poems, and Prose. Biblio Dist. 1972 repr. of 1941 ed. o.p.

BOOKS ABOUT SYNGE

Benson, Eugene. *J. M. Synge*. Macmillan 1982 o.p. A comprehensive overview of Synge and his work.

Gerstenberger, Donna. *John Millington Synge*. Twayne 1990 o.p. Overview of his life; bibliography.

Greene, David H., and Edward M. Stephens. *J. M. Synge, 1871–1909*. NYU Pr. 1989
$35.00. ISBN 0-8147-3028-0. An interesting and readable biography.

Johnson, Toni O'Brien. *Synge, the Medieval and the Grotesque*. Smythe 1982 o.p.
Examines medieval sensibilities in Synge's drama.

Kiberd, Declan. *Synge and the Irish Language*. Rowman 1979 o.p. Study of Synge's Irish
influences.

King, Mary C. *The Drama of J. M. Synge*. Syracuse U. Pr. 1985 $24.95. ISBN 0-8156-
2337-2. Discusses language in Synge's plays, relation between text and world, and
Synge's intellectual background.

Kopper, Edward A., ed. *J. M. Synge: Literary Companion*. Greenwood 1988 $49.95. ISBN
0-313-25173-8. Essays on Irish myth, Christianity versus paganism, and Synge's role
in the Irish literary renaissance.

Mikhail, E. H. *J. M. Synge: Interviews and Recollections*. B & N Imports 1977 $21.50.
ISBN 0-06-494817-X. Colorful anecdotes about Synge by such contemporary figures
as Yeats, Joyce, Colum, and Lady Gregory.

Price, Alan. *Synge and Anglo-Irish Drama*. Methuen 1961 o.p. Explores conflicts between
dream and reality as the basis of Synge's drama.

Thornton, Weldon. *J. M. Synge and the Western Mind*. Smythe 1979 o.p. Assesses Synge's
place in the Western religious tradition.

THOMAS, DYLAN. 1914–1953

The most important Welsh poet of the twentieth century, Thomas was born in
Swansea, about which he remembered unkindly "the smug darkness of a
provincial town." He attended Swansea Grammar School but received his real
education in the extensive library of his father, a disappointed schoolteacher
with higher ambitions. Refusing university study in favor of immediately
becoming a professional writer, Thomas worked first in Swansea and then in
London at a variety of literary jobs, which included journalism and, eventually,
filmscripts and radio plays. In 1936 he began the satisfying but stormy marriage
to the bohemian writer and dancer Caitlin MacNamara that would endure for
the rest of his career. His life fell into a pattern of oscillation between work and
dissipation in London and recovery and relaxation in a rural retreat, usually in
Wales. Thomas worked in a documentary film unit during the war. Besides his
poetry, he wrote plays and fiction. In the early 1950s, he gave three celebrated
poetry-reading tours of the United States, during which his outrageous behavior
vied with his superb reading ability for public attention. Aggravated by chronic
alcoholism, his health collapsed during the last tour, and he died in a New York
City hospital.

In his poetry, Thomas embraced an exuberant romanticism in the encounter
between self and world and a joyous riot in the lushness of language. His work
falls into three periods—an early "womb-tomb" phase during which he
produced a notebook, which he later mined for further poems, a middle one
troubled by marriage and war, and a final acceptance of the human condition.
The exuberant rhetoric of his work belies an equally strong devotion to artistry,
what he once called "my craft or sullen art." His great "Fern Hill," for example,
builds its imagery of the rejoicing innocence of childhood on a strict and
demanding syllabic count. A recollection of boyhood holidays on the farm of his
aunt and uncle, that poem places its emotion within an Edenic framework
typical of Thomas's work. The impressive sonnet sequence "Altarwise by Owl-
Light" (1936) combines the internal quest of romanticism with a more
elaborate religious outlook in tracing the birth and spiritual autobiography of a
poet. Almost at the end of his career he produced the moving elegy "Do Not Go
Gentle into That Good Night" (1952), written during the final illness of his

father. Despite his periods of doubt and dissipation, Thomas celebrated the fullness of life. As he wrote in a note to his *Collected Poems* (1952), "These poems, with all their crudities, doubts, and confusion, are written for the love of Man and in praise of God, and I'd be a damn fool if they weren't."

POETRY BY DYLAN THOMAS

Collected Poems, 1934–1953. 1952. New Dir. Pr. 1971 $8.95. ISBN 0-8112-0205-4
Poems of Dylan Thomas. Ed. by David Jones. New Dir. Pr. 1971 $15.95. ISBN 0-8112-0398-0

SHORT STORY COLLECTIONS BY DYLAN THOMAS

Adventures in the Skin Trade and Other Stories. New Dir. Pr. 1955 $8.95. ISBN 0-8112-0202-X
Collected Stories. New Dir. Pr. 1984 $16.95. ISBN 0-8112-0918-0. With an introduction by Leslie Norris.
Portrait of the Artist as a Young Dog. 1940. New Dir. Pr. 1956 $6.95. ISBN 0-8112-0207-0

PLAYS BY DYLAN THOMAS

The Doctor and the Devils and Other Scripts. New Dir. Pr. 1970 $12.95. ISBN 0-8112-0206-2
Under Milk Wood: A Play for Voices. 1954. New Dir. Pr. 1959 $5.95. ISBN 0-8112-0209-7. Deals with the lives of people in a small Welsh town.

WORKS BY DYLAN THOMAS

A Child's Christmas in Wales. 1954. Godine 1980 $14.95. ISBN 0-87923-339-7
Letters to Vernon Watkins. Ed. by Vernon Watkins. Greenwood 1982 repr. of 1957 ed. $39.75. ISBN 0-313-23746-8
The Notebooks, 1930–1934. Ed. by Ralph Maud. New Dir. Pr. o.p.
Selected Letters. New Dir. Pr. 1967 $10.00. ISBN 0-8112-0399-9. Commentary by Constantine FitzGibbon.

BOOKS ABOUT DYLAN THOMAS

Brinnin, John Malcolm. *Dylan Thomas in America.* Arlington 1988 o.p. Covers the last years of Thomas's life.
Davies, Walford. *Dylan Thomas.* St. Martin 1990 $24.95. ISBN 0-3120-4898-X. General survey.
Gaston, Georg. *Dylan Thomas: A Reference Guide.* Macmillan 1987 $40.00. ISBN 0-8161-8779-7. A useful bibliography and sourcebook on Thomas.
Kidder, Rushworth M. *Dylan Thomas: The Country of the Spirit.* Princeton U. Pr. 1973 o.p. Examines religious elements in Thomas's poetry.
Korg, Jacob. *Dylan Thomas.* Macmillan 1991 $22.95. ISBN 0-8057-7007-0. Overview of his life; with a selected bibliography.
Tremlett, George. *Dylan Thomas: In the Mercy of His Means.* St. Martin 1992 $21.95. ISBN 0-312-06957-X. Biography focusing on the influences on Thomas's work.

THOMAS, EDWARD. 1878–1917

Though Thomas was better known during his lifetime for his literary reviews and criticism, biographies, and nature writing, his reputation today is based on the slender canon of poems he wrote in the last two years of his life. During those last years he was encouraged in his poetry by ROBERT FROST, whom Thomas had met in 1913 while Frost was living in England.

Thomas was among the poets whose lives were tragically cut short by the Great War, yet for decades his reputation languished in the shadows of the group known for their explicit war poetry, such as ISAAC ROSENBERG, WILFRID OWEN, and SIEGFRIED SASSOON. Although Thomas's poetry is discernibly influenced by the upheaval of Europe, the influence is subtle: Poems such as "The Clouds That Are So Light," "The Dark Forest," and "Melancholy" offer delicate portrayals of the dark gloom that pervaded the age but need not manifestly be read through the lens of a world at war. Because they stand on their own as nature poetry, readers for decades missed their relationship to the more mainstream tradition of modernist poetry.

Thomas is recognized as a stylist of acute sensibilities, which were honed in his prose writings on the natural world. His poetry is concise, stripped of the conventional and overwrought timbre that marked much contemporary poetry about nature; yet it retains an appreciation of the intricacy that nature has always afforded the poet. A melancholy human aura pervades the poems, but they do not brood; the infiltration of troubling humanity into the natural realm is handled perhaps more deftly and sensitively than in any other poetry of this period. Thomas enlisted in the British army at age 37 and was killed in action at the battle of Arras on April 9, 1917.

POETRY BY EDWARD THOMAS

Collected Poems. Faber & Faber 1988 $7.95. ISBN 0-571-11368-0. The definitive collection of Thomas's poetic works.

NONFICTION BY EDWARD THOMAS

Edward Thomas on the Countryside: A Selection of His Prose and Verse. Faber & Faber 1977 o.p.
A Language Not to Be Betrayed: Selected Prose of Edward Thomas. Carcanet 1981 o.p. A collection of essays on various subjects.
The South Country. 1909. Hutchinson 1984 o.p. Includes accounts of journeys and essays on natural history.

BOOKS ABOUT EDWARD THOMAS

Coombes, H. *Edward Thomas: A Critical Study*. 1956. B & N Imports 1973 o.p. Surveys Thomas's poetry as well as his prose and criticism.
Kirkham, Michael. *The Imagination of Edward Thomas*. Cambridge U. Pr. 1986 $54.95. ISBN 0-52-132456-4. The definitive critical study, examining Thomas in terms of his imagination and experience.
Marsh, Jan. *Edward Thomas: A Poet for His Country*. B & N Imports 1978 $38.50. ISBN 0-06-494563-4. Biography.
Smith, Stan. *Edward Thomas*. Faber & Faber 1986 o.p. Overview of his life, with bibliography.
Thomas, R. George. *Edward Thomas: A Portrait*. OUP 1985 o.p. Critical biography.

TOLKIEN, J(OHN) R(ONALD) R(EUEL). 1892–1973

A writer of fantasies, Tolkien, a professor of language and literature at Oxford University, was always intrigued by early English and the imaginative use of language. In his greatest book, the trilogy *The Lord of the Rings* (1954–56), Tolkien invented a language with vocabulary, grammar, syntax, even poetry of its own. Though readers have created various possible allegorical interpretations, Tolkien has said: "It is not about anything but itself. (Certainly it has no allegorical intentions, general, particular or topical, moral, religious or political.)" In *The Adventures of Tom Bombadil* (1962), Tolkien tells the story of the "master of wood, water, and hill," a jolly teller of tales and singer of songs, one of the multitude of characters in his romance, saga, epic, or fairy tales about his country of the Hobbits.

Tolkien was also a formidable medieval scholar, as attested to by, among other works, *Beowulf: The Monster and the Critics* (1936) and his edition of *Anciene Wisse: English Text of the Anciene Riwle*.

NOVELS BY TOLKIEN

The Fellowship of the Ring. HM 1992 $30.00. ISBN 0-395-64738-X. The history of the Middle Earth.

The Hobbit. 1937. HM 1989 $16.45. ISBN 0-395-52021-5. Fantasy about a race of creatures known as Hobbits and their adventures.

Lord of the Rings. 1954-56. 3 vols. HM 1992 $90.00. ISBN 0-395-64741-X. Classic fantasy trilogy; includes *The Fellowship of the Ring*, *The Two Towers*, and *The Return of the King*. A story of hobbits, elves, dwarves, and humans and the struggle of good versus evil.

The Return of the King. 1956. HM 1992 $30.00. ISBN 0-395-64740-1

Silmarillion. 1977. Ballantine 1985 $5.95. ISBN 0-345-32581-8

Tree and Leaf. HM 1989 $12.70. ISBN 0-395-50232-2

The Two Towers. 1955. HM 1992 $30.00. ISBN 0-395-64739-8

SHORT STORY COLLECTIONS BY TOLKIEN

The Book of Lost Tales. Ballantine 1992 $5.99. ISBN 0-345-37522-X

Farmer Giles of Ham: A Short Story. HM 1991 repr. $13.45. ISBN 0-395-57645-8

Smith of Wooton Major and *Farmer Giles of Ham*. Ballantine 1986 $4.99. ISBN 0-345-33606-2

Unfinished Tales. Ed. by Christopher Tolkien. HM 1980 $8.70. ISBN 0-395-32441-6

POETRY BY TOLKIEN

Bilbo's Last Song. HM 1990 $14.45. ISBN 0-395-53810-6. Epic fantasy in poem form.

WORKS BY TOLKIEN

The Lost Road and Other Writings: Language and Legend Before the Lord of the Rings. Ed. by Christopher Tolkien. HM 1987 $19.45. ISBN 0-395-45519-7. Collection of earlier manuscripts which lends considerable insight into the evolution of Tolkien's fantastical world.

Tolkien. 4 vols. Ballantine 1986 $23.80. ISBN 0-345-34042-6

BOOKS ABOUT TOLKIEN

Carpenter, Humphrey. *Tolkien: A Biography*. HM 1988 $10.70. ISBN 0-395-48676-9

Day, David. *Tolkien: The Illustrated Encyclopaedia*. Macmillan 1991 $29.95. ISBN 0-02-533431-X. A sourcebook of Tolkien's fantasy worlds.

Isaacs, Neil David. *Tolkien: New Critical Perspectives*. U. Pr. of Ky. 1981 $20.00. ISBN 0-8131-1408-X. Essays on myth, history, and time; the rhetoric of childhood; Tolkien's concept of the hero; folklore and fairy tales.

Johnson, Judith Anne. *J. R. R. Tolkien: Six Decades of Criticism*. Greenwood 1986 $49.95. ISBN 0-3132-5005-7. A comprehensive sourcebook of critical essays on Tolkien and a bibliography of primary and secondary sources.

Purtill, Richard L. *J. R. R. Tolkien: Myth, Morality, and Religion*. HarpC 1984 o.p. Explores ethics and fantasy in Tolkien's work.

Rosebury, Brian. *Tolkien: A Critical Assessment*. Macmillan 1992 o.p. An interesting critical survey of Tolkien's work.

Rossi, Lee D. *The Politics of Fantasy: C. S. Lewis and J. R. R. Tolkien*. Bks. Demand 1984 $41.40. ISBN 0-8357-1597-3. Comparative study of the two writers' political and social views.

West, Richard C. *Tolkien Criticism: An Annotated Checklist*. Bks. Demand repr. of 1981 ed. $52.20. ISBN 0-7837-0572-7. A bibliography of critical writings about Tolkien.

TOMLINSON, CHARLES. 1927–

Distinguished both as poet and painter, Tomlinson was born in Stoke-on-Trent and received his B.A. from Queen's College, Cambridge, in 1948. After a few years of elementary school teaching and a period as private secretary in northern Italy, he returned to study at London University, from which he received an M.A. in 1955. He has taught in the English department at the University of Bristol and visited the United States to teach at the University of New Mexico and at Colgate University.

One of the British poets most open to transatlantic influences, Tomlinson has profited from an array of modern American poets, including MARIANNE MOORE, WALLACE STEVENS, WILLIAM CARLOS WILLIAMS, EZRA POUND, and the objectivist group. Having begun as a painter, he often emphasizes visual elements in his verse. "My theme is relationship," he has said, "a phenomenological poetry, with roots in WORDSWORTH and in RUSKIN, is what I take myself to be writing." Many of Tomlinson's best poems, such as "At Barstow" and "Two Views of Two Ghost Towns," concern the American West. He has also done critical essays and some fine translations of Spanish writers, including the poetry of ANTONIO MACHADO Y RUIZ (see Vol. 2).

POETRY BY TOMLINSON

American Scenes and Other Poems. OUP 1966 o.p.
The Flood. OUP 1981 $11.95. ISBN 0-19-211944-3
The Matachines. San Marcos Pr. 1968 o.p.
Seeing Is Believing. Astor-Honor 1958 $10.95. ISBN 0-8392-1097-3
The Shaft. OUP 1978 o.p.

NONFICTION BY TOMLINSON

Poetry and Metamorphosis. Cambridge U. Pr. 1983 $24.95. ISBN 0-521-24848-5
Some Americans: A Personal Record. U. CA Pr. 1981 $27.50. ISBN 0-520-04037-6
Translations. Contemporary Poetry Ser. OUP 1983 o.p.

WATKINS, VERNON (PHILLIPS). 1906–1967

One of the leading Welsh poets of the twentieth century, Vernon Watkins came from the town of Maesteg, in South Wales. After a series of preparatory schools, he enrolled in Magdalene College, Cambridge, and then withdrew because he felt the intellectual atmosphere threatened his poetry. He returned to Wales, where his father—a branch manager at Lloyd's Bank—got him a job as cashier. During a mental collapse, he experienced a religious vision that provided the ground of much of his later verse. Refusing promotion because it would distract him from poetry, Watkins continued as cashier until retirement from the bank. During World War II, he served first in the home guard and then as a police officer in the Royal Air Force. In the 1960s, he taught poetry both at the University of Washington and at Swansea University, in his native Wales.

Watkins did not publish his first book until his thirty-fifth year. His verse avoids topical subjects (except for tributes to W. B. YEATS and DYLAN THOMAS) in favor of religious or mystical ones, often set in the Welsh countryside. Watkins's particular vision fuses Christian and neo-Platonic traditions in a way that has led critics like Kathleen Raine to value him highly. Influenced early by WILLIAM BLAKE and later by Yeats, he belongs in the ranks of romantic moderns. The most important contemporary poet to Watkins was his great friend Dylan Thomas, whom he met in 1935 and who persuaded Watkins to let his work be published. Watkins also did verse translations, especially of HEINRICH HEINE (see Vol. 2).

POETRY BY WATKINS

Fidelities. 1967. New Dir. Pr. 1969 $5.00. ISBN 0-8112-0404-9
Selected Poems. New Dir. Pr. 1967 $2.25. ISBN 0-8112-0214-3. The definitive edition of Watkins's poetry.
Selected Verse Translations. Small Pr. Dist. 1977 o.p. Introduction by Michael Hamburger.
Unity of the Stream. Lit. Ser. Black Swan 1983 $17.50. ISBN 0-933806-05-1

NONFICTION BY WATKINS

Dylan Thomas: Letters to Vernon Watkins. Ed. by Vernon Watkins. Greenwood 1982 repr. of 1957 ed. $39.75. ISBN 0-313-23746-8

BOOKS ABOUT WATKINS

Mathias, Roland. *Vernon Watkins*. U. of Wales Pr. 1974 o.p. Overview of Watkins's life and work.
Norris, Leslie. *Vernon Watkins*. Faber & Faber 1970 o.p. Biographical reminiscences and tributes from writers including Philip Larkin and Marianne Moore.
Polk, Dora. *Vernon Watkins and the Spring of Vision*. Davies 1977 o.p. Discusses Celtic folk customs and legends and Watkins's use of the past as sources for his poetry.

WAUGH, EVELYN (ARTHUR ST. JOHN). 1903–1966

Evelyn Waugh came from a literary family. His elder brother, Alec, was a novelist and traveler. Their father, Arthur Waugh, was the influential head of the London publishing house Chapman and Hall. Waugh's deeply religious temperament (he later became an ardent Roman Catholic) and literary abilities were occasionally evident during his school days. He joined the Royal Marines at the beginning of World War II and was among the first to volunteer for commando service. In 1944 he survived a plane crash in Yugoslavia and, while hiding in a cave, corrected the proofs of *Brideshead Revisited* (1945). Through conservative eyes looking coldly on the mad scramble of the upper class in the 1930s and the struggle between the young and old generations, Waugh saw his disenchanted world clearly and expressed his cynicism with savage fantasy and satire. His early novels, *Decline and Fall* (1929), *Vile Bodies* (1930), and *A Handful of Dust* (1934), are brilliantly funny; *Decline and Fall* took the British public by storm and made his youthful reputation. In the later, "serious" novels, he became petulant at the disintegration of the staid, stable, indeed snobbish values of the England he imagined to be his; especially interesting in this regard are his novel *Scoop* (1938) and *Waugh in Abyssinia*, journalistic writings of 1936. Evelyn Waugh's novels of the 1920s and 1930s, together with *The Loved One* (1948; an ironic tale of the extravagant and sentimental Forest Lawn Cemetery in California), attack real follies, which can be seen as such from any political or social vantage point. The satire is sharp, unencumbered, and to the point; the stories are furiously witty and inventive. On these he may be judged the outstanding satirist of his day. His greatest works, however, are *Brideshead Revisited*, a nostalgic evocation of halcyon student days at Oxford, and the masterful trilogy of World War II, *Sword of Honor (Men at Arms*, 1952; *Officers and Gentlemen*, 1955; *The End of the Battle*, 1961).

He also wrote impressive biographies of DANTE GABRIEL ROSSETTI and Edmund Campion, the sixteenth-century Roman Catholic martyr. *A Little Learning* (1964), intended as the first volume of several volumes of an autobiography, is "an amusing and thoughtful chronicle of the early years of a man who [had] such a profound influence on the literature and thought of his own day. The prose, as is usual with Mr. Waugh, is elegant and at all times lucid" (*Library Journal*). Waugh died suddenly in Combe Florey in Somerset before completing other volumes in this autobiography. His son, Auberon Waugh, is a journalist.

NOVELS BY WAUGH

Black Mischief. Little 1977 $9.95. ISBN 0-316-92609-4
Brideshead Revisited. 1945. Little 1982 $9.95. ISBN 0-316-92634-5
Decline and Fall. 1929. Little 1977 $15.45. ISBN 0-316-92607-8. Satire on the corruption of the aristocracy.
The End of the Battle. 1961. Little 1979 $7.95. ISBN 0-316-92620-5. Last novel of *Sword of Honor* trilogy.
A Handful of Dust. 1934. Little 1977 $7.95. ISBN 0-316-92605-1
The Loved One. 1948. Little 1977 $8.95. ISBN 0-316-4608-6
Men at Arms. 1952. Little 1979 $8.95. ISBN 0-316-92628-0. Story of a bumbler's military career.
Officers and Gentlemen. 1955. Little 1979 $9.95. ISBN 0-316-92630-2. Second novel of *Sword of Honor* trilogy.
The Ordeal of Gilbert Pinfold. 1957. Little 1979 $8.95. ISBN 0-316-42622-1. Autobiographical story of a writer's breakdown.
Put Out More Flags. Little 1977 $8.95. ISBN 0-316-92612-4
Scoop. 1938. Little 1977 $8.95. ISBN 0-316-92617-5
Vile Bodies. 1930. Little 1977 $8.95. ISBN 0-316-92616-7

SHORT STORY COLLECTIONS BY WAUGH

Charles Ryder's School Days and Other Stories. Little 1982 $7.95. ISBN 0-316-92638-8
Tactical Exercise. Short Story Index Repr. Ser. Ayer repr. of 1954 ed. $18.00. ISBN 0-8369-3997-2. A collection of shorter satiric works, including "Work Suspended" and "Love among the Ruins."

NONFICTION BY WAUGH

The Essays, Articles and Reviews of Evelyn Waugh. Ed. by Donat Gallagher. Little 1984 $40.00. ISBN 0-316-92643-4. Wide-ranging collection touching upon a variety of subjects.
Tourist in Africa. Greenwood 1977 repr. of 1960 ed. $35.00. ISBN 0-8371-9358-3. Travel writings about his experiences in Africa.
When the Going Was Good. Greenwood 1976 repr. of 1946 ed. $35.00. ISBN 0-8371-8253-0

BOOKS ABOUT WAUGH

Blayac, A. *Evelyn Waugh: New Directions*. St. Martin 1991 $49.50. ISBN 0-312-06873-5. Discusses Waugh's humor, his career at the BBC, and the comic structure of his novels.
Davis, Robert Murray. *A Bibliography of Evelyn Waugh*. Whitston Pub. 1986 $35.00. ISBN 0-8787-5313-3. An annotated listing of secondary source materials about Waugh and his work.
Garnett, Robert Reginald. *From Grimes to Brideshead: The Early Novels of Evelyn Waugh*. Bucknell U. Pr. 1990 $29.50. ISBN 0-8387-5170-9. Discusses Waugh's development as a novelist in many of his best-known works.
Lane, Calvin Warren. *Evelyn Waugh*. Macmillan 1981 $19.95. ISBN 0-8057-6793-2. Overview, focusing on Waugh's satire, his Roman Catholic novels, his World War II trilogy, and his criticism.

McCartney, George. *Confused Roaring: Evelyn Waugh and the Modernist Tradition*. Ind. U. Pr. 1987 $25.00. ISBN 0-253-31411-9. Examines Waugh's relationship to his contemporaries.

McDonnell, Jacqueline. *Waugh on Women*. Duckworth 1985 o.p. Studies the roles of women in Waugh's fiction and life.

Morriss, Margaret, and D. J. Dooley. *Evelyn Waugh: A Reference Guide*. G. K. Hall 1984 o.p. A useful sourcebook for the scholar and general reader.

Myers, William. *Evelyn Waugh and the Problem of Evil*. Faber & Faber 1991 $24.95. ISBN 0-57-114094-7. Discusses morality in Waugh's fiction.

Stannard, Martin. *Evelyn Waugh*. Norton 1989 $10.95. ISBN 0-393-30605-4. An interesting, well-written biography.

_____. *Evelyn Waugh: The Critical Heritage*. Routledge 1984 $37.00. ISBN 0-7100-9548-1. General essays and reviews.

WELLS, H(ERBERT) G(EORGE). 1866–1946

Wells wrote (in a very readable, sometimes journalistic style) scientific and fantastic romances, short stories, realistic novels, sociology, history, science, and biography—after 1895, averaging a book or more a year. His sociological works usually take the form of utopias or of prophecies. His *Science of Life* (1931), written with SIR JULIAN HUXLEY (see Vol. 5), is an outline of biology as comprehensive as his *Outline of History* (1920). "He insisted on the importance of science during a long epoch when men of letters were heinously ignorant of it. His sense of the continuity and logical development of human destiny is very valuable, and enabled him to make shrewd guesses at future happenings which sometimes have been impressively right" (Richard Aldington). Wells and Jules Verne wrote the first popular science fiction—and both are still widely read in this vein.

It is the opinion of more than one critic that Wells never wrote anything better than his early science fiction novels and such sociological fiction as *Love and Mr. Lewisham* (1900) and *Kipps* (1905). *Mr. Britling Sees It Through* (1916) was one of the best novels written during World War I. Later novels, many of them devoted to causes he favored, might be less successful as fiction, but they were genuine attempts to reform the novel and will still be interesting to the student of British social history. His frank and brilliant *Experiment in Autobiography* (1934) describes his rise from humble beginnings to world fame and throws interesting light on the literary, social, and political life of his period.

NOVELS BY WELLS

The First Men in the Moon. 1901. Airmont 1965 $1.25. ISBN 0-8049-0078-7

The Food of the Gods. 1904. Airmont 1965 $.95. ISBN 0-8049-0059-0

The History of Mister Polly. 1910. Ed. by Gordon N. Ray. HM 1961 $7.96. ISBN 0-395-05149-5. An average man breaking out of his pedestrian life.

In the Days of the Comet. 1906. Airmont $1.25. ISBN 0-8049-0111-2. With an introduction by Brian Aldiss.

The Invisible Man. 1897. Bantam 1983 $2.15. ISBN 0-553-21155-2

The Island of Dr. Moreau. 1896. Buccaneer Bks. 1983 repr. $16.95. ISBN 0-89966-470-9

The King Who Was a King. Rprt. Serv. 1992 repr. of 1929 ed. $79.00. ISBN 0-7812-7560-1

Little Wars. Da Capo 1977 $4.95. ISBN 0-306-80075-6. A witty parody of militarism.

Mr. Britling Sees It Through. 1979. Buccaneer Bks. 1983 $16.95. ISBN 0-89966-471-7. England during the early years of World War I.

Three Prophetic Novels. Ed. by E. F. Bleiler. Dover $6.95. ISBN 0-4862-0605-X. Contains *When the Sleeper Wakes, A Story of the Days to Come*, and *The Time Machine*.

The Time Machine. 1895. NAL-Dutton 1984 $4.95. ISBN 0-451-52238-9. Futuristic tale of human hedonism and devolution.

Tono-Bungay. 1908. Buccaneer Bks. 1990 $19.95. ISBN 0-89966-691-4. Farcical tale of commerce and imperialism.

The War of the Worlds. 1898. Bantam 1988 $2.25. ISBN 0-553-21338-5. A science fiction tale of a Martian invasion of Earth.

The Wheels of Chance and *The Time Machine.* 1896. Biblio Dist. 1969 repr. of 1935 ed. o.p.

SHORT STORY COLLECTIONS BY WELLS

Best Science Fiction Stories. 1965. Dover $6.95. ISBN 0-486-21531-8

The Country of the Blind, and Other Stories. 1911. *Short Story Index Repr. Ser.* Ayer repr. of 1913 ed. $25.00. ISBN 0-8369-3789-9

Selected Short Stories. Viking Penguin 1990 $4.95. ISBN 0-14-018188-1

Seven Science Fiction Novels. Amereon Ltd. $42.95. ISBN 0-891-90452-2. Contains *The First Men in the Moon, The Food of the Gods, In the Days of the Comet, The Invisible Man, The Island of Dr. Moreau, The Time Machine,* and *The War of the Worlds.*

Thirty Strange Stories. 1897. *Short Story Index Repr. Ser.* Ayer repr. of 1897 ed. $27.50. ISBN 0-8369-3274-9

Twenty-eight Science Fiction Stories. 1905. Dover o.p.

NONFICTION BY WELLS

The Fate of Man. Essay Index Repr. Ser. Ayer repr. of 1939 ed. $19.00. ISBN 0-8369-1487-2

A Modern Utopia. 1905. U. of Nebr. Pr. 1967 $12.95. ISBN 0-8032-5213-7. Introduction by M. R. Hillegas.

BOOKS ABOUT WELLS

Ash, Brian. *Who's Who in H. G. Wells.* Hamilton 1979 o.p. Guide to the characters in Wells's novels.

Bergonzi, Bernard. *The Early H. G. Wells: A Study of the Scientific Romances.* U. of Toronto Pr. 1961 o.p. Discusses Wells as myth maker.

Costa, Richard Hauer. *H. G. Wells.* Macmillan 1985 $18.95. ISBN 0-8057-6887-4. Overview and bibliography; focuses on Wells's scientific romances, comic novels, and feminism.

Hammond, John R. *Herbert George Wells: An Annotated Bibliography of His Works.* Garland 1977 o.p. Comprehensive sourcebook of interest to general readers as well as scholars.

————, ed. *H. G. Wells: Interviews and Recollections.* Macmillan 1980 o.p. Memoirs and interviews that provide great insight into Wells and his work.

Haynes, Roslynn D. *H. G. Wells: Discoverer of the Future.* Macmillan 1980 o.p. Examines influence of science on Wells's writing.

McConnell, Frank. *The Science Fiction of H. G. Wells.* OUP 1981 $6.95. ISBN 0-19-502812-0. Focuses on Wells's science-fiction style.

Parrinder, Patrick, and Christopher Rolfe, eds. *H. G. Wells under Revision: Proceedings of the International H. G. Wells Symposium, London, July 1986.* Susquehanna U. Pr. 1990 $35.00. ISBN 0-945636-05-9. Discusses humor as sociology, Dickensian motifs, feminist reading of Wells's social romances, and Wells and positivism.

Reed, John R. *The Natural History of H. G. Wells.* Ohio U. Pr. 1982 $25.95. ISBN 0-8214-0628-0. Examines Wells's sense of human life as the assertion of will against chaos.

Scheick, William J., and J. Randolph Cox. *H. G. Wells: A Reference Guide.* Macmillan 1988 $50.00. ISBN 0-8161-8946-3. A handy reference sourcebook on Wells.

WESKER, ARNOLD. 1932–

Arnold Wesker grew up in London's Stepney, and after time at the London School of Film Technique and in the Royal Air Force, worked at a number of jobs—carpenter's mate, farm laborer, pastry chef, among others—until *Chicken Soup with Barley* was performed on an Arts Council grant in 1958. Transferred from a theater in Coventry to the Royal Court, it was joined in repertory there by

Roots in 1959 and *I'm Talking about Jerusalem* in 1960. The realistic trilogy centered on the Kahn family and their connections, in London and Norfolk: old Communists, arts-and-crafts idealists, torpid farm workers, young radicals— nothing less than "the working class today." A different sort of play occupied Wesker just before and after the trilogy—the panoramic description of the ordinary activities of a large group of characters. *The Kitchen* (1962) followed the rhythms of calm and crisis in a large restaurant; *Chips with Everything* (1962) dealt with the life of conscripts in an air force training camp. Critic Kenneth Tynan and others welcomed Wesker's microcosms as revelations of the nature of authority and work, and the possibility of collective social action.

But *Chips*, produced in London and New York, was Wesker's last major success. After it, he withdrew temporarily from writing to direct Centre 42, an ambitious worker arts project, the failure of which is memorialized in *Their Very Own and Golden City* (1966), the chronicle of an idealistic city planner's destructive compromises. Wesker's alienation from the radical politics of the 1970s severed his connection with the British left and threatened his relation with the British theater. (Many of his later plays have had their debut abroad, in Sweden and in the United States.) Since *The Four Seasons* (1965), about the growing apart of a couple, Wesker's focus has been personal. *The Merchant* (1976) retells the story of Shylock; *Caritas* (1981) ends with the martyrdom of a nun; *The Old Ones* (1972) are brothers confronting the coming of death.

The change in Wesker's drama has encouraged readers to return to the early plays and recognize that they are less about collective action than its human difficulties. "I would like to think," the playwright explains, "that my plays . . . have a higher proportion of poetry than journalism."

Plays by Wesker

The Merchant. Heinemann Ed. 1983 $5.95. ISBN 0-413-51620-2
The Plays of Arnold Wesker. 2 vols. HarpC 1976–77 o.p. Vol. 1: *The Kitchen, Chips with Everything, The Wesker Trilogy.* Vol. 2: *The Four Seasons, Their Very Own and Golden City, Menace* (television play), *The Friends, The Old Ones.*

Books about Wesker

Leeming, Glenda. *Wesker on File.* Heinemann Ed. 1988 $7.95. ISBN 0-413-58630-8. Surveys Wesker's productions and reviews.
————. *Wesker the Playwright.* Heinemann Ed. 1988 $11.95. ISBN 0-413-49240-3. Focuses on Wesker as strident moralist.
Wilcher, Robert. *Understanding Arnold Wesker.* U. of SC Pr. 1991 $29.95. ISBN 0-8724-9760-7. Examination of Wesker as rebel, his roots, and his solo and mass voices.

WEST, DAME REBECCA (pseud. of Cicily Isabel Fairfield). 1892–1983

Taking her name from one of Henrik Ibsen's (see Vol. 2) strong-minded women, Rebecca West was a politically and socially active feminist all her long life. She had an intense 10-year affair with H. G. Wells, with whom she had a son. A brilliant and versatile novelist, critic, essayist, and political commentator, West's greatest literary achievement is perhaps her travel diary, *Black Lamb and Grey Falcon: A Journey through Yugoslavia* (1942). Five years in the writing, it is the story of an Easter trip that she and her husband, British banker Henry Maxwell Andrews (whom she had married in 1930), made through Yugoslavia in 1937. A historical narrative with excellent reporting, it is essentially an analysis of Western culture. During World War II, she superintended British broadcast talks to Yugoslavia. Her remarkable reports of the treason trials of Lord Haw and John Amery appeared first in the *New Yorker* and are included with other stories about traitors in *The Meaning of Treason* (1947), which was expanded to deal with traitors and defectors since World War II as *The New Meaning of Treason* (1964). *The Birds Fall Down* (1966), which was a bestseller, is the story of a young Englishwoman caught in the grip of Russian terrorists. From a true story told to her more than half a century ago by the sister of FORD MADOX FORD (who had heard it from her Russian husband), West "created a rich and instructive spy thriller, which contains an immense amount of brilliantly distributed information about the ideologies of the time, the rituals of the Russian Orthodox Church, the conflicts of customs, belief, and temperament between Russians and Western Europeans, the techniques of espionage and counter-espionage, and the life of exiles in Paris" (*New Yorker*).

Unlike that of her more famous contemporaries, her fiction is stylistically and structurally conventional, but it effectively details the evolution of daily life amid the backdrop of such historical disasters as the world wars. Her critical works include *Arnold Bennett Himself, Henry James* (1916), *Strange Necessity: Essays and Reviews*, and *The Court and the Castle* (1957), a study of political and religious ideas in imaginative literature. In 1949, she was made a Dame Commander of the Order of the British Empire.

NOVELS BY WEST

Harriet Hume. Trafalgar 1992 $10.95. ISBN 0-86068-145-9. An early feminist novel.

The Judge. Trafalgar 1992 $11.95. ISBN 0-86068-136-X

The Return of the Soldier. Carroll & Graf 1990 $8.95. ISBN 0-88184-658-9. Story about an amnesiac soldier and his homecoming after the Second World War.

The Thinking Reed. AMS Pr. repr. of 1936 ed. $28.00. ISBN 0-404-14630-9

This Real Night. Viking 1986 $6.95. ISBN 0-14-008684-6. First of six announced posthumous works.

WORKS BY WEST

Rebecca West: A Celebration, a Selection of Her Writings Chosen by Her Publishers and Rebecca West. Viking Penguin 1977 o.p. With an introduction by Samuel Hynes.

The Young Rebecca: Writings of Rebecca West, 1911–1917. Ed. by Jane Marcus. Ind. U. Pr. 1989 $12.95. ISBN 0-253-23101-9

BOOKS ABOUT WEST

Deakin, Motley F. *Rebecca West.* Twayne 1980 o.p. Overview and bibliography, with attention to West's career as critic, reviewer, journalist, and historian.

Glendinning, Victoria. *Rebecca West: A Life.* Weidenfeld 1987 o.p. A highly readable biography.

Hammond, J. R. *H. G. Wells and Rebecca West.* St. Martin 1991 $39.95. ISBN 0-312-07163-9. Biographical examination of the relationship and collaboration between the two writers.

Orel, Harold. *The Literary Achievement of Rebecca West.* Macmillan 1986 $25.00. ISBN 0-333-23672-6. Biography, study of West's criticism, and survey of her fiction.

Packer, Jean Garrett. *Rebecca West: An Annotated Bibliography.* Garland 1991 $20.00. ISBN 0-8240-5692-2. A useful and comprehensive sourcebook.

WILSON, ANGUS (ANGUS FRANK JOHNSTONE-WILSON). 1913–1991

Angus Wilson was born in Sussex, the youngest of six sons, and spent several of his childhood years in South Africa. A series of odd jobs was followed by a position in the Department of Printed Books in the British Museum, where he worked on replacing as many as possible of the 300,000 books destroyed during the bombing, and later as deputy superintendent of the reading room. Writing short stories on weekends, he was immediately successful. In 1955 he left the museum to become a full-time writer.

James Gindin has, with some exaggeration, declared that "Angus Wilson is the best contemporary English novelist." *Anglo Saxon Attitudes* (1956) is a long, intricate, and witty novel that satirizes, none too gently, such sacred British institutions as the church, the universities, and Her Majesty's Government. *The Middle Age of Mrs. Eliot* (1958) won the James Tait Black Memorial Award for fiction in 1959. *The Old Men at the Zoo* (1961) is a story of conflict and conscience in a microcosm, the London Zoo in the 1970s. In *Late Call* (1965), a retired couple face problems of readjustment when they go to live with their widowed son. *No Laughing Matter* (1967) traces the fortunes of a British family throughout half a century beginning in 1912.

In addition to short stories and novels, Wilson wrote *Emile Zola: An Introductory Study of His Novels* (1952), *Tempo: The Impact of Television on the Arts* (1966), *The Strange Ride of Rudyard Kipling* (1977), and *The World of Charles Dickens* (1970).

NOVELS BY ANGUS WILSON

As If by Magic. 1973. Viking Penguin 1978 o.p.
Late Call. 1965. Academy Chi. Pubs. 1983 o.p.
No Laughing Matter. 1967. Academy Chi. Pubs. 1983 o.p.
The Old Men at the Zoo. 1961. Academy Chi. Pubs. 1983 o.p.
Setting the World on Fire. Viking Pengin 1980 o.p.
The Wrong Set. Academy Chi. Pubs. o.p. A sharp critique of the social scene.

NONFICTION BY ANGUS WILSON

For Whom the Cloche Tolls: A Scrapbook of the Twenties. 1953. Academy Chi. Pubs. 1983 o.p.

WORK BY ANGUS WILSON

An Anthology: Green River Review, 1968–1973. Green River 1975 $10.00. ISBN 0-940580-01-2. A collection of writings published in the late 1960s and early 1970s.

BOOKS ABOUT ANGUS WILSON

Faulkner, Peter. *Angus Wilson: Mimic and Moralist*. Viking Penguin 1980 o.p. Biographically based critical survey.
Gardner, Averil. *Angus Wilson*. Twayne 1985 o.p. Overview of of his life; bibliography.
Hailo, Jay L. *Critical Essays on Angus Wilson*. G. K. Hall 1985 o.p. Reviews, interviews, and essays, on Wilson's comic mode, his traditionalism, and his critical biographies.
Stape, J. H. *Angus Wilson: A Bibliography*. Mansell 1988 $76.00. ISBN 0-720-11872-7. Comprehensive bibliographic sourcebook on Wilson and his work.

WILSON, COLIN. 1931–

Colin Wilson made his reputation in Britain and the United States on the publication of his first book, *The Outsider* (1956). Sometimes known as the *enfant terrible* of English letters, whose soberer practitioners still do not take him entirely seriously, he has been prolific in many literary fields without ever quite reaching first rank as a novelist. He has written a number of competent thrillers. The Jack the Ripper story was the basis of his first novel, *Ritual in the Dark* (1960). *The Sex Diary of Gerald Sorme*, which is not as sensational as its title, grew out of the author's research for *The Origins of the Sexual Impulse*. *The Violent World of Hugh Greene* is a "good, solid, rather old-fashioned novel of a young man making his way" (*Harper*). In *Necessary Doubt* a German philosopher is plagued by suspicions that a former student is a killer. In *The Glass Cage* (1966), a mystery in which the murderer leaves quotations from WILLIAM BLAKE near his victims is solved by a Blake expert. Wilson has narrative skill, and James Gindin writes that his "heroes are innocents, seeking to understand all the violence and irrationality they find around them. . . . Yet, for all their naiveté, his heroes do reflect something about contemporary Britain; the interest in violence and perversion; . . . the search for order and stability; the feeling that organized society is shallow and hypocritical."

Son of a Leicester factory worker, Colin Wilson left school at 16. After a six-month period in the Royal Air Force, he held a succession of factory, office, hospital, and dishwashing jobs in both London and Paris, worked on the *Paris Review*, and began to write plays, short stories, essays, and poetry. Wilson spent several years in the 1960s as a writer in residence at Hollins College, Virginia.

NOVELS BY COLIN WILSON

The Mind Parasites. 1967. Wingbow Pr. 1975 $7.95. ISBN 0-914728-27-X
The Outsider. 1956. Buccaneer Bks. 1990 $22.95. ISBN 0-89966-670-1. About alienation in the twentieth century.
Ritual in the Dark. 1960. Ronin Pub. 1993 $12.95. ISBN 0-914171-63-1
Schoolgirl Murder Case. Academy Chi. Pubs. 1982 o.p.

NONFICTION BY COLIN WILSON

Mysteries. Putnam Pub. Grp. 1980 o.p.
The Occult: A History. 1971. Random 1973 o.p.

WOOLF, VIRGINIA. 1882–1941

Virginia Woolf was born in London, the daughter of the prominent literary critic Leslie Stephen. She never received a formal university education; her early education was obtained at home through her parents and governesses. After death of her father in 1904, her family moved to Bloomsbury, where they formed the nucleus of the Bloomsbury Group, a circle of philosophers, writers and artists.

As a writer, Woolf was a great experimenter. She scorned the traditional narrative form and turned to expressionism as a means of telling her story. *Mrs. Dalloway* (1925) and *To The Lighthouse* (1927), her two generally acknowledged masterpieces, are stream-of-consciousness novels in which most of the action and conflict occur beneath a surface of social decorum. *Mrs. Dalloway*, set in London shortly after the end of World War I, takes place on a summer's day of no particular significance, except that intense emotion, insanity, and death intrude. *To the Lighthouse*'s long first and third sections, each of which concerns one day 10 years apart, of the same family's summer holidays, are separated and connected by a lyrical short section during which the war occurs, several members of the family die, and decay and corruption run rampant. *Orlando* (1928) is the chronological life story of a person who begins as an Elizabethan gentleman and ends as a lady of the twentieth century; Woolf's friend, VICTORIA SACKVILLE-WEST, served as the principal model for the multiple personalities. (The book was made into a movie in 1993.) *Flush* (1933) is a dog's soliloquy that, by indirection, recounts the love story of ROBERT BROWNING and ELIZABETH BARRETT BROWNING and their elopement and life in Florence. Her last short novel, *Between the Acts* (1941), was left without her final revision, but it is, nonetheless, a major representation of a society on the verge of collapse.

Having had periods of depression throughout her life and fearing a final mental breakdown from which she might not recover, Woolf drowned herself in 1941. Her husband published part of her farewell letter to deny that she had taken her life because she could not face the terrible times of war. Leonard Woolf also edited *A Writer's Diary* (1953), which provides valuable insights into his wife's private thoughts and literary development. Equally informative are his own autobiographies, particularly *Beginning Again* and *Downhill All the Way* (1967), and *The Letters of Virginia Woolf and Lytton Strachey*. Virginia Woolf's *Granite and Rainbow* contains 27 essays on the art of fiction and biography. There are many sidelights on Woolf in the writings, letters, and biographies of other members of her Bloomsbury circle, such as Roger Fry, JOHN MAYNARD KEYNES (see Vol. 3), and LYTTON STRACHEY (see Vol. 3).

Also casting much light on her life, thought, and creative processes are *The Common Reader* (1925), *The Second Common Reader* (1933), *A Room of One's Own* (1929), *Three Guineas* (1938), *The Captain's Death Bed and Other Essays*, *The Death of the Moth and Other Essays* (1942), and various collections of her autobiographical writings, diaries, and letters. In addition, in recent years there has been a veritable industry of writers dealing with Woolf and her work.

NOVELS BY WOOLF

Between the Acts. 1941. HarBraceJ 1970 repr. of 1941 ed. $7.95. ISBN 0-15-611870-X. A country pageant.

Flush: A Biography. 1933. HarBraceJ 1976 $7.95. ISBN 0-15-631952-7. Story of Elizabeth Barrett Browning's dog.

Jacob's Room. 1923. HarBraceJ 1978 $7.95. ISBN 0-15-645742-3. Story about a young man's pointless war death.

Mrs. Dalloway. 1925. HarBraceJ 1990 $7.95. ISBN 0-15-662870-8. A day in the life of an aristocratic socialite.

Orlando: A Biography. 1928. HarBraceJ 1973 ISBN 0-15-670160-X

To the Lighthouse. 1927. HarBraceJ 1990 $15.95. ISBN 0-15-190737-4. Meditation on family, art, philosophy.

The Voyage Out. HarBraceJ 1968 repr. of 1926 ed. $8.95. ISBN 0-15-693625-9. A young woman's quest to discover the self.

The Waves. 1931. Peter Smith 1983 $19.00. ISBN 0-8446-6078-7. Experimental novel chronicling the lives of seven friends.

The Years. HarBraceJ 1969 repr. of 1937 ed. $11.95. ISBN 0-15-699701-0

SHORT STORY COLLECTION BY WOOLF

A Haunted House and Other Short Stories. 1944. HarBraceJ 1966 $5.95. ISBN 0-15-639401-4. Foreword by Leonard Woolf. Includes 12 stories hitherto unpublished in book form.

WORKS BY WOOLF

The Diary of Virginia Woolf. 5 vols. Ed. by Anne Oliver Bell. HarBraceJ 1979–85 $7.95–$10.95 ea. ISBNs 0-15-626036-0, 0-15-626037-9, 0-15-626038-7, 0-15-626039-5, 0-15-626040-9

The Letters of Virginia Woolf. 6 vols. Ed. by Nigel Nicolson. HarBraceJ 1977–82 $5.95–$12.95 ea. ISBNs 0-15-650881-8, 0-15-650882-6, 0-15-650883-4, 0-15-650884-2, 0-15-650886-9, 0-15-650887-7

BOOKS ABOUT WOOLF

Baldwin, Dean R. *Virginia Woolf: A Study of the Short Fiction*. Macmillan 1989 $20.95. ISBN 0-8057-8314-8. Surveys Woolf's short stories.

Batchelor, John. *Virginia Woolf: The Major Novels*. Cambridge U. Pr. 1991 $42.95. ISBN 0-521-32273-1. Examines *Jacob's Room, Mrs. Dalloway, To the Lighthouse, The Waves,* and *Between the Acts*.

Bell, Quentin. *Virginia Woolf: A Biography*. HarBraceJ 1974 repr. $14.95. ISBN 0-15-693580-5. Many previously unknown biographical details, revealed by Woolf's nephew.

Caramagno, Thomas C. *The Flight of the Mind: Virginia Woolf's Art and Manic-Depressive Illness*. U. CA Pr. 1992 $30.00. ISBN 0-520-07280-4. Examines Woolf's medical condition and its effect on her writing.

Caughie, Pamela L. *Virginia Woolf & Postmodernism: Literation in Quest and Question of Itself*. U. of Ill. Pr. 1991 $39.95. ISBN 0-252-01763-3. Feminist and postmodern theoretical approaches to Woolf.

Clements, Patricia, and Isobel Grundy, eds. *Virginia Woolf: New Critical Essays*. B & N Imports 1983 o.p. Discusses Woolf and the specter of domination, narrative voice in her early novels, and memory and the past.

Ferrer, Daniel. *Virginia Woolf and the Madness of Language*. Routledge 1990 $35.00. ISBN 0-415-03194-X. Psychoanalytic study of Woolf's literature and her mental health.

Ginsberg, Elaine K., ed. *Virginia Woolf: Centennial Papers*. Whitston Pub. 1984 $25.00. ISBN 0-878-75242-0. Discusses the intellectual origins of Bloomsbury, Woolf and the problem of the body, and androgyny.

Gordon, Lyndall. *Virginia Woolf: A Writer's Life*. Norton 1986 $8.95. ISBN 0-393-30342-X. A scholarly biography.

Hussey, Mark. *The Singing of the Real World: The Philosophy of Virginia Woolf's Fiction*. Ohio St. U. Pr. 1986 $36.75. ISBN 0-8142-0414-7. Explores the theme of identity and self as well as reality in Woolf's writing.

———. *Virginia Woolf and War: Fiction, Reality, and Myth*. Syracuse U. Pr. 1992 $14.95. ISBN 0-8156-2584-7. Discusses the impact of war on Woolf's writing.

Marcus, Jane. *Virginia Woolf and the Languages of Patriarchy*. Ind. U. Pr. 1987 $29.95. ISBN 0-253-36359-8. Investigates Woolf's confrontation with gender issues in her novels.

McNichol, Stella. *Virginia Woolf and the Poetry of Fiction*. Routledge 1988 $47.50. ISBN 0-415-00329-6. Discusses symbolic intrusions, poetic narratives, rhythmic order, and elegy in Woolf's fiction.

Rice, Thomas Jackson. *Virginia Woolf: A Guide to Research*. Garland 1984 o.p. Bibliography.

Rose, Phyllis. *Woman of Letters: A Life of Virginia Woolf*. HarBraceJ 1987 $8.95. ISBN 0-15-698190-4

Steele, Elizabeth. *Virginia Woolf's Rediscovered Essays: Sources and Allusions*. Garland 1987 o.p. Bibliography of primary sources.

Wheare, Jane. *Virginia Woolf: Dramatic Novelist*. St. Martin 1989 $35.00. ISBN 0-312-02449-5. Examines how some of Woolf's novels exploit the illusion of realist fiction.

YEATS, WILLIAM BUTLER. 1865–1939 (NOBEL PRIZE 1923)

In his 1940 memorial lecture in Dublin, T. S. ELIOT pronounced Yeats "one of those few whose history is the history of their own time, who are a part of the consciousness of an age which cannot be understood without them." Modern readers have increasingly agreed, and some now view Yeats even more than Eliot as the greatest modern poet in our language. Son of the painter John Butler Yeats, the poet divided his early years among Dublin, London, and the port of Sligo in western Ireland. Sligo furnished many of the familiar places in his poetry, among them the mountain Ben Bulben and the lake isle of Innisfree. Important influences on his early adulthood included his father, the writer and artist WILLIAM MORRIS, the nationalist leader John O'Leary, and the occultist Madame Blavatsky. In 1889 he met the beautiful actress and Irish nationalist

Maud Gonne; his long and frustrated love for her (she refused to marry him) would inspire some of his best work. Often and mistakenly viewed as merely a dreamy Celtic twilight, Yeats's work in the 1890s involved a complex attempt to unite his poetic, nationalist, and occult interests in line with his desire to "hammer [his] thoughts into unity."

By the turn of the century, Yeats was immersed in the work with the Irish dramatic movement that would culminate in the founding of the Abbey Theatre in 1904 as a national theater for Ireland. Partly as a result of his theatrical experience, his poetry after 1900 began a complex "movement downwards upon life" fully evident in the *Responsibilities* volume of 1914. After that he published the extraordinary series of great volumes, all written after age 50, that continued until the end of his career. Widely read in various literary and philosophic traditions, Yeats owed his greatest debt to romantic poetry and once described himself, along with his coworkers JOHN SYNGE and LADY ISABELLA AUGUSTA GREGORY, as a "last romantic." Yet he remained resolutely Irish as well and presented in his verse a persona bearing a subtle, idealized relationship to his everyday self. Political events such as the Easter Rising and the Irish civil war found their way into his poetry, as did personal ones such as marriage to the Englishwoman Georgiana "Georgie" Hyde-Lees in 1917, the birth of his children, and his sometime home in the Norman tower at Ballylee. So, too, did his increasing status as a public man, which included both the Nobel Prize in 1923 and a term as senator of the Irish Free State (1922–28).

Yeats's disparate activities led to a lifelong quest for what he called "unity of being," which he pursued by "antinomies," or opposites. These included action and contemplation, life and art, fair and foul, and other famous pairs from his poetry. The most original poet of his age, he was also in ways the most traditional, and certainly the most substantial. His varied literary output included not only poems and plays but an array of prose forms such as essays, philosophy, fiction, reviews, speeches, and editions of folk and literary material. He also frequently revised his own poems, which exist in various published texts helpfully charted in the *Variorum* edition (1957).

POETRY BY YEATS

Collected Poems. Macmillan 1956 o.p. Long the standard collection, with the misleading description on the title page as "Definitive Edition, With the Author's Final Revisions."

The Early Poetry. Ed. by George Bornstein. Cornell Univ. Pr. 1986 o.p.

The Poems of W. B. Yeats. Ed. by Richard J. Finneran. Macmillan 1983 $23.99. ISBN 0-02-632940-9. Contains more than 100 poems not in the *Collected Poems*, together with extensive textual and explanatory notes.

The Variorum Edition of the Poems of W. B. Yeats. Ed. by P. Allt. Macmillan 1987 $65.00. ISBN 0-02-632700-7. Helpful correlation of the various published revisions (often substantial) to Yeats's poems, together with his own notes and prefaces.

SHORT STORY COLLECTIONS BY YEATS

John Sherman and *Dhoya*. 1892. Ed. by Richard J. Finneran. Bks. Demand repr. of 1969 ed. $34.30. ISBN 0-685-16203-6. A novella and a short story.

The Secret Rose: Stories by W. B. Yeats—a Variorum Edition. Ed. by Phillip L. Marcus, Warwick Gould, and Michael J. Sidnell. Cornell Univ. Pr. 1981 o.p.

PLAYS BY YEATS

The Collected Plays of W. B. Yeats. Macmillan 1990 $40.00. ISBN 0-02-632941-7

The Variorum Edition of the Plays of W. B. Yeats. Ed. by Russell K. Alspach. Macmillan 1966 o.p. Helpful correlation of the various published revisions, together with Yeats's own notes and prefaces.

NONFICTION BY YEATS

Autobiographies. 1955. Macmillan 1965 o.p.

Essays and Introductions. Macmillan 1968 $14.95. ISBN 0-02-055610-1. Includes much of Yeats's important literary criticism.

Explorations. Macmillan 1989 $45.00. ISBN 0-02-632942-5. Various prose works, including important section on the Irish dramatic movement.

Memoirs: Autobiography—First Draft and Journal. Ed. by Denis Donoghue. Macmillan 1973 o.p.

The Senate Speeches. Ed. by Donald R. Pearce. Ind. U. Pr. 1960 o.p. A series of political writings.

Uncollected Prose. 2 vols. Ed. by John P. Frayne and Colton Johnson. Col. U. Pr. 1970–76 $100.00. ISBN 0-685-19645-3. Contains material not in the other collections.

WORKS BY YEATS

The Letters of W. B. Yeats. Ed. by Allan Wade. Hippocrene Bks. 1980 repr. of 1955 ed. o.p.

Letters to the New Island. Ed. by Horace Reynolds. HUP 1970 o.p.

BOOKS ABOUT YEATS

Billigheimer, Rachel V. *Wheels of Eternity: A Comparative Study of William Blake and William Butler Yeats.* St. Martin 1990 $39.95. ISBN 0-312-03563-2. Comparative study linking the two poets' uses of apocalypse and prophecy.

Clark, David R. *Yeats at Songs and Choruses.* U. of Mass. Pr. 1983 $30.00. ISBN 0-8702-3358-0. Examines the lyric aspects of Yeats's poetry.

Cullingford, Elizabeth. *Yeats, Ireland and Fascism.* NYU Pr. 1981 o.p. Politically based examination of Yeats's poetry.

Finneran, Richard J. *Critical Essays on W. B. Yeats.* G. K. Hall 1986 $40.00. ISBN 0-8161-8758-4. Looks at Yeats in terms of his Irish heritage.

Hassett, Joseph M. *Yeats and the Poetics of Hate.* Macmillan 1986 o.p. Explores intellectual hatred, spiritual hate, and hatred of God as presented in Yeats's work.

Keane, Patrick J. *Yeats's Interaction with Tradition.* U. of Mo. Pr. 1987 $35.00. ISBN 0-8262-0645-X. Discusses spiritual parables and ghostly paradigms as well as Yeats and the Gregorys.

Krimm, Bernard G. *W. B. Yeats and the Emergence of the Irish Free State, 1918–1939.* Whitston Pub. 1981 $20.00. ISBN 0-87875-200-5. Investigates Yeats's involvement in Irish politics.

Marcus, Philip L. *Yeats and the Beginning of the Irish Renaissance.* Syracuse U. Pr. 1987 repr. of 1970 ed. $14.95. ISBN 0-8156-2398-4. Studies the influence of Celtic culture and mythology on Yeats's work.

Oppel, Frances Nesbitt. *Mask and Tragedy: Yeats and Nietsche, 1902–1910.* U. of Va. Pr. 1987 $27.50. ISBN 0-8139-1104-4. Comparative, philosophically based study.

Orr, Leonard. *Yeats and Postmodernism.* Syracuse U. Pr. 1990 $24.95. ISBN 0-8156-2506-5. Examines Yeats's poetry in light of current critical theories.

Raine, Kathleen. *Yeats the Initiate: Essays on Certain Themes in the Work of W. B. Yeats.* B & N Imports 1990 $76.00. ISBN 0-389-20951-1. Discusses fairy and folk tales, Yeats's debt to Blake, and Yeats and tarot.

Ramazani, Jahan. *Yeats and the Poetry of Death: Elegy, Self-Elegy, and the Sublime.* Yale U. Pr. 1990 $25.00. ISBN 0-300-04804-1. Examines the pervasive motifs of morbidity and elegy in Yeats's poetry.

Wright, David G. *Yeats' Myth of Self: The Autobiographical Prose.* B & N Imports 1987 $45.50. ISBN 0-389-20760-8. Study of the way Yeats presented himself.

CHAPTER 12

British Literature: Popular Modes

Harry Eiss and Gary Hoppenstand

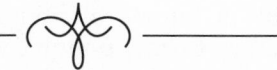

> We who hobnob with hobbits and tell tall tales about little green men are
> quite used to being dismissed as mere entertainers, or sternly disapproved of
> as escapists. But I think that perhaps the categories are changing, like the
> times. Sophisticated readers are accepting the fact that an improbable and
> unmanageable world is going to produce an improbable and hypothetical art.
> At this point, realism is perhaps the least adequate means of understanding or
> portraying the incredible realities of our existence. A scientist who creates a
> monster in his laboratory; a librarian in the library of Babel; a wizard unable
> to cast a spell; a space ship having trouble in getting to Alpha Centauri: all
> these may be precise and profound metaphors of the human condition.
> —URSULA LeGUIN, National Book Award Acceptance Speech

British popular literature and children's literature began as stories that were
told or sung to the masses, and were meant to entertain and be passed down to
future generations. The major early categories consisted of nursery rhymes,
fables, folk tales (sometimes used to include legends and fairy tales; sometimes
strongly separated from or placed under these two categories), ballads, myths,
romances, and epics. All of these categories overlap; and myths, romances, and
epics, depending on their presentation, are sometimes now considered to have
moved beyond popular literature and children's literature into the category of
serious or elitist literature. Further, the language used to categorize and to
discuss this body of literature is often employed differently by scholars, and
other terms are sometimes substituted. In addition, the categories generally
have subcategories. Folk tales, for example, can be divided into such categories
as droll tales, animal tales, cumulative tales, and cautionary tales.

As English society evolved into classes, and as publishing was driven by the
development of the printing press, an elite literature began to distinguish itself
from the popular literature. As time progressed, much of the early popular
literature was placed in the category of children's literature or women's
literature and was considered to be of less value and quality than "serious"
literature. By the time neoclassicism appeared in the 1700s, an embracing of
logic and form had limited serious literature to a strict set of rules, which did
not allow for the inclusion of popular literature.

The great watershed in Western civilization—set in motion by the views of
such theorists as JEAN JACQUES ROUSSEAU (see Vol. 3) and JOHN LOCKE (see Vols.
3 and 4), invigorated by the American Revolution, and taking Europe by storm
with the French Revolution—brought with it a new view of literature. Most
strongly expressed in the romantic movement, it stressed a rejection of the
overcultivated literature of the elite in favor of the more honest, popular
literature of the people. This dramatic shift allowed for the scholarly study of
folk tales as a more correct representation of the culture's heritage and ethos. At
the same time came an acceptance of the child's perspective, since, according

to the new thinking, humans are born with an awareness of truth, beauty, and goodness of nature (and, perhaps, God), and are led astray by a corrupt civilization. The child's perspective and, thus, children's literature suddenly have a theoretical basis. The door has been opened, and definitions and redefinitions of the canon have appeared up to the present day, as strong feminist, Marxist, and multicultural challenges to the traditional elitist categories of literature emerge.

Throughout the eighteenth century, boosted partially by an ever-increasing reading public (especially a female audience) and by the new openness to explore the edges of literary forms, popular and serious writers gave birth to new categories, including the mystery and detective story, fantasy and science fiction, contemporary and historical romance, Gothic and horror tales, and adventure and thriller stories.

Also, new views on myths, especially since the early to mid-twentieth century, have shifted these from the superstitious beliefs of a traditional, tribal people to possibly the highest form of literary expression. Furthermore, the Jungian theories of archetypes, followed by Joseph Campbell's application of them to mythology, have revealed similar psychological concerns in all literature. Indeed, folk tales and dramas by SHAKESPEARE deal with the same concerns of the human condition. While one may be more complex than the other, the themes of fate and free will, birth and death, love and hate, joy and sadness, desire and fulfillment lie at the center of each.

The subsections of children's literature and popular genres within this chapter offer more detailed discussions.

CHILDREN'S LITERATURE

British children's literature precedes American children's literature, but the former and the latter are interwoven, especially since the mid-eighteenth century. The two bodies of literature, in truth, constitute one large, important genre of literature. Each has influenced the other, and all of the major works have been published in both countries.

With this in mind, we can see that several aspects of British children's literature stand out. First, it has its origins in oral literature: folk tales, fables, legends, ballads, nursery rhymes, myths, romances, and epics. Second, its beginnings in written literature are filled with works originally created for adults but adopted by children (e.g., *Robinson Crusoe*, 1719; *Gulliver's Travels*, 1726; *Pilgrim's Progress*, 1678). This pattern continues to the present day (e.g., *The Lord of the Rings*, 1954–56). Interestingly, in addition, a reversal has recently taken place: Some of today's literature for adults is emerging from children's literature (e.g., *The Tin Pot Foreign General and The Old Iron Woman*, 1984, a picture book by Briggs). Third, fantasy has dominated, from the eighteenth century works of GEORGE MACDONALD, LEWIS CARROLL, CHARLES KINGSLEY, JOHN RUSKIN, RUDYARD KIPLING, and others, to the major works of J. R. R. TOLKIEN and C. S. LEWIS (see also Vol. 4) and their followers. Fourth, historical fiction, though not as consistently strong, has produced important writers (e.g., Rosemary Sutcliff, Hester Burton, C. Walter Hodges, and Barbara Willard). The best of these reflect accurate research and solid character development. Fifth, contemporary realistic fiction has only emerged since the early 1960s.

The development of British children's literature followed from the changing views of children. For hundreds of years, children were viewed as "little adults," with no unique psychological or perceptual views, whose sole purpose was to become adults as quickly as possible. Life was short, and survival was based more on physical than mental labor. Since childhood as a separate stage did not exist—or, if it did, it was viewed as a necessary nuisance to be gotten through as quickly as possible—there was no literature, either oral or written, for children. In fact, up until the 1450s, when Johann Gutenberg discovered a practical method for using movable metal type, only a few priests and nobles could obtain the laboriously handwritten parchment manuscripts that contained whatever written literature existed.

However, there was a strong oral tradition, filled with myths and folk tales. According to Robert Leeson in *Children's Books and Class Society* (1977), the oral tradition reached its climax in feudal Europe during the Middle Ages. These tales, sometimes called "castle tales" and "cottage tales," were not meant for children; rather, they comprised the great body of knowledge (tales of the origins of the universe or heroic deeds and ethical truths) that adults passed on to future generations, helping to create and preserve a cultural heritage. Castle tales, as their name suggests, were told by or to the nobility. These tales generally took the form of poetic epics about the great deeds of the lord of the manor (e.g., *Beowulf*). Cottage tales, on the other hand, which were narrated around the hearths of the peasants, offered rewards for kindness or cleverness or honesty or hard work (e.g., *Jack the Giant Killer*).

Although these tales were told by adults (often by traveling bards or minstrels) for the amusement of other adults, children undoubtedly were also in the audience, listening to, being molded by, and revising the tales when they grew old enough to retell them.

With Gutenberg's invention of movable type, mass production of books became possible. In 1476 William Caxton established England's first printing press. Most of the material that he printed relating to children's reading was based on the idea that children should read only what would improve their manners. For example, Caxton's *Book of Curtesye* (1477) contained instruction for combing hair, washing ears, and even cleaning one's nose. He did, however, publish three books for adults that have since become classics in children's literature: *Reynart the Foxe* (*The History of Reynard the Fox*) (1481), *The Book of the Subtyle Historyes and Fables of Esope* (*The Fables of Aesop*) (1484), and *Morte d'Arthur* (*The Death of Arthur*) (1485).

Although Caxton's books were too expensive for the average person, two other types of books were more readily available. Hornbooks, printed sheets of text mounted on wood, usually in the shape of a paddle and covered with translucent animal horn, usually contained the alphabet, a syllabary, numerals, and the Lord's Prayer. They became a popular tool for learning by the end of the 1400s and continued to be used into the 1700s, when the battledore, a lesson book of folded paper consisting of the same material as the hornbook, grew more popular. The battledore was also a form for underground presses, often presenting folk tales and other less scholarly materials. By the eighteenth century, books later referred to as "penny-awfuls" because they cost a penny and contained poor-quality literature, replaced the popular battledores.

The other type of book that appeared in the 1500s and remained popular into the early 1800s was the chapbook. Cheap both in the quality of the printing and in cost, they were also used as lesson books. While they extended the traditional content of the hornbooks to include folk tales and ballads, they still retained a strong dose of religion.

During the 1600s, the Puritan influence, stressing that children were conceived and born in sin and would die in sin unless measures were taken to save them, established the first important view of children as unique—as different from adults and, thus, as an audience needing a literature of its own. This significant new concept was an ironic step forward for children's literature. The Puritan worldview included childhood in it; however, it was a negative perspective of childhood, based on the idea that we are all born in sin. Therefore, children are, in fact, prone to sin; adults must quickly "scare" them into wanting to get to Heaven. It is easy to imagine the dread children had in being forced to read such books as James Janeway's *A Token for Children: Being an Exact Account of the Conversion, Holy and Exemplary Lifes, and Joyful Deaths of Several Young Children* (1677).

The most important book written at this time was JOHN BUNYAN's *Pilgrim's Progress* (1678), an allegory aimed at moral improvement. Because it contained bold action and exciting adventure, however, it was more attractive to children.

In 1693 John Locke's *Some Thoughts Concerning Education* was published. According to Locke, children were not born evil or predestined to sin but were, rather, *tabula rasa* (i.e., blank sheet), on which ideas were to be imprinted. This view stressed a milder, pleasanter approach to teaching children and called for books to provide pleasure (i.e., children were to be enticed to the better path). Locke's notions would open up the philosophical support for the true beginning of children's literature.

Prior to that event, a few other noteworthy publications appeared. In 1697 Charles Perrault, a French aristocrat, published *Contes de ma mère l'oye* (*Tales of Mother Goose*), a major anthology of fairy tales for children. In 1719 DANIEL DEFOE published *Robinson Crusoe*, and in 1726 JONATHAN SWIFT brought out *Gulliver's Travels*. Neither was written for children. Both, in fact, are complex works of satire, difficult reading even for adults. However, children latched on to them. It is easy to understand why, in the midst of literature meant to instruct or moralize, these two great adventure stories found an eager audience.

In the mid-eighteenth century, things began changing. Middle-class life started to center on the home and family, children were beginning to be thought of as something other than little adults, and people had more time and money for books and education. In 1744 John Newbery, an advocate of John Locke's philosophy, initiated the publication of a line of books for the entertainment of children with *A Little Pretty Pocket Book*. This work is generally considered to be the first true work of children's literature as we know it. The volumes that Newbery published were meant not to teach or moralize, although there was a didactic tone about them, but to express ideas about life in the true manner of literature.

Soon after, in 1762, Jean Jacques Rousseau would bring out *Émile*, a book describing the stages of a child's growth. It stressed that children are not only not evil but are not even neutral blank sheets. Rather, they are "little angels," more in tune with nature than adults are. In their growth they should not be led by adults, who have already been corrupted by society, but only accompanied by their elders. This concept helped set the stage for the philosophy of the romantic movement and the view that children, who sprang from nature, purity, love, and truth were closer to the fundamental values of life than were adults, whose purity had been lost or, at least, blunted by civilization.

In 1789 the French Revolution, stimulated by the American Revolution, which was based on the views of such philosophers as Locke and Rousseau, brought with it a new worldview, one embracing the imagination and democracy over logic and aristocracy. In the same year, WILLIAM BLAKE, considered a preromantic, published *Songs of Innocence* (1789), poems expressing a childlike notion of the world. Blake's advocacy of the child's perspective was quickly followed by the romantic movement, which idealized nature, cultural heritage, forms of the Platonic view of a perfect world beyond this from which we originate and, thus, of the closeness of the newborn to the true world. The value of collecting and preserving one's heritage, and the rejection of society as less pure than nature, established a respect for the oral tradition, uncorrupted, pure, offering a more true expression of the human condition than academic literature. Thus, the stage was set for JACOB and WILHELM GRIMM (see Vol. 2), serious, respected scholars, to begin collecting folk tales, stories heretofore considered inferior and not worthy of research. Their two original collections, published in 1812 and 1815, are often thought of as ushering in the Golden Age of children's literature. Now folk tales and similar forms, and a child's perspective, previously considered to be inferior to the adult perspective, could be defended and embraced; and they were.

Soon collectors of folk tales from all of the countries of Europe were publishing the literature of the people. The two most important collectors in England were Joseph Jacobs, known for retaining the language of the people, and Andrew Lang, noted for including colors in the titles of his books (e.g., *The Blue Fairy Book*, 1893; *The Green Fairy Book*, 1893; and so on).

Such literature spawned writers who would extend the genre. In Denmark, HANS CHRISTIAN ANDERSEN (see Vol. 2), who started by collecting and telling traditional folk tales and then moved into writing his own classics, including *The Ugly Duckling*, *The Little Mermaid*, and *The Nightingale* (first published in the late 1830s; all included in the first English translation, 1846), is the most famous. Soon others began experimenting with this new form.

By midcentury, a conservative Victorian England would produce some writers of extended fairy tales, now worthy of the title "fantasies" for children. The leaders included George MacDonald (whose work was a strong influence over the twentieth-century fantasies of C. S. Lewis), Charles Kingsley (now not so highly thought of), and Lewis Carroll (whose work embraced the imagination and purity of the child's view to explore some of the complex logical contradictions of the adult world and may be the best children's fiction ever written). Carroll also initiated, along with EDWARD LEAR, the still healthy genre of nonsense verse in children's literature.

The Victorian Age, 1837–1901, brought with it the Industrial Revolution (a time when children were often forced to work in factories for 70 hours per week) and an emphasis on a strictly controlled social life, centering on the family, and Christian piety. In realistic fiction, children were often depicted either with a great deal of sentimentality or as the victims of the newly formed urban society (e.g., especially in the writings of CHARLES DICKENS). Other writers were producing classics in science fiction (notably, Jules Verne and H. G. WELLS), animal fantasy (Rudyard Kipling), and adventure (ROBERT LOUIS STEVENSON). The number of picture books for children also dramatically exploded into quality literature at this time. With the exception of Thomas Bewick (who brought the art of the woodcut to its highest level), George Cruikshank (who illustrated the first translation of the Brothers Grimm into English), and Edward Lear, illustrations for picture books were generally crude woodcuts. However, in the mid-1800s, Edmund Evans developed better color-printing techniques and gathered together three impressive illustrators who are considered the founders of contemporary picture books. WALTER CRANE, known for his use of color, illustrated such books as *The House That Jack Built* (1865). RANDOLPH CALDECOTT, skillful in depicting people and animals in motion and respected for his ability to extend the story by means of his drawings, illustrated such stories as *The Farmer Went a-Trotting* (1883) and *The Fox Jumps over the Farmer's Gate* (1884). KATE GREENAWAY, whose first book, *Under the Window* (1879), was so successful that 70,000 English copies and over 30,000 French and German copies were sold, continues to be praised for her subtlety and elegance. Her alphabet picture book is still considered a classic. BEATRIX POTTER gave the world an intimate, delicate interplay of precisely chosen words and carefully drawn animals in her small books, most notably *The Tale of Peter Rabbit* (1901).

In 1908 KENNETH GRAHAME brought a fitting close to the Golden Age of children's literature with *The Wind in the Willows*, a book embracing the views of the romantic movement, especially in the brilliant chapter "The Piper at the Break of Dawn."

The first half of the twentieth century saw a great number of sentimental family stories, especially those by Arthur Ransome. However, such classic fantasies as *Mary Poppins* (1934), by P. L. TRAVERS, and *The Story of Dr. Dolittle* (1920) also appeared. Subsequently, there was a surge in popular high fantasy (fantasy dealing with the collision of worlds, the struggle of cosmic good and evil), beginning in 1936 with Tolkien's *The Hobbit*; this title became extremely popular along with his *Lord of the Rings* trilogy and C. S. Lewis's *Chronicles of Narnia* (1950–56). High fantasy remains an important field today, as evidenced by such writers as Susan Cooper, author of *Over Sea, under Stone* (1965).

Overall, British children's literature is a rich tapestry of genres, offering important expressions of the human condition as seen through a child's eyes. Since there is usually a close interweaving of text and illustration in children's literature, both writers and illustrators are represented in this section and the works it includes.

History and Criticism

Bettleheim, Bruno. *The Uses of Enchantment.* Knopf 1989 $11.00. ISBN 0-679-72393-5. Powerful defense of folk tales from a Freudian perspective.

Bottigheimer, Ruth B., ed. *Fairy Tales and Society: Illusion, Allusion, and Paradigm.* U. of Pa. Pr. 1987 $44.95. ISBN 0-8122-8021-0. A scholarly collection of essays exploring folk tales from various perspectives.

Carpenter, Humphrey. *Secret Gardens: The Golden Age of Children's Literature, from Alice's Adventures in Wonderland to Winnie-the-Pooh.* HM 1991 $9.70. ISBN 0-395-57374-2. A discussion of the greatest children's writers, mainly British, between 1860 and 1930.

Cott, Jonathan. *Pipers at the Gates of Dawn: The Wisdom of Children's Literature.* Random 1983 o.p. An excellent discussion of important writers and collectors of children's literature.

Darton, F. J. Harvey. *Children's Books in England: Five Centuries of Social Life.* Ed. by Brian Alderson. 3rd ed. Cambridge U. Pr. 1982 $45.00. ISBN 0-521-24020-4. First published in 1932, considered a classic history, though dated; illustrated.

Eiss, Harry, ed. *Literature for Young People on War and Peace: An Annotated Bibliography.* Greenwood 1989 $35.00. ISBN 0-313-26068-0. Offers unique, qualitative commentary.

Jackson, Mary V. *Engines of Instruction, Mischief, and Magic: Children's Literature in England from Its Beginnings to 1839.* U. of Nebr. Pr. 1989 $16.50. ISBN 0-8032-2570-

6. History in the context of the idea that children were considered resources to be molded; includes bibliography of primary and secondary sources.

Lang, Andrew. *Custom and Myth*. AMS Pr. repr. of 1885 ed. $11.00. ISBN 0-404-03817-4. A discussion of comparative mythology in folk tales, myths, and epics by an important collector.

Luthi, Max. *Once upon a Time: On the Nature of Fairy Tales*. Ind. U. Pr. 1976 $7.95. ISBN 0-253-20203-5. Interesting views of popular oral literature by a highly respected scholar.

Mahony, Bertha E., and Louise Latimer. *Illustrators of Children's Books: 1744–1945*. Vol. 1. Comp. by Beulah Folmsbee. Horn Bk. 1947 $35.95. ISBN 0-87675-015-3. Discusses both British and American books.

Muir, Percy, ed. *Children's Books of Yesterday*. Gale repr. of 1946 ed. o.p.

Norton, Donna. *Through the Eyes of a Child: An Introduction to Children's Literature*. Macmillan 1990. ISBN 0-675-21144-1. An overview containing a brief history, theories of childhood, and discussions of the major genres.

Tolkien, J. R. R. *Tree and Leaf*. HM 1965 $9.70. ISBN 0-395-08253-6. Contains a major discussion of fairy stories by a master of the craft and a short fantasy.

Townsend, John Rowe. *A Sense of Story: Essays on Contemporary Writers for Children*. Horn Bk. 1973 $6.95. ISBN 0-87675-276-8. Nineteen essays on both British and American writers.

Collections

Blishen, Edward, comp. *Oxford Book of Poetry for Children*. OUP 1987 $16.95. ISBN 0-19-276031-90. Traditional poetry for children from Great Britain and the United States; illustrated.

Bogan, Louise, and William Jay Smith, comps. *The Golden Journey: 225 Poems for Young People*. Contemp. Bks. 1989 $9.95. ISBN 0-8092-4249-4. Traditional poems from both England and the United States; illustrated.

Butler, Francelia. *Sharing Literature with Children: A Thematic Anthology*. Waveland Pr. 1989 $24.95. ISBN 0-88133-463-4. A collection of both British and American literature organized by theme; illustrated.

Griffith, John W., and Charles H. Frey. *Classics of Children's Literature*. Macmillan 1991. ISBN 0-02-347290-1. An excellent collection of the best in children's literature, both British and American; illustrated.

Jacobs, Joseph, comp. *English Fairy Tales and More English Fairy Tales*. Amereon Ltd. repr. of 1898 ed. $18.95. ISBN 0-89190-076-4. Republication of several of Jacobs's tales collected in the 1890s; illustrated.

Lang, Andrew, ed. *Blue Fairy Book*. Airmont Classics Ser. Airmont 1969 $2.95. ISBN 0-8049-0196-1. The first and best known of Lang's many collections of folk tales; illustrated.

Opie, Iona, and Peter Opie. *The Classic Fairy Tales*. OUP 1992 $25.00. ISBN 0-19-211559-6. An excellent collection of 24 tales, with bibliographic sources and literary histories; illustrated.

_____. *A Nursery Companion*. OUP 1980 $29.95. ISBN 0-19-212213-4. A reproduction of an excellent collection of nineteenth-century nursery rhymes, alphabets, grammars, and woodcuts; illustrated.

_____. *Oxford Dictionary of Nursery Rhymes*. OUP 1951 $47.50. ISBN 0-19-869111-4. Classic collection and study of the genre; illustrated.

_____. *Oxford Nursery Rhyme Book*. OUP 1955 $29.95. ISBN 0-19-869112-2. An excellent collection put together by highly respected scholars; illustrated.

Saltman, Judith. *The Riverside Anthology of Children's Literature*. HM 1985 $47.56. ISBN 0-395-35773-X. An excellent collection of the major genres of children's literature; includes annotated bibliographies and a brief history.

Sutherland, Zena, and Myra C. Livingston. *The Scott, Foresman Anthology of Children's Literature*. Scott F. 1984 $54.00. ISBN 0-673-15527-7. An excellent collection of representative works from the important genres.

CHRONOLOGY OF AUTHORS

Blake, William. 1757–1827
Dickens, Charles. 1812–1870
Lear, Edward. 1812–1888
MacDonald, George. 1824–1905
Carroll, Lewis. 1832–1898
Crane, Walter. 1845–1915
Caldecott, Randolph. 1846–1886
Greenaway, Kate. 1846–1901
Stevenson, Robert Louis. 1850–1894
Grahame, Kenneth. 1859–1932

Barrie, Sir J(ames) M(atthew).
  1860–1937
Kipling, Rudyard. 1865–1936
Potter, Beatrix. 1866–1943
Milne, A(lan) A(lexander). 1882–1956
Tolkien, J(ohn) R(onald) R(uel).
  1892–1973
Lewis, C(live) S(taples). 1898–1963
Travers, P(amela) L(yndon). 1906–

BARRIE, SIR J(AMES) M(ATTHEW). 1860–1937

[SEE Chapter 10 in this volume for Main Entry.]

CHILDREN'S FANTASY BY BARRIE

Peter Pan. 1904. Bantam 1985 $39.50. ISBN 0-685-00703-0. Classic story of a boy who refuses to grow up.

BLAKE, WILLIAM. 1757–1827

[See Chapter 9 in this volume for Main Entry.]

CHILDREN'S POETRY BY BLAKE

Songs of Innocence and Experience. OUP 1977 $11.95. ISBN 0-19-281089-8. The poems express a childlike worldview while exploring important questions about existence.

CALDECOTT, RANDOLPH. 1846-1886

Heralded as the greatest artist of the triumvirate of modern illustrators that included GREENAWAY and CRANE, Randolph Caldecott is highly praised for introducing techniques of animation into picture book art and for his humorous, satiric extensions of the text in his illustrations.

His fame centers on 16 books, often referred to as the "Toy Books," reprinted by Edmund Evans in his innovative printing techniques, featuring mainly traditional nursery rhymes and songs, and published in pairs. They include *The House That Jack Built* (1865), *The Diverting History of John Gilpin* (written by WILLIAM COWPER) (1878), *Elegy on the Death of a Mad Dog* (written by OLIVER GOLDSMITH) (1979), *Babes in the Wood* (1879), *Sing a Song of Sixpence* (1880), *The Three Jovial Huntsmen* (1880), *The Farmer's Boy* (1881), *The Queen of Hearts* (1881), *The Milkmaid* (1882), *Hey Diddle Diddle with Baby Bunting* (1882), *A Frog He Would a-Wooing Go* (1883), and *The Fox Jumps over the Parson's Gate* (1884).

Caldecott generally drew his illustrations in sepia applied with a brush rather than a pen; he included an average of three uncolored illustrations for each colored one. He has received praise for his fluid style, which created a sense of movement across a page and from one page to another; he is also lauded for his insight into human nature and instinctive grasp of what appeals to children.

The American Library Association each year awards a highly coveted medal in his name to the best illustrated book by an American.

CHILDREN'S PICTURE BOOKS BY CALDECOTT

The Hey Diddle Diddle Picture Book: The Milkmaid, Hey Diddle Diddle, Baby Bunting, A Frog He Would a-Wooing Go, The Fox Jumps over the Parson's Gate. Warne o.p.

The Panjandrum Picture Book: Come Lasses and Lads, Ride a Cock-Horse to Banbury Cross, A Farmer Went Trotting upon His Grey Mare, Mrs. Mary Blaize, The Great Panjandrum Himself. Warne o.p.

Picture Book, No. 1: The Diverting History of John Gilpin, The House That Jack Built, An Elegy on the Death of a Mad Dog, The Babes in the Wood. 1878. Warne o.p.

A Second Collection: Sing a Song of Sixpence, The Three Jovial Hunters. Warne 1986 $4.95. ISBN 0-7232-3433-7. Picture book.

A Third Caldecott Collection: The Queen of Hearts, The Farmer's Boy. Warne 1980 o.p. Picture book.

NONFICTION BY CALDECOTT

Yours Pictorially. Ed. by M. Hatchins. 1976 o.p. Caldecott's letters.

BOOK ABOUT CALDECOTT

Alderson, Brian. *Sing a Song of Sixpence: The English Picture Book Tradition and Randolph Caldecott.* Cambridge U. Pr. 1987 $27.95. ISBN 0-521-33179-X. A scholarly study of Caldecott in the context of his genre; illustrated.

CARROLL, LEWIS (pseud. of Rev. Charles Lutwidge Dodgson). 1832–1898

Born in Daresbury, England, Lewis Carroll became a minister of the Church of England and a professor of mathematics at Christ Church College, Oxford, where he was considered conscientious but often dull. The author took his pseudonym from his own name: Lewis is an anglicized version of Lutwidge, and Carroll is a variant of Charles. In his diary of July 4, 1862, Carroll described "an expedition up the river to Godstowe with the three Lidells," the daughters of the dean of Christ Church College, "on which occasion I told them the fairy tale of 'Alice's Adventures under Ground,' which I undertook to write out for Alice." The original manuscript is on display in the British Museum and has been published in facsimile in the United States.

Carroll's particular talent for mathematical puzzles and paradox, for charming and significant nonsense verse, for verbal ingenuity, and for identification with the distortions and dilemmas of a child's view of the world have made *Alice's Adventures in Wonderland* (1865) and *Through the Looking Glass* (1871) perennial favorites with children. But in recent years Carroll has been taken quite seriously as a major literary artist for adults as well. His works have come under the scrutiny of critics who have explained his permanent attractiveness in terms of existential and symbolic drama: The Alice books dramatize psychological realities in symbolic terms, being commentary on the nature of the human predicament rather than escape from it.

In addition to his writing, Carroll was also a pioneering photographer, and he took many pictures of young children, especially girls, with whom he seemed to empathize.

CHILDREN'S FICTION BY CARROLL

Alice in Wonderland. Buccaneer Bks. 1981 $15.95. ISBN 0-89966-345-1

Alice in Wonderland and Through the Looking Glass. Contemp. Bks. 1988 $7.95. ISBN 0-8092-4488-8. Perhaps the most important children's literature yet written, embracing the imagination and questioning all forms of adult logic; they were a clear breakthrough in children's literature at the time of their writing and are still fresh today.

Alice's Adventures in Wonderland. 1865. HarBraceJ 1991 $16.95. ISBN 0-15-604426-9. The adventures of a young girl who enters a rabbit hole and encounters a strange, wondrous land.

Alice's Adventures in Wonderland: An 1865 Printing Re-described and Newly Identified as the Publisher's "File Copy": with a Revised and Expanded Census of the Suppressed 1865 "Alice" Compiled by Selwin H. Doodacre: To Which Is Added, a Short Title Index Identifying and Locating the Original Preliminary Drawings by John Tenniel for Alice and Looking Glass. Battledore Ltd. 1990 $75.00. ISBN 0-962-71100-4. Facsimile reprint; useful to bibliographers.

Alice's Adventures Under-Ground. 1886. Dover 1965 $2.95. ISBN 0-486-21482-6. Carroll's own neat hand-lettered early version of *Alice's Adventures in Wonderland.*

The Annotated Alice: Alice's Adventures in Wonderland and Through the Looking Glass. NAL-Dutton $11.00. ISBN 0-452-01041-1. Explains, for adults, many now-unfamiliar allusions. Introduction by Martin Gardner.

The Complete Sylvie and Bruno. Mercury House Inc. 1991 $25.00. ISBN 1-56279-009-9. Reissue of one of Carroll's less popular works. Illustrated by Renee Flower.

More Annotated Alice: Alice's Adventures in Wonderland and *Through the Looking-Glass and What Alice Found There.* Random 1990 $35.00. ISBN 0-394-58571-2. A good annotated edition of the two novels; useful to scholars. Illustrated by Peter Newell. Notes by Martin Gardner.

Sylvie and Bruno. Dover 1988 $7.95. ISBN 0-486-25588-3. Introduction by Martin Gardner.

Through the Looking Glass and What Alice Found There. Outlet Bk. Co. 1990 $10.99. ISBN 0-517-03346-1. A sequel to, and usually published with, *Alice in Wonderland.*

CHILDREN'S POETRY BY CARROLL

The Annotated Snark: Full Text of Lewis Carroll's Great Nonsense Epic "The Hunting of the Snark" and the Original Illustrations by Henry Holiday. Ed. by Martin Gardner. Kaufmann 1981 o.p. Includes a bibliography and an interesting appendix.

The Humorous Verse of Lewis Carroll. Amereon Ltd. repr. of 1933 ed. $25.95. ISBN 0-89190-687-8

The Hunting of the Snark: A Musical Comedy. I. E. Clark 1987 $3.00. ISBN 0-88680-273-3. Carroll's "nonsense poem" intended for children, which ultiamtely attracted a very different audience.

WORKS BY CARROLL

The Letters of Lewis Carroll. 2 vols. Ed. by Morton Cohen and Roger L. Green. OUP 1979 $75.00. ISBN 0-19-520090-X. Includes letters covering 1837–1898, a biographical chronology, and a Dodgson family tree.

Lewis Carroll: Interviews and Recollections. Ed. by Morton N. Cohen. U. of Iowa Pr. 1989 $35.00. ISBN 0-87745231-8. Personal reminiscences and interviews with Dodgson.

Looking-Glass Letters. Ed. by Thomas Hind. Collins 1991 o.p. Selection of letters dealing specifically with the Alice novels.

Selected Letters of Lewis Carroll. Macmillan 1989 o.p. Good though unsurprising collection of the letters.

BOOKS ABOUT CARROLL

Aspin, Roy. *Lewis Carroll and His Camera.* Clayhall 1989 $45.00. ISBN 0-948706-04-X. Carroll's photography; especially good for a study of the Alice novels and the drawings.

Cohen, Morton N., and Anita Grandolfo. eds. *Lewis Carroll and the House of Macmillan.* Cambridge U Pr. 1987 $74.95. ISBN 0-52125602-X. Examines Carroll's relationship with his publishers.

Colquhoun, Daryl. *The Alice Concordnace: A Concordance to Lewis Carroll's "Alice in Wonderland" and "Through the Looking-Glass".* U. of Adelaide Pr. 1986 o.p. Useful concordnace of names and terms.

Deleuze, Gilles. *The Logic of Sense*. Ed. by Constantin V. Boundas. Trans. by Mark Lester and Charles Stivale. Col. U. Pr. 1990 $45.00. ISBN 0-824-06457-7

Guiliano, Edward. *Lewis Carroll: An Annotated International Bibliography, 1960–1977*. U. Pr. of Va. 1980 $30.00. ISBN 0-8139-0862-0. Includes more than 1,500 entries (covering 1960 to 1977), filling a critical gap of information about Carroll.

Hudson, Derek. *Lewis Carroll*. Greenwood 1972 repr. of 1954 ed. $45.00. ISBN 0-8371-6439-7

Kelly, Richard Michael. *Lewis Carroll*. Twayne 1990 $19.95. ISBN 0-8057-4988-9. A discussion of the writer's life and his fiction.

Lovett, Charles C. *"Alice" on Stage: A History of the Early Theatrical Adaptations of "Alice in Wonderland"*. Greenwood 1989 $45.00. ISBN 0-313-27681-1. Interesting history of dramatic adaptations of the Alice books.

Phillips, Robert, ed. *Aspects of Alice: Lewis Carroll's Dreamchild as Seen through the Critics' Looking Glasses*. Vanguard 1971 o.p. Interesting collection of essays and poems about the "Alice" books.

Williams, Sidney, and Falconer Madan. *The Lewis Carroll Handbook*. Ed. by Denis Crutch. Shoe String rev. ed. o.p. A new version of *A Handbook of the Literature of the Rev. C. L. Dodgson*, revised, augmented, and brought up to 1960.

CRANE, WALTER. 1845–1915

Crane is considered to be one of the three founders of modern illustration, along with CALDECOTT and GREENAWAY, all of whom had their work reproduced by Edmund Evans, an engraver who developed a process of color printing that revolutionized the field. Crane was born in Liverpool, England, the son of an artist. He married Mary Frances Andrews in 1871, had two sons and one daughter, and made his home in West Kensington, London.

His subject matter came from traditional folk tales, legends, nursery rhymes, and songs. His style was praised for its decorative borders, its control of the entire picture frame, and its use of color. In addition to his prolific output as an illustrator and writer of children's books, Crane lectured and wrote about his profession, was the director of design at the Manchester School of Art, served as principal of the Royal College of Art, and did frieze and mosaic decorations and tapestry designs.

His "Toy Books" (a term used as a series designation by the publisher) include *Absurd ABC*; *Alphabet of Old Friends*; *Beauty and the Beast*; *Bluebeard*; *Chattering Jack*; *Cock Robin*; *Dame Trot and Her Comical Cat*; *Fairy Ship*; *Forty Thieves*; *Frog Prince*; *Goody Two Shoes*; *Grammar in Rhyme*; *Hind in the Wood*; *The House That Jack Built*; *Jack and the Beanstalk*; *Little Red Riding Hood*; *Mother Hubbard*; *Noah's Ark Alphabet*; *Old Courtier*; *One Two, Buckle My Shoe*; *Princess Bell Etoile*; *Puss-in-Boots*; *Sing a Song of Sixpence*; *Sleeping Beauty*; *Three Bears*; *Valentine and Orson*; and *Yellow Dwarf*.

Many of Crane's illustrated books are available in libraries and some of his illustrations have been used in recent titles along with the work of other illustrators. Two books that he wrote about his life and the art of illustrating are currently in print.

NONFICTION BY CRANE

Artist's Reminiscences. Omnigraphics Inc. 1992 repr. of 1907 ed. $40.00. ISBN 1-55888-930-2. Autobiographical, illustrated by the author.

Of the Decorative Illustration of Books Old and New. Omnigraphics Inc. 1968 repr. of 1905 ed. $48.00. ISBN 1-55888-455-6

BOOKS ABOUT CRANE

Engen, Rodney K. *Walter Crane as a Book Illustrator*. St. Martin 1975 o.p.

Spencer, Isobel. *Walter Crane*. Macmillan 1976 o.p. A biography that studies Crane beyond his picture book fame; illustrated.

DICKENS, CHARLES. 1812–1870

[See Chapter 10 in this volume for Main Entry.]

CHILDREN'S FICTION BY DICKENS

A Christmas Carol. Tor Bks. 1990 $2.75. ISBN 0-8125-0434-8. The classic holiday story for all ages, and the Dickens story most often read to or read by children.

GRAHAME, KENNETH. 1859–1932

While employed by the Bank of England, where he rose rapidly to a position of importance, Kenneth Grahame wrote two autobiographical works, *The Golden Age* (1895) and *Dream Days* (1898). Both were written for adults but presented a child's perspective. *Dream Days* included "The Reluctant Dragon," which was later published separately as a story for children. Grahame also edited *Lullaby Land: Songs of Childhood by Eugene Field* (1897) and *The Cambridge Book of Poetry for Children* (1916).

His life was not a happy one. His mother died when he was 5 years old. His father, an attorney, abandoned the family and died, an alcoholic, in France. The third of four children, Kenneth was sent, when he was 5 years old, to live for three years with his grandmother in Cookham Dene, Berkshire, near the Thames and Windsor Forest, where he gained his appreciation for nature and had, for this brief period, his own golden age. The experience served as the basis for his one true classic in children's literature, *The Wind in the Willows* (1908), which began as bedtime stories for his only son, Alistair, of what has been termed a disastrous marriage.

Both praised and condemned for its mixture of adult satire and childish pursuits, its long descriptive passages (often filled with overalliterative, purple prose and trite phrases), and its acceptance of the English "gentleman's club" view of life, *The Wind in the Willows* transcends its faults in a sincere expression of the child's unique unity with nature, love, spirituality, beauty, and a kind of truth with which adults often lose touch (views similar to those expressed by the English romantic poets a century earlier). The chapter titled "The Piper at the Break of Dawn" just might be the most important piece of children's literature yet written.

CHILDREN'S FANTASY BY GRAHAME

The Wind in the Willows. Amereon Ltd. repr. of 1908 ed. $17.95. ISBN 0-88411-877-0. The story of Mole, Rat, Badger, and Toad, as they alternately seek adventure and long for the security of home; illustrated by Ernest H. Shepard.

The Wind in the Willows. Heritage 1944 o.p. Contains the interesting illustrations by the highly respected Arthur Rackham, as well as an introduction by both Theodore Roosevelt and A. A. Milne.

BOOKS ABOUT GRAHAME

Green, Peter. *Kenneth Grahame, 1859–1932: A Study of His Life, Works, and Times*. Trafalgar 1959 o.p. A highly respected biography that speculates on Grahame's psychological state, perhaps dwelling too much on Grahame's marriage.

Kuznets, Lois R. *Kenneth Grahame. Twayne's English Author Ser.* G. K. Hall 1987 $20.95. ISBN 0-8057-6943-9. The most recent critical discussion of Grahame and his work.

GREENAWAY, KATE. 1846–1901

The author and illustrator of many children's books, designer of greeting cards and of the dresses that she used as models for her paintings, Kate Greenaway was born to John (an engraver) and Elizabeth in Frognal, Hampstead, London. She was educated privately and also studied at the Slade School of Art, London. She became a member of the Royal Institute of Painters in Water-Colors in 1889. The Library Association of Great Britain established the Kate Greenaway Medal in 1955, which is awarded annually to the artist who has produced the most distinguished children's illustrations.

Greenaway, who had a happy childhood, became interested in art at a young age. By the time she was 22, she had exhibited her work at the Dudley Gallery and had already won a national bronze medal. After some years spent designing holiday cards and illustrating children's books for others, she was able to get published *Under the Window*, a book she both illustrated and wrote. Its immediate status as a bestseller made a name for Greenaway, and she went to work for Scribner's Sons, publishers.

Her delicate, intimate, flowery style became so popular that some imitators claimed that their work really had been done by her, and others tried to pass themselves off as Kate Greenaway under a pseudonym. Often these copies of her work were so poor that she was forced to protect herself by refusing to part with her copyrights. Not only was her work copied in picture books; it also was used on handkerchiefs, plates, vases, dishes, and even shoes. Its widespread appeal remains even today.

Although her illustrations are sometimes not well balanced and she tends to forget the basic laws of gravity in the anatomical portions of her illustrations, the fine, detailed, Sunday school clothes and the fragile, flower-filled world that she portrays is one of the best conceived in all of children's literature.

The following list of books by her contains only those of which she was also the author, although she illustrated many works written by others.

CHILDREN'S PICTURE BOOKS BY GREENAWAY

An Apple Pie. Outlet Bk. Co. 1993 $4.99. ISBN 0-517-09302-2

Birthday Book for Children. Warne 1963 $6.95. ISBN 0-7232-0216-8. Illustrated; grades 3–6.

The Complete Kate Greenaway. CHP 1967 o.p.

Kate Greenaway's Alphabet. J. Cape repr. of 1885 ed. 1973 o.p.

Kate Greenaway's Birthday Book for Children. Verses by Sale Barker. Warne repr. of 1880 ed. 1937 o.p.

Kate Greenaway's Book of Games. St. Martin 1987 $9.95. ISBN 0-312-01175-X. Illustrated; grade 2 and up.

Kate Greenaway's Mother Goose. Dial Bks. Young 1988 $10.95. ISBN 0-8037-0479-8. Illustrated; preschool and up.

The Kate Greenaway Treasury: An Anthology of the Illustrations and Writings of Kate Greenaway. Ed. by Edward Ernest and Patricia Tracy Lowe. World 1967 o.p.

Mother Goose, or, The Old Nursery Rhymes. Evergreen 1973 repr. of 1890 ed. $3.25. ISBN 0-914510-04-5. Illustrated; grades K–3.

Under the Window: Pictures and Rhymes for Children. Warne repr. of 1879 ed. o.p.

BOOKS ABOUT GREENAWAY

Spielmann, M. H., and G. S. Layard. *Kate Greenaway.* Ayer 1968 repr. of 1905 ed. $29.00. ISBN 0-405-08990-2. An early laudatory biography that deals with both her life and her work; includes many examples of her illustrations.

Taylor, Ina. *The Art of Greenaway: A Nostalgic Portrait of Childhood.* Pelican 1991 $34.95. ISBN 0-88289-867-1

KIPLING, RUDYARD. 1865–1936

[See Chapter 10 in this volume for Main Entry.]

CHILDREN'S FICTION BY KIPLING

The Jungle Books. NAL-Dutton 1961 $3.95. ISBN 0-451-52340-7. Short stories about Mowgli, the boy raised in the jungle by animals.

The Just So Stories. NAL-Dutton 1974 $3.50. ISBN 0-451-52433-0. The classic collection of pourquoi (why) stories filled with humorous wordplay.

Kim. Bantam 1983 $2.50. ISBN 0-553-21332-6. Kipling's best-known longer work, about an Irish orphan who lives by his wits on the streets of India.

LEAR, EDWARD. 1812–1888

Edward Lear was born in Holloway, England, to Jeremiah (a stockbroker) and Ann Lear, tutored at home by his sister, and briefly attended the Royal Academy schools. Both an author and an illustrator, he earned his living as an artist from the age of 15, mainly by doing landscapes. What he is remembered for is his nonsense books, especially his popularization of the limerick. Along with LEWIS CARROLL, he is considered to be the founder of nonsense poetry.

In addition to his limericks, he created longer nonsense poems. The best— and best known—is *The Jumblies*, in which the title characters go to sea in a sieve; it is a brilliant, profound, silly, and sad expression of the need to leave the security of the known world and experience the wonder and danger of the unknown. His other most notable work is *The Owl and the Pussy Cat*, a less complex poem whose title characters also go to sea. Lear produced humorous alphabets and botany books as well.

His wordplay, involving puns, neologisms, portmanteau words, and anticlimax, retains its vitality today and has influenced such contemporary writers of children's nonsense verse as SHEL SILVERSTEIN, Ogden Nash, and Laura Richards.

CHILDREN'S POETRY BY LEAR

The Complete Nonsense of Edward Lear. Dover $5.95. ISBN 0-486-20167-8. Illustrated.

BOOK ABOUT LEAR

Kamen, Gloria. *Edward Lear: King of Nonsense.* Atheneum 1990 $13.95. ISBN 0-689-31419-1. Explores both the serious and fun sides of Lear.

LEWIS, C(LIVE) S(TAPLES). 1898–1963

[See Chapter 11 in this volume for Main Entry.]

CHILDREN'S FANTASY BY LEWIS

The Chronicles of Narnia. 7 vols. Macmillan Child Grp. 1970 $22.95. ISBN 0-02-044280-7. The fantasy world of Narnia, in which Lewis presents a Christian ethos, though not an allegory of Christianity.

MACDONALD, GEORGE. 1824–1905

Praised by C. S. LEWIS as possibly the greatest writer of all time, a friend of LEWIS CARROLL, and a strong influence on J. M. BARRIE, MacDonald brought the writing of fantasy (what has since been called "allegorical fantasy"), into areas that had not yet been explored. He was born in Aberdeenshire and was educated at Aberdeen University. He then worked as a tutor in London, until he became a Congregational minister at Arundel. Since he disagreed with the theology there, he was dismissed for heresy and supported himself through journalism and lecturing, until he was aided financially by LORD BYRON's widow and appointed to a professorship of English literature at Bedford College in 1859.

In his lectures and nonfiction, MacDonald attacked Calvinist ethics and theology. In his fiction, he presented his ethical views in a less strong fashion, but the stories remain moralistic. His longer books for children have been praised for their insight into the child's psyche and for their contributions to the themes and techniques of children's fiction. These works are *At the Back of the North Wind* (1871), in which little Daimond is guided through the world by his friend the North Wind (employing allegory and presenting a moralistic view); *The Princess and the Goblin* (1872), in which Curdie, a miner boy, saves the princess from the wicked goblins; and its sequel, *The Princess and Curdie* (1883), in which the two save the kingdom from evil forces. His shorter fairy tales, especially *The Light Princess* (1890), whose continual punning on the various meanings of *light* keep the story less heavy, and *The Golden Key* (1906), a mystical allegory (both republished with illustrations by MAURICE SENDAK), are better suited to today's audience.

CHILDREN'S FANTASY BY MACDONALD

At the Back of the North Wind. Schocken 1987 $8.95. ISBN 0-8052-0595-0. Illustrated.
The Complete Fairy Tales of George MacDonald. Schocken 1987 $8.95. ISBN 0-8052-0579-9. Illustrated by Arthur Hughes; introduction by Roger Lancelyn Green.
The Golden Key. FS&G 1984 $10.95. ISBN 0-374-32706-8. Contains illustrations by Sendak.
The Light Princess. FS&G 1969 $10.95. ISBN 0-374-34455-8. Contains illustrations by Sendak.
The Light Princess and Other Fantasy Stories. Ed. by George G. Sadler. *Fantasy Stories of George MacDonald Ser.* Eerdmans 1980 $5.95. ISBN 0-8028-1861-7. Contains his shorter allegorical fantasies; introduction by Sadler.
The Princess and Curdie. Buccaneer Bks. 1989 $26.95. ISBN 0-89966-591-8.
The Princess and the Goblin. Dell 1986 $4.95. ISBN 0-440-47189-3

BOOKS ABOUT MACDONALD

Marshall, Cynthia, ed. *Essays on C. S. Lewis and George MacDonald: Truth, Fiction, and the Power of Imagination. Studies in British Literature.* E. Mellen 1991 $49.95. ISBN 0-88946-494-4. Contains excellent recent critical views on MacDonald.
Phillips, Michael. *George MacDonald.* Bethany Hse. 1987 $16.95. ISBN 0-87123-944-2. An in-depth biography.

MILNE, A(LAN) A(LEXANDER). 1882–1956

A prolific writer, A. A. Milne published 35 plays, 6 novels, 3 books of verse, 3 collections of short stories, and several works of nonfiction, including sketches for *Punch* magazine, of which he was the assistant editor. Nevertheless, his fame rests on four books for children: two of whimsical stories about the stuffed animals in his son's bedroom (*Winnie-the-Pooh* and *The House at Pooh Corner*) and two of verse (*When We Were Very Young* and *Now We Are Six*). All are considered classics and have been included among the Children's Literature Association's Touchstone books as the best in children's literature, on the Lewis Carroll Shelf list, and on the *Choice* magazine list of books for the academic library.

He also wrote *Toad of Toad Hall*, a play based on GRAHAME's *The Wind in the Willows*, and *Once upon a Time: A Fairy Tale for Grown-ups*, both of which are sometimes included in volumes with the four classic works.

Milne was born in London, to John Vine Milne, married Dorothy Daphne de Selincourt (also a writer) in 1913, and had a son, Christopher Robin, who served as the model for the little boy in his children's books.

CHILDREN'S FANTASY BY MILNE

House at Pooh Corner. 1928. Dell 1970 $3.25. ISBN 0-440-43795-4. Illustrated. The continued adventures of Christopher Robin, Winnie-the-Pooh, and their friends.

Now We Are Six. 1927. Dell 1970 $3.25. ISBN 0-440-46485-4. Classic collection of childrens verse; illustrated.

When We Were Very Young. 1924. Dell 1970 $3.25. ISBN 0-440-49485-0. Illustrated collection of poems for children.

Winnie-the-Pooh. 1926. Dell 1981 $3.50. ISBN 0-440-49571-7. Classic children's story about the adventures of Christopher Robin and his animal friends; illustrated.

BOOKS ABOUT MILNE

Crews, Frederick C. *The Pooh Perplex: A Freshman Casebook.* NAL-Dutton 1965 $5.95. ISBN 0-525-47160-X. An interesting collection of critiques of Milne.

Milne, A. A. *Autobiography.* NAL-Dutton 1939 o.p. Worth finding, though out of print.

Thwaite, Ann. *A. A. Milne: The Man Behind Winnie-the-Pooh.* Random 1990 $27.95. ISBN 0-394-58724-3. Chronicles Milne's childhood, schooling, and the fame and frustrations that attended his early adulthood.

POTTER, BEATRIX. 1866–1943

Beatrix Potter was born in London to wealthy parents. Because the atmosphere at home was excessively reserved and quiet, she had a lonely, isolated childhood. Supervised by nurses and educated by a governess, Potter spent a great deal of time drawing and painting the many small animals and plants that she saw around her. At one point she became engrossed with fungi and drew hundreds of extremely detailed sketches of them.

Her famous stories of Peter Rabbit and other small animals originated with a letter to Noel Moore, a sick little boy, the son of one of her former governesses. In the letter she wrote: "I don't know what to write to you, so I shall tell you a story about four little rabbits whose names were Flopsy, Mopsy, Cottontail and Peter." Thus began the story of Peter Rabbit and his adventures in Mr. McGregor's garden—both the words and the delicate drawings. Eventually, she had *The Tale of Peter Rabbit* (1893) printed privately and then sold it to Warne publishers. Her second book, *The Tailor of Gloucester* (1902), was also originally printed privately and then bought by Warne. These books are small enough in size, so that they can easily fit into the hands of young children; in the artistic sense, their small size is appropriate to the intimate world Potter created. Her writing style is praised for its economy, precise diction, and avoidance of sentimentality and condescension; her illustrations are praised for the way in which they extend the story, being realistic, and containing both energy and repose. The words and the illustrations are a perfect match.

Her original books were followed by many others. The best known include *The Tale of Benjamin Bunny, The Tale of Two Bad Mice, The Tale of Mrs. Tiggy-Winkle, The Tale of Mr. Jeremy Fisher, The Tale of Tom Kitten, The Tale of Jemima Puddle-Duck, The Roly-Poly Pudding, The Tale of Mrs. Tittlemouse,* and *The Tale of Mr. Tod.* By 1913 Potter had finished her best books. At that time she married William Heelis and settled down to sheep farming in the countryside she loved.

There are many publications of Potter's work. The key is to buy one that has both the original words and illustrations. The year 1993 marked the one-hundredth anniversary of Potter's *The Tale of Peter Rabbit*. To mark this milestone, Potter's long-time publisher, Frederick Warne and Company, brought out a number of special editions, including a special 23-book presentation box set. These books reproduce Potter's original illustrations and her text.

CHILDREN'S PICTURE BOOKS BY POTTER

Beatrix Potter Collection. 3 vols. Warne 1987 $18.95 ea. ISBNs 0-7232-5163-0, 0-7232-5164-9, 0-7232-5165-7

The One Hundredth Anniversary 1–23 Presentation Box: The World of Beatrix Potter. 23 Bks. Warne 1993 $135.00. ISBN 0-7232-4112-0. Illustrated anniversary edition of Potter's stories.

BOOKS ABOUT POTTER

Buchan, Elizabeth. *Beatrix Potter*. Warne 1991 $10.95. ISBN 0-7232-3780-8. Well-written look at Potter's life and work.

Collins, David R. *The Country Artist: A Story About Beatrix Potter*. Carolrhoda Bks. 1989 $4.95. ISBN 0-87614-509-8. Deals with Potter's life as a reflection of her love of the country.

Davies, Hunter. *Beatrix Potter's Lakeland*. Warne 1989 $24.95. ISBN 0-7232-3520-1

Hobbs, Anne S. *Beatrix Potter's Art*. Warne 1990 $24.95. ISBN 0-7232-3598-8. Focuses on the illustrations in Potter's works.

Lane, Margaret. *The Magic Years of Beatrix Potter*. Warne 1978 o.p. A biography with criticism; illustrated.

MacDonald, Ruth. *Beatrix Potter*. Macmillan 1986 $19.95. ISBN 0-8057-6917-X. First book-length, critical study of the written and visual aspects of Beatrix Potter's Peter Rabbit series.

STEVENSON, ROBERT LOUIS. 1850–1894

[See Chapter 10 in this volume for Main Entry.]

CHILDREN'S FICTION BY STEVENSON

Black Arrow. Airmont 1964 $2.95. ISBN 0-8049-0020-5. Historical fiction about the Wars of the Roses.

A Child's Garden of Verses. Airmont 1969 $2.50. ISBN 0-8049-0195-3. A classic collection of poems, stretching beyond the nursery and offering a joyful child's view. Published with many different illustrators; the Jessie Willcox Smith pictures are to be recommended.

Dr. Jekyll and Mr. Hyde. Airmont 1964 $2.50. ISBN 0-8049-0042-6. An exploration of multiple forces in the psyche.

Kidnapped. Airmont 1964 $1.95. ISBN 0-8049-0010-8. A boy's adventures on the sea and in Great Britain, containing a good deal of political commentary.

Treasure Island. Airmont $2.75. ISBN 0-8049-0002-7. Considered by many the best children's adventure story ever; also qualifies as exceptional adult fiction.

TOLKIEN, J(OHN) R(ONALD) R(UEL). 1892–1973

[See Chapter 11 in this volume for Main Entry.]

FANTASY BY TOLKIEN

The Hobbit and *The Lord of the Rings*. HM 1988 $29.95. ISBN 0-395-48907-5. The adventures of Bilbo in *The Hobbit*, as he helps the dwarfs reclaim their treasure from

Smaug, the dragon; and in *The Lord of the Rings*, after Bilbo returns from his adventure and Frodo gains possession of the power ring.

TRAVERS, P(AMELA) L(YNDON). 1906–

Born in Australia to an Irish father and a Scottish mother, P. L. Travers was a voracious reader and began to write while she was still a child. She did some acting but quickly moved into literary and dramatic criticism; she wrote some highly respected poetry as well.

However, it is her series of books for children, starting with *Mary Poppins* (1934), on which her fame rests. The prim, kindly, and enchanting nanny takes charge of the Banks's household and brings the children a seemingly endless stream of fantasy adventures. The book was an immediate success. WALT DISNEY's (see Vol. 3) musical version, in 1964, brought the stories to an even wider audience. Subsequent books about Mary Poppins include *Mary Poppins Comes Back*, *Mary Poppins Opens the Door*, *Mary Poppins in the Park*, *Mary Poppins from A to Z*, and *Mary Poppins and the House Next Door*. Other more recent books include *About Sleeping Beauty* (1975) and *Two Pair of Shoes* (1980).

CHILDREN'S FANTASY BY TRAVERS

Mary Poppins. Dell Rev. Ed. 1991 $3.50. ISBN 0-440-40406-1. Delightful story about a magical nanny.

Mary Poppins from A to Z. HarBraceJ 1962 $10.95. ISBN 0-15-252590-4. Twenty-six brief sketches featuring the irresistible nursemaid Mary Poppins. Wonderful drawings highlight the superb text. Illustrated.

Mary Poppins Comes Back. Dell 1991 $3.50. ISBN 0-440-40418-5. Mary Poppins returns to lead the Banks children through new adventures, including meeting the King of the Castle and the Dirty Rascal.

Mary Poppins in Cherry Tree Lane. Delacorte 1982 $12.95. ISBN 0-385-28601-5. Mary Poppins and the Banks children celebrate Midsummer's Eve in a magical way. Illustrated.

Mary Poppins and the House Next Door. Delacorte 1989 $12.95. ISBN 0-385-29749-1. Illustrated.

Mary Poppins Opens the Door. Buccaneer Bks. 1981 $15.95. ISBN 0-89966-391-5

Mary Poppins in the Park. Dell 1991 $3.50. ISBN 0-440-40452-5. Amusing stories featuring Mary Poppins and the Banks children in various outdoor settings, including their adventures on a summer day and a Halloween night.

POPULAR FICTION

In England, popular fiction began with the Gothic novel *The Castle of Otranto* (1764) by HORACE WALPOLE. This work introduced a type of story previously not published—one that celebrated outrageous sensationalism, two-dimensional characterization, and lurid plotting. In other words, *The Castle of Otranto* appealed to the emotions rather than the intellect, and it attacked moral conventions and social institutions that were emblematic of the elite, noble classes. Prior to Walpole, most of the narrative poetry and other forms of storytelling were concerned with the narrow experiences of the social elite; the lives of the vast majority of people in the lower and middle classes were excluded. In *The Castle of Otranto*, Walpole turned the literary conventions and traditions of the nobility upside down. He celebrated the supernatural over the cerebral, the gross and horrific over the sublime. Before Walpole, most fiction—and, indeed, most books—had been written by and for the wealthy, the powerful, and the educated. Moreover, because books were expensive to produce, only the well-to-do could afford to purchase them. The upper classes were also the only people who possessed the leisure time for education, and the ability to read and write was thus a status symbol of the political and religious aristocracy. After the Middle Ages, however, the advent of a technology made possible mass-production printing and this subsequently lowered the cost of books and increased their availability. As a result, people other than the wealthy could afford to purchase this newfangled thing called a "novel." In addition, improved public education promoted more widespread literacy, and, as a result of an expanding middle class, more people could afford to be educated. As the density of population in urban centers like London increased, it became easier to buy and sell books. And, most important, a larger middle class reflected the growth in leisure time—time that could be spent reading fiction for entertainment.

From its Gothic beginnings, popular fiction proliferated quickly, diversifying and lending itself to new publishing technologies such as the Victorian-era "penny dreadful" (the British equivalent of the American "dime novel") and the serial magazine. Throughout the nineteenth century, from MARY SHELLEY's *Frankenstein* (1818) to BRAM STOKER's *Dracula* (1897), the Gothic narrative evolved into the horror story, a popular staple of a number of important British authors. In the late eighteenth century, ANN RADCLIFFE turned Walpole's Gothic story into popular romance fiction. A century later, ARTHUR CONAN DOYLE took the detective tale from the American EDGAR ALLAN POE—who had himself adopted numerous literary motifs from Walpole's Gothic model—and made it one of England's most popular genres. Masters of the embryonic adventure narrative, such as EDGAR WALLACE and SAX ROHMER, owed their success to the Gothic archetype, as did the early pioneers of high fantasy, WILLIAM MORRIS and LORD DUNSANY, and their more contemporary literary offspring, science fiction authors.

As popular fiction resulted in the evolution of new commercial markets and new formulas, it also resulted in the development of new methods of production. It became the fiction of the Industrial Age—the age of the machine and the factory. With increased demand for more stories, the production and distribution of these stories became an industry—a "fiction factory"—that paralleled the growth of big business. A number of enterprising authors began making a living from their writing, a feat rarely witnessed before mass production printing, and a few became wealthy. Many of these authors throughout the nineteenth century embarked upon the career of the professional author by way of the newspaper, and, hence, the form of the newspaper story became the form of popular fiction. Paragraphs shortened, sentences shrank, and words became simpler. Indeed, authors were streamlining the language of popular stories, making it less obtrusive to the telling of the story, more succinct, easier to digest mentally, and more entertaining for a less-educated and even broader readership. Increased productivity meant increased earnings. The new breed of popular writer became more adept at discovering better ways of making money from his or her writing, first publishing stories in the serial magazines and then collecting those stories into book form, thus earning more than one income for the same piece of fiction. As more authors entered the various popular fiction markets and as publishers challenged each other for dominance of the market, the popular story became more specialized (more fractionalized) in order to sell to a targeted audience. By the end of the nineteenth century, the shape of the popular story was recognizable to the contemporary reader. The formulaic offspring of the Gothic parent—the adventure story, the horror story, the detective story, the science fiction story, and the romance—subdivided themselves into an array of subformulas, each with its own variant of rigidly codified plot structures, character types, and settings.

History and Criticism

Orel, Harold. *Popular Fiction in England, 1914–1918*. U. Pr. of Ky. 1992 $28.00. ISBN 0-8131-1789-5. Despite its highly specific focus, a useful study of British popular fiction.

Raven, James. *Judging New Wealth: Popular Publishing and Responses to Commerce in England, 1750–1800*. OUP 1992 $79.00. ISBN 0-19-820237-7. A revealing look at the commercial side of the British popular press during its formative years.

Richetti, John J. *Popular Fiction before Richardson: Narrative Patterns*. OUP 1992 $18.95. ISBN 0-19-811263-7. A discussion of the early development of British popular fiction.

Roberts, Thomas J. *An Aesthetics of Junk Fiction*. U. of Ga. Pr. 1990 $30.00. ISBN 0-8203-1149-9. The single best theoretical analysis of popular literature.

Adventure/Thriller

An important element of popular fiction is its ability to reflect society. Rarely is this cultural reflection totally accurate, but even in its most exaggerated form, popular fiction may provide the astute observer with useful information about what interests a particular society—such things as what frightens us (horror fiction), what attracts us (romance fiction), and what excites us (adventure fiction). In fact, nowhere is the so-called cultural mirror aspect of popular fiction more evident than in the adventure story. Authors like H. RIDER HAGGARD and RUDYARD KIPLING, for example, wrote adventure fiction that was emblematic of Great Britain's imperialistic and political concerns in Africa and India. Besides his famous Sherlock Holmes series, ARTHUR CONAN DOYLE wrote adventure stories representative of England's preoccupation, during the 1900s, with the exploration of exotic locales. Immediately following the turn of the century, SAX ROHMER's tales of oriental menace—the incorporation of the "yellow peril" stereotype in his adventure fiction—mirrored Great Britain's and Europe's concern with a spirit of nationalism in China and Japan that potentially threatened economic and political holdings in the East. The popular spy fiction of IAN FLEMING and JOHN LE CARRÉ, published during the 1950s and 1960s, symbolized England's involvement in the cold war. The villains of these spy stories frequently were the sociopolitical villains of Western democracy, who heralded the perceived threat of Communist aggression.

As evidenced in the work of the popular writers discussed below, the thematic frame of the typical adventure story is rooted in narrative action. Action predominates; death looms behind every obstacle confronting the protagonist. The protagonist typically undergoes a series of arduous trials and a process of entrapments and escapes that scholar John Cawelti suggests is a celebration of humanity's eventual triumph over death.

HISTORY AND CRITICISM

Atkins, John. *The British Spy Novel*. Riverrun NY 1989 $24.95. ISBN 0-7145-3997-X. The best analysis of the genre.

Denning, Michael. *Cover Stories: Narrative and Ideology in the British Spy Thriller*. Routledge 1987 $11.95. ISBN 0-7100-9642-9. Thought-provoking discussions of writers and their works.

Dove, George N. *Suspense in the Formula Story.* Bowling Green Univ. 1989 $25.95. ISBN 0-87972-455-2. Early chapters analyze the narrative dynamics of popular suspense fiction.

McCormick, Donald, and Katy Fletcher. *Spy Fiction: A Connoisseur's Guide.* Facts on File 1990 $23.95. ISBN 0-8160-2098-1. Lists over 200 British and American spy novels.

Sampson, Robert. *Yesterday's Faces: A Study of Series Characters in the Early Pulp Magazines.* Bowling Green Univ. 1983 $21.95. ISBN 0-87972-217-7. The first volume of a series that examines popular pulp adventure fiction in England and America.

COLLECTION

Bloom, Clive, ed. *Spy Thrillers: From Buchan to Le Carré.* St. Martin 1991 $35.00. ISBN 0-312-04245-0. Representative criticism on neglected subjects and plot overviews.

CHRONOLOGY OF AUTHORS

Haggard, H. Rider. 1856–1925
Wallace, Edgar. 1875–1932
Rohmer, Sax. 1883–1959

Fleming, Ian. 1908–1964
Le Carré, John. 1931–

FLEMING, IAN. 1908–1964

With his suave and debonair character James Bond, Ian Fleming created the world's most famous fictional secret agent. Born in London in 1908, Fleming was educated at Eton College, the Royal Military Academy at Sandhurst, the University of Munich, and the University of Geneva. He worked as a Moscow news correspondent, a banker, a stockbroker, and a publisher. Fleming's experience in naval intelligence during World War II provided him with firsthand insight into the operations of intelligence agencies.

Fleming's first James Bond novel, *Casino Royale* (1954), introduced a series of immensely popular stories that balanced masculine fantasy with precise factual details, all of which were fabricated in narratives that thrived on adventure, graphic sex, and violence. Fleming did not invent the genre of the secret agent thriller; that was accomplished in the pages of the American and British dime novel, and pulp and serial magazines. What Fleming ultimately achieved in his James Bond adventures, however, was something that KINGSLEY AMIS called the "Fleming effect," the ability to describe food, clothing, and exotic settings accurately so that the larger-than-life exploits of Bond and his adversaries were more palatable to the reader's sensibilities. Fleming also wrote one children's book, *Chitty-Chitty-Bang-Bang,* and several travelogues. As ARTHUR CONAN DOYLE created a superhero in Sherlock Holmes that was emblematic of the Victorian era, so Fleming produced in James Bond a slick and sophisticated hero representative of the cold war years. Fleming's Bond found equal success in the popular cinema, and following Fleming's death, accomplished authors such as Kingsley Amis and JOHN GARDNER wrote novels featuring the deathless secret agent.

NOVELS BY FLEMING

Casino Royale. 1955. Berkley Pub. $3.95. ISBN 0-425-08162-1. Bond's first adventure.

Diamonds Are Forever. 1956. Berkley Pub. 1980 $3.95. ISBN 0-425-08986-X. Bond battles a group of American diamond smugglers.

Doctor No. 1958. Berkley Pub. 1980 $3.95. ISBN 0-425-08679-8. The villain is influenced by Sax Rohmer's Fu Manchu character.

For Your Eyes Only. 1960. Diamond 1985 $3.50. ISBN 1-55773-123-3. Bond races to recover a top secret communications device from a sunken ship.

From Russia with Love. 1957. Berkley Pub. 1986 $3.95. ISBN 0-425-08620-8. A violent thriller about love and espionage in Russia.

Goldfinger. 1959. Berkley Pub. 1980 $3.50. ISBN 0-425-08165-6. Bond tries to prevent evil Auric Goldfinger from knocking off Fort Knox.

Live and Let Die. 1955. Diamond 1989 $3.95. ISBN 1-55773-263-9

The Man with the Golden Gun. 1965. NAL-Dutton 1966 $4.50. ISBN 0-451-15855-5. Bond faces off against the insidious Scaramanga, a brilliant madman on the verge of building a new superweapon.

Moonraker. Berkley Pub. 1987 $4.50. ISBN 0-425-13493-8. Villains hijack a space shuttle and intend to depopulate the Earth from a gigantic radar-proof space station.

Octopussy. 1966. NAL-Dutton 1983 $2.50. ISBN 0-451-11878-2. Bond goes off to join the circus, only the clowns are international terrorists.

On Her Majesty's Secret Service. 1963. NAL-Dutton 1964 $3.50. ISBN 0-451-15432-0. Bond prevents villains from releasing a deadly virus over the Earth.

The Spy Who Loved Me. 1962. Diamond $3.95. ISBN 1-55773-300-7. Bond teams up with beautiful Russian agent to crush archvillain Karl Stromberg's plan to hold the world hostage.

Thunderball. 1961. Berkley Pub. 1985 $3.95. ISBN 0-425-08634-8. Villains steal an experimental bomber and hold NATO hostage for 50 million dollars.

You Only Live Twice. 1964. NAL-Dutton 1965 $3.50. ISBN 0-451-15348-0. Bond goes to Japan to stop villains from starting World War III.

BOOKS ABOUT FLEMING

Boyd, Ann. *The Devil with James Bond*. Greenwood 1975 repr. of 1967 ed. $38.50. ISBN 0-8371-7182-2. A solid review of Fleming and James Bond.

Bryce, Ivar. *You Only Live Once: Memories of Ian Fleming*. Greenwood 1975 $42.95. ISBN 0-313-26999-8. A useful, though somewhat limited, discussion of Fleming.

HAGGARD, H. RIDER. 1856–1925

Along with RUDYARD KIPLING, Haggard's friend as well as a professional associate, H. Rider Haggard was one of the most important authors of popular adventure stories in Victorian England. Haggard's popularity—unlike Kipling's—has significantly waned in the twentieth century. Haggard was born in Bradenham, Norfolk. He worked in South Africa between 1875 and 1877 as secretary to Sir Henry Bulwer, the lieutenant-governor of Natal. After returning to England in 1879, Haggard worked in local politics in East Norfolk, became an editor for the *African Review* in 1898, and researched and wrote about agriculture. Toward the end of his life, Haggard spent much of his time in public service and was knighted in 1912.

Haggard's forte as a writer of adventure stories was his ability to combine high fantasy and history. He invented the "lost world" story, which was later imitated in the popular fiction of ARTHUR CONAN DOYLE, EDGAR RICE BURROUGHS, A. Merritt, and Robert E. Howard. Haggard's two series characters were the "great white hunter" Allan Quatermain, who was introduced in the 1885 novel *King Solomon's Mines*, and the immortal goddess Ayesha, who first appeared in *She: A History of Adventure* (1887). Haggard brought together these two popular characters in the adventure novel *She and Allan*. Haggard's skill as a popular storyteller was evidenced by the impact that his fiction had on public perception in England and America before the turn of the century; for many, the "dark continent" was Haggard's Africa. As with Kipling, Haggard, though well liked by the mass readership, was frequently attacked by the literary critics of his time for the unabashed use of adventure in his fiction. During the twentieth century, Kipling's critical reception has warmed somewhat, while Haggard's has not. The fact that much of Haggard's writings remain out of print is a loss for the contemporary reader, since he was perhaps the finest adventure writer of the nineteenth century.

NOVELS BY HAGGARD

Allan Quatermain. 1887. Puffin Bks. 1991 $2.95. ISBN 0-14-035117-5. Adventure in the land of Zu-Vendis ruled by two beautiful queens.
Allan's Wife. Newcastle Pub. 1980 $5.95. ISBN 0-87877-123-9. The fictional tale of Allen Quatermain and his wife Stella, with the history of some further adventures that he encountered.
Ayesha: The Return of She. 1905. Dover 1978 $4.95. ISBN 0-486-23649-8. The sequel to *She*; further episodes in the life of the queen known as She Who Must Be Obeyed.
Eric Brighteyes. Zebra 1982 $2.95. ISBN 0-8217-1042-7
Heart of the World. Newcastle Pub. 1976 $5.95. ISBN 0-87877-109-3. The fantasy story of the Golden City, known as the Heart of the World, and the two men who saw it.
King Solomon's Mines. 1885. Puffin Bks. 1983 $2.25. ISBN 0-14-035014-4. Haggard's most famous adventure story, about the search for treasure in Africa.
Morning Star. Zebra 1978 $2.25. ISBN 0-89083-384-2
Nada the Lily. 1892. Newcastle Pub. 1979 $5.95. ISBN 0-87877-119-0. Umslopgaas, the Zulu chief, is involved in a series of exciting adventures.
The Pearl Maiden. Zebra 1978 $2.50. ISBN 0-89083-352-4
She. 1887. Airmont 1967 $1.95. ISBN 0-8049-0146-5. Perhaps Haggard's best novel; adventure of Leo Vincey, whose quest for revenge leads him to a mysterious queen.

LE CARRÉ, JOHN (pseud. of David John Moore Cornwell). 1931–

John le Carré is the pseudonym of David John Moore Cornwell, who was born in Poole, Dorset. Along with IAN FLEMING, le Carré was one of the most popular and influential authors of the post–World War II secret-agent thriller. Yet, in contrast to Fleming's fantasylike portrayal of spies and their milieu, le Carré's vision of the cold war era is dark, grim, and starkly realistic. Following his education at Berne University in Switzerland and at Oxford University, where he graduated with honors in modern languages in 1956, le Carré was employed as a tutor at Eton College and later worked in the British Foreign Service, served as second secretary at the Bonn Embassy, and was consul in Hamburg.

Le Carré's diverse experience in the worlds of academe and international politics helped him with the writing of his espionage novels. His significant series character is George Smiley, who reminds the reader more of a common bureaucrat than a glamorous spy. Smiley first appeared in the novel *Call for the Dead* (1961). Le Carré's portrayal of espionage examines the moral ambivalence of cold war politics. Clear-cut issues of right and wrong that are easily recognizable in Fleming's work are more muddled in le Carré's fiction. Thus, reading le Carré's work becomes a type of literary existential experience. Of the many writers of spy fiction, le Carré is one of the most highly regarded. He has won considerable recognition for his talents, including the British Crime Novel Award (1963), the Mystery Writers of America "Edgar" Award (1965), and Grand Master Award (1984).

NOVELS BY LE CARRÉ

Call for the Dead. 1961. Bantam 1990 $4.95. ISBN 0-553-26623-3
The Honourable Schoolboy. 1977. Knopf 1977 $24.95. ISBN 0-394-41645-7. An espionage novel featuring series character George Smiley; set in the Far East.
The Little Drummer Girl. 1983. Knopf 1983 $24.95. ISBN 0-394-53015-2. Brilliant spy thriller about Charlie, an actress who becomes a double agent.

Looking Glass War. 1965. Ballantine 1992 $5.99. ISBN 0-345-37736-2
The Naive and Sentimental Lover. 1971. Bantam 1984 $4.50. ISBN 0-553-26821-X
A Perfect Spy. 1986. Knopf 1986 $18.95. ISBN 0-394-55141-9
The Russia House. 1989. Knopf 1989 $19.95. ISBN 0-394-57789-2. A dissident Soviet physicist meets a down-at-the-heels London publisher.
A Small Town in Germany. 1968. Bantam 1990 $5.95. ISBN 0-553-28619-6
Smiley's People. 1979. Knopf 1979 $25.00. ISBN 0-394-50843-2. Concluding volume in the heralded Karla trilogy.
The Spy Who Came in from the Cold. 1963. Ballantine 1992 $5.99. ISBN 0-345-37737-0. The le Carré novel that best embodies the political angst of the cold war era.
Tinker, Tailor, Soldier, Spy. 1974. Knopf 1974 $24.50. ISBN 0-394-49219-6. An intriguing spy fiction novel about betrayal and secrecy in the Cold War era with some series characters found in le Carré's other works.

SHORT STORY COLLECTION BY LE CARRÉ

The Secret Pilgrim. 1990. Knopf 1990 $21.95. ISBN 0-394-58842-8. A collection of superbly crafted stories describing every aspect of security work.

BOOKS ABOUT LE CARRÉ

Barley, Tony. *Taking Sides: The Fiction of John le Carré.* Taylor & Francis 1986 $29.95. ISBN 0-335-15252-X
Lewis, Peter. *John le Carré.* Continuum 1985 $16.95. ISBN 0-8044-2522-1. A study of the novels and their descriptions of espionage, including quotations from interviews between le Carré and the author.
Wolfe, Peter. *Corridors of Deceit: The World of John le Carré.* Bowling Green Univ. 1987 $32.95. ISBN 0-87972-381-5. An exceptional study of le Carré's works by one of the finest scholars of popular adventure and mystery fiction.

ROHMER, SAX (pseud. of Arthur Henry Sarsfield Ward). 1883–1959

Sax Rohmer was born in Birmingham, Warwickshire. At the age of 18, he adopted the name Sarsfield, the name of a famous Irish general admired by Rohmer's mother. He married Rose Elizabeth Knox in 1909 and, at his wife's insistence, began using the name Sax Rohmer for his fiction, eventually employing the pseudonym as his actual name. Rohmer was basically a self-taught scholar. He started writing as a journalist; his beat was the Limehouse underworld in London. Rohmer had a difficult time breaking into the professional fiction markets, but once he did, he became a household name for exotic adventure both in England and in America. Although his writing brought Rohmer success and money, he was never much of a businessman, and most of his wealth was squandered because of his extravagance and through financial mismanagement. Rohmer eventually moved to New York City.

One of Rohmer's great intellectual interests was the occult and supernatural, and these elements frequently appeared as motifs in his fiction. His most famous creation was the evil oriental mastermind, Dr. Fu Manchu, first presented in the novel *The Mystery of Fu Manchu* in 1913 (later retitled *The Insidious Dr. Fu Manchu* for its American publication, also in 1913). Most espionage or adventure fiction exploits the social paranoias of its time, and Rohmer himself effectively tapped the Westerner's fear of the stereotyped "yellow peril" threat—the negatively perceived belief that Orientals will conquer the world. The Fu Manchu adventures were patterned, in part, after ARTHUR CONAN DOYLE's Sherlock Holmes stories. Rohmer's protagonists in these adventures, Sir Denis Nayland Smith and his companion Dr. Petrie, look very much like Doyle's Holmes and Watson, but, whereas Doyle centered his narratives on the heroes and specifically on the elaborate process of detection, Rohmer focused his attention on the villain and on slam-bang action. Fu Manchu was a master of both Western science and Eastern mysticism, and his efforts at world domination caused no end of problems for Smith and Petrie. In Fu Manchu, Rohmer had created the most famous villain in popular fiction (although Rohmer maintained that Fu Manchu was based on an actual Limehouse criminal). Despite Rohmer's use of outrageous racial stereotyping, many of his novels hold up well today and provide superior examples of how to create narrative pacing and suspense.

NOVELS BY ROHMER

The Day the World Ended. Amereon Ltd. 1976 repr. of 1930 ed. $19.95. ISBN 0-89190-804-8

The Emperor of America. Amereon Ltd. 1976 repr. of 1929 ed. $18.95. ISBN 0-89190-805-6

The Golden Scorpion. Amereon Ltd. 1976 repr. of 1920 ed. $19.95. ISBN 0-89190-806-4

The Hand of Fu Manchu. Amereon Ltd. 1976 repr. of 1917 ed. $19.95. ISBN 0-89190-802-1. Nayland Smith and Petrie attempt to apprehend Dr. Fu Manchu in England.

The Insidious Fu Manchu. Lightyear 1976 $13.95. ISBN 0-89968-143-3. The amazing adventures of Nayland Smith as he trails the sinister Dr. Fu Manchu. Reveals some of Rohmer's best work.

The Mask of Fu Manchu. Amereon Ltd. 1976 repr. of 1932 ed. $20.95. ISBN 0-89190-803-X. More adventures of the evil genius of the Orient, Dr. Fu Manchu, who is suspected of using religious furor to further his own evil ends, as Sir Lionel attempts to recover the mask of the prophet El Mokanna.

The Romance of Sorcery. Amereon Ltd. 1976 repr. of 1914 ed. $19.95. ISBN 0-89190-808-0

Tales of Secret Egypt. Amereon Ltd. 1976 repr. of 1918 ed. $19.95. ISBN 0-89190-809-9

BOOK ABOUT ROHMER

Van Ash, Cay, and Elizabeth Sax Rohmer. *Master of Villainy: A Biography of Sax Rohmer.* Bowling Green Univ. 1972 o.p. The essential biography.

WALLACE, EDGAR. 1875–1932

Among the most prolific of all authors of adventure fiction was the redoubtable Edgar Wallace. Born in London, Wallace received his early education at St. Peter's School and the Board School. Wallace served in the Royal West Kent Regiment in England and later as part of the Medical Staff Corps stationed in South Africa. During World War I, Wallace acted as a special interrogator for the War Office. As was the case with a number of successful popular authors, Wallace experienced a rich and diverse life before turning to professional writing. From 1886 to the 1930s, he worked in a printing shop, a shoe shop, and a rubber factory, and served as a merchant sailor and milk deliverer. Beginning in 1899, Wallace became a journalist and wrote variously for the London *Daily Mail* and the *Rand Daily News*, among others; he also worked with the racing periodicals, having founded two of them—*Bibury's Weekly* and *R. E. Walton's Weekly*. Like SAX ROHMER, Wallace earned a fortune from his writings, yet, because of a lack of business sense and a tendency to overspend, he died in debt.

A prodigious writer of fiction, Wallace published, over the course of his professional life, some 173 books and wrote 17 plays. Many of his adventure narratives featured elements of crime or mystery, but they all thrived on action. Although Wallace's handling of plot was superb and he was respected for his ability to blend suspense with humor, he was less successful with his characters, who tended to be two-dimensional and stereotyped. One of his early crime adventures, *The Four Just Men* (1906), introduced what was to become a trademark for Wallace—lurid sensationalism coupled with dramatic violence.

Wallace published in a wide range of genres, including poetry, short fiction, autobiography, and epic political history. Regrettably, much of what he wrote has lapsed into obscurity today. As sometimes is the problem with popular fiction, perhaps it was too hurriedly written—too intimately connected with its contemporary audience—to stand the ultimate test of time. But Wallace's work was highly influential, especially in the American pulp magazine markets of the Great Depression, and stands today, despite its many flaws, as some of the most effective literary adventures ever written.

NOVELS BY WALLACE

Again the Three Just Men. Ayer repr. of 1933 ed. $18.00. ISBN 0-8369-3658-2. Follows the adventures of Manfred, Gonsalez, and Poiccart as they fight for justice.
The Fellowship of the Frog. Curley Pub. 1989 $12.95. ISBN 0-86220-765-7
The Forger. Lightyear 1981 $14.95. ISBN 0-89968-232-4
The Four Just Men. 1906. Lightyear 1976 $14.95. ISBN 0-89968-155-7. A story of people working together to stop passage of a bill that would threaten the life of a just man.
The Murder Book of J. G. Reeder. Dover 1982 $3.95. ISBN 0-486-24374-5

Gothic/Horror

The Gothic story was the first genre of popular fiction in England, and in many ways the most critically suspect. Though the romantic movement in England and the rest of Europe enjoyed substantial critical success in poetry, such as that of WILLIAM WORDSWORTH, SAMUEL TAYLOR COLERIDGE, LORD BYRON, PERCY BYSSHE SHELLEY, and JOHN KEATS, the Gothic novels that were an offshoot, in part, of the same romantic movement engendered considerably more scorn from the critics, despite their popularity with the mass readership. Exotic invention, such as found in the novels of HORACE WALPOLE and MATTHEW GREGORY LEWIS, was then perhaps more intellectually palatable in the guise of poetry, or maybe the Gothic stories of the time were too deeply rooted in folklore and in a culture indigenous to the lower classes. Perhaps Walpole's dark castles suggested entertainment that was more emotional in its appeal than cerebral and thus more suspect to the educated elitist. Whatever the reasons, for nineteenth-century British critics, the fantastic imagination was acceptable in poetry but not in prose. Ironically, the embryonic Gothic imagination in America was better tolerated than in Europe. It was, in fact, the impetus behind much of what was published throughout the literary era known as the American Renaissance. During roughly the same period, while the Gothic in Britain was little more than a guilty pleasure of the English middle-class reader, in the United States the psychological Gothic tale was the narrative form of choice of such talents as CHARLES BROCKDEN BROWN, EDGAR ALLAN POE, NATHANIEL HAWTHORNE, and HERMAN MELVILLE. Unlike the British Gothic, it was the fiction written by the New England cultural elite for the New England elite. It was rarely challenged as being subliterate, as was its European cousin. Although Americans appeared more comfortable with stories of macabre imagination than did their English counterparts, horror and dark fantasy were not beaten into total oblivion in Europe. Instead, the authors of the *fantastique* disguised what they wrote. Some of the finest British horror stories, for example, were written by such authors as MARY SHELLEY and ROBERT LOUIS STEVENSON, who were not limited by the strict confines of genre expectations and who, in fact, were more mainstream (and thus more acceptable in the eyes of the *London Times* literary critic) in their approach to their craft. Rather than being the focus of their stories, horror was only one element from among many they selected to construct their imaginative tales.

HISTORY AND CRITICISM

Barron, Neil, ed. *Horror Literature: A Reader's Guide.* Garland 1990 $55.00. ISBN 0-8240-4347-2. Perhaps the most comprehensive analysis of the genre; an essential reference work.

Heller, Tamar. *Dead Secrets: Wilkie Collins and the Female Gothic.* Yale U. Pr. 1992 $25.00. ISBN 0-300-04574-3. Intended for those conversant with Collins studies.

Heller, Terry. *The Delights of Terror: An Aesthetics of the Tale of Terror.* U. of Ill. Pr. 1987 $11.95. ISBN 0-252-01475-8. Probably the most coherent and well-argued book on the aesthetics of terror.

Kendrick, Walter. *The Thrill of Fear: Two Hundred Fifty Years of Scary Entertainment.* Grove Pr. 1991 $19.95. ISBN 0-8021-1162-9. At time, a wrong-headed but delightful discussion of the social appeal of horror stories.

Twitchell, James B. *Dreadful Pleasures: An Anatomy of Modern Horror.* OUP 1987 $12.95. ISBN 0-19-505067-3. One of the better academic studies of the horror story.

COLLECTIONS

Jones, Stephen, ed. *The Mammoth Book of Terror.* Carroll & Graf 1991 $8.95. ISBN 0-88184-622-8. Ample collection from masters of the genre, including Clive Barker.

Jones, Stephen and Kim Newman, eds. *Horror: The One Hundred Best Books.* Carroll & Graf 1990 $8.95. ISBN 0-88184-594-9. A wide-ranging collection of the works of many writers of the genre.

Morrow, Bradford, and Patrick McGrath. *A Collection of Contemporary Gothic Fiction.* Random 1991 $21.50. ISBN 0-394-58767-7. Collection of stories defining the New Gothic.

CHRONOLOGY OF AUTHORS

Walpole, Horace. 1717–1797	Stoker, Bram. 1847–1912
Lewis, Matthew Gregory. 1775–1818	James, M. R. 1862–1936
Le Fanu, J. Sheridan. 1814–1873	Barker, Clive. 1952–

BARKER, CLIVE. 1952–

Clive Barker frequently has been called the "British STEPHEN KING" by critics of the horror story. Born in Liverpool, Barker attended the University of Liverpool but moved to London in 1977, where he worked as a commercial artist and became involved with the avant-garde theatrical community. Primarily a playwright during this period, he also produced short fiction that he would eventually publish as part of his six-volume *Books of Blood* collection (1984–85).

More than any other author of contemporary horror fiction, Barker has had a tremendous impact on the direction of the genre. He has introduced strong elements of sex and graphic violence into his fiction, but these elements are employed with an artistic objective. As do few of his contemporaries, Barker underscores his work with complex subtextual metaphors and artistic allusions. Preoccupied with the craft of writing and with its effect on the reader, Barker is an innovator of formula and genre, often parodying the former in order to change the philosophical contour of the latter. Barker has achieved commercial success not only with his short fiction but also with his novels. His novels tend to be epic in scope and to blend elements of horror with those of high fantasy. Finally, Barker is one of the more influential voices in horror cinema, having written and directed a number of films.

NOVELS BY BARKER

The Great and Secret Show. HarpC 1990 $5.95. ISBN 0-06-109901-5. The first novel in a projected epic horror-fantasy series.
The Hellbound Heart. HarpC 1991 $4.50. ISBN 0-06-100282-8
Imajica: A Novel. HarpC 1991 $23.00. ISBN 0-06-017922-8. Dazzling metaphysical epic-adventure.
The Inhuman Condition. PB 1991 $4.95. ISBN 0-671-74289-2
In the Flesh. PB 1991 $4.95. ISBN 0-671-74387-2

SHORT STORY COLLECTIONS BY BARKER

Clive Barker's Books of Blood, Volume 1. Berkley Pub. 1986 $4.99. ISBN 0-425-08389-6. Short stories that, some critics say, are his best fiction.
Clive Barker's Books of Blood, Volume 2. Berkley Pub. 1986 $4.99. ISBN 0-425-08739-5
Clive Barker's Books of Blood, Volume 3. Berkley Pub. 1986 $4.95. ISBN 0-425-09347-6. Latest collection of gruesome tales.

BOOKS ABOUT BARKER

Brown, Michael, ed. *Pandemonium: The World of Clive Barker*. Eclipse Bks. 1991 $40.00. ISBN 1-56060-111-6. An intriguing collection of interviews and articles about Barker's work in fiction, film, and comic books.
Jones, Stephen, ed. *Clive Barker's Shadows in Eden*. Underwood-Miller 1991 $39.95. ISBN 0-88733-074-6. Thus far the most comprehensive collection of interviews and essays by and about Barker.

JAMES, M. R. 1862–1936

M. R. James is, along with J. SHERIDAN LE FANU, the finest author of ghost stories in the English language. Although he is somewhat less prolific than Le Fanu, James's handful of elegantly crafted short fiction remains, since first being published, the standard by which all other contemporary ghost stories are judged. James was born in 1862 in Goodnestone, Kent. His early professional interests were in archaeology, later refined to antiquarianism. As a respected academic, he received a fellowship at King's College, Cambridge, in 1887, and later became its provost.

James began writing his ghost stories as an entertainment for his friends; he would read these stories each year at Christmas to his colleagues at King's. The earliest of these tales include "Canon Alberic's Scrap-book" and "Lost Hearts," both of which were later collected in his first anthology of supernatural fiction, *Ghost Stories of an Antiquary* (1904). Perhaps James's single greatest story is the profoundly disturbing "Oh, Whistle, and I'll Come to You, My Lad" (1904). James was a great admirer of the work of Le Fanu and was primarily responsible for resurrecting Le Fanu's work from undeserved obscurity. Like Le Fanu's short stories, James's supernatural fiction is generally understated and powerfully atmospheric.

SHORT STORY COLLECTIONS BY JAMES

The Five Jars. Ayer 1976 repr. of 1922 ed. $14.00. ISBN 0-405-08141-3
Ghost Stories of an Antiquary. 1904. Dover 1971 $3.95. ISBN 0-486-22758-8. First and best collection of James's ghost stories.

More Ghost Stories of an Antiquary. Ayer repr. of 1911 ed. $22.50. ISBN 0-8369-3945-X
Thin Ghost, and Others. Ayer repr. of 1919 ed. $11.00. ISBN 0-8369-3980-8. Fine
    collection of thrilling ghost stories.

LE FANU, J. SHERIDAN. 1814–1873

The greatest author of supernatural fiction during the nineteenth century was
undoubtedly J. Sheridan Le Fanu. Le Fanu was born in Dublin and, as with so
many other English popular fiction authors of his time, entered the genre of
fiction by way of journalism, working on such publications as the *Evening Mail*
and the *Dublin University Magazine*. Le Fanu came from a middle-class
background; his family was of Huguenot descent. He graduated from Trinity
College and married in 1844. After his wife died in 1858, until his own death, Le
Fanu was known as a recluse, creating his ghost fiction late at night in bed.

Probably he began writing ghost fiction in 1838; his earliest supernatural
story is often cited as being either "The Ghost and the Bone-Setter" or the
"Fortunes of Sir Robert Ardagh," both of which were later collected in the
anthology entitled *The Purcell Papers* (1880). Writing most effectively in the
short story form, Le Fanu's tales such as "Carmilla" (a vampire story that is
thought possibly to have influenced BRAM STOKER's *Dracula*) and the problematic "Green Tea" are considered by many literary scholars to be classics of the
supernatural genre. His lengthy Gothic novels, such as *Uncle Silas* (1864),
though less highly regarded than his shorter fiction, are nonetheless wonderfully atmospheric. Le Fanu's particular brand of literary horror tends toward the
refined, subtle fright rather than the graphic sensationalism of MATTHEW
GREGORY LEWIS. His work influenced other prominent horror fiction authors,
including M. R. JAMES.

SHORT STORY COLLECTIONS BY LE FANU

Best Ghost Stories. Dover $7.95. ISBN 0-486-21715-9. One of two books that contain all of
    Le Fanu's short ghost fiction.
The Collected Works of Joseph Sheridan Le Fanu. Ayer 1977 $1,327.50. ISBN 0-405-
    09190-7
Ghost Stories and Mysteries. Dover 1975 $7.95. ISBN 0-486-20715-3. The second volume
    of a comprehensive collection of Le Fanu's short ghost fiction.
The Purcell Papers. 1880. Arkham 1975 $8.95. ISBN 0-87054-072-6

NOVELS BY LE FANU

Uncle Silas. 1864. OUP 1981 $8.95. ISBN 0-19-281541-5. The masterly Goth terror novel
    that explores the ever-present reality of death.
Wylder's Hand. Dover 1978 repr. of 1864 ed. $8.95. ISBN 0-486-23570-X

BOOK ABOUT LE FANU

Begnal, Michael. *Joseph Sheridan Le Fanu*. Bucknell U. Pr. 1975 $4.50. ISBN 0-8387-
    7766-X. A brief but useful analysis of Le Fanu.

LEWIS, MATTHEW GREGORY. 1775–1818

Like HORACE WALPOLE, Matthew Gregory Lewis is primarily known today for
one novel, *The Monk*; yet this single novel garnered much debate, even outrage,
on its initial publication (1796). The poet SAMUEL TAYLOR COLERIDGE, for
example, called the novel "poison," and Lewis was later forced by public
pressure to amend the work. LORD BYRON, on the other hand, was impressed
with *The Monk*, arguing that it was an artistic triumph. As with most other
controversial literary efforts, *The Monk*'s very controversy led it to best-selling

status, and it was subsequently influential in the development of the Gothic story.

Born in London about a year before the American Declaration of Independence, Lewis was inspired during his young adult life by German romanticism, specifically by GOETHE (see Vol. 2), whom Lewis had visited while on a trip to Germany in 1792. Lewis also drew some measure of inspiration from ANN RADCLIFFE's Gothic romance *The Mysteries of Udolpho*. However, Lewis's work differed substantially from that of his peers because of his use of sexual themes. Much of the evil in *The Monk* is sexually motivated: illicit passions manifesting themselves within socially taboo contexts. The Gothic story was generally perceived by its critics as antiestablishment, as a radical branch of its romantic antecedent that, in itself, was viewed suspiciously as too radical. Lewis was the foremost literary extremist in an extreme genre. His blending of sex and the grotesque anticipated contemporary horror fiction trends, such as the hypergraphic fiction written by CLIVE BARKER and the "splatterpunk" school. Yet, aside from the sensational content of his writing, Lewis was an engaging prose stylist, effectively capturing an atmospheric sense of terror and suspense.

NOVELS BY LEWIS

Bravo of Venice, A Romance. Ayer 1972 repr. of 1805 ed. $46.50. ISBN 0-405-00807-4. A tale of treachery and romance in Venice, featuring the dashing Bravo Abellino and his love Rosabella.

The Monk. 1796. OUP 1980 $7.95. ISBN 0-19-281524-5. A Gothic tale about the dissolution of the Abbott Ambrosio, the unhappy love affair of Lorenzo and Antonia, and the adventures of Raymond and Agnes. The definitive critical edition of this important novel.

BOOKS ABOUT LEWIS

Conger, Syndy M. *Matthew G. Lewis, Charles Robert Maturin and the Germans: An Interpretative Study of the Influence of German Literature on Two Gothic Novels.* Ayer 1980 repr. of 1977 ed. $32.50. ISBN 0-405-12652-2. An overly focused analysis, but still useful.

Reno, Robert P. *The Gothic Visions of Ann Radcliffe and Matthew G. Lewis.* Ayer 1980 $28.50. ISBN 0-405-12648-4

STOKER, BRAM. 1847–1912

Bram Stoker's novel *Dracula* has become, since its publication in 1897, one of a handful of the most significant horror stories ever written. As with that other nineteenth-century giant of supernatural fiction, J. SHERIDAN LE FANU, Stoker was born in Dublin. As a child, Stoker listened enrapt while his mother narrated lurid Irish folk tales. Stoker began writing professionally for serial magazines and "penny dreadfuls." His writing ranged in content from somber children's fantasies to short fiction, but it wasn't until *Dracula* was published that he achieved international recognition. Stoker began work on this novel while working as a theater manager for the famous actor Henry Irving. Begun about 1890, the book was finally finished and published in 1897.

Stoker combined in *Dracula* elements of forbidden sexuality barely repressed by a thin Victorian sensibility, thus making *Dracula* symbolically erotic as well as vividly frightening. Focusing on vampires generally and the portrayal of Dracula specifically, Stoker incorporated elements of both folklore and history into his story; within the epistolary structure of the novel, he recounts an epic conflict between traditional evil and contemporary science (represented by the scientist-philosopher Abraham Van Helsing), between Eastern mysticism and

Western pragmaticism, and, ultimately, between the dark past and the enlightened present. In his other occult novels, such as *The Jewel of the Seven Stars* (1903) and *The Lair of the White Worm* (1911), Stoker never seemed to duplicate the success of *Dracula*, yet these works demonstrate his formidable ability as a storyteller. Like MARY SHELLEY's *Frankenstein*, Stoker's *Dracula* has appeared in various popular media reinterpretations through the years, from comic books to movies, becoming in the process one of the archetypal monster figures of the twentieth century.

NOVELS BY STOKER

Dracula. Bantam 1983 $2.95. ISBN 0-553-21271-0. One of the better reprint editions of Stoker's most famous novel.

Dracula's Guest. Zebra 1978 $1.95. ISBN 0-89083-401-6. Less successful sequel to the famous *Dracula*.

The Jewel of the Seven Stars. 1903. Carroll & Graf 1989 $3.95. ISBN 0-88184-501-9. An underestimated novel.

The Lair of the White Worm. 1911. Zebra 1979 $1.95. ISBN 0-89083-519-5. Horror story in which an alluring snake woman lives in a 1000-foot hole on the site of an ancient temple called Diana's Grove.

BOOK ABOUT STOKER

Carter, Margaret. *Dracula: The Vampire and the Critics.* Bks. Demand 1988 $39.95. ISBN 0-8357-1849-1. An anthology of critical essays, with an overview of evaluations of Stoker's work; includes valuable bibliography of studies of Stoker's work.

WALPOLE, HORACE. 1717–1797

For his short novel *The Castle of Otranto*, Horace Walpole is credited with being the creator of the Gothic story in English fiction. In addition, because the Gothic story was literature's first popular formula, he is a founder of the genre of popular fiction itself. At the very least, Walpole's impact on other major Gothic writers, such as ANN RADCLIFFE, William Beckford, MATTHEW GREGORY LEWIS, and MARY SHELLEY, was profound and far-reaching. Walpole was born in London, the third and youngest son of Prime Minister Robert Walpole. Although he was raised in a political family, Walpole demonstrated no interest in choosing a career in politics; instead, he turned to writing. A prolific writer, he is remembered today for only one book, *The Castle of Otranto*, first published in 1764 (some sources give the date as 1765). Walpole claimed that he acquired the idea for this novel during a dream, in which he envisioned a giant armored hand. Yet Walpole's interest in the Gothic, as an architectural style, was evident as early as 1745, when he purchased a cottage at Twickenham, near London, and then enlarged it, transforming it into a Gothic-like castle that he named Strawberry Hill.

Today, *The Castle of Otranto* is nearly unreadable. Its overuse of stilted melodrama, stock characters, and laughable supernatural elements reinforces how dated it is. Historically, however, this Gothic novel is of tremendous importance in understanding the origins of English popular fiction.

NOVEL BY WALPOLE

The Castle of Otranto. 1764. OUP 1982 $3.95. ISBN 0-19-281606-3. The most important Gothic novel in the history of British popular fiction. Set in the Middle Ages, this is the story of an evil usurper, a fateful prophecy, and a mysterious prince and his bride.

Gwynn, Stephen. *The Life of Horace Walpole*. Ayer repr. of 1932 ed. $21.00. ISBN 0-8369-5842-X. A good biography.

Lewis, Wilmarth S. *Rescuing Horace Walpole*. Yale U. Pr. 1978 $45.00. ISBN 0-300-02278-6. The definitive study of Walpole.

Sabor, Peter, ed. *Horace Walpole: The Critical Heritage*. Routledge Chapman & Hall 1988 $69.50. ISBN 0-7100-9956-8

Mystery/Detective

The classic British detective story was, in actuality, invented by an American, EDGAR ALLAN POE, who is generally considered to be the "father" of the genre. British writers like ARTHUR CONAN DOYLE and AGATHA CHRISTIE took Poe's creation, refined it, and remade it as their own, in essence making the classical detective story a specialty of the English popular press. The classic, or British, detective story is most concerned with crime as a form of intellectual puzzle. The hero's generic appellation implies the process of detection of crime and of criminals—and of social taboos. While solving the crime puzzle, the detective searches for useful information and discovers not only the criminal's method and motive but also the relationship between the aberrant individual and society. British detective fiction stages a morality game: The subject of the contest revolves around an individual's violation of taboo (e.g., murder, theft) and society's reaction (as evidenced in the detective hero) to that violation. By successfully completing the game, the detective functions as a metaphoric "doctor" to society, who removes the cancer within that society and restores the validity of a secure moral structure. Some authors of detective fiction find the British model to be too formulaic. In his controversial essay, "The Simple Art of Murder," RAYMOND CHANDLER, an American master of the "hard-boiled" variety of detective fiction, attacks the British detective story as being "dull" and as having an unrealistic view of crime.

HISTORY AND CRITICISM

Barzun, Jacques, and Wendell H. Taylor. *A Catalog of Crime: Being a Reader's Guide to the Literature of Mystery, Detective, and Related Genres*. HarpC 1989 $50.00. ISBN 0-06-010263-2. Lists and describes over 5,000 works.

Binyon, T. J. *Murder Will Out: The Detective in Fiction*. OUP 1990 $8.95. ISBN 0-19-282730-8. Pleasant survey of detective fiction focusing on the detectives themselves.

Haycraft, Howard. *Murder for Pleasure: The Life and Times of the Detective Story*. Carroll & Graf 1984 $10.95. ISBN 0-88184-071-8. The standard history of the genre.

Hoppenstand, Gary. *In Search of the Paper Tiger: A Sociological Perspective of Myth, Formula and the Mystery Genre in the Entertainment Print Mass Medium*. Bowling Green Univ. 1987 $20.95. ISBN 0-87972-355-6. An overview of the various formulas of the mystery genre, including a discussion of the classic British detective story.

Kayman, Martin A. *From Bow Street to Baker Street: Mystery, Detection, and Narrative*. St. Martin 1992 $45.00. ISBN 0-312-06798-4

Oleksiw, Susan P. *A Reader's Guide to the Classic British Mystery*. Macmillan 1988 $35.00. ISBN 0-8161-8787-8. Lists annotations of more than 1440 novels by 121 authors.

Panek, Leroy. *Watteau's Shepherds: The Detective Novel in Britain, 1914–1940*. Bowling Green Univ. 1979 $14.95. ISBN 0-87972-131-6. The single best study written about the British detective story.

COLLECTION

Craig, Patricia. *The Oxford Book of English Detective Stories*. OUP 1990 $25.00. ISBN 0-19-214187-2. A splendid array of 33 prime examples of this genre.

CHRONOLOGY OF AUTHORS

Doyle, Arthur Conan. 1859–1930
Christie, Dame Agatha. 1890–1976
Sayers, Dorothy. 1893–1957

Peters, Ellis. 1913–
Rendell, Ruth. 1930–

CHRISTIE, DAME AGATHA. 1890–1976

Some two decades after her death, Agatha Christie remains one of the most widely read writers of detective fiction in the world. Born in Torquay, Devon, Christie received a private education at home. In 1914 she married her first husband, Colonel Archibald Christie. She later married Sir Max Mallowan, an archaeologist, and her experiences on some trips with him were used as settings for some of her famous mysteries. While working as a volunteer at a hospital, she conceived the idea of writing a mystery novel as a way of escaping the stress of daily life. After several unsuccessful attempts to place her first book with a publisher, she sold it for a meager sum. In 1926 Christie experienced a highly publicized episode, as lurid as anything that appeared in her crime fiction; she seemingly disappeared for some time, afterward claiming that she had been afflicted with amnesia. Such publicity enhanced her already growing popularity. She went on to produce a substantial amount of fiction, both novels and short stories, as well as poetry and drama (some of her work was published under the pseudonym of Mary Westmacott).

Along with DOROTHY SAYERS, Christie heralded what was later regarded as the Silver Age of detective fiction. Her first novel, *The Mysterious Affair at Styles* (1920), introduced one of her two most famous protagonists, Hercule Poirot. The Belgian Poirot takes up residence in England after he has been forced to flee his country during the German invasion in 1914. Christie patterned the egotistical Poirot and his assistant, Captain Hastings, after ARTHUR CONAN DOYLE's Sherlock Holmes and Dr. Watson, but, whereas Doyle wrote most of his Holmes tales in the short novel or short story form, Christie's forte was the detective novel. By the time she published the controversial Poirot mystery *The Murder of Roger Ackroyd* (1926), she had become an acknowledged master of the form. Christie's other famous detective character, the elderly village spinster Miss Jane Marple, was introduced in *The Murder at the Vicarage* (1930). Miss Marple, who resides in the quaint English village of St. Mary Mead, is supposedly patterned after Christie's grandmother. Other protagonists in her prolific canon include Superintendent Battle, who first appears in *The Secret of Chimneys* (1925); Tommy and Tuppence Beresford, who first appeared in *The Secret Adversary* (1922); and Colonel Race, who first appeared in *The Man in the Brown Suit* (1924). Christie's strength as a popular writer of detective fiction was her ability to challenge her reader with a baffling mystery and then, by the conclusion of the story, provide a solution that is both ingenious and perfectly logical.

NOVELS BY CHRISTIE

And Then There Were None. Berkley Pub. 1991 $3.99. ISBN 0-425-12958-6. One of
   Christie's most frequently reprinted novels. Tale is structured around a nursery
   rhyme in which all the characters are eliminated, one by one.

Death on the Nile. 1937. Bantam 1983 $3.50. ISBN 0-553-26138-X. A novel emblematic of
　　Christie's love for exotic settings.
The Man in the Brown Suit. 1924. Berkley Pub. 1987 $3.99. ISBN 0-425-06786-6
The Murder at the Vicarage. 1930. Berkley Pub. 1991 $3.99. ISBN 0-425-09453-7. The first
　　case solved by Miss Marple, a gentle, kind, and shrewd observer of people.
The Murder of Roger Ackroyd. 1926. PB 1989 $3.95. ISBN 0-671-70118-5. One of Hercule
　　Poirot's most baffling cases.
Murder on the Orient Express. 1934. HarpC 1991 $4.99. ISBN 0-06-100274-7. On a train
　　bound for Istanbul, Poirot looks for a killer whom he would rather not find.
The Mysterious Affair at Styles. 1920. Bantam 1983 $3.50. ISBN 0-553-26587-3
The Mysterious Mr. Quin. Berkley Pub. 1984 $3.99. ISBN 0-425-10353-6
Partners in Crime. 1929. Bantam 1990 $4.50. ISBN 0-553-28472-X
The Secret Adversary: A Tommy and Tuppence Mystery. 1922. Berkley Pub. 1991 $3.99.
　　ISBN 0-425-13027-4. Tommy and Tuppence Beresford decide to open a detective
　　agency, with some comic results.
The Secret of Chimneys. 1925. Berkley Pub. 1984 $3.50. ISBN 0-425-06802-1. Superinten-
　　dent Battle of Scotland Yard joins the ranks of Christie's detectives.
The Witness for the Prosecution. 1948. Berkeley Pub. 1987 $4.50. ISBN 0-425-06809-9

SHORT STORY COLLECTIONS BY CHRISTIE

Hercule Poirot's Casebook: Fifty Stories. Putnam Pub. Group 1984 $18.95. ISBN 0-396-
　　08417-6. A comprehensive collection of Poirot short fiction.
Miss Marple: The Complete Short Stories. Putnam Pub. Group 1985 $16.95. ISBN 0-396-
　　08747-7. A comprehensive collection of Miss Marple short fiction; the companion
　　volume to *Hercule Poirot's Casebook*.

PLAY BY CHRISTIE

The Mousetrap and Other Plays. HarpC 1992 $5.99. ISBN 0-06-100374-3

NONFICTION BY CHRISTIE

Agatha Christie: An Autobiography. Berkley Pub. 1991 $12.95. ISBN 0-425-12739-7. An
　　honest self-portrait of the mystery story writer.

BOOKS ABOUT CHRISTIE

Bargainnier, Earl F. *The Gentle Art of Murder*. Bowling Green Univ. 1981 $17.95. ISBN 0-
　　87972-158-8. A superior discussion of Christie's work.
Barnard, Robert. *A Talent to Deceive: An Appreciation of Agatha Christie*. Dodd Mead
　　1980 o.p. Investigates Christie as a "disappearing author" and her strategies of
　　deception.
Gill, Gillian. *Agatha Christie: The Woman and Her Mysteries*. Free Pr. 1990 $24.95. ISBN
　　0-02-911702-X. Examines the mysteries in terms of cultural ideology.
Maida, Patrick D., and Nicholas B. Spornick. *Murder She Wrote: A Study of Agatha
　　Christie's Detective Fiction*. Bowling Green Univ. 1982 $16.95. ISBN 0-87972-216-9.
　　Explores Christie's themes, focusing on her various detectives.
Morgan, Janet P. *Agatha Christie: A Biography*. Collins 1984 o.p. The definitive account of
　　her life.
Sanders, Dennis, and Len Lovallo. *The Agatha Christie Companion: The Complete Guide
　　to Agatha Christie's Life and Work*. Berkley Pub. 1989 $12.95. ISBN 0-425-11845-2.
　　Bibliography, sourcebook, and accumulation of pertinent facts.
Wagoner, Mary S. *Agatha Christie*. Macmillan 1986 $20.95. ISBN 0-8057-6936-6. A good
　　introduction to Christie's fiction.

DOYLE, ARTHUR CONAN. 1859–1930

The most famous fictional detective in the world is Arthur Conan Doyle's
Sherlock Holmes. However, Doyle was, at best, ambivalent about his immensely
successful literary creation and, at worst, resentful that his more "serious"

fiction was relatively ignored. Born in Edinburgh, Doyle studied medicine from 1876 to 1881 and received his M.D. in 1885. He worked as a military physician in South Africa during the Boer War and was knighted in 1902 for his exceptional service. Doyle was drawn to writing at an early age. Although he attempted to enter private practice in Southsea, Portsmouth, in 1882, he soon turned to writing in his spare time; it eventually became his profession. As a Liberal Unionist, Doyle ran, unsuccessfully, for Parliament in 1903. During his later years, Doyle became an avowed spiritualist.

Doyle sold his first story, "The Mystery of the Sasassa Valley," to *Chambers' Journal* in 1879. After trying, without any luck, to sell several novels, he turned to writing a detective novel patterned after EDGAR ALLAN POE's work. When Doyle published the novel *A Study in Scarlet* in 1887, Sherlock Holmes was introduced to an avid public. Doyle is reputed to have used one of his medical professors, Dr. Joseph Bell, as a model for Holmes's character. Eventually, Doyle wrote three additional Holmes novels and five collections of Holmes short stories. A brilliant, though somewhat eccentric, detective, Holmes employs scientific methods of observation and deduction to solve the mysteries that he investigates. Although an "amateur" private detective, he is frequently called upon by Scotland Yard for assistance. Holmes's assistant, the faithful Dr. Watson, provides a striking contrast to Holmes's brilliant intellect and—in Doyle's day, at least—serves as a character with whom the reader can readily identify. Having tired of Holmes's popularity, Doyle even tried to kill the great detective in "The Final Problem" but was forced by an outraged public to resurrect him in 1903. Although Holmes remained Doyle's most popular literary creation, Doyle wrote prolifically in other genres, including historical adventure, science fiction, and supernatural fiction. Despite Doyle's sometimes careless writing, he was a superb storyteller. His great skill as a popular author lay in his technique of involving readers in his highly entertaining adventures.

NOVELS BY DOYLE

Brigadier Gerard. 1887. Gaslight 1992 $24.95. ISBN 0-934468-20-6
Sir Nigel. 1906. Amereon Ltd. $23.95. ISBN 0-88411-538-0
A Study in Scarlet. 1887. Buccaneer Bks $15.95. ISBN 0-89966-231-5
The Valley of Fear. 1915. Viking Penguin 1991 $6.00. ISBN 0-14-005710-2. The final Sherlock Holmes novel, with Holmes more jovial than in previous novels.
The White Company. 1890. Morrow 1988 $17.00. ISBN 0-668-07817-6. An attractive edition of one of Doyle's better historical novels.

SHORT STORY COLLECTIONS BY DOYLE

Best Supernatural Tales of Arthur Conan Doyle. Dover 1979 $6.95. ISBN 0-486-23725-7. An exceptional collection of stories.
Complete Sherlock Holmes. 2 vols. Bantam 1986 $9.90. ISBN 0-553-32825-5. Second best anthology of Sherlock Holmes stories for those unable to acquire *The Annotated Sherlock Holmes.*
The Professor Challenger Adventures: The Lost World and the Poison Belt. Chronicle Bks. 1989 $8.95. ISBN 0-87701-620-8. Some of Doyle's finest imaginative fiction outside of his Sherlock Holmes series.
Tales of Terror and Mystery. Buccaneer Bks. 1982 $16.95. ISBN 0-89966-429-6

WORKS BY DOYLE

The Annotated Sherlock Holmes: The Four Novels and the Fifty-six Short Stories. Outlet Bk. Co. 1992 $29.99. ISBN 0-685-57417-2. The single best collection of Holmes stories.
The Memoirs of Sherlock Holmes. North Bks. 1986 $22.00. ISBN 0-939495-31-7

Memories and Adventures. Rprt. Serv. 1992 repr. of 1924 ed. $99.00. ISBN 0-7812-7522-9. Conan Doyle's memoirs.

Sherlock Holmes: The Complete Novels and Stories. 2 vols. Bantam 1986 Vol. 1 $4.95. ISBN 0-553-21241-9. Vol. 2 $4.95. ISBN 0-553-21242-7. Contains all 56 stories and all 4 of his novels.

BOOKS ABOUT DOYLE

Carr, John. *The Life of Sir Arthur Conan Doyle.* Carroll & Graf 1987 $8.95. ISBN 0-88184-372-5. One of the best standard references.

Hardwick, Michael. *The Complete Guide to Sherlock Holmes.* St. Martin 1986. ISBN 0-312-00580-6. Concordance of names and places in the Sherlock Holmes tales.

Jaffe, Jacqueline A. *Arthur Conan Doyle.* Macmillan 1987 $19.95. ISBN 0-8057-6954-4. A good introduction to Doyle's life and work.

Orel, Harold, ed. *Critical Essays on Sir Arthur Conan Doyle.* G. K. Hall 1992 $40.00. ISBN 0-816-18865-3

Symons, Julian. *Conan Doyle: Portrait of an Artist.* Mysterious Pr. 1988 $9.95. ISBN 0-89296-926-1. The best analysis of Doyle, written by an accomplished mystery writer.

Tracy, Jack, ed. *The Encyclopaedia Sherlockiana.* Doubleday 1977 o.p. Contains 3,500 main entries, 8,000 story citations, over 200 illustrations, and an extensive cross-reference system.

PETERS, ELLIS (pseud. of Edith Pargeter). 1913–

Born in Horsehay, Shropshire, Peters was a chemist's assistant from 1933 to 1940 and participated during World War II in the Women's Royal Navy Service. She came to writing mysteries, she says, "after half a lifetime of novel-writing." Her detective fiction features well-rounded, knowledgeable characters with whom the reader can empathize. Her most famous literary creation is the medieval monk Brother Cadfael. The blend of history and the formula of the detective story gives Peters's works their popular appeal. As detective hero, Brother Cadfael remains faithful to the requirements of the formula, yet the historical milieu in which he operates is both fully realized and well textured. Peters received the Mystery Writers of America's Edgar Award in 1963 and the Crime Writers Association's Silver Dagger Award in 1981.

NOVELS BY PETERS

The Benediction of Brother Cadfael. Mysterious Pr. 1992 $35.00. ISBN 0-89296-449-9. The third mystery/adventure about Brother Cadfael, in which the medieval monk sets out to solve the puzzling murder of a kindly benefactor to his monastery.

Black Is the Color of My True Love's Heart. Warner Bks. 1992 $4.99. ISBN 0-446-40072-6

The Confessions of Brother Haluin. Warner Bks. 1989 $4.99. ISBN 0-445-40855-3. Continuing story of Brother Cadfael as amateur sleuth.

Dead Man's Ransom. Fawcett 1986 $4.95. ISBN 0-449-20819-2. Brother Cadfael solves a political murder mystery.

Flight of a Witch. Mysterious Pr. 1991 $16.95. ISBN 0-89296-404-9. A trio of novels that features Detective Chief Inspector George Felse.

The Heretic's Apprentice. Mysterious Pr. 1990 $16.95. ISBN 0-89296-381-6. Imbues the familiar territory of murder, young love, and odious villainry.

The Hermit of Eyton Forest. Warner Bks. 1989 $4.50. ISBN 0-445-40347-0. In Brother Cadfael's fourteenth appearance, he plays matchmaker, doctor, and shrewd sleuth.

The Knocker on Death's Door. Warner Bks. 1992 $4.99. ISBN 0-446-40016-5

Monk's Hood. Warner Bks. 1992 $4.99. ISBN 0-446-40300-8

A Morbid Taste for Bones. Fawcett 1985 $4.95. ISBN 0-449-20700-5

The Potter's Field. Warner Bks. 1991 $4.99. ISBN 0-446-40058-0. A young woman's body is discovered, and Brother Cadfael must solve the mystery.

Rainbow's End. Warner Bks. 1992 $4.99. ISBN 0-446-40017-3

A Rare Benedictine. Mysterious Pr. 1989 $19.95. ISBN 0-89296-397-2
The Raven in the Foregate. Fawcett 1987 $4.95. ISBN 0-449-21225-4
The Rose Rent. Fawcett 1988 $4.95. ISBN 0-449-21495-8
St. Peter's Fair. Warner Bks. 1992 $4.99. ISBN 0-446-40301-6
The Sanctuary Sparrow. Fawcett 1984 $3.95. ISBN 0-449-20613-0
The Summer of the Danes. Mysterious Pr. 1991 $16.95. ISBN 0-89296-448-0. Brother Cadfael accompanies his former assistant on a mission of church diplomacy.

RENDELL, RUTH. 1930–

In her mystery fiction, Ruth Rendell focuses her formidable creative energies on character. She has discovered that the mystery can be as effectively driven by subtle characterization as by elaborate plot. Born in London, Rendell worked as a newspaper reporter and editor from 1948 to 1952. Her first book, *From Doon with Death* (1964), featured Detective Chief Inspector Reginald Wexford, who became the popular protagonist in a number of Rendell's novels published over the next several decades. Rendell's work is complex, and, even in her more formulaic Inspector Wexford series, she is constantly testing the parameters of the genre. In her fiction, she uses crime as the means by which various characters' motivations may be explored. This later type of crime story profoundly subverts the "cozy" element usually associated with the classic British mystery, but it provides an elegant look into the dark recesses of aberrant human psychology. Rendell was twice the recipient of the Mystery Writers of America's Edgar Award (1975 and 1984) and garnered the Crime Writers Association's Gold Dagger Award in 1977.

NOVELS BY RENDELL

The Best Man to Die. Ballantine 1987 $3.95. ISBN 0-345-34530-4. An excellent mystery story, featuring the series character and protagonist Reginald Wexford.
Death Notes. Ballantine 1986 $4.95. ISBN 0-345-34198-8
From Doon with Death. 1964. Ballantine 1988 $4.95. ISBN 0-345-34817-6
Going Wrong. Mysterious Pr. 1990 $18.95. ISBN 0-89296-389-1. An arresting tale of obsessive love.
Heartstones. Ballantine 1988 $4.95. ISBN 0-345-34800-1. A brief, yet compelling, psychological novel; written in the first-person perspective of a young girl and explores the dark events surrounding her family.
A Judgment in Stone. Bantam 1987 $2.95. ISBN 0-553-26285-8
Master of the Moor. Ballantine 1988 $3.95. ISBN 0-345-00870-7
No More Dying Now. Bantam 1986 $3.50. ISBN 0-553-25968-7
One Across, Two Down. Bantam 1974 $3.50. ISBN 0-553-25975-X
The Secret House of Death. Ballantine 1987 $4.95. ISBN 0-345-34950-4
Talking to Strange Men. Ballantine 1988 $4.99. ISBN 0-345-35174-6. A tale of psychological suspense in which Mungo suspects that a counteragent is betraying London Central.
To Fear a Painted Devil. Ballantine 1987 $3.95. ISBN 0-345-34951-2
An Unkindness of Ravens. Ballantine 1986 $4.95. ISBN 0-345-32746-2
Vanity Dies Hard. Ballantine 1987 $4.95. ISBN 0-345-34952-0
The Veiled One. Ballantine 1989 $4.95. ISBN 0-345-35994-1. The murder of elderly Gwen Robson is investigated.
Wolf to the Slaughter. Ballantine 1987 $4.95. ISBN 0-345-34520-7

SAYERS, DOROTHY. 1893–1957

Dorothy Sayers's impressive reputation as a contemporary master of the classic detective story is eclipsed only by AGATHA CHRISTIE's. Sayers was born in Oxford and attended Somerville College, where she received a B.A. in 1915 and an M.A. in 1920. During that period, Sayers worked as an instructor of modern languages at Hull High School for Girls in Yorkshire and as a reader for a publisher in Oxford. Her early literary work was in poetry; she published several volumes and served as an editor for the journal *Oxford Poetry* from 1917 to 1919. Sayers also worked as a copywriter for a major advertising firm in London. She was president of the Modern Language Association from 1939 to 1945 and of the Detection Club in the 1950s.

Around 1920 Sayers developed the idea for her detective hero Lord Peter Wimsey, and she soon published her first mystery, *Whose Body?* (1923), in which Lord Peter is introduced. For the next dozen or so years, Sayers wrote prolifically about Wimsey, creating in the process what many critics of the genre consider to be the finest detective novels in the English language. Perhaps her most famous Wimsey mystery was *The Nine Tailors* (1934). Although Sayers essentially followed the classic form in her detective fiction—a formula in which the plot assumes a greater importance than do the characters—Sayers maintained that a detective hero's greatness depended on how effectively the character was portrayed. All but one of Sayers's mysteries feature Lord Peter Wimsey. By the late 1930s, Sayers had apparently tired of writing detective fiction. She stated in 1947 that she would write no more mysteries, that she wrote detective fiction only when she was young and in need of money. Thus saying, Sayers turned her attention to her early loves, medieval and religious literature, spending her remaining years lecturing on and translating DANTE (see Vol. 2).

NOVELS BY SAYERS

Busman's Honeymoon. 1937. HarpC 1986 $6.00. ISBN 0-06-080823-3. Lord Peter's honeymoon is interrupted by murder.

Clouds of Witness. 1926. HarpC 1987 $5.95. ISBN 0-06-08035-7. Murder reaches Lord Peter Wimsey in a more personal way when his brother and sister become prime suspects.

Gaudy Night. 1935. HarpC 1986 $6.50. ISBN 0-06-08024-1. Wimsey and his beloved Harriet Vane solve a mystery at Oxford University.

Have His Carcase. 1932. HarpC 1986 $5.95. ISBN 0-06-08027-6. Harriet Vane discovers a body on the beach, and she and Lord Peter must solve the mystery.

Murder Must Advertise. 1933. HarpC 1986 $6.50. ISBN 0-06-080825-X. Murder in an advertising agency.

The Nine Tailors. 1934. HarBraceJ 1966 $5.95. ISBN 0-15-665899-2. The secret is in the ringing church bells.

Strong Poison. 1930. HarpC 1987 $6.00. ISBN 0-06-080826-8. Harriet Vane is accused of murder, and Lord Peter must clear her.

Unnatural Death. 1927 HarpC 1987 $6.50. ISBN 0-06-080840-3. Lord Peter wrestles with his conscience.

The Unpleasantness at the Bellona Club. 1928 HarpC 1987 $6.00. ISBN 0-06-080828-4. Murder strikes at a quiet men's club.

Whose Body? HarpC 1987 $4.95. ISBN 0-06-080829-2. The first novel in which Lord Peter Wimsey appears.

SHORT STORY COLLECTIONS BY SAYERS

Hangman's Holiday. 1933. HarpC 1987 $6.00. ISBN 0-06-080837-3. A dozen stories, some in which Wimsey appears.

In the Teeth of the Evidence. 1939. HarpC 1987 $6.00. ISBN 0-06-080838-1. Seventeen stories of murder and detection, some in which Lord Peter appears.

Lord Peter: A Collection of All the Lord Peter Wimsey Stories. HarpC 1986 $12.00. ISBN 0-06-091380-0. All of the Wimsey short stories in one volume.

Lord Peter Views the Body. 1928. HarpC 1986 $6.50. ISBN 0-06-080839-X. Eleven Wimsey mysteries.

BOOKS ABOUT SAYERS

Brunsdale, Mitzi. *Dorothy L. Sayers: Solving the Mystery of Wickedness.* Berg Pubs. 1990 $39.95. ISBN 0-85496-249-2. An insightful analysis of Sayers's work.

Hone, Ralph E. *Dorothy L. Sayers: A Literary Biography.* Kent St. U. Pr. 1979 $18.00. ISBN 0-87338-228-5. A solid review of Sayers and her work.

Youngberg, Ruth T. *Dorothy L. Sayers: A Reference Guide.* Macmillan 1982 $35.00. ISBN 0-8161-8198-5. A core source of information.

Science Fiction/Fantasy

The British invented the genre of high fantasy. Authors such as WILLIAM MORRIS and LORD DUNSANY helped establish the essential plot motifs that were later duplicated and elaborated on by J. R. R. TOLKIEN in his Lord of the Rings trilogy. What writers like Morris did in the creation of high fantasy during the nineteenth century was to update various elements of traditional medieval legends—such as the tales of King Arthur and the Knights of the Roundtable—being sure, in the process, to emphasize the legends' supernatural and fantastic ingredients. As in most popular fiction, the fundamental narrative conflict in British fantasy is between good and evil. Yet, in the fantasy story, this conflict seems exaggerated, heightened, and taken to the extreme. Good and evil are as diametrically opposed as possible. They are personified in the characters in such a fashion that the typical fantasy narrative often takes on the form of allegory.

Science fiction in England evolved out of the fantasy story in a process that duplicated Britain's developing industrialization. Such authors as H. G. WELLS in his popular early science fantasy novels, like *War of the Worlds* and *The Time Machine*, assisted the transformation of the old genre and the creation of the new science-oriented genre by inventively blending fact and fancy. The author and historian of science fiction BRIAN W. ALDISS defines the genre in his important study *Billion Year Spree: The True History of Science Fiction* (1973). According to Aldiss, "science fiction is the search for a definition of man and his status in the universe which will stand in our advanced but confused state of knowledge (science), and is characteristically cast in the Gothic or post-Gothic mould." Modern-day British science fiction, like its American counterpart, generally has taken two different directions. The one type, as practiced by ARTHUR C. CLARKE, emphasizes the "hard" sciences (physics, mathematics, etc.), whereas the other type, as practiced by Brian Aldiss, stresses the "soft" sciences (sociology, psychology, etc.). Both types of science fiction have proven to be popular in recent years.

HISTORY AND CRITICISM

Aldiss, Brian W. *Trillion Year Spree: The History of Science Fiction.* Avon 1988 $9.95. ISBN 0-380-70461-7. The best study published about the history of the genre.

Barron, Neil, ed. *Anatomy of Wonder: A Critical Guide to Science Fiction.* 3rd ed. Bowker 1987 $48.00. ISBN 0-8352-2312-4. Serves as a unique guide through a maze of literature.

———. *Fantasy Literatuer: A Reader's Guide.* Garland 1990 $55.00. ISBN 0-8240-3148-2. Comprehensive listing of over 1,000 works of fantasy; most with short descriptions.

Ruddick, Nicholas. *British Science Fiction: A Chronology, 1478–1990.* Greenwood 1992 $55.00. ISBN 0-313-28002-9. A comprehensive overview of the genre.

Stableford, Brian. *Scientific Romance in Britain: Eighteen-ninety to Nineteen-fifty*. St. Martin 1985 $29.95. ISBN 0-312-70305-8. A superior analysis of British science fiction.

COLLECTIONS

Aldiss, Brian, and Sam J. Lundwall, eds. *The Penguin World Omnibus of Science Fiction*. Viking Penguin 1987 $4.95. ISBN 0-14-008067-8. Wide-ranging collection from around the world; includes representative works of British writers.

Brown, Charles N., and William G. Contento, eds. *Science Fiction, Fantasy, and Horror: 1990*. Locus Pr. 1991 $50.00. ISBN 0-9616629-8-0. Contains some selections from Great Britain.

Hartwell, David, ed. *The World Treasury of Science Fiction*. Little 1989 $29.95. ISBN 0-685-24900-X. Classic science fiction from around the world.

Williams, Susan, ed. *The Lifted Veil: The Book of Fantastic Literature by Women*. Carroll & Graf 1992 $28.00. ISBN 0-88184-913-8. Eighty science fiction and fantasy stories by women writers from a number of countries, including Great Britain.

CHRONOLOGY OF AUTHORS

Morris, William. 1834–1896
Dunsany, Lord. 1878–1957
Clarke, Arthur C. 1917–

Aldiss, Brian W. 1925–
Moorcock, Michael. 1939–

ALDISS, BRIAN W. 1925–

Brian W. Aldiss is among the most versatile of contemporary science fiction authors. He is also very knowledgeable about the genre, having published in 1973 the highly regarded study *Billion Year Spree: The True History of Science Fiction* (later updated and published as *Trillion Year Spree*). Born in East Dereham, Norfolk, Aldiss attended Framlingham College at Suffolk and West Buckland School. He worked as a bookseller at Oxford University and, later, as editor for the *Oxford Mail* and for Penguin Books. Through the years, Aldiss has been actively involved in various literary and science fiction organizations, and has received numerous prestigious awards for his work, including the Hugo Award, the Nebula Award, and the John W. Campbell Memorial Award.

Aldiss argues that writing is a compulsive act and that he doesn't really think about the reader until the process is completed. He claims that his work focuses on cultural and linguistic diversity, and he suggests that the "necessity of communication" is an integral part of his Helliconia novels. Aldiss published his first science fiction novel *Non-Stop* in 1958 (its American title is *Starship*) and has written prolifically ever since, although he feels somewhat uncomfortable with the label science fiction author. Praised by the literary critics for his seemingly effortless ability to write in a wide variety of styles, Aldiss is more interested in his science fiction novels with human concerns than with technology. He frequently is on the cutting edge of new ideas, as seen in his epic Helliconia series, while also demonstrating an understanding of the genre's traditions, as seen in the reworking of the Frankenstein myth in *Frankenstein Unbound* (1973).

NOVELS BY ALDISS

The Dark Light Years. Carroll & Graf 1991 $3.50. ISBN 0-88184-726-7

Dracula Unbound. HarpC 1991 $18.95. ISBN 0-06-016593-6. Aldiss does for Dracula in this novel what he did for Frankenstein in *Frankenstein Unbound*.

Forgotten Life. Macmillan 1989 $18.95. ISBN 0-689-12041-9

Frankenstein Unbound. 1973. Warner Bks. 1990 $4.95. ISBN 0-446-36036-8. One of Aldiss's best novels.

Helliconia Summer. Ace Bks. 1986 $4.50. ISBN 0-441-32632-3. An installment of Aldiss's epic science fiction series.

Helliconia Winter. Ace Bks. 1987 $3.95. ISBN 0-441-32629-3. Another installment of Aldiss's epic science fiction series.

Last Orders. Carroll & Graf 1990 $3.95. ISBN 0-88184-617-1

The Malacia Tapestry. Berkley Pub. 1985 $3.50. ISBN 0-425-08079-X. An entertaining fictional novel featuring the relationships between various characters in the fictitious geographical area of Malacia.

Non-Stop. 1958. Carroll & Graf 1989 $3.95. ISBN 0-88184-492-6

Starswarm. Baen Bks. 1985 $2.95. ISBN 0-671-55999-0. A novel set in the remote future of a galaxy widely populated by the descendants of humans. Told as a series of interconnecting stories, the events do not occur in a chronological order.

SHORT STORY COLLECTIONS BY ALDISS

Man in His Time: The Best Science Fiction Stories of Brian W. Aldiss. Macmillan 1990 $4.95. ISBN 0-02-030225-8. Highly recommended.

New Arrivals, Old Encounters: Twelve Stories. Ultramarine Pub. 1979 $20.00. ISBN 0-06-010055-9

A Romance of the Equator: The Best Fantasy Stories of Brian W. Aldiss. Macmillan 1990 $18.95. ISBN 0-689-12053-2. Highly recommended.

BOOKS ABOUT ALDISS

Aldiss, Margaret. *The Work of Brian W. Aldiss: An Annotated Bibliography and Guide*. Borgo Pr. 1992 $39.00. ISBN 0-89370-388-5. An essential reference book.

Collings, Michael R. *Brian Aldiss*. Starmont Hse. 1986 $19.95. ISBN 0-916732-99-1. A useful analysis of Aldiss's work.

Mathews, Richard. *Aldiss Unbound: The Science Fiction of Brian W. Aldiss*. Borgo Pr. 1977 $20.00. ISBN 0-89370-113-0. A good, though dated, overview of Aldiss's work.

CLARKE, ARTHUR C. 1917–

One of the most important practitioners of "hard" science in science fiction is Arthur C. Clarke. Drawing upon his experience as a trained scientist, Clarke has published some of the world's most successful contemporary science fiction novels and short fiction. Born in Minehead, Somerset, Clarke was educated at King's College, London, in mathematics and physics, graduating with honors in 1948. Clarke, a lieutenant in the Royal Air Force, was one of the first to work on military radar systems. More recently he has appeared on his own television show, *Arthur C. Clarke's Mysterious World* (1980), and has been a commentator for CBS. He has, in addition, successfully worked the lecture circuit. During the course of his impressive career, Clarke has won a number of honors, including the Hugo Award, the Nebula Award, and the John W. Campbell Award, for his science fiction, as well as numerous awards for his contributions to science.

Whereas a great deal of modern-day science fiction tends to be a variant of the cautionary tale, Clarke's work illustrates a love for—and a fascination with—technology. Clarke does not view technology as humanity's nemesis; rather, he believes that, if it is used properly and in conjunction with a well-placed faith, technology may be humanity's savior. Typically Clarke writes stories with a precise attention to science, and though his characters are sometimes two-dimensional, his mastery of setting and his ingenious utilization of science as an integral aspect of plot are unparalleled. His first published novel was *Prelude to Space* (1951), but his most famous work is his coauthorship with STANLEY KUBRICK (see Vol. 3) of the screenplay for *2001: A Space Odyssey* (and his novelization of that screenplay), as well as his best-selling novels *Childhood's End* (1953) and *Rendezvous with Rama* (1973). Clarke has also written as extensively and as successfully in nonfiction areas, having published an impressive list of articles and books dealing with science and technology. Along with ISAAC ASIMOV, ROBERT HEINLEIN, and a handful of others, Clarke has had a tremendous impact on the direction of Post-World War II science fiction.

NOVELS BY CLARKE

Beyond the Fall of Night. Ace Bks. 1991 $4.95. ISBN 0-441-05612-1

Childhood's End. 1953. Ballantine 1987 $5.95. ISBN 0-345-34795-1. Perhaps Clarke's best work.

The City and the Stars. 1956. NAL-Dutton 1957 $3.50. ISBN 0-451-14822-3. A human venture into outer space produces both surprises and new knowledge.

Deep Range. 1957. Bantam 1991 $4.95. ISBN 0-553-28925-X. Fights with giant squid 12,000 feet beneath the sea.

Fall of Moondust. Bantam 1991 $4.99. ISBN 0-553-28986-1. Science fiction tale of skipper Pat Harris aboard the *Selene*, the only boat on the moon.

Fountains of Paradise. 1979. Bantam 1991 $4.95. ISBN 0-553-28819-9. In the second century, King Kalidasa has a dream that another man tries to fulfill 2,000 years later.

Garden of Rama. Bantam 1991 $20.00. ISBN 0-553-07261-7. A continuing saga of the spacecraft Rama.

The Ghost from the Grand Banks. Bantam 1990 $19.95. ISBN 0-685-38899-9

Glide Path. Bantam 1991 $4.99. ISBN 0-553-29052-5

Imperial Earth. 1976. Bantam 1991 $4.95. ISBN 0-553-28877-6. The saga of a cloned human who returns to Earth for the 500th anniversary of the United States.

Prelude to Space. 1947. Ballantine 1986 $4.95. ISBN 0-345-34102-3. A science fiction novel that examines the concept of space exploration and the absurdity of national rivalries that arise because of it; still relevant in today's world even though the book was written in 1947.

Project Solar Sail. NAL-Dutton 1990 $4.50. ISBN 0-451-45002-7

Rendezvous with Rama. 1973. Bantam 1990 $4.95. ISBN 0-553-28789-3. Winner of the Hugo and Nebula awards. A mission investigates a strange celestial body that appears in the outer reaches of the solar system.

The Sands of Mars. 1951. Bantam 1991 $4.99. ISBN 0-553-29095-9. Science-fictional account of space travel to Mars, and the discovery of life there.

2001: A Space Odyssey. 1968. NAL-Dutton 1968 $4.99. ISBN 0-451-45063-9. Clarke's most famous work. Story of a spaceflight to the planet Jupiter.

2010: Odyssey Two. 1982. Ballantine 1984 $5.95. ISBN 0-345-30306-7. A sequel to *2001: A Space Odyssey*, this story has twists of its own.

2061: Odyssey Three. 1988. Ballantine 1988 $17.95. ISBN 0-345-35173-8. Heywood Floyd begins a new mission.

SHORT STORY COLLECTIONS BY CLARKE

Expedition to Earth. 1953. Ballantine 1985 $5.95. ISBN 0-345-32824-8. Eleven of the very best of Clarke's early stories.

More Than One Universe: The Collected Stories of Arthur C. Clarke. Bantam 1991 $4.99. ISBN 0-553-29189-0. An essential anthology.

Reach for Tomorrow. 1956. Ballantine 1987 $4.95. ISBN 0-345-35376-5. Stories of futures that might be—and should be.

The Wind from the Sun: Stories of the Space Age. 1972. NAL-Dutton 1973 $1.95. ISBN 0-451-11475-2

NONFICTION BY CLARKE

Astounding Days: A Science Fictional Autobiography. Bantam 1990 $8.95. ISBN 0-553-34822-1. A revealing insight into Clarke's life and into the science fiction genre.

BOOKS ABOUT CLARKE

Rabkin, Eric S. *Arthur C. Clarke.* Borgo Pr. repr. of 1979 ed. $19.95. ISBN 0-89370-032-0. A good overview.

Slusser, George E. *The Space Odysseys of Arthur C. Clarke.* Borgo Pr. 1977 $20.00. ISBN 0-89370-212-9. A brief, but interesting, analysis.

DUNSANY, LORD. 1878–1957

Though during his lifetime the Irish nobleman Lord Edward John Moreton Drax Plunkett, the 18th Baron Dunsany, was perhaps regarded as a minor talent, his somber short fantasies and novels had a significant impact on the development of fantasy and horror fiction. Authors including H. P. Lovecraft, L. Sprague de Camp, Clark Ashton Smith, Fritz Leiber, and URSULA LE GUIN were influenced by Lord Dunsany's work. In real life, Dunsany was as interesting and versatile as anyone about whom he wrote. He was an African big-game hunter, a soldier in both the Boer War and World War I, and was wounded in the 1916 Irish Easter Rebellion. He was also the national chess champion of Ireland.

Dunsany's first short story collection, *The Gods of Pegana*, was published in 1905 and was soon followed by other fantasy anthologies, including *Time and the Gods* (1906) and *The Sword of Welleran and Other Stories* (1908), among others. These stories are distinguished by their elegant, fairy tale settings and Dunsany's unique, macabre sense of humor. Dunsany's novels, such as *The King of Elfland's Daughter* (1924) and *The Charwoman's Shadow* (1926), are considered fantasy classics. Although Dunsany wrote prodigiously and with great versatility throughout his life, many regard his early, highly stylized short fiction to be his best work, and his most important.

NOVELS BY DUNSANY

The Curse of the Wise Woman. Amereon Ltd. repr. of 1933 ed. $18.95. ISBN 0-88411-650-6

Last Book of Wonder. Ayer repr. of 1916 ed. $15.00. ISBN 0-8369-3219-6

Plays of Gods and Men. Roth Pub. Inc. 1977 repr. of 1917 ed. $16.50. ISBN 0-8486-2015-1

SHORT STORY COLLECTIONS BY DUNSANY

Book of Wonder. Ayer repr. of 1818 ed. $19.00. ISBN 0-8369-4213-2. One of Dunsany's finer anthologies.

Dreamer's Tales. Ayer repr. of 1910 ed. $17.00. ISBN 0-8369-3191-2. A charming collection of sixteen stories concerned with familiar themes such as the fall of cities and the eventual power of time. This work helped establish Dunsany's reputation.

The Food of Death: Fifty-one Tales. Borgo Pr. 1980 repr. of 1974 ed. $23.00. ISBN 0-89370-502-0. The best collection of Dunsany currently available.

Time and the Gods. 1906. Ayer repr. of 1913 ed. $16.00 ISBN 0-8369-3385-5. Tales about events that happened to men and gods in the imaginary places of Yarnith, Averon, and Zarkandhu.

MOORCOCK, MICHAEL. 1939–

Michael Moorcock is a major contemporary author of science fiction and fantasy. He has published extensively under his own name and also under the pseudonyms Bill Barclay, Edward P. Bradbury, James Colvin, and Desmond Reid. Born in Mitcham, Surrey, Moorcock served as editor for the Liberal party and as editor-publisher of *New Worlds*. He has written for and performed with rock music groups. His fiction has won a host of prizes, including the British Science Fiction Association Award, the Nebula Award, and the World Fantasy Award. Demonstrating his knowledge of the epic fantasy genre, Moorcock published the literary study *Wizardry and Wild Romance* (1987), which stands as the definitive monograph on that subject.

A key influence on Moorcock's early fantasy writings was EDGAR RICE BURROUGHS. From 1956 to 1957, Moorcock was the editor of *Tarzan Adventures*, and several of his seminal novels written under the Bradbury pseudonym were pastiches of Burroughs's John Carter of Mars series. As Moorcock matured in his writing, he pulled away from simple imitation and developed in his several fantasy and science fiction series a somber, elegant style that was distinctive as well as entertaining. The tragic albino sorcerer Elric of Melniboné, parasitically united with his demonic sword "Stormbringer," is perhaps Moorcock's most famous creation. In his various series, the protagonists are merely different incarnations of the same persona: a variant of the character the Eternal Champion. Moorcock's fantasy and science fiction both exhibit a tragic, transcendental quality, in which the protagonists heroically strive against an unrelenting, hostile fate. In the process they often engender their own destruction.

NOVELS BY MOORCOCK

Barbarians of Mars. Ace Bks. 1991 $3.95. ISBN 0-441-04887-0. The third part of the Michael Kane cycle. On his third trip to Mars, Kane searches for a cure to the Green Death. Published under the pseudonym of Edward P. Bradbury.

Behold the Man. Carroll & Graf 1987 $2.95. ISBN 0-88184-369-5. One of Moorcock's more controversial books.

Blades of Mars. Ace Bks. 1991 $3.95. ISBN 0-441-79144-1. Second part of the Michael Kane cycle. Kane returns to Mars to fight a race of massive spiders. Published under the pseudonym of Edward P. Bradbury.

The Brothel in Rosenstrasse. Carroll & Graf 1987 $6.95. ISBN 0-88184-406-3. A doomed aristocracy lives up its last days.

The Chronicles of Corum. Berkley Pub. 1984 $3.95. ISBN 0-425-09533-9. Tells the story of the adventurous prince Corum and his lover Rhalina.

The Cornelius Chronicles, Vol. I. Avon 1977 $4.95. ISBN 0-380-00878-5. Part of a Jerry Cornelius tetralogy; a perilous journey through time and space is undertaken.

The Cornelius Chronicles, Vol. II. Avon 1986 $3.50. ISBN 0-380-75003-1

The Cornelius Chronicles, Vol. III. Avon 1987 $3.50. ISBN 0-380-70255-X

Elric Saga, Book 1: Elric of Melniboné. Ace Bks. 1992 $4.50. ISBN 0-441-20398-1. First part of the Elric cycle, predating *The Stealer of Souls* and *Stormbringer*, which were written earlier. Elric falls in love with Cymoril and begins his rivalry with Yyrkoon. Moorcock's best fantasy series.

Elric Saga, Book 2: Sailor on the Seas of Fate. Ace Bks. 1989 $4.50. ISBN 0-441-74863-5

Elric Saga, Book 3: Weird of the White Wolf. Ace Bks. 1989 $3.95. ISBN 0-441-88805-4

Elric Saga, Book 4: The Vanishing Tower. Ace Bks. 1989 $3.95. ISBN 0-441-86039-7

Elric Saga, Book 5: Bane of the Black Sword. Ace Bks. 1989 $3.95. ISBN 0-441-04885-4

Elric Saga, Book 6: Stormbringer. Ace Bks. 1989 $3.95. ISBN 0-441-78754-1

Elric Saga, Book 7: Fortress of the Pearl. Ace Bks. 1990 $4.50. ISBN 0-441-24866-7

Knight of Swords. Ace Bks. 1987 $2.95. ISBN 0-441-45131-4. First part of the Chronicles of Corum. Corum, the Prince in the Scarlet Robe, is captured and must rescue his lover Rhalina.

Revenge of the Rose. Ace Bks. 1991 $17.95. ISBN 0-441-71844-2. Continuing saga of Elric the Mercenary Prince.

Runestaff, Number 1: Jewel in the Skull. Ace Bks. 1990 $3.50. ISBN 0-441-31847-9. An excellent fantasy series.

Runestaff, Number 2: Mad God's Amulet. Ace Bks. 1990 $3.95. ISBN 0-441-51388-3
Runestaff, Number 3: Sword of the Dawn. Ace Bks. 1990 $3.95. ISBN 0-441-31846-0
Runestaff, Number 4: Runestaff. Ace Bks. 1991 $3.95. ISBN 0-441-31848-7
Warriors of Mars. Ace Bks. 1991 $3.95. ISBN 0-441-87339-1. First part of the Michael
    Kane cycle, written under the pseudonym of Edward P. Bradbury. Scientist Michael
    Kane is transported to ancient Mars.

MORRIS, WILLIAM. 1834–1896

William Morris was one of the most influential nineteenth-century authors of
high fantasy. Born in London, Morris had a significant impact on the world of
art as an early advocate of the pre-Raphaelite movement. A dedicated
antiquarian, he admired the Middle Ages as a philosophical model—one that
denied the mechanized, dehumanized advent of industrialized society. In fact,
Morris was an important social philosopher during his time and an early
communist. Although he was an accomplished poet, editor, and translator of
classical works, it was primarily in his works of high fantasy, published toward
the end of his life, that he most thoroughly expressed his love and respect for the
past. Much of what Morris created in these exquisitely wrought narratives—the
completely realized fantasy universe patterned after a preindustrial society—
would later find their way into the works of E. R. Eddison and J. R. R. TOLKIEN,
among many others. Morris's literary updating of the traditional national epic
saga was his most important contribution to the evolution of fantasy. The
modern reader may find Morris's use of language difficult to approach, but the
reader's efforts are rewarded by Morris's profound sense of imagination and
wonder.

NOVELS BY MORRIS

Child Christopher and Goldilind the Fair. Newcastle Pub. 1977 $5.95. ISBN 0-87877-
    111-5. Imaginary adventure tale of the young King Christopher, denied his birthright
    until he is grown, and his fair maiden Goldilind.
The House of the Wolfings. Newcastle Pub. 1978 $5.95. ISBN 0-87877-115-8. The fantasy
    story of the Wolfings, a group of humans who live by the water.
The Wood Beyond the World. Dover 1972 $8.95. ISBN 0-486-22791-X. The fantasized
    story of Walter, in which his thoughts and feelings are revealed in a distant past time.
    One of Morris's best fantasy stories.

POETRY BY MORRIS

A Book of Verse. Ashgate Pub. Co. 1980 $395.00. ISBN 0-85967-606-4

SHORT STORY COLLECTION BY MORRIS

Golden Wings and Other Stories. Newcastle Pub. 1978 $5.95. ISBN 0-87877-107-7

Romances

Depending on which source you choose, romance fiction accounts for
between 25 and 40 percent of the total English-speaking book publishing
industry, thus making it the most popular of all literary genres. As with the
Gothic horror story and the fantasy story, the British popular press invented
romance fiction. Instrumental in the creation of this genre was the Gothic
romance novelist ANN RADCLIFFE, whose refashioning of the Gothic horror novel
and social melodrama into a romance story introduced many of the literary
devices that are still practiced by popular romance writers today. Radcliffe was
indispensable in bringing both women authors and women readers to the new
literary invention called the novel, which had been created a mere 50 years

earlier by SAMUEL RICHARDSON. Some historians of British literature even argue that Radcliffe's work had an impact on the high, or elite, literature of the subsequent period, including the novels of CHARLOTTE and EMILY BRONTË. Although the genre has been attacked by many critics as mindless entertainment or as a type of literary pornography for women, many feminist scholars recognize in the romance novel numerous instances of significant women's social issues, such as the quest for identity and independence in a male-dominated society. For example, during Radcliffe's time, when women had few options for self-determination, the romance story offered a narrative in which women, not men, took center stage. Proponents of the romance novel cite it as one of the few popular fiction genres that were sympathetic to the woman's point of view and thus among the earliest of feminist writings. Despite its somewhat dubious reputation in the past, the romance novel today continues to gain its share of respect from the literary community.

HISTORY AND CRITICISM

Fallon, Eileen. *Words of Love: A Complete Guide to Romance Fiction*. Garland 1983 o.p. Lists and describes over 1,000 romance novels.

Heller, Tamar. *Dead Secrets: Wilkie Collins and the Female Gothic*. Yale U. Pr. 1992 $25.00. ISBN 0-300-04574-3. Though limited in its focus on the female Gothic genre, a nonetheless interesting analysis of the social and historical context of women's popular fiction.

Modleski, Tania. *Loving with a Vengeance: Mass-Produced Fantasies for Women*. Routledge 1984 $9.95. ISBN 0-415-90136-7. A valuable discussion of this genre.

Radford, Jean. *The Progress of Romance: The Politics of Popular Fiction*. Routledge 1987 $32.50. ISBN 0-7102-0717-4. Analyzes the social and cultural functions of popular romance fiction in its relation to women.

COLLECTIONS

Morrow, Bradford, and Patrick McGrath, eds. *The New Gothic: A Collection of Contemporary Gothic Fiction*. Random 1992 $12.00. ISBN 0-679-73075-3. Masterful, disturbing collection.

CHRONOLOGY OF AUTHORS

Radcliffe, Ann. 1764–1823   Du Maurier, Daphne. 1907–1989
Cartland, Barbara. 1901–   Pilcher, Rosamunde (Scott). 1924–

CARTLAND, BARBARA. 1901–

Barbara Cartland not only is the most prolific romance novelist of all time but also ranks as one of the top five best-selling writers. She has earned the title "the queen of romance." Cartland attended Malvern Girls' College and later wrote anonymous gossip columns for the *Daily News* and later for the *Tattler*. In 1925 Cartland published her first novel, a romance entitled *Jig-Saw*, and thus began her journey to literary fame and infamy. Cartland became a fellow of the Royal Society of Arts in 1984.

There is no question that she is a commercial success as a writer of romances. By 1979 Cartland had published well over 400 books, has sold over 100 million copies of her novels, and has attracted a devoted readership of perhaps four times that number. However, she has frequently been attacked by the critics for writing overly formulaic, mindless escapism—of producing potboilers, written and published with a speed that suggests an element of shoddiness and dreary repetition. (Her work published before World War II is more respected than her recent efforts.) The formula is rigid and highly predictable: Generally a young, sexually innocent heroine falls in love with a powerful, rich hero; following various trials that test the strength of the couple's developing relationship, their love is finally consummated by the end of the story. Basically, Cartland has co-opted the traditional romance narrative as established by ANN RADCLIFFE's Gothic romances and DAPHNE DU MAURIER's highly influential novel *Rebecca*. Cartland's stories are typically set in the past and involve as little explicit sexual content as possible. Although her books are slender, often only 60,000 words in length, Cartland prides herself on the historical research in her writing. Cartland has also published under her married name Barbara McCorquodale.

NOVELS BY CARTLAND

Coronation of Love. Jove Pubns. 1992 $3.50. ISBN 0-515-10883-9
A Dynasty of Love. Jove Pubns. 1992 $3.50. ISBN 0-515-10757-3
Game of Love. Severn Hse. 1991 $17.95. ISBN 0-7278-1769-8
Hiding. Jove Pubns. 1991 $3.50. ISBN 0-515-10601-1
Just Fate. Jove Pubns. 1991 $3.50. ISBN 0-515-10648-8
Love and War. Jove Pubns. 1992 $3.50. ISBN 0-515-10852-9
Love Casts Out Fear. Severn Hse. 1991 $15.95. ISBN 0-7278-1320-X. A story of romance
     and deception in France.
Love Strikes a Devil. Jove Pubns. 1992 $3.50. ISBN 0-515-10835-9
Lovers in Paradise. Severn Hse. 1991 $15.95. ISBN 0-7278-1493-1
Magic from the Heart. Jove Pubns. 1992 $3.50. ISBN 0-515-10793-X
Seek the Stars. Severn Hse. 1991 $18.95. ISBN 0-7278-4225-0
A Tangled Web. Jove Pubns. 1991 $3.50. ISBN 0-515-10617-8
A Theatre of Love. Jove Pubns. 1991 $3.50. ISBN 0-515-10736-0
Warned by a Ghost. Jove Pubns. 1991 $3.50. ISBN 0-515-10692-5
The Windmill of Love. Jove Pubns. 1992 $3.50. ISBN 0-515-10811-1
A Wish Comes True. Jove Pubns. 1992 $3.50. ISBN 0-515-10904-5

DU MAURIER, DAPHNE. 1907–1989

Although not nearly as prolific in her writings as many other romance novelists, Daphne du Maurier was, and is, undoubtedly the most significant. In addition, the romance narrative was only one of several literary genres that du Maurier successfully mastered, including the family drama, the adventure thriller, the horror story, the crime drama, and biography. Born in London, du Maurier was descended from an artistic family; her father, Sir Gerald du Maurier, was an actor, and her grandfather, GEORGE DU MAURIER, was a writer. She was educated privately in Paris, became a fellow of the Royal Society of Literature in 1952, and was made Dame Commander, Order of the British Empire, in 1969. In recognition of her popular mystery fiction, du Maurier was presented the Mystery Writers of America Grand Master Award in 1977.

Du Maurier's most important work in the romance genre was her popular novel *Rebecca* (1938). Patterned somewhat after the work of ANN RADCLIFFE, du Maurier's novel contains a successful blend of romance (the young, innocent woman falling in love with the older, powerful, "dangerous" man), mysterious setting (a seemingly haunted Gothic-like ancestral estate), and intrigue (dark family secrets and murder). Since *Rebecca*, innumerable romance novelists have attempted to duplicate du Maurier's novel, with varying degrees of success.

Du Maurier's writing tends to maintain a consistently high level of quality, and her stories demonstrate a versatility, as well as being entertaining. In addition to her skilled treatment of relationships, du Maurier is a master of narrative irony. Her fiction at times ascends to the lyrical, and frequently a foreboding sense of melancholy evidences itself. She is arguably one of the most talented modern authors of romances and one of those rare popular writers who have enjoyed both critical and commercial success. Du Maurier also wrote competently in other mediums, including the short story, drama, and television. She adapted *Rebecca* for the theater (1940), coauthored the screenplay *Hungry Hill* (1945), and wrote the teleplay *The Breakthrough* (1976).

NOVELS BY DU MAURIER

Frenchman's Creek. 1941. Bentley 1971 repr. of 1941 ed. $20.00. ISBN 0-8376-0412-5. The romantic account of Dona, a woman who subtly, yet surely, grows in spirit and mind.

Jamaica Inn. 1936. Avon 1977 $4.95. ISBN 0-380-00072-5. A superior thriller in which a young woman is forced to live with her estranged aunt and uncle upon her mother's death.

The King's General. 1946. Avon 1978 $3.50. ISBN 0-380-00210-8

Mary Anne. 1954. Dell 1987 $3.95. ISBN 0-440-15208-9. A historical novel featuring the life of Mary Anne Clarke in the late eighteenth and early nineteenth centuries.

My Cousin Rachel. 1952. Bentley 1971 $16.00. ISBN 0-8376-0413-5. A naive young man falls in love with his mysterious cousin.

Rebecca. 1938. Avon 1978 $4.95. ISBN 0-380-00917-X. One of the most important romance novels of the twentieth century.

The Scapegoat. 1957. Carroll & Graf 1988 $4.50. ISBN 0-88184-409-8. The story of a man who is tricked into assuming another man's identity.

BOOK ABOUT DU MAURIER

Shallcross, Martyn. *The Private World of Daphne du Maurier.* St. Martin 1992 $18.95. ISBN 0-312-07072-1. An insightful look into the author's life.

PILCHER, ROSAMUNDE (SCOTT). 1924–

English romance novelist and short story writer Rosamunde Pilcher was born in Lelant, in Cornwall, England. The daughter of a Royal Navy commander, she was educated at public schools in both England and Wales, and served in the Women's Royal Naval Service from 1942 to 1946. After leaving the Naval Service, she married Graham Hope Pilcher in December 1946. The couple have four children.

Pilcher was interested in writing from an early age, and was encouraged by her parents to pursue this interest. At age 16 she submitted a short short to the editor of three women's magazines. Though the story was rejected, the editor told her to keep trying. This contact led to the publication of another story a short time later. She then began a successful career writing what she describes as "sort of mimsy little love stories" under the pseudonym Jane Fraser. Her first novel, *Halfway to the Moon* (1949), was published under that name, and for a number of years she continued to write under that name as well as her own.

Pilcher specializes in "light reading for intelligent ladies," as she has stated in an interview in *Publishers Weekly*. The author of over 20 novels, she has also written numerous short stories, many of which have appeared in *Good Housekeeping* magazine. One of Pilcher's longest and most complex novels, as well as one of her most popular works, is *The Shell Seekers* (1988). The novel focuses on Penelope Keeling, an independent, slightly offbeat woman who

recalls, through flashbacks, her idyllic childhood in Cornwall, her hasty wartime marriage, and her troubled relationship with two of her three children. Now settled in a country cottage filled with reminders of her past, Penelope draws strength and comfort from these mementos, especially a painting entitled "The Shell Seekers," which was painted by her father. Although not autobiographical, the novel loosely parallels Pilcher's own life in a number of ways. Other works include *Sleeping Tiger* (1967), *The End of the Summer* (1971), *Wild Mountain Thyme* (1979), and *Voices in Summer* (1982).

NOVELS BY PILCHER

Another View. 1969. Dell 1989 $4.05. ISBN 0-440-20251-5

The Carousel. Thorndike 1992 $18.95. ISBN 1-56054-148-2. The touching story of Prue Shackleton as she leaves London behind for a holiday trip to Cornwall. The people she meets and the little house where Prue stays will forever change her life.

The Day of the Storm. 1975. Dell 1989 $4.99. ISBN 0-440-20253-1. After her dying mother reveals a family secret that Rebecca knew nothing about, Rebecca Bayliss enters a new world of passion and greed set against the background of a family mystery that she alone must face.

The Empty House. Thorndike 1992 $19.95. ISBN 1-56054-149-0. Virginia Keile gets a second chance in life to find love and happiness after facing loneliness, death, and greed.

The End of the Summer. 1971. St. Martin 1974 o.p. Jane Marsh returns to a remote corner of Scotland to face her past and to discover a new future.

September. St. Martin 1990 $22.95. ISBN 0-312-04467-4. Traditional Pilcher fare set in Scotland, complete with domestic complications, love affairs, estrangements, and reconciliations.

The Shell Seekers. 1988. St. Martin 1988 $19.95. ISBN 0-312-01058-3. Saga depicting one family's relations and emotionally messy lives.

Sleeping Tiger. 1967. Dell 1989 $4.99. ISBN 0-440-20247-7. Selina Bruce leaves behind her lawyer fiancé in London to search for an unknown father on a tiny island off the Spanish coast. Along the way, she finds unexpected truths about herself.

Under Gemini. Thorndike 1993 $19.95. ISBN 1-56054-151-2

Voices in the Summer. 1982. St. Martin 1990 $4.99. ISBN 0-312-92527-1. Newlywed Laura Haverstock discovers truths about herself, her family, and true love during a summer along the Cornwall coast.

Wild Mountain Thyme. 1979. Dell 1989 $4.99. ISBN 0-440-20250-7

SHORT STORY COLLECTIONS BY PILCHER

The Blue Bedroom and Other Stories. 1985. St. Martin 1990 $17.95. ISBN 0-312-05388-6. A collection of stories that shares life's ups and downs. Explores a child's first experience with death and an old woman's new freedom in life.

Flowers in the Rain, and Other Stories. St. Martin 1992 $5.99. ISBN 0-312-92774-6. A heartwarming collection of stories set in England.

RADCLIFFE, ANN. 1764–1823

Ann Radcliffe is generally regarded as the most popular author of her time. One of the first writers to discover the romance story potential in the Gothic tale, she took the narrative model created by HORACE WALPOLE in *The Castle of Otranto* (1765), divested the novel of its overtly supernatural trappings, and injected a female protagonist into this restructured Gothic framework. In the process Radcliffe created a new literary genre—one that looked more like the contemporary romance novel than the traditional Gothic horror story. Radcliffe was born in London to a highly educated family, although her father was a simple businessman. Her husband William, a journalist, encouraged her to write professionally. Ann Radcliffe is noted for having lived as a recluse, and,

when she no longer needed the income from her best-selling novels, she ceased publishing.

Radcliffe's first published novel was *The Castles of Athlin and Dunbayne* (1789), but her two most influential books were *The Mysteries of Udolpho* (1794) and *The Italian* (1797). In their original publication, these massive novels were presented in several volumes. Some critics accuse her writing of being long-winded, overly melodramatic, and, in retrospect, dated. Yet, her status as a seminal romance author is undeniable. What Radcliffe accomplished with her Gothic romance "triple-deckers" (the euphemism employed for multivolume novels) was her recognition of the importance of the role of women. Radcliffe wrote about women, for women. She was one of the first popular authors to wrest the best-selling novel away from the clutches of SAMUEL RICHARDSON, with his male-dominated worldview, and make it a legitimate vehicle for the expression of women's concerns. Although other women authors were paralleling, at another level, Radcliffe's efforts during this period, Radcliffe was the most successful and remains one of the few women writers of the period whose works survive to this day.

NOVELS BY RADCLIFFE

The Castles of Athlin and Dunbayne: A Highland Story. 1789. Ayer repr. of 1821 ed. $46.50. ISBN 0-405-00808-2. The author's first novel, set in the highlands of Scotland during the Dark Ages. A tale of mistaken identity and rewarded virtue.

The Female Advocate. 1799. Coronet Bks. repr. of 1799 ed. $36.50. ISBN 3-487-06724-2

Gaston de Blondeville, or the Court of Henry 3rd, Keeping Festival in Ardenne. 2 vols. Ayer repr. of 1826 ed. $48.50. ISBN 0-405-00815-5

The Italian. 1797. OUP 1981 $7.95. ISBN 0-19-281572-5. A two-volume Gothic romance about the relationship between Ellena and Vivaldi; set in eighteenth-century Italy.

The Mysteries of Udolpho. 1794. OUP 1980 $6.95. ISBN 0-19-281502-4. An enormously popular book when first published, being both a horror novel and a "novel of sentiment." Features the life of protagonist Emily.

The Romance of the Forest. OUP 1986 $7.95. ISBN 0-19-281712-4

Sicilian Romance. Ayer repr. of 1821 ed. $42.00. ISBN 0-405-00809-0

POETRY BY RADCLIFFE

The Poetical Works of Ann Radcliffe. 2 vols. AMS repr. of 1834 ed. $85.00. ISBN 0-686-57611-X

BOOKS ABOUT RADCLIFFE

Cottom, Daniel. *The Civilized Imagination: A Study of Ann Radcliffe, Jane Austen, and Sir Walter Scott.* Cambridge U Pr. 1985 $10.95. ISBN 0-521-30172-6. Effectively places Radcliffe within the literary context of her era.

Durant, David S. *Ann Radcliffe's Novels: Experiments in Setting.* Ayer 1980 $24.50. ISBN 0-405-12665-4. One of the best studies done of Radcliffe.

Garrett, John. *Gothic Strains and Bourgeois Sentiments in the Novels of Mrs. Ann Radcliffe and Her Imitations.* Ayer 1980 $46.00. ISBN 0-405-12668-9. Draws useful parallels between the Gothic and romance narrative motifs in Radcliffe's work.

Part Three

American Literature

CHAPTER 13

Early American Literature: Beginnings to the Nineteenth Century

Emory Elliott

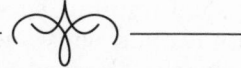

Now shall the adventurous muse attempt a strain
More new, more noble, and more flush of fame
Than all that went before—
. . . what a change is here!—what arts arise!
What towns and capitals! . . . Where silence reign'd before!
    —Hugh Henry Breckenridge and
    Philip Freneau, "The Rising Glory of America"

The first American literature consisted of oral narratives and poetry composed by Native American peoples as early as 3000 B.C. A literary record written in stone dating about A.D.1000 still exists as picture-stories painted on the walls of caves in what is now the southwestern United States. As substantial numbers of Europeans arrived in the Americas in the fifteenth and sixteenth centuries, the explorers began to produce travel narratives, histories, and essays written in several languages for publication in Europe. In the early seventeenth century, books in English by European immigrants to North America began to be published in England and, by mid-century, in Boston.

After the 1620 landing of the first English Puritans in what they named "New England," the number of books and tracts written in America steadily increased. Puritan literature consisted primarily of religious writings: sermons, theological treatises, spiritual autobiographies, spiritualized histories, diaries, and some poetry, usually aimed at religious instruction. By 1650, the colonists were producing an extraordinary amount of writing through which they mainly sought to explain and understand their efforts, accomplishments, and failures in trying to live by divine precepts in their holy community. Because of the intensity of their beliefs and their devotion to education and literacy, they transported from abroad considerable libraries of the classics and works of Renaissance literature as well as religious writings. Despite the pressures of living in a demanding and dangerous frontier society, the journals and histories of colonists such as John Winthrop and William Bradford, the written and oral expressions of leaders like Roger Williams and Anne Hutchinson, and the poetry of Anne Bradstreet and Edward Taylor provide enduring evidence of the power of creative imagination to overcome physical adversity.

By the beginning of the eighteenth century, many of the original doctrines and social controls of the Puritans had declined, while people of other Christian sects had settled in New England. Growing religious and political toleration made Boston and the surrounding towns more cosmopolitan, as the ideas of the

European Enlightenment stressing reason and science opened new intellectual avenues for thought and literature pursued by writers like BENJAMIN FRANKLIN and THOMAS JEFFERSON. Before the demise of Puritanism in America, however, its doctrines were reformulated by the great theologian and thinker, JONATHAN EDWARDS. A scholar who synthesized ideas of both Calvinist theology and Enlightenment philosophies, Edwards created works that are remarkable for their intellectual power and poetic expression.

While the Puritans dominated literature in New England between 1620 and 1750, the English who colonized the southern regions of North America also produced a rich, though somewhat different, literature. The Anglican faith also generated a considerable body of religious literature in the South, and southern authors produced a considerable body of secular writing as well. Written mostly by aristocratic men of classical training, such as Virginia's William Byrd II, the literature of the early South is often witty and sophisticated and more evidently linked than northern texts to the classical and English Renaissance traditions.

In the middle colonies, Philadelphia developed into the cultural center of the colonies as the intellectually liberal spirit of the Friends encouraged the arts. The leading literary figure of Philadelphia was Benjamin Franklin, whose graceful style and wit, both in person and manner and in his writing, typified the cosmopolitan ideal that emerged throughout the colonies during the eighteenth century. While Franklin used his verbal skills and personality to make a mark for American letters abroad, the Quaker author John Woolman combined the traditions of religious writing with a sophisticated Enlightenment rhetoric to preach, lecture, and write about such American social ills as slavery. Meanwhile, William Smith, the head of the College of Philadelphia (later the University of Pennsylvania), was not only an important writer in his own right, but he also inspired such young authors as Thomas Godfrey, whose *The Prince of Parthia* (1765) may have been the first genuine play written and produced in America. Smith also encouraged aspiring poets Jacob Duche and Nathaniel Evans, who styled themselves "the Swains of the Schuykill [River]." By the time of the American Revolution, Philadelphia was the center of the small literary world that was taking shape in the colonies.

During the second half of the eighteenth century, the movement in the colonies toward political unity also contributed to a blending of the cultural elements of the North and South. The prose of the Virginian Thomas Jefferson, the poetry of Connecticut-bred JOEL BARLOW, and the plays of the Bostonian ROYAL TYLER employ stylistic techniques that cross regional borders, creating the beginnings of truly American subjects. Even the Atlantic divide was frequently transcended by the arts as exemplified in the ultimately American works and political visions of the New Jersey-born PHILLIP FRENEAU and the English-born THOMAS PAINE. Similarly cosmopolitan are the novels of the Philadelphia writer CHARLES BROCKDEN BROWN, which vividly depict American natural settings while employing gothic devices to explore radical social and political ideas originating in England, France, and Germany. A genuinely American set of contradictions is represented by the African slave PHILLIS WHEATLEY, who composed poems of biting wit and sometimes bitter, though subtle, irony in English that recalled her African origins and her captivity while representing Anglo-American subjects, such as Harvard students, English preachers, and President George Washington.

What had begun on the shores of New England in 1620 as the tentative notes of William Bradford in his journal had developed by 1800 into a budding national literature that anticipated the nineteenth-century declaration of

America's cultural independence from Europe. American literature was proceeding slowly but surely towards establishing its unique identity.

HISTORY AND CRITICISM

Anderson, Virginia DeJohn. *New England Generation: The Great Migration and the Formation of Society and Culture in the Seventeenth Century*. Cambridge U. Pr. 1991 $34.50. ISBN 0-521-40506-8. A discussion of the ways colonial history shaped the seventeenth century and American culture.

Arieli, Yehoshua. *Individualism and Nationalism in American Ideology*. HUP 1964 o.p. An examination of "rugged individualism" and its impact on literature, culture, and politics.

Bailyn, Bernard. *Education in the Forming of American Society*. Norton 1972 repr. of 1960 ed. $6.95. ISBN 0-393-00643-3. A look at the way literacy and didactic principles influenced society.

Baldwin, Alice. *The New England Clergy and the American Revolution*. Duke 1928 o.p. An analysis of the role of the clergy in the war.

Baritz, Loren. *City on a Hill, A History of Ideas and Myths in America*. Greenwood 1980 repr. of 1964 ed. $35.00. ISBN 0-313-22268-1. An exploration of Winthrop's "city on the hill" and the way this vision resonates in American culture.

Baym, Nina. *Women's Fiction: A Guide to Novels by and about Women in America 1820–1870*. Cornell Univ. Pr. 1980 $12.95. ISBN 0-8014-9184-3. An excellent analysis of women's literature, with theoretical sections of use to anyone working on women's texts.

Bercovitch, Sacvan. *The American Jeremiad*. U. of Wis. Pr. 1980 $12.95. ISBN 0-299-07354-8. A literary analysis that makes the figure of the Jeremiad—the critic—central to American culture.

———. *The American Puritan Imagination: Essays on Revaluation*. Cambridge U. Pr. 1974 $17.95. ISBN 0-521-20392-9. An excellent collection on various literary figures.

———. *The Puritan Origins of the American Self*. Yale U. Pr. 1975 $12.95. ISBN 0-300-02117-8. An exploration of how the paradigms of contemporary American culture can be traced back to Puritan history and theology.

Bercovitch Sacvan, and Myra Jehlen, eds. *Ideology and Classic American Literature*. Cambridge U. Pr. 1987 $49.95. ISBN 0-521-25221-0. A highly useful collection of essays.

Boorstein, Daniel. *The Americans: The Colonial Experience*. Random 1958 o.p. Provides a detailed and popular history of the colonists.

Breitweiser, Mitchell Robert. *American Puritanism and the Defense of Mourning: Religion, Grief and Ethnology in Mary Rowlandson's Captivity Narrative*. U. of Wis. Pr. 1990 $40.00. ISBN 0-299-12650-1. A provocative analysis of a compelling narrative previously read as more generic than subversive.

Bridenbaugh, Carl. *Mitre, Sceptre: Transatlantic Faiths, Ideas, Personalities and Politics, 1689–1775*. OUP 1962 o.p. A good introduction to issues of social history.

Brumm, Ursula. *American Thought and Religious Typology*. Rutgers U. Pr. 1970 o.p. A systematic analysis of the Puritan structure of metaphor and iconography; translated by J. Hooglund.

Cherry, Conrad. *Nature and Religious Imagination: From Edwards to Bushnell*. Fortress 1980 o.p. An examination of the marriage of natural and biblical imagery.

Daly, Robert. *God's Altar: The World and the Flesh in Puritan Poetry*. U. CA Pr. 1978 $37.50. ISBN 0-520-03480-5. An excellent discussion of the paradoxical elements embraced in Puritan verse.

Davis, Richard Beale. *Intellectual Life of Jefferson's Virginia, 1730–1830*. U. of NC Pr. 1964 o.p. A classic study of the subject.

Delbanco, Andrew. *The Puritan Ordeal*. HUP 1989 $30.00. ISBN 0-674-74055-6. Sees Puritans as the first immigrants; a fascinating attempt to add an entirely new dimension to the practice of intellectual history.

Elliott, Emory. *Power in the Pulpit in Puritan New England.* Bks. Demand repr. of 1975 ed. $65.80. ISBN 0-8357-8994-2. An analysis of the social and cultural function of the Puritan sermon.

———. *Revolutionary Writers: Literature and Authority in the New Republic.* OUP 1986 $12.95. ISBN 0-19-503995-5. An analysis of the first writers of the new nation.

———, ed. *The Columbia History of the American Novel.* Col. U. Pr. 1991 $59.95. ISBN 0-231-07360-7. A collection of contemporary essays dealing with the development of American fiction.

———, ed. *The Columbia Literary History of the United States.* Col. U. Pr. 1988 $210.00. ISBN 0-231-06780-1. A comprehensive account of American authors, works, and literary movements.

———, ed. *Puritan Influences in American Literature.* Bks. Demand repr. of 1979 ed. $58.00. ISBN 0-317-28971-3. Essays on Puritan literature and later American writing.

Emerson, Everett. *Puritanism in America, 1620–1750.* Twayne 1977 o.p. A frequently cited, very influential book, useful for any work on Puritan or colonial America.

———, ed. *American Literature, 1764–1789: The Revolutionary Years.* U. of Wis. Pr. 1977 $32.50. ISBN 0-299-07270-3. An extremely useful collection of essays on the colonial and post-Revolutionary period.

———. *Major Writers of Early American Literature: Introductions to Nine Major Writers.* U. of Wis. Pr. 1972 $14.50. ISBN 0-299-06194-9. Contains varied opinions and perceptions regarding colonial authors.

Fiedler, Leslie A. *Love and Death in the American Novel.* Doubleday 1992 $12.00. ISBN 0-385-42417-5. A discussion of images and character configurations traced through the history of the American novel.

Foster, Stephen. *The Long Argument: English Puritanism and the Shaping of New England Culture, 1570–1700.* U. of NC Pr. 1991 $39.95. ISBN 0-8078-1951-4. Explores the development of Puritanism in England.

Gelpi, Albert J. *The Tenth Muse: The Psyche of the American Poet.* Cambridge U. Pr. 1991 $54.50. ISBN 0-521-41339-7. Discusses the unique aspects of the American experience that shaped American poets.

Gilmore, Michael T., ed. *Early American Literature: A Collection of Critical Essays.* P-H 1980 o.p. Essays on various Puritan writers.

Granger, Bruce. *Political Satire in the American Revolution, 1763–1783.* Cornell Univ. Pr. 1960 o.p. An in-depth analysis of its subject.

Hoopes, James. *Consciousness in New England from Puritans and Ideas to Psychoanalysis and Semiotics.* Johns Hopkins 1989 $42.00. ISBN 0-8018-3824-X. A very contemporary and theoretical study of colonial expression and culture.

Kasson, John F. *Civilizing the Machine: Technology and Republican Values in America, 1776–1900.* Viking Penguin 1977 $9.95. ISBN 0-14-004415-9. A discussion of ways technology and the developing industrial revolution shaped American culture.

Ketcham, Ralph L. *From Colony to Country: The Revolution in American Thought, 1750–1820.* Macmillan 1974 o.p. Looks at philosophical developments.

Leary, Lewis. *Soundings: Some Early American Writers.* U. of Ga. Pr. 1975 o.p.

Levin, David. *In Defense of Historical Literature.* Hill & Wang 1967 o.p. An important discussion of early American culture and the significance of history within literary studies.

Lowance, Mason I., Jr. *The Language of Canaan: Metaphor and Symbol in New England from the Puritans to the Transcendentalists.* HUP 1980 $25.50. ISBN 0-674-50949-0. A sweeping argument on language in American history.

Lynen, John F. *The Design of the Present: Essays on Time and Form in American Literature.* Yale U. Pr. 1969 o.p. Focuses especially on Franklin and Edwards.

Martin, Wendy. *An American Triptych: Anne Bradstreet, Emily Dickinson, Adrienne Rich.* U. of NC Pr. 1984 $10.95. ISBN 0-8078-4112-9. A feminist study focusing on the revolutionary aspects of Anne Bradstreet's poetry and examining the ways in which she provided a literary foundation for future American women poets.

Middlekauff, Robert. *The Mathers: Three Generations of Puritan Intellectuals, 1596–1728.* OUP 1971 $7.95. ISBN 0-19-502115-0. A discussion of the power asserted by one

American family, and the way that family's influence manifested itself in theology, literature, and culture.

Miller, Perry. *Errand into the Wilderness.* HUP 1956 $10.95. ISBN 0-674-26155-0. A classic study of Puritan theology, images, and tropes, still greatly influential in contemporary studies of Puritan culture and literature.

———. *The Life of the Mind in America: From the Revolution to the Civil War.* HarBraceJ 1970 $12.95. ISBN 0-15-651990-9. Looks at philosophy in the early nineteenth century.

Morrison, Samuel Eliot. *The Intellectual Life of Colonial New England.* Cornell Univ. Pr. 1960 $11.95. ISBN 0-8014-9011-1. An intriguing historical account by a preeminent intellectual historian.

Nash, Gary B. *Class and Society in Early America.* P-H 1970 o.p. A very readable historical discussion of the ways race, class, and gender shaped colonial America.

Nelson, Dana D. *The Word in Black and White: Writing "Race" in American Literature.* OUP 1992 $35.00. ISBN 0-19-506592-1. A contemporary study examining the ways in which race has historically been reflected in American literature.

Nye, Russell B. *American Literary History: 1607–1830.* Knopf 1970 o.p. A good literary history.

Porterfield, Amanda. *Female Piety in Puritan New England: The Emergence of Religious Humanism.* OUP 1992 $29.95. ISBN 0-19-506821-1. An account of early women writers and the way their work modified the more literal piety of the English Puritans.

Quinn, Arthur Hobson. *American Fiction: An Historical and Critical Survey.* Appleton & Lange 1964 o.p. A useful if necessarily general account of American fiction from its inception to the twentieth century.

———. *A History of the American Drama: From the Beginning to the Civil War.* Irvington 1982 repr. of 1943 ed. $44.50. ISBN 0-89197-218-8. A comprehensive survey.

Regis, Pamela. *Describing Early America: Bartram, Jefferson, Crevecoeur and the Rhetoric of Natural History.* N. Ill. U. Pr. 1992 $30.00. ISBN 0-87580-166-8. A fascinating look at the way that the tropes of geography and natural history came to prefigure American consciousness.

Richards, Jeffrey H. *Theater Enough: American Culture and the Metaphor of the World Stage, 1607–1789.* Duke 1991 $34.95. ISBN 0-8223-1107-0. An account of the way the Renaissance metaphor—"all the world's a stage"—came to shape the performative culture of the colonies.

Rogers, Katherine, ed. *The Meridian Anthology of Early American Women Writers: From Anne Bradstreet to Louisa May Alcott, 1650-1865.* NAL-Dutton 1991 $14.95. ISBN 0-452-01075-0. An excellent compilation and presentation of early American women authors, many of whom are frequently unrepresented in standard anthologies.

Schweitzer, Ivy. *The Work of Self-Representation: Lyric Poetry in Colonial New England.* U. of NC Pr. 1991 $34.95. ISBN 0-8078-1979-4. Examines the role of the self in Puritan poetry.

Scheick, William. *Design in Puritan American Literature.* U. Pr. of Ky. 1992 $25.00. ISBN 0-8131-1775-5. A look at the structuring principles of Puritan literature and their relationship to theology.

Scheick, William, and Joella Doggett. *Guide to Seventeenth-Century American Poetry: A Reference Guide.* G. K. Hall 1977 o.p. A comprehensive listing of colonial poets.

Seelye, John. *Prophetic Waters: The River in Early American Life and Literature.* OUP 1977 $27.95. ISBN 0-19-502047-2. Argues for the importance of the river in the literature.

———. *Beautiful Machine: Rivers and the Republican Plan, 1755-1825.* OUP 1991 $35.00. ISBN 0-19-504551-3. An examination of the way topography shaped culture.

Shea, Daniel B., Jr. *Spiritual Autobiography in Early America.* U. of Wis. Pr. 1988 repr. of 1968 ed. $35.00. ISBN 0-299-11650-6. A classic study of Puritan and Quaker writing.

Silverman, Kenneth, ed. *Colonial American Poetry.* Hafner 1968 o.p. An anthology of early poetry.

Smith, Nigel. *Perfection Proclaimed: Language, Literature and Radical Religion 1640-1660.* OUP 1989 $94.00. ISBN 0-19-812879-7. A highly theoretical discussion, touching on textual deconstruction of Puritan documents.

Spiller, Robert E., ed. *The American Literary Revolution 1783–1837.* Doubleday 1967 o.p.

Stachniewski, John. *The Persecuting Imagination: English Puritanism and the Literature of Religious Despair.* OUP 1991 $95.00. ISBN 0-19-811781-7. A discussion of the bleak and apocalyptic vision often represented in Puritan literature.

Tebbel, John. *A History of Book Publishing in the United States: Volume I, The Creation of an Industry, 1630–1865.* Bowker 1972 o.p. An exploration of the way the publishing industry developed in the United States and the way that industry influenced culture.

Tompkins, Jane. *Sensational Designs: The Cultural Work of American Fiction, 1790–1860.* OUP 1985 $13.95. ISBN 0-19-504119-4. A critical discussion of how an American literary canon was formed and an examination of the ways popular fiction expressed significant cultural anxieties.

Tyler, Moses Coit. *A History of American Literature.* 2 vols. Corner Hse. 1973 repr. of 1878 ed. $40.00. ISBN 0-87928-041-7. A classic survey.

Van Doren, Carl. *The American Novel, 1789–1939.* Macmillan 1940 o.p. A useful early analysis.

Watts, Emily Stipes. *The Poetry of American Women from 1632–1945.* U. of Tex. Pr. 1977 o.p. A comprehensive survey.

Wegelin, O. *Bibliography of Early American Fiction, 1774–1830.* Peter Smith $10.75. ISBN 0-8446-1470-X. Covers works printed before 1831.

Wright, Louis. *American Fiction, 1774–1850: A Contribution Toward a Bibliography.* Huntington Lib. 1969 o.p. A very extensive listing of American literature.

_____. *The Cultural Life of the American Colonies: 1607–1763.* HarpC 1957 o.p. A general overview.

Zakai, Avihu. *Exile & Kingdom: History and Apocalypse in the Puritan Migration to America.* Cambridge U. Pr. 1991 $44.95. ISBN 0-521-40381-2. A discussion of the way Biblical history prefigured the Puritan experience.

Ziff, Larzer. *Literary Democracy: The Declaration of Cultural Independence* in America. Viking Penguin 1981 o.p. A discussion of the unique aspects of American literature.

_____. *Puritanism in America: New Culture in a New World.* Viking Penguin 1973 o.p. The positive and negative aspects of Puritans in America.

Collections of Early American Literature

Ahlsrom, Sydney E., ed. *Theology in America: The Major Protestant Voices from Puritanism to Neo-Orthodoxy.* Bobbs 1967 o.p. Ample selections from Thomas Hooker and Jonathan Edwards as well as later writers.

Burbank, Rex, and Jack B. Moore. *The Literature of Early America.* Charles E. Merrill Bks. 1967 o.p. An anthology of early American literature.

Cady, Edwin H., ed. *Literature of the Early Republic.* HarBraceJ 1969 o.p. An anthology of American literature written between 1763 and 1815.

Demos, John, ed. *Remarkable Providences: Readings on Early American History.* NE U. Pr. 1991 $45.00. ISBN 1-55553-097-4. Selections and commentary defining different areas of colonial life.

Eberwein, Jane Donahue, ed. *Early American Poetry.* U. of Wis. Pr. 1978 $14.50. ISBN 0-299-07444-7. Good selections of Bradstreet, Taylor, Dwight, Freneau, and Bryant.

Gunn, Giles, ed. *New World Metaphysics: Readings on the Religious Meaning of the American Experience.* OUP 1981 o.p. Selections from the colonial period and later.

Meserole, Harrison T., ed. *Seventeenth-Century American Poetry.* Norton 1968 o.p. An anthology of seventeenth-century American poetry.

Miller, Perry, ed. *The American Puritans: Their Prose and Poetry.* Col. U. Pr. 1982 repr. of 1956 ed. $18.00. ISBN 0-231-05419-X. A selection of Puritan poetry and prose.

Miller, Perry, and Thomas H. Johnson, eds. *The Puritans: A Sourcebook of Their Writings.* 2 vols. HarpC 1938 o.p. The standard anthology of Puritan writings. Organized by areas of life: Poetry, Education, Science, etc.

Pearce, Roy Harvey, ed. *Colonial American Writing*. HarBraceJ 1950 o.p. An anthology of colonial American literature.

Collections of Early Travel and Nature Writing

Bourne, Edward Gaylord, and Julius E. Olson, eds. *The Northmen, Columbus, and Cabot, 985–1503*. Scribner's 1906 o.p. Accounts of the voyages of Columbus (all four voyages), John Cabot, and the Norsemen.

Chiapelli, Fredi, ed. *First Images of America: The Impact of the New World Upon the Old*. U. CA Pr. 1976 o.p. A collection of studies of New World exploration.

Cumming, W. P., R. A. Skelton, and D. B. Quinn. *The Discovery of North America*. American Heritage Pr. 1971 o.p. Text about voyages to North America and its subsequent colonization.

Grant, W. L., ed. *Voyages of Samuel de Champlain, 1604–1618*. Rprt. Serv. 1991 repr. of 1907 ed. $89.00. ISBN 0-7812-6351-4. A collection of travel writings by Samuel de Champlain.

Hodge, Frederick W., ed. *Spanish Explorers in the Southern United States, 1528–1543*. Tex. St. Hist. Assn. 1990 repr. of 1984 ed. $24.95. ISBN 0-87611-066-9. Original narratives of De Vaca, De Soto, and Coronado.

Morison, Samuel E. *European Discovery of America: The Northern Voyages*. OUP 1971 $39.95. ISBN 0-19-501377-8. A history of New World Discovery; covers "northern voyages" of 500–1600.

———. *The European Discovery of America: The Southern Voyages*. OUP 1974 $39.95. ISBN 0-19-501823-0. Covers "southern voyages" of 1492–1616.

Palmer, Stanley H., and Dennis Reinhartz, eds. *Essays on the History of North American Discovery and Exploration*. Tex. A&M Univ. Pr. 1988 $17.50. ISBN 0-89096-373-8. A collection of essays on the history of North American exploration.

Quinn, David B. *North America from Earliest Discovery to First Settlements: The Norse Voyages to 1612*. HarpC 1977 o.p. An account of the Norse voyages to North America.

———, ed. *North American Discovery, circa 1000–1612*. U. of SC Pr. 1971 o.p. A collection of annotated primary texts, covering explorations of North America between 1000 and 1612.

———, ed. *New American World: A Documentary History of North America to 1612*. 5 vols. Ayer 1978 $299.50. ISBN 0-405-10759-5. A documentary history of North America up to 1612.

Collections of Early Native American Expressions

Astrov, Margot Luise Therese, ed. *The Winged Serpent: American Indian Prose and Poetry*. Beacon Pr. 1992. ISBN 0-8070-8105-1. An anthology of Native American prose and poetry.

Brumble, H. David. *American Indian Autobiography*. U. CA Pr. 1988 $42.50. ISBN 0-520-06245-0. A study and selection of Native American autobiographies.

Castro, Michael. *Interpreting the Indian: Twentieth-Century Poets and the Native American*. U. of Okla. Pr. 1991 repr. of 1983 ed. $12.95. ISBN 0-8061-2351-6. Native American cultural expressions as they relate to modern poetry.

Dauenhauer, Nora Marks, and Richard Dauenhauer, eds. *Haa Shuka, Our Ancestors: Tlingit Oral Narratives*. U. of Wash. Pr. 1987 $35.00. ISBN 0-295-96495-2. A collection of Tlingit oral narratives.

Krupat, Arnold. *The Voice in the Margin: Native American Literature and the Canon*. U. CA Pr. 1989 $35.00. ISBN 0-520-06669 -3. Native American literature in the context of the literary canon.

Marriott, Alice, and Carol K. Rachlin, eds. *Plains Indian Mythology*. NAL-Dutton 1977 $4.95. ISBN 0-452-00766-6. An anthology of tales and myths of various Plains Indian tribes.

Radin, Paul. *The Trickster: A Study in American Indian Mythology.* Schocken 1987 $12.00. ISBN 0-8052-0351-6. Trickster myths in Native American culture.

Segal, Charles M., and David C. Stineback, eds. *Puritans, Indians & Manifest Destiny.* Putnam Pub. Group 1977 o.p. Exchanges between the Native Americans and the English placed in a historical narrative.

Swann, Brian, and Arnold Krupat, eds. *Recovering the Word: Essays on Native American Literature.* U. CA Pr. 1987 $80.00. ISBN 0-520-05790-2. A collection of essays on Native American literature.

Underhill, Ruth Murray. *Singing for Power: The Song Magic of the Papago Indians of Southern Arizona.* U. CA Pr. 1977 repr. of 1934 ed. $27.50. ISBN 0-520-03310-8. An anthology of songs and ritual speeches of the Papago Indians.

CHRONOLOGY OF AUTHORS

Bradford, William. 1590–1657.
Bradstreet, Anne. c. 1612–1672.
Taylor, Edward. c. 1642–1729.
Edwards, Jonathan. 1703–1758.
Franklin, Benjamin. 1706–1790.
Paine, Thomas. 1737–1809.
Jefferson, Thomas. 1743–1826.
Freneau, Phillip. 1752–1832.

Barlow, Joel. 1754–1812.
Wheatley, Phillis. c. 1754–1784.
Tyler, Royall. 1757–1826.
Rowson, Susanna Haswell. 1762–1824.
Brown, Charles Brockden. 1771–1810.

BARLOW, JOEL. 1754–1812.

Barlow was a member of The Connecticut Wits, a group of nine ambitious young writers determined to celebrate as well as satirize the young American democracy. The two other most famous members of the group—Timothy Dwight and John Trumbull—pursued their satiric inclinations until they became conservative Federalists in the face of Jeffersonian republicanism. But Barlow, who had been born and reared on a Connecticut farm before going to Dartmouth College and then to Yale University, went first to Europe for 17 years. There, despite becoming wealthy, he became a passionate supporter of the French Revolution and saw to the publication of THOMAS PAINE'S *The Age of Reason.*

While running for election as a deputy to the French National Assembly, Barlow wrote his best-known poem, the mock epic "The Hasty Pudding," which brought him celebrity in his native land. When he returned to the United States in 1805, he turned away from his ponderous epic *The Columbiad* (1807), in which he celebrated the United States' future in the context of deploring the European past. As a reward for his support of Jeffersonianism, President James Madison appointed him minister to France. Following Napoleon to Poland in an effort to persuade the emperor to favor U.S. commerce, Barlow narrowly missed Napoleon, who was making his way back to Europe with his defeated army. When Barlow began his own return, he caught pneumonia and died. He was buried in a village near Cracow, Poland.

Barlow is significant for his understanding that the American experience—and its translation into literature and the culture at large—was important in its own right, distinct from European history and aesthetics. His poetry, essays, and orations are infused with his witty perception of the colonialist's mission.

POETRY BY BARLOW

The Anarchiad: A New England Poem. Thomas Pease 1861 o.p. A comic poem on the dangers of political anarchy.

The Columbiad: A Poem. Fry and Kammerer 1807 o.p. An epic revision of the vision of Columbus.

The Conspiracy of Kings; A Poem Addressed to the Inhabitants of Europe from Another Quarter. Walter J. Johnson 1792 o.p. A radical political work addressed to the need for political reform.

The Hasty-Pudding: A Poem in Three Cantos. 1796 o.p. A comic satire.

The Vision of Columbus: A Poem in Nine Books. Hudson & Goodwin 1787 o.p. An epic poem of early American history.

NONFICTION BY BARLOW

A New Translation of Volney's Ruins; or, Meditations on the Revolution of Empires. (coauthored with Thomas Jefferson). Dixon & Sickels 1828 o.p. Reflections on the dangers of political decline.

BOOKS ABOUT BARLOW

Bidwell, John. *The Publication of Joel Barlow's Columbiad.* Am. Antiquarian 1984 o.p. A history of the book.

Ford, Arthur. *Joel Barlow.* Irvington 1971 $17.95. ISBN 0-89197-809-7. An overview of his life and work.

Miller, Victor C. *Joel Barlow: Revolutionist.* De Gruyter 1932 o.p. Barlow as a political reformer.

Zunder, Theodore. *The Early Days of Joel Barlow, A Connecticut Wit: His Life and Works from 1754–1787.* Shoe String 1969 repr. of 1934 ed. $37.50. ISBN 0-208-00769-5. Barlow's early life.

BRADFORD, WILLIAM. 1590–1657.

William Bradford was born in a comfortable Yorkshire yeoman's home, but the family that might have provided him with a nurturing beginning was disrupted and dispersed by the early death of Bradford's parents. Raised by his uncles to be a farmer, Bradford was instead a sickly youth given to private reading. In early adolescence, Bradford first heard the preaching of Richard Clyfton—a nonconformist minister—who converted Bradford to the Separatist movement. A lifelong commitment to that church followed; Bradford first joined the Scrooby congregation, later migrated to Holland in 1608, and sailed with the Pilgrims in 1620. Shortly after his arrival in the New World, Bradford was elected governor of the Plymouth settlement.

Bradford's principal literary contributions lie in the area of history; his account of the Puritans' early settlement provides both an invaluable document of early American life and a powerful example of how Puritan theology found expression in the literal events of history. His lengthy *History of Plymouth Plantation* (1856) has been hailed as a masterpiece by both contemporary critics and Puritan theologian Cotton Mather. Bradford's work frames the development of the New World in biblical terms that illustrate the purposes of an omnipotent God. Bradford also employed verse in his exploration of Providence. His *Collected Verse* consists of largely didactic meditations. Widely read, Bradford's work influenced several generations of Puritan intellectuals.

NONFICTION BY BRADFORD

History of Plymouth Plantation. Rprt. Serv. 1989 repr. of 1856 ed. $99.00. ISBN 0-7812-2037-8

POETRY BY BRADFORD

William Bradford: The Collected Verse. Ed. by Michael G. Runyan. J. Colet Pr. 1974 o.p.

BOOKS ABOUT BRADFORD

Emerson, E. H., ed. *Major Writers of Early American Literature.* U. of Wis. Pr. 1972 $14.50. ISBN 0-299-06194-9. An outstanding collection of essays on Puritan thought, theology, historiography, and iconography; includes an examination of Bradford.

Gay, Peter. *A Loss of Mastery: Puritan Historians in Colonial America.* Bks. Demand repr. of 1966 ed. $44.00. ISBN 0-685-23585-8. A particularly useful text that explores Bradford's work within the context of Puritan historiography, its essential structure and typologies.

Murdock, Kenneth B. *Literature and Theology in Colonial New England.* Greenwood 1970 repr. of 1949 ed. $35.00. ISBN 0-8371-3990-2. An overview of religion and literature in America before 1776.

Westbrook, Perry D. *William Bradford.* Twayne 1978 o.p. General life and work.

BRADSTREET, ANNE. c.1612–1672.

Anne Bradstreet, daughter of one governor of the Massachusetts colony (Thomas Dudley) and wife of another (Simon Bradstreet), was the first woman to be widely recognized as an important and accomplished American poet. Educated at home in England and well-tutored in the classics, Bradstreet married one of her father's assistants and traveled with Simon Bradstreet and her parents to New England in 1630. The ship, *The Arbella*, landed only a decade after the first Pilgrims, and Anne Bradstreet admitted to some discomfiture when she first witnessed the deprivation that the New World required. Nonetheless, Bradstreet settled in what would become Massachusetts and reared her eight children there.

A "good" Puritan—more concerned with the world of God than with the world of humans—Bradstreet was still aware of the sensual power of language and the sway of familial affections. Her poetry explores this paradox through the employment of elegant, lyrical conceits. Her work also probes the position of women within the patriarchal structure of Puritan society. "The Flesh and the Spirit" (1678) explores such contradictory impulses, while "Dialogue between Old and New" (1650) uses the Old and New Worlds as metaphors through which to decry both political upheaval and the tenuous nature of all relationships.

Writing in an era when women's voices were frequently repressed or unrepresented, Bradstreet found a way to be heard; her poetry both reaffirms and reevaluates Puritan values.

POETRY BY BRADSTREET

The Complete Works of Anne Bradstreet. Ed. by Joseph R. McElrath, Jr., and Allan P. Robb. Twayne 1981 o.p. Good edition.

The Tenth Muse Lately Sprung Up in America. Rprt. Serv. 1989 repr. of 1650 ed. $79.00. ISBN 0-7812-2041-6. A collection of early poems.

Works in Prose and Verse. Peter Smith $18.00. ISBN 0-8446-1087-9. Works known by 1867.

The Works of Anne Bradstreet. Ed. by Jeannie Hensley. HUP 1981 o.p. Foreword by Adrienne Rich. The most complete edition of her works.

BOOKS ABOUT BRADSTREET

Campbell, Helen. *Anne Bradstreet and her Time.* Lothrop 1891 o.p. An older study still frequently referred to.

Cowell, Pattie, and Ann Stanford, eds., *Critical Essays on Anne Bradstreet*. G. K. Hall 1983 o.p. A collection of various critical perspectives, containing addresses, essays, and lectures devoted to Bradstreet.

Dolle, Raymond F. *Anne Bradstreet: A Reference Guide*. Macmillan 1990 $40.00. ISBN 0-8161-8974-9. Provides a current and exhaustive bibliography.

Martin, Wendy. *The Lives and Work of Anne Bradstreet, Emily Dickinson and Adrienne Rich*. U. of NC Pr. 1983 o.p. A highly contemporary discussion of feminism and subversive discourse in Bradstreet's work.

――――. "Anne Bradstreet's Poetry: A Study in Subversive Piety." In *Shakespeare's Sisters*. Ed. by Sandra Gilbert and Susan Gubar. Ind. U. Pr. 1979 $35.00. ISBN 0-253-11258-3. Bradstreet as an early feminist.

Rosenmeier, Rosamond. *Anne Bradstreet Revisited*. Macmillan 1991 $22.95. ISBN 0-8057-7625-7. A contemporary perspective of Bradstreet's work and an acknowledgment of the new position Bradstreet holds within the American academy.

Stanford, Anne. *Anne Bradstreet: The Worldly Puritan*. B. Franklin 1974 o.p. A sensitive treatment of the contradictory impulses in Bradstreet's poetry.

White, Elizabeth Wade. *Anne Bradstreet* OUP 1971 o.p. A solid biography.

BROWN, CHARLES BROCKDEN. 1771–1810.

Charles Brockden Brown, the first full-time professional writer in the United States, is considered by many to be the nation's first important novelist. He is noted chiefly for having written four Gothic novels that prefigure one of America's most significant traditions, the sort of psychological-moralistic fiction written by HAWTHORNE, POE, HENRY JAMES, FAULKNER, and FLANNERY O'CONNOR.

Brown was also admired and imitated by English writers such as MARY SHELLEY, PERCY BYSSHE SHELLEY, and THOMAS LOVE PEACOCK. While Brown's texts displayed some of the indulgences inherent in the Gothic tradition, his work is notable for its inventive and sophisticated construction and for what Brown termed "moral painting." Within four years, from 1789 to 1801, he published six novels. *Wieland* (1798), perhaps his best-known work, was based on an actual murder case in New York, but Brown was less interested in the sensational aspects than in the moral and psychological implications of the case. *Ormand* (1799) deals with an attempted seduction but is ultimately about the struggle of conflicting values. *Arthur Mervyn* (1799), the longest of Brown's novels, is a realistic account of the yellow fever plague that occurred in Philadelphia in 1733. *Edgar Huntly* (1799), though occasionally incredible, is a skillful interrogation of moral ambiguities and complexities. Before he abandoned novel writing for a career in journalism in 1804, Brown published two more novels, *Clara Howard* and *Jane Talbot*, both in 1801.

Although for many years Brown's work received relatively limited attention, scholarly interest in his work has increased dramatically in the past 40 years. All of his fiction is once more in print, and carefully edited volumes of his works have recently been published by Kent State University Press.

NOVELS BY BROWN

Edgar Huntly: Memoirs of a Sleep Walker. 1799. Rprt. Serv. 1989 repr. of 1799 ed. $79.00. ISBN 0-7812-2068-8

Jane Talbot. 1801. Rprt. Serv. 1989 repr. of 1804 ed. $79.00. ISBN 0-7812-2072-6

The Novels and Related Works of Charles Brockden Brown: Wieland and Memoirs of Carwin. Ed. by Sydney J. Krause and S. W. Reid. Kent St. U. Pr. 1977 $35.00. ISBN 0-87338-160-2. The definitive edition, still in progress.

Novels of Charles Brockden Brown. 6 vols. B. Franklin 1968 repr. of 1887 ed. o.p. The earlier standard edition.

Ormand, or The Secret Witness. G. Forman 1799 o.p.

Wieland, or, The Transformation. 1798. Ed. by Fred L. Patee. Doubleday 1969 $7.95. ISBN 0-385-03100-9

BOOKS ABOUT BROWN

Axelrod, Alan. *Charles Brockden Brown: An American Tale.* U. of Tex. Pr. 1983 $27.50. ISBN 0-292-71076-3. An interesting study of four Brown novels—*Wieland, Ormond, Arthur Mervyn,* and *Edgar Huntly.*

Clark, David L. *Charles Brockden Brown: Pioneer Voice of America.* Duke repr. of 1952 ed. $22.50. ISBN 0-404-01548-4. A solid biography.

Dunlap, William. *The Life of Charles Brockden Brown.* Rprt. Serv. 1992 repr. of 1815 ed. $75.00. ISBN 0-7812-2718-6. Reissued in 1977, with a text begun by Brown's friend Paul Allen and completed by Dunlap; despite some inaccuracies, the chief source of information about Brown, including letters and fragments of works otherwise unavailable.

Grabo, Norman S. *The Coincidental Art of Charles Brockden Brown.* U. of NC Pr. 1981 $27.50. ISBN 0-8078-1474-1. Critical readings of Brown's works.

Parker, Patricia. *Charles Brockden Brown: A Reference Guide.* G. K. Hall 1980 o.p. A useful bibliography.

Ringe, Donald A. *Charles Brockden Brown. Twayne's US Authors Series.* Macmillan 1991 $22.95. ISBN 0-8057-7606-0. A useful study, including a current bibliographical reference.

Rosenthal, Bernard, ed. *Critical Essays on Charles Brockden Brown.* G. K. Hall 1981 o.p. A new approach to the major and minor works.

Warfel, Harry R. *Charles Brockden Brown: American Gothic Novelist.* Hippocrene Bks. 1974 o.p. Reproduction of the 1949 edition; reliable, useful biography with criticism of the novels.

EDWARDS, JONATHAN. 1703–1758

Born in East Windsor, Connecticut, to Reverend Timothy and Esther Stoddard Edwards—the daughter of the famous liberal cleric Reverend Solomon Stoddard of Massachusetts—Jonathan Edwards seemed from the start predestined to become a preeminent figure among Puritan intellectuals and literary artists. In 1716 Edwards was admitted to Yale at the remarkable age of thirteen. After he graduated in 1722, he spent four years there pursuing theological interests, teaching, and completing his master's degree. In 1727 Edwards complied with his grandfather's request and traveled to Northhampton, Massachusetts to be his assistant in his church. In the same year, Edwards married Sarah Pierrpont, with whom he eventually had eleven children.

A committed scholar of JOHN CALVIN (see Vol. 4) and the early Puritan theologians, as well as of the writings of JOHN LOCKE (see Vols. 3 and 4) and ISAAC NEWTON (see Vols. 4 and 5), Edwards pursued a theology founded on two seemingly contradictory themes—a desire to return to the Calvinist tradition, as well as a desire to include the insights of contemporary Enlightenment philosophy. While Edwards's theological formulations were not completely developed until the 1750s, his lifetime pursuit of these ideas profoundly influenced the Puritan period of religious revival known as the Great Awakening. Though Edwards's provocative theology and sermons occasionally invoked fire and brimstone, as in the famous *Sinners in the Hands of an Angry God* (1741), his sermons generally moved parishioners to faith through the employment of positive imagery, as in *God Glorified in Man's Dependence* (1731).

In spite of his successes during the Great Awakening, Edwards was ultimately involved in a controversy that led to his dismissal at the Northhampton parish in 1750. Viewed as too progressive by a faction of the church known as the Old Lights, Edwards stepped down after delivering his famous *Farewell Sermon*

TYLER, ROYALL. 1757–1826.

When Royall Tyler courted the young Abigail Adams, her father, JOHN ADAMS (see Vol. 3), wrote to his wife that he disapproved of Tyler's suit. He suggested that Tyler drop his literary aspirations and focus on the law. A man of contrasts, Royall Tyler found neither occupation mutually exclusive; he distinguished himself as a lawyer and a military officer, as well as a poet and dramatist. Born William Clark Tyler to a well-established Boston family on July 18, 1757, Tyler was quickly schooled in colonial politics. His father was a member of the Massachusetts House of Representatives and was actively opposed to British interference. When the senior Tyler died in 1771, his fourteen-year-old son adopted his father's name—Royall.

Tyler graduated from Harvard and received an honorary degree from Yale. In 1779 he was awarded a Master of Arts degree from Harvard, and in 1780 he was admitted to the Massachusetts bar. During his college years, Tyler served briefly as a military aide in 1778. During the 1780s, Tyler acted on the government's behalf in quelling Shays's Rebellion, a farmer's revolt in western Massachusetts. Tyler proved himself an excellent counselor and barrister; in 1807 he became chief justice of the Supreme Court of Vermont, as well as a trustee and law professor at the University of Vermont. In 1794 Tyler married Mary Palmer, the daughter of the family with whom he had resided during the time of Shays's Rebellion.

Concurrent with his civic career, Royall Tyler enjoyed another vocation. A prolific writer, particularly of drama, Tyler saw his first play, *The Contrast*, produced in 1787. Like much of his work, this play dealt with the theme of American exceptionalism. Unlike some of his contemporaries, Tyler refused to mimic continental themes and forms and sought to create uniquely American works. Critics have commented at some length on his use of dialect and satire and upon his indictment of duplicitous European influences on the naive and upright American character. Tyler's papers and manuscripts are collected at the Vermont Historical Society, Montpelier, Vermont.

PLAYS BY TYLER

The Algerine Captive; or, the Life and Adventures of Doctor Updike Underhill. NCUP 1970 $16.95. ISBN 0-8084-0048-7. Comic adventure-dramas.
The Chestnut Tree. Driftwood 1931 o.p. A play.
The Contrast: A Comedy in Five Acts. Rprt. Serv. 1992 repr. of 1920 ed. $69.00. ISBN 0-685-51259-2
Four Plays by Royall Tyler. Ed. by Arthur Wallace Peach and George Newbrough. Princeton U. Pr. 1941 o.p. Includes *The Contrast*.

POETRY BY TYLER

The Verse of Royall Tyler. Ed. by Marius B. Peladeau. U. Pr. of Va. 1968 $28.50. ISBN 0-8139-0235-5. Collected poetry.

WORKS BY TYLER

The Prose of Royall Tyler. Ed. by Marius B. Peladeau. VT Hist. Soc. 1972. Collected prose.

BOOKS ABOUT TYLER

Carson, Ada Lou, and Herbert L. Carson. *Royall Tyler*. Twayne 1979 o.p. A general overview of his life and work.
Tanselle, G. Thomas. *Royall Tyler*. HUP 1967 o.p. The best biography of Tyler.

WHEATLEY, PHILLIS. c.1754–1784.

Seized in Senegal/Gambia, West Africa by slave traders, Phillis Wheatley arrived in Boston when she was about seven years old. Purchased as a domestic in 1761, by Susanna and John Wheatley, Phillis Wheatley was frail and asthmatic. Perhaps because of her delicate constitution, she was excused from the most tiring aspects of her domestic duties. Instead, she was taught to read and write and was instructed in the Bible and the classics. Before she was thirteen, Wheatley was writing poetry that gained quick and widespread acclaim; in 1770 she published her first poem—"An Elegiac Poem on the Death of that Celebrated Divine, and Eminent Servant of Jesus Christ, the Reverend and Learned George Whitefield"—a work that touched on the terrible conditions of her own Atlantic crossing.

By 1772 Phillis Wheatley had compiled a collection of verse. Unfortunately, despite the best efforts of John and Susanna Wheatley, no publisher within the colonies was willing to print literature written by an African. Nonetheless, the Wheatleys persisted in their search, and through the intervention of BENJAMIN FRANKLIN and various British sympathizers, including the abolitionist Earl of Dartmouth, they succeeded in finding a publisher for the work. *Poems on Various Subjects, Religious and Moral* was printed in London in 1772; it is the first collection of poetry written by an African American to be published.

Three months before Susanna Wheatley died in 1774 she manumitted (freed) Phillis Wheatley. But with Susanna's death, the Wheatley family disintegrated, and Phillis Wheatley suffered from severe financial difficulties during the Revolutionary War. Despite the voiced misgivings of her friends, Phillis Wheatley married John Peters in 1778. Their marriage was troubled by penury and sickness; in 1784, John Peters was confined to jail because of debt. Wheatley bore three children. Of these, two died in infancy and the third outlived her mother by only a few days. Desperate for assistance, Wheatley worked as a charwoman and maid. Destitute, sick, and alone, Phillis Wheatley died in 1784; she was barely thirty.

Wheatley wrote approximately 145 poems, including the 64-line work "Liberty and Peace," published as a pamphlet under the name of Phillis Peters. Criticized during the early part of this century for not more openly addressing the theme of slavery, Wheatley's work combines Christian imagery and classical typology with an undeniably elegiac tone. Recent scholarship suggests that her Biblical allusions and metaphors demonstrate an antipathy to slavery and that her elegant and educated verse served to undermine colonial institutions of power.

POETRY BY WHEATLEY

The Collected Works of Phillis Wheatley. Ed. by John C. Shields. OUP 1988 $26.00. ISBN 0-19-505241-2. A well-researched and well-edited edition with an extensive bibliography; part of a larger series focusing on nineteenth-century African-American women writers.

An Elegiac Poem on the Death of that Celebrated Divine and Eminent Servant of Jesus Christ the Reverend and Learned George Whitefield. E. Russell & J. Boyles 1770 o.p. A celebration of the life of the famous evangelical preacher.

Liberty and Peace, A Poem. Warden & Russell 1784 o.p. A celebration of American victory.

The Life and Works of Phillis Wheatley. Ed. by G. Herbert Renfro. Ayer 1916 $13.95. ISBN 0-8369-8685-7. A sound biography and early edition of works.

The Poems of Phillis Wheatley. Ed. by Julian D. Mason, Jr. U. of NC Pr. 1989 $27.50. ISBN 0-8078-1835-6. A solid but limited work.

Poems on Various Subjects, Religious and Moral. 1772. AMS Pr. repr. of 1786 ed. $18.00. ISBN 0-404-00126-2

BOOKS ABOUT WHEATLEY

Barker-Barfield, G. J., and Catherine Clinton. *Portraits of American Women.* St. Martin 1991 $35.00. ISBN 0-312-05798-9. Places Wheatley's work within the larger context of women and minority writers.

Graham, Shirley. *The Story of Phillis Wheatley* Messner 1949 o.p. A general, admiring biography.

Richmond, Merle A. *Bid the Vassal Soar: Interpretive Essays on the Life and Poetry of Phillis Wheatley and George Moses Horton.* Howard U. Pr. 1974 $12.95. ISBN 0-88258-001-9. Useful interpretive essays.

Robinson, William H. *Phillis Wheatley in the Black American Beginnings* Broadside Pr. 1975 o.p. A sound general study.

_____. *Phillis Wheatley: A Bio-Bibliography.* Perhaps the most exhaustive account of Wheatley's life and works to date.

CHAPTER 14

Early Nineteenth-Century American Literature

Thomas Wortham

> Give us, then, *nationality*; give us excess of it. Let us love the yet barren hills
> of our own literature, and we shall learn to make them wave and smile with
> harvests. Let our authors strike their roots into their native soil and spread
> themselves to their native sun, and they will flourish.
> —CHARLES INGERSOLL, from a speech in honor of Edwin Forrest

The battle for cultural and artistic independence in the United States took far longer to win than either that for political autonomy or that for economic self-sufficiency. As late as 1820, the English minister and author Sydney Smith could, in annoying fairness, ask: "In the four quarters of the globe, who reads an American book? or goes to an American play? or looks at an American picture or statue?" There can be no question that there exists among many in the United States the desire for a native literature. Hadn't THOMAS PAINE proclaimed, following the American Revolution: "We see [now] with other eyes; we hear with other ears; and think with other thoughts than we formerly used. . . . Every corner of the mind is swept of its cobwebs, poison and dust, and made fit for the reception of generous happiness"? Hadn't Noah Webster already begun his campaign for establishing an American English distinct both in spelling and vocabulary from the language of Great Britain? And hadn't many of the great European philosophers such as JOHANN VON HERDER (see Vol. 2) and poets such as JOHANN VON GOETHE (see Vol. 2) declared that the United States was the land of the future? It is true that America's nationalistic yearnings did at times become mere jingoistic bombast. America's large size, its natural beauty, even its noble ideals of freedom and equality did not necessarily ensure a literature commensurate with these qualities. But, on the whole, the quest for nationality in American literature was remarkably self-critical and restrained in its polemics. As heirs to one of the great literatures of Europe, American writers and critics were both challenged and subdued by the enormity of their task; but, at the same time, enormous political optimism and romantic faith in their mission sustained such individuals as Charles Ingersoll, the Philadelphia lawyer and man of letters whose words preface this chapter, in his belief that, in time, an American literature would flourish and serve the people well.

The United States at the beginning of the nineteenth century enjoyed certain decided advantages for the emergence of a distinctive literary culture, but it still had to contend with a number of barriers to its growth. First was a deeply rooted, native prejudice against the fine arts, a result both of its Puritan heritage and of the realities of frontier life. The familiar story of Captain John Smith's advice to the aristocratic idlers at Jamestown—to eat you must work—reflects that deep devotion to the practical, the utilitarian, that still largely characterizes these United States. As JAMES RUSSELL LOWELL noted in the late 1830s, "New England has written her epic in railroads and commerce. . . . Her people value a new ventilation system more than a great poem."

Difficult, too, for those who would establish a Republic of Arts and Letters in the "New World" was the inability of local economies for many years to support these ambitions. Without great wealth in the hands of a few, the patronage of the arts in the United States was by necessity democratic; artists and writers supported themselves through the purchase of their wares. For printers and publishers, as today, the "bottom line" ruled supreme. Urban centers with printing houses and sufficient population with enough wealth and leisure to support the development of a nonutilitarian literature were long in coming, and, when they finally arrived, American printers found it much more profitable to pirate the works of English authors than to pay royalties to lesser-known native authors. It would be nearly a century before an effective international copyright agreement became law, and the lack of such a law during the nineteenth century kept American authors at a more or less permanent disadvantage.

In the end, however, these disadvantages were outweighed by certain circumstances that did support the emergence of an American literature within a relatively short period of time. For one thing, citizens of the United States were among the most literate people in the world—a political necessity in the view of the country's leaders if the bold project of democratic self-government was to work. Few foreign observers failed to notice how important the printed word was as a force in American society. Then, too, the rapid growth of a market economy during the early nineteenth century enabled an increasing number of Americans, either individually or through library societies, to purchase books and magazines. Also important was the way romanticism—which emerged just as American literature was developing—was in so many ways ideally suited to and, in fact, demanded by, American needs and expectations. The first important generation of American writers—the generation of BRYANT, IRVING, and COOPER—had its origins in a neoclassical, intellectually conservative, provincial society, whose values necessarily saw the newer American literature as inferior to the older British classical culture. In a world adhering to neoclassicism, American literature would always take its cue from elsewhere. But romanticism offered America the artistic and philosophical resources to achieve the literary autonomy desired by so many, the basis on which the next generation, that of EMERSON and HAWTHORNE, would bring the dream of independence to the full light of day.

HISTORY AND CRITICISM

Anderson, Douglas R. *A House Undivided: Domesticity and Community in American Literature*. Cambridge U. Pr. 1990 $37.50. ISBN 0-521-38287-4. A reading of major American literary works in terms of the tradition of domestic and communal discourse originating in Puritan New England.

Anderson, Quentin. *The Imperial Self: An Essay in American Literary and Cultural History*. Knopf 1971 o.p. Argues that an "absolutism of the self" and a rejection of community values distinguishes much nineteenth-century literature, particularly that of Emerson, Whitman, and James.

Andrews, William L., ed. *Literary Romanticism in America.* La. State U. Pr. 1981 $19.95. ISBN 0-8071-0760-3. Seven essays that consider romanticism as "the ability to wonder and to reflect."

Blair, Walter, and Hamlin Hill. *America's Humor: From Poor Richard to Doonesbury.* OUP 1980 $9.95. ISBN 0-19-502756-6. An excellent history of humorous writing in the United States.

Brooks, Van Wyck. *The Flowering of New England, 1815–1865.* AMS Pr. repr. of 1936 ed. $45.00. ISBN 0-404-18007-8. An analysis of "the New England mind," especially as revealed in major literary works.

Brown, Gillian. *Domestic Individualism: Imagining Self in Nineteenth-Century America.* U. CA Pr. 1990 $24.95. ISBN 0-520-06785-1. Considers the implications of gender and domesticity for American views of individualism as reflected in literary works.

Buell, Lawrence. *Literary Transcendentalism: Style and Vision in the American Renaissance.* Cornell Univ. Pr. 1975 $12.95. ISBN 0-8014-9152-5. A fine analysis of the literary art and criticism of such figures as Emerson, Thoreau, Ellery Channing, Jones Very, and Whitman.

———. *New England Literary Culture from Revolution through Renaissance.* Cambridge U. Pr. 1986 $44.50. ISBN 0-521-30206-4. A fine discussion of New England's centrality in American literary culture of the period, 1776–1860.

Chai, Leon. *The Romantic Foundations of the American Renaissance.* Cornell Univ. Pr. 1987 $12.95. ISBN 0-685-18694-6. A comparative study of the literary relationship between the literature of the United States and European romanticism.

Charvat, William. *The Profession of Authorship in America, 1800–1870.* Ed. by Matthew J. Bruccoli. Col. U. Pr. 1992 $42.50. ISBN 0-231-07076-4. A pioneering study of the economic influences upon the development of the literature of the United States.

Conn, Peter. *Literature in America: An Illustrated History.* Cambridge U. Pr. 1989 $29.95. ISBN 0-521-30373-7. An excellent introduction for the general reader.

Coultrap-McQuin, Susan. *Doing Literary Business: American Women Writers in the Nineteenth Century.* U. of NC Pr. 1990 $29.95. ISBN 0-8078-1914-X. A study of the impediments and opportunities for women in the literary marketplace.

Cunliffe, Marcus, ed. *American Literature to Nineteen Hundred.* P. Bedrick Bks. 1987 $39.50. ISBN 0-87226-132-8. A fine general history written by a prominent British critic.

Dekker, George. *The American Historical Romance.* Cambridge U. Pr. 1987 $47.50. ISBN 0-521-33282-6. A study of the impact of Sir Walter Scott's historical novels on the development of fiction in the United States.

Douglas, Ann. *The Feminization of American Culture.* Doubleday 1988 $11.95. ISBN 0-385-24241-7. A groundbreaking study of gender issues in nineteenth-century American literary culture.

Elliott, Emory, ed. *Columbia Literary History of the United States.* Col. U. Pr. 1988 $75.00. ISBN 0-231-05812-8. Standard academic history written by leading specialists.

Feidelson, Charles N., Jr. *Symbolism in American Literature.* U. Ch. Pr. 1983 $17.95. ISBN 0-226-24026-6. Argues that the distinctive quality of mid-nineteenth-century American literature is its writers' "devotion to the possibilities of symbolism."

Ferguson, Robert A. *Law and Letters in American Culture.* HUP 1984 $27.50. ISBN 0-674-51465-3. An excellent study of the relationship between legal theory and literary practice in early nineteenth-century America.

Harbert, Earl N., and Robert A. Rees, eds. *Fifteen American Authors before 1900: Bibliographical Essays on Research and Criticism.* U. of Wis. Pr. 1984 $27.50. ISBN 0-299-09590-8. Bibliographical essays on the criticism and scholarship that has been done on Bryant, Cooper, Holmes, Irving, Longfellow, Lowell, Whittier, and others.

Hart, James D. *The Oxford Companion to American Literature.* OUP 1983 $49.95. ISBN 0-19-503074-5. An excellent dictionary of American authors, books, and literary movements and events.

Horwitz, Howard. *By the Law of Nature: Form and Value in Nineteenth-Century America.* OUP 1991 $39.95. ISBN 0-19-506227-2. A reading of American literature in terms of economic and political developments.

Howe, Irving. *The American Newness: Culture and Politics in the Age of Emerson.* HUP 1986 $15.00. ISBN 0-674-02640-3. Considers the pervasiveness of Emerson in nineteenth-century American literature.

Jones, Howard Mumford. *Revolution and Romanticism.* HUP 1974 $27.95. ISBN 0-674-76710-1. A well-written but fairly old-fashioned reading of American literature between the American Revolution and the Civil War.

Kelley, Mary. *Private Woman, Public Stage: Literary Domesticity in Nineteenth-Century America.* OUP 1984 $12.95. ISBN 0-19-503581-X. An informed and sophisticated historical perspective on the role of several popular women writers in American culture.

Lawrence, D. H. *Studies in Classic American Literature.* Viking Penguin 1977 $6.95. ISBN 0-14-003300-9. An influential modernist reading of American literature by the important British novelist.

Lease, Benjamin. *Anglo-American Encounters: England and the Rise of American Literature.* Cambridge U. Pr. 1982 $49.50. ISBN 0-521-23666-5. Studies the literary relationship between England and the United States.

Leverenz, David. *Manhood and the American Renaissance.* Cornell Univ. Pr. 1989 $35.00. ISBN 0-8014-2281-7. Examines how mid-nineteenth-century American writers struggled with their society's definitions of manhood.

Lewis, R. W. B. *The American Adam: Innocence, Tragedy, and Tradition in the Nineteenth Century.* U. Ch. Pr. 1959 $8.95. ISBN 0-226-47681-2. An examination of the Genesis myth (the new person in a new land) in early nineteenth-century American literature.

Lindberg, Gary. *The Confidence Man in American Literature.* OUP 1982 $29.95. ISBN 0-19-502939-9. A critical history of the use of the "con man" in American literature.

McWilliams, John P., Jr. *The American Epic: Transforming a Genre, 1770–1860.* Cambridge U. Pr. 1989 $34.50. ISBN 0-521-37322-0. A superb analysis of early nineteenth-century American literature in terms of its attempt to refashion the epic for modern usage.

Marchalonis, Shirley, ed. *Patrons and Protégées: Gender, Friendship, and Writing in Nineteenth-Century America.* Rutgers U. Pr. 1988 $28.00. ISBN 0-8135-1270-0. Examines nine important male–female literary relationships.

Marx, Leo. *The Machine in the Garden: Technology and the Pastoral Idea in America.* OUP 1964 $9.95. ISBN 0-19-500738-7. Examines how the pastoral ideal came to be used to define an increasingly technological society.

Matthiessen, F. O. *American Renaissance: Art and Expression in the Age of Emerson and Whitman.* OUP 1968 $18.95. ISBN 0-19-500759-X. A pioneering study of the flowering of American letters between 1850 and 1855.

Miller, Perry. *The Life of the Mind in America, from the Revolution to the Civil War.* HarBraceJ 1970 $12.95. ISBN 0-15-651990-9. Especially good discussion on the American concept of the "sublime" as revealed in literature and art.

———. *The Raven and the Whale: The War of Words and Wits in the Era of Poe and Melville.* Greenwood 1973 repr. of 1956 ed. $45.50. ISBN 0-8371-6707-8. A lively study of the literary and cultural politics in New York during the 1840s and 1850s.

Myerson, Joel, ed. *The Transcendentalists: A Review of Research and Criticism.* Modern Lang. 1984 $34.00. ISBN 0-87352-260-5. Bibliographical essays on the criticism and scholarship devoted to the American Transcendentalists (Emerson, Thoreau, Fuller, etc).

Nelson, Dana. *The Word in Black and White: Writing "Race" in American Literature from Colonization through the Civil War.* OUP 1991 $29.95. ISBN 0-19-506592-1. A critically sophisticated examination of awareness of race in American writing.

Parrington, Vernon Louis. *The Romantic Revolution in America, 1800–1860.* U. of Okla. Pr. 1987 $32.95. ISBN 0-8061-2078-9. The second volume of the author's important liberal interpretation of *Main Currents in American Thought* (1927–1930).

Poirier, Richard. *A World Elsewhere: The Place of Style in American Literature.* OUP 1966 $4.95. ISBN 0-19-500778-6. An examination of the relationship of style to theme and authorial intention.

Porte, Joel. *In Respect to Egotism: Studies in American Romantic Writing.* Cambridge U. Pr. 1991 $44.50. ISBN 0-521-36273-3. Explores various literary responses to Emersonian individualism.

Reynolds, David S. *Beneath the American Renaissance: The Subversive Imagination in the Age of Emerson and Melville.* HUP 1989 $15.95. ISBN 0-674-06565-4. Examines the impact of popular literature on the literature of "high culture" in the mid-nineteenth century.

Reynolds, Larry J. *European Revolutions and the American Literary Renaissance.* Yale U. Pr. 1988 $25.00. ISBN 0-300-04242-6. Studies American responses to the European revolutions of 1848 and 1849.

Rourke, Constance. *American Humor: A Study of the National Character.* U. Press Fla. 1986 $13.00. ISBN 0-8130-0837-9. A pioneering study of an important American literary and cultural tradition—humor.

Rubin, Louis D., Jr., and others. *The History of Southern Literature.* La. State U. Pr. 1990 $16.95. ISBN 0-8071-1643-2. A standard history of the literature of the American South by an impressive group of scholars and critics.

Simpson, David. *The Politics of American English, 1776–1850.* OUP 1986 $36.00. ISBN 0-19-503724-3. An excellent study of the development of an American sense of a national language.

Simpson, Lewis P. *The Man of Letters in New England and the South: Essays on the History of the Literary Vocation in America.* La. State U. Pr. 1973 $32.50. ISBN 0-8071-0216-4. A comparative study of the ideals that informed literary lives in antebellum America.

Slotkin, Richard. *The Fatal Environment: The Myth of the Frontier in the Age of Industrialization, 1800–1890.* U. Pr. of New Eng. 1986 $22.95. ISBN 0-8195-6183-5. A thorough history of the frontier myth as it exists in American culture and literature.

_____. *Regeneration through Violence: The Mythology of the American Frontier, 1600–1860.* U. Pr. of New Eng. 1973 $22.95. ISBN 0-8195-6034-0. Argues that American myths employed violence as a form of renewal and regeneration on the frontier.

Smith, Henry Nash. *Virgin Land: The American West as Symbol and Myth.* HUP 1950 $9.95. ISBN 0-674-93955-7. A classic study of the impact of the American frontier on the development of American literature.

Sundquist, Eric J. *Home as Found: Authority and Genealogy in Nineteenth-Century American Literature.* Johns Hopkins 1979 $32.00. ISBN 0-8018-2241-6. Examines themes of alienation and family in works by Cooper, Thoreau, Hawthorne, and Melville.

Tebbel, John, and Mary Ellen Waller-Zuckerman. *The Magazine in America, 1741–1900.* OUP 1991 $35.00. ISBN 0-19-505127-0. A good narrative history of the emergence of magazines and their impact on American culture.

Tichi, Cecelia. *New World, New Earth: Environmental Reform in American Literature from the Puritans through Whitman.* Yale U. Pr. 1979 $35.00. ISBN 0-300-02287-5. Explores American writers' attitudes toward American physical geography and its uses.

Weisbuch, Robert. *Atlantic Double-Cross: American Literature and British Influence in the Age of Emerson.* U. Ch. Pr. 1989 $29.95. ISBN 0-226-89149-6. A comparative study of major British and American writers of the early nineteenth century.

Woodress, James, ed. *Eight American Authors: A Review of Research and Criticism.* Norton 1971 o.p. Bibliographical essays on the criticism and scholarship done on Emerson, Poe, Thoreau, Whitman, and others.

Woodress, James, and J. Albert Robbins, eds. *American Literary Scholarship.* 27 vols. Duke 1964–1990 $45.00 ea. ISBNs 0-8223-0196-2—0-8223-1234-4. Annual review of current criticism and scholarship on American authors.

COLLECTIONS

Barksdale, Richard, and Kenneth Kinnamon, eds. *Black Writers of America: A Comprehensive Anthology*. Macmillan 1972 $35.25. ISBN 0-02-306080-8. An excellent one-volume collection of African American literature.

Baym, Nina, and others, eds. *The Norton Anthology of American Literature*. 2 vols. Norton 1989 $27.95 ea. ISBNs 0-393-95736-5, 0-393-95740-1. Widely used in college surveys.

Brooks, Cleanth, R. W. B. Lewis, and Robert Penn Warren, eds. *American Literature: The Makers and the Making*. 2 vols. St. Martin 1973 $26.60 ea. ISBNs 0-312-025890-4, 0–312–02660–9. Distinguished by the excellence of the editors' commentaries and introductions.

Butcher, Philip, ed. *The Minority Presence in American Literature 1600–1900*. 2 vols. Howard U. Pr. 1977 $25.00. ISBN 0-88258-103-1. The most comprehensive anthology of "minority" literature in the nineteenth-century United States.

Foerster, Norman, and others, eds. *American Poetry and Prose*. 3 vols. HM 1970 $43.96. ISBN 0-395-04456-1. Somewhat old but still valuable anthology, especially for those writers who are now regarded as "minor."

Lauter, Paul, and others, eds. *The Heath Anthology of American Literature*. 2 vols. Heath 1990 $19.50 ea. ISBNs 0-669-12064-2, 0-669-12065-0. A bold and controversial attempt to expand the canon of American letters in terms of gender, race, and ethnic identity.

McMichael, George, ed. *Anthology of American Literature. Vol. I: Colonial through Romantic*. Macmillan 1989 $24.00. ISBN 0-02-379621-9. A "consensus" anthology that maintains a nice balance between tradition and the reformed canons of American letters.

Turner, Frederick W., III, ed. *The Portable North American Indian Reader*. *Viking Portable Lib*. Viking Penguin 1977 $9.95. ISBN 0-14-015077-3. An excellent collection of Native American literature.

POETRY

Until the early nineteenth century, the writing of verse, as with other arts in the United States, was, for the most part, provincial and imitative. Only with the publication of WILLIAM CULLEN BRYANT's poetry in the 1820s did there appear a voice that was recognized both at home and abroad as distinctively American. Writing after COLERIDGE and WORDSWORTH, Bryant achieved a form that invaded postromantic vision with preromantic diction. His blank verse, in such a poem as "Thanatopsis," echoes the stateliness and sententiousness of the eighteenth-century British poets James Thompson and Edward Young at the same time that it clearly reflects Wordsworth's abiding trust in nature.

Bryant's successful work sets the stage for much of the popular American poetry that followed. HENRY WADSWORTH LONGFELLOW, JOHN GREENLEAF WHITTIER, JAMES RUSSELL LOWELL, and OLIVER WENDELL HOLMES all proved that there were American poets who could hold their own on the terms that English poetry had established for them. For a relatively young nation that had retained the language of its parent, these poets provided models of excellence—proof that Americans would at once accommodate themselves to English forms and at the same time establish American letters as a cultural reality. It is small wonder that they came to be known as the "Schoolroom Poets," for their success both here and abroad was a promise that this nation could, with education and effort, emulate the literature of its parent nation. Longfellow, perhaps more than any of the others, embodied the possibilities of such a poetic identity. Marvelously proficient in European languages, he was at once remarkably popular and extraordinarily urbane.

But because they imagined their poetic roles so much within the terms of a British tradition, there is always an element of competitive imitation in those poets' work. They were trying to be new, yet they were always a bit old-fashioned. The old eighteenth-century didacticism thus stands alongside their nineteenth-century awareness of issues and attitudes. Accomplished though these poets were, their conventionality outweighed their originality. Theirs was the "traditional" tradition: They were quite capable of setting American subject matter to English meters but, for the most part, were unable to discover new forms for their new subject matter. That was the achievement of another group of poets, upholders of the tradition of "the new," true innovators and pioneers. The central "new" figures are RALPH WALDO EMERSON, especially in his writing on poetry, and WALT WHITMAN, whose *Leaves of Grass* revolutionized poetic forms when it was published in 1855, just as earlier the Declaration of Independence had revolutionized political forms.

Insisting that poetry was "a metre making argument," Emerson sought a meter that would be equal to the rude strokes of nature he feared were being lost to the civilizing process of gentility. He realized that blank verse, which was both the natural and the royal line of English poetry, would have to be naturalized and democratized if it was ever to be true to the America he meant to find in the West. More than any other American writer, he called American literature into being. Like the true prophet he was, he did not so much predict the future as he made the future happen.

The poet that Emerson prophesied was Walt Whitman. Releasing himself from the uniformly measured line, Whitman all but broke down the distinction between poetry and prose. He wanted a freedom of verse that would be equal to the freedom of his vision; he wanted the poet to be equal to the reader and was able to imagine the two figures as identical. He thus envisioned himself dying into his words and being reborn as the reader's voice. Realizing that in the English pronominal system, the pronoun *you* retains its form whether it is singular or plural, Whitman made that linguistic fact the heart of his poetic program. Thus, in his poems the *you* always refers to the single reader as well as to the mass of readers Whitman dreamed of as an audience. His poetry is at once incredibly public and wonderfully intimate, just as his vision is at once extraordinarily general and remarkably concrete. In going forward into his free democratic vision, Whitman actually went back beyond both the English and classical masters to a Biblical past. His poetry is more like the Psalms than anything else, which is as it should be, since Whitman imagined himself a god incarnating the word that would in turn embody his readers. In his quest for a national voice that would express the profundities and promises of the American ideal, Whitman was the first poet to speak truly internationally, altering the course of poetry in all languages and literatures ever since.

History and Criticism

Allen, Gay Wilson. *American Prosody*. Hippocrene Bks. 1966 repr. of 1935 ed. $27.50. ISBN 0-374-90133-3. Close analyses of the theory and practice of American poetic technique.

Arms, George. *The Fields Were Green: A New View of Bryant, Whittier, Holmes, Lowell, and Longfellow*. Stanford U. Pr. 1953 $29.50. ISBN 0-8047-0443-0. "New Critical" readings of the Schoolroom Poets.

Duffey, Bernard. *Poetry in America: Expression and Its Values in the Times of Bryant, Whitman, and Pound*. Duke 1978 o.p. Focuses on the changing attitudes toward "the value assumed in poetic composition" from the early nineteenth century to the early twentieth century.

Fussell, Edwin. *Lucifer in Harness: American Meter, Metaphor and Diction*. Princeton U. Pr. 1973 $32.50. ISBN 0-691-06238-2. Examines ways in which American writers have worked within the conventions of traditional English poetics.

Gelpi, Albert. *The Tenth Muse: The Psyche of the American Poet*. Cambridge U. Pr. 1991 $54.50. ISBN 0-521-41339-7. Investigates the "American" quality of such poets as Emerson, Poe, and Whitman.

Kramer, Aaron. *The Prophetic Tradition in American Poetry, 1835–1900*. Fairleigh Dickinson 1975 $35.00. ISBN 0-8386-6774-0. Argues that American poets were influenced by the British romantics during the nineteenth century and were, for the most part, moral and prophetic.

Kreymborg, Alfred. *Our Singing Strength: An Outline of American Poetry (1620–1930)*. AMS Pr. repr. of 1929 ed. $45.00. ISBN 0-404-17123-0. An appreciative and enthusiastic history written for general audiences.

Lee, A. Robert, ed. *Nineteenth-Century American Poetry*. B & N Imports 1985 $38.50. ISBN 0-389-20377-7. A well-balanced collection of original essays appraising the achievements of nineteenth-century American poets.

Loving, Jerome. *Emerson, Whitman, and the American Muse*. U. of NC Pr. 1982 $24.95. ISBN 0-8078-1523-3. Finds in Emerson and Whitman the essence of the American tradition in poetry.

Pearce, Roy Harvey. *The Continuity of American Poetry*. U. Pr. of New Eng. 1987 $35.00. ISBN 0-8195-5155-4. A highly influential history of the role of poetry in American culture.

Sherman, Joan R. *Invisible Poets: Afro-Americans of the Nineteenth Century*. U. of Ill. Pr. 1989 $11.95. ISBN 0-252-06061-X. A pioneering biographical and critical study of African American poets during the nineteenth century.

Shucard, Alan. *American Poetry: The Puritans through Walt Whitman*. G. K. Hall 1988 $23.95. ISBN 0-8057-8450-0. U. of Mass. Pr. 1990 $11.95. ISBN 0-87023-719-5. A solid introductory survey, with separate chapters on Poe, Emerson, and Whitman.

Waggoner, Hyatt H. *American Poets, from the Puritans to the Present*. La. State U. Pr. 1984 $16.95. ISBN 0-8071-1163-5. A fine historical survey that argues Emerson's centrality to the poetry and poetics of the United States.

Walker, Cheryl. *Nightingale's Burden: Women Poets and American Culture before 1900*. Ind. U. Pr. 1983 $22.50. ISBN 0-253-34065-9. Examines how American culture has shaped the literary roles of women poets in the nineteenth century.

Watts, Emily Stipes. *The Poetry of American Women from 1632 to 1945*. U. of Tex. Pr. 1977 o.p. Includes two chapters that examine the rise of female poetry (1800–1850) and the achievements of Lydia Sigourney (1797–1865), Elizabeth Oakes Smith (1806–1893), and Frances Osgood (1811–1850).

Collections

Cook, George W., ed. *Poets of Transcendentalism: An Anthology*. B. Franklin 1971 repr. of 1903 ed. $21.00. ISBN 0-8337-0652-7. Includes a generous selection of poems edited by this early historian of the Transcendental Movement.

Ellman, Richard, ed. *The New Oxford Book of American Verse*. OUP 1976 $39.95. ISBN 0-19-502058-8. A valuable anthology but less thorough in its coverage of nineteenth-century verse than the Matthiessen anthology listed later in this section.

Hall, Donald, ed. *The Oxford Book of Children's Verse in America*. OUP 1985 $29.95. ISBN 0-19-503539-9. A chronological arrangement of poetry written for children from colonial times to the present.

Halpern, Daniel, ed. *The American Poetry Anthology*. Avon 1976 $9.95. ISBN 0-380-00399-6. An inexpensive, compact collection of selections from major poets.

Harmon, William, ed. *Oxford Book of American Light Verse*. OUP 1979 $29.95. ISBN 0-19-502509-1. Appreciative in its selections of the humorous moods of nineteenth-century verse.

Matthiessen, F. O. *Oxford Book of American Verse*. OUP 1950 $45.00. ISBN 0-19-500049-8. Fifty-one poets are arranged chronologically in this excellent anthology; an earlier *Oxford Book of American Verse* was compiled by Bliss Carman in 1927.

Sherman, Joan R. *African-American Poetry of the Nineteenth Century*. U. of Ill. Pr. 1992 $44.95. ISBN 0-252-01917-2. A well-annotated collection of 171 poems by 35 African American men and women.

Stedman, Edmund C., ed. *American Anthology, 1787–1900*. 2 vols. Scholarly 1969 repr. of 1900 ed. $89.00. ISBN 0-403-00057-2. The most comprehensive gathering of American verse of the nineteenth century; especially valuable for its inclusion of many minor writers.

Van Nostrand, Albert, and Charles H. Watts, eds. *The Conscious Voice: An Anthology of American Poetry from the Seventeenth Century to the Present*. *Granger Index Repr. Ser.* Ayer repr. of 1959 ed. $26.50. ISBN 0-8369-6045-9. A thorough and reliable anthology.

FICTION

The earliest American literature in English consisted chiefly of travel books, diaries, sermons, and political writing. Fiction and other imaginative literature was relatively late in development. This was partly because the early Puritan settlers were suspicious of the merely literary but also because this continent was, from a European point of view, a wilderness to be explored, cleared, settled, and governed—all of which meant emphasis on the practical and the utilitarian. This bias was reinforced at the beginning of the nineteenth century by the popularity in American intellectual circles of the Scottish School of Common-sense Philosophers. These followers of the British philosopher JOHN LOCKE (see Vols. 3 and 4) attacked the imagination and argued that novelists, especially, were portrayers of unreality. Mature readers should be given facts and doctrines, not imaginative indulgences in the form of foolish stories. G. Harrison Orians has cleverly summed up the variety of opposition that fiction encountered in press and pulpit at the beginning of the nineteenth century: "The dullest critics contended that novels were lies; the pious, that they served no virtuous purposes; the strenuous, that they softened sturdy minds; the utilitarian, that they crowded out more useful books; the realistic, that they painted adventure too romantic and love too vehement; the patriotic, that, dealing with European manners (as they so often did), they tended to confuse and dissatisfy republican youth."

However, such warnings and objections had, as they so often do, an effect that was just the opposite of the one desired. Though fewer than 100 works of fiction by American writers had been published in the United States before 1820, a readership for British and continental fiction had been created. Then appeared WASHINGTON IRVING and JAMES FENIMORE COOPER, the two writers who more than any others made fiction an American possibility of enormous power and popularity. Irving domesticated the German fairy tale by grounding it in the realities of life along the Hudson River. He also helped make the profession of authorship respectable in a country that still tended to wonder whether storytelling was not a waste of time, if not actually sinful. Irving convinced the English, to whom Americans still looked up in matters of taste and criticism, that the New World was able to produce writers who could write in English almost as well as English natives.

Cooper's novels lacked the grace of Irving's stories and sketches. Indeed, his Leatherstocking Tales strike many modern readers as heavy-handed and tedious. Yet Cooper's rambling melodramatic books about Natty Bumpo and his Indian friends and enemies created a myth about pioneer America that has been heavily exploited by popular and serious writers ever since—as well as criticized as ethnocentric by Native Americans and critics sensitive to their viewpoint.

During the 1830s, particularly in EDGAR ALLAN POE's and NATHANIEL HAWTHORNE's tales and sketches, one sees the beginning of the American short story and the development of an aesthetic that has influenced succeeding generations of short-story writers in Europe as well as in the United States. These early fiction writers did their work well. It was, after all, only 30 years between Sydney Smith's challenging question—"Who reads an American book?"—and the publication of Hawthorne's *The Scarlet Letter* (1850) and HERMAN MELVILLE's *Moby Dick* (1851). By the mid-nineteenth century, it was clear that the United States had learned to play a full part in the concert of Western civilization.

History and Criticism

Baym, Nina. *Woman's Fiction: A Guide to Novels by and about Women in America, 1820–1870.* Cornell Univ. Pr. 1980 $12.95. ISBN 0-8014-9184-3. An excellent critical study of fiction that was previously dismissed as trivial and sentimental.

———. *Novels, Readers, and Reviewers: Responses to Fiction in Antebellum America.* Cornell Univ. Pr. 1984 $32.95. ISBN 0-8014-1709-0. An informative survey of critical responses to American fiction during its formative years.

Bell, Michael D. *The Development of American Romance: The Sacrifice of Relation.* U. Ch. Pr. 1984 $10.95. ISBN 0-226-04213-8. Explores what it meant, psychologically and sociologically, to be a "romancer" in antebellum America.

Bone, Robert. *Down Home: A History of Afro-American Short Fiction, from Its Beginnings to the End of the Harlem Renaissance.* Col. U. Pr. 1988 $51.00. ISBN 0-231-06858-1. A comprehensive overview of genre as practiced by African American writers.

Brown, Herbert R. *The Sentimental Novel in America, 1789–1860.* Ayer repr. of 1940 ed. $22.00. ISBN 0-8369-1490-2. Fairly descriptive survey of popular fiction in America between the American Revolution and the Civil War.

Chase, Richard. *The American Novel and Its Tradition.* Johns Hopkins 1980 $11.95. ISBN 0-8018-2303-X. A discussion of major American novels in light of Chase's controversial thesis that our best novelists have written novel-romances that express the contradictions rather than the unities in American life.

Current-Garcia, Eugene. *The American Short Story before 1850: A Critical History.* Twayne Short Story Ser. G. K. Hall 1985 $22.95. ISBN 0-8057-9359-3. The best historical overview of an important American genre.

Doubleday, Neal Frank. *Variety of Attempt: British and American Fiction in the Early Nineteenth Century.* U. of Nebr. Pr. 1976 $19.95. ISBN 0-8032-0876-6. Traces the development of self-conscious awareness of the craft of fiction during this period.

Dryden, Edgar A. *The Form of American Romance.* Johns Hopkins 1988 $34.00. ISBN 0-8018-3675-1. Another argument for the importance of the generic category of the romance (as opposed to the novel) in American fiction.

Fryer, Judith. *The Faces of Eve: Women in the Nineteenth Century American Novel.* OUP 1976 $22.50. ISBN 0-19-502025-1. Argues that the image of woman in American fiction was created by men in terms of a male-dominated society.

Herzog, Kristin. *Women, Ethnics, and Exotics: Images of Power in Mid-Nineteenth-Century American Fiction.* U. of Tenn. Pr. 1983 $29.50. ISBN 0-87049-372-8. Argues that women and nonwhite characters are portrayed in American literature as the redemptive or demonic power that white males have lost or repressed.

Kaul, A. N. *American Vision: Actual and Ideal Society in Nineteenth Century Fiction.* Greenwood 1980 repr. of 1963 ed. $37.50. ISBN 0-313-22427-7. Explores the imaginative restructuring of society in antebellum American fiction.

Lee, A. Robert, ed. *The Nineteenth-Century American Short Story.* B & N Imports 1986 $38.00. ISBN 0-389-20593-1. An impressive collection of essays that examines Poe, Irving, Hawthorne, and Melville, among others.

Levin, Harry. *Power of Blackness: Hawthorne, Poe, Melville, and the American Character.* Ohio U. Pr. 1980 $9.95. ISBN 0-8214-0581-0. An influential analysis of the tragic theme in the works of three mid-nineteenth-century writers.

Levine, Robert S. *Conspiracy and Romance: Studies in Brockden Brown, Cooper, Hawthorne, and Melville.* Cambridge U. Pr. 1989 $39.50. ISBN 0-521-36654-2. A provocative study of early American novelists' uncertain attempt to recreate community in the New World.

Pattee, Fred L. *The Development of the American Short Story.* Biblo. 1923 $20.00. ISBN 0-8196-0175-6. A study of the short story as used by writers from Irving through O. Henry.

Smith, Henry Nash. *Democracy and the Novel: Popular Resistance to Classic American Writers.* OUP 1978 $7.95. ISBN 0-19-502896-1. Examines how major nineteenth-century novelists responded to the "popular mind" or culture in the United States.

Spengemann, William C. *The Adventurous Muse: The Poetics of American Fiction, 1789–1900.* Yale U. Pr. 1977 o.p. Sees nineteenth-century fiction as a dialectic between the "poetics of adventure" and the "poetics of domesticity."

Tompkins, Jane. *Sensational Designs: The Cultural Work of American Fiction, 1790–1860.* OUP 1985 $11.95. ISBN 0-19-504119-4. Argues that literary texts redefined the social order—a function that modern readers fail to appreciate.

Tuttleton, James W. *The Novel of Manners in America.* Norton 1974 repr. of 1972 ed. $3.45. ISBN 0-393-00717-0. The standard study of an important subgenre of American fiction.

Voss, Arthur. *The American Short Story: A Critical Survey.* U. of Okla. Pr. $14.95. ISBN 0-8061-1644-7. A good general introduction to the literary form that is so distinctively American.

Wright, Lyle H. *American Fiction, 1774–1850: A Contribution toward a Bibliography.* Huntington Lib. 1969 $48.00. ISBN 0-87328-040-7. Lists American editions of prose fiction written for adults by Americans and printed in the United States.

Collections

Stories by American Authors. 10 vols. in 5. Irvington 1972 repr. of 1884 ed. $150.00. ISBN 0-685-36668-5. An anthology of American short fiction edited by the staff of Charles Scribner's Sons during the 1880s.

NONFICTION

American nonfiction of the early nineteenth century was extraordinarily rich and varied. It should be remembered that the American Revolution was also a war of words, an attempt to redefine in language those principles and perceptions by which Americans would live, both individually and communally. The literary legacy of the Revolution—its polemical writings, its political oratory, its public discourses—was something of which no educated person in the United States in the early nineteenth century was unaware. The rules of rhetoric and logical reasoning, the examples of the ancients and the moderns, and the elements of elocution were lessons children were taught in school as a matter of course. It was recognized that in order to succeed in the public arena, one had to be a master of language. The pulpit and the newspaper ruled the social order (though the press soon gained the upper hand), and the effectiveness of an individual was in large part measured by his or her command of the language.

America was also a society eager for instruction. Ambitious to be rid of their provincial image, Americans appeared insatiable in their demand for knowledge; lectures and books on history, science, religion, politics, economy, and agriculture were much in demand. Of course, those instructors who could entertain as well as teach drew the larger audiences, and a greater recognition and response. The emergence of the monthly magazine, especially during the 1830s and 1840s, was primarily the result of this widespread demand for information. Here the realities of the marketplace prevailed, and those prose writers who best manifested in their style the recognized rules of good writing won the day.

The most popular nonfiction writers were the historians and biographers. It might be said that the United States was conceived as a historical text, a national drama whose story and meaning were important for all to consider. This was especially true in antebellum New England, where there appeared a group of historians—WILLIAM HICKLING PRESCOTT (see Vol. 3), George Bancroft, FRANCIS PARKMAN (see Vol. 3), and John Lothrop Motley—who brought to the science of historical fact the art of the romantic novelist. Likewise, books of adventurous travel and exploration were immensely popular during this period, a fact few writers failed to notice, including HENRY DAVID THOREAU, who used the travel narrative in *A Week on the Concord and Merrimack Rivers* (1849) and *Walden* (1854) as a means of transcending the merely physical to reach a higher realm of adventure and discovery.

Sermons and books of moral instruction also held important positions in the literary culture of the day. With the gradual breakup of traditional forms and expressions of religious belief, there appeared, especially among that group of bold thinkers loosely united under the name "Transcendentalists," some who would rewrite scripture to suit the American time and place. Joseph Smith's *Book of Mormon* (1830), RALPH WALDO EMERSON's essays, and, again, Thoreau's celebrations of the universe were, in their various ways, results of this same impulse. Akin to them were those social reformers—Bronson Alcott called them "Apostles of Newness"—who were determined to change the life of humanity on the face of the earth and used as their primary tool the written word. The literature of the antislavery movement, for example, is enormous; but far more important than its quantity is its impressive quality. This generation of literary social agitators, individuals like William Lloyd Garrison, Wendell Phillips, FREDERICK DOUGLASS, Lydia Maria Child, and JAMES RUSSELL LOWELL, further reinforced that strong political commitment found in much of the literature of the United States throughout its history. Emerson defined his "American Scholar" as "Man Thinking" (to say nothing of Woman), but inevitably that thought was translated into text, making early nineteenth-century America one of the leading print cultures in the history of the world.

History and Criticism

Andrews, William L. *To Tell a Free Story: The First Century of Afro-American Autobiography, 1760–1865*. U. of Ill. Pr. 1986 $29.95. ISBN 0-252-01222-4. Traces in detail the history of a major African American literary tradition.

Cox, James M. *Recovering Literature's Lost Ground: Essays in American Autobiography*. La. State U. Pr. 1989 $27.50. ISBN 0-8071-1491-X. Offers insightful readings of the writings of Dana, Emerson, and others within the tradition of American autobiographical writing.

Kagle, Stephen E. *Early Nineteenth-Century Diary Literature. Twayne's United States Authors Ser.* G. K. Hall 1986 $20.95. ISBN 0-8057-7454-8. A valuable survey of the various types of diary literature.

Levin, David. *History as Romantic Art: Bancroft, Prescott, Motley, and Parkman.* AMS Pr. repr. of 1959 ed. $27.50. ISBN 0-404-51830-3. A sophisticated critical reading of mid-nineteenth-century historians as literary artists.

Partridge, Elinor Hughes. *American Prose and Criticism, 1820–1900: A Guide to Information Sources.* Gale 1983 $68.00. ISBN 0-8103-1213-1. Lists both primary and secondary materials relating to the various modes of nonfiction prose writing in the United States.

Payne, William M. *Leading American Essayists: Biographies of Leading Americans.* Ayer repr. of 1910 ed. $25.50. ISBN 0-8369-0778-7. Somewhat pedestrian but useful biographical sketches of prose writers.

Collections

Bronson, Walter C., ed. *American Prose.* Ayer repr. of 1916 ed. $32.00. ISBN 0-888369-3481-4. Includes speeches and essays by prominent writers and orators of the period.

Howard, John R., ed. *Best American Essays.* Ayer repr. of 1910 ed. $21.50. ISBN 0-8369-1140-7. Attempts to be representative of the best American essays in its selection.

Moore, John R., ed. *Representative Essays: English and American.* Ayer repr. of 1930 ed. $20.00. ISBN 0-8369-2808-3. Similar to Howard's anthology but also includes British essays.

CHRONOLOGY OF AUTHORS

Irving, Washington. 1783–1859
Cooper, James Fenimore. 1789–1851
Sedgwick, Catharine Maria. 1789–1867
Longstreet, Augustus Baldwin. 1790–1870
Bryant, William Cullen. 1794–1878
Prescott, William Hickling. 1796–1859
Emerson, Ralph Waldo. 1803–1882
Hawthorne, Nathaniel. 1804–1864
Simms, William Gilmore. 1806–1870
Longfellow, Henry Wadsworth. 1807–1882
Whittier, John Greenleaf. 1807–1892
Holmes, Oliver Wendell. 1809–1894
Poe, Edgar Allan. 1809–1849
Fuller, Margaret. 1810–1850

Fern, Fanny. 1811–1872
Stowe, Harriet Beecher. 1811–1896
Jacobs, Harriet Ann. 1813–1897
Very, Jones. 1813–1880
Harris, George Washington. 1814–1869
Dana, Richard Henry, Jr. 1815–1882
Thorpe, Thomas Bangs. 1815–1878
Thoreau, Henry David. 1817–1862
Douglass, Frederick. 1818–1895
Lowell, James Russell. 1819–1891
Melville, Herman. 1819–1891
Whitman, Walt. 1819–1892
Tuckerman, Frederick Goddard. 1821–1873
Parkman, Francis. 1823–1893
Timrod, Henry. 1828–1867

BRYANT, WILLIAM CULLEN. 1794–1878

Like so many successful New Yorkers during the nineteenth century, Bryant was born and reared in New England. There, in his native Massachusetts, among the beautiful highlands of the Berkshires, he learned early to be a close observer of nature and a careful student of English versification. A child prodigy, he began to make rhymes before his tenth birthday, and in 1808 he gained some fame as the author of *The Embargo, or Sketches of the Time,* a satire in verse in which he echoed the conservative political sentiments of his elders.

Soon, however, he found his own voice and point of view, and the poetry that followed, unlike so much of the literature that was being produced in the United States in the early decades of the nineteenth century, was considered by his contemporaries to be unmistakably American. During his own lifetime and since, his most famous poem has been "Thanatopsis" (from the Greek *thanato* and *opsis*, meaning "a meditation on death"), which was first published in the *North American Review* in 1817. Other poems, such as "Inscription for the Entrance to a Wood" (1817), "A Forest Hymn" (1825), and "To the Fringed Gentian" (1832), printed during the next several decades, brought him recognition both at home and abroad as the leading poet in the United States. Always solemn and stately, his verse seemed cold to JAMES RUSSELL LOWELL, who humorously spoke of Bryant's "iceolation." But others praised Bryant for his careful artisanship, his commitment to romantic aesthetics, his celebration of nature, and his liberal faith in the historical destiny of the United States. MATTHEW ARNOLD called "To a Waterfowl" (1818) one of the finest short lyrics in the English language, and "The Prairies" (1833) and "Earth" (1835) have been seen as noble literary expressions "of the Jacksonian version of the American Dream."

By training a lawyer and by profession a journalist, Bryant was editor-in-chief of the New York *Evening Post* from 1829 until his death in 1878. This position gave him enormous influence on national affairs, and his early support for the fledgling Republican party in the 1850s helped insure that party's success. When he was nearly 80 years old, he translated the *Iliad* and *Odyssey* of HOMER (see Vol. 2) into English blank verse.

POETRY BY BRYANT

The Poetical Works of William Cullen Bryant. AMS Pr. 1969 repr. of 1903 ed. $42.50. ISBN 0-404-01143-8. Inclusive, one-volume "Roslyn Edition" of Bryant's poems, edited by H. C. Sturges and R. H. Stoddard.

The Poetical Works of William Cullen Bryant. Ed. by Parke Godwin. *Life and Works of William Cullen Bryant Ser.* 2 vols. Russell WV 1967 repr. of 1883 ed. o.p. The standard edition of Bryant's poems, edited by his son-in-law.

WORKS BY BRYANT

The Letters of William Cullen Bryant. Ed. by William Cullen Bryant II and Thomas G. Voss. 6 vols. Fordham 1975-1992 $300.00. ISBN 0-8232-0996-2. The definitive edition of Bryant's important correspondence.

The Prose Writings of William Cullen Bryant. Ed. by Parke Godwin. *Life and Works of William Cullen Bryant Ser.* Russell WV 1964 repr. of 1884 ed. o.p. The only collection of Bryant's prose writings that includes his lectures on literature.

BOOKS ABOUT BRYANT

Bigelow, John. *William Cullen Bryant. Amer. Journalists Ser.* Ayer 1970 repr. of 1890 ed. $23.50. ISBN 0-405-01653-0. A reliable account of Bryant's life by one of his associates on the New York *Evening Post*.

Brodwin, Stanley, and Michael D'Innocenzo, eds. *William Cullen Bryant and His America: Centennial Conference Proceedings, 1878–1978.* AMS Pr. 1983 $34.50. ISBN 0-404-61654-2. Fifteen original essays discussing Bryant's poetry as well as his literary and political ideas.

Brown, Charles H. *William Cullen Bryant.* Scribner 1971 o.p. The most factual and thorough account to date of Bryant's life.

Johnson, Curtiss S. *Politics and a Belly-Full: The Journalistic Career of William Cullen Bryant.* Greenwood 1974 repr. of 1962 ed. $35.00. ISBN 0-8371-7246-2. Brief and highly readable.

McLean, Albert F., Jr. *William Cullen Bryant. Twayne's United States Authors Ser.* G. K. Hall 1989 $22.95. ISBN 0-8057-7528-5. *Twayne's United States Authors Ser.* New Coll. U. Pr. 1964 $10.95. ISBN 0-8084-0323-0. The best introduction to Bryant the poet and litterateur.

COOPER, JAMES FENIMORE. 1789–1851

Cooper is best known for his novels of the American frontier and of the sea. *The Spy* (1821), a story of the American Revolution, was the first truly successful work of fiction written in the United States and, along with Cooper's later novels, created an audience both here and abroad for American fiction. Nevertheless, the author was obliged to print his first book at his own expense, since no American publisher would accept it. Its unexpected success turned Cooper, then a cultivated country squire in his early thirties, decisively to authorship. His next work was the first of the five volumes that came to be known as the Leatherstocking Tales—The Pioneers (1823), *The Last of the Mohicans* (1826), *The Prairie* (1827), *The Pathfinder* (1840), and *The Deerslayer* (1841). In this series, Cooper's masterpiece, he portrays the life of Natty Bumpo, a fearless frontier scout who is also known in the tales as Leatherstocking, Deerslayer, Pathfinder, Hawkeye, and *la longue Carabine*. When measured against the more skillfully written and psychologically subtle novels of later American writers, the Leatherstocking Tales seem to many modern readers crude and melodramatic, but historically they are of great importance. In these novels Cooper managed to create an authentic American myth about pioneer life, creating themes and character types still to be found in both the serious and popular literature of today.

Cooper also originated the tale of ships and the sea. [Although Tobias Smollett's *Roderick Random* (1748) and *Peregrine Pickle* (1751) are known as the first sea tales, they are really stories of sailors.] Cooper came well prepared to his task, since he had served as a midshipman in the U.S. Navy for four years and had the knowledge of a professional sailor. *The Pilot* (1824), the first of his sea adventures, was inspired by *The Pirate* (1821) of Sir Walter Scott. Cooper regarded Scott's novel as inaccurate in seamanship, and he wrote *The Pilot* as a correction to Scott.

Among Cooper's publications are 33 substantial works of fiction, 3 books of social and political commentary, 5 travel books, a monumental history of the U.S. Navy (1839), a volume of naval biographies, and an impressive quantity of miscellaneous writings, much of it anonymous and some of it still unknown to scholars. A politically active man of affairs, Cooper used both his novels and his nonfiction to argue the political questions of his day, and through these works helped in the difficult task of defining an American identity. As yet there is no complete edition of his works, but a carefully edited scholarly edition begun under the direction of James F. Beard, editor of Cooper's letters and journals, and published by the State University of New York Press, is well under way with nearly 20 volumes already in print. Most of Cooper's other titles, not yet included in that edition, are available in a variety of single-volume editions.

NOVELS BY COOPER

Afloat and Ashore; or, The Adventures of Miles Wallingford. 1844. Lightyear 1980 repr. of 1844 ed. $18.25. ISBN 0-89968-212-X. Published in two parts; combines sea adventure and social commentary.

The Bravo: A Tale. 1831. Ed. by Donald A. Ringe. *Masterworks of Literature Ser.* New Coll. U. Pr. 1963 $19.95. ISBN 0-8084-0065-7. A political novel set in Venice during the Renaissance.

The Chainbearer; or, The Littlepage Manuscripts. 1845. Scholarly 1981 repr. of 1845 ed. $19.00. ISBN 0-403-00135-8. Continuation of trilogy begun with *Satanstoe.*

The Crater; or, Vulcan's Peak: A Tale of the Pacific. 1847. AMS Pr. repr. of 1896 ed. $37.50. ISBN 0-404-60058-1. A utopian island in the Pacific is brought to ruin by radical democratic developments.

The Deerslayer; or, The First War-Path. 1841. Ed. by Lance Schachterle. *Writings of James Fenimore Cooper Ser.* State U. NY Pr. 1987 $49.50. ISBN 0-87395-361-4. Young Natty Bumpo in upstate New York in the early 1740s.

Home as Found. 1838. Repr. Serv. 1990 repr. of 1838 ed. $79.00. ISBN 0-685-27627-9. Sequel to *Homeward Bound.*

Homeward Bound; or, The Chase: A Tale of the Sea. 1838. Mid-Peninsula Lib. repr. of 1838 ed. $8.50. ISBN 0-933249-11-X. Deals with American family's cultural conflicts upon their return from long sojourn in Europe.

The Last of the Mohicans: A Narrative of 1757. 1826. Ed. by James A. Sappenfield and E. N. Feltskog. *Writings of James Fenimore Cooper Ser.* State U. NY Pr. 1983 $49.50. ISBN 0-87395-362-2. The second, both in composition and chronological sequence, in the series depicting the life of Natty Bumpo.

The Leatherstocking Tales. 2 vols. Ed. by Blake Nevius. Library of America 1985 $32.50 ea. ISBNs 0-940450-20-8, 0-940450-21-6. Attractive and reliable reprint of the five tales.

Lionel Lincoln; or, The Leaguer of Boston. 1825. Ed. by Donald A. Ringe and Lucy B. Ringe. *Writings of James Fenimore Cooper Ser.* State U. NY Pr. 1985 $49.50. ISBN 0-87395-416-5. A historical novel set in Massachusetts during the Revolutionary War.

The Monikins. 1835. Ed. by James S. Hedger. New Coll. U. Pr. 1990 $12.95. ISBN 0-8084-0421-0. Satirical allegory on American follies.

Ned Myers; or, A Life Before the Mast. 1843. *Classics of Naval Literature Ser.* Naval Inst. Pr. 1989 repr. of 1843 ed. $29.95. ISBN 0-87021-417-9. A realistic picture of life at sea during the early years of the nineteenth century.

The Oak Openings; or, The Bee-Hunter. 1848. North Atlantic 1984 repr. of 1848 ed. $40.00. ISBN 0-938190-33-4. Frontier tale set in western Michigan during the War of 1812.

The Pathfinder; or, The Inland Sea. 1840. Ed. by Richard D. Rust. *Writings of James Fenimore Cooper Ser.* State U. NY Pr. 1981 $49.50. ISBN 0-87395-360-6. The third of the Leatherstocking Tales in order of narrative sequence, set in Lake Ontario country during the time of the French and Indian wars.

The Pilot: A Tale of the Sea. 1824. Ed. by Kay S. House. *Writings of James Fenimore Cooper Ser.* State U. NY Pr. 1986 $49.50. ISBN 0-87395-415-7. A sea novel set during the American Revolution and loosely modeled on the career of John Paul Jones.

The Pioneers; or, The Sources of the Susquehanna: A Descriptive Tale. 1823. Ed. by James F. Beard. *Writings of James Fenimore Cooper Ser.* State U. NY Pr. 1980 $49.50. ISBN 0-87395-359-2. The first in composition but the fourth chronologically in Cooper's saga of the life of Natty Bumpo.

The Prairie: A Tale. 1827. Ed. by James P. Elliot. *Writings of James Fenimore Cooper Ser.* State U. NY Pr. 1985 $49.50. ISBN 0-87395-363-0. Natty Bumpo goes farther west and dies.

Precaution: A Novel. 1820. 2 vols. AMS Pr. repr. of 1820 ed. $47.50. ISBN 0-404-01707-X. Cooper's first novel, modeled on Jane Austen's *Persuasion.*

The Red Rover: A Tale. 1828. Ed. by Thomas Philbrick and Marianne Philbrick. *Writings of James Fenimore Cooper Ser.* State U. NY Pr. 1991 $49.50. ISBN 0-7914-0188-X. A sea novel set in the eighteenth century.

The Redskins; or, Indian and Injin: Being the Conclusion of the Littlepage Manuscripts. 1846. Rprt. Serv. 1990 repr. of 1846 ed. $79.00. ISBN 0-685-27636-8. Tales of the anti-rent wars in New York, from 1839 to 1846.

Satanstoe; or, The Littlepage Manuscripts: A Tale of the Colony. 1845. Ed. by Kay S. House. *Writings of James Fenimore Cooper Ser.* State U. NY Pr. 1990 $49.50. ISBN 0-88706-903-7. The first novel of an impressive trilogy dealing with fortunes of a New

York family between the 1740s and 1840s; followed by *The Chainbearer* and *The Redskins*.

The Sea Lions; or, The Lost Sealers. 1849. Ed. by Warren S. Walker. Bks. Demand repr. of 1965 ed. $133.30. ISBN 0-8357-9714-7. A sea story involving whaling and the search for buried treasure.

Sea Tales. Ed. by Kay S. House and Thomas L. Philbrick. Library of America 1991 $35.00. ISBN 0-940450-70-4. Reprint of the texts of *The Pilot* and *The Red Rover*.

The Spy: A Tale of Neutral Ground. 1821. *Masterworks of Literature Ser*. New Coll. U. Pr. 1971 $13.95. ISBN 0-8084-0027-4. An historical novel set in New York during the American Revolution.

Tales for Fifteen; or Imagination and Heart. 1823. Schol. Facsimiles repr. of 1823 ed. $50.00. ISBN 0-8201-1247-X. Two short stories written for young girls.

The Two Admirals: A Tale. 1842. Ed. by Donald A. Ringe. *Writings of James Fenimore Cooper Ser*. State U. NY Pr. 1990 $49.50. ISBN 0-88706-905-3. A novel dealing with British naval exploits during the 1740s.

The Water-Witch; or, The Skimmer of the Seas: A Tale. 1830. AMS Pr. repr. of 1896 ed. $14.50. ISBN 0-404-00629-9. Deals with smuggling in New York Harbor in the time of Queen Anne's War.

The Ways of the Hour: A Tale. 1850. Rprt. Serv. 1990 repr. of 1850 ed. $79.00. ISBN 0-685-27634-1. About a woman on trial for murder, highlighting the problems of American justice.

The Wept of Wish-ton-Wish. 2 vols. AMS Pr. repr. of 1829 ed. $18.00. ISBN 0-404-01715-0. Set in Connecticut during King Philip's War.

The Wing-and-Wing; or, Le Feu-Follet: A Tale. 1842. Rprt. Serv. 1990 repr. of 1842 ed. $79.00. ISBN 0-685-27622-8. An historical novel set at sea during the Napoleonic Wars.

Wyandotté, or, The Hutted Knoll: A Tale. 1843. Ed. by Thomas Philbrick and Marianne Philbrick. *Writings of James Fenimore Cooper Ser*. State U. NY Pr. 1981 $49.50. ISBN 0-87395-414-9. A colonial family is torn apart in New York State during the American Revolution.

NONFICTION BY COOPER

The American Democrat; or, Hints on the Social and Civic Relations of the United States of America. 1838. Ed. by George Dekker and Larry Johnston. Viking Penguin 1989 $6.95. ISBN 0-14-039068-5. A political essay pointing out the destructive tendencies in the American democratic system.

Gleanings in Europe: England. 1837. Ed. by James P. Elliott and Robert D. Madison. *Writings of James Fenimore Cooper Ser*. State U. NY Pr. 1981 $49.50. ISBN 0-87395-367-3

Gleanings in Europe: France. 1837. Ed. by Thomas Philbrick and Constance A. Denne. *Writings of James Fenimore Cooper Ser*. State U. NY Pr. 1983 $49.50. ISBN 0-87395-368-1

Gleanings in Europe: Italy. 1838. Ed. by Constance A. Denne. *Writings of James Fenimore Cooper Ser*. State U. NY Pr. 1981 $49.50. ISBN 0-87395-365-7

Gleanings in Europe: The Rhine. 1836. Ed. by Ernest Redekop and Maurice Geracht. *Writings of James Fenimore Cooper Ser*. State U. NY Pr. 1986 $49.50. ISBN 0-87395-366-5. Originally titled *Sketches of Switzerland: Part Second*.

Gleanings in Europe: Switzerland. 1836. Ed. by Kenneth W. Staggs and James P. Elliot. *Writings of James Fenimore Cooper Ser*. State U. NY Pr. 1980 $18.95. ISBN 0-87395-422-X. Originally titled *Sketches of Switzerland*.

The History of the Navy of the United States of America. 1838. Schol. Facsimiles 1988 $60.00. ISBN 0-8201-1430-8

James Fenimore Cooper: Representative Selections. Ed. by Robert E. Spiller. Greenwood 1977 repr. of 1936 ed. $35.00. ISBN 0-8371-9317-6. A useful early anthology that emphasizes Cooper's social writings.

A Letter to His Countrymen. 1834. Rprt. Serv. 1990 repr. of 1834 ed. $79.00. ISBN 0-685-27804-2. An attack on the American press and a plea for American intellectual independence.

The Letters and Journals of James Fenimore Cooper. 6 vols. Ed. by James F. Beard. HUP Vols. 1–2 1960 o.p. Vols. 3–4 1964 $66.00. ISBN 0-674-52551-5. Vols. 5-6 1968 $70.00. ISBN 0–674–52552–3. The standard edition of Cooper's letters and private writings.

Notions of the Americans: Picked Up by a Travelling Bachelor. 1828. Ed. by Gary Williams. *Writings of James Fenimore Cooper Ser.* State U. NY Pr. 1991 $49.50. ISBN 0-7914-0213-4. A laudatory account of American life and ways, supposedly written by an English aristocrat.

Books about Cooper

Dekker, George, and John P. McWilliams, eds. *Fenimore Cooper: The Critical Heritage.* *The Critical Heritage Ser.* Routledge 1973 $69.50. ISBN 0-7100-7635-5. A collection of criticism mostly published during Cooper's lifetime.

Dyer, Alan Frank. *James Fenimore Cooper: An Annotated Bibliography of Criticism.* Greenwood 1991 $45.00. ISBN 0-313-27919-5. Checklist of nearly 2,000 items published between 1820 and 1990.

Franklin, Wayne. *The New World of James Fenimore Cooper.* U. Ch. Pr. 1982 o.p. Stresses Cooper's importance as an artist rather than as a social thinker or a moral teacher.

Grossman, James. *James Fenimore Cooper.* Stanford U. Pr. 1949 $11.95. ISBN 0-8047-0321-3. A biographical reading of Cooper and his works.

Kelly, William P. *Plotting America's Past: Fenimore Cooper and the Leatherstocking Tales.* S. Ill. U. Pr. 1984 $23.95. ISBN 0-8093-1144-5. A reading of the five tales in terms of Cooper's concept of historical continuity.

McWilliams, John P., Jr. *Political Justice in a Republic: James Fenimore Cooper's America.* U. CA Pr. 1973 $42.50. ISBN 0-520-02175-4. An informed and useful political reading of Cooper's life and works.

Peck, H. Daniel. *A World by Itself: The Pastoral Moment in Cooper's Fiction.* Yale U. Pr. 1977 $27.50. ISBN 0-300-02027-9. Finds Cooper's artistic power in his ability to evoke timeless landscapes of simplicity and childhood wonder.

———, ed. *New Essays on The Last of the Mohicans.* *The American Novel Ser.* Cambridge U. Pr. 1992 $24.95. ISBN 0-521-37414-6. A half-dozen essays by leading Cooper critics evaluating the novel's artistry and impact on American culture.

Ringe, Donald A. *James Fenimore Cooper.* *Twayne's United States Authors Ser.* G. K. Hall 1988 $20.95. ISBN 0-8057-7527-7. *Twayne's United States Authors Ser.* New Coll. U. Pr. 1962 $10.95. ISBN 0-8084-0168-8. An excellent introduction, with close readings of the major novels.

Walker, Warren S. *Plots and Characters in the Fiction of James Fenimore Cooper.* Shoe String 1978 $37.50. ISBN 0-208-01497-7. Contains plot summaries, with a separate list of Cooper's fictional characters.

Wallace, James D. *Early Cooper and His Audience.* Col. U. Pr. 1986 $46.50. ISBN 0-231-06176-5. Argues that in order to write American fiction, Cooper created an American audience for fiction.

DANA, RICHARD HENRY, JR. 1815–1882

Dana is an example of that most curious of literary phenomena, an author of classic stature whose reputation rests solely upon a single book. Born in Cambridge, Massachusetts, Dana was the son of the elder Richard Henry Dana, a minor New England poet and a founder of the *North American Review.* He received a fairly conventional early education in the Boston area and entered Harvard College in 1831. Health and eye problems interrupted his studies several times, and finally, in hopes of regaining his strength, Dana shipped out on the sailing vessel *The Pilgrim* in 1834 as a common sailor. He remained at sea for two years, much of that time gathering hides off the California coast, which was still under Mexican rule. From these experiences he soon produced his great masterpiece, *Two Years Before the Mast* (1840).

A largely autobiographical account, the story tells of a young man's initiation into the responsibilities and uncertainties of adulthood. At times a tale of high adventure, the book provides not only a realistic account of the sailor's hard life at sea but also a picturesque glimpse into the strange culture of what soon would be the southwestern United States. From a strictly literary point of view, the work is seriously flawed, hurriedly written by a young man who still had much to learn about his craft, and at times bogged down in detail and description that Dana had carefully recorded in his journal and in memory. Yet, whatever the book's shortcomings, it has been a perennial favorite, especially of young readers who have been drawn to this account of a young man who is not unlike themselves and his final victories over many of the unexpected challenges of life.

Upon his return to Boston, Dana completed his studies at Harvard and was admitted to the Massachusetts bar in 1840, the same year he completed *Two Years Before the Mast*. Because of his experiences and his passionate commitment to the rights of the common sailor, he specialized in maritime law, soon earning himself the nickname, "the sailors' lawyer." His work on behalf of sailors in both the courts and the popular press led to important reforms in the conditions of their lives and the terms of their employment. Active also in the still unpopular cause of abolition, Dana alienated himself from the rich and powerful, those proper Bostonians who controlled so much of the world to which Dana was drawn by his political ambitions. Prevented by his old enemies from winning those public offices that he believed he deserved, he came to see his life as a failure and, in fact, regretted that his greatest success should have been *Two Years Before the Mast*, "a boy's work, done before I came to the Bar."

NOVEL BY DANA

Two Years before the Mast: A Personal Narrative of Life at Sea. 1840. Ed. by Thomas Philbrick. Viking Penguin 1981 $4.95. ISBN 0-14-039008-1

WORK BY DANA

The Journal of Richard Henry Dana, Jr. 3 vols. Ed. by Robert F. Lucid. HUP 1968 o.p. Well-edited and annotated life record that is quite revealing about its subject and his times.

BOOKS ABOUT DANA

Adams, Charles F., Jr. *Richard Henry Dana: A Biography.* Rprt. Serv. 1989 repr. of 1890 ed. $79.00. ISBN 0-685-27460-8. A sympathetic biography by Dana's contemporary and fellow Bostonian, with liberal quotations from Dana's journal and correspondence.

Gale, Robert L. *Richard Henry Dana, Jr.* Twayne's United States Authors Ser.: G. K. Hall 1969 o.p. Solid and informed; an excellent introduction.

Shapiro, Samuel. *Richard Henry Dana Jr.: 1815–1882.* Mich. St. U. Pr. 1961 $5.00. ISBN 0-87013-062-5. A fine critical study that places Dana solidly in his historical context.

DOUGLASS, FREDERICK. 1818–1895

It might be said that Douglass was born twice: first as Frederick Augustus Washington Bailey, a slave in Tuckahoe, Maryland, the son of a black mother and a white father, the property of another human being; then as Frederick Douglass, a free man after his escape to Massachusetts in 1838, the creation of his own powers and imagination, an abolitionist, orator, writer, and politician who belonged to no one but himself. While the conditions of Douglass's young life as a slave were harsh, he was fortunate in several respects: He learned early to read, which expanded his intellectual horizons, and was sent to live in Baltimore to be trained as a ship's caulker, which allowed him some freedom of movement. Reading was probably more important to Douglass, however. "Ignorance," as Douglass later pointed out, "is a high virtue in a human chattel; and the master studies to keep the slave ignorant." First he read the Bible; later he went on to read writings in defense of liberty, such as the patriotic orations of the American Revolution.

Following his escape to the North, Douglass was enlisted by such leading antislavery advocates as William Lloyd Garrison and Wendell Phillips to take an active role in the abolition movement. This led to the publication in 1845 of the first version of his enormously successful and highly influential autobiography, *Narrative of the Life of Frederick Douglass*. The first edition of 5,000 copies sold out in a few months, and within a year nearly 15,000 copies of the book had been sold.

After his book's publication, Douglass went to England and Ireland, where he stayed two years. In 1847, back in the United States, he founded the *North Star* (later retitled *Frederick Douglass's Paper*), a weekly newspaper that he edited for 17 years, in Rochester, New York. Unlike William Lloyd Garrison's *Liberator* and other radical abolitionist newspapers, Douglass's newspaper favored political methods for freeing the slaves. In 1855 Douglass published the second version of his autobiography, now titled *My Bondage and My Freedom*, which retains the first version's dynamic power but is more artfully done, truly a literary classic of the mid-nineteenth-century American renaissance. During the Civil War, Douglass was active in the recruitment of African American regiments to fight for the Union, and during Reconstruction he was a leading advocate for civil rights. During the last two decades of his life, he served in several government appointments, including that of U.S. minister to Haiti from 1889 to 1891. The final version of his autobiography was published in 1881, *Life and Times of Frederick Douglass*, which includes the texts of many of his distinguished orations.

NONFICTION BY DOUGLASS

The Frederick Douglass Papers: Series 1: Speeches, Debates, and Interviews. Ed. by John W. Blassingame and others. 4 vols. Yale U. Pr. Vol. 1 1979 $70.00. ISBN 0-300-02246-8. Vol. 2 1982 $70.00. ISBN 0-300-02661-7. Vol. 3 1985 o.p. Vol. 4 1991 $85.00. ISBN 0-300-05142-5. When completed, will be the most extensive edition of Douglass's writings available.

Life and Times of Frederick Douglass: The Complete Autobiography. 1881. Ed. by Rayford W. Logan. Macmillan 1962 $14.95. ISBN 0-02-002350-2. The best reprint of the final version of Douglass's autobiography.

The Life and Writings of Frederick Douglass. 5 vols. Ed. by Philip S. Foner. Intl. Pubs. Co. 1975 $70.00. ISBN 0-7178-0119-5. At this time, the standard collection of Douglass's writings, with extensive historical and biographical commentary.

My Bondage and My Freedom. 1855. *Blacks in the New World Ser.* Ed. by William L. Andrews. U. of Ill. Pr. 1988 $34.95. ISBN 0-252-01409-X. A revised text of Douglass's autobiography, considered by many critics to be the best version from a literary point of view.

The Narrative and Selected Writings. Ed. by Michael Meyer. McGraw 1983 $11.50. ISBN 0-07-554-375-3. In addition to the autobiographical writings, reprints a significant selection of Douglass's other writings, including "The Heroic Slave" (1852).

Narrative of the Life of Frederick Douglass, an American Slave. 1845. Ed. by Benjamin Quarles. HUP 1960 $6.95. ISBN 0-674-60101-7. Reprint of the first version of Douglass's autobiography.

BOOKS ABOUT DOUGLASS

Andrews, William L., ed. *Critical Essays on Frederick Douglass. Critical Essays on American Literature Ser.* G. K. Hall 1991 $40.00. ISBN 0-8161-7301-X. Contains both reprinted and newly commissioned essays focusing on Douglass as a writer.

Bloom, Harold, ed. *Frederick Douglass's Narrative of the Life of Frederick Douglass. Modern Critical Interpretation Ser.* Chelsea Hse. 1987 $29.95. ISBN 1-55546-014-3. Reprint of criticism.

Huggins, Nathan I. *Slave and Citizen: The Life of Frederick Douglass.* Little 1980 $14.95. ISBN 0-316-38001-6. A good biography for general audiences.

McFeely, William S. *Frederick Douglass.* Norton 1990 $24.95. ISBN 0-393-02823-2. The fullest and most recent account of Douglass's life by a master biographer.

Martin, Waldo E., Jr. *The Mind of Frederick Douglass.* U. of NC Pr. 1984 $32.50. ISBN 0-8078-1616-7. An intellectual biography that analyzes Douglass's career in terms of the philosophical and social movements of his time.

Preston, Dickson J. *Young Frederick Douglass: The Maryland Years.* Johns Hopkins 1980 $9.95. ISBN 0-8018-2739-6. A thoroughly researched account of Douglass's early life and its relation to the autobiographical writings.

Sundquist, Eric J., ed. *Frederick Douglass: New Literary and Historical Essays.* Cambridge U. Pr. 1990 $39.50. ISBN 0-521-38040-5. An excellent collection of 14 essays of literary appreciation and evaluation.

EMERSON, RALPH WALDO. 1803–1882

Emerson's influence on American literature and culture is pervasive and monumental. THOREAU, WHITMAN, and DICKINSON, to mention only the most brilliant of those younger writers inspired by him during his lifetime, are all startling testimonies to his centrality. Nor did Emerson's influence end with his death in 1882: Poets EDWIN ARLINGTON ROBINSON, ROBERT FROST, and WALLACE STEVENS each in large part defined their role in Emersonian terms. In the other arts and intellectual disciplines, too, Emerson made a decided impact through his writings and example. It is unlikely, for example, that CHARLES IVES (see Vol. 3), in Danbury, Connecticut, during the 1890s, would have created new musical forms that are still revolutionary a century later, had he not been profoundly moved by Emerson. In architecture, LOUIS SULLIVAN (see Vol. 3) and FRANK LLOYD WRIGHT (see Vol. 3) have both paid homage to the "sage of Concord," while philosophers JOSIAH ROYCE (see Vol. 4) and JOHN DEWEY (see Vols. 3 and 4) were in their different ways followers of Emersonian examples. Even WILLIAM JAMES (see Vols. 3, 4, and 5), in his active rejection of so much of what he thought Emerson stood for, still pretty much played the game by the ground rules that Emerson had laid out in his essays and poems. Nor was Emerson's impact just local or national; Europeans as well as Americans read, translated, and responded to his writings in enormously creative ways. Most notable of these was FRIEDRICH NIETZSCHE (see Vol. 4), who was rarely without Emerson's essays near at hand.

Emerson is commonly labeled the leader of the Transcendentalist group in New England. Although this designation is convenient, it is not exactly accurate. One needs only to read Emerson to discover that men and women of his transcendental temperament did not have leaders. Each person was his or her own leader, because, ideally, each person was complete. As Emerson wrote in his journal on April 7, 1840: "In all my lectures, I have taught one doctrine, namely, the infinitude of the private man." Emerson was a challenge to many men and women, but especially to the young. He urged them to seek better things than their fathers and mothers had been content with, since what had been good for their fathers and mothers might not necessarily be good for their sons or daughters.

Born and reared in Boston, Emerson, like generations of his ancestors before him, was educated for the ministry, and in 1829 he was appointed pastor of the Second Church (Unitarian) of Boston. He was, by all accounts, a successful and popular minister, but in 1832 he resigned his pastorate and moved to Concord, a small village a few miles northwest of Boston. He wished to live in terms of an original relationship to nature and to the universe; he wished to think and to write, to become what he later was so brilliantly to define as the "American Scholar": "Man-Thinking." For Emerson this was not a passive action; the motto that he chose for his 1835 journal makes his position clear: "To think is to act." He gave up the Unitarian ministry because the Unitarian church was "freezing him to death." Its intellectual construct emphasized reason, not feeling, with no room for inspiration or miraculous revelation.

Emerson enjoyed much success as a popular lecturer, traveling great distances both at home and abroad. Then in 1836 he published a remarkable little book entitled *Nature*. This essay exemplifies both Emerson's fundamental vision of the beauty of nature and his method of composition, which relied heavily upon the journals be began keeping while still a student at Harvard College. Most of his published essays are revisions of lectures that he developed from journal entries. While eschewing the conventional demands of formal unity, Emerson's essays reveal a firm and consistent commitment to the dignity of human life and to self-reliance.

Emerson's poetry has never enjoyed the popularity of his prose essays, even though he regarded himself as "more of a poet than anything else." He wrote his verse for himself, without regard for an audience, and his poetry has a more spontaneous quality than most of his prose. W. C. Brownell in *American Prose Masters* (1909) speaks of the poems as "a kind of intimate reverberation" of the essays. "They are largely Emerson's communion with himself, as the Essays are his communication with the world." His poems are nearly always short, lyrical, and meditative.

WORKS BY EMERSON

Complete Works of Ralph Waldo Emerson. 12 vols. Ed. by Edward W. Emerson. AMS Pr. repr. of 1904 ed. $468.00. ISBN 0-404-05480-3. Standard edition of Emerson's writings; will be superceded by Harvard University Press edition of *Collected Works.*

Early Lectures of Ralph Waldo Emerson. 3 vols. Ed. by Stephen E. Whicher, Robert E. Spiller, and Wallace E. Williams. HUP. Vol. 1 1959 $35.00. ISBN 0-674-22150-8. Vol. 2 1964 o.p. Vol. 3 1972 $40.00. ISBN 0-674-22152-4. Essential to an understanding of Emerson's early literary career.

Emerson in His Journals. Ed. by Joel Porte. HUP 1982 $35.00. ISBN 0-674-24861-9. A generous and judicious selection from the 16-volume edition of the *Journals and Miscellaneous Notebooks.*

Essays and Lectures. Ed. by Joel Porte. Library of America 1983 $30.00. ISBN 0-940450-15-1. Superb one-volume collection that includes *Nature, Addresses, and Lectures; Essays: First and Second Series; Representative Men; English Traits; The Conduct of Life;* and uncollected prose.

Essays: First Series. 1841. *The Collected Works of Ralph Waldo Emerson.* Vol. 2. Ed. by Joseph Slater and others. HUP 1979 $41.00. ISBN 0-674-13980-1. Well annotated; the standard edition.

Essays: Second Series. 1844. *The Collected Works of Ralph Waldo Emerson.* Vol. 3. Ed. by
    Alfred R. Ferguson and Jean F. Carr. HUP 1983 $32.95. ISBN 0-674-13990-9
The Journals of Ralph Waldo Emerson. Ed. by W. H. Gilman and others. 16 vols. HUP.
    Vol. 1 1960 o.p. Vol. 2 1961 o.p. Vol. 3 1963 o.p. Vol. 4 1964 o.p. Vol. 5 1965 $50.00.
    ISBN 0-674-48454-1. Vol. 6 1966 o.p. Vol. 7 1969 o.p. Vol. 8 1970 $50.00. ISBN 0-674-
    48470-3. Vol. 9 1971 o.p. Vol. 10 1973 $50.00. ISBN 0-674-48473-8. Vol. 11 1975 o.p.
    Vol. 12 1976 o.p. Vol. 13 1977 $61.00. ISBN 0-674-48476-2. Vol. 14 1978 $61.00.
    ISBN 0-674-48477-0. Vol. 15 1982 $61.00. ISBN 0-674-48478-9. Vol. 16 1982 $61.00.
    ISBN 0-674-48479-7. Masterful and comprehensive, the life record of a "man
    thinking."
The Letters of Ralph Waldo Emerson. 8 vols. Ed. by Ralph L. Rusk and Eleanor M. Tilton.
    Col. U. Pr. Vols. 1–6 1939 o.p. Vol. 7 1990 $45.00. ISBN 0-231-06870-0. Vol. 8 1991
    $50.00. ISBN 0-231-07516-2. Rusk's original six-volume edition, to be expanded
    eventually to ten volumes, with the final four by Tilton.
Nature, Addresses, and Lectures. 1849. *The Collected Works of Ralph Waldo Emerson.*
    Vol. 1. Ed. by Robert E. Spiller and Alfred R. Ferguson. HUP 1971 o.p.
Ralph Waldo Emerson. Ed. by Richard Poirier. *The Oxford Authors Ser.* OUP 1990 $45.00.
    ISBN 0-19-254193-5. An excellent selection of Emerson's prose and poetry.
Representative Men. 1850. *The Collected Works of Ralph Waldo Emerson.* Vol. 4. Ed. by
    Wallace E. Williams and Douglas E. Wilson. HUP 1987 $32.95. ISBN 0-674-13991-7.
    Standard edition of one of Emerson's most popular books, in which he considers
    "the uses of great men."

BOOKS ABOUT EMERSON

Allen, Gay Wilson. *Ralph Waldo Emerson: A Biography.* Viking Penguin 1981 o.p. A
    masterful portrait of Emerson that emphasizes his character.
Bishop, Jonathan. *Emerson on the Soul.* AMS Pr. repr. of 1964 ed. $29.50. ISBN 0-404-
    19251-3. A careful and helpful literary analysis of the major works.
Burkholder, Robert E., and Joel Myerson. *Emerson: An Annotated Secondary Bibliogra-
    phy.* U. of Pittsburgh Pr. 1985 $130.00. ISBN 0-8229-3502-3. An annotated checklist
    of nearly 6,000 books and articles about Emerson.
Ellison, Julie. *Emerson's Romantic Style.* Princeton U. Pr. 1984 $37.50. ISBN 0-691-
    006612-4. Argues that Emerson's real power is as an interpreter of texts.
Firkins, Oscar W. *Ralph Waldo Emerson.* AMS Pr. repr. of 1915 ed. $44.50. ISBN 0-404-
    19258-0. Still one of the best critical appreciations of Emerson's writings.
Gougeon, Len. *Virtue's Hero: Emerson, Antislavery, and Reform.* U. of Ga. Pr. 1990
    $45.00. ISBN 0-8203-1193-6. An examination of Emerson's involvement in reform
    movements.
Hopkins, Vivian C. *Spires of Form: A Study of Emerson's Aesthetic Theory.* AMS Pr. repr.
    of 1951 ed. $33.50. ISBN 0-404-19263-7. The most thorough analysis of Emerson's
    theory of art.
Hughes, Gertrude R. *Emerson's Demanding Optimism.* La. State U. Pr. 1984 $25.00. ISBN
    0-8071-1180-5. Emphasizes Emerson's later essays, citing their power and sober
    optimism.
Loving, Jerome. *Emerson, Whitman, and the American Muse.* U. of NC Pr. 1982 $24.95.
    ISBN 0-8078-3024-6. An examination of the personal and literary connections
    between these two great poetic innovators.
Myerson, Joel, ed. *Emerson Centenary Essays.* S. Ill. U. Pr. 1982 $12.95. ISBN 0-8093-
    1023-6. Eleven original essays on a variety of literary and biographical subjects.
Paul, Sherman. *Emerson's Angle of Vision: Man and Nature in American Experience.* AMS
    Pr. repr. of 1952 ed. $33.50. ISBN 0-404-19267-X. Views Emerson's works in terms of
    his idea of sympathetic correspondence.
Porte, Joel. *Representative Man: Ralph Waldo Emerson in His Time.* OUP 1979 $25.00.
    ISBN 0-19-502436-2. An engaging evaluation of Emerson's literary artistry.
Robinson, David. *Apostle of Culture: Emerson as Preacher and Lecturer.* U. of Pa. Pr. 1982
    $33.95. ISBN 0-8122-7824-0. Stresses the importance of Emerson's Unitarian
    background.

Rusk, Ralph L. *The Life of Ralph Waldo Emerson*. Scribner 1949 o.p. The standard biography with an intellectual rather than a psychological emphasis.

Sealts, Merton M., Jr., and Alfred R. Ferguson, eds. *Emerson's "Nature": Origin, Growth, Meaning*. S. Ill. U. Pr. 1979 $9.95. ISBN 0-8093-0900-9. A collection of valuable commentaries from nearly 30 critics—past and present.

Whicher, Stephen E. *Freedom and Fate: An Inner Life of Ralph Waldo Emerson*. U. of Pa. Pr. 1953 o.p. A greatly influential study that argues Emerson's gradual loss of faith.

Yannella, Donald. *Ralph Waldo Emerson. Twayne's United States Authors Ser*. G. K. Hall 1982 $19.95. ISBN 0-8057-7344-4. An intelligent and informed overview of Emerson's life and writings.

FERN, FANNY (SARA PAYSON WILLIS PARTON). 1811–1872

Journalism was in the blood of the Willis family; for generations they had been editors, printers, and publishers. Young Sara Willis was no exception. Still, it took personal tragedy and hardship (the death of her first husband in 1846 and the divorce from her second husband in 1852), and the need to support herself and her children to enable her to overcome the enormous prejudice against women in the world of journalism at that time. But prejudice is quick to bow before the dollar, and Willis's early success as a newspaper writer was soon acknowledged by editors who were eager for her stories and sketches, although they were still unwilling to pay her on equal terms with male writers. In 1852 she became a regular columnist—the first American woman to do so—for the *New York Musical World and Times*, in which her stories, sketches, and essays appeared under the pen name "Fanny Fern." These, along with other writings of hers, were collected a year later in a volume entitled *Fern Leaves from Fanny's Portfolio* (1853). It was a great success, selling over 70,000 copies within one year. When a second series of *Fern Leaves* appeared in 1854, much of the sentimentality that had characterized the first volume (as well as most literature of the time) had vanished, replaced by a vernacular earnestness and satiric wit. These stories and sketches defended the rights of women and children, denounced the social and personal blindness of custom and laws—and sometimes merely entertained.

In 1855 Fern's literary triumph was complete with the signing of a contract to write a weekly column for the popular *New York Ledger* at a salary that made her one of the highest-paid writers in the country. Some were annoyed by her success. NATHANIEL HAWTHORNE complained to his publisher that "the woman writes as if the devil was in her." But most readers were delighted, including her third husband, the popular historian James Parton, and "Fern's" popularity and productivity ended only with her death.

WORKS BY FERN

Fern Leaves from Fanny's Port-Folio. 1853. *American Biography Ser*. Rprt. Serv. 1991 repr. of 1853 ed. $79.00. ISBN 0-7812-8307-8

Fern Leaves from Fanny's Port-Folio: Second Series. 1854. *American Fiction Reprint Ser*. Ayer repr. of 1854 ed. $32.00. ISBN 0-8369-7049-7

Ruth Hall and Other Writings. American Women Writers Ser. Ed. by Joyce W. Warren. Rutgers U. Pr. 1986 $35.00. ISBN 0-8135-1167-4. In addition to the complete text of Fern's 1855 semiautobiographical novel, this volume reprints representative selections from her *Fern Leaves* and other journalistic writings.

BOOKS ABOUT FERN

Warren, Joyce W. *Fanny Fern: An Independent Woman*. Rutgers U. Pr. 1992 $29.95. ISBN 0-8135-1763-X. A critical biography written from the viewpoint of modern feminist theory.

FULLER, (SARAH) MARGARET. 1810–1850

Born in Cambridgeport, Massachusetts, young Fuller was subjected to a severe educational regimen by her father, who was determined to treat his daughter's mind no differently from that of the son he had desired. By the age of eight, Fuller was reading the Latin classics and was soon proficient in several modern European languages. She was especially interested in modern German literature, a passion that brought her to the attention of the New England Transcendentalists, who were attempting at the time to redefine human experiences. With RALPH WALDO EMERSON, she founded, and for a while edited, *The Dial* (1840–1842), the quarterly magazine of literature, philosophy, and religion that had grown out of the meetings of the Transcendental Club in Boston. Also about this time, she began conducting a series of Saturday afternoon "Conversations," discussions of intellectual and literary topics that soon gained great popularity, especially among upper-middle-class Boston women. From these experiences developed her advanced feminist views as elucidated in *Woman in the Nineteenth Century* (1845). In 1844 Horace Greeley, editor of the *New York Tribune*, one of the most important newspapers in the nation, hired her to join his staff, and, during the next two years in New York, Fuller gained national prominence as a critic of art and literature. Some of her essays were reprinted in *Papers on Literature and Art* (1846), one of the most astute works of criticism to appear in the United States before the Civil War.

In August 1846, Fuller sailed for Europe, where she was to act as correspondent for the *Tribune*. These were tumultuous, revolutionary times in Europe, and Fuller soon added her voice to the republican cause that was challenging the established, reactionary political order throughout the Continent. In Italy she met and later married a young aristocrat, Giovanni Angelo, the Marchese Ossoli, a follower of the Italian revolutionary leader, Giuseppe Mazzini. Following the failure of the newly proclaimed Roman Republic in 1849, Fuller, together with her husband and their son, decided to return to the United States, where she could see through the press the history that she had written of the Roman Revolution of 1848–1849. Tragically, however, the family was lost at sea when their vessel sank off Fire Island, near New York, in July 1850.

Fuller's personality and activities generated much interest and strong disagreement, both during her lifetime and since. Her most enduring writing is not her published essays and books but, rather, her personal correspondence, in which the vitality of her mind and the strength of her character are brilliantly revealed.

WORKS BY FULLER

Margaret Fuller: Essays on American Life and Letters. Masterworks of Literature Ser. Ed. by Joel Myerson. New Coll. U. Pr. 1977 $14.95. ISBN 0-8084-0416-4. An excellent topical selection from Fuller's writings, including all of *Woman in the Nineteenth Century*.

The Essential Margaret Fuller. American Women Writers Ser. Ed. by Jeffrey Steele. Rutgers U. Pr. 1992 $50.00. ISBN 0-8135-1777-X. Includes the complete texts of *Woman in the Nineteenth Century* and *Summer on the Lakes, in 1843*, as well as other writings.

The Letters of Margaret Fuller. 5 vols. Ed. by Robert N. Hudspeth. Cornell Univ. Pr. $32.50 ea. Vol. 1 1983. ISBN 0-8014-1386-9. Vol. 2 1983. ISBN 0-8014-1575-6. Vol. 3 1984. ISBN 0-8014-1707-4. Vol. 4 1987. ISBN 0-8014-1972-7. Vol. 5 1988. ISBN 0-8014-2174-8. Meticulously edited and well annotated; Fuller's most enduring literary performances.

Papers on Literature and Art. 1846. Rprt. Serv. 1992 repr. of 1846 ed. $99.00. ISBN 0-7812-6816-8. Trenchant criticism by Fuller, first published in the *New York Tribune*.

Summer on the Lakes, in 1843. 1844. *Prairie State Bk. Ser.* U. of Ill. Pr. 1990 $8.95. ISBN 0-252-06164-0. Impressionistic account of Fuller's travels in the Great Lakes region.

"These Sad but Glorious Days": Dispatches from Europe, 1846–1850. Ed. by Larry J. Reynolds and Susan B. Smith. Yale U. Pr. 1992 $48.75. ISBN 0-300-05038-0. Reports from England, France, and Italy sent to the *New York Tribune*.

Woman in the Nineteen Century. 1845. Norton 1971 $7.95. ISBN 0-393-00615-8. A monumental, sophisticated defense of feminism.

BOOKS ABOUT FULLER

Allen, Margaret V. *The Achievement of Margaret Fuller.* Pa. St. U. Pr. 1979 $24.95. ISBN 0-271-00215-8. A serious intellectual biography, flawed by what appears to some to be an overly high estimation of Fuller's achievement.

Blanchard, Paula. *Margaret Fuller: From Transcendentalism to Revolution.* Addison-Wesley 1987 $12.95. ISBN 0-201-10458-X. A popular rather than scholarly appreciation of Fuller's works.

Brown, Arthur W. *Margaret Fuller.* Twayne's United States Authors Ser. Irvington 1964 $17.95. ISBN 0-8290-1712-7. A useful introduction to Fuller's life and ideas.

Chevigny, Bell Gale. *The Woman and the Myth: Margaret Fuller's Life and Writings.* Feminist Pr. 1977 $8.95. ISBN 0-912670-43-6. An impressively innovative approach, combining generous selections from Fuller's writings, comments by her contemporaries, and analysis by Chevigny.

Stern, Madeleine, B. *The Life of Margaret Fuller.* Greenwood 1991 $45.00. ISBN 0-313-27526-2. A revised edition of a most readable and informed biographical study that first appeared in 1941.

Wade, Mason. *Margaret Fuller: Whetstone of Genius.* Kelley 1973 repr. of 1940 ed. $37.50. ISBN 0-6788-03178-9. A well-researched and thoroughly readable account of Fuller's life and works.

HARRIS, GEORGE WASHINGTON. 1814–1869

Better known to his readers as "Sut Lovingood," Harris was a successful river pilot on the Tennessee River when he published his first sketch in *The Spirit of the Times*, an immensely popular New York magazine that featured in its pages some of the best tall tales and humor of the Old Southwest. As M. Thomas Inge observed, "he quickly developed a facility for local color and dialect and a skill for bringing backwoods scenes and events to life on the printed page." Though considered by many as coarse and even cruel, Harris has had many admirers among his mostly male readers, one of whom was young MARK TWAIN, who regarded him as one of the best of a large number of humorists who wrote in the antebellum South—an estimation that has had some distinguished collaboration during the twentieth century. WILLIAM FAULKNER said that Sut Lovingood was one of his favorite characters in literature: "He had no illusions about himself, did the best he could; at certain times he was a coward and knew it and wasn't ashamed; he never blamed his misfortunes on anyone and never cursed God for them." For F. O. Matthiessen, it was Harris's style that distinguished him from other vernacular humorists—at least before Twain—because he brought "us closer than any other writer to the indigenous and undiluted resources of the American language." Shortly before his death, Harris collected many of his tales and sketches in *Sut Lovingood: Yarns Spun by a "Nat'ral Born Durn'd Fool"* (1867).

WORKS BY HARRIS

High Times and Hard Times: Sketches and Tales by George Washington Harris. Ed. by M. Thomas Inge. B. Franklin 1976 $16.95. ISBN 0-8337-5502-1. Collects all of Harris's known work except for the Sut Lovingood yarns.

Sut Lovingood. Yarns Spun by a "Nat'ral Born Durn'd Fool." 1867. *Masterworks of Literature Ser.* Ed. by M. Thomas Inge. New Coll. U. Pr. 1966 $8.95. ISBN 0-8084-0290-0. A good reprint, with a fine critical introduction.

BOOK ABOUT HARRIS

Rickels, Milton. *George Washington Harris. Twayne's United States Authors Ser.* Irvington 1965 $17.95. ISBN 0-89197-770-8. New Coll. U. Pr. 1965 $10.95. ISBN 0-8084-0144-0. An excellent critical study that locates Harris in his proper historical and literary contexts.

HAWTHORNE, NATHANIEL. 1804–1864

It has seemed appropriate to many that Hawthorne, the first American writer to gain international critical recognition as a great master of prose fiction, should have been born on July 4, the anniversary of his country's independence. America's past, in which Hawthorne's own family had figured so prominently, was essential to the writer's creative imagination. Particularly, it was the stories and legends of New England—of Hawthorne's native Salem and the Puritan experiment in Massachusetts Bay Colony—in which Hawthorne found the inspiration for his best fiction.

Compared to a more prolific writer like JAMES FENIMORE COOPER, Hawthorne's fictional output seems relatively small: only four novels or, as he preferred to call them, "romances"; three collections of short fiction; and several children's books. In quality, however, Hawthorne has no rival in the early and mid-nineteenth century except HERMAN MELVILLE. Such stories as "Young Goodman Brown" (1835), "Rappaccini's Daughter" (1844), and "My Kinsman, Major Molineux" (1832) were remarkable achievements, and Hawthorne has been credited with making a major contribution to the developing art of the American short story. His greatest novel doubtless is *The Scarlet Letter* (1850), a symbolic work of subtle moral and psychological complexity. Though the story is set in Boston during the mid-seventeenth century, it is not in an ordinary sense an historical novel. His interest was rarely in the "pastness" of the past but, rather, in its effect upon the present. In the tragedy of the sinner Hester Prynne, her lover-minister Dimmesdale, and her revenge-seeking husband Chillingworth, Hawthorne uses the past as a metaphor through which to explore the ageless conflict between sacred individualism and community solidarity. The terms in which Hawthorne presents this moral dilemma allow no resolution of the central problem of the novel, so that, like all of Hawthorne's best fiction, it ends—intentionally—in profound ambiguity.

The longer works of fiction that followed *The Scarlet Letter* are all, to various degrees, flawed in their artistry, especially when compared to the early short tales, but, nevertheless, they all possess extraordinary power. *The House of the Seven Gables* (1851) deals mainly with the destructive effects of the past. *The Blithedale Romance* (1852) is a skeptical study of various projects of social reform, including equal rights for women and socialism. *The Marble Faun* (1860), written after Hawthorne's long sojourn in England and Italy from 1853 to 1859, is a modern retelling of the old fable of Adam's fall, dealing like so many of Hawthorne's works with the ambiguous effects of sin. At his death, Hawthorne left several unfinished romances, voluminous private journals, and important correspondence, all of which have been edited and published in the definitive *Centenary Edition of the Works of Nathaniel Hawthorne Series.*

In spite of the introspective character of most of his work and the noted reticence of his personality, Hawthorne was quite active in the life of his times, taking an interest in political affairs, as well as in family and social responsibilities. He was well acquainted with other New England writers, notably his Concord neighbors, RALPH WALDO EMERSON and HENRY DAVID THOREAU, and was a friend and for a short while mentor of Herman Melville, on whose great work *Moby Dick* (1851) Hawthorne exerted an important influence, a debt Melville acknowledged by dedicating the novel to him. But his most intimate friends were his old Bowdoin College classmates, HENRY WADSWORTH LONGFELLOW, Horatio Bridge, and Franklin Pierce. When the latter became president of the United States, he rewarded Hawthorne's loyalty and support by appointing him U.S. consul at Liverpool and Manchester. Hawthorne's experiences and observations abroad later became the basis of his fine book of English sketches, *Our Old Home* (1863).

NOVELS BY HAWTHORNE

The Blithedale Romance. 1852. *Centenary Edition of the Works of Nathaniel Hawthorne Ser.* Vol. 3. Ed. by William Charvat and others. Ohio St. U. Pr. 1965 $47.75. ISBN 0-8142-0061-3

The House of the Seven Gables. 1851. *Centenary Edition of the Works of Nathaniel Hawthorne Ser.* Vol. 2. Ed. by William Charvat and others. Ohio St. U. Pr. 1965 $47.75. ISBN 0-8142-0060-5

The Marble Faun; or, The Romance of Monte Beni. 1860. *Centenary Edition of the Works of Nathaniel Hawthorne Ser.* Vol. 4. Ed. by William Charvat and others. Ohio St. U. Pr. 1968 $62.50. ISBN 0-8142-0062-1. Viking Penguin 1990 $6.95. ISBN 0-14-039077-4

Novels. Ed. by Millicent Bell. Library of America 1983 $30.00. ISBN 0-940450-9. Excellent one-volume edition that reprints *Fanshawe, The Scarlet Letter, The House of the Seven Gables, The Blithedale Romance,* and *The Marble Faun.*

The Scarlet Letter: A Romance. 1850. *Centenary Edition of the Works of Nathaniel Hawthorne Ser.* Vol. 1. Ed. by William Charvat and others. Ohio St. U. Pr. 1963 $36.75. ISBN 0-8142-0059-1

SHORT STORY COLLECTIONS BY HAWTHORNE

Mosses from an Old Manse. 1846. *Centenary Edition of the Works of Nathaniel Hawthorne Ser.* Vol. 10. Ed. by William Charvat and others. Ohio St. U. Pr. 1974 $57.75. ISBN 0-8142-0203-9. Hawthorne's second collection of tales and sketches, including "Young Goodman Brown," "The Birth-mark," "The Artist of the Beautiful," and "Rappaccini's Daughter."

Nathaniel Hawthorne's Tales. Critical Editions Ser. Ed. by James McIntosh. Norton 1987 $24.95. ISBN 0-393-02428-8. A fine edition of Hawthorne's tales, together with valuable critical commentary.

The Snow-Image, and Uncollected Tales. Centenary Edition of the Works of Nathaniel Hawthorne Ser. Vol. 11. Ed. by William Charvat and others. Ohio St. U. Pr. 1974 $52.50. ISBN 0-8142-0204-7. Contains the tales and sketches that Hawthorne collected in 1851 under the title *The Snow-Image and Other Twice-Told Tales,* as well as other tales never gathered in book form during the author's lifetime.

Tales and Sketches. Ed. by Roy H. Pearce. Library of America 1982 $35.00. ISBN 0-940450-03-8. An excellent one-volume edition of all of Hawthorne's important short fiction.

Tanglewood Tales. 1853. Buccaneer Bks. 1990 $21.95. ISBN 0-89966-737-6. Six Greek myths retold for children.

Twice-Told Tales. 1837. *Centenary Edition of the Works of Nathaniel Hawthorne Ser.* Vol. 9. Ed. by William Charvat and others. Ohio St. U. Pr. 1974 $60.50. ISBN 0-8142-0202-0. Hawthorne's first collection of tales and sketches (expanded in 1842), many of which deal with the New England past.

A Wonder Book and Tanglewood Tales. Centenary Edition of the Works of Nathaniel Hawthorne Ser. Vol. 5. Ed. by William Charvat and others. Ohio St. U. Pr. 1972

$47.75. ISBN 0-8142-0158-X. The standard edition of *A Wonder-Book for Girls and Boys* (1852) and its sequel, *Tanglewood Tales* (1853), Hawthorne's two collections of stories from Greek mythology adapted for children.

A Wonder-Book for Girls and Boys. Rprt. Serv. 1992 repr. of 1852 ed. $75.00. ISBN 0-7812-3045-4

WORKS BY HAWTHORNE

The American Claimant Manuscripts. Centenary Edition of the Works of Nathaniel Hawthorne Ser. Vol. 12. Ed. by William Charvat and others. Ohio St. U. Pr. 1978 $62.50. ISBN 0-8142-0251-9. Contains several of Hawthorne's unfinished romances: "The Ancestral Footstep," "Etherege," and "Grimshawe."

American Notebooks. Centenary Edition of the Works of Nathaniel Hawthorne Ser. Vol. 8. Ed. by Claude M. Simpson. Ohio St. U. Pr. 1973 $78.75. ISBN 0-8142-0159-8. Hawthorne's private notebooks, in which he recorded ideas for stories and observations on life.

The Elixir of Life Manuscripts. Centenary Edition of the Works of Nathaniel Hawthorne Ser. Vol. 13. Ed. by William Charvat and others. Ohio St. U. Pr. 1978 $71.00. ISBN 0-8142-0252-7. Critical texts of three other of Hawthorne's fragmentary fictions: "The Dolliver Romance," "Septimius Felton," and "Septimius Norton."

The French and Italian Notebooks. Centenary Edition of the Works of Nathaniel Hawthorne Ser. Vol. 14. Ed. by Thomas Woodson. Ohio St. U. Pr. 1980 $60.50. ISBN 0-8142-0256-X. The standard text of Hawthorne's European journals, written during his travels abroad, from 1858 to 1859.

Letters. 6 vol. *Centenary Edition of the Works of Nathaniel Hawthorne Ser.* Vols. 15–20. Ed. by Thomas Woodson and others. Ohio St. U. Pr. Vol. 15 1985 $52.50. ISBN 0-8142-0363-9. Vol. 16 1985 $52.50. ISBN 0-8142-0364-7. Vol. 17 1987 $65.00. ISBN 0-8142-0363-9. Vol. 18 1987 $55.75. ISBN 0-8142-0383-3. Vol. 19 1988 $55.75. ISBN 0-8142-0384-1. Vol. 20 1988 $65.00. ISBN 0-8142-0462-7. A generously annotated edition of Hawthorne's complete letters, including his diplomatic correspondence.

Life of Franklin Pierce. 1852. Rprt. Serv. 1988 repr. of 1852 ed. $49.00. ISBN 0-317-90298-9. Hawthorne's controversial campaign biography of his friend and Bowdoin classmate.

Our Old Home: A Series of English Sketches. 1863. *Centenary Edition of the Works of Nathaniel Hawthorne Ser.* Vol. 5. Ed. by William Charvat and others. Ohio St. U. Pr. 1970 $40.50. ISBN 0-8142-0002-8. One of the most revealing books about England by an American in the nineteenth century; an artistic reflection of Hawthorne's years in England from 1853 to 1858.

True Stories from History and Biography. 1851. *Centenary Edition of the Works of Nathaniel Hawthorne Ser.* Vol. 6. Ed. by William Charvat and others. Ohio St. U. Pr. 1972 $42.00. ISBN 0-8142-0157-1. Hawthorne's own gathering of three of his earlier books for children: *Grandfather's Chair: A History for Youth* (1841), *Famous Old People: Being the Second Epoch of Grandfather's Chair* (1841), and *Biographical Stories for Children* (1842).

BOOKS ABOUT HAWTHORNE

Baym, Nina. *The Scarlet Letter: A Reading.* G. K. Hall 1986 $20.95. ISBN 0-8057-7959-4. An excellent full-length, general critical introduction to Hawthorne's romance.

Bell, Millicent. *Hawthorne's View of the Artist.* State U. NY Pr. 1962 $49.50. ISBN 0-87395-008-9. A thorough examination of Hawthorne's critical theories.

Cohen, B. Bernard, ed. *The Recognition of Nathaniel Hawthorne: Selected Criticism since 1828.* Bks. Demand repr. of 1969 ed. $80.00. ISBN 0-317-29153-X. A valuable survey, with representative selections of writings about Hawthorne.

Colacurcio, Michael J. *New Essays on "The Scarlet Letter." The Amer. Novel Ser.* Cambridge U. Pr. 1985 $8.95. ISBN 0-521-31998-6. Recent critical methods still find much to reveal about Hawthorne's artistry and creative thought.

———. *Province of Piety: Moral History in Hawthorne's Early Tales.* HUP 1984 $35.00. ISBN 0-674-71957-3. An engaging and demanding reading of Hawthorne's tales in relation to his knowledge of New England history.

Crews, Frederick C. *The Sins of the Fathers: Hawthorne's Psychological Themes.* U. CA Pr. 1989 $10.95. ISBN 0-520-06817-3. A Freudian reading of Hawthorne's work, first published in 1966.

Crowley, J. Donald, ed. *Hawthorne: The Critical Heritage.* Routledge 1978 $69.50. ISBN 0-7100-6886-7. A useful collection of critical responses to Hawthorne's art.

Fogle, Richard H. *Hawthorne's Fiction: The Light and the Dark.* U. of Okla. Pr. 1964 o.p. Revised edition of one of the essential critical studies of Hawthorne's fictional techniques.

Gale, Robert L. *A Nathaniel Hawthorne Encyclopedia.* Greenwood 1991 $75.00. ISBN 0-313-26816-9. Just about everything one might want to know about Hawthorne and his fiction conveniently arranged.

James, Henry. *Hawthorne.* 1879. *English Men of Letters Ser.* AMS Pr. repr. of 1887 ed. $22.50. ISBN 0-404-51715-3. While somewhat revealing of Hawthorne's art and aesthetic, even more revealing of James.

Kesterton, David B. *Critical Essays on Hawthorne's "The Scarlet Letter."* *Critical Essays Ser.* G. K. Hall 1988 $40.00. ISBN 0-8161-8883-1. A collection of mostly previously printed journal articles dealing with Hawthorne's great masterpiece.

Levin, Harry. *The Power of Blackness: Hawthorne, Poe, Melville.* Ohio U. Pr. $9.95. ISBN 0-8214-0581-0. A classic study.

Martin, Terence. *Nathaniel Hawthorne. Twayne's United States Authors Ser.* G. K. Hall 1983 $20.95. ISBN 0-8057-7384-3. Revised edition of one of the best critical studies of Hawthorne's artistry.

Turner, Arlin. *Nathaniel Hawthorne: A Biography.* OUP 1980 $45.00. ISBN 0-19-502547-4. A standard and highly reliable biography.

Von Frank, Albert J. *Critical Essays on Hawthorne's Short Stories. Critical Essays on American Literature Ser.* G. K. Hall 1990 $40.00. ISBN 0-8161-1843-4. A judicious selection of previously published criticism about Hawthorne's short fiction.

Waggoner, Hyatt H. *Hawthorne: A Critical Study.* HUP 1955 o.p. A classic study that is still valuable for its penetrating analysis and insights.

———. *The Presence of Hawthorne.* La. State U. Pr. 1979 $25.00. ISBN 0-8071-0576-7. A collection of eight previously published essays by a master Hawthorne scholar.

HOLMES, OLIVER WENDELL. 1809–1894

A devoted physician and professor of anatomy and physiology at Harvard College for 35 years, Holmes used his literary talents to enhance his life, not to define it. Literary fame came relatively early to Holmes, when in 1830 he published a few lines of verse in a Boston newspaper in which he objected to the dismantling of the frigate *Constitution*, which had served its nation victoriously in the Tripolitan War and the War of 1812. The poem, "Old Ironside," was a great success, both for Holmes as a poet and in saving the frigate. However, his medical studies left Holmes little leisure for literature for the next 25 years.

That changed, however, with the publication of an animated series of essays in the newly founded *Atlantic Monthly* in 1857 and 1858, and afterwards published in book form as *The Autocrat of the Breakfast-Table* (1858). Not only did these essays help secure the magazine's success, but also brought Holmes widespread popularity. Holmes as an essayist has been compared with all of the great writers in that genre, from MICHEL DE MONTAIGNE (see Vols. 2 and 4) to CHARLES LAMB, but his compositions are closer to conversational than to formal prose. Later volumes—*The Professor at the Breakfast-Table* (1860), *The Poet at the Breakfast-Table* (1872), and *Over the Teacups* (1891)—extend the autocrat's delightfully egotistical talks, mainly of Boston and New England, in which Holmes was, by turns, brilliantly witty and extremely serious. During these same years, he also wrote three so-called medicated novels: *Elsie Venner* (1861), *The Guardian Angel* (1867), and *A Mortal Antipathy* (1885). Though undistinguished as literary documents, they are important early studies of that "mysterious borderland which lies between physiology and psychology," and they demonstrate that Holmes was advanced in his conception of the causes and progress of neuroses and mental disease.

Many of Holmes's best poems appeared first in his "Breakfast Table" series. "The Deacon's Masterpiece, or the Wonderful One-Hoss Shay," "The Chambered Nautilus," and "The Living Temple" all may be found in *The Autocrat of the Breakfast-Table* (1858). But the bulk of Holmes's poetry is occasional verse, written "on command" to celebrate "the affairs of men and nations." Indeed, so many events are commemorated in his verses that a social history of the times—at least in Boston—may be read in his complete poems. Much more lasting as literary artifacts, however, are his short, humorous verses, like "The Ballad of the Oysterman" (1830), "The Last Leaf" (1831), and "My Aunt" (1831).

POETRY BY HOLMES

The Complete Poetical Works of Oliver Wendell Holmes. Cambridge Editions Ser. Ed. by Eleanor M. Tilton. HM 1975 o.p. A convenient, well-annotated one-volume edition of Holmes's verse.

NONFICTION BY HOLMES

The Autocrat of the Breakfast-Table. 1858. Airmont 1968 $1.95. ISBN 0-8049-0159-7. The first and most popular of Holmes's "Breakfast Table" series.
Over the Teacups. 1890. Scholarly 1968 repr. of 1892 ed. $39.00. ISBN 0-403-02466-8. Holmes's final and least satisfying volume of conversations.
The Poet at the Breakfast-Table: His Talks with His Fellow-Boarders and the Reader. 1872. Scholarly 1968 repr. of 1895 ed. $18.00. ISBN 0-403-00069-6
The Professor at the Breakfast-Table, with the Story of Iris. 1860. Scholarly 1968 repr. of 1899 ed. $18.00. ISBN 0-403-0068-8

NOVELS BY HOLMES

Elsie Venner: A Romance of Destiny. 1861. *Supernatural and Occult Fiction Ser.* Ed. by R. Reginald and Douglas Menville. Ayer 1976 $38.50. ISBN 0-405-08137-5. A New England novel that examines in psychological terms the issues of predestination and free will.
The Guardian Angel. 1867. Irvington repr. of 1888 ed. $19.00. ISBN 0-8398-0787-2. Another of Holmes's so-called medicated novels, depicting the role of heredity in human behavior.
A Mortal Antipathy: First Opening of the New Portfolio. 1885. Irvington repr. of 1885 ed. $19.00. ISBN 0-8398-0788-0. A psychological novel that considers the later effects of childhood experiences.

WORKS BY HOLMES

The Complete Works of Oliver Wendell Holmes. 13 vols. Scholarly 1972 repr. of 1892 ed. $795.00. ISBN 0-403-00472-1. The standard edition of Holmes's poems and prose.
Oliver Wendell Holmes: Representative Selections. Ed. by S. I. Hayakawa and Howard M. Jones. AMS Pr. repr. of 1939 ed. $34.75. ISBN 0-404-14764-X. A balanced and illuminating selection of Holmes's prose and verse.

BOOKS ABOUT HOLMES

Howe, M. DeWolfe. *Holmes of the Breakfast-Table.* Appel 1976 repr. of 1939 ed. $9.00. ISBN 0-911858-16-4. A sympathetic but still discriminating portrait of Holmes by a fellow Bostonian.

Small, Miriam R. *Oliver Wendell Holmes. Twayne's United States Authors Ser.* G. K. Hall 1962 o.p. Includes a chronology and a selected bibliography.

Tilton, Eleanor M. *Amiable Autocrat: A Biography of Doctor Oliver Wendell Holmes.* Hippocrene Bks. 1976 repr. of 1947 ed. $27.50. ISBN 0-374-97945-6. An excellent critical and thoroughly researched account of Holmes and his works.

IRVING, WASHINGTON. 1783–1859

Irving was the first internationally successful American man of letters, the author of a small group of stories that are still popularly read. The son of a prosperous New York merchant, his life as an author began somewhat casually. With his brother William and their friend, James Kirke Paulding, he amused polite New York society with a series of amusing and satirical essays and poems, the *Salmagundi* papers, which were published serially during 1807 and 1808. Enjoying the fame and attention of his success, Irving went on by himself to write a burlesque *History of New-York* (1809) that has been called "the first great book of comic literature written by an American." However, following the death of his fiancée at this time, Irving abandoned his literary plans and ambitions and he occupied himself by helping his brothers run the family business.

In 1815 Irving sailed to England to look after the family's business affairs there, little realizing that he would not return to the United States for 17 years. When the Irving family firm was forced into bankruptcy in 1818, he gambled his fortune on his being able to write a commercially successful book. The result was *The Sketch Book of Geoffrey Crayon, Gent.* (1819–1820), a series of essays and stories, including the famous "Rip Van Winkle" and "The Legend of Sleepy Hollow." The book was an immediate success, and Irving's future was secure. Until his death he remained one of the most popular writers in the English-speaking world, friend of politicians and poets, honored at home and abroad. His writings are diverse: essays, biographies, histories, short stories, and sketches. The most imaginative works are the short stories; in addition to those collected in *The Sketch Book*, others were published in two volumes that soon followed: *Bracebridge Hall; or, The Humourists: A Medley* (1822) and *Tales of a Traveller* (1824). Irving's contribution to this genre was significant. From him CHARLES DICKENS learned much about characterization, and EDGAR ALLAN POE and NATHANIEL HAWTHORNE appear to have been greatly influenced by his use of atmospheric settings, especially in his Gothic or "supernatural" tales.

While he was in Europe, Irving served as attaché of the U.S. legation in Spain for two years, from 1826 to 1828; later, in 1842, he returned as the U.S. minister to Spain, a post he held for four years. His interest in the Spanish past inspired four works, romantic histories that were popular in his time but are rarely read today: *History of the Life and Voyages of Christopher Columbus* (1828) and its sequel, *Voyages and Discoveries of the Companions of Columbus* (1831); *A Chronicle of the Conquest of Granada* (1829); and *The Alhambra: A Series of Tales and Sketches of the Moors and Spaniards* (1832). Following his triumphant return to the United States in 1832, Irving, as a member of a government commission, made a three-month tour of the American Southwest, about which he later wrote in *A Tour on the Prairies* (1835). His other western writings include *Astoria* (1836), a book done on commission from the Astor family and based upon records furnished by John Jacob Astor, and its sequel, *Adventures of Captain Bonneville, U.S.A.* (1837).

As a biographer, Irving won popular approval in his own day but little lasting distinction. His lives of OLIVER GOLDSMITH (see also Vol. 2) (1840), MUHAMMAD (see Vol. 4) and his successors (1849–50), and GEORGE WASHINGTON (see Vol. 3) (1855–1859), for whom he had been named, are fairly typical examples of romanticized biography. These, along with Irving's other works, are included in a scholarly edition of his writings that was begun by the University of Wisconsin Press and nearly completed in 30 volumes by G. K. Hall (1969–1986), but, unfortunately, most of its titles are already out of print.

SHORT STORY COLLECTIONS BY IRVING

The Alhambra: A Series of Tales and Sketches of the Moors and Spaniards. 1832. Sleepy Hollow 1982 repr. of 1851 ed. $23.95. ISBN 0-9122882-48-4. Exotic tales of Spanish life and history.

Bracebridge Hall: or, The Humourists: A Medley by Geoffrey Crayon, Gent. 1822. AMS Pr. repr. of 1902 ed. $24.00. ISBN 0-404-03508-6. Forty-nine tales and sketches in the manner of *The Sketch Book.*

Bracebridge Hall, Tales of a Traveller, and The Alhambra. Ed. by Andrew B. Myers, Library of America 1991 $35.00. ISBN 0-940450-59-3. A handsome reprint of three important titles.

The Sketch Book of Geoffrey Crayon, Gent. 1819–1820. Viking Penguin 1988 $5.95. ISBN 0-14-039032-4

The Sketch Book of Geoffrey Crayon, Gent. 1819–1820. Sleepy Hollow 1981 repr. of 1852 ed. $23.95. ISBN 0-912882-47-6

Tales of a Traveller by Geoffrey Crayon, Gent. 1824. *Short Story Index Reprint Ser.* Ayer repr. of 1825 ed. $17.00. ISBN 0-8369-4110-1. Thirty-two romantic and gothic tales.

NONFICTION BY IRVING

Adventures of Captain Bonneville, U.S.A.; or, Scenes Beyond the Rocky Mountains of the Far West. 1837. Ed. by Edgeley W. Todd. U. of Okla. Pr. 1986 $14.95. ISBN 0-8061-2015-0. A narrative depicting the exploits of an important soldier–explorer of the American West.

Astoria, or Anecdotes of an Enterprize Beyond the Rocky Mountains. 1836. Ed. by Richard D. Rust. U. of Nebr. Pr. 1982 $9.95. ISBN 0-8032-7450-5. A descriptive and historical account of the Northwest Territory.

A Chronicle of the Conquest of Granada. 1829. 2 vols. AMS Pr. repr. of 1829 ed. $47.50. ISBN 0-404-03532-9. A semifictional account of an important episode in Spanish history.

History of The Life and Voyages of Christopher Columbus. 1828. *Heroes of the Nations Ser.* AMS Pr. repr. of 1893 ed. $49.50. ISBN 0-404-58268-0. An heroic account of Columbus's discoveries.

History of New-York from the Beginning of the World to the End of the Dutch Dynasty. 1809. Sleepy Hollow 1981 repr. of 1854 ed. $23.95. ISBN 0-912882-46-8. Reprints of the revised text of Irving's satirical history of the Dutch origins of New York.

Letters. The Complete Works of Washington Irving Ser. Vols. 23–26. Ed. by Ralph M. Aderman, Herbert L. Kleinfield, and Jenifer S. Banks. G. K. Hall 1979–1982 o.p. The standard edition of Irving's correspondence.

Miscellaneous Writings: 1803–1859. The Complete Works of Washington Irving Ser. Vols. 28–29. Ed. by Wayne R. Kime. G. K. Hall 1981 $90.00. ISBN 0-8057-8520-5. Irving's maverick writings that appeared throughout his career.

Oliver Goldsmith: A Biography. 1849. *English Literature Ser.* Haskell 1972 repr. of 1882 ed. $62.95. ISBN 0-8383-1446-5. A romanticized biography of a popular British writer.

A Tour on the Prairies. 1835. U. of Okla. Pr. 1985 $8.95. ISBN 0-8061-1958-6. An account of Irving's travels in what is now Oklahoma.

Voyages and Discoveries of the Companions of Columbus. 1831. *The Complete Works of Washington Irving Ser.* Vol. 12. Ed. by James W. Tuttleton. Macmillan 1987 $75.00. ISBN 0-8057-8517-5. The sequel to *History of The Life and Voyages of Christopher Columbus.*

WORKS BY IRVING

History, Tales and Sketches. Ed. by James W. Tuttleton. Library of America 1983 $27.50. ISBN 0-940450-14-3. Includes the text of the important 1809 edition of *History of New-York* as well as *Letters of Jonathan Oldstyle, Gent.* (1802–1803), *Salmagundi* (1807–1808), and *The Sketch Book of Geoffrey Crayon, Gent.* (1819–1829).

Washington Irving: Representative Selections. Ed. by Henry A. Pochman. Scholarly 1971 repr. of 1934 ed. $59.00. ISBN 0-403-01039-X. An excellent, compact selection of representative works.

Works of Washington Irving. 14 vols. Rprt. Serv. repr. of 1851 ed. $700.00. ISBN 0-317-90119-2. The edition of his works that Irving saw through the press.

BOOKS ABOUT IRVING

Aderman, Ralph M., ed. *Critical Essays on Washington Irving. Critical Essays on American Literature Ser.* G. K. Hall 1990 $40.00. ISBN 0-8161-8896-3. A judicious selection of both older and more recent critical commentaries on Irving's works.

Antelyes, Peter. *Tales of Adventurous Enterprise: Washington Irving and the Poetics of Western Expansion.* Col. U. Pr. 1990 $37.50. ISBN 0-231-06860-3. A study of the emergence of the western adventure tale in American literature and Irving's role in its development.

Bowden, Mary W. *Washington Irving. Twayne's United States Authors Ser.* G. K. Hall 1981 $19.95. ISBN 0-8057-7314-2. A biographical and critical introduction to Irving and his works.

Brodwin, Stanley, ed. *The Old and New World Romanticism of Washington Irving.* Greenwood 1986 $39.95. ISBN 0-313-25441-9. New essays that attempt to place Irving and his works in their proper critical milieux.

Hedges, William L. *Washington Irving: An American Study, 1802–1832.* Greenwood 1980 repr. of 1965 ed. $45.50. ISBN 0-313-21159-0. The basic critical study of Irving, with an excellent analysis of his American roots and European associations.

Rubin-Dorsky, Jeffrey. *Adrift in the Old World: The Psychological Pilgrimage of Washington Irving.* U. Ch. Pr. 1988 $32.50. ISBN 0-226-73094-8. Brings insightful psychological analysis and broad historical generalizations to bear on Irving's early career (1815–1832).

JACOBS, HARRIET ANN. 1813–1897

Born into slavery in North Carolina, Jacobs's early life was one of abuse and hardship. At the age of 21, she was sent to work on a plantation as penalty for having rejected the sexual advances of her white owner, whereupon she determined to free herself and her children at whatever cost. In 1842 Jacobs escaped to the North and was placed in the home of the popular New York writer, N. P. Willis. Several years later she moved to Rochester, New York, where she became active in a group of antislavery feminists. It was at their urging that she first came to think of writing her autobiography, since slave narratives were found to be an effective means of turning northern sentiment against the cruelties of slavery. Jacobs worked on her book during the next several years, finally finishing it in 1858, but no publisher was willing to publish it. Only after Lydia Maria Child, a leading white abolitionist, agreed to write a preface to Jacobs's autobiography was the book able to find its way into print in 1861. Coming as it did, however, so close to the beginning of the Civil War, *Incidents in the Life of a Slave Girl* (published under the pseudonym "Linda Brent") did not win the enormous popularity that other slave narratives had previously enjoyed, such as FREDERICK DOUGLASS's *Narrative* (1845). Nor was its popularity increased by its frank depiction of the sexual exploitation of female slaves by their masters. However, white women readers especially were moved by the account of a woman who had fought so heroically to free herself and her children from slavery, even at the cost of her "virtue," and were able to identify with her through the perspective of their own situations as wives and mothers. During and after the Civil War, Jacobs traveled and spoke on behalf of the rights of African Americans, her effectiveness enhanced by the recognition that she had earned as an author.

NONFICTION BY JACOBS

Incidents in the Life of a Slave Girl. 1861. Ed. by Jean F. Yellin. HUP 1987 $10.95. ISBN 0-674-44746-8

LONGFELLOW, HENRY WADSWORTH. 1807–1882

During his lifetime Longfellow enjoyed a popularity that few poets have ever known. This has made a purely literary assessment of his achievement difficult, since his verse has had an effect on so many levels of American culture and society. Certainly, some of his most popular poems are, when considered merely as artistic compositions, found wanting in serious ways: the confused imagery and sentimentality of "A Psalm of Life" (1839), the excessive didacticism of "Excelsior" (1841), the sentimentality of "The Village Blacksmith" (1839). Yet, when judged in terms of popular culture, these works are probably no worse—and, in some respects, much better—than their counterparts in our time.

Longfellow was very successful in responding to the need felt by Americans of his time for a literature of their own, a retelling in verse of the stories and legends of these United States, especially New England. His three most popular narrative poems are thoroughly rooted in American soil: *Evangeline: A Tale of Acadie* (1847), an American idyll; *The Song of Hiawatha* (1855), the first genuinely native epic in American poetry; and *The Courtship of Miles Standish* (1858), a Puritan romance of Longfellow's own ancestors, John Alden and Priscilla Mullens. "Paul Revere's Ride," the best known of the *Tales of a Wayside Inn* (1863), is also intensely national. Then there is a handful of intensely personal, melancholy poems that deal in very successful ways with those themes not commonly thought of as Longfellow's: sorrow, death, frustration, the pathetic drift of humanity's existence. Chief among these are "My Lost Youth" (1855), "Mezzo Cammin" (1842), "The Ropewalk" (1854), "The Jewish Cemetery at Newport" (1852), and, most remarkable in its artistic success, "The Cross of Snow," a heartfelt sonnet so personal in its expression of the poet's grief for his dead wife that it remained unpublished until after Longfellow's death. A professor of modern literature at Harvard College, Longfellow did much to educate the general reading public in the literatures of Europe by means of his many anthologies and translations, the most important of which was his masterful rendition in English of Dante's *Divine Comedy* (1865–67).

POETRY BY LONGFELLOW

Evangeline and Selected Tales and Poems. Ed. by Horace Gregory. 1847. NAL-Dutton 1964 $3.95. ISBN 0-451-52003-3. A fine selection of Longfellow's writings by the noted poet and critic.
The Poetical Works of Longfellow. Cambridge Editions Ser. Ed. by George Monteiro. HM 1975 $35.00. ISBN 0-395-188487-8. A revision of the standard, one-volume text of the poems first edited by H. E. Scudder in 1893.
Selected Poems. Ed. by Lawrence Buell. Viking Penguin 1988 $5.95. ISBN 0-14-039064-2. A discriminating selection of Longfellow's best and most familiar verse.

FICTION BY LONGFELLOW

Kavanaugh: A Tale. 1849. *Masterworks of Literature Ser.* Ed. by Jean Downey. New Coll. U. Pr. 1965 $15.95. ISBN 0-8084-0199-8. Meditative romance set in a New England village.

WORKS BY LONGFELLOW

The Letters of Henry Wadsworth Longfellow. 6 vols. Ed. by Andrew Hilen. HUP Vols. 1–2 1967 $80.00. ISBN 0-674-52725-9. Vols. 3–4 1972 $80.00. ISBN 0-674-52728-3. Vols. 5–6 1982 $95.00. ISBN 0-674-52729-1. A superb scholarly edition, with valuable biographical summaries.

The Works of Henry Wadsworth Longfellow. 14 vols. Ed. by Samuel Longfellow. AMS Pr. repr. of 1891 ed. $525.00. ISBN 0-404-04040-3. The standard edition of Longfellow's prose and poetry, compiled by his brother.

BOOKS ABOUT LONGFELLOW

Arvin, Newton. *Longfellow: His Life and Work.* Greenwood 1977 repr. of 1963 ed. $65.00. ISBN 0-8371-9505-5. A critically sophisticated assessment of Longfellow's literary achievement.

Hilen, Andrew, and Tira Gollin. *Papers Presented at the Longfellow Commemorative Conference: April 1–3, 1982.* Longfellow 1983 $5.00. ISBN 0-9610844-0-5. Eight papers of literary comment and analysis, occasioned by the centennial of Longfellow's death.

Longfellow, Samuel. *Life of Henry Wadsworth Longfellow, with Extracts from his Journals and Correspondence.* 3 vols. Scholarly repr. of 1891 ed. $55.00. ISBN 0-403-00078-5. Still valuable for its liberal quotations from Longfellow's private journals.

Thompson, Lawrance. *Young Longfellow (1807–1843).* 1938. Hippocrene Bks. 1969 $27.50. ISBN 0-374-97885-9. An important critical reassessment of Longfellow's formative years as a poet.

Tucker, Edward L. *The Shaping of Longfellow's John Endicott: A Textual History. Including Two Early Versions.* U. Pr. of Va. 1985 $19.95. ISBN 0-8139-1039-0. A detailed account of the genesis of one of Longfellow's *Christus* plays.

Wagenknecht, Edward. *Henry Wadsworth Longfellow: His Poetry and Prose.* Continuum 1986 $18.95. ISBN 0-8044-2960-X. A good, general introduction to Longfellow's works.

Williams, Cecil B. *Henry Wadsworth Longfellow. Twayne's United States Authors Ser.* G. K. Hall 1964 $19.95. ISBN 0-8057-0456-6. Valuable for its summaries of Longfellow's poems and prose works.

LONGSTREET, AUGUSTUS BALDWIN. 1790–1870

Longstreet is remembered for one book, *Georgia Scenes, Characters, Incidents, &c., in the First Half Century of the Republic* (1835), a collection of humorous, racy newspaper sketches of the life of Middle Georgia during the early nineteenth century. Though not the first, it was the most important and most influential early attempt to translate into print those traditions of storytelling and verbal wit that had characterized frontier life in the United States. Here were the beginnings in literature of the vernacular tradition, the humor of the Old Southwest, whose vitality would be one of the mainsprings of the works of MARK TWAIN and WILLIAM FAULKNER. Longstreet, a lawyer, educator, and writer, was in most respects an outsider to the world he so colorfully described in *Georgia Scenes;* an educated, conservative, even moralistic individual, his duties as a circuit court judge had taken him to rural settlements, where he was able to observe the lives of ordinary country people at work and play. His aim in writing down his observations "was to supply a chasm in history which has always been overlooked—the manners, customs, amusements, wit, dialect, as they appear in all grades of society to an eye and ear witness of them." EDGAR ALLAN POE praised Longstreet for his "penetrating understanding of *character* in general, and of Southern character in particular." About *Georgia Scenes*, BERNARD DE VOTO (see Vol. 3), the preeminent historian of the American frontier, had this to say: "In some respects, Longstreet's successors never equalled him, in many respects they never surpassed him, and his book remains today vital and absorbing—the frontier's first permanent work."

NONFICTION BY LONGSTREET

Georgia Scenes, Characters, Incidents, &c., in the First Half Century of the Republic. 1835. Cherokee 1990 $9.95. ISBN 0-87797-213-3

BOOK ABOUT LONGSTREET

King, Kimball. *Augustus Baldwin Longstreet. Twayne's United States Authors Ser.* G. K. Hall 1984 o.p. A good introduction to the man, his times, and his humor.

LOWELL, JAMES RUSSELL. 1819–1891

Essayist, poet, literary critic, humorist, editor, professor, ambassador, letter writer, Lowell was one of the most versatile of nineteenth-century authors. Public recognition of his verse came early in his career, both in the United States and in England, though his lyrical poetry, so greatly honored during his lifetime, is the weakest of his compositions. Only later, when he turned his hand to humorous verse, satire, and public odes, did he achieve distinction. *The Biglow Papers* (1848), occasioned by the war between the United States and Mexico, 1846–48, is a wonderful satiric medley in prose and verse, in vernacular Yankee speech and classic English of the best literary traditions, by far the greatest political satire written during that century. His public poems, such as the "Ode Recited at the Harvard Commemoration" (1867) for Harvard men who died in the Civil War and the "Concord Ode," are fine examples of a form as old as PINDAR (see Vol. 2), designed to give dignity and meaning to the events that bind communities of men and women.

But Lowell's real strengths as a writer are better found in his prose essays than in his verse. A man great in literary learning (he was professor of belles-lettres at Harvard College for many years), wise and passionate in his commitments, he was a great upholder of tradition and value. His essays on the great writers of England and Europe still endure, distinguished not only by their astute insights into the literary classics of Western culture, but also by their spectacular style and stunning wit.

Nor was Lowell merely a dweller in an ivory tower. In his youth he worked passionately for the cause of abolition, risking his literary reputation for a principle that he saw as absolute. In his middle years, he was founding editor of the *Atlantic Monthly* and guided it during its early years toward its enormous success. In his final years, this great example of American character and style represented the United States first as minister to Spain (1877–80), and afterwards to Great Britain (1880–85).

NONFICTION BY LOWELL

Among My Books. 1870. AMS Pr. 1970 repr. of 1870 ed. $11.50. ISBN 0-404-04039-X. A collection of literary and historical essays, including his important essays "Dryden" and "Rousseau and the Sentimentalists."

Literary Criticism of James Russell Lowell. Regents Critics Ser. Ed. by Herbert F. Smith. U. of Nebr. Pr. 1969 $23.50. ISBN 0-8032-0457-4. An excellent anthology of Lowell's best essays on literature.

My Study Windows. 1871. AMS Pr. repr. of 1871 ed. $11.25. ISBN 0-404-04057-8. Another collection by Lowell of his literary and familiar essays.

POETRY BY LOWELL

The Biglow Papers. First Series. 1848. Ed. by Thomas Wortham. N. Ill. U. Pr. 1977 $25.00. ISBN 0-87580-053-X. An annotated critical text of Lowell's satiric masterpiece.

The Biglow Papers. Second Series. 1867. AMS Pr. repr. of 1885 ed. $32.00. ISBN 0-404-04056-X. Lowell's satire on the enemies of right and justice during the American Civil War.

A Fable for Critics. 1848. Ayer 1972 repr. of 1890 ed. $14.00. ISBN 0-8369-7244-9. A long, satiric commentary on American writers and writing.

The Poetical Works of James Russell Lowell. Cambridge Editions Ser. Ed. by Marjorie Kaufman. HM 1978 $15.00. ISBN 0-395-25726-3. Standard and convenient in one volume; an updated edition of work originally edited by H. E. Scudder.

WORKS BY LOWELL

Complete Writings. 16 vols. Ed. by Charles E. Norton. AMS Pr. repr. of 1904 ed. $392.00. ISBN 0-404-04070-5. Standard edition of Lowell's writings, including an expanded edition of the 1894 edition of *Letters.*

Letters of James Russell Lowell. 2 vols. Ed. by Charles E. Norton. AMS Pr. repr. of 1894 ed. $67.50. ISBN 0-404-00080-0. A highly biased selection of Lowell's important correspondence by his friend and literary executor.

BOOKS ABOUT LOWELL

Beatty, Richmond C. *James Russell Lowell.* Shoe String 1969 repr. of 1942 ed. $36.50. ISBN 0-208-00752-0. A generally unsympathetic but still insightful assessment of Lowell by a member of the southern Agrarians.

Duberman, Martin. *James Russell Lowell.* HM 1966 o.p. Well researched and elegantly written; the best of the modern biographies of Lowell.

Howard, Leon. *Victorian Knight-Errant: A Study of the Early Literary Career of James Russell Lowell.* U. CA Pr. 1952 o.p. An intelligent, learned study of young Lowell and his culture.

Scudder, Horace E. *James Russell Lowell: A Biography.* 2 vols. AMS Pr. repr. of 1901 ed. $47.50. ISBN 0-404-05664-4. Still valuable for its generous quotations from Lowell's letters and other writings.

Wagenknecht, Edward C. *James Russell Lowell: Portrait of a Many-Sided Man. Portraits of American Writers Ser.* OUP 1971 $19.95. ISBN 0-19-501376-X. General and interpretive; a fine introduction to the man and his works.

MELVILLE, HERMAN. 1819–1891

Melville was born into a seemingly secure, prosperous world, a descendant of prominent Dutch and English families long established in New York State. That security vanished when first, the family business failed, and then, two years later, in young Melville's thirteenth year, his father died. Without enough money to gain the formal education that professions required, Melville was thrown on his own resources and in 1841 sailed off on a whaling ship bound for the South Seas. His experiences at sea during the next four years were to form in part the basis of his best fiction. Melville's first two books, *Typee* (1846) and *Omoo* (1847), were partly romance and partly autobiographical travel books set in the South Seas. Both were popular successes, particularly *Typee*, which included a stay among cannibals and a romance with a South Sea maiden. During the next several years, Melville published three more romances that drew upon his experiences at sea: *Redburn* (1849) and *White-Jacket* (1850), both fairly realistic accounts of the sailor's life and depicting the loss of innocence of central characters; and *Mardi* (1849), which, like the other two books, began as a romance of adventure but turned into an allegorical critique of contemporary American civilization. *Moby Dick* (1851) also began as an adventure story, based on Melville's experiences aboard the whaling ship. However, in the writing of it—inspired in part by conversations with his friend and neighbor HAWTHORNE and partly by his own irrepressible imagination and reading of SHAKESPEARE and other Renaissance dramatists—Melville turned the book into something so strange that, when it appeared in print, many of his readers and critics were dumbfounded, even outraged. Their misgivings were in no way resolved by the publication in 1852 of his next novel, *Pierre; or, the Ambiguities*, a deeply personal, desperately pessimistic work that tells of the moral ruination of an innocent young man.

By the mid-1850s, Melville's literary reputation was all but destroyed, and he was obliged to live the rest of his life taking whatever jobs he could find and borrowing money from relatives, who fortunately were always in a position to help him. He continued to write, however, and published some marvelous short fiction pieces—"Benito Cereno" (1855) and "Bartleby, the Scrivener" (1853) are the best. He also published several volumes of poetry, the most important of which was *Battle-Pieces and Aspects of the War* (1866), poems of occasionally great power that were written in response to the moral challenge of the Civil War. His posthumously published work, *Billy Budd* (1924), on which he worked up until the time of his death, is Melville's last significant literary work, a brilliant short novel that movingly describes a young sailor's imprisonment and death.

Melville's reputation, however, rests most solidly on his great epic romance, *Moby Dick*. It is a difficult as well as a brilliant book, and many critics have offered interpretations of its complicated ambiguous symbolism. Darrel Abel briefly summed up *Moby Dick* as "the story of an attempt to search the unsearchable ways of God," although the book has historical, political, and moral implications as well.

NOVELS BY MELVILLE

Billy Budd, Sailor. 1924. Ed. by Harrison Hayford and Merton M. Sealts, Jr. U. Ch. Pr. 1962 $5.95. ISBN 0-226-32132-0. An authoritative text of Melville's final work of fiction.

The Confidence-Man: His Masquerade. 1857. *Northwestern-Newberry Edition of the Writings of Herman Melville Ser.* Vol. 10. Ed. by Harrison Hayford and others. Northwestern U. Pr. 1984 $49.95. ISBN 0-8101-0324-9. *Complete Works of Herman Melville Ser.* Ed. by Elizabeth S. Foster. Hendricks House 1979 $20.00. ISBN 0-87532-009-0. A satirical novel set aboard a Mississippi riverboat on April Fool's Day.

Israel Potter, His Fifty Years of Exile. 1855. *Northwestern-Newberry Edition of the Writings of Herman Melville Ser.* Vol. 8. Ed. by Harrison Hayford and others. Northwestern U. Pr. 1982 $39.95. ISBN 0-8101-0552-7. A political novel set primarily during the time of the American Revolution.

Mardi, and a Voyage Thither. 1849. *Northwestern-Newberry Edition of the Writings of Herman Melville Ser.* Vol. 3. Ed. by Harrison Hayford and others. Northwestern U. Pr. 1970 $52.95. ISBN 0-8101-0015-0. A narrative of sea adventure, filled with ruminations on ethics and metaphysics.

Moby Dick; or, The Whale. 1851. *Northwestern-Newberry Edition of the Writings of Herman Melville Ser.* Vol. 6. Ed. by Harrison Hayford and others. Northwestern U. Pr. 1988 $89.95. ISBN 0-8101-0324-9

Omoo: A Narrative of Adventures in the South Seas. 1847. *Northwestern-Newberry Edition of the Writings of Herman Melville Ser.* Vol. 2. Ed. by Harrison Hayford and others. Northwestern U. Pr. 1968 $36.95. ISBN 0-8101-0162-9. A brilliant continuation of the South Seas adventure begun in *Typee*.

Pierre; or, The Ambiguities. 1852. *Northwestern-Newberry Edition of the Writings of Herman Melville Ser.* Vol. 7. Ed. by Harrison Hayford and others. Northwestern U. Pr. 1972 $45.95. ISBN 0-8101-0266-8. A pessimistic tale depicting the woes that transform an innocent youth into a desperate cynic.

Pierre, Israel Potter, The Confidence-Man, Tales, and Billy Budd. Ed. by Harrison Hayford. Library of America 1985 $27.50. ISBN 0-940450-24-0. An attractive reprint of Melville's "social" fiction.

Redburn, His First Voyage: Being the Sailor-boy Confessions and Reminiscences of the Son-of-a-Gentleman, in the Merchant Service. 1849. *Northwestern-Newberry Edition of the Writings of Herman Melville Ser.* Vol. 4. Ed. by Harrison Hayford and others. Northwestern U. Pr. 1969 $39.95. ISBN 0-8101-0013-4. A semiautobiographical novel that follows the wanderings of an American innocent abroad.

Redburn, White-Jacket, Moby Dick. Ed. by G. Thomas Tanselle. Library of America 1983 $30.00. ISBN 0-940450-09-7. An excellent reprint of Melville's sea adventures.

Typee: A Peep at Polynesian Life. 1846. *Northwestern-Newberry Edition of the Writings of Herman Melville Ser.* Vol. 1. Ed. by Harrison Hayford and others. Northwestern U. Pr. 1968 $39.95. ISBN 0-8101-0161-0. A tale of adventure and romance set in the South Seas.

Typee, Omoo, Mardi. Ed. by G. Thomas Tanselle. Library of America 1982 $29.95. ISBN 0-940450-00-3. A reprint of Melville's South Seas romances.

White Jacket; or, The World in a Man-of-War. 1850. *Northwestern-Newberry Edition of the Writings of Herman Melville Ser.* Vol. 5. Ed. by Harrison Hayford and others. Northwestern U. Pr. 1970 $49.95. ISBN 0-8101-0257-9. An adventure story set in a U.S. naval vessel on its voyage from Hawaii to the Atlantic seacoast.

SHORT STORY COLLECTIONS BY MELVILLE

The Piazza Tales. 1856. *Complete Works of Herman Melville Ser.* Ed. by Egbert S. Oliver. Hendricks House 1962 $17.00. ISBN 0-87532-005-8. A collection of six stories, including "Benito Cereno" and "Bartleby, the Scrivener."

The Piazza Tales and Other Prose Pieces, 1839–1860. Northwestern-Newberry Edition of the Writings of Herman Melville Ser. Vol. 9. Ed. by Harrison Hayford and others. Northwestern U. Pr. 1987. $82.95. ISBN 0-8101-0550-0. In addition to the six tales making up *The Piazza Tales* (1856), includes previously uncollected pieces of fiction and nonfiction prose.

POETRY BY MELVILLE

Battle-Pieces and Aspects of the War. 1866. Schol. Facsimilies 1979 repr. of 1966 ed. $50.00. ISBN 0-8201-1252-6. Reflections upon not only the Civil War but also all violent conflicts to which humankind is subject.

Clarel: A Poem and Pilgrimage in the Holy Land. 1876. *Northwestern-Newberry Edition of the Writings of Herman Melville Ser.* Vol. 12. Ed. by Harrison Hayford and others. Northwestern U. Pr. 1991 $82.95. ISBN 0-8101-0906-9. A long meditative poem in which Melville considers the great philosophical and moral problems of his time.

Collected Poems (Except Clarel). Complete Works of Herman Melville Ser. Ed. by Howard P. Vincent. Hendricks House 1992 repr. of 1981 ed. $14.95. ISBN 0-87532-007-4

Poems of Herman Melville. Masterworks of Literature Ser. Ed. by Douglas Robillard. New Coll. U. Pr. 1976 $11.95. ISBN 0-8084-0417-2

Selected Poems of Herman Melville: A Reader's Edition. Ed. by Robert Penn Warren. Random 1970 o.p. An illuminating selection of Melville's verse, with a superb introduction by the great poet–novelist of the twentieth century.

Timoleon Etc. 1891. Gordon Pr. repr. of 1891 ed. $35.00. ISBN 0-8490-1215-5. Melville's final volume of poems—many written decades earlier—that were published shortly before his death.

WORKS BY MELVILLE

Correspondence. Northwestern-Newberry Edition of the Writings of Herman Melville Ser.: Vol. 14. Ed. by Lynn Horth. Northwestern U. Pr. 1989 $89.95. ISBN 0-8101-0981-6. The standard edition of Melville's letters.

Journals. Northwestern-Newberry Edition of the Writings of Herman Melville Ser. Vol. 15. Ed. by Howard C. Horsford and Lynn Horth. Northwestern U. Pr. 1989 $69.95. ISBN 0-8101-0822-4. A critical edition of Melville's extant journals.

BOOKS ABOUT MELVILLE

Arvin, Newton. *Herman Melville.* Greenwood 1973 repr. of 1950 ed. $41.50. ISBN 0-8371-6524-5. A critical biography, with strong emphasis on psychological interpretations.

Auden, W. H. *The Enchafed Flood; or, The Romantic Iconography of the Sea.* U. Pr. of Va. 1979 $15.00. ISBN 0-8139-0827-2. *Moby Dick* is used by this great modern poet to illustrate romantic images of the sea.

Bercaw, Mary K. *Melville's Sources.* Northwestern U. Pr. 1987 $39.95. ISBN 0-8101-0734-1. Lists the literary sources Melville is known or believed to have used in his writings.

Berthoff, Warner. *The Example of Melville.* Princeton U. Pr. 1962 o.p. A survey of the writer as a literary artisan, his use of land- and seascapes, and the vitality of his imagination.

Bickman, Martin, ed. *Approaches to Teaching Melville's Moby Dick.* Modern Lang. 1985 $34.00. ISBN 0-87352-489-6. An excellent collection of essays designed as "a sourcebook of material, information, and ideas" on teaching (and reading) *Moby Dick.*

Bowen, Merlin. *The Long Encounter: Self and Experience in the Writings of Herman Melville.* U. Ch. Pr. 1960 o.p. A reexamination from the viewpoint of Melville's lifelong preoccupation with the riddle of the self and its relation to the world of experience.

Brodhead, Richard H., ed. *New Essays on Moby Dick.* Cambridge U. Pr. 1986 $21.95. ISBN 0-521-30205-6. Five essays that focus on the novel's vision of nature, its social and religious dimensions, and its language.

Bryant, John. *A Companion to Melville Studies.* Greenwood 1986 $95.00. ISBN 0-313-23874-X. Twenty-five leading scholars and critics discuss a great variety of biographical, intellectual, and literary subjects.

Burkholder, Robert E., ed. *Critical Essays on Herman Melville's "Benito Cereno." Critical Essays on American Literature Ser.* G. K. Hall 1992 $45.00. ISBN 0-8161-7317-6. A fine gathering of previously published as well as newly commissioned essays, all providing a good overview of the critical responses to Melville's short story.

Dillingham, William B. *An Artist in the Rigging: The Early Work of Herman Melville.* U. of Ga. Pr. 1972 $18.00. ISBN 0-8203-0276-7. A close, informed reading of Melville's writings up to and including *Mardi.*

———. *Melville's Later Novels.* U. of Ga. Pr. 1986 $37.50. ISBN 0-8203-0799-8. Suggestive and impressive; a reading that stresses the theme of survival in Melville's later fiction.

Dimock, Wai-chee. *Empire for Liberty: Melville and the Poetics of Individualism.* Princeton U. Pr. 1989 $32.50. ISBN 0-691-06758-9. Melville's "authorial enterprise" is viewed in terms of the great national enterprise of his time, Manifest Destiny.

Duban, James. *Melville's Major Fiction: Politics, Theology, and Imagination.* N. Ill. U. Pr. 1983 $25.00. ISBN 0-87580-086-6. A "new historical" reading of Melville's fiction in terms of important political and social concerns of his time.

Franklin, H. Bruce. *The Wake of the Gods: Melville's Mythology.* Stanford U. Pr. 1963 $16.95. ISBN 0-8047-0137-7. A reinterpretation of Melville's major works, demonstrating how mythology determines and defines large parts of their structure and meaning.

Gale, Robert L. *Plots and Characters in the Fiction and Narrative Poetry of Herman Melville*. Archon Bks. 1969 o.p. A convenient list of characters and summaries of the plots of Melville's fiction.

Hillway, Tyrus. *Herman Melville. Twayne's United States Authors Ser.* G. K. Hall rev. ed. 1979 $18.95. ISBN 0-8057-7256-1. A standard introduction to Melville's works.

Howard, Leon. *Herman Melville: A Biography*. U. CA Pr. 1981 $11.95. ISBN 0-5120-00575-9. A standard biography.

Inge, M. Thomas, ed. *Bartleby the Inscrutable: A Collection of Commentary on Herman Melville's Tale "Bartleby, the Scrivener"*. Shoe String 1979 $30.00. ISBN 0-208-01756-9. A fine collection of readings—early and late—of Melville's enigmatic short story.

Kier, Kathleen E. *A Melville Encyclopedia: The Novels*. 2 vols. Whitston Pub. 1990 $120.00. ISBN 0-87875-326-5. Glosses for those persons, places, and things mentioned in Melville's fiction that need to be annotated for many modern readers.

Lee, A. Robert, ed. *Herman Melville: Reassessments*. B & N Imports 1984 $31.50. ISBN 0-389-20376-9. Ten highly readable essays by leading critics that examine the full range of Melville's literary career.

Leyda, Jay. *The Melville Log: A Documentary Life of Herman Melville with Supplementary Chapter*. 2 vols. Gordian 1969 $100.00. ISBN 0-877752-063-1. A great compendium of the facts of Melville's life; contains important supplementary material.

McCall, Dan. *The Silence of Bartleby*. Cornell Univ. Pr. 1989 $29.95. ISBN 0-8014-2320-1. An attractive close reading of Melville's greatest short story, with an appealing defense of the story's narrator.

McSweeny, Kerry. *Moby Dick: Ishmael's Mighty Book. Twayne's Masterwork Studies Ser.* G. K. Hall 1986 $20.95. ISBN 0-8057-7954-X. A fine introductory study, impressive both for its critical sophistication and for its general accessibility.

Milder, Robert. *Critical Essays on Melville's "Billy Budd." Critical Essays on American Literature Ser.* G. K. Hall 1989 $40.00. ISBN 0-8161-8889-0. A collection of some of the most important critical responses to Melville's novella that have appeared since its publication in 1924.

Newman, Lea Bertani Vozar. *A Reader's Guide to the Short Stories of Herman Melville*. G. K. Hall 1986 $45.00. ISBN 0-8161-8653-7. An invaluable study of Melville's short fiction, with well-informed discussions of the stories' genesis, composition, publication, reception, and critical reputation.

Olson, Charles. *Call Me Ishmael*. City Lights 1947 o.p. A highly influential comparative study of *Moby Dick* and Shakespeare by an important twentieth-century poet.

Parker, Hershel. *Reading Billy Budd*. Northwestern U. Pr. 1990 $29.95. ISBN 0-8101-0961-1. An interpretation grounded in a thorough understanding of the compositional history of the text.

Parker, Hershel, ed. *The Recognition of Herman Melville*. U. of Mich. Pr. 1967 o.p. A collection of critical essays from 1846 on, arranged in chronological order.

Parker, Hershel, and Harrison Hayford, eds. *Moby Dick as Doubloon: Essays and Extracts*. Norton 1970 $6.95. ISBN 0-393-09883-4. A collection of critical responses to *Moby Dick* since its publication.

Rogin, Michael P. *Subversive Genealogy: The Politics and Art of Herman Melville*. U. CA Pr. 1985 $12.95. ISBN 0-520-05178-5. Melville's writings viewed in terms of his extended and important family's political views and activities.

Samson, John. *White Lies: Melville's Narratives of Facts*. Cornell Univ. Pr. 1989 $29.95. ISBN 0-8014-2280-9. Studies Melville's "vital rewriting" of his sources in *Typee, Omoo, Redburn, White-Jacket, Israel Potter,* and *Billy Budd*.

Sealts, Merton M. *Melville's Reading*. U. of SC Pr. 1988 $35.00. ISBN 0-87249-515-9. An important study of an author who was influenced as much by what he read as by what he did.

———. *Pursuing Melville: Nineteen Forty to Nineteen Eighty*. U. of Wis. Pr. 1982 $32.50. ISBN 0-299-08870-7. An impressive gathering of essays, introductions, and reviews by a leading Melville scholar–critic.

Tolchin, Neal L. *Mourning, Gender, and Creativity in the Art of Herman Melville.* Yale U.
Pr. 1988 $25.00. ISBN 0-300-03975-1. Sees Melville's work as a series of responses
motivated by his inability to complete the mourning of his father's death.

PARKMAN, FRANCIS. 1823–1893

Early in his youth, this Boston-born historian was infected with what he called
(in language offensive to today's readers) "Injuns on the brain." For the rest of
his life, he dedicated himself to writing what he had called at the age of 18 "a
history of the American forest." In 1846, following the completion of his studies
at Harvard College, he set out in company with a cousin on an expedition from
St. Louis over the Oregon Trail to Fort Laramie, Wyoming, a journey that
brought him into close contact with the Lakota Indians (known to others as
"Sioux"), with whom he lived for several weeks. Back in Boston, he turned the
journal that he had kept on the trail into a series of sketches that were published
in the *Knickerbocker Magazine* and afterwards as a book, *The California and
Oregon Trail, Being Sketches of Prairie and Rocky Mountain Life* (1849), now
better known by the abbreviated title of a later revised edition, *The Oregon Trail.*
By this time, Parkman had well underway the historical work that would occupy
him during the rest of his life, an account of the French and English in North
America, the first installment of which was his *History of the Conspiracy of
Pontiac and the War of the North American Tribes against the English Colonies*,
published in 1851. Even by today's standards of historical scholarship, Parkman's work stands up well, though most agree with FREDERICK JACKSON TURNER
(see Vol. 3) that Parkman was "even greater as an artist than as an historian."

His literary talents were considerable. Largely influenced by the British
writers SIR WALTER SCOTT and LORD BYRON, he always attempted to achieve a
happy balance between "dramatic interest" and "historic proportion." His is
finally a romantic vision of history, with a preference for action and heroic
characters. There were decided biases in Parkman's perception, particularly his
dislike for the Catholicism of the French and his conservative distrust of the
democratic spirit; however, his strengths far outweigh his weaknesses, and he
remains the greatest historian of one of the most crucial periods in North
American history.

NONFICTION BY PARKMAN

France and England in North America. 1865–1892. 2 vols. Ed. by David Levin. Library of
America 1983 $30.00 ea. ISBNs 0-940450-10-0, 0-940450-11-9. A superb reprint of all
seven volumes of Parkman's great history of the European colonization of North
America.
The Oregon Trail. 1849. Ed. by David Levin. Viking Penguin 1982 $4.95. ISBN 0-14-
039042-1. A narrative of Parkman's journey across the prairies of the United States in
1846.
The Oregon Trail and The Conspiracy of Pontiac. Ed. by William R. Taylor. Library of
America 1991 $35.00. ISBN 0-940450-54-2. In addition to *The Oregon Trail*, contains
the complete text of Parkman's other early work, *The Conspiracy of Pontiac and the
Indian War after the Conquest of Canada* (1851).
Some of the Reasons against Woman's Suffrage. 1887. Ed. by Norman E. Tanis. CSUN
1977 $10.00. ISBN 0-937048-07-0. Argues that the right to vote should not be
dissociated from the duty to serve in the armed forces (which women's "higher
duties" prevent).
Works. 20 vols. AMS Pr. repr. of 1902 ed. $770.00. ISBN 0-404-04920-6. A good reprint of
the preferred "Frontenac Edition" of Parkman's historical writings.

WORK BY PARKMAN

Letters of Francis Parkman. 2 vols. Ed. by Wilbur R. Jacobs. Bks. Demand repr. of 1960 ed. Vol. 1 $54.00. ISBN 0-8357-9730-9. Vol. 2 $65.00. ISBN 0-685-07758-6. A standard edition of important correspondence.

BOOKS ABOUT PARKMAN

Doughty, Howard. *Francis Parkman.* HUP 1983 $8.95. ISBN 0-674-31775-0. A fine critical biography.

Farnham, Charles H. *Life of Francis Parkman.* Scholarly 1970 repr. of 1901 ed. $15.00. ISBN 0-403-00208-7. An important, early interpretive biography.

Jacobs, Wilbur R. *Francis Parkman, Historian as Hero: The Formative Years.* Ed. by William H. Goetzmann. U. of Tex. Pr. 1991 $27.50. ISBN 0-292-72467-5. A sound intellectual biography.

Wade, Mason. *Francis Parkman: Heroic Historian.* Shoe String 1972 repr. of 1942 ed. $47.50. ISBN 0-208-01213-3. Makes excellent use of Parkman's private papers and correspondence.

POE, EDGAR ALLAN. 1809–1849

There has never been any doubt about Poe's enormous literary significance, but, with regard to his ultimate artistic merit, there has been considerable disagreement. To some he is little more than a successful charlatan, whose literary performances are only a virtuoso's display of stunning, but finally shallow, effects. Others, however, are struck by Poe's profound probing of the human psyche, his philosophical sophistication, and his revolutionary attitude toward literary language. No doubt both sides of this argument are in part true in their assessments. Poe's work is very uneven, sometimes reaching great literary heights, at other times striking the honest reader as meaningless, bathetic, or simply wrong-headed. This is not surprising, considering the personal turmoil that characterized so much of Poe's short life. Poe was extreme in his literary views and practices; balance and equilibrium were not literary values that he prized.

Scorning the didactic element in poetry, Poe sought to separate beauty from morality. In his best poems, such as "The City in the Sea" (1836), he achieved an intensification of sound sufficient to threaten the common sense of the poetic line and release a buried, even a morbid, sense that would enchant the reader by the sonic pitch of the poem. Defining poetry as "the rhythmic creation of beauty," Poe not only sought the dream buried beneath the poetic vision— COLERIDGE had already done that—but also abandoned the moral rationale that gave the buried dream symbolic meaning. The dream, or nightmare, was itself the content of the verse.

Some readers, however, such as T. S. ELIOT, have found Poe's poetry extremely limited, both in its content and in its technique. While it is true that Poe was one of the few American poets to achieve international fame during the nineteenth century, critics point out that his influence on such literary movements as French symbolism and literary modernism was largely through the superb translations and criticisms of his writings by BAUDELAIRE (see Vol. 2), MALLARMÉ (see Vol. 2), and VALÉRY (see Vol. 2).

Poe's theory of the short story, as well as his own achievements in that genre, contributed substantially to the development of the modern short story, in Europe as well as in the United States. Poe himself regarded his talent for fiction writing as of less importance than his poetry and criticism. His public preferred his detective stories, such as "The Murders in the Rue Morgue" (1841), "The

Mystery of Marie Rogêt" (1842–1843) and "The Gold Bug" (1843); and his analytic tales, such as "A Descent into the Maelstrom" (1841), "The Black Cat" (1843), and "The Premature Burial" (1844). His own preference, however, was for the works of the imagination, such as "Ligeia" (1838), "The Fall of the House of Usher" (1839), and "The Masque of the Red Death" (1842), tales of horror beyond that of the plausible kind found in the analytic stories.

Just as with his poetry, however, readers have been strongly divided in their appreciation of the deeper worth of Poe's fiction. For many, they are at best merely an effective display in Gothicism, good horror stories, an enjoyable experience in vicarious terror, but nothing more. This was the view of HENRY JAMES, that other great nineteenth-century master of the ghost story, who claimed that "an enthusiasm for Poe is the mark of a decidedly primitive stage of reflection." But others have found in these carefully crafted pieces something far more profound, a way of seeing into our unconscious, that place where, for a while at least, terrifying conflicts coexist. As Poe so well put it himself in the preface to his *Tales of the Grotesque and Arabesque* (1840), "If in many of my productions terror has been the basis, I maintain that terror is not of Germany but of the soul."

POETRY BY POE

Poems. Collected Works of Edgar Allan Poe Ser. Vol. 1. Ed. by Thomas O. Mabbott. HUP 1969 $41.00. ISBN 0-674-13935-6. The standard critical edition of Poe's poems, with thorough bibliographical discussions of texts.
Poems of Edgar Allan Poe. Ed. by Floyd Stovall. U. Pr. of Va. 1977 $22.50. ISBN 0-81349-0194-4. An excellent critical edition, with an informative introduction.

SHORT STORY COLLECTIONS BY POE

The Imaginary Voyages. Collected Writings of Edgar Allan Poe Ser. Ed. by Burton R. Pollin. G. K. Hall 1981 o.p. Includes critical texts of *The Narrative of Arthur Gordon Pym* (1838), "The Unparalleled Adventure of One Hans Pfaall" (1835), and "The Journal of Julius Rodman" (1840).
The Narrative of Arthur Gordon Pym of Nantucket. 1838. *Penguin English Library Ser.* Ed. by Harold Beaver. Viking Penguin 1976 $4.95. ISBN 0-14-043097-0. A grotesque and imaginative tale set at sea.
The Science Fiction of Edgar Allan Poe. English Library Ser. Ed. by Harold Beaver. Viking Penguin 1976 $4.95. ISBN 0-14-043106-3. A collection of Poe's contributions to the genre that he helped create.
The Short Fiction of Edgar Allan Poe: An Annotated Edition. Ed. by Stuart Levine and Susan Levine. U. of Ill. Pr. 1990 $19.95. ISBN 0-252-06125-X. A thoroughly successful attempt "to bring together in one convenient edition all of the information one needs to understand Poe's stories."
Tales and Sketches, 1831–1842. Collected Works of Edgar Allan Poe Ser. Vol. 2. Ed. by Thomas O. Mabbott. HUP 1978 o.p. The standard edition of Poe's short writings.
Tales and Sketches, 1843–1849. Collected Works of Edgar Allan Poe Ser. Vol. 3. Ed. by Thomas O. Mabbott. HUP 1978 o.p. The standard edition of Poe's short writings.

NONFICTION BY POE

Essays and Reviews. Ed. by G. R. Thompson. Library of America 1984 $35.00. ISBN 0-940450-19-4. An excellent edition of Poe's important literary criticism.

WORKS BY POE

The Complete Works of Edgar Allan Poe. 17 vols. Ed. by James A. Harrison. AMS Pr. repr. of 1902 ed. $295.00. ISBN 0-404-09400-7. The most complete edition of Poe's writings.

Letters. 2 vols. Ed. by John Ostrom. Gordian 1966 repr. of 1948 ed. $50.00. ISBN 0-87752-085-2. The standard edition of Poe's correspondence.

Poetry and Tales. Ed. by Patrick F. Quinn. Library of America 1984 $35.00. ISBN 0-940450-18-6. A superb one-volume edition of Poe's most important works.

BOOKS ABOUT POE

Baudelaire, Charles. *Baudelaire on Poe: Critical Papers. Bald Eagle Ser.* Trans. by Lois Hyslop and Francis Hyslop. Pa. St. U. Pr. 1952 $20.00. ISBN 0-271-00317-0. Able translations of the great French poet's three essays on Poe, which were first published in the 1850s.

Buranelli, Vincent. *Edgar Allan Poe. Twayne's United States Authors Ser.* G. K. Hall 1977 $18.95. ISBN 0-8057-7189-1. First published in 1961, remains one of the finest introductions to Poe available.

Carlson, Eric W., ed. *Edgar Allan Poe. Critical Essays Ser.* G. K. Hall 1987 $40.00. ISBN 0-8161-8878-5. Reflects an emphasis on Poe's romantic idealism, both in his introduction and in his selection of essays to be reprinted.

———, ed. *The Recognition of Edgar Allan Poe: Selected Criticism since 1829.* U. of Mich. Pr. 1966 o.p. Especially valuable for earlier estimates and the editor's introduction.

Dameron, J. Lasley, and Irby B. Cauthen, Jr., eds. *Edgar Allan Poe: A Bibliography of Criticism, 1827–1967.* U. Pr. of Va. 1974 $35.00. ISBN 0-8139-0498-6. A thorough and well-indexed checklist of criticism on Poe's works.

Davidson, Edward H. *Poe: A Critical Study.* HUP 1957 o.p. A sound and accessible inquiry into Poe's mind and writings.

Dayan, Joan. *Fables of Mind: An Inquiry into Poe's Fiction.* OUP 1987 $34.50. ISBN 0-19-504160-7. Fine discussions of epistemological problems in Poe's writings.

Fisher, Benjamin F., IV, ed. *Poe and His Times: The Artist and His Milieu.* Poe Soc. Baltimore 1990 $25.00. ISBN 0-9616449-2-3. Insightful readings by leading Poe critics and scholars of the writer's career in terms of his culture.

Hammond, J. R. *An Edgar Allan Poe Companion: A Guide to the Short Stories, Romances and Essays.* B & N Imports 1981 $32.50. ISBN 0-389-20172-3. A fairly uncritical but convenient guide for nonspecialists.

Hoffman, Daniel. *Poe Poe Poe Poe Poe Poe Poe.* Paragon Hse. 1990 $12.95. ISBN 0-55778-274-1. A Freudian reading of Poe's life and writings.

Howarth, William L., ed. *Twentieth-Century Interpretations of Poe's Tales.* P-H 1971 $9.95. ISBN 0-13-684654-8. Judicious selection of criticism.

Kennedy, J. Gerald. *Poe, Death, and the Life of Writing.* Yale U. Pr. 1987 $25.00. ISBN 0-300-03773-2. A reading of Poe's letters and fiction in terms of his age's preoccupation with death.

Knapp, Bettina L. *Edgar Allan Poe. Literature and Life Ser.* Continuum 1984 $18.95. ISBN 0-8044-2476-4. A Jungian reading of the tales and poems.

Lee, A. Robert, ed. *Edgar Allan Poe: The Design of Order.* B & N Imports 1986 $38.00. ISBN 0-389-20648-2. Ten essays, united by their worthwhile scope and critical relevance, by diverse authors.

May, Charles E. *Edgar Allan Poe: A Study of the Short Fiction. Twayne's Studies in Short Fiction Ser.* G. K. Hall 1991 $19.95. ISBN 0-8057-8337-7. Detailed discussions of Poe's tales and the critical responses to them.

Parks, Edd W. *Edgar Allan Poe as Literary Critic.* U. of Ga. Pr. 1964 o.p. Argues that Poe's strengths and weaknesses as a critic were in part a result of his work as a magazine editor and writer.

Thomas, Dwight, and David K. Jackson. *The Poe Log: A Documentary Life of Edgar Allan Poe, 1809–1849.* G. K. Hall 1987 $85.00. ISBN 0-8161-8734-7. An impressive and highly accurate gathering of all known life facts about Poe.

Thompson, G. R. *Poe's Fiction: Romantic Irony in the Gothic Tales.* U. of Wis. Pr. 1973 o.p. A valuable study of Poe's most popular works.

Walker, I. M., ed. *Edgar Allan Poe: The Critical Heritage. The Critical Heritage Ser.* Routledge 1986 $69.50. ISBN 0-7100-9855-3. Representative critical estimates arranged chronologically from Poe's time to our own.

gripping story of the warfare between the indigenous Yemassee Indians and the newly arrived European settlers for possession of South Carolina during the early eighteenth century.

Simms was sometimes blinded by his devotion to his region, not only to its strengths, but also to its weaknesses. His defense of slavery, most infamously in *The Pro-Slavery Argument* (1852); of Southern aristocratic ideals, reflected not only in his novels but also in his biographies and essays; and of those principles on which Southern economy depended, has prevented many readers since the Civil War from seeing the merits of his writing, especially the realistic depiction of frontier life, a strong sense of narrative and characterization, and a philosophical view of history that informs his best fiction and stories. These strengths are particularly evident in *The Yemassee* and in the short stories and tales that Simms collected in *The Wigwam and the Cabin* (1845–46), the two works to which anyone wishing to read this unjustly neglected writer should first be directed.

Novels by Simms

Beauchampe; or, The Kentucky Tragedy. 1856. AMS Pr. repr. of 1856 ed. $21.50. ISBN 0-404-06006-4. A novel based on a famous murder case in Kentucky in 1825.

Border Beagles: A Tale of Mississippi. 1840. AMS Pr. repr. of 1855 ed. $24.50. ISBN 0-404-06007-2. A sequel to *Richard Hurdis* (1838).

The Cassique of Kiawah. 1859. Magnolia Pr. 1989 $17.50. ISBN 0-916369-12-9. A novel about colonial life in Charleston.

Charlemont; or, The Pride of the Village: A Tale of Kentucky. 1856. AMS Pr. repr. of 1866 ed. $10.00. ISBN 0-404-06008-0. The first part of the "Kentucky Tragedy," followed by *Beauchampe.*

Confession; or, The Blind Heart: A Domestic Story. 1841. AMS Pr. repr. of 1885 ed. $10.00. ISBN 0-404-06009-9. A story about jealous passions.

Eutaw: A Sequel to the Forayers. 1856. AMS Pr. repr. of 1885 ed. $10.00. ISBN 0-404-06018-8. An adventure novel inspired by an important battle fought in South Carolina during the American Revolution.

The Forayers; or, The Raid of the Dog-Days. 1855. Rprt. Serv. 1976 repr. of 1855 ed. $10.00. ISBN 0-87152-240-3. A Revolutionary War adventure.

Guy Rivers: A Tale of Georgia. 1834. AMS Pr. repr. of 1885 ed. $14.50. ISBN 0-404-06034-X. A novel about gold mining and crime in the wilds of Georgia.

Katharine Walton; or, The Rebel of Dorchester. 1851. Rprt. Serv. 1976 repr. of 1854 ed. $10.00. ISBN 0-87152-238-1. The third novel in the trilogy begun by *The Partisan* (1835).

Martin Faber: The Story of a Criminal. 1833. Ed. by Glenn Reed. New Coll. U. Pr. 1990 $7.95. ISBN 0-8084-0435-0. A psychological study in the Gothic mode of a murderer; Simms's first novel.

Mellichampe: A Legend of the Santee. 1836. AMS Pr. repr. of 1885 ed. $10.00. ISBN 0-404-06039-0. The second part in the trilogy begun by *The Partisan* (1835).

The Partisan: A Tale of the Revolution. 1835. *American Fiction Reprint Ser.* Irvington 1968 $25.00. ISBN 0-8398-1859-9. The first novel in a trilogy depicting the Revolutionary War in South Carolina.

Richard Hurdis; or, The Avenger of Blood. 1838. AMS Pr. repr. of 1890 ed. $10.00. ISBN 0-404-06035-8. Another of the "Border Romances," the story of a bandit on the southern border.

The Scout, or the Black Riders of Congaree. 1854. Irvington 1986 $5.75. ISBN 0-8290-1944-8. Originally titled *The Kinsmen* (1841), a novel dealing with conflicts within a family during the American Revolution.

Vasconselos: A Romance of the New World. 1853. AMS Pr. repr. of 1885 ed. $10.00. ISBN 0-404-06037-4. An historical novel about the explorer Hernando de Soto.

Woodcraft; or, Hawks about the Dovecote. 1854. Irvington repr. of 1856 ed. $20.00. ISBN 0-8398-1862-9. Originally titled *The Sword and the Distaff; or, "Fair, Fat and Forty"* (1852), one of Simms's novels about the American Revolution in the South.

The Yemassee: A Romance of Carolina. 1835. *Masterworks of Literature Ser.* Ed. by Joseph V. Ridgely. New Coll. U. Pr. 1964 $13.95. ISBN 0-8084-0337-0. A frontier romance set in the Carolinas during the early 1700s.

POETRY BY SIMMS

Poems: Descriptive, Dramatic, Legendary and Contemplative. 1854. *The Romantic Tradition in American Literature Ser.* Ayer 1972 repr. of 1853 ed. $47.00. ISBN 0-405-04643-X. The most important collection made by Simms of his verse.

Selected Poems of William Gilmore Simms. Ed. by James E. Kibler, Jr. U. of Ga. Pr. 1990 $50.00. ISBN 0-8203-1188-X. A judicious selection of Simms's verse, together with an excellent introduction

SHORT STORY COLLECTION BY SIMMS

The Wigwam and the Cabin. 1845–46. AMS Pr. repr. of 1885 ed. $15.50. ISBN 0-404-06038–2. A collection of both realistic and Gothic stories set in the Southern frontier.

NONFICTION BY SIMMS

The Life of Captain John Smith, the Founder of Virginia. 1847. Ayer repr. of 1867 ed. $21.50. ISBN 0-8369-5565-X. An appreciative biography of the English explorer and adventurer.

The Life of Francis Marion. 1844. Ayer repr. of 1844 ed. $23.50. ISBN 0-8369-5540-7. A biography of one of Simms's and his region's heroes, the South Carolina military leader during the Revolutionary War.

WORKS BY SIMMS

The Letters of William Gilmore Simms. 6 vols. Ed. by Mary C. Oliphant and T. Duncan Eaves. U. of SC Pr. Vols. 1–4 1952–1956 o.p. Vol. 5 1956 $34.95. ISBN 0-87249-065-3. Vol. 6 1982 $34.95. ISBN 0-87249-438-1. Inclusive and well annotated.

BOOKS ABOUT SIMMS

Guilds, John C. *Long Years of Neglect: The Work and Reputation of William Gilmore Simms.* U. of Ark. Pr. 1988 $20.00. ISBN 1-55728-028-2. A good general appraisal of Simms's major works.

Ridgely, Joseph V. *William Gilmore Simms. Twayne's United States Authors Ser.* New Coll. U. Pr. 1962 $10.95. ISBN 0-8084-0327-3. The best introduction to Simms's life and writings.

Trent, William. *William Gilmore Simms.* Haskell 1969 repr. of 1899 ed. $75.00. ISBN 0-8383-0249-1. An important early critical biography.

Wakelyn, Jon L. *The Politics of a Literary Man: William Gilmore Simms.* Greenwood 1973 $35.00. ISBN 0-8371-6414-1. Discusses Simms's career in terms of the political history of his time.

Wimsatt, Mary A. *The Major Fiction of William Gilmore Simms.* La. State U. Pr. 1989 $35.00. ISBN 0-8071-1459-6. A sophisticated critical reading of Simms's novels and stories.

STOWE, HARRIET BEECHER. 1811–1896

Harriet Beecher was born in Litchfield, Connecticut, one of nine children of the distinguished Congregational minister and stern Calvinist, Lyman Beecher. Of her six brothers, five became ministers, one of whom, Henry Ward Beecher, was considered the finest pulpit orator of his day. In 1832 Harriet Beecher went with her family to Cincinnati, Ohio. There she taught in her sister's school and began publishing sketches and stories. In 1836 she married the Reverend Calvin

E. Stowe, one of her father's assistants at the Lane Theological Seminary and a strong antislavery advocate. They lived in Cincinnati for 18 years, and six of her children were born there. The Stowes moved to Brunswick, Maine, in 1850, when Calvin Stowe became a professor at Bowdoin College.

Long active in abolition causes and knowledgeable about the atrocities of slavery both from her reading and her years in Cincinnati, with its close proximity to the South, Stowe was finally impelled to take action with the passage of the Fugitive Slave Act in 1850. By her own account, the idea of *Uncle Tom's Cabin* (1852) first came to her in a vision while she was sitting in church. Returning home, she sat down and wrote out the scene describing the death of Uncle Tom and was so inspired that she continued to write on scraps of grocer's brown paper after her own supply of writing paper gave out. She then wrote the book's earlier chapters. Serialized first in the *National Era* (1851–52), an important abolitionist journal with national circulation, *Uncle Tom's Cabin* was published in book form in March 1852. It was an immediate international bestseller; 10,000 copies were sold in less than a week, 300,000 within a year, and 3 million before the start of the Civil War. Family legend tells of President ABRAHAM LINCOLN (see Vol. 3) saying to Stowe when he met her in 1862: "So this is the little lady who made this big war?" Whether he did say it or not, we will never know, since Stowe left no written record of her interview with the president. But he would have been justified in saying it. Certainly, no other single book, apart from the Bible, has ever had any greater social impact on the United States, and for many years its enormous historical interest prevented many from seeing the book's genuine, if not always consistent, literary merit.

The fame of the novel has also unfortunately overshadowed the fiction that Stowe wrote about her native New England: *The Minister's Wooing* (1859), *Oldtown Folks* (1869), *Poganuc People* (1878), and *The Pearl of Orr's Island* (1862), the novel that, according to SARAH ORNE JEWETT, began the local-color movement in New England. Here Stowe was writing about the world and its people closest and dearest to her, recording their customs, their legends, and their speech. As she said of one of these novels, "It is more to me than a story. It is my resumé of the whole spirit and body of New England."

NOVELS BY STOWE

Dred: A Tale of the Great Dismal Swamp. 1856. 2 vols. AMS Pr. repr. of 1856 ed. $47.50. ISBN 0-404-06290-3. Stowe's second novel, in which she continued her description of the demoralizing character of slavery in the American South.

The Minister's Wooing. 1859. Stowe-Day 1978 $8.95. ISBN 0-917482-12-3. A surprisingly strong novel set in late eighteenth-century New England.

Oldtown Folks. 1869. *American Women Writers Ser.* Ed. by Dorothy Berkson. Rutgers U. Pr. 1987 $40.00. ISBN 0-8135-1219-0. A classic fictional description of New England provincial life.

The Pearl of Orr's Island: A Story of the Coast of Maine. 1862. Stowe-Day 1979 $8.95. ISBN 0-917482-18-2. Called by Whittier "the most charming New England idyll ever written," a novel about a New England girl.

Pink and White Tyranny, a Society Novel. 1871. NAL-Dutton 1988 $7.95. ISBN 0-452-26177-5. A moralistic tale that attacks divorce and the corruption of polite society.

Poganuc People, Their Loves and Lives. 1878. Stowe-Day 1977 $8.95. ISBN 0-917482-06-9. A fictionalized account of Stowe's own childhood in Litchfield, Connecticut.

Three Novels. Ed. by Kathryn K. Sklar. Library of America 1982 $32.50. ISBN 0-940450–01–1. Contains the complete texts of *Uncle Tom's Cabin, The Minister's Wooing,* and *Oldtown Folks.*

Uncle Tom's Cabin; or Life among the Lowly. 1852. HM 1972 $18.95. ISBN 0-395-08129-7

SHORT STORY COLLECTIONS BY STOWE

Regional Sketches. Masterworks of Literature Ser. Ed. by John R. Adams. New Coll. U. Pr. 1972 $16.95. ISBN 0-8084-0024-X. A selection of some of the best of Stowe's local-color stories about New England.

Sam Lawson's Oldtown Fireside Stories. 1872. *Americans in Fiction Ser.* Irvington repr. of 1872 ed. $27.50. ISBN 0-8398-1874-2. Fifteen local-color sketches.

WORKS BY STOWE

A Key to Uncle Tom's Cabin. 1853. *American Negro: His History and Literature Ser.* Ayer 1968 repr. of 1854 ed. $29.95. ISBN 0-405-01839-8. A defense of Stowe's depiction of slavery in *Uncle Tom's Cabin.*

Writings. 16 vols. AMS Pr. repr. of 1896 ed. $635.00. ISBN 0-404-00220-X. The standard edition of Stowe's works.

BOOKS ABOUT STOWE

Adams, John R. *Harriet Beecher Stowe. Twayne's United States Authors Ser.* G. K. Hall 1989 $19.95. ISBN 0-8057-7532-3. By far the best introduction to Stowe's life and works.

Foster, Charles H. *Rungless Ladder: Harriet Beecher Stowe and New England Puritanism.* Cooper Sq. 1970 repr. of 1954 ed. $28.50. ISBN 0-8154-0319-4. Particularly good on the theological and religious elements in Stowe's fiction.

Gossett, Thomas F. *Uncle Tom's Cabin and American Culture.* SMU Pr. 1985 $29.95. ISBN 0-87074-189-6. A fascinating history of the composition and reception of Stowe's great novel.

Moers, Ellen. *Harriet Beecher Stowe and American Literature.* Stowe-Day 1978 $5.00. ISBN 0-917482-15-8. Defends *Uncle Tom's Cabin* as a great American novel.

Stowe, Charles Edward. *Life of Harriet Beecher Stowe Compiled from Her Letters and Journals.* Rprt. Serv. 1991 repr. of 1889 ed. $99.00. ISBN 0-7812-8370-1. The authorized family biography by Stowe's son, still valuable for its use of private letters and other papers.

Sundquist, Eric, ed. *New Essays on Uncle Tom's Cabin. The American Novel Ser.* Cambridge U. Pr. 1986 $8.95. ISBN 0-521-31786-X. Six important essays by different critics on important themes and elements found in *Uncle Tom's Cabin.*

Wilson, Robert F. *Crusader in Crinoline: The Life of Harriet Beecher Stowe.* Greenwood 1972 repr. of 1941 ed. $45.50. ISBN 0-8371-6191-6. A well-researched and well-written biography that was awarded the Pulitzer Prize in 1942.

THOREAU, HENRY DAVID. 1817–1862

In September 1842, NATHANIEL HAWTHORNE noted this social encounter in his journal: "Mr. Thorow dined with us yesterday. He is a singular character—a young man with much of wild original nature still remaining in him; and so far as he is sophisticated, it is in a way and method of his own. He is as ugly as sin, long-nosed, queer-mouthed, and with uncouth and somewhat rustic, although courteous manners, corresponding very well with such an exterior. But his ugliness is of an honest and agreeable fashion, and becomes him much better than beauty. On the whole, I find him a healthy and wholesome man to know." Most responses to Thoreau's life and writings are as ambiguously respectful as was Hawthorne's. Thoreau was neither an easy person to like nor an easy writer to read.

Thoreau described himself as a mystic, a Transcendentalist, and a natural philosopher. He is a writer of essays about nature—not of facts about nature but of his ideals and emotions in nature's presence. His wish to understand nature led him to Walden Pond, where he lived from 1845 to 1847 in a cabin that he constructed. Though he was an educated man with a Harvard degree, fluent in ancient and modern German, he preferred to study nature by living "a life of simplicity, independence, magnanimity, and trust." Knowing this, we should beware of misreading the book that best reflected this great experience in Thoreau's life: *Walden; or, Life in the Woods* (1854). It is not a handbook of or for the simple life. Though there are elements in the book of a "whole-earth catalogue" mentality, to focus on the radical "economic" aspects of Thoreau's work is to miss much in the book. Nor is it, in the ordinary sense, an autobiography. The right way to read *Walden* is as a "transcendental" narrative prose poem, whose hero is a man named Henry, a modern Odysseus in search of a "true America."

Thoreau left Walden Pond on September 6, 1846, exactly two years, two months, and two days after he had first settled there. As he explained in the pages of *Walden*: "I left the woods for as good a reason as I went to live there. Perhaps it seemed to me that I had several more lives to live, and could not spare any more time for that one." Growth, change, and development were essential to his character. One should not overlook the significance of his selecting July 4 as the day for taking possession of his residence at Walden Pond, a day that celebrates the Declaration of Independence, the establishment of a new form of government whose highest ideal is individual freedom. In terms of Thoreau's redefinition of the nation-idea, "the only true America" is that place where one may grow wild according to one's nature, where one may "enjoy the land, but own it not." Thoreau believed that each person should live according to individual conscience, willing to oppose the majority if necessary. An early proponent of nonviolent resistance, he was jailed briefly for refusing to pay his poll tax to support the Mexican War and the slave system that had promoted that war. His essay "On Civil Disobedience" (1849), which came from this period of passive resistance, was acknowledged by Mahatma Gandhi (who read it in a South African jail) as the basis for his campaign to free India. MARTIN LUTHER KING, JR. (see Vol. 4), later attributed to Thoreau and Gandhi the inspiration for his leadership in the civil rights movement in the United States.

When Thoreau died, he was little known beyond a small circle of friends and admirers. Only two volumes of his writings had been published—*A Week on the Concord and Merrimack Rivers* (1849) and *Walden*. RALPH WALDO EMERSON lamented, "The country knows not yet, or in the least part, how great a son it has lost." But in the twentieth century Thoreau, the "poet-naturalist," began to be recognized as a representative not only of Transcendentalists, naturalists, and dissidents, but also of New England's heritage and tradition. Even more fitting, *Walden* came to be acknowledged as a great masterpiece of American prose writing, the one book, in ROBERT FROST's opinion, in which Thoreau "surpasses everything we have had in America."

NONFICTION BY THOREAU

Cape Cod. 1865. *The Writings of Henry D. Thoreau Ser.* Ed. by Joseph J. Moldenhauer. Princeton U. Pr. 1988 $42.50. ISBN 0-691-06532-2. Ten essays describing the natural environment and the people of the Massachusetts area.

Early Essays and Miscellanies. The Writings of Henry D. Thoreau Ser. Ed. by Joseph J. Moldenhauer and Edwin Moser with Alexander C. Kern. Princeton U. Pr. 1975 $55.00. ISBN 0-691-06286-2. Thoreau's extant writings while he was at Harvard University and his maverick publications before *A Week on the Concord and Merrimack Rivers.*

The Maine Woods. 1864. *The Writings of Henry D. Thoreau Ser.* Ed. by Joseph J. Moldenhauer. Princeton U. Pr. 1972 $45.00. ISBN 0-691-06224-2. Autobiographical narratives of three excursions to Maine, first edited by Sophia Thoreau and William Ellery Channing and published posthumously.

Walden. 1854. *The Writings of Henry D. Thoreau Ser.* Ed. by J. Lyndon Shanley. Princeton U. Pr. 1971 $42.50. ISBN 0-691-06194-7

A Week on the Concord and Merrimack Rivers. 1849. *The Writings of Henry D. Thoreau Ser.* Ed. by Carl Hoyde. Princeton U. Pr. 1980 $50.00. ISBN 0-691-06376-1. Thoreau's first book, written as a memorial to his brother John.

A Week on the Concord and Merrimack Rivers; Walden; The Maine Woods; Cape Cod. Ed. by Robert F. Sayre. Library of America 1985 $30.00. ISBN 0-940450-27-5. An excellent and handy edition of four major works in one attractive volume.

POETRY BY THOREAU

Collected Poems of Henry Thoreau. Ed. by Carl Bode. Johns Hopkins 1970 o.p. The standard edition of Thoreau's verse.

WORKS BY THOREAU

Correspondence. Ed. by Walter Harding and Carl Bode. Greenwood repr. of 1958 ed. $47.50. ISBN 0-8371-7247-0. Well edited, though many letters have been discovered since its publication.

H. D. Thoreau: A Writer's Journal. Ed. by Laurence Stapleton. Dover 1960 $5.95. ISBN 0-486-20678-5. A selection from *Journal* of materials dealing with Thoreau's life and thoughts as a writer.

The Journal of Henry D. Thoreau. Ed. by Bradford Torrey and Francis H. Allen. 14 vols. in 2. Dover repr. of 1906 ed. $60.00 ea. ISBNs 0-486-20312-3, 0-486-20313-1

Portable Thoreau. Ed. by Carl Bode. Viking Penguin 1977 $8.95. ISBN 0-14-015031-5. Excellent selections from Thoreau's various writings.

Reform Papers. The Writings of Henry D. Thoreau Ser. Ed. by Wendell Glick. Princeton U. Pr. 1973 $42.50. ISBN 0-691-06241-2. Gathers together Thoreau's essays and addresses on reform and politics.

Translations. The Writings of Henry D. Thoreau. Ed. by K. P. Van Anglen. Princeton U. Pr. 1986 $29.95. ISBN 0-691-06531-4. Thoreau's translations into English of Latin and Greek works.

The Writings of Henry David Thoreau. Walden Edition. 20 vols. AMS Pr. repr. of 1906 ed. $810.00. ISBN 0-404-59580-4. The standard edition of Thoreau's writing, although it will be superseded by a new Princeton University Press edition of *The Writings of Henry D. Thoreau.*

The Writings of Henry D. Thoreau Ser. Ed. by Robert Sattelmeyer and others. 4 vols. Princeton U. Pr. Vol. 1 1981 $42.50. ISBN 0-691-06361-3. Vol. 2 1984 $42.50. ISBN 0-691-06186-6. Vol. 3 1990 $39.50. ISBN 0-691-06533-0. Vol. 4 1992 $39.50. ISBN 0-691-06535-7. Will eventually replace the 1906 edition of the *Journal.*

BOOKS ABOUT THOREAU

Adams, Stephen, and Donald Ross, Jr. *Revising Mythologies: The Composition of Thoreau's Major Works.* U. Pr. of Va. 1989 $29.50. ISBN 0-81139-1185-0. Argues that the structure of *Walden* during composition was radically changed by Thoreau's further thoughts on romanticism.

Anderson, Charles R. *The Magic Circle of Walden.* H. Holt & Co. 1968 o.p. A careful, formalist reading of the intricate structure of Thoreau's masterpiece.

Bickman, Martin. *Walden: Volatile Truths. Twayne's Masterwork Studies.* Twayne 1992 $20.95. ISBN 0-8057-7958-2. A close reading of key passages from *Walden.*

Bridgman, Richard. *Dark Thoreau.* U. of Nebr. Pr. 1982 $26.50. ISBN 0-8032-1167-8. Focuses on Thoreau's faults as a writer and on his personality.

Cavell, Stanley. *The Senses of Walden.* U. Ch. Pr. 1992 $10.95. ISBN 0-226-09813-3. A philosophical interpretation of *Walden* by an important modern thinker.

Channing, William E. *Thoreau the Poet–Naturalist: With Memorial Verses.* AMS Pr. repr. of 1873 ed. $37.50. ISBN 0-404-19073-1. A biographical account written by Thoreau's close friend.

Christie, John A. *Thoreau as World Traveler.* Col. U. Pr. 1966 $48.00. ISBN 0-231-02833-4. Examines Thoreau's "travels" in his reading and their impact on his writings.

Harding, Walter. *The Days of Henry Thoreau: A Biography.* Princeton U. Pr. 1983 repr. of 1965 ed. $60.00. ISBN 0-691-06555-1. The most detailed and authoritative biography.

———, ed. *Thoreau As Seen by His Contemporaries.* Peter Smith 1991 $17.50. ISBN 0-8446-6465-0. A collection of accounts by those who knew Thoreau.

Harding, Walter, and Michael Meyer. *The New Thoreau Handbook.* NYU Pr. 1980 o.p. A good introduction to Thoreau's life, thoughts, writings, and reputation.

Hildebidle, John. *Thoreau: A Naturalist's Liberty.* HUP 1983 $20.00. ISBN 0-674-88640-2. A study of Thoreau's attitudes toward science and history.

Howarth, William. *The Book of Concord: Thoreau's Life as a Writer.* Viking Penguin 1982 o.p. Uses the *Journal* as a means of discovering Thoreau as a man and a writer.

Johnson, Linck C. *Thoreau's Complex Weave: The Writing of A Week on the Concord and Merrimack Rivers, with the Text of the First Draft.* U. Pr. of Va. 1986 $45.00. ISBN 0-8139-1063-3. An excellent analysis of the composition of Thoreau's first book.

Krutch, Joseph Wood. *Henry David Thoreau.* Greenwood 1976 repr. of 1948 ed. $35.00. ISBN 0-8371-6587-3. Though somewhat outdated in its facts, still greatly insightful as to the meaning of Thoreau's life.

Lebeaux, Richard. *Thoreau's Seasons.* U. of Mass. Pr. 1984 $35.00. ISBN 0-87023-401-3. A continuation of Lebeaux's *Young Man Thoreau.*

———. *Young Man Thoreau.* U. of Mass. Pr. 1989 $14.95. ISBN 0-87023-687-3. A psychological (Eriksonian) interpretation of Thoreau's early life.

Myerson, Joel, ed. *Critical Essays on Henry David Thoreau's Walden. Critical Essays Ser.* G. K. Hall 1988 $40.00. ISBN 0-8161-8885-8. A collection of early and more recent essays and reviews.

Neufeldt, Leonard N. *The Economist: Henry Thoreau and Enterprise.* OUP 1989 $32.50. ISBN 0-19-505789-9. Locates Thoreau's writings within his society's interests in enterprise and business.

Richardson, Robert D., Jr. *Henry Thoreau: A Life of the Mind.* U. CA Pr. 1986 $29.95. ISBN 0-520-05495-4. An intellectual biography of the highest calibre.

Schneider, Richard J. *Henry David Thoreau. Twayne's United States Authors Ser.* G. K. Hall 1987 $19.95. ISBN 0-8057-7495-5. A useful introduction to Thoreau's life and works.

Shanley, J. Lyndon. *The Making of Walden: With the Text of the First Version.* U. Ch. Pr. 1974 $12.00. ISBN 0-226-74956-8. A careful study of the composition and publication of *Walden.*

Wagenknecht, Edward. *Henry David Thoreau: What Manner of Man? New England Writers Ser.* U. of Mass. Pr. 1981 $12.95. ISBN 0-87023-137-5. A lucid and fair-minded introduction to Thoreau's life and writings; excellent for the uninitiated.

THORPE, THOMAS BANGS. 1815–1878

Born in Westfield, Massachusetts, Thorpe's early training was as a painter. However, with the publication in 1839 of his sketch "Tom Owen, the Bee-Hunter," he became recognized both at home and abroad as a leading writer in the school of southwestern humorists. His next success was "The Big Bear of Arkansas," which was printed in the *Spirit of the Times* in 1841, the popular New York magazine devoted to sports and humor of which he later became part owner and editor. These and other tales were collected in *Mysteries of the Backwoods; or, Sketches of the Southwest* (1846), followed a few years later by another collection, *The Hive of the Bee-Hunter: A Repository of Sketches* (1854), but he never again wrote a tale with the power, artistry, and popularity of "The Big Bear of Arkansas." Generally considered the finest tall tale of the pre-Civil

War Southwest, it looks forward to some of the best performances of MARK TWAIN and WILLIAM FAULKNER. Thorpe's other works, *The Master's House: A Tale of Southern Life* (1854), a political novel in which Thorpe examined the conflicts that were leading the nation to civil war, and several histories of the Mexican War, are today forgotten, but the memory of his name seems assured by the continued admiration won by "The Big Bear of Arkansas."

SHORT STORY COLLECTIONS BY THORPE

Mysteries of the Backwoods; or, Sketches of the Southwest. 1846. Irvington repr. of 1846 ed. $22.00. ISBN 0-8398-1958-7. One of Thorpe's own collections of his frontier tales.

A New Collection of Thomas Bangs Thorpe's Sketches of the Old Southwest. Ed. by David Estes. La. State U. Pr. 1989 $40.00. ISBN 0-8071-1457-X. A scholarly and definitive collection of 38 stories and sketches.

BOOK ABOUT THORPE

Rickels, Milton. *Thorpe: Humorist of the Old Southwest.* La. State U. Pr. 1962 o.p. A critical biography.

TIMROD, HENRY. 1828–1867

Timrod was born in Charleston, South Carolina, and attended the University of Georgia (then Franklin College), where he developed an intense interest in the classical writers. This interest was displayed in *Poems*, a small collection of nature lyrics published in 1860, the only volume of his poetry published during his lifetime. Prevented by tuberculosis from serving in the Civil War, Timrod became a war correspondent and rose to the position of editor of the Columbia *South Carolinian*, supporting the Confederate cause with his pen. However, Sherman's capture and burning of Columbia in February 1865 marked the end of any chance Timrod had for a secure life. He died in poverty and despair little more than two years after Lee's surrender at Appomattox.

From the time that another southern poet, Paul H. Hayne (Timrod's friend since their Charleston school days), collected and published *The Poems of Henry Timrod* in 1873, Timrod has been recognized as the "Laureate of the Confederacy." His classical purity of form, coupled with his intellectual and moral austerity, prevent his poetry from becoming mired in the sentimentality that is characteristic of so much nineteenth-century poetry of the American South. Certainly, the best of his poems are those, such as "The Cotton Boll," "A Cry to Arms," and "Ode Sung at the Occasion of Decorating the Graves of the Confederate Dead," that memorialized the losses and sorrows of his region during its long ordeal.

POETRY BY TIMROD

The Poems of Henry Timrod: With a Sketch of the Poet's Life. 1873. Ed. by Paul H. Hayne. Ayer 1972 repr. of 1873 ed. $21.00. ISBN 0-405-04646-4

NONFICTION BY TIMROD

Essays of Henry Timrod. Ed. by Edd W. Parks. U. of Ga. Pr. 1942 $16.00. ISBN 0-8203-0056-X. Includes Timrod's important essays on poetry, written for *Russell's Magazine* during the 1850s.

BOOKS ABOUT TIMROD

Parks, Edd W. *Henry Timrod.* Twayne's United States Authors Ser. New Coll. U. Pr. 1964 $10.95. ISBN 0-8084-0154-8. A fine critical study by the most ardent of Timrod's modern apologists.

Thompson, Henry T. *Henry Timrod: Laureate of the Confederacy.* AMS Pr. repr. of 1928 ed. $16.50. ISBN 0-404-06421-3. The most detailed biography available.

TUCKERMAN, FREDERICK GODDARD. 1821–1873

Tuckerman was little known during his lifetime. After graduating from Harvard Law School in 1842, he settled in Greenfield, Massachusetts, where he carefully observed nature, making notes on eclipses and local fauna, and pursued his literary interests. In 1860 he published *Poems,* a slender volume of sonnets. Although Tuckerman received letters of praise from TENNYSON, EMERSON, and HAWTHORNE, to whom he had sent copies, his work remained practically unknown. It was not until 1931, when Witter Bynner republished the best of *Poems,* together with three unpublished sonnet sequences, that Tuckerman became recognized as a minor master of the sonnet form. A much better edition of Tuckerman's poems was published in 1965 by the modern American poet, N. SCOTT MOMADAY, and for which the eminent critic Yvor Winters wrote a laudatory foreword. There he made this claim: "Tuckerman is flawed by the vices of his century, but *The Cricket,* I feel sure, is the greatest poem in English of the century, and the amount of unforgettable poetry in the sonnets is large." While not all readers agreed with Winters's final estimate of Tuckerman's achievement, it did renew interest in this obscure poet of western Massachusetts.

POETRY BY TUCKERMAN

The Complete Poems of Frederick Goddard Tuckerman. Ed. by N. Scott Momaday. OUP 1965 o.p.

BOOKS ABOUT TUCKERMAN

England, Eugene. *Beyond Romanticism: Tuckerman's Life and Poetry.* State U. NY Pr. $39.50. ISBN 0-7914-0791-8. An excellent critical biography, with detailed analyses of poems.

Golden, Samuel A. *Frederick Goddard Tuckerman. Twayne's United States Authors Ser.* Irvington 1966 $17.95. ISBN 0-89197-764-3. A serviceable introduction to the poet's life and craft.

VERY, JONES. 1813–1880

The son of a sea captain, Very was born in Salem, Massachusetts, and spent much of his early childhood at sea with his father. Following his father's death in 1824, he attended public school in Salem, and later, with the help of a tutor, he gained enough education to take a teaching position in Salem in order to earn money for tuition to attend Harvard College. Graduating in 1836, he continued his studies in the Harvard School of Divinity and at the same time served as Tutor in Greek at the College. While at Harvard, Very was subject to moments of religious ecstasy, so that his sanity was questioned by his superiors, and he was briefly committed to a nearby asylum.

Returning to Salem without taking a degree from the Divinity School, Very led a retired life, devoting more and more of his time to the study of religion and literature. In 1843 he was finally licensed as a Unitarian preacher, but his shy, other-worldly nature made him either unable or unwilling ever to accept a permanent pastorate.

Very was a peripheral follower of Concord Transcendentalism and was much admired by RALPH WALDO EMERSON, who saw in Very's commitment to mysticism and literature both nobility and magnanimity of character. Beyond his admiration of Very's character, Emerson was an enthusiastic supporter of his poetry, recognizing in Very's sonnets the intense love of nature, the mystical humility, and the submissive nature that gave to Very's sonnets mystical intensity coupled with a serene control.

WORK BY VERY

Poems and Essays by Jones Very. Ed. by James Freeman Clark. Ayer 1972 repr. of 1886 ed. $42.00. ISBN 0-405-04649-9. Though not complete, still the most thorough edition of Very's writings.

BOOK ABOUT VERY

Gittleman, Edwin. *Very: The Effective Years 1833–1840.* Col. U. Pr. 1967 o.p. A critical biography focusing on the most important period of Very's creative life.

WHITMAN, WALT. 1819–1892

Whitman once referred to his poetry as "only a language experiment." A true innovator, he has proven to be a great problem as well as a liberating force for poets and readers ever since. Denounced by many in his time as at best a writer of "shredded prose," his stature as a poet was not assured until the twentieth century. EZRA POUND made his famous pact with Whitman in 1926: "It was you that broke the new wood,/Now is a time for carving./We have one sap and one root—/Let there be commerce between us." More recently, PABLO NERUDA (see Vol. 2), the Chilean poet, shortly after receiving the Nobel Prize for literature in 1972, had this to say of the great American writer: "We continue to live in a Whitmanesque age, seeing how new men and new societies rise and grow, despite their birth-pangs. Walt Whitman was the protagonist of a truly geographical personality; the first man in history to speak with a truly continental voice, to bear a truly American name."

Born in West Hills, Long Island, in New York State, Whitman was very much a product of the radical forces of his time. From his working-class father he inherited a commitment to the democratic principles and faith in the common person of THOMAS PAINE (see also Vol. 3) and Andrew Jackson. From his mother he acquired an experiential knowledge of the teachings of the Quakers (Friends), with its emphasis on the individual's direct relationship with the divine—a communication that often manifested itself in mystical experiences. And, like so many young men and women of his time, he was inspired by the writings of RALPH WALDO EMERSON. As he later acknowledged: "I was simmering, simmering—Emerson brought me to a boil."

The first 30 or so years of Whitman's life give little indication of the poetic power and force of personality that would be revealed with the publication in 1855 of the first edition of *Leaves of Grass*. After attending public school in Brooklyn for only a few years, Whitman eventually learned the printing trade. Between 1838 and 1848, he was editor of several newspapers in the New York City area and contributed fairly pedestrian pieces of prose and verse to various newspapers and magazines. Following the Mexican-American War, however, he was forced to give up the prestigious editorship of the Brooklyn *Daily Eagle* because of his disagreement with its owners on the matter of extending slavery to the territories acquired by the United States in its victory.

These events radicalized Whitman and no doubt contributed greatly to his discovery of a truly original poetic voice. No longer did he feel bound by the conventions of traditional English versification, nor limited by those subjects that the nineteenth century believed to be poetic. The verse form he created was at first a stumbling block to many readers, but in time its essential poetic rightness has been justified by poetic practice. The gains made by his literary descendants, the writers of *vers libre*, are gains in which he has shared. The nearest parallel to the verse form of *Leaves of Grass* is found in the poetry of the English Bible, where the structure is based on a symmetry of clauses, called "parallelism." While Whitman's is not a conventional poetic form, it is far from lawless. Its cadence and rhythm are carefully wrought. And, in poetic subject, Whitman was bounded only by the limits of human experiences. As Louis Untermeyer observed of Whitman's great poems: "They shake themselves free from rant and bombastic audacities and rise into the clear air of major poetry. Such poetry is not large but self-assured; it knows, as Whitman asserted, the amplitude of time and laughs at dissolution. It contains continents; it unfolds the new heaven and new earth of the Western world."

POETRY BY WHITMAN

Leaves of Grass. 1891–92. *Critical Editions Ser.* Ed. by Sculley Bradley and Harold W. Blodgett. Norton 1973 $15.95. ISBN 0-39309388-3. Highly reliable edition of the final revised version of Whitman's poems.

Leaves of Grass: The Original 1855 Edition. Ed. by A. S. Ash. Bandanna Bks. 1991 $7.00. ISBN 0-942208-0. A convenient reprint of the first version of the book.

Leaves of Grass by Walt Whitman: Facsimile Edition of the 1860 Text. Ed. by Roy Harvey Pearce. Cornell Univ. Pr. 1961 $12.95. ISBN 0-8014-9095-2. The edition of Whitman's book that many critics believe is aesthetically the strongest.

A Textual Variorum of the Printed Poems. The Collected Writings of Walt Whitman Ser. 3 vols. Ed. by Sculley Bradley. NYU Pr. 1980 o.p. Reflects in notes the revisions Whitman made in the book of poems between 1855 and 1891–92.

Walt Whitman's Blue Book: The 1860–61 Leaves of Grass Containing His Manuscript Additions and Revisions. 2 vols. Ed. by Arthur Golden. NY Pub. Lib. 1968 $60.00. ISBN 0-87104-214-2. An excellent facsimile of Whitman's working copy, providing the reader with insights into the poet at work.

NOVEL BY WHITMAN

Franklin Evans. 1842. *Masterworks of Literature Ser.* Ed. by Jean Downey. New Coll. U. Pr. 1967 $15.95. ISBN 0-8084-0135-1. Temperance novel.

WORKS BY WHITMAN

An American Primer. 1904. Holy Cow 1987 $13.00. ISBN 0-930100-24-7. Made up of notes edited by Whitman's disciple Horace Traubel, arguing for an American English.

Complete Poetry and Selected Prose. Ed. by James E. Miller, Jr. HM 1972 $8.38. ISBN 0-395-05132-0. A convenient one-volume edition of Whitman's writings.

Complete Writings. 1902. Ed. by Richard Maurice Bucke and others. Scholarly repr. of 1902 ed. $695.00. ISBN 0-403-00114-5. Has been replaced by the New York University Press edition of *The Collected Writings of Walt Whitman.*

Correspondence. 5 vols. Ed. by Edwin H. Miller. NYU Pr. Vol. 1 1961 o.p. Vol. 2 1961 o.p. Vol. 3 1964 $95.00. ISBN 0-8147-0437-9. Vol. 4 1969 $125.00. ISBN 0-8147-0438-7. Vol. 5 1969 $125.00. ISBN 0-8147-0439-5. The standard edition of Whitman's letters.

Daybooks and Notebooks. The Collected Writings of Walt Whitman Ser. 3 vols. Ed. by William White. NYU Pr. $425.00. ISBN 0-8147-9191-3. The standard edition of Whitman's journals and diaries.

The Early Poems and the Fiction. The Collected Writings of Walt Whitman Ser. Ed. by Thomas L. Brasher. NYU Pr. 1963 $95.00. ISBN 0-8147-0441-7. Whitman's writings before the publication of *Leaves of Grass.*

Leaves of Grass and Selected Prose. Ed. by Lawrence Buell. Random 1981 $4.25. ISBN 0-685-03397-X. Reprint of final 1891–92 edition of *Leaves of Grass*, together with a good selection of prose writings.

Notebooks and Unpublished Prose Manuscripts. The Collected Writings of Walt Whitman Ser. 6 vols. Ed. by Edward F. Grier and Gay W. Allen. NYU Pr. 1984 $695.00. ISBN 0-8147-2989-4. An excellent edition of Whitman's extant manuscript writings and notations.

Poetry and Prose. Edited by Justin Kaplan. Library of America 1982 $30.00. ISBN 0-94045-02-X. By all accounts, the best one-volume edition of Whitman's writings.

Selected Letters of Walt Whitman. Ed. by Edwin H. Miller. U. of Iowa Pr. 1990 $40.95. ISBN 0-87745-266-0

Books about Whitman

Allen, Gay W. *The New Walt Whitman Handbook.* NYU Pr. 1987 $50.00. ISBN 0-8147-0556-1. An indispensable guide to Whitman's works and ideas.

———. *The Solitary Singer: A Critical Biography of Walt Whitman.* U. Ch. Pr. 1985 $15.95. ISBN 0-226-01435-5. The standard biography, extraordinarily rich in details.

Aspiz, Harold. *Walt Whitman and the Body Beautiful.* U. of Ill. Pr. 1980 $29.95. ISBN 0-252-00799-9. Discusses Whitman's poetry in the light of nineteenth-century pseudo-scientific theories.

Asselineau, Roger. *The Evolution of Walt Whitman.* 2 vols. Trans. by Richard P. Adams and the author. HUP 1960–62 o.p. An insightful study of Whitman's growth and change as a poet.

Bauerlein, Mark. *Whitman and the American Idiom.* La. State U. Pr. 1991 $22.50. ISBN 0-88071-1681-5. Views Whitman as the creator of a new American poetics.

Erkkila, Betsy. *Whitman the Political Poet.* OUP 1989 $32.50. ISBN 0-19-505438-5. An examination of Whitman's views on the political issues of his time.

Greenspan, Ezra. *Walt Whitman and the American Reader.* Cambridge U. Pr. 1990 $39.50. ISBN 0-521-38469-9. A splendid analysis of the impact on Whitman's art of the literary theories and realities of his time.

Hindus, Milton, ed. *Leaves of Grass One Hundred Years After.* Stanford U. Pr. 1955 $19.50. ISBN 0-8047-0464-3. An important collection of essays by leading critics.

———, ed. *Walt Whitman, the Critical Heritage.* Routledge 1971 o.p. Selections of critical responses to Whitman's work from his time to 1970.

Hollis, C. Carroll. *Language and Style in Leaves of Grass.* La. State U. Pr. 1983 $35.00. ISBN 0-8071-1096-5. Uses linguistic theories in its analysis of Whitman's poetry.

Kaplan, Justin. *Walt Whitman: A Life.* S & S Trade 1986 $12.95. ISBN 0-671-62257-9. A good introduction to Whitman's life.

Killingsworth, M. Jimmie. *Whitman's Poetry of the Body: Sexuality, Politics, and the Text.* U. of NC Pr. 1991 $27.50. ISBN 0-8078-1827-5. Examines the sexuality in Whitman's poetry.

Kuebrich, David. *Minor Prophecy: Walt Whitman's New American Religion.* Ind. U. Pr. $29.95. ISBN 0-253-33191-9. Presents the interesting argument that Whitman's ultimate agenda was to provide a scripture for a new American religion.

Kummings, Donald D., ed. *Approaches to Teaching Whitman's Leaves of Grass.* Modern Lang. 1990 $34.00. ISBN 0-87352-537-X. An excellent gathering of views and strategies on reading Whitman's work.

Loving, Jerome. *Emerson, Whitman, and the American Muse.* U. of NC Pr. 1982 $24.95. ISBN 0-8078-1523-3. A careful study of an important literary relationship.

Martin, Robert K., ed. *The Continuing Presence of Walt Whitman: The Life after the Life.* U. of Iowa Pr. 1992 $26.95. ISBN 0-87745-366-7. Various essays that share the view of Whitman's great importance to twentieth-century poetry.

Miller, Edwin Haviland. *Walt Whitman's "Song of Myself": A Mosaic of Interpretations.* U. of Iowa Pr. 1989 $35.00. ISBN 0-87745-227-X. A variorum of critical views and interpretations of Whitman's great poem.

Miller, James E., Jr. *Leaves of Grass: America's Lyric-Epic of Self and Democracy. Twayne's Masterwork Studies Ser.* Twayne 1992 $22.95. ISBN 0-8057-8089-0. One of the best introductions to Whitman's poetry.

Miller, James E., Jr., and Helen Regenstein. *Walt Whitman*. *Twayne's United States Authors Ser.* G. K. Hall 1990 $22.95. ISBN 0-8057-7600-1. An informed overview of Whitman's life and works.

Moon, Michael. *Disseminating Whitman: Revision and Corporeality in Leaves of Grass.* HUP 1991 $32.50. ISBN 0-674-21276-2. Approaches Whitman's poetry from the point of view of contemporary "gay aesthetic" theories.

Myerson, Joel, ed. *Whitman in His Own Time*: *A Biographical Chronicle of His Life, Drawn from the Recollections, Memoirs, and Interviews by Friends and Associates.* Omnigraphics Inc. 1991 $65.00. ISBN 1-55888-424-6. Whitman as his contemporaries saw him.

Price, Kenneth M. *Whitman and Tradition: The Poet in His Century.* Yale U. Pr. 1990 $16.00. ISBN 0-300-04683-9. Examines the literary contexts in which Whitman worked.

Rupp, Richard H., ed. *Critics on Whitman.* U. of Miami Pr. 1972 $10.95. ISBN 0-87024-195-8. A useful gathering of critical views.

Schyberg, Frederik. *Walt Whitman.* Trans. by Evie A. Allen. AMS Pr. repr. of 1961 ed. $24.50. ISBN 0-404-05629-6. An illuminating reading by an important Danish critic.

Stovall, Floyd. *The Foreground of Leaves of Grass.* U. Pr. of Va. 1974 $29.50. ISBN 0-8139-0523-0. An important examination of those various literary and historical forces and events that contributed to Whitman's development as a man and a poet.

Thomas, M. Wynn. *The Lunar Light of Whitman's Poetry.* HUP 1987 $25.50. ISBN 0-674-53952-4. A reading of the poems in terms of nineteenth-century aesthetic theories and practices.

Warren, James Perrin. *Walt Whitman's Language Experiment.* Pa. St. U. Pr. 1990 $27.50. ISBN 0-271-00688-9. Locates Whitman within the nineteenth-century movement to legitimize American English.

Woodress, James, ed. *Critical Essays on Walt Whitman.* G. K. Hall 1983 $45.00. ISBN 0-8161-8632-4. A valuable collection of critical responses to Whitman's writing.

WHITTIER, JOHN GREENLEAF. 1807–1892

Whittier, the Quaker poet, was a "man of peace" but also "the poet militant." While his nonconformist religion demanded passive resistance in the physical arena, he was vigorous in opposition to slavery and the enemies of democratic principles. Born near Haverhill, Massachusetts, and educated at local schools, Whittier became editor of several country newspapers and in 1831 published his first book, *Legends of New England in Prose and Verse.* This was followed by a number of volumes of poetry, nearly 20 between 1836 and the outbreak of the Civil War, but a literary life was not uppermost in Whittier's mind during these turbulent years. Having been drawn into the antislavery movement by William Lloyd Garrison and others, Whittier became one of the most effective voices in the fight against slavery through his poetry and other writings. He himself said that he "set a higher value on his name as appended to the Anti-Slavery Declaration in 1833 than on the title page of any book." It has been said that his *Voices of Freedom* (1846), raised in the cause of abolition, was second only to *Uncle Tom's Cabin* in influencing the public against slavery.

Following the war, Whittier felt free to turn his primary attention from politics to other themes and matters in his poetry, most successfully to the New England folk life that he had known so intimately during his years in rural Massachusetts and which is reflected in *Among the Hills* (1869). *Snow-Bound: A Winter Idyl* (1866) is a long poem celebrating those rural values that Whittier had known in his youth but that were now vanishing before the industrial and urban forces that were transforming the American landscape and, some feared, character. In this, one of the most popular poems of nineteenth-century America, Whittier seeks in his personal past, as ROBERT PENN WARREN pointed out, "not only a sense of personal renewal and continuity, but also a sense of the continuity of the new order with the American past." Other poems of high merit from these later years include "Abraham Davenport" (1866), the exquisite "Prelude" to *Among the Hills* (1868), and "In School-Days" (1870).

POETRY BY WHITTIER

John Greenleaf Whittier's Poetry: An Appraisal and a Selection. Ed. by Robert Penn Warren. U. of Minn. Pr. 1971 o.p. A discriminating selection and commentary by a preeminent poet and critic.

The Poetical Works of Whittier. Cambridge Editions Ser. Ed. by Hyatt H. Waggoner. HM 1975 $29.95. ISBN 0-395-21599-4. Standard one-volume edition based upon Scudder's 1894 "Cambridge Edition."

NOVEL BY WHITTIER

Leaves from Margaret Smith's Journal. 1849. Irvington repr. of 1849 ed. $19.50. ISBN 0-8398-2167-0. A novel in the form of a diary set in colonial New England.

WORKS BY WHITTIER

Legends of New England in Prose and Verse. 1831. Schol. Facsimiles 1972 repr. of 1831 ed. $50.00. ISBN 0-8201-1108-2. Whittier's first book.

The Letters of John Greenleaf Whittier. 3 vols. Ed. by John B. Pickard. HUP 1975 $130.00. ISBN 0-674-52830-1. The standard edition, meticulously edited.

Whittier on Writers and Writing: The Uncollected Critical Writings of John Greenleaf Whittier. Essay Index Reprint Ser. Ed. by Edwin H. Cady and Harry H. Clark. Ayer 1950 $18.00. ISBN 0-8369-2089-9. An excellent introduction to Whittier's critical opinions.

The Writings of John Greenleaf Whittier. 7 vols. Ed. by H. E. Scudder. AMS Pr. repr. of 1894 ed. $280.00. ISBN 0-404-06950-9. The most complete edition of Whittier's writings, edited with Whittier's assistance.

BOOKS ABOUT WHITTIER

Kribbs, Jayne K., ed. *Critical Essays on John Greenleaf Whittier. Critical Essays on American Literature Ser.* G. K. Hall 1980 o.p. A generous selection of recent and older critical assessments.

Leary, Lewis. *John Greenleaf Whittier. Twayne's United States Authors Ser.* New Coll. U. Pr. 1961 $10.95. ISBN 0-8084-0183-1. An excellent, sympathetic introduction to the man and his works.

Pickard, Samuel T. *Life and Letters of John Greenleaf Whittier. American Biography Ser.* 2 vols. Haskell 1969 repr. of 1907 ed. $89.95. ISBN 0-8383-0191-6. The standard biographical study by a close associate of the poet.

Pollard, John A. *John Greenleaf Whittier: Friend to Man.* HM 1949 o.p. The most complete and reliable modern biography of Whittier.

CHAPTER 15

Middle to Late Nineteenth-Century American Literature

Carol Sapora

> Satisfied that the sequence of men led to nothing and that the sequence of
> their society could lead no further, while the mere sequence of time was
> artificial, and the sequence of thought was chaos, he turned at last to the
> sequence of force; and thus it happened that, after ten years' pursuit, he
> found himself lying in the Gallery of machines at the Great Exposition of
> 1900, his historical neck broken by the sudden irruption of forces totally new.
> —HENRY ADAMS, "The Dynamo and the Virgin,"
> *The Education of Henry Adams*

Surely the last half of the nineteenth century was affected by the scientific and
technological force of the "dynamo" that broke HENRY ADAMS's (see also Vol. 3)
historical neck. The steam engine and many other inventions made heavy
industry possible and led to unprecedented economic growth as mills and
factories turned raw materials into steel for bridges, railroads, and skyscrapers.
But, in addition, a complex interweaving of other forces—political, economic,
social, and intellectual—shaped both the people of America and the United
States as a nation. The westward movement that had exploded with the
midcentury rush for gold continued as settlers pushed the frontier toward the
Pacific Ocean, and the search for new markets carried U.S. imperialism to
Hawaii and other islands. Not even the steel rails of the transcontinental
railroad, completed in 1869, could bind the country in face of such expansion.

Although the states had emerged from the Civil War supposedly united, the
regions of the North and the South were irrevocably separated, not only by the
bitterness of the conflict, but also by the political debris left by a Reconstruction
program that collapsed when federal troops were withdrawn in 1877. Share-
cropping and tenant farming kept both freed slaves and poor whites tied to the
land and their landlords; poll taxes and literacy tests effectively denied African
Americans the vote, while "Jim Crow" laws and Ku Klux Klan lynchings further
divided the races.

At the same time, the ethnic composition of the nation's population was
shifting as millions of immigrants arrived in New York and San Francisco.
Recruited to supply industry's almost insatiable demand for cheap labor and
lured by promises of opportunity and citizenship, most of these people came not
from Great Britain and Northern Europe, as before the war, but from the less
familiar countries and cultures of Central and Eastern Europe and Asia.
Spanish-speaking people in the California territory, annexed at the end of the
Mexican War in 1848, were also transformed into U.S. citizens. Meanwhile,
Native Americans were being driven from their land, confined to reservations,
and told that they must assimilate in order to survive. Given the struggles of all

these different populations to enter the "melting pot" of U.S. society—or, in Native Americans' case, to abstain from it—diversity was a fact of life in the United States. Unfortunately, the debate over who were the "true" Americans and who were condemned to remain outsiders or foreigners even after gaining citizenship, sustained the ill effects of prejudice and discrimination well beyond the end of the Civil War.

Fed by abundant natural resources, a supply of cheap labor, and a continuing demand for progress, the U.S. economy boomed, generating huge industrial and business fortunes for a few robber barons—Andrew Carnegie, J. P. Morgan, and John D. Rockefeller—and poverty for many. With wealth came power, the opportunity for philanthropy, and the even greater temptation to graft and corruption. Workers and their families were exploited and their protests ruthlessly quelled, sometimes by the military. The Chicago Haymarket riots in 1886 and the trumped-up conviction of eight "anarchists" accused of planting a bomb in the city suggest both the depth of labor's rebellion and the intensity of capital's efforts to suppress it. Meanwhile the growing middle class, enticed by the luxuries that mass production put within their grasp (even if these were "gilded" imitations), enthusiastically set about the task of "conspicuous consumption." DARWIN's (see Vol. 5) theory of evolution, which had seriously challenged the comfortable absolutes of traditional religion, was also used to assure Wall Street entrepreneurs that the fit would survive in the downtown jungle. Yet, despite the optimistic claims of the Gilded Age, the appearance of prosperity and social justice often substituted for the real thing.

The entire structure of society seemed to buckle under the pressures of the new age. Women, traditionally considered the guardians of traditional civilized values, were not immune to the forces of the changing age. Many chafed under the restrictions of social roles that denied their individuality. The issues were more important than the mere right to shed bulky Victorian dress for the ease and comfort of bloomers; nevertheless, the supposed risk to women's feminine beauty was the focus of many objections to their struggle for greater independence. While some women entered the workplace from necessity, others sought education or fought for such social reforms as suffrage, birth control, and child-labor laws. Many women, of course, remained at home in traditional roles, but the "new woman's" perceived desertion of home and hearth was blamed for all the ills of the family and society.

The literature of the period reflects the results of these complex forces at work in society—the political turmoil, the economic instability, and the social upheaval. Writers wishing to depict their society realistically rejected the romanticism of an earlier age, although Horatio Alger stories of rags-to-riches success remained popular with readers seeking to escape reality. The honest scrutiny of other writers, however, revealed the hollowness at the core of U.S. society. Perhaps the clearest evidence of the shift in the United States' perception of itself is evidenced in the fascination of both readers and writers with the "American girl." Assertive but innocent, she replaced the rugged individual—the Natty Bumppo—of earlier fiction as a seeker of the American dream, and in that role she incarnated both the dream's optimism and its vulnerability. She was seen by some, Howard Chandler Christy in particular, as the "culmination of mankind's long struggle upward from barbarism into civilization." But her failure to survive in the stories written about her—witness HENRY JAMES's Daisy Miller, STEPHEN CRANE's Maggie, KATE CHOPIN's Edna Pontellier, THEODORE DREISER's Carrie Meeber, and EDITH WHARTON's Lily Bart—reveals the crack in the gilded surface of the American dream. Unable to find a place as an individual in a society that conferred her value only as a commodity, the American girl epitomized both the promise and the betrayal of the age. Her apparent freedom was an illusion, and her death (or, in the case of Carrie, her loss of innocence) symbolized the death of the dream itself.

By the end of the century, the aspirations of this age, conceived with such optimism at midcentury, had been crushed by the forces of reality. The promise of the West had disappeared when the frontier closed in 1890. The "United" States had been torn apart by the differences of its people. The "huddled masses yearning to breathe free" had been crowded into city ghettos. And business booms had exploded in the stock market crashes of 1873 and 1893. In literature, realism gave way to the grim necessities of naturalism.

Today, our notions of this volatile period of American literature are undergoing transformations nearly as radical as those of the period itself. Readers are challenging the traditional canon that silenced, and thus by omission denigrated, certain cultures. Authors formerly revered are being eclipsed by writers whose work has been rediscovered or reinterpreted. Readers who value diversity are questioning one of the most long-lived assumptions of literary criticism—that some ideal and unchanging standard of judgment exists. Today's critics, using new historical methods, are examining the contexts of literature and are coming to a clearer vision of that "irruption of forces" that Henry Adams, "lying in the Gallery of machines at the Great Exposition of 1900," found so disturbing—and so compelling.

HISTORY AND CRITICISM

Aaron, Daniel. *The Unwritten War: American Writers and the Civil War.* U. of Wis. Pr. 1987 $37.50. ISBN 0-299-11390-6. Thorough treatment of both Northern and Southern writers and their direct and indirect responses to the Civil War and the material it supplied for writers.

American Literary Scholarship: An Annual. 27 vols. Duke 1965–91 $45.00 ea. Annual selective and evaluative survey of current editions and criticism in American literature.

Bain, Robert, Louis D. Rubin, and Joseph M. Flora, eds. *Southern Writers: A Biographical Dictionary.* L. State U. Pr. 1979 $18.95. ISBN 0-8071-0354-3. Short reliable sketches of writers who were born or lived in the South; includes many lesser known authors.

Bain, Robert, and Joseph M. Flora, eds. *Fifty Southern Writers Before 1900.* Greenwood 1987 $95.00. ISBN 0-313-24518-5. Companion volume to *Fifty Southern Writers After 1900.* Contains biographical and critical essays on major Southern writers.

Banta, Martha. *Imaging American Women: Idea and Ideals in Cultural History.* Col. U. Pr. 1989 $27.50. ISBN 0-231-06127-7. Comprehensive study of the influence of visual and literary images of the American girl and the new woman at the turn of the century.

Bercovitch, Sacvan, ed. *The New Cambridge History of American Literature.* 5 vols. Cambridge U. Pr. o.p. Historical and contextual approach to American literature incorporating ethnic, minority, Native American, and popular literature.

———, ed. *Reconstructing American Literary History. Harvard English Studies.* HUP 1986 $20.00. ISBN 0-674-75085-3. Collection of essays debating the questions of the American literature canon.

Borus, Daniel H. *Writing Realism: Howells, James, and Norris in the Mass Market.* U. of NC Pr. 1989 $37.50. ISBN 0-8078-1869-0. Analyzes social and economic conditions affecting American literary realism after the Civil War.

Bredahl, A. Carl, Jr. *New Ground: Western American Narrative and the Literary Canon.* U. of NC Pr. 1989 $32.50. ISBN 0-8078-1854-2. Argues that the openness of the West has produced writers focused on freedom rather than enclosure and analyzes writers who should be included in the canon of American literature.

Brown, Gillian. *Domestic Individualism: Imagining Self in Nineteenth-Century America. The New Historicism: Studies in Cultural Poetics*. U. CA Pr. 1990 $24.95. ISBN 0-520-06785-1. Study of the rise of nineteenth-century domesticity as a strand of American individualism important to men's as well as to women's sense of self; treats especially Stowe, Hawthorne, and Melville.

Bruce, Dickson D., Jr. *Black American Writing from the Nadir: The Evolution of a Literary Tradition, 1877–1915*. La. State U. Pr. $9.95. ISBN 0-8071-1806-0. Traces the emergence of African American literary tradition in the context of post-Reconstruction racism, considering a wide range of little-known writers.

Buell, Lawrence. *New England Literary Culture: From Revolution through Renaissance*. Cambridge U. Pr. 1986 $34.50. ISBN 0-521-30206-4. Analyzes the society, culture, and ideas that influenced the New England writers.

Chametzky, Jules. *Our Decentralized Literature: Cultural Mediations in Selected Jewish and Southern Writers*. U. of Mass. Pr. 1986 $25.00. ISBN 0-87023-527-3. Collection of essays illustrating the way some marginalized groups have used writing to gain a place in American culture.

Coultrap-McQuin, Susan. *Doing Literary Business: American Women Writers in the Nineteenth Century. Gender & Amer. Culture Ser*. U. of NC Pr. 1990 $29.95. ISBN 0-8078-4284-2. Study of nineteenth-century women writers' professionalism as shaped by society and the publishing industry.

Cunliffe, Marcus, ed. *American Literature to Nineteen Hundred. The New Hist. of Lit. Ser*. P. Bedrick Bks. 1987 $39.50. ISBN 0-87226-132-8. Brief history and selective bibliographies.

De Jackson, J. R. *Historical Criticism and Meaning of Texts*. Routledge 1989 $42.50. ISBN 0-415-00767-4. Argues for an historical approach to literature; i.e., reading texts in the context of their contemporary reception.

DiPietro, J., and Edward Ifkovic, eds. *Ethnic Perspectives in American Literature: Selected Essays on the European Contribution*. Modern Lang. 1983 $37.00. ISBN 0-87352-127-7. Historical overview of the development of literature by European immigrants.

Donovan, Josephine. *Feminist Theory: The Intellectual Tradition of American Feminism*. Continuum 1992 $14.95. ISBN 0-8264-0617-3. Intellectual history focusing on feminism as a political movement.

Draper, James P., ed. *Black Literature Criticism: Excerpts from Criticism of the Most Significant Works of Black Authors over the Past 200 Years*. Gale 1992 $250.00. ISBN 0-8103-7929-5. Comprehensive; complements *African-American Writers Before the Harlem Renaissance* (1986).

Duke, Maurice, Jackson R. Bryer, and M. Thomas Inge, eds. *American Women Writers; Bibliographic Essays*. Greenwood 1983 $49.95. ISBN 0-313-22116-2. Survey of editions and scholarship on 24 women writers.

Elliott, Emory, gen. ed. *Columbia Literary History of the United States*. Col. U. Pr. 1988 $210.00. ISBN 0-231-06780-1. Most recent comprehensive literary history presented through a variety of critical approaches in essays by outstanding scholars; reflects the diversity of American cultural heritage, covering Native American, ethnic, minority, regional, and popular works as well as the traditional canon.

Foerster, Norman, and others, eds. *American Poetry and Prose*. HM 1970 $47.16. ISBN 0-395-04456-1

Foster, M. Marie, ed. *Southern Black Creative Writers, 1829–1953: Biobibliographies, Bibliographies and Indexes in Afro-American and African Studies*. Greenwood 1988 $35.00. ISBN 0-313-26207-1. Bibliography and brief biographical sketches of African-American writers, many of whom are little known.

Fried, Lewis, ed. *Handbook of American-Jewish Literature: An Analytical Guide to Topics, Themes, and Sources*. Greenwood 1988 $75.00. ISBN 0-313-24593-2. Collection of 18 essays considering different aspects of Jewish-American culture from 1880 to the present.

Gilbert, Sandra, and Susan Gubar. *Madwoman in the Attic: The Woman Writer and the Nineteenth-Century Literary Imagination.* Yale U. Pr. 1979 $19.95. ISBN 0-300-02286-7. Influential study of British and American women writers and their conflict with patriarchy.

————. *No Man's Land—The Place of the Woman Writer in the Twentieth Century, Vol. 1: The War of the Words.* Yale U. Pr. 1988 $32.00. ISBN 0-300-04005-9. Revisionist readings of popular and mainstream literature illustrating the "war" between men and women in the nineteenth century.

Hansen, Olaf. *Aesthetic Individualism and Practical Intellect: American Allegory in Emerson, Thoreau, Adams and James.* Princeton U. Pr. 1990 $29.95. ISBN 0-691-06823-2. Original study focusing on texts relevant to contemporary readers: "This book will influence present and future discussion of the evolution of an American 'self'" (Lindborg).

Hapke, Laura. *Tales of the Working Girl: Wage Earning Women in American Literature, 1890-1925.* Twayne's Literature and Society Ser. Twayne 1992 $26.95. ISBN 0-8057-8855-7. Combines literary and social history to examine different representations of the working woman in fiction and nonfiction.

Hart, James D. *The Oxford Companion to American Literature.* OUP 5th ed. 1983 $49.95. ISBN 0-19-503074-5. Encyclopedic entries on authors, major works, historical events, and other topics; includes a chronology of literary and social history.

Horton, Rod W., and Herbert W. Edwards. *Backgrounds of American Literary Thought.* P-H 3rd ed. 1974. ISBN 0-13-056291-2. Offers historical, intellectual, social, and economic backgrounds for American literature; includes suggested readings.

Jackson, Blyden. *A History of Afro-American Literature, Vol. 1: The Long Beginning, 1746–1895.* La. State U. Pr. 1989 $29.95. ISBN 0-8071-1511-8. Complete survey of major and minor African American writers, with bibliography.

Jones, Howard Mumford, and Richard M. Ludwig. *Guide to American Literature and Its Backgrounds Since 1890.* HUP 1972 $18.50. ISBN 0-674-36753-7. Social, intellectual, and cultural backgrounds of American literature; lists works that reflect trends in American literature.

Kazin, Alfred. *American Procession.* Knopf 1984 $18.95. ISBN 0-394-50378-3. Survey of major figures by a distinguished scholar of American literature.

Kolb, Harold H., Jr. *Illusion of Life: American Realism as a Literary Form.* U. Pr. of Va. 1969 o.p. Clearly written, with a new definition of realism.

Kolodny, Annette. *The Lay of the Land: Metaphor As Experience and History in American Life and Letters.* U. of NC Pr. 1975 $22.50. ISBN 0-8078-1241-2. Traces the metaphoric use of the land as a woman in eighteenth through twentieth century American literature.

Krupat, Arnold. *The Voice in the Margin: Native American Literature and the Canon.* U. CA Pr. 1989 $35.00. ISBN 0-520-06669-3. Argues that modern critical theory has marginalized Native American literature, a literature that must be included in the canon of American literature.

Kunitz, Stanley, J., and Howard Haycraft, eds. *American Authors, 1600–1900: A Biographical Dictionary of American Literature.* Wilson Authors Ser. Wilson 8th ed. 1977 $60.00. ISBN 0-8242-0001-2. Contains 1,320 biographies; the standard reference.

Lawrence, D. H. *Studies in Classic American Literature.* Viking Penguin 1977 $6.95. ISBN 0-14-003300-9. Discussions of Whitman, Melville, Benjamin Franklin, Cooper, Poe, Hawthorne, and Dana. Eccentric but perceptive.

Levin, Harry. *The Power of Blackness: Hawthorne, Poe, Melville.* Ohio U. Pr. 1980 repr. of 1958 ed. $9.95. ISBN 0-8214-0581-0. "A remarkable, provocative, astute study attempts to demonstrate that the introspection, tragic awareness, and sense of alienation inherent in the works . . . give a [true] picture of the American mind and milieu" (*Booklist*).

Ling, Amy. *Between Worlds: Woman Writers of Chinese Ancestry.* Athene Ser. Pergamon 1990 $37.50. ISBN 0-08-037464-6. Study of writers of Chinese ancestry writing in English, giving their historical and social backgrounds and a bibliography.

Literary History of the United States. 1948. 3 vols. Macmillan 1953 o.p. This is the standard modern history of American literature and is particularly useful because of its detailed bibliographic entries on all significant American writers. It includes articles in journals and magazines as well as books and lists reprints of authors' works that have now gone out of print.

Littlefield, Daniel F., Jr., and James W. Parins. *A Biobibliography of Native American Writers 1772–1924: A Supplement.* Native Amer. Bib. Ser. Scarecrow 1985 $29.50. ISBN 0-8108-1802-7. Contains biographies and bibliographies of Native American writers.

Lyon, Thomas J., ed. Western Lit. Assn. Staff. *A Literary History of the American West.* Tex. Christian 1986 $79.50. ISBN 0-87565-021-X. Well-organized and focused series of essays treating different categories of the West, with chronologies and bibliographies for included writers.

Marchalonis, Shirley, ed. *Patrons and Protegées: Gender, Friendship, and Writing in Nineteenth-Century America.* Rutgers U. Pr. 1988 $35.00. ISBN 0-8135-1270-0. Considers many little-known women writers and their circles of friends.

Martin, Jay. *Harvests of Change: American Literature, 1865–1914.* P-H 1967 o.p.

Marx, Leo. *Machine in the Garden: Technology and the Pastoral Ideal in America.* OUP 1964 $10.95. ISBN 0-19-500738-7. Classic criticism describing the pastoral ideal and the development of technology as a force in American life and literature.

Matthiessen, F. O. *American Renaissance: Art and Expression in the Age of Emerson and Whitman.* OUP 1968 repr. of 1941 ed. $18.95. ISBN 0-19-500759-X. A major study.

Maxwell, D.E.S. *American Fiction: The Intellectual Background.* Col. U. Pr. 1963 o.p. Chapters on Poe, Cooper, Melville, Hawthorne, and others.

Miller, Perry. *The Raven and the Whale: The War of Words and Wits in the Era of Poe and Melville.* Greenwood 1973 repr. of 1956 ed. $45.50. ISBN 0-8371-6707-8. A lively chronicle of the literary scene in New York in the 1840s and the 1850s and the conflict between American- and foreign-oriented writers.

Mogen, David, Mark Busby, and Paul Bryant, eds. *The Frontier Experience and the American Dream: Essays on American Literature.* TX A & M Univ. Pr. 1989 $29.50. ISBN 0-89096-398-3. Collection of essays using Bakhtin's dialogics in connecting the importance of the frontier to the American literary imagination.

Mott, Frank L. *A History of American Magazines.* Bks. Demand repr. of 1938 ed. Vol. 1 o.p. Vol. 2 $164.20. ISBN 0-7837-3069-1. Vol. 3 $175.30. ISBN 0-7837-3070-5. The standard history.

Parrington, Vernon L. *Main Currents in American Thought.* Vol. 3 *The Beginnings of Critical Realism in America: 1860–1920.* U. of Okla. Pr. 1987 $32.95. ISBN 0-8061-2079-7. Third and last volume, incomplete at Parrington's death, of influential history of American literature. Examines the interconnection between literature and socioeconomic history and culture.

Pattee, Fred L. *The Development of the American Short Story.* Biblo 1923 $20.00. ISBN 0-8196-0175-6. A study of the form as used by writers from Irving through O. Henry.

———. *A History of American Literature Since 1870.* BCL1-PS Amer. Lit. Ser. Rprt. Serv. 1992 $99.00. ISBN 0-7812-6617-3. An early history of American literature first published in 1915, responsible for establishing much of the canon and determining the direction of much scholarship in American literature.

Pizer, Donald. *Realism and Naturalism in Nineteenth-Century Literature.* S. Ill. U. Pr. 1966 o.p. With a preface by Harry T. Moore.

Quinn, Arthur Hobson. *American Fiction: An Historical and Critical Survey.* Appleton & Lange 1964 o.p. A useful, if necessarily general, account of American fiction from the beginning to Willa Cather, with the final chapter "Retrospect and Prospect" and a bibliography.

Rees, Robert A. *Fifteen American Authors Before 1900: Bibliographic Essays on Research and Criticism.* U. of Wis. Pr. rev. ed. 1984 o.p. Surveys by established critics on Adams, Dickinson, Howells, Norris, among others.

Ringe, Donald A. *American Gothic: Imagination and Reason in Nineteenth Century Fiction.* U. Pr. of Ky. 1982 o.p. A useful survey of the important writers of the period.

Rock, Roger O. *The Native American in American Literature: A Selectively Annotated Bibliography. Bib. and Indexes in Amer. Lit. Ser.* Greenwood 1985 $42.95. ISBN 0-313-24550-9. Annotated guide to works by and about Native Americans.

Rubin Louis D., Jr., gen. ed. *The History of Southern Literature.* 1985. La. State U. Pr. 1990 $16.95. ISBN 0-8071-1643-2. Collection of essays covering authors, genres, and topics in Southern literature, including African American literature.

Ruoff, A. LaVonne, Jr. *American Indian Literatures: An Introduction and Selected Bibliography.* Modern Lang. 1990 $45.00. ISBN 0-87352-191-9. Overview and introduction to major Native American authors and literature, both oral and written. Selected bibliography includes material related to Native American literature.

Ruoff, A. LaVonne, Jr., and Jerry W. Ward, eds. *Redefining American Literary History. Comm. on Lit. & Lang. of Amer. Ser.* Modern Lang. 1990 $45.00. ISBN 0-87352-187-0. Argues for expansion and redefinition of American literature to include Hispanic, African American, Native American, Asian American, Chicano, and Puerto Rican literatures.

Schockley, Ann A. *Afro-American Women Writers, 1746–1933: An Anthology and Critical Guide. G. K. Hall Ref. Bks.* Macmillan 1988 $42.50. ISBN 0-8161-8823-8. Useful resource including an overview of African American women's literary traditions as well as long-neglected writers.

Showalter, Elaine, ed. *The New Feminist Criticism: Essays on Women, Literature, and Theory.* Pantheon 1985 $22.95. ISBN 0-394-53913-3. Collection of 18 essays offering an introduction to feminist readings, consideration of the canon, and bibliography.

———. *Sister's Choice: Traditions and Change in American Women's Writing. Clarendon Lectures.* OUP 1991 $21.95. ISBN 0-19-812383-3. Considers Louisa May Alcott, Kate Chopin, and Edith Wharton, among others.

Shulman, Robert. *Social Criticism and Nineteenth-Century American Fictions.* U. of Mo. Pr. 1987 o.p. Examines nineteenth-century mainstream writers' responses to market society, taking into account the effects of capitalism, social change, and American individualism.

Simonson, Harold P. *Beyond the Frontier: Writers, Western Regionalism and a Sense of Place.* Tex. Christian 1989 $15.95. ISBN 0-87565-040-6. Considers the relationship between the frontier and the hope of the American dream in analyzing Western writers.

Spengemann, William C. *A Mirror for Americanists: Reflections on the Idea of American Literature.* U. Pr. of New Eng. 1989 $25.00. ISBN 0-87451-483-5. Essays attempting to define American literature and the criteria used to determine the canon.

Spiller, Robert E. *Cycle of American Literature.* Free Pr. 1967 $15.95. ISBN 0-02-930420-2. A reissue. Essays attempting to define a single, coherent vision of American literature as it illuminates history and social context.

Spiller, Robert E., and others, eds. *Literary History of the United States: History.* Macmillan 1974 o.p. Long the standard literary history, including chronological culture and historical background on major authors, genres, and movements, with a separate bibliographic volume.

Strout, Cushing. *Making American Tradition: Visions and Revisions from Ben Franklin to Alice Walker.* Rutgers U. Pr. 1990 $38.00. ISBN 0-8135-1516-5. Critical approach emphasizing writers' responses to tradition and previous writers.

Taylor, J. Gorden, and others, eds. *A Literary History of the American West.* Tex. Christian 1986 $79.50. ISBN 0-87565-021-X. Covers the history, regions, major writers, genres, and ethnic literature of the West, with bibliographies.

Trachtenberg, Alan. *The Incorporation of America: Culture and Society in the Gilded Age. Amer. Century Ser.* Hill & Wang 1982 $9.95. ISBN 0-8090-5827-8. Examines the influence of business on American social history, values, and culture.

Voloshin, Beverly R., ed. *American Literature, Culture, and Ideology: Essays in Memory of Henry Nash Smith.* P. Lang Pubs. 1990 $16.95. ISBN 0-8204-0850-4. A wide-ranging collection of new and reprinted essays by well-known scholars.

Welter, Barbara. *Dimity Convictions: The American Woman in the Nineteenth Century.* Ohio U. Pr. 1976 $16.95. ISBN 0-8214-0358-3. Examines nineteenth century ideals of womanhood—piety, purity, submissiveness, and domesticity—as reflected in women's lives and literature of the period.

Westbrook, Perry D. *A Literary History of New England.* Lehigh Univ. Pr. 1988 $45.00. ISBN 0-934223-02-5. Distinguishes New England literature and traces its history from the Puritan period to the twentieth century.

Wiget, Andrew, ed. *Critical Essays on Native American Literature. Critical Essays on American Literature.* G. K. Hall 1985 $32.50. ISBN 0-8161-8667-1. Critical views of Native American writing from early myths and legends to contemporary fiction.

Wilson, Edmund. *Patriotic Gore: Studies in the Literature of the American Civil War.* Northeastern U. Pr. 1984 $16.95. ISBN 0-930350-61-8. Influential study of popular writers.

Yeager, Patricia, and Beth Kowateski-Wallace, eds. *Refiguring the Father: New Feminist Readings of Patriarchy.* S. Ill. U. Pr. 1989 $32.50. ISBN 0-8093-1529-7. Essays reconsidering and reevaluating a wide range of standard literary works.

COLLECTIONS

Barksdale, Richard, and Kenneth Kinnamon, eds. *Black Writers of America: A Comprehensive Anthology.* Macmillan 1972 $35.25. ISBN 0-02-306080-8. An excellent one-volume collection of African American literature.

Baym, Nina, and others, eds. *The Norton Anthology of American Literature.* 2 vols. Norton 1989 $27.95 ea. ISBNs 0-393-95736-5, 0-393-95740-1. Widely used in college surveys.

Blanche, Jerry. *Native American Reader: Speeches, Poems and Stories of the American Indian.* Denali Press 1990 $25.00. ISBN 0-938737-20-1

Fetterley, Judith, ed. *Provisions: A Reader from Nineteenth Century American Women.* Ind. U. Pr. 1985 $35.00. ISBN 0-253-17040-0. Anthology providing an overview of the wide range of styles and themes prevailing in women's literature during this period.

Foerster, Norman, and others, eds. *American Poetry and Prose.* 3 vols. HM 1970 $43.96. ISBN 0-395-04456-1. Somewhat old but still valuable anthology, especially for those writers who are now regarded as "minor."

Lauter, Paul, and others, eds. *The Heath Anthology of American Literature.* 2 vols. Heath 1990 $19.50 ea. ISBNs 0-669-12064-2, 0-669-12065-0. A bold and controversial attempt to expand the canon of American letters in terms of gender, race, and ethnic identity.

Masur, Louis P., ed. *Heart-Shaped Leaves: American Writers During the Civil War.* OUP 1993. ISBN 0-19-506868-8

Miller, James E., Jr. *Heritage of American Literature.* 2 vols. HarBraceJ 1990 $29.50 ea. ISBNs 0-15-535697-6, 0-15-535698-4

Rogers, Katharine M., ed. *The Meridian Anthology of Early American Women Writers: From Anne Bradstreet to Louisa May Alcott.* NAL-Dutton 1991 $14.95. ISBN 0-452-01075-6. Excellent collection of fiction, poetry, autobiography, letters, and essays.

POETRY

When RALPH WALDO EMERSON's essay "The Poet" called for an American poet with "a new thought" and "a whole new experience to unfold," American poetry was little more than a subgenre of English poetry. Although the Fireside or Schoolroom poets—LONGFELLOW, WHITTIER, LOWELL, and HOLMES—had produced genteel verse on American subjects, none had broken from the conventions of English meter. Emerson had seen poetry as "a meter making argument," and EDGAR ALLAN POE had emphasized the sensory effects of rhyme and rhythm. Some poets, like JAMES WHITCOMB RILEY, used common American themes and regional dialects; others, like SIDNEY LANIER, experimented with verse forms, drawing on the connection they saw between poetry and music.

But America continued to wait for "its poet," one who would "[unlock] our chains and [admit] us to a new scene." By the end of the nineteenth century, however, two truly American poets had answered Emerson's call, broken the chains of conventional English forms, and, between them, determined the direction of modern poetry.

WALT WHITMAN, with his free verse and his free vision, rejected conventional poetic forms and embraced all subjects. With his expanded line and all-encompassing persona, he "sang America" in ways not heard before. Responding directly to Emerson's call—and later using Emerson's greeting "at the beginning of a great career" to promote his book—Whitman brought out the first of many editions of *Leaves of Grass* (1855). In the preface he describes American bards as "kosmos . . . without monopoly or [secrecy] . . . glad to pass any thing to any one . . . hungry for equals night and day." In his poetry, Whitman speaks, not in a personal voice, but in the voice of all Americans. "What I assume you shall assume," he tells the reader, "For every atom belonging to me as good belongs to you" ("Song of Myself"). In his preface to that work, he asserts that "The proof of a poet is that his country absorbs him as affectionately as he has absorbed it."

At about the same time that Whitman was so boldly claiming his position as poet of all America, EMILY DICKINSON, in an upstairs room of her father's house in Amherst, Massachusetts, was turning out hundreds of poems written in an intensely private, individual voice. The many personal "I's" of Dickinson's poetry—as opposed to the all-encompassing "you" that Whitman uses—describe the experiences of the individual rather than the universal soul. Dickinson's half-rhymes, broken meter, and fractured sentences, as well as her enigmatic images, made most of her poetry unacceptable to her contemporaries. Only 12 of her poems were published during her life, but her poetry touches today's readers with the piercing insight it offers into the human psyche. Without "seeing the ocean" or "venturing very far from home," Dickinson expressed the anxiety and skepticism of her age. Like Whitman, she broke from traditional forms, not by expansion, as he did, but by her own style of compression. Ultimately determined to "select her own Society," Dickinson did not publicly claim a position in the American poetic tradition; rather, she has been awarded her rank by later generations who admire her steadfast refusal to conform as she addressed a world "that never wrote to [me]."

The work of notable minor writers such as HENRY TIMROD, JONES VERY, FREDERICK TUCKERMAN, WILLIAM VAUGHN MOODY, PAUL LAURENCE DUNBAR, and EMMA LAZARUS also found contemporary audiences. Mexican American ballads or *corridos*, Native American songs and legends, as well as dialect and humorous verse by writers such as Riley, BRET HARTE, and JAMES WELDON JOHNSON were popular in the many magazines and newspapers of the time. Whitman and Dickinson, however, remain as the voices of the late nineteenth century who answered Emerson's call to establish a distinctly American poetic idiom, clearing the way for the twentieth-century modernists—T. S. ELIOT (see Vol. 2), EZRA POUND, H. D. (Hilda Doolittle), and others.

History and Criticism

Allen, Gay W. *American Prosody*. Hippocrene Bks. 1966 $27.50. ISBN 0-374-90133-3
Barksdale, Richard, and Kenneth Kinnamon. *Black Writers of America: A Comprehensive Anthology*. Macmillan 1972. ISBN 0-02-306080-8. An excellent anthology of African American writing in America, containing a generous selection of poetry.

Bloom, Harold, ed. *American Poetry Through Nineteen Fourteen. Critical Cosmos Ser.* Chelsea Hse. 1987 $64.95. ISBN 0-87754-951-6. Covers 18 poets beginning with Anne Bradstreet; most essays reprinted from full-length studies.

Day, Arthur G., ed. *The Sky Clears: Poetry of the American Indians.* Greenwood 1983 $38.50. ISBN 0-8032-5047-9

Eberhart, Richard. *Of Poetry & Poets.* U. of Ill. Pr. 1979 $29.95. ISBN 0-252-00630-5

Fussell, Edwin. *Lucifer in Harness: American Meter, Metaphor and Diction.* Princeton U. Pr. 1973 $32.50. ISBN 0-691-06238-2

Gelpi, Albert. *The Tenth Muse: The Psyche of the American Poet.* Cambridge U. Pr. 1991 $54.50. ISBN 0-521-42401-1. Uses the myths of Eros and Psyche to consider five major poets, including Whitman and Dickinson.

Jason, Philip K. *Nineteenth Century American Poetry.* Salem Pr. 1989 $40.00. ISBN 0-89356-651-9. Useful guide to secondary material on major American poets.

Lee, Robert, ed. *Nineteenth-Century American Poetry.* B & N Imports 1985 $28.50. ISBN 0-389-20377-7. Collection offering an overview of poetry delineating the opposing positions of Whitman and Dickinson.

Pearce, Roy Harvey. *The Continuity of American Poetry.* U. Pr. of New Eng. 1987 $40.00. ISBN 0-8195-6198-3. A valuable study of the history of American poetry from the seventeenth century to the age of Eliot.

Perkins, David. *History of Modern Poetry: From the Eighteen Nineties to the High Modernist Mode.* HUP 1976 $33.00. ISBN 0-674-39941-2. A thorough, cautious study.

Sherman, Joan R. *Invisible Poets: Afro-Americans of the Nineteenth Century.* U. of Ill. Pr. 1989 $11.95. ISBN 0-252-01620-3. Essays on 26 neglected African American poets.

Stauffer, Donald Barlow. *A Short History of American Poetry.* NAL-Dutton 1974 o.p. Biographical and historical treatment of individual poets.

Waggoner, Hyatt H. *American Poets: From the Puritans to the Present.* La. State U. Pr. rev. ed. 1984 $35.00. ISBN 0-8071-1146-5. Focuses on Emerson's central position in the development of American poetry.

Walker, Cheryl. *The Nightingale's Burden: Women Poets and American Culture before 1900.* Ind. U. Pr. 1983 $22.50. ISBN 0-253-34065-9. Critical study of Dickinson and Helen Hunt Jackson as well as many often neglected women poets.

Walker, Robert H. *The Poet and the Gilded Age: Social Themes in Nineteenth Century Verse.* Hippocrene Bks. 1969 $27.50. ISBN 0-374-98170-1. Examines the image of America that emerges from the serious, humorous, and didactic verse of major and minor poets of the Gilded Age.

Wallace, Ronald. *God Be with the Clown: Humor in American Poetry.* U. of Mo. Pr. 1984 $27.50. ISBN 0-8262-0422-8. Defines and discusses the theory of the often guarded area of humor in American poetry.

Collections

Allen, Gay W. *American Poetry.* HarpC 1965 o.p. An "impressive volume" of nearly 700 poems from colonial times to the present day, including the much neglected poets Jones Very and Frederick Tuckerman; ". . . sown with a full and generous hand, so the variety and the striking originality of the period's poetry . . . are brilliantly displayed" (*New Yorker*).

Bontemps, Arna, ed. *American Negro Poetry.* Hill & Wang rev. ed. 1974 o.p. Selections from more than 55 poets including Amiri Baraka (LeRoi Jones), Richard Wright, and Langston Hughes, with biographical notes.

Cronyn, George W. *The Path on the Rainbow: An Anthology of Songs and Chants from the Indians of North America.* Arden Lib. 1977 repr. of 1918 ed. o.p.

————, ed. *American Indian Poetry: An Anthology of Songs and Chants.* Fawcett 1992 $10.00. ISBN 0-449-90670-1

Ehrenpreis, Irvin, ed. *American Poetry: Texts & Meanings.* P. Lang Pubs. 1989 $43.80. ISBN 3-631-40652-5

Ellmann, Richard, ed. *The New Oxford Book of American Verse.* OUP 1976 $39.95. ISBN 0-19-502058-8

Gelpi, Albert. *The Poet in America, 1650 to Present*. Heath 1973 o.p.

Halpern, Daniel, ed. *The American Poetry Anthology*. Avon 1976 $9.95. ISBN 0-380-00399-6

Harshaw, Benjamin, and Barbara Harshaw, eds. *American Yiddish Poetry*. Intro. and trans. by Heinz J. Vienken and Daniel Albright. U. CA Pr. 1986 $60.00. ISBN 0-520-04842-3. Includes generous selections from seven important authors.

Hughes, Langston, and Arna Bontemps, eds. *Poetry of the Negro, 1746–1970*. Doubleday 1970 o.p. Contains the works of 147 black poets from prerevolutionary to modern times.

Johnson, James Weldon, ed. *The Book of American Negro Poetry*. HarBraceJ rev. ed. 1969 $10.95. ISBN 0-15-613539-6. Forty writers—biographical and critical sketches.

Matthiessen, F. O., ed. *Oxford Book of American Verse*. OUP 1950 $45.00. ISBN 0-19-500049-8. Fifty-one poets in this excellent anthology from the earlier *Oxford Book of American Verse*, compiled by Bliss Carman in 1927.

Philip, Neil, ed. *A New Treasury of Poetry*. Stewart Tabori & Chang 1990 $25.00. ISBN 1-55670-145-4. Good representation of poetry, including much from this period.

Phillips, Louis, ed. *Random House Treasury of Best Loved Poems*. Random 1990 $9.95. ISBN 0-394-58688-3. Collection of well-known and highly readable works.

Roth Publishing, Inc., Staff, eds. *World's Best Poetry*, Supplement IV. Roth Pub. Inc. 1987 $49.95. ISBN 0-89609-265-8. Includes African American, Native American, and Mexican American poets.

Sherman, Joan R., ed. *Collected Black Women's Poetry. The Schomburg Library of Nineteenth-Century Black Women Writers*. OUP 1988 $29.95. ISBN 0-19-505254-4

Stetson, Erlene, ed. *Black Sister: Poetry by Black American Women, 1746–1980*. Ind. U. Pr. 1981 $29.95. ISBN 0-253-30512-8

Sullivan, Nancy, ed. *The Treasury of American Poetry: A Collection of the Finest by America's Poets*. Doubleday 1978 $21.50. ISBN 0-385-12032-X

Symons, A. J. *An Anthology of Nineties' Verse*. Rprt. Serv. 1988 $49.00. ISBN 0-7812-0044-X

Turner, Frederick W., III, ed. *The Portable North American Indian Reader*. *Viking Portable Lib*. Viking Penguin 1977 $12.00. ISBN 0-14-015077-3. Contains an impressive and discriminating selection of Native American poetry.

Turner, Michael R. *Victorian Parlour Poetry: An Annotated Anthology*. Dover 1992 $9.95. ISBN 0-486-27044-0. Original title: *Parlour Poetry: A Casquet of Gems*. Popular poetry of the period.

Untermeyer, Louis. *An Anthology of the New England Poets from Colonial Times to the Present Day*. Random 1948. o.p. Thirty-three poets from Anne Bradstreet to Robert Lowell, with valuable biographical and critical comments—liberal representation of Longfellow.

Walker, Cheryl, ed. *American Women Poets of the Nineteenth-Century: An Anthology*. *Amer. Women Writers Ser*. Rutgers U. Pr. 1992 $45.00. ISBN 0-8135-1790-7. Volume of 27 women poets including minorities and writers from the Far West.

Whicher, Stephen, and Lars Ahnebrink, eds. *Twelve American Poets*. OUP 1961 o.p. A discriminating selection of poems by Longfellow, Poe, Whitman, Dickenson, and others.

FICTION

By far the most popular type of literature produced during the last half of the nineteenth century was fiction—from sketches and short stories to novellas and novels. Improved printing processes increased the number of available newspapers, magazines, and books. The spread of education expanded both the size and the diversity of the reading public. Reading became both popular entertainment and intellectual enlightenment. Factory workers read dime novels; middle-class women read best-sellers and domestic fiction; "cultured" readers, directed by editors of such magazines as *Harper's Monthly, Atlantic Monthly,* and *The Century,* valued the arts and "high-brow" literature. In short, fiction flourished at least in part because writers of all types could finally make a living from their craft. At the same time, however, they tried to use their art not to romanticize or to idealize, but to represent their age realistically.

Easterner HENRY JAMES and Westerner MARK TWAIN, linked and led by their mutual Midwestern friend WILLIAM DEAN HOWELLS, mark the extremes of the new literary realism and exemplify the diversity of its development in American literature. Between the psychological realism, sophisticated language, and international novels of James and the down-to-earth folk humor, colloquial language, and adventure stories of Twain, lay the many regional writers and realists of this period. After the Civil War, Americans read stories not just to see the reflection of their own lives, but to satisfy their curiosity about other parts of their nation. JOHN WILLIAM DE FOREST and Albion Tourgée realistically described the South of the Civil War and the Reconstruction. MARY WILKINS FREEMAN and SARAH ORNE JEWETT depicted the hardships of rural New England life, while GEORGE WASHINGTON CABLE, Grace King, and KATE CHOPIN told Creole stories set in New Orleans. Mary Murfree recalled the hills of Tennessee; Edith and Maud Eaton wrote of the Chinese American experience in California; BRET HARTE and HELEN HUNT JACKSON told tales and romances of the West; HAMLIN GARLAND and Edward Eggleston filled in the center with Midwestern scenes; and CONSTANCE FENIMORE WOOLSON turned her travels from Michigan to Florida into stories set in the places she visited.

Other writers translated the reality of their experiences of gender, ethnicity, and race into fiction. CHARLOTTE PERKINS GILMAN's and LOUISA MAY ALCOTT's stories revealed the problems of women in a patriarchal society. ABRAHAM CAHAN described the Jewish American immigrant experience in New York ghettos. And African American writers—FRANCES HARPER, CHARLES WADDELL CHESNUTT, GEORGE WASHINGTON HARRIS, and JAMES WELDON JOHNSON—recorded the trials of their race, though many found it more lucrative to satisfy white readers' preference for humor and dialect tales like those of white writer JOEL CHANDLER HARRIS than to challenge racial attitudes in serious fiction.

Late in the century, as writers described life in the cities, the effects of industrialization, and confrontations with the environment, they found that these subjects could not be honestly treated with Howell's brand of optimistic realism. Therefore, they moved toward the more deterministic mode of naturalism. REBECCA HARDING DAVIS had early described the harsh conditions of factory life, but STEPHEN CRANE, THEODORE DREISER, EDITH WHARTON, FRANK NORRIS, AMBROSE BIERCE, and JACK LONDON went further in looking at the grimmer side of existence. Their fiction revealed the materialistic goals of American society and the moral bankruptcy at its core. Finally, the very success of the literary periodicals that led to the growth of American fiction increased its commercialization, as new magazines kept their prices down by selling advertising space and by using their stories to "sell" the market economy to readers. Some writers were rejected by editors and readers who were not prepared to accept their grim, naturalistic visions; other writers refused to compromise their art by selling to popular magazines. Still others managed to maintain their integrity through both popular and critical success.

Having started from opposite extremes of the literary spectrum, Twain and James both entered the twentieth century bitter and disillusioned about American society and the human condition. As the naturalists showed, the nineteenth-century promise of progress was not fulfilled. Twain's late fiction

became increasingly cynical; some of it was too dark to publish during his
lifetime. James left America altogether and settled in England. His monumental
last novels focus on abstract moral decisions made by characters too remote
from life to "live." Fiction had finally confronted the century that would test the
value of art as a constructive and salutary influence in American life.

History and Criticism

Barbour, James, and Tom Quirk. *Writing the American Classics*. U. of NC Pr. 1990 $39.95.
ISBN 0-8078-4280-X. Collection of essays describing the genesis, composition, and
publication of 10 classic American novels.

Bardes, Barbara, and Suzanne Gossett. *Declarations of Independence: Women and
Political Power in Nineteenth-Century American Fiction*. Rutgers U. Pr. 1990 $36.00.
ISBN 0-8135-1500-9. Examines nineteenth-century fiction as it reflected and
influenced society's attitudes toward women's independence; considers neglected
authors and texts.

Bartlett, Irving H. *The American Mind in the Mid-Nineteenth Century*. The Amer. History
Ser. Davidson 1982 ISBN 0-88295-809-7. Examines the influences on writers of the
period.

Baym, Nina. *Women's Fiction. A Guide to Novels By and About Women in America,
1820–1870*. Cornell Univ. Pr. 1978. o.p. A study of fiction that previous critics had
dismissed as trivial or sentimental, but that Baym reevaluates.

Bell, Bernard W. *The Afro-American Novel and Its Tradition*. U. of Mass. Pr. 1987 $32.50.
ISBN 0-87023-568-0. Overview of major and minor African American novels from
the origin of the tradition to the present, noting the double consciousness of African
American experience evident in fiction.

Bewley, Marius. *The Eccentric Design: Form in the Classic American Novel*. Col. U. Pr.
1959 o.p. Able criticism of James, Hawthorne, Cooper, Melville, and Fitzgerald.

Bone, Robert. *Down Home: A History of Afro-American Short Fiction from Its Beginning to
the End of the Harlem Renaissance*. Col. U. Pr. 1988 $54.00. ISBN 0-231-06858-1.
Emphasizes relationship between short fiction and oral tradition.

Cady, Edwin H. *Light of Common Day: Realism in American Fiction*. Ind. U. Pr. 1971 o.p.
A scholarly discussion of the problem of realism and naturalism in writers from
Hawthorne to James; interesting and readable.

Chase, Richard. *The American Novel and Its Tradition*. Johns Hopkins 1980 $12.95. ISBN
0-8018-2303-X. A discussion of major American novels in light of Chase's carefully
worked out thesis that our best novelists have written novel-romances that express
the contradictions in American life rather than the unities.

Coultrap-McQuin, Susan. *Doing Literary Business: American Women Writers in the
Nineteenth Century*. Gender and Amer. Culture Ser. U. of NC Pr. 1990 $29.95. ISBN 0-
8078-1914-X. Focuses on the careers of five literary women and their relationship to
their publishers.

Cowie, Alexander. *The Rise of the American Novel*. Amer. Lit. Ser. Am. Bk. Pubs. 1948 o.p.
Chronological critical history of the development of the American novel during the
eighteenth and nineteenth centuries; dated but still useful, especially for minor
novelists.

Davis, David B. *Homicide in American Fiction, 1798–1860: A Study in Social Values*.
Cornell Univ. Pr. 1968 $12.95. ISBN 0-8014-9066-9. Primarily a study of the early
nineteenth century, but also touches on modern fiction; bibliography and analytical
index.

Denning, Michael. *Mechanic Accents: Dime Novels and Working-Class Culture in
America*. Routledge Chapman & Hall 1987 $39.95. ISBN 0-86091-178-0. Cultural
history and criticism of nineteenth-century popular fiction, including discussions of
writers, publishers, and working-class readers.

Donovan, Josephine. *New England Local Color Literature: A Women's Tradition.* Continuum 1988 $12.95. ISBN 0-8264-0415-4. Examines the influence of New England's people and landscape on women's writing.

Gaston, Edwin W., Jr. *The Early Novel of the Southwest, 1819–1918.* U. of NM Pr. 1961 o.p. A valuable critical study of southwestern fiction of the period, with synopses of the 40 novels discussed and biographical sketches of the authors.

Harris, Susan K. *Nineteenth-Century American Women's Novels: Interpretive Strategies. Studies in Amer. Lit. & Culture.* Cambridge U. Pr. 1990 $39.95. ISBN 0-521-38288-2. Study of both didactic and subversive texts, analyzing social and political implications of plot and style; well documented.

Hilfer, Anthony C. *The Ethics of Intensity in American Fiction.* U. of Tex. Pr. 1981 $22.50. ISBN 0-292-72029-7. Traces the conflict between moral codes imposed from without and the individual's need for emotional self-expression as reflected in fiction by James, Dreiser, Stein, and others.

Holman, C. Hugh. *The American Novel Through Henry James. Goldentree Bib. in Lang. & Lit.* Harlan Davidson 1979. ISBN 0-88295-576-4. Texts, bibliographies, and criticism of 42 novelists.

Howard, June. *Form and History in American Literary Naturalism.* NC U. Pr. 1985 $24.95. ISBN 0-8078-1650-7. Uses contemporary literary theory to redefine naturalism.

Howard, Leon. *Literature and the American Tradition.* Gordian 1972 repr. of 1960 ed. $40.00. ISBN 0-87752-156-5. An examination of the formation of our literary individuality.

Jones, Howard M. *History and the Contemporary: Essays in Nineteenth-Century Literature.* Bks. Demand repr. of 1964 ed. $47.90. ISBN 0-8357-6142-8. Collections of essays by an influential scholar.

Kaplan, Amy. *The Social Construction of American Realism.* U. Ch. Pr. 1988 $24.95. ISBN 0-226-42429-4. Thorough analysis of several classic examples of literary realism balancing conventional definitions with explorations of the deconstructive tendencies of the texts.

Kazin, Alfred. *On Native Grounds: An Interpretation of Modern American Prose Literature.* HarBraceJ 1983 o.p. Brilliant and penetrating literary history of the "relation between American prose and our developing society in the years between 1890 and the present" (*New Yorker*); highly recommended.

Kinney, James. *Amalgamation: Race, Sex, and Rhetoric in the Nineteenth Century American Novel. Contributions in Afro-American & African Studies.* Greenwood 1985 $45.00. ISBN 0-313-25064-2. Study of 63 American novels that treat the subject of interracial relationships.

Kolb, Harold H., Jr. *Illusion of Life: American Realism as a Literary Form.* U. Pr. of Va. 1969 o.p. Clearly written, with a new definition of realism.

Lee, Brian. *American Fiction, Eighteen Sixty-Five to Nineteen Forty. Lit. in Eng. Ser.* Longman 1987 $41.95. ISBN 0-582-49317-X. Introductory survey.

Lee, Robert, ed. *The Nineteenth-Century American Short Story.* B&N Imports 1986 $28.50. ISBN 0-389-20593-1. Fresh perspectives from collection of essays by European scholars of American literature or American Studies.

Lenz, William E. *Fast Talk and Flush Times: The Confidence Man as a Literary Convention.* U. of Mo. Pr. 1985 $26.00. ISBN 0-8262-0450-3. Looks at America's version of the "archetypal trickster," the confidence man, in popular literature and culture.

Martine, James J., ed. *American Novelists.* Gale 1986 $109.00. ISBN 0-8103-2225-0

Michaels, Walter B. *The Gold Standard and the Logic of Naturalism: American Literature at the Turn of the Century.* U. of CA Pr. 1987 $37.50. ISBN 0-520-05982-4. Theoretical discussion of the influence of the marketplace on writers' conceptions of identity.

Mitchell, Lee C. *Determined Fictions: American Literary Naturalism.* Col. U. Pr. 1989 $35.00. ISBN 0-231-06898-0. Discussion of major works of naturalistic writing focusing on the rhetorical style that undermines the notion of an autonomous self.

Pattee, Fred L. *The Development of the American Short Story: An Historical Survey. BCL1-PS Amer. Lit. Ser.* Rprt. Serv. 1992 $89.00. ISBN 0-7812-6638-6. A study of the form as used by writers from Irving through O. Henry.

Payne, Ladel. *Black Novelists and the Southern Literary Tradition.* U. of Ga. Pr. 1981 o.p. Examines common themes and narrative techniques in works of Charles Chesnutt, James Weldon Johnson, and later African American writers.

Pfaelzer, Jean. *The Utopian Novel in America, 1886–1896: The Politics of Form.* U. of Pittsburgh Pr. 1989 $11.95. ISBN 0-8229-5413-3. Considerations of feminist dystopias and utopias as well as the utopian visions of Howells and Bellamy.

Pizer, Donald. *Realism and Naturalism in Nineteenth-Century American Literature.* S. Ill. U. Pr. rev. ed. 1984 $19.95. ISBN 0-8093-1125-9. Classic study of major trends in nineteenth-century literature; the revised edition adds six new essays.

Ringe, Donald A. *American Gothic: Imagination and Reason in Nineteenth Century Fiction.* U. Pr. of Ky. 1982 o.p. A useful survey of the important writers of the period.

Romines, Ann. *The Home Plot: Women, Writing and Domestic Ritual.* U. of Mass. Pr. 1992 $45.00. ISBN 0-87023-783-7. Studies of Stowe, Jewett, Freeman, and others who call attention to the female legacy of domestic ritual.

Scheick, William J. *The Half-Blood: A Cultural Symbol in Nineteenth-Century American Fiction.* U. Pr. of Ky. 1979 $11.00. ISBN 0-8131-1390-3. An interesting account of the creation of mixed-race characters in popular and serious novels.

See, Fred G. *Desire and the Sign: Nineteenth-Century American Fiction.* La. State U. Pr. 1987 $30.00. ISBN 0-8071-1313-1. Focuses on the shift from romanticism to realism and the literary "signs" associated with desire in the work of Harriet Beecher Stowe, Rebecca Harding Davis, and W. D. Howells.

Shapiro, Ann R. *Unlikely Heroines: Nineteenth-Century Women Writers and the Woman Question. Contributions in Women's Studies.* Greenwood 1987 $42.95. ISBN 0-313-25422-2. Basic introduction to issues treated in nineteenth-century American women's novels, finding that "true womanhood" is often rejected in favor of freedom and equality.

Slotkin, Richard. *The Fatal Environment: The Myth of the Frontier in the Age of Industrialization, 1800–1890.* U. Pr. of New Eng. 1986 $22.95. ISBN 0-8195-6183-5. New historical approach tracing writers' uses of the frontier myth.

Stein, Allen F. *After the Vows Were Spoken: Marriage in American Literary Realism.* Ohio St. U. Pr. 1985 $22.50. ISBN 0-8142-0382-5. Investigation of the treatment of marriage by such writers as James, Wharton, Howells, and Chopin.

Sundquist, Eric J. *American Realism: New Essays.* Johns Hopkins 1982 $27.50. ISBN 0-8018-2796-5. Brings together critical discussions of James, Crane, Norris, Wharton, Dreiser, and other novelists.

Taylor, Helen. *Gender, Race and Region in the Writings of Grace King, Ruth McEnery Stuart, and Kate Chopin. Southern Literary Studies.* La. State U. Pr. 1989 $32.50. ISBN 0-8071-1445-6. Sees differences of race and class as more important than gender in selected Southern women writers.

Tuttleton, James W. *The Novel of Manners in America.* Norton 1974 $3.45. ISBN 0-393-00717-0. Analysis of social background of the novel of manners, discussing James, Wharton, and more recent novelists.

Voss, Arthur. *The American Short Story: A Critical Survey.* U. of Okla. Pr. 1980 $14.95. ISBN 0-8061-1644-7. A good general introduction.

Wagenknecht, Edward. *Cavalcade of the American Novel from the Birth of the Nation to the Middle of the Twentieth Century.* H. Holt & Co. 1952 o.p. A comprehensive overview of the novel in the United States.

Walcutt, Charles Child. *American Literary Naturalism, A Divided Stream.* Greenwood 1974 $38.50. ISBN 0-8371-7017-6. Traces naturalism to the influence of transcendentalism and its "divided" romantic and scientific impulses.

Warren, Joyce W. *The American Narcissus: Individualism and Women in Nineteenth-Century American Fiction.* Rutgers U. Pr. 1989 $15.00. ISBN 0-8135-1495-9. Posits that because women were defined as the "other" in nineteenth-century society, their characterizations in literature were weak.

————, ed. *The Other American Traditions: Nineteenth-Century Women Writers.* Rutgers U. Pr. 1993 $45.00. ISBN 0-8135-1911-X

White, Barbara. *American Women's Fiction, 1790–1870: A Reference Guide.* Garland 1989 $48.00. ISBN 0-8240-6673-1. Annotated bibliography of American women writers and list of sources discussing their fiction. Useful for finding material on minor writers.

Woodress, James, ed. *Eight American Authors: A Review of Research and Criticism.* Norton rev. ed. 1972 o.p. Survey of critical research on major authors including Twain and James; useful for reviewing criticism before 1970.

Wright, Lyle H. *American Fiction: A Contribution Towards a Bibliography.* 3 vols. Huntington Lib. 1969–79 $48.00. ISBN 0-87328-043-1. Bibliographies of American editions of prose for adults by Americans printed between 1774 and 1900.

Yancy, Preston M. *The Afro-American Short Story: A Comprehensive, Annotated Index with Selected Commentaries. Bib. & Indexes in Afro-Amer. & Afr. Studies.* Greenwood 1986 $39.95. ISBN 0-313-24355-7

Ziff, Larzer. *The American 1890's: Life and Times of a Lost Generation.* U. of New Eng. Pr. 1979 o.p. Full picture of turn–of–the–century America and the writers who recorded, reflected, and reacted to it.

Zuckert, Catherine H. *Natural Right and the American Imagination: Political Philosophy in Novel Form.* Rowman 1990 $48.00. ISBN 0-8476-7611-0. Examines traditional canon as it comments on and explores the relationship between the individual and society.

Collections

American Short Stories of the Nineteenth Century. Everyman 1967 o.p.

Antler, Joyce, ed. *America and I: Short Stories by American Jewish Women Writers.* Beacon Pr. 1991 $12.95. ISBN 0-8070-3607-2

Barksdale, Richard, and Kenneth Kinnamon. *Black Writers of America: A Comprehensive Anthology.* Macmillan 1972. ISBN 0-02-30608-0

Bellow, Saul, ed. *Great Jewish Short Stories.* Dell 1985 $5.99. ISBN 0-440-33122-6

Botkin, B. A., ed. *Civil War Treasury of Tales.* Amereon Ltd. $31.95. ISBN 0-88411-860-6

Current-Garcia, Eugene, and Bert Hitchcock. *American Short Stories.* Scott F. 1990 $20.95. ISBN 0-673-38568-X. Collection of stories from early to contemporary, including a representative selection from the realistic and naturalistic periods.

Davis, Arthur P., and Joyce A. Joyce, eds. *The New Cavalcade I: African American Writing.* Howard U. Pr. 1991 $32.95. ISBN 0-88258-133-3. Short stories and essays.

Dick, Everett. *Tales of the Frontier: From Lewis and Clark to the Last Roundup.* U. of Nebr. Pr. 1963 $35.00. ISBN 0-8032-5744-9. Collections of tales about the frontier experience by little known writers.

Gates, Louis, ed. *Three Classic African-American Novels.* Vin. 1990 $15.00. ISBN 0-679-72742-6. Includes William Wells Brown's *Clotelle*, Charles Chesnutt's *The Marrow of Tradition*, and Frances E. Harper's *Iola Leroy.*

Mossell, N. F. *The Work of the Afro-American Woman. Schomburg Lib. of Nineteenth-Century Black Women Writers.* OUP 1990 $21.00. ISBN 0-19-506326-0. Essays describing and celebrating the accomplishments of nineteenth century African American women educators, writers, composers, missionaries, and business women.

Peyer, Bernd, ed. *The Singing Spirit: Early Short Stories by North American Indians. Sun Tracks Ser.* U. of Ariz. Pr. 1990 $24.95. ISBN 0-8165-1114-4. Collection of fiction from 1860 to 1930 including biography and bibliography for each author.

Skaggs, Calvin, ed. *The American Short Story.* Dell 1980 $5.95. ISBN 0-440-30297-8

Stegner, Wallace, and Mary Stegner, eds. *Great American Short Stories.* Dell 1985 $5.95. ISBN 0-440-33060-2

Stories by American Authors. 10 vols. in 5. Irvington 1972 repr. of 1884 ed. $150.00. ISBN 0-685-36668-5. An anthology of American short fiction edited by the staff of Charles Scribner's Sons during the 1880s.

NONFICTION

Nonfiction writing of the last half of the nineteenth spans vastly different types of writing, from the intensely private entries in ALICE JAMES's diary and the personal picture of the Confederacy recorded by MARY BOYKIN MILLER CHESTNUT to the philosophical essays of WILLIAM JAMES, JOSIAH ROYCE (see Vol. 4), CHARLES SANDERS PEIRCE (see Vol. 4), and GEORGE SANTAYANA (see Vol. 4). Nonfiction encompasses the economic theories of THORSTEIN VEBLEN (see also Vol. 3) and CHARLOTTE PERKINS GILMAN, JANE ADDAMS's sociological accounts of Chicago settlement houses, and HENRY ADAMS's public and personal histories. It also includes journalism, travel sketches, essays, critical reviews, and literary theory—the Harper's "Editor's Easy Chair" columns of WILLIAM DEAN HOWELLS, the New York Edition Prefaces of HENRY JAMES, and FRANK NORRIS's essays on naturalism.

Autobiography is another major category of late nineteenth-century American nonfiction. Some autobiographies of the time inform readers of the struggles of a particular ethnic group or culture. CHARLES A. EASTMAN's *Indian Boyhood*, SARAH WINNEMUCCA HOPKINS's *Life Among the Piutes*, and MARY AUSTIN's *Earth Horizon* make use of the legends and traditions of Native American cultures. BOOKER T. WASHINGTON's inspirational *Up from Slavery* and W.E.B. DuBois's response, *The Souls of Black Folk*, follow the autobiographical tradition of BENJAMIN FRANKLIN and FREDERICK DOUGLASS. Other autobiographies, like those of Howells, TWAIN, JAMES, and WHARTON, are memoirs—frankly subjective remembrances of incidents selected, perhaps, to control or shape a reputation. Whatever their intent or the result, autobiographies provide both general readers and literary scholars with valuable perspectives about a writer's life and work.

Most writers of this period also wrote numerous letters, many of which have been collected, edited, and published. Rooted in the centuries-old tradition of the art of personal correspondence, these, too, are clearly literature. The correspondence between professional writers is usually interesting and entertaining and often less contrived than autobiography. See particularly the lifelong exchange between Twain and Howells, selections from the voluminous James family correspondence, and the cryptic letters of EMILY DICKINSON. Invaluable sources for critics and literary biographers, letters provide details of everyday life and relationships and allow readers to penetrate a writer's sensibility.

Technically not of the period, literary biographies make extensive use of nonfiction sources, frequently reprinting them. The discovery of new material and the release of previously restricted papers, as well as the development of new critical theories, prompt scholars continually to revise and reinterpret their notions of writers' lives. Ideally, biographers will not merely amass details but will capture the essence of the subject's life and transform it through considerations of personality, psychology, history, and culture into a comprehensive narrative that enables readers to better understand the author, the works, and the time.

History and Criticism

American Literary Critics and Scholars, 1880–1900. Dict. of Lit. Biog. Ser. Vol. 71. Gale 1988 $112.00. ISBN 0-8103-1749-4. Overview of period as well as individual entries.

Couser, G. Thomas. *Altered Egos: Authority in American Autobiography*. OUP 1989 $34.00. ISBN 0-19-505833-X. Notes the difficulty for autobiographers to relate their life stories accurately, but recommends evaluating them on their own terms

Cox, James M. *Recovering Literature's Lost Ground: Essays in American Autobiography*. La. State U. Pr. 1989 $30.00. ISBN 0-8071-1491-X. Covers classic American autobiographies of R.H. Dana, U.S. Grant, Henry James, and Henry Adams.

Culley, Margo, ed. *American Women's Autobiography: Fea(s)ts of Memory*. U. of Wis. Pr. 1992 $42.50. ISBN 0-299-13290-0. Studies of women's autobiographies.

Dawidoff, Robert. *The Genteel Tradition and the Sacred Rage: High Culture vs. Democracy in Adams, James, and Santayana. Cultural Studies of the U.S.* U. of NC Pr. 1992 $32.50. ISBN 0-8078-2017-2. Historical and literary study of the American experience of the split between democracy and intellectualism.

Eakin, Paul J., ed. *American Autobiography: Retrospect and Prospect*. U. of Wis. Pr. 1991 $42.50. ISBN 0-299-12784-2. Collection of essays on American autobiography over four centuries, including those of immigrant, Native American, African American, and women writers.

Edel, Leon. *Writing Lives: Principia Biographica*. 1984 Norton 1987 $15.95. ISBN 0-393-30382-9. Explores the theory and practice of writing literary biographies, especially the relationship between the biographer and the subject.

Fichtelberg, Joseph. *The Complex Image: Faith and Method in American Autobiography*. U. of Pa. Pr. 1989 $28.95. ISBN 0-8122-8146-2. Overview of autobiography, paying particular attention to the role of revision in constructing the "self."

Kagle, Stephen E. *Late Nineteenth-Century American Diary Literature. U.S. Authors Ser.* Macmillan 1988 $22.95. ISBN 0-8057-7504-8. Discussion of nineteenth-century diary literature by Alice James, Richard Henry Dana, and a range of others, chronicling experiences such as Western travel, the Civil War, and transcendentalism.

Krupat, Arnold. *For Those Who Come After: A Study of Native American Autobiography*. U. CA Pr. 1985 $14.95. ISBN 0-520-05307-9. Essays describing Native American autobiographies with attention to correcting the traditional biases of Euro-American editors.

Lee, A. Robert, ed. *First Person Singular: Studies in American Autobiography*. St. Martin 1988 $35.00. ISBN 0-312-02425-8. Considers American autobiography from William Bradford through Norman Mailer.

Partridge, Elinor Hughes. *American Prose and Criticism, 1820–1900: A Guide to Information Sources*. Gale 1983 $68.00. ISBN 0-8103-1213-1. Lists both primary and secondary materials relating to the various modes of nonfiction prose writing in the United States.

Payne, William M. *Leading American Essayists: Biographies of Leading Americans*. Ayer repr. of 1910 ed. $25.50. ISBN 0-8369-0778-7. Somewhat pedestrian but useful biographical sketches of prose writers.

West, Cornel. *The American Evasion of Philosophy: A Genealogy of Pragmatism. Wisconsin Project on American Writers Ser.* U. of Wis. Pr. 1989 $42.50. ISBN 0-299-11960-2. Discusses Emerson, Peirce, W. James, Dewey, and later philosophers, seeing pragmatism as America's most important form of cultural criticism.

Collections

Andrews, William L., ed. *Sisters of the Spirit: Three Black Women's Autobiographies of the Nineteenth Century*. Ind. U. Pr. 1986 $29.95. ISBN 0-253-35260-6. Contains autobiographies of Jarena Lee, Zilpha Elaw, and Julia Foote, all of whom wrote and preached with the purpose of enlightening others about Christ.

Barthelemy, Anthony G., ed. *Collected Black Women's Narratives. Schomburg Lib. of Nineteenth-Century Black Women Writers*. OUP 1990 $10.95. ISBN 0-19-50669-3

Brewer, David J., ed. *The World's Best Essays from the Earliest Period to the Present Time*. 10 vols. Arden Lib. of 1982 repr. of 1900 ed. o.p.

Bronson, Walter C., ed. *American Prose*. Ayer repr. of 1916 ed. $32.00. ISBN 0-888369-3481-4. Includes speeches and essays by prominent writers and orators of the period.

Culley, Margo, ed. *One Day at a Time: The Diary Literature of American Women from 1764 to the Present.* Feminist Pr. 1985 $35.00. ISBN 0-935312-51-X. Excerpts of diaries of "ordinary" American women from different social classes, regions, and periods.

Griswold, Rufus W. *Prose Writers of America.* Irvington 1986 $7.95. ISBN 0-8290-1870-0

Gross, John, ed. *Oxford Book of Essays.* OUP 1991 $30.00. ISBN 0-19-214185-6. Includes several classic essays of the late nineteenth century.

Howard, John R., ed. *Best American Essays.* Ayer repr. of 1910 ed. $21.50. ISBN 0-8369-1140-7. Attempts to be representative of the best American essays in its selection.

Moore, John R., ed. *Representative Essays: English and American.* Ayer repr. of 1930 ed. $20.00. ISBN 0-8369-2808-3. Similar to Howard's anthology but also includes British essays.

Priestley, John B., ed. *Essayists Past and Present. Essay Index Repr. Ser.* Ayer repr. of 1925 ed. $18.00. ISBN 0-8369-0802-3

Pritchard, Francis H., ed. *The World's Best Essays.* Norwood repr. of 1929 ed. o.p.

Sampson, George, ed. *Nineteenth-Century Essays. Essay Index Repr. Ser.* Ayer repr. of 1912 ed. o.p.

Smithberger, Andrew T., ed. *Essays: British and American.* Greenwood repr. of 1953 ed. o.p.

CHRONOLOGY OF AUTHORS

Tuckerman, Frederick Goddard. 1821–1873

Chesnut, Mary Boykin Miller. 1823–1886

Harper, Frances E(llen) W(atkins). 1825–1911

De Forest, John Willima. 1826–1903

Timrod, Henry. 1828–1867

Dickinson, Emily. 1830–1886

Davis, Rebecca Harding. 1831–1910

Jackson, Helen Maria Hunt. 1831–1885

Twain, Mark. 1835–1910

Aldrich, Thomas Bailey. 1836–1907

Harte, Bret(t). 1836?–1902

Howells, William Dean. 1837–1920

Adams, Henry. 1838–1918

Woolson, Constance Fenimore. 1840–1894

Bierce, Ambrose. 1842–1914?

James, William. 1842–1910

Lanier, Sidney. 1842–1881

James, Henry. 1843–1916

Cable, George Washington. 1844–1925

Harris, Joel Chandler. 1848–1908

James, Alice. 1848–1892

Jewett, Sarah Orne. 1949–1909

Lazarus, Emma. 1849–1887

Riley, James Whitcomb. 1849–1916

Bellamy, Edward. 1850–1898

Chopin, Kate. 1851–1904

Freeman, Mary Eleanor. 1852–1930

Washington, Booker T(aliaferro). 1856–1915

Chesnutt, Charles Wadell. 1858–1932

Eastman, Charles A. 1858–1939

Addams, Jane. 1860–1935

Cahan, Abraham. 1860–1951

Garland, Hamlin. 1860–1940

Gilman, Charlotte Perkins. 1860–1935

Wister, Owen. 1860–1938

Henry, O. 1862–1910

Wharton, Edith. 1862–1937

Austin, Mary. 1868–1934

Moody, William Vaughn. 1869–1910

Norris, Frank(lin). 1870–1902

Crane, Stephen. 1871–1900

Johnson, James Weldon. 1871–1938

London, Jack. 1876–1916

ADAMS, HENRY (BROOKS). 1838–1918

Adams was born in Boston, the son of American diplomat Charles Francis Adams and grandson of President John Quincy Adams. Educated at Harvard,

Adams worked in Washington, D.C. as his father's secretary before embarking on careers in journalism and then teaching. A prominent American historian, he wrote several important historical works.

Adams's autobiography, *The Education of Henry Adams* (1907), might be called the story of an education and the recovery from it, although the writer felt that he never in fact recovered. The reader should contrast Adams's earlier work, *Mont-Saint-Michel and Chartres* (privately printed 1904, published 1913), a study of thirteenth-century unity, with the *Education*, a study of twentieth-century multiplicity. It is the multiplicity of modern life, says Adams, that makes education so destructive.

Henry Adams wrote two novels, *Esther* (1884), and the earlier cutting satire on the U.S. government, *Democracy: An American Novel* (1880). In 1905 President THEODORE ROOSEVELT (see Vol. 3) called *Democracy* "that novel which made a great furor among the educated incompetents and the pessimists generally. . . . It had a superficial and rotten cleverness, but it was essentially false, essentially mean and base, and it is amusing to read it now and see how completely events have given it the lie."

NOVELS BY ADAMS

Democracy: An American Novel. 1880. Ed. by Peter Katopes. NCUP 1991 $8.95. ISBN 0-8084-0430-X. Originally published anonymously.

Esther. 1884. Ed. by Robert Spiller. Schol. Facsimiles 1976 $50.00. ISBN 0-8201-1187-2. Originally published under the pseudonym Frances Snow Compton.

Novels, Mont-Saint-Michel, The Education. Ed. by Ernest Samuels and Jayne N. Samuels. Library of America. 1983 $27.50. ISBN 0-940450-12-7. Includes *Democracy, Esther, Mont-Saint-Michel and Chartres, The Education of Henry Adams.*

NONFICTION BY ADAMS

The Correspondence of Henry James and Henry Adams, 1877–1914. Ed. by George Monteiro. La. State U. Pr. 1992 $20.00. ISBN 0-8071-1729-3. Collection of 36 letters (29 from James) illuminating the correspondents, their rivalry and friendship, and the times.

A Cycle of Adams Letters (1861–1865). 2 vols. in 1. Ed. by Worthington C. Ford. Kraus repr. of 1920 ed. o.p. A collection of letters between Adams and his family.

Education of Henry Adams. 1906. *Vintage-Lib. of Amer. Ser.* Random 1990 $14.50. ISBN 0-679-73232-2

Henry Adams and His Friends: A Collection of His Unpublished Letters. Ed. by Harold D. Cater. Hippocrene Bks. repr. of 1970 ed. o.p. A collection of 650 unpublished letters to many different people, edited with a biographical and interpretive introduction by Harold Dean Cater.

Henry Adams: Selected Letters. Ed. by Ernest Samuels. HUP 1992 $29.95. ISBN 0-674-38757-0. Letters illustrating the consistency of Adams's philosophy throughout his life.

History of the U.S. During the Administrations of Jefferson and Madison. 1889–91. Ed. by Earl Harbert. Library of America 1986 $27.50. ISBN 0-840450-35-6. Monumental nine volume study of the United States' transition from European domination to American expansion.

Letters of Henry Adams. 2 vols. Ed. by Worthington C. Ford. Kraus repr. of 1930 ed. o.p.

The Letters of Henry Adams, 1858–1892. Vols. 1–3. Ed. by J. C. Levenson and others. HUP 1983 $150.00. ISBN 0-674-52685-6. Annotated and edited first three volumes of Adam's complete correspondence.

The Letters of Henry Adams: Eighteen Ninety-Two to Nineteen Eighteen. Vols. 4–6. Ed. by Ernest Samuels, Charles Vandersee, and Viola H. Winner. HUP 1988 $175.00. ISBN 0-674-52686-4. Final three volumes of Adams's complete correspondence. Annotated and edited.

Mont-Saint-Michel and Chartres. 1904. *Classics Ser.* Viking Penguin 1986 $7.95. ISBN 0-14-039054-5. Classic study of thirteenth-century buildings that symbolized to Adams humankind's need and search for inner unity.

WORK BY ADAMS

The Works of Henry Adams, 1838–1918. Rprt. Serv. 1987 repr. of 1930 ed. $800.00. ISBN 0-685-18563-X

BOOKS ABOUT ADAMS

Baym, M. I. *French Education of Henry Adams.* Kraus repr. of 1951 ed. o.p. Traces French influence on Adams.

Bishop, Ferman. *Henry Adams. Twayne U.S. Authors Ser.* Twayne 1979 o.p. General introduction to Adams as historian, literary figure, and thinker.

Blackmur, R. P. *Henry Adams.* 1980. Ed. by Veronica A. Makowsky. *Quality Paperbacks Ser.* Da Capo 1984 $10.95. ISBN 0-306-80219-8. Collection of Blackmur's 40-year ongoing study of Adams.

Decker, William M. *The Literary Vocation of Henry Adams.* U. of NC Pr. 1990 $32.50. ISBN 0-8078-1784-7. Surveys the range of Adams's writing, analyzing his rhetorical methods of reaching different readers.

Harbert, Earl N. *The Force So Much Closer Home: Henry Adams and the Adams Family.* NYU Pr. 1977 o.p. Examines relationship between Adams and his family traditions.

———, ed. *Critical Essays on Henry Adams. Critical Essays in Amer. Lit. Ser.* G. K. Hall 1981 o.p. Collection of reprinted reviews and essays.

Levenson, J. C. *The Mind and Art of Henry Adams.* Stanford U. Pr. 1957 $49.50. ISBN 0-8047-0623-9. Sees Adams becoming increasingly pessimistic after completing *The History.*

Lyon, Melvin. *Symbol and Idea in Henry Adams.* U. of Nebr. Pr. 1970 $30.00. ISBN 0-8032-0729-8. Explores Adams's use of various concepts in his writing.

Russell, Francis. *Adams, An American Dynasty.* Amer. Herit. Pubns. 1976 o.p. Provides history of the Adams family and its influence on Henry Adams.

Samuels, Ernest. *Henry Adams.* HUP 1989 $25.00. ISBN 0-674-38735-X. One-volume condensation and revision by author of his earlier three-volume work, separating Adams from the image of failure he projected for himself.

———. *Henry Adams.* 3 vols. HUP. *The Major Phase.* 1964 $40.50. ISBN 0-674-38751-1. *The Middle Years.* 1958 $33.00. ISBN 0-674-38753-8. *The Young Henry Adams.* 1948 $28.00. ISBN 0-674-96630-9. Definitive biography.

Stevenson, Elizabeth. *Henry Adams: A Biography.* Hippocrene Bks. 1977 $31.50. ISBN 0-374-97624-4. "The fullest, finest account yet written of one of the fullest, finest Americans" (Paul Engle), recipient of the Bancroft Prize in 1956.

Wasserstrom, William. *The Ironies of Progress: Henry Adams and the American Dream.* S. Ill. U. Pr. 1984 $28.95. ISBN 0-8093-1155-0. Study of the connection between "founding, flourishing, and failing" in a society as reflected by Adams's life and writings.

ADDAMS, (LAURA) JANE. 1860–1935 (NOBEL PRIZE 1931)

Jane Addams devoted her life to social reform, writing and lecturing about such problems as industrial growth, immigration, child labor, education, prostitution, and women's role in society. Born in Illinois to prosperous parents of Quaker background, Addams received a B.A. from Rockford College in Illinois in 1882. She is best known for her work with Hull House, an immigrant settlement house that she founded in Chicago in 1889. Her autobiographical works, *Twenty Years at Hull-House* (1910) and *The Second Twenty Years at Hull House* (1930), describe not only the people and activities associated with the settlement house but also her own intellectual development and her determined belief in the possibility of social justice which moved beyond the ethic of

American individualism. Addams worked for world peace, writing *Democracy and Social Ethics* (1902), *Newer Ideals of Peace* (1907), and *Peace and Bread in Times of War* (1922). She was also a pacifist during World War I, one of the founders of the Women's International League for Peace and Freedom (WILPF), an active member of the Women Suffrage Association, and co-recipient (with Nicholas Murray Butler) of the Nobel Peace Prize in 1931. In 1912, she seconded the nomination of Theodore Roosevelt for President. Her efforts helped pave the way for the liberal reforms of the Progressive era.

NONFICTION BY ADDAMS

Democracy and Social Ethics. 1902. Rprt. Serv. 1988 $75.00. ISBN 0-7812-0225-6. First study calling attention to the disintegration of modern industrial society.

A New Conscience and an Ancient Evil. 1912. *Family in Amer. Ser*. Ayer 1972 $22.00. ISBN 0-405-03843-7. Concerns prostitution.

Newer Ideals of Peace. 1907. *Peace Movement in Amer. Ser*. Ozer 1972 $24.95. ISBN 0-89198-050-4

Peace and Bread in Time of War. 1922. *Peace Movement in Amer. Ser*. Ozer 1972 $24.95. ISBN 0-89198-051-2

Philanthropy and Social Progress: Seven Essays. *Criminology, Law Enforcement, and Social Problems Ser*. Ed. by Christopher Lasch. Patterson Smith 1970 $15.00. ISBN 0-87585-104-5

Social Thought of Jane Addams. Ed. by Christopher Lasch. Irvington 1982 $16.95. ISBN 0-8290-0338-X. Collection of essays and excerpts from Addams's writing showing her as an intellectual and writer as well as a social reformer.

The Spirit of Youth and the City Streets. 1909. U. of Ill. Pr. 1989 $10.95. ISBN 0-252-00276-8. Views industrialism as the cause of social disintegration.

Twenty Years at Hull-House. 1910. Lightyear 1992 $25.95. ISBN 0-89968-259-6

BOOKS ABOUT ADDAMS

Davis, Allen F. *American Heroine: The Life and Legend of Jane Addams*. Peter Smith 1983 $17.75. ISBN 0-8446-6016-7. An important biographical study.

Deegan, Mary J. *Jane Addams and the Men of the Chicago School, 1892–1918*. Transaction Pubs. 1986 $34.95. ISBN 0-88738-077-8. Discusses the development of American social thought and the intellectual contribution of Jane Addams.

Farrell, John C. *Beloved Lady: A History of Jane Addams's Ideas on Reform and Peace*. Johns Hopkins 1967 o.p.

Lasch, Christopher. *The New Radicalism in America (1899–1963), The Intellectual as a Social Type*. Knopf 1965 o.p.

Levine, Daniel. *Jane Addams and the Liberal Tradition*. Greenwood 1980 $35.00. ISBN 0-313-22691-1

Linn, J. W. *Jane Addams: A Biography*. Greenwood 1968 o.p. A sympathetic look at Addams by her niece. Partly written with Addams's cooperation and contribution.

————, ed. *The Social Thought of Jane Addams*. Irvington 1982 o.p. Examines Addams's ideas on social policy and programs.

ALCOTT, LOUISA MAY. 1832–1888

[SEE Chapter 20 in this volume.]

ALDRICH, THOMAS BAILEY. 1836–1907

A native of New England, happy to belong to genteel Boston society, Thomas Bailey Aldrich lived during a time of great change in American literature. His literary conservatism and his resistance to the harsher outlooks of realism in part account for the neglect of him today. Nevertheless, his poetry and fiction were popular during his day, and he was a conscientious craftsman. At 16 he went to work in his uncle's New York countinghouse, but he spent his free time reading and writing poetry. His first published works, the sentimental "Ballad of Babie Bell" and *The Bells* (1855), a volume of verse, brought him immediate fame. He then devoted himself to literature. He became the editor of the weekly magazine, *Every Saturday*, and eventually of the prestigious *Atlantic Monthly* from 1881 to 1890. His mature lyrics were less sentimental than his early work, though he continued to follow the classical conventions of romantic poetry. His best short stories, particularly those collected in *Marjorie Daw and Other Stories* (1873) and *Two Bites at a Cherry, with Other Tales* (1894), show his use of regional local color, but his romantic plots rely on humor rather than realism for their appeal. His first novel, *The Story of a Bad Boy* (1870), was unique in its depiction not of a "bad boy" but of a "natural boy," a type that anticipated MARK TWAIN's Tom Sawyer. Aldrich's other novels, although popular, were not as successful. Even as he foresaw the change in literary taste that would doom his own reputation, he remained steadfast in preferring the pleasant to the realistic, the conventional to the modern.

NOVEL BY ALDRICH

The Story of Bad Boy. 1870. U. Pr. of New Eng. 1990 $12.95. ISBN 0-87451-534-3. Includes an introduction by David Watters.

SHORT STORY COLLECTIONS BY ALDRICH

Marjorie Daw and Other Stories. 1873. Irvington 1986 $6.95. ISBN 0-8290-1943-X
Two Bites at a Cherry, with Other Tales. 1894. Irvington 1986 $6.95. ISBN 0-8290-2044-6

WORKS BY ALDRICH

The Works of Thomas Bailey Aldrich, 1836–1907. Rprt. Serv. 1987 $500.00. ISBN 0-685-18584-2
Writings of Thomas Bailey Aldrich. AMS Pr. $202.50. ISBN 0-404-03370-2

BOOKS ABOUT ALDRICH

Greenslet, Ferris. *Thomas Bailey Aldrich.* HM 1908 o.p. Official Aldrich biography, including many letters.
Samuels, Charles E. *Thomas Bailey Aldrich. Twayne's U.S. Authors Ser.* NCUP 1965 $10.95. ISBN 0-8084-0297-8. General biographical and thematic introduction to Aldrich and his work.

AUSTIN, MARY (HUNTER). 1868–1934

In her autobiography *Earth Horizon* (1932), Mary Austin refers to herself in the first, second, and third person to reflect the division that she felt as a woman between her true self and the self that conformed to the ideas of her patriarchal society. Born in Carlinville, Illinois, Austin graduated from Blackborn College and moved to the San Joaquin Valley of southern California in 1888. She wrote about the land and people she loved and keenly observed in *The Land of Little Rain* (1903) and *Lost Borders* (1909). Her novel *Outland* (1910) is probably an account of her unhappy marriage. Throughout her life, she devoted herself to environmental issues and championed the Native American and Hispanic traditions of the Southwest. The semiautobiographical *A Woman of Genius* (1912) focuses on the conflicts facing creative women. In *Earth Horizon* (1932) she reports her discovery that women are not limited to "enduring or complaining"; they could get out and "hunt for a remedy." This autobiographical work throws much light on her work, revealing her as a woman who sought an independent philosophy in the spirit of her New England forebears.

NOVEL BY AUSTIN

A Woman of Genius. 1912. Feminist Pr. 1985 $9.95. ISBN 0-935312-44-7

SHORT STORY COLLECTIONS BY AUSTIN

Stories from the Country of Lost Borders. 1909. Ed. by Marjorie Pryse. *Amer. Women Writers Ser.* Rutgers U. Pr. 1987 $35.00. ISBN 0-8135-1217-4. Includes *Land of Little Rain; Lost Borders;* essays; and stories.

Western Trails: A Collection of Short Stories. Ed. by Melody Graulich. U. of Nev. Pr. 1988 o.p. Selection of some of Austin's best work with introduction and notes.

NONFICTION BY AUSTIN

Earth Horizon. 1932. U. of NM Pr. 1991 $16.95. ISBN 0-8263-1316-7. With an afterword by Melody Graulich.

The Land of Journey's Ending. 1923. *BCL1—U.S. Local Hist. Ser.* Rprt. Serv. 1991 $99.00. ISBN 0-7812-6330-1. Sketches.

The Land of Little Rain. 1903. *BCL1—U.S. Local Hist. Ser.* Rprt. Serv. 1991 $79.00. ISBN 0-7812-6331-X. Collection of essays and sketches.

WORK BY AUSTIN

Literary America, Nineteen Hundred and Three to Nineteen Thirty-Four: The Mary Austin Letters. Ed. by T. M. Pearce. *Contributions in Women's Studies Ser.* Greenwood 1979 $42.95. ISBN 0-313-20636-8

BOOKS ABOUT AUSTIN

Doyle, Helen MacKnight. *Mary Austin: Woman of Genius.* Gotham Hse. 1931 o.p. Sympathetic biography written by friend of Austin's.

Fink, Augusta. *I-Mary: A Biography of Mary Austin.* U. of Ariz. Pr. 1983 $29.95. ISBN 0-8165-0789-9. Focuses on Austin's personal relationships.

Pearce, T. M.. *Mary Hunter Austin. Twayne's U.S. Authors Ser.* Irvington 1965 $17.95. ISBN 0-89197-837-2. General biographical and critical introduction.

Stineman, Esther L. *Mary Austin: Song of a Maverick.* Yale U. Pr. 1989 $28.00. ISBN 0-300-04255-8. Places Austin in the tradition of women's writing by focusing on her personal and literary connections.

BELLAMY, EDWARD. 1850–1898

It is as the "humane and romantic Utopian, campaigning for equality and social justice, rather than as a novelist or profound thinker, that Bellamy is remembered and read today." While working as a journalist in Springfield, Massachusetts, he began to write novels and later short stories but did not achieve much success until the publication of *Looking Backward* (1888). The hero of this fantasy falls asleep in 1887 and awakens in the year 2000 to find himself in a humane scientific and socialistic utopia. After selling fewer than 10,000 copies in its first year, *Looking Backward* became enormously popular. Clubs were formed to promote Bellamy's social ideas, and he became a leader of a brief nationalist movement, crusading for "economic equality, human brotherhood, and the progressive nationalization of industry." Americans as diverse as THORSTEIN VEBLEN (see also Vol. 3) and JOHN DEWEY (see Vols. 3 and 4) have been influenced by Bellamy's suggestion that the products of industrial energy, intelligently organized, could be used to obtain a nobler future. His *The Religion of Solidarity* (1940), long out of print, is again available.

Novels by Bellamy

Dr. Heidenhoff's Process. AMS Pr. repr. of 1880 ed. $19.50. ISBN 0-404-00734-1.
Psychological romance demonstrating Bellamy's interest in guilt and psychic
phenomena.

Equality. BLC Ser. II AMS Pr. 1970 repr. of 1887 ed. $24.50. ISBN 0-404-00735-X. Sequel
to *Looking Backward,* though more theoretical and didactic. Attacks the American
pretense of economic equality.

Looking Backward, 2000–1887. 1888. Ed. by John L. Thomas. *John Harvard Lib. Ser.* HUP
1967 o.p.

Short Story Collections by Bellamy

Apparitions of Things to Come: Edward Bellamy's Tales of Mystery and Imagination. Ed. by
Franklin Rosemont. C. H. Kerr 1990 $25.95. ISBN 0-88286-165-4

The Blindman's World and Other Stories. Irvington 1972 repr. of 1898 ed. o.p.

Nonfiction by Bellamy

The Religion of Solidarity. 1940. *Institute of World Culture Ser.* Concord Grove 1984
$8.75. ISBN 0-88695-029-5

Works by Edward Bellamy

The Works of Edward Bellamy 1850–1898. Rprt. Serv. 1987 $600.00. ISBN 0-685-18616-4

Books about Bellamy

Bowman, Sylvia E. *Edward Bellamy. Twayne U.S. Authors Ser.* Macmillan 1986 $19.95.
ISBN 0-8057-7460-2. Basic introduction to Bellamy and his major themes.

———. *Edward Bellamy Abroad.* NCUP 1962 o.p.

———. *Year Two Thousand: A Critical Biography of Edward Bellamy.* Hippocrene Bks.
1979 $29.00. ISBN 0-374-90879-6. Study of Bellamy's life, influences, and ideology,
as expressed in his novels and published articles.

Griffith, Nancy S. *Edward Bellamy: A Bibliography. Scarecrow Author Bib. Ser.* Scarecrow
1987 $25.00. ISBN 0-8108-1932-5. Much needed but not completely satisfactory
bibliography—"to be used with care" (*Choice,* June 1987).

Morgan, Arthur E. *The Philosophy of Edward Bellamy.* Greenwood 1979 $39.75. ISBN 0-
313-21037-3. Comprehensive biography.

Patai, Daphne, ed. *Looking Backward, Nineteen Eighty-Eight to Eighteen Eighty-Eight:
Essays on Edward Bellamy.* U. of Mass. Pr. 1988 $35.00. ISBN 0-87023-633-4. Variety
of approaches demonstrate the complexity of utopian fiction.

Roberts, J. W. *Looking Within: The Misleading Tendencies of Looking Backward Made
Manifest. Utopian Lit. Ser.* Ayer 1971 $22.00. ISBN 0-405-03541-1. A response to
Bellamy's *Looking Backward.*

Widdicombe, Toby, ed. *Edward Bellamy: An Annotated Bibliography of Secondary
Criticism. Ref. Lib. of the Humanities.* Garland 1988 $88.00. ISBN 0-8240-8563-9

BIERCE, AMBROSE (GWINNETT). 1842–1914?

Bierce has been called "bitter," "wicked," and "mysterious," the latter
because of his dramatic disappearance into Mexico in 1913 and his probable
death there the following year. He served with distinction in the Civil War, then
went to San Francisco, where he contributed to periodicals. He was early
known for the vitriolic wit of his journalistic sketches. His short stories, grim
horror tales recalling those of EDGAR ALLAN POE, are his best work. *Can Such
Things Be?,* a collection of supernatural tales, appeared in 1893. His poetry is
epigrammatic, but conventional. His *Fantastic Fables* (1890) and *The Devil's
Dictionary* (1911) display his cynical aversion to "labor unions, democracy and
socialism." Typical of his *Dictionary* definitions are: "Happiness, n. An

agreeable sensation arising from contemplation of the misery of another." "Prejudice, n. A vagrant opinion without visible means of support."

SHORT STORY COLLECTIONS BY BIERCE

Can Such Things Be? 1893. Carol Pub. Group. 1977 $2.95. ISBN 0-8065-0550-8

The Civil War Short Stories of Ambrose Bierce. Ed. by Ernest J. Hopkins. U. of Nebr. Pr. 1988 $6.95. ISBN 0-8032-6087-3

The Complete Short Stories of Ambrose Bierce. Ed. by Ernest J. Hopkins. U. of New Eng. Pr. 1984 $12.95. ISBN 0-8032-6071-7

The Devil's Dictionary (The Cynic's Word Book). 1911. Dell 1991 $5.99. ISBN 0-440-20853-X

Fantastic Fables. 1899. Amereon Ltd. 1976 $15.95. ISBN 0-89190-184-1

Ghost and Horror Stories of Ambrose Bierce. Ed. by E. F. Bleiler. Dover 1964 o.p.

The Secret of Happiness and Other Fantastic Fables. Ed. by Jana Stone. *Belles Lettres Ser.* Stewart Tabori & Chang 1989 $6.95. ISBN 1-55670-117-9

The Stories and Fables of Ambrose Bierce. Ed. by Edward Wagenknecht. Stemmer Hse. 1977 $14.95. ISBN 0-916144-19-4

NONFICTION BY BIERCE

Skepticism and Dissent: Selected Journalism, 1898–1901. Nineteenth-Century Studies. Bks. Demand 1986 $91.00. ISBN 0-8357-1725-7. Journalism satirizing and criticizing society, especially the "rent-seekers."

WORKS BY BIERCE

Collected Works of Ambrose Bierce, 1909–1912. 12 vols. Gordian 1966 $450.00. ISBN 0-87752-010-0

Collected Writings of Ambrose Bierce. Carol Pub. Group 1983 $11.95. ISBN 0-8065-0180-4. A good single volume collection of stories, sketches, essays, and satire.

Letters. BCL1-PS Amer. Lit. Ser. Rprt. Serv. 1992 $79.00. ISBN 0-7812-6675-0

The Principle Works of Ambrose Gwinett Bierce. Rprt. Serv. 1989 o.p.

Twenty-One Letters of Ambrose Bierce. Amer. Biog. Ser. Rprt. Serv. 1991 $59.00. ISBN 0-7812-8019-2

The Works of Ambrose Gwinett Bierce. Rprt. Serv. 1989 $63.00. ISBN 0-685-27260-5

BOOKS ABOUT BIERCE

Davidson, Cathy N. *The Experimental Fictions of Ambrose Bierce: Structuring the Ineffable.* U. of Nebr. Pr. 1984 $16.95. ISBN 0-8032-1666-1. Focuses on Bierce's "surprisingly modern views" on the nature of language.

———, ed. *Critical Essays on Ambrose Bierce.* G. K. Hall 1982 o.p. Collection of early reviews, reprinted essays, and original criticism.

De Castro, Adolph. *Portrait of Ambrose Bierce.* Beekman Pubs. 1974 $25.00. ISBN 0-8464-0737-X. Not completely reliable biography written by friend of Bierce.

Fatout, Paul. *Ambrose Bierce: The Devil's Lexicographer.* U. of Okla. Pr. 1951 o.p. Comprehensive critical biography.

Gaer, Joseph, ed. *Ambrose Gwinnett Bierce: A Bibliography and Biographical Data.* 1935. B. Franklin 1968 o.p. A useful scholarly work.

Grenander, M.E. *Ambrose Bierce. Twayne's U.S. Authors Ser.* G. K. Hall o.p. General introduction using primary sources to avoid perpetuating errors.

McWilliams, Carey. *Ambrose Bierce: A Biography.* Shoe String 1963 repr. of 1929 ed. o.p. Early biography with short-story criticism.

Neale, Walter. *Life of Ambrose Bierce.* AMS Pr. repr. of 1929 ed. $16.00. ISBN 0-0404-04668-1

CABLE, GEORGE WASHINGTON. 1844–1925

Born and raised in New Orleans, Cable left school at age 14 and went to work to support his mother and sisters after his father's death. After serving in the

Confederate Army during the Civil War, Cable worked at a variety of jobs before beginning to write. He is especially well known for his stories about Creole life. He was much attracted to certain aspects of Creole life and anxious to record this life before it entirely disappeared. His sympathies, however, did not extend to what he considered certain moral weaknesses in Creole civilization, particularly in its treatment of African-Americans. As time went on, Cable began to speak out ever more openly on racial injustices in Louisiana and in the South generally. This brought a great deal of bitter criticism from fellow southerners and ultimately resulted in his moving to Massachusetts. His most explicit fictional treatment of racial injustice is probably *John March: Southerner* (1894), which he set in northern Alabama rather than Louisiana to emphasize the regional aspect of the racial problem. He also gave speeches, wrote letters to editors, and published articles on the problems of African-Americans in the South.

Cable's most successful literary work is *The Grandissimes* (1880), which has been compared in power and scope to the fiction of WILLIAM FAULKNER. The novel is somewhat marred by obvious editorializing and some wooden characterization, but it contains powerful scenes and deals with racial injustice, a subject all but taboo in the fiction of the time. Guy A. Cardwell has argued convincingly that Cable significantly altered MARK TWAIN's racial views when the two men were on a lecture tour together. Cable's treatment of race foreshadowed the work of such later Southern writers as Faulkner and ROBERT PENN WARREN.

NOVELS BY CABLE

Bonaventure: A Prose Pastoral of Acadian Louisiana. 1888. Irvington 1986 $5.95. ISBN 0-8290-1866-2. Melodramatic love stories of Cajun society after the Civil War. Depicts the simplicity of this French-speaking people.

Bylow Hill. 1902. Scholarly repr. of 1902 ed. $13.00. ISBN 0-403-00106-4. Unsuccessful novel set in New England. Story of a minister's passion and jealousy of his Southern wife's former suitor.

The Grandissimes. 1880. *Brown Thrasher Bks.* U. of Ga. Pr. 1988 $13.95. ISBN 0-8203-1020-4. With an introduction by Suzanne Jones.

John March: Southerner. 1894. Irvington 1972 $18.50. ISBN 0-8422-8019-7

Madame Delphine. 1881. Scholarly 1986 $11.50. ISBN 0-403-00039-4. Novella dealing with the unhappy life of a quadroon in New Orleans society.

SHORT STORY COLLECTIONS BY CABLE

Old Creole Days. 1883. *Black Heritage Lib. Coll. Ser.* Ayer repr. of 1883 ed. $22.95. ISBN 0-8369-8530-3. Includes some of Cable's best stories: "John-ah-Poquelin," about a former slave trader; "Tite Poulette," about miscegenation; and "Belles Desmoiselles."

Strong Hearts. 1899. Irvington 1986 $8.95. ISBN 0-8290-1865-4. Three of Cable's best stories, including "The Solitary" and "The Entomologist."

NONFICTION BY CABLE

Silent South: Including the Freedman's Case in Equity, the Convict Lease System and to Which Has Been Added Eight Hitherto Uncollected Essays by Cable on Prison and Asylum Reform and an Essay on Cable by Arlin Turner. Criminology, Law Enforcement, and Social Problems Ser. Patterson Smith 1969 o.p. A collection of essays on the plight of the African Americans in the South after the Civil War.

WORKS BY CABLE

Collected Works. Somerset $995.00. ISBN 0-686-01544-4. Reprints of original publications from 1879 to 1918.

The Works of George Washington Cable. Rprt. Serv. 1990 $63.00 ea.

BOOKS ABOUT CABLE

Bikle, Lucy L. *George W. Cable: His Life and Letters.* Russell Sage 1967 repr. of 1928 ed. o.p. Written by Cable's daughter; includes letters and journal entries.

Butcher, Philip. *George Washington Cable. Twayne's U.S. Authors Ser.* Irvington 1962 $17.95. ISBN 0-89197-769-4. General introduction with biography and critical analysis.

Ekstrom, Kjell. *George Washington Cable. Essays & Studies on Amer. Lang. & Lit.* Kraus 1969 repr. of 1950 ed. $15.00. ISBN 0-8115-0190-6. Focuses on Cable's early fiction and his depiction of Creoles as well as their reaction to him.

_____. *George Washington Cable: A Study of His Early Life and Works. Amer. Biog. Ser.* Haskell 1969 $75.00. ISBN 0-8383-0658-6. Biography and critical analysis contending that Cable's early works, "fired with reformatory zeal," were his best.

Richardson, Thomas J. *The Grandissimes: Centennial Essays.* U. Pr. of Miss. 1981 o.p. Collected critical essays, original and reprinted.

Rubin, Louis D. *George Washington Cable: The Life and Times of a Southern Heretic.* Bobbs 1969 o.p. Critical study suggesting that Cable's failure to understand the contradictions in his own life inhibited his ability to create complex characters.

Turner, Arlin. *George W. Cable: A Biography.* La. State U. Pr. 1966 $12.95. ISBN 0-8071-0106-0. Definitive critical biography.

_____, ed. *Critical Essays on George Washington Cable.* G. K. Hall 1980 o.p. Collection of anonymous reviews, early responses, and contemporary criticism.

CAHAN, ABRAHAM. 1860–1951

Born in Russia and trained as a teacher, Abraham Cahan emigrated to New York City in 1882. He documented the immigrant experience in *Yekl: A Tale of the New York Ghetto* (1896) and examined the immigrant's struggle for the American dream of success in *The Rise of David Levinsky* (1917). His work was recognized and praised for its realism by WILLIAM DEAN HOWELLS. In addition to producing a number of short story collections, he worked as a journalist and founded and edited the Yiddish newspaper *Forverts* (*Jewish Daily Forward*). His influence in the Jewish American cultural community has been extensive. Cahan was a committed socialist who fought strongly against communism.

NOVELS BY CAHAN

The Rise of David Levinsky. 1917. HarpC 1976 $12.00. ISBN 0-06-131912-0. With an introduction by J. Higham.

The White Terror and the Red: A Novel of Revolutionary Russia. Modern Jewish Experience Ser. Ayer 1975 $34.50. ISBN 0-405-06699-6

SHORT STORY COLLECTIONS BY CAHAN

The Imported Bridegroom and Other Stories of the New York Ghetto. 1898. Irvington 1972 $36.50. ISBN 0-8422-8021-9

Yekl and The Imported Bridegroom and Other Stories of the New York Ghetto. Dover 1978 $5.95. ISBN 0-486-22427-9. Includes an introduction by Bernard G. Richards.

BOOK ABOUT CAHAN

Chametzky, Jules. *From the Ghetto: The Fiction of Abraham Cahan.* U. of Mass. Pr. 1977 o.p. Biographical and critical analysis of Cahan's work.

CHESNUT, MARY BOYKIN MILLER. 1823–1886

Mary Chesnut was a Southern-aristocrat daughter of the governor of South Carolina and the wife of a U.S. senator who helped draft the South's secession ordinance and then served the Confederate government during the Civil War. Chesnut herself was also a gifted writer. She began her daily journal in 1860 and revised it after the Civil War. While the basis for *A Diary from Dixie* (1905) is her daily journal, her composition process was more akin to that of fiction. She willed her diary to her friend Isabella Martin, who cut it to a third of its original length before publishing it in 1905. Ben Ames Williams, a novelist, edited a more complete version in 1949, including much of the interesting gossip and rumors that had been cut from the first edition. The historian Vann Woodward edited yet another version from original manuscripts, *Mary Chesnut's Civil War* (1981). The *Diary* gives an invaluable record of Confederate society and war efforts, as well as a frank picture of the Chesnuts' marriage. Although her views on African Americans are far from enlightened by modern standards, Mary Chesnut hated slavery and the necessity for women to pretend innocence about the mulatto children in their households. Along with its engaging picture of Confederate life, Chesnut's *Diary* reveals the dilemma of women of wit and intelligence in a repressive society.

NONFICTION BY CHESNUT

Diary from Dixie. 1949. *BCL1-U.S. Hist. Ser.* Ed. by Ben Ames Williams. Rprt. Serv. 1992 $99.00. ISBN 0-7812-6183-X

Mary Chesnut's Civil War. Ed. by Vann Woodward. Yale U. Pr. 1981 o.p. Introduction and annotated edition of Chesnut's *Diary* from original manuscript versions showing Chesnut's work as more fictional than an authentic day-by-day record.

BOOK ABOUT CHESNUT

Wiley, Bell I. *Confederate Women. Contributions in Amer. His. Ser.* Greenwood 1975 $39.95. ISBN 0-8371-8357-X

CHESNUTT, CHARLES WADELL. 1858–1932

An African American born in Ohio, Chesnutt grew up in North Carolina. At age 25, he returned to Cleveland to raise his family and practice legal stenography. Resisting the temptation to "pass" as a white man, he made the issue of race and the inequality of African Americans in the Reconstruction South the primary subject of his fiction, essays, and speeches throughout his life. His first story, "The Goophered Grapevine" (1887), was published in the *Atlantic Monthly*. His major story collections, *The Conjure Woman* (1899) and *The Wife of his Youth and Other Stories of the Color Line* (1899), are local-color stories rich in dialect. Uncle Julius, the ex-slave storyteller, is realistically presented as he tells his Northern white employer tales that show slaves using wit and intelligence to get the best of their masters. Chesnutt's later novels, *The House Behind the Cedars* (1900) and *The Marrow of Tradition* (1901), stories of passing and interracial relationships, speak more boldly and bitterly against the racial injustices of the South. They were not well received and, despite the more conciliatory tone of his last novel, *The Colonel's Dream* (1905), his popularity waned and he returned to his legal business. In 1928 Chesnutt was awarded the Spingarn Medal by the NAACP for "distinguished service" to the "Negro race." Readers today are rediscovering the humor and subtle satire of Chesnutt's stories.

NOVELS BY CHESNUTT

The Colonel's Dream. 1905. Greenwood 1970 $35.00. ISBN 0-8371-2857-9

The House Behind the Cedars. 1900. *Brown Thrasher Bks.* U. of Ga. Pr. 1988 $12.95. ISBN 0-8203-1021-2

The Marrow of Tradition: American Negro. 1901. Ayer 1969 $14.00. ISBN 0-405-01855-X

SHORT STORY COLLECTIONS BY CHESNUTT

The Conjure Woman. 1899. Rprt. Serv. 1988 $59.00. ISBN 0-7812-0047-4

The Short Fiction of Charles Wadell Chesnutt. Ed. by Sylvia L. Render. Howard U. Pr. 1981 o.p. Introduction discusses Chesnutt's themes and style.

The Wife of His Youth and Other Stories. U. of Mich. Pr. 1968 $13.95. ISBN 0-472-06134-8. With an introduction by E. S. Miers.

BOOKS ABOUT CHESNUTT

Andrews, William L. *The Literary Career of Charles W. Chesnutt. Southern Literary Studies* La. State U. Pr. 1980 $37.50. ISBN 0-8071-0673-9. Biographical approach to Chesnutt's fiction.

Chesnutt, Helen M. *Charles Wadell Chesnutt: Pioneer of the Color Line.* U. of NC Pr. 1974 o.p. Biography and memoir by Chesnutt's daughter including passages from journals, letters, and other primary sources.

Ellison, Curtis W., and E. W. Metcalf, Jr. *Charles W. Chesnutt: A Reference Guide.* G. K. Hall 1977 o.p. Annotated bibliography.

Heermance, J. Noel. *Charles W. Chesnutt: America's First Great Black Novelist.* Shoe String 1974 o.p. Biography and critical analysis that considers Chesnutt's cultural, historical, and literary background and speculates about why he stopped writing.

Keller, Frances Richardson. *An American Crusade: The Life of Charles Wadell Chesnutt.* Brigham 1978 o.p. Biography including commentary on journalism and nonfiction as well as on Chesnutt's major fiction.

Render, Sylvia. *Charles Wadell Chesnutt. Twayne's U.S. Authors Ser.* G. K. Hall 1980 o.p. General introduction to Chesnutt's work through thematic study and critical analysis.

CHOPIN, KATE. 1851–1904

Kate Chopin, the daughter of an Irish American merchant father and a French Creole mother, grew up and was educated in St. Louis, Missouri. In 1879 she married Oscar Chopin and moved with him to New Orleans and later to Natchitoches Parish, where many of her stories are set. When her husband died in 1883, she and her five sons rejoined her mother in St. Louis. She began to write essays and stories in order to support her family. Her first novel, *At Fault* (1890), was surpassed by *The Awakening* (1899), which shocked readers and was sharply criticized for its frank treatment of a woman's sensual and sexual nature. After her "awakening," the heroine Edna Pontillier chooses suicide rather than surrender her independence.

The rediscovery of Kate Chopin's fiction was one of the important literary events of the 1970s and 1980s. Historians of American literature had long regarded her as a talented writer of tales about life among Louisiana Creoles, a mere local colorist, and not, therefore, deserving of inclusion in the ranks of major writers of American fiction. With the republication of her novel *The Awakening* (1899) in 1964 and, four years later, of her short story collection *Bayou Folk* (1894), her reputation has steadily grown. Today, *The Awakening* is widely admired both for its subtle artistry and its "stern realism," and a number of her short stories, such as "Desirée's Baby," are frequently singled out for inclusion in anthologies of short fiction and textbooks on American literature. Kate Chopin has now taken her place among the pioneers of the 1890s—

STEPHEN CRANE, THEODORE DREISER, and FRANK NORRIS—as a fiction writer of considerable stature.

NOVELS BY CHOPIN

At Fault. 1890. Somerset Pub. repr. of 1890 ed. $65.00. ISBN 0-403-04558-4. Explores the tensions and stresses within a marriage.
The Awakening. 1899. Knopf 1992 $14.50. ISBN 0-679-41721-4

SHORT STORY COLLECTIONS BY CHOPIN

The Awakening and Selected Stories. Penguin Amer. Lib. Viking Penguin 1984 $5.95. ISBN 0-14-039022-7
Bayou Folk. Gordon Pr. 1974. $250.00. ISBN 0-87968-712-6
Matter of Prejudice and Other Stories. Bantam 1992 $3.95. ISBN 0-553-21405-5
A Night in Acadie. 1897. Gordon Pr. $69.95. ISBN 0-8490-0734-8. Collection of Louisiana and New Orleans stories that first appeared in magazines.
A Vocation and a Voice: Stories. Ed. by Emily Toth. Viking Penguin 1991 $6.95. ISBN 0-14-039078-2. Stories selected and introduced by Chopin's biographer.

BOOKS ABOUT CHOPIN

Bloom, Harold, ed. *Kate Chopin. Modern Critical Views Ser.* Chelsea Hse. 1987 $24.95. ISBN 0-87754-693-2. Collection of reprinted essays by well-known critics.
Bonner, Thomas, Jr. *The Kate Chopin Companion: With Chopin's Translations from French Fiction.* Greenwood 1988 $49.95. ISBN 0-313-25550-4. Chronology and compendium of information useful for reading Chopin; includes bibliography.
Boren, Lynda S., and Sara Davis, eds. *Kate Chopin Reconsidered: Beyond the Bayou. Southern Literary Studies.* La. State U. Pr. 1992 $27.50. ISBN 0-8071-1721-8. Collection of 14 essays that purports to analyze Chopin's life and work from biographical, new historicist, materialist, poststructuralist, and feminist perspectives.
Elfenbein, Anna Shannon. *Women on the Color Line: Evolving Stereotypes and the Writings of George Washington Cable, Grace King, Kate Chopin.* U. Pr. of Va. 1989 $28.50. ISBN 0-8139-1169-9. Contends that Chopin moves from "stereotype to sexual realism" in her depictions of women.
Koloski, Bernard, ed. *Approaches to Teaching Chopin's The Awakening. Approaches to Teaching World Lit. Ser.* Modern Lang. 1988 $34.00. ISBN 0-87352-508-6. Collection of essays using different critical approaches.
Martin, Wendy, ed. *New Essays on The Awakening. The Amer. Novel Ser.* Cambridge U. Pr. 1988 $24.95. ISBN 0-521-31445-3. A useful collection of essays using a variety of critical approaches.
Papke, Mary E. *Verging on the Abyss: The Social Fiction of Kate Chopin and Edith Wharton. Contributions in Women's Studies.* Greenwood 1990 $42.95. ISBN 0-313-26877-0. Good introduction to Chopin's stories. Views the author, and Wharton, as producing "female moral art."
Seyersted, Per. *Kate Chopin: A Critical Biography. Southern Literary Ser.* La. State U. Pr. 1969 $9.95. ISBN 0-8071-0678-X. Readable scholarly work, important and influential in that it aroused interest in Chopin and *The Awakening* as a feminist novel.
———, and Emily Toth. *A Kate Chopin Miscellany.* NSU Pr. LA 1979 $12.95. ISBN 0-917898-02-8
Skaggs, Peggy. *Kate Chopin. U.S. Author Ser.* Macmillan 1985 $19.95. ISBN 0-8057-7439-4. General basic introduction to Chopin's life and work.
Springer, Marlene. *Edith Wharton and Kate Chopin: A Reference Guide.* G. K. Hall 1976 o.p. Annotated bibliographical and critical references.
Toth, Emily. *Kate Chopin: A Life of the Author of The Awakening.* Morrow 1990 $27.95. ISBN 0-688-09707-3. Thorough biography of Chopin's life and relationships using the insights of feminist literary criticism not represented in earlier studies.

CRANE, STEPHEN. 1871–1900

Dead of tuberculosis before he was 30, Crane managed to combine an outstanding literary career with a flamboyant and adventurous life. He was born in New Jersey into a large and devout Methodist family, and attended Syracuse University before beginning his career as a journalist in New York City and becoming a widely traveled newspaper correspondent. He then joined a filibustering expedition to Cuba near the end of 1896 and survived the sinking of the ship that was to take him from Jacksonville to Havana. Crane's newspaper stories about the wreck of the *Commodore* became the basis for his best-known short story, "The Open Boat," a gripping and profound narrative, thought to contain the main ideas of the existential philosophy that became dominant in modern literature several decades after Crane had so brilliantly anticipated it. With Cora Taylor, a hostess of a nightclub brothel, he spent the remaining months of his life in residence at Brede Place in Sussex, where he was a close friend and neighbor of such kindred literary artists as HENRY JAMES, JOSEPH CONRAD, and FORD MADOX FORD. If Crane had lived a normal life span, he might well have become recognized as one of the giants of the modernist tradition.

As it was, Crane made significant contributions. His first book, *Maggie: A Girl of the Streets* (1893), sold so few copies that any original copy is now one of the most highly valued of modern rare books. He wrote this work while a student at Syracuse. *The Red Badge of Courage* (1895), his most famous work, blends a realistic depiction of the Civil War with an impressionistic style and profound religious symbolism. It is a triumph of imaginative evocation as Crane describes with deep psychological insight the experiences of a young recruit, Henry Fleming, who must undergo several baptisms under fire before knowing both shame and triumph. Crane's novel undoubtedly influenced Conrad's *Lord Jim*, as well as ERNEST HEMINGWAY's writings about the war.

Crane's subsequent literary work is uneven in quality, but "The Open Boat," "The Blue Hotel" (1898), and "The Bride Comes to Yellow Sky" (1897) are among the most frequently anthologized stories in American literature. Like *The Red Badge* and the best of his poems, Crane's three most famous short stories reflect an existential view of humans as isolated beings in a meaningless universe, yet capable of defiant heroism.

NOVELS BY CRANE

Maggie: A Girl of the Streets. Random 1989 $6.50. ISBN 0-685-26534-X. Story of a girl turned streetwalker because she is trapped by her environment.

The Red Badge of Courage. Literary Classics Ser. Courage Bks. 1992. $5.95. ISBN 1-56138-115-2. Vividly relates the experiences of a soldier in the Civil War.

POETRY BY CRANE

The Complete Poems of Stephen Crane. Cornell Univ. Pr. 1972 $10.95. ISBN 0-8014-9130-4. Includes a thorough discussion of the poems' texts.

SHORT STORY COLLECTIONS BY CRANE

The Blue Hotel and Other Stories (Maggie and Other Stories). WSP 1982 o.p.

Great Short Works of Stephen Crane. HarpC 1950 $8.00. ISBN 0-06-083032-8. Stories and essays.

Little Regiment: And Other Episodes of the American Civil War. Short Story Index Repr. Ser. Ayer repr. of 1896 ed. $12.50. ISBN 0-8369-3811-9

Men, Women, and Boats. Short Story Index Repr. Ser. Ayer repr. of 1921 ed. $19.00. ISBN 0-8369-3381-8

The Open Boat: And Other Tales of Adventure. Scholarly repr. of 1898 ed. o.p.

Whilomville Stories. Scholarly 1990 $65.00. ISBN 0-403-00013-0. Includes "The Monster," Crane's longest story, a tragedy of a man disfigured rescuing a child from a fire.

Wounds in the Rain: A Collection of Stories Relating to the Spanish American War of 1898. Short Story Index Repr. Ser. Ayer 1972 repr. of 1900 ed. $24.50. ISBN 0-8369-4145-4. Posthumously published collection of some of Crane's best stories and sketches about the Spanish American War.

WORKS BY CRANE

The Correspondence of Stephen Crane. Ed. by Stanley Wertheim and Paul Sorrentino. 3 vols. Col. U. Pr. 1988 $107.00. ISBNs 0-231-06654-6, 0-231-06652-X, 0-231-06002-5. Complete collection of the relatively scarce Crane correspondence along with much additional material.

The Portable Stephen Crane. Ed. by Joseph Katz. *Viking Portable Lib.* Viking Penguin 1977 o.p. Selected novels, stories, and poems with a biographical introduction.

Prose and Poetry. Ed. by J. C. Levenson. Library of America 1984 $27.50. ISBN 0-940450-17-8. Includes: *Maggie: A Girl of the Streets; The Red Badge of Courage; George's Mother; The Third Violet.*

The Works of Stephen Crane. Rprt. Serv. 1990 $63.00. ISBN 0-685-27798-4

The Works of Stephen Crane. 10 vols. Ed. by Fredson Bowers. U. Pr. Va. 1969–76 $15.00–$27.50 ea. Recognized as an approved text by the Center for Editions of American Authors created by the Modern Language Association under the sponsorship of the National Foundation on the Arts and Humanities.

BOOKS ABOUT CRANE

Bassan, M., ed. *Stephen Crane: A Collection of Critical Essays.* P-H 1967 $12.95. ISBN 0-13-188888-9. Useful collection of responses to and critical essays about Crane's work.

Beer, Thomas. *Stephen Crane.* Hippocrene Bks. 1972 repr. of 1923 ed. o.p. A brilliant biography which helped launch the revival of interest in Crane.

Bergon, Frank. *Stephen Crane's Artistry.* Bks. Demand $49.50. ISBN 0-685-20369-7. Acknowledges Crane's limits but praises his use of his imagination to spark his readers.

Berryman, John. *Stephen Crane: A Critical Biography.* 1975. FS&G 1982 $9.25. ISBN 0-374-51732-0. Good critical biography with strong psychological slant.

Bloom, Harold, ed. *Stephen Crane. Modern Critical Views Ser.* Chelsea Hse. 1987 $29.95. ISBN 0-87754-694-0. Collection of essays. Bloom commends Crane's impressionism.

———, ed. *Stephen Crane's The Red Badge of Courage. Modern Critical Interpretations Ser.* Chelsea Hse. 1987 $29.95. ISBN 1-55546-004-6. Solid selection of criticism.

Cady, Edwin H. *Stephen Crane.* Macmillan 1980 $20.95. ISBN 0-8057-7299-5. Solid biocritical study assessing Crane as a modernist.

Crosland, Andrew T. *A Concordance to the Complete Poems of Stephen Crane.* Gale 1975 $90.00. ISBN 0-8103-1006-6

Dooley, Patrick, ed. *Stephen Crane: An Annotated Bibliography of Secondary Scholarship. G. K. Hall Ref. Ser.* Macmillan 1992 $40.00. ISBN 0-8161-7265-X. A thorough listing of English criticism of Crane; supplements Stallman's *Stephen Crane: A Critical Bibliography* (1972).

Gibson, Donald B. *The Red Badge of Courage: Redefining the Hero. Twayne's Masterwork Studies.* Macmillan 1988 $20.95. ISBN 0-8057-7961-2. Useful reading of Crane's text, viewing *The Red Badge of Courage* as pivotal work dividing the nineteenth and the twentieth centuries.

Halliburton, David. *The Color of the Sky: A Study of Stephen Crane. Cambridge Studies in Amer. Lit. & Culture.* Cambridge U. Pr. 1989 $44.95. ISBN 0-521-36274-1. Structuralist approach to Crane's writing.

Hoffman, Daniel G. *Poetry of Stephen Crane.* Col. U. Pr. 1971 $32.00. ISBN 0-231-02195-X. The best available study of Crane's poetry.

Katz, Joseph, ed. *Stephen Crane in Transition: Centenary Essays.* N. Ill. U. Pr. 1972 $22.50. ISBN 0-87580-032-7. Collection of critical essays reassessing Crane's literary position.

Knapp, Bettina L. *Stephen Crane. Lit. & Life Ser.* Continuum 1987 $19.95. ISBN 0-8044-2468-3. Critical study relating Crane's stories to his experience. Views *The Red Badge of Courage* as a rite-of-passage story.

Mitchell, Lee C., ed. *New Essays on the Red Badge of Courage. The Amer. Novel Ser.* Cambridge U. Pr. 1986 $24.95. ISBN 0-521-31512-3. Collection of essays for advanced study of Crane's novel.

Nagel, James. *Stephen Crane and Literary Impressionism.* Pa. St. U. Pr. 1980 $22.50. ISBN 0-271-00267-0

——. *Stephen Crane: A Study of the Short Fiction. Twayne's Studies in Short Fiction.* Twayne 1989 $18.95. ISBN 0-8057-8315-6. Examines the development of Crane's short stories from realism to literary impressionism.

Sherwood, John C. *Stephen Crane: An Annotated Bibliography.* Garland 1983 o.p.

Stallman, Robert W. *Stephen Crane: A Biography.* Braziller 1968 o.p. Most thoroughly researched life of Crane.

——. *Stephen Crane: A Critical Bibliography.* Iowa St. U. Pr. 1972 o.p. Thorough bibliography of Crane's works and early criticism.

Weatherford, Richard M., ed. *Stephen Crane: The Critical Heritage. Critical Heritage Ser.* Routledge 1973 o.p. Collection of early reviews of Crane's fiction and poetry.

Wolford, Chester L. *The Anger of Stephen Crane: Fiction and the Epic Tradition.* U. of Nebr. Pr. 1983 $18.95. ISBN 0-8032-4717-6. Sees *The Red Badge of Courage* as establishing Crane within the epic tradition of Homer, Virgil, and Milton.

DAVIS, REBECCA HARDING. 1831–1910

Rebecca Harding Davis shocked readers with the grim realism of her stories, which appeared during a time when sentimental romances were popular. Her first published story, "Life in the Iron Mills," appeared anonymously in the *Atlantic Monthly* in 1861. The daughter of a prosperous businessman, Rebecca Harding grew up in Wheeling (then in Virginia) on the Ohio River. There she observed the industrial ironworkers' misery and struggle for existence and witnessed the harsh treatment of slaves, which she described in her first novel, *Margaret Howth: A Story of Today* (1862). After her marriage in 1863 to lawyer Clarke Davis, an admirer of her writing, Davis continued to produce stories and serials for popular magazines. Increasingly, however, pressed for time and money by the demands of her growing family, she complied with her editors' calls for happier endings and the quality of her writing declined. She warned her son, writer and journalist Richard Harding Davis, against doing "hack work for money." Rebecca Harding Davis is now recognized for the social history contained in her picture of the exploitation of industrial workers and for the power of her early realism.

NOVELS BY DAVIS

Margaret Howth: A Story of Today. 1862. Ed. by Jean Fagan Yellin. Feminist Pr. 1990 $35.00. ISBN 1-55861-030-8

Waiting for the Verdict. Irvington repr. of 1867 ed. $49.50. ISBN 0-8398-0354-0. Melodramatic story of Philadelphia surgeon who reveals he is part African American.

SHORT STORY COLLECTION BY DAVIS

Life in the Iron Mills and Other Stories. Feminist Pr. 1985 $8.95. ISBN 0-935312-39-0. Moving introduction by writer TILLIE OLSEN gives historical perspective on Davis's work and life as a woman.

Books about Davis

Harris, Sharon M. *Rebecca Harding Davis and American Realism.* U. of Pa. Pr. 1991
$39.95. ISBN 0-8122-3080-9. Examines Davis's work within the context of the
American realist tradition in literature.

Langford, Gerald. *The Richard Harding Davis Years: A Biography of a Mother and Son.*
HR&W Schl. Div. 1961 o.p. Account of Davis's career as a writer and the relationship
between her and her son.

DE FOREST, JOHN WILLIAM. 1826–1903

John William De Forest, long neglected by critics, is described by Robert
Spiller as the "first American writer to deserve the name of realist." His major
novel, *Miss Ravenel's Conversion from Secession to Loyalty* (1867), and two
works, *A Volunteer's Adventures* (published posthumously in 1946) and *A Union
Officer in the Reconstruction* (published posthumously in 1948), which originally appeared in the *Atlantic Monthly* and *Putnam's* magazines, show detailed
pictures of the society and manners of the South during and after the Civil War.
De Forest was born in Seymour, Connecticut, and his first published work was
the *History of the Indians of Connecticut from the Earliest Known Period to 1850*
(1851). He lived with his brother in Syria for several years and traveled widely
through the Near East and Europe. He married and settled in the South but
served with the Connecticut Volunteers in the Civil War. He wrote many novels,
stories, and essays for popular magazines but never succeeded in producing
"The Great American Novel," a work that, as he described in an 1868 article in
the *Nation*, would present "the picture of ordinary emotions and manners of
American existence."

Novels by De Forest

Honest John Vane. 1875. Bald Eagle Pr. 1960 o.p. Story of graft and Congressional
corruption.

Kate Beaumont. Bald Eagle Pr. 1961 o.p. Sentimental story of South Carolina feud.

Miss Ravenel's Conversion from Secession to Loyalty. 1867. Rprt. Serv. 1988 repr. of 1867
ed. $59.00. ISBN 0-7812-1153-0. Story about the Civil War that satirizes New England
puritanism while supporting the Unionist cause.

Playing With Mischief. 1875. Bald Eagle Pr. 1960 o.p. Set in Washington during the Grant
administration.

A Union Officer in the Reconstruction 1948. Ed. by James H. Croushore and David M.
Potter. Yale U. Pr. 1948 o.p.

A Volunteer's Adventures. Ed. by James H. Croushore and David M. Potter. Yale U. Pr.
1946 o.p.

Witching Times. 1856–57. Intro. by Chadwick Hansen. Bald Eagle Pr. 1971 o.p. Set
during Salem witch trials; unpublished during De Forest's lifetime.

Books about De Forest

Gargano, James W. *Critical Essays on John William De Forest.* G. K. Hall 1981 o.p.
Collection of contemporary reviews and twentieth-century essays on De Forest.

Hijiya, James A. *John William De Forest and the Rise of American Gentility.* U. Pr. of New
Eng. 1989 $20.00. ISBN 0-87451-454-1. Useful biography with insight into North-
South relationships at the time of *Miss Ravenel's Conversion.*

Light, James F. *John William De Forest.* Twayne's U.S. Authors Ser. Twayne 1965 o.p.
Introduction with biographical and critical survey of De Forest's work.

Wilson, Edmund. *Patriotic Gore: Studies in the Literature of the American Civil War.*
Northeastern U. Pr. 1984 $16.95. ISBN 0-930350-61-8. Long section devoted to an
affirmative survey of De Forest's work.

DICKINSON, EMILY (ELIZABETH). 1830–1886

Emily Dickinson is considered one of the greatest American poets, and certainly the greatest American woman writer. As Louis Untermeyer put it, "Wholly underivative, her poetry was unique; her influence, negligible at first, is now incalculable." Her verses are all short, but her output was large—a total of 1,775 poems in Thomas H. Johnson's definitive edition. Except for a few poems in magazines, all of Dickinson's work was published after her death, augmented in 1945 by the 650 poems in *Bolts of Melody*. These had remained locked in a camphor wood box since 1896, when Mabel Loomis Todd abruptly ended her painstaking editorial work after the publication of *Poems, Third Series*. Todd edited the first edition of poems in 1890 with Colonel Thomas Wentworth Higginson, a close friend of the Dickinson family, using the manuscripts she had received for the purpose from William Austin and Lavinia, the poet's brother and sister, shortly after Dickinson's death. Todd's daughter, Millicent Todd Bingham, carried on the work after her mother died.

In 1956 Bingham gave to Amherst College one of the largest collections of American literary material ever received by an educational institution up to that time—some 900 manuscript poems, as well as letters and notes of Dickinson, correspondence of other members of the Dickinson family, Bingham's material relating to the work on the poet, first editions of the original volumes, and other Dickinson material.

Readers and critics were quick to appreciate the fine and unusual quality of the first three series of *Poems* when they were first published (1890, 1891, 1896), but public taste changed and the poet's audience grew very slowly during the next 40 years. In 1924, Martha Dickinson Bianchi's *Life and Letters of Emily Dickinson* was published. It was reissued as a centennial edition in 1930. In the same year, the first *Collected Poems* and the first British *Selected Poems*, with a penetrating foreword by CONRAD AIKEN, appeared. The literary excitement revived at that time and has not abated since. She is concerned in her writings with faith, morality, eternity, nature's beauty, love, and often these themes are expressed with simple images of the household, as viewed by a woman who sweeps, dusts, washes clothes, and so on. "The six volumes of the *Poems* and the *Letters*, considered as a unit, contain every word, including prose fragments, that Emily Dickinson is known to have written," commented the *New York Times*.

Dickinson's choice of living a life of extreme privacy and the confused controversial problems of her life and family have been the subject of speculation by many of the admirers of her poetry. Nature, love, and death were her great themes. Her poems are as varied, as baffling as she was and illustrate her love of words, "her insurgent imagination, her unconventional use of rhyme, her audacious experimentation with form and assonance" (Josephine Pollitt). Most of her poems are short, lyrical, with the intellectual precision (in Dickinson's case, rhymed and metered) of the twentieth-century MARIANNE MOORE. Her birthplace in Amherst, Massachusetts, from which she traveled only a few times, was named a national historic landmark in 1964. Her grandfather was a founder of Amherst College, and her family belonged to the intellectual, as well as economic, aristocracy of the town. After completing an excellent education, she returned home until such time as she would marry and leave. However, this never happened.

POETRY BY DICKINSON

Bolts of Melody: New Poems of Emily Dickinson. Ed. by Millicent Todd Bingham and Mabel Loomis Todd. HarpC 1945 o.p.

Collected Works. Rprt. Serv. 1990 $75.00. ea. ISBN 0-7812-2627-9

Complete Poems of Emily Dickinson. Buccaneer Bks. 1990 $25.95. ISBN 0-89966-713-9

The Complete Poems of Emily Dickinson. Ed. by Thomas H. Johnson. Little 1976 $25.00. ISBN 0-316-18414-4. Single volume authoritative edition of Dickinson's poetry based on Johnson's 1955 edition.

Final Harvest: Emily Dickinson's Poems. Ed. by Thomas H. Johnson. Little 1964 $19.95. ISBN 0-316-18416-0

The Manuscript Books of Emily Dickinson: A Facsimile Edition. 2 vols. Ed. by Ralph W. Franklin. HUP 1981 $130.00. ISBN 0-674-54828-0. Presents Dickinson's poems in their original format, providing invaluable context information for critics and scholars.

Poems by Emily Dickinson. Ed. by Martha Dickinson Bianchi and Alfred L. Hampson. Little rev. ed. 1937 $24.95. ISBN 0-316-18417-9. Poems from the manuscript collections of Martha Dickinson Bianchi.

Poems by Emily Dickinson. 3 vols. Ed. by Thomas H. Johnson. HUP 1955 $80.00. ISBN 0-674-67600-9. Authoritative variorum edition.

Selected Poems and Letters. Doubleday 1959 $7.95. ISBN 0-385-09423-X

Selected Poems of Emily Dickinson. Ed. by James Reeves. *Poetry Bookshelf*. B & N Imports 1966 o.p.

WORKS BY DICKINSON

Emily Dickinson Face to Face: The Unpublished Letters, with Reminiscences and Notes by Her Niece. 1932. Ed. by Martha Dickinson Bianchi. Shoe String 1970 o.p.

Emily Dickinson: Selected Letters. Ed. by Thomas H. Johnson. HUP 1971 repr. of 1958 ed. $29.95. ISBN 0-674-25060-5

The Letters of Emily Dickinson. 3 vols. Ed. by Thomas H. Johnson and Theodora Ward. HUP 1958 $65.00. ISBN 0-674-52625-2

The Life and Letters of Emily Dickinson. Ed. by Martha Dickinson Bianchi. Biblo 1970 repr. of 1924 ed. o.p.

The Master Letters of Emily Dickinson. Ed. by R. W. Franklin. Amherst Coll. Pr. 1986 $5.00. ISBN 0-943184-01-0. Edition of the draft letters describing Dickinson's hurt and disappointment. Addressed "Dear Master," the letters are subject of much speculation and critical debate.

BOOKS ABOUT DICKINSON

Anderson, Charles R. *Emily Dickinson's Poetry: Stairway of Surprise*. Greenwood 1982 repr. of 1963 ed. $52.50. ISBN 0-313-23733-6. The first adequate sustained book-length study of Emily Dickinson's poetry; penetrating and discriminating, with 25 poems selected as "great ones" for line-by-line analysis.

Barker, Wendy. *Lunacy of Light: Emily Dickinson and the Experience of Metaphor. Ad Feminam: Women & Lit. Ser*. S. Ill. U. Pr. 1991 $24.50. ISBN 0-8093-1316-2. Investigation of Dickinson's use of a countertradition in literature to undermine the convention linking light with male power and energy.

Benfey, Christopher. *Emily Dickinson: Lives of a Poet*. Braziller 1986 $19.95. ISBN 0-8076-1150-6. Introductory study of Dickinson, including background, reception, photographs, manuscript facsimiles, short bibliography, and brief criticism.

Bingham, Millicent Todd. *Ancestors' Brocades: The Literary Discovery of Emily Dickinson—The Editing and Publication of Her Letters and Poems*. Dover 1945 o.p. The major source of information about the emergence of Dickinson as a poet; documented with poems, letters, reviews, and personal recollections.

———. *Emily Dickinson's Home: The Early Years, as Revealed in Family Correspondence and Reminiscences*. Dover 1967 o.p. Aids in dispelling the many myths about Dickinson.

Blake, Caesar R., ed. *Recognition of Emily Dickinson: Selected Criticism since 1890*. Ed. by Carlton F. Wells. U. of Mich. Pr. 1964 o.p. A selection of critical essays by

American and British writers spanning the past 70 years, including work by Thomas Wentworth Higginson, Conrad Aiken, Sir Herbert Read, and Thomas Johnson.

Bloom, Harold, ed. *Emily Dickinson. Modern Critical Views Ser.* Chelsea Hse. 1985 $29.95. ISBN 0-87754-605-3. Collection of reprinted essays.

Boswell, Jeanetta. *Emily Dickinson: A Bibliography of Secondary Sources, with Selective Annotations, 1890 Through 1987.* McFarland & Co. 1989 $45.00. ISBN 0-89950-368-3

Buckingham, Willis J., ed. *Emily Dickinson's Reception in the 1890s: A Documentary History.* U. of Pittsburgh Pr. 1989 $120.00. ISBN 0-8229-3604-6. Painstaking examination of the reception of Dickinson's poetry and published letters; illustrated.

Cameron, Sharon. *Lyric Time: Dickinson and the Limits of Genre.* Johns Hopkins 1979 $24.00. ISBN 0-8018-2116-9. Examines Dickinson's deviation from temporal order in favor of eternal order of "Immortality," with a look at the ways the poet subverts her text.

Capps, Jack L. *Emily Dickinson's Reading, 1836–1886.* Bks Demand repr. of 1966 ed. $65.00. ISBN 0-8357-3402-1. A close examination of the reading matter (books, periodicals, newspapers, and early school texts) available to Emily Dickinson "to further the understanding of [the poet] and her poetry" (Jack L. Capps); "well documented, with interesting appendixes" (*LJ*).

Cody, John. *After Great Pain: The Inner Life of Emily Dickinson.* Bks. Demand repr. of 1971 ed. $149.00. ISBN 0-7837-1511-0. Maintains Dickinson's relationship with her mother was unsatisfying.

Dickinson, Donna. *Emily Dickinson. Women's Ser.* Berg Pubs. 1987 $19.95. ISBN 0-907582-88-5. Basic introduction to Dickinson's life and the major themes in her poetry.

Dobson, Joanne. *Dickinson and the Strategies of Reticence: The Woman Writer in Nineteenth-Century America.* Ind. U. Pr. 1989 $25.00. ISBN 0-253-31809-2. Uses recent scholarship on nineteenth-century popular writing to illuminate Dickinson, her society, and her poetry.

Eberwein, Jane D. *Dickinson: Strategies of Limitation.* U. of Mass. Pr. 1986 $30.00. ISBN 0-87023-473-0. Introductory study of Dickinson's poetry in nineteenth-century context; uses metaphor of circumference to define boundary between the finite and the infinite in Dickinson's poetry.

Ferlazzo, Paul J. *Critical Essays on Emily Dickinson. Critical Essays on Amer. Lit. Ser.* G. K. Hall 1984 $40.00. ISBN 0-8161-8463-1. Reprints articles, reviews, and excerpts from books; includes some new essays.

————. *Emily Dickinson. U.S. Authors Ser.* G. K. Hall 1984 $19.95. ISBN 0-8057-7180-8. General basic introduction, using thematic organization.

Franklin, R. W. *Editing of Emily Dickinson: A Reconsideration.* U. of Wis. Pr. 1967 o.p. A technical study of the nineteenth- and twentieth-century editions of Emily Dickinson's poems, describing certain inaccuracies, with a discussion of the problems involved in editing Dickinson manuscripts.

Gelpi, Albert J. *Emily Dickinson: The Mind of the Poet.* Norton Lib. 1971 repr. of 1966 ed. o.p. Considers the poet in the overall context of American literature; a brilliant statement of what constitutes poetry."

Higgins, David. *Portrait of Emily Dickinson: The Poet and Her Prose.* Rutgers U. Pr. 1967 o.p. "A solid work of scholarship, carefully documented, that is based in large part on the letters of Emily Dickinson and those of her family and friends" (*LJ*).

Johnson, Thomas H. *Emily Dickinson: An Interpretive Biography.* Atheneum 1967 o.p. By the editor of the three-volume variorum edition of the poems, with an expanded preface for this reliable, scholarly—and fascinating—biography.

Juhasz, Suzanne, ed. *Feminist Critics Read Emily Dickinson.* Ind. U. Pr. 1983 $25.00. ISBN 0-253-32170-0. Essays using feminist critical approaches.

————. *The Undiscovered Continent: Emily Dickinson and the Space of the Mind.* Ind. U. Pr. 1983 $25.00. ISBN 0-253-36164-8. Sees gender as central to Dickinson's identity and argues that she chose the world of the mind over external reality.

Keller, Karl. *The Only Kangaroo Among the Beauty: Emily Dickinson and America*. Johns Hopkins 1980 $27.50. ISBN 0-8018-2174-6. Places Dickinson in context of friends, literary precursors, and contemporary writers, and examines her influence.

Lease, Benjamin. *Emily Dickinson's Readings of Men and Books: Sacred Soundings*. S. Martin 1990 $39.95. ISBN 0-312-03650-7. Uses biography and Dickinson's readings of the King James Bible and seventeenth-century poets to illuminate her poetry.

Leyda, Jay. *The Years and Hours of Emily Dickinson*. 2 vols. Shoe String 1970 repr. of 1960 ed. o.p. A documentary biography that compiles relevant materials without editorial comment; an extraordinary, interesting, and original approach to the poet.

Miller, Cristanne. *Emily Dickinson: A Poet's Grammar*. HUP 1987 $24.95. ISBN 0-674-25035-4. Advanced study focusing on Dickinson's unique manipulation of conventional grammar and syntax.

Mossberg, Barbara. *Emily Dickinson: When a Writer is a Daughter*. Ind. U. Pr. 1983 o.p. Sees Dickinson's relationship with her parents as epitomizing her role as a woman in a patriarchal society.

Phillips, Elizabeth. *Emily Dickinson: Personae and Performance*. Pa. St. U. Pr. 1988 $24.95. ISBN 0-271-00625-0. Reinterprets events of Dickinson's life to challenge the conventional view of her as abnormal.

Porter, David. *Dickinson: The Modern Idiom*. HUP 1981 $26.00. ISBN 0-674-20444-1. Discusses Dickinson's manuscripts in an attempt to reconstruct the composition and revision process.

Rosenbaum, Stanford P., ed. *Concordance to the Poems of Emily Dickinson*. Concordance Ser. Cornell Univ. Pr. 1964 $12.95. ISBN 0-13-208785-5. Concordance to Johnson's 1955 edition.

Salska, Agnieszka. *Walt Whitman and Emily Dickinson: Poetry of the Central Consciousness*. U. of Pa. Pr. 1985 $19.95. ISBN 0-8122-1203-7. Compares Dickinson's and Whitman's divergent responses to the Emersonian idea of the self-reliant individual.

Sewall, Richard B., ed. *Emily Dickinson: A Collection of Critical Essays*. P-H 1963 $12.95. ISBN 0-13-208785-5

——, ed. *The Life of Emily Dickinson*. 2 vols. FS&G 1974 o.p. Comprehensive biography; examines New England culture, Amherst society, Dickinson's family life, and Dickinson's personal world.

——, ed. *The Lyman Letters: New Light on Emily Dickinson and Her Family*. U. of Mass. Pr. 1966 o.p.

Sherwood, William R. *Circumference and Circumstance: Stages in the Mind and Art of Emily Dickinson*. Col. U. Pr. 1968 o.p. Examines the chief influences on the development of Dickinson's ideology.

Small, Judy J. *Positive As Sound: Emily Dickinson's Rhyme*. U. of Ga. Pr. 1990 $35.00. ISBN 0-8203-1227-4. Focuses on Dickinson's poetic technique, demonstrating the connection between sound and meaning.

Ward, Theodore Van. *The Capsule of the Mind: Chapters in the Life of Emily Dickinson*. HUP 1961 o.p. Six essays, of which the first three deal with the poet's emotional life and the last three discuss her friendships; editor is associated with Dickinson's first compiler, T. H. Johnson.

Weisbuch, Robert. *Emily Dickinson's Poetry*. U. Ch. Pr. 1981 o.p. Analysis of Dickinson's poems focusing on the consciousness embodied in them.

Whicher, George F. *This Was a Poet: A Critical Biography of Emily Dickinson*. Shoe String 1980 o.p. Earliest complete biography of Dickinson; influenced direction of later scholarship and study.

Wolff, Cynthia G. *Emily Dickinson*. Knopf 1986 $25.00. ISBN 0-394-54418-8. Important biography exploring the relationship between Dickinson's life and her poetry, offering both interpretation and analysis.

Wolosky, Shira. *Emily Dickinson: A Voice of War*. Yale U. Pr. 1984 $25.00. ISBN 0-300-03109-2. Traces the conflicts in some of Dickinson's poetry to the turmoil of the Civil War.

EASTMAN, CHARLES A. 1858–1939

A Santee Sioux, born in Red Falls, Minnesota, Charles Eastman was raised by his grandmother and uncle in Manitoba, Canada, where he learned Native American traditions and lore. As a teenager he returned to his father's family and attended mission schools and Beloit College. He graduated from Dartmouth College in 1887 and from Boston University School of Medicine in 1890. Although his background made him unwelcome in some parts of white society and his education made him uneasy in Native American cultures, he worked for his people throughout his life as a doctor, as a representative in Washington, D.C., and as a founder of the Society of American Indians. His first published book, *Indian Boyhood* (1902), written for children, tells the stories and traditions of the Sioux nation. *Red Hunters and the Animal People* (1904), *Old Indian Days* (1907), and *Wigwam Evenings* (1909), written with the help of his wife, Elaine Goodale Eastman, continue in this vein, but his later work, including *The Soul of the Indian* (1911), *The Indian Today* (1915), and his autobiography, *From the Deep Woods to Civilization* (1916), attempts to interpret Native American culture for white society, describing the problems of assimilation.

SHORT STORY COLLECTIONS BY EASTMAN

Red Hunters and the Animal People. 1904. AMS Pr. $21.00. ISBN 0-404-11852-6
Wigwam Evenings: Sioux Tales Retold. (with Elaine G. Eastman). 1909. U. of Nebr. Pr. 1990 $28.50. ISBN 0-8032-6717-7. With an introduction by Michael Dorris and Louise Erdrich.

NONFICTION BY EASTMAN

From the Deep Woods to Civilization: Chapters in the Autobiography of an Indian. 1916. U. of Nebr. Pr. 1977 $9.95. ISBN 0-8032-0936-3
Indian Boyhood. 1902. Amer. Biog. Ser. Rprt. Serv. 1991 $69.00. ISBN 0-7812-8120-2. Autobiography and history.
Indian Heroes and Great Chieftains. 1918. U. of Nebr. Pr. 1991 $9.95. ISBN 0-8032-6720-7
The Indian To-Day. 1915. AMS Pr. repr. of 1915 ed. $17.50. ISBN 0-404-11851-8
Old Indian Days. (with LaVonne A. Ruoff). 1907. U. of Nebr. Pr. 1991 $8.95. ISBN 0-8032-6718-5
The Soul of the Indian: An Interpretation. 1911. U. of Nebr. Pr. 1980 $6.95. ISBN 0-8032-6701-0

FREEMAN, MARY ELEANOR (WILKINS). 1852–1930

"I didn't even know that I'm a realist until they wrote and told me," Freeman remarked in 1890. Sometimes dismissed as a local-color writer, Freeman is recognized for the emerging realism of her novels and short stories, which capture the stubborn pride and fierce independence of rural New England women who endure the hardship of farming life, the domination of men, and the censure of their communities.

Mary Wilkins grew up in Randolph, Massachusetts, and Brattleboro, Vermont. Many of her stories, praised by WILLIAM DEAN HOWELLS for their simple directness, appeared in *Harper's Bazaar* and *Harper's Monthly*. Her best-known collections, *A Humble Romance and Other Stories* (1887) and *A New England Nun and Other Stories* (1891), show women who, despite their apparent submissiveness, have a strain of Emersonian self-reliance that gives them the capacity to revolt. Her stories, though softened by her wry humor and her editors' insistence on happy endings, reveal the psychological effects of self-sacrifice, and they question marriage as the only option open to women. Her first novel, *Jane Field* (1892), is an improbable story of a woman, conscience stricken because she has impersonated her sister in order to collect a legacy that she needs to save her daughter's life. *Pembroke* (1894), based on an incident of false pride in her maternal grandmother's family, is more successful. Freeman's biographer, Edward Foster, maintains that at her best she "rivals [NATHANIEL HAWTHORNE] in understanding the dark side of human nature."

Freeman continued writing after her marriage at age 49 to Dr. Charles Freeman, but the disruption of their move to Metuchen, New Jersey, his alcoholism, and the financial pressure on her to produce resulted in a decline in the quality of her work. Freeman and EDITH WHARTON were the first women elected to the National Institute of Arts and Letters, in 1926.

NOVELS BY FREEMAN

Jane Field. 1893. Irvington 1986 $10.95. ISBN 0-8290-1964-2
Pembroke. 1894. Academy Chi. Pubs. 1979 $20.00. ISBN 0-915864-72-X
The Shoulders of Atlas. 1908. *Rediscovery Fiction by Amer. Women Ser.* Ayer repr. of 1977
     ed. $30.00. ISBN 0-405-10044-2. Most financially successful and best of Freeman's
     late novels.

SHORT STORY COLLECTIONS BY FREEMAN

Best Stories of Mary E. Wilkins. Rprt. Serv. 1988 $79.00. ISBN 0-7812-0042-3
A Humble Romance: And Other Stories. 1887. *PS Amer. Lit. Ser.* Rprt. Serv. 1992 $99.00.
     ISBN 0-7812-6713-7
A New England Nun: And Other Stories. 1891. *PS Amer. Lit. Ser.* Rprt. Serv. 1992 $99.00.
     ISBN 0-7812-6714-5
Uncollected Stories. Ed. by Mary Reichardt. U. of Miss. Pr. 1992 $40.00. ISBN 0-87805-
     564-9. Twenty newly collected stories with a useful introduction and bibliography.
The Wind in the Rose-bush: And Other Stories of the Supernatural. 1903. Academy Chi.
     Pubs. 1986 $7.00. ISBN 0-89733-232-6. With an introduction by Alfred Bendixen.

BOOKS ABOUT FREEMAN

Foster, Edward. *Mary E. Wilkins Freeman.* Hendricks House 1956 $12.95. ISBN 0-87532-
     058-9. The only book-length critical biography of Freeman; includes a complete
     listing of her works.
Kendrick, Brent L., ed. *The Infant Sphinx: Collected Letters of Mary E. Wilkins Freeman.*
     Scarecrow 1985 $37.50. ISBN 0-8108-1775-6. Edited and annotated, containing
     business and editorial correspondence and personal letters.
Marchalonis, Shirley, ed. *Critical Essays on Mary Wilkins Freeman. Critical Essays on
     Amer. Lit. Ser.* Macmillan 1991 $40.00. ISBN 0-8161-7306-0. Collection of reprinted
     and original essays.
Reichardt, Mary. *A Web of Relationships: Women in the Short Fiction of Mary Wilkins
     Freeman.* U. of Miss. Pr. 1992 $40.00. ISBN 0-87805-555-X. Studies the conflict in
     Freeman's characters who desire born independence from relationships with others.
     Contains a complete bibliography of Freeman's work.
Westbrook, Perry D. *Mary Wilkins Freeman. U.S. Author Ser.* Macmillan rev. ed. 1988
     $22.95. ISBN 0-8057-7523-4. Critical analysis and survey of major fiction and short
     stories, with bibliography.

GARLAND, (HANNIBAL) HAMLIN. 1860–1940

Garland was born and raised on pioneer farms in the upper Midwest, and his earliest and best fiction (most of it collected in *Main Travelled Roads*, 1891) deals with the unremitting hardship of frontier life—angry, realistic stories about the toil and abuses to which farmers of the time were subjected. As his fiction became more popular and romantic, its quality seriously declined, and Garland is remembered today chiefly for a handful of stories, such as "Under the Lion's Paw" and "Rose of Dutcher's Coolly." His only contribution to literary theory is *Crumbling Idols* (1894), in which he argued for an art that was truthful, humanitarian, and rooted in a specific locale. The first volume of his autobiography, *A Son of the Middle Border* (1917), was followed by the much-admired second volume, *A Daughter of the Middle Border* (1921), which was awarded a Pulitzer Prize. He published several other volumes of reminiscence, all of which are once more available with the reprinting of the 45-volume collection of his works.

NOVELS BY GARLAND

A Member of the Third House. 1892. *The Muckrakers Ser.* Irvington repr. of 1892 ed. $16.00. ISBN 0-8398-0656-6. A story of political corruption.

Rose of Dutcher's Coolly. AMS Pr. repr. of 1899 ed. $12.50. ISBN 0-404-02685-0. Garland's best novel, in which Rose goes to school in Chicago and grows beyond the narrow limits of her valley and her family.

SHORT STORY COLLECTIONS BY GARLAND

Main Travelled Roads. The Collected Works of Hamlin Garland. Rprt. Serv. 1988 $59.00. ISBN 0-7812-1215-4

Prairie Folks. 1892. AMS Pr. rev. ed. repr. of 1899 ed. $16.00. ISBN 0-404-02684-2. Stories of the hardships of farm life and the importance of community in South Dakota, later collected in *Other Main Travelled Roads* (1910).

Prairie Song and Western Story. 1928. *Short Story Index Repr. Ser.* Ayer $20.00. ISBN 0-8369-3940-9

Tales of the Middle Border. Ed. by Joseph McCullough. NCUP 1991 $11.95. ISBN 0-8084-0437-7

Wayside Courtships. 1897. *Short Story Index Repr. Ser.* Ayer repr. of 1897 ed. $18.00. ISBN 0-8369-3251-X. Eleven stories depicting relationships between men and women.

NONFICTION BY GARLAND

A Daughter of the Middle Border. 1921. Peter Smith 1960 o.p. Autobiography.

A Son of the Middle Border. 1917. U. Pr. of New Eng. repr. of 1917 ed. 1979 o.p. Autobiography, with an introduction by Donald Pizer.

WORKS BY GARLAND

Collected Works. The Collected Works of Hamlin Garland. 45 vols. Rprt. Serv. 1988 $1,900.00. ISBN 0-7812-1213-8

Hamlin Garland's Diaries. Ed. by Donald Pizer. Huntington Lib. 1968 $24.95. ISBN 0-87328-034-2. Includes material not in autobiographies.

BOOKS ABOUT GARLAND

Ahnebrink, Lars. *Beginnings of Naturalism in American Fiction, 1891–1903. Essays and Studies on Amer. Lang. and Lit.* Kraus repr. of 1950 ed. o.p. Investigates European as well as American influence on Garland's naturalism.

Bryer, Jackson. *Hamlin Garland and the Critics: An Annotated Bibliography.* Ed. by Eugene Harding and Robert Rees. Whitson Pub. 1973 $12.50. ISBN 0-87875-020-7

Holloway, Jean. *Hamlin Garland: A Biography Select Bib. Repr. Ser.* Ayer repr. of 1960 ed. o.p. Most useful for criticism, analyses, and summaries of Garland's books, and for the bibliography of his publications.

McCullough, Joseph. *Hamlin Garland. Twayne's U.S. Author Ser.* Twayne 1978 o.p. Basic introduction surveying all Garland's works.

Nagel, James. *Critical Essays on Hamlin Garland.* G. K. Hall 1982 o.p. First published collection of essays on Garland.

Pizer, Donald. *Hamlin Garland's Early Work and Career*. Russell Sage 1969 repr. of 1960 ed. o.p. A useful book, particularly for Garland specialists, dealing with Garland's earliest work, some of which is of only minor interest.

Silet, Charles L., Robert E. Welch, and Richard Boudreau. *The Critical Reception of Hamlin Garland, 1891–1978*. Whitston Pub. 1985 $30.00. ISBN 0-87875-274-9. Broad survey of critical writing from early reviews to scholarly essays.

GILMAN, CHARLOTTE PERKINS. 1860–1935

Charlotte Perkins Gilman, perhaps more than any nineteenth-century woman, speaks in both her fiction and nonfiction directly to the issues and problems of women. Born in Hartford, Connecticut, she frequently spent time with her activist great-aunts, including HARRIET BEECHER STOWE. Determined to be independent, she experienced profound frustration in her marriage to fellow artist Charles Walter Stetson. Her best-known work, the chilling story "The Yellow Wallpaper" (1892), is the semiautobiographical narrative of a woman driven mad by her stifling marriage and an S. Weir Mitchell "rest cure," which required women to remain completely isolated and immobilized. Gilman, unlike her heroine, eventually recovered and then left her husband in 1887 (they later divorced) and moved to California, where she became active in feminist publications and helped to found the Women's Peace party. In *Women and Economics* (1898), she argues that, because women's power comes from their ability to attract the opposite sex, they are driven to bargain with men, either in prostitution or marriage, and thus lose their independence. In 1900 Gilman married a cousin, George Houghton Gilman, who supported her feminism. Her satiric female utopian novel, *Herland* (1915), imagines a different solution to the problems of women in a society in which the status of the sexes is reversed. *His Religion and Hers* (1923), her last book except for her autobiography, *The Living of Charlotte Perkins Gilman* (1935), summed up her work with the conclusion that religion had done more disservice to humanity than any other institution or ideology. Although Gilman did not labor over her fiction as she did over her social theory, contemporary critics respect the craft as well as the polemics of her work. The influence of both her fiction and her arguments for nontraditional roles for women is widespread.

NOVELS BY GILMAN

Herland. 1915. Peter Smith 1992 $21.00. ISBN 0-8446-6611-4
Herland: A Lost Feminist Utopian Novel. Pantheon 1979 $12.00. ISBN 0-394-73665-6. With an introduction by Ann J. Lane.

SHORT STORY COLLECTION BY GILMAN

The Charlotte Perkins Gilman Reader. Peter Smith 1992 $21.50. ISBN 0-8446-6618-1. Selected short stories and fragments of novels.
Yellow Wallpaper and Other Writing. 1892. Bantam Bks. 1989 $4.50. ISBN 0-553-21375-X

NONFICTION BY GILMAN

Charlotte Perkins Gilman: A Nonfiction Reader. Ed. by Larry Ceplair. Col. U. Pr. 1991 $65.00. ISBN 0-231-07616-9. Edited collection of Gilman's nonfiction.
His Religion and Hers: A Study of the Faith of Our Fathers and the Work of Our Mothers. 1923. *Pioneers of the Woman's Movement: An International Perspective Ser*. Hyperion Conn. 1985 $26.50. ISBN 0-88355-377-5
The Living of Charlotte Perkins Gilman: An Autobiography. 1935. *Amer. Biog. Ser*. Rprt. Serv. 1991 $79.00. ISBN 0-7812-8146-6. Autobiography published shortly before Gilman's suicide. Tells of her youth, public career, and political struggles with little reference to her personal life.

Women and Economics: The Economic Factor Between Men and Women As a Factor in Social Evolution. 1898. Ed. by Carl N. Degler. HarpC 1966 $11.00. ISBN 0-06-133073-6

BOOKS ABOUT GILMAN

Allen, Polly Wyn. *Building Domestic Liberty: Charlotte Perkins Gilman's Architectural Feminism.* U. of Mass. Pr. 1988 $25.00. ISBN 0-87023-627-X. Argues that Gilman's realistic fiction balances the theoretical excesses of some of her political essays, which she herself considered her best work.

Hill, Mary A. *Charlotte Perkins Gilman: The Making of a Radical Feminist 1860–1896.* Temple U. Pr. 1980 o.p. First major work of Gilman scholarship; useful for the early period of Gilman's life.

Lane, Ann J. *To Herland and Beyond: The Life and Work of Charlotte Perkins Gilman.* NAL-Dutton 1991 $12.95. ISBN 0-452-01080-2. Balanced portrait of Gilman and her feminist rebellion against nineteenth-century society, which summarizes her major works.

Meyering, Sheryl L., ed. *Charlotte Perkins Gilman: The Woman and Her Work.* Challenging the Literary Canon Ser. Univ. Rochester Pr. 1988 $50.00. ISBN 0-8357-1931-6. Collection of reprinted critical essays.

Scharnhorst, Gary. *Charlotte Perkins Gilman.* Twayne U.S. Authors Ser. G. K. Hall 1985 o.p. Study of Gilman's poetry, fiction, and nonfiction and her part in changing nineteenth-century attitudes toward working women.

———. *Charlotte Perkins Gilman: A Bibliography.* Author Bib. Ser. Scarecrow 1985 $20.00. ISBN 0-8108-1780-2. Useful bibliography listing much previously unknown material.

HARPER, FRANCES E(LLEN) W(ATKINS). 1825–1911

Popular with both African American and white audiences, Frances Ellen Harper's poetry, novels, short stories, and lectures reflected her antislavery and antiracist attitudes, going beyond these themes to address broader social issues, such as women's suffrage and temperance. Born to a free family in Baltimore, Harper was encouraged to read and write by her employer, the wife of a bookseller. She moved to the free state of Ohio in 1850, where she taught, spoke for the Anti-Slavery Society of Maine, and published her popular *Poems on Miscellaneous Subjects* (1854). Her novel, *Iola Leroy* (1892), depicts a slave family's effort to reunite after emancipation. It was the first work to chronicle the Reconstruction South from an African American point of view. Although criticized by some as overly sentimental and unrealistic, the novel must be seen in context as an appeal for readers' sympathy and understanding.

NOVELS BY HARPER

The African-American Novel in the Age of Reaction: Three Classics. Ed. by William L. Andrews. NAL-Dutton 1992 $5.99. ISBN 0-451-62849-7. Includes *Iola Leroy* and works by Charles W. Chesnutt and Paul L. Dunbar.

Iola Leroy: or Shadows Uplifted. 1892. The Schomburg Lib. of Nineteenth-Century Black Women Writers. OUP 1990 $23.00. ISBN 0-19-506324-4

POETRY BY HARPER

Atlanta Offering: Poems. 1895. Black Heritage Lib. Coll. Ser. Ayer repr. of 1895 ed. $9.00. ISBN 0-8369-8588-5

Complete Poems of Frances E. W. Harper. The Schomburg Lib. of Nineteenth-Century Black Women Writers. OUP 1988 $28.00. ISBN 0-19-505244-7. With an introduction by Maryemma Graham.

Idylls of the Bible. AMS Pr. repr. of 1901 ed. $11.50. ISBN 0-404-00058-4

Poems. 1871. AMS Pr. $6.50. ISBN 0-404-11387-7

Poems of Frances E. W. Harper. 1895. *Black Heritage Lib. Coll. Ser.* Ayer repr. of 1895 ed.
   $9.00. ISBN 0-8369-8710-1
Poems on Miscellaneous Subjects. B. E. Ser. Kraus 2nd ed. repr. of 1854 ed. $18.00. ISBN
   0-8115-3025-6

Book about Harper

Foster, Frances Smith. *A Brighter Coming Day: A Frances Ellen Watkins Harper Reader.*
   Feminist Pr. 1990 $35.00. ISBN 0-55861-019-7. Contains Harper's verse, many
   letters, and excerpts from her novels.

HARRIS, JOEL CHANDLER. 1848–1908

African-American writer Joel Chandler Harris was a newspaperman whose
stories in black dialect appeared first in the columns of the Atlanta *Constitution,*
with which he was associated for 24 years. His character of Uncle Remus
became immensely popular. The stories, now reprinted in *Notable American
Authors Series,* help to show the literary value of the folklore of the old
plantation and of African American songs and ballads. Harris was the first writer
to make a lasting written local-color literature out of African American oral
culture. With the growth of the civil rights movement, however, dialect stories
have become suspect as patronizing and exploitative; Harris has not escaped the
effects of this critical reevaluation. *On the Plantation* (1892) is the autobiography of his early life.

Novel by Harris

Gabriel Tolliver: A Story of Reconstruction. 1902. *Amer. in Fiction Ser.* Irvington repr. of
   1902 ed. $36.00. ISBN 0-8398-0763-5. Novel about the South during Reconstruction.

Short Story Collections by Harris

Balaam and His Master and Other Sketches and Stories. Short Story Index Repr. Ser. Ayer
   repr. of 1891 ed. $18.00. ISBN 0-8369-3108-4. Stories showing Harris's realistic
   appraisal of Southern life and society.
The Chronicles of Aunt Minervy Ann. Irvington 1972 repr. of 1899 ed. $27.00. ISBN 0-
   0842-8070-7. Reconstruction society seen through the eyes of the title character.
Complete Tales of Uncle Remus. Ed. by Richard Chase. HM 1955 $35.00. ISBN 0-395-
   06799-5
*Daddy Jake, the Runaway, and Short Stories Told after Dark by Uncle Remus. Short Story
   Index Repr. Ser.* Ayer repr. of 1889 ed. $16.00. ISBN 0-8369-4104-7
Favorite Uncle Remus. 1948 Ed. and ill. by George Van Santvoord and Archibald C.
   Coolidge. HM 1948 $17.45. ISBN 0-395-06800-2
Free Joe and Other Georgian Sketches. 1887. *Amer. in Fiction Ser.* Irvington $24.00. ISBN
   0-8398-0762-7. Stories showing the tragic conditions of freed slaves who had no
   place in society after the Civil War.
The Making of a Statesman and Other Stories. 1902. *Short Story Index Repr. Ser.* Ayer
   repr. of 1902 ed. $18.00. ISBN 0-8369-3394-X
Mingo and Other Sketches in Black and White. 1884. *Black Heritage Lib. Coll. Ser.* Ayer
   repr. of 1884 ed. $16.50. ISBN 0-8369-8696-2. Stories about Southern whites and
   blacks showing the contrast between the middle class and the aristocracy.
Nights with Uncle Remus: Myths and Legends of the Old Plantation. Century Bookbindery
   1982 repr. of 1883 ed. o.p. "This collection is the second of Harris's Uncle Remus
   series, valuable because of the introduction in which he gives detail of his methods
   of collection, and a comparison of the stories included here with a volume of South
   African Negro stories" (Publisher's catalog).
On the Wings of Occasions. Short Story Index Repr. Ser. Ayer repr. of 1900 ed. $19.00.
   ISBN 0-8369-3065-7. Popular stories about blockade running and spying during the
   Civil War.

Plantation Pageants. Short Story Index Repr. Ser. Ayer repr. of 1899 ed. $18.00. ISBN 0-8369-3396-6

Stories of Georgia. Omnigraphics Inc. 1992 $34.00. ISBN 1-55888-228-6

Tales of the Home Folks in Peace and War. Short Story Index Repr. Ser. Ayer repr. of 1898 ed. $24.50. ISBN 0-8369-3147-5

Told by Uncle Remus. 1904. *Black Heritage Lib. Coll. Ser.* Ayer $21.00. ISBN 0-8369-9025-0

Uncle Remus: His Songs and His Sayings. 1880. Ed. by Robert Hemenway. *Penguin Amer. Lib. Ser.* Viking Penguin 1982 $5.95. ISBN 0-14-039014-6

Uncle Remus Stories. Amereon Ltd. $17.95. ISBN 0-89190-311-9

NONFICTION BY HARRIS

Joel Chandler Harris, Editor and Essayist. 1931. Ed. by Julia C. Harris. Scholarly 1971 $59.00. ISBN 0-403-01013-6

WORK BY HARRIS

Collected Works. Repr. Serv. 1990 $75.00. ISBN 0-685-47272-8

BOOKS ABOUT HARRIS

Bickley, R. Bruce, Jr. *Critical Essays on Joel Chandler Harris. Critical Essays on Amer. Lit. Ser.* G. K. Hall 1981 o.p. First collection of Harris's criticism.

_____. *Joel Chandler Harris: A Reference Guide.* G. K. Hall 1976 o.p.

_____. *Joel Chandler Harris. Brown Thrasher Bks.* U. of Ga. Pr. 1987 $11.95. ISBN 0-8203-0909-5

_____. *Joel Chandler Harris. Twayne's. U.S. Authors Ser.* G. K. Hall 1978 o.p. General biocritical introduction to Harris and some of his many tales.

Cousins, Paul M. *Joel Chandler Harris: A Biography. Southern Literary Studies.* La. State U. Pr. 1968 o.p. Uses interviews to fill in details of Harris's youth and Georgia background.

Harris, Julia C. *Life and Letters of Joel Chandler Harris.* 1918 *BCL1-PS Amer. Lit. Ser.* Rprt. Serv. 1992 $109.00. ISBN 0-7812-678-8. Sympathetic biography by Harris's daughter-in-law, including unpublished letters and family reminiscences.

HARTE, (FRANCIS) BRET(T). 1836?–1902

Bret Harte's birth year is variously given as 1836 and 1839, and his tombstone bears the date 1837. He is remembered especially for his two short stories, "The Luck of Roaring Camp" (1868) and "The Outcasts of Poker Flat" (1870), both achievements in local color. The former is the story of an orphaned baby adopted by the men in a gold-rush-era mining camp; it was dramatized by Dion Boucicault in 1894. The latter is a tale about four undesirables expelled from a mining camp and their losing battle against a blizzard.

Although he was born in the East and lived there and in Europe most of his life, Harte's 17 years of residence in California have associated him most closely with that state, and the scenes of all his successful stories are set in the West. His contemporary sketches of life in San Francisco during the 1860s, written with MARK TWAIN, were first collected in book form as *Sketches of the Sixties* (1926). When he went east again to settle in Boston in 1871, his talent seems to have deserted him. Much of his later life was spent in England. Today, his formerly out-of-print stories are available in reprint versions from Ayer Publishers.

NOVEL BY HARTE

Gabriel Conroy. 1876. Irvington repr. of 1876 ed. $22.50. ISBN 0-8398-0769-4. Vividly describes the lives of miners and gamblers during the California gold rush.

SHORT STORY COLLECTIONS BY HARTE

Bret Harte the Goldrush Storyteller. Ed. by Henry J. Dam and Lynwood Carrance. Star
    Rover 1986 $9.95. ISBN 0-932458-33-5
Condensed Novels. Ayer repr. of 1871 ed. $14.50. ISBN 0-8369-3548-9. Fourteen novels,
    sketches, and legends that parody writers such as Cooper, Dickens, and Hawthorne.
In a Hollow of the Hills. 1895. Irvington 1987 $19.00. ISBN 0-8398-0770-8
The Luck of Roaring Camp. 1868. Dover 1992 $1.00. ISBN 0-486-27271-0
Openings in the Old Trail. Short Story Index Repr. Ser. Ayer repr. of 1902 ed. o.p.
The Outcasts of Poker Flat, The Luck of Roaring Camp, and Other Sketches. Amereon Ltd.
    1976 repr. of 1869 ed. $17.95. ISBN 0-88411-592-5
Plain Language from Truthful James. Amereon Ltd. $15.95. ISBN 0-88411-593-3
Sketches of the Sixties. (and Mark Twain). Ed. by John Howell. AMS Pr. repr. of 1927 ed.
    $19.50. ISBN 0404-03151-X
*Sketches of the Sixties: Being Forgotten Material Now Collected for the First Time from the
    Californian, 1864–1867. BCL1-PS Amer. Lit. Ser.* Rprt. Serv. 1992 $79.00. ISBN 0-
    7812-6720-X. Humorous narrative poem about a game of euchre.
Tales of the Argonauts and Other Sketches. Short Story Index Repr. Ser. Ayer repr. of 1875
    ed. $16.00. ISBN 0-8369-3802

WORKS BY HARTE

*The Letters of Bret Harte: Assembled and Ed. by Geoffrey Bret Harte. BCL1-PS Amer. Lit.
    Ser.* Rprt. Serv. 1992 $99.00. ISBN 0-7812-6721-8
The Letters of Bret Harte. Amer. Biog. Ser. Rprt. Serv. 1991 $99.00. ISBN 0-7812-8170-9
Works. 25 vols. *BCL1-PS Amer. Lit. Ser.* Rprt. Serv. 1992 repr. of 1889 ed. $1,875.00.
    ISBN 0-7812-6719-6. Newly reprinted edition of Harte's complete works.
The Writings of Bret Harte. 20 vols. AMS Pr. repr. of 1903 ed. $750.00. ISBN 0-404-
    03170-6

BOOKS ABOUT HARTE

Boynton, Henry W. *Bret Harte. Select Bibl. Repr. Ser.* Ayer 1972 repr. of 1903 ed. $10.00.
    ISBN 0-8369-5545-5. Early biography with some critical analysis.
Duckett, Margaret. *Mark Twain and Bret Harte.* Bks. Demand repr. of 1964 ed. $74.10.
    ISBN 0-8357-9734-1. An attempt to offset the damage done to Harte's reputation by
    the derogatory comments about Mark Twain.
Merwin, Henry C. *The Life of Bret Harte: With Some Account of the California Pioneers.*
    Gale 1967 repr. of 1911 ed. o.p. Analyzes Harte's use of humor.
Morrow, Patrick D. *Bret Harte: Literary Critic.* Bowling Green Univ. 1979 o.p. Distin-
    guishes ideas in Harte's literary criticism from those in his fiction.
Pemberton, Thomas E. *The Life of Bret Harte. Select Bibl. Repr. Ser.* Ayer repr. of 1903 ed.
    $21.00. ISBN 0-8369-5562-5. Biography written by friend of Harte's who quotes
    extensively from Harte's letters and other primary sources.
Stewart, George R. *Bibliography of the Writings of Bret Harte.* Folcroft repr. of 1933 ed.
    $30.00. ISBN 0-404-15298-8. Definitive biography that avoids romanticizing Harte's
    life.

HENRY, O. (PSEUD. OF WILLIAM SYDNEY PORTER). 1862–1910

At his death, O. Henry left 250 short stories that filled 15 volumes, an output
of six years. They may be divided into his stories of the Southwest, of Latin
America, and of New York City. *Cabbages and Kings* (1904), his first book, deals
with his South American adventures. *The Four Million* (1906) contains stories of
New York life, a theme continued in *The Trimmed Lamp* (1907) and *Strictly
Business* (1910). The typical O. Henry story is the expanded anecdote, ending in
a sudden, humorous surprise, a formula imitated rather less successfully by
many writers who followed him. Dale Kramer's sympathetic biography, *The
Heart of O. Henry* (1955), recounts the previously untold story of the author's

early love affair and marriage, his conviction for embezzlement, his imprisonment, and the eight remaining years in New York, where his writing made him famous. It is said that the most plausible explanation for his pen name is that he found it in the *U.S. Dispensatory* while serving as prison drug clerk. It was the name of a celebrated French pharmacist, Etienne-Ossian Henry, abbreviated. The authorized biography of O. Henry is *O. Henry Biography* by C. Alphonso Smith (1916); the definitive biography is *Alias O. Henry* by Gerald Langford (1957).

SHORT STORY COLLECTIONS BY O. HENRY

Best of O. Henry. Lit. Classics Ser. Courage Bks. 1992 $5.98 ISBN 1-56138-111-X
Best Short Stories. Buccaneer Bks. 1983 $16.95. ISBN 0-89966-446-6
Collected Stories. Bantam 1991 $4.95. ISBN 0-553-213
Complete Works of O. Henry. Doubleday 1960 $15.95. ISBN 0-385-00961-5. With a foreword by H. Hansen.
Forty-One Stories. NAL-Dutton 1986 $5.95. ISBN 0-451-52254-0. With an introduction by Burton Raffel.
The Gentle Grafter. Lit. of Mystery & Detection. Ayer repr. of 1976 ed. $19.00. ISBN 0-405-07889-7
Gift of the Magi. Berkley Pub. 1990 $3.75. ISBN 0-425-12333-2
O. Henry: Short Stories. C. E. Tuttle 1989 $6.95. ISBN 0-460-87147-1
O. Henry Stories. S & S Trade 1987 $6.98. ISBN 0-671-08619-7
O. Henry's New York. Amereon Ltd. $15.95. ISBN 0-89190-313-5
The Pocket Book of O. Henry Short Stories. Ed. by Harry Hansen. PB 1989 $4.99. ISBN 0-671-68861-8
The Ransom of Red Chief. Amereon Ltd. $15.95. ISBN 0-89190-342-9
Stories by O. Henry. Tor Bks. 1989 $2.50. ISBN 0-8125-0502-6

BOOKS ABOUT O. HENRY

Blansfield, Karen C. *Cheap Rooms and Restless Hearts.* Bowling Green Univ. 1988 $26.95. ISBN 0-87972-420-X. Informative biography of the author and his fiction from his early years to his literary success.
Current-Garcia, Eugene, ed. *O. Henry. U.S. Authors Ser.* Macmillan 1965 $18.95. ISBN 0-8057-0368-3. Thorough introduction and critical study focusing on O. Henry's background and its influence on his stories.
Harris, Richard C. *William Sydney Porter (O. Henry): A Reference Guide.* G. K. Hall 1980 o.p. Comprehensive annotated bibliography.
Langford, Gerald. *Alias O. Henry: A Biography of William Sydney Porter.* Greenwood 1983 repr. of 1957 ed. o.p. Definitive biography that attempts to correct romanticized versions of O. Henry's life.
O'Connor, Richard. *O. Henry: The Legendary Life of William Sydney Porter.* Doubleday 1970 o.p. Analytical and critical biography.
Smith, C. Alphonso. *O. Henry Biography.* Rprt. Serv. 1992 repr. of 1916 ed. $79.00. ISBN 0-7812-6837-0. Earliest full-length biography of Porter, making known for the first time his prison term; examines major themes in O. Henry's fiction.
Stuart, David. *O. Henry: A Biography of William Sydney Porter.* Madison Bks. UPA 1990 $19.95. ISBN 0-8128-3057-1

HOWELLS, WILLIAM DEAN. 1837–1920

An editor of the *Atlantic Monthly* and later *Harper's Magazine*, W. D. Howells exercised a considerable influence on American letters during the latter third of the nineteenth century. He encouraged and helped publish such writers as MARK TWAIN, STEPHEN CRANE, and HENRY JAMES, and for many years carried on a battle with the defenders of sentimental fiction while arguing for the superiority of the new realistic mode. Howells was also a prolific writer, having published more than 100 works of fiction, travel, memoir, poetry, and drama. Among his early works were *Their Wedding Journey* (1872), *A Chance Acquaintance* (1873), *The Lady of the Aroostook* (1879), and *A Modern Instance* (1882), all forerunners of the book for which he is best remembered, *The Rise of Silas Lapham* (1885), a novel about the moral rise of a self-made man who gives up his riches rather than profit from dishonesty. *A Hazard of New Fortunes* (1890) reflects Howells's later concern with social issues. Howells's *Criticism and Fiction and Other Essays* (1891) contains in the long title essay his reflections from his monthly column in *Harper's Magazine* (1869–92). Other nonfiction titles include a facsimile edition of his campaign biography of the *Life of Abraham Lincoln* (1960), annotated in Lincoln's handwriting; the *Life and Character of Rutherford B. Hayes*, another campaign biography; *The Complete Plays of W. D. Howells*; two autobiographical works, once more in print, both dealing with Howells's early life, *A Boy's Town* (1890) and *Years of My Youth*; as well as three literary reminiscences, *My Literary Passions*, *Literary Friends and Acquaintances* (1900), and *My Mark Twain* (1910).

NOVELS BY HOWELLS

Annie Kilburn: A Novel. 1888. Scholarly 1972 repr. of 1891 ed. $14.00. ISBN 0-403-01033-0. Story of a naive New England Crusader. Shows the sociological effects of industry on simple New England people.

A Chance Acquaintance. 1873. Irvington 1987 $13.00. ISBN 0-8398-0796-1

A Foregone Conclusion. Irvington 1987 $6.95. ISBN 0-8290-2111-6. Early novel set in Venice dealing with a priest's unfulfilled passion for an American girl.

A Hazard of New Fortunes. Ed. by Tony Tanner and John Dugdale. *The World's Classics Ser.* OUP 1990 $8.95. ISBN 0-19-282702-2. A novel of New York City life, with implicit social criticism.

Indian Summer. Random 1990 $9.50. ISBN 0-679-72614-4. One of Howells's favorite novels. The story of a journalist who finally realizes his love for the widowed mother of his fiancée.

The Lady of the Aroostook. Greenwood 1970 repr. of 1907 ed. $38.50. ISBN 0-8371-2801-3

A Modern Instance. Intro. by Edwin H. Cady. *Penguin Amer. Lib.* Viking Penguin 1984 $7.95. ISBN 0-14-039027-8

Novels, 1875–1886. Ed. by Edwin H. Cady. Library of America 1982 $27.50. ISBN 0-940450-04-6. Includes *A Foregone Conclusion; A Modern Instance; Indian Summer; The Rise of Silas Lapham.*

Novels, 1886–1888. Ed. Don L. Cook. Library of America 1989 $35.00. ISBN 0-940450-51-8. Includes *The Minister's Charge; April Hopes; Annie Kilburn.*

The Rise of Silas Lapham. 1885. Lightyear 1992 $21.95. ISBN 0-89968-261-8

A Traveler from Altruria. 1894. Hill & Wang 1957 o.p. A utopian novel, pointing out what Howells found wrong with America.

SHORT STORY COLLECTIONS BY HOWELLS

A Pair of Patient Lovers. 1901. *Short Story Index Repr. Ser.* Ayer repr. of 1901 ed. $20.00. ISBN 0-8369-3585-3. Includes "A Difficult Case," one of the author's best stories.

Questionable Shapes. *Short Story Index Repr. Ser.* Ayer repr. of 1903 ed. $17.00. ISBN 0-8369-3049-5

Suburban Sketches. 1871. *Short Story Index Repr. Ser.* Ayer repr. of 1898 ed. $21.00. ISBN 0-8369-3050-9. Howells' first stories using ordinary American life and experience as a subject.

NONFICTION BY HOWELLS

The Ed's Study: A Comprehensive Edition of W.D. Howells' Column. Ed. by James Simpson. Whitston Pub. 1983 $38.50. ISBN 0-87875-213-7. Edited collection of reprints of Howells's editorial columns from *Harpers Magazine*. Shows his influence on writers and literary theory of the period.

My Mark Twain: Reminiscences and Criticisms. 1910. *BCL1-PS Amer. Lit. Ser.* Rprt. Serv. 1992 $69.00. ISBN 0-7812-6690-4

WORKS BY HOWELLS

Collected Works. Rprt. Serv. 1990 $75.00 ea. ISBN 0-7812-3226-0

Life in Letters of William Dean Howells. 1928. *Amer. Biog. Ser.* Rprt. Serv. 1991 repr. of 1928 ed. ISBN 0-7812-8202-0. Originally edited by Howells's daughter, Mildred Howells.

A Selected Edition of W. D. Howells. 12 vols. Ind. U. Pr. 1968–73 o.p.

BOOKS ABOUT HOWELLS

Bennett, George N. *The Realism of William Dean Howells, 1889–1920*. Vanderbilt U. Pr. 1973 $14.95. ISBN 0-8265-1180-5. Overview of Howells's early life and writing career.

Brenni, Vito J. *William Dean Howells: A Bibliography*. *Author Bib. Ser.* Scarecrow 1973 o.p.

Brooks, Van Wyck. *Howells: His Life and World*. NAL-Dutton 1959 o.p. Howells's experiences analyzed for the sources of characters, situations, plots and social philosophy.

Cady, Edwin H. *The Realist at War: The Mature Years 1885–1920 of William Dean Howells*. Greenwood 1986 $65.00. ISBN 0-313-25205-X. Important and influential biography and critical analysis of Howells's literary realism in opposition to romance.

_____. *The Road to Realism: The Early Years 1837–1886 of William Dean Howells*. Greenwood 1986 $57.75. ISBN 0-313-25206-8. Important and influential biography and critical analysis of Howells's early fiction that examines the opposition of literary Easterner and unschooled Westerner.

_____. *Critical Essays on William Dean Howells, 1866–1920*. Ed. by Norma W. Cady. *Critical Essays on Amer. Lit. Ser.* G. K. Hall 1983 o.p.

Carter, Everett. *Howells and the Age of Realism*. Lippincott 1954 o.p. Useful study placing Howells in the larger context of American realism.

Crowley, John W. *The Black Heart's Truth: The Early Career of W. D. Howells*. U. of NC Pr. 1985 $27.50. ISBN 0-8078-1632-9. Psychological study of Howells's youth as it illuminates the interpretation of *A Modern Instance*.

Eble, Kenneth E. *Old Clemens and W.D.H.: The Story of a Remarkable Friendship*. *Southern Lit. Studies.* La. State U. Pr. 1985 $30.00. ISBN 0-8071-1227-5. Based primarily on letters and notebooks, this examines the history of the friendship between Howells and Twain.

_____. *William Dean Howells*. *U.S. Authors Ser.* Macmillan 1982 $19.95. ISBN 0-8057-7372-X. Good overview of Howells. Makes use of material that had been restricted.

_____. *Howells: A Century of Criticism*. Bks. Demand repr. of 1962 ed. $67.40. ISBN 0-8357-8912-8.

Eschholz, Paul A., ed. *Critics on William Dean Howells*. *Readings in Lit. Criticism Ser.* U. of Miami Pr. 1975 $10.95. ISBN 0-87024-271-7. Collection of reprinted essays by major critics and scholars.

Firkins, Oscar W. *William Dean Howells: A Study*. Russell Sage 1963 repr. of 1924 ed. o.p. Early biography studying Howells's life and work and literary standing.

Gibson, William M., and George Arms, eds. *Bibliography of William Dean Howells*. *NY Public Library Pub. in Repr. Ser.* Ayer repr. of 1971 ed. $17.50. ISBN 0-405-01743-X

Kirk, Rudolf, and Clara M. Kirk. *William Dean Howells*. *Twayne's U.S. Authors Ser.* NCUP 1962 $10.95. ISBN 0-8084-0324-9 Useful introduction, biography, and critical study of major work.

McMurray, William. *Literary Realism of William Dean Howells*. *Crosscurrents Modern Critiques Ser.* S. Ill. U. Pr. 1967 o.p. With one chapter devoted to each of 12 of

Howells's novels, discussed in the light of his literary realism and philosophic pragmatism—the latter influenced by William James.

Nolletti, Arthur, Jr., and David Desser, eds. *W. D. Howells: Selected Criticism. William Dean Howells Ser.* Ind. U. Pr. 1992 $39.95. ISBN 0-253-32858-6

Olson, Rodney D. *Dancing in Chains: The Youth of William Dean Howells. Amer. Social Experience Ser.* NYU Pr. 1991 $45.00. ISBN 0-8147-6172-0. Study of Howells's early life using Erik Erikson's theory of identity development.

Pease, Donald E., ed. *New Essays on* The Rise of Silas Lapham. *The Amer. Novel Ser.* Cambridge U. Pr. 1991 $22.95. ISBN 0-521-37898-2. Collection of essays by established scholars and critics.

Wagenknecht, Edward C. *William Dean Howells: The Friendly Eye.* OUP 1969 $19.95. ISBN 0-19-500649-6. Psychological study of the author using his letters, writings, and journal for insight into his life and character.

JACKSON, HELEN MARIA (FISKE) HUNT. 1831–1885

Although Helen Hunt Jackson's works were immensely popular during her lifetime, most are now dismissed for their sentimentality. Born in Amherst, Massachusetts, Helen Fiske began her career writing travel sketches and poetry, which were recognized by Thomas W. Higginson. She later wrote didactic stories for children, as well as novels and stories about strong New England women. She is best known for her indictment of the U.S. government's policies toward Native Americans, which she denounced in *A Century of Dishonor* (1881), in *Report on the Conditions and Needs of the Mission Indians* (1883), and especially in her ever-popular romance novel, *Ramona* (1910), the story of a "half-breed Indian" who with her husband faces land fraud and prejudice in southern California.

NOVELS BY JACKSON

Mercy Philbrick's Choice. 1876. AMS Pr. repr. of 1876 ed. $17.50. ISBN 0-404-03541-8. About a poet who has an unhappy love affair and refuses to publish. Reflects Jackson's experience and friendship with Emily Dickinson.

Ramona. 1884. NAL-Dutton 1988 $4.50. ISBN 0-451-52208-7. Includes an introduction by Michael Dorris.

POETRY BY JACKSON

Poems. 1891. *The Romantic Tradition in Amer. Lit. Ser.* Ayer repr. of 1972 ed. $31.00. ISBN 0-405-04637-5. Poems reflecting Jackson's traditional approach to stanzas and rhythm.

SHORT STORY COLLECTIONS BY JACKSON

Saxe Holm's Stories, First Series. 1874. *Short Story Index Repr. Ser.* Ayer repr. of 1873 ed. $19.00. ISBN 0-8369-3375-3. Early stories about the West Coast, published under the pseudonym Saxe Holm.

Saxe Holm's Stories, Second Series. 1878. Irvington 1988 $5.95. ISBN 0-8290-1946-4

Zeph: A Posthumous Story. 1885. *Amer. Fiction Repr. Ser.* Ayer repr. of 1885 ed. $25.50. ISBN 0-8369-7046-2

NONFICTION BY JACKSON

A Century of Dishonor: A Sketch of the United States Government's Dealings with Some of the Indian Tribes. Rprt. Serv. 1988 $79.00. ISBN 0-7812-0363-5

WORKS BY JACKSON

Collected Works. Rprt. Serv. 1990 $75.00 ea. ISBN 0-7812-3329-1

BOOK ABOUT JACKSON

Mathes, Valerie S. *Helen Hunt Jackson and Her Indian Reform Legacy*. Amer. Studies Ser. U. of Tex. Pr. 1990 $27.95. ISBN 0-292-73056-X. Biography detailing especially the last six years of Jackson's life.

JAMES, ALICE. 1848–1892

"The only thing which survives is the resistance we bring to life, & not the strain life brings to us"—so wrote Alice James in 1890 in her diary. The youngest of five children and the only daughter in the James family, she struggled not only against the repressions common to women in the nineteenth century but also against the intense competition of her famous brothers, WILLIAM JAMES and HENRY JAMES. Suffering from illness and nervous disorders for most of her adult life, Alice James wrote many letters and, while an invalid during the last three years of her life, she kept a journal in which she chronicled the battle between her body and her will in an attempt to bring meaning to her life. Although her journals were ostensibly private, her friend Katharine Loring Peabody indicated that she would have liked to have them published. Alice's brother Henry, however, convinced Peabody that publication would be embarrassing to the family, and so the diary was not published until 1934. Written with directness, humor, and keen observation, James's *Diary* describes the dilemmas facing a woman of sensitivity and intelligence in a patriarchal society.

NONFICTION BY ALICE JAMES

Alice James, Her Brothers—Her Journal. Amer. Biog. Ser. Rprt. Serv. 1991 $69.00. ISBN 0-7812-8210-1

The Diary of Alice James. Amer. Biog. Ser. Rprt. Serv. 1991 $69.00. ISBN 0-7812-8211-X

BOOKS ABOUT ALICE JAMES

Lewis, R.W.B. *The Jameses: A Family Narrative*. FS&G 1991 $35.00. ISBN 0-374-17861-5. Complete story of "remarkable" James family, including a chapter on Alice James.

Mathiesson, F.O. *The James Family: A Group Biography—Together with Selections from the Writings of Henry James Senior, William, Henry, and Alice James*. Random 1980 repr. of 1947 ed. o.p. A classic study of the entire James family.

Strouse, Jean. *Alice James: A Biography*. HM 1980 o.p. Critical biography showing the quandary facing a woman of wit and intelligence in nineteenth-century America.

Yeazell, Ruth B., ed. *The Death and Letters of Alice James: Selected Correspondence*. U. CA Pr. 1980 $29.95. ISBN 0-520-03745-6. Biographical introduction analyzing the slow and deliberate process of James's dying.

JAMES, HENRY. 1843–1916

Born in a wealthy family in New York City, James is one of the most prominent of a number of American writers who chose to live in Europe because it offered, among other things, a much richer texture of manners and morals. In most of his best fiction, James's subject is the contrast between the simplicity (sometimes the simple-mindedness) and naturalness (sometimes the vulgarity) of Americans and the sophistication and decadence of Europeans. From *Daisy Miller* (1878) to the later novels like *The Ambassadors* (1903) and *The Golden Bowl* (1904), James's ultimate concern is with drawing out of this contrast moral distinctions that have seemed too refined for many readers, including H. G. WELLS, who found James tediously complicated. James's reputation has not only survived such criticism but also has continued to grow; today even his detractors acknowledge his importance and influence. He is commonly regarded as our most technically gifted writer. CAROLINE GORDON has referred to him as "the scholar of the novel," for, in addition to writing more than 20 novels and numerous short works of fiction (as well as sketches, plays, and memoirs), James wrote copiously on the art of fiction, on the fiction of other writers, and, most interesting of all, on his own fiction. The prefaces he did for the famous New York Edition of his own work were later edited by R. P. Blackmur and published as *The Art of the Novel* (1934). These prefaces, along with *The Notebooks of Henry James*, provide a fascinating and instructive study of the development of the device of the "central intelligence," which paved the way for the "stream of consciousness" technique developed in the twentieth century by JAMES JOYCE and others.

James was best known for his novels, but he also wrote occasional essays, literary criticism, aesthetic criticism, sketches for the *New York Tribune*, portraits of other novelists and writers, and sufficient letters of merit to fill six volumes. His critical biography *Hawthorne* (1879) is perceptive, particularly about HAWTHORNE's limitations, but it tells a good deal about James as well. His notebooks, edited by Leon Edel and Lyall H. Powers in *The Complete Notebooks of Henry James*, is a major document in the theory and practice of literary composition. James's fine autobiography (1956), edited by F. W. Dupee, consists of three books originally published separately: *A Small Boy and Others* (1913) and *Notes of a Son and Brother* (1914), which relate his childhood in a family blessed with moderate wealth and great understanding, and *The Middle Years* (1917), about his later life. A consummate craftsman devoted to ideals of art, aesthetics, and manners, James was determined to exemplify these ideals in his own work. It may be argued that, because of his formidable style and sentence structure, simply to read with comprehension a novel by James would immensely improve one's grasp of English syntax.

NOVELS BY HENRY JAMES

The Ambassadors. 1903. Buccaneer Bks. 1987 $29.95, ISBN 0-89966-606-X. The story of a man dispatched to Europe by a wealthy New England matriarch to save her son from a presumably disastrous liaison with a woman in Paris.

The American. 1877. Buccaneer Bks. 1990 $26.95. ISBN 0-89966-697-3. Story of a self-made man who confronts sophisticated French aristocrats. Early example of the "international" theme.

The Aspern Papers and The Turn of the Screw. Ed. by Anthony Curtis. *English Lib.* Viking Penguin 1984 $3.95. ISBN 0-14-043224-8. Two popular novellas. The first, a story in which marriage is the price for a poet's papers. The second, a much discussed and debated ghost story about a governess's hold over her two charges.

The Awkward Age. 1899. Viking Penguin 1987 $4.95. ISBN 0-14-043297-3. A complicated social battle among women vying for the same man.

The Bostonians. 1886. Random 1991 $10.50. ISBN 0-679-73381-7. Satire of the competition between a Boston feminist and a Southern lawyer for the loyalty and love of a beautiful woman.

Daisy Miller. 1878. Ed. by Geoffrey Moore. Viking Penguin 1987 $3.95. ISBN 0-14-043262-0. Story of an American girl who, armored and blinded by her innocence, horrifies American expatriates in Rome with her exploits.

The Europeans. 1878. Buccaneer Bks. 1987 $21.95. ISBN 0-89966-608-6. The contrast between European and American cultures becomes clear as a sophisticated baroness and her brother visit their Boston relatives.

The Golden Bowl. 1904. Knopf 1992 $19.50. ISBN 0-679-41733-8. Long, complex novel in which a pair of marriages, consummating a union between Europe and America, are ultimately saved by the story's heroine.

The Great Short Novels of Henry James. Carroll & Graf 1986 $12.95. ISBN 0-88184-247-8

Novels, 1871–1880. Ed. by William T. Stafford. Library of America 1983 $29.95. ISBN 0-940450-13-5. Includes *Watch and Ward; Roderick Hudson; The American; The Europeans; Confidence.*

Novels, 1881–1886. Ed. by William T. Stafford. Library of America 1985 $29.95. ISBN 0-940450-30-5. Includes *Washington Square; The Portrait of a Lady; The Bostonians.*

Novels, 1886–1890. Ed. by Daniel M. Fogel. Library of America 1989 $35.00. ISBN 0-940450-56-9. Includes *The Princess Casamassima; The Reverberator; The Tragic Muse.*

The Portrait of a Lady. 1881. Random 1992 $12.50. ISBN 0-679-73635-2. James's finest and most subtle early novel. Story of a woman whose inheritance, which is meant to free her, is manipulated by others.

The Princess Casamassima. 1886. Knopf 1991 $20.00. ISBN 0-679-40672-7. A woman separates from her husband and becomes involved with a young man torn between the interests of socialism and society. With an introduction by Bernard Richards.

Roderick Hudson. 1876. Ed. by Geoffrey Moore. *Penguin Classics Ser.* Viking Penguin 1986 $5.95. ISBN 0-14-043264-7. James's first, though not fully realized, novel. About an American sculptor who gives up his art to follow the woman he loves.

The Sacred Fount. 1901. Rprt. Serv. 1992 repr. of 1901 ed. $75.00. ISBN 0-7812-3428-X

Sense of the Past. 1917. *BCL1-PS Amer. Lit. Ser.* Rprt. Serv. 1992 $89.00. ISBN 0-7812-6766-8. An incomplete late novel, published posthumously.

The Spoils of Poynton. 1897. Ed. by David Lodge. Viking Penguin 1988 $4.95. ISBN 0-14-043288-4. Story of a woman who passes up the opportunity to break up the engagement between the man she loves and another woman.

The Turn of the Screw. Lightyear 1992 $17.95. ISBN 0-89968-268-5. A governess cares for two mysterious children whom she begins to suspect are possessed by evil spirits.

Washington Square. 1881. *Vintage-Lib. of Amer. Ser.* Random 1990 $8.50. ISBN 0-679-73229-2. Story of a wealthy but plain young woman and a fortune-hunting young man.

What Maisie Knew. 1897. Ed. by Paul Theroux. *Classics Ser.* Viking Penguin 1986 $4.50. ISBN 0-14-043248-5. Masterful use of point of view limited to the consciousness of a twelve-year-old girl observing the sexual intrigues of her parents and stepparents.

The Wings of the Dove. 1902. Ed. by John Bayley. *Penguin Classics Ser.* Viking Penguin 1986 $4.95. ISBN 0-14-043263-9. A complex major novel in which a dying woman defeats a plan by others to gain her fortune.

SHORT STORY COLLECTIONS BY HENRY JAMES

Daisy Miller and Other Stories. Ed. by Jean Gooder. *The World Classics Ser.* OUP 1985 $2.50. ISBN 0-19-281618-7

Embarrassments. Short Story Index Repr. Ser. Ayer repr. of 1896 ed. o.p. Contains title story and "The Figure in the Carpet," "Glasses," "The Next Time," and "The Way It Came."

The Figure in the Carpet and Other Stories. Ed. by Frank Kermode. *Penguin Classics Ser.* Viking Penguin 1986 $6.95 ISBN 0-14-043255-8

An International Episode and Other Stories. Ed. by Gorley S. Putt. *Penguin Classics Ser.* Viking Penguin 1986 $5.95. ISBN 0-14-043227-2

The Jolly Corner: And Other Tales. Ed. by Roger Gard. Viking Penguin 1991 $6.95. ISBN 0-14-043328-7

The Landscape Painter. Short Story Index Repr. Ser. Ayer repr. of 1919 ed. $16.00. ISBN 0-8369-3749-X. Contains four early uncollected stories: the title story; "Poor Richard"; "A Day of Days"; and "A Most Extraordinary Case."

Master Eustace. Short Story Index Repr. Ser. Ayer repr. of 1920 ed. $19.00. ISBN 0-8369-3892-5. Includes four others besides the title story: "Longstaff's Marriage"; "Theodolinde"; "A Light Man"; and "Benvolio."

Real Thing and Other Tales. Short Story Index Repr. Ser. Ayer $18.00. ISBN 0-8369-3979-4

The Soft Side. Short Story Index Repr. Ser. Ayer repr. of 1900 ed. $16.00. ISBN 0-8369-3722-8

Tales of Henry James. Ed. by Christof Weglin. *Critical Ed. Ser.* Norton 1984 $11.95. ISBN 0-393-95359-9

The Tales of Henry James. 3 vols. Ed. by Maqbool Aziz. OUP Vol. 1 1973 $79.00. ISBN 0-19-812457-0. Vol. 2 o.p. Vol. 3 1984 $84.00. ISBN 0-19-812573-9. Complete edited collection of James's 112 works of short fiction.

Terminations. Short Story Index Repr. Ser. Ayer repr. of 1895 ed. o.p. Includes the title story; "The Death of the Lion"; "The Coxon Fund"; "The Middle Years"; and "The Altar of the Dead."

Travelling Companions. Short Story Index Repr. Ser. Ayer repr. of 1919 ed. $17.00. ISBN 0-8369-4111-X. A collection of seven stories written between 1868 and 1874.

NONFICTION BY HENRY JAMES

The American Scene. 1907. St. Martin 1987 $16.95. ISBN 0-312-00409-5. Essays describing the changes James observed between the America of his youth and that of his 1904 visit.

The Art of the Novel: Critical Prefaces. 1934. Northeastern U. Pr. 1984 $14.95. ISBN 0-930350-60-X. With an introduction by Richard Blackmur.

The Art of Travel. Ed. by Morton Zabel. *Essay Index Repr. Ser.* Ayer 1958 $32.00. ISBN 0-8369-1663-8

The Complete Notebooks of Henry James. Ed. by Leon Edel and Lyall H. Powers. OUP 1988 $13.95. ISBN 0-19-504397-9. Biographical material and James's elaboration of ideals, summaries, and outlines give insight into the creative process.

The Critical Muse: Selected Literary Criticism. Viking Penguin 1988 $11.95. ISBN 0-14-043270-1

Essays in London and Elsewhere. Essay Index Repr. Ser. Ayer repr. of 1893 ed. $18.00. ISBN 0-8369-2796-6

Henry James: Autobiography. 1956. Ed. by Frederick W. Dupee. Princeton U. Pr. 1983 $75.00. ISBN 0-691-01408-6. An autobiography not published until 1956.

Italian Hours: Travel Essays. Greenwood 1977 repr. of 1959 ed. $35.00. ISBN 0-8371-8474-6

Literary Criticism. 2 vols. Ed. by Leon Edel and Mark Wilson. Library of America 1984 $32.50 ea. ISBN 0-940450-22-4, 0-940450-23-2

Literary Reviews and Essays on American, English and French Literature. Ed. by Albert Mordell. AMS Pr. repr. of 1957 ed. $17.50. ISBN 0-404-04408-5

Parisian Sketches: Letters to the New York Tribune, 1875–1876. Ed. by Leon Edel and Ilse Dusoir Lind. Greenwood 1978 repr. of 1957 ed. $45.00. ISBN 0-313-20448-9

Selected Literary Criticism. Ed. by Morris Shapira. Cambridge U. Pr. 1981 $21.95. ISBN 0-521-28365-5

The Theory of Fiction: Henry James. Ed. by James E. Miller. Bks. Demand repr. of 1972 ed. $103.70. ISBN 0-7837-1469-6. Excerpts and selections from the prefaces and essays organized topically by the editor.

Transatlantic Sketches. Essay Index Repr. Ser. Ayer repr. of 1875 ed. $21.00. ISBN 0-8369-27974-4

WORKS BY HENRY JAMES

Collected Works. Notable Amer. Authors Ser. Rprt. Serv. 1992 $75.00 ea. ISBN 0-7812-3362-3.

The Complete Plays of Henry James. Ed. by Leon Edel. OUP 1991 $45.00. ISBN 0-19-504379-0. Well-edited edition of James's plays with comment on his "dramatic" years.

Correspondence of Henry James and Henry Adams, 1877–1914. Ed. by George Monteiro. La. State U. Pr. 1992 $20.00. ISBN 0-8071-1729-3. Collection of 36 letters illuminating the correspondents, their rivalry and friendship, and their times.

Henry James and Edith Wharton: Letters, 1900–1915. Ed. by Lyall H. Powers. Scribner 1990 $29.95. ISBN 0-684-19146-6. Complete collection of extant correspondence detailing their friendship.

Henry James: Selected Letters. Ed. by Leon Edel. HUP 1987 $29.95. ISBN 0-674-38793-7. Selection of 166 letters for general readers interested in James's literary career.

Letters. 2 vols. Ed. by Percy Lubbock. Hippocrene Bks. 1969 o.p.

The Letters of Henry James. Ed. by Leon Edel. HUP 1974-84. Vol. 1 *1843–1875.* 1974 $40.00. ISBN 0-674-38780-5. Vol. 2 *1875–1883.* 1975 $41.00. ISBN 0-674-38781-3. Vol. 3 *1883–1895.* 1980 $41.00. ISBN 0-674-38782-1. Vol. 4 *1895–1916.* 1984 $41.00. ISBN 0-674-38783-X. Edited collection of James's vast correspondence.

The Letters of Henry James. BCL1-PS Amer. Lit. Ser. Rprt. Serv. 1992 $150.00. ISBN 0-7812-6768-4

Letters to A. C. Benson and Auguste Monod: Now First Published, and Edited with an Introduction by E. F. Benson. Amer. Biog. Ser. Rprt. Serv. 1991 $59.00. ISBN 0-7812-8212-8

The Novels and Tales of Henry James. BCL1-PS Amer. Lit. Ser. Rprt. Serv. 1992 $1,950.00. ISBN 0-7812-6761-7

Portable Henry James. Ed. by Morton D. Zabel. *Viking Portable Lib.* Viking Penguin rev. ed. 1977 $9.95. ISBN 0-14-015055-2. Manageable selection of novels and stories with biographical introduction.

The Selected Letters of Henry James. Ed. by Leon Edel. Amereon Ltd. $17.95. ISBN 0-89190-316-X

Tragic Muse. 1889. *Novels and Tales of Henry James.* 2 vols. Kelley repr. of 1908 ed. o.p.

BOOKS ABOUT HENRY JAMES

Auchard, John. *Silence in Henry James: The Heritage of Symbolism and Decadence.* Pa. St. U. Pr. 1986 $22.50. ISBN 0-271-00420-7. Considers pairs of James's works and connects "silences" to symbolism and decadence.

Banta, Martha, ed. *New Essays on "The American."* The Amer. Novel Ser. Cambridge U. Pr. 1987 $24.95. ISBN 0-521-30730-9. Different perspectives on the biographical, social, and historical background of the novel and James's art.

Beach, Joseph W. *Method of Henry James.* Saifer rev. ed. 1954 $10.00. ISBN 0-685-42330-1. An old study of James's development as a fictional artist, slightly revised, but one of the best ever written on the subject.

Bell, Millicent. *Meaning in Henry James.* HUP 1991 $45.00. ISBN 0-674-55762-X. Study of the process through which James achieves meaning in his fiction.

Bellringer, Alan W. *Henry James. Modern Novelists Ser.* St. Martin 1988 $24.95. ISBN 0-312-02056-2. Thorough introduction to and analysis of James's fiction and the important scholarship surrounding it.

Blackmur, R.P. *Studies in Henry James.* Ed. Veronica A. Makowsky. New Dir. Pr. 1983 $19.50. ISBN 0-8112-0864-8. Collection of Blackmur's lifelong studies of James.

Bloom, Harold, ed. *Henry James. Modern Critical Views Ser.* Chelsea Hse. 1987 $34.95. ISBN 0-87754-696-7. Collection of reprinted essays on major fiction by established critics; Bloom sees Emerson's influence on James.

———, ed. *Henry James's The Ambassadors. Modern Critical Interpretations Ser.* Chelsea Hse. 1988 $29.95. ISBN 1-55546-006-2. Collection of reprinted essays.

———, ed. *Henry James's Daisy Miller, The Turn of the Screw, and Other Tales. Modern Critical Interpretations Ser.* Chelsea Hse. 1987 $24.95. ISBN 1-55546-007-0. Reprinted essays on James's shorter works.

———, ed. *Henry James's The Portrait of a Lady. Modern Critical Interpretations Ser.* Chelsea Hse. 1987 $24.95. ISBN 1-55546-008-9. Some overlap in introduction and selection of essays with other volumes edited by Bloom.

Brooks, Van Wyck. *The Pilgrimage of Henry James.* Hippocrene Bks. 1972 $18.50. ISBN 0-374-91004-9. Studies James primarily as an expatriate.

Canby, Henry S. *Turn West, Turn East: Mark Twain and Henry James.* Biblo 1951 $20.00. ISBN 0-8196-0154-3. A comparative biography showing two sharply different strains in American culture.

Chapman, Sara S. *Henry James's Portrait of the Writer as Hero.* St. Martin 1990 $35.00. ISBN 0-312-03608-6. Focuses on James's middle period and the relationship between James as artist and critic as reflected in his fiction.

Dupee, Frederick W. *Henry James. Amer. Men of Letters Ser.* Greenwood 1973 repr. of 1951 ed. $35.00. ISBN 0-8371-6566-0. Revised and expanded biography and critical study of James and his work.

_____, ed. *The Question of Henry James.* Hippocrene Bks. 1973 repr. of 1945 ed. o.p. A useful collection of essays dealing with the controversial aspect of James's art.

Edel, Leon. 5 vols. *Henry James: The Untried Years.* 1953. *The Conquest of London.* 1962. *The Middle Years.* 1962. *The Treacherous Years.* 1969. *The Master.* 1972. Avon 1978 o.p. Exhaustive and definitive biography by foremost authority of James.

_____. *Henry James: A Life.* HarpC 1985 o.p. One volume revised and condensed of Edel's five volume work.

_____. *A Bibliography of Henry James.* OUP rev. ed. 1982 $89.00. ISBN 0-19-818186-8. Meticulous and updated bibliography.

Edel, Leon, and Adeline R. Tintner. *The Library of Henry James. Studies in Modern Lit.* Bks. Demand repr. of 1987 ed. $31.40. ISBN 0-8357-1856-5. A useful though incomplete resource for James scholars.

Fogel, Daniel M. *A Companion to Henry James Studies.* Greenwood 1992. ISBN 0-313-25792-2. A useful aid detailing characters and plot outlines of novels and stories.

_____. *Daisy Miller: A Dark Comedy of Manners. Twayne's Masterwork Studies.* Twayne 1990 $17.95. ISBN 0-8057-7975-2. Opens new ways to see the novel by placing it in historical context; argues it is not a tragedy but a "dark comedy of manners."

Freedman, Jonathan. *Professions of Taste: Henry James, British Aestheticism, and Commodity Culture.* Stanford U. Pr. 1990 $29.50. ISBN 0-8047-1784-2. Complex but fresh approach to James examining his connection to modernism.

Funston, Judith. *Henry James: A Reference Guide. Ref. Guide to Lit.* Macmillan 1991 $50.00. ISBN 0-8161-8953-6. An annotated bibliography for the period 1975–1987. Continues the work of Linda J. Taylor (1886–1916), Kristin Pruitt McColgan (1917–1959), and Dorothy McInnis Scura (1960–1974).

Gale, Robert L. *Henry James Encyclopedia.* Greenwood 1989 $95.00. ISBN 0-313-25846-5. "Magisterial compendium of knowledge about Henry James and his intellectual milieu . . . an outstanding research tool" (*Choice*).

Gard, Roger, ed. *Henry James: The Critical Heritage. The Critical Heritage Ser.* Routledge 1968 o.p. Collection of articles by James and contemporary reviews of his works.

Gargano, James W., ed. *Critical Essays on Henry James: The Early Novels.* G. K. Hall 1987 $40.00. ISBN 0-8161-8876-9. Wide-ranging collection of reprinted reviews and original criticism.

_____, ed. *Critical Essays on Henry James: The Late Novels.* G. K. Hall 1987 $40.00. ISBN 0-8161-8877-7. A continued collection of reviews and criticism.

Goetz, William R. *Henry James and The Darkest Abyss of Romance.* La. State U. Pr. 1986 $27.50. ISBN 0-8071-1259-3. Examines the narrative effect of James's authorial presences in certain of his fiction and nonfiction texts.

Greenwald, Elissa. *Realism and the Romance: Nathaniel Hawthorne, Henry James, and American Fiction.* Ed. by Juliet McMaster. *Nineteenth-Century Studies.* Univ. Rochester Pr. 1988 $39.00. ISBN 0-8357-1948-0. Examines Hawthorne's influence on James; sees James as transcending the limits of Hawthorne's romance.

Habegger, Alfred. *Henry James and the "Woman Business."* Cambridge U. Pr. 1989 $34.50. ISBN 0-685-44828-2. Feminist study that considers James's relation to his family and to the popular women writers he reviewed in analyzing his major texts.

Hocks, Richard A. *Henry James: A Study of the Short Fiction. Twayne's Studies in Short Fiction.* Macmillan 1990 $20.95. ISBN 0-8057-8328-8. Goes beyond study of plot and character to analyze major short fiction and novellas; includes relevant excerpts from James's notebooks, letters, and criticism.

Horne, Philip. *Henry James and Revision: The New York Edition.* OUP 1991 $89.00. ISBN 0-19-812871-1. Complex analysis of James's New York Edition revisions in terms of their effect either to clarify or to conceal issues in the original text.

Kastan, Carren. *Imagination and Desire in the Novels of Henry James.* Rutgers U. Pr. 1984 $25.00. ISBN 0-8135-1037-6. Feminist reading of James that questions traditional interpretation of him as an aesthete.

Leavis, F. R. *The Great Tradition: George Eliot, Henry James, Joseph Conrad. Gotham Lib.* NYU Pr. 1963 o.p. Classic study placing James as a major figure in the development of the modern novel.

Lewis, R.W.B. *The Jameses: A Family Narrative.* FS&G 1991 $35.00. ISBN 0-374-17861-5. Story of entire James family. Examines relationships between family members.

McEwen, Fred B. *A Biographical Dictionary of the Characters in the Fiction of Henry James.* Garland 1993 $34.00. ISBN 0-8240-9200-7. In progress.

McWhirter, David. *Desire and Love in Henry James: A Study of the Late Novels.* Cambridge U. Pr. 1989 $44.95. ISBN 0-521-35328-9. Contrasts authentic love to the "imagination of loving" through close readings of James's late fiction.

Matthiessen, F.O. *Henry James: The Major Phase.* OUP 1944 o.p.

Nowell-Smith, Simon, ed. *The Legend of the Master: Henry James as Others Saw Him.* OUP 1986 $10.95. ISBN 0-19-281921-6. Anecdotes about James by friends and fellow writers.

Porte, Joel. *New Essays on The Portrait of a Lady. The Amer. Novel Ser.* Cambridge U. Pr. 1990 $24.95. ISBN 0-521-34508-1. Collection of essays including psychoanalytic and feminist as well as traditional readings of James's novel.

Posnock, Ross. *The Trial of Curiosity: Henry James, William James, and the Challenge of Modernity.* OUP 1991 $45.00. ISBN 0-19-506606-5. Places both Jameses against their contemporaries; especially relevant to Henry James's *The American Scene.*

Powers, Lyall H. *The Portrait of a Lady: Maiden, Woman and Heroine. Twayne's Masterwork Studies.* Macmillan 1991 $21.95. ISBN 0-8057-8066-1. Collection of essays detailing contexts and different critical readings of this thoroughly-studied novel.

Putt, Samuel G. *Henry James: A Reader's Guide.* Cornell Univ. Pr. 1967 o.p. A good, readable introductory work to James's 22 novels and 112 tales.

Seltzer, Mark. *Henry James and the Art of Power.* Cornell Univ. Pr. 1984 o.p. Examines James's depictions of social power in *Princess Casamassima, The Golden Bowl,* and *The American Scene.*

Seymour, Miranda. *A Ring of Conspirators: Henry James and his Literary Circle, 1895–1915.* HM 1989 $19.95. ISBN 0-395-51173-9. Examination of James's life at Lamb House in Rye, England, including the many literary figures who visited him there.

Tanner, Tony. *Henry James: The Writer and His Work.* U. of Mass. Pr. 1989 $12.95. ISBN 0-87023-680-6. General introduction to James. Survey of James's life, summary of major fiction, and comment on selected works.

Tintner, Adeline R. *The Book of Henry James; Appropriating the Classics.* Bks. Demand 1987 o.p. Collection of many previously published articles. Valuable study of influences for reference and resource use.

———. *The Cosmopolitan World of Henry James: An Intertextual Study.* La. State U. Pr. 1991 $39.95. ISBN 0-8071-1663-7. Shows the evolution of James's "cosmopolitan" theme from the international theme of his earlier work.

———. *The Museum World of Henry James. Studies in Modern Lit.* Bks. Demand repr. of 1986 ed. $108.70. ISBN 0-8357-1725-9. Comprehensive study of James, his relation to art, and his use of art in his fiction.

———. *The Pop World of Henry James: From Fairy Tales to Science Fiction.* Ed. by A. Walton Litz. *Studies in Modern Lit.* Bks. Demand 1988 $92.70. ISBN 0-8357-1855-7. Counters the view of James as an elitist. Shows the influence of fairy tales, legends, and scandals on James's writing.

JAMES, WILLIAM. 1842–1910

William James, oldest of five children (including HENRY JAMES and ALICE JAMES) in the extraordinary James family, has had a far-reaching influence on writers and thinkers of the nineteenth and twentieth centuries. Broadly educated by private tutors and through European travel, James initially studied painting. During the Civil War, however, he turned to medicine and physiology, attended Harvard medical school, and became interested in the workings of the mind. His text, *The Principles of Psychology* (1890), presents psychology as a science rather than a philosophy and emphasizes the connection between the mind and the body. James believed in free will and the power of the mind to affect events and determine the future. In *The Will to Believe* (1897) and *The Varieties of Religious Experience* (1902), he explores metaphysical concepts and mystical experiences. He saw truth not as absolute but as relative, depending on the given situation and the forces at work in it. He believed that the universe was not static and orderly but ever-changing and chaotic. His most important work, *Pragmatism* (1907), examines the practical consequences of behavior and rejects the idealist philosophy of the transcendentalists. This philosophy seems to reinforce the tenets of social Darwinism and the idea of financial success as the justification of the means in a materialistic society; nevertheless, James strove to demonstrate the practical value of ethical behavior. Overall, James's lifelong concern with what he called the "stream of thought" or "stream of consciousness" changed the way writers conceptualize characters and present the relationship between humans, society, and the natural world.

NONFICTION BY WILLIAM JAMES

Essays in Pragmatism. Free Pr. 1974 $9.95. ISBN 0-317-30538-7

Pragmatism. 1907. *Great Bks. in Philosophy Ser.* Prometheus Bks. 1990 $7.75. ISBN 0-87975-633-0.

Pragmatism and the Meaning of Truth. 1907. HUP 1978 $11.95. ISBN 0-674-69737-5. With an introduction by A. J. Ayer.

The Principles of Psychology. 1890. Ed. by George A. Miller. HUP 1983 $22.50. ISBN 0-674-70625-0

Psychology: The Briefer Course. Ed. by Gordon Allport. U. of Notre Dame Pr. 1985 $11.95. ISBN 0-268-01557-0. Condensed version of James's *Principles of Psychology.*

The Varieties of Religious Experience: A Study in Human Nature. 1902. Gleneida Pub. 1991 $8.95. ISBN 0-8007-3011-9. With an introduction by R. Niebuhr.

The Will to Believe. 1897. *Works of William James Ser.* HUP 1979 $34.95. ISBN 0-674-95281-2. With an introduction by Edward H. Madden.

The Writings of William James: A Comprehensive Edition. Ed. by John McDermott. U. Ch. Pr. 1978 $19.95. ISBN 0-226-39188-4. Selection of important writings.

WORKS BY WILLIAM JAMES

William James: Selected Unpublished Letters, 1885–1910. Ed. by Frederick J. Scott. Ohio St. U. Pr. 1986 $52.50. ISBN 0-8142-0379-5

The Works of William James. Ed. by Frederick Burkhardt, Fredson Bowers, and others. HUP o.p.

Writings, 1878–1899. Ed. by Gerald E. Myers. Library of America 1992 $35.00. ISBN 0-940450-72-0. Includes: *Psychology; Briefer Course; The Will to Believe; Talks to Teachers; Essays.*

Writings, 1902–1910. Ed. by Bruce Kuklick. Library of America 1988 $27.50. ISBN 0-940450-38-0. Includes: *The Varieties of Religious Experience; Pragmatism; A Pluralistic Universe; The Meaning of Truth; Some Problems of Philosophy.*

BOOKS ABOUT WILLIAM JAMES

Allen, Gay Wilson. *William James: A Biography.* Viking Penguin 1967 o.p. Does not replace Perry's 1938 biography, but makes fuller use of primary material.

Barzun, Jacques. *A Stroll with William James.* U. Ch. Pr. 1984 $25.00. ISBN 0-226-03865-3. Readable exploration of James's intellectual life and ideology.

Bird, Graham. *William James.* Routledge Chapman & Hall 1987 $39.95. ISBN 0-7100-9602-X

Bjork, Daniel W. *William James: The Center of His Vision*. Col. U. Pr. 1988 $47.00. ISBN 0-231-05674-5. Traditional biography making use especially of correspondence between James and his wife; sees James as an interdisciplinary thinker.

Brennan, Bernard P. *William James*. *Twayne's U.S. Authors Ser.* NCUP 1968 $10.95. ISBN 0-8084-0005-3. General introductory study of James's life and thought.

Cotkin, George. *William James, Public Philosopher*. *New Studies in Amer. Intellectual & Cultural Hist.* Johns Hopkins 1989 $32.50. ISBN 0-8018-3878-9

Levinson, Henry S. *Science, Metaphysics, and the Chance of Salvation: An Interpretation of the Thought of William James*. Scholars Pr. GA 1978 $14.95. ISBN 0-89130-234-4. General study of James's philosophy focusing on what questions he asked.

Myers, Gerald E. *William James: His Life and Thought*. Yale U. Pr. 1988 $19.95. ISBN 0-300-04211-6. Comprehensive analysis of James's intellectual development in the context of Western thought.

Perry, Ralph B. *In the Spirit of William James*. 1938. Greenwood 1979 $39.75. ISBN 0-313-20715-1. Long the most comprehensive biography of James detailing James's journey from art to medicine to psychology and finally to philosophy.

Poirier, Richard. *Poetry and Pragmatism*. HUP 1991 $22.95. ISBN 0-674-67990-3

Posnock, Ross. *The Trial of Curiosity: Henry James, William James, and the Challenge of Modernity*. OUP 1991 $45.00. ISBN 0-19-507124-7

Skrupskelis, Ignas K. *William James: A Reference Guide*. G. K. Hall 1974 o.p. Annotated bibliography.

Taylor, Eugene. *William James on Exceptional Mental States: The 1896 Lowell Lectures*. Scribner 1983 o.p. Contends that James did not abandon science to become a mystic.

Wernham, James. *James's Will-to-Believe Doctrine: A Heretical View*. U. of Toronto Pr. 1987 $34.95. ISBN 0-7735-0567-9. Reevaluates the concept of James's "will to believe."

JEWETT, SARAH ORNE. 1849–1909

Although Sarah Orne Jewett spent much of her life in South Berwick, Maine, the locale of many of her short stories, she traveled far beyond the narrow reaches of that New England seaport, both literally and figuratively. Classified as a regional or local-color writer, she produced stories that are among the finest in American literature, notable for their insight into human character and the quiet independence of women who face loneliness and frustration in their lives without giving up. Her most characteristic theme is nostalgic reminiscence. Unable to attend school because of arthritis, Jewett had the opportunity to observe both the landscape and the people of New England as she accompanied her father, a doctor, on his rounds. He encouraged both her reading and her writing. Her first published story appeared in the *Atlantic Monthly* in 1869, and editor WILLIAM DEAN HOWELLS encouraged her to publish her first collection, *Deephaven* (1877), stories set in a fictional town similar to South Berwick. Her first novel, *A Country Doctor* (1884), tells the story of a girl who chooses to become a doctor rather than marry. Other collections of short stories, including *A Marsh Island* (1885), *A White Heron and Other Stories* (1886), *A Native of Winby* (1893), *Tales of New England* (1894), as well as others, continued to detail the Maine countryside and life. *The Country of the Pointed Firs* (1896), her largest and most mature collection of short stories, was considered a masterpiece by WILLA CATHER. In these, the narrator, a summer visitor from Boston, brings the perspective of the outside world to the New England scenes. Although Jewett traveled widely in the United States and Europe, meeting and becoming friends with such writers as Howells, MARK TWAIN, and HENRY JAMES, her strongest friendships and closest affinities were with women. A characteristic thread running through her work is that of female friendships and bondings.

She spent summers and traveled with Annie Fields, the widow of editor James Fields. Without idealizing the past, Jewett's stories capture the vanishing New England rural life and seaport towns and sympathetically portray the lives of the people whose strength she so admired. Jewett's complete collected works are now available in print.

NOVEL BY JEWETT

A Country Doctor. 1884. NAL-Dutton 1986 $5.95. ISBN 0-452-00805-0

SHORT STORY COLLECTIONS BY JEWETT

Best Stories of Sarah Orne Jewett. Ed. by Josephine H. Donovan, Martin H. Greenberg, and Charles G. Waugh. Rodale Pr. Inc. 1988 $10.95. ISBN 0-912769-33-5

Country By-Ways. Rprt. Serv. 1988 repr. of 1881 ed. $59.00. ISBN 0-7812-1304-5. Early stories and sketches of New England, including the humorous "An Autumn Holiday."

The Country of the Pointed Firs. Norton 1982 $7.95. ISBN 0-393-00048-6. With a preface by Willa Cather.

Deephaven. 1877. Lightyear Pr. 1980 $13.50. ISBN 0-89968-211-1

Funeral Seasons. Scream Pr. 1989 $25.00. ISBN 0-910489-22-X

Native of Winby and Other Tales. Short Story Index Repr. Ser. Rprt. Serv. 1988 repr. of 1893 ed. $59.00. ISBN 0-7812-1311-8

Stories and Tales. 7 vol. AMS Pr. repr. of 1910 ed. $185.00. ISBN 0-404-20136-9

Tales of New England. Short Story Index Repr. Ser. Ayer repr. of 1894 ed. o.p. Eight stories reprinted from earlier volumes.

A White Heron. 1886. Tilbury Hse. 1990 $13.95. ISBN 0-88448-082-8

World of Dunnet Landing: A Sarah Orne Jewett Collection. Ed. by David Green. Peter Smith. o.p. Collection of sketches, many originally collected in *The Country of the Pointed Firs.*

WORKS BY JEWETT

Collected Works: The Collected Works of Sarah O. Jewett, 1881–1901. Rprt. Serv. 1988 $700.00. ISBN 0-7812-1301-0

Collected Works. 14 vols. Somerset repr. of 1877–1901 ed. o.p.

Letters. 1911. *Amer. Biog. Ser.* Rprt. Serv. 1991 $59.00. ISBN 0-7812-8219-5

Sarah O. Jewett: Letters. Ed. by Richard Cary. Colby rev. ed. 1967 o.p.

BOOKS ABOUT JEWETT

Cary, Richard. *Sarah Orne Jewett. Twayne's U.S. Authors Ser.* NCUP 1962 $10.95. ISBN 0-8084-0272-2. General biographical and thematic introduction to Jewett's fiction.

Donovan, Josephine L. *Sarah Orne Jewett. Lit. and Life Ser.* Continuum 1980 o.p. A good brief introduction.

Matthiessen, F. O. *Sarah Orne Jewett.* Peter Smith repr. of 1929 ed. $11.25. ISBN 0-8446-1305-3. The first critical biography of Jewett; basis of much later scholarship and interest.

Mobley, Marilyn S. *Folk Roots and Mythic Wings in Sarah Orne Jewett and Toni Morrison: The Cultural Function of Narrative.* La. State U. Pr. 1991 $24.95. ISBN 0-8071-1660-2. Sees Jewett (and Toni Morrison) as "cultural archivists" and "redemptive scribes" of their culture.

Nagel, Gwen L. *Critical Essays on Sarah Orne Jewett. Critical Essays on Amer. Lit. Ser.* G. K. Hall 1984 $40.00. ISBN 0-8161-8422-4. Collection of reprinted and original essays.

Roman, Margaret. *Sarah Orne Jewett: Reconstructing Gender.* U. of Ala Pr. 1992 $28.95. ISBN 0-8173-0533-5. Examines the subversion of conventional gender roles in Jewett's fiction, including lesser-known texts.

Sherman, Sarah W. *Sarah Orne Jewett, an American Persephone.* U. Pr. of New Eng. 1989 $40.00. ISBN 0-87451-484-3. Uses Demeter/Persephone myth to trace the development of feminization in Jewett's fiction.

Westbrook, Perry D. *Acres of Flint: Sarah Orne Jewett and Her Contemporaries.* Scarecrow rev. ed. 1981 $25.00. ISBN 0-8108-1357-2. Critical analysis comparing Jewett, Willa Cather, and Helen Hunt Jackson.

JOHNSON, JAMES WELDON. 1871–1938

James Weldon Johnson, born to a middle-class family and raised in Jacksonville, Florida, was educated so as to become one of the "talented tenth" described by W.E.B. DuBois. Johnson became the first African American admitted to the Florida bar since Reconstruction. However, his experience teaching school in Georgia made him acutely aware of the tensions between African Americans and whites. He wrote poetry, songs, and journalism; practiced law; served in the Venezuelan and Nicaraguan consulates; worked as executive secretary of the National Association for the Advancement of Colored People (NAACP); and held the Spence Chair of Creative Literature at Fisk University. His best-known poem and song is "Lift Every Voice and Sing" (1900), while *God's Trombones: Seven Sermons in Verse* (1927) was his most popular book of poetry. The fictional *Autobiography of an Ex-Colored Man* (1912) documents the experience of an African American man in America. Although Johnson's own thinking had many conservative elements, his work prepared the way for the more radical flowering of African American talent during the Harlem renaissance.

POETRY BY JOHNSON

God's Trombones: Seven Negro Sermons in Verse. Viking Penguin 1990 $5.95. ISBN 0-14-018403-1

Fifty Years and Other Poems. 1917. AMS Pr. repr. of 1917 ed. $15.00. ISBN 0-404-11398-2

NOVEL BY JOHNSON

The Autobiography of an Ex-Colored Man. Viking Penguin 1990 $5.95. ISBN 0-14-018402-3. With an introduction by William L. Andrews.

NONFICTION BY JOHNSON

Along This Way: The Autobiography of James Weldon Johnson. 1933. *Amer. Biog. Ser.* Rprt. Serv. 1991 $89.00. ISBN 0-7812-8221-7

Black Manhattan. 1930. *Da Capo Quality Paperbacks Ser.* Da Capo Pr. 1991 $13.95. ISBN 0-306-80431-X. A collection of essays. Includes an introduction by Sandra K. Wilson.

BOOKS ABOUT JOHNSON

Fleming, Robert E.. *James Weldon Johnson. U.S. Author Ser.* Macmillan 1987 $21.95. ISBN 0-8057-7491-2. General introduction and analysis of major themes.

Levy, Eugene. *James Weldon Johnson: Black Leader, Black Voice.* U. Ch. Pr. 1973 o.p. Critical biography, includes bibliography.

LANIER, SIDNEY. 1842–1881

Lanier was the foremost poet of the nineteenth-century South. Born in Macon, Georgia, he interrupted his education at Oglethorpe University to join the Confederate army. Taken prisoner, he developed tuberculosis, which led to a continual struggle with poor health and, ultimately, to his early death. The novel *Tiger Lilies* (1867) is based on his Civil War experiences. Throughout his life he was interested in both music and poetry. He played first flute in Baltimore's Peabody Symphony Orchestra, and his poetry reflects the connection he saw between music and verse. His greatest poem, "The Marshes of Glynn" (1878), is considered "a symphony without musical score." He lectured on the relationship of music and poetry at Johns Hopkins University and published *The Science of English Verse* (1880), which claimed that the laws of poetry and music were the same. Other lectures, including *Shakespeare and His Forerunners* (1902), were published by his widow. The work Lanier completed and the many fragments he left suggest a far greater potential than he was able to fulfill in his short life.

POETRY BY LANIER

Poems of Sidney Lanier. 1945. U. of Ga. Pr. 1981 $24.95. ISBN 0-8203-0560-X
Selected Poems. AMS Pr. repr. of 1947 ed. $21.50. ISBN 0-404-20151-2. With a preface by Stuart Young.

NONFICTION BY LANIER

Letters. Gordon Pr. $59.95. ISBN 0-8490-0510-8
Letters: Selections from His Correspondence. Select Bib. Repr. Ser. Ed. by Henry W. Lanier. Ayer repr. of 1899 ed. $20.00. ISBN 0-8369-6727-5
Music and Poetry: Essays upon Some Aspects and Interrelations of the Two Arts. Rprt. Serv. 1990 $69.00. ISBN 0-7812-9013-9. Essays and lectures explaining Lanier's theory of the relationship between music and poetry, as exemplified in his poems.
Shakespeare and His Forerunners. BCL1-PR Eng. Lit. Ser. Rprt. Serv. 1992 $99.00. ISBN 0-7812-7289-0

WORKS BY LANIER

Collected Writings. Gordon Pr. 1972 $600.00. ISBN 0-87968-906-4
Sidney Lanier: Poems and Letters. Bks. Demand $59.95. ISBN 0-317-39701-X. Manageable selection of 25 poems and 74 letters related to Lanier's professional life.

BOOKS ABOUT LANIER

De Bellis, Jack. *Sidney Lanier. Twayne's U.S. Authors Ser.* G. K. Hall 1972 o.p. General introduction.
Gabin, Jane S. *A Living Minstrelsy: The Poetry and Music of Sidney Lanier.* Mercer Univ. Pr. 1985 $19.95. ISBN 0-86554-155-8
Graham, Philip, and Joseph Jones. *A Concordance to the Poems of Sidney Lanier: Including the Poem Outlines and Certain Uncollected Items. Eng. Literary Ref. Ser.* Johnson Repr. 1969 repr. of 1939 ed. $45.00. ISBN 0-384-19610-1
Mims, Edwin. *Sidney Lanier.* 1905. Gordon Pr. $59.95. ISBN 0-8490-1052-1. First critical biography of Lanier.
Parks, Edd Winfield. *Sidney Lanier: The Man, the Poet, the Critic.* U. of Ga. Pr. 1968 o.p. Biography including discussion of Lanier's poetry and critical views.
Starke, Aubrey H.. *Sidney Lanier: A Biographical and Critical Study.* Russell Sage 1964 repr. of 1933 ed. o.p. Biography that sees Lanier not solely as a Southern poet.
West, C. *A Sketch of the Life and Writings of Sidney Lanier.* Gordon Pr. 1972 $75.00. ISBN 0-8490-1061-6

LAZARUS, EMMA. 1849–1887

Emma Lazarus is best remembered for her sonnet "The New Colossus" (1883), which is inscribed on the base of the Statue of Liberty. Born in New York City, a precocious child of wealthy and cultured parents, she was an avid reader and student. Her first book of rather conventional poetry, *Poems and Translations* (1866), was published when she was only 17. Her second, *Admetus and Other Poems* (1871), was dedicated to RALPH WALDO EMERSON, who had responded positively to her work. Her many translations—HEINRICH HEINE (see Vol. 2) and FRIEDRICH VON SCHILLER (see Vol. 2) from German, VICTOR HUGO (see

Vol. 2) and Alexandre Dumas (père) (see Vol. 2) from French, and medieval poetry from Hebrew—attest to her scholarship and facility with languages. Some of her best work, included in *Songs of a Semite* (1882), arose from her commitment to her Jewish heritage and her response to the persecution of Jews in Europe, especially the Russian pogroms of 1882.

Poetry by Lazarus

Admetus. 1871. Irvington repr. of 1871 ed. $36.00. ISBN 0-8398-1152-7
Emma Lazarus: Selections from Her Poetry and Prose. Ed. by Morris U. Schappes. Biblio Pr. 1982 $3.75. ISBN 0-685-53371-9
Songs of a Semite: The Dance to Death, and Other Poems. 1882 o.p.

Nonfiction by Lazarus

An Epistle to the Hebrews. Jewish Hist. 1987 $10.00. ISBN 0-916790-02-9. Collected essays.

Work by Lazarus

Letters to Emma Lazarus in the Columbia Univ. Lib. Ed. by Ralph L. Rusk. AMS Pr. 1984 $14.00. ISBN 0-404-05459-5. Collection includes letters from Robert Browning, William Morris, Ralph Waldo Emerson, and others.

Books about Lazarus

Lefer, Diane. *Emma Lazarus. Amer. Women of Achievement Ser.* Chelsea Hse. 1988 $17.95. ISBN 1-55546-664-8
Merrimum, Eve. *Emma Lazarus: Woman with a Torch.* Citadel Pr. 1956 o.p. Biography praising Lazarus.
Vogel, Dan. *Emma Lazarus. Twayne's U.S. Authors Ser.* G. K. Hall 1980 o.p. Study of Lazarus's writing career and her influence on American Jewish writers.
Wagenknecht, Edward. *Daughters of the Covenant: Portraits of Six Jewish Women.* U. of Mass. Pr. 1983 $25.00. ISBN 0-87023-396-3. Considers Lazarus's personality and character in studying her poetry.

LONDON, JACK. 1876–1916

Though Jack London died in his prime, he had already produced an enormous volume of work. He owed his first great success to dog stories: *The Call of the Wild* (1903) is a study of reversion to type, the domesticated dog returning to the wild after performing heroic deeds in the corrupted world of humans, while *White Fang* (1906) reverses that situation by showing the wild dog tamed by kindness. *The Sea Wolf* (1904) is the best known of London's other adventure stories, the exciting tale of the maddest captain in American sea fiction between Herman Melville's Ahab and Herman Wouk's Queeg. The autobiographical *Martin Eden* (1909) stands up as one of the better bildungsromans written at a time when many such self-portraits were being produced, and *The Iron Heel* (1907) remains a vivid novel of social prophecy in which London anticipates the threat of fascism. Of London's many excellent short stories, the often anthologized "To Build a Fire" is considered an impressive classic of literary naturalism.

In *On Native Grounds*, Alfred Kazin writes: "The clue to Jack London's work is certainly to be found in his own turbulent life. . . . The greatest story he ever wrote was the story he lived. . . ." He became an ardent Socialist when, in his oyster pirate days in San Francisco, he read the *Communist Manifesto*. His undoubted skill as a writer and a craftsman of fiction explains why his stock seems to have risen throughout the world in recent years. Critical appreciations appear with increasing regularity, and he continues to be read widely. Students of American literature who want to read only the best and most representative of his literary fiction will find that they cannot do better than to read the two volumes of London's work in the Library of America series edited by Donald Pizer.

NOVELS BY LONDON

The Call of the Wild. 1903. Bantam 1991 $2.95. ISBN 0-553-21233-8

The Iron Heel. 1908. Paul & Co. Pub. 1991 $9.95. ISBN 0-904526-01-1

John Barleycorn: or Alcoholic Memoirs. 1913. *Amer. Biog. Ser.* Rprt. Serv. 1991 $69.00. ISBN 0-7812-8249-7. Fictional memoir supporting the Prohibition movement.

Martin Eden. 1909. Bantam 1986 $3.95. ISBN 0-553-21212-5

White Fang. Berkley Pub. 1990 $3.75. ISBN 0-425-12030-9. Includes an introduction by Abraham Rothberg.

SHORT STORY COLLECTIONS BY LONDON

The Call of the Wild, White Fang, and Other Stories. Ed. by Earle Labor and Robert C. Leitz. *World's Classics Ser.* OUP 1990 $5.95. ISBN 0-19-282709-X

Great Short Works of Jack London: Call of the Wild, White Fang and Six Stories. Ed. by Earle Labor. HarpC 1950 $6.50. ISBN 0-06-083041-7

In a Far Country: Jack London's Western Tales. Ed. by Dale Walker. Green Hill 1987 $8.95. ISBN 0-915463-36-9. Edited collection of London's western stories.

The Sea-Wolf and Other Stories. Ed. by Andrew Sinclair. Viking Penguin 1989 $6.95. ISBN 0-14-018357-4

The Short Stories of Jack London: The Authorized Edition with Definitive Texts Selected by Earle Labor, Robert C. Leitz, III, & I. Milo Shepard. Macmillan 1990 $35.00. ISBN 0-02-567180-4. Stories from 1893 to 1918 showing London's socialist and working-class sympathies.

The Son of the Wolf. 1900. Buccaneer Bks. 1992 $18.95. ISBN 0-89966-953-0. London's first story collection. Includes "The White Silence."

South Sea Tales. 1911. Mutual Pub. HI 1985 $4.95. ISBN 0-935180-14-1. Stories arising from London's experiences in the Pacific Islands.

Tales of the Pacific. Viking Penguin 1989 $6.95. ISBN 0-14-018358-2. Collection of some of London's best tales from his Pacific travels.

NONFICTION BY LONDON

Cruise of the Snark. 1911. Humanities 1984 $12.95. ISBN 0-85036-311-X. Essays.

Jack London Reports: War Correspondence, Sports Articles, and Miscellaneous Writings. Ed. by King Hendricks and Irving Shepard. Doubleday 1970 o.p. Broad sampling of London's diverse nonfiction writings.

The Road. 1907. *Amer. Biog. Ser.* Rprt. Serv. 1991 $69.00. ISBN 0-7812-8250-0. Autobiography.

WORKS BY LONDON

The Kempton-Wace Letters. Ed. by Anna Stunski and Douglas Robillard. NCUP 1991 $7.95. ISBN 0-8084-0436-9

The Letters of Jack London. 3 vols. Ed. by Earle Labor, Robert C. Leitz, and Milo I. Shepard. Stanford U. Pr. 1988 $139.50. ISBN 0-8047-1507-6. Meticulously edited and annotated complete collection of correspondence.

Novels and Social Writings. Ed. by Donald Pizer. Library of America 1982 $27.50. ISBN 0-940450-06-2

Novels and Stories: The Call of the Wild; White Fang; The Sea-Wolf; Short Stories. Ed. by Donald Pizer. Library of America 1982 $27.50. ISBN 0-940450-05-4

BOOKS ABOUT LONDON

Beauchamp, Gorman. *Reader's Guide to Jack London.* Ed. by Roger C. Schlobin. Starmont Hse. 1984 $19.95. ISBN 0-916732-39-8. A useful study and research tool.

Hedrick, Joan D. *Solitary Comrade: Jack London and His Work.* U. of NC Pr. 1982 o.p. Feminist study of London looking at the split between his public and private lives.

Labor, Earle. *Jack London. Twayne's U.S. Authors Ser.* Macmillan 1977 $20.95. ISBN 0-8057-0455-8. Biography and criticism; good basic introduction to London that attempts to separate myth from man.

London, Joan. *Jack London and His Daughters.* Intro. by Bart Abbott. Heyday Bks. 1990 $19.95. ISBN 0-930588-43-6. London's daughter's memoir.

———. *Jack London and His Times: An Unconventional Biography.* U. of Wash. Pr. 1968 o.p. Perceptive study of London by his daughter showing the influence of his family and friends.

Perry, John. *Jack London: An American Myth.* Nelson-Hall 1981 o.p. Biography tracing London's ancestry in an attempt to dispel myths that London and his other biographers have created about his life.

Sherman, Joan R. *Jack London: A Reference Guide.* G. K. Hall 1977 o.p.

Sinclair, Andrew. *Jack: A Biography of Jack London.* HarpC 1977 o.p. Psychological study; first biography to make use of London's personal papers.

Stone, Irving. *Jack London: Sailor on Horseback.* Doubleday 1978 $12.95. ISBN 0-385-14084-3. Unreliable "novel biography" credited with popularizing London.

Tavernier-Courbin, Jacqueline, ed. *Critical Essays on Jack London.* G. K. Hall 1983 o.p. Essays dealing with London's life, works, and writing style.

Walker, Franklin. *Jack London and the Klondike: The Genesis of an American Writer.* Huntington Lib. 1978 repr. of 1966 ed. o.p. Attempts to separate myths from reality of London's Klondike experience.

Watson, Charles N., Jr. *The Novels of Jack London: A Reappraisal.* U. of Wis. Pr. 1983 $25.00. ISBN 0-299-09300-X. Careful examination of major works.

Woodbridge, H. C. *Jack London: A Bibliography.* Kraus rev. ed. 1973 $45.00. ISBN 0-527-97860-4. Indispensable study of primary and secondary material.

MOODY, WILLIAM VAUGHN. 1869–1910

Born in Spencer, Indiana, Moody attended Harvard University before joining the faculty of the University of Chicago. His early poetry, modeled largely on the Elizabethan poets and JOHN MILTON, concentrated primarily on personal themes. But probably under the influence of HAMLIN GARLAND, Moody became passionately interested in political and social issues. His "Gloucester Moors" (1900) displays fine lyric power informing a profound social vision. After writing other poems protesting U.S. imperialism, Moody turned to verse drama, succeeding with his plays, *The Great Divide* (1909) and *The Faith Healer* (1909). His poetry represents a transition from nineteenth-century verse to the twentieth-century work of EDWARD ARLINGTON ROBINSON and ROBERT FROST.

WORKS BY MOODY

Poems and Plays. BCL1-PS Amer. Lit. Ser. Rprt. Serv. 1992 $150.00. ISBN 0-7812-6801-X. Poetry, poetic drama, and plays, including *The Great Divide* and *The Faith Healer.*

Selected Poems of William Vaughn Moody. Ed. by Robert M. Lovett. AMS Pr. repr. of 1931 ed. o.p. Selection of poems and lyrics with introductory memoir.

Some Letters of William Vaughn Moody. BCL1-PS Amer. Lit. Ser. Rprt. Serv. 1992 $69.00. ISBN 0-7812-6802-8

BOOKS ABOUT MOODY

Brown, Maurice F. *Estranging Dawn: The Life and Works of William Vaughn Moody.* S. Ill. U. Pr. 1973 o.p. Thorough critical biography.

Halpern, Martin. *William Vaughn Moody. Twayne's U.S. Authors Ser.* NCUP 1964 $10.95. ISBN 0-8084-0330-3. Biography and critical analysis.

Henry, David D. *William Vaughn Moody: A Study.* Arden Lib. 1978 repr. of 1934 o.p. General introduction and review of early criticism.

NORRIS, (BENJAMIN) FRANK(LIN). 1870–1902

Considered one of the leading pioneers in American naturalism, Frank Norris is read and studied for his vivid and honest depiction of life at the beginning of a lusty and developing new century. Born in Chicago, he moved to San Francisco with his well-to-do family when he was 14 and went on to attend the University of California and Harvard University before becoming a war correspondent in South Africa and Cuba. His early apprentice work consisted mostly of rather unremarkable adventure stories, but, with the long-gestating *McTeague: A Story of San Francisco* (1899), he struck a new note that made him seem to some readers an American ZOLA (see Vol. 2). That powerful study of avarice in a seedy section of the Bay Area may well be Norris's masterpiece.

The Octopus (1901), the first of Norris's projected *Epic of the Wheat* series, deals with the raising of wheat in California and the struggle of ranchers against the railroads, while *The Pit* (1903) is a novel about speculation on the Chicago wheat exchange. Unfortunately, Norris died suddenly after an operation for appendicitis and did not write *The Wolf*, in which the wheat as a symbol of life-force was to feed a famine-stricken village in Europe. *Vandover and the Brute* (1914), the manuscript of which was lost during the San Francisco earthquake and rediscovered for publication in 1914, is an early work admired as representative of American naturalism.

Like STEPHEN CRANE, a writer with whom Norris is frequently compared, Norris died too young to fulfill his considerable promise, but he has more than held his own ground among turn-of-the-century writers whose works have lived. One reason may be that he took his craft as a writer seriously, as is shown by his posthumously published *Responsibilities of the Novelist and Other Literary Essays* (1903) and *The Literary Criticism of Frank Norris*, edited by Donald Pizer.

NOVELS BY NORRIS

Blix. Rprt. Serv. 1992 $89.00. ISBN 0-7812-6807-9. A sentimental love story.

Man's Woman. 1900. Rprt. Serv. 1992 $79.00. ISBN 0-7812-6810-9

McTeague. Norton Critical Ed. Norton 1978 $8.95. ISBN 0-393-04460-2

McTeague: A Story of San Francisco. 1899. Ed. by Kevin Starr. *Penguin Amer. Lib*. Viking Penguin 1982 $5.95. ISBN 0-14-039017-0. Story of a dentist who becomes a drunkard, murders his wife, and is trapped while fleeing across the California desert.

Moran of the Lady Letty: A Story of Adventure off the California Coast. Irvington 1979 repr. of 1898 ed. $11.50. ISBN 0-8398-1351-1. Norris's first novel.

Novels and Essays. Ed. by Donald Pizer. Library of America 1986 $27.50. ISBN 0-940450-40-2. Includes: *Vandover and the Brute; McTeague; The Octopus*.

The Octopus: A Story of California. BCL1-PS Amer. Lit. Ser. Rprt. Serv. 1992 $89.00. ISBN 0-7812-6812-5

The Pit: A Story of Chicago. 1903. BCL1-PS Amer. Lit. Ser. Rprt. Serv. 1992 $99.00. ISBN 0-7812-6813-3

Vandover and the Brute. 1914. BCL1-PS Amer. Lit. Ser. Rprt. Serv. 1992 $89.00. ISBN 0-7812-6814-1

SHORT STORY COLLECTION BY NORRIS

Deal in Wheat and Other Stories of the New and Old West. BCL1-PS Amer. Lit. Ser. Rprt. Serv. 1992 $79.00. ISBN 0-7812-6808-7

Frank Norris of "The Wave": Stories and Sketches from the San Francisco Weekly, 1893 to 1897. Folcroft 1974 repr. of 1931 ed. o.p.

NONFICTION BY NORRIS

Literary Criticism of Frank Norris. Ed. by Donald Pizer. U. of Tex. Pr. 1962 o.p.

WORKS BY NORRIS

The Complete Edition of Frank Norris. 10 vols. 1928 o.p.

The Letters of Frank Norris. Ed. by F. Walker. Book Club of CA 1956 o.p.

A Novelist in the Making: A Collection of Student Themes and the Novels Blix and Vandover and the Brute. Ed. by James D. Hart. *John Harvard Lib. Ser.* HUP 1970 $38.50. ISBN 0-671-62820-9

BOOKS ABOUT NORRIS

Ahnebrink, Lars. *The Influence of Emile Zola on Frank Norris.* Kraus repr. of 1947 ed. $15.00. ISBN 0-8115-0186-8

Dillingham, William B. *Frank Norris: Instinct and Art.* U. of Nebr. Pr. 1969 $19.95. ISBN 0-8032-0039-0. Fills in biography to include the time Norris spent in London studying to be a painter.

French, Warren. *Frank Norris. Twayne's U.S. Author Ser.* NCUP 1962 $10.95. ISBN 0-8084-0134-3. General introduction and critical analysis.

Graham, Don. *Critical Essays on Frank Norris.* G. K. Hall 1980 o.p. A collection of reviews, articles, and essays.

————. *The Fiction of Frank Norris: The Aesthetic Context.* U. of Mo. Pr. 1978 $22.50. ISBN 0-8262-0252-7. Analyzes references to art in Norris's fiction.

Hochman, Barbara. *The Art of Frank Norris, Storyteller.* U. of Mo. Pr. 1988 $22.00. ISBN 0-8262-0663-8. Analysis of the artistic merit in Norris's writing. Goes beyond considerations of literary naturalism.

Marchand, Leslie. *Frank Norris: A Study.* 1942. Hippocrene Bks. 1964 $20.00. ISBN 0-0374-95282-5. Praises Norris for his early naturalism.

Pizer, Donald. *The Novels of Frank Norris. Studies in Fiction Ser.* Haskell 1972 repr. of 1966 ed. $75.00. ISBN 0-8383-1666-2. Sees Norris as struggling to resolve conflicts between religious and scientific ideologies at the end of the nineteenth century.

Walker, Franklin. *Frank Norris: A Biography.* Doubleday 1932 o.p. First Norris biography; used interviews, accounts, letters to present Norris as brash young writer.

RILEY, JAMES WHITCOMB. 1849–1916

Poet, lecturer, and journalist, Riley gained popularity with his series of poems in the Hoosier dialect written under the pseudonym "Benjamin F. Johnson, of Boone." These originally appeared in the Indianapolis *Journal,* where he worked from 1877 to 1885; in 1883 they were published as *The Old Swimmin'-Hole* and *'Leven More Poems.* His most popular poems are "When the Frost is on the Punkin'" and "The Old Man and Jim." Riley went on numerous lecture tours, entertaining as an actor and humorist. Although best known for his dialect poetry—"comforting, familiar platitudes, restated in verse" (Richard Crowder)—Riley also wrote humorous sketches and other poems. He produced more than 90 volumes of popular poetry, some of which are available in reprinted editions.

POETRY BY RILEY

The Best of James Whitcomb Riley. Ed. by Donald C. Manlove. *Midland Bks.* Ind. U. Pr. 1982 $17.95. ISBN 0-253-20299-X. A wide selection from Riley's *Complete Works.*

Book of Joyous Children. 1902. *Granger Index Repr. Ser.* Ayer repr. of 1902 ed. $18.00. ISBN 0-8369-6087-4

Complete Poems. Lightyear 1992 $21.95. ISBN 0-89968-289-8

The Complete Works of James Whitcomb Riley. 6 vols. AMS Pr. repr. of 1913 ed. $270.00. ISBN 0-404-05340-8. The definitive edition of Riley's work.

The Eternal Poetry of Romantic Love. Gloucester Art 1983 $117.50. ISBN 0-86650-082-0

An Old Sweetheart of Mine. Found. Class. Reprints 1991 $99.75. ISBN 0-89901-433-X

Songs of Summer. Folcroft repr. of 1883 ed. o.p.

SHORT STORY COLLECTION BY RILEY

The Boss Girl: A Christmas Story, and Other Sketches. 1885. *Short Story Index Repr. Ser.*
Ayer repr. of 1885. ed. $18.00. ISBN 0-8369-3927-1. Early prose sketches.

WORK BY RILEY

Letters of James Whitcomb Riley. 1930. Ed. by W. L. Phelps. *Amer. Biog. Ser.* Rprt. Serv.
1991 $79.00. ISBN 0-7812-8323-X

BOOKS ABOUT RILEY

Carman, Bliss. *James Whitcomb Riley: An Essay.* Folcroft 1977 repr. of 1925 ed. o.p.
Memoir and assessment of Riley by a friend who considers him "a happy
sentimentalist."
Dickey, Marcus. *The Youth of James Whitcomb Riley.* Richard West 1973 repr. of 1919 ed.
o.p.
Revell, Peter. *James Whitcomb Riley. Twayne's U.S. Authors Ser.* G. K. Hall o.p. One of
the few critical assessments of Riley focusing on his method of achieving popular
success with his poetry.
Russo, Anthony, and Dorothy Russo. *A Bibliography of James Whitcomb Riley. Amer. Lit.
Ser.* Haskell 1972 $69.95. ISBN 0-8383-1418-X

TIMROD, HENRY. 1828–1867

Timrod was born in Charleston, South Carolina. He attended the University of
Georgia (then Franklin College), where he developed an intense interest in the
classical writers—an interest displayed in *Poems,* published in 1859, the one
volume of poetry published during his lifetime. Prevented by tuberculosis from
serving in the Civil War, Timrod became a war correspondent and rose to the
position of editor of the Columbia *South Carolinian,* supporting the Confederate
cause with his pen. But Sherman's capture and burning of Columbia on
February 17, 1865, marked the end of any chance Timrod had for a secure life.
He died in poverty and despair little more than two years after Lee's surrender
at Appomattox.

From the time that Paul Hamilton Hayne, Timrod's friend since their
Charleston school days, collected and published *The Poems of Henry Timrod* in
1873, Timrod has been recognized as the Laureate of the Confederacy. His
classical purity of form, coupled with his intellectual and moral austerity,
prevent his poetry from becoming mired in the sentimentality that was
characteristic of so much southern poetry.

POETRY BY TIMROD

Poems. BCL1-PS Amer. Lit. Ser. Rprt. Serv. 1992 $69.00. ISBN 0-7812-6887-7
The Poems of Henry Timrod: With a Sketch of the Poet's Life. Ed. by Paul Hamilton Hayne.
Romantic Tradition in Amer. Lit. Ser. Ayer 1972 repr. of 1873 ed. $21.00. ISBN 0-405-
04646-4

NONFICTION BY TIMROD

Essays of Henry Timrod. Ed. by Edd W. Parks. U. of Ga. Pr. 1942 $16.00. ISBN 0-8203-
0056-X. Literary criticism found in Timrod's editorials and essays.

BOOKS ABOUT TIMROD

Hubbell, Jay B., ed. *Last Years of Henry Timrod.* AMS Pr. repr. of 1941 ed. $18.50. ISBN
0-404-03374-1. Sympathetic biography using Timrod's correspondence.
Parks, Edd W. *Henry Timrod. Twayne's U.S. Authors Ser.* NCUP 1964 $10.95. ISBN 0-
8084-0154-8. Biography and critical assessment of Timrod's poetry.

Rubin, Louis D., Jr. *The Edge of the Swamp: A Study of the Literature and Society of the Old South.* La. State U. Pr. 1989 $25.00. ISBN 0-8071-1495-2. Study of Southern writers before the Civil War, which seemed to be the catalyst that turned Timrod from a private to a public poet—"the laureate of the Confederacy."

Thompson, H. T. *Henry Timrod: Laureate of the Confederacy.* AMS Pr. repr of 1928 ed. $16.50. ISBN 0-404-06421-3. Biography by the son of one of Timrod's friends. Contains some inaccuracies.

TUCKERMAN, FREDERICK GODDARD. 1821–1873

Tuckerman, who was born in Boston, was little known during his lifetime. After graduating from Harvard University, he settled in Greenfield, Massachusetts, where he carefully observed nature, making notes on eclipses and local fauna. In 1860 he published *Poems,* a slender volume of sonnets. Although Tuckerman received a letter of praise from ALFRED LORD TENNYSON, to whom he had sent a copy, his volume of poems remained practically unknown. It was not until 1931, when Witter Bynner republished the best of *Poems,* together with three unpublished sonnet sequences, that Tuckerman became recognized as a minor master of the sonnet form.

POETRY BY TUCKERMAN

Complete Poems. 1860. Ed. by N. Scott Momaday. OUP 1965 o.p.
The Sonnets of Frederick Goddard Tuckerman. Ed. by Witter Bynner. Knopf 1931 o.p.

BOOKS ABOUT TUCKERMAN

England, Eugene. *Beyond Romanticism: Tuckerman's Life and Poetry.* State U. NY Pr. 1990 $39.50. ISBN 0-7914-0791-8
Golden, Samuel A. *Frederick Goddard Tuckerman.* Irvington 1966 $17.95. ISBN 0-89197-764-3. General introduction to Tuckerman's life and poetry.

TWAIN, MARK (PSEUD. OF SAMUEL LANGHORNE CLEMENS). 1835–1910

Samuel L. Clemens, steamboat pilot, prospector, and newspaper reporter, was born in Florida, Mississippi, the son of a Virginia migrant. When Clemens was four, his family moved to Hannibal, Missouri, a growing port on the Mississippi River. At age 12, Clemens was apprenticed to a printer, and soon after he was writing for a local newspaper owned by his brother Orion. In 1856, he pursued a boyhood ambition to become a steamboat pilot on the Mississippi, but this endeavor was cut short by the Civil War when all riverboats ceased operating. Returning to writing, Clemens adopted the pen name Mark Twain when he began a career as a literary humorist. The pen name—a river pilot's term meaning "two fathoms deep" or "safe water"—appears to have freed him to develop the lecture personality and the deadpan manner that later became an important technique in the creation of his best work.

During his lifetime, Twain wrote a great deal, much of it turned out quickly, like his public lectures, to make money. Even his least significant writing, however, reflects flashes of wit and reveals his marvelous command of colloquial American English still unrivaled in the history of American literature. His best work is his "Mississippi writing"—*Life on the Mississippi* (1883) and, especially, *The Adventures of Huckleberry Finn* (1885), in which he was able to integrate his talent for comic invention with his satirical cast of mind and his tendency toward moral outrage. ERNEST HEMINGWAY declared *Huckleberry Finn* the greatest American book and the source of all modern American fiction. *The Adventures of Tom Sawyer* (1876), although inferior to the two other Mississippi books, is notable for the creation of its hero, one of Twain's most memorable characters. Among his non-Mississippi novels, *A Connecticut Yankee at King Arthur's Court* (1889) and *The Tragedy of Pudd'nhead Wilson* (1894) also belong near the top of the list of Twain's achievements but considerably below his best writings, for in these latter works the satire, moral outrage, and comedy fail to come together as successfully as elsewhere.

WILLIAM DEAN HOWELLS, a friend of Twain's, encouraged him to write for the *Atlantic Monthly* and later wrote an affectionate memoir, *My Mark Twain*, in which he called Twain "the Lincoln of our literature." In 1894 a publishing house in which Twain had invested went bankrupt, and Twain lost a fortune. This was but one of the fortunes he was to lose through attempted moneymaking schemes. His personal life was further blighted with the deaths of an infant son and two grown daughters, and the long illness and death of his wife. These extremes of success, failure, and sorrow may help account for the contrasting extremes of humor and bitterness in his writing. Toward the close of his life, the bitterness predominated and his last writing, (*Letters from the Earth*, c. 1908) became a satirical diatribe against God and humanity, so much so that his surviving daughter, Clara Clemens Samoussoud (d. 1962), refused to allow it to be published until after her death. It appeared in 1963, edited by Bernard DeVoto.

The laureate of the so-called Gilded Age, Twain was among the first of a number of American writers whose works have been edited and published in scholarly editions, including discarded chapters and scenes from earlier works, as well as items left unfinished (and sometimes in multiple versions) at Twain's death and later found among his papers. Among those works appearing in scholarly editions are *Fables of Man*, *Correspondence with Henry Huttleston Rogers*, *Mark Twain's Hannibal, Huck and Tom*, and *What Is Man? and Other Philosophical Writings*. Minor works long out of print have also been reissued in recent years, including *King Leopold's Soliloquy*, *Following the Equator*, and *The American Claimant*.

NOVELS BY TWAIN

The Adventures of Huckleberry Finn. 1885. *Classics Series Stage 4.* Longman 1991 $6.50. ISBN 0-685-53466-9. Sequel to *Tom Sawyer,* in which Huck and the slave Jim float down the Mississippi in an attempt to reach freedom.

The Adventures of Tom Sawyer. 1876. Random 1991 $8.50. ISBN 0-679-73501-1. Imaginative story of Tom Sawyer, his brother Sid, and their friends. Based on Twain's childhood in Hannibal, Missouri.

A Connecticut Yankee at King Arthur's Court. 1889. Tor Bks. 1991 $2.50. ISBN 0-8125-0436-4. Time travel brings a Connecticut engineer to Camelot.

The Gilded Age: A Tale of Today. 1873. NAL-Dutton 1985 $4.95. ISBN 0-452-00779-8. Satire attacking political corruption and business exploitation.

Innocents Abroad. 1869. NTC Pub. Grp. 1989 $11.95. ISBN 0-87052-757-6. Twain's first success. Reports of a simple American's irreverent reactions to the culture and "sights" of Europe.

Joan of Arc: Personal Recollections. 1896. Ignatius Pr. 1989 $29.95. ISBN 0-89870-268-2. Fictional, though serious, biography of Joan of Arc.

Life on the Mississippi. 1883. Viking Penguin 1985 $4.95. ISBN 0-14-039050-2

The Prince and the Pauper. 1882. Tor Bks. 1992 $2.50. ISBN 0-8125-0477-1. Story of what happens when Prince Edward and a pauper boy, identical in appearance, exchange identities.

Pudd'nhead Wilson and Other Tales. 1894. Ed. by R. D. Gooder. *The World's Classics Ser.* OUP 1992 $2.95. ISBN 0-19-281806-6. Lawyer Wilson uses fingerprints to solve a case of murder and mistaken identity.

Roughing It. 1872. Hippocrene Bks. 1988 $9.95. ISBN 0-87052-707-X. Reports of travels and adventures to the Far West and the Sandwich Islands.

Simon Wheeler, Detective. Ed. by Franklin R. Rogers. NY Pub. Lib. 1965 $15.00. ISBN 0-87104-161-8. An uncompleted novel that *Library Journal* finds a good one, with an "illuminating" introduction; first published in 1963.

Tom Sawyer Abroad (and *Tom Sawyer, Detective*). 1894–96. U. CA Pr. 1982 $8.95. ISBN 0-520-04561-0

Traveling with the Innocents Abroad: Mark Twain's Original Reports from Europe and the Holy Land. Ed. by Daniel Morley McKeithan. U. of Okla. Pr. 1958 o.p. A collection of the 58 lively letters sent to American newspapers, describing Twain's experiences on a pleasure excursion to Europe, the Holy Land, and Egypt; revised by Twain to become the basis of *The Innocents Abroad.*

SHORT STORY COLLECTIONS BY TWAIN

The Adam & Eve Diaries: Notes on Courtship and Marriage. Belles Lettres Ser. Stewart Tabori & Chang 1989 $6.95. ISBN 1-55670-089-X. Humorous reconstruction of life in the Garden of Eden.

The Adventures of Thomas Jefferson Snodgrass. Folcroft repr. of 1928 ed. o.p. Ten humorous letters first published in 1861 in the New Orleans *Daily Crescent.*

The Celebrated Jumping Frog of Calaveras County. 1867. *Classic Short Stories Ser.* Creative Ed. 1990 $18.50. ISBN 0-88682-296-3. One of Twain's best known tales.

The Complete Humorous Sketches and Tales. Doubleday 1961 o.p. More than 200 pieces arranged chronologically from 1863.

The Complete Short Stories. Lightyear 1992 $24.95. ISBN 0-89968-272-3

Complete Short Stories of Mark Twain. Bantam 1984 $5.95. ISBN 0-553-21195-1

The Devil's Race-Track: Mark Twain's Great Dark Writings. The Best from "Which Was the Dream?" and "Fables of Man." Ed. by John S. Tuckey. U. CA Pr. 1980 $25.00. ISBN 0-520-03893-2

Diaries of Adam and Eve. Coronado Pr. 1971 $7.50. ISBN 0-87291-012-1

Great Short Works of Mark Twain. Ed. by Justin Kaplan. HarpC 1967 $7.00. ISBN 0-06-083075-1

King Leopold's Soliloquy. Intl. Pubs. Co. 1991 $3.95. ISBN 0-7178-0687-1. Introduction by Stefan Heym.

Mark Twain on Man and Beast. Ed. by Janet Smith. L. Hill Bks. 1972 o.p. Collection of writings about animals.

Mark Twain's Travels with Mr. Brown. Ed. by Franklin Walker and G. Ezra Dane. Russell Sage 1971 o.p. A collection of sketches that Twain wrote for the San Francisco *Alta California,* 1866–67.

Mississippi Writings. Ed. by Guy Cardwell. Library of America. 1982 $29.50. ISBN 0-940450-07-0

Mysterious Stranger and Other Stories. 1916. NAL-Dutton 1962 $2.95. ISBN 0-451-52069-6. Edited and patched version found among Twain's manuscripts and published posthumously.

The Pen Warmed Up in Hell: Mark Twain in Protest. 1972. Ed. by Frederick Anderson. Borgo Pr. 1991 $23.00. ISBN 0-8095-9043-3. Excerpts reflecting Twain's "rage and righteousness."

The Science Fiction of Mark Twain. Ed. by David Ketterer. Shoe String Pr. 1984 $37.50. ISBN 0-208-02036-5. Anthology demonstrating Twain's position as the first science fiction writer.

Selected Shorter Writings of Mark Twain. Ed. by Walter Blair. HM 1972 $9.16. ISBN 0-395-05155-X

The Signet Classic Book of Mark Twain's Short Stories. NAL-Dutton 1989 $4.50. ISBN 0-451-52220-6

The War Prayer. 1923. HarpC 1984 $7.00. ISBN 0-02-069113-1. An antiwar parable that Twain stipulated could be published only after his death.

The Wit and Wisdom of Mark Twain. Ed. by Alex Ayres. NAL-Dutton 1989 $7.95. ISBN 0-452-00982-0. Short quotations from Twain's published and unpublished writings, arranged alphabetically by subject.

NONFICTION BY TWAIN

Autobiography of Mark Twain. 1959. Ed. by Charles Neider. HarpC 1990 $10.00. ISBN 0-06-092025-4. A well-edited version of the mass of material left by Twain to serve as his autobiography.
The Complete Essays of Mark Twain. Ed. by Charles Weider. Doubleday 1985 $15.95. ISBN 0-385-06590-6
Following the Equator. 1897. *Travels Ser.* Ecco Pr. 1992 $12.95. ISBN 0-88001-280-3
Life on the Mississippi. 1883. Random 1991 $10.50. ISBN 0-679-72527-X. A recounting of Twain's experiences on the Mississippi River.

LETTERS BY TWAIN

The Correspondence of Samuel L. Clemens and William D. Howells, 1869–1910. 2 vols. Ed. by Henry Nash Smith and William M. Gibson. HUP 1960 o.p.
Letters from the Sandwich Islands. Haskell 1972 o.p. A collection of Twain's contributions to the Sacramento *Union*, originally edited by G. Ezra Dane.
Mark Twain's Correspondence with Henry Huttleston Rogers, 1893–1909. Ed. by Lewis Leary. *Mark Twain Papers Ser.* U. CA Pr. 1969 $49.95. ISBN 0-520-01467-7
Mark Twain's Letters to His Publishers, 1867–1894. Ed. by Hamlin Hill. *Mark Twain Papers Ser.* U. CA Pr. 1967 o.p. Includes 290 letters, most of them previously unpublished; the MLA-approved text.
Mark Twain's Letters to Mary. Ed. by Lewis Leary. Col. U. Pr. 1961 o.p. These 30-odd letters and notes, characterized by "cheerful affection and prankish good humor," were addressed during the last four years of Twain's life to the young daughter-in-law of Henry H. Rogers, the Standard Oil Company executive who had become Mark Twain's business adviser and close friend.
Mark Twain to Mrs. Fairbanks. Ed. by Dixon Wecter. Huntington Lib. 1949 o.p. "Mother" Fairbanks was one of Twain's early literary mentors.
Mark Twain's Letters to Will Bowen. Haskell 1975 $40.95. ISBN 0-8383-2089-9. Letters to Twain's "first, oldest and dearest friend," first published in a collection edited by Theodore Hornberger.
Mark Twain's Notebooks and Journals. 3 vols. Ed. by Frederick Anderson and others. *Mark Twain Papers Ser.* U. CA Pr. Vol. 1 1975 $50.00. ISBN 0-520-02326-9. Vol. 2 1975 $50.00. ISBN 0-520-02542-3. Vol. 3 1979 $50.00. ISBN 0-520-03383-3. Complete unpublished papers offering scholars insight into the man and the writer.
Selected Mark Twain—Howells Letters. Ed. by Frederick Anderson. Bks. Demand repr. of 1968 ed. $126.10. ISBN 0-7837-2335-0. The *Correspondence* with unimportant matter and canceled words deleted to reduce it to one volume. Contains two new letters; otherwise "substantially the same," with editorial aids virtually unchanged (*LJ*).

WORKS BY TWAIN

Family Mark Twain. *Repr. Ser.* Dorset Pr. 1989 $29.95. ISBN 0-88029-264-4. Full texts of *Life on the Mississippi, Huckleberry Finn, Adventures of Tom Sawyer,* and *Connecticut Yankee.*
Iowa-California Edition of the Works of Mark Twain. U. CA Pr. 1972–88 o.p. Authoritative texts with wealth of notes and resource material. Consult publisher's list for volume contents, titles, editors, and prices.
Mark Twain Papers. U. CA Pr. 1967–79 o.p. Fifteen carefully edited volumes of Twain's unpublished papers. Valuable for scholars.
Portable Mark Twain. Ed. by Bernard A. De Voto. *Viking Portable Lib.* Viking Penguin 1977 $9.95. ISBN 0-14-015020-X. Selected stories, novels, and excerpts; with an introduction.

The Unabridged Mark Twain. Running Press 1988 $15.95. ISBN 0-89471-086-9

BOOKS ABOUT TWAIN

Beaver, Harold. *Huckleberry Finn: Unwin Critical Library.* Unwin Hyman 1987 $34.95. ISBN 0-04-800077-9. General introduction and retrospective look at unresolved problems in the text.

Bloom, Harold, ed. *Mark Twain. Modern Critical Views Ser.* Chelsea Hse. 1986 $29.95. ISBN 0-87754-698-3. Collection of published essays.

_____, ed. *Huck Finn. Major Literary Characters Ser.* Chelsea Hse. 1990 $34.95. ISBN 0-7910-0940-8. Useful sampling of reprinted material, including both standard and revisionist approaches to *Huckleberry Finn.*

_____, ed. *Mark Twain's Adventures of Huckleberry Finn. Modern Critical Interpretations Ser.* Chelsea Hse. 1986 $29.95. ISBN 1-55546-013-5. Collection of reprinted essays reflecting varied responses to this much-studied American classic.

Brooks, Van Wyck. *The Ordeal of Mark Twain.* AMS Pr. repr. of 1933 ed. $37.50. ISBN 0-404-14512-4. The celebrated attack on Twain. Now discredited.

Budd, Louis J. *Critical Essays on Mark Twain, 1867–1910. Critical Essays on Amer. Lit. Ser.* G. K. Hall 1983 $40.00. ISBN 0-8161-8652-9. Collection of reviews and criticism written during Twain's life.

_____. *Our Mark Twain: The Making of His Public Personality.* 1983. Bks. Demand repr. of 1983 ed. $76.20. ISBN 0-8357-3328-9. Examines how Twain established and maintained his image as a cultural hero.

_____, ed. *New Essays on Adventures on Huckleberry Finn. The Amer. Novel Ser.* Cambridge U. Pr. 1985 $24.95. ISBN 0-521-31836-X. Introductory essays dealing with traditional topics, using reader-response criticism, rhetorical theory, and social history.

Cady, Edwin H., and Louis J. Budd, eds. *On Mark Twain: The Best from American Literature.* Duke 1987 $35.00. ISBN 0-8223-0759-6. Collection of previously published essays, including early "classics" as well as recent contributions to Twain scholarship.

Canby, Henry S. *Turn West, Turn East: Mark Twain and Henry James.* Biblo 1951 $18.00. ISBN 0-8196-0154-3. A comparative biography of contrasting contemporaries.

Cardwell, Guy. *The Man Who Was Mark Twain: Images & Ideologies.* Yale U. Pr. 1991 $27.50. ISBN 0-300-04950-1

De Voto, Bernard. *Mark Twain at Work.* AMS Pr. repr. of 1942 ed. o.p.

_____. *Mark Twain's America.* 1932. Greenwood 1978 repr. of 1967 ed. $65.00 ISBN 0-313-20368-7. De Voto's defense of Twain.

Eble, Kenneth E. *Old Clemens and W.D.H.: The Story of a Remarkable Friendship. Southern Literary Studies.* La. State U. Pr. 1985 $30.00. ISBN 0-8071-1227-5. Uses primary sources to trace the lifelong friendship and loyalty between these two men.

Emerson, Everett. *The Authentic Mark Twain: A Literary Biography of Samuel L. Clemens.* U. of Pa. Pr. 1984 o.p. Favors Twain's early, humorous work and comic persona.

Foner, Philip S. *Mark Twain: Social Critic.* Intl. Pub. repr. of 1972 ed. o.p. His thinking on major social, political, and economic issues of his day, based largely on previously unpublished material.

Gibson, William M. *The Art of Mark Twain.* OUP 1976 o.p. A major work on the artistry of Mark Twain.

Gilman, Susan. *Dark Twins: Imposture and Identity in Mark Twain's America.* U. Ch. Pr. 1989 $32.50. ISBN 0-226-29386-6. Examines Twain's dual nature, public and private, as reflected in his fiction.

Gilman, Susan, and Forrest Robinson, eds. *Mark Twain's Pudd'n Head Wilson: Race, Conflict, and Culture.* Duke 1990 $35.00. ISBN 0-8223-1001-5. Collection of essays examining the problems of nineteenth-century culture as reflected in Twain's novel.

Hill, Hamlin. *Mark Twain: God's Fool.* HarpC 1973 o.p. Focuses on the misfortune and pessimism of the last decade of Twain's life.

Hoffman, Andrew J. *Twain's Heroes, Twain's Worlds.* U. of Pa. Pr. 1988 $27.95. ISBN 0-8122-8139-X. Reinterpretations of Huck Finn, Hank Morgan, and David (Pudd'n Head) Wilson.

Inge, M. Thomas, ed. *Huck Finn Among the Critics: A Centennial Selection.* Greenwood 1985 $55.00. ISBN 0-313-27086-4. Sampling from 100 years of criticism, prepared as a tribute to this novel.

Kahn, Sholom J. *Mark Twain's Mysterious Stranger: A Study of the Manuscript Texts.* U. of Mo. Pr. 1978 $30.00. ISBN 0-8262-0236-5. An unpuzzling of the "Mysterious Stranger" manuscripts, concluding that "No. 44" is the most complete and compelling version.

Kaplan, Justin. *Mr. Clemens and Mark Twain.* 1966. S & S Trade 1991 $15.00. ISBN 0-671-74807-6. The best recent biography. Popular Pulitzer Prize-winning biography; psychological study criticized for inadequate documentation.

Kesterson, David B., ed. *Critics on Mark Twain. Readings in Literary Criticism Ser.* U. of Miami Pr. 1979 $10.95. ISBN 0-87024-251-2

Krause, Sydney J. *Mark Twain as Critic.* Bks. Demand repr. of 1967 ed. $83.20. ISBN 0-8357-8214-X. Argues for Twain's value as a literary critic.

Lauber, John. *The Making of Mark Twain. Noonday Ser.* FS&G 1988 $9.95. ISBN 0-374-52130-1. Biography of Twain's early years.

_____. *The Inventions of Mark Twain.* Hill & Wang 1989 $22.95. ISBN 0-8090-5869-3. Study of Twain's entire career, focusing on the writing and reception of *Huckleberry Finn.*

Leonard, James S., Tenney A. Thomas, and Thadious M. Davis, eds. *Satire or Evasion?: Black Perspectives on Huckleberry Finn.* Duke 1991 $45.00. ISBN 0-8223-1163-1. Collection of essays by African American scholars on both sides of the significance of racial issues in *Huckleberry Finn.*

Macnaughton, William R. *Mark Twain's Last Years as a Writer.* U. of Mo. Pr. 1979 $30.00. ISBN 0-8262-0264-0. Analyzes and finds value in Twain's later writings.

Pettit, Arthur G. *Mark Twain and the South.* U. Pr. of Ky. 1974 $22.00. ISBN 0-8131-1310-5. Solid and clearly written on an important subject.

Sanborn, Margaret. *Mark Twain: The Bachelor Years.* Doubleday 1990 $24.95. ISBN 0-385-23702-2. Examination of Twain's young life, including his courtship of Olivia Langdon, using letters, journals, notebooks, and autobiographical writings.

Sattelmeyer, Robert, and J. Donald Crowley, eds. *One Hundred Years of Huckleberry Finn: The Boy, His Book and American Culture. Centennial Essays.* Univ. of Mo. Pr. 1985 $35.00. ISBN 0-8262-0457-0. Essays for scholars.

Scott, Arthur L., ed. *Mark Twain: Selected Criticism.* SMU Pr. rev. ed. 1967 $11.95. ISBN 0-87074-105-5. Traces changes in and growth of Twain's reputation.

Sloane, David E. *Adventures of Huckleberry Finn: American Comic Vision. Masterwork Studies.* Macmillan 1988 $20.95. ISBN 0-8057-7963-9. Accessible close reading of *Huckleberry Finn,* referring to Twain's contemporary sources.

Smith, Henry Nash. *Mark Twain: A Collection of Critical Essays.* P-H 1963 $12.95. ISBN 0-13-933317-7. Collection of essays written after 1950.

_____. *Mark Twain: The Development of a Writer.* HUP 1962 $16.00. ISBN 0-674-54875-2. A standard study of Twain's work.

Steinbrink, Jeffrey. *Getting to Be Mark Twain.* U. CA. Pr. 1991 $22.50. ISBN 0-520-07059-3

Wagenknecht, Edward. *Mark Twain: The Man and His Work.* U. of Okla. Pr. rev. ed. 1967 o.p. Introductory biographical and critical study of Twain; revised to account for new scholarship.

Wecter, Dixon. *Sam Clemens of Hannibal.* AMS Pr. $36.00. ISBN 0-404-15328-3. Meticulously detailed picture of Twain's boyhood and education.

Wilson, James D. *A Reader's Guide to the Short Stories of Mark Twain.* Macmillan 1987 $40.00. ISBN 0-8161-8721-5. Supplies publication history, sources, and analysis of 65 short stories.

VEBLEN, THORSTEIN (BUNDE). 1857–1929

[SEE Volume 3.]

WASHINGTON, BOOKER T[ALIAFERRO]. 1856–1915

Born a slave on a plantation in Hale's Ford, Virginia, Booker T. Washington was considered the "Moses of his Race" for his efforts to lead African Americans out of poverty. After the Civil War, he moved with his mother and brothers to Malden, West Virginia, where through hard work and determination, he eventually gained admission to Hampton Institute in Norfolk, Virginia. He graduated with honors in 1875 and in 1881 was appointed head of the new Tuskegee Institute in Alabama. Throughout his life he wrote, gave lectures, and raised funds for African American education. A realist and a pragmatist, he chose to overlook rather than to confront racial injustices, as evidenced by his 1895 speech, "The Atlanta Compromise." He was well respected and honored in both the African American and the white communities, although he was criticized then as now for his moderate approach and willingness to compromise. Washington wielded enormous power, but the debate between his approach, focusing on vocational training for African Americans, and that of W.E.B. DuBois, stressing higher education and political struggle, shaped black politics in America for several decades. Washington's autobiography, *Up from Slavery* (1901), uses the rhetorical modes of BENJAMIN FRANKLIN (see also Vols. 3 and 5) and FREDERICK DOUGLASS (see also Vol. 3) to chronicle the inspiring story of his own rise from slavery to success.

NONFICTION BY WASHINGTON

Black-Belt Diamonds. 1898. Greenwood 1969 $35.00. ISBN 0-8371-1838-7. Speeches, addresses, and talks to students.

Frederick Douglass. 1907. *BCL1—U.S. History Ser.* Rprt. Serv. 1992 $89.00. ISBN 0-7812-6166-X. A biography of the famous American abolitionist.

The Future of the American Negro. 1899. *BCL1—U.S. Hist. Ser.* Rprt. Serv. 1991 $79.00. ISBN 0-7812-6085-X. Essays and speeches.

My Larger Education. 1911. Mnemosyne Pub. $14.00. ISBN 1-56675-023-7. Sequel to *Up From Slavery* ghost written from Washington's notes and discussions.

Story of My Life and Work. 1900 *Amer. Biog. Ser.* Rprt. Serv. 1991 $89.00. ISBN 0-7812-8402-3. An early autobiography, poorly ghost written and edited.

Up from Slavery: An Autobiography. Amer. Biog. Ser. Rprt. Serv. 1991 $69.00. ISBN 0-7812-8403-1

WORKS BY WASHINGTON

Booker T. Washington Papers. 14 vols. Ed. by Louis R. Harlan. U. of Ill. Pr. 1989 $495.00. ISBN 0-252-01152-X. Edited and introduced by Washington's biographer.

BOOKS ABOUT WASHINGTON

Harlan, Louis R. *Booker T. Washington.* Vol. 1 *The Making of a Black Leader, 1856–1901.* OUP 1972 $39.95. ISBN 0-19-501915-6. Vol. 2 *The Wizard of Tuskegee, 1901–1915.* 1986 $39.95. ISBN 0-19-504229-8. Solid, definitive biography.

Hawkins, Hugh. *Booker T. Washington and His Critics. Problems in Amer. Civilization Ser.* Heath 1974 $8.50. ISBN 0-669-87049-8. Biography of Washington that presents conflicting views of this controversial personality.

Mathews, Basil. *Booker T. Washington, Educator and Interracial Interpreter.* HUP 1948 o.p. Solid biography written by Washington supporter showing Washington as an administrator, political adviser, and foreign traveler.

Meier, August. *Negro Thought in America, 1880–1915: Racial Ideologies in the Age of Booker T. Washington.* U. of Mich. Pr. 1963 $18.95. ISBN 0-472-06118-6. Intellectual and social history of the period.

Schroeder, Alan. *Booker T. Washington. Black Amer. of Achievement Ser.* Chelsea Hse. 1992 $17.95. ISBN 1-55546-616-8. Introduction by Coretta Scott King.

Smock, Raymond W., ed. *Booker T. Washington in Perspective: Essays of Louis R. Harlan.*
U. Pr. of Miss. 1988 $27.50. ISBN 0-87805-374-3. Collection of Harlan's essays
detailing his experience in writing his acclaimed biography of Washington.

Spencer, Samuel R., ed. *Booker T. Washington and the Negro's Place in American Life.*
1955. *The Lib. of Amer. Biog.* Scott F. 1987 $13.00. ISBN 0-673-39352-6. Balanced
assessment of Washington as educator and leader of African Americans.

WHARTON, EDITH (NEWBOLD JONES) 1862–1937

Edith Wharton was a woman of extreme contrasts; brought up to be a leisured
aristocrat, she was also dedicated to her career as a writer. She wrote novels of
manners about the old New York society from which she came, but her attitude
was consistently critical. Her irony and her satiric touches, as well as her insight
into human character, continue to appeal to readers today.

As a child, Wharton found refuge from the demands of her mother's social
world in her father's library and in making up stories. Her marriage at age 23 to
Edward ("Teddy") Wharton seemed to confirm her place in the conventional
role of wealthy society woman, but she became increasingly dissatisfied with the
"mundanities" of her marriage and turned to writing, which drew her into an
intellectual community and strengthened her sense of herself. After publishing
two collections of short stories, *The Greater Inclination* (1899) and *Crucial
Instances* (1901), she wrote her first novel, *The Valley of Decision* (1902), a long,
historical romance set in eighteenth-century Italy. Her next work, the immensely popular *The House of Mirth* (1905), was a scathing criticism of her own
"frivolous" New York society and its capacity to destroy her heroine, the
beautiful Lily Bart.

As Wharton became more established as a successful writer, Teddy's mental
health declined and their marriage deteriorated. In 1907 she left America
altogether and settled in Paris, where she wrote some of her most memorable
stories of harsh New England rural life—*Ethan Frome* (1911) and *Summer*
(1917)—as well as *The Reef* (1912), which is set in France. All describe
characters forced to make moral choices in which the rights of individuals are
pitted against their responsibilities to others. She also completed her most
biting satire, *The Custom of the Country* (1913), the story of Undine Spragg's
climb, marriage by marriage, from a midwestern town to New York to a French
chateau. During World War I, Wharton dedicated herself to the war effort and
was honored by the French government for her work with Belgian refugees.

After the war, the world Wharton had known was gone. Even her Pulitzer
Prize-winning novel, *The Age of Innocence* (1920), a story set in old New York,
could not recapture the former time. Although the new age welcomed her—
Wharton was both a critical and popular success, honored by Yale University
and elected to The National Institute of Arts and Letters—her later novels show
her struggling to come to terms with a new era. In *The Writing of Fiction* (1925),
Wharton acknowledged her debt to her friend HENRY JAMES, whose writings
share with hers the descriptions of fine distinctions within a social class and the
individual's burdens of making proper moral decisions.

R.W.B. Lewis's biography of Wharton, published in 1975, along with a wealth
of new biographical material, inspired an extensive reevaluation of Wharton.
Feminist readings and reactions to them have focused renewed attention on her
as a woman and as an artist. Although many of her books have recently been
reprinted, there is still no complete collected edition of her work.

NOVELS BY WHARTON

The Age of Innocence. 1920. Macmillan 1992 $8.00. ISBN 0-02-026476-3. Conflict between convention and the hope for happiness in the life of a wealthy New York lawyer.

The Buccaneers. Viking Penguin 1993 $22.00. ISBN 0-670-85219-8. Three-fifths of this manuscript was left behind when Wharton died in 1937. It was published (incomplete) in 1938. It has now been completed by scholar Marion Mainwaring.

The Children. 1928. Macmillan 1992 $10.00. ISBN 0-02-026477-1. Story of family of stepchildren determined to stay together.

The Custom of the Country. 1913. Bantam 1991 $4.50. ISBN 0-553-21393-8. A satire about the social climbing of the newly rich.

Ethan Frome and Other Short Fiction. 1911. Macmillan 1987 $6.95. ISBN 0-684-18906-2. *Ethan Frome* recounts the tragic tale of a farmer, his wife, and the woman he comes to love.

The Gods Arrive. 1932. *Hudson River Ed. Ser.* Macmillan 1985 $30.00. ISBN 0-684-18454-0. Last completed novel continues *Hudson River Bracketed,* in which writer Vance Weston and Halo Spear are finally reconciled.

The House of Mirth. 1905. Knopf 1991 $17.00. ISBN 0-679-40667-0. Story of a woman's ambitious attempts to find a suitable husband in old New York.

The House of Mirth. Ed. by Elizabeth Ammons. *Norton Critical Ed. Ser.* Norton 1990 $8.95. ISBN 0-393-95901-5. Includes background and selected critical essays.

Hudson River Bracketed. 1929. Macmillan 1985 $35.00. ISBN 0-684-18455-9. Young Midwesterner Vance Weston struggles to become a writer.

Madame de Treymes and Three Novellas. Twentieth Cent. Classics Ser. Macmillan 1987 $4.95. ISBN 0-02-055420-6. Also includes *Touchstone, Sanctuary,* and "The Bunner Sisters." Introduction by Susan Mary Alsop.

Novellas and Other Writings: Includes Madame de Treymes; Ethan Frome; Summer; Old New York; The Mother's Recompense; Backward Glance. Library of America 1990 $35.00. ISBN 0-940450-53-4

The Mother's Recompense. 1925. Macmillan 1986 $10.95. ISBN 0-684-18737-X. Story of Kate Clephane and her discovery that her former lover is engaged to her daughter.

Novels. Library of America 1986 $35.00. ISBN 0-940450-31-3. Includes: *The House of Mirth; The Reef; The Custom of the Country; The Age of Innocence.*

The Reef. 1912. *Twentieth Cent. Classics Ser.* Macmillan 1987 $3.95. ISBN 0-02-055410-9. Set in France, this is a story about the psychological effects of sexual promiscuity.

Summer. 1917. *Twentieth Cent. Classics Ser.* Macmillan 1987 $4.95. ISBN 0-02-055440-0

Touchstone. 1900. HarpC 1991 $8.95. ISBN 0-06-097379-X. The author's first long fiction; the story of an ethical dilemma.

Valley of Decision. AMS Pr. $14.50. ISBN 0-404-06914-2

SHORT STORY COLLECTIONS BY WHARTON

Lewis, R. W., ed. *The Collected Short Stories of Edith Wharton.* 2 vols. *Hudson River Ed. Ser.* Macmillan 1987 $50.00. ISBN 0-02-570600-4. Complete collection of Wharton's stories, with critical introduction and notes.

―――, ed. *The Selected Short Stories of Edith Wharton: Introduced & Edited by R. W. B. Lewis.* Macmillan 1991 $24.95. ISBN 0-684-19304-3

Crucial Instances. AMS Pr. repr. of 1990 ed. $17.00. ISBN 0-404-06912-6

Ghost Stories of Edith Wharton. 1973. Macmillan 1985 $10.95. ISBN 0-684-18382-X. Collection of previously published ghost stories, including one of Wharton's best late stories, "All Souls."

Old New York. 1924. Berkley Pub. 1981 o.p. Four novellas depicting New York society between 1840 and 1880.

Roman Fever: And Other Stories. Twentieth Cent. Classics Ser. Macmillan 1987 $5.95. ISBN 0-02-059880-7. Includes several of Wharton's best stories.

NONFICTION BY WHARTON

A Backward Glance. 1934. Macmillan 1985 $27.50. ISBN 0-684-15983-X. Memoir.

WORKS BY WHARTON

The Collected Letters of Edith Wharton. Ed. by R.W.B. Lewis and Nancy Lewis. Macmillan 1988 $29.95. ISBN 0-684-18585-7. Fully edited collection of wide range of Wharton's correspondence.
Henry James and Edith Wharton: Letters: 1900–1915. Ed. by Lyall H. Powers. Macmillan 1990 $29.95. ISBN 0-684-19146-6
Letters of Edith Wharton. Ed. by R.W.B. Lewis. Macmillan 1989 $14.95. ISBN 0-02-034400-7

BOOKS ABOUT WHARTON

Ammons, Elizabeth. *Edith Wharton's Argument with America.* U. of Ga. Pr. 1980 o.p. Feminist approach focusing on Wharton's social criticism and her protest against the position of women in society.
Bloom, Harold, ed. *Edith Wharton. Modern Critical Views Ser.* Chelsea Hse. 1986 $24.95. ISBN 0-87754-699-1. Collection of critical essays on novels and short stories.
Fryer, Judith. *Felicitous Space: The Imaginative Structures of Edith Wharton and Willa Cather.* U. of NC Pr. 1986 $34.95. ISBN 0-8078-1655-8. Investigates relationship between physical space and the female imagination.
Goodman, Susan. *Edith Wharton's Women: Friends and Rivals.* U. Pr. of New Eng. 1990 $27.50. ISBN 0-87451-521-1. Emphasizes the relationships and connections rather than the competition among Wharton's female characters.
Goodwyn, Janet. *Edith Wharton: Traveller in the Land of Letters.* St. Martin 1990 $35.00. ISBN 0-312-03200-5. Considers Wharton's travel writing as well as her fiction.
Holbrook, David. *Edith Wharton. Critical Studies.* St. Martin 1991 $39.95. ISBN 0-312-03565-9. Uses Freudian insights to analyze characters' relationships.
Howe, Irving, ed. *Edith Wharton: A Collection of Critical Essays.* P-H 1962 o.p. Useful collection of classic essays on Wharton.
Lauer, Kristin O., and Margaret P. Murray. *Edith Wharton: An Annotated Bibliography.* Garland 1990 $75.00. ISBN 0-8240-4636-6
Lewis, R.W.B. *Edith Wharton: A Biography.* HarpC 1974 o.p. Fromm Int. Pub. Corp. 1985 $12.95. ISBN 0-88064-020-0. Definitive Pulitzer Prize-winning biography; indexed.
Lubbock, Percy. *Portrait of Edith Wharton.* Appleton-Century-Crofts 1947 o.p. Portrait biased by Lubbock's lack of sympathy for Wharton and her position as a serious author.
McDowell, Margaret B. *Edith Wharton. Twayne's U.S. Authors Ser.* Macmillan rev. ed. 1990 $19.95. ISBN 0-8057-7618-4. Survey of major work stressing Wharton as a moralist.
Nevius, Blake. *Edith Wharton: A Study of Her Fiction.* U. CA Pr. 1976 $32.50. ISBN 0-520-03180-6. First critical assessment of Wharton after her death. Describes themes of ."trapped sensibility" and individual responsibility.
Vita-Finzi, Penelope. *Edith Wharton and the Art of Fiction.* St. Martin 1990 $39.95. ISBN 0-312-04187-X. Focuses on Wharton's technique and her depiction of the artist to show the importance of order and inspiration in her fiction.
Wagner-Martin, Linda. *The House of Mirth: A Novel of Admonition. Twayne's Masterwork Studies.* Twayne 1990 $18.95. ISBN 0-8057-9433-1. Basic introduction to the text and context of one of Wharton's most important works.
Walton, Geoffrey. *Edith Wharton: A Critical Interpretation.* Fairleigh Dickinson 1983 $27.50. ISBN 0-8386-3164-9. Compares Wharton's work to that of English novelists.
Wershoven, Carol. *The Female Intruder in the Novels of Edith Wharton.* Fairleigh Dickinson 1983 $29.50. ISBN 0-8386-3126-6. Argues that the outsider serves as critic of society and embodies Wharton's positive values.

Wolff, Cynthia G. *A Feast of Words: The Triumph of Edith Wharton.* OUP 1977 $29.95. ISBN 0-19-502117-7. Biography and critical analysis exploring the psychological tensions released in Wharton's writing.

White, Barbara A. *Edith Wharton: A Study of the Short Fiction. Twayne's Studies in Short Fiction.* Twayne 1991 $26.95. ISBN 0-8057-8340-7. Introduction and story-by-story analysis of Wharton's short fiction.

WISTER, OWEN. 1860–1938

A Philadelphian and grandson of the actress Fanny Kemble, Owen Wister was educated in private schools in the United States and abroad and graduated from Harvard University with highest honors in music. After suffering a nervous breakdown, he traveled to Wyoming to recover his health. He then made frequent trips back to the West. His only well-known novel, *The Virginian* (1902), a bestseller for years, is a pioneer western about a man Wister considered to be the "last heroic figure" of America. It was dedicated to his lifelong friend THEODORE ROOSEVELT (see Vol. 3), another outdoorsman and lover of the West, whom he had met when they were both students at Harvard. Although often ignored as serious literature, Wister's novel with its archetypal hero has widely influenced popular western novels and films. Two of Wister's reprinted books are *Lin McLean* (1898) and *Lady Baltimore* (1906).

NOVELS BY WISTER

Lady Baltimore. BCL1-PS Amer. Lit. Ser. Rprt. Serv. 1992 $99.00. ISBN 0-7812-6907-5
Lin McLean. 1898. Irvington repr. of 1898 ed. $36.50. ISBN 0-8398-2174-3
The Virginian: A Horseman of the Plains. U. of Nebr. Pr. 1992 $12.95. ISBN 0-8032-9736-X. Introduction by Thomas McGuane.

SHORT STORY COLLECTIONS BY WISTER

The Jimmyjohn Boss and Other Stories. Irvington 1972 repr. of 1900 ed. o.p. Second collection of stories, mostly comic, reprinted from magazines.

The West of Owen Wister: Selected Short Stories. U. of Nebr. Pr. 1972 $23.00. ISBN 0-8032-5760-0. With an introduction by Robert L. Hough.

BOOKS ABOUT WISTER

Cobbs, John L. *Owen Wister. Twayne's U.S. Authors Ser.* Twayne 1984 o.p. Biographical and critical introduction to Wister's work.

Payne, Darwin. *Owen Wister: Chronicler of the West, Gentleman of the East.* SMU Pr. 1985 $24.95. ISBN 0-87074-205-1. Biography focusing on Wister's life and relationships rather than on his writing.

Vorpahl, Ben Merchant. *My Dear Wister: The Frederick Remington–Owen Wister Letters.* Amer. W. Bks. 1972 o.p. In-depth analysis of the two men, their friendship, and their respective arts.

White, Edward G. *The Eastern Establishment and the Western Experience: The West of Frederick Remington, Theodore Roosevelt, and Owen Wister.* Yale U. Pr. 1968 o.p. Sees the Virginian as an American hero who embodies the strengths of both the Westerner and the Easterner.

WOOLSON, CONSTANCE FENIMORE. 1840–1894

One of many popular local-color writers, Constance Fenimore Woolson, grand-niece of JAMES FENIMORE COOPER, is best remembered for her short stories, although her good friend HENRY JAMES regarded her as a novelist. She was born in Claremont, New Hampshire, but grew up in the expanding midwestern town of Cleveland. She enjoyed traveling both in the United States and Europe, and many of her stories are set in the places she visited. Summers spent at Mackinac Island in the Great Lakes region provided background for the stories in *Castle Nowhere: Lake-Country Sketches* (1875). Her first novel, *Anne* (1882), serialized in *Harper's,* is a melodramatic story of a love affair and a murder trial.

After the Civil War, Woolson traveled throughout the South, writing *Rodman the Keeper: Southern Sketches* (1880), stories sympathetic to Southern families in the Reconstruction era; *For the Major* (1883), about a Civil War veteran; and *East Angels* (1886), showing a reconciliation between wealthy Northern industrialists and poor Southern aristocrats. In 1879 she moved to Europe, where she continued to write stories and travel sketches, many of which are about Americans abroad. Although her works have been neglected, she is well regarded, especially for her keen observation and her treatment of her female characters.

NOVELS BY WOOLSON

Anne. 1882. *Rediscovered Fiction by Amer. Women.* Ayer 1977 $30.00. ISBN 0-405-10059-0

Horace Chase. 1894. Irvington 1986 $29.50. ISBN 0-8398-2177-8. Last novel showing advances in Woolson's craft.

Jupiter Lights. 1889. *BCL1-PS Amer. Lit. Ser.* Rprt. Serv. 1992 $89.00. ISBN 0-7812-6910-5. Novel set in Georgia and Italy.

SHORT STORY COLLECTIONS BY WOOLSON

Castle Nowhere: Lake-Country Sketches. 1886. *BCL1-PS Amer. Lit. Ser.* Rprt. Serv. 1992 $89.00. ISBN 0-7812-6908-3

For the Major. 1883. *BCL1-PS Amer. Lit. Ser.* Rprt. Serv. 1992 $79.00. ISBN 0-7812-6909-1

For the Major and Selected Short Stories. Ed. by Rayburn S. Moore. *Masterworks of Lit. Ser.* NCUP 1967 $19.95. ISBN 0-8084-0132-7

Front Yard and Other Italian Stories. 1895. *Short Story Index Repr. Ser.* Ayer repr. of 1895 ed. $18.00. ISBN 0-8369-3214-5. Posthumous collection including both early and late stories.

Rodman the Keeper: Southern Sketches. 1880. *BCL1-PS Amer. Lit. Ser.* Rprt. Serv. 1992 $89.00. ISBN 0-7812-6911-3

Women Artists, Women Exiles, "Miss Grief" and Other Stories. Ed. by Joan M. Weimer. *Amer. Women Writers Ser.* Rutgers U. Pr. 1988 $42.00. ISBN 0-8135-1347-2. Well-edited anthology of Woolson's short fiction, with notes and bibliography.

BOOKS ABOUT WOOLSON

Kern, John Dwight. *Constance Fenimore Woolson: Literary Pioneer.* U. of Pa. Pr. 1934 o.p. First full-length scholarly treatment of Woolson's life and works.

Moore, Rayburn S. *Constance F. Woolson. Twayne's U.S. Authors Ser.* NCUP 1963 $10.95. ISBN 0-8084-0092-4. Biography and critical introduction.

Torsney, Cheryl B. *Constance Fenimore Woolson: The Grief of Artistry.* U. of Ga. Pr. 1989 $25.00. ISBN 0-8203-1101-4. Focuses on Woolson's characters who embody the conflict between their roles as women and as artists.

CHAPTER 16

Early Twentieth-Century American Literature

Vareen Bell

It is not a permanent necessity that poets should be interested in philosophy, or in any other subject. We can only say that it appears likely that poets in our civilization, as it exists at present, must be *difficult*. Our civilization comprehends great variety and complexity, and this variety and complexity, playing upon a refined sensibility, must produce various and complex results. The poet must become more and more comprehensive, more allusive, more indirect, in order to force, to dislocate if necessary, language into his meaning.

—T. S. Eliot, *The Metaphysical Poets*

Sir Walter Scott's poetry is like the scenery of a play that has come to an end. It is scenery that has been trucked away and stored somewhere on the horizon or just a little below. In short, the world of Sir Walter Scott no longer exists. It means nothing to compare a modern poet with the poet of a century or more ago. . . . Coleridge and Wordsworth and Sir Walter Scott and Jane Austen did not have to put up with Napoleon and Marx and Europe, Asia and Africa all at one time. It seems possible to say that they knew of the events of their day much as we know of the [events of ours]. . . . [The poet of today] lives in the world of Darwin and not in the world of Plato.

—Wallace Stevens, *Opus Posthumous*

One of the important symbols of American cultural identity in the first half of the twentieth century was the formation of the League of Nations after World War I along with the U.S. Senate's refusal to join it. The League of Nations had been a dream of Woodrow Wilson's and signaled his realization that the United States, having entered a world war and participated decisively in the treaty that resolved it, could no longer withdraw into isolation and disengagement from Europe. But the United States itself—as represented in the Senate—was ambivalent and seemed to wish—partly as a result of the war's appalling human costs—to return to the prewar geopolitical status quo. This ambivalence reflected a knowledge of where the future lay, complicated by a desire to reject that future and to turn inward.

The century's first decade, under the leadership of Theodore Roosevelt (see Vol. 3), had been marked by a spirit of social and political reform intended to bridge the vast gap between the wealthy and the poor and to improve labor conditions. By such means, the middle class was attempting to fend off the social chaos that seemed incipient in the violent, unresolved labor unrest that had accompanied the process of industrialization and the rapid concentration of population in U.S. cities. World War I slowed the process, and the three conservative, laissez-faire Republican administrations that succeeded Wilson's put the brakes on reform as a national agenda. Immigration quotas were also drastically restricted in this decade because of both the labor movement's and the middle class's interest in consolidating and stabilizing internal national resources.

Another symbolic event in a different arena was the opening in 1915 of D. W. GRIFFITH's sensational Civil War epic, *Birth of a Nation*. Here was a masterpiece of American film technology and creative ingenuity, and it was to become one of the most popular films of all time. But *Birth of a Nation* also embodied deep contradictions in the modern American psyche. A technical masterpiece, it was also grotesquely racist and depended exclusively for its compelling melodrama upon already outmoded caricatures of African Americans as either ill-behaved children or bestial sexual predators. Moreover, the African American presence in American life is explicitly represented as the sole cause of division between the otherwise generously disposed white people of the North and South. The movie concludes with an apocalyptic vision of the future in which a gigantic Messiah smiles benignly down upon a peaceful and uniformly white American society.

Birth of a Nation was based on an even more insidiously racist novel called *The Klansman*. Because both celebrated the rise of the Ku Klux Klan after the Civil War—the Klansmen are the heroes of both works—the book and the film became effective recruiting instruments for the Klan itself, which partly because of the disruptions of traditional elements of American society in the previous decades (there were more than 14 million immigrants in the period between 1901 and 1920), grew to a membership strength of over 5 million in the 1920s. In retrospect, it seems clear that the popularity of Griffith's film was due partly to its innovation and cinematic spectacle but also to the suppressed desire of white Americans to blame "outside" elements, a collective "other," for their own anxieties and for all social disorders. Even Woodrow Wilson admired the film. He called it "history written in lightning," which perhaps was more than he meant to say.

Several related forces in the 1920s helped consolidate a national identity. The mass production of automobiles developed by Henry Ford made cars not only available but inexpensive, and this new mobility changed the pace of life and so began to dissolve the barriers between regions, and between city and country. Radio had a similar effect, based as it initially was on the necessity of a national audience. Popular mass-market magazines aimed at and therefore created a nationwide middlebrow audience that had not existed before. The revenues of these magazines were derived largely from advertising. This factor alone generated a new industry known as market research, and market research in turn developed strategies for exploiting the deepest psychological needs of consumers and for manipulating these needs for the benefit of commercial enterprises. By averaging out its audience in this way, modern advertising also therefore created an averaged-out audience, and in effect developed a homogeneous, conservative image of America. Thus the G.I.s represented in patriotic magazine ads during World War II exhibited no trace of disturbing ethnic characteristics, despite the fact that people from all racial and ethnic backgrounds served in the Armed Forces.

So out of America's real diversity after World War I, various interests also worked to create a kind of uniformity of reaction. Management experts had developed progressively more sophisticated techniques for improving efficiency on the assembly line and for optimizing the identity between human and machine. This trend is exemplified by CHARLIE CHAPLIN's film *Modern Times*, which opens with a montage of sheep becoming faceless crowds of people presided over by a giant public clock.

Seen in this context, the counterdevelopments associated with the Jazz Age and the "Lost Generation" in the 1920s were clearly patterns of rebellion against the prevailing drift toward enforced conformity, the greatest single symbol of which was the Prohibition Act of 1918. The energetic hedonism, the daring frankness of the new American woman known as the "flapper," and even jazz itself with its roots in African American culture, all flaunted a new permissiveness in social and sexual attitudes.

The event known now simply as the Armory Show in New York in 1913 introduced another countercultural force at another level. This historic exhibition was the largest presentation ever of modern European and American art. It brought into the foreground of American intellectual life all of the problematic aspects of modern reality, symbolized on the one hand by abstract expressionism and cubism in painting and sculpture, represented on the other by a harsh and grimly representational realism in which art had come to face facts. It was in this cosmopolitan and modernist spirit that many writers and painters in the period during and after World War I turned away from what they perceived to be the increasing uniformity and mediocrity of American cultural life. They became expatriates, literally, intellectually, or both, preferring— whatever their political views might be otherwise—to find their inspiration and identity as artists in the values of an international culture for which Paris had become the mecca. The newest American frontier for the refugees from a mainstream social order had become Europe.

It was largely an inability to come to terms with its internal contradictions, the need to believe that progress could be achieved without destabilizing consequences, that made American society in the first third of the twentieth century more complex than it wished to be. The Great Depression that brought this period to a close radicalized many American writers and intellectuals, but it also abruptly simplified and changed the focus of American life. The interventionist administration of Franklin D. Roosevelt not only transformed the role of government but also forever changed the concept of national identity.

HISTORY AND CRITICISM

Aldridge, John W. *After the Lost Generation: A Critical Study of the Writers of Two Wars.* McGraw 1951 o.p. Studies the contrasting effects of World War I and World War II on the writing of two generations.

———. *The American Novel and the Way We Live Now.* OUP 1983 $25.00. ISBN 0-19-503198-9. Written three decades after *After the Lost Generation*, Aldridge surveyed the contemporary novel and found it even less to his liking.

Baker, Houston A., Jr. *Afro-American Poetics: Revisions of Harlem and the Black Aesthetic.* U. of Wis. Pr. 1988 $19.95. ISBN 0-299-11500-3. A revisionist analysis of African American culture in the twentieth century; focuses on Countee Cullen, Jean Toomer, Amiri Baraka, and Larry Neal.

Bassett, John E. *Harlem in Review: Critical Reactions to Black American Writers, 1917–1939.* Susquehanna U. Pr. 1992 $36.50. ISBN 0-945636-28-8

Booker, M. Keith. *Techniques of Subversion in Modern Literature: Transgression, Abjection, and the Carnivalesque.* U. Press Fla. 1991 $35.95. ISBN 0-8130-1065-9. Analyzes the relationship between poetry and the fallen condition of human language.

Butcher, Philip, ed. *The Ethnic Image in Modern American Literature: 1900–1950.* 2 vols. Howard U. Pr. 1984 $40.95. ISBN 0-88258-110-4. Portrays the realities of ethnic participation in American culture, and examines stereotypical images of non-white Americans.

Cowley, Malcolm. *After the Genteel Tradition: American Writers, 1910–1930*. S. Ill. U. Pr. rev. ed. 1964 o.p. Discusses the literary scene of the 1910–1930 period from the perspective of men and women writing for the *New Republic*.

Davis, Lennard J., ed. *Left Politics and the Literary Profession*. Col. U. Pr. 1990 $39.50. ISBN 0-231-06566-3. Essays on theoretical and existential issues facing the Left in academia.

De Jongh, James. *Vicious Modernism: Black Harlem and the Literary Imagination*. Cambridge U. Pr. 1990 $34.95. ISBN 0-521-32620-6. Focuses on the aesthetic and cultural forces at work in Harlem in the 1920s; examines further transformations through the 1940s and 1960s.

DeKoven, Marianne. *Rich and Strange: Gender, History, Modernism*. Princeton U. Pr. 1992 $39.50. ISBN 0-691-06869-0. Examines the connection between literary modernism and political radicalism; focuses on French post-structuralist theory.

Donoghue, Denis. *Reading America: Essays on American Literature*. Knopf 1987 $22.95. ISBN 0-394-55939-8. Essays on authors such as Thoreau and Whitman; originally published in magazines and literary reviews.

Ellis, William. *Theory of the American Romance: An Ideology in American Intellectual History*. Univ. Rochester Pr. 1989 $39.95. ISBN 0-8357-1984-7

Flora, Joseph M., ed. *Fifty Southern Writers after 1900: A Bio-Bibliographical Sourcebook*. Greenwood 1987 $95.00. ISBN 0-313-24519-3. Presents an overview of writers' lives and works; includes a chronology and bibliography.

Hoffman, Frederick J. *The Twenties: American Writing in the Postwar Decade*. Viking Penguin 1955 o.p. A critical analysis of the value of texts as literature and as representative anecdotes; focuses on authors such as Eliot, Hemingway, and Pound.

Homberger, Eric. *American Writers and Radical Politics, 1900–1939: Equivocal Commitments*. St. Martin 1987 $35.00. ISBN 0-312-02792-3. Traces the evolution of three generations of writers, from Upton Sinclair to the literary class-war writers of the 1930s.

Huggins, Nathan. *The Harlem Renaissance*. OUP 1971 o.p.

Kenner, Hugh. *A Homemade World: The American Modernist Writers*. Johns Hopkins 1988 $12.95. ISBN 0-8018-3839-8. Traces the parallels between the modernism of Pound and Joyce and the American modernism of Faulkner and Stevens.

Kramer, Victor A., ed. *The Harlem Renaissance Re-Examined*. AMS Pr. 1987 $45.00. ISBN 0-404-63202-5. A systematic examination of important aspects of the Harlem Renaissance, including a discussion of the relationship between black and white writers.

Leitch, Vincent B. *American Literary Criticism from the Thirties to the Eighties*. Col. U. Pr. 1989 $67.00. ISBN 0-231-06426-8. Provides accounts of thirteen American critics; covers social and cultural grounds, the main figures, and texts.

Magee, Rosemary M., ed. *Friendship and Sympathy: Communities of Southern Women Writers*. U. Pr. of Miss. 1992 $37.50. ISBN 0-87805-523-1

Margolies, Edward. *Native Sons: A Critical Study of Twentieth-Century Negro American Authors*. Lippincott 1968 o.p. Examines the significance of modern African American writing in terms of its contributions to the quality of American life.

Martin, Stephen-Paul. *Open Form and the Feminine Imagination: The Politics of Reading in Twentieth-Century Innovative Writing*. Maison Neuve Pr. 1988 $19.95. ISBN 0-944624-02-2

Miller, J. Hillis. *Tropes, Parables, Performatives: Essays on Twentieth-Century Literature*. Duke 1991 $47.50. ISBN 0-8223-1111-9

Murphy, James F. *The Proletarian Moment: The Controversy over Leftism in Literature*. U. of Ill. Pr. 1991 $27.50. ISBN 0-252-01788-9

Oliver, Lawrence J. *Brander Matthews, Theodore Roosevelt, and the Politics of American Literature, 1880–1920*. U. of Tenn. Pr. 1992 $29.95. ISBN 0-87049-738-3

Poirier, Richard. *The Performing Self: Compositions and Decompositions in the Languages of Contemporary Life*. Rutgers U. Pr. 1992 $36.00. ISBN 0-8135-1794-X.

Investigates the use of self-parody among some contemporary writers; unifies social, cultural, and literary analyses.

Schneidau, Herbert N. *Waking Giants: The Presence of the Past in Modernism*. OUP 1991 $29.95. ISBN 0-19-506862-9

Slatoff, Walter J. *The Look of Distance: Reflections on Suffering and Sympathy in Modern Literature—Auden to Agee, Whitman to Woolf*. Ohio St. U. Pr. 1985 $36.75. ISBN 0-8142-0385-X. Considers whether the reading of literature can be considered a worthwhile pursuit in a world ordered by suffering.

Sparr, Arnold. *To Promote, Defend and Redeem: The Catholic Literary Revival and the Cultural Transformation of American Catholicism, 1920 through 1960*. Greenwood 1990 $45.00. ISBN 0-313-26391-4

Spencer, Benjamin. *Patterns of Nationality: Twentieth-Century Versions of America*. 1981 o.p. A sequel to *The Quest for Nationality*: assumes that the shape and development of twentieth-century American literature are still in the making.

Tanner, Tony. *Scenes of Nature, Signs of Man: Essays in 19th and 20th Century American Literature*. Cambridge U. Pr. 1989 $18.95. ISBN 0-521-31155-1. Essays, introductions, lectures and a radio-talk on American writers such as Mark Twain and Henry Adams.

Tichi, Cecelia. *Shifting Gears: Technology, Literature, Culture in Modernist America*. U. of NC Pr. 1987 $39.95. ISBN 0-8078-1715-5. Traces the emergence of the principles of technology in the forms of language, art, and popular culture from the 1890s through the 1920s.

Wilson, Christopher P. *The Labor of Words: Literary Professionalism in the Progressive Era*. U. of Ga. Pr. 1987 $15.00. ISBN 0-8203-0940-0. Studies the mass literary marketplace emerging in the United States during the Progressive era (1885–1915).

COLLECTIONS

Bloom, Harold, ed. *Twentieth-Century American Literature*. Chelsea Hse. 1985 $535.00. ISBN 0-87754-800-5. A multivolume portrait of the critical heritage of modern authors from the United States and Canada.

McMichael, George, ed. *Anthology of American Literature*. Vol. 2 *Realism to the Present*. Macmillan 4th ed. 1988. ISBN 0-02-379622-7

McQuade, Donald. *Harper American Literature*. HarpC 1987 $27.50. ISBN 0-06-044367-7

Minnesota Humanities Commission Staff, ed. *Braided Lives: An Anthology of Multicultural American Writing*. MN Humanities 1991 $12.95. ISBN 0-9629298-0-8

Wolfe, Thomas. *A Southern Appalachian Reader*. Appalach. Consortium Pr. 1988 $14.95. ISBN 0-913239-50-X

POETRY

In the two passages that begin this chapter, T. S. ELIOT and WALLACE STEVENS speak of the same crisis, but they responded to it in radically different ways. In his social and political life and writings, Eliot moved away from the historical present into an idealized past defined through what he called "tradition" in Western literature. This withdrawal was an attempt to transcend historical time, his own present in particular. It was represented early in his mature life by his decision to live in England, where his ancestors had lived, and eventually to become an English citizen, an Anglican, and a monarchist, not only reversing the modern tide in his own life but reversing—as it were, rewinding—American history itself. His poems, most notably *The Waste Land* (1930), continue to reflect the cultural complexity he speaks of and show quite honestly that modernist issues remained profoundly disturbing for him, whatever pragmatic decisions *he* may have made to determine the order of *his* personal life.

For Wallace Stevens, the destabilizing aspect of modern experience was also clarifying. He felt that it freed human life from obsolete truths, opening experience to its real aspect as a spectacle of improvisation and change. Reality, he declared, requires perpetual reinvention and rediscovery. Poetry for Stevens was the symbol of the fictions we make from our experience in the world and a consecration of the human power to affirm existence, even in the face of certain tragedy and death. The world, he conceded, exists independently of our conceptions of it—"the nothing that is not there and the nothing that is"—but he argued that we have access to it only through our conceptions. For Stevens, we shape the world. That we pass on a shaping to later generations then means that what we make of experience means something more than just hedonistic self-gratification. Stevens's poetry was abstract and deeply reflective; it was also self-conscious, even exuberantly artificial, as if calling attention to the act of its making. The objects of the world in Stevens's poems tend to lose their status as objects and to become subsumed into the subjective ecology of the mind. In his willing dissociation from the inertia of the past and his affirmation of the freedom of radical subjectivity, Stevens was perhaps the most generically American poet of the modern era, perhaps even of all eras.

The two other claimants to that title, ROBERT FROST and WILLIAM CARLOS WILLIAMS, were quite different from each other in their subject matter and moral concerns. Frost was pre-eminently a poet of nature, and he left indelibly imprinted upon the American consciousness the look and feel of the New England landscape. But his presence as a poet in those landscapes brought to them a modern sense of isolation and anxiety and a normally suppressed American fear of the impersonal vastness of nature, along with the disturbing metaphysical implications of that indifference. With Frost, nature poetry came to the end of its century-long association with the pathetic fallacy, so that human feelings and natural landscapes were decisively separated. Frost's poems are, to be sure, representations of the mind's engagement with nature, but finally, they say more about the mind than about the settings they so lovingly describe. In fact, so described, nature's beauty stands in ironic contrast to the tragedy and loneliness of human life. Poems, Frost said, are momentary stays against confusion, and his own poems were gravely formal precisely in order to oppose the larger disorder that he feared would ultimately prevail.

Williams wished to achieve a break not only with the past and with the old metaphysical order of reality but with "literature" itself, which he believed ignores much of what really counts for human experience and distorts a good bit of the rest. As an exponent of at least one version of imagist poetry, he worked to develop an "unliterary" literary medium through which the world itself—its objects and its people—could find free expression and the commendation they deserved. His long poem *Paterson* (1946–58) was a celebration of a most unpoetic subject, an American industrial city. Yet the industrial city exhilarated Williams and stirred his imagination, and he opened his verse forms wider in order to let it in, in order to make it part of the new affirmative intellectual life of the new century. Williams was American in the tradition of WALT WHITMAN—populist, anti-elitist, celebrating the ordinary life of ordinary people. The demographic complexity that dismayed Eliot—and perhaps Stevens as well—was the true subject of poetry for Williams, because it was the true character of modern American experience.

HART CRANE fit into the Whitman tradition as well, embracing the present and the future of America by seeing in American technology a new birth of the romantic spirit as well as the promise of change. Crane's high modernist visionary poetry sought to generate from otherwise merely material aspects of progress a symbolic spiritual power.

EZRA POUND thought that World War I had also confirmed that European culture had come to an ignominious dead end—"an old bitch gone in the teeth"—and that a crass materialism had sapped Europe of its creative and visionary strength. Gradually, discovering what he was doing as he went along, Pound became a kind of evangelical archeologist searching the surviving artifacts and ideas of earlier cultures for evidence of vital, creative human agency and the intelligent direction of moral and political power. He assembled this evidence in the form of the *Cantos* (1925), a vast ideological epic that was disjunctive and spatial in form rather than progressive and linear, both symbolizing and requiring a radical new way of thinking. This modernist form allowed him to create a model of a historical time in which the values and myths of vastly different periods and cultures could freely coexist with and reinforce each other.

The *Cantos*, unlike *The Waste Land*, was both optimistic and didactic, in that it aimed to revitalize suppressed human achievement to serve as a goal for a new cultural order. These attributes revealed Pound as deeply American: his aggression, his enthusiastic affirmation of the power of change, and his assertion of what is vital against what is obsolete, unexamined, and inert. Temperamentally, he stood between Stevens and Eliot in this respect and became the very symbol of the cosmopolitan spirit of American intellectual life after World War I. Ironically, his very "Americanism" also led him to naively embrace the false promise of European fascism and a dream of the benevolent despotic rule of the educated classes. He ended by turning against the unregulated capitalism and pluralism for which the country of his birth had by then become the supreme international symbol.

One of the effects of that pluralism was the ascendancy after World War I of an intellectually aggressive African American middle class, expressing itself through the fiction and poetry of the Harlem Renaissance. The "Harlem" part of the phrase became a badge of black pride, as the poets of the movement sought to form their own new world by creating a new poetics derived from African American culture. For both COUNTEE CULLEN and LANGSTON HUGHES, vehement protest against racial injustice was crucial, but so was the exploration and creation of a new identity. The poets of the Harlem Renaissance produced out of such conflict a portrait in which public and private crises were fused in a unique and compelling way. The Harlem Renaissance was enacting within the matrix of American racism yet another complex version of the American dream of self-regeneration. By the time of the Great Depression, the story of American life had already become publicly recognized as many stories, and so it would continue to be.

History and Criticism

Altieri, Charles. *Painterly Abstraction in Modernist American Poetry: Infinite Incantations of Ourselves.* Cambridge U. Pr. 1990 $49.50. ISBN 0-521-33085-8. Establishes the context of historical pressures and resources behind modernists such as Eliot, Pound, and Stevens.

Baker, Carlos. *The Echoing Green: Romanticism, Modernism and Phenomena of Transference in Poetry.* Princeton U. Pr. 1984 $45.00. ISBN 0-691-06595-0. Examines the works of Yeats, Frost, Pound, and others in relation to English Romanticism.

Blackmur, Richard. *Language as Gesture: Essays in Poetry.* Greenwood 1977 $49.75. ISBN 0-8371-9782-1. Important collection of essays on modernist poets.

Bloom, Harold, ed. *American Poetry, 1915–1945*. Chelsea Hse. 1987 $64.95. ISBN 0-87754-952-4. Selected critical essays on a variety of related subjects.

Bly, Robert. *American Poetry: Wildness and Domesticity*. HarpC 1990 $22.50. ISBN 0-06-016265-1. Essays written in the 1960s concerned with struggles against the modernist tradition; rallies a new generation of poets.

Borroff, Marie. *Language and the Poet: Verbal Artistry in Frost, Stevens, and Moore*. U. Ch. Pr. 1979 $18.00. ISBN 0-226-06651-7. Analyzes how human experience is given dramatic significance in the poetry of Frost, Stevens, and Moore.

Brooks, Cleanth. *Modern Poetry and the Tradition*. U. of NC Pr. 1970 o.p. Important study of poetry and poets.

———. *Understanding Poetry*. HarBraceJ 1976 $28.00. ISBN 0-03-076980-9. Discusses the genre of poetry and its elements according to the tenets of the "New Criticism."

Candelaria, Cordelia. *Chicano Poetry: A Critical Introduction*. Greenwood 1986 $42.95. ISBN 0-313-23683-6. Overview of Chicano poetry from 1967 to the present; applies a bilingual, multicultural perspective.

Clark, Arthur M. *Realistic Revolt in Modern Poetry*. Haskell 1970 $27.95. ISBN 0-8383-0087-1

Cowan, Louise. *The Fugitive Group: A Literary History*. LSU Pr. 1959 o.p. Examines the poets who published in *The Fugitive* in the early 1920s, including John Crowe Ransom and Robert Penn Warren.

Dembu, L. S. *Conceptions of Reality in Modern American Poetry*. U. CA Pr. 1966 o.p. Philosophical analysis that contends that poets as diverse as Lowell and Pound adhere to a common logic.

Dickie, Margaret. *On the Modernist Long Poem*. U. of Iowa Pr. 1986 $20.00. ISBN 0-87745-140-0. Posits American modernist poetry as both conservative and affirmative; discusses some poets' ambitions to write long public poems.

Diggory, Terrence. *Yeats and American Poetry: The Traditional of the Self*. Princeton U. Pr. 1983 $45.00. ISBN 0-691-06558-6. Shows the influence of Whitman on Yeats, and of Yeats on a wide range of early twentieth-century American poets.

Fairclough, Henry R. *Classics and Our Twentieth Century Poets*. AMS Pr. repr. of 1927 ed. $18.00. ISBN 0-404-51804-4

Fredman, Stephen. *Poet's Prose: The Crisis in American Verse*. Cambridge U. Pr. 2nd ed 1990 $34.50. ISBN 0-521-39098-2. Argues that a poet's prose derives from the question as to whether there is poetry; examines the work of Williams, Creeley, and Ashbery.

Fussell, Edwin. *Lucifer in Harness*. Princeton U. Pr. 1973 o.p. Explores the fundamental dilemma of American poetry in the fields of meter, metaphor, and poetic diction.

Gelpi, Albert. *A Coherent Splendor: The American Poetic Renaissance 1910–1980*. Cambridge U. Pr. 1990 $16.95. ISBN 0-521-38687-X. Argues for a subtle continuity between Romanticism and Modernism.

———. *The Tenth Muse: The Psyche of the American Poet*. HUP 1975 o.p. Contends that there is a debate between intellect and passion in nineteenth-century poets; focuses on Emerson and Poe.

Gilbert, Roger. *Walks in the World: Representation and Experience in Modern American Poetry*. Princeton U. Pr. 1991 $35.00. ISBN 0-691-06858-5

Granger Book Company, Editorial Board Staff. *Survey of American Poetry: Twilight Interval, 1890–1912*. Roth Pub. Inc. 1986 $39.95. ISBN 0-89609-218-6. Anthology of American verse between the passing of the nineteenth century and the arrival of twentieth-century modernism.

Gray, Richard. *American Poetry of the Twentieth Century*. Longman 1990 $27.96. ISBN 0-582-49437-0

Hischak, Thomas S. *Word Crazy: Broadway Lyricists from Cohan to Sondheim*. Greenwood 1991 $19.95. ISBN 0-275-93849-2. Examines the role of American theatre lyricists from the earliest days of operetta up to the conceptual musicals of the last thirty years.

Holden, Jonathan. *The Fate of American Poetry.* U. of Ga. Pr. 1992 $26.00. ISBN 0-8203-1364-5. Demonstrates how postwar American poetry has shed the elitist vestiges of modernism.

Hollander, John, ed. *Modern Poetry: Essays in Criticism.* OUP 1968 $10.95. ISBN 0-19-500757-3. Chronicles the way that modern poetry has been read by critics, scholars, and poets.

Kenner, Hugh. *The Pound Era.* U. CA Pr. 1971 $40.00. ISBN 0-520-01860-5. Examines Pound's exploratory activity as exemplary of other modernist poets.

King, Woodie, ed. *The Forerunners: Black Poets in America.* Howard U. Pr. 1981 $8.95. ISBN 0-88258-015-9. Anthology focusing on the poetic tradition from the Renaissance up to the 1940s and 1950s.

Larrissy, Edward. *Reading Twentieth Century Poetry: The Language of Gender and Objects.* Blackwell Pub. 1991 $47.95. ISBN 0-631-15358-6

Middlebrook, Diane W., ed. *Coming to Light: American Women Poets in the Twentieth Century.* U. of Mich. Pr. 1985 $14.95. ISBN 0-472-08061-X. Discusses contemporary women's poetry in regard to a lack of tradition in a polarized gender system.

Moramarco, Fred. *Modern American Poetry, 1865–1950.* Macmillan 1989 $23.95. ISBN 0-8057-8451-9. Traces the origins and evolution of modernism in American verse from Dickinson to the objectivist movement.

Murphy, Margueritte S. *A Tradition of Subversion: The Prose Poem in English from Wilde to Ashbery.* U. of Mass. Pr. 1992 $25.00. ISBN 0-87023-781-0. Includes chapters on Williams and Stein.

Myers, Jack, ed. *A Profile of Twentieth-Century American Poetry.* S. Ill. U. Pr. 1991 $29.95. ISBN 0-8093-1348-0. Working poets create unique models of their assigned periods and topics; includes a comprehensive and humanistic overview.

Nielsen, Aldon L. *Reading Race: White American Poets and Racial Discourse in the Twentieth Century.* U. of Ga. Pr. 1990 $12.00. ISBN 0-8203-1273-8. A dialectical examination of white discourse on African Americans.

Ostriker, Alicia S. *Stealing the Language: The Emergence of Women's Poetry in America.* Beacon Pr. 1987 $12.95. ISBN 0-8070-6303-7. Views women writers as "thieves of language"; considers the struggle to achieve self-definition in a tradition recalcitrant to women.

Pearce, Roy Harvey. *The Continuity of American Poetry.* U. Pr. of New Eng. 1987 $40.00. ISBN 0-8195-5155-4. A valuable study of the history of American poetry from the seventeenth century to the age of Eliot.

Perkins, David. *A History of Modern Poetry: From the 1890s to the High Modernist Mode.* HUP 1976 $27.50. ISBN 0-674-39941-2. This is a thorough, cautious study.

Perloff, Majorie. *The Poetics of Indeterminacy.* Northwestern U. Pr. 1981 $14.95. ISBN 0-8101-0661-2. Argues that modernism is a time of tension between symbolism and a poetics of indeterminacy.

Pritchard, William. *Lives of the Modern Poets.* OUP 1981 $8.95. ISBN 0-19-502989-5. Critical-biographical studies of such major modernist masters as Frost, Eliot, and Pound.

Quartermain, Peter, ed. *American Poets, 1880 to 1945.* Gale 1985 $112.00. ISBN 0-8103-1723-0. Traces the development of canon and the evolution of reputation in poets such as Frost and Stevens.

Quinn, Sister Bernetta. *Metamorphic Tradition in Modern Poetry: Essays on the Work of Ezra Pound and Other Poets.* Gordian 1966 $40.00. ISBN 0-87752-089-5. Examines the oeuvre of poets who use a predominance of metamorphic themes.

Raiziss, Sona. *Metaphysical Passion: Seven Modern American Poets and the Seventeenth Century Tradition.* Greenwood 1970 $38.50. ISBN 0-8371-3343-2. Reviews American poets extending metaphysical statements into the twentieth century; historical approach.

Rosenthal, Macha L. *Modern Poets: A Critical Introduction.* OUP 1965 $8.95. ISBN 0-19-500718-2. Touches on the continuities with the poetry of the past; surveys the work of great modern poets.

Rosenthal, Macha L. *Sailing into the Unknown: Yeats, Pound, and Eliot.* OUP 1978 $20.00. ISBN 0-19-502318-8. Explores the poems of modern masters; criticism is grounded on the author's experience as a poet.

Ross, Andrew. *The Failure of Modernism.* Col. U. Pr. 1986 $35.00. ISBN 0-231-06330-X. An account of the struggle over subjectivity in modern American poetry, using psychoanalytic and other tools.

Schwartz, Sanford. *The Matrix of Modernism: Pound, Eliot, and Early Twentieth Century Thought.* Princeton U. Pr. 1988 $37.00. ISBN 0-691-06651-5. Examines the ties between individual philosophers and particular poets.

Shucard, Alan. *Modern American Poetry, 1865–1950.* U. of Mass. Pr. 1990 $14.95. ISBN 0-87023-720-9. Reexamines poetry as a reflection of American culture; discusses the origins and evolutions of modernism.

Sitwell, Edith. *Aspects of Modern Poetry.* Ayer repr. of 1934 ed. $17.00. ISBN 0-8369-1684-0

Stanford, Donald. *Revolution and Convention in Modern Poetry.* U. of Delaware Pr. 1983 o.p. Assesses the literary value of experimentalist movements in American poetry.

Steinman, Lisa M. *Made in America: Science, Technology, and American Modernist Poets.* Yale U. Pr. 1989 $10.95. ISBN 0-300-04502-6. A consideration of poets who stayed in America during the early 1900s; examines the influence of science and technology on their work.

Tomlinson, Charles. *Poetry and Metamorphosis.* Cambridge U. Pr. 1983 $22.95. ISBN 0-521-24848-5. Examines the way that fables of metamorphosis have caught the poetic imagination; analyzes translations of Ovid's *Metamorphoses*.

Unger, Leonard, ed. *Seven Modern American Poets: An Introduction.* U. of Minn. Pr. 1967 $19.95. ISBN 0-8166-0416-9. This volume comprises seven numbers from the excellent University of Minnesota Pamphlets on American Writers (Frost, Stevens, Williams, Pound, Ransom, Eliot, and Tate). Under "has written a fine introduction on modern American poetry" (*Library Journal*).

Vendler, Helen. *Part of Nature, Part of Us: Modern American Poets.* HUP 1980 $12.95. IBSN 0-674-65476-5. Scholarly overview of twentieth century poetry; distinguishes successes and failures in a poet's oeuvre.

——, ed. *Voices and Visions: The Poet in America.* Random 1987 $29.95. ISBN 0-394-53520-0. Original essays on thirteen modern American poets including Dickinson and Whitman, with illustrations.

Walker, Cheryl. *Masks Outrageous and Austere: Culture, Psyche, and Persona in Modern Women Poets.* Ind. U. Pr. 1991 $39.95. ISBN 0-253-36322-5. Examines the interrelationships between culture and gender as expressed in poems by American women.

Walker, David. *The Transparent Lyric.* Princeton U. Pr. 1984 $32.50. ISBN 0-691-06606-X. Emphasizes similarities between Stevens and Williams; questions conventional assumptions about dramatic speakers in poetry.

Walker, Jeffrey. *Bardic Ethos and the American Epic Poem: Whitman, Pound, Crane, Williams, Olson.* La. State U. Pr. 1989 $37.50. ISBN 0-8071-1478-2. Argues that Pound, Crane, Williams, and Olson wanted to become American epic bards, and examines Whitman's influence on them.

Collections

Adoff, Arnold, ed. *The Poetry of Black America: Anthology of the Twentieth Century.* HarpC 1973 $25.00. ISBN 0-06-020089-8. An excellent anthology—comprehensive selections from W. B. DuBois and James Weldon Johnson through Richard Wright, Sun Ra, Imamu Amiri Baraka (LeRoi Jones) to Nikki Giovanni and Victor Hernandez Cruz.

Allen, Donald M. *The New American Poetry, 1945–1960.* Grove 1960 o.p.; An important collection of 215 poems by 44 poets, arranged to illuminate some of their differences and similarities. Included are biographies, bibliographies, and statements on poetics by the poets themselves. This anthology had an impact that is hard to overestimate. Reissued in an enlarged edition entitled *The Post Modern Poets*.

Bly, Robert. *Selected from Twentieth-Century American Poetry: An Anthology*. Lit. Vols. NYC 1991 $3.50. ISBN 0-929631-29-3

Carruth, Hayden. *The Voice That Is Great within Us: American Poetry of the Twentieth Century*. Bantam 1983 $6.95. ISBN 0-553-26263-7. An anthology covering sixty years of American verse; its shape and structure attempt to suggest a canon.

DiYanni, Robert. *Modern American Poets*. McGraw 1987 $21.08. ISBN 0-07-554219-6. An anthology featuring the work of thirteen major American poets as well as 36 others; includes critical headnotes to each author. Begins with sections on reading poetry and on various poetic elements, such as voice, imagery, rhyme, and meter.

Ellman, Richard, ed. *Modern Poems: An Introduction to Poetry*. Norton 2nd ed. 1989 $24.95. ISBN 0-393-95907-4

Moser, Barry, illus. *Fifty Years of American Poetry: Anniversary Volume for the Academy of American Poets*. Abrams 1984 $35.00. ISBN 0-8109-0934-0

Oresick, Peter, ed. *Working Classics: Poems on Industrial Life*. U. of Ill. Pr. 1990 $34.95. ISBN 0-252-01730-7

Untermeyer, Louis, ed. *Modern American Poetry*. HarBraceJ 1962 o.p. A critical anthology enlarged to include 772 poems by 76 poets ranging from Whitman to Anne Sexton.

FICTION

The American novel in the twentieth century developed into a fine art the national preoccupation with the meaning and limits of individual freedom as defined by the American experience. RALPH WALDO EMERSON had raised American consciousness on this subject in the nineteenth century by asserting that the individual not only can but must transcend his or her own cultural and historical circumstances, that the only God or law that the individual must answer to is within the self. In the sense that America's very founding was a break with history, with the claims of the European past, and the developing of not only a new country but of a new world, Emersonian individualism could be thought of as an imperative of national destiny.

When Jay Gatsby is told by Nick Carraway that you can't repeat the past, and he responds, "Why of course you can, old sport," Gatsby is imagining a control over the passage of time that amounts to suspending it. Gatsby is said in turn to have been reborn from a Platonic idea of himself, cut off by his own dream from all identification with his family and low social class to become what he wishes to be. In this respect, he is the paragon of American romantic idealism, a new man in a world that in turn always holds forth the promise of a new frontier. The kind of novel Jay Gatsby inhabits is, moreover, an expression of his own understanding of the world. In its most stylized form, this kind of world exemplifies what Richard Chase called "the romance," a symbolic American form because it rises above—or evades—issues of intricate social connections and therefore circumstantial realism, in order to render an idealized presentation of human conflicts and self-realization. The ethos of romance—first so named by HAWTHORNE—is central to the study of the novel in the twentieth century, for modern American fiction both expresses and grimly critiques the naive idealism of that spirit, often—as in *The Great Gatsby* (1925)—within the limits of the same story.

HEMINGWAY's novels and short stories return obsessively, for instance, to the dream of a pure place and a free condition, the private self alone, or with sympathetic male companions, or with an idealized compliant woman, in the mountains, in the snow, on the edge of trout streams, or fishing the Gulf Stream, places where the water is clean and sacramental and where modern war, society, and history do not impinge. But, of course, all of these troubling factors sooner or later do impinge, as they impinge on Jay Gatsby's narcissistic enterprise, and the naive epistemology of the modern novel's romance eventually ensures that novel's turn to the tragic.

The idealized South that recurs in WILLIAM FAULKNER's Yoknapatawpha novels is a projection of nostalgia for his most deeply serious characters, but the region of their imagining never comes into being and perhaps had never been real to begin with. What is then absent from their world and their relationships becomes ironically, what most defines them. Thomas Sutpen, in *Absalom, Absalom!*, tried to achieve the same autonomy and rewriting of his own history that Jay Gatsby had attempted, but was thwarted by his own culturally ingrained racism and was shot ignominiously by an outraged father whose daughter he had exploited and abused.

Edna Pontellier, in KATE CHOPIN's *The Awakening* (1899), dreams of the open spaces of her childhood in Kentucky and of young lovers who will carry her away from the oppression of New Orleans society where she is ruled over by possessions, by reproductive biology, and by an obliviously patriarchal social order. In the end, though, she can fulfill her dream of space and freedom and uncompromised self-presence only by giving herself to the sea.

Those writers of the same period whom we think of now as naturalists—FRANK NORRIS, THEODORE DREISER, NATHANAEL WEST—were influenced by the nineteenth-century human sciences, which systematically demystified human nature, showing it to be wholly driven by economic or biological forces. In America, therefore, the thematic stakes in such novels are always high, and issues of great moment are generated from the most ordinary circumstances. Where built-in character flaws do not cause doom for the protagonists, a random external fate intervenes to ensure it. This causes the characters, sometimes even to themselves, to seem singled out by destiny and to this degree to become larger than life, if only ironically. Happy endings in modern American novels are the exception rather than the rule.

Even in the work of more conventional novelists, such as ELLEN GLASGOW, WILLA CATHER, SHERWOOD ANDERSON, and SINCLAIR LEWIS, unusual individual achievement and autonomy, especially for women, come only at the cost of the individual's becoming socially suspect and alienated from the community. The American ethos plants dreams of autonomy and freedom, and then the conventional American community works insidiously to thwart those dreams. The careers of Cather's protagonists, for example, as they evolve through her novels, move them farther and farther into the austere, unpopulated landscapes of the Southwest and eventually, in their spiritual questing, away not only from America's materialistic culture but from culture and history altogether.

Likewise, Bigger Thomas, the young black man in RICHARD WRIGHT's *Native Son* (1940), dreams of being an aviator, serenely in flight, far above the mean streets of his ghetto; however, in one appalling moment, even his ghetto life is ended when he accidentally kills a young white woman who has befriended him, and he becomes what white culture hounds him into being. His case is taken up by a sympathetic socialist lawyer who argues before the court that Bigger's environment, the effects of poverty and racism, is as much responsible for Bigger's actions as Bigger is himself. But Bigger, in the end, cannot acquiesce even to this claim of society upon him. Although it costs him his life, he claims his own being by taking fully upon himself the responsibility for his actions. Even if we see him as wrong and his lawyer right, it is clear that

Bigger's claim of autonomy is not only an existential but a deeply American moral gesture—and it is all that he has left.

Later in the same decade, during the worst of the Great Depression, when political ideology and economic circumstance militated against personal and individual actions, JOHN STEINBECK's Ma Joad in *The Grapes of Wrath* (1939) collectivizes Bigger's gesture: We are the people, she says, and the people will survive, though at that point there is not even a faint sign that her family— exploited, abused, and all but destroyed by the agents of a powerful fruit growers company—will achieve a happy outcome. Jay Gatsby's success as an entrepreneur and as a beholder of infinite possibility had depended upon his access to a fluid and unlimited money supply. By the end of the 1930s, there was no money supply, and, therefore, there could have been no Gatsby. Instead, capitalism was coming to be seen by JOHN DOS PASSOS, Steinbeck, and other exponents of collective social action, as a system of oppression, depersonalization, and moral decay rather than an agent of autonomy and personal improvement.

EMERSON had optimistically believed that America, come what may, was a continent of privileged possibility, and if the Civil War could not destroy that myth (as MELVILLE thought it had), nothing ever would. But the Great Depression and the subtle psychological attrition of World War II that came after, came close.

History and Criticism

Aaron, Daniel. *Writers on the Left*. Octagon 1974 o.p. A social chronicle of left-wing writers from 1912 to the early 1940s; considers their response to the ideas of communism.

Awkward, Michael. *Inspiriting Influences: Tradition, Revision, and Afro-American Women's Novels*. Col. U. Pr. 1991 $40.00. ISBN 0-231-06806-9. Analyzes recent novels by African American women; establishes a connection between them and the oeuvre of Zora Neale Hurston.

Bakker, J. *The Role of the Mythic West in Some Representative Examples of Classic and Modern American Literature: The Shaping Force of the American Frontier*. E. Mellen 1991 $69.95. ISBN 0-7734-9713-7

Bauer, Dale M., ed. *Feminism, Bakhtin, and the Dialogic*. State U. NY Pr. 1991 $49.50. ISBN 0-7914-0769-1

Blake, Nelson M. *Novelists' America: Fiction as History, 1910–1940*. Syracuse U. Pr. 1969 $5.95. ISBN 0-8156-2147-7. The author, a historian, turns to fiction in the search for historical truth in this rewarding study of three decades of American life as viewed by eight novelists: Lewis, Fitzgerald, Faulkner, Wolfe, Steinbeck, Dos Passos, Farrell, and Wright.

Block, Alan A. *Anonymous Toil: A Reevaluation of the American Radical Novel in the Twentieth Century*. U. Pr. of Amer. 1992 $37.50. ISBN 0-8191-8558-2

Bloom, Harold, ed. *American Fiction, 1914–1945*. Chelsea Hse. 1987 $64.95. ISBN 0-87754-962-1

Blotner, Joseph. *The Modern American Political Novel*. U. of Tex. Pr. 1966 o.p. Attempts to discover the image of American politics as presented in American novels.

Bradbury, Malcolm. *The Modern American Novel*. OUP 1984 $8.95. ISBN 0-19-289044-1. Perhaps the best of the general, nonspecialized introductions to the subject.

Bryer, Jackson R., ed. *Sixteen Modern American Writers: A Survey of Research and Criticism*. Duke 1973 o.p. Prominent academic authorities describe and evaluate biographical, critical, and bibliographic writings on major writers, including Anderson, Cather, Dreiser, Faulkner, Hemingway, Steinbeck, and Wolfe.

Callahan, John F. *In the African-American Grain: Call and Response in Twentieth-Century Black Fiction*. U. Pr. of New Eng. $15.95. ISBN 0-8195-6232-7

―――――. *In the African-American Grain: The Pursuit of Voice in Twentieth-Century Black Fiction.* U. of Ill. Pr. 1988 $24.95. ISBN 0-252-01459-6. Demonstrates the impact of African American oral storytelling techniques on twentieth-century fiction.

Casey, Daniel J., ed. *Modern Irish American Fiction: A Reader.* Syracuse U. Pr. 1989 $34.95. ISBN 0-8156-2462-X. Compelling narration of the Irish People in America; highlights their contribution to American letters.

Conder, John J. *Naturalism in American Fiction: The Classic Phase.* U. Pr. of Ky. 1984 $10.00. ISBN 0-8131-0169-7. Examines naturalism in American fiction; considers the philosophical conceptions of nature.

De Weever, Jacqueline. *Mythmaking and Metaphor in Black Women's Fiction.* St. Martin 1992 $35.00. ISBN 0-312-06532-9

Doan, Laura L., ed. *Old Maids to Radical Spinsters: Unmarried Women in the Twentieth-Century Novel.* U. of Ill. Pr. 1990 $39.95. ISBN 0-252-01731-5

Donovan, Josephine. *After the Fall: The Demeter–Persephone Myth in Wharton, Cather, & Glasgow.* Pa. St. U. Pr. 1989 $23.50. ISBN 0-271-00649-8

Edel, Leon. *The Psychological Novel.* Lippincott 1955 o.p. Discusses how emotional and sensory experience has been rendered in American fiction; analyzes the flow of mental experience.

Fleck, Richard F., ed. *Critical Perspectives on Native American Fiction.* Three Continents 1992 $32.00. ISBN 0-89410-700-3

French, Warren. *The Social Novel at the End of an Era.* S. Ill. U. Pr. 1966 o.p. Excellent study of the way in which social and historical events affected the writing of five novels published around 1940: Steinbeck's *Grapes of Wrath*, Hemingway's *For Whom the Bell Tolls*, Faulkner's *The Hamlet*, Dalton Trumbo's *Johnny Got His Gun*, and Pietro diDonato's *Christ in Concrete*.

Fullbrook, Kate. *Free Women: Ethics and Aesthetics in Twentieth Century Women's Fiction.* Temple U. Pr. 1990 $34.95. ISBN 0-87722-773-X. Discusses women's literary achievements in the modern period; considers the impact of radical new moral principles on their fiction.

Girgus, Sam B. *The New Covenant: Jewish Writers and the American Idea.* U. of NC Pr. 1984 $22.50. ISBN 0-8078-1577-2. Argues that Jewish writers pushed society into cultural renewal.

Goldsmith, Arnold. *The Modern American Urban Novel: Nature as "Interior Structure."* Wayne St. U. Pr. 1991 $29.95. ISBN 0-8143-1994-7. Discusses authors who used images from nature to reinforce the themes of their novels.

Good, Howard. *Acquainted with the Night: The Image of Journalists in American Fiction 1890–1930.* Scarecrow 1986 $20.00. ISBN 0-8108-1889-2. Analyzes the ambivalent portrait of journalists in American fiction from 1890 to 1930.

Hoffman, Frederick J. *The Twenties: American Writing in the Postwar Decade.* Free Pr. 1965 $16.95. ISBN 0-02-914780-8. One of the best surveys of a pivotal period in modern literary history, this sophisticated study balances social awareness with literary values.

Kaplan, Amy. *The Social Construction of American Realism.* U. Ch. Pr. 1988 $24.95. ISBN 0-226-42429-4. Explores how the concept of realism evolves in the works of Howells, Wharton, and Dreiser.

Kazin, Alfred. *The Bright Book of Life: American Novelists and Storytellers from Hemingway to Mailer.* U. of Notre Dame Pr. 1980 repr. of 1971 ed. $11.95. ISBN 0-268-00664-4. An integrated account of American fiction since World War II; views fiction as the embodiment of the American experience.

―――――. *On Native Grounds: An Interpretation of Modern American Prose Literature.* HarBraceJ 1942 o.p. Analyses of American prose from 1890 to 1940; considers such issues as the search for reality and literary crises.

Kelley, Karol L. *Models for the Multitudes: Social Values in the American Popular Novel, 1850–1920.* Greenwood 1987 $32.50. ISBN 0-313-23514-7

Kubitschek, Missy D. *Claiming the Heritage: African-American Women Novelists and History.* U. Pr. of Miss. 1991 $27.50. ISBN 0-87805-456-1. Claims a local, familial, and emotional process in the twentieth-century tradition of African American women's novels.

Lee, A. Robert, ed. *The Modern American Novella*. St. Martin 1989 $35.00. ISBN 0-312-02424-X. Discusses the novella-form and the "Americanness" of the American novella from Henry James onward.

Lynn, David H. *The Hero's Tale: Narration in the Early Modern Novel*. St. Martin 1989 $29.95. ISBN 0-312-01621-2. Analyzes the modern heroic experience; considers both the illusions of conventional beliefs and the hypocrisy of society.

Malmgren, Carl D. *Fictional Space in the Modernist and Postmodernist American Novel*. Bucknell U. Pr. 1985 $35.00. ISBN 0-8387-5067-2. Examines the relationship between fiction and reality, art and life.

Mitchell, Lee C. *Determined Fictions: American Literary Naturalism*. Col. U. Pr. 1989 $35.00. ISBN 0-231-06898-0

Mukherjee, Arun. *The Gospel of Wealth in the American Novel: The Rhetoric of Dreiser and Some of His Contemporaries*. B & N Imports 1987 $45.50. ISBN 0-389-20681-4

Nelson, Robert M. *Place and Vision: The Function of Landscape in Native American Fiction*. Peter Lang 1992 $36.95. ISBN 0-8204-1720-3

Rabinowitz, Paula. *Labor and Desire: Women's Revolutionary Fiction in Depression America*. U. of NC Pr. 1991 $29.95. ISBN 0-8078-1994-8. Discusses the idea of a working class literature as both revolutionary and proto-feminist.

Rowe, Joyce A. *Equivocal Endings in Classic American Novels: The Scarlet Letter, Adventures of Huckleberry Finn, The Ambassadors, The Great Gatsby*. Cambridge U. Pr. 1988 $37.50. ISBN 0-521-33532-9. Analyzes the endings of classical novels such as *Moby Dick* and *The Great Gatsby* in relation to their narratives.

Sundquist, Eric J., ed. *American Realism: New Essays*. Johns Hopkins 1982 $27.50. ISBN 0-8018-2796-5. This collection brings together critical discussions of James, Crane, Norris, Wharton, Dreiser, and other novelists.

Wagner-Martin, Linda. *The Modern American Novel, 1914–1945*. Macmillan 1989 $22.95. ISBN 0-8057-7851-9. A revisionist study that provides an open-ended contribution to the ongoing development of the literary canon.

Wilson, Christopher P. *White Collar Fictions: Class and Social Representation in American Literature, 1885–1925*. U. of Ga. Pr. 1992 $35.00. ISBN 0-8203-1367-X

Woodress, James. *American Fiction, 1900–1950: A Guide to Information Sources*. Gale 1974 $68.00. ISBN 0-8103-1201-8. This useful volume describes literary scholarship devoted to more than 40 of the prominent fiction writers of the early twentieth century, as well as general studies of modern American fiction.

Young, Thomas D., ed. *Modern American Fiction: Form and Function*. La. State U. Pr. 1989 $30.00. ISBN 0-8071-1435-9. Overview of the fiction created in America between 1890 and 1970; discusses issues of quality, technical dexterity, and intention.

Zinsser, William, ed. *Paths of Resistance: The Art and Craft of the Political Novel*. HM 1989 $19.45. ISBN 0-395-51426-6. Five masters of the political novel explain how their writing is impelled by a sense of social responsibility.

Collections

Albert, Richard N., ed. *From Blues to Bop: A Collection of Jazz Fiction*. Doubleday 1992 $12.00. ISBN 0-385-42219-9. Anthology of short stories inspired by the colorful world of jazz music and its protagonists.

Anaya, Rudolfo A., ed. *Cuentos Chicanos: A Short Story Anthology*. U. of NM Pr. 1989 $12.95. ISBN 0-8263-0772-8

Carver, Raymond, ed. *American Short Story Masterpieces*. Dell 1989 $5.95. ISBN 0-440-20423-2

Crane, Milton, ed. *Fifty Great American Short Stories*. Bantam 1984 $4.95. ISBN 0-553-27294-2. Stories dating from the discovery of the American mind and nation to the awareness of an identifiable American literary tradition.

Foley, Martha, ed. *Two Hundred Years of Great American Short Stories*. HM 1975 o.p.

Forkner, Ben, ed. *Stories of the Modern South*. Peter Smith 1984 $20.00. ISBN 0-8446-6171-6. Rich collection of Southern fiction that includes authors such as Agee, Capote, Faulkner and others.

Garcia-Ayvens, Francisco, ed. *The Chicano Anthology Index*. UC Chicano Lib. 1990 $150.00. ISBN 0-918520-13-4

Gold, Herbert, and David L. Stevenson, eds. *Stories of Modern America*. St. Martin 1969 o.p.

Grant, Douglas, ed. *Classic American Short Stories*. OUP 1990 $10.95. ISBN 0-19-282685-9

Modern American Short Stories 1982. Dorrance 1982 $9.95. ISBN 0-8059-2850-2

Prescott, Peter, ed. *The Norton Book of American Short Stories*. Norton 1988 $22.95. ISBN 0-393-02619-1. A collection full of treasures.

Raffel, Burton, ed. *The Signet Classic Book of American Short Stories*. NAL-Dutton 1985 $5.95. ISBN 0-451-52279-6

Skaggs, Calvin, ed. *The American Short Story*. Dell 1980 $5.95. ISBN 0-440-30297-8. Anthology that includes works by Hemingway, Updike, Fitzgerald, and others.

Stegner, Wallace, and Mary Stegner, eds. *Great American Short Stories*. Dell 1985 $6.99. ISBN 0-440-33060-2

Stevick, Philip, ed. *The American Short Story, 1900–1945: A Critical History*. Macmillan 1984 $22.95. ISBN 0-8057-9353-4. Essays that trace the major movements of the short story from the beginning of the century to the end of World War II.

Sullivan, Nancy. *Treasury of American Short Stories*. Doubleday 1981 o.p.

Voss, Arthur. *The American Short Story: A Critical Survey*. U. of Okla. Pr. 1980 $14.95. ISBN 0-8061-1644-7. Provides information and critical opinion about the stories of a particular writer; also includes formal analyses.

Warren, Robert Penn, ed. *Short Story Masterpieces*. Dell 1954 $5.95. A dazzling selection of major short stories from both English and American traditions.

Wolff, Tobias, ed. *Matters of Life and Death: New American Stories*. Wampeter Pr. 1983 $14.95. ISBN 0-931694-14-0

NONFICTION

Of the prose written in the first half of the twentieth century, that which seems to stand out today is the work that in some way questioned the American sense of purpose. Even the New Criticism, largely an American phenomenon, claimed that literature and social action are incompatible, and it therefore promoted a concept of literature that at least pretends to be apolitical and rises above the fray of common life. The New Criticism focused upon the text, placing the highest value upon density of implication, upon irony and complexity in poetic language. As a critical movement, it had an important influence upon the kind of work that such younger poets as ROBERT LOWELL or JOHN BERRYMAN would be producing. It meant also that earlier American writers who qualified by such standards, such as EMILY DICKINSON, could be edged into a parity with older English and European writers, like JOHN DONNE. Modernist poets like ELIOT, STEVENS, POUND, HART CRANE, ALLEN TATE, and JOHN CROWE RANSOM could also then claim a competitive position in a trans-historical tradition as judged by the New Criticism's special criteria. But it also meant that literature is at its best when disengaged from any project identifiable with social disturbance or social change.

It was not a coincidence, then, that many of the most prominent New Critics—Allen Tate, John Crowe Ransom, ROBERT PENN WARREN, and CLEANTH BROOKS—had been professionally associated with the American South. Out of that association had emerged the important collection of essays, *I'll Take My Stand* (1930), in which various social historians and men of letters had urged an agrarian solution to the environmental, social, and moral problems created by unrestrained industrial capitalism. In this argument, the traditional South and its traditional cultural values could be the bastion against America's impending social disintegration. The South would produce a kind of literature in which tradition and individual talent could interact productively. In the larger scheme of things, the Fugitives and Agrarians—as, in different combinations, they were known—could not be an effective force; nevertheless, the publication of *I'll Take My Stand* continues to be regarded as a significant symbolic event because it condensed in one moment the anxiety of many American intellectuals about the increasing disruptions in the social fabric and confusion in the sense of national direction. Although the Fugitives and Agrarians were bitterly opposed to Marxism and Marxist materialism, they were addressing the same problems that KARL MARX (see Vols. 3 and 4) had addressed in the previous century and, perhaps ironically, they had arrived at some of the same conclusions about capitalism's capacity for self-destruction, albeit from a conservative, even a reactionary, point of view.

By far the most dominant polemicist of the period between the wars, however, was H. L. MENCKEN, a cheerfully unassailable iconoclast and acerbic critic not only of American democracy but of the possibilities of a mature democratic culture under any circumstance. In this respect Mencken's role was also significant, since his political skepticism, derived from both PLATO (see Vols. 3 and 4) and NIETZSCHE (see Vol. 4), struck at the very heart of America's abstract image of its own symbolic value in the world. Mencken believed that a democracy was the only form of government that was even tolerable, but he humorously and aggressively debunked all of the shibboleths of American culture, including religion itself, as well as any system of metaphysics or philosophy that could not make its case through scientific proof. The journal that Mencken edited from Baltimore, the *American Mercury*, was one of the most important venues for social and literary criticism in the decades between the two wars. Mencken was critical of racial and ethnic groups to the point of bigotry, but his bigotry was all-inclusive. By comparison, the whimsical, satirical writing of his younger contemporaries who were associated with the *New Yorker* magazine, E. B. WHITE, JAMES THURBER, ROBERT BENCHLEY, and S. J. PERELMAN, seem genteel and harmless; he played the role of JUVENAL (see Vol. 2) in his civilization, they that of HORACE (see Vol. 2). And however invidious many of Mencken's rationalized prejudices seem to us today (his volume of collected essays was forthrightly called *Prejudices*, 1919–27), his challenge to the capacity of Americans for sentimental evasion remains compelling.

A similarly vigorous social criticism from another flank came from W. E. B. DU BOIS, whose angry idealism was as passionate as Mencken's critical nihilism. Du Bois was America's first black militant in the twentieth century. Harvard-educated and a sociologist by profession, Du Bois dedicated his life to the denunciation of racism in America in even its most deceptively benign forms, even in its extensions across the world in the form of American imperialism. In his first distinguished collection of essays, *The Souls of Black Folk* (1903), in many other scholarly studies and political essays, and through the journal *Crisis* that he edited (1910–34), Du Bois tirelessly attacked gradualism and political compromise and promoted the cause of black independence and the full autonomy of black separatism. Du Bois was the most distinguished black intellectual of his day, but his message—which today seems prophetic and which soon became deeply influential—was received with a measure of skepticism in its own time. In any case, it was clearly a criticism of American democracy that could not be compatible with the nostalgic critiques of the Agrarians or the elitist cynicism of Mencken and the *Mercury*.

Besides the *Mercury*, the chief literary journals of the period were the *Dial*, *Nation*, and *New Republic*, as well as, in the 1930s, the *New Masses* and *Partisan Review*. The controversies that animated these magazines tended to focus on the contrast between traditional religious humanism, identified with Irving Babbitt and Paul Elmer Moore, and a freer modernist experimentalism—in life as well as in art—associated with EDMUND WILSON, MALCOLM COWLEY, and R. P. BLACKMUR. Such issues converged in the 1930s, when the apparent failure of traditional Western capitalism caused many writers and intellectuals to question the very purpose of literature, as in the socialist Max Eastman's *The Literary Mind: Its Place in an Age of Science*. Much of the dispute during this period centered on the issue of whether international communism should be thought of as a redeeming force or as an oppressive one, and if the latter, which if any of its social ideals could be put into a credible form while still holding a vision of American democracy intact. These political debates about literature and culture remained unresolved, eventually dissipating under the tragic influence of World War II. Perhaps naturally enough, only the New Criticism, with its aestheticist detachment, survived these world conflicts intact.

Du Bois, meanwhile, was unappeased and unregenerate to the end, and in any case he had never been a part of the liberal mainstream to begin with. He joined the Communist party in 1963 at the age of 93 and left the United States to go to Africa, where he died.

History and Criticism

Adams, Timothy D. *Telling Lies in Modern American Autobiography*. U. of NC Pr. 1990 $27.50. ISBN 0-8078-1888-7. Discusses the possibility of a truly objective autobiography and its value from critical and historical standpoints.

Andrews, William L. *African American Autobiography: A Collection of Critical Essays*. P-H 1992 $12.95. ISBN 0-13-019845-5

Barrett, Eileen. *American Women Writers: Diverse Voices in Prose Since 1845*. St. Martin 1992 $30.65. ISBN 0-312-04121-7

Brier, Peter A., ed. *American Prose and Criticism, Nineteen Hundred to Nineteen Fifty: A Guide to Information Sources*. Gale 1981 $68.00. ISBN 0-8103-1214-X. Concentrates on expository prose writers who transcended the domain of purely journalistic or academic writing.

Eakin, Paul J., ed. *American Autobiography: Retrospect and Prospect*. U. of Wis. Pr. 1991 $42.50. ISBN 0-299-12780-X. Essays surveying the development and varieties of nineteenth-century autobiography.

Sims, Norman, ed. *Literary Journalism in the Twentieth Century*. OUP 1990 $14.95. ISBN 0-19-505965-4. Addresses the history of literary journalism and some of the issues of literary theory surrounding it.

Stepto, Robert B. *From Behind the Veil: A Study of Afro-American Narrative*. U. of Ill. Pr. 1991 $11.95. ISBN 0-252-06211-6. Discusses how twentieth century African American writing is intrinsically connected to slave narrative.

Collections

Clifford, John, and Robert DiYanni. *Modern American Prose: A Reader for Writers*. Random 2nd ed. 1987.

Fuller, Margaret. *Essays in American Life and Letters.* NCUP 1977 $15.95. ISBN 0-8084-0416-4. Wide-ranging collection.

Gross, John, ed. *The Oxford Book of Essays.* OUP 1991 $30.00. ISBN 0-19-214185-6

Muir, Frank, ed. *The Oxford Book of Humorous Prose.* OUP 1992 $17.95. ISBN 0-19-282959-9. Gathers humorous prose from over two hundred writers from every English-speaking country.

Whittemore, Katharine, ed. *Voices in Black and White: Writings on Race in America from Harper's Magazine, 1850–1992.* Harpers Mag. Found. 1992 $21.95. ISBN 0-879957-07-8

CHRONOLOGY OF AUTHORS

Masters, Edgar Lee. 1869–1950
Du Bois, W(illiam) E(dward) B(urghardt). 1868–1963
Robinson, Edwin Arlington. 1869–1935
Dreiser, Theodore. 1871–1945
Frost, Robert. 1874–1963
Glasgow, Ellen. 1874–1945
Lowell, Amy. 1874–1925
Stein, Gertrude. 1874–1946
Anderson, Sherwood. 1876–1941
Cather, Willa. 1876–1947
Sandburg, Carl. 1878–1967
Sinclair, Upton. 1878–1968
Lindsay, Vachel. 1879–1931
Stevens, Wallace. 1879–1955
Mencken, H(enry) L(ouis). 1880–1956
Roberts, Elizabeth Madox. 1881–1941
Williams, William Carlos. 1883–1963
Lardner, Ring(gold Wilmer). 1885–1933
Lewis, Sinclair. 1885–1951
Pound, Ezra. 1885–1972
H. D. 1886–1961
Jeffers, Robinson. 1887–1962
Moore, Marianne. 1887–1972
Ransom, John Crowe. 1888–1974
Aiken, Conrad. 1889–1973
Benchley, Robert. 1889–1945
McKay, Claude. 1889–1948
Porter, Katherine Anne. 1890–1980
Larsen, Nella. 1891–1964
Miller, Henry. 1891–1980
Barnes, Djuna. 1892–1982
MacLeish, Archibald. 1892–1982
Millay, Edna St. Vincent. 1892–1950
Parker, Dorothy. 1893–1967

Cummings, E(dward) E(stlin). 1894–1962
Thurber, James. 1894–1961
Toomer, Jean. 1894–1967
Schuyler, George, 1895–1977
Wilson, Edmund. 1895–1972
Dos Passos, John. 1896–1970
Fitzgerald, F(rancis) Scott. 1896–1940
Burke, Kenneth. 1897–
Faulkner, William. 1897–1962
Wilder, Thornton. 1897–1975
Benét, Stephen Vincent. 1898–1943
Cowley, Malcolm. 1898–1989
Crane, Hart. 1899–1932
Hemingway, Ernest. 1899–1961
Tate, Allen. 1899–1979
White, E(lwyn) B(rooks). 1899–1985
Wolfe, Thomas. 1900–1938
Hurston, Zora Neale. 1901–1960
Riding, Laura. 1901–1991
Bontemps, Arna. 1902–1973
Hughes, Langston. 1902–1967
Steinbeck, John. 1902–1968
Caldwell, Erskine. 1903–1987
Cullen, Countee. 1903–1946
Nin, Anaïs. 1903–1977
Blackmur, R(ichard) P(almer). 1904–1965
Farrell, James T(homas). 1904–1979
Perelman, S(idney) J(oseph). 1904–1979
West, Nathanael. 1904–1940
O'Hara, John. 1905–1970
Warren, Robert Penn. 1905–1989
Barzun, Jacques. 1907–
Wright, Richard. 1908–1960
Welty, Eudora. 1909–

AIKEN, CONRAD. 1889–1973

Born in Georgia, Conrad Aiken graduated from Harvard University and for several years lived alternately in England and the United States. Although he knew all the major modernist poets, for many years he himself was comparatively unknown. He won the Pulitzer Prize (1930), the Bollingen Prize (1956), and a gold medal (1958) from the National Institute of Arts and Letters, among many other awards. He was also consultant in poetry at the Library of Congress (1950–52). ALLEN TATE once described him as the "perfection of a vanishing American type: the complete man of letters." His autobiographical work *Ushant: An Essay* (1952) is of considerable historical interest for the student of modernism.

POETRY BY AIKEN

The Charnel Rose, Senlin: A Biography and Other Poems. Haskell 1972 $75.00. ISBN 0-8383-1247-0. Long metaphysical poems initially published in Aiken's early years.
Collected Poems, 1916–1970. OUP 2nd ed. 1970 o.p.
Jig of Forslin. Branden Pub. Co. 1964 $3.95. ISBN 0-8283-1443-8. A five-part poem abundant with symbolist imagery; from early in Aiken's career.
Selected Poems. Schocken 1982 o.p. Representative of his most important work since 1917.

NONFICTION BY AIKEN

Collected Criticism. OUP 1968 $4.50. ISBN 0-19-500445-0. Includes articles on literature and authors such as Dostoevsky, James, and Williams; initially published as *A Reviewer's ABC*.
Ushant: An Essay. 1952. OUP 1971 o.p.

WORKS BY AIKEN

Selected Letters of Conrad Aiken. Bks. Demand $103.00. ISBN 0-8357-3749-7. Selection intended to reflect Aiken in the variety of his interests and styles.
Silent Snow, Secret Snow. Creative Ed. 1983 $15.65.

BOOKS ABOUT AIKEN

Bonnell, F.C. *Conrad Aiken: A Bibliography*. Huntington Lib. 1983 $34.95. ISBN 0-87328-118-7
Butscher, Edward. *Conrad Aiken: Poet of White Horse Vale*. U. of Ga. Pr. 1988 $34.95. ISBN 0-8203-0760-2. Examines Aiken's youth and early childhood in Savannah, Georgia, and his move to Massachusetts at the age of 11.
Lorenz, Clarissa M. *Lorelei Two: My Life with Conrad Aiken*. U. of Ga. Pr. 1983 $27.50. ISBN 0-8203-0661-4. A presentation by Aiken's second wife of her ten years with the poet.
Marten, Harry. *The Art of Knowing: The Poetry and Prose of Conrad Aiken*. U. of Mo. Pr. 1988 $22.00. ISBN 0-8262-0654-9. Aims to provide a reading of selected works of Aiken's prose and poetry in order to shed light on his search to understand human knowing.
Seigel, Catharine F. *The Fictive World of Conrad Aiken: A Celebration of Consciousness*. N. Ill. U. Pr. 1992 $27.00. ISBN 0-87580-172-2
Spivey, Ted R. *The Writer As Shaman: The Pilgrimages of Conrad Aiken and Walker Percy*. Mercer Univ. Pr. 1986 $24.95. ISBN 0-86554-199-X. Argues that for both Aiken and Percy, childhood traumas (parental suicide) and resultant alienation became the essential spur to a shamanistic quest or pilgrimage in their lives and writings toward an affirmation of God through human love.
Spivey, Ted R., ed. *A Priest of Consciousness: Essays on Conrad Aiken*. AMS Pr. 1988 $45.00. ISBN 0-404-63206-8. Looks into Aiken's need to bring about a constant search for a higher consciousness throughout his poetry.

ANDERSON, SHERWOOD. 1876–1941

The important but often misunderstood role that Sherwood Anderson played in modern literary history has tended to obscure his distinctive merits as a writer. In different ways he served as a catalyst for HEMINGWAY and FAULKNER at the beginnings of their careers, and, although both repaid him with satiric mockery in early novels, Faulkner was generous enough to acknowledge in 1956 that "he was the father of my generation of American writers and the tradition of American writing which our successors will carry on. He has never received his proper evaluation."

Born in Camden, Ohio, of Scottish-American parents, Anderson led a varied, restless life as laborer, soldier, businessman, and newspaper proprietor. A highlight of *Sherwood Anderson's Memoirs: A Critical Edition*, edited by Ray L. White, is Anderson's account of the pivotal moment in 1912 when he spontaneously walked away from the Ohio paint factory that he managed in order to begin a precarious new career in Chicago as a writer. His father served as the model for Windy in *Windy McPherson's Son* (1916), his first novel, and many of his later works of fiction are based on autobiographical experience. *Marching Men* (1917) established a main theme: the conflict between one's own instincts and the stultifying effects of industry and society. *Poor White*, which first appeared in 1920 and is available in *The Portable Sherwood Anderson* (1977), is generally considered the best of his novels. Such others as *Many Marriages* (1923), *Dark Laughter* (1925), and *Kit Brandon* (1936), which seemed daring and progressive in their frank depiction of sex and in their author's probing of the subconsciousness of his characters, now appear somewhat wooden and dated, and most critics agree that he was at his best as a writer of short fiction.

Largely because of *Winesburg, Ohio* (1919), Anderson's place in literary history owes much to his association with the revolt-from-the-village tradition of writers like SINCLAIR LEWIS and EDGAR LEE MASTERS. Too often overlooked are the books in which Anderson presented a much more sympathetic view of small-town life. They include *Mid American Chants* (1918), which uses somewhat Whitmanesque free verse to celebrate the Midwest and the "common man," and *The Buck Fever Papers*, which brings together rather whimsical and good-humored news stories Anderson wrote under the Buck Fever pseudonym for two newspapers he owned in southwestern Virginia.

SHORT STORY COLLECTIONS BY ANDERSON

Death in the Woods: And Other Stories. Norton 1986 $7.95. ISBN 0-87140-140-1. Collects the best of Anderson's short fiction written until 1933.

Portable Sherwood Anderson. Viking Penguin 1977 $9.95. ISBN 0-14-015076-5

A Story Teller's Story. Viking Penguin 1989 $6.95. ISBN 0-14-009443-1. Explores the author's world view in an ever-changing American landscape, including the advent of an industrial society.

The Triumph of the Egg. FWEW 1988 $8.95. ISBN 0-941423-11-5. A major literary achievement; focuses upon the lives of people who become grotesques.

Winesburg, Ohio. 1919. Viking Penguin 1988 $3.95. ISBN 0-14-043304-X. A poignant collection of stories about yearning, lonely people in a small Ohio town.

NOVEL BY ANDERSON

Dark Laughter. 1925. Amereon Ltd. $19.95. ISBN 0-88411-277-2

WORKS BY ANDERSON

The Sherwood Anderson Diaries, 1936–1941. Ed. by Hilbert H. Campbell. U. of Ga. Pr. 1987 $35.00. ISBN 0-8203-0908-7. Record of Sherwood's daily activities during the last five years of his life.

Sherwood Anderson: Selected Letters. U. of Tenn. Pr. 1983 $32.50. ISBN 0-87049-404-X
The Writer at His Craft. Appel 1978 $22.50. ISBN 0-911858-37-7. Anthology of previously
   uncollected works; focuses on Anderson's contribution to periodicals in the 1930s.

BOOKS ABOUT ANDERSON

Burbank, Rex. *Sherwood Anderson.* G. K. Hall 1964 o.p.
Crowley, John W., ed. *New Essays on Winesburg, Ohio.* Cambridge U. Pr. 1990 $22.95.
   ISBN 0-521-38283-1. Puts forth interesting and provocative viewpoints.
Rideout, Walter B., ed. *Sherwood Anderson: A Collection of Critical Essays.* P-H 1974
   $12.95. ISBN 0-13-036558-0. Discusses several aspects of Anderson's life and work;
   Winesburg, Ohio is given special attention.
Rogers, Douglas. *Sherwood Anderson: A Selective, Annotated Bibliography.* Scarecrow
   1976 $17.50. ISBN 0-8108-0900-1
Weber, Brom. *Sherwood Anderson: A Biographical and Critical Study.* Stanford U. Pr.
   1966 o.p. Still the best-balanced account of Anderson's life and writing career.
White, Ray L. *Winesburg, Ohio: An Exploration.* Macmillan 1990 $20.95. ISBN 0-8057-
   8097-1. Clear and sensitive exploration of Anderson's remarkable story-cycle.
White, Ray L., ed. *The Achievement of Sherwood Anderson: Essays in Criticism.* U. of NC
   Pr. 1966 o.p. Covers fifty years of critical articles and essays on Anderson.
Williams, Kenny J. *A Storyteller and a City: Sherwood Anderson's Chicago.* N. Ill. U. Pr.
   1988 $28.50. ISBN 0-87580-135-8. Focuses on Sherwood's Chicago sojourn in the
   early years of this century, and his two Chicago novels, *Windy McPherson's Son* and
   Marching Men.

BARNES, DJUNA. 1892–1982

Although Djuna Barnes was a New Yorker who spent much of her long life in
Greenwich Village, where she died a virtual recluse in 1982, she resided for
extended periods in France and England. Her writings, too, are representative
modernist works in that they seem to transcend all national boundaries to take
place in a land peculiarly her own. Deeply influenced by the French symbolists
of the late nineteenth century and by the surrealists of the 1930s, she wrote also
as a liberated woman, whose unconventional way of life is reflected in the
uncompromising individuality of her literary style. Her dreamlike and haunted
writings have never found a wide popular audience, but they have strongly
influenced such writers as WEST, ALGREN, Dahlberg, Lowry, MILLER, and
especially NIN, in whose works a semifictional character named Djuna
sometimes appears.

Barnes published *The Book of Repulsive Women* anonymously in 1915. Not
long afterward she moved to Paris and became associated with the colony of
writers and artists who made that city the international center of culture during
the 1920s and early 1930s. Her *Ladies Almanack* was privately printed there in
1928, the same year that Liveright in America published her first novel, *Ryder.*
The book on which her fame largely depends is *Nightwood* (1936), a surrealistic
story set in Paris and the United States, dealing with the complex relationships
among a group of strangely obsessed characters, most of them homosexuals and
lesbians.

She wrote little after *Nightwood*. In fact, she professed to Malcolm Lowry in
1952 that she had been so frightened by the experience of writing that searing
work that she could not write anything afterward. Fortunately, her literary
talents revived with *The Antiphon*, a verse-drama originally published in 1958,
which is now available in *Selected Works* (1962). EDWIN MUIR described that
ambitious experimental work as "one of the greatest things that have been
written in our time."

NOVELS BY BARNES

Nightwood. 1936. New Dir. Pr. 1946 o.p. According to T. S. Eliot, in his introduction, a book with "the great achievement of a style, the beauty of phrasing, the brilliance of wit and characterization, and a quality of horror and doom very nearly related to that of Elizabethan tragedy."

Ryder. 1928. Dalkey Arch. 2nd ed. 1990 $9.95. ISBN 0-916583-55-4

SHORT STORY COLLECTION BY BARNES

Smoke and Other Early Stories. Sun & Moon CA 2nd rev. ed. 1988 $9.95. ISBN 1-55713-014-0. Fourteen short stories initially published in American newspapers.

WORKS BY BARNES

The Book of Repulsive Women: Eight Rhymes and Five Drawings. Sun & Moon CA 1989 $5.00. ISBN 1-55713-087-6

Interviews. Sun & Moon CA 1985 $16.95. ISBN 0-940650-36-3

Ladies Almanack. Dalkey Archive Pr. 1992 $9.95. ISBN 0-916583-88-0

New York. Sun & Moon CA 1989 $12.95. ISBN 0-940650-99-1

Selected Works of Djuna Barnes. FS&G 1962 o.p.

BOOKS ABOUT BARNES

Broe, Mary L., ed. *Silence & Power: A Reevaluation of Djuna Barnes.* S. Ill. U. Pr. 1991 $29.95. ISBN 0-8093-1250-6. Essays that resituate Barnes in the context of literary theory and feminist revisions of modernism.

Field, Andrew. *Djuna: The Life and Times of Djuna Barnes.* Putnam Pub. Group 1983 o.p.

Kaivola, Karen. *All Contraries Confounded: The Lyrical Fiction of Virginia Woolf, Djuna Barnes, & Marguerite Duras.* U. of Iowa Pr. 1991 $22.95. ISBN 0-87745-323-3

Kannenstine, Louis. *The Art of Djuna Barnes: Duality and Damnation.* NYU Pr. 1977 o.p. Establishes the literary context within which Barnes's work belongs; recognizes her formal achievement and thematic consistency.

O'Neel, Hank. *Life Is Painful, Nasty and Short . . . In My Case It Has Only Been Painful and Nasty: Djuna Barnes, 1978–1981: An Informal Memoir.* Paragon Hse. 1990 $19.95. ISBN 1-55778-394-2

Plumb, Cheryl J. *Fancy's Craft: Art and Identity in the Early Works of Djuna Barnes.* Susquehanna U. Pr. 1987 $26.50. ISBN 0-941664-17-1. Presents a succinct introductory analysis to Barnes's early work.

BARZUN, JACQUES. 1907–

Barzun, born in France and educated in America, became professor of history at Columbia University in 1945 and served as dean of faculties and provost there until 1967. He has written with wisdom and tact on history, criticism, education, and musicology. He calls himself a "student of cultural history," but his learned interpretations of historical fact and critical theory, educational policy, and research techniques demonstrate a penetrating grasp of relevant issues. His *Teacher in America* (1945) was called "one of the few volumes on education by which no intelligent reader can be bored." He writes of his adopted country, America, with humor and perception in *God's Country and Mine* (1954). He is frank and genial, but ready to challenge the establishment: In *The House of Intellect* (1959), he attacks the whole intellectual (or pseudointellectual) world for its betrayal of true intellect in such areas as public administration, communications, conversation and home life, education, business, and scholarship. Included among later works are *The Use and Abuse of Art* (1974), the highly acclaimed *Simple and Direct: A Rhetoric for Writers* (1975), and *A Stroll with William James* (1982).

NONFICTION BY BARZUN

Classic, Romantic and Modern. U. Ch. Pr. 1975 $10.95. ISBN 0-226-03852-1

Clio and the Doctors: History, Psycho-History, Quanto History. U. Ch. Pr. 1989 repr. of 1974 ed. $14.95. ISBN 0-226-03851-3. Discusses the interaction between historical and psychological discourses in contemporary historiography.

Critical Questions: On Music and Letters, Culture and Biography. Ed. by Bea Friedland. U. Ch. Pr. 1984 $22.50. ISBN 0-226-03863-7. Diverse collection of essays intended to show Barzun's broad cultural concerns.

Darwin, Marx, Wagner: Critique of a Heritage. 1958. U. Ch. Pr. 2nd ed. 1981 $13.95. ISBN 0-226-03859-9. Questions the contribution of these three leading nineteenth-century thinkers in science, political philosophy, and music; considers the ideas of progress and perfection.

The Energies of Art: Studies of Authors Classic and Modern. Greenwood 1975 repr. of 1956 ed. $76.50. ISBN 0-8371-6856-2

God's Country and Mine. 1954. Greenwood 1973 repr. of 1954 ed. $35.00. ISBN 0-8371-6860-0

The House of Intellect. 1959. Greenwood 1978 repr. of 1959 ed. $35.00. ISBN 0-313-20071-8

Of Human Freedom. Greenwood 1977 repr. of 1964 ed. 2nd rev. ed. $38.50. ISBN 0-8371-9321-4. Discusses ideas of culture and democracy as they frame our conception of freedom.

On Writing, Editing and Publishing: Essays Explicative and Hortatory. U. Ch. Pr. 1986 $20.00. ISBN 0-226-03857-2. Looks into the notion of authorship, including how authors and publishers interact.

Teacher in America. 1945. U. Pr. of Amer. 1986 repr. of 1944 ed. $14.75. ISBN 0-8191-5447-4

The Use and Abuse of Art. 1974. Princeton U. Pr. 1974 $9.95. ISBN 0-691-01804-9. Critical analysis of twentieth-century artistic production; discusses the origins of art and its interaction with religious practices.

BENCHLEY, ROBERT. 1889–1945

Known today primarily for his humorous essays for the *New Yorker* and other journals, Robert Benchley had other literary talents, too. He was an influential drama critic first for *Life* magazine (1920–29) and then for the *New Yorker* (1929–40). He was also a stage actor and a radio personality and played in Hollywood films as well.

His humorous essays are marked by their sense of whimsy; the writer frequently becomes truly silly and invites the reader to become so, too. The generous, light-hearted quality of Benchley's writing belies the darker side of his own life, in which, among other things, he wrestled with a serious drinking problem. He was a member of the famous Algonquin Round Table, among whom he and his good friend DOROTHY PARKER were two of the brightest and wittiest lights.

NONFICTION BY BENCHLEY

Benchley at the Theatre. Ipswich Pr. 1985 $14.95. ISBN 0-938864-05-X

Benchley Beside Himself. Amereon Ltd. 1976 $18.95. ISBN 0-88411-307-8

Benchley Lost and Found. Dover 1970 $4.95. ISBN 0-486-22410-4

Benchley or Else. Amereon Ltd. 1976 $18.95. ISBN 0-88411-306-X

The Benchley Roundup: A Selection by Nathaniel Benchley of His Favorites. U. Ch. Pr. 1983 $12.95. ISBN 0-226-04218-9. Ninety pieces chosen by Benchley's son from thirty years (1915–1945) of humorous writing.

Chips off the Old Benchley. Amereon Ltd. 1976 $18.95. ISBN 0-88411-301-9. A posthumous selection of Benchley's writing for periodicals and other sources.

A Good Old-Fashioned Christmas. Ipswich Pr. 1981 $8.95. ISBN 0-938864-02-5

Inside Benchley. Amereon Ltd. 1976 $19.95. ISBN 0-88411-302-7
My Ten Years in a Quandary. 1936. Amereon Ltd. 1976 $21.95. ISBN 0-88411-305-5
Penguin Psychology: or, The Mystery of Bridge Building. Amereon Ltd. $14.95. ISBN 0-88411-299-3
Pluck and Luck. Amereon Ltd. $18.95. ISBN 0-88411-308-6
The Robert Benchley Omnibus. Amereon Ltd. $21.95. ISBN 0-8488-0069-9
The Treasurer's Report: And Other Aspects of Community Singing. Amereon Ltd. 1976 $17.95. ISBN 0-88411-304-3
Twenty Thousand Leagues Under the Sea or David Copperfield. 1928. Amereon Ltd. 1976 $18.95. ISBN 0-88411-305-1. Collection of Benchleyana originally published in 1928; includes pieces for *The New Yorker, The Yale Review,* and other publications.

BOOKS ABOUT BENCHLEY

Altman, Bill. *Robert Benchley: A Biography.* Norton $17.95. ISBN 0-393-02397-4
Rosmond, Babette. *Robert Benchley: His Life and Good Times.* Paragon Hse. 1989 $12.95. ISBN 1-55778-169-9. An informal biographical account of Benchley; attempts to capture his joie de vivre.

BENÉT, STEPHEN VINCENT. 1898–1943

A poet, dramatist, and short story writer, Benét was born in Pennsylvania and attended Yale University. His career as a writer began quite modestly with the publication of several collections of verse. But *John Brown's Body* (1928), which won the Pulitzer Prize for poetry in 1929 and brought Benét instant popularity, is a history of the Civil War in rhyme and blank verse—a history told from the point of view of ordinary people, a rank-and-file history, of both the North and the South. This narrative of "the rich man's war and the poor man's fight" is a remarkable epic of the United States. Although he was enormously influential on other poets, notably Harlem Renaissance writer Anne Spencer, and despite his wide popular audience, Benét has not received high praise from academic critics.

POETRY BY BENÉT

America. H. Holt & Co. 1944 $5.00. ISBN 0-03-028535-6
Book of Americans. H. Holt & Co. 1984 $12.95. ISBN 0-8050-0284-7. Fifty-six poems about the lives of famous men and women from Columbus to Woodrow Wilson.
By the Waters of Babylon. Creative Ed. 1990 $15.65. ISBN 0-685-28209-0
The Devil and Daniel Webster. Creative Ed. 1990 $15.65. ISBN 0-685-28210-4
James Shore's Daughter. Scholarly 1934 $39.00. ISBN 0-403-00507-8
John Brown's Body. 1928. H. Holt & Co. 1984 $25.00. ISBN 0-8050-1318-0. A long poem about the Civil War and its effects on various kinds of Americans.
Last Circle. Ayer 1973 $20.00. ISBN 0-8369-4217-5
Spanish Bayonet. Scholarly 1926 $29.00. ISBN 0-685-27275-3
Zero Hour: A Summons to the Free. Ayer repr. of 1940 ed. $18.00. ISBN 0-8369-2341-3. Discusses moral obligation in relation to World War II.

SHORT STORY COLLECTION BY BENÉT

Thirteen O'Clock, Stories of Several Worlds. Ayer repr. of 1937 ed. $24.50. ISBN 0-8369-3793-7

WORKS BY BENÉT

Selected Letters of Stephen Vincent Benét. Elliots Bks. 1960 $49.50. ISBN 0-685-26661-3

BOOKS ABOUT BENÉT

Benét, William R. *Stephen Vincent Benét.* Porter 1979 o.p.

Fenton, Charles A. *Stephen Vincent Benét: The Life and Times of an American Man of Letters, 1898–1943.* Greenwood 1978 repr. of 1958 ed. $37.50. ISBN 0-313-20200-1. Emphasizes Benét's American spirit; some attention to his works.

BLACKMUR, R(ICHARD) P(ALMER). 1904–1965

R. P. Blackmur, a native of Massachusetts, was one of America's foremost critics. Though lacking a college education, he was on the Princeton faculty from 1940 until his death, and in 1961–62 was Pitt Professor of American History and Institutions at Cambridge University. He contributed criticism to literary journals and "little" magazines, chiefly on nineteenth- and twentieth-century novelists and poets. As a leader in the New Criticism—an academic movement that advocated close rhetorical analysis of texts—he rejected the traditional historicism of literary criticism. In *A Burden for Critics* (1948), he called for "modern criticism to enlarge its scope, and to add to analysis, elucidation, and comparison the important function of judgment based on rational standards." Blackmur's development of a New Critical theory depended in large part on MATTHEW ARNOLD's conviction that literary study was and should be the pivotal feature of "culture."

NONFICTION BY BLACKMUR

Anni Mirabiles, 1921–1925: Reason in the Madness of Letters. Folcroft 1974 repr. of 1956 ed. o.p. Lectures on twentieth-century literature; explores the idea of contemplation and metaphysics in writing.
The Double Agent: Essays in Craft and Elucidation. 1935. Peter Smith 1962 $11.50. ISBN 0-8446-1080-1. A selection of essays on twentieth-century American literature; discusses authors such as Pound, Stevens, and Lawrence.
The Expense of Greatness. Somerset 1980 repr. of 1940 ed. $49.00. ISBN 0-7812-0271-X
Henry Adams. Da Capo 1984 $10.95. ISBN 0-306-80219-8. A hymn to Adams's concept of the imagination as the embodiment of human energy; intensely personal and critical.
Language as Gesture: Essays in Poetry. Greenwood 1977 repr. of 1952 ed. $49.75. ISBN 0-8371-9782-1. Essays published from 1935 through 1952 on poets such as Dickinson, Yeats, and Pound.
The Lion and the Honeycomb: Essays in Solicitude and Critique. Greenwood 1977 repr. of 1955 ed. $38.50. ISBN 0-8371-9799-6. Reflections on criticism, the condition of the artist, and on writers such as Dante and Melville.
Selected Essays of R. P. Blackmur. Ecco Pr. 1986 $17.50. ISBN 0-88001-083-5. Essays published from 1930 to 1964 on prose writers such as James and Mann and on poets such as Stevens and Crane.

BOOKS ABOUT BLACKMUR

Fraser, Russell A. *A Mingled Yarn: The Life of R. P. Blackmur.* HarBraceJ 1981 o.p. A chronological account of Blackmur's early years up to the Princeton period; includes a critical discussion of his writings.
Pannick, Gerald J. *Richard Palmer Blackmur.* Twayne 1981 o.p.

BONTEMPS, ARNA. 1902–1973

Arna Bontemps was one of many African American writers associated with Fisk University, where he taught for 20 years and then returned (after a visiting professorship at Yale University) to spend the last years of his life. Bontemps grew up in the South and wrote of the condition and spirit of the southern black in memoirs and in fiction. His historical and topical novel *Black Thunder* (1936) is perhaps his best known, along with *Drums at Dusk* (1935). As an active leader in the Harlem Renaissance, however, Bontemps wrote prolifically in all genres, for children as well as adults. He produced several important collections of slave narratives and black folk tales, was a major anthologizer of Harlem Renaissance work, and helped shape the new black writing as theoretician and critic.

NOVELS BY BONTEMPS

Black Thunder: Gabriel's Revolt: Virginia, 1800. 1936. Beacon Pr. 1992 $12.00. ISBN 0-8070-6337-1
God Sends Sunday. AMS Pr. repr. of 1931 ed. $15.00. ISBN 0-404-00137-8
Lonesome Boy. Beacon Pr. 1988 $12.95. ISBN 0-8070-8306-2. A lonely river boy with a silver trumpet follows his music through a series of adventures.

WORKS BY BONTEMPS

Great Slave Narratives. Beacon Pr. 1969 $15.95. ISBN 0-8070-5473-9. An anthology intended to suggest the continuing relevance of chronicles of a half-forgotten history.
One Hundred Years of Negro Freedom. Greenwood 1980 $45.00. ISBN 0-313-22218-5. A reflection about the ambiguity of Negro emancipation in the United States.

BOOKS ABOUT BONTEMPS

Fleming, Robert E. *James Weldon Johnson and Arna Wendell Bontemps: A Reference Guide.* G. K. Hall 1978 o.p. Lists and annotates every book and periodical that discuss the two authors.
Jones, Kirkland C. *Renaissance Man from Louisiana: A Biography of Arna Wendell Bontemps.* Greenwood 1992 $47.95. ISBN 0-313-28013-4. Nine chapters that cover everything from Bontemps's family background to his friendship with Langston Hughes.

BURKE, KENNETH. 1897–

Born in Pittsburgh, Burke was educated at Ohio State and Columbia universities. During his early career, he became involved with a number of little magazines, including *Broom* and *Secession*. He also wrote for *The Dial* and *The Nation* as a music critic. His greatest fame, however, has been as a literary critic.

Omnivorously eclectic, Burke has found in the analysis of human symbolic activities a key to the largest cultural issues. For Burke, literature is the most prominent and sophisticated form of "symbolic action," one that provides "equipment for living" by allowing us to try out hypothetical strategies for dealing with the endless variety of human situations and experiences. Human society demands some principle of order, but the language and reason that create order can fall into rigid abstractions that can be destructive and violently imposed. Literature shows us an image of sacrifice, forgiveness, and flexibility that plays an important role in keeping society functioning flexibly. Burke's writing is extensive, complex and wide ranging, but also unique and uniquely important among current critical approaches.

NONFICTION BY BURKE

Attitudes Toward History. U. CA Pr. 3rd ed. 1984 $45.00. ISBN 0-520-04145-3
Language As Symbolic Action: Essays on Life, Literature, and Method. U. CA Pr. 1966 $15.95. ISBN 0-520-00192-3. Exemplifies the author's theory of literature as a symbolic mode of action, applied to writers such as Aeschylus, Shakespeare, and William Carlos Williams; includes notes and a very useful index.
On Symbols and Society. U. Ch. Pr. 1989 $39.95. ISBN 0-226-08077-3
Permanence and Change: An Anatomy of Purpose. U. CA Pr. 3rd ed. 1984 $45.00. ISBN 0-520-04144-5

The Philosophy of Literary Form. U. CA Pr. 1974 $15.95. ISBN 0-520-02483-4. Considers art as "biological (and sociological) adaptation."

The Rhetoric of Religion: Studies on Logology. U. CA Pr. 1970 $12.95. ISBN 0-520-01610-6

Surrealism Pro and Con. Gotham 1973 $4.50. ISBN 0-910664-27-7

POETRY BY BURKE

Collected Poems. 1915–1967. U. CA Pr. 1968 $39.95. ISBN 0-520-00195-8

SHORT STORY COLLECTION BY BURKE

The Complete White Oxen: Collected Short Fiction. U. CA Pr. 1968 $5.95. ISBN 0-520-00155-9

BOOKS ABOUT BURKE

Frank, Armin P. *Kenneth Burke.* Irvington 1969 $17.95. ISBN 0-89197-816-X

Henderson, Greig E. *Kenneth Burke: Literature and Language as Symbolic Action.* U. of Ga. Pr. 1989 $27.50. ISBN 0-8203-1037-9. Examines the importance of rhetoric and Burke's view of language as highlighted against a backdrop of other, recent, influential views.

Rueckert, William H. *Kenneth Burke and the Drama of Human Relations.* U. CA Pr. 2nd rev. ed. 1981 $29.95. ISBN 0-520-03199-7. A comprehensive, thorough, and useful guide to understanding Burke as a critic, linguist, and philosopher; includes a bibliography and index.

———. *Critical Responses to Kenneth Burke. 1924–1966.* Bks. Demand repr. of 1969 ed. $135.30. ISBN 0-317-29493-8

Simons, Herbert W., ed. *The Legacy of Kenneth Burke.* U. of Wis. Pr. 1988 $37.50. ISBN 0-299-11830-4

Southwell, Samuel B. *Kenneth Burke and Martin Heidegger: With a Note Against Deconstructionism.* U. Pr. Fla. 1988 $16.95. ISBN 0-8130-0872-7. Shows how the central issue structuring Burke's thought is "the question of being," using concepts of philosopher Martin Heidegger; includes an appendix.

CALDWELL, ERSKINE. 1903–1987

Although Erskine Caldwell was for years one of the most popular American writers, he once complained, "I'm not read very much in the South because they are very touchy about what they regard as unkind criticism, and I'm not thought much of in the North either." He may well have thought of himself as a prophet without honor in his home country, for his fame elsewhere was quite spectacular. His more than 50 books were translated into more than 40 languages and have sold more than 75 million copies. But he was hardly neglected in his home country either. His third novel, *Tobacco Road* (1932), was both a bestselling book and, in a stage adaptation by John Kirkland, one of the most successful American plays. That work, a seriocomic portrayal of a rural southern family struggling to eke out a living in an impoverished backwoods area, set the pattern for much of the fiction about the South that followed, and although sophisticated southern readers may have resented the implication that the South was populated mostly by ignorant, degraded people like the Lesters, the rest of the country found his books both amusing and shockingly realistic. His popularity and his preference for "low-life" subjects may help to explain why he has been more or less steadily ignored by the critical establishment, but now that the weakest of his many books have quietly gone out of print, it seems clear that what remains is likely to last. *Tobacco Road, God's Little Acre* (1933), and the best of his short stories show a highly original talent that managed to capture definitively what much of America was like during the Great Depression and perhaps thereafter. Caldwell was ahead of his time in his frank treatment of sex and in his mixture of the funny with the vulgar and grotesque in a way that anticipated the black humor of the 1960s.

Caldwell has never quite managed to live down the image of a man confused with his fictional characters, but after graduating from the University of Virginia, he lived the cosmopolitan life of a reporter and correspondent, working in many sections of America and traveling widely abroad. He provided the text for several books of photographs by his then-wife Margaret Bourke-White (he was married four times), including *You Have Seen Their Faces* (1937), which ranks among the best documentary accounts of Depression America.

NOVELS BY CALDWELL

God's Little Acre. 1933. Buccaneer Bks. 1991 $22.95. ISBN 0-89966-869-0
This Very Earth. Amereon Ltd. $12.95. ISBN 0-89190-164-7
Tobacco Road. 1932. Bentley 1978 $14.00. ISBN 0-8376-0422-2

SHORT STORY COLLECTIONS BY CALDWELL

The Black and White Stories of Erskine Caldwell. Peachtree Pubs. 1984 $12.95. ISBN 0-931948-63-0. Twenty-two stories examining relationships between poor rural black and white folks in the South in the early and mid 1900s.
Midsummer Passion and Other Tales of Maine Cussedness. Yankee 1990 $11.95. ISBN 0-89909-214-4. Collection of 20 short stories offering a mosaic of Maine living.

NONFICTION BY CALDWELL

Call It Experience. 1951. A mid-life autobiography.
With All My Might: An Autobiography. Peachtree Pubs. 1987 $19.95. ISBN 0-934601-11-9
You Have Seen Their Faces. 1937. Ayer 1975 $20.00. ISBN 0-405-06769-0

BOOKS ABOUT CALDWELL

Arnold, Edwin T., ed. *Conversations with Erskine Caldwell*. U. Pr. of Miss. 1988 $30.00. ISBN 0-87805-343-3. Thirty-two interviews ranging chronologically from 1929 to just before her 1987 death.
Cook, Sylvia J. *Erskine Caldwell and the Fiction of Poverty: The Flesh and the Spirit*. La. State U. Pr. 1991 $37.50. ISBN 0-8071-1645-9. Presents a chronological analysis of Caldwell's prolific writings.
Devlin, James E. *Erskine Caldwell*. Macmillan 1984 $19.95. ISBN 0-8057-7410-6. A welcome and balanced analysis of Caldwell's early and most critically successful novels; with notes and bibliography.
Klevar, Harvey L. *Erskine Caldwell*. U. of Tenn. Pr. 1993 $37.95. ISBN 0-87049-774-X. Finally, here is the "authorized biography"; a "respectable job." (*Booklist*)
Lindberg, Stanley W. *The Legacy of Erskine Caldwell*. U. of Ga. Pr. 1989 $9.95. ISBN 0-8203-1315-7. Absorbing glimpses into the writer's personal life.

CATHER, WILLA (SIBERT). 1876–1947

Of American women novelists of her time, none is more highly regarded than Willa Cather. Most of her books are written in a style of disarming simplicity, and she usually preferred to write about quite ordinary people, but her work has proved lasting because of her delicate craft, artistic honesty, and ability to create memorable characters. Her best novels have, in fact, seemed to grow richer with the passing years, as may be suggested by the amount of criticism and the number of differing interpretations they continue to receive. *The Professor's House* (1925), for example, contrasts the life of a burnt-out middle-aged historian with that of a creative young inventor named Tom Outland who died in the war but left a positive legacy of integrity by which other lives are to be measured. This novel, with its mythical overtones and its symmetrical contrasts, seems to be interpreted variously by each of its readers.

The most popular of Cather's novels and the most widely taught is *My Antonia* (1918), the vivid life story of a farm woman of the prairie country, admired not only for its warm depiction of a remarkably human character but also for the subtlety of a narrator's point of view that lends a sort of double perspective to her portrait—she is always viewed from outside but her own inner life is suggested. *Death Comes for the Archbishop* (1927), Cather's own choice as her best book, is a fictionalized account of the first bishop appointed to the New Mexico Territory after its annexation. By means of loosely structured episodes covering more than 40 years, she raised a historical narrative to the level of a legend and wrote what is generally considered her masterpiece. Her other novels, from *Alexander's Bridge* (1912) and *O Pioneers!* (1913) to *Sapphira and the Slave Girl*, vary in quality, but none is a shoddy piece of work and the total corpus of writings she left behind is clearly that of a dedicated professional writer. In addition to her work as a novelist, Cather served as an editor of *McClure's* magazine, produced journalism of various kinds, and wrote a number of short stories for the popular magazines of her day. Of her shorter fiction, "The Sculptor's Funeral," "Neighbor Rosicky," and the frequently reprinted "Paul's Case" are generally considered the most worthy.

In telling the story of Thea Kronberg, a Swedish girl from Colorado who becomes a great Wagnerian soprano in *The Song of the Lark* (1915), Cather gave a veiled history of her own development from her childhood in rural Nebraska to her triumphant years in New York. In a groundbreaking and controversial biography, Phyllis C. Robinson claimed that Cather was a lesbian and that her long-term, lifelong partnerships with women, as well as her perceived need to hide the sexual nature of these relationships, helped to shape her work. In fact, Cather's will contained an unqualified prohibition against the publication of any of her letters.

NOVELS BY CATHER

Alexander's Bridge. 1912. NAL-Dutton 1988 $6.00. ISBN 0-452-00875-1
Death Comes for the Archbishop. 1927. Knopf 1992 $16.50. ISBN 0-679-41319-7
A Lost Lady. 1923. Random 1990 $9.00. ISBN 0-679-7288-2. An enduring portrait of Cather's life, originally published in 1923.
Lucy Gayheart. 1935. Random 1976 $6.95. ISBN 0-394-71756-2
My Antonia. 1918. Buccaneer Bks. 1992 $19.95. ISBN 0-89966-977-8. Highly suggested reading for young adults; resembles an autobiographical style. Poignant story of Czech immigrants in America, most notably the title character, Antonia Shimerda, who in real life was a close friend of Cather's.
My Mortal Enemy. 1926. Random 1990 $8.95. ISBN 0-679-73179-2
Neighbor Rosicky. Creative Ed. 1986 $15.65. ISBN 0-685-12414-2
One of Ours. 1922. Random 1991 $12.00. ISBN 0-679-73744-8. Pulitzer Prize-winning story of a boy from the Western plains who joins the army and is killed in France in World War I.
O Pioneers! 1913. Viking Penguin 1992 $4.95. ISBN 0-14-016928-8
O Pioneers! 1913. U. of Nebr. Pr. 1992 $40.00. ISBN 0-8032-1457-X
The Professor's House. 1925. Random 1973 $4.95
Sapphira & the Slave Girl. 1940. Random 1975 $7.95. ISBN 0-394-71434-2
Shadows on the Rock. 1931. Random 1971 $9.00. ISBN 0-394-71680-9
The Song of the Lark. 1915. NAL-Dutton 1991 $4.95. ISBN 0-421-52533-7

SHORT STORY COLLECTIONS BY CATHER

The Old Beauty and Others. 1948. Random 1976 $7.00. ISBN 0-394-72122-5

The Troll Garden. 1905. NAL-Dutton 1984 $3.95. ISBN 0-452-00714-3. Cather's first collection; contains the famous story "Paul's Case."

Obscure Destinies. 1932. Random 1974 $8.00. ISBN 0-394-71179-3

Uncle Valentine and Other Stories: Willa Cather's Uncollected Short Fiction, 1915–1929. U. of Nebr. Pr. 1973 $17.95. ISBN 0-8032-0820-0

Willa Cather's Collected Short Fiction 1892–1912. U. of Nebr. Pr. 1970 $35.00. ISBN 0-8032-0770-0

Youth and the Bright Medusa. 1920. Random 1975 $7.95. ISBN 0-394-71684-1

NONFICTION BY CATHER

The Kingdom of Art: Willa Cather's First Principles and Critical Statements, 1893–1896. U. of Nebr. Pr. 1967 $40.00. ISBN 0-8032-0012-9. Pieces Cather wrote for the *Nebraska State Journal* during 1895–96; includes a checklist and index.

Willa Cather in Person: Interviews, Speeches, and Letters. U. of Nebr. Pr. 1990 $17.95. ISBN 0-8032-1184-8. Collection of ephemeral materials that helps complete our picture of a major American novelist.

Willa Cather on Writing: Critical Studies on Writing As an Art. U. of Nebr. Pr. 1988 $6.95. ISBN 0-8032-6332-5

POETRY BY CATHER

April Twilights. 1903. U. of Nebr. Pr. 1990 $20.00. ISBN 0-8032-1448-0

WORKS BY CATHER

Early Novels & Stories. Library of America 1987 $27.50. ISBN 0-940450-39-9

Not under Forty. 1936. U. of Nebr. Pr. 1988 $6.95. ISBN 0-8032-6331-7

Willa Cather: Stories, Poems, and Other Writings. Library of America 1992 $35.00. ISBN 0-940450-71-2

Willa Cather: Three Volumes in One: Alexander's Bridge, O Pioneers, The Sons of the Lark. Outlet Bk. Co. 1992 $9.99. ISBN 0-517-06493-6

BOOKS ABOUT CATHER

Ambrose, Jamie. *Willa Cather.* Berg Pubs. 1989 $24.95. ISBN 0-85496-152-6. A brief but trenchant critical introduction to Cather, drawing a distinct connection between the writer's life and her art.

Bloom, Harold, ed. *Willa Cather.* Chelsea Hse. 1986 $29.95. ISBN 0-87754-623-1. Selection of critical essays.

———, ed. *Willa Cather's My Antonia.* Chelsea Hse. 1987 $24.95. ISBN 1-55546-035-6. Essays dealing with many aspects of the novel—its structure, themes, imagery, mythic elements, treatment of time and history, the role and character of the narrator, and its relation to Cather's other works.

Brown, E. K. *Willa Cather: A Critical Biography.* U. of Nebr. Pr. 1987 $9.95. ISBN 0-8032-6084-9

Gerber, Philip L. *Willa Cather.* Macmillan 1975 $19.95. ISBN 0-8057-7155-7. A general study of Cather's life and works.

Lee, Hermione. *Willa Cather: Double Lives.* Random 1991 $15.00. ISBN 0-679-73649-2. Argues that the lucidity of Cather's prose belies the complexity of her sensibilities.

Lewis, Edith. *Willa Cather Living: A Personal Record.* Ohio U. Pr. 1989 $22.95. ISBN 0-8214-0913-1

Middleton, Jo A. *Willa Cather's Modernism: A Study of Style of Technique.* Fairleigh Dickinson 1990 $32.50. ISBN 0-8386-3385-4. Offers occasional insights into Cather's artistic processes, with extensive quotations from traditional interpretations.

Murphy, John J. *My Antonia: The Road Home.* Macmillan 1989 $20.95. ISBN 0-8057-7986-8. Excellent study that introduces the new or developing Cather scholar to the major issues in what is perhaps Cather's most widely read novel.

Robinson, Phyllis C. *Willa: The Life of Willa Cather.* Doubleday 1983 o.p.

Rosowski, Susan J. *The Voyage Perilous: Willa Cather's Romanticism*. U. of Nebr. Pr. 1986 $25.00. ISBN 0-8032-3874-6. Provides a forum for all aspects of Cather scholarship and criticism, including biography, various critical approaches, and her literary relationships and reputation.

————, ed. *Cather Studies*. U. of Nebr. Pr. 1990 $26.50. ISBN 0-685-33072-9

Sergeant, Elizabeth S. *Willa Cather: A Memoir*. Ohio U. Pr. 1992 $14.95. ISBN 0-8214-1009-1. Highly personal memoir of Sergeant's relationship with Cather from 1910 until the great novelist's death in 1947.

Shaw, Patrick W. *Willa Cather and the Art of Conflict: Re-visioning Her Creative Imagination*. Whitston Pub. 1992 $23.50. ISBN 0-87875-423-7. Considers tensions in Cather's fiction and relates them to tensions within Cather's personal life.

Skaggs, Merrill M. *After the World Broke in Two: The Later Novels of Willa Cather*. U. Pr. of Va. 1990 $25.00. ISBN 0-8139-1300-4. An intellectual history of Cather's work, primarily derived from her published work.

Thomas, Susie. *Willa Cather*. B & N Imports 1989 $36.50. ISBN 0-389-20882-5. Interesting overview of Cather's work.

Wasserman, Loretta. *Willa Cather: A Study of the Short Fiction*. Macmillan 1991 $20.95. ISBN 0-8057-8330-X. Presents a compact, accessible overview of Cather's short fiction.

Woodress, James. *Willa Cather: A Literary Life*. U. of Nebr. Pr. 1987 $40.00. ISBN 0-8032-4734-6. Discusses the author's life as it relates to the characters and plots of her novels and stories.

COWLEY, MALCOLM. 1898–1989

Malcolm Cowley, critic, poet, editor, and translator, has long been an influential figure in American letters. The son of a Pittsburgh physician, Cowley studied at Harvard University and the University of Montpelier, "starved" in Greenwich Village ("and that's no figure of speech"), and lived in France, where he met the Dada crowd and worked on two expatriate magazines, *Secession* and *Broom*. From 1929 to 1944, he was associate editor of *The New Republic*. His book *The Faulkner-Cowley File: Letters and Memories, 1944–1962* documents his early recognition of WILLIAM FAULKNER. *The Portable Faulkner* was published at Cowley's instigation and under his editorship in 1946, when all 17 of Faulkner's books were out of print. Its publication had a profound effect—virtually creating Faulkner's literary revival. Cowley is probably the critic who was most influential in analyzing and promoting the writers of the Lost Generation.

NONFICTION BY COWLEY

Books That Changed Our Minds. Ayer repr. of 1939 ed. $20.00. ISBN 0-8369-1912-2

The Dream of the Golden Mountains: Remembering the 1930s. Viking Penguin 1981 $8.95. ISBN 0-14-005919-9. Concise and vital survey of an overwhelmingly turbulent period, consistently readable and admirably fair; illustrated and indexed.

Exile's Return: A Literary Odyssey of the 1920s. Viking Penguin 1976 $9.95. ISBN 0-14-004392-6. Cowley's groundbreaking analysis of the cultural experience of the "Lost Generation" and how it affected their art.

The Faulkner-Cowley File: Letters and Memories, 1944–1962. Viking Penguin 1978 o.p.

Many-Windowed House: Collected Essays on American Writers and American Writing. Ed. by Henry Dan Piper. S. Ill. U. Pr. 1970 o.p. Fourteen lucid and straightforward essays on nineteenth- and early twentieth-century American writers.

The Portable Faulkner. 1946. Viking Penguin rev. ed. 1977 $9.95. ISBN 0-14-015018-8

A Second Flowering: Works and Days of the Lost Generation. Viking Penguin 1980 $7.95. ISBN 0-14-005498-7. Focuses on eight representatives of the Lost Generation: Faulkner, Hemingway, Dos Passos, Cummings, Wilder, Fitzgerald, Wolfe, and Crane; well unified by an excellent introduction.

The View from Eighty. Viking Penguin 1980 o.p. Crisp and critical account of aging and its many implications.

BOOKS ABOUT COWLEY

Faulkner, Donald W., ed. *The Portable Malcolm Cowley.* Viking Penguin 1990 $9.95. ISBN 0-14-015101-X

Kempf, James M. *The Early Career of Malcolm Cowley: A Humanist Among the Moderns.* La. State U. Pr. 1985 $25.00. ISBN 0-8071-1217-8. Critical biography that, for the first time, makes full use of the early years of the Cowley papers.

Young, Thomas D., ed. *Conversations with Malcolm Cowley.* U. Pr. of Miss. 1986 $32.50. ISBN 0-87805-290-9. Interviews conducted by various writers and critics on literature, communism, and religion.

CRANE, (HAROLD) HART. 1899–1932

Born in Ohio, Hart Crane's early life was filled with change and trauma. His family's many moves and his parents' divorce turned him to writing at age 13. Some critics say it also contributed to emotional instability. In 1923, Crane moved to New York, where he published his first book of poetry, *White Buildings*, in 1926. In 1930 he published *The Bridge*, considered by most to be his best work. That same year he won the Levinson Prize from *Poetry* magazine; he was awarded a Guggenheim Fellowship in 1931. Crane's tortured, rootless life, with its moments of mystic vision and inspired writing, ended in 1932 when he committed suicide by drowning. He jumped from a ship as he was returning to the United States from a trip to Mexico. Crane's stature as a modernist remains great, despite his relatively small output of works.

POETRY BY CRANE

The Bridge. 1930. Norton 1970 $8.95. ISBN 0-87140-225-4
White Buildings. 1926. Liveright 1986 $3.95. ISBN 0-87140-272-6

WORKS BY CRANE

Complete Poems and Selected Letters and Prose of Hart Crane. Liveright 1946 $19.95. ISBN 0-87140-959-3

Letters of Hart Crane and His Family. Col. U. Pr. 1974 $91.50. ISBN 0-231-03740-6. Allows the reader to participate in the excitement of Crane's professional and private lives; with detailed index, useful chronology, and annotations.

BOOKS ABOUT CRANE

Berthoff, Warner. *Hart Crane: A Re-Introduction.* U. of Minn. Pr. 1989 $34.95. ISBN 0-8166-1700-7. Finds sanity, shrewdness, and a sense of purpose in Crane's poems.

Bloom, Harold, ed. *Hart Crane.* Chelsea Hse. 1986 $34.95. ISBN 0-87754-654-1

Brunner, Edward J. *Splendid Failure: Hart Crane and the Making of The Bridge.* U. Ill. Pr. 1985 $29.95. ISBN 0-252-01094-9

Edelman, Lee. *Transmemberment of Song: Hart Crane's Anatomies of Rhetoric and Desire.* Stanford U. Pr. 1987 $32.50. ISBN 0-8047-1413-4. Examines "the allegory of rhetoric" that Crane's poetry enacts, concentrating on the major poems; includes insight that startles in its aptness and simplicity.

Giles, Paul. *Hart Crane: The Contexts of The Bridge.* Cambridge U. Pr. 1986 $49.95. ISBN 0-521-32074-7. Discusses Hart's dexterity with pun, ambiguity, paradox, oxymoron, and metonymy.

Simon, Marc. *Poems of Hart Crane.* Liveright 1989 $8.95. ISBN 0-87140-139-8

Unterecker, John. *Voyager: A Life of Hart Crane.* Liveright 1987 $14.95. ISBN 0-87140-143-6

Uroff, Margaret. *Hart Crane: The Patterns of His Poetry*. Bks. Demand repr. of 1974 ed. $61.50. ISBN 0-317-28980-2. Remarkably insightful analyses through reflective reference, with full footnoting.

Yingling, Thomas E. *Hart Crane and the Homosexual Text: New Thresholds, New Anatomies*. U. Ch. Pr. 1990 $39.95. ISBN 0-226-95634-2. Precise and expansive in its outlook; clearly one of the most important critical works of recent years.

CULLEN, COUNTEE. 1903–1946

Born in New York City, Countee Cullen was separated from his mother in early childhood. He was raised in part by the Reverend Frederick Cullen, a Methodist minister. In high school, Cullen was already praised for his poetry. The poem "Life's Rendezvous" was published in a high school literary magazine and won first prize in a citywide contest. Educated at New York University and Harvard University, Cullen worked as an assistant editor on the Urban League's *Opportunity: A Journal of Negro Life*, writing a monthly literary column. His many awards for poetry included the first Harmon Prize for distinguished achievement in literature by a black writer, and a Guggenheim Fellowship. He taught junior high school in New York City until his death.

POETRY BY CULLEN

Color. 1925. Ayer 1970 repr. of 1925 ed. $14.00. ISBN 0-405-01919-X

NOVEL BY CULLEN

One Way to Heaven. 1931. AMS Pr. repr. of 1931 ed. $19.00. ISBN 0-404-11383-4. Comedy about life in Harlem.

WORKS BY CULLEN

Lost Zoo. 1940. Silver Burdett Pr. 1991 $12.95. ISBN 0-382-24256-4. Rhymed-verse children's story in which a few strange animals fail to get into Noah's Ark; with humorous and imaginative illustrations.

My Soul's High Song: The Collected Writings of Countee Cullen. Doubleday 1991 $14.95. ISBN 0-385-41295-9. Contains the very best of Cullen's poetry and prose.

BOOKS ABOUT CULLEN

Baker, Houston. *A Many Colored Coat: Countee Cullen*. Broadside Pr. 1974 $3.00. ISBN 0-910296-36-7. A well-balanced, concise introduction to the career and works of an important American poet.

Bronz, Stephen H. *Roots of Negro Racial Consciousness*. Libra 1964 $10.00. ISBN 0-87212-019-8. Discusses the authors James Weldon Johnson, Countee Cullen, and Claude McKay.

Perry, Margaret. *Bio-Bibliography of Countee P. Cullen, 1903–1946*. Greenwood 1970 $39.95. ISBN 0-8371-3325-4. Includes a brief life of Cullen, notes on his poetry, and selections from contemporary criticism; includes a substantial bibliography, including a few unpublished works.

Shucard, Alan R. *Countee Cullen*. G. K. Hall 1984 $17.95. ISBN 0-8057-7411-4. A good general introduction to Cullen's life and art.

CUMMINGS, E(DWARD) E(STLIN). 1894–1962

A Harvard University graduate, E. E. Cummings, who styled himself e. e. cummings, lived in Greenwich Village and spent his summers on a farm in New Hampshire. While working for the American Red Cross in France in 1917, Cummings was mistakenly imprisoned for several months; this experience resulted in the publication of a novel, *The Enormous Room* (1922). Although he went on to write other prose, it is for his poetry that he is best known. He also published plays, wrote a ballet, and was a respected painter. He was awarded many honors for his work, including the 1958 Bollingen Prize for poetry and the National Book Award in 1955.

In describing Cummings's poem *i: six nonlectures* (1953), the *Atlantic* wrote: "Full of originality, high spirits, and aphoristic dicta, they express a credo of intense individualism." Although he used many techniques to stress his meaning, he wrote about the traditional subjects of love, nature, and the corrupting influence of materialism. Cummings delivered these unconventional lectures while at Harvard in 1952. He also wrote the delightful commentaries for the 50 photographs in *Adventures in Value* by his wife, Marion Morehouse, a fine and sensitive photographer. For a generation or so, Cummings was the very model of the "modern poet"—a difficult, experimenting bohemian. His playful, innovative work remains admired by critics and beloved by readers of poetry.

POETRY BY CUMMINGS

The Complete Poems 1913–1962. Lightyear 1992 $27.95. ISBN 0-89968-267-7. A definitive collection, with some 250 pages added to the previous edition; includes Cummings's translation of Louis Aragon's "Le Front Rouge"; indexed.
Concordance to the Complete Poems of E. E. Cummings. Cornell Univ. Pr. 1988 $58.50. ISBN 0-8014-2239-6
Hist Whist and Other Poems for Children. Liveright 1983 $12.95. ISBN 0-87140-640-3. Excellent introduction for children to Cummings's work and a springboard to other modern, more experimental poets; irresistibly vivid word divisions, letter play, and sound bouncing.
In Just-Spring. Little 1988 $14.95. ISBN 0-316-16390-2. Three brief poems of childhood images, made accessible to young children through the spare but attractive illustrations.
Is Five . . . 1926. Liveright 1985 $14.95. ISBN 0-87140-648-9
Little Tree. Crown Bks. Yng. Read. 1988 $10.95. ISBN 0-517-56598-9. The theme of the humble-made-beautiful by love and care transcends this Christmas poem; Ray's drawings echo the poem's inherent warmth and simplicity.
No Thanks. 1935. Liveright 1978 $9.95. ISBN 0-87140-631-4. Seventy-one poems, including some of Cummings's most exciting linguistic and typographical play, crude wit, and stinging satire.
One Hundred Selected Poems. Grove Pr. 1988 $6.95. ISBN 0-8021-3072-0
Seventy Three Poems. HarBraceJ 1971 $5.95. ISBN 0-15-680676-2
Spooky Poems. Little 1989 $13.95. ISBN 0-316-08987-7
Viva. 1931. Liveright 1970 $6.00. ISBN 0-87140-528-8. Includes some of Cummings's most experimental work and several of his best-known poems.
Xaipe. 1950. Liveright 1979 $9.95. ISBN 0-87140-633-0. A lyrical volume of poems, including several of his finest; provides satires on war and insights into religious kinds of experience.

WORKS BY CUMMINGS

The Enormous Room. 1922. Liveright 1978 $12.95. ISBN 0-87140-630-6. An account of the author's wartime internment in France.
Fairy Tales. HarBraceJ 1975 $3.95. ISBN 0-15-629895-3. Four quiet bedtime tales for the very young; "The Old Man Who Said Why" is especially full of imagery and imagination.
i: six nonlectures. HUP 1953 $4.50. ISBN 0-686-82914-X

BOOKS ABOUT CUMMINGS

Cohen, Milton A. *Poet and Painter: The Aesthetics of E. E. Cummings's Early Work*. Wayne St. U. Pr. 1987 $34.95. ISBN 0-8143-1845-2

Friedman, Norman. *Cummings: The Growth of a Writer*. S. Ill. U. Pr. 1980 $9.95. ISBN 0-8093-0978-5

Kennedy, Richard S. *Dreams in the Mirror: A Biography of E. E. Cummings*. Liveright 1982 $8.95. ISBN 0-87140-130-4

Lane, Gary. *I Am: A Study of E. E. Cummings' Poems*. U. Pr. of KS 1976 $9.95. ISBN 0-7006-0144-9. Explications of 25 of Cummings's poems, showing the poems to be evolutions from various traditions going back to the classics.

Marks, Barry A. *E. E. Cummings*. Macmillan 1965 $19.95. ISBN 0-8057-0176-1. A comprehensive general introduction to the life and works of Cummings for the beginning student.

DOOLITTLE, HILDA, known as H. D. 1886–1961

Born in Bethlehem, Pennsylvania, Hilda Doolittle was educated at Bryn Mawr College. In 1911, after a visit abroad, she helped to organize the imagists with EZRA POUND. She married Richard Aldington, the English poet and novelist, whom she later divorced. Written in poetic prose, her poignant and subtle *Tribute to Freud: With Unpublished Letters by Freud to the Author* (1965) is a record of her memories of her analytical experiences in 1933–34, a memoir of FREUD (see Vols. 3 and 5) in London in 1938–39, and a description of the impact of his unique personality. In *Palimpsest* (1926), she explores the difficulties that a woman finds herself in as she tries to cultivate both love and art in a world that is ugly, vulgar, and violent. Her novel *Bid Me To Live: A Madrigal* (1960), about a woman's loneliness and self-discovery during World War I, is a poetic stream-of-consciousness study. She lived in London from 1911 through the bombings of two world wars and spent her later years in Zurich, Switzerland, coming to New York only for brief visits. She received the Brandeis University Creative Arts Award (1959) and the award of merit medal for poetry (1960) from the American Academy of Arts and Letters—the first time the latter was awarded to a woman. Her importance as a model for women writers has grown steadily, and her stature as a modernist innovator, as well as a foremost imagist poet, is assured.

POETRY BY H. D.

By Avon River. Black Swan CT 1989 $20.00. ISBN 0-933806-39-6

Collected Poems, 1912-1944. New Dir. Pr. 1986 $19.95. ISBN 0-8112-0971-7. Contains poems about Greece and its culture, love and death, and a series of simple yet telling conversations between mother and daughter.

Helen in Egypt. New Dir. Pr. 1974 $12.95. ISBN 0-8112-0543-6

Hermetic Definition. New Dir. Pr. 1972 $6.95. ISBN 0-8112-0453-7

Priest and A Dead Priestess Speaks. Copper Canyon 1983 $125.00. ISBN 0-914742-79-5

Red Roses for Bronze. AMS Pr. o.p.

Trilogy. New Dir. Pr. 1973 $8.95. ISBN 0-8112-0491-X. The first of H. D.'s three autobiographies to appear in print; demonstrates her wit, sense of rhythm, and control of language.

Vale Ave. Black Swan CT 1991 $20.00. ISBN 0-933806-64-7

NOVELS BY H. D.

Bid Me to Live. 1960. Black Swan CT 1983 $20.00. ISBN 0-933806-19-1

Hedylus. Black Swan CT 1980 $17.50. ISBN 0-933806-00-0. H. D.'s second novel, a landmark in imagist prose; with an afterpiece by her daughter, and a list of textual notes.

Hermione. New Dir. Pr. 1971 $9.95. ISBN 0-8112-0817-6

PLAYS BY H. D.

Hippolytus Temporizes. Black Swan CT 1985 $20.00. ISBN 0-933806-23-X. Adapts material and themes from ancient Greek myth and literature—an innocent young man is falsely accused by his lovesick stepmother of sexual assault upon her.

WORKS BY H. D.

End to Torment: A Memoir of Ezra Pound. New Dir. Pr. 1979 $6.95. ISBN 0-8112-0720. Incisive and enigmatic recollections and interpretations of H. D.'s relationship with Ezra Pound; includes useful annotations.

The Gift. New Dir. Pr. 1982 $14.95. ISBN 0-8112-0853-2. A memoir of the poet's childhood in a series of impressionistic essays.

Notes on Thought and Vision. City Lights 1983 $9.95. ISBN 0-87286-142-2. Two essays examining artistic sensibility and an attempt to capture Sappho's personal and poetic essence; with a helpful introduction and brief glossary.

Paint It Today. NYU Pr. 1972 $35.00. ISBN 0-8147-3487-1

Tribute to Freud: Writing on the Wall. 1965. New Dir. Pr. 1984 $9.95. ISBN 0-8112-0897-4

BOOKS ABOUT H. D.

Buck, Claire. *H. D. and Freud: Bi-Sexuality and a Feminine Discourse.* St. Martin 1991 $35.00. ISBN 0-312-01958-0. Offers new insights into the writing of H. D. that break away from the established school of feminist critical analysis.

Collecott, Diana, ed. *H. D.* Black Swan CT 1988 $17.50. ISBN 0-933806-51-5

Friedman, Susan S. *Psyche Reborn: The Emergence of H. D.* Ind. U. Pr. 1981 $29.95. ISBN 0-253-37826-5. A prodigiously informative book about Doolittle's psychological and psychic makeup.

Fritz, Angela DiPace. *Thought and Vision: A Critical Reading of H. D.'s Poetry.* Cath. U. Pr. 1988 $34.95. ISBN 0-8132-0642-1. Presents a chronological study of Hilda Doolittle's poetic quest for a synthesis between objective reality and spirituality.

Kloepfer, Deborah K. *The Unspeakable Mother: Forbidden Discourse in Jean Rhys and H. D.* Cornell Univ. Pr. 1989 $25.95. ISBN 0-8014-2306-6. Perceptive reading of five prose works by H. D.

Robinson, Janice S. *H. D., The Life and Work of an American Poet.* HM 1982 o.p. The first full-length study of Hilda Doolittle, part biography, part analysis of the poetry and prose; contains a chronology, photographs, notes, and a selected bibliography.

Swann, Thomas Burnett. *The Classical World of H. D.* U. of Nebr. Pr. 1962 o.p.

DOS PASSOS, JOHN (RODERIGO). 1896–1970

Of Portuguese descent, Dos Passos was born in Chicago of well-to-do parents and attended Choate and Harvard University. It is as a social chronicler that Dos Passos is most admired, for in addition to a large quantity of writing depicting his personal response to the events of his times, his best-known works of fiction are in general "documentary" accounts that mix the lives of real people with those of his fictional characters. The *U.S.A.* trilogy, consisting of *The 42nd Parallel* (1930), *1919* (1932), and *The Big Money* (1936), remains his most impressive achievement. Distributed through that work are 68 Newsreel sections composed of newspaper headlines and lines from popular songs as well as other materials; 27 short biographies of such people as Eugene Debs, Henry Ford, ISADORA DUNCAN, and the WRIGHT brothers; and 51 Camera Eye sections in which Dos Passos attempts a kind of kaleidoscopic view of experiences recounted by a poetic speaker who is different from the impersonal narrator of the other sections. The lives of 12 main fictional characters representing various walks of life are traced in the three volumes, and although *U.S.A.* may not be the Great American Novel, it comes close to living up to its title. A second trilogy, comprised of *Adventures of a Young Man* (1939), *Number One* (1943), and *The*

Grand Design (1949) grouped under the title *District of Columbia* (1952), lacks the cohesiveness of *U.S.A.* but finds a loosely linked kind of unity through Dos Passos's use of members of the same family in the three volumes.

Aside from his two trilogies, Dos Passos wrote eight individual novels. *One Man's Initiation—1917* (1917) is a highly subjective record of his experiences in the French ambulance service in World War I, while *Three Soldiers* (1921) is one of the first novels to reveal the sordidness of military life. *Manhattan Transfer* (1925) anticipates some aspects of the later style, and its comparatively shorter length makes it more accessible for college courses than *U.S.A.*

During and following World War II as a correspondent for *Life*, he reported on the various theaters of war, U.S. occupation of Germany, the Nuremberg trials, Socialist England, and the industrial United States. Books collecting some of those observations include *Journey between Wars* (1938), *Brazil on the Move* (1963), *Orient Express* (1927), *The Prospect before Us* (1927), and *Tour of Duty* (1946).

Most critics agree that Dos Passos's literary powers declined after the 1930s. Married twice, his last years were spent writing at his father's old farm in Virginia.

NOVELS BY DOS PASSOS

The Big Money. 1936. NAL-Dutton 1989 $5.95. ISBN 0-317-02795-6
Century's Ebb. Harvard Common Pr. 1975 $9.95. ISBN 0-87645-089-3
Chosen Country. Amereon Ltd. $25.95. ISBN 0-685-10848-1
First Encounter. AMS Pr. repr. of 1945 ed. $19.50. ISBN 0-404-20083-4
The Forty Second Parallel. 1930. NAL-Dutton 1983 $4.50. ISBN 0-451-52045-9
Manhattan Transfer. 1925. HM 1991 $9.70. ISBN 0-395-57423-4
Nineteen Nineteen. 1932. NAL-Dutton $4.95. ISBN 0-451-52248-6
One Man's Initiation: Nineteen Seventeen: A Novel by John Dos Passos. 1917. U. Pr. of Amer. 1986 $13.25. ISBN 0-8191-9360-5. His first novel, this work has a bitter anti-war sentiment; the work is primarily of historical and biographical significance.
Theme is Freedom. Ayer 1956 $22.00. ISBN 0-8369-1460-0
Three Soldiers. 1921. Carroll & Graf 1988 $9.95. ISBN 0-88184-413-6. The futility of war expressed through the sad stories of three soldiers of World War I.

WORKS BY DOS PASSOS

Brazil on the Move. 1963. Paragon Hse. 1991 $10.95. ISBN 0-55778-359-4
Facing the Chair: Story of the Americanization of Two Foreign-Born Workmen. Da Capo 1970 $19.50. ISBN 0-306-71871-5. Dos Passos's impassioned story of Sacco and Vanzetti.
State of the Nation. Greenwood 1973 $38.50. ISBN 0-8371-6782-5. Gives a vivid sense of the years 1937–68; effective use of fictional narrative, brief biographies, journalism, and blank verse.

BOOKS ABOUT DOS PASSOS

Belkind, Allen. *Dos Passos: The Critics and the Writer's Intention.* Bks. Demand repr. of 1971 ed. $91.60. ISBN 0-317-58108-2. Seventeen essays, all published before mid-1960, that provide a glimpse of various facets of John Dos Passos.
Carr, Virginia S. *Dos Passos: A Life.* Doubleday 1984 o.p. The most thorough and authoritative biography of Dos Passos available.
Clark, Michael. *Dos Passos's Early Fiction, 1912–1938.* Susquehanna U. Pr. 1987 $29.50. ISBN 0-941664-18-X. Sensible and well-written study emphasizing the specifically American dimension of the novelist's thought; with a bibliography and index.
Hook, Andrew, ed. *Dos Passos: A Collection of Critical Essays.* P-H 1974 $2.45. ISBN 0-13-218859-7
Maine, Barry, ed. *Dos Passos.* Routledge 1988 $49.50. ISBN 0-415-00229-X

Pizer, Donald. *Dos Passos' U.S.A.: A Critical Study.* Bks. Demand repr. of 1988 ed. $60.00. ISBN 0-8357-2570-7. Analyzes the genesis and meaning of this trilogy against the backdrop of Dos Passos's artistic and political development during the 1920s; a straightforward, wide-ranging, and informative study.

Rosen, Robert C. *John Dos Passos: Politics and the Writer.* U. of Nebr. Pr. 1981 $19.95. ISBN 0-8032-3860-6

Wagner, Linda W. *Dos Passos: Artist as American.* U. of Tex. Pr. 1979 $16.95. ISBN 0-292-74011-5. Succinct assessment of all of Dos Passos's works, fully introduced and documented with end notes; excellent bibliography of primary and secondary sources.

DREISER, THEODORE. 1871–1945

Hardly anyone these days questions the stature of Theodore Dreiser as a major writer, but only because he has survived decades of begrudging and patronizing criticism from readers and critics who have found his ideas unsophisticated and his style fumbling and "elephantine." For all his flaws— perhaps no other major novelist since DOSTOEVSKY (see Vol. 2) has suffered from as many imperfections as Dreiser—there is a raw narrative force in his better works that makes them compelling reading. His first two novels—*Sister Carrie* (1900) and *Jennie Gerhardt* (1911), stories of young women from the Midwest who learn some of life's bitter lessons—are considered landmark contributions to American literary naturalism, and the number of editions of *Sister Carrie* in print testifies to the rank of that novel as a modern classic widely taught in schools and universities. However, *An American Tragedy* (1925) is usually considered Dreiser's best book. Based on an actual murder case, it is the story of a young man, Clyde Griffiths, who finds himself in such a tangled web of social and psychological forces beyond his control that his tragic fate seems to carry with it a relentless inevitability that keeps the story both tough-minded and compassionate.

As an indictment of American social and business values, *An American Tragedy* develops themes all too apparent in Dreiser's trilogy of works—*The Financier* (1912), *The Titan* (1914), and *The Stoic* (published posthumously in 1947)—about an unscrupulous and successful businessman named Frank Cowperwood whose fictional story provides a vivid but devastating record of the boom period in American industry.

Dreiser was born in Terre Haute, Indiana, a member of a large, poor, and religious immigrant family that included several sisters whose experiences provided models for his first novels and a brother who, as Paul Dresser, was to achieve fame as the composer of "On the Banks of the Wabash" and other popular songs. Dreiser attended the University of Indiana and worked as a newspaper reporter and magazine editor before moving to New York in 1894. Among his several works of autobiography, *A Traveler at Forty* (1913), *A Book about Myself* (1922), and *Dawn* (1931) are currently out of print, but available are *A Hoosier Holiday* (1916) and *Newspaper Days* (1931). *Notes on Life* consists of reflections selected and edited by Marguerite Tjader and John McAleer. *The American Diaries, 1902–1926* is one of three titles published by the University of Pennsylvania Press. The others are *The Pennsylvania Edition of Sister Carrie* and the first publication of an unfinished work of mixed autobiography and fiction written early in Dreiser's career and published as *An Amateur Laborer*.

NOVELS BY DREISER

An American Tragedy. 1925. Buccaneer Bks. 1990 $31.95. ISBN 0-89966-709-0. Story of Clyde Griffiths, whose burning ambition to achieve the American Dream through upward mobility leads to the tragedy of a young woman's murder.

The Financier. 1912. NAL-Dutton 1967 $5.95. ISBN 0-452-00825-5
The Genius. NAL-Dutton 1981 $5.95. ISBN 0-452-00753-4
Jennie Gerhardt. 1911. OUP 1991 $5.95. ISBN 0-19-282743-X
Sister Carrie. 1900. OUP 1991 $7.95. ISBN 0-19-282742-1. The saga of a young woman
    who achieves greatness as she loses her innocence.
The Stoic. 1947. NAL-Dutton 1981 o.p. Introduction by Richard Lingerman.
The Titan. 1914. AMS Pr. repr. of 1946 ed. $27.50. ISBN 0-404-20084-2
Twelve Men. Scholarly 1971 repr. of 1919 ed. $46.00. ISBN 0-403-00914-6 .

Nonfiction by Dreiser

American Diaries, 1902–1926. U. of Pa. Pr. 1983 $21.95. ISBN 0-8122-1148-0
Newspaper Days. 1931. U. of Pa. Pr. 1991 $49.95. ISBN 0-8122-3095-7. Record of
    Dreiser's early venture into journalism.

Short Story Collections by Dreiser

The Best Short Stories of Theodore Dreiser. I. R. Dee 1989 $9.95. ISBN 0-929587-03-0
Fulfilment and Other Stories of Women & Men. Black Sparrow 1992 $25.00. ISBN 0-
    87685-882-5

Plays by Dreiser

Plays of the Natural and Supernatural. AMS Pr. 1969 $18.00. ISBN 0-404-02179-4

Work by Dreiser

An Amateur Laborer. 1904. U. of Pa. Pr. 1984 $29.95. ISBN 0-8122-7890-9. The first
    printing of Dreiser's 1904 manuscript, complete with historical notes and illustra-
    tions, and an informative and scholarly introduction.

Books about Dreiser

Boswell, Jeanetta. *Theodore Dreiser and the Critics, 1911–1982: A Bibliography with
    Selective Annotations.* Scarecrow 1986 $32.50. ISBN 0-8108-1837-X. Annotated,
    alphabetical listing of 1,719 entries of Dreiser's books, dissertations, articles, and
    reviews.
Gerber, Philip L. *Theodore Dreiser.* G. K. Hall 1963 o.p.
Hussman, Lawrence E. *Dreiser and His Fiction: A Twentieth Century Quest.* U. of Pa. Pr.
    1983 o.p. Examines the religious awe before the modern secular world as depicted
    by Dreiser; particularly helpful in clarifying the nature of Dreiser's naturalism.
Lehan, Richard. *Theodore Dreiser: His World and His Novels.* S. Ill. U. Pr. 1974 $9.95.
    ISBN 0-8093-0663-8. Systematic and careful study utilizing Dreiser's autobiographies
    and letters; draws conclusions about the relationship between the author's life and
    his fictional world.
Lingeman, Richard. *Theodore Dreiser, Vol. 1: At the Gates of the City, 1871–1907.* Putnam
    Pub. Group 1986 $22.95. ISBN 0-399-13147-7. A massive biography of Dreiser's early
    years, focusing on Dreiser's journalist background and his ultimate success with
    Sister Carrie.
———. *Theodore Dreiser, Vol. 2: An American Journey, 1908–1945.* Putnam Pub. Group
    1990 $39.95. ISBN 0-399-13520-0. Impressive second volume of the definitive
    biography of Dreiser, focusing on the last troubled years of his life.
Lundquist, James. *Theodore Dreiser.* Continuum 1974 $18.95. ISBN 0-8044-2563-9. A
    general study of Dreiser's life and works, including a bibliography and chronology as
    well as in-depth discussions of each major novel.
Mukherjee, Arun. *The Gospel of Wealth in the American Novel: The Rhetoric of Dreiser
    and Some of His Contemporaries.* B & N Imports 1987 $45.50. ISBN 0-389-20681-4.
    Examines Dreiser's autobiographies and major novels, viewing the author as an
    acute social philosopher and a moral satirist.

Pizer, Donald, ed. *New Essays on Sister Carrie*. Cambridge U. Pr. 1991 $22.95. ISBN 0-521-38278-5. Collection of thoughtful, readable, persuasive essays; includes notes, select bibliography, and background on the essayists.

_____. *The Novels of Theodore Dreiser: A Critical Study*. Bks. Demand $102.50. ISBN 0-8357-6536-9. Provides a detailed account of each novel's development, and a critical analysis of structural and thematic patterns; with an index and chapter notes.

Swanberg, W. A. *Dreiser*. Scribner 1965 o.p. "Unquestionably . . . the definitive biography of [a] major novelist . . . [P]rodigious research . . . [using] the most obscure sources, . . . thousands of letters, and . . . scores of men and women who knew Dreiser, and with this massive detail he has constructed a fascinating story" (*Library Journal*).

DU BOIS, W(ILLIAM) E(DWARD) B(URGHARDT). 1868–1963

W. E. B. Du Bois was a modern successor to FREDERICK DOUGLASS as the leading spokesman for African American equality, and he became a dominant voice for civil rights in the twentieth century. He had been born and raised in western Massachusetts, innocent of the most virulent form of racial prejudice and segregation in the South, but he became enlightened and gradually radicalized after he attended Fisk University in Nashville, Tennessee. He eventually went on to be educated at Harvard University, where he earned a second B.A. (cum laude), an M.A., and a Ph.D. Early in his career, he established a reputation as one of the most uncompromising of black leaders, almost an anachronism in his clear-sighted unwillingness to make any concessions to racism. He rejected the gradualism of BOOKER T. WASHINGTON and other conservative black leaders. He was one of the early founders of the National Association for the Advancement of Colored People but became disillusioned even with that organization's cautious positions. Du Bois's writings were both scholarly and polemical and set a militant tone for civil rights discourse that did not wholly materialize elsewhere until the 1960s. His promotion of a form of black nationalism and pan-Africanism and his scathing attacks on white imperialism, in both Europe and the United States, caused him to come under continuous surveillance as a subversive during the McCarthy era and throughout the early Cold War period. Eventually, after traveling and studying around the world, he embraced communism officially—at age 93—and became a citizen of Ghana, where he died in 1963. Du Bois was an inexhaustibly prolific writer and published six novels and numerous poems in addition to his many studies of black culture in America and of African history. He is known today more for *The Souls of Black Folk* (1903), in which he described the terrible psychological costs of racism in America and urged strong measures for confronting this issue, which he predicted would be the central crisis in American political and moral life in the twentieth century.

NONFICTION BY DU BOIS

ABC of Color. Intl. Pubs. 1989 $4.95. ISBN 0-7178-0391-0

Against Racism: Unpublished Essays, Papers, Addresses, 1887–1961. U. of Mass. Pr. 1985 $15.95. ISBN 0-87023-624-5. The most significant of Du Bois's previously unpublished writings, organized chronologically; with helpful footnotes and introductions to entries.

The Autobiography of W. E. B. Du Bois: A Soliloquy on Viewing My Life from the Last Decade of Its First Century. 1968. Kraus 1976 $20.00. ISBN 0-527-25262-X. Written with grace and clarity; includes valuable reference notes, chronology, and a selected bibliography.

Black Folk Then and Now: An Essay in the History and Sociology of the Negro Race. Kraus 1975 $24.00. ISBN 0-527-25275-1

Black Reconstruction in America, 1860–1880. 1935. Macmillan 1972 $16.95. ISBN 0-689-70063-6

The Common School and the Negro American. Kraus 1911 $15.00. ISBN 0-527-03117-8

Dusk of Dawn: An Essay Toward an Autobiography of a Race Concept. 1940. Transaction Pubs. 1991 $19.95. ISBN 0-87855-917-5

The Gift of Black Folk: The Negroes in the Making of America. 1935. Kraus 1975 $21.00. ISBN 0-527-25310-3

Negro-American Family. Greenwood 1970 $35.00. ISBN 0-8371-1342-3. Reissue of a 1909 publication with a foreword by Daniel P. Moynihan and an introduction by James E. Conyers.

The Souls of Black Folk. 1903. Random 1990 $9.50. ISBN 0-679-72519-9. First published in 1947, this work is important as a key to understanding the aspirations and the quest for identity of black Americans of the time.

World and Africa: Inquiry into the Part Which Africa Has Played in World History. Intl. Pubs. Co. 1965 $7.95. ISBN 0-7178-0221-3

Writings. Library of America 1987 $27.50. ISBN 0-940450-33-X

NOVELS BY DU BOIS

The Black Flame: A Trilogy. 3 vols. Kraus 1976 $55.00. ISBN 0-527-25286-7

WORKS BY DU BOIS

The Correspondence of W.E.B. Du Bois. U. of Mass. Pr. Vol. 1 1973 $35.00. ISBN 0-87023-131-6. Vol. 2 1976 $35.00. ISBN 0-87023-132-4. Vol. 3 1978 $35.00. ISBN 0-87023-133-2. Arranged chronologically; demonstrates Du Bois's interests in all aspects of black American life; succinct and illuminating introductions and notes.

Prayers for Dark People. U. of Mass. Pr. 1980 $9.95. ISBN 0-87023-303-3. Seventy-one short lessons for daily discipline intended to inspire black students to struggle against diversity; includes a few notes and a brief introduction.

The Quest of the Silver Fleece. NE U. Pr. 1989 $15.95. ISBN 1-55553-064-8

BOOKS ABOUT DU BOIS

De Marco, Joseph P. *The Social Thought of W. E. B. Du Bois.* U. Pr. of Amer. 1983 $45.00. ISBN 0-8191-3235-7. Interprets and surveys the structure, rationale, and development of Du Bois's social philosophy as presented in his nonfiction writing.

Marable, Manning. *W. E. B. Du Bois: Black Radical Democrat.* Macmillan 1987 $12.95. ISBN 0-8057-7771-7

McKissack, Patricia. *W. E. B. Du Bois.* Watts 1990 $13.90. ISBN 0-531-10939-9. Biography giving important insight into the life and times of the great African American journalist and author; includes source notes and a valuable appendix.

Partington, Paul G. *W.E.B. Du Bois: A Bibliography of Writings about Him.* P. G. Partington 1989 $20.00. ISBN 0-9602538-5-8. Includes journal articles, book chapters or brief biographical entries, and dissertations and master's theses.

Rampersad, Arnold. *Art and Imagination of W.E.B. Du Bois.* Schocken 1990 $14.95. ISBN 0-8052-0985-9

Stafford, Mark. *W. E. B. Du Bois.* Chelsea Hse. 1989 $17.95. ISBN 1-55546-582-X. A sound portrait of Du Bois, balancing his strengths and weaknesses; profusely illustrated with photographs, and includes a bibliography.

ELIOT, T. S. 1888–1965

[SEE Chapter 11 in this volume.]

FARRELL, JAMES T(HOMAS). 1904–1979

If there is an American author of this century who has suffered from overexposure, it is James T. Farrell. Resisting commercial pressures and testing the patience of critics, he was too fiercely independent to compromise his personal standards in order to reach a wide audience. Yet he managed to publish more than 50 books, including 28 novels and 16 collections of short stories. Almost all of his novels form a part of four series on which his reputation largely rests, but the fact that only *Studs Lonigan: A Trilogy* (1932–35) remains in print would suggest that his place in literature is still to be determined. His second major cycle is the out-of-print Danny O'Neill pentalogy published between 1936 and 1953—*A World I Never Made*, *No Star Is Lost*, *Father and Son*, *My Days of Anger*, and *The Face of Time*. The Bernard Carr trilogy (1946–52) consists of *Bernard Clare*, *The Road Between*, and *Yet Other Waters*, all of which are out of print. All three series are semiautobiographical works, with the first two set in Chicago, where Farrell grew up in the Irish slums of the South Side, and the third showing how the central figure achieves success as a writer in New York City from 1927 to 1936.

After 1958 Farrell was engaged primarily in writing a new series called *The Universe of Time*, which also has a central autobiographical character, Eddie Ryan, but which Farrell envisioned as "a relativistic panorama of our times" dealing with "man's creativity and his courageous acceptance of impermanence." Of some 30 projected volumes in the series, 10 were published in Farrell's lifetime. They are *Boarding House Blues* (1961), *The Silence of History* (1963), *What Time Collects* (1964), *When Time Was Born* (1966), *New Year's Eve 1929* (1967), *A Brand New Life* (1968), *Judith* (1969), *Invisible Swords* (1970), *The Dunne Family* (1976), and *The Death of Nora Ryan* (1978). In his review of the second volume, Robert Gorham Davis commented: "It is an effort to recapture the sounds and inner rhythms of an American experience now gone forever. Sooner or later Farrell will be given his place as a sort of WILLIAM DEAN HOWELLS of Jackson Park in recognition of the scope and faithfulness with which he recorded the day-to-day, almost hour-to-hour, suffering, sentimentality, dignity, coarseness and despair of an important part of the Nation's population at a time of decisive change in its psyche" (*N.Y. Times*).

Only *Studs Lonigan*, however, has captured a wide audience to date. That series is read largely for its historical interest as a vivid period piece of "slice-of-life" realism. Farrell's objective method of presenting experience, his reluctance to point a moral, and his naturalistic philosophy have offended some readers and critics, but time may show that it is Farrell's freedom from moralism and transient commitments that make him capable of seeing individual experience in broad and universal terms.

NOVELS BY FARRELL

Father and Son. 1940. Ayer 1976 repr. of 1940 ed. $38.50. ISBN 0-405-09335-7
New Year's Eve—1929. 1967. The Smith $6.00. ISBN 0-912292-02-4
Sam Holman. Prometheus 1983 $24.95. ISBN 0-87975-202-5. Very believable depiction of a minor intellectual's copings with 1930s political ideals, personal skepticism, loneliness, sexual appetite, and a need to love.
Studs Lonigan: A Trilogy. 1932-35. Vanguard 1979 o.p. *Young Lonigan* (1932), *The Young Manhood of Studs Lonigan* (1934), *Judgment Day* (1935). With a new introduction by the author.
What Time Collects. 1964. Woodhill repr. of 1974 ed. o.p.
When Time Was Born. 1966. The Smith 1966 $35.00. ISBN 0-912292-05-9. Splendidly comic treatment of the Garden of Eden story.

SHORT STORY COLLECTION BY FARRELL

Eight Short, Short Stories and Sketches. Arts End 1981 $10.00. ISBN 0-933292-07-4

NONFICTION BY FARRELL

Reflections at Fifty and Other Essays. Vanguard 1954 o.p.

BOOKS ABOUT FARRELL

Fried, Lewis. *Makers of the City.* U. of Mass. Pr. 1990 $30.00. ISBN 0-87023-693-8.
   Examines the portrayal of the American city in the writings of Farrell and others.
Phelps, Donald, ed. *Hearing Out James T. Farrell.* The Smith 1985 $12.95. ISBN 0-912292-
   75-X. Collection of lectures about literature, society, politics, and Farrell's attitude
   toward the art of fiction.
Wald, Alan M. *James T. Farrell: The Revolutionary Socialist Years.* NYU Pr. 1978 o.p.

FAULKNER, WILLIAM. 1897–1962 (NOBEL PRIZE 1949)

William Faulkner was awarded the 1949 Nobel Prize for literature "for his
powerful and artistically independent contribution to the new American novel,"
but it would appear now that he also deserved to win that honor for his
contribution to world literature. Only a few American writers of the twentieth
century really qualify as international modernists, and there can be little doubt
that Faulkner is one of them. When reporting his death, the *Boston Globe*
quoted Faulkner's having once told an interviewer: "Since man is mortal, the
only immortality for him is to leave something behind him that is immortal
since it will always move. That is the artist's way of scribbling 'Kilroy was here'
on the wall of the final and irrevocable oblivion through which he must some
day pass." In those terms, Faulkner left an ineradicable mark deeper than that
of almost any other writer of his times.

Faulkner was a Mississippi writer of great power who was drawn to portraits
of abnormality and decadence. His novels are intense in their character
portrayals of disintegrating southern aristocrats, poor whites, and African
Americans. A complex stream-of-consciousness rhetoric often involves Faulkner in lengthy sentences of anguished power. Most of his tales are set in the
mythical Yoknapatawpha County, Mississippi—a place not found on any map—
and are characterized by the use of many recurring characters from families of
different social levels spanning more than a century. His best subjects are the
old, dying South and the newer materialistic South.

After a brief stint as a flier in the Royal Canadian Air Force near the end of
World War I, Faulkner returned to his home in Oxford, Mississippi. Unable at
first to make a living from his writing, he worked as night superintendent at a
power plant, carpenter, roof painter, and postmaster at the local University of
Mississippi until his growing reputation finally enabled him to place stories in
such popular magazines as the *Saturday Evening Post* and brought him
opportunities to write lucrative Hollywood screenplays. *The Sound and the Fury*
(1929) is considered his first major work. It is told from multiple viewpoints, as
is *As I Lay Dying* (1930), a grotesquely tragicomic story about a family of poor
southern whites. Less experimental in technique than these two works and
therefore an easier introduction to the Yoknapatawpha saga is *Light in August*
(1932), a novel of sure-handed craftsmanship, which successfully blends
violence with pathos. With *Absalom, Absalom!* (1936); the difficult parts of his
famous short novel "The Bear" (as published in *Go Down, Moses,* 1942); and the
allegorical *A Fable* (1954), a non-Yoknapatawpha novel set in France during
World War I; Faulkner returned to an innovative and difficult style that most
readers have trouble with. Yet, interspersed with such works are collections of
easily readable stories originally published in popular magazines, and there
seems to be a growing sentiment among critics that the Snopes trilogy—*The*

Hamlet (1940), *The Town* (1957), and *The Mansion* (1959)—for the most part an example of Faulkner's "moderate" style, could well be among his most important works.

In addition to the Nobel Prize, Faulkner received the Howells Medal of the American Academy of Arts and Letters in 1950, and in 1951 he was given the National Book Award for his *Collected Stories*. For his novel *A Fable* he received the National Book Award for the second time, as well as the Pulitzer Prize in 1955. *The Reivers* (1962) was awarded the Pulitzer Prize in 1963. In 1957 and 1958, he was the University of Virginia's first writer-in-residence, and in January 1959 he accepted an appointment as consultant on contemporary literature to the Alderman Library of that university.

Considering that Faulkner was not without honors in his lifetime and in light of the world recognition that has come to him since then, it is surprising to learn that, when MALCOLM COWLEY edited *The Portable Faulkner* in 1946, he found that almost all of Faulkner's books were out of print. By arranging selections from the works with intelligence and ingenuity to form a continuous chronicle, Cowley deserves much of the credit for making readers aware of the way in which Faulkner was creating a fictive world on a scale grander than that of any novelist since BALZAC (see Vol. 2).

NOVELS BY FAULKNER

Absalom, Absalom! 1936. Random 1991 $10.95. ISBN 0-679-73218-7

As I Lay Dying. 1930. Random 1991 $8.95. ISBN 0-679-73225-X

A Fable. 1954. Random 1977 repr. of 1954 ed. $8.00. ISBN 0-394-72413-5

Flags in the Dust. Random 1974 $9.00. ISBN 0-394-71239-0

The Hamlet: A Novel of the Snopes Family. 1940. Random 1991 $10.00. ISBN 0-679-73653-0. The uncut 1929 novel, compiled from a composite manuscript; adds another chapter to the Faulkner legend and his cosmos of Yoknapatawpha.

Intruder in the Dust. 1948. Random 1991 $9.00. ISBN 0-679-73651-4

Knight's Gambit. Random 1978 $4.95. ISBN 0-394-72729-0

Light in August. 1932. Random 1991 $9.95. ISBN 0-679-73226-8

The Mansion. 1959. Random 1965 $9.00. ISBN 0-394-70282-4

Mosquitoes. 1927. Liveright 1955 $6.95. ISBN 0-685-03090-3

New Orleans Sketches. Random 1968 $13.95. ISBN 0-394-43818-3

Pylon. Random 1987 $4.95. ISBN 0-394-74741-0

Reivers. Random 1966 $8.95. ISBN 0-394-70339-1

Requiem for a Nun. 1951. Random 1975 $9.00. ISBN 0-394-71412-1

Sanctuary. Random 1987 $7.00. ISBN 0-394-74744-5. Throws some light on Faulkner's creative process after the writing of "Sartoris" and "The Sound and the Fury"; of interest mainly to Faulkner specialists.

Sartoris. NAL-Dutton 1983 $3.50. ISBN 0-452-00646-5

Soldiers' Pay. 1926. Liveright 1954 o.p.

The Sound and the Fury. 1929. Random 1991 $8.95. ISBN 0-679-73224-1

Three Famous Short Novels: Spotted Horses, Old Man, and The Bear. Random 1958 $9.00. ISBN 0-394-70149-6. *Spotted Horses:* hilarious account of a horse auction; *Old Man:* story of a convict adrift with a pregnant woman during a flood; *The Bear:* story of a boy coming to terms with the adult world.

The Town. 1957. Random 1961 $7.95. ISBN 0-394-70184-4

The Unvanquished. Random 1991 $9.00. ISBN 0-679-73652-2

Wild Palms. Random 1984 $14.95. ISBN 0-394-60513-6

SHORT STORY COLLECTIONS BY FAULKNER

Collected Stories of William Faulkner. Random 1977 $18.00. ISBN 0-394-72257-4. Forty-two stories from Faulkner's earliest works through 1948.

Go Down, Moses and Other Stories. Random 1991 $9.95. ISBN 0-679-73217-9. Interrelated stories about African Americans in the South.

Selected Short Stories of William Faulkner. Random 1993 $14.50. ISBN 0-679-42478-4

Uncollected Stories of William Faulkner. Random 1981 $17.95. ISBN 0-394-40044-5

POETRY BY FAULKNER

Marble Faun, and a Green Bough. Random 1965 $10.95. ISBN 0-394-40385-1. Faulkner at the beginning of his career; heavily influenced by the Imagists. Includes a fine introduction by Phil Strong.

WORKS BY FAULKNER

The Faulkner Reader. Random 1989 $8.95. ISBN 0-685-28565-0

Portable Faulkner. 1946. Viking Penguin rev. ed. 1977 $9.95. ISBN 0-14-015018-8. The famous volume edited by Malcolm Cowley that turned Faulkner's reputation around.

BOOKS ABOUT FAULKNER

Adams, Richard P. *Faulkner: Myth and Motion.* Princeton U. Pr. 1968 o.p.

Bleikasten, Andre. *The Ink of Melancholy: Faulkner's Novels from "The Sound and the Fury" to "Light in August."* Ind. U. Pr. 1990 $37.95. ISBN 0-253-31200-0. Records 30 years of close reading of four of Faulkner's finest novels.

Bloom, Harold, ed. *William Faulkner.* Chelsea Hse. 1986 $34.95. ISBN 0-87754-652-5. Excellent selection of critical essays.

Blotner, Joseph. *Faulkner: A Biography.* Random 1991 $16.95. ISBN 0-679-73053-2

Brodhead, Richard. *Faulkner: A Collection of Critical Essays.* P-H 1983 $16.50. ISBN 0-13-308288-1. A well-chosen collection of essays by major critics, including Cleanth Brooks on good and evil in Faulkner, Irving Howe on Faulkner's treatment of black people, and Hugh Kenner on Faulkner and the avant-garde.

Brooks, Cleanth. *William Faulkner: First Encounters.* Yale U. Pr. 1985 $11.95. ISBN 0-300-03399-0. Good introduction to Faulkner for the uninitiated.

———. *William Faulkner: The Yoknapatawpha Country.* La. State U. Pr. 1990 $16.95. ISBN 0-8071-1601-7. An analysis of the stories and novels that take place in Faulkner's imaginary country.

———. *William Faulker: Toward Yoknapatawpha and Beyond.* La. State U. Pr. 1990 $16.95. ISBN 0-8071-1602-5

Budd, Louis J., ed. *On Faulkner: The Best from American Literature.* Duke 1989 $33.50. ISBN 0-8223-0960-2

Connolly, Thomas E. *Faulkner's World: A Directory of His People and Synopses of Actions in His Published Works.* U. Pr. of Amer. 1988 $56.75. ISBN 0-8191-5703-1. Includes all characters of any significance, named and unnamed, with chronological arrangement by conception or execution; detailed introduction and indexes of titles and characters.

Davis, Thadious M. *Faulkner's "Negro": Art and the Southern Context.* La. State U. Pr. 1983 $25.00. ISBN 0-8071-1047-7

Dowling, David. *William Faulkner.* St. Martin 1989 $24.95. ISBN 0-312-02058-9. A general introduction to Faulkner, with bibliography and index; appendix of the history of Yoknapatawpha County.

Ford, Margaret P., and Suzanne Kincaid. *Who's Who in Faulkner.* La. State U. Pr. 1966 o.p.

Fowler, Doreen, ed. *Faulkner and Women.* U. Pr. of Miss. 1986 $35.00. ISBN 0-87805-311-5. Provides a very broad range of critical approaches and equally diverse interpretations.

———. *Faulkner and Race.* U. Pr. of Miss. 1988 $35.00. ISBN 0-87805-328-X. Fifteen critics enthusiastically cover Faulkner's writing as it deals with race.

Friedman, Alan W. *William Faulkner.* Continuum 1985 $18.95. ISBN 0-8044-2218-4. A useful general study of Faulkner's life and works.

Gresset, Michael. *A Faulkner Chronology.* U. Pr. of Miss. 1985 $10.95. ISBN 0-87805-229-1

————. *Fascination: Faulkner's Fiction, 1919–1936*. Duke 1988 $45.00. ISBN 0-8223-0811-8. Shows how certain image patterns of Faulkner's poetry are transformed in the early novels of 1924–32 into brilliant scenes charged with emotion and symbolism.

Guerard, Albert T. *The Triumph of the Novel: Dickens, Dostoevsky, Faulkner*. U. Ch. Pr. 1982 $9.50. ISBN 0-226-31034-5

Gwin, Minrose C. *The Feminine and Faulkner: Reading (Beyond) Sexual Difference*. U. of Tenn. Pr. 1990 $24.50. ISBN 0-87049-619-0. Draws on a wide range of contemporary criticism and shows that Faulkner sensed more about women than he knew.

Harrington, Gary. *Faulkner's Fables of Creativity: The Non-Yoknapatawpha Novels*. U. of Ga. Pr. 1990 $30.00. ISBN 0-8203-1098-0. Helps to interpret Faulkner outside the "landscape" of the Yoknapatawpha novels.

Hoffman, Daniel. *Faulkner's Country Matters: Folklore and Fable in Yoknapatawpha*. La. State U. Pr. 1989 $22.50. ISBN 0-8071-1562-2. Focuses on Faulkner's use of folklore and fable in his fiction.

Hoffmann, Frederick J. *William Faulkner*. Macmillan 1966 $19.95. ISBN 0-8057-0244-X. One of the best introductions to Faulkner's work.

Howe, Irving. *William Faulkner: A Critical Study*. I. R. Dee 4th ed. 1991 $12.95. ISBN 0-929587-69-3. An early (1952) and basic study.

Karl, Frederick R. *William Faulkner: American Writer*. Fawcett 1990 $16.95. ISBN 0-449-90352-4. Focuses on Faulkner's family background and incidents from all stages of his development.

Kreiswirth, Martin. *William Faulkner: The Making of a Novelist*. U. of Ga. Pr. 1984 $22.50. ISBN 0-8203-0672-X

Kuyk, Dirk, Jr. *Sutpen's Design: Interpreting Faulkner's "Absalom, Absalom!"* U. Pr. of Va. 1990 $24.50. ISBN 0-8139-1260-1. Perceives Sutpen, the protagonist of *Absalom, Absalom!*, as author of his own convoluted and misperceived narrative, as his quest for dynasty leads to one failure after another.

Lockyer, Judith. *Ordered by Words: Language and Narration in the Novels of William Faulkner*. S. Ill. U. Pr. 1991 $27.50. ISBN 0-8093-1702-8

Matthews, John T. *The Play of Faulkner's Language*. Cornell Univ. Pr. 1982 $32.50. ISBN 0-8014-1413-X. An intricate, specialized study of the way Faulkner's language works in four of his major fictions: *The Sound and The Fury, Absalom, Absalom!, The Hamlet*, and *Go Down Moses*, and, less fully, in *Mosquitoes* and *Sartoris*.

Millgate, Michael. *The Achievement of William Faulkner*. U. of Ga. Pr. 1989 $14.95. ISBN 0-8203-1142-1. One of the best studies of Faulkner's style and themes.

Minter, David. *William Faulkner: His Life and Work*. Johns Hopkins 1982 $15.95. ISBN 0-8018-2463-X. An important psychological biography.

Moreland, Richard C. *Faulkner and Modernism: Revision and Rewriting*. U. of Wis. Pr. 1990 $37.50. ISBN 0-299-12500-9. Suggests the ways in which Faulkner's use of previously silenced voices—"white trash," blacks and women—begins to articulate alternatives to his culture's dominant discourses.

Morris, Wesley. *Reading Faulkner*. U. of Wis. Pr. 1989 $24.95. ISBN 0-299-12220-4. Emphasizes Faulkner's interest in narration.

Morris, Willie. *Faulkner's Mississippi*. Oxmoor Hse. 1990 $50.00. ISBN 0-8487-1052-5

Parker, Robert D. *Faulkner and the Novelistic Imagination*. U. of Ill. Pr. 1985 $19.95. ISBN 0-252-01155-4. Skillfully written and convincing biographical analysis of four novels: *As I Lay Dying, Sanctuary, Light in August*, and *Absalom, Absalom!*

Pearce, Richard. *The Politics of Narration: James Joyce, William Faulkner and Virginia Woolf*. Rutgers U. Pr. 1991 $37.00. ISBN 0-8135-1656-0. Argues that dominant cultures reshape such features as narrative voice and the implied contract between narrator and audience.

Pilkington, John. *The Heart of Yoknapatawpha*. U. Pr. of Miss. 1981 $10.95. ISBN 0-87805-179-1. A solid and intelligent reading of the chosen works.

Putzel, Max. *Genius of Place: William Faulkner's Triumphant Beginnings*. La. State U. Pr. 1985 $37.50. ISBN 0-8071-1183-X. Examines the growth of Faulkner's art through a reconstruction of the chronology of his writing, showing how Faulkner's concern with short fiction allowed him to write his best novels.

Ricks, Beatrice, ed. *William Faulkner: A Bibliography of Secondary Works*. Scarecrow 1981 $49.50. ISBN 0-8108-1323-8. Over 8,000 entries, intelligently organized, with annotations and topical index.

Ross, Stephen. *Fiction's Inexhaustible Voice: Speech and Writing in Faulkner*. U. of Ga. Pr. 1989 $35.00. ISBN 0-8203-1045-X

Schwartz, Lawrence H. *Creating Faulkner's Reputation: The Politics of Modern Literary Criticism*. U. of Tenn. Pr. 1988 $32.50. ISBN 0-87049-565-8. Carefully documents the factors that brought about the wide acceptance now bestowed upon Faulkner.

Shead, James A. *Figures of Division: William Faulkner's Major Novels*. Routledge Chapman & Hall 1987 $29.50. ISBN 0-416-01261-2. Examines rhetorical plays that underlie the natural division of the races throughout Faulkner's novels.

Sundquist, Eric J. *Faulkner: The House Divided*. Johns Hopkins 1985 $11.95. ISBN 0-8018-3164-4

Taylor, Walter. *Faulkner's Search for a South*. U. of Ill. Pr. 1982 $27.50. ISBN 0-252-00943-6

Urgo, Joseph R. *Faulkner's Apocrypha: A Fable, Snopes, and the Spirit of Human Rebellion*. U. Pr. of Miss. 1989 $30.00. ISBN 0-87805-404-9. Study that reflects some of the best characteristics of Faulkner criticism.

Vickery, Olga W. *Novels of William Faulkner: A Critical Interpretation*. La. State U. Pr. rev. ed. 1964 $32.50. ISBN 0-8071-0817-0. An unsurpassed pioneer interpretation.

Volpe, Edmond. *A Reader's Guide to William Faulkner*. Hippocrene Bks. 1975 o.p.

Wadlington, Warwick. *Reading Faulknerian Tragedy*. Cornell Univ. Pr. 1987 $28.95. ISBN 0-8014-2011-3. Focuses on the aesthetics of Faulkner's tragedy and the reader's active collaboration with the multiple voices created by Faulkner in his works.

Welshimer, Linda. *William Faulkner: Four Decades of Criticism*. Mich. St. U. Pr. 1973 o.p. The first important collection of Faulkner criticism.

FITZGERALD, F(RANCIS) SCOTT (KEY). 1896–1940

F. Scott Fitzgerald remains one of the best-known American authors of the twentieth century in spite of the fact that only occasionally did he write works of genuine distinction. The uneven quality of his output may be attributed in part to his desiring fame, wealth, and a good time at least as much as he wanted to be a literary artist. Fitzgerald was born in St. Paul, Minnesota, spent much of his childhood in upstate New York, and attended private schools in St. Paul and New Jersey before enrolling at Princeton University in 1913. He left in 1917 without taking a degree. While serving as an army lieutenant at Camp Sheridan near Montgomery, Alabama, he met and fell in love with Zelda Sayre, a beautiful and popular southern belle who had many suitors. When their engagement was broken because it seemed unlikely that Scott could support Zelda in her accustomed style, he wrote in cynical despair *This Side of Paradise* (1920). The spectacular success of this first of the lost-generation novels enabled Scott and Zelda to marry not long after its publication. They then embarked on a glamorous and well-publicized way of life that saw them traveling back and forth between the best hotels and speakeasies of America and the most fashionable resorts of Europe. Somehow Fitzgerald managed to write his best novel, *The Great Gatsby* (1925), in spite of the many distractions around him, but the wild lifestyle of the Fitzgeralds took its inevitable toll. Zelda gradually lapsed into incurable mental illness. After 1930 she spent much of her life in mental sanitariums before finally dying in an asylum fire in 1948.

Fitzgerald's writings after *Gatsby* are of uneven quality. *Tender Is the Night* (1934), his most ambitious novel, is a moving psychological narrative but one so close to the Fitzgeralds' own experiences that it lacks the detachment that is probably necessary for full artistic control. To pay for Zelda's medical expenses and their daughter's education in private schools, not to mention his own indulgences, Fitzgerald turned out numerous stories and articles for popular magazines between the time of the stock market crash in 1929 and his own fatal heart attack in 1940. While in Hollywood in 1937, he met the columnist Sheila Graham, and it was she who helped him combat his alcoholism and encouraged him to write *The Last Tycoon* (published posthumously in 1941). Only occasionally did Fitzgerald's talent rise to the potential suggested by *The Great Gatsby*. His short story "Babylon Revisited" (1930) may convey better than any other work of fiction the atmosphere of Paris before and after the Fall; and some critics feel that *The Last Tycoon* might have been equal to *Gatsby* if Fitzgerald had lived long enough to polish and resolve the story. That short novel was edited by Fitzgerald's friend from Princeton days, EDMUND WILSON, who later collected other late pieces, notebook entries, and letters to and from Fitzgerald in a volume appropriately called *The Crack-up* (1945). JOHN CHEEVER wrote that "In Fitzgerald there is a thrilling sense of knowing exactly where one is—the city, the resort, the hotel, the decade and the time of day. His greatest innovation was to use social custom, clothing, overheard music, not as history but as an expression of his acute awareness of the meaning of time."

The tormented yet glamorous lives of Scott and Zelda Fitzgerald have intrigued readers of several generations—so much so that they themselves have become semifictional characters whose lives have been dramatized in movies and television specials as well as depicted in fiction by other writers. And every few years it seems that a new biography promising fresh revelations is published to critical acclaim and wide public interest. The popular attractiveness of the Fitzgeralds has tended to obscure the fact that Scott was indeed a writer of considerable talent who occasionally flashed into genius. His best works have been mainstays in college classrooms for half a century and have thus evoked almost as much criticism and scholarship as has been devoted to any American writer of the modern period.

NOVELS BY FITZGERALD

The Beautiful and the Damned. 1921. Macmillan 1988 $6.95. ISBN 0-02-019970-8
The Great Gatsby. 1925. Macmillan 1992 $8.95. ISBN 0-02-019881-7. Jay Gatsby's saga as the paradigm for the quintessential American story—the mysterious stranger's rise from rags to riches and his clash with those who are already very rich.
The Last Tycoon. 1941. Macmillan 1988 $4.95. ISBN 0-02-019950-3
Taps at Reveille. 1936. Macmillan 1976 $37.50. ISBN 0-684-14742-4
Tender Is the Night. 1954. Macmillan 1988 $5.95. ISBN 0-02-019930-9
This Side of Paradise. 1920. Macmillan 1988 $6.95. ISBN 0-02-019920-1

POETRY BY FITZGERALD

Poems, 1911 to 1940. Bruccoli 1981 $11.95. ISBN 0-89723-026-4. Over 200 poems, with six manuscript pages in facsimile, notes, and an incisive, valuable introductory essay by poet James Dickey.

SHORT STORY COLLECTIONS BY FITZGERALD

Babylon Revisited and Other Stories. Macmillan 1988 $5.95. ISBN 0-02-019980-5
The Basil and Josephine Stories. Macmillan 1987 $4.95. ISBN 0-02-019870-1
The Pat Hobby Stories. 1962. Macmillan 1988 $5.95. ISBN 0-02-019910-4. Humorous stories of a fading filmscript writer in Hollywood.
Six Tales of the Jazz Age and Other Stories. Macmillan 1966 $8.95. ISBN 0-684-71762-X
Stories of F. Scott Fitzgerald. Macmillan 1988 $7.95. ISBN 0-02-019940-6

Works by Fitzgerald

Afternoon of an Author: A Selection of Uncollected Stories and Essays. Scribner 1981
$22.50. ISBN 0-684-16469-8. With an introduction by Arthur A. Mizener.
The Crack-Up. New Dir. Pr. 1956 $9.95. ISBN 0-8112-0051-5
The Cruise of the Rolling Junk. Bruccoli 1976 $25.00. ISBN 0-89723-008-6
The Letters of F. Scott Fitzgerald. Macmillan 1981 $55.00. ISBN 0-684-16476-0
The Vegetable. Macmillan 1987 $4.95. ISBN 0-02-019880-9

Books about Fitzgerald

Allen, Joan M. *Candles and Carnival Lights: The Catholic Sensibility of F. Scott Fitzgerald.*
NYU Pr. 1978 o.p. Intelligent study of the effects of Fitzgerald's Catholic upbringing
on his life and art; with index and copious footnotes.
Bloom, Harold, ed. *F. Scott Fitzgerald.* Chelsea Hse. 1986 $29.95. ISBN 0-87754-650-9.
Eight essays providing a useful introduction to the novel for undergraduates; with a
chronology and selected bibliography.
———, ed. *F. Scott Fitzgerald's The Great Gatsby.* Chelsea Hse. 1986 $24.95. ISBN 0-
87754-901-X. Excellent selection of critical essays.
Bruccoli, Matthew J. *The Last of the Novelists: F. Scott Fitzgerald and "The Last Tycoon."*
S. Ill. U. Pr. 1977 o.p.
———. *Scott and Ernest: The Authority of Failure and the Authority of Success.* S. Ill. U.
Pr. 1980 o.p. Comparative study of Fitzgerald and Hemingway.
———. *Some Sort of Epic Grandeur: The Life of F. Scott Fitzgerald.* Carroll & Graf 1993
$16.95. ISBN 0-88184-907-3. ". . . a single, authoritative record that deserves to be
called 'definitive'" (*Journal of Modern Lit.*).
———, ed. *New Essays on "The Great Gatsby."* Cambridge U. Pr. 1985 $22.95. ISBN 0-
521-26589-4. Six essays that assess *Gatsby*'s greatness.
———. *F. Scott Fitzgerald: A Descriptive Bibliography.* U. of Pittsburgh Pr. 1988 $100.00.
ISBN 0-8229-3560-0. Expanded bibliography that includes 331 original periodical
appearances in addition to the 42 volumes published during Fitzgerald's life and
posthumously.
Buttitta, Tony. *The Lost Summer: A Personal Memoir of F. Scott Fitzgerald.* St. Martin 1987
$7.95. ISBN 0-312-01061-3. Memoir of Buttitta's short-lived friendship with Fitzger-
ald that documents the novelist's views of other big-name authors and his feelings of
inadequacy and guilt regarding Zelda.
Chambers, John B. *The Novels of F. Scott Fitzgerald.* St. Martin 1989 $35.00. ISBN 0-312-
02803-2. Interesting and useful study of the four novels Fitzgerald published in his
lifetime.
Donaldson, Scott, ed. *Critical Essays on F. Scott Fitzgerald's "The Great Gatsby."* G. K.
Hall 1984 $35.00. ISBN 0-8161-8679-0. Twenty-three essays covering just about every
conceivable topic and approach; includes correspondence with Fitzgerald discussing *Gatsby* and Seides's review of the book.
Eble, Kenneth. *F. Scott Fitzgerald.* Macmillan 1977 $19.95. ISBN 0-8057-7183-2. A broad
examination of Fitzgerald's life and works, focusing on his major themes and
development as a writer.
Gallo, Rose A. *F. Scott Fitzgerald.* Continuum 1978 o.p. A general introduction to
Fitzgerald's life and works; appropriate for general readers.
Kuehl, John. *Dear Scott Dear Max: The Fitzgerald-Perkins Correspondence.* Macmillan
1991 $65.00. ISBN 0-02-538481-3
———. *F. Scott Fitzgerald.* Macmillan 1991 $20.00. ISBN 0-8057-8332-6. Offers a richness
and new dimension to our understanding of Fitzgerald's fiction and of the writer
himself.
Lee, A. Robert, ed. *Scott Fitzgerald: The Promises of Life.* St. Martin 1989 $35.00. ISBN 0-
312-02423-1. Contains nine essays, all written by established British critics, that treat
in turn all of his novels.
Mellow, James R. *Invented Lives: The Marriage of F. Scott and Zelda Fitzgerald.* HM 1984
o.p.

Mizener, Arthur, ed. *F. Scott Fitzgerald: A Collection of Critical Essays*. P-H 1963 $19.95. ISBN 0-13-320853-2

_____. *The Far Side of Paradise: A Biography of F. Scott Fitzgerald*. Avon 1984 o.p. A biography that does full justice to the writer as a man representative of his times.

Turnbull, Andrew. *Scott Fitzgerald*. Scribner 1982 o.p. "First-rate biography which displaces every work before it, including the earnest and admirable pioneering effort of Arthur Mizener a decade ago" (*Atlantic*). Written by a man who knew Fitzgerald and who interviewed everyone he could find who had known him.

Way, Brian. *F. Scott Fitzgerald and the Art of Social Fiction*. St. Martin 1980 $25.00. ISBN 0-312-27950-7. A brilliantly perceptive study of Fitzgerald's fiction, stressing the social context of his art; particularly useful are Way's comparisons with Henry James and Edith Wharton.

FROST, ROBERT (LEE). 1874–1963

Frost was, in a sense, our national poet laureate. Not only was he made Vermont's official poet laureate, but he received a special congressional medal during the Eisenhower administration and was invited to read a poem at the inauguration of President John F. Kennedy in January 1961. Such official recognition was ironic in view of the fact that his first books of poetry had to be published in England. But this says as much about the moribund state of poetry in the United States at the turn of the century as it does about any experimentalism on Frost's part. Such ironies involved with the line between innovation and official recognition are very much part of Frost's career. Frost's poetry is written in traditional language and form, but its content is often at odds with its surface features. Despite the easily recognizable subjects of pastoral quietism and New England dutifulness, Frost's poetry is often entangled with the issues of nihilism and despair. Frost did win recognition, however, including the Pulitzer Prize in 1924, 1931, 1937, and 1943, and honorary degrees from 17 colleges.

Although descended from New Englanders, Frost was born and raised in San Francisco; he returned to New England in 1885 after his father's death. He studied at Dartmouth College and Harvard University, but gave up college for teaching. In 1912 he went to England, where he lived for three years. It was there that he published *A Boy's Will* (1913) and *North of Boston* (1914). After his return to the United States in 1915, he taught at various colleges and helped found the Bread Loaf School in Middlebury, Vermont. Frost's reputation grew after 1915 and he was much sought after as a speaker and a teacher. His outward appearance as a simple country sage concealed a poet and craftsman of considerable talent filled with pain and ambiguity. Peter Davison writes that "His [Frost's] was the poetry of experience, and it came hard and late." Poverty and disaster marked much of his life: his only sister was mentally ill; his wife was unhappy in their marriage; two children died in infancy, one by suicide, one after childbirth, and at least one was mentally ill.

Frost will no doubt be read first as a traditional poet, but the discriminating will also continue to turn to him as the representative of a special brand of modernist irony. His prose writings about the art and craft of poetry, although limited in volume, have had a considerable influence, and they contain many clues to his elaborate cunning and quick imagination, as well as his use of colloquial rhythms and conscious artifice. He was an artist who took great pains to hide his pain and still continue to speak truthfully about what he had seen. Both President Kennedy and ARCHIBALD MACLEISH spoke on October 26, 1963, at a special Amherst College convocation held in conjunction with the dedication of the $3.5 million library built in honor of the poet.

POETRY BY FROST

The Poetry of Robert Frost. H. Holt & Co. 1979 $12.95. ISBN 0-8050-0501-3. Selection of Frost's most popular poems, spanning his entire career.

Selected Poems. Ed. by Robert Graves. HarBraceJ 1963 $18.00. ISBN 0-03-012060-8

WORKS BY FROST

The Selected Letters of Robert Frost. Comp. by Lawrence Thompson. H. Holt & Co. 1964 o.p.

BOOKS ABOUT FROST

Bloom, Harold, ed. *Robert Frost.* Chelsea Hse. 1986 $29.95. ISBN 0-87754-626-6

Bober, Natalie S. *A Restless Spirit: The Story of Robert Frost.* H. Holt & Co. 1991 $19.95. ISBN 0-8050-1672-4. Chronicles the struggles and the triumphs that shaped Pulitzer Prize-winning poet Robert Frost.

Burnshaw, Stanley. *Robert Frost Himself.* Braziller 1989 $12.95. ISBN 0-8076-1234-0. Provides a view of the complex, elusive Frost, as poet and person, that is at once searching and balanced.

Gerber, Philip L., ed. *Critical Essays on Robert Frost.* G. K. Hall 1982 $45.00. ISBN 0-8161-8442-9

———. *Robert Frost.* Macmillan 1982 $19.95. ISBN 0-8057-7348-7. A good general introduction to Frost's life and poetry, with discussions of the major work.

Holland, Norman N. *The Brain of Robert Frost: A Cognitive Approach to Literature.* Routledge 1988 $39.50. ISBN 0-415-90023-9. Attempts to make connections between what physiologists tell us about the brain and what might be going on there when we read and interpret a poem.

Lathem, Edward C. *Robert Frost Poetry and Prose.* H. Holt & Co. 1984 $13.95. ISBN 0-8050-0245-6

Marcus, Mordecai. *Poems of Robert Frost: An Explication.* Macmillan 1991 $35.00. ISBN 0-8161-7267-6. Analyzes all of the 355 poems that appear in *The Poetry of Robert Frost.*

Monteiro, George. *Robert Frost and the New England Renaissance.* U. Pr. of Ky. 1988 $19.00. ISBN 0-8131-1649-X. Fresh treatment of the influence of Dickinson, Thoreau, and Emerson on the poetry and thought of Robert Frost.

Oster, Judith. *Toward Robert Frost: The Reader and the Poet.* U. of Ga. Pr. 1991 $45.00. ISBN 0-8203-1322-X. Focuses on Frost as a poet who needed readers yet feared what their interpretations would do to his creations.

Poirier, Richard. *Robert Frost: The Work of Knowing.* Stanford U. Pr. 1990 $42.50. ISBN 0-8047-1741-9. Poirier's work is reissued with a new afterword by the author and a new foreword by John Hollander.

Pritchard, William H. *Frost: A Literary Life Reconsidered.* OUP 1985 $8.95. ISBN 0-19-503730-8. An admirable study, gracefully written by a critic who is a sensitive reader of poetry; deftly moves between Frost's life and art.

Tharpe, Jac, ed. *Frost: Centennial Essays.* U. Pr. of Miss. 1974 $10.00. ISBN 0-87805-055-8

Thompson, Lawrence. *Robert Frost: A Biography.* H. Holt & Co. 1981 $25.00. ISBN 0-03-050921-1. The official biography on Frost, well researched and heavily documented.

Trikha, Manorama, ed. *Robert Frost: An Anthology of Recent Criticism.* Advent NY 1990 $30.00. ISBN 81-85433-01-1

Vail, Dennis. *Robert Frost's Imagery and the Poetic Consciousness.* Tex. Tech. Univ. Pr. 1976 $8.00. ISBN 0-89672-022-5

Wilcox, Earl J., ed. *Robert Frost: The Man and the Poet.* Univ. Central AR Pr. 2nd ed. 1989 $36.25. ISBN 0-944436-08-0. Twelve essays, many by distinguished critics; essentially fresh studies despite a turbulent decade of metacriticism.

GLASGOW, ELLEN. 1874–1945

Born in Richmond, Virginia, of a mother who traced her ancestry to the Cavalier settlers of Tidewater Virginia and a father who descended from the

Scotch-Irish of the Shenandoah Valley, Ellen Glasgow was a writer whose divided background helps explain her ability to combine romantic sensibility with tough-minded realism. For the Virginia Edition of her works, published by Scribner in 1938 and now out of print, she chose 12 of her 18 novels and divided them into two main groups. What she called novels of character and comedies of manners consist of five works: *The Battle-Ground* (1902); *The Deliverance* (1904); *They Stooped to Folly* (1929); *Virginia* (1913); and *Barren Ground* (1925). The remaining seven novels she grouped under the heading "social history in the form of fiction." Covering almost 100 years of life in the Old Dominion, they are perhaps better read in historical sequence than in the order in which they were originally published: *The Miller of Old Church* (1911); *The Romantic Comedians* (1926); *The Voice of the People* (1900); *The Romance of a Plain Man* (1909); *Life and Gabriella* (1916); *The Sheltered Life* (1932); and *Vein of Iron* (1935). The new prefaces that she wrote for each volume of the Virginia Edition form a valuable record of her literary growth and a treatise on novel writing that compares favorably with the prefaces that HENRY JAMES wrote for the New York Edition of his works. With the addition of an introduction to the one novel she published subsequently, the Pulitzer Prize-winning *In This Our Life* (1941), these prefaces were brought together and published as *A Certain Measure* (1943). *The Woman Within* (1954), her own story of her inner life, parallels her fiction in its account of a courageous woman who refused to become a victim of the outmoded codes of chivalry and male domination that characterized the Old South of her heritage. She remains a transitional figure of considerable importance in the literary history of America, not only because she was a conscious craftsperson with high standards for her art, but also because, as the first Southern woman writer to break through from romantic conventions to high-quality ironic and realistic literature, she showed the way for many of the southern women writers who have followed her.

NOVELS BY GLASGOW

Barren Ground. 1925. HarBraceJ 1985 $12.95. ISBN 0-15-610685-X
The Descendant. 1897. Ed. by Elizabeth Hardwick. Ayer 1977 repr. of 1926 ed. $26.00. ISBN 0-405-10046-9. Glasgow's first novel, originally published anonymously, republished with an introduction by Elizabeth Hardwick.
In This Our Life. 1941. Amereon 1981 $19.95. ISBN 0-89190-152-3
The Romantic Comedians. 1926. Ed. by Elizabeth Hardwick. Ayer 1977 repr. of 1926 ed. $30.00. ISBN 0-405-10047-7
The Sheltered Life. 1932. Amereon repr. of 1932 ed. $19.95. ISBN 0-88411-646-8
Vein of Iron. 1935. HarBraceJ 1967 $7.95. ISBN 0-15-693476-0
Virginia. 1913. Viking Penguin 1989 $4.95. ISBN 0-14-039072-3
The Voice of the People. 1900. NCUP 1972 $17.95. ISBN 0-8084-0030-4

POETRY BY GLASGOW

The Freeman and Other Poems. Americanist 1973 $4.85. ISBN 0-910120-00-5

BOOKS ABOUT GLASGOW

Auchincloss, Louis. *Ellen Glasgow.* Bks. Demand repr. of 1964 ed. $20.00. ISBN 0-317-29467-9. Perceptive commentary on Glasgow's 19 novels, recognizing the author as a transitional figure in the development of realism in Southern literature.
Godbold, E. Stanly, Jr. *Ellen Glasgow and the Woman Within.* La. State U. Pr. 1972 $37.50. ISBN 0-8071-0040-4. Furnishes a complete portrait of Glasgow as she relates to the backdrop of Southern literary history; with a bibliography and index.
McDowell, Frederick P. *Ellen Glasgow and the Ironic Art of Fiction.* U. of Wis. Pr. 1962 $6.95. ISBN 0-299-02114-9

Richards, Marion K. *Ellen Glasgow's Development As a Novelist.* Mouton 1971 $34.70.
ISBN 90-2791-606-3. Discusses Glasgow's early novels against a background of her
life and career; includes a selected bibliography.
Rouse, Blair. *Ellen Glasgow.* Irvington 1962 $17.95. ISBN 0-89197-745-7. Highlights
Glasgow's artistic skills and her ability to evoke life in Virginia.
Saunders, Catherine E. *Writing the Margins: Edith Wharton, Ellen Glasgow, and the
Literary Tradition of the Ruined Woman.* HUP 1987 $5.00. ISBN 0-674-96235-4
Thiebaux, Marcelle. *Ellen Glasgow.* Continuum 1982 $18.95. ISBN 0-8044-2872-7. An
analysis of Glasgow's fiction, with a biography, chronology, and bibliography.

H. D.

[SEE Doolittle, Hilda in this chapter.]

HEMINGWAY, ERNEST. 1899–1961 (NOBEL PRIZE 1954)

The announcement in early 1985 that an annual Ernest Hemingway Award
would be presented for the best novel published in English anywhere in the
world seemed fitting recognition for this great American author; as Charles
Poore said, Hemingway "may be the strongest influence in literature that this
age will give to posterity." Today, it seems apparent that Hemingway was one of
the literary giants of the twentieth century. Only WILLIAM FAULKNER among
American writers after HENRY JAMES can claim equal stature with Hemingway,
but, whereas Faulkner made Yoknapatawpha County of Mississippi seem
universal and mythical in the broadest sense, Hemingway quite literally was an
international writer, taking most of the world as his range of coverage, from
Upper Michigan to "the green hills of Africa." Some members of the academic
and literary establishments have long taken a somewhat patronizing attitude
toward Hemingway, questioning the validity of his macho image and finding his
ideas either too conservative or too superficial. Nevertheless, he seems more
firmly entrenched than ever as one of the modern masters.

Hemingway was born in Oak Park, near Chicago, the son of a doctor who
loved outdoor sports and instilled in his son what were long considered
masculine values. After graduation from high school, Hemingway gave up
college to serve a journalistic apprenticeship with the *Kansas City Star*. He went
to Italy as an ambulance driver in World War I, joined the Italian infantry, and
was severely wounded. As a correspondent, he covered disturbances in the Near
East, and about 1921 settled with other American expatriates in Paris. His first
books were published there. *The Torrents of Spring* (1926), a satiric burlesque of
SHERWOOD ANDERSON's style, really acknowledges his debt to Anderson, who
with GERTRUDE STEIN was his teacher in the natural rhythms of American
speech. His first successful novel, *The Sun Also Rises* (1926), is made up almost
entirely of the conversations of a group of the "lost generation" artists and
writers in Paris. *Men without Women* (1927) deals with deadpan gangsters and
matadors. He used the Italy of World War I as the background for the love story
of an English nurse and an American soldier in *A Farewell to Arms* (1929).

In 1927 Hemingway returned to America and in 1930 bought a home in Key
West, the scene of *To Have and Have Not* (1937), which he considered "not so
good." In 1936 he went to Spain at the beginning of the bloody civil war. His
play *The Fifth Column* (1938) and his greatest novel, *For Whom the Bell Tolls*
(1940), were the matured results of his Spanish experiences. For his many and
varied services in World War II, he was decorated with a Bronze Star. While on
assignment for *Look* magazine in 1954, he and his wife (he was married four
times) had two narrow escapes when two planes on which they were traveling

crashed in Africa. Seven years later, in declining health, partly as a result of injuries suffered in these crashes, he shot himself in his home in Ketchum, Idaho. With hindsight it is impossible to avoid the knowledge that Hemingway had always been preoccupied with the theme of self-destruction.

In addition to his steady production of fiction, Hemingway wrote such distinguished works of nonfiction as *Death in the Afternoon* (1932), a vigorous account of bullfighting in Spain; *The Green Hills of Africa* (1935), memorable not only for descriptions of big game hunting on an African safari but for campfire discussions on life and literature; and *A Moveable Feast* (1964), a series of vivid character sketches about people he knew in Paris during the 1920s. In his foreword, Hemingway admitted that much of *A Moveable Feast* might be considered semifictional, but his portraits of Scott and Zelda Fitzgerald, Gertrude Stein, FORD MADOX FORD, and others are generally considered psychologically accurate. Almost all of Hemingway's fugitive journalistic writings from his high school days through two world wars to his last years were collected in three volumes—*Ernest Hemingway's Apprenticeship*; *Ernest Hemingway, Cub Reporter*; and *By Line: Ernest Hemingway*.

NOVELS BY HEMINGWAY

Across the River and into the Trees. 1950. Macmillan 1988 $5.95. ISBN 0-02-051920-6

A Farewell to Arms. 1929. Macmillan 1987 $10.95. ISBN 0-317-56218-5

For Whom the Bell Tolls. 1940. Macmillan 1987 $6.95. ISBN 0-02-051850-1. Hemingway's Spanish Civil War experiences transmuted into this novel.

The Garden of Eden. 1987. Macmillan 1987 $18.95. ISBN 0-684-18693-4. Posthumously published novel based loosely on certain autobiographical aspects of Hemingway's young manhood and his first two marriages; highly readable.

Islands in the Stream. Bantam 1984 $4.50. ISBN 0-553-25007-8. Hemingway's last novel, about an aging man spending his last years in Cuba.

The Old Man and the Sea. 1952. Macmillan 1987 $4.95. ISBN 0-02-051910-9. Allegorical tale of human desire and disappointment told through the story of an old man's efforts to bring in a giant tuna.

The Sun Also Rises. 1926. Macmillan 1987 $5.95. ISBN 0-02-051870-6

To Have and Have Not. 1937. Macmillan 1987 $5.95. ISBN 0-02-051880-3

The Torrents of Spring. 1926. Macmillan 1987 $30.00. ISBN 0-02-550750-8

SHORT STORY COLLECTIONS BY HEMINGWAY

The Complete Short Stories of Ernest Hemingway. Macmillan 1991 $16.95. ISBN 0-02-033200-9

In Our Time. Macmillan 1987 $3.95. ISBN 0-02-051810-2. Collection of stories of the Michigan wilderness, focusing on physical action, outdoor adventure, and the brutality of natural forces.

Men Without Women. Macmillan 1988 $4.95. ISBN 0-02-051890-0

Nick Adams Stories. Macmillan 1987 $40.00. ISBN 0-02-550780-X. Stories of the young Nick Adams's passage into manhood; includes "The Killers," in which Nick, working in a diner, overhears two hired killers planning to murder an ex-boxer.

The Snows of Kilimanjaro and Other Stories. 1961. Macmillan 1987 $4.95. ISBN 0-02-051830-7

Winner Take Nothing. 1933. Scribner 1981 $4.95. ISBN 0-684-17426-X. Short stories.

NONFICTION BY HEMINGWAY

A Moveable Feast. 1964. Macmillan 1987 $5.95. ISBN 0-02-051960-5

Death in the Afternoon. 1932. Macmillan 1978 $45.00. ISBN 0-684-15750-0

Green Hills of Africa. 1935. Macmillan 1987 $5.95. ISBN 0-02-051930-3

Men at War. Outlet Bk. Co. 1991 $12.99. ISBN 0-517-06660-2

POETRY BY HEMINGWAY

Complete Poems. U. of Nebr. Pr. rev. ed. 1992 $9.95. ISBN 0-8032-7259-6

WORKS BY HEMINGWAY

The Enduring Hemingway: An Anthology of a Lifetime in Literature. Ed. by Charles Scribner, Jr. Kelley 1974 o.p. *A Farewell to Arms* and *The Old Man and the Sea* as well as a generous selection of other writings.

Ernest Hemingway: Selected Letters, 1917–1961. Macmillan 1989 $50.00. ISBN 0-02-550941-1

The Fifth Column and Four Stories of the Spanish Civil War. Macmillan 1978 $35.00. ISBN 0-684-15815-9. Embodies the author's faith in the Spanish Loyalist cause and the destiny of the individual; of the stories, "The Denunciation" stands out.

Hemingway Reader. Macmillan 1977 $50.00. ISBN 0-684-15164-2

BOOKS ABOUT HEMINGWAY

Baker, Carlos. *Ernest Hemingway: A Life Story.* Macmillan 1988 $12.95. ISBN 0-02-001690-5. The definitive biography and one of the best of any modern writer.

———. *Hemingway, the Writer As Artist.* Princeton U. Pr. 1972 $42.00. ISBN 0-691-06231-5

Benson, Jackson J., ed. *New Critical Approaches to the Short Stories of Ernest Hemingway.* Duke 1991 $19.95. ISBN 0-8223-1067-8. Valuable as one of the few studies of Hemingway's short fiction.

Burgess, Anthony. *Ernest Hemingway and His World.* Macmillan 1985 $10.95. ISBN 0-684-18504-0. Contains an illustrated biographical introduction.

Fenton, Charles A. *The Apprenticeship of Ernest Hemingway.* Octagon 1975 repr. of 1954 ed. o.p. Scholarly study of the Kansas City and Toronto years.

Gilmore. *Hemingway.* St. Martin 1988 $3.50. ISBN 0-312-91175-0

Griffin, Peter. *Along with Youth: Hemingway, the Early Years.* OUP 1987 $22.95. ISBN 0-19-503680-8. Traces Hemingway from boyhood through World War I and his first marriage.

———. *Less Than a Treason: Hemingway in Paris.* OUP 1990 $17.95. ISBN 0-19-505332-X. Second volume of a multivolume biography that recreates the period 1922–1929.

Hamod, Syed A. *The Short Fiction of Ernest Hemingway: A Study in Major Themes.* Nataraj Bks. 1985 $16.50. ISBN 0-81-7024-008-5

Hotchner, A. E. *Hemingway and His World.* Vendome 1990 $45.00. ISBN 0-86565-082-9. A photographic extravaganza; the text offers a working knowledge of Hemingway's life; includes a bibliography and index.

Kert, Bernice. *The Hemingway Women.* Norton 1986 $12.95. ISBN 0-393-30270-9

Lee, A. Robert, ed. *Ernest Hemingway: New Critical Essays.* B & N Imports 1983 $40.00. ISBN 0-389-20284-3. Refreshing new essays by British and American scholars; with an intelligent introduction and "Notes on Contributors."

Lewis, Robert, Jr. *Hemingway on Love.* Haskell 1972 $75.00. ISBN 0-8383-1650-6. Traces the development of two concepts of love, eros and agape, through the five stages of Hemingway's development; includes a bibliography and a thorough index.

Lynn, Kenneth S. *Hemingway.* Fawcett 1988 $14.95. ISBN 0-449-90308-7. An intelligent, lively, but mean-spirited biography of Hemingway; includes a bibliography and index.

Meyers, Jeffrey, ed. *Hemingway: The Critical Heritage.* Routledge Chapman & Hall 1982 $65.00. ISBN 0-7100-0929-1. A detailed scrutiny of Hemingway's life and work, with a bibliography and index.

———. *Hemingway: A Biography.* HarpC 1986 $12.95. ISBN 0-06-091364-9

Nagel, James, ed. *Ernest Hemingway: The Writer in Context.* U. of Wis. Pr. 1984 $27.50. ISBN 0-299-09740-4. Produced by a symposium of Hemingway scholars, adding new insight into other critical works on the author.

Nahal, Chaman. *The Narrative Pattern in Ernest Hemingway's Fiction*. Fairleigh Dickinson 1975 $27.50. ISBN 0-8386-7795-9. Studies Hemingway's use of suspended moments of passive activity in which characters become aware of inclusive rhythms of the universe; includes an index and a bibliography limited to books.

Reynolds, Mike. *Hemingway's First War*. Blackwell Pubs. 1987 $14.95. ISBN 0-631-15826-X

_____. *Hemingway's Reading, Nineteen Ten to Nineteen Forty: Commentary and Inventory*. Princeton U. Pr. 1981 $37.50. ISBN 0-691-06447-4

_____. *Hemingway: The Paris Years*. Blackwell Pubs. 1989 $24.95. ISBN 0-631-15352-7

_____. *The Young Hemingway*. Blackwell Pubs. 1987 $12.95. ISBN 0-631-14787-X

Scafella, Frank, ed. *Hemingway: Essays of Reassessment*. OUP 1990 $29.95. ISBN 0-19-506546-8. Provides potent and persuasive evidence to justify reconsidering beliefs about the man and his work.

Selkirk, Errol. *Hemingway for Beginners*. Writers & Readers 1992 $8.95. ISBN 0-86316-128-6

Smith, Paul. *Reader's Guide to the Short Stories of Ernest Hemingway*. Macmillan 1989 $60.00. ISBN 0-8161-8794-0. Examines 55 of Hemingway's short stories.

Spilka, Mark. *Hemingway's Quarrel with Androgyny*. U. of Nebr. Pr. 1990 $41.50. ISBN 0-8032-4127-5. Hypothesizes that Ernest was subconsciously androgynous because his mother dressed him like a girl until he was two or three years old.

Stanton, Edward F. *Hemingway and Spain: A Pursuit*. U. of Wash. Pr. 1989 $22.50. ISBN 0-295-96710-2. A personal journey in search of Hemingway's Spain—using description, biography, criticism, and conversations with Hemingway's friends.

Tavernier-Courbin, Jacqueline. *Ernest Hemingway's A Moveable Feast: The Making of Myth*. NE U. Pr. 1991 $35.00. ISBN 1-55553-103-2. Provides a detailed account of the book's construction from conception and creation to posthumous editing and publication.

Villard, Henry Serrano, and James Nagel. *Hemingway in Love and War: The Lost Diary of Agnes von Kurowsky, Her Letters, and Correspondence of Ernest Hemingway*. NE U. Pr. 1989 $25.00. ISBN 1-55553-057-5. Discusses how Hemingway's romanticized *Farewell to Arms* differs from his actual experiences.

Wagner, Linda, ed. *Ernest Hemingway: Six Decades of Criticism*. Mich. St. U. Pr. 1987 $18.00. ISBN 0-87013-250-4

Weber, Ronald. *Hemingway's Art of Nonfiction*. St. Martin 1990 $29.95. ISBN 0-312-03592-6. Well presented and documented study of Hemingway's nonfiction.

Whitlow, Roger. *Cassandra's Daughters: The Women in Hemingway*. Greenwood 1984 $42.95. ISBN 0-313-24488-X

Wilkinson, Myler. *Hemingway and Turgenev: The Nature of Literary Influence*. Bks. Demand repr. of 1986 ed. $35.90. ISBN 0-8357-1748-8. Compares primarily *The Sportsman Sketches* and *Fathers and Sons*.

Young, Philip. *Ernest Hemingway*. Bks. Demand repr. of 1965 ed. $20.00. ISBN 0-685-15931-0. Important biographical study of Hemingway and his work.

_____. *Ernest Hemingway: A Reconsideration*. Pa. St. U. Pr. 1966 $28.50. ISBN 0-271-73060-9. Early critical study with psychological interpretations that proved to be prophetic.

HUGHES, LANGSTON. 1902–1967

Langston Hughes was born in Joplin, Mississippi, into an African American family once zealous in the cause of abolitionism. He grew up in Lawrence, Kansas, and Cleveland, Ohio, where his first verse and fiction were published in his high school magazine. In 1921 he entered Columbia University but left in 1922, spending the next few years working at odd jobs. During this time, his poetry also began appearing in magazines. Two books of verse, *The Weary Blues* (1926) and *Fine Clothes to the Jew* (1927), confirmed his talent and gave him a reputation as an important chronicler of Harlem. When compared with many African American writers who came after him, "Hughes' approach to racial matters was more wry than angry, sly than militant" (*Publishers Weekly*). But he helped set the mood for the present assertiveness and determination of the African American people and deserves credit for improvements in their condition. He was in no sense a traditional poet, taking his poetic form and material from folk sources, with a great deal of his work expressing the spirit of the blues. With COUNTEE CULLEN and ZORA NEALE HURSTON, Hughes was outstanding in the Harlem Renaissance of the 1920s.

POETRY BY HUGHES

Selected Poems of Langston Hughes. 1959. Random 1990 $9.95. ISBN 0-679-72818-X. Hughes's personal selection of his best poems.

SHORT STORY COLLECTIONS BY HUGHES

The Best of Simple. FS&G 1961 $9.95. ISBN 0-374-52133-6. Tales of Jesse B. Semple— "Simple"—a Harlem worker who has humorous and insightful conversations with a black intellectual on a wide range of issues.

Simple Speaks His Mind. Amereon Ltd. $17.95. ISBN 0-88411-061-3. More Simple stories.

Simple Takes a Wife. Amereon Ltd. $17.95. ISBN 0-88411-062-1. The continuation of Simple's life story.

Simple's Uncle Sam. 1965. Amereon Ltd. repr. of 1965 ed. $15.95. ISBN 0-88411-709-X. Simple's insights into politics and other issues.

Something in Common and Other Stories. 1963. Hill & Wang 1963 $7.95. ISBN 0-8090-0057-1. Warm, generous stories about Harlem residents, a Cuban spy, slumming white folks, and other fascinating characters.

The Sweet Flypaper of Life. Howard U. Pr. 1985 $24.95. ISBN 0-88258-152-X

The Ways of White Folks. 1934. Random 1990 $9.00. ISBN 0-679-72817-1. Sardonic but ultimately open-hearted collection of stories about white folks and their strange and often painful treatment of African Americans.

PLAYS BY HUGHES

Five Plays by Langston Hughes. 1963. Ind. U. Pr. 1963 $20.00. ISBN 0-253-32230-8

Mule Bone: A Comedy of Negro Life in Three Acts. HarpC 1991 $9.95. ISBN 0-06-096885-0. African American folklore fashioned into a play.

WORKS BY HUGHES

Book of Negro Humor. Buccaneer Bks. 1990 $25.95. ISBN 0-89966-733-3. Highly recommended collection of humorous pieces pointing out the incongruities that existed in American life for blacks in the 1960s.

The Langston Hughes Reader. Braziller 1981 $17.50. ISBN 0-8076-0057-1

The Negro Mother: And Other Dramatic Recitations. Ayer repr. of 1931 ed. $9.95. ISBN 0-88143-070-6

BOOKS ABOUT HUGHES

Barksdale, Richard K. *Langston Hughes: The Poet and His Critics.* Bks. Demand repr. of 1977 ed. $41.80. ISBN 0-317-27976-9

Bloom, Harold, ed. *Langston Hughes.* Chelsea Hse. 1990 $24.95. ISBN 1-55546-376-2. A collection of modern critical essays by such distinguished scholars as Hughes biographer Arnold Rampersad ("The Origin of Poetry in Langston Hughes"), Onwuchekwa Jemie ("Jazz, Jive, and Jam") and Irwin T. Turner, on Hughes as a playwright.

Jemie, Onwuchekwa. *Langston Hughes: An Introduction to the Poetry.* Col. U. Pr. 1985 $21.50. ISBN 0-231-03780-5

Mikolyzk, Thomas A., ed. *Langston Hughes: A Bio-Bibliography.* Greenwood 1990 $45.00. ISBN 0-313-26895-9. Guide to Hughes's published works that includes a 30-page biographical summary and succinct and well-written annotations.

Miller, R. Baxter. *The Art and Imagination of Langston Hughes.* U. Pr. of Ky. 1989 $16.00. ISBN 0-8131-1662-7. Offers a biocritical reading of Hughes's writings.

Mullen, Edward J. *Critical Essays on Langston Hughes.* G. K. Hall 1986 $40.00. ISBN 0-8161-8697-9. Contains 35 reviews from 1936 to 1968 on Hughes's career as poet, prose writer, and dramatist.

Nichols, Charles H., ed. *Arna Bontemps—Langston Hughes: Letters, 1925–1967.* Paragon Hse. 1990 $14.95. ISBN 1-55778-391-8

Rampersad, Arnold. *The Life of Langston Hughes.* Vol. 1 *1902–1941: I, Too, Sing America.* OUP 1988 $13.95. ISBN 0-19-505426-1. Combines an illuminating biographical study with some of the most insightful critical commentary to appear on Hughes's writing.

HURSTON, ZORA NEALE. 1901–1960

Zora Neale Hurston, ALICE WALKER has said, "went forth into the world with one dress to her name . . . rescued and recreated a world which she labored to hand us whole, never underestimating the value of her gift if at times doubting the good sense of its recipients. . . . And of all people in the world to be she chose to be herself. . . ." Hurston was a controversially independent black woman who worked both as a writer and as a resourceful field anthropologist. She was a friend and collaborator of prominent figures in the Harlem Renaissance, most notably LANGSTON HUGHES, but she was attacked by other African American writers—male ones in particular—for celebrating the traditional African American community rather than joining the black protest movement associated with social realism. She was trained in anthropology at Columbia University and later supported in her field research by successive grants from the Guggenheim Foundation. She became an enthusiastic student of and spokeswoman for black folk culture, which she had experienced firsthand in a particularly empowering form in the all-black community, Eatonville, Florida, in which she was born and raised and where her father was the mayor. Yet late in her career, 1950, she was working as a maid in Florida, and she died penniless in a welfare home in St. Lucie County. Until Alice Walker found it in 1972, Hurston was buried in an unmarked grave. Her work was perhaps undervalued in her own lifetime because it was of the black woman's crises of which she wrote and the black woman's search for an uncompromised identity. The white community—even as an oppressive force—scarcely exists in her fiction or her autobiographical prose. She has been an inspiration and influence for contemporary African American women writers, most notably Alice Walker, who edited an important collection of Hurston's work in 1979, and TONI MORRISON. Her most widely read novel, *Their Eyes Were Watching God* (1937), was out of print for four decades but is now a standard text in many American literature courses.

NOVELS BY HURSTON

Jonah's Gourd Vine. HarpC 1990 $11.00. ISBN 0-06-091651-6. The author's first novel, originally published in 1934, launching her long, illustrious career. Story of a black preacher who owes his reputation largely to the wife he treats badly.

Moses, Man of the Mountain. HarpC 1991 repr. of 1939 ed. $11.00. ISBN 0-06-091994-9. Moses' story told as though Moses and the Hebrews were contemporary (to Hurston) African Americans.

Seraph on the Suwanee: A Novel. HarpC 1991 $9.95. ISBN 0-06-097359-5. A charming and readable chronicle of the life of poor Southern whites.

Their Eyes Were Watching God. 1937. HarpC 1990 $9.95. ISBN 0-06-091650-8. Love story that is also a loving tribute to African American culture.

SHORT STORY COLLECTIONS BY HURSTON

The Complete Stories. HarpC 1992 $22.50. ISBN 0-06-016732-7

Spunk: The Selected Stories of Zora Neale Hurston. Turtle Isl. Foun. 1985 $9.95. ISBN 0-913666-79-3. Collection of eight stories originally published between 1924 and 1942.

NONFICTION BY HURSTON

Dust Tracks on a Road: An Autobiography. HarpC 1991 $11.00. ISBN 0-06-09657-3. More Hurston's creation of her own myth than a factual autobiography—but a fascinating myth!

I Love Myself When I am Laughing . . . And Then Again When I am Looking Mean and Impressive: A Zora Neale Hurston Reader. Ed. by Alice Walker. Feminist Pr. 1979 $10.95. ISBN 0-912670-66-5. Collection of Hurston's groundbreaking writing on color.

Mules and Men. HarpC 1990 $11.00. ISBN 0-06-091648-6. Hurston's collection of African American folklore.

The Sanctified Church. Turtle Isl. Foun. 1983 $9.95. ISBN 0-913666-44-0

Tell My Horse. HarpC 1990 $9.95. ISBN 0-06-091649-4. More folklore.

WORKS BY HURSTON

Three Classic Works by Zora Neale Hurston: Their Eyes Were Watching God, Dust Tracks on a Road, Mules and Men. HarpC 1991 $30.00. ISBN 0-06-092099-8

BOOKS ABOUT HURSTON

Awkward, Michael. *New Essays on Their Eyes Were Watching God.* Cambridge U. Pr. 1991 $9.95. ISBN 0-521-38775-2. Collection of five essays by established scholars in African American and women's literary studies.

Bloom, Harold, ed. *Zora Neale Hurston.* Chelsea Hse. 1986 $24.95. ISBN 0-87754-627-4. From the *Modern Critical Views* series, with an introduction by Bloom; includes a bibliography, chronology, and index.

————, ed. *Zora Neale Hurston's Their Eyes Were Watching God.* Chelsea Hse. 1987 $24.95. ISBN 0-55546-054-2. Eight essays that focus on Hurston's use of language, metaphor, metonymy, and voice.

Colbert, Roz. *Zora Neale Hurston.* Chelsea Hse. 1993 $12.95. ISBN 0-7910-1766-4

Glassman, Steve, and Kathryn Lee Seidel, eds. *Zora in Florida.* U. Press Fla. 1991 $29.95. ISBN 0-8130-1050-0. Groundbreaking collection of 15 essays that discusses Hurston's lesser-known works.

Hemenway, Robert. *Zora Neale Hurston: A Literary Biography.* U. of Ill. Pr. 1980 $12.95. ISBN 0-252-00807-3. Definitive work on Hurston, relating her work and life to demonstrate her groundbreaking contribution to African-American culture.

Holloway, Karla F. *The Character of the Word: The Texts of Zora Neale Hurston.* Greenwood 1987 $42.95. ISBN 0-313-25264-5. First book-length analysis of Hurston's use of language in her four major novels.

Lyons, Mary E. *Sorrow's Kitchen: The Life and Folklore of Zora Neale Hurston.* Macmillan 1990 $13.95. ISBN 0-684-19198-9. Explores Hurston's life and works; contains detailed and unobtrusive documentation.

Nathiri, N. Y., ed. *Zora! Zora Neale Hurston: A Woman and Her Community.* Tribune 1991 $24.95. ISBN 0-941263-21-5. Gracious tribute to Hurston that remembers her as liberated, flamboyant, and enigmatic.

Newson, Adele S. *Zora Neale Hurston: A Reference Guide.* Macmillan 1987 $30.00. ISBN 0-8161-8902-1. Excellent annotated bibliography that charts the development of Hurston's reputation.

Porter, A. P. *Jump at de Sun: The Story of Zora Neale Hurston.* Carolrhoda Bks. 1992 $11.95. ISBN 0-87614-667-1. Chronology of the events of Hurston's life punctuated by selections from her letters and works.

Witcover, Paul. *Zora Neale Hurston*. Chelsea Hse. 1991 $17.95. ISBN 0-7910-1129-1.
Focuses on Hurston's awareness of the individual struggle within the folk community, which both suffocates and empowers its members.

Yates, Janelle. *Zora Neale Hurston: A Storyteller's Life*. Ward Hill Pr. 1991 $9.95. ISBN 0-
9623380-7-9. Highly readable, sometimes lyrical account that conveys Hurston's
remarkable spirit.

JEFFERS, (JOHN) ROBINSON. 1887–1962

Born in Pennsylvania, the son of a Presbyterian minister and Old Testament
scholar, Jefferson attended school in Germany and Switzerland. After moving
with his family to California in 1903, he graduated from Occidental College and
also studied at the University of Southern California, the University of Zurich,
and the University of Washington. Finally, after years of traveling, Jeffers settled
with his wife on a wild, sea-beaten cliff at Carmel, California, in what was
virtually a literary hermitage. There he set down the tragic folktales of northern
California in ironic epic. Jeffers was a poet concerned with cruelty and horror,
whose dramatic narratives are filled with scenes of blood and lust, and whose
verse shows vigorous beauty and great originality. He was a poet who is not
easily contained within the regular framework of literary history.

POETRY BY JEFFERS

The Alpine Christ and Other Poems. Cayucos 1974 $20.00. ISBN 0-9600372-4-1. Poems
fraught with moments of eloquence and power, frequently anticipating the poet's
later work in form, style, and subject.

Collected Poetry of Robinson Jeffers. 2 vols. Stanford U. Pr. Vol. 1 *1920–1928*. 1988
$60.00. ISBN 0-8047-1414-2. Vol. 2 *1928–1938*. 1989 $60.00. ISBN 0-8047-1723-0.
Jeffers's engaging style and iconoclastic subjects offer a rich matrix for studying an
alternative to the modernist tradition.

Rock and Hawk: A Selection of Shorter Poems by Robinson Jeffers. Random 1987 $19.95.
ISBN 0-394-55769-7. Chronological arrangement of poems showing Jeffers's development through fury to diversity; has an outstanding introduction by Robert Hass.

Selected Poetry. Random 1938 $24.95. ISBN 0-394-40442-4

WORKS BY JEFFERS

Cawdor and Medea. New Dir. Pr. 1970 $10.95. ISBN 0-8112-0073-6

BOOKS ABOUT JEFFERS

Boswell, Jeanetta. *Robinson Jeffers and the Critics, 1912–1983: A Bibliography of Secondary
Sources with Selective Annotations*. Scarecrow 1986 $20.00. ISBN 0-8108-1914-7.
Covers 12 more years of criticism than any other full bibliographic study of Jeffers.

Carpenter, Frederic I. *Robinson Jeffers*. NCUP 1962 $10.95. ISBN 0-8084-0269-2. A
general study of Jeffers's life and work, including a chronology, bibliography, and
one-chapter biography; most of the book focuses on the relationship between
Jeffers's life and his major works.

Everson, William. *The Excesses of God: Robinson Jeffers As a Religious Figure*. Stanford U.
Pr. 1988 $29.50. ISBN 0-8047-1415-0. Argues that Jeffers was a religious poet, in the
sense that his poetry extols an awestruck state of mind in confrontation with an
uncaring universe.

Karman, James. *Critical Essays on Robinson Jeffers*. G. K. Hall 1990 $45.00. ISBN 0-8161-
8897-1. Refines the body of material available on Jeffers into an invaluable anthology
of articles and reviews, both early and modern.

Powell, Lawrence C. *Robinson Jeffers: The Man and His Work*. Gordon Pr. 1973 $59.95.
ISBN 0-8490-0966-9

Zaller, Robert, ed. *Centennial Essays for Robinson Jeffers*. U. of Delaware Pr. 1991 $39.50.
    ISBN 0-87413-414-5. Keenly drawn assessment in Jeffers's current but long-overdue
    rejuvenation.

LARDNER, RING(GOLD WILMER). 1885–1933

In the literary history of America, along with the creators of Huck Finn, Nick
Adams, and Holden Caulfield, the creator of Jack Keefe occupies an important
place. Ring Lardner was for many years a sports reporter in Chicago who wrote
in a distinctive style that was known as Lardner's Ringlish. Young HEMINGWAY,
growing up in nearby Oak Park, greatly admired Lardner's work, and later
fiction about sports by such writers as Mark Harris and Dan Jenkins might never
have been written if the imaginary letters that Lardner composed for a brash
and uneducated bush-league baseball player named Jack Keefe had not made
You Know Me, Al (1916) an American classic of its kind. Lardner's most famous
short story is "Haircut," a frequently anthologized tale in which an ignorant and
naive barber tells a horror story as if it were funny. There came to be a
repetitious quality about Lardner's later work as he fell increasingly under "the
spell of the misspelled" and "the lure of the illiterate," but in the comic
tradition of American fiction, he has long been assured a permanent niche.

SHORT STORY COLLECTIONS BY LARDNER

The Best Short Stories of Ring Lardner. Macmillan 1985 $22.50. ISBN 0-685-04559-5
Haircut and Other Stories. Random 1984 $6.95. ISBN 0-394-72610-3
Ring Around the Bases: The Complete Baseball Stories of Ring Lardner. Macmillan 1992
    $35.00. ISBN 0-684-19374-4. Collects Lardner's 46 baseball-related tales, displaying
    the writer's excellence in capturing the idiom and nuances of baseball talk.
Ring Lardner Reader. Macmillan 1977 $40.00. ISBN 0-684-15365-3
Some Champions: Previously Uncollected Autobiographical Sketches and Fiction. Macmil-
    lan 1977 $3.95. ISBN 0-684-15065-4. Seventeen sketches and nine short stories; of
    particular interest for the Lardner buff and scholars.
You Know Me Al: A Busher's Letters. 1916. Macmillan 1991 $9.95. ISBN 0-02-022342-0

NONFICTION BY LARDNER

The Story of a Wonder Man: Being the Autobiography of Ring Lardner. Greenwood 1975
    $38.50. ISBN 0-8371-8414-2

WORKS BY LARDNER

Letters from Ring. Walden Pr. 1979 $10.95. ISBN 0-685-05275-3. Carefully edited, annotated,
    and thoroughly indexed collection of witty and entertaining correspondence.

BOOKS ABOUT LARDNER

Evans, Elizabeth. *Ring Lardner*. Continuum 1990 $18.95. ISBN 0-8044-2185-4
Friedrich, Otto. *Ring Lardner*. Bks. Demand $20.00. ISBN 0-317-29459-8
Patrick, Walton R. *Ring Lardner*. NCUP 1963 $10.95. ISBN 0-8084-0261-7
Yardley, Jonathan. *Ring: A Biography of Ring Lardner*. Atheneum 1984 o.p. Carefully
    researched biography, particularly good on Lardner's early development; with a
    bibliography and index.

LARSEN, NELLA. 1891–1964

Nella Larsen was associated with the Harlem Renaissance. She also worked as
a librarian and a nurse in New York City, pursuing nursing after her brief,
successful writing career until her death in 1964. Larsen's mother was Danish,
and her father was West Indian; she used her experience as the child of middle-
class parents in a mixed marriage to create characters in two novels who are

stranded, caught between two cultures and unable to feel wholly at home in either. In each of Larsen's novels, the heroine suffers suffocating constrictions of her identity in both African American and white European culture. These crises in both *Quicksand* (1928) and *Passing* (1929) are further complicated by the heroine's quest for sexual as well as social identity, and both novels end without hopeful resolution. Both contain autobiographical elements, but *Quicksand*, the more successful, reproduced in fictional form many of the circumstances of Larsen's own early life. Although her work had been out of print for many years, she has recently been rediscovered.

NOVELS BY LARSEN

Passing. 1929. Ayer 1970 $19.95. ISBN 0-405-01930-0. The story of an upper-class Harlem doctor's wife and her strange fascination with a friend who is passing for white.
Quicksand. 1928. Greenwood 1970 $35.00. ISBN 0-8371-1127-7. Helga Crane's search for her own identity in a world determined to deny, constrict, or distort who she is.

LEWIS, SINCLAIR. 1885–1951 (NOBEL PRIZE 1930)

The first American to win the Nobel Prize for literature, Sinclair Lewis was a busy and popular writer whose novels chronicle the social history of his time and constitute what Maxwell Geismar called "a remarkable diary of the middle class mind in America." The work that won him the Nobel Prize was a group of novels that realistically depicted various aspects of American life. *Main Street* (1920), his first important work, is a scathing picture of provincialism in the small town of Gopher Prairie, Minnesota, which Lewis modeled on his hometown of Sauk Centre, while *Babbitt* (1922), a moving account of midlife crisis experienced by an average American businessman, actually succeeded in adding a new word to the American dictionary—*babbitry*, or the ultimate in shallow, middle-brow materialism. Continuing a blend of social criticism with sympathy, Lewis wrote *Arrowsmith* (1925), in which the idealism of a devoted scientist and physician is contrasted with the materialistic forces that try to capitalize on his discoveries. Though offered the Pulitzer Prize for this novel, he refused it. *Elmer Gantry* (1927) is a portrait of a dissolute but successful evangelist, while *Dodsworth* (1929) deals with a retired industrialist whose material success and ambitious wife have failed to provide emotional suste-nance. Lewis succeeded in bringing to life the talk and actions common to the middle classes of America. Although some of the conditions he describes now seem peculiarly dated, his people remain convincingly real.

Lewis's sense of responsibility to society seemed to become all the stronger after his Nobel Prize, and some of the books he wrote afterward have topical subjects that now seem rather dated. *It Can't Happen Here* (1935) forecast an imaginary coming of fascism to the United States, *Gideon Planish* (1943) exposed corruption in organized philanthropy, *Kingsblood Royal* (1947) was one of the first novels to deal with the evils of racial prejudice, and *Cass Timberlane* (1945), originally subtitled *A Novel of Husbands and Wives*, gave a long, clear look at the institution of marriage in its story of a Minnesota judge and his young second wife.

If American novelists of this century can be divided into opposing camps of social historians and literary artists, Lewis clearly belongs to the former group. As a result, he has seemed to fade further into the past as writer after writer has taken his place as an authoritative observer of the times. However, the characters he created and the human situations he has depicted have sometimes caused him to be compared to DICKENS. He remains one of the great portrayers of American middle-class life in the 1920s.

NOVELS BY LEWIS

Ann Vickers. 1933. AMS Pr. repr. of 1933 ed. $44.50. ISBN 0-404-20157-1. Story of a woman reformer, from childhood through her coming of age to her ultimate career as prison administrator.

Arrowsmith. 1925. HarBraceJ 1990 $15.95. ISBN 0-15-108216-2. Poignant saga of a doctor dedicated to humanitarian research while all about him care only for money.

Babbitt. 1922. HarBraceJ 1989 $15.95. ISBN 0-15-110421-2. George Babbitt, ultimate mid0dle-class "boosler," and his gradual—partial—realization of his life's emptiness.

Cass Timberlane. 1945. Buccaneer Bks. 1982 $18.95. ISBN 0-89966-401-6. About a middle-aged judge, his efforts to stay married to his lovely young wife—and related stories about every unhappy marriage in town.

Dodsworth. 1929. NAL-Dutton 1971 o.p.

Elmer Gantry. 1927. NAL-Dutton 1967 $4.95. ISBN 0-451-52251-6

Free Air. Scholarly 1971 $59.00. ISBN 0-403-01071-3

Gideon Planish. 1943. Woodhill 1974 o.p. Phony philanthropist discovering some real feelings.

The God-Seeker. 1949. Woodhill 1975 o.p.

It Can't Happen Here. 1935. NAL-Dutton 1970 $4.95. ISBN 0-451-15936-5. Chilling if slightly dated portrait of how fascism could take root in the United States.

Main Street. 1920. HarBraceJ 1989 $15.95. ISBN 0-15-155547-8. Classic story of spirited woman and the narrow small town that closes in around her.

Storm in the West. Madison Bks. UPA 1981 $5.95. ISBN 0-8128-6079-9

Work of Art. AMS Pr. $37.50. ISBN 0-404-20159-8

World So Wide. 1950. Woodhill 1974 o.p.

SHORT STORY COLLECTION BY LEWIS

Selected Short Stories of Sinclair Lewis. I. R. Dee 1990 $12.95. ISBN 0-929587-22-7

BOOKS ABOUT LEWIS

Bloom, Harold, ed. *Sinclair Lewis.* Chelsea Hse. 1987 $24.95. ISBN 0-87754-628-2. A collection of modern critical essays covering most aspects of Lewis's work.

Bucco, Martin, ed. *Critical Essays on Sinclair Lewis.* G. K. Hall 1986 $40.00. ISBN 0-8161-8698-7. Balanced view of Lewis's uneven career.

Grebstein, Sheldon N. *Sinclair Lewis.* NCUP 1962 $10.95. ISBN 0-8084-0278-1. A general study of Lewis's life and fiction, focusing on the relation of his life and works, and including a one-chapter biography, a chronology, and a bibliography.

Lundquist, James. *Sinclair Lewis.* Continuum 1974 $16.95. ISBN 0-8044-2563-0. A general introduction to Lewis's life and works, with extensive discussion of the major novels; includes chronology and bibliography.

Parrington, Vernon L. *Sinclair Lewis: Our Own Diogenes.* Haskell 1974 $75.00. ISBN 0-8383-1720-0

Schorer, Mark. *Sinclair Lewis, an American Life.* McGraw 1961 o.p.

LINDSAY, (NICHOLAS) VACHEL. 1879–1931

From Springfield, Illinois, Lindsay studied at Hiram College, the Chicago Art Institute, and the New York Art School, turning to poetry only after he had no success as an artist. The appeal of Vachel Lindsay's poetry is first and foremost one of sound. Many of his poems are meant to be chanted aloud, intoned, or sung. The poet was a phenomenon in his day, who became famous for the recitation of his poems. He preached a gospel of beauty expressed in almost primitive cadences. His early art studies under Robert Henri gave him the ability to illustrate his own poems, and he developed an elaborate theory of art that has gone largely ignored. Among his best-known works are *General William Booth Enters Heaven*, published in *Poetry* magazine in 1913, and *The Congo* (1914).

POETRY BY LINDSAY

Collected Poems. 1923. Macmillan rev. ed. 1925 o.p. Illustrated by Lindsay.
Johnny Appleseed and Other Poems. 1928. Buccaneer Bks. repr. of 1981 ed. $23.95. ISBN 0-89966-365-6. A selection made chiefly with children in mind.
The Poetry of Vachel Lindsay. Spoon River 1984 $24.95. ISBN 0-933180-45-4. Consists of about 350 poems, some not published before, from 1920 through 1931.
Selected Poems. Ed. by Mark Harris. Macmillan 1963 o.p.

WORKS BY LINDSAY

Letters of Vachel Lindsay. Ed. by Marc Chenetier. B. Franklin 1979 o.p. An important volume.
The Prose of Vachel Lindsay. Spoon River 1989 $24.95. ISBN 0-944024-08-4. A delightful book that includes Lindsay's film criticism.

BOOKS ABOUT LINDSAY

Hallwas, John E., ed. *The Vision of This Land: Studies of Vachel Lindsay, Edgar Lee Masters, and Carl Sandburg.* WIU Essays Lit. 1976 $5.00. ISBN 0-934312-00-1. Valuable insights by various critics, written primarily for scholars; includes extensive footnotes.
Harris, Mark. *City of Discontent: An Interpretive Biography of Vachel Lindsay, Being Also the Story of Springfield, Illinois, U.S.A.* Hippocrene Bks. 1975 $27.50. ISBN 0-374-93676-5
Masters, Edgar Lee. *Vachel Lindsay: A Poet in America.* Biblo 1969 repr. of 1935 ed. $25.00. ISBN 0-8196-0239-6. A sensitively written and informative biography that is more personal than critical.

LOWELL, AMY. 1874–1925

Although Amy Lowell did not look like the stereotypical poet—she was of ample build and enjoyed smoking large black cigars in public—she did write verse that was revolutionary in its time. When *Sword Blades and Poppy Seed* (1914) was published, she emerged as the leader of the new poetry movement called the imagist school, and so thoroughly was she identified with this new precise and delicate style that EZRA POUND jokingly proposed to retitle it "Amygism." "*Patterns*" (1915) and "*A Lady*" (1914) are frequently anthologized, both demonstrating her vivid depiction of color, agility with sharp images, and precise use of words.

Lowell came from a well-known and established Boston family that included JAMES RUSSELL LOWELL as one of her predecessors and was later to produce another well-known poet in the person of ROBERT LOWELL. Louis Untermeyer said of Amy Lowell, in his introduction to *The Complete Poetical Works* (1955), that "her final place in the history of American literature has not been determined, but the importance of her influence remains unquestioned. Underneath her preoccupation with the need for novelty . . . she was a dynamic force." She did much to introduce French literary figures to an American audience with her essays and wrote a major biography of KEATS. For many people, Lowell was the very figure of the avant-garde poet, bohemian and yet with respect for tradition, apparently experimental yet fully conscious of the need to create a public role for herself as a tastemaker and trendsetter. Her posthumous volume, *What's O'Clock* (1925), was awarded the Pulitzer Prize for poetry in 1926.

POETRY BY LOWELL

The Complete Poetical Works of Amy Lowell. HM 1955 o.p. Introduction by Louis Untermeyer.

A Dome of Many-Coloured Glass. 1912. AMS Pr. repr. of 1921 ed. $20.00. ISBN 0-404-17127-3. Collection of poetry that is heavily influenced by the poetic style of the nineteenth century.

Selected Poems. Scholarly 1971 $29.00. ISBN 0-403-00657-0

WORKS BY LOWELL

A Critical Fable. 1922. AMS Pr. repr. of 1922 ed. $17.50. ISBN 0-404-17126-5. Humorous and light-hearted survey, in rhymed couplets, of leading poets of her time and herself.

Tendencies in Modern American Poetry. Rprt. Serv. 1992 $89.00. ISBN 0-7812-6629-7. A definitive work on the early years of the "new poetry" movement; views poetry as reflecting patterns of social change.

BOOKS ABOUT LOWELL

Benvenuto, Richard. *Amy Lowell.* Macmillan 1985 $20.95. ISBN 0-8057-7436-X. Offers a clear, sensible, balanced combination of fact and interpretation of the works and days of a neglected modernist.

Gregory, Horace. *Amy Lowell.* Ayer repr. of 1958 ed. $25.00. ISBN 0-8369-5008-9. Highly critical analysis of Lowell's poetic style.

Ruihley, Glenn R. *The Thorn of a Rose: Amy Lowell Reconsidered.* Shoe String 1975 $29.50. ISBN 0-208-01458-6. Traces the development of the poet's life and her literary accomplishments.

MCKAY, CLAUDE. 1889–1948

Claude McKay was born in Jamaica of a poor farming family and came to America as a student when he was 23 years old. He therefore experienced American racial prejudice for the first time as an immigrant, and the shock of that experience continued to affect his themes as a poet and a novelist until the end of his career. He attended Tuskeegee Institute and Kansas State College and eventually migrated to New York, where he became one of the earliest contributors to the literature of the Harlem Renaissance. In both his poems and his novels, McKay sought to express realistically and without sentimentality the common spirit of identity of ordinary people of the Harlem working classes. He wrote under the pseudonym of Eli Edwards. After publication of his most important volume of poems, *Harlem Shadows* (1922), he spent 12 years as a wandering exile in Europe, Russia, and Morocco. During that period he wrote four novels, the first of which, *Home to Harlem* (1928), was the first novel by an African American writer to become a national bestseller.

NOVELS BY MCKAY

Banana Bottom. 1933. HarBraceJ 1974 $7.95. ISBN 0-15-610650-7. A novel about a young woman who returns to her Jamaican homeland in search of her roots.

Banjo. 1929. HarBraceJ 1970 $9.95. ISBN 0-15-610675-2. The story of a group of musicians living a hand-to-mouth existence on the waterfront.

Harlem Glory. C. H. Kerr 1990 $20.95. ISBN 0-88286-162-X. Tells the story of a black bon vivant who returns to Harlem and faces his frustrations, loneliness, fears, and anger.

Home to Harlem. 1929. NE U. Pr. 1987 $35.00. ISBN 1-55553-023-0. A novel about the joys of life in Harlem.

POETRY BY MCKAY

Constab Ballads. 1912. Gordon Pr. 1977 $59.95. ISBN 0-8490-1666-5. A recollection of
the bigotry and discord McKay found in urban Kingston.
The Dialect Poetry of Claude McKay. 1912. 2 vols. Ayer repr. of 1912 ed. $21.00. ISBN 0-
8369-8982-1. Includes *Songs of Jamaica* (1912) and *Constab Ballads* (1912).
Selected Poems of Claude McKay. HarBraceJ 1969 $5.95. ISBN 0-15-680649-5

SHORT STORY COLLECTION BY MCKAY

Gingertown. 1932. Ayer repr. of 1932 ed. $16.00. ISBN 0-8369-4113-6. Short stories on
black issues, with social and psychological overtones.

NONFICTION BY MCKAY

Long Way from Home. HarBraceJ 1970 $5.95. ISBN 0-15-653145-3. The author's
autobiography.

BOOKS ABOUT MCKAY

Bronz, Stephen H. *Roots of Negro Racial Consciousness.* Libra 1964. $10.00. ISBN 0-
87212-019-8. An in-depth study of three Harlem renaissance writers; Countee Cullen,
James Weldon Johnson, and Claude McKay.
Cooper, Wayne F. *Claude McKay: Rebel Sojourner in the Harlem Renaissance: A
Biography.* La. State U. Pr. 1987 $29.95. ISBN 0-8071-1310-7. Offers a rich,
comprehensive view of a talented, complex, and mercurial personality.
Giles, James Richard. *Claude McKay.* Twayne 1975 o.p. History of the author's life, with
an in-depth review of his poetry, prose, and his critics.
McLeod, A. L., ed. *Claude McKay: Centennial Studies.* Apt Bks. 1992 $35.00. ISBN 81-
207-1403-2
Tillery, Tyrone. *Claude McKay: A Black Poet's Struggle for Identity.* U. of Mass. Pr. 1992
$24.95. ISBN 0-87023-762-4. Well-documented and cautious biography of a tough,
angry, and mercurial Jamaican writer during the interwar years in America.

MACLEISH, ARCHIBALD. 1892–1982

Son of a Chicago businessman, MacLeish was born in Glencoe, Illinois,
graduated from Yale University in 1915, was married in 1916, and graduated
from Harvard Law School in 1919. During his undergraduate years, he began
writing poetry and in 1923 decided to give up law and devote himself to being a
poet. He took his family to Europe, mostly to France, and did not return to the
United States until 1928. From 1939 to 1944, MacLeish was librarian of
Congress. During World War II, he was director of O.F.F. (the first U.S. ministry
of information) and later assistant secretary of state (1944–45). In November
1945, he went to London as chair of the U.S. delegation to the first general
conference of UNESCO in Paris (1946), a position he resigned in 1947. Clearly,
throughout his life, MacLeish played a public role as well as a private one and
was fearless in battles against censorship, intimidation, and violations of civil
liberties. In 1949, he became Boylston Professor of Rhetoric and Oratory at
Harvard. *J.B.: A Play in Verse* (1958), the story of Job transferred to contemporary life, won the 1958 Pulitzer Prize for drama. The world premiere of the play
was at Yale, his alma mater. MacLeish had already won two previous Pulitzer
Prizes in 1932 (for *Conquistador*) and in 1953. In 1953 he was also awarded the
Bollingen Prize in poetry and the National Book Award.

POETRY BY MACLEISH

New and Collected Poems: 1917–1984. HM 1985 $14.95. ISBN 0-395-39569-0. An expanded
volume of MacLeish's poetry, containing eight previously unpublished poems.

PLAYS BY MACLEISH

J.B.: A Play in Verse. 1958. HM $6.70. ISBN 0-395-08353-2
Six Plays. HM 1980 $9.75. ISBN 0-395-28419-8

NONFICTION BY MACLEISH

Freedom Is the Right to Choose. Ayer 1951 $17.00. ISBN 0-8369-2172-0
Poetry and Opinion. Haskell 1974 $75.00. ISBN 0-8383-2043-0. Attempts to relate Pound's
    work to "an accepted theory of poetic function."
Riders on the Earth: Essays and Recollections. HM 1978 $8.95. ISBN 0-395-26382-4.
    Collection of articles, essays, and memoirs about the 1960s and early 1970s.
Time to Act. Ayer 1943 $18.00. ISBN 0-8369-1713-8

WORKS BY MACLEISH

Letters of Archibald MacLeish 1907–1892. HM $20.00. ISBN 0-317-05480-5

BOOKS ABOUT MACLEISH

Drabeck, Bernard A., ed. *Archibald MacLeish: Reflections.* U. of Mass. Pr. 1988 $30.00.
    ISBN 0-87023-5117. Series of interviews that traces MacLeish's career as poet,
    Librarian of Congress, Statesman, and man of letters.
Falk, Signi L. *Archibald MacLeish.* NCUP 1965 $10.95. ISBN 0-8084-0054-1. A general
    introduction to MacLeish's life and works, focusing on how the two relate and
    including a chronology and a bibliography.
Mullaly, Edward J. *Archibald MacLeish: A Checklist.* Bks. Demand repr. of 1973 ed.
    $28.40. ISBN 0-8357-5576-2
Smith, Grover. *Archibald MacLeish.* U. of Minn. Pr. 1971 $1.25. ISBN 0-8166-0618-8. A
    pamphlet providing a brief summary of MacLeish's life and works, with particular
    attention to his themes of political and personal freedom.

MASTERS, EDGAR LEE. 1869–1950

The Kansas-born poet of *Spoon River Anthology* (1915), Edgar Lee Masters,
wrote almost 50 volumes but continues to be known for only that one, so great
was its extraordinary success. The character of the verses—short postmortem
monologues in a cemetery in epitaph form—is borrowed from the old *Greek
Anthology*. By invading the realm of social criticism usually reserved for prose
fiction, *Spoon River* anticipated the mood of SHERWOOD ANDERSON's *Winesburg,
Ohio* and SINCLAIR LEWIS's *Main Street.* For 11 years, he lived near the Spoon
River, his source of inspiration for this work. The 244 characters in the
Anthology lay bare, in their own epitaphs, the hypocrisies, jealousies, frustrations, and infrequent triumphs of their lives. Masters is often regarded as the last
best-selling American poet. *Spoon River* has been adapted into a popular stage
version that is frequently performed at colleges, high schools, and community
theater.

POETRY BY MASTERS

The Enduring River: Edgar Lee Masters' Uncollected Spoon River Poems. S. Ill. U. Pr. 1991
    $16.95. ISBN 0-8093-1685-4. Third collection of Spoon River poems.
Spoon River Anthology. 1915. NAL-Dutton 1992 $4.95. ISBN 0-451-52530-2. Collection of
    narrative poems in which deceased residents of Spoon River review their lives.

NONFICTION BY MASTERS

Across Spoon River: An Autobiography. Rprt. Serv. 1991 $89.00. ISBN 0-7812-8276-4

BOOKS ABOUT MASTERS

Flanagan, John T. *Edgar Lee Masters: The Spoon River Poet and His Critics.* Scarecrow 1974 $20.00. ISBN 0-8108-0741-6. Surveys the critical reception to Master's poetry and prose.

Masters, Hardin W. *Edgar Lee Masters: A Biographical Sketchbook about a Great American Author.* Fairleigh Dickinson 1978 $24.50. ISBN 0-8386-2031-0. Provides keen and warm insight into the life and personality of Masters.

Primeau, Ronald. *Beyond Spoon River: The Legacy of Edgar Lee Masters.* U. of Tex. Pr. 1981 $22.50. ISBN 0-292-70731-2. Examines the major influences of the author, including his Midwestern heritage.

Wrenn, John H. *Edgar Lee Masters.* Macmillan 1983 $19.95. ISBN 0-8057-7396-7. A useful introduction to Master's life and works for the general reader, discussing how Master's life affected his poetry; includes a chronology and bibliography.

MENCKEN, H(ENRY) L(OUIS). 1880–1956

The great Baltimore iconoclast, lexicographer, and journalist made his *American Mercury* a famous battleground for culture, politics, and fashion in the 1920s. His apprenticeship was as a contentious local reporter. Eventually he became an editor, a war correspondent, and finally a literary critic for *The Smart Set* in 1908. Mencken's collaboration with the drama critic George Jean Nathan began at *The Smart Set* and survived the first few years of the *Mercury.* The *N.Y. Times* described Mencken's prolific writings as "a great stream of literally millions of words of reporting, editorials, essays, commentary, articles, and books, all of it bearing the unmistakable stamp of individuality possessed by a master craftsman who was also a man of honor, of intellectual curiosity, of humanity and of superb wit." Mencken was wildly popular—and unpopular— and was widely influential. In 1950, he received the National Institute and American Academy of Arts and Letters Gold Medal.

NONFICTION BY MENCKEN

The American Language. 1919. Knopf 1977 $22.95. ISBN 0-394-73315-0. Theorizes about the cultural ties between the American and British forms of the English language.

An American Scene: A Reader. Random 1982 $12.95. ISBN 0-394-75214-7

A Carnival of Buncombe: Writings on Politics. U. Ch. Pr. 1984 $12.95. ISBN 0-226-51977-5

Days of H. L. Mencken: Three Volumes in One: Happy Days, Newspaper Days, and Heathen Days. Dorset Pr. 1990 $29.95. ISBN 0-88029-417-5. Three volumes that include *Happy Days,* Mencken's boyhood memoirs; *Newspaper Days,* memoirs from his days as a reporter; and *Heathen Days,* random recollections from his past.

Diary of H. L. Mencken. Random 1991 $16.95. ISBN 0-679-73176-8

Happy Days, 1880–1892. AMS Pr. repr. of 1940 ed. $37.50. ISBN 0-404-20174-1

Heathen Days, 1890–1936. AMS Pr. repr. of 1940 ed. $37.50. ISBN 0-404-20175-X

Mencken Chrestomathy. Pantheon 1982 $14.95. ISBN 0-394-75209-0. A comprehensive anthology of Mencken's work.

Newspaper Days, 1899–1906. AMS Pr. $37.50. ISBN 0-404-20176-8

Vintage Mencken. Random 1990 $9.95. ISBN 0-679-72895-3. Selection of Mencken's writings culled from books, magazines and newspapers.

BOOKS ABOUT MENCKEN

Bode, Carl. Johns Hopkins 1986 $12.95. ISBN 0-8018-3404-X

Bulsterbaum, Allison, ed. *H. L. Mencken.* Garland 1988 $48.00. ISBN 0-8240-6634-0. A selective bibliography useful to the general reader.

Douglas, George. *H. L. Mencken: Critic of American Life.* Shoe String 1978 $27.50. ISBN 0-208-01693-7. Introduces a new generation to the man who wrote, "Democracy is the theory that the common people know what they want and deserve to get it good and hard."

Fitzpatrick, Vincent. *H. L. M.—The Mencken Bibliography: A Second Ten-Year Supplement, 1972–1981.* Enoch Pratt 1986 $17.95. ISBN 0-910556-25-3. Examines Mencken's influence on American life and letters by discussing his most influential writings.

———. *H. L. Mencken.* Continuum 1989 $19.95. ISBN 0-8264-0419-7

Hobson, Fred C., Jr. *Serpent in Eden: H. L. Mencken and the South.* La. State U. Pr. 1974 $9.95. ISBN 0-8071-0455-8

Manchester, William. *Disturber of the Peace: The Life of H. L. Mencken.* U. of Mass. Pr. 2nd ed. 1986 $16.95. ISBN 0-87023-544-3

Rodgers, Marion, ed. *Mencken and Sara: A Life in Letters.* McGraw 1987 $22.95. ISBN 0-07-041505-6. A record of the brief but loving marriage between the middle-aged Mencken and the young Sara that ended with Sara's death from tuberculosis in 1935; perhaps the best source for learning about Mencken's extraordinary wife.

Scruggs, Charles. *The Sage in Harlem: H. L. Mencken and the Black Writers of the 1920s.* Johns Hopkins 1983 $28.00. ISBN 0-8018-3000-1

Singleton, Marvin. *H. L. Mencken and the American Mercury Adventure.* Duke 1962 $14.95. ISBN 0-8223-0351-5. Examines Mencken's entry into mass-market publishing and his support of such young writers as Sinclair Lewis and Theodore Dreiser.

Stenerson, Douglas C. *Critical Essays on H. L. Mencken.* G. K. Hall 1987 $40.00. ISBN 0-8161-8694-4. Attempts to cover all the aspects of Mencken's career as editor, critic, journalist, analyst of the American language, and personality.

MILLAY, EDNA ST. VINCENT. 1892–1950

Edna St. Vincent Millay was born in Maine and graduated from Vassar College in 1917. She then joined the Provincetown Players, acting many leading roles, including those of her own plays. Like most of her Greenwich Village peers, the poet lived a poor, but happy existence. Her earliest poem, "Renascence," written when she was 19, first appeared in *The Lyric Year* (1912), an anthology of competitive poems. Its philosophy marked it as one of the most thoughtful poems in the collection. Although known among literary circles for her early work, she did not become well known among the general reading public until the publication of her second work, *A Few Figs From Thistles* (1920). She was awarded the Pulitzer Prize for poetry in 1923 for *The Ballad of the Harp Weaver.* As the bohemian spokeswoman for early twentieth-century youth, she won further fame with her poetry of love and gaiety and longing and death, especially her sonnets. A delight in beauty and nature and the wonders of the world are recurring themes in her early works. As Millay approached her middle years, her writing became more serious, especially when war erupted in Europe. Among her works at this time are *Make Bright the Arrow* (1940) and *Collected Sonnets* (1941).

Millay married Eugen Boissevain, a New York importer, in 1923. Shortly after, they purchased a farm in upstate New York, which they called Steepletop after an abundant wildflower in the region. Millay lived here for the rest of her life, composing some of her finest work in a little shack separate from the main house.

POETRY BY MILLAY

Collected Lyrics. 1943 HarpC 1981 $11.00. ISBN 0-06-090863-7. Millay's own selection.
Collected Poems. Lightyear 1992 $24.95. ISBN 0-89968-266-9
Collected Sonnets. HarpC 1988 $9.00. ISBN 0-06-091091-7.
Renascence and Other Poems. Ayer repr. of 1917 ed. $10.75. ISBN 0-8369-8245-2
Selected Poems: Edna St. Vincent Millay. HarpC 1991 $18.00. ISBN 0-06-016733-5

WORK BY MILLAY

The Letters of Edna St. Vincent Millay. Ed. by Allan Ross McDougall. Greenwood 1973 repr. of 1952 ed. o.p.

BOOKS ABOUT MILLAY

Britten, Norman A. *Edna St. Vincent Millay.* Macmillan 1967 $10.95. ISBN 0-8084-0114-9. Compact examination of Millay's life and work, including consideration of her feminism and her relationship to "High Modernism."

Daffron, Carolyn. *Edna St. Vincent Millay.* Chelsea Hse. 1990 $17.95. ISBN 1-55546-668-0. Includes an all-encompassing look at the poet's happy childhood, the brazen young adult's feminism, and the shy reclusiveness of the later years.

MILLER, HENRY. 1891–1980

The apparent heir of D. H. LAWRENCE in championing the natural in humans and hailed by NORMAN MAILER as one of the most vital writers of the century, Henry Miller had some 30 years of underground fame before Grove Press successfully fought off the censors in 1961 and published *Tropic of Cancer* (1934)—the first volume in the trilogy for which Miller is best known—for the first time legally in the United States.

Born and raised in New York City, the young Miller worked at various menial jobs before going to Paris as a nearly penniless and unproven writer. Because of his choice of subjects and the frankness of his treatment, his early picaresque novels were published only in Paris, although several of them were read in the United States in smuggled copies. *The Cosmological Eye* (1939), a collection of stories, essays, and other prose pieces that defies conventional classification, was the first book that an American publisher dared to publish, and Laughlin's New Directions went on to bring out such similar volumes as *The Wisdom of the Heart, Sunday after the War* (1944), *The Air-Conditioned Nightmare* (1945–47), *Remember to Remember*, and *Stand Still Like the Hummingbird*.

The Rosy Crucifixion, the collective title for the novels *Sexus* (1949), *Plexus* (1953), and *Nexus* (1960), is his second major trilogy. These provide yet more fictional autobiography covering, in his usual ribald fashion, the years of his "crucifixion" in the United States before he went to France.

Miller's busy writing hand and the complicated publication history of his works make it difficult to establish a canon of his writings. Among his works are three installments of *Book of Friends: A Tribute to Friends of Long Ago*; such literary criticism as *Henry Miller on Writing, Books in My Life, Time of the Assassins: A Study of Rimbaud* (1956), and *The World of Lawrence: A Passionate Appreciation*; travel books such as *The Colossus of Maroussi* (1941), *Big Sur and the Oranges of Hieronymus Bosch* (1957), *Quiet Days in Clichy*, and *Under the Roofs of Paris. Just Wild about Harry* is a play, and some of Miller's work as a watercolor artist is available in *The Paintings of Henry Miller*.

NOVELS BY MILLER

Black Spring. 1936. Grove Pr. 1989 $8.95. ISBN 0-8021-3182-4. A continuation of *Tropic of Cancer* in which Miller explores the past of the protaganist.

Crazy Cock. Grove Pr. 1991 $18.95. ISBN 0-8021-1412-1. A novel in tortured prose, about an author trying to find his voice.

Nexus: The Rosy Crucifixion III. 1960. Grove Pr. 1987 $7.95. ISBN 0-8021-5178-7

Plexus: The Rosy Crucifixion II. 1953. Grove Pr. 1987 $9.95. ISBN 0-8021-5179-5

The Rosy Crucifixion: Sexus, Plexus, and Nexus. 3 vols. Grove Pr. 1980 o.p.

Sexus. 1949. Grove Pr. 1987 $12.95. ISBN 0-8021-5180-9

Tropic of Cancer. 1934. Grove Pr. 1987 $10.95. ISBN 0-8021-3178-6. The story of an artist who has given up living in a conventional manner. Largely autobiographical, it covers the artist's years spent bumming around in Paris.

Tropic of Capricorn. 1938. Grove Pr. 1987 $9.95. ISBN 0-8021-5182-5. Beginning of a triad of autobiographical novels in which Miller is a central character. Covers the period from 1920 through 1923 when he met June Smith to 1928 when they left for Europe. The two other works include *Tropic of Cancer* and *Black Spring*.

Nonfiction by Miller

Big Sur and the Oranges of Hieronymus Bosch. 1957. New Dir. Pr. 1964 $12.95. ISBN 0-8112-0107-4. Chronicles Miller's life in the Big Sur coastal area of southern California.

The Books in My Life. New Dir. Pr. 1969 $9.95. ISBN 0-8112-0108-2

The Colossus of Maroussi. 1941. New Dir. Pr. 1958 $8.95. ISBN 0-8112-0109-0

Gliding into the Everglades: And Other Essays. Borgo Pr. 1989 $23.00. ISBN 0-8095-4065-7

Letters to Anais Nin. Paragon Hse. 1988 $12.95. ISBN 1-55778-146-X

A Literate Passion: Letters of Anais Nin and Henry Miller, 1932–1953. HarBraceJ 1987 $19.95. ISBN 0-15-152729-6. Letters revealing the private friendship between Miller and Anais Nin.

Henry Miller on Writing. New Dir. Pr. 1964 $9.95. ISBN 0-8112-0112-0

Henry Miller's Book of Friends: A Trilogy. Borgo Pr. 1988 $30.00. ISBN 0-8095-4031-2

Henry Miller's Hamlet Letters. Capra Pr. 1988 $8.95. ISBN 0-88496-269-5. Collection of essay-type letters in which Miller discusses the metaphysical problems of the time.

Quiet Days in Clichy. Grove Pr. 1987 $7.95. ISBN 0-8021-3016-X. Anecdotal reflections about Miller's post-*Tropic of Cancer* Parisian period.

The Time of the Assassins: A Study of Rimbaud. 1956. New Dir. Pr. 1962 $8.95. ISBN 0-8112-0115-5

Under the Roofs of Paris. Grove Pr. 1985 $3.95. ISBN 0-394-62030-5

Play by Miller

Just Wild about Harry. New Dir. Pr. 1979 $4.95. ISBN 0-8112-0724-2

Works by Miller

The Air-Conditioned Nightmare. 1945–47. New Dir. Pr. 1970 $10.95 ISBN 0-8112-0106-6

Aller Retour New York. New Dir. Pr. 1993 $8.95. ISBN 0-8112-1226-2

The Cosmological Eye. 1939. New Dir. Pr. 1969 $10.95. ISBN 0-8112-0319-0. Collection of shorter prose writings taken from *Black Spring, Max,* and *The White Phagocytes.*

Henry Miller Reader. New Dir. Pr. 1969 $12.95. ISBN 0-8112-0111-2

Into the Heart of Life: Henry Miller at One Hundred. New Dir. Pr. 1991 $10.95. ISBN 0-8112-1185-1. An anthology of Miller's work that fully represents his distinctive literary characteristics.

The Nightmare Notebook. New Dir. Pr. 1975 $150.00. ISBN 0-8112-0576-2

Nothing but the Marvelous: The Wisdoms of Henry Miller. Capra Pr. 1990 $10.95. ISBN 0-88496-313-6. Short excerpts from periodicals and published works on a variety of subjects.

Sextet: His Later Writings Under One Cover. Borgo Pr. 1988 $25.00. ISBN 0-8095-4046-0

Stand Still Like the Hummingbird. New Dir. Pr. 1967 $8.95. ISBN 0-8112-0322-0

Books about Miller

Brown, J. D. *Henry Miller.* Continuum 1986 $18.95. ISBN 0-8044-2077-7. Displays a deep sensitivity for and appreciation of Miller while acknowledging his shortcomings as a writer.

Durrell, Lawrence, illustrator. *Henry Miller—The Paintings: A Centennial Retrospective.* Coast Pub. 1991 $25.00. ISBN 0-9600554-2-8. Published to commemorate the centenary of Miller's birth.

Ferguson, Robert. *Henry Miller: A Life*. Norton 1991 $24.95. ISBN 0-393-02978-6. Detailed study of Miller's experiences.

Moss, Leonard. *Henry Miller*. Macmillan 1990 $20.95. ISBN 0-8057-7607-9. Covers Miller's late years and works.

Parkin, John. *Henry Miller: The Modern Rabelais*. E. Mellen 1990 $59.95. ISBN 0-88946-628-9

Shifreen, Lawrence J. *Henry Miller: A Bibliography of Secondary Sources*. Scarecrow 1979 $39.50. ISBN 0-8108-1171-5. An annotated bibliography of commentary and criticism of Miller.

Wicks, George, ed. *Henry Miller and the Critics*. S. Ill. U. Pr. 1967 $12.95. ISBN 0-8093-0102-4. Interesting selection of essays appraising Miller's work and the man himself.

Widmer, Kingsley. *Henry Miller*. Macmillan 1990 $19.95. ISBN 0-685-46982-4. A scholarly, critical study of Miller's writings.

MOORE, MARIANNE. 1887–1972

Born in St. Louis, the "first lady of American poetry," Marianne Moore, graduated from Bryn Mawr College in 1909. In 1918 she moved to New York City with her mother, remaining there for the rest of her life. She became a well-known character in her Brooklyn Heights neighborhood, easily recognizable in a large black hat and rather eccentric style. In 1921 a few of her friends pirated her work and published it under the title *Poems*. On her seventy-fifth birthday, November 15, 1962, she was honored by the National Institute of Arts and Letters, and in a special interview for the *N.Y. Times*, she spoke of her feelings concerning the treatment of poetry: "I'm very doubtful about scholasticizing poetry," she said. "I feel very strongly that poetry should not be an assignment but a joy." Five years later she said: "I wonder that I can bear myself to be in a world where they don't outlaw war." In 1967 Moore received both the MacDowell Medal and a Gold Medal. Mayor John Lindsay of New York City hailed her as "truly the poet laureate of New York City." The famed Rosenbach Museum in Philadelphia has a collection devoted to her work and a detailed replica of a room in her Brooklyn home.

Moore brought to her work a prodigious knowledge and passionate interest in many diverse fields, including the arts, natural history, and public affairs. Her use of the images and language of these fields in her poetry enabled her to offset traditional poetic tones with the cadences of prose rhetoric and everyday speech. This talent, coupled with her precision and intricate metrics, make her one of the leading modernist poets.

POETRY BY MOORE

The Complete Poems of Marianne Moore. Viking Penguin 1987 $9.95. ISBN 0-14-058601-6. A collection that reveals the full scope of Moore's work; includes her final revisions made after 1967.

WORK BY MOORE

The Complete Prose of Marianne Moore. Viking Penguin 1986 $24.95. ISBN 0-670-80451-7. Collection of Moore's reviews from *The Dial*, and long critical essays on William Carlos Williams and Ezra Pound.

BOOKS ABOUT MOORE

Bloom, Harold, ed. *Marianne Moore*. Chelsea Hse. 1986 $24.95. ISBN 0-87754-631-2. Contains important critical essays.

Engel, Bernard F. *Marianne Moore*. Macmillan 1988 $22.95. ISBN 0-8057-7525-0. A solid general introduction to Moore's life and works.

Erickson, Darlene W. *Illusion Is More Precise Than Precision: The Poetry of Marianne Moore.* U. of Ala. Pr. 1982 $29.95. ISBN 0-8173-0570-X. Insightful study focusing on Moore's poetic creativity.

Goodridge, Celeste. *Hints and Disguises: Marianne Moore and Her Contemporaries.* U. of Iowa Pr. 1989 $18.95. ISBN 0-87745-239-3. Exploration of Moore's prose that focuses on her private and public critical exchanges with Stevens, Pound, Williams, and Eliot.

Holley, Margaret. *The Poetry of Marianne Moore: A Study in Voice and Value.* Cambridge U. Pr. 1988 $37.50. ISBN 0-521-33284-2. Throws light on the pervasive moralism of Moore's poetry.

Merrin, Jeredith. *An Enabling Humility: Marianne Moore, Elizabeth Bishop, and the Uses of Tradition.* Rutgers U. Pr. 1990 $35.00. ISBN 0-8135-1547-5. Examines Moore's debts to and feminist departures from Renaissance and romantic models.

Molesworth, Charles. *Marianne Moore: A Literary Life.* Macmillan 1990 $29.95. ISBN 0-689-11815-5. Noteworthy biography that focuses on Moore's poetry and her relationships with other writers.

Phillips, Elizabeth. *Marianne Moore.* Continuum 1982 $18.95. ISBN 0-8044-2698-8. A useful study of Moore's life and works with special attention to her poetic techniques; includes a chronology, bibliography, and concise biographical sketch.

Schulman, Grace. *Marianne Moore: The Poetry of Engagement.* U. of Ill. Pr. 1987 $24.95. ISBN 0-252-01270-4. Study of the changing rhetorical patterns of Moore's poetry.

Stapleton, Laurence. *Marianne Moore: The Poet's Advance.* Princeton U. Pr. 1978 $42.50. ISBN 0-691-06373-7. Presents a full-scale interpretation of Moore's poetry and prose.

Willis, Patricia C. *Marianne Moore: Vision into Verse.* U. Pr. of Va. 1988 $18.50. ISBN 0-939084-21-X. Exhibition of the Marianne Moore collection that includes a thoughtful and sensitive essay of the poet's life and works as well as numerous illustrations of artifacts, curiosities, and newspaper clippings that teased the author's imagination into poetry.

NIN, ANAÏS. 1903–1977

Anaïs Nin was a neglected and almost legendary figure in the history of modern art and letters until selections from her monumental diary—drawn from an original 150 volumes comprising 15,000 pages of typescript—began to appear in 1966. She was born in 1903, the daughter of a well-known Spanish pianist and composer who separated from his wife and daughter when Nin was 11 years old. Brought to the United States, she attended public schools only briefly before embarking on a remarkable program of self-education that included starting her diary as an unmailed letter to her lost father. Creating a special persona for herself, she returned to Paris during the early 1930s, supporting herself as an artist's model and Spanish dancer while continuing to write. By 1939 she had published in Paris *D. H. Lawrence: An Unprofessional Study*, a prose poem called *House of Incest* (1936) and three novelettes gathered under the title *Winter of Artifice* (1939). She had become close friends with many leading figures of the Parisian artistic and social scene, including the then-struggling writer HENRY MILLER; the young surrealist poet ANTONIN ARTAUD (see Vol. 2); and the psychiatrist Otto Rank. She returned to the United States at the outbreak of World War II in 1939. Because she could not place her writings with commercial publishers, she bought her own printing press and in 1944 produced a small, hand-set edition of her stories, *Under a Glass Bell*. Praised by EDMUND WILSON in the *New Yorker*, it was republished four years later by Dutton, and from then on she was able to publish regularly, although she found only a small, discriminating audience until the publication of her diary. Then the representative role she seemed to play in the feminist movement helped to arouse interest in her creative work.

Anaïs Nin's fiction is marked by a dreamlike sensibility. Probably the best entry into her fictive world is the omnibus volume *Cities of the Interior* (1946–58), which brings together five short novels to create a sustained narrative. Even the erotica she wrote on commission for a wealthy gentleman during her Paris years—published after her death in *Delta of Venus* (1977) and *Little Birds* (1979)—has a poetic and transcendent aura.

NOVELS BY NIN

Children of the Albatross. Ohio U. Pr. 1959 $4.95. ISBN 0-8040-0039-5. A novel, divided into two sections, about a woman and the men who encircle her.

Cities of the Interior. Introduction by Sharon Spencer. Ohio U. Pr. 1974 $19.95. ISBN 0-8040-0665-2. An omnibus volume containing *Ladders to Fire*, *Children of the Albatross*, *The Four-Chambered Heart*, *A Spy in the House of Love*, and *The Seduction of the Minotaur*.

Collages. Ohio U. Pr. 1964 $3.95. ISBN 0-8040-0045-X. A portfolio of characters who have some flaw which makes them interesting.

Four-Chambered Heart. Ohio U. Pr. 1959 $5.95. ISBN 0-8040-0121-9. A story about a woman and her relationships with men, particularly one who is a guitar player.

House of Incest. 1936. Ohio U. Pr. 1958 $4.95. ISBN 0-8040-0148-0

Ladders to Fire. Ohio U. Pr. 1959 $5.95. ISBN 0-8040-0181-2. A novel about an actress who is successful in her career, but is filled with self-doubt about her work and life.

Seduction of the Minotaur. Ohio U. Pr. 1961 $6.95. ISBN 0-8040-0268-1. Tells about the development of a woman from an unsettled past to a more fulfilled and contented life.

A Spy in the House of Love. 1954. Bantam 1986 $3.95. ISBN 0-553-26391-9. A novel about a woman's anguish in grasping the nature of her difficulties.

Winter of Artifice. 1939. Ohio U. Pr. 1961 $5.95. ISBN 0-8040-0322-X

NONFICTION BY NIN

The Novel of the Future. Ohio U. Pr. 1986 $10.95. ISBN 0-8040-0879-5. Discusses techniques and approaches to writing and literature.

WORKS BY NIN

Anais Nin Reader. Ed. by Philip K. Jason, intro. by Anna Balakian. Ohio U. Pr. 1973 o.p. Selections from both her fiction and her nonfiction—a good introduction to this not easily classified writer.

Delta of Venus. 1977. Bantam 1978 $4.50. ISBN 0-553-26911-9

D. H. Lawrence: An Unprofessional Study. Ohio U. Pr. 1964 $4.95. ISBN 0-8040-0067-0

The Diary of Anais Nin, 1966–1974. HarBraceJ 1981 $10.95. ISBN 0-15-626035-2. Reveals Nin's quest for independence, and her own psychological acceptance of a feminine identity.

The Early Diary of Anais Nin: Vol. 1, 1914–1920. HarBraceJ 1980 $7.50. ISBN 0-15-652386-8. Covers Nin's thoughts and feelings from the time she moved to New York at age 11 until age 17.

The Early Diary of Anais Nin. Vol. 2, 1920–1923. HarBrace J 1983 $12.95. ISBN 0-15-627248-2. Continues Nin's diary memoirs as she made the transition to the world of artists and models.

The Early Diary of Anais Nin. Vol. 3, 1923–1927. HarBrace J 1985 $12.95. ISBN 0-15-627250-4. Third volume of Nin's diary, which begins a month after her marriage to French banker Hugh Guiler; comments primarily on her marriage, her parents, and her experiences in Paris.

The Early Diary of Anais Nin. Vol. 4, 1918–1927. HarBrace J 1986 $12.95. ISBN 0-15-627251-2. The fourth volume of Nin's diary reveals her feelings about married life, her life in Paris, and her obsession with John Erskine.

Henry and June: From the Unexpurgated Diary of Anais. HarBraceJ 1986 $14.95. ISBN 0-15-140003-2. Used as the basis for a film made in 1991.

In Favor of the Sensitive Man and Other Essays. HarBrace J 1976 $7.95. ISBN 0-15-644445-3. Essays sharing her perceptions of people, places, and the arts.
Little Birds. 1979. PB 1990 $4.95. ISBN 0-671-68011-0
Under a Glass Bell. 1944. Ohio U. Pr. 1948 $4.95. ISBN 0-8040-0302-5
Waste of Timelessness: And Other Early Stories. Ohio U. Pr. 1980 $6.00. ISBN 0-685-03709-6. Series of vignettes detailing Paris life with its cafes, theaters, and artists.

Books about Nin

Franklin, Benjamin. *Anais Nin: An Introduction.* Ohio U. Pr. 1980 $20.00. ISBN 0-8214-0395-8. A comprehensive analysis of Nin's work.
———. *Anais Nin: A Bibliography.* Bks. Demand repr. of 1973 ed. $31.30 ISBN 0-317-10335-0
Knapp, Bettina L. *Anais Nin.* Continuum 1978 $18.95. ISBN 0-8044-2481-0. Examines Nin's fiction in the context of French culture and the arts of her time.
Pine, Richard. *The Dandy and the Herald.* St. Martin 1988 $35.00. ISBN 0-312-00521-0
Scholar, Nancy. *Anais Nin.* G. K. Hall 1984 o.p.
Spencer, Sharon. *College of Dreams: The Writings of Anais Nin.* Ohio U. Pr. 1977 $12.95. ISBN 0-8040-0760-8. In-depth examination of Nin's fiction and nonfiction.
———, ed. *Anais Nin, Art and Artists: A Collection of Essays.* Penkevill 1987 $20.00. ISBN 0-913283-11-8. Collection of essays attempting to place Nin's work in the context of modern feminism and the arts.

O'HARA, JOHN. 1905–1970

Working comfortably within the tradition of social realism, John O'Hara turned out more than 20 novels and 200 short stories. According to Charles Bassett (*Dictionary of Literary Biography*), O'Hara "claimed to be the hardest working author in the United States." The eldest of eight children of a physician in Pottsville, Pennsylvania, whose sudden death seemed to make college impossible for his children, O'Hara, deeply disappointed, used journalism as his path to a writing career, working as a Hollywood press agent, serving as secretary to Heywood Broun, and writing regularly for the *N.Y. Herald Tribune* and the *New Yorker* before his first novel, *Appointment in Samarra* (1934), brought him immediate fame. Although its successor, *Butterfield 8* (1935), was less of a critical success, it too found a wide audience. These first two novels, comparatively short and more tightly constructed than most of his later works, are still thought to be among his best works, although in retrospect it now seems that his career reached its peak with two long novels published during the mid-1950s. *Ten North Frederick*, published in 1955, was given the National Book Award in that year. O'Hara may have liked *From the Terrace* (1958) best of all his novels because it deals with a favorite theme—the emotional poverty of a man who in the eyes of the world is a great success.

Novels by O'Hara

Appointment in Samarra. 1934. Random 1982 $9.00. ISBN 0-394-71192-0
Butterfield 8. 1935. Buccaneer Bks. 1991 $22.95. ISBN 0-89966-871-2
The Ewings. Random 1972 $14.95. ISBN 0-394-47404-X. Posthumously published novel about a married woman and mother who discovers her lesbianism.
From the Terrace. 1958. Carroll & Graf 1984 $5.95. ISBN 0-88184-105-6
Hope of Heaven. Carroll & Graf 1985 $3.95. ISBN 0-88184-149-8. A romantic love story tinged with fatalism.
The Lockwood Concern. Carroll & Graf 1986 $4.95. ISBN 0-88184-217-6. Novel about a family's moral history, its egotism, and its isolation.
Lovey Childs: A Philadelphian's Story. Random 1969 o.p. Tale of a young girl who is anxious to come of age, but whose initiation into life is too much for her to bear.

Pal Joey. 1940. Random 1983 repr. of 1976 ed. o.p. Tale of a brash and egotistical second-rate night-club entertainer; it was made into a successful musical and movie.

A Rage to Live. Carroll & Graf 1986 $4.95. ISBN 0-88184-216-8. The story of a woman whose inability to control her sexual passions results in the destruction of her marriage.

The Second Ewings. Bruccoli 1977 $40.00. ISBN 0-89723-012-4. A 74-page fragment, published posthumously, that begins to expand the story of the family in *The Ewings*. In this fragment, Bill Ewing becomes a chairman of a company.

Sermons and Soda Water. Carroll & Graf 1986 $4.95. ISBN 0-88184-271-0. Three novellas about the passing of youth and the middle-aged aftermath of happier times.

Ten North Frederick. 1955. Carroll & Graf 1985 $4.50. ISBN 0-88184-173-0. Novel about a successful family man who faces failure and isolation late in life.

Waiting for Winter. Random 1966 o.p. Series of tales on diverse subjects, taking place in both the past and present and on all levels of society.

SHORT STORY COLLECTIONS BY O'HARA

Collected Stories of John O'Hara. Random 1985 $19.95. ISBN 0-394-54083-2

The Time Element and Other Stories. Random 1972 $14.95. ISBN 0-394-48211-5

BOOKS ABOUT O'HARA

Grebstein, Sheldon N. *John O'Hara.* NCUP 1966 $10.95. ISBN 0-8084-0187-4. Candid, comprehensive critique of O'Hara's writings.

Long, Robert E. *John O'Hara.* Continuum 1983 $18.95. ISBN 0-8044-2541-8. A comprehensive, up-to-date account of O'Hara's life and career.

MacShane, Frank. *The Life of John O'Hara.* NAL-Dutton 1981 o.p. Vivid portrait of O'Hara that views him as one of the great popular writers of the century.

PARKER, DOROTHY. 1893–1967

Poet and short story writer Dorothy Parker was born in New Jersey. When she was 5, her mother died and her father, a clothes salesman, remarried. Parker had a great antipathy toward her stepmother and refused to speak to her. She attended parochial school and Miss Dana's school in Morristown, New Jersey for a brief time before dropping out at age 14. A voracious reader, she decided to pursue a career in literature. She began her career by writing verse as well as captions for a fashion magazine.

During the years of her greatest fame, Dorothy Parker was known primarily as a writer of light verse, an essential member of the Algonquin Round Table, and a caustic and witty critic of literature and society. She is remembered now as an almost legendary figure of the 1920s and 1930s. Her reviews and staff contributions to three of the most sophisticated magazines of this century, *Vanity Fair*, the *New Yorker*, and *Esquire*, were notable for their put-downs; and many of the most famous bright remarks of the time were attributed to her—only some of them justly so. For all her highbrow wit, however, Dorothy Parker was liberal, even radical, in her political views, and the hard veneer of brittle toughness that she showed to the world was often a shield for frustrated idealism and soft sensibilities. The best of her fiction is marked by a balance of ironic detachment and sympathetic compassion, as in "Big Blonde," which won the O. Henry Award for 1929 and is still her best-remembered and most frequently anthologized story.

Parker was twice married, once to SINCLAIR LEWIS. Her private life did not mirror her public one. Besides her foundered marriages, she had a number of unhappy love affairs and one-night stands. There were also abortive suicide attempts, abortions, and great bouts of drinking. She died alone in her New York apartment.

The best of Dorothy Parker is readily and compactly accessible in *The Portable Dorothy Parker*. Her own selection of stories and verse for the original edition of that compilation, published in 1944, remains intact in the revised edition, but included also are additional stories, reviews, and articles.

PLAY BY PARKER

The Coast of Illyria. A Play in Three Acts. U. of Iowa Pr. 1990 $26.00. ISBN 0-87745-273-3. The story of a man whose guardianship of his unstable sister allows him no other personal attachments.

WORKS BY PARKER

At Her Best. Amereon Ltd. $18.95. ISBN 0-8488-0117-2
The Portable Dorothy Parker. 1944. Viking Penguin rev. ed. 1976 $12.00. ISBN 0-14-015074-9. Contains all of Parker's major works, revealing her caustic wit and sharp, critical mind.

BOOKS ABOUT PARKER

Keats, John. *You Might As Well Live: The Life and Times of Dorothy Parker*. Paragon Hse. 1986 $12.95. ISBN 0-913729-49-3
Kinney, Arthur F. *Dorothy Parker*. G. K. Hall 1978 o.p. A comprehensive introduction to Parker's life and works, with extensive discussion of how the two relate; includes chronology and bibliography.
Meade, Marion. *Dorothy Parker: What Fresh Hell Is This?* Random 1987 $22.50. ISBN 0-394-54440-4. Recounts the unhappy life of the wise-cracking versifier.

PERELMAN, S(IDNEY) J(OSEPH). 1904–1979

S. J. Perelman—called the king of the "dementia praecox field" by fellow humorist ROBERT BENCHLEY—was a prolific humorist and satirist at the *New Yorker* for almost half a century. His contributions had a surrealistic quality in style and in subject that elicited from DOROTHY PARKER the judgment that he had "a disciplined eye and a wild mind" and "a magnificent disregard" for his reader. His raillery was aimed at popular fiction, motion pictures, advertising, and similar features of our transient culture. In his preferred form, a short drama, Perelman excelled in the unconventional, the concentrated, the sophisticated in humor.

NONFICTION BY PERELMAN

Baby, It's Cold Inside. Viking Penguin 1987 $6.95. ISBN 0-14-008042-2. A series of satires revealing Perelman's amusement at human failings.
Crazy Like a Fox. 1944. Random 1973 o.p. Contains 46 short pieces.
Don't Tread on Me: The Selected Letters of S. J. Perelman. Ed. by Prudence Crowther. Viking Penguin 1988 $10.95. ISBN 0-14-009482-2. Collection of 51 years of letters from the American humorist.
Eastward Ha! S & S Trade 1983 o.p. Humorous reflections on Perelman's journeys around the globe, including trips to Scotland and the Pacific.
The Last Laugh. S & S Trade 1982 o.p. Includes fourteen stories from the *New Yorker* and four chapters from his autobiography.
The Rising Gorge. Viking Penguin 1987 $6.95. ISBN 0-14-008041-4
The Swiss Family Perelman. Viking Penguin 1987 $6.95. ISBN 0-14-008040-6. Chronicles Perelman's globe-trotting escapades with his family.
Westward, Ha!: Around the World in 80 Clichés. Da Capo 1984 $7.95. ISBN 0-306-80229-5. More globe-trotting commentary, including descriptions and comments on various locales.

BOOKS ABOUT PERELMAN

Gale, Steven H., ed. *S. J. Perelman: Critical Essays*. Garland 1991 $45.00. ISBN 0-8240-3422-8. Includes interviews with Perelman, anthology introductions, reviews, a chronology, and a selected primary bibliography.

PORTER, KATHERINE ANNE. 1890–1980

Katherine Anne Porter is known for her subtle and delicate perception; her careful, disciplined technique; and her precision of word and phrase. She wrote slowly and with restraint but achieved an impression of ease and naturalness that is close to perfection. She was born in Texas, schooled in Louisiana convents, and, working as a newspaper reporter and freelance journalist, traveled to such places as Paris, Majorca, Berlin, Vienna, and Mexico. Her *Collected Stories* (1965), which won both the Pulitzer Prize and the National Book Award in 1966, was written over a long lifetime. It includes works that have been a standard part of high school and college literature courses for a half-century. Among the best are "Noon Wine," "The Jilting of Granny Weatherall," and "Flowering Judas." "Pale Horse, Pale Rider," long enough to be considered a novelette, is one of several stories about a character named Miranda who as a girl and young woman undergoes experiences not unlike those of Porter. Other Miranda stories are "Old Mortality" and a group of seven gathered under the title "The Old Order" that deal with her childhood.

Her one and only full-length novel, *Ship of Fools* (1962), 20 years in the writing, "is the story of a voyage. . . . A novel of character rather than of action, it has as its main purpose a study of the German ethos shortly before Hitler's coming to power in Germany. . . . 'Ship of Fools' is also a human comedy and a moral allegory" (*New Yorker*). To some critics, the book was a disappointment, but all recognized its importance and it appeared on the bestseller list for 28 weeks in 1962.

"In my view," wrote ROBERT PENN WARREN in a tribute published in *Saturday Review* after Porter's death in 1980, "the final importance of Katherine Anne Porter is not merely that she has written a number of fictions which have enlarged and deepened the nature of the story, both short and long, in our time, but that she has created an *oeuvre*—a body of work including fiction, essays, letters, and journals—that bears the stamp of a personality, distinctive, delicately perceptive, keenly aware of the depth and darkness of human experience, delighted by the beauty of the world and the triumphs of human kindness and warmth, and thoroughly committed to a quest for meaning in the midst of the ironic complexities of man's lot." Much of the nonfictional part of that body of work was gathered into *The Collected Essays and Occasional Writings of Katherine Anne Porter*.

NOVEL BY PORTER

Ship of Fools. 1962. Little 1984 $11.95. ISBN 0-316-71390-2. Diverse collection of ship's passengers enriching this allegorical tale of pre-Hitler Germany.

SHORT STORY COLLECTION BY PORTER

The Collected Stories of Katherine Anne Porter. 1964. HarBraceJ 1979 $10.95. ISBN 0-15-618876-7

NONFICTION BY PORTER

Collected Essays and Occasional Writings of Katherine Anne Porter. HM 1990 $12.70. ISBN 0-395-53362-7

This Strange Old World and Other Book Reviews by Katherine Anne Porter. U. of Ga. Pr. 1991 $25.00. ISBN 0-8203-1331-9. Collection of previously unpublished reviews from newspapers, revealing Porter's positions on social issues.

WORK BY PORTER

Letters of Katherine Anne Porter. Atlantic Monthly 1981 $16.95. ISBN 0-87113-453-5. Letters to friends, family, publishers, editors, and lovers, covering the years from 1930 to 1963.

BOOKS ABOUT PORTER

Bloom, Harold, ed. *Katherine Anne Porter.* Chelsea Hse. 1986 $24.95. ISBN 0-87754-657-6. Contains critical essays, a chronology, and a bibliography.

Givner, Joan. *Katherine Anne Porter: A Life.* U. of Ga. Pr. 1991 repr. of 1982 ed. $19.95. ISBN 0-8203-1348-3. "A judicious and balanced portrait" by a biographer chosen by Porter (*Journal of Modern Lit.*).

_____. *Katherine Anne Porter: Conversations.* U. Pr. of Miss. 1987 $30.00. ISBN 0-87805-266-6. Interviews with Katherine Anne Porter that reveal some facet of her life and career.

Hendrick, George. *Katherine Anne Porter.* Macmillan 1988 $19.95. ISBN 0-8057-7513-7. Explication of both those moments in Porter's work that show brilliance and those less frequent occasions that reveal flaws.

Machann, Clinton, ed. *Katherine Anne Porter and Texas: An Uneasy Relationship.* Texas A & M Univ. Pr. 1990 $29.50. ISBN 0-89096-441-6. Contains essays on Porter divided into three sections—personal recollections written by a scholar, friends, and a nephew of the author; critical essays discussing the imprint of Texas on Porter's fiction; and an annotated bibliography of letters, articles, and other writing by or about Porter.

Mooney, Harry J., Jr. *The Fiction and Criticism of Katherine Anne Porter.* U. of Pittsburgh Pr. rev. ed. 1962 $4.95. ISBN 0-8229-5018-9

Schwartz, Edward. *Katherine Anne Porter: A Critical Biography.* Folcroft 1953 o.p.

Unrue, Darlene H. *Truth and Vision in Katherine Anne Porter's Fiction.* U. of Ga. Pr. 1985 $30.00. ISBN 0-8203-0768-8

_____. *Understanding Katherine Anne Porter.* U. of SC Pr. 1988 $24.95. ISBN 0-87249-583-3. Perceives Porter to be critical of institutional religions, dictatorial societies, and environments restrictive of women.

Vanashree. *Feminine Consciousness in the Fiction of Katherine Anne Porter.* Advent NY 1990 $17.95. ISBN 81-7045-069-1

Walsh, Thomas F. *Katherine Anne Porter and Mexico: The Illusion of Eden.* U. of Tex. Pr. 1992 $37.50. ISBN 0-292-74311-4. Attempts a full account of Porter's experience in Mexico and an interpretation of her works in the light of her experiences there.

Warren, Robert Penn. *Katherine Anne Porter: A Collection of Critical Essays.* P-H 1978 o.p.

POUND, EZRA (LOOMIS). 1885–1972

With T. S. ELIOT, Ezra Pound was one of the two main influences on British and U.S. poetry between the two world wars. The collection of his *Letters, 1907–1941* revealed the great erudition of this most controversial expatriate poet. Born in Idaho, Pound graduated from the University of Pennsylvania and went abroad to live in 1908. His first book, *A Lume Spento,* a small collection of poems, was published in Venice in 1908. With the publication of *Personae* in London in 1909, he became the leader of the imagists abroad.

Pound's writings have been subject to many foreign influences. First he imitated the troubadours; then he came under the influence of the Chinese and Japanese poets. *The Cantos* (1925–60), his major work, to which he added for many years, is a mixture of modern colloquial language and classical quotation.

The Pisan Cantos (1948), written during his imprisonment in Italy, is more autobiographical.

Pound's prose, as well as his poetry, has been extremely influential. *The Spirit of Romance* (1910) is a revision of his studies of little-known romance writers. *ABC of Reading* (1934) is an exposition of his critical method. His critical writings include *Literary Essays of Ezra Pound* (1954), *Instigations* (1920), and *Guide to Kulchur* (1938).

Pound was a linguist, whom Eliot called "the inventor of Chinese poetry for our time." His greatest translating achievements from Japanese, Chinese, Anglo-Saxon, Italian, Provençal, and French are collected in *The Translations of Ezra Pound* (1933). Among his other writings are *Make It New: Essays*; *Jefferson and/or Mussolini*, a discussion of American democracy and capitalism and fascism; and *The Classic Noh Theatre of Japan*, with Ernest Fenollosa.

Living in Italy, Pound felt that some of the practices of Mussolini were in accord with the doctrines of social credit, in which he had become interested in the 1920s and 1930s. He espoused some of the general applications of fascism and also was a strong advocate of anti-Semitism. During World War II, he broadcast a pro-Fascist series of programs addressed to the Allied troops on Italian radio. Indicted for treason and brought to the United States to stand trial in 1946, he was judged mentally incompetent to prepare a defense and was committed to St. Elizabeth's Hospital in Washington, D.C. in what is now considered less of a reflection on his sanity than on his politics. After a concerted appeal to the federal government by American poets, led by ROBERT FROST, Pound was at last released in 1958 and returned to Italy. Critics have recently begun to face squarely the connections between his fascism and his poetry; facts of his life and work continue to arouse mixed feelings.

POETRY BY POUND

Cantos of Ezra Pound: Nos. 1–117. 1925–60. New Dir. Pr. 1970 $31.95. ISBN 0-8112-0350-6

The Collected Early Poems of Ezra Pound. New Dir. Pr. 1982 $11.95. ISBN 0-8112-0843-5. Complete texts of the poet's first 6 texts and 25 poems originally published in periodicals.

Drafts and Fragments, Cantos 110–117. New Dir. Pr. 1969 o.p. The final Volume of Pound's *Cantos*.

A Draft of XXX Cantos. Haskell 1974 $75.00. ISBN 0-8383-1997-1

Lustra. Haskell 1973 $75.00. ISBN 0-8383-1688-3. Collection of poems that displays his mastery over the "modern poem".

Personae: Collected Poems. 1909. New Dir. Pr. o.p. All the early work Pound cared to preserve.

Selected Cantos. New Dir. Pr. 1970 $6.95. ISBN 0-8112-0160-0. Pound's own selection from the monumental *Cantos*. Of use to the general poetry reader and beginning Pound student.

Selected Poems. New Dir. Pr. rev. ed. 1957 $6.95. ISBN 0-8112-0162-7

NONFICTION BY POUND

ABC of Reading. New Dir. Pr. 1960 $9.95. ISBN 0-8112-0151-1

Antheil and the Treatise on Harmony. Da Capo 2nd ed. 1968 $25.00. ISBN 0-306-70981-3. A study of music based partly on the notes on music from the American composer George Antheil.

Ezra Pound and the Visual Arts. New Dir. Pr. 1980 $25.95. ISBN 0-8112-0772-2

Gaudier-Brzeska: A Memoir. 1916. New Dir. Pr. 1970 $7.95. ISBN 0-8112-0527-4. This remarkable French sculptor was killed in World War I at age 24.

Guide to Kulchur. New Dir. Pr. 1968 $11.95. ISBN 0-8112-0156-2. A work of criticism about the "Kultur" of various groups from Chinese philosophers to modern poets.

Literary Essays of Ezra Pound. 1953. New Dir. Pr. 1968 $12.95. ISBN 0-8112-0157-0. With an introduction by T. S. Eliot.

Make It New: Essays. Scholarly 1971 $59.00. ISBN 0-403-01158-2

Pavannes and Divagations. New Dir. Pr. 1975 $9.95. ISBN 0-8112-0575-4

Selected Prose, 1909–1965. Ed. by William Cookson. New Dir. Pr. 1975 $12.95. ISBN 0-8112-0574-6. Gathers Pound's previously uncollected prose pieces, including pieces on religion, Confucius, America, economics, and history.

Signs in Action. Red Dust 1987 $4.00. ISBN 0-87376-057-3

Spirit of Romance. New Dir. Pr. 1968 $7.75. ISBN 0-8112-0163-5. Discussion of the art of writing, which is years ahead of his contemporaries.

WORKS BY POUND

Confucian Analects. Dufour 1980 $26.00. ISBN 0-7206-1850-9. Pound's translation and study of the analects, or sayings, of Confucius.

Ezra Pound and Japan: Letters and Essays. Black Swan CT 1986 $25.00. ISBN 0-933806-27-2. Meticulous tracing of Pound's fascination with Japan.

Letters of Ezra Pound. Haskell 1974 $75.00. ISBN 0-8383-1991-2

The Letters of Ezra Pound to James Joyce, with Pound's Essays on Joyce. Ed. by Forrest Read. New Dir. Pr. 1970 o.p.

Letters to John Theobald. Black Swan CT 1984 $22.50. ISBN 0-933806-02-7

Letters to Tom Carter. Black Swan CT 1989 $25.00. ISBN 0-933806-25-6

Pound-Ford: The Story of a Literary Friendship. New Dir. Pr. 1982 $22.95. ISBN 0-8112-0833-8

Pound-Lewis: The Letters of Ezra Pound and Wyndham Lewis. New Dir. Pr. 1985 $37.50. ISBN 0-8112-0932-6

Pound-The Little Review: The Letters of Ezra Pound to Margaret Anderson. New Dir. Pr. 1988 $37.50. ISBN 0-8112-1059-6. Pound's letters to the open-minded founder of the *Little Review*.

Selected Letters of Ezra Pound, 1907–1941. New Dir. Pr. 1971 $6.95. ISBN 0-8112-0161-9. Correspondence to friends, colleagues, and unknowns who wrote for advice.

The Translations of Ezra Pound. New Dir. Pr. 1953 o.p. A collection of Pound's translations of original poetry.

BOOKS ABOUT POUND

Ackroyd, Peter. *Ezra Pound.* Thames Hudson 1987 $9.95. ISBN 0-500-26025-7

Alexander, Michael. *The Poetic Achievement of Ezra Pound.* U. CA Pr. 1979 $42.50. ISBN 0-520-03739-1. Useful introduction to Pound's poetry that identifies its basic qualities and characteristics.

Bernstein, Michael A. *The Tale of the Tribe: Ezra Pound and the Modern Verse Epic.* Princeton U. Pr. 1980 $55.00. ISBN 0-691-06434-2. A systematic analysis of the tradition of modern epic poetry using *Cantos* as a model.

Bloom, Harold, ed. *Ezra Pound.* Chelsea Hse. 1987 $34.95. ISBN 0-87754-634-7

Bornstein, George, ed. *Ezra Pound Among the Poets.* U. Ch. Pr. 1988 $17.95. ISBN 0-226-06640-1. Crash course in Pound's literary ancestry, sponsorship, and legacies.

Brooker, Peter, ed. *A Student's Guide to the Selected Poems of Ezra Pound.* Faber & Faber 1979 $15.95. ISBN 0-571-11011-8

Bush, R. *The Genesis of Ezra Pound's Cantos.* Princeton U. Pr. 1989 $50.00. ISBN 0-691-06308-7. Traces the development of *Cantos*, and analyzes its similarities with the poetry of Pound's contemporaries.

Carpenter, Humphrey. *A Serious Character: The Life of Ezra Pound.* Delacorte 1990 $19.95. ISBN 0-385-29996-6. Detailed, comprehensive biography of Pound.

Casillo, Robert. *The Genealogy of Demons: Anti-Semitism, Fascism, and the Myths of Ezra Pound.* Northwestern U. Pr. 1988 o.p. Thought-provoking study of the relationship between fascist and anti-Semitic thought and Pound's work.

Childs, John S. *Modernist Form: Pound's Style in the Early Cantos*. Susquehanna U. Pr. 1986 $32.50. ISBN 0-941664-15-5. Full-length structuralist study of the *Cantos* packed with arcane terminology and dense readings.

Cookson, William. *A Guide to the Cantos of Ezra Pound*. Persea Bks. 1985 $24.95. ISBN 0-89255-081-3. Useful work that determines the general themes of the poem; identifies people, places, abbreviations, and unusual expressions; and translates quotations in foreign languages.

Davie, Donald. *Ezra Pound*. U. Ch. Pr. 1982 $4.95. ISBN 0-226-13753-8

Davis, Kay. *Fugue and Fresco: Structures in Pound's Cantos*. Natl. Poet. Found. 1984 $18.00. ISBN 0-915032-07-4

Doolittle, Hilda. *End to Torment: A Memoir of Ezra Pound*. New Dir. Pr. 1979 $6.95. ISBN 0-8112-0720-X. Recollections of Pound by one of his lifelong friends; includes 25 new poems by Pound entitled "Hilda's Book".

Edwards, John H. *Annotated Index to the Cantos of Ezra Pound: Cantos I–LXXXIV*. U. CA Pr. 1971 $49.95. ISBN 0-520-01923-7. Helpful guide to understanding the *Cantos*.

Ellmann, Maud. *The Poetics of Impersonality: T. S. Eliot and Ezra Pound*. HUP 1988 $22.50. ISBN 0-674-678858-3. Discusses the contradictions inherent in the theory of artistic personality that both Pound and Eliot advanced.

Flory, Wendy S. *Ezra Pound and the Cantos: A Record of Struggle*. Yale U. Pr. 1980 $35.00. ISBN 0-300-02392-8. Comprehensive study that examines the autobiographical aspects of *Cantos*.

——. *The American Ezra Pound*. Yale U. Pr. 1989 $30.00. ISBN 0-300-04236-1. Discusses the poet's anti-Semitism, political loyalties, and mental instability.

Gallup, Donald. *Ezra Pound: A Bibliography*. U. Pr. of Va. 1983 $50.00. ISBN 0-8139-0976-7

Hamilton, Scott. *Ezra Pound and the Symbolist Inheritance*. Princeton U. Pr. 1992 $35.00. ISBN 0-691-06924-7. Most scrupulous and scholarly study thus far of symbolist poets and their relationship to Ezra Pound.

Homberger, Eric, ed. *Ezra Pound: The Critical Heritage*. Routledge Chapman & Hall 1972 $69.50. ISBN 0-7100-7260-0

Kaye, Jacqueline. *Ezra Pound and America*. St. Martin 1991 $12.95. ISBN 0-312-06832-8. Collection of 11 essays exploring the little-studied theme of Pound's Americanness.

Kayman, Martin A. *The Modernism of Ezra Pound: The Science of Poetry*. St. Martin 1986 $35.00. ISBN 0-312-54295-X. Addresses the dilemma of many Pound studies: How can one praise the poetry that celebrates such odious politics?

Kearns, George. *Guide to Ezra Pound's Selected Cantos*. Rutgers U. Pr. 1980 $15.00. ISBN 0-8135-0887-8

——. *Pound: The Cantos*. Cambridge U. Pr. 1990 $22.95. ISBN 0-521-33373-3

Kenner, Hugh. *The Pound Era*. U. CA Pr. 1971 $16.95. ISBN 0-520-02427-3

——. *The Poetry of Ezra Pound*. U. of Nebr. Pr. 1985 $8.95. ISBN 0-8032-7756-3

Lindberg, Kathryne V. *Reading Pound Reading: Modernism after Nietzsche*. OUP 1987 $37.00. ISBN 0-19-504165-8. Establishes Pound's links to nineteenth-century thought and the modern critical movement by examining his critical writing.

Makin, Peter. *Pound's Cantos*. Johns Hopkins 1992 $12.95. ISBN 0-8018-4371-5. Offers a guide to the literary and intellectual background of the Cantos, followed by an extended, systematic critical discussion of the work itself and a historical survey of its critical reception.

McGann, Jerome J. *Towards a Literature of Knowledge*. U. Ch. Pr. 1989 $24.95. ISBN 0-226-55839-8. Final work in a five-part project on literature textuality and ideology.

——. *The Textual Condition*. Princeton U. Pr. 1991 $29.95. ISBN 0-691-06931-X

Nassar, Eugene Paul. *The Cantos of Ezra Pound: The Lyric Mode*. Johns Hopkins 1975 $23.00. ISBN 0-8018-1703-X. Provides a coherent overview and detailed analysis of passages in the *Cantos*.

Oderman, Kevin. *Ezra Pound and the Erotic Medium*. Duke 1986 $25.00. ISBN 0-8223-0672-7. Critical look at the sexuality found in Pound's poetry and prose.

Rabate, Jean-Michael. *Language, Sexuality, and Ideology in Ezra Pound's Cantos*. State U. NY Pr. 1986 $49.50. ISBN 0-88706-036-6

Rainey, Lawrence S. *Ezra Pound and the Monument of Culture: Text, History, and the Malatesta Cantos.* U. Ch. Pr. 1991 $29.95. ISBN 0-226-70316-9

Redman, Tim. *Ezra Pound and Italian Fascism.* Cambridge U. Pr. 1991 $34.50. ISBN 0-521-37305-0. Explorative study about the evolution of Pound's political thought and the reaction to it by the literary community.

Russell, Peter. *Examination of Ezra Pound: A Collection of Essays by T. S. Eliot and Others.* Gordian 1973 $40.00. ISBN 0-87752-141-7. Collection of essays on Pound by Eliot, Hemingway, and others.

Ruthven, K. K. *Ezra Pound As Literary Critic.* Routledge 1990 $47.50. ISBN 0-415-02074-3. Analyzes key episodes in Pound's career as a literary critic, thereby revealing how Pound invented, manipulated, and dominated the early and historical discourses of modernism.

———. *A Guide to Pound's Personae.* U. CA Pr. 1969 $10.95. ISBN 0-520-04960-8

Sicari, Stephen. *Pound's Epic Ambition: Dante and the Modern World.* State U. NY Pr. 1991 $44.50. ISBN 0-7914-0699-7. Shows how Pound's fragments achieve tentative coherence through the increasingly complex journey of a wandering epic hero.

Terrell, Carroll F. *A Companion to the Cantos of Ezra Pound, Vol. II: Cantos 74–120.* U. CA Pr. 1984 $49.95. ISBN 0-520-04731-1

Wilheim, J. J. *Ezra Pound in London and Paris, 1908–1925.* Pa. St. U. Pr. 1990 $32.50. ISBN 0-271-00682-X. Traces Pound's career from his arrival in London in 1908 to his departure from Paris in 1924.

RANSOM, JOHN CROWE. 1888–1974

A Rhodes scholar who went to Oxford University from Vanderbilt University, John Crowe Ransom later taught at Vanderbilt University from 1914 to 1937. While there, he became mentor to a number of individuals, including ROBERT PENN WARREN and CLEANTH BROOKS, who later became involved in the New Criticism with Ransom. Professor of poetry at Kenyon College, Ohio, from 1937 to 1958, Ransom founded *The Kenyon Review* in 1939. He was also one of the seven residents of Nashville, Tennessee, who founded and edited *The Fugitive* (1922–25) and, according to Louis Untermeyer, "He more than any of the others was responsible for the new awakening of poetry in the South." He won the Academy of American Poets' $5,000 fellowship prize (1962) for his "distinguished poetic achievement." He also won the Bollingen Prize in poetry and the Loines Award for poetry. By writing a handful of lyrics remarkable for their irony and structural tensions, as well as critical essays that praised just these virtues in the name of New Criticism, Ransom had an influence far beyond many of his peers.

POETRY BY RANSOM

Selected Poems. Knopf 1991 $21.50. ISBN 0-679-40257-8. Selection of poems that have been revised from earlier editions and original manuscript, as well as several new poems with the poet's own commentary.

NONFICTION BY RANSOM

Beating the Bushes: Selected Essays, 1941–1970. Bks. Demand repr. of 1972 ed. $46.50. ISBN 0-8357-7086-9. Selection of Ransom's unpublished essays from the *Kenyon Review*.

College Primer of Writing. R. S. Barnes 1943 $15.00. ISBN 0-686-17405-4

The New Criticism. Greenwood 1979 $65.00. ISBN 0-8371-9079-7. An account of the poetic process and composition, the title of which came to be identified with the new philosophy of criticism and approach to literature that dominated the period between the 1940s and 1960s.

Selected Essays of John Crowe Ransom. La. State U. Pr. 1984 $37.50. ISBN 0-8071-1130-9

WORK BY RANSOM

Selected Letters of John Crowe Ransom. La. State U. Pr. 1985 $40.00. ISBN 0-8071-1168-6. Selection of letters covering the period from the early 1900s, when Ransom was a Rhodes scholar, until the late 1960s.

BOOKS ABOUT RANSOM

Buffington, Robert. *Equilibrist: A Study of John Crowe Ransom's Poems 1916–1963*. Vanderbilt U. Pr. 1967 $9.95. ISBN 0-8265-1107-4. Probing analysis of Ransom's poetry.

Quinlan, Kieran. *John Crowe Ransom's Secular Faith*. La. State U. Pr. 1989 $22.50. ISBN 0-8071-1471-5. Lucid and persuasive study that traces the evolution of John Crowe Ransom's youthful Christian doubts into a fully formed agnosticism.

Young, Thomas D. *Gentleman in a Dustcoat: A Biography of John Crowe Ransom*. La. State U. Pr. 1976 $40.00. ISBN 0-8071-0190-7. Readable biography of Ransom focusing on his life as a poet, critic, and editor.

_____, ed. *John Crowe Ransom: Critical Essays and a Bibliography*. La. State U. Pr. 1968 $35.00. ISBN 0-8071-0842-1. Interesting collection of essays assessing Ransom's work in relation to the work of other writers.

RIDING, LAURA (LAURA [RIDING] JACKSON). 1901–1991

Laura Riding is surely one of the most mysterious and neglected poets of the twentieth century. Although she is unknown to most casual readers of poetry, KENNETH REXROTH has said that "Laura Riding is the greatest lost poet in American literature."

Riding was born in New York City and educated at Cornell University. Her work appeared in the 1920s in numerous small literary magazines, including *The Fugitive*. In 1925 she went to Europe, where she and ROBERT GRAVES ran the Seizin Press in Majorca. In 1939 she returned to the United States, renounced poetry, and since then has lived in Florida writing studies on the nature of language with her husband, Schuyler Jackson.

POETRY BY RIDING

Selected Poems: In Five Sets. Persea Bks. 1993 repr. of 1970 ed. $9.95. ISBN 0-89255-189-5. All the poems Riding wishes to have preserved are included in this volume.

NONFICTION BY RIDING

Survey of Modernist Poetry. Scholarly 1971 $19.00. ISBN 0-403-01178-7

Voltaire: A Biographical Fantasy. Norwood 1978 repr. of 1927 ed. o.p.

ROBERTS, ELIZABETH MADOX. 1881–1941

Elizabeth Madox Roberts has not received much critical attention in recent years, although three book-length studies of her life and work were published during the late 1950s and 1960s. Her achievement was still sufficiently recognized in 1946 for Viking Press to publish a deluxe anniversary edition of her distinguished novel, *The Time of Man* (1926), four years after she had died of Hodgkin's disease. Roberts entered college late in life, enrolling at the University of Chicago at age 36 and graduating with honors at age 40. Her novels are set in Kentucky, where she was born and grew up and where her ancestors had been pioneers. These works focus upon women characters who strive to come to terms imaginatively and spiritually with the hardships and deprivations of their isolated rural existence. Her other important novel, *The Great Meadow* (1930), is set during the time of the Revolutionary War.

NOVELS BY ROBERTS

Black Is My Truelove's Hair. Ayer 1977 $30.00. ISBN 0-405-10053-1. Tale of a woman's
return to her village after a failed love.
The Great Meadow. J. S. Sanders 2nd ed. 1992 $10.95. ISBN 1-879941-07-4
The Time of Man. 1926. U. Pr. of Ky. 1982 $23.00. ISBN 0-8131-1467-5

SHORT STORY COLLECTIONS BY ROBERTS

The Haunted Mirror. 1932. AMS Pr. repr. of 1932 ed. $23.50. ISBN 0-404-15236-8.
Roberts's first volume of short stories.
Not by Strange Gods. 1941. AMS Pr. $20.50. ISBN 0-404-15237-6. The second short story
collection.

POETRY BY ROBERTS

Under the Tree. 1922. U. Pr. of Ky. 1985 $9.00. ISBN 0-8131-1561-2. A volume of poems,
one of her earliest publications.

BOOKS ABOUT ROBERTS

Campbell, H. M., and R. Foster. *Elizabeth Madox Roberts: American Novelist.* 1956 o.p.
The first critical study of her work.
McDowell, Frederick P. *Elizabeth Madox Roberts.* NCUP 1963 $10.95. ISBN 0-8084-
0119-X. An insightful study of Roberts's life and work.
Rovit, E. H. *Herald to Chaos: The Novels of Elizabeth Madox Roberts.* 1960 o.p. The most
perceptive of the three critical studies.

ROBINSON, EDWIN ARLINGTON. 1869–1935

Born in Maine, Robinson grew up in Gardiner, the "Tilbury Town" of his
verses. His family's finances were almost gone by the time he graduated from
high school in 1889. He had started writing poems at age 11, but he kept this a
secret from family and friends. In 1891 he entered Harvard University as a
special student, thanks to the help of sympathetic townspeople; but, after two
years of ill health and lack of funds, he was forced to return to Gardiner.

After the death of his mother (his father had died earlier), Robinson left
Gardiner and went to New York City, arriving in 1896. He took a succession of
ill-paying jobs while he pursued his writing. Eventually, his work came to the
attention of President THEODORE ROOSEVELT (see Vol. 3), who appointed him to a
permanent job in the New York Customs House. After that his writing
increased, and he published *The Outlook* (1905) to good reviews. He resigned
from his job at the Customs House in 1910; from 1911 on he wrote mostly at the
McDowell Colony in New Hampshire. He never married.

AMY LOWELL spoke of Edwin Arlington Robinson's "difficult and beautiful
poetry" and considered him "one of the most intellectual poets in America." He
was a slow writer and waited long for recognition. His gift is for the delineation
of character; his study of SHAKESPEARE in the volume *The Man against the Sky*
(1916) won much praise in its time. Robinson is especially interested in the
contrast between human hopes and fate, and is concerned with the lives of
failures, depicting a kind of "quiet desperation" of frustrated characters. This is
somehow always accompanied by a hint of hopefulness.

Robinson won the Pulitzer Prize in 1922, 1925, and 1928. The third Pulitzer
was for one of his most intricate works, *Tristram* (1927), a single poem of more
than 40,000 words. It was a bestseller and, with the later works, established the
poet in popular favor. Robinson's work is represented in many anthologies,
such as Louis Untermeyer's *Modern American Poetry* and Gerald De Witt
Sanders's *Chief Modern Poets.*

POETRY BY ROBINSON

Collected Poems. Macmillan 1937 o.p. A number of shorter poems and long narrative poems, not previously included in a book.

Selected Poems of E. A. Robinson. Macmillan 1966 $12.95. ISBN 0-02-070530-1. A selection of eight of Robinson's best-known poems.

WORKS BY ROBINSON

Selected Early Poems and Letters. Ed. by Charles Davis. H. Holt & Co. 1960 o.p.

Selected Letters of Edwin Arlington Robinson. Greenwood 1980 $38.50. ISBN 0-313-21266-X

BOOKS ABOUT ROBINSON

Barnard, Ellsworth. *Edwin Arlington Robinson: A Critical Study.* Hippocrene Bks. 1969 $26.00. ISBN 0-374-90380-8. The best general introduction to Robinson's work.

Bloom, Harold, ed. *Edwin Arlington Robinson.* Chelsea Hse. 1987 $24.95. ISBN 1-55546-322-3. A collection of critical essays, including some by well-known poets, on Robinson's development and accomplishments.

Burton, David. *Edwin Arlington Robinson: Stages in a New England Poet's Search.* E. Mellen Pr. 1986 $59.95. ISBN 0-88946-557-6. An examination of Robinson's life and work, focusing on his response to the major events of his time.

Carley, James P., ed. *Arthurian Poets: Edwin Arlington Robinson.* Boydell & Brewer 1990 $21.00. ISBN 0-85115-545-6. Discusses Robinson's work in relation to the Arthurian tradition.

Lippincott, Lillian. *A Bibliography of the Writings and Criticisms of Edwin Arlington Robinson.* Haskell 1974 $49.95. ISBN 0-8383-2049-X

Redman, Ben. *Edwin Arlington Robinson.* Haskell 1974 $34.95. ISBN 0-8383-2045-7. A critical study of Robinson's poetry, with special attention to his themes and longer works.

Van Doren, Mark. *Edwin Arlington Robinson.* Haskell 1975 $75.00. ISBN 0-8383-2103-8

SANDBURG, CARL. 1878–1967

The son of Swedish immigrants, Sandburg was born in Galesburg, Illinois. At age 13 he left school to roam the Midwest; he remained on the road for six years, working as a day laborer. Sandburg served in the Spanish-American War and then, from 1898 to 1902, attended Lombard College in Galesburg. After college, he went to Milwaukee, where he worked as a journalist; he also married Lillian Steichen there in 1908. During World War I, he served as a foreign correspondent in Stockholm; after the war he returned to Chicago and continued to write about America, especially the common people.

Sandburg's first poems to gain wide recognition appeared in *Poetry* magazine in 1914. Two years later he published his *Chicago Poems* (1916), and *Cornhuskers* appeared in 1918. Meanwhile, Sandburg set out to become an authority on ABRAHAM LINCOLN (see Vol. 3). His exhaustive biography of the president, which took many years to complete, appeared as *Abraham Lincoln: The Prairie Years* (2 vols., 1926) and *Abraham Lincoln: The War Years* (4 vols., 1939), which won a Pulitzer Prize.

Sandburg's poetry is untraditional in form. Drawing on WHITMAN as well as the imagists, its rhymeless and unmetered cadences reflect Midwestern speech, and its diction ranges from strong rhetoric to easygoing slang. Although he often wrote about the uncouth, the muscular, and the primitive, there was a pity and loving kindness that was a primary motive for his poetry.

At Sandburg's death, Mark Van Doren, ARCHIBALD MACLEISH, and President Lyndon Johnson delivered eulogies. In his tribute, President Johnson said that

"Carl Sandburg was more than the voice of America, more than the poet of its strength and genius. He was America. . . . He gave us the truest and most enduring vision of our own greatness." The *N.Y. Times* described Sandburg as "poet, newspaper man, historian, wandering minstrel, collector of folk songs, spinner of tales for children, [whose] place in American letters is not easily categorized. But it is a niche that he has made uniquely his own." Sandburg was the labor laureate of the United States.

Sandburg received the Pulitzer Prize for poetry in 1951 for his *Complete Poems* (1950). Among his many other awards were the gold medal for history and biography (1952) from the American Academy of Arts and Letters; the Poetry Society of America's gold medal (1953) for distinguished achievement; and the Boston Arts Festival Award (1955) in recognition of "continuous meritorious contribution to the art of American poetry." In 1959 he traveled under the auspices of the Department of State to the U.S. Trade Fair in Moscow, and to Stockholm, Paris, and London. In 1960 he received a citation from the U.S. Chamber of Commerce as a great living American for the "significant and lasting contribution which he has made to American literature."

POETRY BY SANDBURG

The Complete Poems of Carl Sandburg. 1950. HarBraceJ 1970 $27.95. ISBN 0-15-120773-9

The People, Yes. 1936. HarBraceJ 1990 $9.95. ISBN 0-15-671665-8. Panoramic view of American people expressed through folklore.

Selected Poems of Carl Sandburg. Outlet Bk. Co. 1992 $5.99. ISBN 0-517-07244-0

SHORT STORY COLLECTION BY SANDBURG

Rootabaga Stories. HarBraceJ 1990 $3.95. ISBN 0-15-269065-4. A collection of tales for children.

NONFICTION BY SANDBURG

Abraham Lincoln: The Prairie Years. 1929. Rprt. Serv. 1992 $150.00. ISBN 0-7812-6171-6. Exhaustive biography of the great Civil War president.

Prairie-Town Boy. HarBraceJ 1990 $4.95. ISBN 0-15-263332-4

WORKS BY SANDBURG

The American Songbag. 1927. HarBraceJ 1990 $16.95. ISBN 0-15-605650-X. Collection of ballads that were an important contribution to American folklore; includes accounts of their origins.

The Poet and the Dream Girl: The Love Letters of Lilian Steichen and Carl Sandburg. Ed. by Margaret Sandburg. U. of Ill. Pr. 1987 $24.95. ISBN 0-252-01386-7. Collection of 134 letters written during the winter and spring of 1908 between Carl Sandburg and his future wife, Lilian Steichen.

Sandburg Treasury: Prose and Poetry for Young People. HarBraceJ 1970 $24.95. ISBN 0-15-270180-X

BOOKS ABOUT SANDBURG

Allen, Gay W. *Carl Sandburg. Pamphlets on Amer. Writers Ser.* U. of Minn. Pr. 1972 o.p. A good introduction to the poetry of Sandburg, with a selected bibliography; useful to the beginning student.

Callahan, North. *Carl Sandburg: His Life and Works.* Pa. St. U. Pr. 1987 $29.75. ISBN 0-271-00486-X. Definitive biography of Sandburg's life.

Crowder, Richard. *Carl Sandburg.* Macmillan 1964 $18.95. ISBN 0-8057-0648-8. General study of Sandburg's poetry and prose and his role in American letters.

Niven, Penelope. *Carl Sandburg: A Biography*. Macmillan 1991 $35.00. ISBN 0-684-19251-9. Attempts to resurrect Sandburg's declining literary reputation as poet, biographer, and journalist.

Salwak, Dale. *Carl Sandburg: A Reference Guide*. Macmillan 1988 $40.00. ISBN 0-8161-8821-1. Provides more than 1,000 selections from critical opinion in order to reflect the fluctuations of Sandburg's reputation.

SCHUYLER, GEORGE. 1895–1977

George Schuyler was an African American professional journalist of considerable distinction who served as an officer in the army in World War I and later made a name for himself as a satirical polemicist, attacking both white and black positions in the racial politics of this country. He carved out a position for himself as a conservative spokesman within the African American community, particularly as an ardent anti-Communist. His ingenious Swiftian fantasy, *Black No More* (1934), tells the story of a miracle cure for black skin color by means of which, to the great discomfort of the white population, the black and white "races" become indistinguishable.

NOVEL BY SCHUYLER

Black No More: Being an Account of the Strange and Wonderful Workings of Science in the Land of the Free. 1934. NE U. Pr. 1989 $11.95. ISBN 1-55553-063-X

NONFICTION BY SCHUYLER

Hunger in a Land of Plenty. Schenkman Bks. Inc. 1980 $13.95. ISBN 0-87073-870-4

Slaves Today: A Story of Liberia. AMS Pr. 1969 $29.50. ISBN 0-404-00209-9. Novel about two Liberian natives who are sold into slavery; dramatizes the theme of man's inhumanity to man.

SINCLAIR, UPTON (BEALL). 1878–1968

Sinclair, a lifelong vigorous socialist, first became well known with a powerful muckraking novel, *The Jungle*, in 1906. Refused by five publishers and finally published by Sinclair himself, it became an immediate bestseller, and inspired a government investigation of the Chicago stockyards, which led to much reform. In 1967 he was invited by President Lyndon Johnson to "witness the signing of the Wholesome Meat Act, which will gradually plug loopholes left by the first Federal meat inspection law" (*N.Y. Times*), a law Sinclair had helped to bring about. Newspapers, colleges, schools, churches, and industries have all been the subject of a Sinclair attack, analyzing and exposing their evils. Sinclair was not really a novelist, but a fearless and indefatigable journalist-crusader. All his early books are propaganda for his social reforms. When regular publishers boycotted his work, he published himself, usually at a financial loss. His 80 or so books have been translated into 47 languages, and his sales abroad, especially in the former Soviet Union, have been enormous.

Dragon's Teeth (1942), a "Lanny Budd" novel, won the Pulitzer Prize in 1942. With *World's End* (1940), his sixty-fifth novel and a Literary Guild selection, Sinclair had started his series of best-selling volumes in the ambitious saga of his hero Lanny Budd—a fictional history of contemporary world events told through the events and people that cluster around Lanny, a rich young man with socialist principles. *Presidential Mission* (1947) brings Lanny up to the invasion of North Africa and the Casablanca Conference with Franklin D. Roosevelt, WINSTON CHURCHILL (see Vol. 3), and others; and the eleventh volume, *The Return of of Lanny Budd* (1953) concerns the growth of the Soviet menace from 1946 through 1949. More than a million copies of the Lanny Budd novels have been sold, and they have been translated into more than 20 languages. Today, Sinclair's works are out of fashion, and with the exception of *The Jungle*, they are seldom read.

NOVELS BY SINCLAIR

Boston: A Documentary Novel of the Sacco-Vanzetti Case. 1928. Bentley 1978 repr. of 1928 ed. $32.00. ISBN 0-8376-0420-6. A novel tracing the history of the Sacco-Vanzetti case.

The Coal War. U. Pr. Colo. 1976 $25.00. ISBN 0-87081-067-7

Dragon's Teeth. 1942. Buccaneer Bks. 1992 $18.95. ISBN 0-89966-956-5

The Jungle. 1906. Berkley Pub. 1991 $3.95. ISBN 0-425-12527-0

King Coal: A Novel. 1917. AMS Pr. 1980 repr. of 1921 ed. $30.00. ISBN 0-404-58469-1. The story of a mine-owner's son who spends a summer in a mining camp and finds himself championing the miner's cause. With an introduction by George Brandes.

Manassas: A Novel of the War. Scholarly 1969 $39.00. ISBN 0-403-00060-2. Novel about a Southerner who becomes an antislavery advocate and the Civil War hostilities between the North and South.

Oil! 1927. Bentley 1981 repr. of 1927 ed. $32.00. ISBN 0-8376-0444-3. Story about the son of an oil magnate who is torn between his upper-class roots and the socialist movement.

Prince Hagen: A Phantasy. Ed. by R. Reginald and Douglas Melville. Ayer 1978 repr. of 1903 ed. $20.00. ISBN 0-405-11008-1

Springtime and Harvest. Buccaneer Bks. 1992 $18.95. ISBN 0-89966-955-7

Sylvia: A Novel. Scholarly 1971 repr. of 1913 ed. $49.00. ISBN 0-403-00291-5. Novel about the life of a Virginia belle.

PLAYS BY SINCLAIR

Plays of Protest. Scholarly 1970 $39.00. ISBN 0-403-00293-1

WORKS BY SINCLAIR

The Brass Check: A Study of American Journalism. 1918. Ayer 1970 repr. of 1919 ed. $25.50. ISBN 0-405-01696-4. A highly critical and scathing view of journalism.

Little Steel. AMS Pr. repr. of 1938 ed. $29.00. ISBN 0-404-58470-5. Story about the determination of steel company owners and managers to keep the labor unions out of their industry.

Mammopart: An Essay in Economic Interpretation. Hyperion Conn. 1975 $25.85. ISBN 0-88355-249-3

BOOKS ABOUT SINCLAIR

Bloodworth, William, Jr. *Upton Sinclair.* Macmillan 1977 $19.95. ISBN 0-8057-7197-2. Balanced analysis of Sinclair's place in American letters; contains a chronology and a bibliography.

Dell, Floyd. *Upton Sinclair: A Study in Social Protest.* AMS Pr. $24.50. ISBN 0-404-02076-3. By Sinclair's contemporary and fellow socialist journalist.

Mookerjee, R. N. *Art for Social Justice: The Major Novels of Upton Sinclair.* Scarecrow 1988 $20.00. ISBN 0-8108-2066-8. Attempt at a revaluation of *The Jungle, King Coal, Oil!,* and *Boston.*

Yoder, Jon A. *Upton Sinclair.* Continuum 1975 $18.95. ISBN 0-8044-2989-8

STEIN, GERTRUDE. 1874–1946

A dominant figure in modern cultural history, Gertrude Stein "left behind her the memory of a personage—not a great writer but a bold experimenter and a great woman" (MALCOLM COWLEY). She was born in Pennsylvania to an upper-middle-class Jewish family (originally from Germany). As an infant she traveled abroad with her family; the family then moved to Oakland, California in 1879 and she spent most of her childhood and early youth there. After graduating from Radcliffe College, where she was strongly influenced by the philosopher WILLIAM JAMES (see Vols. 3, 4, and 5), she studied medicine for four years at Johns Hopkins University (1897–1902) but took no degree. In 1903 she went to Paris with her brother Leo.

From 1907 until her death, Stein lived in France with her lover and secretary, Alice B. Toklas. Their apartment in Paris became renowned as one of the most celebrated and long-lived cultural salons in our century. Toklas, who died in 1967, described in her autobiography, *What Is Remembered* (1963), their long friendship and the procession of artists, writers, philosophers, and critics who were their friends. Stein returned to the United States only once, in 1934, to give a lecture tour and to see her opera "Four Saints in Three Acts" performed with music by VIRGIL THOMSON (see Vol. 3). During World War II, Stein lived at a country home while France was occupied by the Germans; from this experience she wrote *Wars I Have Seen* (1944), *Yes Is For a Very Young Man* (1944), and *Brewsie and Willie* (1946).

Stein was a master of words and used them evocatively, bringing out their tonal and associational qualities. Such sentences as "Rose is a rose is a rose is a rose" baffled many of her contemporaries but seem less strange, and often masterly, in the light of today's changed taste, which she helped to mold. Her most ambitious novel was *The Making of Americans* (1925); ERNEST HEMINGWAY corrected the original proofs. Her plays, *In Circles* and *What Happened*, have had great success in the New York off-Broadway theater. *What Happened* won an Obie Award in 1964. With the chief exception of *The Autobiography of Alice B. Toklas* (1933), her most widely read work, and *Three Lives* (1909), which includes *Melanctha*, a brilliant portrait of a young African American woman, most of Gertrude Stein's writings are too difficult and experimental for general readers, but she has had considerable influence on other writers from the time of Ernest Hemingway and other members of what she called "the lost generation" to the present postmodernist period. Today's avant-garde writers often discover that their most daring innovations of language and style were anticipated by Gertrude Stein. She has often been called a "Cubist writer."

NOVELS BY STEIN

Blood on the Dining-Room Floor: A Murder Mystery. Creative Arts 1982 $12.95. ISBN 0-916870-50-2. A murder mystery that focuses on French provincial families and the consequences that a violent death has on them.

A Book Concluding with As a Wife Has a Cow: A Love Story. Ultramarine Pub. 1973 $12.50. ISBN 0-87110-092-4

Ida: A Novel. Random 1972 $8.95. ISBN 0-394-71797-X. Novel about the effects that publicity has on a woman's identity and her personality. Considered Stein's witty response to James Joyce's heroines.

Lucy Church Amiably. Ultramarine Pub. 1972 repr. of 1930 ed. $30.00. ISBN 0-89366-110-4. A full-length prose fiction that is an extended meditation on landscape.

Mrs. Reynolds. Sun & Moon CA 1987 $15.95. ISBN 1-55713-022-1. A tale of two powerful men in war-torn Europe during the second World War.

Novel of Thank You. Ayer 1958 $27.50. ISBN 0-8369-5164-6. Written as a hermetic diary consisting largely of remembered conversations and experiences.

Three Lives. 1909. Viking Penguin 1990 $7.95. ISBN 0-14-018184-9. Stein's first book.

POETRY BY STEIN

Alphabets and Birthdays. Ayer 1957 $27.50. ISBN 0-8369-5160-3. Poems celebrating intimacy and connection with the body.

Four in America. 1947. Ayer 1947 $19.50. ISBN 0-8369-1381-7. Poems about four leading American historical figures: Ulysses S. Grant, George Washington, Henry James, and Wilbur Wright or the Wright brothers.

Lifting Belly. Naiad Pr. 1989 $14.95. ISBN 0-941483-53-3. An erotic poem about lesbianism.

Painted Lace and Other Pieces, 1914–1937. Ayer 1955 $27.50. ISBN 0-8369-5165-4. A series of poems revealing much about Stein's personality and habits.

Stanzas in Meditation and Other Poems (Nineteen Twenty-Nine to Nineteen Thirty-Three). Ayer 1956 $27.50. ISBN 0-8369-5166-2

Tender Buttons. 1914. Sun & Moon CA 1990 $9.95. ISBN 1-55713-093-0. Stein's groundbreaking—and coded—exploration of female sexuality in poetry.

NONFICTION BY STEIN

The Autobiography of Alice B. Toklas. 1933. Random 1990 $9.00. ISBN 0-679-72463-X. Stein's own autobiography composed as though written by her companion.

Everybody's Autobiography. 1932. Cooper Sq. 1971 $32.50. ISBN 0-8154-0386-0. An account of her American lecture tour.

How to Write. 1931. Dover 1975 $6.95. ISBN 0-486-23144-5. An exploration of language that focuses on vocabulary, sentences, and paragraphs.

Paris, France. 1940. Liveright 1970 $7.95. ISBN 0-87140-231-9. A sympathetic study of French customs.

Picasso. Dover 1984 $4.95. ISBN 0-486-24715-5. Meditative reminiscences and anecdotes about the great Spanish artist.

WORKS BY STEIN

As Fine As Melanctha (Nineteen Fourteen to Nineteen Thirty). Ayer 1954 $27.50. ISBN 0-8369-5161-1

Geography and Plays. 1922. Ultramarine Pub. 1968 $40.00. ISBN 0-89366-109-0

The Gertrude Stein First Reader and Three Plays. Haskell repr. of 1948 ed. $39.95. ISBN 0-8383-0074-X. Plays for children that at times resemble nursery rhymes, songs, and games.

Selected Writings of Gertrude Stein. Random 1990 $14.95. ISBN 0-679-72464-8

Useful Knowledge. Station Hill Pr. 1988 $19.95. ISBN 0-88268-075-7. Shorter pieces about "redress" and "excess" in the sexual imagination.

The World Is Round. Haskell 1965 $75.00. ISBN 0-8383-0629-2. A child's tale about two children who have a number of enigmatic experiences.

BOOKS ABOUT STEIN

Bloom, Harold, ed. *Gertrude Stein.* Chelsea Hse. 1986 $29.95. ISBN 0-87754-668-1. A representative selection of essays about Stein and her work.

Bowers, Jane P. *They Watch Me As They Watch This: Gertrude Stein's Metadrama.* U. of Pa. Pr. 1991 $22.95. ISBN 0-8122-3057-4. A discerning study focusing on Stein's plays.

Brinnin, John M. *The Third Rose: Gertrude Stein and Her World.* Addison-Wesley 1987 $14.38. ISBN 0-201-05880-4. Provides stimulating insights on Stein's life and art.

DeKoven, Marianne. *A Different Language: Gertrude Stein's Experimental Writing.* U. of Wis. Pr. 1983 $25.00. ISBN 0-299-09210-1. A feminist analysis of Stein's experimental writings; provides an alternative to patriarchal literary traditions.

Fifer, Elizabeth. *Rescued Readings: A Reconstruction of Gertrude Stein's Difficult Texts.* Wayne St. U. Pr. 1992 $29.95. ISBN 0-8143-2340-5. Examines the relationship between Stein's lesbianism and her art.

Hobhouse, Janet. *Everybody Who Was Anybody: A Biography of Gertrude Stein.* Doubleday 1989 $8.95. ISBN 0-385-26331-7. Highly readable biography featuring many photographs and reproductions of artworks associated with Stein.

Hoffman, Michael J., ed. *Critical Essays on Gertrude Stein*. G. K. Hall 1986 $40.00. ISBN 0-8161-8696-0. A careful selection of analytical essays dealing with Stein's fiction and her literary style.

Knapp, Bettina L. *Gertrude Stein*. Continuum 1990 $18.95. ISBN 0-8264-0458-8. Dwells on Stein's circle—Alice, Pablo, Bertrand, Henri, Sherwood, Ernest, Guillaume, Virgil.

Kostelanetz, Richard, ed. *Gertrude Stein Advanced: An Anthology of Criticism*. McFarland & Co. 1990 $37.50. ISBN 0-89950-433-7. Twenty-seven previously published articles proceeding from the general to the more specific.

La Farge, Ann. *Gertrude Stein*. Chelsea Hse. 1988 $17.95. ISBN 1-55546-678-8. Combines candid views of Stein's personal life with discussion of her work and her relation to the important artistic movement of her time.

Liston, Maureen. *Gertrude Stein: An Annotated Critical Bibliography*. Bks. Demand repr. of 1979 ed. $63.50. ISBN 0-8357-5573-8

Mellow, James R. *Charmed Circle: Gertrude Stein and Company*. HM 1991 $12.70. ISBN 0-395-47982-7

Neuman, Shirley, ed. *Gertrude Stein and the Making of Literature*. NE U. Pr. 1988 $30.00. ISBN 1-55553-025-7. Major contribution to Stein scholarship.

Ruddick, Lisa. *Reading Gertrude Stein: Body, Text, Gnosis*. Cornell Univ. Pr. 1990 $34.95. ISBN 0-8014-2364-3. Interpretive study of Gertrude Stein that breaks new ground in both Stein studies and poststructural theory.

Souhami, Diana. *Gertrude and Alice*. Thorsons SF 1992 $26.00. ISBN 0-04-440833-1. Focuses on the "devoted marriage" of Gertrude Stein and Alice B. Toklas.

Stewart, Allegra. *Gertrude Stein and the Present*. HUP 1967 o.p. Traces Stein's theories of writing as applied to her work.

Walker, Jayne L. *The Making of a Modernist: Gertrude Stein from "Three Lives" to "Tender Buttons."* U. of Mass. Pr. 1984 $22.50. ISBN 0-87023-323-8

STEINBECK, JOHN (ERNST). 1902–1968

In recent years Steinbeck has been elevated to a more prominent status among American writers of his generation. If not quite at the world-class artistic level of a HEMINGWAY or a FAULKNER, he is nonetheless read very widely throughout the world by readers of all ages who consider him one of the most "American" of writers.

Born in Salinas County, California, Steinbeck was of German-Irish parentage. After four years as a special student at Stanford University, he went to New York, where he worked as a reporter and as a hod carrier. Returning to California, he devoted himself to writing, with little success; his first three books sold fewer than 3,000 copies. *Tortilla Flat* (1935), dealing with the *paisanos*, California Mexicans whose ancestors settled in the country 200 years ago, established his reputation. *In Dubious Battle* (1936), a labor novel of a strike and strike-breaking, won the gold medal of the Commonwealth Club of California. *Of Mice and Men* (1937), a long short story that turns upon a melodramatic incident in the tragic friendship of two farm hands, written almost entirely in dialogue, was an experiment and was dramatized in the year of its publication, winning the New York Drama Critics Circle Award. It brought him fame.

Out of a series of articles that he wrote about the transient labor camps in California came the inspiration for his greatest book, *The Grapes of Wrath* (1939), the odyssey of the Joad family, dispossessed of their farm in the Dust Bowl and seeking a new home, only to be driven on from camp to camp. The fiction is punctuated at intervals by the author's voice explaining this new sociological problem of homelessness, unemployment, and displacement. As the American novel "of the season, probably the year, possibly the decade," it won the Pulitzer Prize. It roused America and won a broad readership by the

unusual simplicity and tenderness with which Steinbeck treated social questions. Even today, *The Grapes of Wrath* remains alive as a vivid account of
believable human characters seen in symbolic and universal terms as well as in
geographically and historically specific ones. Ma Joad is one of the most
memorable characters in twentieth-century American fiction. It is her courage
that sustains the family. Steinbeck's best and most ambitious novel after *The
Grapes of Wrath* is *East of Eden* (1952), a saga of two American families in
California from before the Civil War through World War I. *Cannery Row* (1945),
The Wayward Bus (1947), and *Sweet Thursday* (1955) are lighter works that find
Steinbeck returning to the lighthearted tone of *Tortilla Flat* as he recounts
picaresque adventures of modern-day picaros. *The Winter of Our Discontent*
(1961) struck some reviewers as being appropriately titled because of its
despairing treatment of humanity's fall from grace in a wasteland world where
money is king.

Steinbeck also wrote important nonfiction, including *Russian Journal* (1948)
in collaboration with the photographer Robert Capa; *Once There Was a War*
(1958) and *America and Americans* (1966), which features pictures by 55 leading
photographers and a 70-page essay by Steinbeck. His interest in marine biology
led to two books primarily about sea life, *Sea of Cortez* (1941) (with Edward F.
Ricketts) and *The Log from the Sea of Cortez* (1951). *Travels with Charley* (1952)
is an engaging account of his journey of rediscovery of America, which took him
through approximately 40 states.

NOVELS BY STEINBECK

Acts of King Arthur and His Noble Knights. Ballantine 1986 $5.95. ISBN 0-345-34512-6.
    Based on Malory's *Le Morte D'Arthur*; An Arthurian adventure tale.
Cannery Row. 1945. Bantam 1982 $2.95. ISBN 0-553-27823-1
A Cup of Gold. Viking Penguin 1976 $5.95. ISBN 0-14-004234-2. Tale of a pirate and his
    adventures on the Caribbean.
East of Eden. 1952. Viking Penguin 1979 $5.95 ISBN 0-14-004997-5
The Grapes of Wrath. 1939. Viking Penguin 1977 $10.95. ISBN 0-14-015508-2
In Dubious Battle. 1936. Viking Penguin 1979 $5.95. ISBN 0-14-004888-X
The Moon Is Down. 1942. Viking Penguin 1982 $4.95. ISBN 0-14-006222-X
Of Mice and Men. 1937. Bantam 1983 $3.50. ISBN 0-553-27824-X
The Pastures of Heaven. Viking Penguin 1982 $4.95. ISBN 0-14-004998-3. Novel about the
    unintentional effects a family has on a new town, including murders and a suicide.
The Pearl. 1947. Bantam 1986 $2.50. ISBN 0-553-26261-0. Allegorical study of a priceless
    treasure that brings only unhappiness to the people who find it.
The Red Pony. 1933. Bantam 1986 $2.50. ISBN 0-553-26444-3. Poignant tale of a boy's
    love for his horse and his coming of age through learning to feel for others more
    than for himself.
*The Short Novels of John Steinbeck: Tortilla Flat, Of Mice and Men, The Red Pony, The
    Moon Is Down, Cannery Row, The Pearl.* Viking Penguin 1963 o.p.
Short Reign of Pippin IV: A Fabrication. Viking Penguin 1977 $4.95. ISBN 0-14-004290-3
Sweet Thursday. 1955. Viking Penguin 1979 repr. of 1955 ed. $4.95. ISBN 0-14-004889-8
To a God Unknown. Viking Penguin 1976 $5.95. ISBN 0-14-004233-4. Story of a man who
    becomes a fisher king in order to save his land from drought.
Tortilla Flat. 1935. Viking Penguin 1977 $5.95. ISBN 0-14-004240-7
The Wayward Bus. 1947. Viking Penguin 1979 repr. of 1947 ed. $6.00. ISBN 0-14-
    005001-9
The Winter of Our Discontent. 1961. Viking Penguin 1982 $5.95. ISBN 0-14-006221-1

SHORT STORY COLLECTION BY STEINBECK

The Long Valley. 1938. Viking Penguin 1986 $4.95. ISBN 0-14-008038-4. Thirteen short
    stories, including "The Chrysanthemums" and "Flight."

PLAY BY STEINBECK

Burning Bright: A Play in Story Form. Viking Penguin 1979 repr. of 1950 ed. $4.95. ISBN 0-14-004999-1

NONFICTION BY STEINBECK

The Harvest Gypsies: On the Road to the Grapes of Wrath. Heyday Bks. 1988 $7.95. ISBN 0-930588-38-X
The Log from the Sea of Cortez. 1951. Viking Penguin 1977 $5.95. ISBN 0-14-004261-X
Once There Was a War. 1958. Viking Penguin 1977 $4.95. ISBN 0-14-004291-1
A Russian Journal. 1948. Paragon Hse. 1990 $10.95. ISBN 1-55778-225-3
Sea of Cortez: A Leisurely Journal of Travel and Research. 1941. Appel $40.00. ISBN 0-911858-08-3
Travels with Charley in Search of America. 1952. Viking Penguin 1980 $5.95. ISBN 0-14-005320-4

WORKS BY STEINBECK

John Steinbeck: A Life in Letters. Ed. by Elaine Steinbeck and Robert Wallsten. Viking Penguin 1975 $22.50. ISBN 0-670-66961-X. A partially annotated collection of Steinbeck's letters.
Journal of a Novel: The "East of Eden" Letters. Viking Penguin 1990 $8.95. ISBN 0-14-014418-8. Day-by-day account on the writing of *East of Eden*, written in the form of letters to Pascal Covici.
The Portable Steinbeck. Viking Penguin 1976 $9.95. ISBN 0-14-015002-1. Collection of Steinbeck's best work, including excerpts from his novels and short stories and two uncollected short stories.
Working Days: The "Journals of the Grapes of Wrath." Viking Penguin 1990 $8.95. ISBN 0-14-014457-9. Revealing account of Steinbeck's painful struggle to create his literary masterpiece.

BOOKS ABOUT STEINBECK

Bennett, Robert. *Wrath of John Steinbeck.* Gordon Pr. repr. of 1972 ed. $59.95. ISBN 0-8490-1337-2. Anecdotal account of Steinbeck in his teens.
Benson, Jackson J. *Looking for Steinbeck's Ghost.* U. of Okla. Pr. 1988 $24.95. ISBN 0-8061-2155-6. Contains interviews with Steinbeck's ex-wives, lost correspondence, and material on the migrant worker who supplied him with much of his information for *The Grapes of Wrath.*
———. ed. *The Short Novels of John Steinbeck: Critical Essays.* Duke 1990 $39.50. ISBN 0-8223-0988-2. Decent checklist of criticism on the short novels.
———. *The True Adventures of John Steinbeck, Writer: A Biography.* Viking Penguin 1990 $16.95. ISBN 0-14-014417-X. Forthright and thorough biography of Steinbeck, with consideration of his major works.
Bloom, Harold, ed. *John Steinbeck's The Grapes of Wrath.* Chelsea Hse. 1988 $24.95. ISBN 1-55546-050-X. Useful collection of critical interpretations of *The Grapes of Wrath.*
Chadha, Rajni. *Social Realism in the Novels of John Steinbeck.* Advent NY 1991 $30.00. ISBN 81-85151-31-8
Davis, Robert M., ed. *Steinbeck: A Collection of Critical Essays.* P-H 1972 o.p. Fine collection of critical essays on Steinbeck the man and his novels.
Ditsky, John. *Critical Essays on Steinbeck's "The Grapes of Wrath."* G. K. Hall 1989 $40.00. ISBN 0-8161-8887-4. Contains early reviews of the novel, some maps, and nine essays, four of the written for this volume.
Ferrell, Keith. *John Steinbeck: The Voice of the Land.* M. Evans 1986 $11.95. ISBN 0-87131-480-0
French, Warren G., ed. *Companion to the Grapes of Wrath.* Kelley 1963 o.p. Criticism, newspaper articles, and essays elucidating the social, historical, and literary background of Steinbeck's classic novel.

———. *John Steinbeck*. Macmillan 1975 $16.95. ISBN 0-672-61501-0. Relates Steinbeck's work to the literary and social criticism of the 1970s.

Levant, Howard. *The Novels of John Steinbeck: A Critical Study*. U. of Mo. Pr. 1983 $20.00. ISBN 0-8262-0164-4. Critical study of Steinbeck's major novels.

McCarthy, Paul. *John Steinbeck*. Lit. and Life Ser. Continuum 1980 o.p. Interesting study of the Steinbeck's life, focusing on the places and people who helped shape his writing.

Millichap, Joseph R. *Steinbeck and Film*. Continuum 1983 o.p.

Noble, Donald, ed. *The Steinbeck Question: New Essays in Criticism*. Whitston Pub. 1992 $29.50. ISBN 0-87875-424-5

Owens, Louis. *John Steinbeck's Re-Vision of America*. U. of Ga. Pr. 1985 $27.50. ISBN 0-8203-0736-X. Emphasizes the central importance of the California setting of much of Steinbeck's fiction.

———. *The Grapes of Wrath: Trouble in the Promised Land*. Macmillan 1989 $9.95. ISBN 0-8057-8047-5

St. Pierre, Brian. *John Steinbeck: The California Years*. Chronicle Bks. 1984 o.p.

Tetsumaro, Hayashi, ed. *Steinbeck's The Grapes of Wrath: "Essays in Criticism."* Ball State Univ. 1990 $20.00. ISBN 0-937994-16-2

Timmerman, John H. *John Steinbeck's Fiction: The Aesthetics of the Road Taken*. U. of Okla. Pr. 1986 $27.95. ISBN 0-8061-1998-5. Appraisal of Steinbeck's philosophical beliefs and their appearance in his novels and stories.

———. *The Dramatic Landscape of Steinbeck's Short Stories*. U. of Okla. Pr. 1990 $27.95. ISBN 0-8061-2258-7. Examines the decade that began while Steinbeck was a writer at Stanford, and continues through 1934, when Steinbeck drafted the stories of "The Long Valley" collection.

STEVENS, WALLACE. 1879–1955

Born in Pennsylvania, Stevens attended Harvard University and New York Law School. He was admitted to the bar in 1904, was associated with the Hartford Accident and Indemnity Company after 1916, was made a company vice-president in 1934, and was also vice-president of the Hartford Livestock Insurance Company. He believed that his character as a poet was enhanced by this daily contact with a regular job. Nearly as important to his poetic development during these years was his marriage, in 1909, to a young woman from his hometown named Elsie Viola Kachel. Stevens did not gain general recognition until Harriet Monroe included four of his poems in the war number of *Poetry* in 1914. In 1915, *Poetry* awarded him a prize for his *Three Travelers Watch a Sunrise*, a one-act play in free verse. His first book of poems was *Harmonium* (1923), which contains one of his best-known poems, "Sunday Morning." He received the Bollingen Prize in poetry (1949) and the National Book Award for poetry (1950) for *The Auroras of Autumn* (1949). In 1955 he received the National Book Award for the second time for *The Collected Poems* (1954) as well as the Pulitzer Prize. *The Necessary Angel: Essays on Reality and the Imagination* (1951) stands as his poetic credo. Although it is easy to say his great theme is the shaping power of the imagination, it is considerably more difficult to say how various are Stevens's inventive explorations and restatements of this theme. His stature as one of the select modern masters grows more secure each year, and he is perhaps at once the most philosophical and the most sensuous poet in the American tradition.

POETRY BY STEVENS

The Collected Poems. Random 1990 $14.00. ISBN 0-679-72669-1. Contains all but three of his previously published works and 25 later poems.

WORKS BY STEVENS

Letters of Wallace Stevens. Ed. by Holly Stevens. Knopf 1966 o.p. More than 800 letters selected by Stevens's daughter, who has, in addition, supplied extracts from his unpublished private journal and letters to him from his father.

The Necessary Angel: Essays on Reality and the Imagination. 1951. Random 1965 $8.00. ISBN 0-394-70278-6

Opus Posthumous. Ed. by Samuel French Morse. Random 1990 $14.95. ISBN 0-679-72534-2. Includes poems, plays, and prose works.

The Palm at the End of the Mind: Selected Poems and a Play. Ed. by Holly Stevens. Shoe String 1984 $37.50. ISBN 0-208-02058-6

BOOKS ABOUT STEVENS

Axelrod, Steven G., ed. *Critical Essays on Wallace Stevens.* G. K. Hall 1988 $40.00. ISBN 0-8161-8886-6. Contains a sizeable gathering of early reviews and a broad selection of more recent scholarship.

Baird, James R. *The Dome and the Rock: Structure in the Poetry of Wallace Stevens.* Bks. Demand repr. of 1968 ed. $92.00. ISBN 0-317-30116-0

Bates, Milton J. *Wallace Stevens: A Mythology of Self.* U. CA Pr. 1985 $37.50. ISBN 0-520-04909-8. Valuable for the light it throws on Stevens the man, and, so far as his poetry is autobiographical, on Stevens the poet as well.

Berger, Charles. *Forms of Farewell: The Late Poetry of Wallace Stevens.* U. of Wis. Pr. 1985 $22.50. ISBN 0-299-09920-2. Examines the major poems and guiding themes of Stevens's last decade.

Bevis, William. *Mind of Winter: Wallace Stevens, Meditation, and Literature.* U. of Pittsburgh Pr. 1989 $29.95. ISBN 0-8229-3598-8. Provides an alternative reading to the generally accepted one that the poet's meditative verse coincides with Christian meditative poetry.

Bloom, Harold, ed. *Wallace Stevens.* Chelsea Hse. 1985 $29.95. ISBN 0-87754-607-X. Wide-ranging selection of critical responses to the poet's work.

Brogard, Jacqueline V. *Stevens and Simile: A Theory of Language.* Princeton U. Pr. 1986 $35.00. ISBN 0-691-06689-2. Analyzes Stevens's use of simile in his poetry.

Carroll, Joseph. *Wallace Stevens' Supreme Fiction: A New Romanticism.* La. State U. Pr. 1987 $42.50. ISBN 0-8071-1367-0. Links Stevens to developments in romantic and Victorian poetry.

Doggett, Frank, ed. *Wallace Stevens: A Celebration.* Princeton U. Pr. 1980 $55.00. ISBN 0-691-06414-8

Doyle, Charles. *Wallace Stevens: The Critical Heritage.* Routledge Chapman & Hall 1985 $69.50. ISBN 0-7100-9647-X. Brings together reviews and essays covering several decades of criticism.

Enck, John J. *Wallace Stevens: Images and Judgments.* S. Ill. U. Pr. 1964 $7.95. ISBN 0-8093-0120-2

Filreis, Alan. *Wallace Stevens and the Actual World.* Princeton U. Pr. 1991 $35.00. ISBN 0-691-06864-X. New investigation of imagination versus reality in Stevens.

Fisher, Barbara M. *Wallace Stevens: The Intensest Rendezvous.* U. Pr. of Va. 1990 $28.50. ISBN 0-8139-1248-2. Approaches the poet's work as a constellation of various forms of desire.

Fuchs, Daniel. *The Comic Spirit of Wallace Stevens.* Bks. Demand repr. of 1963 ed. $52.80. ISBN 0-317-42195-6

Gelpi, Albert, ed. *Wallace Stevens: The Poetics of Modernism.* Cambridge U. Pr. 1985 $29.95. ISBN 0-521-30201-3. Selection of critical essays examining Stevens's impact on America's poetic tradition.

———. *Wallace Stevens: The Poetics of Modernism.* Cambridge U. Pr. 1990 $13.95. ISBN 0-521-38699-3

Grey, Thomas C. *The Wallace Stevens Case: Law and the Practice of Poetry.* HUP 1991 $24.95. ISBN 0-674-94577-8

Halliday, Mark. *Stevens and the Interpersonal.* Princeton U. Pr. 1991 $29.95. ISBN 0-691-06548-9

Kermode, Frank. *Wallace Stevens: A Faber Student Guide.* Faber & Faber 1990 $9.95. ISBN 0-571-14079-3

Kessler, Edward. *Images of Wallace Stevens.* Gordian 1983 $35.00. ISBN 0-87752-226-X. Examines the major and controlling images found in the poet's later poetry.

Leggett, B. J. *Early Stevens: The Nietzschean Intertext.* Duke 1992 $34.95. ISBN 0-8223-1201-8. Draws together texts of Stevens and Nietzsche to produce new and surprising readings of the poet's early work.

_____. *Wallace Stevens and Poetic Theory: Conceiving the Supreme Fiction.* U. of NC Pr. 1987 $24.95. ISBN 0-8078-1718-X. Important book for Stevens scholars and for students of aesthetics.

Lensing, George S. *Wallace Stevens: A Poet's Growth.* La. State U. Pr. 1991 $9.95. ISBN 0-8071-1671-8. The most intimate portrait of Stevens to date.

Litz, A Walton. *Introspective Voyager: The Poetic Development of Wallace Stevens.* OUP 1972 $19.95. ISBN 0-19-501518-5

Longenbach, James. *Wallace Stevens: The Plain Sense of Things.* OUP 1991 $39.95. ISBN 0-19-506863-7. Establishes the thesis that Stevens's great gift is to reveal the extraordinary in the ordinary.

Morris, Adelaide K. *Wallace Stevens: Imagination and Faith.* Princeton U. Pr. 1974 $32.50. ISBN 0-691-06265-X

Patke, Rajeev S. *The Long Poems of Wallace Stevens: An Interpretive Study.* Cambridge U. Pr. 1985 $44.50. ISBN 0-521-30126-2. Developed dissertation on the seven long poems.

Richardson, Joan. *Wallace Stevens: The Early Years, 1879–1923.* Morrow 1986 $21.95. ISBN 0-688-05401-3. Reveals Stevens the man and Stevens the artist and reconciles with grace and authority these seemingly opposite extremes.

_____. *Wallace Stevens: The Later Years, 1925–1955.* Morrow 1988 $27.95. ISBN 0-688-06860-X. The birth of Stevens's daughter and his own death form the chronological bookends in this second volume of Richardson's biography.

Riddel, Joseph N. *The Clairvoyant Eye: The Poetry and Poetics of Wallace Stevens.* La. State U. Pr. 1991 $10.95. ISBN 0-8071-0716-6

Sukenick, Ronald. *Wallace Stevens: Musing the Obscure.* In Pr. Co. 1991 $9.95. ISBN 0-9626530-1-2. Useful guide to understanding Stevens's poetry.

Vendler, Helen H. *On Extended Wings: Wallace Stevens' Longer Poems.* HUP 1969 $21.00. ISBN 0-674-63435-7. Chronological approach to Stevens's work; very useful for understanding the poet's longer poems.

_____. *Wallace Stevens.* HUP 1986 $5.95. ISBN 0-674-94575-1

TATE, ALLEN. 1899–1979

Tate—poet, essayist, novelist, biographer, and critic—began his literary career in 1922 as an editor of *The Fugitive,* a magazine of southern poets and critics, many of them associated with Vanderbilt University. As editor and in his own works, Tate advocated regionalism, explaining that "only a return to the provinces, to the small self-contained centers of life, will put the all-destroying abstraction America safely to rest." In 1943 he held the chair of poetry in the Library of Congress. From 1944 to 1947, he edited another important journal of literary criticism, *Sewanee Review.* Tate claimed to be "on record as a casual essayist of whom little consistency can be expected." Nevertheless, as editor of *The Fugitive* and the *Sewanee Review,* he had a dramatic impact on the availability and evaluation of poets and prose writers. He made significant contributions to modern poetry and modern literary criticism. His poetry, usually identified as "modern metaphysical," he described as "gradually circling round a subject, threatening it and using the ultimate violence upon it." As a critic, he is generally placed with the "new" or formalist critics, though he adds a strong strain of religious humanism, reflected by his conversion in 1950 to Roman Catholicism. Tate was elected to the National Institute of Arts and Letters in 1949 and won the Bollingen Prize in poetry in 1956.

POETRY BY TATE

Collected Poems, 1919–1976. La. State U. Pr. 1989 $9.95. ISBN 0-8071-1533-9. Wide-ranging collection of poems representing the poet's earliest to latest periods.

NONFICTION BY TATE

Hovering Fly and Other Essays. Ayer 1968 $16.00. ISBN 0-8369-0923-2

Jefferson Davis: His Rise and Fall. Rprt. Serv. 1992 $89.00. ISBN 0-7812-6176-7. Strong biography of the Confederate leader, exploring his character and his ultimate downfall.

On the Limits of Poetry: 1928 to 1948. Ayer 1948 $23.00. ISBN 0-8369-1484-8. Series of essays reflecting Tate's attitudes and ideas on poetry.

The Poetry Reviews of Allen Tate, 1924–1944. La. State U. Pr. 1983 $27.50. ISBN 0-8071-1057-4

Reactionary Essays on Poetry and Ideas. Ayer 1968 $18.00. ISBN 0-8369-0924-0. Essays on the technique of writing poetry, as well as illuminating social criticism.

Reason in Madness: Critical Essays. Ayer 1968 $21.95. ISBN 0-8369-0925-9

Stonewall Jackson: The Good Soldier. J. S. Sanders 1991 $10.95. ISBN 1-879941-02-3

BOOKS ABOUT TATE

Carrithers, Gale H. *Mumford, Tate, Eiseley: Watchers in the Night*. La. State U. Pr. 1991 $29.95. ISBN 0-8071-1650-5. Comparative study of pinpointing a distinctive American identity in the three men as reflected in their writing.

Dupree, Robert S. *Allen Tate and the Augustinian Imagination: A Study of the Poetry*. La. State U. Pr. 1983 $35.00. ISBN 0-8071-1100-7. Compares Tate's quest for wholeness to the life and writings of St. Augustine of Hippo.

Meiners, R. K. *Everything to Be Endured: An Essay on Robert Lowell and Modern Poetry*. U. of Mo. Pr. 1970 $9.95. ISBN 0-8262-0093-1. Long essay focusing on Lowell's relationship to modern poetry and the poetic tradition.

——. *Last Alternatives: Allen Tate*. Haskell 1972 $75.00. ISBN 0-8383-1594-1

Sullivan, Walter. *Allen Tate: A Recollection*. La. State U. Pr. 1988 $16.95. ISBN 0-8071-1481-2. Written by a teenaged disciple of Tate; fixes a clear eye on the poet's public persona and private life.

Young, Thomas D., ed. *The Lytle-Tate Letters: The Correspondence of Andrew Lytle and Allen Tate*. U. Pr. of Miss. 1987 $39.50. ISBN 0-87805-326-3. Collection of Tate's 40-year correspondence with Andrew Lytle that illuminates the marriage from Tate's perspective.

THURBER, JAMES. 1894–1961

Born in Columbus, Ohio, Thurber was blinded in one eye in a childhood accident. He attended Ohio State University but left without earning a degree. In 1925 he moved to New York City, where he joined the staff of the *New Yorker* in 1927 at the urging of his friend E. B. WHITE. For the rest of his lifetime, Thurber contributed to the magazine his highly individual pieces and those strange, wry, and disturbing pen-and-ink drawings of "huge, resigned dogs, the determined and sometimes frightening women, the globular men who try so hard to think so unsuccessfully." The period from 1925, when the *New Yorker* was founded, until the death of its creator-editor, Harold Ross, in 1951, was described by Thurber in delicious and absorbing detail in *The Years with Ross* (1959). Of his two great talents, Thurber preferred to think of himself primarily as a writer, illustrating his own books. He published "fables" in the style of AESOP (see Vol. 2) and LA FONTAINE (see Vol. 2)—usually with a "barbed tip of

contemporary significance"—children's books, several plays (two Broadway
hits, one successful musical revue), and endless satires and parodies in short
stories or full-length works. "The Secret Life of Walter Mitty," included in *My
World—and Welcome to It* (1942), is probably his best-known story and
continues to be frequently anthologized. T. S. ELIOT described Thurber's work
as "a form of humor which is also a way of saying something serious."

SHORT STORY COLLECTIONS BY THURBER

James Thurber: Ninety-Two Stories. Outlet 1992 $8.99. ISBN 0-517-45999-X

The Last Flower. 1939. Amereon Ltd. $11.95. ISBN 0-89190-270-8. An ironic parable of
modern war.

The Secret Life of Walter Mitty. Creative Ed. 1983 $18.50. ISBN 0-87191-961-3. Thurber's
most famous story—of a man who escapes his miserable life and his domineering
wife through heroic fantasies.

NONFICTION BY THURBER

Collecting Himself: James Thurber on Writing and Writers, Humor and Himself. HarpC
1990 $8.95. ISBN 0-06-092017-3. Collection of Thurber's work that humorously
illuminates his views on writing and on himself.

My Life and Hard Times. 1933. HarpC 1990 $7.95. ISBN 0-06-091642-7. Hilarious group of
reminiscences—one brilliantly crafted story per chapter—about Thurber's family
and childhood.

The Years with Ross. 1959. Amereon Ltd. $18.95. ISBN 0-89190-257-0. An amusing
depiction of a modern man's attempt at maintaining order.

WORKS BY THURBER

*The Beast in Me and Other Animals: A Collection of Pieces and Drawings about Human
Beings and Less Alarming Creatures.* 1948. HarBraceJ 1973 $5.95. ISBN 0-15-610850-
X. Thurber's whimsical drawings enliven this collection of stories and essays.

Fables for Our Time. 1940. HarpC 1983 $10.00. ISBN 0-06-090999-4. Lessons-in-prose
dedicated to conventional sinners; with pictorial interpretations.

Is Sex Necessary? or: Why You Feel the Way You Do. (with E. B. White). 1929. HarpC
1984 $8.95. ISBN 0-06-091102-6. Playful satire of 1920s Freudian psychology.

*Lanterns and Lances: A Variety of Encounters with Women, Men, and Other Children As
Well As Less Confusing Creatures.* 1961. D. Fine 1992 $10.00. ISBN 1-55611-299-8.
Humorous pieces about the frightful losses that the English language has suffered.

Let Your Mind Alone. 1937. Queens Hse.-Focus Serv. 1977 $19.95. ISBN 0-89244-058-9.
Humorous criticism of science and modern technology.

Many Moons. 1943. HarBraceJ 1973 $5.95. ISBN 0-15-656980-9. Children's fable about a
jester and a princess.

Men, Women and Dogs. 1943. Amereon Ltd. $17.95. ISBN 0-89190-267-8. Witty
depictions of the chaos of human life.

The Middle-Aged Man on the Flying Trapeze. 1935. Queens Hse.-Focus Serv. 1977 $19.95.
ISBN 0-89244-059-7. Depictions of the problems of human communication, told in
Thurber's inimitable comic style.

My World and Welcome to It. 1942. HarBraceJ 1969 $7.95. ISBN 0-15-662344-7

Thirteen Clocks. 1950. Dell 1992 $3.50. ISBN 0-440-40582-3. Children's fairy tale about a
poet who must journey through the labyrinth of this world in order to win his lady's
hand.

Thurber Carnival. 1945. Random 1979 $12.95. ISBN 0-394-60474-1. A retrospective
collection of the satirist's work and world.

Thurber Country. 1953. S & S Trade 1982 $16.50. ISBN 0-671-45931-7. Collection of witty
essays, conversation pieces and memoirs.

Thurber on Crime. Mysterious Pr. 1991 $18.95. ISBN 0-89296-450-2. Views on crime
through Thurber's satiric eyes.

Thurber's Dogs. S & S Trade 1992 $12.00. ISBN 0-671-79219-9. A humorous collection of pieces about dogs and how their treatment reflects the human condition.

White Deer. 1945. HarBraceJ 1968 $4.95. ISBN 0-15-696264-0. Children's fantasy.

The Wonderful O. 1957. Dell 1992 $3.50. ISBN 0-440-40579-3. Essays and doodles.

BOOKS ABOUT THURBER

Fensch, Thomas, ed. *Conversations with James Thurber.* U. Pr. of Miss. 1989 $32.50. ISBN 0-87805-409-X. Delightful book, both for the hardened Thurberites and those who need an introduction to him.

Long, Robert E. *James Thurber.* Continuum 1988 $19.95. ISBN 0-8044-2546-9. Concise account of Thurber's life, his writing, and art; also considers his times and his relationship with other writers.

Morsberger, Robert E. *James Thurber.* NCUP 1964 $10.95. ISBN 0-8084-0174-2. Among the first book-length studies of Thurber's life and writing; still highly regarded.

TOOMER, JEAN. 1894–1967

Jean Toomer is known today for the one successful book of his career, the novel *Cane*, published in 1923. Based in part upon his brief experience in the South as a school teacher, *Cane* was perhaps the first genuinely experimental novel by an African American writer responding to the liberating form of modernist narrative techniques as well as to the deepest and most primal roots of black folk culture in both the South and the North. As such, it reflects in its form the identity conflict that the novel's interwoven stories and poems address. *Cane* is unique for its blend of poetic language and psychological and moral realism; it established Toomer as one of the leading figures of the Harlem Renaissance. However, Toomer soon was absorbed in his own spiritual education. He eventually became a Quaker and spent most of the last part of his life in seclusion.

NOVEL BY TOOMER

Cane. 1923. Norton 1987 $7.95. ISBN 0-393-95600-8. Contains critical essays and an excellent introduction by Darwin T. Turner.

POETRY BY TOOMER

The Collected Poems of Jean Toomer. U. of NC Pr. 1988 $17.95. ISBN 0-8078-1773-2

WORK BY TOOMER

Essentials. U. of Ga. Pr. 1991 $18.50. ISBN 0-8203-1333-5. A collection of aphorisms and definitions.

BOOKS ABOUT TOOMER

Benson, Brian Joseph, and Mabel Mayle Dillard. *Jean Toomer.* Twayne 1980 o.p. Discusses Toomer's literary achievements and relevance to American literature.

Byrd, Rudolph P. *Jean Toomer's Years with Gurdjieff: Portrait of an Artist, 1923–1936.* U. of Ga. Pr. 1990 $30.00. ISBN 0-8203-1248-7. Examines Toomer's largely unknown and often unpublished later work.

Kerman, Cynthia Earl, and Richard Eldridge. *The Lives of Jean Toomer: A Hunger for Wholeness.* La. State U. Pr. 1987 $12.95. ISBN 0-8071-1548-7. Interesting biography focusing on Toomer's many passions.

McKay, Nellie Y. *Jean Toomer, Artist: A Study of His Literary Life and Work, 1894–1936.* U. of NC Pr. 1984 $29.95. ISBN 0-8078-1583-7. Examines the growth, development, and decline of Toomer as a literary artist.

Turner, Darwin T. *In a Minor Chord: Three Afro-American Writers and Their Search for Identity.* S. Ill. U. Pr. 1971 o.p. Surveys the lives and the works of Jean Toomer, Countee Cullen, and Zora Neale Hurston.

WARREN, ROBERT PENN. 1905–1989

Robert Penn Warren, the first Poet Laureate of the United States, was an unusually versatile writer who tried his hand at almost every kind of literature. In all of these forms, he achieved recognition and distinction, but it is as a poet, critic, and novelist that he was most widely known.

Writing almost always about his native South, Warren produced 10 novels and a collection of short stories, *The Circus in the Attic and Other Stories* (1948). By far the most successful of his novels is *All the King's Men* (1946), the story of a southern politician and demagogue named Willie Stark, which Warren based on the rise and fall of Huey Long. Warren was considered one of the most influential of the New Critics, whose influence on the teaching of literature in American schools and universities during the late 1940s and 1950s could scarcely be overestimated. Because *All the King's Men* seemed to be the very epitome of what a good work of literature should be in New Critical terms—a complicated but highly readable narrative filled with irony and ambiguity—the novel came to be used widely in courses on modern fiction. It won both the Pulitzer Prize and the Southern Authors Award in 1947.

Warren's other novels are disappointing by comparison. Following the success of *All the King's Men*, however, Warren seemed to turn to more loosely told stories about dramatic and romantic subjects, such as the interracial theme of *Band of Angels* (1955) or the natural catastrophes that serve as the crisis background for *The Cave* (1959) and *Flood: A Romance of Our Time* (1964). *Wilderness: A Tale of the Civil War* (1961) is an allegory of a man's spiritual quest for truth about himself and the world. *Meet Me in the Green Glen* (1971), the story of a tragic love affair, seemed to mark a return to the tighter structure and more complex artistry of Warren's earlier novels, but *A Place to Come To* (1977), his last novel, in which an elderly and renowned scholar who seems to owe much to Warren himself looks back on his family's past in an effort to find the meaning of his life, struck some reviewers as a confused and tired work. Sometime midway through his career as a novelist it is as if Warren stopped thinking of himself as a southern writer in the tradition of WILLIAM FAULKNER and turned instead to THOMAS WOLFE for inspiration. Although in retrospect that switch must be regretted, no one can deny the immense influence of Robert Penn Warren on modern letters. Warren's poetry is intellectual, rich in powerful images, and has its roots in the pre-Civil War South. He continued to write impressive poetry almost until the time of his death.

NOVELS BY WARREN

All the King's Men. 1946. HarBraceJ 1983 $8.95. ISBN 0-15-604762-4
At Heaven's Gate. 1943. New Dir. Pr. 1985 $11.95. ISBN 0-8112-0933-4. Novel about a
    family in decline.
The Cave. 1959. Random 1959 o.p.
Night Rider. 1939. Random 1979 o.p. A story about a lawyer who starts a movement to
    intimidate tobacco growers, which causes the destruction of his public and personal
    life.
A Place to Come To. 1977. Random 1977 $12.95. ISBN 0-394-41064-5
World Enough and Time. 1950. Random 1979 o.p. Novel about a politician destroyed by
    the Southern tradition of personal honor and violence.

POETRY BY WARREN

Audubon: A Vision. Random 1969 o.p. A beautifully produced series of poems suggested
    to the poet by episodes from the life and reading of John James Audubon.
Being Here: Poetry 1977–1980. Random 1980 $10.95. ISBN 0-394-51304-5

Brother to Dragons: A New Version. 1953. Random 1979 $12.95. ISBN 0-394-50551-4. Verse-novel that reconstructs a fact-based violent death of a black slave.

Incarnations: Poems, 1966–68. Random 1968 o.p. Thirty-four new poems never before in book form, with photographs of the author.

New and Selected Poems, 1923–1985. 1985. Random 1985 $19.95. ISBN 0-394-54380-7

Now and Then: Poems 1976–1978. Random 1978 $11.95. ISBN 0-394-50164-0

Or Else: Poems 1968–1973. Random 1974 $10.95. ISBN 0-394-49448-2

Rumor Verified: Poems, 1979–1980. Random 1981 $9.95. ISBN 0-394-52136-6

Selected Poems, 1923–1975. Random 1976 $17.95. ISBN 0-394-40531-5. Wide collection of previously published poems.

SHORT STORY COLLECTION BY WARREN

The Circus in the Attic: And Other Stories. 1947. HarBraceJ 1968 $5.95. ISBN 0-15-618002-2

WORKS BY WARREN

Democracy and Poetry. HUP 1975 $9.95. ISBN 0-674-19626-0. Argues that the erosion of individual worth in a commercial society may be halted by the power of poetry.

John Brown: The Making of a Martyr. Rprt. Serv. 1992 $99.00. ISBN 0-7812-6165-1

The Legacy of the Civil War. HUP 1983 $6.95. ISBN 0-674-52175-7. Long essay focusing on the injustices in American society both before and immediately following the Civil War.

New and Selected Essays. Random 1989 $24.95. ISBN 0-394-57516-4. Collection of essays on several authors, including Twain, Faulkner, and Hemingway.

A Robert Penn Warren Reader. Random 1987 $22.50. ISBN 0-394-55896-0

BOOKS ABOUT WARREN

Bedient, Calvin. *In the Heart's Last Kingdom.* HUP 1984 $10.95. ISBN 0-674-44547-3. Critical analysis of Warren's *Audubon* and other poems.

Bloom, Harold, ed. *Robert Penn Warren.* Chelsea Hse. 1986 $34.95. ISBN 0-87754-662-2. Important critical essays that present a complete analysis of Warren's fiction, poetry, and criticism.

———, ed. *Robert Penn Warren's All the King's Men.* Chelsea Hse. 1987 $29.95. ISBN 1-55546-063-1

Bohner, Charles. *Robert Penn Warren.* Macmillan 1981 $19.95. ISBN 0-8057-7345-2. Revised and updated analysis of Warren's poetry and prose; contains a chronology and a bibliography.

Burt, John. *Robert Penn Warren and American Idealism.* Yale U. Pr. 1988 $25.00. ISBN 0-300-04067-9. Intelligent discussion of the American ideal manifested in Warren's works as the internal struggle of romantic selfhood.

Chambers, R., ed. *Twentieth Century Interpretations of All the Kings Men.* P-H 1977 $9.95. ISBN 0-13-022434-0

Clark, William B. *Critical Essays on Robert Penn Warren.* G. K. Hall 1981 o.p. Reviews and critical essays about Warren's many achievements; includes the text of an interview.

Gray, Richard, ed. *Robert Penn Warren: A Collection of Critical Essays.* Greenwood 1979 repr. of 1965 ed. $35.00. ISBN 0-313-20807-7

Grimshaw, James A., Jr. *Robert Penn Warren: A Descriptive Bibliography, 1922–1979.* U. Pr. of Va. 1981 $40.00. ISBN 0-8139-0891-4

———, ed. *Time's Glory: Original Essays on Robert Penn Warren.* Univ. Central AR Pr. 1986 $19.95. ISBN 0-9615143-2-9. More useful sections of this little volume include Richard Law's long and provocative essay on *World Enough and Time* and the "Bibliographical Note" by the book's editor.

Justus, James H. *The Achievement of Robert Penn Warren.* La. State U. Pr. 1981 $35.00. ISBN 0-8071-0875-8

Runyon, Randolph P. *The Braided Dream: Robert Penn Warren's Late Poetry*. U. Pr. of Ky. 1990 $26.00. ISBN 0-8131-1722-4. Examines Runyon's late four publications of poetry and convinces us that each set of poems forms a remarkably interrelated sequence.

_____. *The Taciturn Text: The Fiction of Robert Penn Warren*. Ohio St. U. Pr. 1990 $35.00. ISBN 0-8142-0530-5. Close reading of each of Warren's ten novels, preceded by a detailed synopsis of the plot.

Ruppersburg, Hugh. *Robert Penn Warren and the American Imagination*. U. of Ga. Pr. 1990 $27.50. ISBN 0-8203-1215-0. Studies Warren by exploring his expression of the myth of America—the gap between American ideals and the actualities of American life—in both poetry and prose written during his 65-year career.

Snipes, Katherine. *Robert Penn Warren*. Continuum 1984 $18.95. ISBN 0-8044-2828-X

Strandberg, Victor H. *The Poetic Vision of Robert Penn Warren*. U. Pr. of Ky. 1977 $27.00. ISBN 0-8131-1347-4. Elucidates, through an evaluation of his poetry, Warren's three major themes: passage, the undiscovered self, and mysticism.

Watkins, Floyd C. *Then and Now: The Personal Past in the Poetry of Robert Penn Warren*. U. Pr. of Ky. 1982 $15.00. ISBN 0-8131-1456-X. Interesting study analyzing Warren's use of his past in his poetry.

_____, ed. *Talking with Robert Penn Warren*. U. of Ga. Pr. 1990 $45.00. ISBN 0-8203-1219-3. Collection of interviews, with racism at the heart of the tangle.

WELTY, EUDORA. 1909–

One of the most admired American writers, Eudora Welty has steadily gone on writing short stories and novels that are entirely original, sometimes melodramatic, occasionally fantastic, and often concerned with psychological aberration. She has a fine ear for dialogue and a sense of style that elevates her fiction above the ordinary. Born in Jackson, Mississippi, she attended the Mississippi State College for Women before going north to the University of Wisconsin and Columbia University. She worked for a while in advertising, then returned to Jackson to take a government publicity job. She has remained in Jackson since then, living quietly with her family and pursuing a literary career that has brought her several awards and much critical attention. Some of her better-known short stories, frequently anthologized and thus widely taught and studied in classrooms, are "Why I Live at the P.O.," "Death of a Traveling Salesman," "Petrified Man," and "A Worn Path."

Although Welty's critical reputation remains largely dependent upon her excellent short stories, she has also written four full-length novels, which have been well received. *Delta Wedding* (1946) is a densely plotted novel with many characters told from multiple points of view. It explores with intelligence and subtlety problems of domestic relationships and the mixing of social classes. *The Ponder Heart* (1954), a more simply told story, centers on the murder trial of a man unjustly accused of killing his young wife. With *Losing Battles* (1970), Welty deals again with the complexities of a large family gathering. *The Optimist's Daughter* (1972) is the story of tangled relationships between a 71-year-old judge undergoing a critical eye operation in a New Orleans hospital, his daughter, a withdrawn widow summoned from Chicago, and the judge's second wife of "coarse breeding," younger than his daughter. Gradually, this subtle story of father-daughter and husband-wives begins to reverberate with further complications. Howard Moss called the book "a miracle of compression. . . . The best book Eudora Welty has ever written" (*N.Y. Times*).

One Writer's Beginnings (1984), an engaging volume of reminiscences originally given as lectures at Harvard University, had the unusual distinction (for a serious work of literary nonfiction published by a university press) of climbing high on the bestseller lists during 1984. Her other nonfiction includes *One Time, One Place: Mississippi in the Depression* (1972), *A Snapshot Album* (1971), and *The Eye of the Storm: Selected Essays and Reviews* (1977).

Welty will perhaps be best remembered for her highly eclectic and original voice, her brilliant style and revealing dialogue, her humane celebration of characters, and her visionary outlook and playful exuberance.

NOVELS BY WELTY

Delta Wedding. 1946. HarBraceJ 1979 $7.95. ISBN 0-15-625280-5

Losing Battles. 1970. Random 1990 $8.95. ISBN 0-679-72882-1. Welty's best and most robust novel.

Optimist's Daughter. 1972. Random 1990 $9.00. ISBN 0-679-72883-X

The Ponder Heart. 1954. HarBraceJ 1967 $6.95. ISBN 0-15-672915-6

The Robber Bridegroom. 1942. HarBraceJ 1978 repr. of 1948 ed. $6.95. ISBN 0-15-676807-0. Tale of two lovers living in a "fairyland" that is threatened by a wicked stepmother and vengeful Indians.

SHORT STORY COLLECTIONS BY WELTY

The Bride of Innisfallen and Other Stories. Amereon Ltd. $15.95. ISBN 0-89190-515-4

The Collected Stories of Eudora Welty. 1980. HarBraceJ 1982 $12.95. ISBN 0-15-618921-6

A Curtain of Green and Other Stories. 1941. HarBraceJ 1979 $7.95. ISBN 0-15-623492-0. Stories about black life in the South.

The Golden Apples. HarBraceJ 1956 $8.95. ISBN 0-15-63609-X. Short stories dramatizing the changes of a Mississippi town as it moves into modern times.

Selected Stories. Random 1978 $12.95. ISBN 0-394-60445-8. Contains an introduction by Katherine Anne Porter.

Thirteen Stories. 1956. Ed. by Ruth M. Vande Kieft. HarBraceJ 1965 $6.95. ISBN 0-15-689969-8

The Wide Net and Other Stories. HarBraceJ 1974 repr. of 1943 ed. $7.95. ISBN 0-15-696610-7. Stories depicting the pioneer heritage of the South.

PLAY BY WELTY

The Hitch-Hikers. Dramatists Play 1986 $3.95. ISBN 0-317-44294-5

NONFICTION BY WELTY

Eye of the Story: Selected Essays and Reviews. Random 1990 $8.95. ISBN 0-679-73004-4. Useful as an access to Welty's own theory of fiction writing.

One Time, One Place. 1971. Random 1971 $12.95. ISBN 0-394-47308-6

One Writer's Beginnings. Warner Bks. 1991 $6.99. ISBN 0-446-39328-2. An intriguing autobiographical memoir of Welty's early life.

BOOKS ABOUT WELTY

Black, Patti C., ed. *Welty.* U. Pr. of Miss. 1977 $6.95. ISBN 0-87805-337-9

Bloom, Harold, ed. *Eudora Welty.* Chelsea Hse. 1986 $24.95. ISBN 0-87754-718-1. Essays that run the gamut from interview to explication of individual works.

Carson, Barbara H. *Eudora Welty: Two Pictures at Once in Her Frame.* Whitston Pub. 1992 $23.50. ISBN 0-87875-422-9

Desmond, John F., ed. *A Still Moment: Essays on the Art of Eudora Welty.* Scarecrow 1978 $20.00. ISBN 0-8108-1129-4. Collection of critical essays about Welty's fiction.

Devlin, Albert J., ed. *Eudora Welty's Chronicle: A Story of Mississippi Life.* U. Pr. of Miss. 1983 $27.50. ISBN 0-87805-176-7. Discusses the reflection of Mississippi history in Welty's work.

————, ed. *Welty: A Life in Literature.* U. Pr. of Miss. 1987 $29.50. ISBN 0-87805-315-8. Broad collection of critical essays celebrating Welty's achievements as a literary artist.

Gygax, Franziska. *Serious Daring from Within: Female Narrative Strategies in Eudora Welty's Novels*. Greenwood 1990 $35.00. ISBN 0-313-26865-7. Examines the different female narrators found in Welty's novels.

Kreyling, Michael. *Author and Agent: Eudora Welty and Diarmuid Russell*. FS&G 1991 $22.95. ISBN 0-374-10727-0. Documents the three-decade-long association and friendship between Welty and Russell.

MacNeil, Robert. *Eudora Welty: Seeing Black and White*. U. Pr. of Miss. 1990 $9.95. ISBN 0-87805-471-5

Manning, Carol S. *With Ears Opening Like Morning Glories: Eudora Welty and the Love of Storytelling*. Greenwood 1985 $42.95. ISBN 0-313-24776-5. Attempts to unify Welty's work as a vision of Southern culture.

Marrs, Suzanne. *The Welty Collection: A Guide to the Eudora Welty Manuscripts and Documents at the Mississippi Department of Archives and History*. U. Pr. of Miss. 1988 $30.00. ISBN 0-87805-366-2. Expertly catalogs Welty's manuscripts, photos, correspondence, publications, and memorabilia.

Prenshaw, Peggy W., ed. *Eudora Welty: Thirteen Essays*. U. Pr. of Miss. 1983 $12.95. ISBN 0-87805-187-2. Fine selection of critical essays on Welty and her work.

Randisi, Jennifer L. *A Tissue of Lies: Eudora Welty and the Southern Romance*. U. Pr. of Amer. 1982 $47.75. ISBN 0-8191-2451-6

Swearingen, Bethany C. *Eudora Welty: A Critical Bibliography, 1936–58*. U. Pr. of Miss. 1984 o.p.

Trouard, Dawn, ed. *Eudora Welty: The Eye of the Storyteller*. Kent St. U. Pr. 1989 $24.00. ISBN 0-87338-384-2. Sixteen essays that examine the breadth of Welty's talent and expand the range of critical approaches to her fiction.

Turner, W. Craig. *Critical Essays on Eudora Welty*. G. K. Hall 1989 $40.00. ISBN 0-8161-8888-2. Includes original and reprinted essays and reviews arranged by literary works followed by a section on her work in general.

Vande Kieft, Ruth M. *Eudora Welty*. Macmillan 1987 $20.95. ISBN 0-8057-7487-4. Offers close explication of Welty's short stories and novels.

Westling, Louise. *Eudora Welty*. B & N Imports 1989 $42.00. ISBN 0-389-20867-1

WEST, NATHANAEL (pseud. of Nathan Wallenstein Weinstein). 1904–1940

American novelist Nathanael West was born in New York City, the son of a prosperous building contractor. He began his college education at Tufts University but transferred to Brown University, from which he graduated in 1924. After graduation, West went to Europe and lived in Paris for a few years, where he wrote the short novel *The Dream Life of Balso Snell* (1931), an avant–garde work that reflected his concern with the emptiness of contemporary life. West's modest legacy of completed works reached its peak of recognition during the period when later Jewish American writers were discovering black humor. Among novels that chronicle the wasteland despair and grotesque comedy of the time between the wars, West's *Miss Lonelyhearts* (1933) and *The Day of the Locust* (1939) stand out as remarkable examples. The first is about a young man conducting a column of advice to the lovelorn who finds it increasingly impossible not to share the problems of his readers. *The Day of the Locust* is a surrealistic story about a riot that ends with the burning of Los Angeles. If FRANZ KAFKA (see Vol. 2) had lived to come to the United States and become a screenwriter, he might have written a book like *The Day of the Locust*, which MALCOLM COWLEY called the best novel ever written about Hollywood. West's other short novel, *A Cool Million* (1934), is, like *The Dream Life of Balso Snell*, an experimental work that offers variations on the theme of reality and illusion; both works look toward a literature of the absurd and deserve their place in literary history as influences on a school of American writers that came into prominence during the 1960s.

West's own life had aspects of tragic absurdity. He was married to Eileen McKenney, the original of the central figure in *My Sister Eileen*, while his own sister became the wife of humorist S. J. PERELMAN. After writing *Miss Lonelyhearts*, West and his wife went to Hollywood and remained there until they were both killed in a car accident in 1940.

NOVELS BY WEST

The Day of the Locust. 1939. NAL-Dutton 1983 $3.95. ISBN 0-451-52348-2
The Dream Life of Balso Snell and *A Cool Million: Two Novels by West.* 1931. FS&G 1963 $8.95. ISBN 0-374-50292-7
Miss Lonelyhearts and *The Day of the Locust.* New Dir. Pr. 1962 $6.95. ISBN 0-8112-0215-1

WORKS BY WEST

The Complete Works of Nathanael West. Introduction by Alan Ross. Hippocrene Bks. 1979 repr. of 1957 ed. o.p. Includes four of West's novels: *The Dream Life of Balso Snell, Miss Lonelyhearts, A Cool Million,* and *The Day of the Locust,* as well as other assorted works.

BOOKS ABOUT WEST

Comerchero, Victor. *Nathanael West: The Ironic Prophet.* U. of Wash. Pr. 1967 o.p. Critical study analyzing the factors that influenced West and shaped his novels.
Long, Robert Emmet. *Nathanael West.* Continuum 1985 o.p. Critical study that examines West's themes and techniques.
Martin, Jay. *Nathanael West: The Art of His Life.* Carroll & Graf 1984 $8.95. ISBN 0-88184-030-0. The standard biography.
Vannatta, Dennis P. *Nathanael West: An Annotated Bibliography.* Garland 1975 o.p. Bibliography of secondary sources to West's work; includes pamphlets, periodicals, reviews, books, and biographies.
Widmer, Kingsley. *Nathanael West.* G. K. Hall 1982 o.p. Scholarly study of West's life and a review of his novels.
Wisker, Alistair. *The Writings of Nathanael West.* St. Martin 1990 $35.00. ISBN 0-312-04014-8. Explores the works of West and traces his literary development.

WHITE, E(LWYN) B(ROOKS). 1899–1985

Born in Mount Vernon, New York, E. B. White was educated at Cornell University and served as a private in World War I. After several years as a journalist, he joined the staff of the *New Yorker*, then in its infancy. For 11 years he wrote most of the "Talk of the Town" columns, and it was White and JAMES THURBER who can be credited with setting the style and attitude of the magazine. In 1938 he retired to a saltwater farm in Maine, where he wrote essays regularly for *Harper's Magazine* under the title "One Man's Meat." Like THOREAU, White preferred the woods; he also resembled Thoreau in his impatience and indignation.

White received several prizes: in 1960, the gold medal of the American Academy of Arts and Letters; in 1963, the Presidential Medal of Freedom, the nation's highest civilian award (he was honored along with THORNTON WILDER and EDMUND WILSON); and in 1978, a special Pulitzer Prize. His verse is original and witty but with serious undertones. His friend James Thurber described him as "a poet who loves to live half-hidden from the eye." Three of his books have become children's classics: *Stuart Little* (1945), about a mouse born into a human family, *Charlotte's Web* (1952), about a spider who befriends a lonely pig, and *The Trumpet of the Swan* (1970). Among his best-known and most widely used books is *The Elements of Style* (1959), a guide to grammar and rhetoric based on a text written by one of his professors at Cornell, William Strunk, which White revised and expanded. White was married to Katherine Angell, the first fiction editor of the *New Yorker*.

CHILDREN'S FICTION BY WHITE

Charlotte's Web. 1952. Buccaneer Bks. 1990 $21.95. ISBN 0-89966-696-5
Stuart Little. 1945. G. K. Hall 1988 $13.95. ISBN 0-8161-4490-7
The Trumpet of the Swan. 1970. HarpC 1973 $3.95. ISBN 0-06-440048-4

WORKS BY WHITE

The Elements of Style. 1959. (co-authored with William Strunk, Jr.) Macmillan 1979 $5.95. ISBN 0-02-418200-1
Essays of E. B. White. HarpC 1979 $9.95. ISBN 0-06-090662-6
Here Is New York. Warner Bks. 1988 $5.95. ISBN 0-446-38829-7. Observations on life in New York.
Letters of E. B. White. HarpC 1989 $14.95. ISBN 0-06-091517-X Comprehensive collection of letters written between 1908 and 1976.
One Man's Meat. HarpC 1983 $13.00. ISBN 0-06-091081-X. Essays on a variety of subjects, including his love for Maine.
The Second Tree from the Corner. HarpC 1989 $9.95. ISBN 0-06-091516-1. Many works here originally published in the *New Yorker*'s "Talk of the Town" column, along with some poignant short stories about lonely men leading narrow lives.
Writings from the New Yorker: 1927–1976. HarpC 1991 $11.00. ISBN 0-06-092123-4. Diverse selection of writings written for the *New Yorker*.

BOOK ABOUT WHITE

Gherman, Beverly. *E. B. White: Some Writer!* Atheneum 1992 $13.95. ISBN 0-689-31672-0. Straightforward account of White's childhood, marriage, work, and friendships.

WILDER, THORNTON. 1897–1975

One of the most honored and versatile of modern writers, Thornton Wilder combined a career as a successful novelist with work for the theater that made him one of this century's outstanding dramatists. It was an early short novel, however, that first brought him fame. *The Bridge of San Luis Rey* (1927), a bestseller that won the Pulitzer Prize in 1927, is the story of a group of assorted people who happen to be on a bridge in Peru when it collapses. Ingeniously constructed and rich in its philosophical implications about fate and synchronicity, Wilder's book would seem to be the first well-known example of a formula that has become a cliché in popular literature. His attraction to classical themes is manifested in *The Woman of Andros* (1930), a tragedy about young love in pre-Christian Greece, and *The Ides of March* (1948), set in the time of JULIUS CAESAR (see Vol. 3) and told in letters and documents covering a long span of years. *Heaven's My Destination* (1934), is a seriocomic and picaresque story about a young book salesman traveling through the Midwest during the early years of the Great Depression. *Theophilus North* (1973), Wilder's last novel, disappointed many reviewers, but it provided its author with opportunities to offer some wry observations on the life of the idle rich in Newport during the summer of 1926 and to ponder in the story of his alter ego what might have happened if Wilder had stayed home, so to speak, instead of becoming Thornton Wilder. As a serious writer of fiction, Wilder's main claim rests on *The Eighth Day* (1967), an intellectual thriller, which the *N.Y. Times* called "the most substantial fiction of his career." It won the National Book Award for fiction in

1968. For more on Wilder's contributions as a playwright, see Chapter 18 in this volume.

NOVELS BY WILDER

The Bridge of San Luis Rey. 1927. HarpC 1986 $8.00. ISBN 0-06-091341-X. Novel about why the particular people on a bridge that collapsed had the bad luck—or divine destiny—to die when they did.

The Cabala. Carroll & Graf 1987 $3.95. ISBN 0-88184-295-8. Tale of a young American in Rome and his inability to relate to a different culture.

The Eighth Day. 1967. Carroll & Graf 1987 $4.95. ISBN 0-88184-339-3

Theophilus North. 1973. Carroll & Graf 1988 $4.95. ISBN 0-88184-382-2

PLAYS BY WILDER

Three Plays. HarpC 1985 $10.95. ISBN 0-06-091293-6. Includes *Our Town, The Skin of Our Teeth*, and *The Matchmaker*. Wilder's American classics—a portrait of small-town life, an allegory about humanity's evils, and a Moliere-style comedy about a wealthy bachelor and a clever woman.

Our Town: A Play in Three Acts. 1938. HarpC 1985 $5.00. ISBN 0-06-080779-2. Wilder's renowned play about life and death in a small New England town; centers on the love of Emily and George and Emily's death.

WORK BY WILDER

The Journals of Thornton Wilder. Yale U. Pr. 1987 $18.00. ISBN 0-300-04054-7

BOOKS ABOUT WILDER

Bryer, Jackson, ed. *Conversations with Thornton Wilder*. U. Pr. of Miss. 1991 $32.50. ISBN 0-87805-513-4. Interviews with Wilder that were done at different periods of his life.

Burbank, Rex J. *Thornton Wilder*. Macmillan 1978 $19.95. ISBN 0-8057-7223-5. Dated but nonetheless useful account of Wilder's life and work.

Castronovo, David. *Thornton Wilder*. Continuum 1986 $18.95. ISBN 0-8044-2119-6. Brings considerable background in modern literature to this study of Wilder.

Harrison, Gilbert A. *The Enthusiast: A Life of Thornton Wilder*. Fromm Intl. Pub. 1986 $12.95. ISBN 0-88064-053-7. A candid account of Wilder, the creative performer versus Wilder, the writer.

Walsh, Claudette M. *Thornton Wilder: A Reference Guide*. Macmillan 1991 $45.00. ISBN 0-8161-8790-8

Wilder, Amos N. *Thornton Wilder and His Public*. Fortress Pr. 1980 o.p.

WILLIAMS, WILLIAM CARLOS. 1883–1963

Poet, artist, and practicing physician of Rutherford, New Jersey, William Carlos Williams wrote poetry that was experimental in form, ranging from imagism to objectivism, with great originality of idiom and human vitality. Credited with changing and directing American poetry toward a new metric and language, he also wrote a large number of short stories and novels. *Paterson* (1946–58), about the New Jersey city of that name, was his epic and places him with EZRA POUND of the *Cantos* as one of the great shapers of the long poem in this century.

National recognition did not come early, but eventually Williams received many honors, including a vice-presidency of the National Institute of Arts and Letters (1952); the Bollingen Prize (1953); the $5,000 fellowship of the Academy of American Poets; the Loines Award for poetry of the National Institute of Arts and Letters (1948); and the Brandeis Award (1957). Book II of *Paterson* received the first National Book Award for poetry in 1949. Williams was named consultant in poetry in English to the Library of Congress for 1952–53.

Williams's continuously inventive style anchored not only objectivism, the school to which he most properly belongs, but also a long line of subsequent poets as various as ROBERT LOWELL, FRANK O'HARA, and ALLEN GINSBERG. With Stevens, he forms one of the most important sources of a specifically American tradition of modernism.

In addition to his earlier honors, Williams received two important awards posthumously, the Pulitzer Prize for Poetry (1963) and the Gold Medal for Poetry from the National Institute of Arts and Letters (1963).

POETRY BY WILLIAMS

The Collected Poems of William Carlos Williams. 2 vols. New Dir. Pr. 1991. Vol. 1 *1909–1939* $35.00. ISBN 0-8112-0999-7. Vol. 2 *1939–1962* $35.00. ISBN 0-8112-1063-4

Paterson. New Dir. Pr. 1963 $8.95. ISBN 0-8112-0233-X

Selected Poems. New Dir. Pr. 1985 $8.95. ISBN 0-8112-0958-X

NOVEL BY WILLIAMS

A Voyage to Pagany. 1928. Rprt. Serv. 1988 $49.00. ISBN 0-317-90788-3. Story about Dr. Evans and his search for his heritage, which takes him to Rome, Vienna, and France.

PLAYS BY WILLIAMS

Many Loves and Other Plays. New Dir. Pr. 1961 $9.95. ISBN 0-8112-0232-1. Also includes *A Dream of Love* and *Tituba's Children.*

NONFICTION BY WILLIAMS

The American Idiom: A Correspondence. Bright Tyger Pr. 1991 $21.95. ISBN 0-944378-80-3. Brings together the 83 extant letters of the Williams-Norse correspondence.

Autobiography of William Carlos Williams. New Dir. Pr. 1967 $12.95. ISBN 0-8112-0226-7. An informal and chatty memoir that reveals a great deal about Williams's life and work.

Embodiment of Knowledge. New Dir. Pr. 1974 $18.75. ISBN 0-8112-0553-3

I Wanted to Write a Poem. New Dir. Pr. 1978 $4.95. ISBN 0-8112-0707-2

A Recognizable Image: William Carlos Williams on Art and Artists. New Dir. Pr. 1978 $16.00. ISBN 0-8112-0704-8

Selected Essays. New Dir. Pr. 1969 $10.95. ISBN 0-8112-0235-6

The Selected Letters of William Carlos Williams. New Dir. Pr. 1985 $9.95. ISBN 0-8112-0934-2

WORK BY WILLIAMS

William Carlos Williams Reader. New Dir. Pr. 1969 $11.95. ISBN 0-8112-0239-9

BOOKS ABOUT WILLIAMS

Bloom, Harold, ed. *William Carlos Williams.* Chelsea Hse. 1986 $24.95. ISBN 0-87754-637-1. Collection of essays presenting a complete critical portrait of Williams.

Breslin, James E. *William Carlos Williams: An American Artist.* U. Ch. Pr. 1985 $9.95. ISBN 0-226-07407-2

Callan, Ron. *William Carlos Williams and Transcendentalism: Fitting the Crab in a Box.* St. Martin 1992 $35.00. ISBN 0-312-07596-0. Study of William Carlos Williams and his relation to American transcendentalism.

Conrad, Bryce. *Refiguring America: A Study of William Carlos Williams' In the American Grain.* U. of Ill. Pr. 1990 $29.95. ISBN 0-252-01704-8. First book-length study of a still-controversial collection of historical essays by Williams.

Diggory, Terence. *William Carlos Williams and the Ethics of Painting.* Princeton U. Pr. 1991 $27.50. ISBN 0-691-06852-6. Explores Williams's use of the paradigm of a marriage that can acknowledge and withstand infidelity to challenge the assumption that violence and oppression are inherent in all relationships.

Doyle, Charles. *William Carlos Williams: The Critical Heritage.* Routledge Chapman & Hall 1980 $69.50. ISBN 0-7100-8987-2

Duffey, Bernard. *A Poetry of Presence: The Writing of William Carlos Williams.* U. of Wis. Pr. 1986 $23.75. ISBN 0-299-10470-2. Treats both the poetry and the prose.

Fisher-Wirth, Ann W. *William Carlos Williams and Autobiography: The Woods of His Own Nature.* Pa. St. U. Pr. 1989 $24.95. ISBN 0-271-00653-6. Examines Williams's works for what they reveal about his conception of self and his public and private desires.

Lloyd, Margaret G. *William Carlos Williams' Paterson: A Critical Appraisal.* Fairleigh Dickinson 1979 $35.00. ISBN 0-8386-2152-X. Fine general study of *Paterson* with an emphasis on the structure of the poem.

Mariani, Paul J. *William Carlos Williams: A New World Naked.* Norton 1990 $14.95. ISBN 0-393-30672-0

———. *William Carlos Williams: The Poet and His Critics.* Bks. Demand $71.00. ISBN 0-317-27974-2. Cogent, well-written biography of Williams and his art.

Rapp, Carl. *William Carlos Williams and Romantic Idealism.* U. Pr. of New Eng. 1984 $25.00. ISBN 0-87451-290-5. Alternative view of Williams's work as representing, rather than refuting, and extending romanticism.

Riddel, Joseph N. *The Inverted Bell: Modernism and the Counterpoetics of William Carlos Williams.* La. State U. Pr. 1991 $10.95. ISBN 0-8071-1697-1. A critical attempt to apply "post-structuralist" European thought upon Williams's work.

Schmidt, Peter. *William Carlos Williams, the Arts, and Literary Tradition.* La. State U. Pr. 1988 $35.00. ISBN 0-8071-1406-5. Attempts to synthesize two dominant views of Williams.

Terrell, Carroll F., ed. *William Carlos Williams: Man and Poet.* Natl. Poet. Foun. 1983 $45.00. ISBN 0-915032-57-0

Weaver, M. *William Carlos Williams.* Cambridge U. Pr. 1977 $39.50. ISBN 0-521-08072-X

Whitaker, Thomas. *William Carlos Williams.* Macmillan 1989 $20.95. ISBN 0-8057-7541-2. Comprehensive analysis of Williams's life and work with an emphasis on his poetry.

WILSON, EDMUND. 1895–1972

Wilson roamed the world and read widely in many languages. He was a journalist for leading literary periodicals: *Vanity Fair*, where he was briefly managing editor; *The New Republic*, where he was associate editor for five years; and the *New Yorker*, where he was book reviewer in the 1940s. These varied experiences were typical of Wilson's range of interests and ability. Eternally productive and endlessly readable, he conquered American literature in countless essays. If he is idiosyncratic and lacks a rigid mold, that probably contributes to his success as a literary critic, since he was not committed to interpretation in the straitjacket of some popular approach or dogma. His critical position suits his cosmopolitan background—historical and sociological considerations prevail. He went through a brief Marxist period and experimented with Freudian criticism. *Axel's Castle* (1931), a penetrating analysis of the symbolist writer, has exerted a great influence on contemporary literary criticism. Its dedication, to Christian Gauss of Princeton, reads: "It was principally from you that I acquired . . . my idea of what literary criticism ought to be—a history of man's ideas and imaginings in the setting of the conditions which have shaped them." His volume of satiric short stories, *Memoirs of Hecate County* (1946), with its frankly erotic passages, was the subject of court cases in a less tolerant decade than the present one. It was

Wilson's own favorite among his writings, but he complained that those individuals who like his other work tend to disregard it.

NONFICTION BY WILSON

American Earthquake: A Documentary of the Jazz Age, the Great Depression and the New Deal. FS&G 1979 o.p. Essays from periodicals.

Apologies to the Iroquois: The Iroquois and Their Neighbors. Syracuse U. Pr. 1992 $15.95. ISBN 0-8156-2564-2

Axel's Castle. 1931. Macmillan 1991 $12.95. ISBN 0-02-012871-1. A study in the imaginative literature of 1870–1930.

The Devils and Canon Barham: Essays on Poets, Novelists and Monsters. FS&G 1973 o.p. With a foreword by Leon Edel.

The Fifties: From Notebooks and Diaries of the Period. FS&G 1986 $25.00. ISBN 0-374-15486-4

The Forties: From Notebooks and Diaries of the Period. FS&G 1984 $9.25. ISBN 0-374-51835-1. Notes on Wilson's observations during travels to Europe, New Mexico, and Haiti.

Letters on Literature and Politics, 1912–1972. Ed. by Elena Wilson. FS&G 1977 o.p. An engrossing collection of letters reflecting Wilson's views on literature and politics.

Patriotic Gore: Studies in the Literature of the American Civil War. NE U. Pr. 1984 $16.95. ISBN 0-930350-61-8. Excellent discussions of the lives and works of some 30 persons.

The Portable Edmund Wilson. Ed. by Lewis M. Dabney. Viking Penguin 1983 o.p. Essays on a great range of subjects, including critical looks at Dickens, Marx, Engels, Hemingway, and other writers; also includes correspondence and autobiographical writings.

The Shock of Recognition. 1943. Hippocrene Bks. repr. of 1974 ed. o.p. A valuable collection of American literary documents, edited by Wilson.

The Shores of Light: A Literary Chronicle of the 1920s and 1930s. NE U. Pr. 1985 $16.95. ISBN 0-930350-68-5. Includes personal impressions, memoirs of important writers, sketches of life in the 1920s, imaginary dialogues, personal letters, and satire.

The Sixties: From Notebooks and Diaries of the Period. FS&G 1993 $30.00. ISBN 0-374-26554-2

The Thirties: From Notebooks and Diaries of the Period. Ed. by Leon Edel. FS&G 1980 o.p. Wilson's account of his travels and events in America in the 1930s.

The Triple Thinkers and The Wound and the Bow: A Combined Volume. Foreword by Frank Kermode. NE U. Pr. 1984 o.p. Altogether 19 essays on literary subjects and critical theory.

The Twenties: From Notebooks and Diaries of the Period. Ed. by Leon Edel. FS&G 1975 o.p. Thoughts on the grim side of the Roaring Twenties, the mad side of Hollywood, and gossip and anecdotes about his peers.

Upstate: Records and Recollections of Northern New York. Syracuse U. Pr. 1990 $15.95. ISBN 0-8156-2499-9

SHORT STORY COLLECTION BY WILSON

Memoirs of Hecate County. Transaction Pubs. 1990 $22.95. ISBN 0-85290-020-2

BOOKS ABOUT WILSON

Castronovo, David. *Edmund Wilson.* Continuum 1984 $19.95. ISBN 0-8044-2116-1. Critical study scrutinizing Wilson's life and work from literary, cultural, and psychological viewpoints.

Douglas, George H. *Edmund Wilson's America.* U. Pr. of Ky. 1983 $23.00. ISBN 0-8131-1494-2. Surveys Wilson's mordant observations on the 1920s, the Depression, sex, the Vietnam War, and other subjects.

Groth, Janet. *Edmund Wilson: A Critic for our Time.* Ohio U. Pr. 1989 $29.95. ISBN 0-8214-0919-0. Insightful study focusing on Wilson's critical preoccupations with style and the progress of his literary career.

WOLFE, THOMAS (CLAYTON). 1900–1938

When WILLIAM FAULKNER was asked to rate his contemporaries, he put Thomas Wolfe at the top of the list—not so much for what Wolfe accomplished, Faulkner said, but for the magnitude of what he tried to do. Wolfe was born in Asheville, North Carolina, received his M.A. from Harvard University, taught at New York University (1924-30), and traveled abroad when he could. His long autobiographical series of novels begins with *Look Homeward, Angel* (1929), perhaps the best American *Bildungsroman* ever written, the account of a sensitive young man named Eugene Gant. Eugene's story is continued in *Of Time and the River* (1935), in which a publisher's note announced that "this novel is the second in a series of six" and gave the six titles. Wolfe lived to complete only four. Hurt and troubled by widespread rumors that his undisciplined manuscripts had been shaped into publishable form by Scribner's famous editor Maxwell Perkins, Wolfe changed publishers, moving from Scribner to Harper, and for legal reasons found it necessary to change the name of his fictional surrogate. The George Webber of *The Web and the Rock* (1939) and *You Can't Go Home Again* (1940) is essentially Eugene Gant continuing his search for the meaning of life. Wolfe traces the turbulent path of his hero through his European experiences, which have shown George the beginnings of Hitlerism, so that he tells his editor that henceforth he will write fiction of social protest. Sadly, Wolfe did not live to write the books so bravely announced. From an early bout with pneumonia, he suffered from tuberculosis of the lungs, which led to a fatal tuberculosis of the brain. He died following brain surgery at age 38.

In addition to the four installments of the one long autobiographical novel on which his reputation must chiefly rest, Wolfe wrote some short stories that are collected in *The Hills Beyond* (1941) and *From Death to Morning* (1935). As a student in the famous 47 Workshop at Harvard, and afterward on his own, Wolfe wrote several plays, including *Welcome to Our City.* Wolfe's own plays were not as successful in the theater as Ketti Frings's adaptation of *Look Homeward, Angel* as a comedy-drama in three acts; that work won a Pulitzer Prize in 1958 as well as the New York Drama Critics Circle Award as the best play of the season.

One of Wolfe's defining characteristics is an insatiable desire to "tell all"; indeed, his memoirs are unforgettable to the reader. Although often criticized for the wordiness of his sprawling manuscripts, his writing evoked the sights, sounds, and shapes of things in his experience with concrete clarity.

NOVELS BY WOLFE

Look Homeward, Angel. 1929. Macmillan 1982 $9.95. ISBN 0-684-17616-5
Of Time and the River. 1935. Macmillan 1980 $22.95. ISBN 0-684-16649-6
The Short Novels of Thomas Wolfe. Macmillan 1976 $25.00. ISBN 0-684-14554-5
You Can't Go Home Again. 1940. HarpC 1989 $6.95. ISBN 0-06-080986-8
The Web and the Rock. 1939. HarpC 1973 repr. of 1939 ed. o.p.

SHORT STORY COLLECTIONS BY WOLFE

Complete Short Stories of Thomas Wolfe. Macmillan 1989 $12.95. ISBN 0-02-040891-9
From Death to Morning. 1935. Macmillan 1983 $20.00. ISBN 0-684-17980-6
The Hills Beyond. 1941. I. R. Dee 1991 $14.95. ISBN 0-929587-72-3

POETRY BY WOLFE

A Stone, a Leaf, a Door: Poems. Macmillan 1991 $9.95. ISBN 0-684-19313-2

PLAYS BY WOLFE

Mannerhouse: A Play in a Prologue and Four Acts. La. State U. Pr. 1985 $22.50. ISBN 0-8071-1242-9. Set during the Civil War, this play follows the dissolution of an aristocratic Southern family.

Welcome to Our City: A Play in Ten Scenes. La. State U. Pr. 1983 $22.50. ISBN 0-8071-1085-X

WORKS BY WOLFE

The Autobiography of an American Novelist. Ed. by Leslie A. Field. HUP 1983 $7.95. ISBN 0-674-05317-6. Combines *The Story of a Novel* (1936) and *Writing and Living* (1964).

Beyond Love and Loyalty: The Letters of Thomas Wolfe and Elizabeth Nowell. Ed. by Richard S. Kennedy. U. of NC Pr. 1983 $22.50. ISBN 0-8078-1545-4. Correspondence between Wolfe and his agent/biographer, together with a previously unpublished story, "No More Rivers."

My Other Loneliness: Letters of Thomas Wolfe and Aline Bernstein. Ed. by Suzanne S. Stutman. U. of NC Pr. 1983 $34.95. ISBN 0-8078-1543-8. Correspondence with Aline Bernstein, the woman who served as the model for Esther Jack in Wolfe's fiction.

The Notebooks of Thomas Wolfe. Bks. Demand $117.60. ISBN 0-8357-3861-2

A Southern Appalachian Reader. Appalach. Consortium 1988 $14.95. ISBN 0-913239-50-X

A Western Journal. U. of Pittsburgh Pr. 1968 $6.95. ISBN 0-8229-5121-5. Full of Wolfe's hurried, vivid phrases, this journal reflects the author's continuing relish for new experiences.

BOOKS ABOUT WOLFE

Bloom, Harold, ed. *Thomas Wolfe.* Chelsea Hse. 1987 $24.95. ISBN 0-87754-638-X. Important critical essays probing the connection between Wolfe's life and work.

Donald, David H. *Look Homeward: A Life of Thomas Wolfe.* Fawcett 1988 $12.95. ISBN 0-449-90286-2. Definitive and highly readable biography of Thomas Wolfe; contains photographs.

Field, Leslie. *Thomas Wolfe and His Editors: Establishing a True Text for the Posthumous Publications.* U. of Okla. Pr. 1988 $22.95. ISBN 0-8061-2095-9. Exhausting and tedious study.

Harper, Margaret M. *Aristocracy of Art in Joyce and Wolfe.* La. State U. Pr. 1990 $27.50. ISBN 0-8071-1596-7. Shows how both Joyce and Wolfe used their novels to reinvent themselves as members of an exclusive group among whom order and beauty prevail as the dominant forces of life.

Holman, C. Hugh. *Three Modes of Modern Southern Fiction: Ellen Glasgow, William Faulkner, Thomas Wolfe.* U. of Ga. Pr. 1966 $12.00. ISBN 0-8203-0185-X. Explores Southern life and writing through an analysis of three writers, including Wolfe.

———. *The Loneliness at the Core: Studies in Thomas Wolfe.* La. State U. Pr. 1975 o.p.

Idol, John L., Jr. *A Thomas Wolfe Companion.* Greenwood 1987 $49.95. ISBN 0-313-23829-4. Miscellany of information about Wolfe's life and work.

Kennedy, Richard S. *The Window of Memory: The Literary Career of Thomas Wolfe.* U. of NC Pr. 1968 $12.95. ISBN 0-8078-4030-0. A penetrating, scholarly and critical study of the genesis and composition of Wolfe's fiction.

Lanzinger, Klaus. *Jason's Voyage: The Search for the Old World in American Literature. A Study of Melville, Hawthorne, Henry James, and Thomas Wolfe.* P. Lang Pubs. 1989 $40.50. ISBN 0-8204-0975-8. Offers a new synthesis that might permit insights into an old story—the American fascination with Europe.

Johnson, Elmer D. *Thomas Wolfe: A Checklist.* Kent St. U. Pr. 1970 o.p.

Magi, Aldo P., ed. *Thomas Wolfe Interviewed, 1929–1938*. La. State U. Pr. 1985 $19.95. ISBN 0-8071-1229-1. Consists of twenty-five newspaper interviews and one magazine article with an introduction and notes.

McElderry, Bruce R., Jr. *Thomas Wolfe*. NCUP 1964 $10.95. ISBN 0-8084-0299-4. Competent and careful study of Wolfe's life and work.

Nowell, Elizabeth. *Thomas Wolfe: A Biography*. Greenwood 1973 $38.50. ISBN 0-8371-6519-9

Phillipson, John S. *Thomas Wolfe: A Reference Guide*. G. K. Hall 1977 o.p.

Rubin, Louis D., Jr., ed. *Thomas Wolfe: A Collection of Critical Essays*. P-H 1973 o.p. Series of scholarly, critical essays on Wolfe's writing, some dealing with the major influences on his work.

WRIGHT, RICHARD. 1908–1960

Richard Wright was generally thought of as one of the most gifted contemporary African American writers until the rise of JAMES BALDWIN. "With Wright, the pain of being a Negro is basically economic—its sight is mainly in the pocket. With Baldwin, the pain suffuses the whole man. . . . If Baldwin's sights are higher than Wright's, it is in part because Wright helped to raise them" (*Time*). Wright was born on a plantation near Natchez, Mississippi, the son of a sharecropper. At the age of 15, he started to work in Memphis, then in Chicago, then "bummed all over the country," supporting himself by various odd jobs. His early writing was in the smaller magazines—first poetry, then prose. He won *Story*'s $500 prize—for the best story written by a worker on the Writer's Project—with "Uncle Tom's Children" in 1938, his first important publication. He wrote *Native Son* (1940) in eight months, and it made his reputation. Based in part on the actual case of a young black murderer of a white woman, it was one of the first of the African American protest novels, violent and shocking in its scenes of cruelty, hunger, rape, murder, flight, and prison.

Black Boy (1945) is the simple, vivid, and poignant story of Wright's early years in the South. It appeared at the beginning of a new postwar awareness of the evils of racial prejudice and did much to call attention to the plight of the African American. *The Outsider* (1953) is a novel based on Wright's own experience as a member of the Communist party, an affiliation he terminated in 1944. He remained politically inactive thereafter and from 1946 until his death made his principal residence in Paris. His nonfiction writings on problems of his race include *Black Power: A Record of Reactions in a Land of Pathos* (1954), about a visit to the Gold Coast, *White Man, Listen* (1957), and *Twelve Million Black Voices: A Folk History of the Negro in the United States*.

NOVELS BY WRIGHT

The Long Dream. 1958. Borgo Pr. 1991 $20.00. ISBN 0-8095-9068-9. Novel about the South.

Native Son. 1940. HarpC 1989 $6.00. ISBN 0-06-080977-9

The Outsider. 1953. HarpC 1989 $6.00. ISBN 0-06-080976-0

Savage Holiday. 1954. Chatham o.p. Psychological thriller.

Uncle Tom's Children: Four Novellas. 1938. HarpC 1989 $5.00. ISBN 0-06-080988-4

NONFICTION BY WRIGHT

American Hunger. 1977. Borgo Pr. 1991 $23.00. ISBN 0-8095-9067-0. Continuation of autobiography started with *Black Boy*; published posthumously.

Black Boy: A Record of Childhood and Youth. 1945. HarpC 1989 $6.00. ISBN 0-06-080987-6. Well-known, highly respected autobiography of Wright's experiences growing up black in the South during the era of the Jim Crow laws.

Black Power: A Record of Reactions in a Land of Pathos. Greenwood 1974 $48.50. ISBN 0-8371-7136-9
Eight Men. 1961. Thunder's Mouth Pr. 1987 $11.95. ISBN 0-938410-39-3
Twelve Million Black Voices. Thunders Mouth 1988 $15.95. ISBN 0-938410-44-X
White Man, Listen! 1957. Greenwood 1978 $38.50. ISBN 0-313-20533-7

WORKS BY WRIGHT

Richard Wright Reader. Ed. by Ellen Wright and Michel Fabre. HarpC 1978 $7.95. Wide-ranging collection of fiction, poetry, essays, and criticism; includes excerpts from *Native Son* and *Black Boy.*
Richard Wright: Works. Library of America 1991 $70.00. ISBN 0-940450-75-5

BOOKS ABOUT WRIGHT

Bloom, Harold, ed. *Richard Wright's Native Son.* Chelsea Hse. 1988 $24.95. ISBN 1-55546-055-0. Critical essays dealing with Wright's novels and short stories, as well as his role in the black literary tradition.
Fabre, Michel. *The Unfinished Quest of Richard Wright.* U. of Ill. Pr. 1992 $54.95. ISBN 0-252-01985-7
_____. *The World of Richard Wright.* U. Pr. of Miss. 1985 $35.00. ISBN 0-87805-258-5. Offers serious and detailed examination of Richard Wright's poetry, fiction, and essays.
_____. *Richard Wright: Books and Writers.* U. Pr. of Miss. 1990 $37.50. ISBN 0-87805-403-0. Provides a crucial tool for students exploring Richard Wright's intellectual context and development.
Felgar, Robert. *Richard Wright.* Macmillan 1980 $19.95. ISBN 0-8057-7320-7. Excellent general introduction to Wright's life and work.
Gayle, Addison. *Richard Wright: Ordeal of a Native Son.* Peter Smith 1983 $20.00. ISBN 0-8446-6000-0
Gounard, Jean-François. *The Racial Problem in the Works of Richard Wright and James Baldwin.* Greenwood 1992. ISBN 0-313-27308-1
Hakutani, Yoshinobu. *Critical Essays on Richard Wright.* Macmillan 1982 $35.00. ISBN 0-8161-8425-9. Interesting collection of criticism comprised of 18 essays dealing with Wright's fiction, nonfiction, and poetry.
Joyce, Joyce A. *Richard Wright's Art of Tragedy.* U. of Iowa Pr. 1991 $7.95. ISBN 0-87745-320-9. Focuses specially on the stylistic characteristics of Wright's most successful novel to show how his language merges with his subject matter to illuminate *Native Son* as a tragedy.
Kinnamon, Keneth, ed. *New Essays on Native Son.* Cambridge U. Pr. 1990 $22.95. ISBN 0-521-34319-4
_____, ed. *A Richard Wright Bibliography: Fifty Years of Criticism and Commentary, 1933–1982.* Greenwood 1988 $99.50. ISBN 0-313-25411-7. Lists public appearances, public statements, and critical reaction to Wright's writing in the print media of 54 nations.
Miller, Eugene E. *Voice of a Native Son: The Poetics of Richard Wright.* U. Pr. of Miss. 1990 $32.50. ISBN 0-87805-399-9. Taps a rich stock of unpublished material to give credence to Wright's lasting intellectual search into the substance of his vision (or self) and the resolution of his dual background as an African American.
Reilly, John M., ed. *Richard Wright: The Critical Reception.* B. Franklin 1978 o.p.
Trotman, James C. *Richard Wright: Myths and Realities.* Garland 1989 $29.00. ISBN 0-8240-7839-X Collection of critical essays first presented to the Richard Wright Literary Symposium held in October 1985. Provides fresh perspectives on the major works.

Urban, Joan. *Richard Wright*. Holloway 1990 $3.95. ISBN 0-87067-562-1. Excellent introduction to Wright for young adult readers.

Walker, Margaret. *The Daemonic Genius of Richard Wright*. Howard U. Pr. 1984 o.p. Written by a fellow African American novelist who was one of Wright's closest friends in his youth—until a mysterious final break in their relationship.

CHAPTER 17

Middle to Late Twentieth-Century American Literature

Jennifer B. Fleischner

> The American writer in the middle of the twentieth century has his hands full in trying to understand and then describe, and then make *credible* much of the American reality. It stupefies, it sickens, it infuriates, and finally it is even a kind of embarrassment to one's meager imagination. The actuality is continually outdoing our talents and the culture tosses up figures almost daily that are the envy of any novelist.
>
> —PHILIP ROTH

It was a common lament of nineteenth-century American authors, self-consciously comparing their nation to those of Europe, that America lacked sufficient material for the writer of fiction to write about. Because of this, so the argument ran, the genre for the new nation would be the romance, a form of the novel that was not tethered to actuality, which was felt to be so woefully thin in America.

However, the American writer in the late twentieth century is more likely to feel in competition with an actuality that has thickened immeasurably. Indeed, as theorists caution, even to speak of a single actuality is misleading; *actualities* more accurately describes the situation. The nation has become more urban and its population more diverse. In addition, writers have had to confront a bombardment of staggering events: three major wars (World War II, Korea, and Vietnam) and many skirmishes and invasions; the explosion of the first atomic bomb (1945); the Holocaust; the production of the first electronic computer (1946); the start of full-time television broadcasting (1948); the explosion of the first hydrogen bomb (1952); the decoding of DNA (1953); the civil rights revolution of the 1950s and 1960s; the women's movement of the 1960s and 1970s; the rapid exploration of space; the explosion in computer technology; Watergate; Irangate; the rise and the collapse of communism in Eastern Europe; answering machines; MTV; and sound bites and a host of other world-transforming technologies.

From the first, imaginative writing in America has been linked closely to the nation's historical task of self-creation. American fictions and history have always been interconnected. This dynamic, however, has assumed different proportions when, as JOHN UPDIKE asserts, "so-called non-fiction dominates" the publishing world, "and the dominant mass medium is television," featuring events rather than fictions—"the sports event, the panel discussion, the talk show, the quiz show." For Updike, the turning point was 1959, when NORMAN MAILER published *Advertisements for Myself* (104 years after WALT WHITMAN's "Song of Myself"). Having begun as a novelist, Mailer turned to nonfiction and then to a hybrid form of fiction and nonfiction, redefining American literature through the creation of a new relation between the imagination and actuality. In Mailer's view, the two major "impulses in American letters had failed"—the "realistic impulse," or the effort to reflect life, and the "aristocratic impulse," or the attempt to transform life through the order and beauty of art. The self-conscious play of history and fiction is an evident trend that extends across a range of writers, from DONALD BARTHELME, E. L. DOCTOROW, JOYCE CAROL OATES, JOAN DIDION, and THOMAS PYNCHON to such younger postmodernists as MAX APPLE or T. CORAGHESSAN BOYLE. Another kind of mix of fiction and reality, descended from the self-conscious narratives of VLADIMIR NABOKOV, are the metafictions of JOHN BARTH and PHILIP ROTH, in which the author himself is a character in the fiction.

Not all writers responded to the shifting relation between actuality and fiction by questioning the status of each. For some, the challenge for the postmodern American writer became to clear out a space for the imagination amid the reported events that clamored for a limited audience's limited attention and to give vital presence to the human, emotional life in a world more and more animated by push buttons and dials. Such writers, among them JOHN UPDIKE, JOHN CHEEVER, ANNE TYLER, JANE SMILEY, and RUSSELL BANKS, have been committed to the making of literature out of the stuff of ordinary family life. They have found deep emotional resonance in the everyday, the seemingly small. Other writers, such as SAUL BELLOW and WALKER PERCY, have adhered to another tradition, shaping their works around philosophical investigations of existence in America today.

Poetry's response to the seeming conflation of history and fiction in everyday experience has been varied. Beginning in the fifties, the Beats (so named by journalists, to suggest what was jazzy, beaten down, and beatified) wrote poetry that broke with traditional forms and included revelations about the actuality of contemporary culture (including drugs, homosexuality, sexual promiscuity, and disillusionment with the government) that shocked some and exhilarated others. Most important of these, and still being declaimed to a wide audience, is ALLEN GINSBERG. At the same time, confessional poets (among them THEODORE ROETHKE, RANDALL JARRELL, JOHN BERRYMAN, ROBERT LOWELL, ANNE SEXTON, and SYLVIA PLATH), who were influenced by psychoanalysis, began reworking the relation between the actual and fantasy by exploring childhood memories and dreams.

In poetry, as in prose, the problem of articulating experience, whether internal or external, encouraged a range of linguistic and formal experimentation. The "Black Mountain" poets, named for an avant-garde college in North Carolina with which they were associated, followed from EZRA POUND and built their poems out of a montage of images and phrases instead of logically unfolding ideas or symbols. Most recently, questions about the adequacy of language to capture the new conceptual models, the new pace of change, and the new forms of media preoccupy American poets. For JOHN ASHBERY, probably the boldest poet today, there was an urgency about this search for words because of the instability of experience: "[T]he naming of all the new things we now possessed had become our chief occupation; . . . very little time for the mere tasting and having of them was left over, and . . . even these simple, tangible experiences were themselves subject to description and enumeration, or else they too became fleeting and transient. . . ."

Yet, although most contemporary poets are given to speculations about the power of language, acknowledgment of the force of words finally underlies the commitment of anyone who makes writing his or her lifetime's work. Poetry's present task is to translate the seemingly random complexity of the "actualities" of American life into the concentrated moments of poetic experience. "To be 'capable of being in uncertainties,'" asserts CHARLES SIMIC, quoting JOHN KEATS, "is to be literally in the midst. The poet is in the midst. The poem, too, is in the midst, a kind of magnet for complex historical, literary, and psychological forces, as well as a way of maintaining oneself in the face of that multiplicity."

Perhaps the most significant change in American letters to have occurred in the last half of the twentieth century is its diversification: Perspectives that might once have been relegated to the margins began to be accepted into the "mainstream," changing the very definitions of *marginal* and *central* in American literature. The contributions of African American, Asian American, Hispanic American, Native American, and women writers to the development of literary styles as well as to the foregrounding of certain themes and concerns has changed the face of twentieth-century American literature. The stylistic experimentation of TONI CADE BAMBARA, the postmodern efforts of OSCAR HIJUELOS, and the utopian explorations of ALICE WALKER, have expanded the possibilities of the American novel, while the new female language of ADRIENNE RICH, the jazz riffs of GWENDOLYN BROOKS, and the political musings of AMIRI BARAKA and AUDRE LORDE have broadened our notion of American poetry. The addition of working-class, gay, and lesbian perspectives to the literary canon further enriches modern literature by creating new styles as well as broadened content. Literary criticism in turn has come to deal with class, race, gender, and sexuality in new and exciting ways, promising still further developments for the next century.

HISTORY AND CRITICISM

Baker, Houston A. *Afro-American Poetics: Revisions of Harlem and the Black Aesthetic.* Univ. of Wis. Pr. 1988 $19.95. ISBN 0-299-11500-3. Addresses a distinct aesthetic in literature written by African Americans.

Berthoff, Warner. *A Literature Without Qualities: American Writing Since 1945.* U. CA Pr. 1979 $35.00. ISBN 0-520-03696-4. Analysis of contemporary literature by a leading critic.

Braxton, Joanne. *Wild Women in the Whirlwind: Afra-American Culture and the Contemporary Literary Renaissance.* Rutgers U. Pr. 1990 $45.00. ISBN 0-8135-1441-X. Examination of contemporary African American women's writing; makes the claim for a separate tradition.

Clarke, Graham. *New American Writing: Essays on American Literature Since 1970.* St. Martin 1990 $35.00. ISBN 0-312-03566-7. Part of Critical Studies Series.

Foster, Edward Halsey. *Understanding the Beats.* U. of SC Pr. 1992 $29.95. ISBN 0-87249-798-4. Part of the Understanding Contemporary American Literature series.

Hassan, Ihab Habib. *Contemporary American Literature, 1945–1972: An Introduction.* Continuum 1973 $2.50. ISBN 0-8044-3121-3. Compact survey of the major genres with particular emphasis on fiction; offers a sense of connections among writers previously viewed in isolation.

Hickey, Morgen. *The Bohemian Register: An Annotated Bibliography of the Beat Literary Movement.* Scarecrow 1990 $32.50. ISBN 0-8108-2397-7. Good bibliography on history and criticism of Beats and bohemians in America.

Hobson, Fred. C. *The Southern Writer in the Postmodern World.* U. of Ga. Pr. 1991 $19.95. ISBN 0-8203-1275-4. Lectures about intellectual life in the contemporary South.

Kiernan, Robert F. *American Writing Since 1945: A Critical Survey.* Continuum 1983 $24.95. ISBN 0-8044-2458-6. Excellent survey of some 300 writers organized by genre; discusses the movements and groups within genres; includes selected bibliography and index.

Klinkowitz, Jerome. *The American 1960s: Imaginative Acts in a Decade of Change*. Bks. Demand repr. of 1980 ed. $33.60. ISBN 0-8357-5384-0. Sees the 1960s as a watershed for social, political, and literary change.

Kostelanetz, Richard. *American Writing Today*. Whitston Pub. 1991 $65.00. ISBN 0-87875-379-6. Contains good bibliography of contemporary writers, as well as of essays in history and criticism.

Lauter, Paul. *Canons and Context*. OUP 1991 $38.00. ISBN 0-19-505593-4. Essays addressing recent conflict in universities over the study and teaching of literature.

Lucas, John. *Moderns and Contemporaries: Novelists, Poets, and Critics*. B & N Imports 1985 o.p. Accessible collection of essays and lectures.

McCaffery, Larry. *Alive and Writing: Interviews with American Authors of the 1980s*. U. of Ill. Pr. 1987 $29.95. ISBN 0-252-01385-9. Thirteen contemporary fiction writers respond with candor in these interviews.

Pearlman, Mickey, and Katherine Henderson, eds. *Inter–view: Talks With America's Writing Women*. U. Pr. of Ky. 1990 $25.00. ISBN 0-8131-1780-1. Collection of revealing interviews.

Pinsker, Sanford. *Bearing the Bad News: Contemporary American Literature and Culture*. U. of Iowa Pr. 1990 $24.95. ISBN 0-87745-292-X. Examines literature as it deals with social problems.

POETRY

There is no one way to characterize recent American poetry: It is too diverse, taking too many forms, emanating from every corner of the country and tending toward a multiplicity of ends. Perhaps in the three decades following World War II one could point to definite "schools" of poetry: the confessional poets (ROBERT LOWELL, JOHN BERRYMAN, SYLVIA PLATH, ANNE SEXTON); the Beats (ALLEN GINSBERG, GARY SNYDER); the Black Mountain school (CHARLES OLSON, ROBERT CREELEY, ROBERT DUNCAN); and the New York school (JOHN ASHBERY, KENNETH KOCH). It would be difficult to categorize poets in such clear-cut ways today.

It is, however, possible to identify certain tasks and tendencies in recent American poetry. It is clear, for instance, that for many poets the diversification of poetry means that one speaks not simply as a poet but as a member of a group. Older poets, such as GWENDOLYN BROOKS and ADRIENNE RICH, were transformed by the consciousness-raising of the black power and women's movements of the 1960s and 1970s, beginning as poets identified with a particular poetic tradition and emerging as poets identified with African American women (in Brooks's case) or with feminists and lesbians (in Rich's case). This mode of self-definition is taken for granted today among many younger poets and has, to some extent, been critically sanctioned, as a glance at any anthology or reference book will show.

Another striking direction in recent poetry follows current thinking about the nature of reality and the relation of words to things. Recent theorists argue that we can never get "outside" language to a prior reality; language, alone, constitutes a world. Marjorie Perloff has called the poetry based on such an axiom a "poetry of indeterminacy" and has identified the avant-garde poet JOHN ASHBERY as its leading practitioner. Rather than viewing this as a crisis for poetry, Ashbery sees language and poetry as "an open field of . . . possibilities." Ashbery has experimented with discontinuity, fragmentation, and enigmatic imagery to loosen poetry from its usual structures. His verse is frequently self-reflective, offering his view of an artist, not modeled on God the creator: "[We] left/Our trash, sperm and excrement everywhere, smeared/On the landscape, to make of us what we could." Speculations about the power of language and its relation to reality preoccupy several contemporary poets, including W. S. MERWIN, MARK STRAND, and ALBERT GOLDBARTH.

Recently, too, poetry has been transformed by being intermixed with prose, music, photography, stage performance, and video. "Performance poetry" and "language poetry" enable a further exploration of the dislocation of language, discontinuous form, and fragmentation.

History and Criticism

Allen, Don Cameron, ed. *The Moment of Poetry*. Greenwood 1980 repr. of 1962 ed. $39.75. ISBN 0-313-22406-4. The reflections of five poet-professors (May Sarton, Richard Eberhart, Richard Wilbur, Randall Jarrell, and John Holmes) on their craft.

Allen, Donald M., and Warren Taliman, eds. *The Poetics of the New American Poetry*. Grove Pr. 1989 $14.95. ISBN 0-8021-5113-2. A collection of statements by 25 major poets.

Altieri, Charles. *Enlarging the Temple: New Directions in American Poetry during the 1960's*. Bucknell U. Pr. 1979 $29.50. ISBN 0-8387-2127-3. Offers a crucial theoretical background for contemporary poetry.

_____. *Self and Sensibility in Contemporary American Poetry*. Cambridge Studies in Amer. Lit. and Culture. Cambridge U. Pr. 1984 o.p. Focuses on Creeley, Rich, and Ashbery but deals with other figures as well.

Bellamy, Joe David. *American Poetry Observed: Poets on Their Work*. U. of Ill. Pr. 1988 $12.95. ISBN 0-252-06010-5. Interesting interviews that reflect both the diversity and the underlying assumptions behind the work of many contemporary poets.

Bennett, Paula. *My Life A Loaded Gun: Dickinson, Plath, Rich, and Female Creativity*. U. of Ill. Pr. 1990 $12.95. ISBN 0-252-06117-9. Argues for feminist tradition in poetry.

Boyers, Robert, ed. *Contemporary Poetry in America: Essays and Interviews*. Schocken 1974 o.p. A useful collection with important essays on such poets as James Wright, Sylvia Plath, Adrienne Rich, and others.

Breslin, James. *From Modern to Contemporary: American Poetry, 1945–1965*. U. Ch. Pr. 1985 $9.95. ISBN 0-226-07409-9. Close readings of works from such poets as Lowell, O'Hara, Levertov, and Ginsberg along with a historical framework.

Brooks, Cleanth. *Modern Poetry and the Tradition*. U. of NC Pr. 1970 o.p. One of the classic works of the New Criticism; close textual analysis of Yeats, Auden, Eliot, and others, with emphasis on form.

Charters, Samuel. *Some Poems and Some Poets: Studies in American Underground Poetry since 1945*. Oyez 1971 o.p. Group of essays on Jack Spicer, Robert Duncan, Allen Ginsberg, Lawrence Ferlinghetti, Charles Olson, Robert Creeley, and Gary Snyder.

Cook, Bruce. *The Beat Generation: The Tumultuous '50's Movement and Its Impact on Today*. Greenwood 1983 repr. of 1971 ed. o.p. A chatty, casual, but comprehensive history of the Beat Generation from its New York-San Francisco genesis to the Woodstock aftermath.

Cowan, Louise. *The Fugitive Group: A Literary History*. La. State U. Pr. 1959 o.p. An examination of the poets who published in *The Fugitive* in Nashville in the early 1920s: John Crowe Ransom, Allen Tate, and Robert Penn Warren.

Day, A. Grove. *The Sky Clears: Poetry of the American Indians*. Greenwood 1983 repr. of 1951 ed. $38.50. ISBN 0-8032-5047-9. A discussion for the general reader of the best available translations of Native American poetry.

Dickey, James. *Babel to Byzantium: Poets and Poetry Now*. Ecco Pr. 1981 o.p. Highly partisan criticism and appreciation, mostly on Dickey's contemporaries.

Eberhart, Richard. *Of Poetry and Poets*. U. of Ill. Pr. 1979 $29.95. ISBN 0-252-00630-5. An excellent overview of modern poetry that includes essays on poetics and on individual poets and a series of interviews with the author.

Fass, Ekbert, ed. *Towards a New American Poetics, Essays and Interviews: Olson, Duncan, Snyder, Creeley, Bly, Ginsberg.* Black Sparrow 1979 o.p. Important source material about the Black Mountain and Beat poets.

Feder, Lillian. *Ancient Myth in Modern Poetry.* Princeton U. Pr. 1972 $17.95. ISBN 0-691-01336-5. An exhaustive analysis of the use of Greek and Roman myth in the poetry of Yeats, Eliot, Pound, Auden, and other modern poets.

Fredman, Stephen. *Poet's Prose: The Crisis in American Verse.* Cambridge U. Pr. 1990 $37.95. ISBN 0-521-39098-2. Studies on prose poems of Williams, Ashbery, and Creeley.

Friebert, Stuart, and David Young. *A Field Guide to Contemporary Poetry and Poetics.* Longman 1980 o.p. An uneven collection that has some interesting essays.

Fussell, Edwin. *Lucifer in Harness: American Meter, Metaphor and Diction.* Princeton U. Pr. 1973 $32.50. ISBN 0-691-06238-2. A clearly written book about the forms and apparent formlessness of American poetics in the twentieth century.

Gayle, Addison, Jr. *The Black Aesthetic.* Doubleday 1972 o.p. Anthology of essays that approach black culture through aesthetics; offers a variety of critical views.

Gibson, Donald B. *Modern Black Poets: A Collection of Critical Essays.* P-H 1973 o.p. Excellent collection of articles by well-known black critics, including paired essays on the hate/humanism motif; good bibliography that deals specifically with eight important poets.

Heller, Michael. *Conviction's Net of Branches.* S. Ill. U. Pr. 1985 $9.95. ISBN 0-8093-1188-7. Essays on the objectivists, especially Oppen and Rakoski.

Howard, Richard. *Alone with America: Essays on the Art of Poetry in the United States since 1950.* Atheneum 1980 o.p. An approach to a whole generation of poets, including A. R. Ammons, James Wright, James Dickey, James Logan, Mark Strand, Anne Sexton, and 35 others.

Jackson, Richard. *Acts of Mind: Conversations with Contemporary Poets.* U. of Ala. Pr. 1983 $12.50. ISBN 0-8173-0228-X. Another collection of interviews, including several "younger" poets.

Johnson, Joyce. *Minor Characters.* PB 1990 $7.95. ISBN 0-671-72790-7. A memoir by a woman who knew many of the Beat poets during the 1950s.

Kalstone, David. *Five Temperaments: Elizabeth Bishop, Robert Lowell, James Merrill, Adrienne Rich, John Ashbery.* Norton 1985 o.p. Criticism that is almost exclusively positive along with some useful information on the poets.

Kherdian, David. *Six Poets of the San Francisco Renaissance: Portraits and Checklists.* Giligia o.p. Interesting portraits, or bio-bibliographies, of Ferlinghetti, Gary Snyder, Philip Whalen, David Meltzer, Michael McClure, and Brother Antoninus.

Larrissy, Edward. *Reading Twentieth-Century Poetry: The Language of Gender and Objects.* Blackwell Pubs. 1991 $47.95. ISBN 0-631-15358-6. Studies in post-modernism in English and American poetry.

Lieberman, Lawrence. *Unassigned Frequencies: American Poetry in Review, 1964–1977.* U. of Ill. Pr. 1977 o.p. Useful information about single volumes of poetry by a wide range of contemporary poets.

Mazzaro, Jerome. *Postmodern American Poetry.* U. of Ill. Pr. 1980 $24.95. ISBN 0-252-00759-X. A solid intellectual history of the postmodern period; traces the origins of postmodernism from the early poetry of Auden through Bishop's *Geography III.*

Middlebrook, Diane Wood, and Marilyn Yalom, eds. *Coming to Light: American Women Poets in the Twentieth Century.* U. of Mich. Pr. 1985 $14.95. ISBN 0-472-08061-X. Sixteen essays on such poets as H. D. Bishop, Plath, and Rich.

Molesworth, Charles. *The Fierce Embrace: A Study of Contemporary American Poetry.* U. of Mo. Pr. 1979 $27.50. ISBN 0-8262-0278-0. Treats several poets in depth, as well as such topics as the little poetry magazines and the poet's sense of belonging to a specific generation.

Murphy, Margueritte S. *A Tradition of Subversion: The Prose Poem in English From Wilde to Ashbery.* U. of Mass. Pr. 1992 $25.00. ISBN 0-87023-781-0. Prose poems of Williams, Gertrude Stein, and Ashbery.

Nelson, Cary. *Our Last First Poets: Vision and History in Contemporary American Poetry*. U. of Ill. Pr. 1984 $11.95. ISBN 0-252-01140-6. A searching book that asks serious questions about the poets' views.

Oberg, Arthur. *Modern American Lyric: Lowell, Berryman, Creeley and Plath*. Rutgers U. Pr. 1978 o.p. Sensitive readings that are especially alert to tones and emotional struggles in the poems.

Ostroff, Anthony, ed. *The Contemporary Poet as Artist and Critic: Eight Symposia*. Little 1964 o.p. A close-up look at how poets read other poets and how they respond to criticism; the essays show the New Criticism in practice.

Perloff, Marjorie. *Radical Artifice: Writing Poetry in the Age of Media*. U. Ch. Pr. 1992 $27.50. ISBN 0-226-65733-7. Experimental poetry analyzed by a leading contemporary critic.

Pinsky, Robert. *The Situation of Poetry: Contemporary Poetry and Its Traditions*. Princeton Essays in Lit. Ser. Princeton U. Pr. 1977 $12.95. ISBN 0-691-01352-7. An excellent critique of assumptions that animate—and deaden—much of contemporary poetry.

Reinfeld, Linda. *Language Poetry: Writing as Rescue*. La. State U. Pr. 1992 $25.00. ISBN 0-8071-1698-X. Collection about the founders of the avant-garde movement, popular in the seventies.

Rosenthal, M. L. *The Modern Poets: A Critical Introduction*. OUP 1965 o.p. An early study.

Ross, Andrew. *The Failure of Modernism*. Col. U. Pr. 1986 $35.00. ISBN 0-231-06330-X. Essays on poetry from modernism through Olson and Ashbery, focusing on subjectivity in literature.

Simpson, Eileen. *Poets in Their Youth: A Memoir*. FS&G 1990 $10.95. ISBN 0-374-52261-8. A revealing look at Berryman, Lowell, and others by a woman who was married to Berryman.

Smith, Dave. *Local Assays: On Contemporary American Poetry*. U. of Ill. Pr. 1985 $27.50. ISBN 0-252-01134-1. Readable collected essays.

Sutton, Walter. *American Free Verse: The Modern Revolution in Poetry*. New Dir. Pr. 1973 $3.95. ISBN 0-8112-0473-1. The development of free verse by American poets, with much explication and interpretation; provides a historical and critical survey of both old and new poets.

Turner, Alberta, ed. *Fifty Contemporary Poets: The Creative Process*. Longman 1977 $25.95. ISBN 0-582-28025-7. The origins, changes, and principles of technique used by fifty poets to bring their writings into final form.

Vendler, Helen. *Part of Nature, Part of Us: Modern American Poets*. Harvard Pap. Ser. HUP 1980 $22.00. ISBN 0-674-65475-7. Miscellaneous reviews and essays on a wide range of poets, with little theoretical or contextual argument.

Wagner, Jean. *Black Poets of the United States: From Paul Laurence Dunbar to Langston Hughes*. Trans. by Kenneth Douglas. U. of Ill. Pr. 1973 o.p. The best full-length study of these writers; thorough and sensitive to the black experience; includes 32 pages of valuable bibliographical data.

Whittemore, Reed. *Little Magazines*. Pamphlets on Amer. Writers Ser. Bks. Demand repr. of 1963 ed. $25.00. ISBN 0-7837-2854-9. A historical survey of the little poetry magazines of the twentieth century; a good general outline.

Wildman, Eugene, ed. *Anthology of Concretism*. Ohio U. Pr. 2nd ed. 1969 o.p. An introduction to concretism, an international movement once in vogue in the United States, presenting poetry in graphic design.

Williamson, Alan. *Introspection and Contemporary Poetry*. HUP 1984 $22.50. ISBN 0-674-46276-9. Sensitive readings of Plath, as well as of several "younger" poets, such as Louise Glück.

Collections

Adoff, Arnold, ed. *The Poetry of Black America: Anthology of the Twentieth Century*. HarpC. 1973 $25.00. ISBN 0-06-020089-8. An excellent anthology—comprehensive selections from W. E. B. DuBois and James Weldon Johnson through Richard

Wright, Sun Ra, Imamu Amiri Baraka (LeRoi Jones) to Nikki Giovanni and Victor Hernandez Cruz.

Allen, Donald M. *The New American Poetry, 1945–1960.* Grove Pr. 1960 o.p. An important collection of 215 poems by 44 poets, arranged to illuminate their differences and similarities, including biographies, bibliographies, and statements by the poets; had an impact that is hard to overestimate. Reissued in an enlarged edition entitled *The Post Modern Poets.*

Berg, Stephen, and Robert Mezey, eds. *Naked Poetry: Recent American Poetry in Open Forms.* Macmillan 1969 $11.49. ISBN 0-02-308280-1. An anthology of the work of 19 major poets with brief biographical sketches and photographs of the poets, including Levertov, Creeley, Rexroth, Roethke, Patchen, Berryman, and Snyder.

Brooks, Gwendolyn. *A Broadside Treasury, 1965–1970.* Broadside Pr. o.p. Poems by 50 African-American poets from the Broadside Press series, including work by Gwendolyn Brooks, LeRoi Jones, Nikki Giovanni, Lance Jeffers, Don L. Lee, and Sonia Sanchez, among others.

Carruth, Hayden. *The Voice That Is Great within Us: American Poetry of the Twentieth Century.* Bantam Class. Ed. Ser. Bantam 1983 $6.95. ISBN 0-553-26263-7. Anthology of over 130 poets, including Frost, Jeffers, Cummings, Rexroth, Patchin; includes a bibliography and notes.

DiYanni, Robert. *Modern American Poets: Their Voices and Visions.* Random 1987 $22.37. ISBN 0-394-36279-9. A survey with helpful introductory essays on understanding poetry, along with biographical information.

Hall, Donald, ed. *Contemporary American Poetry.* Poets Ser. Viking Penguin rev. ed. 1963 $5.95. ISBN 0-14-042067-3. Second edition includes works by poets such as Sylvia Plath, Frank O'Hara, Allen Ginsburg, and Ann Sexton.

Heyen, William. *The Generation of 2000: Contemporary American Poets.* Ontario Rev. NJ 1984 $14.95. ISBN 0-86538-043-0. A recent collection that makes several younger poets' work available, with short prose statements by each poet.

Padgett, Ron, and David Shapiro. *Anthology of New York Poets.* Random 1970 o.p. Important for the student of the New York school; sizable selections from the work of James Schuyler, Clark Coolidge, Kenward Elmslie, and Ted Berrigan, among others.

Pearson, Norman Holmes. *Decade: A Collection of Poems from the First Ten Years of the Wesleyan Poetry Program.* Bks. Demand repr. of 1969 ed. $81.60. ISBN 0-7837-0218-3. A collection of 33 poets published by Wesleyan up to 1968, including John Ashbery, Robert Bly, James Dickey, and James Wright.

Poulin, A., Jr. *Contemporary American Poetry.* HM 1991 $16.50. ISBN 0-395-43231-6. One of the anthologies most often used in college courses.

Sanders, Gerald De Witt, and others, eds. *Chief Modern Poets of Britain and America.* 2 vols. Macmillan 5th ed. 1970 $23.95 ea. ISBNs 0-02-405890-4, 0-02-405900-5

Strand, Mark, ed. *Contemporary American Poets: American Poetry since 1940.* NAL-Dutton 1969 $4.95. ISBN 0-451-62488-2. Selections from 92 poets published since the 1940s.

Untermeyer, Louis, ed. *Modern American Poetry.* HarBraceJ 1962 o.p. A critical anthology enlarged to include 772 poems by 76 poets ranging from Whitman to Anne Sexton.

Wolff, Tobias. *Matters of Life and Death: New American Series.* Wampeter Pr. 1983 $14.95. ISBN 0-931694-14-0

FICTION

Modern American fiction has borne witness to the traumas of recent history and to that history's threat to literature. But today's fiction has also been focused and energized by the very forces of change—social, political, and technological—that have challenged its existence. Modern American fiction has asserted an indomitable vitality, reflective of the human spirit.

Since World War II, American literature has been marked by a number of seemingly opposing trends. It has become more socially and politically aware and concerned with group identity; yet this very engagement with history also gave rise to an intensified interest in personal histories and local heritages. It was marked by narrative experiments—fragmented or multiple narratives, inner monologues, self-referentiality, a surrealistic mix of history and fiction— intended to map the uncertainties of modern reality; but realism, with its traditional focus on the feelings and furniture of ordinary life, has emerged stronger than ever in the 1990s.

The popularity of the "nonfiction novel," in which sophisticated literary techniques are used to narrate actual events, indicates the degree to which writers have begun to experience fiction as history and history as fiction. TRUMAN CAPOTE's *In Cold Blood* (1966) and NORMAN MAILER's *Armies of the Night* (1968) broke the ground for this new kind of mix. From this grew the "new journalism" of such writers as Tom Wolfe and JOAN DIDION. Soon, another kind of historical involvement found expression in the works of women and minority writers, whose concern with the particular experiences of marginalized Americans has reshaped ideas about American history and literary tradition. For instance, in *Beloved* (1987), TONI MORRISON drew upon the narratives of slave women to create a novel about the fugitive slaves' experience.

The self-reflexive narrative fictions of JOHN BARTH, DONALD BARTHELME, and WILLIAM GASS, popular in the 1970s, may have inspired GORE VIDAL to lament, in a famous 1976 essay, "Plastic Fiction," that novels had become mere "teaching-tools, artifacts. . . . " The rise (and fall) of minimalism in the 1980s seemed to suggest that literature was more dead than alive. Minimalists ANN BEATTIE and RAYMOND CARVER depict a flat, enigmatic world indifferent to art, disassociated from feeling. Yet richly imagined worlds continue to be the writer's gift to readers: RUSSELL BANKS's semirural New Hampshire; JOHN UPDIKE's Eastern suburbs; TONI MORRISON's small-town Ohio; SAUL BELLOW's Chicago; I. B. SINGER's immigrant New York City.

Perhaps the most striking quality of modern American fiction, then, is its vitality. Whether it draws upon stylistic innovation, nonfiction styles, realist traditions, or worlds rarely portrayed in mainstream literature, American fiction in the late twentieth century offers readers a rich variety of choices and experiences.

History and Criticism

Aldridge, John W. *After the Lost Generation.* Ayer repr. of 1951 ed. $20.00. ISBN 0-8369-2141-0. A pioneer study that remains of more than historical interest; contrasts the writers of the Lost Generation, principally Hemingway, Fitzgerald, and Dos Passos, with the then-new writers of the 1940s.

———. *The American Novel and the Way We Live Now.* OUP 1983 $25.00. ISBN 0-19-503198-9. Aldridge's growing criticism of the contemporary novel.

Allen, Mary. *The Necessary Blankness: Women in Major American Fiction of the Sixties.* U. of Ill. Pr. 1976 $24.95. ISBN 0-252-00519-8. Studies the portrayal of women by Barth, Pynchon, Kesey, Roth, Updike, and others; connects the weakness of the 1960s hero with the "blankness" of women in fiction of the time.

Balakian, Nona, and Charles Simmons, eds. *The Creative Present: Notes on the Contemporary American Novel.* Gordian 1973 $40.00. ISBN 0-87752-158-1. Leading critics' evaluations of the work of 17 writers; a valuable and absorbing book with a moderately conservative view.

Baumbach, Jonathan. *The Landscape of Nightmare: Studies in the Contemporary American Novel*. NYU Pr. 1965 $20.00. ISBN 0-8147-0032-2. Perceptive analyses and interpretations of individual novels by Bellow, Ellison, Malamud, Morris, O'Connor, Salinger, Styron, Edward Lewis Wallant, and Warren.

Bluefarb, Sam. *The Escape Motif in the American Novel: Mark Twain to Richard Wright*. Ohio St. U. Pr. 1972 o.p. Clear and concise analysis of characters and motives in relation to the changing "escape motif" found in American novels.

Bradbury, Malcolm. *The Modern American Novel*. Viking Penguin 1993 $25.00. ISBN 0-670-84515-9. Representative novels used as illustrations of prevailing movements and themes from the time of the naturalists to the present.

Byerman, Keith Eldon. *Fingering the Jagged Grain: Tradition and Form in Recent Black Fiction*. U. of Ga. Pr. 1986 $35.00. ISBN 0-8203-0789-0. Traces line of descent in twentieth-century African-American literature.

Butler-Evans, Elliott. *Race, Gender, and Desire: Narrative Strategies in the Fiction of Toni Cade Bambara, Toni Morrison, and Alice Walker*. Temple U. Pr. 1989 $34.95. ISBN 0-87722-608-3. Reflects interest in political implications of narrative.

Callahan, John F. *In the African-American Grain: The Pursuit of Voice in Twentieth-Century Black Fiction*. U. of Ill. Pr. 1988 $24.95. ISBN 0-252-01459-6. Argues for a distinctive "voice" in recent African American fiction.

Caramello, Charles. *Silverless Mirrors: Book, Self and Postmodern American Fiction*. U. Press Fla. 1983 $24.95. ISBN 0-685-07498-6. A provocative study that discusses Barth and Gass, as well as some lesser known contemporary experimental writers.

Coindreau, Maurice Edgar. *The Time of William Faulkner: A French View of Modern American Fiction*. Ed. and trans. by George McMillan Reeves. U. of SC Pr. 1971 o.p. A collection by Coindreau, popularizer of modern American fiction in Europe, bringing together 11 commentaries on Faulkner as well as translated prefaces to French editions of books by Caldwell, Capote, William Goyen, O'Connor, and William Maxwell.

Davis, Thadious M., and Trudier Harris, eds. *Afro-American Fiction Writers after 1955*. Volume 33 in *Dictionary of Literary Biography*. Gale 1984 $113.00. ISBN 0-8103-1711-7. Part of the generously illustrated *Dictionary of Literary Biography* series, featuring authoritative biographical and critical introductions to 49 established and promising writers.

Frohock, W. M. *The Novel of Violence in America*. 1950. SMU Pr. 5th ed. 1971 o.p.

Galloway, David D. *The Absurd Hero in American Fiction: Updike, Styron, Bellow, Salinger*. U. of Tex. Pr. 1981 $10.95. ISBN 0-292-70355-4. A perceptive critic's look at how four American novelists have used the novel to portray the absurd man in four aspects: as saint, as tragic hero, as picaro, as seeker for love.

Gardner, John. *On Moral Fiction*. Basic 1979 $14.00. ISBN 0-465-05226-6. A controversial polemic that draws a line between the traditionalists and the formalists among contemporary writers.

Girgus, Sam B. *The New Covenant: Jewish Writers and the American Idea*. U. of NC Pr. 1984 $24.95. ISBN 0-8078-1577-2. Patriotic immigrant aspirations fulfilled by "New Puritan" writers such as Brandeis, Cahan, Malamud, Roth, Bellow, Mailer, and Doctorow; well-documented with chapter notes and a comprehensive bibliography.

Godden, Richard. *Fictions of Capital: The American Novel From James to Mailer*. Cambridge U. Pr. 1990 $44.95. ISBN 0-521-38131-2. Capitalism as a theme in literature in the United States.

Harper, Howard M., Jr. *Desperate Faith: A Study of Bellow, Salinger, Mailer, Baldwin, and Updike*. Bks. Demand repr. of 1967 ed. $54.10. ISBN 0-8357-4410-8. Examines the five authors' views of man in relation to God, the universe, his fellow man, and himself; includes an abbreviated index.

Hassan, Ihab. *Radical Innocence: Studies in the Contemporary Novel*. Princeton U. Pr. 1961 o.p. An exhaustive probing, by a distinguished critic, of McCullers, Mailer, Salinger, and others.

Helterman, Jeffrey, and Richard Layman, eds. *American Novelists since World War II*. Volume 2 in *Dictionary of Literary Biography*. Gale 1978 $113.00. ISBN 0-8103-0914-9. Standard reference work.

Hendin, Josephine. *Vulnerable People: A View of American Fiction since 1945*. OUP 1978 $7.95. ISBN 0-19-502620-9. The relation of life and literature in the modern novel; includes an index.

Karl, Frederick R. *American Fictions, 1940–1980: A Comprehensive History and Critical Evaluation*. HarpC 1983 o.p. A solid and lengthy survey dealing with types and trends as well as with the work of the most seriously committed writers of literary fiction during four decades.

Kazin, Alfred. *Bright Book of Life: American Novelists and Storytellers from Hemingway to Mailer*. U. of Notre Dame Pr. 1980 repr. of 1971 ed. $11.95. ISBN 0-268-00664-4. Less ambitious than *On Native Grounds*, but a more than worthy continuation of that classic of modern criticism; a personal response to the post-Hemingway generation of American fiction writers.

Kibler, James E., Jr. *American Novelists since World War II: Second Series*. Vol. 6 in *Dictionary of Literary Biography*. Gale 1980 $113.00. ISBN 0-8103-0908-4. Supplements the volume edited by Helterman and Layman listed above.

Klein, Marcus. *After Alienation*. Ayer 1964 $20.00. ISBN 0-8369-1969-6. An important analysis of Bellow, Ellison, Baldwin, Morris, and Malamud.

Klinkowitz, Jerome. *The Life of Fiction*. U. of Ill. Pr. 1977 $19.95. ISBN 0-252-00643-7. With graphics by Roy R. Behrens; an innovative introduction to the work of 12 experimental writers.

———. *Literary Disruptions: The Making of a Post-Contemporary American Fiction*. U. of Ill. Pr. 1980 $11.95. ISBN 0-252-00810-3. Discusses the works of "literary disruptionists," including Vonnegut, Baraka, Federman, Barthelme, J.P. Sloan, Sorrentino, and Ishmael Reed; excellent separate bibliographies of original works by, and criticism on, each writer.

———. *Structuring the Void: The Struggle for Subject in Contemporary American Fiction*. Duke 1992 $29.95. ISBN 0-8223-1205-0. Written from a postmodernist perspective to examine the nature of identity or the "subject" in a world that no longer believes in a stable subject.

LeClair, Tom. *The Art of Excess: Mastery in Contemporary American Fiction*. U. of Ill. Pr. 1989 $15.95. ISBN 0-252-06102-0. Studies American contemporary fiction as well as "systems" of physics, cybernetics, history and more.

Lynn, Kenneth Schuyler. *The Dream of Success: A Study of the Modern American Imagination*. Greenwood 1972 repr. of 1955 ed. o.p.

Lyons, John O. *The College Novel in America*. S. Ill. U. Pr. 1962 o.p. A first major attempt to bring the literature of college life together, covering more than 200 novels from the early nineteenth century to the present.

Madden, David E. *American Dreams, American Nightmares*. S. Ill. U. Pr. 1972 $9.95. ISBN 0-8093-0600-X. Specially commissioned essays on the theme of the American dream and the awakening therefrom in representative literary texts, including novels by Ellison, Faulkner, Fitzgerald, Mailer, Miller, and Wolfe.

———. *Proletarian Writers of the Thirties*. Crosscurrents Modern Critiques Ser. S. Ill. U. Pr. 1979 repr. of 1968 ed. $9.95. ISBN 0-8093-0895-9. Fifteen essays that serve as introductions to Michael Gold, Jack Conroy, John Dos Passos, Robert Cantwell, and other "proletarians"; a companion document to Madden's *Tough Guy Writers of the Thirties*.

———. *Tough Guy Writers of the Thirties*. Crosscurrents Modern Critiques Ser S. Ill. U. Pr. 1968 $16.95. ISBN 0-8093-0287-X. A unique and valuable look at such writers as Hemingway, O'Hara, James M. Cain, Dashiell Hammett, and Raymond Chandler; includes essays on special genres, individual novels, and the entire subject.

Malin, Irving. *New American Gothic*. Crosscurrents Modern Critiques Ser. S. Ill. U. Pr. 1962 o.p. Examines fiction marked by intensity of character, fierce struggle between self and antiself, and an unresolved blur of identity banging against walls of complex and equally unresolved reality; includes Capote, McCullers, Salinger, O'Connor, Hawkes, and Purdy.

Malmgren, Carl Darryl. *Fictional Space in the Modernist and Post-modernist American Novel.* Bucknell U. Pr. 1985 $35.00. ISBN 0-8387-5067-2. Semiotic readings of a range of twentieth-century novels.

Martine, James J., ed. *American Novelists, 1910–1945.* Vol. 9 in *Dictionary of Literary Biography.* 3 vols. Gale 1981 $339.00. ISBN 0-8103-0931-9. Generously illustrated volumes covering 140 novelists who came to prominence between the two world wars; for succeeding installments, see listings above for Helterman and Layman and for Kibler.

May, John R. *Toward a New Earth: Apocalypse in the American Novel.* U. of Notre Dame Pr. 1973 $10.95. ISBN 0-268-00513-3. Traces the theme of judgment, catastrophe, and renewal in 12 novels from Hawthorne to Vonnegut, among them works by Faulkner, West, O'Connor, Ellison, Barth, and Pynchon.

Mellard, James M. *The Exploded Form: The Modernist Novel in America.* U. of Ill. Pr. 1980 $24.95. ISBN 0-252-00801-4. Excellent insights on William Faulkner, Joseph Heller, and Richard Brautigan; includes a useful index and notes.

Milne, Gordon. *The American Political Novel.* U. of Okla. Pr. 1966 $10.95. ISBN 0-8061-1050-3. A chronological look at American political novels from the 18th century to the mid-1960s, from Hopkinson and Brackenridge to Knebel-Bailey and Scaevola.

Nadeau, Robert L. *Readings from the New Book of Nature: Physics and Metaphysics in the Modern Novel.* U. of Mass. Pr. 1981 $25.00. ISBN 0-87023-331-9. How the New Physics has influenced some modern writers, particularly Barth, Updike, Pynchon, and Vonnegut.

Olderman, Raymond. *Beyond the Waste Land: The American Novel in the Nineteen-Sixties.* Bks. Demand repr. of 1972 ed. $70.00. ISBN 0-8357-8042-2. Another demonstration that American novelists have moved toward a more affirmative vision of life; a worthwhile critical study particularly rich on Kesey, Heller, Barth, Pynchon, Hawkes, and Vonnegut.

Payne, Ladell. *Black Novelists and the Southern Literary Tradition.* U. of Ga. Pr. 1981 o.p. Examines the importance of the "Southernness" of most black writers' literary ancestry.

Peden, William. *The American Short Story: Continuity and Change, 1940–1975.* HM 1975 o.p. Standard critical survey that discusses more than 100 writers of short fiction.

Pinsker, Sanford. *Between Two Worlds: The American Novel in the 1960s.* Whitston Pub. 1980 $7.50. ISBN 0-87875-169-6. A clear and well-supported thesis that the novel of the 1960s was in a period of transition; includes useful notes and selected bibliographies; examines Barth, Madden, Malamud, Oates, and Vonnegut.

———. *The Schlemiel as Metaphor: Studies in the Yiddish and American Jewish Novel.* *Crosscurrents Modern Critiques Ser.* S. Ill. U. Pr. 1991 $29.95. ISBN 0-8093-1581-5. Interesting and insightful look into the literature of some Yiddish and English-writing Jewish authors and their characterizations of "schlemielhood."

Pizer, Donald. *Twentieth-Century American Literary Naturalism: An Interpretation.* S. Ill. U. Pr. 1982 $19.95. ISBN 0-8093-1027-9. A leading scholar's readings of six novels from the tradition of literary naturalism: Farrell, Dos Passos, Steinbeck, Mailer, Styron, and Bellow.

Pizer, Donald, and Earl N. Harbert, eds. *American Realists and Naturalists.* Volume 12 in *Dictionary of Literary Biography.* Gale 1982 $113.00. ISBN 0-8103-1149-6

Rubenstein, Roberta. *Boundaries of the Self: Gender, Culture, Fiction.* U. of Ill. Pr. 1987 $29.95. ISBN 0-252-01355-7. Feminist criticism, including special focus on literature of minority women.

Rubin, Louis D., Jr. *The Curious Death of the Novel.* La. State U. Pr. 1967 $35.00. ISBN 0-8071-0723-9. A "sharp, funny, rabbit-punching" title essay about a fallow period for American fiction.

———. *Writers of the Modern South: The Faraway Country.* U. of Wash. Pr. 1966 o.p. Discusses Faulkner, Wolfe, Warren, Welty, Ransom, Tate, and Styron.

Rupp, Richard H. *Celebration in Postwar American Fiction, 1945–1957*. U. of Miami Pr. 1970 $11.95. ISBN 0-87024-145-1. A critical study of ten contemporary novelists that sees a swing away from the alienation and despair of earlier periods; deals with Agee, Baldwin, Bellow, Cheever, Ellison, Malamud, O'Connor, Salinger, Updike, and Welty.

Safer, Elaine B. *The Contemporary American Comic Epic: The Novels of Barth, Pynchon, Gaddis, and Kesey*. Wayne St. U. Pr. 1988 $14.95. ISBN 0-8143-2050-3. Part of the humor in life and letters series.

Schaub, Thomas. *American Fiction in the Cold War*. U. of Wis. Pr. 1991 $35.00. ISBN 0-299-12840-7. An analysis of liberalism and the Cold War and their impact on American literature.

Schumacher, Michael. *Reasons to Believe: New Voices in American Fiction*. St. Martin 1988 $9.95. ISBN 0-312-01811-8. Interviews and criticism.

Schulz, Max F. *Black Humor Fiction of the Sixties: A Pluralistic Definition of Man and His World*. Ohio U. Pr. 1973 o.p. A comprehensive exploration of the enigmatic, multi-faceted black humor of the 1960s; fully footnoted and indexed, with summaries of 26 works.

Smith, Valerie. *Self-Discovery and Authority in Afro-American Narrative*. HUP 1987 $24.95. ISBN 0-674-80087-7. Critical study showing patterns in African American literature from slave narratives to Toni Morrison.

Sullivan, Walter. *Death by Melancholy: Essays on Modern Southern Fiction*. La. State U. Pr. 1972 $22.50. ISBN 0-8071-0236-9. Several general essays accompany studies of Faulkner, Porter, Warren, O'Connor, and others.

Tanner, Tony. *City of Words: American Fiction, 1950–1970*. HarpC 1971 o.p. A fresh-eyed look at contemporary American fiction with perceptive discussions of Mailer, Purdy, Hawkes, Heller, Roth, Pynchon, Vonnegut, Barth, Barthelme, and Gass.

Vinson, James, and Daniel Kirkpatrick, eds. *Contemporary Novelists*. St. Martin 3rd ed. 1982 o.p. An ambitious and useful reference work representing some 600 American and British novelists, usually including a list of writings, a personal statement by the author, and a signed critical commentary from a prominent contributor for each author.

Walden, Daniel, ed. *Twentieth-Century American-Jewish Fiction Writers*. Vol. 28 in *Dictionary of Literary Biography*. Gale 1984 o.p. An addition to the *Dictionary of Literary Biography* series including entries on 51 writers.

Wallace, Ronald. *The Last Laugh: Form and Affirmation in the Contemporary American Comic Novel*. U. of Mo. Pr. 1979 $22.50. ISBN 0-8262-0274-8. Works by Barth, Hawkes, Kesey, and Coover, among others, placed against the literary traditions to which they belong.

Walsh, Jeffrey. *American War Literature: 1914 to Vietnam*. St. Martin 1982 $35.00. ISBN 0-312-03128-9. An absorbing survey of writings on war in the 20th century; includes a helpful preface and introduction.

Werner, Craig H. *Paradoxical Resolutions: American Fiction since James Joyce*. U. of Ill. Pr. 1982 $24.95. ISBN 0-252-00931-2. Traces the pervasive influence of Joyce on American fiction since the time of Faulkner and Wright.

Witham, W. Tasker. *The Adolescent in the American Novel, 1920–1960*. Continuum 1975 o.p. Chronological list of American novels dealing with problems of adolescents; includes a bibliography.

Woodress, James. *American Fiction, 1900–1950: A Guide to Information Sources*. Gale 1974 $68.00. ISBN 0-8103-1201-8. A useful volume describing the literary scholarship devoted to more than 40 prominent fiction writers of the early twentieth century as well as to general studies of modern American fiction.

Young, Thomas Daniel. *The Past in the Present: A Thematic Study of Modern Southern Fiction*. La. State U. Pr. 1981 $27.50. ISBN 0-8071-0768-9. Seven books of fiction analyzed in terms of their dominant themes, discussing Faulkner, Tate, Warren, Welty, O'Connor, Percy, and Barth.

Zavarzdeh, Mas'ud. *The Mythopoeic Reality: The Postwar American Nonfiction Novel.* U. of Ill. Pr. 1976 $11.95. ISBN 0-252-00645-3. Works by Capote and Mailer, among others, considered in this somewhat theoretical study of a new kind of American fiction.

Collections

Abrahams, William. *Prize Stories 1988: The O. Henry Awards.* Doubleday 1988 $9.95. ISBN 0-385-24184-4. Includes stories by Alice Adams, Ann Beattie, Joyce Carol Oates, John Updike, and others.

Angus, Douglas, and Sylvia Angus, eds. *Contemporary American Short Stories.* Fawcett 1986 $4.95. ISBN 0-449-30049-8

Bellow, Saul, ed. *Great Jewish Short Stories.* Dell 1985 $5.99. ISBN 0-440-33122-6

Clarke, John H., ed. *American Negro Short Stories.* Hill & Wang 1966 o.p. A wide-ranging anthology of representative works from the turn of the century to the 1960s.

Current-Garcia, Eugene, and Walton R. Patrick, eds. *American Short Stories.* Scott F. 1989 $23.00. ISBN 0-673-38568-X

Elkin, Stanley, and Shannon Ravenel, eds. *The Best American Short Stories, 1980.* Viking Penguin 1981 o.p.

Foley, Martha, ed. *Two Hundred Years of Great American Short Stories.* HM 1975 o.p. A chronological survey of familiar and lesser-known authors; selections are preceded by facts about the writers and stories.

Gold, Herbert, and David L. Stevenson, eds. *Stories of Modern America.* St. Martin 1969 o.p.

Henry, Dewitt, ed. *The Ploughshares Reader: New Fiction for the 80's.* Pushcart Pr. 1985 $24.95. ISBN 0-916366-30-8. Offers 33 of the "best" stories appearing in 15 years of Ploughshares Magazine.

Hills, L. Rust, and P. C. Hills. *How We Live.* 2 vols. Macmillan 1971 o.p. Fifty-six short stories by 48 American writers, with each story followed by informative comments on its author; includes an appendix listing 300 American fictionists.

Killens, John O., and Jerry W. Ward. *Black Southern Voices: An Anthology of Fiction, Poetry, Nonfiction, Drama and Critical Essays.* NAL-Dutton 1992 $15.00. ISBN 0-452-01096-9

Kostelanetz, Richard. *Breakthrough Fictioneers.* A-R Eds. 1978 repr. of 1973 ed. $50.00. ISBN 0-932360-17-3. Imaginative selection of highly experimental fiction.

Martin, Russell, and Marc Barasch. *Writers of the Purple Sage: An Anthology of Recent Western Writing.* Viking Penguin 1984 $9.95. ISBN 0-14-007370-1. Stories chapters-from-novels, memoirs, and essays depicting the poignant and ordinary events of life in the intermountain West.

Messerli, Douglas. *The Contemporary American Fiction.* Sun & Moon CA. 1983 o.p. An exciting array of out-of-the-ordinary work by both well-known and newer writers, including Tom Ahern, John Ashbery, Michael Andre, and Roberta Allen.

Murphy, George E., Jr. *The Editor's Choice: New American Stories.* Bantam 1986 $8.95. ISBN 0-553-34221-5. First in a projected series of stories selected by editors of leading magazines and literary reviews.

Oates, Joyce Carol. *Scenes from American Life: Contemporary Short Fiction.* Random 1972 o.p. Fine collection of 20 stories produced by leading American writers, including Oates, Eudora Welty, John Updike, and Flannery O'Connor.

Sklar, Mary, and Robert Peters. *Editor's Choice III: Fiction, Poetry and Art from the U.S. Small Press, 1984–1990.* Spirit That Moves 1992 $18.50. ISBN 0-930370-40-6. Top-of-the-line anthology drawn from hundreds of nominating magazines and small presses.

Solomon, Barbara H. *American Wives: Thirty Short Stories By Women.* NAL-Dutton 1986 $4.95. ISBN 0-451-02505-6. More than a century of stories by women about marriage.

Stegner, Wallace, and Mary Stegner. *Great American Short Stories.* Dell 1985 $6.99. ISBN 0-440-33060-2

Stevick, Philip. *Anti-Story: An Anthology of Experimental Writing*. Free Pr. 1971 $14.95.
    ISBN 0-02-931500-X. Excellent selection of unusual stories by various contemporary
    writers, mostly American.
Sullivan, Nancy. *Treasury of American Short Stories*. Doubleday 1981 o.p. Anthology of
    63 short stories that matches standard anthologized figures such as Poe, Faulkner,
    Hemmingway, Crane, and Updike with lesser-known writers of quality, such as
    Curtis Harnack, Josephine Jacobsen, and James Allen McPherson.
Wolff, Tobias. *Matters of Life and Death: New American Stories*. Wampeter Pr. 1983
    $14.95. ISBN 0-931694-17-5. Seventeen stories by Raymond Carver, Ann Beattie,
    John Gardner, Stanley Elkin, and others.

NONFICTION

In a review about literary essays, critic Arthur Krystal quotes Cyril Connolly's
contention that "it should be possible to learn as much about an author's
income and sex-life from one paragraph of his writing as from his cheque stubs
and his love letters." Krystal comments: "Though this is probably more of a
conceit than a firm conviction . . . Connolly was expressing a general
confidence in style's transparency."

Perhaps no form of essay has undergone more transformation in the last 25
years than the literary essay. Connolly divided literary styles into the Mandarin
and the Vernacular, the former exulting in elaboration and eloquence, the latter
sticking to the rhythms of ordinary speech and journalism. Another division
often made is between the formal and the informal. The first, exemplified by
FRANCIS BACON (see also Vol. 4), is a tightly argued, logical, studied style; the
second, after MICHEL MONTAIGNE (see Vols. 2 and 4) is looser, relaxed, highly
confidential, even musing. Today's literary essay is more likely to be highly
theoretical and technical—a style that might only be called difficult. Furthermore, the subject and the goal of the literary essay has changed radically. Once
critics wrote about character development, plot, imagery, and irony and argued
about the relation between form and content. Now critics are more likely to
explore the literary work as it constructs gender, class, or race relations. And a
literary critic writing today will probably be more concerned with how the
"text" either subverts or is complicit with the dominant social or political
power structures than with how light and dark imagery are used throughout to
convey meaning.

To get an idea of the shift, one might first read more traditional critics, such
as LIONEL TRILLING, CLEANTH BROOKS, or M. H. ABRAMS and then turn to the
poststructuralists, such as PAUL DE MAN, FREDRIC JAMESON, EDWARD SAID, SACVAN
BERCOVITCH, or Peggy Kamuf. Literary theorists today are likely to argue for the
necessity of their difficult style: they are trying to say highly precise, complex,
and hard-to-understand things about the way that literary texts operate in the
world. Perhaps, however, their difficulty reflects a shift in approach that in turn
reflects contemporary views about the disjunction between word and thing,
literature and reality. This "new" view about literature is not merely highly
skeptical about style's transparency, but rejects an earlier age's confidence in
language's power to represent anything outside of itself at all.

To some extent, the gap between these divergent views is bridged by a new
generation of feminist and antiracist critics who use poststructuralist and
structuralist techniques to interrogate race, gender, and class within literature.
Critics such as Nancy K. Miller, Barbara Christian, Barbara Smith, and HENRY
LOUIS GATES, JR., offer new readings of old texts as well as new attention to

works once considered marginal, opening up new realms of understanding and criticism.

Another literary form of nonfiction that deserves special mention is literary biography and autobiography. First, what makes good literary biography? Primarily, the essential element is one few can achieve: to capture the imagination, the essence or substance, of the subject. Whatever the precise method or blending of methods that a writer uses to achieve this, the biographer must integrate the life, so that we comprehend how that author wrote those books, poems, or plays, or committed those acts and behaved in that way. All biography must achieve this, literary and otherwise, but the literary biographer has an additional task: to penetrate the avalanche of words pouring from his or her subject and to create a particular order. That order will provide a road into the subject's imagination. It will be based on various insights—psychological, historical, sociological, personal and sexual, broadly cultural. These are the elements and modes we have in mind when we speak of literary biography. More than any other kind of biography, it must pursue two goals: the recreation of broad contexts and the trenchant integration of imaginative materials.

By its very nature, literary autobiography (as distinct from other kinds of autobiography) is far rarer than literary biography. The latter requires that a professional author research a subject and become familiar with it, but literary autobiography requires not only a writer's creative temperament but a life of sufficient interest or variety to sustain self-examination. It is, in reality, a different enterprise, in that it requires personal achievement and confession, whereas literary biography demands objectivity, a critical and historical acumen. When the "he" or "she" of biography becomes the "I" of autobiography, even the sense of historical and present time alters from something outside to an inside phenomenon.

Other kinds of biography and autobiography have their own integrity and literary value. Their subjects may be figures from any field of achievement. Biographies and autobiographies appear throughout *The Reader's Adviser* in connection with profiled individuals.

Contemporary Criticism

Abel, Elizabeth, ed. *Writing and Sexual Difference*. U. Ch. Pr. 1982 $13.95. ISBN 0-226-00076-1. Anthology of essays on issues of writing and gender.

Abel, Elizabeth, and Emily K. Abel, eds. *The Signs Reader: Women, Gender, and Scholarship*. U. Ch. Pr. 1983 $25.00. ISBN 0-226-00075-3. Essays from the prominent feminist journal *Signs*.

Altieri, Charles. *Act and Quality: A Theory of Literary Meaning and Humanistic Understanding*. U. of Mass. Pr. 1981 $35.00. ISBN 0-87023-327-0. Draws on Wittgenstein and language analysis to link meaning to use and action; analyzes poetry by William Carlos Williams.

Bakhtin, Mikhail. *The Dialogic Imagination: Four Essays*. Trans. by Caryl Emerson and Michael Holquist. Ed. by Michael Holquist. U. of Tex. Pr. 1981 $14.95. ISBN 0-292-71534-X. Important essays on time, language, and the novel.

Barfield, Owen. *Poetic Diction: A Study in Meaning*. U. Pr. of New Eng. 1984 $14.95. ISBN 0-8195-6026-X

———. *Saving the Appearances: A Study in Idolatry*. HarBraceJ 1988 $12.95. ISBN 0-8195-6205-X

Bernikow, Louise. *Among Women*. HarpC 1981 o.p. Wide-ranging essays on women in literature.

Bleich, David. *Subjective Criticism*. Johns Hopkins 1978 $14.95. ISBN 0-8018-2093-6. An important, challenging treatment that draws upon extensive reading in psychology, epistemology, linguistics, and literature; has many implications for teachers of literature, language, reading, or writing.

Bleicher, Josef. *Contemporary Hermeneutics: Hermeneutics as Method, Philosophy and Critique.* Routledge 1980 $14.95. ISBN 0-7100-0552-0. Discusses general issues and history of reflections on how the reader understands texts.

Booth, Wayne. *Critical Understanding: The Power and Limits of Pluralism.* U. Ch. Pr. 1982 $22.50. ISBN 0-226-06554-5. An impressive attempt to understand the anarchic state of American criticism; influenced by the critical intelligence of the journal *Critical Inquiry.*

———. *The Rhetoric of Fiction.* 1961. U. Ch. Pr. 1983 $30.00. ISBN 0-226-06556-1. A ground-breaking analysis of major writers and literary critics; makes significant points about the nature of rhetoric in fiction and levels of speaking voices within fiction.

Borkland, Elmer. *Contemporary Literary Critics.* Gale 1982 $64.00. ISBN 0-8103-0443-0. Short essays and bibliographies of 124 British and American critics.

Bradbrook, Muriel C. *Women and Literature. 1779–1982.* B & N Imports 1983 $37.50. ISBN 0-389-20295-9. Essays on literature by and about women and on lives led by women in fiction and reality.

Brooks, Cleanth. *Modern Poetry and the Tradition.* 1939. U. of NC Pr. 1970 o.p. Essays applying close attention to language and imagery in Elizabethan and modern poems.

———. *The Well-Wrought Urn: Studies in the Structure of Poetry.* HarBraceJ 1956 o.p. Presents and applies a method of "close reading" to a variety of English poems.

Bruns, Gerald L. *Inventions: Writing, Textuality, and Understanding in Literary History.* Yale U. Pr. 1982 o.p. A brilliant collection of essays, wide ranging in topic and texts discussed.

Butler, Christopher. *Interpretation, Deconstruction and Ideology: An Introduction to Some Current Issues in Literary Theory.* OUP 1984 $24.95. ISBN 0-19-815792-4. Interpretive approaches based on linguistics and stylistics; a pragmatic look at theory, with examples of deconstruction and ideology.

Christian, Barbara. *Black Feminist Criticism: Perspectives on Black Women Writers.* Pergamon 1985 $50.00. ISBN 0-08-031956-4. A comprehensive, critical review, ranging from common stereotypes of black women in the antebellum period to more recent works by Ntozake Shange, Alice Walker, and others.

Culler, Jonathan. *On Deconstruction: Theory and Criticism After Structuralism.* Cornell Univ. Pr. 1982 $35.00. ISBN 0-8014-1322-2. Good introduction to this important and difficult modern critical movement.

———. *The Pursuit of Signs: Semiotics, Literature, Deconstruction.* Cornell Univ. Pr. 1981 $29.95. ISBN 0-8014-1417-2. Eleven essays that assess the import of semiotics, deconstruction, and post-structuralism in French and American literary theory.

———. *Structuralist Poetics: Structuralism, Linguistics, and the Study of Literature.* Cornell Univ. Pr. 1976 $10.95. ISBN 0-8014-9155-X. Good introduction to structuralism.

Dickstein, Morris. *The Critic and Society: From Matthew Arnold to the New Historicism.* OUP 1992 $22.00. ISBN 0-19-507399-1. Essays dealing with function of literary criticism in society.

Donaldson, Laura E. *Decolonizing Feminisms: Race, Gender, and Empire-Building.* U. of NC Pr. 1992 $29.95. ISBN 0-8078-2044-X. Reflects recent tendency in feminist criticism to acknowledge "feminisms"—the differences between women that have necessitated a complex view of the feminist project.

Donoghue, Denis. *Ferocious Alphabets.* Col. U. Pr. 1984 repr. of 1981 ed. $16.50. ISBN 0-231-05823-3. Critical study of contemporary criticism, especially deconstruction.

Donovan, Josephine, ed. *Feminist Literary Criticism: Explorations in Theory.* U. Pr. of Ky. 1989 $7.00. ISBN 0-8131-0190-5. Six essays, one bibliographic.

Eagleton, Terry. *Criticism and Ideology: A Study in Marxist Literary Theory.* Routledge Chapman & Hall 1978 $13.95. ISBN 0-86091-707-X. Studies of F. R. Leavis, Raymond Williams, French Marxism, and Marxist literary history in England from 1860 to 1930 ranging from George Eliot to James Joyce.

———. *Literary Theory: An Introduction.* U. of Minn. Pr. 1983 $29.50. ISBN 0-8166-1238-2. Surveys contemporary criticism from a Marxist perspective.

———. *Marxism and Literary Criticism.* U. of CA Pr. 1976 $9.95. ISBN 0-520-03243-8.

Eisenstein, Hester. *Contemporary Feminist Thought.* G. K. Hall 1984 $9.95. ISBN 0-8161-9048-8. An intellectual history.

Empson, William. *Seven Types of Ambiguity.* New. Dir. Pr. 1947 $10.95. ISBN 0-8112-0037-X. Intense concentration on ambiguous language in poetry.

———. *Some Versions of Pastoral.* New Dir. Pr. 1960 $8.95. ISBN 0-8112-0038-8. Broadens the concept of pastoral and extends it to nineteenth- and twentieth-century works.

———. *The Structure of Complex Words.* HUP 1989 repr. of 1951 ed. $12.95. ISBN 0-674-84375-4. On key words in literary contexts, including "wit," "sense," "honest," in Pope, Shakespeare, and others.

French, Marilyn. *Beyond Power: On Women, Men, and Morals.* Ballantine 1986 $11.95. ISBN 0-345-33405-1. Far-ranging historical discussion by the noted novelist.

Frye, Marilyn. *The Politics of Reality: Essays in Feminist Theory.* Crossing Pr. 1983 $10.95. ISBN 0-89594-099-X. An alternative to mainstream liberal feminism; aimed at redefining the current political economy and social hierarchy of male dominance.

Gates, Henry Louis, Jr. *Loose Canons: Notes of the Culture Wars.* OUP 1992 $19.95. ISBN 0-19-507519-6. Balanced essays considering the impact of multiculturalism on the ideas of "canon" and "culture."

Gilbert, Sandra M., and Susan Gubar. *The Madwoman in the Attic: A Study of the Women and the Literary Imagination in the Nineteenth Century.* Yale U. Pr. 1979 $19.95. ISBN 0-300-02596-3. One of the most widely influential studies.

Graff, Gerald. *Literature against Itself: Literary Ideas in Modern Society.* U. Ch. Pr. 1981 $10.00. ISBN 0-226-30598-8. A controversial polemic on political grounds against the pretenses of modernist literature and critical theory.

Hardwick, Elizabeth. *Seduction and Betrayal: Women and Literature.* Random 1990 $8.95. ISBN 0-679-72427-3. Accessible and literary.

Harari, Josue V., ed. *Textual Strategies: Perspectives in Post-Structuralist Criticism.* Cornell Univ. Pr. 1979 $49.95. ISBN 0-8014-1218-8. Well-chosen introductory anthology with excellent bibliography.

Heilbrun, Carolyn G. *Reinventing Womanhood.* Norton 1981 $10.95. ISBN 0-393-00997-1. A synthesis of material from literature, folklore, mythology, and psychology in support of the integration of achievement and womanhood.

———. *Toward a Recognition of Androgyny.* Norton 1982 repr. of 1973 ed. $8.95. ISBN 0-393-30025-0. Heilbrun is one of the founders of feminist criticism.

Hirsch, E. D. *The Aims of Interpretation.* U. Ch. Pr. 1978 $8.95. ISBN 0-226-34241-7. Essays, including reconsiderations of his earlier theories.

Hornby, Nick. *Contemporary American Writing.* St. Martin 1992 $35.00. ISBN 0-312-04213-2

Howard, Roy J. *Three Faces of Hermeneutics: An Introduction to Current Theories of Understanding.* U. CA Pr. 1982 $10.95. ISBN 0-520-04689-7. Describes analytic, Marxist, and phenomenological hermeneutics.

Hoy, David Couzens. *The Critical Circle: Literature, History, and Philosophical Hermeneutics.* U. CA Pr. 1978 $11.95. ISBN 0-520-04639-0. Excellent introduction to hermeneutics in relation to contemporary philosophy and criticism.

Kahn, Coppelia, and Gayle Green, eds. *Making a Difference: Feminist Literary Criticism.* Routledge Chapman & Hall 1985 $14.95. ISBN 0-416-37470-0. Ten wide-ranging essays introducing the field.

Kurzweil, Edith, and William Phillips, eds. *Literature and Psychoanalysis.* Col. U. Pr. 1983 o.p. Traces psychoanalytic criticism from Freud to the present.

Lawall, Sarah. *Critics of Consciousness: The Existential Structures of Literature.* HUP 1968 $20.50. ISBN 0-674-17750-9. General introduction to critics who describe how an author's consciousness structures the world presented in the work.

Leavis, F. R. *The Great Tradition: George Eliot, Henry James, Joseph Conrad. Gotham Lib.* NYU Pr. 1963 o.p. A landmark in the criticism of the novel; a work of judicial criticism.

Lentricchia, Frank. *After the New Criticism.* U. Ch. Pr. 1981. $21.00. ISBN 0-226-47197-7. Reflections on developments in literary theory since the 1960s, emphasizing the social and political context of key issues.

———. *Criticism and Social Change.* U. Ch. Pr. 1985 $15.00. ISBN 0-226-47199-3

Levin, Harry. *Grounds for Comparison. Studies in Comparative Lit.* HUP 1972 $30.50. ISBN 0-674-36335-3. Collected essays.

———. *Refractions: Essays in Comparative Literature.* OUP 1966 o.p. A collection of 18 lectures and essays marked by the author's wit and talent for recalling analogies in themes and phrases; includes an index of authors.

Marks, Elaine, and Isabelle de Courtivron, eds. *New French Feminisms: An Anthology.* Schocken 1987 $14.00. ISBN 0-8052-0681-7. Excellent selections, many first translated here.

Miller, Nancy K., ed. *The Poetics of Gender.* Col. U. Pr. 1987 $42.00. ISBN 0-231-06310-5. Essays from the second wave of feminist criticism with its focus on gender studies.

Moi, Toril. *Sexual/Textual Politics.* Routledge Chapman & Hall 1985 $13.95. ISBN 0-416-02974-0. Comprehensive survey of feminist criticism through 1985.

Natoli, Joseph P., ed. *Psychological Perspectives on Literature: Freudian Dissidents and Non-Freudian, A Casebook.* Shoe String 1984 o.p.

Nicholson, Linda, ed. *Feminism/Postmodernism.* Routledge 1989 $45.00. ISBN 0-415-90058-1. Important, thoughtful collection.

Norris, Christopher. *Deconstruction: Theory and Practice.* Routledge Chapman & Hall 1982 $13.95. ISBN 0-416-32070-8. Good introduction to the background and ideas of deconstruction.

Olsen, Tillie. *Silences.* Peter Smith 1984 $20.00. ISBN 0-8446-6091-4. Essays by the distinguished short-story writer.

Ostriker, Alicia. *Writing Like a Woman. Poets on Poetry Ser.* U. of Mich. Pr. 1983 $11.95. ISBN 0-472-06347-2

Richards, I. A.. *Practical Criticism: A Study of Literary Judgment.* HarBraceJ 1956 $9.95. ISBN 0-15-673626-8. Influential manifesto for "close reading" instead of impressionistic criticism.

———. *Principles of Literary Criticism.* HarBraceJ 1961 $7.95. ISBN 0-15-674592-5. Influential in the founding of modern approaches to reading poetry.

Rosen, Norma. *Accidents of Influence: Writing as a Woman and a Jew in America.* State U. NY Pr. 1992 $34.50. ISBN 0-7914-1091-9. Literate, meditative, and personal essays examining the life of the mind of Rosen, a prolific novelist.

Ruthven, K. K.. *Feminist Literary Studies: An Introduction.* Cambridge U. Pr. 1990 $7.95. ISBN 0-521-39852-5. Useful survey dealing with various types of feminist criticism and their disagreements with "non-feminist" approaches; considers the impact of structuralism and post-structuralism.

Said, Edward. *Beginnings: Intention and Method.* Col. U. Pr. 1985 repr. of 1975 ed. $48.50. ISBN 0-231-05936-1. A wide-ranging discourse on literary and nonliterary topics; contains useful sections on Freud, Conrad, Vico, and Foucault; a companion to Frank Kermode's *The Sense of An Ending.*

———. *The World, the Text, and the Critic.* HUP 1983 $9.95. ISBN 0-674-96187-0. Broad survey and critique of contemporary critical movements.

Scholes, Robert. *Structuralism in Literature: An Introduction.* Yale U. Pr. 1974 $11.95. ISBN 0-300-01850-9. Good introduction to an important contemporary critical approach.

Showalter, Elaine, ed. *The New Feminist Criticism: Essays on Women, Literature, and Theory.* Pantheon 1985 $12.76. ISBN 0-394-72647-2. Eighteen essays that reveal the evolution of feminist literary scholarship from the 1960s to the 1980s; includes a useful introduction and comprehensive bibliography.

Skura, Meredith. *The Literary Use of the Psychoanalytic Process.* Yale U. Pr. 1983 o.p. A landmark in the theory and practice of psychoanalytic criticism; includes an index.

Smith, Barbara. *Toward a Black Feminist Criticism.* Crossing Pr. 1977 $3.00. ISBN 0-918314-14-3

Strelka, Joseph, ed. *Literary Criticism and Myth.* Pa. St. U. Pr. 1980 $25.00. ISBN 0-271-00225-5

Suleiman, Susan R., and Inge Crosman, eds. *The Reader in the Text: Essays on Audience and Interpretation.* Princeton U. Pr. 1980 o.p. Stimulating collection of essays by leading critics with bibliography.

Tompkins, Jane P., ed. *Reader-Response Criticism: From Formalism to Structuralism.* Johns Hopkins 1981 $11.95. ISBN 0-8018-2401-X. A collection of key essays with an excellent introduction and analysis by the editor and an annotated bibliography.

Warhol, Robyn R., and Diane Price Herndl, eds. *Feminisms: An Anthology of Literary Theory and Criticism.* Rutgers U. Pr. 1991 $55.00. ISBN 0-8135-1731-1. Comprehensive collection of essays providing an excellent overview; contains many well-known essays, along with new contributions.

Wellek, Rene. *The Attack on Literature and Other Essays.* U. of NC Pr. 1982 $10.95. ISBN 0-8078-4090-4. Eleven essays that reaffirm Wellek's belief in literary scholarship and criticism as well as in a systematic theory of literature.

———. *Concepts of Criticism.* Ed. by Stephen G. Nichols, Jr. Bks. Demand repr. of 1963 ed. $108.50. ISBN 0-8357-8079-1. Collection of fourteen essays that survey the methods of criticism in Europe and America; includes a bibliography of Wellek's writings.

———. *Discriminations: Further Concepts of Criticism.* Bks. Demand repr. of 1970 ed. $103.30. ISBN 0-8357-8097-X. Eight published and six unpublished articles complementing Wellek's *Concepts of Criticism;* examines the theory of comparative literature, the discrimination of critical terms, and the aesthetics of Kant.

Wilentz, Gay. *Binding Cultures: Black Women Writers in Africa and the Diaspora.* Ind. U. Pr. 1992 $29.95. ISBN 0-253-36585-6. Part of a series concerned with the connections among African people who have been scattered.

Wimsatt, W. K. *Days of the Leopards: Essays in Defense of Poems.* Bks. Demand repr. of 1976 ed. $70.80. ISBN 0-8357-3761-6

———. *Hateful Contraries: Studies in Literature and Criticism.* U. Pr. of Ky. 1965 $12.00. ISBN 0-8131-0110-7

———. *The Verbal Icon: Studies in the Meaning of Poetry.* U. Pr. of Ky. 1954 $13.00. ISBN 0-8131-0111-5. One of the great books of contemporary reflections on poetry and criticism.

Winters, Yvor. *In Defense of Reason: Three Classics of Contemporary Criticism.* Swallow 1986 $17.95. ISBN 0-8040-0151-0. Includes "Primitivism and Decadence" and other essays and studies of poetry, mostly modern and American.

Wright, Elizabeth. *Psychoanalytic Criticism: Theory in Practice.* Routledge Chapman & Hall 1985 $13.95. ISBN 0-416-32660-9. Broad survey of psychoanalytic critical theory through the mid-1980s.

General Works on Literary Autobiography

Bruss, Elizabeth W. *Autobiographical Acts: The Changing Situation of a Literary Genre.* Bks. Demand repr. of 1976 ed. $50.00. ISBN 0-8357-5905-9

Clark, Arthur. *Autobiography: Its Genesis and Phases.* Folcroft 1935 o.p.

Couser, G. Thomas. *Altered Egos: Authority in American Autobriography.* OUP 1989 $36.00. ISBN 0-19-505833-X. Excellent chapters examining the ways American autobiographers have tended to refashion themselves rhetorically.

Eakin, Paul J., ed. *American Autobiography: Retrospect and Prospect.* U. of Wis. Pr. 1991 $42.50. ISBN 0-299-12780-X. Strong collection of essays.

Lejeune, Philippe. *On Autobiography.* Trans. by Katherine Leary. U. of Minn. Pr. 1989 $49.95. ISBN 0-8166-1631-0. An oft-cited theoretical work on the nature of autobiography.

Miller, Nancy K. *Getting Personal: Feminist Occasions and Other Autobiographical Acts.* Routledge 1991 $39.95. ISBN 0-415-90323-8. Concerned with women's acts of self-definition as related to their socially constructed identities.

Olney, James. *Autobiography: Essays Theoretical and Critical.* Princeton U. Pr. 1980 $40.00. ISBN 0-691-06412-1. Recommended are essays by Louis A. Renza, "The Veto of the Imagination: A Theory of Autobiography"; Roger Rosenblatt, "Black Autobiography: Life as the Death Weapon"; Jean Starobinski, "The Style of Autobiography"; and Olney, "Autobiography and the Cultural Moment: A Thematic, Historical, and Bibliographcal Introduction."

———. *Metaphors of Self: The Meaning of Autobiography.* Princeton U. Pr. 1972 $44.00. ISBN 0-691-06221-8. An important work, with application to several varieties of autobiography.

Pascal, Roy. *Design and Truth in Autobiography.* Ed. by Robin W. Wicks, *History and Historiography Ser.* Garland 1985 o.p.

Smith, Sidonie, and Julia Watson. *Decolonizing the Subject: The Politics of Gender in Women's Autobiography.* U. of Minn. Pr. 1992 $44.95. ISBN 0-8166-1991-3. $19.95. ISBN 0-8166-1992-1. Theoretically sophisticated essays exploring ways women's identities have been "colonized," and the ways in which they and critics have sought to "decolonize" their identities in autobiographical writings.

Stepto, Robert B. *From Behind the Veil: A Study of Afro-American Narrative.* U. of Ill. Pr. 1991 $11.95. ISBN 0-252-06211-6. Reissue of excellent, standard work.

General Works on Literary Biography

Aaron, Daniel, ed. *Studies in Biography. Harvard Eng. Studies* HUP 1978 $16.00. Some good general essays on biographical problems and theories, along with individual essays on literary subjects including Emerson.

Altick, Richard D. *Lives and Letters: A History of Literary Biographies in England and America.* Greenwood 1979 repr. of 1965 ed. $38.50. ISBN 0-313-21116-7. Altick's book is a general guide to literary biographical writing, with emphasis on theories and trends. The reader's attention is also directed to Altick's *The Scholar Adventurers.*

Bowen, Catherine. *Biography: The Craft and the Calling.* Greenwood 1978 repr. of 1969 ed. o.p. The well-known biographer has written a "how-to" guide for present and future biographers.

Clifford, James L. *From Puzzles to Portraits: Problems of a Literary Biographer.* U. of NC Pr. 1970 o.p. A pioneering book in dealing with biographical problems.

Edel, Leon. *Literary Biography.* Ind. U. Pr. 1973 o.p. Having grown out of Edel's Alexander Lectures at the University of Toronto in 1956, this is the first book to deal fully with literary biography as an art form.

———. *Writing Lives: Principia Biographica.* Norton 1987 o.p. Edel here is concerned with what he calls the New Biography, which he finds in myth, archives narrative forms, and the question of transference or the writer's emotional involvement with his subject. This is an updating of *Literary Biography,* plus six new chapters.

Kendall, Paul M. *The Art of Biography.* Norton 1985 repr. of 1965 ed. $4.95. ISBN 0-393-00411-2. A study mainly of biographical theory. Kendall deals with different types of the genre at different times, among them interpretive biography, the biography of recollection, the several-volumed work, and the relationship between author and work.

Petrie, Dennis W. *Ultimately Fiction: Design in Modern American Literary Biography.* Purdue U. Pr. 1981 $10.95. ISBN 0-911198-62-8. Petrie discusses how aesthetic truth can be incorporated into historical truth in the biographical process.

Strout, Cushing. *The Veracious Imagination: Essays on American History, Literature, and Biography.* Wesleyan U. Pr. 1981 $14.95. ISBN 0-8195-6136-3. Essays on American history, literature, and biography as they cross each other, with some biographical theory on literary figures: Ellison, Mailer, Doctorow, and others.

Veninga, James F., ed. *The Biographer's Gift: Life, Histories, and Humanism.* Tex. A & M Univ. Pr. 1983 $11.50. ISBN 0-89096-168-9. Discussion about the connection between humanism and biography, with some relevance to literary biography in particular.

Weintraub, Stanley. *Biography and Truth. Composition and Rhetoric Ser.* Macmillan 1967 $2.50. ISBN 0-672-60901-0. Problems in literary biography are linked to the need to extract the truth from an individual life.

CHRONOLOGY OF AUTHORS

Gordon, Caroline. 1895–1981.
Bogan, Louise. 1897–1970.
Burke, Kenneth. 1897–
Nabokov, Vladimir. 1899–1977.
Brown, Sterling Allen. 1901–1989
Johnson, Edgar. 1901–
Cozzens, James Gould. 1903–1978
Eberhart, Richard. 1904–
Singer, Isaac Bashevis. 1904–1991
Zukofsky, Louis. 1904–1978
Kunitz, Stanley. 1905–
Rexroth, Kenneth. 1905–1983
Trilling, Lionel. 1905–1975
Brooks, Cleanth. 1906–
Roth, Henry. 1906–
Edel, Leon. 1907–
Petry, Ann. 1908–
Roethke, Theodore. 1908–1963
Agee, James. 1909–1955
Stegner, Wallace. 1909–1993
Morris, Wright. 1910–
Olson, Charles. 1910–1970
Bishop, Elizabeth. 1911–1979
Patchen, Kenneth. 1911–1972
Abrams, M. H. 1912–
Cheever, John. 1912–1982
Frye, Northrop. 1912–1991
McCarthy, Mary. 1912–1989
Hayden, Robert E(arl). 1913–1980
Olsen, Tillie. 1913–
Rukeyser, Muriel. 1913–1980
Schwartz, Delmore. 1913–1966
Shapiro, Karl. 1913–
Berryman, John. 1914–1972
Burroughs, William S. 1914–
Ellison, Ralph. 1914–
Ignatow, David. 1914–
Jarrell, Randall. 1914–1965
Malamud, Bernard. 1914–1986
Stafford, William. 1914–
Bellow, Saul. 1915–
Kazin, Alfred. 1915–
Percy, Walker. 1916–
Auchincloss, Louis. 1917–
Brooks, Gwendolyn. 1917–

Fiedler, Leslie A(aron). 1917–
Lewis, R(ichard) W(arrington) B(aldwin). 1917–
Lowell, Robert. 1917–1977
McCullers, Carson. 1917–1967
Powers, J(ames) F(arl). 1917–
Ellmann, Richard. 1918–
De Man, Paul. 1919–1983
Duncan, Robert. 1919–
Jackson, Shirley. 1919–1965
Salinger, J(erome) D(avid). 1919–
Swenson, May. 1919–1989
Clampitt, Amy. 1920–
Howe, Irving. 1920–1993
Nemerov, Howard. 1920–1991
Jones, James. 1921–1977
Van Duyn, Mona. 1921–
Wilbur, Richard. 1921–
Gaddis, William. 1922–
Kerouac, Jack. 1922–1969
Vonnegut, Kurt, Jr. 1922–
Dickey, James. 1923–
Dugan, Alan. 1923–
Hecht, Anthony. 1923–
Hugo, Richard. 1923–1982
Levertov, Denise. 1923–
Logan, John. 1923–
Mailer, Norman. 1923–
Purdy, James. 1923–
Simpson, Louis. 1923–
Baldwin, James. 1924–1987
Berger, Thomas. 1924–
Capote, Truman. 1924–1984
Gass, William. 1924–
Hawkes, John. 1925–
Justice, Donald. 1925–
Kizer, Carolyn. 1925–
Koch, Kenneth. 1925–
Merrill, James. 1925–
O'Connor, Flannery. 1925–1965
Styron, William. 1925–
Vidal, Gore. 1925–
Ammons, A(rchie) R(andolph). 1926–
Bly, Robert. 1926–
Creeley, Robert. 1926–

Ginsberg, Allen. 1926–
Lurie, Alison. 1926–
O'Hara, Frank. 1926–1966
Snodgrass, W(illiam) D(ewitt). 1926–
Ashbery, John. 1927–
Kinnell, Galway. 1927–
Merwin, W(illiam) S(tanley). 1927–
Wright, James. 1927–1980.
Angelou, Maya. 1928–
Hall, Donald. 1928–
Kennedy, William. 1928–
Levine, Philip. 1928–
Ozick, Cynthia. 1928–
Sexton, Anne. 1928–1977
Wiesel, Elie. 1928–
Dorn, Edward. 1929–
Howard, Richard. 1929–
Kennedy, X. J. 1929–
Marshall, Paule. 1929–
Potok, Chaim. 1929–
Rich, Adrienne. 1929–
Steiner, George. 1929–
Barth, John. 1930–
Corso, Gregory. 1930–
Elkin, Stanley. 1930–
Snyder, Gary. 1930–
Barthelme, Donald. 1931–
Doctorow, E(dgar) L(aurence). 1931–
McPhee, John. 1931–
Morrison, Toni. 1931–
Coover, Robert. 1932–
Heller, Joseph. 1932–
McClure, Michael. 1932–
Plath, Sylvia. 1932–1963
Updike, John. 1932–
Bercovitch, Sacvan. 1933–
Gardner, John. 1933–1982
Kosinski, Jerzy. 1933–1991
Roth, Philip. 1933–
Sontag, Susan. 1933–
Baraka, Imamu Amiri. 1934–
Didion, Joan. 1934–

Momaday, N. Scott. 1934–
Sanchez, Sonia. 1934–
Strand, Mark. 1934–
Allen, Woody. 1935–
Kesey, Ken. 1935–
Said, Edward W. 1935–
Wright, Charles. 1935–
Baym, Nina. 1936–
McMurtry, Larry. 1936–
Silverman, Kenneth. 1936–
Pynchon, Thomas. 1937–
Stone, Robert. 1937–
Carver, Raymond. 1938–1988.
Fish, Stanley. 1938–
Harper, Michael. 1938–
Oates, Joyce Carol. 1938–
Reed, Ishmael. 1938–
Simic, Charles. 1938–
Bambara, Toni Cade. 1939–
Banks, Russell. 1940–
Kingston, Maxine Hong. 1940–
Pinsky, Robert. 1940–
Apple, Max. 1941–
Hass, Robert. 1941–
Showalter, Elaine. 1941–
Tyler, Anne. 1941–
Irving, John. 1942–
Rose, Phyllis. 1942–
Baker, Houston A. Jr. 1943–
Glück, Louise. 1943–
Tate, James. 1943–
Walker, Alice. 1944–
Strouse, Jean. 1945–
Beattie, Ann. 1947–
Ackerman, Diane. 1948–
Boyle, T. Coraghessan. 1948–
Goldbarth, Albert. 1948–
Silko, Leslie Marmon. 1948–
Smiley, Jane. 1949–
Naylor, Gloria. 1950–
Hijuelos, Oscar. 1951–
Dove, Rita. 1952–

ABRAMS, M. H. 1912–

Born in Long Branch, New Jersey, and educated at Harvard and Cambridge, M. H. Abrams is currently Professor of English Emeritus at Cornell University. Before the subjectivity of the critic had become the *sine qua non* of literary theory, Abrams argued that there were four different possibilities, or "orientations" that have always been available to literary critics: the mimetic, which sees the work primarily as a mirror of reality; the pragmatic, which is concerned with the effects of the work on the audience; the objective, which isolates the work as a complex object unto itself; and finally, the expressive, which deals with the qualities of the artist's mind and soul. A pluralist by nature, however, Abrams does not see these modes as mutually exclusive; rather, they describe critical tendencies that can be incorporated into the overall purpose of the critic.

Abrams introduced this theory in *The Mirror and the Lamp* (1953), the first of his two highly influential works on English romanticism. The second, *Natural Supernaturalism* (1971), established Abrams in the tradition of humanistic scholarship, which locates a natural connection between the human spirit and the world it inhabits.

NONFICTION BY ABRAMS

Doing Things with Texts: Essays in Criticism and Critical Theory. Norton 1991 $14.95. ISBN 0-393-30747-6. Argues for a critical pluralism while registering important effects of new theoretical and critical directions.

The Mirror and the Lamps: Romantic Theory and the Critical Tradition. OUP 1971 repr. of 1953 ed. $12.95. ISBN 0-19-501471-5. Deals primarily with the differences between Romantic theory and its predecessors.

Natural Supernaturalism: Tradition and Revolution in Romantic Literature. Norton 1973 repr. of 1971 ed. $14.95. ISBN 0-393-00609-3. Traces the metaphors and archetypal actions that persist throughout Romantic poetry, revealing its links to Christian concerns.

ACKERMAN, DIANE. 1948–

Like the poets of the seventeenth and eighteenth centuries, Diane Ackerman bridges the "two cultures" of science and art in her poetry and prose. An enthusiastic explorer of the world, which means for her "the full sum of Creation," Ackerman joyfully pursues the course of her changing passions throughout her work, rejoicing in aviation, astronomy, the senses, bats, quasars, and corpuscles. "I suppose the key to my work is that it is never what occasions it, or what it pretends to be about," Ackerman has commented. "I give myself passionately, totally to whatever I'm observing, with as much affectionate curiosity as I can muster, but only as a means to release in me thoughts about what being human means, and what it was like to have once been alive on the planet, how it felt in one's sense, passions, contemplations."

After receiving her M.F.A. in creative writing from Cornell University in 1973 (winning, among other prizes, the Academy of American Poets Award), she received her Ph.D. in English in 1978. She then worked briefly as a social worker in New York City before returning to academia as a professor and writer-in-residence at several colleges and universities. Since 1988, Ackerman has been a staff writer at the *New Yorker*. She has twice received National Endowment for the Arts fellowships (1976, 1986).

POETRY BY ACKERMAN

Jaguar of Sweet Laughter: New and Selected Poems. Random 1993 $11.00. ISBN 0-679-74304-9. Shows the full range of Ackerman's wit and ingenuity, as well as the seemingly limitless scope of her interests and voices.

Lady Faustus. Morrow 1983 o.p. Collection of short poems about the desire to know and what it means to know something.

The Planets: A Comic Pastoral. Morrow 1976 o.p. Poetic explorations and meditations on the planets, Cape Canaveral, the asteroids, and Comet Kahoutek.

Wife of Light. Morrow 1978 o.p. Collection of short poems.

NONFICTION BY ACKERMAN

The Moon by Whalelight & Other Adventures Among Bats, Penguins, Crocodilians & Whales. Random 1991 $19.50. ISBN 0-394-58574-7. A choice treat for both nature lovers and general readers.

A Natural History of the Senses. Random 1990 $19.95. ISBN 0-394-57335-8. An in-depth study of the history, poetry, and meaning of the senses.
On Extended Wings. Atheneum 1985 $7.95. Memoir about learning to fly.
Twilight of the Tenderfoot: A Western Memoir. Morrow 1980 o.p. Recounts Ackerman's experiences on a cattle ranch.

PLAY BY ACKERMAN

Reverse Thunder. Lumen Inc. 1988 $7.95. ISBN 0-930829-09-3. Verse play produced in 1982 about Juana Ines de la Cruz, a late seventeenth-century Mexican who was a poet, scientist, and independent thinker.

AGEE, JAMES. 1909–1955

Tennessee born and Harvard educated, Agee crowded a lot of versatile literary activity into his short and troubled life. In addition to two novels, he wrote short stories, essays, poetry, and screenplays; and he worked professionally as a journalist and film critic. Appropriately, he is best remembered for a work that combines several genres and literary approaches. *Let Us Now Praise Famous Men,* a documentary report on sharecropper life accompanied by vividly realistic photographs by Walker Evans, has been called "a great Moby-Dick of a book" (*N.Y. Times Bk. Review*). It may be considered an important precursor of the so-called nonfiction novel that was to gain prominence during the 1960s.

Belonging to more conventional types of fiction are *The Morning Watch* (1954), a novel in the tradition of portraits of artists-to-be, and *A Death in the Family,* a moving account of domestic life based on the loss of his father, for which Agree was posthumously awarded the Pultizer Prize in 1958. The 1960 dramatization by Tad Mosel, *All the Way Home,* also won a Pulitizer Prize and the New York Drama Critics Circle Award and was cited by *Life* as the "Best American Play of the Season."

Agee's work for the screen was highlighted by his scripts for *The African Queen* and *The Night of the Hunter. Agee on Film* (1958–60) consists of a gathering of reviews and comments as well as five scripts.

Prior to Laurence Bergreen's well-received 1984 biography of Agee, the principal source of information about his life was *Letters of James Agee to Father Flye,* which consists of 70 letters written by Agee to his instructor at St. Andrew's School, a close and trusted friend throughout his life. They show Agee most often in a reflective, self-condemning mood. The final letters, written from the hospital where he was battling daily heart attacks, are touching, as are his sad reflections on the work he yet wanted to do.

NOVEL BY AGEE

A Death in the Family. 1959. Bantam 1983 $4.95. ISBN 0-553-27011-7

WORKS BY AGEE

Collected Short Prose. 1969. Ed. by Robert Fitzgerald. Berg Pubs. 1978 o.p. Features a valuable memoir by Fitzgerald as well as a selection of Agee's short stories, satiric pieces, movie scripts, and miscellanea.
James Agee: Selected Journalism. U. of Tenn. Pr. 1985 $24.95. ISBN 0-87049-466-X. Selections from Agee's contributions to *Fortune* and *Time;* with photographs and a bibliography.
Letters of James Agee to Father Flye. 1962. Berg Pubs. 1978 o.p.
Let Us Now Praise Famous Men. (coauthored with Walker Evans). 1941. HM 1989 $24.45. ISBN 0-395-48901-6. The centerpiece of Agee's career, a poetic re-creation of tenant

farmers' lives through such experimental techniques as a shifting point of view, several narrative levels and time schemes, and an evocative structure.

BOOKS ABOUT AGEE

Barson, Alfred T. *A Way of Seeing: A Critical Study of James Agee*. U. of Mass. Pr. 1972 o.p. Traces Agee's development as an artist, including his writings as a teenager; includes a bibliography and index.

Bergreen, Laurence. *James Agee*. NAL-Dutton 1984 o.p. Important biography.

Doty, Mark A. *Tell Me Who I Am: James Agee's Search for Selfhood*. La. State U. Pr. 1981 $25.00. ISBN 0-8071-0758-1

Larsen, Erling. *James Agee*. Pamphlets on Amer. Writers Ser. U. of Minn. Pr. 1971 o.p.

Madden, David, ed. *Remembering James Agee*. La. State U. Pr. 1974 o.p. Thirteen essays that examine Agee's life and work.

Ohlin, Peter. *Agee*. Astor-Honor 1965 $19.95. ISBN 0-8392-5011-8. The first booklength study of Agee's work, offering valuable insight into screenwriting and film criticism; includes a bibliography of primary and secondary works.

ALLEN, WOODY. 1935–

Allen's favorite personality—the bemused neurotic, the perpetual worry-wart, the born loser—dominates his plays, his movies, and his essays. A native New Yorker, Allen attended local schools and despised them, turning early to essay writing as a way to cope with his personal (and apparently self-imposed) isolation and to distinguish himself at school. Since his apprenticeship, writing gags for comedians such as Sid Caesar and Garry Moore, the image he projects—of a "nebbish from Brooklyn"—has developed into a personal metaphor of life as a concentration camp from which no one escapes alive. Allen wants to be funny, but isn't afraid to be serious either—even at the same time. His film *Annie Hall*, co-written with Marshall Brickman and winner of four Academy Awards, was a subtle, dramatic development of the contemporary fears and insecurities of American life. In her review of *Love and Death*, Judith Crist wrote that Allen goes "for the character rather than the cartoon, the situation rather than the set-up, the underlying madness rather than the surface craziness." Later Allen films, such as *Crimes and Misdemeanors* or *Husbands and Wives*, take on a far more somber and philosophic tone, which has delighted some critics and appalled others. In Allen's essays and fiction reprinted from the *New Yorker*, *Getting Even* (1971), *Without Feathers* (1975), and *Side Effects* (1980), the situations and characters don't just speak to us, they are us.

WORKS BY ALLEN

Getting Even. Random 1971 $10.95. ISBN 0-394-47348-5. An early collection of previously published pieces.

Without Feathers. 1986 $5.99. ISBN 0-345-33697-6

Woody Allen: A New Collection: Without Feathers, Getting Even, Side Effects. Outlet Bk. Co. 1991 $9.99. ISBN 0-517-07229-7.

AMMONS, A(RCHIE) R(ANDOLPH). 1926–

Considered by Daniel Hoffman to be an "American Romantic in the Tradition of EMERSON and WHITMAN," Ammons easily communicates to men and women of science as well as those of letters. After attending Wake Forest College, he studied at the University of California, Berkeley, and later became an executive in the biological glass industry. Since 1964 he has taught at Cornell University, and his *Collected Poems, 1915–1971* won a National Book Award (1973). In

1981, he was granted a MacArthur fellowship, and in 1982 he received the National Book Critics Circle Award.

Ammons's use of images of nature to impart his perception of human ambiguity is similar to that of ROBERT FROST. He is one of the most prolifically inventive poets of recent times, and he has an astonishing range of moods, from philosophical to playful. He has remained a singular poet while being influenced by such diverse sources as EMERSON, MARIANNE MOORE, and WILLIAM CARLOS WILLIAMS.

POETRY BY AMMONS

Briefings. Norton 1971 $6.00. ISBN 0-393-04326-6. A cool and intellectual dialogue between the poet and nature.

A Coast of Trees. Norton 1981 o.p. Thirty-seven poems, primarily meditations on the natural world.

Collected Poems, 1951–1971. Norton 1972 o.p.

Corson's Inlet. Norton 1965 o.p. Sharp observations of natural objects, rich in verbal and technical resources.

Diversifications: Poems. Norton 1975 o.p. Examines the relationship between the mind that knows and the senses that perceive.

Lake Effect Country: Poems. Norton 1983 $15.50. ISBN 0-393-01702-8. Reminiscent of Ammons' earlier work, with an added earnestness.

Northfield Poems. Norton 1966 $5.95. ISBN 0-393-04462-9. Crisp and unadorned natural descriptions and unpretentious anecdotes.

Selected Poems, 1951–1977. Norton 1977 o.p. Demonstrates the poet's remarkable style and exhaustive range.

The Snow Poems. Norton 1977 o.p. Keen observations, metaphysical musings, and wordplay in this description of winter.

Sphere: The Form of a Motion. Norton 1974 o.p. An important long poem that extends the tradition of Williams's *Paterson* and Merrill's *Changing Light.*

Sumerian Vistas. Norton 1987 $15.95. ISBN 0-393-02468-7. Captures the immediacy of humans in nature: employs the symbolism of opposing forces.

Worldly Hopes: Poems. Norton 1982 $12.95. ISBN 0-393-01518-1. Austere in diction, Ammon's reflective impulses are restrained in favor of worldly observations.

ANGELOU, MAYA. 1928–

Author, poet, playwright, singer, and dancer, Angelou's autobiographies have been nominated for a National Book Award and a Pulitzer Prize. She began writing books after friends, among them JAMES BALDWIN, encouraged her to write down the stories she was always telling about her childhood that was spent shuttling between the segregated, rural Arkansas town where her grandmother ran the general store, and St. Louis, where her more sophisticated and glamorous mother lived. "Her genius as a writer is her ability to recapture the texture of the way of life in the texture of its idioms, its idiosyncratic vocabulary, and especially in its process of image-making," critic Sidonie Smith wrote of Angelou's first book, *I Know Why the Caged Bird Sings* (1970). Although praised by critics, none of her subsequent autobiographies achieved quite the commercial success of this first one. A professor at Wake Forest University in North Carolina, Angelou participated at the inauguration of President Bill Clinton in January 1993 by composing and reciting a poem for the occasion.

NONFICTION BY ANGELOU

All God's Children Need Traveling Shoes. Random 1991 $9.00. ISBN 0-679-73404-X. Angelou's four-year stay in Ghana, during the period when Africa was claiming its independence from European colonialism; the "hidden history of a people both African and American."

Gather Together in My Name. Bantam 1985 $4.95. ISBN 0-553-26066-9. Angelou's late adolescence and brief flirtation with prostitution and drug addiction.

The Heart of a Woman. Random 1981 $24.95. ISBN 0-394-51273-1. Angelou's participation in the civil rights activism of the 1960s here and abroad, and her love affair with African activist Vusumzi Make.

I Know Why the Caged Bird Sings. Bantam 1983 $4.99. ISBN 0-553-27937-8. Covers Angelou's life up to the age of 16; a great commercial and critical success.

Singin' and Swingin' and Gettin Merry Like Christmas. Bantam 1985 $4.95. ISBN 0-553-25199-6. Angelou's life as she establishes a reputation as an avant-garde performer during the 1950s.

APPLE, MAX. 1941–

"It was my fascination itself with the English language that made me a writer," Apple wrote in an essay for the *New York Times Book Review.* "Its endless suggestiveness has carried me through many a plot, entertained me when nothing else could." Growing up in a Yiddish-speaking family, being "surprised" in kindergarten "that everything happened in English," Apple writes a prose that is remarkably attuned to America's cultural and linguistic clichés as, perhaps, only someone "surprised" by English could be. With the 1976 publication of *The Oranging of America, and Other Stories* Apple established himself as one of America's most affectionate, humorous, and astute critics. Like other postmodernist writers, Apple describes famous historical figures and American pop cultural heroes mingling with his fictional characters: Howard Johnson, NORMAN MAILER, Fidel Castro, and J. Edgar Hoover, among others, have all turned up in Apple's fiction. In the words of one critic, Apple creates "the literary equivalent of a Magritte painting where surrealism emerges less from subject than from juxtaposition." Apple is currently a professor of English at Rice University.

NOVELS BY APPLE

Zip: A Novel of the Left and the Right. Viking Penguin 1978 o.p. About a Jewish Detroiter who manages a Puerto Rican heavyweight named Jesus Goldstein.

SHORT STORY COLLECTIONS BY APPLE

Free Agents. HarpC 1985 $6.95. ISBN 0-06-091140-9.

The Oranging of America, and Other Stories. Grossman 1976 o.p. Postmodernist tales satirizing American culture.

ASHBERY, JOHN. 1927–

A contemporary and fellow classmate of KENNETH KOCH at Harvard University, John Ashbery has been one of the most experimental of the New York school of poets. Noted for his mixture of unusual diction and elegant wit, he was influenced by early W. H. AUDEN, LAURA RIDING, and WALLACE STEVENS.

Born in Rochester, New York, Ashbery grew up near Lake Ontario. After graduation from Harvard University, he studied at Columbia University, where he obtained his M.A. In 1955 he was awarded a Fulbright Scholarship to study in France, where he wrote art criticism for the Paris edition of the *N.Y. Herald Tribune.* Like others in the New York school, Ashbery was closely associated with art and artists and wrote for *Art News.* His first book, which contained a preface by Auden, won the *Yale Series of Younger Poets* prize. In 1991 he became Professor of English at Bard College.

Ashbery's plays *The Heroes* and *The Compromise or Queen of the Caribou* have both been produced—the former by the Living Theatre and the latter at the Poet's Theatre in Cambridge, Massachusetts. It is now virtually impossible to overstate Ashbery's influence and the fervor of his partisans. Since the death of LOWELL, he has been the most discussed (and praised) of all American poets. Although his poetry is imbued with anxiety and uncertainty (or perhaps because of this), Ashbery has become the dominant poet of both the avant-garde and academic criticism—a position not held by one poet since T. S. ELIOT in the 1930s and 1940s. Ashbery has received numerous awards, among them the Bollingen prize (1985) and a MacArthur Fellowship (1985).

POETRY BY ASHBERY

April Galleons. Viking Penguin 1988 $7.95. ISBN 0-14-058603-2. Rich in language, imagery, tone, and style, these poems include lyric moments, flat assertations, oracular pronouncements, and wonderful humor.

As We Know. Penguin Poets Ser. Viking Penguin 1986 $15.00. ISBN 0-14-058591-5. Examines faith and belief; an observation of the physical and metaphysical worlds.

Double Dream of Spring. 1970. *Amer. Poetry Ser.* Ecco Pr. 1976 $12.95. ISBN 0-912946-30-X. Twenty eight poems, mostly impersonal intellectual reflections.

Flow Chart. McKay 1991 $19.50. ISBN 0-679-40201-2. Smoothly and deceptively cast in the syntax of discourse and persuasion, Ashbery pursues the unknown.

Houseboat Days. Penguin Poets Ser. Viking Penguin 1977 o.p. Inspired conversations that move into a world where everything may be seen as new.

The Ice Storm. Hanuman Bks. 1987 $5.95. ISBN 0-937815-07-1

Rivers and Mountains. 1966. *Amer. Poetry Ser.* Ecco Pr. 1977 repr. of 1967 ed. $9.95. ISBN 0-88001-190-4

Selected Poems. Viking Penguin 1986 $12.95. ISBN 0-14-058553-2

Self-Portrait in a Convex Mirror. Viking Penguin 1990 $10.00. ISBN 0-14-058668-7. Winner of three national awards; the book that secured the poet's reputation.

Shadow Train: Fifty Lyrics. Penguin Poets Ser. Viking Penguin 1981 o.p. A book of 16-line sonnets.

Some Trees. Ecco Pr. 1978 $9.95. ISBN 0-88001-243-9

The Tennis Court Oath: A Book of Poems. U. Pr. of New Eng. 1962 $10.95. ISBN 0-8195-1013-0

Three Poems. Ecco Pr. 1989 $8.95. ISBN 0-88001-227-7. Written in prose of great flexibility, this important book is central to Ashbery's canon.

A Wave. Viking Penguin 1984 o.p. Explores the mysteries of personal art, change, and perception.

NONFICTION BY ASHBERY

Reported Sightings. Knopf 1989 $35.00. ISBN 0-394-57387-0. Rich, reflective essays discussing everything from nineteenth-century Romanticism to today's Abstract Expressionism.

BOOKS ABOUT ASHBERY

Lehman, David, ed. *Beyond Amazement: New Essays on John Ashbery.* Cornell Univ. Pr. 1980 $39.95. ISBN 0-8014-1235-8. A significant collection of essays, offering fresh ideas on the philosophical and political dimensions of Ashbery's work; includes a short bibliography.

Shapiro, David. *John Ashbery: An Introduction to the Poetry. Intro. to 20th-Century Amer. Poetry Ser.* Col. U. Pr. 1979 o.p. Traces Ashbery's development from ordered nonsense to significant expressions of nature and art; notes the influences of Chirico, Raymond Roussel, and Pierre Reverdy.

AUCHINCLOSS, LOUIS. 1917–

A practicing lawyer who has found time to write more than 35 books, 27 of them works of fiction, Louis Auchincloss calls himself a Jacobite who is proud to be an author in the tradition of HENRY JAMES and EDITH WHARTON. He followed in his family's solid tradition by attending Groton, Yale, and the University of Virginia Law School before serving in the Pacific during World War II. His first novel, *The Indifferent Children* (1947), was published under the pseudonym Andrew Lee, but its successful reception encouraged him to publish under his own name from then on. *Sybil*, a novel about an unhappy socialite in search of a real identity beneath the roles that have been imposed upon her, established Auchincloss as a male writer with a special understanding of feminine psychology. He has maintained that reputation throughout his career, even though several of his most recent books are explorations of different kinds of women portrayed with something less than complete sympathy. Another theme frequently explored by Auchincloss is the moral, legal, and psychological crises faced by his lawyer characters in works like *The Embezzler* (1966), *The Country Cousin* (1978), and the related stories about a law firm told in *The Partners* (1974). In what is generally thought to be his most successful novel, *The Rector of Justin* (1964), Auchincloss offers a somewhat ambiguous portrait of a deeply committed headmaster and good man whom no one ever sees truly or clearly. When Auchincloss returned to the theme of the dedicated man in *The House of the Prophet* (1980), Robert Kiely (*NY Times*) suggested that the book has a fatal weakness in offering as central character a "genius" with "mundane" ideas. In addition to his fiction, Auchincloss has written biographical and critical portraits of EDITH WHARTON, HENRY ADAMS, ELLEN GLASGOW, and other writers.

NOVELS BY AUCHINCLOSS

The Country Cousin. HM 1978 o.p.

The Dark Lady. HM 1977 o.p. Theme similar to *The House of the Prophet.*

The Embezzler. HM 1964 o.p. Deals with the corruption of lawyer with superficial values.

False Gods. HM 1992 $20.50. ISBN 0-395-60475-3. An insider's understanding of the sins and vanities of upper-class Manhattanites.

The Great World and Timothy Colt. HM 1956 o.p.

The House of the Prophet. HM 1990 $19.95. ISBN 0-88738-857-4. Closed aristocratic world threatened by outsiders—in this case, Jews.

The Partners. HM 1974 o.p. About a law firm.

Pursuit of the Prodigal. HM 1959 o.p. Portrays one of Auchincloss's more rebellious characters.

The Rector of Justin. HM 1964 o.p. About the ambiguities of commitment to an Old World institution.

Sybil. 1952. Greenwood 1972 repr. of 1952 ed. $35.00. ISBN 0-8371-3728-4

A World of Profit. HM 1968 o.p. A story of failed and failing aristocracy.

BAKER, HOUSTON A., JR. 1943–

Baker is one of the most persistent voices in African American literary criticism, one that has helped to establish a tradition in black literature from slave narratives and spirituals to blues and modern African American writing. He is a frequent contributor to literary journals, author and editor of numerous books, and a leading mover in the diversification of American literature.

NONFICTION BY BAKER

Blues, Ideology, and Afro-American Literature: A Vernacular Theory. U. Ch. Pr. 1987 $11.95. ISBN 0-226-03538-7. Provocative study that charts new territory in contemporary literature theory.

The Journey Back: Issues in Black Literature and Criticism. U. Ch. Pr. 1984 $11.95. ISBN 0-226-03535-2. Traces tradition "back" into the past of African American literature.

Long Black Song: Essays in Black American Literature and Culture. U. Pr. of Va. 1990 $9.95. ISBN 0-8139-1301-2. Collection of essays based on lectures to the Yale Faculty Wives.

Modernism and the Harlem Renaissance. U. Ch. Pr. 1989 $9.95. ISBN 0-226-03525-5. Mostly devoted to the examination of the rhetorical strategies employed by pre-Renaissance writers.

Workings of the Spirit: The Poetics of Afro-American Women's Writing. U. Ch. Pr. 1992 $12.95. ISBN 0-226-03523-9. Examines the intellectual life and works of various African American women writers; includes bibliographical references and an index.

BALDWIN, JAMES. 1924–1987

EDMUND WILSON (in *The Bit between My Teeth*) described James Baldwin as "not only one of the best black writers that we have ever had in this country, [but] one of the best writers that we have. He has mastered a taut and incisive style . . . and in writing about what it means to be a Negro he is writing about what it means to be a man." Looking back on Baldwin's career several decades after Wilson made his comment, it seems increasingly clear that, if the main theme of Baldwin's writings is what it means to be a man, he has approached that theme from the perspective of an outsider. His novels, plays, short stories, and essays are concerned again and again with problems of racial, sexual, and personal identity; and what makes those works especially remarkable is the uncompromising honesty of their author.

Baldwin emerged to prominence during the 1950s and 1960s, when for the first time there was a large receptive audience ready to listen to articulate spokespeople from black America. His first novel, *Go Tell It on the Mountain* (1953), describes the growing up of a young man in Harlem. Clearly fictional, yet autobiographical in its setting and dominant psychological themes, the work raised expectations that Baldwin would serve as a leading force in a postmodern literature marked by passion and commitment to activist causes.

That promise was only partly fulfilled. Baldwin left the United States for Paris in 1948 and spent many of his subsequent years living abroad, but another explanation for the direction of his writing may be found in his increasing concern with questions of personal rather than racial identity. His second and third novels, *Giovanni's Room* (1956) and *Another Country* (1962) are remembered largely for what was considered a daring and advanced depiction of homosexuals. And although *If Beale Street Could Talk* (1974) was one of the bestsellers of 1975, its story of a young African American couple victimized by the American judicial system ends on such a note of uncertainty that the book seems ineffective as an activist statement. Baldwin's last novel, *Just Above My Head* (1979), is a more ambitious, complex work. Baldwin commented, "What I've really been feeling is that I've come full circle. From 'Go Tell It on the Mountain' to 'Just Above My Head' sums up something of my experience—it's difficult to articulate—that sets me free to go someplace else" (*Dictionary of Literary Biography*).

Baldwin has written several plays. *Blues for Mister Charlie* (1964), which received mixed reviews on Broadway, is a powerful study of racial conflict in a southern town, while *The Amen Corner* (1968) movingly describes the desperate struggle of a woman minister in Harlem to keep her church and hold her family together.

NOVELS BY BALDWIN

Another Country. 1962. Dell 1985 $5.95. ISBN 0-440-30200-5
Giovanni's Room. 1956. Dell 1985 $5.99. ISBN 0-440-32881-0. Explores homosexual love.
Go Tell It on the Mountain. 1953. Dell 1985 $5.99. ISBN 0-4403-3307-6. Baldwin's first
and finest novel, about the conversion of John Grimes.
If Beale Street Could Talk. 1974. Dell 1986 $5.99. ISBN 0-440-34060-8. Narrated by
women in Harlem; suggests new cynicism and complexity.
Just Above My Head. 1979. Dell 1990 $5.95. ISBN 0-440-20599-9

SHORT STORY COLLECTION BY BALDWIN

Going to Meet the Man. 1965. Dell 1986 $5.99. ISBN 0-440-32931-0. Eight stories.

PLAYS BY BALDWIN

The Amen Corner. 1968. Dell 1990 $5.99. ISBN 0-440-20662-6
Blues for Mr. Charlie. 1964. Dell 1985 $4.95. ISBN 0-440-30637-X

POETRY BY BALDWIN

Jimmy's Blues: Selected Poems. St. Martin 1990 $9.95. ISBN 0-312-05104-2. Lyrics against
racism and oppression with a streetwise yet visionary poetic voice.

NONFICTION BY BALDWIN

The Evidence of Things Not Seen. 1985. H. Holt & Co. 1986 $7.95. ISBN 0-8050-0138-7.
An extended essay on the conviction of Wayne Williams for the Atlanta child
murders.
Notes of a Native Son. 1955. Beacon Pr. 1990 $11.00. ISBN 0-8070-6431-9. Among the
most powerful indictments of racial tyranny ever written.
The Price of the Ticket: Collected Nonfiction 1948–1985. 1986. St. Martin 1985 $29.95.
ISBN 0-312-64306-3. A collection of Baldwin's most noted essays including the
famous *Notes of a Native Son.*

BOOKS ABOUT BALDWIN

Rossett, Lisa. *James Baldwin.* Chelsea Hse. 1989 $17.95. ISBN 1-55546-572-2. Sets
Baldwin's life and ideals in the context of the civil rights movement and identifies his
conflicts with other writers and activists.
Troupe, Quincy, ed. *James Baldwin: The Legacy.* S&S Trade 1989 $12.95. ISBN 0-671-
67651-2. Contains memorial tributes from Baldwin's family and friends along with
several lengthy interviews with Baldwin.
Weatherby, W. J. *James Baldwin: Artist on Fire.* Dell 1990 $5.95. ISBN 0-440-20573-5.
Connects events in Baldwin's life with incidents in his stories and essays.

BAMBARA, TONI CADE. 1939–

Bambara emerged from the 1960s as a civil rights activist, community
organizer, teacher, and chronicler of the lives of African Americans living in big
cities. Her first two collections of short stories, *Gorilla, My Love* (1972) and *The
Sea Birds Are Still Alive* (1977), struck reviewers as containing "among the best
portraits of black life to have appeared in some time." Avoiding the linear
development of plot, Bambara writes stories that build improvisationally out of
situations, dealing with the basic emotions binding together her communities of
characters. Most striking and beautiful is her characters' speech; as one critic
commented, "conversations [are] conducted in a rhythmic, black-inflected,
sweet-and-sour language." In addition to her fiction, Bambara has written
numerous screenplays for television, edited two anthologies of African American literature, and led numerous workshops on writing and community
organizing for community centers, museums, prisons, libraries, and universi-

ties. In addition, three of her short stories, "Gorilla, My Love," "Medley," and "Witchbird," have been adapted for film.

SHORT STORY COLLECTIONS BY BAMBARA

Gorilla, My Love. 1972. Random 1992 $9.00. ISBN 0-679-73898-3. Engaging stories, with convincing use of street dialect.

The Sea Birds Are Still Alive. 1977. Random 1982 $10.00. ISBN 0-394-71176-9. Stories about African American neighborhoods in big cities, with occasional trips South.

NOVEL BY BAMBARA

The Salt Eaters. 1980. Random 1992 $10.00. ISBN 0-679-74076-7. Relationships among the various women in a community, creating a complex portrait of African-American women's lives.

BANKS, RUSSELL. 1940–

Like many of his characters, Banks is a New Englander drawn to the warmth and mystery of the Caribbean, where he once lived for a year and a half. In his widely acclaimed novel *Continental Drift* (1985), Banks juxtaposes the lives of two people seeking the American dream—one, a New Hampshire oil-burner repairman who moves his family to Florida where he hopes to become a successful businessman; the other, a Haitian woman who emigrates to America to start a new life. A vigorous, realistic novelist, Banks makes almost a nineteenth-century use of a moralizing, engaged narrator. "I'm really interested in re-inventing the narrator," he has commented. "I want to feel I have my arm around a shoulder of this reader and I'm explaining, narrating, telling a wonderful story to this person that I've stopped, like the wedding guest in COLERIDGE's 'The Ancient Mariner.'" Banks's fiction has been contrasted to the minimalist fiction popular in the 1970s and 1980s. Unlike their small canvases, Banks's fiction presents a broad overview of contemporary America recognizable in all its promise and failure. He deals persuasively with America's "drift"—with its uprootedness, its disassociation from the past, its free-floating greed.

NOVELS BY BANKS

Affliction. 1989. HarpC 1990 $10.00. ISBN 0-06-092007-6. Examines the macho tradition and brutality through the eyes of a young American male.

The Book of Jamaica. 1980. Ballantine 1986 $5.95. ISBN 0-345-33074-9. The story of a 35-year-old college professor who travels to the Caribbean to finish a novel.

Continental Drift. 1985. Ballantine 1986 $4.95. ISBN 0-345-33021-8. The disastrous convergence of two seekers of the American dream.

Hamilton Stark. 1978. Ballantine 1986 $5.95. ISBN 0-345-33077-3. The story of a misanthropic New Hampshire pipefitter.

The Sweet Hereafter: A Novel. HarpC 1991 $20.00. ISBN 0-06-016703-3. The after-effects of a tragic school-bus crash.

SHORT STORY COLLECTION BY BANKS

Trailerpark. 1981. Ballantine 1986 $5.95. ISBN 0-345-33077-3. Lucid characterizations of people living in a trailerpark.

BARAKA, IMAMU AMIRI (LEROI JONES). 1934–

Baraka is so powerful, accomplished, and versatile in so many literary fields that he quickly made himself a name in literature; then he became a militant against the oppression of African Americans. Baraka's early poems were often personal, uncommitted, and diffuse; even in these, he showed a strong lyric talent.

Baraka was sentenced to prison in connection with the Newark, New Jersey, riots of 1967. Before serving his term of imprisonment, however, he and other black militants were instrumental in helping maintain order in Newark at the time of MARTIN LUTHER KING, JR.'s (see Vol. 4) assassination in 1968. Since then, he has become more active in the black nationalist movement, more recently espousing revolutionary Marxist-Leninist principles. The major African American poet of the postwar era, Baraka has refused in the last two decades to separate his revolutionary commitment and his literary art. This vision informs his work.

POETRY BY BARAKA

Black Magic Poetry: Collected Poetry, 1961–67. Bobbs 1970 o.p. Includes the following volumes: *Sabotage; Target Study; Black Art.*

Preface to a Twenty Volume Suicide Note. Corinth Bks. 1961 o.p. Baraka's preoccupation with death.

PLAY BY BARAKA

The Baptism (and The Toilet). Grove Pr. 1967 $3.95. ISBN 0-802-17253-1

NONFICTION BY BARAKA

The Autobiography of LeRoi Jones/Amiri Baraka. Freundlich 1984 $16.95. ISBN 0-88191-000-7. Details Baraka's artistic and political views as well as his personal life.

Home: Social Essays. 1964. Morrow 1972 o.p. Essays on race relations in the United States.

Raise Race Rays Raze: Essays since 1965. Univ. Place 1971 $20.00. ISBN 0-685-77057-5. Compilation of essays including: "Work Notes 1966," "Poetry and Karma," and "What the Arts Need Now." All essays deal with African American relations in the United States.

WORKS BY BARAKA

Daggers and Javelins: Essays, 1974–1979. Morrow 1984 o.p. A compilation of essays, articles, and speeches by the author.

The LeRoi Jones-Amiri Baraka Reader. Ed. by William J. Harris. Thunders Mouth 1991 $14.95. ISBN 1-56025-007-0. Samplings of his writing from the 1950s to the present.

The Music: Reflections on Jazz and Blues. Morrow 1987 $22.95. ISBN 0-688-04388-7. Collection of miscellaneous pieces of poetry, reviews, speeches, and interviews.

The System of Dante's Hell, The Dead Lecturer, and Tales. Grove Pr. 1976 o.p.

BOOKS ABOUT BARAKA

Harris, William J. *The Poetry and Poetics of Amiri Baraka: The Jazz Aesthetic.* U. of Mo. Pr. 1985 $20.00. ISBN 0-8262-0483-X. Shows the influence of jazz music on Baraka's poetic principles.

Hudson, Theodore. *From LeRoi Jones to Amiri Baraka: The Literary Works.* Duke 1973 $23.95. ISBN 0-8223-0296-9. Scholarly analysis and criticism of Baraka's early work.

Sollars, Werner. *Amiri Baraka-LeRoi Jones: The Quest for "Popular Modernism."* Col. U. Pr. 1978 o.p. An important critical study.

BARTH, JOHN. 1930–

John Barth published an essay in the August 1967 issue of *Atlantic Monthly* called "The Literature Of Exhaustion," which has become a classic of contemporary criticism. While describing the kind of self-consciously reflective fiction that helps to distinguish the latest period of high modernism, Barth identified his own antecedents and set down some cautionary principles that help to explain his work and that of other members of his generation. He is often considered an American leader of the metafictional writers. Robert Scholes called him "the best writer of fiction we have at present, and one of the best we have ever had."

Born in Cambridge, Maryland, Barth attended the Juilliard School of Music, but went on to Johns Hopkins for an M.A., became addicted to the academic life while working in the classics library, and now holds a professorship in creative writing at Johns Hopkins. His first novel, *The Floating Opera* (1956), is an existentialist tale that is cynical, readable, funny, relatively brief. His fourth novel, *Giles Goat-Boy* (1966), is also picaresque—a 700-page allegorical fantasy set in the present.

Barth's later fiction is even more experimental than his two long novels. The stories in *Lost in the Funhouse* (1968) are reflexive to an extreme, self-consciously concerned as they are with technical problems of storytelling. Yet for all their difficulty, Barth's humor and virtuosity make his stories immediately enjoyable. His interest in classical themes and subjects is utilized in *Chimera* (1972), which consists of retellings of the legends of Scheherazade, Perseus, and Bellerophon interlocked in such a way that the artist-as-storyteller begins to take on the stature of a mythical hero. Most reviewers in the commercial press found the book confusing and annoying, but it is filled with the kinds of labyrinthine riddles and indigenous tricks that make Barth's writings especially attractive to college audiences. In fact, to judge from the sometimes hostile reception of two of Barth's later novels, *Letters*, and *Sabbatical: A Romance* (1982) the academic appeal of his kind of writing has started to lose favor with some reviewers. Of *Letters* (1979), Barth's attempt to revive the epistolary novel in the form of another long and complicated work, both John Leonard in the *N.Y. Times* and Robert Towers in the *N.Y. Review of Books* suggested that it seemed to have been written only for "graduate students and other masochists" (Leonard) or "that little band of academic scholar-critics, now mostly middle-aged, who, having locked themselves into a room with POUND's 'Cantos' and 'Finnegans Wake,' glare balefully through barred windows at the rest of the literary scene" (Towers). On the other hand, Philip Stevick, a professor-critic writing in the *Nation*, found *Letters* to be "an extraordinary exercise in intersecting perspectives, intersecting rhetorics, intersecting ways of organizing the world. . . . It is a book that confirms one's conviction that, for pure talent, the ability to do anything with words, nobody is better than Barth."

NOVELS BY BARTH

The Floating Opera and *The End of the Road*. 1956 and 1958. Doubleday 1988 $10.95. ISBN 0-385-24089-9

Giles Goat-Boy; or The Revised New Syllabus. 1978. Doubleday 1987 $11.95. ISBN 0-385-24086-4. An experimental picaresque novel.

Last Voyage of Somebody the Sailor. Little 1991 $22.95. ISBN 0-316-08251-1. Twelve stories that make up a metafictional journal.

The Sot-Weed Factor. 1960. Doubleday 1987 $11.95. ISBN 0-385-24088-0. Wordplay, gags—a metafictional feast.

The Tidewater Tales: A Novel. Fawcett 1988 $12.95. ISBN 0-449-90293-5. Novel set on a Chesapeake Bay sailboat.

SHORT STORY COLLECTIONS BY BARTH

Chimera. 1972. Fawcett 1985 $4.95. ISBN 0-449-21113-4

Lost in the Funhouse: Fiction for Print, Tape, Live Voice. 1968. Doubleday 1988 $8.95. ISBN 0-385-24087-2. Barth's parodic rage finding a new expression.

BOOKS ABOUT BARTH

Fogel, Stan. *Understanding John Barth.* U. of SC Pr. 1990 $29.95. ISBN 0-87249-660-0. Covers Barth's works, written over a twenty-five year period.

Harris, Charles B. *Passionate Virtuosity: The Fiction of John Barth.* U. of Ill. Pr. 1983 $24.95. ISBN 0-252-01037-X

Morrell, David. *John Barth: An Introduction.* Pa. St. U. Pr. 1976 o.p. Analyzes six of Barth's major novels.

Tharpe, Jac. *John Barth: The Comic Sublimity of Paradox. Crosscurrents Modern Critiques Ser.* S. Ill. U. Pr. 1974 o.p.

Vine, Richard A. *John Barth: An Annotated Bibliography. Author Bibliographies Ser.* Scarecrow 1977 $22.50. ISBN 0-8108-1003-4

Walkiewicz, E. P. *John Barth.* Macmillan 1986 $21.95. ISBN 0-8057-7461-0. Provides critical commentaries, brief biographical remarks, and a chronology.

Weixlmann, Joseph. *John Barth: An Annotated Bibliography. Reference Lib. of the Humanities.* Garland 1976 o.p. An annotated bibliography of Barth and his critics.

BARTHELME, DONALD. 1931–1989

Barthelme is considered by many critics to be one of the most influential fiction writers in America. Born in Philadelphia, he served in the army, worked as a museum director in Houston during the mid-1950s, and did editorial work before establishing himself as a writer. His novel *Snow White* (1967) took up almost an entire issue of the *New Yorker*. Few works have received such distinction, and Barthelme is the youngest writer to be so honored.

Snow White is hardly the typical *New Yorker* story. More surreal than realistic, more cynical than sensitive, it updates the fairy tale in startling ways. Barthelme's Snow White shares an apartment with seven short businessmen who have grown prosperous manufacturing Asian baby foods such as Baby Dim Sum and Baby Dow Shew. The evil stepmother is named Jane Villiers de l'Isle Adam, the prince-hero turns out to be a real frog, and the story ends in a way that will surprise readers of the BROTHERS GRIMM (see Vol. 2). Whereas much modern fiction is reflexive in the sense that it deals with its own composition, making us conscious of the artist behind the work, Barthelme takes us a step further by pulling the reader into his stories. Thus, for example, *Snow White* is interrupted with a questionnaire in which the author solicits advice from his readers as to how his story should proceed.

Sixty Stories (1982), which comprises approximately half of the short fiction Barthelme wrote between 1961 and 1981, offers what he and his editors consider the best of his shorter works. Most of those works are at least as experimental as his novel—so much so that it is perhaps more convenient to see them as exercises in verbal and visual effects than to view them as traditional short stories. He likes to pepper his sketches with erudite literary references. He makes use of real people as fictional characters—as in the startling reversal of nonfiction fiction shown in "Robert Kennedy Saved from Drowning." He likes to break down barriers of time, as in "The Indian Uprising," in which an old-fashioned cowboys-and-Indians formula is used to tell about guerrilla warfare in a modern urban ghetto. Because he has been strongly influenced by the visual arts, including film, it is not surprising that he turned to breaking down the usual distinctions between the verbal and visual genres of art. *The Dead Father* (1975) and other key works combined illustrations with text in an unusually effective way, which found some imitators. Among Barthelme's last works was a novel, *The King* (1990), published after his death in 1989. His death was widely mourned, especially by those writers and critics who admired his experimental art.

SHORT STORY COLLECTIONS BY BARTHELME

Come Back, Dr. Caligari. 1964. Little 1971 $7.95. ISBN 0-316-08254-6. Good examples of early Barthelme.
Forty Stories. 1989. Viking Penguin 1989 $7.95. ISBN 0-14-011245-6
Sixty Stories. 1981. NAL-Dutton 1981 $10.95. ISBN 0-525-48328-4
Unspeakable Practices, Unnatural Acts. 1968. PB 1978 $2.25. ISBN 0-671-82306-X. Kafkaesque landscapes comprised of brand products.

NOVELS BY BARTHELME

The Dead Father. 1975. Viking Penguin 1986 $8.00. ISBN 0-14-008667-6. Satire of patriarchy.
Snow White. 1967. Macmillan 1972 $7.95. ISBN 0-689-70331-7

BOOKS ABOUT BARTHELME

Gordon, Louis. *Donald Barthelme. Twayne's U.S. Authors Ser.* G. K. Hall 1982 $14.50. ISBN 0-8057-7347-9. General introduction to Barthelme's life and fiction with discussions of individual works.
Klinkowitz, Jerome, and others. *Donald Barthelme: A Comprehensive Bibliography and an Annotated Secondary Checklist.* Shoe String 1977 $27.50. ISBN 0-208-01712-7
McCaffery, Larry. *The Metafictional Muse: The Work of Robert Coover, Donald Barthelme, and William Gass. Critical Essays in Modern Lit. Ser.* U. of Pittsburgh Pr. 1982 $32.95. ISBN 0-8229-3462-0. Interprets three major writers; includes commentary on the nature of language and the self.
Molesworth, Charles F. *Donald Barthelme's Fiction: The Ironist Saved from Drowning. Literary Frontier Ed.* U. of Mo. Pr. 1982 $8.95. ISBN 0-8262-0338-8. Important criticism of Barthelme and his work; includes bibliographical references.
Roe, Barbara. *Donald Barthelme: A Study of the Short Fiction.* Macmillan 1992 $22.95. ISBN 0-8057-8338-5. Serves as a useful general handbook.
Trachtenberg, Stanley. *Understanding Donald Barthelme.* U. of SC Pr. 1990 $29.95. ISBN 0-87249-711-9. Examines both his fiction and nonfiction and identifies his major themes.

BAYM, NINA. 1936–

Born in Princeton, New Jersey, and educated at Cornell University and Harvard, literary critic Nina Baym's career revolves around what she considers to be the necessary project of making the "minor" nineteenth-century American women writers into an area of literary study. Noting that theories of nineteenth-century American literature tended to exclude women, Baym explains that her writing centers not only on the works of women writers, but on the "matter of major and/versus minor authors, the contexts of authorship, the constitution of the canon, and other matters concerning the way in which we make our literary choices and, having made them, justify them." A recipient of a Guggenheim fellowship (1975–76) and a fellowship from the National Endowment for the Humanities (1982–83), she is teaching at the University of Illinois.

NONFICTION BY BAYM

Novels, Readers, and Reviewers: Responses to Fiction in Antebellum America. Cornell Univ. Pr. 1984 $34.95. ISBN 0-8014-1709-0. Considers American readers' responses to fiction written a generation before the Civil War; examines reviews of novels from this era.

The Scarlet Letter: A Reading. Macmillan 1986 $17.95. ISBN 0-685-19706-9. Easy-to-read critical commentary.

The Shape of Hawthorne's Career. Cornell Univ. Pr. 1976 o.p.

Women's Fiction: A Guide to Novels by and about Women in America, 1820–1870. U. of Ill. Pr. 1993 $15.95. ISBN 0-252-06285-X. A useful guide to nineteenth-century women's writing.

BEATTIE, ANN. 1947–

Born in Washington, D.C., Beattie was educated at the University of Connecticut and American University. In recent years she has taught at both Harvard and the University of Virginia. Noted for her minimalist style—short declarative sentences, an accretion of detail, non sequiturs—Beattie has published numerous stories in the *New Yorker*, as well as several collections and novels. Her characters tend to be baby boomers, disillusioned in a post-sixties world, unable to sustain fulfilling connections to humanity. Critics have reacted variably to Beattie's flattened, affectless portrayals of flattened, affectless 20-to-30-somethings: yet most have recognized a haunting quality in Beattie's tales, as she depicts an America that—as JOHN UPDIKE put it—"is like the America one pieces together from the *National Enquirers* that her characters read—a land of pathetic monstrosities, of pain clothed in clichés, of extraterrestrial trivia." Beattie herself simply says, "I write in those flat simple sentences because that's the way I think."

SHORT STORY COLLECTIONS BY BEATTIE

Distortions. 1976. Random 1991 $9.95. ISBN 0-679-73235-7. Called "still lifes," stories depicting an eerie state of existence.

Secrets and Surprises. 1979. McKay 1991 $10.00. ISBN 0-679-73193-8

What Was Mine & Other Stories. Random 1991 $19.50. ISBN 0-679-40007-X. Quick studies of the lives of middle-class Americans caught in the kind of self-examination that exposes the frailties and limitations of their perceptions.

NOVEL BY BEATTIE

Chilly Scenes of Winter. 1976. Random 1990 $10.00. ISBN 0-679-73234-9. People who came of age in the 1960s, lost and disillusioned in the 1970s.

BELLOW, SAUL. 1915– (NOBEL PRIZE 1976)

Even before Saul Bellow won the Nobel Prize, *Newsweek* in a cover story of September 1, 1975, had called him "the most honored American novelist of his age." By then he had received several Guggenheim Fellowships, a Pulitzer Prize, and no less than three National Book Awards in addition to other recognitions. Perhaps a major reason for his high respectability may be found in the representative nature of his work. Bellow has always seemed to exist comfortably between extremes. Neither too liberal nor too conservative in his politics but very much aware of changing social conditions, on occasion very funny and often quite profound, sophisticated in his literary knowledge yet sometimes loose and sprawling in his literary forms, Bellow has epitomized American literary culture of his time. *Newsweek* noted, "PHILLIP ROTH put it nicely when he referred to Bellow as 'closing the gap, as it were, between Damon Runyon and THOMAS MANN.'"

He was born Solomon Bellows in a small town in Quebec, of Russian Jewish parents. His family moved to Chicago when he was 9. A graduate of Northwestern University, he did graduate work in anthropology at the University of Wisconsin until he decided to devote himself to writing. He served in the merchant marine during World War II and worked on the fringes of the New York publishing scene before returning to the Middle West and settling into an academic career. In 1962 he became a member and chairperson of the University of Chicago's Committee on Social Thought, a flexible department with restricted enrollment for people with broad intellectual interests. In 1993 Bellow accepted a new position on the faculty of Boston University.

The Adventures of Augie March (1953) is generally considered the pivotal book in Bellow's career as a writer. It was preceded by *Dangling Man* (1944) and *The Victim* (1947), comparatively short novels, which were well received by some of the most influential critics of the time and praised for the way in which they seemed to reflect the existential mood of the postwar years. With *Augie March*, a long picaresque novel centered on the misadventures of a kind of "Chicago Tom Jones" (Albert J. Guerard), Bellow began to develop what IRVING HOWE has called "the first major new style in American prose fiction since those of HEMINGWAY and FAULKNER." It is a style that combines the rhythms and energy of urban street talk with the plain speech of the Middle West and the bookish consciousness of an intellectual. *Augie March* brought Bellow not only the first of his National Book Awards, but wide public acceptance as a writer to be enjoyed as well as respected. However, Bellow turned back to shorter, tighter forms with his next book, and the novelette of the same title in his *Seize the Day* (1956) volume is generally considered one of his two or three outstanding works. *Henderson the Rain King* (1959) marked a return to the picaresque with its zesty account of the African adventure of the only WASP hero in the Bellow gallery of main characters, a larger-than-life Yankee millionaire.

Herzog (1964), the most autobiographical of his novels, is generally considered the best of his longer novels. It is the story of Moses Herzog (a name borrowed, significantly, from JOYCE's *Ulysses*), a kind of Leopold Bloom in reverse whose life seems to be one long anxiety attack as he looks back on the most recent of his domestic crises and what led to it. Herzog's letters to all sorts of people are included in the loosely structured novel, and its encyclopedic quality makes it seem in some ways as representative in its depiction of midcentury Chicago as *Ulysses* was in its coverage of Dublin in 1904. Bellow's next full-length novel, which also won a National Book Award, was *Mister Sammler's Planet* (1970), the story of an elderly man whose experiences and attitudes also suggest the collective unconsciousness of the century in which we live. *Humboldt's Gift* (1975), Bellow's Pulitzer Prize-winning novel, is a story told by a writer not unlike Bellow who looks back on the tragic career of a poet friend with traits reminiscent of both JOHN BERRYMAN and DELMORE SCHWARTZ. *The Dean's December* (1982), on the other hand, depressed some reviewers because of what they considered its reflection of Bellow's own world-weary attitudes at a low point in his personal life. Fortunately, that mood seems to have been a passing one. Of *Him with His Foot in His Mouth and Other Stories* (1984), Robert M. Adams said, "Of all the American novelists who don't have a foot in their mouth, he remains one of the most rewarding; and the new collection of stories provides encouraging evidence that this state of things is not about to change" (*N.Y. Review of Books*). Since then, Bellow has returned to an exploration of the short novel form while continuing to publish short stories and nonfiction.

NOVELS BY BELLOW

The Adventures of Augie March. 1953. Viking Penguin 1984 $11.00. ISBN 0-14-007272-1
Dangling Man. 1944. Viking Penguin 1988 $8.95. ISBN 0-14-001862-X

Henderson the Rain King. 1959. Viking Penguin 1984 $10.00. ISBN 0-14-007269-1

Herzog. 1964. Viking Penguin 1984 $9.00. ISBN 0-14-007270-5

Humboldt's Gift. 1975. Viking Penguin 1984 $10.00. ISBN 0-14-007271-3. Autobiographical, comic look at a writer's life in America.

Mister Sammler's Planet. 1970. Viking Penguin 1984 $8.95. ISBN 0-14-007317-5

Something to Remember Me By—Three Tales: The Bellarosa Connection; A Theft; Something to Remember Me By. Viking Penguin 1991 $21.95. ISBN 0-670-84216-8. Novellas; *The Bellarosa Connection* and *A Theft* originally published individually in 1989.

The Victim. 1947. Viking Penguin 1988 $8.95. ISBN 0-14-002493-X

SHORT STORY COLLECTIONS BY BELLOW

Great Jewish Short Stories. Dell 1985 $6.95. ISBN 0-440-33122-6

Mosby's Memoirs and Other Stories. 1969. Viking Penguin 1984 $5.95. ISBN 0-14-007318-3

Seize the Day, with Three Short Stories and a One-Act Play. 1957. Viking Penguin 1984 $7.95. ISBN 0-14- 007285-3

NONFICTION BY BELLOW

To Jerusalem and Back: A Personal Account. Viking Penguin 1985 $6.95. ISBN 0-14-007273-X

BOOKS ABOUT BELLOW

Bradbury, Malcolm. *Saul Bellow. Contemporary Writers Ser.* Routledge Chapman & Hall 1982 o.p. Looks at Bellow as a leading figure in the development of contemporary fiction, and how his work is challenged by "post-modernism."

Braham, Jeanne. *A Sort of Columbus: The American Voyages of Saul Bellow's Fiction.* U. of Ga. Pr. 1984 o.p. Convincing case for Bellow's place in American literature; examines how his fiction is rooted in American consciousness.

Clayton, John J. *Saul Bellow: In Defense of Man.* Bks. Demand $90.00. ISBN 0-8357-6692-6. A study of Bellow's ideas in light of past literary traditions.

Dutton, Robert R. *Saul Bellow.* 1971. *Twayne's U.S. Authors Ser.* G. K. Hall 1982 $20.00. ISBN 0-8057-7353-3. An overview of Bellow's life and work with discussions of individual titles.

Fuchs, Daniel. *Saul Bellow: Vision and Revision.* Duke 1984 o.p. First scholarly study of Bellow's text.

Goldman, L. H. *Saul Bellow's Moral Experiences: A Critical Study of the Jewish Experience.* Irvington 1983 $29.50. ISBN 0-8290-1535-3

Harris, Mark. *Saul Bellow: Drumlin Woodchuck.* U. of Ga. Pr. 1980 o.p. Candid biography of Bellow's personal life; discusses some of his work.

Hollahan, Eugene, ed. *Saul Bellow and the Struggle at the Center.* AMS Pr. 1992 $45.00. ISBN 0-404-63212-2. Collection of critical essays.

Malin, Irving. *Saul Bellow's Fiction.* Pref. by Harry T. Moore. *Crosscurrents Modern Critiques Ser.* Southern Ill. U. Pr. 1969 o.p. Detailed discussion of Bellow's intertextual and fictive world; examines his main themes.

Nault, Marianne. *Saul Bellow: His Works and His Critics—An Annotated International Bibliography. Reference Lib. of the Humanities* Garland 1977 o.p. Annotated bibliography with international coverage.

Newman, Judie. *Saul Bellow and History.* St. Martin 1984 $29.95. ISBN 0-312-69981-6. Persuasive study of how Bellow incorporates history into his fiction.

Opdahl, Keith. *Novels of Saul Bellow: An Introduction.* Pa. St. U. Pr. 1967 $22.50. ISBN 0-271-73118-4. Scholarly study of Bellow's work that reveals much about his creative process.

Porter, M. Gilbert. *Whence the Power: The Artistry and Humanity of Saul Bellow.* U. of Mo. Pr. 1974 $25.00. ISBN 0-8262-0165-2. A formalist study of Bellow's use of imagery in his work.

Rodrigues, Eusebio L. *Quest for the Human: An Exploration of Saul Bellow's Fiction*.
 Bucknell U. Pr. 1982 $35.00. ISBN 0-8387-2368-3. Examines Bellow's ideas about the
 search for the human spirit.
Scheer-Schaezler, Brigitte. *Saul Bellow*. *Lit. and Life Ser*. Continuum 1972 o.p.
 Chronological study of the author's life and major works.
Sokoloff, B. A. *Saul Bellow: A Comprehensive Bibliography*. Folcroft 1972 o.p.
Trachtenberg, Stanley, ed. *Critical Essays on Saul Bellow*. *Critical Essays on Amer. Lit.
 Ser*. G. K. Hall 1979 o.p.

BERCOVITCH, SACVAN. 1933–

Bercovitch, who is a professor at Harvard University, is probably the most
influential critic in American studies today. Tracing the function of rhetoric in
American writing from the Puritans through the nineteenth century, Bercovitch
has argued that the persuasiveness of rhetoric is "in proportion to its capacity to
help men [*sic*] act in history." In his books, Bercovitch has revealed the power
of American rhetoric as it creates a myth of America that conflates religious and
political issues, transforming even the most despairing and critical energies into
affirmations of the American way. Among his major arguments is the idea that
the rhetoric of America's colonial sermons and histories, founding documents
(such as the Declaration of Independence), and novels of the American
Renaissance, all participate in the project of transforming what he calls
"dissensus" into "rituals of consensus."

NONFICTION BY BERCOVITCH

The American Jeremiad. U. of Wis. Pr. 1978 $32.50. ISBN 0-299-07350-5. Prose study of
 preaching and oratory in the United States.
The Office of the Scarlet Letter. Johns Hopkins 1991 $22.95. ISBN 0-8018-4203-4. Traces
 the mediatory functions of American liberal ideology in the romance.
The Puritan Origins of the American Self. Yale U. Pr. 1975 $25.00. ISBN 0-300-01754-4.
 Examines the theology and intellectual life of New England Puritans; includes a
 bibliography and index.
The Rites of Assent. Routledge 1992 $49.95. ISBN 0-415-90014-X

BERGER, THOMAS (LOUIS). 1924–

Thomas Berger has been gradually building a reputation as a comic and
satiric novelist of exceptional gifts. Born in Cincinnati, he served in the army
from 1943 to 1946, graduated from the University of Cincinnati in 1948, did
graduate work at Columbia, and held several editorial and librarian positions
while beginning his writing career. His Reinhart series—*Crazy in Berlin* (1958),
Reinhart in Love (1962), *Vital Parts* (1970), and *Reinhart's Women* (1981)—
which the *Washington Post* called "a great and unique achievement," follows
the central character, big and clumsy Carlo Reinhart, from youth to middle age.
  Like other writers of black humor, Berger sometimes slips into presenting life
as such a horror that any laughter it may evoke is strained and hollow. For
example, *Killing Time* (1967) is the story of a murderer who thinks that he is
doing his victims a favor by killing them; and *Regiment of Women* (1973) is an
unpleasant fantasy set in a future time when women roam the world like fierce
Amazons raping and abusing men in a not very convincing thesis-novel about
what would happen if the Women's Liberation movement did indeed triumph. A
much more successful blend of horror and comedy is *Little Big Man* (1964),
which won the Rosenthal award of the National Institute of Arts and Letters in
1965. In this best-known of Berger's novels—a fame due in large part to a
successful movie adaptation starring Dustin Hoffman—the author makes good

use of the tall tale. It is a big, sprawling novel about life in the Old West during the nineteenth century. This mock-hero saga gave Berger ample range and scope for his gifts as a satirist. Few writers since the time of SWIFT and POPE have made better use of extravagant caricature and wild exaggeration to expose the foibles and evils of what humanity has done in the name of civilization.

Although Berger claims that he wrote each book in a different style, most of them have in common a strong element of satire and parody. Among his novels, *Who Is Teddy Villanova?* (1977) takes off as a spoof of popular detective novels; *Arthur Rex* (1978) is an irreverent retelling of the Camelot legend, which *Kirkus Reviews* called "the first really astute reworking of the Arthurian story in decades"; and *Neighbors* (1980), one of Berger's personal favorites among his books, is like KAFKA's (see Vol. 2) *The Trial* in showing how "at any moment banality might turn sinister." Berger said of *Neighbors*, "It is for me the absolutely pure fiction that I have lately aspired to, with no taint of journalism, sociology, and the other corruptions." Berger continued his exposé of suburban and small-town America with *The Feud* (1982), a story set in the 1930s.

NOVELS BY BERGER

Arthur Rex. Delacorte 1979 $5.95. ISBN 0-385-28005-X. Comedic reappraisal of the Arthurian legend.

Crazy in Berlin. 1958. Delacorte 1982 o.p.

The Feud. 1982. Delacorte 1983 o.p. A tale about small town life in the late 1930s—families, feuds, and the passions all people hide.

Killing Time. 1967. Little 1990 $9.95. ISBN 0-316-09147-2

Little Big Man. 1964. Delacorte 1989 $9.95. ISBN 0-385-29829-3

Meeting Evil. Little 1992 $19.95. ISBN 0-316-09258-4. Story of suburban realtor John Felton.

Neighbors. 1980. Doubleday 1989 $8.95. ISBN 0-685-52494-9. A morality play about domestic realities.

Nowhere. Delacorte 1985 o.p. The travails of Detective Russell Wren and his investigations.

Orrie's Story. Viking Penguin 1992 $10.00. ISBN 0-14-014994-5. Muddled, modernized tale of the *Oresteia*, casting Agamemnon as a returning World War II veteran ambushed by his murderous wife.

Regiment of Women. 1973. Delacorte 1991 $9.95. ISBN 0-385-28833-6

Reinhart in Love. 1962. Delacorte 1982 o.p.

Reinhart's Women. Delacorte 1981 o.p.

Sneaky People. Little 1990 $10.95. ISBN 0-316-09222-3. A comedic portrait of three people's lives.

Vital Parts. 1970. Little 1982 $10.95. ISBN 0-316-09225-8

Who Is Teddy Villanova? 1977. Delacorte 1989 $8.95. ISBN 0-385-29149-3. Introduces the character of Detective Wren and his investigation of murder in the big city.

BERRYMAN, JOHN. 1914–1972

John Berryman's poetry has a depth and obscurity that discourages readers while it entices critics. His major work, *The Dream Songs* (1969), forms a poetic notebook that captures the ephemera of mood and attitude of this most mercurial of poets. Born John Smith in McAlester, Oklahoma, and educated at Columbia University and Clare College, Cambridge, he later taught at several universities. He received the Shelley Memorial Award (1948), the Harriet Monroe Award (1957), the Loines Award for poetry of the National Institute of Arts and Letters (1964), and the fellowship of the Academy of American Poets (1966). In 1964 he won the Pulitzer Prize in poetry for *77 Dream Songs* (1964). His short story "The Imaginary Jew" received the Kenyon-Doubleday Award and was listed in *Best American Short Stories, 1946*. He also wrote *Stephen Crane* (1950) and is the author of a novel, *Recovery* (1973). In 1972 Berryman committed suicide. Often listed along with SYLVIA PLATH and ANNE SEXTON as a major confessional poet, he was as much concerned with literary artifice as he was with personal revelation.

POETRY BY BERRYMAN

Berryman's Sonnets. FS&G 1967 o.p.

Collected Poems. FS&G 1989 $25.00. ISBN 0-374-12619-4. Contains an introductory essay by Charles Thornbury that provides a biological context for the sonnets, satires, and confessionals.

The Dream Songs. FS&G 1982 $4.95. ISBN 0-374-51670-7

The Freedom of the Poet. FS&G 1976 o.p. Essays about poets and poetry, with a preface by Robert Giroux.

Homage to Mistress Bradstreet and Other Poems. 1956. FS&G 1968 o.p.

Love and Fame. FS&G 1970 o.p. Berryman annotated the second edition, explaining the deletion of some poems and voicing thoughts on the poems in general.

Short Poems. FS&G 1967 o.p. A collection of 64 poems, including "The Dispossessed" (1948) and "Formal Elegy," written in 1963 on the occasion of John F. Kennedy's death.

BOOKS ABOUT BERRYMAN

Haffenden, John. *John Berryman: A Critical Commentary.* NYU Pr. 1980 o.p. A probing look at John Berryman and his work; includes a bibliography and index.

————. *The Life of John Berryman.* Routledge 1982 o.p. An exhaustive—and exhausting—biography.

Kelley, Richard. *John Berryman: A Checklist.* Scarecrow 1972 $20.00. ISBN 0-8108-0552-9. Bibliographic reference tool.

Martz, William J. *John Berryman. Pamphlets on Amer. Writers Ser.* Bks. Demand repr. of 1969 ed. $25.00. ISBN 0-7837-2875-1. An introduction to Berryman's poetry.

BISHOP, ELIZABETH. 1911–1979

In his *N.Y. Times* column, the late Harvey Breit applauded the awarding of the Pulitzer Prize for 1956 to "the peripatetic Massachusetts-born poet, Elizabeth Bishop, Vassar '34, traveler through Europe and Africa, ex-resident of Key West and Mexico, and present dweller in Brazil. We applauded because she . . . once said she was opposed 'to making poetry monstrous or boring and proceeding to talk the very life out of it.' " About *Questions of Travel* (1965), Philip Booth said, "No poet now writing achieves more naturally right notes or greater flexibility in formally structured poems. . . . Bishop's skill is lyrically demonstrated by the 47 quatrains of 'The Burglar of Babylon,' and by the marvelous ease of 'Sestina.' . . . Bishop is not only our most valuable export to Brazil, she is one of the true poets of this, or any, hemisphere" (*Christian Science Monitor*). The *Complete Poems* (1969) won the National Book Award (1970). She also wrote the nonfiction *Brazil* (1967) and with Emanuel Brasil edited *An Anthology of Twentieth Century Brazilian Poetry* (1972) (translated by Paul Blackburn and others). Her influence on other poets was not obvious during her life, but many have tried to emulate her distinctive talent, and her reputation continues to grow.

POETRY BY BISHOP

Complete Poems. FS&G 1969 o.p. Includes: "North and South," "A Cold Spring," "Questions of Travel," "Elsewhere," "Translations from the Portuguese," and new and uncollected works.

The Complete Poems, 1927–1979. FS&G 1984 $11.00. ISBN 0-374-51817-3. Includes the same books of poems as *Complete Poems* plus "Geography III."

WORK BY BISHOP

The Collected Prose. Ed. by Robert Giroux. FS&G 1984 $17.50. ISBN 0-374-12628-3. Contains essays and stories of startling precision and ironic dryness.

BOOKS ABOUT BISHOP

Schwartz, Lloyd, and Sylvia P. Estees. *Elizabeth Bishop and Her Art. Under Discussion Ser.* U. of Mich. Pr. 1983 $32.50. ISBN 0-472-09343-6. An insightful group of essays on Elizabeth Bishop's life and work; includes a foreword by Harold Bloom.

Stevenson, Anne. *Elizabeth Bishop. Twayne's U.S. Authors Ser.* NCUP 1966 $10.95. ISBN 0-8084-0118-1. Comprehensive overview of Bishop's life and work.

BLY, ROBERT. 1926–

Robert Bly lives on a farm in his native state of Minnesota; in Madison, Wisconsin, he edited *The Seventies* magazine, which he founded as *The Fifties* and in the next decade called *The Sixties.* In 1966, with David Ray, he organized American Writers against the Vietnam War. "A pungent critic, an undaunted moralist, a hackled dissenter, he is the sworn enemy of worldliness in the conduct of life and in the conduct of poetry" (*Atlantic*). *The Light around the Body*, which won the National Book Award in 1968, "is strongly critical of the war in Vietnam, of the callousness of American foreign policy in other areas and of the general tenor of American life" (*NY Times*). Since publication of *Iron John: A Book About Men* (1990), his response to the women's movement, Bly has been immensely popular, appearing on talk shows and advising men to retrieve their primitive masculinity through "wildness."

Bly is also a translator of Scandinavian literature, such as *Twenty Poems of Tomas Transtromer.* Through the Sixties Press and the Seventies Press, he has introduced little-known European and South American poets to American readers. His magazines have been the center of a poetic movement involving the poets DONALD HALL, LOUIS SIMPSON, and JAMES WRIGHT.

POETRY BY BLY

American Poetry: Wildness and Domesticity. HarpC 1990 $22.50. ISBN 0-06-016265-1

Iron John: A Book About Men. Addison-Wesley 1990 $19.18. ISBN 0-201-51720-5

The Light around the Body. HarBraceJ 1985 $9.95. ISBN 0-06-090786-X

Loving a Woman in Two Worlds: Love Poems. HarpC 1987 $10.00. ISBN 0-06-097083-9. Poems that examine grief with a gentle honesty.

The Man in the Black Coat Turns: Poems. 1981. HarpC 1988 $10.00. ISBN 0-06-097186-X. Includes 24 introspective, masculine works.

The Morning Glory: Prose Poems. 1969. HarpC 1975 o.p. Twelve prose poems with drawings by Tomi de Paola.

Old Man Rubbing His Eyes. 1973. Unicorn Pr. 4th ed. 1975 $17.50. ISBN 0-87775-050-5. Twenty new poems with 20 drawings by Franz Richter.

The Sea and the Honeycomb. Beacon Pr. 1971 o.p. A book of tiny poems by Quasimodo, D. H. Lawrence, Machado, and Issa, with originals of foreign-language poems at the back of the volume.

Selected Poems. HarpC 1986 $10.00. ISBN 0-06-096048-5. Collection of works inspired by the physical and spiritual nature of living things.

Silence in the Snowy Fields. U. Pr. of New Eng. 1962 $10.95. ISBN 0-8195-1015-7. A collection of delicate nature poems about the Minnesota landscape.

Sleepers Joining Hands (Shadow Mothers). 1970. HarpC 1985 $10.00. ISBN 0-06-090785-1. Poems constructed around the matriarchal consciousness and the idea of motherhood.

This Body Is Made of Camphor and Gopherwood. HarBraceJ 1977 o.p.
This Tree Will Be Here for a Thousand Years. HarBraceJ 1992 $10.00. ISBN 0-06-092278-8. The sequel to *Silence in the Snowy Fields*; includes 44 works.

NONFICTION BY BLY

Talking All Morning. Poets on Poetry Ser. U. of Mich. Pr. 1980 $11.95. ISBN 0-472-15760-4. A collection of essays and interviews.

BOOKS ABOUT BLY

Nelson, Howard. *Robert Bly: An Introduction to the Poetry.* Ed. by John Unterecker. Col. U. Pr. 1984 $31.50. ISBN 0-231-05310-X
Peseroff, Joyce, ed. *Robert Bly: When Sleepers Awake.* U. of Mich. Pr. 1985 $13.95. ISBN 0-472-06354-5. A collection of essays by various critics.

BOGAN, LOUISE. 1897–1970

The cowinner with Leonie Adams of the Bollingen Prize in poetry (1954), Louise Bogan also won the Academy of American Poets Fellowship (1959) and the Brandeis Prize for poetry (1961). Her *Achievement in American Poetry, 1900–1950* (1950) is a spirited book of criticism. Bogan was for many years the poetry critic for the *New Yorker* magazine.

POETRY BY BOGAN

Blue Estuaries: Poems. 1923–1968. *Amer. Poetry Ser.* Ecco Pr. 1977 $8.50. ISBN 0-88001-192-0. Contributions from five decades of her poetry, representing various themes and writing styles.
Poet's Alphabet. McGraw 1970 o.p.

BOOK ABOUT BOGAN

Frank, Elizabeth. *Louise Bogan: A Portrait.* Knopf 1985 $24.95. ISBN 0-394-52484-5. Detailed, insightful, superior full-length biography of Bogan.

BOYLE, T. CORAGHESSAN. 1948–

Born in Peekskill, New York, Boyle originally chose to pursue a career in music. While pursuing his studies, however, he encountered the absurdist, antiheroic works of writers such as EUGENE IONESCO (see Vol. 2), JEAN GENET (see Vol. 2), THOMAS PYNCHON, and JOHN BARTH. As a result, he decided to pursue a literary career instead. Admired for his energetic language, his daring, and his invention, Boyle is considered by many critics to be among the great American humorists writing today. Crafting his novels and stories with a lexicon that has reminded readers of S. J. PERELMAN, Boyle tends to create bizarre situations out of the mundane: in "The Hector Quesadilla Story," published in *Greasy Lake and Other Stories* (1985), Boyle depicts an aging baseball player in a never-ending game; another tale, "Ike and Nina," relates an imaginary love affair between President Eisenhower and Nikita Khrushchev's wife. Like other postmodernists, Boyle mixes history with fantasy, high with low culture, to create a sometimes surrealistic stew. Early criticism of his work faulted Boyle for what some perceived as a superficial quality; more recent novels, however, such as *World's End* and *East is East* reveal Boyle's development as a writer of rich, complex, hilarious worlds.

NOVELS BY BOYLE

Budding Prospects: A Pastoral. 1984. Viking Penguin 1985 $8.95. ISBN 0-14-008151-8. Man involved in multimillion-dollar marijuana-growing scheme.

East is East. Viking Penguin 1990 $19.95. ISBN 0-670-83220-0. The escape of a Japanese
man to America, where he finds himself in a writers' colony.
The Road to Wellsville. 1993. Viking Penguin 1993 $22.50. ISBN 0-670-84334-2. A satire
on America's national obsession with health and nutritional fads.
Water Music. 1981. Viking Penguin 1983 $9.95. ISBN 0-14-006550-4. First novel, about
Mungo Park and a con man in Africa.
World's End. Viking Penguin 1990 $9.95. ISBN 0-14-029993-9. Intersplicing of past and
present history of Dutch family in Westchester.

SHORT STORY COLLECTIONS BY BOYLE

The Descent of Man. 1979. Viking Penguin 1990 $7.95. ISBN 0-14-029994-7. Includes a
title story about the love affair between a woman and a brilliant Nietzshe-reading
chimpanzee.
Greasy Lake and Other Stories. 1985. Viking Penguin 1986 $8.95. ISBN 0-14-007781-2
If the River Was Whiskey: Stories. 1989. Viking Penguin 1990 $8.95. ISBN 0-14-011950-7.
Sixteen tragicomic short stories depicting extremes of social conditions.

BROOKS, CLEANTH. 1906–

Educator and critic Cleanth Brooks was born in Kentucky and educated at
Vanderbilt, Tulane, and Oxford (as a Rhodes scholar). From 1932 to 1947, he
taught English at Louisiana State University and then moved on to Yale. At Yale,
Brooks helped to articulate the principles of New Criticism, which dominated
literary studies in the 1940s and 1950s. The New Criticism argued that the
literary work was an organic, complex whole to be evaluated on its own terms,
without reference to "extraliterary" concerns such as biography, authorial
intention, or historical and social context. Brooks claims that literature's
powers are unique: "The poem is not only the linguistic vehicle that conveys the
thing communicated most 'poetically' . . . it is also the sole linguistic vehicle
which conveys the thing communicated accurately." In Brooks's view, what
determines the force and specialness of literature is irony, created primarily
through paradox and metaphor.

While at Yale, Brooks coedited the journal *Southern Review* with ROBERT
PENN WARREN. He also wrote several classic titles in collaboration with Warren,
including *Understanding Poetry* (1938) and *Understanding Fiction* (1943). A third
work, *Understanding Drama* (1945) was done in collaboration with Robert
Heilman.

NONFICTION BY BROOKS

The Hidden God: Studies in Hemingway, Faulkner, Yeats, Eliot, and Warren. Yale U. Pr.
1963 o.p. Argues that these authors can only be understood "by reference to
Christian premises."
Literary Criticism: A Short History (coauthored with W. K. Wimsatt). 2 vols. U. Ch. Pr.
1983 repr. of 1957 ed. Vol. 1 $17.95. ISBN 0-226-90175-0. Vol. 2 $19.95. ISBN 0-226-
90176-9. A major achievement, giving an informed account of the development of
literary criticism up to its time.
A Shaping Joy: Studies in the Writer's Craft. HarBraceJ 1971 o.p. Relatively straightforward miscellany, mostly lectures.
The Well-Wrought Urn: Studies in the Structure of Poetry. HarBraceJ 1947 o.p. Classic of
literary criticism, in which Brooks reads ten poems, testing for irony, including
Donne's "The Canonization" and Keats's "Ode on a Grecian Urn."

BROOKS, GWENDOLYN. 1917–

Gwendolyn Brooks was born in Topeka, Kansas, and published her first poem
in a children's magazine at age 13. After the publication of her first book of

poetry, *A Street in Bronzeville* (1945), she was chosen as one of 10 Women of the Year by *Mademoiselle* magazine. In 1946 she received an award for creative writing from the American Academy of Arts and Letters and a Guggenheim Fellowship. Early in 1968, Governor Otto Kerner of Illinois appointed her to succeed the late CARL SANDBURG as state poet laureate. Her second book of poems, *Annie Allen* (1949), won the 1950 Pulitzer Prize. A turning point in Brooks's career came with her attendance in 1967 at the Second Black Writers' Conference at Fisk University, where she met AMIRI BARAKA, among others. After that, according to Brooks, she entered a "new consciousness." She moved from her earlier work, which has drawn comparisons to WALLACE STEVENS and EMILY DICKINSON, to a voice that she sees as connecting her to recent African American poets. Brooks won a National Endowment for the Arts award in 1989.

POETRY BY BROOKS

Aloneness. 1971. Broadside Pr. 1971 $5.00. ISBN 0-910296-55-3. Poems for young people about the African American experience.

Annie Allen. 1949. Greenwood 1972 $35.00. ISBN 0-8371-5561-4

Beckonings. Broadside Pr. 1975 $3.00. ISBN 0-910296-37-5. Twelve poems of African American women's experiences.

Blacks. Third World 1991 $36.95. ISBN 0-88378-105-0. Portraits of African Americans in everyday social situations.

Bronzeville Boys and Girls. HarpC 1967 $12.89. ISBN 0-06-020651-9. Thirty-four poems dedicated to the author's children.

Family Pictures. 1970. Broadside Pr. 1970 $5.00. ISBN 0-685-24799-6. Eight poems reflecting familial interpretations of African American consciousness.

Gottschalk and the Grande Tarantelle. Third World 1988 o.p.

In the Mecca. HarpC 1968 o.p. Poems in novelistic form written about the author's secretarial experiences.

The Near-Johannesburg Boy. Third World 1991 $8.95. ISBN 0-88378-055-0

Selected Poems. 1963. HarpC 1963 $6.95. ISBN 0-06-090989-7. This volume includes some poems previously unpublished in book form.

Winnie. Third World 1991 $6.95. ISBN 0-88378-050-X. Reflects Brooks's interest in South Africa.

World of Gwendolyn Brooks. HarpC 1971 o.p. Five notable works by Pulitzer Prize-winner Brooks.

NONFICTION BY BROOKS

Report from Part I. Broadside Pr. 1972 $17.95. ISBN 0-910296-82-0. An autobiography describing significant influences on Brooks's art and life.

BOOKS ABOUT BROOKS

Melhem, D. H. *Gwendolyn Brooks: Poetry and the Heroic Voice.* U. Pr. of Ky. 1987 $12.00. ISBN 0-8131-1605-8. A close reading of Brooks's poetry with emphasis on her themes.

Stanford, Barbara Dodds, and Karima Amin. *Black Literature for High School Students.* NCTE 1978 o.p. Contains a chapter on Brooks, including an interview.

BROWN, STERLING ALLEN. 1901–1989

Brown's contribution to the study of African American culture and literature can hardly be overestimated. He devoted his life as a writer to a development of an authentic black folk literature and his career as a teacher to the education of African American students, especially at Howard University, where he taught for 40 years. He was one of the first to identify folklore as central to the black aesthetic. Brown published his first book of poetry, *Southern Road*, in 1932, but, although this book was well-received, Brown met critical and publishing resistance to his next collection. Discouraged, Brown turned his energies to producing a steady stream of essays, reviews, and sketches about African American life. *Negro Poetry and Drama* and *The Negro in American Fiction*, both published in 1938, are seminal studies; and his anthology of African American literature, *The Negro Caravan* (1941), defined the field as a scholarly and academic discipline. *The Collected Poems* (1980), which contains many early poems never before published, assures Brown's fame as a poet at the same time that it serves as a painful reminder of a gift that was stunted because it was ignored. A first-rate narrative poet and a master of the folk idiom, Brown was, for many, a bridge between nineteenth- and twentieth-century Africans American literature—a writer who helped to define African American literature and experience for blacks and whites alike.

POETRY BY BROWN

The Collected Poems of Sterling A. Brown. 1980. HarpC 1980 $15.95. ISBN 0-06-010517-8. The important collection of a long-neglected poet.

The Last Ride of Wild Bill, and Eleven Narrative Poems. Broadside Pr. 1975 $5.00. ISBN 0-9192906-02-2. Brown's strength as a narrative poet showcased here.

NONFICTION BY BROWN

The Negro in American Fiction. 1937. Ayer 1972 repr. of 1937 ed. $15.00. ISBN 0-405-01851-7

The Negro Caravan. 1941. Ayer 1978 repr. of 1941 ed. $52.95. ISBN 0-405-01852-5

The Negro Newcomers in Detroit and The Negro in Washington (coauthored with George E. Haynes). Ayer 1970 repr. of 1918 ed. $11.00. ISBN 0-405-01926-2

BOOKS ABOUT BROWN

Gabbin, Joane V. *Sterling A. Brown: Building the Black Aesthetic Tradition*. Greenwood 1985 $36.95. ISBN 0-313-23720-4. A critical biography with a comprehensive bibliography.

Wagner, Jean. *Black Poets of the United States*. Trans. by Kenneth Douglas. U. of Ill. Pr. 1973 $12.50. ISBN 0-252-00341-1. Includes an unusually comprehensive chapter on Brown.

BURKE, KENNETH. 1897–

Omnivorously eclectic, Burke has found in the analysis of human symbolic activities a key to the largest cultural issues. For Burke, literature is the most prominent and sophisticated form of "symbolic action," one that provides "equipment for living" by allowing us to try out hypothetical strategies for dealing with the endless variety of human situations and experiences. Human society demands some principle of order, but the language and reason that create order can fall into rigid abstractions that can be destructive and violently imposed. Literature shows us an image of sacrifice, forgiveness, and flexibility that plays an important role in keeping society functioning flexibly. Burke's writing is extensive, complex, and wide ranging, but also unique and uniquely important among current critical approaches.

NONFICTION BY BURKE

Dramatism and Development. Clark U. Pr. 1972 o.p.

A Grammar of Motives. U. CA Pr. 1969 repr. of 1945 ed. $14.95. ISBN 0-520-01544-4. Examines theories of reasoning, knowledge, and semantics.

Language as Symbolic Action: Essays on Life, Literature, and Method. U. CA Pr. 1966
$15.95. ISBN 0-520-00192-3. An annotated collection of essays published over 16
years.
On Symbols and Society. U. Ch. Pr. 1989 $15.95. ISBN 0-226-08078-1. Selections that
consider the relation of Burke's ideas to sociological thought and practice.
Perspectives by Incongruity: Studies in Symbolic Action and Terms for Order. Ed. by
Stanley Edgar Hyman and Barbara Karmiller. Ind. U. Pr. 1964 o.p. Selections from
his criticism and creative writing.
The Philosophy of Literary Form: Studies in Symbolic Action. U. CA Pr. rev. ed. 1974 repr.
of 1941 ed. $15.95. ISBN 0-520-02483-4. A methodical study of issues in literature
and language.
A Rhetoric of Motives. U. CA Pr. 1969 repr. of 1950 ed. $12.95. ISBN 0-520-01546-0.
Continues Burke's ideology of ritualistic drama begun in *Philosophy of Literary Form.*
The Rhetoric of Religion: Studies in Logology. 1961. U. CA Pr. 1970 $12.95. ISBN 0-520-
01610-6. Analyses of Biblical and theological tracts.
Terms for Order. Ed. by Stanley Edgar Hyman and Barbara Karmiller. Bks. Demand repr.
of 1964 ed. $51.50. ISBN 0-685-43702-7. Discusses humankind's use of terminology
and symbols.
Towards a Better Life: Being a Series of Epistles, or Declamations. U. CA Pr. 1966 $32.50.
ISBN 0-520-04638-2. Eloquent introspections on life.

BOOKS ABOUT BURKE

Frank, Armin Paul. *Kenneth Burke. Twayne's U.S. Authors Ser.* Irvington 1969 $17.95.
ISBN 0-89197-996-4. Analyzes Kenneth Burke's works, attempting to find common
themes in his writings.
White, Hayden, and Margaret Brose, eds. *Representing Kenneth Burke: Selected Papers
from the English Institute.* Johns Hopkins 1983 $30.00. ISBN 0-8018-2877-5. An
interesting collection of essays on Burke's writings and personal life.

BURROUGHS, WILLIAM S. 1914–

From hipster to so-called Godfather of Punk, William Burroughs has lived a
controversial life as a leading member of the Beat Generation and a daring
writer of psychedelic literary experiments, but, when he reached his seventieth
birthday in 1984, it was almost as if he had been overtaken by respectability.

Burroughs was born in St. Louis as the grandson of the man who invented the
adding machine and a descendant of the Robert E. Lee of Civil War fame. After
attending Harvard University and while living a bohemian life in association
with such Beat writers as ALLEN GINSBERG and JACK KEROUAC (Burroughs
appears as a character named Old Bull Lee in *On the Road*), he became addicted
to morphine and under the pseudonym William Lee published his first novel,
Junkie, in 1953 as half of an Ace Double Books paperback. Described on the
jacket as "Confessions of an Unredeemed Drug Addict," it escaped critical
notice but may be seen now as the forerunner of his later fiction with its
introduction of many of the themes, settings, characters, and amoral postures
that became prominent with *Naked Lunch* (1959) and its successors. Refused by
the American publishers to whom Burroughs submitted the manuscript, *Naked
Lunch* first appeared in Paris under the Olympia Press imprint in 1959, the same
year that Burroughs was permanently cured of his addiction, and, although the
introduction to the regular Grove Press edition continues to claim that the work
was composed from "a stack of crazed scribblings" that Burroughs found he
had written under the influence of heroin, he admitted to Jennifer Crichton in
Publisher's Weekly, "That was an exaggeration, . . . an *allegory.*" It now seems
apparent that much of the psychedelic effect of Burroughs's fiction is an illusion
that masks rather deliberate methods of composition, which include "cut-out"

techniques, pastiche, and the deliberate trying-out of styles derived from popular fiction genres to create literary montages that owe as much to fantasy and science as to the surrealism of avant-garde literature.

Naked Lunch might have remained ignored if both MARY MCCARTHY and NORMAN MAILER had not called attention to the work at the International Writers Conference held in Edinburgh in 1962. The difficulties experienced by Grove Press as it fought censorship of its first U.S. edition of the work, an important episode of modern literary history fully recounted in a book by Michael Barry Goodman cited below, helped to call public attention to the work, and, although Burroughs's raw subject matter and seeming lack of discipline have alienated some of the more academic and genteel literary critics, he has been assured a loyal audience of appreciative readers ever since. *Naked Lunch* was followed by three additional novels about the Nova crime syndicate—*The Soft Machine* (1961), *The Ticket That Exploded* (1962), and *Nova Express* (1964)—which make use of overlapping characters and motifs. With *The Wild Boys* of 1971, Burroughs began to develop a new style more accessible to the general reader, and, although *Cities of the Red Night* (1981) received mixed reviews, it was praised by such Burroughs experts as Jennie Skerl and Robert Burkholder (*Dictionary of Literary Biography*) as perhaps the best of his more recent novels. Of *The Place of Dead Roads* (1983), Jennifer Crichton said that it "gives no indication of being the work of an older writer. Set in the nineteenth-century West, the novel is true to Burroughs's various obsessions: guns, homosexuality, the writer as 'shootist' blasting into his readers' heads and the terror produced by those addicted to power and control."

NOVELS BY BURROUGHS

Ah Pook Is Here. Riverrun NY 1982 $9.95. ISBN 0-7145-3859-0. Three short stories about time travel and death.

Blade Runner: A Movie. Blue Wind 1979 $6.95. ISBN 0-912652-46-2

The Cat Inside. Viking Penguin 1992 $12.50. ISBN 0-670-84465-9. Full of sentimental anecdotes and bizarre pseudo-scholarly lore.

Cities of the Red Night. H. Holt & Co. 1982 $9.95. ISBN 0-8050-1763-1

Exterminator. 1973. Viking Penguin 1979 $10.00. ISBN 0-14-005003-5. A collection of short pieces examining art as aggressive action and the writer's quest for freedom.

Junky. 1953. Viking Penguin 1977 $10.00. ISBN 0-14-004351-9

The Last Words of Dutch Schultz. Seaver Bks. 1987 $6.95. ISBN 0-8050-0179-4. Compelling portrait of a gangster's last days.

Naked Lunch. 1959. Grove Pr. 1992 $11.95. ISBN 0-8021-3295-2

Nova Express. 1964. Grove Pr. 1992. ISBN 0-8021-3330-4

The Place of Dead Roads. H. Holt & Co. 1985 $9.95. ISBN 0-8050-1541-8

Port of Saints. 1975. Blue Wind 1980 $12.95. ISBN 0-912652-65-9. A fantasy about a man with alternate selves who journeys into space, time, and sexuality.

Roosevelt after Inauguration. City Lights 1979 o.p.

The Soft Machine. 1961. Grove Pr. 1992. ISBN 0-8021-3329-0

(and Brion Gysin). *The Third Mind.* Grove Pr. 1982 o.p. Interview with Burroughs; poems written in different formats.

The Ticket That Exploded. 1962. Grove Pr. 1967 $7.95. ISBN 0-8021-5150-7

The Wild Boys: A Book of the Dead. Grove Pr. 1992. ISBN 0-8021-3331-2. Coolly brilliant, futuristic tale of global warfare.

Three Novels. Grove Pr. 1981 o.p. *The Soft Machine*, bound with *Nova Express* and *The Wild Boys*.

(and Allen Ginsberg). *Yage Letters.* City Lights 1963 $6.95. ISBN 0-87286-004-3

WORKS BY BURROUGHS

The Burroughs File. City Lights 1984 $19.95. ISBN 0-87286-152-X. Miscellaneous essays and sketches.

The Letters of William S. Burroughs, 1945–1959. Ed. by Oliver C. Harris. Viking Penguin 1993 $25.00. ISBN 0-670-81348-6

BOOKS ABOUT BURROUGHS

Burroughs, William S., Jr. *Kentucky Ham.* Overlook Pr. 1984 $15.95. ISBN 0-87951-956-8. Includes reminiscences about his father by a promising writer who died young (1947–1981).

Goodman, Michael Barry. *William S. Burroughs: An Annotated Bibliography of His Works and Criticism. Reference Lib. of the Humanities.* Garland 1975 o.p.

Maynard, Joe, and Barry Miles, eds. *William S. Burroughs, 1953–1973: A Bibliography.* U. Pr. of Va. 1978 $27.50. ISBN 0-8139-0710-1. With an introduction by Allen Ginsberg.

Mottram, Eric. *William Burroughs: Algebra of Need. Critical Appraisals Ser.* Humanities 1977 o.p.

Odier, Daniel. *The Job: Interviews with William Burroughs.* Viking Penguin 1989 $11.00. ISBN 0-14-011882-9. Revised and enlarged edition.

CAPOTE, TRUMAN. 1924–1984

Truman Capote made his special province the exploration of the dividing line between dream and reality, fiction and truth. Even before his first novel, *Other Voices, Other Rooms* (1948), brought him international recognition, he had written several memorable short stories, such as "A Tree of Night," "Master Misery," and "Miriam," which combine romantic pathos with nightmarish horror. The short novel *Breakfast at Tiffany's* (1958), which introduced the delightfully free-spirited Holly Golightly, also marks the transition in Capote's career from his early preoccupation with southern locales and themes to a concern with the sometimes campy, sometimes sophisticated, lives of people associated with the arts, the theater, and high society.

Long before his *In Cold Blood* (1966) helped to make "nonfiction novel" a catchphrase of modern criticism, Capote was experimenting with in-depth reportage through his profiles of celebrities or vividly personal descriptions of interesting places from New Orleans to Soviet Russia. Although such high-level journalism helped develop some of the techniques he was to use in *In Cold Blood*, his previous choice of subjects and his own well-publicized life with "the beautiful people" could not prepare readers for the startling impact of his nonfiction novel. In order to write *In Cold Blood*, the story of a senseless murder of a Kansas family and the background of the two murderers, Capote spent considerable time in the Midwest researching the lives of the victims and becoming close friends with both the police officer credited with solving the crime and the two young men responsible for it. The result is a remarkable and dramatic work. Although *Book Week* was justified in calling it "talented, powerful, and enigmatic" and finding that "the enigma lies in Capote's curious neutrality, in the blank eyes that stare up from the book's pages," it is also true that Capote's seemingly objective detachment only masks a deep compassion for human suffering and weakness. Capote's subsequent campaign against capital punishment testifies to his personal involvement, and Richard Brooks's vivid movie adaptation of *In Cold Blood* was faithful to the novel in emphasizing America's social responsibility for crime as well as the stupidity of this particular killing.

Capote was frequently in the limelight, partly through his appearances on talk shows, partly because of the widely publicized episodes involving drugs and drinking, and when he died suddenly in August 1984 there was much speculation about the unknown whereabouts of a long Proustian novel to be called "Answered Prayers," on which he said he had been working for years. That unfinished manuscript published in 1988 as *Answered Prayers*, as well as the experimental stories in *Music for Chameleons* (1980) will testify to the nature of the new style he was struggling to develop. To the end, Capote was a literary artist who kept challenging himself to find new forms of expression, and it is as one of the finest stylists of twentieth-century American prose literature that he will be remembered.

Novels by Capote

Answered Prayers: The Unfinished Novel. NAL-Dutton 1988 $8.95. ISBN 0-452-26137-6. Treasure trove of gossip about the real-life jetsetters Capote ran with. A novel about an amoral bisexual who has been living on the run.

Breakfast at Tiffany's. Random 1958 $13.95. ISBN 0-394-41770-4

A Christmas Memory. Random 1966 $19.95. ISBN 0-394-41931-6. Traces a month of pre-Christmas doings in Capote's parentless, poor household.

In Cold Blood. Random 1966 $24.95. ISBN 0-394-43023-9

Music for Chameleons. Random 1980 $11.95. ISBN 0-394-50826-2

Other Voices, Other Rooms. 1948. Random 1968 $19.95. ISBN 0-394-43949-X

Works by Capote

The Grass Harp (and *A Tree of Night and Other Short Stories*). 1941–51. NAL-Dutton 1956 $4.95. ISBN 0-451-16777-7. A novel about childhood in a fairy tale atmosphere; also includes romantic short stories exploring the human psyche.

The Selected Writings of Truman Capote. Random 1963 $16.95. ISBN 0-394-44467-1. A selection of 117 titles representing 20 years of his writing, including *Breakfast at Tiffany's*, *The Muses Are Heard*, and parts of *A Tree of Night* and *Local Color*.

Books about Capote

Clarke, Gerald. *Capote: A Biography.* Ballantine 1989 $12.95. ISBN 0-345-36078-8. Depicts the sad sequence of sparkling achievements and overwhelming despair that marked the life of Truman Capote.

Garson, Helen S. *Truman Capote. Lit. and Life Ser.* Continuum 1980 $19.95. ISBN 0-8044-6172-4. Insightful study of Capote's life and literary accomplishments.

Rudisill, Marie, and James C. Simmons. *Truman Capote.* Morrow 1983 o.p.

Stanton, Robert J. *Truman Capote: A Reference Guide.* G. K. Hall 1980 o.p.

Windham, Donald. *Footnote to a Friendship: A Memoir of Truman Capote and Others.* S. Campbell 1983 $40.00. ISBN 0-917366-06-9. A memoir of Capote and others by friends and associates.

CARVER, RAYMOND. 1938–1988

Born in an Oregon logging town, Carver grew up in Yakima, Washington. After marrying at age 19, he moved to California with his wife to attend college there. From California he went to Iowa to attend the Iowa Writers Workshop. Soon, however, he returned to California, where he worked at a number of unskilled jobs before getting a job teaching.

Widely acclaimed as the most important short story writer of his generation, Carver writes about the kind of lower-middle-class people whom he knew growing up. His characters, critic Thomas R. Edwards writes, "are waitresses, mechanics, postmen, high school teachers, factory workers, door-to-door salesmen" with never enough money, leading drab lives. "Of all the writers at work today," observed Ray Anello in *Newsweek*, "Carver may have the most distinctive vision of the working class." Nominated posthumously for both a National Book Critics Circle Award (1988) and a Pulitzer Prize (1989) for *Where I'm Calling From: New and Selected Stories* (1988), Carver is one of a handful of writers credited with reviving the short story form. IRVING HOWE put Carver in the tradition of ERNEST HEMINGWAY and perhaps STEPHEN CRANE, chroniclers of "the American voice of loneliness and stoicism, the native soul locked in this continent's space." Carver's stories tend to be brief, with enigmatic endings; although never erupting, violence is often just below the surface. An air of quiet desperation pervades his stories, as Carver explores the collapse of human relationships in bleak circumstances. In later works, Carver strikes a note of redemption, unheard at the beginning of his career. But for readers who are not attuned to Carver's voice of resignation, these moments may sound sentimental and unconvincing. He died of lung cancer in 1988.

SHORT STORY COLLECTIONS BY CARVER

What We Talk About When We Talk About Love. 1981. Random 1989 $8.95. ISBN 0-679-72305-6. Variations on the theme of marriage and love.

Where I'm Calling From. Random 1989 $11.00. ISBN 0-679-72231-9. Posthumous collection, striking for its less austere style.

Will You Please Be Quiet, Please? 1976. McKay 1992 $10.00. ISBN 0-679-73569-0. Introduces reader to Carver's world, peopled with ordinary characters desperate to break free of their confines.

WORKS BY CARVER

Fires: Essays, Poems, Stories. Random 1989 $9.00. ISBN 0-679-72230-4. A collection of essays, poems, and stories.

No Heroics, Please: Uncollected Writings. Random 1992 $10.00. ISBN 0-679-74007-4

CHEEVER, JOHN. 1912–1982

Although John Cheever's first full-length novel won a National Book Award and his last one a Pulitzer Prize, the publication of *The Stories of John Cheever* in 1978 seemed to cap his career and to establish his reputation as a writer who was at his best with shorter forms of fiction. It was largely on the strength of the collected edition of his stories that he was given the National Medal for Literature at the American Book Awards in 1982. Accepting the award, Cheever said that he had always been devoted to one fundamental thing—the creation of "a page of good prose."

A few months after that presentation Cheever died of cancer. An obituary notice in *Publishers Weekly* offers this summary: "Cheever began his writing career early, moving to New York at age 17 to write fiction rather than attend college. The *New Yorker* accepted his first short story in 1935, and he soon became a regular contributor to that magazine. Altogether he published more than one hundred short stories, in which he explored the personalities and social life of upper-middle-class characters who lived in Manhattan's Upper East Side and the Westchester County and Connecticut suburbs. The stories revolved around spacious homes and apartments, Ivy League schools, the better families, hired help, well-paying jobs, alcohol, adultery, and a simmering but resigned, almost disappointed approach to that life."

Cheever's first novel, *The Wapshot Chronicle* (1958), and its sequel, *The Wapshot Scandal* (1965), evoke his family and youth in New England. Whereas the Wapshot novels celebrate life with reservations, *Bullet Park* (1969) descends to a much more sinister and apocalyptic vision as it centers on the attempted immolation of a child on a church altar. Regeneration is the theme of *Falconer* (1978), a widely acclaimed novel that won a Pulitzer Prize, written after Cheever had been hospitalized following a period of heavy drinking. The book is also the first to reflect his bisexuality, which he openly confessed in his *Journals*, published posthumously in 1991. Cheever's last book, *Oh What a Paradise It Seems* (1983), is a novelette that some critics found a fitting summation of his work. Paul Gray in *Time* saw the book as a kind of "coda" that provides final variations of themes seen in earlier stories, and JOHN UPDIKE, a writer with whom Cheever is frequently compared, classified the work as "an ecological romance, a parable and a tall tale" that reestablished Cheever's links to an American transcendentalist tradition of qualified idealism: "Ever more boldly the celebrant of the grand poetry of life, Cheever, once a taut and mordant chronicler of urban and suburban disappointments, now speaks in the cranky, granular, impulsive, confessional style of our native wise men and exhorters since Emerson" (*New Yorker*).

Susan Cheever's memoir of her father, *Home before Dark*, based in large part on 30 volumes of intimate journals kept by Cheever, became one of the nonfiction bestsellers of 1984. It was praised by reviewers for what Elizabeth Hardwick (*N.Y. Review of Books*) called its "tone of elegiac candor."

NOVELS BY CHEEVER

Bullet Park. 1969. Ballantine 1987 $3.95. ISBN 0-345-35006-5. A philosophical novel examining suburbia.

Falconer. 1977. Ballantine 1985 $3.95. ISBN 0-345-33145-1

Oh What a Paradise It Seems. Random 1992 $8.00. ISBN 0-679-43785-5

The Wapshot Scandal. 1965. HarpC 1989 $7.95. ISBN 0-06-091617-6. Praised for its rich descriptions of contemporary life and its profound, unsentimental portrayal of ugliness, pain, loneliness, and horror.

SHORT STORY COLLECTIONS BY CHEEVER

Some People, Places, and Things That Will Not Appear in My Next Novel. 1961. *Short Story Index Repr. Ser.* Ayer 1961 $15.00. ISBN 0-8369-3449-0. Short stories depicting suburban life.

The Stories of John Cheever. 1978. Ballantine 1985 $6.95. ISBN 0-345-33567-8

WORK BY CHEEVER

The Journals of John Cheever. Knopf 1991 $24.50. ISBN 0-394-57274-2. Drawn from 29 loose-leaf notebooks; spans 35 or so years. Edited by Robert Gottlieb, who had worked closely with Cheever on a number of his novels.

BOOKS ABOUT CHEEVER

Bosha, Francis J. *John Cheever: A Reference Guide*. G. K. Hall 1981 o.p. An annotated bibliography of works discussing Cheever's literature.

Cheever, Susan. *Home Before Dark: A Biographical Memoir of John Cheever*. HM 1984 $15.95. ISBN 0-395-35297-5. A sensitive and revealing portrait of the man and the writer; written by Cheever's daughter and based on 30 volumes of intimate journals kept by Cheever.

Coale, Samuel. *John Cheever*. Continuum 1977 $16.95. ISBN 0-8044-2126-9. A general introduction to Cheever's life and works appropriate for college undergraduates and general readers; contains a bibliography and chronology as well as discussions of major works.

Collins, Robert G. *Critical Essays on John Cheever*. *Critical Essays on Amer. Lit. Ser.* G. K. Hall 1982 $40.00. ISBN 0-8161-8623-5. A collection of essays, analyzing and interpreting Cheever's work and style; includes interviews with Cheever.

Donaldson, Scott. *John Cheever: A Biography*. Random 1988 $22.50. ISBN 0-394-54921-X. Covers in depth the contradictory aspects of the writer's personal life, while also celebrating his achievement as a novelist and writer of short stories.

Hunt, George W. *John Cheever: The Hobgoblin Company of Love*. Bks. Demand repr. of 1983 ed. $87.00. ISBN 0-317-36144-6. An analysis of Cheever's work and style.

Waldeland, Lynne. *John Cheever*. G. K. Hall 1979 $15.95. ISBN 0-8057-7251-0. An introduction to Cheever's life and works with emphasis on his major themes, development as a writer, and literary reputation; contains a chronology and bibliography.

CLAMPITT, AMY. 1920–

Clampitt was born in Iowa and educated at Grinnell College and Columbia University. While honing her craft, she worked in New York City for Oxford University Press, the National Audubon Society, and E. P. Dutton. Clampitt's first full-length poetry collection, *The Kingfisher* (1983), appeared when she was 63 years old. It was a dazzling debut, inspiring critics to rank her with EMILY DICKINSON and ELIZABETH BISHOP. Elegant, erudite, and allusive, Clampitt's poetry is characterized by a profusion of unusual words used in unusual ways. Clampitt engages in a kind of romance with language, so that even the best educated reader may need to keep a dictionary handy while reading her work. Modern critics agree, however, that Clampitt's work is well worth the effort.

POETRY BY CLAMPITT

Archaic Figure. Knopf 1987 $15.95. ISBN 0-394-55010-3. Inspired by figures of Greek myth.

The Kingfisher. Knopf 1983 $15.95. ISBN 0-394-52840-9

What the Light Was Like. Knopf 1985 $14.95. ISBN 0-394-54318-1. Ranged around images of light and darkness.

COOVER, ROBERT. 1932–

Robert Coover is a midwesterner who has earned a reputation as one of the most innovative of contemporary writers of fiction. Coover likes to experiment with an abundance of differing styles, and his stories are marked by clever ingenuity and sometimes dizzying displays of verbal pyrotechnics. *The Origin of the Brunists* (1966), his first novel, is a religious parable heavily loaded with symbolism and mythical parallels. It deals with the rise following an Appalachian coal-mine disaster of a sect of worshipers made up of fundamentalists and theosophists whose leader, Giovanni Bruno, is less a preacher than a silent enigma. The principal analogue is apparently meant to be the founding of the Christian religion, but Coover's extensive irony requires that he reverse many of the traditional features of the Christian legend. *The Universal Baseball Association* (1968), Coover's most accessible novel to date, is also dominated by religious symbolism. Over the years, J. Henry Waugh, a middle-aged bachelor and accountant, has developed an elaborately structured game, which he plays with dice. His game is based on the mathematical probabilities of baseball. Every evening Henry plays his game and maintains his extensive record books. "There are box scores to be audited," he explains to a friend, "trial balances of averages along the way, seasonal inventories, rewards and punishments to be meted out, life histories to be overseen." J. Henry Waugh is thus a surrogate for God, and the participants in his imaginary baseball league seem almost to come to life, raising as they do age-old questions about fate and free will, success and failure, games and religions.

Coover's *Pricksongs and Descants* (1969) is a collection of 20 short pieces and a theoretical "Prologo" in which the author states his belief that contemporary fiction should be based on familiar historical or mythical forms not in the way of modernist works like JAMES JOYCE's *Ulysses* or T. S. ELIOT's *The Waste Land*, which simply use myths as a means of providing an arbitrary, skeletal framework. This framework has no particular thematic importance but is used only in order to break through the mythical forms and thus expose them, leading the reader to a kind of revelation. Most of the stories in this volume, which was well received by critics, are based on biblical episodes or classical fairy tales retold in startling new ways.

The Public Burning (1977), based on the controversial trial of the Rosenbergs, is a hard-to-classify work in which an essentially tragic story is told in a broadly comic manner. *A Political Fable* is "a kind of warm-up exercise for 'The Public Burning,' " though it did not appear until afterward: "Published in book form by Viking to coincide with the 1980 election year, 'A Political Fable' remains a dazzling, often hilarious spoof of America's circuslike political operations" (*Dictionary of Literary Biography Yearbook*).

With the exception of a novel, *A Night at the Movies* (1992), Coover's publications in recent years have consisted mainly of shorter works, written at various stages of his career, published in limited editions to appeal to collectors.

NOVELS BY COOVER

The Origin of the Brunists. 1966. Norton 1989 $10.95. ISBN 0-393-30600-3
Pinocchio in Venice: A Novel. S & S Trade 1991 $19.95. ISBN 0-671-64471-8
The Universal Baseball Association, J. Henry Waugh, Prop. 1968 NAL-Dutton 1971 $8.95.
    ISBN 0-452-26030-2

SHORT STORY COLLECTIONS BY COOVER

In Bed One Night and Other Brief Encounters. Burning Deck 1983 o.p.
A Night at the Movies: or You Must Remember This. Dalkey Arch. 1992 repr. of 1987 ed.
    $9.95. ISBN 1-56478-016-3. A collection of short fiction depicting various scenes in
    movies.
Pricksongs and Descants. 1969. NAL-Dutton 1989 $7.95. ISBN 0-317-02809-X. A collec-
    tion of fictional narration.

BOOKS ABOUT COOVER

Andersen, Richard. *Robert Coover*. Twayne's U.S. Authors Ser. G. K. Hall 1981 o.p. An
    analysis of Coover's work.
Gordon, Lois. *Robert Coover: The Universal Fictionmaking Process*. Crosscurrents Modern
    Critiques New Ser. S. Ill. U. Pr. 1983 $16.95. ISBN 0-8093-1092-9. A review of
    Coover's work.
McCaffery, Larry. *The Metafictional Muse: The Work of Robert Coover, Donald Barthelme,
    and William Gass*. Critical Essays in Modern Lit. Ser. U. of Pittsburgh Pr. 1982 $32.95.
    ISBN 0-8229-3462-0. Interprets the works of three writers of experimental fiction.

CORSO, GREGORY. 1930–

In 1957 ALLEN GINSBERG wrote of Corso, "He's probably the greatest poet in America, and he's starving in Europe." According to Derek Parker, Corso is a "more introverted poet than Ginsberg. . . . [He] combines in his work an unlikely mixture of street language and slang with lofty poetic rhetoric." KENNETH REXROTH describes Corso as "a genuine naif. A real wildman with all the charm of a hoodlum . . . a wholesome Antonin Artaud, or a 'sincere' Tristan Tzara." Corso's themes are death and beauty, always in American terms.

Virtually an orphan, Corso was born on Bleecker Street in New York's Greenwich Village. He spent his childhood and youth in and out of foster homes. During his numerous prison terms, he was introduced to literature by a fellow convict. On his release, he met Ginsberg, who immediately recognized his talent and helped him.

POETRY BY CORSO

Elegiac Feelings American. New Dir. Pr. 1970 $3.95. ISBN 0-8112-0026-4. A collection of poems.

Gasoline, The Vestal Ladies on Brattle. Pocket Poets Ser. City Lights 1992 repr. of 1958 ed. $6.95. ISBN 0-87286-088-4. A volatile and combustible collection of "New American Poetry"; includes an introduction by Allen Ginsberg.

The Happy Birthday of Death. New Dir. Pr. 1960 $5.95. ISBN 0-8112-0027-2. A collection of poems.

Long Live Man. New Dir. Pr. 1962 $7.95. ISBN 0-8112-0025-6. Poems celebrating the wonders of being alive.

COZZENS, JAMES GOULD. 1903–1978

Cozzens had earned a solid reputation as a novelist before the appearance of *By Love Possessed* (1957), but that bestseller and Book-of-the-Month Club selection seemed to establish him as a major American writer. In 1960 he was awarded the Howells Medal of the American Academy of Arts and Letters for *By Love Possessed*. In the years since then, however, Cozzens has seemed to "plateau out"; his works may deserve respect for their craft and moral vision, but Cozzens's critical stature has not grown appreciably. The fact that he was guilty of writing a bestselling novel with "love" in its title may have caused some reviewers of his later works to question his artistic integrity, but a more likely explanation for the decline of readership is that, because Cozzens usually chose to write on topical subjects, his novels now seem dated.

Whatever the reasons, several of his main works of fiction have been allowed to go out of print. His first novel, *Confusion* (1924), is a romantic story written when Cozzens was a sophomore at Harvard University. He left college without graduating, produced three more youthful adventure stories, and then produced *S.S. San Pedro* in 1931. The first of his works that Cozzens saw as deserving of serious attention, that novel is the story of how disaster at sea tests the seamanship and character of his protagonists.

Even before he wrote his sea novel, Cozzens had been concerned with what was to be his main theme—how people are tested by their professions. Both *Cock Pit* (1928) and *The Son of Perdition* (1929) deal with the Cuban sugar industry, while Cozzens's later "occupational" novels include *The Last Adam* (1933), which is devoted to medicine; *Men and Brethren* (1936), about the ministry; *The Just and the Unjust* (1942) and *By Love Possessed*, about the law; the Pulitzer Prize-winning *Guard of Honor* (1948) about the army air force; and *Morning, Noon and Night* (1968), about the business world.

NOVELS BY COZZENS

By Love Possessed. 1957. HarBraceJ 1957 $8.50. ISBN 0-15-115113-X

A Flower in Her Hair. Bruccoli 1974 $45.00. ISBN 0-89723-011-6. About a girl's resentment that her older sister has become interested in boys.

Guard of Honor. 1948. HarBraceJ 1964 $8.95. ISBN 0-15-637609-1

The Last Adam. 1933. Carroll & Graf 1986 $4.95. ISBN 0-88184-210-9

Men and Brethren. 1936. I. R. Dee 1989 $7.95. ISBN 0-929587-08-1

A Rope for Dr. Webster. Bruccoli 1976 $55.00. ISBN 0-89723-010-8. Deals with the 1849 execution of Harvard professor John Webster for the murder of Dr. George Parkman.

BOOKS ABOUT COZZENS

Bracher, Frederick G. *The Novels of James Gould Cozzens.* Greenwood 1972 repr. of 1959 ed. o.p. An analysis of Cozzens's novels and technique.

Bruccoli, Matthew J. *James Gould Cozzens: A Descriptive Bibliography. Pittsburgh Ser. in Bibliography.* U. of Pittsburgh Pr. 1981 $65.00. ISBN 0-8229-3435-3. A comprehensive bibliography of all books, pamphlets, periodicals, translations, movies, and books about Cozzens.

_____. *James Gould Cozzens: A Life Apart.* HarBraceJ 1984 $9.95. ISBN 0-15-645952-3. Standard biography by the scholar and bibliophile who has done most to keep Cozzens's reputation alive.

_____, ed. *James Gould Cozzens: New Acquist of True Experience. Crosscurrents Modern Critiques Ser.* S. Ill. U. Pr. 1979 o.p. Critical appreciations and studies.

CREELEY, ROBERT. 1926–

Robert Creeley belongs to the Black Mountain group of poets, who came to know each other while teaching or studying at Black Mountain College. He is a former editor of the *Black Mountain Review.*

Creeley was born in Massachusetts, attended Harvard University, and has lived abroad in France, Spain, and Guatemala. During World War II, he served in the American Field Service in India and Burma. In 1960 he won the Levinson Prize for a group of 10 poems published in *Poetry.* He has also won the Shelley Award (1981) and the Frost Medal (1987), both from the Poetry Society of America. Creeley has written a novel, *The Island* (1963), concerning the shifting marital moods of an American husband and wife in Mallorca, where Creeley himself once ran Divers Press; as well as a collection of short stories, *The Gold Diggers* (1954). He also has taught English at the University of New Mexico in Albuquerque and at the State University of New York at Buffalo. Creeley's work has allegiances to the indigenous American tradition that reaches back to EMILY DICKINSON and HENRY DAVID THOREAU. His *Selected Poems* (1991) is an important testament to a career of integrity molded out of self-doubt and self-knowledge. Few other poets have so trusted their voice, in the physical and psychological sense, to provide them with their only theme and their only defense.

POETRY BY CREELEY

Charm: Early and Uncollected Poems. Writing Ser. Four Seasons Foun. 1969 o.p. Contains 75 poems and a preface by Creeley.

Collected Poems. U CA Pr. 1983 o.p. A collection of poems, including "The Charm," "Words," "In London," and "For Love and Pieces."

For Love: Poems, 1950–1960. Scribner 1962 o.p. Poems focusing on use of language and human relationships.

Later. New Dir. 1979 $5.95. ISBN 0-8112-0736-6. Poems of interior exploration rooted in everyday sights and sounds.

Memory Gardens. New Dir. Pr. 1986 $15.95. ISBN 0-8112-0973-3. Poems about recollections of life.

Mirrors. New Dir. 1983 $6.95. ISBN 0-8112-0877-X. Poems about love and loss, birth and death.

Selected Poems. New Dir. Pr. 1991 $25.00. ISBN 0-5200-6935-8

WORKS BY CREELEY

Hello: A Journal, Feb. 29–May 3, 1976. New Dir. Pr. 1978 o.p. An unusual and experimental book.

A Quick Graph: Collected Notes and Essays. Four Seasons Foun. 1970 o.p. Nonfictional prose, with notes on Creeley's poetry.

BOOKS ABOUT CREELEY

Ford, Arthur L. *Robert Creeley.* Twayne 1978 o.p.

Novik, Mary. *Robert Creeley: An Inventory.* Bks. Demand repr. of 1973 ed. $59.30. ISBN 0-8357-5578-9. A bibliographical catalog of all writings by and about Creeley.

Wilson, John, ed. *Robert Creeley's Life and Work: A Sense of Increment.* U. of Mich. Pr. 1988 $32.50. ISBN 0-472-09374-6. A collection of responses to Creeley's work over the last 40 years by other poets, reviewers, and critics.

DE MAN, PAUL. 1919–1983

Born and educated in Europe, De Man moved to the United States in 1947 and earned his doctorate at Harvard University. His critical essays of the 1950s are chiefly indebted to the existential philosophy of JEAN-PAUL SARTRE (see Vols. 2 and 4). During the early 1960s, he gradually developed the view that the operations of language, especially devices like metaphor and irony, subvert a text's apparent statement. Literature differed from other kinds of language in its awareness of this fact, in its recognition of its own "fictional" status. Other kinds of writers, he argued, struggle endlessly to fix their meaning in words, which despite their efforts endlessly give rise to varying understanding. The whole point of literature, on the other hand, is to create exactly this endless stream of reading, re-reading, and interpretation. De Man's critical position came to be called "deconstruction," and is strikingly similar to the views of the prominent French philosopher JACQUES DERRIDA (see Vol. 4). His essays are difficult and closely argued, but penetrating and widely influential. After De Man's death, revelations about early writings that were sympathetic to the Nazis shattered his reputation. Critics of deconstruction claimed a connection between De Man's revision of his own past with his literary theories about the absence of reality outside of texts.

BOOKS BY DE MAN

Allegories of Reading. Yale U. Pr. 1979 $15.00. ISBN 0-300-02845-8. An analysis of romanticism in the literature of Rilke, Rousseau, Nietzsche, and Proust.

Blindness and Insight: Essays in the Rhetoric of Contemporary Criticism. Theory and History of Lit. Ser. U. of Minn. Pr. 2nd rev. ed. 1983 $15.95. ISBN 0-8166-1135-1. Essays on American and European critics and issues.

The Rhetoric of Romanticism. Col. U. Pr. 1986 $16.50. ISBN 0-231-05527-7. A collection of essays on European romantic and postromantic literature.

DICKEY, JAMES. 1923–

James Dickey is an eccentric personality and one of the most audible voices in poetry the United States produced in the 1960s. Born in Atlanta, Georgia, Dickey was a pilot in World War II and the Korean War. He spent six years in advertising and gave it up in 1961. He was educated at Vanderbilt University and has taught at Rice University and the University of Florida. He has been poet-in-residence at Reed and San Fernando State colleges, writer-in-residence at the University of Wisconsin, and consultant in poetry in English to the Library of Congress (1966–68). He has received honorary degrees from 13 American universities.

In addition to poetry, Dickey is the author of several collections of critical essays, among them *The Suspect in Poetry* (1964); *Babel to Byzantium: Poets and Poetry Now*, which discusses some 80 contemporary British and American poets; *The Self as Agent* (1970); *Sorties: Journals and New Essays* (1972). Recent works collect his interviews, essays, conversations, and commencement addresses. Dickey's first novel, *Deliverance* (1969), became a major motion picture, featuring an appearance by Dickey himself as a backwoods sheriff. In 1976, Dickey composed a poem for the inauguration of President Jimmy Carter. A daring poet, who reminds some readers of MELVILLE in his strivings for an epic quality, Dickey tries "to give each cluster of words its own fierce integrity."

POETRY BY DICKEY

Buckdancer's Choice. Wesleyan U. Pr. 1965 $10.95. ISBN 0-8195-1028-9

The Central Motion: Poems, 1968–1983. Wesleyan U. Pr. 1983 $30.00. ISBN 0-8195-5091-4. Three major works: "Eye-beaters," "Zodiac," and "Strength of Fields."

Drowning with Others. Wesleyan U. Pr. 1962 o.p. Poems about Dickey's own life, his obsessions, possessions, and renunciations.

Falling: May Day Sermon and Other Poems. Wesleyan U. Pr. 1982 $17.00. ISBN 0-8195-5060-4. A collection of new long-line verse poems.

Helmets. Wesleyan U. Pr. 1964 o.p. Poems about life experiences.

Poems 1957–1967. 1968. Wesleyan U. Pr. 1978 $12.95. ISBN 0-8195-6055-3. Selections of poems from major works, including "Into the Stone," "Drowning with Others," "Helmets," and "Buckdancers Choice."

Puella. Doubleday 1982 o.p. Poems recreating the childhood of Dickey's wife.

The Strength of Fields. Doubleday 1979 o.p. Includes a title poem written for President Carter's inauguration; shows Dickey's populist spirit in its purest form.

Whole Motion: Collected Poems, 1945–1992. U. Pr. of New Eng. $29.95. ISBN 0-8195-2202-3. Poems that praise the landscape of Dickey's native South, linger over memories of war, and relish the contest of hunting and the pleasure of sleeping outdoors.

The Zodiac. Doubleday 1976 o.p. Poems about the experiences of a real-life Dutch sailor who was possessed by the mysteries of the zodiac.

NONFICTION BY DICKEY

Self-Interviews. 1970. Ed. by Barbara Reiss and James Reiss. La. State U. Pr. 1984 $9.95. ISBN 0-8071-1141-4. The poet's criticism of his own work and his opinions on the work of others.

Sorties. La. State U. Pr. 1984 $9.95. ISBN 0-8071-1140-6. More of Dickey's opinions about other writers.

BOOKS ABOUT DICKEY

Ashley, Franklin. *James Dickey: A Checklist*. Bruccoli o.p. A list of all of the books and pamphlets by Dickey up to 1972.

Bowers, Neal. *James Dickey: The Poet as Pitchman*. U. of Mo. Pr. 1985 $8.95. ISBN 0-8262-0459-7. Brief and often insightful introduction to the major features of Dickey's poems.

Bruccoli, Matthew J., and Judith S. Baughman. *James Dickey: A Descriptive Bibliography*. U. of Pittsburgh Pr. 1990 $95.00. ISBN 0-8229-3629-1. Identifies the first appearance in print of everything he wrote, and includes descriptive information essential to establishing the pedigree of the editions.

Kirschten, Robert. *James Dickey and the Gentle Ecstasy of Earth: A Reading of the Poems*. La. State U. Pr. 1988 $30.00. ISBN 0-8071-1405-7. Endeavors to provide a satisfactory account of the multiple sources of the energy and power of Dickey's poetic vision.

Weigl, Bruce, and T. R. Hammer, eds. *The Imagination as Glory: Essays on the Poetry of James Dickey*. Madison Bks. UPA 1984 $24.95. ISBN 0-252-01101-5. Writings on Dickey and his work.

DIDION, JOAN. 1934–

A novelist and essayist known for her clear-eyed analyses of the American social and political scene, Didion is probably best understood as a moralist. Her characters always realize a moral dimension in their lives, even as they flirt with chaos. A major theme in Didion's work is the disintegration of order, associated with the past and tradition, as suggested by her taking W. B. YEATS's famous phrase—"slouching towards Bethlehem"—as the title of a collection of essays. Newspaper headlines, popular ballads, Hollywood jargon, and the symbols of a Christian upbringing (again, as indicated by her use of Yeats) recur throughout her work. Born in California, Didion set her earliest novels there; later, her evocations of other countries—notably Latin America and Southeast Asia—are haunted by the policies and culture of the United States. She is married to the writer John Gregory Dunne.

Novels by Didion

A Book of Common Prayer. 1977. FS&G 1977 o.p. Experiences of a San Francisco Pollyana in an archetypal banana republic.
Play It As It Lays. 1970. FS&G 1990 $8.95. ISBN 0-374-52171-9. Corrosion of culture in Los Angeles, portrayed through the disintegration of one woman's life.

Nonfiction by Didion

After Henry. S & S Trade 1992 $22.00. ISBN 0-671-71731-1. What it's like for Didion to write after the death of her longtime editor.
Slouching Towards Bethlehem. 1968. FS&G 1990 $10.00. ISBN 0-374-52171-7. Short essays, concerning film, the West, the 1960s.
The White Album. 1979. FS&G 1990 $10.00. ISBN 0-374-52221-9. Recollection of the 1960s and the events that shaped that generation.

DOCTOROW, E(DGAR) L(AURENCE). 1931–

That E. L. Doctorow is a professional writer in the best sense may be indicated by the fact that he has yet to write two books alike. A New Yorker by birth and schooling, he prepared himself for the writing trade by attending Kenyon College when its literary program under JOHN CROWE RANSOM was at full crest, going on to graduate work at Columbia University, and working as a script reader for Columbia Pictures before becoming an editor with New American Library and Dial Press. Among other works, he has written a serious western novel, a science fiction fantasy, a play, a collection of short stories, and three novels of quite different types, one of which includes a considerable amount of poetry.

The practice in mixing the real with the fictional that Doctorow gained by writing *The Book of Daniel* (1971) was put to effective and spectacular use in *Ragtime* (1975). He interweaves the stories of three families, one WASP, one Jewish, and one African American, with one another and with such historical figures as J. P. Morgan, Houdini, FREUD (see Vols. 3 and 5), JUNG (see Vol. 5), SCOTT JOPLIN (see Vol. 3), and Thomas Edison. These real people involve themselves with the problems of the fictional people, and by the time the novel is concluded most readers feel that the fictional character Coalhouse Walker, for instance, must have actually existed since he was so dramatically involved with people we remember from the history books. This ingenious fusion of fact and fiction annoyed such readers as Paul Levy (*Books and Bookmen*), who found that the characters who bear the famous names in the novel "are not historical personages; they are merely pawns in Doctorow's particularly dotty and tasteless game of chess." But other reviewers and a multitude of plain readers seemed to agree with Eliot Fremont-Smith (*The Village Voice*), who called the book "a bag of riches, totally lucid and accessible, full of surprises, epiphanies, little time-bombs that alter one's view of things, and enormous fun to read."

Doctorow's more recent books of fiction have not had the impact of *Ragtime*, but they show him continuing to experiment with form and style. *Loon Lake* (1980), set in the time of the Great Depression, takes a young drifter named Joe Korzeniowski (JOSEPH CONRAD's original name in Poland) to an opulent residence in the Adirondacks of an industrial magnate and his wife, a famous aviator. Joe's tale of his picaresque wanderings among carnival people is juxtaposed with the questionable stability of the Loon Lake resort, and the novel seems rather heavily loaded with symbols of rebirth and regeneration. Doctorow's frequent shifting point of view as well as his juggling of prose, poetry, and "computerese" make *Loon Lake* sometimes seem rather like the joint effort of a very talented class in creative writing. It may be no accident that Doctorow next tried his hand at a series of carefully wrought and deceptively simple short fiction that seems very traditional by comparison. The novella and six stories in *Lives of the Poets* (1984) are almost Chekhovian in their quiet, muted tone, but their use of recurring images and other interweaving devices would suggest that much is operating beneath the surface. *World's Fair* (1985) is an autobiographical novel, and *Billy Bathgate* (1991), about gangster Dutch Schultz, are Doctorow's most recent works.

NOVELS BY DOCTOROW

Billy Bathgate. HarpC 1991 $5.99. ISBN 0-06-100331-X
The Book of Daniel. Random 1971 $14.95. ISBN 0-394-46271-8
Lives of the Poets: Six Stories and a Novella. Random 1984 $14.95. ISBN 0-394-52530-2
Loon Lake. Random 1992 $10.00. ISBN 0-679-73625-5
Ragtime. Random 1975 $21.95. ISBN 0-394-46901-1
Welcome to Hard Times. 1960. Random 1975 $9.95. ISBN 0-394-73107-7. An ironic tale of life on the American frontier.
World's Fair. Random 1992 $11.00. ISBN 0-679-73628-X

BOOK ABOUT DOCTOROW

Trenner, Richard, ed. *E. L. Doctorow: Essays and Conversations*. Ontario Rev. NJ 1983 $9.95. ISBN 0-86538-024-4. Nine critical assessments in addition to several personal statements by Doctorow and three interviews.

DORN, EDWARD. 1929–

One of the "younger" Black Mountain poets, Edward Dorn was a student of ROBERT CREELEY and CHARLES OLSON. His work is not so much influenced by the Black Mountain school as it is integral to it. A deep sense of the necessities of speech patterns transmitted by projective verse and geography, myth, and prehistoric times puts Dorn particularly close to the work and thought of Olson. In fact, Olson compiled his *Bibliography for Ed Dorn* to reflect this interest in the latter three subjects. Like Olson, Dorn finds his greatest challenge and accomplishment in the long poem. His *Gunslinger* (1968–69) series of books—a continuing epic of the American West ostensibly in a satiric-comic mode but actually a deep expression of the poet's concern with the idea of hero and "free ego"—is already a landmark.

POETRY BY DORN

The Collected Poems, 1956–1974. *Writing Ser.* Four Seasons Foun. 1975 $15.00. ISBN 0-87704-029-X. A collection of sketches, narratives, travelogues, lyrics, and satires.
Geography. Telegraph Bks. 1964 o.p. Poems about American politics.
Gunslinger. 1968–69. Duke 1989 $24.95. ISBN 0-8223-0964-5
Hands Up. Ed. by LeRoi Jones. Corinth Bks. 1964 o.p. Poems on American culture.
The North Atlantic Tribune. Telegraph Bks. 1967 o.p. Political poems about the struggle to come to terms with Western civilization.

NONFICTION BY DORN

Interviews. Ed. by Donald Allen. *Writing Ser.* Four Seasons Foun. 1980 $5.00. ISBN 0-87704-038-9. Very distinctive views about contemporary poetry.

DOVE, RITA. 1952–

A concern with history underlies Dove's poetry. Figures such as Schumann, Catherine of Alexandria, BOCCACCIO (see Vol. 2), and SHAKESPEARE make their appearance in her works. She also explores the history of the African American experience from slavery to the present. Using the individual to explore the collective history of African Americans, Dove wrote about the lives of her grandparents from courtship to death in the Pulitzer Prize-winning *Thomas and Beulah* (1986). In these and other works, she depicts the African American's determination and spirit in the face of racism.

A recipient of numerous awards and fellowships, Dove is currently a professor of English at the University of Virginia and, since 1987, has served as commissioner at the Schomburg Center for the Preservation of Black Culture, New York Public Library. In 1993 she was named to the post of Poet Laureate.

POETRY BY DOVE

Grace Notes. Norton 1989 $16.95. ISBN 0-393-02719-8. Poems that blend chiseled imagery, everyday observation, private dramas, and political comment.
Thomas and Beulah. Carnegie-Mellon 1987 $6.95. ISBN 0-88748-021-7. The story of Dove's grandparents, from courtship to death.
The Yellow House on the Corner. Carnegie-Mellon 1989 $10.95. ISBN 0-88748-092-6. Explores history of African American experience.

SHORT STORY COLLECTION BY DOVE

Fifth Sunday. U. Pr. of Va. 1985 $8.95. ISBN 0-8139-1308-X. Fictional accounts of the struggles of African Americans.

DUGAN, ALAN. 1923–

The *Saturday Review* said of *Poems* (1961), the first volume by the native New Yorker Alan Dugan: "His poetry is a special way of looking at things. . . . Through personal experience of war he shapes universal messages, while he takes history, religion, and mythology and gives them an intimate meaning." This book won the National Book Award and the Pulitzer Prize in 1962, and in the same year the poet won a fellowship in literature at the American Academy in Rome. The *New York Times* found that in *Poems 2* (1963), Dugan reveals "a sharp eye for the sights and sounds of New York." In *Poems 3*, Dugan "writes with an anger at society that moves from artless outcry to black resignation in the face of the world's evils, and back again" (*Saturday Review*).

POETRY BY DUGAN

New and Collected Poems, 1961–1983. Amer. Poetry Ser. Ecco Pr. 1985 $9.50. ISBN 0-88001-085-1. Poems from three earlier books: *Poems, Poems 2,* and *Poems 3.*

Poems. Yale Ser. of Younger Poets. AMS Pr. repr. of 1961 ed. $18.00. ISBN 0-404-53857-6. Foreword by Dudley Fitts.

Poems 6. Ecco Pr. 1989 $17.95. ISBN 0-88001-199-8

DUNCAN, ROBERT (EDWARD). 1919–

A leading poet of the San Francisco renaissance, Robert Duncan is a member of the international avant-garde. Born in Oakland, California, he has been an editor, a teacher at Black Mountain College, and assistant director of the Poetry Center at San Francisco State College. Highly regarded by fellow nonacademic poets, Duncan's poetry is at once learned and spontaneous. Its form seems at once innate and wrought, complex, and wonderfully musical.

He received the Harriet Monroe Memorial Prize (1960); a Guggenheim Memorial Award (1963); the Levinson Poetry Prize (1964); a National Endowment for the Arts grant (1967); and the Eunice Tietjens Memorial Prize (1967). After a self-imposed silence of many years, Duncan published a challenging volume in 1984, *The Ground Work,* a book he designed himself. He continues to be one of the chief advocates for the poem as "wisdom literature" and not just personal expression or artifact.

POETRY BY DUNCAN

Bending the Bow. New Dir. Pr. 1968 $4.95. ISBN 0-8112-0033-7. Personal epic of humankind's spirit in history.

The Ground Work: Before the War. New Dir. Pr. 1984 $10.50. ISBN 0-8112-0896-6

The Ground Work II: In the Dark. New. Dir. Pr. 1988 $19.95. ISBN 0-8112-1042-1. Poems that speak directly about childhood.

The Opening of the Field. 1960. New Dir. Pr. rev. ed. 1973 $6.95. ISBN 0-8112-0480-4. A collection of short lyrics.

Roots and Branches. 1964. New Dir. Pr. 1969 $4.95. ISBN 0-8112-0034-5. Lyrics about the monarch butterfly.

Selected Poems. New Dir. Pr. 1993 $22.95. ISBN 0-8112-1227-0

The Years as Catches: First Poems. 1966. Oyez 1977 $3.00. ISBN 0-685-80007-5. Duncan's first poems (1939–1946) with a retrospective introduction by the poet.

BOOKS ABOUT DUNCAN

Bertholf, Robert. *Robert Duncan: A Descriptive Biography.* Black Sparrow 1986 $65.00. ISBN 0-87685-620-2. Reveals Duncan's major contribution to poetry and his versatility.

Bertholf, Robert, and Ian W. Reid, eds. *Robert Duncan: Scales of the Marvelous.* New Dir. Pr. 1979 $5.95. ISBN 0-8112-0735-8. Essays and tributes to Duncan and his work.

Ironwood 22: Robert Duncan—A Special Issue. Includes part of Duncan's book on H. D. (Hilda Doolittle), plus important Duncan letters and essays by several critics.

EBERHART, RICHARD. 1904–

Born in Minnesota and educated at Dartmouth College and Cambridge (on a Rhodes Scholarship) and Harvard universities, Richard Eberhart has served as consultant in poetry at the Library of Congress (1959–66), and has won the Bollingen Prize (1962) and the Pulitzer Prize (1966). DAME EDITH SITWELL remarked of his poems that they have "strong intellectual sinews, are poems of ideas, but have a warmth of humanity as strong as their intellect." He is a member of the National Institute of Arts and Letters.

POETRY BY EBERHART

Collected Poems 1930–1986. OUP 1988 $35.00. ISBN 0-19-504055-4. Fifty poems that find Eberhart as philosophical, as romantic, as readable as ever.

The Long Reach: New and Uncollected Poems 1948–1984. New Dir. Pr. 1984 $17.95. ISBN 0-8112-0885-0

New and Selected Poems, 1930–1990. Blue Moon Pr. 1990 $16.95. ISBN 0-929654-95-1. Short collection containing a sampling of better-known work plus 11 hitherto unpublished poems.

BOOK ABOUT EBERHART

Wright, Stuart. *Richard Eberhart: A Descriptive Bibliography, 1921–1987.* Greenwood 1989 $75.00. ISBN 0-313-27708-7

EDEL, (JOSEPH) LEON. 1907–

Leon Edel, Canadian-born biographer and critic, has been Henry James Professor of English and American Literature at New York University and is now Citizen Professor of English Emeritus at the University of Hawaii. His *Henry James* (1953–72) has been considered among the finest biographies by and about an American author. Two of the volumes won the National Book Award and the Pulitzer Prize in biography. Edel has also edited JAMES's plays and short fiction, as well as a four-volume edition of James's letters. Also notable is his group biography of Bloomsbury figures in *A House of Lions* (1979) and his edited editions of EDMUND WILSON's journals. An interesting analysis of his craft is found in *Telling Lives* (1979), in which he argues that biography is a legitimate literary form in its own right.

NONFICTION BY EDEL

Henry James: The Conquest. Avon 1978 $2.95. ISBN 0-380-39651-3

Henry James: The Master. Lippincott 1972 $13.95. ISBN 0-397-00733-7

Henry James: The Middle Years. Avon 1978 $2.95. ISBN 0-380-39669-6

Henry James: The Treacherous Years. Avon 1978 $2.95. ISBN 0-380-39677-7

Henry James in Westminster Abbey: The Address. Petronium Pr. 1976 $7.00. ISBN 0-932136-02-8

(and Edward K. Brown). *Willa Cather.* Knopf 1953 o.p. A biography completed by Edel after the death of Brown.

Writing Lives: Principia Biographia. Norton 1987 $15.95. ISBN 0-393-01882-2. Essays on the writing of biography as a literary form.

ELKIN, STANLEY. 1930–

Without a bestseller to his credit or a lot of critical attention, Stanley Elkin has steadily, quietly worked his way into the higher ranks of contemporary American novelists. He was born in New York, but grew up in Chicago and has spent most of his life since in the Midwest, receiving his Ph.D. in English from the University of Illinois with a dissertation on WILLIAM FAULKNER and teaching since 1960 at Washington University in St. Louis. John Ditsky (*Hollins Critic*) places Elkin's fiction in these terms: "If Elkin seems to be some sort of spiritual descendant of NATHANIEL WEST in the ways in which he attaches out-loud, falling-on-the-floor humor to reflections on the human state as a steady downward plunge to death, he is nevertheless very much his own man in the manner in which he explores and develops that tradition." His novel *George Mills* (1983), provides a kind of hindsight focus on what makes Elkin's fiction peculiarly his own. The George Mills of this title is not one man, but a whole series of men named George Mills whose lives bridge centuries of time and repeat much the same fate as again and again they are destined to serve as "God's blue collar worker." As if to deliberately confound those critics who had objected to Elkin's neglect of plot in his earlier novels, these George Millses go astray like sparks from an anvil as their author displays his stylistic virtuosity, yet taken together the many George Millses become an Everyman with mythical dimensions whose all-encompassing humanity remains after the laughter and the cleverness are stilled.

Reviewers found Elkin's first novel, *Boswell: A Modern Comedy* (1964), the story of an uninhibited modern-day counterpart of the eighteenth-century biographer, hilarious and promising, while the stories in *Criers and Kibitzers, Kibitzers and Criers* (1966) established Elkin as a writer capable of writing short stories of textbook-anthology quality. The ironically entitled *A Bad Man* (1967) is about a Jewish department store magnate who deliberately arranges to have himself convicted of several misdeeds so that he can experience the real world of a prison and carry on his own war with the warden in what takes on the dimensions of a burlesque existential allegory. *The Dick Gibson Show* (1971) uses the host of a radio talk show as a way of showing fancifully what it means to live "at sound barrier," and both *Searchers and Seizures* (1973) and *The Living End* (1979) are triptychs of related stories verging on surrealism. *The Franchiser* (1976), generally considered Elkin's best novel before *George Mills*, uses the story of a traveling salesman of franchises to show the flattening homogenization of American life. But as usual, what happens in this Elkin novel is less important than the way in which the story is told. As Thomas LeClair put it in *Contemporary Literature*, "Sentence for sentence, nobody in America writes better than Stanley Elkin. For him the novel is primarily a place for language, energized and figurative language, to happen."

NOVELS BY ELKIN

A Bad Man. 1967. *Obelisk Ser.* NAL-Dutton 1984 o.p.
Criers and Kibitzers, Kibitzers and Criers. 1966. Thunders Mouth 1990 $12.95. ISBN 1-56025-005-4
The Dick Gibson Show. 1971. NAL-Dutton 1983 o.p.
The Franchiser. Godine 1980 repr. of 1976 ed. $10.95. ISBN 0-87923-323-0
George Mills. Thunders Mouth 1991 repr. of 1983 ed. $12.95. ISBN 1-56025-019-4
The MacGuffin: A Novel. Viking Penguin 1992 $10.00. ISBN 0-14-017234-3. About a 58-year-old man named Druff, Commissioner of Struts.
The Magic Kingdom. Thunders Mouth 1991 repr. of 1986 ed. $12.95. ISBN 1-56025-018-6
Searchers and Seizures. 1973. Godine 1978 $10.95. ISBN 0-87923-253-6. Three novellas.

ELLISON, RALPH (WALDO). 1914–

Ralph Ellison has the distinction of being one of the few writers who has established a firm literary reputation on the strength of a single work of long fiction. Writer and teacher, Ralph Ellison was born in Oklahoma City, studied at Tuskegee Institute, and has lectured at New York, Columbia, and Fisk universities and at Bard College. He received the Prix de Rome from the Academy of Arts and Letters in 1955, and in 1964 he was elected a member of the National Institute of Arts and Letters. He has contributed short stories and essays to various publications.

Invisible Man (1952), his first novel, won the National Book Award for 1952 and is considered an impressive work. "Ellison's sensibility is unique and his novel is original—not because he has created a new form (in that sense he has written a traditional novel), but rather because he holds a view we have not known before, or only half knew, because he has managed to penetrate to a heart of our society which we have hidden, or half hidden, from ourselves. It is a vision of the underground man who is also the invisible African American, and its possessor has employed this subterranean view and viewer to so extraordinary an advantage that the impression of the novel is that of a pioneer work. This impression was corroborated by JAMES BALDWIN, who in *Notes of a Native Son* wrote, "Mr. Ellison, by the way, is the first Negro novelist I have ever read to utilize in language, and brilliantly, some of the ambiguity and irony of Negro life" (*The Creative Present*). A book of essays, *Shadow and Act*, which discusses the African American in America and Ellison's Oklahoma boyhood, among other topics, appeared in 1964.

NOVEL BY ELLISON

Invisible Man. 1952. Random 1989 $6.95. ISBN 0-679-72313-7

BOOKS ABOUT ELLISON

Hersey, John, ed. *Ralph Ellison: A Collection of Critical Essays. Twentieth-Century Views Ser.* P-H 1973 $12.95. ISBN 0-13-274357-4. A good general collection.
Nadel, Alan. *Invisible Criticism: Ralph Ellison and the American Canon.* U. of Iowa Pr. 1991 repr. of 1988 ed. $8.95. ISBN 0-87745-321-7. Exposes some of the ways Ellison situates *Invisible Man* in regard to the American literary tradition.
O'Meally, Robert G. *The Craft of Ralph Ellison.* HUP 1980 $18.95. ISBN 0-674-17548-4

ELLMANN, RICHARD. 1918–

Richard Ellmann, American teacher and scholar, has been Goldsmith Professor of English at New College, Oxford University, since 1968. His research and writing have been primarily identified with turn-of-the-century Irish writers, especially JOYCE, YEATS, and WILDE. His *James Joyce* (1959) received the National Book Award for biography. In *Ulysses on the Liffey* (1972), a biographical-critical examination of Joyce's masterwork, the novel "is seen to work as the most complex fictional structure of all time, but, through that, it is seen to work also as a great testament to human love" (Anthony Burgess). Of *Yeats* (1948) Sean O'Faolain has said: "This is the first lucid interpretation we have had of Yeats's literary pilgrimage and poetic metabolisms. It is a masterly book, thoroughly documented, sensitive and sure-footed." Because Yeats attained literary eminence early in life and kept it so long, he became a focal center for disciples and rebels. In *Eminent Domain* (1967), Ellmann examines the complicated interactions among selected writers who responded literarily to them. *Golden Codgers* (1973) is a volume of biographical-critical speculative essays on writers from GEORGE ELIOT to T. S. ELIOT.

With Ellsworth Mason, Ellmann edited *The Critical Writing of James Joyce*. He has also edited Volume 2 of the *Letters of James Joyce*, Stanislaus Joyce's *My Brother's Keeper: James Joyce's Early Years* (1958), and *Edwardians and Late Victorians: Essays of the English Institute* (1960). His Wilde editions include *Oscar Wilde: A Collection of Critical Essays* and *The Artist as Critic: Critical Writings of Oscar Wilde*.

NONFICTION BY ELLMANN

Eminent Domain: Yeats among Wilde, Joyce, Eliot and Auden. OUP 1967 o.p.
Identity of Yeats. 1954. OUP 2nd ed. 1964 o.p.
Golden Codgers: Biographical Speculations. OUP 1973 o.p.
James Joyce. 1959. OUP 1982 o.p.
Ulysses on the Liffey. OUP 1972 o.p.

Yeats: The Man and the Masks. 1948. *Norton Lib.* Norton 1978 $11.95. ISBN 0-393-00859-2. Based on both published works and unpublished manuscripts, a good study of Yeats's personae.

FIEDLER, LESLIE A(ARON). 1917–

Fiedler, a literary critic and professor of English at the State University of New York, Buffalo, since 1965, has (according to Saul Maloff in the *N.Y. Times*) "a voice like that of no one else: swashbuckling, hectoring, raucous, calculatedly outrageous—and, at his best, brilliant, wonderfully suggestive, not in the way of most criticism but in the way of imaginative literature." Fiedler's well-known preoccupation with social and psychological issues emerged with *Love and Death in the American Novel* (1960), which became a major critical text of the 1960s. In this book he argues that American writing has been shaped by an inability to portray mature sexual relationships and by an underlying fear of death. He admonishes critics, teachers, and readers of literature to connect text and context—to consider a poem, for example, as the sum of many contexts, including its genre, the other works of the author, the other works of his time, and so forth. Fiedler's notions of moral ambiguity echo MATTHEW ARNOLD's focus on art as criticism of life, but with an energy and style peculiar to himself. He depends a lot on generalizations (usually unexpected), making his critical remarks reflect broader considerations.

NONFICTION BY FIEDLER

Collected Essays. 2 vols. Madison Bks. UPA 1971 $12.50 ea. ISBNs 0-8128-1333-2, 0-8128-1352-9
An End to Innocence. 1955. Madison Bks. UPA 1972 $4.95. ISBN 0-8128-1478-9. Essays on culture and politics, some reprinted from *Commentary* and *Partisan Review.*
Fiedler on the Roof: Apostle to the Gentiles. Godine 1991 $19.95. ISBN 0-87923-859-3. Twelve essays, all previously published over the last 20 years.
A Fiedler Reader. Madison Bks. UPA 1977 $6.95. ISBN 0-8128-2192-0
Freaks: Myths and Images of the Secret Self. Anch. 1993 repr. of 1978 ed. $12.95. ISBN 0-385-47013-4
Love and Death in the American Novel. 1960. Madison Bks. UPA rev. ed. 1975 $12.95. ISBN 0-8128-1799-0
No! In Thunder: Essays on Myth and Literature. 1960. Madison Bks. UPA 1972 o.p.
What Was Literature? Class, Culture and Society. S & S Trade 1984 o.p.

FISH, STANLEY. 1938–

Fish is the most prominent and controversial of those critics who have focused attention on the reader and the reader's response to a literary work. In his earlier writings, he emphasized the way readers form expectations about what will come next in a work—how a sentence will end, a character act, a plot turn out. The author, he argued, played on and especially against these expectations, producing new and unexpected outcomes. More recently, Fish argued that readers create the meaning of a work on the basis of codes or ways of reading they have learned from an "interpretive community" (their teachers in English class, for instance). The reader will think the work simply "means" what he or she thinks it does, but, in fact, the "meaning" is a product of his or her own socially determined activity. Fish has argued his views with clarity, verve, and polemic vigor in a series of books and essays on literature from the Renaissance onward. Most recently, Fish has turned his attention to the law, teaching at Duke University Law School as well as holding an appointment in Duke's English Department.

NONFICTION BY FISH

Doing What Comes Naturally: Change, Rhetoric, and the Practice of Theory in Literary and Legal Studies. Duke 1990 $37.50. ISBN 0-8223-0859-2. Argues that while we can never separate our judgments from the contexts in which they are made, those judgments are nevertheless authoritative and even objective.

Is There a Text in This Class? The Authority of Interpretive Communities. HUP 1980 $11.95. ISBN 0-674-46726-4. Collects 15 years of essays, showing Fish's evolution from formalist reader-response to "interpretive communities" theory.

The Living Temple: George Herbert and Catechizing. U. CA Pr. 1978 $37.50. ISBN 0-520-02657-8. Analyzes the seventeenth-century poet in the light of Fish's theories.

Self-Consuming Artifacts: The Experience of Seventeenth-Century Literature. U. CA Pr. 1973 $10.95. ISBN 0-520-02764-7. Analyzes literary works as subverting readers' expectations.

Surprised by Sin: The Reader in Paradise Lost. U. CA Pr. 1971 $12.95. ISBN 0-520-01897-4. Milton's epic lures the reader into "sinful" expectations, then subverts them to impel the growth of religious and moral insight.

FRYE, (HERMAN) NORTHROP. 1912–1991

Educated at Oxford and a professor at the University of Toronto for many years, Northrup Frye's interest was in the human imagination and its power to create patterns or shapes that guide our individual and social lives and our interaction with nature. These patterns are "myths" or "archetypes," and the entire mass of literature is a vast treasure house of patterns, sometimes in disguised or "displaced" form. The critic's job, according to Frye, is to provide a precise and comprehensive classification of the forms of literature. Critics thus educate and liberate our imaginations from the narrow range of our own present-day culture and show both the limited myths that organize our immediate society and the much broader range of myths that can be seen throughout human history.

NONFICTION BY FRYE

Anatomy of Criticism. Princeton U. Pr. 1957 $12.95. ISBN 0-691-01298-9. His magnum opus, a comprehensive system embracing the varieties of literature.

The Bush Garden: Essays on the Canadian Imagination. U. of Toronto Pr. 1971 o.p. Essays on twentieth-century Canadian literature.

Creation and Recreation. U. of Toronto Pr. 1980 $12.95. ISBN 0-8020-6422-1. Links theological with artistic creation.

The Critical Path: An Essay on the Social Context of Literary Criticism. Bks. Demand repr. of 1971 ed. $47.00. ISBN 0-7837-3703-3

The Double Vision: Language and Meaning in Religion. U. of Toronto Pr. 1991 $35.00. ISBN 0-8020-5925-2. A study of the language of religion and the religious aspects of language.

The Eternal Act of Creation: Essays 1979–1990. Ed. by Robert D. Denham. Ind. U. Pr. 1993 $25.00. ISBN 0-253-32516-1

Fearful Symmetry: A Study of William Blake. Princeton U. Pr. 1947 $15.95. ISBN 0-691-01291-1. A seminal study of Blake's cosmology.

The Great Code: The Bible and Literature. HarBraceJ 1983 $9.95. ISBN 0-15-636480-8. Archetypal readings of literature.

A Natural Perspective. HarBraceJ 1969 $6.95. ISBN 0-15-665414-8. Development of Shakespearean comedy and romance.

Northrop Frye: Myth and Metaphor, Selected Essays 1974–1988. Ed. by Robert D. Denham. U. of Va. Pr. 1992 repr. of 1990 ed. $40.00. ISBN 0-8139-1261-X. Twenty-four collected essays focusing on the fundamental themes that have dominated Frye's career.

Reading the World: Selected Writings, 1935–1976, Vol. 1. P. Lang Pubs. 1990 $70.00.
    ISBN 0-8204-1214-7
The Secular Scripture: A Study of the Structure of Romance. HUP 1976 $17.00. ISBN 0-
    . 674-79675-6
Spiritus Mundi: Essays on Literature, Myth, and Society. Bks. Demand repr. of 1976 ed.
    $84.30. ISBN 0-7837-3704-1
A Study of English Romanticism. U. Ch. Pr. 1983 o.p.
Words With Power: Being a Secondary Study of the Bible and Literature. HarBraceJ 1992
    $10.95. ISBN 0-15-698365-6. Analyzes the Bible's imagery, narrative structure, and
    literary classics.

BOOKS ABOUT FRYE

Cook, Eleanor, and others, eds. *Centre and Labyrinth: Essays in Honour of Northrop Frye*.
    U. of Toronto Pr. 1982 $17.95. ISBN 0-8020-2496-3
Denham, Robert D. *Northrop Frye: An Enumerative Bibliography. Author Bibliographies
    Ser.* Scarecrow 1974 o.p.
―――――. *Northrop Frye and Critical Method.* Pa. St. U. Pr. 1978 o.p. Focuses chiefly on
    Anatomy of Criticism.
Krieger, Murray, ed. *Northrop Frye in Modern Criticism: Selected Papers from the English
    Institute.* AMS Pr. repr. of 1966 ed. o.p. Essays collected from an important annual
    conference at Harvard.

GADDIS, WILLIAM. 1922–

In Recognition of William Gaddis (1984) is a collection of essays supporting
the view that Gaddis is the HERMAN MELVILLE of the twentieth century. The
comparison may prove justified, not only because of artistic similarities, but
also because both writers suffered from years of neglect before achieving fame.
Gaddis's novel *The Recognitions* (1955) baffled and angered most of its initial
reviewers, but it has slowly, steadily attracted a growing number of appreciative
readers willing to work through its more than 900 demanding pages. Its length
and encyclopedic complexity caused some critics mistakenly to hail it as the
American *Ulysses*, but Gaddis disclaimed much knowledge of JAMES JOYCE. His
central figure, Wyatt, is a painter who finds his natural talent misdirected away
from original creation toward the forging of old masterpieces. Scores of other
characters appear, and almost all of them are also forgers, imposters,
counterfeiters, and plagiarists, for *The Recognitions* is essentially a deeply
religious work about the nature of reality and creativity.

As if to make amends for the neglect of *The Recognitions*, most reviewers
greeted Gaddis's second novel, *JR* (1975), with respectful attention. Although
not a popular success, it won the National Book Award. Of *Carpenter's Gothic*
(1985), *Publishers Weekly* wrote that readers "familiar with his virtuosity . . . will
find his gifts very much intact here; the narrative spins and swirls at high voltage
and with unflagging energy. Of the many pleasures the novel affords, however,
the principal one remains Gaddis's eerily uncanny ear for American speech in
all its broken rhythms, violence, expressiveness, booming narrative power."

NOVELS BY GADDIS

Carpenter's Gothic. Viking Penguin 1986 $6.95. ISBN 0-14-008993-4
JR. 1975. Viking Penguin 1985 o.p. A novel written almost entirely in dialogue.
The Recognitions. 1955. Avon 1974 o.p. Wyatt Gwyon attempts to find truth in the field of
    art, without losing his own integrity.

BOOKS ABOUT GADDIS

Kuehl, John, and Steven Moore. *In Recognition of William Gaddis*. Syracuse U. Pr. 1984
    $29.95. ISBN 0-8156-2306-2

Moore, Steven. *A Reader's Guide to William Gaddis's "The Recognitions."* U. of Nebr. Pr.
    1982 $35.00. ISBN 0-8032-3072-9. Annotations based on newly discovered source
    books belonging to Gaddis.

GARDNER, JOHN (C.). 1933–1982

One of the most lively literary controversies of recent years was stirred up by
the publication of John Gardner's *On Moral Fiction* (1978). He attacked many of
his leading contemporaries for their world-weary despair, smart-alecky cleverness, and excessive concern for ingenious literary techniques at the expense of
those solid human values that Gardner insisted lay at the core of the art of
fiction. Whether or not one agreed with its main thesis, *On Moral Fiction* (the
title essay won a Pushcart Prize) clearly stated the artistic credo of its author,
and, when Gardner's literary career was brought to a premature end several
years later, critics found it tempting to evaluate his total output in terms of his
own standards. The authors of the first full-length critical studies of Gardner
would seem to agree wholeheartedly with David Cowart's statement that "the
remarkable thing about Gardner's fiction is its consistent clarity of purpose and
moral vision" (*Dictionary of Literary Biography*). It is important to realize,
however, that by "moral" Gardner did not mean didactic, and the eight major
novels he left behind offer no easy affirmations. "What is there in this world but
accident?" asks one of his principal characters, and those works contain many
instances of gratuitous violence and senseless sudden endings not unlike
Gardner's own death in a motorcycle accident four days before he was to be
married.

Gardner was born in Batavia, New York, and attended both DePauw
University and Washington University of St. Louis before attaining a Ph.D. in
English from the State University of Iowa in 1958, which qualified him for a
career as a teacher of creative writing and a scholar of medieval literature. He
taught and lectured at a number of schools and universities, but his main
academic affiliations were at Southern Illinois University and, from 1978 until
his death, the State University of New York at Binghamton, where he founded
the creative writing department. An extremely productive and versatile writer,
he published scholarly work on the medieval period as well as several study
guides, and his creative efforts included not only adult fiction, but children's
books, poetry, libretti for operas, and radio plays.

Gardner published two philosophical novels—*The Resurrection* (1966) and
The Wreckage of Agathon (1970)—without attracting much notice before
Grendel (1975) established him as a major new talent. Already considered a
modern classic, that short novel retells the Old English epic of *Beowulf* from
the point of view of the dragon rather than the hero. The success of *Grendel*
enabled Gardner to revise and publish several longer novels on which he had
been working during the 1960s. *The Sunlight Dialogues* (1972) is a lengthy novel
that deals with the conflict between an earnest but bumbling police chief in
upstate New York and a bearded, mysterious transient who calls himself The
Sunlight Man and epitomizes the spirit of freedom and anarchy as emphatically
as the police chief represents law and order. Some critics think that it is
Gardner's best novel set in contemporary times. *Nickel Mountain* (1973), which
Gardner called in a subtitle *A Pastoral Novel*, is the story of a developing love
affair between a middle-aged man and a young woman in a somber country

setting. *October Light* (1976), which won the National Book Critics Circle Award in 1976, includes a novel within a novel. Gardner's next full-length novel, *Freddy's Book* (1980), is also a kind of double novel in that it provides at least a half-frame for its central narrative, a fablelike tale called *King Gustav and the Devil* set in sixteenth-century Scandinavia. What proved to be Gardner's last novel, *Mickelson's Ghosts* (1982), is a lengthy, somewhat tortured account of the several crises faced by a middle-aged philosophy professor at SUNY-Binghamton. The reviews were largely negative, with the principal complaint being the seeming lack of distance between the novel's hero and its author.

Gardner is a collectible author whose first editions and small-press publications have considerable appeal in the rare book market. One reason may be that he worked in several attractive and unusual genres.

Novels by Gardner

Death Is Forever. Putnam Pub. Group 1992 $14.95. ISBN 0-399-13716-5. Gardner's eleventh Bond book, just after the reunification of Germany.
Freddy's Book. Knopf 1980 o.p.
Grendel. Random 1989 $8.00. ISBN 0-679-72311-0
Mickelson's Ghosts. Knopf 1982 o.p.
Never Send Flowers. Putnam Pub. Group 1993 $18.95. ISBN 0-399-13809-9. Reincarnation of James Bond examines a string of serial killings.
Nickel Mountain. Random 1989 $12.00. ISBN 0-394-74393-8
October Light. 1976. Ballantine 1985 $4.95. ISBN 0-345-32448-X
The Sunlight Dialogues. 1972. Ballantine 1982 $6.95. ISBN 0-685-00684-0

Short Story Collection by Gardner

The Art of Living and Other Stories. Random 1989 $8.95. ISBN 0-679-72350-1

Nonfiction by Gardner

On Becoming a Novelist. HarpC 1985 $10.00. ISBN 0-06-091126-3. Meditations on how to become a novelist, offering guidance and advice to aspiring authors.
On Moral Fiction. 1970. Basic 1979 $14.00. ISBN 0-465-05226-6

Books about Gardner

Butts, Leonard. *The Novels of John Gardner: Making Life as a Moral Process.* La. State U. Pr. 1988 $27.50. ISBN 0-8071-1392-1. Critical assessment of the novels of John Gardner.
Cowart, David. *Arches and Light: The Fiction of John Gardner.* S. Ill. U. Pr. 1983 o.p.
Morace, Robert A. *John Gardner: An Annotated Secondary Bibliography. Reference Lib. of the Humanities.* Garland 1984 o.p.
———, ed. *John Gardner: Critical Perspectives.* Ed. by Kathryn Vanspanckeren. *Crosscurrents Modern Critiques New Ser.* S. Ill. U. Pr. 1982 $19.95. ISBN 0-8093-1031-7. Afterword by John Gardner.
Morris, Gregory L. *A World of Order and Light: The Fiction of John Gardner.* U. of Ga. Pr. 1984 o.p.
Winther, Per. *The Art of John Gardner: Introduction and Exploration. SUNY Series in American Literature.* State U. NY Pr. 1992 $39.50. ISBN 0-7914-1113-3. Emphasizes Gardner's compositional method as manifested in *Grendel*.

GASS, WILLIAM. 1924–

William Gass is known as one of our most interesting stylists, an experimental writer willing to take chances as he explores new dimensions of fictional form. He was born in Fargo, North Dakota, and after attending Kenyon College at a time when that school was in its heyday as a literary center, he went on to graduate study in philosophy at Cornell University, receiving his Ph.D. in 1954. From then until 1969 he taught at Purdue, and he now holds a distinguished professorship at Washington University in St. Louis.

His writing talent was first recognized in 1958, when the editors of *Accent* invited him—an unprecedented honor—to fill an entire issue of that distinguished little magazine with some of his stories and essays, but nine more years passed before he published his first book. His novel *Omensetter's Luck* (1966) was well received by critics, who praised it for its exceptional style and its rich evocation of a particular time and place. *Newsweek* described it as "a dense, provoking, vastly rewarding and very beautiful first novel." Then his collection of stories, *In the Heart of the Heart of the Country* (1968), attracted additional readers. The title story of that volume and several others, in particular the brilliant "The Pedersen Kid," have evoked considerable critical interest. So has his short novel, *Willie Master's Lonesome Wife* (1968), a wildly bawdy and richly allusive interior monologue by a latter-day Molly Bloom, which appeared originally as a special supplement to *Tri-Quarterly*. In recent years Gass has devoted himself to the writing of an ambitious longer work, which remains unpublished. In addition, he has become a busy contributor of essay-reviews and other prose pieces to the *New York Review of Books* and other literary journals. Some of his reviews of individual writers and essays on the theory of fiction are collected in *Fiction and Figures of Life* (1970), *The World within the Word* (1978), and *The Habitations of the Word* (1985). Difficult to classify is *On Being Blue: A Philosophical Inquiry* (1978), though one might say that it is as brilliant and witty an exposition of the many meanings of the word "blue" as one would expect from a very bright professor of philosophy who loves languages.

NOVELS BY GASS

In the Heart of the Heart of the Country. Godine 1981 $10.95. ISBN 0-87923-374-5
Omensetter's Luck. NAL-Dutton 1966 o.p.

NONFICTION BY GASS

On Being Blue: A Philosophical Inquiry. Godine 1978 $10.95. ISBN 0-87923-237-4.

BOOK ABOUT GASS

McCaffery, Larry. *The Metafictional Muse: The Work of Robert Coover, Donald Barthelme, and William Gass.* U. of Pittsburgh Pr. 1982 $32.95. ISBN 0-8229-3462-0. Critical essays on twentieth-century metafiction, with historical survey.

GEERTZ, CLIFFORD. 1926–

[SEE Volumes 4 and 5.)

GINSBERG, ALLEN. 1926–

"I saw the best minds of my generation destroyed by madness. . . ." So begin the prophetic intonations of *Howl*, Ginsberg's strong indictment of his society. *Howl*, now acclaimed as *The Waste Land* of our time, was first published in 1956 with an introduction by WILLIAM CARLOS WILLIAMS, and it created an immediate sensation. The first edition, printed in England for Lawrence Ferlinghetti's City Lights Books, was seized by customs and impounded until cleared of obscenity charges by a San Francisco court. This publishing event, coupled with the appearance of JACK KEROUAC's novel *On the Road*, brought into focus a new movement in the literary world—Beat writing. In the tradition of WHITMAN, Beat was timely, spontaneous, and expansive.

Ginsberg described himself as "the son of Naomi Ginsberg, Russian émigré, and Louis Ginsberg, lyric poet and school teacher." Born in Newark, New Jersey, Ginsberg was educated at Columbia University. Early on, he decided on a career as a poet, and in the 1940s and 1950s he began associating with Kerouac and others of the Beat Generation. During that time he gained a reputation that made him a character in the writings of others. Real celebrity came with the publication of *Howl* and the notoriety it caused.

Ginsberg's later poetry is concerned with political subjects, including drugs, sexual disorder, voluntary poverty, and rejection of society. His is the voice of a public figure, increasingly interested in bringing poetry to the mass audience.

POETRY BY GINSBERG

Collected Poems, 1947–1980. HarpC 1988 $15.95. ISBN 0-06-091494-7. Includes annotations and photographs, as well as the important prefaces and afterword to the separate volumes.

The Empty Mirror: Early Poems. Corinth Bks. 1961 o.p.

The Fall of America: Poems of These States, 1965–1971. Pocket Poets Ser. City Lights 1972 $7.95. ISBN 0-87286-063-9. Continuation of *Planet News* with afterwords by Ginsberg. Winner of the National Book Award (1974).

Howl and Other Poems. Pocket Poets Ser. City Lights 1956 $4.95. ISBN 0-87286-017-5

Kaddish and Other Poems, 1958–1960. Pocket Poets Ser. City Lights 1961 $3.95. ISBN 0-87286-019-1. Includes perhaps the most important elegy by a postwar American poet, the title poem.

Mind Breaths: Poems, 1972–1977. City Lights 1978 $7.95. ISBN 0-87286-092-2

Planet News: Poems, 1961–1964. City Lights 1968 $7.95. ISBN 0-87286-020-5. Forty poems on the United States, Indian religions, and cosmology.

Reality Sandwiches: Poems, 1953–1960. City Lights 1963 $6.95. ISBN 0-87286-021-3 (and William Burroughs). *The Yage Letters.* City Lights 1963 $6.95 ISBN 0-87286-004-3. Written in 1953 when Burroughs was in South America.

White Shroud: Poems, 1980–1985. HarpC 1987 $11.00. ISBN 0-06-091429-7

WORKS BY GINSBERG

Indian Journals: March 1962–May 1963. City Lights 1970 o.p. With drawings and photographs by Ginsberg; journal of a trip through northern India.

Journals: Early Fifties–Early Sixties. Grove Pr. 1977 o.p. Gives an inside view of the Beats and the American scene.

BOOKS ABOUT GINSBERG

Kramer, Jane. *Allen Ginsberg in America.* Random 1970 o.p. An interesting journalistic book about the poet.

Merril, Thomas F. *Allen Ginsberg.* G. K. Hall 1988 $19.95. ISBN 0-8057-7510-2. An overview of and introduction to Ginsberg's life and poetry.

GLÜCK, LOUISE. 1943–

Born in New York City and raised on Long Island, Glück studied at Sarah Lawrence College and Columbia University. She has won numerous awards, including grants from the Rockefeller Foundation, the National Endowment for the Arts, and the Guggenheim Foundation. She lives in Vermont and teaches at Goddard College. Glück's poetry originally resembled the work of such poets as PLATH and SEXTON, emphasizing sexual violence and male mental cruelty. More recently, her concern has been with myth and transcendental longings, taking as her starting points the Old Testament and classical myth.

POETRY BY GLÜCK

Descending Figure. 1980. *Amer. Poetry Ser.* Ecco Pr. 1983 $9.95. ISBN 0-912946-71-7
Firstborn. Amer. Poetry Ser. Ecco Pr. 1983 $5.95. ISBN 0-912946-93-8
The House on Marshland. Amer. Poetry Ser. Ecco Pr. 1976 $7.95. ISBN 0-912946-19-9
The Tongues We Speak: New and Selected Poems. Milkweed Ed. 1989 $9.95. ISBN 0-915943-34-4

GOLDBARTH, ALBERT. 1948–

Born in Chicago and educated at the University of Illinois and University of Iowa, Goldbarth has taught at various schools, including the University of Texas. Prolific and wide-ranging in content, Goldbarth writes against the grain of much contemporary poetry, which aims to strip language to its barest essentials. His verse, by contrast, is baroque, florid, even—as his critics would have it—cluttered. The effect of his virtuoso verbal performance is to suggest how intensely is the human need for explanation and connection with the vast storehouse of culture within which we live. In his recent works, Goldbarth has pursued his theory that life is a Moebius strip, continually repeating itself, with no discernible beginning or end.

POETRY BY GOLDBARTH

Comings Back: A Sequence of Poems. Doubleday 1976 o.p. Treats theme of history's repetitiveness.
Curve: Overlapping Narratives. New Rivers Pr. 1977 o.p. Reflects Goldbarth's interest in narrative and history.
Different Fleshes. Hobart and William Smith College Pr. 1979 o.p. A novel/poem with alternating prose and poetry sections.
Original Light: New and Selected Poems 1973–1983. Ontario Rev. NJ 1983 $12.95. ISBN 0-86538-031-7
Popular Culture. Ohio St. U. Pr. 1989 $17.95. ISBN 0-8142-0498-8. Goldbarth's fourth volume of poems, in which he reveals himself as a descendant of Walt Whitman.

GORDON, CAROLINE. 1895–1981

Caroline Gordon's controlled use of her craft as well as her conservative attitudes stamped her as a traditionalist among modern writers. Born in Kentucky as the daughter of a classics teacher and graduated from Bethany College in 1916, she married the poet Allen Tate in 1924 and became an associate of the Fugitives and Southern Agrarian groups that helped to make Nashville a vital mecca for southern intellectuals during the 1970s. Her first novel, *Penhally* (1931), traces the decline brought about by pride and jealousy as well as the devastation of the Civil War. *None Shall Look Back* (1937), which had the misfortune to appear shortly after MARGARET MITCHELL's *Gone with the Wind*, is a distinguished but neglected novel with a theme similar to her first. Against the story of the Allard family, which, like the house of Penhally, deteriorates through internal weaknesses as well as because of the Civil War, Gordon sets off the heroic figure of the Confederate General Nathan Bedford Forrest. *The Garden of Adonis* (1937) picks up the story of the Allards, this time during the depression of the 1930s, and shows how social conditions as well as the family's own incapacities have put the men of the family at the mercy of their spoiled and neurotic women.

Aleck Maury, Sportsman (1934), like Gordon's most famous short story "Old Red," is remarkable for its vivid hunting scenes. Probably no other woman has written so knowledgeably and sympathetically about the outdoor man's love of the fields and streams of his native region and the almost sacramental view of nature that accompanies such allegiance. *Green Centuries* (1941) is a novel about a pioneer couple who settle near the Cumberland Gap during the American Revolution. *The Women on the Porch* (1944), *The Strange Children* (1951), and *The Malefactors* (1956) are novels about modern intellectuals found wanting when tested by nature and their own raw emotions.

NOVELS BY GORDON

Aleck Maury, Sportsman: A Novel. S. Ill. U. Pr. 1980 repr. of 1934 ed. $12.95. ISBN 0-8039-0988-2
The Garden of Adonis. Cooper Sq. 1972 repr. of 1937 ed. o.p.
Green Centuries. J. S. Sanders 1992 repr. of 1941 ed. $10.95. ISBN 1-879941-05-8
The Women on the Porch. J. S. Sanders 1992 repr. of 1944 ed. $10.95. ISBN 1-879941-20-1
The Strange Children. Cooper Sq. 1972 repr. of 1951 ed. o.p.

SHORT STORY COLLECTION BY GORDON

The Collected Stories of Caroline Gordon. La. State U. Pr. 1990 $16.95. ISBN 0-8071-1630-0. Brings together all of Gordon's short fiction.

WORK BY GORDON

The Southern Mandarins: Letters of Caroline Gordon to Sally Wood, 1924–1937. Ed. by Sally Wood. La. State U. Pr. 1984 $27.50. ISBN 0-8071-1137-6

BOOKS ABOUT GORDON

Fraistat, Rose A. *Caroline Gordon as Novelist and Woman of Letters.* La. State U. Pr. 1984 o.p. Illuminating on Gordon's contribution to Southern literature.
Landess, Thomas H., ed. *The Short Fiction of Caroline Gordon: A Symposium.* U. of Dallas Pr. 1972 o.p. Symposium occasioned by Gordon's visit in 1991 to the University of Dallas.
Makowsky, Veronica A. *Caroline Gordon: A Biography.* OUP 1989 $25.00. ISBN 0-19-505718-X. Brief biography and literary study of Caroline Gordon.

HALL, DONALD. 1928–

Donald Hall was born in New Haven, Connecticut, and attended Harvard and Oxford universities. The poem "Exile" from his first collection, *Exile and Marriages* (1955), won the Newdigate Prize in England.

Hall has been poetry editor for the *Paris Review*. He has edited *Contemporary American Poetry* and (with Robert Pack) *New Poets of England and America.* He is also the editor of numerous anthologies, including *Modern Stylists: Writers on the Art of Writing*; and he is also the author of *Henry Moore: The Life and Work of a Great Sculptor.* He lives on a farm in New Hampshire that his family has occupied for generations.

POETRY BY HALL

Kicking the Leaves. HarpC 1978 o.p. Poems about life on the family farm and other rural topics.
Old and New Poems. Ticknor & Fields 1990 $12.95. ISBN 0-89919-954-2. Most recent collection of poems, showing continuity and development in Hall's works; serves as a superb introduction to newcomers.

Nonfiction by Hall

Goatfoot Milktongue Twinbird. Poets on Poetry Ser. U. of Mich. Pr. 1978 $11.95. ISBN 0-472-40000-2. Essays on many topics, especially the sources of poetry.

Remembering Poets: Reminiscences and Opinions. HarpC 1979 o.p. Deals with Dylan Thomas, Pound, and Eliot.

String Too Short to Be Saved: Recollections of Summers on a New England Farm. 1961. Godine 1979 $10.95. ISBN 0-87923-282-X. About Hall's childhood on his grandfather's farm; in prose.

HARPER, MICHAEL. 1938–

Though Brooklyn-born, Harper grew up in Los Angeles in a household filled with jazz and blues. As he recounts, "Billie Holiday played piano in my family's house when I was 12." Difficult to characterize, his poetry is driven by intensely personal rhythms rooted in the music he heard growing up. Concerned with his identity as an African American whose origins are in both African and American cultures, Harper says that he writes about the "relationships between speech and body, between men, between men and cosmology . . ."

Poetry by Harper

Dear John, Dear Coltrane. U. of Ill. Pr. 1985 $10.95. ISBN 0-252-01193-7

Debridement. Doubleday 1973 o.p.

Healing Song for the Inner Ear. U. of Ill. Pr. 1985 $14.95. ISBN 0-252-01128-7. Confirms Harper's status as a poet of consummate skill and grace; poems steeped in African American history.

Images of Kin: New and Selected Poems. U. of Ill. Pr. 1977 o.p.

HASS, ROBERT. 1941–

Robert Hass was born in San Francisco and studied at St. Mary's College and Stanford University. He has taught at the State University of New York in Buffalo and the University of California, Berkeley. He has been awarded a MacArthur Foundation fellowship, and his book of prose, *Twentieth Century Pleasures* (1985), was the winner in the criticism category of the 1985 National Book Critics Circle Award. It contains some very interesting writing about contemporary poetry and other subjects. Hass's poetry combines great skill with intelligence and lyric grace. Few of his contemporaries can match his use of cultural allusion meshed with a sensitivity to shades of feeling and tenuous but deep moments of meditative insight. His first book was a selection in the *Yale Series of Younger Poets.*

Poetry by Hass

Field Guide. Yale Ser. of Younger Poets. Yale U. Pr. 1973 $14.95. ISBN 0-300-01650-6

Human Wishes. Ecco Pr. 1989 $17.95. ISBN 0-88001-211-0. A collection of short poems and prose pieces.

Praise. Amer. Poetry Ser. Ecco Pr. 1980 $8.95. ISBN 0-88001-242-0

Nonfiction by Hass

Twentieth Century Pleasures. Ecco Pr. 1985 $12.95. ISBN 0-88001-046-0

HAWKES, JOHN. 1925–

Robert Coover is quoted on the jacket of *Virginie: Her Two Lives* (1982) with the suggestion that those discovering John Hawkes for the first time "might as well begin right here with this lush, erotic masterpiece." However, for readers not already acquainted with Hawkes's singular writings, probably the best entry is through *Humors of Blood and Skin: A John Hawkes Reader* (1984). From his novels and other writings, Hawkes selected representative passages, which he linked together to form a sort of literary montage. WILLIAM GASS in his introduction praises the book as "the joyful showing forth and celebration of Hawkes's healing art" and says of Hawkes's style, *"It is a prose that breathes what it sees."*

If Hawkes is an American writer whose works seem to put him in the company of such international modernists as NABOKOV (see also Vol. 2) and BECKETT, it is partly because he has himself traveled widely yet taken as part of his imaginative luggage a strange and interior country of his own. After an early childhood in Connecticut and New York City, Hawkes moved to Juneau, Alaska at the age of 10. He spent his formative years there before attending schools in New England and graduating from Harvard College. He served as an ambulance driver in Germany during World War II, and he has spent considerable time in the south of France, where he has done much of his writing.

The Cannibal (1949), his short first novel, struck its readers as suggestive of KAFKA's (see Vol. 2) stories, DJUNA BARNES's *Nightwood*, and the work of the French surrealists; and although a similar vein of plotless narratives set in strange and macabre landscapes is characteristic of his books through *The Lime Twig* (1951) and *Second Skin* (1964), he began to place more emphasis on story with *The Blood Oranges* (1971). Hawkes moved even further in that direction when he changed publishers from New Directions to Harper & Row in a frankly acknowledged effort to reach a wider audience. *The Passion Artist* (1979), the story of a celibate forced to purge the repressed traumas of his youth through sex and violence in middle age, was described by JOHN BARTH as "severe, horrific, and yet somberly hilarious; Hawkes's best since 'Second Skin,' " though Josephine Hendin entitled her review in the *N.Y. Times Book Review* "A Detour to Nihilism" and Paul Gray in *Time* said that the book "does not so much explore sex as mime its mysteries." *Virginie: Her Two Lives* is a kind of feminine counterpart of *The Passion Artist*, which, like *The Blood Oranges*, contrasts two historical periods. The heroine is an 11-year-old girl who lives both in the eighteenth century and in Paris after World War II. She is purged of innocence while remaining strangely invulnerable in her double lives, saved in each story by the *deus ex machina* of a maternal figure who puts an abrupt end to the "phallocentric" proceedings that have entrapped her.

NOVELS BY HAWKES

The Beetle Leg. 1951. New Dir. Pr. 1967 $5.95. ISBN 0-8112-0062-0
The Blood Oranges. New Dir. Pr. 1972 $9.95. ISBN 0-8112-0061-2
The Cannibal. New Dir. Pr. 1949 $8.95. ISBN 0-8112-0063-9
Death, Sleep and the Traveler. New Dir. Pr. 1974 $6.95. ISBN 0-8112-0522-3
The Lime Twig. New Dir. Pr. 1960 $9.95. ISBN 0-8112-0065-5
The Owl. 1953 New Dir. Pr. 1977 o.p.
The Passion Artist. New Dir. Pr. 1979 $50.00. ISBN 0-8112-0750-1
Second Skin. New Dir. Pr. 1964 $10.95. ISBN 0-8112-0067-1
Travesty. New Dir. Pr. 1976 $5.95. ISBN 0-8112-0640-8
Virginie: Her Two Lives. Carroll & Graf 1983 $7.95. ISBN 0-88184-054-8

WORKS BY HAWKES

Humors of Blood and Skin: A John Hawkes Reader. New Dir. Pr. 1984 $22.50. ISBN 0-8112-0906-7, With an introduction by William Gass.
Lunar Landscapes. New Dir. Pr. 1969 o.p. Contains *Charivari, The Goose on the Grave, The Owl,* and short stories.

BOOKS ABOUT HAWKES

Berry, Eliot. *A Poetry of Force and Darkness: The Fiction of John Hawkes.* Borg. Pr. 1979 $20.00. ISBN 0-89370-132-7

Busch, Frederick. *Hawkes: A Guide to His Fictions.* Syracuse U. Pr. 1973 $14.95. ISBN 0-8156-0089-5. Essays on eight novels.

Greiner, Donald J. *Understanding John Hawkes.* U. of SC Pr. 1985 $24.95. ISBN 0-87249-460-8. Provides detailed commentaries on all of Hawkes's works.

Hryciw, Carol A. *John Hawkes: An Annotated Bibliography.* Author Bibliographies Ser. Scarecrow 1977 $20.00. ISBN 0-8108-1024-7

Kuehl, John. *John Hawkes and the Craft of Conflict.* Rutgers U. Pr. 1975 o.p. Close readings of forms and content in the novels; last section records some of Hawkes's own comments.

O'Donnell, Patrick. *John Hawkes.* Twayne's U.S. Authors Ser. G. K. Hall 1982 o.p. A good literary biographical essay.

Santore, Anthony C., ed. *A John Hawkes Symposium: Design and Debris.* Ed. by Michael N. Pocalyko. New Dir. Pr. 1977 o.p.

Scotto, Robert M. *Three Contemporary Novelists: An Annotated Bibliography of Works by and about John Hawkes, Joseph Heller and Thomas Pynchon.* Reference Lib. of the Humanities. Garland 1977 o.p.

HAYDEN, ROBERT E(ARL). 1913–1980

Hayden's poetry is informed by, indeed haunted by, the history of the African American experience. Thus, Hayden saw history "as a long, tortuous, and often bloody process of becoming, of psychic evolution." Hayden's immersion in history began in the 1930s, when he researched African American history for the Federal Writers' Project in his native Detroit. Some of his best poems are about such black historical figures as Nat Turner, FREDERICK DOUGLASS, Malcolm X, and Harriet Tubman, and he is noted for his ability to combine the historical with the personal. Another source for Hayden's poetry was his adherence to the Baha'i faith, an Eastern religion that sees human history as evolving toward a coming world civilization. Such a universal outlook was behind Hayden's desire to be judged as "a poet among poets," not as an African American poet. This position was criticized sharply by other African Americans during the 1960s, and it cost Hayden some of his popularity. Yet from the 1960s through the 1970s, his star rose steadily until, in 1976, he was appointed Consultant in Poetry to the Library of Congress.

POETRY BY HAYDEN

American Journal. 1978. Liveright 1982 $12.95. ISBN 0-87140-642-X. Poems, many on historical black figures, such as Phyllis Wheatley and Paul Laurence Dunbar.

Robert Hayden: Collected Poems. Liveright 1985 $16.70. ISBN 0-87140-138-X

NONFICTION BY HAYDEN

The Collected Prose. Ed. by Frederick Glaysher. U. of Mich. Pr. 1984 $11.95. ISBN 0-472-06351-0. An important collection of essays, mostly on poetry.

BOOK ABOUT HAYDEN

Williams, Pontheolla T. *Robert Hayden: A Critical Analysis of His Poetry.* U. of Ill. Pr. 1987 $21.95. ISBN 0-252-01289-5. Reveals details of the poet's life and skillfully connects them to his poetry.

HECHT, ANTHONY. 1923–

Educated at Bard College and Columbia University, Hecht is a skilled poetic artisan whose work is rich in texture and verbal music. Hecht's use of varied metrical patterns and stanzaic forms as well as his frequent literary allusions create a poetry that is eloquent and serious. His works explore the classical subjects: birth and death; the relationship between art and life; memory and aspiration. He received a Pulitzer Prize for *Millions of Strange Shadows* (1977) in 1978.

POETRY BY HECHT

Collected Earlier Poems. Knopf 1990 $22.95. ISBN 0-394-58505-4
Millions of Strange Shadows. OUP 1977 o.p.
The Transparent Man. Knopf 1990 $18.95. ISBN 0-394-58506-2. Delightful collection including some longer poems.
The Venetian Vespers. Macmillan 1979 o.p. Contains several long poems.

BOOK ABOUT HECHT

Lea, Sydney, ed. *The Burdens of Formality: Essays on the Poetry of Anthony Hecht.* U. of Ga. Pr. 1989 $30.00. ISBN 0-8203-1091-3. First important book-length contribution to the critical assessment of Anthony Hecht.

HELLER, JOSEPH. 1932–

Even if *Catch-22* (1961), Heller's first and most successful novel, had no other merits to keep it alive, it would well be remembered for introducing a new phrase into the English language. As explained by Captain Yossarian, the antihero of this darkly comic and absurdist antiwar novel, the catch goes like this: "Anyone who is crazy must be grounded; anyone who is willing to fly combat missions must be crazy; ergo, anyone who flies should be grounded. But [you have to] request grounding; no one crazy enough to fly missions would ask; and if one should there's a catch: anyone who wants to get out of combat duty isn't really crazy." Nelson Algren wrote of the book in the *Nation*: "Below its hilarity, so wild that it hurts, . . . this novel is not merely the best American novel to come out of World War II; it is the best American novel that has come out of anywhere in years." Some critics did find Heller's satiric method repetitive and ultimately tiresome—but they were well in the minority. Seven years later, after 2 million copies had been sold in paperback with total copies approaching 3½ million, *Catch-22* was again reviewed in the *N.Y. Times*. Josh Greenberg wrote, "I found the antic humor of Catch-22 . . . robustly fresh [and] sidesplittingly funny. I know of no book written in the last 20 years that continues to make me laugh out loud so much."

Like Yossarian, the Brooklyn-born Heller was a B-25 bombardier during World War II. He graduated from New York University, received an M.A. from Columbia, and attended Oxford University on a Fulbright Scholarship. He began *Catch-22* in 1953 and finished it in 1961 by working after his hours at advertising jobs at *McCall's, Look, Time,* and Remington Rand. He capitalized on his experience in the worlds of business and publishing in his second novel, *Something Happened* (1974), in which another unheroic hero, Bob Slocum, expresses the author's ideas in a gloomy, wry, and humorous story about the moral bankruptcy of middle-class American life in the postwar years. In *Good as Gold* (1979) the Heller surrogate is a writer and college professor named Bruce Gold, the first Jewish protagonist in a Heller novel. If this book was less than enthusiastically received by some critics, that may have been partly because yet another novel about identity crises seemed rather passé after a whole decade of such Jewish black humor as PHILIP ROTH's *Portnoy's Complaint*. Heller continued his exploration of ethnic identity with *God Knows*, one of the bestsellers of 1984.

NOVELS BY HELLER

Catch-22. 1961. Dell 1989 $4.95. ISBN 0-440-11120-X
God Knows. 1984. Dell 1989 $5.95. ISBN 0-440-20438-0
Good as Gold. 1979. PB 1980 $2.95. ISBN 0-671-82388-4
Picture This. 1988. Ballantine 1989 $4.95. ISBN 0-345-35886-4
Something Happened. 1974. Dell 1988 $5.95. ISBN 0-440-20441-0

BOOKS ABOUT HELLER

Pinsker, Sanford. *Understanding Joseph Heller.* U. of SC Pr. 1991 $24.95. ISBN 0-87249-
    751-8
Potts, Stephen W. *From Here to Absurdity: The Moral Battlefields of Joseph Heller.* Borgo
    Pr. 1992 $25.00. ISBN 0-89370-318-4. Introduction to first three novels.
Seed, David. *The Fiction of Joseph Heller: Against the Grain.* St. Martin 1989 $24.95. ISBN
    0-312-02795-8. A thoughtful and useful analysis of Heller's works and themes.

HIJUELOS, OSCAR. 1951–

Oscar Hijuelos, winner of the 1990 Pulitzer Prize for fiction, was born in New
York City and educated at the City College of New York. Hijuelos's novels *Our
House in the New World* (1983) and *The Mambo Kings Play Songs of Love*
(winner of the Pulitzer Prize), deal with the Cubans who immigrated to America
in the 1940s. Concerned with questions of identity and perspective, both novels
attempt, in Hijuelos's words, to "commemorate at least a few aspects of the
Cuban psyche (as I know it)." Hijuelos's writing is emotional, generous, and
elegant; although his novels are in one sense realistic, they also reflect the
magic-realist tradition of Latin American writing. Unlike many of his contemporaries, Hijuelos's imagination is epic—he follows his characters' lives from their
origins in Cuba, often remembered or misremembered, to their final days of
squalor in Spanish Harlem. Hijuelos portrays with clarity and sympathy
characters who succumb to the pressures that "work against the [American]
dream of upward mobility." Hijuelos's most recent novel, *The Fourteen Sisters
of Emilio Montez O'Brien* (1993), is quite different from his prize-winning *The
Mambo Kings Play Songs of Love.* While that earlier work focused on Cuban-
American fraternal machismo, the latter work celebrates femininity in a
Pennsylvania family of mixed Cuban and Irish descent. Though displaying some
aspects of magic-realism, the work is, in most respects, a realistic account of the
lives of its characters. Winner of numerous awards, Hijuelos has been
recognized as introducing a new, strong voice to contemporary American
fiction.

NOVELS BY HIJUELOS

Fourteen Sisters of Emilio Montez O'Brien. 1993. FS&G 1993 $27.00. ISBN 0-374-15815-0.
    An old-fashioned family saga spanning 100 years; a hymn to the feminine spirit and
    the power of women.
The Mambo Kings Play Songs of Love. 1989. HarpC 1992 $12.00. ISBN 0-06-097451-6. The
    rise and fall of two brothers as they dream of meeting Desi Arnaz and playing in their
    own mambo band; made into a film in 1991.
Our House in the Last World. 1983. Persea Bks. $18.95. ISBN 0-89255-069-4. Follows a
    New York Cuban family from the father's death to the family's near collapse.

HOWARD, RICHARD. 1929–

Richard Howard was born in Cleveland and educated at Columbia University
and the Sorbonne. Noted for his translations of French literature, including the
works of ROBBE-GRILLET (see Vol. 2) and the memoirs of Charles de Gaulle,

Howard is also the author of one of the more important books on contemporary American poetry, *Alone with America* (1969) as well as a reviewer and critic for *Poetry* magazine. He was awarded a Guggenheim Fellowship for poetry in 1966–67.

Howard's most notable poetic achievement is his fine adaptation of BROWNING's dramatic monologues, first compiled in *Untitled Subjects* (1969). Harold Bloom writes of them: "Richard Howard's dramatic monologues with their intricate blendings of our emergent sensibility and the anguish and splendor of the great Victorians represent one of the handful of surprising and refreshing inventions in American poetry of the Sixties."

POETRY BY HOWARD

Alone with America. Atheneum 1980 o.p.

The Damages. Wesleyan Poetry Program. Wesleyan U. Pr. 1967 o.p.

Fellow Feelings. Atheneum 1976 o.p.

Findings: A Book of Poems. Atheneum 1971 o.p.

Lining Up. Atheneum 1984 o.p.

Misgivings. Atheneum 1979 o.p. Includes a series of poems about the subjects of the great French photographer Nadar.

No Traveller. Knopf 1989 $18.95. ISBN 0-679-57466-4

Quantities. Wesleyan Poetry Program. Wesleyan U. Pr. 1962 o.p.

Two-Part Inventions. Atheneum 1974 o.p. Poems built out of dialogues between famous people, most of them writers.

Untitled Subjects. 1969. Atheneum 1983 o.p.

HOWE, IRVING. 1920–1993

A self-styled "democratic socialist," founder and editor of the radical journal *Dissent*, and a regular contributor to *The New Republic*, Howe was professor of English at Hunter College. His first book, *Sherwood Anderson* (1951), made a substantial impression on his contemporaries and firmly established his reputation as a critic. He wrote several volumes of essays on literary topics— some of these with an emphasis on political commitments—all informed by a sensitive critical intellect. He felt that the fundamental problem with modern culture is that we look for meaning of life outside of it, rather than engaging with social and cultural issues as concerned citizens, active members of civil society. Howe insisted that moderation threatens our social order as much as radicalism because it is "passive, indifferent and atomized." His valuable introduction to *The Idea of the Modern in Literature and the Arts* (1971) reveals an uncomfortable awareness of the difficulties of modernism and a deep dissatisfaction with the limited role of the contemporary critic. By contrast, Howe wanted criticism to form our tastes, to come to the defense of literacy, and to confirm the ideal of individual imagination. Another of Howe's works, *World of Our Fathers* (1976), is a look at the lives of Jewish immigrants in New York during the early years of the century.

NONFICTION BY HOWE

Bridges and Boundaries: African Americans and American Jews. (coauthored with Gretchen Sorin and Marlene Park). Braziller 1992 $45.00. ISBN 0-8076-1279-0. Published in conjunction with an exhibit at the New York Historical Society exploring the often conflicted historical alliance between African Americans and American Jews.

Celebrations and Attacks: Thirty Years of Literary and Cultural Commentary. HarBraceJ 1980 $4.95. ISBN 0-15-616248-2. Reprinted essays and book reviews.

The Decline of the New: A Collection of Essays on Modern Writers and Their Books.
Horizon Pr. AZ 1970 o.p.
The Idea of the Modern in Literature and the Arts. 1971. Horizon Pr. AZ 1977 o.p. A study
of society and modernism in the arts.
A Margin of Hope: An Intellectual Autobiography. HarBraceJ 1984 $7.95. ISBN 0-15-
657245-1. A discussion of Howe's life as a critic among Jewish radicals in New York
City during midcentury.
Politics and the Novel. Col. U. Pr. 1992 $30.00. ISBN 0-231-07994-X. Essays on Stendhal,
Dostoyevsky, Conrad, Malraux, and others.
Selected Writings, 1950–1990. HarBraceJ 1990 $34.95. ISBN 0-15-180390-0. Essays
whose subject areas range from T. E. Lawrence to Ronald Reagan, anarchy to styles
in leftism.
World of Our Fathers. HarBraceJ 1989 $34.95. ISBN 0-15-146353-0. Jewish immigrants in
New York City, their social conditions and intellectual life.

HUGO, RICHARD. 1923–1982

Born in Seattle, Washington, Richard Hugo served in the army in World War
II. Some of his experiences are recounted in his book of prose, *The Triggering
Town: Lectures and Essays on Poetry and Writing* (1979). His work was twice
nominated for the National Book Award and he has received the Theodore
Roethke Prize. He worked for the Boeing Company in Seattle for more than a
decade before directing the Creative Writing Program at the University of
Montana. Shortly before his death, he was named the judge in the *Yale Series of
Younger Poets.*

Hugo's poetry is plainspoken and almost shy of any literary overtones. "I had
the need to relive over and over my early personal sense of defeat to some sort
of poetic fulfillment," he claimed, and his poetry often deals with anguished
loneliness and social failure. It has more affinity with the fiction of SHERWOOD
ANDERSON and even BRET HARTE than with the verbal dexterity of high
modernism.

POETRY BY HUGO

The Lady in Kicking Horse Reservoir. Norton 1973 o.p.
Making Certain It Goes On: The Collected Poems of Richard Hugo. Norton 1984 $25.00.
ISBN 0-393-01784-2
The Right Madness on Skye: Poems. Norton 1980 $5.95. ISBN 0-393-00982-3
Selected Poems. Norton 1979 $9.95. ISBN 0-393-00936-X
31 Letters and 13 Dreams: Poems. Norton 1977 o.p.

NONFICTION BY HUGO

The Triggering Town: Lectures and Essays on Poetry and Writing. Norton repr. of 1982 ed.
$7.95. ISBN 0-393-30057-9

IGNATOW, DAVID. 1914–

David Ignatow has been an instructor at the New School for Social Research
(1964–65) and a lecturer at the universities of Kentucky and Kansas and Vassar
College. He was poet-in-residence at York College of the City University of New
York in 1969, after which he joined the faculty of Columbia University, where he
still teaches. He is the recipient of the National Institute of Arts and Letters
Award (1964), a Guggenheim Fellowship (1965–66), a Shelley Memorial Prize
(1966), and a Rockefeller grant (1968–69). An early interest in realism, as in the
style of WILLIAM CARLOS WILLIAMS, gave way to Ignatow's later fascination with
surrealism. As Ignatow has said, "My form is usually very free, content and/or
idea determining it. . . ." In his *Notebooks* (1974) as much as in his poems,

Ignatow is the recorder of the anxieties of middle-class life in an urbanized, industrialized world.

POETRY BY IGNATOW

New and Collected Poems 1970–1985. Wesleyan U. Pr. 1986 $35.00. ISBN 0-8195-5169-4
Poems, 1934–1969. Wesleyan U. Pr. 1970 $14.95. ISBN 0-8195-6059-6. The collected poems to date, including *Poems* (1948), *The Gentle Weight Lifter* (1955), *Say Pardon* (1961), *Figures of the Human* (1964), and *Rescue the Dead* (1968).
Rescue the Dead. 1968. Wesleyan U. Pr. 1968 $22.50. ISBN 0-8195-2037-3
Whisper to the Earth. Little 1981 $10.95. ISBN 0-316-41494-8

WORK BY IGNATOW

Notebooks. 1974. Ed. by Ralph J. Mills, Jr. Sheep Meadow 1981 $9.75. ISBN 0-935296-23-9

IRVING, JOHN. 1942–

John Irving has been one of the most visible and successful members of a postwar generation of American writers whose main literary lineage can be traced back to the black humor of the 1960s and from there perhaps back to the *Mad* magazine of their adolescent years. Irving's novels are filled with grotesque and bizarre characters, ranging from bespectacled bears in the Vienna Zoo to a transsexual tight end for the Philadelphia Eagles, but, although he is capable of finding humor in such subjects as castration, speech impediments, and crippled ballerinas, there is an underlying humane seriousness in Irving's fiction. *The World according to Garp* (1978) went quickly from cult status to bestsellerdom; *The Hotel New Hampshire* (1981) rapidly became the second bestselling book of 1981. Irving's three earlier novels found only respectful attention from a few reviewers, but became more popular after *Garp*'s spectacular rise to fame.

Irving grew up in New Hampshire, attending Exeter Academy, going on to the universities of Pittsburgh and New Hampshire, and then attending the Iowa Writers Workshop, where KURT VONNEGUT, JR., was one of his teachers. Crucial to his development was a period spent in Vienna in 1963–64, a city that became a presence in virtually all of his novels.

Setting Free the Bears (1968), a first novel written while Irving was in Iowa, introduces many of his later concerns and themes in its farcical and extravagant account of what happens when the animals in the Vienna Zoo are freed from their cages by the idealistic Siggy Javotnik. *The Water-Method Man* (1972) is Fred "Bogus" Trumper, who can neither urinate nor have sexual intercourse without experiencing excruciating pain unless he can bring himself to face an operation even more acutely painful. Trumper finds some solace by translating for his dissertation an "Old Low Norse" epic, finding it so dull that he keeps improving upon the original until he becomes its real author. Thus Irving introduces a reflexive fiction-within-fiction device that becomes increasingly central in his fiction after *The 158-Pound Marriage* (1974), a book about the consequences of wife-and-husband swapping.

The main appeal of Irving's work is his zestful view of the more trendy interests of contemporary society. However, after *Garp*, Irving's critical reputation declined, partly out of disappointment with how later work failed to live up to *Garp*'s promise. His popularity has likewise diminished.

NOVELS BY IRVING

The Cider House Rules. Bantam 1986 $5.95. ISBN 0-553-25800-1
The Hotel New Hampshire. Dutton 1981 o.p.

The 158-Pound Marriage. Ballantine 1990 $5.95. ISBN 0-345-36743-X. Deals with the consequences of wife-and-husband swapping.

A Prayer for Owen Meany. Morrow 1989 $19.95. ISBN 0-688-07708-0. Relates the story of Owen Meany, who believes he is God's instrument.

Setting Free the Bears. Ballantine 1990 $5.95. ISBN 0-345-36741-3 Account of what happens when the animals in the Vienna Zoo are freed from their cages by the idealistic Siggy Zavotnik.

The Water-Method Man. 1972. PB 1982 o.p. Story of Fred "Bogus" Trumper, who can neither urinate nor have sexual intercourse without experiencing excruciating pain.

The World according to Garp. Ballantine 1990 $5.95. ISBN 0-345-36676-X

JACKSON, SHIRLEY. 1919–1965

Shirley Jackson's literary reputation rests firmly but not solely on a short story that is considered a modern American classic. From the time of its first appearance in the June 28, 1948, issue of the *New Yorker*, "The Lottery" has been much discussed and often anthologized. The story of an ancient scapegoat ritual reenacted in a community of modern times, it offers a chilling and cynical view of human nature. Along with the other stories collected in *The Lottery; or The Adventures of James Harris*, it provides evidence that Shirley Jackson was "a literary sorceress of uncanny prowess" (Orville Prescott, *N.Y. Times*). Most of Jackson's longer fiction combines an interest in abnormal mental states with a sense of the uncanny and the supernatural. After her first novel, *The Road through the Wall* (1948), a somewhat satiric account of suburban life in California, she wrote *Hangsaman* (1951), about a woman on the verge of mental collapse; *The Bird's Nest* (1954), a dramatic tale of suspense based on a real-life case study of a woman afflicted with multiple personalities; and *The Sundial* (1958), a story about religious zealots awaiting the end of the world. The best known of her full-length novels are *The Haunting of Hill House* (1959), which as *The Haunting* became a classic movie chiller starring Julie Harris, and *We Have Always Lived in the Castle* (1962), a frightening psychological portrait of a disturbed and isolated young girl.

The somber side of Jackson's stories and novels is balanced to some extent by the lighthearted nature of two volumes of personal memoirs. *Life among the Savages* (1953) and *Raising Demons* (1957) are humorous chronicles of life in an intellectual family of a small Vermont town, based on Jackson's experiences as the wife of the critic Stanley Edgar Hyman and the mother of four children. Jackson died suddenly of heart failure at age 47. Her husband edited the posthumous *Come Along With Me* (1968)—three lectures on the craft of writing along with the novel she was working on at the time of her death.

SHORT STORY COLLECTION BY JACKSON

The Lottery: And Other Stories. 1949. FS&G 1992 $8.95. ISBN 0-374-51681-2

NOVELS BY JACKSON

The Haunting of Hill House. 1959. Viking Penguin 1984 $6.95. ISBN 0-14-007108-3

The Sundial. 1958. Viking Penguin 1986 $5.95. ISBN 0-14-008317-0

We Have Always Lived in the Castle. 1962. Viking Penguin 1986 $5.95. ISBN 0-14-007107-5

NONFICTION BY JACKSON

Life Among the Savages. 1953. Academy Chi. Pubs. 1989 $8.95. ISBN 0-89733-342-X. Hilarious account of Jackson's family life in Vermont.

BOOK ABOUT JACKSON

Friedman, Lenemaja. *Shirley Jackson. Twayne's U.S. Authors Ser.* G. K. Hall 1975 $14.95. ISBN 0-8057-0402-7. A good general introduction to Jackson's life and works, including a bibliography, a chronology, a one-chapter biography, and extensive discussion of how Jackson's works relate to her life.

JAMESON, FREDRIC. 1934–

[SEE Chapter 19 in this volume.]

JARRELL, RANDALL. 1914–1965

In 1961 Randall Jarrell's *The Woman at the Washington Zoo* (1960) won the National Book Award. The poems collected there displayed Jarrell's characteristic expert technical skill with rhyme, assonance, meter, and imagery.

Poet, critic, novelist, and teacher, Jarrell was born in Nashville, Tennessee. He graduated from Vanderbilt University, where he received his M.A., and taught at the University of Texas, Sarah Lawrence College, and the Woman's College of the University of North Carolina. He won a Guggenheim Fellowship (1947) and was awarded a grant from the National Institute of Arts and Letters (1951). In 1956–58, Jarrell served as poetry consultant at the Library of Congress; later he became literary editor of *The Nation* and poetry editor for the *Partisan Review* and the *Yale Review.*

Jarrell's fictional comedy *Pictures from an Institution* (1954) is a brilliant comment on college faculty capers. *A Sad Heart at the Supermarket: Essays and Fables* (1962) contains his ironic observations on the decline in taste, learning, and culture in the United States. He was also the author of a number of children's books. Fatally injured when hit by a car in Chapel Hill, North Carolina, in October 1965, Jarrell was one of the finest of the poet-critics who flourished during the era of new critical formalism.

POETRY BY JARRELL

Complete Poems. FS&G 1981 $45.00. ISBN 0-374-12716-6
Selected Poems. FS&G 1990 $17.95. ISBN 0-374-25867-8
Selected Poems, Including The Woman at the Washington Zoo. Atheneum 1964 o.p.

NONFICTION BY JARRELL

Kipling, Auden & Co.: Essays and Reviews, 1935–1964. FS&G 1980 $17.95. ISBN 0-374-18153-5. This selection demonstrates Jarrell's critical acuity.

BOOKS ABOUT JARRELL

Bryant, Joseph A. *Understanding Randall Jarrell.* U. of SC Pr. 1986 $24.95. ISBN 0-87249-487-X. Offers stimulating exchanges on one of the best poets of the century.
Ferguson, Suzanne. *Poetry of Randall Jarrell. Southern Literary Studies.* La. State U. Pr. 1971 o.p. The first major critical study of Jarrell; a chronological survey.
Flynn, Richard. *Randall Jarrell and The Lost World of Childhood.* U. of Ga. Pr. 1990 $25.00. ISBN 0-8203-1243-6. Relates Jarrell's preoccupation with the experience of childhood to events in his own early life.
Jarrell, Mary, ed. *Randall Jarrell's Letters: An Autobiographical and Literary Selection.* HM 1985 o.p. Posthumous collection.
Pritchard, William H. *Randall Jarrell: A Literary Life.* FS&G 1990 $25.00. ISBN 0-374-24677-7. Attempts to read both the written part and the lived part of Jarrell's life.

JOHNSON, EDGAR. 1901–

Johnson is one of the preeminent biographers of the twentieth century; his industriousness and thoroughness place him in the tradition of the multivolume writers of the nineteenth century who were his subjects. He began research for a biography on SIR WALTER SCOTT in 1956, started writing in 1961, and ended up at the end of the decade with a manuscript of 500,000 words in 78 chapters. *Sir Walter Scott: The Great Unknown* (1970) was awarded the American Heritage biography prize in 1969, at $20,000 considered the largest award in the U.S. for a literary work. Some critics preferred Johnson's biography to Scott's works; all agreed that it was a definitive account of a major author. Johnson is notable, also, as the biographer of CHARLES DICKENS.

NONFICTION BY JOHNSON

Charles Dickens: His Tragedy and Triumph. Viking Penguin 1986 $12.95. ISBN 0-14-058027-1
Sir Walter Scott: The Great Unknown. Macmillan 1970 o.p.

JONES, JAMES. 1921–1977

Born in Illinois, Jones was unable to afford college, so he enlisted in the Army in 1939. With the publication of *Whistle* (1978), it became apparent that Jones's main achievement was a trilogy of novels about U.S. Army life during World War II that may well stand among the best war fiction of all time. Jeffrey Helterman (*Dictionary of Literary Biography*) has said that Jones may well have "produced an immense, vital trilogy on men at war which should earn him the place he had always wanted—to be the THOMAS WOLFE of his generation." The same main characters appear in *From Here to Eternity* (1951), *The Thin Red Line* (1962), and *Whistle*, though their names are changed. The first novel of the trilogy, *From Here to Eternity*, which won the National Book Award, was a controversial bestseller that was made into one of the best movies of 1953. Jones's novel is a brutal, almost ugly, picture of the peacetime army in Hawaii until the attack on Pearl Harbor. *The Thin Red Line* describes the Guadalcanal campaign, while *Whistle*, which was edited by Willie Morris from a nearly completed manuscript, shows Mort Winch ("Milt Warden" of *From Here to Eternity*) returning wounded to the United States with three of his men and discovering that neither the army nor their country has any significant place for them.

Jones's other fiction is considered less successful. *Some Came Running* (1957) is an autobiographical novel about a veteran who returns to Illinois to write a war novel; it was condemned for its undisciplined length, verbal excesses, and naive philosophizing. The deliberately short and much tighter *The Pistol* (1959) proved to be the first of several works in which an almost obsessive concern with heavy symbolism suggested to some readers that Jones had veered too far away from the raw naturalism of his first novel. *Go to the Widow-Maker* (1967), about a civilian's effort to prove his masculinity and courage in skin diving and shark shooting, was likewise poorly received. Nevertheless, Jones's achievements in his trilogy continue to be admired by critics and eagerly read by new generations of readers.

NOVELS BY JONES

From Here to Eternity. 1951. Dell 1991 $5.99. ISBN 0-440-32770-9
Go to the Widow-Maker. 1967. Dell 1967 o.p.
The Pistol. 1959. Dell 1979 o.p.

The Thin Red Line. 1962. Dell 1991 $5.99. ISBN 0-440-38876-7
Whistle: Chapter One of a Work-in-Progress. Bruccoli 1974 $35.00. ISBN 0-89723-017-5

Books about Jones

Garrett, George. *James Jones.* HarBraceJ 1984 o.p.
Giles, James R. *James Jones. Twayne's U.S. Authors Ser.* G. K. Hall 1981 o.p. Readable, interpretive criticism.
Hopkins, John R., ed. *James Jones: A Checklist.* Gale 1974 o.p.

JUSTICE, DONALD. 1925–

Donald Justice studied at the universities of Miami, Iowa, and Stanford, and has taught at the universities of Missouri, Syracuse, and California at Irvine and the Writers Workshop of the University of Iowa, where he exercised great influence on a whole generation of poets, including MARK STRAND and CHARLES WRIGHT. Justice currently teaches at the University of Florida. He has edited the *Collected Poems of Weldon Kees.* The Pulitzer Prize was awarded to his *Selected Poems* (1979) and he has won the Lamont Prize (1960) and the Harriet Monroe Memorial Prize, as well as grants from the Rockefeller and Guggenheim Foundations. A noted translator of French writings, Justice has been influenced by French literature as well as by the American and British traditions. Justice's poems are generally short and ironic. A formalist, Justice moves with ease among a variety of verse forms. He sees life through the frame of a certain American survivalism; his sensibility is singular, yet representative of his time and culture.

POETRY BY JUSTICE

Departures. Atheneum 1973 o.p.
A Donald Justice Reader. U. Pr. of New Eng. 1991 $19.95. ISBN 0-87451-567-X. Reader-friendly sampler of Justice's work.
Night Light. 1967. Wesleyan U. Pr. rev. ed. 1981 $22.50. ISBN 0-8195-2106-X
Selected Poems. Atheneum 1979 o.p.
The Summer Anniversaries. Wesleyan U. Pr. rev. ed. 1981 $10.95. ISBN 0-8195-1105-6
The Sunset Maker: Poems/Stories/A Memoir. Atheneum 1987 o.p. Many of these works have an elegiac quality.

KAZIN, ALFRED. 1915–

Alfred Kazin, a literary critic and professor of English literature, was born in Brooklyn and educated at City College and Columbia University. Kazin established his own critical reputation in the mid-1940s with *On Native Grounds* (1942), a study of American literature. He started work on it at the suggestion of Carl Van Doren in 1939 while, he explains, "half-heartedly doing a master's essay at Columbia on Gibbon and wondering what would ever become of me or of the maddening age." His later work, *Bright Book of American Life* (1973), is both a recapitulation of modernism and an evaluation of American writers who have achieved prominence since 1945. Modernism, a favorite topic of Kazin, is in his view a literary revolution marked by spontaneity and individuality but lacking in precisely the mass culture appeal necessary to its survival. *Contemporaries* (1962) includes reflective essays on travel, five essays on Freud, and some very perceptive essays on literary and political matters. The final section, "The Critic's Task," concerns itself with the critic's function within a popular and an academic context and with critical theory and principles. *Starting Out in the Thirties* (1965) describes Kazin's early years with *The New Republic* as book reviewer and evaluates his contemporaries—MALCOLM COWLEY, MARY MC-

CARTHY, Philip Rahv, Granville Hicks, and others—in a period when the depression and radical political thought, pro and con, deeply affected literary production. In the midst of the current antihumanistic trend in literary theory, Kazin remains a literary critic of the old school, believing in the relevance of literature to modern life.

NONFICTION BY KAZIN

An American Procession. Knopf 1984 $18.95. ISBN 0-394-50378-3

Bright Book of Life: American Novelists and Storytellers from Hemingway to Mailer. 1973. U. of Notre Dame Pr. 1980 $11.95. ISBN 0-268-00664-4

Contemporaries, from the Nineteenth Century to the Present. 1962. Horizon Pr. rev. ed. 1981 o.p.

The Inmost Leaf: A Selection of Essays. HarBraceJ 1979 $4.95. ISBN 0-15-644398-8

On Native Grounds: An Interpretation of Modern American Prose Literature. 1942. HarBraceJ 1983 o.p.

New York Jew. Knopf 1978 o.p.

Starting Out in the Thirties. 1965. Cornell Univ. Pr. 1989 $7.95. ISBN 0-8014-9562-8. Sequel to *A Walker in the City.*

A Walker in the City. 1951. HarBraceJ 1969 $9.95. ISBN 0-15-694176-7. Autobiographical memories and reflections.

A Writer's America: Landscape in Literature. Knopf 1988 $24.95. ISBN 0-394-57142-8. Considers the impact of the American landscape on the country's writers from Thomas Jefferson and St. John de Crèvecoeur to Dashiell Hammett and Adrienne Rich.

KENNEDY, WILLIAM. 1928–

When *Ironweed* won both the Pulitzer Prize and the National Book Critics Circle Award in 1983, recognition came to a writer who had quietly produced a small body of significant work that SAUL BELLOW had praised in these terms: "These Albany novels will be memorable, a distinguished group of books." The Albany Cycle, as it is now called, consists so far of three novels set in the upstate capital of New York during the 1920s and 1930s with emphasis on the seamy side of Albany—its crooked politicians, gangsters, gamblers, and Depression-era tramps. Good as the first two novels in the cycle are, *Ironweed* is artistically a much more assured performance. A wanderer's-return sort of mellowness replaces the wisecracks and the cynical tone of *Legs* (1975) while reinforcing the human values of *Billy Phelan's Greatest Game* (1978). The progression of Kennedy's development as a writer is all the more apparent when one compares *Ironweed* with Kennedy's first novel, *The Ink Truck* (1969). The success of the Albany Cycle encouraged Viking Press to reissue in 1984 the novel first published in 1969, and in a new author's note Kennedy conceded that the unidentified locale of this novel about a newspaper strike is indeed Albany. The *Washington Post Book World* was no doubt prescient when it called the book "a fine debut by a writer of obvious talent and much promise." Kennedy has provided his own background gloss to the cycle with *O Albany! An Urban Tapestry* (1983). In addition to teaching at the State University of New York in Albany, Kennedy worked as a journalist and free-lance writer until his success. The award of a MacArthur "genius grant" enabled him to devote himself full time to such writing chores as the screenplay for Francis Ford Coppolla's film, *The Cotton Club,* and the continuation of the Albany Cycle. A recent work, *Quinn's Book* (1989), deals with the ancestors of some of the characters already introduced.

NOVELS BY KENNEDY

Billy Phelan's Greatest Game. Viking Penguin 1983 $7.95. ISBN 0-14-006340-4

The Ink Truck. 1969. Viking Penguin 1985 $8.95. ISBN 0-14-007674-3

Ironweed. Contemporary Amer. Fiction Ser. Viking Penguin 1988 $4.50. ISBN 0-14-008103-8

Legs. Viking Penguin 1983 $10.00. ISBN 0-14-006484-2

Quinn's Book. 1988. Viking Penguin 1989 $10.95. ISBN 0-14-007737-5. Set in Albany, descendants of characters introduced in trilogy.

Very Old Bones. Viking Penguin 1992 $22.00. ISBN 0-670-83457-2. Kennedy's most recent and experimental novel.

KENNEDY, X. J. 1929–

According to Kennedy: "Nearly always write in rime and metre. Favor narratives, lyrics to be sung." Widely anthologized, Kennedy's poetry may not be as influential among contemporary poets as others' because of his preference for, in his words, "old-fangled structures most poets have junked these days." As Kennedy's comments on his verse suggest, his poetry is witty, concise, and unpretentious. His subject matter is drawn from the everyday—his Catholic background, middle-class suburban life. Yet his concerns can be profound—death, violence, suicide, Genesis.

POETRY BY KENNEDY

Brats. Atheneum 1986 $11.95. ISBN 0-689-50392-X. Forty-two humorous poems about horrible children written for children.

Cross Ties: Selected Poems. U. of Ga. Pr. 1985 $9.95. ISBN 0-8203-0738-6. Organized around longer poems, 1956–84, and songs, light verse, epigrams, and children's verses.

Dark Horses, New Poems. Johns Hopkins 1992 $26.00. ISBN 0-8018-4484-3

Hangover Mass. Bits Pr. 1981 o.p. Kennedy looks at Catholicism before Vatican II.

Nude Descending a Staircase: Poems, Song, A Ballad. Doubleday 1961 o.p. Title poem inspired by a Duchamp painting that scandalized the Armory Art Show viewers in 1913.

BOOK ABOUT KENNEDY

Prundy, Wyatt. *Fallen from the Symboled World.* OUP 1990 $35.00. ISBN 0-19-505786-4. Concentrates on how Kennedy and others employ rhetorical figures.

KEROUAC, JACK. 1922–1969

Now that *On the Road* (1957) has been sanctified as a *Penguin Modern Classic* and honored by inclusion in the *Viking Critical Library*, we must see Jack Kerouac as more than the representative of the Beat Generation, a latter-day bohemian, and a social rebel. Now we can also see Kerouac as a major postwar American writer.

Kerouac coined the phrase "Beat Generation" in 1952, and several years later the *American College Dictionary* used his definition: *"Beat Generation*—members of the generation that came of age after World War II who espouse mystical detachment and relaxation of social and sexual tensions, supposedly as a result of disillusionment stemming from the cold war." But when Kerouac himself protested, "I'm king of the beats, but I'm not a beatnik," he may have wanted to disclaim responsibility for the next generation—the hippies who took to the road even while he stayed at home during the late sixties and early seventies. Kerouac himself was a conservative in both politics and religion, and if he was a revolutionary at all, it was in the tradition of romantic American individualism of a Thoreauvian kind. Nonetheless, his three best-selling works—*On the Road, The Dharma Bums* (1958), and *The Subterraneans* (1958)—attracted hundreds of thousands of readers and remain social documents of great historical significance as manifestos of new attitudes that profoundly affected young people throughout the Western world.

Born in Lowell, Massachusetts, of French-Canadian extraction (he was christened Jean Louis Lebris De Kerouac), Kerouac interrupted his education at Columbia University to serve in the merchant marine during World War II and spent his postwar years roaming the United States and Mexico, often in association with other writers who later became famous, such as ALLEN GINSBERG, WILLIAM BURROUGHS, and GARY SNYDER, as well as the almost legendary Neal Cassaday, whom he was to immortalize as the Dean Moriarty of *On the Road* and the Cody of *Visions of Cody* (1972). Kerouac's first novel, *The Town and the City* (1950), is a rather conventional story of family disintegration written under the influence of THOMAS WOLFE, but he found his own characteristic voice in his next work. *On the Road* was the first of his books to reflect his method of "spontaneous prose." Written in 20 days on a single 120-foot roll of teletype paper, it makes use of free association in a way that Kerouac likened to improvised jazz. He saw that novel and most of his subsequent works as installments in one vast autobiographical testament, which he hoped to see eventually published in a uniform edition as *The Legend of Duluoz* with the names of the real-life models for his characters substituted for their varying fictional names. According to Ann Charters (*Dictionary of Literary Biography*), one can read the whole Kerouac saga in 12 stages corresponding to the chronological periods in his life.

Kerouac's first book of poetry, *Mexico City Blues* (1959), consists of 242 jazz poems on such subjects as Zen, drug addiction, and childhood. He also authored several other volumes of poetry as well as a collection of travel sketches called *Lonesome Traveler* (1960).

NOVELS BY KEROUAC

Big Sur. Viking Penguin 1992 $10.00. ISBN 0-14-016812-5
The Book of Dreams. City Lights 1961 $7.95. ISBN 0-87286-027-2
The Dharma Bums. 1958. Viking Penguin 1971 $6.95. ISBN 0-14-004252-0. Two rebels on
    a wild march for experience from San Francisco's swinging bars to the top of the
    snow-capped Sierras.
Doctor Sax. 1959. Buccaneer Bks. 1976 $21.95. ISBN 0-89966-133-5
Maggie Cassidy. Viking Penguin 1993 $10.00. ISBN 0-14-017906-2
On the Road. 1957. Viking Penguin 1976 $5.95. ISBN 0-14-004259-8
Pic. Grove Pr. 1971 o.p. Story about a black baseball player.
Satori in Paris. Grove Pr. 1988 $8.95. ISBN 0-8021-3061-5
The Subterraneans. 1958. Grove Pr. 1989 $6.95. ISBN 0-8021-3186-7
The Town and the City. HarBraceJ 1970 repr. of 1950 ed. $12.95. ISBN 0-15-690790-9
Tristessa. Viking Penguin 1992 $9.00. ISBN 0-14-016811-7
Visions of Cody. 1972. McGraw 1976 $6.95. ISBN 0-07-034204-0
Visions of Gerard. McGraw 1990 $8.95. ISBN 0-07-034241-5

POETRY BY KEROUAC

Poems All Sizes. City Lights 1992 $8.95. ISBN 0-87286-269-0. A good collection, with an
    introduction by Allen Ginsberg.

BOOKS ABOUT KEROUAC

Challis, Chris. *Quest for Kerouac.* Faber & Faber 1984 o.p. A retracing of Kerouac's paths
    across the United States by a British author.

Charters, Ann. *Kerouac: A Biography*. St. Martin 1987 $10.95. ISBN 0-312-06617-9. Detailed, thoroughly researched biography of Kerouac heavily dependent on primary sources.

Clark, Tom. *Jack Kerouac*. HarBraceJ 1984 o.p.

Gifford, Barry, and Lawrence Lee. *Jack's Book: An Oral Biography of Jack Kerouac*. St. Martin 1978 o.p. On Kerouac at center of American bohemianism.

Hipkiss, Robert A. *Jack Kerouac, Prophet of the New Romanticism: A Critical Study of the Published Works of Kerouac and a Comparison of Them to Those of J. D. Salinger, James Purdy, John Knowles and Ken Kesey*. U. Pr. of KS 1976 o.p. Argues Kerouac's centrality to literary movement.

Hunt, Tina. *Kerouac's Crooked Road: Development of a Fiction*. Shoe String 1981 $27.50. ISBN 0-208-01871-9. An analysis of the various influences that shaped Kerouac's work.

McNally, D. *Desolate Angel: Jack Kerouac, the Beat Generation and America*. McGraw 1980 o.p. The Beats as "psychic pioneers"; necessary for an understanding of post-World War II America.

Milewski, Robert J., and others. *Jack Kerouac: An Annotated Bibliography of Secondary Sources, 1944–1979*. Author Bibliographies Ser. Scarecrow 1981 $27.50. ISBN 0-8108-1378-5

Nicosia, Gerald. *Memory Babe: A Critical Biography of Jack Kerouac*. Viking Penguin 1988 $9.95. ISBN 0-14-058016-6. A major study of Kerouac's life and work.

Weinreich, Regina. *The Spontaneous Poetics of Jack Kerouac; A Study of The Fiction*. Paragon Hse. 1990 $9.95. ISBN 0-55778-285-7

KESEY, KEN. 1935–

Born in Colorado, graduated from the University of Oregon, and since then a sometimes vagabond resident of the West Coast, Kesey has published only two full-length novels, but they have helped to give him a cult following. *One Flew over the Cuckoo's Nest* (1962) owes much to Kesey's own experience as a ward attendant in a mental hospital. This exciting first novel is told from the point of view of a half-Indian man who thinks of himself as the Big Chief pictured on the writing tablets of everybody's school days looking out at the other inmates in a Disneylike world. Its portrayal of the doomed but heroic rebel McMurphy stood for a particular kind of American individualism.

Sometimes a Great Notion (1964) is a long, complex novel that troubled many of Kesey's earlier readers. For although this story of a lumbering family dynasty in the Northwest exalts the romantic values of nature and emotion over the feeble representatives of the establishment depicted in the story, it also seems to champion strong, arrogant individualism against anything that smacks of conformity or easy concessions to group approval. The Ken Kesey who wrote *Sometimes a Great Notion* would not have been likely to attend the festivities at Woodstock. Yet, after publishing that daring and misunderstood novel, Kesey publicly renounced "literature" for "life" and allowed himself to become a cult hero precisely for the Woodstock generation. Now married and the father of four children, he has served as a kind of guru for an Oregon commune since his second novel was published. Kesey's most recent novel is *Demon Box* (1987); although it was somewhat well received, it was still compared unfavorably to his earlier works.

NOVELS BY KESEY

Demon Box. Viking Penguin 1987 $9.95. ISBN 0-14-008530-0
One Flew over the Cuckoo's Nest. 1962. Viking Penguin 1977 $12.00. ISBN 0-14-015509-0
Sometimes a Great Notion. 1964. Viking Penguin 1977 $12.00. ISBN 0-14-004529-5

BOOKS ABOUT KESEY

Leeds, Barry H. *Ken Kesey*. *Lit. and Life Ser.* Continuum 1981 o.p.
Porter, M. Gilbert. *The Art of Grit: Ken Kesey's Fiction. Literary Frontiers Ser.* U. of Mo. Pr. 1982 o.p. A good study by the author of several books about Kesey.
Tanner, Stephen L. *Ken Kesey. Twayne's U.S. Authors Ser.* Macmillan 1983 $20.95. ISBN 0-8057-7383-5

KINGSTON, MAXINE (TING TING) HONG. 1940–

Born in California to immigrant Chinese parents, Kingston was educated at the University of California at Berkeley. Kingston soared to literary celebrity upon the publication of her autobiographical *The Woman Warrior: Memoirs of a Girlhood among Ghosts* (1976). Writes critic Henry Allen: "In a wild mix of myth, memory, history and a lucidity which verges on the eerie," Kingston describes the experiences of the women in her family "as women, as Chinese coming to America and as Americans." *The Woman Warrior* is dominated by Kingston's mother; her next work, *China Men* (1980), although not autobiographical in the manner of her previous book, is focused on her father and on the other men in her family, giving fictionalized, poetic versions of their histories. The combination of fiction, nonfiction, memoir, and myth in both books create a form of balanced opposites that one critic has likened to yin and yang. Her first novel, *Tripmaster Monkey: His Fake Book*, was published in 1989.

NONFICTION BY KINGSTON

China Men. Random 1989 $10.00. ISBN 0-679-72328-5. Chinese men in North America and Hawaii.
The Woman Warrior: Memoirs of a Girlhood among Ghosts. Random 1977 $4.95. ISBN 0-394-72392-9. Susan Currier describes this work as "an effort to reconcile American and Chinese female identities" (The Dictionary of Literary Biography Yearbook: 1980).

NOVEL BY KINGSTON

Tripmaster Monkey: His Fake Book. 1989. Knopf 1989 $19.95. ISBN 0-394-56831-1. Follows the life of a young Chinese-American man in San Francisco in the 1960s. Features the hero as the legendary monkey troublemaker of Chinese mythology, and considers the question of whether an oriental can assimilate into an occidental society.

KINNELL, GALWAY. 1927–

A New Englander by birth, Galway Kinnell is a poet who eludes easy categorization. His poetry at its height speaks of city as well as country. Indeed, his "The Avenue Bearing the Initial of Christ into the New World" is a kind of literary landmark for New York City's Lower East Side. At his best in long poems—his masterly *The Book of Nightmares* (1971) is one 75-page poem—Kinnell is most famous for his masterpiece "The Bear," in which a hunter unites with the hunted and the poet unites with the prey and the predator. The largeness of his vision is coupled with an intense ability to weave a detailed tapestry out of American life and experience.

Kinnell has also written a novel, *Black Light* (1980), set in the Middle East. He has traveled extensively in Europe and the Middle East and has taught in Grenoble, France. Educated at Princeton University and the University of Rochester, Kinnell was the winner of a Fulbright Fellowship to study in Paris. His awards include a Guggenheim Fellowship (1961–62), a National Institute of Arts and Letters grant (1961), a Rockefeller grant (1967–68), the American Book

Award (1983), a Pulitzer Prize (1983), and a MacArthur Fellowship (1984). He has also translated poetry from the French.

POETRY BY KINNELL

The Avenue Bearing the Initial of Christ into the New World: Poems, 1946–1964. HM 1974 $12.70. ISBN 0-395-18628-5. Early poetry, demonstrating a strong narrative impulse.
The Book of Nightmares. HM 1973 $9.70. ISBN 0-395-12098-5. A book-length poem.
Mortal Acts, Mortal Words: A Collection of Poems. HM 1980 $10.95. ISBN 0-395-29125-9
The Past. HM 1986 1985 $13.45. ISBN 0-395-39385-X
Selected Poems. HM 1983 $12.50. ISBN 0-395-32046-1. This book won the Pulitzer Prize and the American Book Award.

WORK BY KINNELL

Walking Down the Stairs: Selections from Interviews. Ed. by Donald Hall. *Poets on Poetry Ser.* U. of Mich. Pr. 1978 $11.95. ISBN 0-472-52530-1

BOOKS ABOUT KINNELL

Nelson, Howard, ed. *On the Poetry of Galway Kinnell: The Wages of Dying.* U. of Mich. Pr. 1988 $32.50. ISBN 0-472-09376-2. Brings together a broad spectrum of critical views on Kinnell's work.
Zimmerman, Lee. *Intricate and Simple Things: The Poetry of Galway Kinnell.* U. of Ill. Pr. 1987 $27.50. ISBN 0-252-01375-1. Follows Kinnell's development book by book.

KIZER, CAROLYN. 1925–

Poet and critic Carolyn Kizer was born in Spokane, Washington, and educated at Sarah Lawrence College. She has spent a great deal of time studying in China. Influenced by the Chinese belief in yin and yang, Kizer writes about life's dualities—old and young, past and present, male and female. Exploring the woman poet's dilemma—women writers' contradictory position as "handmaidens/To our own goddess"—Kizer also celebrates the paradoxes felt by women in a modern world. She has been awarded a Pulitzer Prize (1985) and a Poetry Society of America Frost Medal (1988). A skilled translator, she has done translations from Urdu, Macedonian, Yiddish, and, most notably, from the Chinese—the great Tang poet TU FU and the love poems of a modern woman poet, Shu Ting.

POETRY BY KIZER

Mermaids in the Basement: Poems for Women. Copper Canyon 1984 $14.00. ISBN 0-914742-80-9. Along with *Poems for Men*, explores tensions between men and women.
Midnight Was My Cry: New and Selected Poems. Doubleday 1971 o.p.
The Nearness of You: Poems for Men. Copper Canyon 1986 $15.00. ISBN 0-914742-96-5. Companion to *Poems for Women.*
Yin: New Poems. BOA Edns. 1984 $18.00. ISBN 0-918526-44-2. Contains two autobiographical reveries.

KOCH, (JAY) KENNETH. 1925–

Born in Cincinnati, Ohio, Kenneth Koch began to write at age 5 and became serious about it at age 17. After serving in the army, he received his B.A. from Harvard University and, later, his Ph.D. from Columbia University, where he now teaches. He has taught creative writing to children and, using works of his own pupils as examples, has written several books on the subject, notably *Wishes, Lies and Dreams: Teaching Children to Write Poetry* (1970) and *Rose, Where Do You Get That Red?* (1973). Koch is the recipient of a Fulbright

Fellowship (1950–51), a Guggenheim Fellowship (1961), and an Ingram-Merrill Foundation Fellowship (1969).

Koch is associated with the New York school of poets of the 1950s, a group that included JOHN ASHBERY and FRANK O'HARA. Much of his early work was influenced largely by JACQUES PRÉVERT (see Vol. 2), among others, but his poetry has since taken on a simpler and more realistic style. Like other New York poets, Koch has been actively interested in theater, and many of his plays, including *Little Red Riding Hood, The Election,* and *Perides,* have been performed by off-Broadway groups.

POETRY BY KOCH

Days and Nights. Random 1982 o.p.
Selected Poems 1950–82. Random 1985 $9.95. ISBN 0-394-73771-7. A representative collection.

NONFICTION BY KOCH

Rose, Where Did You Get That Red? Teaching Great Poetry to Children. Random 1973 $5.95. ISBN 0-394-71885-2
Wishes, Lies and Dreams: Teaching Children to Write Poetry. HarpC 1980 repr. of 1970 ed. $6.00. ISBN 0-06-080530-7

KOSINSKI, JERZY. 1933–1991

Jerzy Kosinski, whose *Steps* won the National Book Award for fiction in 1968, grew up in Poland but emigrated to the United States in 1957 and became a naturalized citizen in 1965. His first two novels are set in Europe, with European themes and concerns. *The Painted Bird* (1965) is the story of a young boy wandering through Eastern Europe during the years of World War II. Looking on scenes of devastation and violence, the mute young observer somehow conveys a sense of mingled horror and compassion for the human condition. *Steps* presents even more neutralized vignettes of abuse, rape, and mutilation, achieving a kind of poetic grandeur in its unstated assumption that it is better to see horror than to see nothing at all. A novel without conventional narration, point of view, or dialogue, it harks back to works like DJUNA BARNES's *Nightwood* in its surrealistic view of human bestiality, but it offers hope nonetheless if only in its demonstration that destruction must precede creation.

In the works after *Steps,* Kosinski has sometimes succeeded in combining experimental techniques with popular appeal. Kosinski's name stayed prominently before the public when he was made the target of a *Village Voice* exposé in 1982, in which he was accused of being a CIA agent and writing his books with unacknowledged collaboration from paid helpers. Those charges have been more or less satisfactorily refuted, but not without apparent damage to Kosinski's reputation. Even before the furor caused by the *Voice* piece and reactions to it elsewhere in the media, *Pinball* (1982), like the novel before it, *Passion Play* (1979), had received a largely negative response from critics. Presumably a fair assessment of Kosinski cannot be made until the critical climate has time to cool. In any case, Kosinski is an author with a distinctive voice of his own that also echoes some main currents of international modernism. Tragically, Kosinski committed suicide in 1991.

NOVELS BY KOSINSKI

Being There. 1971. Bantam 1980 $3.95. ISBN 0-553-26780-9. Turned into a popular film.
Blind Date. Arcade Pub. Inc. 1989 $8.95. ISBN 1-55970-003-3
Cockpit. Arcade Pub. Inc. 1989 $8.95. ISBN 1-55970-022-X

The Devil Tree. HarBraceJ 1973 o.p.
The Painted Bird. 1965. Bantam 1983 $5.99. ISBN 0-553-26520-2
Pinball. 1982. Arcade Pub. Inc. 1989 repr. of 1982 ed. $8.95. ISBN 1-55970-004-1
Steps. Random 1988 $9.00. ISBN 0-394-75716-5

BOOKS ABOUT KOSINSKI

Bruss, Paul. *Victims: Textual Strategies in Recent American Fiction.* Bucknell U. Pr. 1981 $32.50. ISBN 0-8387-5006-0. A reading of Kosinski alongside Nabokov and Barthelme.
Cronin, Gloria L., and Blaine H. Hall. *Jerzy Kosinski: An Annotated Bibliography.* Greenwood 1991 $35.00. ISBN 0-313-27442-8. A model of bibliography devoted to the writings of Kosinski.
Lavers, Norman. *Jerzy Kosinski. Twayne's U.S. Authors Ser.* G. K. Hall 1982 o.p. Criticism and interpretation of Kosinski's works; includes a brief biography.

KUNITZ, STANLEY (JASSPON). 1905–

Since his *Selected Poems* (1959), Kunitz has moved from the intricate, highly intellectual poems that placed him in the tradition of JOHN DONNE and T. S. ELIOT, to a more simple, realistic style. "Maybe age itself compels me to embrace the great simplicities," he has commented, "as I struggle to free myself from the knots and complications, the hang-ups, of my youth."

Kunitz served in World War II as a private and later taught at Bennington College in Vermont. He translated works from the Russian and did much to popularize the work of the poets YEVTUSHENKO (see Vol. 2) and VOZNESENSKY (see Vol. 2). His *Selected Poems* won the Pulitzer Prize (1958,) and he has been elected to the National Institute of Arts and Letters. ROBERT LOWELL said of him, "He has been one of our masters for years."

POETRY BY KUNITZ

Interviews and Encounters. Sheep Meadow 1992 $22.50. ISBN 0-935296-79-4. Functions as an oral history of American art and letters.
Selected Poems, 1928–1978. Atlantic Monthly 1979 o.p.
Testing-Tree: Poem. Atlantic Monthly 1971 o.p. Thirty new poems including the four-page title poem.
The Wellfleet Whale and Companion Poems. Sheep Meadow 1983 $7.95. ISBN 0-935296-36-0

NONFICTION BY KUNITZ

A Kind of Order, A Kind of Folly: Essays and Conversations. Little 1975 o.p. Useful commentary on his distinctive poetic vision.

LEVERTOV, DENISE. 1923–

Born in Essex, England, Denise Levertov became a U.S. citizen after her marriage to Mitchell Goodman, the writer who was indicted, with BENJAMIN SPOCK (see Vol. 5) and the Rev. William Sloane Coffin, for his antiwar activities. She came to New York to live in 1948.

Levertov acknowledges that her writing was influenced by WILLIAM CARLOS WILLIAMS, CHARLES OLSON, and ROBERT DUNCAN. After her first book, *The Double Image* (1946), was published in England in 1946, she did not produce another volume until 1957, when City Lights brought out *Here and Now*. In 1961 she was poetry editor for the *Nation*, and in 1965 she received the grant in literature from the National Institute of Arts and Letters. Her essays collected in *The Poet in the World* (1973) and *Light Up the Cave* are written with a penetrating intelligence. Winner of numerous awards and prizes, she is a poet of reverence and fierce moral drive.

POETRY BY LEVERTOV

Candles in Babylon. New Dir. Pr. 1982 $5.95. ISBN 0-8112-0909-1. Poems about art's purpose in the modern world.
Collected Earlier Poems, 1940–1960. New Dir. Pr. 1979 $9.50. ISBN 0-8112-0717-X
Life in the Forest. New Dir. Pr. 1978 $5.95. ISBN 0-8112-0692-0. Poems concerned with the effects of the myth of "the Garden."
Poems 1968–1972. New Dir. Pr. 1987 $19.95. ISBN 0-8112-1004-9

BOOKS ABOUT LEVERTOV

Atchity, John K. *Denise Levertov: An Interview*. New London Pr. 1980 o.p.
Marten, Harry. *Understanding Denise Levertov*. U. of SC Pr. 1989 $12.95. ISBN 0-87249-579-5. Aimed at readers who are coming to the work for the first time.
Wagner, Linda W. *Denise Levertov. Twayne's U.S. Authors Series*. NCUP 1967 o.p. Readable interpretations and biographical essay.
Wagner-Martin, Linda. *Critical Essays on Denise Levertov*. G. K. Hall 1990 $45.00. ISBN 0-8161-8899-8

LEVINE, PHILIP. 1928–

As a poet, Levine has been preoccupied with domestic and modern urban life, loneliness, and love. His poetry is somber, reflective, and restrained; his language simple and direct. His take on the modern world is dark and unsentimental. Born in Detroit, Levine has taught writing at a number of universities, including Berkeley, Princeton, and Columbia.

POETRY BY LEVINE

New Selected Poems. McKay 1991 $23.50. ISBN 0-679-40165-2. The latest collection of Levine's works.
Not This Pig: Poems. U. Pr. of New Eng. 1968 $10.95. ISBN 0-8195-2038-1

NONFICTION BY LEVINE

Don't Ask. U. of Mich. Pr. 1981 $11.95. ISBN 0-472-06327-8. Gives insight into the poet's methods.

LEWIS, R(ICHARD) W(ARRINGTON) B(ALDWIN). 1917–

Noted as the biographer of EDITH WHARTON, Lewis is also recognized as a literary critic concerned with the history of ideas in American culture. Revising the old view of Wharton as *"grande dame,"* Lewis has given readers a new Wharton, "a connoisseur of friendship, struggling to create a 'republic of the spirit' among those she was most attracted to." Using material never before available, uncovering the facts of her one great love affair, and publishing as an appendix a piece of pornography by Wharton, Lewis treated Wharton as a devoted artist and sexually alive woman, awakening readers to a new appreciation of her place in the female literary tradition.

NONFICTION BY LEWIS

Edith Wharton: A Biography. Fromm Intl. Pub. 1985 repr. of 1975 ed. $12.95. ISBN 0-88064-020-0
Literary Reflections: A Shoring of Images, 1960–1993. NE U. Pr. 1993 $24.95. ISBN 1-55553-160-1. First collection of Lewis's essays in almost 30 years; covers such various writers as Toni Morrison, Poe, and Albert Camus.

LOGAN, JOHN. 1923–

Born in Red Oak, Iowa, educated at Coe College; the University of Iowa, Iowa City; and Georgetown University, John Logan found inspiration for his early poetical works in his conversion to Catholicism. Influenced primarily by RAINER MARIA RILKE (see Vol. 2), his poetry has moved from a religious formalistic style to a freedom of line and voice.

Editor of *Choice*, a major magazine of poetry and photography, Logan has received the Indiana School Letters Fellowship (1965, 1969); the Miles Modern Poetry Award (1967); and a Rockefeller grant (1968). He presently resides in Buffalo, New York, where he teaches at the State University. He has read at the Poetry Center of the YMHA in New York City, where he has also taught poetry workshops from time to time.

POETRY BY LOGAN

The Collected Poems. BOA Edns. 1989 $30.00. ISBN 0-918526-64-7
Only the Dreamer Can Change the Dream. Ecco Pr. 1982 $7.95. ISBN 0-912946-78-4.
 Collection of poems.

SHORT STORY COLLECTION BY LOGAN

The Collected Fiction. BOA Edns. 1991 $25.00. ISBN 0-685-46261-7

LORDE, AUDRE GERALDINE. 1934–1992

[SEE Chapter 19 in this volume.]

LOWELL, ROBERT. 1917–1977

Born in Boston, Robert Lowell, great-grandnephew of JAMES RUSSELL LOWELL and distant cousin of AMY LOWELL, was a brilliant—and rebellious—member of that distinguished family. He received his B.A. in 1940 from Kenyon College, where he had studied under JOHN CROWE RANSOM and came to know ALLEN TATE. In 1940 he also converted to Catholicism. During World War II he tried twice to enlist, but by the time he was called, his strong feelings against the bombing of civilians had made him a conscientious objector. He was married for a time to Elizabeth Hardwick, editor of the *N.Y. Review of Books*. His subject matter includes New England and its traditions, colored in the early poems by an intellectualized religious symbolism and a savage satire against the material-ism of modern American life.

Lowell won the 1947 Pulitzer Prize for poetry for *Lord Weary's Castle* (1946), in which religion was beginning to fade as a source of his symbolism. In *Life Studies*, which won the National Book Award for poetry in 1960, he offers portraits of his New England relatives, through whom he studies himself and his origins. It was with this volume that critics began to speak of Lowell as a confessional poet. *For the Union Dead* (1964), another collection, continued the exploration of his own and the United States' past and present. Among Lowell's other prizes were the Harriet Monroe Memorial Prize (1961) and the 1962 Bollingen Prize of $2,500, which he shared with Richmond Lattimore, for *Imitations*.

Lowell was also well known for his active political concerns. Bitterly opposed to the Vietnam War, he caused a sensation in 1965 when he rejected a White House invitation to appear at a festival of the arts. In his letter to President Johnson, he wrote: "Every serious artist knows that he cannot enjoy public celebration without making subtle public commitments." He demonstrated against the war (notably with NORMAN MAILER at a vast gathering at the Pentagon in 1967), spoke repeatedly in favor of peace, and accompanied Senator Eugene McCarthy during his antiwar campaign for the 1968 presidential nomination. Lowell's thoughtful and visionary genius was clearly a response and a challenge to his times, as well as a reflection of deep-seated historical anxieties. The poetry of Lowell's late period, especially the *Notebook* (1969) volumes, portrays the agonies of failed heroic values and the debilitating effects of historical irony. This late poetry shows how all of Lowell's idealism was an inescapable struggle, with only tenuous victories. The self-consciousness and autobiographical shorthand of his final volume, *Day by Day* (1977), give off an uncanny glow of sadness and weary acceptance fitting for a person who was the leading poet of his generation.

POETRY BY LOWELL

Day by Day. FS&G 1977 $5.95. ISBN 0-374-51471-2

The Dolphin. FS&G 1973 o.p. Thirty-two-page poems sequence.

For Lizzie and Harriet. FS&G 1973 $2.95. ISBN 0-374-51291-4. Contains in complete form poems that were published earlier in *Notebook* (1967–68).

History. FS&G 1973 o.p. Approximately 400 poems, 80 of which had not previously appeared in book form, the remainder of which appeared in *Notebook* (1967–68).

Imitations. FS&G rev. ed. 1990 $10.95. ISBN 0-374-50260-9. English versions, not translations, of 66 poems by authors ranging from Homer to Pasternak.

Life Studies and for the Union Dead. FS&G 1967 $7.95. ISBN 0-374-50628-0

Lord Weary's Castle and the Mills of the Kavanaughs. 1946. 2 vols. HarBraceJ 1968 $3.95. ISBN 0-15-653500-9

Notebook. 1969. FS&G rev. ed. 1970 o.p. The new expanded edition of the original *Notebook*, including changes in the original poems and 90 new poems.

Selected Poems. FS&G 1977 $10.95. ISBN 0-374-51400-3

PLAY BY LOWELL

The Old Glory. 1965. FS&G rev. ed. 1968 o.p. Three plays: *Benito Cereno; My Kinsman Major Molineux;* and *Endecott and the Red Cross.*

WORK BY LOWELL

The Collected Prose. FS&G 1987 $25.00. ISBN 0-374-12625-9. Pulls together Lowell's disparate prose works.

BOOKS ABOUT LOWELL

Axelrod, Steven Gould. *Robert Lowell: Life and Art.* Princeton U. Pr. 1978 o.p. First biography to appear after Lowell's death.

Hamilton, Ian. *Robert Lowell: A Biography.* Random 1983 $19.95. ISBN 0-394-50965-X. A massive work that sheds important light on Lowell's extremely troubled life.

Hobsbaum, Philip. *A Reader's Guide to Robert Lowell.* Thames Hudson 1988 $10.95. ISBN 0-500-15020-6

Martin, Jay. *Robert Lowell.* Bks. Demand repr. of 1970 ed. $25.00. ISBN 0-7837-2876-X. A readable nonscholarly introduction to Lowell's poetry, with selected bibliography on plays, prose, and critical studies.

Meiners, Roger K. *Everything to Be Endured: An Essay on Robert Lowell and Modern Poetry.* Literary Frontiers Ser. U. of Mo. Pr. 1970 $9.95. ISBN 0-8262-0093-1. Lowell and Allen Tate in the context of twentieth-century American poetry.

Meyers, Jeffrey, ed. *Robert Lowell: Interviews and Memoirs.* U. of Mich. Pr. 1988 $29.95. ISBN 0-472-10089-0

Rudman, Mark. *Robert Lowell: An Introduction to the Poetry.* Col. U. Pr. 1983 $32.00. ISBN 0-231-04672-3. Makes ample use of the poems themselves to explain Lowell's art and vision.

Williamson, Alan. *Pity the Monsters: The Political Vision of Robert Lowell.* Greenwood 1986 repr. of 1974 ed. $43.75. ISBN 0-313-25135-5. A clear and useful study.

LURIE, ALISON. 1926–

Lurie was born in Chicago and educated at Radcliffe. An academic with a specialty in children's literature whose fictional protagonists are usually academics, Lurie won the Pulitzer Prize in 1985 for her novel *Foreign Affairs* (1984), about a middle-aged English professor doing research in England who has an affair with a bluff Texan businessman. Her characters often teach at Corinth College—a thinly disguised Cornell University, where Lurie has been a professor since 1976. As a writer she is often compared to JANE AUSTEN; like Austen, she focuses on the concerns of a small community and the growth and development of an individual character within it. Lurie's comic gifts and the structures of her novels also recall Austen's. Her ironic view of campus life—its silliness, pretensions, pettiness—put her works on a par with those of DAVID LODGE as among the best in the genre of the academic novel.

NOVELS BY LURIE

Foreign Affairs. 1984. Avon 1990 $10.00. ISBN 0-380-70990-2. Love affair between two unlikely people.

Imaginary Friends. 1967. Avon 1991 $8.95. ISBN 0-380-71136-2. A sociologist's comic infiltration of a cult group.

The Nowhere City. Avon 1992 $9.00. ISBN 0-380-71936-3. Traces the breakdown of Paul and Katharine's marriage and follows Katharine as she finally establishes her own identity.

The War Between the Tates. 1974. Avon 1990 $8.95. ISBN 0-380-71135-4. Recent divorcees and their children trying to sort out complicated relationships.

NONFICTION BY LURIE

Don't Tell the Grownups: Why Kids Love the Books They Do. Avon 1991 $9.95. ISBN 0-380-71402-7. Essays that cite the popularity of certain authors as proof that children prefer books that feature disobedient characters.

CHILDREN'S FICTION BY LURIE

Clever Gretchen and Other Forgotten Folktales. HarpC 1980 $12.89. ISBN 0-690-03944-1. Collection of folk tales chosen for their active female protagonists.

McCARTHY, MARY. 1912–1989

Before *Cannibals and Missionaries* was published in 1979, Mary McCarthy announced that it would be her last novel. Appropriately, that last novel raises serious questions about the value of art in a world full of social injustice, for when one looks back on McCarthy's career as a writer of fiction, no theme seems more dominant than the conflict between aesthetics and morals. After a promising first novel, *The Company She Keeps* (1942), and a short *conte philosophique* called *The Oasis* (1949), McCarthy brought together some of the stories she had written for literary magazines. Her next book, *The Groves of Academe* (1952), is an effective satire about a typical American college's crisis of hypocrisy brought about by the pressures of the Senator McCarthy era. *A Charmed Life* (1955) deals with an intellectual woman at odds with herself and seems to look back obliquely on McCarthy's own failed marriage with EDMUND WILSON. *The Group* (1963), which became a bestseller almost immediately, tells of eight Vassar students, class of 1933, and the seven eventful years that followed their commencement. *Birds of America* (1971), the story of a sensitive young man and his harpsichordist mother in a world they never made, caused Helen Vendler to write that "Mary McCarthy, for all her cold eye and fine prose, is an essayist, not a novelist. But then, if we can have nonfiction novels, why not a new McCarthy genre, the fictional essay? It is not an unworthy form, taken for what it is" (*N.Y. Times*).

Nonetheless, some readers continue to feel that McCarthy's best writing is her nonfiction. The best of her literary criticism appears in *The Writing on the Wall and Other Literary Essays* and *Ideas and the Novel*. *On the Contrary* is a collection of articles on politics and the social scene, women, and literature and the arts. Her art-history-travel books, *Venice Observed* (1956) and *The Stones of Florence* (1959), are notable for combining sharp observation with personal intensity.

NOVELS BY MCCARTHY

Birds of America. HarBraceJ 1992 $10.95. ISBN 0-15-612630-3
Cannibals and Missionaries. HarBraceJ 1979 $10.95. ISBN 0-15-115387-6
A Charmed Life. HarBraceJ 1955 $15.95. ISBN 0-15-116907-1. A wordly, vivid novel about the inhabitants of an artist's colony in a bleak New England seacoast town.
The Company She Keeps. 1942. HarBraceJ 1967 $5.95. ISBN 0-15-620085-6. Six brilliantly written episodes that create a fascinating portrait of a New York social circle of the 1930s.
The Group. HarBraceJ 1991 $8.95. ISBN 0-15-637208-8
The Groves of Academe. HarBraceJ 1992 $9.50. ISBN 0-15-637211-8. A satiric novel of scandal and subterfuge in a progressive New England college.
The Oasis. 1949. Avon 1981 o.p.

SHORT STORY COLLECTION BY MCCARTHY

The Hounds of Summer and Other Stories. Avon 1981 o.p. Two previously uncollected stories in addition to some from *Cast a Cold Eye* (1950).

NONFICTION BY MCCARTHY

Intellectual Memoirs: New York 1936–1938. HarBraceJ 1992 $15.95. ISBN 0-15-144820-5. Vibrates with the wicked wit and moral astringency that made the author a giant of American belles-lettres.

BOOKS ABOUT MCCARTHY

Gelderman, Carol. *Mary McCarthy: A Life*. St. Martin 1989 $12.95. ISBN 0-312-03482-2. First comprehensive biography of the prominent American literary figure.
McKenzie, Barbara. *Mary McCarthy*. Twayne's U.S. Authors Ser. NCUP 1966 $10.95. ISBN 0-8084-0215-3
Stock, Irvin. *Mary McCarthy*. Pamphlets on Amer. Writers Ser. Bks. Demand repr. of 1968 ed. $25.00. ISBN 0-7837-2861-1. A standard approach.

McCLURE, MICHAEL. 1932–

A native midwesterner, Michael McClure is associated with the San Francisco renaissance of the mid-1950s, and his work in the tradition of BLAKE and ARTAUD is prophetic in tone and usually quite experimental on the printed page. His plays, *The Beard* (1965) and *The Tooth of Crime* are underground theater classics. He is part of the poet's-theater movement that was revived in San Francisco in the 1980s.

POETRY BY MCCLURE

Antechamber and Other Poems. New Dir. Pr. 1978 $2.95. ISBN 0-8112-0682-3
Fragments of Perseus. New Dir. Pr. 1983 $6.25. ISBN 0-8112-0755-2

Jaguar Skies. New Dir. Pr. 1975 $7.95. ISBN 0-8112-0579-7
September Blackberries. New Dir. Pr. 1974 $7.50. ISBN 0-8112-0523-1

PLAY BY McCLURE

Gorf. New Dir. Pr. 1976 $8.50. ISBN 0-8112-0630-0

NONFICTION BY McCLURE

The Tracery Gleam: Selected Prose. U. of NM Pr. 1992 $19.95. ISBN 0-9629172-5-7

McCULLERS, CARSON. 1917–1967

Born in Columbus, Georgia, where she finished high school at a very early age, McCullers began to write seriously from age 16. She ventured to New York in 1934 and studied at intervals at Columbia and New York universities while beginning a literary career that saw her first short stories accepted by *Story. The Heart Is a Lonely Hunter* (1940), her first novel, is the story of a deaf-mute to whom secrets are confided by a number of sharply drawn characters. RICHARD WRIGHT wrote of "the astonishing humanity that enabled a white writer, for the first time in Southern fiction, to handle Negro characters with as much ease and justice as those of her own race." The domestic tragedy of an army officer in a southern camp in peacetime is the main subject of *Reflections in a Golden Eye* (1941), but again it is a gallery of supporting characters that stands out as the trademark of her distinctive art. *The Member of the Wedding* (1946), which also became a successful Broadway play, is a psychological study of a 12-year-old girl. Her second play, *The Square Root of Wonderful* (1958), was not as well received, and when her novella *The Ballad of the Sad Cafe* (1951) was adapted by EDWARD ALBEE (1963) and produced on Broadway, the *N.Y. Times* felt that a prose poem that seemed strangely tender had been transformed into "a play flecked with weird, halting poetry." *Clock without Hands* (1961) is a perceptive and poignant study of the change in Southern mores brought about by the 1954 Supreme Court decision declaring public school segregation unconstitutional. McCullers suffered a series of debilitating strokes that made her last years a constant agony and cut short prematurely a career that seemed about to break through to the higher ranks of international fame. French and British critics in particular found her work close to FAULKNER's in quality and tone.

NOVELS BY McCULLERS

The Ballad of the Sad Cafe and Other Stories. Bantam 1967 o.p.
The Heart Is a Lonely Hunter. Random 1993 $15.50. ISBN 0-679-42474-1
The Member of the Wedding. Bantam 1985 $3.99. ISBN 0-553-25051-5

BOOKS ABOUT McCULLERS

Carr, Virginia. *Understanding Carson McCullers.* U. of SC Pr. 1989 $24.95. ISBN 0-87249-661-9. Provides a basic and readable study.
Spencer-Carr, Virginia. *The Lonely Hunter: A Biography of Carson McCullers.* Carrol & Graf 1985 $12.95. ISBN 0-88184-123-4

McMURTRY, LARRY. 1936–

Born in Texas, McMurtry grew up on a family ranch, surrounded by the life and landscape that would play such an important part in his writing. In most of his work, he rewrites the myth of the West, using the cowboy as the reference point to trace change. In *Horseman, Pass By* (1961), McMurtry uses the government-ordered destruction of an elderly man's herd of diseased cattle, and his stepson Hud's resistance to the order, to pinpoint the calamitous passing of a way of ranching and a way of life. The novel became the moving Hollywood film *Hud*, starring Paul Newman and Patricia Neal. In his novels of the 1970s, McMurtry writes about the future of men like Hud, adrift in the cities amid mass culture. Although McMurtry focuses on a conventionally male world, he has been praised for his portrayal of female characters, particularly in *Leaving Cheyenne* (1963) and *Terms of Endearment* (1975). McMurtry's bittersweet tales of mortality have proven to be particularly well-suited to dramatization: His novels *The Last Picture Show* (1966) and *Terms of Endearment* were also made into popular films.

NOVELS BY MCMURTRY

All My Friends Are Going to be Strangers. 1972. PB 1992 $5.99. ISBN 0-671-75871-3. Tragic story about a restless, rootless man.
Anything For Billy. PB 1991 $5.95. ISBN 0-671-74605-7
The Evening Star. S & S Trade 1992 $23.00. ISBN 0-671-75871-3
Horseman, Pass By. 1961. Touchstone 1991 $9.00. ISBN 0-671-75499-8
The Last Picture Show. 1966. Touchstone Bks. 1992 $10.00. ISBN 0-671-75487-4. The coming-of-age of teen-aged boys in a small dusty town, while adults flounder.
Leaving Cheyenne. 1963. Touchstone 1992 $10.00. ISBN 0-671-75490-4. From boyhood to old age in the lives of a genuine cowboy and a rancher.
Lonesome Dove. PB 1993 $6.99. ISBN 0-671-79589-9. Ambitious, epic novel about a cattle drive from Texas to Montana, set in the year of the national centennial, the year of Custer's last stand.
Terms of Endearment. 1975. PB 1992 $5.99. ISBN 0-671-75872-1. Dominated by Aurora Greenway, one of McMurtry's most vivid female characters, the story of a mother and a daughter.

McPHEE, JOHN. 1931–

McPhee was born in Princeton, New Jersey, and educated at Princeton University. A staff writer for the *New Yorker* since 1964, McPhee is known for his nonfiction books and essays about offbeat subjects and people who still care about what they do and are committed to doing it well. His wide-ranging curiosity has led him to write about such diverse topics as oranges, canoemakers, basketball players, Alaska, American geology, restauranteurs, backyard inventors, and vegetable growers. McPhee came of age as a writer during the 1960s, when writers were becoming increasingly interested in nonfiction as a literary form, and when a dissatisfied "younger generation" sought sustenance in meaningful work and traditional skills.

NONFICTION BY MCPHEE

Assembling California. FS&G 1993 $20.00. ISBN 0-374-10645-2. Summarizes 15 years of revelatory theories about the nature of the geologic process known as plate tectonics.
Coming into the Country. FS&G 1991 $9.95. ISBN 0-374-52287-1. Insider's view of Alaska.
The Control of Nature. FS&G 1990 $10.00. ISBN 0-374-52259-6. About environmental protection.
Giving Good Weight. FS&G 1980 $11.95. ISBN 0-374-51600-6. Collection containing McPhee's notorious *New Yorker* piece about a talented chef so publicity-shy he would not allow his name to be mentioned for fear he'd be overrun by *New Yorker*-reading gourmands.
In Suspect Terrain. FS&G 1983 $19.95. ISBN 0-374-51794-0. Chronicles a journey amidst great Western rock formations, in which McPhee is accompanied by an accomplished geologist.

Levels of the Game. FS&G 1979 $9.00. ISBN 0-374-51526-3. About basketball players, focusing on the Knicks' Bill Bradley, later a New Jersey senator.

Looking For a Ship. FS&G 1991 $9.95. ISBN 0-374-52319-3. About the seafaring life aboard the merchant marine ship, *Stella Dykes.*

Oranges. FS&G 1967 $7.95. ISBN 0-374-51297-3. The history, growth, life cycles, and harvesting of oranges.

The Survival of the Bark Canoe. FS&G 1975 $18.95. ISBN 0-374-27207-7. A combination of shop manual, history, and character sketch.

WORK BY MCPHEE

Howarth, William, ed. *The McPhee Reader.* FS&G 1977 o.p. Selections from McPhee's books.

MAILER, NORMAN. 1923–

Norman Mailer has been very much in the public eye ever since his first novel, *The Naked and the Dead,* was a bestseller of 1948 that seemed to many readers the best novel likely to come out of World War II. Prior to bursting in on the literary scene, Mailer had synthesized a Brooklyn childhood, a Harvard education, and a two-year stint in the army to create a unique perspective on the postwar world. In the years since, he has increasingly placed himself within the history that he has recorded, so that his fiction and his nonfiction have moved ever closer.

After *The Barbary Shore* (1951) and *The Deer Park* (1955), two fairly short novels of contemporary life, the turning point in Mailer's career came with *Advertisements for Myself* in 1959. In that bulky work, he reprinted practically everything he had written. He has gone on to write works of semipure fiction such as the traumatic *An American Dream* (1966), the long-awaited historical novel *Ancient Evenings,* and the ersatz thriller *Tough Guys Don't Dance* (1984), but he has seemed at his best in crossover books like *Why Are We in Vietnam?* (1967) and *The Executioner's Song* (1979). The former is generally thought to be Mailer's best novel after *The Naked and the Dead,* but it made its chief impact as social commentary. Called by its author a true-life novel, *The Executioner's Song* recounts vividly the last year in the life of the murderer Gary Gilmore before his execution.

Beginning with *The Armies of the Night: History as a Novel, the Novel as History* (1968), a book published the same year that he ran unsuccessfully for mayor of New York City, Mailer has turned his considerable talents to his own particular brand of the New Journalism. Mailer has not been content to investigate the events of his time from the point of view of a detached observer. Instead, he has placed himself squarely in the center of the history he has traced. Books like *Some Honorable Men, The Fight,* and *Of a Fire on the Moon* (1971) are examples of what Richard Poirier calls narrative-journals, in which Mailer described his own presence at national political conventions, the heavyweight fight between Muhammad Ali and George Foreman, and U.S. space-program preparations at Cape Canaveral. With *The Prisoner of Sex* (1971), he took on the critiques that had been made of him and his style by various feminists. Providing a counterpart to the earlier summation of *Advertisements for Myself* is *Pieces and Pontifications* (1982), consisting of previously uncollected articles and reflections, as well as 20 interviews on a wide variety of subjects. Among his more recent novels is *Ancient Evenings* (1983), a story about reincarnation in ancient Egypt, and *Harlot's Ghost* (1992).

NOVELS BY MAILER

Advertisements for Myself. 1959. Putnam Pub. Group 1992 $15.95. ISBN 0-674-00590-2
Ancient Evenings. Little 1983 $19.95. ISBN 0-316-54410-8
The Barbary Shore. Fertig 1980 repr. of 1951 ed. $45.00. ISBN 0-86527-218-2
The Deer Park. Fertig 1980 repr. of 1955 ed. o.p.
The Executioner's Song. Little 1979 $25.00. ISBN 0-316-54417-5
Harlot's Ghost. Random 1992 $30.00. ISBN 0-394-58915-7. On the C.I.A. and the paranoid
    style.
The Naked and the Dead. 1948. H. Holt & Co. 1990 $30.00. ISBN 0-8050-1273-7
Tough Guys Don't Dance. Random 1984 $16.95. ISBN 0-394-53786-6
A Transit to Narcissus: A Facsimile of the Original Typescript. Fertig 1978 $49.50. ISBN 0-
    86527-315-4. Previously unpublished apprentice work.
Why Are We in Vietnam? A Novel. 1967. H. Holt & Co. 1982 $5.95. ISBN 0-03-059977-6

NONFICTION BY MAILER

Armies of the Night. 1968. NAL-Dutton 1968 $5.99. ISBN 0-451-14070-2. About the 1968
    Democratic Convention.
Pieces and Pontifications. Little 1982 o.p.

BOOKS ABOUT MAILER

Adams, Laura. *Existential Battles: The Growth of Norman Mailer.* Ohio U. Pr. 1976 o.p.
    Discussion of Mailer as a philosophical moralist.
Begiebing, Robert J. *Acts of Regeneration: Allegory and Archetype in the Works of Norman
    Mailer.* Bks. Demand 1980 $60.30. ISBN 0-7837-2361-X. A study of symbolism in
    Mailer's work.
Braudy, Leo, ed. *Norman Mailer: A Collection of Critical Essays.* P-H 1972 $1.95. ISBN 0-
    13-545541-3. A good collection of essays on a range of topics.
Bufithis, Philip H. *Norman Mailer. Lit. and Life Ser.* Continuum 1978 o.p.
Manso, Peter. *Mailer: His Life and Times.* 1984. S & S Trade 1985 o.p. A major biography.
Merrill, Robert. *Norman Mailer. Twayne's U.S. Authors Ser.* G. K. Hall 1978 $16.95. ISBN
    0-8057-7254-5
Mills, Hilary. *Mailer: A Biography.* Empire Bks. 1982 o.p. Fast-paced reportage in a highly
    readable book.
Poirier, Richard. *Norman Mailer.* Ed. by Frank Kermode. *Modern Masters Ser.* Viking
    Penguin 1972 o.p. A study of Mailer by a leading literary critic.

MALAMUD, BERNARD. 1914–1986

With the exception of *The Natural* (1953), almost all of Bernard Malamud's
works of fiction deal with Jewish characters, "because," he said, "I know them.
But more important I write about them because the Jews are absolutely the very
stuff of drama." Born in Brooklyn of immigrant parents, he graduated from City
College of New York and received his M.A. in English from Columbia.
Beginning in 1949 he taught for 12 years at Oregon State University while he
wrote his first four books, including *A New Life* (1961), a black-comedy account
of a Jewish intellectual from New York who accepts a teaching appointment in
the Northwest. Partly because his lack of a Ph.D. prevented him from teaching
advanced literature courses at Oregon State in spite of his growing literary
fame, he left Corvallis in 1961 to accept an appointment at Bennington College
in Vermont, where he taught until retirement. He served as a visiting lecturer at
Harvard University from 1966 to 1968 and was elected a member of the
National Institute of Arts and Letters in 1964.

Interest in his first novel, *The Natural*, was revived in 1983 when a movie
starting Robert Redford brought to life the highly symbolic story of baseball
player Roy Hobbs and his homemade bat Wonderboy. *The Assistant* (1957),

much of which takes place in a grocery store owned by a poor Jew named Morris Bober, also makes use of mythical themes, as does *The Fixer* (1966), which Malamud based on the case of a Kiev brickworker who was arrested in 1911 for the alleged ritual murder of a Christian boy. *The Fixer* had the unusual distinction of winning both the National Book Award for fiction and the Pulitzer Prize. It was Malamud's second National Book Award; *The Magic Barrel* (1958), his first collection of short stories, was also granted that recognition.

In his later novels, Malamud became concerned with the relation of art to life and love. The tone of *Pictures of Fidelman* (1969), a loosely constructed gathering of episodes in the life of an unsuccessful painter, is largely comic and satiric. However, *The Tenants* (1971) marks a return to the profound compassion found in works like *The Assistant* and *The Fixer*. *Dubin's Lives* (1979) is a novel about an aging biographer who lives in New England and finds himself challenged to live passionately when he starts to write a book about D. H. LAWRENCE. Dubin's affair with a young woman is marked by comic misadventure, much more characteristic of Malamud's novels than Lawrence's, but there is a tone of mellow compassion in the book that keeps it from seeming to be a satire on the male climacteric. Malamud's last novel, *God's Grace* (1983), is a fantasy on the theme of the last survivor on Earth. Alan Lelchuk (*N.Y. Times Book Review*) called it "a fable by turns charming and foolish, topical and far-fetched, provocative and innocent."

NOVELS BY MALAMUD

The Assistant. 1957. Avon 1980 $3.95. ISBN 0-380-51474-5

Dubin's Lives. 1979. FS&G 1979 $10.00. ISBN 0-374-14414-2. A tragicomic novel about a successful biographer.

The Fixer. 1966. PB 1982 $3.95. ISBN 0-671-46075-7. A powerful novel about faith and society based on the Berliss case.

God's Grace. 1982. Avon $3.95. ISBN 0-380-64519-X

The Natural. 1953. Avon 1960 $3.95. ISBN 0-380-50609-2

A New Life. 1961. FS&G 1988 $8.95. ISBN 0-374-52103-4

Pictures of Fidelman: An Exhibition. FS&G 1969 o.p.

The Tenants. FS&G 1988 $8.95. ISBN 0-374-52102-6

SHORT STORY COLLECTIONS BY MALAMUD

Idiots First. 1963. FS&G $8.95. ISBN 0-374-52010-0

The Magic Barrel. 1958. FS&G 1958 $14.95. ISBN 0-374-19576-5

A Malamud Reader. FS&G 1967 o.p. Includes *The Assistant*; ten stories from *The Magic Barrel* and *Idiots First*; excerpts from *The Natural, A New Life,* and *The Fixer.*

Rembrandt's Hat. 1973. FS&G 1986 $8.95. ISBN 0-374-52034-8

The Stories of Bernard Malamud. 1983. NAL-Dutton 1984 $9.95. ISBN 0-452-26354-9

BOOKS ABOUT MALAMUD

Alter, Iska. *The Good Man's Dilemma: Social Criticism in the Fiction of Bernard Malamud. Studies in Modern Lit.* AMS Pr. 1981 $29.50. ISBN 0-404-18038-8. Deals with Malamud's concern with everyday events and social relations in his work.

Helterman, Jeffrey. *Understanding Bernard Malamud.* U. of SC Pr. 1985 $12.95. ISBN 0-87249-470-5. Useful guide for students and nonacademic readers who desire a short but skillful overview of Malamud's fiction.

Hershinow, Sheldon J. *Bernard Malamud. Lit. and Life Ser.* Continuum 1980 $16.95. ISBN 0-8044-2377-6. A general survey of Malamud's life and works, with extensive discussion of how the life can be used to illuminate the work; includes a useful chronology and bibliography.

Kosofsky, Rita N. *Bernard Malamud: An Annotated Checklist*. Bks. Demand repr. of 1969 ed. $25.00. ISBN 0-7837-0571-9

Ochshorn, Kathleen. *The Heart's Essential Landscape: Bernard Malamud's Hero*. P. Lang Pubs. 1990 $55.95. ISBN 0-8204-1269-4. Presents a comprehensive analysis of Malamud's heroes, noting the novelist's emphasis on the potential for redemptive change and fulfillment in love.

Richman, Sidney. *Bernard Malamud. Twayne's U.S. Authors Ser.* Macmillan 1966 $9.95. ISBN 0-8057-0472-8. Accessible interpretive criticism and biography.

MARSHALL, PAULE (BURKE). 1929–

Born in Brooklyn, New York, Paule Marshall was educated at Brooklyn College. Marshall has said that her work sprang from a childhood spent listening to her mother's friends talk as they sat around the kitchen table in their Brooklyn brownstone home. These women were, in Marshall's view, "unknown bards" whose West Indian dialect was their nurturing connection to their original homes in Barbados. Invisible in their adopted country by virtue of their race, nationality, and gender, these women preserved their identities—and their spirits—by talking. This inheritance both sustains and weighs upon Marshall in her fiction. Thus, in *Brown Girl, Brownstones* (1959), about the coming of age of West Indian Brooklynite Selina Boyce, Marshall's use of Barbados as well as Brooklyn dialects indicates the price of Boyce's hard-won autonomy in America—the sense of rootlessness. In some way, all of Marshall's work explores the conflicts of people trying to win selfhood as self-consciously "modern" Americans whose ancestors come from an Afro-Caribbean background. In a sense, Marshall argues that every woman needs to gain the power to speak the language of her elder kinswomen in order to finally create her own voice. Among her more recent works is *Daughters* (1991).

NOVELS BY MARSHALL

Brown Girl, Brownstones. 1959. Feminist Pr. 1981 $8.95. ISBN 0-912670-96-7. Semiautobiographical coming-of-age novel.

The Chosen Place, the Timeless People. 1969. Random 1984 $13.00. ISBN 0-394-72633-2. Encounter between an American research team and the people of an island resembling Barbados, revealing the effects of colonialism on a native culture.

Daughters. Macmillan 1991 $19.95. ISBN 0-689-12139-3. Explores the psyche of Marshall's own personal archetype: a black woman torn between her West Indian roots and the demands of life in America.

Praisesong for the Widow. 1983. NAL-Dutton 1984 $9.00. ISBN 0-452-26711-0. A 64-year-old widow goes on a cruise, her voyage out into the future through the memories of the past.

SHORT STORY COLLECTIONS BY MARSHALL

Reena and Other Stories. 1983. Feminist Pr. 1984 $11.95. ISBN 0-93531-24-2. Tales of African-American and Afro-Caribbean girls and women searching for ways to construct or reconstruct their identities.

Soul Clap Hands and Sing. 1961. Howard U. Pr. 1988 $7.95. ISBN 0-88258-155-4. Four stories of elderly, wasted men and their efforts to find meaning even at life's end.

MERRILL, JAMES. 1925–

James Merrill was born in New York and attended Amherst College, where he later spent a year teaching English. An extensive traveler, he has lived in Italy and now divides his time between Stonington, Connecticut, and Greece. In *First Poems* (1951), "Merrill's images derive from both Symbolist and metaphysical sources—substances such as glass, crystal, and flint are linked with apparatuses of one kind or another (compasses, barometers, spectrums, and hourglasses)—and he speaks of the 'machinery of light' and the 'machinery of decay' " (LOUISE BOGAN, *New Yorker*). *Nights and Days* (1966) won Merrill a 1967 National Book Award for "his scrupulous and uncompromising cultivation of the poetic art, evidenced in his refusal to settle for an easy and profitable stance."

Merrill's play *The Immortal Husband* has been performed off-Broadway. He has also written two novels, *The Seraglio* (1957), about an aging businessman, and *The (Diblos) Notebook* (1965), which was a runner-up for the 1966 National Book Award in fiction. His epic poem *The Changing Light at Sandover* (1982) is one of the most impressive long poems written since the era of the modernist masters. It secures Merrill's place as one of the preeminent poets of his generation and certainly one of the most ambitiously inventive writers of the postwar decades.

POETRY BY MERRILL

Braving the Elements. Atheneum 1972 o.p.

Divine Comedies. Atheneum 1976 o.p.

The Changing Light at Sandover. McKay 1992 $29.50. ISBN 0-679-41083-X. Includes "Scripts for the Pageant" and "Mirabell: Books of Number" to form an epic-length poem.

From the First Nine: Poems, 1946–1976. Macmillan 1983 $20.00. ISBN 0-689-11280-7. Merrill's selections from his books of lyric poems.

The Inner Room—Poems. Atheneum 1988 $16.95. ISBN 0-394-57248-3

BOOKS ABOUT MERRILL

Lehman, David, and Charles Berger, eds. *James Merrill: Essays in Criticism*. Cornell Univ. Pr. 1982 $36.95. ISBN 0-8014-1404-0. An important collection of essays.

Moffett, Judith. *James Merrill: An Introduction to the Poetry*. Col. U. Pr. 1984 $34.00. ISBN 0-231-05210-3. A good aid to readers of Merrill's poetry.

MERWIN, W(ILLIAM) S(TANLEY). 1927–

Born in New York City and educated at Princeton University, W. S. Merwin has lived in Boston, Spain, France, and England. In a short space of time, he published four volumes of verse and three of translations from the Spanish. Later, he also did translations from the French. His first book of poetry, *A Mask for Janus* (1952), was sponsored by the *Yale Series of Younger Poets*; his second, *The Dancing Bears* (1954), won the Kenyon Review Fellowship; and his third, *Green with Beasts* (1960), won a British Poetry Book Society award.

In his early work, Merwin "wrote . . . with a verse technique as dazzling as that of any poet of his generation" (Peter Davison, *Atlantic*). Merwin has remained loyal to the modernist dicta to "make it new" and to use no superfluous verbiage. His surrealistic style has brought comparisons to PLATH, ROETHKE, OLSON; but his apocalyptic visions have been said to be unique to him.

POETRY BY MERWIN

Finding the Islands. North Point Pr. 1982 $11.00. ISBN 0-86547-088-X

The Lost Upland. Knopf 1992 $21.50. ISBN 0-679-40526-7

Selected Poems. Atheneum 1988 $22.95. ISBN 0-689-11970-4

NONFICTION BY MERWIN

Selected Translations 1948–1968. Atheneum 1979 o.p.

WORK BY MERWIN

Unframed Originals: Recollections. Macmillan 1983 $14.95. ISBN 0-689-11284-X. A book
of prose memoirs, beautifully written and truly haunting in their nostalgic accuracy.

MOMADAY, N. SCOTT. 1934–

A member of the Kiowa tribe, Momaday was born in Oklahoma but grew up
on reservations in the Southwest. He was educated at the University of New
Mexico and Stanford University, and later taught at Berkeley, Stanford, and the
University of Arizona. Momaday lives two lives—as a professor of English and
Comparative Literature and as a Kiowa tribal dancer and recorder of the Native
American experience in this country. "None but an Indian, I think," he has said,
"knows so much what it is like to have existence in two worlds and security in
neither." This is a theme that runs through his fiction and nonfiction, including
his Pulitzer prize-winning first novel, *House Made of Dawn* (1968). Yet, as a
Native American and a writer, Momaday finds two sources of identity—the land
and the language. The former gives strength to the American Indian, whose
sense of identification comes from a closeness to the land. The latter connects
humankind to ourselves and our world. "[M]an's idea of himself" finds "old and
essential being in language," Momaday has written. Acts of naming, of
remembering—these are "legendary as well as historical, personal as well as
cultural."

NOVELS BY MOMADAY

The Ancient Child: A Novel. Doubleday 1989 $18.95. ISBN 0-385-27972-8
House Made of Dawn. 1968. HarpC 1989 $10.00. ISBN 0-06-091633-8. About a man who
survives World War II to discover he can neither go back to his tribal identity nor
relinquish the American culture of his upbringing.

NONFICTION BY MOMADAY

The Way to Rainy Mountain. U. of NM Pr. 1976 $8.95. ISBN 0-8263-0436-2. A portrait of
Rainy Mountain, "the immense landscape of the continental interior" which "lay
like memory in [my grandmother's] blood."

BOOKS ABOUT MOMADAY

Nelson, Robert M. *Place and Vision: The Function of Landscape in Native American
Fiction.* P. Lang Pubs. 1992 $36.95. ISBN 0-8204-1720-3
Woodard, Charles L. *Ancestral Voice: Conversations With N. Scott Momaday.* U. of Nebr.
Pr. 1989 $21.50. ISBN 0-8032-4749-4

MORRIS, WRIGHT. 1910–

Early in his career, Wright Morris was called by Mark Schorer "probably the
most original young novelist writing in the United States." In 1968 Leon
Howard wrote: "Wright Morris has been the most consistently original of
American novelists for a quarter of a century." Since then, the University of
Nebraska Press has brought out new editions of his first 17 novels. Although
both critical and popular appreciation of his work continues to grow slowly,
there is a general consensus that he ranks high among contemporary American
novelists. Born in Central City, Nebraska, the Lone Tree of his fiction, Morris
attended Pomona College in California and had an academic career chiefly at
San Francisco State University until his retirement in 1975. Nebraska and
California have provided the main settings for his work, but he has traveled
widely here and abroad, and some of his best novels relate the picaresque
odysseys made by engaging characters. For instance, his first novel, *My Uncle*

Dudley (1942), is a fictionalized account of a trip to California with his father that motherless Morris made as a youth. When almost 30 years later Morris wrote about another east-to-west journey in *Fire Sermon* (1971), in which an old man and a boy encounter three young hippies, Granville Hicks called the book "simon-pure, dyed-in-the-wool honest-to-God Wright Morris of the very highest grade" (*N.Y. Times*). *The Field of Vision* (1956), which deals with "innocents abroad in Mexico," won the National Book Award for fiction in 1957 and ranks behind only *Ceremony in Lone Tree* (1960) as his most successful novel. *Ceremony* involves four generations at a family reunion as Morris ingeniously reconciles the past, present, and future in a story that avoids both nostalgia and the disillusionment of the you-can't-go-home-again theme that appears quite often in his other fiction. Critics attempting to define Morris's originality have emphasized his distinctive style—a Faulkner-like ability to draw characters that come alive as individuals, his cross-country Americanness, and a strong sense of place that may owe something to Morris's considerable gifts as a photographer.

Morris's fine feeling for the conjunction of time and place is evident in his several books of photographs with text: *The Inhabitants* (1946), *The Home Place* (1948), *God's Country and My People* (1968), *Photographs and Words*, and *Picture America* (1982). Other nonfiction includes a collection of essays on contemporary social and political problems—*A Bill of Rites, a Bill of Wrongs, a Bill of Goods* (1967)—and two widely praised volumes of criticism—*The Territory Ahead: Critical Iinterpretations in American Literature* (1958) and *Earthly Delights, Unearthly Adornments: American Writers as Image Makers*. Two volumes of personal memoirs are *Will's Boy* (1981) and *Solo: An American Dreamer in Europe, 1933–1934* (1983).

NOVELS BY MORRIS

Cause for Wonder. U. of Nebr. Pr. 1978 repr. of 1963 ed. $22.50. ISBN 0-8032-0966-5
Ceremony in Lone Tree. U. of Nebr. Pr. 1973 repr. of 1960 ed. $9.95. ISBN 0-8032-5782-1
The Deep Sleep. U. of Nebr. Pr. 1975 repr. of 1953 ed. $5.95. ISBN 0-8032-5823-2
The Field of Vision. U. of Nebr. Pr. 1974 repr. of 1956 ed. $22.00. ISBN 0-8032-3060-5
Fire Sermon. U. of Nebr. Pr. 1979 repr. of 1971 ed. $3.50. ISBN 0-8032-8104-8
The Fork River Space Project. U. of Nebr. Pr. 1981 repr. of 1977 ed. $5.95.ISBN 0-8032-8112-9
The Huge Season. U. of Nebr. Pr. 1975 repr. of 1954 ed. $6.50. ISBN 0-8032-5805-4
In Orbit. U. of Nebr. Pr. 1976 repr. of 1967 ed. o.p.
A Life. U. of Nebr. Pr. 1980 repr. of 1973 ed. $3.95. ISBN 0-8032-8106-4
Love among the Cannibals. U. of Nebr. Pr. 1977 repr. of 1957 ed. $8.95. ISBN 0-8032-5842-9
Man and Boy. U. of Nebr. Pr. 1974 repr. of 1951 ed. $5.25. ISBN 0-8032-5787-2
The Man Who Was There. U. of Nebr. Pr. 1977 repr. of 1945 ed. $4.95. ISBN 0-8032-5813-5
My Uncle Dudley. U. of Nebr. Pr. 1975 repr. of 1942 ed. $4.50. ISBN 0-8032-5804-6
One Day. U. of Nebr. Pr. 1976 repr. of 1965 ed. $33.50. ISBN 0-8032-0879-0
Plains Song. Godine 1991 repr. of 1980 ed. $10.95. ISBN 0-87923-835-6. Links three generations of Midwestern women.
What a Way to Go. U. of Nebr. Pr. 1979 repr. of 1962 ed. $25.95. ISBN 0-8032-0915-0
The Works of Love. U. of Nebr. Pr. 1972 repr. of 1952 ed. $6.95. ISBN 0-8032-5767-8
The World in the Attic. U. of Nebr. Pr. 1971 repr. of 1949 ed. $18.95. ISBN 0-8032-3053-2

BOOKS ABOUT MORRIS

Bird, Roy K. *Wright Morris: Memory and Imagination.* P. Lang Pubs. 1985 $23.30. ISBN 0-8204-0181-1

Crump, G. B. *The Novels of Wright Morris: A Critical Interpretation.* U. of Nebr. Pr. 1978
    $30.00. ISBN 0-8032-0962-2
Knoll, Robert E., ed. *Conversations with Wright Morris: Critical Views and Responses.*
    U. of Nebr. Pr. 1977 $25.00. ISBN 0-8032-0904-5
Madden, David. *Wright Morris. Twayne's U.S. Authors Ser.* NCUP 1964 $10.95. ISBN 0-
    8084-0336-2. A good interpretive approach to Morris's work.

MORRISON, TONI. 1931–

Pulitzer Prize-winner Toni Morrison is one of today's leading novelists, as well
as a writer whose African American identity has helped shape her impressive
literary contributions. As Jean Strouse, who wrote a *Newsweek* cover story
about her, says, "Morrison hates it when people say she is not a 'black writer.' "
"Of course I'm a black writer. That's like saying Dostoevski's not a Russian
writer. They mean I'm not *just* a black writer, but categories like black writer,
woman writer, and Latin American writer aren't marginal anymore. We have to
acknowledge that the thing we call 'literature' is pluralistic now, just as society
ought to be."

Toni Morrison's novels show a steady progression not only in artistic skill but
also in the range and scope of her subjects and settings. The first three take
place in African American communities in dominantly white Lorain, Ohio,
where Toni Morrison, as Chloe Anthony Wofford, grew up as a member of a
stable family of six headed by a father who often worked three jobs simultaneously in order to support his family during the Depression years. She
graduated from Howard University and received a master's degree from Cornell
University with her thesis on the theme of suicide in modern literature. She
teaches writing at Princeton University.

Her first novel, *The Bluest Eye* (1970), is an experimental work that begins
haltingly with the Dick-and-Jane language of a grade school primer and slowly
develops into a poetically tragic story of a little African American girl, and, by
extension, the tragedy of racism, sexual violence, and black self-hatred. Her
second novel, *Sula* (1973), is the story of two women whose deep early
friendship is severely tested when one of them returns after a 10-year absence as
"a classic type of evil force" to disrupt the community. *Song of Solomon* (1977)
has as central characters a young man named Milkman and his nemesis, Guitar,
whose fates are as inextricably linked as those of the young women in *Sula*.
Song of Solomon is a thoughtful work rich in symbols and mythical in its
implications as it portrays the complicated hidden histories of African Americans. Yet the book is readable enough to have been chosen a main selection of
the Book-of-the-Month Club and as winner of the National Book Critics Circle
Award for 1977. In *Tar Baby* (1981) Morrison extends her range to an island in
the Caribbean and for the first time allows white characters to play prominent
roles along with the black. *Tar Baby* is essentially a novel of ideas, but the ideas
again are conveyed along with a fast-moving narrative with credible characters.
She was awarded the Pulitzer Prize for *Beloved* (1987), a brilliant novel about a
fugitive slave woman who murders her infant, Beloved, so that the child will not
grow up to become a slave. Her most recent novel, *Jazz* (1990), continues her
powerful explorations of African American communities.

NOVELS BY MORRISON

Beloved. 1987. NAL-Dutton 1988 $9.95. ISBN 0-452-26446-4
The Bluest Eye. 1970. WSP 1972 $3.95. ISBN 0-671-53146-8
Jazz. McKay 1992 $21.00. ISBN 0-679-41167-4
Song of Solomon. 1977. Signet 1978 $4.50. ISBN 0-451-15828-8

Sula. 1973. NAL-Dutton 1987 $6.95. ISBN 0-452-26010-8
Tar Baby. 1981. Signet 1983 $4.95. ISBN 0-451-16639-6

BOOKS ABOUT MORRISON

Harris, Trudie. *Fiction and Folklore: The Novels of Toni Morrison.* U. of Tenn. Pr. 1991 $28.50. ISBN 0-87049-708-1. Blends fictive and folkloric approaches to illuminate the depth and complexity of the African American literary heritage.

McKay, Nellie Y. *Critical Essays on Toni Morrison.* G. K. Hall 1988 $40.00. ISBN 0-8161-8884-X. Her works are examined and cross-examined.

Mbalia, Doreatha D. *Toni Morrison's Developing Class Consciousness.* Susquehanna U. Pr. 1991 $28.50. ISBN 0-945636-17-2. Traces and discusses Morrison's increasing awareness of class in her novels and the unity that exists between them.

Samuels, Wilfred D., and Clenora Hudson-Weems. *Toni Morrison.* G. K. Hall 1990 $17.95. ISBN 0-8057-7601-X. A new and comprehensive study of Morrison's life and works.

Tate, Claudia, ed. *Black Women Writers at Work.* Crossroad NY 1984 $9.95. ISBN 0-8264-0243-7. Contains an excellent chapter on Morrison's works and literary principles.

NABOKOV, VLADIMIR. 1899–1977

"I am an American writer, born in Russia and educated in England, where I studied French literature, before spending fifteen years in Germany. I came to America in 1940 and decided to become an American citizen and made America my home." So writes Nabokov—novelist, dramatist, poet, essayist, English teacher (famous for his incredibly difficult exams), literary critic, translator, and lepidopterist. Nabokov is considered one of the most brilliant and fascinating writers of the twentieth century. His mixed identities have contributed to his reputation as one of the most unsettling and difficult writers of his time. "The best writer of English prose at present holding American citizenship," was JOHN UPDIKE's description of Nabokov. Although he began his literary career as a poet, Nabokov is probably best known for his novels, most notoriously *Lolita* (1955). "He is a major force in the contemporary novel" wrote Anthony Burgess in *The Novel Now: A Guide to Contemporary Fiction.*

Although some critics find his work so distinctive that they consider it to comprise its own species of novel, Nabokov's work is more usefully seen as a self-conscious extension and reinvention of a European novelistic tradition, from DICKENS, FLAUBERT, TOLSTOY, DOSTOEVSKY, through PROUST and JOYCE, with whom he shared a taste for elaborate wordplay and arcane allusion. Nabokov's works have tended to provoke the awe as well as the discomfort of numerous critics. ALFRED KAZIN, for instance, described himself as "floundering and traveling in the mind of that American genius" during his bout with *Ada or Ardor: A Family Chronicle* (1969), Nabokov's most ambitious novel. "In that novel, as in almost all of his works," Kazin wrote, "Nabokov intentionally laced the narrative with obscure literary allusions and tri-lingual puns that pivot on an understanding of Russian, and to a lesser degree French, language and culture. Though helpful, even a broad knowledge of European literature would not make Nabokov's creations entirely clear for, as an artist, he enjoyed playing tricks on the reader." What has been called his "artistic duplicity" is perhaps explained by Nabokov's theory of narrative as being an intricate interplay between author and reader. " . . . [R]ead books for the sake of their form, their visions, their art," he advised in a series of lectures at Cornell; one reads "to share not the emotions of the people in the book but the emotions of its author. . . ." The discomfort provoked by Nabokov's works was not due solely to his technique, however; *Lolita*, about a middle-aged man's passion for and seduction of 12-year-old Lolita ("the loveliest nymphet")—all in obsessive, hilarious detail—struggled into print after being rejected on both sides of the Atlantic. Shocking to many, *Lolita*, like JAMES JOYCE's *Ulysses*, is the author's masterpiece, a work that continues to generate contradictory interpretations and open-mouthed astonishment.

NOVELS BY NABOKOV

Ada or Ardor. 1969. Random 1990 $15.00. ISBN 0-679-72522-9. Intricately structured narratives-within-narratives about an incestuous relationship, exploring Nabokov's preoccupation with time and memory.

Lolita. 1955. Knopf 1992 $16.50. ISBN 0-679-41043-0

Pale Fire. McKay 1992 $16.50. ISBN 0-679-41077-5. Written as a 999-line poem, composed by the late John Shade, with foreword and commentary by Dr. Charles Kinbote, an emigré scholar of dubious sanity; called by Mary McCarthy "a trap to catch reviewers."

Pnin. 1957. Random 1989 o.p.

NONFICTION BY NABOKOV

Conclusive Evidence: A Memoir. 1951 o.p. Published as *Speak Memory: A Memoir*, in England, 1951; as experimental as his novels.

The Nabokov-Wilson Letters: Correspondence between Vladimir Nabokov and Edmund Wilson, 1940–1971. Ed. by Simon Karlinsky. 1969 o.p.

Lectures on Literature. Ed. by Fredson Bowers. HarBraceJ 1982 $12.95. ISBN 0-15-649589-9. Letters by two twentieth-century greats.

BOOKS ABOUT NABOKOV

Appel, Alfred, Jr., ed. *The Annotated Lolita*. Random 1991 $19.00. ISBN 0-679-72729-9. Contains helpful annotations.

Field, Andrew. *Nabokov: His Life in Art*. Little 1967 o.p. A critical narrative of Nabokov's life.

———. *Nabokov: His Life in Part*. Viking Penguin 1977 o.p. The second book by Field about Nabokov.

Juliar, Michael. *Vladimir Nabokov: A Descriptive Bibliography*. Garland 1986 $94.00. ISBN 0-8240-8590-6. A comprehensive descriptive listing of Nabokov's varied literary appearances in books and serials.

Schuman, Samuel. *Vladimir Nabokov: A Reference Guide*. G. K. Hall 1979 o.p.

Sharpe, Tony. *Vladimir Nabokov*. Routledge Chapman & Hall 1991 $10.95. ISBN 0-7131-6575-8

NAYLOR, GLORIA. 1950–

Born in New York City, Gloria Naylor was educated at both Brooklyn College and Yale University. Naylor is best known for the novel that won the American Book Award, *The Women of Brewster Place* (1982), which she described as a "love letter to the black women of America—a celebration of their strength and endurance." Set within the decaying apartment complex of Brewster Place, the novel is structured by seven narratives, each about the past and present of a different woman in the neighborhood; yet it achieves unity by its focus on a single community and the final tragic but regenerative event that causes the women's paths to cross. Naylor's novels reveal a dual interest in narrative form and content: She frequently plays with perspective and intercutting narrative lines while addressing the experience of African Americans.

NOVELS BY NAYLOR

Bailey's Cafe. HarBraceJ 1992 $19.95. ISBN 0-15-110450-6. Revolves around Bailey's Cafe, an enigmatic little 1940's eatery somewhere in the U.S.

Linden Hills. Viking Penguin 1986 $10.00. ISBN 0-14-008829-6. Intricate narrative structure, depicting the pressures on middle-class black people to assimilate into white society.

Mama Day. G. K. Hall 1989 $19.95. ISBN 0-8161-4692-6. A spiritual and often frightening novel about two women struggling for love and life on a Georgia sea island.

The Women of Brewster Place: A Novel in Seven Stories. Viking Penguin 1988 $4.50. ISBN 0-318-37688-1

NEMEROV, HOWARD. 1920–1991

Nemerov's poetry is known for its wit and intelligence. His poetry is stoical and ironical. In his essays, he has argued against both what he considers to be the slackness of "free form" and the rigidity of prescriptive measures from the past. Nemerov's first book of poetry, *The Image and Law* (1947), was well received by critics, while *The Salt Garden* (1955) reflects the themes he was to develop in his writing, especially a concern for nature. *The Blue Swallows* (1967) received mixed reviews but won him the first Roethke Memorial Prize. He also received the Oscar Blumenthal Prize (1958), the Harriet Monroe Memorial Prize (1959), the National Institute and American Academy Award in literature (1961), and the Pulitzer Prize (1978). A lively and uncompromising critic, he has selected for his *Poetry and Fiction: Essays* essays of the 1970s emphasizing twentieth-century literature and the contemporary stance of the critic. *Journal of the Fictive Life* (1965) is Nemerov's somewhat grim introspective search for the conditions that make a writer most creative. He became the third poet laureate of the United States in 1988. His sister was the well-known photographer Diane Arbus.

POETRY BY NEMEROV

The Collected Poems of Howard Nemerov. U. Ch. Pr. 1981 $16.95. ISBN 0-226-57259-5
Inside the Onion. U. Ch. Pr. 1985 $9.95. ISBN 0-226-57244-7
Trying Conclusions: New and Selected Poems. 1961–1991. U. Ch. Pr. 1991 $18.95. ISBN 0-226-57263-3. Good, wide-ranging selection.

NOVELS BY NEMEROV

The Homecoming Game. U. of Mo. Pr. 1992 $12.95. ISBN 0-8262-0870-3. A professor flunks the college football star.

The Melodramatists. 1949. U. of Mo. Pr. 1992 $14.95. ISBN 0-8262-0846-0. Traces the lives of two sisters after their father is sent away to the funny farm.

WORK BY NEMEROV

A Howard Nemerov Reader. U. of Mo. Pr. 1991 $24.95. ISBN 0-8262-0776-6. Contains a soupçon of Nemerov's poetry, a few short stories, snippets from his various critical collections, and one complete novel—*Federigo, or, The Power of Love.*

BOOK ABOUT NEMEROV

Labrie, Ross. *Howard Nemerov.* Twayne's U.S. Authors Ser. G. K. Hall 1980 o.p. A useful approach to Nemerov's work.

OATES, JOYCE CAROL. 1938–

Joyce Carol Oates would seem to live the life of a person of letters more fully than anyone else at this time. By the time she was 47 years old, she had published at least that many separate books, including 16 full-length novels and more than a dozen collections of short stories. She has also written numerous poems collected in several volumes, at least three plays, many critical essays, and articles and reviews on various subjects while fulfilling her obligations as a professor of English at the University of Windsor, where with her husband Raymond Smith she edited the *Ontario Review*, which the couple has continued since moving to Princeton in 1978. She has earned a reputation as indubitably one of our most prolific writers and very likely one of our best.

Her fiction alone demonstrates considerable variety, ranging from direct naturalism to complex experiments in form. However, what chiefly makes her work her own is a quality of psychological realism, an uncanny ability to bring to the surface an underlying sense of foreboding or a threat of violence that seems to lurk just around the corner from the everyday domestic lives she depicts so realistically. Her first six novels, including *Them* (1969), which won the National Book Award, express these qualities in varying ways.

Since 1975 her novels have shown her experimenting with several genres, ranging from such Gothic romances as *Bellefleur* (1980), *A Bloodsmoor Romance* (1982), and *Mysteries of Winterthur* (1984) at one pole to her more Joycean books at the other. Of *Childworld* (1976), which makes use of stream of consciousness, shifting chronology, and other sophisticated techniques reminiscent of *Ulysses*, Irene Chayes (*New Republic*) wrote: "This is a novel that at last is comparable to the best of her short stories and by an evolutionary leap has already moved beyond them, into the tradition of literature, going back at least as far as the Romantics, in which the philosophical problems of man's existence and his destiny are bound up with the problems of art." *The Assassins: A Book of Hours* (1975), a rather heavy treatment of politics, seemed to most reviewers a less successful experiment. Likewise, *Son of the Morning* (1978), which the author described as "a first person narration by a man addressing himself throughout to God . . . the whole novel is a prayer," was only respectfully received. *Unholy Loves* (1979) is an academic novel set at a university in upstate New York that caters to Ivy League rejects and, with the cutting and catty remarks of the novel's narrator, provides abundant material for a satiric view of college and sexual politics. Both *Cybele* (1979) and *Angel of Light* (1981) are renderings of ancient myths in contemporary terms, the former about orgiastic rites performed by a kind of modern-day eunuch and the second a story set in our nation's capital loosely based on the story of the house of Atreus. *Solstice* (1985) examines a close friendship between two women and seems to show Oates returning to the rich psychological penetration that has marked her best work.

Recently, Oates caused a minor scandal by publishing under a pseudonym because she was so prolific that publishers could not keep up with her output. Oates has also published many volumes of poetry and literary criticism.

Novels by Oates

Angel of Light. 1981. Warner Bks. 1982 o.p.

The Assassins: A Book of Hours. Vanguard 1975 o.p.

Because It Is Bitter, and Because It Is My Heart. NAL-Dutton 1991 $10.00. ISBN 0-452-26581-9. Story of the love that binds a black man and a white woman in an upstate New York industrial town wracked by violence and murder.

Bellefleur. NAL-Dutton 1991 $15.00. ISBN 0-452-26794-3

Black Water: A Novel. NAL-Dutton 1992 $17.00. ISBN 0-525-93455-3. The drowning at Chappaquiddick.

A Bloodsmoor Romance. NAL-Dutton 1982 o.p.

Expensive People. Fawcett 1982 $2.95. ISBN 0-449-20012-4

Mysteries of Winterthur. NAL-Dutton 1984 o.p.

Solstice. NAL-Dutton 1985 o.p.

Them. Fawcett 1984 $5.95. ISBN 0-449-20692-0

Unholy Loves. Vanguard 1979 o.p.

Wonderland. 1971. Ontario Rev. NJ 1992 repr. of 1971 ed. $12.95. ISBN 0-86538-075-9. Reissued version of 1971 masterpiece with a new afterword.

SHORT STORY COLLECTIONS BY OATES

By The North Gate. Vanguard 1963 o.p.

Crossing the Border. Fawcett 1978 $2.50. ISBN 0-449-23751-6

The Goddess and Other Women. Vanguard 1974 o.p. Stories.

Heat: And Other Stories. NAL-Dutton 1992 $12.00. ISBN 0-452-26646-7. Twenty-five stories including several prize winners.

Last Days: Stories. NAL-Dutton 1984 o.p.

Marriages and Infidelities. Vanguard 1972 o.p. Stories.

Night-Side. Fawcett 1980 $2.50. ISBN 0-449-24206-4

The Seduction and Other Stories. 1975. Black Sparrow 1976 o.p.

Upon the Sweeping Flood and Other Stories. Vanguard 1966 o.p. Stories with themes of death and dying.

Wheel of Love and Other Stories. Vanguard 1970 o.p.

Where Are You Going, Where Have You Been? Stories of Young America. Fawcett 1979 $1.75. A selection of stories from previous collections.

BOOKS ABOUT OATES

Bastian, Katherine. *Joyce Carol Oates's Short Stories between Tradition and Innovation.* P. Lang Pubs. 1982 $30.75. ISBN 3-8204-7215-0. Oates's reimaginings of stories by Chekhov, Kafka, James, Joyce, and Thoreau.

Creighton, Joanne V. *Joyce Carol Oates. Twayne's U.S. Authors Ser.* G. K. Hall 1979 o.p. A good overview.

———. *Joyce Carol Oates: Novels of the Middle Years.* Macmillan 1992 $21.95. ISBN 0-8057-7647-8. Concentrates on only a few of Oates's novels.

Friedman, Ellen G. *Joyce Carol Oates. Lit. and Life Ser.* Continuum 1980 o.p.

Milazzo, Lee, ed. *Conversations With Joyce Carol Oates.* U. Pr. of Miss. 1989 $14.95. ISBN 0-87805-412-X

Wagner, Linda W. *Critical Essays on Joyce Carol Oates. Critical Essays on Amer. Lit. Ser.* G. K. Hall 1979 o.p. A good place to begin reading about Oates's work.

O'CONNOR, FLANNERY. 1925–1965

Although Flannery O'Connor produced only a small body of work during her short life, no other American writer of her generation has received more critical attention. Her creative work was largely compressed within the decade of the 1950s, and, according to Frederick R. Karl (*American Fictions, 1940–1980*), hers was "the most singularly unique voice" of the period: "Her mixture of wit, irony, paradox, and traditional belief in the devil and God gave her prose a maturity that belied the age at which most of her fiction was written." The victim of an inherited lupus disease that eventually crippled her and cut short her life, she had a quiet, bookish life as a child before attending Georgia State College for Women and going on to the Writers Workshop at the State University of Iowa, where she earned an M.F.A.

Her 1949 dissertation consisted of six short stories, one of which was developed into her first novel, *Wise Blood* (1952). That highly symbolic story of a fanatical itinerant preacher who sets out to found a "church of truth without Jesus Christ crucified" introduces some of the religious themes that pervade her later work. *The Violent Bear It Away* (1960), her second novel, is a story of murder involving a Tennessee backwoods preacher and a small boy. Here O'Connor again exhibits her interest in the strange forms religion can take and in aberrant human personality; here, too, she shows herself a writer concerned with the oppressive mores of the Deep South in the FAULKNER tradition.

As powerful as her novels are, they are in some ways less impressive than her short fiction. Her best-known story is "A Good Man Is Hard to Find," a psychological horror story about the murder of a family on vacation by an escaped convict called The Misfit. Frequently used in college textbooks, this story of grace and redemption is considered a modern American classic. Other stories frequently anthologized are "The Artificial Nigger," "Good Country People," and "Everything That Rises Must Converge."

Most critics who write about Flannery O'Connor emphasize her religious themes or her relation to a school of southern writers who favored the grotesque, seeing her as in some ways an American GRAHAM GREENE or a younger WILLIAM FAULKNER. But thanks in part to a current of comedy that runs through her writings, she is also unique enough to defy easy labeling. As she explained in a letter to Andrew Lytle, "To my way of thinking, the only thing that keeps me from being a regional writer is being a Catholic and the only thing that keeps me from being a Catholic writer (in the narrow sense) is being a Southerner."

NOVELS BY O'CONNOR

Three by Flannery O'Connor: Wise Blood; The Violent Bear It Away; A Good Man Is Hard to Find. NAL-Dutton 1983 $4.95. ISBN 0-451-52101-3

*Wise Blood (*and *The Violent Bear It Away* and *Everything That Rises Must Converge).* FS&G 1962 $10.95. ISBN 0-374-29128-4

SHORT STORY COLLECTION BY O'CONNOR

The Complete Stories of Flannery O'Connor. FS&G 1971 o.p. Supersedes other collections.

NONFICTION BY O'CONNOR

Mystery and Manners: Occasional Prose. Ed. by Robert Fitzgerald and Sally Fitzgerald. FS&G 1969 $9.00. ISBN 0-374-50804-6

WORK BY O'CONNOR

The Habit of Being: Letters. Ed. by Sally Fitzgerald. FS&G 1979 $30.00. ISBN 0-374-16769-9. Provides insight into O'Connor's life and thoughts.

BOOKS ABOUT O'CONNOR

Asals, Frederick. *Flannery O'Connor: The Imagination of Extremity.* U. of Ga. Pr. 1982 $13.00. ISBN 0-8203-0839-0

Brinkmeyer, Robert H., Jr. *The Art and Vision of Flannery O'Connor.* La. State U. Pr. 1990 $25.00. ISBN 0-8071-1492-8. Invaluable in illuminating the source of the bizarre and violent in O'Connor's fiction.

Friedman, Melvin J., ed. *The Added Dimension: The Art and Mind of Flannery O'Connor.* 1966. Fordham 2nd ed. 1977 $20.00. ISBN 0-8232-0711-0. A collection of original critical pieces by various authors; offers a range of critical opinions.

Giannone, Richard. *Flannery O'Connor and the Mystery of Love.* U. of Ill. Pr. 1989 $29.95. ISBN 0-252-01606-8. Explores the fictional world of Flannery O'Connor in the light of her religious beliefs.

Grimshaw, James A., Jr. *The Flannery O'Connor Companion.* Greenwood 1981 $55.00. ISBN 0-313-21086-1. A compendium of information.

Kinney, Arthur F. *Flannery O'Connor's Library: Resources of Being.* U. of Ga. Pr. 1985 o.p. An interesting study of O'Connor's library and its relation to her work.

McFarland, Dorothy T. *Flannery O'Connor. Lit. and Life Ser.* Continuum 1976 $16.95. ISBN 0-8044-2609-0. A useful critical study of O'Connor's life and works.
McKenzie, Barbara. *Flannery O'Connor's Georgia.* U. of Ga. Pr. 1980 o.p.
Magee, Rosemary M. *Conversations with Flannery O'Connor.* U. Pr. of Miss. 1987 $32.50. ISBN 0-87805-264-X. Provides rewarding insights for students of literature.
Miller, Gilbert H. *Nightmares and Visions: Flannery O'Connor and the Catholic Grotesque.* U. of Ga. Pr. 1972 o.p.

O'HARA, FRANK. 1926–1966

Frank O'Hara was born in Baltimore, Maryland, and raised in Worcester, Massachusetts. After serving in the navy during World War II, he graduated from Harvard University, where he met KENNETH KOCH and John Ashbery and helped found the Poet's Theatre. He later studied at the University of Michigan. In 1951 he moved to New York City, where he became involved with the burgeoning art scene. He was an art critic, worked for *Art News*, and later became associate curator for exhibitions of paintings and sculpture. In the early 1960s, he became the center of a group known as the New York school of poets.

O'Hara's poetry features dreamlike, irrational sequences of images; one of the dominant qualities of his work is its visual imagery, influenced to some degree by the leading painters of the decade, Pollack, Kline, and de Kooning. His work also reflected the pop art culture manifested in movies, advertising, and billboards. At times, however, an almost classic simplicity appears in his verse; "To the Harbormaster" is a good example, beginning simply, "I wanted to be sure to reach you,/though my ship was on the way/it got caught/in some moorings. . . ." O'Hara was one of a number of gay poets whose sexual identity is now generally recognized as a key element in his poetry.

O'Hara died tragically when a dune buggy ran over him on Fire Island. In 1972, he was posthumously given the National Book Award for his *Collected Poems* (1971).

POETRY BY O'HARA

Art Chronicles, 1954–1966. Braziller 1990 $14.95. ISBN 0-8076-0756-8
Collected Poems of O'Hara. 1971 Knopf 1971 o.p.
Selected Poems. Ed. by Donald M. Allen. Random 1974 $14.00. ISBN 0-394-71973-5
Standing Still and Walking in New York. Ed. by Donald M. Allen. Grey Fox 1983 repr. of 1975 ed. $6.95. ISBN 0-912516-12-7

BOOK ABOUT O'HARA

Elledge, Jim, ed. *Frank O'Hara: To Be True to a City.* U. of Mich. Pr. 1990 $32.50. ISBN 0-472-09408-4. Essential collection of reviews and essays on O'Hara's poetry, prose, and plays.
Perloff, Marjorie. *Frank O'Hara: Poet among Painters.* U. of Tex. Pr. 1979 $7.95. ISBN 0-292-72429-7. A leading critical work.

OLSEN, TILLIE (LERNER). 1913–

Born in Omaha, Nebraska, Tillie Olsen received only a high school education. But because of her success as a writer, she has served as a visiting lecturer and writer-in-residence at a number of colleges, including Amherst College, Stanford University, and MIT. She has received numerous awards for her work, including an O. Henry Award for best American short story (1961) and a Guggenheim fellowship (1976–77).

The widely anthologized "I Stand Here Ironing" (1961), in the circumstances of its publication and its voice and subject, embodies the concerns of Olsen's literary career. In this monologue of a woman reviewing her relationship to her 19-year-old daughter, Olsen suggests the themes of the blighted potential and wasted talent of working-class women that have preoccupied her throughout her career. As she irons, the woman mournfully meditates on how she may have prevented her daughter's full "flowering"—a flowering that she herself has never had. Most intensely recalled is how she had to leave her infant daughter to go to work after her husband abandoned them. A mother herself by age 19, Olsen did not publish her first work until she was in her forties (though she began to write in her teens) when the pressures of supporting herself and her four children lessened and she felt she had written something worthy of publication. At times considered unrelenting in the despair that she attributes to her characters, Olsen's style is marked by a rhythmic, hypnotic lyricism and an evocative use of language.

Olsen later published an introductory essay to the reprint of Rebecca Harding Davis's nineteenth-century novel, *Life in the Iron Mills*. In *Silences* (1978), a collection of essays, she addresses directly the various cultural, political, and economic forces that silence women writers and writers from working-class or minority backgrounds.

SHORT STORY COLLECTION BY OLSEN

Tell Me a Riddle: A Collection. 1961. Delacorte 1989 $7.95. ISBN 0-440-55010-6. Stories about marriage, familial relations, friendship. The title story describes an elderly couple re-examining their lives as the wife faces imminent death.

NOVEL BY OLSEN

Yonnondio: From the Thirties. 1974. Dell 1975 $1.95. ISBN 0-440-39881-9. "Mislaid" for 35 years, an incomplete Depression novel, divided between the voices of the child Maizie and her mother.

NONFICTION BY OLSEN

Silences. 1978. Delacorte 1989 $9.95. ISBN 0-440-55011-4. Essays about the ways that women and other artists are silenced.

OLSON, CHARLES. 1910–1970

The "elder statesman" of the Black Mountain school of poets, Charles Olson directly affected the work of fellow teachers ROBERT DUNCAN and ROBERT CREELEY, as well as students including John Wieners, Jonathan Williams, Joel Oppenheimer, and Edward Dorn. His catalytic theory of poetry, expounded in the essay *Projective Verse* (1950), was reprinted in part in WILLIAM CARLOS WILLIAMS's *Autobiography* and in Donald M. Allen and Warren Taliman, eds., *The New Poetics of the New American Poetry, 1945–1960*. In his *Selected Writings* (1967), Olson emphasizes "how to restore man to his 'dynamic.' There is too much concern, he feels, with end and not enough with instant. It is not things that are important, but what happens between them. . . . He thinks of poetry as transfers of energy and he reminds us that dance is kinesis, not mimesis" (*N.Y. Times*). *Human Universe and Other Essays* is a collection of interesting pieces on subjects ranging from HOMER (see Vol. 2) to YEATS. *Proprioception* is one of Olson's seminal essays on verse and the poet's awareness.

Born in Worcester, Massachusetts, Olson attended Wesleyan, Harvard, and Yale universities. He taught at Harvard University and Clark and Black Mountain colleges. He received two Guggenheim Fellowships and a grant from the Wenner-Gren Foundation to study Mayan hieroglyphs in the Yucatan. His involvement with early Indian societies stimulated his interest in mysticism and the drug culture.

Poetry by Olson

The Complete Maximus Poems. 1960. Ed. by George F. Butterick. U. CA Pr. 1983 $49.95. ISBN 0-520-04015-5

Selected Writings. Ed. by Robert Creeley. New Dir. Pr. 1967 $9.95. ISBN 0-8112-0128-7. Poetry and criticism, including selections from *The Maximus Poems, Projective Verse,* and *Human Universe.*

Work by Olson

Charles Olson and Robert Creeley: The Complete Correspondence. 6 vols. Ed. by George F. Butterick. Black Sparrow 1980–84 $20.00 ea. ISBNs 0-87685-441-2, 0-87685-400-5, 0-87685-483-8, 0-87685-486-2

Books about Olson

Butterick, George F. *A Guide to the Maximus Poems of Charles Olson.* U. CA Pr. 1978 $25.00. ISBN 0-520-04270-0

Byrd, Don. *Charles Olson's Maximus.* U. of Ill. Pr. 1980 $24.95. ISBN 0-252-00779-4. A strong, sympathetic reading.

Von Hallberg, Robert. *Charles Olson: The Scholar's Art.* HUP 1978 $22.50. ISBN 0-674-11130-3

OZICK, CYNTHIA. 1928–

Novelist, short story writer, and essayist, Cynthia Ozick was born in the Bronx, New York. She is a writer who blossomed late, not finishing her first novel until 1966. Ozick has recounted how she began this first novel, *Trust* (1966), as an American writer in the tradition of Henry James and completed it six and a half years later as a Jewish writer in another tradition. Unlike many contemporary American Jewish writers, she brings a wealth of Jewish learning to her work. For Ozick, the artist's urge for beauty necessitates a central paradox for the Jewish artist. "The single most serviceable description of a Jew—as defined 'theologically'— . . . is someone who shuns idols," she has written; but to create art is to position oneself "in competition, like a god, with the Creator," so that "[art] too is turned into an idol." Throughout her works Ozick explores characters for whom the tensions of identity revolve around their Jewish heritage and the issue, as Ozick puts it, "of Hellenism-versus-Hebraism." Most importantly, for Ozick, the Holocaust is the defining experience for contemporary Jewish identity, exerting an inexorable force on survivors and their children. Yet Ozick is careful to avoid romanticizing suffering: as a Holocaust survivor in *Bloodshed* (1976) tells the Jewish protagonist whom he rescues from suicide, "despair must be earned."

Novels by Ozick

The Messiah of Stockholm. Knopf 1987 $15.95. ISBN 0-394-54701-2

Trust. 1966. o.p. Ironically named Jamesian novel set in Europe and in America, about a wealthy American family.

Short Story Collections by Ozick

Bloodshed and Three Novellas. 1976. o.p. Unified by theme of the futility of the efforts of post-Holocaust Jews to flee their Jewish heritage.

Levitation: Five Fictions. 1982. o.p. Story of a female golem who is chanted into existence by Puttermesser, a middle-aged Jewish woman living in New York City.

The Pagan Rabbi and Other Stories. 1971. Viking Penguin 1991 $8.95. ISBN 0-14-015343-8. Explorations of Ozick's "Pan-Moses" theme.

The Shawl. Knopf 1989 $12.95. ISBN 0-394-57976-3. Unrelentingly painful stories about the survival and death of a mother, her infant, and her daughter, victims of the Holocaust.

NONFICTION BY OZICK

Metaphor and Memory. Random 1991 $12.00. ISBN 0-679-73425-2. A mix of critical essays on literature and personal reminiscences.

BOOKS ABOUT OZICK

Lowin, Joseph. *Cynthia Ozick.* Macmillan 1988 $21.95. ISBN 0-8057-7526-9. Traces Ozick's movement from a Yiddish family background to scholarly pursuits in Western literature to mastering the Jewish textual tradition.

Pinsker, Sanford. *The Uncompromising Fictions of Cynthia Ozick.* U. of Mo. Pr. 1987 $9.95. ISBN 0-8262-0635-2. A highly readable, chronologically organized critical summary of Ozick's work.

PATCHEN, KENNETH. 1911–1972

"One of America's most unusual and powerful contemporary poets," said the *San Francisco Chronicle* of this versatile West Coast poet, writer, and painter. Born in Niles, Ohio, Patchen worked in all sorts of jobs before settling in California. In 1957 he pioneered in the "public birth of poetry—jazz" by reading his poems to the accompaniment of the Chamber Jazz Sextet in nightclubs and concert halls on the West Coast, breaking attendance records in San Francisco and Los Angeles. In 1954 he received the Shelley Memorial Award. Patchen died in 1972 after a prolonged illness, during which he continued to write prolifically.

POETRY BY PATCHEN

Awash With Roses: The Collected Love Poems of Kenneth Patchen. Bottom Dog Pr. 1991 $19.95. ISBN 0-933087-19-5

Collected Poems. New Dir. Pr. 1969 $15.95. ISBN 0-8112-0140-6. Patchen's own choice; shows a wide range of techniques and ideas.

The Journal of Albion Moonlight. New Dir. Pr. 1961 $9.95. ISBN 0-8112-0144-9. Written in the 1940s.

Selected Poems. New Dir. Pr. 1958 $9.95. ISBN 0-8112-0146-5. Some 130 poems chosen from ten volumes published during the last 20 years.

BOOKS ABOUT PATCHEN

Morgan, Richard G., ed. *Kenneth Patchen: A Collection of Essays. AMS Studies in Modern Lit.* AMS Pr. 1977 $29.50. ISBN 0-404-16005-0. A good general collection.

Nelson, Raymond. *Kenneth Patchen and American Mysticism.* U. of NC Pr. 1984 $24.95. ISBN 0-8078-1610-8. An interesting interpretation of Patchen in light of a tradition of mysticism in American literature.

PERCY, WALKER. 1916–1990

Walker Percy, born in Alabama, raised in Mississippi, and a former resident of Louisiana, was a member of a prominent Southern family who lost his parents at an early age and grew up as the foster son of his father's cousin. Percy graduated from the University of North Carolina and received his M.D. from Columbia, but was a nonpracticing physician who devoted much of his life to his writing. ALFRED KAZIN wrote that "the lean, subtle Percy style, the unmistakable breeding behind the style, puts Percy among the 'dandys' now when there are so many real and would-be roughnecks" (*Harper's*). However, it is not so much Percy's genteel style that attracted a steadily growing critical audience, as the profoundly humanistic views and conservative tone of a writer who described himself as a southern "philosophical Catholic existentialist" (*Dictionary of Literary Biography*).

Percy's witty and provocative first novel, *The Moviegoer* (1961), won the 1962 National Book Award, but Charles Poore considers *The Last Gentleman* (1966) "an even better book." *Love in the Ruins* (1971) marks a sharp change in method and subject from the first two novels. A doomsday story set "at the end of the Auto Age," it exposes many foibles and abuses in contemporary life through sharp satire and extravagant fantasy. Whereas *Love in the Ruins* is funny, Percy's next novel, *Lancelot* (1977) is the rather bleak and pessimistic story of a deranged man who blows up his home when he finds proof of his wife's infidelities and then tells his story in an asylum for the mentally disturbed. Its apocalyptic vision is expressed in a more positive and affirmative way in *The Second Coming* (1980), which takes its title from the fact that it resurrects the character of Will Barret from *The Last Gentleman* and locates him, a quarter-century older, finding love and meaning in a cave.

NOVELS BY PERCY

Lancelot. Ivy Bks. 1989 $3.95. ISBN 0-8041-0380-1
The Last Gentleman. Ivy Bks. 1989 $4.95. ISBN 0-8041-0379-8
Love in the Ruins. Ivy Bks. 1989 $4.95. ISBN 0-8041-0378-X
The Moviegoer. Ivy Bks. 1988 $3.95. 8041-0290-2
The Second Coming. Ivy Bks. 1990 $4.95. ISBN 0-8041-0542-1
Signposts in a Strange Land. FS&G 1991 $25.00. ISBN 0-374-26391-1

BOOKS ABOUT PERCY

Bloom, Harold. *Walker Percy.* Chelsea Hse. 1986 $24.95. ISBN 0-87754-714-9
Broughton, Panthea Reid, ed. *The Art of Walker Percy: Stratagems for Being. Southern Literary Studies.* La. State U. Pr. 1979 $37.50. ISBN 0-8071-0560-01. Covers five major novels.
Coles, Robert. *Walker Percy: An American Search.* 1978. Little 1979 o.p. On Christian and existential elements in Percy's fiction; written by an eminent psychiatrist.
Lawson, Lewis A., and Victor A. Kramer. *Conversations with Walker Percy.* U. Pr. of Miss. 1985 $14.95. ISBN 0-87805-252-6. Collection of 27 interviews.
Poteat, Patricia Lewis. *Walker Percy and the Old Modern Age: Reflections on Language, Argument, and the Telling of Stories.* La. State U. Pr. 1985 $27.50. ISBN 0-8071-1187-2. On connections between philosophy and literature.
Wright, Stuart. *Walker Percy, Nineteen Thirty to Nineteen Eighty-Four: A Bibliography.* Greenwood 1986 $29.50. ISBN 0-313-27709-5

PETRY, ANN (LANE). 1908–

The recent reissue of Petry's first novel, *The Street* (1946), has enabled contemporary readers to rediscover an important voice in African American literature. In the tradition of RICHARD WRIGHT's *Native Son*, *The Street* tells the story of an African American woman's attempts to protect herself and her young son from the violence and degradation of the racist country in which she lives. Occasionally criticized as overwritten and thesis-driven, Petry's novel nevertheless moved one early reviewer to acclaim her as "the most exciting new Negro writer in the last decade." Although in her later works she departs from racial themes, Petry is probably most important for her treatment of the particular impact on African American women of America's racial tensions. She also writes books for children, including *The Drugstore Cat* (1949). Petry was born in Connecticut.

NOVELS BY PETRY

Country Place. 1947. o.p. Set in a New England town, the story of a returning war veteran and marital infidelity.

The Narrows. 1953. o.p. Set in an African American neighborhood in Connecticut, about love and betrayal.

The Street. 1946. HM 1992 $9.70. ISBN 0-395-57380-7. About being trapped in a Harlem ghetto.

SHORT STORY COLLECTION BY PETRY

Miss Muriel and Other Stories. Beacon Pr. 1989 repr. of 1971 ed. $10.00. ISBN 0-8070-8311-9

PINSKY, ROBERT. 1940–

Robert Pinsky was born in Long Branch, New Jersey, and studied at Rutgers and Stanford universities. He has taught at the University of Chicago, Wellesley College, and the University of California, Berkeley. For several years the poetry editor of *The New Republic*, he has won the Oscar Blumenthal Prize (1978) and Woodrow Wilson and Fulbright grants. His book of criticism, *The Situation of Poetry: Contemporary Poetry and Its Traditions* (1976), is referred to often. He has argued for, and written, a poetry of discursiveness—one that can treat abstract thought and social reality as well as subjectivity and deep emotion.

POETRY BY PINSKY

An Explanation of America. Princeton Ser. of Contemporary Poets. Princeton U. Pr. 1979 $8.95. ISBN 0-691-01360-8. An impressive poem of great scope and inventive form.

History of My Heart. Amer. Poetry Ser. Ecco Pr. 1985 $9.95. ISBN 0-88001-048-7

Sadness and Happiness: Poems. Princeton Ser. of Contemporary Poets. Princeton U. Pr. 1975 $12.00. ISBN 0-691-06295-1

The Want Bone. Ecco Pr. 1991 $9.95. ISBN 0-88001-251-X

NONFICTION BY PINSKY

The Situation of Poetry: Contemporary Poetry and Its Traditions. Princeton U. Pr. 1976 $21.00. ISBN 0-691-06314-1. Attempts to situate modern poetry in a historical context.

PLATH, SYLVIA. 1932–1963

Plath's best poetry was produced, tragically, as she pondered self-destruction—in her poems as well as her life—and she eventually committed suicide. She had an extraordinary impact on British as well as American poetry in the few years before her death, and affected many poets, particularly women, in the generation after. She is a confessional poet, influenced by the approach of ROBERT LOWELL.

Born in Boston, a graduate of Smith College, Plath attended Newnham College, Cambridge University, on a Fulbright Fellowship and married the British poet TED HUGHES. Of her first collection, *The Colossus and Other Poems* (1962), the *Times Literary Supplement* remarked, "Plath writes from phrase to phrase as well as with an eye on the larger architecture of the poem; each line, each sentence is put together with a good deal of care for the springy rhythm, the arresting image and—most of all, perhaps—the unusual word."

Plath's second book of poetry, *Ariel*, written in 1962 in a last fever of passionate creative activity, was published posthumously in 1965 and explores dimensions of women's anger and sexuality in groundbreaking new ways. Plath's struggles with women's issues, in the days before the second wave of American feminism, became legendary in the 1970s, when a new generation of women readers and writers turned to her life as well as her work to understand the contradictory pressures of ambitious and talented women in the 1950s. *The Bell Jar*—first published under a pseudonym in 1963 and later issued under Plath's own name in England in 1966—is an autobiographical novel describing an ambitious young woman's efforts to become a "real New York writer" only to sink into mental illness and despair at her inability to operate within the narrow confines of traditional feminine expectations. Plath was posthumously awarded the Pulitzer Prize for poetry in 1982. In recent years, there have been a number of biographies and critical evaluations of Plath's work.

POETRY BY PLATH

Ariel: Poems. 1965. Borgo Pr. 1991 $20.00. ISBN 0-8095-9056-5. An important early collection, published in 1965.
The Collected Poems of Sylvia Plath. HarpC 1981 $11.95. ISBN 0-06-090900-5
The Colossus and Other Poems. 1962. Random 1968 $3.95. ISBN 0-394-70466-5
Crossing the Water. Borgo Pr. 1991 $20.00. ISBN 0-8095-9058-1. Poems written between 1960 and 1965.

NOVEL BY PLATH

The Bell Jar. 1963. Bantam 1975 $4.50. ISBN 0-553-26008-1. Based on Plath's experiences in New York City after college; classic story of young woman's work conflicts before feminism.

WORKS BY PLATH

Johnny Panic and the Bible of Dreams: Short Stories, Prose, and Diary Excerpts. 1979. HarpC 1980 $7.95. ISBN 0-06-132062-5
Letters Home: Correspondence 1950–1963. HarpC 1992 $15.00. ISBN 0-06-097491-5. Reveals Plath's early concerns and burgeoning talent.

BOOKS ABOUT PLATH

Alexander, Paul. *Rough Magic: A Biography of Sylvia Plath.* Viking Penguin 1991 $24.95. ISBN 0-670-81812-7. A comprehensive, well-researched biography focusing on Plath's creative drive and poetic talent.
Axelrod, Stephen G. *Sylvia Plath: The Wound and the Cure of Words.* Johns Hopkins 1992 $12.95. ISBN 0-8018-7374-X
Butscher, Edward. *Sylvia Plath: Method and Madness.* WSP 1977 o.p. Focuses on her creative powers and her mental illness.
Holbrook, David. *Sylvia Plath: Poetry and Existence.* Humanities 1988 repr. of 1976 ed. $19.95. ISBN 0-485-12062-3. A "depth-psychology" study.
Lane, Gary, ed. *Sylvia Plath: New Views on the Poetry.* Bks. Demand repr. of 1979 ed. $10.00. ISBN 0-685-15476-9. An excellent example of post-structuralist criticism.
Rose, Jacqueline. *The Haunting of Sylvia Plath.* HUP 1992 $24.95. ISBN 0-674-38225-0. Offers extraordinary insight.
Rosenblatt, Jon. *Sylvia Plath: The Poetry of Initiation.* U. of NC Pr. 1982 o.p. A thematic reading of Plath's work.
Steiner, Nancy H. *A Closer Look at Ariel: A Memory of Sylvia Plath.* HarpC 1973 o.p. A biographical description and character analysis of Plath with critical introduction and biographical survey by George Stade.

Wagner-Martin, Linda. *Sylvia Plath: A Biography*. St. Martin 1988 $12.95. ISBN 0-312-02325-1. A detailed and readable biography tracing the whole of Plath's life and writing.

POTOK, CHAIM. 1929–

Born in New York City and educated at Yeshiva University and the University of Pennsylvania, Potok trained to be a rabbi and served as an army chaplain. His writings deal with the incompatibility of religious and artistic life, especially in the context of Jewish experience in America. Potok's characteristic subject is the struggle of the young Jewish male to reconcile an orthodox faith with a modern, secular world. His first and perhaps best novel, *The Chosen* (1967), follows the relationship between the son of a progressive but still Orthodox Talmudic scholar and the son of a Hassidic rabbi. In his third novel, *My Name Is Asher Lev* (1972), Potok deals with the conflicts between art and faith, as the Hassidic protagonist must break with his background to become an artist, whose masterpieces turn out to be two paintings of Crucifixions. Criticized for being schematic, a writer more at ease with philosophical dialogues and Talmudic lessons than everyday experience, Potok nonetheless has earned a following for his uncompromising exploration of the intellectual problems of American Orthodox Judaism.

NOVELS BY POTOK

The Book of Light. Knopf 1981 $19.95. ISBN 0-394-52031-9

The Chosen. 1967. Knopf 1992 $29.50. ISBN 0-679-40222-5. Reveals two vastly different Jewish cultures, the Hasidic and Orthodox, through the friendship of two boys.

Davita's Harp. Knopf 1985 $16.95. ISBN 0-394-54290-8. A female protagonist, though Potok's themes of religious–secular conflict remain the same.

The Gift of Asher Lev. Knopf 1990 $19.95. ISBN 0-394-57212-2. Sequel to *My Name Is Asher Lev*.

In the Beginning. 1975. Fawcett 1986 $5.95. ISBN 0-449-20911-3. As an adult and a teacher, David looks back to his childhood and tells his story of growing up Jewish in New York.

My Name Is Asher Lev. 1972. Fawcett 1984 $4.95. ISBN 0-449-20714-5. Traces the life of a Jewish boy from Brooklyn—Asher Lev—who must overcome strife in order to become a renowned painter and find peace within himself.

The Promise. 1969. Fawcett 1985 $4.95. ISBN 0-449-20910-5. Continues the story of Danny Saunders and Reuvan Malter, the two boys in *The Chosen*, as they start their professional lives.

NONFICTION BY POTOK

Wanderings: Chaim Potok's History of the Jews. Knopf 1978 $40.00. ISBN 0-394-50110-1

BOOK ABOUT POTOK

Abramson, Edward A. *Chaim Potok*. G. K. Hall 1986 $17.95. ISBN 0-8057-7463-7. Concise critical introduction to Potok and his complete works.

POWERS, J(AMES) F(ARL). 1917–

"Powers is among the greatest of living storytellers," said FRANK O'CONNOR—and his modest production has been chiefly in the medium of the short story. He has contributed to the *New Yorker* and other magazines. Early in his career he wrote with anger at the plight of the African American as well as his own humiliation during the Depression at being forced to accept jobs as salesclerk and insurance sales agent. Later, although "neither a determined and conscious apologist for the church of Rome, nor blindly revolting against her" (*SR*), he found his subjects in the lives of priests and their parishes, which he has treated with gentle irony.

The *New Yorker* called *Prince of Darkness* (1947), his first collection, "varied and fresh stories, written in delightfully firm and straightforward prose, in which Mr. Powers proves that he has few rivals at creating characters with more than superficial reality." The *N.Y. Times* said of *Presence of Grace* (1956), "J. F. Powers is a largely endowed, careful and important short-story writer, one of the best in America. Some of the nine stories in his new collection are distinguished by a high astringent hilarity, and some are filled with terror and pity." His first novel, *Morte d'Urban* (1962), won him the 1963 National Book Award. Its "prose is clear, lean, and supple: it is the work of a master who has achieved virtuosity. . . . The gaiety of his wit . . . is pertinent here because *Morte d'Urban* could have been bitter, even savage, in its ridicule of a certain kind of priest" (*Commonweal*).

SHORT STORY COLLECTIONS BY POWERS

Presence of Grace. Ayer repr. of 1956 ed. $17.00. ISBN 0-8369-3037-1
Prince of Darkness and Other Stories. 1947. Random 1979 o.p.

NOVELS BY POWERS

Morte d'Urban. 1962. Random 1979 o.p.
Wheat That Springeth Green. 1988. Knopf 1988 $18.95. ISBN 0-394-49609-4. A satiric
    story about a Roman Catholic priest assigned to a suburban parish who struggles to
    resist his own skepticism and various secular enthusiasms.

BOOK ABOUT POWERS

Hagopian, John V. *J. F. Powers. Twayne's U.S. Authors Ser.* NCUP 1968 $10.95. ISBN 0-
    8084-0341-9. A good, helpful interpretive approach.

PURDY, JAMES. 1923–

"The American dream turned nightmare" is how Warren French and Donald Pease (*Dictionary of Literary Biography*) characterize the strange Gothic world of James Purdy's fiction. The "special kind of literary imagination" that David Daiches praised in his preface to *Malcolm* (1959), Purdy's first novel, runs like a current through the nine novels and several volumes of short stories that have followed, but it is Purdy's earliest works that have made the greatest impact. Reticent about his personal life, Purdy has revealed little about his past, but it is known that he was born in Ohio and educated in Mexico before taking an M.A. in Romance languages at the University of Chicago and spending some time at the University of Madrid. He has lived quietly in Brooklyn Heights for the past several decades.

Color of Darkness (1957), his first collection of stories, was printed privately, then brought out in England before being published in his own country. In her introduction to the American edition, DAME EDITH SITWELL wrote: "Purdy does more in a whisper than most novelists do by yelling at the tops of their voices. . . . There is never a sentence too much, never a word too much. . . . He is a superb writer, using all the fires of the heart and the crystallizing powers of the brain." *Malcolm* is the story of a confused boy abandoned by his father in a sort of existential allegory. *The Nephew* (1960) depicts a woman in rural Ohio who tries to write a memorial to her orphaned nephew, missing in action in Korea, only to discover after her researches into his life that he is as faceless and absent as ever. *Cabot Wright Begins* (1964) is the tale of a convicted rapist whose story is pieced together by a group of predatory writers who are trying to commercialize it into a best-selling sex novel.

Jeremy's Version (1970), *The House of the Solitary Maggot* (1974), and *Mourners Below* (1981) comprise the trilogy called *Sleepers in Moon-Crowned Valleys.* They have little in common with each other except as depictions of dying rural communities, but their somber, mellow tone may be contrasted with the grotesque and sometimes precious exoticism of such later works as *I Am Elijah Thrush* (1972), *In a Shallow Grave* (1976), and *Narrow Rooms* (1977).

Purdy remains a writer with a distinctive voice that not everyone hears clearly, but he has found an audience, mainly academic critics who are willing to respond to the challenge of novels and stories that seem to cry out for analysis and interpretation.

NOVELS BY PURDY

In a Shallow Grave. City Lights 1988 repr. of 1975 ed. $8.95. ISBN 0-87286-234-8
The Mourners Below. Contemporary Amer. Fiction Ser. Dufour 1984 $28.00. ISBN 0-7206-0621-7
Narrow Rooms. Arbor Hse. 1977 o.p. Concerns homosexuality.
The Nephew. 1960. Penguin 1980 o.p. Introduction by Edward Albee.
Old Glory's Course. Viking Penguin 1984 o.p.
Proud Flesh. Lord John 1981 o.p.

SHORT STORY COLLECTIONS BY PURDY

The Candles of Your Eyes. 1985. City Lights Books 1991 $7.95. ISBN 0-87286-256-9
Dream Palaces: Malcolm, The Nephew and 63 Dream Palace. Viking Penguin 1980 o.p.
Sixty-Three: Dream Palace, Selected Stories, 1956–1987. Black Sparrow 1992 $25.00. ISBN 0-87685-845-0. Includes 26 short stories and one novella.

BOOK ABOUT PURDY

Schwarzchild, Bettina. *The Not-Right House: Essays on James Purdy. Literary Frontiers Ser.* U. of Mo. Pr. 1968 o.p. Sees Purdy as prose poet of the grotesque and the alienated.

PYNCHON, THOMAS (RUGGLES). 1937–

If there is a legitimate American heir to JAMES JOYCE, it would appear to be Thomas Pynchon, and it is probably no accident that some of the same academic minds that have devoted years to the explication of *Ulysses* and *Finnegans Wake* have also turned their attention to Pynchon's fiction. He has steadfastly avoided personal publicity, and little is known of him other than that he was born in Glen Cove, New York, and graduated from Cornell, where he took VLADIMIR NABOKOV's famous course in modern literature. George Plimpton (*N.Y. Times*) has commented, "Pynchon's remarkable ability includes a vigorous and imaginative style, a robust humor, a tremendous reservoir of information (one suspects he could churn out a passable almanac in a fortnight's time) and, above all, a sense of how to use and balance these talents."

In 1963 Pynchon won the Faulkner First Novel Award with *V* (1963). The main character, Benny Profane, is determined to learn the identity of a woman identified in the diary of his late father only as "V." MARY MCCARTHY suggests that the book could rank as "one of the most encyclopedic founts of fact in the history of the novel," with its detailed descriptions of a nose operation, the intricacies of British espionage in the Middle East, the history of Malta, and similar abstruse subjects.

The Crying of Lot 49 (1966) is the story of how Oedipa Maas discovers a world within her world, an antiworld, an adversary world—or perhaps a world that she has invented in her imagination. The novel makes use of information and communications theory à la Norbert Wiener, among other subjects. Here again the symbolism, the commentary on the United States and on human isolation are intricate and masterly—though some reviewers found the book overingenious and maddeningly dense. With this book, Pynchon won the Rosenthal Foundation Award.

Gravity's Rainbow (1973), winner of the National Book Award for fiction in 1974, is considered Pynchon's greatest fictional achievement to date. In part a fictional elegy and meditation on death, it is an encyclopedic work that jumps through time and is loaded with references to a multitude of topics ranging from light bulbs to a schematic history of German thought. The novel was enthusiastically received by most reviewers, with Edward Mendelson announcing (*Yale Review*) "that few books in this century have achieved the range and depth of this one." After a hiatus of over a decade, Pynchon published his latest novel, *Vineland* (1990). Although favorably reviewed, it has not made nearly the impact of his earlier work.

Pynchon won a MacArthur Foundation Award in 1988. Perhaps the most reclusive of all American writers, he gives no interviews, allows no photographs of himself, and keeps his address secret.

NOVELS BY PYNCHON

The Crying of Lot 49. Borgo Pr. 1991 $20.00. ISBN 0-8095-9030-1
Gravity's Rainbow. Viking Penguin 1991 $12.95. ISBN 0-14-099699-0. About a group of conspirators known as "The M."
V. HarpC 1986 repr. of 1963 ed. $12.00. ISBN 0-06-091308-8
Vineland. Little 1990 $19.95. ISBN 0-316-72444-0

SHORT STORY COLLECTION BY PYNCHON

Slow Learner: Early Stories. 1984. Bantam 1985 $4.95. ISBN 0-553-24962-2

BOOKS ABOUT PYNCHON

Chambers, J. *Thomas Pynchon*. Macmillan 1992 $21.95. ISBN 0-8057-3960-2
Clerc, Charles. *Approaches to "Gravity's Rainbow."* Ohio St. U. Pr. 1983 o.p. Useful interpretations of this difficult novel.
Cooper, Peter L. *Signs and Symptoms: Thomas Pynchon and the Contemporary World*. U. CA Pr. 1983 $37.50. ISBN 0-520-04537-8
Cowart, David. *Thomas Pynchon: The Art of Allusion. Crosscurrents Modern Critiques New Ser*. S. Ill. U. Pr. 1980 $18.95. ISBN 0-8093-0944-0. Treats allusion as theme and technique.
Dugdale, John. *Thomas Pynchon: Allusive Parables of Power*. St. Martin 1990 $39.95. ISBN 0-312-04630-8
Hite, Molly. *Ideas of Order in the Novels of Thomas Pynchon*. Ohio St. U. Pr. 1983 $31.00. ISBN 0-8142-0350-7. Philosophical ideal of order in Pynchon's novels.
Mendelson, Edward, ed. *Pynchon: A Collection of Critical Essays. Twentieth-Century Views Ser*. P-H 1978 $12.95 o.p. A good critical collection.
Pearce, Richard. *Critical Essays on Thomas Pynchon. Critical Essays on Amer. Lit. Ser*. G. K. Hall 1981 o.p.
Schaub, Thomas H. *Pynchon: The Voice of Ambiguity*. U. of Ill. Pr. 1981 $19.95. ISBN 0-252-00816-2
Stark, John O. *Pynchon's Fictions: Thomas Pynchon and the Literature of Information*. Ohio U. Pr. 1980 $18.95. ISBN 0-8214-0419-9

Weisenburger, Steven C. *A Gravity's Rainbow Companion: Sources and Contexts for Pynchon's Novel.* U. of Ga. Pr. 1988 $ 32.00. ISBN 0-8203-1025-5. Offers fresh insights into the novel's relations with history and intertexts; incorporates the best of previous research.

REED, ISHMAEL. 1938–

Poet and novelist Ismael Reed was born in Chattanooga, Tennessee, and grew up in Buffalo, New York. After attending the State University of New York at Buffalo, he moved to New York City, where he became a co-founder of the *East Village Other,* a journal of experimental writing. From New York, he moved to Berkeley, California, and started the Yardbird Publishing Company. Reed's fiction draws upon myth, magic, and ritual to produce a literature that attempts to be larger than life. He has been called an ironist, whose explorations of United States history in general and African American history in particular reveal deep scars in the culture that no amount of technology can heal. Reed tries to incorporate multimedia and nonlinear techniques into his writing style. He has defended his eclectic techniques with spirit, however: "Many people call my fiction muddled, crazy, incoherent because I've attempted in fiction the techniques and forms painters, dancers, film makers, musicians in the West have taken for granted for at least fifty years, and the artists of many other cultures, for thousands of years."

NOVELS BY REED

Flight to Canada. 1976. Macmillan 1989 $11.00. ISBN 0-689-70733-9. History and mythos of slavery and the Civil War.

The Last Days of Louisiana Red. Macmillan 1989 $8.95. ISBN 0-689-70731-2. Brings characters and ideas of *Mumbo-Jumbo* to Berkeley in the 1970s.

Mumbo-Jumbo. 1972. Macmillan 1989 $9.95. ISBN 0-689-7030-4. Interweaves hoodoo/voodoo and African American religious cults into a portrayal of the Jazz Age and the Harlem renaissance.

The Terrible Threes. Macmillan 1989 $16.95. ISBN 0-689-11893-7. A jazzlike, surreal phantasmagoria set in America in the late 1990s, in which millions of homeless forage for food, while the President is manipulated by a televangelist.

The Terrible Twos. Macmillan 1988 $9.95. ISBN 0-689-70727-4. Satire on greed and racism in the United States, portrayed as a grasping two-year old.

REXROTH, KENNETH. 1905–1982

Kenneth Rexroth was born in South Bend, Indiana, and worked at a wide variety of jobs, being largely self-educated. In the late 1950s, he won a number of awards, including an Amy Lowell Travelling Fellowship, the Shelley Memorial Award, and a National Institute of Arts and Letters Literature Award. He translated widely, mainly from the Japanese, and wrote a lively account of his life, *An Autobiographical Novel.* His work influenced many younger poets, such as SNYDER, and continued in part the traditions of imagism and objectivism. A critic as well as a poet, his collections of essays include *American Poetry in the Twentieth Century* (1971) and *Communalism: From Its Origins to the Twentieth Century* (1975).

POETRY BY REXROTH

The Collected Longer Poems. 1968. New Dir. 1970 $8.25. ISBN 0-8112-0368-9

The Collected Shorter Poems. New Dir. Pr. 1967 $12.75. ISBN 0-8112-0367-0

Flower Wreath Hill: Later Poems. New Dir. Pr. 1991 $9.95. ISBN 0-8112-1178-9. Combines *New Poems* and *The Morning Star.*

RICH, ADRIENNE. 1929–

On her graduation from Radcliffe in 1951, Adrienne Rich found that her first book of poems, *A Change of World* (1951), had been chosen by W. H. Auden for the *Yale Series of Younger Poets*. Both Auden and Rich's father, who had encouraged her writing throughout her childhood, strongly influenced her early writing. At this point, Rich's poetry was relatively traditional, largely in emulation of Auden. When *The Diamond Cutters* (1955) came out, she was married, had three children, and was struggling with being a woman and a poet in the American environment of that time. Her poetry started to change remarkably in the 1960s, when she started writing directly as a woman and a lesbian. She moved to New York City, where she became involved in antiwar activities. Her poems now manifest a merging between highly personal experience and social themes, in which, she says, "at last the woman in the poem and the woman writing the poem become the same person."

Poetry by Rich

An Atlas of the Difficult World: Poems 1988–1991. Norton 1991 $17.95. ISBN 0-393-03069-5. Her most recent collection.

A Change of World. Yale Ser. of Younger Poets. AMS Pr. repr. of 1951 ed. $18.00. ISBN 0-404-53848-7. The author's first book, which won the *Yale Series of Younger Poets* prize. Foreword by W. H. Auden.

Diving into the Wreck: Poems 1971–72. 1973. Norton 1973 $5.95. ISBN 0-393-04384-3. New poems with an intense personal and feminist slant; winner of the National Book Award (1974).

The Dream of a Common Language: Poems, 1974–1977. 1978. Norton 1978 $5.95. ISBN 0-393-04510-2. Within the tradition of feminist writing.

The Fact of a Door Frame: Poems Selected and New, 1950–1984. 1984. Norton 1984 $19.70. ISBN 0-393-30204-0

Leaflets: Poems 1965–68. 1969. Norton 1969 $4.95. ISBN 0-393-0419-3

Necessities of Life. 1966. o.p. A reissue of the author's first book.

Snapshots of a Daugher-in-Law. 1963. Norton rev. ed. 1967 $4.95. ISBN 0-393-04146-8. Attacks traditional feminine mystique.

A Wild Patience Has Taken Me This Far: Poems, 1978–1981. 1981. Norton 1981 $17.95. ISBN 0-393-00072-9

The Will to Change: Poems 1968–70. Norton 1971 $7.95. ISBN 0-393-04361-4

Nonfiction by Rich

Of Woman Born: Motherhood as Experience and Institution. Norton 1986 $17.95. ISBN 0-393-02379-6. An important book in the new feminism.

On Lies, Secrets, and Silence: Selected Prose, 1966–1978. Norton 1980 $18.95. ISBN 0-393-00942-4. Ground-breaking essays that have become well known for their exploration of feminism and literature.

Work by Rich

Adrienne Rich's Poetry and Prose. Norton 1993 $8.95. ISBN 0-393-96147-8. A good collection showing development of Rich's career, from writing in her father's house to having a room of her own.

Books about Rich

Cooper, Jane R., ed. *Reading Adrienne Rich: Reviews and Revisions, 1951–81*. U. of Mich Pr. 1984 $13.95. ISBN 0-472-06350-2

Keyes, Claire. *The Aesthetics of Power: The Poetry of Adrienne Rich*. U. of Ga. Pr. 1986 $22.50. ISBN 0-8203-0803-X. A feminist interpretation of Rich's poetry, examining the accepted uses of power and the shape and scope of female aesthetics.

Rich, Adrienne, and Barbara Gelphi, eds. *Adrienne Rich's Poetry. Norton Critical Eds.*
  Norton 1975 $7.95. ISBN 0-393-09241-0. Contains good essays by and about Rich.
Warner, Craig. *Adrienne Rich.* ALA 1988 $19.95. ISBN 0-8389-0487-4. An examination of
  Rich's poetry in the context of the criticism it has produced.

ROETHKE, THEODORE. 1908–1963

The Waking (1953) brought Theodore Roethke the Pulitzer Prize in 1954. In
1959 his *Words for the Wind* (1958) won the National Book Award for poetry,
the Bollingen Prize, the Millay Memorial Award, and the Borestone Mountain
Poetry Award. He won the Poetry Society of America annual award and the
Shelley Award in 1962.

Roethke spent his childhood in Saginaw, Michigan, was educated at the
University of Michigan and at Harvard University, taught at a number of colleges
and universities, and was a professor of English at the University of Washington
at the time of his death. A Theodore Roethke Memorial Foundation to aid
American poets has since been established in his honor.

On the Poet and His Craft (1965) contains Roethke's analyses of some of his
own work as well as essays on DYLAN THOMAS and LOUISE BOGAN. Roethke
argued that it was necessary to "stand up against" a great style, and by wrestling
with his influences, especially YEATS, he became one of the most distinctive and
important poets since World War II. His work centers on the themes of the self-
generating energies of the embattled ego, as well as the ecstatic occasions of
nature.

POETRY BY ROETHKE

Collected Poems. Doubleday 1975 $7.95. ISBN 0-385-08601-6
Words for the Wind: The Collected Verse of Theodore Roethke. 1958. U. of Wash. Pr. 1981
  o.p. Generally considered his best work.

WORKS BY ROETHKE

On the Poet and His Craft: Selected Prose of Theodore Roethke. Ed. by Ralph J. Mills, Jr.
  U. of Wash. Pr. 1965 $7.95. ISBN 0-295-74003-5
Selected Letters. Ed. by Ralph J. Mills, Jr. U. of Wash. Pr. 1968 $20.00. ISBN 0-295-
  97892-9
Straw from the Fire: From the Notebooks of Theodore Roethke, 1943–1963. Ed. by David
  Wagoner. U. of Wash. Pr. 1980 o.p. A selection from the notebooks, including poems
  and fragments, with reproductions of manuscript pages and illustrations.

BOOKS ABOUT ROETHKE

Blessing, Richard. *Theodore Roethke's Dynamic Vision.* Ind. U. Pr. 1974 o.p.
Bowers, Neal. *Theodore Roethke: The Journey from I to Otherwise.* Univ. of Mo. Pr. 1982
  $26.00. ISBN 0-8262-0347-1
LaBelle, Jenijoy. *The Echoing Wood of Theodore Roethke. Princeton Essays in Lit. Ser.*
  Princeton U. Pr. 1976 $29.95. ISBN 0-691-06312-5. Explores ways in which Roethke
  creates a tradition for himself.
Parini, Jay. *Theodore Roethke: An American Romantic.* U. of Mass. Pr. 1979 $25.00. ISBN
  0-87023-270-3. Sees Roethke in the tradition of American romanticism.
Seager, Allen. *The Glass House: The Life of Theodore Roethke.* U. of Mich. Pr. 1990
  $34.50. ISBN 0-472-09454-8. This deeply informed and moving biography retains its
  power since it was first published in 1968.
Sullivan, Rosemary. *Theodore Roethke: The Garden Master.* U. of Wash. Pr. 1975 $25.00.
  ISBN 0-295-95429-9. An excellent, influential study.
Williams, Harry. *The Edge Is What I Have: Theodore Roethke and After.* Bucknell U. Pr.
  1976 $24.50. ISBN 0-8387-1706-3. Interpretation of Roethke that makes claims for
  his influence on later poets.

ROSE, PHYLLIS. 1942–

Of her approach to biography, Rose has said: "Most people think of a biographer as somebody who accumulates facts about people's lives. . . . But I think of myself as somebody who puts the facts of people's lives into different contexts, or emphasizes shape somehow, and puts facts into new structures." A feminist critic, Rose's work has focused primarily on the lives of women. In *Women of Letters: A Life of Virginia Woolf* (1978), which was nominated for a National Book Award, Rose explores the relationship among Woolf's writing, recurring bouts of mental illness, and sexuality. Her most popular work to date has been *Parallel Lives: Five Victorian Marriages* (1983), a highly readable and penetrating study of the marriages of several famous nineteenth-century writers. Her latest biography *Jazz Cleopatra* (1989), is a compelling study of the jazz singer and performer Josephine Baker. A collection of essays, *Never Say Goodby*, was published in 1991.

NONFICTION BY ROSE

Jazz Cleopatra: Josephine Baker in Her Time. Doubleday 1989 $22.50. ISBN 0-385-24891-1. Most recent biography, emphasizing Baker as a figure of exotic desire and her use of humor.

Never Say Goodby. Doubleday 1991 $18.95. ISBN 0-385-41692-X. A series of essays that consider a number of universal and philosophical questions; splendid examples of the classic essay.

Parallel Lives: Five Victorian Marriages. Random 1984. $11.00. ISBN 0-394-72580-0. Thomas Carlyle and Jane Welsh, John Ruskin and Effie Gray, John Stuart Mill and Harriet Taylor, Charles Dickens and Catherine Hogarth, George Eliot and George Henry Lewes.

Woman of Letters: A Life of Virginia Woolf. HarBraceJ 1987. $8.95. ISBN 0-15-698190-4

ROTH, HENRY. 1906–

Roth's family immigrated from Austria-Hungary to New York City in 1908, where, like other sons of Jewish immigrants, Roth went to public schools, graduating from City College ("the poor man's Harvard") in 1928. While at City College, Roth's writing skills came to the attention of Eda Lou Walton, a member of the faculty. In 1928 Roth began living with Walton, and during this period he wrote his only novel, which he dedicated to her. This novel, *Call It Sleep* (1934), is recognized as one of the finest American works of the century. It explores the urban immigrant experience through the childhood experiences of David Schearl, growing up on the Lower East Side, from the time he is slightly less than 2 years old until he is 8. Rivalling DICKENS and DOSTOEVSKY (see Vol. 2) as a portrayal of the pathos of childhood, *Call It Sleep* is both a psychological novel and a social novel. Yet, recalling his writing of the novel nearly 40 years earlier, Roth has commented ". . . I had no thesis whatever to advance (that I was aware of), only to convey what it felt to be alive, in my time." Between 1940 and the early 1960s he worked in many jobs. He never completed another novel after his first, publishing only a few short stories over the years. *Henry Roth: The Man and His Work* (1977), a good biography by B. Lyons, is unfortunately out of print.

NOVEL BY HENRY ROTH

Call It Sleep. 1934. FS&G 1991 $30.00. ISBN 0-374-11819-1. "Rediscovered" in the 1960s, when it acquired the popularity and critical stature it now enjoys.

SHORT STORY COLLECTIONS BY HENRY ROTH

Boundaries of Love: And Other Stories. British Amer. Pub. 1990 $17.95. ISBN 0-945167-
    31-8. Nineteen energetic tales affirming that most aspects of love are slightly skewed.
Shifting Landscape. JPS Phila. 1987 $19.95. ISBN 0-8276-0292-8. a collection of short
    writings, all previously published. Roth's second book, published at the age of 81.

ROTH, PHILLIP. 1933–

"'Goodbye, Columbus' is a first book but it is not the book of a beginner.
Unlike those of us who come howling into the world, blind and bare, Mr. Roth
appears with nails, hair, and teeth, speaking coherently. At 26 he is skillful,
witty, and energetic and performs like a virtuoso"—so wrote SAUL BELLOW when
Philip Roth made a loud entry onto the literary scene with *Goodbye, Columbus*
(1960), a novella and short stories that won the 1960 National Book Award.
Roth, born and raised in Newark, New Jersey, attended the public schools of
that city and went on to Bucknell University before receiving his M.A. from the
University of Chicago and publishing stories about contemporary Jewish life in
such prestigious literary magazines as *Paris Review*, the *New Yorker*, and
Commentary. Of *Letting Go* (1962), a novel about young university teachers in
the 1950s, the *Atlantic* said that "the sharply observant qualities of his first book
have been expanded and enriched; he has become more probing, tentative,
complex"; and "When She Was Good," his story of a gentile girl of the Midwest
who in striving for moral perfection destroys her family and ultimately herself,
was described by Raymond Rosenthal in the *New Leader*: "With a simplicity and
modesty that are in the end lethal, Roth has written the most violently satiric
book about American life since EVELYN WAUGH's 'The Loved One.'"

The bestselling *Portnoy's Complaint* (1969) caused a greater stir than any
other novel of its time. Told in the form of a confession by Alexander Portnoy to
his psychiatrist Dr. Spielvogel, this outrageous novel centers around the
character of Alexander's archetypal Jewish mother. Virtually the apotheosis of
the American Jewish novel, *Portnoy's Complaint* seems almost to have killed off
the form it represents, and even Roth himself has been hard put to match or
surpass this blackest of comedies. *Our Gang* (1971) is a clever political satire
directed at President Nixon and his pre-Watergate associates, but those
prominent targets of Roth's venomous scorn seem pale and feeble when
compared with the formidable mother in *Portnoy's Complaint*. *The Breast*
(1972) finds Roth rather pathetically groping for a subject equally spectacular.

Roth has continued to produce novels at the rate of about one every two
years, but none has come close to matching the impact of *Portnoy's Complaint*.
In fact, Roth has linked together several of his recent works by means of a
central character named Nathan Zuckerman, who seems to be Philip Roth
looking back on his literary career and wondering where he goes from there.
Zuckerman is introduced in *My Life as a Man* (1974) and takes the central role
in *The Ghost Writer* (1979), *Zuckerman Unbound* (1981), and *The Anatomy
Lesson* (1983). In addition to the Zuckerman saga, Roth has produced several
independent novels. Recent work, such as *Deception* (1991), deals further with
the interplay of truth and fiction in the "author's" life. In his most recent work,
Patrimony: A True Story (1991), winner of a National Book Critics Circle Award,
Roth recounts his father's illness and death. Roth has also taken an active
interest in the work of Eastern European writers, such as MILAN KUNDERA, (see
Vol. 2) and has helped bring their work to the West's attention.

NOVELS BY PHILIP ROTH

The Anatomy Lesson. FS&G 1983 $14.95. ISBN 0-374-10491-3
The Breast. 1972. Viking Penguin 1985 $5.95. ISBN 0-14-007679-4
The Counterlife. FS&G 1987 $18.95. ISBN 0-374-13026-4
Deception. S & S Trade 1991 $18.95. ISBN 0-685-37883-7
The Facts: A Novelist's Autobiography. FS&G 1988 $17.95. ISBN 0-374-15212-8
The Ghost Writer. FS&G 1979 o.p.
Goodbye Columbus and Five Short Stories. 1959. Random 1979 $13.00. ISBN 0-394-60470-9
The Great American Novel. H. Holt & Co. 1991 $35.00. ISBN 0-8050-1734-8
Letting Go. Random 1962 $12.50. ISBN 0-394-43305-X. Concerns the agonies of graduate students.
Portnoy's Complaint. Random 1983 $6.95. ISBN 0-394-60810-0
The Professor of Desire. FS&G 1977 o.p.
When She Was Good. Viking Penguin 1985 $5.95 ISBN 0-14-007676-X
Zuckerman Bound: A Trilogy and Epilogue. FS&G 1985 $22.50. ISBN 0-374-29943-9. Brings together the three Zuckerman novels along with a wild short novel, "The Prague Orgy," bleak and funny.
Zuckerman Unbound. FS&G 1981 o.p.

NONFICTION BY PHILIP ROTH

Patrimony: A True Story. S & S Trade 1992 $10.00 ISBN 0-671-75862-4

WORK BY ROTH

A Philip Roth Reader. FS&G 1980 o.p. Introduction by Martin Green.

BOOKS ABOUT PHILIP ROTH

Baumgarten, Murray, and Barbara Gottfried. *Understanding Philip Roth.* U. of SC Pr. 1990 $29.95. ISBN 0-87249-685-6. Analytic study that elaborates the course of Roth's career.
Jones, Judith, and Nancy Guinevera. *Philip Roth. Lit and Life Ser.* Continuum 1981 $19.95. ISBN 0-8044-2438-1
Lee, Hermione. *Philip Roth. Contemporary Writers Ser.* Routledge Chapman & Hall 1982 o.p. A good reading by a contemporary critic.
Milbauer, Asher Z., and Donald G. Watson, eds. *Reading Philip Roth.* St. Martin 1988 $27.50. ISBN 0-312-00934-8. Thirteen essays written specifically for this volume useful to Roth scholars as well as the general public.
Pinsker, Sanford. *The Comedy That "Hoits": An Essay on the Fiction of Philip Roth. Literary Frontiers Ser.* U. of Mo. Pr. 1975 o.p. Deals with Jewishness and dark humor.
————. *Critical Essays on Philip Roth. Critical Essays on Amer. Lit. Ser.* G. K. Hall 1982 o.p. A collection covering a range of responses.
Rodgers, Bernard F., Jr. *Philip Roth: A Bibliography. Author Bibliographies Ser.* Scarecrow 1984 $32.50. ISBN 0-8108-1699-7
Searles, George J. *The Fiction of Philip Roth and John Updike.* S. Ill. U. Pr. 1984 $19.95. ISBN 0-8093-1175-5

RUKEYSER, MURIEL. 1913–1980

During her five-decade literary career, Rukeyser provoked varying critical response; yet her passionate contribution to the contemporary literary and political scene cannot be doubted. An outspoken "spokespoet," she was always where the political action was. As a young reporter from Vassar, she covered the 1932 Scottsboro Trial; some forty years later, she was jailed for her anti-Vietnam protests in Washington, D.C. So closely aligned is her activism to her art that several reviewers believe that the history of midcentury America can be garnered from her poetry. Yet, along with her outrage, Rukeyser's poetry is marked by optimism in a way that is reminiscent of WALT WHITMAN's verse. It is as though she believed that out of the pain of conflict will come a healing and transforming revelation. During her career, Rukeyser moved from a reliance on simple declaratives to a more sophisticated, private use of language; and, though she continued to deal with politics all her life, later poems also treat personal subjects—her role as mother and daughter, her sexual feelings for women and men, the illness that led to her death. From beginning to end, she was honored for her contribution to poetry: with the Yale Younger Poets Prize in 1935 for *Theory of Flight* to the tribute paid her at the annual *New York Quarterly* Poetry Day in 1977.

POETRY BY RUKEYSER

Breaking Open: New Poems. Random 1973 o.p. Contains translations of Eskimo songs; calls for universal fellowship.

The Collected Poems of Muriel Rukeyser. McGraw 1978 o.p. Shows the development of Rukeyser's poetry.

Waterlily Fire: Poems 1935–1962. Macmillan 1962 o.p. Includes the group of poems entitled "The Speaking Tree," called by critics "Whitmanesque."

BOOK ABOUT RUKEYSER

Kertesz, Louise. *The Poetic Vision of Muriel Rukeyser.* La. State U. Pr. 1979 $42.50. ISBN 0-8071-0552-X. The first full-length study of Rukeyser's work.

SAID, EDWARD E. 1935–

Said's interests as a literary critic have always been political. Literature, he believes, does not exist in a realm that transcends the politics of worldly existence. Rather, a literary text is always situated within a particular historical context, and it expresses a relation to society that Said likens to that of colonizer to colonized—a "self-confirming will to power" in the face of social oppression. Literature may also reinforce existing power relations. For instance, in his ground-breaking *Orientalism* (1978), Said studied how European views of the East have structured Western prejudices by creating the East as exotic, mysterious—and, ultimately, inferior. Literary criticism, therefore, becomes a political act that must avoid complicity with the colonizing voice of the dominant culture.

NONFICTION BY SAID

Beginnings: Intention and Method. Col. U. Pr. 1985 repr. of 1975 ed. $48.50. ISBN 0-231-05936-1. An important critical book on authority in literature.

Musical Elaborations. Col. U. Pr. 1991 $19.95. ISBN 0-231-07318-6. The musical speculation of Said, an accomplished pianist and music critic, whose reviews have appeared in *The Nation.*

Orientalism. Random 1979 $12.00. ISBN 0-394-74067-X

The World, the Text, and the Critic. HUP 1983 $9.95. ISBN 0-674-96187-0. Relationship among the three.

SALINGER, J(EROME) D(AVID). 1919–

More than 20 years of seclusion and silence have taken their toll on J. D. Salinger's literary reputation, but the impact made by *The Catcher in The Rye* (1951) and the Glass family stories was deep enough to make a lasting impression and to assure his continued readership. Salinger was born in New York City of Jewish and Scottish-Irish extraction. He attended Manhattan public schools, a military academy in Pennsylvania, and three colleges, but received no degrees. "A happy tourist's year in Europe," he wrote in 1955, "when I was eighteen and nineteen. In the Army from '42 to '46, most of the time with the Fourth Division. . . . I've been writing since I was fifteen or so. My short stories have appeared in a number of magazines over the last ten years, mostly—and most happily—in the *New Yorker*. I worked on "The 'Catcher in the Rye,' on and off, for ten years" (*Twentieth Century Authors*). "Remarkable and absorbing . . . profoundly moving . . . magic," Harrison Smith called this story. *The Catcher* has been an extremely popular book among young people ever since its appearance and has brought Salinger an international reputation. *Franny and Zooey* (1961) is composed of two long *New Yorker* stories, which appeared in 1955 and 1957, recording a significant weekend in the lives of Franny Glass, a troubled 20-year-old college student, and her brother Zooey, a television actor. *Raise High the Roof Beam, Carpenters* (1963) is another story of the Glass family. There are seven Glass children, "two of whom are now dead and all of whom were child prodigies."

Salinger gradually withdrew from public life and the literary scene during the 1950s. He had discovered Zen during his days in Greenwich Village after the war, and that philosophy may have encouraged his deeper immersion in meditation and writing. Unfortunately, however, Salinger's withdrawal has not led to increased creativity—at least not visibly. As of 1992, his years of seclusion since 1963 had produced only silence, and his critical reputation, which peaked in the early 1960s, has suffered accordingly. *The Catcher in the Rye*, however, remains a standard text in high school and college classrooms, and a loyal following of readers continues to hope for a continuation of the Glass family saga. They feel that, when and if that work is completed, it will be one of the masterworks of twentieth-century fiction. Salinger now lives a somewhat reclusive life in Cornish, New Hampshire, where he may still be writing. He has occasionally been involved in lawsuits concerning unauthorized use of his writings.

NOVEL BY SALINGER

The Catcher in the Rye. 1951. Bantam 1984 $2.95. ISBN 0-553-25025-6

SHORT STORY COLLECTIONS BY SALINGER

Franny and Zooey. 1961 Bantam 1984 $3.50. ISBN 0-553-20348-7
Nine Stories. Little 1991 $4.99. ISBN 0-316-76950-9
Raise High the Roof Beam, Carpenters and Seymour: An Introduction. 1963. Bantam 1984 $3.95. ISBN 0-553-26255-6. Two novellas.

BOOKS ABOUT SALINGER

Alsen, Eberhard. *Salinger's Glass Stories as a Composite Novel*. Whitston Pub. 1984 $22.50. ISBN 0-87875-243-9
French, Warren. *J. D. Salinger*. 1963. G. K. Hall 1988 $16.95. ISBN 0-8057-7522-6. Contains a useful overview of Salinger criticism.
Gwynn, Frederick L. and Joseph Blotner. *The Fiction of J. D. Salinger. Critical Essays in Modern Lit. Ser*. U. of Pittsburgh Pr. 1958 $4.95. ISBN 0-8229-5019-7. An early study.
Hamilton, Ian. *In Search of J. D. Salinger*. Random 1989 $17.95. ISBN 0-685-25524-7. A very public lawsuit against Hamilton was waged by Salinger regarding alleged unauthorized use of the author's letters.
Lundquist, James. *J. D. Salinger. Lit. and Life Ser*. Continuum 1978 $16.95. ISBN 0-8044-2560-4. Penetrating and objective assessment of the writer and his ideas; focuses on the themes of alienation and isolation in Salinger's work.
Starosciak, Kenneth. *J. D. Salinger: A Thirty Year Bibliography, 1938–1968*. Ross 1971 $6.95. ISBN 0-87018-072-X

SANCHEZ, SONIA. 1934–

Born in Alabama, educated in New York City, Sanchez is a leading poet of the Black Arts Movement, whose poetry is written from political, economic, and social concerns as well as literary ones. Although her literary focus has been primarily to express her experience as an African American woman, Sanchez claims, "if you write from a black experience, you're writing from a universal experience as well." Sanchez's poems are direct, colloquial, and often militant. Many of her works are for children, such as her *"poems for young brothas and sistuhs,"* as she puts it in *It's a New Day* (1971). Yet she also writes with tenderness about love. As academic interest in the voices of women and African Americans has intensified, critical interest in and acceptance of Sanchez's work has increased.

POETRY BY SANCHEZ

Homegirls and Handgrenades. Thunders Mouth 1984 $8.95. ISBN 0-938410-23-7.
Homecoming. Broadside Pr. 1969 $3.00. ISBN 0-685-00866-5. A young poet's struggling with self, others, and the world.
It's a New Day: Poems for Young Brothas and Sistuhs. Broadside Pr. 1971 $3.00. ISBN 0-9120296-60-X. A call for unity, wholeness of spirit, and purity of purpose and action.
Love Poems. Okpaku Communications 1973 $15.00. ISBN 0-8938-8104-X. Explores relationships among African Americans.

SCHWARTZ, DELMORE. 1913–1966

Born in Brooklyn, New York, Delmore Schwartz was educated at Columbia University, the University of Wisconsin, and New York University. He taught at Harvard University (1940–47) and lectured at various other universities. He was also associated with *Partisan Review* (1943–55), served as literary consultant for *New Directions*, and was poetry editor of *The New Republic* (1955–57). His first volume of short stories, *In Dreams Begin Responsibilities* (1938) received praise from many critics. He received the Bollingen Prize, the Shelley Memorial Prize, and two other poetry awards after the publication of *Summer Knowledge: New and Selected Poems, 1938–1958* in 1959. The youngest winner of the Bollingen Prize since its establishment, Schwartz had already received a Guggenheim Fellowship when only 26 years old.

Until a year before his death from a heart attack, he was teaching at Syracuse University. He is immortalized, after a fashion, as the main figure in SAUL BELLOW's novel *Humboldt's Gift*.

POETRY BY SCHWARTZ

Last and Lost Poems. Ed. by Robert Phillips. New Dir. Pr. rev. ed. 1989 $9.95. ISBN 0-8112-1096-0
Selected Poems: Summer Knowledge (Summer Knowledge: Selected Poems). 1959. New Dir. Pr. 1967 $5.95. ISBN 0-8112-0191-0

SHORT STORY COLLECTION BY SCHWARTZ

In Dreams Begin Responsibilities. 1938. Ed. by James Atlas. New Dir. Pr. 1978 $6.25. ISBN 0-8112-0680-7

WORKS BY SCHWARTZ

Letters. Ed. by Robert Phillips. Ontario Rev. NJ 1984 $14.95. ISBN 0-86538-048-1
Selected Essays. Ed. by Donald A. Dike and David H. Zucker. U. Ch. Pr. 1970 $15.00. ISBN 0-226-74214-8

SEXTON, ANNE. 1928–1974

Anne Sexton's painful personal experiences form the subject matter of most of her poetry, which is often called confessional because of its frank approach and compulsive energy. Her first collection, *To Bedlam and Part Way Back* (1960), focuses on her mental illness and subsequent hospitalization. *Live or Die* (1966) also "palpates human suffering, personal, physical, psychic" (*Library Journal*).

Sexton was born in Newton, Massachusetts. She won the Robert Frost Fellowship in poetry (1959), became a scholar at the Radcliffe Institute (1961–63), received a fellowship from the American Academy of Arts and Letters (1963–64), and was awarded a Ford Foundation grant (1965). In 1965 she also won the first literary magazine travel grant from the Congress for Cultural Freedom and was elected a fellow of the Royal Society of Literature in London. In 1967 she received the Shelley Award for the excellence of her total work and the Pulitzer Prize for *Live or Die*.

Sexton later became an inspiring figure to a younger generation of women poets for her frank explorations of women's sexuality and anger, exemplified in such groundbreaking work as *Transformations* (1972), her feminist readings of old fairy tales. Sexton's suicide was associated with that of SYLVIA PLATH as evidence of the unusual pressures on contemporary women poets.

POETRY BY SEXTON

All My Pretty Ones. HM 1962 o.p.
The Awful Rowing toward God. HM 1975 o.p.
The Complete Poems, 1981. HM 1982 $29.95. ISBN 0-395-29475-4
Live or Die. HM 1966 o.p.
Love Poems. HM 1969 $4.95. ISBN 0-395-51760-5. Twenty-five poems.
The Selected Poems of Anne Sexton. HM 1988 $21.45. ISBN 0-395-44595-7
To Bedlam and Part Way Back. HM 1960 o.p.
Transformations. HM 1972 $6.95. ISBN 0-395-12721-1. Poem-stories derived from Grimm's fairy tales, with a preface by Kurt Vonnegut, Jr.

BOOKS ABOUT SEXTON

McClatchy, J. D., ed. *Anne Sexton: The Artist and Her Critics.* Ind. U. Pr. 1978 o.p.
Sexton, Linda, ed. *Anne Sexton: A Self-Portrait in Letters.* HM 1992 repr. of 1977 ed. $24.95. ISBN 0-395-63118-1. Arresting, disturbing portrait of Anne Sexton based on her letters.
Middlebrook, Diane. *Anne Sexton: A Biography.* HM 1991 $24.45. ISBN 0-395-35362-9. A controversial biography using tapes of Sexton's psychoanalytic sessions.
Wagner-Martin, Linda. *Critical Essays on Anne Sexton.* G. K. Hall 1989 $40.00. ISBN 0-8161-8891-2. Traces the critical reputation of the poet.

SHAPIRO, KARL (JAY). 1913–

Karl Shapiro won the Pulitzer Prize in 1945 for *V-Letter and Other Poems* (1944). Born in Baltimore, he attended the University of Virginia and Johns Hopkins University. After service in the army, he was appointed consultant in poetry at the Library of Congress in 1946 and joined the faculty of Johns Hopkins. There he taught writing courses until his resignation in 1950 to become editor, for a period, of *Poetry*. Shapiro is an accomplished poet in a wide variety of styles. Like others of his generation, his early work displays a concern with life and institutions of modern society. His later work included a series of bold love poems, *The White-Haired Lover* (1968). Typical of critics' response to Shapiro is Ralph J. Mills, Jr.'s assessment of *The Bourgeois Poet*

(1964), in which Shapiro "breaks with accepted metrical patterns to attempt a poetry of direct speech. . . . 'The Bourgeois Poet' definitely has about it the air of a new imaginative release. Irony and social criticism are still there, but autobiography, invective, heavy doses of sexuality. . . and an occasional prophetic note are now blended together" (*Contemporary American Poetry*).

POETRY BY SHAPIRO

Collected Poems, 1940–1978. Random 1978 o.p. The poet's choice of the contents of three previous books with 18 unpublished poems.

NONFICTION BY SHAPIRO

Reports of My Death: An Autobiography. Algonquin 1990 $22.95. ISBN 0-945575-28-9. Shapiro writes in the third person about his life, career, and travels.

BOOK ABOUT SHAPIRO

Reino, Joseph. *Karl Shapiro.* Twayne 1981 o.p. A straightforward interpretation of the man and his work.

SHOWALTER, ELAINE. 1941–

In 1977, Showalter published *A Literature of Their Own: British Women Novelists from Bronte to Lessing.* It was one of the most influential works in feminist criticism, as it sought to establish a distinctive tradition for women writers. In later essays, Showalter helped to develop a clearly articulated feminist theory with two major branches: the special study of works by women and the study of all literature from a feminist perspective. In all of her recent writing, Showalter has sought to illuminate a "cultural model of female writing," distinguishable from male models and theories. Her role as editor bringing together key contemporary feminist criticism has been extremely influential on modern literary study.

NONFICTION BY SHOWALTER

The Female Malady: Women, Madness, and English Culture, 1930–1980. Viking Penguin 1987 $9.95. ISBN 0-14-010169-1. Study of Victorian England's association of female sexuality with women's insanity.

A Literature of Their Own: British Women Novelists From Bronte to Lessing. Princeton U. Pr. 1976. $14.95. ISBN 0-691-01343-8. A groundbreaking feminist study, arguing for distinctly female tradition.

Sexual Anarchy: Gender and Culture at the Fin de Siècle. Viking Penguin 1991 $11.00. ISBN 0-14-011587-0. Cultural interpretation of the construction of gender.

Sister's Choice: Traditions and Change in American Women's Writing. OUP 1991 $21.95. ISBN 0-19-812383-3. Collected Clarendon lectures delivered in 1989.

Showalter, Elaine, ed., *The New Feminist Criticism: Essays on Women, Literature, and Theory.* Pantheon 1985 $12.76. ISBN 0-394-72647-2. Important collection of essays by American feminist critics.

———, ed., *Speaking of Gender.* Routledge 1988 $39.50. ISBN 0-415-90026-3. An argument for gender studies, exploring the ways in which gender identity for men as well as for women is socially constructed.

———, ed., *These Modern Women: Autobiographical Essays from the Twenties.* Feminist Pr. 1989 $8.95. ISBN 1-55861-007-3

SILKO, LESLIE MARMON. 1948–

Silko's identity as a Laguna informs her writing. Born in Albuquerque and educated at Board of Indian Affairs schools in New Mexico, Silko explores her Native American heritage through characters in conflict between their Anglo side and their Native American side. Her novel *Ceremony* (1977) is ranked with N. Scott Momaday's *House Made of Dawn* as the two most important novels in modern Native American literature. In *Ceremony*, Silko traces the struggles of her half-Anglo, half-Native American protagonist as he attempts to realign himself with his Native American heritage upon his return to his New Mexico reservation just after World War II. Silko's use of her Native American culture does not just contribute themes and characters to her work; she also attempts to convey the American Indian's particular experience of time and reality through the techniques of her narrative structure. So she begins *Ceremony* with the *Thought-Woman*, a spider, "sitting in her room/thinking of a story now/I'm telling you the story she is thinking."

In 1981, Silko was granted a MacArthur Foundation Fellowship, which enabled her to take a leave of absence from her teaching responsibilities at the University of Arizona and concentrate on her writing.

Novel by Silko

Ceremony. Viking Penguin 1977 o.p.

Work by Silko

Storyteller. 1981. Arcade Pub. Inc. 1989 $14.95. ISBN 1-55970-005-X. Anthology of tribal folk tales, short stories, family anecdotes, photographs, and poems.

Books about Silko

Seyersted, Per. *Leslie Marmon Silko.* Boise St. U. W. Writ. Ser. 1980 $3.95. ISBN 0-88430-069-2
Velie, Alan R. *Four American Indian Masters.* U. of Okla. Pr. 1982 o.p.

SILVERMAN, KENNETH. 1936–

A specialist in American culture and literature, Silverman received a Pulitzer Prize in biography and a Bancroft Prize in American history, both in 1985, for *The Life and Times of Cotton Mather* (1984). His most recent biography is a psychological portrait of Edgar Allan Poe. Critics have consistently noted Silverman's masterful range and his skill at presenting his figures as complex human beings of great depth.

Nonfiction by Silverman

Edgar A. Poe: Mournful and Never-ending Remembrance. HarpC 1991 $27.50. 0-06-016715-7. Argues that a key to Poe's imagination and psyche is his mother's death when Poe was 2 years old, and that in his life and works he "re-enacts the loss of the mother."
The Life and Times of Cotton Mather. Col. U. Pr. 1985 $20.00. ISBN 0-231-06125-0

SIMIC, CHARLES. 1938–

Charles Simic was born in Belgrade, Yugoslavia, immigrated with his family to Chicago in 1954, and was educated at New York University. Although his native language was Serbian, he began writing in English. Some of his work reflects the years he served in the U.S. Army (1961–63). He has been awarded a MacArthur Foundation fellowship, a Guggenheim Foundation grant, and a National Endowment for the Arts award. "My poetry always had surrealistic tendencies, which were discouraged a great deal in the '50's," the poet said, but such tendencies were applauded in the 1970s and his reputation consequently flourished. His poems are about obsessive fears and often depict a world that resembles the animism of primitive thought. His work has affinities with that of MARK STRAND and has in its turn produced several imitators.

POETRY BY SIMIC

Austerities. Braziller Poetry Ser. Braziller 1982 $7.95. ISBN 0-8076-1043-7
Charon's Cosmology. Braziller Poetry Ser. Braziller 1977 $6.95. ISBN 0-8076-0842-4
Classic Ballroom Dances. Braziller 1980 $6.95. ISBN 0-8076-0973-0
Dismantling the Silence. Ed. by Richard Howard. *Braziller Poetry Ser.* Braziller 1971 $6.95. ISBN 0-8076-0590-5
Selected Poems, 1963–1983. Braziller 1990 $10.95. ISBN 0-8706-1240-5
The World Doesn't End: Prose Poems. HarBraceJ 1989 $9.95. ISBN 0-15-698350-8. Pulitzer Prize-winning collection of poems; attempts to redefine human experience and reveal the absurdity of everyday life.

NONFICTION BY SIMIC

Wonderful Words, Silent Truths: Essays on Poetry and a Memoir. U. of Mich. Pr. 1990 $32.50. ISBN 0-472-09421-1

SIMPSON, LOUIS. 1923–

Born in the British West Indies, Louis Simpson became a U.S. citizen after volunteering for service in the U.S. Army in 1943. He draws his material from the daily events of his own life, and several of his best-known poems are war poems that deal with the hardness and brutality of what he calls "the other side of glory." He cites as influences "many poets, English and American— particularly ELIOT and WHITMAN. His basically realistic verse has strains of imagism and surrealism. With Robert Pack and Donald Hall, he edited *New Poets of England and America* (1957) and is well known for his *An Introduction to Poetry*. His awards include a Hudson Review Fellowship (1957); the Millay Award (1960); Guggenheim Fellowships (1962, 1970); and the Pulitzer Prize for poetry (1964) for *At the End of the Open Road* (1963).

POETRY BY SIMPSON

At the End of the Open Road. Wesleyan Poetry Program. Wesleyan U. Pr. 1963 $10.95. ISBN 0-8195-1020-3. Reveals greater flexibility of style and growth of themes.
The Best Hour of the Night. Ticknor & Fields 1983 o.p. Continued exploration of Jamaican childhood, mother's Russian tales.
Collected Poems. Paragon 1990 $12.95. ISBN 1-5577-8411-6. A good overview of Simpson's works.
A Dream of Governors. Wesleyan Poetry Program. Wesleyan U. Pr. 1959 $22.50. ISBN 0-8195-2003-9. Penetrating poems about America.
People Live Here: Selected Poems, 1949–1983. BOA Edns. 1983 $25.00. ISBN 0-918526-42-6

BOOK ABOUT SIMPSON

Lazer, Hank, ed. *On Louis Simpson: Depths Beyond Happiness.* U. of Mich. Pr. 1988 $13.95. ISBN 0-472-06382-0. Surveys Simpson's work and gives a good overview of major reviews and essays.

SINGER, ISAAC BASHEVIS. 1904–1991 (NOBEL PRIZE 1978)

Nobel Prize winner I. B. Singer was born in Radzymin, Poland, the son of a rabbi. He came from a thoroughly traditional background, descended from rabbis on both sides of his family. Singer lived in a *shtetl* and also in Warsaw, where he attended the Tachkemoni Rabbinical Seminary from 1920 to 1922. He worked for 10 years as a proofreader and translator before emigrating to the

United States in 1935 with the help of his brother Israel Joshua Singer, who was a writer and journalist there. (Their sister Esther Singer was a Yiddish novelist as well.) Upon arriving in the United States, Singer settled in New York City and joined his brother as a journalist for the *Jewish Daily Forward*, a famous Jewish newspaper.

Even though Singer lived in the United States for more than a half century, he always composed his stories in Yiddish and translated himself into English. Because of this close connection to Yiddish, Singer's works retain a rhythm and flavor that recall the Old World of his youth and early manhood. Singer typically writes about one of two topics: some of his fiction portrays the lives of Polish Jews living within the Pale; other works, primarily later ones, explore the conflicts of displaced Jews after the Holocaust, cut off from their past and stranded in America.

Singer is an ironist who explores the complicated intertwinings of passion, intellect, and faith that comprise human experience. A strong believer in storytelling rather than commentary, he set many of his works among the Jews of Poland, Germany, and America. Many critics feel that his best work is his short stories and tales, many of which resemble folk tales, treating a time and a place that are untouched by contemporary life. These and other works are rich in vivid detail, humor, and drama. He is especially skillful at providing psychological insight into the characters he creates. His vital and colorful characters have also been brought to the stage and screen in such adaptations as the film *Enemies: A Love Story*, a tale of a survivor of the Holocaust who lives in Brooklyn with his Polish wife, but becomes involved with another woman, also a Holocaust survivor.

Considered by many to be the last and greatest Yiddish writer, Singer was awarded the Nobel Prize in 1978, the first Yiddish writer to receive the award. In addition to his many works of fiction for adults, he also wrote a play, *Schlemiel the First* (1974) and numerous tales for children. In recognition for the latter, he received the National Book Award for children's literature in 1970. In 1964 he was elected to the National Institute of Arts and Letters. His autobiography, *In My Father's Court*, was published in 1966.

SHORT STORY COLLECTIONS BY SINGER

A Friend of Kafka and Other Stories. FS&G 1970 o.p. Stories translated by Singer, among others.

The Collected Stories. FS&G 1982 $30.00. ISBN 0-374-12631-3

The Death of Methuselah and Other Stories. 1988. NAL-Dutton 1989 $10.00. ISBN 0-452-26215-1

Gimpel the Fool and Other Stories. Trans. by SAUL BELLOW and others. FS&G 1988 $11.00. ISBN 0-374-50052-5. Fantasy and reality, characteristically, meet.

Short Friday and Other Stories. FS&G 1964 o.p.

The Spinoza of Market Street and Other Stories. FS&G 1961 o.p.

NOVELS BY SINGER

Enemies: A Love Story. FS&G 1988. $11.00. ISBN 0-374-51522-0. Made into a film.

The Family Moskat. FS&G 1985 $16.00. ISBN 0-374-50392-3. Tale of a Jewish family in Poland.

The Manor. FS&G 1967 o.p. Two-part historical novel set in late nineteenth-century Russia about the son of a rabbi who becomes an "enlightened" doctor.

Satan in Goray. FS&G 1955 o.p. Impact of a false Messiah on Jews in Poland during the mid-seventeenth century.

CHILDREN'S FICTION BY SINGER

The Golem. FS&G o.p. Based on folk tale tradition.
Stories for Children. FS&G 1985 $12.95. ISBN 0-374-446498-8
Why Noah Chose the Dove. FS&G 1974 o.p. A story explaining why Noah chose the dove
    to search for dry land after the flood.

NONFICTION BY SINGER

In My Father's Court. Fawcett 1980 $2.50. ISBN 0-449-24074-6

WORK BY SINGER

Isaac Bashevis Singer on Literature and Life: An Interview. (coauthored with Paul
    Rosenblatt and Gene Koppel). U. of Ariz. Pr. 1979 o.p.

BOOKS ABOUT SINGER

Alexander, Edward. *Isaac Bashevis Singer: A Study of the Short Fiction.* Twayne 1990
    $18.95. ISBN 0-8057-8329-6. Individual chapters explore the stories by theme,
    including supernaturalism, morality, love, sex and perversion, vegetarianism, and
    the Holocaust.
Farrell Lee, Grace. *From Exile to Redemption: The Fiction of Isaac Bashevis Singer.* S. Ill.
    U. Pr. 1987 $16.95. ISBN 0-8093-1330-8. Well-written, intelligent study of Singer's
    views of exile and redemption.
Kresh, Paul. *Isaac Bashevis Singer: The Story of a Storyteller.* NAL-Dutton 1984 $13.95.
    ISBN 0-525-67156-0
Miller, David N. *A Bibliography of Isaac Bashevis Singer 1924–1949.* P. Lang Pubs. 1984.
    $28.95. ISBN 0-8204-0002-5

SMILEY, JANE. 1949–

Jane Smiley was born in Los Angeles and educated at Vassar College and the
University of Iowa. She is currently a professor of English at Iowa State
University. Her first critically acclaimed novel, *The Greenlanders* (1988), was
preceded by three other novels and a highly regarded short story collection, *The
Age of Grief* (1987). Smiley's novel *A Thousand Acres* (1991) received both the
National Book Critics Circle Award and the Pulitzer Prize. Like *King Lear*, to
which it invites comparisons, the novel deals with the division of property, a
father, three daughters, and the powerful feelings and secret crimes that bind
them. Familial relations preoccupy Smiley throughout her works. "I think the
tensions of family life are the interesting things to talk about since I accept the
closeness of family as a given," she commented in an interview. She eyes the
shifting ground of love relations without illusion, yet with sympathy: her
portrait of marriage through the meditations of a 35-year-old dentist and father
of three girls in *The Age of Grief* (1987) conveys beautifully the compromises of
closeness and the intensities and confusions of ordinary life. "Everything I
write, I write in a sort of investigative mode," Smiley has said, "and to me an
interesting character is a person who is trying to figure out what's right and
trying to reconcile everything that they are told with what their feelings are. I
think my characters are usually trying to come up with some right way to act, or
even to think or be, in the face of a lot of confusing input."

NOVELS BY SMILEY

At Paradise Gate. S & S Trade 1981 o.p. Elderly woman faces the imminent death of her
    husband as her daughters and granddaughter face crises of their own.
Barn Blind. HarpC 1980 o.p. Pastoral novel about rancher's family in the Midwest.
Duplicate Keys. Knopf 1984 o.p. Mystery—about marriages, affairs, friendships—set in
    New York City, on the Upper West Side.

The Greenlanders. Knopf 1988 $19.95. ISBN 0-394-55120-6. Historical saga of Scandina-
vian life in the fourteenth century.
Ordinary Love and Good Will. Knopf 1989 $17.95. ISBN 0-394-57772-8. Two novellas.
A Thousand Acres. Fawcett 1992 $12.00. ISBN 0-449-90748-1

SHORT STORY COLLECTION BY SMILEY

The Age of Grief. Knopf 1987 $15.95. ISBN 0-394-55848-0. Novella and five stories about
marriage and friendship.

SNODGRASS, W(ILLIAM) D(EWITT). 1926–

Born and educated in Pennsylvania, W. D. Snodgrass has taught at a number
of colleges. His work has been compared to that of ROBERT LOWELL. With the
publication of *Heart's Needle* (1959) a collection of confessional poetry that won
the 1960 Pulitzer Prize, Snodgrass gained immediate fame as one of the best
poets to come out of the 1950s. According to one critic, Snodgrass "spoke in a
distinctive voice. It was one that was jaunty and assertive on the surface . . . but
somber and hurt beneath. His work had a colloquial ease but was traditional in
form. It was one of the few books that successfully bridged the directness of
contemporary free verse with the demands of the academy. His poetry was
appealing in that the poet stood in front of the work." Snodgrass's later poetry is
much less directly personal, as he learned to deal with some of the major
historical events of his time.

POETRY BY SNODGRASS

After Experience: Poems and Translations. Ultramarine Pub. 1968 o.p. Poems that elevate
personal sorrow through symbols to universals of experience.
The Führer Bunker: A Cycle of Poems in Progress. Amer. Poets Continuum Ser. BOA Edns.
1977 $12.95. ISBN 0-918526-00-0. Confronts the "banality of evil."
Heart's Needle. 1959. Knopf 1983 o.p.
Selected Poems, 1957–1987. Soho Pr. 1987 $19.95. ISBN 0-939149-61-3. Reveals
Snodgrass's impressive array of dramatic powers.

SNYDER, GARY. 1930–

Gary Snyder was born in San Francisco and received a B.A. in anthropology
at Reed College. He attended Indiana University and pursued the study of
oriental languages at the University of California at Berkeley. When he was 18,
he shipped out of New York as a sailor. He later worked as a logger and forest
lookout in Oregon, Washington, and California. Before moving to Japan to
study in a Zen monastery under a Bollingen Foundation grant, Snyder worked
on an American tanker in the Persian Gulf and South Pacific Islands, then spent
four months in India (1961–62).

Snyder is one of the most famous Beat poets, along with ALLEN GINSBERG and
GREGORY CORSO. He is the most controlled and concise of that school; yet his
adventurous life has given his verse a unique range of subject and feeling. Close
to nature since childhood, he also is the most widely known poet of the ecology
movement. Often his poems have a Zen-like stillness and sharpness of
perception, which serves to define the connective web between humanity and
the natural universe.

Snyder is deeply interested in the American Indian and the idea of the tribe as
an alternative to modern culture, or at least an an example for modern culture.
Besides receiving the first Zen Institute of America Award in 1956, Snyder was
the recipient of an American Academy of Arts and Sciences poetry prize in 1966.

His essays, *Earth House Hold* (1969), composed of journal notes and diary excerpts, have become a classsic in the underground ecology movement.

POETRY BY SNYDER

Axe Handles. N. Point Pr. 1983 $20.50. ISBN 0-86547-119-3
Back Country. New Dir. Pr. 1968 $7.95. ISBN 0-8112-0194-5. Experiences in nature.
No Nature: New and Selected Poems. Pantheon 1992 $24.50. ISBN 0-679-41385-5
Riprap and Cold Mountain Poems. N. Point Pr. 1940 repr. of 1958 ed. $19.95. ISBN 0-86547-455-9
Six Sections from Mountains and Rivers without End Plus One. Writing Ser. Four Seasons Foun. 1970 o.p. Contains the newest section of this continuing series, which is likely to be one of the major poems of our time.

NONFICTION BY SNYDER

The Real Work: Interviews and Talks, 1964–1978. Ed. by Scott McLean. New Dir. Pr. 1980 $10.00. ISBN 0-8112-0760-9

BOOKS ABOUT SNYDER

Harper, Jon. *Gary Snyder: Dimensions of a Life.* Sierra 1991 $17.00. ISBN 0-87156-616-8. Explores Snyder's contribution to contemporary literature and thought.
Molesworth, Charles. *Gary Snyder's Vision: Poetry and the Real Work. Literary Frontiers Ser.* U. of Mo. Pr. 1983 $9.95. ISBN 0-8262-0414-7. Attempts to explain Snyder's "alternate vision" as poet.

SONTAG, SUSAN. 1933–

Sontag, an influential cultural critic with a Harvard master's degree in philosophy, is noted for taking radical positions and venturing outrageous interpretations. Proclaiming a "new sensibility," she supported the cause of pop art and underground films in the 1960s. Her reputation as a formidable critic has been established by numerous reviews, essays, and articles in the *New York Review of Books*, the *N.Y. Times*, *Harper's*, and other periodicals. *Against Interpretation* (1966) includes her controversial essay "Notes on Camp," first published in *Partisan Review*. The title of the book introduces her argument against what she sees as the distortion of an original work by the countless critics who bend it to their own interpretations. "The aim of all commentary on art," she writes, "should be to make works of art—and, by analogy, our own experience—more, rather than less, real to us." Sontag has a mature modernist sensibility, but manages to depict the avant-garde in language accessible to any reader. She has lectured extensively around the United States and has taught philosophy at Harvard, Sarah Lawrence, and Columbia. She is a frequent and popular television discussion personality, particularly on contemporary issues of illness or feminism, although many feminists are unhappy that she does not declare herself to be a "feminist critic." She is also, less successfully, a fiction writer.

NONFICTION BY SONTAG

Against Interpretation. 1966. Hippocrene Bks. repr. of 1978 ed. $20.50. ISBN 0-807052-352-X. A selection of critical writings, 1961–65, on modern novels, films, and theater and a nominee for the 1967 National Book Award.
Illness as Metaphor. 1978. Doubleday 1990 $8.95. ISBN 0-385-26705-3. Written out of Sontag's own experience as a cancer patient.
A Susan Sontag Reader. FS&G 1982 o.p. A good collection of essays and fiction.
Styles of Radical Will. 1969. Delacorte 1978 $5.75. ISBN 0-385-28909-X
The Way We Live Now. FS&G 1991 $35.00. ISBN 0-374-52305-3. Deals with AIDS.

NOVELS BY SONTAG

The Benefactor. 1963. Doubleday 1991 $11.00. ISBN 0-385-26710-X
Death Kit. 1967. Doubleday 1991 $9.95. ISBN 0-385-26711-8
The Volcano Lover. 1992. FS&G 1992 $22.00. ISBN 0-374-28516-0. Historical novel set in eighteenth-century Italy; about a refined British ambassador named Cavaliere, whose true loves are art collecting and the volcano Vesuvius.

STAFFORD, WILLIAM (EDGAR). 1914–

Born in Kansas, William Stafford was educated in the Midwest and has taught at Lewis and Clark College in Oregon. He is a consciously "Western poet, a word-painter of Western landscapes. He is often linked with ROBERT BLY and JAMES WRIGHT as a poet of deep imagery. He has said: "My poetry seems to me direct and communicative, with some oddity and variety. It is usually not formal. It is much like talk, with some enhancement."

POETRY BY STAFFORD

The Long Sigh the Wind Makes: Poems by William Stafford. Adrienne Lee 1991 $15.00. ISBN 0-9629194-0-3
My Name is William Tell. Confluence Pr. 1992 $11.00. ISBN 0-917652-96-7. Nature, story, and social values.
Password: Poems. HarpC 1991 $11.00. ISBN 0-06-055293-X

STEGNER, WALLACE. 1909–1993

In 1972, Stegner won a Pulitzer Prize for *Angle of Repose* (1971), a novel about a wheelchair-bound man's re-creation of his New England grandmother's experience in a late nineteenth-century frontier town. As a result, Stegner is undergoing something of a revival. His work enjoys a new appreciation for its traditional narrative forms, its use of rich detail, and the unpretentious way it treats general social and psychological issues. For readers tired or confused by postmodernist fiction, Stegner offers relief.

Stegner may also be the beneficiary of a quickening of interest in the latest literary westward expansion that includes such diverse writers as JANE SMILEY and LARRY MCMURTRY. Stegner's novels and stories are profoundly influenced by the American West where he grew up, and he wants to construct the history of a place where people went, often trying to escape the past. Moving between Eastern "cultivation" and Western "nature," Stegner's novels trace various stages in the Westward movement of the American experience. Against this broad cultural landscape, showing the modern betrayal of the past, Stegner details individual human behavior through a range of fully conceived and finely drawn characters. He is a master at tracing the changes over time in marriages and friendships, as well as at depicting the poignant tensions between a mind that remains strong in a body that is succumbing to illness.

NOVELS BY STEGNER

All the Little Live Things. Viking Penguin 1991 $10.00. ISBN 0-14-015441-8. A retired academic in present-day California measures the failed promises of Westward expansion.
Angle of Repose. Viking Penguin 1992 $12.00. ISBN 0-14-016930-X. The story of a historian considering his own life in contemporary California while uncovering his grandmother's history.
The Big Rock Candy Mountain. Viking Penguin 1991 $11.00. ISBN 0-14-013939-7. About a family wandering on the western frontiers.

Crossing to Safety. Viking Penguin 1990 $11.00. ISBN 0-14-013348-8. Follows the friendship of two academic couples over the course of many years.
Remembering Laughter. Little 1937 o.p.
The Spectator Bird. Viking Penguin 1990 $10.00. ISBN 0-14-013940-0. About a retired literary agent who meditates on death, life, literature, love.

SHORT STORY COLLECTION BY STEGNER

The Collected Stories of Wallace Stegner. Viking Penguin 1991 $11.95. ISBN 0-14-014774-8. A recent collection revealing pathos and the range of Stegner's writing.

STEINER, GEORGE. 1929–

Son of a Jewish father who left Vienna in 1924, Steiner was brought up in France and came to the United States in 1940. After a period as a Rhodes Scholar at Oxford, he worked for the London *Economist*. Since 1974 he has been professor of English and comparative literature at the University of Geneva in Switzerland. Though he commands respect—and occasionally awe at his astonishing polymathic proficiency—from critics and academics in America and abroad, he belongs to no critical "school" (though he calls himself a radical humanist), nor is his writing "academic" in the strict sense. He is seeking, he says, a "philosophy of language" that can help rescue people from the cheapening torrent of words with which they are assaulted by Marshall McLuhan's "media" and from a diminution of intellectual, political, and humane values that threaten us with the silence of total ruin. In *After Babel* (1975) he defends precisely those simple contextual linguistic relationships that modern language studies ignore or dismiss. In this "bestial" age, Steiner mourns the idealism and literacy that were lost in World War II and the Holocaust. Steiner has written for *The New Yorker* many years.

NONFICTION BY STEINER

After Babel: Aspects of Language and Translation. OUP 1975 $13.95. ISBN 0-19-502048-0
Antigones. OUP 1986 $29.95. ISBN 0-19-812665-4. Sophocles's Antigone as a legendary character in art.
The Death of Tragedy. OUP 1980 repr. of 1961 ed. $9.95. ISBN 0-19-502702-7. A study of tragedy as a dramatic mode.
Extraterritorial: Papers on Literature and the Language Revolution. Atheneum 1971 o.p. Work on psycholinguistics.
George Steiner: A Reader. 1984. OUP 1987 $35.00. ISBN 0-19-520458-1
In Bluebeard's Castle: Some Notes toward the Redefinition of Culture. Yale U. Pr. 1971 $10.00. ISBN 0-300-01710-3
Language and Silence: Essays on Language, Literature and the Inhuman. 1967 Athenaeum 1970 o.p. Lectures and essays on moral implications of silence and language.
On Difficulty and Other Essays. OUP 1978 $21.95. ISBN 0-19-212208-8. Makes use of discourse analysis and philology.
Real Presences: Is There Anything in What We Say? U. Ch. Pr. 1989 $19.95. ISBN 0-226-77233-0. Passionately argued essay that ranges fluently over esthetics, linguistics, philosophy, and post-structuralism.

STONE, ROBERT. 1937–

Born in Brooklyn, New York, Robert Stone is often compared to CONRAD and MELVILLE because he combines an ability to write compelling adventure stories with a concern for the moral dilemmas confronting human beings in history. Never one to avoid a conflict, he writes about the historical and political events that have structured contemporary American experience—racism, the Vietnam War, American involvement in Latin American revolutions—and creates characters who wrestle with the timeless problems of personal responsibility and commitment. Stone served in the U.S. Navy in the mid-1950s, then went to Stanford University, where he became politically active in the 1960s. He draws on these experiences to explore the motives of characters who become involved in the historical and political events of their age.

NOVELS BY STONE

Children of Light. Knopf 1986 $17.95. ISBN 0-394-52573-6. Screenwriter Gordon Walker seeks out his old lover LuAnne in Mexico.
Dog Soldiers. 1974. Viking Penguin 1987 $10.00. ISBN 0-14-009835-6. Winner of the National Book Award. The horrific aftereffects of Vietnam, showing its relation to America's drug culture.
A Flag for Sunrise. Knopf 1981 $15.95. ISBN 0-394-40757-1. Probably Stone's most successful integration of political issues with personal ones; questions U.S. role in Latin America.
Hall of Mirrors. 1967. Viking Penguin 1987 $10.00. ISBN 0-14-009834-8. Story of three drifters meeting in New Orleans in the 1960s as Stone criticizes the right-wing extremism he sees infecting American society.
Outerbridge Reach. Ticknor & Fields 1992 $21.45. ISBN 0-395-58781-6. Brought comparisons with Melville and Conrad—sea story.

STRAND, MARK. 1934–

Although not associated with any one school of poetry, Mark Strand's work seems to possess qualities of the European and Latin American surrealists. As Strand is a translator of PAZ (see Vol. 2), BORGES (See Vol. 2), GUILLÉN (see Vol. 2), and QUASIMODO (see Vol. 2), this is not surprising. His poetry, though written in a matter-of-fact style, seems singularly removed from the here and now, filled with the impossibilities of the restless world lying between dream and wakefulness. Strand also writes children's stories.

This Canadian-born U.S. poet received his degree from Antioch College, attended Yale University, studied in Florence on a Fulbright grant (1960–61), and later studied at the University of Iowa. He was a Fulbright lecturer in 1965 and 1966, and during 1966–67 he held an Ingram Merrill Fellowship and taught at Mount Holyoke College. His prizes include an award from the National Council on the Arts (1967–68) and a Rockefeller Fellowship (1968–1969). In 1990 Strand was named the fourth Poet Laureate of the United States.

POETRY BY STRAND

Continuous Life. Random 1990 $20.00. ISBN 0-394-58817-7. Contains 30 poems and 6 prose-poems bathed in the moonlight of imagination.
Reasons for Moving. Atheneum 1968 $4.95. ISBN 0-689-10262-3
Selected Poems. Atheneum 1980 $10.95. ISBN 0-689-11088-X. A collection of some of Strand's best early work.

NONFICTION BY STRAND

The Monument. Ecco Pr. 1978 $7.95. ISBN 0-912946-50-4. A book of prose.

SHORT STORY COLLECTION BY STRAND

Mr. and Mrs. Baby and Other Stories. 1985. Knopf 1985 $11.45. ISBN 0-394-51359-2. A collection for children.

STROUSE, JEAN. 1945–

A journalist and general editor at *Newsweek,* Strouse has written a biography of ALICE JAMES, the sister of HENRY and WILLIAM JAMES, that one critic observed to be "more than a biography, a complicated work of social history." In *Alice James: A Biography* (1980), Strouse presents James as a potentially brilliant woman who was emotionally crippled by the conventions of nineteenth-century society. Denied the opportunities available to her brothers, Alice "made a career of emotional collapse." The biography won the Bancroft Prize in American history and was nominated for a National Book Critics Circle Award.

NONFICTION BY STROUSE

Alice James: A Biography. 1980. HM 1991 $10.70. ISBN 0-395-59773-0

STYRON, WILLIAM. 1925–

When William Styron's first novel appeared in 1951, it seemed to some critics that the young author was the likely heir to WILLIAM FAULKNER. The story of a family doomed to decline and tragedy like Faulkner's Compsons, *Lie Down in Darkness* (1951) is a highly charged book that carries a quality of poetic brooding that seems both Southern in the Faulkner sense and very modern in the way of a KAFKA (see Vol. 2) or CAMUS (see Vol. 2).

Born in Newport News, Virginia, Styron served in the U.S. Marine Corps before completing his studies at Duke University. Not long after *Lie Down in Darkness* (1951) was accepted for publication, Styron was recalled to active duty because of the Korean War. He used some of his military experiences in *The Long March* (1953), a short novel about individuality and authority in the military that was well received critically. His next full-length novel, *Set This House on Fire* (1960), is a tragicomedy, a satire, a *bildungsroman*, a portrait of the artist, and a whopping big novel in the THOMAS WOLFE tradition that seemed to elevate Styron to the rank of major novelist.

Styron's bestseller, *The Confessions of Nat Turner* (1967), received almost universal praise by the literary establishment before winning the Pulitzer Prize in 1967. Styron based his novel on a contemporary 20-page pamphlet about the actual Turner uprising published by a lawyer named Thomas Gray and hit upon the fictional device of having Turner dictate his account of the affair to Gray so that the rebellion is seen both from within and outside. Clifton Fadiman thought that Styron had "somehow thought himself inside the skin of one of the most remarkable, appalling and tragic figures in the entire chronicle of the American Negro." However, that judgment was severely contradicted by the contributions to *William Styron's Nat Turner: Ten Black Writers Respond*, in which such prominent African American writers as John Oliver Killens and John Williams accused Styron of helping to perpetuate "just about every myth with which the black man has been shackled since slavery" (*Publishers Weekly*).

Styron turned to another moral issue in *Sophie's Choice* (1979), a novel about the after-effects of the Holocaust that illustrates Styron's themes of the nature of evil, life in the military, and the effects of being dominated. Sophie Zawistowska tells her story to a young Southern writer named Stingo who appears to be a surrogate for Styron himself. Reviewer Edith Milton (*Yale Review*), for instance, found it "an ambiguous, masterful, and enormously satisfying novel" whereas Benjamin Demott (*Atlantic*) called it "an over-reaching blockbuster."

NOVELS BY STYRON

The Confessions of Nat Turner. Random 1967 $24.95. ISBN 0-394-42099-3
Lie Down in Darkness. 1951. Random 1979 $24.95. ISBN 0-394-50659-6. A dark view of suburban life.
The Long March. Random 1953 o.p. About life in the Marine Corps.

Set This House on Fire. 1960. Random 1968 $10.95. ISBN 0-394-43387-4. About a murder and some Americans in Italy.
Sophie's Choice. Random 1979 $29.95. ISBN 0-394-46109-6

NONFICTION BY STYRON

Darkness Visible: A Memoir of Madness. Random 1990 $15.95. ISBN 0-394-58888-6. Styron's struggle with depression.

WORK BY STYRON

This Quiet Dust: And Other Writings. Random 1982 $17.50. ISBN 0-394-50934-X. A potpourri of reminiscences, essays, and reflections on the themes of Styron's fiction.

BOOKS ABOUT STYRON

Casciato, Arthur D., and James L. West, III. *Critical Essays on William Styron.* G. K. Hall 1982 o.p. A collection of valuable essays.
Friedman, Melvin J. *William Styron.* Bowling Green Univ. 1974 $3.50. ISBN 0-87972-071-9
Morris, Robert K., and Irving Malin, eds. *The Achievement of William Styron.* U. of Ga. Pr. 1975 o.p.
Pearce, Richard. *William Styron. Pamphlets on Amer. Writers Ser.* Bks. Demand repr. of 1971 ed. $25.00. ISBN 0-7837-72868-9
Ruderman, Judith. *William Styron.* HarpC 1987 $15.95. ISBN 0-8044-2781-X. Offers a compact yet discerning tribute to the literary accomplishment of a Southern novelist whose reputation is tinged with controversy.

SWENSON, MAY. 1919–1989

May Swenson was born in Utah and educated at Utah State University, Logan. A former editor at New Directions Publishing Corporation, she has been a poet-in-residence at Purdue University in Indiana and has taught poetry seminars at the University of North Carolina, Greensboro (1968–69). Twice a recipient of a Rockefeller Fellowship (1955 and 1967), Swenson has also been awarded a Guggenheim Fellowship (1959); a National Institute of Arts and Letters Award (1969); a Ford Foundation grant (1964); a Lucy Martin Donnelly Fellowship from Bryn Mawr College (1968); and a Shelley Memorial Award (1968). Her poetry is remarkable for its agility, its intensity, and its consistency. Swenson's poems have been published in such popular magazines as *Harper's, The Atlantic,* and *The New Yorker.* She is also noted for her translations of contemporary Swedish poetry.

POETRY BY SWENSON

In Other Words. Knopf 1992 $12.00. ISBN 0-679-73356-6. New poems.
New and Selected Things Taking Place. Atlantic Monthly 1978 o.p.
The Love Poems of May Swenson. HM 1991 $9.70. ISBN 0-395-59222-4

TATE, JAMES. 1943–

Born in Kansas City, Tate erupted upon the poetry scene when, in 1967, at the age of 23, he received the Yale Series of Young Poets award for *The Lost Pilot* (1967). Within two years of his stunning debut, Tate had another dozen collections in print or accepted for publication. Remarkable for his originality and control, Tate has declared himself to be "in the tradition of the Impurists: WHITMAN, WILLIAMS, NERUDA [see Vol. 2] . . . I am trying to combine words in such a way as to lend a new life, a new hope, to that which is lifeless and hopeless." He has taken as his themes the agony of communication and the difficulties of having been treated as a poetic prodigy.

POETRY BY TATE

Absences. 1972. Carnegie-Mellon 1990 $9.95. ISBN 0-88748-091-8
Distance from Loved Ones. Wesleyan U. Pr. 1990 $22.50. ISBN 0-8195-1191-9
The Lost Pilot. 1967. Yale U. Pr. 1982 $5.95. ISBN 0-912946-65-2. An elegy to his father, in
    the title poem.
Selected Poems. Wesleyan U. Pr. 1991 $30.00. ISBN 0-8195-1192-7. First collection of
    Tate's work, showing his development over two decades.

TRILLING, LIONEL. 1905–1975

Trilling has exerted a wide influence upon literature and criticism: as
university professor at Columbia, where he taught English literature, and in his
long association with *Partisan Review, Kenyon Review,* and the Kenyon School
of English (now the School of Letters, Indiana University). He considered
himself a true "liberal"—having a "vision of a general enlargement of
[individual] freedom and rational direction in human life. Yet even liberalism,
Trilling insisted, was simply one of several ways of organizing the complexity of
life; however, it can reveal "variousness and possibility" just as literature, its
subject, does. Trilling was viewed as a genteel moralist, but never would settle
for mere simplification in literary analysis even if it led to understanding.

NONFICTION BY TRILLING

Beyond Culture. HarBraceJ 1978 $10.95. ISBN 0-15-111987-2
Last Decade: Essays and Reviews, 1965–1975. Ed. by Diana Trilling. HarBraceJ 1981
    $7.95. ISBN 0-15-648892-2. Essays and reviews collected by Trilling's wife.
The Liberal Imagination: Essays on Literature and Society. 1950. HarBraceJ 1979 $10.00.
    ISBN 0-15-151197-7. The great humanists, with essays on Freud, Wordsworth, and
    American literature.
The Opposing Self: Nine Essays in Criticism. 1955. HarBraceJ 1979 $13.95. ISBN 0-15-
    670065-4. Romantic image of the self in Keats, Austen, Wordsworth, Tolstoy,
    Dickens, Flaubert, Howells, Henry James, and Orwell.
Prefaces to the Experience of Literature. HarBraceJ 1979 $12.95. ISBN 0-15-173915-3
Sincerity and Authenticity: Six Lectures. HUP 1971 $6.95. ISBN 0-674-80861-4. The
    Charles Eliot Norton Lectures for 1969–70.
Speaking of Literature and Society. Ed. by Diana Trilling. HarBraceJ 1980 $17.95. ISBN
    0-15-184710-X. Focuses on Trilling's belief in literature as social criticism.

TYLER, ANNE. 1941–

Novelist and short-story writer Anne Tyler was born in Minnesota, grew up in
North Carolina, and was educated at Duke University. Since 1965 she has lived
in Baltimore, the setting for much of her work. With wry humor and sympathy,
Tyler writes about the ambivalence of family relations, focusing on ordinary
characters, most of whom live in Baltimore or in small Southern towns. Her
concerns are with the human need to belong and to be loved, the necessity of
making imperfect choices, and the acceptance of mortality. Beginning with her
ninth novel, *Dinner at the Homesick Restaurant* (1982), which won the PEN
Faulkner Award, Tyler has gained the wider audience she deserves. This novel
shows Tyler's development as a writer: here, she is able to delineate family
tensions over several generations. Tyler's feel for the oddities of families and the
strange configurations of which they are made comes through vividly in *The
Accidental Tourist* (1985).

NOVELS BY TYLER

The Accidental Tourist. 1985 Berkeley Pub. 1988 $4.95. ISBN 0-425-11423-6. Unexpected love affair between a travel writer and a single mother.

Breathing Lessons. 1988. Berkley Pub. 1989 $5.50. ISBN 0-425-11774-X. Examines themes of love, marriage, and regret.

Celestial Navigation. 1974. Ivy Bks. 1993 $5.99. ISBN 0-8041-0888-9. Story of an artist who needs to make contact with others.

Dinner at the Homesick Restaurant. 1982. Berkley Pub. 1989 $4.95. ISBN 0-425-09868-0. Her finest novel. About the tensions in a family that tries to eat in harmony.

Saint Maybe: A Novel. Knopf 1991 $24.50. ISBN 0-679-40771-5. A story about four generations of an eccentric Baltimore family.

UPDIKE, JOHN. 1932–

American novelist, poet, and critic John Updike was born in Shillington, Pennsylvania, and studied at Harvard (which he attended on a scholarship) and the Ruskin School Drawing and Fine Art in Oxford, England. After returning from England in 1955, he worked for two years on the staff of *The New Yorker*. This marked the beginning of a long relationship with the magazine, during which he has contributed numerous short stories, poems, and book reviews.

Although Updike's first published book was a collection of verse, *The Carpentered Hen and Other Tame Creatures* (1958), his renown as a writer is based on his fiction, beginning with *The Poorhouse Fair*, published in 1959. When *Couples* was published in 1968, Wilfred Sheed (*N.Y. Times*) looked back on Updike's career to that time and commented, "Updike can be quite a virtuoso. But with each book, his position seems a little less flashy and more solid." The mixture of flashy versatility and solid achievement has been apparent in Updike's writing since that judgment was made, and his deep artistic commitment is apparent not only in the abundance of his works in several genres, but also by his willingness to experiment with new forms and themes. Updike has shifted directions with each decade as he has responded to the changing times, while at the same time maintaining a basic, if sometimes ambiguous, personal integrity.

Updike's work, sophisticated and inventive, focuses on middle-class America and their major concerns—marriage, divorce, religion, materialism, and sex. Among his best-known works are the Rabbit tetrology—*Rabbit, Run* (1960), *Rabbit Redux* (1971), *Rabbit Is Rich* (1981), and *Rabbit at Rest* (1988). *Rabbit Run* introduces Harry "Rabbit" Angstrom as a 26-year-old salesman of dime-store gadgets trapped in an unhappy marriage in a dismal Pennsylvania town, looking back wistfully on his days as a high school basketball star. *Rabbit Redux* takes up the story 10 years later, and Rabbit's relationship with representative figures of the 1960s enables Updike to provide social commentary in a story marked by mellow wisdom and compassion in spite of some shocking jolts. In *Rabbit Is Rich*, Harry is comfortably middle-aged and complacent. Much of the book seems to satirize the country-club set and the swinging sexual/social life of Rabbit and his friends, but Updike again moves the story onto a higher plain, which would seem to justify those critics who think that his vision is unquestionably religious in its essential nature. Finally, in *Rabbit at Rest*, Harry arrives at the age where he must confront his mortality.

Updike's other novels range widely in subject and locale, from *The Poorhouse Fair*, about a home for the aged that seems to be a microcosm for society as a whole, through *The Court* (1978), about a revolution in Africa, to *The Witches of Eastwick* (1984), in which Updike tries to write from inside the sensibilities of three witches in contemporary New England. *The Centaur* (1963) is a subtle, complicated allegorical novel that won Updike the National Book Award in 1964. Another recent trilogy includes *A Month of Sundays* (1975), *Roger's Version* (1986), and *S* (1988).

In addition to his novels, Updike also has written short stories, poems, critical essays, and reviews. His short fiction is notable for the crisps, efficient way in which he treats a wide variety of subjects. *Self-Consciousness*, a memoir of his early life, his thoughts on issues such as the Vietnam War, and his attitude toward religion, was published in 1989. Updike currently lives near Boston with his second wife. He was elected to the American Academy of Arts and Letters in 1977.

NOVELS BY UPDIKE

Bech: A Book. 1970. Random 1980 $5.95. ISBN 0-394-74509-4
Bech is Back. 1982. Fawcett 1983 $2.95. ISBN 0-499-20277-1
The Centaur. 1963. Fawcett 1988 $4.95. ISBN 0-449-21522-9
The Coup. 1978. Fawcett 1985 $4.50. ISBN 0-449-24259-5
Couples. 1968. Fawcett 1985 $4.95. ISBN 0-449-20797-8
Marry Me. 1976. Fawcett 1983 $3.95. ISBN 0-449-20795-1
A Month of Sundays. 1975. Fawcett 1985 $3.50. ISBN 0-449-20795-1
Of the Farm. 1965. Fawcett 1987 $3.95. ISBN 0-449-21451-6
The Poorhouse Fair. 1959. Fawcett 1985 $3.50. ISBN 0-449-21213-6
Rabbit at Rest. Knopf 1988 $21.95. ISBN 0-394-58815-0. Last in the "Rabbit" series.
Rabbit Is Rich. 1981. Fawcett 1982 $4.95. ISBN 0-449-24548-8
Rabbit Redux. 1971. Fawcett 1985 $4.95. ISBN 0-449-20934-2
Rabbit Run. 1960. Fawcett 1983 $4.95. ISBN 0-449-20506-1
Roger's Version. 1986. Fawcett 1987 $4.95. ISBN 0-449-21652-7. Roger Chillingworth's version of *The Scarlet Letter*.
S. 1988. Knopf 1988 $17.95. ISBN 0-394-56835-4
The Witches of Eastwick. Fawcett 1985 $5.95. ISBN 0-449-20647-5

SHORT STORY COLLECTIONS BY UPDIKE

Museums and Women and Other Stories. 1972 Random 1981 $7.95 ISBN 0-394-74762-3
The Music School. 1966. Random 1980 $10.00. ISBN 0-394-74510-8. An important early collection of stories.
Pigeon Feathers and Other Stories. 1962. Fawcett 1986. $3.95. ISBN 0-449-21332-0
Problems and Other Stories. 1979. Fawcett 1985 $3.50. ISBN 0-449-21103-7
Same Door. 1959. Random 1981 $7.95. ISBN 0-395-74763-1
Too Far to Go. 1979. Fawcett 1982 $2.75. ISBN 0-449-20016-7. A selection of stories.

NONFICTION BY UPDIKE

Self-Consciousness: Memoirs. 1989. Knopf 1989 $18.95. ISBN 0-394-57222-X

BOOKS ABOUT UPDIKE

Burchard, Rachael C. *John Updike: Yea Sayings. Crosscurrents Modern Critiques Ser.* S. Ill. U. Pr. 1971 o.p. An early attempt to account for Updike's popularity.
Detweiler, Robert. *John Updike. Twayne's U. S. Authors Ser.* G. K. Hall 1977 $16.95. ISBN 0-8057-7422-X. Appreciative analysis of Updike's narrative art.
Greiner, Donald J. *John Updike's Novels*. Ohio U. Pr. 1984 $23.95. ISBN 0-8214-0780-5. Complements *The Other John Updike* (below) as a serviceable critical assessment of Updike's literary career.
————. *The Other John Updike: Poems, Short Stories, Prose, Play*. Ohio U. Pr. 1981 $24.95. ISBN 0-8214-0585-3
Leonard, J. S., and C. E. Wharton. *John Updike: The Cipher of the World*. St. Martin 1988 $19.95. ISBN 0-312-01342-6. Close readings that throw new light on Updike's novels.

MacNaughton, William R. *Critical Essays on John Updike. Critical Essays on Amer. Lit. Ser.* G. K. Hall 1982 $36.50. ISBN 0-8161-8467-4. Well-chosen collection of essays by scholars and critics with differing viewpoints on Updike's art.

Markle, Joyce B. *Fighters and Lovers: Theme in the Novels of John Updike.* NYU Pr. 1973 o.p. Focuses on familial and love relationships in the novels.

Olivas, Michael A. *Annotated Bibliography of John Updike Criticism.* Garland 1974 o.p.

Sokoloff, B. A. *John Updike: A Comprehensive Bibliography.* Folcroft 1972 o.p.

VAN DUYN, MONA. 1921–

The sixth Poet Laureate of the Library of Congress, Van Duyn is the author of seven books of poetry, most recently, *Near Changes* (1990), for which she won the 1991 Pulitzer Prize for poetry. Born in Waterloo, Iowa, Van Duyn has lived in St. Louis since 1950. She was a lecturer at Washington University from 1950 to 1967. Noted for her subtle intelligence, her humor and satire, her formal elegance, and her compassionate attentiveness to the human heart, Van Duyn takes as her theme "the wintry work of living, our flawed art." Her work was slow to receive the recognition it deserved. However, in 1971 she won the Bollingen Prize; several major awards and grants soon followed.

POETRY BY VAN DUYN

Firefall: Poems. Knopf 1992 $19.50. ISBN 0-679-41897-0. Contains a charming poem about setting the VCR to record an old movie and somehow losing the coveted conclusion.

If It Be Not I: Collected Poems. Knopf 1992 $24.50. ISBN 0-679-41902-0. A kaleidoscope of poems about nature, growth, birds, neighbors, and death.

Letters from a Father and Other Poems. 1982. Macmillan 1982 $6.95. ISBN 0-689-11287-4

Merciful Disguises: Poems Published and Unpublished. 1973. Macmillan 1982 $9.95. ISBN 0-689-11294-7. A wonderful collection of moving poetry.

Near Changes. Knopf 1990. $18.95. ISBN 0-394-58444-9

VIDAL, GORE. 1925–

When Gore Vidal's nineteenth novel, *Lincoln*, was published in 1984, Harold Bloom used it as the occasion to look back respectfully at Vidal's career as a writer. In Bloom's view, Vidal has been most "gifted at re-imagining history" so that such books as *Julian* (1964), about the pagan ruler of Rome in the fourth century, *Burr* (1973), about America during the revolutionary period, and *1876*, about America 100 years later, are probably the best achievements in fiction before *Lincoln*. In *Lincoln*, Vidal "found his truest subject, which is our national political history during precisely those years when our political and military histories were as one, one thing and one thing only: the unwavering will of Abraham Lincoln to keep the states united" (*N.Y. Review of Books*).

Gore Vidal was born at West Point, site of the U.S. Military Academy, and spent much of his childhood in Washington, D.C., with his maternal grandfather, Senator Thomas Gore, a scholarly and witty senator from Oklahoma. His first book, *Williwaw* (1946), reflected his own experiences on an army freight-supply ship in the Aleutian Islands during World War II, while *The City and the Pillar* (1948) drew attention as one of the first honest and serious depictions of homosexuality in fiction. *Washington, D.C.,* (1967) is a novel about corruption in that city from about 1937 to 1954 as seen from the perspective of a senator, and *Myra Breckenridge* (1968) achieved a certain notoriety both as a novel and a film dealing with the life of a transvestite. Other recent novels include Empire (1987), a story of the Gilded Age, and *Hollywood* (1990), about Hollywood in the 1920s. While well known as a novelist, it is as an essayist that Vidal finds his other chief distinction as a writer. He says of himself, "I am at heart a propagandist, a tremendous hater, a tiresome nag, complacently positive that there is no human problem which could not be solved if people would simply do as I advise." Vidal spends most of his time at his villa in Italy.

NOVELS BY VIDAL

Burr: A Novel. Ballantine 1988 $4.95. ISBN 0-345-00884-7
Creation. Random 1981 $45.00. ISBN 0-394-50015-6
Duluth. Ballantine 1984 $4.95. ISBN 0-345-31220-1
1876. 1976. Ballantine 1987 $5.95. ISBN 0-345-34626-2. Focuses on the Tilden-Hayes presidential election in the year of the novel's title.
Hollywood. 1990. Ballantine 1991 $5.95. ISBN 0-345-37013-9
Julian. Ballantine 1985 $5.95. ISBN 0-345-32908-2
Kalki. Random 1978 $14.95. ISBN 0-394-42053-5
Lincoln: A Novel. Random 1993 $19.00. ISBN 0-679-60048-5
Live from Golgatha. Random 1992 $21.50. ISBN 0-679-41611-0. Rather irreverent depiction of life and times during early Christianity.
Myron: A Novel. Random 1974 $6.95. ISBN 0-394-49477-6
Washington, D.C. 1967 Ballantine 1988 $4.95. ISBN 0-345-00887-1. About the New Deal and McCarthyism.
Williwaw: A Novel. AMS Pr. repr. of 1946 ed. $23.50. ISBN 0-404-20276-4

SHORT STORY COLLECTION BY VIDAL

A Thirsty Evil: Seven Short Stories. Gay Sunshine 1981 repr. of 1956 ed. $20.00. ISBN 0-917342-83-6

NONFICTION BY VIDAL

At Home: Essays 1982–1988. 1988. Random 1990 $9.95. ISBN 0-679-72528-8
Homage to Daniel Shays: Collected Essays, 1952–1972. 1973. Random 1973 o.p.
Screening History. HUP 1992 $14.95. ISBN 0-674-79586-5. Lectures on the value of films in teaching Americans history.

PLAYS BY VIDAL

The Best Man. 1960. Dramatists Play 1990 $4.75. ISBN 0-8222-0107-0
Visit to a Small Plant. 1956. Dramatists Play 1990 $4.75. ISBN 0-8222-1211-0

BOOKS ABOUT VIDAL

Kiernan, Robert F. *Gore Vidal. Lit. and Life Ser.* Continuum 1982 $19.95. ISBN 0-8044-2461-6. A fine introduction to Vidal.
Stanton, Robert J. *Gore Vidal: A Primary and Secondary Bibliography.* G. K. Hall 1980 o.p.
————, ed. *Views from a Window: Conversations with Gore Vidal.* Carol Pub. Group 1980 $14.95. ISBN 0-8184-0302-0. Vidal as a witty, irreverent raconteur.
White, Ray L. *Gore Vidal, U.S. Authors Ser.* NCUP 1968 $10.95. ISBN 0-8084-0007-X

VONNEGUT, KURT, JR. 1922–

The appeal of Kurt Vonnegut, Jr., especially to bright younger readers of the past few decades, may be attributed partly to the fact that he is one of the few writers who have successfully straddled the imaginary line between science-fiction/fantasy and "real literature." He was born in Indianapolis and attended Cornell University, but his college education was interrupted by World War II. Captured during the Battle of the Bulge and imprisoned in Dresden, he received a Purple Heart for what he calls a "ludicrously negligible wound." After the war he returned to Cornell and then earned his M.A. at the University of Chicago. He worked as a police reporter and in public relations before placing several short stories in the popular magazines and beginning his career as a novelist.

His first novel, *Player Piano* (1952), is a highly credible account of a future mechanistic society in which people count for little and machines for much. *The Sirens of Titan* (1959), is the story of a playboy whisked off to Mars and outer space in order to learn some humbling lessons about Earth's modest function in the total scheme of things. *Mother Night* (1962) satirizes the Nazi mentality in its narrative about an American writer who broadcasts propaganda in Germany during the war as an Allied agent. *Cat's Cradle* (1963) makes use of some of Vonnegut's experiences in General Electric laboratories in its story about the discovery of a special kind of ice that destroys the world. *God Bless You, Mr. Rosewater* (1965) satirizes a benevolent foundation set up to foster the salvation of the world through love, an endeavor with, of course, disastrous results.

Slaughterhouse-Five; or *The Children's Crusade* (1969) is the book that marked a turning point in Vonnegut's career. Based on his experiences in Dresden, it is the story of another Vonnegut surrogate named Billy Pilgrim who travels back and forth in time and becomes a kind of modern-day Everyman. The novel was something of a cult book during the Vietnam era for its antiwar sentiments. *Breakfast of Champions* (1973), the story of a Pontiac dealer who goes crazy after reading a science fiction novel by "Kilgore Trout," received generally unfavorable reviews but was a commercial success. *Slapstick* (1976), dedicated to the memory of Laurel and Hardy, is the somewhat wacky memoir of a 100-year-old ex-president who thinks he can solve society's problems by giving everyone a new middle name. In addition to his fiction, Vonnegut has published nonfiction on social problems and other topics, some of which is collected in *Wampeters, Foma and Granfalloons* (1974).

NOVELS BY VONNEGUT

Breakfast of Champions. Dell 1975 $4.95. ISBN 0-440-13148-5
Cat's Cradle. 1963. Dell 1970 $4.95. ISBN 0-440-11149-8
God Bless You, Mr. Rosewater. 1965. Dell 1978 $4.95. ISBN 0-440-12929-X
Mother Night. 1962. Dell 1988 $4.95. ISBN 0-440-15853-2
Player Piano. 1952. Dell 1974 $4.95. ISBN 0-440-17037-0
The Sirens of Titan. 1959. Dell 1970 $4.95. ISBN 0-440-17948-3
Slapstick; or Lonesome No More. 1976. Dell 1977 $4.95. ISBN 0-440-18009-0
Slaughterhouse-Five; or The Children's Crusade. 1969. Dell 1978 $4.95. ISBN 0-440-18029-5

SHORT STORY COLLECTION BY VONNEGUT

Welcome to the Monkey House. 1968. Dell 1979 $4.95. ISBN 0-440-19478-4. His second collection.

PLAY BY VONNEGUT

Between Time and Timbuktu; or Prometheus Five: A Space Fantasy. 1969. Delacorte 1972 $4.95. ISBN 0-385-28079-3. Teleplay based on excerpts of short stories and novels.

NONFICTION BY VONNEGUT

Palm Sunday: An Autobiographical Collage. 1982. Dell 1984 $4.95. ISBN 0-440-36906-1. Autobiographical collage of speeches, letters, fiction, and articles that reveal Vonnegut, the man.
Wampeters, Foma and Granfallons. 1974. Dell 1979 $4.95. ISBN 0-440-18533-5. Reviews, essays, and speeches.

BOOKS ABOUT VONNEGUT

Hudgens, Betty L., ed. *Kurt Vonnegut, Jr.: A Checklist. Modern Authors Checklist Ser.* Gale 1972 o.p.
Klinkowitz, Jerome. *Kurt Vonnegut. Contemporary Writers Ser.* Routledge Chapman & Hall 1982 $8.50. ISBN 0-416-33480-6. Deals with Vonnegut's "formula" novels and his "personal" novels.
Lundquist, James. *Kurt Vonnegut. Lit. and Life Ser.* Continuum 1977 $16.95. ISBN 0-8044-2564-7. Critical study of Vonnegut's life and writings.
Reed, Peter J. *Kurt Vonnegut, Jr. Writers for the Seventies Ser.* T. Y. Crowell 1976 o.p.
Schatt, Stanley. *Kurt Vonnegut, Jr.* G. K. Hall 1976 $17.95. ISBN 0-8057-7176-X. Describes and analyzes Vonnegut's best-known work.

WALKER, ALICE. 1944–

Novelist, poet, short-story writer, and essayist Alice Walker was born in Eatonton, Georgia, and was educated at Spellman College and Sarah Lawrence. Her early work draws heavily on her Southern childhood and on her civil rights activism and experiences in Africa. Her concerns as a "womanist"—a version of African American feminism centered on an idea of female utopianism—also informs all of her writing. Perhaps as a result, she was for a time a target of criticism, mostly by African American men, for what was seen as her negative portrayal of them in her novel *The Color Purple* (1982), which won both the Pulitzer Prize and the American Book Award. In that book, after a lifetime of abuse at the hands of men, beginning with her rape by her father, Celie finds love, self, and spiritual liberation through her emotional/sexual relationship with her husband's longtime mistress, Shug Avery. Drawing upon African American vernacular, culture, and myth, reaching back to her culture's roots in Africa, Walker creates fictional worlds that are in touch with the metaphysical as she deals with black female identity and struggle.

NOVELS BY WALKER

The Color Purple. 1982. HarBraceJ 1982 $12.95. ISBN 0-15-119153-0. Epistolary novel made into a movie in 1985.
Meridian. 1976. HarBraceJ 1976 $14.95. ISBN 0-15-119153-0. Moves back and forth between the 1960s and 1970s in its harrowing portrait of the Civil Rights movement and its aftereffects.
Possessing the Secret of Joy. HarBraceJ 1992 $19.95. ISBN 0-15-173512-7. A story about female circumcision in an African tribe and its effect on women and their sexuality.
The Temple of My Familiar. 1989. PB 1990 $5.99. ISBN 0-671-68399-3. Thrilled some, maddened others with its ambitions ranging across metaphysics and myths.

WIESEL, ELIE. 1928–   (NOBEL PRIZE 1986)

Born in Sighet, Romania, Elie Wiesel was the son of a grocer. In 1944 he and his family were deported, along with other Jews, to the Nazi death camps. His father died in Buchenwald and his mother and his younger sisters at Auschwitz. (Wiesel did not learn until after the war that his older sisters had also survived.) Upon liberation from the camps, Wiesel boarded a train for Western Europe with other orphans. The train arrived in France, where he chose to remain. He settled first in Normandy and later in Paris, where he completed his education at the Sorbonne (from 1948 to 1951). To support himself, he did whatever he could, including tutoring, directing a choir, and translating. Eventually he began working as a reporter for various French and Jewish publications. Emotionally unable at first to write about his experience of the Holocaust, in the mid-1950s the novelist FRANCOIS MAURIAC (see Vol. 2) urged him to speak out and tell the world of his experiences. The result was *La Nuit* (1958), later translated as *Night* (1960), the story of a teenage boy plagued with guilt for having survived the death camps and for questioning his religious faith. Before the book was published, Wiesel had moved to New York (in 1956), where he continued writing and eventually began teaching. He became a naturalized American citizen in 1963, following a long recuperation from a car accident.

Since the publication of *Night*, Wiesel has become a major writer, literary critic, and journalist. As a writer steeped in the Hasidic tradition and concerned with the Holocaust he survived, he has written on the problem of persecution and the meaning of being a Jew. *Dawn* (1960) is an illuminating document about terrorists in Palestine. In *The Accident* (1961), Eliezer, a Holocaust survivor, can not seem to escape the past. Other notable works include *The Gates of the Forest* (1964) and *Twilight* (1988), which explore the themes of human suffering and a belief in God. Wiesel has received a number of awards and honors for his literary work, including the William and Janice Epstein Fiction Award in 1965, the Jewish Heritage Award in 1966, the Prix Medicis in 1969, and the Prix Livre-International in 1980. As a result of his work in combating human cruelty and in advocating justice, Wiesel was awarded the Nobel Peace Prize in 1986. He has also served as chairman of the U.S. Holocaust Memorial Council and spoke at the dedication of the Holocaust Museum in Washington, D.C., in 1993.

WORKS BY WIESEL

A Beggar in Jerusalem. Schocken 1989 $8.95. ISBN 0-8052-0887-6

Dawn. 1960. Trans. by Frances Frenaye. Bantam 1982 $3.95. ISBN 0-553-22536-7

The Fifth Son. Warner Bks. 1991 $7.99. ISBN 0-446-39329-0

From the Kingdom of Memory: Reminiscences. Summit Bks. 1990 $19.45. ISBN 0-671-52332-5

The Gates of the Forest. 1964. Trans. by Frances Frenaye. Schocken 1989 $13.00. ISBN 0-8052-0896-8

The Jews of Silence: A Personal Report on Soviet Jewry. Schocken rev. ed. 1987 $8.95. ISBN 0-8052-0826-7

Messengers of God: Biblical Portraits and Legends. Summit Bks. 1985 $8.95. ISBN 0-671-54134-X

Night. 1958. Bantam 1982 $2.95. ISBN 0-553-20807-1

The Night Trilogy: Night, Dawn, The Accident. Hill & Wang 1989 $9.95. ISBN 0-374-52140-9

One Generation After. Schocken 1982 $6.95. ISBN 0-8092-0713-9

Sages and Dreamers: Portraits and Legends from the Bible, the Talmud and the Hasidic Tradition. Summit Bks. 1991 $24.50. ISBN 0-671-74679-0. A retelling of fascinating tales from Jewish history and legend.

Souls on Fire: Portraits and Legends of Hasidic Masters. 1972. Trans. by Marion Wiesel. Summit Bks. 1982 $9.95. ISBN 0-671-44171-X

The Town beyond the Wall. 1967. Schocken 1982 $8.95. ISBN 0-8052-0697-3

Zalmen, or the Madness of God. Schocken 1985 $7.95. ISBN 0-8052-0777-5

BOOKS ABOUT WIESEL

Abrahamson, Irving. *Against Silence: The Voice and Vision of Elie Wiesel*. 3 vols. Holocaust Pbns. 1985 $95.00. ISBN 0-685-08779-4

Berenbaum, Michael. *The Vision of the Void: Theological Reflections on the Works of Elie Wiesel*. U. Pr. of New Eng. 1979 $12.95. ISBN 0-8175-6189-4

Rittner, Carol. *Elie Wiesel: Between Memory and Hope*. NYU Pr. 1989 $40.00. ISBN 0-8147-7410-5. Collection of essays that spans Wiesel's 30-year writing career.

Walker, Graham B., Jr. *Elie Wiesel: A Challenge to Theology*. McFarland & Co. 1988
    $18.95. ISBN 0-89950-298-9

WILBUR, RICHARD. 1921–

When Richard Wilbur's *Things of This World* (1956) won the 1957 Pulitzer
Prize and the National Book Award the same year, the *N.Y. Times* commented
editorially: "A seemingly effortless craftsman, Mr. Wilbur reveals a fine lyrical
gift, a searching wit and, in his translations, a sympathetic kinship to the works
of others."

Wilbur was born in New York City and educated at Amherst College and
Harvard University. During the late 1950s he taught at Wesleyan University. He
has also been on the English faculty at Harvard and Wellesley College, and he is
a member of both the American Academy of Arts and Sciences and the National
Institute of Arts and Letters. With LILLIAN HELLMAN he wrote the libretto for the
opera *Candide*. He also is one of the premier translators of his generation. He
has translated MOLIÈRE's (see Vol. 2) *Tartuffe* and *Misanthrope* and many poems
of ANDREI VOZNESENSKY (see Vol. 2) and others. Co-recipient of the Bollingen
Translation Prize in 1963, he was made the second Poet Laureate of the United
States in 1987.

POETRY BY WILBUR

The Mind-Reader. HarBraceJ 1977 o.p. Maintains the subject of poetry to be the play of
    the mind on any object.
New and Collected Poems. HarBraceJ 1989. $10.95. ISBN 0-15-665491-1
Opposites: Poems and Drawings. 1973. HarBraceJ 1991 $11.95. ISBN 0-15-258720-9. For
    children.
The Poems of Richard Wilbur. HarBraceJ 1963 $6.95. ISBN 0-15-672251-8

NONFICTION BY WILBUR

Responses: Prose Pieces, 1948–1976. HarBraceJ 1976 $3.95. ISBN 0-15-676550-0.
    Collection of criticism.

WORK BY WILBUR

The Whale and Other Uncollected Translations. New Amer. Trans. Ser. BOA Edns. 1982
    $14.00. ISBN 0-918526-32-9

BOOKS ABOUT WILBUR

Bixler, Frances. *Richard Wilbur: A Reference Guide*. Macmillan 1991 $44.95. ISBN 0-
    8161-7262-5. Provides a record of critical work relating to Wilbur now in print.
Salinger, Wendy, ed. *Richard Wilbur's Creation*. Under Discussion Ser. U. of Mich. Pr.
    1983 $12.95. ISBN 0-472-06348-0. A survey of the critical reception of Wilbur's
    poetry.

WRIGHT, CHARLES. 1935–

Charles Wright was born in a small town in Tennessee and took his degrees
from Davidson College and the University of Iowa. He has won the American
Book Award (1982) for *Country Music* (1982), which contains poems from his
first four books. He has also won the Edgar Allan Poe Award from the Academy
of American Poets. His poetry is dense with an imagistic texture derived from
POUND and the great Italian modernist MONTALE (see Vol. 2). Themes of
redemption, memory, and the haunting spirits of place combine to make Wright
one of the most lyric of poets.

POETRY BY CHARLES WRIGHT

Country Music: Selected Early Poems. 1982. Wesleyan U. Pr. 1991 $14.95. ISBN 0-8195-1201-X. Brings together the work from the first several books.

The World of the Ten Thousand Things: Poems 1980–1990. FS&G 1992 $12.95. ISBN 0-374-52326-6.

WRIGHT, JAMES. 1927–1980

James Wright's work is typified by a humanitarian tenderness, compassion, and a keen sense of man's alienation. He wrote of his efforts: "I have written about the things I am deeply concerned with—crickets outside my window, cold and hungry old men . . . a feeling of desolation in the fall, some cities I have known." His work presents an unusual vision of middle America: the decayed and yet beautiful landscapes of train yards, bars, and red-light districts in Minneapolis. Stylistically, Wright moved from a traditional rhymed and metered verse, drawing on the techniques of the now classic modernists—ROBINSON, MASTERS, FROST, and even THOMAS HARDY—to experimentalism in form and language. His later poems exhibit a certain delicacy, yet retain the colloquial sense of the native American idiom.

Born in Martin's Ferry, Ohio, Wright attended Kenyon College and the University of Washington. Recipient of a Fulbright Scholarship to study in Vienna, he was awarded a National Institute of Arts and Letters grant, a Guggenheim grant, the Oscar Blumenthal Award, and a Pulitzer Prize for his *Collected Poems* in 1972.

POETRY BY JAMES WRIGHT

Above the River: The Complete Poetry. FS&G 1990 $27.95. ISBN 0-374-12749-2. A thorough, fine collection.

The Branch Will Not Break. Wesleyan Poetry Program. Wesleyan U. Pr. 1963 $10.95. ISBN 0-8195-1018-1

Collected Poems. Wesleyan U. Pr. 1971 $30.00. ISBN 0-8195-4031-5.

Saint Judas. Wesleyan Poetry Program. Wesleyan U. Pr. 1959 $10.95. ISBN 0-8195-1110-2. Poems collected from the following volumes: *The Green Wall, St. Judas, The Branch Will Not Break,* and *Shall We Gather at the River?*

Shall We Gather at the River? Wesleyan Poetry Program. Wesleyan U. Pr. 1968 $22.50. ISBN 0-8195-2043-8

This Journey. 1982 $10.50. ISBN 0-394-52365-2

NONFICTION BY WRIGHT

Collected Prose. Ed. by Anne Wright. *Poets on Poetry Ser.* U. of Mich. Pr. 1982 $11.00. ISBN 0-492-06344-8

ZUKOFSKY, LOUIS. 1904–1978

Louis Zukofsky first achieved a reputation in the literary world during the 1920s, when EZRA POUND published his work in *Exile*. Later he became editor of *Poetry*, in which, in 1931, he actively promoted the as yet relatively unknown WILLIAM CARLOS WILLIAMS and KENNETH REXROTH, among others. Zukofsky was born in New York City and received both his A.B. and M.A. degrees from Columbia University and taught for two years at the Brooklyn Polytechnic Institute. Zukofsky's poetry is notoriously difficult, although it continues to generate its defenders and a small but gallant group of explainers.

POETRY BY ZUKOFSKY

A. 1972. U. CA Pr. 1978 $27.50. ISBN 0-520-03223-3. The epic-length poem.

All: The Collected Short Poems, 1923–1958. Norton 1965 o.p.
All: The Collected Short Poems, 1956–1964. Norton 1971 $4.50. ISBN 0-393-04266-9
Complete Short Poetry. Johns Hopkins 1991 $34.95. ISBN 0-8018-4103-8. An excellent
    collection of shorter works.

SHORT STORY COLLECTION BY ZUKOFSKY

Collected Fiction. Archive Pr. 1990 $9.95. ISBN 0-916583-59-7

NONFICTION BY ZUKOFSKY

Autobiography. Grossman 1970 o.p. In prose and poetry, with music scores by Celia
    Zukofsky.
Prepositions: The Collected Critical Essays of Louis Zukofsky. U. CA Pr. 1981 $10.95. ISBN
    0-520-04361-8. Reprint of the 1967 edition.

BOOK ABOUT ZUKOFSKY

Ahearn, Barry. *Zukofsky's "A." An Introduction.* U. CA Pr. 1983 $27.50. ISBN 0-520-
    04378-2. Introduction and guide to reading Zukofsky's epic-length poem.

CHAPTER 18

Twentieth-Century American Drama

C. Warren Robertson

> The first efforts at dramatic literature in this country were wild—the essays of
> youth not sufficiently instructed in anything and deficient in literary
> education.
>
> —WILLIAM DUNLAP, *A History of the American Theatre*

The earliest prerevolutionary American producers presented works by English
playwrights such as THOMAS OTWAY (see Vol. 2), GEORGE FARQUHAR (see Vol. 2),
and WILLIAM SHAKESPEARE, with Shakespeare's magnificent *Richard III* being the
most popular script. Although the imitation of English and European literature
continued for more than half a century, plays presenting distinctive American
qualities eventually began to emerge as well. Three indigenous themes
predominated: the American Yankee; the American Indian (as the Native
American was called); and the African American. ROYALL TYLER's *The Contrast*
(1787), a comedy, was the first play written by an American on a native subject
and produced by a professional company. It introduced the stage Yankee as less
sophisticated than a European counterpart, but set apart by the possession of
such virtues as integrity, honesty, and bravery. The frontier Yankee was a
recurring type, achieving its greatest fame in DION BOUCICAULT's dramatization
of *Rip Van Winkle* (1865). Joseph Jefferson III, one of the best loved actors of
the nineteenth century, played the role well over 2,500 times between 1865 and
the turn of the century.

In addition to popularizing the Yankee, early nineteenth-century drama
presented the American Indian in the romantic—and condescending—tradition of the "noble savage." The actor Edwin Forrest won fame for his lofty
portrayal of the Indian chief in John Augustus Stone's *Metamora* (1829).
Ironically, while Indians were being idealized on stages in New York and
Philadelphia, they were being brutally killed in the West.

The other character type to evolve was the "stage Negro." This type began
with an image that is not acceptable today, particularly because the original
stage Negroes were invariably portrayed by whites in blackface. To white
audiences, these caricatures may have seemed endearing and humorous, but
even at the time, many African Americans were offended by the image of "black
folk" as perpetually happy, simple singers and dancers.

The portrayal of African Americans on stage began in 1828, when an itinerant
white actor named Thomas Dartmouth Rice was walking behind a hotel in
Louisville, Kentucky. Rice was an unhappy-looking African American with a
deformed shoulder and rheumatism, singing a song as he curried a horse.

Turn about and wheel about and do just so.
And everytime I wheel about I jump Jim Crow.

Rice borrowed the clothes from the old man and began to perform the song and
dance in blackface between the acts of a play in which he had a part. His success
in both England and America was astounding and his Jim Crow routine earned
"Daddy" Rice the title of the father of American minstrelsy. Minstrel shows—in
which whites in blackface spoke in exaggerated dialect, sang, danced, and told
jokes—became a popular form.

The first serious treatment of the African American, however, was the
dramatization of HARRIET BEECHER STOWE's novel, *Uncle Tom's Cabin* (1852).
Quickly adapted into several play versions, it became the most popular drama of
the nineteenth century. Stowe's work was a forceful indictment of slavery, and
while the craze for the play died down before 1860, the show was revived in the
1870s with as many as 50 traveling companies performing it. Members of
theater companies that played *Uncle Tom's Cabin* were known as "Tommers"
and their plays were called "Tom Shows."

During the second half of the nineteenth century, realism came back into
fashion, but for the most part plays did not grapple with complex social issues.
Dion Boucicault's *The Octoroon* (1859) touched on the evils of slavery, but his
formulaic melodrama relied more on sentimentality, sensationalism, and local
color than on in-depth analysis. James A. Herne's *Margaret Fleming* (1890) is a
remarkable piece for its time because it dealt with a husband's infidelities;
perhaps its unique qualities were responsible for its lack of success. Unfortunately, the transformation taking place in European drama with writers such as
IBSEN (see Vol. 2) had little impact on American drama. America's version of the
new realism was seen primarily not in the writing, but in the carefully detailed
settings offered by such producers as David Belasco.

American drama did not achieve its renaissance until after World War I, when
writers and producers turned to the theater to produce art rather than profit.
Their way was paved by GEORGE PIERCE BAKER, whose 47 Workshop at Harvard
University was to have such illustrious students as PHILIP BARRY, S. N. Behrman,
Sidney Howard, and EUGENE O'NEILL; and by the "little theater" movement that
produced the Provincetown Players, which presented O'Neill's first plays, and the
Washington Square Players, which later became the Theatre Guild. The true
source of this renaissance, however, was the dramatists' discovery of European
drama. Ibsen was finally allowed to exert his valuable influence, and by then his
work of making modern drama a major art form had been forwarded by
STRINDBERG (see Vol. 2), CHEKHOV, SHAW, SYNGE, and the German expressionists.

The 1920s was a period of considerable experimentation in American drama.
Writers like Barry and Howard helped develop a polished brand of realism in
both comedy and serious drama, while others, especially O'Neill and ELMER
RICE, alternated between realism and more experimental forms, especially
expressionism. O'Neill's experimentation was the most ambitious; besides
expressionism he tried poetic fantasy, pageantry, myth, and various kinds of
tragedy—in all lengths. Also by the mid-1920s, Baker had left Harvard for New
Haven to establish the prestigious Yale School of Drama, a source for new
theater talent from that time to the present.

The interest in experimentation continued into the 1930s with MAXWELL
ANDERSON's attempts to produce modern verse tragedy and with the plays of
THORNTON WILDER (whose most experimental work, *The Skin of Our Teeth*, was
produced as late as 1942). For the most part, however, the dominant style of the

drama of the 1930s was realism. In keeping with the times (a decade that began in a Depression and ended with the rise of fascism), the preoccupation of the most significant plays of the 1930s (especially those of Paul Green, Lillian Hellman, and Clifford Odets) was social protest.

The theater since World War II has been marked by several important trends. First, there has been a tremendous flowering of playwriting talent with the creation of such world-class American writers as Tennessee Williams, Arthur Miller, Lorraine Hansberry, Edward Albee, David Rabe, Sam Shepard, August Wilson, and David Henry Hwang. Second, there has been a major shift in focus away from the commercial theaters of Broadway to such regional theaters as the Guthrie Theatre in Minneapolis, the Arena Stage in Washington, D.C., the Alley Theatre in Houston, the Mark Taper Forum in Los Angeles, the Alabama Shakespeare Festival in Montgomery, and the Actors Theatre of Louisville. While Broadway has contributed uniquely to world theater with the American musical, much of America's serious drama is being done by regional and repertory companies from coast to coast. Some of these theaters have or have had important playwrights-in-residence: Preston Jones at the Dallas Theatre Center, Megan Terry at the Omaha Magic Theatre, and Lanford Wilson at the Circle Repertory Company in New York City. A new interest in plays by African Americans has made space for works by such writers as Imamu Amiri Baraka, James Baldwin, Ed Bullins, and Alice Childress, expanding both the content and the formal possibilities for post-World War II theater. Such playwrights as Beth Henley, Marsha Norman, Suzan-Lori Parks, and Pulitzer Prize-winner Wendy Wasserstein have chronicled women's concerns from the consciousness-raising 1960s to the present. Comic talent—often in bittersweet or black comedy form—also flourished with such writers as John Guare, Christopher Durang, Terrence McNally, and Neil Simon. In short, the theater since World War II has been characterized by its increasing diversification, its range and depth of writing, and its inventiveness in staging and design. The American theater is currently enjoying unprecedented national and international acclaim and shows vibrant signs of continued growth and development.

HISTORY AND CRITICISM

Abramson, Doris E. *Negro Playwrights in the American Theatre, 1925–1959.* Bks. Demand 1969 $87.80. ISBN 0-317-29442-3. Analyzes 20 plays from Garland Anderson's *Appearances* to Lorraine Hansberry's *A Raisin in the Sun*; "the most comprehensive survey of 20th century Negro literature to date" (*Choice*).

Anderson, Maxwell. *Off Broadway: Essays About the Theatre.* Da Capo repr. of 1947 ed. $21.50. ISBN 0-306-71337-3. Critical essays by America's premier verse dramatist.

Atkinson, Brooks, and Al Hirschfeld. *The Lively Years, 1920–1973.* Da Capo 1984 $9.95. ISBN 0-306-802-34-1. From Brooks Atkinson, former drama critic of the *New York Times*, comments on 82 dramas, many American, which he covered on opening nights; accompanied by sketches by the Broadway caricaturist Hirschfeld.

Barlow, Judith E. *Final Acts: The Creation of Three Late O'Neill Plays.* U. of Ga. Pr. 1985 $25.00. ISBN 0-8203-0759-9

Bentley, Eric. *What is Theatre?: Incorporating—the Dramatic Event.* Limelight Edns. 1984 $10.95. ISBN 0-87910-012-5. Reviews written mostly for the *New Republic* by the author of *The Life of the Theatre*.

Bernstein, Samuel J. *The Strands Entwined: A New Direction in American Drama.* Northeastern U. Pr. 1980 o.p. Emphasizes Rabe's *Sticks and Bones*, Guare's *The House of Blue Leaves*, Bullins's *The Taking of Miss Janie*, Robert Anderson's *Double Solitaire*, and Albee's *Seascape*.

Bigsby, C. W. *A Critical Introduction to Twentieth-Century American Drama.* 3 vols. Cambridge U. Pr. Vol. 1 1982 $19.95. ISBN 0-521-27116-9. Vol. 2 1985 $19.95. ISBN 0-521-27717-5. Vol. 3 1985 $59.95. ISBN 0-521-26256-9. Vol. 1 on U.S. drama from 1900 to 1940; Vol. 2 on Miller, Williams, and Albee; and Vol. 3 on the non-Broadway theater. An important survey by a major British critic of U.S. drama.

Bock, Hedwig, and Albert Wertheim, eds. *Essays on Contemporary American Drama.* Adlers Foreign Bks. 1981 $29.75. ISBN 3-19-002232-1. Representative collection of critical essays.

Bogard, Travis, Richard Moody, and Walter J. Meserve. In *Revels History of Drama in English, American Drama.* Routledge Chapman & Hall 1978 $59.95. ISBN 0-416-13090-9. The relevant volume in an important series, written by three major authorities on American drama and theater.

Bonin, Jane F. *Prize-Winning American Drama: A Bibliographical and Descriptive Guide.* Scarecrow 1973 $13.00. ISBN 0-8108-0607-X. Describes plays that have won one or more of the five major American drama awards.

Bordman, Gerald. *The Oxford Companion to American Theatre.* OUP 1984 $55.00. ISBN 0-19-503443-01. Three thousand entries on playwrights, plays, performers, producers and directors, lyricists and composers, theaters, etc.

Brockett, Oscar G., and Robert R. Findlay. *Century of Innovation: A History of European and American Theatre and Drama.* Allyn 1990 $48.00. ISBN 0-205-12878-5

Bronner, Edwin. *The Encyclopedia of the American Theatre, 1900–1975.* A. S. Barnes 1980 o.p. Important reference work covering all aspects of theater in America.

Brown, Janet. *Feminist Drama: Definition and Critical Analysis.* Scarecrow 1979 o.p. Discusses feminist theater groups and plays by Alice Childress, Rosalyn Drexler, Tina Howe, David Rabe, and Ntozake Shange.

———. *Taking Center Stage: Feminism in Contemporary U.S. Drama.* Scarecrow 1991 $22.50. ISBN 0-8108-2448-5. Up-to-date analysis of feminist trends in American drama.

Brown, John Russell, and Bernard Harris, eds. *American Theatre.* Holmes & Meier 1967 o.p. Covers writers, influences, ideological and social conditions, theatrical idioms, from British and American contributors.

Buttitta, Tony. *Uncle Sam Presents: A Memoir of the Federal Theatre, 1935–1939.* U. of Pa. Pr. 1982 $39.95. ISBN 0-8122-7826-7. Solid introduction to this WPA-funded project, with interesting primary material.

Clurman, Harold. *The Fervent Years: The Group Theatre and the Thirties. Quality Pap. Ser.* Da Capo 1983 repr. of 1945 ed. $10.95. ISBN 0-306-80186-8. An articulate record from one of the founders of the Group Theatre, including memories of playwrights Clifford Odets, Irwin Shaw, and William Saroyan.

Cohn, Ruby. *Dialogue in American Drama.* Ind. U. Pr. 1971 o.p. An important study of the language of America's leading dramatists by a major scholar.

———. *New American Dramatists, 1960–1990.* Grove Pr. 1991 $19.95. ISBN 0-312-04249-3. Indispensable for the study of the more-recent American dramatists.

Cole, Toby, ed. *Playwrights on Playwriting: The Meaning and Making of Modern Drama. Drama Bk. Ser.* Hill & Wang 1961 $9.95. ISBN 0-8090-0529-8. Intro. by John Gassner. Including material on American playwrights O'Neill, Wilder, and Williams.

Cooper, T. G., and Carole Singleton. *On Stage in America.* Cloverdale Lib. 1987 $27.95. ISBN 0-685-17904-4

Craig, E. Quita. *Black Drama of the Federal Theatre Era: Beyond the Formal Horizons.* U. of Mass. Pr. 1980 $25.00. ISBN 0-87023-294-0. " . . . valuable insights into an era and dramatic form" (*Choice*).

Downer, Alan S., ed. *American Drama and Its Critics: A Collection of Critical Essays.* U. Ch. Pr. 1976 $15.00. ISBN 0-226-16061-0

Dukore, Bernard F. *American Dramatists, 1918–1945.* Grove Pr. 1984 o.p. Good brief survey, emphasizing important plays of major dramatists (excluding O'Neill) and productions.

Dunlap, William. *The History of the American Theatre and Anecdotes of the Principal Actors.* 3 vols. Rprt. Serv. 1992 repr. of 1832 ed. $75.00. ISBN 0-7812-2719-4. The first history of the American theater and its playwrights by the notable nineteenth-century playwright and stage manager.

Eaton, Walter P. *The Theatre Guild: The First 10 Years, with Articles by the Directors.* Ayer repr. of 1929 ed. $26.50. ISBN 0-8369-5180-8

Eddleman, Floyd E. *American Drama Criticism: Interpretations, 1890–1977.* Shoe String 1979 $45.00. ISBN 0-208-01713-5

Engel, Lehman. *The American Musical Theatre: A Consideration.* 1967 Macmillan rev. ed. o.p. Both a history and an analysis of the making of a musical, including a discography and a list of published librettos and vocal scores.

Flanagan, Hallie. *Arena: The History of the Federal Theatre.* Ayer repr. of 1940 ed. $32.00. ISBN 0-405-08521-4. A firsthand account by the woman who headed the government-established theatre; "As exciting as a novel and twice as provocative" (John Gassner, *NY Times*).

Flexner, Eleanor. *American Playwrights, 1918–1938.* Ayer repr. of 1938 ed. $32.00. ISBN 0-8369-1412-0. Biographical and critical look at early twentieth-century playwrights.

Garfield, David. *The Actors Studio: A Player's Place.* Macmillan 1984 o.p. Pref. by Ellen Burstyn. ". . . A sober, well-balanced study of the place" (John Lahr, *NY Times*).

Goldman, William. *The Season: A Candid Look at Broadway.* Limelight Edns. rev. ed. 1984 repr. of 1969 ed. $8.95. ISBN 0-87910-023-0

Goldstein, Malcolm. *The Political Stage: American Drama and Theater of the Great Depression.* OUP 1974 o.p. ". . . a solidly researched work that will serve as a useful introduction to the American drama and theater of this turbulent decade" (Stephen Grecco, *Modern Drama*).

Green, Stanley. *Broadway Musicals of the Thirties.* Da Capo 1982 $14.95. ISBN 0-306-80165-5. Discusses 175 musicals produced on Broadway during the 1930s, presented chronologically.

———. *The World of Musical Comedy.* A. S. Barnes repr. of 1980 ed. $22.50. ISBN 0-306-80207-4

Hartman, John G. *The Development of American Social Comedy from 1787 to 1936.* Hippocrene Bks. 1970 repr. of 1939 ed. $16.00. ISBN 0-374-93708-7. Comprehensive look at American comedic theater from colonial times to the 1930s.

Havens, Daniel F. *The Columbian Muse of Comedy: The Development of a Native Tradition in Early American Social Comedy, 1787–1845.* S. Ill. U. Pr. 1973 o.p. For serious students of American playwriting in its early stages.

Heilman, Robert B. *The Iceman, the Arsonist, and the Troubled Agent: Tragedy and Melodrama on the Modern Stage.* U. of Wash. Pr. 1973 o.p. Major chapters on O'Neill, Miller, and Williams by an important drama scholar.

Hill, Errol, ed. *The Theatre of Black Americans.* 2 vols. Applause Theatre Bk. Pubs. 1986 $14.95. ISBN 0-936839-27-9. Vol. 1 stresses drama; Vol. 2, theater.

Hirsch, Foster. *A Method to Their Madness: The History of the Actors Studio.* Da Capo 1986 $11.95. ISBN 0-306-80268-6. Describes the Actors Studio's founding and growth, focusing on its animating force, Lee Strasberg.

Huerta, Jorge A. *Chicano Theater: Themes and Forms.* Biling Rev-Pr. 1982 $24.00. ISBN 0-916950-26-3. "An excellent account of the first 15 years of the current Chicano theater movement in this country, placing it in theatrical, social, and historic context" (*Choice*).

Hughes, Glenn. *History of the American Theatre, 1700–1950.* French 1951 o.p. A chronological review of American theater.

Jones, Robert Edmond. *The Dramatic Imagination.* Routledge Chapman & Hall 1941 $9.95. ISBN 0-87830-035-X. Famous treatise by the "new stagecraft" designer.

———. *Towards a New Theatre: The Lectures of Robert Edmond Jones.* Ed. by Delbert Unruh. Limelight Edns. 1992 $8.95. ISBN 0-87910-152-0

Kauffmann, Stanley. *Persons of the Drama: Theatre Criticism and Comment.* HarpC 1976 o.p. More than 80 reviews of productions, most of which originally appeared in the *New Republic*, as well as a group of essays on broader topics.

———. *Theater Criticisms.* PAJ Pubns. 1984 $34.50. ISBN 0-933826-57-5. Reviews and essays originally published between 1975 and 1983.

Kaye, Phyllis J., ed. *The National Playwrights Directory.* E. O'Neill 1982 $35.00. ISBN 0-9605160-0-X. Bibliographies of living American playwrights.

Kernan, Alvin, ed. *The Modern American Theater: A Collection of Critical Essays.* P-H 1967 o.p. Includes Tynan on Miller, Guthrie on Wilder, Kaprow on "Happenings," and several essays by and about Albee.

Kernodle, George R., and Portia Kernodle. *Invitation to the Theatre.* HarBraceJ 1985 $21.00. ISBN 0-15-546924-X

Keyssar, Helene. *The Curtain and the Veil: Strategies in Black Drama.* B. Franklin 1981 o.p. Analyzes plays by Hughes, Richardson, Ward, Hansberry, Baraka, Bullins, and Shange.

_____. *Feminist Theatre.* St. Martin 1990 $12.95. ISBN 0-312-04129-2. Assesses contributions made by Megan Terry and others.

Kinne, Wisner P. *George Pierce Baker and the American Theatre.* Greenwood 1969 repr. of 1954 ed. $49.75. ISBN 0-8371-0129-8. "A real contribution to theatrical history" (*Nation*).

Kirkpatrick, Daniel, ed. *Contemporary Dramatists.* St. James Pr. 1988 $115.00. ISBN 0-912289-62-7

Kolin, Phillip C., ed. *American Playwrights Since 1945: A Guide to Scholarship, Criticism, and Performance.* Greenwood 1989 $85.00. ISBN 0-313-25543-1. Excellent bibliographical and critical study of 40 major American playwrights.

Long, E. Hudson, comp. *American Drama from Its Beginning to the Present.* Harlan Davidson 1970 $6.95. ISBN 0-88295-522-5

Ludlow, Noah M. *Dramatic Life As I Found It.* Ayer 1966 repr. of 1880 ed. $27.50. ISBN 0-405-08755-1. The frontier theater of the early nineteenth century.

MacGowan, Kenneth, and Robert Jones. *Continental Stagecraft.* Ayer repr. of 1922 ed. $18.00. ISBN 0-405-08765-9. Although not about American drama, a very influential book in America, based on the authors' observations of some 60 productions by Appia, Reinhardt, Craig, Stanislavsky, Copeau, and others.

MacNicholas, John, ed. *Twentieth-Century American Dramatists.* 2 vols. Gale 1981 $224.00. ISBN 0-8103-0928-9. Excellent brief biographies with extensive lists of productions and publications by and about the dramatists.

Mantle, Burns, ed. *The Best Plays Series.* Ayer 1976 $27.50 ea. *The Best Plays of 1919–1920.* ISBN 0-405-09168-0. *The Best Plays of 1928–1929.* ISBN 0-405-09169-9. *The Best Plays of 1929–1930.* ISBN 0-405-09170-2. *The Best Plays of 1930–1931.* ISBN 0-405-09171-0. *The Best Plays of 1938–1939.* ISBN 0-405-091745-5. With a summary and excerpts of the ten best plays of the Broadway season in each volume, plus invaluable statistics: complete listings of New York productions with dates, theaters, and casts; important premieres of plays in the United States and Europe; lists of drama awards; necrology.

Marranca, Bonnie. *Theatrewritings.* PAJ Pubns. 1984 $28.50. ISBN 0-933826-67-2. Essays by a leading American theater critic.

Marranca, Bonnie, and Gautam Dasgupta. *American Playwrights: A Critical Survey.* Drama Bk. 1981 o.p. Discusses 18 contemporary playwrights associated with the off-Broadway theater, including Kopit, Wilson, Guare, Van Itallie, Shepard, Baraka, and others; indispensable for dramatists of the past two decades.

Mathews, Jane D. *The Federal Theatre, 1935–1939: Plays, Relief and Politics.* Hippocrene Bks. 1980 repr. of 1967 ed. $21.50. ISBN 0-374-95311-2. "A consistently engrossing account of the W.P.A. Theatre Project" (*PW*).

Meserve, Walter J. *An Emerging Entertainment: The Drama of the American People to 1828.* Ind. U. Pr. 1977 o.p. An important study by a major historian of American drama.

_____. *Heralds of Promise: The Drama of the American People During the Age of Jackson, 1829–1849. Contributions in American Studies.* Greenwood 1986 $42.95. ISBN 0-313-25015-4

_____. *An Outline History of American Drama.* Rowman 1965 o.p. From colonial theater to Albee.

Meserve, Walter J., and Mollie A. Meserve. *A Chronological History of World Theatre.* 1992 Feedback Thea. Bks. ISBN 0-937657-12-3

Moody, Richard. *America Takes the Stage.* Kraus repr. of 1955 ed. $29.00. ISBN 0-527-64750-0. An important study of the beginnings of American drama and theater by a major historian of American drama.

Mordden, Ethan. *The American Theatre.* OUP 1981 $32.95. ISBN 0-19-502959-3. Selective overview for the general reader.

———. *Broadway Babies: The People Who Made the American Musical.* OUP 1983 $24.95. ISBN 0-19-503345-0

Moses, Montrose. *The American Dramatist.* Ayer rev. ed. repr. of 1925 ed. $22.00. ISBN 0-405-08800-0. By one of the best editors of eighteenth-, nineteenth-, and early twentieth-century American drama.

———. *Famous Actor Families in America.* Ayer 1968 repr. of 1906 ed. $20.00. ISBN 0-405-08800-0. Biographical look at some of the first families of the American theater.

———. *Famous Actor Families in America. Library of Literature, Drama and Criticism.* Johnson Repr. 1969 repr. of 1906 ed. $24.00. ISBN 0-384-40215-1

Moses, Montrose, and John Mason Brown. *American Theatre as Seen by Its Critics, 1752–1934.* Cooper Sq. repr. of 1934 ed. o.p.

The New York Times Directory of the Theater. Times Bks. 1973 o.p. Intro. by Clive Barnes. Cites, but does not print, actual reviews and articles on actors, actresses, playwrights, producers, directors, and others, that appeared from 1920 to 1970.

Odell, George C. *Annals of the New York Stage.* 15 vols. AMS Pr. 1970 $95.00 ea. ISBN 0-404-07830-3. A valuable history, covering opera, concerts, burlesque, and circus, as well as the theater.

Paris Review. *Writers at Work: Third Series.* Viking Penguin 1977 $9.95. ISBN 0-14-004542-2. Lively and fascinating interviews with contemporary authors, including Hellman, Miller, and Albee.

Quinn, Arthur H. *A History of the American Drama: From the Beginning to the Civil War.* Irvington 1982 repr. of 1943 ed. $44.50. ISBN 0-89197-218-8. Provides thorough history of American theater from revolutionary times to the Civil War.

———. *A History of the American Drama: From the Civil War to the Present Day.* Irvington 1982 repr. of 1946 ed. $44.50. ISBN 0-89197-219-6

Rabkin, Gerald. *Drama and Commitment. Studies in Drama.* Haskell 1972 repr. of 1964 ed. $75.00. ISBN 0-8383-1659-X. Examines theatrical developments during the Depression—the Theater Union, the Group Theatre, and the Federal Theatre—as well as the effect of political commitment on five playwrights of the period: Lawson, Odets, Behrman, Rice, and Maxwell Anderson.

Rahill, Frank. *World of Melodrama.* Pa. St. U. Pr. 1967 o.p. Scholarly study that follows the development of melodrama in France, England, and the United States, documenting stock characters and situations.

Rigdon, Walter, and Raymond D. McGill, eds. *Notable Names in the American Theatre.* 1966. Gale 2nd ed. 1976 o.p. Includes sections on New York productions, premieres of American plays at home and abroad, theater-group biographies, theater-building biographies, awards, biographical bibliography, necrology, and who's who listings.

Sarlos, Robert K. *Jig Cook and the Provincetown Players: Theatre in Ferment.* U. of Mass. Pr. 1982 $27.50. ISBN 0-87023-349-1. Winner of the American Theater Association's Barnard Hewett Award for distinguished achievement in theater history: " . . . an important contribution to American theatre history, filling in details about the Provincetown experiment" (Linda Benzvi, *Modern Drama*).

Scanlan, Tom. *Family, Drama, and American Dreams.* Greenwood 1978 $47.95. ISBN 0-8371-9827-5. Concentrates on selected plays by O'Neill, Miller, and Williams.

Seller, Maxine S., ed. *Ethnic Theatre in the United States.* Greenwood 1983 $55.00. ISBN 0-313-21230-9. Essays and information on the full range of ethnic theater.

Shaland, Irene. *American Theater & Drama Research: An Annotated Guide to Information Sources, 1945–1990.* McFarland & Co. 1991 $29.95. ISBN 0-89950-626-7

Shank, Theodore. *American Alternative Theatre. Modern Dramatists Ser.* St. Martin 1988
$14.95. ISBN 0-312-02126-7. Discusses the Living Theatre, the San Francisco Mime
Troupe, Schechner's Performance Group, Richard Foreman, etc.

Sievers, David. *Freud on Broadway.* Cooper Sq. 1971 repr. of 1955 ed. $35.00. ISBN 0-
8154-0366-6. The influence of Freud on dramatists from Glaspell to the early Miller
and Williams.

Szilassy, Zoltan. *American Theater of the 1960s. Crosscurrents-Modern Critiques Ser.*
S. Ill. U. Pr. 1986 $15.95. ISBN 0-8093-1227-1

Taylor, Thomas J. *American Theater History.* Salem Pr. 1992 $40.00. ISBN 0-89356-672-1

Vardac, A. Nicholas. *Stage to Screen: Theatrical Method from Garrick to Griffith.* Ayer
1968 repr. of 1949 ed $18.00. ISBN 0-405-09039-0. Shows how American and British
theater evolved cinematic methods and production techniques that were borrowed
by early filmmakers.

Vinson, James, ed., *Contemporary Dramatists.* St Martin 1973 $30.00. ISBN 0-312-16660-
5

Williams, Henry B., ed. *The American Theater: A Sum of Its Parts.* French 1972 $12.00.
ISBN 0-573-69002-2. Excellent collection of essays by theater scholars on the
development of U.S. drama.

Willis, John. *Theatre World.* Crown 1973–92 $19.95–$40.00 ea.

Wilson, Garff B. *Three Hundred Years of American Drama and Theatre: From Ye Bear and
Ye Cubb to Chorus Line.* P-H 1982 $28.95. ISBN 0-13-920330-3. A popular overview.

Young, Stark. *The Flower in Drama and Glamour: Theatre Essays and Criticism.*
Hippocrene Bks. 1973 repr. of 1955 ed. $19.00. ISBN 0-374-98840-4

——. *Immortal Shadows.* Hippocrene Bks. 1973 repr. of 1948 ed. $20.50. ISBN 0-374-
98844-7. A selection from 25 years of criticism by one of America's finest drama
critics.

——. *The Theatre.* Limelight Edns. 1986 $5.95. ISBN 0-87910-046-X

COLLECTIONS

Baitz, Jon R., and others, eds. *New Plays U.S.A., No. 4.* Theatre Comm. 1988 $24.95. ISBN
0-930452-80-1

Ballet, Arthur H., ed. *Playwrights for Tomorrow: A Collection of Plays.* 13 vols. Bks.
Demand. Vol. 1 $72.80. ISBN 0-8357-6528-8. Vol. 3 $91.60. ISBN 0-8357-6529-6. Vol.
4 $90.80. ISBN 60-8357-6530-X. Vol. 5 $41.50. ISBN 0-317-41782-7. Vol. 6 $37.00.
ISBN 0-317-41783-5. Vol. 7 $57.50. ISBN 0-8357-6531-8. Vol. 8 $57.20. ISBN 0-8357-
6532-6. Vol. 9 $56.20. ISBN 0-8357-6533-4. Vol. 10 $52.30. ISBN 0-8357-6534-2. Vol.
11 $61.70. ISBN 0-8357-6525-3. Vol. 12 $71.30. ISBN 0-8357-6526-1. Vol. 13 $81.70.
ISBN 0-8357-6527-X

Barlow, Judith, ed. *Plays by American Women: 1900–1930.* Applause Theatre Bk. Pubs.
1985 repr. of 1981 ed. $24.95. ISBN 1-55783-007-X

Clurman, Harold, ed. *Famous American Plays of the Nineteen Sixties.* Dell 1972 $6.95.
ISBN 0-440-32609-5

——, ed. *Famous American Plays of the Nineteen Thirties. American Drama Ser.* Dell
1980 $6.99. ISBN 0-440-32478-5. Odets, *Awake and Sing*; Behrman, *End of Summer*;
Sherwood, *Idiot's Delight*; Steinbeck, *Of Mice and Men*; Saroyan, *The Time of Your
Life.*

——, ed. *The Fervent Years: The Group Theatre and the Thirties. Quality Paperbacks
Ser.* Da Capo 1983 $10.95. ISBN 0-306-80186-8

Corbin, Richard, and Miriam Balf, eds. *Twelve American Plays, 1920–1960.* Macmillan
1969. ISBN 0-02-325180-8. Includes plays by Albee, Chase, Hellman, Kesselring,
Nash, O'Neill, Patrick, Rodgers and Hammerstein, Serling, Sherwood, Wilder, and
Williams.

Garza, Roberto J., ed. *Contemporary Chicano Theatre.* U. of Notre Dame Pr. 1975 o.p.
Valdez, *Los Perdidos* and *Bernabe*; Sierra, *La Raza Pura; or Racial, Racial*; Alurista,

Dawn; Macias, *The Ultimate Pandejadu* and *Martir Montezuma*; Garza, *No Nos Venceremos*; Portillo, *The Day of the Swallows.*

Gassner, John, ed. *Best American Plays: 5th Series, 1957–1963*. Crown 1963 $19.95. ISBN 0-517-50860-5. Includes works by Albee, Chayefsky, Frings, Gardner, Inge, Kopit, O'Neill, Saroyan, Vidal, Williams, and others.

———, ed. *Best American Plays: 4th Series, 1952–1957*. Crown 1958 $35.00. ISBN 0-517-50436-7. Among the works included are Anderson's *Tea and Sympathy*, Axelrod's *The Seven Year Itch*, Inge's *Bus Stop* and *Picnic*, Levin's *No Time for Sergeants*, Miller's *The Crucible* and *A View from the Bridge*, O'Neill's *A Moon for the Misbegotten*, Wilder's *The Matchmaker*, and Wouk's *The Caine Mutiny.*

———, ed. *Best American Plays: 3rd Series, 1941–1951*. Crown 1987 $35.00. ISBN 0-517-50950-4. Includes *Anne of the Thousand Days; Billy Budd; Mister Roberts; Come Back, Little Sheba; The Member of the Wedding; Death of a Salesman; The Iceman Cometh; Bell, Book and Candle; A Streetcar Named Desire*, and others.

———, ed. *Best American Plays: 6th Series, 1963–1967*. Crown 1971 $35.00. ISBN 0-517-50591-2. Among the works included are Albee's *Tiny Alice*, Baldwin's *Blues for Mister Charlie*, Duberman's *In White America*, Gilroy's *The Subject Was Roses*, Hanley's *Slow Dance on the Killing Ground*, Hansberry's *The Sign in Sidney Brustein's Window*, Lowell's *Benito Cereno*, and Simon's *The Odd Couple.*

———, ed. *Best American Plays: Supplementary Volume, 1918–1958*. Crown 1961 $23.95. ISBN 0-517-50450-2. Among the works included are Chase's *Harvey*, Green's *The House of Connelly*, Kingsley's *Men in White*, Mayer's *Children of Darkness*, Patrick's *The Teahouse of the August Moon*, and Tarkington's *Clarence.*

———, ed. *Best Plays of the Early American Theatre: From the Beginning to 1916*. Crown 1967 $27.95. ISBN 0-517-50949-0. Includes *Uncle Tom's Cabin, Superstition, The Octoroon, The Count of Monte Cristo, The Truth, The Scarecrow, The Great Divide, The Witching Hour*, and others.

———, ed. *Best Plays of the Modern American Theatre: 2nd Series, 1939–1946*. Crown 1947 $23.95. ISBN 0-517-50948-2. Among the plays included are Hellman's *Watch on the Rhine*, Kanin's *Born Yesterday*, Kesselring's *Arsenic and Old Lace*, Saroyan's *The Time of Your Life*, Sherwood's *Abe Lincoln in Illinois*, and Van Druten's *I Remember Mama.*

———, ed. *Twenty Best Plays of the Modern American Theatre*. Crown 1939 o.p. Includes works by Abbott and Holm, Anderson, Barry, Behrman, Booth, Connelly, Ferber and Kaufman, Green, Hart and Kaufman, Hellman, Kingsley, Kirkland and Caldwell, MacLeish, Odets, Reed, Shaw, Sherwood, B. and S. Spewack, and Steinbeck.

———, ed. *Twenty-Five Best Plays of the Modern American Theatre: Early Series*. Crown 1949 o.p. Among the plays included are Bladerston's *Berkeley Square*, Barry's *Paris Bound*, Behrman's *The Second Man*, Glaspell's *Trifles*, Green's *White Dresses*, Howard's *They Knew What They Wanted*, Kelley's *Craig's Wife* and *Poor Aubrey*, Millay's *Aria da Capo*, Rice's *Street Scene*, Sherwood's *The Road to Rome*, Sturges's *Strictly Dishonorable*, and Treadwell's *Machinal.*

Gassner, John, and Clive Barnes, eds. *Best American Plays: 7th Series, 1967–1973*. Crown 1975 $35.00. ISBN 0-517-51387-0. Includes plays by Albee, Crowley, Elder, Feiffer, Guare, Kopit, Rabe, Simon, and Wilson, among others.

Gates, Robert A., ed. *Eighteenth and Nineteenth Century American Drama*. Irvington 1985 text ed. $36.50. ISBN 0-8290-1151-X

Gaver, Jack, ed. *Critics' Choice: New York Drama Critics' Circle Prize Plays, 1935–55*. Play Anthology Repr. Ser. Ayer repr. of 1955 ed. $43.00. ISBN 0-8369-8221-S. Includes plays by M. Anderson, Steinbeck, Saroyan, Hellman, Kingsley, Williams, Miller, McCullers, Van Druten, Inge, and Patrick.

Gerould, Daniel, ed. *American Melodrama: Plays and Documents*. PAJ Pbns. 1983 $13.95. ISBN 0-933826-21-4. Boucicault, *The Poor of New York*; Aiken, *Uncle Tom's Cabin*; Daly, *Under the Gaslight*; Belasco, *The Girl of The Golden West.*

Halline, Allan G., ed. *American Plays*. AMS Pr. repr. of 1935 ed. $44.50. ISBN 0-404-14763-1. Among the plays included are Tyler's *The Contrast*, Dunlap's *Andre*, Barker's *Superstition*, Bird's *The Gladiator*, Mowatt's *Fashion*, Boker's *Francesca da*

Rimini, Miller's *The Danites in the Sierras*, Mitchell's *The New York Idea*, Barry's *You and I*, O'Neill's *The Great God Brown*, and Green's *The Field God.*

————, ed. *Six Great American Plays.* Random 1978 $13.95. ISBN 0-394-60457-1

————, ed. *Six Modern American Plays. Modern Lib. College Ed. Ser.* McGraw 1966 $7.88. ISBN 0-07-553-660-9. O'Neill, *The Emperor Jones*; M. Anderson, *Winterset*; Kaufman and Hart, *The Man Who Came to Dinner*; Hellman, *The Little Foxes*; Williams, *The Glass Menagerie*; Heggen and Logan, *Mister Roberts.*

Hatch, James V., and Ted Shine, eds. *Black Theater, U.S.A.: Forty-Five Plays by Black Americans, 1847–1974.* Macmillan 1974 $36.95. ISBN 0-02-914160-5. The widest historical representation; includes bibliographies.

Hewes, Henry, ed. *Famous American Plays of the Nineteen Forties.* Dell 1960 $6.95. ISBN 0-440-32490-4. Wilder, *The Skin of Our Teeth*; Laurents, *Home of the Brave*; Miller, *All My Sons*; Anderson, *Lost in the Stars*; McCullers, *The Member of the Wedding.*

Hoffman, Ted, ed. *Famous American Plays of the Nineteen Seventies.* Dell 1981 $6.95. ISBN 0-440-32537-4

Jacobus, Lee, ed. *Longman Anthology of American Drama.* Longman 1982 $34.95. ISBN 0-582-28348-5. Includes works by Tyler, Mowatt, Aiken, Boucicault, Howard, Glaspell, Rice, Connelly, Odets, Wilder, Inge, Hansberry, Van Itallie, Bullins, Kopit, Gordone, and Rabe, among others.

Kozelka, Paul, ed. *Fifteen American One-Act Plays.* PB 1984 $4.95. ISBN 0-671-54313-X. Among the plays included are Goodman's *Dust of the Road*, Ehlert's *The Undercurrent*, Hughes's *Red Carnations*, Fletcher's *Sorry, Wrong Number*, Kaufman's *The Still Alarm*, Glaspell's *Trifles*, Tarkington's *The Trysting Place*, and Benet's *The Devil and Daniel Webster.*

Leverett, James, ed. *New Plays U.S.A., No. 1.* Theatre Comm. 1982 o.p. Breuer, *A Prelude to Death in Venice*; Cole, *Dead Souls*; Hwang, *FOB*; Mann, *Still Life*; Oyama, *The Resurrection of Lady Lester*; Shank, *Winterplay.*

————, ed. *New Plays U.S.A., No. 2.* Theatre Comm. 1984 $17.95. ISBN 0-930452-35-6

Leverett, James, and Elizabeth M. Osborn, eds. *New Plays U.S.A., No. 3.* Theatre Comm. 1986 $22.50. ISBN 0-930452-53-4

McGowan, Kenneth, ed. *Famous American Plays of the Nineteen Twenties.* Dell 1980 $6.99. ISBN 0-440-32466-1. O'Neill, *The Moon of the Caribbees*; M. Anderson and Stallings, *What Price Glory?*; Howard, *They Knew What They Wanted*; Heyward and Heyward, *Porgy*; Barry, *Holiday*; Rice, *Street Scene.*

Marx, Robert, ed. *Famous American Plays of the Nineteen Eighties.* Dell 1988 $6.95. ISBN 0-440-20150-0. Lowell, *Benito Cereno*; Alfred, *Hogan's Goat*; Heller, *We Bombed in New Haven*; Horovitz, *The Indian Wants the Bronx*; Crowley, *The Boys in the Band.*

Matlaw, Myron, ed. *Nineteenth-Century American Plays.* Applause Theatre Bk. Pubs. 1988 $24.95. ISBN 1-55783-017-7. Mowatt, *Fashion*; Boker, *Francesca da Rimini*; Boucicault, *The Octoroon*; Jefferson, *Rip Van Winkle*; Barras, *The Black Crook*; Howard, *Shenandoah*; Herne, *Margaret Fleming.*

Moore, Honor, ed. *The New Women's Theatre: Ten Plays by Contemporary American Women.* Random 1977 o.p. Jacker, *Bits and Pieces*; Russ, *Window Dressing*; Molinaro, *Breakfast Past Noon*; Howe, *Birth and After Birth*; Moore, *Mourning Pictures*; Childress, *Wedding Band*; Wolff, *The Abdication*; Kraus, *The Ice Wolf*; Lamb, *I Lost a Pair of Gloves Yesterday*; *Out of Our Father's House* (arranged for the stage by Merriam, Wagner, and Hoffsiss).

Moses, Montrose, ed. *Representative Plays by American Dramatists.* 3 vols. Ayer repr. of 1972 ed. $132.00. ISBN 0-685-43147-9. Volume 1 includes plays written between 1765 and 1819 by the following dramatists: Godfrey, Rogers, Warren, Brackenridge, Leacock, Low, Tyler, Dunlap, Barker, and Noah. Volume 2 includes plays written between 1815 and 1858 by the following dramatists: Hutton, Payne, Brown, Wallis, Jones, Conrad, Mowatt, Aiken, Bateman, and Tayleure. Volume 3 includes plays written between 1856 and 1911 by the following dramatists: Burke, Boker, Bunce, Mackaye, Howard, Thomas, Fitch, Mitchell, Walter, and Belasco.

Nelson, Stanley, ed. *The Scene-Four*. The Smith 1977 $8.00. ISBN 0-912292-42-3. Plays by Vallejo, Horovitz, Tolnay, and Shea. This and the three other books by Nelson include original casts, performance dates, and information on rights.

————, ed. *The Scene-One: Plays from Off-Off Broadway*. The Smith 1973 o.p. Plays by Newgurge, Greth, Bailey, Nelson, Bradford, Lohman, Reinhold, and Garcia.

————, ed. *The Scene-Three: Annual Anthology of Off-Off Broadway Plays*. The Smith 1975 $8.00. ISBN 0-912292-38-5. Plays by Houston, Reinhold, Herron, Roth, Bailey, Gilbert, Chappart, Garcia, Lengyel, Gauthier, Wilbert, O'Reilly, Gonzalez, Lazarus.

————, ed. *The Scene-Two*. The Smith 1974 $8.00. ISBN 0-912292-34-2. Plays by McGrinder, Kushner, Ordway, Thie, Sainer, Mandel, and Patrick.

New American Plays. Hill & Wang 1965–1971 Vol. 1 Ed. by Robert Corrigan. o.p. Vol. 4 Ed. by William Hoffman. o.p. Volume 1 includes the following plays: *The Death and Life of Sneaky Fitch, Socrates Wounded, Constantinople Smith, The Hundred and First, Ginger Anne, Pigeons, The Golden Bull of Boredom, Blood Money, Mr. Biggs*, and *A Summer Ghost*. Volume 4 includes the following plays: *Slaughterhouse Play, At War with the Mongols, Captain Jack's Revenge, African Medea, Icarus*, and *Moby Tick*.

New American Plays One. Ed. by Richard Strand and others. Heinemann Ed. 1992 $15.95. ISBN 0-435-08604-9

New American Plays Two. Ed. by Janet Noble and others. Heinemann Ed. 1992 $15.95. ISBN 0-435-08605-7

Richards, Stanley. *The Most Popular Plays of the American Theater*. Madison Bks. UPA 1979 $24.95. ISBN 0-8128-2682-5

Sills, Stephanie, and Clinton S. Oliver, eds. *Contemporary Black Drama*. Macmillan 1971. ISBN 0-02-410490-6. Includes *A Raisin in the Sun, Purlie Victorious, Funnyhouse of a Negro, Dutchman, Blues for Mister Charlie, Day of Absence, Happy Ending, The Gentleman Caller, No Place to be Somebody*.

Strasberg, Lee, ed. *Famous American Plays of the Nineteen Fifties*. American Drama Ser. Dell 1963 $6.95. ISBN 0-440-32491-2. Williams, *Camino Real*; Hellman, *The Autumn Garden*; Anderson, *Tea and Sympathy*; Albee, *The Zoo Story*; Gazzo, *A Hatful of Rain*.

Wordplays Two: New American Drama. PAJ Pubns. 1982 o.p. Owens, *Chucky's Hunch*; Shawn, *A Thought in Three Parts*; Jenkens, *Dark Ride*; Kondoleon, *The Brides*; O'Keefe, *All Night Long*.

Wordplays Five: New American Drama. Wordplays Ser. Ed. by James Lapine and others PAJ Pubns. 1986 $22.95. ISBN 1-55554-006-6

CHRONOLOGY OF AUTHORS

Kelly, George Edward. 1887–1974
Anderson, Maxwell. 1888–1959
O'Neill, Eugene. 1888–1953
Kaufman, George S. 1889–1961
Rice, Elmer. 1892–1967
Green, Paul. 1894–1981
Barry, Philip. 1896–1949
Wilder, Thornton. 1897–1975
Hellman, Lillian. 1905–1984
Odets, Clifford. 1906–1963
Saroyan, William. 1908–1981
Williams, Tennessee. 1911–1983
Inge, William. 1913–1973
Miller, Arthur. 1915–
Anderson, Robert. 1917–
McCullers, Carson. 1917–1967
Baldwin, James. 1924–1987
Simon, Neil. 1927–

Albee, Edward. 1928–
Gurney, A. R., Jr. 1930–
Hansberry, Lorraine. 1930–1965
Linney, Romulus. 1930–
Terry, Megan. 1932–
Baraka, Imamu Amiri (LeRoi Jones). 1934–
Bullins, Ed. 1935–
Van Itallie, Jean-Claude. 1935–
Jones, Preston. 1936–1979
Zindel, Paul. 1936–
Kopit, Arthur. 1937–
Wilson, Lanford. 1937–
Guare, John. 1938–
Horovitz, Israel. 1939–
McNally, Terrence. 1939–
Rabe, David. 1940–
Shepard, Sam. 1943–

ALBEE, EDWARD. 1928–

Edward Albee was the pampered adopted son of millionaire parents. An indifferent, rebellious student, he attended various private schools and—briefly—Trinity College, then quit home and schooling at age 21 to live in New York City. For nearly a decade, he worked at odd jobs, writing poetry, attempting novels, publishing nothing. Just before his thirtieth birthday, he sat down and wrote *The Zoo Story* (1959) in two weeks. *The Sandbox* (1960), *Fam and Yam* (1960), *The American Dream* (1960), and *The Death of Bessie Smith* (1960) followed rapidly, and the fame of the young dramatist was established.

Although these one-act plays linked Albee to the Theater of the Absurd, *Who's Afraid of Virginia Woolf?*, his Broadway debut in 1962, was by contrast naturalistic. The evening-long argument between a married couple is a strong denunciation of modern marital relationships, amusingly bitchy on the surface but murderously vicious underneath. "The heart of his technique is an archetypal family unity in which the defeats, hopes, dilemmas, and values of our society (as Albee sees it) are tangibly compressed" (Lee Baxandall, *The Theater of Edward Albee*).

The Ballad of the Sad Cafe, Albee's adaptation of the novella by CARSON McCULLERS, was less successful in 1963. *Tiny Alice* (1965) had elements of the Theater of the Absurd and appeared to many as an allegory about spiritual versus secular elements in American society. *A Delicate Balance* (1967), a more conventional black comedy of serious intent, is, Albee says, "about how as you get older the freedom of choices becomes less and less, and you are left only with the illusion of freedom of actions and you become a slave of compromise." *Seascape* (1975), intended as a comedy and a balance to the view of life expressed in *All Over* (1971), has a middle-aged couple at the shore meeting a reptile. Their conversation reveals common problems in life. Some of his later plays reflect a growing alienation of Albee from his public. This is especially true of *The Lady from Dubuque* (1980), which makes self-reference the sole motive of performance.

Albee won the Pulitzer Prize for drama for *A Delicate Balance* and *Seascape* and the New York Drama Critics Circle Award for *Who's Afraid of Virginia Woolf?*

PLAYS BY ALBEE

All Over. French 1971 o.p. Eloquent death watch.

The American Dream and *The Zoo Story*. NAL-Dutton 1960 $4.99. ISBN 0-451-16643-4. Two outstanding one-acts in the absurdist tradition.

The Ballad of the Sad Cafe. Dramatists Play 1963 o.p. An adaptation from Carson McCullers's novella. Grotesque Southern tale about a love triangle.

A Delicate Balance. French 1966 o.p. Pulitzer Prize-winning story about sanity, madness, and a desperate search for identity.

Fam and Yam. Dramatists Play 1960 o.p. Absurdist one-act about a young American playwright (Yam) and a famous American playwright (Fam).

The Lady from Dubuque. Dramatists Play $3.95. ISBN 0-686-69575-5. Provocative examination of death and loss.

The Sandbox and *The Death of Bessie Smith*. NAL-Dutton 1988 $7.95. ISBN 0-452-26083-3. Two more absurd and moving one-acts.

Seascape. Dramatists Play 1975 o.p. Pulitzer Prize-winning play on evolution and the meaning of life.

Tiny Alice. Dramatists Play 1964 o.p. Compelling drama about a lawyer, a church cardinal, and the world's richest woman.

Who's Afraid of Virginia Woolf? NAL-Dutton 1983 $4.99. ISBN 0-451-15871-7. Shattering drama about a college professor, his domineering wife, and a younger couple who stop by for drinks.

Books about Albee

Amacher, Richard E. *Edward Albee*. Twayne's U.S. Authors Ser. G. K. Hall 1982 $17.95. ISBN 0-8057-5349-5. Rates the one-act plays and the full-length tragedies as the best.

Bigsby, C.W.E. *Albee*. Writers and Critics Ser. Chips 1978 $24.50. ISBN 0-912378-08-5. One of the most astute critics on Albee.

Bloom, Harold, ed. *Edward Albee*. Chelsea Hse. 1987 $19.95. ISBN 0-87754-707-6. A collection of modern critical essays including a useful description of Albee's techniques.

Esslin, Martin. *The Theater of the Absurd*. Overlook Pr. 1973 $35.00. ISBN 0-87951-005-6. Definitive work on absurdism showing Albee's place in the movement.

Green, Charles I. *Edward Albee: An Annotated Bibliography, 1968–1977*. AMS Pr. 1980 $29.50. ISBN 0-404-18014-0

ANDERSON, MAXWELL. 1888–1959

After some years as a teacher and a journalist, Anderson turned to drama in 1923, achieving his first success with *What Price Glory?* in 1924, a World War I comedy cowritten with Laurence Stallings. During his long and successful career as a dramatist (his last play premiered in 1958), Anderson produced historical dramas, patriotic plays, musicals, fantasies, and a thriller. Perhaps his best piece is *Winterset* (1935). Inspired by the Sacco and Vanzetti case, it dramatizes the efforts of Mio, the son of a man executed ostensibly for murder but actually for his radical ideas, to clear his father's name. Anderson's first play was a verse drama, and beginning with *Elizabeth the Queen* (1940), his most famous historical drama, he employed for many years an irregular blank verse, typical—like his preoccupation with traditional tragic form—of his attempt to bring high seriousness to the Broadway stage. Critics have not been enthusiastic about Anderson's work, and his plays are seldom revived today, but in his heyday—especially the 1930s—his plays, verse and all, repeatedly succeeded in the commercial theater.

Anderson won the Pulitzer Prize for drama for *Both Your Houses* (1933) and the New York Drama Critics Circle Award for *Winterset* (1935) and *High Tor* (1937).

Plays by Anderson

The Bad Seed. Dramatists Play 1955 o.p. Psychological drama about an innately evil child.

Both Your Houses. French 1933 o.p. Critiques American political system.

Elizabeth the Queen. French 1930 o.p. Story of love and power centering on Elizabeth the queen and her favorite general, Essex.

Joan of Lorraine. Dramatists Play 1946 o.p. Theatrical version of Joan of Arc focusing on the meaning of faith.

Mary of Scotland. French 1934 o.p. The story of Mary Queen of Scots' bewilderment by her cousin Elizabeth's intrigues, which slowly close in on her.

Winterset. Dramatists Play 1935 o.p. Verse drama about a son's efforts to clear his radical father's name.

WORKS BY ANDERSON

Dramatist in America: Letters of Maxwell Anderson, 1912–1958. Ed. by Laurence G. Avery.
  U. of NC Pr. 1977 $39.95. ISBN 0-8078-1309-5. Epistles by the playwright covering
  46-year period.
Notes on a Dream. Ed. by Laurence G. Avery. U. of Tex. Pr. 1971 $10.00. ISBN 0-87959-
  056-4. Ruminations of a playwright.

BOOKS ABOUT ANDERSON

Shivers, Alfred S. *The Life of Maxwell Anderson.* Stein & Day 1983 o.p. Trenchant
  biography of the playwright that also sheds light on American theater history.
_____. *Maxwell Anderson. Twayne's U.S. Authors Ser.* G. K. Hall 1976 o.p. Especially
  useful for the new biographical material it provides.
_____. *Maxwell Anderson: An Annotated Bibliography of Primary and Secondary Works.*
  Scarecrow 1985 $29.50. ISBN 0-8108-1833-7. Includes extensive, annotated material
  written by and about the playwright.

ANDERSON, ROBERT. 1917–

Anderson was born in New York City, moved with his family to New Rochelle,
New York, while attending grade school, and completed his secondary
education at Exeter Academy in New Hampshire. In 1935 he entered Harvard
University, where he joined the drama club, wrote musicals, and was elected
class poet. He graduated *magna cum laude* in 1939 with a B.A. in English.

It was not until he was commissioned an ensign in the U.S. Navy that
Anderson began to pursue seriously his goal of becoming a playwright, and his
unpublished script, *Come Marching Home* (1945), won a contest sponsored by
the army and navy. During the postwar period, he continued writing original
scripts and made numerous adaptations for radio and television. His most
famous original play, *Tea and Sympathy*, was produced in the fall of 1953 by The
Playwrights' Company with Elia Kazan as director and Jo Mielziner as designer.
The story concerns a wretched boy at boarding school who is persecuted by the
other students and wrongly accused of homosexuality. An older woman, the
wife of a housemaster at the school, offers to have sex with the boy to reassure
him of his normalcy. The play, which ran on Broadway for 712 performances
and was later made into a film, was noted for the sensitivity of its direction and
the evocativeness of its setting.

An evening of one-acts, *You Know I Can't Hear You When The Water's
Running* (1967), ran on Broadway for 755 performances. *I Never Sang for My
Father* (1968) ran for 124 performances on Broadway. His *Solitaire/Double
Solitaire* (1971), another evening of one-acts, ran for only 36 performances in its
New York production, though it doubtless deserved a longer run.

Anderson's plays are carefully crafted works that treat the subject of marriage
with insight, compassion, and perhaps a measure of sorrow. Husbands and
wives with incompatible sexual drives find themselves increasingly isolated and
lonely. Fathers who confuse aggression with manliness and who fail to teach
sensitivity and compassion damage and alienate their sons. Aging family
members find that their choices are increasingly diminished with the passage of
time. In spite of these uncertainties, the consolations of family are seen as the
best, perhaps the only ones we have.

Six of Anderson's plays have appeared on Broadway, two have been named
Best Plays, and two of his films have received Academy Award nominations. In
1981 he was inducted into the Theatre Hall of Fame.

PLAYS BY ANDERSON.

Famous American Plays of the Nineteen Fifties. Ed. by Lee Strasberg. Dell 1963 $6.95. ISBN 0-440-32491-2. Includes *Tea and Sympathy* as well as plays by Williams, Hellman, Albee, and Gazzo.

I Never Sang for My Father. Dramatists Play 1968 o.p. Probes the unsettling alienation between a grown son and his 80-year-old father.

Silent Night, Lonely Night. French 1960 o.p. About an unhappy married man and an unhappy woman who meet in a New England inn.

Solitaire/Double Solitaire. Dramatists Play 1972 o.p. Two short plays; one set in the computerized future where marriage has been abolished, the other set in the present.

Tea and Sympathy. French 1953 o.p. Story of a hazed schoolboy who is comforted by an older woman.

You Know I Can't Hear You When the Water's Running. Dramatists Play 1967 o.p. Four short plays, warm-hearted, hilarious, and occasionally despairing, about sex.

BOOK ABOUT ANDERSON

Adler, Thomas P. *Robert Anderson.* Twayne 1978 o.p. Each of Anderson's plays analyzed in sequence, with an emphasis on autobiographical and thematic elements.

BALDWIN, JAMES. 1924–1987

Born in New York's Harlem, Baldwin was the oldest of nine children and had the responsibility of looking out for his younger brothers and sisters. Legend has it that he would often have a baby in one hand and a book, *Uncle Tom's Cabin*, in the other. His mother raised her children in accordance with the strict moral standards associated with the family's southern religious background. His father, a minister from New Orleans, was a bitter, paranoid man, not well liked by the children.

As a teenager, Baldwin became a minister in Harlem's Fireside Pentecostal Church and for three emotion-packed years reveled in the fact that he was a better preacher than his father. While attending De Witt Clinton High School, however, he became editor of the school's literary magazine and discovered his preference for writing over preaching. He graduated in 1942.

Following his father's death, Baldwin realized that to become a successful writer, he would have to move away from his family. He chose Greenwich Village and for the next five years supported himself in a variety of office, factory, and restaurant jobs. He spent his evenings writing reviews of books on African-American topics and began work on his first novel.

In 1948 Baldwin received a fellowship that enabled him to move to Paris. In this climate more congenial to his race, Baldwin was able to develop himself as a literary artist. His essays, novels, and plays brought him distinction as one of America's finest writers. He also became a civil-rights advocate, maintaining the position that these issues did not reflect a problem of black people so much as it did an illness of white people. A central theme in Baldwin's works has been that racism dehumanizes white people as well as black. Another related theme is that religion, properly understood, requires that the members of any one race love and accept people of all other races.

The Amen Corner (1955) and *Blues for Mr. Charlie* (1964) are regarded as Baldwin's major dramatic achievements. Set in a store-front church in Harlem, *The Amen Corner* is concerned with the way impoverished African Americans use religion as a means of escape. *Blues for Mr. Charlie* depicts the trial and acquittal of a southern racist white who has killed a caustic black man. The play,

which throbs with fires of racial fury, was roughly based on the murder of
Emmett Till, a black teenager killed in Mississippi in 1955.

Baldwin received numerous awards and fellowships, including the Eugene
Saxton Memorial Trust Award (1945), a Rosenwald Foundation Fellowship
(1948), a Guggenheim Fellowship (1954), a National Institute of Arts and Letters
Award (1956), a *Partisan Review* Fellowship (1956), and a Ford Foundation
Fellowship (1958). In 1964 he received the Foreign Drama Critics Award for the
sensational *Blues for Mr. Charlie*. The University of British Columbia and
Morehouse College both awarded him honorary doctorates, the first in 1963 and
the latter in 1976. In 1978 he won the Martin Luther King, Jr., award from the
City College of the State University of New York.

PLAYS BY BALDWIN

The Amen Corner. Dell 1990 $5.99. ISBN 0-440-20662-6. About a self-appointed woman
     preacher and her store-front church in Harlem.
Blues for Mr. Charlie. Dell 1965 o.p. The trial and acquittal of a southern white racist,
     with a compelling eulogy for his victim.

NONFICTION BY BALDWIN

Another Country. 1962. Dell 1985 $5.95. ISBN 0-440-30200-5. Concerned with whatever
     demeans black people in a predominantly white society.
The Fire Next Time. 1963. Dell 1985 $5.99. ISBN 0-440-32542-0. Talks about the Black
     Muslim movement and sums up Baldwin's views on race relations in the United
     States.
Nobody Knows My Name. Dell 1961 o.p. A collection of magazine articles dealing with
     literary issues and expressing Baldwin's much-dreaded first trip to the South.

NOVEL BY BALDWIN

Giovanni's Room. 1962. Dell 1985 $5.99. ISBN 0-440-32881-0. Deals with homosexuality
     and reveals the persecution of this minority group.

BOOKS ABOUT BALDWIN

Pratt, Louis. *James Baldwin. Twayne's U.S. Authors Ser.* Macmillan 1978 $19.95. ISBN 0-
     8057-7193-X. The best existing biographical treatment of Baldwin, probing the
     themes of his writings.
Standley, Fred L., and Nancy V. Burt. *Critical Essays on James Baldwin. Critical Essays
     Ser.* G. K. Hall 1988 $40.00. ISBN 0-8161-8879-3. With an introduction that provides
     an excellent, carefully detailed discussion of bibliographies and anthologies.
Standley, Fred L., and Louis H. Pratt, eds. *Conversations with James Baldwin.* U. Pr. of
     Miss. 1989 $32.50. ISBN 0-87805-388-3. Collection of Baldwin interviews by Studs
     Terkel, Ben Shahn, Nat Hentoff, David Frost, and others.
Troupe, Quincy, ed. *James Baldwin: The Legacy.* S & S Trade 1989 $12.95. ISBN 0-671-
     67651-2. Contains memorial tributes from Baldwin's family and friends along with
     several lengthy interviews with Baldwin.
Weatherby, W. J. *James Baldwin: Artist on Fire.* Dell 1990 $5.95. ISBN 0-440-20573-5.
     Connects events in Baldwin's life with incidents in his stories and essays.

BARAKA, IMAMU AMIRI (LEROI JONES). 1934–

Born LeRoi Jones in Newark, New Jersey, Baraka graduated from Howard
University and then taught at Columbia University, the New School for Social
Research, and San Francisco State College. Baraka has been involved in a
number of theater and education projects designed to improve conditions for
African Americans. In 1968, he assumed his new name and became a minister

of the Kawaida faith. In 1974 he renounced black nationalism for Marxist-Leninist thought with an internationalist emphasis.

With *Dutchman* (1964), a controversial one-act play about a provocative white woman who alternately entices, belittles, and finally kills a young African-American man in the subway, Baraka emerged as an important black dramatic voice. In *The Slave* (1964), a black revolutionary confronts his former wife, a white woman, and kills their two children. In *The Toilet* (1967), a black youth beats a white youth who has made homosexual advances, but in the absence of others returns to comfort the white youth. *Slave Ship* (1967) is an indictment of white imperialism. *The Motion of History* is epic drama seeking to write African-American history from a Marxist point of view.

Baraka's plays are bold in concept, strong in language, and committed to revolutionary racial and social change, but his later plays have tended to be excessively didactic. In recent years, however, Baraka has focused more on poetry and nonfiction prose, which have helped balance the negative critical reception of his later plays. Baraka's importance as a catalyst of the African-American arts movement is secure.

PLAYS BY BARAKA

The Baptism (and *The Toilet*). Grove Pr. 1967 o.p. Produced in 1964, the plays expressed both humor and rage with regard to the subject of race.

Dutchman. French 1964 o.p. A white woman attempts to seduce an African American man, fails, humiliates him, succeeds, murders him, then primps for her next black victim.

Dutchman and The Slave: Two Plays. Morrow 1971 $8.45. ISBN 0-688-21084-8. Plays from the 1960s that brought the playwright critical acclaim.

Four Black Revolutionary Plays. Macmillan 1969 $4.50. ISBN 0-672-50672-6. Contains *Experimental Death Unit #1, A Black Mass, Great Goodness of Life: A Coon Show*, and *Madheart.*

The Slave. French 1964 o.p. Black people rise up and begin to burn white America.

BOOKS ABOUT BARAKA

Benston, Kimberly W. *Baraka: The Renegade and the Mask.* Yale U. Pr. 1976 o.p. Examines Baraka's plays as products of two cultural traditions, the Western and the African-American.

Bernotas, Bob. *Amiri Baraka.* Chelsea Hse. 1991 $17.95. ISBN 0-7910-1117-8. Biography of Baraka with an introduction by Coretta Scott King.

Hudson, Theodore R. *From LeRoi Jones to Amiri Baraka: The Literary Works.* Duke 1973 $18.75. ISBN 0-8223-0296-9. Scholarly analysis and criticism of Baraka's early work.

Sollers, Werner. *Amiri Baraka/LeRoi Jones: The Quest for "Popular Modernism."* Col. U. Pr. 1978 o.p. An important study of Baraka by a major black scholar.

BARRY, PHILIP. 1896–1949

Barry, a product of Baker's 47 Workshop, is best remembered for his witty and elegant comedies about marriage among the well-to-do. His most noted play is *The Philadelphia Story* (1939), about a wealthy young woman who on her wedding day switches from a dull social climber to remarry her first husband. Other drawing room successes include *Paris Bound* (1929) and *Holiday* (1928). Barry also wrote plays of greater seriousness, but with less critical and popular success. *Hotel Universe* (1930), in which a group of strangers relive personal crises in their lives, and *Here Come the Clowns* (1938) are experimental dramas with a mystical side, reflecting a Freudian interpretation of character and existential doubt. In *Tomorrow and Tomorrow* (1931) a man discovers that his mistress is more his wife in behavior and love than the woman to whom he is legally married.

Of Barry, Brendan Gill wrote, "No matter how ambitious the intentions of his plays, he kept the plays themselves modest in scale. He wrote often in the now unfashionable genre of high comedy but his comedies strove to be deeper than they were high."

PLAYS BY BARRY

Holiday. French 1928 o.p. About a young man who prefers enjoying life as a holiday over "making good" with his rich fiancée's father.

Hotel Universe. French 1930 o.p. Modern morality play about the meaning of life.

The Philadelphia Story: A Comedy in Three Acts. AMS Pr. repr. of 1939 ed. $24.50. ISBN 0-404-20018-4. Romantic smash hit about a strong woman who needs to learn compassion and humility. Later made into a successful film.

BOOK ABOUT BARRY

Roppolo, Joseph P. *Philip Barry. Twayne's U.S. Authors Ser.* N.C.U.P. Inc. 1965 $10.95. ISBN 0-8084-0243-9

BULLINS, ED. 1935–

Born in the African-American slums of Philadelphia, Bullins was raised with a knowledge of the streets. In time he became an active participant in the black nationalist movement. As he became increasingly mistrustful of ideologies, however, he turned his focus almost entirely to the theater as a means of expressing the needs and aspirations of his people. By the mid-1960s, he had established himself, along with IMAMU AMIRI BARAKA, as a leading playwright in America's black theater.

In works such as *Clara's Ole Man* (1965), *Goin'a Buffalo* (1968), and *In the Wine Time* (1968), Bullins depicts the lives of people in the ghetto and shows himself able to turn even their obscene talk into a special kind of poetry. *The Fabulous Miss Marie* (1971) depicts the black middle class with equal poignancy and was awarded an Obie. *The Taking of Miss Janie* (1975), a study of American race relations, won the New York Drama Critics Award.

Bullins has received two Guggenheim fellowships, three Rockefeller grants, and a Creative Artists' Public Service Program Award. In 1976 he received an honorary doctorate from Columbia College in Chicago.

PLAYS BY BULLINS

Five Plays: Goin'a Buffalo. In the Wine Time. The Electronic Nigger. A Son, Come Home. Clara's Ole Man. Bobbs 1969 o.p. Depicts the lives of ghetto folk. Revised as *The Electronic Nigger and Other Plays.*

The New Lafayette Theatre Presents the Complete Plays and Aesthetic Comments by Six Black Playwrights. Ed. by Ed Bullins. Doubleday 1974 o.p. Contains *The Fabulous Miss Marie.*

The Taking of Miss Janie. In *Famous American Plays of the 1970s.* Dell 1981 $6.95. ISBN 0-440-32537-4. Dissects American race relations.

DURANG, CHRISTOPHER. 1949–

Reared in Berkeley Heights, New Jersey, Christopher Durang spent his childhood acting out plays that he based on television and movie characters. His 12 years in repressive Roman Catholic schools as well as traumatic elements in his home life became the basis for the dark humor of his later plays.

Known as one of America's angry young playwrights, Durang has focused his satirical wit on Hollywood's myth-making cinemas, the Catholic church, contemporary psychoanalytic practices, and the problems of individual and family identity. His combining of farce and philosophical despair places him in the absurdist tradition of IONESCO (see Vol. 2) and BECKETT (see Vol. 2). Although he has enjoyed only limited success on Broadway, he has become a major voice off-Broadway and in America's burgeoning regional and university theaters.

Durang developed as a playwright during the early 1970s while working under Robert Brustein at the Yale Repertory Theatre. Much of his work during this period brought him little critical attention. However, in 1976 his satirical play, *A History of the American Film*, was read at the O'Neill National Playwrights Conference. The following year the play was premiered at the Hartford Stage Company, the Mark Taper Forum in Los Angeles, and the Arena Stage in Washington. By the close of the decade, the play had become a regional theatre favorite.

Sister Mary Ignatius Explains It All for You opened in 1979 at the Ensemble Studio Theatre in New York as a companion piece to works by DAVID MAMET, MARSHA NORMAN, and TENNESSEE WILLIAMS. The play begins with a simple catechism delivered by a seven-year-old student but soon turns into a deadly confrontation between the nun, Sister Mary Ignatius, and a number of her former students. The play, which is concerned with censorship, won the coveted Obie in 1980. The wildly humorous *The Actor's Nightmare* served as a curtain raiser for the controversial *Sister Mary Ignatius* when these two plays were presented in 1981 at off-Broadway's Playwrights Horizons.

Beyond Therapy opened off-Broadway in 1981 and enjoyed a less successful run the following year on Broadway. This screwball comedy concerns two people who are seeking meaningful relationships but who are hampered by the efforts of their respective therapists. The story shows the patients sorting it out and learning to live *beyond* therapy. As with other Durang plays, it has enjoyed strong regional support.

The Marriage of Bette and Boo, first produced in 1973, was rewritten to open at the Public Theatre in 1985. A brilliant and satirical dissection of the modern American family, the play is Durang's most autobiographical work. Durang himself played the role of Matt, Bette and Boo's son, in the New York production. The play, which earned an Obie, enjoyed critical and popular success and has been viewed as an important breakthrough in Durang's career.

PLAYS BY DURANG

The Actor's Nightmare. In *Two Plays.* Dramatists Play 1981 o.p. Spoof about a stranger who is suddenly pushed on stage to replace a sick actor.

Beyond Therapy. French 1983 o.p. Screwball comedy that satirizes psychiatry.

A History of the American Film. French 1978 o.p. Parodies American films, especially those from the 1930s through the 1950s.

Identity Crisis. In *Three Short Plays.* Dramatists Play 1979 o.p. Black comedy dealing with the pretensions of modern psychiatry.

Laughing Wild. Dramatists Play 1988 $4.50. ISBN 0-8222-0644-7. A humorous and provocative study of the perils of contemporary city life.

Laughing Wild and *Baby with the Bathwater.* Grove Pr. 1989 $8.95. ISBN 0-8021-3130-1. Thought-provoking comedies on contemporary life.

The Marriage of Bette and Boo. Grove Pr. 1987 $7.95. ISBN 0-394-62347-9. A brilliant dissection of marriage and the family in contemporary America.

The Nature and Purpose of the Universe. In *Three Short Plays.* Dramatists Play 1979 o.p.
   Absurdist comedy dealing with the problem of blind religious faith.
Sister Mary Ignatius Explains It All For You. In *Two Plays.* Dramatists Play 1979 o.p.
   Biting and uproariously funny satire aimed at organized religion.
The Vietnamization of New Jersey. Dramatists Play 1978 o.p. A satiric, wildly comic
   portrait of post-Vietnam America.

NONFICTION BY DURANG

Christopher Durang Explains It All For You. Grove Pr. 1990 $12.95. ISBN 0-8021-3232-4.
   With an introduction that contains an informative autobiography.

GREEN, PAUL. 1894–1981

   Born on a North Carolina farm, Green studied philosophy at the University of
North Carolina. He began to write plays as a freshman under the guidance of
Frederic Koch, whose Carolina playmakers staged Green's first works. An
important regional dramatist, Green portrays the plight of black and white
oppressed Southerners of both the old South and the new. His dramas feature
interpolations of folk songs along with authentic North Carolina dialect. Among
Green's finest achievements are *The House of Connelly* (1931) and *Johnny
Johnson* (1936). John Gassner described the first as "the most poignant drama of
the postbellum South" and the second as "the most imaginative and affecting
antiwar full-length play in the American Theatre." *In Abraham's Bosom* (1926)
shows the failure of a mulatto to achieve status. This later work, performed by
the Provincetown Players in New York City, won the Pulitzer Prize for drama in
1926.
   Green is also largely responsible for the development of pageants or
symphonic dramas, as he terms them, the only dramatic writing he did after
1936. *The Lost Colony* (1937) was his first outdoor drama and was written to
commemorate the three hundred fiftieth anniversary of Raleigh's colony at
Roanoke, Virginia. It has been performed with a cast of 150 every summer
since. Other popular Green pageants, derived from the life and history of the
people or single individuals from a particular locale, are *The Common Glory*
(1948) and *The Stephen Foster Story* (1959).

PLAYS BY GREEN

The Common Glory. Greenwood repr. of 1948 ed. $35.00. ISBN 0-8371-7080-X. Outdoor
   historic drama.
The Confederacy. French 1958 o.p. Outdoor drama about General Robert E. Lee.
The Field God (and *In Abraham's Bosom*). AMS Pr. repr. of 1927 ed. $29.50. ISBN 0-404-
   20112-1. Portrays the plight of oppressed Southerners.
The Founders. Boulevard Bks. 1957 $12.95. ISBN 0-910278-22-9. Outdoor drama about
   early English colonization.
The Highland Call. French 1939 o.p. Drama about conflicting loyalties during Revolu-
   tionary War era.
The Honeycomb. French 1972 o.p. Folk tragedy set on a southern farm.
Johnny Johnson. French 1936 o.p. Antiwar play with music by Kurt Weill.
The Lost Colony. French 1937 o.p. The story of the first English settlement in America.
Native Son. French rev. ed. 1941 o.p. Adapted from Richard Wright's novel; the story of a
   black youth seeking his way in a white world.
The Stephen Foster Story. French 1959 o.p. Outdoor musical drama about the American
   composer.
Texas. French 1959 o.p. Outdoor drama focusing on historic conflict between farmers
   and ranchers.

Trumpet in the Land. French 1972 o.p. Outdoor drama about eighteenth-century Moravian missionaries to the American Indians.

Wide Fields. AMS Pr. repr. of 1928 ed. $14.50. ISBN 0-404-00625-6. Poignant drama of the South.

Wilderness Road. Boulevard Bks. 1956 $10.95. ISBN 0-910278-23-7. Outdoor drama dealing with the impact of the Civil War on mountain folk.

WORKS BY GREEN

Hawthorne Tree: Some Papers and Letters on Life and the Theatre. Ayer repr. of 1943 ed. $15.00. ISBN 0-8369-2228-X. Thoughts from America's premier author of outdoor dramas.

BOOKS ABOUT GREEN

Clark, Barrett H. *Paul Green*. Haskell 1974 $29.95. ISBN 0-8383-2016-3. By one of America's best critics.

Kenny, Vincent S. *Paul Green. Twayne's U.S. Authors Ser*. Irvington 1971 $17.95. ISBN 0-8290-0007-0

GUARE, JOHN. 1938–

Born of Irish Catholic parents in New York City, Guare was an only child. His parents led intense but somewhat separate lives and young Guare found himself increasingly alone as he grew up. He spent his childhood reading, listening to albums of Broadway musicals, and writing plays. His first play was presented in a neighbor's garage when he was eleven.

After graduating from Georgetown University in Washington, D.C., Guare went on to the School of Drama at Yale University where he studied playwriting. After completing his M.F.A. in 1963, he had a short stint with the Air Force Reserve, then worked briefly in England as a reader for a London publishing house. During this period, Guare hitchhiked around Europe while continuing to write plays.

Guare first came to public attention with his one-act play *Muzeeka* (1968), a biting social satire about an ambitious man who works for a canned-music company that inflicts its banal arrangements on the entire country. The hero, Jack Argue, is a modern guilt-ridden "Everyman" who has sold himself out to the system. The play was first performed at Connecticut's Eugene O'Neill Memorial Theatre, then at the Mark Taper Forum in Los Angeles. On April 28, 1968, it opened off-Broadway at the Provincetown Playhouse on a double bill with SAM SHEPARD's *Red Cross. Muzeeka* ran for 65 performances and earned its author an Obie Award that year.

The House of Blue Leaves (1971), Guare's first full-length play, is set in a Queens apartment on the day the Pope is making his first visit to New York City. It is the story of Artie Shaughnessy, an Irish-American middle-aged zoo-keeper and would-be songwriter, who wants to commit his wife, Bananas, to a mental hospital. Artie's son shows up with a bomb that he intends to use on the Pope. The characters are so caught up in their own peculiar dreams of salvation, fame, or fortune that they are unable to relate to the needs of others.

A savage farce, *The House of Blue Leaves* presents an unrelenting attack on lower middle-class values. It shows the emptiness of the characters' inner lives and the horror of their senseless acts of violence. The play won both an Obie and the New York Drama Critics Circle Award in 1971. In 1986 it enjoyed a highly successful revival at New York's Lincoln Center, which further established Guare as a unique and critically acclaimed American playwright.

Guare's freewheeling, somewhat autobiographical works are filled with bizarre characters and situations and are often concerned with family relationships. Although his plays have not always enjoyed commercial success, he is a high-risk farceur whose works have earned him steady critical acclaim. His more recent plays, such as *Six Degrees of Separation* (1990), show the playwright turning toward a more tragic outlook. The play, which is about a wealthy couple fooled by a young man, exposes the gap between blacks and whites and between parents and their children.

Critics have been almost universal in their praise of Guare's screenplay for Louis Malle's film, *Atlantic City* (1981). Although not published in book form, the Canadian-French film has been distributed by Paramount in the United States. It is a bittersweet, Runyonesque tale about a small-time numbers runner, played by Burt Lancaster, and a small-town waitress, played by Susan Sarandon. *Atlantic City* received a number of honors, including best-screenplay awards by the National Society of Film Critics, the Los Angeles Film Critics Society, and the New York Film Critics Circle.

PLAYS BY GUARE

Bosoms and Neglect. Dramatists Play 1980 o.p. Painful comedy about neglect and guilt between parents and children.

Gardenia. Dramatists Play 1982 o.p. Set on a deserted Nantucket beach, a compelling history of romantic intrigue, murder, and failed utopian dreams.

The House of Blue Leaves. NAL-Dutton 1971 $9.95. ISBN 0-452-26459-6. Farce about a frustrated songwriter and his crazy wife, whom he strangles.

Landscape of the Body. Dramatists Play 1978 o.p. Bizarre story of a young woman blamed for the savage murder of her son.

Lydie Breeze. Dramatists Play 1982 o.p. Continues the twisted history of an idealistic nineteenth-century commune destroyed by adultery, murder, and suicide.

Marco Polo Sings a Solo. Dramatists Play 1977 o.p. Set on an island off the coast of Norway, an absurdist comedy with a disturbing glimpse of the future.

Muzeeka. Dramatists Play 1968 o.p. Satire depicting a financially successful man who has sold his soul to a piped-in music corporation.

Rich and Famous. Dramatists Play 1977 $3.95. ISBN 0-685-81648-6. A madcap satire about the world's oldest living promising young playwright.

Six Degrees of Separation. Random 1990 $19.95. ISBN 0-679-40161-X. Affecting piece about a con artist who turns out to give more than he takes.

GURNEY, A. R., JR. 1930–

Born into a well-to-do family in Buffalo, New York, Albert Ramsdell Gurney began writing plays and musical sketches while a student at Williams College in the 1950s. During the 1960s he wrote a number of one-act dramas including *The Comeback* (1964), *The Rape of Bunny Stuntz* (1964), *The David Show* (1966), and *The Golden Fleece* (1968).

Gurney's first full-length play, *Scenes from American Life* (1970), is a collection of numerous vignettes depicting the lives of wealthy Anglo-Saxon Protestants in Buffalo from the time of the Depression to a futuristic police state. Although the play has over one hundred characters, they are played by a cast of only four men and four women. Normally staged on a stark set, the only indispensable scenic element is a piano, which remains throughout the play and serves to place each scene and comment on and evaluate the action of the play. The play's central theme is the decline of a culture-bound elite society in an America that is becoming increasingly egalitarian.

Gurney's play *The Dining Room* (1982) is also a series of connected vignettes dramatizing the changing manners of elitist Northeasterners. The unifying visual motif of this play is an elegant dining suite, which is the focal point in the lives of various family members from the Depression years to the 1980s. The play's themes touch on the decline of the nuclear family, the loss of traditional values, and the conflict between the old and the new. The play was Gurney's first important critical and commercial success.

During the 1980s, Gurney wrote a number of plays that were produced in regional, off-Broadway, and London theaters. *The Perfect Party* (1986) draws a metaphorical comparison between a professor who attempts to create a perfect party and a dramatist who longs to stage a perfect play. *Sweet Sue* (1986), which is reminiscent of the ancient play *Hippolytus* by EURIPIDES (see Vol. 2), is about a middle-aged woman who wants to have an affair with her son's college roommate. *Another Antigone* (1988) is about a college professor who rejects a student's updated version of SOPHOCLES' (see Vol. 2) tragedy when it is submitted as a term paper. The play's themes touch on the nuclear arms race, anti-Semitism, and academic freedom.

Gurney received the Award of Merit from the American Academy and Institute of Arts and Letters in 1987. He is noted for his ability to combine social criticism with both comic and affecting dramatic situations. While his plays have received mixed reviews, he has established himself as an important and talented contemporary dramatist.

Plays by Gurney

Children. Dramatists Play 1977 $3.95. ISBN 0-685-81642-7. Study of a well-to-do New England family forced to deal with challenges to its comfortable way of life.

The Cocktail Hour and Two Other Plays: The Perfect Party and Another Antigone. NAL-Dutton 1989 $8.95. ISBN 0-452-26338-7. Three comedies by one of our most adroit theatrical magicians.

The Comeback. Dramatists Play 1964 o.p. A witty and perceptive retelling of the Odysseus legend in a modern setting.

The David Show. French 1966 o.p. A modern, comic version of the Biblical story of David and Bathsheba.

The Golden Fleece. French 1968 o.p. A comic here-and-now version of the ancient tragedy *Medea* of Euripides.

Love Letters and Two Other Plays: The Golden Age and What I Did Last Summer. NAL-Dutton 1990 $8.95. ISBN 0-452-26501-0. This companion to *The Cocktail Hour* offers three more comic dramas by one of the most readable contemporary American playwrights.

The Middle Ages. Dramatists Play 1978 o.p. Romantic comedy set in the trophy room of a snobbish men's club.

The Rape of Bunny Stuntz. French 1964 o.p. A suburban matron is lured into a liaison with an underworld intruder.

Scenes from American Life. French 1970 o.p. A critically acclaimed look at American hypocrisy.

Sweet Sue. Dramatists Play 1986 o.p. A comic tour de force in which two actors and two actresses portray various aspects of the same two characters.

The Wayside Motor Inn. Dramatists Play 1978 $3.95. ISBN 0-685-08727-1. Set in an antiseptic motel outside Boston, the play is an indictment of the impersonality and futility of modern American life.

HANSBERRY, LORRAINE. 1930–1965

The daughter of a well-to-do Chicago real estate man, Hansberry studied painting before venturing to New York in 1950, where she worked as a saleswoman, cashier, and assistant to an off-Broadway producer. She took courses in playwriting at the New School for Social Research and began to write seriously after her marriage to producer Robert Nemiroff. *A Raisin in the Sun* (1959), which brought her sudden success, was the warmly human story of an African-American family moving into a white neighborhood (as her father had done when she was eight). The title refers to LANGSTON HUGHES's poem: "What happens to a dream deferred? Does it dry up like a raisin in the sun?" *The Sign in Sidney Brustein's Window* (1965), about the moral problems of a Jewish intellectual in Greenwich Village, was written during Hansberry's final illness. She died of cancer.

PLAYS BY HANSBERRY

Les Blancs. French 1970 o.p. Confronts the effects of white colonialism in Africa.

Lorraine Hansberry: The Collected Last Plays. Ed. by Robert Nemiroff. NAL-Dutton 1983 $8.95. ISBN 0-452-25414-0. Three provocative and powerful dramas (*Les Blancs, The Driving Gourd,* and *What Use Are Flowers?*) edited by Hansberry's husband, Robert Nemiroff.

A Raisin in the Sun. NAL-Dutton 1959 $3.99. ISBN 0-451-16137-8. Story of a black family moving into a white neighborhood.

A Raisin in the Sun and The Sign in Sidney Brustein's Window. NAL-Dutton 1987 $8.95. ISBN 0-452-25942-8. Expanded twenty-fifth anniversary edition of Hansberry's two full-length plays.

The Sign in Sidney Brustein's Window. French 1965 o.p. A Jewish intellectual and his actress wife find meaning through commitment and activism.

To Be Young, Gifted and Black. NAL-Dutton 1989 $4.95. ISBN 0-317-02801-4. Biography adapted for the stage by Robert Nemiroff, reflecting the African-American experience.

BOOK ABOUT HANSBERRY

Cheney, Anne. *Lorraine Hansberry. Twayne's U.S. Authors Ser.* Macmillan 1984 $19.95. ISBN 0-8057-7365-7. A comprehensive overview of and introduction to Hansberry's life and work.

HELLMAN, LILLIAN. 1905–1984

Born in New Orleans, Hellman was educated at New York and Columbia universities and worked as a publisher's reader, book reviewer, and theater publicist before DASHIELL HAMMETT, her longtime friend and companion, encouraged her to write plays. The immediate result was her first success, *The Children's Hour* (1934), which was based on a nineteenth-century Scottish trial and concerned the financial and psychological destruction of two teachers at a girls' boarding school after a malicious child convinces her wealthy grandmother that they are lesbians. In subsequent plays Hellman focuses on antilabor violence—*Days to Come* (1936)—and the threat of fascism—*Watch on the Rhine* (1941) and *The Searching Wind* (1944). Her best plays, *The Little Foxes* (1939) and *Another Part of the Forest* (1946), brilliantly combine comedy and melodrama to attack greed and rapacity through the story of the avaricious Hubbard clan of the turn-of-the-century South. Hellman's other important plays include *The Autumn Garden* (1951), a Chekhovian play about people with unfulfilled lives, and *Toys in the Attic* (1960), which dramatizes a young man's difficult escape from his possessive sisters. In later years Hellman became a distinguished memoirist. Concerning her plays, Robert Corrigan wrote, "In a realistic style, characteristic of Ibsen, she writes of the conflicts of personal morality and their public consequences. . . . In each of her plays she raspingly attacks both the doers of evil and those who stand by and watch them do it."

Hellman won the New York Drama Critics Circle Award for *Watch on the Rhine* and *Toys in the Attic*.

PLAYS BY HELLMAN

Another Part of the Forest. Dramatists Play 1946 o.p. Revenge on a family tyrant in this hard-hitting sequel to *The Little Foxes*.

The Children's Hour. Dramatists Play 1934 o.p. The story of a malicious child's lies and the two schoolteachers whose lives are ruined by them.

The Collected Plays. Little 1972 $25.00. ISBN 0-316-35519-4. Includes *The Children's Hour* (1934); *Days to Come* (1936); *The Little Foxes* (1939); *Watch on the Rhine* (1941); *The Searching Wind* (1944); *Another Part of the Forest* (1946); *Montserrat* (a 1950 adaptation of a play by Emmanuel Robles); *The Autumn Garden* (1951); *The Lark* (a 1955 adaptation of a play by JEAN ANOUILH); *Candide* (a 1956 book of a coauthored musical); *Toys in the Attic* (1960); *My Mother, My Father and Me* (1963).

The Little Foxes. Dramatists 1939 o.p. Members of a post-Civil War family struggle unscrupulously with one another for the family wealth.

Six Plays by Lillian Hellman: The Children's Hour, Days to Come, The Little Foxes, Watch on the Rhine, Another Part of the Forest, The Autumn Garden. Random 1979 $13.00. ISBN 0-394-74112-9

Toys in the Attic. Dramatists Play 1960 o.p. About two sisters who dream of touring Europe and the ne'er-do-well brother who ruins their plans.

Watch on the Rhine. Dramatists Play 1941 o.p. Story of a leader of the anti-Nazi underground who is forced to kill a Nazi agent.

NONFICTION BY HELLMAN

Three: An Unfinished Woman, Pentimento, Scoundrel Time. Little 1980 $18.95. ISBN 0-316-35511-9. The complete texts of her important memoirs, with new commentaries by the author.

BOOKS ABOUT HELLMAN

Falk, Doris V. *Lillian Hellman*. Continuum 1978 o.p. A comprehensive overview and introduction to Hellman's plays and memoirs.

Lederer, Katherine. *Lillian Hellman*. Macmillan 1979 $21.95. ISBN 0-8057-7275-8. An excellent introduction to Hellman's life and works, with corrections of previous misreadings.

HENLEY, BETH. 1952–

Henley was born in Jackson, Mississippi, and received a B.F.A. in drama from Southern Methodist University. She achieved popular and critical success with *Crimes of the Heart*, which was produced at the Actors Theatre in Louisville in 1979, off-Broadway in 1980, and on Broadway in 1981. It concerns a "bad day" in the lives of three eccentric sisters, Meg, Lenny, and Babe, the last of whom has shot her husband because she "didn't like his looks." Henley's blend of naturalism combined with absurdist comedy and off-beat humor is also evident in *The Miss Firecracker Contest* (1979), in which members of a small-town family become embroiled in the efforts of one of them to win a beauty contest. Henley won the Pulitzer Prize for drama and the New York Drama Critics Circle Award for *Crimes of the Heart*.

Henley's later work includes *Abundance*, a much wider-ranging play than her earlier efforts. Its chronicle of women's lives in the Old West takes on the ugly side of Manifest Destiny, including the brutal treatment of Native Americans, the casualties of individualism, and the oppression of women.

PLAYS BY HENLEY

Abundance. Dramatists Play 1990 $4.75. ISBN 0-8222-0005-8. Deceptively optimistic story of women in the Old West.

Am I Blue. Dramatists Play 1972 o.p. Offbeat one-act in which a college freshman is accosted by a tantalizing young student.

Crimes of the Heart. Dramatists Play 1982 $3.95. ISBN 0-686-92580-7. Hilarious family troubles including Babe being out on bail after shooting her husband.

The Miss Firecracker Contest. Dramatists Play 1985 $3.95. ISBN 0-317-19748-7. The hilarious but ultimately bittersweet preparations for a Fourth of July beauty competition.

The Wake of Jamey Foster. Dramatists Play 1982 o.p. Offbeat humor at the wake of a man killed by a cow.

HOROVITZ, ISRAEL. 1939–

Born in Wakefield, Massachusetts, Horovitz completed an unpublished novel at the tender age of 13. Since then he has written some four dozen plays that have been translated into many languages. *The Indian Wants the Bronx* (1968) won an Obie and the Vernon Rice Award and established him as an absurdist in the Beckett–Ionesco tradition. His more recent plays have focused less on urban violence and more on Jewish family life and small-town problems. His plays have been frequently produced both internationally and in America's regional and college theaters. He is the first American to have been honored as playwright-in-residence at the Royal Shakespeare Company in England.

PLAYS BY HOROVITZ

The Chopin Playoffs. Dramatists Play 1987 o.p. The third play of the poignant Torgov trilogy, with young piano prodigies competing for a non-Jewish girl.

The Indian Wants the Bronx. Dramatists Play 1968 o.p. A powerful study of pointless violence directed toward a foreigner.

The Primary English Class. Dramatists Play 1976 $3.95. ISBN 0-685-77039-7. Hilarious comedy about a young teacher trying to teach basic English to a class of immigrants.

A Rosen by Any Other Name. Dramatists Play 1987 $3.95. ISBN 0-317-60251-9. The second of the Torgov trilogy, focusing on anti-Semitism.

Today, I Am a Fountain Pen. Dramatists Play 1987 o.p. Based on stories by Morley Torgov, the first of a trilogy dealing with Jewish home life in Ontario.

HWANG, DAVID HENRY. 1957–

The son of immigrant Chinese parents, Hwang attended Stanford University and the Yale Drama School and has been a director and a teacher of playwriting. *FOB* (1981), which stands for "Fresh off the boat,'" explores the conflicts between two Chinese Americans and a Chinese exchange student still steeped in the customs and beliefs of the old world. It won an Obie Award in 1981. *The Dance and the Railroad* (1982) concerns an artist and his fellow workers who stage a strike to protest the inhuman conditions suffered by Chinese railroad workers in the American West in the nineteenth century. *M Butterfly* (1988), about the relationship between an American man and a Chinese transvestite, won the Tony Award as best play of the year. MAXINE HONG KINGSTON wrote, "David Hwang has an ear for Chinatown English, the language of childhood and the subconscious, the language of emotion, the language of home."

PLAYS BY HWANG

The Dance and the Railroad and *Family Devotions*. Dramatists Play 1983 o.p. *Devotions* deals with the conflict between a Christianized Chinese-American family and a "pagan" relative.

FOB and *The House of Sleeping Beauties*. Dramatists Play 1983 o.p. *Sleeping Beauties* is a brilliant fantasy set in a bizarre brothel.

M Butterfly. NAL-Dutton 1989 $7.95. ISBN 0-452-26230-5. Strange tale of a French diplomat who carries on a twenty-year relationship with a Chinese opera star who turns out to be a man.

The Sound of a Voice. Dramatists Play 1984 o.p. One-act about a love affair between a samurai and a mysterious woman who gives him shelter.

INGE, WILLIAM (MOTTER). 1913–1973

Inge was born in Independence, Kansas, attended the University of Kansas and Peabody College in Nashville, Tennessee, and studied theater with Maude Adams at Stephens College in Columbia, Missouri. He taught drama for some years and then served as drama critic for the St. Louis *Star Times* before becoming a playwright. *Come Back, Little Sheba* (1950), his first success on Broadway, is about an aging couple, the wife clinging to the past, the husband an alcoholic. His next play was *Picnic* (1953, later revised as *Summer Brave*), about a virile young drifter and his effect on women in a small town. *Bus Stop* (1955) involves stranded people—each reveals his or her loneliness, and in the end an aspiring singer accepts the attention of a naive but rough cowboy. *The Dark at the Top of the Stairs* (1958) portrays a frustrated family in which a stranger's suicide inspires a new understanding between the mother and father and more confidence on the part of the son and daughter.

Inge was immensely popular in the 1950s. In most of his plays, the characters live a humdrum existence, usually in the Kansas-Oklahoma region of 50 years ago. Behind the naturalistic dialogue is an inner softness, and the main figures are prone to confession. His works have been called "psycho-dramas involving the solution of personal and social problems by introspection and togetherness" (Eric Mottram).

Inge won the Pulitzer Prize for drama and the New York Drama Critics Circle Award for *Picnic*. The later part of Inge's career as a dramatist was not successful. He took his own life in 1973.

PLAYS BY INGE

Bus Stop. Dramatists Play 1955 o.p. A rough-hewn cowboy must learn how to woo and win a woman.

Come Back, Little Sheba. French 1950 o.p.

The Dark at the Top of the Stairs. Dramatists Play 1958 o.p. A family story set in Oklahoma showing the power of tolerance, compassion, and love.

Eleven One-Act Plays. Dramatists Play 1962 o.p. Contains *To Bobolink, for Her Spirit; A Social Event; The Boy in the Basement; The Tiny Closet; Memory of Summer; The Rainy Afternoon; The Mall; An Incident at the Standish Arms; People in the Wind; Bus Riley's Back in Town; The Strains of Triumph*.

Four Plays. Grove Pr. 1990 $9.95. ISBN 0-8021-3209-X. Contains *Come Back, Little Sheba; Picnic; Bus Stop; The Dark at the Top of the Stairs*.

A Loss of Roses. Dramatists Play 1960 o.p. A midwestern Depression story of lost love.

Picnic. Dramatists Play 1953 o.p.

Summer Brave. Dramatists Play 1962 $3.95. ISBN 0-686-62807-1. The rewritten and final version of the romantic comedy *Picnic*.

JONES, PRESTON. 1936–1979

Texas playwright Preston Jones was one of the more important figures who, in the 1970s, helped to break New York's grip on the American theater. His acting, directing, and playwriting career at the Dallas Theatre Center was one part of a national mosaic of regional theatres that were successfully rebelling against the commercial offerings of Broadway. His best known work, *A Texas Trilogy* (1976), received rave reviews from audiences in Dallas and in Washington, D.C., before moving on to other major cities. Jones received national attention in September 1976 with the repertory presentation of *A Texas Trilogy* on Broadway.

Set in Bradleyville, a small town in West Texas, the three plays show the effects of time on the people who are caught there. *The Last Meeting of the Knights of the White Magnolia* (1976) is a comic masterpiece depicting the final throes of an outmoded and racist fraternal order. *Lu Ann Hampton Laverty Oberlander* (1977) is the epic story of a woman who sacrifices her dreams of faraway places for the realities of life in a small town. *The Oldest Living Graduate* (1976) depicts a cantankerous veteran of World War I who resents growing old and who resists the loss of ideals to expediency.

Jones's other plays also focus on the theme of time. *A Place on the Magdalena Flats* (1976) explores the growing discord between a hard-working rancher and his misfit younger brother. *Santa Fe Sunshine* (1977) is a warm-hearted comedy about an untalented sculptor who believes that at long last he has created a great work of art. Jones's final play, *Remember,* focuses on the experiences of a single day in the life of an aging actor. This unpublished work, which raises philosophical questions about mortality, opened just over a month before the playwright's own untimely death at the age of 43.

During his career, Preston Jones received the Rockefeller Foundation Playwright-in-Residence Fellowship (1975), the Golden Apple Award from *Cue* (1976), the Outer Critics Circle Award (1977), and the Drama Desk Award (1977). His plays continue to be popular in community, university, and regional theaters.

PLAYS BY JONES

The Last Meeting of the Knights of the White Magnolia. Dramatists Play 1976 $3.95. ISBN 0-685-81643-5. A comic masterpiece about a fraternity of aging "good ole boys."
Lu Ann Hampton Laverty Oberlander. Dramatists Play 1977 $3.95. ISBN 0-685-081645-1. Epic tale of a small-town woman who sacrifices her dreams.
The Oldest Living Graduate. Dramatists Play $3.95. ISBN 0-685-81647-8. A humorous portrait of a cantankerous but lovable World War I veteran.
A Place on the Magdalena Flats. Dramatists Play 1984 o.p. A gripping story about a stern rancher and his misfit brother.
Santa Fe Sunshine. Dramatists Play 1977 o.p. A warm-hearted comedy about a not-so-talented sculptor and a bumbling painter.

BOOK ABOUT JONES

Bennett, Patrick, *Talking with Texas Writers: Twelve Interviews.* TX A&M U. Pr. 1980 $9.95. ISBN 0-89096-105-0. Discusses Jones's writing habits and includes anecdotal material about his life.

KAUFMAN, GEORGE S. 1889–1961

Kaufman, who was born in Pittsburgh, attended law school for two years, failed as a business person, and became a humorist for Franklin P. Adams's column before joining the *New York Times,* whose drama editor he became in the 1920s. Kaufman was sole author of one long play and two one-act plays, including the popular *The Butter and Egg Man* (1926), but he collaborated on more than 25 plays, most importantly with Moss Hart, but also with Marc Connelly, Edna Ferber, and others, including RING LARDNER and John P. Marquand. These plays range from the hilarious madness of *Cocoanuts* (1929) and *Animal Crackers* (1928), two MARX BROTHERS (see Vol. 3) shows that Kaufman worked on, to the comic pathos of *Stage Door* (1936) (with Edna Ferber). In all of them, Kaufman's distinctive touch was what Brooks Atkinson called "the destructive wisecrack" or "the verbal ricochet." John Gassner wrote of Kaufman and his collaborators that they "have been marvelous recorders of American surfaces" but in their critical outlook they "were either disinclined or unable to carry it to conclusions. . . . Their flippancy [was] amusing and at worst just a trifle too empty." Commenting on why he did not write true satire, Kaufman said, "Satire is what closes Saturday night." Kaufman, Morris Ryskind, and Ira Gershwin won the Pulitzer Prize for drama for *Of Thee I Sing* (1932) and Kaufman and Hart for *You Can't Take It with You* (1937).

PLAYS BY KAUFMAN

Animal Crackers. French 1928 o.p. Musical collaboration with Morris Ryskind featuring Marx Brothers lunacy.

Dinner at Eight. French 1932 o.p. An Edna Ferber collaboration showing the jealousy, greed, and ruin beneath the upper-class characters' suave exteriors.

Dulay. French 1921 o.p. A Marc Connelly collaboration about a disastrous, comic weekend party.

George S. Kaufman and His Collaborators: Three Plays. Performing Arts 1984 o.p. Contains *June Moon* (with RING LARDNER); *Bravo* (with Edna Ferber); *The Late George Apley* (with John P. Marquand).

George Washington Slept Here. Dramatists Play 1940 o.p. Moss Hart collaboration; concerns the tribulations of a family that buys a little place out in the country.

Merton of the Movies. French 1922 o.p. A Marc Connelly collaboration that presents a comic commentary on motion pictures.

Once in a Lifetime, You Can't Take It with You, The Man Who Came to Dinner: Three Plays. Grove Pr. 1980 o.p. Collaborations with Moss Hart.

Of Thee I Sing. French 1932 o.p. A Pulitzer prize-winning musical collaboration with Morris Ryskind and Ira Gershwin.

The Royal Family. French 1928 o.p. Interesting collaboration with Edna Ferber about a great family of the American stage and their manic adventures.

The Solid Gold Cadillac. Dramatists Play 1954 o.p. Howard Teichman collaboration that comically critiques the management of a large corporation.

Stage Door. Dramatists Play 1936 o.p. Edna Ferber collaboration about a boarding house full of women who have come to New York to become actors.

You Can't Take It with You. Dramatists Play 1937 o.p. Moss Hart collaboration about the Sycamores—a delightful madcap family.

BOOK ABOUT KAUFMAN

Goldstein, Malcolm. *George S. Kaufman: His Life, His Theater*. OUP 1979 o.p. "A substantial, diligently researched work . . . certain to prove valuable to students of the American theater . . . " (Seymour Peck, *NY Times*).

KELLY, GEORGE EDWARD. 1887–1974

A member of Philadelphia's famous Kelly clan and the uncle of the late Princess Grace of Monaco, Kelly's reputation was made by three of his plays from the 1920s. *The Torch-Bearers* (1922) pokes fun at amateur theater groups; *The Show-Off* (1924) is a classic presentation of the bragger; *Craig's Wife* (1926) is a study of a woman who loves her home and position more than she does her husband. "Kelly points out the follies and ludicrous behavior of his times with a crabbed cynicism that would do credit to BEN JONSON if it did not lack Jonson's raucous gusto" (*Sievers*). Kelly won a Pulitzer Prize for drama for *Craig's Wife*.

PLAYS BY KELLY

Craig's Wife. French 1926 o.p. A selfish woman who succeeds in driving her husband, friends, and relatives out of her home.

Daisy Mayme. French 1926 o.p. Delightful comedy about an unmarried woman who comes into a man's home, teaches him how to have fun, then marries him.

The Fatal Weakness. French 1947 o.p. Urbane comedy that criticizes romantic love, marriage, and infidelity.

The Show-Off. French 1924 o.p. Comedy of character about an obnoxious egoist.

The Torch-Bearers. French 1922 o.p. Clever satire on amateur dramatics.

KOPIT, ARTHUR. 1937–

Born in New York, Kopit won a scholarship to Harvard University to study electrical engineering but found that his main interest was playwriting. Shortly after graduation, he wrote *Oh Dad, Poor Dad, Mamma's Hung You in the Closet and I'm Feeling So Sad* (1960), an absurdist play about an overprotective mother who travels not only with her son, but with two Venus's-flytraps and the remains of her husband, in an obvious parody of TENNESSEE WILLIAMS's *Suddenly Last Summer*. *Indians* (1969), a more ambitious play, depicts in epic style Buffalo Bill who, caught in an ambivalent position between the government and the Indians, comes to represent both the nemesis of the American Indian and the untroubled American conscience. *Wings* (1978) concerns a former aviatrix and stunt pilot who suffers a stroke and gradually regains language and, through it, contact with the world. Kopit has also written the book for the successful musical *Nine* (1983) and adapted IBSEN's *Ghosts* for Liv Ullman. Gautam Dasgupta has observed of Kopit, "Like the absurdists before him, he chooses to depict a horrific world where logic holds no sway."

PLAYS BY KOPIT

The Day the Whores Came Out to Play Tennis and Other Plays. Hill & Wang 1965 o.p. Contains *Chamber Music; The Questioning of Nick; Sing to Me through Open Windows; The Hero; The Conquest of Everest*.

The End of the World. Hill & Wang 1984 $8.95. ISBN 0-8090-1247-2. Comic play about the nuclear peril.

Indians. Hill & Wang 1969 $5.70. ISBN 0-8090-1218-9. About a Wild West show that offers America's apology to the Indians for having exploited them.

Nine. French 1983 o.p. Musical based on Fellini's classic movie *8 ½*, with score and lyrics by Maury Yeston.

Oh Dad, Poor Dad, Mamma's Hung You in the Closet and I'm Feeling So Sad. Hill & Wang 1960 $7.95. ISBN 0-8090-1202-2. Absurdist comedy about a wealthy widow and her son who arrive at a hotel with a ton of luggage, priceless plants, a coffin, and a fish bowl with a live piranha.

Road to Nirvana. Hill & Wang 1991 $18.95. ISBN 0-8090-8242-X. A thinly disguised Madonna (Nirvana) wants her life story on film.

Wings. Hill & Wang 1978 $7.95. ISBN 0-8090-1239-1. Powerful drama from the point of view of a stroke victim who has lost contact with the world.

LINNEY, ROMULUS. 1930–

Born in Philadelphia and reared in North Carolina, Linney is an actor, director, novelist, and playwright who has achieved wide respect if not fame. His plays are often produced off-Broadway and in America's burgeoning regional theaters. He has also enjoyed success in Great Britain, Canada, Germany, and Austria.

A number of Linney's plays are set in the South and are noted for their Faulknerian humor. Other of his works focus on historical figures such as Jesus Christ, Frederick the Great, and LORD BYRON. His themes deal with social and personal values, religion, and death. Although his plots are sometimes melodramatic, his accurate and perceptive portrayals of the human condition have earned him praise.

Linney's first stage play, *The Sorrows of Frederick* (1967), is a psychological study of the historic figure Frederick William II, the eighteenth-century king of Prussia. *The Love Suicide at Schofield Barracks* (1972) is about an army general and his wife who commit suicide as a protest against the Vietnam War. Linney's first southern play, *Holy Ghosts* (1974), focuses on a Pentecostal sect that requires its members to handle poisonous snakes. *Laughing Stock* (1984) is set in different regions of the South and is composed of three one-acts: *Goodbye, Howard* portrays a North Carolina hospital where several quarrelsome sisters await the death of their brother; *Tennessee* dramatizes a woman's return to her childhood home; and *F.M.* depicts a young writer enrolled in an Alabama college.

Linney's most recent plays have been lighthearted in tone and have been mounted with simplicity and economy. *Pops* (1986) is composed of six vignettes dealing with romantic love and structured around six famous melodies performed by the Boston Pops Orchestra. *Heathen Valley*, adapted from his first novel, was performed in 1987 as a part of the Philadelphia Festival for New Plays. The work, which is set in the mountains of North Carolina, was staged very simply with fiddles and dulcimers providing a musical background and the actors evoking the landscape.

Linney's critical recognition includes a 1974 National Endowment for the Arts Fellowship in playwriting, a 1980 Guggenheim Fellowship, a 1984 Award in Literature from the American Academy and Institute of Arts and Letters, and a 1986 Rockefeller Foundation Fellowship. Linney also received the coveted Obie Award in 1980 for his play *Tennessee*. In 1990 a number of his plays were featured at a New York theater, the first time this had been done for a playwright.

PLAYS BY LINNEY

Childe Byron. Dramatists Play 1981 o.p. A brilliant, searing, and witty portrait of the controversial historical figure Lord Byron.

Holy Ghosts. Dramatists Play 1976 o.p. A striking, often humorous, and moving study of a snake-handling cult.

Laughing Stock. Dramatists Play 1984 $3.95. ISBN 0-317-17219-0. Three highly entertaining short plays set in the South.

The Love Suicide at Schofield Barracks. A Play in Two Acts. Dramatists Play 1976 $4.50. A probing courtroom drama that makes a profound statement about war.

Old Man Joseph and His Family. Dramatists Play 1978 o.p. A warm-hearted, amusing, and colorful interpretation of Biblical figures and events.

Pops. Dramatists Play 1987 $4.75. ISBN 0-8222-0906-3. Popular music underscores this collection of short plays dealing with love.

The Sorrows of Frederick. Dramatists Play 1968 o.p. A psychological tour de force presenting high points from the life of a philosopher-king.

The Sorrows of Frederick and *Holy Ghosts*. HarBraceJ 1977 $3.95. ISBN 0-15-683848-6. Two of Linney's most popular plays

A Woman Without a Name. Dramatists Play 1986 $3.95. ISBN 0-317-52991-9

NOVELS BY LINNEY

Heathen Valley. Atheneum 1962 o.p. An absorbing picture of nineteenth-century life in the western mountains of North Carolina.

Jesus Tales. North Point Pr. 1980 o.p. A humorous and perceptive view of the story of Jesus.

Slowly, By Thy Hand Unfurled. HarBraceJ 1965 o.p. Lays bare the tormented soul of a woman whose love for her children was ignorant, possessive, and perhaps destructive.

McCULLERS, CARSON. 1917–1967

Born Lula Carson Smith, McCullers grew up in Columbus, Georgia, and began writing at age 16. Well known for her early novels written in her twenties, she also composed two plays: *The Member of the Wedding* (1951) and *The Square Root of Wonderful* (1958).

Based on her 1946 novel, *The Member of the Wedding* is a poignant study of a motherless 12-year-old, Frankie Addams, who lives in a small southern town. Ignored by her peers, she spends her summer afternoons with her seven-year-old cousin, John Henry, and with the earthy African-American maid, Berenice. Troubled by being "just an 'I' person," Frankie longs to belong to a "we." The theme of the play is loneliness and its central action is Frankie's struggle to make a connection with others. In the third act Frankie is ejected from her brother's car as he and his bride leave on their honeymoon. John Henry dies. By the end of the play, the girl has made friends with her peers, but Berenice is left alone in an empty kitchen, her own sense of loneliness irrevocably heightened as Frankie's unique individuality appears to be slipping away.

A beautiful and powerful piece in the tradition of CHEKHOV (see Vol. 2), *The Member of the Wedding* enjoyed tremendous popular success. In 1950, the New York Drama Critics Circle voted it the best play of the season. Critics praised the play for its haunting evocation of adolescence and saw it as reflecting the theater's general trend toward mood and away from action.

In *The Square Root of Wonderful*, McCullers again pursued the theme of loneliness and the need for acceptance, but the play was not so successful as the earlier work. The play's life–death theme, moreover, may have been an attempt to exorcise the playwright's guilt over the death of her husband, Reeves McCullers, who committed suicide in France in 1953.

While *The Square Root of Wonderful* suggested that McCullers was a better novelist than playwright, the continuing success of *The Member of the Wedding* has assured her permanent recognition as an American dramatist.

PLAYS BY MCCULLERS

The Member of the Wedding. Dramatists Play 1951 $5.95. Portrait of an adolescent girl in Georgia.

The Square Root of Wonderful. French 1958 $15.00. Shows that offered love cannot always save a person who chooses death.

NOVELS BY MCCULLERS

The Ballad of the Sad Cafe. Bantam 1991 $8.50. ISBN 0-553-35423-X. A grotesque novella of love and violence in a small southern town; adapted for the stage by EDWARD ALBEE in 1963.

The Heart Is a Lonely Hunter. Bantam 1970 $3.95. ISBN 0-553-25481-2. A realistic portrayal of a small mill town in the South.

The Member of the Wedding. 1951 New. Dir. Pr. 1963 $5.95. ISBN 0-8112-0093-0. Southern in setting, the novel deals with solitude.

BOOKS ABOUT MCCULLERS

Carr, Virginia Spencer. *The Lonely Heart: A Biography of Carson McCullers*. Doubleday 1975 o.p. Exhaustive amount of biographical material.

―――. *Understanding Carson McCullers*. *Understanding Contemporary American Literature Series*. U. of SC Pr. 1989 $24.95. ISBN 0-87249-661-9. Provides an overall view of the career of McCullers.

Evans, Oliver. *The Ballad of Carson McCullers*. Coward 1966 o.p. Excellent analysis of the author's works.

McNALLY, TERRENCE. 1939–

Born in St. Petersburg, Florida, and raised in Corpus Christi, Texas, McNally majored in journalism at Columbia University. Following graduation, he turned to playwriting and by the 1968–1969 season had established himself as a major comic writer. His bleak outlook and biting humor were not always appreciated by the critics, however. His early works, such as *And Things Go Bump in the Night* (1966), exhibit anger and frustration and are often about violence and cruelty. More recent works such as *Frankie and Johnny in the Claire de Lune* (1987), while still humorous, have tended toward lyricism and joy. *Lips Together, Teeth Apart* (1992) is more naturalistic than McNally's previous works. It affords greater space for the actors' interpretation and provides an emotional seesaw for audiences despite its rather prosaic and somber appearance on the written page. As a social satirist, McNally is considered one of America's most brilliant and original playwrights.

PLAYS BY McNALLY

And Things Go Bump in the Night. In *Playwrights for Tomorrow: A Collection of Plays, I*. U. of MN Pr. 1966; Dramatists Play 1966 $4.50 o.p. Bizarre story of a family that seeks sanctuary from a sinister world by barricading itself in a cellar.

Frankie and Johnny in the Claire de Lune. NAL-Dutton 1991 $6.95. ISBN 0-452-26884-2. A bittersweet comedy about an unlikely romance between two middle-aged "failures."

It's Only a Play. Dramatists Play 1982 o.p. A bizarre and humorous sendup of show business.

Lips Together, Teeth Apart. NAL-Dutton 1992 $8.00. ISBN 0-452-26807-9. Two couples, related by marriage, spend a July 4 weekend at the Fire Island Beach House that one of them has inherited from a brother who recently died of AIDS.

Sweet Eros. In *Off-Broadway Plays 2*. Viking Penguin 1972 o.p. Explores the dark mind of a man who kidnaps and enslaves an innocent girl.

MAMET, DAVID. 1947–

Mamet was born in Chicago and while still in high school worked as a busboy at Chicago's famed Second City, a comedy improvisation cabaret. He was educated at Goddard College, where, as drama instructor and artist-in-residence, he subsequently produced some of his early plays. Others were produced in Chicago, and he still tends to present his work there first, especially at the Goodman Theatre, for which he became associate director and playwright-in-residence in 1978.

Mamet's work reached New York in 1975 with an off-off-Broadway production of two short plays, *The Duck Variations* (1977), in which two old men sit on a park bench and discuss ducks and life, and *Sexual Perversity in Chicago* (1977), concerned with the fundamental emptiness in the sexual relations of four pseudosophisticated young people. Mamet has subsequently produced a number of significant works, among them *American Buffalo* (1976), in which three small-time crooks plot in a Chicago junkshop to rob a man of his coin collection; *A Life in the Theatre* (1977), in which two actors—one old, the other young—perform, rehearse, discuss, and debate their work; and *Glengarry Glen Ross* (1984), which shows real-estate men hustling and competing with one another for sales leads. Most of Mamet's plays explore the pervasiveness and destructiveness of the American dream. He has been praised for the economy and marvelous accuracy of his dialogue and faulted for his lack of control over plot and structure.

Mamet won the Pulitzer Prize for drama in 1984 for *Glengarry Glen Ross* and the New York Drama Critics Circle Award in 1977 for *American Buffalo*. Among his most recent plays is the well-received drama, *Speed-the-Plow* (1988), a powerful satire of Hollywood and American culture.

PLAYS BY MAMET

American Buffalo. Grove Pr. 1988 $6.95. ISBN 0-8021-5057-8. Award-winning play about three small-time crooks in a Chicago junk shop.

Dramatic Sketches and Monologues. French 1985 o.p. Includes *Five Unrelated Pieces, The Power Outage, The Dog, Film Crew, 4 A.M., Food, Pint's a Pound the World Around, Deer Dogs, Columbus Avenue, Conversations with the Spirit World, Maple Sugaring, Morris and Joe, Steve McQueen, Yes, Dowsing, In the Mall, Cross Patch, Goldberg Street.*

The Duck Variations. French 1977 o.p. Comedy about two old men who discuss the ways of ducks.

Edmond. French 1983 o.p. A reverse-image morality play in which Edmond descends into big-city degradation in search of sexual gratification.

Five Television Plays. Grove Pr. 1990 $12.95. ISBN 0-8021-3171-9. Contains *A Waitress in Yellowstone, Bradford, The Museum of Science and Industry Story, A Wasted Weekend, We Will Take You There.*

Glengarry Glen Ross. Grove Pr. 1988 $7.95. ISBN 0-8021-3091-7. Pulitzer Prize-winning, scalding drama about real estate sales agents.

Goldberg Street: Short Plays and Monologues. Grove Pr. 1989 $9.95. ISBN 0-8021-5104-3. Contains *Goldberg Street, Cross Patch, Two Conversations, Two Scenes, Yes But So What, Conversations with the Spirit World, Pint's a Pound the World Around, Dowsing, Deer Dogs, In the Mall, Maple Sugaring, Morris and Joe, The Dog, Film Crew, Four A.M., The Power Outage, Food, Columbus Avenue, Steve McQueen, Yes, The Blue Hour, City Sketches, A Sermon, Shoeshine, Litko: A Dramatic Monologue, In Old Vermont, All Men Are Whores: An Inquiry.*

Homicide: A Screenplay. Grove Pr. 1992 $8.95. ISBN 0-8021-3308-8

Lakeboat. French 1981 o.p. Poetic vignettes focusing on the crew aboard a Great Lakes steamer.

A Life in the Theatre. Grove Pr. 1977 $9.95. ISBN 0-8021-5067-5. A comedy about an older actor and an eager novice.

Mr. Happiness. French 1978 $4.50. Curtain-raiser to *The Water Engine*, the play is set in a 1930s radio station.

Reunion and *Dark Pony.* Grove Pr. 1990 $8.95. ISBN 0-8021-5171-X. A bill of one-acts about the dislocation of male/female relationships.

Sexual Perversity in Chicago. French 1977 o.p. "A glittering mosaic of tiny, deadly muzzle-flashes from the war between men and women among the filing cabinets and single bars" (*NY Times*).

Sexual Perversity in Chicago and *The Duck Variations.* Grove Pr. 1977 $7.95. ISBN 0-8021-5011-X. Two short plays.

The Shawl & Prairie du Chien. Grove Pr. 1985 $6.95. ISBN 0-8021-5172-8. Includes *The Shawl*, the story of a medium who is also a charlatan, and *Prairie du Chien*, a short play for six men.

Some Freaks. Viking Penguin 1991 $7.95. ISBN 0-14-012434-9

Speed-the-Plow. Grove Pr. 1988 $6.95. ISBN 0-8021-1028-2

Squirrels. French 1982 o.p. A one-act; "rollicking, frolicking, nonetheless tender excursion into the forbidding realm of literary creativity" (Mamet).

Three Children's Plays. Grove Pr. 1986 $8.95. ISBN 0-8021-5173-6. Includes *The Poet and the Rent*, *The Frog Prince*, and *The Revenge of the Space Pandas*.

The Water Engine: An American Fable. French 1978 o.p. Brilliant radio play within a play about the murder of a young inventor.

We're No Angels. Grove Pr. 1990 $17.95. ISBN 0-8021-3202-2

The Woods. French 1979 o.p. About two lovers who spend the night in a cabin, grow apart, quarrel, then cling to each other from need.

The Woods, Lakeboat, and *Edmond*. Grove Pr. 1987 $10.95. ISBN 0-8021-5109-4

POETRY BY MAMET

The Hero Pony. Grove Pr. 1991 $16.95. ISBN 0-8021-1221-8. Collection of poetry that should be of interest to Mamet fans as a gloss to his career as a playwright.

MILLER, ARTHUR. 1915–

The son of a well-to-do New York Jewish family, Miller graduated from high school and then went to work in a warehouse. His plays have been called "political," but he considers the areas of literature and politics to be quite separate and has said, "The only sure and valid aim—speaking of art as a weapon—is the humanizing of man." The recurring theme of all his plays is the relationship between a man's identity and the image that society demands of him. After two years, he entered the University of Michigan, where he soon started writing plays.

All My Sons (1947), a Broadway success that won the New York Drama Critics Circle Award in 1947, tells the story of a son, home from the war, who learns that his brother's death was due to defective airplane parts turned out by their profiteering father. *Death of a Salesman* (1949), Miller's experimental yet classical American tragedy, received both the Pulitzer Prize and the New York Drama Critics Circle Award in 1949. It is a poignant statement of a man facing himself and his failure. In *The Crucible* (1953), a play about bigotry in the Salem witchcraft trials of 1692, Miller brings into focus the social tragedy of a society gone mad, as well as the agony of a heroic individual. The play was generally considered to be a comment on the McCarthyism of its time. Miller himself appeared before the Congressional Un-American Activities Committee and steadfastly refused to involve his friends and associates when questioned about them.

His screenplay for *The Misfits* (1961), from his short story, was written for his second wife, actress MARILYN MONROE (see Vol. 3); *After the Fall* (1964) has clear autobiographical overtones and involves the story of this ill-fated marriage as well as further dealing with Miller's experiences with McCarthyism. In the one-act *Incident at Vichy* (1964), a group of men are picked off the streets one morning during the Nazi occupation of France. *The Price* (1968) is a psychological drama concerning two brothers, one a police officer, one a wealthy surgeon, whose long-standing conflict is explored over the disposal of their father's furniture. *The Creation of the World and Other Business* (1973) is a retelling of the story of Genesis, attempted as a comedy. *The American Clock* (1980) explores the impact of the Depression on the nation and its individual citizens.

Among Miller's most recent works is *Danger: Memory!* (1987), a study of two elderly friends. During the 1980s, almost all of Miller's plays were given major

British revivals, and the playwright's work has been more popular in Britain than in the United States of late.

Plays by Miller

After the Fall. 1964. Viking Penguin 1980 $6.00. ISBN 0-14-048162-1. Powerful study of a contemporary man struggling to come to terms with himself.

All My Sons. Dramatists Play 1947 o.p. Powerful drama of war deaths caused by defective airplane parts.

The American Clock and *The Archbishop's Ceiling.* Grove Pr. 1980 $19.95. ISBN 0-8021-1085-1. A study of America's Great Depression; and an exploration of the problem of being an artist in a totalitarian country.

The Creation of the World and Other Business. Boulevard 1973 $16.95. ISBN 0-670-24616-6. Biblical parable that goes to the roots of human guilt and responsibility.

The Crucible. 1953. Viking Penguin 1976 $5.95. ISBN 0-14-048138-9

Danger: Memory! Grove Pr. 1987 $5.95. ISBN 0-8021-5176-0. Contains two one-acts: *I Can't Remember Anything*, a study of two elderly friends; and *Clara*, about an aging father's attempt to come to grips with his daughter's murder.

Death of a Salesman. 1949. Viking Penguin 1976 $5.95. ISBN 0-14-048134-6. Modern tragedy about the life of a failing salesman.

Elegy for a Lady. Dramatists Play 1982 o.p. Evocative one-act about the pain of love, loss, and rejection.

Everybody Wins. Grove Pr. 1990 $7.95. ISBN 0-8021-3200-6. Deals with a miscarriage of justice.

Incident at Vichy. 1964. Viking Penguin 1985 $4.95. ISBN 0-14-048193-1. An intense play dealing with the Nazis' mistreatment of the Jews.

A Memory of Two Mondays. 1955. Dramatists Play o.p. A long one-act set in an auto-parts warehouse; a mood piece.

The Price. 1968. Viking Penguin 1985 $6.00. ISBN 0-14-048194-X. Examines with compassion the relationship of two long-estranged brothers.

Some Kind of Love Story. Dramatists Play 1982 o.p. One-act naturalistic study of a detective, a prostitute, and undisclosed corruption in high places.

Up From Paradise. French 1974 o.p. Musical about Adam and Eve; music by Stanley Silverman.

A View from the Bridge. 1955. Viking Penguin 1977 $5.95. ISBN 0-14-048135-4. Tragedy about a longshoreman who opposes the marriage of his niece because of his own warped love for her.

Works by Miller

The Portable Arthur Miller. Ed. by Harold Clurman. Viking Penguin 1977 $9.95. ISBN 0-14-015071-4. Contains *Death of a Salesman; The Crucible;* selections from *The Misfits;* essays and poetry; critical introduction, chronology, bibliography and notes.

Books about Miller

Carson, Neil. *Arthur Miller.* St. Martin 1988 $12.95. ISBN 0-312-02381-2. A general study; opening chapter outlines Miller's life while subsequent chapters discuss his works.

Corrigan, Robert W., ed. *Arthur Miller: A Collection of Critical Essays.* P-H 1969 $12.95. ISBN 0-13-582973-9

Evans, Richard I. *Psychology and Arthur Miller.* Greenwood 1981 $38.50. ISBN 0-275-90620-5. A discussion between a psychologist and the dramatist.

Martine, James J. *Critical Essays on Arthur Miller.* Macmillan 1979 $40.00. ISBN 0-8161-8258-2

Moss, Leonard. *Arthur Miller. Twayne's U.S. Authors Ser.* Macmillan rev. ed. 1980 $19.95. ISBN 0-8057-7311-8. A view of Miller as more than a purely "social dramatist," who tries "to unify social and psychological perspectives" with mixed success.

Schlueter, June, and James K. Flanagan. *Arthur Miller.* Continuum 1987 $16.95. ISBN 0-8044-2797-6. A good general introduction to Miller's life and works, especially useful to the first-time reader of Miller, with a brief biography, a chronology, a bibliography, and extensive discussion of Miller's major plays.

NORMAN, MARSHA. 1947–

Norman was born in Louisville and educated at Agnes Scott College, the University of Louisville, and the Center for Understanding Media in New York City. She has been a schoolteacher and a journalist as well as a playwright. She wrote her first play, *Getting Out* (1978), a study of a woman ex-convict, for the Actors Theatre of Louisville, which also produced other plays of hers, including *Third and Oak* (1978) (consisting of two one-act plays, *The Laundromat* and *The Pool Hall*) and *The Circus Valentine* (1979). Her most successful play has been *'night, Mother* (1983), in which a mother and daughter examine the daughter's determination to kill herself. In 1985, *The Laundromat* was produced as a filmed drama for Home Box Office. Norman won the Pulitzer Prize for drama for *'night, Mother*.

PLAYS BY NORMAN

Four Plays. Theatre Comm. 1988 $10.95. ISBN 0-930452-84-4
Getting Out. Dramatists Play 1979 o.p. A young woman's attempts to cope following her release from prison.
The Holdup. Dramatists Play 1987 $3.95. ISBN 0-317-59787-6. Antic tale about an aging outlaw during World War I era.
'night, Mother. FS&G 1988 $8.95. ISBN 0-374-52138-7. A young woman's decision that life is no longer worth living, and her mother's attempts to keep her alive.
Third and Oak: The Laundromat. Dramatists Play 1980 o.p. A probing study of two lonely women who meet in a late-night laundromat.
Third and Oak: The Pool Hall. Dramatists Play 1985 o.p. A successful young African American, an aging white pool-hall owner, and the confrontation they work through.

ODETS, CLIFFORD. 1906–1963

With LILLIAN HELLMAN, Odets remains one of the foremost U.S. dramatists of the 1930s. Born in Philadelphia, he became an actor about 1923 and joined the Group Theatre upon its founding in 1930. From then until its collapse in 1940, the Group Theatre produced seven plays by Odets, all of which reflect the Depression era in which they· were written. His first play, *Waiting for Lefty* (1935), an agitprop play about strikers, was an enormous success. Most of his other plays of the 1930s, most notably *Awake and Sing* (1935) and *Paradise Lost* (1935), concern the economic and psychological plight of poor New York City Jewish families and heighten middle-class Jewish speech into a kind of poetry. After the collapse of the Group Theatre, Odets produced only four more plays. Malcolm Goldstein wrote, "The plays of Odets are marked by a strong social sympathy that tended, no matter the political fashion of the year, to divide humanity into two classes: the exploiters and the exploited." Harold Clurman observed that Odets's "central theme was the difficulty of attaining maturity in a world where money as a token of success . . . plays so dominant a role." Odets was criticized, however, for betraying his leftist sympathies when he named names before the House Un-American Activities Committee during the McCarthy era.

PLAYS BY ODETS

The Big Knife. Dramatists Play 1949 o.p. Tells of the last days of a movie star whose years of compromise have slowly destroyed him.

The Country Girl. Dramatists Play 1950 o.p. A loving wife's long years of devotion to her
   actor husband—which nearly destroy her.
The Flowering Peach. Dramatists Play 1954 o.p. A folk poem—a retelling of the Biblical
   story of Noah and the ark.
Golden Boy. Dramatists Play 1935 o.p. Tragedy about a young Italian American who plays
   the violin but ruins his hands in a prizefight.
Six Plays of Clifford Odets. Grove Pr. 1988 $10.95. ISBN 0-8021-5060-8. Contains *Waiting
   for Lefty, Awake and Sing, Golden Boy, Rocket to the Moon, Till the Day I Die,* and
   Paradise Lost.
Waiting for Lefty. Dramatists Play 1935 o.p. Famous agitprop play of the Depression that
   ends with workers calling for a strike.

Books about Odets

Miller, Gabriel. *Clifford Odets.* Continuum 1989 $18.95. ISBN 0-8044-2632-5. A compre-
   hensive study of Odets and his plays, focusing on how Odets's fascination with
   socialism and political issues informed his work.
Murray, Edward. *Clifford Odets: The Thirties and After.* Continuum 1968 o.p. Examines
   the structure of three of the early and five of the later plays; probing, original
   evaluations.

O'NEILL, EUGENE. 1888–1953. (Nobel Prize 1936)

O'Neill was America's first major dramatist and remains its finest—the one
American dramatist whose reputation is secure worldwide. Born in New York
City, the son of the famous actor James O'Neill, the tormented circumstances of
his family life are well known to those familiar with his late, great autobiographical drama *Long Day's Journey into Night* (1950). After being suspended from
Princeton University in 1907, O'Neill spent several years in various pursuits,
including prospecting for gold, shipping out as a merchant sailor, acting in his
father's company, writing for newspapers, and drifting. Some of his disillusionment of this period is captured in *The Iceman Cometh* (1946).

In 1912 O'Neill was hospitalized for tuberculosis, and during his six months in
a sanitorium he read widely in the world's dramatic literature. By 1913 he was
writing plays of his own, and in 1916 his first plays were produced by the
Provincetown Players.

O'Neill's first commercial successes, *Beyond the Horizon* (1920) and *Anna
Christie* (1921), were realistic, but most of his plays written in the next 12 or so
years were relentlessly experimental, employing expressionistic techniques
(*The Emperor Jones*, 1921, and *The Hairy Ape*, 1922), symbolism (*The Fountain*,
1925), masks (*The Great God Brown*, 1925), and interior monologues (*Strange
Interlude*, 1928). *Mourning Becomes Electra* (1931) was an attempt to combine
Greek tragedy (it is based on Aeschylus's *Oresteia*) and Freudian psychology.

In 1934 O'Neill ceased his direct involvement with the commercial theater
and devoted his remaining years to writing a projected mammoth cycle of plays
on U.S. history (only *A Touch of the Poet*, 1957, *More Stately Mansions*, 1964, and
some fragments survive), a projected series of one-act plays (of which only
Hughie, 1959, survives), and the intense, brooding autobiographical plays, *The
Iceman Cometh, Long Day's Journey into Night,* and *A Moon for the Misbegotten*
(1952). The plays O'Neill wrote during this final period constitute his lasting
achievement.

John Gassner wrote of O'Neill that "despite his not always trustworthy flair
for theatricality . . . much of his best work seemed wrung from him rather than
contrived or calculated. In it, a uniquely tormented spirit subsumed much of

the twentieth century's dividedness and anguish, largely existential rather than topical."

O'Neill won the Pulitzer Prize for drama for *Beyond the Horizon* in 1920, *Anna Christie* in 1922, *Strange Interlude* in 1928, and *Long Day's Journey into Night* in 1957. He also won the New York Drama Critics Circle Award for *Long Day's Journey into Night*, as well as the Nobel Prize for Literature in 1936.

PLAYS BY O'NEILL

Anna Christie (with *The Emperor Jones* and *The Hairy Ape*). Random 1972 $7.00. ISBN 0-394-71855-0. *The Emperor Jones*, originally produced in 1920; *Anna Christie* in 1921; *The Hairy Ape* in 1922.

Children of the Sea. Ed. by Jennifer Atkinson. Bruccoli 1972 $15.00. ISBN 0-910972-14-1. Contains *Children of the Sea; Bread and Butter; Now I Ask You; Shell Shock.*

Chris Christofferson: A Play in Three Acts. Random 1982 $15.00. ISBN 0-394-52531-0. An early version of *Anna Christie.*

Complete Plays. 3 vols. Ed. by Travis Bogard. Library of America 1988. Vol. 1 1913–1920 $35.00. ISBN 0-940450-48-8. Vol. 2 1920–1931 $35.00. ISBN 0-940450-49-6. Vol. 3 1932–1943 $35.00. ISBN 0-940450-50-X. Contains the full canon of O'Neill's drama—50 plays plus his only short story, "Tomorrow."

The Emperor Jones. 1920. Ed. by Max J. Herzberg. P-H 1960 $8.95. ISBN 0-13-274902-5. An expressionist drama about the disintegration of the mind of a black dictator.

Hughie. Yale U. Pr. 1959 $5.95. ISBN 0-300-02881-4. A one-act play, one of O'Neill's last works, set in the lobby of a seedy Times Square Hotel.

The Iceman Cometh. Random 1957 $8.00. ISBN 0-394-70018-X. Produced in 1946, the story of a group of social misfits unable to live without illusions.

The Later Plays. Ed. by Travis Bogard. McGraw 1967 $7.88. ISBN 0-07-553664-1. Contains *Ah, Wilderness!; A Touch of the Poet; Hughie; A Moon for the Misbegotten.*

Long Day's Journey Into Night. Yale U. Pr. 1950 $18.50. ISBN 0-300-04600-6. Powerful autobiographical play first produced in 1956.

The Long Voyage Home: Seven Plays of the Sea. Amereon Ltd. repr. of 1972 ed. $16.95. ISBN 0-89190-369-0. Contains *The Moon of the Caribbees; Bound East for Cardiff; The Long Voyage Home; In the Zone; Ile; Where the Cross Is Made; The Rope;* many set on board the *S.S. Glencairn,* based on O'Neill's own experiences as a sailor.

A Moon for the Misbegotten. Random 1974 $7.00. ISBN 0-394-71236-6. Family tragedy first produced in 1957.

More Stately Mansions. Ed. by Donald Gallup. Yale U. Pr. 1964 $9.95. ISBN 0-300-00177-0. Produced in 1967, intended as the fourth play in the cycle on U.S. history.

Nine Plays of Eugene O'Neill. Random 1977 $14.95. ISBN 0-394-60416-4. Contains *Mourning Becomes Electra; Strange Interlude; The Emperor Jones; Marco Millions; The Great God Brown; All God's Chillun Got Wings; Lazarus Laughed; The Hairy Ape; Desire Under the Elms.*

Six Short Plays of Eugene O'Neill. Random 1965 $7.00. ISBN 0-394-70276-X. Includes *The Dreamy Kid; Before Breakfast; Diff'rent; Welded; The Straw; Gold.*

Three Plays. Random 1959 $8.00. ISBN 0-394-70165-8. Contains *Desire under the Elms; Strange Interlude; Mourning Becomes Electra.*

The Unknown O'Neill: Unpublished & Unfamiliar Writings of Eugene O'Neill. Ed. by Travis Bogard. Yale U. Pr. 1988 $45.00. ISBN 0-300-03985-9. Includes three full-length plays, two short stories, an unpublished love poem, brief theatrical pieces, extracts from a working diary kept in the late 1920s, and a few fugitive essays.

WORKS BY O'NEILL

Selected Letters of Eugene O'Neill. Ed. by Travis Bogard & Jackson Bryer. Yale U. Pr. 1988 $45.00. ISBN 0-300-04374-0. Includes letters spanning 50 years.

The Theatre We Worked For: The Letters of Eugene O'Neill to Kenneth MacGowan. Ed. by Jackson R. Bryer. Yale U. Pr. 1982 $35.00. ISBN 0-300-02583-1. Indispensable reflections of the quality of Off-Broadway theater in the 1920s.

BOOKS ABOUT O'NEILL

Berlin, Normand. *Eugene O'Neill*. St. Martin 1988 $10.95. ISBN 0-312-02125-9. A general study of O'Neill's life and works, relating events of his life to the incidents and characters of his plays.

Bogard, Travis. *Contour in Time: The Plays of Eugene O'Neill*. OUP 1988 $12.95. ISBN 0-19-504548-3. An important study; shows the way O'Neill interwove his life into his dramatic constructs.

Carpenter, Frederic I. *Eugene O'Neill*. Twayne's U.S. Authors Ser. Macmillan 1979 $20.95. ISBN 0-8057-4267-7. Superb brief treatment of O'Neill; highly recommended.

Chothia, Jean. *Forging a Language: A Study of the Plays of Eugene O'Neill*. Cambridge U. Pr. 1982 $17.95. ISBN 0-521-28523-2. No new evaluations, but good explications of O'Neill's linguistic devices.

Falk, Doris V. *Eugene O'Neill and the Tragic Tension: An Interpretive Study of the Plays*. Gordian 1982 repr. of 1958 ed. $40.00. ISBN 0-87752-222-7. A neo-Freudian interpretation.

Floyd, Virginia. *The Plays of Eugene O'Neill: A New Assessment*. Lit. and Life Ser. Continuum 1984 $24.95. ISBN 0-8044-2206-0. Most thorough study to date of O'Neill's plays.

Manheim, Michael. *Eugene O'Neill's New Language of Kinship*. Syracuse U. Pr. 1982 $12.95. ISBN 0-8156-2277-5. Sees O'Neill's plays as disguised autobiography; literary survey as psychobiography.

Martine, James J. *Critical Essays on Eugene O'Neill*. G. K. Hall 1984 $35.00. ISBN 0-8161-8683-9. All new essays with valuable new material, offering an excellent contemporary perspective on O'Neill criticism.

Miller, Jordan Y. *Eugene O'Neill and the American Critic: A Bibliographical Checklist*. Shoe String rev. ed. 1974 o.p. Essential for the serious student.

Raleigh, John H. *The Plays of Eugene O'Neill*. S. Ill. U. Pr. 1972 o.p. Analyzes three periods in O'Neill's career, relating them to specific American cultural strands; a detailed and major study.

Sheaffer, Louis. *O'Neill: Son and Artist*. AMS Pr. repr. of 1973 ed. $75.00. ISBN 0-404-20322-1. The second half of the monumental Sheaffer opus.

———. *O'Neill: Son and Playwright*. Paragon Hse. 1989 repr. of 1968 ed. $16.95. ISBN 1-55778-185-0. The most important O'Neill biography.

Winter, S. K. *Eugene O'Neill: A Critical Study*. Russell 1961 o.p. The main ideas behind O'Neill's plays in the context of his times.

RABE, DAVID. 1940–

Born in Dubuque, Iowa, Rabe was educated at Loras College and Villanova. His service in Vietnam has had a major influence on his work, particularly in his early plays. In 1971 both *The Basic Training of Pavlo Hummel*, which traces a soldier's life from basic training to an ugly and ironic death in Vietnam, and *Sticks and Bones*, a slightly absurdist play that combines broad satire of U.S. family life with a realistic portrayal of the suffering of a blind veteran, were produced at Joseph Papp's New York Shakespeare Festival. Rabe's other plays of the 1970s were also produced there. *Streamers* (1976), which won the New York Drama Critics Circle Award, is the most notable of his Vietnam plays. Set in an army barracks, it is a powerful presentation of the destruction that can result from blind, uncontrolled rage. *Hurlyburly* (1985), which concerns the hollow lifestyle of a group of hip southern California men, began a long run on Broadway in 1984. As with many of Rabe's other plays, it explores the horrors that can result from distorted ideas of masculinity. Another recent play, *Goose and Tomtom* (1987), is a forceful drama about two small-time jewel thieves. In it, Rabe explores the theme of the illusory nature of reality.

PLAYS BY RABE

The Basic Training of Pavlo Hummel. French 1972 o.p. About a "poor soul" who is drafted into the army, finds himself in constant trouble, and finally goes into battle and meets his destiny in death.

Goose and Tomtom. Grove Pr. 1987 $7.95. ISBN 0-8021-5193-0

Hurlyburly. Grove Pr. 1985 $7.95. ISBN 0-8021-5097-7. Riveting drama about Hollywood's decadent cocaine-riddled culture, and about men lost in the feminist era.

In the Boom Boom Room. Grove Pr. 1986 $8.95. ISBN 0-8021-5194-9. Bizarre masterpiece about a go-go dancer.

The Orphan: A Play in Two Acts. French 1975 o.p. Explores the exploitations of Vietnam by America and completes Rabe's "Vietnam trilogy."

Sticks and Bones. French 1972 o.p. A strikingly original and powerful antiwar play.

Streamers. Knopf 1977 $10.95. ISBN 0-394-73314-2. Explores the inner furies of an African-American soldier in a barracks community.

RICE, ELMER. 1892–1967

A native of New York City, Rice studied law and passed his bar exams. However, he immediately began writing, and *On Trial* (1914), which employed a flashback technique, made Rice an important playwright at age 22. He proceeded to study under Hatcher Hughes at Columbia University, where he also directed. He helped found the Playwrights' Company in 1938, the Dramatists Guild, and other groups. In 1951 he came to the defense of actors whose allegedly left-wing associations were causing them to lose their jobs. During his 45 years in the theater, Rice wrote 50 full-length plays, 4 novels, and several film and television scripts, as well as his autobiography and *The Living Theater* (1939), which appraises the theater in terms of the social and economic forces affecting its development.

His two masterpieces are *The Adding Machine* (1923), an expressionistic comedy wherein the hero remains a cipher in mechanized society, and *Street Scene* (1929), which was originally entitled *Landscape with Figures* because Rice considered "the [tenement] house as the real protagonist of the drama." The plot's *crime passionel* is but one aspect of the crowded panorama of tenement life. Robert Hogan writes in assessing Rice's career, "Rice has produced a remarkable body of work—large, varied, experimental and honest . . . . As a consistently experimental playwright he is rivalled in our theater only by O'Neill." Rice won the Pulitzer Prize for drama for *Street Scene*.

PLAYS BY RICE

The Adding Machine. French 1923 o.p. Expressiodist fantasy satirizing the dehumanizing effects of machines.

Court of Last Resort. Proscenium 1985 $3.95. ISBN 0-912262-87-7. Published as part of the Lost Play Series.

Dream Girl. Dramatists Play 1945 o.p. About an overimaginative young woman who inefficiently runs a bookstore.

Elmer Rice: Three Plays. Hill & Wang 1965 $9.95. ISBN 0-8090-0735-5. Includes *The Adding Machine, Street Scene*, and *Dream Girl*.

Street Scene. French 1929 o.p. Pulitzer Prize-winning portrait of New York City slums.

BOOKS ABOUT RICE

Durham, Frank. *Elmer Rice. Twayne's U.S. Authors Ser*. Irvington 1970 $17.95. ISBN 0-8057-0616-X

Hogan, Robert. *Independence of Elmer Rice. Crosscurrents Modern Critiques Ser*. S. Ill. U. Pr. 1965 o.p.

Palmieri, Anthony F. *Elmer Rice: A Playwright's Vision of America*. Fairleigh Dickinson 1970 $29.50. ISBN 0-8386-2333-6. Not exactly the "pathfinding project" the author imagines, but nevertheless a valuable and insightful critical survey of Rice's work.

SAROYAN, WILLIAM. 1908–1981

An Armenian American with little formal education, Saroyan was a dramatist who disparaged the usual conventions of the form: "Plot, atmosphere, style, and all the rest of it," he wrote, "may be regarded as so much nonsense" (*Three Times Three*). His plays have been criticized as formless and his writing as undisciplined; yet his work is imbued with fondness for the human race and contains an infectious enthusiasm for society's misfits and innocents. Saroyan's dramatic career was launched with *My Heart's in the Highlands* (1939), a fantasy. The following year, *The Time of Your Life* (1939) was awarded the Pulitzer Prize—which Saroyan publicly refused on the grounds that commerce had no right to patronize art. This play, undoubtedly Saroyan's one enduring piece, takes place in a waterfront saloon where vivid characters wander in and out to come into contact with the philosophical Joe, a man of unending generosity.

PLAYS BY SAROYAN

The Beautiful People. French 1941 o.p. A beguiling comedy, innocent and a little deranged.
The Cave Dwellers. French 1957 o.p. Records the adventures of some poor people camping out on the stage of an abandoned theater.
Get Away Old Man. French 1944 o.p. About an old, wealthy Hollywood producer who tries but fails to buy a young writer's heart.
Hello, Out There. French 1941 o.p. One-act play about an itinerant gambler falsely charged with rape.
My Heart's in the Highlands. French 1939 o.p. A play of wonderment about the innocents of this world.
The Time of Your Life. French 1939 o.p. Pulitzer Prize-winning mood piece set in Nick's waterfront saloon.

BOOKS ABOUT SAROYAN

Lee, Lawrence, and Barry Gifford. *Saroyan: A Biography*. HarpC 1984 o.p.
Saroyan, Aram. *Last Rites: The Death of William Saroyan*. Morrow 1982 o.p.

SHEPARD, SAM. 1943–

Shepard, one of the best dramatists currently writing in the United States, was born on an army base in Illinois and grew up mainly on a ranch in California. His first play was produced off-off-Broadway when he was 19, and he won the first of his 8 Obie Awards when he was 23. A rock lyricist and film actor as well as a dramatist, Shepard has written more than 40 plays, winning the Pulitzer Prize for drama with *Buried Child* (1981) in 1978.

Shepard's plays show the impact of a variety of influences, including rock music, old movies, popular myths of the Old West, and the 1960s drug culture. His early plays, produced off- and off-off-Broadway, are short, bizarre, surrealistic pieces that tend to project images rather than provide ordered reflections of reality; they are characterized by compelling monologues. These plays culminate in his early masterpiece *The Tooth of Crime* (1981), a cross between rock concert and classical tragedy, which pits Hoss, the reigning superstar, in a verbal shoot-out against the challenger, Crow.

Shepard's later work has become more realistic and more responsive to such traditional concepts of drama as plot, character, and theme. It has also brought to the forefront his previously occasional concern for the collapse of the American dream. *True West* (1980) is concerned with the tension between individuals, especially fathers and sons and brothers, and their struggle to define and assert their identities. *Fool for Love* (1983) is a masterfully constructed, searingly intense study of love, hate, and the dying myths of the Old West. And *A Lie of the Mind* (1986) is a landmark play revealing the mental and physical abuse that occurs in two desperate families. Bonnie Marranca has written that, "Shepard is the quintessential American playwright. His plays are American landscapes reflecting the country's iconography, myths, entertainments, archetypes, and—in a less glowing light—the corruption of its revolutionary ideals, and the disorientation of its times."

Plays by Shepard

Buried Child. Dramatists Play 1981 o.p. Pulitzer Prize-winning vision of American disintegration as seen on a squalid Midwestern farm.

Fool for Love. Dramatists Play 1984 o.p.

Fool for Love and Other Plays. Bantam 1984 $7.95. ISBN 0-553-34339-4. Contains *Melodrama Play; Cowboy Mouth; Geography of a Horse-Dreamer; Action; Angel City; Suicide in B-Flat; Seduced; Fool for Love*.

Fool for Love and *The Sad Lament of Pecos Bill on the Eve of Killing His Wife*. City Lights 1984 $8.95. ISBN 0-87286-150-3

A Lie of the Mind. NAL-Dutton 1987 $6.95. ISBN 0-452-25869-3

Seven Plays. Bantam 1984 $10.00. ISBN 0-553-34611-3. Contains *La Turista; The Tooth of Crime; Curse of the Starving Class; Buried Child; Savage/Love; Tongues; True West*.

The Tooth of Crime. French 1981 o.p. About a rock star who battles to protect his kingdom against a young gypsy marauder.

True West. French 1981 o.p. Brilliantly funny, surrealistic play about a Hollywood screenwriter and his drifting alcoholic older brother.

The Unseen Hand and Other Plays. Bantam 1986 $8.95. ISBN 0-553-34263-0. Contains *The 4-H Club; Forensic and the Navigators; The Unseen Hand; The Holy Ghostly; Shaved Splits; Back Bog Beast Bait*.

Books about Shepard

Auerbach, Doris. *Sam Shepard, Arthur Kopit, and the Off-Broadway Theater*. Twayne's *U.S. Authors Ser*. G. K. Hall 1982 o.p. A useful introduction, but uneven and too broad in its coverage.

Marranca, Bonnie, ed. *American Dreams: The Imagination of Sam Shepard*. PAJ Pubns. 1981 $12.95. ISBN 0-933826-13-3. A collection of new and reprinted essays on several Shepard plays.

Mottram, Ron. *Inner Landscapes: The Theater of Sam Shepard*. U. of Mo. Pr. 1984 o.p. The first full-length study devoted to Shepard.

SIMON, NEIL. 1927–

Born in the Bronx, Simon had childhood ambitions to be a doctor, but after attending New York University and the University of Denver, he turned instead to television, writing comedy for Sid Caesar, Phil Silvers, and others. His first play, *Come Blow Your Horn* (1958), about a young rebel who moves into the luxurious apartment of his older brother, is partly autobiographical. Since then, Simon has written numerous successful comedies. Most are about the middle class, the comedy deriving from situations of personal frustration.

Although detractors have accused him of superficiality, today Simon is widely considered one of the world's most successful playwrights. His plays have been produced in community theaters throughout the country and have also been made into films. He is so well known that when he opens a new play on Broadway his name is often put in larger letters than the title of his work.

A master at comedy, Simon gets laughs not just from clever gags and one-liners, but also by presenting deviations from the normal in character, situation, and thought. Although he seems to espouse conventional values, it is the dramatic deviation from these social norms that make his works so funny.

Some of Simon's most commercially successful plays include *Barefoot in the Park* (1963), *The Odd Couple* (1965), *Plaza Suite* (1968), *The Last of the Red-Hot Lovers* (1969), *The Sunshine Boys* (1972), and *California Suite* (1976). But Simon has also been willing to experiment. *The Good Doctor* (1973) is based on humorous stories by ANTON CHEKHOV (see Vol. 2). *God's Favorite* (1974) is adapted from the Biblical story of Job, and *Fools* (1981) is set in an idyllic Russian hamlet where the villagers suffer from chronic stupidity.

In recent years, Simon's plays have become increasingly autobiographical, reflecting both his Jewish background and events from his later life. *Chapter Two* (1977) was written in agonized response to the death of his first wife, Joan, and his subsequent courtship of and marriage to actress Marsha Mason. *Brighton Beach Memoirs* (1983), the first of an autobiographical trilogy, is set in Brooklyn in 1937 with the teenaged hero, aspiring writer Eugene, modeled on the young Neil Simon. *Biloxi Blues* (1985) shows Eugene learning about life and developing his writing skills while at boot camp during World War II. *Broadway Bound* (1986), the most successful of the trilogy, is vaguely reminiscent of a TENNESSEE WILLIAMS memory play: Eugene and his older brother attempt to break into the world of professional comedy writing while coping with their parents' impending divorce. The figure of the mother, Kate, is one of Simon's finest achievements.

Over the years, Neil Simon's plays have matured artistically and philosophically, and he has begun to gain the admiration not just of his audiences, but also of theater artists, critics, and scholars. The themes about which he writes are important ones: sibling rivalry, the crises of puberty, and the frustrations of sexual awakening; the values of friendship, love, marriage, and family; midlife problems associated with infidelity, divorce, and death; and, finally, the importance of individual dignity.

Neil Simon's reputation has been enhanced by numerous awards. He received an Emmy in 1957 and again in 1959 for his television work. He received the Tony in 1963, 1965, 1970, and 1985. He was given the Writer's Guild of America West Award for his screenplays in 1969, 1971, 1972, and 1976. In 1983 he received the New York Drama Critics Circle Award. In 1983 and again in 1985 he received the Outer Circle Award.

PLAYS BY SIMON

Barefoot in the Park. Random 1964 $11.95. ISBN 0-394-40515-3. Popular and critically successful comedy about the trials of a newlywed couple.

Biloxi Blues. Random 1986 $11.95. ISBN 0-394-55139-7. The continuing saga of young Eugene Morris Jerome, the would-be writer, as a World War II army recruit.

Brighton Beach Memoirs. Random 1984 $14.95. ISBN 0-394-53739-4. Autobiographical memory play portraying the writer as a Brooklyn teenager in 1937.

Broadway Bound. Random 1987 $13.95. ISBN 0-394-56395-6. The third part of Simon's autobiographical trilogy, in which the writer upsets his family by writing about them.

California Suite. Random 1977 $9.95. ISBN 0-394-41284-2. Four comic one-acts set in a Beverly Hills hotel.

Chapter Two. Random 1978 $11.95. ISBN 0-394-50293-0. A partially autobiographical story about a writer's new life and love after the death of his wife.

The Collected Plays of Neil Simon. Random 1979 $29.95. ISBN 0-394-50770-3. Includes *The Sunshine Boys; The Good Doctor; God's Favorite; California Suite; Little Me;* and *Chapter Two.*

The Collected Plays of Neil Simon, Vol. II. NAL-Dutton 1986 $12.95. ISBN 0-452-25871-5. Includes eight plays produced between 1970 and 1979.

The Collected Plays of Neil Simon, Vol. III. Random 1992 $34.50. ISBN 0-679-40889-4. Includes Simon's later plays.

Come Blow Your Horn. French 1958 o.p. About a playboy and his assertive younger brother who move into an apartment of their own.

Comedy of Neil Simon. Random 1971 $25.00. ISBN 0-394-47364-7. Includes *Come Blow Your Horn; The Star-Spangled Girl; Barefoot in the Part; The Odd Couple; Plaza Suite; Last of the Red-Hot Lovers; The Gingerbread Lady;* and *The Prisoner of Second Avenue.*

Fools. Random 1982 $10.50. ISBN 0-394-52390-3. Love story set in a Russian village that has been plagued with chronic stupidity for 200 years.

The Gingerbread Lady. French 1970 o.p. A touching story about an alcoholic singer and other misfits.

God's Favorite. French 1974 o.p. A play based on the Biblical story of Job.

The Good Doctor. French 1973. Humorous vignettes based on some of Anton Chekhov's finest stories.

I Ought to Be in Pictures. Random 1981 $9.95. ISBN 0-394-51774-1. Poignant, yet humorous story of a father and daughter who pick up the pieces of their relationship.

Last of the Red-Hot Lovers. French 1969 o.p. Amusing story about a middle-aged man who tries unsuccessfully to have an affair.

Lost in Yonkers. Random 1992 $16.50. ISBN 0-679-40890-8. Painful story of two orphans raised by difficult relatives.

The Odd Couple. Random 1966 $10.95. ISBN 0-394-40649-4. About a messy bachelor and a meticulous fellow who try to live together

Plaza Suite. Random 1969 $9.95. ISBN 0-394-40667-2. Three hilarious one-acts set in the Plaza Hotel.

The Prisoner of Second Avenue. Random 1972 $9.95. ISBN 0-394-48259-X. Economic and other pressures drive the protagonist into a nervous breakdown.

The Sunshine Boys. Random 1973 $9.95. ISBN 0-394-48808-3. Two old vaudevillians' natural antipathy and residual camaraderie.

Books about Simon

Johnson, Robert K. *Neil Simon. Twayne's U.S. Authors Ser.* Macmillan 1983 $20.95. ISBN 0-8057-7387-8. "An effective attempt to bring Simon's work the serious critical attention it deserves" (*Choice*).

McGovern, Edythe M. *Neil Simon: A Critical Study.* Continuum 1979 o.p. Contains useful summaries of the plays.

_____. *Not So Simple Neil Simon.* Perivale Pr. 1978 o.p. Intro. by Neil Simon. Traces Simon's growth as a literary artist.

TERRY, MEGAN. 1932–

Born in Seattle, Washington, Terry received her B.Ed. degree from the University of Washington in 1956. In the 1960s she became internationally prominent as a playwright with the Open Theatre and as the author of the first rock musical, *Viet Rock* (1966). In 1974 she joined the Omaha Magic Theatre as literary manager and playwright-in-residence. Many of her plays, which are experimental and avant-garde, criticize stereotyped gender roles while creatively affirming the strength of women. Over the years, Terry has created approximately 70 plays that have changed the course of contemporary drama and established her as a key figure in America's alternative theatre.

PLAYS BY TERRY

Approaching Simone. French 1973 o.p. Powerful drama about Simone Weil, a French philosopher who died of starvation in 1943 because she refused to eat while soldiers were starving on the front.

Hothouse. French 1974 o.p. Set in the heartland of America; a story about matriarchal love.

Viet Rock: A Folk War Movie. In *Four Plays.* S&S Trade 1967 o.p. Popular 1960s rock musical designed to stop the war in Vietnam.

VAN ITALLIE, JEAN-CLAUDE. 1935–

Van Itallie was born in Brussels and grew up in Great Neck, New York, which, he says, "left me with a horror of the American suburbs." After graduating from Harvard University, he got involved with the Open Theatre group under the direction of Joe Chaikin, producing as a result some of the most stunning and innovative experimental theater work of the 1960s, especially *America Hurrah*, a 1965 trilogy consisting of *Interview*, *TV*, and *Motel*, and *The Serpent*, a 1968 ritualistic and largely mimed theatrical piece that grew out of improvisations on *Genesis* and juxtaposes biblical events with current ones. Van Itallie's plays of the 1970s, which include *A Fable* and *Bag Lady*, have been more traditional in form and simpler in scope, and he has also adapted several of CHEKHOV's (see Vol. 2) plays. In 1983 he returned to the mode of *The Serpent* in *The Tibetan Book of the Dead*, but with notably less success.

PLAYS BY VAN ITALLIE

America Hurrah. Dramatists Play 1965 o.p. Consists of *Interview*, a satire of an employment interview; *TV*, a view of the unreal world of a broadcasting studio; and *Motel*, an absurdist excursion into an antiseptically stark motel.

America Hurrah and Other Plays. Grove Pr. 1978 $5.95. ISBN 0-394-17039-3. Includes *Almost Like Being: A Fable; The Hunter and the Bird; The Serpent.*

Bag Lady. Dramatists Play 1980 $1.95. ISBN 0-686-68847-3. An articulate evocation of big-city life captured through the character of a "bag lady."

Early Warnings: Three Related Short Plays. Dramatists Play 1979 o.p. Contains *Sunset Freeway; Bag Lady;* and *Final Orders.*

A Fable. Dramatists Play 1976 $3.95. ISBN 0-685-67168-2. An allegorical journey through life in search of the beast that is stifling the kingdom.

Five Short Plays. Dramatists Play 1967 o.p. Contains *War; Where Is De Queen; Almost Like Being; The Hunter and the Bird; I'm Really Here.*

Mystery Play. Dramatists Play 1973 o.p. A farcical murder mystery set in the posh living room of a U.S. senator.

The Serpent. Dramatists Play 1965 o.p. Improvisational tour de force explores the Book of Genesis.

Seven Short and Very Short Plays. Dramatists Play 1973 o.p. Contains *Eat Cake; Harold; Take a Deep Breath; Photographs: Mary and Howard; Thoughts on the Instant of Greeting a Friend on the Street; The Girl and the Soldier; Rosary.*

The Tibetan Book of the Dead. Dramatists Play 1983 o.p. An innovative performance piece tracing the Buddhist concept of the transmigration of the soul from life to death to eventual rebirth.

WASSERSTEIN, WENDY. 1950–

Although she is one of several female playwrights currently enjoying popular success, Wasserstein has succeeded in establishing herself commercially as the preeminent chronicler of recent changes in the women's movement. Her first off-Broadway success, *Uncommon Women and Others* (1977), is an affectionate comedy portraying the aspirations of a group of seniors at a prestigious women's college. *Isn't It Romantic* (1979) is a sequel that examines the lives of two friends as they come to terms with their personal and professional lives in the years following their graduation. Her most ambitious play, *The Heidi Chronicles* (1989), traces the history of the women's movement from the consciousness-raising 1960s through the social changes of the 1980s. It not only received the prestigious Pulitzer Prize but virtually every other major award: the Tony, the New York Drama Critics Circle, Outer Critics Circle, Drama Desk, the Susan Smith Blackburn Prize for most outstanding play by a woman, and the Hull-Warriner Award for the best play dealing with a controversial subject. Feminists, however, criticized the play as part of an anti-feminist "backlash."

Wasserstein was born in Brooklyn, New York, the youngest child of Jewish immigrants. After attending Mount Holyoke College, Wasserstein completed an M.A. at City College of New York and continued her studies at Yale University's School of Drama. A one-act play not only served as her M.F.A. thesis but became the basis for her successful full-length work, *Uncommon Women and Others*. The success of the play lay in its perceptiveness, warm humor, and sympathetically drawn characters.

Wasserstein's next play, *Isn't It Romantic*, opened in May 1981 to mixed reviews. While praised for its contemporary jargon, antic poetry, and urbane wit, it was criticized for its lack of organization. With the support of the British American Arts Association, Wasserstein spent nearly two years working on her next major play, *The Heidi Chronicles*. The story, which employs flashbacks, focuses on the life of an art history professor who delivers a lecture on female artists who have been ignored by art historians. After a three-month run at Playwrights Horizons, the play was transferred to Broadway, where it became a big hit. The key to the play's popular and critical success lay in its ability to induce laughter while provoking the audience to examine its own preconceptions.

Wasserstein's plays have been staged in university and regional theaters throughout the country. In spite of the relatively small number of her plays, she holds great promise for continuing as a major voice in the American theater.

PLAYS BY WASSERSTEIN

The Heidi Chronicles. Dramatists Play 1989 $4.50. ISBN 0-8222-0510-6
The Heidi Chronicles and Other Plays. HarBraceJ 1990 $17.95. ISBN 0-15-139985-9. Also includes *Uncommon Women and Others* and *Isn't It Romantic*.
Isn't It Romantic. Avon 1979 o.p. Witty exploration of the conflict between independence and romantic fulfillment.
Uncommon Women and Others. Dramatists Play 1978 o.p. Collage of scenes reflecting on the world faced by young women graduating from college in the 1960s.

NONFICTION BY WASSERSTEIN

Bachelor Girls. Random 1991 $9.00. ISBN 0-679-76062-1. Collection of 29 semi-humorous essays that expatiate on topics including manicures and body-hair waxing, relationships between men and women, and Wasserstein's love of plaid.

WILDER, THORNTON. 1897–1975

Wilder, also a Pulitzer Prize-winning novelist, was born in Wisconsin and educated at Oberlin College and Yale and Princeton universities. His drama, which consistently celebrates human existence, reflects his vast learning in its allusions, borrowings, and experimentation. But it also captures a basic simplicity that has made one of his plays, *Our Town* (1938), one of the most popular and enduring works of the American theater. He made use of antinaturalistic Eastern and classical dramatic traditions and European mystery plays in order to free his work from the conventions of realism and to experiment with stage space and time.

Our Town is a tender portrait of small-town people, oblivious, except for the heroine (who dies at the end of the play), to what it is to be alive. *The Matchmaker* (1938), a comedy, later formed the basis for the popular musical, *Hello, Dolly. The Skin of Our Teeth* (1942) is an expressionist fantasy depicting a suburban family and its freewheeling maid, surviving through war, the Great Flood, and the Ice Age. Much of the material for this play is derived from JAMES JOYCE's experimental novel *Finnegans Wake,* but Wilder quite reasonably argued that "literature has always more resembled a torch race than a furious dispute among heirs." Wilder won the Pulitzer Prize for *Our Town* and *The Skin of Our Teeth.*

PLAYS BY WILDER

The Alcestiad or A Life in the Sun: A Play in Three Acts with a Satyr Play, The Drunken Sisters. French 1977 o.p. Adapted from Euripides' *Alcestis.*

The Matchmaker. French 1938 o.p. About a rich old merchant who decides to take a wife—and all the romantic complications that ensue.

Our Town: A Play in Three Acts. HarpC 1985 $5.00. ISBN 0-06-080779-2. Depicts the life of a New Hampshire village with humor and pathos.

The Skin of Our Teeth. French 1942 o.p. Satiric story of the Antrobus family down through the ages.

Three Plays: Our Town, The Skin of Our Teeth, The Matchmaker. HarpC 1985 $12.00. ISBN 0-06-091293-6. With an author's preface that makes an important contribution to our understanding of dramatic technique and theater history.

WORKS BY WILDER

The Journals of Thornton Wilder. Ed. by Donald Gallup. Yale U. Pr. 1987 $18.00. ISBN 0-300-04054-7. Adroitly selected passages, including two scenes from an uncompleted play.

_____. *The Journals of Thornton Wilder: With Two Scenes of an Uncompleted Play, The Emporium.* Ed. by Donald Gallup. Yale U. Pr. $40.00. ISBN 0-300-033375-3. Represents a judicious calling from Wilder's papers in the Yale Library collection.

BOOKS ABOUT WILDER

Burbank, Rex J. *Thornton Wilder. Twayne's U.S. Authors Ser.* Macmillan 1978 $19.95. ISBN 0-8057-7223-5. Dated, but nonetheless useful, account of Wilder's life and work.

Goldstein, Malcolm. *The Art of Thornton Wilder.* Bks. Demand repr. of 1965 ed. $49.70. ISBN 0-8357-6835-X. An excellent book on the highlights of Wilder's thought, but not enough about his art.

Harrison, Gilbert A. *The Enthusiast: A Life of Thornton Wilder.* Fromm Intl. 1986 $12.95. ISBN 0-88064-053-7. A candid account of Wilder, the creative performer vs. Wilder, the writer.

Wilder, Amos N. *Thornton Wilder and His Public.* Bks. Demand repr. of 1980 ed. $25.50. ISBN 0-685-23665-X. A brief book by Wilder's older brother, a Harvard emeritus professor of divinity, with valuable personal reminiscences and other material not available elsewhere.

WILLIAMS, TENNESSEE. 1911–1983

After O'NEILL, Williams is perhaps the best dramatist the United States has yet produced. Born in his grandfather's rectory in Columbus, Mississippi, Williams and his family later moved to St. Louis. There Williams endured many bad years caused by the abuse of his father and his own anguish over his introverted sister, who was later permanently institutionalized. Williams attended the University of Missouri, and, after time out to clerk for a shoe company and for his own mental breakdown, also attended Washington University of St. Louis and the University of Iowa, from which he graduated in 1938.

Williams began to write plays in 1935. During 1943 he spent six months as a contract screenwriter for MGM but produced only one script, *The Gentleman Caller*. When MGM rejected it, Williams turned it into his first major success, *The Glass Menagerie* (1945). In this intensely autobiographical play, Williams dramatizes the story of Amanda, who dreams of restoring her lost past by finding a gentleman caller for her crippled daughter, and of Amanda's son Tom, who longs to escape from the responsibility of supporting his mother and sister.

After *The Glass Menagerie*, Williams wrote his masterpiece, *A Streetcar Named Desire* (1947), along with a steady stream of other plays, among them such major works as *Summer and Smoke* (1948), *Cat on a Hot Tin Roof* (1954), and *Suddenly Last Summer* (1958). His plays celebrate the "fugitive kind," the sensitive outcasts whose outsider status allows them to perceive the horror of the world and who often give additional witness to that horror by becoming its victims. Stephen S. Stanton has summed up Williams's "virtues and strengths" as "a genius for portraiture, particularly of women, a sensitive ear for dialogue and the rhythms of natural speech, a comic talent often manifesting itself in 'black comedy,' and a genuine theatrical flair exhibited in telling stage effects attained through lighting, costume, music, and movements." After *The Night of the Iguana* (1961), Williams continued to write profusely—and constantly to revise his work—but it became more difficult to get productions of his plays and, if they were produced, to win critical or popular acclaim for them.

Williams won the Pulitzer Prize for drama for *A Streetcar Named Desire* and *Cat on a Hot Tin Roof*. He won the New York Drama Critics Circle Award for these two and for *The Glass Menagerie* and *The Night of the Iguana*.

PLAYS BY WILLIAMS

American Blues: Five One-Act Plays. Dramatists Play 1948 o.p. *Moony's Kid Don't Cry; Ten Blocks on the Camino Real; The Case of the Crushed Petunias; The Dark Room; The Long Stay Cut Short*.

Battle of Angels. Dramatists Play 1940 o.p. An early version of *Orpheus Descending*.

Camino Real. New Dir. Pr. 1970 $7.95. ISBN 0-8112-0218-6. A strange fantasy set in a walled community from which only Don Quixote and Kilroy are able to escape.

Cat on a Hot Tin Roof. New Dir. Pr. rev. ed. 1975 $7.95. ISBN 0-8112-0567-3. About the members of a southern family gathering at the plantation house to help Big Daddy celebrate his sixty-fifth birthday, while old evils poison the gaiety.

Four Plays. NAL-Dutton 1976 $5.95. ISBN 0-451-52015-7. Includes *Summer and Smoke; Orpheus Descending; Suddenly Last Summer; Period of Adjustment*.

The Glass Menagerie. New Dir. Pr. 1949 $4.95. ISBN 0-8112-0220-8. Painful study of lost illusions in a decaying southern family.

Night of the Iguana. Dramatists Play 1961 o.p. Powerful drama of loneliness and despair set at a cheap Mexican resort hotel.

Orpheus Descending. Dramatists Play 1957 o.p. About a guitar-playing youth who comes in off the highway to help a woman storekeeper.

The Rose Tattoo. Dramatists Play 1951 o.p. About Serafina delle Rose, a restless widow whose instinct for love drives love away.

Small Craft Warnings. New Dir. Pr. 1972 $6.95. ISBN 0-8112-0461-8. A group of lonely individuals, rejected by society, and how they come together to seek human contact in a rundown bar.

A Streetcar Named Desire. New Dir. Pr. 1980 $5.95. ISBN 0-8112-0765-X. About Blanche du Bois and her romantic illusions, which lead tragically to delusions and madness.

Suddenly Last Summer. Dramatists Play 1958 o.p. Story of Anne Meacham, who has witnessed her cousin's unbelievably shocking death and is brought under intense pressure to deny the lurid tale she has told.

Summer and Smoke. Dramatists Play 1948 o.p. A spiritual young woman and worldly young doctor's unsuccessful search for love.

Sweet Bird of Youth. New Dir. Pr. 1975 $6.95. ISBN 0-8112-0596-7. Story of an aging motion-picture actress, in flight from her latest failure, who hooks up with a good-looking young hustler.

The Theatre of Tennessee Williams. Vol. I. New Dir. Pr. 1971 $35.00. ISBN 0-8112-0417-0. Contains *Battle of Angels, A Streetcar Named Desire, The Glass Menagerie.*

The Theatre of Tennessee Williams. Vol. II. New Dir. Pr. 1971 $35.00. ISBN 0-8112-0418-9. Contains *The Eccentricities of a Nightingale, Summer and Smoke, The Rose Tattoo, Camino Real.*

The Theatre of Tennessee Williams. Vol. III. New Dir. Pr. 1971 $35.00. ISBN 0-8112-0419-7. Contains *Cat on a Hot Tin Roof, Orpheus Descending, Suddenly Last Summer.*

The Theatre of Tennessee Williams. Vol. IV. New Dir. Pr. 1972 $35.00. ISBN 0-8112-0422-7. Contains *Sweet Bird of Youth, Period of Adjustment, Night of the Iguana.*

The Theatre of Tennessee Williams. Vol. V. New Dir. Pr. 1976 $35.00. ISBN 0-8112-0593-2. Contains *The Milk Train Doesn't Stop Here Anymore; Kingdom of Earth; Small Craft Warnings; The Two-Character Play.*

The Theatre of Tennessee Williams. Vol. VI. New Dir. Pr. 1992 $19.95. ISBN 0-8112-1215-7. Contains several short plays including *27 Wagons Full of Cotton; The Purification; The Lady of Larkspur Lotion; The Last of My Solid Gold Watches; Portrait of a Madonna; Auto-Da-Fe; Lord Byron's Love Letters; The Strangest Kind of Romance; The Young Goodbye; Hello from Bertha; This Property is Condemned; Talk to Me Like the Rain . . .; Something Unspoken.*

The Theatre of Tennessee Williams. Vol. VII. New Dir. Pr. 1981 $35.00. ISBN 0-8112-0795-1. Contains *In the Bar of a Tokyo Hotel* and other plays: *I Rise in Flame, Cried the Phoenix; The Mutilated; I Can't Imagine Tomorrow; Confessional; The Frosted Glass Coffin; The Gnädiges Fräulein; A Perfect Analysis Given by a Parrot; Lifeboat Drill; Now the Cats with Jewelled Claws; This is the Peaceable Kingdom.*

The Theatre of Tennessee Williams. Vol. VIII. New Dir. Pr. 1992 $35.00. ISBN 0-8112-1201-7. Contains *Vieux Carre; A Lovely Sunday for Creve Coeur; Clothes for a Summer Hotel; The Red Devil Battery Sign.*

Three Plays. NAL-Dutton 1976 $5.95. ISBN 0-451-52149-8. Includes *Sweet Bird of Youth; The Rose Tattoo; Night of the Iguana.*

Books about Williams

Falk, Signi L. *Tennessee Williams. Twayne's U.S. Authors Ser.* Macmillan 1978 $19.95. ISBN 0-8057-7202-2. Scholarly examination of Williams's life and works.

Gunn, Drewey W. *Tennessee Williams: A Bibliography.* Scarecrow 1991 $49.50. ISBN 0-8108-2495-7. A major work, indispensable for any devotee of Williams and his plays.

Hirsch, Foster. *A Portrait of the Artist: The Plays of Tennessee Williams.* Assoc. Fac. Pr. 1979 o.p. Emphasizes the homosexual dimension in Williams's plays.

Londre, Felicia H. *Tennessee Williams. Lit. and Life Ser.* Continuum 1980 o.p. An adequate compilation of the facts about Williams's work, but offers no consistent statement about the content of his oeuvre.

Nelson, Benjamin. *Tennessee Williams.* Astor-Honor 1961 $20.00. ISBN 0-8392-1111-2. A solid, important study.

Rader, Dotson. *Tennessee: Cry of the Heart.* Doubleday 1985 o.p. An intimate memoir by a close friend.

Stanton, Stephen S., ed. *Tennessee Williams: A Collection of Critical Essays. Twentieth Century Interpretations Ser.* P-H 1977 o.p. An excellent collection of major essays, old and new, on Williams's plays.

Williams, Dakin, and Shepherd Mead. *Tennessee Williams: An Intimate Biography.* Arbor Hse. 1983 o.p. An anecdotal account, largely drawn from existing sources, by Williams's brother.

WILSON, AUGUST. 1945–

Wilson was born in Pittsburgh, Pennsylvania, and grew up in the city's African-American Hill district. His mother supported the family with a cleaning job and raised her six children in a two-room apartment. When they tried to move into a predominantly white neighborhood, young Wilson was greeted with racist notes on his desk at school and bricks through a window at home. Discouraged, the would-be poet dropped out of school in the ninth grade but continued his education at the public library by reading such African-American writers as LANGSTON HUGHES and RICHARD WRIGHT. From this discouraging and somewhat unlikely background, August Wilson has risen to the position of being one of America's leading dramatists, having twice won the Pulitzer Prize—first for *Fences* (1987) and again for *The Piano Lesson* (1988).

Wilson wrote his earliest plays for Pittsburgh's Black Horizons on the Hill, a theater that he helped found in 1968. During this period he was active in the Black Power movement. In 1978 Wilson moved to St. Paul, Minnesota, and wrote scripts for the Science Museum, also becoming involved with the Playwrights Center in Minneapolis. In this new environment, his plays began to echo the rhythmic language of his old neighborhood haunts in Pittsburgh.

Moved by the life of the legendary blues singer Bessie Smith, who had studied music under Ma Rainey, he penned his first major critical and popular success, *Ma Rainey's Black Bottom* (1985). Set in a rundown recording studio in Chicago, the play is a carefully crafted portrait of black jazz musicians in the 1920s, complete with genuine music from the period. Presented first on April 6, 1984, at the Yale Repertory Theater in New Haven, Connecticut, the play was successfully moved to the Cort Theater in New York, where it ran for 267 performances. The play presents a searing account of racism and also shows black prejudice against other black people—a concept long understood by sociologists but so poorly understood generally as to result in Wilson's historic vision being labeled "revisionist."

Fences was first presented at the O'Neill Center in 1983 as a staged reading and then premiered at the Yale Repertory Theatre in 1985. After a pre-Broadway run in San Francisco, *Fences* opened on March 26, 1987, at the Forty-Sixth Street Theater in New York. The play starred James Earl Jones as Troy Maxson, a former star of a Negro baseball league who has been reduced to working as a garbage collector. Maxson now sees the world in terms of the "fences" that have held him back, and he discourages his son who wants to try his luck in the newly integrated professional sports world. James Earl Jones's powerful performance has left its mark on *Fences* in much the same way that Marlon Brando's portrayal of Stanley Kowalski left its mark on *A Streetcar Named Desire*. In addition to the Pulitzer Prize, *Fences* won the other major awards in 1987—the Drama Desk, Outer Critics Circle, New York Drama Critics, and the Tony.

Joe Turner's Come and Gone (1984) is set in a black boardinghouse in Pittsburgh in 1911 and shows each resident's different relationship with his past of slavery and his urban present. *The Piano Lesson* (1987) is set in 1936. In this play, Boy Willie is driven to sell the family piano to secure the future, while his defiant sister, Bernice, is determined to preserve the heirloom as a symbol of their family's past.

Both of these plays premiered at the Yale Repertory Theater in New Haven and are a part of Wilson's projected cycle of ten plays showing, decade by decade, the evolving twentieth-century African-American experience.

August Wilson's vision is authentic and monumental. He is an impassioned and compelling storyteller who holds promise as a continuing major voice in the American theater.

PLAYS BY WILSON

August Wilson: Three Plays. U. of Pittsburgh Pr. 1991 $24.95. ISBN 0-8229-3666-6. With preface by the author.

Fences. NAL-Dutton 1986 $6.95. ISBN 0-452-26048-5. Story of a former baseball star with a Negro league who now works as a garbage collector.

Joe Turner's Come and Gone. NAL-Dutton 1988 $7.95. ISBN 0-452-26009-4. Chronicles the African-American search for identity—and jobs.

Ma Rainey's Black Bottom. NAL-Dutton 1985 $7.95. ISBN 0-452-26113-9. Brilliant portrayal of 1920s black jazz musicians.

The Piano Lesson. NAL-Dutton 1990 $16.95. ISBN 0-525-24926-5. Haunting drama dealing with black life in America.

Two Trains Running. NAL-Dutton 1992 $18.00. ISBN 0-525-48607-0. Continues Wilson's chronicle of the African-American experience.

WILSON, LANFORD. 1937–

Wilson was born in Lebanon, Missouri, and began to write plays while at the University of Chicago. In 1969 he helped found the off-Broadway Circle Repertory Company, becoming its chief playwright. He thus has had the rare opportunity to develop his craft in collaboration with a permanent company of actors and a theater where he could try out and, if necessary, revise his plays. Like *The Hot l Baltimore* (1973), which ran for 1,166 performances and set an off-Broadway record for a nonmusical, many of Wilson's plays are vaguely realistic in manner, emphasizing characters over plot, and featuring likeable misfits and deviants.

Fifth of July (1978), *Talley's Folly* (1979), and *Talley and Son* (1981) are all about the Talley family of Lebanon, Missouri. *Fifth of July*, a Broadway smash hit, deals with people who were "burned" physically and psychologically by the 1960s but who can still dream of a democratic America. *Talley's Folly*, another Broadway hit, is an unabashed love story about the Jewish outsider, Matt, and the misfit of the Protestant Talley family, Sally. *Talley and Son* tells of the financial and other machinations of three generations of Talleys. This story of meanness and greed has often been compared with LILLIAN HELLMAN's *The Little Foxes*.

Angels Fall (1982) concerns a group of people brought together in a mission in northwestern New Mexico by a nuclear accident. Although it seems at first that the play will comment on an impending apocalypse, its actual themes deal with daily questions: how to live and love, how to teach and learn, and how to find one's vocation.

Burn This (1987) is the story of a young dancer, Anna, who is profoundly distressed by the death of her gay collaborator. Her life is transformed by the bizarre and explosive arrival of Pale, the dead man's older brother. Shocking, outrageous, and larger than life, the play presents Wilson's views on art, human sexuality, and love. It is a poetic and cataclysmic work in which art is seen as a sacrament, as an outward sign for inward, chaotic, and exhilarating truths. *Burn This*, which opened on Broadway in the fall of 1987, is Wilson's masterpiece.

Lanford Wilson is a distinctly American playwright whose works reflect his roots in the Ozarks as well as in his adopted home, New York City. The esteem in which he is held is attested to by the respect of numerous critics and by the many awards he has received: a Vernon Rice Award, several Rockefeller and

Guggenheim fellowships, the Brandeis University Creative Arts Award, Obies for *The Hot l Baltimore* and *The Mound Builders* (1976), and a Pulitzer Prize and New York Drama Critics Circle Award in 1980 for *Talley's Folly*.

PLAYS BY WILSON

Angels Fall. FS&G 1983 $9.95. ISBN 0-374-52231-6. Absorbing drama about six people trapped by a nuclear accident in a mission church in New Mexico.

Balm in Gilead. Dramatists Play 1965 o.p. Illuminates the bleak world of outcasts in New York City.

Balm in Gilead and Other Plays. FS&G 1965 $8.95. ISBN 0-374-52156-5. Includes *Balm in Gilead; Home Free;* and *Ludlow Fair.*

Brontosaurus. Dramatists Play 1978 o.p. Remarkable one-act about the conflict between a cynical New York antique dealer and her taciturn nephew, a student of theology.

Burn This. FS&G 1988 $9.95. ISBN 0-374-52158-1. A cataclysmic work about a young dancer who is devastated by the death of her gay roommate and artistic collaborator.

The Fifth of July. Hill & Wang 1979 $24.95. ISBN 0-8090-4455-2. Set in a farmhouse in rural Missouri, about people who were "burned" physically and psychologically by the 1960s.

The Gingham Dog. Dramatists Play 1969 o.p. Shows the disintegration of an interracial marriage.

Home Free. Dramatists Play 1964 o.p. Haunting two-character play about incestuous siblings living in an isolated, make-believe world.

The Hot l Baltimore. FS&G 1973 $9.95. ISBN 0-374-52165-4. Set in the lobby of a run-down urban hotel; a study of society's lost souls.

Lemon Sky. Dramatists Play 1970 o.p. An autobiographical play showing an adult trying to make peace with his parents and his past.

Ludlow Fair. Dramatists Play 1964 o.p. A bedtime story about two female roommates.

The Madness of Lady Bright. Dramatists Play 1964 o.p. Depicts the psychological disintegration of an aging homosexual male.

The Mound Builders. Dramatists Play 1976 o.p. Epic drama about an archeological team's race with time to uncover the secrets of an American Indian tribe.

Redwood Curtain. Hill & Wang 1992 $19.95. ISBN 0-8090-8052-4

The Rimers of Eldritch. Dramatists Play 1967 o.p. Poetic and evocative play portraying intolerance and scapegoating in a small midwestern town.

The Rimers of Eldritch and Other Plays. FS&G 1967 $7.95. ISBN 0-374-52168-9. Includes *The Rimers of Eldritch; This Is the Rill Speaking; Wandering; Days Ahead;* and *The Madness of Lady Bright.*

Serenading Louie. Dramatists Play 1976 $3.95. ISBN 0-685-74730-1. Two modern couples at a crisis point in their lives.

Talley and Son. Hill & Wang 1986 $15.95. ISBN 0-8090-1251-0. A story of meanness and greed, about the financial and other machinations of three generations of Talleys.

Talley's Folly. FS&G 1980 $7.95. ISBN 0-374-52157-3. An American "melting-pot" love story set in a deserted Victorian-style boathouse.

This Is the Rill Speaking. Dramatists Play 1967 o.p. A touching view of small-town life.

Thymus Vulgaris. Dramatists Play 1982 $1.95. ISBN 0-686-83804-1. A one-act about two women of easy virtue whose fortunes improve.

BOOKS ABOUT WILSON

Barnett, Gene A. *Lanford Wilson. Twayne's U.S. Authors Ser.* Macmillan 1987 $23.95. ISBN 0-8057-7498-X. Contains chapters on all of the major plays through *Talley and Son.*

Busby, Mark. *Lanford Wilson.* Boise St. U. Pr. 1987 $3.95. ISBN 0-88430-080-3. Informative and evaluative essay on Wilson, with a selected bibliography of primary and secondary sources.

ZINDEL, PAUL. 1936–

Born on Staten Island, New York, Zindel was raised by a single mother who pursued a variety of odd and mostly unsuccessful jobs and took in terminally ill patients to supplement the family income. Due to her eccentricity and restlessness, the mother moved the family from one apartment to another, making it difficult for Zindel to form lasting friendships. As a consequence, the boy lived in the world of his imagination, developing interests in both science and writing.

Zindel majored in chemistry at Wagner College on Staten Island, completing both bachelors and masters degrees. During this period he also took a creative-writing course offered by the playwright EDWARD ALBEE. After college he worked briefly as a technical writer for a chemical company and then discovered a more fulfilling vocation as a teacher of chemistry and physics at a Staten Island high school. It was during this period in the early 1960s that Zindel was able to develop his potential as a playwright by drawing on his own background as well as the experiences of his young students.

The Effect of Gamma Rays on Man-in-the-Moon Marigolds premiered at the Alley Theater in Houston in 1965, was presented in a condensed version on television the following year, and finally opened off-Broadway at the Mercer-O'Casey Theater in 1970. Because of a fire in the theater, the play was moved, with a new cast, to the New Theater on Broadway, where it ran for a total of 819 performances. In addition to being enormously popular, *Gamma Rays* earned in 1970 an Obie Award as the best play of the season, the New York Drama Critics Circle Award as the best American play, and the Vernon Rice Drama Desk Award for most promising playwright. In 1971 the play was awarded the Pulitzer Prize in Drama.

Gamma Rays is the story of an embittered, half-mad widow, Beatrice Hunsdorfer; her teenaged daughters, Ruth and Tillie; and Nanny, a decrepit old woman who boards with them. The family lives in chaos, with Beatrice dealing out petty vengeance to everyone. Nanny has been abandoned by her daughter. Ruth is wanton, untidy, and subject to seizures. Tillie, however, has become interested in science and enters her marigold experiment in the science fair; by exposing the marigold seeds to radiation, she shows that some produce normal plants, others produce mutations with beautiful double blooms, while still others die. The metaphor, of course, is that Tillie has emerged from her chaotic environment as a beautiful and whole person, a human "double bloom."

Zindel's other plays include *And Miss Reardon Drinks a Little* (1971), *The Secret Affairs of Mildred Wild* (1973), *Let Me Hear You Whisper* (1973), and *Ladies at the Alamo* (1975). While these plays continue to show Zindel's skill in writing excellent roles for women, none of them have matched the critical and popular success of *Gamma Rays*.

Since the late 1960s, Zindel has also written several novels for young adults. *The Pigman* (1968), which is about a lonely widower and two destructive teenagers, has sold more than 1 million copies. His other novels include *My Darling, My Hamburger* (1969), *I Never Loved Your Mind* (1970), *Pardon Me, You're Stepping on My Eyeball* (1976), *Confessions of a Teenage Baboon* (1977), and *The Undertaker's Gone Bananas* (1978). As in *Gamma Rays*, these works display not only a penchant for grotesque humor but an uncanny awareness of the problems of teenagers.

Zindel's works, which also include several screenplays, explore the themes of loneliness, escapism, and eccentricity. His best works are humorous, perceptive, and warm; they present an affirmation of life emerging from desperate and grotesque circumstances. He is especially noted for his excellent women's roles, which has helped sustain him as a best-selling playwright for school and community groups.

PLAYS BY ZINDEL

And Miss Reardon Drinks a Little. Dramatists Play 1971 o.p. Portrait of three wacky sisters who have been psychologically damaged by a domineering mother.

The Effect of Gamma Rays on Man-in-the-Moon Marigolds. Bantam 1984 $3.95. ISBN 0-553-28028-7. Compassionate, award-winning story of adolescent trauma and success.

Ladies at the Alamo. Dramatists Play 1975 o.p. About five fiery women who fight for control of a Texas theater.

Let Me Hear You Whisper. Dramatists Play 1974 o.p. Humorous play about a cleaning woman who saves the life of a dolphin.

The Secret Affairs of Mildred Wild. Dramatists Play 1973 o.p. Portrait of an eccentric woman who lives a life of movie-induced fantasies.

NOVELS BY ZINDEL

Confessions of a Teenage Baboon. Bantam 1984 $2.95. ISBN 0-553-27190-3. Story of a fatherless teenager and a strange mother.

I Never Loved Your Mind. HarpC 1970 $12.89. ISBN 0-06-026822-0. About a dropout who falls for a flower child, who eventually leaves him.

My Darling, My Hamburger. Bantam 1984 $3.50. ISBN 0-553-27324-8. Presents a creative approach to dealing with the problem of adolescent sex.

Pardon Me, You're Stepping on My Eyeball. Bantam 1976 $12.89. ISBN 0-06-026838-1. Story of two teenagers who are the victims of the bizarre adults in charge of them.

The Pigman. Bantam 1983 $3.50. ISBN 0-553-26321-8. Novel for grades seven and up about a lonely widower with a prized collection of ceramic pigs.

The Undertaker's Gone Bananas. Bantam 1984 $3.50. ISBN 0-553-27189-X. Mystery story about loving parents and misfit teenagers.

BOOK ABOUT ZINDEL

Forman, Jack J. *Presenting Paul Zindel*. Macmillan 1988 $19.95. ISBN 0-8057-8206-0. First full-length study of Paul Zindel; presents never-before published biographical information from interviews and a complete analysis of Zindel's works.

CHAPTER 19

American Literature: Some New Directions

Carole-Anne Tyler

> There's a broad body of people in this country across lines of race, religion, regions, and sex who desperately want that new direction within this country and new connections with other people and forms of government in the world.
>
> —Jesse Jackson, *Marxism Today*

Since the 1960s, American literature has been in state of flux. Indeed, it is now rather commonplace to speak of a crisis in literary studies, one brought about by the impact of "theory" on the discipline and of various political activisms effecting it. No longer is there a general consensus about what American literature is or how it should be taught. For many in the field, the old canon, the "Great Tradition of American literature" whose works were considered representative of the best American thought and writing, can no longer be taught or written about as such; not in the wake of critiques of American culture by activists of the so called "New Left," who are dedicated to reconstructing the democratic ideals and values that lie at the center of traditional American literary studies. The Great Tradition, composed chiefly of works by white, Anglo-Saxon protestant, middle-class men is now being reconsidered from the perspective of those dissatisfied with the failure of the United States to ensure freedom and equality for all Americans as promised by the country's founding ideals. The Great Tradition is thus being supplemented with works by women, lesbians and gays, people of color, religious and ethnic minorities, and members of the working class. These groups have, of course, contributed to American literature in the past, but it is only recently that their status as distinct literary voices has come to the fore.

As a result of recent criticism, the notion of a Great Tradition is now rather suspect by some Americans, on the grounds of being elitist and ideologically conservative, constructed to preserve the values and assumptions of only certain groups of Americans and maintain their hegemony over others. Efforts to reinstate the Great Tradition, such as E. D. Hirsch's *Cultural Literacy: What Every American Needs to Know* (1987) and Allan Bloom's *The Closing of the American Mind* (1987), as well as the recent debates within and about the National Endowment of the Arts and National Endowment of the Humanities, are part of a backlash by the "New Right" against what they consider political correctness." These conservative critics are defending what they see as "timeless" or genuinely and universally valuable. Current new directions in American literature and literary studies question and challenge the very notion of timeless or universal values, recognizing the diversity of American hopes,

1124

dreams, fears, and fascinations as they have been expressed in literary and cultural productions.

The change in direction in American studies has been motivated by changes in the people who teach and write about American culture—changes that can be traced to the 1960s and the rise of the social movements of the New Left among many intellectuals, academics, and educators. New Left movements had led many individuals to think critically about the function of education and educational institutions in the United States, as well as of other institutions such as museums and grant agencies. Turning a critical eye to their own disciplines in particular, these scholars investigated how both their object of study—a book, a painting, an historical movement—and their very methodology for analyzing it helped to reproduce the American society that they hoped to transform. In the field of literature, this investigation took the form of questioning both the literary canon itself and the values its works were thought to embody, as well as the principles by which these works were evaluated. As these investigations proceeded, a number of literary critics concluded that literary values themselves were suspect, and that literature and literary analysis were neither personal nor disinterested, but were, in fact, quite political and ideological.

This new thinking about literature owed much to the reconceptualization of ideology by neo-Marxist critics like Louis Althusser, who had himself been influenced by the structuralist and psychoanalytic theory of CLAUDE LEVI-STRAUSS (see Vol. 3) and Jacques Lacan, as well as by the work of the Frankfurt School of Marxist cultural theory. Early Marxists had theorized ideology as "false consciousness"—wrong-headed ideas that were part of the cultural superstructure, determined by the economic base that they helped reproduce by legitimizing ruling-class values and assumptions. According to Althusser, ideology was "overdetermined" in the manner of a neurotic symptom, the result of a confluence of contradictory impulses, some of which might not be consistent with capitalism. He also redefined ideology as a process of "subjectification" rather than as a set of lies. For Althusser, "Ideological State Apparatuses" (ISAs) were those institutions and practices that treated individuals as subjects of a capitalist society, one in which assumptions, beliefs, values, and desires had been shaped to secure its own existence. Schools and universities, including English departments, were ISAs, as were leisure industries such as the cinema, television, record companies, and the popular press. In this schema, reading a book, watching a film, or listening to a pop song were thus both personal and political activities, since they could reaffirm one's identity as a certain kind of person with a certain kind of politics (although this generally took place at the unconscious rather than conscious level). In light of this, the job of the American studies scholar-critic was therefore to teach and to write about literature and culture in a new way: to explicate how particular literary works, the literary canon, and even literary study itself were ideological, and to locate those works and methodologies that were critical or subversive of the dominant culture. The job of American studies was thus to expose the political unconscious of American culture—and thereby to try to change it.

The desire to change the political consciousness of American culture has fueled the current interest in Continental literary and cultural theory, which was first imported into foreign language and comparative literature departments, brought later into English departments, and then carried into American studies programs. Throughout this process, literary and cultural theory has been seen by many as an antidote to the naive historicism and populism of much earlier work on American literature and culture. This earlier work had, almost from the beginning, an organicist impulse to connect literature to American society, but its literary histories were not informed by the problems of treating historiography as an empirical social science. These earlier American studies also sought to bridge the gap between high and popular culture, again because of an impulse to understand how all the expressions of American society were linked. Too often, however, a combination of populist description and historicism was substituted for an ideological analysis of popular and mass culture.

The three areas briefly explored in this chapter—literary theory, film studies, and gay and lesbian literature—are the newest of the new directions that a more critical democratic impulse has taken within American literary studies. They have not yet secured as firm a place as feminist studies, African American studies, and studies of other ethnic American literatures and cultures (Asian American, Chicano, Jewish, Latino, Native American, etc.). Already, many critics are heading in even newer directions, such as the study of colonialism and postcolonialism, performance theory, television studies, and cultural studies, all of which continue to challenge the divisions between history, theory, and literature, and between high and popular culture. Some critics even challenge the distinctions between and within the "new directions" themselves, questioning the objects of inquiry and methodologies just as those of the old American studies had been called into question.

Today, many Americans are striving to renew the democratic ideal, to head in new directions in order to forge connections with other Americans and peoples of the world. Newer "new directions" in literary studies are part of that ongoing process, a process in which American studies scholars and critics have participated by writing and revising literary canons and methodologies so as to challenge old ideas and fully realize democratic ideals and values both in the United States and abroad.

HISTORY AND CRITICISM

Althusser, Louis. *Lenin and Philosophy and Other Essays.* Trans. by Ben Brewster. Monthly Rev. 1972 $12.00. ISBN 0-85345-213-X. Includes the important essay on ISAs.

Baldick, Christopher. *The Social Mission of English Criticism.* OUP 1983 $59.00. ISBN 0-19-812821-5. Considers the role of criticism and the notion of the literary in England from Arnold to Leavis.

Bloom, Alan. *The Closing of the American Mind.* 1987. S&S Trade 1988 $10.95. ISBN 0-671-65715-1. Asserts that America has declined because students lack an awareness of "mainstream" culture.

Brantlinger, Patrick. *Crusoe's Footprints: Cultural Studies in Britain and America.* Routledge 1990 $39.50. ISBN 0-415-90146-4. An overview of the movement that challenges traditional humanities and social-science scholarship.

D'Souza, Dinesh. *Illiberal Education: The Politics of Race and Sex on Campus.* Free Pr. 1991 $19.95. ISBN 0-02-908100-9. A polemic by a highly vocal conservative participant in the "political correctness" debates about the multicultural curriculum.

Eagleton, Terry. *The Function of Criticism: From the Spectator to Post-Structuralism.* Routledge Chapman & Hall 1984 $12.95. ISBN 0-86091-799-1. Links criticism to the bourgeois public sphere and argues that its disintegration has generated the crisis in criticism.

————. *The Significance of Theory*. Blackwell Pubs. 1990 $15.95. ISBN 0-631-17269-6. Essays exploring the changes in literary studies in response to the rise of theory.

Easthope, Antony. *Literary into Cultural Studies*. Routledge 1991 $49.95. ISBN 0-415-06640-9. Details the transformation of English literary studies into cultural studies.

Elbow, Peter. *What is English?* Modern Lang. 1990 $37.00. ISBN 0-87352-381-4. With the National Council of Teachers of English 1990, reflections on the 1987 English Coalition Conference, with "interludes" by others who attended.

Fish, Stanley. *Doing What Comes Naturally: Change, Rhetoric, and the Practice of Theory in Literary and Legal Studies*. Duke 1990 $37.50. ISBN 0-8223-0859-2. Develops ideas from his previous books about criticism, professionalism, and "interpretative communities."

Frow, John. *Marxism and Literary History*. HUP 1986 $22.00. ISBN 0-674-55096-X. Proposes a Marxist reconciliation of formalism and historicism for a history of literature.

Gates, Henry Louis, Jr. *Loose Canons: Notes on the Culture Wars*. OUP 1992 $19.95. ISBN 0-19-507519-6. Essays on multiculturalism in the academy by the renowned African - American theorist.

Gramsci, Antonio. *Selections from Cultural Writings*. Ed. by David Forgacs and Geoffrey Nowell-Smith. Trans. by William Boelhower. HUP 1985 $25.00. ISBN 0-674-79985-2. Includes most of this major Marxist theorist's important reflections on literature and popular culture.

Hirsch, E. D., Jr. *Cultural Literacy: What Every American Needs to Know*. HM 1987 $19.45. ISBN 0-395-43095-X. Recognizes that schooling is always political but makes an argument like Bloom's, providing lists of the missing "mainstream" knowledge.

Gunn, Giles. *The Culture of Criticism and the Criticism of Culture*. OUP 1988 $12.95. ISBN 0-19-505642-6. A reevaluation of American moral pragmatism, with discussions of Geertz, Rorty, Burke, Bakhtin, Wilson, and Trilling.

Lovell, Terry. *Consuming Fiction*. Routledge Chapman & Hall 1987 $44.95. ISBN 0-86091-173-X. Marxist-feminist analysis of how the novel was transformed from a commodity into "literature."

Macherey, Pierre. *A Theory of Literary Production*. Trans. by Geoffrey Wall. Routledge 1978 $15.95. ISBN 0-7100-0087-1. Althusserian Marxist analysis of literature and criticism.

Merod, Jim. *The Political Responsibility of the Critic*. Cornell Univ. Pr. 1987 $29.95. ISBN 0-8014-1976-X. Examines the role of the literary critic and the way U.S. culture limits the production of critical knowledge.

Miller, Nancy K. *Getting Personal: Feminist Occasions and Other Autobiographical Acts*. Routledge 1991 $39.95. ISBN 0-415-90323-8. An autobiographical perspective on institutional politics by a well-known feminist critic.

Ohmann, Richard. *English in America: A Radical View of the Profession*. OUP 1976 o.p. Argues that the teaching of literature has served the interests of capitalism.

Resing, Russell. *The Unusable Past: Theory and the Study of American Literature*. Routledge Chapman & Hall 1986 $35.00. ISBN 0-416-01311-2. Critical examination of the history and contexts of major schools of theorizing about American studies.

Ross, Andrew. *No Respect: Intellectuals and Popular Culture*. Routledge 1989 $32.50. ISBN 0-415-90036-0. Considers the responses of American intellectuals (Sontag, Baraka, and others) to various popular cultural phenomena.

Scholes, Robert. *Textual Power: Literary Theory and the Teaching of English*. Yale U. Pr. 1985 $10.00. ISBN 0-300-03726-0. The third in his useful series of books on theory, concentrating on pedagogy.

Sherry, Ruth. *Studying Women's Writing: An Introduction*. Routledge Chapman & Hall 1988 $9.95. ISBN 0-7131-6566-9. An introduction to the major issues confronting the teacher of women's writing and feminist theory.

Weber, Samuel. *Institution and Interpretation*. U. of Minn. Pr. 1987 $34.95. ISBN 0-8166-1297-8. Argues that boundaries between fields are continually reinstituted through conflictual processes of interpretation.

Williams, Raymond. *Marxism and Literature*. OUP 1977 $9.95. ISBN 0-19-876061-2. Classic Marxist analysis of literature and ideology that displays no poststructuralist influence).

———. *Problems in Materialism and Culture*. Routledge Chapman & Hall 1985 $16.95. ISBN 0-86091-729-0. Develops the Marxist analysis of literature and culture laid out in *Marxism and Literature*.

COLLECTIONS

Allen, Paula Gunn, ed. *Studies in American Indian Literature: Critical Essays and Course Designs*. Modern Lang. 1983 $37.00. ISBN 0-87352-354-7. Particularly useful for its suggestions for syllabi.

Atkins, C. Douglas, and Michael Johnson, eds. *Writing and Reading Differently: Deconstruction and the Teaching of Composition and Literature*. U. Pr. of KS 1985 $12.95. ISBN 0-7006-0283-6. Essays on deconstruction and pedagogy, composition, and literature by well-known theorists.

Aufderheide, Patricia, ed. *Beyond P. C. Toward a Politics of Understanding*. Graywolf 1992 $9.00. ISBN 1-55597-164-4. Represents a spectrum of positions in the "political correctness" debates about the multicultural curriculum.

Baker, Houston A., Jr., ed. *Three American Literatures*. Modern Lang. 1982 $37.00. ISBN 0-87352-352-0. Essays on Asian-American, Chicano, and Native American literature for American studies teachers.

Bercovitch, Sacvan, and Myra Jehlen, eds. *Ideology and Classic American Literature*. Cambridge U. Pr. 1987 $49.95. ISBN 0-521-25221-0. Essays on the history and theory of American literary studies by noted scholars in the field.

Berman, Paul, ed. *Debating P. C.* Dell 1992 $8.00. ISBN 0-440-50466-X. Scholarly essays, journalism, and interviews on the "political correctness" debates about the multicultural curriculum.

Crew, Louie, ed. *The Gay Academic*. ETC Pubns. 1978 $23.95. ISBN 0-88280-036-1. An early collection of essays about lesbians and gays in academia.

Cruikshank, Margaret, ed. *Lesbian Studies: Present and Future*. Feminist Pr. 1982 $15.95. ISBN 0-935312-07-2. Includes sample syllabi and reading lists for a range of university courses, as well as essays on teaching and research.

Culley, Margo, and Catherine Portuges, eds. *Gendered Subjects: The Dynamics of Feminist Teaching*. Routledge 1985 o.p. Essays on women's studies, feminist pedagogy, and sexual and racial difference.

Dynes, Wayne R., ed. *Homosexuality: A Research Guide*. Garland 1987 $56.00. ISBN 0-8240-8692-9. An annotated bibliography covering a range of disciplines.

Fisher, Dexler, and Robert B. Stepto, eds. *Afro-American Literature: The Reconstruction of Instruction*. Modern Lang. 1979 $19.50. ISBN 0-87352-351-2. Essays by well-known African-Americanist scholars.

Gibaldi, Joseph, ed. *Introduction to Scholarship in Modern Languages and Literatures*. Modern Lang. 1992 $37.00. ISBN 0-87352-385-7. Fifteen new essays on gender studies, minority literature, cultural studies, the canon, and related topics in criticism.

Graff, Gerald, and Reginald Gibbons. *Criticism in the University*. Northwestern U. Pr. 1985 o.p. Essays on the university, the development of literary studies, pedagogy, and theory.

Greenblatt, Stephen, and Giles Gunn, eds. *Redrawing the Boundaries: The Transformation of English and American Literary Studies*. Modern Lang. 1992 $45.00. ISBN 0-87352-395-4. Essays on major historical periods and on new directions in literary and composition theory.

Grossberg, Lawrence, and others. *Cultural Studies*. Routledge 1991 $59.50. ISBN 0-415-90351-3. The most important cultural studies anthology, including essays by internationally renowned scholars on a range of topics from a variety of perspectives.

Langland, Elizabeth, and Walter Gore. eds. *A Feminist Perspective in the Academy: The Difference It Makes.* U. Ch. Pr. 1983 $5.95. ISBN 0-226-46875-5. Essays on feminism and various disciplines.

Mitchell, W.J.T., ed. *Against Theory: Literary Studies and the New Pragmatism.* U. Ch. Pr. 1985 $7.50. ISBN 0-226-53227-5. The well-known debate from the journal *Critical Inquiry* about poststructuralist theory, initiated by Steven Knapp and Walter Benn-Michaels.

Nelson, Cary, ed. *Theory in the Classroom.* U. of Ill. Pr. 1986 $29.95. ISBN 0-252-01265-8. Essays on theory and pedagogy, including deconstruction, feminism, and psychoanalysis.

Robbins, Bruce, ed. *Intellectuals: Aesthetics, Politics, Academics.* U. of Minn. Pr. 1990 $39.95. ISBN 0-685-4579-3. Essays on the political role of intellectuals and academics by important cultural theorists.

Ruoff, A. LaVonne Brown. *American Indian Literatures: An Introduction, Bibliographic Review and Selected Bibliography.* Modern Lang. 1990 $45.00. ISBN 0-87352-191-9. The most comprehensive introduction to the major genres and authors in the field.

Ruoff, A. LaVonne Brown, and Jerry W. Ward, Jr., eds. *Redefining American Literary History.* Modern Lang. 1990 $45.00. ISBN 0-87352-187-0. Essays and bibliographies focusing primarily on the literatures and cultures of ethnic minorities.

LITERARY THEORY

Not so long ago, "literature" was an unproblematic category and "literary criticism," a matter of common-sense assumptions about the relation between a text and its author, the author's times, and "human nature." In the nineteenth century, Victorian poet and critic MATTHEW ARNOLD had argued that literature exerted a civilizing influence, rather like religion once had. The function of criticism, according to Arnold, was the disinterested examination of the literary object in order to identify and discuss its literary qualities, such as its moral vision or tone. Its success or failure hinged on the character of its author, whose insights into the truths of life literature was thought to express. A great author, like "myriad-minded SHAKESPEARE," was one who could transcend the petty concerns of his era and class to embrace universal human values and timeless truths, seeing and representing the world from an unbiased, cosmic perspective.

Arnold's program of liberal humanism continued to dominate in the early twentieth century as "English" (which eventually came to include American literature as well, although not without a struggle) was institutionalized in universities as a valid field of study like classics. Two of the most important critics and editors of the time, F. R. Leavis and T. S. ELIOT, endorsed it, asserting that close analysis of a literary text was a way of combating the debilitating effects of modern commercial culture. However, Eliot's methodology placed so much importance on the literary object's formal qualities that his thinking constituted something of a break with the liberal humanist assumption that literature was to be evaluated as "expressive realism," mimetic of reality and expressive of an author's "vital experience" of that reality. Eliot contributed to the elaboration of what was to become the most important critical paradigm of the midcentury, the New Criticism. This New Criticism rejected some of the central tenets of Matthew Arnold's approach, in particular, the authority of the author, whose intentions and sincerity were of no concern to the New Critic. What mattered instead were formal qualities, particularly unity, tension, irony, and complexity. The New Critics, therefore, reconceived the role of the author well before poststructuralist thinkers like MICHEL FOUCAULT (see Vols. 2, 4, and

5) and ROLAND BARTHES (see Vol. 2) did so. While some critics endorsed methodologies besides New Criticism at midcentury (most notably those promoting Marxist and psychoanalytic approaches), New Criticism was the dominant methodology. It was not as incompatible with the liberal humanist ethos of the United States as Marxism and psychoanalysis were, and it was also eminently teachable—no small matter for English professors confronting the large numbers of students with uneven educational backgrounds who were beginning to attend college under the G.I. bill.

A more definitive break with liberal humanism did not occur until the 1960s, when structuralism was introduced to the American academy. Although it was not the first school of Continental theory to have an impact on the United States, it proved to be the most influential, its formalism having been prepared for by New Criticism and the criticism of NORTHROP FRYE. Like New Criticism, structuralism was concerned with the formal properties of texts. However, like Russian formalism, which developed in the Slavic countries at about the same time as New Criticism, it sought to explain literature as a whole as much as to explicate individual texts. Structuralism proposed that it was possible to analyze the cultural foundations of literature by exposing the layers of buried meaning in literary texts. For example, structuralists have shown how stories may spring from what they call an "ur-narrative," a sort of grand story that a people or culture has without realizing it. The notion of "progress" and the hopes and dreams it inspires is an example of an ur-narrative. Structuralists did not entirely break with the assumptions of their predecessors, however. Like Matthew Arnold's adherents and New Critics, they believed in unitary meaning (the ur-narrative) and the disinterested pursuit of it.

Poststructuralism, which for most critics begins with the work of deconstructive philosopher JACQUES DERRIDA (see Vol. 4), rejects the notion of timeless and universal unitary meanings. Like literary modernism, deconstruction undermines the notion of objectivity and of language as a medium for reflecting universal truths. Rather, deconstruction insists that there is no way to prove, in an objective way, that there is any relation between a cultural product, such as a book, and the ideas or feelings of the person who produced it or the elements of its cultural context. Some scholars have seen deconstruction as yet another ahistorical and apolitical formalism, but others have found its insights helpful for elaborating politicized critiques of mainstream literature and culture. Deconstruction has been used to undermine the apparent identities structuring a discourse so that the discourse can be examined from fresh perspectives. There are therefore a variety of poststructuralisms (Marxist, psychoanalytic, feminist, etc.) that have developed from revisions to theoretical paradigms, which have preceded or arisen in isolation from structuralism and the deconstructive critiques of it, many of which are incompatible with one another. Although liberal humanist and other resistances to this theory continue, its impact has been such that neither "literature" nor critical methodologies can ever again be taken for granted.

History and Criticism

Allen, Paula Gunn. *The Sacred Hoop: Recovering the Feminine in American Indian Traditions*. Beacon Pr. 1992 $14.00. ISBN 0-8070-4617-5. The most important work by the best-known theorist of Native American literature.

Anzaldua, Gloria. *Borderlands—La Frontera: The New Mestiza*. Aunt Lute Bks. 1987 $19.95. ISBN 1-879960-13-3. Combines prose, poetry, and autobiography, as well as English and Spanish, to articulate a theory of border subjectivity.

Ashcroft, Bill, and others, eds. *The Empire Writes Back: Theory & Practice in Post-Colonial Tradition*. Routledge 1989 $39.95. ISBN 0-415-01208-2. A survey of the major issues and theorists in colonial and postcolonial studies, concentrating on language.

Baker, Houston. *Blues, Ideology, and Afro-American Literature: A Vernacular Theory*. U. Ch. Pr. 1987 $22.00. ISBN 0-226-03536-0. Argues that the blues voice is central to American and African-American culture.

Belsey, Catherine. *Critical Practice*. Routledge Chapman & Hall 1980 $13.95. ISBN 0-416-72950-9. A useful, short, and highly readable introduction to poststructuralism by a poststructuralist Marxist feminist.

Bennett, Tony. *Formalism and Marxism*. Routledge Chapman & Hall 1979 $12.95. ISBN 0-416-70880-3. The best overview of the topic, and a very readable introduction to poststructuralist Marxism.

Brantlinger, Patrick. *Crusoe's Footprints: Cultural Studies in Britain and America*. Routledge 1990 $39.50. ISBN 0-415-90146-4. The best introduction to cultural studies theory in the United States; also an introduction to poststructuralism.

Buci-Glucksmann, Christine. *Gramsci and the State*. Trans. by David Fernbach 1980 o.p. The best critical work on the Italian Marxist who has been so important to cultural studies.

Cixous, Hélène, and Catherine Clement. *The Newly Born Woman*. Trans. by Betsy Wing. U. of Minn. Pr. 1986 $34.95. ISBN 0-8166-1465-2. Essays by two important French feminists, including Cixous's well-known "Sorties."

Collins, Patricia Hill. *Black Feminist Thought: Knowledge, Consciousness, and the Politics of Empowerment*. Unwin Hyman 1990 $49.95. ISBN 0-04-445137-7. The first synthetic overview of African-American feminism, concentrating on Angela Davis, bell hooks, Alice Walker, and Audre Lorde.

Culler, Jonathan. *Roland Barthes*. OUP 1983 $25.00. ISBN 0-19-520420-4. A very readable basic introduction to the works of Barthes.

———. *Structuralist Poetics: Structuralism, Linguistics, and the Study of Literature*. Cornell Univ. Pr. 1976 $10.95. ISBN 0-8014-9155-X. One of the first, and still useful, surveys of literary structuralism and poststructuralism.

D'Amico, Robert. *Historicism and Knowledge*. Routledge 1988 $35.00. ISBN 0-415-90032-8. A critical account of historicist discourse from Popper to Foucault.

De Man, Paul. *The Resistance to Theory*. U. of Minn. Pr. 1986 $29.95. ISBN 0-8166-1293-5. Arguably the most important collection of essays by the American deconstructive literary theorist.

Deleuze, Gilles. *Foucault*. Trans. by Sean Hand. U. of Minn. Pr. 1988 $29.95. ISBN 0-8166-1674-4. The first analysis by a major poststructuralist theorist in his own right.

Derrida, Jacques. *A Derrida Reader: Between the Blinds*. Ed. by Peggy Kamuf. Col. U. Pr. 1991 $68.50. ISBN 0-231-06658-9. An excellent introduction to the work of French poststructuralist deconstructive philosopher Jacques Derrida.

Dews, Peter. *Logics of Disintegration: Post-Structuralist Thought and the Claims of Critical Theory*. Routledge Chapman & Hall $50.00. ISBN 0-86091-105-5. Draws on Adorno to compare Frankfurt school Marxist cultural theory with poststructuralist theory.

Eagleton, Terry. *Literary Theory: An Introduction*. U. of Minn. Pr. 1983 $29.95. ISBN 0-8166-1238-2. Now the classic introduction to structuralist and poststructuralist theory, despite a sometimes old-style Marxist bias.

Freund, Elizabeth. *The Return of the Reader: Reader-Response Criticism*. Routledge Chapman & Hall 1987 $37.50. ISBN 0-416-34400-3. Explores all the major schools and theorists, from Richards to Culler, Fish, Holland, and Iser.

Geertz, Clifford. *The Interpretation of Cultures*. Basic 1977 $16.00. ISBN 0-465-09719-7. An influential theory of cultural analysis of constitutive "symbolic forms."

Gilbert, Sandra, and Susan Gubar. *The Madwoman in the Attic: A Study of Women and the Literary Imagination in the Nineteenth Century*. Yale U. Pr. 1979 $19.95. ISBN 0-300-02596-3. Classic feminist-humanist criticism adapting Bloom's theory to articulate a female literary tradition.

Grosz, Elizabeth. *Jacques Lacan: A Feminist Introduction*. Routledge 1990 $45.00. ISBN 0-415-01399-2. A good introduction to Lacanian psychoanalytic theory and the best feminist overview of Lacan's work.

Haraway, Donna. *Simians, Cyborgs, and Women: The Reinvention of Nature*. Routledge 1990 $55.00. ISBN 0-415-90386-6. Essays elaborating the poststructuralist ideas that nature is constructed, not discovered, and that knowledge is inextricable from power.

Hawkes, Terence. *Structuralism and Semiotics*. U. CA Pr. 1977 $10.95. ISBN 0-520-03422-8. A good introduction to Saussure and semiotics, to structuralist anthropology, and to their impact on literary studies.

Horkheimer, Max, and Theodor W. Adorno. *Dialectic of Enlightenment*. Trans. by John Cumming. Continuum 1975 $16.95. ISBN 0-8164-9153-4. The classic statement about mass culture from the Frankfurt School of Marxist cultural theory.

Jameson, Fredric. *The Political Unconscious: Narrative As a Socially Symbolic Act*. Cornell Univ. Pr. 1982 $11.95. ISBN 0-8014-9222-X. Still the most important of the books by the influential Marxist literary theorist.

Lacan, Jacques. *Ecrits: A Selection*. Trans. by Alan Sheridan. Norton 1982 $12.95. ISBN 0-393-30047-1. Still the most important work of poststructuralist psychoanalyst Lacan available in English.

Laclau, Ernesto, and Chantal Mouffe. *Hegemony and Socialist Strategy: Towards a Radical Democratic Politics*. Routledge Chapman & Hall 1985 $15.95. ISBN 0-86091-769-X. Discusses the new social movements and their vision of a radically pluralist democracy.

Leitch, Vincent B. *American Literary Criticism: From the 30s to the 80s*. Col. U. Pr. 1989 $67.00. ISBN 0-231-06426-8. The best and most complete introduction to and survey of criticism and theory in America.

———. *Deconstructive Criticism: An Advanced Introduction*. Col. U. Pr. 1982 $50.50. ISBN 0-231-05472-6. The most thorough overview of deconstruction's philosophical background.

Martin, Wallace. *Recent Theories of Narrative*. Cornell Univ. Pr. 1986 $33.95. ISBN 0-8014-1771-6. The best overview of narrative theory and of key issues in narrative studies, such as realism.

Moi, Toril, ed. *The Kristeva Reader*. Col. U. Pr. 1986 $47.50. ISBN 0-231-06324-5. An excellent introduction to the work of the French feminist semiotician and psychoanalyst.

Rorty, Richard. *Contingency, Irony, and Solidarity*. Cambridge U. Pr. 1989 $42.95. ISBN 0-521-35381-5. Articulates a poststructuralist pragmatist philosophy.

Said, Edward. *Orientalism*. Random 1979 $12.00. ISBN 0-394-74067-X. A seminal text in postcolonial studies.

Saldivar, Ramon. *Chicano Narrative: The Dialectics of Difference*. U. of Wis. P. 1990 $30.00. ISBN 0-299-12470-3. A theoretically informed work on Chicano literature.

Sedgwick, Eve. *Epistemology of the Closet*. U. CA Pr. 1990 $24.95. ISBN 0-520-07042-9. Argues that "the closet" is a structural relation of knowledge and ignorance constitutive of homophobic culture.

Showalter, Elaine. *A Literature of Their Own: British Women Novelists from Bronte to Lessing*. Princeton U. Pr. 1977 $14.95. ISBN 0-691-01343-8. Classic feminist-humanist criticism privileging realism and "strong" female characters.

Silverman, Kaja. *The Subject of Semiotics*. OUP 1983 $35.00. ISBN 0-19-503177-6. An advanced introduction to poststructuralist theory, especially psychoanalysis and cine-semiotics.

Spivak, Gayatri. *In Other Worlds: Essays in Cultural Politics*. Routledge Chapman & Hall 1987 $35.00. ISBN 0-416-01651-0. Essays on feminism, pedagogy, imperialism, and historiography by a major theorist.

Turner, Graeme. *British Cultural Studies*. Unwin Hyman 1990 $39.95. ISBN 0-04-445424-4. A useful (if obviously biased) introduction to a field that is currently having an impact on American studies.

Wittig, Monique. *The Straight Mind: and Other Essays*. Beacon Pr. 1992 $24.95. ISBN 0-8070-7916-2. Essays by the influential French lesbian-feminist materialist theorist.

Wright, Elizabeth. *Psychoanalytic Criticism: Theory in Practice*. Routledge Chapman & Hall 1985 $13.95. ISBN 0-416-32660-9. A good overview of a variety of psychoanalytic theories and reading methodologies.

Young, Robert. *White Mythologies: Writing History and the West*. Routledge 1991 $74.50. ISBN 0-415-05371-4. A history of histories from Hegel and Marx to Althusser and Foucault that critiques Marxist Eurocentrism.

Collections

Adams, Hazard, ed. *Critical Theory Since Plato*. HarBraceJ 1971 $48.00. ISBN 0-15-516142-3. The standard anthology for survey courses, including excerpts of theorists from Plato to the poststructuralists.

Arac, Jonathan, and others, eds. *The Yale Critics: Deconstruction in America*. U. of Minn. Pr. 1983 o.p. Essays considering deconstruction in the context of politics.

Bhabha, Homi, ed. *Nation and Narration*. Routledge 1990 $46.00. ISBN 0-415-01482-4. Essays focusing on the constitution of the nation as an imagined community through literature.

Bloom, Harold, and others, eds. *Deconstruction and Criticism*. Continuum 1979 $11.95. ISBN 0-8264-0010-8. Something of a manifesto for the "Yale School" of American deconstruction, also including an essay by Derrida.

Butler, Judith, ed. *Feminists Theorize the Political*. Routledge 1992 $55.00. ISBN 0-415-90273-8. The most important collection of poststructuralist feminist essays on political science and politics in the broadest sense.

Clifford, James, and George E. Marcus, eds. *Writing Culture: The Poetics and Politics of Ethnography*. U. CA Pr. 1986 $42.50. ISBN 0-520-05729-5. The first collection of poststructuralist-influenced essays theorizing (and critiquing) anthropology and ethnography.

Collier, Peter, and Helga Geyer-Ryan, eds. *Literary Theory Today*. Cornell Univ. Pr. 1990 $49.95. ISBN 0-8014-2526-3. A superb collection of essays by such major theorists as Gayatri Spivak.

De Lauretis, Teresa, ed. *Feminist Studies/Critical Studies*. Ind. U. Pr. 1986 $29.95. ISBN 0-253-32171-9. An important interdisciplinary anthology of feminist essays informed by poststructuralism.

Donald, James, ed. *Psychoanalysis and Cultural Theory: Thresholds*. St. Martin 1991 $39.95. ISBN 0-312-05232-4. Essays by well-known psychoanalytic critics of culture and cultural theory.

Ferguson, Russell, and others, eds. *Out There: Marginalization and Contemporary Cultures*. The New Museum of Contemporary Art and MIT Pr. 1990 o.p. A very diverse collection, representing lesbian and gay, African-American, postcolonial, feminist, and poststructuralist theory.

Foster, Hal. *The Anti-Aesthetic: Essays on Postmodern Culture*. Bay Pr. 1983 $9.95. ISBN 0-941920-01-1. One of the first and most important anthologies on poststructuralism and postmodernism.

Fuss, Diana, ed. *Inside/Out: Lesbian Theories, Gay Theories*. Routledge 1991 $59.50. ISBN 0-415-90236-3. A theoretically sophisticated collection of essays on a range of topics, from sexuality and identity to AIDS.

Gates, Henry Louis, Jr., ed. *Reading Black, Reading Feminist: A Critical Anthology*. NAL-Dutton 1990 $14.95. ISBN 0-452-01045-4. An important anthology of essays and excerpts from books on black feminism and black women's writing.

———. *Black Literature and Literary Theory*. Routledge Chapman & Hall 1984 $15.95. ISBN 0-416-37240-6. The first—and still important—anthology of African-American poststructuralist literary and cultural theory.

Goldberg, David Theo, ed. *Anatomy of Racism*. U. of Minn. Pr. 1990 $14.95. ISBN 0-8166-1804-6. Essays by major poststructuralist, postcolonial, and African-Americanist theorists on race and ethnicity in a range of discourses.

Greene, Gayle, and Coppelia Kahn. *Making a Difference: Feminist Literary Criticism.* Routledge Chapman & Hall 1985 o.p. A still-useful collection surveying a variety of feminist theories, including "French," lesbian, and African-American.

Gunew, Sneja, ed. *Feminist Knowledge: Critique and Construct.* Routledge 1990 $55.00. ISBN 0-415-01226-0. A very useful collection of international essays discussing feminism along with a variety of disciplines and issues.

Harrari, Josue, ed. *Textual Strategies: Perspectives in Post-Structuralist Criticism.* Cornell Univ. Pr. 1979 $49.95. ISBN 0-8014-1218-8. One of the earliest collections of essays by major poststructuralists on a range of topics.

Jardine, Alice, and Paul Smith, eds. *Men in Feminism.* Routledge Chapman & Hall 1987 $35.00. ISBN 0-416-01591-3. A most important collection of essays about men and feminist theory, many of which address each other.

Kreiswirth, Martin, and Mark A. Cheetham, eds. *Theory between the Disciplines: Authority/Vision/Politics.* U. of Mich. Pr. 1990 $37.50. ISBN 0-472-10165-X. Interdisciplinary essays about the politics of poststructuralist theory and theorists.

LaCapra, Dominick, ed. *The Bounds of Race: Perspectives on Hegemony and Resistance.* Cornell Univ. Pr. 1991 $41.50. ISBN 0-8014-2553-0. Essays on African and African-American literatures and on racism.

Lentricchia, Frank, and Thomas McLaughlin, eds. *Critical Terms for Literary Study.* U. Ch. Pr. 1989 $45.00. ISBN 0-226-47201-9. Brief but not reductive essays by important theorists and critics on major concepts in literary theory today.

Macksey, Richard, and Eugenio Donato, eds. *The Structuralist Controversy: The Languages of Criticism and the Sciences of Man.* Johns Hopkins 1970. The most important early collection of essays on structuralism.

Natoli, Joseph. *Tracing Literary Theory.* U. of Ill. Pr. 1987 $14.95. ISBN 0-252-01384-0. A useful introduction to and commentary on theory from Bakhtin to phenomenology to poststructuralism.

Parker, Andrew, and others, eds. *Nationalisms and Sexualities.* Routledge 1991 $49.95. ISBN 0-415-90432-3. Essays focusing on nationalism, sexuality, gender, and dress and the complexities of their articulation.

Rice, Philip, and Patricia Waugh, eds. *Modern Literary Theory: A Reader.* Routledge Chapman & Hall 1992 $17.95. ISBN 0-340-57599-9. A good selection of twentieth-century theory.

Showalter, Elaine, ed. *The New Feminist Criticism: Essays on Women, Literature, and Theory.* Pantheon 1985 $22.95. ISBN 0-394-53913-3. Essays and excerpts from books about feminist theory and criticism, most of which are uninformed by poststructuralism.

Tompkins, Jane P., ed. *Reader-Response Criticism: From Formalist to post-Structuralism.* Johns Hopkins 1980 $11.95. ISBN 0-8018-2401-X. With the Suleiman and Crosman collection, one of the two most important collections of reader-response theory.

Wall, Cheryl A., ed. *Changing Our Own Words: Essays on Criticism, Theory, and Writing by Black Women.* Rutgers U. Pr. 1989 $36.00. ISBN 0-8135-1462-2. Includes essays by most of the major black feminist literary and cultural theorists.

Warhol, Robyn, and Diane Price Herndl, eds. *Feminisms: An Anthology of Literary Theory and Criticism.* Rutgers U. Pr. 1991 $55.00. ISBN 0-8135-1731-1. The biggest and best general collection of essays by feminists representing a variety of approaches.

CHRONOLOGY OF AUTHORS
(Literary Theory)

Wimsatt, William Kurtz, Jr. 1907–1975
De Man, Paul. 1919–1983
Booth, Wayne. 1921–
Hirsch, Edward D. 1928–

Miller, Joseph Hillis. 1928–
White, Hayden V. 1928–
Bloom, Harold. 1930–
Jameson, Fredric. 1934–
Gilbert, Sandra Mortola. 1936–

Allen, Paula Gunn. 1939–
Anzaldua, Gloria. 1942–
Spivak, Gayatri Chakravorty. 1942–
Baker, Houston. 1943–
Chodorow, Nancy Julia. 1944–
Culler, Jonathan. 1944–

Gubar, Susan. 1944–
Haraway, Donna Jeanne. 1944–
Carby, Hazel. 1948–
Radway, Janice A. 1949–
Gates, Henry Louis, Jr. 1950–
Gallop, Jane. 1952–

ALLEN, PAULA GUNN. 1939–

Of Laguna Pueblo and Sioux descent, Allen is one of the best-known Native American writers and critics and cousin to another, LESLIE MARMON SILKO. She has published numerous volumes of her own poetry, fiction, and nonfiction, edited two important collections of Native American writing, and received grants from the National Endowment for the Arts, the Ford Foundation, and the University of California at Los Angeles, where she was a postdoctoral fellow in American Indian Studies. She is currently a professor of Native American Studies and Ethnic Studies at the University of California at Berkeley. As a woman, a lesbian, and a Native American in a culture that is all too often sexist, homophobic, and racist, Allen knows what it is to be oppressed. She has devoted much of her work to combating that oppression by critiquing the ideas that have sanctioned it and by affirming her identities. For example, in *The Woman Who Owned the Shadows* (1983), a novel about a woman who comes to realize that she is a lesbian, Allen explores and affirms for women and lesbians the ideas of Spider Grandmother, in many Native American traditions the creator of the heavens, the earth, and all the spirit beings, and an icon of female power. In *The Sacred Hoop* (1986), she collects essays written over a number of years that explicitly argue what is implicit in the earlier novel—that Native American literature, traditions, mythology, and spirituality can be powerful antidotes to white racism, sexism, and homophobia.

POETRY BY ALLEN

Shadow Country. U. CA Pr. 1982 $7.50. ISBN 0-935626-26-3. Part of their Native American Series.
Skins and Bones: Poems 1979–87. West End 1988 $6.95. ISBN 0-931122-50-3. Poems about Native American and feminist concerns.

NOVEL BY ALLEN

The Woman Who Owned the Shadows. Aunt Lute Bks. 1983 $9.95. ISBN 0-933216-07-6

NONFICTION BY ALLEN

The Sacred Hoop: Recovering the Feminine in American Indian Traditions. Beacon Pr. 1986 $24.95. ISBN 0-8070-4600-0. Includes "*Hwame, Koshkalaka*, and the Rest: Lesbians in American Indian Cultures."
Studies in American Indian Literature: Critical Essays and Course Designs. Modern Lang. 1983 $35.00. ISBN 0-87352-354-7. Introduction and two essays by Allen, including "The Sacred Hoop."

WORK BY ALLEN

Spider Woman's Granddaughters: Traditional Tales and Contemporary Writing by Native American Women. Fawcett 1989 $19.95. ISBN 0-8070-8100-0. Introduction and one story by Allen. Allen edited the remaining traditional tales and modern works.

Book about Allen

Hanson, Elizabeth I. *Paula Gunn Allen*. Boise St. U. W. Writ. Ser. 1990 $3.95. ISBN 0-88430-095-1. A short volume (really an essay) in the Boise State Western Writers Series.

ANZALDUA, GLORIA. 1942–

A native of the Southwest, Anzaldua is a Chicana lesbian feminist theorist, creative writer, editor, and activist. She has taught Chicano studies, feminist studies, and writing at a number of universities; has conducted writing workshops around the world; and has been a contributing editor for the feminist literary journal *Sinister Wisdom* since 1984. She has also been active in the migrant farm workers movement. Anzaldua first came to critical attention with an anthology she co-edited with another Chicana lesbian feminist theorist and writer, Cherrie Moraga, *This Bridge Called My Back: Writings by Radical Women of Color* (1981). This important collection includes poetry, fiction, autobiographical writing, criticism, and theory by and about women of color (Chicanas, African Americans, Asian Americans, and Native Americans, both heterosexual and lesbian) who advocate change in academia and the culture at large.

Anzaldua is perhaps best known for her second book, *Borderlands—La Frontera* (1987), which like the others combines prose and poetry, history, autobiography, fiction and criticism, Spanish and English (as well as Tex-Mex and Nahautl) to interrogate, deconstruct, and undermine the "borders" of each as well as the U.S.-Mexican border by exploring border subjectivities along with sexual, psychological, and spiritual borderlands. The "new mestiza," she argues, challenges regimes of exclusion and exploitation by problematizing the notion of unitary identity wherever it is found, wherever the space between two or more cultures "shrinks with intimacy." As they negotiate multiple identities, border subjects practice "code-switching," which revitalizes cultures, awakens dormant areas of consciousness, and prepares us for the necessary meeting of diverse cultures in the next century.

Anzaldua currently resides in Santa Cruz, where she is at work on both an autobiographical volume and a collection of Chicana-Mexicana theory.

Nonfiction by Anzaldua

Borderlands—La Frontera: The New Mestiza. Aunt Lute Bks. 1987 $19.95. ISBN 1-879960-13-3

Making Face, Making Soul—Haciendo Caras: Creative and Critical Perspectives by Women of Color. Aunt Lute Bks. 1990 $24.95. ISBN 0-933-21674-2

This Bridge Called My Back: Writings by Radical Women of Color. 1981. Kitchen Table 1984 $21.95. ISBN 0-913175-18-8. Winner of the Before Columbus Foundation American Book Award.

BAKER, HOUSTON. 1943–

Professor of English and Human Relations at the University of Pennsylvania, where he also directs the Center for the Study of Black Literature and Culture, Baker is one of the best-known and most influential African American literary and cultural theorists. He has published many books of criticism and theory, as well as several volumes of poetry; has won a number of prestigious awards; and has been actively involved in the leadership of the Modern Language Association, the largest and most important organization for literary scholars.

Since the 1980s, Baker has engaged the issues, politics, and methodologies of what would seem to be contradictory theoretical impulses: the Black Aesthetic movement, which concentrated on articulating a distinctively black style, criticism, ethics, and politics; and poststructuralism, which questions the very notion of fixed identities whose essence is directly expressed in distinctive cultural productions. In his work of the 1970s, inspired by black nationalism and the Black Aesthetic movement, Baker was interested in reviving and revaluing the literature he saw as part of a black American tradition different from those of white America and Africa, one that has been influenced by folk tales, sermons, spirituals, jazz, and blues. In *The Journey Back* (1980), this goal was recast in structuralist terms as an "anthropology" of black art, which Baker asserted must be studied in the context of African American culture as a whole.

Baker's more recent work includes an incisive analysis of the Harlem Renaissance and a lavishly illustrated book on African American women writers and African American female creativity. In *Modernism and the Harlem Renaissance* (1987), he argues that the Harlem Renaissance was a movement as modernist as imagism, cubism, and surrealism, which were dominated by white artists and writers whose work has served as the paradigm of modernism. If the Harlem Renaissance has not been seen as modernist, he argues, it is only because African American modernism is different from the modernism of white Anglo-America and Europe. In *Workings of the Spirit: The Poetics of Afro-American Women's Writing* (1991), Baker incorporates feminist theory into his analysis. He also argues for the utility of poststructuralist theory for African American studies, including African American "womanist" studies. As Baker sees it, African American critics must refigure theory, black and white, to make it speak black (and black womanist) concerns, since every critical practice has a theory, even if it is not consciously articulated.

NONFICTION BY BAKER

Afro-American Literary Study in the 1990s. (coedited with Patricia Redmond). U. Ch. Pr. 1989 $24.95. ISBN 0-226-03537-9. Essays by major African-Americanists, including Gates, McDowell, Yarborough, Benston, and Baker.

Blues, Ideology, and Afro-American Literature: A Vernacular Theory. U. Ch. Pr. 1984 $11.95. ISBN 0-226-03538-7

The Journey Back: Issues in Black Literature and Criticism. U. Ch. Pr. 1984 $11.95. ISBN 0-226-03535-2

Modernism and the Harlem Renaissance. U. Ch. Pr. 1989 $9.95. ISBN 0-226-03525-2

Workings of the Spirit: The Poetics of Afro-American Women's Writing. U. Ch. Pr. 1990 $24.95. ISBN 0-226-03522-0. With a phototext by Elizabeth Alexander and Patricia Redmond.

BLOOM, HAROLD. 1930–

Born in New York City, Bloom was educated at Cornell and Yale. A longtime proponent of romanticism, he began his challenge to the New Criticism with *Shelley's Mythmaking* (1959) and *The Visionary Company* (1961).

Bloom's central idea has been that poets must struggle against the existing body of poetry in order to make room for their own writings and personal style. In various works, he has elaborated the steps or stages in this struggle, which can be interpreted as psychological moments in the poet's career, but also as poetic images and devices, which Bloom believes are found in a specific sequence in all great lyric poetry in English after MILTON. Only poets who pass through all the stages and record that passage in their lyric poetry achieve greatness or "strength," in Bloom's term. He has applied his ideas in books on YEATS and WALLACE STEVENS and in essays on many other poems and poets.

NONFICTION BY BLOOM

Agon: Towards a Theory of Revisionism. 1981. OUP 1982 $27.95. ISBN 0-19-502945-3
The American Religion: The Emergence of the Post-Christian Nation. S&S Trade 1992 $22.00. ISBN 0-671-67997-X. Reconstructs a remarkable diagram of the religious imagination.
The Anxiety of Influence: A Theory of Poetry. 1973. OUP 1973 $8.95. ISBN 0-19-501896-6
The Book of J. Random 1991 $12.00. ISBN 0-679-73624-7. Controversial collaboration of one woman's interpretations of texts within Genesis, Exodus, Numbers and Deuteronomy.
British Modern Fiction, 1920–1945. Chelsea Hse. 1987 $54.95. ISBN 0-87754-987-7
Deconstruction and Criticism. Continuum 1979 $11.95. ISBN 0-8264-0010-8
Kabbalah and Criticism. 1975. Continuum 1975 $9.95. ISBN 0-8264-0242-9. Draws on Gershom Scholem's studies of Jewish mystical writings to extend Bloom's theories on poetic creation.
A Map of Misreading. 1975. OUP 1975 $9.95. ISBN 0-19-502809-0. Elaborates Bloom's theory of poetic creation on imagistic, rhetorical, and psychological dimensions.
Ruin the Sacred Truths: Poetry and Belief from the Bible to the Present. HUP 1989 $20.00. ISBN 0-674-78027-2. Bloom presents his personal encounter with Western authors.

BOOK ABOUT BLOOM

Fite, David. *Harold Bloom: The Rhetoric of Romantic Vision.* U. of Mass. Pr. 1985 $25.00. ISBN 0-87023-484-6. Narrates Bloom's critical progress from the early work.

BOOTH, WAYNE. 1921–

A graduate student at the University of Chicago in the late 1940s, when the English Department was dominated by members of the "Chicago School" of criticism, Booth returned to his alma mater in the early 1960s and became perhaps the best-known exponent of its critical methodology. Because the Chicago Critics were influenced by the formalist, rhetorical analysis of ARISTOTLE'S (see Vols. 3, 4, and 5) *Poetics*, which was concerned with the principles of literary construction and literary esthetics, they were also known as the neo-Aristotelians. However, unlike the New Critics, who shared their interest in formalist analysis of texts, the Chicago Critics emphasized the importance of knowledge about the author and his or her historical context. They believed that New Criticism, which had developed at about the same time, was too restrictive in its bracketing of that information as "external" to the text and therefore incidental to understanding and evaluating it. The Chicago Critics were pluralists; they thought that different texts demanded different critical approaches, and they argued that the history of literary theory and practice clearly demonstrated the correctness of their position. For them, nothing could be bracketed in advance as irrelevant. They also believed that texts have determinable meanings, so that some readings are simply wrong, an idea at odds with much contemporary poststructuralist literary theory.

The first generation of Chicago School critics, Booth's teachers, did not have much impact beyond the university itself; nationwide, the New Criticism they critiqued was in the ascendant. But Booth's continued advocacy of pluralism in books like *Critical Understanding: The Powers and Limits of Pluralism* (1979) has helped revitalize and popularize Chicago School principles. Booth is also associated with two other movements in contemporary literary theory: reader-response criticism and narratology. The former includes a very heterogeneous group of reader-oriented (rather than text-oriented) methodologies. The latter is usually seen as a type of structuralist or proto-structuralist literary study, since it focuses on the function and "grammar" or structure of narrative. Linked with both is Booth's *Rhetoric of Fiction* (1962), which concentrates on the analysis of point of view and how writers manipulate it so that readers accept the values of "the implied author" of a text's narration. Booth's work has increasingly emphasized reading, ethics, and the rhetoric of persuasion—a concern already implicit in this early book.

NONFICTION BY BOOTH

The Company We Keep: An Ethics of Fiction. U. CA Pr. 1988 $13.95. ISBN 0-520-06210-8. Makes ethics, including the ethics of feminism, an explicit concern for literary critics.

Critical Understanding: The Powers and Limits of Pluralism. U. Ch. Pr. 1979 $8.95. ISBN 0-226-06555-3

Modern Dogma and the Rhetoric of Assent. U. Ch. Pr. 1974 $10.00. ISBN 0-226-06572-3

Now Don't Try to Reason with Me: Essays and Ironies for a Credulous Age. 1972. U. Ch. Pr. 1972 $2.95. ISBN 0-226-06580-4

Rhetoric of Fiction. 1961. U. Ch. Pr. rev. ed. 1983 $12.95. ISBN 0-226-06558-8. Still his best-known work.

A Rhetoric of Irony. 1974. U. Ch. Pr. 1975 $12.95. ISBN 0-226-06553-7

CARBY, HAZEL. 1948–

Carby is a British-born critic of African American literature, whose work is informed by that of Stuart Hall and other scholars affiliated with the Centre for Contemporary Cultural Studies at the University of Birmingham in England, where she studied during the 1970s. In her influential *Reconstructing Womanhood* (1987), which focuses on the fiction and journalism of African American women writing from the mid-to-late nineteenth to the early twentieth centuries, Carby demonstrates that African American women of that period articulated a distinctive black feminist discourse and politics in response to the sexism of American culture and the racism of the white feminist movements that arose to combat that sexism. She suggests that the racism of white feminist theory has resulted from a failure to see "whiteness" as a racial (and historical) category, rather than as a universal (and ahistorical) norm that would guarantee that all women, regardless of differences of race, are "sisters in struggle" because they share an essential femininity or experience of oppression. Carby urges African American feminists not to make the same mistake by assuming that all African American women share some universal experience of black femininity and oppression that is expressed in the black female literary tradition as a black female aesthetic. The production of an essential black literary tradition or literary aesthetic always necessitates the suppression of differences, including the different aesthetics that may arise in response to different experiences and histories. Carby argues that the current African American literary canon is the product of just such a suppression, because it highlights texts that focus on and even romanticize black southern, rural culture at the expense of northern, urban, working- and middle-class black culture. She calls for a reevaluation of the output of such authors as NELLA LARSEN and Jessie Redmond Fauset, whose work has been dismissed or ignored because it does not participate in the perpetuation of the myth of "the folk."

NONFICTION BY CARBY

Reconstructing Womanhood: The Emergence of the Afro-American Woman Novelist. OUP
    1989 $14.95. ISBN 0-19-506071-7

CHODOROW, NANCY JULIA. 1944–

Chodorow's *The Reproduction of Mothering: Psychoanalysis and the Sociology
of Gender* (1978) helped rehabilitate psychoanalytic theory for feminism, which
had rejected it on the grounds that SIGMUND FREUD's (see Vols. 3 and 5) sexism
invalidated all psychoanalytic insights, particularly those about women, femininity, and culture. Chodorow's book served as an introduction to object-
relations theory and the work of Melanie Klein, D. W. Winnicott, W. R. D.
Fairbairn, and others. Object-relations theory focuses on the child's early
relations to objects—persons, parts of the body, and toys or other "comforting"
things. The most significant of these for object-relations analysts is the mother.
Object-relations theory concentrates on the importance of the child's relation to
the mother before it has a fully developed sense of self. The theory derived from
the work of Melanie Klein, one of Freud's disciples. Klein theorized that
children of both sexes must struggle to separate themselves from the mother
and develop a distinct identity, a task that is doubly difficult for the boy because
he must repudiate his original feminine attachment to, and identification with,
the female parent.

Whereas Klein emphasized the importance of fantasy and unconscious
aggressive drives, Winnicott and Fairbairn stress the significance of "real"
relations between the child and the mother (and other objects), as if these were
direct and immediate rather than mediated by unconscious, repressed desires.
The result is that the mother is made almost entirely responsible for the child's
development. It is this emphasis on the woman's total responsibility for child
care that Chodorow critiques. She argues that this is what reproduces the
gender differences of patriarchy. Because girls are mothered by someone of the
same sex, their egos are more fluid than those of boys, and they experience a
sense of connection with other people. Boys must exaggerate their differences
from mothers and other women in order to develop a separate and masculine
self; consequently, they have trouble feeling a sense of connection with other
people and tend to denigrate the feminine as a defense against being engulfed
by it.

Many feminists have been persuaded by Chodorow's argument and have
sought to apply her ideas to literature and popular culture. Critics, however,
have been disturbed by Chodorow's retention of what is problematic about
object-relations theory, its failure to address the importance of fantasy and the
unconscious. Furthermore, Chodorow's call for joint parenting by men and
women is seen by some as heterocentric, if not homophobic. Finally, she fails to
attend to the importance of other differences between women, for example, of
race and class, which must obviously impact on their sense of "connectedness."

NONFICTION BY CHODOROW

Feminism and Psychoanalytic Theory. Yale U. Pr. 1991 repr. of 1989 ed. $14.00. ISBN 0-
    300-05116-6. Essays written between 1971 and 1986.
The Reproduction of Mothering: Psychoanalysis and the Sociology of Gender. U. CA Pr.
    1978 $32.50. ISBN 0-520-03133-4

CULLER, JONATHAN. 1944–

Professor of English and Comparative Literature at Cornell University, Culler
has played an important role in the dissemination of structuralist and

poststructuralist theory in the U.S. academy. His *Structuralist Poetics* (1975) was one of the first books to survey the new continental theory, and it included a bibliography with all the English translations of that work then available. As the title suggests, Culler's book concentrates on structuralist literary analysis, explicating in particular what various continental critics had to say about the "deep structures" or codes governing literary production as a mode of discourse with an apparent radical diversity of texts and "surface structures." He also covers some of the background to structuralist literary theory, such as the work of the early Russian formalists and structural anthropologists like CLAUDE LÉVI-STRAUSS (see Vol. 3), and the work of people who are now identified as poststructuralists, including JACQUES DERRIDA (see Vol. 4) and Julia Kristéva. Interestingly, Culler also develops in this book a theory of reading that is not quite structuralist, although it does make use of a structuralist vocabulary and some structuralist ideas.

The Pursuit of Signs (1981) is, in effect, the second in his trilogy of introductions to this theory. It offers explanations of poststructuralist theory, which is as much a response to as a development of structuralist theory, whose premises it frequently rejects. Just one year later, Culler published a supplement to this volume, *On Deconstruction* (1982), devoted not only to the work of Derrida but also to the work of American deconstructionists, who were sometimes elaborating deconstruction in more obviously political directions; for example, by generating feminist deconstructive analyses.

Culler has continued to interpret Continental theory and theorists for U.S. audiences in his more recent publications. A prolific author, he has also published books about nineteenth-century French literature and culture, the field in which he did his graduate work, and books or essays on a range of other topics which he addresses from the perspective of poststructuralist theory, including puns, tourism, and trash.

NONFICTION BY CULLER

On Deconstruction: Theory and Criticism after Structuralism. Cornell Univ. Pr. 1982 $35.00. ISBN 0-8014-1322-2
The Pursuit of Signs: Semiotics, Literature, Deconstruction. Cornell Univ. Pr. 1981 $10.95. ISBN 0-8014-1417-2
Structuralist Poetics: Structuralism, Linguistics, and the Study of Literature. Cornell Univ. Pr. 1976 $10.95. ISBN 0-8014-9155-X

DE MAN, PAUL. 1919–1983

The most important of the Yale University critics, and one of the most influential literary theorists in America, de Man was the son of a manufacturer whose family was very prominent in Belgium. He attended the University of Brussels from 1939 to 1942, studying science and philosophy; upon completing his degree, he worked in publishing. In 1947 he moved to the United States and taught French before pursuing a Ph.D. in comparative literature at Harvard University, which he received in 1960. His renown as a teacher was established at Cornell University and increased during his years at Johns Hopkins University and Yale, where he was a professor of comparative literature from 1970 until his death. At Yale he was also the nucleus of the rather heterogeneous group of critics (including JOSEPH HILLIS MILLER), called the "Yale School"—which is not a school in the traditional sense since most are no longer at Yale—who are interested in Continental theory, particularly PAUL DERRIDA's theory of deconstruction.

De Man's work centers on the critique based on the redemptive possibilities attributed to literature since the nineteenth century, in particular the idea that it can reconcile subject and object, spirit and matter, or humankind and "nature" through a special use of language (the "symbol" or "image"). His first essays are phenomenological, focusing on ontological questions and on the implications of Heidegger's philosophy with regard to literature. According to de Man's early theories, language is constitutive and not reflective. The symbol, like all language, identifies the impossibility of immediate "being" and the subject's inevitable division from its objects or "nature," as well as its "self." De Man's first book, *Blindness and Insight* (1971), develops these ideas in a deconstructive rather than phenomenological direction, focusing on textuality or rhetoric, rather than "being." De Man's argument is that critics "owe their best insights to assumptions these insights disprove." Paradoxically, real critical insights are implicit, the result of close readings of the rhetoric of the critic's claims or explicit insights, whose conceptual limits are exposed by the language in which they are not just named but constructed. According to de Man, literary language is self-deconstructing. It has no blind spots, because it signals its literariness and allegorically prefigures its misunderstanding as literal. Allegory is de Man's privileged trope, because it acknowledges the effects of meaning as conventional and constitutive, rather than natural.

Blindness and Insight had a tremendous impact on the literary community, generating interest in, and resistance to, Continental theory, in particular, deconstruction. Resistance has been especially strong among Marxist and historicist critics, who have argued that deconstruction denies the possibility of historical explanation and is nihilistic. De Man addresses this resistance to theory in his book *The Resistance to Theory* (1986). He defines "theory" as language's power to resist interpretive closure, and emphasizes how texts undermine the very meaning that they produce. For de Man, the resistance to theory arises from a fear of it, because it upsets ideologies by "revealing the mechanics of their workings."

Many critics who are resistant to theory have found proof that deconstruction is not only nihilist but also Fascist in the recent revelation that from 1940 to 1942 de Man wrote book and music reviews for two newspapers whose regular staff had been replaced by Nazi collaborators. Undoubtedly some of these early essays are anti-Semitic, perhaps most notoriously "Jews in Contemporary Literature," which suggests that German literature remained "healthy," despite the influence of Jews and other "outsiders" on its development. However, the de Man of these reviews embraces the schemes of literary history that the later de Man insistently critiques as the sign of a resistance to theory. The early and the later work of de Man therefore cannot be combined. The later, deconstructive work can even be read as a response—or resistance—to his earlier resistance to theory.

NONFICTION BY DE MAN

Aesthetic Ideology. Ed. by Andrzej Warminski. U. of Minn. Pr. 1988 o.p. Essays on Kant, Hegel, and others who were critical of aesthetic ideology.   '
Allegories of Reading: Figural Language in Rousseau, Nietzsche, Rilke and Proust. Yale U. Pr. 1979 o.p. Argues that texts generate allegories of their own undecidability.
Blindness and Insight: Essays in the Rhetoric of Contemporary Criticism. 1971. Ed. by Wlad Godzich. U. of Minn. Pr. 2nd rev. ed. 1983 $15.95. ISBN 0-8166-1135-1
Critical Writings, 1953–1978. Ed. by Lindsay Waters. U. of Minn. Pr. 1989 $15.95. ISBN 0-8166-1695-5. Primarily essays and reviews written before 1970, many for *Critique* and *Monde Nouveau.*

The Resistance to Theory. Ed. by Wlad Godzich. U. of Minn. Pr. 1986 $29.95. ISBN 0-8166-1293-5

The Rhetoric of Romanticism. Col. U. Pr. 1984 $46.50. ISBN 0-231-05526-9. Argues that romanticism explores the figurality of all language and critiques nostalgia for the natural object.

Wartime Journalism, 1939–1943. Ed. by Werner Hamacher and others. U. of Nebr. Pr. 1988 $40.00. ISBN 0-8032-1684-X. De Man's student writings, written during the Nazi occupation of Belgium.

BOOKS ABOUT DE MAN

Brooks, Peter, and others, eds. *The Lesson of Paul de Man. Yale French Studies.* Yale U. Pr. 1985 o.p. Includes tributes, as well as essays, a bibliography, and de Man's last lecture.

de Graef, Ortwin. *Serenity in Crisis: A Preface to Paul de Man, 1939–1960.* U. of Nebr. Pr. 1993 $35.00. ISBN 0-8032-1694-7. An analysis of de Man's writings by the Belgian who discovered his wartime journalism.

Derrida, Jacques. *Memories for Paul de Man.* Col. U. Pr. 1986 $33.00. ISBN 0-231-06232-X. Discusses memory and friendship, as well as historical memory and a deconstructive sense of temporality.

Hamacher, Werner, and others, eds. *Responses: On Paul de Man's Wartime Journalism.* U. of Nebr. Pr. 1989 $42.50. ISBN 0-8032-2352-8. A companion volume of responses to de Man's wartime journalism.

Norris, Christopher. *Paul de Man: Deconstruction and the Critique of Aesthetic Ideology.* Routledge Chapman & Hall 1988 $13.95. ISBN 0-416-01972-4. An analysis by an important deconstructive critic, with a summary of responses to the wartime journalism.

FISH, STANLEY. 1938–

[SEE Chapter 17 in this volume.]

GALLOP, JANE. 1952–

Professor of English and Comparative Literature at the University of Wisconsin at Milwaukee, Gallop has been associated with the dissemination of "French feminist" poststructuralist theory in the United States. Whereas "Anglo-American feminists" like ELAINE SHOWALTER, SANDRA MORTOLA GILBERT, and SUSAN GUBAR were sociohistorical, empiricist, and reformist in their orientation, "French feminists" like HÉLÈNE CIXOUS (see Vol. 2), Luce Irigaray, and Julia Kristéva were interested in issues raised by structuralist and poststructuralist theory, which was severely critical of empiricism and had far more radical implications for culture and change. Anglo-American feminists focused on women's experience and history and on "realistic" images of women in literature. French feminists theorists, on the other hand, explored feminine subjectivity and the use of "woman" in language, philosophy, and psychoanalysis. Anglo-American feminists searched out literary foremothers; French feminists elaborated a utopian and modernist or avant-garde writing of the feminine body and desire. Anglo-American feminists called for women to make themselves "whole"; French feminists theorized a feminine subject who was inescapably split, gloriously multiple, uncontained by a unitary self.

Gallop's second book, *The Daughter's Seduction: Feminism and Psychoanalysis* (1982), was published shortly after the first translated works of French feminists appeared. Hers was therefore one of the first American feminist overviews of French feminist deconstructive and psychoanalytic theory. As such, it had a significant impact on the way in which the French theorists were read, and it participated in what was becoming a division within the feminist community between those for or against "theory."

All of Gallop's books, even her first, *Intersections* (1981), strategically engage French theory and questions of sexuality. Typically, Gallop demystifies texts by doing "symptomatic readings" of them, drawing on psychoanalytic and deconstructive methodologies to reveal a work's "'perversities"—the contradictions, blind spots, and slips that arise from its rootedness in history and ideological conflicts. She seeks to expose these so as to betray the text's (or author's) interests. Her own work is frequently autobiographical, full of puns and other literary gestures that call into question its claims to knowledge—a process she terms "dephallicization." Gallop has published four books and has been the recipient of several fellowships, including a Guggenheim.

NONFICTION BY GALLOP

Around 1981: Academic Feminist Literary Theory. Routledge 1991 $42.50. ISBN 0-415-90189-8. A history of feminist theory structured around what Gallop sees as 12 crucial anthologies published from 1972 to 1987.

The Daughter's Seduction: Feminism and Psychoanalysis. Cornell Univ. Pr. 1982 $28.50. ISBN 0-8014-1493-8

Intersections: A Reading of Sade, with Bataille, Blanchot, and Klossowski. U. of Nebr. Pr. 1981 $25.00. ISBN 0-8032-2110-X. In the tradition of French philosophical privileging of perversion as transgressive of oppressive norms.

Thinking through the Body. Col. U. Pr. 1990 $30.00. ISBN 0-231-06610-4. Essays originally published from 1977 through 1986, combining theory and autobiography and focusing on French theory and sexuality.

GATES, HENRY LOUIS, JR. 1950–

Henry Louis Gates was born in Keyser, West Virginia and educated at Yale University and Clare College, Cambridge. Early in his career he worked as staff correspondent for *Time* magazine at their London bureau and as a public relations representative for the American Cyanamid Company. Since 1975, however, he has taught at a number of universities, including Yale, Cornell, and Duke, where he is currently the John Spencer Bassett Professor of English and Literature.

Gates, an African American, is well known for his work in literary theory. His edited volume of essays, *Black Literature and Literary Theory* (1984), is considered by many to be one of the most important contributions to the study of black literature. According to Reed Dasenbrock, it is "an exciting, important volume . . . that attempts to explore the relevance of contemporary literary theory, especially structuralism and poststructuralism, to African and Afro-American literature." (*World Literature Today*). In the book, Gates brings together 13 essays that apply modern literary theory to the literary production of Africans and African Americans. In attempting to enrich the understanding of black literary works, the essays also question the authoritarianism of a literary canon.

In 1983 Gates published a new edition of a pre–Civil War novel entitled *Our Nig*, which was written by Harriet Wilson and published in 1859. Shortly before, he had established that Harriet Wilson was a black woman, and the novel thus became recognized as the first American novel written by a black woman, supplanting the novel *Iola Leroy* (also known as *Shadows Uplifted*), written by Frances E. W. Harper in 1892.

Winner of a MacArthur Foundation Award (1981–86), the Zora Neale Hurston Society Award for Creative Scholarship (1986) and the American Book Award

(1989), Gates has contributed articles and reviews to a number of periodicals and journals, including *Black World. Black American Literature Forum*, the *Yale Review*, the *Antioch Review*, and the *New York Times Book Review*. Among his more recent books are *Figure in Black: Words, Signs, and the Racial Self* (1987) and *The Signifying Monkey: Theory of Afro-American Literary Criticism* (1988).

BOOKS BY GATES

Black Literature and Literary Theory. 1984. Routledge Chapman & Hall 1984 $15.95. ISBN 0-416-37240-6

Figures in Black: Words, Signs, and the Racial Self. 1987. OUP 1987 $38.00. ISBN 0-19-503564-X

The Signifying Monkey: Towards a Theory of Afro-American Literary Criticism. 1988. OUP 1989 $36.00. ISBN 0-19-503463-5

GEERTZ, CLIFFORD. 1926–

[SEE Volumes 3 and 4.]

GILBERT, SANDRA MORTOLA. 1936–

A poet, feminist critic, and professor of English at the University of California at Davis, Gilbert received her Ph.D. from Columbia University in 1968. Her early work addressed canonical male figures, but in the 1970s she began to focus on women writers from a feminist perspective, teaming up with SUSAN GUBAR, a professor of English at Indiana University, in what has proven to be a very influential collaboration. In 1979 they published their first joint efforts, a collection of feminist essays on women poets, *Shakespeare's Sisters*, and *The Madwoman in the Attic*, an exploration of major nineteenth-century women writers, which has had a major role in defining feminist scholarship. This massive volume takes its title from Jane Eyre's "mad" and monstrous double, Bertha, hidden away in the attic by Jane's would-be lover, Rochester; Gilbert and Gubar see figures like Bertha as resisting patriarchy, subversive surrogates for the docile heroines who populate nineteenth-century fiction by women.

Their book elaborates a theory of female authorship and a female literary tradition that draws on but modifies Harold Bloom's Freudian oedipal model of literary influence. In this model, the "strong poet" who strives to be unique must write so as to revise previous writers, who serve as father figures, at once empowering and repressive. The "son" writer must somehow overthrow the "father," which he does by utilizing rhetorical strategies that operate like psychic defense mechanisms. Gilbert and Gubar, applying this paradigm to women writers, suggest that the nineteenth-century woman writer must address a patriarchal tradition that reduces her to stereotypes; she therefore suffers not so much from an anxiety of influence as an anxiety of authorship. To resist men's readings of her and her work, which would deny her ability to write, she must seek out female precursors who demonstrate that revolt against sexist repression is indeed possible. Nevertheless, the nineteenth-century woman is never entirely comfortable with her role as author. The female literary tradition is testimony to the patriarchal double bind in which women find themselves: They can be ill and monstrous (like Bertha) or ill and angelic (like Jane Eyre's Helen), claustrophobic or agoraphobic, aphasic or amnesiac, but they can never simply take their right to write for granted. In essays on a range of nineteenth-century women writers, Gilbert and Gubar find recurrent themes and images of escape and enclosure, clear vision and eye trouble, hunger and anorexia, which they argue are the marks of female literary imaginations. Women writers, they assert, at once counter and express anger and fear that they are aberrations. Their texts are therefore like palimpsests; the feminist reader's job is to uncover the rage beneath what may be a patriarchal veneer—in effect, to find the mad woman in the attic.

Although Gilbert and Gubar's ideas have been very influential, many critics, particularly poststructuralists, have taken issue with them. For Gilbert and Gubar, a woman writer is by definition angry, and her text will express that anger, albeit in disguised or distorted form. Reading hinges on knowing the sex of the author, rather than on a careful analysis of the text itself and the multivalency of its language. Gilbert and Gubar's work is part of a debate about essentialist and antiessentialist feminist theories, which has addressed issues like "the signature" (the significance of knowledge about the author and authorial intentions) and gendered expression in general. Are all women—and only women—"feminine"—and feminine in the same way? Is femininity necessarily expressed in a specific "style," an "essentially feminine" way of relating to words, to the body, and to other people? Is being feminine the same as being feminist? These are the questions poststructuralist feminists ask, which Gilbert and Gubar find less relevant than an historical exploration of particular women's experiences.

Gilbert and Gubar's more recent work, the multivolume series *No Man's Land* (Vol. 1, 1988; Vol. 2, 1989; Vol. 3, available in 1994), focuses on sexual and textual politics from the midnineteenth century to the present and so is a sequel to *Madwoman in the Attic*. It, too, has been criticized as essentialist: Gilbert and Gubar analyze modernism as a largely misogynist response to "the women question," inevitably finding a sexist reinscription of patriarchal roles and ideas in male modernist texts and a liberating androgyny or transvestism in female modernist texts.

Nonfiction by Gilbert and Gubar

The Madwoman in the Attic: A Study of Women and the Literary Imagination in the Nineteenth Century. Yale U. Pr. 1979 $19.95. ISBN 0-300-02596-3

No Man's Land. 2 vols. Yale U. Pr. Vol. 1 *The War of the Words.* 1989 $14.00. ISBN 0-300-04587-5. Vol. 2 *Sexchanges.* 1991 $20.00. ISBN 0-300-05025-9. A massive projected trilogy, with the first volume concentrating on the conflicts between male and female modernists and the second exploring the trope of transvestism.

Shakespeare's Sisters: Feminist Essays on Women Poets. Ind. U. Pr. 1979 $35.00. ISBN 0-253-20263-9.

GUBAR, SUSAN. 1944–

[SEE Main Entry for Gilbert, Sandra Mortola.]

HARAWAY, DONNA JEANNE. 1944–

An influential historian of science and cultural studies theorist, Haraway attended Colorado College and then Yale University, where she received a Ph.D. in biology in 1972. She currently teaches at the University of California at Santa Cruz. Haraway draws on poststructuralist, Marxist, feminist, postcolonial, and cultural studies theory to explore the political and social dimensions of science in order to reclaim it for ends other than social control. Axiomatic for her is that nature is not discovered and then objectively observed and described, but rather that it is actively constructed by a culture so as to serve certain political ends, even if these are not consciously articulated or known. Like MICHEL

FOUCAULT (see Vols. 2, 4, and 5), Haraway believes that discourses of knowledge are always also discourses of pleasure and power.

Haraway's first book, *Crystals, Fabrics, and Fields* (1976), is not as theoretically sophisticated as her next two books, which have had a significant impact on cultural, feminist, and postcolonial studies, and have been the subject of some controversy amongst traditionally trained scientists and historians of science. *Primate Visions* (1989) is an analysis of the gender and racial politics of primatology, the study of "man's closest relatives in the animal kingdom." Haraway argues that primatology is, in effect, simian orientalism (a reference to the ground-breaking term "orientalism"—the West's patronizing and oppressive view of the East—developed by critic EDWARD SAID). In this view, apes are constituted as the white man's "other," a "self" at an earlier stage of development, not quite civilized or fully human, like so many of the white, middle-class man's "others," all of which help to naturalize his domination. As Haraway persuasively argues, in primatology, as in Western culture in general, apes are a signifier for dark-skinned humans. Therefore, a complex politics shapes the activities of white women in the field, as well as the ways white women are viewed, a politics that has to do with notions of white femininity in relation both to white masculinity and to the masculinity and femininity attributed to people of color. Primatology texts therefore condense meanings, anxieties, and desires about gender and race relations in which miscegenation, the return to nature, and the colonial "civilizing mission" all figure.

One of Haraway's recent books, *Simians, Cyborgs, and Women* (1991), collects essays written between 1978 and 1989, including the important "Cyborg Manifesto," which argues for the necessity of a feminist science and technology, rather than the rejection of both fields, as advocated by many feminist utopians. Instead, Haraway calls for the further development of the "cyborg," a hybrid subject who deconstructs by combining distinct and unitary identities (human-machine, human-animal, etc.). Haraway's cyborg functions something like the "border subject" theorized by Chicana lesbian feminist GLORIA ANZALDUA and is a figure for a politics based on "affinities" or shared goals rather than identities. Haraway also theorizes what she terms "situated knowledges," which seem to be like the products of what feminist psychoanalytic theorist JANE GALLOP describes as the "dephallicization" of discourses of knowledge through revealing the location and desires of the body behind the "truth."

NONFICTION BY HARAWAY

Crystals, Fabrics, and Fields: Metaphors of Organicism in Twentieth-Century Developmental Biology. Yale U. Pr. 1976 $35.00. ISBN 0-300-01864-9

Primate Visions: Gender, Race, and Nature in the World of Modern Science. Routledge 1989 $35.00. ISBN 0-415-90114-6. Named one of the 25 outstanding books of 1989 by the *Village Voice.*

Simians, Cyborgs, and Women: The Reinvention of Nature. Routledge 1990 $55.00. ISBN 0-415-90386-6

HIRSCH, EDWARD D. 1928–

Hirsch is a conservative critic best known for his repudiation of critical approaches to literature (chiefly poststructuralism and New Criticism) that assume that the author's intentions do not determine readings. He argues that any such methodology is guilty of "the organic fallacy," the belief that the text leads a life of its own. For Hirsch, the author's authority is the key to literary interpretation: The critic's job is to reproduce textual meaning by recovering the author's consciousness, which guarantees the validity of an interpretation. In his two most important books, *Validity in Interpretation* (1967) and its sequel, *The Aims of Interpretation* (1976), Hirsch warns against the "critical anarchy" that follows from the "cognitive atheism" of both relativism and subjectivism, which for him result from a corollary of the organic fallacy, the thesis that meaning is ultimately indeterminate because it changes over time or with the differing interests and values of different readers. According to Hirsch, meaning does not change; only value or significance does, as readers relate a text's fixed meaning to their cultures. If there is more than one valid interpretation of a text, it is because literature may be reduced to more than one "intrinsic genre" or meaning type—the particular set of conventions governing ways of seeing and of making meaning at the time the author was writing.

Many critics suggest that the intentions Hirsch recovers in intrinsic genres are really his own, rather than those of the author, because no one, including Hirsch, can escape his or her historically conditioned frame of reference when developing interpretations of literature. Hirsch's recent books, including *Cultural Literacy* (1987), are seen as proof of those flaws by those who are troubled by the history and values of the dominant culture that Hirsch insists is the only culture. Hirsch argues that "common knowledge" is being denied minority students and others by feminists and other "radicals" who have undermined the authority of its great texts.

NONFICTION BY HIRSCH

The Aims of Interpretation. U. Ch. Pr. 1978 repr. of 1976 ed. $8.95. ISBN 0-226-34241-7
Cultural Literacy: What Every American Needs to Know. HM 1987 $19.95. ISBN 0-395-43095-X. Maintains that American schools fail to acquaint students with the common knowledge of American culture; proposes curricular revision to restore cultural content to education.
Validity in Interpretation. Yale U. Pr. 1973 $13.00. ISBN 0-300-01692-1

JAMESON, FREDRIC. 1934–

The leading Marxist literary theorist in the United States, Jameson has been an influential disseminator and critic of Continental theory. He received his Ph.D. from Yale University in 1960. Since then he has taught and lectured at a number of universities in the United States and abroad, most recently at the University of California at Santa Cruz and at Duke University, where he is currently the William A. Lane professor of comparative literature. Jameson has won a number of prestigious awards, among them Rotary, Woodrow Wilson, Fulbright, and Guggenheim fellowships. He is also a coeditor of the leftist periodical *Social Text* and cofounder of the Marxist Literary Group, both of which have been important for the renewal of Marxist theory in America. Jameson's interests are extremely wide-ranging, including film, architecture, music, psychoanalysis, historiography, nineteenth- and twentieth-century literature, surrealism, structuralism and poststructuralism, existentialism, postcolonialism, and Marxism. His writings on these topics reflect a continuing concern for developing a Marxist analysis of modern and contemporary "culture," in the broadest sense of that term, and to effect social change.

Jameson's first book, *Sartre: The Origins of a Style* (1961), was not Marxist, but SARTRE's (see Vols. 2 and 4) Marxist allusions prompted him to explore Marxist theory. This led to Jameson's second book, *Marxism and Form* (1971), much of which is again devoted to Sartre but which also serves as an introduction to the work of a number of other Western Marxists. Jameson's third book, *The Prison-House of Language* (1972), develops his interest in form, which was found in his earlier books, by addressing and critiquing formalism and structuralism. In it he argues that, for structuralists, history has no meaning because it is a discontinuous succession of discursive systems that have no referential reality, no existential link to the real world and history, as they do for Marxists, for whom history is a meaningful sequence of modes of production. Structuralism is therefore an effect of the very economic realm that it purports to explain, which reifies all social relations, abstracting them from "history."

Jameson's nostalgia for a utopian, precapitalist, and unalienated culture and a premodernist faith in totalizing—and allegorizing—theories is quite marked in this and succeeding books, of which the most important is *The Political Unconscious* (1981). In it Jameson develops the notion of "transcoding" that he articulated in *The Prison-House of Language*. Transcoding understands art as encoding real ideological contradictions in disguised form so as to provide imaginary resolutions to them. Art is like a dream—the effect of an unconscious, but a political unconscious. According to Jameson, all interpretation is allegorical—a "strategy of containment" that forecloses on the ambiguous meanings of texts and history to favor one mode of understanding. Jameson's basic premise is Marxism: He argues that the results of a structuralist or psychoanalytic analysis of a text need to be historicized; that is, linked to the history that a work expresses by means of transcoding. However, he recognizes that history itself is always an effect of such transcoding and cannot be known outside the texts and narratives that mediate it. Nevertheless, his faith in human ability to understand history and in its utopian drive or *telos*, meaning "completion," persists.

Jameson's more recent work has focused on postmodernity, which he sees as distinctly different from modernity. According to Jameson, while modernism mistakenly divorces art from history, postmodernism undermines any sense not only of a meaningful history but also of a knowable space, like the nation-state, and of such unifying identifications as gender, race, and class. In a recent essay, Jameson argues that only the "national allegory" of the literature of developing nations can offer a critical perspective on and alternative to industrialized postmodern capitalism. Many critics have since criticized this as an extremely reductive reading of the culture of developing nations.

NONFICTION BY JAMESON

The Geopolitical Aesthetic: Cinema and Space in the World System. Ind. U. Pr. and the British Film Institute 1992 $25.00. ISBN 0-253-33093-9. An account of film in postmodernity, drawing on the ideas of *The Political Unconscious.*

Late Marxism: Adorno, or the Persistence of the Dialectic. Routledge Chapman & Hall 1990 $50.00. ISBN 0-86091-270-1. Focuses on one of the leading theorists of the Marxist "Frankfurt School."

Marxism and Form: 20th Century Dialectical Theories of Literature. Princeton U. Pr. 1971 $16.95. ISBN 0-691-01311-X

The Political Unconscious: Narrative as a Socially Symbolic Act. Cornell Univ. Pr. 1982 $11.95. ISBN 0-8014-9222-X

Postmodernism, or, the Cultural Logic of Late Capitalism. Duke 1991 $34.95. ISBN 0-8223-0929-7. Essays on theory, architecture, film, and other topics; includes "The Cultural Logic of Late Capitalism."

The Prison-House of Language: A Critical Account of Structuralism and Russian Formalism. Princeton U. Pr. 1972 $10.95. ISBN 0-691-01316-0

Sartre: The Origins of a Style. Yale U. Pr. 1961 o.p.

Signatures of the Visible. Routledge 1990 $25.00. ISBN 0-415-9011-5. Essays on film in postmodern culture; includes "Reification and Utopia in Mass Culture."

BOOKS ABOUT JAMESON

Dowling, William C., and Althusser Jameson. *Marx: An Introduction to "The Political Unconscious."* Cornell Univ. Pr. 1984 $27.95. ISBN 0-8014-1714-7. Introduction to Jameson and to the structuralist Marxist theory upon which he draws.

Kellner, Douglas, ed. *Postmodernism/Jameson/Critique.* Maisonneuve Pr. 1989 $29.95. ISBN 0-944624-06-5. Includes a useful essay by the editor, a well-known Marxist and postmodernist critic, and a bibliography.

LORDE, AUDRE GERALDINE. 1934–1992

[SEE Main Entry under Gay and Lesbian Literature in this chapter.]

MILLER, JOSEPH HILLIS. 1928–

An important literary critic associated with the so-called Yale School of literary criticism, Miller received his Ph.D. in English from Harvard University in 1952. After close to 20 years as an eminent professor of English at Johns Hopkins University, he joined other faculty at Yale who were interested in Continental philosophy and criticism, particularly deconstruction, and remained there until his move to the University of California at Irvine in 1986. With his colleagues PAUL DE MAN, HAROLD BLOOM, Geoffrey Hartman, and Barbara Johnson, he formed "the Yale School." Although each "Yale School" critic worked on different material with different concerns, the Yale critics all helped make influential the work of deconstructive philosopher JACQUES DERRIDA (see Vol. 4), who for a time spent a portion of each year at Yale.

Miller was initially associated with the "Geneva School" of phenomenological criticism, the best-known practitioners of which were Georges Poulet, Jean-Pierre Richard, and Jean Starobinski. These critics aimed at an "immanent" reading of the text, one that discounted the contexts of its production or reception as factors in its analysis. But this was not a formalist reading either, since phenomenology understood a work to be an embodiment of its author's consciousness, rather than an artifact that is a beginning and an end in itself. Therefore, the critic's goal is to grasp an author's subjectivity by reading all of his or her works and discovering the "deep structures" of his or her mind, revealed in recurrent themes and patterns of imagery. These recurring elements are signs of the phenomenological relations between the author as subject and the world as object, the way he or she lived some aspect of reality. Miller's first book, *Charles Dickens: The World of His Novels* (1958), was in this mode. In it Miller argues that all of DICKENS's works center on "a single problem: the search for viable identity." Miller's next four books were also phenomenological in approach, although the last two, *The Form of Victorian Fiction* (1968) and *Thomas Hardy* (1970), already displayed a structuralist and poststructuralist concern with language.

Miller's interest in poststructuralism, particularly deconstruction, developed after his exposure to it in 1966 at Johns Hopkins, where the conference that initiated the "structuralist revolution" in America took place. By 1970 Miller had rejected the phenomenological belief in language as the pure reflection of the presence of authorial consciousness, accepting the critique of it that he found in the work of FRIEDRICH NIETZSCHE (see Vol. 4), Ferdinand de Saussure, SIGMUND FREUD (see Vols. 3 and 5), MARTIN HEIDEGGER (see Vol. 4), Jacques Derrida, and PAUL DE MAN. By 1975 Miller had publicly identified this critique with his colleagues at Yale, who four years later published what has come to be regarded as a manifesto of sorts, *Deconstruction and Criticism*.

Like de Man, Miller argues that literature does not have to be deconstructed because it deconstructs itself, a claim made in part to defuse the charge that deconstructive critics "read into" a text, although, like formalism, such a claim also works to obscure the critic's labor—and biases. Miller's practice is to locate a work's structuring "webs" or "labyrinths" of figurative language, which can never simply be opposed to the "literal" (since all language is fundamentally rhetorical), nor unified into a single and originary meaning (since all language also has a diversity of meanings). In *Fiction and Repetition* (1982), for example, Miller discusses two kinds of repetition of tropes (themes), one centered on language and one that takes language apart and exposes its units. Together, these themes make a text's meaning "undecidable," not because it oscillates between the two themes but because each recalls the other, thereby subverting or deconstructing its own identity. Miller therefore cannot offer a definitive explication of any of the seven novels he reads, since each is ambiguously full of many contradictory impulses and structures.

Miller's work has earned him several awards, among them Guggenheim, National Endowment for the Humanities, Carnegie, and Whitney Humanities Center Fellowships, as well as a distinguished teaching award from the Danforth Foundation. He has also served on the editorial boards of several journals and as president of the Modern Language Association, the most important professional society for literary scholars.

NONFICTION BY MILLER

Ariadne's Thread: Story Lines. Yale U. Pr. 1992 $30.00. ISBN 0-300-05216-2
Charles Dickens: The World of His Novels. HUP 1958 o.p.
Deconstruction and Criticism. Continuum 1979 $11.95. ISBN 0-8264-0010-8
The Ethics of Reading: Kant, de Man, Eliot, James, and Benjamin. Col. U. Pr. 1989 $33.00.
    ISBN 0-231-06334-2. Addresses the ethics of deconstructive reading.
Fiction and Repetition: Seven English Novels. HUP 1982 $18.95. ISBN 0-674-29925-6
The Form of Victorian Fiction. Bellflower 1980 $17.50. ISBN 0-934958-00-9. Discusses the
    rhetoric of fiction and the Victorian response to the "death" of God.
Illustration. HUP 1992 $35.00. ISBN 0-674-44357-8
Theory Now and Then. Duke 1991 $47.50. ISBN 0-822-31112-7
Thomas Hardy: Distance and Desire. HUP 1970 o.p. Argues that Hardy's narrators reflect
    his detachment from a world without God and the belief in love.

RADWAY, JANICE A. 1949–

Educated at Michigan State University, Radway was for several years a professor of American Civilization at the University of Pennsylvania and has recently moved to Duke University. Her *Reading the Romance* (1984) builds on Tania Modleski's work on women's popular culture in *Loving with a Vengeance* (1981). Both Radway and Modleski reevaluate romance, which feminists have read with suspicion on the grounds that it helps reproduce women's oppression by reproducing patriarchal ideology, fostering assumptions, values, and desires which are complicit with it rather than critical of it. Radway and Modleski argue otherwise, asserting that romance can be a form of protest against the restrictive roles imposed on women in patriarchy. Like British Cultural Studies theorists, they are opposed to the pessimistic views about mass culture associated with the Frankfurt School of Marxist cultural theory (particularly THEODOR W. ADORNO [see Vol. 4]) and elitist literary theorists like F. R. Leavis and T. S. ELIOT. For both Radway and Modleski, women's popular culture, like all mass culture, is never purely complicit with dominant ideology; it is also subversive. But even its moments of resistance, which express women's unhappiness with patriarchy, are at least partially recuperable, according to Modleski. For Modleski, romance expresses the contradictions of patriarchy but in order to reconcile women to it rather than to inspire their resistance.

Radway is far more optimistic about the subversive possibilities of romance, although, by utilizing the psychoanalytic and sociological theory of NANCY CHODOROW, she, too, recognizes that some of romance's pleasures have the double effect outlined by Modleski. Nevertheless, she stresses that the resistance to patriarchal ideology can be quite literally a matter of reading, which always entails a refusal to care for others in the home while one does something (*i.e.,* reading) for oneself.

Radway's book grew out of her analysis of responses by 42 midwestern women to a questionnaire she designed and so falls into the ethnographic tradition that has become a key methodology in Cultural Studies, in large part because of the impact her work has had on the field. Some critics have raised questions about ethnographic approaches (including Modleski); Radway has herself acknowledged that she unfairly extrapolated from white middle-class women to all women in her assertions about romance reading.

NONFICTION BY RADWAY

Reading the Romance: Women, Patriarchy, and Popular Literature. U. of NC Pr. 1991 repr. of 1984 ed. $10.95. ISBN 0-8078-4349-0. Early and important feminist ethnographic study of women's popular culture. Reissued with a new introduction.

SAID, EDWARD W. 1935–

[SEE Chapter 17 in this volume.]

SHOWALTER, ELAINE. 1941–

[SEE Chapter 17 in this volume.]

SPIVAK, GAYATRI CHAKRAVORTY. 1942–

Born in Calcutta, Spivak attended the University of Calcutta and Cornell University, where she studied with PAUL DE MAN and completed a Ph.D. in comparative literature (1967). She has since taught at a number of academic institutions worldwide, most recently at Columbia University. Her critical interests are wide-ranging: she has written on literature, film, Marxism, feminism, deconstruction, historiography, psychoanalysis, colonial discourse and postcolonialism, translation, and pedagogy East and West. She argues forcefully that these disciplinary and theoretical categories must each be articulated in ways that do not "interrupt" each other, bringing them to "crisis." Spivak's own work is resistant to any easy categorization. Her first book, *Myself I Must Remake: Life and Poetry of W. B. Yeats* (1974), did not have the impact of her second publication, the 1976 translation and long foreword to deconstructive philosopher JACQUES DERRIDA's (see Vol. 4) *De la grammatologie (Of Grammatology)*, which established her as a theorist of note. Since then Spivak has concentrated on examining deconstruction and postcolonialism, and its implications for feminist and Marxist theory. She engages not so much the specifics of colonial rule as the forms that neocolonialism currently assumes, both in the intellectual exchanges of the First World academy and in the socioeconomic traffic between the industrialized and developing nations.

In the last decade, Spivak has been associated with revisionist, post-Marxist historians who have sought to challenge the elitist presuppositions of South Asian history, whether colonial or nationalist. Her contributions include theoretical essays and translations of the Bengali writer Mahasweta Devi.

Most recently, Spivak has published essays on translation and more translations of Mahasweta Devi's stories. She has also given a number of important interviews on political and theoretical issues, many of which have been collected in *The Post-Colonial Critic* (1990).

NONFICTION BY SPIVAK

In Other Worlds: Essays in Cultural Politics. Routledge 1987 $13.95. ISBN 0-415-90002-6. Essays on feminism, pedagogy, imperialism, and historiography written from 1977 through 1987.

Selected Subaltern Studies: Writings on South Asian History and Society. Ed. by Ranajit Guha and G. C. Spivak. OUP 1988 $9.95. ISBN 0-19-505289-7. Selections from the first five volumes (1982–87) of *Subaltern Studies*.

The Post-Colonial Critic: Interviews, Strategies, Dialogues. Ed. by Sarah Harasym. Routledge 1990 $39.50. ISBN 0-415-90170-7. Addresses pedagogy, multiculturalism, representation, and the politics of location.

WHITE, HAYDEN V. 1928–

Educated at Wayne State University and the University of Michigan, White currently holds a university professorship in the department of the History of Consciousness at the University of California at Santa Cruz. The author of many important books in the field of intellectual history, White is best-known for his work critiquing traditional historiography, which he has reconceptualized in the wake of structuralist and poststructuralist theory.

In the nineteenth century, historians had begun to distance themselves from *belles lettres* by emulating a scientific model. By 1940, however, the scientific status of history was being questioned in some quarters. The French *Annales* School, for example, argued that histories were not scientific, objective, disinterested analysis and reportage but, rather, narratives constructed from an interested perspective, in which the selection and description of events, the constitution of causal networks, and even the delimiting of a temporal series by fixing beginning and end points for a process were all governed by ideology. It was possible, therefore, to have very different histories of the same time and place, depending on one's ideology—which might not even be held consciously (i.e., the historian might not be fully aware of the values and assumptions governing his or her writing).

For those who accepted these notions, history began to look more like literature than social science. As such, it was subject to the same kind of rhetorical and narratological analyses that literature was, in addition to an ideological analysis. It was exactly this assumption that led to White's first and ground-breaking book on the narrative strategies of nineteenth-century history, *Metahistory* (1973). In it White draws on the work of structuralist narratologists, on NORTHROP FRYE's proto-structuralist theory of archetypal literary modes, and on KENNETH BURKE's theory of rhetorical figures to analyze the forms of various historical discourses and to link them with particular ideologies. He suggests that the plots of histories fall into one of four generic modes (romance, tragedy, comedy, or satire), each of which can be correlated with an ideological mode (anarchist, radical, conservative, or liberal), an argumentative mode (formist, mechanistic, organicist, or contextualist), and a tropological mode (metaphor, metonymy, synecdoche, or irony). According to White, these modes comprise the underlying "deep structure" of all histories, whose "surface structure" (the aesthetic, moral, and cognitive levels of plot, ideology, and explanation) is merely an arrangement of these more profound levels. White's later work in *Tropics of Discourse* (1978) and *The Content of the Form* (1987) further develops this poetics of historiography.

Nonfiction by White

The Content of the Form: Narrative Discourse and Historical Representation. Johns Hopkins Pr. 1987 $35.00. ISBN 0-8018-2937-2
Metahistory: The Historical Imagination in Nineteenth-Century Europe. Johns Hopkins 1974 $14.95. ISBN 0-8018-1761-7. His masterwork.
Tropics of Discourse: Essays in Cultural Criticism. Johns Hopkins 1985 repr. of 1978 ed. $13.95. ISBN 0-8018-2741-8. Essays that supplement *Metahistory*, discussing historians before and after the nineteenth century.

WIMSATT, WILLIAM KURTZ, JR. 1907–1975

Wimsatt, Sterling Professor of English at Yale, where he taught for over 35 years, was one of the most important literary critics of his generation. He and Yale colleague CLEANTH BROOKS were arguably the key disseminators of the New Criticism, which was extremely influential from the 1940s through the 1960s. The basic tenets of New Criticism were outlined in England during the 1920s and 1930s by T. S. ELIOT, William Empson, and I. A. Richards, and in America at about the same time by a group of southern writers, among them Cleanth Brooks. Wimsatt's 1954 collection of essays, *The Verbal Icon*, was one of the most important statements of New Critical methodology, and along with the works of Brooks, was frequently taught in college and university courses as New Criticism became the standard approach to literature, virtually synonymous with criticism itself.

Two essays from the volume, coauthored with Monroe Beardsley, have provided particularly enduring catch phrases and key indicators of New Critical assumptions. "The Intentional Fallacy" describes what Wimsatt and Beardsley saw as an excessive emphasis on the author's psyche and self-expression at the expense of the work itself, so that the critic reduces the meaning of a text to the author's ostensible intentions, the feelings or ideas he or she meant it to convey (if these can even be discovered). "The Affective Fallacy" describes the opposite, the mistake of determining the meaning and success of a work by its emotional or didactic effect on the reader, again at the expense of a close reading of the text itself. For New Critics like Wimsatt, a work of literature should be a self-contained, organic whole to be understood and evaluated "objectively," as a linguistic structure apart from its production or consumption, according to formal and supposedly internal criteria, such as complexity, irony, and unity. To consider the feelings or ideas presumed to be expressed in a work or to result from reading it is, according to New Criticism, to be swayed by moral, philosophical, or sociological criteria external and therefore extraneous to the work.

Many literary theorists now suggest that the objectivity and apoliticism for which formalist New Criticism strove is impossible and actually resulted in biased, politically conservative readings of literature. However, most contemporary critics still find close reading and explication of textual elements as crucial to the critical activity as the biographical, psychobiographical, historical, and ethico-philosophical studies whose importance they have renewed.

NONFICTION BY WIMSATT

Day of the Leopards: Essays in Defense of Poems. Yale U. Pr. 1976 $30.00. ISBN 0-300-
01960-2. More essays on New Critical concepts like The Intentional Fallacy.

Hateful Contraries: Studies in Literature and Criticism. With an essay on English meter
written in collaboration with Monroe C. Beardsley. U. Pr. of Ky. 1965 $8.00. ISBN 0-
8131-0110-7. The sequel to *The Verbal Icon.*

Literary Criticism: A Short History. (coauthered with Cleanth Brooks.) 2 vols. U. Ch. Pr.
1983 repr. of 1957 ed. Vol. 1 $17.95. ISBN 0-226-90175-0. Vol. 2 $19.95. ISBN 0-226-
90176-9. Much praised in the heyday of New Criticism.

The Verbal Icon: Studies in the Meaning of Poetry. 1954. U. Pr. of Ky. 1967 $10.00. ISBN 0-
813-0111-5. Two preliminary essays written in collaboration with Monroe C.
Beardsley.

BOOK ABOUT WIMSATT

Brady, Frank, and others, eds. *Literary Theory and Structure: Essays in Honor of William
K. Wimsatt.* Yale U. Pr. 1973 o.p. Series of scholarly essays examining various facets
of Wimsatt's ideas and work.

FILM STUDIES

Film was the twentieth century's first original art form. Since it was
developed for a paying mass audience, its conventions inevitably owe something to the need for commercial viability. The history of film studies,
institutionalized as a discipline since the 1960s, is a history of at least a double
perspective on film: one that saw film as an art amenable to aesthetic analysis
and one that saw it as a commodity, whose meaning and value was constrained
by its commercial status. The aesthetic approach to film has been concerned
chiefly with evaluation, as determined by the film critic's beliefs about a film's
"essence" and purpose. Modernists argue that film should explore its own
formal properties (*mise-en-scène,* or staging; cinematography; and *montage,* or
editing), while realists assert that it should reflect the world. Aesthetic histories
of the medium, therefore, tend to center on progress in filmmaking: either
greater and greater modernism (with European art or avant-garde cinemas as
the epitome of achievement) or greater and greater illusionism (with cinema
verité or Italian Neo-Realism as the epitome). The alternative approach to film
has often avoided the question of evaluation altogether and has focused instead
on the role of film in society, generating ideological analyses of the industry, of
important genres, and of individual film texts. Whereas the aesthetic approach
has scorned commercial products with mass appeal, the ideological approach
has focused on them just because of their popularity and status as commodities.

The earliest aesthetic approaches to film are associated with German
expressionism and the Soviet montage technique of SERGEI EISENSTEIN (see
Vol. 3). Expressionist filmmakers sought to create a stylized symbolic world in
their films rather than to reflect reality, and they manipulated staging to achieve
that end. Eisenstein also emphasized film as an expressive medium but
concentrated on montage, which he believed created new ideas about reality by
joining two separate shots and the realities they represent. According to
Eisenstein, montage was quintessentially cinematic, because film was a kind of
writing, like the Chinese ideogram. The Italian Neo-Realists and the leading
theorist of that style, André Bazin, argued that the quintessential cinematic form
was *mise-en-scène* rather than montage. Bazin believed that film was inherently
mimetic. He found montage too manipulative, an imposition of the filmmaker's

meaning upon a world already meaningful in itself. For Bazin, a film should simply reflect reality, a goal best accomplished by means of long shots and deep camera focus. Bazin is also associated with *auteur* theory, which identified a film with its director, despite the fact that a film is a collaborative production. The *auteur*, in this view, is able to realize his or her personal vision of the world, expressing it in a unique style. *Auteur* critics like Bazin and Andrew Sarris began arguing in the 1950s that even some Hollywood directors, such as ALFRED HITCHCOCK and JOHN FORD, were *auteurs*, which helped legitimize the analysis of popular as well as "art" films. *Auteur* theory also directed attention to the details of a film's style, inaugurating close textual analysis.

During the 1960s, structuralism's impact on the new discipline of film studies was as great as its impact on literary studies. Beginning with the work of Christian Metz, critics analyzed the "grammar" of the film medium, film genres, and individual films. Such analyses were based on the antirealist idea that cinema never simply reflects reality, but substitutes for it. Meaning arises from the ways in which cinematic elements are linked together, rather than from an essential link between film and the real world. During the 1970s, film studies increasingly focused on the "subject effects" of cinema, demonstrating that the popular classic, realist films of Hollywood reproduced bourgeois subjects and capitalist ideology. At the same time, feminist theories and ideas also became enormously influential in the field.

More recently, film study has been criticized for its pessimism about Hollywood cinema and for its inattentiveness to the importance of differences among its audience. Much of this criticism grows out of recent developments, including postcolonial, African American, and lesbian and gay theory, as well as a rethinking of psychoanalytic theory. Just as important, however, have been analyses articulating the challenge of traditional hegemony by subcultures as a way of countering dominant ideology and mass cultural forms. Such analyses have been particularly influential in the growing field of television studies, where it has frequently taken the form of ethnographic studies of audience response. Today, film studies is as heterogeneous an enterprise as literary studies, comprising several variations of ideological analysis, as well as a range of aesthetic and more traditional empiricist and historicist approaches.

The individuals discussed later in this chapter are those who have played a seminal role in the development of film in the United States as initiators or innovators. Additional people involved in the film industry, both in the United States and abroad, are included in Volume 3 in the chapter on the Mass Media.

History and Criticism

Allen, Robert, and Douglas Gomery. *Film History: Theory and Practice*. McGraw 1985 $19.32. ISBN 0-07-554871-2. A good overview; encyclopedic in its reference.

Andrew, Dudley. *Concepts in Film Theory*. OUP 1984 $32.00. ISBN 0-19-503394-9. A useful survey of film studies methodologies and key concepts.

Andrew, Dudley. *The Major Film Theories: An Introduction*. OUP 1976 $10.95. ISBN 0-19-501991-1. His first book, focusing on major (primarily prestructuralist) theorists, rather than on concepts, as in his second book.

Armes, Roy. *Third World Film Making and the West*. U. CA Pr. 1987 $65.00. ISBN 0-520-05690-6. A survey of Third World films and film theory.

Bazin, André. *What Is Cinema?* 2 Vols. Ed. and trans. by Hugh Gray. Vol. 1 1967 $29.95. ISBN 0-520-00091-9. Vol. 2 1971 $29.95. ISBN 0-520-02255-6. The most important essays by the renowned *auteur* theorist and advocate of film realism.

Bordwell, David, and Kristin Thompson. *Film Art: An Introduction.* 1979. McGraw 1992 $30.00. ISBN 0-07-006446-6. The best of the introductions to film studies, despite its formalist bias.

Bordwell, David, Janet Staiger, and Kristin Thompson. *The Classical Hollywood Cinema: Film Style and Mode of Production to 1960.* Col. U. Pr. 1987 $29.50. ISBN 0-231-06055-6. Seminal history of the rise to dominance of classic realist film from a neo-formalist perspective.

Burch, Noel. *Life to Those Shadows.* U. CA Pr. 1991 $45.00. ISBN 0-520-07143-3. Analyzes the hegemony of the classic realist Hollywood film.

Carroll, Noel. *Mystifying Movies: Fads and Fallacies in Contemporary Film Theory.* Col. U. Pr. 1991 $39.00. ISBN 0-231-05954-X. Critical review of the rise of cinesemiotics, which Carroll sees as overly totalizing, leading him to call for "local theories."

Cripps, Thomas. *Slow Fade to Black: The Negro in American Film, 1900–1942.* OUP 1977 o.p. Seminal study of racism and images of African Americans in cinema.

Doane, Mary Ann. *The Desire to Desire: The Woman's Film of the 1940s.* Ind. U. Pr. 1987 $35.00. ISBN 0-253-31682-0. An important feminist psychoanalytic account of the repression of woman in and by Hollywood cinema.

Dyer, Richard. *Now You See It: Studies on Lesbian and Gay Film.* Routledge 1990 $59.95. ISBN 0-415-03555-4. Analyzes overt lesbian and gay films in their historical contexts, including that of the subculture and of cinema history.

Eisenstein, Sergei. *Film Form.* HarBraceJ 1969 repr. of 1949 ed. $14.95. ISBN 0-15-630920-3. Essays by the famous Soviet director and advocate of montage.

Ellis, John. *Visible Fictions.* Routledge 1983 $13.95. ISBN 0-7100-9304-7. A classic introduction to film and television studies.

Heath, Stephen. *Questions of Cinema.* Ind. U. Pr. 1981 $12.95. ISBN 0-253-15914-8. An important collection of the essays of the well-known film theorist.

Kuhn, Annette. *Women's Pictures: Feminism and Cinema.* Thorsons SF 1982 $13.50. ISBN 0-04-440678-9. The best introduction to film studies from a feminist perspective.

Metz, Christian. *Film Language: A Semiotics of the Cinema.* Trans. by Michael Taylor. OUP 1974 $35.00. ISBN 0-19-501762-5. The most important cinesemiotic text, in which Metz outlines *la grande syntagmatique.*

———. *The Imaginary Signifier: Psychoanalysis and the Cinema.* 1977. Trans. by Celia Britton and Annwyl Williams. Ind. U. Pr. 1982 $27.95. ISBN 0-253-33105-6. A psychoanalytic exploration of cinematic spectatorship that had a dramatic impact on cinesemiotics.

Monaco, James. *How to Read a Film: The Art, Technology, Language, History, and Theory of Film and Media.* OUP 1981 $40.00. ISBN 0-19-502802-3. A useful introduction to film and media studies, with a good bibliography and glossary.

Nichols, Bill. *Ideology and the Image: Social Representation in the Cinema and Other Media.* Ind. U. Pr. 1981 $29.95. ISBN 0-253-18287-5. An analysis of how ideology informs images in film, advertising, painting and photography.

Noriega, Chon A., ed. *Chicanos and Film: Essays on Chicano Representation and Resistance.* Garland 1991 $50.00. ISBN 0-8240-7439-4. Essays covering a range of methodological approaches and issues, including alternative film production.

Penley, Constance. *The Future of an Illusion: Film, Feminism, and Psychoanalysis.* U. of Minn. Pr. 1989 $35.95. ISBN 0-8166-1771-6. An analysis of the developments in feminist film theory by a woman who helped formulate the methodologies of feminist criticism.

Rodowick, D. N. *The Crisis of Political Modernism: Criticism and Ideology in Contemporary Film Theory.* U. of Ill. Pr. 1988 $29.95. ISBN 0-252-01533-9. Details the impact on film studies of the redefinition of modernism to accord with structuralist Marxism.

Ryan, Michael, and Douglas Kellner. *Camera Politica: The Politics and Ideology of Contemporary Hollywood Film.* Ind. U. Pr. 1988 $47.95. ISBN 0-253-31334-1. Combines history, politics, and film studies to analyze the movement from the 1960s New Left to today's New Right.

Sarris, Andrew. *The American Cinema: Directors and Directions: 1929–1968*. U. Ch. Pr. 1968 $11.95. ISBN 0-226-73500-1. A discussion of his pantheon of great directors by the well-known American *auteur* critic.

Schatz, Thomas. *Hollywood Genres: Formulas, Filmmaking, and the Studio System*. Random 1981 o.p. The classic book on the subject, although it only addresses six genres.

Silverman, Kaja. *The Acoustic Mirror: The Female Voice in Psychoanalysis and Cinema*. Ind. U. Pr. 1988 $39.95. ISBN 0-253-30284-6. A feminist psychoanalytic analysis of sexual difference, focusing on sound and the voice in film and theory.

Sitney, P. Adams. *Visionary Film, The American Avant-Garde*. OUP 1979 $27.50. ISBN 0-19-502485-0. The classic text on the genre.

Stam, Robert, and others, eds. *New Vocabularies in Film Semiotics: Structuralism, Poststructuralism & Beyond*. Routledge 1992 $52.50. ISBN 0-415-06594-1. The best guide to the concepts of cinesemiotics by important theorists.

Turner, Graeme. *Film as Social Practice*. Routledge 1988 $47.50. ISBN 0-415-00734-8. Cultural studies introduction to film and film studies.

Wollen, Peter. *Signs and Meaning in the Cinema*. 1969. Ind. U. Pr. rev. ed. 1973 $10.95. ISBN 0-253-18141-0. An important text, with chapters on Eisenstein, *auteur* theory, and cinesemiotics.

Collections

Caughie, John, ed. *Theories of Authorship*. Routledge 1981 $15.95. ISBN 0-7100-0650-0. Essays debating auteur theory and the poststructuralist critiques of authorship.

Cook, Pam, ed. *The Cinema Book*. Ind. U. Pr. 1992 $35.00. ISBN 0-85170-144-2. An indispensable comprehensive overview of cinema, film history, and film studies.

Doane, Mary Ann, and others, eds. *Re-Vision: Essays in Feminist Film Criticism*. Greenwood 1984 $42.95. ISBN 0-313-27010-4. A wide-ranging anthology of feminist film theory representing a variety of approaches.

Erens, Patricia. *Issues in Feminist Film Criticism*. Ind. U. Pr. 1990 $45.00. ISBN 0-253-31964-1. The most representative collection of feminist approaches to film, with good introductions to sections.

Gehring, Wes D., ed. *Handbook of American Film Genres*. Greenwood 1988 $59.95. ISBN 0-313-24715-3. A wide-ranging collection of essays about various film genres.

How Do I Look: Queer Film and Video. Ed. by Bad Object-Choices staff. Bay Pr. 1991 $16.95. ISBN 0-941920-20-8. Essays on film and video representation and sexual and racial identification.

MacCabe, Colin, ed. *High Theory/Low Culture*. St. Martin 1986 $12.95. ISBN 0-312-37230-2. Analyses of mass culture theory, film, television, and video games by important critics.

Mast, Gerald, and Marshall Cohen, eds. *Film Theory and Criticism: Introductory Readings*. OUP 1992 $21.95. ISBN 0-19-506398-8. Essays on wide-ranging topics, including classical film theory (studies of Eisenstein, Bazin, formalism, etc.).

Nichols, Bill, ed. *Movies and Methods*. Vol. 1 U. CA Pr. 1977 $47.50. ISBN 0-520-02890-2. Primarily includes the approaches dominant before cinesemiotics—genre theory, historical criticism, etc.

_____. *Movies and Methods*. Vol. 2 U. CA Pr. 1985 $55.00. ISBN 0-520-05408-3. The companion to the first volume, demonstrating the shift in film studies to semiotic and psychoanalytic approaches.

Penley, Constance, ed. *Feminism and Film Theory*. Routledge 1988 $13.95. ISBN 0-415-90108-1. Essays—many of them classics—in the tradition of feminist psychoanalytic cinesemiotics.

Pines, Jim, and Paul Willemen. *Questions of Third Cinema*. Ind. U. Pr. 1989 $29.95. ISBN 0-85170-262-7. Essays by filmmakers and scholars interested in Third World cinema's challenge to First World cinema practices and politics.

Pribram, E. Deidre, ed. *Female Spectators: Looking at Film and Television.* Routledge Chapman & Hall 1988 $39.95. ISBN 0-86091-204-3. Essays in the feminist cultural studies tradition.

Rosen, Philip. *Narrative, Apparatus, Ideology: A Film Theory Reader.* Col. U. Pr. 1986 $19.50. ISBN 0-231-05881-0. Includes many of the most important cinesemiotic essays.

CHRONOLOGY OF AUTHORS
(Film Studies)

Porter, Edwin Stanton. 1870–1941
Griffith, D(avid) Lewelyn W(ark). 1875–1948
Micheaux, Oscar. 1884–1951
Stroheim, Erich von. 1885–1957
Chaplin, Charlie. 1889–1977
Sternberg, Josef von. 1894–1969
Ford, John. 1895–1973
Hitchcock, (Sir) Alfred (Joseph). 1899–1980

Sirk, Douglas. 1900–1987
Disney, Walt(er) Elias. 1901–1966
Welles, (George) Orson. 1915–1985
Deren, Maya. 1917–1961
Brakhage, Stan. 1933–
Rainer, Yvonne. 1934–
Lucas, George Walton, Jr. 1944–
Dash, Julie. 1950–
Lee, Spike. 1957–

BRAKHAGE, STAN. 1933–

A major figure in American avant-garde films, Brakhage made his first film, *Interim*, at the age of 18, after having a nervous breakdown and dropping out of college. Most of his experimental films since then have been shorts that explore the film medium, offering a modernist critique of Renaissance realist space. He frequently alters the strip of film itself by making scratches in the emulsion after recording images on it, disrupting the effect of the real by recalling the two-dimensionality of what appears to be three-dimensional. Sometimes these scratches have a symbolic dimension as well: In *Reflections on Black* (1955), he scratches out a blind man's eyes. Even more inventive is the collage technique of *Mothlight* (1963), made as a collage of bits of leaves, seeds, ferns, flowers, and moth wings, attached not onto film celluloid but onto splicing tape, which is then run through an optical printer. *Mothlight* is therefore a film made without a camera and even without film! Because the objects in it have not been photographed, they appear more as abstract shapes—blotches and scratches on celluloid—than as natural things; due to the effects of motion achieved by linking still frames, they also seem to "dance," rather like the shapes and objects of Fernand Leger's and Dudley Murphy's Cubist film, *Ballet Mecanique (Mechanical Ballet)*, (1924).

Other aspects of Brakhage's short films include accelerated and slow motion shots; optical distortions such as tinting, overexposure, and underexposure; alternation between monochrome and color stock or negatives and positives; superimpositions; and the presence of film leader and the dots that end a roll of film, as well as frames marked by the flare that results when film is exposed as the camera is being loaded or unloaded. These techniques, too, may have a symbolic or visionary dimension, as when a superimposition suggests something about the allegorical or psychological significance of an action or character trait, or when editing suggests a metaphoric transformation or link. For example, *The Wonder Ring* (1955) includes some surrealist effects of superimposition achieved very simply while filming in a subway car: Sometimes the viewer can see both the reflections on the window glass and what is behind the glass in the landscape through which the train passes.

Many of Brakhage's films do have characters and stories; however, they are not realistic. *Dog Star Man* (1965) has no coherent narrative, with continuity achieved instead through recurring patterns and motifs. The dog star man of the title climbs a snow-covered hill with a dog, occasionally falling. At the end he chops wood. In between, there are repeated shots of the sun, trees, different seasons, an infant, and sexual organs, all linked metaphorically through juxtaposition and repetition. Such a film constitutes what Brakhage called "an adventure of perception," one in which the eye sees reality outside the convention of realism, with its laws of composition and perspective. Such adventures are always his guiding principle in filmmaking. As the legend goes, Brakhage threw away his glasses when he began to make films.

NONFICTION BY BRAKHAGE

The Brakhage Lectures. Good Lion Pr. 1972 o.p. A discussion of his work and theories.
Metaphors on Vision. Anthology Film 1963 $12.00. ISBN 0-317-55956-7. A special issue. Discusses his early work and the theory behind it; with a striking cover.

BOOK ABOUT BRAKHAGE

Rich, Donald. *Stan Brakhage—A Retrospective.* Museum Mod. Art 1970 o.p. The exhibit catalogue for the MOMA film retrospective.

CHAPLIN, CHARLIE (SIR CHARLES SPENCER). 1889–1977

Charlie Chaplin's London childhood was marked by what were to become the themes of his silent comedies: poverty, cruelty, and loneliness. His parents were music hall entertainers; when his father died of alcoholism and his mother became insane, he and his brother were forced into a workhouse, which Chaplin escaped by entering the theater. While on tour in the United States with a music hall revue, he was spotted and hired by Mack Sennett, a film producer for Keystone Studio, which specialized in broad comic spectacles of anarchic violence. It was a style at odds with that which Chaplin had perfected in his vaudeville routines, so, when he began to direct himself in his own films a few months after he was hired, he made changes in Keystone's frenetic world of farce, developing recurring characters to create comedies filled with emotion and slapstick pathos. One of his signature characters was the rake he played in his very first film, *Making a Living* (1914), but the best known and loved of them was "the little tramp," whose fussy mustache, walking stick, worn bowler hat, and baggy pants with oversized tails suggested both personal dignity and poverty. The tramp made his film debut in *Kid Auto Races at Venice* (1914). Chaplin used him and other characters to generate comedy out of the widening social gap of the post–World War I period between rich and poor, rural and urban, immigrant and native, in such films as *The Tramp* (1915), *The Immigrant* (1917), *The Kid* (1920), *The Gold Rush* (1925), and *The Circus* (1928), which won him a special Oscar.

Mime was perhaps Chaplin's most powerful tool: He used it to give voice to those who could not speak, illustrating their deprivation, as in the boot-eating scene in *The Gold Rush*. It was an important part of his subtle acting style, which eschewed the techniques of melodramatic stage acting to psychologize action, showing it as motivated by character rather than by an external force or a plot device like a "gag." He helped center comedy on characters and performers, rather than on the events that befell them, paving the way for such comedians as Buster Keaton and Harold Lloyd. Chaplin also favored a "comedy of space," developing narrative—and humor—not through montage or editing, as with D. W. GRIFFITH or SERGEI EISENSTEIN (see Vol. 3), but through *mise-en-scène* or composition, building the story and jokes around the little tramp's interactions with the objects in his world in each scene.

Chaplin was one of the key figures of the first generation of Hollywood stars. He joined with D. W. Griffith, Mary Pickford, and Douglas Fairbanks to form United Artists in 1919 in order to be able to compete more effectively in the big-business environment of Hollywood under the studio system. But, although he was an internationally beloved celebrity, he was also notorious for his penchant for beautiful teenagers (he married and divorced several) and, increasingly, for his left-wing political views. His refusal to give his comedies typically happy endings, in which the little tramp would gain fame or fortune, put him at odds with Hollywood.

By the 1930s, the political bite of Chaplin's social satire had become quite sharp, even if it was also accompanied by sentimentality. *Modern Times*, released in 1936 during the depths of the Depression, put the little tramp in overalls as a displaced worker abused by both the bosses and the machines of the factory. His first full-length sound film, *The Great Dictator* (1940), took advantage of the odd resemblance between Adolf Hitler and the little tramp, with Chaplin playing the double parts of a Nazi-like leader and a Jewish barber; it earned several Academy Award nominations. Chaplin's representation of the conditions of his characters' social and economic displacement made him an increasingly controversial figure, drawing the attention of the House Un-American Activities Committee during the 1950s. In 1953 Chaplin, who had never become an American citizen, took up residency in Switzerland, after being informed by the U.S. State Department that he would be investigated for "political and moral turpitude." He returned to the United States briefly before his death to receive a Lifetime Achievement Award from the Motion Picture Academy in 1972, but his exile in many ways marked the political boundaries of traditional Hollywood cinema. He was knighted two years before he died.

NONFICTION BY CHAPLIN

Charlie Chaplin's Own Story. Ed. by Harry M. Geduld. Ind. U. Pr. 1985 $20.00. ISBN 0-253-11179-X. Enables readers to discover how at age 27 Chaplin wished to be viewed by the public.

My Autobiography. NAL-Dutton 1992 Focuses on the events of Chaplin's life without really providing much insight into his thoughts about them or his films.

My Life in Pictures. 1974. G & D 1978 o.p. His autobiography in pictures, designed by David King.

BOOKS ABOUT CHAPLIN

Bazin, André, and others. *Essays on Chaplin.* Trans. by Jean Bodon. U. New Haven Pr. 1985. ISBN 0-936285-00-1. Essays by well-known *auteur* critics and filmmakers, such as Rohmer and Truffaut.

Geduld, Harry M. *Chaplinana: A Commentary on Charlie Chaplin's 81 Movies.* Vol. 1 *The Keystone Films.* Ind. U. Pr. 1987 $49.95. ISBN 0-253-31336-8. The first of three volumes reconstructs the "best text" for each film and provides critical overviews of them.

Gehring, Wes. *Charles Chaplin: A Bio-Bibliography.* Greenwood 1983 $38.95. ISBN 0-313-23288-1. Includes a useful filmography and a discography.

Haining, Peter, ed. *Charlie Chaplin: A Centenary Celebration.* Trans-Atl. Phila. 1989
    $32.50. ISBN 0-572-01318-3. Essays collected by a Chaplin expert.
Huff, Theodore. *Charles Chaplin.* 1951. Arno 1972 o.p. Still one of the most important
    discussions of Chaplin.
Robinson, David. *Chaplin, the Mirror of Opinion.* Ind. U. Pr. 1984 $12.95. ISBN 0-253-
    21160-3. Follows Chaplin's rise to fame, interweaving reviews, journalism, and
    memoirs.
Tyler, Parker. *Chaplin: Last of the Clowns.* 1948. Garland 1985 $16.00. ISBN 0-8240-
    5781-3. An overview by the well-known film critic; part of the Cinema Classics series.

DASH, JULIE. 1950–

A graduate of the American Film Institute and the University of California at
Los Angeles film programs, Dash is perhaps the best-known African American
female filmmaker in America. Her critical acclaim is founded on the success of
her 1982 short, *Illusions*, which won Best Film of the Decade from the Black
Filmmaker Foundation, as well as several other national and international
awards. The film's protagonist is an African American female executive in the
film industry of the 1940s, Mignon Dupree, who is passing as white without
making an effort to do so; her coworkers simply assume that she is white. She is
also imitating a masculine identity to the degree that she dresses and acts to
discourage being eroticized by the white men with whom she must work as an
equal. Mignon wants to produce real life dramas about ordinary people, rather
than the usual industry fantasies about extraordinary people; however, her
suggestions about films are generally blocked or incorporated so as to defuse
their critical potential. During the course of the film, Mignon finds that passing
for white is oppressive, and she begins to assert her identity as an African
American.

More recently, Dash has made her first feature-length film, *Daughters of the
Dust* (1991), which has been widely exhibited and also broadcast on public
television's *American Playhouse* series. Like *Illusions*, it is concerned with the
articulation and affirmation of African American identity. It focuses on—and in
some critics' view, romanticizes—the turn-of-the-century Gullah culture of the
Sea Islands off the South Carolina coast, which has retained many West African
traditions, particularly religious and occult practices. Dash sees this film and
Illusions as part of a series that she hopes to make on the experiences of African
American women in the United States in the twentieth century.

NONFICTION BY DASH

Daughters of the Dust: The Making of an African American Woman's Film. New Pr. 1992
    $27.95. ISBN 1-56584-029-1. Coauthored with Toni C. Bambara and Bell Hooks.

DEREN, MAYA (ELEANORA DERENKOWSKY). 1917–1961

Sometimes called "the mother of the American avant-garde cinema," Deren
was born in Kiev in the Soviet Union. At age 5, she fled the country with her
parents and settled in New York. She attended Syracuse University, where she
majored in journalism and became involved in political activism of the Left. She
also studied at New York University and at Smith College, where she received
an M.A. in English.

In 1941 Deren took a job with choreographer Katherine Dunham and became
fascinated by dance and movement, which was to serve as a subject for some of
her films and inspired her thinking about camera movement as an art of dance.
Her interest in film was sparked by Czech filmmaker Alexander Hammid, who
became her second husband in 1942. They collaborated on her first two films,

Meshes of the Afternoon (1943) and *At the Land* (1944). Both films use slow motion and subjective camera angles to disrupt the realist conventions of narrative film, undermining the coherency and continuity of time and space. *Meshes of the Afternoon* explores irrational violence, the unconscious, and female subjectivity in surrealist fashion, whereas *At the Land* more overtly manipulates time and space. *A Study in Choreography for Camera* (1945), *Ritual in Transfigured Time* (1946), and *Meditation on Violence* (1948) are all "dance films," in which the camera's constitutive role for film is explored through camera movement. Particularly striking is the use of the camera as a sparring partner for the boxer featured in *Meditation on Violence.*

Throughout the 1940s, Deren worked in independent, experimental cinema, lecturing extensively and developing a network of nontheatrical exhibit spaces across the country. She also wrote a theoretical tract in *An Anagram of Ideas on Art, Form and Film* (1946), which is testimony to her dictum that artists need to educate themselves in old and new knowledge—what she called philosophy. The fruit of her efforts was the Creative Film Foundation, which she established in 1954. Four years later, Deren made her last film, *The Very Eye of Night*, which she described as cool and classicist, contrasting it with the romanticism that she had come to despise in the work of some other avant-garde filmmakers.

NONFICTION BY DEREN

An Anagram of Ideas on Art, Form and Film. 1946. Univ. Microfilms 1982 o.p. Film theory.
The Divine Horseman: The Voodoo Gods of Haiti. 1953. Chelsea Hse. 1970 o.p. The result of a trip to Haiti and her interest in ritual. Includes a preface by Joseph Campbell.

BOOK ABOUT DEREN

Clark, VeVe A., and others. *The Legend of Maya Deren: A Documentary Biography and Collected Works.* 2 Vols. Anthology Film 1984–1988 Vol. 1 1984 $40.00. ISBN 0-911688-16-8. Vol. 2 1988 $40.00. ISBN 0-911689-18-4. Multivolume set.

DISNEY, WALT(ER) ELIAS. 1901–1966

After driving an ambulance for the Red Cross in France during the final months of World War I, Disney went to work as a commercial artist in Kansas City, where he met Ub Iwerks, another artist who became his lifelong collaborator. In 1923 they moved to Hollywood where, with Disney's older brother, Roy, they produced a series of cartoons called *Alice in Cartoonland.* Mickey Mouse was born in 1928, the star of two silent cartoons, *Plane Crazy* and *Gallopin' Gaucho*, and then the sound experiment, *Steamboat Willie* (1928), in which Disney himself supplied Mickey's high, squeaky voice. Minnie Mouse, Goofy, Donald Duck, and Pluto soon followed, helping the Disney name become a household word across America long before Disney's death in 1966, of complications from lung surgery.

Disney is especially known for his innovations in animation. In his *Silly Symphonies* series, he matched the action to the beat of prerecorded music, rather than the other way around. The most popular of these was *The Three Little Pigs* (1933), which included what became a hit song, "Who's Afraid of the Big Bad Wolf?" Another cartoon in the series, *Flowers and Trees* (1933), was the first film done in full Technicolor. Disney also made the first feature-length animated film, *Snow White and the Seven Dwarfs* (1937). A smashing success, it ensured the viability of the animated motion picture in America and was quickly followed by such other Disney feature-length productions as *Pinocchio* (1939) and *Bambi* (1943). The more experimental *Fantasia* (1940) created some controversy by "animating" classical music with popular images, which enraged musical purists and bored the general public, although film buffs loved it. It has gone on to become a big moneymaker through rereleases. In *The Three Caballeros* (1944), Disney once again combined cartoons with live action, as he had in *Alice in Cartoonland*, anticipating more recent films such as *Who Framed Roger Rabbit* (1988) directed by Robert Zemekis. The Disney team also developed the multiplane camera, which enabled them to make animated films with more intricate action and a greater illusion of depth.

The years of World War II were difficult for the Disney company, for a number of reasons. The government imposed production restrictions and recruited Disney to make propaganda films. The company was also affected by worker unrest. In 1941 Disney animators went on strike to protest Disney's autocratic rule and insistence on a naturalistic drawing style. Eventually, there was a mass resignation from the studio, and the protestors formed United Productions of America (UPA). This was perhaps the beginning of a recognition that a Disney film could be propaganda even if Disney was not making propaganda films per se. Disney films embody certain values and assumptions, not only about drawing style and narrative, but also about the world that the cartoons represent, however indirectly and humorously. Disney offers family entertainment with a distinct view of the family and the proper behavior of family members (parent-child relationships, gender roles), as well as of America and the proper American.

By the postwar years, this ideology was being exported worldwide, not just in Disney's animated features. In the 1950s the company began to make live-action films, following the success of the first such effort, *Treasure Island* (1950); other hits included such children's classics as *Mary Poppins* (1964) (which incorporated animation into a primarily live-action film). Disney also expanded into the production of nature documentaries and developed an immensely popular weekly television show; more recently, his company purchased a cable station. Last but not least, in 1955, Disneyland was opened in Anaheim, California, followed by similar amusement parks in Florida, Japan,.and in 1992, in Europe. Perhaps even more than the films, these amusement parks have provoked critical commentary about Disney's marketing of a fantasy of American life and the family, which many in Europe, in particular, have decried as cultural imperialism.

Disney himself and the Disney company have won numerous awards over the years, including several Academy Awards, although they have all been special awards or awards for shorts (no animated feature-length film has ever won the Oscar for "Best Picture"). Disney was also twice honored by the U.S. government for contributing to "the American dream." Since Disney's death, his company has continued carrying on his tradition for quality family entertainment, perhaps best embodied by such recent animated features as *Beauty and the Beast* (1991), which was nominated for an Academy Award for Best Picture, and *Aladdin* (1992).

NONFICTION BY DISNEY

The Art of Animation. Amer. Fed. Arts 1958 o.p. Issued for an exhibit tracing the history of animation through *Sleeping Beauty*.

BOOKS ABOUT DISNEY

Dorfman, Ariel, and Armand Mattelart. *How to Read Donald Duck: Imperialist Ideology in the Disney Comic.* Trans. by David Kunzle. Intl. General 1991 $11.95. ISBN 0-88477-

023-0. An ideological analysis of Disney by two important Marxist critics of mass culture. Includes an appendix by John Shelton Lawrence.

Eisenstein, Sergei. *Eisenstein on Disney*. Ed. by Jay Leyda. Trans. by Alan Upchurch. S. Asia 1986 o.p. Comments on Disney by the famed early Soviet film director with an introduction by Naum Kleiman.

Holliss, Richard, and Brian Sibley. *The Disney Studio Story*. Crown Pub. Group 1988 $24.99. ISBN 0-517-57078-5. History of the Disney company.

Leebron, Elizabeth, and Lynn Gartley. *Walt Disney: A Guide to References and Resources*. G. K. Hall 1979 o.p. A useful guide to the huge volume of material on Disney and the Disney studio.

Miller, Diane (Disney), with Pete Martin. *The Story of Walt Disney*. H. Holt & Co. 1957 o.p. Disney's daughter's version of her father's story, as told to Pete Martin.

Schickel, Richard. *The Disney Version: The Life, Times, Art, and Commerce of Walt Disney*. S & S Trade 1985 $10.95. ISBN 0-671-54714-3. The best-known biography of Disney.

Sinyard, Neil. *The Best of Disney*. Crown Pub. Group 1988 o.p. A chronicle of Disney movies from the early cartoons to recent films such as *Never Cry Wolf*.

Thomas, Bob. *Walt Disney, The Art of Animation*. S & S Trade 1958 o.p. The Disney staff's version of their studio's contribution to animation.

Kurtz, Bruce D., ed. *Haring, Warhol, Disney*. TeNeues 1992 $45.00. ISBN 3-791-31146-8. Catalog of the exhibition organized by the Phoenix Art Museum March 23–May 12, 1991.

FORD, JOHN (SEAN ALOYSIUS O'FEENEY or O'FEARNA). 1895–1973

Ford was the thirteenth and youngest child of Irish immigrants. He grew up in Portland, Maine, where his father owned a saloon, and moved to Hollywood after high school in 1913, joining his brother Francis, who was a director, writer, and actor at Universal Studios. While working on Broadway, Francis had changed his name to Ford; John followed suit and Anglicized his first name as well, although he was known as Jack rather than John until 1923. He began as a set laborer and assistant propman, and occasionally acted—he was an extra in D. W. GRIFFITH's *Birth of a Nation* (1915) and frequently served as a stunt double for his brother. By 1915 he was an assistant director and feature player in his brother's films, and two years later he was directing his own films, the first of which was *Tornado* (1917). Before he moved to Fox in 1920, during the formative years of the classical Hollywood cinema, he had made over 30 films, mostly westerns.

At Fox, Ford directed two important silent films, *The Iron Horse* (1924) and *Four Sons* (1928). His fame, however, rests on his many sound productions over the next three decades, particularly the films of the 1930s and 1940s, including such classics as *The Informer* (1935), which won him his first Academy Award for best director; *Stagecoach* (1939); *Young Mr. Lincoln* (1939); *The Grapes of Wrath* (1941), which won him his second Academy Award; *How Green Was My Valley* (1941), another Academy Award winner; *My Darling Clementine* (1946); *Fort Apache* (1948); and *She Wore a Yellow Ribbon* (1949). Although his later films were not quite as critically acclaimed, several of them are now also regarded as classics: *Wagonmaster* (1950); *Rio Grande* (1950); *The Quiet Man* (1952), an Academy Award winner; *The Searchers* (1956); and *The Man Who Shot Liberty Valance* (1962). These films frequently starred the same actors: John Wayne, Ward Bond, James Stewart, Henry Fonda, Harry Carey, Sr. and Jr., and Victor McLaglen, as well as the same stunning southwestern scenery— Monument Valley, on the Arizona-Utah border.

Ford's westerns are generally about a tough but somewhat naive loner living in the apparently vast and open American frontier. This mythic space, often filmed in panoramic long shots, is always already occupied by the "wrong" sort of community—the Indians—although the hero can never quite be comfortable with the white community and its values either. He seems to want to join the white community but ultimately rejects it, as signified by his interest in a woman with whom he never can bring himself to settle down. Even the apparently homoerotic male friendships that he has forged, usually after fights or while drunk, turn out to be short-lived. These stories, and the visual style of Ford's films, as well as the soundtracks, have seemed so distinctive to critics that Ford, like ALFRED HITCHCOCK, has been considered one of the great *auteurs*, despite the fact that his were almost all genre films that closely followed the conventions of the western—which, after all, he helped create.

Ford's last films were *Seven Women* (1965) and *Chesty: A Tribute to a Legend* (1970), a documentary. In addition to the Academy Awards he won for his features, he was awarded two Oscars for propaganda documentaries that he made during World War II: *The Battle of Midway* (1942) and *December 7th* (1943). He also received four New York Film Critics Awards, a Golden Lion at the 1971 Venice Film Festival, and the American Film Institute's first Life Achievement Award in 1973, just before he died.

FILMS BY FORD

The Selected Plays: The Broken Heart, 'Tis Pity She's a Whore, Perkin Warbeck. Ed. by C. Gibson. Cambridge U. Pr. 1986 $69.95. ISBN 0-521-22543-4

Stagecoach: A Film by John Ford and Dudley Nichols. S & S Trade 1971 o.p. Screenplay by Nichols, based on Ernest Haycox's *Stage to Lordsburg*.

BOOKS ABOUT FORD

Anderson, Lindsay. *About John Ford*. McGraw 1983 o.p. By the noted British filmmaker and *auteurist*, with a filmography.

Buscombe, Edward. *Stagecoach: BFI Film Classics*. Ind. U. Pr. 1992 $9.95. ISBN 0-85170-299-6. An expert on the western discussing the elements that make this film a classic.

Ford, Dan. *Pappy: The Life of John Ford*. P-H 1979 o.p. A biography by his son.

Place, Janey Ann. *The Non-Western Films of John Ford*. Carol Pub. Group 1979 $17.95. ISBN 0-8065-0643-1. The sequel to *The Western Films of John Ford*.

———. *The Western Films of John Ford*. Carol Pub., Group 1974 $12.00. ISBN 0-8065-0445-5. Based on a dissertation.

Sarris, Andrew. *The John Ford Movie Mystery*. Ind. U. Pr. 1975 o.p. By the noted American *auteurist* critic.

Sinclair, Andrew. *John Ford*. Continuum 1984 o.p. Includes an extensive filmography.

GRIFFITH, D(AVID) LEWELYN W(ARK). 1875–1948

D. W. Griffith has been credited with inventing Hollywood, not only as the location for the institution of American filmmaking, but also as a significant commercial element of American culture and as an identifiable set of formal and narrative conventions. However, he only turned to the motion picture industry in 1907, after a career as a stage actor and journalist, when the Edison Company hired him to write scenarios and act in a film directed by the influential Edwin S. Porter. Later that year, he got his own chance to direct, and by 1908 Griffith was a full-time director with American Biograph, a rival of the Edison Company, for whom he made some 450 movies by 1913, when he left the company because it would not let him do a feature-length film.

When Griffith first began to direct, most films consisted of a series of static scenes, single takes in long shot, usually of events from the popular press or stage, which might be linked by intertitles. Narrative details were difficult to discern, and clear, logical connections between shots or scenes were virtually nonexistent. Although Porter had pioneered montage in America, combining shots to make a multiscene story in *The Life of an American Fireman* (c. 1903) and *The Great Train Robbery* (1903), he did not employ it consistently. Griffith much more regularly made use of expressive devices like close-ups, cross-cutting between parallel stories or simultaneous actions, and flashbacks. He also hired younger actors who were able to adapt to a style of acting that was better suited to the camera than the broad style then popular on the stage. Film directors in France and Denmark were making similar decisions at this time, and their films were screened in the United States, just as Griffith's films were being exported. Critics therefore continue to debate the originality of Griffith's use of the techniques that became those of classic realist Hollywood cinema, although they all acknowledge that he had a key role in disseminating them.

In any case, by 1915 Griffith was making full use of classic techniques, as can be seen in his first feature-length film, the sentimental and melodramatic *Birth of a Nation*, which captured an unprecedented mass audience. However, it also generated considerable controversy because of the racism espoused by the film, which credits the Ku Klux Klan with rescuing white America from a freed degenerate African American population during the Reconstruction era. For many years, film critics attempted to solve this "problem" by separating form and content, celebrating Griffith the technician while explaining, if not excusing, Griffith the nostalgic son of a Confederate soldier as a historical anomaly. More recently, critics have suggested that race was one of the few issues around which a mass audience could be formed in early twentieth-century America. The resonance of "the ride to the rescue" associated with Griffith's endings, which became a stock Hollywood convention, undoubtedly gained power by positing an ideology of absolute difference between protagonist and antagonist—whether black and white, or later, in the western, Indians and cavalry.

In 1916 Griffith tried to better his own accomplishment with *Intolerance*, a mammoth epic that sought to recreate Babylon itself as the setting for one of four historical plots. An epic depiction of the Manichean struggle between hate and intolerance against love and charity, *Intolerance* was, in effect, Griffith's response to the charges of racism leveled at *Birth of a Nation*. But the conscious suppression of the immediate, emotive appeals of the characters that had characterized *Birth of a Nation* spelled box office disaster, although the movie continues to fascinate film historians. Griffith directed 26 more feature-length films following *Intolerance*, including the critically acclaimed *Broken Blossoms* (1919) and the popular success, *Way Down East* (1920), which were made by United Artists, the studio that he formed with CHARLIE CHAPLIN, Mary Pickford, and Douglas Fairbanks. His last film, one of only two sound productions that he directed, was *The Struggle* (1931). Although most of these later films were either commercial or critical hits, Griffith has continued to be defined by both the successes and failures of *Birth of a Nation*.

NONFICTION BY GRIFFITH

D. W. Griffith Papers, 1897–1954. Ed. by Eileen Bowser. U. Pubns. Amer. 1982 o.p. Catalogues his papers chronologically.

The Man Who Invented Hollywood: The Autobiography of D. W. Griffith. Ed. by James Hart. Tourmaline Pub. Co. 1972 o.p. Griffith's unfinished memoir and his notes, with annotations by Hart.

BOOKS ABOUT GRIFFITH

Gish, Lillian. *The Movies, Mr. Griffith, and Me*. Mercury Hse. Inc. 1988 repr. of 1969 ed.
    $9.95. ISBN 0-916515-40-0. An autobiography and memoir about Griffith by the
    silent screen actress whom he made a star.
Schickel, Richard. *Griffith: An American Life*. S & S Trade 1984 o.p. A biography and
    critical commentary on the films, with a bibliography and filmography.

HITCHCOCK, (SIR) ALFRED (JOSEPH). 1899–1980

The London-born son of a grocer, Hitchcock attended the London School of
Engineering and Navigation. His first job was as a technical estimator of electric
cables, but he enrolled in art classes and soon found himself in the British film
industry, illustrating title cards for silent films. By 1922 he was an assistant
director (as well as an art director and screenwriter); his first production, *Mrs.
Peabody* (also known as *No. 13*), was never finished. His real directorial debut
was not until 1925, with *The Pleasure Garden*, which was filmed in Munich. It
was there that he developed an appreciation of German expressionist cinema.
Hitchcock himself, however, considered his third film, *The Lodger* (1926) (U.S.
title, *The Case of Jonathan Drew*) to be his first real film. The story of a man who
is falsely suspected of being Jack the Ripper, the film utilizes expressionist
techniques and themes, and Soviet montage (his famous point-of-view shot-
reverse shot structures that generate suspense). This film was the first of many
successful thrillers that earned him the title, "the Master of Suspense." It was
also the first in which Hitchcock himself made a cameo appearance, a
trademark gesture initially motivated by superstition but continued as a joke.

Hitchcock's next few productions were not hits as *The Lodger* had been, but
Blackmail (1929), his—and Britain's—first talking film, was a critical success
that further revealed Hitchcock's technical virtuosity as well as his obsessions.
The story of a woman who stabs an artist to death when he tries to rape her, the
film features an early use of subjective sound: In one scene, Hitchcock
emphasizes the woman's anxiety by gradually distorting all but a single word of
a neighbor's conversation the morning after the killing—the word "knife."
Blackmail also includes brilliant montage editing that builds up the suspense.

The Man Who Knew Too Much (1934) was the first of a series of 1930s
thrillers, which include *The 39 Steps* (1935) and *The Lady Vanishes* (1938), that
were to make Alfred Hitchcock the foremost director in England. On the
strength of this success, Hitchcock was approached by producer David O.
Selznick to direct in the United States. Hitchcock accepted the offer so that he
could take advantage of the better-equipped American studios. His very first
American film, *Rebecca* (1940), won the Academy Award for best picture and
earned him a nomination for best director, as well as winning him the
enthusiastic support of the American public, which continues to be fascinated
by the technically brilliant suspense films he directed in the United States,
including *Shadow of a Doubt* (1943), *Spellbound* (1945), *Rope* (1940), *Rear
Window* (1954), *Vertigo* (1958), *Psycho* (1960), and *The Birds* (1963), several of
which were nominated for Academy Awards.

Hitchcock has been of major importance in the history of film studies as well
as the history of films. His famous "obsessions"—recurring narrative or visual
themes and motifs—as well as his technical virtuosity, made him a favorite of
auteurist critics like FRANÇOIS TRUFFAUT (see Vol. 3). He is said to have edited *in*
the camera, shooting long, complicated takes that would have to be used so as
to circumvent studio control over the final cut and to realize his personal vision.
His thematization of the gaze, particularly evident in *Rear Window* and *Vertigo*,

has been of great interest in film studies, because Hitchcock seems to address film spectatorship itself as part of his exploration of the medium. More recently, his representation of women has been the focus of feminist debates about whether he participates in misogyny or critiques it in his many movies about women who are violently punished for resisting male authority or for acting on their own desires. A film like *Vertigo*, for example, appears to be about masculine voyeurism and fetishism as much as it is about investigating the guilty woman, which undermines any certainty about who is really criminal and perverse.

Although some of Hitchcock's later films, like *Topaz* (1976), were rather dull, his final two, *Frenzy* (1972) and *Family Plot* (1976), exhibit the familiar Hitchcock obsessions. In 1979 Hitchcock was awarded the American Film Institute Life Achievement Award and in 1980, just before he died, he was knighted.

SHORT STORY COLLECTIONS BY HITCHCOCK

Alfred Hitchcock Presents Stories to be Read with the Door Locked. Ed. by Hitchcock. Random 1975 o.p. One of many anthologies of horror and thrillers edited or endorsed by "the Master of Suspense."

Alfred Hitchcock's Tales to Fill you with Fear and Trembling. Ed. by Eleanor Sullivan. Dial Pr. 1980 o.p. Another anthology of horror in a series endorsed by Hitchcock.

FILMS BY HITCHCOCK

Alfred Hitchcock's Psycho. Ed. by Richard J. Anobile. Avon 1974 o.p. Screenplay by Joseph Stefano, from an original story by Robert Bloch. The original dialogue with 1400 frame blowups.

Alfred Hitchcock's Rope. Dell 1948 o.p. Screenplay by Arthur Laurents, from the original play by Patrick Hamilton, *Rope's End.* Based on the Leopold and Loeb story.

Alfred Hitchcock's Vertigo. Screenplay by Alec Coppel and Samuel Taylor, from an original story by Pierre Boileau, *D'entre les morts (Between the Deaths).* Script City 1957 o.p. A chilling tale of a man obsessed with a dead woman—and with the live woman who resembles her.

The Lady Vanishes. Screenplay by Frank Launder and Sidney Gilliat, from an original novel by Ethel Lina White, *The Wheel Spins.* Continuum 1984 o.p. Suspense and humor in this spy story set on a European train.

BOOKS ABOUT HITCHCOCK

Deutelbaum, Marshall, and Leland Pogue, eds. *A Hitchcock Reader.* Iowa St. U. Pr. 1986 $36.95. ISBN 0-8138-0891-X. Pieces by Richard Abel, Lindsay Anderson, and Patrice Petro.

Freeman, David. *The Last Days of Alfred Hitchcock: A Memoir Featuring the Screenplay of "Alfred Hitchcock's The Short Night".* Overlook Pr. 1988 $9.95. ISBN 0-87951-318-7. A memoir by Freeman, with Hitchcock's screenplay and a filmography.

La Valley, Albert J., ed. *Focus on Hitchcock.* P-H 1972 o.p. Includes an essay by André Bazin, as well as one by Hitchcock on the role of the director.

Modleski, Tania. *The Women Who Knew Too Much: Hitchcock and Feminist Theory.* Routledge Chapman & Hall 1987 $35.00. ISBN 0-416-01701-0. Argues that Hitchcock exposes rather than reproduces the predicaments of women in patriarchy.

Naremore, James. *Filmguide to Psycho.* Ind. U. Pr. 1973 o.p. A useful overview of the film.

Rohmer, Eric, and Claude Chabrol. *Hitchcock: The First Forty-Four Films.* Continuum 1979 o.p. By the noted French New Wave directors and auteurist critics who were influenced by Hitchcock.

Rothman, William. *Hitchcock: The Murderous Gaze.* HUP 1982 $15.95. ISBN 0-674-40411-4. An *auteur* theory argument about Hitchcock's masterful control over theatricality as style.

Spoto, Donald. *The Dark Side of Genius: The Life of Alfred Hitchcock*. Ballantine 1984
    $5.95. ISBN 0-345-31462-X. Suggests that Hitchcock's obsession with tormented and
    victimized women is sadistic.

Truffaut, Francois. *Hitchcock*. S & S Trade 1985 $17.95. ISBN 0-671-60429-5. By the
    noted French New Wave director and *auteur* critic who was influenced by
    Hitchcock.

Weis, Elizabeth. *The Silent Scream: Alfred Hitchcock's Sound Track*. Fairleigh Dickinson
    1982 $24.50. ISBN 0-8386-3079-0. A study of Hitchcock's often innovative uses of
    sound.

Wood, Robin. *Hitchcock's Films*. A. S. Barnes 1977 o.p. Argues that Hitchcock is as
    serious an *auteur* as Shakespeare because his works show characters overcoming
    their weaknesses.

Yacowar, Maurice. *Hitchcock's British Films*. Archon Bks. 1977 $32.50. ISBN 0-208-
    01635-X. A somewhat conservative discussion of the early films.

LEE, SPIKE. 1957–

Directing, writing, and starring in his own films, as did CHARLIE CHAPLIN and
ORSON WELLES before him, Lee has arguably had almost as profound an
influence on American filmmaking as his predecessors, although in very
different ways. In his own words, he is good at "marketing," and what he has
marketed is a highly politicized African American cinema that is also commercially viable. Many critics credit Lee with paving the way for a new wave of
mass-market yet socially conscious filmmakers, including John Singleton,
Charles Lane, and Carl Franklin.

The eldest of six children, Lee was educated first at Morehouse College and
then at New York University's film school. His first feature release, *She's Gotta
Have It* (1986), won the Prix de Jeunesse at Cannes and was both critically
acclaimed and commercially successful in the United States. Lee went on to
make *School Daze* (1988) and *Do the Right Thing* (1989), a technically
sophisticated film that addressed racism in a complex and controversial fashion.
The film constructs a narrative that leaves it to the viewer to decide whether its
protagonist, Mookie, has done the right thing when he responds to the death of
one of his friends at the hands of the police by throwing a trash can through the
window of his employer, who had called the police in the first place. Because a
riot ensues, many (white) critics argued that the film celebrated violence, and
the press suggested that it would incite black spectators to riot (it did not).
Other critics suggested that Mookie actually defuses a riot, by directing the
community's anger toward property and away from the police.

Two years later, Lee tackled the subject of interracial relationships in another
hotly debated film, *Jungle Fever* (1991), which some saw as preachy and sexist
and others praised as bold and complex. However, his most recent and
ambitious film, *Malcolm X* (1992), has been almost universally acclaimed.

Lee has published a companion text for each film that includes biographies of
all of the principals, essays on such topics as guerilla filmmaking, production
stills, details of salaries and finances, excerpts from his journal or production
notes, and the script. These materials demystify production, advertise the
talents of the people who work for him, and promote his political positions,
particularly his commitment to black entrepreneurship and cultural self-
expression.

NONFICTION BY LEE

Do the Right Thing. S & S Trade 1989 $10.95. ISBN 0-671-68265-2. Includes the tale of
    Lee's jump from acclaimed independent to successful commercial filmmaker.

Five for Five: The Films of Spike Lee. Stewart Tabori & Chang 1991 $35.00. ISBN 0-55670-216-7. Includes screenplays of *She's Gotta Have It, School Daze, Do the Right Thing, Mo' Better Blues,* and *Jungle Fever.*

Mo' Better Blues. S & S Trade 1990 $12.95. ISBN 0-671-72570-X. Lee's story of jazz musicians; screenplay and memoirs of growing up a musician's son.

Spike Lee's Gotta Have It: Inside Guerilla Filmmaking. S & S Trade 1987 $9.95. ISBN 0-671-64417-3. Story of Lee's first, extremely low-budget film.

Uplift the Race: The Construction of School Daze. S & S Trade 1988 o.p. With commentary from many of the cast and crew.

BOOKS ABOUT LEE

Patterson, Alex. *Spike Lee*. Avon 1992 $4.99. ISBN 0-380-76994-8. An unauthorized biography with some critical commentary on the films and media wars.

LUCAS, GEORGE WALTON, JR. 1945–

As a graduate of the prestigious Cinema Studies program of the University of Southern California, George Lucas represents the movie-educated generation of American filmmakers, which emerged in the 1970s, including Francis Ford Coppola, Steven Spielberg, Martin Scorsese, and Brian DePalma. Lucas's award-winning 20-minute student science fiction film, *THX-1138*, and a student fellowship to work with Coppola, launched a career of unprecedented financial success. Backed by Coppola, he made a feature-length version of *THX-1138* (1971), then gained wide recognition with the release of *American Graffiti* (1973), a look at high school in 1962, whose rock-and-roll soundtrack set off a wave of 1950s nostalgia. Made for $750,000, *American Graffiti* grossed nearly $50 million. However, Lucas's next feature dwarfed this success. *Star Wars* (1977) broke all box-office records and defined the basic terms of Lucas's legacy: spectacular technical effects and a comic-book sense of adventure.

With the profits from *Star Wars* and the massive merchandising campaign around it, Lucas built Skywalker ranch in Marin County, California, home to Industrial Light and Magic, the premier special-effects laboratory in the world. Lucas wrote the scenarios for the *Star Wars* sequels, *The Empire Strikes Back* (1980) and *Return of the Jedi* (1983), and later for the Indiana Jones films, but he handed over directing to others, as he had sworn he would after completing *Star Wars*. In renouncing the director's role, the ultimate gesture of the anti-*auteur*, Lucas exemplifies Hollywood since the late 1970s, which has focused on high-concept formulas with pyrotechnic displays of special effects, a sure-fire recipe for commercial success.

FICTION BY LUCAS

The Star Wars: From the Adventures of Luke Skywalker. Ballantine 1986 $4.99. ISBN 0-345-34146-5

BOOK ABOUT LUCAS

Pollock, Dale. *Skywalking: The Life and Films of George Lucas*. French 1990 repr. of 1973 ed. $14.95. ISBN 0-573-60606-4. Includes a biography and a discussion of the films, as well as a bibliography and filmography.

MICHEAUX, OSCAR. 1884–1951

Micheaux is the most prolific African American filmmaker—and perhaps independent filmmaker—in the history of American cinema. He wrote, produced, and directed nearly 40 features between 1919 and 1948, although few of them have survived. Most of his movies, like those of other early African

American filmmakers, were independently made "race films," made for a African animate and largely urban audience. They featured African American actors in major roles, unlike the all-white-produced studio films of the time, which employed white actors in blackface, as D. W. GRIFFITH had done in *The Birth of a Nation*. In fact, the racism of Griffith's film, in particular, prompted the formation of many all-black companies, including the Lincoln Film Company of Nebraska, which first sparked Micheaux's interest in the cinema.

Micheaux worked shining shoes, doing farm labor, and as a Pullman porter until 1904, when he purchased a homestead in South Dakota. By 1913 he owned 500 acres and had written and published the first of 10 semiautobiographical novels, *The Conquest: The Story of a Negro Pioneer* (1913), which he sold successfully door-to-door. In 1918 the Lincoln Film Company approached him about filming his 1917 novel, *The Homesteader*. When the company refused to produce the film on the scale he wanted, Micheaux decided he would do it himself. He founded his own production company and shot the movie in an abandoned studio in Chicago, where it opened in 1919, inaugurating a decade of successful filmmaking for Micheaux. Much of this success can be credited to the promotional strategies that he developed while selling his novels. Micheaux toured theaters in African American neighborhoods across the country, soliciting advances from owners and securing screening dates, thereby circumventing the cash flow and distribution problems that other African American companies encountered. He also employed relatively cheap, nonprofessional actors, although some of them became famous, like Paul Robeson, who made his debut in Micheaux's *Body and Soul* (1924). He also billed actors as black counterparts to white stars. Micheaux was virtually the only African American filmmaker to survive the 1930s and the Depression, the skyrocketing of production costs with the advent of sound, and the entry of Hollywood into the "race" market with all-black musicals—produced, directed, and written by whites.

Micheaux's films have been controversial from the beginning. Because his budgets were always minimal, the movies have poor production values: poor acting, cheap sets, poor lighting, and amateurish editing, with frequent violations of continuity—coherent spatial and temporal relations from shot to shot. Perhaps most distressing to modern viewers, his stories are melodramatic rather than realistic. Recently, however, some film theorists have come to see these "flaws" as virtues, the elements of a perhaps self-conscious aesthetic critical of the Hollywood paradigm. They argue that classic realism and continuity may be complicit with oppressive ideologies in a way that more stylized genres like melodrama are not. Such forms can provoke thought by distancing the viewer from the characters and actions instead of soliciting identification and overinvolvement, as realism does; "poor" production values, like avant-garde techniques, can also have this effect.

At least as controversial as his aesthetics is Micheaux's version of "racial uplift." His audiences were frequently ambivalent about the bourgeois ideology of the self-made man that Micheaux seemed to represent in his films, in which only light-skinned blacks succeeded, often by passing as whites. His characters seemed to live in a separate but equal world, as if black poverty and white racism did not exist. Micheaux argued that his films represented a range of images of African American life, rather than reproducing white stereotypes or limiting black actors to roles as servants.

In 1948, after a 10-year absence from the industry, Micheaux staged a disastrous comeback with *The Betrayal*, which was extensively and negatively reviewed in both the black and white press. Its failure permanently ended his career. He died three years later while on a promotional tour for one of his books.

FICTION BY MICHEAUX

The Conquest: The Story of a Negro Pioneer. Ayer repr. of 1913 ed. $16.00. ISBN 0-8369-8632-6

BOOK ABOUT MICHEAUX

Young, Joseph A. *Black Novelist as White Racist: The Myth of Black Inferiority in the Novels of Oscar Micheaux.* Greenwood 1989 $39.95. ISBN 0-313-25749-3. Part of the Greenwood series on African American and African literature.

PORTER, EDWIN STANTON. 1870–1941

Porter is the first important American director and one of the most influential of all early filmmakers, often ranked in importance with the French directors Georges Méliès and Auguste and Louis Lumière; the former pioneered the fantasy film and the latter, the realist film. Porter is in the tradition of the Lumière brothers, but his contribution to realist film production depended on an insight he shared with Méliès—that editing was crucial for narrative cinema. While Méliès discovered how editing could be used to achieve the special effects so central to the fantasy films he made, Porter concentrated on using editing to make realistic events more dramatic and so more like stories than the "slices of life" filmed by the Lumières. He introduced many of the editing techniques that are the backbone of what is called the continuity system—the conventions for linking shots in realist narrative cinema to maintain continuous story action and clear space-time and causal relations between the events depicted.

Porter, a mechanic, began as a general handyman for the Edison Company in 1896 and then graduated to camera operator and, finally, director, in which role he helped make Edison one of the major studios. Initially, he made films like those of other early directors, which were generally little more than moving tableaux in long shot, so that scenes unfolded in single, panoramic takes, with important narrative details difficult to discern and links between shots and scenes virtually nonexistent. After Porter saw Méliès's films, however, he realized that he could combine or edit together shots of events by cutting and joining them in order to make a more complex scene as well as a multiscene story, in which each shot contributed to the narrative as a whole and could not be fully understood apart from the others. His first experiment with editing was the revolutionary *The Life of an American Fireman* (c. 1903). The film Porter made about a year later, *The Great Train Robbery* (1903), was to be even more successful and influential: It was the most widely exhibited of all nickelodeon movies and the model for many a filmmaker until D. W. GRIFFITH, who further developed Porter's editing principles (indeed, Griffith eventually eclipsed Porter in importance). *The Great Train Robbery* heightens the drama of the capture of the train robbers by cross-cutting between the robbers on the run and the posse that is closing in on them. It also contains one of the first uses of match-on-action (or a near match)—a cut to a different framing of the same action but at the same moment, so that the narrative appears to continue without a break.

Of the several hundred (mostly brief) films that Porter made, a few others are particularly noteworthy. In *The Ex-Convict* (1905), he developed contrast editing—cutting between scenes to create thought-provoking comparisons of the contrasting social situations they represented. In *The Kleptomaniac* (1905), he refined contrast editing and developed parallel editing—cutting between two different stories of shoplifting so that they commented on each other by virtue of their similarities as well as their differences. In *The Dream of a Rarebit Fiend* (1906), he elaborated on some of the special effects that had been developed by Meliès. In *The Eternal City* (1915), he made what was only America's second big film spectacle (Griffith had made the first). But he lost most of his money in the crash of 1929 and spent many of his last years working in a machine shop, forgotten by the industry that he had influenced so profoundly.

BOOKS ABOUT PORTER

Musser, Charles. *Before the Nickelodeon: Edwin S. Porter and the Edison Manufacturing Company.* U. CA Pr. 1990 $60.00. ISBN 0-520-06080-6. Part of the UCLA Film and Television Archive Studies in History, Criticism, and Theory Series.

RAINER, YVONNE. 1934–

Like two other well-known, avant-garde filmmakers, British director Sally Potter and American STAN BRAKHAGE, Rainer began as a performer before shifting her attention to film. Her Judson Dance Performances in the mid-1960s made her one of the best-known women in the New York avant-garde art world. Rainer brought this avant-garde sensibility to film when, in the early 1970s, she began creating what have been described as cubist melodramas. All of her films, beginning with the first, *Lives of Performers* (1972), are the product of an antihumanist and modernist/avant-garde interest in form and the properties of film as a medium. Nevertheless, Rainer's films are not just about film form; they also reveal an enduring humanist and realist interest in content, particularly the experiences of women.

Because of this double focus, many feminist film theorists have found Rainer's work to be exemplary. They argue that its modernist self-reflexivity disrupts the viewer identification with female characters that are typical of Hollywood realist cinema and some feminist documentaries, allowing for a more politically effective distance and analytical relationship to what is represented. For example, one of her most critically acclaimed films, *Film about a Woman Who . . .* (1974), is a story of a woman whose unhappiness arises from her inability to have the kind of relationship with a man that she wants. However, Rainer uses a number of distancing devices throughout the film to prevent the spectator from becoming totally immersed in the story and the protagonist's emotions; these devices serve as a constant reminder that the film is a film—a construction of a reality—rather than a window on to some actual reality that is merely reflected. Rainer's distancing techniques include unusual compositions and points of view, a disjunction between the voice-over and the image, the use of intertitles or frames of written text, and the fracturing of the space-time relations of the narrative, which is presented in disjointed fragments. Rather than doing all the work of making connections and sense, as the director does in a realist film, Rainer forces the spectator to do that work and, in the process, causes him or her to ask questions about love between men and women in our culture. Thus, while the film is not explicitly feminist (Rainer did not think of her early films as such, although she was interested in many of the issues associated with feminism), the spectator is led to ask the kinds of questions that feminists believe must be addressed in a sexist culture. Rainer has since come to identify herself as a feminist and to collaborate with other women who wish to address feminist issues in the medium of film. A key concern of her later films is the objectification of women and the politics of vision in cinema.

NONFICTION BY RAINER

The Films of Yvonne Rainer. Ind. U. Pr. 1989 $35.00. ISBN 0-253-34906-0. Critical essays by Rainer, B. Ruby Rich, and others; includes filmography.
Work 1961–73. NYU Pr. 1974 o.p. Covers Rainer's work in dance and her first two films, including shooting scripts.

SIRK, DOUGLAS (SIERCK, CLAUS DETLEF). 1900–1987

Born in Denmark, Sirk went to Germany in his teens to study law, philosophy, art, and drama. While there, he became involved in theater, spending many years as a successful stage producer and director before making his first feature-length film, *April, April* (1935). Sirk found himself at odds with the Nazi regime, which exerted rigorous control over the theater. But because film had an international market, film directors had more freedom than directors in the theater, and this prompted Sirk's switch to movies. He finally fled Germany in 1937, working throughout Europe, South Africa, and Australia before emigrating to Hollywood, where he arrived in 1939. Despite his reputation in Europe, Sirk virtually had to start all over in the United States and he changed his name, Americanizing it to avoid the liability of a German name during the war years.

Sirk's first American film was *Hitler's Madman* (1943), which was followed by the moderately popular thrillers *Lured* (1947) and *Sleep My Love* (1948); thus was inaugurated Sirk's association with the genres of the thriller and melodrama. Time and again he was assigned scripts in these popular forms and given ridiculously small budgets with which to work. Yet he produced films that many critics now regard as brilliant, partly because of the reevaluation of the melodrama form during the 1970s by literary and film scholars. Such melodramas as *All That Heaven Allows* (1955), *Written on the Wind* (1956), and *Imitation of Life* (1959) are now seen as offering compelling critiques of conservative patriarchal and racist American values. Critics argue that melodrama achieves its effects through the very stylization that has provoked its denigration when it is compared to realism. Because the staging is more often symbolic than realistic, it can comment on character and action in the manner of a parallel story; in effect, the setting and style express what the characters are unable to, either because they are unaware or because they do not have a language adequate to their emotions. Thus, women's entrapment by bourgeois domesticity is often represented visually in Sirk films by framing women behind stair rails or hemming them in by the excessive furnishings of a middle-class home.

Claiming ill health, Sirk retired from the film industry in 1959 and returned to Germany, where he resumed the work in the theater that had been his first enthusiasm. He died in Switzerland.

NONFICTION BY SIRK

Imitation of Life. ed. by Lucy Fischer. Rutgers U. Pr. 1991 $37.00. ISBN 0-8135-1644-7. A well-rounded study of the film by the same name that includes interviews, biographical information and source material.

STERNBERG, JOSEF VON. 1894–1969

Sternberg was born to a middle-class Jewish family in Vienna and emigrated to the United States at the age of 17. During World War I, he produced training films for the U.S. Army Signal Corps. After the war ended, he worked in various menial positions in the film industry before becoming an assistant director in 1921 and a director a few years later. At that time, the aristocratic *von* was attached to his name by a producer who thought it would add class. His directorial debut was in 1925, with the low-budget but very successful *The Salvation Hunters*; however, Sternberg only really made a name for himself with *Underworld* (1926), the first of several gangster films featuring George Bancroft. These were especially remarkable for their cinematography and lighting, which revealed the influence of expressionism in their play with light and dark. Sternberg never made a color film, but he exploited the medium of black and white to create textured spaces of light and shadow, smoke and mist, and screens and veils, which were symbolically and emotionally resonant. Although critics have sometimes found his narratives thin, they have agreed that his visuals are stunning.

While Sternberg was considered one of Hollywood's most important directors in his own day, he is now remembered chiefly for his seven films with Marlene Dietrich. He discovered her in a cabaret in Berlin, where he had gone to film *The Blue Angel* (1930), Germany's first sound production; she was cast as the provocative singer Lola-Lola, a role that made her a star. Sternberg carefully managed her screen image in the six other films that he made with her: *Morocco* (1930), *Dishonored* (1931), *Shanghai Express* (1932), *Blonde Venus* (1932), *The Scarlet Empress* (1934), and *The Devil Is a Woman* (1935).

Sternberg was notoriously imperious and autocratic, with a fondness for jodhpurs and riding boots, and was thought of as something of a caricature of the Hollywood director. The role he envisioned for Dietrich was that of the *femme fatale*, the desirable but enigmatic and even dangerous lady who seems to symbolize the "eternal feminine" and the attraction, mystery, and threat that that image holds for men. Feminist film theorists have suggested that Sternberg's visual style, as well as Dietrich's acting style, work to expose and critique the sexism of this archetype of femininity.

Sternberg's difficulties with *I, Claudius* (unfinished, 1937) damaged his reputation in Hollywood, and he worked irregularly thereafter. His last film—his favorite project—was *Anatahan* (1953), about Japanese soldiers isolated on an island at the close of World War II. Although he traveled to international film festivals and occasionally lectured in the years that followed, he never made another film.

NONFICTION BY STERNBERG

Fun in a Chinese Laundry. 1965. Mercury Hse. Inc. 1988 repr. of 1965 ed. $9.95. ISBN 0-916515-37-0. His colorful—and bitter—autobiography.
Marlene Dietrich: Portraits. (with Klaus-Jurgen Sembach.) Trans. by Arthur S. Wensinger and Richard H. Wood. Grove Pr. 1984 o.p. Photos of Dietrich by Kenneth Alexander and others, with an introduction by Sembach and an epilogue by Sternberg.

BOOKS ABOUT STERNBERG

Harrington, Curtis. Ed. by Herman G. Weinberg. *An Index to the Films of Josef von Sternberg.* Gordon Pr. 1976 $59.95. ISBN 0-8490-2051-4
Sarris, Andrew. *The Films of Josef von Sternberg.* Doubleday 1966 o.p. Commentaries by the well-known *auteurist* film critic.
The Cinema of Josef von Sternberg, a Compendiumn of Critical Commentary, Opinion, and Historical Notes on Von Sternberg and His Work. U. of Minn. Pr. 1964 o.p. Dated; useful for early material only.

Studlar, Gaylyn. *In the Realm of Pleasure: Von Sternberg, Dietrich, and the Masochistic Aesthetic*. U. of Ill. Pr. 1988 $29.95. ISBN 0-252-01536-3. A feminist analysis of Sternberg's films and his creation of Dietrich's image that critiques the reigning psychoanalytic paradigm.

STROHEIM, ERICH VON. 1885–1957

Born in Vienna of bourgeois Prussian Jewish and Polish parents, Erich Oswald Stroheim emigrated to the United States in 1909, changing his identity en route: He called himself a decorated military officer, renamed himself Erich von Stroheim, and gave himself aristocratic parents, as *von* suggests. In this guise, he presented himself to Hollywood and quickly advanced from studio extra to military advisor, assistant art director, art director, scriptwriter, and finally to director in D. W. GRIFFITH's (see also Vol. 3) production company. He also frequently acted the role of a sinister or seductive continental military officer, billed by the studio as "the man you love to hate"—a part rather similar to the one he had played behind the cameras since he had left Europe. His finest performance in that type of role was the role of von Rauffenstein in Jean Renoir's *La Grande Illusion* (1936); it won him the French Legion of Honor.

However, Stroheim is best remembered as a gifted but uncompromising director who was forcibly retired from directing in 1932. Believing that film was an art form, he toiled over his nine productions, refusing to conform to studio timetables or budgets. His work anticipated the aesthetics of sound film (although he never made one), using composition and realistic details of *mise-en-scène* rather than montage or pantomime to suggest character. Stroheim's first important film, which established his reputation as a creative genius and profligate spendthrift, was *Foolish Wives* (1921). It explored the sexual awakening of a neglected American wife in Europe, who responds to the attentions of a sophisticated continental gentleman, played by Stroheim himself. Because Stroheim insisted on authentic detail—for example, demanding that the studio build a life-size replica of Monte Carlo—the film went over budget and cost close to $1 million, an incredible sum for that time. Stroheim's masterpiece about human degradation, *Greed* (1924), was also made at considerable expense, in large part because of location shooting, including scenes in Death Valley. The original ran 10 hours, much too long for commercial release; an inexperienced studio cutter reduced it to an hour and a half, and the work print was destroyed, as were Stroheim's versions of almost all of his films. Stroheim's extravagance ensured the demise of his directing career, although his acting career as a monocled seducer continued to flourish long after he had ceased to direct.

SCREENPLAY BY STROHEIM

The Complete Greed of Erich von Stroheim. Arno Pr. 1972 o.p. The script for the original uncut film. Compiled and annotated with a foreword by Herman G. Weinberg.

BOOKS ABOUT STROHEIM

Koszarski, Richard. *The Man You Loved to Hate: Erich von Stroheim and Hollywood*. OUP 1983 $29.95. ISBN 0-19-503239-X. Includes a biography plus critical commentary on the film; exposes Stroheim's self-mythologizing.

Noble, Peter. *Hollywood Scapegoat: The Biography of Erich von Stroheim*. Ayer 1972 repr. of 1950 ed. $18.00. ISBN 0-405-03922-0. Accepts Stroheim's stories about himself at face value.

WELLES, (GEORGE) ORSON. 1915–1985

Welles, who cowrote, produced, directed, and starred in the acclaimed movie *Citizen Kane*, was only 26 years old when the film was released in May 1941. When he arrived in Hollywood just two years earlier, he was already an international celebrity, having been active in New York theater and radio for almost a decade as an actor, director, and writer. He started the Mercury Theatre with John Houseman in 1937, and the critical acclaim that followed their productions of *Julius Caesar* (1937) and *Housebreak House* (1938) led to a contract with CBS radio. From 1938 to 1940, Welles wrote, directed, and acted in the *Mercury Theatre of the Air*, and as part of its programming, he broadcast H. G. WELLS's *War of the Worlds* on the eve of Halloween 1938. The uproar that ensued made Welles famous worldwide and prompted Hollywood to take notice. Of the studios competing for him, RKO offered Welles the most appealing contract, a six-picture deal that gave him control over every aspect, except budget, of the films he made. This creative freedom, unprecedented in the film industry, together with the talent that Welles gathered around him, resulted in the production of *Citizen Kane*.

The film was years ahead of its time. Its narrative structure was very sophisticated, incorporating parodic newsreel footage and a series of flashbacks depicting various characters' memories of Charles Foster Kane, introducing subtle questions about representation, truth, objectivity, memory, and media. The film's style was very innovative, combining dramatic chiaroscuro lighting; extraordinary depth of field and almost "universal focus" cinematography; long takes, composition in depth, and complicated camera movements; expressionistic sets; and striking new uses of sound, such as the lightning mix, which some said made it the first modern sound film.

Citizen Kane had a profound impact on the way in which films were made in Hollywood and abroad, influencing American *film noir*, the French New Wave, and Bazinian "realism," the aesthetic articulated by *auteur* theorist André Bazin. Although critics realized the value of the film when it was released (it won an unprecedented four Oscar nominations), it did very poorly at the box office because of adverse publicity by the newspapers owned by William Randolph Hearst, who was clearly the model for Kane.

Welles was never again to enjoy the freedom and resources he had while making *Citizen Kane*. His second feature for RKO, *The Magnificent Ambersons* (1942), is considered by many critics to be a lost masterpiece: The studio cut Welles's version from 132 to 88 minutes and shot a new ending for the film. It lost money, as did *The Lady from Shanghai* (1948), another Welles film that is now highly regarded. After a 10-year exile from directing films in Hollywood, Welles returned to make *Touch of Evil* (1958), a tour de force that nearly rivals *Citizen Kane* in its technical mastery and thematic sophistication. Although it won the Grand Prix at Cannes, it did not do well financially. *Chimes at Midnight* (1966), Welles's last completed feature, was made in Europe and has been highly acclaimed.

Welles continued to act even after directing became his primary interest, often in his own films but also in other films and even television commercials. He made his last film appearance in Henry Jaglom's bittersweet comedy, *Someone to Love* (1987). Welles received a Special Oscar in April 1971 for "superlative artistry and versatility" and a Life Achievement Award from the American Film Institute in 1975.

FICTION BY WELLES

Mr. Arkadin, a Novel. Crowell 1956 o.p. The basis for a Welles film.

SCREENPLAYS BY WELLES

The Cradle Will Rock. Script City 1984 o.p. Written with John Houseman. A W.P.A. script that created an uproar because of its socialist themes.

Orson Welles on Shakespeare: The W.P.A. and Mercury Theater Playscripts. Greenwood 1990 $45.00. ISBN 0-313-27334-0. Includes his famous adaptations of *Macbeth, Julius Caesar,* and *The Tempest.*

BOOKS ABOUT WELLES

Bazin, André. *Orson Welles: A Critical View.* Trans. by Jonathan Rosenbaum. Acrobat 1991 repr. of 1978 ed. $13.95. ISBN 0-918226-28-7. By the noted *auteurist* critic.

Carringer, Robert. *The Making of Citizen Kane.* U. CA Pr. 1985 $37.50. ISBN 0-520-05367-2. The most comprehensive production record.

Kael, Pauline. *The Citizen Kane Book: Raising Kane.* Limelight Edns. 1984 $16.95. ISBN 0-87910-016-8. Calls into question Welles's genius as an *auteur* by giving credit to others who worked with Welles on the film.

Leaming, Barbara. *Orson Welles: A Biography.* Viking Penguin 1989 $10.95. ISBN 0-14-012762-3. The definitive biography.

Naremore, James. *The Magic World of Orson Welles.* Rev. ed. U. Pr. 1989 repr. of 1978 ed. $14.95. ISBN 0-87074-299-X. The best all-around critical work on Welles.

GAY AND LESBIAN LITERATURE

Gay and lesbian studies, like women's and black studies, arose in response to the political activism of the 1960s. Its institutionalization, however, has come about more slowly; indeed, most university programs in gay and lesbian studies are less than five years old. Theory, therefore, had an impact on the field even before its inception, generating debates that have centered on the issue of identity politics or essentialist and antiessentialist/social-constructionist theories of homosexuality. Essentialist positions hold that there is some (perhaps biological) "essence" to homosexuality that ensures that one is gay or lesbian from birth, so that one's social situation does not influence one's sexual identity except insofar as it promotes self-hatred or denial through homophobic oppression. Stories of "coming out" are often characterized by an essentialism of this sort, in which the narrator affirms that he or she was always "different." The corollary to essentialism on the personal level is essentialism on the world-historical level, in which the presence of a more or less constant number of gays and lesbians in all places at all times is affirmed. This results in histories like Jonathan Boswell's *Christianity, Social Tolerance, and Homosexuality* (1980), which assume that historical or geographical differences in sexual practices are not essential and do not challenge the premise that sexuality is naturally divided into two and only two orientations and identities. Literary histories in this mode uncover a homosexual tradition that begins with the lyrics of SAPPHO (see Vol. 2) and the pederastic poems of ancient Greece.

The antiessentialist or social-constructionist position is much more or radically historicist. Drawing on the work of poststructuralist historian MICHEL FOUCAULT (see Vols. 2, 4, and 5), social constructionists argue that sexuality and therefore sexual identities are not "natural," the expression of some biological instinct, but are instead social constructs, different in different times and places. Both heterosexuality and homosexuality, therefore, have a history, which, according to Foucault, begins some time in the nineteenth century. In this view, to describe Greek pederastic poetry as "gay" is to misconstrue it, since sexuality was very differently organized in ancient Greece, structured around activity and passivity rather than object choice, as in the modern West. The strength of antiessentialism is just this historicism, which counters the Western ethnocentric tendency to universalize and to naturalize our institutions, practices, and ideas. It also enables a deconstruction of identity as bounded and fixed, opening it to the notion of multiple identities in one person as well as to change. This seems necessary in light of critiques of identity politics (whether gay, feminist, or black) as exclusionary and oppressive because it is blind to the heterogeneity of a supposedly homogeneous group. On the other hand, many activists see a continued need for politics that rest on a stable notion of identity because they have been the foundation for civil rights demands and public policies like affirmative action. Some also fear that antiessentialism deconstructs away identities that still function as such in an oppressive society and that they have struggled to be affirmed in the face of that oppression.

Clearly, this debate has implications for all of gay and lesbian studies, including the critique or affirmation of gay and lesbian representations. Critiques in the field concentrate on exposing homophobia in straight literature and literary theory, as well as revealing "heterocentrism," the assumption of heterosexuality as a norm, which naturalizes and universalizes it. These critiques frequently examine images of lesbians and gays, assuming that the reader has no problem identifying a character's sexual identity, a premise antiessentialism would question. Similarly, affirmation involves two strategies, both of which would be called into question by antiessentialism. The effort to articulate a lesbian or gay "specificity"—locating a gay difference in lesbian and gay sexuality, gender roles, literature, music, filmmaking and so on—is obviously problematic from an antiessentialist perspective. Potentially just as problematic from that point of view are the recovery and revaluation of lesbian and gay texts, because they beg the question of what counts as lesbian and gay in the first place. Is a lesbian or gay text one by a self-identified homosexual? Or is it one by an author who can be "outed" on the basis of some biographical evidence, even if his or her work has no explicitly gay themes or characters? And just what is a gay theme or character? What counts as evidence for an author's lesbian or gay sexual activity? Are lesbian or gay fantasies enough? And which fantasies or desires are gay? Can texts that are read and enjoyed by lesbian and gay readers express those desires, even when they have been written by straight authors or seem to be directed to straight readers? Recently, some critics who have considered these questions have begun to elaborate a version of "queer theory" and "queer identities," recognizing the variety of sexual practices and the variability of sexual identities based on them.

Theory has impacted not only on the issue of gay and lesbian identities, but also on a host of other issues of concern to the gay community, most importantly, AIDS. Discourses about AIDS have been analyzed using poststructuralist theory to uncover their representational strategies as well as the ideological interests they serve, with the hope of influencing government policies about AIDS and AIDS research. Clearly, both theory and political activism have deeply influenced the structure of the field itself, which, unlike literary studies, has from the first been organized around issues and debates in the community, rather than canonical texts or authors.

History and Criticism

Allen, Paula Gunn. *The Sacred Hoop: Recovering the Feminine in American Indian Traditions*. Beacon Pr. 1992 $14.00. ISBN 0-8070-4617-5. Essays by the Native American scholar, poet, and novelist, including two that focus at length on homosexuality.

Altman, Dennis. *Homosexual: Oppression and Liberation*. Avon 1973 o.p. Groundbreaking study from a Marxist perspective of the oppression of lesbians and gays in America.

Bergman, David. *Gaiety Transfigured: Gay Self-Representation in American Literature*. U. of Wis. Pr. 1993 repr. of 1991 ed. $12.95. ISBN 0-299-13054-1. A critical survey of writing by gay men from Walt Whitman to the present.

Boswell, John. *Christianity, Social Tolerance, and Homosexuality: Gay People in Western Europe from the Beginning of the Christian Era to the Fourteenth Century*. U. Ch. Pr. 1981 $18.95. ISBN 0-226-06711-4. Contains information about gay men in the pre-Christian era as well as the Christian Middle Ages.

Bright, Susie. *Susie Sexpert's Lesbian Sex World*. Cleis Pr. 1991 $24.95. ISBN 0-939416-34-4. The editor of *On Our Backs* discusses the 1980s lesbian sex wars, AIDS in the lesbian community, and so on.

Bronski, Michael. *Culture Clash: The Making of a Gay Sensibility*. South End Pr. 1984 $30.00. ISBN 0-89608-218-0. Argues for a (largely "camp") gay sensibility in Victorian through contemporary gay subcultures.

Butler, Judith. *Gender Trouble: Feminism and the Subversion of Identity*. Routledge 1989 $32.50. ISBN 0-415-90042-5. An influential and sophisticated Foucaultian analysis of gender and sexuality as constructed—through performance.

Crimp, Douglas, with Adam Rolston. *AIDS Demo Graphics*. Bay Pr. 1990 $13.95. ISBN 0-941920-16-X. Discusses Queer Nation and the ACT UP movement.

D'Emilio, John. *Sexual Politics, Sexual Communities: The Making of a Homosexual Minority in the United States, 1940–1970*. U. Ch. Pr. 1984 $10.95. ISBN 0-226-14266-3. Traces the development of an urban lesbian and gay culture before the Stonewall riots.

Dollimore, Jonathan. *Sexual Dissidence: Augustine to Wilde, Freud to Foucault*. OUP 1991 $35.00. ISBN 0-19-811225-4. An important Renaissance and gay studies scholar considers the role of sexuality in resistance to domination.

Dyer, Richard. *Now you See It: Studies on Lesbiain and Gay Film*. Routledge 1990 $59.95. ISBN 0-415-03555-4. Working in the cultural studies tradition, Dyer analyzes lesbian and gay themes in films by lesbian and gay filmmakers.

Dynes, Wayne R. *Homosexuality: A Research Guide*. Garland 1987 $56.00. ISBN 0-8240-8692-9. An annotated bibliography.

Faderman, Lillian. *Odd Girls and Twilight Lovers: A History of Lesbian Life in Twentieth Century America*. Col. U. Pr. 1991 $29.95. ISBN 0-231-07488-3. Continues the history begun in *Surpassing the Love of Men* by chronicling explicitly lesbian American culture.

Faderman, Lillian. *Surpassing the Love of Men: Romantic Friendship and Love between Women from the Renaissance to the Present*. Morrow 1981 $15.45. ISBN 0-688-00396-6. A ground-breaking history of lesbianism which argues that "romantic friendships" among apparently straight women were actually lesbian.

Foucault, Michel. *The History of Sexuality: An Introduction*. Vol. 1. Trans. by Robert Hurley. Random 1980 $6.95. ISBN 0-394-74026-2. An enormously influential discussion of the social construction of sexuality and sexual identities.

Freud, Sigmund. *Leonardo da Vinci and a Memory of His Childhood*. Ed. by James Strachey. Trans. by Alan Tyson. Norton 1990 $5.95. ISBN 0-393-00149-0. Freud's important discussion of da Vinci's homosexuality.

———. *Three Essays on the Theory of Sexuality*. Basic 1976 $13.00. ISBN 0-465-08606-3. Includes Freud's influential discussion of inversion.

Garber, Marjorie. *Vested Interests: Cross-Dressing and Cultural Anxiety*. Routledge 1991 $35.00. ISBN 0-415-90072-7. A wide-ranging discussion of various practices of transvestism, which is defined as inherently subversive.

Grahn, Judy. *Another Mother Tongue: Gay Words, Gay Essays*. Beacon Pr. 1990 $15.95. ISBN 0-8070-7911-1. A wide-randing account of lesbian and gay culture by the well-known lesbian poet.

Halperin, David M. *One Hundred years of Homosexuality and Other Essays on Greek Love*. Routledge 1989 $39.95. ISBN 0-415-90096-4. A Foucaultian discussion of classical Greek literatures and sexualities.

Irigaray, Luce. *This Sex Which Is Not One*. Trans. by Catherine Porter with Carolyn Burke. Cornell Univ. Pr. 1985 $33.50. ISBN 0-8014-1546-2. Essays by the French feminist theorist which sometimes argue that feminine desire is lesbian.

Katz, Jonathan. *Gay American History: Lesbians and Gay Men in the U.S.A.* NAL-Dutton 1992 $20.00. ISBN 0-452-01092-6. A well-known history of lesbians and gays in America from the colonial era to the present.

Kitzinger, Celia. *The Social Construction of Lesbianism*. Sage 1988 $45.00. ISBN 0-8039-8116-3. Critiques current as well as older lesbian studies methodologies.

Koestenbaum, Wayne. *Double Talk: The Erotics of Male Literary Collaboration*. Routledge 1989 $39.50. ISBN 0-415-90109-X. Focuses on the homoerotics of collaboration by such pairs as Freud and Fleiss.

Lorde, Audre. *Sister/Outsider: Essays and Speeches*. Crossing Pr. 1984 $22.95. ISBN 0-89594-142-2. Critical prose by the important African American lesbian feminist poet.

Martin, Robert K. *The Homosexual Tradition in American Poetry*. U. of Tex. Pr. 1979 o.p. Argues that many important poets have been misread because their gay sexuality has been ignored.

Meese, Elizabeth. *(Sem)Erotics: Theorizing Lesbian: Writing*. NYU Pr. 1992 $40.00. ISBN 0-8147-5469-4. Uses poststructuralist theory to discuss experimental lesbian writing in a critical form that is itself experimental.

Newton, Esther. *Mother Camp: Female Impersonators in America*. U. Ch. Pr. 1979 $5.95. ISBN 0-226-57760-0. A classic anthropological analysis of drag in the mid-1960s.

Patton, Cindy. *Inventing AIDS*. Routledge 1990 $42.50. ISBN 0-415-90256-8. An ideological analysis of the representation of AIDS in a range of discourses by an activist and scholar.

Roof, Judith. *A Lure of Knowledge: Lesbian Sexuality and Theory*. Col. U. Pr. 1991 $40.00. ISBN 0-231-07486-7. A theoretically sophisticated analysis of lesbian representation in theory, film, and literature.

Rule, Jane. *Lesbian Images*. Doubleday 1982 $8.95. ISBN 0-89594-088-4. A classic volume of critical essays on lesbian representation in literature by the well-known lesbian novelist.

Russo, Vito. *The Celluloid Closet: Homosexuality in the Movies*. HarpC 1987 $13.00. ISBN 0-06-096132-5. Documents the homophobic representation of homosexuality in Hollywood cinema.

Sedgwick, Eve Kosofsky. *Between Men: English Literature and Male Homosocial Desire*. Col. U. Pr. 1986 $15.50. ISBN 0-231-05861-6. A very influential and theoretically sophisticated analysis of male triangles of desire in English literature.

———. *Epistemology of the Closet*. U. CA Pr. 1990 $24.95. ISBN 0-520-07042-9. A theoretically sophisticated analysis of gay male sexuality in a range of discourses by an important gay studies scholar.

Summers, Claude J. *Gay Fictions: Studies in a Male Homosexual Literary Tradition*. Continuum 1990 $22.95. ISBN 0-8264-0466-9. Discusses Anglo-American gay fiction from Wilde to the year of the Stonewall riots.

Weeks, Jeffrey. *Sexuality and Its Discontents: Meanings, Myths, and Modern Sexualities*. Routledge 1985 $35.00. ISBN 0-7102-0564-3. A cultural materialist analysis of the sexual revolution.

Wittig, Monique. *The Straight Mind and Other Essays*. Beacon Pr. 1992 $24.95. ISBN 0-8070-7916-2. The essays of an important French lesbian materialist theorist and novelist.

Wittig, Monique, and Sande Zeig. *Lesbian Peoples: Material for a Dictionary*. Bard 1976 o.p. A creative "dictionary" of lesbian concepts, characters, and people.

Yingling, Thomas E. *Hart Crane and the Homosexual Text: New Thresholds, New Anatomies*. U. Ch. Pr. 1990 $39.95. ISBN 0-226-95634-2. A theoretically sophisticated analysis of the work of the gay poet.

Zimmerman, Bonnie. *A Safe Sea of Women: Lesbian Fiction 1969–1989*. Beacon Pr. 1990 $24.95. ISBN 0-8070-7904-9. Examines popular and literary lesbian fiction in its social and literary contexts.

Collections

Allen, Jeffner, ed. *Lesbian Philosophy and Cultures*. State U. NY Pr. 1990 $44.50. ISBN 0-7914-0383-1. Discussions of lesbian feminism, multi-cultural politics, and lesbian sexuality and desire.

Beck, Evelyn Torton, ed. *Nice Jewish Girls: A Lesbian Anthology*. Beacon Pr. 1989 $15.00. ISBN 0-8070-7905-7. Essays considering what it means to be both lesbian and Jewish and having to confront anti-Semitism and homophobia.

Boone, Joseph, ed. *Engendering Men: The Question of Male Feminist Criticism*. Routledge 1990 $35.00. ISBN 0-415-90254-1. Essays by gay male feminists, including Cohen, Edelman, Koestenabaum, and Warner.

Brandt, Kate. *Happy Endings: Lesbian Writers Talk about Their Lives and Work*. Naiad 1993 $10.95. ISBN 1-56280-050-7. Twenty-two of Brandt's interviews, covering forty years of lesbian writing and publishing.

Bristow, Joseph, ed. *Sexual Sameness: Textual Differences in Lesbian and Gay Writing*. Routledge 1992 $49.95. ISBN 0-415-06936-X. Essays by important lesbian and gay literary and cultural theorists.

Bulkin, Elly, and Joan Larkin, eds. *Lesbian Poetry: An Anthology*. Persephone Pr. 1981 o.p. Includes poems by such well-known lesbian feminists as Susan Griffin, Rita Mae Brown, Audre Lorde, and Judy Grahn.

Butters, Ronald R., and others, eds. *Displacing Homophobia: Gay Male Perspectives on Literature and Culture*. Duke 1990 $40.00. ISBN 0-8223-0962-9. Originally a special issue of *South Atlantic Quarterly* focusing on a range of issues in different historical moments.

Coote, Stephen, ed. *The Penguin Book of Homosexual Verse*. Viking Penguin 1987 $10.95. ISBN 0-14-058551-6. Homoerotic poetry through the ages.

Cruikshank, Margaret, ed. *Lesbian Studies: Present and Future*. Feminist Pr. 1982 $15.95. ISBN 0-935312-07-2. Includes sample syllabi and reading lists for lesbian studies in the university, as well as essays on pedagogy and research.

Davis, Jill, ed. *Lesbian Plays*. Heinemann Ed. 1987 $13.95. ISBN 0-413-15310-X. Plays by Posner, Kay, Fleming, Klein, and others.

Duberman, Martin, and others. *Hidden from History: Reclaiming the Gay and Lesbian Past*. NAL-Dutton 1990 $15.00. ISBN 0-452-01067-5. An important collection of essays addressing such key issues as the controversy about essentialism and social constructionism.

Dyer, Richard, ed. *Gays and Films*. British Film Inst. UK 1980 o.p. Essays by Dyer on stereotypes, Jack Babuscio on camp, and Caroline Sheldon on lesbian images.

Dynes, Wayne R., ed. *The Encyclopedia of Homosexuality*. 2 Vols. Garland 1990 $150.00. ISBN 0-8240-6544-1. Covers a truly encyclopedic range of topics, although not all of the entries are equally sophisticated.

Epstein, Julia, and Kristina Straub, eds. *Body Guards: The Cultural Politics of Gender Ambiguity*. Routledge 1991 $52.50. ISBN 0-415-90388-2. An important anthology addressing a wide range of "gender ambiguities," including homosexuality, from late antiquity to the present.

The Faber Book of Gay Short Fiction. Faber & Faber 1991 $24.95. ISBN 0-571-14472-1. A stellar collection of short stories by gay men, including James, Isherwood, Burroughs, and Cooper.

Fuss, Diana, ed. *Inside/Out: Lesbian Theories, Gay Theories*. Routledge 1991 $59.50. ISBN 0-415-90236-3. Theoretically sophisticated essays addressing a range of issues, including gender, drag, pornography, and AIDS.

Gay Left Collective, eds. *Homosexuality: Power and Politics*. Allison & Busby 1980 o.p. Essays selected by an early and influential British Marxist group of gay academics, with contributions by lesbians.

Glasgow, Joanne, and Karla Jay. *Lesbian Texts and Contexts*. NYU Pr. 1990 Essays on lesbian identities, subcultures, and literature from a variety of theoretical perspectives.

Hoffman, William M. *Gay Plays: First Collection*. Avon 1979 $4.95. ISBN 0-380-42788-5. Plays by Hoffman, Orton, and the like.

How Do I Look? Queer Film and Video. Ed. by Bad Object-Choices staff. Bay Pr. 1991 $16.95. ISBN 0-941920-20-8. Essays, followed by discussions, on such topics as activism and the academy, AIDS, race and the gay community, and pornography.

Jay, Karla, and Allen Young, eds. *Out of the Closet: Voices of Gay Liberation, Twentieth-Anniversary Edition*. NYU Pr. 1992 $45.00. ISBN 0-8147-4182-7. A reissue of the 1972 collection, including essays that articulate approaches for lesbian and gay studies.

Leyland, Winston, ed. *Gay Sunshine Interviews*. 2 Vols. Gay Sunshine Vol. 1 1978 $25.00. ISBN 0-917342-60-7. Vol. 2 1982 $25.00. ISBN 0-917342-62-3. Interviews with gay poets, novelists, and playwrights, including Burroughs, Genet, and Isherwood.

McEwen, Christian, and Sue O'Sullivan, eds. *Out the Other Side*. Crossing Pr. 1989 o.p. American and British contributors addressing the effects of coming out, in interviews, essays, letters and journal entries.

Moraga, Cherie, and Gloria Anzaldua, eds. *This Bridge Called My Back: Writing by Radical Women of Color*. Kitchen Table 1984 repr. of 1981 ed. $21.95. ISBN 0-913175-18-8. An early (1981) and still important multicultural anthology, covering a range of genres and topics, including lesbianism.

Nestle, Joan, ed. *The Persistent Desire: A Femme-Butch Reader*. Alyson Pubns. 1992 $14.95. ISBN 1-55583-190-7. Stories, poems, and essays about butch-femme roles.

Nestle, Joan, and Naomi Holoch, eds. *Women on Women: An Anthology of American Lesbian Short Fiction*. NAL-Dutton 1990 $11.00. ISBN 0-452-26388-3. Includes fiction by noted writers Jewell Gomez and Sarah Schulman.

Plummer, Kenneth, ed. *The Making of the Modern Homosexual*. B & N Imports 1981 $38.50. ISBN 0-389-20159-6. An important collection of essays focusing on gay male identity, including early social-construction arguments.

Ramos, Juanita, ed. *Companeras: Latina Lesbians (An Anthology)*. LLHP 1987 $8.95. ISBN 0-9619450-0-1. Oral histories, essays, poems, short stories, and art by and about Latina lesbians.

Smith, Barbara, ed. *Home Girls: A Black Feminist Anthology*. Kitchen Table 1983 $9.95. ISBN 0-913175-14-5. Incorporates a section on African-American lesbians, with contributions by the noted writers Jewell Gomez and Audre Lorde.

Snitow, Ann, and others, eds. *Powers of Desire: The Politics of Sexuality*. Monthly Rev. 1983 $25.00. ISBN 0-85345-609-7. Now a classic feminist and lesbian collection of poetry and essays on sexual politics.

Stambolian, George, and Elaine Marks, eds. *Homosexualities and French Literature: Cultural Contexts/Critical Texts*. Cornell Univ. Pr. 1990 repr. of 1979 ed. $14.95. ISBN 0-8014-9766-3. Includes a number of important theoretical essays, as well as literary criticism, by major lesbian and gay theorists and writers.

Stein, Edward, ed. *Forms of Desire: Sexual Orientation and Social Constructionist Controversy*. Routledge 1992 $15.95. ISBN 0-415-90485-4. A collection focused on this divisive issue, with essays by Foucault, McIntosh, Boswell, Davidson, and Epstein, among others.

Trujillo, Carla, ed. *Chicana Lesbians: The Girls Our Mothers Warned Us About*. Third Woman 1991 $10.95. ISBN 0-943219-06-X. Poetry and prose by Chicana lesbians addressing racism, sexism, and homophobia.

Vance, Carole, ed. *Pleasure and Danger: Exploring Female Sexuality.* Thorsons SF 1993 $20.00. ISBN 0-04-440867-6. Poetry and prose from the 1982 Barnard feminist conference; controversy erupted over the issue of nontraditional sexualities.

White, Edmund. *The Faber Book of Gay Short Fiction.* Faber & Faber 1991 $24.95. ISBN 0-571-14472-1. Fiction from Henry James to the present.

Young, Ian. *The Male Muse: A Gay Anthology.* Crossing Pr. 1973 o.p. Poetry by and about gay men.

————. *Son of the Male Muse: New Gay Poetry.* Crossing Pr. 1983 o.p. An update of the first volume, *The Male Muse.*

CHRONOLOGY OF AUTHORS
(Gay and Lesbian Literature)

Daly, Mary. 1928–
Lorde, Audre Geraldine. 1934–1992
Rechy, John. 1934–
Allen, Paula Gunn. 1939–

Grahn, Judy Rae. 1940–
Cooper, Dennis. 1953–
Hemphill, Essex. 1957–
Anzaldua, Gloria. n.d.–

ALLEN, PAULA GUNN. 1939–

[See Main Entry under Literary Theory in this chapter.]

ANZALDUA, GLORIA. 1942–

[See Main Entry under Literary Theory in this chapter.]

BALDWIN, JAMES. 1924–1987

[SEE Chapter 17 in this volume.]

BARNES, DJUNA. 1892–1982

[SEE Chapter 16 in this volume.]

BURROUGHS, WILLIAM S. 1914–

[SEE Chapter 17 in this volume.]

CAPOTE, TRUMAN. 1924–1984

[SEE Chapter 17 in this volume.]

CATHER, WILLA SIBERT. 1873–1947

[SEE Chapter 16 in this volume.]

COOPER, DENNIS. 1953–

An increasingly prominent gay writer, Cooper grew up in Southern California and currently lives in West Los Angeles. His first literary success was a collection of verse and prose poetry, *The Tenderness of the Wolves* (1982), which was nominated for a *Los Angeles Times* Book Prize for poetry in 1982. Since then, he has curated a multimedia exhibition, coauthored a performance project, written a number of novels and short stories, and continued to write and publish poetry in his own poetry magazine, *Little Caesar*, and in other journals. His work examines the extremes of gay identity and the dark side of contemporary life, particularly the icons and rituals of consumer culture. Many of his characters are media stars, groupies, hustlers, serial killers, athletes, and/or drug addicts, the subjects or objects of obsessive behaviors that seem to be both subversive of, and complicit with, dominant culture.

POETRY BY COOPER

The Tenderness of the Wolves. Crossing Pr. 1982 o.p.
Tiger Beat. Little Caesar Pr. 1978 o.p. Published by his own press.

NOVEL BY COOPER

Frisk: A Novel. Grove Pr. 1992 $9.95. ISBN 0-8021-3289-8. A novel about a man who becomes fascinated with mutilation.

SHORT STORY COLLECTION BY COOPER

Wrong: Stories. Grove Pr. 1992 $9.95. ISBN 0-8021-1401-6. Short fiction.

CRANE, (HAROLD) HART. 1899–1932

[SEE Chapter 16 in this volume.]

DALY, MARY. 1928–

A radical feminist theorist and theologian, Daly was educated at Catholic schools in the United States and the University of Fribourg in Switzerland. She has also taught at Boston College since 1969. Shortly after she received her advanced degrees, Daly ceased to be a traditional Catholic and began challenging the church's conservatism from a feminist and radical or "new Catholic" perspective. She finally broke completely with the church during a period of profound disillusionment following the events of the Second Vatican Council, in which significant feminist and other liberal reforms were not enacted. This disillusionment is reflected in the influential *The Church and the Second Sex* (1968), which articulates a critique of the systemic sexism and intolerance of the church as an institution and a body of doctrinal texts. Patriarchy, she argues, relies on Christianity. Drawing on DE BEAUVOIR's (see Vol. 2) feminist existentialism as expressed in her *The Second Son*, Daly advocates a feminist spiritual revolution in which women refuse old stereotypes.

Realizing that her feminism and lesbianism would never find an effective voice within the confines of the church or within the society at large, Daly began to purge what she saw as the influence of patriarchy in her language and her spiritual beliefs. Her first "post-Christian" book, *Beyond God the Father* (1973), takes as its starting point a rejection of the essential misogyny of Western Christianity in favor of a broader-based spirituality that allows for women's expression, including lesbian expression. Although Daly sees the possibility of a feminist revolution as dependent upon the physical, emotional, and spiritual connections among women, she is nevertheless somewhat suspicious of the notion of lesbianism, because it may be a limiting definition imposed upon women's experience by patriarchal culture. Indeed, for Daly, all language is suspect because it embodies a patriarchal vision of reality that it therefore helps to reproduce. She argues that female spirituality and sexuality cannot be reconstructed unless language itself is reconstructed and suggests that vocabulary should replace the masculinist vocabulary that paralyze feminine spirituality.

Daly's theses about language are most forcefully presented in her best-known work, *Gyn/Ecology* (1978), in which she asserts that women must create a "gynomorphic" language in order to cultivate "gynaesthesia," the ability to perceive the interrelatedness of things that women develop when they become feminists and work in women-only collectives. "Gyn/Ecology" is Daly's name for the new kind of knowledge that results; it replaces the patriarchal medicalization and objectification of the female body. Daly's insistence that women have been robbed of the human power of naming of the self, the world, and God, which they must reclaim in order to realize their human potential, informs her later works, in which her feminist wordplay intensifies: *Pure Lust* (1984) and *Webster's First New Intergalactic Wickedary of the English Language* (1987).

NONFICTION BY DALY

Beyond God the Father: Toward a Philosophy of Women's Liberation. Beacon Pr. 1985 $13.95. ISBN 0-8070-1503-2

The Church and the Second Sex: Including the Feminist Postchristian. 1968 Beacon Pr. 1985 $13.00. ISBN 0-8070-1101-0

Gyn/Ecology: The Metaethics of Radical Feminism. Beacon Pr. 1978

Pure Lust: Elemental Feminist Philosophy. Beacon Pr. 1984 $15.95. ISBN 0-8070-1505-9. Discusses "wild, weird women," who are "metapatriarchal mutations of self-creation and a new language."

Webster's First New Intergalactic Wickedary of the English Language. (coauthored with Jane Caputi) Beacon Pr. 1987 $18.00. ISBN 0-8070-6733-4. A radical feminist dictionary that includes such words for women in patriarchy as *fembot*, defined as "the totaled woman."

H. D. (DOOLITTLE, HILDA). 1886–1961

[SEE Chapter 16 in this volume.]

GINSBERG, ALLEN. 1926–

[SEE Chapter 17 in this volume.]

GRAHN, JUDY RAE. 1940–

Grahn is a lesbian feminist poet, fiction writer, publisher, and cultural critic of note. Born in Chicago, she grew up in New Mexico and at age 21 was expelled from the Air Force for being a lesbian. Over the years she attended six colleges, where she studied poetry, and she completed her B.A. at San Francisco State University in 1984. She has taught lesbian and gay studies and women's writing, cofounded a women's press (The Women's Press Collective of Oakland), and was at the forefront of a West Coast poetry "renaissance" of the 1970s, along with Susan Griffin, Pat Parker, and Alta.

In her work, Grahn seeks to link various oppressions in order to facilitate the emergence of coalitions of the oppressed. She draws her themes and images from ancient myths, Western literary and philosophical traditions, and histori-cal and social trends, defining—or redefining—them as expressing feminine and homoerotic desire and then appropriating them for their subversive potential. For example, she invents a new, more expressive "American sonnet" for "The Common Woman" sequence in *Edward the Dyke and Other Poems* (1971), which celebrates both women's differences and commonalities. In *She, Who* (1977), she rewrites scripture as feminist experimental verse. These two volumes have been collected with later poems as *The Work of a Common Woman* (1978), with an introduction by ADRIENNE RICH. *The Queen of Wands* (1982), the first of a projected four-part *Chronicle of Queens* is loosely based on the Tarot and Greek mythology; it focuses, like H. D.'s *Helen in Egypt* (1961), on Helen of Troy, who is abducted and robbed of her power to create civilization. In the second volume in the series, *The Queen of Swords* (1987), Helen encounters the queen of the underworld. The last two books (the queens of cups and diamonds) are still in progress.

Although she first came to critical attention with her poetry, Grahn is now also known for her cultural and literary criticism. Her two editions of *Another Mother Tongue* (1979, 1984) offer a wealth of information about gay identities throughout history, which Grahn links to a number of myth systems and languages in a form that blends poetry, legend, autobiography, and etymology. In effect, she imaginatively retrieves and invents gay cultural history, mythology, and language (the "other mother tongue" of the title). *The Highest Apple* (1985) constructs a lesbian poetic tradition in Europe that begins with Sappho (see Vol. 2). *Really Reading Gertrude Stein* (1989), an anthology with critical essays, addresses sexuality in the work of the acclaimed lesbian modernist writer.

Grahn has also written fiction, including the novel-length *Mundane's World* (1988), which narrates in a playful and punning style the protagonist Ernesta's passage to womanhood in a gynocentric society. In addition, Grahn is the editor of a two-volume anthology of short tales, *True to Life Adventure Stories* (1978, 1981), in which ordinary women speak about their experiences.

POETRY BY GRAHN

Edward the Dyke and Other Poems. Women's Pr. Collective 1971 o.p.
She, Who: A Graphic Book of Poems. Diana Pr. 1972 o.p. With illustrations.
The Queen of Swords. Beacon Pr. 1990 $10.95. ISBN 0-8070-6803-9
The Queen of Wands. Crossing Pr. 1982 $8.95. ISBN 0-89594-094-9
The Work of a Common Woman: The Collected Poetry of Judy Grahn 1964–1977. Crossing Pr. 1984 $8.95. ISBN 0-89594-155-4. With an introduction by Adrienne Rich.

NOVEL BY GRAHN

Mundane's World. The Crossing Pr. 1988 o.p.

SHORT STORY COLLECTION BY GRAHN

True to Life Adventure Stories. 2 Vols. Ed. by Grahn. Crossing Pr. Vol. 1 1978 o.p. Vol. 2 1981 o.p.

NONFICTION BY GRAHN

Another Mother Tongue: Gay Words, Gay Worlds. 1979. Beacon Pr. 1990 $15.95. ISBN 0-8070-7911-1
The Highest Apple: Sappho and the Lesbian Poetic Tradition. Spinsters 1985 o.p.
Really Reading Gertrude Stein. The Crossing Pr. 1989 o.p.

HEMPHILL, ESSEX. 1957–

One of the most important new voices on the gay literary scene, Hemphill has published poetry in several anthologies and essays in the gay press, most of which have been collected in his three books. The merits of his work have been rewarded with several fellowships, including one from the National Endowment for the Arts. Hemphill has also been involved in the production of three gay African American films: *Looking for Langston*, which is about Langston Hughes; *Tongues Untied*, a celebration of African American gay identity; and *Out of the Shadows*, an AIDS documentary.

Hemphill says that his work has been informed by his efforts to "integrate all of my identities into a functioning self" and to "articulate and politicize my sexuality" (*Ceremonies* 53). As he makes clear, it is not easy to accomplish this in a racist and homophobic society. He deplores the racism that he finds in the gay community, in particular the sexual objectification of black men by white men, which he argues characterizes the art of the celebrated photographer Robert Mapplethorpe. He is equally critical of the sexism and homophobia of the African American community, which he believes informs the rhetoric of the key movement, Black Nationalism. But Hemphill also celebrates his sexual and racial identities, affirming his participation in both the gay and black communities even as he critiques them and American society at large, whose prejudices they sometimes share.

POETRY BY HEMPHILL

Earth Life. 1985. Be Bop Bks. 1988 o.p. Poems affirming his African-American and gay identities.

NONFICTION BY HEMPHILL

Brother to Brother: New Writings by Black Gay Men. Ed. by Hemphill. Conceived by Joseph Beam. Alyson Pubns. 1991 $8.95. ISBN 1-55593-146-X. An important collection of poetry and prose by gay African American men, with an introduction and several poems and essays by Hemphill.

Ceremonies. NAL-Dutton 1992 $10.00. ISBN 0-452-26817-6. Prose and poetry, including previously published material.

HUGHES, JAMES LANGSTON. 1902–1967

[SEE Chapter 16 in this volume.]

LORDE, AUDRE GERALDINE. 1934–1992

An African American lesbian feminist critic and writer, Lorde was born in Harlem and educated at National University of Mexico, Hunter College, and Columbia University. She married in 1962 and divorced in 1970, after having two children. Lorde first came to critical attention with her poetry. Her first poem was published in *Seventeen* magazine while she was in high school; it had been rejected by her high school newspaper because it was "too romantic" (Lorde considered her "mature" poetry, which focuses on her lesbian relationships, to be romantic also). Other early poems were published in many different journals, many of them under the pseudonym Rey Domini. Her first volume of poetry, *The First Cities*, was published in 1968. Lorde then quit her job as head librarian at a school in New York City in order to devote her time to teaching and writing. She was a professor of English at Hunter College from 1980 until her untimely death from cancer in 1992.

Although many of Lorde's poems are about love, many are about anger, particularly anger about racism, sexism, and homophobia in America. "The Brown Menace or Poem to the Survival of Roaches" likens African Americans to cockroaches—hated, feared, and poisoned by whites but survivors nevertheless. Other poems express a daughter's anger toward her mother; still others eschew anger for affirmation and inspiration, which are represented as coming from lesbian love and traditional African myths because, as Lorde has said, "the master's tools will not dismantle the master's house." Lorde is also well-known for her prose. Her courageous account of her struggle with breast cancer and the mastectomy that she underwent is movingly chronicled in *The Cancer Journals* (1980), her first major prose publication. *Zami, a New Spelling of My Name* (1982) is, in Lorde's words, a "biomythography," combining history, biography, and myth. In *Zami* Lorde focuses on her developing lesbian identity and her response to racism in the white feminist and gay communities, and to sexism and homophobia in the African American community. Lorde's critical essays, collected in *Sister/Outsider* (1984) and *A Burst of Light* (1988), have been quite influential, particularly "Uses of the Erotic: The Erotic as Power," in which she discusses the relationship of poetry to politics and the erotic.

Lorde was the recipient of several grants—from the National Endowment for the Arts in 1968 and 1981 and from the Creative Artists Public Service in 1972—as well as the Borough of Manhattan President's Award for Literary Excellence in 1987. She was also nominated for the National Book Award for poetry in 1974 for her third volume of verse, *From a Land Where Other People Live* (1973).

POETRY BY LORDE

The Black Unicorn. Norton 1978 $8.95. ISBN 0-393-04516-1. The mythical beast is given an African as well as feminine connection in these poems, several of which focus on Africa.

The First Cities. The Poet's Pr. 1968 o.p.

From a Land Where Other People Live. Broadside Pr. 1973 $5.00. ISBN 0-910296-97-9

Our Dead Behind Us: Poems. Norton 1986 $14.95. ISBN 0-393-02329-X. Poems that derive inspiration but also grief from African myths and writings.

NONFICTION BY LORDE

The Cancer Journals. Aunt Lute Bks. 1980 $7.00. ISBN 0-879960-26-5

A Burst of Light. Firebrand Bks. 1988 $16.95. ISBN 0-932379-40-0. A story of spiritual victory—renewed life in the face of death despite the return of cancer.

Sister/Outsider: Essays and Speeches. Crossing Pr. 1984 $22.95. ISBN 0-89594-142-2

WORK BY LORDE

Zami, a New Spelling of My Name. Crossing Pr. 1982 $23.95. ISBN 0-89594-123-6

O'HARA, FRANK. 1926–1966

[SEE Chapter 17 in this volume.]

RECHY, JOHN. 1934–

Rechy is an important gay writer also linked to the Beat Movement, whose work has been recognized by a number of prestigious grant nominations or awards, including one from the National Endowment for the Arts. He grew up in El Paso, Texas, in a poor, Mexican American family. Because of his poverty and his ethnic heritage, he learned very early in life to feel himself an outsider, which was intensified by his later experiences as a gay hustler traveling America in search of his social and sexual identity. He came to popular and critical attention with his first published novel, *City of Night* (1963), which was a bestseller and was nominated for the International Prix Formentor. A fictionalized account of his travels, the novel focuses on the people whom the unnamed narrator encounters on the hustling scene in a number of cities, including New York, San Francisco, New Orleans, Chicago, and Los Angeles. Together, these cities make up the titular "city of night," or, as Rechy writes, "the city of night of the soul." A state of mind rather than a particular place, this "city"—modern America—is where hypocrisy and homophobia are reconciled with the fact of homosexuality in various forms, and poverty may be more spiritual than material. The book owes something to two classics: JACK KEROUAC's Beat novel, *On the Road*, which celebrates countercultural alternatives to middle-class culture and lifestyles, including bourgeois marriage and family life, and DJUNA BARNES's modernist novel *Nightwood*, which explores a tragic gay "nightworld" as a symbol of the modern urban wasteland.

Rechy addresses similar themes in a later work that is equally well known, *The Sexual Outlaw* (1977), which he has described as an experiment with the novel form. Ostensibly a documentary of the life of a gay man, the book is also a critique of American values and morality. Commentaries throughout the text are really journalistic essays that expose the double standards and double binds of a "closeted" culture, in which many fear to be openly gay because of homophobic reprisals. Rechy has suggested that all of his work (which includes plays, essays, and reviews, as well as novels) articulates the need to preserve gay "difference," which he associates with "abundant sexuality," in the face of increasing "heterofascism."

NOVELS BY RECHY

Bodies and Souls. Carroll & Graf 1983 $17.95. ISBN 0-88184-003-3. About three runaways whose lives prove only as lonely as those of other Los Angeles residents.
City of Night. 1963. Grove Pr. 1988 $9.95. ISBN 0-8021-3083-6. Contains a new introduction by Rechy.
Marilyn's Daughter. Carroll & Graf 1988 $18.95. ISBN 0-88184-272-9. About a woman who travels to Los Angeles to find out if she really is Monroe's daughter.
Rushes. Grove Pr. 1979 o.p. Set in a leather bar, the novel's Christian symbolism includes parallel "crucifixions."
The Sexual Outlaw: A Documentary. Grove Pr. 1990 $9.95. ISBN 0-8021-3163-8

RICH, ADRIENNE. 1929–

[SEE Chapter 17 in this volume.]

STEIN, GERTRUDE. 1874–1946

[SEE Chapter 16 in this volume.]

VIDAL, GORE. 1925–

[SEE Chapter 17 in this volume.]

WILLIAMS, TENNESSEE. 1911–1983.

[SEE Chapter 20 in this volume.]

CHAPTER 20

American Literature: Popular Modes

Harry Eiss and Candace Klaschus

> NOTICE: Persons attempting to find a motive in this narrative will be prosecuted; persons attempting to find a moral in it will be banished; persons attempting to find a plot in it will be shot. BY ORDER OF THE AUTHOR Per G.G., CHIEF OF ORDNANCE.
> —MARK TWAIN, *The Adventures of Huckleberry Finn*

American popular literature and children's literature began as an extension of British literature. Yet American literature was popular from its inception: Elitist literature was of little interest to the colonists, who were preoccupied with practical matters and the Puritan religion.

The first American literature consisted of accounts of voyages, such as John Brereton's *Brief and True Relation of the Discoverie of the North Part of Virginia* (1602). Although such accounts were meant to inform, they were generally very personal and displayed simple, even crude, yet endearing fictional qualities. Other early works included promotions of the territory, such as John Smith's *Description of New England* (1612); histories and biographies, such as Cotton Mather's biographies in *Magnalia Christi Americana* (1702), which generally included a defense of the subject's religious views; diaries and autobiographies, such as those of Jonathan Edwards, which, once again, were mainly concerned with religious matters; and sermons, which were the most highly developed literary type. Early popular poetry is generally considered very crude today; it too frequently dealt with religion. Overall, very little really imaginative popular literature was produced in early America, no doubt because such literature was viewed with a great deal of suspicion.

The American Revolution brought forth a great deal of political literature, though, once again, not much imaginative writing. During the years following the Revolution, easily three-fourths of the printed material in America, including most of the imaginative writing, was still being brought in from England. However, American writers began to emerge toward the middle of the century. PHILIP FRENEAU, WILLIAM CULLEN BRYANT, WASHINGTON IRVING, JAMES FENIMORE COOPER, and EDGAR ALLAN POE led an American romantic movement, reliant on the British movement, but added to it and developed new American versions of popular fiction, for example, the detective story, the horror story, and science fiction.

By the mid-eighteenth century, the American Renaissance had begun, led by WALT WHITMAN, JAMES RUSSELL LOWELL, OLIVER WENDELL HOLMES, HENRY DAVID THOREAU, RALPH WALDO EMERSON, HERMAN MELVILLE, and HENRY WADSWORTH LONGFELLOW. Also, high-culture writers were developing the precursors to later popular modes: NATHANIEL HAWTHORNE, for example, created early versions of the horror tale and the romance, quickly followed by a surge of local-color writers, led by SAMUEL CLEMENS (Mark Twain), GEORGE WASHINGTON HARRIS, BRET HARTE, GEORGE WASHINGTON CABLE, JOEL CHANDLER HARRIS, JOHN GREENLEAF WHITTIER, and SARAH ORNE JEWETT. From these, the American tall tale was born, and American folk songs—spirituals, cowboy songs, and railroad songs—found their way into literature. LOUISA MAY ALCOTT added to the popular lexicon by writing several thrillers; she also began the family novel for children with *Little Women* (1868). Another popular mode was the Horatio Alger success story, promoting riches and the virtues of honest labor.

By the turn of the century, American high-culture forms had developed a dark tone. STEPHEN CRANE's *Red Badge of Courage* (1895) led the way to a form of irony implying that humans had little control over their lives. Even the humor of Samuel Clemens became a disparaging cry against human failings.

On the popular front, the serials came into their own, especially within what has since been called the Stratemeyer Syndicate, which produced endless and endlessly popular series such as Nancy Drew and the Hardy Boys. Comic strips began and would develop into big business by the 1930s. Such magazines as *Amazing Stories* began to publish science fiction, and by the middle of the twentieth century, RAY BRADBURY, ISAAC ASIMOV, and others were leading the way in a popular genre that would soon gain a strong push in the world of film. American writers and illustrators of children's fiction also rose to the cutting edge, especially by the 1960s. Hard-hitting writers of novels for adolescents were led by J. D. SALINGER and Robert Cormier.

Behind it all, the oral tradition, which American literature inherited both from England and from Native Americans, has continued to feed the thematic and stylistic explorations of American writers. The same archetypes found in HERMAN MELVILLE, ERNEST HEMINGWAY, and WILLIAM FAULKNER can be found in the simple folk songs and tall tales of the American frontier, and the greatest of the American writers have combined the oral tradition with the elitist literature imported from England. Samuel Clemens's *The Adventures of Huckleberry Finn* (1885) captured the late eighteenth-century American world better than any other work by combining the picaresque novel developed in Europe with the superstitions of the American frontier, satirizing the American con artists via a delightfully jumbled pastiche of SHAKESPEARE, and condemning American politics and ethics with a deftness surpassing that of DICKENS.

If the real flowering of American children's literature took place at the end of the nineteenth century, popular literature came into its own in the twentieth century. Although each type of writing had its roots in higher-culture forms, high and popular modes grew further and further apart for some time. Now, perhaps ironically, both children's literature and popular literature have come to be recognized and taken seriously in new ways.

CHILDREN'S LITERATURE

As we might expect, American children's literature was first born out of British children's literature, of which it is an extension. Together, American and British literature form one important expression of the culture and values of Western civilization.

The early books for children in America were brought over by the Puritans. As early as 1632, there are references to children's hornbooks from England—with the crosses scratched off, as the Puritans objected to crosses. The most famous of the English Puritan books, JOHN BUNYAN's *Pilgrim's Progress* (1678), was a staple of eighteenth- and nineteenth-century American children's literature.

The first book for children actually published in America was written by John Cotton, titled *Milk for Babes, Drawn out of the Breasts of Both Testaments, Chiefly for the Spiritual Nourishment of Boston Babes in either England, but may be of like Use for any Children* (1646); even its title clearly reveals the strong didactic purpose of this body of literature. The *New England Primer*, published at least as early as 1691, continued this moralistic thrust. Its famous alphabet began, "In Adam's fall/We sinned all." This strong didacticism continued during the eighteenth century with such books as Perkins and Marvin's *Mary Lathrop/Who Died In/Boston/1831*, a book devoted to Mary's "pious" death, meant to lead children into paths of righteousness.

Samuel G. Goodrich (1793–1860), writing under the pseudonym of Peter Parley, produced seemingly endless biographies of famous men and various other nonfiction works, all written in a pedantic manner. Jacob Abbot (1803–75) wrote about a boy named Rollo who bore up remarkably well under endless moralizing as he was dragged from one location to another.

During the second half of the century, the field of didactic children's literature was dominated by Martha Farquharson, pseudonym for Martha Finley (1828–1909). Her Elsie Dinsmore books ran to 26 volumes; in each, Elsie's overly dramatic fainting and tears and martyrdom were used to preach Christianity.

However, a new strand of children's literature was edging its way into American culture. In 1822, an American professor, Clement Moore, wrote "A Visit from St. Nicholas," still the classic Christmas poem for children. Lucretia Hale (1820–1900) published a humorous series of magazine stories about the Peterkin family which were eventually collected into a book in 1880. NATHANIEL HAWTHORNE (1804–64) published his children's versions of Greek mythology, *A Wonder-Book for Girls and Boys* (1852) and *Tanglewood Tales for Girls and Boys* (1853). These works are not highly respected today because they talk down to children and because the gods and heroes they portray are pictured as overly childish; at the time they were a refreshing antidote to the strong moralizing of the age. In the same vein, William Taylor Adams (1822–97), writing under the pseudonym of Oliver Optic, produced adventure stories for boys; Horatio Alger (1834–99) wrote *Ragged Dick* (1867) and other stories that popularized the "rags-to-riches" genre. Meanwhile, JOEL CHANDLER HARRIS's Uncle Remus stories began a serious use of American racial folklore in literature for children—although today Harris's work is considered a patronizing and somewhat offensive view of African American culture.

The first American illustrator was HOWARD PYLE, whose best-known writing and illustration was a retelling of the Robin Hood stories, done in 1883, and whose Brandywine School of art produced several important illustrators. WANDA GÁG's *Millions of Cats* (1928) was the first actual picture book published in America, leading to an explosion of excellent illustration in a tradition carried on by such great illustrators as Robert Lawson, Robert McCloskey, DR. SEUSS, James Daugherty, and Garth Williams earlier in the century, and Arnold and Anita Lobel, Barbara Cooney, CHRIS VAN ALLSBURG, and MAURICE SENDAK in recent times.

American fantasy, though at first overshadowed by British fantasy, came into its own at the turn of the century with L. FRANK BAUM's *The Wizard of Oz* (1900), going on to include E. B. WHITE's *Charlotte's Web* (1952), Madeleine L'Engle's *A*

Wrinkle in Time (1962) trilogy, and Lloyd Alexander's five-book high-fantasy saga beginning with *The Book of Three* (1963). American children's poetry also came out of the British tradition, but its distinctive qualities were developed by such notables as ROBERT FROST, LANGSTON HUGHES, David McCord, John Ciardi, Nancy Willard, and SHEL SILVERSTEIN.

However, it is in realistic fiction that American children's writers first came to the forefront, where they still remain. LOUISA MAY ALCOTT's *Little Women* (1867), which contained masterful characterizations, led the way, followed by the greatest writer of his time, SAMUEL CLEMENS, who wrote under the name Mark Twain. Clemens carried Alcott's realist tradition into a more blunt realism beyond the security of the traditional family structure, offering children main characters who went against the rules of society and yet remained attractive and morally good.

LAURA INGALLS WILDER's Little House series led a group of excellent realistic historical fiction books in the 1930s and 1940s, including Carol Ryrie Brink's *Caddie Woodlawn* (1935) and ESTHER FORBES's *Johnny Tremain* (1943), portraying the American Revolution. Eleanor Estes's series beginning with *The Moffats* (1941–43) began a trend toward contemporary family-oriented fiction.

Since the early 1960s, American realistic fiction has moved into a more hard-hitting realism dealing with important issues—death, sex, AIDS, divorce, and abortion—in an honest manner. KATHERINE PATERSON leads a group of excellent writers, including Betsy Byars, Patricia MacLachlan, Virginia Hamilton, Beverly Cleary, Paula Fox, Vera and Bill Cleaver, Louise Fitzhugh, Norma Klein, Norma Fox Mazer, and for older children, Robert Cormier, PAUL ZINDEL, M. E. Kerr, and Sandra Scoppetone. This realistic fiction is closely related to biography, and some excellent works have been written for children and young adults, most notably CARL SANDBURG's *Abe Lincoln Grows Up* (1928), the many books by Jean Fritz, and Russell Freedman's photo-biography of Lincoln.

History and Criticism

Bettelheim, Bruno. *The Uses of Enchantment*. Knopf 1989 $11.00. ISBN 0-679-72393-5. Powerful study of folk tales analyzed from a Freudian perspective.

Carpenter, Humphrey. *The Oxford Companion to Children's Literature*. OUP 1984 $49.95. ISBN 0-19-211582-0

Carruth, Gorton. *The Young Reader's Companion*. Bowker 1993 $39.95. ISBN 0-8352-2765-0. Single-volume encyclopedia; contains more than 2,000 entries on titles, authors, concepts, places, and characters.

Eiss, Harry. *Literature for Young People on War and Peace: An Annotated Bibliography*. Greenwood 1989 $35.00. ISBN 0-313-26068-0. Good resource for locating important books dealing with conflict in children's literature.

Fakih, Kimberly Olson. *The Literature of Delight: A Critical Guide to Humorous Books for Children*. Bowker 1993 $35.00. ISBN 0-8352-3027-9

Gillespie, John T. *Best Books for Junior High Readers*. Bowker 1991 $43.00. ISBN 0-8352-3020-1. A very thorough volume for ages 12-15.

_____. *Best Books for Senior High Readers*. Bowker 1991 $48.00. ISBN 0-8352-3021-X. Annotates material appropriate for ages 15-18.

Gillespie, John T. and Corinne Naden. *Best Books for Children: Preschool Through Grade 6*. 4th ed. Bowker 1990 $48.00. ISBN 0-8352-2668-9. Lists some 11,000 titles.

Immel, Myra, and Marion Sader, eds. *The Young Adult Reader's Adviser*. 2 vols. Bowker 1992 $79.95. ISBN 0-8352-3068-6. Developed by a panel of distinguished educators and librarians, it features 17,000 bibliographic entries and over 850 bibliographic profiles.

Kingman, Lee, ed. *The Illustrator's Notebook.* Horn Bk. 1978 $28.95. ISBN 0-87675-013-7. Children's illustrators discuss their craft.

————, ed. *Newbery and Caldecott Medal Books: 1956–1965.* Horn Bk. 1975 $22.95. ISBN 0-87675-003-X. Biographical sketches and acceptance speeches of award-winning authors.

————, ed. *Newbery and Caldecott Medal Books: 1976–1985.* Horn Bk. 1986 $24.95. ISBN 0-87675-004-8. Biographical sketches and acceptance speeches of award-winning authors.

Kunitz, Stanley J., and Howard Haycroft. *The Junior Book of Authors.* Wilson 2nd rev. ed. 1951 $32.00. ISBN 0-8242-0028-4. Biographical material on children's authors.

Lima, Carolyn W., and John A. Lima. *A to Zoo: Subject Access to Children's Picture Books.* 4th ed. Bowker 1993 $49.95. ISBN 0-8352-3201-8. Almost 12,000 picture books are indexed by subject, title, author, and illustrator.

Lynn, Ruth, ed. *Fantasy Literature for Children and Young Adults.* 3rd ed. Bowker 1989 $48.00. ISBN 0-8352-2347-7. An annotated bibliography of 3,300 fantasy novels and story collections.

Lystad, Mary. *From Dr. Mather to Dr. Seuss: 200 Years of American Books for Children.* Schenkman Bks. Inc. 1980 $15.95. ISBN 0-87073-210-2. An examination of the changing values expressed in American children's literature.

Meigs, Cornelia. *A Critical History of Children's Literature.* Macmillan 1953 o.p.

Nodelman, Perry. *Words about Pictures: The Narrative Art of Children's Picture Books.* U. of Ga. Pr. 1989 $35.00. ISBN 0-8203-1271-1. Contemporary American view of how pictures and text produce a unique art form.

————. *The Pleasures of Children's Literature.* Longman 1992 $19.95. ISBN 0-8013-0219-6. An attempt to bring together the various disciplines studying children's literature.

Norton, Donna. *Through the Eyes of a Child: An Introduction to Children's Literature.* Merrill 3rd ed. 1990 $37.95. ISBN 0-675-21144-1. An introduction containing a brief history, a selection guide, discussions of the major genres, and several indexes.

Pearson, Carol S. *The Hero Within: Six Archetypes We Live By.* HarpC 1989 $9.95. ISBN 0-06-254862-X. An attempt to combine theories of male and female hero myths and offer expanded types of heroes.

Stephens, John. *Language and Ideology in Children's Fiction.* Longman 1992 $19.96. ISBN 0-582-07063-5. A study of the uses of language in children's literature.

Sutherland, Zena, and Myra C. Livingston. *The Scott, Foresman Anthology of Children's Literature.* Scott F. 1984 $56.50. ISBN 0-673-15527-7

Townsend, John Rowe. *A Sense of Story: Essays on Contemporary Writers for Children.* Horn Bk. 1973 $6.95. ISBN 0-87675-276-8. Nineteen essays on British and American writers.

Yolan, Jane. *Touch Magic: Fantasy, Faerie and Folklore in the Literature of Childhood.* Putnam Pub. Group o.p. Collection of essays on the importance of folk tales and fantasy in children's cognitive and emotional growth.

Collections

Adoff, Arnold, ed. *I Am the Darker Brother: An Anthology of Modern Poems by Negro Americans.* Macmillan 1970 $4.95. ISBN 0-02-041120-0. One of several collections by Adoff of African-American poetry for children.

————, ed. *My Black Me, a Beginning Book of Black Poetry.* Dutton Child. Bks. 1974 $12.95. ISBN 0-525-35460-3. More poems for children by African Americans.

————, ed. *The Poetry of Black America: An Anthology of the 20th Century.* HarpC Child. Bks. 1973 $24.95. ISBN 0-06-020089-8. Poems by African Americans.

Bierhorst, John, ed. *In the Trail of the Wind, American Indian Poems and Ritual Orations.* FS&G 1987 $4.95. ISBN 0-374-43576-6. Poems from the oral traditions of several Native American and Inuit tribes.

Blishen, Edward, comp. *Oxford Book of Poetry for Children.* OUP 1987 $16.95. ISBN 0-19-276031-9. British and American poetry for children.

Bogan, Louise, and William Jay Smith, comps. *The Golden Journey: Two Hundred Twenty-Five Poems for Young People*. Contemp. Bks. 1989 $9.95. ISBN 0-8092-4249-4. Traditional collection of English and American poetry.

Brewton, Sara, and John E. Brewton, comps. *Laughable Limericks*. HarpC Child. Bks. 1990 $12.89. ISBN 0-690-04887-4. A collection of contemporary limericks for children.

————, comps. *They've Discovered a Head in a Box for the Bread & Other Laughable Limericks*. HarpC Child. Bks. 1978 $13.89. ISBN 0-690-03883-6. More contemporary limericks for children.

Butler, Francelia. *Sharing Literature with Children: A Thematic Anthology*. Waveland Pr. 1989 $24.95. ISBN 0-88133-463-4. A collection organized by important themes, compiled by an important contemporary critic.

Emrich, Duncan. *American Folk Poetry: An Anthology*. Little 1974 $35.00. ISBN 0-316-23722-1. An excellent complete collection of a wide range of songs, riddles, tales, legends, superstitions, and other folk literature.

Griffith, John W., and Charles H. Frey, eds. *Classics of Children's Literature*. Macmillan 3rd rev. ed. 1991. ISBN 0-02-347290-1. Excellent collection of the best in children's literature, both British and American.

Saltman, Judith. *The Riverside Anthology of Children's Literature*. HM 6th ed. 1985 $47.56. ISBN 0-395-35773-X. Excellent collection of both British and American literature separated into the important genres; includes a brief history and several indexes.

Sutherland, Zena, and Myra C. Livingston. *The Scott, Foresman Anthology of Children's Literature*. Scott F. 1984 $54.00. ISBN 0-673-1-15527-7. Excellent collection of works from important genres.

CHRONOLOGY OF AUTHORS

Alcott, Louisa May. 1832–1888
Clemens, Samuel Langhorn. 1835–1910
Burnett, Frances Hodgson. 1849–1924
Pyle, Howard. 1853–1911
Baum, L(yman) Frank. 1856–1919
Wilder, Laura Ingalls. 1867–1957
Frost, Robert. 1874–1963
Sandburg, Carl. 1878–1967

Forbes, Esther. 1891–1967
Gág, Wanda. 1893–1946
White, E(lwyn) B(rooks). 1899–1985
Geisel, Theodor Seuss. 1904–1991
Sendak, Maurice. 1928–
Paterson, Katherine. 1932–
Silverstein, Shel(by). 1932–
Van Allsburg, Chris. 1949–

ALCOTT, LOUISA MAY. 1832–1888

Louisa May Alcott, generally considered to be a writer of sentimental children's fiction, has received renewed critical attention from scholars examining her adult fiction and previously uncredited gothic thrillers. These works reveal a darker, more complex side of this author. Born in Germantown, Pennsylvania, Alcott moved to Boston in 1834 and then in 1840 to Concord, which was to remain her family home for the rest of her life. Her father Bronson Alcott was a transcendentalist and friend of RALPH WALDO EMERSON and HENRY DAVID THOREAU. Alcott early realized that her father could not be counted on as sole support of his family, and so she sacrificed much of her own pleasure to earn money by sewing, teaching, and churning out potboilers. Her reputation was established with *Hospital Sketches* (1863), an account of her work as a volunteer nurse in Washington. Her first works were indeed written for children, including her best-known *Little Women* (1868–69) and *Little Men: Life at Plumfield with Jo's Boys* (1871). *Moods* (1864), however, a "passionate conflict," was written for adults. Alcott's writing eventually became the family's main source of income.

Throughout her life, Alcott continued to produce highly popular and idealistic literature for children. *An Old-Fashioned Girl* (1870), *Eight Cousins* (1875), *Rose in Bloom* (1876), *Under the Lilacs* (1878), and *Jack and Jill* (1881) also enjoyed wide popularity. At the same time, her adult fiction—such as the autobiographical novel *Work: A Story of Experience* (1873) and *A Modern Mephistopheles* (1877), a story based on the Faust legend—shows her deeper concern with social issues such as education, prison reform, and women's suffrage. She realistically depicts the problems of adolescents and working women, the difficulties of relationships between men and women, and the values of the single women's life.

CHILDREN'S FICTION BY ALCOTT

Aunt Jo's Scrapbag (The Works of Louisa May Alcott). Rprt. Serv. 1989 repr. of 1871 ed. $79.00. ISBN 0-685-27392-X. A six-volume series of stories, essays, and sketches.
Eight Cousins. Little 1974 $17.95. ISBN 0-316-03091-0. Stories of a young girl and her seven cousins.
Jo's Boys. 1886. NAL-Dutton 1987 $2.25. ISBN 0-451-52089-0. Sequel to *Little Women*; depicts the careers and marriages of the March sisters' children and their schoolmates.
Jo's Boys and How They Turned Out. Little 1986 $17.95. ISBN 0-316-03093-7. Sequel to *Jo's Boys.*
Little Men. 1871. Dell 1991 $3.99. ISBN 0-440-40152-6. Story about Jo March and her husband and their efforts running a school for boys.
Little Women. Viking Penguin 1989 $5.95. ISBN 0-14-039009-3. The book that Alcott's fame rests on, though she herself called it "moral pap for children." Story of the March family and the four sisters in the family—Meg, Jo, Beth, and Amy.
An Old Fashioned Thanksgiving. Applewood 1990 $5.95. ISBN 1-55709-135-8. About seven children who prepare for Thanksgiving with mother away caring for grandmother.
Rose in Bloom. Little 1976 $16.95. ISBN 0-316-03098-8. Sequel to *Eight Cousins.*

ADULT NOVELS BY ALCOTT

A Modern Mephistopheles. 1877. *Classics Ser.* Bantam 1987 $3.50. ISBN 0-553-21266-4
Moods. 1864. *Amer. Women Writers Ser.* Ed. by Sarah Elbert. Rutgers U. Pr. 1991 $35.00. ISBN 0-8135-1669-2. Includes 1882 revisions.
Work: A Story of Experience. 1873. Ed. by Elizabeth Hardwick. *Rediscovered Fiction by Amer. Women Ser.* Ayer 1977 $27.00. ISBN 0-405-10042-6

SHORT STORIES BY ALCOTT

Alternative Alcott. Amer. Women Writers Ser. Ed. by Elaine Showalter. Rutgers U. Pr. 1988 $40.00. ISBN 0-8135-1271-9
Behind a Mask: The Unknown Thrillers of Louisa May Alcott. Amereon Ltd. $19.95. ISBN 0-88411-096-6. Eerie and blood-curdling tales of a mansion encircled by screaming peacocks and a female Dr. Jekyll and Mr. Hyde.
A Double Life: Newly Discovered Thrillers by Louisa May Alcott. Ed. by Madeleine B. Stern, Joel Myerson, and Daniel Shealy. Little 1988 $17.95. ISBN 0-316-03101-1. Stories that reveal Alcott's feminism and her "double" literary life.
Hospital Sketches. 1863. Applewood 1988 $6.95. ISBN 0-918222-78-8. Stories written from Alcott's experience as a nurse in the Civil War.

Transcendental Wild Oats. Intro. by William H. Harrison. Harvard Common Pr. 1981 $6.95. ISBN 0-916782-21-2. Stories written about Alcott family experience in transcendental colony, Fruitlands.

WORKS BY ALCOTT

The Journals of Louisa May Alcott. Ed. by Joel Myerson, Daniel Shealy, and Madeleine B. Stern. Little 1989 $24.95. ISBN 0-316-59362-1. Includes all known manuscripts and journals written from 1843 to 1888.
Louisa May Alcott: Her Life, Letters and Journals. Amer. Biog. Ser. Rprt. Serv. 1991 $89.00. ISBN 0-7812-8009-5
The Selected Letters of Louisa May Alcott. Ed. by Joel Myerson, Daniel Shealy, and Madeleine B. Stern. Little 1987 $24.95. ISBN 0-316-59361-3. Selection of 271 letters, half newly published, enriched with chronology, photographs, and notes.
The Works of Louisa May Alcott, 1832–1888. Rprt. Serv. 1987 $800.00. ISBN 0-685-18574-5

BOOKS ABOUT ALCOTT

Anthony, Katharine S. *Louisa May Alcott.* 1937–38. Greenwood 1977 $35.00. ISBN 0-8371-9552-7. Early biography serialized in *Woman's Home Companion* examining Alcott's family life.
Burke, Kathleen. *Louisa May Alcott. Amer. Women of Achievement Ser.* Chelsea Hse. 1988 $17.95. ISBN 1-55546-637-0. A readable biography; illustrated with historical prints.
Elbert, Sarah. *A Hunger for Home: Louisa May Alcott and Little Women.* Temple U. Pr. 1984 $34.95. ISBN 0-87722-317-3. First full-length critical treatment of Alcott.
_____. *Hunger for Home: Louisa May Alcott's Place in American Culture.* Rutgers U. Pr. 1987 $14.00. ISBN 0-8135-1199-2. Traces Alcott's feminist perspective in her major fiction.
Gulliver, Lucille. *Louisa May Alcott: A Bibliography.* Gordon Pr. 1972 $59.95. ISBN 0-8490-0559-0. Describes all known editions of Alcott's work.
MacDonald, Ruth K. *Louisa May Alcott. U.S. Authors Ser.* Macmillan 1983 $19.95. ISBN 0-8057-7397-5. General introduction.
Marsella, Joy A. *The Promise of Destiny: Children and Women in the Stories of Louisa May Alcott. Contributions to the Study of Childhood and Youth Ser.* Greenwood 1983 $38.50. ISBN 0-313-23603-8. Examines the tension between women's public and private roles in Alcott's stories.
Payne, Alma. *Louisa May Alcott: A Reference Guide.* G. K. Hall 1980 o.p. Knowledgeable introduction and review of criticism.
Saxton, Martha. *Louisa May: A Modern Biography of Louisa May Alcott.* HM 1977 o.p. Psychoanalytical study focusing on Alcott's adult fiction. A feminist biography.
Shealy, Daniel. *Freaks of Genius. Contributions to the Study of Popular Culture Ser.* Greenwood 1991 $42.95. ISBN 0-313-27627-7. Examines Alcott's gothic romances demonstrating her interest in themes of darkness.
Stern, Madeleine B. *Critical Essays on Louisa May Alcott. Critical Essays on Amer. Lit.* G. K. Hall 1984 o.p. Reprinted and original essays supplying a thorough overview of Alcott's work, especially *Little Women.*
_____. *Louisa May Alcott.* U. of Okla. Pr. 1985 $14.95. ISBN 0-8061-0938-6. Critical biography responsible for much modern Alcott scholarship.

BAUM, L(YMAN) FRANK. 1856–1919

L. Frank Baum was a prolific writer of novels, plays, and nonfiction for adults, and of several forms of children's literature, including one of the first science fiction novels, *The Master Key: An Electric Fairy Tale.* However, Baum is now remembered almost exclusively for his series of books about the fantastic land of Oz, mainly the first and best of them, *The Wonderful Wizard of Oz* (1900), later republished as *The Wizard of Oz.*

Baum wrote several sequels recounting further adventures in Oz, which he portrayed as a magical land full of such fantastic creatures as a talking Tin Man, a live Scarecrow, and a Saw Horse that could gallop and trot. In the original Oz book, Dorothy is catapulted from the real world into Oz and, for most of the book, tries to get home again. Later Oz stories lose the sense of interplay between Oz and the real world, featuring lifelong Oz inhabitants; later, Dorothy and her family come to take up permanent residence in the magical kingdom.

The Oz books proved to be extremely popular, and other writers took up the series after Baum's death. Although their works have not lasted, Baum's work has. All but one of Baum's 16 Oz books, published between 1900 and 1921, have been reissued in modern editions. Many of the Oz books have been turned into movies, although the first movie of *The Wizard of Oz*, famous as the first film to incorporate color photography, remains the most beloved.

Baum was born in Chittenango, New York, and died in Hollywood, where he had made his home for many years. After being tutored at home and attending Peekskill (New York) Military Academy, he worked, generally unsuccessfully, at many jobs, including actor, producer, journalist, and storekeeper. His first book for children was *Mother Goose in Prose* (1897), but it was *The Wizard of Oz* that made his career.

Critics have praised his originality and have condemned his style.

CHILDREN'S FICTION BY BAUM

Dorothy and the Wizard. 1908. Troll Assocs. 1980 $2.50. ISBN 0-89375-192-8
The Emerald City of Oz. 1910. Dover 1988 $6.95. ISBN 0-486-25681-2
Glinda of Oz. 1920. Ballantine 1985 $3.95. ISBN 0-345-33394-2
The Magic of Oz. 1919. Ballantine 1985 $3.95. ISBN 0-345-33288-1
The Marvelous Land of Oz. 1904. Morrow 1985 $15.00. ISBN 0-688-05439-0
Ozma of Oz. 1907. Morrow 1989 $19.95. ISBN 0-688-06632-1
The Road to Oz. 1909. Dover 1986 $4.95. ISBN 0-486-25208-6
The Tin Woodman of Oz. Ballantine 1985 $3.50. ISBN 0-345-33436-1
The Wizard of Oz. Ballantine 1986 $3.95. ISBN 0-345-33590-2

BOOKS ABOUT BAUM

Baum, F. J., and Russell P. MacFall. *To Please a Child: A Biography of L. Frank Baum, Royal Historian of Oz.* Reilly & Lee 1961 o.p. Favorable biography.
Gardner, Martin, and Russell B. Nye. *The Wizard of Oz and Who He Was.* Mich. St. U. Pr. 1957 o.p. Biography and critique.
Moore, Raylyn. *Wonderful Wizard Marvelous Land.* Bowling Green Univ. 1974 o.p. Introduction by Ray Bradbury. A strong defense of Baum's writing, including a selected bibliography of critical and biographical writings.

BURNETT, FRANCES HODGSON. 1849–1924

An English-born American author of plays, fiction, and journalism, Burnett is praised for her strength as a storyteller, her understanding of young people, and her authentic characterizations. Although she was a popular author of adult fiction during her lifetime, today she is remembered mainly for her children's fiction. The most famous of her works include *The Secret Garden* (1909), the classic story of an angry little rich girl who softens when she discovers a beautiful garden; *Little Lord Fauntleroy* (1886), about an American boy who discovers he is heir to an English fortune; and *The Little Princess* (1905), in which a little girl is transformed from favored heiress to drudge before she finally regains a fortune and a loving family.

Burnett was born to Edwin and Eliza Hodgson. In 1873 she married Swan M. Burnett, a physician, whom she divorced in 1898. In 1900, she married Stephen Townesend, another physician, whom she also divorced, in 1901. She had two sons with her first husband—Lional, who died in 1890, and Vivian. Burnett lived much of her life in Long Island, New York.

Drawing on her own childhood and the works of the Brontës, Burnett wrote *The Secret Garden* to express her love of nature as well as her strong wish for happiness. The book is the story of Mary Lennox, a disagreeable orphan, who arrives at her uncle's mansion in Yorkshire, where she befriends her cousin Colin, a spoiled invalid, and the Pan-like Dickon, brother of the maid. With Dickon's help, Mary and Colin bloom into loving healthy children through nature's healing powers and through the warmth and wisdom of Dickon's family. The book strongly stresses the unity and importance of love, family, nature, beauty, and health—standard in realistic fiction for children at the time.

CHILDREN'S FICTION BY BURNETT

Little Lord Fauntleroy. 1886. Buccaneer Bks. 1981 $21.95. ISBN 0-89966-288-9
The Little Princess. 1905. Buccaneer Bks. 1981 $15.95. ISBN 0-89966-327-3
The Secret Garden. 1909. Buccaneer Bks. 1981 $19.95. ISBN 0-89966-326-5

NONFICTION BY BURNETT

The One I Know Best of All. Ayer 1980 repr. of 1893 ed. $36.00. ISBN 0-405-12828-2. The author's autobiography.

BOOKS ABOUT BURNETT

Burnett, Constance Buel. *Happily Ever After: A Portrait of Frances Hodgson Burnett*. Vanguard 1965 o.p. Aimed at ages 11 to 16, written by Burnett's son's wife.
Burnett, Vivian. *The Romantic Lady: Frances Hodgson Burnett, the Life Story of an Imagination*. Macmillan Child. Grp. 1927 o.p. Vivian Burnett's views on his mother, making much use of her own letters.
Thwaite, Ann. *Waiting for the Party: The Life of Frances Hodgson Burnett*. Godine 1989 $13.95. ISBN 0-87923-790-2. Proposes the theory that Burnett wanted all of life to be a party, though hers wasn't.

CLEMENS, SAMUEL LANGHORN (Mark Twain; Thomas Jefferson Snodgrass). 1835–1910

[SEE Chapter 15 in this volume for Main Entry.]

CHILDREN'S FICTION BY CLEMENS

Works of Mark Twain: Prince and the Pauper, Tom Sawyer, Huckleberry Finn, A Connecticut Yankee. Longmeadow Pr. 1990 $17.95. ISBN 0-681-41002-7. Includes Twain's major stories for younger audiences.

POETRY BY CLEMENS

The War Prayer. HarpC 1984 $5.95. ISBN 0-06-091113-1. Twain's highly acclaimed and controversial antiwar poem, often introduced to children in schools.

FORBES, ESTHER. 1891–1967

Forbes was the author of six historical novels and four books of nonfiction for adults, as well as the recipient of the Pulitzer Prize in history in 1942 for her adult biography, *Paul Revere and the World He Lived In* (1942). Yet Forbes's reputation is primarily as a children's writer, resting particularly on *Johnny Tremain* (1942), an offshoot of her research for the adult Paul Revere biography and considered by many the best example of historical fiction ever written for children.

Johnny Tremain follows the story of a silversmith's apprentice as he stumbles into the American Revolution and gains insight into his own character. In writing about the life of an ordinary citizen of Boston at that time, Forbes wanted to show, in her words, "not merely what was done but why and how people felt." Originally intending to keep Johnny neutral during the Revolution, she changed her mind as a result of the advent of World War II, because she saw parallels between the two wars and wanted to show young readers those parallels. Although this may have resulted in some pushing of contemporary ideology onto a historical setting, most critics have praised the story's accuracy. It was and remains an important book for promoting the idea that young readers can grasp mature writing.

Forbes's only other book for children, *America's Paul Revere*, summarizes that man's life. It is also noteworthy for its excellent illustrations by Lynd Ward.

CHILDREN'S FICTION BY FORBES

Johnny Tremain. 1942. Buccaneer Bks. 1981 $21.95. ISBN 0-89966-306-0

CHILDREN'S NONFICTION BY FORBES

America's Paul Revere. HM 1990 $4.95. ISBN 0-395-24907-4

FROST, ROBERT. 1874–1963

[SEE Chapter 16 in this volume for Main Entry.]

POETRY BY FROST

Stopping by Woods on a Snowy Evening. Dutton Child. Bks. 1978 $12.95. ISBN 0-525-40115-6. An illustrated version of his famous poem, suitable for children.
A Swinger of Birches: Poems of Robert Frost for Young People. Stemmer Hse. 1982 $21.95. ISBN 0-916144-92-5. A collection of Frost's most famous poems.

GÁG, WANDA (HAZEL). 1893–1946

A highly touted writer and illustrator of children's picture books, Gág was born in New Ulm, Minnesota, to Anton Gág, also an artist, and Lisse Gág. She married Earle Marshall Humphreys in 1930. She studied art at the St. Paul Institute of Arts, the Minneapolis School of Art, and the Art Students League in New York City.

Gág began her career illustrating for the children's section of the *Minneapolis Journal*; first had her works exhibited at the Weyrhe Gallery, New York City, 1926; and created the text and drawings for her most famous work, *Millions of Cats*, in 1928. The book was a runner-up for the John Newbery Medal in 1929, won first prize at the Philadelphia Lithograph Show in 1930, and won the Lewis Carroll Shelf Award in 1958. Other important works include *ABC Bunny* (1933), another runner-up for the Newbery award in 1934; *Snow White and the Seven Dwarfs*, a runner-up for the Caldecott award in 1939; and *Nothing at All*, also a runner-up for the Caldecott award in 1942. In 1993, the centennial of her birth was celebrated with special exhibits of her art and a number of evaluative articles.

CHILDREN'S PICTURE BOOKS BY GÁG

ABC Bunny. 1933. Putnam Pub. Group 1978 $8.95. ISBN 0-698-20000-4. An alphabet book.

Millions of Cats. 1928. Putnam Pub. Group 1977 $77.95. ISBN 0-698-20091-8. Story of a couple who gathers more and more cats but ends up with only one. A repetitive and cumulative illustrated tale.

Nothing at All. Putnam Pub. Group 1941 o.p. Story about a dog that is brought to life.

Snow White and the Seven Dwarfs. Putnam Pub. Group 1938 o.p. Translated retelling of the famous fairy tale with black-and-white liner illustrations.

BOOK ABOUT GÁG

Scott, Alma O. *Wanda Gág: The Story of an Artist*. U. of Minn. Pr. 1949 o.p. Complimentary biography.

GEISEL, THEODOR SEUSS (Dr. Seuss; Theo LeSieg). 1904–1991

Certainly the most popular of all American writers and illustrators of picture books, Geisel made his pseudonym Dr. Seuss famous to several generations of children and their parents. Geisel developed a rhythmic form of poetry that relied on quick rhymes and wordplay reminiscent of Mother Goose rhymes. He combined this with exaggerated cartoonlike illustrations of fantasy characters to entice children into stories that contained important messages, often presented with a great deal of irony and satire.

Geisel always embraced the imagination of children and condemned adults' inability to join into it, using the child's view to reveal the flaws in society. His first picture book, *And to Think That I Saw It on Mulberry Street* (1937), describes a child's adding more and more imaginative elements to the story that he plans to tell about what he saw on the way home, only to end with the child actually telling the truth: he saw only a very uninteresting horse and cart. *The Cat in the Hat* (1957), written as a beginning reader, portrays two children having a magical afternoon with a strange cat while their mother is away, complete with a frantic cleanup before their mother can find out what they have done. This is probably his most famous work.

Geisel's later books took on social questions more directly. *The Butter-Battle Book* (1984) condemned the cold war, and it is often removed from children's sections of libraries for political reasons. Likewise, *The Lorax* (1971), which condemned the destruction of the ecology, has also been banned.

Altogether, Geisel wrote and illustrated 47 books, which have sold more than 100 million copies in 18 languages. In 1984 he received a Pulitzer Prize for his contributions to children's literature. More than a dozen of his books are still in print.

CHILDREN'S PICTURE BOOKS BY GEISEL

Bartholomew and the Oobleck. 1980. Random Bks. Yng. Read. 1980 $8.95. ISBN 0-394-80075-3

The Butter-Battle Book. 1984. Random Bks. Yng. Read. 1984 $12.00. ISBN 0-394-86580-4

The Cat in the Hat. 1957. Random Bks. Yng. Read. 1987 $6.95. ISBN 0-394-89218-6

Green Eggs and Ham. 1960. Random Bks. Yng. Read. 1987 $6.95. ISBN 0-394-89220-8. The story of Sam, who doesn't like green eggs and ham—at first.

Horton Hatches the Egg. 1940. Random Bks. Yng. Read. 1991 $10.95. ISBN 0-394-82956-5

Horton Hears a Who. 1962. Random Bks. Yng. Read. 1990 $10.95. ISBN 0-679-80003-4. Fabulous story about a rhyming elephant who tries to save the tiny residents of Whoville.

How the Grinch Stole Christmas. 1957. Random Bks. Yng. Read. 1988 $9.95. ISBN 0-394-81339-1. Classic Christmas story made into television holiday show.

The Lorax. Ed. by Ted Danson. Random Bks. Yng. Read. 1992 $13.00. ISBN 0-394-82237-9

There a Wocket in My Pocket. 1974. Random Bks. Yng. Read. 1974 $6.95. ISBN 0-394-82920-4

Yertle the Turtle and Other Stories. 1958. Ed. by John Lithgow. Random Bks. Yng. Read. 1992 $14.00. ISBN 0-679-83229-7

PATERSON, KATHERINE. 1932–

Perhaps the best writer of historical and contemporary realistic fiction for children over 10 years of age, Paterson was born in Qing Jiang, Jiangsu, China, daughter of George Raymond, a minister, and Mary Womeldorf. She married John Barstow Paterson, also a minister, in 1962.

After spending her childhood in China and the United States, Paterson attended King College and received her M.A. from Presbyterian School of Christian Education. She later studied at Naganuma School of Japanese Language in Kobe, Japan, and at Union Theological Seminary, New York. She was a missionary in Japan from 1957 to 1962, and she taught school in Lovettsville, Virginia, and Pennington, New Jersey.

Paterson's first three books are set in ancient Japan. *The Sign of the Chrysanthemum* (1973) is a coming-of-age story that follows Muno in search of his samurai father. *Of Nightingales That Weep* (1974) depicts a young girl's conflict between loyalty to her family and personal love. *The Master Puppeteer* (1976), a National Book Award winner, is a mystery centering on Osaka, the mysterious puppeteer bandit. These books are followed by Paterson's two best works, *Bridge to Terabithia* (1977), a Newbery Award winner about the loss of a friend and the need to take responsibility for oneself (a major theme in Paterson's works); and *The Great Gilly Hopkins* (1978), a Newbery honor book about a foster child who learns that life is tough, but not necessarily bad. *Jacob Have I Loved* (1980), set mainly on an island in Chesapeake Bay during World War II, deals once again with the theme of responsibility—this time through the struggle of a twin to realize her own worth. *Rebels of the Heavenly Kingdom* (1983), set in nineteenth-century China, deals with two youths during the Taiping Rebellion. *Come Sing, Jimmy Jo* (1985) is about a boy with the gift of a great singing voice and how he deals with it. *Park's Quest* (1988) concerns a boy who learns to deal with his Vietnamese half-sister. *Lyddie* (1991) follows a young girl as she grows up in nineteenth-century America and must learn (once again) that she is responsible for herself.

Although Paterson has a strong Christian background, her books are never preachy and more often attack phony religious views than offer positive preaching. Her themes center on the belief that life is tough but that it is up to the individual to make the best of it, which, in fact, is exactly what makes life a good thing—the change to do a good job at something that is difficult.

CHILDREN'S FICTION BY PATERSON

Bridge to Terabithia. 1977. HarpC Child. Bks. 1977 $13.95. ISBN 0-690-01359-0

Come Sing, Jimmy Jo. 1985. Dutton Child. Bks. 1985 $12.95. ISBN 0-525-67167-6

The Great Gilly Hopkins. 1978. HarpC Child. Bks. 1978 $13.95. ISBN 0-690-03837-2

Jacob Have I Loved. 1980. Avon 1980 $2.95. ISBN 0-3890-56499-8

Lyddie. 1991. Dutton Child. Bks. 1991 $14.95. ISBN 0-525-67338-5

The Master Puppeteer. 1976. Avon 1981 $2.95. ISBN 0-380-53322-7

Of Nightingales That Weep. 1974. HarpC Child. Bks. 1974 $13.95. ISBN 0-690-00485-0

Park's Quest. 1988. Dutton Child. Bks. 1988 $12.95. ISBN 0-525-67258-3

Rebels of the Heavenly Kingdom. 1983. Dutton Child. Bks. 1983 $11.95. ISBN 0-525-66911-6

The Sign of the Chrysanthemum. 1973. HarpC Child. Bks. 1976 $13.95. ISBN 0-690-73625-8

The Tale of the Mandarin Ducks. Dutton Child. Bks. 1990 $14.95. ISBN 0-525-67283-4. A folk tale translated by Paterson.

PYLE, HOWARD. 1853–1911

Called the father of American illustration, Pyle is praised for his writing and rewriting, as well as for his brilliant illustrating techniques. He is considered a pioneer in bringing text, illustrations, and design together in works mainly aimed at middle grades through high school. Pyle is also the founder of the Brandywine School of art, which produced such noted illustrators as N. C. Wyeth, Maxfield Parrish, Jessie Willcox Smith, Frank Schoonover, and Violet Oakley.

Besides illustrating many books and stories written by others, Pyle's own writings include a classic four-volume retelling of the King Arthur stories, as well as two novels, *Otto of the Silver Hand* (1888) and *Men of Iron* (1892). However, he is best known for his first work, *The Merry Adventures of Robin Hood of Great Renown, in Nottinghamshire* (1883), generally regarded as the best book ever done on the subject.

Pyle's most famous style consists of decorative black-and-white line drawings that include panels, headpieces, and tailpieces, done with a bold, forceful control of anatomy and movement. Later he experimented with a more impressionistic style, which was up to the standards of the fine artists of the time.

CHILDREN'S FICTION BY PYLE

Men of Iron. 1892. Troll Assocs. 1990 $12.89. ISBN 0-8167-1871-7. Adventures of a young English squire during the time of Henry IV.

The Merry Adventures of Robin Hood. 1883. Dover 1968 $6.95. ISBN 0-486-22043-5

The Story of King Arthur and His Knights. Dover $6.95. ISBN 0-486-21445-1

Otto of the Silver Hand. 1888. Dover 1967 $5.95. ISBN 0-486-21784-1. Excellent historical fiction, taking place in twelfth-century Germany.

BOOK ABOUT PYLE

Agosta, Lucien L. *Howard Pyle. Twayne's U.S. Authors Ser.* G. K. Hall 1987 $22.95. ISBN 0-8057-7493-9. A good critical assessment of Pyle's work.

SANDBURG, CARL. 1878–1967.

[SEE Chapter 16 in this volume for Main Entry.]

CHILDREN'S FICTION BY SANDBURG

Rootabaga Stories, Pt. 1. HarBraceJ 1988 $19.95. ISBN 0-15-269061-1. Sandburg's first collection of humorous stories for children.

Rootabaga Stories, Pt. 2. HarBraceJ 1989 $19.95. ISBN 0-15-269062-X. Sandburg's second collection of humorous children's fiction.

CHILDREN'S NONFICTION BY SANDBURG

Abe Lincoln Grows Up. 1928. HarBraceJ 1975 $19.95. ISBN 0-15-201037-8. First part of his famous imaginative biography, generally the one introduced to children.

Abe Lincoln; The Prairie Years & the War Years. 1929, 1939. HarBraceJ 1974 $18.95. ISBN 0-15-602611-2. The complete biography.

SENDAK, MAURICE. 1928–

Perhaps the best-known and most highly respected illustrator of his generation, Sendak is credited with bringing into the picture book a highly complex dimension of child psychology. Drawing on memories of his own childhood, Sendak explores openly the deepest emotions of children: fear, sexuality, jealousy, grief, anger, and the need for approval.

Sendak's illustrating technique is praised for its versatility, its control of the medium, its use of contrast, and its page design. He employs humorous line drawings, impressionistic watercolors, bright posterlike images, and detailed black-and-white drawings. His writing is praised for its economy and expressiveness.

Sendak began his career illustrating for such other noted writers of children's picture books as Ruth Sawyer, Beatrice Schenk de Regniers, and Mendert DeJong, and gained his first wide audience illustrating *A Hole Is to Dig* (1952) for Ruth Krauss. He has continued to illustrate books written by others, including some classics by GEORGE MacDONALD (see Vol. 2) and HANS CHRISTIAN ANDERSEN (see Vol. 2). His most famous work, however, consists of a trilogy that he wrote and illustrated himself: *Where the Wild Things Are* (1963); *In the Night Kitchen* (1970); and *Outside Over There* (1981). In each one of these stories, a child is separated from his parents in a traumatic situation, solves the problem in a dream or fantasy world, and returns successfully to the security of home. *The Nutshell Library* is another well-known group of books that Sendak wrote and illustrated—this one a boxed set of four small books including an alphabet book, a poem about the seasons, a cautionary tale, and a counting rhyme. Most recently, Sendak is co-founder of a children's theater in New York.

CHILDREN'S PICTURE BOOKS BY SENDAK

In the Night Kitchen. HarpC Child. Bks. 1970 $14.95. ISBN 0-06-025489-0
Nutshell Library. HarpC Child. Bks. 1962 $10.95. ISBN 0-06-025500-5. Includes *Alligators All Around; Chicken Soup with Rice; One Was Johnny; Pierre.*
Outside Over There. HarpC Child. Bks. 1981 $19.95. ISBN 0-06-025523-4. An Ursula Nordstrom book.
Where the Wild Things Are. HarpC Child. Bks. 1988 $13.95. ISBN 0-06-025492-0. Twenty-fifth anniversary edition.

BOOK ABOUT SENDAK

Lanes, Selma. *The Art of Maurice Sendak.* Abrams 1984 $34.98. ISBN 0-8109-8063-0. A good discussion of Sendak's work.

SEUSS, DR. 1904–1991

[See GEISEL, THEODOR SEUSS]

SILVERSTEIN, SHEL(BY) (Uncle Shelby). 1932–

The most popular current writer of humorous verse for children, Silverstein was born in Chicago, Illinois, has been married and divorced, has one daughter, and currently lives in Brooklyn, New York. His career includes composing popular songs, drawing cartoons, writing many adult articles (several for *Playboy*), and acting. However, he is best known for his self-illustrated children's poetry.

His first such book was *Uncle Shelby's Story of Lafcadio, the Lion Who Shot Back* (1963), the humorous tale of a lion who turns the tables on hunters. It was followed by *The Giving Tree* (1964), a story of a parentlike tree that gives endlessly and is endlessly used by its son. Several other such picture books followed, including *The Missing Piece* (1976), about a circle that goes in search of a missing piece, and its sequel, *The Missing Piece Meets the Big O* (1981). However, two collections of poetry are probably his best-loved work: *Where the Sidewalk Ends: The Poems and Drawings of Shel Silverstein* (1974), and *A Light in the Attic* (1981).

All of Silverstein's poetry for children employs the language play common to LEWIS CARROLL and EDWARD LEAR. Silverstein is probably the best of the contemporary nonsense poets for children.

CHILDREN'S PICTURE BOOKS BY SILVERSTEIN

Giraffe and a Half. 1964. HarpC Child. Bks. 1964 $14.00. ISBN 0-06-025655-9. Humorous picture book about an unusual giraffe.
The Giving Tree. 1964. HarpC Child. Bks. 1964 $12.00. ISBN 0-06-025665-6
Lafcadio, the Lion Who Shot Back. 1963. HarpC Child. Bks. 1963 $14.00. ISBN 0-06-025675-3
The Missing Piece. 1976. HarpC Child. Bks. 1976 $14.00. ISBN 0-06-025671-0
The Missing Piece Meets the Big O. 1981. HarpC Child. Bks. 1981 $14.00. ISBN 0-06-025657-5
Who Wants a Cheap Rhinoceros? Macmillan rev. ed. 1983 $12.95. ISBN 0-02-782690-2. Humorous story for young children.

POETRY BY SILVERSTEIN

A Light in the Attic. 1981. HarpC Child. Bks. 1981 $15.00. ISBN 0-06-025673-7
Where the Sidewalk Ends: The Poems and Drawings of Shel Silverstein. 1974. HarpC Child. Bks. 1974 $15.00. ISBN 0-06-025667-2

VAN ALLSBURG, CHRIS. 1949–

Considered to be one of the foremost authors and illustrators of surrealistic fantasy for children, Van Allsburg was born in Grand Rapids, Michigan, to Richard, a dairy owner, and Chris Van Allsburg. He married Lisa Morrison and currently teaches at the Rhode Island School of Design.

Van Allsburg's work is highly praised for the excellent artisanship of his illustrations, which combine a realistic style with a dark tonality, often with a surreal element as well. His first book, *The Garden of Abdul Gasazi* (1979), concerning a lost dog found by a magician, and his second book, *Jumanji* (1981), about a strange board game that comes to life, brought him quick attention for their mysterious and original tone. *Jumanji* won the Caldecott Medal. *Ben's Dream* (1982) follows a boy's imaginary journey around the world; the story is told through black-and-white line drawings. *The Wreck of the Zephyr* (1983) offers a curious, mythical journey by a boy who sails into another reality. *The Mysteries of Harris Burdick* (1984) is a collection of separate stories— consisting only of their titles and first lines—accompanied by one strange picture each. *The Polar Express* (1985), Van Allsburg's most popular book, deals with the idea that the ability to believe in things beyond one's experiences helps to keep a person young. It also won a Caldecott Medal. Other books by Van Allsburg include *The Z was Zapped*, an alphabet book, and *Just a Dream*, a story about a boy who learns to be ecological.

CHILDREN'S PICTURE BOOKS BY VAN ALLSBURG

Ben's Dream. 1982. HM 1982 $14.95. ISBN 0-395-32084-4
The Garden of Abdul Gasazi. 1979. HM 1979 $15.95. ISBN 0-395-27804-X
Jumanji. 1981. HM 1981 $15.95. ISBN 0-395-30448-2

Just a Dream. 1990. HM 1990 $17.95. ISBN 0-395-53308-2
The Mysteries of Harris Burdick. 1984. HM 1984 $15.95. ISBN 0-395-35393-5
Polar Express. 1985. HM 1985 $17.95. ISBN 0-395-38949-6
The Stranger. 1986. HM 1986 $16.95. ISBN 0-395-42331-7
Two Bad Ants. 1988. HM 1988 $16.95. ISBN 0-395-48668-8
The Wreck of the Zephyr. 1983. HM 1983 $15.95. ISBN 0-395-33075-0
The Z Was Zapped: A Play in Twenty-Six Acts. 1987. HM 1987 $16.95. An alphabet book.

WHITE, E(LWYN) B(ROOKS). 1899–1985

[See Chapter 16 for Main Entry.]

CHILDREN'S FICTION BY WHITE

E. B. White Boxed Set. Includes *Charlotte's Web; The Trumpet of the Swan; Stuart Little*.
   HarpC Child Bks. 1974 $11.40. ISBN 0-06-440061-1. Contains White's three major
   books for children: *Charlotte's Web*, about a pig who is saved from slaughter through
   the clever writings of a spider; *The Trumpet of the Swan*, about a trumpeter swan
   who makes up for his birth defect by learning to play a real trumpet; and *Stuart
   Little*, about a humanlike mouse who has a series of adventures.

WILDER, LAURA INGALLS. 1867–1957

Wilder was born near Pepin, Wisconsin; attended school in DeSmet, South
Dakota; and became a teacher before she was 16, teaching for seven years in
Dakota Territory schools. She and her husband, Almanzo Wilder, farmed near
DeSmet for about nine years and then moved to Mansfield, Missouri, where they
lived out the rest of their days.

Wilder did not write her first book, *Little House in the Big Woods*, about her
early years in Wisconsin, until late in life, on the urging of her daughter, Rose
Wilder Lane. It was first published in 1932. She followed this with *Farmer Boy*
(1933), a book about her husband's childhood in New York State. She then
completed a series of books about her life as she and her family moved
westward along the frontier. *Little House on the Prairie* (1935) records the
family's move to Kansas. *On the Banks of Plum Creek* (1937) describes the
family's move to Minnesota. *By the Shores of Silver Lake* (1939) records the
family's move to South Dakota, as do the final three books in the series: *The
Long Winter, Little Town on the Prairie* (1941), and *These Happy Golden Years*
(1943), which ends with her marriage to Almanzo Wilder. Three of Wilder's
books were published posthumously: *On the Way Home*, a diary of her trip to
Mansfield; *The First Four Years*, an unfinished book about her first four years of
marriage; and *West from Home*, letters she wrote on a visit to her daughter in
San Francisco, none of them up to the quality of her earlier books.

At her best, Wilder employs a clear, simple style, a wealth of fascinating
detail, and a straightforward narrative style. Her tales of a strong, traditional
frontier family that endures the hardships of the late eighteenth century are
seen through the eyes of a child, which endears them to young readers. Her
work is possibly the best example of historical realistic fiction for children.

CHILDREN'S FICTION BY WILDER

By the Shores of Silver Lake. 1939. Bantam 1990 $15.95. ISBN 1-55736-176-2
Farmer Boy. 1933. HarpC Child. Bks. 1961 $15.00. ISBN 0-06-026425-X
The First Four Years. HarpC Child. Bks. 1971 $15.00. ISBN 0-06-026426-8
Little House in the Big Woods. 1932. HarpC Child. Bks. 1961 $15.00. ISBN 0-06-026430-6
Little House on the Prairie. 1935. Bucaneer Bks. 1991 $19.95. ISBN 0-89966-868-2
Little Town on the Prairie. 1941. HarpC Child. Bks. 1961 $15.00. ISBN 0-06-026450-0
The Long Winter. 1941. HarpC Child. Bks. 1961 $15.00. ISBN 0-06-026460-8

On the Banks of Plum Creek. 1937. HarpC Child. Bks. 1961 $15.00. ISBN 0-06-026470-5
These Happy Golden Years. 1943. HarpC Child. Bks. 1961 $15.00. ISBN 0-06-026480-2

BOOKS ABOUT WILDER

Anderson, William T. *Laura Ingalls Wilder Country: The People and Places in Laura Ingalls Wilder's Life and Books.* HarpC 1990 $19.95. ISBN 0-06-097346-3. A good recent discussion of Wilder's life and works.
———. *The Story of the Ingalls.* Anderson MI 1971 $3.95. ISBN 0-9610088-0-6. Biography for children.
Blair, Gwenda. *Laura Ingalls Wilder.* Putnam Pub. Group 1981 $6.99. ISBN 0-399-61139-8. A good introduction to Wilder for younger children.
Spaeth, Janet. *Laura Ingalls Wilder.* Twayne's U.S. Author Ser. G. K. Hall 1987 $18.95. ISBN 0-8057-7501-3. An excellent analysis of Wilder and her work.
Zochert, Donald. *Laura: The Life of Laura Ingalls Wilder.* Avon 1977 $4.95. ISBN 0-380-01636-2. An inexpensive biography of Wilder; worthwhile.

POPULAR FICTION

Since the eighteenth century, American popular literature has developed alongside high literature, but only in the last several decades has popular literature become the subject of scholarly research. The inclusion of excerpts from such books as SUSANNA HASWELL ROWSON's *Charlotte Temple* (1791) and CATHERINE SEDGWICK's *Hope Leslie* (1827) in some of the major literary anthologies used in college courses demonstrates that the canon is broadening to include authors of popular works whose names had previously been known to only a few literary historians.

All of the genres covered in this chapter—westerns, romances, mystery/detective, horror, historical fiction, and science fiction—can trace their beginnings back to British and American high literature. Westerns, some assert, have their roots partly in such texts as the 1682 captivity narrative of Mary Rowlandson, as well as the frontier novels of JAMES FENIMORE COOPER, particularly his Leatherstocking saga. Romances, too, stretch back at least as far as SAMUEL RICHARDSON's *Pamela* (1740) and *Clarissa Harlowe* (1747). EDGAR ALLAN POE is often cited as the inventor of the detective story, and horror, too, can tip its literary hat to Poe, as well as to MARY SHELLEY's *Frankenstein* (1818). The influence of SIR WALTER SCOTT was widespread among nineteenth-century American historical novelists; indeed, the historical novel became immensely popular in the late nineteenth century and dominated the popular fiction market until well into the twentieth century. Finally, science fiction was a reaction to the increasingly technological societies of America and Europe in the late nineteenth century, with Jules Verne and H. G. WELLS leading the way for the American EDGAR RICE BURROUGHS.

These six broad divisions are only the major groupings of popular fiction. Each category contains specialized types: Romances may be sentimental, historical, or sexually explicit; detective stories may be classical or hard-boiled; and so on. Whatever the category, it is certain that readers of popular fiction are looking for entertainment as well as a certain kind of aesthetic pleasure when they dip into ISAAC ASIMOV's robot stories, LOUIS L'AMOUR's frontier tales, or RAYMOND CHANDLER's hard-boiled detective novels, to name only a few of the hundreds of authors who have devoted their lives to writing popular fiction.

History and Criticism

Cawelti, John. *Adventure, Mystery, and Romance: Formula Stories as Art and Popular Culture*. U. Ch. Pr. 1977 $10.95. ISBN 0-226-09867-2. Brilliant study of the aesthetics of several popular genres, seeing them as works of art revealing much about American culture.

Hart, James D. *The Popular Book: A History of America's Literary Taste*. Greenwood 1976 repr. of 1950 ed. $35.00. ISBN 0-8371-8694-3. Though 40 years old, still a very useful and entertaining, scholarly look at the history of popular fiction in America; a seminal work.

Inge, Thomas, ed. *Handbook of American Popular Literature*. Greenwood 1988 $57.95. ISBN 0-313-25405-2. Anthology of essays by experts in many popular genres; an excellent place to begin the study of popular literature.

Radway, Janice. *Reading the Romance: Women, Patriarchy and Popular Literature*. U. of NC Pr. 1991 $10.95. ISBN 0-8078-4349-0. A scholarly book that provides a brilliant model for studying popular literature, even if one is not interested in romances.

Roberts, Thomas. *An Aesthetics of Junk Fiction*. U. of Ga. Pr. 1990 $30.00. ISBN 0-8203-1149-9. A scholarly look at popular fiction that counters some of the theories of Cawelti and others; very fine exploration of several genres, including science fiction.

Rosenberg, Betty. *Genreflecting*. Libs. Unl. 1987 $30.00. ISBN 0-87287-530-X. Extremely useful set of lists and bibliographies, some annotated, in the major divisions of popular literature.

Westerns

Scholars who study westerns face two problems at the outset. First, how is the western to be defined? Second, what are the origins of this most American of genres? Western historian Richard Etulain, wrestling with the problem of definition, says that it is "like trying to shovel fleas through a barn door—more escape than are captured." Still, it is possible to begin a definition based on geography. A western takes place west of the Mississippi River. Even this may be immediately challenged, however, since many writers of westerns, most prominently LOUIS L'AMOUR, use locales in the eastern and southern United States. Thus, one option is to say that a western is set on America's frontier, since that changed as the continent was settled by Americans and European immigrants. Another, perhaps more useful approach, is that of critic John Cawelti, who neatly sidesteps the dilemma of place: "The element that most clearly defines the western is the symbolic landscape in which it takes place and the influence on the character and actions of the hero." Shifting the focus from the actual to the imaginary provides flexibility, a key in dealing with popular literature. While authors of popular literature, including westerns, do use formulaic structures of plot and characterizations, it is the variations of those formulas that sustain the reader's interest and the vitality of the genre. In American popular literature, the western formula has proven to be one of the most adaptable to the changing social, cultural, economic, and historical forces shaping society.

A second part of the definition of westerns has to do with when the action takes place. Again, problems arise, since in the twentieth century most westerns have been set in the era between 1865 and 1890—the time of the great cattle drives, of the wars between the military and Native Americans on the Plains and in the Southwest, of rapid railroad expansion—in short, those years when the movement across North America was reaching its peak. *The Virginian* (1902), *Riders of the Purple Sage* (1912), and *Shane* (1949), among many other classic westerns, are set in this era. But to limit the historical period in this way leaves out far too much, including the work of JAMES FENIMORE COOPER, whose five Leatherstocking Tales—*The Pioneers* (1823), *The Last of the Mohicans* (1826), *The Prairie* (1827), *The Pathfinder* (1840), and *The Deerslayer* (1841)—are often cited as the forerunners of the western, along with the later dime novels. Also excluded from the strict 1865–1890 time frame are the many early narratives of travel and exploration, as well as texts such as Mary Rowlandson's captivity narrative (1682), which not only sows the seeds for one of the genre's most enduring plots, the captivity of white women by Native Americans, but also provides a close look at America's indigenous peoples, whose legends and histories would become a genre staple. Once again, John Cawelti cuts through the problem to provide a useful and flexible framework: "Historically, the western represents a moment when the forces of civilization and wilderness life are in balance, the epic moment at which the old life and the new confront each other and individual actions may tip the balance one way or another, thus shaping the future history of the whole settlement." If we use Cawelti's notion that the western captures a recurring moment in history, then we may consider westerns as responses to an ongoing process, into which Mary Rowlandson, Natty Bumppo (the dime novel hero), *The Virginian*, and *Shane* may all be placed.

Paradoxically, readers of this historical genre have not always demanded that the accouterments—weapons, horses, saddles, clothing—be represented with historical accuracy. The demand for apparent authenticity has taken place gradually. It is generally acknowledged that Cooper's depiction of Native Americans is inaccurate, and, naturally, dime novels are not realistic, but attitudes began to change in the twentieth century as the Old West in fact disappeared. Readers began seeking verisimilitude, and such writers as ZANE GREY, Clarence Mulford (of Hopalong Cassidy fame), and ERNEST HAYCOX did historical research in order to give their works substance, nevertheless maintaining—with some tinkering here and there—the formulaic plots and stereotyped characterizations. Thus, it seems as if fans of westerns get historical and geographic accuracy while reading about a West that never was. Evidently, the highly adaptable western form is able to accommodate widely varying times, places, peoples, and events and yet somehow retain its identity, even into the late twentieth century.

CHRONOLOGY OF AUTHORS

Wister, Owen, 1860–1938
Grey, Zane. 1872–1939
Brand, Max. 1892–1944
Haycox, Ernest. 1899–1950
Guthrie, A. B., Jr. 1901–1991

Schaefer, Jack. 1907–1990
L'Amour, Louis Dearborn. 1908–1988
Short, Luke. 1908–1975
Fisher, Clay/Henry, Will. 1912–1991
Manfred, Frederick. 1912–

BRAND, MAX (pseud. of Frederick Schiller Faust). 1892–1944

Although he was born in Seattle, Washington, and raised in Modesto, California, Frederick Faust was famous for his dislike of the real West. He much preferred Italy, where he lived from 1926 to 1938, and where much of his writing was done. Faust, who wrote under more than a dozen pseudonyms, was an extremely prolific writer, not only of westerns, but also of hundreds of other novels and books, including the popular "Dr. Kildare" series. He was also a screenwriter for several Hollywood studios, including MGM, Warner Brothers, and Columbia. Faust had no interest in trying to create an accurate historical West and generally had little regard for his own work. He said of his westerns: "The basic formula I use is simple: good man turns bad, bad man turns good. Naturally, there is considerable variation on the theme. . . . There has to be a woman, but not much of a one. A good horse is much more important." His first novel *The Untamed* (1918) was a success and introduced a semimythical character, Whistlin' Dan Barry, who travels the West following the wild geese, accompanied by a black wolf. Faust's characters, who often have a mythic quality, are memorable, and his books are always entertaining.

NOVELS BY BRAND

Dan Barry's Daughter. 1924. Berkley Pub. 1987 $2.75. ISBN 0-425-10190-8. About the beautiful daughter of the legendary Dan Barry who must grow up in the tough West.
Destry Rides Again. 1930. PB 1991 $2.95. ISBN 0-671-73543-8. The story of Harry Destry, wrongly imprisoned, and his search for revenge on the jury who sent him to jail.
Singing Guns. 1928. S&S Trade 1991 $2.95. ISBN 0-671-73542-X. About the former outlaw Annan Rhiannon, who reforms under the tutelage of Sheriff Caradac, returns to his outlaw ways, and is finally tamed for good.
Wild Freedom. 1922. Warner Bks. 1985 $2.50. ISBN 0-446-32769-7. The story of 12-year-old orphan Tommy Parks, who lives in the wilderness with grizzlies until an encounter with an outlaw forces him to return to civilization.

BOOK ABOUT BRAND

Nolan, William F. *Max Brand, Western Giant: The Life and Times of Frederick Faust.* Bowling Green Univ. 1986 $22.95. ISBN 0-87972-291-6. An interesting and thorough look at the complex Faust and his incredibly prolific career.

FISHER, CLAY/HENRY, WILL (pseud. of Henry Wilson Allen). 1912–1991

Henry Wilson Allen held many jobs—gold miner, blacksmith, house mover, sugar mill worker, and newspaper columnist—before he became a novelist. He has called himself "a man born into the wrong century," and his work shows his fascination with the history and people of the nineteenth-century American West. Whether he is writing about Jesse James as a psychotic gunman in *Death of a Legend* (1954), Native Americans in *From Where the Sun Now Stands* (1960), or the explorers Lewis and Clark in *Gates of the Mountains* (1963), Allen's careful historical research is evident. He often uses such devices as the alleged discovery of old diaries or family papers to make the reader think that the book is history rather than fiction, as in *No Survivors* (1950). His books are solidly crafted and always of high quality.

NOVELS BY FISHER

Red Blizzard and The Oldest Maiden Lady in New Mexico. Tor Bks. 1990 $3.50. ISBN 0-8125-0532-8. Fictionalized account of the Fetterman Massacre and the courageous ride of "Portugee" Phillips to bring aid to an army besieged by two thousand Native Americans; includes the short story "Oldest Maiden Lady in New Mexico."

The Tall Men. 1954. Bantam 1989 $2.95. ISBN 0-553-727644-1. The story of Nathan Stark setting out to make big money by taking Texas cattle to Montana; features a cattle drive, Indian attacks, troubles with the military, and romance.

Yellowstone Kelly. 1957. Bantam 1989 $2.95. ISBN 0-553-28026-0. The story of Luther "Yellowstone" Kelly learning to be a mountain man and falling in love with an Absaroka girl.

NOVELS BY HENRY

From Where the Sun Now Stands. 1960. Bantam 1991 $3.99. ISBN 0-553-29084-3. An accurate fictional account of the retreat of the Nez Percé from the American military in 1877.

Gates of the Mountains. 1963. Bantam 1991 $7.00. ISBN 0-553-29181-5. The story of adventures on the Lewis and Clark expedition, told by Francois Rivet.

Who Rides With Wyatt? 1955. Bantam 1990 $2.95. ISBN 0-553-25002-7. Fictionalized, ambiguous portrait of lawman Wyatt Earp as he battles internal and external forces in Tombstone, Arizona.

BOOK ABOUT FISHER/HENRY

Gale, Robert. *Will Henry-Clay Fisher.* Boise St. U. *Western Writers Ser.* 1982 $3.95. ISBN 0-88430-026-9. Short but clear introduction to Henry Wilson Allen's life and work.

GREY, ZANE. 1872–1939

The fan of westerns can turn to Zane Grey for books about almost every aspect of the American West, be it cattle drives, railroads, range wars, cowboys, Indians, Mormons, or desert life. Grey, who spent part of his adult life as a dentist, gave up that profession to research and write about the West he loved. He began publishing in 1910 with the story "Heritage of the Desert," and his blockbuster novel *Riders of the Purple Sage* followed in 1913. According to critic Lawrence Clark Powell, this book, "more than any other . . . determined the universal stereotype of the West." Literary historians look to Grey as the author whose popularization of the American West firmly established the western as a genre. Grey's heroes are often king-sized, and his prose is rich and descriptive. His West is a romantic place, where easterners, fatigued by the corruption and unhealthy atmosphere of the East, can go to be rejuvenated and healed. His novels are regularly reissued, and he remains one of the most popular writers of westerns, even more than 50 years after his death.

NOVELS BY GREY

Heritage of the Desert. 1910. PB 1985 $2.95. ISBN 0-671-60674-3. Hardworking Mormon ranch family and their trouble with outlaws, while a hero and outsider saves the innocent from the wicked.

Riders of the Purple Sage. 1912. Bantam 1990 $2.95. ISBN 0-553-28308-1. Story of a gentile gunman, Lassiter, who fights to save Mormon Jane Withersteen's Utah ranch; the two then fall in love and must flee civilization.

The U.P. Trail. 1918. HarpC 1991 $3.50. ISBN 0-06-100176-7. Technology and manifest destiny versus the Native American way of life in a story about building the transcontinental railroad.

The Vanishing American. 1925. HarpC 1991 $3.99. ISBN 0-06-100295-X. Native American Nophaie, raised and educated by whites, and his struggles between the need to help his people and his love for a white woman.

Western Union. 1939. HarpC 1991 $3.50. ISBN 0-06-100222-4. About New Englander Wayne Cameron going West to find adventure building the Western Union telegraph; with Indian battles, prairie fires, buffalo stampedes, and romance.

Wildfire. 1916. HarpC 1990 $3.50. ISBN 0-06-100081-7. About eighteen-year-old ranch-er's daughter Lucy Bostil taming a wild mustang, racing against her father's favorite thoroughbred and winning, and nearly dying in the process.

BOOKS ABOUT GREY

Gruber, Frank. *Zane Grey: A Biography.* Amereon Ltd. 1970 $18.95. ISBN 0-89190-756-4. Not as critical as might be wished, but good for basic information; uses material from Grey's diaries and letters.

Jackson, Carlton. *Zane Grey. Twayne's U.S. Authors Ser.* G. K. Hall rev. ed. 1989 $20.95. ISBN 0-8057-7543-9. Well-researched and well-written account of Grey's life and work.

Ronald, Ann. *Zane Grey.* Boise St. U. *Western Writers Ser.* 1975 $3.95. ISBN 0-88430-016-1. Short but solid introduction; an excellent place to begin research on Grey.

GUTHRIE, A. B., Jr. 1901–1991

Winner of many awards for his writing about the American West, including the Distinguished Achievement Award from the Western Literature Association (1972), the Golden Saddleman from the Western Writers of America, and the Pulitzer Prize in 1949 for *The Way West* (1949), Guthrie is recognized as one of the finest writers about the West. As critic Wayne Chatterton has noted, "from the beginning he has tried to show that, by the process of winning the West, the frontiersmen and the settlers have been losing it forever." The success of *The Big Sky* (1947) allowed Guthrie to quit his job at the Lexington, Kentucky, *Leader* to become a full-time novelist. Guthrie knew the land firsthand, having been raised in Montana. He did extensive historical research and worked to create memorable characters dealing with difficult situations, as in *The Way West*, a novel about pioneers in a wagon train crossing the continent to what they hope will be a better life in Oregon. In his work, Guthrie shows not only the beauty of the West but also the harshness of western life; his is a balanced view of humans and nature.

NOVELS BY GUTHRIE

The Big Sky. 1947. Bantam 1984 $4.95. ISBN 0-553-26683-7. Fine mountain-man novel centering on the paradox of whites coming into a pristine wilderness, thus beginning its ruination.

Fair Land, Fair Land. 1982. Bantam 1984 $3.95. ISBN 0-553-26118-5. Sequel to *The Big Sky* and *The Way West*, in which mountain man Dick Summers returns to the mountains; richly explored is the theme of the changing West.

The Way West. HM 1993 $9.95. ISBN 0-395-65662-1

BOOK ABOUT GUTHRIE

Milton, John. *The Novel of the American West.* U. of Nebr. Pr. 1980 $29.95. ISBN 0-8032-0980-0. Contains an excellent chapter discussing the work of Guthrie and Frederick Manfred.

HAYCOX, ERNEST. 1899–1950

A native of Oregon, an area that became the setting of one of his finest novels, *The Earthbreakers* (1952), Haycox served an apprenticeship writing for pulp western magazines before his novels and short stories began to sell. Haycox is generally credited for introducing a more complex, brooding hero into the western genre; many of his heroes frequently question themselves and often are torn about the correct action to take. Haycox's heroes are loyal, fair, and tough, but they seem almost fatalistic as they face the many dangers in tough western towns. His stories often have two female characters—a "good woman" whose passions sometimes overwhelm her and a "bad woman" who is good inside. Haycox did careful historical research, and his books are accurate, if fictionalized, depictions of western history.

NOVELS BY HAYCOX

Bugles in the Afternoon. 1944. Windsor NY 1990 $3.95. ISBN 1-55817-455-9. Professional soldier Kern Shafter, his fights with the ill-fated Seventh Cavalry, and his return to the woman he loves.

Free Grass. 1928. Windsor NY 1989 $2.95. ISBN 1-55817-207-6. The story of Tom Gillette, cheated by gunman San Saba and vowing revenge; meanwhile, he must fight hired claim jumpers in a land war.

Saddle and Ride. 1939. Windsor NY $2.95. ISBN 1-55817-085-5. The clash between antagonists Clay Morgan and Ben Herendeen over ranch lands as Herendeen hires rustlers to drive Morgan out.

The Silver Desert. 1935. Windsor NY 1989 $2.95. ISBN 1-55817-259-9. Tom Sebastian fighting for his cattle and his life after threats to his Barrier Ranch.

Trail Town. 1944. Windsor NY 1989 $2.95. ISBN 1-55817-293-9. River Bend Sheriff Dan Mitchell (based on the historical figure Bear River Tom Smith), tough enough to fight rowdy cowboys but gentle for the woman he loves.

BOOK ABOUT HAYCOX

Etulain, Richard. *Ernest Haycox.* Boise St. U. *Western Writers Ser.* 1988 $3.95. ISBN 0-88430-085-4. Succinct but thorough introduction to Haycox's work by a leading Haycox scholar.

L'AMOUR, LOUIS DEARBORN. 1908–1988

Born in Jamestown, North Dakota, L'Amour's adventurous life could have been the subject of one of his novels. Striking out on his own in 1923, at age 15, L'Amour began a peripatetic existence, taking whatever jobs were available, from skinning dead cattle to being a sailor. L'Amour knew early in life that he wanted to be a writer, and the experiences of those years serve as background for some of his later fiction. During the 1930s he published short stories and poetry; his career was interrupted by army service in World War II. After the war, L'Amour began writing for western pulp magazines and wrote several books in the Hopalong Cassidy series using the pseudonym Tex Burns; these are now being reissued under L'Amour's name. His first novel, *Westward the Tide* (1950), serves as an example of L'Amour's frontier fiction, for it is an action-packed adventure story containing the themes and motifs that he uses throughout his career. His fascination with history and his belief in the inevitability of manifest destiny are clear. Also present and typical of L'Amour's work are the strong, capable, beautiful heroine who is immediately attracted to the equally capable hero; a clear moral split between good and evil; reflections on the Native Americans, whose land and ways of life are being disrupted; and a happy ending. Although his work is somewhat less violent than that of other western writers, L'Amour's novels all contain their fair share of action, usually in the form of gunfights or fistfights (L'Amour was a professional boxer).

L'Amour's major contribution to the western genre is his attempt to create, in 40 or more books, the stories of three families whose histories intertwine as the generations advance across the American frontier. The novels of the Irish Chantry, English Sackett, and French Talon families are L'Amour's most ambitious project, and sadly were left unfinished at his death. Although L'Amour did not complete all of the novels, enough of the series exists to demonstrate his vision.

L'Amour's strongest attribute is his ability to tell a compelling story; readers do not mind if the story is similar to one they have read before, for in the telling, L'Amour adds enough small twists of plot and detail to make it worth the reader's while. L'Amour fans also enjoy the bits of information he includes about everything from wilderness survival skills to finding the right person to marry. These lessons give readers the sense that they are getting their money's worth, that there is more to a L'Amour novel than sheer escapism. With over 200 million copies of his books in print worldwide, L'Amour must be counted as one of the most influential writers of westerns in this century.

NOVELS BY L'AMOUR

Conagher. 1969. Bantam 1982 $2.95. ISBN 0-553-25770-6. About a lonely, hard-working cowboy who yearns for a home and finds adventure and love on the western plains; more muted and thoughtful than some L'Amour westerns.

The Daybreakers. 1960. Bantam 1984 $2.95. ISBN 0-553-27674-3. The story of Orrin and Tyrel Sackett, who leave Tennessee for a better life out West in a tale about cattle drives, gunfights, and the importance of making the West safe for families.

Fair Blows the Wind. 1976. Bantam 1978 $2.95. ISBN 0-553-25612-2. The first Chantry family novel: Tatton Chantry—writer, soldier, merchant—battles pirates and finally gets to America with much swordplay, as well as a romance with a woman who is part-Inca.

Hondo. 1953. Fawcett 1981 $2.25. ISBN 0-449-14255-8. Half-Indian, half-white Hondo Lane's love story with rancher Angie Lowe; the action revolves around battles with Apache, whom Lane greatly respects. One of L'Amour's best.

Rivers West. Bantam 1983 $3.99. ISBN 0-553-25436-7. The first Talon family novel: Jean Talon leaves Quebec in 1821 to seek his fortune in the Louisiana Territory.

Sackett's Land. Bantam 1984 $2.95. ISBN 0-553-25271-2. Chronologically the first Sackett family tale, in which Barnabas Sackett escapes enemies in England, sails to America, and founds a dynasty.

NONFICTION BY L'AMOUR

Education of a Wandering Man. Bantam 1989 $16.95. ISBN 0-553-05703-0. Close to being an autobiography; interesting for its insight into L'Amour's informal education, listing the books he read and offering much personal reminiscence.

Frontier. Bantam 1984 $34.95. ISBN 0-553-05078-8. Stunning photos by David Muench complementing a wide-ranging text about the American frontier.

The Sackett Companion: A Personal Guide to the Sackett Novels. Bantam 1988 $19.95. ISBN 0-553-05305-1. Often ponderously written but useful for those wanting details and further background on the Sacketts.

BOOKS ABOUT L'AMOUR

Gale, Robert. *Louis L'Amour. Twayne's U.S. Authors Ser.* G. K. Hall rev. ed. 1992 $20.95. ISBN 0-8057-7649-4. Well-researched, balanced, scholarly study of L'Amour's life and work.

Hall, Halbert. *The Works of Louis L'Amour: An Annotated Bibliography and Guide.* Borgo Pr. 1991 $20.00. ISBN 0-8095-1510-5. Indispensable for anyone doing research on L'Amour.

L'Amour, Angelique. *A Trail of Memories: The Quotations of Louis L'Amour.* Bantam 1988 $12.95. ISBN 0-553-05271-3. L'Amour's daughter's collection of her father's most memorable comments on a vast array of topics.

Phillips, Robert. *Louis L'Amour: His Life and Trails.* Knightsbridge Pub. 1990 o.p. A mostly laudatory, unauthorized biography that collects much material to survey L'Amour's life and work; adds little to L'Amour scholarship.

Weinberg, Robert. *The Louis L'Amour Companion.* Andrews & McMeel 1992 $12.95. ISBN 0-8362-7996-4. Includes rare interviews with and about L'Amour and essays about his work, including audio and video adaptations.

MANFRED, FREDERICK. (pseud. of Feike Feikema). 1912–

Born in Iowa, Manfred has lived much of his life in southern Minnesota. Most of his novels are set in southern Minnesota and the Dakotas, and his Native American characters are usually Sioux. A fine storyteller, Manfred does extensive historical research, which gives his books a sense of authenticity. He is also interested in psychology and human sexuality, and many of his books have Freudian or Jungian overtones. Manfred often focuses on the importance of the land in shaping his characters: frequently in his books, a man must test himself against the wilderness in order to discover his true nature.

NOVELS BY MANFRED

Conquering Horse. 1965. U. of Nebr. Pr. 1983 $10.95. ISBN 0-8032-8119-6. The story of Sioux No Name's search for a white stallion to fulfill his vision, in which he finds a horse and returns to replace his father as leader.

King of Spades. 1966. U. of Nebr. Pr. 1983 $7.95. ISBN 0-8032-8121-8. Oedipal tale in which Earl Ransom sleeps with his mother and eventually commits suicide.

Lord Grizzly. 1954. U. of Nebr. Pr. 1983 $7.95. ISBN 0-8032-8118-8. Story of a hero based on the historical figure Hugh Glass, in which the hero is left for dead after being attacked by a grizzly but survives to seek revenge on those who abandoned him.

Riders of Judgment. 1957. U. of Nebr. Pr. 1982 $6.95. ISBN 0-8032-8117-X. Based on the 1892 Johnson County War, a story of conflicts between older pioneers and new ranchers leading to bloodshed.

Silver Plume. 1964. U. of Nebr. Pr. 1983 $10.95. ISBN 0-8032-8120-X. Uses the hanging of 38 Sioux to explore cultural relations between Sioux and white settlers, including a romance between a Sioux warrior and a white woman.

BOOKS ABOUT MANFRED

Flora, Joseph. *Frederick Manfred.* Boise St. U. *Western Writers Ser.* 1974 $3.95. ISBN 0-88430-012-9. A clear and scholarly study of Manfred's major works; a good introduction to his career.

Mulder, Rodney, and John H. Timmerman. *Frederick Manfred: A Bibliographic and Publication History.* Ctr. Western Studies 1981 $16.95. ISBN 0-931170-15-X. The most complete listing of Manfred's publications; a must for Manfred scholars.

SCHAEFER, JACK. 1907–1990

After receiving his B.A. from Oberlin College and doing graduate work at Columbia University, Schaefer spent most of his adult life working as a journalist. His first novel, *Shane* (1949), a portrait of a gunfighter trying to escape his violent past, was a success. Schaefer covers a variety of themes in his work, including the relationship of the individual to the community and how people overcome obstacles while maintaining their integrity. His characterizations are often memorable, and he has a gift for writing dialogue that sounds realistic. Critic Fred Erisman has remarked that "Schaefer brings to his writing a clear-cut sense of professionalism, a deeply felt commitment to the storyteller's craft, and a keen ear for the spoken word."

NOVELS BY SCHAEFER

Monte Walsh. 1963. U. of Nebr. Pr. 1981 $31.00. ISBN 0-8032-4124-0. Episodes in the life of a cowboy drifter that show the changing West.

Shane. 1949. Bantam 1980 $2.95. ISBN 0-553-26262-9. Based on the short story "Rider from Nowhere," in which a gunman trying to escape his past helps small ranchers fight big ranchers; told from a small boy's point of view.

Shane: The Critical Edition. Ed. by James C. Work. U. of Nebr. Pr. 1984 $10.95. ISBN 0-8032-9142-6. A fine edition of the novel; includes essays about the novel and the film by leading scholars and an interview with Schaefer. Very useful for scholars working on Schaefer.

BOOK ABOUT SCHAEFER

Haslam, Gerald. *Jack Schaefer.* Boise St. U. *Western Writers Ser.* 1980 $3.95. ISBN 0-88430- 019-6. A concise, well-written survey of Schaefer's major work along with a brief discussion of his life.

SHORT, LUKE (pseud. of Frederick D. Glidden). 1908–1975

Along with his brother Jonathan Glidden, Frederick Glidden, whose most popular pseudonym was Luke Short, wrote more than 50 novels and over 100 short stories. Frederick Glidden was, among other things, a trapper, so he knew the life and land of the West. He was also a professional journalist, as were so many of the writers of westerns. Like ERNEST HAYCOX and CLAY FISHER/WILL HENRY, Glidden spent time doing historical research, and his novels reflect a sense of the realities of western living changing from the "lone riding gunman" syndrome, in which every man takes care of himself, to a West where the importance of the community comes to the fore.

NOVELS BY SHORT

And the Wind Blows Free. Thorndike Pr. 1989 repr. of 1955 ed. $15.95. ISBN 0-89621-869-4. The story of a young man growing up in Oklahoma in the 1880s and working in the beef industry.

Hard Money. 1940. Dell 1990 $2.95. ISBN 0-440-20503-4. Published in 1939 as *Flood-Water*, a fast-paced action story about mining life in the California Mother Lode.

WISTER, OWEN. 1860–1938

It may be ironic that this easterner, a Pennsylvania native, is responsible for creating the prototypical cowboy hero in his most famous novel, *The Virginian: A Horseman of the Plains* (1902). According to critic Ben Merchant Vorpahl, "Wister was a myth-maker of considerable skill and determination who set out, in a calculated way, to fashion the cowpuncher into a hero on the model of a Gawain, a Tristan or—to use one of his favorite analogies—a prodigal son. How well he succeeded may be judged partly on the basis of the hundreds of horse operas in print, film, and television that have sprung more or less directly from his vision of what happened when people were transplanted from eastern cities, where they could not help being 'all varnished over with Europe,' to the wide open spaces of the western plains, where they became 'real Americans.'" Wister's first trip West, in 1885, was taken to improve his health. Enchanted by what he saw, he began to write about western life. In *The Virginian*, Wister creates a hero whose good looks, strength, courage, integrity, and skill combine to win the heroine's love, vanquish the villain and—most importantly—serve as a model for future heroes of western fiction.

NOVELS BY WISTER

Lin McLean. Irvington repr. of 1898 ed. $36.50. ISBN 0-8398-2174-3. More readily seen as a collection of short stories than as a novel. Tells of Wyoming cowboy life—a forerunner of *The Virginian*.

The Virginian: A Horseman of the Plains. 1902. NAL-Dutton 1979 $4.50. ISBN 0-451-52325. In which the narrator, an easterner, learns about manhood and friendship as he tells the story of the Virginian and Vermont teacher Molly Wood. Contains many now-familiar western motifs, including the showdown between the hero and the villain.

SHORT STORY COLLECTION BY WISTER

The West of Owen Wister: Selected Short Stories. U. of Nebr. Pr. 1972 $21.00. ISBN 0-8032-0808-1. Contains Wister's early and more famous short stories; useful for those tracing Wister's development as a craftsman.

BOOKS ABOUT WISTER

Etulain, Richard. *Owen Wister.* Boise St. U. Western Writers Ser. 1973 $3.95. ISBN 0-88430-006-4. A discussion of Wister's life and work in a clear, thorough survey, by one of the foremost scholars of popular westerns.

Frantz, Joe B. and Julian E. Choate, Jr. *The American Cowboy: The Myth and the Reality.* Greenwood 1981 repr. of 1955 ed. $41.50. ISBN 0-313-23109-5. Contains an interesting discussion of Wister and *The Virginian.*

Payne, Darwin. *Owen Wister: Chronicler of the West, Gentleman of the East.* SMU Pr. 1985 $24.95. ISBN 0-807074-205-1. The most complete biography of Wister, offering a thorough, scholarly discussion of his life and work.

Romances

Romances are the most female-oriented form of popular fiction, because, according to Kay Mussell, "the tensions and issues inherent in love stories are traditionally women's concerns." In the romance, love, courtship, and marriage are key elements. As with other popular literary forms, such as westerns, mysteries, and science fiction, romances may be written to include accurate historical or practical details; readers may demand that the ballgowns worn and dances performed fit into the era in which the novel is set. The critic Betty Rosenberg remarks that in these period romances, the "intent is the creation of a dream of romance safely in another time far distant from the mundane present." Women do not read romances primarily to learn history, however. The most significant element of the romance is that true love is the key to happiness. According to Mussell, "the plot of a romantic novel begins with an assumption—unquestioned and unexamined except in a few books—that the necessary, preordained, and basic goal of any woman is to achieve a satisfying, mature, and all-fulfilling marriage. The primacy of romantic love, in defining a woman's place and value in the world, is rarely in doubt in the books. The plot may appear diffuse, but it never loses sight of that goal." While such a specific goal might seem to limit the adaptability and variety of the genre, such is not the case. Writers of romances, most—though not all—of them women, have responded to social change just as have writers of other popular genres.

The late eighteenth century first saw the beginning of the romance novel in America with the publication of SUSANNA HASWELL ROWSON's *Charlotte Temple* (1791). This book—in which the unmarried heroine becomes pregnant, is abandoned by the father, and dies after giving birth—sets the stage for the many seduced-and-abandoned heroines who followed, even into the twentieth century. Other authors, including CATHERINE SEDGWICK (*Hope Leslie,* 1827), Susan Warner (*The Wide, Wide World,* 1850), E.D.E.N. SOUTHWORTH (*Retribution,* 1849), and Maria Cummins (*The Lamplighter,* 1854), produced dozens of popular books—most of them set in the domestic sphere of women and focusing on relationships between women and men. These women writers were very successful, and their books were routinely among the bestsellers of their day, which is no small achievement, given that they were competing with such male authors as NATHANIEL HAWTHORNE and HERMAN MELVILLE.

As with westerns, dime novels helped perpetuate the romance form. Into the twentieth century, information culled from bestseller lists demonstrates that romance has maintained its popularity, with perhaps the high point coming in 1936, with MARGARET MITCHELL's *Gone with the Wind*.

The romance is similar to the mystery and science fiction genres in that all three always have been written by both British and American authors, and it would be misleading to strictly separate the two branches. They have in common a focus on the intricacies of negotiating the often rocky path of love that leads, inevitably, to marriage. In recent years, romances from both sides of the Atlantic have shown certain shifts in plot, mostly having to do with sexual explicitness. According to Janice Radway, the sexually explicit *The Flame and the Flower* (1972) by KATHERINE WOODIWISS enabled romance authors "to treat their heroines as sexual creatures capable of arousal and carnal desire." Radway goes on to point out that her studies indicate that "this change in sexual mores was and still is tolerable only within very strict limits." The romantic heroine may have sexual relations while unmarried, but the underlying—and sometimes overt—message of romances is that the most satisfying physical relationship is to be found within marriage. It is probable that these beliefs will continue to inform and to shape the romance genre in years to come.

CHRONOLOGY OF AUTHORS

Southworth, E.D.E.N. 1819–1899
Slaughter, Frank G. 1908–
Robbins, Harold. 1916–
Yerby, Frank. 1916–1992
Sheldon, Sidney. 1917–
Woodiwiss, Kathleen. 1939–

Michaels, Fern (pseud. of
    Roberta Anderson, 1942–
    and Mary Kuczkir, 1939–)
Dailey, Janet. 1947–
Deveraux, Jude. 1947–
Steel, Danielle. 1947–

DAILEY, JANET. 1947–

Dailey's midwestern values (she was born in Iowa) and her unpretentious writing style endear her to millions of fans worldwide—fans whom she respects as intelligent, thoughtful readers who know a good story and want to lose themselves in a romance for a few hours. She knew early in life that she wanted to be a writer, and she began her career as a romance writer publishing with Harlequin Books, for whom she wrote more than 50 novels. Now, with more than 80 books to her credit, she still works almost every day, using in many of her stories the research that her husband does for her. *The Janet Dailey Newsletter* is a quarterly publication for fans to learn the latest news about Dailey and her upcoming books. A straightforward, skillful stylist, Dailey does most of her manuscript revisions in her head rather than on paper. She has said of writing: "The first thing is story. The second thing is traditional values. . . . A writer must write it so the reader will feel it, to the point where he hurts and cries and he laughs and he feels the warmth in it." Her characters are usually attracted to each other's strengths, and they typically go through much turmoil before getting together for a happy ending.

NOVELS BY DAILEY

The Hostage Bride. 1981. PB 1984 $4.50. ISBN 0-671-73693-0. Love at first sight for Tamara James and Bick Rutledge but she, desperate for money to pay her mother's medical bills, embezzles company funds, before the ultimate happy ending.

Masquerade. 1990. G. K. Hall 1991 $14.95. ISBN 0-8161-5060-5. The story of amnesia victim Remy Jardin, who teams up with her former lover to find out who she is and solve the mystery surrounding her family's shipping business.

Reilly's Woman. 1977. Harlequin Bks. 1987 $2.75. ISBN 0-373-89828-2. About a plane crash in the Nevada desert that forces Leah Talbot to learn to understand Native American hero Reilly Smith.

The Rogue. PB 1988 $4.95. ISBN 0-671-68142-7. Desert setting for romance between rancher's daughter Diana Somers and ranch hand Holt Mallory, in which a search for missing horses makes them allies and finally lovers.

Tangled Vines. Little 1992 $21.95. ISBN 0-316-17156-5. Kelly Douglas, prime-time television show host, involved with Napa Valley vintner Sam Rutledge; includes a murder by Kelly's abusive father.

This Calder Sky. 1981. PB 1990 $5.50. ISBN 0-671-70881-3. The story of Montana rancher Chase Calder who loves but cannot tame beautiful Maggie O'Rourke, focusing on their struggle to understand and accept one another.

DEVERAUX, JUDE (pseud. of Jude Gilliam White). 1947–

Deveraux, a former elementary school teacher, is not only a writer of romances but also a staunch defender of the genre. Indignant at critics' denigration of romances, she contends that writing them takes hard work and dedication, and her many fans would certainly agree that she has demonstrated both in more than 20 novels. Deveraux considers herself a feminist and likes to create women characters who can take charge and run their careers successfully. She told *Contemporary Authors:* "I wanted to write about women who had some power, who could create things, could make things happen." In her own successful writing career, Deveraux is a living example of this philosophy.

NOVELS BY DEVERAUX

The Conquest. PB 1991 $5.50. ISBN 0-671-64447-5. The story of the Peregrine and Howard families' feud as Zared Peregrine, disguised as a boy to keep her from the Howards, falls in love with Tearle Howard, who sets out to woo her.

Counterfeit Lady. PB 1984 $5.50. ISBN 0-671-73976-X. Nicole Courtalain—mistaken for a titled lady, kidnapped and taken to colonial Virginia, and wooed by Clayton Armstrong, who had been engaged to the lady for whom Nicole is mistaken.

Mountain Laurel. 1990. PB 1991 $5.50. ISBN 0-671-68976-2. The story of Captain Ring Montgomery escorting opera singer Madelyn Worth into Colorado Territory to sing for miners; after an initial animosity, they fall in love.

Twin of Ice. PB 1985 $5.50. ISBN 0-671-73971-9. How newly wealthy Kane Taggart determined to win beautiful Houston Chandler in the Colorado mining territory.

MICHAELS, FERN. (pseud. of Roberta Anderson, 1942–, and Mary Kuczkir, 1939–)

As the joint authors of more than 20 romances and thrillers under the pseudonym Fern Michaels, Roberta Anderson and Mary Kuczkir are one of the most successful writing teams currently working. Not college educated and without literary backgrounds, they have nevertheless created a series of steamy, well-constructed novels about strong women and men trying to create successful lives in modern America. They are particularly known for the creation of the Colemans, a Texas ranching and business family.

NOVELS BY MICHAELS

Sins of Omission. Ballantine 1989 $5.95. ISBN 0-345-34120-1. A 1920s story in which Reuben Tarz and Daniel Bishop are taken to a French chateau, where Reuben falls in love with Michelene Fousard; the story continues in Hollywood.

Texas Fury. Ballantine 1989 $5.95. ISBN 0-345-31375-5. Third in the Coleman family saga, in which Amelia Coleman Assante may lose her husband to another, and Sawyer successfully runs Coleman Aviation.

Texas Heat. 1986. Ballantine 1989 $4.95. ISBN 0-345-01028-0. Fireworks between Maggie Coleman Tanner and the rest of the Coleman clan after an invitation to a family reunion at their Texas ranch starts the sparks flying.

Texas Rich. 1985. Ballantine 1987 $5.95. ISBN 0-345-33540-6. More on the rise of the Coleman dynasty as Seth Coleman's son marries Billie Ames, who struggles to remain true to herself while she becomes a part of the Coleman clan.

ROBBINS, HAROLD. 1916–

A tough childhood in New York's Hell's Kitchen made Harold Robbins an ambitious young man. During the Great Depression, he became a food vendor, selling farmers' crops to wholesale grocers and canners; he was a millionaire by the age of 20, but the vagaries of Depression economics led to his bankruptcy by 1939. Robbins then worked for Universal Pictures, and he was promoted after uncovering corruption within the company. He began his enormously successful writing career in the 1940s, with *Never Love a Stranger* (1948), his first novel. His international settings; wealthy, powerful characters; and plots of intrigue; plus a large helping of sex, have made his novels huge bestsellers, with more than 250 million copies in print worldwide. Justifiably proud of his success, Robbins, on the basis of his sales figures, claims to be one of the world's best writers.

NOVELS BY ROBBINS

The Adventurers. 1966. PB 1984 $4.95. ISBN 0-671-53151-4. Settings include Paris, London, the Riviera, China, New York, Hollywood, and Texas in this story about Diogenes Alejandro Xenos (Dax), playboy and diplomat, torn between the violent life he knew as a boy and the glittering international scene.

The Betsy. 1971. PB 1982 $5.50. ISBN 0-671-73553-5. About the dynasty founded by auto baron Loren Hardeman, in which three generations of Hardemans struggle to build and maintain the company—romance, high finance, sex, in international settings (also a movie starring Laurence Olivier).

The Storyteller. 1985. Curley Pub. 1987 $20.95. ISBN 1-55504-244-9. The story of a young man, born in poverty, who struggles to become a famous writer in Hollywood and Europe, where he finds, loses, and then regains, love and fame.

SHELDON, SIDNEY. 1917–

Multitalented Sidney Sheldon not only writes best-selling romances, but also has written and produced several successful television series, including "The Patty Duke Show," "I Dream of Jeannie," and "Hart to Hart." He won an Oscar, in 1948, for the original screenplay of *The Bachelor and the Bobby-Soxer*, a Tony Award for the book for the musical, *Redhead*, and an Edgar for the best mystery novel of 1970, *The Naked Face*. One of the world's best-selling writers, Sheldon decided to try writing a novel when he got an idea that he could not adapt to a play or a screenplay. The millions of fans who enjoy his fast-paced plots and their beautiful heroines, who are usually bent on revenge for having been hurt, are grateful that this prolific author turned to novels.

NOVELS BY SHELDON

Memories of Midnight. 1990. Warner Bks. 1991 $5.99. ISBN 0-446-35467-8. Sequel to *The Other Side of Midnight* (1974), in which Constantine Demiris, murderer of his former mistress and still obsessed with revenge, plots to kill Catherine Douglas.

The Other Side of Midnight. Warner Bks. 1988 $5.99. ISBN 0-446-35740-5. Story of murder and intrigue, focusing on the life of Constantine Demiris.

Rage of Angels. 1980. Warner Bks. 1988 $5.95. ISBN 0-446-35661-1. The story of attorney Jennifer Parker, who struggles to regain her reputation and career after being duped by the Mafia.

The Sands of Time. Warner Bks. 1989 $5.95. ISBN 0-446-35683-2. About four nuns forced to flee their Spanish convent, caught between the warring forces of underground Basque revolutionaries and the Spanish government.

The Stars Shine Down. Morrow 1992 $23.00. ISBN 0-688-08490-7. About a terrible secret that threatens the well-being of tycoon Lara Cameron.

Windmills of the Gods. Warner Bks. 1987 $5.95. ISBN 0-446-35010-9. The story of university professor Mary Ashley, appointed American ambassador to a communist country and targeted for assassination.

SLAUGHTER, FRANK G. 1908–

The medical background of Frank Slaughter is evident in much of his work; he received his medical degree from Johns Hopkins University in 1930. He uses medical terminology to give his books authenticity. Slaughter began writing as a hobby—first short stories and then novels—and he has also written nonfiction. A fascination with biblical stories led him to write *The Road to Bithynina* (1951), a book about St. Luke, who was also a physician. Slaughter enjoys research and does many revisions of his manuscripts, and his hard work shows in the well-crafted books he produces. Having more than 60 million books in print testifies to Slaughter's long-lasting popularity in America and abroad.

NOVELS BY SLAUGHTER

East Side General. Am. Repr.-Rivercity Pr. 1975 repr. of 1952 ed. $16.95. ISBN 0-89190-282-1. The story of a patient, badly burned by radioactivity, who becomes the focus of an FBI investigation as doctors try to save him while unknown others try to keep him from surviving.

A Savage Place. 1964. Ulverscroft 1971 $12.00. ISBN 0-85456-651-1. The story of surgeon Mike Constant, who returns to his boyhood town to find himself in a complicated web of relationships as an outbreak of hepatitis threatens many.

Sword and Scalpel. 1957. Ulverscroft 1979 $12.00. ISBN 0-7089-0386-X. About army surgeon Paul Scott, who is captured and imprisoned during the Korean War and then accused of collaborating with the enemy so that he must prove his innocence.

Tomorrow's Miracle. 1962. Ulverscroft 1978 $12.00. ISBN 0-7089-0091-7. Tale of mission doctor Benson Ware, who works in French Guiana to combat disease and improve people's lives, until his former mistress and her husband appear to wreak havoc.

STEEL, DANIELLE. 1947–

After having worked in public relations and advertising, Steel was encouraged to try writing a novel. Luckily for her millions of fans, she did, and today has more than 125 million books in print worldwide. She has written more than 25 novels for adults, 8 for juveniles, and a good deal of poetry. Steel's goal is to write entertaining fiction that is also thought-provoking. Her heroines are often successful, powerful women who must try to balance, and sometimes choose between, career and romance—a dilemma with which many female readers can sympathize. Steel cares about her readers and their opinions, and she tries to answer all of their letters while juggling her own large family and writing career. Several of her novels have been made into television movies, including *Kaleidoscope* (1987) and *Jewels* (1992).

NOVELS BY STEEL

Changes. 1983. Dell 1984 $5.99. ISBN 0-440-11181-1. About successful television producer Melanie Adams, who seems content until she meets famous heart surgeon Peter Hallan; then the two must learn to trust and love one another.

Fine Things. 1987. Dell 1988 $5.95. ISBN 0-440-20056-3. About successful businessman Bernie Fine, dissatisfied with jet-set life, and his search for commitment with a young girl and her mother.

Jewels. Delacorte 1992 $23.00. ISBN 0-385-30490-0. Sarah Whitfield remembers her shameful 1930 divorce, her trip to Europe and love for the Duke of Whitfield, with whom she buys jewels from World War II survivors to start a successful jewelry business.

Kaleidoscope. 1987. Dell 1988 $5.95. ISBN 0-440-20192-6. Three orphaned Walker sisters' search for each other and their struggle to face old family tragedies and secrets.

The Ring. 1980. Dell 1983 $5.95. ISBN 0-440-17392-2. Set in Hitler's Germany, where Kassandra von Gotthard sets off a series of tragic events by her involvement with a Jewish novelist; her daughter must live with the pain of her mother's secret.

Secrets. 1985. Dell 1986 $5.95. ISBN 0-440-17648-4. Television industry backdrop for a story about the cast of *Manhattan,* featuring the passions, egos, and romances of cast members as each tries to find fame.

SOUTHWORTH, E.D.E.N. 1819–1899

As would be the case with many of the female romance writers who followed her, Emma Dorothy Eliza Nevitte Southworth began writing because she needed the money to support her family after she separated from her husband, Frederick Southworth, in 1843. Her first novel, *Retribution* (1849), was a success, and Southworth eventually published more than 60 novels and many short stories during her long and prolific career.

NOVEL BY SOUTHWORTH

Retribution; or the Vale of Shadows. AMS Pr. repr. of 1849 ed. $37.50. ISBN 0-404-17395-0. Wealthy Hester Gray, befriended by poor, beautiful, scheming Juliette Summers, marries her guardian Ernest Dent, who lusts after Juliette.

BOOK ABOUT SOUTHWORTH

Baym, Nina. *Woman's Fiction: A Guide to Novels by and about Women in America, 1820–1870.* Cornell Univ. Pr. 1978 o.p. Scholarly study of early women's fiction, including an excellent chapter on Southworth.

WOODIWISS, KATHLEEN. 1939–

Woodiwiss is not as prolific as some authors, but her loyal fans eagerly await her well-researched historical romances. She was first encouraged by friends to finish her first novel *The Flame and the Flower* (1977), which she began writing because she could not find a romance that suited her taste. The novel, which combined a new eroticism with the conventional historical romance formula, was a success and influenced the entire genre to be more sexually explicit. As a busy mother who has raised three sons, Woodiwiss knows that her readers are seeking entertainment and escape, but the research she does also results in novels that portray historical periods with rich detail and fidelity. Woodiwiss's *Shanna* (1978) was the first historical romance to appear in trade paperback. More than 10 million copies of her books are currently in print.

NOVELS BY WOODIWISS

A Rose in Winter. 1982. Avon 1983 $5.50. ISBN 0-380-84400-1. A tale of eighteenth-century England, in which Erienne Fleming must wed Lord Saxton to save her father from financial ruin.

Ashes in the Wind. Avon 1979 $5.50. ISBN 0-380-76984-0. Love between Alaina MacGaren, a southerner, and Captain Cole Latimer, a northerner, despite political enmity during the Civil War.

The Flame and the Flower. 1972. Avon 1977 $5.99. ISBN 0-380-00525-5. The story of Heather Summers, escaping a life of drudgery, who accidentally kills a man and takes up with an adventurous ship's captain.

Forever in Your Embrace. Avon 1992 $12.50. ISBN 0-380-8981-7. The temptation of British colonel Tyrone Rycroft by Russian Synnovea Zenkovna, who then finds she is unable to control subsequent events.

Shanna. Avon 1978 $5.50. ISBN 0-380-38588-0. About Ruark Beauchamp, first desiring revenge on Shanna Trahern, then falling in love with her while on a Caribbean island.

So Worthy, My Love. Avon 1989 $5.95. ISBN 0-380-76148-3. Elizabethan England setting in which wealthy Elise Radborne is kidnapped and imprisoned by Maxim Seymour, and then comes to love her captor.

YERBY, FRANK. 1916–1992

Although Yerby's novels have sold more than 55 million copies during the past 40 years, critics either have paid little attention to his work or have attacked him for writing romantic tales of adventure when, according to some, the part African, part American Yerby should have been writing about race relations and African Americans. Yerby, however, did not believe in using his fiction as a pulpit; that, he thought, was for ministers. Instead, he concentrated on producing novels with complex plots and many well-conceived characters. His first published story, "Health Card," won the O. Henry Memorial Prize in 1946.

Yerby, who had always wanted to be a writer, enjoyed the research he did in order to make his books plausible. He did write one race-related novel, *The Dahomean* (1971), about an African who becomes governor of his province but is sold into slavery by jealous relatives. The critics praised this work, which shows the complexity and richness of African culture.

NOVELS BY YERBY

Foxes of Harrow. 1946. Buccaneer Bks. 1976 $20.94. ISBN 0-89966-210-2. Set in 1825 New Orleans, where charming gambler Stephen Fox is rescued from a Mississippi River sandbar and gambles his way to fortune and into the heart of Creole Odalie Arceneaux.

The Serpent and the Staff. 1958. Ulverscroft 1978 $12.00. ISBN 0-7089-241-3. About Duncan Childers, raised in poverty, who rejects the life of a physician to the wealthy to dedicate his career to healing the poor but runs into opposition from society and his family.

The Vixens. Ulverscroft 1981 $12.50. ISBN 0-7089-0628-1. The story of the Fournois brothers Laird and Phillip, who, having fought on opposite sides in the Civil War, return to Louisiana to rebuild their lives.

Mystery/Detective

Crime has probably always fascinated people, perhaps because we instinctively feel that, given the proper circumstances, most people are capable of committing crimes. Mystery and detective fiction enables readers to explore safely the darker side of human nature. "Without exaggeration one can say that crime and literature have been in it together from the beginning" (John Cawelti). Some critics even go back as far as ancient Greece for the roots of mysteries. Certainly SHAKESPEARE was interested in plots dealing with crime, including murder, and, through the seventeenth and eighteenth centuries, writers of picaresque novels often thrust their protagonists into criminal activities. However far back we wish to go, one thing is certain: Readers of mysteries are interested in the how, why, and who—how a crime has been committed, what the motivation has been, and who has done the heinous deed. Critic Betty Rosenberg remarks that "Suspense is the code word for the thriller: the characters and the reader are in a constant state of uneasy anticipation of the worst, which all too often happens. Why this worst looms—threatening happiness and often life—lies in the mystery to be analyzed or the adventure to be pursued."

Most scholars trace the beginning of the modern mystery and detective novels to EDGAR ALLAN POE, to the beginning of an investigative police unit in Paris in 1817, and the creation of Britian's Scotland Yard in 1829. Poe's stories, "The Murders in the Rue Morgue" (1841), "The Mystery of Marie Rôget" (1842–43), and "The Purloined Letter" (1844) feature detectives who use reason and logic to solve crimes. Critic Larry Landrum has stated that "Throughout much of the rest of the nineteenth century, the narrative form in which the detective appeared remained relatively open, as if writers were willing to concede the field of the closed form to Poe. The detective's investigation tended to merge in most novels with themes from Gothic fiction, domestic romance, courtroom exposition, social exposés, and picaresque adventure stories." SIR ARTHUR CONAN DOYLE is, of course, the other great name in detective fiction, whose famous character Sherlock Holmes, like Poe's detectives, uses logic to find the solution to the mystery. According to critic Russel B. Nye, "The conventions of the detective story had taken rather clear shape by 1900. Its point was the puzzle; the crime existed to be solved; the approach of both writer and reader to crime . . . was detached, neutral, removed. Whatever the crime (even murder, the worst one), the point was that it disturbed and threatened social order and security. The detective's function, in which the reader shared, was to set the balance right again by solving the crime and repairing the intrusion."

The dime novel, in which form hundreds of mysteries were published, gave way after World War I to pulp magazines. The post-World War I era also saw a major shift in the tenor of detective fiction with the appearance of the hard-boiled sleuth in works by DASHIELL HAMMETT, who introduced his character the Continental Op in *Red Harvest* (1929). The legendary Sam Spade followed in *The Maltese Falcon* (1930). RAYMOND CHANDLER in *The Big Sleep* (1939), and other books; ROSS MACDONALD (Kenneth Millar); MICKEY SPILLANE; and JOHN D. MACDONALD all followed in Hammett's literary footsteps. As Russel B. Nye points out, in the hard-boiled detective novel, murder is removed from the upper classes and set in the streets. The scene and situation, rather than the plot, are in the foreground, and danger is everywhere. Rational solutions often fail to suffice against the irrationality stemming from twentieth-century alienation symbolized by the concrete canyons of urban America.

Fictional detectives do not necessarily represent reality any more than do the cowboys in westerns or the heroines in romances. Critic Larry Landrum remarks that "Instead, they seem to represent a way of reflecting upon the darker metaphors of life and problems in the way to their understanding." As mystery and detective novels continue to flourish, they will inevitably continue to attempt to explain that ultimate puzzle, the human psyche and its propensity for evil.

CHRONOLOGY OF AUTHORS

Stout, Rex. 1886–1975
Chandler, Raymond. 1888–1959
Gardner, Erle Stanley. 1889–1979
Cain, James M. 1892–1977
Hammett, Dashiell. 1894–1961
Whitney, Phyllis A. 1903–
Queen, Ellery. (pseud. of Frederic Dannay, 1905–1982, and Manfred Lee, 1905–1971)
Macdonald, Ross. 1915–1983

MacDonald, John D. 1916–1986
Spillane, Mickey. 1918–
Sanders, Lawrence. 1920–
Highsmith, Patricia. 1921–
Hillerman, Tony. 1925–
Leonard, Elmore. 1925–
McBain, Ed. 1926–
Grafton, Sue. 1940–
Paretsky, Sara. 1947–

CAIN, JAMES M. 1892–1977

A journalist who was once managing editor of *The New Yorker*, Cain's successful transition to mystery writer eventually brought him the Grand Master Award from the Mystery Writers of America. He wrote 17 novels, as well as many short plays and short stories; he also worked as a Hollywood screenwriter. Cain's first novel, *The Postman Always Rings Twice* (1934), was a huge bestseller and was critically well received. It is in the hard-boiled tradition, with a gritty realism and a good deal of overt sexuality. The characters in Cain's work are always everyday people who, through circumstances mostly beyond their control, become involved in violent, criminal activities; often, rather than being immoral, Cain's characters seem amoral and alienated from middle-class American life. Although critics disagree about the quality of his work, new generations of readers continue to enjoy Cain's best novels.

NOVELS BY CAIN

Cloud Nine. Mysterious Pr. 1987 $14.95. ISBN 0-89296-079-5. About rival brothers' struggle over a young pregnant woman and a million dollars.
Mildred Pierce. 1941. Random 1989 $6.95. ISBN 0-679-72321-8. The story of divorcée Mildred Pierce and her obsession with achieving success for herself and her daughter, who is more interested in men than in her domineering mother.
The Postman Always Rings Twice. 1934. Random 1989 $7.95. ISBN 0-679-72325-0. A transient's affair with the wife of a restaurant owner and the lovers' plot to murder him for his insurance money.

BOOKS ABOUT CAIN

Hooper, Roy. *Cain: The Biography of James M. Cain.* U. of Ill. Pr. 1987 $16.95. ISBN 0-8093-1361-8. An interesting scholarly look at Cain's life and career.
Madden, David. *Cain's Craft.* Scarecrow 1985 $20.00. ISBN 0-8108-1750-0. A discussion of Cain's skill as detective fiction writer.
_____. *James M. Cain.* Twayne's U.S. Authors Ser. Irvington 1974 $17.95. ISBN 0-8057-0128-1. Biographical, critical, and bibliographical information.

CHANDLER, RAYMOND. 1888–1959

Born in Chicago but raised in England, where he studied the classics, Chandler had early jobs as a reporter for English newspapers. He also had other jobs—accountant, bookkeeper, and auditor among them. But his first love was writing, and, from 1933 to his death, Chandler was a professional writer. Besides novels and short stories, he wrote screenplays; he won two academy awards, for *Double Indemnity* (1944) and *The Blue Dahlia* (1946). Urban America's darker side fascinated Chandler as a place where the promise of America has gone wrong, corrupted by greed, money, and power. Into this setting Chandler places detective Philip Marlowe, a disillusioned idealist made cynical by what he sees on the streets of Los Angeles. According to critic Lianna Babener, in his work Chandler demonstrates "the imaginative possibilities of the detective story" as he transforms "the genre from formulaic puzzlement to cultural inquiry."

NOVELS BY CHANDLER

The Big Sleep. 1939. Random 1992 $9.00. ISBN 0-394-75828-5. Chandler's first novel in which private eye Philip Marlowe takes a case involving a paralyzed millionaire, his two mentally unbalanced daughters, blackmail, and murder (became a 1946 movie starring Humphrey Bogart and Lauren Bacall).

Farewell, My Lovely. 1940. Random 1992 $10.00. ISBN 0-394-75827-7. Philip Marlowe involved with the gambling underworld in a murder case where three beautiful women are suspects (several film adaptations).

The High Window. 1942. Random 1988 $8.95. ISBN 0-394-75826-9. Philip Marlowe's investigation of a murder involving a stolen coin and the secretary of an old woman with much to hide.

The Lady in the Lake. 1943. Random 1992 $10.00. ISBN 0-394-75825-0. The mountains north of Los Angeles as the setting for Philip Marlowe's search for a missing woman.

The Long Goodbye. 1953. Random 1992 $10.00. ISBN 0-394-75768-8. Philip Marlowe, war-scarred veteran Terry Lennox, and alcoholic writer Roger Wade trail victims of a deceptive woman (several film adaptations).

The Raymond Chandler Omnibus. Random 1980 $13.95. ISBN 0-394-60492-X. Contains four classic Chandler novels: *The Big Sleep, Farewell, My Lovely, The High Window, The Lady in the Lake.*

BOOKS ABOUT CHANDLER

Brewer, Gay. *The Detective in Distress: Philip Marlowe's Domestic Dream.* Borgo Pr. 1990 $10.00. ISBN 0-941028-08-9. A short but intriguing look at the Marlowe character's longing for a different life.

Bruccoli, Matthew. *Raymond Chandler: A Checklist.* Bks. Demand $15.00. ISBN 0-8357-9373-7. Useful for those doing research on Chandler.

———. *Raymond Chandler: A Descriptive Bibliography.* U. of Pittsburgh Pr. 1979 $60.00. ISBN 0-8229-3382-9

Marling, William H. *Raymond Chandler. Twayne's U.S. Authors Ser.* Macmillan 1980 $20.95. ISBN 0-8057-7472-6. A survey of Chandler's life and work; a clear, succinct, and perceptive study.

Skinner, Robert E. *The Hard-Boiled Explicator: A Guide to the Study of Dashiell Hammett, Raymond Chandler, and Ross Macdonald.* Scarecrow 1985 $20.00. ISBN 0-8108-1749-7. A very useful place for those interested in hard-boiled detective fiction to begin their research.

GARDNER, ERLE STANLEY. 1889–1970

Gardner successfully pursued two demanding careers—law and writing. An attorney and member of the California bar, he also was given the Grand Master Award by the Mystery Writers of America in 1961. By using his own law background as the basis for some of his plots, Gardner gives a sense of authenticity to his mysteries, particularly when super-lawyer Perry Mason is in charge. As an attorney, Gardner often defended poor people and minorities, and he founded the "Court of Last Resort" to take on apparently hopeless cases. As a writer, Gardner was just as dedicated: He disciplined himself to write 4,000 words every evening. He published his first story in 1921 and his first Perry Mason novel in 1933. It was then that Gardner's career took off, and the Perry Mason character became the basis for a radio series as well as a television series that is still being broadcast. Gardner's stated aims were to make money and to provide his readers with pleasure, and he was hugely successful in both endeavors.

NOVELS BY GARDNER

The Case of the Daring Divorcee. 1964. Ballantine 1984 $3.95. ISBN 0-345-32003-4. A case in which client Adelle Hastings seeks Perry Mason's protection but ends up being charged with murder so that Mason must find the real culprit.

The Case of the Fabulous Fake. Ballantine 1986 $3.95. ISBN 0-345-33548-1. The case of a female client, known only to Perry Mason as 36-24-36, who wants him to help her disappear without leaving any trace.

The Case of the Mythical Monkeys. Bentley 1981 repr. of 1959 ed. $14.95. ISBN 0-8376-0398-6. Perry Mason dealing with uncooperative witnesses to solve the murder of which client Gladys Doyle is wrongfully accused.

The Case of the Phantom Fortune. 1946. Ballantine 1986 $3.50. ISBN 0-345-33191-5. A command invitation to the buffet dinner of a wealthy client that involves Perry Mason and secretary Della Street in a murder investigation.

The Case of the Swinging Skirt. Bentley 1981 repr. of 1959 ed. $14.00. ISBN 0-8376-0399-4. In which Perry Mason must determine whether Ellen Robb is telling the truth in claiming she is being framed for murdering the wife of a customer in the casino where she works.

BOOK ABOUT GARDNER

Mundell, E. H. *Erle Stanley Gardner: A Checklist.* Bks. Demand repr. of 1968 ed. $27.10. ISBN 0-8357-5577-0. A useful bibliography of a very prolific author; very handy for those doing research.

GRAFTON, SUE. 1940–

One of the new generation of mystery/detective novelists, Grafton is also one of a group of women who have successfully created female detectives in the hard-boiled tradition. Along with SARA PARETSKY, Grafton has managed to introduce this new element into the genre without changing the traditional parameters of the classic detective story: She writes well-crafted, exciting suspense novels whose heroine, private investigator Kinsey Millhone, is brave, intelligent, good at her work, and possesses integrity. Grafton's fans may look forward to many more fine books from this talented author, as she makes her way through the alphabet in titling her works.

NOVELS BY GRAFTON

E Is for Evidence. 1988. Bantam 1989 $5.99. ISBN 0-553-27955-6. In which Kinsey Millhone takes herself as a client to solve the mystery that threatens her license and her life.

F Is for Fugitive. H. Holt & Co. 1989 $15.95. ISBN 0-8050-0460-2. Old secrets revealed, leading to chaos as Kinsey Millhone investigates a 17-year-old murder.

G Is for Gumshoe. Fawcett 1991 $5.95. ISBN 0-449-21936-4. Kinsey Millhone's love affair with the bodyguard she hires for protection from the hit man who stalks her as she searches for an old woman living in the Mojave Desert.

H Is for Homicide. Fawcett 1992 $5.99. ISBN 0-449-21946-1. Kinsey Millhone's foray into the Los Angeles barrio to investigate the death of an insurance claims adjustor.

HAMMETT, DASHIELL. 1894–1961

Among the many jobs Dashiell Hammett had, his stint as detective for the Pinkerton Agency may have been the one that best prepared him for his later career as a writer of detective novels. Hammett is generally considered to be responsible for inventing the character of the hard-boiled detective, an innovation that greatly influenced the genre: RAYMOND CHANDLER, ROSS MACDONALD, SUE GRAFTON, and SARA PARETSKY are among Hammett's descendants. Between 1923 and 1927, 32 stories by Hammett appeared in *Black Mask*, the mystery magazine started by George Jean Nathan and H. L. MENCKEN. An often brilliant writer of dialogue, Hammett's character studies are realistic, tough, and perceptive; he created some of the most memorable characters in the genre, such as Sam Spade, private eye of *The Maltese Falcon* (1930).

Politically, Dashiell Hammett was on the left. A member of the Communist party, he was often outspokenly critical of it, as well as of mainstream politics. He spent six months in federal prison for refusing to testify before the New York Supreme Court concerning a case involving violation of bail bonds by other Communist party members. He considered it against his principles to help the U.S. government persecute Communists—or anyone else. Long a companion of the playwright LILLIAN HELLMAN, Hammett died in 1961.

NOVELS BY HAMMETT

The Maltese Falcon. 1930. Random 1972 $4.95. ISBN 0-394-71772-4. The story of Sam Spade's search for his partner's killer, with the statue of a black falcon as the clue; involvement with Brigid O'Shaugnessy almost proves Spade's undoing.

The Novels of Dashiell Hammett. Knopf rev. ed. 1965 $30.00. ISBN 0-394-43860-4. Contains *Red Harvest* (1929), *The Dain Curse* (1929), *The Maltese Falcon* (1930), *The Glass Key* (1931), and *The Thin Man* (1934).

Red Harvest. 1929. Random 1989 $6.95. ISBN 0-679-72261-0. A tale about small-town corruption, in which the Continental Op seeks to punish those guilty of murders in Personville, or Poisonville.

The Thin Man. 1934. Random 1992 $9.00. ISBN 0-394-23905-9. About Nick and Nora Charles, a rich, glamorous couple who investigate mysteries in this hard-boiled novel of manners.

SHORT STORY COLLECTIONS BY HAMMETT

The Big Knockover. 1962. Ed. by Lillian Hellman. Random 1989 $8.95. ISBN 0-679-72259-9. Contains the title story as well as "The Gutting of Couffignal," "Fly Paper," "The Scorched Face," "This King Business," "The Gatewood Caper," "Dead Yellow Woman," "Corkscrew," "Tulip," and "$106,000 Blood Money."

The Continental Op. Random 1989 $7.95. ISBN 0-679-72258-0. Seven early stories introducing Hammett's hard-boiled detective, including "The Tenth Clew," "The Golden Horseshoe," "The Girl with the Silver Eyes," "The House in Turk Street," "The Whosis Kid," "The Main Death," and "The Farewell Murder."

BOOKS ABOUT HAMMETT

Dooley, Dennis. *Dashiell Hammett*. Continuum 1984 $18.95. ISBN 0-8044-2141-2. Useful study of Hammett's life and work.

Johnson, Diane. *Dashiell Hammett: A Life*. Fawcett 1987 $8.95. ISBN 0-449-90223-4. Solid biography; a good starting place for work on Hammett.

Layman, Richard. *Dashiell Hammett: A Descriptive Bibliography*. U. of Pittsburgh Pr. 1979 $60.00. ISBN 0-8229-3394-2. Necessary for anyone doing work on Hammett.

HIGHSMITH, PATRICIA. 1921–

As a writer of novels, short stories, and teleplays, Highsmith is known for her character studies exploring people's darker side—the side of an apparently moral person who is capable of murder. Highsmith likes to examine the ways in which people can get to the point at which they are capable of murder, as well as who they become after they have committed a crime. In carefully constructed stories and novels, she integrates this scrutiny of the human psyche into complex plots that often take unexpected twists. An example is her first novel, *Strangers on a Train* (1950), in which architect Guy Haines meets Charles Bruno on a train. Bruno conceives of a plan to have Haines kill Bruno's father, while Bruno will kill Haines's wife. The effect that this plan has on Haines is the focus of the story. Highsmith does not publish a great amount of fiction, but when she does, her work is always among the best in the genre.

NOVELS BY HIGHSMITH

The Mysterious Mr. Ripley. Random 1992 $10.00. ISBN 0-679-74229-8. Includes three of Highsmith's novels about Tom Ripley: *The Talented Mr. Ripley*, *Ripley Underground*, and *Ripley's Cane*.

Ripley Underground. Random 1970 $10.00. ISBN 0-679-74230-1. In which the wealthy, well-married, psychotic Tom Ripley will do anything, including evil, to keep what he has.

Ripley Under Water. Knopf 1992 $21.00. ISBN 0-679-41677-3. About Tom Ripley finding himself stalked by someone who knows about his past crimes.

The Talented Mr. Ripley. 1955. Random 1992 $10.00. ISBN 0-679-74229-8. Tom Ripley's efforts to get Dickie Greenleaf to return to his father's control, as Ripley finds himself wanting to become Dickie.

SHORT STORY COLLECTION BY HIGHSMITH

Slowly, Slowly in the Wind. Penzler Bks. o.p. Twelve suspense stories, including the title story as well as "The Man Who Wrote Books in His Head," "The Network," "The Pond," "Woodrow Wilson's Neck-Tie," and others.

HILLERMAN, TONY. 1925–

As a journalist, Hillerman has worked for newspapers in Oklahoma and for UPI. He has been a political reporter in Santa Fe, a professor of journalism and chair of the journalism department at the University of New Mexico, and assistant to the president of that university. The American Southwest and its landscape and peoples, particularly the Navajo, are the focus for many of Hillerman's mysteries. He hopes that people learn more about Native Americans and their cultures by reading his books, and he draws upon their many traditions and stories for his novels. Thus, as people read Hillerman's work, they are learning about another culture and history as well as enjoying a finely crafted mystery. His two detectives—Officer Jim Chee and Lieutenant Joe Leaphorn—first came together in *Skinwalkers* (1987).

NOVELS BY HILLERMAN

The Blessing Way. 1970. HarpC 1990 $5.99. ISBN 0-06-100001-9. Tale of Lieutenant Joe Leaphorn's suspicions of a supernatural killer as he investigates a murder and follows Wolf-Witch throughout Navajo country.

Coyote Waits. 1990. HarpC 1992 $5.99. ISBN 0-06-109932-5. A story of evil in which Jim Chee and Joe Leaphorn investigate the murder of Navajo tribal policeman Delbert Nez, wondering why the man who is arrested will neither confess to nor deny the crime.

Dance Hall of the Dead. 1973. HarpC 1990 $5.99. ISBN 0-06-100002-7. Lieutenant Joe Leaphorn's investigation of the disappearance of two boys, one a Zuni; an archeological dig and the laws of the Zuni complicate the case.

Leaphorn and Chee. HarpC 1992 $19.00. ISBN 0-06-016909-5. Contains three novels: *Skinwalkers, Talking God,* and *The Thief of Time.*

Listening Woman. 1978. HarpC 1990 $5.99. ISBN 0-06-100029-9. The murders of a teenage girl and an old man, in which Leaphorn uncovers a kidnapping and an old conspiracy.

Talking God. 1989. HarpC 1991 $5.95. ISBN 0-06-109918-X. Joe Leaphorn and Jim Chee confronting terrorism and assassination in Washington, D.C. as they look for a villainous museum conservator.

A Thief of Time. HarpC 1990 $4.95. ISBN 0-06-100004-3. Lieutenant Joe Leaphorn and Officer Jim Chee's joint investigation of the disappearance of an anthropologist from an ancient Anasazi archeological site, in which the discovery of two corpses leads to buried secrets amid ancient indigenous ruins.

Book about Hillerman

Talking Mysteries: A Conversation with Tony Hillerman. U. of NM Pr. 1991 $16.95. ISBN 0-06-100004-3. Very useful for anyone wanting to know how Hillerman researches and writes his mysteries.

LEONARD, ELMORE. 1925–

An advertising copywriter who hated copywriting but needed to make a living, Leonard worked for years writing short stories for pulp magazines during the 1950s, determined to make a living as a writer. His persistence paid off, for in 1977 the Western Writers of America named his western novel *Hombre* (1961) one of the 25 best westerns of all time.

The early 1980s finally brought him recognition in the mystery genre with the publication of *Stick* (1982). Leonard strives in his fiction to push past the formulaic to a level of social commentary, but his tight prose and excellent ear for diction, as well as his talent for suspenseful plotting, produce entertaining novels that weave sex, violence, and tension into the ultimate lesson that it is worthwhile taking risks for good causes.

Novels by Leonard

Cat Chaser. 1982. Avon 1983 $3.95. ISBN 0-380-64642-0. The story of ex-marine George Moran, who falls in love with the wife of a Dominican mobster and becomes involved in the seamy Miami underworld.

City Primeval: High Noon in Detroit. 1982. Avon 1983 $3.95. ISBN 0-380-56952-3. Detroit homicide detective Raymond Cruz's investigation of a pair of Bonnie-and-Clyde-type murderers.

Get Shorty. Delacorte 1990 $18.95. ISBN 0-385-30141-3. Film industry setting in which loan shark Chili Palmer goes to Las Vegas and Hollywood trying to recover payments and partnership with film producer Harry Zimm leads to danger.

Killshot. 1989. Warner Bks. 1990 $5.95. ISBN 0-446-35041-9. Wayne and Carmen Olson, in the Federal Witness Security Program, for witnessing a murder, pursued by killers, Armand Degas and Richie Nix.

La Brava. 1983. Avon 1984 $4.95. ISBN 0-380-69237-6. The involvement of free-lance photographer and former secret service agent Joe LaBrave with an extortionist, a murderous Cuban refugee, and a faded movie actress.

The Moonshine War. Dell 1985 $4.99. ISBN 0-440-15807-9. A tale set during Prohibition, in which Kentucky moonshiner Son Martin gets involved in a war with local authorities over $125,000 worth of illegally brewed sour-mash whiskey.

MCBAIN, ED (pseud. of Evan Hunter). 1926–

Although his odd jobs include having sold lobsters and answering the phone for the American Automobile Association, writing is Evan Hunter's true profession. He has wanted to be a writer since his college days and wrote detective stories for pulp magazines. As Evan Hunter, he has written well-known novels, including *The Blackboard Jungle* (1950); screenplays, such as for *The Birds* (1963); and a television series, "The Chisholms" (1979–80). But he has a second, separate identity—Ed McBain, author of mystery novels about police officers at the 87th Precinct. Hunter does research in actual police precincts, which gives his novels a feeling of authenticity. The reader can feel the frustration, tedium, anger, and compassion in the police officers as they attempt to solve crimes. Although these are books written according to a formula and are not meant to provide social commentary, readers do feel as if they have been brought into the inner sanctum of a working police unit. McBain's novels are also highly entertaining page-turners that keep fans waiting for the next installment.

NOVELS BY MCBAIN

Beauty and the Beast. 1982. Windsor NY 1992 $3.99. ISBN 1-55817-662-4. Matthew Hope's efforts to prove that George Harper did not kill his wife Michelle and to find out who did.

Eight Black Horses. Avon 1986 $4.50. ISBN 0-380-70029-8. An 87th Precinct mystery in which The Deaf Man returns to wreak havoc on precinct cops; Steve Carella and fellow police must solve murders and find The Deaf Man.

Lightning. 1984. Avon 1985 $4.95. ISBN 0-380-69974-5. A story of murders and rapes of women in the 87th Precinct, which have police thinking The Deaf Man is back; rape squad decoy Eileen Burke must put her life in jeopardy to solve crimes.

Snow White and Rose Red. 1985. Mysterious Pr. 1986 $3.95. ISBN 0-445-40513-9. Matthew Hope's efforts to free Sarah Whitaker from the psychiatric home to which she claims to have been wrongly committed by family members seeking her inheritance.

Ten Plus One. 1963. NAL-Dutton 1982 $3.50. ISBN 0-451-16367-2. Apparently random sniper shootings investigated by the 87th Precinct detectives.

Three Blind Mice. 1990. Mysterious Pr. 1991 $4.95. ISBN 0-446-40035-1. Matthew Hope's investigation of the brutal murder of three Vietnamese men after they are acquitted of raping the wealthy Jessica Leeds, whose husband is a murder suspect.

MACDONALD, JOHN D. 1916–1986

It seems that when one discusses the creators of memorable detective heroes, three names inevitably arise: DASHIELL HAMMETT, RAYMOND CHANDLER, and John D. MacDonald. Winner of the Grant Master Award from the Mystery Writers of America in 1972, MacDonald began writing for pulp mystery magazines in the 1940s and also wrote science fiction and several nonfiction books. But it is his hard-boiled detective character Travis McGee, a descendant of The Continental Op (Operative), Sam Spade, and Philip Marlowe, who epitomizes the MacDonald themes. McGee lives on a houseboat in Florida but works as a freelance private investigator. No matter how much danger he faces, McGee always survives and wins. But he is also concerned with modern culture's obsession with junk—junk food, junk culture—a seemingly unstoppable decline. Sex also plays a role in the well-plotted novels of MacDonald. Critic Francis Nevins has remarked, "Indeed MacDonald portrayed more vividly and knowledgeably than any other crime writer the readjustment of American business from a war footing to a consumer-oriented peacetime economy which would soon be spewing out megatons of self-destructing plastic junk and incurring the wrath of the later MacDonald and his beach-bum-philosopher-adventurer-hero Travis McGee."

NOVELS BY JOHN D. MACDONALD

Bright Orange for the Shroud. 1965. Fawcett 1987 $4.95. ISBN 0-449-13358-3. Story of Travis McGee's aid to Arthur Wilkinson, whose cunning wife has broken Wilkinson and gotten hold of his money.

Cinnamon Skin. 1982. Fawcett 1986 $5.95. ISBN 0-449-12873-3. The mysterious death of the niece of Travis McGee's friend Meyer, killed when a yacht mysteriously explodes; McGee must investigate and possibly find that his friend is guilty.

The Empty Copper Sea. Amereon Ltd. 1978 $16.95. ISBN 0-89190-778-5. Travis McGee's investigation when friend Van Harder is blamed for a death; how—or if—Hub Lawless really did it is the mystery to be solved.

One More Sunday. 1984. Fawcett 1985 $4.95. ISBN 0-449-20703-X. Religion as high-tech business: the founder of the Church of the Eternal Believer, Matthew Meadows, is dying and his not-so-Christian son John readies to take over.

SHORT STORY COLLECTION BY JOHN D. MACDONALD

More Good Old Stuff. Knopf 1984 $15.95. ISBN 0-394-53898-6. Stories from the 1940s, some updated, including "Deadly Damsel," "State Police Report That . . .," "I Accuse Myself," "Verdict," and others.

BOOK ABOUT JOHN D. MACDONALD

Hirschberg, Edgar W. *John D. MacDonald. Twayne's U. S. Authors Ser.* G. K. Hall 1990 $20.00. ISBN 0-8057-7440-8. A fact-filled, intelligent discussion of MacDonald's life and career, as well as of the themes and style in his work.

MACDONALD, ROSS (pseud. of Kenneth Millar). 1915–1983

A difficult and peripatetic childhood, coupled with dual American and Canadian citizenship, caused Kenneth Millar to feel for many years as if the world were an unstable place; certainly, he was unsure of his own place in it. A one-time high school English and history teacher, the successful writing career of his wife Margaret Millar allowed him to leave teaching and enter graduate school at the University of Michigan in Ann Arbor. There he wrote his first novel, *The Dark Tunnel* (1944). His own psychotherapy helped relieve him of his childhood neuroses, and what he called his "breakthrough novel," *The Galton Case* (1959), is written with a new, strong, and confident voice. Along with DASHIELL HAMMETT and RAYMOND CHANDLER, Millar is considered one of America's finest writers of detective fiction. His primary protagonist, Lew Archer, often becomes involved in the psychological dimensions of his cases. The plots of his novels are complex, and he focuses on southern California as a beautiful land where people's actions corrupt the naturally peaceful setting. Critic John Vermillion has noted that "Over a span of more than thirty years, Millar has created a large body of fiction informed by acute observation, significant ideas, integrity, wisdom, and craftsmanship. Within and above these qualities he has found the elusive tension, emotional and imaginative, which molds the novel into an active experience. But equally important is that he has written popular fiction which may be read by a cross section of the reading public."

NOVELS BY ROSS MACDONALD

Archer in Jeopardy. Knopf 1979 $24.95. ISBN 0-394-50804-1. Set of three Lew Archer novels: *The Doomsters* (1958), *The Zebra-Striped Hearse* (1962), and *The Instant Enemy* (1968).

The Blue Hammer. 1976. Bantam 1988 $3.95. ISBN 0-553-27548-8. Lew Archer on the trail of a stolen painting by a vanished artist; fifty years of complicated secrets must be unraveled before the mystery is solved.

The Far Side of the Dollar. Warner Bks. 1990 $3.95. ISBN 0-446-35890-8. Lew Archer hired to find a missing boy in what begins as an apparently simple case of a bad child and leads to a complex maze of extortion and murder.

The Goodbye Look. 1969. Warner Bks. 1992 $4.50. ISBN 0-446-35894-0. Initially a routine burglary investigation for Lew Archer, then, a murder case as Archer becomes involved with a wealthy Georgia family.

The Zebra-Striped Hearse. 1962. Bantam 1984 $3.95. ISBN 0-553-27362-0. Lew Archer's efforts to discover whether three apparently different men are in fact all the same person.

SHORT STORY COLLECTION BY ROSS MACDONALD

Lew Archer, Private Investigator. Mysterious Pr. 1977 $10.00. ISBN 0-89296-033-7. Nine Lew Archer stories, including "Find the Woman," "The Beaded Lady," "The Suicide," "Guilt-Edged Blonde," and "Sleeping Dog."

BOOK ABOUT ROSS MACDONALD

Schopen, Bernard A. *Ross Macdonald (Kenneth Millar). Twayne U.S. Authors Ser.* Macmillan 1990 $20.95. ISBN 0-8057-7548-X. Excellent, concise introduction to Macdonald's life and major themes.

PARETSKY, SARA. 1947–

Her own background as an enthusiastic reader of mysteries has given Paretsky an almost intuitive feel for the conventions of detective fiction. Like SUE GRAFTON, Paretsky does not violate the formula for hard-boiled detective stories; she has intentionally set out to create a Raymond Chandler-type character in her protagonist V. I. Warshawsky. Paretsky wants to show a woman succeeding in a traditional male role. In Warshawsky, Paretsky has an attractive, realistic female character whose integrity frequently leads her into trouble, but that steadfastness in the face of obstacles is also why Warshawsky is so appealing. Warshawsky's troubled past and her loving, eccentric friends make for stories that are emotionally engaging as well as intellectually intriguing.

NOVELS BY PARETSKY

Bitter Medicine. 1987. Ballantine 1988 $5.95. ISBN 0-345-34722-6. V. I. Warshawsky's efforts to prove malpractice after her friend dies in a hospital emergency room; murder and violence, including an attack on Warshawsky, complicate the investigation.

Blood Shot. 1988. Dell 1989 $4.95. ISBN 0-440-20420-8. V. I. Warshawsky hired by a childhood friend to find the father she never knew, with the death of another friend prompting a murder investigation.

Burn Marks. 1990. Dell 1991 $4.95. ISBN 0-440-20845-9. V. I. Warshawsky's investigation of a fire at her aunt's SRO hotel and a subsequent murder, leading to a deeper look at the problems of the homeless and the shady real-estate deals that create homelessness.

Deadlock. Ballantine 1984 $5.95. ISBN 0-345-31954-0. V. I. Warshawsky's investigation of the death of her cousin and her discovery that his murder is linked to criminal activity in the shipping business.

Guardian Angel. Delacorte 1992 $20.00. ISBN 0-385-29931-1. V. I. Warshawsky's involvement in neighbor Hattie Frizell's legal affairs and her investigation of one of Chicago's leading families as she uncovers a scandal linked to union fraud and the banking industry.

Indemnity Only. 1982. Dell 1991 $4.95. ISBN 0-440-21069-0. The first V. I. Warshawsky novel in which she investigates a case of a missing coed for a client who will not say who he is.

QUEEN, ELLERY. (pseud of Frederic Dannay, 1905–1982, and Manfred Lee, 1905–1971)

An unsuccessful entry in a mystery story contest turned into a career for Frederic Dannay and his cousin Manfred Lee. The story was picked up for publication in 1929, and the career of Ellery Queen, the pseudonym that Dannay and Lee chose, was off and running. The two wrote countless novels and short stories about Ellery Queen, a young detective who used reason to solve complex puzzles. Their emphasis was always on the intellectual rather than the emotional or intuitive capacities of the detective. Dannay and Lee founded *Ellery Queen's Mystery Magazine* in 1941, and it proved to be important in keeping the genre vital. Ellery Queen has won numerous awards, including the Grand Master Award in 1960 from the Mystery Writers of America. More than 150 million Ellery Queen books are in print, and there have been Ellery Queen radio and television shows, as well as movies.

NOVELS BY QUEEN

And on the Eighth Day. 1964. Ballantine 1983 $1.95. ISBN 0-345-31742-4. Ellery Queen's cross-country trip, complicated by several mysterious and eccentric people in what seems to be another world.
The Player on the Other Side. Curley Pub. 1990 $18.95. ISBN 0-89340-107-2. The threat of a mysterious "Y" to several members of the York family; Ellery Queen must find "Y" before it is too late.

SHORT STORY COLLECTION BY QUEEN

Ellery Queen's Circumstantial Evidence. Amereon Ltd. $18.95. ISBN 0-89190-790-4. Twenty-two stories from *Ellery Queen's Mystery Magazine* in 1978, with each story involving questions about the nature of evidence.

SANDERS, LAWRENCE. 1920–

After years of working as an editor for a number of magazines, including *Mechanix Illustrated* and *Science and Mechanics*, Lawrence Sanders wrote and published his first novel, *The Anderson Tapes* (1970), at the age of 50. It was made into a film in 1971, as was *The First Deadly Sin* (1973). Sanders loves to write; it has become nearly an obsession with him. Although he lives in Florida, he is not interested in outdoor hobbies, such as fishing; he would rather write. His fans are certainly glad about that, because his readable, tautly plotted novels are well crafted, and, although his detectives may not be as memorable as some of the more hard-boiled characters, they are highly believable as they attempt to solve the various crimes that Sanders devises.

NOVELS BY SANDERS

The Eighth Commandment. Berkley Pub. 1985 $4.95. ISBN 0-425-10005-7. Mary Lou Bateson, who is accused of stealing a priceless Greek coin and has to prove her innocence as she digs into the background of the fabulously wealthy Haustock family.
The Fourth Deadly Sin. Putnam Pub. Group 1985 $17.95. ISBN 0-399-13062-4. The murder of gentle psychiatrist Simon Ellerby, bringing former chief of detectives Edward X. Delaney out of retirement; suspects include the doctor's client and his widow.

The Seventh Commandment. Putnam Pub. Group 1991 $22.95. ISBN 0-399-13611-8. The
  story of Hartford insurance investigator Dora Conti, who finds more than she
  bargained for as she looks into the murder of a jewelry magnate with the help of a
  NYPD detective.

The Timothy Files. 1987. Berkley Pub. 1988 $4.95. ISBN 0-425-10924-0. Three cases to be
  solved by private eye Timothy Cone, concerning a real-estate firm, a fertility clinic
  that may be involved with murder, and shady Middle Eastern businessmen.

SHORT STORY COLLECTION BY SANDERS

Tales of the Wolf. 1968. Avon 1986 $4.50. ISBN 0-380-75145-3. Thirteen stories about
  claims investigator Wolf Lannihan, including "Manhattan After Dark," "The Death of
  a Model," and "The Case of the Missing Nude."

SPILLANE, MICKEY (pseud. of Frank Morrison Spillane). 1918–

Early in the 1940s, Spillane began writing comic books, but, because he
needed more money, he began writing novels. *I, the Jury* (1946), Spillane's first
novel, has sold more than 8 million copies. Two film versions have been made,
in 1953 and 1981. Other writing projects have included short stories, children's
books, and television and film scripts. Mike Hammer, Spillane's detective hero,
is a big, tough private investigator who kills when necessary and always gets his
man—or woman—in the end. Sex and violence characterize his books, but
apparently Spillane's work appeals to readers; 7 of his books have been among
the top 15 all-time bestsellers during the last 50 years. Spillane has said that he
writes for the public, not for the critics, and his formula is a very successful one.

NOVELS BY SPILLANE

I, the Jury. 1947. NAL-Dutton 1948 $3.95. ISBN 0-451-16592-6. Story of hard-boiled
  private eye Mike Hammer investigating the murder of his best friend and following
  the trail to a beautiful, deadly woman.

The Killing Man. NAL-Dutton 1989 $17.95. ISBN 0-525-24827-7. Mike Hammer's search
  for a killer after he finds a dead man in his chair and the man's secretary beaten
  almost to death.

The Snake. NAL-Dutton 1964 $3.95. ISBN 0-451-13715-9. Crooked politics and under-
  world crime in a case about a beautiful blond in danger from her rich stepfather.

STOUT, REX. 1886–1975

A child prodigy with a gift for mathematics, Stout drifted as he became an
adult, holding odd jobs in many places—cook, cabinetmaker, bellhop, hotel
manager, salesman, bookkeeper, and even a guide in a pueblo. But his true
talent lay in storytelling; he sold his first story, about William Howard Taft, in
1912. His most famous creation is Nero Wolfe, a 286-pound detective genius
who, with sidekick Archie Goodwin, can often solve a case without leaving his
room. It is the way in which the puzzle is solved that intrigues Nero Wolfe, who
is much like Sherlock Holmes in his ability to use deductive reasoning. More
than 60 million copies (in 24 languages) of Stout's books have been sold. Stout
writes quickly, drawing upon a lifetime of impressions. He neither uses an
outline nor revises; he lets his characters take over as the story develops. The
classy, erudite Nero Wolfe presents for readers an alternative to the hard-boiled
branch of the genre.

NOVELS BY STOUT

Death of a Doxy. 1966. Bantam 1991 $3.95. ISBN 0-553-27606-9. Nero Wolfe's efforts to
  free an employee who has been jailed for murder while keeping a wealthy client's
  name out of the press and finding the real murderer.

Death of a Dude. 1969. Bantam 1990 $3.95. ISBN 0-553-27422-8. The murder of dude
    Philip Brodell on a Montana ranch with Archie and Nero on the case.
The Father Hunt. 1968. Bantam 1991 $3.95. ISBN 0-553-24728-X. The case of Amy
    Denovo, who hires Rex Stout and Archie Goodwin to find her father, whom she has
    never seen, heard of, or met, though he has left her money.
Five of a Kind: The Third Nero Wolfe Omnibus. Ayer repr. of 1961 ed. $29.95. ISBN 0-
    8369-4136-5. Includes two novels, *The Rubber Band* and *In the Best Families,* as well
    as three short stories.

BOOK ABOUT STOUT

McAleer, John J. *Rex Stout: A Biography.* Borgo Pr. 1992 $57.00. ISBN 0-941028-09-7. A
    hefty, thorough biography of Stout examining his life and career.

WHITNEY, PHYLLIS A. 1903–

Phyllis A. Whitney moved around quite a bit during her youth, from Japan to
China, the Philippines, and the United States. Her first novel, for adolescents,
was *A Place for Ann* (1942). Winner of the Grand Master Award from the Mystery
Writers of America, Whitney mixes an intriguing blend of mystery and romance
that has kept her fans happy for many years. Often her stories have the feel of
Gothic thrillers, with brooding castles and old family secrets hidden away. Often
her protagonists are strong, even liberated, women who are intent on
uncovering the mysteries. Whitney, who loves writing, strives to create escapist
plots but balances them with realistic female characters with whom her readers
can identify.

NOVELS BY WHITNEY

Blue Fire. 1961. Fawcett 1985 $3.95. ISBN 0-449-20868-0. A South African setting for
    mystery and romance with a heroine struggling to recall her past and her father's
    involvement in a diamond smuggling ring.
Columbella. 1966. Fawcett 1982 $2.75. ISBN 0-449-20220-8. Two beautiful women
    engaging in struggle for the love of one man in an exotic Virgin Island setting.
Flaming Tree. 1985. Fawcett 1986 $4.95. ISBN 0-449-20914-8. Story of a recent divorcée
    seeking refuge in Carmel, California, and becoming involved with a badly injured
    boy in what first appears to have been an accident but then turns out to be a
    deliberate injury.
Lost Island. 1970. Fawcett 1985 $3.95. ISBN 0-449-21099-5. Lacey Ames's return to
    Hampton Island and the mansion ruled by the Severen dynasty—and the resulting
    upheaval that threatens to uncover dark, old secrets.
Poinciana. 1980. Fawcett 1984 $4.95. ISBN 0-449-20439-1. Sharon Hollis's marriage to
    wealthy Ross Logan and her arrival at the Palm Beach estate Poinciana, which
    produces mysterious events that turn her newly-found bliss into a nightmare.
Rainbow in the Mist. 1989. Fawcett 1990 $5.95. ISBN 0-449-21742-6. The story of
    clairvoyant Christy Loren, seeking to flee her fame as a psychic in the peaceful Blue
    Ridge mountains—but a mystery unfolds as she joins the search for missing writer
    Deidre Mitchell.
The Turquoise Mask. 1973. Fawcett 1981 $4.95. ISBN 0-449-23470-3. Amanda Austin's
    travels to New Mexico to uncover a mystery about her past, including the truth about
    her mother's murder.

Horror

Why do people seem to enjoy being frightened by a book or a movie? What is
it in such tales that keeps them reading or watching, even as their hearts pound
and their palms sweat? Perhaps part of the answer lies in just those physical
reactions: The adrenalin that surges while waiting for the approaching monster

to attack makes them feel more vital. In being frightened of death, people are paradoxically affirming that they are very much alive. Critic John Cawelti notes that "On the face of it, horror is a most puzzling sort of entertainment, yet, judging from the popularity of the formula and the great enjoyment audiences derive from it, people take enormous delight in being scared out of their wits, at least in fantasy." Just as readers of westerns may escape for a time into the imaginary dangers and adventures of the Wild West, so the readers of horror fiction may vicariously thrill to blood curdling depictions of monsters or may feel the mental anguish of psychological terror—all from the safety of their armchairs.

For the roots of popular horror fiction in America, we must look back to several different sources. During the eighteenth century, horror novels were often considered Gothics, but then the Gothic became more sentimental and romantic. The novels of CHARLES BROCKDEN BROWN, including *Wieland* (1798), *Ormand* (1799), and *Edgar Huntly* (1799), have some of the characteristics of the horror genre, particularly in the way in which they attempt to examine how fear affects people's psychology or frame of mind. But the Gothic and the horror forms came together most brilliantly in the work of EDGAR ALLAN POE. His well-known (and still frightening) stories, such as *"The Tell-Tale Heart"* (1838) and *"The Fall of the House of Usher"* (1839), with their blending of supernatural phenomena and psychological terror, provide models that still hold up well, even for today's audiences. MARY SHELLEY's *Frankenstein* (1818) and BRAM STOKER's *Dracula* (1897) also serve as prototypes for modern horror fiction. Certainly, the vampire novels of ANNE RICE owe a debt to Stoker, whose original novel is still being used as the source for films, the most recent of which was a version by Francis Ford Coppola (1992).

Such contemporary writers as DEAN KOONTZ, PETER STRAUB, and, of course, the very successful and prolific STEPHEN KING have brought the genre of horror fiction to new heights, and its popularity appears to be greater than ever.

CHRONOLOGY OF AUTHORS

Andrews, V(irginia) C(leo). ?–1986
Rice, Anne. 1941–
Saul, John. 1942–
Straub, Peter. 1943–

Koontz, Dean. 1945–
King, Stephen. 1947–
McCammon, Robert R. 1952–

ANDREWS, V(IRGINIA) C(LEO). ?–1986

As a result of medical neglect when she was a child, V. C. (Virginia Cleo) Andrews spent her life on crutches and in a wheelchair. A commercial artist before she published the highly successful *Flowers in the Attic* (1979), she let her imagination run free as she wrote, becoming almost obsessed with her writing. Andrews did not shy away from such controversial themes as incest and misygony, and although her work has not been critically acclaimed, she has been noted for her ability to keep her readers enthralled. Andrews's books have proved especially popular with adolescent girls, for she excels at being able to express the adolescent point of view.

NOVELS BY ANDREWS

Dawn. Ed. by Linda Morrow. PB 1990 $5.95. ISBN 0-671-67068-9. The story of poor
  Dawn and Jimmy Longchamp and their chance to go to a good school, until the
  death of their mother sets in motion events that separate brother and sister and
  uncover evil secrets.
Dark Angel. 1986. PB 1991 $5.95. ISBN 0-671-72939-X. Second in the Casteel family
  trilogy: Heaven, living with her wealthy grandparents, slowly learns that serious
  problems exist beneath the luxurious veneer.
Fallen Hearts. 1989. PB 1991 $5.95. ISBN 0-671-72940-3. The story of Heaven Casteel,
  newly married to Logan Stonewall, and her struggles to put her family's shameful
  past behind her and live a normal life. Third in the Casteel trilogy.
Flowers in the Attic. 1979. PB 1991 $5.95. ISBN 0-671-72941-1. Tale of children whose
  father dies and whose mother takes them to live with their grandparents, who hate
  them; the mother hides the children in the attic and even tries to kill them, so she
  can inherit her father's money.
Heaven. 1986. PB 1989 $5.95. ISBN 0-671-72944-6. The efforts of the Casteel family, in
  the West Virginia mountains, trying to rise out of poverty; although Heaven's abusive
  father and stepmother prevent her happiness, she is finally able to leave and go to
  her grandparents' home. First in the Casteel trilogy.
Petals on the Wind. PB 1991 $5.95. ISBN 0-671-72947-0. Tale of Cathy Dollganger, who
  escapes from the locked attic with her siblings and then seeks revenge on her mother
  and grandmother for their abuse.

KING, STEPHEN. 1947–

King is one of the most prolific, and certainly the most famous, writer of
horror novels working today. He is almost an industry in his own right, and his
legions of loyal fans eagerly await each new novel. Before he began writing
professionally, King worked at odd jobs as a janitor and as a laborer in an
industrial laundry and in a knitting mill; he also taught high school English. He
was raised by his mother after his father deserted the family when King was only
2 years old. Life for the King family was not easy, and King remembers always
feeling different as a child. He began writing at the age of 7 and published his
first story at the age of 18.

To put it simply, King has a talent for scaring people. His stories often begin
with a setting that seems serene—often small towns in New England—but he is
able to portray the nightmare world of everyday people with troubled marriages
and adolescent worries that are overshadowed when some horror begins to
control their lives. King can get deep inside his characters' minds and souls to
their central core, where their deepest fears lie. His readers, identifying with the
characters, can thus be terrified while sitting safely in their living room chairs.
Critic Sharon Malinowski notes that "Throughout a prolific array of novels,
short stories, and screenwork in which elements of horror, fantasy, science
fiction, and humor meld, King deftly arouses fear from dormancy. The breadth
and durability of his popularity alone evinces his mastery as a compelling
storyteller." King also wrote early stories under the pseudonym Richard
Bachman and won Hugo and Nebula awards for his novel *The Shining* (1978).

NOVELS BY KING

The Bachman Books: Four Early Novels by Stephen King. NAL-Dutton 1986 $5.99. ISBN 0-
  451-14736-7. Includes *Rage* (1977), *The Long Walk* (1979), *Road Work* (1981), and
  The Running Man (1982); with King's "Why I Was Bachman" (1985).
Christine. NAL-Dutton 1983 $5.99. ISBN 0-451-16044-4. An unlikely tale of teenage
  horror as a 1958 Plymouth begins to have a life and mind of its own.

Cujo. 1981. NAL-Dutton 1982 $5.99. ISBN 0-451-16135-1. The story of an apparently friendly St. Bernard who turns into a demon after an encounter with sick bats and goes on to terrorize a rural Maine town.

Firestarter. 1980. NAL-Dutton 1981 $5.99. ISBN 0-451-16780-5. The government's hunt for little Charlie McGee, who has the ability to set anything on fire; then Charlie decides to take revenge.

Gerald's Game. Viking Penguin 1992 $23.50. ISBN 0-670-84650-3. The story of Jessie Burlingame's accidental murder of her husband Gerald during a sex game; handcuffed to the bed, she is trapped, and her internal fears take over.

Needful Things. Viking Penguin 1991 $24.95. ISBN 0-670-83953-1. The final Castle Rock, Maine, story: for a price, one can buy anything he or she needs in a shop called Needful Things.

The Shining. NAL-Dutton 1978 $5.99. ISBN 0-451-16091-6. Jack Torrance and his family's move into a Colorado resort hotel as winter caretakers, where Jack goes crazy and son Danny senses evil in both the place and his father.

BOOKS ABOUT KING

Beahm, George. *The Stephen King Story: A Literary Profile.* Andrews & McMeel 1991 $16.95. ISBN 0-8362-7989-1. Examines King's amazing success from his early years to the present; essays include a critical look at King's work, personal anecdotes from friends, King's current and forthcoming projects, and an annotated checklist of his fiction.

Spignesi, Stephen J. *The Complete Stephen King Encyclopedia.* Contemp. Bks. 1992 $35.00. ISBN 0-8092-3911-6. Details from published and unpublished King texts, a concordance, a biography of King, interviews, annotations of all film and audio adaptations, and an index of the first lines of every novel and short story. Extremely useful for King fans and researchers.

KOONTZ, DEAN. 1945–

A former high school English teacher as well as a teacher-counselor with the Appalachian Poverty Program, Koontz began writing as a child to escape an ugly home life caused by his alcoholic father. A prolific writer at a young age, Koontz had sold a dozen novels by the age of 25. Plots that make the character think and feel have always been important to Koontz. In his more recent work, he has begun spending more time on characterization and setting. Basically an optimist, Koontz does not want to promote a sense of disaster or doom for humankind; rather, he wants to show that people can be strong and noble. Koontz believes that the world can be improved, and he sees his novels as bearing that upbeat message, in spite of their horrific events.

NOVELS BY KOONTZ

The Bad Place. Berkley Pub. 1990 $5.95. ISBN 0-425-12434-7. The story of Bobby and Julie Dakota and their investigation of Frank Pollard, an amnesiac who apparently commits crimes as he sleeps; they are drawn into a world of evil and their lives are threatened.

Darkfall. 1984. Berkley Pub. 1989 $4.95. ISBN 0-425-10434-6. About a series of vicious murders that has the police puzzled: as the city lies paralyzed by a blizzard, an evil life form stalks terrorized residents, searching for young victims.

Lightning. 1988. Berkley Pub. 1989 $4.95. ISBN 0-425-11580-1. The story of Laura Shane, plagued from birth with something trying to kill her, rescued many times by a stranger, then finally aware of her destiny and the danger it will cause her.

Phantoms. 1983. Berkley Pub. 1987 $4.95. ISBN 0-425-10145-2. Gruesome murders in a small California mountain town that terrorize residents, who try to find the cause of the horrible deaths—a maniac, a disease, or something more evil.

MCCAMMON, ROBERT R. 1952–

As have so many writers of popular fiction, McCammon worked in advertising, in his case, for department stores and the B. Dalton bookstore chain. He was also a copy editor. In his horror fiction, McCammon wants to explore the concept of fear—how it works and what it does to people. He endeavors in his fiction to go below the surface to a deeper level in people's conscious and unconscious selves. Although he is one of the newer writers in the horror genre, his well-written, compelling novels have already made him one of the major writers in the field.

NOVELS BY MCCAMMON

Boy's Life. PB 1992 $5.99. ISBN 0-671-74305-8. Follows a boy and his father as they seek a killer in Alabama in 1964.

Gone South. PB 1992 $22.00 ISBN 0-671-74306-6. After accidentally killing a man, a Vietnam veteran flees south to the Louisiana bayous, pursued by an odd assemblage of characters.

Mine: A Novel of Terror. PB 1990 $18.95. ISBN 0-671-66486-7. About the infant son of journalist Laura Clayborne, kidnapped by former 1960s terrorist Mary Terrell ("Terror"); Laura, tracking Mary and her son, finds herself becoming more like the terrorist as the chase goes on.

They Thirst. Dark Harvest 1991 $22.95. ISBN 0-913165-60-3. The Undead's descent on Los Angeles to feast—a vampire invasion that terrorizes the city.

RICE, ANNE. 1941–

Three literary personae inhabit the body of Anne Rice: As Anne Rampling, she writes contemporary, mainstream fiction; as A. N. Roquelaure, she publishes sadomasochistic novels; as Anne Rice, she writes about the bizarre and supernatural. Her storytelling skills include an ability to construct complex, rich, and exotic settings, peopled with wonderfully strange characters, such as the Vampire Lestat, antiheroic protagonist of several of Rice's novels. Rice had difficulty getting *Interview with a Vampire* (1976) published, and it was not an immediate success; however, it did eventually attract a kind of cult following. Some see Rice's vampire characters as metaphors for the marginalized "other" in American culture.

NOVELS BY RICE

Cry to Heaven. Ballantine 1991 $12.00. ISBN 0-345-37370-7. An eighteenth-century setting for this tale of castrated male sopranos—Tonio Treschi, possessed by love of music and revenge for those who ruined him, and Guido Maffeo, who becomes Tonio's mentor.

Interview with a Vampire. 1976. Buccaneer Bks. 1991 $29.95. ISBN 0-89966-781-3. Story of the Vampire, once heir to a Louisiana plantation, now talking about his initiation to vampirism and his life since, telling how he made young Claudia a vampire, and describing his journeys to Europe to find others like himself. First in the Vampire Chronicles.

The Queen of the Damned. Ballantine 1989 $5.95. ISBN 0-345-35152-5. Third in the Vampire Chronicles. The intertwining of three stories—of Vampire Lestat, rock star; of a mysterious dream haunting certain people; and of Akasha, Queen of the Damned.

The Vampire Lestat. Ballantine 1986 $5.99. ISBN 0-345-31386-0. The story of Lestat's search for his origins and the meaning of immortality, in which he becomes a rock star and decides to tell his story.

The Tale of the Body Thief. Knopf 1992 $24.00. ISBN 0-679-40528-3. Vampire Lestat's trading of his body for a mortal one and his dislike of being human; the story of how he must regain his vampire self from an evil psychic.

SAUL, JOHN. 1942–

Saul has several major themes in his horror fiction; children as victims, and sometimes perpetrators, of evil; technology used for horrific ends; and occult occurrences (is it something external or internal that causes the horrible things to happen to his characters?). While Saul's earlier work has been noted for its extremely gruesome quality, in his later writing Saul is trying to restrain that aspect of his fiction. Often his plots revolve around hidden, secret evil that is discovered by an innocent person, who must then battle against seemingly impossible odds to defeat the demon.

NOVELS BY SAUL

Creature. 1989. Bantam 1990 $5.95. ISBN 0-553-28411-8. The story of Silverdale, Colorado, which seems like paradise for the Tanner family until secret rituals, the sudden violence of innocent children, and the discovery of hidden secret cages make Sharon Tanner realize an evil presence is in the town.

Darkness. Bantam 1991 $17.50. ISBN 0-553-07373-7. About a secret society practicing blood rites in a Florida swamp, bringing the innocent Anderson family into its circle of terror.

Shadows. Bantam 1992 $19.50. ISBN 0-553-07474-1. In which young Josh MacCallum uncovers the secret of the evil intelligence who runs the Academy and uses brilliant children in its schemes.

Suffer the Children. Dell 1986 $5.95. ISBN 0-440-18293-X. A story of children disappearing from Port Arbello and of history repeating itself as the 100-year-old-murder of a child comes back to haunt the town.

The Unwanted. Bantam 1987 $5.99. ISBN 0-553-26657-8. About Cassie Winslow, who has psychic powers, predicting her mother's death and going to live with her father as her powers strengthen.

STRAUB, PETER. 1943–

Straub taught English in Milwaukee, Wisconsin, and worked for a time on his doctorate in Ireland; he has been writing since 1969. His novel *Julia* (1975) was an attempt to find a successful genre in which to work, after his first novel, *Marriages* (1973), did not sell well. He found that he had a talent for writing horror thrillers in the Gothic tradition. His stories are complex and well paced, with authentic settings that add to the believability of the plot. Straub is particularly good at creating grotesque characters and gruesome situations; the eeriness of his work is captivating. His novels are entertaining and extremely scary, and he doubtless has a long career ahead of him as he develops his talent.

NOVELS BY STRAUB

Floating Dragon. 1983. Berkley Pub. 1985 $5.50. ISBN 0-425-09725-0. Story of the yuppie town of Hampstead, engulfed in mystery and terror, as four townspeople discover an evil presence and fight to save the town.

Koko. 1988. NAL-Dutton 1989 $5.95. ISBN 0-451-16214-5. Horrible murders in Asia, leading four Vietnam veterans to the Far East in search of the killer whose signature is Koko.

Mystery. NAL-Dutton 1990 $19.95. ISBN 0-525-24818-8. About Tom Pasmore, nearly killed in a fire and obsessed with two unsolved murders; also involved is detective Lamont von Helitz, "The Shadow."

•

SHORT STORY COLLECTION BY STRAUB

Houses Without Doors. NAL-Dutton 1991 $5.99. ISBN 0-451-17082-2. Includes "Blue
  Rose," "The Juniper Tree," "A Short Guide to the City," "The Buffalo Hunter," and
  others.

Historical Fiction

Any examination of historical fiction must turn first to the great English
author SIR WALTER SCOTT, who, while he may not have invented the form,
certainly popularized it and according to critic R. Gordon Kelly, "effectively
established a model adhered to by writers for nearly a century afterward." In its
broadest sense, the historical novel is a novel in which the action occurs at an
earlier time. While such a definition may seem to contain too much, the
historical novel is one in which historical persons and events are highlighted,
and the fictitious characters are involved with those persons and events.

Scott's novels were very popular in America, and JAMES FENIMORE COOPER
successfully adapted Scott's model to American history, with *The Spy* (1821)
and *The Pilot* (1823). Another of Cooper's lesser-known historical novels, *The
Wept of Wishton-Wish* (1829), tells of the capture of a white girl during King
Philip's War (1675–76). Although it is not one of Cooper's finest literary efforts,
it is interesting for the view it portrays of relations between English settlers and
Native Americans.

Just as Cooper imitated Scott, so numerous authors hurried to copy Cooper
by using American history as the basis for fiction. Critics may have questioned
whether the young nation had seen enough history of its own to form a basis for
a new genre, but the writers were undaunted. Southern romance novelists,
foremost among them WILLIAM GILMORE SIMMS with books such as *The
Yemassee* (1835), were enthusiastically received by the reading public, who
perhaps wanted to prove to themselves that their new nation did indeed have a
history worth examining. Both *The Yemassee* and Robert Montgomery Bird's
Nick of the Woods (1837) explore relations between white settlers and American
Indians, a theme that continues in popularity to the present; for example, James
Alexander Thom's *From Sea to Shining Sea* (1984) focuses on the Lewis and
Clark expedition, and his *Panther in the Sky* (1989) is about Tecumseh.

Another bestseller in antebellum America was Judge Daniel P. Thompson's
The Green Mountain Boys (1859), which provides a model for novels with
Revolutionary War settings; JOHN JAKES's eight-volume *The Kent Family
Chronicles* is the modern equivalent. Finally, Joseph Holt Ingraham's *The
Prince of the House of David* (1855) gives us the third strand of historical fiction:
religious history, specifically the life of Christ. LEW WALLACE's *Ben-Hur* (1880) is
in this tradition, as is Thomas Costain's *The Silver Chalice* (1953).

The blending of romance with historical fiction proved to be a boon in the
late nineteenth century, as Anthony Hope's *The Prisoner of Zenda* (1894),
F. Marion Crawford's *In the Palace of the King* (1900), and Charles Major's *When
Knighthood Was in Flower* (1898) provided real or imaginary European settings
and plenty of adventure, spiced by romance.

The historical romance continued its popularity into the early twentieth
century. After a brief decline, it regained steam when HERVEY ALLEN published
Anthony Adverse in 1933. Of course, the most famous example from this era—
and perhaps the most well-known of all American historical novels—is
MARGARET MITCHELL's *Gone with the Wind* (1936). War has always been a
favorite topic for novelists, and this richly detailed epic, which also qualifies as a

romance, was a sensation as both novel and film; it continues to capture a worldwide audience, (as well as to be criticized for its pro-Confederacy politics and its patronizing, if not racist, portraits of African Americans).

Historical fiction remains a popular genre. The prolific JAMES MICHENER publishes regularly, and his novels seem sure-fire bets for the bestseller list. Perhaps historical fiction fills a need in people to learn about their own nation's history, as well as the histories of other nations. Given the growing sense of global community and people's increasing awareness of world events, it will not be surprising if the historical novel continues to hold a solid position in popular literature.

CHRONOLOGY OF AUTHORS

Wallace, Lew. 1827?–1905
Allen, Hervey. 1889–1949
Mitchell, Margaret. 1900–1949.
Stone, Irving. 1903–
Michener, James. 1907–

Fast, Howard. 1914–
Wallace, Irving. 1916–1990
Jakes, John. 1932–
Holland, Cecelia. 1943–

ALLEN, HERVEY. 1889–1949

Novelist, poet, and biographer, native Pennsylvanian Allen began writing poetry while a student but did not start writing professionally until after his service in World War I, when he was teaching in South Carolina. His biography *Israfel: The Life and Times of Edgar Allan Poe* was published in 1926. His novel *Anthony Adverse* (1933) is one of the best-selling historical novels of all time, with nearly 3 million copies in print to date. Allen's works of historical fiction are set all over the world and in eras ranging from the eighteenth through the twentieth centuries. "That he was able to keep his novels from becoming merely costume romances attests to Allen's eye for accurate detail and his skill in ordering vast amounts of material in such a way that the reader never ceases to be an interested participant" (Wilton Eckley). In spite of his use of rich details and historical background, Allen's focus is always on the people in his writing. Nor is he interested in examining the neuroses of characters but rather in portraying them in a romantic, colorful, and exciting way that sweeps the reader along.

NOVELS BY ALLEN

Anthony Adverse. 1933. H. Holt & Co. 1991 $37.50. ISBN 0-8050-1731-3. About picaresque hero Anthony Adverse, illegitimate son of Marquise Maria da Umcitata, who travels the globe seeking adventure and fortune, while his travels lead him through a maze of jealousy, greed, lust, and vengeance.

FAST, HOWARD. 1914–

The grandson of Jewish immigrants from the Ukraine, Fast was raised in a poor family, and his politics have always been an important part of his life and work. A fighter for anti-Fascist causes and a one-time member of the Communist party, he was jailed for three months during the 1950s for refusing to testify about his political activity. Blacklisted as a result, he founded his own publishing house, Blue Heron Press, which released his novel *Spartacus* (1951); it was made into a popular film in 1960. Fast's first novel was published in 1933 during the Great Depression, and he has had a solidly successful career ever since. Considered to be one of the world's most widely read writers, his books have been translated into a staggering 82 languages. More than 10 of his novels have been made into films, and *The Immigrants* (1977) was made into a television miniseries in 1979. His novels are page-turners, in which characters struggle with personal, political, and religious questions in their lives. The female characters—a number of his books have female protagonists—are strong, intelligent, and capable people who must fight to maintain their families and their fortunes amidst the tumultuous events of the twentieth century.

Novels by Fast

The Establishment. HM 1979 $11.95. ISBN 0-395-28160-1. Journalist Barbara Lavette's involvement in the McCarthy congressional hearings.

The Immigrants. 1977. Dell 1987 $5.95. ISBN 0-440-14175-3. First in the Lavette family saga, in which Daniel Lavette, son of immigrant parents, grows up in San Francisco, rises to wealth, and loses his fortune.

The Immigrant's Daughter. 1980. Dell 1987 $4.50. ISBN 0-440-13988-0. Last in the Lavette family saga, in which Barbara Lavette runs for Congress and becomes involved in Central American politics.

The Legacy. 1981. Dell 1987 $5.95. ISBN 0-440-14720-4. Continuation of the Lavette family saga: Barbara Lavette in the turbulent 1960s and 1970s, with the women's movement, racial tensions, Nixon years, and the Vietnam war as backdrop.

Second Generation. 1978. Dell 1987 $4.50. ISBN 0-440-17915-7. Second in the Lavette family saga, in which Dan Lavette's daughter becomes a journalist before World War II and falls in love; with Egypt, Paris, and San Francisco as settings.

Book about Fast

Fast, Howard. *Being Red: A Memoir.* Dell 1991 $13.00. ISBN 0-440-50412-0. Fast taking a look at his own life and recounting how his political activities affected his career.

HOLLAND, CECELIA. 1943–

Born in Henderson, Nevada, Cecelia Holland was educated at Pennsylvania State University and Connecticut College, where she received her B.A. degree. While currently a resident of California, she has served as a visiting professor of English at Connecticut College since 1979.

Holland's historical novels have received broad critical acclaim. According to one critic, she "proves that there can be more to historical thrillers than swordplay and seduction." (*Time*) Among her novels are *City of God* (1979), which is set in Rome during the period of the Borgia family. Told from the point of view of Nicolas, a secretary to the Florentine ambassador to Rome, this novel brings to life the period of the Renaissance, including the political intrigue that characterized Rome at the time. Other works include *Until the Sun Falls* (1969), a story of the ancient Mongols and their empire, *The Firedrake* (1966), her first published novel, *Great Maria* (1974), *The Bear Flag* (1990), and *Pacific Street* (1991).

Holland is very adept at capturing the period she writes about, including the clothing, furnishings, and customs of the time. One critic has noted that Holland "is never guilty of the fatuity which plagues most historical fiction: she never nudges the reader into agreeing that folks way back then were really just like you and me, only they bathed less often."

Novels by Holland

The Bear Flag. HM 1990 $19.45. ISBN 0-395-48886-9. A story of frontier California pitting homesteaders and misfits against powerful Spanish landholders.

City of God. 1979. Knopf 1979 o.p.

The Firedrake. 1966. Atheneum 1966 o.p.

Great Maria. 1974. Soho Pr. 1993 $12.00. ISBN 0-939149-84-2

Pacific Street. HM 1991 $21.45. ISBN 0-395-56144-2. Set in San Francisco in the mid-nineteenth-century, an explosive mingling of races and allegiances played out against the violence and adventure of a frontier society.

Until the Sun Falls. 1969. Atheneum 1969 o.p.

Pillar of the Sky. Knopf 1985 $17.95. ISBN 0-394-53538-3

JAKES, JOHN. 1932–

Jakes's first ambition was to be an actor, but writing has turned out to be a better career choice for this prolific historical novelist, whose Kent Family Chronicles have sold almost 40 million copies. Jakes has been writing since the 1950s and has published several novels under the pseudonym Jay Scotland, including *I, Barbarian* (1959), and *Strike the Black Flag* (1961). In the seven generations contained in the Kent Family Chronicles, Jakes gives his readers straightforward, enjoyable, popularized history that gives a sense of being in the place and time, whether it is America during the Revolutionary War, the Civil War, or the Wild West.

NOVELS BY JAKES

The Americans. 1980. Jove Pubns. 1986 $5.50. ISBN 0-515-09133-2. Last in the Kent Family Chronicles, in which a dying Gideon Kent sees his dynasty slipping away as Eleanor falls in love with immigrant Leo Goldman, and Will Kent must put family back on top.

The Furies. 1976. Jove Pubns. 1986 $5.50. ISBN 0-515-09157-X. The fourth Kent Family saga, set during America's westward movement, in which Amanda strives to restore the family's fame and fortune, while Jephtha seeks solace in religion, and Jared searches for gold.

The Rebels. 1975. Jove Pubns. 1983 $4.95. ISBN 0-515-09206-1. Battles in war and in the halls of State as Philip Kent joins the American revolutionary cause as a patriot. Second in the Kent Family saga.

The Titans. 1976. Jove Pubns. 1989 $5.50. ISBN 0-515-09928-7. Fifth Kent Family story, with Louis Kent rapidly ruining the family fortune as the Civil War breaks out, tearing the family apart; Jephtha writing for a Northern newspaper; and his sons fighting for the South.

The Warriors. 1977. Jove Pubns. 1986 $5.50. ISBN 0-515-09209-6. The Kent family trying to reunite during the Gilded Age, as Southerner Jeremiah goes west, while Louis becomes a robber baron. Sixth Kent Family novel.

MICHENER, JAMES. 1907–

Unsure of his birthdate and knowing nothing of his background, Michener was an adopted child raised in Buck's County, Pennsylvania. He attended Swarthmore College on a sports scholarship, receiving his B.A. summa cum laude in 1929, and an M.A. from Colorado State College of Education in 1937. He taught there for three years and published numerous articles on teaching social studies. He was a visiting professor at Harvard University in 1940 and 1941, and then took a job on the editorial staff of the Macmillan Publishing Company in New York City. Although Michener had been raised in the Quaker faith, he joined the navy in 1942 and was posted in the South Pacific. It was there that Michener began collecting material for his first book, *Tales of the South Pacific* (1947), which won a Pulitzer Prize in 1948. It became the basis for the Rodgers and Hammerstein musical *South Pacific* in 1949.

Michener is an immensely prolific writer. His novels are popularizations of history; he thoroughly immerses the reader in the subject through details of history, geography, geology, archeology, anthropology, and many other disciplines. He has covered enormous spans of time and place, from ancient Israel to outer space. Although his characters may at times lack deep development, the situations into which they are placed makes such development seem almost unimportant. Michener's readers have the pleasure of learning about countless subjects as they read competent, enjoyable novels that invite them into exotic places and times. Critic A. Grove Day notes that, "As a scholarly novelist, Michener has won wide popularity without stooping to cheap melodrama. He may best be remembered for his family saga in which men and women intermingle in far-off places."

NOVELS BY MICHENER

Alaska. Random 1988 $22.50. ISBN 0-394-55154-0. A mixture of historical and fictional characters and events about Alaska's settlement from prehistoric times to the present.

The Bridges at Toko-ri. Random 1953 $16.95. ISBN 0-394-41780-1. A Korean War story, in which a naval task force must destroy bridges at Toko-ri.

Caravans. Random 1963 $29.95. ISBN 0-394-41849-2. The story of American embassy official Mark Miller, who in 1946 must find Ellen Jaspar, an American senator's daughter who has disappeared in Afghanistan among the merchant caravans that crisscross the Middle East.

Caribbean: A Novel. Random 1989 $22.95. ISBN 0-394-56561-4. Begins with the pre-Columbian history of native peoples and goes through Columbus's arrival, buccaneer days, sugar plantations, and slave revolts up to the twentieth century and current events.

Centennial. Random 1974 $34.50. ISBN 0-394-47970-X. In which Professor Lewis Vernor researches Centennial, Colorado, as a microcosm of the history of the American West.

Chesapeake. Random 1978 $39.45. ISBN 0-394-50079-2. Maryland's Eastern Shore is the setting for an epic about the settling of the New World, mingling Native Americans, English, Catholics, Quakers, African slaves, and Irish immigrants.

The Fires of Spring. Random 1966 $22.95. ISBN 0-394-42487-5. Autobiographical second novel in which a young boy grows up orphaned in a poor house, wants to be a writer, and after much struggle becomes a success.

Mexico. Random 1992 $25.00. ISBN 0-679-41449-8. Norman Clay, American journalist, in Mexico City investigating his family's past as Mexican history unfolds from A.D. 500 to the present.

The Source. Fawcett 1986 $6.95. ISBN 0-449-21147-9. Archaeology in Israel at center stage of these layered stories of the Holy Land, revealing how families and historical events intertwine.

BOOKS ABOUT MICHENER

Becker, George J. *James Michener*. Continuum 1983 $19.95. ISBN 0-8044-2044-0. Clear, well-developed biography of Michener; good place to begin research.

Day, A. Grove. *James Michener*. Macmillan 1977 $20.95. ISBN 0-8057-7184-0. Excellent sources, biographic and bibliographical material.

MITCHELL, MARGARET. 1900–1949

Atlanta-born Margaret Mitchell published only one book, *Gone with the Wind* (1936), but with that single work she became one of America's best-known authors. *Gone with the Wind* is one of the best-selling books of all time, and it has been translated into 27 languages. The story it tells has become part of American culture: The heroine Scarlett O'Hara and hero Rhett Butler have come to symbolize America's white antebellum South, even to those who feel alienated by Mitchell's proslavery views.

Mitchell's mother Maybelle was a suffragist, and Margaret was raised to be determined and to overcome adversity. Her Catholic upbringing made her different from the other children in their neighborhood. Young Margaret was also a tomboy gifted with an active imagination; she began writing as a teenager. Her first love, Clifford Henry, died of wounds received in World War I, and Mitchell finally married Red Upshaw, whose background made him an unsuitable husband for her in the eyes of many. The marriage lasted only briefly and was annulled. Finally, she married John Marsh and settled into a career with the *Atlanta Journal.*

Mitchell began writing *Gone with the Wind* in 1927, beginning with stories she had heard since childhood about the South before and during the Civil War. She also did intensive historical research and wrote the book in sections, keeping each section in an envelope. The novel was an immediate success, winning a Pulitzer Prize in 1937, and the film rights to the novel were sold to David O. Selznick. The making of the film, released in 1939, has become part of Hollywood legend.

Critics still debate the literary status of *Gone with the Wind.* Is it just a trashy romance? Is it a racist defense of slavery and a demeaning portrayal of African Americans? Or is it a *Bildungsroman*—a novel about the coming to maturity of a young woman who must face dark and desperate times as she struggles to save her family and her home? Whatever one decides, it is certain that millions now and in the future will continue to read this significant novel.

NOVEL BY MITCHELL

Gone with the Wind. 1936. Macmillan 1975 $37.50. ISBN 0-02-585350-3. Scarlett O'Hara's struggle to survive during and after the Civil War. Romance with the scoundrel-hero Rhett Butler gives continuity to this sweeping historical saga.

BOOKS ABOUT MITCHELL

Edwards, Anne. *The Road to Tara: The Life of Margaret Mitchell.* Dell 1991 $5.99. ISBN 0-440-37438-3. An excellent biographer's well-researched account of Mitchell's life and work.

Hanson, Elizabeth I. *Margaret Mitchell.* Twayne 1991 $18.95. ISBN 0-8057-7608-7. Sympathetic treatment of Mitchell that includes both standard biographical information as well as critical discussions of her work.

Pyron, Darden Asbury. *Southern Daughter: The Life of Margaret Mitchell.* OUP 1991 $26.00. ISBN 0-19-505276-5. Well-documented biography that includes much previously unpublished material.

STONE, IRVING. 1903–

One-time instructor of economics, Stone's prolific career also has brought him lectureships at several American universities. The reigning king of the biographical novel form, Stone's first such work, *Lust for Life* (1934), was just the beginning of a long line of well-researched and entertaining books. Stone abandoned his studies in economics and political science, moved to Europe, and began writing plays, essays, and fiction. He supported himself by penning detective stories. His biographical novels bring to life the eras and personalities of the world's great figures, including VINCENT VAN GOGH (see Vol. 3), JACK LONDON, Clarence Darrow, Rachel and Andrew Jackson, Mary Todd and ABRAHAM LINCOLN (see Vol. 3), MICHELANGELO (see Vol. 3), FREUD (see Vols. 3 and 5), and DARWIN (see Vol. 5), to name only some of his many subjects.

NOVELS BY STONE

Adversary in the House. Doubleday 1947 $15.95. ISBN 0-385-04003-2. Life of labor leader Eugene V. Debs, from the early years in Indiana, where he falls in love, through the turmoil of labor strife in late nineteenth- and twentieth-century America.

The Agony and the Ecstasy. Doubleday 1961 $19.95. ISBN 0-385-01092-3. Italian Renaissance genius Michelangelo Buonarotti's life as painter, sculptor, poet, engineer, and architect, tracing his career from his apprenticeship through his greatest achievements.

Lust for Life. 1934. Doubleday 1959 $17.95. ISBN 0-385-04270-1. Tragic life of the Dutch painter Vincent Van Gogh, struggling against the artistic establishment and mental instability to become one of the world's most famous painters.

The Origin. 1980. NAL-Dutton 1987 $5.95. ISBN 0-451-16810-0. Cambridge graduate Charles Darwin and the 1832 voyage that changes his life and the history of world science as he develops his theory of origin of the species.

The Passions of the Mind. NAL-Dutton 1972 $5.95. ISBN 0-451-16307-9. Sigmund Freud's rise as one of the world's most famous psychiatrists, in which he gives up a safe and predictable life as a physician to develop the science of psychoanalysis.

WALLACE, IRVING. 1916–1990

It seems mind-boggling, but Irving Wallace has been estimated to have 1 billion readers worldwide, making him one of the world's all-time best-selling authors. He began writing in 1931 and worked as a screenwriter for a number of Hollywood studios—Columbia, Fox, Warner Brothers, Universal, and MGM. A great deal of research goes into his novels, which cover a wide variety of subjects, from the presentation of the Nobel Prize to political scenarios. His plots are complicated but entertaining; his characters sometimes lead glamorous lives, but just as often they are hard-working professionals, such as lawyers or journalists who find themselves caught up in the social and political turmoil around them. Several of his novels have been made into films, including *The Chapman Report* (1962) and *The Prize* (1963).

NOVELS BY IRVING WALLACE

The Guest of Honor. Delacorte 1989 $18.95. ISBN 0-385-29742-4. U.S. President Matt Underwood's romance with the woman president of an East Asian country, as their enemies and the press work to expose the affair and ruin both presidencies.

The Man. 1964. Ulverscroft 1977 $12.50. ISBN 0-85456-55802. African-American Douglas Dilman's rise to the U.S. presidency, and the story of the great opposition and, finally, impeachment that he faces.

The Miracle. NAL-Dutton 1985 $4.95. ISBN 0-451-15896-2. The story of the Vatican's announcement that the Virgin Mary will return to Lourdes to perform a miracle, featuring an international cast of characters as publicity grows in anticipation of the event.

The Prize. 1961. NAL-Dutton 1969 $4.95. ISBN 0-451-13759-0. The Nobel Prize ceremony as backdrop for international glitz and intrigue, as winners gather in Stockholm from around the world to receive their prizes.

The Second Lady. 1980. NAL-Dutton 1981 $4.95. ISBN 0-451-15745-1. A Cold War story in which Russians create a First Lady impostor to take the place of the real First Lady in order to learn state secrets.

WALLACE, LEW. 1827?–1905

Attorney, soldier, politician, and writer, Lew Wallace fought in both the Mexican and Civil wars, after which he returned to practicing law and then entered politics. He wrote his epic *Ben-Hur* (1880) while serving as territorial governor in New Mexico. A biography of General Benjamin Harrison followed in 1888. Wallace also wrote plays and poetry.

NOVEL BY LEW WALLACE

Ben-Hur. 1880. Barbour & Co. 1985 $7.95. ISBN 0-916441-11-3. The story of Ben Hur who becomes a slave after his enemy Messala ruins his family; Ben-Hur becomes a hero again, as well as a disciple of Jesus, finally building catacombs in Rome to shelter persecuted Christians.

NONFICTION BY LEW WALLACE

An Autobiography. 2 vols. Irvington 1972 repr. of 1906 ed. $48.95. ISBN 0-8422-8121-5. Interesting not only for Wallace's version of his life but also as a look at nineteenth-century American culture.

Science Fiction

Science fiction is perhaps the most difficult to define of all popular genres. Although it is fiction, it often contains (and some would assert *must* contain) the facts of science. But others point out that what is called science fiction may not have much to do with science at all; rather, what is truly at the heart of science fiction is the search for knowledge about humankind's place in, and relationship to, the universe. According to critic Marshall B. Tymn, "The seeds of science fiction were planted thousands of years ago, as the human species dreamed of the great unknown." Another critic, Betty Rosenberg, points out, "Science fiction has been labeled a fiction of questions. What if . . . ? If only . . . ? If this goes on . . . ?" Using these questions as an analytical framework, we may see science fiction developing through history as a literary mode that enables writers to construct an infinite variety of plots and characters in order to explore the larger questions of existence. Or perhaps it is best to put it as critic E. F. Bleiler has done: "Science fiction, to make a truistic statement, is what is accepted as science fiction by readers and writers." Such a definition certainly gives us latitude in tracing the genre's history.

Doing double duty as the progenitor of horror fiction and science fiction is MARY SHELLEY's *Frankenstein* (1818). Its theme—that the advances of science must be handled with care and forethought—is still popular among science fiction writers. EDGAR ALLAN POE's interest in science and pseudoscience also qualifies his work as early science fiction. Rapid industrialization during the nineteenth century brought with it optimism about the possibilities of the future but also warnings about the adverse effects of technological progress. Jules Verne and H. G. WELLS both concerned themselves with new technologies. Critic Tymn notes that, "With Wells, science fiction began to take form and direction, becoming more a medium of ideas than a variety of adventure. . . . He not only showed that fiction can anticipate the power of science to change the world; he also predicted that scientific discoveries would change people's view of their place in the universe." As with science fiction writers who would follow him, Wells used his stories as forums for social commentary, to criticize what he perceived were the growing inequities of the class system; his fiction often had a pessimistic tone.

Although a number of motifs, including interplanetary travel and discoveries of exotic lost people, were developed early in the twentieth century by EDGAR RICE BURROUGHS and others, it was not until the 1920s that Hugo Gernsback (after whom the Hugo Award is named) began regularly to publish and promote what he first called "scientifiction." Beginning in 1926, his pulp magazine *Amazing Stories* was a place where eager young writers could polish their skills. Naturally, equally eager readers turned to *Amazing Stories* to fulfill their desire for what finally came to be called science fiction. John W. Campbell continued the trend in 1937, when he became editor of *Astounding Stories*. "Campbell, a regular contributor to that magazine, recruited writers who could write more realistically about science and scientists and demanded from them greater sophistication of style and technique, and greater rigor of ideas. Writers refined their plots and characters, while emphasizing human relationships, and were encouraged by Campbell to tap psychology, philosophy, politics, and other soft sciences and areas of specialization" (Marshall B. Tymn). The work of such writers as ISAAC ASIMOV, CLIFFORD SIMAK, and ROBERT A. HEINLEIN all appeared in *Astounding Stories*, and the years from 1938 to 1950 are often referred to as the Golden Age of science fiction.

The end of World War II and the disclosure of the Holocaust of course affected all literature; in science fiction, writers turned to closer examination of humankind's use and abuse of technology. Continuing to use the disciplines of social science, authors such as FREDERICK POHL and Cyril Kornbluth with *The Space Merchants* (1953), RAY BRADBURY with *The Martian Chronicles* (1950) and *Fahrenheit 451* (1953), and Arthur C. Clarke with *Childhood's End* (1953) explored in increasing depth the possible futures facing humanity. The New Wave sci-fi authors of the mid-1960s and 1970s—SAMUEL R. DELANEY, Harlan Ellison, JOANNA RUSS, and Thomas M. Disch among them—not only continued to expand on these ideas but also often used new techniques of postmodern fiction, presenting their readers with work that challenged them, not only thematically but also stylistically.

A number of motifs have emerged in science fiction that seem effective in dealing with those "what if" and "if only" questions: space and time travel, the promise and problems of science and technology, and the discovery of other worlds. The critic Russel Nye remarks that, "Beneath the plots lie certain value patterns which seem to hold consistently throughout the spectrum of modern science fiction. They have deep faith in man's ability to improve his world and his future, an almost eighteenth-century, deistic conviction that science means progress, if properly used. . . . There is also in the more thoughtful stories a recognition of the need for human values in a nonhumanistic world, and sometimes, too, a sense of the pathos of human existence." Science fiction is one of the most popular literary genres, and the amount of criticism is extensive. As the world continues to depend more and more on science and technology for survival, it seems inevitable that science fiction will continue to ask questions about humankind's use of those technologies.

CHRONOLOGY OF AUTHORS

Burroughs, Edgar Rice. 1875–1950
Simak, Clifford. 1904–1988
Heinlein, Robert A. 1907–1988
Farmer, Philip Jose. 1918–
Pohl, Frederick. 1919–
Asimov, Isaac. 1920–1992
Bradbury, Ray. 1920–
Herbert, Frank. 1920–1986

Miller, Walter M., Jr. 1923–
Dick, Philip K. 1928–1982
Le Guin, Ursula. 1929–
Anthony, Piers. 1934–
Russ, Joanna. 1937–
Zelazny, Roger. 1937–
Niven, Larry. 1938–
Delaney, Samuel R. 1942–

ANTHONY, PIERS (PIERS ANTHONY JACOB). 1934–

Piers Anthony Jacob Dillingham was born in England but became a U.S. citizen in 1958. He tried being an English teacher, a technical writer, and a freelance writer before he turned to writing novels; his first published book was *Chthon* (1967). According to critics Stephen Buccleugh and Beverly Rush, "In Anthony's best fiction, questions of man's place in the ecology of the natural universe blend with considerations of the individual's role in providing satisfactory and humane answers." Anthony is a careful writer who often plays with language. He likes to make the process of reading fun, so his books are entertaining, but Anthony also focuses on serious themes dealing with the relation of humans to their social and physical environment.

NOVELS BY ANTHONY

Battle Circle. Avon 1978 $4.95. ISBN 0-380-01800-4. Trilogy of *Sos the Rope* (1968), *Var the Stick* (1972), and *Neq the Sword* (1975). Story of the aftermath of a nuclear holocaust, with America as an underground society and nomadic barbarians threatening those who live underground.

God of Tarot. 1979. Ace Bks. 1989 $3.95. ISBN 0-441-29470-7. Brother Paul's struggles with conflicting religious sects after he is sent to Tarot to investigate strange events about the tarot.

Macroscope. 1969. Avon 1976 $4.95. ISBN 0-380-00209-4. The story of macroscope, which makes it possible to see all space and time, so that humans can no longer protect their individual thoughts, and the universe's secrets are revealed.

Omnivore. 1968. Avon 1978 $3.95. ISBN 0-380-00262-0. Cal, Veg, and Aquilar's investigation of a mushroom jungle on planet Nacre, from which they bring back a funguslike being who threatens earth.

Orn. 1970. Avon 1978 $3.95. ISBN 0-380-00266-3. Cal, Veg, and Aquilar's trip back to prehistoric earth to protect the Orn, a bird whose extinction is threatened.

ASIMOV, ISAAC. 1920–1992

Widely regarded as one of the world's finest writers of science fiction, Asimov has written countless science fiction novels, as well as factual science books for adults and juveniles, history books, mysteries, and guides to the Bible and SHAKESPEARE—a truly mind-boggling display of writing. A native of Russia, Asimov came to the United States at the age of 3 and became a citizen in 1928. An early fan of science fiction in magazines, Asimov began writing at the early age of 11 and continued throughout high school.

Asimov coined the word "robotics" and devised the "Three Laws of Robotics": first, a robot may not injure a human being, or, through inaction, allow a human being to come to harm; second, a robot must obey the orders given it by human beings, except in such instances when such orders would conflict with the First Law; third, a robot must protect its own existence as long as such protection does not conflict with the First or Second Laws. Many see these laws, and Asimov's robot characters, as a metaphor for human behavior. Of all Asimov's work, he is perhaps best known for his Foundation series, which began as a group of short stories published in the 1940s and collected in the 1950s. The stories concern themselves with future history in a galactic empire of 25 million worlds—all populated by humans. These books have been extremely influential in the history of science fiction. The critic Stephen H. Goldman notes that, "in aggregate they present a view of sheer galactic magnitude and multiplicity unsurpassed by any science-fiction work yet produced. Asimov did his work so well that later writers simply built on his 'Foundation'." Winner of numerous Hugo and Nebula awards for his achievements in science fiction, Asimov's reputation as one of the geniuses of science fiction is assured. (See Vol. 5 for more on Asimov.)

NOVELS BY ASIMOV

Foundation. 1951. Ballantine 1986 $5.95. ISBN 0-345-33637-5. Began as a series of eight stories in which Galactic Empire, analogous to Rome, falls, and the Seldon plan is proposed to establish two Foundations, one where all human knowledge will be collected, and one a group of psychohistorians.

Foundation and Earth. 1986. Ballantine 1987 $5.95. ISBN 0-345-33996-7. Golan Trevize's continued search for Earth, not satisfied with a comfortable conventional life on Gaia where progress has halted; final novel in the Foundation series.

Foundation's Edge. 1982. Doubleday 1982 $14.95. ISBN 0-385-17725-9. The Seldon Plan five hundred years later: hero Golan Trevize, refusing to believe Earth and Second Foundation were destroyed, searches for Earth but ends up on Gaia, a world colonized by humans.

Foundation and Empire. 1952. Ballantine 1986 $4.95. ISBN 0-345-33628-3. Two-part story in which the Foundation is threatened by a military leader and a mutant, and the threat can be only temporarily halted.

The Gods Themselves. 1973. Bantam 1990 $4.95. ISBN 0-553-28810-5. The discovery of a physically impossible substance which leads to a parallel universe, while the invention of Electron Pump creates an unlimited power source that poses a danger to solar system.

SHORT STORY COLLECTION BY ASIMOV

The Early Asimov. Ballantine 1986 $3.95. ISBN 0-345-32590-7. Contains most early science fiction not in the Foundation or robot series; demonstrates the subjects and themes that Asimov developed in later fiction: how humans react to space travel, difficulties with systems of government, and the use of scientific fact in fiction.

BOOKS ABOUT ASIMOV

Gunn, James. *Isaac Asimov: The Foundation of Science Fiction.* OUP 1982 $4.95. ISBN 0-19-503059-1. Examines Asimov as a science-fiction pioneer who created many common motifs and themes of the genre.

Miller, Marjorie M. *Isaac Asimov: A Checklist of Works Published in the United States, March 1939–May 1972.* Bks. Demand $29.70. ISBN 0-8357-5575-4. Indispensable for those doing research on Asimov.

Touponce, William F. *Isaac Asimov. Twayne's U.S. Authors Ser.* Macmillan 1991 $19.95. ISBN 0-8057-7623-0. A good introduction to Asimov's work. Briefly examines Asimov's life, major phases, and works; with a critical summary and selected bibliography.

BRADBURY, RAY. 1920–

More than 500 stories, poems, essays, plays, television screenplays, and motion picture screenplays have been produced by the prolific Bradbury, who began writing before the age of 15. His first professional story was published in 1941, and his reputation grew throughout the 1940s. Bradbury's work appeared frequently in *Weird Tales,* but he also broke into the slick magazine market, publishing in *The New Yorker, Harpers,* and *Mademoiselle.* His work has been included in collections of *The Best American Short Stories.* Television scripts for "Alfred Hitchcock Presents," "Steve Canyon," and "The Twilight Zone" also occupied Bradbury, as did writing the screenplay for the film version of *Moby Dick* (1956).

In his best writing, Bradbury is concerned with themes of alienation from oneself and from the community at large. He also seems to have a preoccupation with death and decay, and the importance of considering the dangers and consequences of technology. In his stories about space, Bradbury has created his own version of a frontier thesis. Critic Willis McNelly says that "It is almost as though Bradbury were appealing to some Jungian collective unconscious in all of us, recalling the dim ancestral memories of how we feared by land the saber-toothed tiger and eventually conquered it, and looking ahead at how we will fear but face the expanses of space and eventually conquer its vastness." Although critics disagree about Bradbury's importance to the genre, he certainly has added a number of unforgettable books to the canon, and his millions of loyal fans regard him as one of the best science fiction writers that America has produced.

NOVELS BY BRADBURY

Fahrenheit 451. 1953. Ballantine 1987 $3.95. ISBN 0-345-34296-8. About a world in which books have been outlawed and are regularly burned, and a group has formed to remember and recreate the books.

The Martian Chronicles. 1950. Bantam 1980 $3.95. ISBN 0-553-27822-3. Originally a collection of short stories, now unified in a novel, in which Earthlings colonize the frontier on Mars and transport American values and culture to outer space.

Something Wicked This Way Comes. 1962. Bantam 1983 $4.50. ISBN 0-553-28032-5. Carnival acts and sideshows as the opportunity for metamorphoses in this story of a carnival that is evil incarnate.

SHORT STORY COLLECTIONS BY BRADBURY

The Golden Apples of the Sun. 1971 Greenwood repr. of 1953 ed. $37.50. ISBN 0-8371-5160-0. Contains "The Foghorn" and "A Sound of Thunder," two of Bradbury's finest stories.

The Illustrated Man. 1951. Bantam 1983 $4.50. ISBN 0-553-27449-X. Tattooed illustrations on man's body inspire stories, including "The Veldt," "The Exiles," "The Highway," "The City," and "Kaleidoscope."

BOOKS ABOUT BRADBURY

Albright Donn. *Bradbury Bits and Pieces: The Ray Bradbury Bibliography, 1974–88.* Starmont Hse. $25.95. ISBN 1-55742-151-X. Information on Bradbury's later publications.

Mogen, David. *Ray Bradbury. Twayne's U.S. Authors Ser.* Macmillan 1986 $19.95. ISBN 0-8057-7464-5. The life and work of Bradbury, including poetry, films, dramas, and detective fiction; an excellent critical survey of his work and career.

BURROUGHS, EDGAR RICE. 1875–1950

An enormously varied background may have helped prepare Burroughs to become a writer. He was a railroad police officer, a member of the Seventh Cavalry, the owner of a stationery store, the mayor of Malibu Beach, California, in 1933, and a war correspondent for United Press in the Pacific during World War II. But when Burroughs needed financial security, he began to write, and his character Tarzan, Lord of the Apes is enshrined in American popular culture. The novel *Tarzan of the Apes* (1914) has sold 25 million copies and by 1946 had been translated into 56 languages. Although Burroughs cannot be considered strictly a science fiction writer, he did write many novels about space travel. Burroughs's work is often rather too fanciful, especially for today's more sophisticated audiences, yet his work still has its attractions, for it is often exciting and rapidly captures the reader's imagination.

Novels by Burroughs

The Gods of Mars. 1913. P. Hunt 1975 $35.00. ISBN 0-940724-03-0. In which John Carter tries, but fails, to recapture his wife on Mars.

A Princess of Mars. 1917. Carroll & Graf 1985 $2.95. ISBN 0-88184-462-4. Revision of an earlier novel, *Under the Moons of Mars* (1912), in which Virginian John Carter is mysteriously taken to Mars, where after many battles, he wins princess Dejah Thoris only to lose her at the end of the book.

Tarzan of the Apes. 1914. Ballantine 1984 $3.95. ISBN 0-345-31977-X. The story of Lord Greystoke, raised by apes in Africa, showing his natural nobility as he deals with his jungle environment.

The Warlord of Mars. 1914. Buccaneer Bks. 1976 repr. of 1919 ed. $18.95. ISBN 0-89966-045-2. John Carter's continued quest to find his wife, in which he finally wins the title "Warlord of Mars."

Books about Burroughs

Holtsmark, Erling B. *Edgar Rice Burroughs. Twayne's U.S. Authors Ser.* Macmillan 1986 $19.95. ISBN 0-8057-7459-9. Examines closely Burroughs's major work, offering a succinct introduction to this early science fiction writer.

————. *Tarzan and Tradition: Classical Myth in Popular Literature.* Greenwood 1981 $39.95. ISBN 0-313-22530-3. Interesting study of the role of classical myth in the Tarzan character and how it is part of popular culture.

DELANEY, SAMUEL R. 1942–

Part of the "New Wave" of science fiction writers that includes JOANNA RUSS and URSULA LE GUIN, Delaney began writing while in junior high school. His first novel, *The Jewels of Aptor* (1962), demonstrated that he was a new talent to be reckoned with. People's relationship to culture, particularly to art, is a main theme of Delaney's. According to critic Peter S. Alterman, "His are stories in which the creative experience of the reader is as important as the narrative. They invite, wheedle, and bully the reader into confronting the process of his reading and thereby participating in both the creation and the experience of the story." As a critic and writer, Delaney has helped bring a postmodern consciousness to science fiction. Along with such writers as Octavia Butler, he is also part of a "New Wave" of African American science fiction writers.

Novels by Delaney

Dhalgren. 1975. Bantam 1983 $4.95. ISBN 0-553-25391-3. Story of an amnesiac who finds himself in Bellona, which is near collapse; a self-reflexive narrative forces the reader to constantly shift and engage with the text.

Nova. 1968. Bantam 1983 $4.50. ISBN 0-553-23621-0. Story of a band led by Lorq Von Ray that battles enemies while searching for Illyrian, an energy source.

DICK, PHILIP K. 1928–1982

"What is reality?" is one of the main themes of author Philip K. Dick's work. Dick sold his first short story in 1952, and, although he is not as prolific as some writers, his novels have had an important impact on the genre. Dick did not believe that the world could or should be viewed rationally. In his novels the world often seems an illusion, and his characters must struggle to remain human while trying to cope with the increasing desolation of their planets. His novel *Do Androids Dream of Electric Sheep?* (1968) was made into the movie *Blade Runner* (1982). Although his work has been criticized as being uneven, Dick was, according to critic Brian M. Stableford, "a novelist of considerable power. He has done more than anyone else to open up metaphysical questions to science fiction analysis. His sympathy for the plight of his characters lends his work a human dimension that is too often lacking in works whose primary interest is metaphysics, and it is his most valuable asset."

NOVELS BY DICK

Blade Runner (Do Androids Dream of Electric Sheep?). 1968. Ballantine 1987 $4.95. ISBN 0-345-35047-2. Tale of androids in which caring for humans is the only quality by which one can distinguish them, and Rick Deckard has to find escaped androids.

Eye in the Sky. 1957. Macmillan 1989 $4.50. ISBN 0-02-031590-2. Story of eight people who find themselves trapped in another dimension, created and recreated by the mental world of each.

The Man in the High Castle. 1962. Berkley Pub. 1984 $2.95. ISBN 0-679-74067-8. Allied loss in World War II leading to the Axis division of America into German and Japanese zones, while the discovery of a science-fiction novel that suggests America might have won the war precipitates action.

BOOK ABOUT DICK

Mackey, Douglas A. *Philip K. Dick. Twayne's U.S. Authors Ser.* Macmillan 1988 $21.95. ISBN 0-8057-7515-3. A scholarly examination of Dick's novels, his life, and his influence on the genre.

FARMER, PHILIP JOSE. 1918–

One of the most startling innovations in the genre of science fiction came with the publication of Farmer's story "The Lovers" in 1952, in which a human has sex with an alien. His Riverworld series began in 1952 as well, but a string of misfortunes eventually forced him to take jobs as a manual laborer. He did technical writing from 1956 to 1970, but continued writing science fiction, increasingly winning a name for himself. Success has finally come with the Riverworld series, in which the characters—many famous historical people— are in search of the headwaters of the River. Farmer is known as a writer who breaks taboos, making fun of the solemn and sacred. As critic Roald D. Tweet notes, "He is also a mocker of traditions, an upsetter of the conventions that come to surround every culture, a court jester whose antics turn society topsy-turvy—not to destroy that society but to examine it and keep it healthy."

NOVELS BY FARMER

The Dark Design. 1977. Berkley Pub. 1984 $3.50. ISBN 0-425-08678-X. Riverworld series: Samuel Clemens again builds a riverboat and goes in search of the Dark Tower to get revenge on King John.

The Fabulous Riverboat. 1971. Berkley Pub. 1985 $3.50. ISBN 0-425-09958-X. Riverworld series: A reincarnated Samuel Clemens builds a riverboat to challenge the river, but England's King John steals it.

The Lovers. 1961. Ballantine 1980 $2.25. ISBN 0-345-28691-X. Expansion of a short story in which Hal Yarrow seeks escape from totalitarian earth, finds love and full sexual expression, and finally tragedy, with alien Jeannette.

The Magic Labyrinth. 1980. Berkley Pub. 1984 $3.50. ISBN 0-425-09550-9. Riverworld series: in which the remaining humans begin to die, the Dark Tower is finally located, and the ethicals who control the planet are defeated for the moment.

HEINLEIN, ROBERT A. 1907–1988

Heinlein was a good student who attended the U.S. Naval Academy and finished at the top of his class. His first publication of a science fiction story was in 1939, and he is considered by many to be one of the most innovative among the early group of science fiction writers. Heinlein's innovation was to publish

stories in which seemingly outrageous or improbable things like space travel
were made to seem plausible, even normal. He accomplished this by peopling
his books with characters who were quite normal in most ways, but who had the
capacity to adapt to the new, exciting challenges of the high-tech future.
Stranger in a Strange Land (1961) was the first of his novels to appear on
bestseller lists; it was a great success and continues to enchant each new
generation of science fiction fans. Critical acclaim has been elusive for
Heinlein, however. His work has always been controversial, and he is both one
of the most loved and the most disliked of science fiction writers. The reasons
for this dichotomy may lie in Heinlein's using his stories as teaching tools. His
themes often focus on such controversial issues as racism, gender roles, sexual
mores and values, and control by governments—and the stance that Heinlein
takes on these issues is definitely not welcomed by some. Peter Nicholls
maintains that "Although Heinlein is regarded as one of the most 'scientific' of
science fiction writers, as a 'nuts-and-bolts' man, the emotional center of his
work has always been the political and social nature of man [sic], and the
cultures he builds and lives in." Thus Heinlein's work, while troubling to some,
both entertains readers and makes them think more deeply about the
importance of the ideas he so elegantly creates.

NOVELS BY HEINLEIN

Beyond this Horizon. NAL-Dutton 1960 $3.95. ISBN 0-451-16676-0. About a government-
controlled breeding program that eliminates many negative human characteristics
and increases intelligence; explores the question of one's reason for living to old age
after the causes of death have been removed.

I Will Fear No Evil. 1970. Berkley Pub. 1986 $4.95. ISBN 0-425-09554-1. A story of gender
roles and sexual assumptions as the brain of a dying man is transplanted into a
woman.

Rocket Ship Galileo. 1947. Ballantine 1986 $3.95. ISBN 0-345-33660-7. Juvenile novel in
which teenagers travel to the moon and learn through experience that reason, not
emotion, will best serve them.

Space Cadet. Ballantine 1987 $4.95. ISBN 0-345-35311-0. Venus as the setting for a story
about the irrationality of racism in which a cadet learns how to accept the life forms
on the planet Venus.

Stranger in a Strange Land. 1961. Ace Bks. 1987 $5.99. ISBN 0-441-79034-8. The story of
Valentine Michael Smith, born on Mars of human parents, precipitating major
changes in Earth culture, particularly in sexual values.

Time Enough for Love. 1973. Berkley Pub. 1986 $4.95. ISBN 0-425-10224-6. About the
nearly immortal Lazarus Long's series of sexual liaisons that raise questions about
contemporary American sexual mores.

BOOKS ABOUT HEINLEIN

Beason, Gordon, Jr. *Robert Anson Heinlein.* Borgo Pr. 1990 $25.00. ISBN 0-8095-4741-1.
Well-written, careful study of Heinlein's life and work. Considers his impact on the
genre and his critical reception.

Franklin, H. Bruce. *Robert A. Heinlein: America as Science Fiction.* OUP 1980 $7.95.
ISBN 0-19-502747-7. Discusses Heinlein's use of American cultural conventions and
the ways that he comments on American culture through his work.

HERBERT, FRANK. 1920–1986

Frank Herbert worked originally as a journalist, but then turned to science
fiction. His Dune series has had a major impact on that genre. Some critics
assert that Herbert is responsible for bringing in a new branch of ecological
science fiction. Herbert had a personal interest in world ecology, and consulted

with the governments of Vietnam and Pakistan about ecological issues. The length of some of his novels also helped make it acceptable for science fiction authors to write longer books. It is clear that, if the reader is engaged by the story—and Herbert certainly has the ability to engage his readers—length is not important. As is usually the case with popular fiction, it comes down to whether or not the reader is entertained, and Herbert is, above all, an entertaining and often compelling writer. His greatest talent is his ability to create new worlds that are plausible to readers, in spite of their alien nature, such as the planet Arrakis in the Dune series.

NOVELS BY HERBERT

Children of Dune. 1976. Ace Bks. 1987 $4.95. ISBN 0-441-10402-9. The story of Paul Muad' Dib's children, Leto and Ghanima, who are born knowing the past and future and must overcome political intrigues; Leto ascends the throne to establish the Golden Path knowing it, too, will eventually fall.

Dune. 1965. Ace Bks. 1990 $5.99. ISBN 0-441-17271-7. The desert planet Dune as the setting for the struggles of Paul Atreides and his mother Jessica to free Arrakis from the evil Harkonnens; giant sandworms make fascinating monsters.

Dune Messiah. 1969. Ace Bks. 1987 $5.99. ISBN 0-441-17269-5. In which Paul Atreides has become imperial leader Muad' Dib, despite the increasing corruption of people; the struggle to tame the desert planet Dune is central to the plot.

God Emperor of Dune. Ace Bks. 1987 $4.95. ISBN 0-441-29467-7. With no characters remaining from previous Dune novels, the planet is excavated by archeologists; with the message that nothing lasts forever in spite of human machinations.

BOOKS ABOUT HERBERT

Benson, Gordon, Jr. *Frank Herbert.* Borgo Pr. 1990 $18.00. ISBN 0-8095-4734-1. A leading science-fiction critic's look at Herbert's life and work.

Levack, Daniel J. *Dune Master: A Frank Herbert Bibliography.* Greenwood 1988 $49.95. ISBN 0-313-27679-X. Invaluable for anyone interested in serious study of Herbert's work.

Touponce, William F. *Frank Herbert. Twayne's U.S. Authors Ser.* Macmillan 1988 $19.95. ISBN 0-8057-75145. A careful study of the impact of Herbert's work on the genre.

LE GUIN, URSULA. 1929–

Born and raised in Berkeley, California, Ursula Le Guin began writing after first establishing her family. Her unique blend of fantasy, science fiction, and social commentary give her stories the unmistakable flavor of intelligent, imaginative, poetic writing. Although her tales may be set in outer space or distant times, they almost always reflect the problems of contemporary Earth. The plots emphasize personal relationships and human problems, and the themes suggest that the solutions to these problems will come through integration—the bringing together of things that are normally thought of as separate. Le Guin's works also explore social and political concerns. She questions, for instance, whether fear and insecurity will undermine democracies and lead to dictatorship. She constantly calls attention to the creative power of language—the ability of words not only to describe reality but also to create or modify it. Le Guin is also very concerned with the concept of balance—the need for opposing forces to be brought into equilibrium with each other. But, above all, as she noted in her acceptance speech for the National Book Award for *The Farthest Shore* (1972), she believes that the work of the fantasist is to talk "about human life as it is lived, and as it might be lived, and as it ought to be lived."

NOVELS BY LE GUIN

Always Coming Home. 1985. Bantam 1987 $4.95. ISBN 0-553-26280-7. The history, adventures, customs, language, and art of the Kesh, an imaginary, ancient people discovered on the Pacific Coast.

The Dispossessed. 1974. Avon 1976 $3.95. ISBN 0-380-00382-1. A fantasy set on an anarchist moon colony and its capitalist mother planet.

The Farthest Shore. 1972. Bantam 1984 $3.50. ISBN 0-553-26847-3. Third book in the Earthsea trilogy; an aging leader sets off with a young prince to discover whether magic still remains in the land.

The Left Hand of Darkness. 1969. Ace Bks. 1983 $3.95. ISBN 0-441-47812-3. Story of a planet populated by "androgynes," beings who periodically change from male to female.

The Tombs of Atuan. 1971. Bantam 1984 $3.95. ISBN 0-553-27331-0. Second book in the Earthsea trilogy; Ged becomes the archmage (head magician) of the archipelago, and Arha gives up everything to become a high priestess.

Very Far Away from Anywhere Else. 1976. Bantam 1982 $2.50. ISBN 0-553-25376-4. Story of a gifted, but lonely, high school boy who meets an equally gifted young woman.

A Wizard of Earthsea. 1968. Bantam 1984 $3.95. ISBN 0-553-26250-5. Ged, the boy wizard, brings forth from the shadow a beast that wants to destroy his soul.

SHORT STORY COLLECTIONS BY LE GUIN

Buffalo Gals and Other Animal Presences. 1987. Bantam 1987 $7.95. ISBN 0-452-26480-4. Collection of stories that presents our planet through the eyes of animals.

Orsinian Tales. 1976. HarpC 1987 $6.95. ISBN 0-06-091433-5. Tales of an alternate universe.

BOOKS ABOUT LE GUIN

Bloom, Harold, ed. *Ursula K. Le Guin.* Chelsea Hse. 1986 $27.50. ISBN 0-87754-659-2. A collection of modern critical essays encompassing a wide range of perspectives on Le Guin's work.

Spivak, Charlotte. *Ursula K. Le Guin.* G. K. Hall 1984 $7.95. ISBN 0-8057-7430-0. A general introduction to Le Guin's life and work, with extensive discussion of how the two relate; includes a one-chapter biography, chronology, and bibliography.

MILLER, WALTER M., JR. 1923–

Miller's participation in the bombing of Casino, Italy, during World War II apparently had a lasting impact on the writer, for his only novel, *A Canticle for Leibowitz* (1960), is rife with images of massive destruction caused by war. Miller began writing short stories in 1950 while recovering from an automobile accident, and most of his writing was done between 1950 and 1960. Often regarded as one of the best science fiction novels ever written, *A Canticle for Leibowitz* is a complex, beautifully written book that traces human history from a twentieth-century nuclear war forward to another war in A.D. 3781. It stands as one of the best examples of the fear that millions of people have of the power of nuclear weapons and the aftermath of nuclear holocaust. Richly symbolic and multilayered, the novel lends itself to critical commentary more than do most popular works of literature. Critic John B. Ower remarks that, perhaps because of his conversion to Catholicism, "Miller's religious belief is complex and comprehensive enough to contain within itself the dark misgivings, the ironies, and the ambiguities of our deeply disturbed century."

NOVEL BY MILLER

A Canticle for Leibowitz. 1960. Bantam 1984 $4.95. ISBN 0-553-27381-7. The story of Isaac Edward Leibowitz, survivor of a nuclear holocaust, who founds a monastery;

different sections of the novel go through the development of earth up to another war.

NIVEN, LARRY. 1938–

An interest in mathematics and technology—Niven received his B.A. in mathematics in 1962—has given Niven a background that has proved useful in his career as a writer of science fiction. During his first year of writing, all he received were rejection slips, but his first novel, *World of Ptavvs* (1966), was a success and launched his career. Niven has won five Hugos and one Nebula award—testimony that his colleagues in the science fiction world respect his work. Perhaps Niven's most well-known creation is Ringworld, a distant planet that may be taken as a metaphor for Earth, as it was once great but has since fallen into decay.

NOVELS BY NIVEN

Ringworld. 1970. Ballantine 1985 $5.95. ISBN 0-345-33392-6. About a team of explorers—two humans and two aliens—who, after crashlanding on Ringworld, try to discover why the once-great civilization has fallen into decadence.

The Ringworld Engineers. 1979. Ballantine 1985 $4.95. ISBN 0-345-33430-2. Sequel to *Ringworld*, in which an engineer discovers that the orbit of the ring is becoming unstable and must try to correct the problem.

World of Ptavvs. 1966. Ballantine 1986 $3.95. ISBN 0-345-34508-0. Story of a human, who, after a memory transfer, thinks he is an alien planning to enslave all of earth; he recovers but vows to travel to alien worlds to facilitate interplanetary communication.

POHL, FREDERICK. 1919–

Pohl has had a lifelong interest in science fiction, first as a fan, then as a writer, editor, and agent. His work for an advertising firm showed him how easily people can be manipulated, which is a major theme in his science fiction. For Pohl, advertising is dangerous; he believes that it rots people's minds and turns them into unthinking automatons. He has won several Hugo and Nebula awards for his writing and editing; as an editor, Pohl has been a major influence on the development of science fiction.

NOVELS BY POHL

Gateway. Ballantine 1977 $4.95. ISBN 0-345-34690-4. Adventures of a lottery winner who leaves earth for Gateway; told in flashbacks during his psychiatric therapy as he tries to face what he has done.

The Space Merchants. (Collaboration with C. M. Kornbluth.) 1953. St. Martin 1987 $3.50. ISBN 0-312-90655-2. The story of Hero, an ad man, who gradually becomes aware of the damage he has done through advertising and decides to help the world instead of hurting it.

BOOK ABOUT POHL

Pohl, Frederick. *The Way the Future Was: A Memoir.* 1978. Ballantine 1979 $1.95. ISBN 0-345-26059-7. Personal anecdotes about this influential writer and editor; an entertaining autobiography in lively style.

RUSS, JOANNA. 1937–

A lifelong interest in science led to Russ's winning the Westinghouse Science Talent Search in 1953, her senior year of high school. Russ also has an MFA in playwriting from the Yale Drama School, and she is a professor of English at the University of Washington. Thus, she blends her many interests to create some of the most intriguing science fiction being written in a field that is still dominated by male authors. Russ finds in the science fiction genre the freedom to explore strong, active, successful female characters in ways that other, more conventional forms of fiction may not allow. Her essay, "What Can a Heroine Do? Or Why Women Can't Write" (1972) explains her theory that fiction too often must take as its basis myths that give men power while they subordinate women. Her dedication to the craft of writing, combined with a strong commitment to feminism, identifies her with such writers as Octavia Butler, URSULA LE GUIN, and a growing number of women science fiction and fantasy writers.

NOVELS BY RUSS

The Female Man. 1975. Beacon Pr. 1987 $8.95. ISBN 0-8070-6313-4. Four different female voices used to narrate, thus exploring gender relations in four parallel worlds, showing the connections between women even across worlds.

We Who Are About To. . . Dell 1977 $1.50. ISBN 0-440-19428-8. Shipwrecked space travelers' efforts to survive on an uncharted planet, with a female protagonist who resists the group's insistence on survival and kills them, then devotes her remaining time to learning how to die.

SHORT STORY COLLECTION BY RUSS

The Adventures of Alyx. 1976. Baen Bks. 1986 $2.95. ISBN 0-671-65601-5. Short stories and a novella about heroine Alyx, an ancient Greek whose disillusion with religion causes her to seek adventure.

SIMAK, CLIFFORD. 1904–1988

Simak's distinguished career as a science fiction writer spanned 50 years; he has been called the dean of science fiction writers. His first story, "The World of the Red Sun," was published in 1931, in the early years of the development of the genre. Simak studied journalism and worked as a reporter, but his main love was always science fiction. He often used, in fantasy form, his own boyhood Wisconsin landscape. The critic Thomas D. Clareson notes that, "Simak seems to have realized that, aesthetically, the use of the village-rural midwestern setting not only ties his work to the main body of American fiction but also helps his reader to make the necessary transition from a familiar, everyday world to the unknown world or worlds of science fiction."

NOVELS BY SIMAK

The Visitors. 1980. Ballantine 1988 $2.95. ISBN 0-345-00761-1. About the havoc caused by the landing of aliens near a small Minnesota town.

Way Station. Bentley 1980 repr. of 1963 ed. $14.00. ISBN 0-8376-0440-0. The story of Enoch Wallace, 124 years old, who uses his Wisconsin farm as a stop for galactic travelers; his task is to prove humans are worthy to join an intergalactic brotherhood.

SHORT STORY COLLECTION BY SIMAK

City. 1952. Macmillan 1991 $4.95. ISBN 0-02-02539-5. Eight related stories, including the title tale in which survivors of future earth hide among ruins of great cities; includes "Huddling Place," about an agoraphobic who cannot bring himself to help the friend who could save humankind.

ZELAZNY, ROGER. 1937–

After receiving his B.A. from Case Western Reserve University and his M.A. from Columbia University, Zelazny began publishing science fiction stories in 1962. His reputation has gone through ups and downs, but he was given a

Nebula award in 1966 for *And Call Me Coward* (1965), in a tie with *Dune* by FRANK HERBERT. A prolific writer, Zelazny's works focus on the relationship between illusion and reality. He always pays close attention to his craft, and his stories are intelligent, occasionally sentimental, often romantic and, to his many fans, very satisfying.

NOVELS BY ZELAZNY

The Dream Master. 1966. S&S Trade 1990 $3.50. ISBN 0-671-69874-5. Story of psychiatrist Charles Render, who tries to restore sight to the woman he loves; his failure causes him to go insane as he is trapped in her delusional world.

Immortal. 1966. Baen Bks. 1989 $3.95. ISBN 0-671-69848-6. In which post-nuclear holocaust Earth's used by Vegans as resort, while an immortal and former rebel leader must save a Vegan from assassins.

SHORT STORY COLLECTION BY ZELAZNY

Four for Tomorrow. 1967. PB 1991 $3.95. ISBN 0-671-72051-1. Contains "A Rose for Ecclesiastes," in which a Martian poet helps revive life on Mars, and "The Doors of His Face, the Lamps of His Mouth," a 1966 Nebula winner.

Name Index

In addition to authors of books, this index includes the names of persons mentioned in introductory essays, section introductions, biographical profiles, general bibliographic entries, and "Books about" sections. Throughout, however, persons mentioned only in passing—to indicate friendships, relationships, and so on—are generally not indexed. Editors, translators, and compilers are not indexed unless there is no specific author given for the work in question. Writers of the introductions, forewords, afterwords, and similar parts of works are not indexed. The names of individuals who are represented by separate biographical profiles appear in boldface, as do the page numbers on which their profiles appear.

Miller, Stuart W., 93
Miller, Victor C., 633
Miller, Walter M., Jr., 1260
Millett, Bella, 147
Millgate, Jane, 300
Millgate, Michael, 363, 837
Millichap, Joseph R, 886
Mills, David, 159
Mills, Hilary, 1012
Mills, Howard W., 297
Mills, Maldwyn, 147
Mills, Sara, 325
**Milne, A(lan) A(lexander),
587**, 588
Milne, Gordon, 919
Milton, John, 57, 162, 164,
166, 188, **190**, 243, 251,
267, 277, 311, 324, 644,
775, 1137, 1214
Milton, Mary Lee, 288
Milward, Peter, 219
Mims, Edwin, 772
Miner, Earl, 242
Minnis, A. J., 152
Minter, David, 837
Mintz, Alan, 354
Miola, Robert S., 213, 219
Miriam Joseph, Sister, 217
Mitchell, Edwin Valentine,
32
Mitchell, Lee C., 723, 743,
805
Mitchell, Margaret, 982,
1220, 1244, **1248**
Mitchell, Sally, 312
Mitchell, Susan L., 381
Mitchell, W.J.T., 1129
Miura, Akira, 100
Miura, Kerstin Tini, 25
Mizener, Arthur, 476, 841
Mobley, Marilyn S., 770
Moddelmog, Debra, 464
Modleski, Tania, 618, 1169
Moers, Ellen, 699
Moffat, Mary J., 130
Moffett, Judith, 1015
Mogen, David, 715, 1255
Moglen, Helen, 259
Moi, Toril, 926, 1132
Mole, John, 418
Moler, Kenneth L., 276
Molesworth, Charles F., 864,
913, 944, 1052
Molière, 254, 263, 1066
Momaday, N. Scott, 704,
1016
Monaco, James, 1157
Monaghan, David, 276
Monod, Sylvère, 350
Monroe, Marilyn, 1103
Monsman, Gerald, 296, 387
Montagnes, Ian, 47

**Montagu, Lady Mary Wort-
ley, 250**
Montague, John, 418
Montaigne, Michel Eyquem
de, 677, 922
Montale, Eugenio, 1066
Monteiro, George, 842
Montgomery, Guy, 242
Moody, Marily, 108
Moody, Richard, 1072, 1075
**Moody, William Vaughn,
775**
Mookerjee, R. N., 880
Moon, Eric, 57
Moon, Michael, 708
Mooney, Harry J., Jr., 870
Mooney, James E., 68
Moorcock, Michael, 615
Moore, Clement, 1194
Moore, Don, 201
Moore, Emerson, Marianne,
934
Moore, George, 380
Moore, Harry T., 510
Moore, Honor, 1078
Moore, Jack B., 630
Moore, John Hammond, 45
Moore, John R., 660, 728
Moore, Marianne, 560, 745,
863
Moore, Michael, 196
Moore, Rayburn S., 790
Moore, Raylyn, 1200
Moore, Steven, 978, 978
Moore-Gilbert, B. J., 372
Moorman, Frederick, 182
Moorman, Mary, 307
Morace, Robert A., 448, 515,
979
Moraga, Cherie, 1184
Moramarco, Fred, 799
Moran, James, 9
Moran, Mary Hurley, 468
Morante, Pedro Díaz, 18
Mordden, Ethan, 1075
More, Sir Thomas, 166,
193, 445
Morehead, Joe, 108
Morehead, Philip D., 94
Moreland, Richard C., 837
Morgan, Arthur E., 734
Morgan, Janet P., 606
Morgan, Richard G., 1028
Morgan, Ted, 521
Morison, Samuel E., 631
Morison, Stanley, 9, 18, 63
Morley, Christopher, 33
Morley, Sheridan, 465
Morpurgo, J. E., 42
Morrell, David, 943
Morrell, Jack, 312
Morris, Adelaide K., 888
Morris, Brian, 201

Morris, David B., 252
Morris, Gregory L., 979
Morris, Jan, 312
Morris, Mary, 92, 96
Morris, Robert K., 1057
Morris, Wesley, 837
Morris, William, 10, 92, 96,
309, 314, 367, **382**, 397,
570, 591, 611, **617**
Morris, Willie, 837
Morris, Wright, 1016
Morrison, Blake, 415
Morrison, Samuel Eliot, 629
Morrison, Toni, 849, 916,
1018
Morriss, Margaret, 563
Morrow, Bradford, 514, 599,
618
Morrow, Patrick D., 756
Morsberger, Robert E., 891
Mortimer, John, 481
Morton, J. B., 443
Moseley, E. M., 167
Moser, Barry, 801
Moser, Thomas, 476
Moses, Montrose, 1075, 1078
Mosher, Frederic J., 77
Mosimann, Elizabeth A., 22
Moss, Leonard, 863, 1104
Moss, Norman, 91
Moss, Robert F., 372
Mossberg, Barbara, 748
Mossell, N. F., 725
Motion, Andrew, 508
Mott, Frank Luther, 51, 715
Mottram, Eric, 958
Mottram, Ron, 1111
Mouffe, Chantal, 1132
Moulton, Charles A., 134
Moulton, Charles W., 430
Mowat, Barbara A., 211
Mowery, J. Franklin, 22
Moxon, Joseph, 10
Moynahan, Julian, 510
Mozart, Wolfgang Amadeus,
543
Mudrick, Marvin, 276
Mueller, Janet M., 167
Muendel, Renate, 379
Muggeridge, Malcolm, 342
Muhammad, 679
Muir, Edwin, 521, 812
Muir, Frank, 809
Muir, Kenneth, 201, 205,
213, 215, 218, 219, 222
Muir, Percy, 7, 579
Muir, P. H., 33
Mukherjee, Arun, 805, 830
Mulder, Rodney, 1217
Mullaly, Edward J., 858
Mullaney, Stephen, 209
Mullen, Edward J., 849
Muller, Robert H., 72

Title Index

Titles of all books discussed in *The Reader's Adviser* are indexed here, except broad generic titles such as "Complete Works," "Selections," "Poems," "Correspondence." Also omitted is any title written by a profiled author that also includes that author's full name or last name as part of the title, such as *Complete Works of Ralph Waldo Emerson*. The only exception to this is Shakespeare (Volume 1), where *all* works by and about him are indexed. To locate all titles by and about a profiled author, the user should refer to the Name Index for the author's primary listing (given in boldface). In general, subtitles are omitted unless two or more works have the same main title, or the main title consists of an author's full or last name (e.g., *Stephen Crane: A Critical Biography* and *Stephen Crane: An Annotated Bibliography*. When two or more works by different authors have the same title, the authors' last names will appear in parentheses following the title.

THE READER'S ADVISER

Subject Index

This index provides detailed, multiple-approach access to the subject content of the volume. Arrangement is alphabetical. The names of profiled, main-entry authors are not included in this index; the reader is reminded to use the Name Index to locate these individuals. For additional information, the reader should refer to the detailed Table of Contents at the front of the volume.